The New Routledge
Dutch Dictionary

The New Routledge Dutch Dictionary

Dutch-English/English-Dutch

N. Osselton and R. Hempelman

Routledge
Taylor & Francis Group

LONDON AND NEW YORK

First published 2001 by Van Dale Lexicografie bv as
Ster Woordenboek Engels-Nederlands/Nederlands-Engels Third edition,
R. Hempelman and N. E. Osselton

English edition first published 2003 by Routledge
2 Park Square, Milton Park, Abingdon, Oxon, OX14 4RN

Editorial consultant for English edition: Sarah Butler.

Simultaneously published in the USA and Canada
by Routledge, 270 Madison Avenue, New York, NY 10016

Reprinted 2005, 2006, 2007 (twice), 2008 (twice)

Routledge is an imprint of the Taylor & Francis Group, an informa business

© 2003 Van Dale Lexicografie bv, Utrecht-Antwerpen

Typeset in Minion and Myriad by PlantijnCasparie, Heerhugowaard, Holland
Printed and bound in Great Britain by MPG Books Ltd, Bodmin, Cornwall

British Library Cataloguing in Publication Data
A catalogue record for this book is available from the British Library

Library of Congress Cataloging-in-Publication Data
Osselton, N. E.
   The new Routledge Dutch dictionary: Dutch-English-English-Dutch / N.
Osselton and R. Hempelman.
      p. cm.
   ISBN 0-415-30040-1 — ISBN 0-415-30041-X (pbk.)
   1. Dutch language—Dictionaries—English.   2. English
language—Dictionaries—Dutch.   I. Title: Routledge Dutch dictionary.
II. Hempelman, R.   III. Title
   PF640.O77 2003
   439.31'321—dc21

                              2002153868

ISBN 10: 0-415-30040-1 (hbk)
ISBN 10: 0-415-30041-X (pbk)

ISBN 13: 978-0-415-30040-7 (hbk)
ISBN 13: 978-0-415-30041-4 (pbk

Foreword

For this edition the selection of entries has been fine-tuned to meet the requirements of modern language learners and users. It therefore includes words such as *snailmail, wimp, truant* and *chatline, rokade, mobieltje, frietje oorlog* and *f-sleutel*. Many Belgian-Dutch words are now easily accessible, so *appelsien, inkom* and *melk in brik* are listed here.

The dictionary also includes the past tense and past participle forms of Dutch irregular verbs.

In this dictionary all words appear in British spelling. To avoid confusion, American spellings have not been included. However, in many cases American spellings can easily be predicted on the basis of British spellings. For example, many words ending in *-our* (*humour*) and *-tre* (*centre*) are spelt *-or* (*humor*) and *-ter* (*center*) in American English. Also, unlike British spelling, American spelling does not always double consonants, thus American English has "trave*l*er" and "jewe*l*er" rather than British "trave*ll*er" and "jewe*ll*er".

However, where British and American English differ lexically, there are entries for both: so for *apotheek* both chemist's, and *Am* drugstore are given.

The pronunciation of entries is represented by means of easy-to-understand symbols.

Detailed information about the layout of this dictionary is to be found in the Guide to the dictionary.

To make it easy to look up words, each entry appears at the beginning of a new line; in addition, all entries are printed in full.

List of abbreviations

A

adj	adjective
adv	adverb
Am	American, in the USA
art	article
Austr	Australian, in Australia
aux vb	auxiliary verb

B

Belg	Belgian, in Belgium
bijv.	bijvoorbeeld
bldg	building

C

chem	chemistry
com	commerce
comp	computer
conj	conjunction
cop	copula

D

dem pron	demonstrative pronoun
depr	depreciatory

E

econ	economics
educ	education
eg	for example
elec	electricity
esp	especially
euph	euphemism

F

fig	figurative
form	formal

I

iem	iemand
ind pron	indefinite pronoun
inform	informal
int	interjection
iron	ironical

M

maths	mathematics
mbt	met betrekking tot
med	medical
mil	military
mus	music

N

num.	numeral

O

oft	often

P

pers	person
pers pron	personal pronoun
pl	plural
pol	politics
poss pron	possessive pronoun
pron	pronoun
prep.	preposition

R

ref pron	reflexive pronoun
ref vb	reflexive verb
rel	religion

S

shipp	shipping
sing	singular
s.o.	someone
socc	soccer
sth.	something

T

traf	traffic

V

vb	verb
vd	van de
ve	van een
vh	van het
vulg	vulgar

Guide to the dictionary

The abbreviations used in this dictionary are explained in the *List of abbreviations* on the preceding pages.

All entries appear in bold type

aunt [a:nt] tante
aandenken [andɛŋkə(n)] *het* keepsake, memento: *iets bewaren als* ~ keep sth as a keepsake

The vowel or vowels of stressed syllables are underlined

absent-minded verstrooid, afwezig
kartel [kartɛl] *het* cartel, trust*een* ~ *vormen, zich aansluiten tot een* ~form a cartel

In most cases the pronunciation of the entries appears between square brackets

abolition [æbəlisjən] afschaffing
aircraft vliegtuig[h]
achteruit [aχtərœyt] *adv* back(wards)

Entries with identical spellings but different stress, pronunciation patterns or grammar are identified by a superscript numeral 1, 2 etc. at the beginning of the line

[1]**accent** [æksnt] *n* accent[h] *(also fig)*, klemtoon, uitspraak: *the* ~ *is on exotic flowers* de nadruk ligt op exotische bloemen
[2]**accent** [əksɛnt] *vb* accentueren *(also fig)*, de klemtoon leggen op, (sterk) doen uitkomen
[1]**aas** [as] *het* bait: *levend* ~ live bait; *van* ~ *voorzien* bait (the hook, trap)
[2]**aas** [as] *het, de (cards)* ace

The grammatical information is given after the pronunciation patterns
In Dutch nouns the article and, if applicable, plural form are given

aalbes [albɛs] *de (~sen)* currant: *rode* (or: *witte*) ~*sen* red (*or:* white) currants

In the translation of English nouns the Dutch neuter nouns are marked with a superior *h* to mark the use of the Dutch article *het*
In case the articles *het* and *de* are both allowed, the nouns are marked with +*h*

abscess [æbses] abces[h], ettergezwel[h]
ace [ees] 1 *(cards)* aas[+h], één, *(fig)* troef; 2 *(sport, esp tennis)* ace; 3 *(inf)* uitblinker: *an* ~ *at arithmetic* een hele piet in het rekenen

Commas are used to separate translations which are very close in meaning

aboveboard eerlijk, openlijk, rechtuit

Semi-colons are used to separate translations which are less close in meaning. In many cases information about this small difference in meaning appears in brackets

adulterate [ədultəreet] vervalsen; versnijden
shrimp [sjrimp] garnaal; *(inf)* klein opdondertje[h]

If the entry has very different translations, these are numbered 1, 2 etc.

abbreviate [əbrie:vie·eet] 1 inkorten, verkorten; 2 afkorten

In some cases a translation requires clarification: eg restrictions as to the usage of a word, a field label, a brief explanation. This additional information is printed in italics and appears between brackets

alderman [o:ldəmən] *(roughly)* wethouder, gedeputeerde, *(Belg)* schepen

In a number of cases the translation is followed by examples and expressions. These are italicised; the entry is represented by the symbol ~. Examples and expressions are always followed by a translation

absolute [æbsəloe:t] 1 absoluut, geheel, totaal: ~ *proof* onweerlegbaar bewijs; 2 onvoorwaardelijk: ~ *promise* onvoorwaardelijke belofte

For some entries no translations are given; they appear in one or more expressions. In these cases the expression is preceded by a colon

amok [amɔk] ‖ ~ *maken* run amok

Expressions which do not clearly fit any of the given translations of an entry are dealt with at the end, after the ‖ symbol

breakage [breekidzj] breuk, het breken, barst ‖ *£10 for* ~ £10 voor breukschade

In entries which are abbreviations, the explanation is given first, printed in italics

a.s. *aanstaande* next: ~ *maandag* next Monday

Alternative forms appear between brackets and are introduced by *or*. Thus the expressions *feel affinity for* and *feel affinity with* may both be translated as *sympathie voelen voor*

affinity [əfinnittie] 1 (aan)verwantschap[h]; 2 affiniteit, overeenkomst, sympathie: *feel* ~ *with (*of: *for)* sympathie voelen voor

In many cases a translation is given for an alternative form, also introduced by *or*. So *nieuwe aanplant* is translated as *new plantings* and *jonge aanplant* as *young plantings;* similarly *an all-time high* is translated as *een absoluut hoogtepunt* and *an all-time low* as *een absoluut dieptepunt*

aanplant [amplant] *de* plantings, plants: *nieuwe* (or: *jonge)* ~ new (*or:* young) plantings
all-time van alle tijden: *an* ~ *record* een (langdurig) ongebroken record; *an* ~ *high* een absoluut hoogtepunt

Some entries are only used in fixed combinations with another word. In these cases the latter word is introduced by "with"

accessible [əksessibl] (with *to)* toegankelijk (voor), bereikbaar (voor), *(fig)* begrijpelijk (voor)

Translations which are mainly used in American English are preceded by the abbreviation *Am.* This notation is also used in compounds. The example appearing on the right says that *apartment* is mainly used in American English

appartement [apartəmɛnt] *het (~en)* flat, *(Am)* apartment: *een driekamerappartement* a 2-bedroom flat

Pronunciation symbols Dutch:

ɑ *as in French* chat
a *as in* after
ɛ *as in* bed
e *as in* late
ə *as in* about
ɪ *as in* bid
i *as in French* ici
ɔ *as in* lot
o *as in German* Boot
ʏ *as in* sun
y *as in French* fumé
u *as in* foot

b *as in* back
c *as in* cheek
d *as in* door
f *as in* far
ɣ *as in* loch (but voiced)
χ *as in* loch
g *as in* goal
h *as in* help
j *as in* yet
k *as in* car
l *as in* like
m *as in* milk
n *as in* nose
ŋ *as in* wrong
ɲ *as in* canyon
p *as in* paper
r *as in* room
s *as in* son
ʃ *as in* fish
ʒ *as in* pleasure
t *as in* town
v *as in* verb
w *as in* wax
z *as in* zip

ø *as in German* schön
ɛi *approx as in* table, vein
œi *as in Latin* neutrum
ɑu *as in* mouth
œː *as in* nurse
ɑ̃ *as in French* chanson
ɛ̃ *as in French* chien
ɔ̃ *as in French* chanson

: lengthening symbol, lengthens the preceding vowel
ɑ: *as in* barbecue
ɛ: *as in* wear
i: *as in* jeans
ɔ: *as in* corner
u: *as in* jury
ʏ: *as in* service
y: *as in French* pur

Pronunciation symbols English:

aj *as in* idea
æ *as in* abolition
ã *as in* mange-tout
au *as in* power
b *as in* book
ch *as in* loch
d *as in* dark
ə *as in* assume
e *as in* academic
ee *as in* late
f *as in* front
g *as in* goal
h *as in* horse
i *as in* accessible
ie *as in* hungry
j *as in* you
k *as in* cable
l *as in* look
m *as in* more
n *as in* not
ng *as in* going
o *as in* long
oe *as in* pull
oo *as in* behold
p *as in* part
r *as in* road
s *as in* song
t *as in* tongue
ð *as in* the, their
θ *as in* thriller
õ *as in* restaurant
u *as in* bus
v *as in* view
w *as in* world
z *as in* zero

: lengthening symbol, lengthens the preceding vowel
a: *as in* balm
ɔ: *as in* verb
ie: *as in* field
o: *as in* all
oe: *as in* roof

· pause symbol: əs·joe:m

Dutch irregular verbs

infinitive	imperfect sing	imperfect pl	past participle
bakken	(bakte)		gebakken
bannen	(bande)		gebannen
barsten	(barstte)		gebarsten
bederven	bedierf	bedierven	bedorven
bedriegen	bedroog	bedrogen	bedrogen
beginnen	begon	begonnen	begonnen
begrijpen	begreep	begrepen	begrepen
belijden	beleed	beleden	beleden
bergen	borg		geborgen
bevelen	beval	bevalen	bevolen
bewegen	bewoog	bewogen	bewogen
bezwijken	bezweek	bezweken	bezweken
bidden	bad	baden	gebeden
bieden	bood	boden	geboden
bijten	beet	beten	gebeten
binden	bond		gebonden
blazen	blies	bliezen	geblazen
blijken	bleek	bleken	gebleken
blijven	bleef	bleven	gebleven
blinken	blonk		geblonken
braden	(braadde)		gebraden
breken	brak	braken	gebroken
brengen	bracht		gebracht
brouwen	(brouwde)		gebrouwen
buigen	boog	bogen	gebogen
delven	dolf/(delfde)	dolven	gedolven
denken	dacht		gedacht
dingen	dong		gedongen
doen	deed	deden	gedaan
1. doe 2. doet 3. doet			
dragen	droeg		gedragen
drijven	dreef	dreven	gedreven
dringen	drong		gedrongen
drinken	dronk		gedronken
druipen	droop	dropen	gedropen
duiken	dook	doken	gedoken
dunken	(dunkte)/docht		(gedunkt)/gedocht
durven	(durfde)/dorst		(gedurfd)
dwingen	dwong		gedwongen
eten	at	aten	gegeten
fluiten	floot	floten	gefloten
gaan	ging		gegaan
1. ga 2. gaat 3. gaat			
gelden	gold		gegolden
genezen	genas	genazen	genezen
genieten	genoot	genoten	genoten
geven	gaf	gaven	gegeven
gieten	goot	goten	gegoten
glijden	gleed	gleden	gegleden
glimmen	glom	glommen	geglommen
graven	groef	groeven	gegraven
grijpen	greep	grepen	gegrepen

infinitive	imperfect sing	imperfect pl	past participle
hangen	hing		gehangen
hebben	had	hadden	gehad
1. heb 2. hebt 3. heeft			
heffen	hief	hieven	geheven
helpen	hielp		geholpen
heten	(heette)		geheten
hijsen	hees	hesen	gehesen
houden	hield		gehouden
houwen	hieuw		gehouwen
jagen	(jaagde)/joeg		(gejaagd)
kerven	(kerfde)/korf	kerfden/korven	(gekerfd)/gekorven
kiezen	koos	kozen	gekozen
kijken	keek	keken	gekeken
kijven	(kijfde)/keef	kijfden/keven	(gekijfd)/gekeven
klimmen	klom	klommen	geklommen
klinken	klonk		geklonken
kluiven	kloof	kloven	gekloven
knijpen	kneep	knepen	geknepen
komen	kwam	kwamen	gekomen
kopen	kocht		gekocht
krijgen	kreeg	kregen	gekregen
krijsen	(krijste)/krees	krijsten/kresen	(gekrijst)/gekresen
krijten	kreet	kreten	gekreten
krimpen	kromp		gekrompen
kruipen	kroop	kropen	gekropen
kunnen	kon	konden	(gekund)
1. kan 2. kan/kunt 3. kan			
kwijten	kweet	kweten	gekweten
lachen	(lachte)		gelachen
laden	(laadde)		geladen
laten	liet		gelaten
leggen	(legde)/lei		(gelegd)
lezen	las	lazen	gelezen
liegen	loog	logen	gelogen
liggen	lag	lagen	gelegen
lijden	leed	leden	geleden
lijken	leek	leken	geleken
lopen	liep		gelopen
luiken	look	loken	geloken
malen	(maalde)		gemalen
melken	molk/(melkte)		gemolken
meten	mat	maten	gemeten
mijden	meed	meden	gemeden
moeten	moest		gemoeten
mogen	mocht		gemogen
1. mag 2. mag 3. mag			
nemen	nam	namen	genomen
nijgen	neeg	negen	genegen
nijpen	neep	nepen	genepen
ontginnen	ontgon	ontgonnen	ontgonnen
plegen			
−be in habit of	placht		-
−commit	(pleegde)		(gepleegd)
pluizen			
−fluff	ploos	plozen	geplozen
−give off fluff	(pluisde)		(gepluisd)

infinitive	imperfect sing	imperfect pl	past participle
prijzen			
-praise	prees	prezen	geprezen
-price	(prijsde)		(geprijsd)
raden			
-guess	(raadde)		geraden
-advise	(raadde)/ried		geraden
rieken	(riekte)/rook		geroken
rijden	reed	reden	gereden
rijgen	reeg	regen	geregen
rijten	reet	reten	gereten
rijzen	rees	rezen	gerezen
roepen	riep		geroepen
ruiken	rook	roken	geroken
scheiden	(scheidde)		gescheiden
schelden	schold		gescholden
schenden	schond		geschonden
schenken	schonk		geschonken
scheppen			
-create	schiep		geschapen
-shovel	(schepte)		(geschept)
scheren			
-shave	schoor	schoren	geschoren
-skim	(scheerde)		(gescheerd)
schieten	schoot	schoten	geschoten
schijnen	scheen	schenen	geschenen
schijten	scheet	scheten	gescheten
schrijden	schreed	schreden	geschreden
schrijven	schreef	schreven	geschreven
schrikken			
-be scared	schrok	schrokken	geschrokken
-be quenched	(schrikte)		(geschrikt)
schuilen			
-hide	school	scholen	gescholen
-shelter	(schuilde)		(geschuild)
schuiven	schoof	schoven	geschoven
slaan	sloeg		geslagen
1. sla 2. slaat 3. slaat			
slapen	sliep		geslapen
slijpen	sleep	slepen	geslepen
slijten	sleet	sleten	gesleten
slinken	slonk		geslonken
sluipen	sloop	slopen	geslopen
sluiten	sloot	sloten	gesloten
smelten	smolt		gesmolten
smijten	smeet	smeten	gesmeten
snijden	sneed	sneden	gesneden
snuiten	snoot	snoten	gesnoten
snuiven	snoof	snoven	gesnoven
spannen	(spande)		gespannen
spijten	speet	speten	gespeten
spinnen	spon	sponnen	gesponnen
splijten	spleet	spleten	gespleten
spreken	sprak	spraken	gesproken
springen	sprong		gesprongen
spugen	(spuugde)/spoog	spuugden/spogen	(gespuugd)/gespogen
spruiten	sproot	sproten	gesproten

infinitive	imperfect sing	imperfect pl	past participle
spuiten	spoot	spoten	gespoten
staan	stond		gestaan
1. sta 2. staat 3. staat			
steken	stak	staken	gestoken
stelen	stal	stalen	gestolen
sterven	stierf	stierven	gestorven
stijgen	steeg	stegen	gestegen
stijven			
−starch	steef	steven	gesteven
−stiffen	(stijfde)		(gestijfd)
stinken	stonk		gestonken
stoten	(stootte)/stiet		gestoten
strijden	streed	streden	gestreden
strijken	streek	streken	gestreken
stuiven	stoof	stoven	gestoven
treden	trad	traden	getreden
treffen	trof	troffen	getroffen
trekken	trok	trokken	getrokken
tijgen	toog	togen	getogen
vallen	viel		gevallen
vangen	ving		gevangen
varen	voer		gevaren
vechten	vocht		gevochten
verdrieten	verdroot	verdroten	verdroten
verdwijnen	verdween	verdwenen	verdwenen
vergeten	vergat	vergaten	vergeten
verliezen	verloor	verloren	verloren
verschuilen	verschool	verscholen	verscholen
verslinden	verslond		verslonden
vinden	vond		gevonden
vlechten	vlocht		gevlochten
vlieden	vlood	vloden	gevloden
vliegen	vloog	vlogen	gevlogen
vlieten	vloot	vloten	gevloten
vouwen	(vouwde)		gevouwen
vragen	vroeg		gevraagd
vreten	vrat	vraten	gevreten
vriezen	vroor	-	gevroren
waaien	(waaide)/woei		gewaaid
wassen			
−grow	wies		gewassen
−wash	(waste)/wies		gewassen
wegen	woog	wogen	gewogen
werpen	wierp		geworpen
werven	wierf	wierven	geworven
weten	wist		geweten
weven	weefde		geweven
wezen	was	waren	(geweest)
wijken	week	weken	geweken
wijten	weet	weten	geweten
wijzen	wees	wezen	gewezen
willen	(wilde)/wou	wilden/wouden	(gewild)
1. wil 2. wilt 3. wil			
winden	wond		gewonden
winnen	won	wonnen	gewonnen
worden	werd		geworden

infinitive	imperfect sing	imperfect pl	past participle
wreken	(wreekte)		gewroken
wrijven	wreef	wreven	gewreven
wringen	wrong		gewrongen
zeggen	zei/(zegde)	zeiden/zegden	(gezegd)
zenden	zond		gezonden
zieden	(ziedde)/zood	ziedden/zoden	(gezied)/gezoden
zien	zag	zagen	gezien
1. zie 2. ziet 3. ziet			
zijgen	zeeg	zegen	gezegen
zijn	was	waren	geweest
1. ben 2. bent 3. is			
zingen	zong		gezongen
zinken	zonk		gezonken
zinnen	zon/(zinde)	zonnen/zinden	gezonnen
zitten	zat	zaten	gezeten
zoeken	zocht		gezocht
zouten	(zoutte)		gezouten
zuigen	zoog	zogen	gezogen
zuipen	zoop	zopen	gezopen
zullen	zou	zouden	
1. zal 2. zult 3. zal			
zwelgen	zwolg		gezwolgen
zwellen	zwol	zwollen	gezwollen
zwemmen	zwom	zwommen	gezwommen
zweren			
−swear	zwoer		gezworen
−fester	zwoor/(zweerde)	zworen/zweerden	gezworen
zwerven	zwierf	zwierven	gezworven
zwijgen	zweeg	zwegen	gezwegen

Dutch-English

a

a [a] *de (~'s)* a, A: *van ~ tot z kennen* know from A to
Z (*or:* from beginning to end); *wie ~ zegt, moet ook
b zeggen* in for a penny, in for a pound

à [a] *prep* **1** (*roughly*) (*from …*) to, or: *2 ~ 3 maal 2*
or 3 times; *er waren zo'n 10 ~ 15 personen* there were
some 10 to 15 people; **2** at (the rate of): *5 meter ~ 6
euro, is 30 euro* 5 metres at 6 euros is 30 euros

A4 [avir] *de* **1** A4; **2** side

AA [aa] *Anonieme Alcoholisten* Alcoholics
Anonymous

aaien [aja(n)] *vb* stroke, caress

aak [ak] *de (aken)* barge

aal [al] *de (alen)* eel

aalbes [albɛs] *de (~sen)* currant: *rode* (or: *witte)
~sen* red (*or:* white) currants

aalmoes [almus] *de (aalmoezen)* alms

aalscholver [alsχɔlvər] *de (~s)* cormorant

aambeeld [ambelt] *het (~en)* anvil

aambeien [ambɛiə(n)] *de* piles

¹aan [an] *prep* **1** on, at, by: *vruchten ~ de bomen* fruit
on the trees; *~ een verslag werken* work on a report;
~ zee (or: *de kust) wonen* live by the sea (*or:* on the
coast); **2** by, with: *dag ~ dag* day by day; *doen ~* do,
go in for; *twee ~ twee* two by two; **3** to: *hij geeft les
~ de universiteit* he lectures at the university; *~ wal
gaan* go ashore; *hoe kom je ~ dat spul?* how did you
get hold of that stuff?; **4** of, from: *sterven ~ een ziekte* die of a disease; **5** of: *een tekort ~ kennis* a lack of
knowledge; **6** up to: *het is ~ mij ervoor te zorgen dat
… it* is up to me to see that …; *dat ligt ~ haar* that's
her fault; *hij heeft het ~ zijn hart* he has got heart
trouble; *hij is ~ het joggen* he's out jogging; *hij is ~
het strijken* he's (busy) ironing; *ze zijn ~ vakantie
toe* they could do with (*or:* are badly in need of) a
holiday

²aan [an] *adj* on: *een vrouw met een groene jurk ~* a
woman in (*or:* wearing) a green dress; *de kachel is
~* the stove is on; *het is weer dik ~ tussen hen* it's on
again between them; *daar is niets ~: a)* there's
nothing to it, it's dead easy; *b)* it's a waste of time

³aan [an] *adv* (with *wat) about, around, away: *ik rotzooi maar wat ~* I'm just messing about; *stel je niet
zo ~!* stop carrying on like that!; *daar heeft zij niets
~* that's no use to her; *daar zijn we nog niet ~ toe* we
haven't got that far yet; (*fig) zij weet niet waar zij ~
toe is* she doesn't know where she stands; *rustig ~!*

calm down!, take it easy!; *van nu af ~* from now on;
van voren af ~ from the beginning; *van jongs af ~*
from childhood; *jij kunt ervan op ~ dat …* you can
count on it that …

aanbakken [ambakə(n)] *vb* burn, get burnt

aanbellen [ambɛlə(n)] *vb* ring (at the door): *bij
iem ~* ring s.o.'s doorbell

aanbesteding [ambəstedɪŋ] *de (~en)* tender, contract: *inschrijven op een ~* (submit a) tender for a
contract

aanbetaling [ambətalɪŋ] *de (~en)* down payment,
deposit: *een ~ doen van 200 euro* make a down payment of 200 euros

aanbevelen [ambəvelə(n)] *vb* recommend: *dat
kan ik je warm ~* I can recommend it warmly to you

aanbeveling [ambəvelɪŋ] *de (~en)* recommendation

aanbidden [ambɪdə(n)] *vb* **1** worship, venerate; **2**
(*fig) worship, adore: *Jan aanbad zijn vrouw* Jan
worshipped (*or:* adored) his wife

aanbidder [ambɪdər] *de (~s)* **1** worshipper; **2** admirer: *een stille ~* a secret admirer

aanbieden [ambidə(n)] *vb* **1** offer, give: *iem een geschenk ~* present a gift to s.o.; *hulp* (or: *diensten) ~*
offer help (*or:* services); *zijn ontslag ~* tender one's
resignation; *zijn verontschuldigingen ~* offer one's
apologies; **2** offer: *iets te koop* (or: *huur) ~* put sth
up for sale (*or:* rent)

aanbieding [ambidɪŋ] *de (~en)* special offer, bargain: *goedkope* (speciale*) ~* special offer, bargain;
koffie is in de ~ deze week coffee is on special offer
this week, coffee's reduced this week

aanblijven [amblɛivə(n)] *vb* stay on: *zij blijft aan
als minister* she is staying on as minister

aanblik [amblɪk] *de* **1** sight, glance: *bij de eerste ~* at
first sight (*or:* glance); **2** sight, (*pers) appearance:
een troosteloze ~ opleveren be a sorry sight, make a
sorry spectacle

aanbod [ambɔt] *het* **1** offer: *iem een ~ doen* make
s.o. an offer; *zij nam het ~ aan* she accepted (*or:*
took up) the offer; *zij sloeg het ~ af* she rejected the
offer; **2** supply: *vraag en ~* supply and demand

aanbouw [ambau] *de* **1** building, construction: *dit
huis is in ~* this house is under construction; **2** extension, annexe: *een ~ aan een huis* an extension
(*or:* annexe) to a house

aanbouwen [ambauwə(n)] *vb* build on, add: *een
aangebouwde keuken* a built-on kitchen

aanbranden [ambrandə(n)] *vb* burn (on): *laat de
aardappelen niet ~* mind the potatoes don't boil
dry (*or:* get burnt)

¹aanbreken [ambrekə(n)] *vb* come, break, dawn,
fall: *het moment was aangebroken om afscheid te
nemen* the moment had come to say goodbye

²aanbreken [ambrekə(n)] *vb* break into, break (into), open (up): *er staat nog een aangebroken fles*
there's a bottle that's already been opened

aanbrengen [ambrɛŋə(n)] *vb* **1** put in, put on, install, introduce, apply: *verbeteringen ~* make im-

provements; *een gat in de muur ~* make a hole in the wall; **2** inform on; report: *een zaak ~* report a matter

aandacht [ɑndɑχt] *de* attention, notice: *(persoonlijke) ~ besteden aan* give (*or:* pay) (personal) attention to; *aan de ~ ontsnappen* escape notice; *al zijn ~ richten op ...* focus all one's attention on ...; *iemands ~ trekken* attract s.o.'s attention, catch s.o.'s eye; *de ~ vestigen op* draw attention to; *onder de ~ komen* (or: *brengen*) *van* come (*or:* bring) to the attention of

aandachtig [ɑndɑχtəχ] *adj, adv* attentive, intent: *~ luisteren* listen attentively (*or:* intently)

aandeel [ɑndel] *het (aandelen)* **1** share, portion: *~ hebben in een zaak* (or: *de winst)* have a share in a business (*or:* the profits); **2** contribution, part: *een actief ~ hebben in iets* take an active part in sth; **3** share (certificate), *(Am)* stock (certificate): *~ op naam* nominative share, registered share

aandeelhouder [ɑndelhɑudər] *de (~s)* shareholder

aandenken [ɑndɛŋkə(n)] *het* keepsake, memento: *iets bewaren als ~* keep sth as a keepsake

aandoen [ɑndun] *vb* **1** put on; **2** do to, cause: *iem een proces ~* take s.o. to court; *iem verdriet, onrecht ~* cause s.o. grief, do s.o. an injustice; *dat kun je haar niet ~!* you can't do that to her!; **3** turn on, switch on

aandoening [ɑndunɪŋ] *de (~en)* disorder, complaint: *een lichte ~ van de luchtwegen* a touch of bronchitis

aandoenlijk [ɑndunlək] *adj, adv* moving, touching

aandraaien [ɑndrajə(n)] *vb* tighten, screw tighter

aandragen [ɑndraɣə(n)] *vb* carry, bring (up, along, to)

aandrang [ɑndrɑŋ] *de* insistence, instigation: *~ uitoefenen op* exert pressure on; *op ~ van mijn vader doe ik het* I'm doing it at my father's insistence

aandrijven [ɑndrɛivə(n)] *vb* drive: *door een elektromotor aangedreven* driven by an electric motor

aandringen [ɑndrɪŋə(n)] *vb* **1** urge: *niet verder ~* not press the point, not insist; *bij iem op hulp ~* urge s.o. to help; **2** insist: *er sterk op ~ dat* strongly insist that; *~ op iets* insist on sth

aanduiden [ɑndœydə(n)] *vb* indicate: *niet nader aangeduid* unspecified; *iem ~ als X* refer to s.o. as X

aandurven [ɑndʏrvə(n)] *vb* dare to (do); feel up to: *een taak ~* feel up to a task; *het ~ om* dare (*or:* presume) to

aaneengesloten [ɑnenɣəslotə(n)] *adj* unbroken, connected, continuous, *(fig)* united

aaneenschakelen [ɑnensχakələ(n)] *vb* link up (*or:* together), join together, couple

aaneenschakeling [ɑnensχakəlɪŋ] *de (~en)* chain, succession, sequence: *een ~ van ongelukken* a series (*or:* sequence) of accidents

aaneensluiten [ɑnenslœytə(n)] *ref vb* join together, merge, *(fig also)* join forces, *(fig also)* unite: *zich ~ tot* join together in

aanfluiting [ɑnflœytɪŋ] *de (~en)* mockery

¹aangaan [ɑŋɡan] *vb* **1** go (towards), head (for, towards): *achter iem (iets) ~: a)* chase s.o. (sth) (up); *b) (fig)* go after s.o., go for sth; **2** go on, switch on, light

²aangaan [ɑŋɡan] *vb* **1** enter into, contract: *een lening ~* contract a loan; **2** concern: *dat gaat hem niets aan* that's none of his business; *wat mij aangaat* as far as I'm concerned

aangapen [ɑŋɡapə(n)] *vb* gape (at), gawp at, gawk at: *sta me niet zo dom aan te gapen!* stop gaping at me like an idiot!

aangeboren [ɑŋɡəborə(n)] *adj* innate, inborn, *(med)* congenital

aangedaan [ɑŋɡədan] *adj* **1** moved, touched; **2** affected

aangeklaagde [ɑŋɡəklaɣdə] *de (~n)* accused; defendant

aangelegd [ɑŋɡələχt] *adj* -minded: *artistiek ~ zijn* have an artistic bent

aangelegenheid [ɑŋɡələɣənhɛit] *de (-heden)* affair, business, matter

aangenaam [ɑŋɡənam] *adj, adv* pleasant, pleasing, congenial: *ze was ~ verrast* she was pleasantly surprised; *~ (met u kennis te maken)* pleased to meet you; *het was me ~* it was nice (*or:* a pleasure) meeting you

aangenomen [ɑŋɡənomə(n)] *adj* || *een ~ kind* an adopted child; *~ werk* contract work

aangepast [ɑŋɡəpɑst] *adj* (specially) adapted; adjusted: *een ~e versie* an adapted version; *goed ~ zijn* be well-adapted (*or:* well-adjusted); *slecht ~ zijn* be poorly adapted (*or:* adjusted)

aangeschoten [ɑŋɡəsχotə(n)] *adj* **1** under the influence, tipsy; **2** unintentional: *~ hands* unintentional hands

aangeslagen [ɑŋɡəslaɣə(n)] *adj* affected, shaken: *de bokser maakte een ~ indruk* the boxer looked unsteady

aangetekend [ɑŋɡətekənt] *adj* registered: *je moet die stukken ~ versturen* you must send those items by registered mail

aangetrouwd [ɑŋɡətrɑut] *adj* related by marriage: *~e familie* in-laws

aangeven [ɑŋɡevə(n)] *vb* **1** hand, pass; **2** indicate, declare: *de trein vertrok op de aangegeven tijd* the train left on time; *tenzij anders aangegeven* except where otherwise specified, unless stated otherwise; **3** report, notify, declare: *een diefstal ~* report a theft (to the police); *een geboorte* (or: *huwelijk) ~* register a birth (*or:* marriage); *hebt u nog iets aan te geven?* do you have anything (else) to declare?; **4** indicate, mark: *de thermometer geeft 30 graden aan* the thermometer is registering 30 degrees; *de maat ~* beat time; **5** *(socc)* feed; *(volleyball)* set

aangewezen [ɑŋɡəwezə(n)] *adj* || *de ~ persoon* the obvious (*or:* right) person (for the job); *op iets ~ zijn* rely on sth; *op zichzelf ~ zijn* be left to one's own devices

aangezicht [ɑŋɡəzɪχt] *het (~en)* countenance, face

aangezien [aŋɣəzin] *conj* since, as, seeing (that)
aangifte [aŋɣɪftə] *de (~n)* declaration; report; registration: ~ *inkomstenbelasting* income tax return; ~ *doen van een misdrijf* report a crime; ~ *doen* make a declaration; ~ *doen van geboorte* register a birth; *bij diefstal wordt altijd ~ gedaan* shoplifters will be prosecuted
aangifteformulier [aŋɣɪftəfɔrmylir] *het (~en)* tax form; declaration; registration form
aangrenzend [aŋɣrɛnzənt] *adj* adjoining, adjacent, neighbouring
aangrijpen [aŋɣrɛipə(n)] *vb* **1** grip; move, make a deep impression on: *dit boek heeft me zeer aangegrepen* this book has made a deep impression on me; **2** seize (at, upon), grip: *een gelegenheid met beide handen ~* seize (at, upon) an opportunity with both hands
aangrijpend [aŋɣrɛipənt] *adj, adv* moving, touching, poignant
aanhalen [anhalə(n)] *vb* **1** caress, fondle; **2** quote: *als voorbeeld (or: bewijs) ~* quote as an example (*or:* as evidence); **3** pull in; haul in: *de teugels ~* tighten the reins
aanhalig [anhaləχ] *adj, adv* affectionate: *hij kon zeer ~ doen* he could be very affectionate
aanhaling [anhalɪŋ] *de (~en)* quotation, *(inf)* quote
aanhalingsteken [anhalɪŋstekə(n)] *het (~s)* quotation mark, *(inf)* quote, inverted comma: *tussen ~s* in quotation marks, in inverted commas
aanhang [anhaŋ] *de* following; supporters: *over een grote ~ beschikken* have a large following; *veel ~ vinden onder* find considerable support among, have a large following among
aanhangen [anhaŋə(n)] *vb* adhere to, be attached to, support: *een geloof ~* adhere to a faith; *een partij ~* support a party
aanhanger [anhaŋər] *de (~s)* follower; supporter: *een vurig (or: trouw) ~ van* an ardent (*or:* a faithful) supporter of
aanhangig [anhaŋəχ] *adj* pending, before the courts: *een kwestie ~ maken bij de autoriteiten* take a matter up with the authorities
aanhangsel [anhaŋsəl] *het (~s)* appendix: *een ~ bij een polis* an appendix to a policy
aanhangwagen [anhaŋwaɣə(n)] *de (~s)* trailer
aanhankelijk [anhaŋkələk] *adj, adv* affectionate, devoted
aanhebben [anhɛbə(n)] *vb* have on, be wearing
aanhechten [anhɛχtə(n)] *vb* attach, fasten on, affix
aanhechting [anhɛχtɪŋ] *de (~en)* attachment
aanhef [anhɛf] *de* opening words, *(letter)* salutation
aanheffen [anhɛfə(n)] *vb* start, begin, break into, raise
aanhoren [anhorə(n)] *vb* listen to, hear: *iemands relaas geduldig ~* listen patiently to s.o.'s story
¹**aanhouden** [anhaudə(n)] *vb* **1** stop, arrest, hold: *een verdachte ~* take a suspect into custody; **2** hold on to, keep, continue, stick to; **3** keep on; **4** keep on,

keep up, leave on, keep going: *als je het recept aanhoudt, kan er niets misgaan* if you stick to the recipe, nothing can go wrong
²**aanhouden** [anhaudə(n)] *vb* **1** keep on, go on, persist (in): *blijven ~* persevere, insist; *je moet niet zo ~* you shouldn't keep going on about it (like that); **2** go on, continue; hold, last, keep up; **3** *(with op)* keep *(left or right);* make (for), head (for): *links* (or: *rechts) ~* keep to the left (*or:* right), bear left (*or:* right)
aanhoudend [anhaudənt] *adj, adv* **1** continuous, persistent, constant, all the time: *een ~e droogte* a prolonged period of drought; **2** continual, repeated, time and again, always
aanhouding [anhaudɪŋ] *de (~en)* arrest
aankijken [aŋkɛikə(n)] *vb* look at: *elkaar veelbetekenend ~* give each other a meaningful look; *het ~ niet waard* not worth looking at
aanklacht [aŋklaχt] *de (~en)* charge, indictment, complaint: *een ~ indienen tegen iem (bij)* lodge a complaint against s.o. (with); *de ~ werd ingetrokken* the charge was dropped
aanklagen [aŋklaɣə(n)] *vb* bring charges against, lodge a complaint against: *iem ~ wegens diefstal* (or: *moord)* charge s.o. with theft (*or:* murder)
aanklager [aŋklaɣər] *de (~s)* accuser; complainant; plaintiff, prosecutor: *openbare ~* public prosecutor, Crown Prosecutor
aankleden [aŋkledə(n)] *vb* dress, get dressed, clothe, fit out: *je moet die jongen warm ~* you must wrap the boy up well; *zich ~* get dressed
aankleding [aŋkledɪŋ] *de (~en)* furnishing; decor, furnishings; decor, set(ting)
aanklikken [aŋklɪkə(n)] *vb* click (on)
aankloppen [aŋklɔpə(n)] *vb* knock (at the door), *(fig)* come with a request, appeal (to): *tevergeefs bij iem ~ om hulp* appeal to s.o. for help in vain
aanknopen [aŋknopə(n)] *vb* **1** tie on: *(fig) we hebben er nog maar een dagje aangeknoopt* we're staying on another day (*or:* a day extra); **2** enter into: *betrekkingen ~ met* establish relations with; *onderhandelingen ~ met* enter into negotiations with
aanknopingspunt [aŋknopɪŋspynt] *het (~en)* clue, lead; starting point
¹**aankomen** [aŋkomə(n)] *vb* **1** arrive, reach, come in, pull in, finish: *de trein kan elk ogenblik ~* the train is due at any moment; *daar komt iem aan* s.o. is coming; *als derde ~* come in third; **2** hit hard: *de klap is hard aangekomen: a)* it was a heavy blow; *b) (fig)* it was a great blow to him; **3** come (with): *en daar kom je nu pas mee aan?* and now you tell me!; *je hoeft met dat plan bij hem niet aan te komen* it's no use going to him with that plan; **4** come (along), approach: *ik zag het ~* I could see it coming; **5** touch, hit, come up (against): *niet (nergens) ~!* don't touch!, hands off!; **6** put on weight
²**aankomen** [aŋkomə(n)] *vb* come (down) (to): *als het op betalen aankomt* when it comes to paying; *waar het op aankomt* what really matters; *als het*

erop aan komt when it comes to the crunch

aankomend [aŋkomənt] *adj* prospective, future; budding; apprentice, trainee: *een ~ actrice* a starlet, an up-and-coming actress; *een ~ schrijver* a budding author

aankomst [aŋkɔmst] *de* arrival, coming (in), finish(ing), landing: *in volgorde van ~* in (the) order of finishing; *bij ~* on arrival

aankomsttijd [aŋkɔmstɛit] *de (~en)* time of arrival

aankondigen [aŋkɔndəɣə(n)] *vb* announce: *de volgende plaat ~* announce (*or:* introduce) the next record; *~ iets te zullen doen* announce that one will do sth

aankondiging [aŋkɔndəɣɪŋ] *de (~en)* announcement, notice, signal, foreboding, proclamation: *tot nadere ~* until further notice

aankopen [aŋkopə(n)] *vb* buy, purchase, acquire

aankrijgen [aŋkrɛiɣə(n)] *vb* get going: *ik krijg de kachel niet aan* I can't get the stove to burn (*or:* light)

aankruisen [aŋkrœysə(n)] *vb* tick: *~ wat van toepassing is* tick where appropriate

aankunnen [aŋkʏnə(n)] *vb* **1** be a match for, (be able to) hold one's own against: *het alleen ~* hold one's own; **2** be equal (*or:* up) to, be able to manage (*or:* cope with): *zij kon het werk niet aan* she couldn't cope (with the work); *kan ik ervan op aan, dat je komt?* can I rely on your coming?

aanlanden [aŋlɑndə(n)] *vb* land (up), arrive at: *waar zijn we nu aangeland?* where have we got to now?

aanleg [aŋlɛχ] *de* **1** construction, building, laying, digging, layout: *in ~* under construction; *~ van elektriciteit* installation of electricity; **2** talent; aptitude: *~ tonen voor talen* show an aptitude for languages; *~ voor muziek* a talent for music; **3** tendency, predisposition, inclination: *~ voor griep hebben* be susceptible to flu; *(Belg) rechtbank van eerste ~ (roughly)* county court

¹aanleggen [aŋlɛɣə(n)] *vb* **1** construct, build, lay, dig, lay out, install, build up: *een spoorweg (or: weg) ~* construct a railway (*or:* road); *een nieuwe wijk ~* build a new estate (*or Am:* development); **2** aim: *leg aan!* take aim!

²aanleggen [aŋlɛɣə(n)] *vb (shipp)* moor, tie up; touch (at), berth

aanlegplaats [aŋlɛχplats] *de (~en)* landing stage (*or:* place), mooring (place), berth

aanleiding [aŋlɛidɪŋ] *de (~en)* occasion, reason, cause: *er bestaat geen ~ om (or: tot)* there is no reason to (*or:* for); *iem (geen) ~ geven* give s.o. (no) cause; *~ geven tot klachten* give cause for complaints; *~ zijn (geven) tot* give rise to; *naar ~ van* as a result of; *naar ~ van uw schrijven* in reply (*or:* with reference) to your letter

aanlengen [aŋlɛŋə(n)] *vb* dilute

aanleren [aŋlerə(n)] *vb* **1** learn, acquire: *slechte manieren ~* acquire bad manners; **2** teach: *een hond kunstjes ~* teach a dog tricks

aanlijnen [aŋlɛinə(n)] *vb* leash: *aangelijnd houden* keep on the leash (*or:* lead)

aanlokkelijk [aŋlɔkələk] *adj* tempting, alluring, attractive

aanloop [aŋlop] *de (aanlopen)* **1** run-up: *een ~ nemen* take a run-up; *een sprong met (or: zonder) ~* a running (*or:* standing) jump; **2** visitors, callers, customers: *zij hebben altijd veel ~* they always have lots of visitors

aanlopen [aŋlopə(n)] *vb* **1** walk (towards), come (towards); drop in, drop by: *tegen iets ~: a)* walk into sth; *b) (fig)* chance (*or:* stumble) on sth; **2** rub, drag; **3** turn ... (in the face): *rood ~* turn red in the face

aanmaken [amakə(n)] *vb* **1** mix; prepare: *sla ~* dress a salad; **2** light: *een vuur (or: de kachel) ~* light a fire (*or:* the stove)

aanmanen [amanə(n)] *vb* **1** urge: *tot voorzichtigheid ~* urge caution; **2** order: *iem tot betaling ~* demand payment from s.o.

aanmaning [amanɪŋ] *de (~en)* **1** reminder: *een vriendelijke ~* a gentle reminder; **2** request for payment, notice to pay

aanmelden [amɛldə(n)] *vb* **1** announce, report; **2** present, enter forward (s.o.'s name), put forward (s.o.'s name)

aanmelding [amɛldɪŋ] *de (~en)* entry; application; enlistment, enrolment: *de ~ is gesloten* applications will no longer be accepted

aanmeren [amerə(n)] *vb* moor, tie up

aanmerkelijk [amɛrkələk] *adj, adv* considerable; appreciable, marked, noticeable: *een ~ verschil met vroeger* a considerable change from the past; *het gaat ~ beter* things have improved noticeably

aanmerken [amɛrkə(n)] *vb* comment, criticize: *op zijn gedrag valt niets aan te merken* his conduct is beyond reproach

aanmerking [amɛrkɪŋ] *de (~en)* comment, criticism, remark: *~en maken (hebben) op* find fault with, criticize; *in ~ nemen* consider; *in ~ komen voor* qualify for

aanmodderen [amɔdərə(n)] *vb* muddle on: *maar wat ~* mess around

aanmoedigen [amudəɣə(n)] *vb* encourage, cheer on: *iem tot iets ~* encourage s.o. to do sth

aanmoediging [amudəɣɪŋ] *de (~en)* encouragement, cheers: *onder ~ van het publiek* while the spectators cheered him (*or:* her, them) on

aanmonsteren [amɔnstərə(n)] *vb* sign on

aannemelijk [anemələk] *adj* **1** plausible: *een ~e verklaring geven voor iets* give a plausible explanation for sth; **2** acceptable, reasonable: *tegen elk ~ bod* any reasonable offer accepted

aannemen [anemə(n)] *vb* **1** take, accept, pick up, answer: *kan ik een boodschap ~?* can I take a message?; **2** accept, take (on), pass, carry: *een aanbod met beide handen ~* jump at an offer; *een opdracht (or: voorstel) ~* accept a commission (*or:* proposal); *met algemene stemmen ~* carry unanimously; **3** accept, believe: *stilzwijgend* ~ tacitly accept; *u kunt het van mij* ~ you can take it from me; **4** assume, suppose: *algemeen werd aangenomen dat* ... it was generally assumed that ...; *als vaststaand (vanzelfsprekend)* ~ take for granted; **5** undertake, contract for: *de bouw van een blok woningen* ~ contract for (the building of) a block of houses; **6** engage, take on: *iem op proef* ~ appoint s.o. for a trial period

aannemer [ạnemər] *de (~s)* (building) contractor, builder

aanpak [ạmpɑk] *de* approach: *de* ~ *van dit probleem* the way to deal with (*or:* tackle) this problem

aanpakken [ạmpɑkə(n)] *vb* **1** take, take, catch, get hold of; **2** go (*or:* set) about (it), deal with, handle, tackle, seize, take: *een probleem* ~ tackle a problem; *hoe zullen we dat* ~? how shall we set about it?; *een zaak goed* (or: *verkeerd)* ~ go the right (*or:* wrong) way about a matter; *hij weet van* ~ he's a tremendous worker; **3** deal with, attack, *(law)* proceed against: *iem flink* ~ take a firm line with s.o., be tough on s.o.

aanpappen [ạmpɑpə(n)] *vb* chum (*or:* pal) up (with)

¹aanpassen [ạmpɑsə(n)] *vb* **1** try on, fit on: *een nieuwe jas* ~ try on a new coat; **2** adapt (to), adjust (to), fit (to): *de lonen zullen opnieuw aangepast worden* wages will be readjusted

²aanpassen [ạmpɑsə(n)] *ref vb* adapt oneself (to)

aanpassing [ạmpɑsɪŋ] *de (~en)* adaptation (to), adjustment (to)

aanplakbiljet [ạmplɑgbɪljɛt] *het (~ten)* poster, bill

aanplakbord [ạmplɑgbɔrt] *het (~en)* notice board; boarding, *(Am)* billboard

aanplakken [ạmplɑkə(n)] *vb* affix, paste (up), post (up): *verboden aan te plakken* no billposting

aanplant [ạmplɑnt] *de* plantings, plants: *nieuwe* (or: *jonge)* ~ new (*or:* young) plantings

aanplanten [ạmplɑntə(n)] *vb* plant (out), cultivate, grow, afforest

aanpoten [ạmpotə(n)] *vb* hurry (up), slog away

aanpraten [ạmprɑtə(n)] *vb* palm off on, talk into: *iem iets* ~ talk s.o. into (doing) sth, palm sth off on s.o.

aanprijzen [ạmprɛizə(n)] *vb* recommend, praise

aanraakscherm [ạnrɑksχɛrm] *het (~en) (comp)* touchscreen

aanraden [ạnrɑdə(n)] *vb* advise, recommend, suggest: *de dokter ried hem rust aan* the doctor advised him to take rest; *iem dringend* ~ *iets te doen* advise s.o. urgently to do sth

aanraken [ạnrɑkə(n)] *vb* touch: *verboden aan te raken* (please) do not touch; *met geen vinger* ~ not lay a finger on

aanranden [ạnrɑndə(n)] *vb* assault

aanrander [ạnrɑndər] *de (~s)* assailant

aanranding [ạnrɑndɪŋ] *de (~en)* (criminal, indecent) assault

aanrecht [ạnrɛχt] *het, de (~en)* kitchen (sink) unit

aanrechtblad [ạnrɛχtblɑt] *het (~en)* worktop, working top

aanrichten [ạnrɪχtə(n)] *vb* cause, bring about: *een bloedbad* ~ *(onder)* bring about a massacre (among); *grote verwoestingen* ~ *(bij)* create (*or:* wreak) havoc (on)

aanrijden [ạnrɛidə(n)] *vb* collide (with), crash (into), run into: *hij heeft een hond aangereden* he hit a dog; *tegen een muur* ~ run (*or:* crash) into a wall

aanrijding [ạnrɛidɪŋ] *de (~en)* collision, crash: *een* ~ *hebben* be involved in a collision (*or:* crash)

aanroeren [ạnrurə(n)] *vb* **1** touch: *het eten was nauwelijks aangeroerd* the food had hardly been touched; **2** touch upon

aanrommelen [ạnrɔmələ(n)] *vb* mess around

aanschaf [ạnsχɑf] *de* purchase, buy, acquisition

aanschaffen [ạnsχɑfə(n)] *vb* purchase, acquire

aanscherpen [ạnsχɛrpə(n)] *vb* **1** sharpen; **2** *(fig)* accentuate, highlight

aanschieten [ạnsχitə(n)] *vb* **1** hit: *een aangeschoten hert* a wounded deer; **2** buttonhole, accost: *een voorbijganger* ~ buttonhole a passer-by

aanschouwen [ạnsχɑuwə(n)] *vb* behold, see: *het levenslicht* ~ (first) see the light

aanschuiven [ạnsχœyvə(n)] *vb* draw up, pull up

¹aanslaan [ạnslan] *vb* **1** touch, strike, hit: *een toets* ~ strike a key; *een snaar* ~ touch a string; **2** estimate, assess, tax: *iem hoog* ~ think highly of s.o.

²aanslaan [ạnslan] *vb* **1** start; **2** catch on, be successful: *dat plan is bij hen goed aangeslagen* that plan has caught on (well) with them

aanslag [ạnslɑχ] *de (~en)* **1** *(mus)* touch: *een lichte* (or: *zware)* ~ a light (*or:* heavy) touch; **2** ready: *met het geweer in de* ~ with one's rifle at the ready; **3** attempt, attack, assault: *een* ~ *op iemands leven plegen* make an attempt on s.o.'s life; **4** deposit; moisture: *een vieze* ~ *op het plafond* a filthy (smoke) deposit on the ceiling; **5** assessment: *een* ~ *van €1000,- ontvangen* get assessed €1000.00

aanslagbiljet [ạnslɑχbɪljɛt] *het (~ten)* assessment (notice); (income) tax return (*or:* form)

aanslibben [ạnslɪbə(n)] *vb* form a deposit: *aangeslibd land* alluvium, alluvial land

¹aansluiten [ạnslœytə(n)] *vb* connect, join, link: *een nieuwe abonnee* ~ connect a new subscriber; *wilt u daar* ~? will you queue up there, please?

²aansluiten [ạnslœytə(n)] *ref vb* join (in), become a member of: *zich bij de vorige spreker* ~ agree with the preceding speaker; *zich bij een partij* ~ join a party; *daar sluit ik me graag bij aan* I would like to second that

aansluiting [ạnslœytɪŋ] *de (~en)* **1** joining, association (with): ~ *vinden bij iem (iets)* join in with s.o. (sth); *(fig)* ~ *zoeken bij* seek contact with; **2** *(traf)* connection: *de* ~ *missen* miss the connection; **3** connection: ~ *op het gasnet* connection to the gas mains

aansmeren [ạnsmerə(n)] *vb* palm off (on): *iem een veel te dure auto* ~ cajole s.o. into buying far too expensive a car

aansnijden [ɑnsnɛidə(n)] *vb* **1** cut (into); **2** *(fig)* broach, bring up

aanspannen [ɑnspɑnə(n)] *vb* institute: *een proces (tegen iem)* ~ institute (legal) proceedings (against s.o.)

aanspoelen [ɑnspulə(n)] *vb* wash ashore, be washed ashore: *er is een fles met een briefje erin aangespoeld* a bottle containing a letter has been washed ashore

aansporen [ɑnsporə(n)] *vb* urge (on), spur (on): *iem ~ tot grotere inspanning* incite s.o. to greater efforts

aansporing [ɑnsporɪŋ] *de (~en)* incentive: *die beloning was een echte ~ voor hem* that reward was a real incentive to him

aanspraak [ɑnsprak] *de (aanspraken)* **1** claim: *geen ~ kunnen doen gelden op iets)* not be able to lay any claim (to sth); *~ maken op iets* lay claim to sth; **2** contacts: *weinig ~ hebben* have few contacts

aansprakelijk [ɑnsprakələk] *adj* responsible (for), *(law)* liable (for): *zich voor iets ~ stellen* take responsibility for sth; *iem ~ stellen voor iets* hold s.o. responsible for sth

aansprakelijkheid [ɑnsprakələkhɛit] *de (-heden)* liability (for); responsibility: *wettelijke ~, (Belg) burgerlijke ~* (legal) liability, liability in law; *~ tegenover derden* third-party liability

aanspreken [ɑnsprekə(n)] *vb* **1** draw on, break into: *zijn kapitaal ~* break into one's capital; *een spaarrekening ~* remove (*or:* withdraw) money from a savings account; **2** speak to, talk to, address: *iem (op straat) ~* approach s.o. (in the street); *ik voel mij niet aangesproken* it doesn't concern me; *iem met mevrouw (or: meneer) ~* address s.o. as madam (*or:* sir); *iem over zijn gedrag ~* talk to s.o. about his conduct; **3** appeal to

aanstaan [ɑnstan] *vb* **1** please: *zijn gezicht staat mij niet aan* I do not like the look of him; **2** be running; be (turned) on

¹aanstaande [ɑnstandə] *adj* **1** next; this: *~ vrijdag* this Friday; **2** (forth)coming; approaching: *een ~ moeder* an expectant mother, a mother-to-be

²aanstaande [ɑnstandə] *de (~n)* fiancé, fiancée

aanstalten [ɑnstɑltə(n)] || *~ maken om te vertrekken* get ready to leave; *geen ~ maken (om)* show no sign (*or:* intention) (of)

aanstaren [ɑnstarə(n)] *vb* stare at, gaze at: *iem met open mond ~* stare open-mouthed at s.o., gape at s.o.; *iem vol bewondering ~* gaze at s.o. admiringly

aanstekelijk [ɑnstekələk] *adj, adv* infectious, contagious, catching

aansteken [ɑnstekə(n)] *vb* **1** light, kindle, turn on, switch on: *die brand is aangestoken* that fire was started deliberately; *een kaars ~* light a candle; **2** infect, contaminate: *(fig) ze steken elkaar aan* they are a bad (*or:* good) influence on one another

aansteker [ɑnstekər] *de (~s)* (cigarette) lighter

¹aanstellen [ɑnstɛlə(n)] *vb* appoint: *iem vast ~* appoint s.o. permanently

²aanstellen [ɑnstɛlə(n)] *ref vb* show off, put on airs, act: *zich belachelijk ~* make a fool of oneself; *stel je niet aan!* be your age!, stop behaving like a child!

aansteller [ɑnstɛlər] *de (~s)* poseur; *(someone behaving childishly)* baby

aanstellerig [ɑnstɛlərəχ] *adj* affected, theatrical

aanstellerij [ɑnstɛlɛrɛi] *de (~en)* affectation, pose, showing off || *is het nu uit met die ~?* are you quite finished?

aanstelling [ɑnstɛlɪŋ] *de (~en)* appointment: *een vaste (or: tijdelijke) ~ hebben* have a permanent (*or:* temporary) appointment

aansterken [ɑnstɛrkə(n)] *vb* get stronger, recuperate, regain one's strength

aanstichten [ɑnstɪχtə(n)] *vb* instigate

aanstippen [ɑnstɪpə(n)] *vb* **1** mention briefly, touch on; **2** *(med)* dab

aanstoken [ɑnstokə(n)] *vb* stir up, incite

aanstoot [ɑnstot] *de* offence: *~ geven* give offence; *~ nemen aan* take offence at

aanstootgevend [ɑnstotχevənt] *adj, adv* offensive, objectionable, *(stronger)* scandalous, *(stronger)* shocking: *~e passages in een boek* offensive passages in a book

¹aanstoten [ɑnstotə(n)] *vb* knock (against), bump (into): *hij stootte tegen de tafel aan* he bumped into the table

²aanstoten [ɑnstotə(n)] *vb* nudge: *zijn buurman ~* nudge one's neighbour

aanstrepen [ɑnstrepə(n)] *vb* mark, check (off), tick (off): *een plaats in een boek ~* mark a place in a book

aansturen [ɑnstyrə(n)] *vb* (with *op*) aim for, aim at, steer towards, drive at: *ik zou niet weten waar hij op aanstuurt* I don't know what he is driving at

aantal [ɑntɑl] *het (~len)* number: *een ~ jaren lang* for a number of years; *een ~ gasten kwam te laat* a number of guests were late; *een flink ~ boeken* quite a few books; *het totale ~ werkende kinderen* the total number of working children

aantasten [ɑntɑstə(n)] *vb* **1** affect, harm, attack: *dit zuur tast metalen aan* this acid corrodes metals; *die roddels tasten onze goede naam aan* those rumours damage (*or:* harm) our reputation; **2** attack: *door een ziekte aangetast worden* be stricken with a disease

aantekenen [ɑntekənə(n)] *vb* **1** take (*or:* make) a note of, note down, write down, record, register: *brieven laten ~* have letters registered; **2** comment, note, remark: *daarbij tekende hij aan, dat ...* he further observed that ...

aantekening [ɑntekənɪŋ] *de (~en)* note: *~en maken* take notes

aantocht [ɑntoχt] || *in ~ zijn* be on the way

aantonen [ɑntonə(n)] *vb* demonstrate, prove, show: *er werd ruimschoots aangetoond dat ...* ample evidence was given to show that ...

aantreffen [ɑntrɛfə(n)] *vb* **1** meet, encounter, find: *iem in bed ~* find s.o. in bed; *iem niet thuis ~* find s.o. out; **2** find, come across

aantrekkelijk [antrɛ̯kələk] *adj* attractive, inviting: *ik vind ze erg ~* I find them very attractive

¹aantrekken [ạntrɛkə(n)] *vb* **1** attract, draw: *de aarde wordt door de zon aangetrokken* the earth gravitates towards the sun; **2** tighten: *een knoop ~* tighten a knot; **3** draw, attract: *zich aangetrokken voelen door/tot iem (iets)* feel attracted to s.o. (sth); *dat trekt mij wel aan* that appeals to me; **4** attract, draw: *nieuwe medewerkers ~* take on (*or:* recruit) new staff; **5** put on: *andere kleren ~* change one's clothes; *ik heb niets om aan te trekken* I have nothing to wear

²aantrekken [ạntrɛkə(n)] *ref vb* be concerned about, take seriously: *zich iemands lot ~* be concerned about s.o.('s fate); *trek het je niet aan* don't let that worry you; *zich alles persoonlijk ~* take everything personally

aantrekkingskracht [ạntrɛkiŋskraχt] *de* **1** attraction, appeal: *een grote ~ bezitten voor iem* hold (a) great attraction for s.o.; *~ uitoefenen op iem* attract s.o.; **2** (force of) attraction, gravitational force

aanvaardbaar [anvạrdbar] *adj* acceptable: *~ voor* acceptable to

aanvaarden [anvạrdə(n)] *vb* **1** accept, agree to, take: *ik aanvaard uw aanbod* I accept your offer; *de consequenties ~* take (*or:* accept) the consequences; *een voorstel ~* accept a proposal; **2** accept, assume: *de verantwoordelijkheid ~* assume the responsibility

aanval [ạnval] *de* (*~len*) **1** attack, assault, offensive: *een ~ ondernemen* (*or: afslaan*) launch (*or:* beat off) an attack; *tot de ~ overgaan* take the offensive; *in de ~ gaan* go on the offensive; *de ~ is de beste verdediging* attack is the best form of defence; **2** (*med*) attack, fit: *een ~ van koorts* an attack of fever; *een ~ van woede* an attack of anger

aanvallen [ạnvalə(n)] *vb* attack, assail, assault: *de vijand in de rug ~* attack (*or:* take) the enemy from the rear

aanvallend [ạnvalənt] *adj, adv* offensive, aggressive

aanvaller [ạnvalər] *de* (*~s*) **1** assailant, attacker; **2** (*sport*) attacker, (*socc*) forward, striker

aanvangen [ạnvaŋə(n)] *vb* begin, start, commence: *met die jongen is niets aan te vangen* that boy is hopeless

aanvankelijk [anvạŋkələk] *adv* initially, at first, in (*or:* at) the beginning

aanvaren [ạnvarə(n)] *vb* run into, collide with: *een ander schip ~* collide with another ship

aanvaring [ạnvariŋ] *de* (*~en*) collision, crash: *in ~ komen met* collide with

aanvechtbaar [anvɛχtbar] *adj* contestable, disputable: *een ~ standpunt* a debatable point of view

aanvechten [ạnvɛχtə(n)] *vb* dispute: *een beslissing ~* challenge a decision

aanvechting [ạnvɛχtiŋ] *de* (*~en*) (*fig*) temptation, impulse: *een ~ van (de) slaap* an attack of sleepiness

aanvegen [ạnveɣə(n)] *vb* sweep, sweep out

aanverwant [ạnvərwant] *adj* related; allied: *de geneeskunde en ~e vakken* medicine and related professions

¹aanvliegen [ạnvliɣə(n)] *vb* fly at, attack: *de hond vloog de postbode aan* the dog flew at the postman

²aanvliegen [ạnvliɣə(n)] *vb* fly (towards): *tegen iets ~* fly (towards) against sth, crash into sth

aanvoelen [ạnvulə(n)] *vb* feel, sense: *iem ~* understand s.o., (*stronger*) empathize with s.o.; *een stemming ~* sense an atmosphere; *elkaar goed ~* speak the same language; *het voelt koud aan* it feels cold

aanvoer [ạnvur] *de* supply, delivery: *de ~ van levensmiddelen* food supplies

aanvoerder [ạnvurdər] *de* (*~s*) leader, captain

aanvoeren [ạnvurə(n)] *vb* **1** lead, command, captain: *een leger ~* command an army; **2** supply, import: *hulpgoederen werden per vliegtuig aangevoerd* relief supplies were flown in; **3** bring forward, advance, produce, argue: *hij voerde aan dat …* he argued that …

aanvoering [ạnvuriŋ] *de* command, leadership, captaincy: *onder ~ van* under the command (*or:* leadership) of

aanvraag [ạnvraχ] *de* (*aanvragen*) **1** application, request, inquiry: *een ~ indienen* submit an application; *op ~ te vertonen* to be shown on demand; *~ voor een uitkering* application for social welfare payment; **2** request, demand, order: *wij konden niet aan alle aanvragen voldoen* we couldn't meet the demand; *op ~ verkrijgbaar* available on request

aanvragen [ạnvraɣə(n)] *vb* **1** apply for, request: *ontslag ~* apply for permission to make redundant; *een vergunning ~* apply for a licence; **2** request, order: *vraag een gratis folder aan* send for free brochure; *informatie ~ over treinen in Engeland* inquire about trains in England

aanvrager [ạnvraɣər] *de* (*~s*) applicant

aanvullen [ạnvylə(n)] *vb* complete, finish, fill (up): *de voorraad ~* replenish stocks; *zij vullen elkaar goed aan* they complement each other well

aanvullend [anvỵlənt] *adj* supplementary, additional: *een ~e cursus* a follow-up course; *een ~ pensioen* a supplementary pension

aanvulling [ạnvylɪŋ] *de* (*~en*) supplement, addition

aanvuren [ạnvyrə(n)] *vb* fire; rouse; incite: *iemands ijver ~* fire s.o.'s zeal; *de troepen ~* rouse the troops

aanwaaien [ạnwajə(n)] *vb* come naturally to: *alles waait hem zo maar aan* everything just falls into his lap

aanwakkeren [ạnwakərə(n)] *vb* **1** stir up: *het vuur ~* fan the fire; **2** stimulate, stir up: *de kooplust ~* stimulate buying

aanwas [ạnwas] *de* (*~sen*) growth, accretion

aanwenden [ạnwɛndə(n)] *vb* apply, use: *zijn gezag ~* use one's authority; *zijn invloed ~* exert one's influence

aanwennen [ˈɑnwɛnə(n)] *ref vb* get into the habit of: *zich slechte gewoonten* ~ fall into (*or:* acquire) bad habits

aanwezig [ɑnwe̯zəχ] *adj* present: *Trudie is vandaag niet* ~ Trudie is not in (*or:* here) today; ~ *zijn bij* be present at; *niet* ~ absent

aanwezigheid [ɑnwe̯zəχhɛit] *de* presence, attendance: *uw* ~ *is niet noodzakelijk* your presence is not necessary (*or:* required); *in* ~ *van* in the presence of

aanwijzen [ˈɑnwɛizə(n)] *vb* **1** point to, point out, indicate, show: *een fout* ~ point out a mistake; *gasten hun plaats* ~ show guests to their seats; **2** designate, assign, allocate: *een acteur* ~ *voor een rol* cast an actor for a part; *een erfgenaam* ~ designate an heir; **3** indicate, point to, show: *de klok wijst de tijd aan* the clock shows the time

aanwijzing [ˈɑnwɛizɪŋ] *de* (~*en*) **1** indication, sign, clue: *er bestaat geen enkele* ~ *dat* ... there is no indication whatever that ...; **2** instruction, direction: *hij gaf nauwkeurige* ~*en* he gave precise instructions; *de* ~*en opvolgen* follow the directions; ~*en voor het gebruik* directions for use

aanwinst [ˈɑnwɪnst] *de* (~*en*) **1** acquisition, addition: *een mooie* ~ *voor het museum* a beautiful acquisition for the museum; **2** gain, improvement, asset: *de computer is een* ~ *voor ieder bedrijf* the computer is an asset in every business

aanzet [ˈɑnzɛt] *de* (~*ten*) start, initiative: *de (eerste)* ~ *geven tot iets* initiate sth, give the initial impetus to sth

aanzetten [ˈɑnzɛtə(n)] *vb* **1** put on, sew on, stitch on: *een mouw* ~ sew on (*or:* set in) a sleeve; **2** start up, turn on: *de radio* ~ turn on the radio; **3** spur on, urge, incite: *iem tot diefstal* ~ incite s.o. to steal; *ergens laat komen* ~ turn up late somewhere; *met iets komen* ~ turn up with sth, come up with sth

aanzicht [ˈɑnzɪχt] *het* (~*en*) aspect, look, view: *nu krijgt de zaak een ander* ~ that puts a different light on the matter

¹**aanzien** [ˈɑnzin] *vb* **1** look at, watch, see: *die film is niet om aan te zien* it's an awful film; *ik kon het niet langer* ~ I couldn't bear to watch it any longer; **2** consider, regard: *waar zie je mij voor aan?* what do you take me for?; *iem voor een ander* ~ (mis)take s.o. for s.o. else; *ik zie haar er best voor aan* I think she's quite capable of it

²**aanzien** [ˈɑnzin] *het* **1** looking (at), watching: *dat is het* ~ *waard* that is worth watching (*or:* looking at); *ten* ~ *van* with regard (*or:* respect) to; **2** look, aspect, appearance: *iets een ander* ~ *geven* put a different complexion on sth; **3** standing, regard: *een man van* ~ a man of distinction; *hij is sterk in* ~ *gestegen* his prestige has risen sharply

aanzienlijk [ˈɑnzinlək] *adj, adv* considerable, substantial: ~*e schade* serious damage; *een* ~*e verbetering* a substantial improvement

aanzoek [ˈɑnzuk] *het* (~*en*) proposal: *de knappe prins deed het meisje een* ~ the handsome prince proposed to the girl

aanzwellen [ˈɑnzwɛlə(n)] *vb* swell (up, out), rise

aap [ap] *de (apen)* monkey; ape

aapmens [ˈapmɛns] *de* (~*en*) apeman

aar [ar] *de (aren)* ear

aard [art] *de* **1** nature, disposition, character: *zijn ware* ~ *tonen* show one's true character; **2** nature, sort, kind: *schilderijen van allerlei* ~ various kinds (*or:* all kinds) of paintings

aardappel [ˈardɑpəl] *de* (~*s*, ~*en*) potato: *gekookte* (*or:* *gebakken*) ~*s* boiled (*or:* fried) potatoes

aardappelmesje [ˈardɑpəlmɛʃə] *het* (~*s*) potato peeler

aardappelpuree [ˈardɑpəlpyre] *de* mashed potato(es)

aardas [ˈardɑs] *de* (~*sen*) axis of the earth

aardbei [ˈardbɛi] *de* (~*en*) strawberry

aardbeving [ˈardbevɪŋ] *de* (~*en*) earthquake

aardbodem [ˈardbodəm] *de* surface (*or:* face) of the earth: *honderden huizen werden van de* ~ *weggevaagd* hundreds of houses were wiped off the face of the earth

aardbol [ˈardbɔl] *de* (~*len*) earth, world, globe

aarde [ˈardə] *de* **1** earth, world: *in een baan om de* ~ in orbit round the earth; *op* ~ on earth, under the sun; **2** ground, earth (*electricity*); **3** earth, soil: *dat zal bij haar niet in goede* ~ *vallen* she is not going to like that; *het plan viel in goede* ~ the plan was well received

¹**aarden** [ˈardə(n)] *adj* earthen, clay: ~ *potten* earthenware pots

²**aarden** [ˈardə(n)] *vb* thrive: *zij kan hier niet* ~ she can't settle in here, she can't find her niche; *ik aard hier best* I fit in here, I feel at home here; *dit diertje aardt hier goed* this animal thrives here

³**aarden** [ˈardə(n)] *vb* (*electricity*) earth

¹**aardewerk** [ˈardəwɛrk] *het* earthenware, pottery

²**aardewerk** [ˈardəwɛrk] *adj* || *een* ~ *schotel* an earthenware dish

aardgas [ˈartχɑs] *het* natural gas

¹**aardig** [ˈardəχ] *adj* **1** nice, friendly: (*iron*) *wat doe je* ~ (how) charming (you are)!; *dat is* ~ *van je!, wat* ~ *van je!* how nice of you; **2** nice, pretty: *het is een* ~*e meid* she's a nice girl; *een* ~ *tuintje* a nice (*or:* pretty) garden; **3** fair, nice: *een* ~ *inkomen* a nice income

²**aardig** [ˈardəχ] *adv* nicely, pretty, fairly: *dat komt* ~ *in de richting* that's more like it; ~ *wat mensen* quite a few people; *hij is* ~ *op weg om* ... *te worden* he is well on his way to becoming ...

aardigheid [ˈardəχhɛit] *de* (*-heden*) small present: *ik heb een* ~*je meegebracht* I have brought a little something

aardolie [ˈartoli] *de* (*-oliën*) petroleum

aardrijkskunde [ˈardrɛikskʏndə] *de* geography

aardrijkskundig [ˈardrɛikskʏndəχ] *adj* geographic(al)

aards [arts] *adj* earthly, worldly: ~*e machten* earthly powers; *een* ~ *paradijs* paradise on earth; ~*e genoegens* worldly pleasures

aardworm [ɑrtwɔrm] *de (~en)* (earth)worm

aars [ars] *de (aarzen)* arse

aartsbisschop [ɑrtsbisχɔp] *de (~pen)* archbishop

aartsengel [ɑrtsɛŋəl] *de (~en)* archangel

aartshertog [ɑrtshɛrtɔχ] *de (~en)* archduke

aartsvijand [ɑrtsfɛiɑnt] *de (~en)* arch-enemy

aarzelen [ɑrzələ(n)] *vb* hesitate: ~ *iets te doen* hesitate about doing sth; *ik aarzel nog* I am still in doubt

aarzeling [ɑrzəliŋ] *de (~en)* hesitancy, hesitation; shilly-shallying, doubt: *na enige* ~ after some hesitation

¹**aas** [as] *het* bait: *levend* ~ live bait; *van* ~ *voorzien* bait (the hook, trap)

²**aas** [as] *het, de (cards)* ace

aasgier [asχir] *de (~en)* vulture

abattoir [ɑbɑtwɑr] *het (~s)* abattoir, slaughterhouse

abc [abese] *het (~'s)* ABC

abdij [ɑbdɛi] *de (~en)* abbey

ABN [abeɛn] *het Algemeen Beschaafd Nederlands* (received) standard Dutch

abnormaal [ɑpnɔrmɑl] *adj, adv* abnormal; deviant, aberrant; deformed: *een* ~ *groot hoofd* an abnormally large head

abonnee [ɑbɔne] *de (~s)* subscriber (to)

abonneenummer [ɑbɔnenymər] *het (~s)* subscriber('s) number

abonnement [ɑbɔnəmɛnt] *het (~en)* 1 subscription (to); taking (or: buying) a season ticket: *een* ~ *nemen op ...* subscribe to ...; *een* ~ *opzeggen* (or: *vernieuwen)* cancel (or: renew) a subscription; 2 season ticket

abonneren [ɑbɔnerə(n)] *ref vb* subscribe (to), take out a subscription (to)

abortus [ɑbɔrtʏs] *de (~sen)* abortion; miscarriage

abrikoos [ɑbrikos] *de* apricot

abrupt [ɑprʏpt] *adj, adv* abrupt, sudden: ~ *halt houden* stop abruptly (or: suddenly)

absent [ɑpsɛnt] *adj* absent

absentie [ɑpsɛnsi] *de (~s)* absence

absoluut [ɑpsolyt] *adj, adv* absolute, perfect: ~ *gehoor* perfect pitch; *dat is* ~ *onmogelijk* that's absolutely impossible; ~ *niet* definitely (or: absolutely) not; *ik heb* ~ *geen tijd* I simply have no time; *weet je het zeker?* ~! are you sure? absolutely!

absorberen [ɑpsɔrberə(n)] *vb* absorb: ~*d middel* absorbent, absorbing agent

abstract [ɑpstrɑkt] *adj, adv* abstract: ~*e denkbeelden* abstract (or: theoretical) ideas; ~ *schilderen* paint abstractly

absurd [ɑpsʏrt] *adj, adv* absurd, ridiculous, ludicrous: ~ *toneel* theatre of the absurd

abt [ɑpt] *de (~en)* abbot

¹**abuis** [ɑbœys] *het* mistake: *per (bij)* ~ by mistake

²**abuis** [ɑbœys] *adj* mistaken: *u bent* ~ you are mistaken

abusievelijk [ɑbysivələk] *adv* mistakenly, erroneously

acacia [akɑsia] *de* locust (tree), (false) acacia

academie [akɑdemi] *de (~s)* university, college: *pedagogische* ~ college of education; *sociale* ~ college of social studies

academisch [ɑkɑdemis] *adj, adv* academic, university: *een* ~*e graad* a university degree; ~ *ziekenhuis* university (or: teaching) hospital

acceleratie [ɑksɛlərɑ(t)si] *de* acceleration

accelereren [ɑksəlererə(n)] *vb* accelerate

accent [ɑksɛnt] *het (~en)* accent, stress *(also fig)*: *een sterk* (or: *licht) noordelijk* ~ a strong (or: slight) northern accent; *het* ~ *hebben op de eerste lettergreep* have the accent on the first syllable; *het* ~ *leggen op* stress

accentueren [ɑksɛntywerə(n)] *vb* stress, emphasize, accentuate

acceptabel [ɑksɛptɑbəl] *adj, adv* acceptable

accepteren [ɑksɛptərə(n)] *vb* accept, take: *een wissel* ~ accept a bill (of exchange); *zijn gedrag kan ik niet* ~ I can't accept (or: condone) his behaviour

accessoire [ɑsəswɑrə] *het (~s)* accessory

accijns [ɑksɛins] *de (accijnzen)* excise (duty, tax): *accijnzen heffen (op)* charge excise (on)

acclimatiseren [ɑklimatizerə(n)] *vb* acclimatize, become acclimatized

accolade [ɑkolɑdə] *de (~s)* brace, bracket

accommodatie [ɑkomodɑ(t)si] *de (~s)* accommodation; facilities: *er is* ~ *voor tien passagiers* there are facilities for ten passengers

accordeon [ɑkɔrdejɔn] *het, de (~s)* accordion

accordeonist [ɑkɔrdejɔnist] *de (~en)* accordionist

accountant [ɑkɑuntənt] *de (~s)* accountant, auditor

accu [ɑky] *de (~'s)* battery: *de* ~ *is leeg* the battery is dead

accuraat [ɑkyrɑt] *adj, adv* accurate, precise, meticulous: ~ *werken* work accurately

accuratesse [ɑkyratɛsə] *de* accuracy, precision, meticulousness

ace [es] *de (~s)* ace

ach [ɑχ] *int* oh, ah: ~ *wat, ik doe het gewoon!* oh who cares, I'll just do it!; ~, *je kunt niet alles hebben!* oh well, you can't have everything!

achillespees [ɑχiləspes] *de (-pezen)* Achilles tendon

¹**acht** [ɑχt] *de (~en)* attention, consideration: ~ *slaan op: a)* pay attention to; *b)* take notice of; *de regels in* ~ *nemen* comply with (or: observe) the rules; *voorzichtigheid in* ~ *nemen* take due care

²**acht** [ɑχt] *num* eight: *nog* ~ *dagen* another eight days, eight more days; *iets in* ~*en breken* break sth into eight pieces; *zij kwamen met hun* ~*en* eight of them came; *zij zijn met hun* ~*en* there are eight of them

achtbaan [ɑχtban] *de (-banen)* roller coaster

achteloos [ɑχtəlos] *adj, adv* careless, negligent; inconsiderate

achten [ɑχtə(n)] *vb* 1 esteem, respect; 2 consider, think

¹achter [ɑχtər] *prep* **1** behind, at the back (*or:* rear) of: ~ *het huis* behind (*or:* at the back of) the house; ~ *haar ouders' rug om* behind her parents' back; *zet een kruisje* ~ *je naam* put a tick against your name; ~ *zijn computer* at his computer; **2** after: ~ *elkaar* one after the other, in succession, in a row; ~ *iets komen* find out about sth, get to the bottom of sth; ~ *iem staan* stand behind s.o.; ~ *iets staan* approve of sth, back sth; *er zit (steekt) meer* ~ there is more to it

²achter [ɑχtər] *adv* **1** behind, at the rear (*or:* back): ~ *in de tuin* at the bottom of the garden; **2** slow, behind(hand); *jouw horloge loopt* ~ your watch is slow; *ik ben* ~ *met mijn werk* I am behind(hand) with my work; *(sport)* ~ *staan* be behind (*or:* trailing); *(sport) vier punten* ~ *staan* be four points down

achteraan [ɑχtəraṇ] *adv* at the back, at (*or:* in) the rear: *wij wandelden* ~ we were walking at the back; ~ *in de zaal* at the back of the hall

achteraangaan [ɑχtəraṇɣan] *vb* go after: *ik zou er maar eens* ~ you'd better look into that, I'd do sth about it if I were you

achteraankomen [ɑχtəraṇkomə(n)] *vb* come last: *wij komen wel achteraan* we'll follow on after

achteraanlopen [ɑχtəraṇlopə(n)] *vb* walk on behind

achteraanzicht [ɑχtəranziχt] *het* (~en) rear view

achteraf [ɑχtərɑf] *adv* **1** at the back, in (*or:* at) the rear, *(remote)* out of the way: ~ *wonen* live out in the sticks, live in the middle of nowhere; **2** afterwards, later (on), now, as it is: ~ *bekeken zou ik zeggen dat* … looking back I would say that …; ~ *is het makkelijk praten* it is easy to be wise after the event; ~ *ben ik blij dat* … now I'm glad that …

achterbak [ɑχtərbɑk] *de* (~ken) boot

achterbaks [ɑχtərbɑks] *adj, adv* underhand, sneaky

achterban [ɑχtərbɑn] *de* (~nen) supporters, backing, grassroots (support)

achterblijven [ɑχtərblɛivə(n)] *vb* **1** stay behind, remain (behind); **2** be (*or:* get) left (behind); **3** be left: *zij bleef achter met drie kinderen* she was left with three children

achterbuurt [ɑχtərbyrt] *de* (~en) slum

achterdeur [ɑχtərdør] *de* (~en) back door, rear door *(car)*

achterdocht [ɑχtərdɔχt] *de* suspicion (of, about): *hij begon* ~ *te krijgen* he began to get suspicious

achterdochtig [ɑχtərdɔχtəχ] *adj, adv* suspicious

achtereenvolgend [ɑχtərenvɔlɣənt] *adj* successive, consecutive

achtereenvolgens [ɑχtərenvɔlɣəns] *adv* successively

achtereind [ɑχtərɛint] *het* (~en) rear end; hindquarters

achteren [ɑχtərə(n)] *adv* (the) back: *verder naar* ~ further back(wards); *van* ~ from behind

achtergebleven [ɑχtərχəblevə(n)] *adj* backward, underdeveloped: ~ *gebieden* backward (*or:* underdeveloped) areas

achtergrond [ɑχtərɣrɔnt] *de* (~en) background: *de* ~*en van een conflict* the background to (*or:* of) a dispute; *zich op de* ~ *houden* keep in the background

achterhaald [ɑχtərhalt] *adj* out of date, irrelevant

achterhalen [ɑχtərhalə(n)] *vb* **1** overtake; catch up with: *de politie heeft de dief kunnen* ~ the police were able to run down the thief; **2** retrieve: *die gegevens zijn niet meer te* ~ those data can no longer be accessed (*or:* retrieved); *die gegevens zijn al lang achterhaald* that information is totally out of date

achterhoede [ɑχtərhudə] *de* (~s) *(sport)* defence

achterhoedespeler [ɑχtərhudəspelər] *de* (~s) defender, back

achterhoofd [ɑχtərhoft] *het* (~en) back of the head: *iets in zijn* ~ *hebben* have sth at the back of one's mind

achterhouden [ɑχtərhaudə(n)] *vb* **1** keep back, withhold; **2** hold back

achterin [ɑχtərɪn] *adv* in the back (*or:* rear), at the back (*or:* rear)

achterkant [ɑχtərkɑnt] *de* (~en) back, rear (side), reverse (side): *op de* ~ *van het papier* on the back of the paper

achterkleindochter [ɑχtərklɛindɔχtər] *de* (~s) great-granddaughter

achterkleinkind [ɑχtərklɛiŋkɪnt] *het* (~eren) great-grandchild

achterkleinzoon [ɑχtərklɛinzon] *de* (-zonen, ~s) great-grandson

achterklep [ɑχtərklɛp] *de* (~pen) lid of the boot *(car)*; hatchback, liftback

achterlaten [ɑχtərlatə(n)] *vb* leave (behind): *een bericht* (or: *boodschap*) ~ leave (behind) a note (*or:* message)

achterliggen [ɑχtərlɪɣə(n)] *vb* lie behind, lag (behind): *drie ronden* ~ be three laps behind, be trailing by three laps

achterlijf [ɑχtərlɛif] *het* (-lijven) **1** rump; abdomen; **2** back

¹achterlijk [ɑχtərlək] *adj* backward, (mentally) retarded: *hij is niet* ~ he's no fool

²achterlijk [ɑχtərlək] *adv* like a moron, like an idiot: *doe niet zo* ~ don't be such a moron

achterlopen [ɑχtərlopə(n)] *vb* **1** be slow, lose time, be behind, lag behind; **2** be behind the times

achterna [ɑχtərna] *adv* **1** after, behind; **2** afterwards, after the event

achternaam [ɑχtərnam] *de* (-namen) surname, last name, family name

achternagaan [ɑχtərnaɣan] *vb* go after, follow (behind)

achternazitten [ɑχtərnazɪtə(n)] *vb* chase: *de politie zit ons achterna* the police are after us (*or:* on our heels, on our tail)

achterneef [ɑχtərnef] *de* (-neven) second cousin; great-nephew

achternicht [ɑχtərnɪχt] *de (~en)* second cousin; great-niece

achterom [ɑχtərɔm] *adv* round the back: *een blik ~ a* backward glance

achterop [ɑχtərɔp] *adv* 1 at (*or:* on) the back: *spring maar ~!* jump on behind me!; 2 behind: ~ *raken: a)* drop behind; *b)* fall (*or:* get) behind

achterover [ɑχtərɔvər] *adv* back(wards): *hij viel ~ op de stenen* he fell back(wards) onto the stones

achteroverdrukken [ɑχtərɔvərdrʏkə(n)] *vb* pinch

achteroverhellen [ɑχtərɔvərhɛlə(n)] *vb* tilt, slope backwards

achterplaats [ɑχtərplats] *de (~en)* courtyard, backyard

achterpoot [ɑχtərpot] *de (-poten)* hind leg

achterruit [ɑχtərœyt] *de (~en)* rear window, back window

achterruitverwarming [ɑχtərœytfərwɑrmɪŋ] *de* (rear window) demister

achterspeler [ɑχtərspelər] *de (~s)* back

achterst [ɑχtərst] *adj* back, rear, hind(most): *de ~e rijen* the back rows

achterstallig [ɑχtərstɑləχ] *adj* back, overdue, in arrears: *~e huur* rent arrears, back rent; *~ onderhoud* overdue maintenance

achterstand [ɑχtərstɑnt] *de* arrears: *(sport) een grote ~ hebben* be well down (*or:* behind); *de ~ inlopen* make up arrears; *een ~ oplopen* fall behind; *de ploeg probeerde de ~ weg te werken* the team tried to draw level

achterstandswijk [ɑχtərstɑn(t)swɛik] *de (~en)* disadvantaged urban area

¹**achterste** [ɑχtərstə] *het (~n)* 1 back (part); 2 backside, rear (end): *op zijn ~ vallen* fall on one's bottom

²**achterste** [ɑχtərstə] *het, de (~n)* back one, hindmost one, rear(most) one

achterstellen [ɑχtərstɛlə(n)] *vb* slight, neglect: *hij voelde zich achtergesteld* he felt discriminated against

achtersteven [ɑχtərstevə(n)] *de (~s)* stern

achterstevoren [ɑχtərstəvorə(n)] *adv* back to front

¹**achteruit** [ɑχtərœyt] *adv* back(wards)

²**achteruit** [ɑχtərœyt] *de* reverse (gear): *een auto in zijn ~ zetten* put a car into reverse (gear)

achteruitgaan [ɑχtərœytχan] *vb* 1 go back(wards), go astern (*ship*), reverse (*car*), back (*car*): *ga eens wat achteruit!* stand back a little!; 2 (*fig*) decline, get worse, grow worse, fail: *zijn prestaties gaan achteruit* his performance is on the decline; *haar gezondheid gaat snel achteruit* her health is failing rapidly; *ik ben er per maand honderd euro op achteruitgegaan* I am a hundred euros worse off per month

¹**achteruitgang** [ɑχtərœytχɑŋ] *de* back exit, rear exit, back door

²**achteruitgang** [ɑχtərœytχɑŋ] *de* decline: *de huidige economische ~* the present economic decline

achteruitkijkspiegel [ɑχtərœytkɛikspiɣəl] *de (~s)* rear-view mirror

achteruitrijden [ɑχtərœytrɛidə(n)] *vb* reverse (into), back (into)

achteruitwijken [ɑχtərœytwɛikə(n)] *vb* back away; step back, fall back

achtervolgen [ɑχtərvɔlɣə(n)] *vb* 1 follow: *die gedachte achtervolgt mij* that thought haunts (*or:* obsesses) me; 2 pursue, persecute

achtervolging [ɑχtərvɔlɣɪŋ] *de (~en)* pursuit, chase, persecution: *de ~ inzetten* pursue, set off in pursuit (of)

¹**achterwaarts** [ɑχtərwarts] *adv* back(wards): *een stap ~* a step back(wards)

²**achterwaarts** [ɑχtərwarts] *adj* backward, rearward: *een ~e beweging* a backward movement

achterwand [ɑχtərwɑnt] *de (~en)* back wall, rear wall

achterwege [ɑχtərweɣə] *adv* ‖ *een antwoord bleef ~* an answer was not forthcoming; ~ *laten* omit, leave undone

achterwerk [ɑχtərwɛrk] *het (~en)* backside, rear (end)

achterwiel [ɑχtərwil] *het (~en)* back wheel, rear wheel

achterzijde [ɑχtərzɛidə] *de (~n)* back, rear

achthoek [ɑχthuk] *de (~en)* octagon

achting [ɑχtɪŋ] *de* regard, esteem: ~ *voor iem hebben* have respect for s.o.; *in (iemands) ~ dalen* come down in s.o.'s estimation; *in (iemands) ~ stijgen* go up in s.o.'s estimation

achtste [ɑχtstə] *adj* eighth: *een ~ liter* one eighth of a litre

achttien [ɑχtin] *num* eighteen

achttiende [ɑχtində] *num* eighteenth

achttiende-eeuws [ɑχtindəews] *adj* eighteenth-century

acne [ɑkne] *de* acne

acquisitie [akwizi(t)si] *de (~s)* acquisition

acrobaat [akrobat] *de (acrobaten)* acrobat

acrobatisch [akrobatis] *adj, adv* acrobatic

acryl [akril] *het* acrylic (fibre)

acteren [aktera(n)] *vb* act, perform

acteur [ɑktør] *de (~s)* actor, performer

actie [ɑksi] *de (~s)* 1 action, activity: *er zit geen ~ in dat toneelstuk* there's no action in that play; *in ~ komen* go into action; 2 (protest) campaign: ~ *voeren (just once)* hold a demonstration; ~ *voeren tegen* campaign against

actief [ɑktif] *adj, adv* active (*finance*), busy, energetic: *in actieve dienst: a)* on active duty; *b) (mil)* on active service; *een actieve handelsbalans* a favourable balance of trade; *iets ~ en passief steunen* support sth (both) directly and indirectly; *actieve handel* export (trade)

actievoerder [ɑksivurdər] *de (~s)* campaigner, activist

activa [ɑktiva] *de* assets: ~ *en passiva* assets and liabilities; *vaste ~* fixed assets; *vlottende ~* current assets

activeren [ɑktivɛrə(n)] *vb* activate

activiteit [ɑktiviteit] *de (~en)* activity: *~en ont-plooien* undertake activities

actrice [ɑktrisə] *de (~s)* actress

actualiteit [ɑktywaliteit] *de (~en)* topical matter *(or:* subject), current event, *(pl also)* news, *(pl also)* current affairs

actueel [ɑktywel] *adj* current, topical: *een ~ onder-werp* a topical subject, *(pl also)* current affairs

acupunctuur [akypyŋktyr] *de (acupuncturen)* acupuncture

¹**acuut** [ɑkyt] *adj* acute, critical: *~ gevaar* acute danger

²**acuut** [ɑkyt] *adv* immediately, right away, at once

A.D. *anno Domini* AD

adamsappel [ɑdɑmsɑpəl] *de (~s)* Adam's apple

adder [ɑdər] *de (~s)* viper, adder: *(fig) er schuilt een ~(tje) onder het gras* there's a snake in the grass, there's a catch in it somewhere

adel [ɑdəl] *de* nobility, peerage: *hij is van ~* he is a peer, he belongs to the nobility

adelaar [ɑdəlar] *de (~s)* eagle

adellijk [ɑdələk] *adj* noble: *van ~e afkomst* of noble birth; *~ bloed* noble blood

adem [ɑdəm] *de* breath: *de laatste ~ uitblazen* breathe one's last; *slechte ~* bad breath; *zijn ~ in-houden (also fig)* hold one's breath; *naar ~ happen* gasp for breath; *buiten ~ zijn* be out of breath; *in één ~* in the same breath; *weer op ~ komen* catch one's breath

adembenemend [ɑdəmbənemənt] *adj, adv* breathtaking: *een ~ schouwspel* a breathtaking scene

ademen [ɑdəmə(n)] *vb* breathe, inhale: *vrij ~ (also fig)* breathe freely; *de lucht die we hier ademen is verpest* the air we are breathing here is poisoned

ademhalen [ɑdəmhalə(n)] *vb* breathe: *weer adem kunnen halen* be able to breathe again; *haal eens diep adem* take a deep breath

ademhaling [ɑdəmhalɪŋ] *de (~en)* breathing, respiration: *kunstmatige ~* artificial respiration; *een onrustige ~* irregular breathing

ademloos [ɑdəmlos] *adj, adv* breathless: *een ademloze stilte* a breathless hush

ademtest [ɑdəmtɛst] *de (~s)* breath test: *iem de ~ afnemen* breathalyse s.o.

adequaat [ɑdəkwat] *adj, adv* appropriate, effective; adequate: *~ reageren* react appropriately *(or:* effectively)

ader [ɑdər] *de (~s, ~en)* vein, blood vessel, artery: *een gesprongen ~* a burst blood vessel

aderverkalking [ɑdərvərkɑlkɪŋ] *de* arteriosclerosis, hardening of the arteries

adhesie [ɑthezi] *de* adherence

adjudant [ɑtjydɑnt] *de (~en)* **1** adjutant, aide(-de-camp); **2** *(roughly)* warrant officer

adjunct-directeur [ɑtjʏŋɡdirɛktør] *de (~en)* deputy director *(or:* manager); *(educ)* deputy headmaster

administrateur [ɑtministratør] *de (~en, ~s)* administrator: *de ~ van een universiteit* the administrative director of a university

administratie [ɑtministra(t)si] *de (~s)* **1** administration, management, accounts: *de ~ voeren* do the administrative work, keep the accounts; **2** administrative department; *(bldg)* administrative building *(or:* offices): *hij zit op de ~* he's in the administrative *(or:* clerical) department

administratief [ɑtministratif] *adj, adv* administrative, clerical: *~ personeel* administrative *(or:* clerical) staff; *(Belg) ~ centrum* administrative centre

administratiekosten [ɑtministra(t)sikɔstə(n)] *de* administrative costs, service charge(s)

admiraal [ɑtmiral] *de (~s)* admiral

adopteren [adɔptɛrə(n)] *vb* adopt

adoptie [adɔpsi] *de (~s)* adoption

adoptiekind [adɔpsikɪnt] *het (~eren)* adopted child

adoptieouder [adɔpsiaudər] *de (~s)* adoptive parent

adrenaline [adrenalinə] *de* adrenaline

adres [adrɛs] *het (~sen)* address, (place of) residence: *(fig) je bent aan het juiste ~* you've come to the right place; *hij verhuisde zonder een ~ achter te laten* he moved without leaving a forwarding address; *per ~* care of, *(abbr)* c/o

adresseren [adrɛsɛrə(n)] *vb* address: *een brief ver-geten te ~* forget to address a letter

adreswijziging [adrɛsweizəɣɪŋ] *de (~en)* change of address

Adriatisch [adrijatis] *adj* Adriatic: *~e Zee* Adriatic Sea

adv [adevɛ] *de arbeidsduurverkorting* shorter working hours

advent [ɑtfɛnt] *de* Advent

adverteerder [ɑtfərtɛrdər] *de (~s)* advertiser

advertentie [ɑtfərtɛnsi] *de (~s)* advertisement, ad(vert): *een ~ plaatsen* put an advertisement in the paper(s)

adverteren [ɑtfərtɛrə(n)] *vb* advertise, announce: *er wordt veel geadverteerd voor nieuwe computerspelletjes* new computer games are being heavily advertised

advies [ɑtfis] *het (adviezen)* advice: *~ geven* give advice; *iemands ~ opvolgen* follow s.o.'s advice; *iem om ~ vragen* ask s.o.'s advice; *een ~* a piece of advice, a recommendation

adviseren [ɑtfizɛrə(n)] *vb* **1** recommend, advise (s.o.): *hij adviseerde mij de auto te laten repareren* he advised me to have the car mended; **2** advise, counsel: *ik kan je in deze lastige kwestie niet ~* I can't offer you advice in this complicated matter

adviseur [ɑtfizør] *de (~s)* adviser, advisor, counsellor, consultant: *rechtskundig ~* legal advisor, lawyer, solicitor

advocaat [ɑtfokat] *de (advocaten)* lawyer, barrister, solicitor: *een ~ nemen* engage a lawyer

aerobics [ɛːrɔ̯bɪks] *de* aerobics

¹af [ɑf] *adv* **1** off, away: *mensen liepen ~ en aan* people came and went; *~ en toe* (every) now and then; *klaar? ~!* ready, steady, go!, get set! go!; **2** (with *van*) from: *van die dag ~* from that day (on, onwards); *van kind ~ (aan) woon ik in deze straat* since I was a child I have been living in this street; *van de grond ~* from ground level; **3** away, off: *(fig) dat kan er bij ons niet ~* we can't afford that; *de verf is er ~* the paint has come off; *ver ~* a long way off; *hij woont een eindje van de weg ~* he lives a little way away from the road; *van iem ~ zijn* be rid of s.o.; *u bent nog niet van me ~* you haven't seen (*or:* heard) the last of me, I haven't finished with you yet; **4** down: *de trap ~* down the stairs; **5** to, towards, up to: *ze komen op ons ~* they are coming towards us; *goed* (*or: beter, slecht*) *~ zijn* have come off well (*or:* better, badly); *ik weet er niets van ~* I don't know anything about it; *van voren ~ aan beginnen* start from scratch, start all over again

²af [ɑf] *adj* **1** finished, done, completed, polished, well-finished: *het werk is ~* the work is done (*or:* finished); **2** (*game*) out: *je bent ~* you're out; *teruggaan naar ~* go back to square one

afbakenen [ɑ̯vbakənə(n)] *vb* mark out, stake out, define, demarcate, mark off

afbeelden [ɑ̯vbeldə(n)] *vb* depict, portray, picture

afbeelding [ɑ̯vbeldɪŋ] *de (~en)* picture, image, illustration, figure

afbellen [ɑ̯vbɛlə(n)] *vb* **1** cancel (by telephone); **2** ring round: *hij belde de halve stad af om een taxi* he rang round half the city for a taxi

afbetalen [ɑ̯vbətalə(n)] *vb* pay off; pay for (*goods*): *het huis is helemaal afbetaald* the house is completely paid for

afbetaling [ɑ̯vbətalɪŋ] *de (~en)* hire purchase, payment by instalment (*or:* in instalments): *op ~ on* hire purchase

afbijten [ɑ̯vbɛitə(n)] *vb* **1** bite off; **2** strip, remove || *van zich ~* stick up for oneself

afbladderen [ɑ̯vblɑdərə(n)] *vb* flake (off), peel (off): *de verf bladdert af* the paint is flaking (*or:* peeling) off

afblazen [ɑ̯vblazə(n)] *vb* blow off (*or:* away): *stof van de tafel ~* blow the dust off the table; *de scheidsrechter had (de wedstrijd) al afgeblazen* the referee had already blown the final whistle

afblijven [ɑ̯vblɛivə(n)] *vb* keep off, leave alone, let alone, keep (*or:* stay) away (from): *blijf van de koekjes af* leave the biscuits alone

afboeken [ɑ̯vbukə(n)] *vb* **1** transfer; **2** write off

afborstelen [ɑ̯vbɔrstələ(n)] *vb* brush (down): *zijn kleren ~* give one's clothes a brush

afbouwen [ɑ̯vbɑuwə(n)] *vb* **1** cut back (on), down (on), phase out: *we zijn de therapie aan het ~* we're phasing out the therapy; **2** complete, finish

afbraak [ɑ̯vbrak] *de* demolition

afbranden [ɑ̯vbrɑndə(n)] *vb* burn down

afbreekbaar [ɑvbre̯gbar] *adj* decomposable, degradable, biodegradable: *biologisch afbreekbare wasmiddelen* biodegradable detergents

¹afbreken [ɑ̯vbrekə(n)] *vb* break off (*or:* away), snap (off): *de punt brak (van de stok) af* the end broke off (the stick); *een draad ~* break a thread

²afbreken [ɑ̯vbrekə(n)] *vb* **1** break off, interrupt, cut short: *onderhandelingen ~* break off negotiations; *de wedstrijd werd afgebroken* the game was stopped; **2** pull down, demolish, break down, tear down; break up, dismantle: *de boel ~* smash the place up; **3** decompose, degrade: *afvalstoffen worden in het lichaam afgebroken* waste-products are broken down in the body

afbrengen [ɑ̯vbrɛŋə(n)] *vb* put off: *ze zijn er niet van af te brengen* they can't be put off (*or:* deterred); *het er goed ~* do well; *het er levend ~* escape with one's life; *het er heelhuids ~* come out of it unscathed

afbrokkelen [ɑ̯vbrɔkələ(n)] *vb* crumble (off, away), fragment: *het plafond brokkelt af* the ceiling is crumbling

afbuigen [ɑ̯vbœyɣə(n)] *vb* turn off, bear off, branch off: *hier buigt de weg naar naar rechts af* here the road bears (to the) right

afdak [ɑ̯vdɑk] *het (~en)* lean-to

afdalen [ɑ̯vdalə(n)] *vb* go down, come down, descend: *een berg ~* go (*or:* come) down a mountain

afdaling [ɑ̯vdalɪŋ] *de (~en)* **1** descent; **2** (*skiing*) downhill

afdanken [ɑ̯vdɑŋkə(n)] *vb* **1** discard, cast off; (send for) scrap; **2** dismiss, disband: *personeel ~* pay off staff

afdankertje [ɑ̯vdɑŋkərcə] *het (~s)* cast-off, hand-me-down

afdekken [ɑ̯vdɛkə(n)] *vb* cover (over, up)

afdeling [ɑ̯vdelɪŋ] *de (~en)* department, division, section, ward: *de ~ Utrecht van onze vereniging* the Utrecht branch of our society; *Kees werkt op de ~ financiën* Kees works in the finance department

afdingen [ɑ̯vdɪŋə(n)] *vb* bargain (*or:* haggle) (with s.o.)

afdoen [ɑ̯vdun] *vb* **1** take off, remove: *zijn hoed ~* take off one's hat; **2** take off: *iets van de prijs ~* knock a bit off the price, come down a bit (in price)

afdoend [ɑvdu̯nt] *adj, adv* sufficient, adequate, effective: *een ~ middel* an effective method

afdraaien [ɑ̯vdrajə(n)] *vb* twist off: *de dop van een vulpen ~* unscrew the cap of a fountain pen; *hier moet u rechts afdraaien* you turn right (*or:* turn off to the right) here

afdragen [ɑ̯vdraɣə(n)] *vb* **1** make over, transfer, hand over, turn over; **2** wear out: *afgedragen schoenen* worn-out shoes

afdrijven [ɑ̯vdrɛivə(n)] *vb* drift off, (*shipp*) go adrift || *de bui drijft af* the shower is blowing over

afdrogen [ɑ̯vdroɣə(n)] *vb* dry (up), wipe dry: *zijn handen ~* dry one's hands (on a towel); *zich ~* dry oneself (off)

afdroogdoek [ɑ̯vdroɣduk] *de (~en)* tea towel

afdruk [ɑvdrγk] *de* (~*ken*) print, imprint; mould, cast: *de wielen lieten een* ~ *achter* the wheels left an impression

afdrukken [ɑvdrγkə(n)] *vb* print (off), copy, run off

afdwalen [ɑvdwalə(n)] *vb* stray (off) (from), go astray, wander (off): *zijn gedachten dwaalden af naar haar* his thoughts wandered off to her; *van zijn onderwerp* ~ stray from one's subject

afdwingen [ɑvdwɪŋə(n)] *vb* exact (from); extort (from)

affaire [ɑfɛ:rə] *de* (~*s*) affair

affiche [ɑfiʃə] *het, de* (~*s*) poster, (play)bill

afgaan [ɑfχan] *vb* **1** go down, descend: *de trap* ~ go down the stairs; **2** (with *op*) *(fig)* rely on, depend on: ~*de op wat hij zegt* judging by what he says; *op zijn gevoel* ~ play it by ear; **3** come off, be deducted: *daar gaat 10 % van af* 10 % is taken off that; **4** go off: *een geweer doen* ~ fire a rifle; **5** lose face, flop, fail

afgang [ɑfχaŋ] *de* (~*en*) (embarrassing) failure, flop

afgeladen [ɑfχəladə(n)] *adj* (jam-)packed, crammed

afgelasten [ɑfχəlastə(n)] *vb* cancel, call off; *(sport)* postpone

afgelegen [ɑfχəleyə(n)] *adj, adv* remote, far(-away), far-off: *een* ~ *dorp* a remote (*or:* an out-of-the-way) village

afgeleid [ɑfχəlɛit] *adj* diverted, distracted: *hij is gauw* ~ he is easily distracted

afgelopen [ɑfχəlopə(n)] *adj* last, past: *de* ~ *maanden hadden wij geen woning* for the last few months we haven't had anywhere to live; *de* ~ *tijd* recently; *de* ~ *weken* the past weeks, the last few weeks; ~*!* stop it!, that's enough!

afgemeten [ɑfχəmetə(n)] *adj, adv* measured (off, out): *met* ~ *passen* with measured steps

afgepeigerd [ɑfχəpɛiγərt] *adj* knackered, exhausted

afgericht [ɑfχərɪχt] *adj* (well-)trained

afgerond [ɑfχərɔnt] *adj* **1** (well-)rounded: *het vormt een* ~ *geheel* it forms a complete whole; **2** round

afgesproken [ɑfχəsprokə(n)] *adj* agreed, settled || *dat is dan* ~ it's a deal!

afgestompt [ɑfχəstɔmt] *adj* dull(ed), deadened

afgestudeerde [ɑfχəstyderdə] *de* (~*n*) graduate

afgetakeld [ɑfχətakəlt] *adj* decrepit: *er* ~ *uitzien* look decrepit

afgevaardigde [ɑfχəvardəɣdə] *de* (~*n*) delegate, representative, member (of parliament): *de geachte* ~ the honourable member

¹afgeven [ɑfχevə(n)] *vb* **1** run; **2** (with *op*) run down: *op iem (iets)* ~ run s.o. (sth) down

²afgeven [ɑfχevə(n)] *vb* **1** hand in, deliver, leave; hand over, give up: *hij weigerde zijn geld af te geven* he refused to part with his money; *een pakje bij iem* ~ leave a parcel with s.o.; **2** give off: *de kachel geeft veel warmte af* the stove gives off a lot of heat

afgewerkt [ɑfχəwɛrkt] *adj* used (up), spent: ~*e olie* used oil

afgewogen [ɑfχəwoγə(n)] *adj* balanced

afgezaagd [ɑfχəzaχt] *adj (fig)* stale; hackneyed

afgezant [ɑfχəzant] *de* (~*en*) envoy, ambassador

afgezien [ɑfχəzin] || ~ *van* besides, apart from; ~ *van de kosten* (*or: moeite*) apart from the cost (*or:* trouble)

afgezonderd [ɑfχəzɔndərt] *adj, adv* isolated, cut off, segregated, remote

Afghaan [ɑfχan] *de (Afghanen)* Afghan

Afghaans [ɑfχans] *adj* Afghan

Afghanistan [ɑfχanistan] *het* Afghanistan

afgieten [ɑfχitə(n)] *vb* pour off, strain, drain: *aardappels* ~ drain potatoes; *groente* ~ strain vegetables

afgietsel [ɑfχitsəl] *het* (~*s*) cast, mould

afgifte [ɑfχɪftə] *de* delivery; issue *(tickets etc)*

afgod [ɑfχɔt] *de* (~*en*) idol

afgooien [ɑfχojə(n)] *vb* throw down, fling down: *pas op dat je het er niet afgooit* take care that you don't knock it off

afgraven [ɑfχravə(n)] *vb* dig up, dig off, level

afgrendelen [ɑfχrɛndələ(n)] *vb (fig)* seal off, close off; *(literally)* bolt up

afgrijselijk [ɑfχrɛisələk] *adj, adv* **1** horrible, horrid, atrocious: *een* ~*e moord* a gruesome murder; **2** hideous, ghastly

afgrijzen [ɑfχrɛizə(n)] *het* horror, dread: *met* ~ *vervullen* horrify

afgrond [ɑfχrɔnt] *de* (~*en*) abyss, chasm

afgunst [ɑfχγnst] *de* envy, jealousy

afhaken [ɑfhakə(n)] *vb* pull out, drop out

afhakken [ɑfhakə(n)] *vb* chop off, cut off

afhalen [ɑfhalə(n)] *vb* **1** collect, call for; **2** collect, meet: *ik kom je over een uur* ~ I'll pick you up in an hour; *iem van de trein* ~ meet s.o. at the station

afhandelen [ɑfhandələ(n)] *vb* settle, conclude, deal with, dispose of: *de spreker handelde eerst de bezwaren af* the speaker first dealt with the objections

afhandeling [ɑfhandəlɪŋ] *de* settlement, transaction

afhandig [ɑfhandəχ] *adj* || *iem iets* ~ *maken* trick s.o. out of sth

afhangen [ɑfhaŋə(n)] *vb* depend (on): *hij danste alsof zijn leven ervan afhing* he danced for dear life (*or:* as though his life depended on it); *het hangt van het weer af* it depends on the weather

afhankelijk [ɑfhaŋkələk] *adj* dependent (on), depending (on): *ik ben van niemand* ~ I am quite independent; *de beslissing is* ~ *van het weer* the decision is dependent on (*or:* depends on) the weather

afhankelijkheid [ɑfhaŋkələkhɛit] *de* dependence

afhouden [ɑfhaudə(n)] *vb* **1** keep off, keep out: *zij kon haar ogen niet van de taart* ~ she couldn't keep her eyes off the cake; *iem van zijn werk* ~ keep s.o. from his work; **2** keep back: *een deel van het loon* ~ withhold a part of the wages

afhuren [ɑfhyrə(n)] *vb* hire, rent

afijn [ɑfɛin] *int* so, well

afkammen [ɑfkɑmə(n)] *vb* run down, tear (to pieces), *(book also)* slash (to shreds), slate

afkeer [ɑfker] *de* aversion (to), dislike (of): *een ~ hebben* (or: *tonen)* have (*or:* display) an aversion (to)

afkeren [ɑfkerə(n)] *vb* turn away (*or:* aside), avert: *het hoofd ~* turn one's head away; *zich ~ van iem (iets)* turn away from s.o.

¹**afketsen** [ɑfkɛtsə(n)] *vb* **1** bounce off, glance off; **2** *(fig)* fall through, fail: *het plan is afgeketst op geldgebrek* the plan fell through because of a lack of money

²**afketsen** [ɑfkɛtsə(n)] *vb (fig)* reject, defeat, frustrate

afkeuren [ɑfkørə(n)] *vb* **1** reject, turn down, declare unfit: *hij is voor 70 % afgekeurd* he has a 70 % disability; **2** disapprove of, condemn: *een doelpunt ~* disallow a goal

afkeuring [ɑfkørɪŋ] *de (~en)* disapproval, condemnation: *zijn ~ uitspreken over* express one's disapproval of

afkickcentrum [ɑfkɪksɛntrʏm] *het (-centra)* drug rehabilitation centre

afkicken [ɑfkɪkə(n)] *vb* kick the habit, dry out: *hij is afgekickt* he has kicked the habit

afkijken [ɑfkɛikə(n)] *vb* **1** copy, crib; **2** see out, see to the end: *we hebben die film niet afgekeken* we didn't see the film out; *bij* (or: *van) zijn buurman ~ copy* (*or:* crib) from one's neighbour

afkloppen [ɑfklɔpə(n)] *vb* knock on wood, touch wood: *even ~!* touch wood!

afknappen [ɑfknɑpə(n)] *vb* break down, have a breakdown: *~ op iem (iets)* get fed up with s.o. (sth)

afknippen [ɑfknɪpə(n)] *vb* cut (off), trim

afkoelen [ɑfkulə(n)] *vb* cool (off, down), chill, refrigerate: *iets laten ~* leave sth to cool

afkomen [ɑfkomə(n)] *vb* **1** (with *op)* come up to (*or:* towards): *(dreigend) op iem ~* approach s.o. (menacingly); *zij zag de auto recht op zich ~* she saw the car heading straight for her (*or:* coming straight at her); *get rid of, be done* (*or:* finished) with; get off (*or:* away), get out of: *er gemakkelijk ~* get off easily (*or:* lightly)

afkomst [ɑfkɔmst] *de* descent, origin, birth, *(word)* derivation: *Jean is van Franse ~* Jean is French by birth

afkomstig [ɑfkɔmstəх] *adj* **1** from, coming (from), originating (from): *~ uit Spanje* of Spanish origin; **2** originating (from), derived (from): *dat woord is ~ uit het Turks* that word is derived (*or:* borrowed) from Turkish

afkondigen [ɑfkɔndəɣə(n)] *vb* proclaim, give notice of

afkondiging [ɑfkɔndəɣɪŋ] *de (~en)* proclamation, declaration

afkopen [ɑfkopə(n)] *vb* buy (from), purchase (from), buy off, redeem; ransom: *een hypotheek ~*

redeem a mortgage; *een polis ~* surrender a policy

afkoppelen [ɑfkɔpələ(n)] *vb* uncouple; disconnect

afkorten [ɑfkɔrtə(n)] *vb* shorten, abbreviate

afkorting [ɑfkɔrtɪŋ] *de (~en)* abbreviation, shortening

afkrabben [ɑfkrɑbə(n)] *vb* scratch off, scrape off (*or:* from)

afkraken [ɑfkrakə(n)] *vb* run down: *de criticus kraakte haar boek volledig af* the reviewer ran her book into the ground

afkrijgen [ɑfkrɛiɣə(n)] *vb* **1** get off, get out: *hij kreeg de vlek er niet af* he couldn't get the stain out; **2** get done (*or:* finished): *het werk op tijd ~* get the work done (*or:* finished) in time

afleggen [ɑflɛɣə(n)] *vb* **1** take off, lay down; **2** make; take: *een bezoek ~* pay a visit; *een examen ~* sit (for) an examination; **3** cover: *500 mijl per dag ~* cover 500 miles a day

afleiden [ɑflɛidə(n)] *vb* **1** lead (*or:* guide) away (from), divert (from) *(road etc),* conduct *(lightning): de stroom ~* divert the stream; **2** divert, distract: *ik leidde hem af van zijn werk* I kept him from doing his work; **3** trace back (to); derive (from): *'spraak' is afgeleid van 'spreken'* 'spraak' is derived from 'spreken'

afleiding [ɑflɛidɪŋ] *de (~en)* distraction, diversion: *ik heb echt ~ nodig* I really need sth to take my mind off it (*or:* things); *voor ~ zorgen* take s.o.'s mind off things

afleren [ɑflerə(n)] *vb* unlearn, get out of (a habit): *ik heb het stotteren afgeleerd* I have overcome my stammer; **2** cure of, break of: *ik zal je dat liegen wel ~* I'll teach you to tell lies; *nog eentje om het af te leren* one for the road

afleveren [ɑfleverə(n)] *vb* deliver: *de bestelling is op tijd afgeleverd* the order was delivered on time

aflevering [ɑfleverɪŋ] *de (~en)* **1** delivery: *bij ~ betalen* cash on delivery; **2** episode

aflezen [ɑflezə(n)] *vb* **1** read out (the whole of): *een lijst ~* read out a list; **2** read (off)

aflikken [ɑflɪkə(n)] *vb* lick: *zijn vingers* (or: *een lepel) ~* lick one's fingers (*or:* a spoon)

afloop [ɑflop] *de (aflopen)* **1** end, close: *na ~ van de voorstelling* after the performance; **2** result, outcome: *ongeluk met dodelijke ~* fatal accident

aflopen [ɑflopə(n)] *vb* **1** (come to an) end, finish, expire: *de cursus is afgelopen* the course is finished; *dit jaar loopt het huurcontract af* the lease expires this year; *het verhaal liep goed af* the story had a happy ending; *het loopt af met hem* he is sinking fast (*or:* is near the end); **2** run (*or:* go, walk) down

aflopend [ɑflopənt] *adj* || *het is een ~e zaak* we're fighting a losing battle

aflossen [ɑflɔsə(n)] *vb* **1** relieve: *laten we elkaar ~* let's take turns; **2** pay off: *een bedrag op een lening ~* pay off an part of a loan

aflossing [ɑflɔsɪŋ] *de (~en)* **1** changing, change: *de ~ van de wacht* the changing of the guard; **2** (re)payment; **3** (re)payment (period), instalment:

een maandelijkse (or: *jaarlijkse*) ~ a monthly (or: an annual) payment

afluisteren [ɑflœystərə(n)] *vb* eavesdrop (on), listen in to (or: in on), monitor, (wire-)tap: *iem ~* eavesdrop on s.o., monitor s.o.; *een telefoongesprek ~* listen in to a phone call

¹afmaken [ɑfmakə(n)] *vb* **1** finish, complete: *een werkje ~* finish (or: complete) a bit of work; **2** kill: *ze hebben de hond moeten laten ~* they had to have the dog put down

²afmaken [ɑfmakə(n)] *ref vb* ‖ *hij maakte er zich met een grap van af* he brushed it aside with a joke; *zich er wat al te gemakkelijk van ~* shrug sth off too lightly

afmatten [ɑfmɑtə(n)] *vb* exhaust, wear out, tire out

afmelden [ɑfmɛldə(n)] *vb* cancel: *zich ~* check (or: sign) (oneself) out

afmeten [ɑfmetə(n)] *vb* measure, judge: *de kwaliteit van een opleiding ~ aan het aantal geslaagden* judge the quality of a course from (or: by) the number of passes

afmeting [ɑfmetɪŋ] *de (~en)* dimension, proportion, size: *de ~en van de kamer* the dimensions (or: size) of the room

afname [ɑfnamə] *de* **1** purchase: *bij ~ van 25 exemplaren* for quantities of 25, if 25 copies are ordered (or: bought); **2** sale; **3** decline, decrease: *de ~ van de werkloosheid* the reduction in unemployment

afneembaar [ɑfnembar] *adj* detachable, removable

¹afnemen [ɑfnemə(n)] *vb* **1** take off (or: away), remove (from): *zijn hoed ~* take off one's hat, raise one's hat; *het kleed van de tafel ~* take (or: remove) the cloth from the table; **2** remove: *iem bloed ~* take blood (or: a blood sample); **3** clean: *de tafel met een natte doek ~* wipe the table with a damp cloth; **4** deprive: *iem zijn rijbewijs ~* take away s.o.'s driving licence; **5** hold, administer: *iem de biecht ~* hear s.o.'s confession; *iem een eed ~* administer an oath to s.o., swear s.o. in; *iem een examen ~* examine s.o.; **6** buy, purchase

²afnemen [ɑfnemə(n)] *vb* decrease, decline: *onze belangstelling nam af* our interest faded; *in gewicht ~* lose weight

afnemer [ɑfnemər] *de (~s)* buyer, customer: *Duitsland is onze grootste ~ van snijbloemen* Germany is our largest customer for cut flowers

afpakken [ɑfpɑkə(n)] *vb* take (away), snatch (away): *iem een mes ~* take away a knife from s.o.

afpersen [ɑfpɛrsə(n)] *vb* extort (or: wring), force: *iem geld ~* extort money from s.o.

afperser [ɑfpɛrsər] *de (~s)* blackmailer

afpersing [ɑfpɛrsɪŋ] *de (~en)* extortion, blackmail

afpingelen [ɑfpɪŋələ(n)] *vb* haggle: *proberen af te pingelen* try to beat down the price

afplakken [ɑfplɑkə(n)] *vb* tape up, cover with tape

afplukken [ɑfplʏkə(n)] *vb* pick, pluck: *de veren van een kip ~* pluck a chicken

afpoeieren [ɑfpujərə(n)] *vb* brush off, put off

afprijzen [ɑfprɛizə(n)] *vb* reduce, mark down: *alles is afgeprijsd* everything is reduced (in price)

afraden [ɑfradə(n)] *vb* advise against: *(iem) iets ~* dissuade (or: discourage) s.o. from (doing) sth

afraffelen [ɑfrɑfələ(n)] *vb* rush (through): *zijn huiswerk ~* rush (through) one's homework

aframmeling [ɑfrɑməlɪŋ] *de (~en)* beating, hiding

afranselen [ɑfrɑnsələ(n)] *vb* beat (up), flog, cane

afrastering [ɑfrɑstərɪŋ] *de (~en)* fencing, fence, railings

afreageren [ɑfrejaɣerə(n)] *vb* work off (or: vent) one's emotions, let off steam: *iets op iem ~* take sth out on s.o.

afrekenen [ɑfrekənə(n)] *vb* settle (up), settle (or: pay) one's bill, settle one's account(s): *ober, mag ik ~!* waiter, the bill please!

afrekening [ɑfrekənɪŋ] *de (~en)* **1** payment; **2** receipt, statement

afremmen [ɑfrɛmə(n)] *vb* **1** slow down, brake, put the brake(s) on: *hij kon niet meer ~* it was too late for him to brake; *voor een bocht ~* slow down to take a curve; **2** (*fig*) curb, check: *iem in zijn enthousiasme ~* curb s.o.'s enthusiasm

africhten [ɑfrɪχtə(n)] *vb* train: *valken ~ voor de jacht* train falcons for hunting

¹afrijden [ɑfrɛidə(n)] *vb* drive down, ride down (on horseback): *een heuvel ~* ride (or: drive) down a hill

²afrijden [ɑfrɛidə(n)] *vb* drive to the end of, ride to the end of: *de hele stad ~* ride (or: drive) all over town

Afrika [afrika] *het* Africa

Afrikaan [afrikan] *de (Afrikanen)* African

Afrikaans [afrikans] *adj, adv* **1** African; **2** South African

afrikaantje [afrikancə] *het (~s) (bot)* African marigold

Afrikaner [afrikanər] *de* Afrikaner, Boer

afrit [ɑfrɪt] *de (~ten)* exit: *op- en ~ten* slip roads; *bij de volgende ~* at the next exit

afroep [ɑfrup] *de* ‖ *op ~ beschikbaar* available on demand, on call

afroepen [ɑfrupə(n)] *vb* call out, call off

afrollen [ɑfrələ(n)] *vb* **1** unwind; unroll; **2** roll down

afromen [ɑfromə(n)] *vb* **1** skim; **2** cream off

afronden [ɑfrɔndə(n)] *vb* **1** wind up, round off: *wilt u (uw betoog) ~?* would you like to wind up (what you have to say)?; *een afgerond geheel vormen* form a complete whole; **2** round off: *naar boven* (or: *beneden*) ~ round up (or: down); *een bedrag op hele euro ~* round off an amount to the nearest euro

afronding [ɑfrɔndɪŋ] *de (~en)* winding up, rounding off, completion, conclusion: *als ~ van je studie moet je een werkstuk maken* to complete your study, you have to do a project

afruimen [ɑfrœymə(n)] *vb* clear (away), clear the table

afschaffen [ɑfsχɑfə(n)] *vb* abolish, do away with:

de doodstraf ~ abolish capital punishment
afschaffing [ɑfsχɑfɪŋ] *de* abolition: *de* ~ *van de sla-vernij* the abolition of slavery
afscheid [ɑfsχɛit] *het* parting, leaving, farewell, departure: *van iem* ~ *nemen* take leave of s.o.; *offici-eel* ~ *nemen (van)* take formal leave (of); *bij zijn* ~ *kreeg hij een gouden horloge* when he left he received a gold watch
afscheiden [ɑfsχɛidə(n)] *vb* **1** divide (off), partition off: *een ruimte met een gordijn* ~ curtain off an area; **2** discharge; secrete: *sommige bomen scheiden hars af* some trees secrete (*or:* produce) resin
afscheiding [ɑfsχɛidɪŋ] *de (~en)* **1** separation, secession, schism; demarcation; **2** partition, dividing line: *een* ~ *aanbrengen* put up a partition; **3** discharge, secretion
afschepen [ɑfsχepə(n)] *vb* (*with met)* palm (sth) off on (s.o.), fob (s.o.) off with (sth): *zij laat zich niet zo gemakkelijk* ~ she is not so easily put off; *zich niet laten* ~ *(met een smoesje)* not be fobbed off (with an excuse)
afscheren [ɑfsχerə(n)] *vb* shave (off); shear (off)
afschermen [ɑfsχɛrmə(n)] *vb* screen, protect (from)
afscheuren [ɑfsχørə(n)] *vb* tear off
afschieten [ɑfsχitə(n)] *vb* **1** fire (off), discharge: *een geweer* ~ fire a gun; **2** shoot: *wild* ~ shoot game
afschilderen [ɑfsχɪldərə(n)] *vb* **1** paint; **2** portray, depict: *iem* ~ *als* portray s.o. as, make s.o. out to be
afschrapen [ɑfsχrapə(n)] *vb* scrape off
afschrift [ɑfsχrɪft] *het (~en)* copy: *een* ~ *van een (lopende) rekening* a current account statement
afschrijven [ɑfsχrɛivə(n)] *vb* **1** debit: *geld van een rekening* ~ withdraw money from an account; **2** write off: *die auto kun je wel* ~ you might as well write that car off; *we hadden haar al afgeschreven* we had already written her off; **3** write down, write off (as depreciation)
afschrijving [ɑfsχrɛivɪŋ] *de (~en)* **1** debit; **2** *(fixed assets)* depreciation, write-off, *(intangible assets)* amortization: *voor* ~ *op de machines* for depreciation of the machines
afschrikken [ɑfsχrɪkə(n)] *vb* deter, put off, frighten off, scare off: *zo'n benadering schrikt de mensen af* an approach like that scares (*or:* puts) people off; *hij liet zich door niets* ~ he was not to be put off (*or:* deterred)
afschrikkingsmiddel *het* deterrent
afschudden [ɑfsχʏdə(n)] *vb* shake off, cast off: *een tegenstander van zich* ~ shake off an opponent
afschuiven [ɑfsχœyvə(n)] *vb* pass (on to s.o.): *de verantwoordelijkheid op een ander* ~ pass the buck; *zijn verantwoordelijkheid van zich* ~ shirk one's responsibility
afschuren [ɑfsχyrə(n)] *vb* rub down, sand down
afschuw [ɑfsχyw] *de* horror, disgust: *een* ~ *hebben van iets* loathe (*or:* detest) sth; *van* ~ *vervuld* horrified, appalled
afschuwelijk [ɑfsχywələk] *adj, adv* **1** horrible; **2**

shocking, awful, appalling: *ik heb een* ~*e dag gehad* I've had an awful day; *die rok staat je* ~ that dress looks awful on you
¹afslaan [ɑfslan] *vb* **1** turn (off): branch off; **2** cut out, stall || *van zich* ~ hit out
²afslaan [ɑfslan] *vb* turn down; refuse, decline: *nou, een kopje koffie sla ik niet af* I won't say no to a cup of coffee; *een thermometer* ~ shake down a thermometer
afslachten [ɑfslɑχtə(n)] *vb* slaughter, massacre
afslag [ɑfslɑχ] *de (~en)* **1** turn(ing), exit: *de volgen-de* ~ *rechts nemen* take the next turning on the right; **2** Dutch auction: ~ *van vis* fish auction; *bij* ~ *veilen* sell by Dutch auction
afslanken [ɑfslɑŋkə(n)] *vb* slim (down), trim down: *het bedrijf moet aanzienlijk* ~ the company has to slim down considerably
¹afslijten [ɑfslɛitə(n)] *vb* wear (off, down)
²afslijten [ɑfslɛitə(n)] *vb* wear out, wear off
afsluitdijk [ɑfslœydɛik] *de (~en)* dam, causeway: *de* ~ *(van het IJsselmeer)* the IJsselmeer Dam
afsluiten [ɑfslœytə(n)] *vb* **1** close (off, up): *een weg* ~ *voor verkeer* close a road to traffic; **2** lock (up), close: *heb je de voordeur goed afgesloten?* have you locked the front door?; **3** cut off, shut off, turn off, disconnect, exit: *de stroom* ~ cut off the electricity; **4** conclude, enter into, negotiate: *een levensverze-kering* ~ take out a life insurance policy; **5** close, conclude: *een (dienst)jaar* ~ close a year; *zich* ~ cut oneself off
afsluiting [ɑfslœytɪŋ] *de (~en)* **1** closing off, closing up; **2** locking (up, away); **3** shut-off, cut-off, disconnection; **4** conclusion; **5** closing, close, balancing; **6** seclusion, isolation
afsnijden [ɑfsnɛidə(n)] *vb* **1** cut off: *bloemen* ~ cut flowers; **2** cut off: *de bocht* ~ cut the corner; *een stuk (weg)* ~ take a short cut
¹afspelen [ɑfspelə(n)] *ref vb* happen, take place, occur: *waar heeft het ongeluk zich afgespeeld?* where did the accident take place (*or:* occur)?
²afspelen [ɑfspelə(n)] *vb* play: *een bandje op een bandrecorder* ~ play a tape on a tape recorder
afspiegelen [ɑfspiɣələ(n)] *vb* depict, portray: *men spiegelt hem af als een misdadiger* he is represented as a criminal
afspiegeling [ɑfspiɣəlɪŋ] *de (~en)* reflection, mirror image
afspoelen [ɑfspulə(n)] *vb* rinse (down, off), wash (down, off): *het stof van zijn handen* ~ rinse the dust off one's hands
afspraak [ɑfsprak] *de (afspraken)* appointment; engagement; agreement: *een* ~ *maken* (or: *hebben) bij de tandarts* make (*or:* have) an appointment with the dentist; *een* ~ *nakomen, zich aan een* ~ *houden: a)* keep an appointment; *b)* stick to an agreement
afspraakje [ɑfsprakjə] *het (~s)* date
¹afspreken [ɑfsprekə(n)] *vb* agree (on), arrange: *een plan* ~ agree on a plan; *dat is dus afgesproken* that's a deal, that's settled then; ~ *iets te zullen doen*

agree to do sth; *zoals afgesproken* as agreed

²**afspreken** [ɑfspreka(n)] *vb* make an appointment

afstaan [ɑfstan] *vb* give up, hand over: *zijn plaats ~ (eg to a younger colleague)* step down

afstammeling [ɑfstɑmǝlɪŋ] *de (~en)* descendant

afstammen [ɑfstɑmǝ(n)] *vb* descend (from)

afstamming [ɑfstɑmɪŋ] *de* descent: *van Italiaanse ~* of Italian extraction

afstand [ɑfstɑnt] *de (~en)* 1 distance (to, from): *een ~ afleggen* cover a distance; *~ houden (bewaren)* keep one's distance, *(fig also)* keep aloof; *~ nemen van een onderwerp* distance oneself from a subject; *op een ~: a)* at a distance; *b)* distant, aloof; *iem op een ~ houden (fig also)* keep s.o. at arm's length; *erg op een ~ zijn tegen iem* be very standoffish to s.o.; 2 renunciation: *~ doen van* renounce, disclaim, give up; *~ doen van zijn bezit* part with one's possessions

afstandelijk [ɑfstɑndǝlǝk] *adj, adv* distant, aloof

afstandsbediening [ɑfstɑntsbǝdinɪŋ] *de* remote control (unit)

afstandsonderwijs [ɑfstɑntsɔndǝrwɛis] *het* distance learning

afstapje [ɑfstɑpjǝ] *het (~s)* step: *denk om het ~* mind the step

afstappen [ɑfstɑpǝ(n)] *vb* step down, come down, come off, dismount, get off (one's bike)

¹**afsteken** [ɑfsteka(n)] *vb* stand out: *de kerktoren stak (donker) af tegen de hemel* the church tower stood out against the sky

²**afsteken** [ɑfsteka(n)] *vb* 1 let off: *vuurwerk ~* let off fireworks; 2 deliver: *een speech ~* hold forth, make a speech

afstel [ɑfstɛl] *het* cancellation

afstellen [ɑfstɛlǝ(n)] *vb* adjust (to), set, tune (up)

afstemmen [ɑfstɛmǝ(n)] *vb* 1 tune; 2 tune (to), tune in (to): *een radio op een zender ~* tune a radio in to a station; 3 tune (to): *alle werkzaamheden zijn op elkaar afgestemd* all activities are geared to one another

afstempelen [ɑfstɛmpǝlǝ(n)] *vb* stamp, cancel, postmark: *een paspoort* (or: *kaartje) ~* stamp a passport (or: ticket)

afsterven [ɑfstɛrvǝ(n)] *vb* die (off), *(bot also)* die back

afstevenen [ɑfstevǝnǝ(n)] *vb (with op)* make for, head for (or: towards)

afstoffen [ɑfstɔfǝ(n)] *vb* dust (off)

¹**afstompen** [ɑfstɔmpǝ(n)] *vb* blunt, dull, numb

²**afstompen** [ɑfstɔmpǝ(n)] *vb* become blunt(ed) (or: numb)

afstoten [ɑfstotǝ(n)] *vb* 1 dispose of, reject, hive off: *arbeidsplaatsen ~* cut jobs; 2 repel: *zo'n onvriendelijke behandeling stoot af* such unfriendly treatment is off-putting

afstraffen [ɑfstrɑfǝ(n)] *vb* punish

afstrijken [ɑfstrɛikǝ(n)] *vb* 1 strike, light; 2 wipe off, level (off): *een afgestreken eetlepel* a level tablespoonful

afstropen [ɑfstropǝ(n)] *vb* 1 strip (off): *een haas de huid ~* skin a hare; 2 pillage, ransack: *enkele benden stroopten het platteland af* a few bands pillaged the countryside

afstudeerrichting [ɑfstyderɪχtɪŋ] *de (~en)* main subject

afstuderen [ɑfstyderǝ(n)] *vb* graduate (from), complete (or: finish) one's studies (at)

afstuiten [ɑfstœytǝ(n)] *vb* rebound, be frustrated: *de bal stuit af tegen de paal* the ball rebounds off the post; *het voorstel stuitte af op haar koppigheid* the proposal fell through owing to her obstinacy

afstuiven [ɑfstœyvǝ(n)] *vb (with op)* rush, dash

afsturen [ɑfstyrǝ(n)] *vb (with op)* send (towards): *de hond op iem ~* set the dog on s.o.

aftakelen [ɑftakǝlǝ(n)] *vb* go (or: run) to seed, go downhill: *hij begint al flink af te takelen* he really is starting to go downhill, *(mentally)* he is really starting to lose his faculties

aftakeling [ɑftakǝlɪŋ] *de (~en)* deterioration, decline

aftands [ɑftɑnts] *adj* broken down, worn out: *een ~e piano* a worn-out (or: dilapidated) piano

aftappen [ɑftɑpǝ(n)] *vb* 1 draw off, drain: *als het hard vriest, moet je de waterleiding ~* when it freezes hard you have to drain the pipes; *een telefoonlijn ~* tap a telephone line; 2 tap: *de benzine ~* siphon (off) the petrol

aftasten [ɑftɑstǝ(n)] *vb* 1 feel, sense: *een oppervlak ~* explore a surface with one's hands; 2 feel out, sound out

¹**aftekenen** [ɑftekǝnǝ(n)] *vb* 1 outline, mark off: *de plattegrond van een plein ~* map out a (town) square; 2 register, record: *ik heb mijn gewerkte uren laten ~* I've had my working hours registered

²**aftekenen** [ɑftekǝnǝ(n)] *ref vb* stand out, become visible: *zich ~ tegen* stand out against

aftellen [ɑftelǝ(n)] *vb* count (out, off): *de dagen ~* count the days

aftershave [aftǝrʃef] *de (~s)* aftershave

aftikken [ɑftɪkǝ(n)] *vb* tag (out)

aftiteling [ɑftitǝlɪŋ] *de (~en)* credit titles, credits

aftocht [ɑftɔχt] *de (~en)* retreat: *de ~ slaan* (or: *blazen)* beat a retreat

aftrap [ɑftrɑp] *de (~pen)* kick-off: *de ~ doen* kick off

aftreden [ɑftredǝ(n)] *vb* resign (one's post)

aftrek [ɑftrɛk] *de* 1 deduction: *~ van voorarrest* reduction in sentence for time already served; *na ~ van onkosten* less expenses; 2 deduction, allowance

aftrekbaar [ɑftrɛgbar] *adj* deductible, tax-deductible

aftrekken [ɑftrɛkǝ(n)] *vb* 1 subtract: *als je acht van veertien aftrekt houd je zes over* if you take eight from fourteen you have six left; 2 deduct; 3 masturbate

aftrekpost [ɑftrɛkpɔst] *de (~en)* deduction, tax-deductible item (or: expense)

aftreksom [ɑftrɛksɔm] *de (~men)* subtraction

(sum)

aftroeven [ɑftruvə(n)] *vb* score (points) off

aftroggelen [ɑftrɔɣələ(n)] *vb* wheedle out of: *iem iets weten af te troggelen* succeed in wheedling sth out of s.o.

aftuigen [ɑftœyɣə(n)] *vb* beat up, mug

afvaardigen [ɑfardəɣə(n)] *vb* send (*or:* appoint) as delegate: *hij was naar de leerlingenraad afgevaardigd* he had been appointed as delegate to the students' council

afvaardiging [ɑfardəɣɪŋ] *de* (*~en*) delegation

afval [ɑfɑl] *het, de* waste (matter), refuse, rubbish: *radioactief ~* radioactive waste

afvalbak [ɑfɑlbɑk] *de* litter bin (*or:* basket), dustbin, rubbish bin

afvalbedrijf [ɑfɑlbədrɛif] *het* waste-processing firm

afvallen [ɑfɑlə(n)] *vb* **1** fall off (*or:* down): *de bladeren vallen af* the leaves are falling; **2** drop out: *dat alternatief viel af* that option was dropped (*or:* was no longer available); **3** lose weight: *ik ben drie kilo afgevallen* I've lost three kilos

afvalproduct [ɑfɑlprodʏkt] *het* (*~en*) by-product, waste product

afvalrace [ɑfɑlres] *de* (*~s*) elimination race

afvalstof [ɑfɑlstɔf] *de* (*~fen*) waste product, (*pl also*) waste (matter): *schadelijke ~fen* harmful (*or:* noxious) waste

afvalverwerking [ɑfɑlvərwɛrkɪŋ] *de* (*~en*) processing of waste, waste disposal (*or:* treatment)

afvalwater [ɑfɑlwatər] *het* waste water

afvegen [ɑfeɣə(n)] *vb* wipe (off), brush away, wipe away: *de tafel ~* wipe (off) the table

afvloeien [ɑflujə(n)] *vb* be made redundant, be laid off, be given early retirement

afvloeiing [ɑflujɪŋ] *de* (*~en*) release, gradual dismissal (*or:* discharge)

afvoer [ɑfur] *de* **1** transport, conveyance: *de ~ van goederen* transport (*or:* removal) of goods; **2** drain(pipe), outlet, exhaust (pipe): *de ~ is verstopt* the drain is blocked

afvoeren [ɑfurə(n)] *vb* **1** transport, drain away, drain off, lead away; **2** carry off (*or:* down), lead down

afvragen [ɑfraɣə(n)] *ref vb* wonder, ask oneself, (be in) doubt (as to): *ik vraag mij af, wie ...* I wonder who ...; *ik vraag mij af of dat juist is* I wonder if (*or:* whether) that is correct

afvuren [ɑfyrə(n)] *vb* fire, let off, discharge, launch

afwachten [ɑfwɑχtə(n)] *vb* wait (for), await, anticipate: *zijn beurt ~* wait (for) one's turn; *we moeten maar ~* we'll have to wait and see

afwachting [ɑfwɑχtɪŋ] *de* expectation, anticipation: *in ~ van uw antwoord* we look forward to receiving your reply

afwas [ɑfwɑs] *de* **1** dishes, washing-up; **2** doing (*or:* washing) the dishes, washing-up: *hij is aan de ~* he is washing up (*or:* doing) the dishes

afwasbaar [ɑfwɑzbar] *adj* washable

afwasborstel [ɑfwɑzbɔrstəl] *de* (*~s*) washing-up brush

afwasmachine [ɑfwɑsmaʃinə] *de* (*~s*) dishwasher, washing-up machine

afwasmiddel [ɑfwɑsmɪdəl] *het* (*~en*) washing-up liquid; (*Am*) dishwashing liquid

¹afwassen [ɑfwɑsə(n)] *vb* **1** wash (up); **2** wash off (*or:* away): *bloed van zijn handen ~* wash blood from his hands

²afwassen [ɑfwɑsə(n)] *vb* do (*or:* wash) the dishes

afwatering [ɑfwatərɪŋ] *de* (*~en*) **1** drainage; **2** drainage, drains

afweer [ɑfwer] *de* defence

afwegen [ɑfweɣə(n)] *vb* **1** weigh; **2** weigh (up), consider: *de voor- en nadelen (tegen elkaar) ~* weigh the pros and cons (against each other)

¹afweken [ɑfwekə(n)] *vb* soak off

²afweken [ɑfwekə(n)] *vb* come off, come unstuck (*or:* undone): *de pleister is afgeweekt* the plaster has come off

afwenden [ɑfwɛndə(n)] *vb* **1** turn away (*or:* aside), avert: *het hoofd* (*or:* de ogen*) *~* turn one's head (*or:* eyes) away, look away; *de ogen niet ~ van iem (iets)* not take one's eyes off s.o. (sth); **2** avert, ward off, stave off, parry

afwennen [ɑfwɛnə(n)] *vb* cure of, break of: *iem het nagelbijten proberen af te wennen* try to get s.o. out of the habit of biting his nails

afwentelen [ɑfwɛntələ(n)] *vb* shift, transfer

afweren [ɑfwerə(n)] *vb* keep off (*or:* away), hold off, (*fig*) fend off, ward off: *nieuwsgierigen ~* keep bystanders at a distance; *een aanval* (or: *aanvaller*) *~* repel an attack (*or:* attacker)

afwerken [ɑfwɛrkə(n)] *vb* **1** finish (off): *een opstel* (or: *roman*) *~* add the finishing touches to an essay (*or:* a novel); **2** finish (off), complete: *een programma ~* complete a programme

afwerking [ɑfwɛrkɪŋ] *de* (*~en*) finish(ing), finishing touch

afweten [ɑfwetə(n)] *vb* || *het laten ~* fail, refuse to work, not show up

afwezig [ɑfwezəχ] *adj* **1** absent, away, gone: *Jansen is op het ogenblik ~* Jansen is away at the moment; **2** absent-minded, preoccupied

afwezigheid [ɑfwezəχhɛit] *de* **1** absence: *tijdens Pauls ~* during Paul's absence; *in (bij) ~ van* in the absence of; **2** absent-mindedness: *in een ogenblik van ~* in a forgetful moment, in a momentary fit of absent-mindedness

afwijken [ɑfwɛikə(n)] *vb* **1** deviate (from) (*also fig*), depart (from), diverge (from): *doen ~* divert, turn (away), *van het rechte pad ~* deviate from the straight and narrow; **2** differ, deviate, vary, disagree (with)

afwijkend [ɑfwɛikənt] *adj* different: *~ gedrag* abnormal behaviour; *~e mening* different opinion

afwijking [ɑfwɛikɪŋ] *de* (*~en*) **1** defect, abnormality, aberration: *een geestelijke ~* a mental abnormality; *een lichamelijke ~* a physical defect; **2** difference, deviation: *dit horloge vertoont een ~ van één seconde* this watch is accurate to within one second

afwijzen [ɑfwɛizə(n)] *vb* **1** not admit, turn away: *een bezoeker ~* turn away a visitor; *iem als lid (van een vereniging) ~* refuse s.o. membership (of an association); **2** refuse, decline, reject, repudiate: *een kopje thee ~* refuse a cup of tea

afwijzing [ɑfwɛizɪŋ] *de (~en)* refusal, rejection, repudiation

afwikkelen [ɑfwɪkələ(n)] *vb* complete, settle: *een contract* (or: *kwestie*) *~* settle a contract (*or:* question)

afwisselen [ɑfwɪsələ(n)] *vb* **1** alternate with, take turns, relieve: *elkaar ~* take turns; **2** vary: *zijn werk ~ met ontspanning* alternate one's work with relaxation

¹afwisselend [ɑfwɪsələnt] *adj* **1** alternate; **2** varied

²afwisselend [ɑfwɪsələnt] *adv* alternately, in turn

afwisseling [ɑfwɪsəlɪŋ] *de (~en)* variety, variation, change: *een welkome ~ vormen* make a welcome change; *voor de ~* for a change

afzeggen [ɑfsɛɣə(n)] *vb* cancel, call off: *de staking werd afgezegd* the strike was called off

afzender [ɑfsɛndər] *de (~s)* sender, shipper *(goods): ~ …* (*on letter*) from …

afzet [ɑfsɛt] *de* **1** sale, market; **2** sales

afzetten [ɑfsɛtə(n)] *vb* **1** switch off, turn off, disconnect; **2** cut off, amputate; **3** cheat, swindle, overcharge: *een klant voor tien euro ~* cheat a customer out of ten euros; **4** enclose, fence off, fence in, block off, close off: *een bouwterrein ~* fence off a building site; **5** push off: *zich ~ tegen (iets, iem)* react against (sth, s.o.); *zich ~ voor een sprong* take off; **6** dismiss, remove: *een koning ~* depose a king; **7** drop, set down, put down: *een vriend thuis ~* drop a friend at his home; *dat moet je van je af (kunnen) zetten* (you should be able to) get that out of your mind

afzetter [ɑfsɛtər] *de (~s)* cheat, swindler

afzetting [ɑfsɛtɪŋ] *de (~en)* enclosure, fence, cordon

afzichtelijk [ɑfsɪχtələk] *adj, adv* ghastly, hideous

afzien [ɑfsin] *vb* **1** (with *van*) abandon, give up, renounce: *naderhand zagen ze toch van samenwerking af* afterwards they decided not to cooperate; **2** have a hard time (of it), sweat it out: *dat wordt ~* we'd better roll up our sleeves

afzijdig [ɑfsɛidəχ] *adj* aloof: *zich ~ houden van, ~ blijven van* keep aloof from

afzonderen [ɑfsɔndərə(n)] *ref vb* separate (*or:* seclude) oneself (from), retire (from), withdraw (from): *zich van de wereld ~* withdraw from the world

afzondering [ɑfsɔndərɪŋ] *de (~en)* separation, isolation, seclusion: *in strikte (strenge) ~* in strict isolation

afzonderlijk [ɑfsɔndərlək] *adj* separate, individual, single: *de keuze wordt aan ieder ~ kind overgelaten* the choice is left to each individual child

afzuigkap [ɑfsœyχkɑp] *de (~pen)* (cooker) hood

afzwemmen [ɑfswɛmə(n)] *vb* take a swimming test

afzweren [ɑfswerə(n)] *vb* renounce, forswear: *de drank ~: a)* give up drink(ing); *b)* swear off drink(ing); *zijn geloof* (or: *beginselen*) *~* renounce one's faith (*or:* principles)

agenda [aɣɛnda] *de (~'s)* **1** (*notebook*) diary; **2** agenda: *op de ~ staan* be on the agenda

agent [aɣɛnt] *de (~en)* **1** policeman, constable: *een stille ~, een ~ in burger* a plain-clothes policeman; **2** agent: *een geheim ~* a secret agent

agglomeratie [aɣloməra(t)si] *de (~s)* conurbation

aggregatietoestand [aɣreɣa(t)situstɑnt] *de (~en)* physical state

agrariër [aɣrarijər] *de (~s)* farmer

agrarisch [aɣraris] *adj* agrarian, agricultural, farming: *~e school* school of agriculture

agressie [aɣrɛsi] *de (~s)* aggression: *een daad van ~* an act of aggression; *~ opwekken* provoke aggression

agressief [aɣrɛsif] *adj, adv* aggressive: *een agressieve politiek voeren* pursue an aggressive policy

ah [a] *int* ah, oh

ai [ɑj] *int* ouch, ow; ah, oh || *~!, dat was maar net mis* oops! that was a close shave

aids [ets] *de* Aids

air [ɛːr] *het (~s)* air, look: *met het ~ van* with an air of

airconditioning [ɛːrkɔndɪʃənɪŋ] *de* air-conditioning

ajuin [ajœyn] *de (~en) (Belg)* onion

akelig [akələχ] *adj* **1** unpleasant, nasty, dismal, dreary, bleak, ghastly: *een ~ gezicht* (or: *beeld*) a nasty sight (*or:* picture); *een ~ verhaal* a ghastly story; *~ weer* nasty weather; **2** ill, sick: *ik word er ~ van* it turns my stomach

akker [ɑkər] *de (~s)* field

akkerbouw [ɑkərbɑu] *de* (arable) farming, agriculture

akkoord [ɑkort] *het (~en)* **1** agreement, arrangement, settlement, bargain: *een ~ aangaan* (or: *sluiten*) come to an arrangement; *tot een ~ komen* reach an agreement; **2** (*mus*) chord: *~ gaan (met)* agree (to), be agreeable (to); *niet ~ gaan (met)* disagree (with)

akoestiek [akustik] *de* acoustics

akte [ɑktə] *de (~n, ~s)* **1** deed; contract: *~ van geboorte* (or: *overlijden, huwelijk*) birth (*or:* death, marriage) certificate; *een ~ opmaken* draw up a deed; *~ opmaken van* make a record of; **2** certificate, diploma; licence; **3** (*theatre, film*) act

aktetas [ɑktətɑs] *de (~sen)* briefcase

¹al [ɑl] *adv* **1** yet; already: *~ een hele tijd* for a long time now; *~ enige tijd, ~ vanaf juli* for some time past (*or:* now), (ever) since July; *dat dacht ik ~* I thought so; *is zij er nu ~?* is she here already?; *is Jan er ~?* is John here yet?; *ik heb het altijd ~ geweten* I've known it all along; *daar heb je het ~* there you are; **2** all: *dat alleen ~* that alone; *~ te snel* (or: *spoe-*

dig) far too fast (*or:* soon); *ze weten het maar ~ te goed* they know only too well; *hij had het toch ~ moeilijk* he had enough problems as it was; *het is ~ laat* (*or: duur)* it is late (*or:* expensive) enough as it is; *dat lijkt er ~ meer op, dat is ~ beter* that's more like it

²**al** [ɑl] *ind pron* **1** all, whole: *~ de moeite* all our (*or:* their) trouble; *het was één en ~ geweld op tv gisteren* there was nothing but violence on TV yesterday; **2** all (of)

³**al** [ɑl] *num* all (of), every, each: *~ zijn gedachten* his every thought; *~ de kinderen* all (of) the children

⁴**al** [ɑl] *conj* though, although, even though, even if: *~ ben ik arm, ik ben gelukkig* I may be poor, but I'm happy; *~ zeg ik het zelf* even though I say so myself; *~ was het alleen maar omdat* if only because; *ook ~ is het erg* bad as it is (*or:* may be); *ik deed het niet, ~ kreeg ik een miljoen* I wouldn't do it for a million pounds

alarm [alɑrm] *het* alarm: *groot ~* full (*or:* red) alert; *loos (vals) ~* false alarm; *een stil ~* a silent alarm; *~ slaan* (*or: geven)* give (*or:* sound) the alarm

alarmcentrale [alɑrmsɛntralə] *de (~s)* emergency centre, (general) emergency number

alarmeren [alɑrmɛrə(n)] *vb* **1** alert, call out: *de brandweer ~* call (out) the fire brigade; **2** alarm: *~de berichten* disturbing reports

alarmlichten [alɑrmlɪxtə(n)] *de* hazard warning lights

alarmnummer [alɑrmnʏmər] *het (~s)* emergency number

alarmsignaal [alɑrmsɪɲal] *het (-signalen)* alarm, alert

¹**Albanees** [ɑlbanes] *de (Albanezen) (person)* Albanian

²**Albanees** [ɑlbanes] *het (language)* Albanian

³**Albanees** [ɑlbanes] *adj* Albanian

Albanië [ɑlbanijə] *het* Albania

albast [ɑlbɑst] *het (~en)* alabaster

albatros [ɑlbatrɔs] *de (~sen)* albatross

albino [ɑlbino] *de (~'s)* albino

album [ɑlbʏm] *het (~s)* album

alchemie [ɑlxemi] *de* alchemy

alcohol [ɑlkohɔl] *de* alcohol: *pure ~* pure alcohol; *verslaafd aan ~* addicted to alcohol

alcoholisch [ɑlkoholis] *adj* alcoholic: *~e dranken* alcoholic drinks; *een niet ~ drankje* a non-alcoholic drink

alcoholisme [ɑlkoholɪsmə] *het* alcoholism

alcoholist [ɑlkoholɪst] *de (~en)* alcoholic

alcoholvrij [ɑlkohɔlvrɛi] *adj* non-alcoholic, soft: *~e dranken* non-alcoholic beverages, soft drinks

aldaar [ɑldar] *adv* there, at (*or:* of) that place

alert [alɛrt] *adj* alert: *~ zijn op spelfouten* be on the alert (*or:* lookout) for spelling mistakes

alfa [ɑlfa] *de (~'s) (educ) (roughly)* languages, humanities, arts || *zij is een echte ~* all her talents are on the arts side

alfabet [ɑlfabɛt] *het (~ten)* alphabet: *alle letters van het ~* all the letters in the alphabet; *de boeken staan op ~* the books are arranged in alphabetical order

alfabetisch [ɑlfabɛtis] *adj, adv* alphabetical: *een ~(e) gids* (*or: ~ spoorboekje)* an ABC, an A to Z; *in ~e volgorde* in alphabetical order

alfabetiseren [ɑlfabɛtizɛrə(n)] *vb* alphabetize

alfanumeriek [ɑlfanymerik] *adj* alphanumeric(al)

algebra [ɑlɣəbra] *de* algebra

algeheel [ɑlɣəhel] *adj* complete, total: *met algehele steun* with (everyone's) full support; *met mijn algehele instemming* with my wholehearted consent; *tot algehele tevredenheid* to everyone's satisfaction

algemeen [ɑlɣəmen] *adj, adv* **1** public, general, universal, common: *een algemene regel* a general rule; *voor ~ gebruik* for general use; *algemene ontwikkeling* general knowledge; *in algemene zin* in a general sense; *algemene middelen* public funds; *het is ~ bekend* it is common knowledge; *~ beschouwd worden als* be generally known as; **2** general(ized), broad: *in algemene bewoordingen* in general terms; *in het ~ hebt u gelijk* on the whole, you're right; *zij zijn in het ~ betrouwbaar* for the most part they are reliable; *in (over) het ~* in general

algemeenheid [ɑlɣəmenhɛit] *de (-heden)* generality; indefiniteness || *(Belg) met ~ van stemmen* unanimously

algen [ɑlɣə(n)] *de* algae

Algerije [ɑlɣɛrɛiə] *het* Algeria

Algerijn [ɑlɣɛrɛin] *de (~en)* Algerian

Algerijns [ɑlɣɛrɛins] *adj* Algerian

alhoewel [ɑlhuwɛl] *conj* although

alias [alijas] *adv* alias, also (*or:* otherwise) known as

alibi [alibi] *het, de (~'s)* alibi, excuse: *iem een ~ bezorgen (geven)* cover up for s.o.

alimentatie [alimɛnta(t)si] *de* maintenance (allowance, money), alimony

alinea [alineja] *de (~'s)* paragraph: *een nieuwe ~ beginnen* start a new paragraph

Allah [ɑla] *de* Allah

allang [ɑlɑŋ] *adv* for a long time, a long time ago: *ik ben ~ blij dat je er bent* I'm pleased that you're here at all

¹**alle** [ɑlə] *ind pron* all, every, each: *uit ~ macht iets proberen* try one's utmost; *hij had ~ reden om* he had every reason to; *boven ~ twijfel* beyond all doubt; *voor ~ zekerheid* to make quite (*or:* doubly) sure

²**alle** [ɑlə] *num* all, every, each, everyone, everybody: *van ~ kanten* from all sides, from every side; *in ~ opzichten* in all respects; *zij gingen met hun ~n naar het zwembad* they went all together to the swimming pool; *geen van ~n wist het* not one of them knew

allebei [ɑləbɛi] *num* both; either: *~ de kinderen waren bang* both (of the) children were afraid; *het was ~ juist geweest* either would have been correct

alledaags [alədaxs] *adj* daily, everyday: *de ~e be-*

slommeringen day-to-day worries; *de kleine, ~e dingen van het leven* the little everyday things of life; *dat is niet iets ~* that's not an everyday occurrence

¹**alleen** [alɛn] *adj, adv* 1 alone, by oneself, on one's own: *hij is graag ~* he likes to be alone (*or:* by himself); *het ~ klaarspelen* manage it alone (*or:* on one's own); *helemaal ~* all (*or:* completely) alone; *een kamer voor hem ~* a room (all) to himself; **2** only, alone: *~ in het weekeinde geopend* only open at weekends

²**alleen** [alɛn] *adv* only, merely, just: *de gedachte ~ al* the mere (*or:* very) thought; *ik wilde u ~ maar even spreken* I just wanted to talk to you; *~ maar aan zichzelf denken* only think of oneself

alleenheerschappij [alɛnhersχapɛi] *de* absolute power, (*fig*) monopoly: *de ~ voeren (over)* reign supreme (over)

alleenrecht [alɛnrɛχt] *het (~en)* exclusive right(s)

alleenstaand [alɛnstant] *adj* single: *een ~e ouder* a single parent

alleenverdiener [alɛnvərdinər] *de (~s)* sole wage-earner

allegorie [aləɣori] *de (~ën)* allegory

¹**allemaal** [aləmal] *adv* all, only: *hij zag ~ sterretjes* all he saw was little stars

²**allemaal** [aləmal] *num* all, everybody, everyone, everything: *beste van ~* best of all; *~ onzin* all nonsense; *ik houd van jullie ~* I love you all; *zoals wij ~* like all of us; *~ samen (tegelijk)* all together; *tot ziens ~* goodbye everybody

allemachtig [aləmaχtəχ] *adv* amazingly: *een ~ groot huis* an amazingly big house

allerbest [alərbɛst] *adj, adv* very best: *zijn ~e vrienden* his very best friends; *ik wens je het ~e* I wish you all the best

allereerst [alərerst] *adj, adv* first of all, very first: *vanaf het ~e begin* from the very beginning

allergie [alɛrɣi] *de (~ën)* allergy

allergisch [alɛrɣis] *adj* allergic (to)

allerhande [alərhandə] *adj* all sorts (of), all kinds (of)

Allerheiligen [alərhɛiləɣə(n)] *de* All Saints' (Day)

allerhoogst [alərhoχst] *adj* highest of all, very highest; supreme, paramount; maximum; top: *van het ~e belang* of supreme (*or:* paramount) importance; *het is de ~e tijd* it's high time

allerlaatst [alərlatst] *adj, adv* last of all, very last, very latest: *de ~e bus* the (very) last bus; *de ~e mode* the very latest style; *op het ~* at the very last moment; *tot op het ~* right up to the (very) end

allerlei [alərlɛi] *adj* all sorts (*or:* kinds) of: *~ speelgoed* all sorts of toys

allerliefst [alərlifst] *adj, adv* **1** (very) dearest (*or:* sweetest): *een ~ kind* a very dear (*or:* sweet) child; **2** more than anything: *hij wil het ~ acteur worden* he wants to be an actor to be an actor more than anything

allerminst [alərmɪnst] *adj* **1** least (of all): *ik heb er* niet het ~e op aan te merken I don't have the slightest objection; **2** (very) least, (very) slightest: *op zijn ~* at the very least

Allerzielen [alərzilə(n)] *de* All Souls' (Day)

alles [aləs] *ind pron* everything, all, anything: *hij heeft (van) ~ geprobeerd* he has tried everything; *is dat ~?* will that be all?; *dat is ~* that's it (*or:* everything); *ik weet er ~ van* I know all about it; *(het is) ~ of niets* (it's) all or nothing; *~ op ~ zetten* go all out; *van ~ (en nog wat)* all sorts of things; *~ bij elkaar viel het mee* all in all (*or:* all things considered) it was better than expected; *~ op zijn tijd* all in due course, all in good time

allesbehalve [aləzbəhalvə] *adv* anything but: *het was ~ een succes* it was anything but a success; *~ vriendelijk* anything but friendly

alleseter [aləsetər] *de (~s)* omnivore

allesomvattend [aləsomvatənt] *adj* all-embracing, comprehensive, universal

allesoverheersend [aləsovərhersənt] *adj* overpowering: *een ~e smaak van knoflook* an overpowering taste of garlic

allesreiniger [aləsrɛinəɣər] *de (~s)* all-purpose cleaner

alliantie [alijansi] *de (~s)* alliance

allicht [alɪχt] *adv* most probably (*or:* likely), of course: *ja ~* yes, of course

alligator [aliɣatɔr] *de (~s)* alligator

¹**allochtoon** [aloχton] *de (allochtonen)* immigrant, foreigner

²**allochtoon** [aloχton] *adj* foreign

all-risk [ɔːlrɪsk] *adj, adv* comprehensive: *~ verzekerd zijn* have a comprehensive policy

allure [alyrə] *de (~s)* air, style: *~ hebben* have style; *iem van ~* a striking personality; *een gebouw met ~* an imposing building

almaar [almar] *adv* constantly; continuously, all the time: *kinderen die ~ om snoep vragen* children who are always asking for sweets

almachtig [almaχtəχ] *adj* almighty, all-powerful: *de Almachtige* the Almighty

almanak [almanak] *de (~ken)* almanac

alo [alo] *de academie voor lichamelijke opvoeding* college of physical education

alom [alɔm] *adv* everywhere, on all sides: *~ gevreesd* (*or:* bekend) generally feared (*or:* known)

alp [alp] *de (~en)* alp

alpino [alpino] *de (~'s)* (Basque) beret

als [als] *conj* **1** like, as: *zich ~ een dame gedragen* behave like a lady; *hetzelfde ~ ik* the same as me, just like me; *hij is even groot ~ jij* he is as tall as you; *de brief luidt ~ volgt* the letter reads as follows; *zowel in de stad ~ op het land* both in the city and in the country; **2** as, as if: *~ bij toverslag veranderde alles* as if by magic everything changed; *~ ware het je eigen kind* as if it were your own child; **3** for, as: *poppen ~ geschenk* dolls for presents; *ik heb die man nog ~ jongen gekend* I knew that man when he was still a boy; *~ vrienden uit elkaar gaan* part as friends; **4** when: *telkens ~ wij elkaar tegenkomen keert hij zich af* whenever we meet, he turns away; **5** if, as long as: *~ zij er niet geweest was …* if she had not been there …; *maar wat ~ het regent, ~ het nu eens regent?* but what if it rains?; *~ het mogelijk is* if possible; *~ ze al komen* if they come at all

alsmaar [ɑlsmar] *adv* constantly, all the time: *~ praten* talk constantly

alsnog [ɑlsnɔχ] *adv* still, yet: *je kunt ~ van studie veranderen* you can still change your course

alsof [ɑlsɔf] *conj* as if: *je doet maar ~* you're just pretending; *hij keek ~ hij mij niet begreep* he looked as if he didn't understand me

¹alstublieft [ɑlstyblift] *adv* please: *een ogenblikje ~* just a minute, please; *wees ~ rustig* please be quiet

²alstublieft [ɑlstyblift] *int* please; here you are: *~, dat is dan* €6,50 (thank you,) that will be €6.50

¹alt [ɑlt] *de (mus) (singer)* alto

²alt [ɑlt] *de (mus) (voice)* alto

altaar [ɑltar] *het, de (altaren)* altar

alternatief [ɑltɛrnatif] *het (alternatieven)* alternative: *er is geen enkel ~* there is no alternative; *als ~* as an alternative

altijd [ɑltɛit] *adv* always, forever: *ik heb het ~ wel gedacht* I've thought so all along, I've always thought so; *je kunt niet ~ winnen* you can't win them all; *~ weer* again and again; *wat je ook doet, je verliest ~* no matter what you do, you always lose; *bijna ~* nearly always; *wonen ze nog ~ in Almere?* are they still living in Almere?; *voor eens en ~* once and for all; *hetzelfde als ~* the same as always, the usual; *ze ging ~ op woensdag winkelen* she always went shopping on Wednesdays

altsaxofoon [ɑltsɑksofon] *de (~s, -saxofonen)* alto saxophone

aluin [ɑlœyn] *de (~en)* alum

¹aluminium [ɑlymɪnijym] *het* aluminium

²aluminium [ɑlymɪnijym] *adj* aluminium

alvast [ɑlvɑst] *adv* meanwhile, in the meantime: *jullie hadden ~ kunnen beginnen zonder mij* you could have started without me

alvleesklier [ɑlvlesklir] *de (~en)* pancreas

alweer [ɑlwer] *adv* again, once more: *het wordt ~ herfst* autumn has come round again

alzheimer [ɑltshɛimər] *de* Alzheimer's (disease)

amalgaam [ɑmɑlɣam] *het (amalgamen)* amalgam

amandel [ɑmɑndəl] *de (~en)* **1** almond; **2** tonsil: *zijn ~en laten knippen* have one's tonsils (taken) out

amanuensis [amanywɛnsɪs] *de (~sen, amanuenses)* laboratory assistant

amateur [amatør] *de (~s)* amateur

amateuristisch [amatørɪstis] *adj, adv* amateur(ish): *~e sportbeoefening* amateur sports; *dat is zeer ~ gedaan* that was done very amateurishly

amazone [amazɔːnə] *de (~s)* horsewoman

Amazone [amazɔːnə] *de* Amazon

ambacht [ɑmbaχt] *het (~en)* trade, (handi)craft: *het ~ uitoefenen van …* practise the trade of …

ambassade [ɑmbɑsadə] *de (~s)* embassy

ambassadeur [ɑmbɑsadør] *de (~s)* ambassador

amber [ɑmbər] *de* amber

ambiëren [ɑmbijɛrə(n)] *vb* aspire to: *een baan ~* aspire to a job

ambitie [ɑmbi(t)si] *de (~s)* ambition: *een man van grote ~* a man with great ambitions

ambitieus [ɑmbi(t)ʃøs] *adj* ambitious: *ambitieuze plannen* ambitious plans

¹Ambonees [ɑmbones] *de (Ambonezen)* Amboinese, Moluccan

²Ambonees [ɑmbones] *adj* Amboinese, Moluccan

ambt [ɑmt] *het (~en)* office: *een ~ uitoefenen* carry out one's duties

ambtelijk [ɑmtələk] *adj, adv* official: *~e stukken* official documents

ambtenaar [ɑmtənar] *de (ambtenaren)* official, civil servant, public servant: *~ van de burgerlijke stand* registrar, (Am) county clerk; *burgerlijk ~* civil (or: public) servant

ambtenarij [ɑmtənarɛi] *de* bureaucracy, red tape

ambtsperiode [ɑmtsperijodə] *de (~s)* term of office: *de ~ van de burgemeester loopt binnenkort af* the mayor's term of office is drawing to a close

ambulance [ɑmbylɑsə] *de (~s)* ambulance

amen [amə(n)] *het* amen || *(Belg) ~ en uit* that's enough!, stop it!

Amerika [amerika] *het* America

Amerikaan [amerikan] *de (Amerikanen)* American: *tot ~ naturaliseren* naturalize as an American

Amerikaans [amerikans] *adj* American: *de ~e burgeroorlog* the American Civil War; *het ~e congres* Congress; *~e whiskey* bourbon, rye, corn whiskey

Amerikaanse [amerikansə] *de* American (woman)

amfetamine [ɑmfetaminə] *het, de (~n)* amphetamine

amfibie [ɑmfibi] *de (~ën)* amphibian

aminozuur [amɪnozyr] *het (-zuren)* amino acid

ammonia [amɔnija] *de* ammonia (water)

amnestie [ɑmnɛsti] *de (~ën)* amnesty: *~ verlenen (aan)* grant an amnesty (to)

amoebe [amøbə] *de (~n)* amoeba

amok [amɔk] || *~ maken* run amok

amoreel [amorel] *adj, adv* amoral

amper [ɑmpər] *adv* scarcely, barely, hardly: *hij kon ~ schrijven* he could barely write

ampère [ɑmpɛːrə] *de (~s)* ampere

ampul [ɑmpyl] *de (~len)* ampoule

amputatie [ɑmpyta(t)si] *de (~s)* amputation

amputeren [ɑmpytɛrə(n)] *vb* amputate

amulet [amylɛt] *de (~ten)* amulet

amusant [amyzɑnt] *adj, adv* amusing: *een ~ verhaal* an amusing story; *iets ~ vinden* find sth amusing (or: entertaining)

amusement [amyzəmɛnt] *het (~en)* amusement, entertainment

amusementshal [amyzəmɛn(t)shɑl] *de (~len)* amusement arcade

amuseren [amyzɛrə(n)] *ref vb* amuse oneself, entertain oneself, enjoy oneself: *zich kostelijk (uitstekend)* ~ thoroughly enjoy oneself

anaal [anal] *adj, adv* anal

anabool [anabol] *adj* anabolic: *anabole steroïden* anabolic steroids

anachronisme [anaχronɪsmə] *het (~n)* anachronism

analfabeet [analfabet] *de (analfabeten)* illiterate

analfabetisme [analfabetɪsmə] *het* illiteracy

analist [analɪst] *de (~en)* (chemical) analyst, lab(oratory) technician

analoog [analoχ] *adj, adv* analogue

analyse [analizə] *de (~s)* analysis: *een kritische ~ van een roman* a critical analysis of a novel

analyseren [analizɛrə(n)] *vb* analyse: *grondig ~: a)* analyse thoroughly; *b)* dissect

analytisch [analitɪs] *adj, adv* analytical: *~ denken* think analytically

ananas [ananɑs] *de (~sen)* pineapple

anarchie [anarχi] *de* anarchy

anarchisme [anarχɪsmə] *het* anarchism

anarchist [anarχɪst] *de (~en)* anarchist

anatomie [anatomi] *de* anatomy

anatomisch [anatomɪs] *adj* anatomical

ancien [ãsjɛ̃] *de (~s) (Belg)* veteran, ex-serviceman

Andalusië [andalysijə] *het* Andalusia

¹ander [andər] *adj* **1** other, another: *aan de ~e kant* on the other hand; *een ~e keer misschien!* maybe some other time!; *(de) een of ~e voorbijganger* some passer-by; *met ~e woorden* in other words; *om de één of ~e reden* for some reason, for one reason or another; **2** different: *ik voel me nu een ~ mens* I feel a different man (*or:* woman) now; *dat is een heel ~e zaak* that's quite a different matter, that's a different matter altogether

²ander [andər] *ind pron* **1** another, *(pl)* others: *de een of ~* somebody, someone; *sommigen wel, ~en niet* some do (*or:* are), some don't (*or:* aren't); *de ene of de ~e* (choose) one thing or the other; **2** another matter (*or:* thing), *(pl)* other matters (*or:* things): *je hebt het een en ~ nodig om te …* you need a few things in order to …; *onder ~e* among other things, including; *of het één, of het ~!* you can't have it both ways

³ander [andər] *num* next, other: *om de ~e dag* every other day, on alternative days

anderhalf [andərhalf] *num* one and a half: *~ maal zoveel* half as much (*or:* many) again; *~ maal zo hoog* one and a half times as high; *~ uur* an hour and a half

¹anders [andərs] *adv* **1** normally, differently: *het ~ aanpakken* handle it differently; *~ gezegd, …* in other words …; *in jouw geval liggen de zaken ~* in your case things are different; *(zo is het) en niet ~* that's the way it is (*or:* how things are); *net als ~* just as usual; *niet meer zo vaak als ~* less often than usual; **2** otherwise, else: *wat kon ik ~ (doen) (dan …)?* what else could I do (but …); *~ niets?* will that be

all?; *ergens ~* somewhere else

²anders [andərs] *adj* different (from): *niemand ~* nobody else; *wilt u nog iets ~?* do you want anything else?; *over iets ~ beginnen (te praten)* change the subject; *er zit niets ~ op dan …* there is nothing for it but to …

andersom [andərsɔm] *adv* the other way round

anderstalige [andərstaləɣə] *de* non-native speaker

anderzijds [andərzɛits] *adv* on the other hand

andijvie [andɛivi] *de* endive

andreaskruis [andrejaskrœys] *het (~en)* cross of St Andrew

anekdote [anɛgdotə] *de (~s)* anecdote

anemoon [anəmon] *de (anemonen)* anemone

anesthesie [anɛstezi] *de* anaesthesia: *lokale (or: totale)* ~ local (*or:* general) anaesthesia

anesthesist [anɛstezɪst] *de (~en)* anaesthetist

angel [aŋəl] *de (~s)* sting

Angelsaksisch [aŋəlsaksis] *adj* **1** English(-speaking); **2** Anglo-Saxon

angina [aŋɣina] *de* tonsillitis

anglicaan [aŋχlikan] *de (anglicanen)* Anglican

anglicaans [aŋχlikans] *adj* Anglican: *de anglicaanse Kerk* the Church of England

anglist [aŋχlɪst] *de (~en)* specialist (*or:* student) of English (language and literature)

Angola [aŋɣola] *het* Angola

Angolees [aŋɣoles] *de* Angolan

angst [aŋst] *de (~en)* fear (of) (*oft pl*), dread, terror (of), *(psychology)* anxiety: *~ aanjagen* frighten, *(stronger)* terrify; *~ hebben voor* be afraid (*or:* scared) of; *uit ~ voor straf* for fear of punishment; *verlamd van ~* numb with fear

angstaanjagend [aŋstanjaɣənt] *adj, adv* terrifying, frightening

angstig [aŋstəχ] *adj* **1** anxious; *(after vb)* afraid: *een ~e schreeuw* an anxious cry; *dat maakte mij ~* that frightened me, that made me afraid; **2** fearful, anxious, terrifying: *~e gedachten* anxious thoughts; *het waren ~e tijden* those were anxious times

angstvallig [aŋstfaləχ] *adj, adv* **1** scrupulous, meticulous; **2** anxious, nervous: *~ keek hij om* he glanced back anxiously

angstzweet [aŋstswet] *het* cold sweat

anijs [anɛis] *de* aniseed

animatie [anima(t)si] *de (~s)* animation: *(Belg) kinder~* children's activities (during an event)

animo [animo] *het, de* zest (for): *met ~ iets doen* do sth with gusto

anjer [aɲər] *de (~s)* carnation

anker [aŋkər] *het (~s)* anchor: *het ~ lichten* raise (the) anchor, *(also fig)* get under way

ankerplaats [aŋkərplats] *de (~en)* anchorage, berth

annexatie [anɛksa(t)si] *de (~s)* annexation, incorporation *(esp municipalities)*

annexeren [anɛksɛrə(n)] *vb* annex, incorporate *(esp municipalities)*

anno [ɑno] *prep* in the year: ~ *1981* in the year 1981

annonce [ɑnõsə] *de (~s)* advertisement, announcement

annuleren [ɑnylɛrə(n)] *vb* cancel: *een bestelling ~* cancel an order

annulering [ɑnylɛrɪŋ] *de (~en)* cancellation: ~ *van een reservering* cancellation of a reservation

anoniem [anonim] *adj* anonymous, nameless, incognito

anorak [ɑnorɑk] *de (~s)* anorak

ANP [aɛnpe] *het Algemeen Nederlands Persbureau* Dutch press agency

ansichtkaart [ɑnzɪχtkart] *de (~en)* (picture) postcard

ansjovis [ɑnʃovɪs] *de (~sen)* anchovy

Antarctica [ɑntɑrktika] *het* Antarctica

antecedent [ɑntəsədɛnt] *het (~en)* antecedent: *iemands ~en natrekken* look into s.o.'s past record

antenne [ɑntɛnə] *de (~s)* aerial; antenna

antibioticum [ɑntibijotikʏm] *het (antibiotica)* antibiotic: *ik neem antibiotica* I'm taking antibiotics

anticiperen [ɑntisipɛrə(n)] *vb* anticipate

anticlimax [ɑntiklimɑks] *de (~en)* anticlimax

anticonceptie [ɑntikɔnsɛpsi] *de* contraception, birth control

anticonceptiemiddel [ɑntikɔnsɛpsimɪdəl] *het (~en)* contraceptive

¹antiek [ɑntik] *het* antiques *(pl)*

²antiek [ɑntik] *adj* antique, ancient: *~e meubels* antique furniture

Antillen [ɑntɪlə(n)] *de* (the) Antilles: *de Nederlandse ~* the Netherlands Antilles

Antilliaan [ɑntɪl(i)jan] *de (Antillianen)* Antillean

antilope [ɑntilopə] *de (~n)* antelope

antipathie [ɑntipati] *de (~ën)* antipathy (towards)

antiquair [ɑntikɛːr] *de (~s)* antique dealer

anti-semitisme [ɑntisemitɪsmə] *het* anti-Semitism

antiseptisch [ɑntisɛptis] *adj* antiseptic

antistof [ɑntistɔf] *de (~fen)* antibody

antivries [ɑntivris] *het, de* antifreeze

antraciet [ɑntrasit] *het, de* anthracite (coal)

antropologie [ɑntropoloɣi] *de* anthropology: *culturele ~* cultural anthropology, ethnology

antropoloog [ɑntropoloχ] *de (-logen)* anthropologist

Antwerpen [ɑntwɛrpə(n)] *het* Antwerp

antwoord [ɑntwort] *het (~en)* answer, reply: *een afwijzing (ontkennend) ~* a negative answer; *een bevestigend ~* an affirmative answer; *een positief ~* a favourable answer; *~ geven op* reply to, answer; *een ~ geven* give an answer; *in ~ op uw brief (schrijven)* in reply to your letter; *dat is geen ~ op mijn vraag* that doesn't answer my question

antwoordapparaat [ɑntwortaparat] *het (-apparaten)* answering machine, answerphone

antwoorden [ɑntwordə(n)] *vb* answer, reply, respond: *bevestigend (positief) ~* answer in the affirmative; *ik antwoord niet op zulke vragen* I don't answer such questions

antwoordnummer [ɑntwortnʏmər] *het (~s) (roughly)* Freepost

anus [ɑnʏs] *de* anus

ANWB [aɛnwebe] *de Algemene Nederlandse Wielrijdersbond (roughly)* Dutch A.A. *(or Am: A.A.A.)*, Royal Dutch Touring Club

aorta [aɔrta] *de (~'s)* aorta

AOW [aowe] *de* 1 *Algemene Ouderdomswet* general retirement pensions act; 2 (old-age retirement) pension

AOW'er [aowejər] *de (~s)* OAP (old-age pensioner), senior citizen

apart [apɑrt] *adj, adv* 1 separate, apart: *elk geval ~ behandelen* deal with each case individually; *iem ~ nemen (spreken)* take s.o. aside; *onderdelen ~ verkopen* sell parts separately; 2 special, exclusive: *zij vormen een klasse ~* they are in a class of their own; 3 different, unusual: *hij ziet er wat ~ uit* he looks a bit unusual

apartheid [apɑrtheit] *de* apartheid

apegapen [apəɣapə(n)] || *op ~ liggen* be at one's last gasp

apenkop [apə(n)kɔp] *de (~pen)* monkey, brat

Apennijnen [apɛnɛinə(n)] *de* Apennines

apennoot [apənot] *de* peanut, monkey nut

apenstaartje [apə(n)starcə] *het (~s)* at sign

aperitief [aperitif] *het, de (aperitieven)* aperitif

APK-keuring [apekakørɪŋ] *de (~en)* motor vehicle test, MOT test

Apocalyps [apokalɪps] *de* Apocalypse

apostel [apɔstəl] *de (~en)* apostle

apostrof [apostrɔf] *de (~s)* apostrophe

apotheek [apotek] *de (apotheken)* (dispensing) chemist's, *(Am)* drugstore

apparaat [apɑrat] *het (apparaten)* machine, appliance, device: *huishoudelijke apparaten* household appliances

apparatuur [apɑratyr] *de* apparatus, equipment, machinery, hardware

appartement [apɑrtəmɛnt] *het (~en)* flat, *(Am)* apartment: *een driekamerappartement* a 2-bedroom flat

appartementsgebouw [apɑrtəmɛntsχəbau] *het (~en) (Belg)* block of flats

appel [ɑpəl] *de (~s)* apple

appelflap [ɑpəlflɑp] *de (~pen)* apple turnover

appelgebak [ɑpəlɣəbɑk] *het (roughly)* apple tart

appelmoes [ɑpəlmus] *het, de* apple-sauce

appelsien [ɑpəlsin] *de (~en) (Belg)* orange

appelstroop [ɑpəlstrop] *de* apple spread

appendix [apɛndɪks] *het, de (appendices)* appendix

applaudisseren [aplaudisɛrə(n)] *vb* applaud, clap: *~ voor iem* applaud s.o.

applaus [aplɑus] *het* applause, clapping: *de motie werd met ~ begroet* the motion was received with applause; *een ~je voor Marleen!* let's give a big hand to Marleen!

april [aprɪl] *de (~s)* April: *één ~* April Fools' Day

aprilgrap [aprɪlɣrɑp] *de (~pen)* April Fool's joke

apropos [apropo̱] ‖ *van zijn ~ raken (zijn)* lose the thread of one's argument

à propos [apropo̱] *int* apropos, by the way, incidentally

aquaduct [akwady̱kt] *het (~en)* aqueduct

aquarel [akwarε̱l] *de (~len)* water colour, aquarelle

aquarium [akwa̱rijʏm] *het (~s, aquaria)* aquarium

Arabië [ara̱bijə] *het* Arabia

Arabier [arabi̱r] *de (~en)* **1** Saudi (Arabian); **2** Arab

¹Arabisch [ara̱bis] *het* Arabic: *in het ~* in Arabic

²Arabisch [ara̱bis] *adj* Arabic; Arabian; Arab: *de ~e literatuur* Arabic literature

arbeid [arbεit] *de* labour, work: *de Dag van de Arbeid* Labour Day; *de Partij van de Arbeid* the Labour Party; *(on)geschoolde ~* (un)skilled labour *(or: work)*; *~ verrichten* labour, work

arbeider [arbεidər] *de (~s)* worker, workman: *landarbeiders* agricultural labourers; *geschoolde ~s* skilled workers; *ongeschoolde ~s* unskilled workers

arbeiderspartij [arbεidərspartεi] *de (~en)* Labour Party, Socialist Party

arbeidsbureau [arbεitsbyro] *het (~s)* employment office, jobcentre: *zich inschrijven bij het ~* sign on at the employment office

arbeidsintensief [arbεitsintεnzi̱f] *adj* labour-intensive

arbeidsmarkt [arbεitsmarkt] *de (~en)* labour market, job market: *de situatie op de ~* the employment situation

arbeidsongeschikt [arbεitsoŋɣəsx̱ɪkt] *adj* disabled, unable to work: *gedeeltelijk ~ verklaard worden* be declared partially disabled

arbeidsovereenkomst [arbεitsovəreɛ̱nkɔmst] *de (~en)* employment contract: *een collectieve ~* a collective agreement; *een individuele ~* an individual employment contract

arbeidstijdverkorting [arbεitstεitfərkɔrtɪŋ] *de* reduction of working hours, shorter working week

arbeidsvoorwaarde [arbεitsforwardə] *de (~n)* term *(or: condition)* of employment: *secundaire ~n* fringe benefits

arbiter [arbi̱tər] *de (~s) (sport)* referee, umpire

Arbowet [a̱rbowεt] *de* (Dutch) occupational health and safety act; Factories Act; *(Am; roughly)* Labor Law

arceren [arsε̱rə(n)] *vb* shade: *het gearceerde gedeelte* the shaded area

archaïsch [arx̱ais] *adj* archaic, antiquated

archeologie [arx̱eoloɣi] *het* archaeology

archeologisch [arx̱ejoloɣ̱is] *adj, adv* archaeological: *~e opgravingen* archaeological excavation(s)

archeoloog [arx̱ejoloɣ̱] *de (-logen)* archaeologist

archief [arx̱if] *het (archieven)* archives *(pl)*, record office, registry (office), files: *iets in het ~ opbergen* file sth (away)

archiefkast [arx̱i̱fkast] *de (~en)* filing cabinet

archipel [a̱rx̱ipεl] *de (~s)* archipelago

architect [arʃitε̱kt] *de (~en)* architect

architectuur [arʃitεkty̱r] *de* architecture, building

(style): *voorbeelden van moderne ~* examples of modern architecture

archivaris [arx̱iva̱rɪs] *de (~sen)* archivist, keeper of the archives *(or: records)*, registrar

Ardennen [ardε̱nə(n)] *de* (the) Ardennes

are [a̱rə] *de (~n)* are: *één ~ is honderd vierkante meter* one are is a hundred square metres

arena [arε̱na] *de (~'s)* arena

arend [a̱rənt] *de (~en)* eagle

argeloos [a̱rɣələos] *adj, adv* unsuspecting, innocent

Argentijn [arɣəntεi̱n] *de (~en)* Argentine, Argentinian

Argentinië [arɣəntinijə] *het* Argentina

arglistig [arx̱lɪstəx̱] *adj, adv* crafty, cunning

argument [arɣymε̱nt] *het (~en)* argument: *een steekhoudend ~* a watertight argument; *~en aanvoeren voor iets* make out a case for sth; *~en voor en tegen* pros and cons; *dat is geen ~* that's no reason

argumentatie [arɣymεnta(t)si] *de (~s)* **1** argumentation, reasoning, line of reasoning; **2** argument

argwaan [a̱rx̱wan] *de* suspicion: *~ koesteren tegen iem (omtrent iets)* be suspicious of s.o. (sth); *~ krijgen* grow suspicious

argwanend [arx̱wa̱nənt] *adj, adv* suspicious: *een ~e blik* a suspicious look

aria [a̱rija] *de (~'s)* aria

aristocraat [arɪstokra̱t] *de (aristocraten)* aristocrat

aristocratie [arɪstokra(t)si̱] *de (~ën)* aristocracy

ark [ark] *de (~en)* **1** houseboat; **2** Ark: *de ~ van Noach* Noah's Ark

¹arm [arm] *de (~en)* **1** arm: *een gebroken ~* a broken *(or: fractured)* arm; *met open ~en ontvangen* receive *(or: welcome)* with open arms; *hij sloeg zijn ~en om haar heen* he threw his arms around her; *zij liepen ~ in ~* they walked arm in arm; *een advocaat in de ~ nemen* consult a solicitor; **2** arm, sleeve: *de ~ zit niet goed* the arm doesn't fit well

²arm [arm] *adj* **1** poor: *de ~e landen* the poor countries; *de ~en en de rijken* the rich and the poor; **2** poor (in), lacking; **3** poor, wretched: *het ~e schaap* the poor thing *(or: soul)*

armatuur [armaty̱r] *de (armaturen)* fitting, bracket

armband [a̱rmbant] *de (~en)* bracelet

¹Armeens [armε̱ns] *het* Armenian

²Armeens [armε̱ns] *adj* Armenian

Armenië [armε̱nijə] *het* Armenia

Armeniër [armε̱nijər] *de (~s)* Armenian

armetierig [armətie̱rəx̱] *adj, adv* miserable, paltry

armleuning [a̱rmlønɪŋ] *de (~en)* arm(rest)

armoede [a̱rmudə] *de* poverty, *(stronger)* destitution: *geestelijke ~* intellectual *(or: spiritual)* poverty; *schrijnende (or: bittere) ~* abject *(or: grinding)* poverty

armoedig [armu̱dəx̱] *adj, adv* poor, shabby: *~ gekleed* shabbily dressed; *dat staat zo ~* that looks so shabby

armsgat [a̱rmsx̱at] *het (~en)* armhole

armslag [a̱rmslax̱] *de (~en)* elbow room

armzalig [ɑrmzɑ̯lə χ] *adj, adv* poor, paltry, miserable: *een ~ pensioentje* a meagre pension

aroma [arọma] *het* aroma, flavour

arrangement [arɑʒəmɛnt] *het (~en)* arrangement, format, order: *een ~ voor piano* an arrangement for piano

arrangeren [arɑʒẹrə(n)] *vb* 1 arrange, set out; 2 arrange, organize, get up; 3 arrange, score: *voor orkest ~* orchestrate, score

arrenslee [ɑrə(n)sle] *de (~ën)* horse sleigh

arrest [arɛst] *het (~en)* arrest, detention, custody: *u staat onder ~* you are under arrest

arrestant [arɛstɑnt] *de (~en)* arrested man (*or:* woman), detainee; prisoner

arrestatie [arɛstɑ(t)si] *de (~s)* arrest: *een ~ verrichten* make an arrest

arrestatiebevel [arɛstɑ(t)sibəvɛl] *het (~en)* arrest warrant

arresteren [arɛstẹrə(n)] *vb* arrest, detain: *iem laten ~* have s.o. arrested, place s.o. in charge

arriveren [arivẹrə(n)] *vb* arrive

arrogant [aroɣɑnt] *adj, adv* arrogant, superior: *een ~e houding hebben* have a haughty manner

arrondissement [arɔndisəmɛnt] *het (~en)* district

arrondissementsrechtbank [arɔndisəmɛntsrɛχtbɑŋk] *de (~en)* district court

arsenaal [ɑrsenạl] *het (arsenalen)* arsenal

arsenicum [ɑrsẹnikʏm] *het* arsenic

articuleren [ɑrtikylẹrə(n)] *vb* articulate, enunciate: *goed* (or: *duidelijk*) *~* articulate well (*or:* distinctly); *slecht ~* articulate badly (*or:* poorly)

artiest [ɑrtịst] *de (~en)* artist, entertainer, performer

artikel [ɑrtịkəl] *het (~en)* 1 article, paper, story: *een redactioneel ~* an editorial; *de krant wijdde er een speciaal ~ aan* the newspaper ran a feature on it; 2 article, item: *huishoudelijke ~en* household goods (*or:* items); 3 (*law*) article, section, clause: *~ 80 van de Grondwet* section 80 of the constitution

artillerie [ɑrtɪlərị] *de (~ën)* artillery: *lichte* (or: *zware*) *~* light (*or:* heavy) artillery

¹**artisanaal** [ɑrtizanạl] *adj (Belg)* craft-

²**artisanaal** [ɑrtizanạl] *adv (Belg)* by craftsmen, by traditional methods

artisjok [ɑrtiʃɔk] *de (~ken)* artichoke

artistiek [ɑrtɪstịk] *adj, adv* artistic: *een ~e zin voor verhoudingen* an artistic feeling for proportions

arts [ɑrts] *de (~en)* doctor, physician: *zijn ~ raadplegen* consult one's doctor

Aruba [arụba] *het* Aruba

¹**as** [ɑs] *de (~sen)* 1 axle, shaft; 2 (*geometry*) axis: *om zijn ~ draaien* revolve on its axis

²**as** [ɑs] *de (~sen)* ashes, ash: *gloeiende ~* (glowing) embers

a.s. *aanstaande* next: *~ maandag* next Monday

asbak [ɑzbɑk] *de (~ken)* ashtray

asbest [ɑzbɛst] *het* asbestos

asfalt [ɑsfɑlt] *het (~en)* asphalt

asiel [azịl] *het (~en)* 1 asylum, sanctuary: *politiek ~*

vragen (or: *krijgen*) seek (*or:* obtain) political asylum; 2 animal home (*or:* shelter); pound

asielzoeker [azịlzukər] *de (~s)* asylum seeker

asjemenou [aʃəmənɑu̯] *int* oh dear!, my goodness!

a.s.o. [aɛsọ] *het (Belg) algemeen secundair onderwijs* general secondary education

asociaal [asoʃɑ̯l] *adj* antisocial, unsociable, asocial: *~ gedrag* antisocial behaviour

aspect [ɑspɛkt] *het (~en)* aspect: *we moeten alle ~en van de zaak bestuderen* we must consider every aspect of the matter

asperge [ɑspɛrʒə] *de (~s)* asparagus

aspirant [ɑspirɑnt] *de (~en)* 1 trainee, student; 2 junior: *hij speelt nog bij de ~en* he is still (playing) in the junior league

assemblage [asɛmblɑʒə] *de (~s)* assembly, assembling

assembleren [asɛmblẹrə(n)] *vb* assemble

assenstelsel [ɑsə(n)stɛlsəl] *het (~s)* co-ordinate system

Assepoester [ɑsəpustər] *de* Cinderella

assertief [asɛrtịf] *adj* assertive: *~ gedrag* assertive behaviour

assertiviteit [asɛrtivitɛi̯t] *de* assertiveness

Assisen [asịzə(n)] *de (Belg)* || *Hof van ~* (roughly) Crown Court

assistent [asistɛnt] *de (~en)* assistant, aid, helper

assistentie [asistɛnsi] *de* assistance, aid, help: *~ verlenen* give assistance; *de politie verzocht om ~* the police asked for assistance

assisteren [asistẹrə(n)] *vb* assist, help, aid

associatie [asoʃɑ(t)si] *de (~s)* association

associëren [asoʃẹrə(n)] *vb* associate (with) || *zich ~ met* associate with

assortiment [asɔrtimɛnt] *het (~en)* assortment, selection: *een ruim* (or: *beperkt*) *~ hebben* have a broad (*or:* limited) assortment

assurantie [asyrɑnsi] *de (assurantiën)* insurance

aster [ɑstər] *de (~s)* aster

asterisk [ɑstərɪsk] *de (~en)* asterisk

astma [ɑsma] *het, de* asthma: *~ hebben* suffer from (*or:* have) asthma

astmatisch [ɑsmɑ̯tis] *adj* asthmatic

astrologie [ɑstroloɣị] *de* astrology

astroloog [ɑstrolọχ] *de (-logen)* astrologer

astronaut [ɑstronɑu̯t] *de (~en)* astronaut

astronomie [ɑstronomị] *de* astronomy

astronomisch [ɑstronọmis] *adj* 1 astronomical: *~e kijker* astronomical telescope; 2 astronomic(al): *~e bedragen* astronomic amounts

astronoom [ɑstronọm] *de (-nomen)* astronomer

Aswoensdag [ɑswṵnzdɑχ] *de* Ash Wednesday

asymmetrisch [asimẹtris] *adj, adv* asymmetric(al)

atalanta [atalɑnta] *de (~'s) (zoology)* red admiral

atechnisch [atɛχnis] *adj* untechnical

atelier [atəljẹ] *het (~s)* studio; workshop: *werken op een ~* work in a studio

Atheens [atẹns] *adj* Athenian

atheïsme [atejɪsmə] *het* atheism

atheïst [atejɪst] *de (~en)* atheist
Athene [atɛnə] *het* Athens
atheneum [atənejʏm] *het (~s) (Dutch; roughly)* grammar school, *(Am)* high school: *op het ~ zitten (roughly)* be at grammar school
Atlantisch [atlɑntis] *adj* Atlantic: *de ~e Oceaan* the Atlantic (Ocean)
atlas [ɑtlɑs] *de (~sen)* atlas
atleet [atlɛt] *de (atleten)* athlete
atletiek [atletik] *de* athletics
atletisch [atlɛtis] *adj* athletic
atmosfeer [atmɔsfɛr] *de (atmosferen)* atmosphere, environment: *de hogere* (or: *lagere*) *~* the upper (or: lower) atmosphere
atmosferisch [atmɔsfɛris] *adj* atmospheric: *~e storing* static interference, atmospheric disturbance
atol [atɔl] *het (~len)* atoll
atoom [atom] *het (atomen)* atom
atoombom [atombɔm] *de (~men)* atom bomb, A-bomb
attaché [ataʃɛ] *de (~s) (Belg)* ministerial adviser
attenderen [atɛndɛrə(n)] *vb* point out, draw attention to: *ik attendeer u erop dat …* I draw your attention to (the fact that) …
attent [atɛnt] *adj, adv* **1** attentive: *iem ~ maken op iets* draw s.o.'s attention to sth; **2** considerate, thoughtful: *hij was altijd heel ~ voor hen* he was always very considerate towards them
attentie [atɛnsi] *de (~s)* attention, mark of attention, present: *ik heb een kleine ~ meegebracht* I've brought a small present; *ter ~ van* for the attention of
attest [atɛst] *het (~en)* certificate
attractie [atrɑksi] *de (~s)* attraction: *zij is de grootste ~ vanavond* she is the main attraction this evening
attractiepark [atrɑksipark] *het (~en)* amusement park
attribuut [atribyt] *het (attributen)* attribute, characteristic
atv [ateve] *de arbeidstijdverkorting* reduction of working hours
au [ɑu] *alstublieft* please
a.u.b. [aybɛ] *alstublieft* please
aubergine [obərʒinə] *de (~s)* aubergine, eggplant
audiëntie [aud(i)jɛnsi] *de (~s)* audience: *~ geven (verlenen)* grant an audience (to s.o.)
audiovisueel [audijovizywɛl] *adj* audio-visual
auditie [audi(t)si] *de (~s)* audition, try-out, screen test: *een ~ doen* (do an) audition
auditor [auditɔr] *de (~en)* (student) listener
auditorium [auditorijʏm] *het (auditoria, ~s)* auditorium
augurk [auɣʏrk] *de (~en)* gherkin
augustus [auɣʏstʏs] *de* August
aula [aula] *de (~'s)* great hall, auditorium
au pair [opɛːr] *de (~s)* au pair
ausputzer [ausputsər] *de (~s)* sweeper
Australië [australijə] *het* Australia

Australiër [australijər] *de (~s)* Australian
Australisch [australis] *adj* Australian
auteur [autør] *de (~s)* author, writer
auteursrecht [autørsrɛxt] *het (~en)* copyright: *overtreding van het ~* infringement of copyright
authentiek [autɛntik] *adj* authentic, legitimate, genuine: *een ~e tekst* an authentic text; *een ~ kunstwerk* an original (or: authentic) work of art
autistisch [autɪstis] *adj* autistic
auto [auto] *de (~'s)* car: *in een ~ rijden* drive, go by car; *het is een uur rijden met de ~* it's an hour's drive by car
autobiografie [autobijoɣrafi] *de (~ën)* autobiography
autobotsing [autobɔtsɪŋ] *de (~en)* car crash
autobus [autobʏs] *de (~sen)* bus
autochtoon [autɔxton] *adj* autochthonous, indigenous, native
autodidact [autodidɑkt] *de (~en)* autodidact, self-taught person
autodiefstal [autodifstal] *de (~len)* car theft
autogas [autoɣas] *het (~sen)* LPG *(liquefied petroleum gas)*
autogordel [autoɣɔrdəl] *de (~s)* seat belt, safety belt: *het dragen van ~s is verplicht* the wearing of seat belts is compulsory
autohandelaar [autohandəlar] *de (~s, -handelaren)* car dealer
autokaart [autokart] *de (~en)* road map, road atlas
autokerkhof [autokɛrkhɔf] *het (-hoven)* junkyard, (used) car dump
automaat [automat] *de (automaten)* **1** automaton, robot; **2** slot machine, vending machine; ticket machine: *munten in een ~ gooien* feed coins into a slot machine
automatenhal [automatə(n)hal] *de (~len) (roughly)* amusement arcade
automatiek [automatik] *de (~en)* automat
automatisch [automatis] *adj, adv* automatic: *machtiging voor ~e afschrijving* standing order; *een ~e piloot* an automatic pilot, an autopilot; *iets ~ doen* do sth automatically; *~ sluitende deuren* self-closing doors
automatiseren [automatizɛrə(n)] *vb* automate, automatize, computerize: *een administratie ~* computerize an accounting department
automatisering [automatizɛrɪŋ] *de* automation, computerization
automobiel [automobil] *de (~en)* (motor) car
automobilist [automobilɪst] *de (~en)* motorist, driver
automonteur [automɔntør] *de (~s)* car mechanic
auto-ongeluk [autoɔŋɣəlʏk] *het (~ken)* car crash, (road) accident: *bij het ~ zijn drie mensen gewond geraakt* three people were injured in the car crash
autopapieren [autopapirə(n)] *de* car (registration) papers
autopech [autopɛx] *de* breakdown, car trouble
autoped [autopɛt] *de (~s)* scooter

autopsie [autɔpsi] *de (~s, ~ën)* autopsy: *(een) ~ verrichten op* perform an autopsy on
autorace [autores] *de (~s)* car race
autorijschool [autorɛisχol] *de (-scholen)* driving school
autorisatie [autoriza(t)si] *de (~s)* authorization, sanction, authority: *de ~ van de regering verkrijgen om* be authorized by the government to
autoritair [autoritɛːr] *adj, adv* authoritarian
autoriteit [autoritɛit] *de (~en)* authority: *de plaatselijke ~en* the local government; *een ~ op het gebied van slakken* an authority on snails
autoruit [autorœyt] *de (~en)* car window, windscreen
autosloperij [autosloporɛi] *de (~en)* breaker's yard, wrecker's yard
autosnelweg [autosnɛlwɛχ] *de (~en)* motorway
autostop [autostɔp] *de (Belg)* ‖ *~ doen* hitch-hike
autostrade [autostradə] *de (Belg)* motorway
autoverkeer [autovərker] *het* car traffic
autoweg [autowɛχ] *de (~en)* motorway
avenue [avəny] *de (~s)* avenue
¹**averechts** [avərɛχts] *adv* **1** back-to-front, inside out, upside down; **2** (all) wrong: *het valt ~ uit* it goes all wrong
²**averechts** [avərɛχts] *adj* **1** misplaced, wrong: *een ~e uitwerking hebben* have a contrary effect, be counter-productive; **2** unsound, contrary, wrong
averij [avərɛi] *de (~en)* damage, average: *zware ~ oplopen* sustain heavy damage
avocado [avokado] *de (~'s)* avocado
avond [avɔnt] *de (~en)* evening, night: *in de loop van de ~* during the evening; *de hele ~* all evening, the whole evening; *het is zijn vrije ~* it is his night off; *een ~je tv kijken* (or: *lezen*) spend the evening watching TV (or: reading); *een ~je uit* a night out, an evening out; *tegen de ~* towards the evening; *de ~ voor de grote wedstrijd* the eve of the big match; *'s ~s* at night, in the evening
avondcursus [avɔntkʏrzʏs] *de (~sen)* evening classes
avondeten [avɔntetə(n)] *het* dinner, supper, evening meal: *het ~ klaarmaken* prepare dinner (or: supper)
avondkleding [avɔntkledɪŋ] *de* evening dress (or: wear)
avondklok [avɔntklɔk] *de (~ken)* curfew
avondmaal [avɔntmal] *het* dinner, supper: *het Laatste Avondmaal* the Last Supper; *het Avondmaal vieren* celebrate (Holy) Communion
Avondmaal [avɔntmal] *het* (Holy) Communion
avondschool [avɔntsχol] *de (-scholen)* night school, evening classes: *op een ~ zitten* go to night school
avondspits [avɔntspɪts] *de (~en)* evening rush-hour
avonturier [avɔntyrir] *de (~s)* adventurer, adventuress
avontuur [avɔntyr] *het (avonturen)* **1** adventure:

een vreemd ~ beleven have a strange adventure; **2** venture: *niet van avonturen houden* not like risky ventures; **3** luck, chance: *het rad van ~* the wheel of fortune
avontuurlijk [avɔntyrlək] *adj, adv* **1** adventurous; **2** full of adventure, exciting
avontuurtje [avɔntyrcə] *het (~s)* affair: *een ~ hebben met …* have an affair with …
axioma [aks(i)joma] *het (~'s)* axiom
azalea [azaleja] *de (~'s)* azalea
Azerbeidzjaan [azɛrbɛidʒan] *de* Azerbaijani
Azerbeidzjaans [azɛrbɛidʒans] *adj* Azerbaijani
Azerbeidzjan [azɛrbɛidʒan] *het* Azerbaijan
Aziaat [azijat] *de (Aziaten)* Asian
Aziatisch [azijatis] *adj* Asian
Azië [azijə] *het* Asia
azijn [azɛin] *de (~en)* vinegar
Azteken [astekə(n)] *de* Aztecs
azuur [azyr] *het* azure

b

baai [baj] *de (~en)* bay, *(small)* cove, inlet
baal [bal] *de (balen)* bag, sack, bale: *een ~ katoen* a
   bale of cotton
baaldag [baldɑχ] *de (~en)* off-day
baan [ban] *de (banen)* 1 job: *een vaste ~ hebben*
   have a permanent job; 2 path; lane: *iets op de lange
   ~ schuiven* shelve sth; 3 *(sport)* track; court; rink;
   speed-skating track; course: *starten in ~ drie* start
   in lane three; 4 orbit: *een ~ om de aarde maken* orbit the earth
baanbrekend [bambrekənt] *adj* pioneering,
   groundbreaking, pathbreaking: *~ werk verrichten*
   do pioneering work, break new ground
baanvak [banvɑk] *het (~ken)* section (of track)
baar [bar] *de* 1 litter, stretcher; 2 ingot, bar: *een ~
   goud* a gold bar *(or: ingot)*
baard [bart] *de (~en)* beard: *hij krijgt de ~ in de keel*
   his voice is breaking; *zijn ~ laten staan* grow a
   beard
baarmoeder [barmudər] *de (~s)* womb
baars [bars] *de (baarzen)* perch, bass
baas [bas] *de (bazen)* 1 boss: *de situatie de ~ zijn* be
   in control of the situation; 2 boss, owner
baat [bat] *de (baten)* 1 benefit, advantage; 2 prof-
   it(s), benefit
babbel [bɑbəl] *de (~s)* chat: *hij heeft een vlotte ~*
   he's a smooth talker
babbelen [bɑbələ(n)] *vb* chatter; chat
babbellijn [bɑbəlɛin] *de (~en)* chatline
baby [bebi] *de (~'s)* baby: *een te vroeg geboren ~* a
   premature baby
babybedje *het* (baby's) cot
babydoll [bebidɔl] *de (~s)* baby-doll (nightdress)
babyfoon [bebifɔn] *de (~s)* baby alarm
babysit [bebisɪt] *de (~s)* babysitter
babysitten [bebisɪtə(n)] *vb* babysit
bacil [basɪl] *de (~len)* bacillus, bacterium, germ,
   bug
bacterie [bɑktɛri] *de (bacteriën)* bacterium, microbe
bad [bɑt] *het (~en)* 1 bath; 2 pool
¹baden [bɑdə(n)] *vb* 1 bath, *(Am)* bathe; (go for a)
   swim, bathe, take a dip; 2 roll (in), wallow (in),
   swim (in)
²baden [bɑdə(n)] *vb* bath
badgast [bɑtχɑst] *de (~en)* seaside visitor; bather

badge [bɛdʒ] *het, de (~s)* (name) badge, (name)
   tag; insignia
badjas [bɑtjɑs] *de (~sen)* (bath)robe, bath(ing)
   wrap
badjuffrouw [bɑtjʏfrɑu] *de (~en)* female bath attendant
badkamer [bɑtkamər] *de (~s)* bathroom
badkleding [bɑtkledɪŋ] *de* swimwear, bathing
   wear *(or:* gear)
badkuip [bɑtkœyp] *de (~en)* bathtub, bath
badmeester [bɑtmestər] *de (~s)* bath superintendent *(or:* attendant), lifeguard
badminton [bɛtmɪntɔn] *het* badminton
badpak [bɑtpɑk] *het (~ken)* swimsuit, bathing suit
badplaats [bɑtplats] *de (~en)* seaside resort
badstof [bɑtstɔf] *de (~fen)* towelling, terry (cloth)
   (or: towelling)
bagage [bɑɣaʒə] *de (~s)* 1 luggage; 2 intellectual
   baggage, stock-in-trade
bagagedrager [bɑɣaʒədraɣər] *de (~s)* (rear) carrier
bagagekluis [bɑɣaʒəklœys] *de (-kluizen)* (luggage) locker
bagageruimte [bɑɣaʒərœymtə] *de (~n, ~s)* boot,
   (Am) trunk
bagatel [bɑɣatɛl] *het, de (~len)* bagatelle, trifle
bagger [bɑɣər] *de (~s)* mud; dredgings
baggeren [bɑɣərə(n)] *vb* dredge
bah [bɑ] *int* ugh!, yuck!
Bahama's [bahamas] *de* the Bahamas
bahco [bako] *de (~'s)* adjustable spanner
bajes [bajəs] *de* can, cooler, jug, stir
bajesklant [bajəsklɑnt] *de (~en)* jailbird, lag, con
bajonet [bajɔnɛt] *de (~ten)* bayonet
bak [bɑk] *de (~ken)* 1 (storage) bin; cistern; tank;
   tray; trough; dish, bowl; tray; 2 joke: *een goede (or:
   schuine) ~* a good *(or:* dirty) joke; 3 can, jug, clink;
   4 cup (of coffee)
bakbeest [bɑɡbest] *het (~en)* whopper, monster
bakblik [bɑɡblɪk] *het (~ken)* baking tin, cake tin
bakboord [bɑɡbort] *het* port
bakeliet [bakəlit] *het* bakelite
baken [baka(n)] *het (~s) (shipp)* beacon
bakermat [bakərmɑt] *de (~ten)* cradle, origin
bakfiets [bɑkfits] *de (~en)* 1 carrier tricycle; 2 delivery bicycle, carrier cycle
bakkebaard [bɑkəbart] *de (~en)* (side) whiskers,
   sideboards, muttonchop, muttonchop whisker
bakken [bɑkə(n)] *vb* 1 bake: *vers gebakken brood*
   freshly-baked bread; 2 fry, deep-fry: *friet ~*
   deep-fry chips
bakker [bɑkər] *de (~s)* 1 baker; 2 bakery, baker's
   shop: *een warme ~* a fresh bakery; *(dat is) voor de
   ~* that's settled *(or:* fixed)
bakkerij [bɑkərɛi] *de (~en)* bakery, baker's shop
bakkie [bɑki] *het (~s)* rig
bakmeel [bɑkmel] *het* self-raising flour
bakoven [bɑkovə(n)] *de (~s)* oven
baksteen [bɑksten] *de (bakstenen)* brick: *(exam)*

zakken als een ~ fail (abysmally)

bakstenen [bɑkstenə(n)] *adj* brick

bakvorm [bɑkfɔrm] *de (~en)* baking tin, cake tin

¹bal [bɑl] *de (~len)* **1** *(sport)* ball: *(fig) een ~letje over iets opgooien* put out feelers about sth; *een ~(letje) gehakt* a meatball; *een ~letje slaan* hit a ball; **2** snob

²bal [bɑl] *het (~len)* ball: *gekostumeerd ~* fancy-dress ball

balanceren [bɑlɑnsɛrə(n)] *vb* balance: *~ op de rand van de dood* hover between life and death

balans [bɑlɑns] *de (~en)* **1** balance, equilibrium; **2** (pair of) scales, balance; **3** balance sheet, audit (report): *de ~ opmaken: a)* draw up the balance sheet; *b) (fig)* take stock (of sth)

baldadig [bɑldadəχ] *adj, adv* rowdy, boisterous

baldakijn [bɑldakɛin] *het, de (~en)* canopy, baldachin

balein [balɛin] *de (~en)* whalebone, rib

balen [balə(n)] *vb* be fed up (with), be sick (and tired) (of)

balg [balχ] *de (~en)* bellows

balie [bali] *de (~s)* **1** counter, desk: *aan de ~ verstrekt men u graag alle informatie* you can obtain all the information you need at the desk; **2** bar

baliemedewerker [balimedəwɛrkər] *de (~s)* desk clerk, receptionist

balk [bɑlk] *de (~en)* beam ‖ *het geld over de ~ gooien* spend money like water

Balkan [bɑlkɑn] *de* (the) Balkans

balken [bɑlkə(n)] *vb* bray

balkon [bɑlkɔn] *het (~s)* **1** balcony; **2** *(theatre)* balcony, (dress) circle, gallery; **3** platform

ballade [baladə] *de (~n, ~s)* ballad

ballast [bɑlɑst] *de* **1** ballast; **2** lumber, dead weight, *(of people)* dead wood

¹ballen [bɑlə(n)] *vb* play (with a) ball

²ballen [bɑlə(n)] *vb* clench: *de vuist(en) ~* clench one's fist(s)

ballerina [balərina] *de* ballerina

ballet [balɛt] *het (~ten)* ballet: *op ~ zitten* take ballet lessons

balletdanseres [balɛtdɑnsərɛs] *de (~sen)* ballet dancer

balletje-balletje [baləcəbaləcə] *het* shell game

balling [bɑlɪŋ] *de (~en)* exile

ballingschap [bɑlɪŋsχɑp] *de* exile, banishment: *in ~ gaan* go into exile

ballon [balɔn] *de (~nen)* balloon: *een ~ opblazen* blow up a balloon

ballpoint [bɔlpɔjnt] *de (~s)* ballpoint

balpen [bɑlpɛn] *de (~nen)* ballpoint (pen)

balsem [bɑlsəm] *de (~s)* balm, balsam, ointment, salve

balsemen [bɑlsəmə(n)] *vb* embalm, mummify

Baltisch [bɑltis] *adj* Baltic: *~e Zee* Baltic (Sea), the Baltic

balts [bɑlts] *de* display, courtship

balustrade [balystradə] *de (~s)* balustrade, railing, banister(s)

balzaal [bɑlzal] *de (balzalen)* ballroom

¹bamboe [bɑmbu] *de, het* bamboo

²bamboe [bɑmbu] *adj* bamboo

bami [bami] *de* chow mein: *~ goreng* chow mein, fried noodles

ban [bɑn] *de (~nen)* **1** excommunication, ban; **2** spell, fascination: *in de ~ van iets raken* fall under the spell of sth

banaal [banal] *adj, adv* banal, trite

banaan [banan] *de (bananen)* banana

banaliteit [banalitɛit] *de (~en)* platitude, cliché

bananenschil [banana(n)sχɪl] *de (~len)* banana peel *(or:* skin): *uitglijden over een ~* slip on a banana skin

¹band [bɑnt] *de (~en)* **1** band, ribbon, tape, *(karate, judo)* belt: *een ~ afspelen* play a tape back; *iets op de ~ opnemen* tape sth; *zwarte ~* black belt; **2** tyre: *een lekke ~* a flat tyre, a puncture; **3** conveyor (belt): *de lopende ~* the conveyor belt; *aan de ~ staan* work on the assembly line; **4** tie, bond, link, alliance, association: *~en van vriendschap* ties of friendship; **5** (wave)band, wave: *27 MC-band* citizens band; **6** cushion, bank: *aan de lopende ~ doelpunten scoren* pile on scores; *uit de ~ springen* get out of hand

²band [bɑnt] *het (~en)* tape, ribbon, string, band

³band [bɛnt] *de (~en)* band, orchestra, group, combo

bandage [bɑndaʒə] *de (~s)* bandage

bandenlichter [bɑndə(n)lɪχtər] *de (~s)* tyre lever

bandenpech [bɑndə(n)pɛχ] *de* tyre trouble, flat (tyre), puncture

bandiet [bɑndit] *de (~en)* **1** bandit, brigand; **2** hooligan

bandje [bɑncə] *het (~s)* **1** band, strip, ribbon, string; **2** tape; **3** tape recording; **4** strap

bandleider [bɛntlɛidər] *de (~s)* bandleader

bandrecorder [bɑntrikɔ:rdər] *de (~s)* tape recorder

bang [bɑŋ] *adj* **1** afraid (of); frightened (of), scared (of), terrified (of): *~ maken* scare, frighten; *~ in het donker* afraid of the dark; **2** frightening, anxious, scary; **3** timid, fearful; **4** afraid, anxious: *ik ben ~ dat het niet lukt* I'm afraid it won't work; *wees daar maar niet ~ voor* don't worry about it

bangerd [bɑŋərt] *de (~s)* coward, chicken

banier [banir] *de (~en)* banner

banjo [bɑŋo] *de (~'s)* banjo

bank [bɑŋk] *de (~en)* **1** bench; couch, settee, sofa; seat; **2** bank: *geld op de ~ hebben* have money in the bank; **3** desk: *ga in je ~ zitten* sit down at your desk; **4** pew; **5** bank, shoal: *door de ~ (genomen)* on average

bankbiljet [bɑŋbɪljɛt] *het (~ten)* (bank)note, *(pl also)* paper currency

bankemployé [bɑŋkɑmplwaje] *de (~s)* bank employee

banket [bɑŋkɛt] *het (~ten)* **1** banquet, feast; **2** *(roughly)* (almond) pastry

banketbakker [bɑŋkɛdbɑkər] *de (~s)* confectioner, pastry-cook

banketbakkerij [baŋkɛdbɑkərɛi] *de (~en)* confectionery, patisserie, confectioner's (shop)

banketletter [baŋkɛtlɛtər] *de (~s)* (almond) pastry letter

bankier [baŋkir] *de (~s)* banker

bankkluis [baŋklœys] *de (-kluizen)* bank vault (*or:* strongroom), *(for client)* safe-deposit box

bankoverval [baŋkovərval] *de (~len)* bank hold-up, bank robbery

bankpas [baŋkpas] *de (~sen)* bank(er's) card

bankrekening [baŋkrekənɪŋ] *de (~en)* bank account: *~ openen bij een bank* open an account with a bank

¹**bankroet** [baŋkrut] *het (~en)* bankruptcy

²**bankroet** [baŋkrut] *adj* bankrupt, broke, bust: *~ gaan* go bankrupt, (go) bust

bankroof [baŋkrof] *de* bank robbery

bankschroef [baŋksχruf] *de (-schroeven)* vice

bankspeler [baŋkspelər] *de* reserve, substitute (player)

bankstel [baŋkstɛl] *het (~len)* lounge suite

banneling [banəlɪŋ] *de (~en)* exile

bannen [banə(n)] *vb* exile (from), expel (from), banish: *ban de bom* ban the bomb

bantamgewicht [bantamɣəwɪχt] *het* bantam(weight)

¹**bar** [bɑr] *de (~s)* bar: *aan de ~ zitten* sit at the bar; *wie staat er achter de ~?* who's behind the bar?; *hakkenbar* heel bar

²**bar** [bɑr] *adj* **1** barren; **2** severe: *~ weer* severe weather; **3** rough, gross: *jij maakt het wat al te ~* you are carrying things too far; *~ en boos* really dreadful

³**bar** [bɑr] *adv* extremely, awfully

barak [barɑk] *de (~ken)* shed, hut, barracks

barbaar [bɑrbar] *de (barbaren)* barbarian

barbaars [bɑrbars] *adj, adv* barbarian, barbarous, barbaric, savage

barbecue [bɑːrbəkju] *de (~s)* barbecue (party)

barbecueën [bɑːrbəkjuwə(n)] *vb* barbecue

barbediende [bɑrbədində] *de (~n, ~s)* barman, barwoman

bareel [barel] *de (barelen) (Belg)* barrier

barema [barema] *het (~'s) (Belg)* wage scale, salary scale

baren [barə(n)] *vb* bear, give birth to

baret [barɛt] *de (~ten)* beret, (academic) cap

¹**Bargoens** [barɣuns] *het* **1** (thieves') slang, argot; **2** jargon

²**Bargoens** [barɣuns] *adj* slangy

bariton [baritɔn] *de (~s)* baritone (singer)

barjuffrouw [bɑrjʏfrɑu] *de (~en)* barmaid

barkeeper [bɑrkipər] *de (~s)* barman

barmhartig [bɑrmhɑrtəχ] *adj, adv* merciful, charitable: *de ~e Samaritaan* the Good Samaritan

barmhartigheid [bɑrmhɑrtəχhɛit] *de (-heden)* mercy, clemency, charity

¹**barok** [barɔk] *de, het* baroque

²**barok** [barɔk] *adj* baroque

barometer [barometər] *de (~s)* barometer: *de ~ staat op mooi weer* (or: *storm*): *a)* the barometer is set fair (or: is pointing to storm); *b) (fig)* things are looking good (or: bad)

baron [barɔn] *de (~nen)* baron: *meneer de ~* his (or: your) Lordship

barones [barɔnɛs] *de (~sen)* baroness

barracuda [bɑrakuda] *de (~'s)* barracuda

barrage [barɑʒə] *de (~s) (sport)* decider, play-off

barre [bɑːr] *de (~s)* barre; parallel bar: *oefeningen aan de ~* exercises at the bar

barricade [barikɑdə] *de (~n)* **1** barricade: *voor iets op de ~ gaan staan (fig)* fight on the barricades for sth; **2** *(fig)* barrier

barricaderen [barikadɛrə(n)] *vb* barricade, bar

barrière [bɑrijɛːrə] *de (~s)* barrier: *een onoverkomelijke ~* an insurmountable barrier

bars [bɑrs] *adj, adv* stern, grim, forbidding, harsh

barsheid [bɑrshɛit] *de* sternness, grimness, harshness, gruffness

barst [bɑrst] *de (~en)* crack, chap: *er komen ~en in* it is cracking

barsten [bɑrstə(n)] *vb* **1** crack, split, burst *(also fig)*; chap, get chapped; **2** burst, explode ‖ *het barst hier van de cafés* the place is full of pubs

bas [bas] *de (~sen)* **1** bass (singer, player), basso; **2** double bass, (contra)bass: *~ spelen* play the bass; **3** bass (guitar)

baseballen [bɛzbɔlə(n)] *vb* play baseball

¹**baseren** [bazɛrə(n)] *vb* base (on), found (on)

²**baseren** [bazɛrə(n)] *ref vb* base oneself on, go on: *we hadden niets om ons op te ~* we had nothing to go on

basgitaar [basχitar] *de (basgitaren)* bass (guitar)

basilicum [bazilikʏm] *het* basil

basiliek [bazilik] *de (~en)* basilica

basis [bazɪs] *de (bases)* **1** basis, foundation: *de ~ leggen voor iets* lay the foundation of sth; **2** base, basis

basisbeurs [bazɪzbørs] *de (-beurzen)* basic grant

basiscursus [bazɪskʏrzʏs] *de (~sen)* basic course, elementary course

basisonderwijs [bazɪsɔndərwɛis] *het* primary education

basisopstelling [bazɪsɔpstɛlɪŋ] *de (~en)* (the team's) starting line-up

basisschool [bazɪsχol] *de (-scholen)* primary school

basisvorming [bazɪsfɔrmɪŋ] *de* basic (secondary school) curriculum

Baskenland [baskə(n)lant] *het* the Basque Country

basketbal [bɑːskədbal] *het* basketball

Baskisch [baskis] *het* Basque

bassin [basɛ̃] *het (~s)* **1** (swimming) pool; **2** basin

bassist [basɪst] *de (~en)* bass player

bast [bast] *de (~en)* **1** bark, husk; **2** *(inf)* skin, hide

basta [bɑsta] *int* stop!, enough!: *en daarmee ~!* and there's an end to it!

bastaard [bɑstart] *de (~s)* **1** bastard; **2** mongrel; cross-breed; **3** hybrid, cross(-breed)

bastaardhond [bɑstarthɔnt] *de (~en)* mongrel

basterdsuiker [bɑstərtsœykər] *de* soft brown sugar

bastion [bɑstijɔn] *het (~s)* bastion

bataljon [bɑtɑljɔn] *het (~s)* battalion

Batavier [bɑtavir] *de (~s)* Batavian

bate [bɑtə] ǁ *ten ~ van* for the benefit of

baten [bɑtə(n)] *vb* avail: *wij zouden erbij gebaat zijn* it would be very helpful to us; *baat het niet, dan schaadt het niet* no harm in trying

batig [bɑtəχ] *adj* ǁ *~ saldo* surplus, credit balance

batikken [bɑtɪkə(n)] *vb* batik: *gebatikte stoffen* batiks

batje [bɛcə] *het* bat

batterij [bɑtərɛi] *de (~en)* battery: *lege ~* dead battery

bauxiet [bɑuksit] *het* bauxite

baviaan [bavijan] *de (bavianen)* baboon

baxter [bɛkstər] *de (~s) (Belg; med)* drip

bazaar [bazar] *de (~s)* bazaar, (fancy)fair

bazelen [bazələ(n)] *vb* drivel (on), waffle

bazig [bazəχ] *adj, adv* overbearing, domineering, bossy

bazin [bazɪn] *de (~nen)* **1** mistress; **2** lady of the house

beademen [bəadəmə(n)] *vb* **1** breathe air into; **2** apply artificial respiration to

beademing [bəadəmɪŋ] *de (~en)* **1** breathing of air into; **2** artificial respiration

beambte [bəɑmtə] *de (~n, ~s)* functionary, (junior) official

beamen [bəamə(n)] *vb* endorse, agree (with): *een bewering ~* endorse a claim

beangstigen [bəɑŋstəχə(n)] *vb* alarm; frighten

¹beantwoorden [bəɑntwordə(n)] *vb* answer, meet, comply with: *aan al de vereisten ~* meet all the requirements; *niet ~ aan de verwachtingen* fall short of expectations

²beantwoorden [bəɑntwordə(n)] *vb* answer, reply to

beargumenteren [bəɑryymɛntərə(n)] *vb* substantiate: *zijn standpunt kunnen ~* be able to substantiate one's point of view

beautycase [bju:tikes] *de (~s)* vanity case

bebloed [bəblut] *adj* bloody, blood-stained: *zijn gezicht was geheel ~* his face was completely covered in blood

beboeten [bəbutə(n)] *vb* fine: *beboet worden* be fined, incur a fine; *iem ~ met 100 euro* fine s.o. 100 euros

bebossen [bəbɔsə(n)] *vb* (af)forest: *bebost terrein* woodland

bebouwd [bəbɑut] *adj* built-on: *de ~e kom* the built-up area

bebouwen [bəbɑuwə(n)] *vb* **1** build on; **2** cultivate, farm: *de grond ~* cultivate the land

bebouwing [bəbɑuwɪŋ] *de (~en)* buildings

becijferen [bəsɛifərə(n)] *vb* calculate, compute, estimate: *de schade valt niet te ~* it is impossible to calculate the damage

becommentariëren [bəkɔmɛntarijɛrə(n)] *vb* comment (on)

beconcurreren [bəkɔŋkyrɛrə(n)] *vb* compete with: *de banken ~ elkaar scherp* there is fierce competition among the banks

bed [bɛt] *het (~den)* bed: *het ~ (moeten) houden* be confined to bed; *zijn ~je is gespreid* he has got it made; *het ~ opmaken* make the bed; *naar ~ gaan* go to bed; *naar ~ gaan met iem* go to bed with s.o.; *hij gaat ermee naar ~ en staat er weer mee op* he can't stop thinking about it; *dat is ver van mijn ~* that does not concern me; *een ~ rozen* a bed of roses

bedaard [bədart] *adj, adv* **1** composed, collected; **2** calm, quiet: *~ optreden* act calmly

bedacht [bədɑχt] *adj* prepared (for): *op zoveel verzet waren ze niet ~ geweest* they had not bargained for so much resistance

bedachtzaam [bədɑχtsam] *adj, adv* cautious, circumspect; deliberate: *heel ~ te werk gaan* set about sth with great caution

bedankbrief [bədɑŋgbrif] *de (-brieven)* letter of thanks

¹bedanken [bədɑŋkə(n)] *vb* thank: *iem voor iets ~* thank s.o. for sth

²bedanken [bədɑŋkə(n)] *vb* decline, refuse

bedankje [bədɑŋkjə] *het (~s)* thank-you, letter of thanks, word of thanks: *er kon nauwelijks een ~ af!* (and) small thanks I got (for it)!

bedankt [bədɑŋkt] *int* thanks: *reuze ~* thanks a lot

bedaren [bədarə(n)] *vb* quiet down, calm down: *iem tot ~ brengen* calm (or: quieten) s.o. down

beddengoed [bɛdə(n)yut] *het* (bed)clothes, bedding

beddensprei [bɛdə(n)sprɛi] *de (~en)* bedspread

bedding [bɛdɪŋ] *de (~en)* bed, channel

bedeesd [bədest] *adj* shy, diffident, timid

bedekken [bədɛkə(n)] *vb* cover, cover up, cover over: *geheel ~ met iets* cover in sth

bedekking [bədɛkɪŋ] *de (~en)* cover(ing)

bedekt [bədɛkt] *adj* **1** overcast; **2** covert: *in ~e termen* in guarded terms

bedelaar [bedəlar] *de (~s)* beggar

bedelarij [bedəlarɛi] *de* begging

bedelarmband [bedəlɑrmbɑnt] *de (~en)* charm bracelet

bedelen [bedələ(n)] *vb* beg (for)

bedelven [bədɛlvə(n)] *vb* bury, *(fig also)* swamp: *zij werden door het puin bedolven* they were buried under the rubble

bedenkelijk [bədɛŋkələk] *adj, adv* **1** worrying, dubious, questionable, serious: *een ~ geval* a worrying (or: serious) case; **2** doubtful, dubious: *een ~ gezicht* a doubtful (or: serious) face

¹bedenken [bədɛŋkə(n)] *vb* **1** think (about), consider: *als je bedenkt, dat ...* considering (or: bearing in mind) (that) …; **2** think of, think up, invent, devise

²bedenken [bədɛŋkə(n)] *ref vb* **1** think (about), consider: *zij zal zich wel tweemaal ~ voordat …* she'll think twice before …; *zonder zich te ~* without a moment's thought; **2** change one's mind, have second thoughts

bedenking [bədɛŋkɪŋ] *de (~en)* objection: *~en hebben tegen iets* have objections to sth

bederf [bədɛrf] *het* decay, rot

bederfelijk [bədɛrfələk] *adj* perishable: *~e goederen* perishables

¹bederven [bədɛrvə(n)] *vb* decay, rot

²bederven [bədɛrvə(n)] *vb* spoil: *die jurk is totaal bedorven* that dress is completely ruined; *iemands plezier ~* spoil s.o.'s fun

bedevaart [bedəvart] *de (~en)* pilgrimage: *een ~ doen* make (*or:* go) on a pilgrimage

bedevaartganger [bedəvartxaŋər] *de (~s)* pilgrim

bedevaartsoord [bedəvartsort] *het (~en)* place of pilgrimage

bediende [bədində] *de (~n, ~s)* **1** employee, clerk, assistant, attendant: *jongste ~: a)* office junior; *b)* dogsbody; **2** servant: *eerste ~* butler; **3** (*Belg*) official

¹bedienen [bədinə(n)] *vb* **1** serve: *iem op zijn wenken ~* wait on s.o. hand and foot; *aan tafel ~* wait at (the) table; **2** operate

²bedienen [bədinə(n)] *ref vb* use, make use of

bediening [bədinɪŋ] *de (~en)* **1** service: *al onze prijzen zijn inclusief ~* all prices include service (charges); **2** operation: *de ~ van een apparaat* the operation of a machine

bedieningspaneel [bədinɪŋspanel] *het (-panelen)* control panel, dash(board), (*comp*) console

beding [bədɪŋ] *het (~en)* condition, stipulation: *onder geen ~* under no circumstances

bedingen [bədɪŋə(n)] *vb* stipulate (for, that), insist on, require, agree (on)

bedlampje [bɛtlampjə] *het (~s)* bedside lamp, bedhead light

bedlegerig [bɛtleɣərəx] *adj* ill in bed, bedridden

bedoeïen [beduwin] *de (~en)* Bedouin

bedoelen [bədulə(n)] *vb* mean, intend: *wat bedoel je?* what do you mean?; *het was goed bedoeld* it was meant well (*or:* well meant); *~ met* mean by

bedoeling [bədulɪŋ] *de (~en)* **1** intention, aim, purpose, object: *dat was niet de ~* that was not intended (*or:* the intention); *met de ~ om te …* with a view to (…ing); **2** meaning, drift

bedoening [bədunɪŋ] *de (~en)* to-do, job, fuss: *het was een hele ~* it was quite a business

bedolven [bədɔlvə(n)] *adj* **1** covered (with); **2** snowed under (with), swamped (with): *~ onder het werk* snowed under with work, up to one's ears in work

bedompt [bədɔmt] *adj* stuffy; close, airless, stale: *een ~e atmosfeer* a stuffy atmosphere

bedorven [bədɔrvə(n)] *adj* bad, off, (*fig*) spoilt: *de melk is ~* the milk has gone off

bedotten [bədɔtə(n)] *vb* fool, take in

bedplassen [bɛtplasə(n)] *vb* bed-wetting

bedrading [bədradɪŋ] *de (~en)* wiring, circuit

bedrag [bədraχ] *het (~en)* **1** amount; **2** sum: *een rond ~* a round sum; *een ~ ineens* a lump sum

bedragen [bədraɣə(n)] *vb* amount to, number; come to be

bedreigen [bədrɛiɣə(n)] *vb* threaten: *bedreigde (dier- of planten)soorten* endangered species

bedreiging [bədrɛiɣɪŋ] *de (~en)* threat: *onder ~ van een vuurwapen* at gunpoint

bedreven [bədreivə(n)] *adj* adept (at, in), skilled (in), skilful (in), (well-)versed (in): *niet ~ zijn in iets* lack experience in sth

bedrevenheid [bədreivə(n)hɛit] *de* expertise, proficiency, skill

bedriegen [bədriɣə(n)] *vb* deceive, cheat, swindle: *hij bedriegt zijn vrouw* he cheats on his wife

bedrieger [bədriɣər] *de (~s)* cheat, fraud, impostor, swindler

bedrieglijk [bədriχlək] *adj, adv* deceptive, false, deceitful, fraudulent: *dit licht is ~* this light is deceptive

bedrijf [bədrɛif] *het (bedrijven)* **1** business, company, enterprise, firm, (*large*) concern, farm: *gemengd ~* mixed farm; *openbare bedrijven* public services; **2** act; **3** operation, (working) order: *buiten ~ zijn* be out of order

bedrijfsadministratie [bədrɛifsɑtministra(t)si] *de* business administration, business accountancy, industrial accountancy

bedrijfscultuur [bədrɛifskʏltyr] *de (-culturen)* corporate culture

bedrijfseconomie [bədrɛifsekonomi] *de* business economics, industrial economics

bedrijfskapitaal [bədrɛifskapital] *het (-kapitalen)* working capital

bedrijfskunde [bədrɛifskʏndə] *de* business administration, management

bedrijfsleider [bədrɛifslɛidər] *de (~s)* manager

bedrijfsleiding [bədrɛifslɛidɪŋ] *de (~en)* management, board (of directors)

bedrijfsleven [bədrɛifsleivə(n)] *het* business, trade and industry: *het particuliere ~* private enterprise

bedrijfsrevisor [bədrɛifsrevizɔr] *de (~s, ~en)* (*Belg*) auditor

bedrijfssluiting [bədrɛifslœytɪŋ] *de (~en)* shutdown, close-down

bedrijfsvereniging [bədrɛifsfərenəɣɪŋ] *de (~en)* industrial insurance board

bedrijfsvoering [bədrɛifsfurɪŋ] *de* management

bedrijven [bədrɛivə(n)] *vb* commit, perpetrate

bedrijvend [bədrɛivənt] *adj* ‖ *de ~e vorm van een werkwoord* the active voice of a verb

bedrijvig [bədrɛivəχ] *adj* active, busy, industrious, bustling: *een ~ type* an industrious type

bedroefd [bədruft] *adj* sad (about), dejected, upset

(about), distressed (about)

bedroefdheid [bədrufthɛit] *de* sadness, sorrow, dejection, distress

¹bedroevend [bədruvənt] *adj* **1** sad(dening), depressing; **2** pathetic: *~e resultaten* pitiful results

²bedroevend [bədruvənt] *adv* pathetically, miserably: *zijn werk is ~ slecht* his work is lamentable

bedrog [bədrɔχ] *het* **1** deceit, deception, fraud, swindle: *~ plegen* cheat, swindle, deceive, commit fraud; **2** deception, delusion: *optisch ~* optical illusion

bedrukken [bədrykə(n)] *vb* print, inscribe

bedrukt [bədrykt] *adj* dejected, depressed

bedrust [bɛtryst] *de* bedrest

bedtijd [bɛtɛit] *de* bedtime

beduidend [bədœydənt] *adj, adv* significant, considerable: *~ minder* considerably less

beduusd [bədyst] *adj* taken aback, flabbergasted

bedwang [bədwɑŋ] *het* control, restraint: *iem in ~ houden* keep s.o. in check

bedwelmd [bədwɛlmt] *adj* **1** stunned, dazed, knocked out: *door alcohol ~* intoxicated; **2** anaesthetized, drugged

bedwelmen [bədwɛlmə(n)] *vb* stun, stupefy, intoxicate

bedwingen [bədwɪŋə(n)] *vb* suppress, subdue, restrain: *zijn tranen ~* hold back one's tears

beëdigd [bəədəχt] *adj* sworn, chartered: *~ getuige* sworn witness

beëdigen [bəədəɣə(n)] *vb* swear (in), administer an oath to: *een getuige ~* swear (in) a witness

beëdiging [bəədəχɪŋ] *de (~en)* **1** swearing, confirmation on oath; **2** swearing (in), administration of the oath

beëindigen [bəəindəɣə(n)] *vb* **1** end, finish, complete: *een vriendschap ~* break off a friendship; **2** end, close; discontinue, terminate

beek [bek] *de (beken)* brook, stream

beeld [belt] *het (~en)* **1** statue, sculpture; **2** picture, image, view, illustration: *in ~ zijn* be on (the screen); *in ~ brengen* show (a picture, pictures of); **3** picture, description

beeldbuis [beldbœys] *de (-buizen)* **1** cathode ray tube; **2** screen, box: *elke avond voor de ~ zitten* sit in front of the box every evening

beeldenstorm [beldə(n)stɔrm] *de (~en)* **1** *(fig)* image breaking; **2** iconoclasm

beeldhouwen [belthauwə(n)] *vb* sculpture, sculpt, carve

beeldhouwer [belthauwər] *de (~s)* sculptor, sculptress, woodcarver

beeldhouwkunst [belthaukynst] *de* sculpture

beeldhouwwerk [belthauwɛrk] *het (~en)* sculpture, carving

beeldmerk [beltmɛrk] *het (~en)* logo(type)

beeldpunt [beltpʏnt] *het, de (~en)* pixel

beeldscherm [beltsχɛrm] *het (~en)* (TV, television) screen, *(comp)* display

beeldschrift [beltsχrɪft] *het* pictography, picture writing

beeldspraak [beltsprak] *de (-spraken)* metaphor, imagery, metaphorical language, figurative language

beeldtelefoon [belteləfon] *de (~s)* videophone

beeldverhaal [beltfərhal] *het (-verhalen)* comic strip

been [ben] *het (benen)* **1** leg, *(in expressions often)* foot: *op eigen benen staan* stand on one's own (two) feet; *hij is met het verkeerde ~ uit bed gestapt* he got out of bed on the wrong side; *de benen nemen* run for it; *met beide benen op de grond staan (fig)* have one's feet firmly on the ground; **2** leg; **3** bone; **4** bones *(pl)*; **5** *(maths)* side, leg: *de benen van een driehoek* the sides of a triangle; *(Belg) het (spek) aan zijn ~ hebben* be deceived, be had

beenbeschermer [bembəsχɛrmər] *de (~s)* leg-guard, pad

beenhouwer [benhauwər] *de (~s) (Belg)* butcher

beenhouwerij [benhauwərɛi] *de (~en) (Belg)* butcher's shop

beer [ber] *de (beren)* **1** bear, (bear) cub; **2** boar

beerput [berpʏt] *de (~ten)* cesspool, cesspit *(also fig)*: *(fig) de ~ opentrekken* blow (or: take) the lid off

beest [best] *het (~en)* **1** beast, animal: *(fig) het ~je bij zijn naam noemen* call a spade a spade; **2** animal, beast, cattle; **3** creepy-crawly

¹beestachtig [bestɑχtəχ] *adj* bestial, brutal, savage

²beestachtig [bestɑχtəχ] *adv* terribly, dreadfully

beet [bet] *de (beten)* bite

¹beethebben [bethɛbə(n)] *vb* **1** have (got) (a) hold of; **2** take in, cheat, fool, make a fool of

²beethebben [bethɛbə(n)] *vb (fishing)* have a bite

¹beetje [becə] *het (~s)* (little) bit, little: *een ~ Frans kennen* know a little French, have a smattering of French; *~ melk graag* a little milk (or: a drop of milk), please; *bij stukjes en bij ~s* bit by bit, little by little; *alle ~s helpen* every little helps

²beetje [becə] *adv* (a) (little) bit, (a) little, rather: *dat is een ~ weinig* that's not very much; *een ~ vervelend zijn: a)* be a bit of a nuisance, be rather annoying; *b)* be rather boring, be a bit of a bore; *een ~ opschieten* get a move on

beetnemen [betnemə(n)] *vb* take in, make a fool of, fool: *je bent beetgenomen!* you've been had!

beetpakken [betpɑkə(n)] *vb* lay hold of, get one's (or: lay) hands on

befaamd [bəfamt] *adj* famous, renowned

begaafd [bəɣaft] *adj* **1** gifted, talented; **2** gifted (with), endowed (with)

begaafdheid [bəɣafthɛit] *de (-heden)* **1** talent, ability, intelligence, genius; **2** talent (for), gift (for)

¹begaan [bəɣan] *vb* do as one likes (or: pleases)

²begaan [bəɣan] *vb* commit, *(mistakes also)* make

begaanbaar [bəɣambar] *adj* passable, practicable

begeerte [bəɣertə] *de (~n)* desire (for), wish (for), craving (for)

begeleiden [bəɣəlɛidə(n)] *vb* **1** accompany, escort; **2** guide, counsel, support, supervise, coach; **3** ac-

company *(mus also)*, go with
begeleidend [bəɣəlɛidənt] *adj* accompanying, attendant: *~e muziek* incidental music
begeleider [bəɣəlɛidər] *de (~s)* 1 companion, escort; 2 guide, counsellor, supervisor, coach; 3 *(mus)* accompanist
begeleiding [bəɣəlɛidɪŋ] *de (~en)* 1 accompaniment, accompanying, escort(ing); 2 guidance, counselling, support, supervision, coaching: *de ~ na de operatie was erg goed* the follow-up care after the operation was very good; *onder ~ van* under the guidance of; 3 *(mus)* accompaniment
begeren [bəɣerə(n)] *vb* desire, crave, long for: *alles wat zijn hartje maar kon ~* all one could possibly wish for
begerenswaardig [bəɣerənswardəɣ] *adj* desirable, eligible, enviable
begerig [bəɣerəɣ] *adj, adv* desirous (of), longing (for), eager (for), hungry (for): *~e blikken* hungry looks
¹**begeven** [bəɣevə(n)] *vb* 1 break down, fail, collapse, give way: *de auto kan het elk ogenblik ~* the car is liable to break down any minute; 2 forsake, leave, fail: *zijn stem begaf het* his voice broke
²**begeven** [bəɣevə(n)] *ref vb* proceed, embark (on, upon), adjourn (to): *zich op weg ~ (naar)* set out (for)
begin [bəɣɪn] *het* beginning, start, opening: *~ mei* early in May, (at) the beginning of May; *een veelbelovend ~* a promising start; *dit is nog maar het ~* this is only the beginning; *een ~ maken met iets* begin *(or:* start) sth; *(weer) helemaal bij het ~ (moeten) beginnen* (have to) start from scratch; *in het ~* at the beginning, at first, initially; *een boek van ~ tot eind lezen* read a book from cover to cover
beginletter [bəɣɪnlɛtər] *de (~s)* initial letter, first letter, initial
beginneling [bəɣɪnəlɪŋ] *de (~en)* beginner, novice
¹**beginnen** [bəɣɪnə(n)] *vb* begin, start, open: *een gesprek ~* begin *(or:* start) a conversation; *een zaak ~* start a business
²**beginnen** [bəɣɪnə(n)] *vb* 1 begin, start (to do sth, doing sth), commence, set about (doing): *(inf) begin maar!* go ahead!, fire away!; *laten we ~* let's get started; *het begint er op te lijken* that's more like it; *weer van voren af aan moeten ~* go back to square one; *hij begon met te zeggen ...* he began by saying ...; *het begint donker te worden* it is getting dark; *je weet niet waar je aan begint* you don't know what you are letting yourself in for; 2 (with *over*) bring up, raise: *over politiek ~* bring up politics; *over iets anders ~* change the subject; *daar kunnen we niet aan ~* that's out of the question; *om te ~ ...* for a start ...; *voor zichzelf ~* start one's own business
beginner [bəɣɪnər] *de (~s)* beginner: *beginnerscursus* beginners' course
beginpunt [bəɣɪmpʏnt] *het (~en)* starting point, point of departure
beginsel [bəɣɪnsəl] *het (~en)* principle, rudiment:

in ~ in principle
beglazing [bəɣlazɪŋ] *de (~en)* glazing
begoed [bəɣut] *adj (Belg)* well off
begraafplaats [bəɣrafplats] *de (~en)* cemetery, graveyard, burial ground
begrafenis [bəɣrafənɪs] *de (~sen)* 1 funeral; 2 burial
begrafenisondernemer [bəɣrafənɪsɔndərnemər] *de (~s)* undertaker, funeral director
begrafenisstoet [bəɣrafənɪstut] *de (~en)* funeral procession
begraven [bəɣravə(n)] *vb* bury: *dood en ~ zijn* be dead and gone
begrensd [bəɣrɛnst] *adj* limited, finite, restricted
begrenzen [bəɣrɛnzə(n)] *vb* 1 border: *door de zee begrensd* bordered by the sea; 2 *(fig)* define; 3 limit, restrict
¹**begrijpelijk** [bəɣrɛipələk] *adj* 1 understandable, comprehensible, intelligible; 2 natural, obvious: *dat is nogal ~* that is hardly surprising; *het is heel ~ dat hij bang is* it's only natural that he should be frightened
²**begrijpelijk** [bəɣrɛipələk] *adv* clearly
begrijpen [bəɣrɛipə(n)] *vb* 1 understand, comprehend, grasp: *hij begreep de hint* he took the hint, he got the message; *dat kan ik ~* I (can) understand that; *o, ik begrijp het* oh, I see; *laten we dat goed ~* let's get that clear; *begrijp je me nog?* are you still with me?; *dat laat je voortaan, begrepen!* I'll have no more of that, is that clear? *(or:* do you hear?); *als je begrijpt wat ik bedoel* if you see what I mean; 2 understand, gather: *begrijp me goed* don't get me wrong; *iem (iets) verkeerd ~* misunderstand s.o. (sth)
begrip [bəɣrɪp] *het (~pen)* 1 understanding, comprehension, conception: *vlug van ~* quick-witted; 2 concept, idea, notion; 3 understanding, sympathy: *~ voor iets kunnen opbrengen* appreciate; *ze was vol ~* she was very understanding
begroeid [bəɣrujt] *adj* grown over (with), overgrown (with), wooded
begroeten [bəɣrutə(n)] *vb* greet, hail, salute: *elkaar ~* exchange greetings; *het voorstel werd met applaus begroet* the proposal was greeted with applause
begroeting [bəɣrutɪŋ] *de (~en)* greeting, salutation
begroten [bəɣrotə(n)] *vb* estimate (at), cost (at): *de kosten van het gehele project worden begroot op 12 miljoen* the whole project is costed at 12 million
begroting [bəɣrotɪŋ] *de (~en)* estimate, budget: *een ~ maken* make an estimate
begrotingstekort [bəɣrotɪŋstəkɔrt] *het (~en)* budget deficit
begunstigde [bəɣʏnstəɣdə] *de (~n)* beneficiary, payee
beha [beha] *de (~'s)* bra
behaaglijk [bəhaɣlək] *adj, adv* 1 pleasant, comfortable: *een ~ gevoel* a comfortable feeling; 2 com-

fortable, relaxed; **3** cosy, snug

behalen [bəhaːlə(n)] *vb* gain, obtain, achieve, score, win: *een hoog cijfer ~* get (*or:* obtain) a high mark

behalve [bəhɑlvə] *prep* **1** except (for), but (for), with the exception of, excepting: *~ mij heeft hij geen enkele vriend* except for me he hasn't got a single friend; **2** besides, in addition to

behandelen [bəhɑndələ(n)] *vb* **1** handle, deal with, treat, attend to: *dergelijke aangelegenheden behandelt de rector zelf* the director attends to such matters himself; *eerlijk behandeld worden* be treated fairly; *de dieren werden goed behandeld* the animals were well looked after; *iem oneerlijk ~* do s.o. (a) wrong; *iem voorzichtig ~* go easy with s.o.; **2** treat (of), discuss, deal with: *een onderwerp ~* discuss a subject; **3** treat, nurse

behandeling [bəhɑndəlɪŋ] *de (~en)* **1** treatment, use, handling, operation; handling, management: *een wetsontwerp in ~ nemen* discuss a bill; *in ~ nemen* deal with; **2** treatment, discussion; **3** *(med)* treatment, attention: *zich onder ~ stellen* go to a doctor

behandelkamer [bəhɑndəlkaːmər] *de (~s)* surgery

behang [bəhɑŋ] *het* wallpaper

¹behangen [bəhɑŋə(n)] *vb* (wall)paper (a room), hang (wallpaper)

²behangen [bəhɑŋə(n)] *vb* hang (with), drape (with)

behanger [bəhɑŋər] *de (~s)* paperhanger

behartigen [bəhɑrtəʝə(n)] *vb* look after, promote

behartiging [bəhɑrtəʝɪŋ] *de* promotion (of), protection (of)

beheer [bəheːr] *het* **1** management, control, supervision: *de penningmeester heeft het ~ over de kas* the treasurer is in charge of the funds; **2** administration, management, rule: *dat eiland staat onder Engels ~* that island is under British administration

beheerder [bəheːrdər] *de (~s)* **1** administrator, trustee; **2** manager

beheersen [bəheːrsə(n)] *vb* control, govern, rule, dominate: *die gedachte beheerst zijn leven* that thought dominates his life; *een vreemde taal ~* have a thorough command of a foreign language

beheersing [bəheːrsɪŋ] *de* control, command: *de ~ over zichzelf verliezen* lose one's self-control

beheerst [bəheːrst] *adj, adv* controlled, composed

behelpen [bəhɛlpə(n)] *ref vb* manage, make do: *hij weet zich te ~* he manages, he can make do

behendig [bəhɛndəχ] *adj, adv* dexterous, adroit, skilful, clever, smart: *een ~e jongen* an agile boy; *~ klom ze achterop* she climbed nimbly up on the back

behendigheid [bəhɛndəχhɛit] *de* dexterity, agility, skill

beheren [bəheːrə(n)] *vb* **1** manage, administer: *de financiën ~* control the finances; **2** manage, run

behoeden [bəhuːdə(n)] *vb* **1** guard (from), keep (from), preserve (from): *iem voor gevaar ~* keep s.o. from danger; **2** guard, watch over: *God behoede*

ons (may) God preserve us

behoedzaam [bəhuːtsaːm] *adj, adv* cautious, wary

behoefte [bəhuːftə] *de (~n)* need (of, for), demand (for): *in eigen ~ (kunnen) voorzien* be self-sufficient; *~ hebben aan rust* have a need for quiet; *zijn ~ doen* relieve oneself

behoeve [bəhuːvə] || *ten ~ van* for the benefit of

¹behoorlijk [bəhoːrlək] *adj* **1** decent, appropriate, proper, fitting: *producten van ~e kwaliteit* good quality products; **2** adequate, sufficient; **3** decent, respectable, presentable; **4** considerable, substantial: *dat is een ~ eind lopen* that's quite a distance to walk

²behoorlijk [bəhoːrlək] *adv* **1** decently, properly: *gedraag je ~* behave yourself; **2** adequately, enough; **3** pretty, quite: *~ wat* a fair amount (of); **4** decently, well (enough): *je kunt hier heel ~ eten* you can get a very decent meal here

behoren [bəhoːrə(n)] *vb* **1** belong (to), be owned by, be part of: *dat behoort nu tot het verleden* that's past history; **2** require, need, be necessary, be needed: *naar ~* as it should be; **3** should, ought (to): *jongeren ~ op te staan voor ouderen* young people should stand up for older people; **4** belong (to), go together (*or:* with): *een tafel met de daarbij ~de stoelen* a table and the chairs to go with it; *hij behoort tot de betere leerlingen* he is one of the better pupils

behoud [bəhaut] *het* **1** preservation, maintenance, conservation; **2** preservation, conservation, care

behouden [bəhaudə(n)] *vb* **1** preserve, keep, conserve, retain: *zijn zetel ~* retain one's seat; **2** maintain, keep: *zijn vorm ~* keep fit

behuizing [bəhœyzɪŋ] *de (~en)* housing, accommodation, house, dwelling: *passende ~ zoeken* look for suitable accommodation

behulp [bəhʏlp] || *met ~ van iets* with the help (*or:* aid) of sth

behulpzaam [bəhʏlpsaːm] *adj* helpful: *zij is altijd ~* she's always ready to help

beiaard [bɛiart] *de (~s)* carillon

beide [bɛidə] *num* both, either (one), two: *het is in ons ~r belang* it's in the interest of both of us; *een opvallend verschil tussen hun ~ dochters* a striking difference between their two daughters; *in ~ gevallen* in either case, in both cases; *ze zijn ~n getrouwd* they are both married, both (of them) are married; *wij ~n* both of us, the two of us; *ze weten het geen van ~n* neither of them knows

¹beige [bɛːʒə] *het* beige

²beige [bɛːʒə] *adj* beige

beïnvloeden [bəɪnvludə(n)] *vb* influence, affect: *zich door iets laten ~* be influenced by sth

beïnvloeding [bəɪnvludɪŋ] *de* || *~ van de jury* influencing the jury

Beiroet [bɛirut] *het* Beirut

beitel [bɛitəl] *de (~s)* chisel

beits [bɛits] *het, de (~en)* stain

bejaard [bəjart] *adj* elderly, aged, old

bejaarde [bəjɑrdə] *de (~n)* elderly (*or:* old) person, senior citizen

bejaardentehuis [bəjɑrdə(n)təhœys] *het (-tehuizen)* old people's home, home for the elderly

bejaardenverzorger [bəjɑrdə(n)vərzɔrɣər] *de (~s)* geriatric helper

bek [bɛk] *de (~ken)* **1** bill; beak; **2** snout, muzzle; **3** mouth, trap, gob: *een grote ~ hebben* be loud-mouthed; *hou je grote ~* shut up!; **4** mug: *(gekke) ~ken trekken* make (silly) faces

bekaf [bɛkɑf] *adj* all-in, knackered, dead tired

bekakt [bəkɑkt] *adj, adv* affected, snooty

bekeken [bəkɑkə(n)] *adj* **1** settled; **2** well-judged

bekend [bəkɛnt] *adj* **1** known: *dit was mij ~* I knew (of) this; *het is algemeen ~* it's common knowledge; *voor zover mij ~* as far as I know; *voor zover ~* as far as is known; **2** well-known, noted (for), known (for), notorious (for): *~ van radio en tv* of radio and TV fame; **3** familiar: *u komt me ~ voor* haven't we met (somewhere) (before)?

bekende [bəkɛndə] *de (~n)* acquaintance

bekendheid [bəkɛnthɛit] *de* **1** familiarity (with), acquaintance (with), experience (of); **2** reputation, name, fame

bekendmaken [bəkɛntmakə(n)] *vb* **1** announce; **2** publish, make public (*or:* known): *de verkiezingsuitslag ~* declare the results of the election; **3** familiarize (with), acquaint

bekendmaking [bəkɛntmakɪŋ] *de (~en)* **1** announcement; **2** publication, notice, declaration

bekennen [bəkɛnə(n)] *vb* **1** *(law)* confess, plead guilty (to): *schuld ~* admit one's guilt; **2** confess, admit, acknowledge: *schuld ~* admit one's guilt; *je kunt beter eerlijk ~* you'd better come clean; **3** see, detect: *hij was nergens te ~* there was no sign (*or:* trace) of him (anywhere)

bekentenis [bəkɛntənɪs] *de (~sen)* confession, admission, acknowledgement, plea of guilty: *een volledige ~ afleggen* make a full confession

beker [bekər] *de (~s)* beaker, cup, mug: *de ~ winnen* win the cup

bekeren [bəkerə(n)] *vb* convert, reform

bekerfinale [bekərfinalə] *de (~s)* cup final

bekering [bəkerɪŋ] *de (~en)* conversion

bekerwedstrijd [bekərwɛtstrɛit] *de (~en)* cup-tie

bekeuren [bəkørə(n)] *vb* fine (on the spot): *bekeurd worden voor te hard rijden* be fined for speeding

bekeuring [bəkørɪŋ] *de (~en)* (on-the-spot) fine, ticket

bekijken [bəkɛikə(n)] *vb* **1** look at, examine: *iets vluchtig ~* glance at sth; *van dichtbij ~* take a close(r) look at; **2** look at, consider; **3** see, look at, consider, view: *hoe je het ook bekijkt* whichever way you look at it; *je bekijkt het maar!* please yourself!; *goed bekeken!* well done!, good thinking!

bekken [bɛkə(n)] *het (~s)* **1** basin; **2** *(biology)* pelvis; **3** *(mus)* cymbal

beklaagde [bəklɑɣdə] *de (~n)* accused, defendant, prisoner (at the bar)

beklaagdenbank [bəklɑɣdə(n)bɑŋk] *de (~en)* dock

bekladden [bəklɑdə(n)] *vb* blot; daub; plaster

beklag [bəklɑχ] *het* complaint

¹beklagen [bəklɑɣə(n)] *vb* pity

²beklagen [bəklɑɣə(n)] *ref vb* complain (to s.o.), make a complaint (to s.o.)

bekleden [bəkledə(n)] *vb* **1** cover, coat, line: *een kamer ~* carpet a room; **2** hold, occupy: *een hoge positie ~* hold a high position

bekleding [bəkledɪŋ] *de (~en)* covering, coating, lining

beklemd [bəklɛmt] *adj* jammed, wedged, stuck, trapped

beklemtonen [bəklɛmtonə(n)] *vb* stress, accent(uate), emphasize *(also fig)*

beklimmen [bəklɪmə(n)] *vb* climb, ascend, scale

beknellen [bəknɛlə(n)] *vb* trap: *door een botsing bekneld raken in een auto* be trapped in a car after a collision

beknopt [bəknɔpt] *adj, adv* brief(ly-worded), concise, succinct ‖ *een ~e uitgave* an abridged edition

bekoelen [bəkulə(n)] *vb* **1** cool (off, down); **2** *(fig)* cool (off), dampen

bekogelen [bəkoɣələ(n)] *vb* pelt, bombard

bekomen [bəkomə(n)] *vb* **1** agree with, suit; disagree with: *dat zal je slecht ~* you'll be sorry (for that); **2** recover, get over; come round, come to: *van de (eerste) schrik ~* get over the (initial) shock

bekommerd [bəkɔmərt] *adj* concerned (about), worried (about)

bekommeren [bəkɔmərə(n)] *ref vb* worry (about), bother (about), concern (*or:* trouble) oneself (with, about)

bekopen [bəkopə(n)] *vb* pay for

bekoring [bəkorɪŋ] *de (~en)* charm(s), appeal

bekostigen [bəkɔstəɣə(n)] *vb* bear the cost of, pay for, fund: *ik kan dat niet ~* I can't afford that

bekrachtigen [bəkrɑχtəɣə(n)] *vb* ratify, confirm, pass; assent to: *bekrachtigd worden* be passed

bekrachtiging [bəkrɑχtəɣɪŋ] *de (~en)* **1** ratification, confirmation; **2** upholding ‖ *stuurbekrachtiging* power steering

bekritiseren [bəkritizerə(n)] *vb* criticize, find fault with

bekrompen [bəkrɔmpə(n)] *adj, adv* narrow(-minded), petty, blinkered, *(stronger)* bigoted

bekronen [bəkronə(n)] *vb* award a prize to: *een bekroond ontwerp* a prizewinning design, an award-winning design

bekroning [bəkronɪŋ] *de (~en)* award

bekruipen [bəkrœypə(n)] *vb* come over, steal over: *het spijt me, maar nu bekruipt me toch het gevoel dat …* I'm sorry, but I've got a sneaking feeling that …

bekvechten [bɛkfɛχtə(n)] *vb* argue, bicker

bekwaam [bəkwam] *adj* competent, capable, able

bekwaamheid [bəkwamhɛit] *de (-heden)* competence, (cap)ability, capacity, skill

bekwamen [bəkwa̱mə(n)] *ref vb* qualify, train (oneself), study, teach: *zich in iets ~* train for sth

bel [bɛl] *de (~len)* **1** bell, chime, gong (bell): *de ~ gaat* there's s.o. at the door; *op de ~ drukken* press the bell; **2** bubble: *~len blazen* blow bubbles

belabberd [bəla̱bərt] *adj, adv* rotten, lousy, rough: *ik voel me nogal ~* I feel pretty rough (or: lousy)

belachelijk [bəla̱χələk] *adj, adv* ridiculous, absurd, laughable, ludicrous: *op een ~ vroeg uur* at some ungodly hour; *doe niet zo ~* stop making such a fool of yourself

¹beladen [bəla̱də(n)] *adj* emotionally charged

²beladen [bəla̱də(n)] *vb* load *(also fig)*, burden

belagen [bəla̱ɣə(n)] *vb* **1** beset, *(stronger)* besiege; **2** menace, endanger

belanden [bəla̱ndə(n)] *vb* land (up), end up, finish, find oneself: *~ bij* end up at, finish at; *waardoor hij in de gevangenis belandde* which landed him in prison

belang [bəla̱ŋ] *het (~en)* **1** interest, concern, good: *het algemeen ~* the public interest; *~ bij iets hebben* have an interest in sth; *in het ~ van uw gezondheid* for the sake of your health; **2** interest (in): *~ stellen in* be interested in, take an interest in; **3** importance, significance: *veel ~ hechten aan iets* set great store by sth

belangeloos [bəla̱ŋəlos] *adj, adv* unselfish, selfless: *belangeloze hulp* disinterested help

belangenvereniging [bəla̱ŋə(n)vərenəɣɪŋ] *de (~en)* interest group, pressure group, lobby

belanghebbend [bəla̱ŋhɛbənt] *adj* interested, concerned

belanghebbende [bəla̱ŋhɛbəndə] *de (~n)* interested party, party concerned

belangrijk [bəla̱ŋrɛik] *adj* **1** important: *de ~ste gebeurtenissen* the main (or: major) events; *zijn gezin ~er vinden dan zijn carrière* put one's family before one's career; *en wat nog ~er is …* and, more importantly), …; **2** considerable, substantial, major: *in ~e mate* considerably, substantially

¹belangstellend [bəla̱ŋstɛlənt] *adj* interested: *ze waren heel ~* they were very attentive

²belangstellend [bəla̱ŋstɛlənt] *adv* interestedly, with interest

belangstellende [bəla̱ŋstɛləndə] *de* person interested, interested party

belangstelling [bəla̱ŋstɛlɪŋ] *de* interest (in): *in het middelpunt van de ~ staan* be the focus of attention; *een man met een brede ~* a man of wide interests; *zijn ~ voor iets verliezen* lose interest in sth; *daar heb ik geen ~ voor* I'm not interested in (that)

belast [bəla̱st] *adj* responsible (for), in charge (of)

belastbaar [bəla̱stbar] *adj* taxable: *~ inkomen* taxable income

belasten [bəla̱stə(n)] *vb* **1** load: *iets te zwaar ~* overload sth; **2** (place a) load (on); **3** make responsible (for), put in charge (of): *iem te zwaar ~* overtax s.o.; **4** tax

belastend [bəla̱stənt] *adj* aggravating; *(law)* incriminating; damning, damaging

belasteren [bəla̱stərə(n)] *vb* slander, *(written)* libel

belasting [bəla̱stɪŋ] *de (~en)* **1** load, stress: *~ van het milieu met chemische producten* burdening of the environment with chemicals; **2** burden, pressure: *de studie is een te grote ~ voor haar* studying is too much for her; tax, taxation, rate(s): *~ heffen* levy taxes; *~ ontduiken* evade tax

belastingaangifte [bəla̱stɪŋaŋɣɪftə] *de (~n)* tax return

belastingaanslag [bəla̱stɪŋanslaχ] *de (~en)* tax assessment

belastingaftrek [bəla̱stɪŋaftrɛk] *de* tax deduction

belastingdienst [bəla̱stɪŋdinst] *de (~en)* tax department, Inland Revenue, *(Am)* IRS, Internal Revenue Service

belastingheffing [bəla̱stɪŋhɛfɪŋ] *de (~en)* taxation, levying of taxes

belastingontduiking [bəla̱stɪŋɔndœykɪŋ] *de (~en)* tax evasion; tax dodging

belastingstelsel [bəla̱stɪŋstɛlsəl] *het (~s)* tax system, system of taxation

belastingvrij [bəla̱stɪŋvrɛi] *adj* tax-free, duty-free, duty-paid, untaxed

belazeren [bəla̱zərə(n)] *vb* cheat, make a fool of

beledigen [bəle̱dəɣə(n)] *vb* offend, *(stronger)* insult: *zich beledigd voelen door* be (or: feel) offended by

beledigend [bəle̱dəɣənt] *adj, adv* offensive (to), insulting (to), abusive

belediging [bəle̱dəɣɪŋ] *de (~en)* insult, affront: *een grove (zware) ~* a gross insult

beleefd [bəle̱ft] *adj, adv* polite, courteous, well-mannered, civil: *dat is niet ~* that's bad manners, that's not polite

beleefdheid [bəle̱fthɛit] *de (-heden)* politeness, courtesy

beleg [bəlɛχ] *het* **1** siege: *de staat van ~ afkondigen* declare martial law; **2** (sandwich) filling

belegen [bəle̱ɣə(n)] *adj* mature(d), ripe, *(fig)* stale: *jong (licht) ~ kaas* semi-mature(d) cheese

belegeren [bəle̱ɣərə(n)] *vb* besiege, lay siege to

belegering [bəle̱ɣərɪŋ] *de (~en)* siege

¹beleggen [bəlɛɣə(n)] *vb* invest: *in effecten ~* invest in stocks and shares

²beleggen [bəlɛɣə(n)] *vb* **1** convene, call: *een vergadering ~* call a meeting; **2** cover, fill, put meat (or: cheese) on *(slice of bread)*: *belegde broodjes* (ham, cheese etc.) rolls

belegger [bəlɛɣər] *de (~s)* investor

belegging [bəlɛɣɪŋ] *de (~en)* investment

beleid [bəlɛit] *het* **1** policy *(oft pl)*: *het ~ van deze regering* the policies of this government; *verkeerd (slecht) ~* mismanagement; **2** tact, discretion: *met ~ te werk gaan* handle things tactfully

belemmeren [bəlɛmərə(n)] *vb* hinder, hamper, *(stronger)* impede, interfere with, *(stronger)* obstruct, block: *iem het uitzicht ~* obstruct (*or:* block) s.o.'s view

belemmering [bɔlɛmərɪŋ] *de (~en)* hindrance, impediment, interference, obstruction: *een ~ vormen voor* stand in the way of

beletsel [bɔlɛtsɔl] *het (~s)* obstacle, impediment

beletten [bɔlɛtə(n)] *vb* prevent (from), obstruct

beleven [bɔlevə(n)] *vb* go through, experience: *de spannendste avonturen ~* have the most exciting adventures

belevenis [bɔlevənɪs] *de (~sen)* experience, adventure

Belg [bɛlχ] *de (~en)* Belgian

België [bɛlɣijə] *het* Belgium

Belgisch [bɛlɣis] *adj* Belgian

Belgrado [bɛlɣrado] *het* Belgrade

belichamen [bɔlɪχamə(n)] *vb* embody

belichaming [bɔlɪχamɪŋ] *de (~en)* embodiment

belichten [bɔlɪχtə(n)] *vb* **1** illuminate, light (up); **2** discuss, shed (*or:* throw) light on: *een probleem van verschillende kanten ~* discuss different aspects of a problem; **3** expose

belichting [bɔlɪχtɪŋ] *de* lighting

¹believen [bɔlivə(n)] *vb* please

²believen [bɔlivə(n)] *vb* want, desire: *wat belieft u?* (I beg your) pardon?

belijden [bɔlɛidə(n)] *vb* profess; avow

belijdenis [bɔlɛidənɪs] *de (~sen)* confession (of faith), confirmation

¹bellen [bɛlə(n)] *vb* ring (the bell): *de fietser belde* the cyclist rang his bell

²bellen [bɛlə(n)] *vb* ring (up), call: *kan ik even ~?* may I use the (tele)phone?

bellenblazen [bɛlə(n)blazə(n)] *vb* blow bubbles

belletje [bɛləcə] *het (~s)* buzz, call, ring

bellettrie [bɛlɛtri] *de* belles-lettres, literature

belofte [bɔlɔftə] *de (~n)* promise, pledge: *iem een ~ doen* make s.o. a promise; *zijn ~ (ver)breken* break one's promise

belonen [bɔlonə(n)] *vb* pay, reward, repay

beloning [bɔlonɪŋ] *de (~en)* reward, pay(ment): *als ~ (van, voor)* in reward (for)

beloop [bɔlop] *het (belopen)* course, way: *iets op zijn ~ laten* let sth take (*or:* run) its course, let things slide

beloven [bɔlovə(n)] *vb* promise, vow, pledge: *dat belooft niet veel goeds* that does not augur well; *het belooft een mooie dag te worden* it looks as if it'll be a lovely day

beluisteren [bɔlœystərə(n)] *vb* **1** listen to; listen in to: *het programma is iedere zondag te ~* the programme is broadcast every Sunday; **2** hear, overhear

belust [bɔlʏst] *adj (*with *op)* bent (on), out (for)

bemachtigen [bəmɑχtəɣə(n)] *vb* **1** get hold of, get (*or:* lay) one's hands on: *een zitplaats ~* secure a seat; **2** seize, capture, take (possession of), acquire

bemannen [bəmɑnə(n)] *vb* man, staff, crew: *een bemand ruimtevaartuig* a manned spacecraft

bemanning [bəmɑnɪŋ] *de (~en)* crew; ship's company, complement; garrison

bemanningslid [bəmɑnɪŋslɪt] *het (-leden)* crewman, member of the crew, hand

bemerken [bəmɛrkə(n)] *vb* notice, note

bemesten [bəmɛstə(n)] *vb* manure, fertilize

bemiddelaar [bəmɪdəlar] *de (~s)* intermediary, mediator, go-between

bemiddeld [bəmɪdəlt] *adj* affluent, well-to-do

bemiddelen [bəmɪdələ(n)] *vb* mediate: *~d optreden (in)* act as a mediator (*or:* an arbitrator) (in)

bemiddeling [bəmɪdəlɪŋ] *de* mediation

bemind [bəmɪnt] *adj* dear (to), loved (by), much-loved: *door zijn charme maakte hij zich bij iedereen ~* his charm endeared him to everyone

beminde [bəmɪndə] *de (~n)* beloved, sweetheart

beminnelijk [bəmɪnələk] *adj* amiable

beminnen [bəmɪnə(n)] *vb* love, hold dear

bemoedigen [bəmudəɣə(n)] *vb* encourage, hearten

bemoeial [bəmujal] *de (~len)* busybody

bemoeien [bəmujə(n)] *ref vb* (with *met*) meddle (in), interfere (in): *bemoei je niet overal mee!* mind your own business!; *daar bemoei ik me niet mee* I don't want to get mixed up in that

bemoeilijken [bəmujləkə(n)] *vb* hamper, hinder, impede; aggravate, complicate

benadelen [bənadelə(n)] *vb* harm, put at a disadvantage, handicap, *(law)* prejudice: *iem in zijn rechten ~* infringe s.o.'s rights

benaderen [bənadərə(n)] *vb* **1** approach, *(fig also)* approximate to, come close to: *moeilijk te ~* unapproachable; **2** approach, get in touch with: *iem ~ over een kwestie* approach s.o. on a matter; **3** calculate (roughly), estimate (roughly)

benadering [bənadərɪŋ] *de (~en)* **1** approach, *(fig also)* approximation (to); **2** (rough) calculation, (rough) estimate, approximation ‖ *bij ~* approximately, roughly

benadrukken [bənadrʏkə(n)] *vb* emphasize, stress, underline

benard [bənɑrt] *adj* awkward; perilous; distressing

benauwd [bənɑut] *adj* **1** short of breath; **2** close, muggy, stuffy: *een ~ gevoel op de borst* a tight feeling in one's chest; *~ warm* close, muggy, oppressive; **3** anxious, afraid: *het ~ krijgen* feel anxious; **4** upsetting; **5** narrow, cramped

benauwdheid [bənɑutɦɛit] *de (-heden)* **1** tightness of the chest; **2** closeness, stuffiness; **3** fear, anxiety

bende [bɛndə] *de (~s)* **1** mess, shambles; **2** mass, swarm, crowd; **3** gang, pack

¹beneden [bənedə(n)] *adv* down, below, downstairs, at the bottom: *(via de trap) naar ~ gaan* go down(stairs); *de vijfde regel van ~* the fifth line up, the fifth line from the bottom

²beneden [bənedə(n)] *prep* under, below, beneath: *kinderen ~ de zes jaar* children under six (years of age)

benedenste [bənedə(n)stə] *adj* lowest, bottom,

undermost

benedenverdieping [bɔnɛdə(n)vərdipɪŋ] *de* (~*en*) ground floor, lower floor

benedenwinds [bɔnedə(n)wɪnts] *adj* leeward

Benelux [benəlyks] *de* Benelux, the Benelux countries

benemen [bɔnɛmə(n)] *vb* take away (from)

benen [benə(n)] *adj* bone

benepen [bɔnɛpə(n)] *adj* **1** small-minded, petty; **2** anxious, timid

benevelen [bɔnɛvələ(n)] *vb* cloud, (be)fog: *licht(elijk) beneveld* tipsy, woozy

Bengaals [bɛnɣals] *adj* Bengal, Bengali

bengel [bɛŋəl] *de* (~*s*) (little) rascal, scamp, (little) terror

bengelen [bɛŋələ(n)] *vb* dangle, swing (to and fro)

benieuwd [bəniwt] *adj* curious: *ik ben* ~ *wat hij zal zeggen* I wonder what he'll say; *ze was erg* ~ *(te horen) wat hij ervan vond* she was dying to hear what he thought of it

benieuwen [bɔniwə(n)] *vb* arouse curiosity: *het zal mij* ~ *of hij komt* I wonder if he'll come

benijden [bɔnɛidə(n)] *vb* envy, be envious (of), be jealous (of): *al onze vrienden* ~ *ons om ons huis* our house is the envy of all our friends

benijdenswaardig [bɔnɛidənswardəχ] *adj, adv* enviable

benodigd [bɔnodəχt] *adj* required, necessary, wanted

benodigdheden [bɔnodəχthedə(n)] *de* requirements, necessities

benoemen [bɔnumə(n)] *vb* appoint, assign (to), nominate: *iem tot burgemeester* ~ appoint s.o. mayor

benoeming [bɔnumɪŋ] *de* (~*en*) appointment, nomination

benul [bɔnyl] *het* notion, inkling, idea: *hij heeft er geen (flauw)* ~ *van* he hasn't got the foggiest idea

benutten [bɔnytə(n)] *vb* utilize, make use of: *een strafschop* ~ score from a penalty

benzine [bɛnzinə] *de* petrol, *(Am)* gas(oline): *gewone (normale)* ~ two star petrol; *loodvrije* ~ unleaded petrol

benzinemotor [bɛnzinəmotər] *de* (~*en*) petrol engine

benzinepomp [bɛnzinəpɔmp] *de* (~*en*) **1** petrol station, filling station; **2** fuel pump

beoefenaar [bɔufənar] *de* (~*s*) student; practitioner

beoefenen [bɔufənə(n)] *vb* practise, pursue, follow, study, go in for: *sport* ~ go in for sports

beoordelaar [bɔordelar] *de* (~*s*) judge, assessor, reviewer

beoordelen [bɔordelə(n)] *vb* judge, assess: *een boek* ~ criticize a book; *dat kan ik zelf wel* ~! I can judge for myself (, thank you very much)!; *dat is moeilijk te* ~ that's hard to say; *iem verkeerd* ~ misjudge s.o.

beoordeling [bɔordelɪŋ] *de* judg(e)ment, assess-

ment, evaluation, *(educ)* mark, review

¹bepaald [bəpalt] *adj* **1** particular, specific: *heb je een* ~ *iemand in gedachten?* are you thinking of anyone in particular?; **2** specific, fixed, set, specified, given: *vooraf* ~ predetermined; **3** certain, particular: *om* ~*e redenen* for certain reasons

²bepaald [bəpalt] *adv* definitely: *niet* ~ *slim* not particularly clever

bepakking [bəpɑkɪŋ] *de* (~*en*) pack, (marching) kit

bepalen [bəpalə(n)] *vb* **1** prescribe, lay down, determine, stipulate: *zijn keus* ~ make one's choice; *vooraf* ~ predetermine; *de prijs werd bepaald op* €100,- the price was set at 100 euros; **2** determine, ascertain: *u mag de dag zélf* ~ (you can) name the day; *het tempo* ~ set the pace

bepaling [bəpalɪŋ] *de* (~*en*) **1** definition; **2** provision, stipulation, regulation: *een wettelijke* ~ a legal provision (*or:* stipulation); **3** condition; **4** determination

¹beperken [bəpɛrkə(n)] *vb* **1** limit, restrict; **2** (with *tot*) restrict (to), limit (to), confine (to), keep (to): *de uitgaven* ~ keep expenditure down; *tot het minimum* ~ keep (down) to a minimum

²beperken [bəpɛrkə(n)] *ref vb* restrict (oneself to), confine (oneself to)

beperking [bəpɛrkɪŋ] *de* (~*en*) **1** limitation, restriction: *zijn* ~*en kennen* know one's limitations; **2** reduction, cutback

beperkt [bəpɛrkt] *adj, adv* limited, restricted, confined, reduced: ~ *blijven tot* be restricted to; *een* ~*e keuze* a limited choice

beplanten [bəplɑntə(n)] *vb* plant (with), sow (with)

beplanting [bəplɑntɪŋ] *de* (~*en*) planting, plants, crop(s)

bepleiten [bəplɛitə(n)] *vb* argue, plead, advocate: *iemands zaak* ~ *(bij iem)* plead s.o.'s case (with s.o.)

beproeven [bəpruvə(n)] *vb* (put to the) test, try: *zijn geluk* ~ try one's luck

beproeving [bəpruvɪŋ] *de* (~*en*) **1** testing; **2** ordeal, trial

beraad [bərat] *het* consideration, deliberation, consultation *(oft pl)*: *na rijp* ~ after careful consideration

beraadslagen [bəratslaɣə(n)] *vb* deliberate (upon), consider: *met iem over iets* ~ consult with s.o. about sth

beraadslaging [bəratslaɣɪŋ] *de* (~*en*) deliberation, consideration, consultation

beraden [bəradə(n)] *ref vb* consider, think over: *zich* ~ *over (op)* deliberate about

beramen [bəramə(n)] *vb* **1** devise, plan: *een aanslag* ~ plot an attack; **2** estimate, calculate

beraming [bəramɪŋ] *de* (~*en*) **1** planning, design; **2** estimate, calculation, budget

berde [bɛrdə] ‖ *iets te* ~ *brengen* bring up a matter, raise a point

berechten [bərɛχtə(n)] *vb* try

berechting **44**

berechting [bərɛχtɪŋ] *de (~en)* trial, judgement, adjudication
bereden [bəredə(n)] *adj* mounted
beredeneren [bərədənɛrə(n)] *vb* argue, reason (out)
bereid [bərɛit] *adj* **1** prepared; **2** ready, willing, disposed: *tot alles ~ zijn* be prepared to do anything
bereiden [bərɛidə(n)] *vb* prepare, get ready, cook, make, fix: *iem een hartelijke (warme) ontvangst ~ give s.o.* a warm welcome
bereidheid [bərɛithɛit] *de (-heden)* readiness, preparedness, willingness
bereiding [bərɛidɪŋ] *de (~en)* preparation, making, manufacture, production
bereidingswijze [bərɛidɪŋswɛizə] *de (~n)* method of preparation, process of manufacture, procedure
bereik [bərɛik] *het* reach, range: *buiten (het) ~ van kinderen bewaren* keep away from children
bereikbaar [bərɛiɡbar] *adj* accessible, attainable, within reach: *bent u telefonisch bereikbaar?* can you be reached by phone?
bereiken [bərɛikə(n)] *vb* **1** reach, arrive in, arrive at, get to; **2** reach, achieve, attain, gain: *zijn doel ~* attain one's goal; **3** reach, contact, get through (to)
berekend [bərekənt] *adj* meant for, designed for; equal to, suited to: *hij is niet ~ voor zijn taak* he is not up to his job
berekenen [bərekənə(n)] *vb* **1** calculate, compute, determine, figure out, add up; **2** charge: *iem te veel (or: weinig) ~* overcharge (or: undercharge) s.o.
berekenend [bərekənənt] *adj* calculating, scheming
berekening [bərekənɪŋ] *de (~en)* **1** calculation, computation: *naar (volgens) een ruwe ~* at a rough estimate; **2** calculation, evaluation, assessment: *een huwelijk uit ~* a marriage of convenience
berg [bɛrχ] *de (~en)* mountain, hill: *~en verzetten* move mountains
bergachtig [bɛrχaχtəχ] *adj* mountainous, hilly
bergafwaarts [bɛrχɑfwarts] *adv* downhill
bergbeklimmen [bɛrɣbəklɪmə(n)] *vb* mountaineering, (rock-)climbing
bergbeklimmer [bɛrɣbəklɪmər] *de (~s)* mountaineer, (mountain-)climber
¹bergen [bɛrɣə(n)] *vb* **1** store, put away, stow (away): *mappen in een la ~* put files away in a drawer; **2** *(shipp)* salvage; **3** rescue, save, shelter, recover
²bergen [bɛrɣə(n)] *ref vb* get out of harm's (or: the) way, take cover
berghelling [bɛrχhɛlɪŋ] *de (~en)* mountain slope, mountainside
berghok [bɛrχhɔk] *het (~ken)* shed, storeroom, boxroom
berging [bɛrɣɪŋ] *de (~en)* **1** *(shipp)* salvage, recovery; **2** storeroom, boxroom; shed
bergkam [bɛrχkɑm] *de (~men)* (mountain) ridge
bergketen [bɛrχketə(n)] *de (~s)* mountain range (or: chain)
bergkristal [bɛrχkrɪstɑl] *het* rock-crystal, rhinestone

bergop [bɛrχɔp] *adv* uphill
bergpas [bɛrχpɑs] *de (~sen)* (mountain) pass, col
bergplaats [bɛrχplats] *de (~en)* storage (space), storeroom; shed
bergsport [bɛrχspɔrt] *de* mountaineering, (mountain) climbing, alpinism
bergtop [bɛrχtɔp] *de (~pen)* summit, mountain top, peak, pinnacle
bergwand [bɛrχwɑnt] *de (~en)* mountain side, face of a mountain, mountain wall
bericht [bərɪχt] *het (~en)* message, notice, communication, report, news: *volgens de laatste ~en* according to the latest reports; *tot nader ~* until further notice; *u krijgt schriftelijk ~* you will receive written notice (*or:* notification); *~ achterlaten dat* leave a message that
berichten [bərɪχtə(n)] *vb* report, send word, inform, advise
berichtgeving [bərɪχtχevɪŋ] *de* reporting, (news) coverage, report(s)
berijden [bərɛidə(n)] *vb* **1** ride; **2** ride (on), drive (on)
berijder [bərɛidər] *de* rider
berispen [bərɪspə(n)] *vb* reprimand, admonish
berisping [bərɪspɪŋ] *de (~en)* reprimand, reproof
berk [bɛrk] *de (~en)* birch
Berlijn [bɛrlɛin] *het* Berlin
berm [bɛrm] *de (~en)* verge, roadside, shoulder
bermuda [bɛrmyda] *de (~'s)* Bermuda shorts, Bermudas
beroemd [bərumt] *adj* famous, renowned, celebrated, famed: *~ om* famous for
beroemdheid [bərumthɛit] *de (-heden)* **1** fame, renown; **2** celebrity
beroemen [bərumə(n)] *ref vb* boast (about), take pride (in), pride oneself (on)
beroep [bərup] *het (~en)* **1** occupation, profession, vocation, trade, business: *in de uitoefening van zijn ~* in the exercise of one's profession; *wat ben jij van ~?* what do you do for a living?; **2** appeal: *raad van ~: a)* Court of Appeal; *b) (Am)* Court of Appeals; *een ~ doen op iem (iets)* (make an) appeal to s.o. (sth)
beroepen [bərupə(n)] *ref vb* (with *op*) call (upon), appeal (to), refer (to)
beroeps [bərups] *adj* professional: *~ worden* turn professional
beroepsbevolking [bərupsbəvɔlkɪŋ] *de* employed population, working population, labour force
beroepshalve [bərupshɑlvə] *adv* professionally, in one's professional capacity
beroepskeuze [bərupskøzə] *de* choice of (a) career (*or:* of profession): *begeleiding bij de ~* careers counselling
beroepskeuzeadviseur [bərupskøzəatfizør] *de (~s)* counsellor, careers master
beroepsonderwijs [bərupsɔndərwɛis] *het* vocational training, professional training

beroepsopleiding [bərupsɔplɛidɪŋ] *de (~en)* professional (*or:* vocational, occupational) training

beroepsschool [bərupsχol] *de (-scholen) (Belg)* technical school

beroerd [bərurt] *adj, adv* 1 miserable, wretched, rotten: *ik word er ~ van* it makes me sick; *hij ziet er ~ uit* he looks terrible; 2 lazy: *hij is nooit te ~ om mij te helpen* he is always willing to help me

beroeren [bərurə(n)] *vb* 1 touch; 2 trouble, agitate

beroering [bərurɪŋ] *de (~en)* trouble, agitation, unrest, commotion

beroerte [bərurtə] *de (~s)* stroke

berooid [bərojt] *adj* destitute

berouw [bərau] *het* remorse: *~ hebben over* regret

berouwen [bərauwə(n)] *vb* regret, rue, feel sorry for

beroven [bərovə(n)] *vb* 1 rob: *iem ~ van iets* rob s.o. of sth; 2 deprive of, strip: *iem van zijn vrijheid ~* deprive s.o. of his freedom

beroving [bərovɪŋ] *de (~en)* robbery

berucht [bərʏχt] *adj* notorious (for), infamous

berusten [bərʏstə(n)] *vb* 1 (with *op*) rest on, be based on, be founded on: *dit moet op een misverstand ~* this must be due to a misunderstanding; 2 resign oneself to; 3 rest with, be deposited with: *de wetgevende macht berust bij het parlement* legislative power rests with parliament

berusting [bərʏstɪŋ] *de* resignation, acceptance, acquiescence

bes [bɛs] *de* 1 berry, currant; 2 (*mus*) B-flat

beschaafd [bəsχaft] *adj* cultured, civilized, refined, well-bred

beschaamd [bəsχamt] *adj, adv* ashamed, shamefaced

beschadigd [bəsχadəχt] *adj* damaged

beschadigen [bəsχadəyə(n)] *vb* damage: *door brand beschadigde goederen* fire-damaged goods

beschadiging [bəsχadəyɪŋ] *de (~en)* damage

beschamen [bəsχamə(n)] *vb* 1 (put to) shame; 2 disappoint, betray: *iemands vertrouwen (niet) ~* (not) betray s.o.'s confidence

beschamend [bəsχamənt] *adj* shameful, humiliating, ignominious: *een ~e vertoning* a humiliating spectacle

beschaving [bəsχavɪŋ] *de (~en)* 1 civilization; 2 culture, refinement, polish

bescheiden [bəsχɛidə(n)] *adj, adv* 1 modest, unassuming: *zich ~ terugtrekken* withdraw discreetly; *naar mijn ~ mening* in my humble opinion; 2 modest, unpretentious: *een ~ optrekje* a modest little place

bescheidenheid [bəsχɛidə(n)hɛit] *de* modesty, unpretentiousness: *valse ~* false modesty

beschermeling [bəsχɛrməlɪŋ] *de (~en)* ward; protégé

beschermen [bəsχɛrmə(n)] *vb* protect, shield, preserve, (safe)guard, shelter: *een beschermd leventje* a sheltered life; *~ tegen de zon* screen from the sun

beschermengel [bəsχɛrmɛŋəl] *de (~en)* guardian angel

beschermer [bəsχɛrmər] *de (~s)* defender, guardian, protector

beschermheer [bəsχɛrmher] *de (-heren)* patron

beschermheilige [bəsχɛrmhɛiləyə] *de (~n)* patron saint, patron, patroness

bescherming [bəsχɛrmɪŋ] *de (~en)* protection, (safe)guarding, shelter, cover: *~ bieden aan* offer protection to

beschermlaag *de* protective layer (*or:* coating)

beschieten [bəsχitə(n)] *vb* fire on, fire at, shell, bombard, pelt

beschikbaar [bəsχɪgbar] *adj* available, at one's disposal, free

beschikbaarheid [bəsχɪgbarhɛit] *de* availability

beschikken [bəsχɪkə(n)] *vb* (with *over*) dispose of, have (control of), have at one's disposal: *over genoeg tijd ~* have enough time at one's disposal; *over iemands lot ~* determine s.o.'s fate

beschikking [bəsχɪkɪŋ] *de (~en)* disposition, disposal: *ik sta tot uw ~* I am at your disposal

beschilderen [bəsχɪldərə(n)] *vb* paint

beschildering [bəsχɪldərɪŋ] *de (~en)* painting

beschimmeld [bəsχɪməlt] *adj* mouldy: *~e papieren* musty papers

beschouwen [bəsχauwə(n)] *vb* 1 consider, contemplate; 2 consider, regard as, look upon as: *iets als zijn plicht ~* consider sth (as, to be) one's duty

beschouwing [bəsχauwɪŋ] *de (~en)* consideration, view: *iets buiten ~ laten* leave sth out of account, ignore sth

beschrijven [bəsχrɛivə(n)] *vb* 1 write (on); 2 describe, portray: *dat is met geen pen te ~* it defies description; 3 describe, trace: *een baan om de aarde ~* trace a path around the earth

beschrijving [bəsχrɛivɪŋ] *de (~en)* description, depiction, sketch: *dat gaat alle ~ te boven* that defies description

beschroomd [bəsχromt] *adj* timid, diffident, bashful

beschuit [bəsχœyt] *de (~en)* Dutch rusk, biscuit rusk, zwieback

beschuldigde [bəsχʏldəyə] *de (~n)* accused, defendant

beschuldigen [bəsχʏldəyə(n)] *vb* accuse (of), charge (s.o. with sth), blame (s.o. for sth): *ik beschuldig niemand, maar ...* I won't point a finger, but ...

beschuldigend [bəsχʏldəyənt] *adj* accusatory, denunciatory

beschuldiging [bəsχʏldəyɪŋ] *de (~en)* accusation, imputation, charge, indictment: *iem in staat van ~ stellen (wegens)* indict s.o. (for); *onder (op) ~ van diefstal (gearresteerd)* (arrested) on a charge of theft

beschut [bəsχʏt] *adj* sheltered, protected

beschutten [bəsχʏtə(n)] *vb* (with *tegen*) shelter (from), protect (from, against), shield (from)

beschutting [bəsχχytɪŋ] *de (~en)* shelter, protection: *(geen)* ~ *bieden* offer (no) protection; ~ *tegen de regen* protection from the rain

besef [bəsɛf] *het* understanding, idea, sense: *tot het* ~ *komen dat* come to realize that

beseffen [bəsɛfə(n)] *vb* realize, be aware (of), grasp, be conscious (of): *voor ik het besefte, had ik ja gezegd* before I knew it, I had said yes

¹beslaan [bəslan] *vb* mist up *(or:* over), steam up *(or:* over): *toen ik binnenkwam, besloeg mijn bril* when I entered, my glasses steamed up

²beslaan [bəslan] *vb* **1** take up, cover, run to: *deze kast beslaat de halve kamer* this cupboard takes up half the room; **2** shoe

beslag [bəslɑχ] *het (~en)* **1** batter; **2** fitting(s), ironwork, metalwork, shoe; **3** possession: *iemands tijd in* ~ *nemen* take up s.o.'s time; *deze tafel neemt te veel ruimte in* ~ this table takes up too much space; **4** attachment: *smokkelwaar in* ~ *nemen* confiscate contraband

beslaglegging [bəslɑχlɛɣɪŋ] *de (~en)* attachment, seizure, distress (on)

beslissen [bəslɪsə(n)] *vb* decide, resolve: *dit doelpunt zou de wedstrijd* ~ this goal was to decide the match

beslissend [bəslɪsənt] *adj* decisive, conclusive, final, crucial: *in een* ~ *stadium zijn* have come to a head, be at a critical stage

beslissing [bəslɪsɪŋ] *de (~en)* decision, ruling

¹beslist [bəslɪst] *adj* **1** definite; **2** decided

²beslist [bəslɪst] *adv* certainly, definitely

besloten [bəslotə(n)] *adj* closed, private: *een* ~ *vergadering* a meeting behind closed doors

besluipen [bəslœypə(n)] *vb* steal up on, creep up on, stalk: *de vrees besloop hen* (the) fear crept over them

besluit [bəslœyt] *het (~en)* **1** decision, resolution, resolve: *een* ~ *nemen* take a decision; *mijn* ~ *staat vast* I'm quite determined; **2** conclusion; **3** order, decree

besluiten [bəslœytə(n)] *vb* **1** conclude, close, end; **2** decide, resolve

besluitvaardig [bəslœytfardəχ] *adj* decisive, resolute

besmeren [bəsmerə(n)] *vb* butter; daub *(with paint)*

besmet [bəsmɛt] *adj* **1** infected, contaminated; **2** tainted, contaminated, polluted

besmettelijk [bəsmɛtələk] *adj* **1** infectious, contagious, catching: *een ~e ziekte* an infectious disease; **2** (be) easily soiled

besmetten [bəsmɛtə(n)] *vb* **1** infect (with), contaminate (with): *met griep besmet worden (door iem)* catch the flu (from s.o.); **2** taint, soil

besmetting [bəsmɛtɪŋ] *de (~en)* infection, contagion; disease: *radioactieve* ~ radioactive contamination

besneden [bəsnedə(n)] *adj* circumcised

besnijden [bəsnɛidə(n)] *vb* circumcise

besnijdenis [bəsnɛidənɪs] *de* circumcision

¹besnoeien [bəsnujə(n)] *vb* **1** trim (off, down), cut (down, back), curtail: *uitgaven* ~ cut down (on) expenses; **2** prune, lop; trim

²besnoeien [bəsnujə(n)] *vb* cut down (on)

bespannen [bəspɑnə(n)] *vb* **1** stretch, string; **2** harness (a horse to a cart): *een rijtuig met paarden* ~ put horses to a carriage

bespanning [bəspɑnɪŋ] *de (~en)* stringing

besparen [bəsparə(n)] *vb* **1** save; **2** spare, save: *de rest zal ik je maar* ~ I'll spare you the rest

besparing [bəsparɪŋ] *de (~en)* **1** saving, economy; **2** saving(s), economies: *een* ~ *op* a saving on

bespelen [bəspelə(n)] *vb* **1** *(sport)* play on, play in *(field);* **2** *(mus)* play (on); **3** manipulate; play on: *een gehoor* ~ play to an audience

bespeuren [bəspørə(n)] *vb* sense, notice, perceive, find

bespieden [bəspidə(n)] *vb* spy (on), watch

bespioneren [bəspijonerə(n)] *vb* spy on

bespoedigen [bəspudəɣə(n)] *vb* accelerate, speed up

bespottelijk [bəspɔtələk] *adj, adv* ridiculous, absurd: *een* ~ *figuur slaan* (make oneself) look ridiculous

bespotten [bəspɔtə(n)] *vb* ridicule, mock, deride, scoff at

bespreken [bəsprekə(n)] *vb* **1** discuss, talk about, consider: *een probleem* ~ go into a problem; **2** discuss, comment on, examine, review; **3** book, reserve: *kaartjes (plaatsen)* ~ make reservations

bespreking [bəsprekɪŋ] *de (~en)* **1** discussion, talk; **2** meeting, conference, talks; **3** review; **4** booking, reservation

besprenkelen [bəsprɛŋkələ(n)] *vb* sprinkle

bespringen [bəsprɪŋə(n)] *vb* pounce on, jump

besproeien [bəsprujə(n)] *vb* **1** sprinkle; **2** irrigate, spray, water

¹best [bɛst] *adj* **1** best, better, optimum: *met de ~e bedoelingen* with the best of intentions; *~e maatjes zijn met* be very thick with; *Peter ziet er niet al te ~ uit* Peter is looking the worse for wear; *hij kan koken als de ~e* he can cook with the best of them; *op een na de ~e* the second best; *het ~e ermee!* good luck!, best wishes!; **2** well, all right: *(het is) mij ~* I don't mind; **3** dear, good: *Beste Jan* Dear Jan; *hij overnacht niet in het eerste het ~e hotel* he doesn't stay at just any (old) hotel

²best [bɛst] *adv* **1** best: *jij kent hem het ~e* you know him best; **2** fine; **3** sure: *je weet het* ~ you know perfectly well; *het zal* ~ *lukken* it'll work out (all right); **4** really; **5** possibly, well: *dat zou* ~ *kunnen* that's quite possible; *ze zou* ~ *willen …* she wouldn't mind …; *zijn* ~ *doen* do one's best; *hij is op zijn* ~ he is at his best; *ze is op haar* ~ *(gekleed)* she looks her best

¹bestaan [bəstan] *het* **1** existence: *die firma viert vandaag haar vijftigjarig* ~ that firm is celebrating its fiftieth anniversary today; **2** living, livelihood

²**bestaan** [bəstan] *vb* **1** exist, be (in existence): *laat daar geen misverstand over* ~ let there be no mistake about it; *onze liefde zal altijd blijven* ~ our love will live on forever; *ophouden te* ~ cease to exist; **2** *(with uit)* consist (of), be made up (of): *dit werk bestaat uit drie delen* this work consists of three parts; **3** be possible: *hoe bestaat het!* can you believe it!

bestaand [bəstant] *adj* existing, existent, current

bestaansminimum [bəstansminimʏm] *het (-minima)* subsistence level

¹**bestand** [bəstant] *het (~en)* **1** truce, armistice; **2** file

²**bestand** [bəstant] *adj* ‖ ~ *zijn tegen* withstand, resist, be immune to; *tegen hitte* ~ heat-resistant

bestanddeel [bəstandel] *het (-delen)* constituent, element, component (part), ingredient

besteden [bəstedə(n)] *vb* **1** spend, devote (to), give (to), employ for: *geen aandacht* ~ *aan* pay no attention to; *zorg* ~ *aan (werk)* take care over (work); **2** spend (on): *ik besteed elke dag een uur aan mijn huiswerk* every day I spend one hour on my homework

besteedbaar [bəstedbar] *adj* disposable

bestek [bəstɛk] *het (~ken)* **1** cutlery: *(een) zilveren* ~ a set of silver cutlery; **2** specifications: *iets in kort* ~ *uiteenzetten* explain sth in brief

bestel [bəstɛl] *het* (established) order

bestelbusje [bəstɛlbʏʃə] *het (~s)* delivery van

besteldatum [bəstɛldatʏm] *de* order date, date of order(ing)

bestelen [bəstelə(n)] *vb* rob

bestellen [bəstɛlə(n)] *vb* **1** order, place an order (for), send for: *een taxi* ~ call a taxi; *iets* ~ *bij* order sth from; **2** deliver; **3** book; reserve

besteller [bəstɛlər] *de (~s)* **1** delivery man; postman; **2** customer

bestelling [bəstɛlɪŋ] *de (~en)* **1** delivery; **2** order; **3** order, goods ordered: *~en afleveren* deliver goods ordered

bestemmeling [bəstɛmelɪŋ] *de (~en) (Belg)* addressee

bestemmen [bəstɛmə(n)] *vb* mean, intend; design: *dit boek is voor John bestemd* this book was meant for John

bestemming [bəstɛmɪŋ] *de (~en)* **1** intention, purpose, allocation; **2** destination: *hij is met onbekende* ~ *vertrokken* he has gone without leaving a forwarding address; **3** destiny

bestendig [bəstɛndəχ] *adj, adv* **1** durable; lasting, enduring: *~e vrede* lasting peace; **2** stable, steady: *~ weer* settled weather; **3** -proof, -resistant: *hittebestendig* heat-resistant

bestijgen [bəstɛiɣə(n)] *vb* **1** mount, ascend; **2** climb, ascend

bestijging [bəstɛiɣɪŋ] *de (~en)* **1** mounting, ascent, accession (to); **2** climbing, ascent

bestoken [bəstokə(n)] *vb* harass, press, shell; bomb(ard): *iem met vragen* ~ bombard s.o. with questions

bestormen [bəstɔrmə(n)] *vb* storm

bestorming [bəstɔrmɪŋ] *de (~en)* storming, assault

bestraffen [bəstrafə(n)] *vb* punish

bestraffing [bəstrafɪŋ] *de (~en)* punishing, chastisement

bestralen [bəstralə(n)] *vb* give radiation treatment *(or:* radiotherapy)

bestraling [bəstralɪŋ] *de (~en)* irradiation, radiotherapy, radiation treatment

bestraten [bəstratə(n)] *vb* pave, surface, cobble

bestrating [bəstratɪŋ] *de (~en)* pavement, paving, surface, cobbles

bestrijden [bəstrɛidə(n)] *vb* **1** dispute, challenge, contest, oppose, resist; **2** combat, fight, counteract, control: *het alcoholisme* ~ combat alcoholism

bestrijdingsmiddel [bəstrɛidɪŋsmɪdəl] *het (~en)* pesticide; herbicide, weed killer

bestrijken [bəstrɛikə(n)] *vb* **1** cover: *deze krant bestrijkt de hele regio* this newspaper covers the entire area; **2** spread; coat

bestrooien [bəstrojə(n)] *vb* sprinkle (with); cover (with), spread (with); powder (with), dust (with): *gladde wegen met zand* ~ sand icy roads

bestuderen [bəstyderə(n)] *vb* **1** study, pore over; **3** study, investigate, explore

bestuiven [bəstœyvə(n)] *vb* pollinate; dust, powder

besturen [bəstyrə(n)] *vb* **1** drive, steer, navigate: *een schip* ~ steer a ship; **2** control, operate; **3** govern, administrate, manage, run

besturing [bəstyrɪŋ] *de (~en)* control(s), steering, drive

besturingssysteem [bəstyrɪŋsistem] *het (-systemen)* operating system

bestuur [bəstyr] *het (besturen)* **1** government, rule; administration; management: *de raad van* ~ *van deze school* the Board of Directors of this school; **2** administration, government, management; **3** government; council, corporation: *iem in het* ~ *kiezen* elect s.o. to the board

bestuurbaar [bəstyrbar] *adj* controllable, manageable, navigable: *gemakkelijk* ~ *zijn* be easy to steer *(or:* control); *niet meer* ~ *zijn* be out of control

bestuurder [bəstyrdər] *de (~s)* **1** driver; pilot; operator; **2** administrator, manager: *de ~s van een instelling* the governors *(or:* managers) of an institution; **3** director, manager

bestuurlijk [bəstyrlək] *adj* administrative, governmental, managerial

bestuurslid [bəstyrslɪt] *het (-leden)* member of the board; committee member

bestwil [bɛstwɪl] *de* ‖ *ik zeg het voor je (eigen)* ~ I'm saying this for your own good

bèta [bɛːta] *de* science (side, subjects)

betaalbaar [bətalbar] *adj* affordable, reasonably priced

betaalcheque [bətalʃɛk] *de (~s)* (bank-)guaranteed cheque

betaald [bətalt] *adj* paid (for), hired, professional: ~ *voetbal* professional soccer

betaalkaart [bətɑlkɑrt] *de (~en)* (guaranteed) giro cheque

betaalmiddel [bətɑlmɪdəl] *het (~en)* tender, currency, circulating medium

betaalpas [bətɑlpɑs] *de (~sen)* cheque card

betalen [bətɑlə(n)] *vb* pay; pay for: *de kosten ~* bear the cost; *(nog) te ~* balance due; *contant ~* pay (in) cash; *die huizen zijn niet te ~* the price of these houses is prohibitive; *met cheques ~* pay by cheque; *dit werk betaalt slecht* this work pays badly

betaler [bətɑlər] *de (~s)* payer

betaling [bətɑlɪŋ] *de (~en)* payment, reward, remuneration, settlement: *~ in termijnen* payment in instalments

betalingsbalans [bətɑlɪŋzbɑlɑns] *de (~en)* balance of payments

betalingsbewijs [bətɑlɪŋzbəwɛis] *het (-bewijzen)* receipt

betalingstermijn [bətɑlɪŋstɛrmɛin] *de (~en)* instalment

betamelijk [bətɑmələk] *adj, adv* decent, fit(ting), seemly, proper

betasten [bətɑstə(n)] *vb* feel, finger

betegelen [bəteɣələ(n)] *vb* tile

betekenen [bətekənə(n)] *vb* 1 mean, stand for, signify: *wat heeft dit te ~?* what's the meaning of this?; *wat betekent NN?* what does N.N. stand for?; 2 mean, count, matter: *mijn auto betekent alles voor mij* my car means everything to me; *niet veel (weinig) ~* be of little importance; *die baan betekent veel voor haar* that job means a lot to her; 3 mean, entail: *dat betekent nog niet dat ...* that does not mean that ...

betekenis [bətekənɪs] *de (~sen)* 1 meaning, sense; 2 significance, importance: *van doorslaggevende ~* of decisive importance

beter [betər] *adj, adv* 1 better: *het is ~ dat je nu vertrekt* you'd better leave now; *ze is ~ in wiskunde dan haar broer* she's better at maths than her brother; *dat is al ~* that's more like it; *~ maken* improve; *~ worden* improve; *wel wat ~s te doen hebben* have better things to do; *~ laat dan nooit* better late than never; *hij is weer helemaal ~* he has completely recovered; *~ maken, weer ~ maken* cure; *~ worden, weer ~ worden* recover, get well again; *het ~ doen (dan een ander)* do better than s.o. else; *je had ~ kunnen helpen* you would have done better to help; *de leerling kon ~* the student could do better; *John tennist ~ dan ik* John is a better tennis-player than me; *(iron) het ~ weten* know best; *ze weten niet ~ of ... for* all they know ...; *des te ~ (voor ons)* so much the better (for us); *hoe eerder hoe ~* the sooner the better; *de volgende keer ~* better luck next time; 2 better (class of), superior: *uit ~e kringen* upper-class

beterschap [betərsχɑp] *de* recovery (of health): *~!* get well soon!

beteuterd [bətøtərt] *adj* taken aback, dismayed: *~ kijken* look dismayed

betichte [bətɪχtə] *de (~n) (Belg; law)* accused, defendant

betimmeren [bətɪmərə(n)] *vb* board; panel

betoelaging [bətulaɣɪŋ] *de (Belg)* subsidy

betogen [bətoɣə(n)] *vb* demonstrate, march

betoger [bətoɣər] *de (~s)* demonstrator, marcher

betoging [bətoɣɪŋ] *de (~en)* demonstration, march

beton [bətɔn] *het* concrete: *gewapend ~* reinforced concrete; *~ storten* pour concrete

betonen [bətonə(n)] *vb* show, display, extend

betonnen [bətɔnə(n)] *adj* concrete

betoog [bətoχ] *het (betogen)* argument, plea

betoveren [bətovərə(n)] *vb* 1 put (*or:* cast) a spell on, bewitch: *betoverd door haar ogen* bewitched by her eyes; 2 enchant

betovering [bətovərɪŋ] *de (~en)* 1 spell, bewitchment; 2 enchantment, charm

betrachten [bətrɑχtə(n)] *vb* practise, exercise, observe, show

betrachting [bətrɑχtɪŋ] *de (~en) (Belg)* aim, intention

betrappen [bətrɑpə(n)] *vb* catch, surprise: *op heterdaad betrapt* caught redhanded

betreden [bətredə(n)] *vb* 1 enter: *het is verboden dit terrein te ~* no entry, keep out (*or:* off); 2 tread: *nieuwe paden ~* break new (*or:* fresh) ground

betreffen [bətrɛfə(n)] *vb* 1 concern, regard: *waar het politiek betreft* when it comes to politics; *wat mij betreft is het in orde* as far as I'm concerned it's all right; *wat betreft je broer* with regard to your brother; 2 concern, relate to

betreffende [bətrɛfəndə] *prep* concerning, regarding

¹betrekkelijk [bətrɛkələk] *adj* relative: *dat is ~* that depends (on how you look at it); *alles is ~* everything is relative

²betrekkelijk [bətrɛkələk] *adv* relatively, comparatively

betrekkelijkheid [bətrɛkələkhɛit] *de* relativity

¹betrekken [bətrɛkə(n)] *vb* involve, concern: *zij deden alles zonder de anderen erin te ~* they did everything without consulting the others

²betrekken [bətrɛkə(n)] *vb* 1 become overcast (*or:* cloudy), cloud over; 2 cloud over, darken

betrekking [bətrɛkɪŋ] *de (~en)* 1 post, job, position, office: *iem aan een ~ helpen* engage s.o., help s.o. find a job; 2 relation(ship): *nauwe ~en met iem onderhouden* maintain close ties (*or:* connections) with s.o.; 3 relation, connection: *met ~ tot* with regard to, with respect to

betreuren [bətrørə(n)] *vb* 1 regret, be sorry for: *een vergissing ~* regret a mistake; 2 mourn (for, over), be sorry for

betreurenswaardig [bətrørənswardəχ] *adj* regrettable, sad

betrokken [bətrɔkə(n)] *adj* 1 concerned, involved: *de ~ docent* the teacher concerned; 2 overcast, cloudy

betrokkenheid [bətrɔkənhɛit] *de* involvement, commitment, concern

betrouwbaar [bətrɑubar] *adj* reliable, trustworthy, dependable: *uit betrouwbare bron* on good authority

betrouwbaarheid [bətrɑubarhɛit] *de* reliability, dependability, trustworthiness

betuigen [bətœyɣə(n)] *vb* express: *iem zijn deelneming* (or: *medeleven*) ~ express one's condolences (or: sympathy) to s.o.

betwijfelen [bətwɛifələ(n)] *vb* doubt, (call in) question: *het valt te ~ of ...* it is doubtful whether ...

betwisten [bətwɪstə(n)] *vb* dispute, contest, challenge

beu [bø] *adj* || *iets ~ zijn* be sick of sth

beugel [bøɣəl] *de* (~s) brace: *een ~ dragen* wear braces, wear a brace

beuk [bøk] *de* (~en) beech

¹**beuken** [bøkə(n)] *adj* beech

²**beuken** [bøkə(n)] *vb* batter, pound, lash: *op* (or: *tegen*) *iets ~* hammer on sth, batter (away) at sth

beul [bøl] *de* (~en) 1 executioner, hangman; 2 *(fig)* tyrant, brute

beunhaas [bønhas] *de* (-hazen) moonlighter

¹**beurs** [børs] *de* (beurzen) 1 scholarship, grant: *een ~ hebben, van een ~ studeren* have a grant; *een ~ krijgen* get a grant; 2 exchange, market; *(bldg)* Stock Exchange; 3 fair, show, exhibition: *antiekbeurs* antique(s) fair; 4 purse

²**beurs** [børs] *adj* overripe, mushy

beursnotering [børsnoterɪŋ] *de* (~en) quotation, share price; foreign exchange rate

beurt [børt] *de* (~en) turn: *een goede ~ maken* make a good impression; *een grote ~ (car)* a big service; *de kamer een grondige ~ geven* give the room a good cleaning; *hij is aan de ~* it's his turn, he's next; *om de ~ iets doen* take turns doing sth; *om de ~* in turn

beurtelings [børtəlɪŋs] *adv* alternately, by turns, in turn: *het ~ warm en koud krijgen* go hot and cold (all over)

beurtrol [børtrɔl] *de* (~len) *(Belg) see* toerbeurt

bevaarbaar [bəvarbar] *adj* navigable

bevallen [bəvɑlə(n)] *vb* 1 give birth (to): *zij is van een dochter ~* she gave birth to a daughter; 2 please, suit, give satisfaction: *hoe bevalt het je op school?* how do you like school?

bevalling [bəvɑlɪŋ] *de* (~en) delivery, childbirth

bevangen [bəvɑŋə(n)] *vb* seize, overcome: *hij werd door angst ~* he was panic-stricken

bevaren [bəvarə(n)] *vb* navigate, sail

bevattelijk [bəvɑtələk] *adj, adv* intelligible, comprehensible

bevatten [bəvɑtə(n)] *vb* 1 contain, hold; 2 comprehend, understand: *niet te ~* incomprehensible

beveiligen [bəvɛiləɣə(n)] *vb* protect, secure, *(fig also)* safeguard

beveiliging [bəvɛiləɣɪŋ] *de* (~en) 1 protection, security, *(fig also)* safeguard(s); 2 safety (or: protective, security) device

bevel [bəvɛl] *het* (~en) order, command, warrant: *~ geven tot* give the order to; *het ~ voeren over een leger* be in command of an army

bevelen [bəvelə(n)] *vb* order, command

bevelhebber [bəvɛlhɛbər] *de* (~s) commander, commanding officer

beven [bevə(n)] *vb* 1 shake, tremble, shiver: *~ van kou* shiver with cold; 2 tremble, quake

bever [bevər] *de* (~s) beaver

bevestigen [bəvɛstəɣə(n)] *vb* 1 fix, fasten, attach; 2 confirm; affirm: *de uitzondering bevestigt de regel* the exception proves the rule

bevestigend [bəvɛstəɣənt] *adj, adv* affirmative

bevestiging [bəvɛstəɣɪŋ] *de* (~en) 1 fixing, fastening, attachment; 2 confirmation; 3 affirmation, confirmation

¹**bevinden** [bəvɪndə(n)] *vb* find: *gezien en goed bevonden* seen and approved; *schuldig ~ (aan een misdaad)* find guilty (of a crime)

²**bevinden** [bəvɪndə(n)] *ref vb* be, find oneself: *zich in gevaar ~* be in danger

bevinding [bəvɪndɪŋ] *de* (~en) finding, result, experience, conclusion

beving [bevɪŋ] *de* (~en) trembling, shiver

bevlekken [bəvlɛkə(n)] *vb* soil, stain, spot: *met bloed bevlekt* bloodstained

bevlieging [bəvliɣɪŋ] *de* (~en) whim, impulse

bevlogen [bəvloɣə(n)] *adj* animated, inspired, enthusiastic

bevochtigen [bəvɔxtəɣə(n)] *vb* moisten, wet, humidify

bevochtiger [bəvɔxtəɣər] *de* (~s) humidifier

bevoegd [bəvuxt] *adj* competent, qualified, authorized: *de ~e overheden (autoriteiten)* the proper authorities; *~e personen* authorized persons; *~ zijn* be qualified

bevoegdheid [bəvuxthɛit] *de* (-heden) competence, qualification, authority, jurisdiction: *de bevoegdheden van de burgemeester* the powers of the mayor; *de ~ hebben om* have the power to; *zonder ~* unauthorized

bevolken [bəvɔlkə(n)] *vb* populate, people

bevolking [bəvɔlkɪŋ] *de* (~en) population, inhabitants: *de inheemse ~* the native population

bevolkingsdichtheid [bəvɔlkɪŋzdɪxthɛit] *de* population density

bevolkingsgroep [bəvɔlkɪŋsxrup] *de* (~en) community, section of the population

bevolkingsregister [bəvɔlkɪŋsrəɣɪstər] *het* (~s) register (of births, deaths and marriages)

bevolkt [bəvɔlkt] *adj* populated: *een dicht- (or: dunbevolkte) streek* a densely (or: sparsely) populated region

bevoordelen [bəvordelə(n)] *vb* benefit, favour: *familieleden ~ boven anderen* favour relatives above others

bevooroordeeld [bəvorordelt] *adj* prejudiced, bias(s)ed: ~ *zijn tegen* (or: *voor*) be prejudiced against (or: in favour of)

bevoorraden [bəvo̲radə(n)] *vb* provision, supply, stock up

bevoorrechten [bəvo̲rɛχtə(n)] *vb* privilege, favour: *een bevoorrechte positie innemen* occupy a privileged position

bevorderen [bəvo̲rdərə(n)] *vb* 1 promote, further, advance, boost, aid, encourage, stimulate, lead to, be conducive to: *dat bevordert de bloedsomloop* that stimulates one's blood circulation; *de verkoop van iets* ~ boost the sale of sth, push sth; 2 promote: *bevorderd worden* go up (to the next class); *een leerling naar een hogere klas* ~ move a pupil up to a higher class; *hij werd tot kapitein bevorderd* he was promoted to (the rank of) captain

bevordering [bəvo̲rdərɪŋ] *de* (~en) 1 promotion, advancement, encouragement; 2 promotion: *voor* ~ *in aanmerking komen* be eligible for promotion

bevorderlijk [bəvo̲rdərlək] *adj* beneficial (to), conducive (to), good (for): ~ *zijn voor: a)* promote, further, advance; *b)* boost, aid; *c)* lead to, be conducive to

bevredigen [bəvre̲dəɣə(n)] *vb* satisfy, gratify: *zijn nieuwsgierigheid* ~ gratify one's curiosity; *moeilijk te* ~ hard to please

bevredigend [bəvre̲dəɣənt] *adj* satisfactory, satisfying, gratifying: *een* ~*e oplossing* a satisfactory solution

bevrediging [bəvre̲dəɣɪŋ] *de* (~en) satisfaction, fulfilment, gratification: ~ *in iets vinden* find satisfaction in sth

bevreesd [bəvre̲st] *adj* afraid, fearful

bevriend [bəvri̲nt] *adj* friendly (with): *een* ~*e mogendheid* a friendly nation (or: power); *goed* ~ *zijn (met iem)* be close friends (with s.o.)

bevriezen [bəvri̲zə(n)] *vb* 1 freeze (up, over), become (or: be frozen) (up, over): *het water is bevroren* the water is frozen; *alle leidingen zijn bevroren* all the pipes are (or: have) frozen (up); 2 frost (up, over), become frosted; 3 freeze, block

bevriezing [bəvri̲zɪŋ] *de* 1 freezing (over), frost, frostbite; 2 freeze: ~ *van het aantal kernwapens* nuclear freeze

bevrijden [bəvrɛi̲də(n)] *vb* free (from), liberate, release, set free; rescue, emancipate: *een land* ~ free (or: liberate) a country; *iem uit zijn benarde positie* ~ rescue s.o. from a desperate position

bevrijding [bəvrɛi̲dɪŋ] *de* 1 liberation, release, rescue, emancipation: ~ *uit slavernij* emancipation from slavery; 2 (*fig*) relief: *een gevoel van* ~ a feeling of relief

bevrijdingsdag [bəvrɛi̲dɪŋzdɑχ] *de* liberation day

bevruchten [bəvrʏχtə(n)] *vb* fertilize, impregnate, inseminate

bevruchting [bəvrʏχtɪŋ] *de* (~en) fertilization, impregnation, insemination: *kunstmatige* ~ artificial insemination; ~ *buiten de baarmoeder* in vitro fertilization

bewaarder [bəwa̲rdər] *de* (~s) 1 keeper, guardian, jailer, warder: *ordebewaarder* keeper of the peace; 2 keeper

bewaarmiddel [bəwa̲rmɪdəl] *het* (~en) (*Belg; culinary*) preservative

bewaarplaats [bəwa̲rplats] *de* (~en) depository, repository, store(house)

bewaken [bəwa̲kə(n)] *vb* guard, watch (over), monitor, watch, mind: *het budget* ~ watch the budget; *een gevangene* ~ guard a prisoner; *een terrein* ~ guard (over) an area; *zwaar* (or: *licht*) *bewaakte gevangenis* maximum (or: minimum) security prison

bewaker [bəwa̲kər] *de* (~s) 1 guard; 2 security guard

bewaking [bəwa̲kɪŋ] *de* guard(ing), watch(ing), surveillance, control: *onder strenge* ~ *staan* be kept under strict surveillance

bewandelen [bəwɑndələ(n)] *vb* 1 walk (on, over); 2 (*fig*) take (or: follow, steer) a … course: *de middenweg* ~ steer a middle course; *de officiële weg* ~ take the official line

bewapenen [bəwa̲pənə(n)] *vb* arm: *zich* ~ arm; *zwaar bewapend* heavily armed

bewapening [bəwa̲pənɪŋ] *de* armament, arms

bewaren [bəwa̲rə(n)] *vb* 1 keep, save; 2 keep, store, stock (up): *appels* ~ store apples; *een onderwerp tot de volgende keer* ~ leave a topic for the next time; ~ *voor later* save up for a rainy day; 3 keep, maintain: *zijn kalmte* ~ keep calm; 4 preserve (from), save (from), guard (from, against)

bewaring [bəwa̲rɪŋ] *de* 1 keeping, care, storage, custody: *in* ~ *geven (aan, bij)* deposit (at, with), entrust (to), leave (with); 2 custody, detention: *huis van* ~ house of detention

beweegbaar [bəwe̲ɣbar] *adj* movable: *beweegbare delen* moving parts

beweeglijk [bəwe̲χlək] *adj* agile, lively, active: *een zeer* ~ *kind* a very active child

beweegreden [bəwe̲χredə(n)] *de* (~en) motive, (*pl also*) grounds: *de* ~*en van zijn gedrag* the motives underlying his behaviour

bewegen [bəwe̲ɣə(n)] *vb* move, stir: *op en neer* (or: *heen en weer*) ~ move up and down (or: to and fro); *zich* ~ move, stir; *ik kan me nauwelijks* ~ I can hardly move; *geen blad bewoog* not a leaf stirred; ~*de delen* moving parts; *niet* ~! don't move!

beweging [bəwe̲ɣɪŋ] *de* (~en) movement, move, motion, gesture: *een verkeerde* ~ *maken* make a wrong move; *er is geen* ~ *in te krijgen* it won't budge (or: move); *in* ~ *brengen, in* ~ *zetten* set in motion, start; *in* ~ *blijven* keep moving; *in* ~ *zijn* be moving, be in motion; *de vredesbeweging* the peace movement

bewegingloos [bəwe̲ɣɪŋlos] *adj* motionless, immobile

bewegingsvrijheid [bəwe̲ɣɪŋsfrɛihɛit] *de* freedom of movement

beweren [bəwe̲rə(n)] *vb* claim, contend, allege:

durven te ~ dat dare to claim that; *dat zou ik niet willen ~* I wouldn't (go as far as to) say that; *zij beweerde onschuldig te zijn* she claimed to be innocent; *dat is precies wat wij ~* that's the very point we're making; *hij beweert dat hij niets gehoord heeft* he maintains that he did not hear anything

bewering [bəwɛrɪŋ] *de (~en)* assertion, statement, allegation, claim, contention: *bij zijn ~ blijven* stick to one's claim; *kun je deze ~ hard maken?* can you substantiate this claim?

bewerken [bəwɛrkə(n)] *vb* treat, work, process; edit, rewrite, revise, adapt: *een studieboek voor het Nederlandse taalgebied* ~ adapt a textbook for the Dutch user; *de grond ~* till the land (*or:* soil); *geheel opnieuw bewerkt door* completely revised by; *~ tot een film* adapt for the screen

bewerking [bəwɛrkɪŋ] *de (~en)* 1 treatment, cultivation, process(ing), manufacturing, editing: *de derde druk van dit schoolboek is in ~* the third edition of this textbook is in preparation; 2 adaptation, version; arrangement; revision: *de Nederlandse ~ van dit boek* the Dutch version of this book; *~ voor toneel* (or: *de film*) adaptation for stage (*or:* the screen); 3 manipulation, influencing; 4 processing

bewerkstelligen [bəwɛrkstɛləɣə(n)] *vb* bring about, effect, realize: *een ontmoeting* (or: *verzoening*) ~ bring about a meeting (*or:* reconciliation)

bewijs [bəwɛis] *het (bewijzen)* 1 proof, evidence: *(Belg) ~ van goed gedrag en zeden* (roughly) certificate of good character; *het ~ leveren (dat, van)* produce evidence (that, of); *als ~ aanvoeren* quote (in evidence); 2 proof, evidence, sign: *als ~ van erkentelijkheid* as a token of gratitude; 3 proof, certificate: *betalingsbewijs* proof of payment, receipt; *~ van goed gedrag* certificate of good conduct

bewijsbaar [bəwɛizbar] *adj* demonstrable, provable: *moeilijk ~* hard to prove

bewijslast [bəwɛislɑst] *de (~en)* burden of proof

bewijsmateriaal [bəwɛismaterijal] *het* evidence, proof

bewijzen [bəwɛizə(n)] *vb* 1 prove, establish, demonstrate: *dit bewijst dat* this proves that; 2 render, show, prove: *zichzelf moeten ~* have to prove oneself

bewind [bəwɪnt] *het* 1 government, regime, rule: *aan het ~ komen* come to power; 2 administration, government

bewindvoerder [bəwɪntfurdər] *de (~s)* administrator, director

bewogen [bəwoɣə(n)] *adj* 1 moved: *tot tranen toe ~* moved to tears; 2 stirring, eventful

bewolking [bəwɔlkɪŋ] *de (~en)* cloud(s): *laaghangende ~* low cloud(s)

bewolkt [bəwɔlkt] *adj* cloudy, overcast

bewonderaar [bəwɔndərar] *de (~s)* admirer, *(inf)* fan

bewonderen [bəwɔndərə(n)] *vb* admire, look up to

bewonderenswaardig [bəwɔndərənswardəχ] *adj, adv* admirable, wonderful

bewondering [bəwɔndərɪŋ] *de* admiration, wonder

bewonen [bəwonə(n)] *vb* inhabit; occupy, live in

bewoner [bəwonər] *de (~s)* inhabitant, occupant, resident

bewoning [bəwonɪŋ] *de* occupation, residence

bewoonbaar [bəwombar] *adj* (in)habitable, liveable

bewoording [bəwordɪŋ] *de* wording, phrasing, (*pl*) terms: *in krachtige ~en* strongly worded, warmly expressed

¹bewust [bəwɪst] *adj* 1 concerned, involved: *op die ~e dag* on the day in question; 2 aware, conscious: *ik ben me niet ~ van enige tekortkomingen* I am not aware of any shortcomings

²bewust [bəwɪst] *adv* consciously, knowingly

bewusteloos [bəwɪstəlos] *adj* unconscious, senseless: *~ raken* pass out

bewusteloosheid [bəwɪstəloshɛit] *de* unconsciousness

bewustzijn [bəwɪstsɛin] *het* consciousness, awareness: *zijn ~ verliezen* lose consciousness

bezaaien [bəzajə(n)] *vb* strew, stud: *bezaaid met* strewn with, studded with, littered with, dotted with

bezadigd [bəzadəχt] *adj* sober, level-headed, dispassionate

bezegelen [bəzeɣələ(n)] *vb* seal

bezem [bezəm] *de (~s)* broom

bezemsteel [bezəmstel] *de (-stelen)* broomstick, broomhandle

¹bezeren [bəzerə(n)] *ref vb* hurt oneself, get hurt, *(stronger)* injure oneself

²bezeren [bəzerə(n)] *vb* hurt, bruise

bezet [bəzɛt] *adj* 1 occupied, taken: *~ gebied* occupied territory; *geheel ~* full (up); 2 taken up, occupied; 3 engaged, occupied, busy: *de lijn is ~* the line is engaged, busy

bezeten [bəzetə(n)] *adj* 1 possessed (by): *als een ~e tekeergaan* go berserk; 2 obsessed (by)

bezetten [bəzɛtə(n)] *vb* occupy, take, fill: *een belangrijke plaats ~ in* occupy an important place in, feature in

bezetter [bəzɛtər] *de (~s)* occupier(s), occupying force(s)

bezetting [bəzɛtɪŋ] *de (~en)* 1 occupation, sit-in, filling, filling up; 2 (*theatre*) cast

bezichtigen [bəzɪχtəɣə(n)] *vb* (pay a) visit (to), see, tour, inspect: *een huis ~* view a house

bezichtiging [bəzɪχtəɣɪŋ] *de (~en)* visit, view, inspection, tour

bezielen [bəzilə(n)] *vb* inspire, animate: *wat bezielt je!* what has got into you!

bezien [bəzin] *vb* see, consider, look on

bezienswaardig [bəzinswardəχ] *adj* worth seeing

bezienswaardigheid [bəzinswardəχhɛit] *de (-heden)* place of interest, sight

bezig [bɛzəχ] *adj* busy (with sth, doing sth), working (on), preoccupied (with), engaged (in): *de wedstrijd is al ~* the match has already started; *als je er toch mee ~ bent* while you are at it (*or:* about it); *vreselijk lang met iets ~ zijn* be an awful long time over sth; *waar ben je eigenlijk mee ~!* what do you think you're up to?; *hij is weer ~* he's at it again
bezigheid [bɛzəχhɛit] *de (-heden)* activity, occupation, work
¹bezighouden [bɛzəχhaudə(n)] *vb* occupy, keep busy
²bezighouden [bɛzəχhaudə(n)] *ref vb* occupy (*or:* busy) oneself (with), engage (oneself) (in)
bezinken [bəzɪŋkə(n)] *vb* **1** settle (down), sink (to the bottom); **2** clarify, settle (out)
bezinksel [bəzɪŋksəl] *het (~s)* sediment, deposit, residue
bezinnen [bəzɪnə(n)] *ref vb* **1** contemplate, reflect (on): *bezint eer ge begint* look before you leap; **2** change one's mind
bezinning [bəzɪnɪŋ] *de* reflection, contemplation
bezit [bəzɪt] *het* possession, property: *in ~ houden* keep in one's possession
bezitten [bəzɪtə(n)] *vb* possess, own, have
bezitter [bəzɪtər] *de (~s)* owner, holder, possessor
bezitting [bəzɪtɪŋ] *de (~en)* property, possession, belongings, estate: *waardevolle ~en* valuables
bezocht [bəzɔχt] *adj* visited, attended, frequented: *een druk ~e receptie* a busy reception
bezoek [bəzuk] *het (~en)* **1** visit, call: *op ~ gaan bij iem* pay s.o. a visit; **2** visitor(s), guest(s), caller(s)
bezoeken [bəzukə(n)] *vb* visit, pay a visit to: *een school ~* attend a school
bezoeker [bəzukər] *de (~s)* visitor, guest
bezondigen [bəzɔndəɣə(n)] *ref vb* be guilty of
bezopen [bəzopə(n)] *adj* **1** sloshed, plastered; **2** absurd
bezorgd [bəzɔrχt] *adj, adv* **1** concerned (for, about): *de ~e moeder* the caring mother; **2** worried (about): *wees maar niet ~* don't worry
bezorgdheid [bəzɔrχthɛit] *de (-heden)* concern (for, about), worry
bezorgen [bəzɔrɣə(n)] *vb* **1** get, provide: *iem een baan ~* get s.o. a job; *dat bezorgt ons heel wat extra werk* that lands us with a lot of extra work; **2** give, cause: *iem een hoop last ~* put s.o. to great inconvenience; **3** deliver
bezorger [bəzɔrɣər] *de (~s)* delivery man (*or:* woman)
bezorging [bəzɔrɣɪŋ] *de (~en)* delivery
bezuinigen [bəzœynəɣə(n)] *vb* economize, save
bezuiniging [bəzœynəɣɪŋ] *de (~en)* **1** economy, cut(back); **2** saving(s)
bezwaar [bəzwar] *het (bezwaren)* **1** drawback; **2** objection, scruple: *zonder enig ~* without any objection
bezwaard [bəzwart] *adj* troubled
bezwaarlijk [bəzwarlək] *adj* troublesome
bezwaarschrift [bəzwarsχrɪft] *het (~en)* protest, petition

bezweet [bəzwɛt] *adj* sweaty, sweating
bezweren [bəzwɛrə(n)] *vb* **1** implore; **2** avert
bezwijken [bəzwɛikə(n)] *vb* **1** give (way, out); **2** succumb, yield: *voor de verleiding ~* yield to (*or:* give in) to the temptation; **3** go under: *aan een ziekte ~* succumb to a disease
bh [beha] *de (~'s) bustehouder* bra
bibberen [bɪbərə(n)] *vb* shiver (with)
bibliografie [biblijoɣrafi] *de (~ën)* bibliography
bibliothecaris [biblijotekarəs] *de (~sen)* librarian
bibliotheek [biblijotek] *de (bibliotheken)* library
bidden [bɪdə(n)] *vb* **1** pray, say one's prayers: *de rozenkrans ~* say the rosary; **2** implore
biecht [biχt] *de (~en)* confession: *iem de ~ afnemen* hear s.o.'s confession
biechten [biχtə(n)] *vb* confess, go to confession
bieden [bidə(n)] *vb* **1** offer, present; **2** (*cards*) bid: *het is jouw beurt om te ~* it's your (turn to) bid now; **3** (make an) offer, (make a) bid: *ik bied er twintig euro voor* I'll give you twenty euros for it
bieder [bidər] *de (~s)* bidder
biefstuk [bifstʏk] *de (~ken)* steak: *~ van de haas* fillet steak
biels [bils] *de (bielzen)* (railway) sleeper, (*Am*) railroad tie
bier [bir] *het (~en)* beer: *(Belg) klein ~* small beer; *~ van het vat* draught beer
bierbrouwerij [birbrauwərɛi] *de (~en)* brewery
bierviltje [birvɪlcə] *het (~s)* beer mat, coaster
bies [bis] *de (biezen)* **1** piping, border, edging; **2** rush ‖ *zijn biezen pakken* make oneself scarce
biet [bit] *de (~en)* beet
bietsen [bitsə(n)] *vb* scrounge, cadge
bietsuiker [bitsœykər] *de* beet sugar
biezen [bizə(n)] *adj* rush: *een ~ zitting* a rush(-bottomed) seat
big [bɪχ] *de (~gen)* piglet, piggy
biggelen [bɪɣələ(n)] *vb* trickle
¹bij [bɛi] *de (~en)* (honey) bee
²bij [bɛi] *prep* **1** near (to), close (by, to): *~ iem gaan zitten* sit next to s.o.; *ik woon hier vlak ~* I live nearby (*or:* close by); **2** at, to: *~ een kruispunt komen* come to an intersection; **3** to, with: *alles blijft ~ het oude* everything stays the same; *we zullen het er maar ~ laten* let's leave it at that; **4** while, during: *~ zijn dood* at his death; **5** at: *zij was ~ haar tante* she was at her aunt's; *er niet ~ zijn met zijn gedachten* have only half one's mind on it; **6** for, with: *~ een baas werken* work for a boss; *~ de marine* in the navy; *~ ons* at our house, back home, in our country (*or:* family); **7** with, along: *zij had haar dochter ~ zich* she had her daughter with her; *ik heb geen geld ~ me* I have no money on me; **8** with, to: *inlichtingen ~ de balie inwinnen* request information at the desk; *~ zichzelf (denken, zeggen)* (think, say) to oneself; **9** by: *iem ~ naam kennen* know s.o. by name; **10** by, at, in: *~ het lezen van de krant* (when) reading the newspaper; *~ het ontbijt* at breakfast;

11 in case of, if; **12** for, in the eyes of: *zij kan ~ de buren geen goed doen* she can do no good as far as the neighbours are concerned; *de kamer is 6 ~ 5* the room is 6 by 5; *je bent er ~* the game is up, gotcha!

³bij [bɛi] *adj* **1** up-to-date: *de leerling is weer* (or: *nog niet*) *~ met wiskunde* the pupil has now caught up on (or: is still behind in) mathematics; **2** up-to-date: *(goed) ~ zijn* be (thoroughly) on top of things

bijbehorend [bɛibəhorənt] *adj* accompanying, matching

bijbel [bɛibəl] *de (~s)* Bible

bijbels [bɛibəls] *adj* biblical

bijbenen [bɛibenə(n)] *vb* keep up (with)

bijbestellen [bɛibəstɛlə(n)] *vb* reorder, order a further (or: fresh) supply (of)

bijbetalen [bɛibətalə(n)] *vb* pay extra, pay an additional (or: extra) charge

bijblijven [bɛiblɛivə(n)] *vb* **1** keep pace, keep up; **2** stick in one's memory: *dat zal mij altijd ~* I shall never forget it

bijbrengen [bɛibrɛŋə(n)] *vb* impart (to), convey (to), instil (into): *iem bepaalde kennis ~* convey (certain) knowledge to s.o.

bijdehand [bɛidəhɑnt] *adj* bright, sharp

bijdrage [bɛidraɣə] *de (~n)* contribution, offering

bijdragen [bɛidraɣə(n)] *vb* contribute, add: *zijn steentje ~* do one's bit

bijeen [bɛien] *adv* together

bijeenbrengen [bɛiembrɛŋə(n)] *vb* bring together, get together, raise

bijeenkomen [bɛienkomə(n)] *vb* meet, assemble

bijeenkomst [bɛienkɔmst] *de (~en)* meeting, gathering

bijeenroepen [bɛienrupə(n)] *vb* call together, convene

bijenhouder [bɛiə(n)hɑudər] *de (~s)* beekeeper

bijenkoningin [bɛiə(n)koniŋin] *de (~nen)* queen bee

bijenkorf [bɛiə(n)kɔrf] *de (-korven)* (bee)hive

bijenteelt [bɛiə(n)telt] *de* apiculture

bijenvolk [bɛiə(n)vɔlk] *het (~en)* (swarm of, hive of) bees

bijenwas [bɛiə(n)wɑs] *het, de* beeswax

bijgebouw [bɛiɣəbɑu] *het (~en)* annex, outbuilding

bijgedachte [bɛiɣədɑχtə] *de (~n)* **1** association; **2** ulterior motive (or: design)

bijgeloof [bɛiɣəlof] *het* superstition

bijgelovig [bɛiɣəlovəχ] *adj, adv* superstitious

bijgelovigheid [bɛiχələvəχɛit] *de (-heden)* superstition, superstitiousness

bijgenaamd [bɛiɣənamt] *adj* called, nicknamed

bijhouden [bɛihɑudə(n)] *vb* **1** hold out (or: up) (to): *houd je bord bij* hold out your plate; **2** keep up (with), keep pace (with): *het onderwijs niet kunnen ~* be unable to keep up at school; **3** keep up to date: *de stand ~* keep count (or: the score)

bijhuis [bɛihœys] *het (bijhuizen)* (Belg) branch

bijkantoor [bɛikɑntor] *het (bijkantoren)* branch (office)

bijkeuken [bɛikøkə(n)] *de (~s)* scullery

bijklussen [bɛiklʏsə(n)] *vb* have a sideline

bijkomen [bɛikomə(n)] *vb* **1** come to (or: round); **2** (re)gain (one's) breath, recover (oneself): *niet meer ~ (van het lachen)* be overcome (with laughter)

bijkomend [bɛikomənt] *adj* additional, incidental, subordinate

bijkomstig [bɛikɔmstəχ] *adj* accidental, incidental; inessential; secondary, subordinate

bijkomstigheid [bɛikɔmstəχɛit] *de (-heden)* incidental circumstance

bijl [bɛil] *de (~en)* axe || *het ~tje erbij neerleggen* knock off, call it a day, call it quits

bijlage [bɛilaɣə] *de (~n)* **1** enclosure, appendix, supplement; **2** *(comp)* attachment

bijleggen [bɛilɛɣə(n)] *vb* **1** contribute, pay, make up; **2** settle: *het ~* make up

bijles [bɛilɛs] *de (~sen)* coaching, tutoring

bijleveren [bɛilevərə(n)] *vb* supply (in addition, extra)

bijna [bɛina] *adv* almost, nearly, close on, near: *nooit* (or: *geen*) almost never (or: none), hardly ever (or: any)

bijnaam [bɛinam] *de (bijnamen)* nickname

bijou [biʒu] *het (~s)* jewel

bijouterie [biʒutəri] *de (-ën)* jewellery

bijpassend [bɛipɑsənt] *adj* matching, to match

bijscholen [bɛisχolə(n)] *vb* give further training

bijscholing [bɛisχoliŋ] *de (extra)* training

bijschrift [bɛisχrɪft] *het (~en)* **1** caption, legend; **2** note

bijschrijven [bɛisχrɛivə(n)] *vb* enter, include

bijschrijving [bɛisχrɛiviŋ] *de (~en)* **1** entering (in the books); **2** amount entered, item entered

bijsluiter [bɛislœytər] *de (~s)* information leaflet, instruction leaflet

bijsmaak [bɛismak] *de (bijsmaken)* taste: *deze soep heeft een ~je* this soup has a funny taste to it, this soup doesn't taste right

bijspijkeren [bɛispɛikərə(n)] *vb* brush up: *een zwakke leerling ~* bring a weak pupil up to standard

bijspringen [bɛisprɪŋə(n)] *vb* support, help out

¹bijstaan [bɛistan] *vb* assist, aid

²bijstaan [bɛistan] *vb* dimly recollect: *er staat me iets bij van een vergadering waar hij heen zou gaan* I seem to remember that he was to go to a meeting

bijstand [bɛistɑnt] *de* **1** assistance, aid, social security: *hij leeft van de ~* he's on social security; **2** Social Security

bijstandsmoeder [bɛistɑntsmudər] *de (~s)* mother on social security

bijstandsuitkering [bɛistɑntsœytkeriŋ] *de (~en)* social security (payment)

bijstandswet [bɛistɑntswɛt] *de* social security act

bijstelling [bɛistɛliŋ] *de (~en)* (re-)adjustment

bijster [bɛistər] *adv* unduly, (none) too: *de tuin is niet ~ groot* the garden is none too large; *het spoor*

~ *zijn* have lost one's way

bijsturen [bɛistyrə(n)] *vb* **1** steer (away from, clear of, towards); **2** *(fig)* steer away from (*or:* clear of), adjust

bijt [bɛit] *de* (*~en*) hole (in the ice)

bijten [bɛitə(n)] *vb* **1** bite: *van zich af* ~ give as good as one gets, stick up for oneself; **2** sting, smart

bijtend [bɛitənt] *adj, adv* biting, corrosive

bijtijds [bɛitɛits] *adv* **1** early; **2** early, (well) in advance

bijtrekken [bɛitrɛkə(n)] *vb* **1** straighten (out), improve; **2** come (a)round

bijv. *bijvoorbeeld* e.g.

bijvak [bɛivɑk] *het* (*~ken*) subsidiary (subject)

bijval [bɛivɑl] *de* approval, support

bijverdienen [bɛivərdinə(n)] *vb* have an additional income: *een paar pond* ~ earn a few pounds extra (*or:* on the side)

bijverdienste [bɛivərdinstə] *de* (*~n*) extra earnings, extra income, additional income

bijverschijnsel [bɛivərsχɛinsəl] *het* (*~en*) side effect

bijvoegen [bɛivuɣə(n)] *vb* add, enclose, attach

bijvoeglijk [bɛivuɣlək] *adj* || ~ *naamwoord* adjective

bijvoegsel [bɛivuɣsəl] *het* (*~s*) supplement, addition

bijvoorbeeld [bɛivorbelt] *adv* for example, for instance, e.g.

bijvullen [bɛivʏlə(n)] *vb* top up (with), fill up (with)

bijwedde [bɛiwɛdə] *de (Belg)* salary supplement for highly qualified teachers

bijwerken [bɛiwɛrkə(n)] *vb* improve, catch up (on), bring up to date, update

bijwerking [bɛiwɛrkɪŋ] *de* (*~en*) side effect

bijwonen [bɛiwonə(n)] *vb* attend, be present at

bijwoord [bɛiwort] *het* (*~en*) adverb

bijzaak [bɛizak] *de (bijzaken)* side issue, (minor) detail

bijzetten [bɛizɛtə(n)] *vb* **1** add; **2** inter, bury

bijziend [bɛizint] *adj* short-sighted

bijziendheid [bɛizinthɛit] *de* short-sightedness

bijzijn [bɛizɛin] *het* || *in (het)* ~ *van* in the presence of

bijzin [bɛizɪn] *de* (*~nen*) (subordinate) clause: *betrekkelijke* ~ relative clause

¹bijzonder [bizɔndər] *adj* **1** particular: *in het* ~ in particular, especially; **2** special, especially; **3** strange, peculiar; **4** private

²bijzonder [bizɔndər] *adv* **1** very (much); **2** particularly, in particular, especially

bijzonderheid [bizɔndərhɛit] *de (-heden)* detail, particular

bikini [bikini] *de* (*~'s*) bikini

bikken [bɪkə(n)] *vb* chip (away)

bil [bɪl] *de* (*~len*) buttock: *dikke* (or: *blote*) *~len* a fat (*or:* bare) bottom

biljart [bɪljɑrt] *het* (*~s*) billiards; billiard table

biljarten [bɪljɑrtə(n)] *vb* play billiards

biljarter [bɪljɑrtər] *de* billiards player

biljartkeu [bɪljɑrtkø] *de* (*~s, ~en*) billiard cue

biljet [bɪljɛt] *het* (*~ten*) **1** ticket; bill, poster; **2** note, *(Am)* bill

biljoen [bɪljun] *het* (*~en*) **1** trillion *(10¹²);* **2** billion *(10⁹)*

billijk [bɪlək] *adj, adv* fair, reasonable, moderate

billijkheid [bɪləkhɛit] *de* fairness, reasonableness

binair [binɛːr] *adj* binary

¹binden [bɪndə(n)] *vb* **1** tie (up), knot, bind, fasten, strap; **2** tie (up); **3** bind: *door voorschriften gebonden zijn* be bound by regulations; **4** bind; **5** thicken

²binden [bɪndə(n)] *ref vb* commit oneself (to), bind (*or:* pledge) oneself (to)

bindend [bɪndənt] *adj* binding

binding [bɪndɪŋ] *de* (*~en*) bond, tie

bingo [bɪŋgo] *het* bingo

bink [bɪŋk] *de* (*~en*) hunk: *de* ~ *uithangen* show off, play the tough guy

¹binnen [bɪnə(n)] *adv* inside, in, indoors: *hij is* ~ he has got it made; *daar* ~ inside, in there; *naar* ~ *gaan* go in, go inside, enter; *het wil me niet te* ~ *schieten* I can't bring it to mind; *van* ~ (on the) inside; *'~!'* come in!

²binnen [bɪnə(n)] *prep* inside, within: *het ligt* ~ *mijn bereik (also fig)* it is within my reach

binnenband [bɪnə(n)bɑnt] *de* (*~en*) (inner) tube

binnenbrengen [bɪnə(n)brɛŋə(n)] *vb* bring in, take in, carry in

binnendoor [bɪnə(n)dor] *adv* || ~ *gaan* take the direct route

binnendringen [bɪnə(n)drɪŋə(n)] *vb* penetrate (into), enter, break in(to), force one's way in(to)

binnendruppelen [bɪnə(n)drʏpələ(n)] *vb (also fig)* trickle in(to)

binnengaan [bɪnə(n)ɣan] *vb* enter, go in(to), walk in(to)

binnenhalen [bɪnə(n)halə(n)] *vb* fetch in; bring in, land

binnenhaven [bɪnə(n)havə(n)] *de* (*~s*) inland harbour (*or:* port), inner harbour

binnenhouden [bɪnə(n)hɑudə(n)] *vb* keep in(doors)

binnenin [bɪnə(n)ɪn] *adv* inside

binnenkant [bɪnə(n)kɑnt] *de* (*~en*) inside, interior

binnenkomen [bɪnə(n)komə(n)] *vb* come in(to), walk in(to), enter, arrive: *zij mocht niet* ~ she was not allowed (to come) in

binnenkomst [bɪnə(n)kɔmst] *de* entry, entrance, arrival

binnenkort [bɪnə(n)kɔrt] *adv* soon, shortly, before (very) long

binnenkrijgen [bɪnə(n)krɛiɣə(n)] *vb* **1** get down, swallow; **2** get, obtain

binnenland [bɪnə(n)lɑnt] *het* (*~en*) **1** interior, inland; **2** home

binnenlands [bɪnə(n)lɑnts] *adj* home, internal, domestic

binnenlaten [bɪnə(n)latə(n)] *vb* let in(to), admit (to), show in(to), usher in(to)

binnenlopen [bɪnə(n)lopə(n)] *vb* go in(to), walk in(to): *de trein kwam het station ~ the train drew into the station*

binnenmuur [bɪnə(n)myr] *de (-muren)* interior wall, inside wall

binnenplaats [bɪnə(n)plats] *de (~en)* (inner) court(yard), yard

binnenpretje [bɪnə(n)prɛcə] *het (~s)* secret amusement

binnenscheepvaart [bɪnə(n)sχepfart] *de* inland navigation, inland shipping

binnenschipper [bɪnə(n)sχɪpər] *de (~s)* skipper of a barge

binnenshuis [bɪnənshœys] *adv* indoors, inside, within doors

binnensmonds [bɪnənsmɔnts] *adv* inarticulately, indistinctly

binnensport [bɪnə(n)spɔrt] *de (~en)* indoor sport

binnenstad [bɪnə(n)stɑt] *de (-steden)* town centre, city centre, inner city

binnenste [bɪnə(n)stə] *het* inside, in(ner)most part, inner part

binnenstebuiten [bɪnənstəbœytə(n)] *adv* inside out, wrong side out

binnenstromen [bɪnə(n)stromə(n)] *vb (also fig)* pour in(to), flow in(to), rush in(to), surge in(to)

binnenvaart [bɪnə(n)vart] *de* inland shipping

binnenvallen [bɪnə(n)vɑlə(n)] *vb* burst in(to), barge in(to), invade: *bij iem komen ~ descend on s.o.*

binnenvetter [bɪnə(n)vɛtər] *de (~s)* introvert

binnenwater [bɪnə(n)watər] *het (~en)* **1** inland waterway, canal, river; **2** polder water

binnenweg [bɪnə(n)wɛχ] *de (~en)* byroad, short cut

binnenzak [bɪnə(n)zɑk] *de (~ken)* inside pocket

binnenzee [bɪnə(n)ze] *de (~ën)* inland sea

bint [bɪnt] *het (~en)* beam, joist

biobak [bijobɑk] *de (~ken)* compost bin

biochemicus [bijoχemikʏs] *de (-chemici)* biochemist

biochemie [bijoχemi] *de* biochemistry

biograaf [bijoγraf] *de (biografen)* biographer

biografie [bijoγrafi] *de (~ën)* biography

biografisch [bijoγrafis] *adj* biographic(al)

bio-industrie [bijoɪndʏstri] *de (~ën)* factory farming, agribusiness

biologie [bijoloγi] *de* biology

biologisch [bijoloγis] *adj, adv* biological; organic

bioloog [bijoloχ] *de (biologen)* biologist

bioscoop [bijoskop] *de (bioscopen)* cinema

Birma [bɪrma] *het* Burma

Birmaans [bɪrmans] *adj* Burmese

bis [bɪs] *adv* (once) again, encore

biscuit [bɪskwi] *het, de (~s)* biscuit, *(Am)* cookie

bisdom [bɪzdɔm] *het (~men)* diocese, bishopric

biseksueel [bɪsɛksywel] *adj* bisexual

biskwietje [bɪskwicə] *het* biscuit, *(Am)* cookie

bisschop [bɪsχɔp] *de (~pen)* bishop

bissen [bɪsə(n)] *vb (Belg; educ)* repeat (the year)

bisser [bɪsər] *de (~s) (Belg; educ)* pupil who repeats a class

bistro [bistro] *de (~'s)* bistro

¹bit [bɪt] *het* bit

²bit [bɪt] *de* bit

bits [bɪts] *adj, adv* snappish, short(-tempered)

¹bitter [bɪtər] *adj* **1** bitter; **2** bitter, sour

²bitter [bɪtər] *de, het* (gin and) bitters

bitterheid [bɪtərhɛit] *de (-heden)* bitterness

bivak [bivɑk] *het (~ken)* bivouac: *zijn ~ opslaan (fig)* pitch one's tent

bivakkeren [bivɑkerə(n)] *vb* **1** bivouac; **2** lodge, stay

bizar [bizɑr] *adj, adv* bizarre

bizon [bizɔn] *de (~s)* bison

blaadje [blɑcə] *het (~s)* **1** leaf(let), sheet (of paper), piece (of paper), paper, tray; **2** *(bot)* leaflet; petal ‖ *bij iem in een goed ~ staan* be in s.o.'s good books

blaam [blam] *de* blame

blaar [blar] *de (blaren)* blister

blaas [blas] *de (blazen)* bladder, cyst

blaasinstrument [blasɪnstrymɛnt] *het (~en)* wind instrument

blaasorkest [blasɔrkɛst] *het (~en)* wind orchestra, brass band

blaaspijpje [blaspɛipjə] *de (~s)* breathalyser

blabla [blabla] *de* **1** blah(-blah); **2** fuss

blad [blɑt] *het (~en, ~eren)* **1** *(bot)* leaf, petal; **2** tray; **3** sheet, leaf, page; **4** (news)paper; magazine; **5** sheet, top, blade

bladderen [blɑdərə(n)] *vb* blister, bubble, flake, peel

bladeraar [blɑdərar] *de (~s)* browser

bladerdeeg [blɑdərdeχ] *het* puff pastry *(or:* paste)

bladeren [blɑdərə(n)] *vb* thumb, leaf

bladgroen [blɑtχrun] *het* chlorophyll

bladgroente [blɑtχruntə] *de (~n, ~s)* green vegetables

bladluis [blɑtlœys] *de (-luizen)* greenfly, blackfly, aphis

bladmuziek [blɑtmyzik] *de* sheet music

bladnerf [blɑtnɛrf] *de (-nerven)* vein (of a leaf)

bladrand [blɑtrɑnt] *de (~en)* margin of a leaf

bladwijzer [blɑtwɛizər] *de (~s)* bookmark(er)

bladzijde [blɑtsɛidə] *de (~n)* page: *ik sloeg het boek open op ~ 58* I opened the book at page 58

blaffen [blɑfə(n)] *vb* bark

blaken [blakə(n)] *vb* burn (with), glow (with)

blamage [blamaʒə] *de (~s)* disgrace

blancheren [blɑ̃ʃerə(n)] *vb* blanch

blanco [blɑnko] *adj, adv* blank

blank [blɑŋk] *adj* **1** white: *~ hout* natural wood; **2** flooded: *de kelder staat ~* the cellar is flooded

blanke [blɑŋkə] *de (~n)* white (man, woman): *de ~n* the whites

blaten [blatə(n)] *vb* bleat

blauw [blɑu] *adj* **1** blue: *in het ~ gekleed* dressed in blue; **2** black, dark: *een ~e plek* a bruise; *iem bont en ~ slaan* beat s.o. black and blue

blauwbaard [blɑubart] *de (~en)* bluebeard

blauwdruk [blɑudrʏk] *de (~ken)* blueprint

blauwhelm [blɑuhɛlm] *de (~en)* blue helmet

¹**blazen** [blɑzə(n)] *vb* **1** blow: *op de trompet* (or: *de fluit, het fluitje, de hoorn) ~* sound the trumpet, play the flute, blow the whistle, play the horn; **2** breathe into a breathalyser: *katten ~ als ze kwaad zijn* cats hiss when they are angry

²**blazen** [blɑzə(n)] *vb* blow ‖ *het is oppassen geblazen* we (or: you) need to watch out

blazer [blɑzər] *de (~s)* player of a wind instrument

bleek [blek] *adj* **1** pale, wan: *~ zien* look pale (or: wan); **2** pale, white

bleekheid [blekhɛit] *de* paleness, pallor

bleekmiddel [blekmɪdəl] *het (~en)* bleach, bleaching agent

bleekselderij [bleksɛldərɛi] *de* celery

bleekwater [blekwatər] *het* bleach, bleaching agent

bleken [blekə(n)] *vb* bleach

blèren [blɛːrə(n)] *vb* **1** squall, howl; **2** bleat

bles [blɛs] *de (~sen)* blaze, star

blesseren [blɛsɛrə(n)] *vb* injure, hurt, wound

blessure [blɛsyrə] *de (~s)* injury

blessuretijd [blɛsyrətɛit] *de* injury time

bleu [blø] *adj* timid

blij [blɛi] *adj* **1** glad, happy, pleased, cheerful, merry: *daar ben ik ~ om* I'm pleased about it; *~ zijn voor iem* be glad for s.o.'s sake; **2** happy, joyful, joyous

blijdschap [blɛitsχap] *de* joy, gladness, cheer(fulness), happiness

blijf [blɛif] *(Belg)* ‖ *geen ~ met iets weten* be at a loss, not know what to do about sth

blijheid [blɛihɛit] *de* gladness, joy, happiness

blijk [blɛik] *het (~en)* mark, token: *~ geven van belangstelling* show one's interest

¹**blijkbaar** [blɛigbar] *adj* evident, obvious, clear

²**blijkbaar** [blɛigbar] *adv* apparently, evidently

blijken [blɛikə(n)] *vb* prove, turn out: *doen ~ van* show, express; *hij liet er niets van ~* he gave no sign of it; *dat moet nog ~* that remains to be seen

blijven [blɛivə(n)] *vb* **1** remain: *het blijft altijd gevaarlijk* it will always be dangerous; *rustig ~* keep quiet; *deze appel blijft lang goed* this apple keeps well; *jong ~* stay young; **2** remain (doing), stay (on) (doing), continue (doing), keep (doing): *~ logeren* stay the night (in the house); *blijft u even aan de lijn?* hold the line, please; *blijf bij de reling vandaan* keep clear of the railings; *je moet op het voetpad ~* you have to keep to the footpath; **3** be, keep: *~ staan: a)* stand still, stop; *b)* remain standing; *waar zijn we gebleven?* where were we?; *waar is mijn portemonnee gebleven?* where has my purse got to?; **4** perish, be left (or: remain) behind: *ergens in ~ (van het lachen): a)* choke; *b) (fig)* die (laughing)

blijvend [blɛivənt] *adj* lasting; enduring; permanent, durable

¹**blik** [blɪk] *de* **1** look, glance; **2** look (in one's eyes), expression; **3** view, outlook ‖ *een geoefende (or: scherpe) ~* a trained (or: sharp) eye

²**blik** [blɪk] *het* **1** tin(plate): *in ~* tinned; **2** tin, *(Am)* can; **3** dustpan

blikgroente [blɪkχruntə] *de (~n, ~s)* tinned vegetables

¹**blikken** [blɪkə(n)] *adj* tin: *~ doosjes* tin boxes (or: canisters)

²**blikken** [blɪkə(n)] *vb* ‖ *zonder ~ of blozen* without batting an eyelid

blikopener [blɪkopənər] *de (~s)* tin-opener

blikschade [blɪksχadə] *de* bodywork damage

bliksem [blɪksəm] *de (~s)* lightning: *als door de ~ getroffen* thunderstruck; *de ~ slaat in* lightning strikes; *er als de gesmeerde ~ vandoor gaan* take off like greased lightning

bliksemafleider [blɪksəmɑflɛidər] *de (~s)* lightning conductor

bliksembezoek [blɪksəmbəzuk] *het (~en)* flying visit, lightning visit

bliksemen [blɪksəmə(n)] *vb* flash, blaze

bliksemflits [blɪksəmflɪts] *de (~en)* (flash of) lightning

blikseminslag [blɪksəmɪnslɑχ] *de (~en)* stroke (or: bolt) of lightning, thunderbolt

bliksemsnel [blɪksəmsnɛl] *adj, adv* lightning; at (or: with) lightning speed, quick as lightning, like greased lightning

bliksemstart [blɪksəmstart] *de* lightning start

blikvanger [blɪkfɑŋər] *de (~s)* eye-catcher

blikvoer [blɪkfur] *het* tinned food, *(Am)* canned food

¹**blind** [blɪnt] *adj* blind: *zich ~ staren (op)* concentrate too much on sth; *~ typen* touch-type; *zij is aan één oog ~* she is blind in one eye

²**blind** [blɪnt] *de (~en)* (window) shutter, blind

blinddoek [blɪnduk] *de (~en)* blindfold

blinddoeken [blɪndukə(n)] *vb* blindfold

blinde [blɪndə] *de (~n)* blind person, blind man, blind woman: *de ~n* the blind

blindedarm [blɪndədɑrm] *de (~en)* appendix

blindelings [blɪndəlɪŋs] *adv* blindly: *~ volgen* follow blindly

blindengeleidehond [blɪndə(n)χəlɛidəhɔnt] *de (~en)* guide dog (for the blind)

blindheid [blɪnthɛit] *de* blindness

blinken [blɪŋkə(n)] *vb* shine, glisten, glitter: *alles blinkt er* everything is spotless (or: spick and span)

blits [blɪts] *adj* trendy, hip

blocnote [blɔknot] *de (~s)* (writing) pad

bloed [blut] *het* blood: *mijn eigen vlees en ~* my own flesh and blood; *~ vergieten* shed (or: spill) blood; *geen ~ kunnen zien* not be able to stand the sight of blood

bloedarmoede [blutɑrmudə] *de* anaemia

bloedbad [bludbɑt] *het (~en)* bloodbath, massacre: *een ~ aanrichten onder de inwoners* massacre

bloedbank [blu̯dbɑŋk] *de (~en)* blood bank
bloedcel [blu̯tsɛl] *de (~len)* blood cell (*or:* corpuscle)
bloeddorstig [blu̯dɔrstəχ] *adj, adv* bloodthirsty
bloeddruk [blu̯dryk] *de* blood pressure: *de ~ meten* take s.o.'s blood pressure
bloeden [blu̯də(n)] *vb* bleed
bloederig [blu̯dərəχ] *adj* bloody, gory
bloederziekte [blu̯dərziktə] *de* haemophilia
bloedgroep [blu̯tχrup] *de (~en)* blood group (*or:* type)
bloedheet [bluthe̯t] *adj* sweltering (hot), boiling (hot)
bloedhond [blu̯thɔnt] *de (~en)* bloodhound
bloedig [blu̯dəχ] *adj* bloody, gory
bloeding [blu̯dɪŋ] *de (~en)* bleeding, haemorrhage
bloedlichaampje [blu̯tlɪχampjə] *het (~s)* blood corpuscle (*or:* cell)
bloedneus [blu̯tnøs] *de (-neuzen)* bloody nose
bloedonderzoek [blu̯tɔndərzuk] *het (~en)* blood test(s)
bloedproef [blu̯tpruf] *de (-proeven)* blood test
bloedrood [blu̯trot] *adj, adv* blood-red
bloedsomloop [blu̯tsɔmlop] *de* (blood) circulation
bloedstollend [blu̯tstɔlənt] *adj* blood-curdling
bloedtransfusie [blu̯transfyzi] *de (~s)* (blood) transfusion
bloeduitstorting [blu̯tœytstɔrtɪŋ] *de (~en)* extravasation (of blood)
bloedvat [blu̯tfɑt] *het (~en)* blood vessel
bloedvergieten [blu̯tfərɣitə(n)] *vb* bloodshed: *een revolutie zonder ~* a bloodless revolution
bloedvergiftiging [blu̯tfərɣɪftəɣɪŋ] *de (~en)* blood poisoning
bloedverlies [blu̯tfərlis] *het* loss of blood
bloedverwant [blu̯tfərwɑnt] *de (~en)* (blood) relation, relative, kinsman, kinswoman: *naaste ~en* close relatives, next of kin
bloedworst [blu̯twɔrst] *de (~en)* black pudding
bloedwraak [blu̯tvrak] *de* blood feud, vendetta
bloedzuiger [blu̯tsœyɣər] *de (~s)* leech, bloodsucker
bloei [bluj] *de* bloom, flower(ing), blossoming: *iem in de ~ van zijn leven* s.o. in the prime of (his) life
bloeien [blujə(n)] *vb* 1 bloom, flower, blossom; 2 (*fig*) prosper, flourish
bloeiperiode [blujperijodə] *de (~n, ~s)* 1 (*bot*) flowering time (*or:* season); 2 (*fig*) prime
bloem [blum] *de (~en)* 1 flower, bloom, blossom; 2 flour
bloembak [blumbɑk] *de (~ken)* planter, flower box, window box
bloembed [blumbɛt] *het (~den)* flowerbed
bloemblad [blumblɑt] *het (~en)* petal
bloembol [blumbɔl] *de (-len)* bulb
bloemenhandelaar [blumə(n)hɑndəlar] *de (~s, -handelaren)* florist

bloemenstalletje [blumə(n)stɑlərə] *het (~s)* flower stand, flower stall
bloemenvaas [blumə(n)vas] *de (-vazen)* (flower) vase
bloemenwinkel [blumə(n)wɪŋkəl] *de (~s)* florist's (shop), flower shop
bloemetje [blumərə] *het (~s)* 1 (little) flower; 2 flowers, nosegay: *iem in de ~s zetten* (*fig*) fête s.o.; *de ~s buiten zetten* paint the town red
bloemist [blumɪst] *de (~en)* florist
bloemkool [blumkol] *de (-kolen)* cauliflower
bloemkroon [blumkron] *de (-kronen)* corolla
bloemkwekerij [blumkwekərɛi] *de (~en)* 1 nursery, florist's (business); 2 floriculture, flower-growing industry
bloemlezing [blumlezɪŋ] *de (~en)* anthology
bloempot [blumpɔt] *de (~ten)* flowerpot
bloemschikken [blumsχɪkə(n)] *het* (art of) flower arrangement
bloemstuk [blumstyk] *het (~ken)* flower arrangement
bloemsuiker [blumsœykər] *de (Belg)* icing sugar
bloes [blus] *de (bloezen)* blouse; shirt
bloesem [blusəm] *de (~s)* blossom, bloom, flower
blok [blɔk] *het (~ken)* 1 block, chunk, log: *slapen als een ~* sleep like a log; *een ~je omlopen* walk around the block; *een doos met ~ken* a box of building blocks; 2 block, check; 3 (*pol*) bloc(k)
blokfluit [blɔkflœyt] *de (~en)* recorder
blokhut [blɔkhyt] *de (~ten)* log cabin
blokje [blɔkjə] *het (~s)* cube, square
blokkade [blɔkadə] *de (~s)* blockade
blokken [blɔkə(n)] *vb* cram, swot: *~ voor een tentamen* cram for an examination
blokkendoos [blɔkə(n)dos] *de (-dozen)* box of building blocks
blokkeren [blɔkerə(n)] *vb* 1 blockade, block; 2 freeze: *een cheque ~* stop a cheque; 3 block, jam, lock; 4 (*sport*) block, obstruct
blokletter [blɔklɛtər] *de (~s)* block letter, printing
blokletteren [blɔklɛtərə(n)] *vb (Belg)* headline, splash (news on the front page)
blokuur [blɔkyr] *het (-uren)* (roughly) double period (*or:* lesson)
blond [blɔnt] *adj* 1 blond, fair; 2 golden
blondine [blɔndinə] *de (~s)* blonde
¹bloot [blot] *het* nudity
²bloot [blot] *adj* bare, naked, nude: *op blote voeten lopen* go barefoot(ed); *uit het blote hoofd spreken* speak off the cuff, speak extempore; *met het blote oog iets waarnemen* observe sth with the naked eye; *onder de blote hemel* in the open (air); *een jurk met blote rug* a barebacked dress
blootgeven [blotχevə(n)] *ref vb* 1 expose oneself; 2 give oneself away: *zich niet ~* not commit oneself, be non-committal
blootje [blorə] *het* || *in zijn ~* in the nude
blootleggen [blotlɛɣə(n)] *vb* lay open (*or:* bare), expose; (*fig also*) reveal

blootshoofds [blotshofts] *adv* bareheaded

blootstaan [blotstan] *vb* be exposed (to), be subject (to), be open (to)

blootstellen [blotstɛlə(n)] *vb* expose (to): *zich aan gevaar* ~ expose oneself to danger

blos [blɔs] *de (~sen)* 1 bloom: *een gezonde* ~ a rosy complexion; 2 flush; blush

blouse [bluzə] *de (~s)* blouse

blozen [blozə(n)] *vb* 1 bloom (with); 2 flush (with); blush (with)

blubber [blʏbər] *de* mud

bluf [blʏf] *de* 1 bluff(ing); 2 boast(ing), brag(ging), big talk

bluffen [blʏfə(n)] *vb* bluff; boast, brag, talk big

bluffer [blʏfər] *de (~s)* bluffer, boaster, braggart

blufpoker [blʏfpokər] *het* || *hij speelde een partijtje* ~ he tried to brazen it out (*or:* bluff his way out)

blunder [blʏndər] *de (~s)* blunder

blunderen [blʏndərə(n)] *vb* blunder, make a blunder

blusapparaat [blʏsɑparat] *het (-apparaten)* fire extinguisher

blussen [blʏsə(n)] *vb* extinguish (*also fig*), put out

blut [blʏt] *adj* broke, skint: *volkomen* ~ stony-broke, flat broke

blz. *bladzijde* p.; pp. *(pl)*

b.o. *het (Belg) bijzonder onderwijs* special needs education

boa [bowa] *de (~'s)* boa

board [bɔːrd] *het (~s)* hardboard, (fibre)board

bobbel [bɔbəl] *de (~s)* bump, lump

bobslee [bɔpsle] *de (~ën)* bob(sleigh)

bobsleeën [bɔpslejən] *vb* bobsleigh

bochel [bɔχəl] *de (~s)* hump; hunchback

bocht [bɔχt] *de* bend, curve: *zich in allerlei ~en wringen* try to wriggle one's way out of sth; *uit de ~ vliegen* run off the road

bochtig [bɔχtəχ] *adj* winding

bod [bɔt] *het* offer, bid: *niet aan* ~ *komen* not get a chance

bode [bodə] *de (~n, ~s)* messenger, postman

bodem [bodəm] *de (~s)* 1 bottom, base: *een dubbele* ~ a hidden meaning; 2 ground, soil; 3 territory, soil: *producten van eigen* ~ home-grown products; *op de ~ van de zee* at the bottom of the sea

bodemverontreiniging [bodəmvərɔntrɛinəyɪŋ] *de (~en)* soil pollution

Boedapest [budapɛst] *het* Budapest

Boeddha [buda] *de* Buddha

boeddhisme [budɪsmə] *het* Buddhism

boeddhist [budɪst] *de (~en)* Buddhist

boeddhistisch [budɪstis] *adj* Buddhist

boedel [budəl] *de (~s)* property, household effects

boef [buf] *de (boeven)* scoundrel, rascal

boeg [buχ] *de (~en)* bow(s), prow: *het over een andere* ~ *gooien* change (one's) tack, change the subject

boei [buj] *de (~en)* 1 buoy: *een kop* (or: *een kleur*) *als een* ~ (a face) as red as a beetroot; 2 chain, hand-cuff

boeien [bujə(n)] *vb* 1 chain, (hand)cuff; 2 fascinate, captivate: *het stuk kon ons niet (blijven)* ~ the play failed to hold our attention

boeiend [bujənt] *adj, adv* fascinating, gripping, captivating

boek [buk] *het (~en)* book: *altijd met zijn neus in de ~en zitten* always have one's nose in a book, always be at one's books; *een* ~ *over* a book on

Boekarest [bukarɛst] *het* Bucharest

boekbespreking [bugbəsprekɪŋ] *de (~en)* book review

boekbinden [bugbɪndə(n)] *het* (book)binding

boekbinder [bugbɪndər] *de (~s)* (book)binder

boekbinderij [bugbɪndərɛi] *de (~en)* bindery, (book)binder's

boekdeel [bugdel] *het (-delen)* volume

boekdrukkerij [bugdrʏkərɛi] *de (~en)* 1 printing house (*or:* office), print shop; 2 printer's

boekdrukkunst [bugdrʏkʏnst] *de* (art of) printing, typography

boeken [bukə(n)] *vb* book, post, enter (up)

boekenbeurs [bukə(n)børs] *de (-beurzen)* book fair

boekenbon [bukə(n)bɔn] *de (~nen)* book token

boekenfonds [bukə(n)fɔn(t)s] *het (~en)* (educational) book fund

boekenkast [bukə(n)kɑst] *de (~en)* bookcase

boekenlegger [bukə(n)lɛɣər] *de (~s)* bookmark(er)

boekenlijst [bukə(n)lɛist] *de (~en)* (required) reading list, booklist

boekenrek [bukə(n)rɛk] *het (~ken)* bookshelves

boekensteun [bukə(n)støn] *de (~en)* bookend

boekentaal [bukə(n)tal] *de* 1 literary language; 2 bookish language

boekentas [bukə(n)tɑs] *de (~sen)* briefcase, school bag, satchel

boekenweek [bukə(n)wek] *de (-weken)* book week

boekenwurm [bukə(n)wʏrm] *de (~en)* bookworm

boeket [bukɛt] *het, de (~ten)* bouquet (*also of wine*): *een ~je* a posy, a nosegay

boekhandel [bukhɑndəl] *de (~s)* bookshop

boekhandelaar [bukhɑndəlar] *de (~s, -handelaren)* bookseller

¹boekhouden [bukhɑudə(n)] *het* bookkeeping, accounting

²boekhouden [bukhɑudə(n)] *vb* keep the books, do the accounting, do (*or:* keep) the accounts

boekhouder [bukhɑudər] *de (~s)* accountant, bookkeeper

boekhouding [bukhɑudɪŋ] *de (~en)* 1 accounting, bookkeeping; 2 accounting department (*or:* section), accounts department

boekhoudkundig [bukhɑutkʏndəχ] *adj, adv* accounting, bookkeeping

boeking [bukɪŋ] *de (~en)* 1 booking, reservation; 2 (*socc*) booking, caution; 3 entry

boekjaar [bukjar] *het (-jaren)* fiscal year, financial

year

boekje [bukjə] *het (~s)* (small, little) book, booklet || *buiten zijn ~ gaan* exceed one's authority

boekwaarde [bukwardə] *de* book value, balance sheet value

boekweit [bukwɛit] *de* buckwheat

boekwinkel [bukwɪŋkəl] *de (~s)* bookshop

boel [bul] *de* 1 things, matters, mess: *hij kan zijn ~tje wel pakken* he can (*or:* might) as well pack it in (now); *de ~ aan kant maken* straighten (*or:* tidy) things up; 2 affair, business, matter, situation: *er een dolle ~ van maken* make quite a party of it; *een mooie ~* a fine mess; *het is er een saaie (dooie) ~* it's a dead-and-alive place; 3 a lot, heaps, lots, loads

boeman [bumɑn] *de (~nen)* bogeyman

boemel [buməl] *de (~s)* || *aan de ~ gaan* go (out) on the razzle

boemeltrein [buməltrɛin] *de (~en)* slow train, stopping train

boemerang [bumərɑŋ] *de (~s)* boomerang

boender [bundər] *de (~s)* scrubbing brush; *(Am)* scrub-brush

boenen [bunə(n)] *vb* 1 polish; 2 scrub

boenwas [bunwɑs] *het, de* beeswax, wax polish

boer [bur] *de (~en)* 1 farmer, peasant, rancher; 2 boor, (country) bumpkin; 3 burp, belch; 4 jack

boerderij [burdərɛi] *de (~en)* farm

boeren [burə(n)] *vb* 1 farm, run a farm; 2 burp, belch || *hij heeft goed (or: slecht) geboerd dit jaar* he has done well (*or:* badly) this year

boerenknecht [burə(n)knɛχt] *de (~en)* (farm)hand

boerenkool [burə(n)kol] *de (-kolen)* kale

boerenverstand [burə(n)vərstɑnt] *het* horse sense

boerenwagen [burə(n)waχə(n)] *de (~s)* cart

boerenzwaluw [burə(n)zwalyw] *de (~en)* swallow

boerin [burɪn] *de (~nen)* 1 farmer's wife; 2 woman farmer

boers [burs] *adj, adv* rustic, rural, peasant: *een ~ accent* a rural accent

boete [butə] *de (~s)* 1 fine: *een ~ krijgen van €100* be fined 100 euros; *iem een ~ opleggen* fine s.o.; 2 (*rel*) penance; 3 penalty

boeten [butə(n)] *vb* pay ((the penalty, price) for), (*rel*) atone (for), (*rel*) do penance (for): *zwaar voor iets ~* pay a heavy penalty for sth

boetiek [butik] *de (~s)* boutique

boetseren [butserə(n)] *vb* model

boezem [buzəm] *de (~s)* 1 bosom, breast: *een zware (flinke) ~ hebben* be full-bosomed; 2 bosom, heart

boezemvriend [buzəmvrint] *de (~en)* bosom friend

bof [bɔf] *de (~fen)* 1 (good) luck: *wat een ~, dat ik hem nog thuis tref* I'm lucky (*or:* what luck) to find him still at home; 2 mumps: *de ~ hebben* have mumps

boffen [bɔfə(n)] *vb* be lucky

bofkont [bɔfkɔnt] *de (~en)* lucky dog

Bohemen [bohemə(n)] *het* Bohemia

boiler [bɔjlər] *de (~s)* water heater, boiler

bok [bɔk] *de (-ken)* 1 (male) goat, billy goat; buck, stag; 2 buck

bokaal [bokal] *de (bokalen)* 1 goblet; 2 beaker

bokkensprong [bɔkə(n)sprɔŋ] *de (~en)* caper || *(rare) ~en maken* behave unpredictably (*or:* in a ridiculous way)

bokking [bɔkɪŋ] *de (~en)* smoked herring

boksbal [bɔksbɑl] *de (~len)* punchball

boksbeugel [bɔksbøγəl] *de (~s)* knuckleduster

boksen [bɔksə(n)] *vb* box

bokser [bɔksər] *de (~s)* boxer

bokshandschoen [bɔkshɑntsχun] *de (~en)* boxing glove

bokspringen [bɔksprɪŋə(n)] *vb* 1 (play) leapfrog; 2 (squat) vaulting, vaulting exercise

bokswedstrijd [bɔkswɛtstrɛit] *de (~en)* boxing match, (prize)fight

¹bol [bɔl] *de (~len)* 1 ball, bulb; 2 (*maths*) sphere

²bol [bɔl] *adj, adv* round: *een ~le lens* a convex lens

boleet [bolet] *de (boleten)* boletus

bolero [bolero] *de* bolero

bolhoed [bɔlhut] *de (~en)* bowler (hat)

bolide [bolidə] *de* racing car

Bolivia [bolivija] *het* Bolivia

Boliviaan [bolivijan] *de (Bolivianen)* Bolivian

bolknak [bɔlknɑk] *de (~ken)* big cigar, fat cigar, Havana

bolleboos [bɔləbos] *de (-bozen)* high-flyer

bollenkweker [bɔlə(n)kwekər] *de (~s)* bulb grower

bollenteelt [bɔlə(n)telt] *de* bulb-growing (industry)

bollentijd [bɔlə(n)tɛit] *de* bulb season

bollenveld [bɔlə(n)vɛlt] *het (~en)* bulb field

bolletje [bɔləcə] *het (~s)* 1 (little) ball, globule; 2 (soft) roll

bolster [bɔlstər] *de (~s)* shell: *ruwe ~, blanke pit* a rough diamond

bolwassing [bɔlwɑsɪŋ] *de (~en)* (*Belg*) dressing down

bolwerk [bɔlwɛrk] *het (~en)* bulwark, (*fig also*) stronghold, bastion

bolwerken [bɔlwɛrkə(n)] *vb* manage, pull off; stick it out, hold one's own: *het (kunnen) ~* manage (it), pull it off, stick it out

bom [bɔm] *de (~men)* bomb: *het bericht sloeg in als een ~* the news came like a bombshell

bomaanslag [bɔmanslɑχ] *de (~en)* bomb attack, bombing, bomb outrage

bomalarm [bɔmalɑrm] *het* bomb alert, air-raid warning, bomb scare

bombardement [bɔmbɑrdəmɛnt] *het (~en)* bombardment

bombarderen [bɔmbɑrderə(n)] *vb* 1 bomb; 2 bombard, shell; 3 (*fig*) bombard, shower

bombrief [bɔmbrif] *de (bombrieven)* letter bomb, mail bomb

bommelding [bɔmɛldɪŋ] *de (~en)* bomb alert

bommenwerper [bɔmə(n)wɛrpər] *de (~s)* bomber

bommetje [bɔməcə] *het (~s)* cannonball

bomvol [bɔmvɔl] *adj* chock-full, cram-full, packed

bon [bɔn] *de (~nen)* **1** bill, receipt, cash-register slip; **2** voucher, coupon, token, credit slip; **3** ticket

bonbon [bɔmbɔn] *de (~s)* chocolate, bonbon

bond [bɔnt] *de (~en)* **1** (con)federation, confederacy, alliance, union; **2** union

bondgenoot [bɔntχənot] *de (-genoten)* ally, confederate

bondgenootschap [bɔntχənotsχap] *het (~pen)* alliance, confederacy, (con)federation

bondig [bɔndəχ] *adj, adv* concise, terse, pithy

bondscoach [bɔntskotʃ] *de (~es)* national coach

bondselftal [bɔn(t)sɛlftal] *het (~len)* national team

bondskanselier [bɔntskansəlir] *de (~s)* Federal Chancellor

Bondsrepubliek [bɔntsrepyblik] *de* Federal Republic (of Germany)

bonenstaak [bonə(n)stak] *de (-staken)* beanpole

bonje [bɔɲə] *de* rumpus, row

bonk [bɔŋk] *de (~en)* lump: *één ~ zenuwen* a bundle of nerves

bonken [bɔŋkə(n)] *vb* **1** crash (against, into), bump (against, into); **2** bang, pound

bonnefooi [bɔnəfoj] *de || op de ~ ergens heen gaan* go somewhere on the off chance

bons [bɔns] *de (bonzen)* **1** thud, thump; **2** (big) boss || *iem de ~ geven* give s.o. the push

¹bont [bɔnt] *het (~en)* fur: *met ~ gevoerd* fur-lined

²bont [bɔnt] *adj, adv* **1** multicoloured, variegated: *~e kleuren* bright colours; *iem ~ en blauw slaan* beat s.o. black and blue; **2** colourful: *een ~ gezelschap: a)* a colourful group of people; *b) (depr)* a motley crew; *het te ~ maken* go too far

bontgoed [bɔntχut] *het* (cotton) prints

bonthandel [bɔnthandəl] *de* fur trade

bonthandelaar [bɔnthandəlar] *de (~s, -handelaren)* furrier

bontjas [bɔntjas] *de (~sen)* fur coat

bontmuts [bɔntmyts] *de (~en)* fur cap, fur hat

bonus [bonys] *de (~sen)* bonus, premium

bonzen [bɔnzə(n)] *vb* **1** bang, hammer; **2** bump (against, into), crash (against, into): *tegen iem aan ~* bump into s.o., crash against (*or:* into) s.o.; **3** pound

boodschap [botsχap] *de (~pen)* **1** purchase *(oft pl): die kun je wel om een ~ sturen (fig)* you can leave things to him (*or:* her); **2** message: *een ~ voor iem achterlaten* leave a message for s.o.; *een ~ krijgen* get a message; **3** errand, mission

boodschappendienst [botsχapə(n)dinst] *de (~en)* messenger service

boodschappenlijstje [botsχapə(n)lɛiʃə] *het (~s)* shopping list

boodschappenmand [botsχapəmant] *de (~en)* shopping basket

boodschappentas [botsχapə(n)tas] *de (~sen)* shopping bag

boodschapper [botsχapər] *de (~s)* messenger, courier

boog [boχ] *de (bogen)* **1** bow: *met pijl en ~* with bow and arrow; **2** arch, span; **3** arc, curve: *met een (grote) ~ om iets heenlopen* go out of one's way to avoid sth

boogbal [boχbal] *de (~len)* lob

boogscheut [boχsχøt] *de (~en) (Belg)* stone's throw: *op een ~* a stone's throw from

boogschieten [boχsχitə(n)] *vb* archery

boogschutter [boχsχytər] *de (~s)* archer

Boogschutter [boχsχytər] *de (~s)* Sagittarius

boom [bom] *de (bomen)* **1** tree: *ze zien door de bomen het bos niet meer* they can't see the wood for the trees; **2** bar, barrier, gate

boomgaard [bomγart] *de (~en)* orchard

boomkwekerij [bomkwekərɛi] *de (~en)* tree nursery

boomschors [bomsχɔrs] *de (~en)* (tree) bark

boomstam [bomstam] *de (~men)* (tree) trunk

boomstronk [bomstrɔŋk] *de (~en)* tree stump

boon [bon] *de (bonen)* bean: *witte bonen* haricot beans

boontje [boncə] *het (~s) || ~ komt om zijn loontje* serves him right

boor [bor] *de (boren)* **1** brace; **2** bit; **3** drill

boord [bort] *het, de (~en)* **1** band, trim; **2** collar; **3** board: *van ~ gaan* disembark; *(Belg) iets goed (or: slecht) aan ~ leggen* set about it in the right (*or:* wrong) way

boordevol [bordəvɔl] *adj* full (*or:* filled) to overflowing: *~ nieuwe ideeën* bursting with new ideas; *~ mensen* packed (*or:* crammed) with people

booreiland [borɛilant] *het (~en)* drilling rig (*or:* platform); oilrig

boormachine [bormaʃinə] *de (~s)* (electric) drill

boortoren [bortorə(n)] *de (~s)* derrick, drilling rig

boos [bos] *adj, adv* **1** angry, cross, hostile: *~ kijken (naar iem)* scowl (at s.o.); *~ worden op iem* get angry at s.o.; **2** evil, bad, malicious, wicked, vicious: *het was geen boze opzet* no harm was intended; *de (grote) boze wolf* the big bad wolf; **3** evil, foul, vile: *de boze geesten* evil spirits

boosaardig [bosardəχ] *adj, adv* **1** malignant; **2** malicious, vicious

boosdoener [bozdunər] *de (~s)* wrongdoer

boosheid [boshɛit] *de (-heden)* anger, fury

boot [bot] *de (boten)* boat, vessel, *(large)* steamer, *(large)* ship, ferry: *de ~ missen (also fig)* miss the boat

bootreis [botrɛis] *de (-reizen)* voyage, cruise

bootsman [botsman] *de (bootslui, bootslieden)* boatswain

boottocht [botɔχt] *de (~en)* boat trip (*or:* excursion)

bootwerker [botwɛrkər] *de (~s)* docker, dockhand

bord [bɔrt] *het (~en)* **1** plate: *alle probleemgevallen komen op zijn ~je terecht* he ends up with all the difficult cases on his plate; *van een ~ eten* eat off a plate; **2** sign, notice: *de hele route is met ~en aangegeven* it is signposted all the way; **3** board; (black)board; notice board: *een ~ voor zijn kop hebben* be thick-skinned

bordeaux [bɔrdo̱] *de (~s)* bordeaux, claret

bordeel [bɔrde̱l] *het (bordelen)* brothel, whorehouse

bordenwarmer [bɔrdə(n)wɑrmər] *de (~s)* plate warmer

bordenwasser [bɔrdə(n)wɑsər] *de (~s)* dishwasher

border [bɔːrdər] *de (~s)* border

bordes [bɔrdɛs] *het (~sen) (roughly)* steps

bordkrijt [bɔrtkrɛit] *het* chalk

borduren [bɔrdyrə(n)] *vb* embroider

borduurnaald [bɔrdyrnalt] *de (~en)* embroidery needle

borduurwerk [bɔrdyrwɛrk] *het (~en)* embroidery

boren [bo̱rə(n)] *vb* bore, drill

borg [bɔrχ] *de (~en)* **1** surety, bail: *zich ~ stellen voor een gevangene* stand bail for a prisoner; **2** security, deposit

borgsom [bɔrχsɔm] *de (~men)* deposit; security (money)

borgtocht [bɔrχtɔχt] *de (~en)* bail, recognizance

boring [bo̱rɪŋ] *de (~en)* boring, drilling

borrel [bɔrəl] *de (~s)* drink || *iem voor een ~ uitnodigen* ask s.o. round (*or*: invite s.o.) for a drink

borrelen [bɔrələ(n)] *vb* **1** bubble, gurgle; **2** have a drink

borrelhapje [bɔrəlhɑpjə] *het (~s)* snack, appetizer

borst [bɔrst] *de* **1** chest: *uit volle ~ zingen* sing lustily; **2** breast: *een kind de ~ geven* breastfeed a child

borstcrawl [bɔrstkrɔːl] *de (front)* crawl

borstel [bɔrstəl] *de (~s)* brush || *(Belg) ergens met de grove ~ door gaan* tackle sth in a rough-and-ready way

borstelen [bɔrstələ(n)] *vb* brush

borstelig [bɔrstələχ] *adj* bristly, bushy

borstkanker [bɔrstkɑŋkər] *de* breast cancer

borstkas [bɔrstkɑs] *de (~sen)* chest

borstslag [bɔr(st)slɑχ] *de (~en)* breaststroke; (front) crawl

borstvin [bɔrs(t)fɪn] *de (~nen)* pectoral fin

borstvoeding [bɔrstfudɪŋ] *de (~en)* breastfeeding

borstwijdte [bɔrstwɛitə] *de (~s)* (width of the) chest, bust (measurement)

borstzak [bɔrstsɑk] *de (~ken)* breast pocket

¹**bos** [bɔs] *de* bundle, bunch: *een flinke ~ haar* a fine head of hair

²**bos** [bɔs] *het* wood(s); forest

bosbeheer [bɔzbəher] *het* forestry

bosbes [bɔzbɛs] *de (~sen)* bilberry, *(Am)* blueberry

bosbouwschool [bɔzbɑusχol] *de (-scholen)* school of forestry

bosbrand [bɔzbrɑnt] *de (~en)* forest fire

bosje [bɔʃə] *het (~s)* **1** bundle, tuft, wisp; **2** grove, coppice; **3** bush, shrub

Bosjesman [bɔʃəsmɑn] *de (~nen)* Bushman

bosklas [bɔsklɑs] *de (~sen) (Belg)* nature class (in the woods)

bosneger [bɔsneɣər] *de (~s)* maroon

Bosnië-Hercegovina [bɔsnijəhɛrtʃegovina] *het* Bosnia-Herzegovina

Bosnisch [bɔsnis] *adj* Bosnian

bospad [bɔspɑt] *het (~en)* woodland path, forest path (*or*: trail)

Bosporus *de* Bosp(h)orus

bosvrucht [bɔsfrʏχt] *de* forest fruit, fruit of the forest

boswachter [bɔswɑχtər] *de (~s)* forester, *(Am)* (forest) ranger, gamekeeper

¹**bot** [bɔt] *de* flounder || *(fig) ~ vangen* draw a blank, come away empty-handed

²**bot** [bɔt] *het* bone: *tot op het ~ verkleumd zijn* chilled to the bone

³**bot** [bɔt] *adj* **1** blunt, dull; **2** blunt, curt: *iets ~ weigeren* refuse sth flat(ly)

botanicus [botɑnikʏs] *de (botanici)* botanist

botanisch [botɑnis] *adj* botanic(al)

boter [botər] *de (~s)* butter: *~ bij de vis* cash on the nail; *hij heeft ~ op zijn hoofd* listen who's talking

boterbloem [botərblum] *de (~en)* buttercup

boterbriefje [botərbrifjə] *het (~s)* marriage lines, marriage certificate

boteren [botərə(n)] *vb* || *het wil tussen hen niet ~* they can't get on

boterham [botərhɑm] *de (~men)* **1** slice (*or*: piece) of bread: *(fig) iets op zijn ~ krijgen* get sth on one's plate; *een ~ met ham* a ham sandwich; **2** living, livelihood: *zijn ~ verdienen met …* earn one's living by …

boterhamtrommeltje [botərhɑmtrɔmələ] *het (~s)* sandwich box, lunch box

boterhamworst [botərhɑmwɔrst] *de (roughly)* luncheon meat

boter-kaas-en-eieren [botərkasɛnɛijərə(n)] *het* noughts and crosses, *(Am)* tic-tac-toe

botermelk [botərmɛlk] *de* buttermilk

botervloot [botərvlot] *de (-vloten)* butter dish

botheid [botɛit] *de* **1** bluntness, dullness; **2** bluntness, gruffness

botkanker [botkɑŋkər] *de* bone cancer

botontkalking [botɔntkɑlkɪŋ] *de* osteoporosis

botsautootje [bɔtsautoːə] *het (~s)* dodgem (car), bumper car

botsen [bɔtsə(n)] *vb* **1** collide (with), bump into (*or*: against), crash into (*or*: against): *twee wagens botsten tegen elkaar* two cars collided; **2** *(fig)* clash (with)

botsing [bɔtsɪŋ] *de (~en)* collision, crash: *met elkaar in ~ komen* collide with one another, run into one another

bottelen [bɔtələ(n)] *vb* bottle

botter [bɔtər] *de (~s)* smack, fishing boat
botulisme [botylɪsmə] *het* botulism
botweg [bɔtwɛχ] *adv* bluntly, flatly
bougie [buʒi] *de (~s)* sparking plug
bouillon [bujɔn] *de (~s)* broth
bouillonblokje [bujɔmblɔkjə] *het (~s)* beef cube
boulevard [buləvar] *de (~s)* **1** boulevard, avenue; **2** promenade
boulevardblad [buləvarblat] *de (~en) (roughly)* tabloid
boulimia nervosa [bulimijanɛrvoza] *de* bulimia nervosa, *(Am)* bulimarexia
bourgogne [burgɔɲə] *de (~s)* burgundy
Bourgondiër [burɣɔndijər] *de (~s)* Burgundian
bourgondisch [burχɔndis] *adj, adv* exuberant
bout [baut] *de (~en)* **1** (screw) bolt, pin; **2** leg, quarter, drumstick
bouvier [buvje] *de (~s)* Bouvier des Flandres
bouw [bau] *de* **1** building, construction; **2** building industry (*or:* trade); **3** structure, construction, build
bouwbedrijf [baubədrɛif] *het (-bedrijven)* construction firm, builders
bouwdoos [baudos] *de (-dozen)* (do-it-yourself) kit
¹bouwen [bauwə(n)] *vb* build, construct, erect, put up
²bouwen [bauwə(n)] *vb (with op)* rely on
bouwer [bauwər] *de (~s)* builder, (building) contractor, shipbuilder
bouwgrond [bauɣrɔnt] *de (~en)* building land
bouwjaar [baujar] *het (-jaren)* year of construction (*or:* manufacture): *te koop: auto van het ~ 1981* for sale: 1981 car
bouwkunde [baukyndə] *de* architecture
bouwkundig [baukyndəχ] *adj, adv* architectural, constructional, structural: *~ ingenieur* structural engineer
bouwkundige [baukyndəɣə] *de (~n)* architect, structural engineer
bouwkunst [baukynst] *de* building, construction, architecture
bouwmaatschappij [baumatsχapɛi] *de (~en)* (property) development company, building company
bouwmateriaal [baumaterijal] *het (-materialen)* building material
bouwpakket [baupakɛt] *het (~ten)* (do-it-yourself) kit
bouwpromotor [baupromotər] *de (~en, ~s) (Belg)* (property) developer
bouwput [baupYt] *de (~ten)* (building) excavation
bouwsteen [bausten] *de (-stenen)* **1** brick; **2** building block
bouwstof [baustɔf] *de (~fen)* building material; *(fig)* material(s)
bouwtekening [bautekənɪŋ] *de (~en)* floor plan, drawing(s)

bouwterrein [bautɛrɛin] *het (~en)* **1** building land; **2** building site, construction site
bouwvakker [bauvakər] *de (~s)* construction worker
bouwval [bauval] *de (~len)* ruin
bouwvallig [bauvaləχ] *adj* crumbling, dilapidated, rickety
bouwwerk [bauwɛrk] *het (~en)* building; structure, construction
¹boven [bovə(n)] *prep* **1** above, over: *hij woont ~ een bakker* he lives over a baker's shop; *~ water komen: a)* surface, come up for air; *b) (fig)* turn up; *de flat ~ ons* the flat overhead; **2** above, beyond: *dat gaat ~ mijn verstand* that is beyond me; **3** above, over: *hij stelt zijn carrière ~ zijn gezin* he puts his career before his family; *er gaat niets ~ Belgische friet* there's nothing like Belgian chips; *veiligheid ~ alles* safety first; **4** over, above, beyond: *kinderen ~ de drie jaar* children over three; *~ alle twijfel* beyond (all) doubt
²boven [bovə(n)] *adv* **1** above, up, upstairs: *(naar) ~ brengen* take (*or:* carry) up, bring back; *woon je ~ of beneden?* do you live upstairs or down(stairs)?; *naar ~ afronden* round up; **2** on top: *dat gaat mijn verstand (begrip) te ~* that is beyond me, that's over my head; *de vierde regel van ~* the fourth line from the top; **3** above; **4** (with *aan*) on top, at the top: *~ aan de lijst staan* be at the top (*or:* head) of the list
bovenaan [bovə(n)an] *adv* at the top: *~ staan* be (at the) top
bovenarm [bovə(n)arm] *de (~en)* upper arm
bovenbeen [bovə(n)ben] *het (-benen)* upper leg, thigh
bovenbouw [bovə(n)bau] *de* **1** *(educ)* last 2 or 3 classes (of secondary school); **2** superstructure
bovendien [bovəndin] *adv* moreover, in addition, furthermore, besides: *~, hij is niet meerderjarig* besides, he's a minor
bovengenoemd [bovə(n)ɣənumt] *adj* above(-mentioned), mentioned above, stated above, *(law)* (afore)said
bovengrens [bovə(n)ɣrɛns] *de (-grenzen)* upper limit
bovengronds [bovə(n)ɣrɔnts] *adj, adv* aboveground, surface, overhead
bovenkant [bovə(n)kant] *de (~en)* top
bovenkleding [bovə(n)kledɪŋ] *de* outer clothes, outerwear
bovenkomen [bovə(n)komə(n)] *vb* **1** come up, come to the surface, break (the) surface, surface; **2** come up(stairs)
bovenlaag [bovə(n)laχ] *de (-lagen)* upper layer, surface layer, top coat
bovenlijf [bovə(n)lɛif] *het (-lijven)* upper part of the body: *met ontbloot ~* stripped to the waist
bovenlip [bovə(n)lɪp] *de (~pen)* upper lip
bovenmenselijk [bovə(n)mɛnsələk] *adj, adv* superhuman
bovenmodaal [bovə(n)modal] *adj* above-average
bovennatuurlijk [bovənatyrlək] *adj, adv* supernat-

ural

bovenop [bovə(n)ɔp] *adv* **1** on top: *(fig) ergens ~ springen* pounce on sth; **2** on one's feet: *de zieke kwam er snel weer ~* the patient made a quick recovery

bovenst [bovənst] *adj* top, topmost, upper(most): *van de ~e plank* first class; *de ~e verdieping (also fig)* the top storey

bovenstaand [bovə(n)stant] *adj* above, above-mentioned

bovenstuk [bovə(n)stʏk] *het (~ken)* top, top part, upper part

bovenuit [bovə(n)œyt] *adv* above: *zijn stem klonk overal ~* his voice could be heard above everything

bovenverdieping [bovə(n)vərdipɪŋ] *de (~en)* upper storey, upper floor, top floor *(or:* storey)

bovenwinds [bovə(n)wɪnts] *adj, adv* windward

bovenwoning [bovə(n)wonɪŋ] *de (~en)* upstairs flat

bovenzijde [bovə(n)zɛidə] *de (~n) see* bovenkant

bowl [bowl] *de (~s)* punch

bowlen [bowlə(n)] *vb* bowl

bowlingbaan [bolɪŋban] *de (-banen)* bowling alley

box [bɔks] *de (~en)* **1** (loud)speaker; **2** (loose) box, stall; **3** storeroom; **4** (play)pen

boxer [bɔksər] *de (~s)* boxer

boxershort [bɔksərʃɔːrt] *de (~s)* boxer shorts

boycot [bɔjkɔt] *de (~s)* boycott

boycotten [bɔjkɔtə(n)] *vb* boycott, freeze out

braadpan [bratpan] *de (~nen)* casserole

braadworst [bratwɔrst] *de (~en)* **1** (frying) sausage; **2** German sausage

braaf [braf] *adj, adv* **1** good, honest, *(oft iron)* respectable, decent; **2** well-behaved, obedient

braafheid [brafhɛit] *de* goodness, decency, honesty, *(sometimes iron)* respectability, obedience

braak [brak] *adj* **1** waste; fallow: *~ laten liggen* leave *(or:* lay) fallow; **2** *(fig)* fallow, undeveloped, unexplored

braakliggend [braklɪɣənt] *adj* fallow

braaksel [braksəl] *het* vomit

braam [bram] *de (bramen)* blackberry, bramble

braden [bradə(n)] *vb* roast; fry; pot-roast; grill

braderie [bradəri] *de (~ën)* fair

braille [brajə] *het* braille

braken [brakə(n)] *vb* vomit, be sick, throw up, regurgitate

brallen [bralə(n)] *vb* brag, boast

brancard [braŋkar] *de (~s)* stretcher

branche [brɑ̃ʃ] *de (~s)* branch, department, line (of business), (branch of) trade

brand [brant] *de (~en)* fire, blaze: *er is gevaar voor ~* there is a fire hazard; *~ stichten* commit arson; *in ~ staan* be on fire; *in ~ vliegen* catch fire, burst into flames, ignite; *iets in ~ steken* set sth on fire, set fire to sth

brandbaar [brantbar] *adj* combustible, (in)flammable

brandblusinstallatie [brantblʏsɪnstala(t)si] *de*

(~s) sprinkler system

brandblusser [brantblʏsər] *de (~s)* (fire) extinguisher

¹branden [brandə(n)] *vb* burn, be on fire, blaze: *de lamp brandt* the lamp is on; *de kachel laten ~* leave the (gas) fire burning; *ze was het huis niet uit te ~* there was no way of getting her out of the house

²branden [brandə(n)] *vb* burn, scald, roast: *zich de vingers ~ (fig)* burn one's fingers

branderig [brandərəχ] *adj* irritant, caustic

brandewijn [brandəwɛin] *de (~en)* brandy

brandgevaar [brantχəvar] *het* fire hazard, fire risk

brandgevaarlijk [brantχəvarlək] *adj* flammable

brandglas [brantχlas] *het (-glazen)* burning-glass

brandhout [branthaut] *het (~en)* firewood

branding [brandɪŋ] *de (~en)* surf, breakers

brandkast [brantkast] *de (~en)* safe

brandladder [brantladər] *de (~s)* escape ladder

brandmerk [brantmɛrk] *het (~en)* brand

brandmerken [brantmɛrkə(n)] *vb* brand

brandnetel [brantnetəl] *de (~s)* nettle

brandpunt [brantpʏnt] *het (~en)* **1** focus *(also maths);* **2** *(fig)* centre

brandschoon [brantsχon] *adj* spotless

brandslang [brantslaŋ] *de (~en)* fire hose

brandspiritus [brantspiritʏs] *de* methylated spirit(s)

brandstapel [brantstapəl] *de (~s)* stake

brandstichten [brantstɪχtə(n)] *vb* commit arson

brandstichter [brantstɪχtər] *de (~s)* arsonist

brandstichting [brantstɪχtɪŋ] *de (~en)* arson

brandstof [brantstɔf] *de (~fen)* fuel

brandtrap [brantrap] *de (~pen)* fire escape

brandweer [brantwer] *de* fire brigade

brandweerauto [brantwerauto] *de (~'s)* fire engine

brandweercommandant [brantwerkɔmandant] *de (~en)* (senior) fire officer

brandweerkazerne [brantwerkazɛrnə] *de (~s)* fire station

brandweerman [brantwerman] *de (-lieden)* fireman

brandwond [brantwɔnt] *de (~en)* burn

brasserie [brasəri] *de (~ën)* brasserie

bravo [bravo] *int* bravo!, hear! hear!

bravoure [bravur] *de* bravura: *met veel ~* dashing

Braziliaan [brazilijan] *de (Brazilianen)* Brazilian

Braziliaans [brazilijans] *adj* Brazilian

Brazilië [brazilijə] *het* Brazil

breakdancen [breɡdɛːnsə(n)] *vb* break-dance

¹breed [bret] *adj* wide, broad: *de kamer is 6 m lang en 5 m ~* the room is 6 metres (long) by 5 metres (wide); *niet breder dan twee meter* not more than two metres wide *(or:* in width)

²breed [bret] *adv* widely, loosely: *een ~ omgeslagen kraag* a wide *(or:* loose) collar

breedband [bredbant] *de (comp)* broadband

breedbeeldtelevisie [bredbɛltələvizi] *de (~s)* wide-screen TV

breedgebouwd [bretχəbaut] *adj* broad(ly-built), square-built

breedte [bretə] *de (~s)* **1** width, breadth: *in de ~* breadthways; **2** *(geog)* latitude

breedtegraad [bretəɣrat] *de (-graden)* parallel, degree of latitude

breeduit [bretœyt] *adv* **1** spread (out): *~ gaan zitten* sprawl (on); **2** out loud

breekbaar [breɡbar] *adj* fragile, brittle

breekijzer [brekɛizər] *het (~s)* crowbar

breekpunt [brekpʏnt] *het (~en)* breaking point *(also fig)*

breien [brɛiə(n)] *vb* knit

brein [brɛin] *het* brain, *(fig also)* brains: *het ~ zijn achter een project* be the brain(s) behind a project, mastermind a project

breinaald [brɛinalt] *de (~en)* knitting needle

breiwerk [brɛiwɛrk] *het (~en)* knitting

¹**breken** [brekə(n)] *vb* break, *(light)* refract || *een record ~* break a record; *de betovering* (or: *het verzet*) *~* break the spell *(or:* resistance)

²**breken** [brekə(n)] *vb* break, *(med also)* fracture || *met iem ~* break off (relations) with s.o., break up with s.o.; *met een gewoonte ~* break a habit

brem [brɛm] *de* broom

brengen [brɛŋə(n)] *vb* **1** bring, take: *mensen (weer) bij elkaar ~* bring (or: get) people together (again); *naar huis ~* take home; *een kind naar bed ~* put a child to bed; **2** bring, take, give: *zijn mening naar voren ~* put forward, come out with one's opinion; *iets naar voren ~* bring sth up; *een zaak voor het gerecht ~* take a matter to court; **3** bring, send, put: *iem tot een daad ~* drive s.o. to (sth); *iem aan het twijfelen ~* raise doubt(s) in s.o.'s mind; *het ver ~* go far

bres [brɛs] *de (~sen)* breach, hole *(also fig): voor iem in de ~ springen* step into the breach for s.o.

Bretagne [brətaɲə] *het* Brittany

bretel [brətɛl] *de (~s)* braces, *(Am)* suspenders

breuk [brøk] *de (~en)* **1** break(ing), breakage; **2** crack, split, fault; **3** *(med)* fracture, hernia; **4** rift, breach; **5** *(maths)* fraction: *decimale (tiendelige) ~* decimal fraction; *samengestelde ~* complex *(or:* compound) fraction

brevet [brəvɛt] *het (~ten)* certificate, *(aviation)* licence

bridgen [brɪdʒə(n)] *vb* play bridge

brief [brif] *de (brieven)* letter: *aangetekende ~* registered letter; *in antwoord op uw ~ van de 25e* in reply to your letter of the 25th

briefhoofd [brifhoft] *het (~en)* letterhead, letter-heading

briefje [brifjə] *het (~s)* note: *dat geef ik je op een ~* you can take it from me

briefkaart [brifkart] *de (~en)* postcard

briefpapier [brifpapir] *het* writing paper, stationery

briefwisseling [brifwɪsəlɪŋ] *de (~en)* correspondence: *een ~ voeren (met)* correspond (with)

bries [bris] *de* breeze

briesen [brisə(n)] *vb* roar; snort

brievenbus [brivə(n)bʏs] *de (~sen)* **1** postbox, letter box; **2** letter box, *(Am)* mailbox

brigade [briɣadə] *de (~s)* **1** brigade; **2** squad, team

brigadier [briɣadir] *de (~s)* **1** police sergeant; **2** (school) crossing guard

brij [brɛi] *de* **1** pulp; **2** porridge || *om de hete brij heen draaien* beat about the bush

brik [brɪk] *de (~ken) (Belg)* || *melk in ~* milk in cartons

bril [brɪl] *de (~len)* **1** (pair of) glasses, (pair of) goggles: *alles door een donkere* (or: *roze*) *~ zien* take a gloomy *(or:* rosy) view of everything; **2** (toilet) seat

¹**briljant** [brɪljɑnt] *de (~en)* (cut) diamond

²**briljant** [brɪljɑnt] *adj, adv* brilliant

brillantine [brɪljɑntinə] *de* brilliantine

brilmontuur [brɪlmɔntyr] *het, de (-monturen)* glasses frame

brilslang [brɪlslɑŋ] *de (~en)* (spectacled) cobra

Brit [brɪt] *de (~ten)* Briton, Brit

brits [brɪts] *de (~en)* plank bed, wooden bed

Brits [brɪts] *adj* British

broccoli [brɔkoli] *de* broccoli

broche [brɔʃ] *de (~s)* brooch

brochure [brɔʃyrə] *de (~s)* pamphlet

broeden [brudə(n)] *vb* brood || *hij zit op iets te ~* he is working on sth

broeder [brudər] *de (~s)* **1** brother; **2** *(Roman Catholicism)* brother, friar; **3** (male) nurse

broederschap [brudərsχɑp] *de (~pen)* brotherhood, fraternity

broedmachine [brutmaʃinə] *de (~s)* incubator, brooder

broedplaats [brutplats] *de (~en)* breeding ground *(also fig)*

broeien [brujə(n)] *vb* **1** heat, get heated, get hot; **2** be sultry || *er broeit iets* there is sth brewing

broeierig [brujərɔχ] *adj, adv* **1** sultry, sweltering, muggy; **2** sultry, sensual

broeikas [brujkɑs] *de (~sen)* hothouse, greenhouse

broeikaseffect [brujkɑsɛfɛkt] *het* greenhouse effect

broek [bruk] *de (~en)* (pair of) trousers, shorts || *een proces aan zijn ~ krijgen* get taken to court

broekje [brukjə] *het (~s)* briefs; panties, knickers

broekpak [brukpɑk] *het (~ken)* trouser suit

broekriem [brukrim] *de (~en)* belt: *(also fig) de ~ aanhalen* tighten one's belt

broekspijp [brukspɛip] *de (~en)* (trouser-)leg

broekzak [bruksɑk] *de (~ken)* trouser(s) pocket: *iets kennen als zijn ~* know sth inside out *(or:* like the back of one's hand)

broer [brur] *de (~s)* brother

broertje [brurcə] *het (~s)* little brother || *een ~ dood aan iets hebben* hate sth, detest sth

brok [brɔk] *het, de (~ken)* piece, fragment, chunk: *~ken maken: a)* smash things up; *b) (fig)* mess things up; *hij had een ~ in zijn keel* he had a lump in his throat

brokaat [brokat] *het* brocade

brokkelen [brɔkələ(n)] *vb* crumble

brokstuk [brɔkstʏk] *het (~ken)* (broken) fragment, piece, *(pl also)* debris

brom [brɔm] *de* buzz

bromfiets [brɔmfits] *de (~en)* moped

bromfietscertificaat [brɔmfitsɛrtifikat] *het* moped licence

bromfietser [brɔmfitsər] *de (~s)* moped rider *(or:* driver)

bromfietshelm [brɔmfitshɛlm] *de (~en)* crash helmet, moped helmet

bromfietsplaatje *het* moped number plate

bromfietsrijbewijs *het* moped licence

brommen [brɔmə(n)] *vb* **1** hum, growl; **2** mutter; **3** ride a moped

brommer [brɔmər] *de (~s)* moped

bromscooter [brɔmskutər] *de (~s)* (motor) scooter

bromvlieg [brɔmvliχ] *de (~en)* bluebottle, blowfly

bron [brɔn] *de (~nen)* **1** well, spring: *hete ~* hot springs; **2** source, spring, cause: *~nen van bestaan* means of existence; *hij heeft het uit betrouwbare ~* he has it from a reliable source; *een rijke (onuitputtelijke) ~ van informatie* a mine of information

bronchitis [brɔŋχitəs] *de* bronchitis

brons [brɔns] *het (bronzen)* bronze

bronstijd [brɔnstɛit] *de* Bronze Age

bronwater [brɔnwatər] *het (~en)* spring water; *(in bottle)* mineral water

bronzen [brɔnzə(n)] *adj* bronze: *een ~ medaille* a bronze (medal)

brood [brot] *het (broden)* **1** bread: *daar is geen droog ~ mee te verdienen* you won't *(or:* wouldn't) make a penny out of it; *(fig) ~ op de plank hebben* be able to make ends meet; **2** loaf (of bread): *een snee ~* a slice of bread; *twee broden* two loaves (of bread); **3** living

broodbeleg [brodbələχ] *het* sandwich filling

brooddeeg [brodeχ] *het* (bread) dough

broodje [broсə] *het (~s)* (bread) roll, bun

broodje-aap [brocaap] *het* monkey's sandwich

broodjeszaak [brocəzak] *de (~zaken)* sandwich bar

broodkruimel [brotkrœyməl] *de (~s)* breadcrumb

broodmaaltijd [brotmaltɛit] *de (~en)* cold meal *(or:* lunch)

broodmager [brotmaγər] *adj* skinny, bony

broodnodig [brotnodəχ] *adj* much-needed, badly needed, highly necessary

broodrooster [brotrostər] *het, de (~s)* toaster

broodtrommel [brotrɔməl] *de (~s)* **1** breadbin; **2** lunch box

broodwinner [brotwinər] *de (~s)* breadwinner

broodwinning [brotwinɪŋ] *de (~en)* livelihood

broos [bros] *adj, adv* fragile, delicate, frail

bros [brɔs] *adj* brittle, crisp(y)

brossen [brɔsə(n)] *vb (Belg)* play truant, skip classes

brouwen [brɑuwə(n)] *vb* brew; mix, concoct

brouwer [brɑuwər] *de (~s)* brewer

brouwerij [brɑuwərɛi] *de (~en)* brewery

brouwsel [brɑusəl] *het (~s)* brew, concoction

brug [brʏχ] *de (~gen)* **1** bridge; **2** bridge(work); **3** *(sport)* parallel bars; **4** *(shipp)* bridge || *hij moet over de ~ komen* he has to deliver the goods *(or:* pay up)

Brugge [brʏγə] *het* Bruges

brugklas [brʏχklɑs] *de (~sen)* first class *(or:* form) (at secondary school)

brugklasser [brʏχklɑsər] *de (~s)* first-former

brugleuning [brʏχlønɪŋ] *de (~en)* bridge railing, parapet

brugwachter [brʏχwɑχtər] *de (~s)* bridgekeeper

brui [brœy] *de* || *er de ~ aan geven* chuck it (in)

bruid [brœyt] *de (~en)* bride

bruidegom [brœydəγɔm] *de (~s)* (bride)groom

bruidsboeket [brœytsbukɛt] *het, de (~ten)* bridal bouquet

bruidsjapon [brœytsjapɔn] *de (~nen)* bridal gown, wedding dress

bruidsmeisje [brœytsmɛiʃə] *het* bridesmaid

bruidsnacht [brœytsnɑχt] *de (~en)* wedding night

bruidspaar [brœytspar] *het (-paren)* bride and (bride)groom, bridal couple

bruidssuite [brœytswitə] *de (~s)* bridal suite

bruidstaart [brœytstart] *de (~en)* wedding cake

bruikbaar [brœygbar] *adj* usable, useful, serviceable, employable

bruikleen [brœyklen] *het, de (-lenen)* loan: *iets aan iem in ~ geven* lend sth to s.o.

bruiloft [brœylɔft] *de (~en)* wedding

bruin [brœyn] *adj, adv* brown || *wat bak je ze weer ~* you're really going to town on it

bruinbrood [brœymbrot] *het (-broden)* brown bread

bruinen [brœynə(n)] *vb* brown, tan, bronze: *de zon heeft zijn vel gebruind* the sun has tanned his skin

bruinkool [brœyŋkol] *de (-kolen)* brown coal, lignite

bruinvis [brœynvɪs] *de (~sen)* porpoise

bruisen [brœysə(n)] *vb* foam, effervesce: *~ van geestdrift (or: energie)* bubble with enthusiasm *(or:* energy)

bruisend [brœysənt] *adj* exuberant

brullen [brʏlə(n)] *vb* roar, bawl, howl: *~ van het lachen* roar *(or:* howl) with laughter

brunch [brʏnʃ] *de (~es)* brunch

brunette [brʏnɛtə] *de (~s)* brunette

Brussel [brʏsəl] *het* Brussels

Brussels [brʏsəls] *adj* Brussels

brutaal [brytal] *adj, adv* **1** insolent, cheeky, impudent: *zij was zo ~ om ...* she had the cheek *(or:* nerve) to ...; **2** bold, forward

brutaliteit [brytalitɛit] *de (~en)* cheek, impudence

bruto [bryto] *adv* gross: *het concert heeft ~ €1100 opgebracht* the concert raised 1100 euros gross

brutogewicht [brytoγəwɪχt] *het (~en)* gross weight

brutoloon [brytolon] *het (-lonen)* gross income

brutosalaris [brytosalarıs] *het* gross salary

brutowinst [brytowınst] *de (~en)* gross profit

bruut [bryt] *adj, adv* brute, brutal

bso [beeso] *het (Belg) beroepssecundair onderwijs* secondary vocational education

btw [betewe] *de belasting op de toegevoegde waarde* VAT, value added tax

bubbelbad [bybəlbɑt] *het (~en)* whirlpool, jacuzzi

budget [bydʒɛt] *het (~ten)* budget

budgettair [bydʒɛtɛːr] *adj* budgetary

budgetteren [bydʒɛtɛrə(n)] *vb* budget

buffel [byfəl] *de (~s)* buffalo

buffer [byfər] *de (~s)* buffer

buffervoorraad [byfərvorat] *de (-voorraden)* buffer stock

buffet [byfɛt] *het (~ten)* sideboard, buffet

buggy [bygi] *de (~'s)* buggy

bui [bœy] *de (~en)* **1** shower, (short) storm: *schuilen voor een ~* take shelter from a storm; *de ~ zien hangen (fig)* see the storm coming; *hier en daar een ~* scattered showers; **2** mood: *in een driftige ~* in a fit of temper

buidel [bœydəl] *de (~s)* **1** purse; **2** pouch

buideldier [bœydəldir] *het (~en)* marsupial

¹buigen [bœyɣə(n)] *vb* bend: *het hoofd ~ (fig)* bow (to), submit (to); *de weg buigt naar links* the road curves (or: bends) to the left; *zich over de balustrade ~* lean over the railing

²buigen [bœyɣə(n)] *vb* **1** bow: *voor iem ~* bow to s.o.; **2** (with *voor*) bow (to), bend (before); **3** bend (over)

buiging [bœyɣıŋ] *de (~en)* **1** bend, curve: *de weg maakt hier een ~* the road bends here; **2** bow, curtsy

buigzaam [bœyχsam] *adj* **1** flexible, supple; **2** *(fig)* flexible, adaptable, compliant

buiig [bœyəχ] *adj* showery, gusty

buik [bœyk] *de (~en)* belly, stomach, abdomen: *(fig) er de ~ van vol hebben* be fed up (with it), be sick and tired of it

buikdanseres [bœyɡdɑnsərɛs] *de (~sen)* belly dancer

buikholte [bœykhɔltə] *de (~n, ~s)* abdomen

buikje [bœykjə] *het (~s)* paunch, pot belly

buiklanding [bœyklɑndıŋ] *de (~en)* pancake landing, belly landing

buikpijn [bœykpɛin] *de (~en)* stomach-ache, belly-ache

buikriem [bœykrim] *de (~en)* belt

buikspier [bœykspir] *de (~en)* stomach muscle, abdominal muscle

buikspreken [bœyksprekə(n)] *vb* ventriloquize, throw one's voice

buikspreker [bœyksprekər] *de (~s)* ventriloquist

buikvin [bœykfın] *de (~nen)* pelvic fin

buikvliesontsteking [bœykflisɔntstekıŋ] *de (~en)* peritonitis

buil [bœyl] *de (~en)* bump

buis [bœys] *de (buizen)* **1** tube, pipe, valve; **2** box, TV; **3** *(Belg; inf)* fail (mark)

buit [bœyt] *de* **1** booty, spoils, loot; **2** catch: *met een flinke ~ thuiskomen* come home with a big catch

buitelen [bœytələ(n)] *vb* tumble, somersault

¹buiten [bœytə(n)] *prep* **1** outside, beyond: *~ het bereik van* out of reach of; *hij was ~ zichzelf van woede* he was beside himself with anger; **2** out of: *iets ~ beschouwing laten* leave sth out of consideration; **3** without: *het is ~ mijn medeweten gebeurd* it happened without my knowledge

²buiten [bœytə(n)] *adv* outside, out, outdoors: *een dagje ~* a day in the country; *daar wil ik ~ blijven* I want to stay out of that; *naar ~ gaan: a)* go outside (*or:* outdoors); *b)* go into the country (*or:* out of town); *naar ~ brengen* take out, lead (*or:* show) out (*pers*); *een gedicht van ~ leren* (*or:* kennen) learn (*or:* know) a poem by heart

buitenaards [bœytə(n)arts] *adj* extraterrestrial

buitenaf [bœytənɑf] *adv* outside, external, from (*or:* on) the outside

buitenbaan [bœytə(n)ban] *de (-banen)* outside lane

buitenband [bœytə(n)bɑnt] *de (~en)* tyre

buitenbeentje [bœytə(n)bencə] *het (~s)* odd man out, outsider

buitenbocht [bœytə(n)bɔχt] *de (~en)* outside curve (*or:* bend)

buitenboordmotor [bœytə(n)bortmotər] *de (~en)* outboard motor

buitendeur [bœytə(n)dør] *de (~en)* front door, outside door

buitenechtelijk [bœytə(n)ɛχtələk] *adj* extramarital: *~ kind* illegitimate child

¹buitengewoon [bœytə(n)ɣəwon] *adj* special, extra; exceptional, unusual

²buitengewoon [bœytə(n)ɣəwon] *adv* extremely, exceptionally

buitenhuis [bœytə(n)hœys] *het (-huizen)* country house

buitenkansje [bœytə(n)kɑnʃə] *het (~s)* stroke of luck

buitenkant [bœytə(n)kɑnt] *de (~en)* outside, exterior: *op de ~ afgaan* judge by appearances

buitenland [bœytə(n)lɑnt] *het* foreign country (*or:* countries): *van (or: uit) het ~ terugkeren* return (*or:* come back) from abroad

buitenlander [bœytə(n)lɑndər] *de (~s)* foreigner, alien

buitenlands [bœytə(n)lɑnts] *adj* foreign, international: *een ~e reis* a trip abroad

buitenlucht [bœytə(n)lyχt] *de* open (air); country air

buitenshuis [bœytənshœys] *adv* outside, out(side) of the house, outdoors: *~ eten* eat out

buitensluiten [bœytə(n)slœytə(n)] *vb* shut out, lock out

buitenspel [bœytə(n)spɛl] *het* offside || *(fig) hij werd ~ gezet* he was sidelined

buitensporig [bœytənsporəχ] *adj, adv* extravagant, excessive, exorbitant, inordinate

buitenst [bɶytə(n)st] *adj* out(er)most, exterior, outer

buitenstaander [bɶytə(n)standər] *de (~s)* outsider

buitenwacht [bɶytə(n)waχt] *de* outside world, public, outsiders

buitenwereld [bɶytə(n)werəlt] *de* public (at large), outside world

buitenwijk [bɶytə(n)wɛik] *de (~en)* suburb, *(pl also)* outskirts

buitenwipper [bɶytə(n)wɪpər] *de (~s) (Belg)* bouncer

buitenzijde [bɶytə(n)zɛidə] *de (~n)* outside, exterior, surface

buitmaken [bɶytmakə(n)] *vb* seize, capture *(ship)*

buizen [bɶyzə(n)] *vb (Belg; inf)* fail

buizerd [bɶyzərt] *de (~s)* buzzard

¹bukken [bʏkə(n)] *vb* stoop, duck: *hij gaat gebukt onder veel zorgen* he is weighed down by many worries

²bukken [bʏkə(n)] *ref vb* stoop, bend down

buks [bʏks] *de (~en)* (short) rifle

bul [bʏl] *de* degree certificate

bulderen [bʏldərə(n)] *vb* roar, bellow

buldog [bʏldɔχ] *de (~gen)* bulldog

Bulgaar [bʏlɣar] *de (Bulgaren)* Bulgarian

Bulgaars [bʏlɣars] *adj* Bulgarian

Bulgarije [bʏlɣarɛiə] *het* Bulgaria

bulkgoederen [bʏlkχudərə(n)] *de* bulk goods

bulldozer [bʏldozər] *de (~s)* bulldozer

bullebak [bʏləbak] *de (~ken)* bully, ogre

bulletin [bʏlətɛ] *het (~s)* bulletin, report

bult [bʏlt] *de (~en)* 1 lump, bump; 2 hunch, hump: *met een ~* hunchbacked, humpbacked

bumper [bʏmpər] *de (~s)* bumper

bundel [bʏndəl] *de (~s)* 1 bundle, sheaf; 2 collection, volume

bundelen [bʏndələ(n)] *vb* bundle, cluster, combine: *krachten ~* join forces

bungalow [bʏŋgalow] *de (~s)* bungalow; (summer) cottage, chalet

bungalowpark [bʏŋgalowpark] *het (~en)* holiday park

bungalowtent [bʏŋgalowtɛnt] *de (~en)* family (frame) tent

bungelen [bʏŋələ(n)] *vb* dangle, hang

bunker [bʏŋkər] *de (~s)* bunker, bomb shelter, air-raid shelter

bunkeren [bʏŋkərə(n)] *vb* 1 refuel; 2 stoke up, stuff oneself

bunsenbrander [bʏnzə(n)brandər] *de (~s)* Bunsen burner

bunzing [bʏnzɪŋ] *de (~s, ~en)* polecat

burcht [bʏrχt] *de (~en)* castle, fortress, citadel, stronghold

bureau [byro] *het (~s)* 1 (writing) desk, bureau; 2 office, bureau, department, (police) station, agency

bureaucraat [byrokrat] *de (bureaucraten)* bureaucrat

bureaucratie [byrokra(t)si] *de (~ën)* bureaucracy, officialdom

bureaucratisch [byrokratis] *adj, adv* bureaucratic: *~e rompslomp* red tape

bureaula [byrola] *de (~'s, ~den)* (desk) drawer

bureaulamp [byrolamp] *de (~en)* desk lamp

bureauredacteur [byroredaktør] *de (~en, ~s)* copy editor

bureaustoel [byrostul] *de* office chair, desk chair

burgemeester [bʏrɣəmɛstər] *de (~s)* mayor, *(Scotland)* provost: *~ en wethouders* mayor and aldermen, municipal executive

burger [bʏrɣər] *de (~s)* 1 citizen; 2 civilian: *militairen en ~s* soldiers and civilians

burgerlijk [bʏrɣərlək] *adj, adv* 1 middle-class, bourgeois; 2 *(depr)* bourgeois, conventional, middle-class, philistine, smug; 3 civil, civic: *~e stand* marital status; *(bureau van de) ~e stand* Registry of Births, Deaths and Marriages, Registry Office; 4 civil(ian)

burgeroorlog [bʏrɣərorlɔχ] *de (~en)* civil war

bus [bʏs] *de (~sen)* 1 bus, coach: *met de ~ gaan* go by bus; *~je* minibus, van; 2 tin; *(large)* drum; 3 box: *u krijgt de folders morgen in de ~* you will get the brochures in the post tomorrow; *niemand weet wat er uit de ~ komt* nobody knows what the result will be

buschauffeur [bʏsʃofør] *de (~s)* bus driver, coach driver

busdienst [bʏzdinst] *de (~en)* bus service, coach service

bushalte [bʏshaltə] *de (~n, ~s)* bus stop, coach stop

buskruit [bʏskrɶyt] *het* gunpowder

buslichting [bʏslɪχtɪŋ] *de (~en)* collection

buste [bʏstə] *de (~s, ~n)* bust, bosom

butagas [bytaɣas] *het* butane (gas)

butler [bʏtlər] *de (~s)* butler

button [bʏtən] *de (~s)* badge

buur [byr] *de (buren)* neighbour: *de buren* the (next-door) neighbours

buurland [bʏrlant] *het (~en)* neighbouring country

buurman [bʏrman] *de (buurlieden)* (next-door) neighbour, man next door

buurt [bʏrt] *de (~en)* neighbourhood, area, district: *rosse ~* red-light district; *de hele ~ bij elkaar schreeuwen* shout the place down; *in (or: uit) de ~ wonen* live nearby (*or:* a distance away); *je kunt maar beter bij hem uit de ~ blijven* you'd better give him a wide berth

buurtbewoner [bʏrtbəwonər] *de (~s)* local resident

buurthuis [bʏrthɶys] *het (-huizen)* community centre

buurtvereniging [bʏrtfərenəɣɪŋ] *de (~en)* residents' association

buurvrouw [bʏrvrau] *de (~en)* neighbour, woman next door

bijv. *bijvoorbeeld* e.g.
BV [beve̱] *de (~'s) Besloten Vennootschap* PLC, *(Am)* Inc.
BVD [bevede̱] *de Binnenlandse Veiligheidsdienst* (Dutch) National Security Service, Dutch Secret Service
Byzantijns [bizɑntɛ̱ins] *adj* Byzantine

C

ca. *circa* approx., ca.
cabaret [kabarɛ(t)] *het (~s)* cabaret
cabaretier [kabarɛce] *de (~s)* cabaret performer, cabaret artist(e)
cabine [kabinə] *de (~s)* **1** cabin; **2** booth
cabriolet [kabrijolɛt] *de (~s)* convertible, drophead coupé
cacao [kakau] *de* cocoa, (drinking) chocolate
cactus [kaktʏs] *de (~sen)* cactus
CAD [seadɛ] *het (~'s) Computer Assisted Design* CAD
cadans [kadɑns] *de (~en)* cadence, rhythm
cadeau [kado] *het (~s)* present, gift: *iem iets ~ geven* give a person sth as a present; *(iron) dat krijg je van me ~!* you can keep it!; *iets niet ~ geven* not give sth away
cadeaubon [kadobɔn] *de (~nen)* gift voucher
cadet [kadɛt] *de (~ten, ~s) (Belg)* junior member of sports club
café [kafɛ] *het (~s)* café, pub, bar
cafeïne [kafejinə] *de* caffeine
cafeïnevrij [kafejinəvrɛi] *adj* decaffeinated
cafetaria [kafetarija] *de (~'s)* cafeteria, snack bar
cahier [kajɛ] *het (~s)* exercise book
caissière [kaʃɛːrə] *de (~s)* cashier, check-out assistant
cake [kek] *de (~s)* (madeira) cake
calamiteit [kalamitɛit] *de (~en)* calamity, disaster
calcium [kɑlsijʏm] *het* calcium
calculatie [kɑlkyla(t)si] *de (~s)* calculation, computation
calculator [kɑlkylatɔr] *de (~s)* calculator
calculeren [kɑlkylɛrə(n)] *vb* calculate, compute
caleidoscoop [kalɛidoskop] *de (-scopen)* kaleidoscope
Californië [kalifɔrnijə] *het* California
calorie [kalori] *de (~ën)* calorie
caloriearm [kaloriɑrm] *adj* low-calorie, low in calories
calorierijk *adj* high-calorie, rich in calories
calvinist [kɑlvinɪst] *de (~en)* Calvinist
Cambodja [kɑmbɔca] *het* Cambodia
Cambrium [kɑmbrijʏm] *het* Cambrian (period)
camera [kaməra] *de (~'s)* camera: *verborgen ~* hidden camera, candid camera
camouflage [kamuflaʒə] *de (~s)* camouflage, *(fig)* cover, front
camoufleren [kamuflɛrə(n)] *vb* camouflage, cover up, disguise
campagne [kɑmpɑɲə] *de (~s)* campaign, drive: *~ voeren (voor, tegen)* campaign (for, against)
camper [kɛmpər] *de (~s)* camper
camping [kɛmpɪŋ] *de (~s)* camping site
campus [kɑmpʏs] *de (~sen)* campus
Canada [kanada] *het* Canada
Canadees [kanadɛs] *de* Canadian
canapé [kanapɛ] *de (~s)* sofa, settee, couch
Canarische Eilanden [kanarisəɛilandə(n)] *de* (the) Canaries, (the) Canary Islands
cannabis [kɑnabɪs] *de* cannabis, hemp, marijuana
canon [kanɔn] *de (~s)* round, canon: *in ~ zingen* sing in a round (*or:* in canon)
cantharel [kɑntarɛl] *de (~len)* chanterelle
canvas [kɑnvas] *het* canvas, tarpaulin
cao [seao] *de (~'s) collectieve arbeidsovereenkomst* collective wage agreement
capabel [kapabəl] *adj* capable, able, competent, qualified: *voor die functie leek hij uiterst ~* he seemed very well qualified for the job; *hij is niet ~ om te rijden* he's in no shape (*or:* condition) to drive; *ik acht hem ~ om die klus uit te voeren* I reckon he can cope with that job
capaciteit [kapasitɛit] *de (~en)* **1** capacity, power: *een motor met kleine ~* a low-powered engine; **2** ability, capability: *Ans is een vrouw van grote ~en* Ans is a woman of great ability
cape [kep] *de (~s)* cape
capitulatie [kapityla(t)si] *de (~s)* capitulation, surrender
capituleren [kapitylɛrə(n)] *vb* capitulate, surrender
capriool [kaprijol] *de (capriolen)* prank, caper
capsule [kɑpsylə] *de (~s)* capsule
capuchon [kapyʃɔn] *de (~s)* hood
carambole [karɑmbol] *de (~s)* cannon
caravan [kɛravɛn] *de (~s)* caravan, *(Am)* trailer (home)
carburator [kɑrbyratɔr] *de (~en)* carburettor
cardiogram [kɑrdijoɣrɑm] *het (~men)* cardiogram
cardioloog [kɑrdijoloɣ] *de (-logen)* cardiologist
Caribisch [karibis] *adj* Caribbean: *het ~ gebied* the Caribbean
cariës [karijɛs] *de* caries, tooth decay, dental decay
carillon [karɪljɔn] *het, de (~s)* carillon, chimes: *het spelen van het ~* the ringing of the bells
carnaval [kɑrnaval] *het (~s)* carnival (time)
carnavalsvakantie [kɑrnavalsfakɑn(t)si] *de* carnival holiday, Shrovetide holiday
carnivoor [kɑrnivor] *de (carnivoren)* carnivore
carpoolen [kɑːrpulə(n)] *vb (Am)* carpool
carport [kɑːrpɔːrt] *de (~s)* carport
carrière [karijɛːrə] *de (~s)* career
carrosserie [karɔsəri] *de (~ën)* body, bodywork
cartoon [kartuːn] *de (~s)* cartoon
casco [kɑsko] *het (~'s)* body, vessel, hull

¹cash [kɛʃ] *de* cash

²cash [kɛʃ] *adv* cash

cashewnoot [kɛʃunɔt] *de (-noten)* cashew (nut)

casino [kazino] *het (~'s)* casino

cassatie [kɑsa(t)si] *de (~s)* annulment: *hof van ~* court of appeal

cassette [kɑsɛtə] *de (~s)* **1** box, casket, coffer, slip case, money box; **2** cassette

cassetteband [kɑsɛtəbɑnt] *de (~en)* cassette (tape)

cassettedeck [kɑsɛtədɛk] *de (~s)* cassette deck, tape deck

cassis [kɑsɪs] *de* cassis, black currant drink

castagnetten [kɑstɑɲɛtə(n)] *de* castanets

castreren [kɑstrɛrə(n)] *vb* castrate, neuter, doctor

catacombe [katakɔmbə] *de (~n)* catacombs

Catalaans [katalɑns] *adj* Catalan, Catalonian

catalogiseren [kataloɣizɛrə(n)] *vb* catalogue, record

catalogus [kataloɣʏs] *de (catalogi)* catalogue

Catalonië [katalonijə] *het* Catalonia

catamaran [katamɑrɑn] *de (~s)* catamaran

catastrofaal [katastrofal] *adj, adv* catastrophic, disastrous

catastrofe [katastrɔːfə] *de (~s, ~n)* catastrophe, disaster

catechismus [katəχɪsmʏs] *de (~sen)* catechism

categorie [katəyori] *de (~ën)* category, classification, bracket: *in drie ~ën indelen* distinguish into three categories

categoriseren [katəyorizɛrə(n)] *vb* categorize, class

cateren [ketərə(n)] *vb* cater (for)

catheter [katetər] *de (~s)* catheter: *een ~ inbrengen bij* catheterize

causaal [kɑuzal] *adj* causal, causative: *~ verband* causal connection

cavalerie [kavalɛri] *de (~s)* cavalry, tanks

cavia [kavija] *de (~'s)* guinea pig, cavia

cc [sese] **1** *kubieke centimeter* cc; **2** *kopie conform (roughly)* certified copy

cd [sede] *de compact disc* CD

cd-i [sedei] *de (~'s) compact disc interactief* CD-I

cd-i-speler [sedeispelər] *de* CD-I-player

cd-r [sedeːr] *de (~'s) compact disc-recordable* CD-R

cd-romspeler [sederɔmspelər] *de (~s)* CD-ROM drive, CD-ROM player

cd-single [sedesɪŋəl] *de* CD single

cd-speler [sedespelər] *de (~s)* CD player

ceder [sedər] *de (~s)* cedar

ceintuur [sɛntyr] *de (ceinturen)* belt, waistband

cel [sɛl] *de (~len)* cell, (call) box, booth: *hij heeft een jaar ~ gekregen* he has been given a year; *in een ~ opsluiten* lock up in a cell

celdeling [sɛldelɪŋ] *de (~en)* fission, cell division

celibaat [selibat] *het* celibacy

cellist [sɛlɪst] *de (~en)* cellist

cello [sɛlo] *de (~'s)* (violon)cello

cellulair [sɛlylɛːr] *adj* cellular

¹celluloid [sɛlylɔjt] *het* celluloid

²celluloid [sɛlylɔjt] *adj* celluloid

Celsius [sɛlsijʏs] *de* Celsius, centigrade

cement [səmɛnt] *het, de* cement

censureren [sɛnzyrɛrə(n)] *vb* censor, *(fig)* black out

censuur [sɛnzyr] *de* censorship

cent [sɛnt] *de (~en)* **1** cent: *iem tot op de laatste ~ betalen* pay s.o. to the full; **2** *(inf)* penny, farthing: *ik geef geen ~ meer voor zijn leven* I wouldn't give a penny for his life; *ik vertrouw hem voor geen ~* I don't trust him an inch; **3** money, cash: *zonder een ~ zitten* be penniless

centiliter [sɛntilitər] *de (~s)* centilitre

centime [sɛntim] *de (~s)* centime

centimeter [sɛntimetər] *de (~s)* **1** centimetre: *een kubieke ~* a cubic centimetre; *een vierkante ~* a square centimetre; **2** tape-measure

centraal [sɛntral] *adj, adv* central: *(fig) een centrale figuur* a central *(or:* key) figure; *een ~ gelegen punt* a centrally situated point

centrale [sɛntralə] *de (~s)* **1** power station, powerhouse; **2** (telephone) exchange, switchboard

centralisatie [sɛntraliza(t)si] *de (~s)* centralization

centreren [sɛntrɛrə(n)] *vb* centre

centrifuge [sɛntrifyːʒə] *de (~s)* centrifuge, spin-dryer

centrum [sɛntrʏm] *het (centra)* centre: *in het ~ van de belangstelling staan* be the centre of attention; *(pol) links (or: rechts) van het ~* left *(or:* right) of centre

centrumspits [sɛntrʏmspɪts] *de (~en)* centre forward

ceremonie [serəmoni] *de (~s, ceremoniën)* ceremony

ceremonieel [serəmon(i)jɛl] *adj, adv* ceremonial, formal: *een ceremoniële ontvangst* a formal reception

ceremoniemeester [serəmonimestər] *de (~s)* Master of Ceremonies, best man

certificaat [sɛrtifikɑt] *het (certificaten)* certificate

Ceylon [sɛilɔn] *het* Ceylon, Sri Lanka

cfk [seɛfka] *de (~'s) chloorfluorkoolwaterstof* CFC

chagrijnig [ʃɑɣrɛinəχ] *adj, adv* miserable, grouchy: *doe niet zo ~* stop being such a misery; *~ zijn* sulk

chalet [ʃalɛ] *het, de (~s)* chalet, Swiss cottage

champagne [ʃɑmpɑɲə] *de (~s)* champagne

champignon [ʃɑmpijɔn] *de (~s)* mushroom

chantage [ʃɑntaʒə] *de (~s)* blackmail

chanteren [ʃɑntɛrə(n)] *vb* blackmail

chaos [χaɔs] *de* chaos, disorder, havoc: *er heerst ~ in het land* the country is in chaos

chaotisch [χaotis] *adj, adv* chaotic

chaperon [ʃapərɔn] *de (~s)* chaperon(e)

charcuterie [ʃɑrkytəri] *de (Belg)* cold cooked meats

charisma [χarɪsma] *het (~'s)* charisma

charmant [ʃɑrmɑnt] *adj* charming, engaging, winning, delightful, attractive: *een ~e jongeman* a charming young man

charme [ʃɑrmə] *de (~s)* charm

charter [tʃɑːrtər] *het (~s)* **1** charter flight; charter(ed) plane; **2** charter

charteren [ʃɑrtərə(n)] *vb* charter; enlist, commission

chartervliegtuig [tʃɑːrtərvliːxtœyx] *het (~en)* charter(ed) aircraft

chassis [ʃɑsi] *het* chassis

chatten [tʃɛtə(n)] *vb* chat

chaufferen [ʃofɛrə(n)] *vb* drive

chauffeur [ʃofør] *de (~s)* driver, chauffeur

chauvinisme [ʃovinɪsmə] *het* chauvinism

chauvinist [ʃovinɪst] *de (~en)* chauvinist

checken [tʃɛkə(n)] *vb* check (up, out), verify

chef [ʃɛf] *de (~s)* leader, boss; head, chief, superior (officer), manager, stationmaster: *~ van een afdeling* head (*or:* manager) of a department; *~ d'équipe* team manager; *~ de mission* head of the delegation

chef-kok [ʃɛfkɔk] *de (~s)* chef

chemicaliën [xemikɑlijə(n)] *de* chemicals, chemical products

chemicus [xemikʏs] *de (chemici)* chemist

chemie [xemi] *de* chemistry

chemotherapie [xemoterapi] *de* chemotherapy

cheque [ʃɛk] *de (~s)* cheque: *een ongedekte ~* a dud cheque; *een ~ innen* cash a cheque

chequeboek [tʃɛgbuk] *het (~en)* chequebook

¹**chic** [ʃik] *adj, adv* **1** chic, stylish, smart: *er ~ uitzien* look (very) smart; **2** elegant, distinguished, fashionable

²**chic** [ʃik] *de* chic, stylishness, elegance

Chileen [ʃilen] *de (Chilenen)* Chilean

Chileens [ʃilens] *adj* Chilean

chili [ʃili] *de* chilli, hot pepper

Chili [ʃili] *het* Chile

chimpansee [ʃɪmpɑnse] *de (~s)* chimpanzee, chimp

China [ʃina] *het* China

¹**Chinees** [ʃines] *de (Chinezen)* **1** Chinese, Chinaman; **2** Chinese restaurant; Chinese takeaway

²**Chinees** [ʃines] *het (language)* Chinese

³**Chinees** [ʃines] *adj* Chinese: *Chinese wijk (buurt)* Chinatown

Chinese [ʃinesə] *de* Chinese (woman)

chip [tʃɪp] *de (~s)* **1** chip, integrated circuit; **2** chip, microprocessor

chipkaart [tʃɪpkart] *de (~en)* smart card, intelligent card

chipknip [tʃɪpknɪp] *de (~pen)* smart card (for small amounts)

chips [ʃɪps] *de* (potato) crisps, *(Am)* chips

Chiro [xiro] *de (Belg)* Christian youth movement

chirurg [ʃirʏrx] *de (~en)* surgeon

chirurgie [ʃirʏrxi] *de* surgery

chirurgisch [ʃirʏrxis] *adj, adv* surgical: *een ~e ingreep* a surgical operation, surgery

chloor [xlor] *het, de* **1** chlorine; **2** bleach

chloroform [xlorofɔrm] *de* chloroform

chocolaatje [ʃokolaːcə] *het (~s)* chocolate

chocolade [ʃokolɑdə] *de* **1** chocolate, choc: *pure ~* plain chocolate; **2** (drinking) chocolate, cocoa

chocolademelk [ʃokolɑdəmɛlk] *de* (drinking) chocolate, cocoa

chocoladepasta [ʃokolɑdəpɑsta] *de (~'s)* chocolate spread

choke [ʃok] *de (~s)* choke

cholera [xoləra] *de* cholera

cholesterol [xolɛstərɔl] *de* cholesterol

choqueren [ʃɔkerə(n)] *vb* shock, give offence: *gechoqueerd zijn (door)* be shocked (at, by)

choreograaf [xorejoyraf] *de (-grafen)* choreographer

¹**christelijk** [krɪstələk] *adj* Christian: *een ~e school* a protestant school

²**christelijk** [krɪstələk] *adv* decently

christen [krɪstə(n)] *de (~en)* Christian

christen-democraat [krɪstə(n)demokrat] *de (-democraten)* Christian Democrat

christendom [krɪstə(n)dɔm] *het* Christianity

Christus [krɪstʏs] *de* Christ || *na ~* A.D., after Christ; *voor ~* B.C., before Christ

chromosoom [xromozom] *het (chromosomen)* chromosome

chronisch [xronis] *adj, adv* chronic, lingering, recurrent: *een ~ zieke* a chronically sick patient

chronologie [xronoloxi] *de* chronology

chronologisch [xronoloyis] *adj, adv* chronological

chronometer [xronometər] *de (~s)* stopwatch, chronograph

chroom [xrom] *het* chrome

chrysant [xrizɑnt] *de (~en)* chrysanthemum

CID *de Criminele Inlichtingendienst* criminal investigation department

cider [sidər] *de* cider

cijfer [sɛifər] *het (~s)* **1** figure, numeral, digit, cipher: *Romeinse ~s* Roman numerals; *twee ~s achter de komma* two decimal places; *getallen die in de vijf ~s lopen* five-figure numbers; **2** mark, grade: *het hoogste ~* the highest mark

cijferlijst [sɛifərlɛist] *de (~en)* list of marks, (school) report

cilinder [silɪndər] *de (~s)* cylinder

cineast [sinejɑst] *de (~en)* film maker (*or:* director)

cipier [sipir] *de (~s)* warder, jailer

cipres [siprɛs] *de (~sen)* cypress

circa [sɪrka] *adv* approximately, about, circa

circuit [sɪrkwi] *het (~s)* **1** *(sport)* circuit, (race)track; **2** scene: *het zwarte ~* the black economy

circulatie [sɪrkyla(t)si] *de (~s)* circulation: *geld in ~ brengen* put money into circulation

circuleren [sɪrkylerə(n)] *vb* circulate; distribute: *geruchten laten ~* put about (*or:* circulate) rumours

circumcisie [sɪrkʏmsizi] *de (~s)* circumcision

circumflex [sɪrkʏmflɛks] *het, de (~en)* circumflex (accent)

circus [sɪrkʏs] *het, de (~sen)* circus
cirkel [sɪrkəl] *de (~s)* circle: *halve* ~ semicircle; *een vicieuze* ~ a vicious circle
cirkeldiagram [sɪrkəldijaɣrɑm] *het (~men)* pie chart, circle graph
cirkelen [sɪrkələ(n)] *vb* circle, orbit
cirkelomtrek [sɪrkəlɔmtrɛk] *de (~ken)* perimeter
citaat [sitat] *het (citaten)* quotation, quote; citation: *einde* ~ unquote, close quotes
citer [sitər] *de (~s)* zither
citeren [sitɛrə(n)] *vb* quote; cite
Citotoets [sitotuts] *de (~en)* secondary education aptitude test
citroen [sitrʏn] *de (~en)* lemon
citrusvrucht [sitrʏsfrʏχt] *de (~en)* citrus fruit
city [sɪti] *de (~'s)* city centre
civiel [sivil] *adj, adv* civil, civilian: *een politieman in* ~ plain-clothes officer
civiel-ingenieur [sivilɪnʒeɲør] *de (~s)* civil engineer
civilisatie [siviliza(t)si] *de (~s)* civilization
claim [klem] *de (~s)* claim: *een* ~ *indienen (bij)* lodge a claim (with)
claimen [klɛmə(n)] *vb* (lay) claim (to), file (*or:* lodge) a claim: *een bedrag* ~ *bij de verzekering* claim on one's insurance
clan [klɛn] *de (~s)* clan, clique, coterie
clandestien [klɑndɛstin] *adj, adv* clandestine; illicit: *de* ~*e pers* underground press; ~ *gestookte whisky* bootleg whiskey, moonshine
clark [klɑːrk] *de (~s) (Belg)* fork-lift truck
classeur [klɑsør] *de (~s) (Belg)* file
classicus [klɑsikʏs] *de (classici)* classicist
classificatie [klɑsifika(t)si] *de (~s)* classification, ranking, rating
classificeren [klɑsifisɛrə(n)] *vb* classify, class, rank
claustrofobie [klɑustrofobi] *de* claustrophobia
clausule [klɑuzylə] *de (~s)* clause, proviso, stipulation: *een* ~ *opnemen in* build a clause into
claxon [klɑksɔn] *de (~s)* (motor) horn: *op de* ~ *drukken* sound one's horn
claxonneren [klɑksɔnɛrə(n)] *vb* sound one's horn; hoot
cliché [kliʃe] *het (~s)* 1 cliché; 2 plate, block
clichématig [kliʃematəχ] *adj, adv* cliché'd, commonplace, trite
cliënt [klijɛnt] *de (~en)* 1 client; 2 customer, patron
clientèle [klijɛntɛːlə] *de* clientele, custom(ers)
climax [klimɑks] *de (~en)* climax: *naar een* ~ *toe werken* build (up) to a climax
clip [klɪp] *de (~s)* 1 paper clip, *(large)* bulldog clip; 2 clip, pin; 3 (video)clip
clitoris [klitɔrɪs] *de (clitores)* clitoris
closet [klozɛt] *het (~s)* lavatory, toilet
closetpot [klozɛtpɔt] *de (~ten)* lavatory pan
clou [klu] *de* point, essence, punch line: *de* ~ *van iets niet snappen* miss the point (of sth)
clown [klɑun] *de (~s)* clown, buffoon: *de* ~ *uithangen* clown around

clownesk [klɑunɛsk] *adj, adv* clownish: *een* ~ *gebaar* a comic(al) gesture
club [klʏp] *de (~s)* 1 club *(also golf)*, society, association; 2 crowd, group, gang
clubhuis [klʏphœys] *het (-huizen)* 1 club(house), pavilion; 2 community centre, youth centre
clubkas [klʏpkɑs] *de (~sen)* club funds
cluster [klʏstər] *de (~s)* cluster
cm *centimeter* cm
coach [kotʃ] *de (~es)* coach, trainer, supervisor, tutor
coachen [kotʃə(n)] *vb* coach, train; tutor
coalitie [kowali(t)si] *de (~s)* coalition
coassistent [koɑsistɛnt] *de (~en)* (assistant) houseman, *(Am)* intern(e)
cobra [kobra] *de (~'s)* cobra
cocaïne [kokainə] *de* cocaine: ~ *snuiven* snort (*or:* sniff) cocaine
cockpit [kɔkpɪt] *de (~s)* cockpit, flight deck
cocktail [kɔktel] *de (~s)* cocktail
cocktailbar [kɔktelbɑːr] *de (~s)* cocktail lounge
cocon [kokɔn] *de (~s)* cocoon, pod
code [kodə] *de (~s)* code, cipher: *een* ~ *ontcijferen* crack a code
coderen [kodɛrə(n)] *vb* (en)code, encipher
codicil [kodisɪl] *het (~len)* codicil
coëfficiënt [koɛfiʃɛnt] *de (~en)* coefficient
coffeeshop [kɔfiʃɔp] *de (~s)* coffee shop
cognac [kɔɲɑk] *de (~s)* cognac
cognitief [kɔɣnitif] *adj, adv* cognitive
cognossement [kɔχnɔsəmɛnt] *het (~en)* bill of lading, B/L
coherent [kohɛrɛnt] *adj, adv* coherent, consistent
cohesie [kohɛzi] *de* cohesion
coke [kok] *de* coke; snow
cokes [koks] *de* coke
col [kɔl] *de (~s)* 1 roll-neck, polo neck; 2 col, (mountain) pass
cola [kola] *de (~'s)* coke
cola-tic [kolatɪk] *de* rum (*or:* gin) and coke
colbert [kɔlbɛːr] *het, de (~s)* jacket
collaborateur [kɔlaboratør] *de (~s)* collaborator, quisling
collaboratie [kɔlabora(t)si] *de* collaboration
collaboreren [kɔlaborɛrə(n)] *vb* collaborate, work together
collage [kɔlaʒə] *de (~s)* collage, montage, paste-up
collectant [kɔlɛktɑnt] *de (~en)* collector, sidesman
collecte [kɔlɛktə] *de (~s)* collection, whip-round
collecteren [kɔlɛktɛrə(n)] *vb* collect, make a collection, *(in church)* take the collection
collecteur [kɔlɛktør] *de (~s)* collector
collectie [kɔlɛksi] *de (~s)* 1 collection, show: *een fraaie* ~ *schilderijen* a fine collection of paintings; 2 collection, accumulation
¹collectief [kɔlɛktif] *adj, adv* collective, corporate, joint, communal: *collectieve arbeidsovereenkomst* collective wage agreement; *collectieve uitgaven* public expenditure

²**collectief** [kɔlɛktif] *het (collectieven)* collective

collega [kɔleɣa] *de (~'s, ~e)* colleague, associate, workmate

college [kɔleɣə] *het (~s)* 1 college; (university) class, (formal) lecture: *de ~s zijn weer begonnen* term has started again; *~ geven (over)* lecture (on), give lectures (on); *~ lopen* attend lectures; 2 board: *~ van bestuur: a)* Board of Governors (or *Am:* Regents); *b)* Board of Directors; *het ~ van burgemeester en wethouders* the (City, Town) Council

collegedictaat [kɔleɣədɪktat] *het (-dictaten)* lecture notes

collegiaal [kɔleɣ(i)jal] *adj, adv* fraternal, brotherly, comradely: *zich ~ opstellen* be loyal to one's colleagues

collie [kɔli] *de (~s)* collie

collier [kɔljeː] *het, de (~s)* necklace

collo [kɔlo] *het (colli)* package

colofon [kolofɔn] *het, de (~s)* colophon

Colombia [kolɔmbija] *het* Colombia

Colombiaan [kolɔmbijan] *de (Colombianen)* Colombian

Colombiaans [kolɔmbijans] *adj* Colombian

colonnade [kolɔnadə] *de (~s, ~n)* colonnade, portico

colonne [kolɔnə] *de (~s)* column

colporteren [kɔlpɔrteːrə(n)] *vb* sell door-to-door, hawk

coltrui [kɔltrœy] *de (~en)* roll-neck (pullover, sweater), *(Am)* turtleneck (pullover, sweater)

coma [koma] *het (~'s)* coma: *in (een) ~ raken* lapse into a coma

comapatiënt [komapaʃɛnt] *de (~en)* comatose patient, patient in a coma

combi [kɔmbi] *de (~'s)* estate car, station wagon

combikaart [kɔmbikart] *de (~en)* all-in-one ticket, combined ticket, train plus admission to an event

combinatie [kɔmbina(t)si] *de (~s)* combination

combinatietang [kɔmbina(t)sitaŋ] *de (~en)* combination pliers, electrician's pliers

combine [kɔmbɑjn] *de (~s)* combine (harvester)

¹**combineren** [kɔmbineːrə(n)] *vb* go (together), match: *deze kleuren ~ niet* these colours don't go (together) (or: don't match), these colours clash

²**combineren** [kɔmbineːrə(n)] *vb* 1 combine (with): *twee banen ~* combine two jobs; 2 associate (with), link (with)

combo [kɔmbo] *het, de (~'s)* combo

comeback [kɔmbɛk] *de (~s)* comeback: *een ~ maken* make (or: stage) a comeback

comfort [kɔmfɔːr] *het* comfort *(oft pl)*, convenience *(oft pl)*: *dit huis is voorzien van het modernste ~* this house is fully equipped with the latest conveniences

comfortabel [kɔmfɔrtabəl] *adj, adv* comfortable

comité [komiteː] *het (~s)* committee: *uitvoerend ~* executive committee

commandant [komandɑnt] *de (~en)* 1 commander, commandant; 2 chief (fire) officer, (fire) chief

commanderen [komandeːrə(n)] *vb* 1 command, be in command (of); 2 give orders, *(depr)* boss about, order about

commanditair [komanditɛːr] *adj* || *~ vennootschap* limited partnership

commando [komando] *het (~'s)* 1 command: *het ~ voeren (over)* be in command (of); 2 (word of) command, order; *(comp)* command: *iets op ~ doen* do sth to order; *huilen op ~* cry at will; 3 *(mil)* commando

commentaar [komɛntaːr] *het, de (commentaren)* 1 comment(s), remark(s), observation(s), commentary (on): *~ op iets geven* (or: *leveren*) comment (or: make comments) on sth; *geen ~* no comment; 2 (unfavourable) comment, criticism: *een hoop ~ krijgen* receive a lot of unfavourable comment; *rechtstreeks ~* (running) commentary

commentaarstem [komɛntarstɛm] *de (~men)* voice-over

commentator [komɛntatɔr] *de (~en)* commentator

commercie [komɛrsi] *de* commerce, trade

commercieel [komɛrʃel] *adj, adv* commercial: *op niet-commerciële basis* on a non-profit(-making) basis

commissariaat [komɪsarijat] *het (commissariaten)* 1 commissionership: *een ~ bekleden bij een bedrijf* sit on the board of a company; 2 commissioner's office

commissaris [komɪsarɪs] *de (~sen)* 1 commissioner; governor: *~ van de Koningin* (Royal) Commissioner, governor; *~ van politie* Chief Constable, Chief of Police, police commissioner; *raad van ~sen* board of commissioners; 2 official, officer

commissie [komɪsi] *de (~s)* 1 committee, board, commission: *de Europese Commissie* the European Commission; *een ~ instellen* appoint (or: set up) a committee; 2 *(com)* commission

commode [komodə] *de (~s)* chest of drawers

commune [komynə] *de (~s)* commune

communicant [komynikɑnt] *de (~en)* 1 s.o. making his (or: her) first Communion; 2 communicant

communicatie [komynika(t)si] *de (~s)* communication

communicatief [komynikatif] *adj, adv* communicative

communicatiemiddel [komynika(t)simɪdəl] *het (~en)* means of communication

communiceren [komyniseːrə(n)] *vb* communicate (with): *~ de vaten* communicating vessels

communie [komyni] *de (~s)* (Holy) Communion: *eerste* (or: *plechtige*) *~* first (or: solemn) Communion

communiqué [komynikeː] *het (~s)* communiqué, statement: *een ~ uitgeven* issue a communiqué, put out a statement

communisme [komynɪsmə] *het* Communism

communist [komynɪst] *de (~en)* Communist

compact [kɔmpɑkt] *adj, adv* compact
compact disc [kɔmpɑkdɪsk] *de (~s)* compact disc
compagnie [kɔmpɑɲi] *de (~s)* company, partnership: *de Oost-Indische Compagnie* the Dutch East India Company
compagnon [kɔmpɑɲɔn] *de (~s)* **1** partner, (business) associate: *de ~ van iem worden* go into partnership with s.o.; **2** pal, buddy, chum
compartiment [kɔmpɑrtimɛnt] *het (~en)* compartment
compatibel [kɔmpɑtibəl] *adj* compatible
compensatie [kɔmpɛnzɑ(t)si] *de (~s)* compensation: *als ~ voor, ter ~ van* by way of compensation for
compenseren [kɔmpɛnserə(n)] *vb* compensate for, counterbalance, make good: *dit compenseert de nadelen* this outweighs the disadvantages; *een tekort ~* make good a deficiency (*or:* deficit)
competent [kɔmpətɛnt] *adj* **1** competent, able, capable: *hij is (niet) ~ op dat gebied* he is (not) competent in that field; **2** competent, qualified, authorized: *dit hof is in deze kwestie niet ~* this court is not competent to settle this matter
competentie [kɔmpətɛnsi] *de (~s)* competence, capacity
competitie [kɔmpəti(t)si] *de (~s)* league
competitiewedstrijd [kɔmpəti(t)siwɛtstrɛit] *de (~en)* league match; league game
compilatie [kɔmpilɑ(t)si] *de (~s)* compilation
compleet [kɔmplet] *adj, adv* **1** complete: *deze jaargang is niet ~* this volume is incomplete; **2** complete, total, utter: *complete onzin* utter (*or:* sheer) nonsense; *ik was ~ vergeten de oven aan te zetten* I'd clean (*or:* completely) forgotten to switch the oven on
complement [kɔmpləmɛnt] *het (~en)* complement
complementair [kɔmplemɛntɛːr] *adj* complementary
¹**complex** [kɔmplɛks] *het (~en)* complex; aggregate: *een heel ~ van regels* a whole complex of rules
²**complex** [kɔmplɛks] *adj* complex, complicated, intricate: *een ~ probleem* a complex problem; *een ~ verschijnsel* a complex phenomenon
complicatie [kɔmplikɑ(t)si] *de (~s)* complication: *bij dit soort operaties treden zelden ~s op* with this type of surgery complications hardly ever arise
compliceren [kɔmpliserə(n)] *vb* complicate: *een gecompliceerde breuk* a compound fracture
compliment [kɔmplimɛnt] *het (~en)* **1** compliment: *iem een ~ maken over iets* pay s.o. a compliment on sth, compliment s.o. on sth; **2** regard, respect: *de ~en van vader en of u even wilt komen* father sends his regards and would you mind calling around
complimenteren [kɔmplimɛnterə(n)] *vb* compliment: *iem ~ met iets* compliment s.o. on sth
complimenteus [kɔmplimɛntøs] *adj, adv* complimentary
complot [kɔmplɔt] *het (~ten)* **1** plot: *een ~ smeden*

hatch a plot, conspire; **2** conspiracy
component [kɔmponɛnt] *de (~en)* component
componeren [kɔmponerə(n)] *vb* compose
componist [kɔmponɪst] *de (~en)* composer
compositie [kɔmpozi(t)si] *de (~s)* composition
compost [kɔmpɔst] *het, de* compost
composteren [kɔmpɔsterə(n)] *vb* compost
compote [kɔmpɔːt] *de (~s)* stewed fruit
compressor [kɔmprɛsɔr] *de (~en)* compressor
comprimeren [kɔmprimerə(n)] *vb* compress, condense
compromis [kɔmprɔmi] *het (~sen)* compromise: *een ~ aangaan (or: sluiten)* come to (*or:* reach) a compromise
compromitteren [kɔmpromiterə(n)] *vb* compromise
compromitterend [kɔmpromiterənt] *adj* compromising, incriminating: *~e verklaringen (or: papieren)* incriminating statements (*or:* documents)
computer [kɔmpjutər] *de (~s)* computer: *gegevens invoeren in een ~* feed data into a computer
computeren [kɔmpjutərə(n)] *vb* be at (*or:* work on, play on) the computer
computerfanaat [kɔmpjutərfanat] *de* computer fanatic (*or:* freak)
computergestuurd [kɔmpjutərɣəstyrt] *adj* computer-controlled
computerkraker [kɔmpjutərkrakər] *de (~s)* hacker
computerprogramma [kɔmpjutərproɣrama] *het (~'s)* computer program
computerprogrammeur [kɔmpjutərproɣramør] *de (~s)* computer programmer
computertijd [kɔmpjutərtɛit] *de* machine time, run time
concentraat [kɔnsɛntrat] *het (concentraten)* concentrate, extract
concentratie [kɔnsɛntrɑ(t)si] *de (~s)* concentration: *~ van het gezag* concentration of authority; *zijn ~ verliezen* lose one's concentration
concentratiekamp [kɔnsɛntrɑ(t)sikɑmp] *het (~en)* concentration camp
concentratieschool [kɔnsɛntrɑ(t)sisχol] *de (-scholen) (Belg)* school for ethnic minority children
¹**concentreren** [kɔnsɛntrerə(n)] *ref vb* concentrate (on): *zijn hoop concentreerde zich op de zomervakantie* his hopes were pinned on the summer holidays
²**concentreren** [kɔnsɛntrerə(n)] *vb* concentrate, centre, mass, strengthen: *een geconcentreerde oplossing* a concentrated solution
concentrisch [kɔnsɛntris] *adj, adv* concentric
concept [kɔnsɛpt] *het (~en)* **1** (rough, first) draft, outline: *een ~ maken van* draft; **2** concept
conceptie [kɔnsɛpsi] *de (~s)* conception
concern [kɔnsyːrn] *het (~s)* group
concert [kɔnsɛrt] *het (~en)* **1** concert, recital: *naar een ~ gaan* go to a concert; **2** concerto

concertgebouw [kɔnsɛrtxǝbɑu] *het (~en)* concert hall

concertpodium [kɔnsɛrtpodijʏm] *het (~s, -podia)* concert platform

concertzaal [kɔnsɛrtsal] *de (-zalen)* concert hall, auditorium

concessie [kɔnsɛsi] *de (~s)* concession, franchise, licence || ~*s doen aan iem* make concessions to s.o.

conciërge [kɔnʃɛːrʒǝ] *de (~s)* caretaker, janitor, porter

concluderen [kɔŋklydɛrǝ(n)] *vb* conclude, deduce: *wat kunnen we daaruit ~?* what can we conclude from that?

conclusie [kɔŋklyzi] *de (~s)* conclusion, deduction, findings: *de ~ trekken* draw the conclusion

concours [kɔŋkur] *het, de (~en)* competition, contest

concreet [kɔŋkret] *adj, adv* **1** concrete, material, real, actual, tangible: *een ~ begrip* a concrete term; *een ~ geval van* a specific case of; **2** definite: *concrete toezeggingen* definite promises; *het overleg heeft niets ~s opgeleverd* the discussion did not result in anything concrete

concurrent [kɔŋkyrɛnt] *de (~en)* competitor, rival

concurrentie [kɔŋkyrɛnsi] *de* competition, contest, rivalry

concurrentiepositie [kɔŋkyrɛnsipozi(t)si] *de (~s)* competitive position, competitiveness

concurreren [kɔŋkyrɛrǝ(n)] *vb* compete

concurrerend [kɔŋkyrɛrǝnt] *adj, adv* competitive *(price);* competing, rival; conflicting

condens [kɔndɛns] *het* condensation

condenseren [kɔndɛnzɛrǝ(n)] *vb* condense, boil down, evaporate

conditie [kɔndi(t)si] *de (~s)* **1** condition, proviso, *(pl also)* terms: *een ~ stellen* make a condition; *onder (op) ~ dat* on (the) condition that; **2** condition, state, form, shape: *de speler is in goede ~* the player is in good shape *(or:* is fit); *je hebt geen ~* you're (badly) out of condition

conditietraining [kɔndi(t)sitrenɪŋ] *de* fitness training: *aan ~ doen* work out

condoléance [kɔndolejɑsǝ] *de (~s)* condolence, sympathy: *mag ik u mijn ~s aanbieden* may I offer my condolences

condoleren [kɔndolɛrǝ(n)] *vb* offer one's condolences (to s.o.)

condoom [kɔndom] *het (~s)* condom; rubber

condor [kɔndɔr] *de (~s)* (Andean) condor

conducteur [kɔndʏktør] *de (~s)* conductor, ticket collector

confectie [kɔnfɛksi] *de* ready-to-wear clothes, ready-made clothes

confederatie [kɔnfedǝra(t)si] *de (~s)* confederation, confederacy

conference [kɔnferɑsǝ] *de* **1** (solo) act, (comic) monologue; **2** talk

conferencier [kɔnferɑʃe] *de (~s)* entertainer

conferentie [kɔnferɛnsi] *de (~s)* conference, meeting

confessie [kɔnfɛsi] *de (~s)* confession, admission

confessioneel [kɔnfɛʃonel] *adj* confessional, denominational

confetti [kɔnfɛti] *de* confetti

confidentieel [kɔnfidɛnʃel] *adj, adv* confidential

confisqueren [kɔnfiskɛrǝ(n)] *vb* confiscate

confituren [kɔnfityrǝ(n)] *de* conserves

confituur [kɔnfityr] *de (confituren) (Belg)* jam

conflict [kɔnflɪkt] *het (~en)* conflict, clash: *in ~ komen met* come into conflict with

conform [kɔnfɔrm] *adj, adv* in accordance with

conformeren [kɔnfɔrmɛrǝ(n)] *refvb* conform (to), comply (with): *zich ~ aan de publieke opinie* bow to public opinion

confrontatie [kɔnfrɔnta(t)si] *de (~s)* confrontation

confronteren [kɔnfrɔntɛrǝ(n)] *vb* confront (with): *met de werkelijkheid geconfronteerd worden* be faced *(or:* confronted) with reality

conglomeratie [kɔŋxlomǝra(t)si] *de (~s)* conglomeration

congres [kɔŋɣrɛs] *het (~sen)* conference, congress

congrescentrum [kɔŋɣrɛsɛntrʏm] *het (-centra)* conference centre

congresgebouw [kɔŋɣrɛsxǝbɑu] *het* conference hall

conifeer [konifer] *de (coniferen)* conifer

conjunctuur [kɔnjʏŋktyr] *de (conjuncturen)* economic situation, market conditions, trade cycle

connectie [kɔnɛksi] *de (~s)* connection, link || *goede ~s hebben* be well connected

corrector [kɔnrɛktɔr] *de (~s) (roughly)* deputy headmaster

consciëntieus [kɔnʃɛnʃøs] *adj, adv* conscientious, scrupulous, painstaking

consecratie [kɔnsekra(t)si] *de (~s)* consecration

consensus [kɔnsɛnzʏs] *de* consensus

consequent [kɔnsǝkwɛnt] *adj, adv* **1** logical: *~ handelen* act logically, be consistent; **2** consistent (with)

consequentie [kɔnsǝkwɛnsi] *de (~s)* implication, consequence: *de ~s trekken* draw the obvious conclusion

¹conservatief [kɔnsɛrvatif] *de (conservatieven)* conservative, Tory

²conservatief [kɔnsɛrvatif] *adj, adv* conservative; *(pol)* Conservative: *de conservatieve partij* the Conservative *(or:* Tory) Party

conservator [kɔnsɛrvatɔr] *de (~s, ~en)* curator, keeper, custodian

conservatorium [kɔnsɛrvatoriʏm] *het (conservatoria)* academy of music, conservatory

conserven [kɔnsɛrvǝ(n)] *de* canned food(s), tinned food(s), preserved food(s)

conservenblik [kɔnsɛrvǝ(n)blɪk] *het (~ken)* can, tin (can)

conserveren [kɔnsɛrvɛrǝ(n)] *vb* preserve, conserve; can, tin: *goed geconserveerd zijn* be well preserved

conservering [kɔnzɛrvɛrɪŋ] *de* **1** preservation; conservation; **2** preserving, canning

conserveringsmiddel [kɔnsɛrvɛrɪŋsmɪdəl] *het (~en)* preservative

consignatie [kɔnsiɲa(t)si] *de (~s)* consignment

consolideren [kɔnsolidɛrə(n)] *vb* **1** consolidate, strengthen; **2** consolidate, fund

consorten [kɔnsɔrtə(n)] *de* confederates, associates, buddies: *Hans en ~* Hans and his pals

consortium [kɔnsɔr(t)sijʏm] *het (~s)* consortium, syndicate

constant [kɔnstɑnt] *adj, adv* constant, steady, continuous, staunch, loyal: *een ~e grootheid* (or: *waarde)* a constant quantity (or: value); *hij houdt me ~ voor de gek* he is forever pulling my leg (or: making a fool of me)

constante [kɔnstɑntə] *de (~n)* constant

constateren [kɔnstatɛrə(n)] *vb* establish, ascertain, record; detect, observe: *ik constateer slechts het feit dat* I'm merely stating the fact that, all I'm saying is that

constatering [kɔnstatɛrɪŋ] *de (~en)* observation, establishment

consternatie [kɔnstɛrna(t)si] *de (~s)* consternation, alarm: *dat gaf heel wat ~* it caused quite a stir

constipatie [kɔnstipa(t)si] *de* constipation: *last hebben van ~* be constipated

constitutie [kɔnstitʏ(t)si] *de (~s)* **1** constitution, physique: *een slechte ~ hebben* have a weak constitution; **2** constitution

constitutioneel [kɔnstity(t)ʃonel] *adj, adv* constitutional: *constitutionele monarchie* constitutional monarchy

constructeur [kɔnstrʏktør] *de (~s)* designer

constructie [kɔnstrʏksi] *de (~s)* construction, building, erection, structure

constructief [kɔnstrʏktif] *adj, adv* **1** constructive, useful: *~ te werk gaan* go about sth in a constructive way; **2** constructional, structural

construeren [kɔnstrywɛrə(n)] *vb* construct, build, erect, design

consul [kɔnsʏl] *de (~s)* consul

consulaat [kɔnsʏlat] *het (consulaten)* consulate

consulent [kɔnsʏlɛnt] *de (~en)* consultant, adviser

consult [kɔnsʏlt] *het (~en)* consultation, visit

consultatiebureau [kɔnsʏlta(t)sibyro] *het (~s)* clinic, health centre: *~ voor zuigelingen* infant welfare centre, child health centre, well-baby clinic

consulteren [kɔnsʏltɛrə(n)] *vb* **1** consult; **2** confer, discuss

consument [kɔnsʏmɛnt] *de (~en)* consumer

consumentenbond [kɔnsʏmɛntə(n)bɔnt] *de (~en)* consumers' organization

consumeren [kɔnsʏmɛrə(n)] *vb* **1** consume; eat, drink; **2** deplete, exhaust

consumptie [kɔnsʏmpsi] *de (~s)* **1** consumption: *(on)geschikt voor ~* (un)fit for (human) consumption; **2** food, drink(s), refreshment(s)

consumptiebon [kɔnzʏmsibɔn] *de (~nen)* food voucher

consumptief [kɔnsʏmptif] *adj* consumptive: *~ krediet* consumer credit

consumptiegoederen [kɔnsʏmpsiɣudərə(n)] *de* consumer goods: *duurzame ~* consumer durables

contact [kɔntɑkt] *het (~en)* **1** contact, connection, touch: *telefonisch ~ opnemen* get in touch by phone; *~ opnemen met iem (over iets)* contact s.o., get in touch with s.o.; *in ~ blijven met* keep in touch with; **2** contact, terms: *een goed ~ met iem hebben* have a good relationship with s.o.; **3** contact (man), connection: *~en hebben in bepaalde kringen* have connections in certain circles; **4** contact, switch, ignition: *het sleuteltje in het ~ steken* put the key in(to) the ignition

contactadvertentie [kɔntɑktɑtfərtɛnsi] *de (~s)* personal ad(vert), advert in the personal column

contactdoos [kɔntɑɡdos] *de (-dozen)* socket; appliance inlet

contactlens [kɔntɑktlɛns] *de (-lenzen)* contact lens, *(pl also, inf)* contacts

contactlijm [kɔntɑktleim] *de* contact adhesive

contactsleutel [kɔntɑktsløtəl] *de (~s)* ignition key

contactueel [kɔntɑktywel] *adj, adv* contactual

container [kɔntenər] *de (~s)* **1** container; **2** (rubbish) skip

containerpark [kɔntenərpɑrk] *het (~en) (Belg)* recycling centre, amenity centre

contant [kɔntɑnt] *adj, adv* cash, ready: *tegen ~e betaling* on cash payment, cash down; *~ geld* ready money

contanten [kɔntɑntə(n)] *de* cash, ready money, cash in hand

content [kɔntɛnt] *adj* content (with), satisfied (with)

context [kɔntɛkst] *de (~en)* context, framework, background: *je moet dat in de juiste ~ zien* you must put that into its proper context

continent [kɔntinɛnt] *het (~en)* continent

contingent [kɔntiŋɣɛnt] *het (~en)* **1** contingent; **2** quota, share, proportion, allocation, allotment

¹continu [kɔntiny] *adj* continuous, unbroken

²continu [kɔntiny] *adv* continuously: *hij loopt ~ te klagen* he is always complaining

continueren [kɔntinywɛrə(n)] *vb* **1** continue (with), carry on (with); **2** continue, retain

continuering *de* continuation

continuïteit [kɔntinywiteit] *de* **1** continuity; **2** continuation

conto [kɔnto] *het (~'s)* account: *(fig) iets op iemands ~ schrijven* hold s.o. accountable for sth

contour [kɔntur] *de (~en)* contour

contra [kɔntra] *prep* contra, against, *(law)* versus: *alle argumenten pro en ~ bekijken* consider all the arguments for and against

contrabas [kɔntrabɑs] *de (~sen)* (double) bass

contraceptie [kɔntrasɛpsi] *de* contraception

contract [kɔntrɑkt] *het (~en)* contract, agreement: *zijn ~ loopt af* his contract is running out; *een ~ op-*

zeggen (or: verbreken) terminate (or: break) a contract; volgens ~ according to contract

contracteren [kɔntrɑktɛrə(n)] vb 1 engage, sign (up, on); 2 contract: ~de partijen contracting parties

contradictie [kɔntradɪksi] de (~s) contradiction

contraspionage [kɔntraspijonaʒə] de (~s) counter-espionage

contrast [kɔntrɑst] het (~en) contrast: een schril ~ a harsh contrast

contreien [kɔntrɛiə(n)] de parts, regions

contributie [kɔntribyˌ(t)si] de (~s) subscription; contribution

controle [kɔntrɔːlə] de (~s) 1 check (on), checking, control, supervision (of, over); (med) check-up, monitoring: ~ van de bagage baggage check; de ~ van de boekhouding the audit of accounts, the examination of the books; de ~ over het stuur verliezen lose control of the steering-wheel; 2 control (point), checkpoint, (ticket) gate: zijn kaartje aan de ~ afgeven hand in one's ticket at the gate

controleerbaar [kɔntrolɛrbar] adj verifiable

controleren [kɔntrolɛrə(n)] vb 1 supervise, superintend, monitor: ~d geneesheer (roughly) medical officer; 2 check (up, on), inspect, examine, verify: de boeken ~ audit the books (or: accounts); kaartjes ~ inspect tickets; iets extra (dubbel) ~ double-check sth

controleur [kɔntrolør] de (~s) inspector, controller, checker, ticket inspector (or: collector), auditor

controverse [kɔntrovɛrsə] de (~n, ~s) controversy

convent [kɔnvɛnt] het (~en) monastery; convent

conventie [kɔnvɛnsi] de (~s) convention: in strijd met de ~ zijn go against the accepted norm

conventioneel [kɔnvɛnʃonɛl] adj, adv conventional

conversatie [kɔnvɛrsaˌ(t)si] de (~s) conversation, talk

converseren [kɔnvɛrsɛrə(n)] vb converse (with), engage in conversation (with)

converteren [kɔnvɛrtɛrə(n)] vb convert (into, to)

coöperatie [koopəraˌ(t)si] de (~s) 1 cooperation, collaboration; 2 cooperative (society)

coöperatief [koopəratif] adj, adv cooperative

coördinatie [koɔrdinaˌ(t)si] de (~s) coordination

coördinator [koɔrdinatɔr] de (~en) coordinator

coördineren [koɔrdinɛrə(n)] vb coordinate, arrange, organize: werkzaamheden ~ supervise work

copiloot [kopilot] de (copiloten) co-pilot

coproductie [koprodʏksi] de (~s) joint production, co-production

copulatie [kopylaˌ(t)si] de (~s) copulation, sexual intercourse

copyright [kɔpirɑjt] het (~s) copyright

corduroy [kɔrdyrɔj] adj cord(uroy), corded

cornedbeef [kɔrnɛdbif] het corned beef, bully (beef)

corner [kɔːrnər] de (~s) corner

corporatie [kɔrporaˌ(t)si] de (~s) corporation, corporate body

corps [kɔːr] het (corpora) corps

corpsstudent [kɔːrstydɛnt] de (~en) member of a student association

corpulent [kɔrpylɛnt] adj corpulent

correct [kɔrɛkt] adj, adv 1 correct; right, exact: ~ antwoorden get the answer(s) right, answer correctly; 2 correct, right, proper: ~e houding proper conduct (or: behaviour); ~e kleding suitable dress

correctheid [kɔrɛkthɛit] de (-heden) 1 correctness, precision; 2 correctness, propriety

correctie [kɔrɛksi] de (~s) correction, adjustment, revision; (educ also) marking: ~s aanbrengen make corrections, adjust, make adjustments

correctiewerk [kɔrɛksiwɛrk] het correction, correcting, (educ) marking: ik moet nog een hoop ~ doen I still have a lot of correcting (or: marking) to do

correctioneel [kɔrɛkʃonɛl] adj (Belg) criminal: correctionele rechtbank (roughly) Crown Court

correlatie [kɔrelaˌ(t)si] de (~s) correlation

correspondent [kɔrɛspɔndɛnt] de (~en) correspondent: van onze ~ in Parijs from our Paris correspondent

correspondentie [kɔrɛspɔndɛnsi] de (~s) correspondence: een drukke ~ voeren carry on a lively correspondence

correspondentievriend [kɔrɛspɔndɛnsivrint] de (~en) penfriend

corresponderen [kɔrɛspɔndɛrə(n)] vb 1 correspond (with), write (to); 2 correspond (to, with), match (with), agree (with)

corrigeren [kɔriʒɛrə(n)] vb 1 correct, adjust; 2 correct, (educ also) mark

corrumperen [kɔrʏmpɛrə(n)] vb corrupt, pervert: macht corrumpeert power corrupts

corrupt [kɔrʏpt] adj, adv corrupt, dishonest

corruptheid [kɔrʏpthɛit] de corruptness

corruptie [kɔrʏpsi] de (~s) corruption

corsage [kɔrsaʒə] het, de (~s) corsage

Corsica [kɔrsika] het Corsica

corso [kɔrso] het (~'s) pageant, parade, procession

corvee [kɔrveˌ] de (~s) (household) chores: ~ hebben do the chores

coryfee [korifeˌ] de (~ën) star, lion, celebrity

cosinus [kosinʏs] de cosine

cosmetica [kɔsmɛtika] de cosmetics

cosmetisch [kɔsmɛtis] adj cosmetic

coulant [kulɑnt] adj, adv accommodating, obliging, reasonable

coulisse [kulɪsə] de (~n) (side) wing (oft pl)

counter [kɑuntər] de (~s) counter-attack, countermove: op de ~ spelen rely on the counter-attack

counteren [kɑuntərə(n)] vb counter(-attack)

countrymuziek [kɑuntrimʏzik] de country music

coup [kup] de (~s) coup (d'état): een ~ plegen stage a coup

coupe [kup] de (~s) 1 cut, style; 2 coupe: ~ royale (roughly) sundae

coupé [kupe] *de (~s)* **1** compartment; **2** coupé

couperen [kupɛrə(n)] *vb* cut: *een hond ~* dock a dog's tail

coupe soleil [kupsolɛi] *de (coupes soleils)* highlights

couplet [kuplɛt] *het (~ten)* stanza, verse, couplet

coupon [kupɔn] *de (~s)* **1** remnant; **2** coupon

coupure [kupyrə] *de (~s)* **1** cut, deletion; **2** *(finance)* denomination

courant [kurɑnt] *adj* current

coureur [kurør] *de (~s)* (racing) cyclist; racing motorcyclist; racing car driver

courgette [kurʒɛt(ə)] *de (~s)* courgette

courtage [kurtaʒə] *de (~s)* brokerage, (broker's) commission

couture [kutyrə] *de* couture, dressmaking

couturier [kutyrjɛ] *de (~s)* couturier, (fashion) designer

couvert [kuvɛːr] *het (~s)* **1** cover, envelope; **2** cover, cutlery

couveuse [kuvøzə] *de (~s)* incubator

cover [kɔvər] *het, de (~s)* cover (version), remake

cowboy [kɑubɔj] *de (~s)* cowboy

coyote [kojotə] *de (~s)* coyote

c.q. [seky] *casu quo* and, or

cracker [krɛkər] *de (~s)* cracker

crashen [krɛʃə(n)] *vb* **1** crash: *het toestel crashte bij de landing* the plane crashed on landing; **2** crash, go bankrupt

crawl [krɔːl] *de* crawl

crawlen [krɔːlə(n)] *vb* do the crawl

creatie [kreja(t)si] *de (~s)* creation: *de nieuwste ~s van Dior* Dior's latest creations

creatief [krejatif] *adj, adv* creative, original, imaginative: *~ bezig zijn* do creative work

creativiteit [krejativitɛit] *de* creativity, creativeness: *(fig) haar oplossingen getuigen van ~* her solutions show creative talent

crèche [krɛʃ] *de (~s)* crèche, day-care centre, day nursery

credit [krɛdɪt] *het* credit: *debet en ~* debit and credit; *iets op iemands ~ schrijven (also fig)* put sth to s.o.'s credit, credit s.o. with sth

creditcard [krɛdɪtkɑːrt] *de (~s)* credit card

crediteren [krɛdɪtɛrə(n)] *vb* credit

crediteur [krɛditør] *de (~en)* creditor, *(pl: bookkeeping)* accounts payable

crediteurenadministratie [krɛditørə(n)ɑtministra(t)si] *de* accounts payable

creditpost [krɛdɪtpɔst] *de (~en)* credit item *(or: entry)*, asset

credo [krɛdo] *het (~'s)* **1** credo, creed; **2** Credo, Creed

creëren [krejɛrə(n)] *vb* create

crematie [krema(t)si] *de (~s)* cremation

crematorium [krematɔrijʏm] *het (crematoria)* crematorium

crème [krɛːm] *de (~s)* **1** cream: *~ op zijn gezicht smeren* rub cream on one's face; **2** crème: *een ~ ja-*

pon a cream(-coloured) dress

cremeren [krəmɛrə(n)] *vb* cremate

creool [krejɔl] *de (creolen)* Creole

¹**creools** [krejɔls] *het* creole

²**creools** [krejɔls] *adj* creole

crêpepapier [krɛːpapir] *het* crêpe paper

creperen [krepɛrə(n)] *vb* **1** die: *ze lieten haar gewoon ~* they let her die like a dog; **2** suffer: *~ van de pijn* be racked with pain

cricketen [krɪkətə(n)] *vb* play cricket

crime [krim] *de* disaster: *het is een ~* it is a disaster

criminaliteit [kriminalitɛit] *de (~en)* criminality: *de kleine ~* petty crime

criminologie [kriminoloʏi] *de* criminology

crisis [krizɪs] *de (crises)* crisis: *de ~ van de jaren dertig* the depression of the 1930s; *een ~ doormaken* go through a crisis; *een ~ doorstaan* weather a crisis

criterium [kritɛrijʏm] *het (criteria)* **1** criterion: *aan de criteria voldoen* meet the criteria; *een ~ vaststellen* lay down a criterion; **2** *(cycling)* criterium

criticus [kritikʏs] *de (critici)* critic, reviewer: *door de critici toegejuicht worden* receive critical acclaim

croissant [krwasɑ] *de (~s)* croissant

croque-monsieur [krɔkməsjø] *de (~s)* *(Belg)* toasted ham and cheese sandwich

cross [krɔs] *de (~es)* cross

crossen [krɔsə(n)] *vb* **1** take part in a cross-country (event), do cross-country, do autocross *(or: rallycross)* *(car)*; **2** tear about: *hij crost heel wat af op die fiets* he is always tearing about on that bike of his

crossfiets [krɔsfits] *de (~en)* cyclo-cross bike; BMX bike

crossmotor [krɔsmotər] *de* cross-country motorcycle

¹**cru** [kry] *de (~'s)* vintage

²**cru** [kry] *adj, adv* **1** crude, rude, rough: *dat klinkt misschien ~, maar …* that sounds a bit harsh, but …; **2** blunt; cruel

cruciaal [krysi(j)al] *adj* crucial

crucifix [krysifɪks] *het (~en)* crucifix

cruise [kruːs] *de (~s)* cruise

cryptisch [krɪptis] *adj, adv* cryptic(al), obscure

cryptogram [krɪptoʏrɑm] *het (~men)* cryptogram

CS [sɛs] *het centraal station* Central Station

Cuba [kyba] *het* Cuba

Cubaan [kyban] *de (Cubanen)* Cuban

Cubaans [kybans] *adj* Cuban

culinair [kylinɛːr] *adj* culinary

cultiveren [kʏltivɛrə(n)] *vb* **1** cultivate, till; **2** cultivate, improve: *gecultiveerde kringen* cultured *(or: sophisticated)* circles

cultureel [kʏltyrɛl] *adj, adv* cultural: *~ werk* cultural activities, social and creative activities

cultus [kʏltʏs] *de (culten)* cult

cultuur [kʏltyr] *de (culturen)* **1** culture, cultivation: *een stuk grond in ~ brengen* bring land into cultivation; **2** culture, civilization: *de oosterse ~* eastern civilization

cultuurgrond [kʏltyryrɔnt] *de (~en)* arable land,

cultivated land

cum laude [kumlаudǝ] *adv* with distinction

cumulatief [kymylatif] *adj* cumulative

cup [kʏp] *de (~s)* cup

Cupido [kypido] *de* Cupid, Eros

curatele [kyratelǝ] *de* legal restraint, wardship; receivership

curator [kyratɔr] *de (~s, ~en)* curator ‖ *de firma staat onder het beheer van een ~* the firm is in receivership

curieus [kyrijøs] *adj, adv* curious, strange: *ik vind het maar ~* I find it rather strange

curiositeit [kyrijozitɛit] *de (~en)* curiosity, oddity, strangeness: *… en andere ~en …* and other curiosities (*or:* curiosa)

curriculum [kyrikylʏm] *het (curricula)* curriculum: *~ vitae* curriculum vitae

cursief [kʏrsif] *adj, adv* italic, italicized, cursive: *~ drukken* print in italics

cursist [kʏrsɪst] *de (~en)* student

cursor [kʏrsɔr] *de (~s)* cursor

cursus [kʏrzʏs] *de (~sen)* course (of study, lectures): *zich opgeven voor een ~ Frans* sign up for a French course; *een schriftelijke ~* a correspondence course

cursusboek [kʏrzʏzbuk] *het (~en)* textbook, coursebook

cursusjaar [kʏrzʏsjar] *het (-jaren)* year, school year, academic year

curve [kʏrvǝ] *de (~n)* curve

custard [kʏstɑrt] *de* custard (powder)

cut [kʏt] *de (~s)* cut(ting)

cutter [kʏtǝr] *de (~s)* **1** slicer; **2** cutter, editor

¹cv [seve] *de centrale verwarming* central heating

²cv [seve] *het curriculum vitae* cv

CV [seve] *de (~'s)* **1** *Commanditaire Vennootschap* Limited (*or:* Special) Partnership; **2** *coöperatieve vereniging* co-op

cyanide [sijanidǝ] *het (~n)* cyanide

cybernetica [sibɛrnetika] *de* cybernetics

cyclaam [siklam] *de (cyclamen)* cyclamen

cyclisch [siklis] *adj, adv* cyclic(al): *~e verbindingen* cyclic compounds

cyclocross [siklokrɔs] *de (~es)* cyclo-cross

cycloon [siklon] *de (cyclonen)* cyclone, hurricane

cycloop [siklop] *de (cyclopen)* Cyclops

cyclus [siklʏs] *de (cycli)* cycle

cynisch [sinis] *adj, adv* cynical

cynisme [sinɪsmǝ] *het* cynicism

Cyprioot [siprijot] *de (Cyprioten)* Cypriot

Cyprus [siprʏs] *het* Cyprus

cyrillisch [sirɲlis] *adj* Cyrillic

d

daad [dat] *de (daden)* act(ion), deed, activity: *een goede ~ verrichten* do a good deed

daadwerkelijk [datwɛrkələk] *adj, adv* actual, active, practical

¹daags [daχs] *adj* daily, everyday

²daags [daχs] *adv* a day, per day, daily: *tweemaal ~* twice a day

¹daar [dar] *adv* **1** (over) there: *zie je dat huis ~* (do you) see that house (over there)?; *tot ~* up to there; **2** (just, over, right) there: *wie is ~?* who is it? (*or:* there?)

²daar [dar] *conj* as, because, since

daaraan [daran] *adv* on (to) it (*or:* them): *wat heb je ~* what good is that

daarachter [daraχtər] *adv* **1** behind (it, that, them, there): *(fig) wat zou ~ zitten?* I wonder what's behind it; **2** beyond (it, that, them, there)

daarbeneden [darbənedə(n)] *adv* down there, below

daarbij [darbɛi] *adv* **1** with it (*or:* that); with these (*or:* those): *~ blijft het* that's how it is, we'll keep it like that; **2** besides, moreover, furthermore: *~ komt, dat …* what's more …

daarbinnen [darbɪnə(n)] *adv* in there, inside, in it (*or:* that), in these (*or:* those): *~ is het warm* it's warm in there

daarboven [darbovə(n)] *adv* up there, above it

daardoor [dardor] *adv* **1** through it (*or:* that); through these (*or:* those); **2** therefore, so, consequently, by this (*or:* that) means: *zij weigerde, en ~ gaf zij te kennen …* she refused, and by doing so made it clear …; *~ werd hij ziek* that is (*or:* was) what made him ill, because of this (*or:* that) he became ill

daarentegen [darənteɣə(n)] *adv* on the other hand: *hij is zeer radicaal, zijn broer ~ conservatief* he is a strong radical, his brother, on the other hand, is conservative

daarheen [darhen] *adv* (to) there: *wij willen ~* we want to go (over) there

daarin [darɪn] *adv* **1** in there (*or:* it, those); **2** in that: *hij is ~ handig* he is good at it

daarlangs [darlɑŋs] *adv* by (*or:* past, along) that: *we kunnen beter ~ gaan* we had better go that way

daarmee [darme] *adv* with, by that (*or:* it, those): *~ kun je het vastzetten* you can fasten it with that (*or:*

those); *en ~ uit!* and that's that! (*or:* all there is to it!)

daarna [darna] *adv* after(wards), next, then: *de dag ~* the day after (that); *snel (*or:* kort) ~ soon (*or:* shortly) after (that); *eerst … en ~ …* first … and then …

daarnaar [darnar] *adv* **1** at (*or:* to, for) that; **2** accordingly, according to that: *~ moet je handelen* you must act accordingly

daarnaast [darnast] *adv* **1** beside it, next to it; **2** besides, in addition (to this): *~ is hij nog brutaal ook* what's more he is cheeky (too)

daarnet [darnɛt] *adv* just now, only a little while ago, only a minute ago

daarom [darɔm] *adv* **1** around it; **2** therefore, so, because of this (*or:* that), for that reason: *hij wil het niet hebben, ~ doe ik het juist* he doesn't like it, and that's exactly why I do it; *waarom niet? ~ niet!* why not? because (I say so)!, that's why!

daaromheen [darɔmhen] *adv* around it (*or:* them): *een tuin met een hek ~* a garden with a fence around it

daaronder [darɔndər] *adv* under(neath) it

daarop [darɔp] *adv* **1** (up)on that; on top of that (*or:* those): *de tafel en het kleed ~* the table and the cloth on top of it; **2** on that, to that: *uw antwoord (*or:* reactie) ~* your reply (*or:* reaction) (to that); **3** thereupon: *de dag ~* the next (*or:* following) day, the day after (that); *kort ~* shortly afterwards, soon after (that)

daaropvolgend [darɔpfɔlɣənt] *adj, adv* next, following: *hij kwam in juli en vertrok in juni ~* he arrived in July and left the following June

daarover [darovər] *adv* **1** on top of it, on (*or:* over, above) that: *~ lag een zeil* there was a tarpaulin on top of (*or:* over, across) it; **2** about that: *genoeg ~* enough said, enough of that

daartegen [darteɣə(n)] *adv* **1** against it, next to it; **2** against it (*or:* them): *eventuele bezwaren ~* any objections to it

daartegenaan [darteɣə(n)an] *adv* (right) up against it (*or:* them), (right) onto it (*or:* them): *onze schuur is ~ gebouwd* our shed is built up against (*or:* onto) it

daartegenover [darteɣə(n)ovər] *adv* **1** opposite (*or:* facing) it/them: *de kerk met de pastorie ~* the church with the vicarage opposite it (*or:* facing it); **2** on the other hand, (but) then again …: *~ staat dat dit systeem duurder is* (but) on the other hand this system costs more

daartoe [dartu] *adv* **1** for that, to that; **2** for that (purpose), to that end: *~ gemachtigd zijn* be authorized to do it

daartussen [dartʏsə(n)] *adv* **1** between them, among them: *die twee ramen en de ruimte ~* those two windows and the space between (them); **2** between them: *wat is het verschil ~?* what's the difference (between them)?

daaruit [darœyt] *adv* **1** out of that (*or:* those): *het* *water spuit* ~ the water spurts out of it; **2** from that: ~ *kan men afleiden dat ...* from this it can be deduced that ...

daarvan [darvɑn] *adv* **1** from it (*or:* that, there); **2** of it (*or:* that), thereof; **3** of it (*or:* that): ~ *maakt men plastic* plastic is made of that, that is used for making plastic; *niets* ~ nothing of the sort

daarvandaan [darvɑndan] *adv* **1** (away) from there, away (from it); **2** hence, therefore

daarvoor [darvor] *adv* **1** in front of it, before that (*or:* those); **2** before (that): *de week* ~ the week before (that), the previous week; **3** for that (purpose): ~ *heb ik geen tijd* I've no time for that; **4** for it (*or:* them): ~ *(in de plaats) heb ik een boek gekregen* I got a book instead; **5** that's why: ~ *ben ik ook gekomen* that's what I've come for; *daar zijn het kinderen voor* that's children for you

dadel [dadəl] *de* date

dadelijk [dadələk] *adv* **1** immediately, at once, right away: *kom je haast? ja,* ~ are you coming now? yes, in a minute; **2** directly, presently: *ik kom (zo)* ~ *bij u* I'll be right with you

dadelpalm [dadəlpɑlm] *de (~en)* date palm

dader [dadər] *de (~s)* perpetrator, offender: *de vermoedelijke* ~ the suspect

¹dag [dɑχ] *de (~en)* **1** day; daybreak; daytime: ~ *en nacht bereikbaar* available day and night; *bij klaarlichte* ~ in broad daylight; *het is kort* ~ time is running out (fast), there is not much time (left); *het is morgen vroeg* ~ we must get up early (*or:* an early start) tomorrow; *iem de* ~ *van zijn leven bezorgen* give s.o. the time of his life; *lange ~en maken* work long hours; *er gaat geen* ~ *voorbij of ik denk aan jou* not a day passes but I think of you; *het is vandaag mijn* ~ *niet* it just isn't my day (today); *wat is het voor* ~? what day (of the week) is it?; *morgen komt er weer een* ~ tomorrow is another day; ~ *in,* ~ *uit* day in day out; ~ *na* ~ day by day, day after day; *het wordt met de* ~ *slechter* it gets worse by the day; *om de drie ~en* every three days; *24 uur per* ~ 24 hours a day; *van* ~ *tot* ~ daily, from day to day; *van de ene* ~ *op de andere* from one day to the next; *over veertien ~en* in two weeks' time, in a fortnight; **2** daylight: *voor de* ~ *komen* come to light, surface, appear; *met iets voor de* ~ *komen: a)* come up with sth; *b)* come forward, present oneself; *voor de* ~ *ermee!: a)* out with it!; *b)* show me!; *goed voor de* ~ *komen* make a good impression; **3** day(s), time: *ouden van ~en* the elderly; **4** hello, hi (there); bye(-bye), good-bye

²dag [dɑχ] *int* hello, hi; bye(-bye), goodbye: *dáág!* bye(-bye)!, bye then; *ja, dáág!* forget it!

dagafschrift [dɑχɑfsχrɪft] *het (~en)* daily statement (of account)

dagblad [dɑχblɑt] *het (~en)* (daily) newspaper, (daily) paper

dagboek [dɑχbuk] *het (~en)* diary, journal: *een* ~ *(bij)houden* keep a diary

dagdagelijks [dɑχdaɣələks] *adj (Belg)* daily, everyday

dagdeel [dɑχdel] *het (-delen)* part of the day; shift, morning, afternoon, evening, night

dagdienst [dɑχdinst] *de (~en)* daywork, day duty, days, day shift: ~ *hebben* be on days

dagdromen [dɑχdromə(n)] *vb* daydream

¹dagelijks [daɣələks] *adj* **1** daily: *zijn ~e bezigheden* his daily routine; *voor* ~ *gebruik* for everyday use; **2** everyday, ordinary: ~ *bestuur* executive (committee); *in het* ~ *leven* in everyday life; *dat is* ~ *werk voor hem* that's his routine for him

²dagelijks [daɣələks] *adv* daily, each day, every day: *dat komt* ~ *voor* it happens every day

dagen [daɣə(n)] *vb* **1** summon(s), subpoena: *iem voor het gerecht* ~ summon(s) s.o.; **2** dawn: *het begon mij te* ~ it began to dawn on me

dageraad [daɣərat] *de* dawn, daybreak, break of day

dagje [dɑχjə] *het (~s)* day: *een* ~ *ouder worden* be getting on (a bit); *een* ~ *uit* a day out

dagjesmensen [dɑχjəsmɛnsə(n)] *de* (day) trippers

dagkaart [dɑχkart] *de (~en)* day-ticket

dagkoers [dɑχkurs] *de (~en)* current rate (of exchange)

daglicht [dɑχlɪχt] *het* daylight; light of day: *bij iem in een kwaad* ~ *staan* be in s.o.'s bad books; *iem in een kwaad* ~ *stellen* put s.o. in the wrong (with)

dagonderwijs [dɑχɔndərwɛis] *het* daytime education

dagopleiding [dɑχɔplɛidɪŋ] *de (~en)* daytime course (*or:* study)

dagopvang [dɑχɔpfɑŋ] *de* day nursery; day-care centre

dagprijs [dɑχprɛis] *de* current (market) price

dagretour [dɑχrətur] *het (~s)* day return, day (return) ticket

dagschotel [dɑχsχotəl] *de (~s)* plat du jour; today's special

dagtaak [dɑχtak] *de (dagtaken)* **1** daily work; **2** day's work: *daar heb ik een* ~ *aan* that is a full day's work (*or:* a full-time job)

dagtocht [dɑχtɔχt] *de (~en)* day trip

dagvaarding [dɑχfardɪŋ] *de (~en)* (writ of) summons, writ; subpoena

dagverblijf [dɑχfərblɛif] *het (dagverblijven)* **1** day room: *een* ~ *voor kinderen* a day-care centre, a day nursery, a crèche; **2** outdoor enclosure, outside cage, outside pen

dahlia [dalija] *de (~'s)* dahlia

dak [dɑk] *het (~en)* roof: *auto met open* ~ convertible, soft-top; *een* ~ *boven het hoofd hebben* have a roof over one's head; *iets van de ~en schreeuwen* shout sth from the rooftops

dakbedekking [dɑgbədɛkɪŋ] *de (~en)* roofing material

dakgoot [dɑkχot] *de (dakgoten)* gutter

dakkapel [dɑkapɛl] *de (~len)* dormer (window)

dakloos [dɑklos] *adj* homeless; (left) without a roof

over one's head

dakloze [dɑklozə] *de* homeless person; *(pl)* street people

dakpan [dɑkpɑn] *de (~nen)* (roof(ing)) tile

dakraam [dɑkram] *het (dakramen)* skylight, attic window, garret window

dal [dɑl] *het (~en)* valley; dale || *hij is door een diep ~ gegaan* he has had a very hard *(or:* rough) time

dalen [dɑlə(n)] *vb* 1 descend, go down, come down, drop, fall: *het vliegtuig daalt* the (aero)plane is descending; *de temperatuur daalde tot beneden het vriespunt* the temperature fell below zero; 2 fall, go down, come down, drop, decline, decrease: *de prijzen zijn een paar euro gedaald* prices are down by a couple of euros

daling [dɑliŋ] *de (~en)* 1 descent, fall(ing), drop: *~ van de zeespiegel* drop in the sea level; 2 slope, incline, descent, drop, *(small)* dip; 3 decrease, drop, slump: *de ~ van het geboortecijfer* the fall in the birth rate

dalmatiër [dɑlmɑtsijər] *de (~s)* Dalmatian

daluren [dɑlyrə(n)] *de* off-peak hours

dam [dɑm] *de* 1 dam: *een ~ leggen* build a dam; 2 *(draughts)* king, crowned man: *een ~ halen (maken)* crown a man

damast [dɑmɑst] *het (~en)* damask

dambord [dɑmbɔrt] *het (~en)* draughtboard

dame [dɑmə] *de (~s)* 1 lady; 2 *(chess, cards)* queen: *een ~ halen* queen a pawn

dameskapper [dɑməskɑpər] *de (~s)* ladies' hairdresser

damesmode [dɑməsmodə] *de (~s)* 1 ladies' fashion; 2 ladies' clothing

damesslipje [dɑməslɪpjə] *het* pair of briefs, (pair of) knickers: *een ~* a pair of briefs

damestoilet [dɑməstwalɛt] *het (~ten)* ladies' toilet

damhert [dɑmhɛrt] *het (~en)* fallow deer

dammen [dɑmə(n)] *vb* play draughts

damp [dɑmp] *de (~en)* 1 steam, vapour, mist; 2 smoke, *(oft pl)* fume: *schadelijke ~en* noxious fumes

dampen [dɑmpə(n)] *vb* 1 steam; 2 smoke

dampkap [dɑmpkɑp] *de (~pen) (Belg)* cooker hood, extractor hood

dampkring [dɑmpkrɪŋ] *de (~en)* (earth's) atmosphere

damschijf [dɑmsχɛif] *de (damschijven) (draughts)* draught(sman)

damspel [dɑmspɛl] *het (~(l)en)* 1 draughts; 2 set of draughts

¹**dan** [dɑn] *adv* 1 then: *morgen zijn we vrij, ~ gaan we uit* we have a day off tomorrow, so we're going out; *nu eens dit, ~ weer dat* first one thing, then another; *tot ~* till then, see you then; *hij zei dat hij ~ en ~ zou komen* he said he'd come at such and such a time; *en je broer ~?* and what about your brother then?; *wat ~ nog?* so what!; *ook goed, ~ niet* all right, we won't then; *al ~ niet groen* green or otherwise, whether green or not; *en ~ zeggen ze nog dat …* and

still they say that …; *hij heeft niet gewerkt; hij is ~ ook gezakt* he didn't work, so not surprisingly he failed; 2 then, besides: *eerst werken, ~ spelen* business before pleasure; *zelfs ~ gaat het niet* even so it won't work; *en ~?* and then what?

²**dan** [dɑn] *conj* than: *hij is groter ~ ik* he is bigger than me; *een ander ~ hij heeft het me verteld* I heard it from s.o. other than him

danig [dɑnəχ] *adv* soundly, thoroughly, well: *~ in de knoei zitten* be in a terrible mess

dank [dɑŋk] *de* thanks, gratitude: *iets niet in ~ afnemen* take sth in bad part; *geen ~* you're welcome; *stank voor ~ krijgen* get little thanks for one's pains; *bij voorbaat ~* thank you in advance

dankbaar [dɑŋgbar] *adj, adv* 1 grateful, thankful: *ik zou u zeer ~ zijn als …* I should be most grateful to you *(or:* obliged) if …; 2 rewarding, grateful: *een dankbare taak* a rewarding task

dankbaarheid [dɑŋgbarhɛit] *de* gratitude, thankfulness: *uit ~ voor* in appreciation of

¹**danken** [dɑŋkə(n)] *vb* 1 thank: *ja graag, dank je* yes, please, thank you; *niet(s) te ~* not at all, you're welcome; 2 owe, be indebted: *dit heb ik aan jou te ~* I owe this to you, I have you to thank for this

²**danken** [dɑŋkə(n)] *vb* decline (with thanks)

dankwoord [dɑŋkwort] *het (~en)* word(s) of thanks

dankzij [dɑŋksɛi] *prep* thanks to

dans [dɑns] *de (~en)* dance, dancing || *de ~ ontspringen* get off scot-free

dansen [dɑnsə(n)] *vb* dance: *uit ~ gaan* go (out) dancing; *~ op muziek* (or: *een plaat)* dance to music *(or:* a record)

danser [dɑnsər] *de (~s)* dancer

dansje [dɑnʃə] *het (~s)* dance; hop

dansorkest [dɑnsɔrkɛst] *het (~en)* dance band

dansvloer [dɑnsflur] *de (~en)* dance floor

danszaal [dɑnsal] *de (-zalen)* dance hall, ballroom

dapper [dɑpər] *adj, adv* 1 brave, courageous: *zich ~ verdedigen* put up a brave fight; 2 plucky, tough: *klein maar ~* small but tough

dapperheid [dɑpərhɛit] *de* bravery, courage

dar [dɑr] *de (~ren)* drone

darm [dɑrm] *de (~en)* intestine, bowel: *blinde ~* appendix; *twaalfvingerige ~* duodenum

dartelen [dɑrtələ(n)] *vb* romp, frolic, gambol

das [dɑs] *de* 1 badger; 2 tie: *dat deed hem de ~ om* that did for him, that finished him; 3 scarf

dashboard [dɛʒbɔːrt] *het (~s)* dashboard

dashboardkastje [dɛʒbɔːrtkɑʃə] *het (~s)* glove compartment

¹**dat** [dɑt] *dem pron* that: *ben ik ~?* is that me?; *~ is het hem nu juist* that's just it, that's the problem; *ziezo, ~ was ~* right, that's that (then), so much for that; *~ lijkt er meer op* that's more like it; *mijn boek en ~ van jou* my book and yours; *~ mens* that (dreadful) woman

²**dat** [dɑt] *pron* 1 that, which; *(of pers)* that, who, whom: *het bericht ~ mij gebracht werd …* the mes-

sage that (*or:* which) was brought me ...; *het jonge-tje ~ ik een appel heb gegeven* the little boy (that, who) I gave an apple to; **2** which; *(of pers)* who; *(of pers)* whom: *het huis, ~ onlangs opgeknapt was, werd verkocht* the house, which had recently been done up, was sold

³dat [dɑt] *conj* **1** that *(usually not translated):* *in plaats (van) ~ je me het vertelt ...* instead of telling me, you ...; *de reden ~ hij niet komt is ...* the reason (why) he is not coming is ...; *ik denk ~ hij komt* I think (that) he'll come; *zonder ~ ik het wist* without me knowing; *het regende ~ het goot* it was pouring (down); **2** that, because: *hij is kwaad ~ hij niet mee mag* he is angry that (*or:* because) he can't come; **3** so that: *doe het zo, ~ hij het niet merkt* do it in such a way that he won't notice; **4** as far as: *is hier ook een bioscoop? niet ~ ik weet* is there a cinema here? not that I know; **5** that: *~ mij nu juist zoiets moest overkomen!* that such a thing should happen to me now!

data [dɑta] *de* **1** data; **2** dates

databank [dɑtabɑŋk] *de (~en)* data bank

datacommunicatie [dɑtakɔmynika(t)si] *de* data communication(s)

¹dateren [datera(n)] *vb* date

²dateren [datera(n)] *vb* date (from), go back (to): *het huis dateert al uit de veertiende eeuw* the house goes all the way back to the fourteenth century; *de brief dateert van 6 juni* the letter is dated 6th June

datgene [dɑtxenə] *dem pron* what, that which: *~ wat je zegt, is waar* what you say is true

dato [dɑto] *adv* date, dated: *drie weken na ~* three weeks later

datum [dɑtʏm] *de (data)* date, time: *zonder ~* undated; *er staat geen ~ op* there is no date on it

dauw [dɑu] *de* dew || *(Belg) van de hemelse ~ leven* live the life of Riley

dauwdruppel [dɑudrʏpəl] *de (~s)* dewdrop

daveren [dɑvərə(n)] *vb* thunder, shake, roar, resound: *de vrachtwagen daverde voorbij* the truck thundered (*or:* roared) past

daverend [dɑvərənt] *adj, adv* resounding; thunderous: *een ~ succes* a resounding success

davidster [dɑvɪtstər] *de (~ren)* Star of David

de [də] *art* the: *eens in ~ week* once a week; *ze kosten twintig euro ~ kilo* they are twenty euros a kilo; *dat is dé man voor dat karwei* he is (just) the man for the job

debacle [debɑkəl] *het, de (~s)* disaster, failure, downfall

debat [dəbɑt] *het (~ten)* debate; argument

debatteren [debɑtera(n)] *vb* debate; argue

debet [debɛt] *het* debit(s), debtor side, debit side: *~ en credit* debit(s) and credit(s)

¹debiel [dəbil] *de (~en)* mental defective, moron, imbecile, cretin

²debiel [dəbil] *adj, adv* mentally deficient, feeble-minded

debiteren [debitera(n)] *vb* debit, charge

debiteur [debitør] *de (~en)* debtor, debt receivable,

account(s) receivable

debutant [debytɑnt] *de (~en)* novice; newcomer

debuut [debyt] *het (debuten)* debut: *zijn ~ maken* make one's debut (*or:* first appearance)

decaan [dekɑn] *de (decanen)* **1** dean; **2** student counsellor

decadent [dekadɛnt] *adj* decadent

decafeïne [dekɑfejinə] *de* decaffeinated (coffee)

december [desɛmbər] *de* December

decennium [desɛnijʏm] *het (decennia)* decade

decentraal [desɛntrɑl] *adj, adv* decentralized, local

decentralisatie [desɛntraliza(t)si] *de* decentralization, deconcentration, localization

decentraliseren [desɛntralizera(n)] *vb* decentralize, deconcentrate, localize

decibel [desibɛl] *de (~s)* decibel

deciliter [desilitər] *de (~s)* decilitre

¹decimaal [desimɑl] *de (decimalen)* decimal (place): *tot op zes decimalen uitrekenen* calculate to six decimal places

²decimaal [desimɑl] *adj* decimal: *decimale breuk* decimal fraction, decimal

decimaalpunt [desimɑlpʏnt] *het (~en)* decimal point

decimeter [desimetər] *de (~s)* decimetre

declameren [deklɑmera(n)] *vb* declaim, recite

declaratie [deklɑra(t)si] *de (~s)* expenses claim; account; claim (form): *zijn ~ indienen* put in one's claim

declareren [deklarera(n)] *vb* declare: *een bedrag (or: driehonderd euro) ~* charge an amount (*or:* three hundred euros); *heeft u nog iets te ~?* have you anything to declare?

decoderen [dekodera(n)] *vb* decode

decolleté [dekɔlətə] *het (~s)* low neckline, cleavage

decor [dekɔːr] *het (~s)* **1** decor, scenery, setting(s), *(film)* set: *~ en kostuums* scenery and costumes; **2** *(fig)* background

decoratie [dekɔra(t)si] *de (~s)* decoration, adornment

decoratief [dekɔratif] *adj, adv* decorative, ornamental

decoreren [dekɔrera(n)] *vb* decorate

decreet [dəkret] *het (decreten)* decree

deeg [dex] *het (degen)* dough; pastry

deegrol [dexrɔl] *de (~len)* rolling pin

deel [del] *het* **1** part, piece: *één ~ bloem op één ~ suiker* one part (of) flour to one part (of) sugar; *voor een groot ~* to a great extent; *voor het grootste ~* for the most part; *~ uitmaken van* be part of, belong to; **2** share: *zijn ~ van de winst* his share of the profits; **3** volume

deelbaar [delbar] *adj* divisible: *tien is ~ door twee* ten is divisible by two

deelcertificaat [delsɛrtifikat] *het (-certificaten)* credit, subject certificate

deelnemen [delnemə(n)] *vb* participate (in), take part (in), attend, enter, compete (in), join (in): *aan een wedstrijd ~* take part in a contest; *~ aan een* *examen* take an exam

deelnemend [dɛlnɛmənt] *adj* participating: *de ~e landen van de EU* the member countries of the EU

deelnemer [dɛlnemər] *de (~s)* participant; conferee; competitor, entrant; contestant: *een beperkt aantal ~s* a limited number of participants

deelneming [dɛlnemɪŋ] *de* **1** participation, attendance, entry: *bij voldoende ~* if there are enough entries; **2** sympathy, condolence(s): *zijn ~ betuigen* extend one's sympathy

deelregering [dɛlrəɣerɪŋ] *de (~en) (Belg)* regional government (*or:* administration)

deels [dels] *adv* partly, part

deelsom [dɛlsɔm] *de (~men)* division (sum)

deelstaat [dɛlstat] *de (-staten)* (federal) state

deelteken [dɛltekə(n)] *het (~s)* division sign

deeltijd [dɛltɛit] *de* part-time, half-time

deeltijdbaan [dɛltɛidban] *de (-banen)* part-time job

deeltijdonderwijs [dɛltɛitɔndərwɛis] *het* part-time education

deeltijdstudie [dɛltɛitstydi] *de (~s)* part-time course

deeltje [dɛlcə] *het (~s)* particle

deelwoord [dɛlwort] *het (~en)* participle: *het onvoltooid ~* the present participle; *het voltooid ~* the past participle

Deen [den] *de (Denen)* Dane

¹**Deens** [dens] *het* Danish

²**Deens** [dens] *adj* Danish

¹**defect** [defɛkt] *het (~en)* fault, defect; flaw: *we hebben het ~ aan de machine kunnen verhelpen* we've managed to sort out the trouble with the machine

²**defect** [defɛkt] *adj* faulty, defective, out of order, damaged: *~ out of order

defensie [defɛnsi] *de* defence: *de minister van ~* the Minister of Defence

defensief [defɛnsif] *het* defensive

deficiënt [defiʃɛnt] *adj* deficient

defilé [defile] *het (~s)* parade

definiëren [defin(i)jerə(n)] *vb* define: *iets nader ~* define sth more closely, be more specific about sth

definitie [defini(t)si] *de (~s)* definition: *per ~* by definition

definitief [definitif] *adj, adv* definitive, final: *de definitieve versie* the definitive version

deflatie [defla(t)si] *de (~s)* deflation

deftig [dɛftəχ] *adj, adv* distinguished, fashionable, stately: *een ~e buurt* a fashionable quarter

¹**degelijk** [deɣələk] *adj* **1** reliable, respectable, solid, sound: *een ~ persoon* a respectable person; **2** sound, reliable, solid: *een ~ fabrikaat* a reliable product

²**degelijk** [deɣələk] *adv* thoroughly, soundly, very much ‖ *wel ~* really, actually, positively; *ik meen het wel ~* I am quite serious

degelijkheid [deɣələkhɛit] *de* **1** soundness, thoroughness; **2** reliability, solidity, respectability

degen [deɣə(n)] *de (~s)* sword, foil

degene [dəɣenə] *dem pron* he, she; those: *degene die ... he* who, she who

degeneratie [deɣenəra(t)si] *de (~s)* degeneration

degradatie [deɣrada(t)si] *de (~s) (esp mil)* demotion; *(esp sport)* relegation

¹**degraderen** [deɣradɛrə(n)] *vb* degrade, downgrade (to), *(esp mil)* demote (to), *(esp sport)* relegate (to)

²**degraderen** [deɣradɛrə(n)] *vb* be relegated (to), be downgraded (to)

deinen [dɛinə(n)] *vb* **1** heave: *de zee deinde sterk* the sea surged wildly; **2** bob, roll

deining [dɛinɪŋ] *de (~en)* **1** swell, roll; **2** rocking motion; **3** commotion: *~ veroorzaken* cause a stir

dek [dɛk] *het (~ken)* **1** cover(ing), horse-cloth; **2** *(shipp)* deck: *alle hens aan ~* all hands on deck

dekbed [dɛgbɛt] *het (~den)* continental quilt, duvet

deken [dekə(n)] *de* **1** blanket: *onder de ~s kruipen* pull the blankets over one's head; **2** dean

dekenaat [dekənat] *het (dekenaten)* deanery

dekhengst [dɛkhɛŋst] *de (~en)* stud(-horse), (breeding) stallion

dekken [dɛkə(n)] *vb* **1** cover, coat: *de tafel ~* set the table; **2** agree (with), correspond (with, to); **3** cover (for), protect: *iem in de rug ~* support s.o., stand up for s.o.; *zich ~* cover (*or:* protect) oneself; **4** cover, meet: *deze cheque is niet gedekt* this cheque is not covered; *de verzekering dekt de schade* the insurance covers the damage; **5** cover, service

dekking [dɛkɪŋ] *de* **1** *(mil)* cover, shelter: *~ zoeken* seek (*or:* take) cover (from); **2** service; **3** cover; **4** cover: *ter ~ van de (on)kosten* to cover (*or:* meet, make up) the expenses; **5** coverage; **6** *(socc)* marking; cover; guard (*boxing etc*)

dekmantel [dɛkmantəl] *de (~s)* cover, cloak, blind, front: *iem (iets) als ~ gebruiken* use s.o. (sth) as a front

dekschaal [dɛksχal] *de (dekschalen)* tureen, covered dish

dekschuit [dɛksχœyt] *de (~en)* barge (with a deck)

deksel [dɛksəl] *het, de (~s)* lid, top, cover: *het ~ op zijn neus krijgen* get the door slammed in one's face

dekzeil [dɛksɛil] *het (~en)* tarpaulin, canvas

delegatie [deleɣa(t)si] *de (~s)* delegation

delen [delə(n)] *vb* **1** divide, split; **2** share, divide: *het verschil ~* split the difference; *je moet kiezen of ~* take it or leave it; *eerlijk ~* share and share alike; *samen ~* go halves; **3** divide, *(educ)* do division: *honderd ~ door tien* divide one hundred by ten; *een mening ~* share an opinion; *iem in zijn vreugde laten ~* share one's joy with s.o.

deler [delər] *de (~s)* divisor

delfstof [dɛlfstɔf] *de (~fen)* mineral

delicatesse [delikatɛsə] *de (~n)* delicacy

delict [delɪkt] *het (~en)* offence; indictable offence

delinquent [delɪŋkwɛnt] *de (~en)* delinquent, offender

delirium [delirijʏm] *het (deliria)* delirium

delta [dɛlta] *de (~'s)* **1** delta; **2** delta wing
deltavliegen [dɛltavliyə(n)] *vb* hang-gliding
delven [dɛlvə(n)] *vb* **1** dig; **2** extract: *goud (or: grondstoffen)* ~ mine gold *(or:* raw materials)
demagoog [demaɣoꭓ] *de (demagogen)* demagogue
demarreren [demarɛrə(n)] *vb* break away, take a flyer
dement [demɛnt] *adj* demented
dementeren [demɛntɛrə(n)] *vb* grow demented, get demented
dementie [demɛnsi] *de* dementia
demobilisatie [demobiliza(t)si] *de* demobilization
democraat [demokrat] *de (democraten)* democrat
democratie [demokra(t)si] *de (~ën)* democracy, self-government
democratisch [demokratis] *adj, adv* democratic
demografie [demoɣrafi] *de* demography
demografisch [demoɣrafis] *adj, adv* demographic
demon [demɔn] *de (~en)* demon, devil, evil spirit
demonstrant [demɔnstrɑnt] *de (~en)* demonstrator, protester
demonstratie [demɔnstra(t)si] *de (~s)* **1** demonstration, display, show(ing), exhibition; **2** demonstration, (protest) march: *een ~ tegen kernwapens* a demonstration against nuclear arms
demonstratief [demɔnstratif] *adj, adv* ostentatious, demonstrative, showy: *zij liet op demonstratieve wijze haar ongenoegen blijken* she pointedly showed her displeasure
¹demonstreren [demɔnstrerə(n)] *vb* demonstrate, display, show, exhibit
²demonstreren [demɔnstrerə(n)] *vb* demonstrate, march, protest: *~ tegen (or: voor) iets* demonstrate against *(or:* in support of) sth
demontage [demɔntaʒə] *de (~s)* dismantling, disassembling, taking apart, removal, defusing
demonteren [demɔntɛrə(n)] *vb* **1** disassemble, dismantle, take apart, remove; knock down; **2** deactivate, defuse, disarm
demotiveren [demotivɛrə(n)] *vb* remove *(or:* reduce) (s.o.'s) motivation, discourage, dishearten
dempen [dɛmpə(n)] *vb* **1** fill (up, in), close (up), stop (up); **2** subdue, tone down; muffle, deaden, dim, shade *(light): gedempt licht* subdued *(or:* dimmed, soft) light
demper [dɛmpər] *de (~s)* silencer, *(Am)* muffler
den [dɛn] *de (~nen)* pine (tree), fir
denderen [dɛndərə(n)] *vb* rumble, thunder, hurtle, roar
Denemarken [denəmɑrkə(n)] *het* Denmark
denigrerend [deniɣrɛrənt] *adj, adv* disparaging, belittling
denkbaar [dɛŋgbar] *adj* conceivable, imaginable, possible
denkbeeld [dɛŋgbelt] *het (~en)* **1** concept, idea, thought, notion: *zich een ~ vormen van* form some idea of; *een verkeerd ~ hebben van* have a wrong conception *(or:* idea) of; **2** opinion, idea, view: *hij*

houdt er verouderde ~en op na he has some antiquated ideas
denkbeeldig [dɛŋgbeldəꭓ] *adj* **1** notional, theoretical, hypothetical; **2** imaginary, illusory, unreal, fictitious: *het gevaar is niet ~ dat ...* there's a (very) real danger that ...
¹denken [dɛŋkə(n)] *vb* **1** think, consider, reflect, ponder: *het doet ~ aan* it reminds one of ...; *dit doet sterk aan omkoperij ~* this savours strongly of bribery; *waar zit je aan te ~?* what's on your mind?; *ik moet er niet aan ~* I can't bear to think about it; *ik denk er net zo over* I feel just the same about it; *ik zal eraan ~* I'll bear it in mind; *nu ik eraan denk* (now I) come to think of it; *aan iets ~* think *(or:* be thinking) of sth; *ik probeer er niet aan te ~* I try to put it out of my mind; *iem aan het ~ zetten* set s.o. thinking; *ik dacht bij mezelf* I thought *(or:* said) to myself; *denk om je hoofd* mind your head; *er verschillend (anders) over ~* take a different view (of the matter); *zij denkt er nu anders over* she feels differently about it (now); *dat had ik niet van hem gedacht* I should never have thought it of him; **2** think of *(or:* about), intend (to), plan (to): *ik denk erover met roken te stoppen* I'm thinking of giving up smoking; *geen ~ aan!* it's out of the question!
²denken [dɛŋkə(n)] *vb* **1** think, be of the opinion, consider: *ik weet niet wat ik ervan moet ~* I don't know what to think; *wat dacht je van een ijsje?* what would you say to an ice cream?; *dat dacht je maar, dat had je maar gedacht* that's what you think!; *ik dacht van wel (or: van niet)* I thought it was *(or:* wasn't); *wie denk je wel dat je bent?* (just) who do you think you are?; **2** think, suppose, expect, imagine: *wie had dat kunnen ~* who would have thought it?; *u moet niet ~ (dat) ...* you mustn't suppose *(or:* think) (that) ...; *dat dacht ik al* I thought so; *dacht ik het niet!* just as I thought!; **3** think, understand, imagine, appreciate, consider: *de beste arts die men zich maar kan ~* the best (possible) doctor; *denk eens (aan)* imagine!, just think of it!; **4** think of *(or:* about), intend, be going (to), plan: *wat denk je nu te doen?* what do you intend to do now?
denker [dɛŋkər] *de (~s)* thinker
denkfout [dɛŋkfaut] *de (~en)* logical error, error of reasoning
denkpiste [dɛŋkpistə] *de (~s, ~n) (Belg)* cast of mind
denksport [dɛŋksport] *de (~en)* puzzle solving, problem solving
denkwijze [dɛŋkwɛizə] *de (~n)* way of thinking, mode of thought
dennen [dɛnə(n)] *adj* pine(wood)
dennenappel [dɛnə(n)ɑpəl] *de (~s)* pine cone; fir cone
deodorant [dejodorɑnt] *de (~s, ~en)* deodorant
depanneren [depanɛrə(n)] *vb (Belg)* repair, put back on the road
departement [depɑrtəmɛnt] *het (~en)* department, ministry

dependance [depɛndɑ̯s] *de (~s)* annex(e)

deponeren [depoˈnɛrə(n)] *vb* **1** deposit, place, put (down): *documenten bij de notaris* ~ deposit documents with the notary's; **2** file, lodge

deporteren [depɔrˈtɛrə(n)] *vb* deport; transport: *een gedeporteerde* a deportee (*or:* transportee)

deposito [depoˈzito] *het (~'s)* deposit

depot [depoˈ] *het, de (~s)* **1** deposit(ing), committing to safe keeping; **2** (goods on) deposit, deposited goods (*or:* documents); **3** depot, store

deppen [dɛpə(n)] *vb* dab, pat (dry)

depressie [deprɛsi] *de (~s)* depression

depressief [deprɛsif] *adj* depressed, depressive, low, dejected

deprimeren [deprimɛrə(n)] *vb* depress, deject, oppress, dishearten

der [dɛr] *art* of (the)

derby [dɛrbi] *de (derbies)* local derby

¹derde [dɛrdə] *het (~n)* third: *twee ~ van de kiezers* two thirds of the voters

²derde [dɛrdə] *de (~n)* **1** third party: *in aanwezigheid van ~n* in the presence of a third party; **2** third form: *in de ~ zitten* be in the third form

³derde [dɛrdə] *num* third: *de ~ mei* the third of May

derdemacht [dɛrdəmɑχt] *de (~en)* cube, third power, power of three: *tot de ~ verheffen* raise to the third power

derde wereld [dɛrdəwɛrəlt] *de* Third World

derdewereldland [dɛrdəwɛrəltlɑnt] *het* Third World country

derdewereldwinkel [dɛrdəwɛrəltwɪŋkəl] *de (~s)* Third-World shop

deren [dɛrə(n)] *vb* hurt, harm, injure

dergelijk [dɛrɣələk] *dem pron* similar, (the) like, such(like): *wijn, bier en ~e dranken* wine, beer and drinks of that sort; *iets ~s heb ik nog nooit meegemaakt* I have never experienced anything like it

dermate [dɛrmatə] *adv* so (much), to such an extent, such (that)

dermatologie [dɛrmatoloɣi] *de* dermatology

dertien [dɛrtin] *num* thirteen; *(in dates)* thirteenth: *~ is een ongeluksgetal* thirteen is an unlucky number; *zo gaan er ~ in een dozijn* they are two a penny

dertiende [dɛrtində] *num* thirteenth

dertig [dɛrtəχ] *num* thirty; *(in dates)* thirtieth: *zij is rond de ~* she is thirtyish

dertigste [dɛrtəχstə] *num* thirtieth

derven [dɛrvə(n)] *vb* lose, miss

¹des [dɛs] *adv* wherefore, on that (*or:* which) count ‖ *~ te beter* all the better; *hoe meer mensen er komen, ~ te beter ik me voel* the more people come, the better I feel

²des [dɛs] *art* of (the), (the) …'s: *de heer ~ huizes* the master of the house

desalniettemin [dɛsɑlnitəmɪn] *adv* nevertheless, nonetheless

desastreus [dezɑstrøs] *adj, adv* disastrous: *de wedstrijd verliep* ~ the match turned into a disaster

desbetreffend [dɛzbətrɛfənt] *adj* relevant, appropriate; respective: *de ~e afdelingen* the departments concerned (*or:* in question)

deserteren [dezɛrtɛrə(n)] *vb* desert: *uit het leger ~* desert (the army)

desertie [dezɛr(t)si] *de (~s)* desertion

desgewenst [dɛsχəwɛnst] *adv* if required (*or:* desired)

desillusie [dɛsɪlyzi] *de (~s)* disillusion, disillusionment

desinfecteren [dɛsɪnfɛktɛrə(n)] *vb* disinfect

desintegratie [dɛsɪntəɣra(t)si] *de* disintegration, decomposition

desinteresse [dɛsɪntərɛsə] *de* lack of interest

deskundig [dɛskʏndəχ] *adj, adv* expert (in, at), professional: *een zaak ~ beoordelen* judge a matter expertly; *zij is zeer ~ op het gebied van* she's an authority on

deskundige [dɛskʏndəɣə] *de (~n)* expert (in, at), authority (on), specialist (in)

deskundigheid [dɛskʏndəχhɛit] *de* expertise, professionalism: *zijn grote ~ op dit gebied* his great expertise in this field

desnoods [dɛsnots] *adv* if need be, if necessary; in an emergency, at a pinch

desondanks [dɛsɔndɑŋks] *adv* in spite of this, in spite of (all) that, all the same, for all that: *~ protesteerde hij niet* in spite of all that he did not protest

desoriëntatie [dɛsorijɛnta(t)si] *de* disorientation

despoot [dɛspot] *de (despoten)* despot, autocrat, tyrant

dessert [dɛsɛːr] *het (~en)* dessert, pudding: *wat wil je als ~?* what would you like for dessert?

dessin [dɛsɛ̃] *het (~s)* design, pattern

destijds [dɛstɛits] *adv* at the (*or:* that) time, then, in those days

destructie [dɛstrʏksi] *de (~s)* destruction

destructief [dɛstrʏktif] *adj, adv* destructive

detacheren [detaʃɛrə(n)] *vb* **1** second, send on secondment; **2** attach (to), second, post (to)

detail [detɑj] *het (~s)* detail, particular, specifics: *in ~s treden* go into detail

detailhandel [detɑjhɑndəl] *de* retail trade

detailhandelsschool [detɑjhɑndəlsχol] *de* training school for retail trade

detaillist [detɑjɪst] *de (~en)* retailer

detective [ditɛktɪf] *de (~s)* **1** detective: *particulier ~* private detective (*or:* investigator); **2** detective novel, whodunit

detentie [detɛnsi] *de (~s)* detention, arrest, custody

determineren [detɛrminɛrə(n)] *vb* **1** determine, establish; **2** *(biology)* identify

detineren [detinɛrə(n)] *vb* detain: *in Scheveningen gedetineerd zijn* be on remand in Scheveningen (prison)

deugd [døχt] *de (~en)* **1** virtuousness, morality; **2** virtue, merit

deugdelijk [døɣdələk] *adj* sound, good, reliable

deugdelijkheid [dø̞χdələkhɛit] *de* soundness, good quality, reliability
deugdzaam [dø̞χtsam] *adj, adv* virtuous, good, upright, honest
deugdzaamheid [dø̞χtsamhɛit] *de* virtuousness, uprightness, honesty
deugen [dø̞ɣə(n)] *vb* **1** be no good, be good for nothing: *die jongen heeft nooit willen ~* that boy has always been a bad lot; **2** be wrong (*or:* unsuitable, unfit): *die man deugt niet voor zijn werk* that man's no good at his job
deugniet [dø̞χnit] *de (~en)* rascal, scamp, scallywag
deuk [dø̞k] *de (~en)* **1** dent; **2** *(fig)* blow, shock: *zijn zelfvertrouwen heeft een flinke ~ gekregen* his self-confidence took a terrible knock; **3** fit: *we lagen in een ~* we were in stitches
deuken [dø̞kə(n)] *vb* dent, *(fig)* damage
deun [dø̞n] *de (~en)* tune
deur [dø̞r] *de (~en)* door: *voor een gesloten ~ komen* find no one in; *de ~ voor iemands neus dichtdoen (dichtgooien)* shut (*or:* slam) the door in s.o.'s face; *zij komt de ~ niet meer uit* she never goes out any more; *iem de ~ uitzetten* turn s.o. out of the house; *aan de ~ kloppen* knock at (*or:* on) the door; *vroeger kwam de bakker bij ons aan de ~* the baker used to call at the house; *buiten de ~ eten* eat out; *met de ~en gooien* slam doors; *met de ~ in huis vallen* come straight to the point
deurbel [dø̞rbɛl] *de (~len)* doorbell
deurknop [dø̞rknɔp] *de (~pen)* doorknob
deuropening [dø̞ropənɪŋ] *de (~en)* doorway
deurpost [dø̞rpɔst] *de (~en)* doorpost
deurwaarder [dø̞rwardər] *de (~s)* process-server; bailiff, usher
devaluatie [devalywa̠(t)si] *de (~s)* devaluation
devies [dəvis] *het (deviezen)* motto, device
deviezen [dəvizə(n)] *de (pl)* (foreign) exchange
devotie [devo̠(t)si] *de (~s)* devotion
deze [dezə] *dem pron* this; these; this one; these (ones): *wil je ~ (hier)?* do you want this one? (*or:* these ones?)
dezelfde [dəzɛlvdə] *dem pron* the same: *van ~ datum* of the same date; *wil je weer ~?* (would you like the) same again?; *op precies ~ dag* on the very same day
dhr. *de heer* Mr
dia [dija] *de (~'s)* slide, transparency
diabetes [dijabɛtəs] *de* diabetes
diabeticus [dijabɛtikʏs] *de (diabetici)* diabetic
diadeem [dijadem] *het, de (diademen)* diadem
diafragma [dijafraɣma] *het (~'s)* diaphragm, stop
diagnose [dijaɣno̠zə] *de (~n, ~s)* diagnosis
¹**diagonaal** [dijaɣona̠l] *de* diagonal
²**diagonaal** [dijaɣona̠l] *adj* diagonal
diagram [dijaɣram] *het (~men)* diagram, graph, chart
diaken [dijakə(n)] *de (~s, ~en)* deacon
dialect [dijalɛkt] *het (~en)* dialect

dialoog [dijalo̠χ] *de (dialogen)* dialogue
dialyse [dijalizə] *de (~n)* dialysis; (haemo)dialysis
diamant [dijamɑnt] *het, de (~en)* diamond: *~ slijpen* polish (*or:* cut) a diamond
diamanten [dijamɑntə(n)] *adj* diamond: *een ~ broche* a diamond brooch
diameter [dijametər] *de (~s)* diameter
diaraampje [dijarampjə] *het (~s)* slide frame
diarree [dijarɛ] *de* diarrhoea
¹**dicht** [dɪχt] *adj* **1** closed, shut, drawn, off: *mondje ~* mum's the word; *de afvoer zit ~* the drain is blocked (up); **2** tight; **3** close-lipped, tight-lipped, close(-mouthed); **4** close, thick, dense, compact: *een gebied met een ~e bevolking* a densely populated area; *~e mist* thick (*or:* dense) fog
²**dicht** [dɪχt] *adv* close (to), near: *ze zaten ~ opeengepakt* they sat tightly packed together; *hij woont ~ in de buurt* he lives near here
dichtbegroeid [dɪχtbəɣruit] *adj* thick, dense, thickly wooded
dichtbevolkt [dɪχtbəvɔlkt] *adj* densely populated
dichtbij [dɪχtbɛi] *adv* close by, near by, nearby: *van ~* from close up
dichtbundel [dɪχtbʏndəl] *de (~s)* collection of poems, book of poetry
dichtdoen [dɪɣdun] *vb* close, shut, draw: *geen oog ~* not sleep a wink
dichtdraaien [dɪɣdrajə(n)] *vb* turn off, close
dichten [dɪχtə(n)] *vb* **1** write poetry, compose verses; **2** stop (up), fill (up), seal: *een gat ~* stop a gap, mend a hole
dichter [dɪχtər] *de (~s)* poet
dichterbij [dɪχtərbɛi] *adv* nearer, closer
dichterlijk [dɪχtərlək] *adj, adv* poetic(al): *~e vrijheid* poetic licence
dichtgaan [dɪχtχan] *vb* close, shut, heal: *de deur gaat niet dicht* the door won't shut; *op zaterdag gaan de winkels vroeg dicht* the shops close early on Saturdays
dichtgooien [dɪχtχojə(n)] *vb* **1** slam (to, shut), bang; **2** fill up, fill in
dichtgroeien [dɪχtχrujə(n)] *vb* close, heal (up); grow thick
dichtheid [dɪχthɛit] *de* density, thickness, compactness
dichtklappen [dɪχtklɑpə(n)] *vb* snap shut, snap to; slam (shut)
dichtknijpen [dɪχtknɛipə(n)] *vb* squeeze
dichtknopen [dɪχtknopə(n)] *vb* button (up), fasten
dichtkunst [dɪχtkʏnst] *de* (art of) poetry
dichtmaken [dɪχtmakə(n)] *vb* close, fasten
dichtnaaien [dɪχtnajə(n)] *vb* sew up, stitch up
dichtplakken [dɪχtplɑkə(n)] *vb* seal (up); stick down; close, stop
¹**dichtslaan** [dɪχtslan] *vb* slam shut, bang shut
²**dichtslaan** [dɪχtslan] *vb* bang (shut), slam (shut), snap shut: *de deur voor iemands neus ~* slam the door in s.o.'s face

dichtslibben [dɪχtslɪbə(n)] *vb* silt up, become silted up

dichtsmijten [dɪχ(t)smɛitə(n)] *vb* slam (to, shut), bang

dichtspijkeren [dɪχtspɛikərə(n)] *vb* nail up (*or:* down), board up

dichtstbijzijnd [dɪχstbɛizɛint] *adj* nearest

dichtstoppen [dɪχtstɔpə(n)] *vb* stop (up), fill (up), plug (up)

dichttrekken [dɪχtrɛkə(n)] *vb* close, draw: *de deur achter zich ~* pull the door to behind one

dichtvallen [dɪχtfɑlə(n)] *vb* fall shut, swing to, close

dichtvouwen [dɪχtfɑuwə(n)] *vb* fold up

dichtvriezen [dɪχtfrizə(n)] *vb* freeze (over, up), be frozen (up), be frozen over

dichtzitten [dɪχtsɪtə(n)] *vb* be closed, be blocked (*or:* locked): *mijn neus zit dicht* my nose is blocked up

dictaat [dɪktat] *het (dictaten)* 1 (lecture) notes; 2 dictation

dictafoon [dɪktafon] *de (~s)* dictaphone

dictator [dɪktatɔr] *de (~s)* dictator

dictatoriaal [dɪktatorijal] *adj, adv* dictatorial

dictatuur [dɪktatyr] *de (dictaturen)* dictatorship

dictee [dɪktɛ] *het (~s)* dictation

dicteren [dɪktɛrə(n)] *vb* dictate

didactiek [didɑktik] *de* didactics

didactisch [didɑktis] *adj, adv* didactic

¹**die** [di] *dem pron* 1 that; those; that one; those (ones): *heb je ~ nieuwe film van Spielberg al gezien?* have you seen this new film by Spielberg?; *~ grote of ~ kleine?* the big one or the small one?; *niet deze maar ~ (daar)* not this one, that one; *mevrouw ~ en ~* Mrs so and so, Mrs such and such; 2 that; those; that one; those (ones): *mijn boeken en ~ van mijn zus* my books and my sister's (*or:* those of my sister); *~ tijd is voorbij* those times are over; *~ van mij/jou/hem/haar* (*or:* ons, jullie, hen) mine, yours, his, hers, ours, yours, theirs; *ze draagt altijd van ~ korte rokjes* she always wears (those) short skirts; *ken je ~ van die Belg die …* do you know the one about the Belgian who …?; *~ is goed* that's a good one; *o, ~!* oh, him! (*or:* her!); *waar is je auto? ~ staat in de garage* where's your car? it's in the garage; *~ zit!* bullseye!, touché!

²**die** [di] *pron* that, *(pers also)* who, whom, which: *de kleren ~ u besteld heeft* the clothes (that, which) you ordered; *de man ~ daar loopt, is mijn vader* the man (that is, who is) walking over there is my father; *de mensen ~ ik spreek, zijn heel vriendelijk* the people (who, that) I talk to are very nice; *dezelfde ~ ik heb* the same one (as) I've got; *zijn vrouw, ~ arts is, rijdt in een grote Volvo* his wife, who's a doctor, drives a big Volvo

dieet [dijɛt] *het (diëten)* diet: *op ~ zijn* be on a diet

dief [dif] *de (dieven)* thief, robber, burglar: *houd de ~!* stop thief!

diefstal [difstɑl] *de (~len)* theft, robbery, burglary

diegene [diɣɛnə] *pron* he, she: *diegenen die* those who

dienaar [dinar] *de (dienaren)* servant

dienblad [dimblɑt] *het (~en)* (dinner-)tray, (serving) tray

¹**dienen** [dinə(n)] *vb* 1 serve: *dat dient nergens toe* that is (of) no use; 2 serve as, serve for, be used as (*or:* for): *vensters ~ om licht en lucht toe te laten* windows serve the purpose of letting in light and air; 3 need, should, ought to: *u dient onmiddellijk te vertrekken* you are to leave immediately

²**dienen** [dinə(n)] *vb* 1 serve, attend (to), minister: *dat dient het algemeen belang* it is in the public interest; 2 serve, help: *waarmee kan ik u ~?* are you being served?; *iem van advies ~* give s.o. advice

diens [dins] *dem pron* his

dienst [dinst] *de (~en)* 1 service: *zich in ~ stellen van* place oneself in the service of; *ik ben een maand geleden als verkoper in ~ getreden bij deze firma* a month ago I joined this company as a salesman; *in ~ nemen* take on, engage; *in ~ zijn* do one's military service; 2 duty: *ik heb morgen geen ~* I am off duty tomorrow; 3 service, department: *de ~ openbare werken* the public works department; 4 service, office: *iem een goede ~ bewijzen* do s.o. a good turn; *je kunt me een ~ bewijzen* you can do me a favour; 5 place, position: *in vaste* (*or:* tijdelijke) *~ zijn* hold a permanent (*or:* temporary) appointment; *iem in ~ hebben* employ s.o.; *in ~ zijn bij iem* be in s.o.'s service; *~ doen (als)* serve (as, for); *de ~ uitmaken* run the show, call the shots; *tot uw ~* you're welcome; *iem van ~ zijn met* be of service to s.o. with

dienstbetrekking [dinstbətrɛkɪŋ] *de (~en)* employment

dienstbode [dinstbodə] *de (~n, ~s)* servant (girl), maid(servant)

dienstdoend [dinzdunt] *adj* on duty; in charge; acting

dienstensector [dinstə(n)sɛktɔr] *de* services sector, service industries

dienstjaar [dinstjar] *het (-jaren)* year of service, *(pl also)* seniority

dienstknecht [dinstknɛχt] *de (~en)* man(servant), servant

dienstlift [dinstlɪft] *de (~en)* service lift

dienstmededeling [dinstmedədəlɪŋ] *de (~en)* staff announcement

dienstmeisje [dinstmɛiʃə] *het* maid(servant), housemaid

dienstplicht [dinstplɪχt] *de* (compulsory) military service, conscription: *vervangende ~* alternative national service, community service

dienstplichtig [dinstplɪχtəχ] *adj* eligible for military service: *de ~e leeftijd bereiken* become of military age; *niet ~* exempt from military service

dienstplichtige [dinstplɪχtəɣə] *de* conscript

dienstregeling [dinstreɣəlɪŋ] *de (~en)* timetable: *een vlucht met vaste ~* a scheduled flight

diensttijd [dịnstɛit] *de* (period, length of) service, term of office: *buiten* (or: *onder*) ~ when off (*or:* on) duty

dienstverband [dịnstfərbɑnt] *het* employment: *in los* (or: *vast*) ~ *werken* be employed on a temporary (*or:* permanent) basis

dienstverlening [dịnstfərlenıŋ] *de* service(s)

dienstweigeraar [dịnstwɛiɣərar] *de (~s)* conscientious objector

dientengevolge [dintɛŋɣəvɔlɣə] *adv* consequently, as a consequence

¹diep [dip] *adj* deep, *(fig also)* profound, total, impenetrable: *twee meter* ~ two metres deep; *~er maken* deepen; *in het ~e gegooid worden* be thrown in at the deep end; *een ~e duisternis* utter darkness; *in* ~ *gepeins verzonken* (sunk) deep in thought; *alles was in ~e rust* everything was utterly peaceful; *een ~e slaap* a deep sleep; ~ *in zijn hart* deep (down) in one's heart; *uit het ~ste van zijn hart* from the bottom of one's heart; *een ~e stem* a deep voice; ~ *blauw* deep blue

²diep [dip] *adv* **1** deep(ly), low: ~ *zinken (vallen)* sink low; ~ *ongelukkig zijn* be deeply unhappy; *hij is ~ verontwaardigd* he is deeply (*or:* mortally) indignant; *een keer ~ ademhalen* take a deep breath; ~ *nadenken* think hard; **2** deep, far

diepgaand [dipχant] *adj, adv* profound, searching, in-depth: *~e discussie* in-depth (*or:* deep) discussion

diepgang [dipχaŋ] *de* **1** draught; **2** depth, profundity

diepte [diptə] *de (~n, ~s)* **1** depth; depth(s), profundity; **2** trough, hollow

dieptepunt [diptəpynt] *het (~en)* **1** (absolute) low; **2** all-time low; rock bottom: *een ~ in een relatie* a low point in a relationship

diepvries [dipfris] *de* deep-freeze, freezer

diepvriezen [dipfrizə(n)] *vb* (deep-)freeze

diepzeeduiken [dipsɛdœykə(n)] *vb* deep-sea diving

diepzinnig [dipsınəχ] *adj, adv* **1** profound, discerning; **2** profound, pensive: *een ~e blik* a thoughtful (*or:* pensive) look

diepzinnigheid [dipsınəχhɛit] *de* profundity, profoundness, depth

dier [dir] *het (~en)* animal, creature, beast

dierbaar [dịrbar] *adj* dear, much-loved, beloved

dierenarts [dịrə(n)ɑrts] *de (~en)* veterinary surgeon, vet

dierenasiel [dịrə(n)azil] *het (~en)* animal home (*or:* shelter)

dierenbescherming [dịrə(n)bəsχɛrmıŋ] *de* animal protection, prevention of cruelty to animals

dierenbeul [dịrə(n)bøl] *de (~en)* s.o. who is cruel to animals

dierendag [dịrə(n)dɑχ] *de (roughly)* animal day, pets' day

dierenmishandeling [dịrə(n)mıshɑndəlıŋ] *de* cruelty to animals, maltreatment of animals

dierenpension [dịrə(n)pɛnʃɔn] *het (~s)* (boarding) kennel(s)

dierenriem [dịrə(n)rim] *de* zodiac

dierentemmer [dịrə(n)tɛmər] *de (~s)* animal trainer, lion-tamer

dierentuin [dịrə(n)tœyn] *de (~en)* zoo, animal park

dierenverzorger [dịrə(n)vərzɔrɣər] *de (~s)* animal keeper, zookeeper

dierenwinkel [dịrə(n)wıŋkəl] *de (~s)* pet shop

diergeneeskunde [dịrɣəneeskyndə] *de* veterinary medicine

dierlijk [dịrlək] *adj* animal, *(depr)* bestial, brute, brutish: *de ~e aard (natuur)* animal nature

diersoort [dịrsort] *de (~en)* animal species: *bedreigde ~en* endangered species (of animals)

diesel [dịzəl] *de (~s, ~s)* diesel (oil, fuel), derv: *op ~ rijden* take diesel

diëtist [dijetıst] *de (~en)* dietitian

dievegge [divɛɣə] *de (~s)* thief, shoplifter

diezelfde [dizɛlvdə] *dem pron* the same, this same, that same

differentiaal [dıfərɛnʃal] *de (differentialen)* differential

differentiëren [dıfərɛnʃərə(n)] *vb* differentiate (between), distinguish (between)

diffusie [dıfyzi] *de* diffusion; mixture

diffuus [dıfys] *adj* diffuse, scattered

difterie [dıftəri] *de* diphtheria

digestie [diɣɛsti] *de* digestion

diggelen [dıɣələ(n)] || *aan ~ slaan* smash to smithereens

digibeet [diɣibet] *de (digibeten)* computer illiterate

digitaal [diɣital] *adj, adv* digital

digitaliseren [diɣitalizərə(n)] *vb* digit(al)ise

dij [dɛi] *de (~en)* thigh, ham

dijbeen [dɛibən] *het (dijbenen)* thigh bone

dijk [dɛik] *de (~en)* bank, embankment, *(in the Netherlands)* dike: *een ~ (aan)leggen* throw up a bank (*or:* an embankment); *iem aan de ~ zetten* sack s.o., lay s.o. off

¹dik [dık] *adj* **1** thick: *10 cm ~* 10 cm thick; *de ~ke darm* the large intestine; *ze stonden tien rijen ~* they stood ten (rows) deep; ~ *worden* thicken, set, congeal; **2** thick, fat, bulky: *een ~ke buik* a paunch; **3** fat, stout, corpulent: *een ~ke man* a fat man; **4** swollen: *~ke vingers* plump fingers; **5** thick, close, great: *~ke vrienden zijn* be great (*or:* close) friends; ~ *doen* swank, swagger, boast

²dik [dık] *adv* **1** thick, ample, good: ~ *tevreden (zijn)* (be) well-satisfied; ~ *onder het stof* thick with dust; *het er ~ bovenop leggen* lay it on thick; *dat zit er ~ in* that's quite on the cards; **2** thick, heavy, dense: *door ~ en dun gaan* go through thick and thin

dikkop [dıkɔp] *de (~pen)* tadpole

dikoor [dıkor] *de* mumps

dikte [dıktə] *de (~s)* **1** fatness, thickness; **2** thickness, gauge: *een ~ van vier voet* four feet thick; **3** thickness, density

dikwijls [dɪkwəls] *adv* often, frequently
dikzak [dɪksɑk] *de (~ken)* fatty, fatso
dilemma [dilɛma] *het (~'s)* dilemma
diligence [diliʒɑsə] *de (~s)* (stage)coach
dimensie [dimɛnsi] *de (~s)* **1** dimension, measurement, meaning; **2** dimension, perspective
dimlicht [dɪmlɪχt] *het (~en)* dipped headlights
¹dimmen [dɪmə(n)] *vb* dip (the headlights), shade
²dimmen [dɪmə(n)] *vb* cool it: *effe ~, da's niet leuk meer* cool it, it's not funny any more
diner [dine] *het (~s)* dinner: *aan het ~* at dinner
dineren [dinerə(n)] *vb* dine, have dinner
ding [dɪŋ] *het (~en)* **1** thing, object, gadget: *en (al) dat soort ~en* and (all) that sort of thing; **2** thing, matter, affair: *doe geen gekke ~en* don't do anything foolish; *de ~en bij hun naam noemen* call a spade a spade
dinges [dɪŋəs] *de* thingummy, what's-his-name, what's-her-name
dinosaurus [dinosɑurʏs] *de (~sen)* dinosaur
dinsdag [dɪnzdɑχ] *de (~en)* Tuesday: *(Belg) vette ~* Shrove Tuesday
dinsdags [dɪnzdɑχs] *adj* Tuesday
diode [dijodə] *de (~n, ~s)* diode
dioxide [dijɔksidə] *het (~n)* dioxide
diploma [diplomɑ] *het (~'s)* diploma, certificate: *een ~ behalen* qualify, graduate
diplomaat [diplomɑt] *de (diplomaten)* diplomat
diplomatenkoffertje [diplomɑtə(n)kɔfərcə] *het (~s)* attaché case
diplomatie [diploma(t)si] *de* **1** diplomacy; **2** diplomatic corps, diplomats: *hij gaat in de ~* he is going to enter the diplomatic service
diplomatiek [diplomɑtik] *adj, adv* **1** diplomatic: *langs ~e weg* by diplomacy; **2** diplomatic, tactful
diplomeren [diplomerə(n)] *vb* certificate: *niet gediplomeerd* unqualified, untrained
¹direct [dirɛkt] *adj* **1** direct, immediate, straight: *zijn ~e chef* his immediate superior; *de ~e oorzaak* the immediate cause; *~e uitzending* live broadcast; **2** prompt, immediate: *~e levering* prompt delivery
²direct [dirɛkt] *adv* **1** direct(ly), at once: *kom ~* come at once (*or:* straightaway); **2** presently, directly: *ik ben ~ klaar* I'll be ready in a minute; *niet ~ vriendelijk* not exactly kind
directeur [dirɛktør] *de (~en, ~s)* manager; (managing) director; principal; headmaster; superintendent; governor
directheid [dirɛktheɪt] *de* directness, straightforwardness, bluntness
directie [dirɛksi] *de (~s)* management
directiekamer [dirɛksikɑmər] *de (~s)* boardroom
directielid [dirɛksilɪt] *het* member of the board (of directors)
dirigeerstok [diriɣerstɔk] *de (~ken)* baton
dirigent [diriɣɛnt] *de (~en)* conductor; choirmaster
dirigeren [diriɣerə(n)] *vb* conduct; control
discipel [disipəl] *de (~en)* disciple, follower

discipline [disiplɪnə] *de* discipline
discman [dɪskmɛːn] *de (~s)* discman
disco [dɪsko] *de (~'s)* disco
disconteren [dɪskɔntərə(n)] *vb* discount
disconto [dɪskɔnto] *het (~'s)* discount
discotheek [dɪskotɛk] *de (discotheken)* **1** record library (*or:* collection); **2** record library; **3** discotheque
discreet [dɪskret] *adj, adv* **1** discreet, delicate, tactful; **2** discreet, unobtrusive: *een ~ tikje op de kamerdeur* a discreet tap on the door; **3** delicate, secret
discrepantie [dɪskrepɑnsi] *de* discrepancy
discretie [dɪskreti] *de* **1** discretion; tact; **2** discretion, secrecy
discriminatie [dɪskrimina(t)si] *de* discrimination
discrimineren [dɪskriminerə(n)] *vb* discriminate (against), (*with direct object*) segregate
discus [dɪskʏs] *de (~sen)* discus; disc
discussie [dɪskʏsi] *de (~s)* discussion, debate: *(het) onderwerp van ~ (zijn)* (be) under discussion; *een hevige (verhitte) ~* a heated discussion; *ter ~ staan* be under discussion, be open to discussion
discussiëren [dɪskʏʃerə(n)] *vb* discuss, debate, argue
discuswerpen [dɪskʏswɛrpə(n)] *vb* discus throwing
discutabel [dɪskytɑbəl] *adj* debatable, dubious, disputable
disk [dɪsk] *de (~s)* disk
diskette [dɪskɛtə] *de (~s)* diskette, floppy (disk)
diskjockey [dɪskdʒɔki] *de (~s)* disc jockey
diskrediet [dɪskrədit] *het* discredit: *in ~ geraken* fall into discredit
diskwalificeren [dɪskwalifisərə(n)] *vb* disqualify
display [dɪsplɛj] *de (~s)* display
dispuut [dɪspyt] *het (disputen)* debating society
dissertatie [dɪsɛrta(t)si] *de (~s)* (doctoral) dissertation, (doctoral) thesis
¹dissident [dɪsidɛnt] *de (~en)* dissident
²dissident [dɪsidɛnt] *adj* dissident
distantiëren [dɪstɑnʃerə(n)] *ref vb* distance, dissociate
distel [dɪstəl] *de (~s)* thistle
distilleren [dɪstilerə(n)] *vb* **1** distil; **2** deduce, infer: *iets uit iemands woorden ~* deduce sth from what s.o. says
distribueren [dɪstribywerə(n)] *vb* distribute, dispense, hand out
district [dɪstrɪkt] *het (~en)* district, county
dit [dɪt] *dem pron* this; these: *in ~ geval* in this case; *wat zijn ~?* what are these?
ditmaal [dɪtmal] *adv* this time, for once
diva [divɑ] *de (~'s)* diva
divan [divɑn] *de (~s)* divan, couch
divers [divɛrs] *adj* **1** diverse, various; **2** various, several
diversen [divɛrsə(n)] *de* sundries, miscellaneous
diversiteit [divɛrsitɛit] *de* diversity, variety

dividend [dividɛnt] *het (~en)* dividend

divisie [diviːzi] *de (~s)* division; league, class

dm *decimeter* dm

d.m.v. *door middel van* by means of

DNA-onderzoek [deːnaːɔndərzuk] *het* DNA-test

do [do] *de (~'s)* do(h)

dobbelen [dɔbələ(n)] *vb* dice, play (at) dice

dobbelspel [dɔbəlspɛl] *het (~len)* dicing, game of dice

dobbelsteen [dɔbəlsten] *de (-stenen)* **1** dice: *met dobbelstenen gooien* throw the dice; **2** dice, cube

dobber [dɔbər] *de (~s)* float || *hij had er een zware ~ aan* he found it a tough job

dobberen [dɔbərə(n)] *vb* float, bob: *op het water ~* bob up and down on the water

dobermannpincher [dobərmɑnpɪnʃər] *de (~s)* Doberman(n)(pinscher)

docent [dosɛnt] *de (~en)* teacher, instructor: *~ aan de universiteit* university lecturer

docentenkamer [dosɛntə(n)kamər] *de (~s)* staffroom

doceren [dosɛrə(n)] *vb* teach, lecture

dochter [dɔχtər] *de (~s)* daughter, (little) girl

doctor [dɔktɔr] *de (~en, ~s)* doctor

doctoraat [dɔktɔraːt] *het (doctoraten)* doctorate

doctorandus [dɔktɔrɑndʏs] *de (~sen, doctorandi)* (title of) university graduate

doctrine [dɔktrinə] *de (~s)* doctrine, dogma

document [dokymɛnt] *het (~en)* document, paper

documentair [dokymɛntɛːr] *adj* documentary

documentaire [dokymɛntɛːrə] *de (~s)* documentary

documentatie [dokymɛnta(t)si] *de* documentation

documenteren [dokymɛntɛrə(n)] *vb* document, support with evidence

dode [dodə] *de (~n)* dead person, the deceased

dodelijk [dodələk] *adj, adv* **1** deadly, mortal, lethal, fatal: *een ~ ongeluk, een ongeval met ~e afloop* a fatal accident; **2** dead(ly), deathly, killing: *~ vermoeid* dead beat, dead tired

doden [dodə(n)] *vb* kill, murder, slay

dodenherdenking [dodə(n)hɛrdɛŋkɪŋ] *de (~en)* commemoration of the dead

dodental [dodə(n)tɑl] *het (~len)* number of deaths (*or:* casualties), death toll

doedelzak [dudəlzɑk] *de (~ken)* bagpipes: *op een ~ spelen* play the bagpipes

doe-het-zelfzaak [duətsɛlfsak] *de (doe-het-zelfzaken)* do-it-yourself shop, D.I.Y. shop

doek [duk] *het, de* **1** cloth, fabric; **2** screen: *het witte ~* the silver screen; **3** canvas, painting; **4** curtain, backcloth: *het ~ gaat op* the curtain rises; *iets uit de ~en doen* disclose sth

doekje [dukjə] *het (~s)* (piece of) cloth, tissue

doel [dul] *het (~en)* **1** target, purpose, object(ive), aim, goal, destination; **2** goal, net: *in eigen ~ schieten* score an own goal; *zijn ~ bereiken* achieve one's aim; *het ~ heiligt de middelen (niet)* the end justi-

fies (*or:* does not justify) the means

doelbewust [dulbəwʏst] *adj, adv* determined, resolute

doeleinde [dulɛində] *het (~n)* **1** purpose, aim, design; **2** end, aim, purpose, destination: *voor eigen* (*or: privé) ~n* for one's own (*or:* private) ends

doelgebied [dulɣəbit] *het (~en)* goal area

doelgericht [dulɣərɪχt] *adj, adv* purposeful, purposive

doelloos [dulos] *adj, adv* aimless, idle, pointless

doelman [dulmɑn] *de (~nen)* goalkeeper

doelmatig [dulmatəχ] *adj, adv* suitable, appropriate, functional, effective

doelmatigheid [dulmatəχhɛit] *de* suitability, expediency, effectiveness

doelpaal [dulpal] *de (doelpalen)* (goal)post

doelpunt [dulpʏnt] *het (~en)* goal, score: *een ~ afkeuren* disallow a goal; *een ~ maken* kick (*or:* score) a goal; *met twee ~en verschil verliezen* lose by two goals

doelschop [dulsχɔp] *de (~pen)* goal kick

doelstelling [dulstɛlɪŋ] *de (~en)* aim, object(ive)

doeltreffend [dultrɛfənt] *adj, adv* effective, efficient

doelwit [dulwɪt] *het (~ten)* target, aim, object: *een dankbaar ~ vormen* make an easy victim (*or:* target)

doem [dum] *de* doom

doemdenken [dumdɛŋkə(n)] *vb* doom-mongering, defeatism

doemen [dumə(n)] *vb* doom, destine

¹doen [dun] *vb* **1** do, make, take: *een oproep ~* make an appeal; *uitspraak ~* pass judgement; *doe mij maar een witte wijn* for me a white wine, I'll have a white wine; *wat kom jij ~?* what do you want?; *wat doet hij (voor de kost)?* what does he do (for a living)?; **2** put: *iets in zijn zak ~* put sth in one's pocket; **3** make, do: *dat doet me plezier* I'm glad about that; *iem verdriet (or: pijn) ~* hurt s.o., cause s.o. grief (*or:* pain); **4** (with *het*) work: *de remmen ~ het niet* the brakes don't work; **5** make: *we weten wat ons te ~ staat* we know what (we have, are) to do; *anders krijg je met mij te ~* or else you'll have me to deal with; *dat doet er niet(s) toe* that's beside the point; *niets aan te ~* can't be helped

²doen [dun] *vb* **1** do, act, behave: *gewichtig ~* act important; *~ alsof* pretend; *je doet maar* go ahead, suit yourself; *je doet, en be: ik doe er twee uur over it* takes me two hours; *aan sport ~* do sport(s), take part in sport(s); *dat is geen manier van ~* that's no way to behave

dof [dɔf] *adj, adv* **1** dim, dull, mat(t); tarnished: *~fe tinten* dull (*or:* muted) hues/tints; **2** dull, muffled: *een ~fe knal (dreun)* a muffled boom

dofheid [dɔfhɛit] *de* dullness, dimness

dog [dɔχ] *de (~gen)* mastiff

dogma [dɔɣma] *het (~'s)* dogma

dok [dɔk] *het (~ken)* dock(yard)

doka [doka] *de (~'s)* darkroom

dokken [dɔkə(n)] *vb* fork out, cough up

dokter [dɔktər] *de (~s, doktoren)* doctor, GP: *een ~ roepen (laten komen)* send for (*or:* call in) a doctor; *~tje spelen* play doctors and nurses

doktersadvies [dɔktərsatfis] *het (-adviezen)* doctor's advice, medical advice

doktersassistente [dɔktərsasistɛntə] *de* (medical) receptionist

doktersbehandeling [dɔktərzbəhandəliŋ] *de* medical treatment

doktersrecept [dɔktərsrəsɛpt] *het* (medical) prescription

doktersvoorschrift [dɔktərsforsxrɪft] *het* medical instructions, doctor's orders

dokwerker [dɔkwɛrkər] *de (~s)* dockworker, docker

dol [dɔl] *adj* **1** mad, crazy: *het is om ~ van te worden* it is enough to drive you crazy; *~ op iets (iem) zijn* be crazy about sth (s.o.); **2** mad, wild, crazy: *door het ~le heen zijn* be beside oneself with excitement (*or:* joy); **3** foolish, silly, daft: *~le pret hebben* have great fun; **4** worn, slipping, stripped: *die schroef is ~* the screw is stripped (*or:* slipping); **5** crazy, whirling (round in circles): *het kompas is ~* the compass has gone crazy; **6** mad, rabid

¹**doldraaien** [dɔldrajə(n)] *vb* **1** (have) strip(ped), slip: *de schroef is dolgedraaid* the screw has slipped; **2** *(fig)* run away with itself; go off the rails *(pers)*

²**doldraaien** [dɔldrajə(n)] *vb* drive (*or:* push, turn) too far, overload

dolen [dolə(n)] *vb* wander (about), roam

dolfijn [dɔlfɛin] *de (~en)* dolphin

dolgraag [dɔlɣraχ] *adv* with the greatest of pleasure: *ga je mee?* ~ are you coming? I'd love to

dolk [dɔlk] *de (~en)* dagger

dollar [dɔlar] *de (~s)* dollar

dolleman [dɔləman] *de (~nen)* madman, lunatic

dollen [dɔlə(n)] *vb* lark about, horse around

¹**dom** [dɔm] *de (~men)* cathedral

²**dom** [dɔm] *adj, adv* **1** stupid, simple, dumb: *zo ~ als het achtereind van een varken* as thick as two (short) planks; **2** silly, daft: *sta niet zo ~ te grijnzen!* wipe that silly grin off your face!; **3** sheer, pure: *~ geluk* sheer luck, a fluke; **4** ignorant: *zich van de ~me houden* play ignorant, play (the) innocent

domein [dɔmɛin] *het (~en)* domain, territory

domheid [dɔmhɛit] *de (-heden)* stupidity, idiocy

dominant [dominɑnt] *adj* dominant, overriding

dominee [domine] *de (~s)* minister

domineren [dominerə(n)] *vb* dominate

domino [domino] *het (~'s)* dominoes

dominosteen [dominosten] *de (-stenen)* domino

dommelen [dɔmələ(n)] *vb* doze, drowse

domoor [dɔmor] *de (domoren)* idiot, fool, blockhead, dunce

dompelen [dɔmpələ(n)] *vb* plunge, dip, immerse

domper [dɔmpər] *de (~s)* ‖ *dit onverwachte bericht zette een ~ op de feestvreugde* this unexpected news put a damper on the party

dompteur [dɔmtør] *de (~s)* animal trainer (*or:* tamer)

domweg [dɔmwɛχ] *adv* (quite) simply, without a moment's thought, just

donateur [donatør] *de (~s)* donor, contributor, supporter

donatie [dona(t)si] *de (~s)* donation, gift

Donau [donau] *de* Danube

donder [dɔndər] *de (~s)* **1** thunder; **2** carcass, *(pers)* devil: *op zijn ~ krijgen* get a roasting; **3** hell, damn(ation)

donderbui [dɔndərbœy] *de (~en)* thunderstorm, thunder-shower

donderdag [dɔndərdaχ] *de (~en)* Thursday: *Witte Donderdag* Maundy Thursday

donderdags [dɔndərdaχs] *adj* Thursday

¹**donderen** [dɔndərə(n)] *vb* thunder

²**donderen** [dɔndərə(n)] *vb* thunder away, bluster

donderjagen [dɔndərjaɣə(n)] *vb* be a nuisance, be a pain (in the neck)

donderslag [dɔndərslaχ] *de (~en)* **1** thunderclap, thunderbolt, roll (*or:* crack) of thunder; **2** *(fig)* thunderbolt, bombshell: *als een ~ bij heldere hemel* like a bolt from the blue

doneren [donerə(n)] *vb* donate

¹**donker** [dɔŋkər] *het* dark(ness), gloom

²**donker** [dɔŋkər] *adj* **1** dark, gloomy; **2** dark, dismal, gloomy: *een ~e toekomst* a gloomy future; **3** dark, dusky; **4** low(-pitched)

³**donker** [dɔŋkər] *adv* dismally, gloomily: *de toekomst ~ inzien* take a gloomy view of the future

donor [donɔr] *de (~en)* donor

donorcodicil [donɔrkodisil] *het (~len)* donor card

dons [dɔns] *het* down, fuzz

donsdeken [dɔnzdekə(n)] *de (~s)* eiderdown, (down) quilt, duvet, (continental) quilt

¹**dood** [dot] *de* death; end: *aan de ~ ontsnappen* escape death; *dat wordt zijn ~* that will be the death of him; *iem ter ~ veroordelen* condemn (*or:* sentence) s.o. to death; *de een zijn ~ is de ander zijn brood* one man's death is another man's breath; *(zo bang) als de ~ voor iets zijn* be scared to death of sth

²**dood** [dot] *adj* **1** dead, killed: *hij was op slag ~* he died (*or:* was killed) instantly; **2** dead, extinct: *een dooie boel* a dead place; *op een ~ spoor zitten* be at a dead end; *een dode vulkaan* an extinct volcano; *op zijn dooie gemak* at one's leisure

doodbloeden [dodbludə(n)] *vb* **1** bleed to death; **2** *(fig)* run down, peter out

doodeenvoudig [dotenvɑudəχ] *adj, adv* perfectly simple, quite simple

doodernstig [dotɛrnstəχ] *adj* deadly serious, solemn

doodgaan [dotχan] *vb* die: *van de honger ~* starve to death

doodgeboren [dotχəborə(n)] *adj* stillborn

doodgewoon [dotχəwon] *adj, adv* perfectly common (ordinary): *iets ~s* sth quite ordinary

doodgooien [dotχojə(n)] *vb* bombard, swamp

doodgraver [do̱tχravər] *de (~s)* gravedigger, sexton

doodkist [do̱tkɪst] *de (~en)* coffin

doodklap [do̱tklɑp] *de (~pen)* **1** death blow, final blow, coup de grâce; **2** almighty blow

doodlachen [do̱tlɑχə(n)] *ref vb* kill oneself (laughing), split one's sides: *het is om je dood te lachen* it's a scream

doodleuk [do̱tløk] *adv* coolly, blandly

doodlopen [do̱tlopə(n)] *vb* **1** come to an end (*or:* a dead end), peter out: *~d steegje* blind alley; *een ~de straat* a dead end; **2** lead nowhere, lead to nothing

doodmoe [do̱tmu] *adj* dead tired, dead on one's feet, worn out

doodongerust [dotɔŋɣəry̱st] *adj* worried to death, worried sick

doodop [do̱tɔp] *adj* worn out, washed-out

doodrijden [do̱trɛidə(n)] *vb* run over and kill

doods [dots] *adj* **1** deathly, deathlike: *een ~e stilte* a deathly silence; **2** dead, dead-and-alive

doodsangst [do̱tsɑŋst] *de (~en)* agony, mortal fear

doodsbang [do̱tsbɑŋ] *adj, adv* (with *voor*) terrified (of), scared to death: *iem ~ maken* terrify s.o.

doodschamen [do̱tsχamə(n)] *ref vb* be terribly embarrassed

doodseskader [do̱tsɛskadər] *het (~s)* death squad

doodsgevaar [do̱tsχavar] *het (-gevaren)* deadly peril, mortal danger: *in ~ zijn (verkeren)* be in mortal danger

doodshoofd [do̱tshoft] *het (~en)* skull

doodskist [do̱tskɪst] *de (~en)* coffin

doodslaan [do̱tslan] *vb* kill, beat to death, strike dead: *een vlieg ~* swat a fly

doodslag [do̱tslɑχ] *de (~en)* manslaughter

doodsoorzaak [do̱tsorzak] *de (-oorzaken)* cause of death

doodsteken [do̱tstekə(n)] *vb* stab to death, stab and kill

doodstil [do̱tstɪl] *adj* deathly quiet (*or:* still); quite still; dead silent: *het werd opeens ~ toen hij binnenkwam* there was a sudden hush when he came in

doodstraf [do̱tstrɑf] *de (~fen)* death penalty: *hier staat de ~ op* this is punishable by death

doodsvijand [do̱tsfɛiant] *de (~en)* mortal enemy, arch-enemy

doodvonnis [do̱tfɔnɪs] *het (~sen)* death sentence

doodziek [do̱tsik] *adj* **1** critically ill; terminally ill; **2** sick and tired: *ik word ~ van die kat* I'm (getting) sick and tired of that cat

¹doodzonde [do̱tsɔndə] *de* **1** mortal sin; **2** mortal sin, deadly sin

²doodzonde [dots̠ɔndə] *adj* a terrible pity; a terrible waste

doof [dof] *adj, adv* deaf: *~ blijven voor* turn a deaf ear to; *~ aan één oor* deaf in one ear

doofheid [do̱fhɛit] *de* deafness

doofpot [do̱fpɔt] *de (~ten)* extinguisher; cover-up: *die hele zaak is in de ~ (gestopt)* that whole business has been hushed up

doofstom [dofsto̱m] *adj* deaf-and-dumb, deaf mute

doofstomme [dofsto̱mə] *de (~n)* deaf mute

dooi [doj] *de* thaw

dooien [do̱jə(n)] *vb* thaw: *het begon te ~* the thaw set in

dooier [do̱jər] *de (~s)* (egg) yolk

doolhof [do̱lhɔf] *de (doolhoven)* maze, labyrinth

doop [dop] *de (dopen)* **1** christening, baptism; **2** *(fig)* inauguration, christening: *de ~ van een schip* the naming of a ship; **3** *(Belg)* initiation (of new students)

doopceel [do̱psel] *de, het (doopcelen)* ‖ *iemands ~ lichten* bring out s.o.'s past

doopnaam [do̱pnam] *de (doopnamen)* Christian name, baptismal name, given name

doopsel [do̱psəl] *het (~s)* baptism, christening

doopvont [do̱pfɔnt] *het (~en)* font

¹door [dor] *prep* **1** through: *~ heel Europa* throughout Europe; *~ rood (oranje) rijden* jump the lights; **2** through, into: *zout ~ het eten doen* mix salt into the food; *alles lag ~ elkaar* everything was in a mess; **3** by (means of): *~ ijverig te werken, kun je je doel bereiken* you can reach your goal by working hard; *~ haar heb ik hem leren kennen* it was thanks to her that I met him; **4** because of, owing to, by, with: *~ het slechte weer* because of (*or:* owing to) the bad weather; *~ ziekte verhinderd* prevented by illness from coming (*or:* attending, going); *dat komt ~ jou* that's (all) because of you; **5** by: *zij werden ~ de menigte toegejuicht* they were cheered by the crowd; *~ wie is het geschreven?* who was it written by?; *~ de jaren heen* over the years; *~ de week* through the week

²door [dor] *adv* through: *de hele dag ~* all day long, throughout the day; *het kan ermee ~* it's passable; *de tunnel gaat onder de rivier ~* the tunnel passes under the river; *tussen de buien ~* between showers; *ik ben ~ en ~ nat* I'm wet through (and through); *~ en ~ slecht* rotten to the core

doorbakken [dorbɑ̱kə(n)] *adj* well-done

doorberekenen [do̱rbərekənə(n)] *vb* pass on, on-charge

doorbetalen [do̱rbətalə(n)] *vb* keep paying, continue paying

doorbijten [do̱rbɛitə(n)] *vb* **1** bite (hard): *de hond beet niet door* the dog didn't bite hard; **2** keep biting, continue biting (*or:* to bite), *(fig)* keep trying, *(fig)* keep at it: *even ~!* just grin and bear it!

doorbladeren [do̱rbladərə(n)] *vb* leaf through, glance through, thumb through

doorboren [dorbo̱rə(n)] *vb* drill (through), bore (a hole in), tunnel; pierce, stab

doorbraak [do̱rbrak] *de (doorbraken)* **1** bursting, collapse; **2** breakthrough; *(sport)* break: *~ van een politieke partij* the breakthrough of a political party

doorbranden [do̱rbrɑndə(n)] *vb* **1** burn through, burn properly; **2** burn out: *een doorgebrande lamp* a blown (light) bulb

¹doorbreken [dorbrɛkə(n)] *vb* break (through), burst (through), breach *(also fig): de sleur* ~ get out of the rut

²doorbreken [dɔ̱orbrɛkə(n)] *vb* **1** break (apart, in two), break up, burst, perforate: *het gezwel brak door* the swelling ruptured; **2** break through, come through: *de tandjes zullen snel* ~ the teeth will come through fast; **3** break through, make it

³doorbreken [dɔ̱orbrɛkə(n)] *vb* break (in two), snap (in two): *ze brak zijn wandelstok door (in tweeën)* she broke his walking stick in two

doorbrengen [dɔ̱orbrɛŋə(n)] *vb* spend: *ergens de nacht* ~ spend the night *(or:* stay overnight) somewhere

doorbuigen [dɔ̱orbœyɣə(n)] *vb* **1** bend, sag: *de vloer boog sterk door* the floor sagged badly; **2** bend further (over), bow deeper: *die jongen kan wel dieper* ~ that boy must be able to bend further

doordacht [dordɑ̱xt] *adj* well-thought-out, well-considered

doordat [dordɑ̱t] *conj* because (of the fact that), owing to, as a result of, on account of (the fact that), in that: ~ *er gebrek aan geld was* through lack of money

doordenken [dɔ̱ordɛŋkə(n)] *vb* reflect, think, consider: *als je even doordenkt* (or: *door had gedacht)* if you think *(or:* had thought) for a moment

doordeweeks [dordəwe̱ks] *adj* weekday, workaday

doordraaien [dɔ̱ordrajə(n)] *vb* **1** keep turning, continue turning *(or:* to turn), *(fig)* go on, *(fig)* keep moving: *de motor laten* ~ keep the engine running *(or:* on); **2** slip, not bite, have stripped, be stripped

doordrammen [dɔ̱ordrɑmə(n)] *vb* nag, go on: ~ *over iets* keep harping on (about) sth

doordrammer [dɔ̱ordrɑmər] *de (~s)* nagger, pest

doordraven [dɔ̱ordravə(n)] *vb* rattle on

doordrenken [dordrɛ̱ŋkə(n)] *vb* soak (through), saturate, drench

¹doordrijven [dɔ̱ordrɛivə(n)] *vb* push through, force through, enforce, impose: *iets te ver* ~ carry things too far

²doordrijven [dɔ̱ordrɛivə(n)] *vb* nag: *je moet niet zo* ~ stop nagging!

¹doordringen [dordrɪ̱ŋə(n)] *vb* **1** penetrate, permeate; **2** persuade, convince: *doordrongen zijn van de noodzaak ...* be convinced of the necessity of ...

²doordringen [dɔ̱ordrɪŋə(n)] *vb* penetrate, get through, occur: ~ *in* penetrate, permeate, filter through; *het drong niet tot me door dat hij mij wilde spreken* it didn't occur to me that he wanted to see me; *niet tot iem kunnen* ~ not be able to get through to s.o.

doordringend [dordrɪ̱ŋənt] *adj* piercing, penetrating, pungent: *iem* ~ *aankijken* give s.o. a piercing look

doordrukken [dɔ̱ordrʏkə(n)] *vb* push through, force through: *zijn eigen mening* ~ impose one's own view

dooreen [dorɛ̱n] *adv* jumbled up, higgledy-piggledy

¹doorgaan [dɔ̱orɣan] *vb* **1** go on, walk on, continue: *deze trein gaat door tot Amsterdam* this train goes on to Amsterdam; **2** continue (doing, with), go *(or:* carry) on (doing, with), persist (in, with), proceed (with): *hij bleef er maar over* ~ he just kept on about it; *dat gaat in één moeite door* we can do that as well while we're about it; **3** continue, go on, last; **4** go through, pass through, pass; **5** take place, be held: *het feest gaat door* the party is on; *niet* ~ be off; **6** pass for, pass oneself off as, be considered (as): *zij gaat voor erg intelligent door* she is said to be very intelligent

²doorgaan [dɔ̱orɣan] *vb* go through, pass through

doorgaand [dɔ̱orɣant] *adj* through: ~ *verkeer* through traffic

doorgaans [dɔ̱orɣans] *adv* generally, usually

doorgang [dɔ̱orɣɑŋ] *de (~en)* **1** occurrence: *(geen)* ~ *hebben* (not) take place; **2** passage(way), way through, gangway, aisle

doorgedraaid [dɔ̱orxədrajt] *adj* exhausted, worn out

doorgeven [dɔ̱orɣevə(n)] *vb* **1** pass (on, round), hand on *(or:* round): *geef de fles eens door* pass the bottle round *(or:* on); **2** pass (on): *een boodschap aan iem* ~ pass a message on to s.o.; **3** pass on, hand on, hand over; **4** pass on, let (s.o.) know about: *dat zal ik moeten* ~ *aan je baas* I will have to tell your boss about this

doorgewinterd [dɔ̱orɣəwɪntərt] *adj* seasoned, experienced

doorgronden [dorɣrɔ̱ndə(n)] *vb* fathom, penetrate

doorhalen [dɔ̱orhalə(n)] *vb* cross out, delete

doorhebben [dɔ̱orhɛbə(n)] *vb* see (through), be on to: *hij had het dadelijk door dat ...* he saw at once that ...

doorheen [dorhɛ̱n] *adv* through: *zich er* ~ *slaan* get through (it) somehow or other

doorkijken [dɔ̱orkɛikə(n)] *vb* look through

doorkneed [dorkne̱t] *adj* experienced

doorknippen [dɔ̱orknɪpə(n)] *vb* cut through, cut in half *(or:* in two)

doorkomen [dɔ̱orkomə(n)] *vb* **1** come through *(or:* past, by), pass (through, by): *de stoet moet hier* ~ the procession must come past here; **2** get through (to the end): *de dag* ~ make it through the day; *er is geen* ~ *aan: a) (book, work etc)* there is no way I'm going to get this finished; *b) (crowd, traffic)* I don't stand a hope of getting through; **3** come through, get through: *de zon komt door* the sun is breaking through

doorkruisen [dorkrœysə(n)] *vb* **1** traverse, roam, scour: *hij heeft heel Frankrijk doorkruist* he has travelled all over France; **2** thwart: *dat voorstel doorkruist mijn plannen* that proposal has thwarted my plans

doorlaten [dɔ̱orlatə(n)] *vb* let through *(or:* pass), allow through (or: to pass): *geen geluid ~ be sound-proof*

doorleefd [dorlēft] *adj* wrinkled; aged

doorleren [dōrlerə(n)] *vb* keep (on) studying, continue with one's studies, stay on at school

doorlichten [dōrlɪχtə(n)] *vb* investigate, examine carefully, screen *(pers)*

doorliggen [dōrlɪɣə(n)] *vb* have bedsores, get bedsores: *zijn rug is doorgelegen* he has (got) bedsores on his back

¹**doorlopen** [dorlōpə(n)] *vb* **1** walk through, go through, pass through; **2** go through, pass through, complete: *alle stadia ~* pass through (or: complete) every stage; **3** run through, glance through

²**doorlopen** [dōrlopə(n)] *vb* **1** walk (or: go, pass) through: *hij liep tussen de struiken door* he walked (or: went) through the bushes; **2** keep (on) walking (or: going, moving), continue walking/moving (or: to walk, to move), walk on, go on, move on: *~ a.u.b.!* move along now, please!; **3** run: *het blauw is doorgelopen* the blue has run; **4** run on, carry on through, continue, be consecutive: *de eetkamer loopt door in de keuken* the dining room runs through into the kitchen; **5** hurry up

doorlopend [dorlōpənt] *adj, adv* continuous, continuing; continual; consecutive: *hij is ~ dronken* he is constantly drunk

doormaken [dōrmakə(n)] *vb* go through, pass through, live through, experience, undergo: *een moeilijke tijd ~* have a hard time (of it)

doormidden [dormɪdə(n)] *adv* in two, in half

doorn [dorn] *de (~en)* thorn: *dat is mij een ~ in het oog* that is a thorn in my flesh

doornemen [dōrnemə(n)] *vb* **1** go through (or: over): *een artikel vluchtig ~* skim through an article; **2** go over: *iets met elkaar ~* go over sth together

Doornroosje [dornrōʃə] Sleeping Beauty

doorprikken [dōrprɪkə(n)] *vb* burst, prick, puncture

¹**doorreizen** [dōrɛizə(n)] *vb* continue one's journey, continue travelling: *ze reist vandaag nog door naar Tilburg* she is going on to Tilburg today

²**doorreizen** [dōrɛizə(n)] *vb* travel through: *ik heb heel Europa doorgereisd* I have travelled all over Europe

doorrijden [dōrɛidə(n)] *vb* **1** keep on (or: continue) driving/riding: *rijdt deze bus door naar het station?* does this bus go on to the station?; **2** drive on, ride on, proceed, continue: *~ na een aanrijding* fail to stop after an accident; **3** drive faster, ride faster, increase speed: *als we wat ~, zijn we er in een uur* if we step on it, we will be there in an hour

doorrijhoogte [dōrɛihoχtə] *de (~n)* clearance, headway

doorschemeren [dōrsχemərə(n)] *vb* be hinted at, be implied: *hij liet ~ dat hij trouwplannen had* he hinted that he was planning to marry

doorscheuren [dōrsχørə(n)] *vb* tear up, tear in half

doorschieten [dōrsχitə(n)] *vb* shoot through (or: past)

doorschijnen [dōrsχɛinə(n)] *vb* **1** be translucent; **2** show through, shine through: *haar slipje schijnt door* her panties are showing (through her dress)

doorschijnend [dōrsχɛinənt] *adj, adv* translucent, see-through, transparent

doorschuiven [dōrsχœyvə(n)] *vb* pass on

doorslaan [dōrslan] *vb* **1** tip, dip: *de balans doen ~* tip the scales; **2** blow, melt, fuse, break down: *de stop is doorgeslagen* the fuse has blown; **3** talk

doorslaand [dōrslant] *adj* conclusive, decisive: *een ~ succes* a resounding success

doorslag [dōrslaχ] *de (~en)* **1** turn (or: tip) (of the scale): *dat gaf bij mij de ~* that decided me; *dat geeft de ~* that settles it; **2** carbon (copy), duplicate

doorslaggevend [dōrslaχɣevənt] *adj* decisive: *van ~ belang* of overriding importance

doorslapen [dōrslapə(n)] *vb* sleep on (or: through): *de dag ~* sleep through the day

doorslikken [dōrslɪkə(n)] *vb* swallow

doorsmeren [dōrsmerə(n)] *vb* lubricate: *de auto laten ~* have the car lubricated

doorsnede [dōrsnedə] *de (~n)* **1** section, cross-section, profile: *een ~ van een bol maken* make a cross-section of a sphere; **2** diameter: *die bal heeft een ~ van 5 cm* this ball has a diameter of 5 cm

doorsnee [dōrsne] *adj* average, mean

¹**doorsnijden** [dōrsnɛidə(n)] *vb* cut, sever, cut in(to) two, bisect: *hij heeft alle banden met zijn familie doorgesneden* he has severed (or: cut) all ties with his family

²**doorsnijden** [dōrsnɛidə(n)] *vb* cut (through)

¹**doorspelen** [dōrspelə(n)] *vb* play on, continue to play: *het orkest speelde door alsof er niets gebeurd was* the orchestra played on as if nothing had happened

²**doorspelen** [dōrspelə(n)] *vb* pass on, leak: *informatie aan een krant ~* pass on information to a newspaper; *de bal ~ naar ...* pass (the ball) to ...

doorspoelen [dōrspulə(n)] *vb* **1** wash down (or: out, through): *je eten ~ met wijn* wash down your food with wine; **2** flush out; flush; **3** wind on

doorspreken [dōrsprekə(n)] *vb* discuss, go into (in depth)

doorstaan [dorstan] *vb* endure, bear, (with)stand, come through: *een proef ~* come through a test

doorstart [dōrstart] *de (~s)* **1** aborted landing; **2** *(economics)* new start

doorstarten [dōrstartə(n)] *vb* start up again

doorsteken [dorstekə(n)] *vb* stab, run through, pierce, knife

doorstoten [dōrstotə(n)] *vb* **1** keep on (or: continue) pushing; **2** advance, push on (or: through), break through, burst through: *~ tot de kern van de zaak* get to the heart of the matter

doorstrepen [dōrstrepə(n)] *vb* cross out, delete, strike out (or: through)

doorstromen [dorstromə(n)] *vb* **1** move up, move

on; **2** flow (through)

doorstroming [dọrstromıŋ] *de* **1** moving up, moving on; **2** flow, circulation: *een vlottere ~ van het verkeer* a freer flow of traffic

doorstuderen [dọrstyderə(n)] *vb* continue (with) one's studies

doorsturen [dọrstyrə(n)] *vb* send on, send away: *een brief ~* forward a letter; *een patiënt naar een specialist ~* refer a patient to a specialist

doortastend [dortạstənt] *adj, adv* vigorous, bold

doortocht [dortɔχt] *de (~en)* **1** crossing, passage through, way through; **2** passage, thoroughfare: *de ~ versperren* block the way through

doortrapt [dortrɑpt] *adj, adv* **1** cunning, crafty; **2** base, villainous

¹doortrekken [dọrtrɛkə(n)] *vb* **1** extend, continue: *een lijn ~* follow the same line (*or:* course); *een vergelijking ~* carry a comparison (further); **2** flush

²doortrekken [dọrtrɛkə(n)] *vb* travel through, pass through, journey through, roam: *de verkiezingskaravaan trekt het hele land door* the election caravan is touring the whole country

doorverbinden [dọrvərbındə(n)] *vb* connect, put through (to)

doorvertellen [dọrvərtɛlə(n)] *vb* pass on: *aan niemand ~, hoor!* don't tell anyone else!

doorverwijzen [dọrvərwɛizə(n)] *vb* refer

doorweekt [dorwẹkt] *adj* wet through, soaked, drenched

¹doorwerken [dọrwɛrkə(n)] *vb* **1** go (*or:* keep) on working, continue to work, work on, work overtime: *er werd dag en nacht doorgewerkt* they worked night and day; **2** make headway, get on (with the job): *je kunt hier nooit ~* you can never get on with your work here; **3** affect sth, make itself felt: *zijn houding werkt door op anderen* his attitude has its effect on others

²doorwerken [dọrwɛrkə(n)] *vb* work (one's way) through, get through, go through: *een heleboel stukken door moeten werken* have to plough through a mass of documents

¹doorzagen [dọrzaɣə(n)] *vb* saw (sth) through, saw in two ‖ *iem over iets blijven ~* force sth down s.o.'s throat, question s.o. closely, grill s.o.

²doorzagen [dọrzaɣə(n)] *vb* keep (*or:* go, moan) on (about sth)

doorzakken [dọrzɑkə(n)] *vb* **1** sag, give (way); **2** go on drinking (*or:* boozing), make a night of it

¹doorzetten [dọrzɛtə(n)] *vb* **1** become stronger, become more intense: *de weeën zetten door* the contractions are increasing (in intensity); **2** persevere: *nog even ~!* don't give up now!; *van ~ weten* not give up easily

²doorzetten [dọrzɛtə(n)] *vb* **1** press (*or:* go) ahead with; **2** go through with: *iets tot het einde toe ~* see sth through

doorzetter [dọrzɛtər] *de (~s)* go-getter, stayer

doorzettingsvermogen [dọrzɛtıŋsfərmoɣə(n)] *het* perseverance, drive

doorzichtig [dorzıχtəχ] *adj* **1** transparent, see-through: *gewoon glas is ~, matglas doorschijnend* plain glass is transparent, frosted glass is translucent; **2** *(fig)* transparent, thin, obvious

doorzichtigheid [dorzıχtəχhɛit] *de* transparency

doorzien [dorzịn] *vb* see through, be on to *(pers)*: *hij doorzag haar bedoelingen* he saw what she was up to

doorzoeken [dorzụkə(n)] *vb* search through, go through, ransack: *zijn zakken ~* turn one's pockets (inside) out

doos [dos] *de (dozen)* box, case: *(aviation) de zwarte ~* the black box

dop [dɔp] *de (~pen)* **1** shell; pod; husk; **2** cap, top; **3** *(Belg; inf)* dole, unemployment benefit: *van de ~ leven* be on benefit (*or:* on the dole); *kijk uit je ~pen!* watch where you're going!

dope [dop] *de* dope

dopen [dopə(n)] *vb* **1** sop, dunk (in): *zijn pen in de inkt ~* dip one's pen in the ink; **2** *(rel)* baptize, christen: *iem tot christen ~* baptize s.o.; **3** *(Belg)* initiate, rag

doper [dopər] *de (~s)* baptizer: *Johannes de Doper* John the Baptist

doperwt [dɔpɛrt] *de (~en)* green pea

doping [dopıŋ] *de* drug(s)

dopingcontrole [dopıŋkɔntro:lə] *de (~s)* dope test

dopje [dɔpjə] *het (~s)* cap, top

¹doppen [dɔpə(n)] *vb* (un)shell, pod, hull, peel, (un)husk, hull

²doppen [dɔpə(n)] *vb (Belg)* be on benefit, be on the dole

dor [dɔr] *adj* **1** barren, arid; **2** withered

dorp [dɔrp] *het (~en)* village, *(Am)* town: *het hele ~ weet het* it's all over town

dorpel [dɔrpəl] *de (~s)* threshold, doorstep

dorpeling [dɔrpəlıŋ] *de (~en)* villager, *(pl also)* village people

dorpsbewoner [dɔrpsbəwonər] *de (~s)* villager

dorpshuis [dɔrpshœys] *het (-huizen)* community centre

dorsen [dɔrsə(n)] *vb* thresh

dorst [dɔrst] *de* thirst: *ik verga van de ~* I'm dying of thirst

dorstig [dɔrstəχ] *adj* thirsty, parched

doseren [dozerə(n)] *vb* dose

dosering [dozerıŋ] *de (~en)* quantity; dose, dosage

dosis [dozıs] *de (doses)* dose; measure: *een flinke ~ gezond verstand* a good measure of common sense

dossier [dɔʃe] *het (~s)* file, documents, records: *een ~ bijhouden van iets (iem)* keep a file on sth (s.o.)

dot [dɔt] *de (~ten)* tuft: *een flinke ~ slagroom* a dollop of cream

douane [duwanə] *de (~n, ~s)* customs

douanebeambte [duwanəbəamtə] *de (~n)* customs officer

douanerechten [duwanərɛχtə(n)] *de* customs duties

double [dɑbəl] *de (~s)* double

doubleren [dublɛrə(n)] *vb* repeat (a class)

doubleur [dublør] *de (~s) (roughly)* non-promoted pupil

douche [duʃ] *de (~s)* shower: *(fig) een koude ~* a rude awakening

douchen [duʃə(n)] *vb* shower, take *(or:* have) a shower

douwen [dɑuwə(n)] *vb* shove, push, crowd

dove [dovə] *de (~n)* deaf person

doven [dovə(n)] *vb* extinguish, put out, turn out, turn off *(light)*

dovenetel [dovənetəl] *de (~s)* dead nettle

doveninstituut [dovə(n)ɪnstityt] *het (-instituten)* institute for the deaf

doventaal [dovə(n)tal] *de (-talen)* sign language

downloaden [dɑunlodə(n)] *vb* download

dozijn [dozɛin] *het* dozen: *een ~ eieren* one dozen eggs

draad [drat] *de (draden)* **1** thread; fibre: *tot op de ~ versleten* worn threadbare; *de ~ weer opnemen* pick up the thread; *de ~ kwijt zijn* flounder; **2** fibre, string

draadje [dracə] *het (~s)* **1** thread, strand, fibre: *aan een zijden ~ hangen* hang by a thread; *er zit een ~ los bij hem* he has a screw loose; **2** wire, piece of wiring

draadloos [dratlos] *adj, adv* wireless: *draadloze telefoon* cellular (tele)phone

draagbaar [draɣbar] *adj* portable, transportable

draagmoeder [draɣmudər] *de (~s)* surrogate mother

draagstoel [draɣstul] *de (~en)* sedan (chair)

draagvlak [draɣflɑk] *het (~ken) (literal)* bearing surface, basis, support *(also fig)*: *het maatschappelijk ~ van een wetsontwerp* the public support for a bill

draai [draj] *de (~en)* **1** turn, twist, bend: *een ~ van 180° maken* make an about-turn; **2** turn, twist, screw: *iem een ~ om de oren geven* box s.o.'s ears; *hij kon zijn ~ niet vinden* he couldn't settle down

draaibaar [drajbar] *adj* revolving, rotating, swinging: *een draaibare (bureau)stoel* a swivel chair

draaiboek [drajbuk] *het (~en)* script, screenplay, scenario

draaicirkel [drajsɪrkəl] *de (~s)* turning circle

draaideur [drajdør] *de (~en)* revolving door

¹draaien [drajə(n)] *vb* **1** turn (around), twirl, spin: *het gas hoger* (or: *lager) ~* turn the gas up (or: down); *een deur op slot ~* lock a door; **2** turn (around), swerve; **3** roll, turn: *een film ~* shoot a film; **4** dial; **5** play: *een film ~* show a film; *een nachtdienst ~* work a night shift

²draaien [drajə(n)] *vb* **1** turn (around), revolve, rotate, orbit, pivot: *een ~de bal* a spinning ball; *in het rond ~* turn round, spin round; *daar draait het om* that's what it's all about; **2** turn, swerve: *de wind draait* the wind is changing; **3** work, run, do: *met winst* (or: *verlies) ~* work at a profit (or: loss); *die*

film draait nog steeds that film is still on; *aan de knoppen ~* turn the knobs; *er omheen ~* evade the question

draaierig [drajərəχ] *adj* dizzy

draaihek [drajhɛk] *het* turnstile, swing gate

draaikolk [drajkɔlk] *de (~en)* whirlpool

draaikruk [drajkrʏk] *de (~ken)* revolving stool

draaimolen [drajmolə(n)] *de (~s)* merry-go-round

draaiorgel [drajɔrɣəl] *het (~s)* barrel organ, hand organ: *de orgelman speelde zijn ~* the organgrinder was grinding his barrel organ

draaischijf [drajsχɛif] *de (-schijven)* **1** dial; **2** potter's wheel

draaistoel [drajstul] *de (~en)* swivel chair, revolving chair

draaitafel [drajtafəl] *de (~s)* turntable

draak [drak] *de (draken)* dragon

drab [drɑp] *het, de* **1** dregs, sediment; **2** ooze

drachme [drɑχmə] *het, de (~n)* drachma

dracht [drɑχt] *de (~en)* **1** gestation, pregnancy; **2** costume, dress

drachtig [drɑχtəχ] *adj* with young, bearing: *~ zijn* be with young

draf [drɑf] *de* trot: *in volle ~* at full trot; *op een ~je lopen* run along, trot

¹dragen [draɣə(n)] *vb* **1** support, bear, carry, *(fig also)* sustain: *iets bij zich ~* have sth on one; **2** wear, have on: *die schoenen kun je niet bij die jurk ~* those shoes don't go with that dress; **3** take, have: *de gevolgen ~* bear *(or:* take) the consequences; **4** bear, endure: *de spanning was niet langer te ~* the tension had become unbearable

²dragen [draɣə(n)] *vb* rest on, be supported: *een ~de balk* a supporting beam

drager [draɣər] *de (~s)* bearer, carrier

dralen [dralə(n)] *vb* linger, hesitate

drama [drama] *het (~'s)* **1** tragedy, drama: *de Griekse ~'s* the Greek tragedies; *een ~ opvoeren* perform a tragedy; **2** tragedy, catastrophe: *een ~ van iets maken* make a drama of sth

dramatisch [dramatis] *adj, adv* **1** dramatic: *~e effecten* theatrical effects; **2** tragic; theatrical: *doe niet zo ~* don't make such a drama of it

dramatiseren [dramatizɛrə(n)] *vb* **1** dramatize, make a drama of; **2** dramatize, adapt for the stage

drammen [dramə(n)] *vb* nag, go on

drammerig [dramərəχ] *adj, adv* nagging, insistent, tiresome

drang [drɑŋ] *de* **1** urge, instinct: *de ~ tot zelfbehoud* the survival instinct; **2** pressure, force: *met zachte ~* with gentle insistence

dranghek [drɑŋhɛk] *het (~ken)* barrier

drank [drɑŋk] *de (~en)* drink, beverage: *alcoholhoudende ~en* alcoholic beverages; *(Belg) korte ~* spirits, liquor

drankgebruik [drɑŋkχəbrœyk] *het* consumption of alcohol, drinking

drankje [drɑŋkjə] *het (~s)* drink: *een ~ klaarmaken* mix a drink

drankmisbruik [drɑŋkmɪzbrœyk] *het* alcohol abuse

drankorgel [drɑŋkɔrɣəl] *het (~s)* drunk(ard), hard drinker

drankprobleem [drɑŋkproblem] *het (-problemen)* alcohol problem, drinking problem

drankvergunning [drɑŋkfərɣynɪŋ] *de (~en)* liquor licence

drankwinkel [drɑŋkwɪŋkəl] *de (~s)* off-licence, *(Am)* liquor store

draperen [draperə(n)] *vb* drape

drassig [drɑsəɣ] *adj* boggy, swampy

drastisch [drɑstis] *adj, adv* drastic: *de prijzen (or: belastingen) ~ verlagen* slash prices *(or:* taxes)

draven [dravə(n)] *vb* **1** trot; **2** hurry about

dreef [dref] *de (dreven)* **1** (with *op)* in form, in one's stride: *niet op ~ zijn* be off form; *hij is aardig (or: geweldig) op ~* he's in good *(or:* splendid) form; **2** avenue, lane

dreggen [drɛɣə(n)] *vb* drag

dreigement [drɛiɣəmɛnt] *het (~en)* threat

¹**dreigen** [drɛiɣə(n)] *vb* **1** threaten, menace: *~ met straf* threaten punishment; **2** threaten, be in danger: *de vergadering dreigt uit te lopen* the meeting threatens to go on longer than expected

²**dreigen** [drɛiɣə(n)] *vb* threaten

dreigend [drɛiɣənt] *adj* **1** threatening, ominous, menacing: *iem ~ aankijken* scowl at s.o.; **2** imminent, threatening

dreiging [drɛiɣɪŋ] *de (~en)* threat, menace

drek [drɛk] *de* dung, muck, manure

drempel [drɛmpəl] *de (~s)* **1** threshold, doorstep; **2** threshold, barrier

drenkeling [drɛŋkəlɪŋ] *de (~en)* drowning person, drowned body *(or:* person)

drenken [drɛŋkə(n)] *vb* drench, soak, saturate

drentelen [drɛntələ(n)] *vb* saunter, stroll

dresseren [drɛserə(n)] *vb* train

dresseur [drɛsør] *de (~s)* (animal) trainer

dressoir [drɛswar] *het, de (~s)* sideboard, buffet

dressuur [drɛsyr] *de* training, drilling, dressage, schooling

dreumes [drøməs] *de (~en)* toddler, tot

dreun [drøn] *de (~en)* **1** boom, rumble, drone: *er klonk een doffe ~* there was a dull boom *(or:* rumble); **2** drone, monotone; **3** blow, thump: *iem een ~ verkopen (geven)* sock s.o. one

dreunen [drønə(n)] *vb* **1** hum, drone, rumble: *het hele huis dreunt ervan* the whole house is rocking with it; **2** boom, crash, thunder, roar: *hij sloeg de deur ~d dicht* he slammed the door shut

dribbelen [drɪbələ(n)] *vb* dribble

drie [dri] *num* three; *(in dates)* third: *een auto in z'n ~ zetten* put a car into third gear; *met ~ tegelijk* in threes; *zij waren met hun ~ën* there were three of them; *het is tegen (or: bij) ~ën* it's almost three o'clock; *met 3-0 verliezen* lose by three goals to nil

driedaags [dridaɣs] *adj* three-day

driedelig [drideləɣ] *adj* tripartite, three-piece

driedimensionaal [dridimɛnʃonal] *adj* three-dimensional

driedubbel [dridʏbəl] *adj, adv* **1** threefold, triple; **2** treble, triple

driegen [driɣə(n)] *vb (Belg)* baste, tack

driehoek [drihuk] *de (~en)* triangle

driehoekig [drihukəɣ] *adj, adv* triangular, three-cornered

driehonderd [drihɔndərt] *num* three hundred

driejarig [drijarəɣ] *adj* **1** three-year-old: *op ~e leeftijd* at the age of three; **2** three-year

driekleur [driklør] *de* tricolour

Driekoningen [drikɔnɪŋə(n)] *de* (feast of (the)) Epiphany, Twelfth Night

driekwart [drikwart] *adj, adv* three-quarter: *(voor) ~ leeg* three parts empty; *(voor) ~ vol* three-quarters full

driekwartsmaat [drikwartsmat] *de* three-four (time)

drieling [drilɪŋ] *de (~en)* (set of) triplets: *de geboorte van een ~* the birth of triplets

driemaal [drimal] *adv* three times: *~ zo veel (groot) geworden* increased threefold; *~ is scheepsrecht* third time lucky

driemaandelijks [drimandələks] *adj, adv* quarterly, three-monthly: *een ~ tijdschrift* a quarterly

driemaster [drimastər] *de (~s)* three-master

driepoot [dripot] *de (-poten)* tripod

driesprong [drisprɔŋ] *de (~en)* three-forked road

drietal [drital] *het (~len)* threesome, trio, triad

drietand [dritant] *de (~en)* **1** trident: *de ~ van Neptunus* Neptune's trident; **2** three-pronged, three-tined fork

drietjes [dricəs] *num* the three of ...: *wij ~* the three of us, we three; *ze kwamen met z'n ~* three of them came

drievoud [drivaut] *het (~en)* **1** treble, triplicate: *een formulier in ~ ondertekenen* sign a form in triplicate; **2** multiple of three

drievoudig [drivaudəɣ] *adj* treble, triple: *we moesten het ~e (bedrag) betalen* we had to pay three times as much

driewieler [driwilər] *de (~s)* tricycle; *(car)* three-wheel car

driezijdig [drizɛidəɣ] *adj* three-sided, triangular

drift [drɪft] *de (~en)* **1** (fit of) anger, (hot) temper, rage: *in ~ ontsteken* fly into a rage; **2** passion, urge; **3** drift

driftbui [drɪftbœy] *de (~en)* fit *(or:* outburst) of anger

¹**driftig** [drɪftəɣ] *adj* **1** angry, heated: *je moet je niet zo ~ maken* you must not lose your temper; **2** short-tempered

²**driftig** [drɪftəɣ] *adv* **1** angry, hot-headed: *~ spreken* speak in anger; **2** vehement, heated: *hij stond ~ te gebaren* he was making vehement gestures; *zij maakte ~ aantekeningen* she was busily taking notes

driftkop [drɪftkɔp] *de (~pen)* hothead

drijfkracht [drɛifkraχt] *de* **1** driving power, motive power (*or:* force), drive; **2** driving force, moving spirit

drijfnat [drɛifnɑt] *adj* soaking wet, sopping wet, drenched, soaked

drijfveer [drɛifer] *de (-veren)* motive, mainspring

drijfzand [drɛifsɑnt] *het* quicksand(s)

¹drijven [drɛivə(n)] *vb* **1** float, drift: *het pakje bleef ~* the package remained afloat; **2** float, drift, glide; **3** be soaked: *~ van het zweet* be dripping with sweat

²drijven [drɛivə(n)] *vb* **1** drive, push, move: *de menigte uit elkaar ~* break up the crowd; **2** drive, push, compel: *iem tot het uiterste ~* push s.o. to the extreme; **3** run, conduct, manage: *handel ~ met een land* trade with a country; *de spot met iem ~* make fun of s.o.; **4** drive, propel, operate: *door stoom gedreven schepen* steam-driven (*or:* steam-propelled) ships

drijvend [drɛivənt] *adj* floating, drifting, afloat

drijver [drɛivər] *de (~s)* **1** driver, drover; beater; **2** float: *~s van een watervliegtuig* floats of a seaplane

drilboor [drɪlbor] *de (-boren)* drill

drillen [drɪlə(n)] *vb* drill

¹dringen [drɪŋə(n)] *vb* **1** push, shove, penetrate: *hij drong door de menigte heen* he pushed (*or:* elbowed, forced) his way through the crowd; *naar voren ~* push forward; **2** push, press: *het zal wel ~ worden om een goede plaats* we'll probably have to fight for a good seat; **3** press, urge, compel: *de tijd dringt* time is short

²dringen [drɪŋə(n)] *vb* push, force

¹dringend [drɪŋənt] *adj* **1** urgent; pressing; acute, dire; **2** urgent, earnest, insistent, pressing: *op ~ verzoek van* at the urgent request of

²dringend [drɪŋənt] *adv* urgently; acutely, direly: *ik moet u ~ spreken* I must speak to you immediately

drinkbaar [drɪŋgbar] *adj* drinkable; potable

drinken [drɪŋkə(n)] *vb* **1** drink, sip: *wat wil je ~?, wat drink jij?* what are you having?, what'll it be?; *ik drink op ons succes* here's to our success!; **2** soak (up); **3** drink: *te veel ~* drink (to excess)

drinker [drɪŋkər] *de (~s)* drinker

drinkplaats [drɪŋkplats] *de (~en)* watering place

drinkwater [drɪŋkwatər] *het* drinking water, potable water

drinkyoghurt [drɪŋkjɔɣʏrt] *de (~s)* drinking yoghurt

droef [druf] *adj, adv* sad, sorrowful

droefheid [drufhɛit] *de* sorrow, sadness, grief

¹droevig [druvəχ] *adj* **1** sad, sorrowful, miserable; **2** sad, melancholy: *een ~e blik* a sad (*or:* melancholy) look; **3** depressing, saddening: *een ~ lied* a sad (*or:* melancholy) song; **4** depressing, miserable

²droevig [druvəχ] *adv* **1** sadly, dolefully, sorrowfully; **2** depressingly, pathetically: *het is ~ gesteld met hem* he's in a distressing situation

¹drogen [droɣə(n)] *vb* dry: *de was te ~ hangen* hang out the laundry to dry

²drogen [droɣə(n)] *vb* dry, air, wipe: *iets laten ~*

leave sth to dry

droger [droɣər] *de (~s)* drier

drogist [droɣɪst] *de (~en)* **1** chemist; **2** chemist's

drogisterij [droɣɪstərɛi] *de (~en)* chemist's

drol [drɔl] *de (~len)* turd

drom [drɔm] *de (~men)* crowd, horde, throng

dromedaris [drɔmədarəs] *de (~sen)* dromedary, (Arabian) camel

¹dromen [dromə(n)] *vb* **1** dream; **2** (day)dream, muse

²dromen [dromə(n)] *vb* dream, imagine

dromer [dromər] *de (~s)* dreamer, stargazer, rainbow chaser

¹dromerig [dromərəχ] *adj* **1** dreamy, faraway; **2** dreamy, dreamlike, illusory: *een ~e sfeer* a dreamlike feeling

²dromerig [dromərəχ] *adv* dreamily: *~ uit zijn ogen kijken* gaze dreamily

dronk [drɔŋk] *de (~en)* **1** toast; **2** drinking

dronken [drɔŋkə(n)] *adj* drunken; drunk: *de wijn maakt hem ~* the wine is making him drunk

dronkenschap [drɔŋkənsχɑp] *de* drunkenness, intoxication, inebriety: *in kennelijke staat van ~ (verkeren)* (be) under the influence of drink

droog [droχ] *adj* dry, arid, dried out: *hij zit hoog en ~* he is sitting high and dry

droogbloem [droɣblum] *de (~en)* dried flower

droogdoek [droɣduk] *de (~en)* tea towel

droogkap [droχkɑp] *de (~pen)* (hair)dryer (hood)

droogkuis [droχkœys] *de (Belg)* dry-cleaning

droogleggen [droχlɛɣə(n)] *vb* reclaim, *(esp in the Netherlands)* impolder

droogte [droχtə] *de (~n)* dryness, aridity, drought

droogtrommel [droχtrɔməl] *de (~s)* dryer, drying machine, tumble(r) dryer

droogzwemmen [droχswɛmə(n)] *vb* **1** practise swimming on (dry) land; **2** do a dry run

droogzwierder [droχswirdər] *de (~s)* (*Belg*) spin-dryer

droom [drom] *de (dromen)* dream, fantasy: *het meisje van zijn dromen* the girl of his dreams; *een natte ~* a wet dream; *iem uit de ~ helpen* disillusion (*or:* disenchant) s.o.

droomprins [dromprɪns] *de (~en)* Prince Charming

droomwereld [dromwerəlt] *de* dream-world, fantasy world, fool's paradise

drop [drɔp] *het, de* liquorice: *Engelse ~* liquorice all-sorts

droppen [drɔpə(n)] *vb* drop off

dropping [drɔpɪŋ] *de (~s)* drop

drug [drʏɣ] *de (~s)* drug, narcotic: *handelen in ~s, ~s verkopen* deal in (*or:* sell) drugs

drugsbeleid [drʏɣksbəlɛit] *het* drug policy, policy on drugs

drugsdealer [drʏɣksdiːlər] *de (~s)* (drug) dealer, pusher

drugsgebruik [drʏɣksχəbrœyk] *het* use of drugs, drug abuse

drugshandel [drʏkshɑndəl] *de* dealing (in drugs), drug trade

drugshandelaar [drʏkshɑndəlar] *de (~s)* drug trafficker, drug dealer

drugsverslaafde [drʏksfərslavdə] *de (~n)* drug addict, junkie

druïde [drywidə] *de (~n)* druid

druif [drœyf] *de* grape: *een tros druiven* a bunch of grapes

druilerig [drœylərəχ] *adj* drizzly

druiloor [drœylor] *de (-oren)* mope(r)

druipen [drœypə(n)] *vb* drip, trickle

druipnat [drœypnɑt] *adj* soaking wet, soaked through

druipsteen [drœypsten] *het, de* stalactite; *(hanging)* stalagmite *(standing)*

druivenoogst [drœyvə(n)oχst] *de (~en)* grape harvest, vintage

druivensap [drœyvə(n)sɑp] *het* grape-juice

druivensuiker [drœyvə(n)sœykər] *de* grape sugar, dextrose

¹druk [drʏk] *de (~ken)* **1** pressure: *~ uitoefenen (op)* exert pressure (on); **2** strain, stress; **3** edition: *een herziene ~* a revised edition

²druk [drʏk] *adj* **1** busy, demanding, active, lively: *een ~ke baan* a demanding job; *een ~ leven hebben* lead a busy life; **2** active, lively, boisterous: *~ke kinderen* boisterous children; *zich ~ maken over iets* worry about sth

³druk [drʏk] *adv* **1** busily: *~ bezet* busy; *~ bezig zijn (met iets)* be very busy (with, doing sth); **2** busily, noisily, excitedly

drukfout [drʏkfɑut] *de (~en)* misprint, printing error, erratum

¹drukken [drʏkə(n)] *vb* press, push

²drukken [drʏkə(n)] *vb* **1** push, press: *iem de hand ~* shake hands with s.o.; **2** force: *iem tegen zich aan drukken* hold s.o. close (to oneself); **3** push down: *de prijzen (or: kosten) ~* keep down prices (or: costs); **4** print: *10.000 exemplaren van een boek ~* print (or: run off) 10,000 copies of a book; **5** stamp, impress

drukkend [drʏkənt] *adj* **1** oppressive, heavy, burdensome; **2** sultry, close

drukker [drʏkər] *de (~s)* printer

drukkerij [drʏkərɛi] *de (~en)* printer, printing office (or: business), printer's

drukkingsgroep [drʏkɪŋsχrup] *de (~en) (Belg)* pressure group

drukknoop [drʏknop] *de (-knopen)* press stud, press fastener, popper

drukknop [drʏknɔp] *de (~pen)* push-button

drukletter [drʏklɛtər] *de (~s)* **1** (block, printed) letter; **2** type, letter

drukpers [drʏkpɛrs] *de (~en)* printing press

drukproef [drʏkpruf] *de (-proeven)* proof, galley (proof), printer's proof

drukte [drʏktə] *de* **1** busyness, pressure (of work): *door de ~ heb ik de bestelling vergeten* it was so busy

(or: hectic) I forgot the order; **2** bustle, commotion, stir: *de ~ voor Kerstmis* the Christmas rush; **3** fuss, ado: *veel ~ over iets maken* make a big fuss about sth

druktemaker [drʏktəmakər] *de (~s)* noisy (or: rowdy) person, show-off

druktoets [drʏktuts] *de (~en)* (push-)button

drukwerk [drʏkwɛrk] *het (~en)* printed matter (or: papers)

drum [drʏm] *de (~s)* drum

drumband [drʏmbɛnt] *de (~s)* drum band

drummer [drʏmər] *de (~s)* drummer

drumstel [drʏmstɛl] *het (~len)* drum set, (set of) drums

druppel [drʏpəl] *de (~s)* drop(let), bead: *alles tot de laatste ~ opdrinken* drain to the (very) last drop

druppelen [drʏpələ(n)] *vb* drip, trickle, ooze: *iets in het oog ~* put drops in one's eye

ds. *dominee* (the) Rev(erend)

¹dubbel [dʏbəl] *adj* **1** double, duplicate, dual: *een ~e bodem* a double (or: hidden) meaning; **2** double (the size), twice (as big): *een ~ leven leiden* lead a double life

²dubbel [dʏbəl] *adv* **1** double, twice: *ik heb dat boek ~* I have two copies of that book; *~ liggen* be doubled up; **2** doubly, twice: *dat is ~ erg* that's twice as bad; *hij verdient het ~ en dwars* he deserves every bit of it

dubbelboeking [dʏbəlbukɪŋ] *de (~en)* double booking

dubbel-cd [dʏbəlsede] *de (~'s)* double CD

dubbeldekker [dʏbəldɛkər] *de (~s)* double-deck(er) (bus)

dubbelepunt [dʏbələpʏnt] *de (~en)* colon

dubbelganger [dʏbəlɣɑŋər] *de (~s)* double, lookalike, doppelgänger

dubbelklikken [dʏbəlklɪkə(n)] *vb* double-click

dubbelnummer [dʏbəlnʏmər] *het (~s)* double issue

dubbelop [dʏbələp] *adv* double

dubbelrol [dʏbəlrɔl] *de (~len)* double role, twin roles

dubbelspel [dʏbəlspɛl] *het (~en) (sport)* doubles

dubbelspion [dʏbəlspijɔn] *de (~nen)* double agent

dubbeltje [dʏbəlcə] *het (~s)* ten-cent piece: *zo plat als een ~* (as) flat as a pancake

dubbelvouwen [dʏbəlvɑuwə(n)] *vb* fold in two, bend double (or: in two)

dubbelzinnig [dʏbəlzɪnəχ] *adj* **1** ambiguous: *een ~ antwoord* an ambiguous (or: evasive) answer; **2** suggestive, with a double meaning

dubbelzinnigheid [dʏbəlzɪnəχhɛit] *de (-heden)* **1** ambiguity; **2** ambiguous remark, suggestive remark

dubben [dʏbə(n)] *vb* brood, ponder: *~ over iets* brood about sth

dubieus [dybijøs] *adj* **1** dubious, doubtful; **2** dubious, questionable

duchten [dʏχtə(n)] *vb* fear

duel [dywɛl] *het (~s)* duel, fight, single combat
duelleren [dywɛlɛrə(n)] *vb* duel, fight
duet [dywɛt] *het (~ten)* duet, duo
duf [dʏf] *adj, adv* **1** musty, stuffy, mouldy: *het rook daar ~* it smelled musty; **2** *(fig)* stuffy, stale
dug-out [dʏgaut] *de (~s)* dugout
duidelijk [dœydələk] *adj, adv* **1** clear, clear-cut, plain: *zich in ~e bewoordingen (taal) uitdrukken* speak plainly; *ik heb hem ~ gemaakt dat …* I made it clear to him that …; *om ~ te zijn, om het maar eens ~ te zeggen* to put it (quite) plainly; **2** clear, distinct, plain: *een ~e voorkeur hebben voor iets* have a distinct preference for sth; *~ zichtbaar* (or: *te merken) zijn* be clearly visible (or: noticeable)
duidelijkheid [dœydələkhɛit] *de* clearness, clarity, obviousness
duiden [dœydə(n)] *vb* **1** point (to, at); **2** point (to), indicate: *verschijnselen die op tuberculose ~* symptoms that indicate tuberculosis
duif [dœyf] *de (duiven)* pigeon, dove
duik [dœyk] *de (~en)* dive, diving, plunge: *een ~ nemen* take a dip
duikboot [dœygbot] *de (-boten)* submarine, sub, U-boat
duikbril [dœygbrɪl] *de (~len)* diving goggles
duikelen [dœykələ(n)] *vb* **1** (turn a) somersault, go (*or*: turn) head over heels, tumble; **2** (take a) tumble, fall head over heels; **3** drop, dive, plunge (downward)
duikeling [dœykəlɪŋ] *de (~en)* **1** somersault, roll; **2** fall, tumble
duiken [dœykə(n)] *vb* **1** dive, plunge, duck, go under, submerge: *(sport) naar een bal ~* dive for (*or*: after) a ball; **2** duck (down, behind): *in een onderwerp ~* go (deeply) into a subject
duiker [dœykər] *de (~s)* diver
duikerpak [dœykərpɑk] *het (~ken)* wetsuit, diving suit
duiksport [dœykspɔrt] *de* diving
duim [dœym] *de (~en)* **1** thumb: *de ~ opsteken* give the thumbs up; *onder de ~ houden* keep under one's thumb; **2** inch: *(Belg) de ~en leggen* surrender, throw in the sponge; *iets uit zijn ~ zuigen* dream sth up
duimen [dœymə(n)] *vb* **1** keep one's fingers crossed; **2** suck one's thumb
duimpje [dœympjə] *het (~s)* || *Klein Duimpje* Tom Thumb; *iets op zijn ~ kennen* know sth like the back of one's hand, know sth (off) by heart
duimschroef [dœymsχruf] *de (-schroeven)* thumbscrew: *(iem) de duimschroeven aandraaien* tighten the screws (on s.o.), turn on the heat on (s.o.)
duimstok [dœymstɔk] *de (~ken)* folding ruler
duin [dœyn] *het, de (~en)* (sand) dune, sand hill
Duinkerken [dœyŋkɛrkə(n)] *het* Dunkirk
¹duister [dœystər] *het* dark, darkness: *in het ~ tasten* be in the dark
²duister [dœystər] *adj, adv* **1** dark, gloomy, *(fig)* dim, black; **2** shady, dubious

duisternis [dœystərnɪs] *de (~sen)* darkness, dark
duit [dœyt] *de (~en)* || *ook een ~ in het zakje doen* put in a word
Duits [dœyts] *adj* German || *~e herdershond* Alsatian
Duitse [dœytsə] *de* German woman, German girl: *zij is een ~* she is German
Duitser [dœytsər] *de (~s)* German
Duitsland [dœytslɑnt] *het* Germany
Duitstalig [dœytstaləχ] *adj* **1** German-speaking; **2** German
duivel [dœyvəl] *de (~s)* **1** *(rel)* devil; **2** demon
duivels [dœyvəls] *adj, adv* **1** diabolic(al), devilish, demonic: *een ~ plan* a diabolical plan; **2** livid, (raving) mad, furious
duivelskunstenaar [dœyvəlskʏnstənar] *de (~s)* wizard
duiveltje [dœyvəlcə] *het (~s)* imp, little devil
duivenhok [dœyvə(n)hɔk] *het (~ken)* dovecote
duivenmelker [dœyvə(n)mɛlkər] *de (~s)* pigeon fancier; pigeon flyer
duiventil [dœyvə(n)tɪl] *de (~len)* dovecote, pigeon house
duizelen [dœyzələ(n)] *vb* become dizzy, reel: *het duizelt mij* my head is spinning (*or*: swimming)
duizelig [dœyzələχ] *adj* dizzy (with), giddy (with): *de drukte maakte hem ~* the crowds made his head spin
duizeligheid [dœyzələχhɛit] *de* dizziness
duizeling [dœyzəlɪŋ] *de (~en)* dizziness, dizzy spell, vertigo: *soms last hebben van ~en* suffer from dizzy spells
duizelingwekkend [dœyzəlɪŋwɛkənt] *adj, adv* dizzy, giddy, staggering
duizend [dœyzənt] *num* (a, one) thousand: *~ pond* (*or*: dollar) a thousand pounds (*or*: dollars); *dat werk heeft (vele) ~en gekost* that work cost thousands; *~ tegen één* a thousand to one; *hij is er één uit ~(en)* he is one in a thousand
duizend-en-een-nacht [dœyzəntənenaχt] *de* the Thousand and One Nights, the Arabian Nights
duizendpoot [dœyzəntpot] *de (-poten)* **1** centipede; **2** jack of all trades
duizendste [dœyzəntstə] *num* thousandth
duizendtal [dœyzəntɑl] *het (~len)* **1** thousand; **2** *(pl)* thousands
dukaat [dykɑt] *de (dukaten)* ducat
dulden [dʏldə(n)] *vb* **1** endure, bear, put up with: *geen tegenspraak ~* not bear being contradicted; **2** tolerate, permit, allow: *de leraar duldt geen tegenspraak* the teacher won't put up with any contradiction
dumpen [dʏmpə(n)] *vb* dump
¹dun [dʏn] *adj* **1** thin, slender, fine: *~ne darm* small intestine; **2** sparse, light, fine, scant; **3** thin, light, runny
²dun [dʏn] *adv* thinly, sparsely, lightly, meanly
dunbevolkt [dʏmbəvɔlkt] *adj* thinly populated, sparsely populated

dunk [dʏŋk] *de* **1** opinion; **2** *(basketball)* dunk (shot)

duo [dywo] *het (~'s)* duo, pair

duobaan [dywoban] *de (-banen)* shared job

dupe [dypə] *de* victim, dupe: *wie zal daar de ~ van zijn?* who will be the one to suffer for it? (*or:* pay for it?)

duperen [dype̱rə(n)] *vb* let down, fail

duplicaat [dyplika̱t] *het (duplicaten)* duplicate (copy), transcript, facsimile

duren [dy̱rə(n)] *vb* last, take, go on: *het duurt nog een jaar* it will take another year; *het duurde uren* (*or: eeuwen, een eeuwigheid)* it lasted hours (*or:* ages, an eternity); *het duurt nog wel even (voor het zover is)* it will be a while yet (before that happens); *de tentoonstelling duurt nog tot oktober* the exhibition runs until October; *zo lang als het duurt* as long as it lasts

durf [dʏrf] *de* daring, nerve, guts

durven [dʏ̱rvə(n)] *vb* dare, venture (to, upon): *hoe durf je!* how dare you!; *als het erop aan kwam durfde hij niet* he got cold feet when it came to the crunch

dus [dʏs] *conj* so, therefore, then: *ik kan ~ op je rekenen?* I can count on you then?

dusdanig [dʏ̱zdanəχ] *adv* so, in such a way (*or:* manner), to such an extent

dusver [dʏsfe̱r] *adv* ǁ *tot ~* so far, up to now; *tot ~ is alles in orde* so far so good

dutje [dʏ̱cə] *het* nap, snooze, forty winks

duts [dʏts] *de (~en) (Belg)* duffer, dunce

dutten [dʏ̱tə(n)] *vb* (take a) nap, snooze

¹duur [dyr] *de* duration, length, life, term: *van korte ~* short-lived; *op de lange ~* in the long run, finally

²duur [dyr] *adj* expensive, dear, costly: *die auto is ~ (in het gebruik)* that car is expensive to run; *hoe ~ is die fiets?* how much is that bicycle?; *dat is te ~ voor mij* I can't afford it

³duur [dyr] *adv* expensively, dearly: *iets ~ betalen* pay a high price for sth, pay dearly for sth

duursport [dy̱rspɔrt] *de (~en)* endurance sport

¹duurzaam [dy̱rzam] *adj* **1** durable, hard-wearing; (long-)lasting, enduring, permanent: *duurzame kleuren* permanent (*or:* fast) colours; *duurzame verbruiksgoederen* durable consumer goods; **2** permanent, (long-)lasting: *voor ~ gebruik* for permanent use

²duurzaam [dy̱rzam] *adv* permanently, durably: *~ gescheiden* permanently separated

duurzaamheid [dy̱rzamhɛit] *de* durability; endurance, (useful, service) life

duw [dyw] *de (~en)* push, shove, nudge, poke, jab, dig: *hij gaf me een ~ (met de elleboog)* he nudged me; *de zaak een ~tje geven* help the matter along; *iem een ~tje (omhoog, in de rug) geven* give s.o. a boost

duwboot [dy̱wbot] *de (duwboten)* pusher tug

¹duwen [dy̱wə(n)] *vb* **1** push, shove, wheel: *een kinderwagen ~* wheel (*or:* push) a pram; **2** push, thrust,

shove, nudge: *iem opzij ~* push (*or:* elbow) s.o. aside

²duwen [dy̱wə(n)] *vb* press, push, jostle: *een ~de en dringende massa* a jostling crowd

dwaalspoor [dwa̱lspor] *het (-sporen)* wrong track, false scent: *iem op een ~ brengen* mislead (*or:* misguide) s.o.

¹dwaas [dwas] *de (dwazen)* fool, idiot, ass, dope, dummy, nincompoop

²dwaas [dwas] *adj* foolish, silly, stupid: *een ~ idee* a crazy idea

³dwaas [dwas] *adv* foolishly, stupidly, crazily

dwaasheid [dwa̱shɛit] *de (-heden)* foolishness, folly, stupidity

dwalen [dwa̱lə(n)] *vb* **1** stray, wander; **2** wander, roam: *wij dwaalden twee uur in het bos* we wandered through the forest for two hours; **3** stray, travel

dwaling [dwa̱lɪŋ] *de (~en)* error, mistake: *een rechterlijke ~* a miscarriage of justice

dwang [dwɑŋ] *de* compulsion, coercion, force, obligation, pressure: *met zachte ~* by persuasion

dwangarbeid [dwɑ̱ŋɑrbɛit] *de* hard labour, forced labour

dwangarbeider [dwɑ̱ŋɑrbɛidər] *de (~s)* convict

dwangbuis [dwɑ̱ŋbœys] *het (-buizen)* straitjacket

dwarrelen [dwɑ̱rələ(n)] *vb* whirl, twirl, swirl, flutter

dwars [dwɑrs] *adj, adv* transverse, diagonal, crosswise: *~ tegen iets ingaan* go right against sth; *ergens ~ doorheen gaan* go right through (*or:* across) sth; *~ door het veld* straight across the field; *~ door iem heen kijken* look straight through s.o.

dwarsbeuk [dwɑ̱rzbøk] *de (~en)* transept

dwarsbomen [dwɑ̱rzbomə(n)] *vb* thwart, frustrate

dwarsdoorsnede [dwɑ̱rzdorsnedə] *de (~n)* cross-section

dwarsfluit [dwɑ̱rsflœyt] *de (~en)* flute

dwarslaesie [dwɑ̱rslezi] *de* spinal cord lesion, paraplegia

dwarsliggen [dwɑ̱rslɪɣə(n)] *vb* be obstructive, be contrary, be a troublemaker

dwarsstraat [dwɑ̱rsstrat] *de (-straten)* side street: *ik noem maar een ~* just to give an example

dwarszitten [dwɑ̱rsɪtə(n)] *vb* cross, thwart, hamper: *iem ~* frustrate s.o.('s plans); *wat zit je dwars?* what's worrying (*or:* bugging) you?

dweil [dwɛil] *de (~en)* (floor-)cloth, rag, mop

dweilen [dwɛ̱ilə(n)] *vb* mop (down), mop (up): *dat is ~ met de kraan open* it's like swimming against the tide

dweilorkest [dwɛ̱ilɔrkɛst] *het (~en)* Carnival band, Oompah band

dwepen [dwe̱pə(n)] *vb* be enthusiastic: *~ met* be enthusiastic about

dwerg [dwɛrχ] *de (~en)* **1** gnome, dwarf, elf: *Sneeuwwitje en de zeven ~en* Snow White and the Seven Dwarfs; **2** dwarf, midget

dwingen [dwɪ̱ŋə(n)] *vb* force, compel, oblige, coerce, make (s.o. do sth): *hij was wel gedwongen (om) te antwoorden* he was obliged to answer; *iem ~ een overhaast besluit te nemen* rush s.o. into making a hasty decision; *niets dwingt je daartoe* you are not obliged to do it; *iem ~ tot gehoorzaamheid* force s.o. to obey

¹dwingend [dwɪŋənt] *adj* compelling, compulsory: *~e redenen* compelling reasons

²dwingend [dwɪŋənt] *adv* authoritatively: *iem iets ~ voorschrijven* make sth compulsory for s.o.

d.w.z. *dat wil zeggen* i.e.

dynamica [dinamika] *de* dynamics

dynamiek [dinamik] *de* dynamics, vitality, dynamism

dynamiet [dinamit] *het* dynamite

dynamisch [dinamis] *adj* dynamic, energetic, forceful

dynamo [dinamo] *de (~'s)* dynamo, generator

dynastie [dinɑsti] *de* dynasty

dysenterie [dɪsɛntəri] *de* dysentery

dyslectisch [dɪslɛktis] *adj* dyslexic

dyslexie [dɪslɛksi] *de* dyslexia

e

e [e] *de (~'s)* e, E: *E groot* (or: *klein) E major (or: minor)*

e.a. *en andere(n)* et al.

eau de cologne [odəkolɔ̯nə] *de (eaux de cologne)* cologne, eau de Cologne

eau de toilette [odətwalɛt] *de (eaux de toilette)* eau de toilette, toilet water

eb [ɛp] *de* **1** ebb(-tide), outgoing tide: *het is ~ the tide is out;* **2** low tide

ebbenhout [ɛbə(n)hɑut] *het* ebony

echo [ɛχo] *de (~'s)* echo, reverberation, blip: *de ~ weerkaatste zijn stem* his voice was echoed

echoën [ɛχowə(n)] *vb* echo, reverberate, resound, ring

echoscopie [ɛχoskopi] *de (~ën)* ultrasound scan

¹echt [ɛχt] *adj* **1** real, genuine, authentic, true, actual: *een ~e vriend* a true (or: real) friend; **2** real, regular, true (blue, born): *het is een ~ schandaal* it's an absolute scandal; **3** legitimate

²echt [ɛχt] *adv* **1** really, truly, genuinely, honestly: *dat is ~ Hollands* that's typically Dutch; *dat is ~ iets voor hem* that's him all over; *ik heb het ~ niet gedaan* I honestly didn't do it; **2** real, genuine(ly)

echtelijk [ɛχtələk] *adj* conjugal, marital: *een ~e ruzie* a domestic quarrel

echter [ɛχtər] *adv* however, nevertheless, yet, but: *dat is ~ niet gebeurd* however, that did not happen

echtgenoot [ɛχtχənot] *de (-genoten)* husband: *de aanstaande echtgenoten* the husband and wife to be

echtgenote [ɛχtχənotə] *de (~n, ~s)* wife

echtheid [ɛχthɛit] *de* authenticity, genuineness

echtpaar [ɛχtpar] *het (-paren)* married couple: *het ~ Keizers* Mr and Mrs Keizers

echtscheiding [ɛχtsχɛidɪŋ] *de (~en)* divorce

eclips [eklɪps] *de (~en)* eclipse

ecologie [ekoloɣi] *de* ecology

ecologisch [ekoloɣis] *adj, adv* ecological, biological

econometrie [ekonometri] *de* econometry

economie [ekonomi] *de (~ën)* **1** economy; **2** economy, frugality, thrift; **3** economics, political economy

economisch [ekonɔmis] *adj, adv* **1** economical, frugal, thrifty; **2** economic: *de ~e aspecten van het uitgeversbedrijf* the economics of publishing

econoom [ekonom] *de (economen)* economist

ecu [ɛky] *de (~'s)* ecu

Ecuador [ɛkwadɔr] *het* Ecuador

eczeem [ɛksem] *het (eczemen)* eczema

e.d. *en dergelijke* and the like

edammer [edɑmər] *de* Edam (cheese)

edel [edəl] *adj, adv* **1** noble, aristocratic: *van ~e geboorte* high-born; **2** noble, magnanimous

edelachtbaar [edəlɑχtbar] *adj* || *Edelachtbare* Your Honour

edelgas [edəlɣas] *het (~sen)* inert gas

edelhert [edəlhɛrt] *het (~en)* red deer

edelman [edəlmɑn] *de (edellieden)* noble, nobleman, peer

edelmetaal [edəlmetal] *het (-metalen)* precious metal

edelmoedig [edəlmudəχ] *adj, adv* noble, generous, magnanimous

edelmoedigheid [edəlmudəχhɛit] *de* generosity, magnanimity, nobility

edelsteen [edəlsten] *de (-stenen)* precious stone, gem(stone)

Eden [edə(n)] *het* Eden

editie [edi(t)si] *de (~s)* edition, issue, version

educatie [edyka(t)si] *de (~s)* education

educatief [edykatif] *adj, adv* educational

eed [et] *de (eden)* oath, vow: *iets onder ede verklaren* declare sth on oath

e.e.g. [eeɣe] *het (~'s)* elektro-encefalogram E.E.G.

EEG [eeɣe] *de Europese Economische Gemeenschap* E.E.C.

eekhoorn [ekhorn] *de (~s)* squirrel

eekhoorntjesbrood [ekhorncɑzbrot] *het* cep, boletus

eelt [elt] *het* hard skin; callus

¹een [ən] *art* **1** a, an: *op ~ (goeie) dag* one (fine) day; *neem ~ Oprah Winfrey* take s.o. like an Oprah Winfrey; **2** a, some: *over ~ dag of wat* in a few days; **3** a, some: *wat ~ mooie bloemen!* what beautiful flowers!; *wat ~ idee!* what an idea!

²een [en] *num* one: *het ~ en ander* this and that; *van het ~ komt het ander* one thing leads to another; *op één dag* in one day, on the same day; *~ en dezelfde* one and the same; *de weg is ~ en al modder* the road is nothing but mud; *op ~ na de laatste* the last but one; *op ~ na de beste* the second best; *~ voor ~* one by one, one at a time; *~ april* April Fools' Day; *hij gaf hem er ~ op de neus* he gave him one on the nose; *geef me er nog ~* give me another (one), give me one more; *zich ~ voelen met de natuur* be at one with nature

eenakter [enɑktər] *de (~s)* one-act play

eencellig [ensɛləχ] *adj* unicellular, single-celled

eend [ent] *de (~en)* **1** duck, duckling, drake: *zich een vreemde ~ in de bijt voelen* feel the odd man out; **2** (Citroën) 2 CV, deux-chevaux

eendagsvlieg [endɑχsfliχ] *de (~en)* **1** mayfly; **2** nine days' wonder

¹eender [endər] *adj* (the) same, alike, equal: *geen twee mensen zijn ~* no two people are alike

²**eender** [ɛndər] *adv* alike, equally
eendje [encə] *het (~s)* duckling
eendracht [ɛndraχt] *de* harmony, concord
eenduidig [endœydəχ] *adj, adv* unequivocal, unambiguous
eeneiig [enɛiəχ] *adj* monovular, monozygotic: *een ~e tweeling* identical twins
eenentwintigen [enəntwɪntəʏə(n)] *vb* play blackjack (*or:* pontoon)
eengezinswoning [eŋʏəzɪnswonɪŋ] *de (~en)* (small) family dwelling
eenheid [ɛnhɛit] *de (-heden)* **1** unity, oneness, uniformity: *de ~ herstellen* (or: *verbreken*) restore (or: destroy) unity; **2** unit: *eenheden en tientallen* units and tens; **3** unit, entity: *de mobiele ~* riot police; *een (hechte, gesloten) ~ vormen* form a (tight, closed) group
eenheidsprijs [ɛnhɛitsprɛis] *de (-prijzen)* **1** unit price, price per unit; **2** uniform price
eenhoorn [ɛnhorn] *de (~s)* unicorn
eenjarig [enjarəχ] *adj* **1** one-year(-old), yearling; **2** one-year('s): *een ~e plant* an annual
eenkennig [eŋkɛnəχ] *adj* shy
eenling [ɛnlɪŋ] *de (~en)* (solitary) individual, lone wolf, loner
eenmaal [ɛmal] *adv* **1** once, one time: *~, andermaal, voor de derdemaal, verkocht* going, going, gone!; **2** once; one day, some day: *als het ~ zover komt* if it ever comes to it; **3** just, simply: *dat is nu ~ zo* that's just the way it is; *ik ben nu ~ zo* that's the way I am
eenmalig [emaləχ] *adj* once-only, one-off: *een ~ optreden (concert)* a single performance
eenmanszaak [ɛmɑnsak] *de (-zaken)* one-man business
eenoudergezin [enɑudərʏəzɪn] *het (~nen)* single-parent family
eenpersoonsbed [empɛrsɔnzbɛt] *het (~den)* single bed
eenpersoonskamer [empɛrsɔnskamər] *de (~s)* single room, single
eenrichtingsverkeer [enrɪχtɪŋsfərker] *het* one-way traffic: *straat met ~* one-way street
¹**eens** [ens] *adv* **1** once: *voor ~ en altijd* once and for all; *~ in de week* (or: *drie maanden*) once a week (*or:* every three months); **2** some day, one day, sometime; once: *kom ~ langs* drop in (*or:* by) sometime; *er was ~* once upon a time there was; **3** just: *denk ~ even (goed) na* just think (carefully); *niet ~ tijd hebben om* not even have the time to; *nog ~* once more, (once) again; *wel ~* once in a while, sometimes
²**eens** [ens] *adj* agreed, in agreement: *het over de prijs ~ worden* agree on a (or: about the) price; *het niet ~ zijn met iem* disagree with s.o.
eensgezind [ensχəzɪnt] *adj, adv* unanimous, united, concerted: *~ voor* (or: *tegen*) *iets zijn* be unanimously for (*or:* against) sth
eensgezindheid [ensχəzɪnthɛit] *de* unanimity,

consensus, harmony, accord
eensklaps [ensklɑps] *adv* suddenly, all of a sudden
eenstemmig [enstɛmməχ] *adj, adv* **1** unanimous, by common assent (*or:* consent); **2** in unison, for one voice
eentje [encə] *ind pron* one: *neem er nog ~* have another (one, glass); *op* (or: *in*) *z'n ~* (by) oneself, (on) one's own
eentonig [entonəχ] *adj, adv* monotonous, monotone, drab, dull: *een ~ leven (bestaan) leiden* lead a humdrum (*or:* dull) existence; *~ werk* tedious (*or:* monotonous) work, drudgery
eentonigheid [entonəχhɛit] *de* monotony, monotonousness, tedium
een-tweetje [entweːcə] *het (~s)* one-two, wall pass
eenvoud [ɛnvɑut] *de* **1** simplicity, simpleness, plainness; **2** simplicity, straightforwardness, naivety, innocence: *hij zei dat in zijn ~* he said that in his naivety (*or:* innocence)
¹**eenvoudig** [ɛnvɑudəχ] *adj* **1** simple, uncomplicated, plain; easy: *dat is het ~ste* that's the easiest way; *zo ~ ligt dat niet* it's not that simple; **2** simple, unpretentious, ordinary; **3** simple, plain, ordinary, low(ly), humble, modest, unpresuming, simple-hearted
²**eenvoudig** [ɛnvɑudəχ] *adv* **1** simply, plainly: *(al) te ~ voorstellen* (over)simplify; **2** simply, just
eenvoudigweg [ɛnvɑudəχwɛχ] *adv* simply, just
eenzaam [ɛnzam] *adj, adv* **1** solitary, isolated, lonely, lone(some): *een ~ leven leiden* live a solitary life; **2** solitary, isolated, lonely, secluded
eenzaamheid [ɛnzamhɛit] *de* solitude, solitariness, loneliness, isolation, retirement, seclusion
eenzijdig [enzɛidəχ] *adj, adv* **1** one-sided, unilateral, limited: *hij is erg ~* he is very one-sided; **2** one-sided, biased, partial
eenzijdigheid [enzɛidəχhɛit] *de* **1** one-sidedness, bias, partiality; **2** imbalance, one-sidedness
eer [er] *de* **1** honour, respect: *de ~ redden* save one's face; *aan u de ~ (om te beginnen)* you have the honour (of starting); *naar ~ en geweten antwoorden* answer to the best of one's knowledge; *op mijn (woord van) ~* I give you my word (of honour); **2** honour(s), credit: *iem de laatste ~ bewijzen* pay s.o. one's last respects; *het zal me een (grote, bijzondere) ~ zijn* I will be (greatly) honoured; *ter ere van* in honour of (s.o., sth)
eerbied [erbit] *de* respect, esteem, regard, reverence, veneration, worship: *iem ~ verschuldigd zijn* owe s.o. respect
eerbiedig [erbidəχ] *adj, adv* respectful
eerbiedigen [erbidəʏə(n)] *vb* respect, regard, observe: *de mening van anderen ~* respect the opinions of others
eerbiedwaardig [erbitwardəχ] *adj* respectable
¹**eerder** [erdər] *adj* earlier
²**eerder** [erdər] *adv* **1** before (now), sooner, earlier: *ik heb u al eens ~ gezien* I have seen you (somewhere) before; *hoe ~ hoe beter (liever)* the sooner

the better; **2** rather, sooner, more (likely): *ik zou ~ denken dat* I am more inclined to think that

eergevoel [ˈeːrɣəvul] *het* (sense, feeling of) honour, pride

eergisteren [eːrˈɣɪstərə(n)] *adv* the day before yesterday

eerherstel [ˈeːrhɛrstɛl] *het* rehabilitation

¹eerlijk [ˈeːrlək] *adj* **1** honest, fair, sincere: *~ is ~* fair is fair; **2** honest, true, genuine: *een ~e zaak* a square deal; **3** fair, square, honest: *~ spel* fair play

²eerlijk [ˈeːrlək] *adv* **1** sincerely; honestly, frankly: *~ gezegd* to be honest; **2** honestly, really and truly: *ik heb het niet gedaan, ~ (waar)!* honestly, I didn't do it!; **3** fairly, squarely: *~ delen!* fair shares!

eerlijkheid [ˈeːrləkhɛit] *de* honesty, fairness, sincerity

eerroof [ˈeːrof] *de (Belg; law)* libel: *laster en ~* defamation of character

eerst [eːrst] *adv* **1** first: *hij zag de brand het ~* he was the first to see the fire; *(het) ~ aan de beurt zijn* be first (*or:* next); **2** first(ly), at first: *~ was hij verlegen, later niet meer* at first he was shy, but not later

eerste [ˈeːrstə] *num* first, chief, prime, senior, earliest: *de ~ vier dagen* (for) the next four days; *informatie uit de ~ hand* first-hand information; *de ~ die aankomt krijgt de prijs* the first to get there gets the prize; *één keer moet de ~ zijn* there's a first time for everything; *van de ~ tot de laatste* down to the last one, every man jack (of them); *hij is niet de ~ de beste* he is not just anybody

eerstegraads [eːrstəˈɣraːts] *adj, adv* first-degree

eerstehulppost [eːrstəˈhʏlpɔst] *de (~en)* first-aid post (*or:* station)

eerstehulpverlening [eːrstəˈhʏlpfərleːnɪŋ] *de* first aid

eerstejaars [ˈeːrstəjaːrs] *adj* first-year

Eerste-Kamerlid [eːrstəˈkaːmərlɪt] *het (-leden)* Member of the Upper Chamber (*or:* Upper House) (of the Dutch Parliament)

eersteklas [eːrstəˈklɑs] *adj, adv* first-rate, first-class

eersteklasser [eːrstəˈklɑsər] *de (~s)* first-former

eersterangs [eːrstəˈrɑŋs] *adj* first-rate, top-class

eerstgenoemd [eːrstˈχənuːmt] *adj* first; former

eerstvolgend [eːrstˈfɔlɣənt] *adj* next: *de ~e trein* the next train due

¹eervol [ˈeːrvɔl] *adj* **1** honourable, glorious, creditable: *de ~le verliezers* the worthy losers; **2** with honour, without loss of face: *een ~le vrede sluiten* conclude a peace with honour

²eervol [ˈeːrvɔl] *adv* honourably, worthily, gloriously, creditably

eerzaam [ˈeːrzaːm] *adj, adv* respectable, virtuous, decent, honest

eerzucht [ˈeːrzʏχt] *de* ambition

eerzuchtig [eːrˈzʏχtəχ] *adj, adv* ambitious, aspiring

eetbaar [ˈeːdbaːr] *adj* edible, fit for (human) consumption, fit to eat, eatable, palatable

eetgerei [ˈeːtχərɛi] *het* cutlery, tableware

eetgewoonte [ˈeːtχəwoːntə] *de (~n, ~s)* eating habit, diet

eethoek [ˈeːthuk] *de (~en)* **1** dinette; **2** dining table and chairs

eethuis [ˈeːthœys] *het (eethuizen)* eating house, (small) restaurant

eetlepel [ˈeːtleːpəl] *de (~s)* soup spoon, dessertspoon, tablespoon(ful)

eetlust [ˈeːtlʏst] *de* appetite

eetservies [ˈeːtsɛrvis] *het (-serviezen)* dinner service, dinner set, tableware

eetstokje [ˈeːtstɔkjə] *het (~s)* chopstick

eetwaar [ˈeːtwaːr] *de (eetwaren)* foodstuff(s), eatables, food

eetzaal [ˈeːtsaːl] *de (eetzalen)* dining room (*or:* hall), canteen

eeuw [eːw] *de (~en)* **1** century: *in de loop der ~en* through the centuries (*or:* ages); *in het Londen van de achttiende ~* in eighteenth-century London; **2** ages, (donkey's) years: *het is ~en geleden dat ik van haar iets gehoord heb* I haven't heard from her for ages; *dat heeft een ~ geduurd* that took ages; **3** age, era, epoch: *de gouden ~* the golden age

eeuwenlang [ˈeːwə(n)lɑŋ] *adv* for centuries (*or:* ages)

eeuwenoud [ˈeːwə(n)ɑut] *adj* age-old, centuries-old

¹eeuwig [ˈeːwəχ] *adj* **1** eternal, everlasting, perennial, perpetual, never-ending: *~e sneeuw* perpetual snow; **2** lifelong, undying: *~e vriendschap* undying (*or:* lifelong) friendship; **3** endless, incessant, interminable, never-ending: *een ~e optimist* an incorrigible optimist

²eeuwig [ˈeːwəχ] *adv* **1** forever, eternally, perpetually; **2** forever, incessantly, endlessly, interminably, eternally

eeuwigdurend [eːwəˈdyːrənt] *adj* perpetual, everlasting

eeuwigheid [ˈeːwəχhɛit] *de (-heden)* ages, eternity: *ik heb je in geen ~ gezien* I haven't seen you for ages

eeuwwisseling [ˈeːwɪsəlɪŋ] *de (~en)* turn of the century

effect [ɛfɛkt] *het (~en)* **1** effect, result, outcome, consequence; **2** spin, side: *een bal ~ geven* put spin on a ball; **3** *(com)* stock, share, security

effectenbeurs [ɛfɛktə(n)børs] *de (-beurzen)* stock exchange

effectief [ɛfɛktif] *adj, adv* **1** real, actual, effective, active; **2** effective, efficacious; **3** *(Belg; law)* non-suspended

effen [ˈɛfə(n)] *adj, adv* **1** even, level, smooth; **2** plain, uniform, unpatterned: *~ rood* solid red

effenen [ˈɛfənə(n)] *vb* level, smooth: *de weg ~ voor iem* pave the way for s.o.

efficiënt [ɛfiʃɛnt] *adj, adv* efficient, businesslike

efficiëntie [ɛfiʃɛn(t)si] *de* efficiency

eg [ɛχ] *de (~gen)* harrow

EG [eːˈɣeː] *de Europese Gemeenschap* E.C.

egaal [eˈɣaːl] *adj, adv* even, level, smooth, uniform, solid

egaliseren [eɣaliˈzeːrə(n)] *vb* level, equalize, smooth

Egeïsch [eɣɛis] *adj* Aegean

egel [eɣəl] *de (~s)* hedgehog

eggen [ɛɣə(n)] *vb* harrow

ego [eɣo] *het* ego

¹**egocentrisch** [eɣosɛntris] *adj* egocentric, self-centred

²**egocentrisch** [eɣosɛntris] *adv* in an egocentric (*or*: a self-centred) way

egoïsme [eɣowɪsmə] *het* egoism, selfishness

egoïst [eɣowɪst] *de (~en)* egoist

Egypte [eɣɪptə] *het* Egypt

Egyptenaar [eɣɪptənar] *de (Egyptenaren)* Egyptian

Egyptisch [eɣɪptis] *adj* Egyptian

eh [ə] *int* er

EHBO [ehabeo] *de Eerste Hulp Bij Ongelukken* first aid; first-aid post (*or*: station); accident and emergency ward (*or*: department)

ei [ɛi] *het (~eren)* **1** egg: *een hard(gekookt) ~* a hard-boiled egg; *dat is voor haar een zacht(gekookt) ~tje* it's a piece of cake for her; *dat is het hele ~eren eten* that's all there is to it; *een ~ leggen* (or: *uitbroeden*) lay (*or*: hatch) an egg; **2** ovum, egg: *(Belg) ~ zo na* very nearly

eicel [ɛisɛl] *de (~len)* egg cell, ovum, female germ cell

eiderdons [ɛidərdɔns] *het* eider(down)

eierdooier [ɛiərdojər] *de (~s)* egg yolk

eierdop [ɛiərdɔp] *de (~pen)* **1** eggshell; **2** eggcup

eierschaal [ɛiərsχal] *de (-schalen)* eggshell

eierstok [ɛiərstɔk] *de (~ken)* ovary

eierwekker [ɛiərwɛkər] *de (~s)* egg-timer

Eiffeltoren [ɛifəltorə(n)] *de* Eiffel Tower

eigen [ɛiɣə(n)] *adj* **1** own, private, personal: *voor ~ gebruik* for one's (own) private use; *mensen met een ~ huis* people who own their own house; *wij hebben ieder een ~ (slaap)kamer* we have separate (bed)rooms; *~ weg* private road; *op zijn geheel ~ wijze* in his very own way; *bemoei je met je ~ zaken* mind your own business; **2** typical, characteristic, individual: *bier met een geheel ~ smaak* beer with a distinctive taste; **3** own, native, domestic

eigenaar [ɛiɣənar] *de (eigenaren)* owner, possessor, holder: *deze auto is drie keer van ~ veranderd* this car changed hands three times

¹**eigenaardig** [ɛiɣənardəχ] *adj* **1** peculiar, personal, idiosyncratic: *een ~ geval* a peculiar case; **2** peculiar, strange, odd, curious: *hij was een ~e jongen* he was a strange boy

²**eigenaardig** [ɛiɣənardəχ] *adv* peculiarly, oddly

eigenbelang [ɛiɣə(n)bəlaŋ] *het* self-interest

eigendom [ɛiɣəndɔm] *de (~men)* **1** ownership, title: *in ~ hebben* own (sth); **2** property, possession, belongings: *dat boek is mijn ~* that book belongs to me

eigendomsbewijs [ɛiɣə(n)dɔmzbəwɛis] *het* title deed, proof of ownership (to, of)

eigendunk [ɛiɣə(n)dʏŋk] *de* (self-)conceit, self-importance, arrogance

eigengemaakt [ɛiɣə(n)ɣəmakt] *adj* home-made

eigengereid [ɛiɣə(n)ɣərɛit] *adj* headstrong, self-willed

eigenhandig [ɛiɣə(n)hɑndəχ] *adj, adv* (made, done) with one's own hand(s), (do sth) oneself, personally

¹**eigenlijk** [ɛiɣə(n)lək] *adj* real, actual, true, proper: *de ~e betekenis van een woord* the true meaning of a word

²**eigenlijk** [ɛiɣə(n)lək] *adv* really, in fact, exactly, actually: *u heeft ~ gelijk* you are right, really; *wat is een pacemaker ~?* what exactly is a pacemaker?; *~ mag ik je dat niet vertellen* actually, I'm not supposed to tell you

eigennaam [ɛiɣənam] *de (-namen)* proper name

eigenschap [ɛiɣənsχɑp] *de (~pen)* quality, property, (*comp*) attribute: *goede ~pen* qualities (*or*: strong points, strengths)

eigentijds [ɛiɣə(n)tɛits] *adj* contemporary, modern

eigenwaarde [ɛiɣə(n)wardə] *de* self-respect, self-esteem

eigenwijs [ɛiɣə(n)wɛis] *adj, adv* cocky, conceited, pigheaded: *doe niet zo ~* don't think you know it all

eigenzinnig [ɛiɣə(n)zɪnəχ] *adj, adv* self-willed, stubborn, obstinate, unamenable, wayward

eigenzinnigheid [ɛiɣə(n)zɪnəχhɛit] *de* wilfulness, obstinacy

eik [ɛik] *de (~en)* oak (tree)

eikel [ɛikəl] *de (~s)* **1** acorn; **2** (*anatomy*) glans penis

¹**eiken** [ɛikə(n)] *het* oak

²**eiken** [ɛikə(n)] *adj* oak

eikenboom [ɛikə(n)bom] *de (-bomen)* oak (tree)

eiland [ɛilɑnt] *het (~en)* island: *op het ~ Man* on (*or*: in) the Isle of Man; *een kunstmatig ~* an artificial island, a man-made island

eilandengroep [ɛilɑndə(n)ɣrup] *de (~en)* archipelago, group of islands

eileider [ɛilɛidər] *de (~s)* Fallopian tube

eind [ɛint] *het (~en)* **1** way, distance; piece: *een ~ touw* a length of rope, a piece of string; *het is een heel ~* it's a long way; *het is nog een heel ~* it's still a long way; *daar kom ik een heel ~ mee* that will go a long way; **2** end, extremity, ending: *~ mei* at the end of May; *het andere ~ van de stad* the other end of the town; *het bij het rechte ~ hebben* be right

eindbestemming [ɛindbəstɛmɪŋ] *de (~en)* final destination, terminal

eindcijfer [ɛintsɛifər] *het (~s)* final figure, grand total, final mark

einddiploma [ɛindiploma] *het (~'s)* diploma, certificate, certificate of qualification

einde [ɛində] *het (~n)* **1** end: *er komt geen ~ aan* there's no end to it; **2** end, ending: *een verhaal met een open ~* a story with an open ending; *aan zijn ~ komen* meet one's end; *laten we er nu maar een ~ aan maken* let's finish off now; *aan het ~ van de middag* in the late afternoon; *ten ~ raad zijn* be at one's wits' end; *van het begin tot het* ~ from beginning to end; *eind goed, al goed* all's well that ends well

eindelijk [ɛindələk] *adv* finally, at last, in the end

eindeloos [ɛindəlos] *adj, adv* **1** endless, infinite, interminable; **2** endless, perpetual, interminable, unending: *ik moest* ~ *lang wachten* I had to wait for ages

einder [ɛindər] *de* horizon

eindexamen [ɛintɛksamə(n)] *het (~s)* final exam: *voor zijn* ~ *slagen (*or: *zakken)* pass *(or:* fail) one's final exams

eindexamenkandidaat [ɛintɛksamə(n)kandidat] *de (-kandidaten)* examinee, A-level candidate

eindexamenvak [ɛintɛksamə(n)vak] *het (~ken)* final examination subject, school certificate subject

eindgebruiker [ɛintχəbrœykər] *de* end-user

eindig [ɛindəχ] *adj* **1** finite: ~*e getallen (*or: *reeksen)* finite numbers *(or:* progressions); **2** limited

¹eindigen [ɛindəγə(n)] *vb* **1** end, finish, come to an end, stop: ~ *waar men begonnen is* end up where one started (from); **2** end, finish, come to an end, terminate, run out, expire: *dit woord eindigt op een klinker* this word ends in a vowel; *zij eindigde als eerste* she finished first

²eindigen [ɛindəγə(n)] *vb* finish (off), end, bring to a close, terminate

eindje [ɛincə] *het (~s)* **1** piece, bit: *een* ~ *touw* a length of rope, a piece of string; **2** short distance: *een* ~ *verder* a bit further; **3** (loose) end: *de* ~*s met moeite aan elkaar kunnen knopen* be hardly able to make (both) ends meet

eindklassement [ɛintklasəmɛnt] *het (~en)* overall standings

eindlijst [ɛintlɛist] *de (~en)* final list

eindmeet [ɛintmet] *de (-meten) (Belg)* finishing line

eindproduct [ɛintprodykt] *het (~en)* final product, end-product, final result, end-result

eindpunt [ɛintpynt] *het (~en)* end, terminus

eindrapport [ɛintrapɔrt] *het (~en)* **1** (school) leaving report; **2** final report

eindredacteur [ɛintredaktør] *de (~en, ~s) (roughly)* editor-in-chief

eindresultaat [ɛintrezyltat] *het* final result, end result, conclusion, final total

eindsaldo [ɛintsaldo] *het* final balance, closing balance

eindsignaal [ɛintsɪnal] *het (-signalen)* final whistle

eindsprint [ɛintsprɪnt] *de (~s)* final sprint

eindstadium [ɛintstadiʏm] *het (-stadia)* final stage, terminal stage

eindstand [ɛintstant] *de (~en)* final score

eindstation [ɛintsta(t)ʃɔn] *het (~s)* terminal (station)

eindstreep [ɛintstrep] *de (-strepen)* finish(ing line): *de* ~ *niet halen (fig)* not make it

eindstrijd [ɛintstrɛit] *de* final(s), final contest

eindterm [ɛintɛrm] *de* final attainment level

eindtotaal [ɛintotal] *het* grand total, final total

einduitslag [ɛintœytslaχ] *de (~en)* final results, final score, (list of) results

eindverslag [ɛintfərslaχ] *het (~en)* final report

eindwerk [ɛintwɛrk] *het (~en) (Belg)* dissertation submitted at end of course

eindzege [ɛintseγə] *de (~s)* first place

eis [ɛis] *de (~en)* **1** requirement, demand, claim: *hoge ~en stellen aan iem* make great demands of s.o.; *iemands ~en inwilligen* comply with s.o.'s demands; **2** demand, terms: *akkoord gaan met iemands ~en* agree to s.o.'s demands; **3** *(law)* claim, suit, sentence demanded

eisen [ɛisə(n)] *vb* **1** demand, require, claim: *iets van iem* ~ demand sth from s.o.; **2** *(law)* demand, sue for: *schadevergoeding* ~ claim damages

eiser [ɛisər] *de (~s)* **1** requirer, claimer; **2** *(law)* plaintiff, prosecutor, claimant

eitje [ɛicə] *het (~s, eiertjes)* (small) egg, ovum: *(fig) een zacht(gekookt)* ~ a soft-boiled egg

eivormig [ɛivɔrməχ] *adj* egg-shaped, oval

eiwit [ɛiwɪt] *het (~ten)* **1** egg white, white of an egg; **2** protein, albumin

ejaculatie [ejakyla(t)si] *de (~s)* ejaculation

EK [eka] *de, het Europees kampioenschap* European Championship

ekster [ɛkstər] *de (~s)* magpie

elan [elɑ̃] *het* élan, panache, zest

eland [elant] *de (~en)* elk, moose

elasticiteit [elastisitɛit] *de* elasticity

elastiek [elastik] *het (~en)* **1** rubber, elastic; **2** rubber band, elastic band

elastisch [elastis] *adj* elastic

elders [ɛldərs] *adv* elsewhere

eldorado [ɛldorado] *het* eldorado

electoraat [elɛktorat] *het (electoraten)* electorate

elegant [eləγɑnt] *adj, adv* elegant, refined

elegantie [eləγɑnsi] *de* elegance

elektra [elɛktra] *het, de* electricity

elektricien [elɛktriʃɛ̃] *de (~s)* electrician

elektriciteit [elɛktrisitɛit] *de* electricity: *de* ~ *is nog niet aangesloten* we aren't connected to the mains yet

elektriciteitscentrale [elɛktrisitɛitsɛntralə] *de* power station

elektrisch [elɛktris] *adj, adv* electric(al): *een* ~*e centrale* a power station; *een* ~*e deken* an electric blanket; ~ *koken* cook with electricity

elektrocardiogram [elɛktrokardijoγrɑm] *het (~men)* electrocardiogram

elektrocutie [elɛktrokγ(t)si] *de (~s)* electrocution

elektrode [elɛktrodə] *de (~n, ~s)* electrode

elektromagneet [elɛktromaγnet] *de (-magneten)* electromagnet

elektromonteur [elɛktromɔntør] *de (~s)* electrical fitter, electrician

elektromotor [elɛktromotər] *de (~en, ~s)* electric motor

elektron [elɛktrɔn] *het (~en)* electron
elektronica [elɛktronika] *de* electronics
elektronisch [elɛktronis] *adj, adv* electronic: *~e post* electronic mail, e-mail
elektrotechnisch [elɛktrotɛχnis] *adj* electrical: *~ ingenieur* electrical engineer
element [eləmɛnt] *het (~en)* element, component
elementair [eləmɛntɛːr] *adj* elementary, fundamental, basic
¹**elf** [ɛlf] *de (~en, elven) (-en)* elf, pixie, fairy
²**elf** [ɛlf] *num* eleven; *(in dates)* eleventh: *het is bij elven* it's close on eleven
elfde [ɛlvdə] *num* eleventh
elfje [ɛlfjə] *het* fairy
elfstedentocht [ɛlfstedə(n)tɔχt] *de (~en)* 11-city race, skating marathon in Friesland
elftal [ɛlftɑl] *het (~len)* team: *het tweede ~* the reserves
eliminatie [eliminα(t)si] *de (~s)* elimination, removal
elimineren [eliminerə(n)] *vb* eliminate, remove
elitair [elitɛːr] *adj* elitist
elite [elitə] *de* elite
elixer [elɪksər] *het (~s)* elixir
elk [ɛlk] *ind pron* **1** each (one); every one: *van ~ vier (stuks)* four of each; **2** everyone, everybody: *~e tweede* every other one; **3** each; every; any: *ze kunnen ~e dag komen* they can come any day; *ze komen ~e dag* they come every day; *~e keer dat hij komt* every time he comes
elkaar [ɛlkαr] *ref pron* each other, one another: *in ~s gezelschap* in each other's company; *uren achter ~* for hours on end; *vier keer achter ~* four times in a row; *bij ~ komen* meet, come together; *meer dan alle anderen bij ~* more than all the others put together; *wij blijven bij ~* we stick (*or:* keep) together; *door ~ raken* get mixed up (*or:* confused); *zij werden het met ~ eens* they came to an agreement; *naast ~ zitten* (or: *liggen*) sit (*or:* lie) side by side; *op ~ liggen* lie one on top of the other; *die auto valt bijna (van ellende) uit ~* that car is dropping to bits; *(personen of zaken) (goed) uit ~ kunnen houden* be able to tell (people, things) apart; *uit ~ gaan: a)* break up; *b)* split up, break up; *zij zijn familie van ~* they are related; *iets niet voor ~ kunnen krijgen* not manage (to do) sth
elleboog [ɛlaboχ] *de (ellebogen)* **1** elbow: *mijn trui is door aan de ellebogen* my sweater is (worn) through at the elbows; **2** forearm: *ze moesten zich met de ellebogen een weg uit de winkel banen* they had to elbow their way out of the shop
ellende [ɛlɛndə] *de* **1** misery; **2** trouble, bother: *dat geeft alleen maar (een hoop) ~* that will only cause (a lot of) trouble
¹**ellendig** [ɛlɛndəχ] *adj* **1** awful, dreadful, miserable: *ik voelde me ~* I felt rotten; **2** wretched, miserable; **3** awful, dreadful: *ik kan die ~e sommen niet maken* I can't do those awful sums
²**ellendig** [ɛlɛndəχ] *adv* awfully, miserably

ellips [ɛlɪps] *de (~en)* ellipse, oval
els [ɛls] *de (elzen)* alder
Elzas [ɛlzɑs] *de* Alsace
elzenhout [ɛlzə(n)hαut] *het* alder-wood
email [emɑj] *het* enamel
e-mail [imel] *de* e-mail
e-mailen [imelə(n)] *vb* e-mail
emancipatie [emɑnsipα(t)si] *de (~s)* emancipation, liberation
emballage [ɑmbɑlaʒə] *de* packing, packaging
embargo [ɛmbɑrɣo] *het (~'s)* (trade) embargo ‖ *een ~ opheffen* lift an embargo
embleem [ɛmblem] *het (emblemen)* emblem
embolie [ɛmboli] *de* embolism
embryo [ɛmbrijo] *het (~'s)* embryo
emigrant [emiɣrɑnt] *de (~en)* emigrant
emigratie [emiɣrα(t)si] *de (~s)* emigration
emigreren [emiɣrerə(n)] *vb* emigrate
eminent [eminɛnt] *adj* eminent, distinguished
emir [emir] *de (~s)* emir
emissie [emɪsi] *de (~s)* emission, issue
emmer [ɛmər] *de (~s)* bucket, pail: *met hele ~s tegelijk* by the bucketful
emoe [emu] *de (~s)* emu
emotie [emo(t)si] *de (~s)* emotion, feeling, excitement: *~s losmaken* release emotions; *zij liet haar ~s de vrije loop* she let herself go
¹**emotioneel** [emo(t)ʃonel] *adj* emotional, sensitive: *een emotionele benadering vermijden* avoid an emotional approach
²**emotioneel** [emo(t)ʃonel] *adv* emotionally
emplacement [ɑplɑsəmɛnt] *het (~en)* yard
employé [ɑmplwaje] *de (~s)* employee
EMU [eemy] *de Economische en Monetaire Unie* EMU, Economic and Monetary Union
en [ɛn] *conj* **1** and, plus: *twee ~ twee is vier* two and two is four, two plus two is four; **2** and: *én boete én gevangenisstraf krijgen* get both a fine and a prison sentence; **3** and, but, so: *~ waarom doe je het niet?* so why don't you do it?; *~ toch* and still; *nou ~?* so what?, and …?; *vind je het fijn? (nou) ~ of!* do you like it? I certainly do!, I'll say!
encyclopedie [ɑ̄sikloped̪i] *de (~ën)* encyclopaedia
ene [enə] *ind pron* a, an, one: *woont hier ~ Bertels?* does a Mr (*or:* Ms) Bertels live here?
energie [enɛrʒi] *de (~ën)* energy; power: *overlopen van ~* be bursting with energy
energiebedrijf [enɛrʒibədrɛif] *het (-bedrijven)* electricity company, power company
energiebesparend [enɛrʒibəsparənt] *adj, adv* energy-saving, low-energy
energiebesparing [enɛrʒibəspɑrɪŋ] *de* energy saving
energiebewust [enɛrʒibəwʏst] *adj* energy-conscious
energiebron [enɛrʒibrɔn] *de (~nen)* source of energy (*or:* power)
energiek [enɛrʒik] *adj, adv* energetic, dynamic
energieverspilling [enɛrʒivərspɪlɪŋ] *de* waste of

energy

energievoorziening [enɛrʒivorziniŋ] *de* power supply

energiezuinig [enɛrʒizœynəχ] *adj* low-energy

enerverend [enɛrvɛrənt] *adj* exciting, nerve-racking

enerzijds [ɛnərzɛits] *adv* on the one hand: ~ ..., *anderzijds* ... on the one hand ..., on the other (hand) ...

eng [ɛŋ] *adj, adv* 1 scary, creepy: *een ~ beest* a nasty (*or:* creepy, scary) animal, a creepy-crawly; 2 narrow

engagement [aŋgaʒəmɛnt] *het (~en)* commitment, involvement

engel [ɛŋəl] *de (~en)* angel

Engeland [ɛŋəlɑnt] *het* England

engelbewaarder [ɛŋəlbəwardər] *de (~s)* guardian angel

Engels [ɛŋəls] *adj* English || *iets van het Nederlands in het ~ vertalen* translate sth from Dutch into English

Engelse [ɛŋəlsə] *de* Englishwoman: *zij is een ~* she is English

Engelsman [ɛŋəlsmɑn] *de (Engelsen)* Englishman

Engelstalig [ɛŋəlstaləχ] *adj* 1 English-language, English; 2 English-speaking

engte [ɛŋtə] *de (~n, ~s)* narrow(s)

¹**enig** [enəχ] *adj* only, sole: *~ erfgenaam* sole heir; *dit was de ~e keer dat* ... this was the only time that ...; *hij is de ~e die het kan* he is the only one who can do it; *het ~e wat ik kon zien was* all I could see was

²**enig** [enəχ] *adj, adv* wonderful, marvellous, lovely

³**enig** [enəχ] *ind pron* 1 some: *enige moeite doen* go to some trouble; *zonder ~e twijfel* without any doubt; 2 any, a single: *zonder ~ incident* without a single incident; 3 some, a few: *er kwamen ~e bezoekers* a few visitors came

enigszins [enəχsɪns] *adv* 1 somewhat, rather: *hij was ~ verlegen* he was rather (*or:* somewhat) shy; 2 at all, in any way: *indien (ook maar) ~ mogelijk* if at all possible

¹**enkel** [ɛŋkəl] *de (~s)* ankle: *een verstuikte ~* a sprained ankle

²**enkel** [ɛŋkəl] *adj* single: *een kaartje ~e reis* a single (ticket)

³**enkel** [ɛŋkəl] *adv* 1 singly; 2 only, just: *hij doet het ~ voor zijn plezier* he only does it for fun; *ik doe het ~ en alleen om jou* I'm doing it simply and solely for you

⁴**enkel** [ɛŋkəl] *num* 1 sole, solitary, single: *in één ~e klap* at one blow; *er is geen ~ gevaar* there is not the slightest danger; *geen ~e kans hebben* have no chance at all; *op geen ~e manier* (in) no way; 2 a few: *in slechts ~e gevallen* in only a few cases; 3 (*pl*) a few: *in ~e dagen* in a few days

enkelspel [ɛŋkəlspɛl] *het (~en)* singles

enkeltje [ɛŋkəlcə] *het (~s)* single (ticket)

enkelvoud [ɛŋkəlvɑut] *het (~en)* singular

enkelzijdig [ɛŋkəlzɛidəχ] *adj, adv* one-sided

enorm [enɔrm] *adj, adv* 1 enormous, huge: *een ~ succes* an enormous success; 2 tremendous: *~ groot* gigantic, immense

enquête [ɑŋkɛːtə] *de (~s)* 1 poll, survey: *een ~ houden naar* conduct (*or:* do, make) a survey of; 2 inquiry, investigation

enquêteformulier [ɑŋkɛːtəfɔrmylir] *het (~en)* questionnaire

ensceneren [ɑ̃sənerə(n)] *vb* stage, put on

ensemble [ɑ̃sɑ̃blə] *het (~s)* ensemble, company, troupe

ent [ɛnt] *de (~en)* graft

enten [ɛntə(n)] *vb* graft

enteren [ɛntərə(n)] *vb* board

entertoets [ɛntərtuts] *de (~en)* enter (key)

enthousiasme [ɑntuʒɑsmə] *het* enthusiasm

enthousiast [ɑntuʒɑst] *adj, adv* enthusiastic

entourage [ɑnturaʒə] *de (~s)* entourage

entrecote [ɑntrəkɔt] *de (~s)* entrecôte

entree [ɑ̃tre] *het, de (~s)* 1 entrance, entrance hall; 2 entry, entrance, admission: *vrij ~* admission free, free entrance; 3 admission: *~ heffen* charge for admission

entreegeld [ɑ̃treɣɛlt] *het (~en)* admission charge, entrance fee

enveloppe [ɛnvəlɔp] *de (~n)* envelope

enz. *enzovoort* etc.

enzovoorts [ɛnzovorts] et cetera, and so on, etc.

enzym [ɛnzim] *het (~en)* enzyme

epicentrum [episɛntrʏm] *het* epicentre

epidemie [epidemi] *de (~ën)* epidemic

epilepsie [epilɛpsi] *de* epilepsy

epileptisch [epilɛptis] *adj* epileptic

epiloog [epilɔχ] *de (epilogen)* epilogue

episode [epizɔdə] *de (~n, ~s)* episode

epistel [epɪstəl] *de, het (~s)* epistle

epos [ɛpɔs] *het (epen)* epic (poem), epos

equator [ekwatɔr] *de* equator

equipe [ekip] *de (~s)* team

¹**equivalent** [ek(w)ivalɛnt] *het (~en)* equivalent: *een ~ vinden voor* find an equivalent for

²**equivalent** [ek(w)ivalɛnt] *adj* equivalent (to)

¹**er** [ɛr] *pron* of them (*often not translated*): *ik heb ~ nog* (or: *nóg*) *twee* I have got two left (*or:* more); *ik heb ~ geen (meer)* I haven't got any (left); *hij kocht ~ acht* he bought eight (of them); *er zijn ~ die* ... there are those who ...

²**er** [ɛr] *adv* 1 there: *ik zal ~ even langsgaan* I'll just call in (*or:* look in, drop in); *dat boek is ~ niet* that book isn't there; *wie waren ~?* who was (*or:* were) there?; *we zijn ~* here we are, we've arrived; 2 (*often not translated*): *~ gebeuren rare dingen* strange things (can) happen; *heeft ~ iem gebeld?* did anybody call?; *wat is ~?* what is it?, what's the matter?; *is ~ iets?* is anything wrong? (*or:* the matter?); *~ is* (or: *zijn*) ... there is (*or:* are) ...; *~ wordt gezegd dat* ... it is said that ...; *~ was eens een koning* once upon a time there was a king; *het ~ slecht*

afbrengen make a bad job of it; ~ *slecht afkomen* come off badly; *ik zit ~ niet mee* it doesn't worry me

eraan [ɛrᾳn] *adv* on (it), attached (to it): *kijk eens naar het kaartje dat ~ zit* have a look at the card that's on it (*or:* attached to it); *de hele boel ging ~* the whole lot was destroyed; *wat kan ik ~ doen?* what can I do about it?; *ik kom ~* I'm on my way

erachter [ɛrᾳχtər] *adv* behind (it): *het hek en de tuin ~* the hedge and the garden behind (it)

eraf [ɛrᾳf] *adv* off (it): *het knopje is ~* the button has come off; *de lol is ~* the fun has gone out of it

erbarmelijk [ɛrbᾳrmələk] *adj, adv* abominable, pitiful, pathetic

erbij [ɛrbɛi̯] *adv* **1** there, included at (*or:* with) it; **2** at it, to it: *ik blijf ~ dat …* I still believe (*or:* maintain) that …; *zout ~ doen* add salt; *hoe kom je ~!* the very idea!, what can you be thinking of!; *het ~ laten* leave it at that (*or:* there); *je bent ~* your game (*or:* number) is up

erboven [ɛrbᴑvə(n)] *adv* above, over (it)

erbovenop [ɛrbᴑvə(n)ᴑp] *adv* on (the) top, on top of it (*or:* them) ‖ *nu is hij ~: a)* he has got over it now; *b)* he has pulled through; *c) (financially)* he is on his feet again

erdoor [ɛrdᴑr] *adv* **1** through it: *die saaie zondagen, hoe zijn we ~ gekomen?* those boring Sundays, however did we get through them?; **2** by (*or:* because) of it: *hij raakte zijn baan ~ kwijt* it cost him his job; *ik ben ~* I've passed; *ik wil ~* I'd like to get past (*or:* through)

erdoorheen [ɛrdᴑrhɛn] *adv* through, through it

erecode [ɛrəkodə] *de (~n, ~s)* code of honour

erectie [ɛrɛksi] *de (~s)* erection

eredienst [ɛrədinst] *de (~en)* worship, service

eredivisie [ɛrədivizi] *de* premier league

eredoctoraat [ɛrədᴑktᴑrat] *het (eredoctoraten)* honorary doctorate

eregalerij [ɛrəᵧɑlərɛi] *de (~en)* hall of fame

eregast [ɛrəᵧɑst] *de (~en)* guest of honour

erekruis [ɛrəkrœys] *het (~en)* cross of honour

erelid [ɛrəlɪt] *het (ereleden)* honorary member

ereloon [ɛrəlon] *het (erelonen) (Belg)* fee

eren [ɛrə(n)] *vb* honour

ereplaats [ɛrəplats] *de (~en)* place of honour: *een ~ innemen* have an honoured place

erepodium [ɛrəpodijʏm] *het (erepodia)* rostrum, podium

ereteken [ɛrətekə(n)] *het (~s, ~en)* decoration, badge (*or:* mark) of honour

eretribune [ɛrətribynə] *de* seats of honour

erewoord [ɛrəwort] *het* word of honour

erf [ɛrf] *het (erven)* **1** property; **2** (farm)yard, estate, grounds: *huis en ~ property*

erfdeel [ɛrvdel] *het (erfdelen)* inheritance, portion: *het cultureel ~* the cultural heritage

erfelijk [ɛrfələk] *adj, adv* hereditary

erfelijkheid [ɛrfələkhɛit] *de* heredity

erfelijkheidsleer [ɛrfələkhɛitsler] *de* genetics

erfenis [ɛrfənɪs] *de (~sen)* **1** inheritance, heritage:

een ~ krijgen be left an inheritance (*or:* a legacy); **2** legacy, inheritance, estate

erfgenaam [ɛrfχənam] *de (erfgenamen)* heir: *iem tot ~ benoemen* appoint s.o. (one's) heir

erfgoed [ɛrfχut] *het (~eren)* inheritance

erfpacht [ɛrfpɑχt] *de (~en)* (roughly) long lease

erfstuk [ɛrfstʏk] *het (~ken)* (family) heirloom

erfzonde [ɛrfsᴑndə] *de* original sin

¹erg [ɛrχ] *adj* bad: *in het ~ste geval* if the worst comes to the worst; *vind je het ~ als ik er niet ben?* do you mind if I'm not there?; *wat ~!* how awful!; *het is (zo) al ~ genoeg* it's bad enough as it is

²erg [ɛrχ] *adv* very: *een ~e grote* (*or:* mooie) a very big (*or:* beautiful) one; *het spijt me ~* I'm very sorry; *hij ziet er ~ slecht uit* he looks awful (*or:* dreadful, terrible)

ergens [ɛrᵧəns] *adv* **1** somewhere, anywhere: *~ anders* somewhere else; **2** somewhere: *ik heb dat ~ gelezen* I've read that somewhere; **3** somehow: *ik kan hem ~ toch wel waarderen* (I have to admit that) he has his good points; **4** something: *hij zocht ~ naar* he was looking for sth (*or* other)

¹ergeren [ɛrᵧərə(n)] *vb* annoy, irritate

²ergeren [ɛrᵧərə(n)] *ref vb* feel (*or:* get) annoyed (at), be shocked, take offence: *zich dood ~* be extremely annoyed

ergerlijk [ɛrᵧərlək] *adj, adv* annoying, aggravating

ergernis [ɛrᵧərnɪs] *de (~sen)* annoyance, irritation: *tot (grote) ~ van de aanwezigen* to the (great) annoyance of those present

ergonomisch [ɛrᵧonᴑmis] *adj, adv* ergonomic, (*Am*) biotechnological

ergotherapeut [ɛrᵧoterapœyt] *de (~en)* occupational therapist

ergotherapie [ɛrᵧoterapi] *de (~ën)* occupational therapy

erheen [ɛrhɛn] *adv* there

erin [ɛrɪn] *adv* in(to) it, (in) there: *~ lopen (fig)* walk right into it, fall for it

erkend [ɛrkɛnt] *adj* **1** recognized, acknowledged; **2** recognized, authorized, certified: *een internationaal ~ diploma* an internationally recognized certificate

erkennen [ɛrkɛnə(n)] *vb* recognize, acknowledge, admit: *zijn ongelijk ~* admit to being (in the) wrong; *iets niet ~* disown sth; *een natuurlijk kind ~* acknowledge a natural child; *een document als echt ~* recognize a document as genuine

erkenning [ɛrkɛnɪŋ] *de (~en)* recognition, acknowledgement

erkentelijk [ɛrkɛntələk] *adj* thankful, grateful

erker [ɛrkər] *de (~s)* bay (window)

erlangs [ɛrlɑŋs] *adv* past (it), alongside (it): *wil je deze brief even op de bus doen als je ~ komt?* could you pop this letter in the (post)box when you're passing?

erlenmeyer [ɛrlə(n)mɛi̯ər] *de (~s)* Erlenmeyer flask

ermee [ɛrme] *adv* with it: *hij bemoeide zich ~* he

concerned himself with it, he interfered with it; *wat doen we ~?* what shall we do about (*or:* with) it?

erna [ɛrnɑ] *adv* afterwards, after (it), later: *de morgen ~* the morning after

ernaar [ɛrnɑr] *adv* to (*or:* towards, at) it: *~ kijken* look at it

ernaast [ɛrnɑst] *adv* 1 beside it, next to it: *de fabriek en de directeurswoning ~* the factory and the manager's house next to it; 2 off the mark: *~ zitten* be wide of the mark, be wrong

ernst [ɛrnst] *de* 1 seriousness, earnest(ness): *in volle (alle) ~* in all seriousness; *het is bittere ~* it is dead serious, a serious matter; 2 seriousness, gravity: *de ~ van de toestand inzien* recognize the seriousness of the situation

¹ernstig [ɛrnstəχ] *adj* 1 serious, grave: *de situatie wordt ~* the situation is becoming serious; 2 serious, earnest, sincere: *dat is mijn ~e overtuiging* that is my sincere conviction; 3 serious, severe, grave: *~e gevolgen hebben* have grave (*or:* serious) consequences

²ernstig [ɛrnstəχ] *adv* 1 seriously, gravely: *iem ~ toespreken* have a serious talk with s.o.; 2 seriously, earnestly, sincerely: *het ~ menen* be serious

erom [ɛrɔm] *adv* 1 around it, round (about) it: *een tuin met een schutting ~* a garden enclosed by a fence; 2 for it: *als hij ~ vraagt* if he asks for it; *denk je ~?* you won't forget, will you?; *het gaat ~ dat …* the thing is that …

eromheen [ɛrɔmhɛn] *adv* around it, round (about) it

eronder [ɛrɔndər] *adv* 1 under it, underneath (it), below it: *hij zat op een bank en zijn hond lag ~* he sat on a bench and his dog lay underneath (*or:* under) it; 2 as a result of it, because of it, under it: *hij lijdt ~* he suffers from it

eronderdoor [ɛrɔndərdor] *adv* underneath it: *~ gaan: a)* go to pieces; *b)* go bust

eronderop [ɛrɔndərɔp] *adv* underneath (it), on the bottom

eronderuit [ɛrɔndərœyt] *adv* out (from) under it: *(fig) ~ kunnen* get out of sth

erop [ɛrɔp] *adv* 1 on it; on them: *~ of eronder* all or nothing; 2 up it; up them; on(to) it: *~ slaan* hit it, bang on it, hit out; 3 up it; up then: *~ klimmen* climb up it, mount it; 4 to it: *het vervolg ~* the sequel to it; *de dag ~* the following day; *~ staan* insist on it; *het zit ~* that's it (then)

eropaan [ɛrɔpan] *adv* to(wards) it || *als het ~ komt* when it comes to the crunch; *u kunt ~* you can depend on it

eropaf [ɛrɔpɑf] *adv* to (it): *~ gaan* go towards it

eropin [ɛrɔpɪn] *adv* in(to) || *~ gaan* take it up, consider it

eropuit [ɛrɔpœyt] *adv* || *een dagje ~ gaan* go off (*or:* away) for the day; *hij is ~ mij dwars te zitten* he is out to frustrate me

erosie [ɛrozi] *de* (*~s*) erosion

erotiek [erotik] *de* eroticism

erotisch [erotis] *adj, adv* erotic

erover [ɛrovər] *adv* 1 over it, across it: *het kleed dat ~ ligt* the cloth which covers it; 2 over it: *hij gaat ~* he is in charge of it; 3 about it, of it: *hoe denk je ~?* what do you think about it?

eroverheen [ɛrovərhɛn] *adv* over it, across it: *het heeft lang geduurd eer ze ~ waren* it took them a long time to get over it

ertegen [ɛrteɣə(n)] *adv* 1 against it, at it: *hij gooide de bal ~* he threw the ball at it; 2 against (it): *ik ben ~* I am against it; *~ vechten* fight (against) it, oppose it; *~ kunnen* feel up to it, be able to put up with it

ertegenaan [ɛrteɣə(n)an] *adv* onto it, against it: *~ lopen* run into it; *~ gaan* get down to it, tackle it, get going

ertegenop [ɛrteɣə(n)ɔp] *adv* 1 up it: *~ zien* dread sth; 2 against it: *~ kunnen* be able to cope with it

ertegenover [ɛrteɣə(n)ovər] *adv* 1 opposite (to) it: *het huis ~* the house opposite; 2 against it; towards it: *~ staat dat … *on the other hand …; *hoe sta je ~?* where do you stand on that?

ertoe [ɛrtu] *adv* 1 to: *de moed ~ hebben* have the courage for it (*or:* to do it); *iem ~ brengen om iets te doen* persuade s.o. to do sth; *~ komen* get round to it; *hoe kwam je ~ ?* what made you do it?; 2 to (it): *de vogels die ~ behoren* the birds which belong to it; *wat doet dat ~?* what does it matter?, what has that got to do with it?

erts [ɛrts] *het* (*~en*) ore

ertussen [ɛrtɣsə(n)] *adv* 1 (in) between (it): *het lukte me niet ~ te komen* I couldn't get a word in (edgeways); 2 in the middle, among other things

ertussendoor [ɛrtɣsə(n)dor] *adv* 1 through (it), between (it); 2 mixed in: *een grapje ~ gooien* throw in the occasional joke; 3 (in) between, meanwhile: *dat kunnen wij wel even ~ doen* we can do that as we go along

ertussenin [ɛrtɣsə(n)ɪn] *adv* 1 (in) between (it): *hij is de oudste, zij is de jongste en ik zit ~* he is the eldest, she is the youngest, and I come in between; 2 in the middle, among other things

ertussenuit [ɛrtɣsə(n)œyt] *adv* 1 out (of it); 2 out, loose: *een dagje ~ gaan (knijpen)* slip off for the day

eruit [ɛrœyt] *adv* 1 out: *eruit!* (get) out!; 2 out, gone: *~ liggen* be out of favour, *(sport)* be eliminated

eruitzien [ɛrœytzin] *vb* 1 look; 2 look like, look as if: *hij is niet zo dom als hij eruitziet* he's not as stupid as he looks; 3 look a mess

eruptie [erɣpsi] *de* (*~s*) eruption

ervan [ɛrvɑn] *adv* from it, of it: *dat is het aantrekkelijke ~* that's what is so attractive about it; *ik ben ~ overtuigd* I am convinced of it; *ik schrok ~* it gave me a fright

ervandaan [ɛrvɑndan] *adv* 1 away (from there); 2 from there: *hij woont dertig kilometer ~* he lives twenty miles from there

ervandoor [ɛrvɑndor] *adv* off: *met het geld ~ gaan* make off with the cash; *zij ging ~ met een zeeman*

she ran off with a sailor
¹ervaren [ɛrvɑ̯rə(n)] *adj* experienced (in), skilled (in)

²ervaren [ɛrvɑ̯rə(n)] *vb* experience, discover

ervaring [ɛrvɑ̯rɪŋ] *de (~en)* experience: *veel ~ hebben* be highly experienced; *de nodige ~ opdoen* (or: *missen*) gain (or: lack) the necessary experience

erven [ɛ̯rvə(n)] *vb* inherit: *iets (van iem) ~* inherit sth (from s.o.)

ervoor [ɛrvo̯r] *adv* **1** in front (of it); **2** before (it); **3** for it: *dat dient ~ om ...* that is for ..., that serves to ...; *hij moet ~ boeten* he will pay for it (or: this); *~ zorgen dat ...* see to it that ...; **4** for it, in favour (of it): *ik ben ~* I am in favour of it; **5** for it, instead (of it): *~ doorgaan* pass for (sth else); *wat krijg ik ~?* what will I get for it?; *er alleen voor staan* be on one's own; *zoals de zaken ~ staan* as things stand

erwt [ɛrt] *de (~en)* pea

erwtensoep [ɛ̯rtə(n)sup] *de* pea soup

es [ɛs] *de* ash

escalatie [ɛskalɑ̯(t)si] *de (~s)* escalation

¹escaleren [ɛskalȩrə(n)] *vb* escalate, rocket, shoot up

²escaleren [ɛskalȩrə(n)] *vb* (cause to) escalate, force up

escapade [ɛskapɑ̯də] *de (~s)* escapade

escorte [ɛsko̯rtə] *het (~s)* escort

esculaap [ɛskylɑp] *de (esculapen)* staff of Aesculapius

esdoorn [ɛ̯zdorn] *de (~s)* maple; sycamore

eskader [ɛskɑ̯dər] *het (~s)* squadron

eskimo [ɛ̯skimo] *de (~'s)* Eskimo

esp [ɛsp] *de (~en)* aspen

Esperanto [ɛsperɑ̯nto] *het* Esperanto

espresso [ɛsprȩso] *de (~'s)* espresso

espressobar [ɛsprȩsobɑːr] *de* café, coffee bar

essentie [ɛsȩnsi] *de* essence

essentieel [ɛsɛnʃȩl] *adj, adv* essential: *een ~ verschil* a fundamental difference

Est [ɛst] *de (~en)* Estonian

estafette [ɛstafȩtə] *de (~s)* relay (race)

estafettestokje [ɛstafȩtəstɔkjə] *het (~s)* baton

esthetisch [ɛstȩtis] *adj, adv* aesthetic

Estland [ɛ̯stlɑnt] *het* Estonia

etage [etɑ̯ʒə] *de (~s)* floor, storey: *op de eerste ~* on the first (or Am: second) floor

etalage [etalɑ̯ʒə] *de (~s)* shop window, display window: *~s (gaan) kijken* (go) window-shopping

etalagepop [etalɑ̯ʒəpɔp] *de (~pen)* (shop-window) dummy, mannequin

etaleren [etalȩrə(n)] *vb* display

etaleur [etalø̯r] *de (~s)* window dresser

etappe [etɑ̯pə] *de (~s)* **1** stage, lap; **2** (sport) stage, leg

etc. *et cetera* etc.

¹eten [e̯tə(n)] *vb* eat: *het is niet te ~* it's inedible, it tastes awful; *wat ~ we vandaag?* what's for dinner today?; *je kunt hier lekker ~* the food is good here; *eet smakelijk* enjoy your meal

²eten [e̯tə(n)] *vb* eat, dine: *blijf je ~?* will you stay for dinner?; *wij zitten net te ~* we've just sat down to dinner; *uit ~ gaan* go out for a meal

³eten [e̯tə(n)] *het* **1** food: *hij houdt van lekker ~* he is fond of good food; **2** meal, dinner: *warm ~* hot meal, dinner; *het ~ is klaar* dinner is ready; *ik ben niet thuis met het ~* I won't be home for dinner

etensbak [e̯tə(n)zbɑk] *de* trough, food bowl

etensresten [e̯tənsrɛstə(n)] *de* leftovers

etenstijd [e̯tənstɛit] *de* dinnertime, time for dinner

etentje [e̯təncə] *het (~s)* dinner, meal

eter [e̯tər] *de (~s)* eater

ether [e̯tər] *de* **1** ether; **2** air: *in de ~ zijn* be on the air

ethiek [etik] *de* ethics

Ethiopië [etijo̯pijə] *het* Ethiopia

Ethiopiër [etijo̯pijər] *de (~s)* Ethiopian

ethisch [e̯tis] *adj, adv* ethical, moral

etiket [etikȩt] *het (~ten)* label, ticket, tag, sticker

etiquette [etikȩtə] *de* etiquette, good manners

etmaal [ɛ̯tmal] *het (etmalen)* twenty-four hours

etnisch [ȩtnis] *adj* ethnic

ets [ɛts] *de (~en)* etching

etsen [ɛ̯tsə(n)] *vb* etch

ettelijke [ȩtələkə] *num* dozens of, masses of

etter [ȩtər] *de* pus

etterbuil [ȩtərbœyl] *de (~en)* abscess

etteren [ȩtərə(n)] *vb* fester

etude [ety̯də] *de (~s)* étude

etui [etwi̯] *het (~s)* case

etymologie [etimoloɣi̯] *de (~ën)* etymology

etymologisch [etimolo̯ɣis] *adj, adv* etymological

EU [ey̯] *de Europese Unie* EU

eucalyptus [œykalɪ̯ptʏs] *de (~sen)* eucalyptus (tree)

eucharistie [œyχarɪsti̯] *de* Eucharist, celebration of the Eucharist, (esp Roman Catholicism) (the) Mass, (Anglican Church) (Holy) Communion

eufemisme [œyfemɪsmə] *het (~n)* euphemism

Eufraat [ø̯frat] *de* Euphrates

eunuch [œynyχ] *de (~en)* eunuch

euro [ø̯ro] *de* euro

eurocent [ø̯rosɛnt] *de (~en)* (Euro) cent

eurocheque [ø̯roʃɛk] *de (~s)* Eurocheque

eurocommissie [ø̯rokɔmɪsi] *de (~s)* European Commission

euroland [ø̯rolɑnt] *het* Euroland; Euro country

Europa [ørɑ̯pa] *het* Europe

Europacup [ørɑ̯pakʏp] *de (~s)* European Cup

europarlement [øropɑrləmɛnt] *het* European Parliament

Europeaan [øropejɑn] *de (Europeanen)* European

Europees [ørope̯s] *adj, adv* European

Eurovisie [ørovi̯zi] *de* Eurovision

Eurovisiesongfestival [ørovizisɔ̯ŋfɛstival] *het (~s)* Eurovision Song Contest

eustachiusbuis [œystɑ̯χijvzbœys] *de (-buizen)* Eustachian tube

euthanasie [œytanazi̯] *de* euthanasia

euvel [ǿvəl] *het (~s)* fault, defect: *een ~ verhelpen* remedy a fault (*or:* defect)

Eva [éva] *de* Eve

evacuatie [evakywa(t)si] *de (~s)* evacuation

evacué [evakywé] *de (~s)* evacuee

¹evacueren [evakywéra(n)] *vb* be evacuated

²evacueren [evakywéra(n)] *vb* evacuate

evaluatie [evalywa(t)si] *de (~s)* **1** evaluation, assessment; **2** evaluation

evalueren [evalywéra(n)] *vb* evaluate, assess

evangelie [evɑŋɣéli] *het (evangeliën)* **1** gospel; **2** Gospel: *het ~ van Marcus* the Gospel according to St Mark

evangelist [evɑŋɣelɪst] *de (~en)* evangelist

¹even [éva(n)] *adv* **1** (just) as: *ze zijn ~ groot* they're equally big; *in ~ grote aantallen* in equal numbers; *hij is ~ oud als ik* he is (just) as old as I am; **2** just: *zij is altijd ~ opgewekt* she's always nice and cheerful; **3** just, just a moment (*or:* while): *het duurt nog wel ~* it'll take a bit (*or:* while) longer; *mag ik u ~ storen?* may I disturb you just for a moment?; *eens ~ zien* let me see; *heel ~* just for a second (*or:* minute); *~ later (daarna)* shortly afterwards; **4** (only) just, barely; **5** just (a bit): *nog ~ doorzetten* go on for just a bit longer; *als het maar éven kan* if it is at all possible

²even [éva(n)] *adj* even ‖ *om het ~ wie* whoever, no matter who

evenaar [évanar] *de (~s)* equator

evenals [eva(n)ɑls] *conj* (just) like, (just) as: *hun zaak ging failliet, ~ die van veel andere kleine ondernemers* their business went bankrupt, just like many other small businesses

evenaren [evanára(n)] *vb* equal, (be a) match (for)

eveneens [eva(n)éns] *adv* also, too, as well

evenement [evanamɛnt] *het (~en)* event

evengoed [eva(n)ɣút] *adv* **1** just as: *jij bent ~ schuldig als je broer* you are just as guilty as your brother; **2** just as well: *je kunt dat ~ zo doen* you can just as well do it like this; **3** all the same, just the same: *ik weet van niets, maar word er ~ wel op aangekeken* I know nothing about it, but I am suspected all the same

evenmin [eva(n)mɪn] *adv* (just) as little as, no(t any) more than, neither, nor: *ik kom niet en mijn broer ~* I am not coming and neither is my brother

evenredig [eva(n)rédaɣ] *adj, adv* proportional (to), commensurate (with): *het loon is ~ aan de inspanning* the pay is in proportion to the effort; *(maths) omgekeerd ~ met* inversely proportional to

¹eventueel [eva(n)tywél] *adv* possibly, if necessary, alternatively: *alles of ~ de helft* all of it, or alternatively half; *wij zouden ~ bereid zijn om ...* we might be prepared to ...

²eventueel [eva(n)tywél] *adj* any (possible), such ... as, potential: *eventuele klachten indienen bij ...* (any) complaints should be lodged with ...; *eventuele klanten* prospective (*or:* potential) customers

evenveel [eva(n)vél] *num* as much, just as,

equally: *iedereen heeft er ~ recht op* everyone is equally entitled to it; *ieder krijgt ~* everyone gets the same amount

evenwicht [éva(n)wɪχt] *het* balance: *wankel ~* unsteady balance; *zijn ~ bewaren* (*or:* *verliezen*) keep (*or:* lose) one's balance; *het juiste ~ vinden* achieve the right balance; *de twee partijen houden elkaar in ~* the two parties balance each other out; *in ~ zijn* be well-balanced, be in equilibrium; *zijn ~ kwijt zijn* have lost one's balance

¹evenwichtig [eva(n)wɪχtaɣ] *adj* (well-)balanced, steady, stable, (*fig*) level-headed

²evenwichtig [eva(n)wɪχtaɣ] *adv* evenly, equally, uniformly

evenwichtigheid [evanwɪχtaɣhɛit] *de* balance, equilibrium, stability, poise, composure

evenwichtsbalk [éva(n)wɪχtsbalk] *de (~en)* (balance) beam

evenwichtsgevoel [éva(n)wɪts̠χavul] *het* sense of balance

evenwijdig [eva(n)wɛídaχ] *adj, adv* parallel (to, with)

evenzo [eva(n)zó] *adv* likewise

evenzogoed [eva(n)zoɣút] *adv* **1** just as well, equally well: *het had ~ mis kunnen gaan* it could just as well have gone wrong; **2** just (*or:* all) the same, nevertheless: *hij had er totaal geen zin in, ~ ging hij* he didn't feel like it at all, but he still went (*or:* went all the same)

everzwijn [évarzwɛin] *het (~en)* wild boar

evident [evidɛnt] *adj, adv* obvious, (self-)evident, *(as adverb also)* clearly

evolueren [evolywéra(n)] *vb* evolve

evolutie [evoly(t)si] *de (~s)* evolution

¹exact [ɛksɑkt] *adj* exact, precise: *~e wetenschap* (exact) science

²exact [ɛksɑkt] *adv* accurately, precisely

ex aequo [ɛksékwo] *adv* joint: *Short en Anand eindigden ~ op de tweede plaats* Short and Anand finished joint second

examen [ɛksáma(n)] *het (~s)* exam(ination): *mondeling* (*or:* *schriftelijk*) *~* oral (*or:* written) exam; *een ~ afleggen, ~ doen* take (*or:* sit) an exam

examengeld [ɛksáma(n)χɛlt] *het* examination fee

examenvak [ɛksáma(n)vɑk] *het (~ken)* examination subject

examinator [ɛksáminatǝr] *de (~en)* examiner

excellent [ɛksɛlɛnt] *adj, adv* excellent, splendid

excellentie [ɛksɛlɛnsi] *de (~s)* Excellency

excentriek [ɛksɛntrik] *adj, adv* eccentric

excentriekeling [ɛksɛntríkalɪŋ] *de (~en)* eccentric, crank, crackpot

exces [ɛksɛs] *het (~sen)* excess, extravagance

¹exclusief [ɛksklyzíf] *adj* exclusive

²exclusief [ɛksklyzíf] *adv* excluding; excl.: *~ btw* excluding VAT, plus VAT

excursie [ɛkskyrsi] *de (~s)* **1** excursion; **2** (study) visit; field trip

excuseren [ɛkskyzéra(n)] *vb* excuse, pardon: *Jack*

vraagt of we hem willen ~, hij voelt zich niet lekker Jack asks to be excused, he is not feeling well; *wilt u mij even ~* please excuse me for a moment; *zich ~ voor* one's excuses (*or:* apologies) for

excuus [ɛkskys] *het (excuses)* **1** apology: *zijn excuses aanbieden* apologize; **2** excuse: *een slap ~* a poor excuse

executeren [ɛksekytɛrə(n)] *vb* execute

executie [ɛksekɥ(t)si] *de (~s)* execution: *uitstel van ~* stay of execution

exemplaar [ɛksɛmplar] *het (exemplaren)* **1** specimen, sample; **2** copy

exercitie [ɛksɛrsi(t)si] *de (~s)* exercise, drill

exhibitionisme [ɛksibi(t)ʃonɪsmə] *het* exhibitionism

exhibitionist [ɛksibiʃonɪst] *de (~en)* exhibitionist

exotisch [ɛksotis] *adj* exotic

expediteur [ɛkspeditør] *de (~en)* shipping agent, forwarding agent, shipper, carrier

expeditie [ɛkspedi(t)si] *de (~s)* **1** shipping department, forwarding department; **2** expedition: *op ~ gaan (naar)* go on an expedition (to); **3** dispatch, shipping, forwarding: *voor een snelle ~ van de goederen zorgen* ensure that the goods are forwarded rapidly

experiment [ɛksperimɛnt] *het (~en)* experiment: *een wetenschappelijk ~ uitvoeren (op)* perform a scientific experiment (on)

experimenteel [ɛksperimɛntel] *adj, adv* experimental

experimenteren [ɛksperimɛntɛrə(n)] *vb* experiment

expert [ɛkspɛːr] *de (~s)* expert

expertise [ɛkspɛrtiːzə] *de (~s, ~n)* (expert's) assessment

expliciet [ɛksplisit] *adj, adv* explicit

exploderen [ɛksplodɛrə(n)] *vb* explode

exploitatie [ɛksplwata(t)si] *de (~s)* exploitation, development

exploiteren [ɛksplwatɛrə(n)] *vb* exploit, develop: *een stuk grond ~* develop a plot of land

explosie [ɛksplozi] *de (~s)* explosion

¹explosief [ɛksplozif] *adj, adv* explosive: *explosieve stoffen* explosives

²explosief [ɛksplozif] *het (explosieven)* explosive

exponent [ɛkspongnt] *de (~en)* exponent

export [ɛkspɔrt] *de* export

exporteren [ɛkspɔrtɛrə(n)] *vb* export

exporteur [ɛkspɔrtør] *de (~s)* exporter

exposeren [ɛkspozɛrə(n)] *vb* exhibit, display, show

expositie [ɛkspozi(t)si] *de (~s)* exhibition, show

expres [ɛksprɛs] *adv* on purpose, deliberately

expresse [ɛksprɛsə] *de (~n)* express (delivery)

expressie [ɛksprɛsi] *de (~s)* expression

expressionisme [ɛksprɛʃonɪsmə] *het* expressionism

expressionist [ɛksprɛʃonɪst] *de (~en)* expressionist

expresweg [ɛksprɛswɛχ] *de (~en) (Belg) (roughly)*

major arterial road

extase [ɛkstazə] *de* ecstasy, rapture

¹exterieur [ɛkster(i)jør] *het (~en)* exterior

²exterieur [ɛkster(i)jør] *adj* exterior, external, outside

extern [ɛkstɛrn] *adj* **1** non-resident; living-out; **2** external, outside

¹extra [ɛkstra] *adv* **1** extra: *hij kreeg 20 euro ~* he got 20 euros extra; **2** specially: *de leerlingen hadden ~ hun best gedaan* the pupils had made a special effort

²extra [ɛkstra] *adj* extra, additional: *er zijn geen ~ kosten aan verbonden* there are no extras (involved); *iets ~'s* sth extra

extraatje [ɛkstracə] *het (~s)* bonus

extra's [ɛkstras] *de* **1** bonuses, perquisites, perks; **2** extras

extravagantie [ɛkstravaɣɑnsi] *de (~s)* extravagance

extravert [ɛkstravɛrt] *adj* extrovert(ed), outgoing

¹extreem [ɛkstrem] *adj* extreme

²extreem [ɛkstrem] *adv* **1** extremely; **2** ultra-, far: *~-links* extreme left-wing

extremisme [ɛkstremɪsmə] *het* extremism

extremist [ɛkstremɪst] *de (~en)* extremist

ezel [ezəl] *de (~s)* **1** donkey: *zo koppig als een ~* be as stubborn as a mule; *een ~ stoot zich in 't gemeen niet tweemaal aan dezelfde steen* once bitten, twice shy; **2** easel

ezelsbruggetje [ezəlzbrɣɣəcə] *het* memory aid, mnemonic

ezelsoor [ezəlsor] *het (-oren)* dog-ear

f

fa [fa] *de (~'s) (mus)* fa(h)
faalangst [f̪a̠lɑŋst] *de* fear of failure
faam [fam] *de* fame, renown
fabel [f̪ab̪əl] *de (~s)* fable, fairy-tale
fabelachtig [f̪ab̪əlɑχtəχ] *adj, adv* fantastic, incredible
fabricage [fab̪rik̪a̠ʒ̪ə] *de* manufacture, production
fabriceren [fabris̪e̠rə(n)] *vb* 1 manufacture, produce; 2 make, construct
fabriek [fab̪rik̪] *de (~en)* factory
fabrieksfout [fab̪rik̪sf̪aut] *de (~en)* manufacturing fault
fabrieksterrein [fab̪rik̪st̪ərɛin] *het* factory site
fabrikaat [fab̪rik̪a̠t] *het (fabrikaten)* manufacture, make: *Nederlands* ~ made in the Netherlands
fabrikant [fab̪rik̪ɑnt] *de (~en)* manufacturer, producer, factory owner
façade [fasa̠də] *de (~s)* façade, front
facet [fas̪ɛt] *het (~ten)* aspect, facet
faciliteit [fasilit̪ɛit] *de (~en)* facility, convenience, amenity
factor [f̪ɑkt̪ɔr] *de (~en)* factor
factureren [f̪ɑkt̪yre̠rə(n)] *vb* invoice, bill
factuur [f̪ɑkt̪yr] *de (facturen)* invoice, bill
facultatief [f̪ɑkyltat̪if̪] *adj* optional, elective
faculteit [f̪ɑkylt̪ɛit] *de (~en)* faculty
fagot [f̪ay̪ɔt] *de (~ten)* bassoon
Fahrenheit [f̪a̠rənhɑjt] *de* Fahrenheit
failliet [f̪ajit] *adj, adv* bankrupt: ~ *gaan* go bankrupt
faillissement [fajisəmɛnt] *het (~en)* bankruptcy
fakir [f̪ak̪ir] *de (~s)* fakir
fakkel [f̪ɑk̪əl] *de (~s)* torch
falen [f̪a̠lə(n)] *vb* fail, make an error (of judgment), make a mistake
faling [f̪a̠lŋ] *de (Belg)* bankruptcy
falsetstem [fals̪ɛt̪st̪ɛm] *de* falsetto
fameus [famøs] *adj, adv* famous, celebrated
familiaal [familijal] *adj* || *(Belg)* ~ *helpster* home help
familie [famili] *de (~s)* 1 family: *(fig) het is één grote* ~ they are one great big happy family; *bij de* ~ *Jansen* at the Jansens; 2 family, relatives, (blood) relations: *wij zijn verre* ~ *(van elkaar)* we are distant relatives; *het zit in de* ~ it runs in the family
familiekwaal [famili̪kwal] *de (-kwalen)* hereditary disease *(or:* illness)
familielid [f̪amili̪lɪt] *het (-leden)* member of the family, relative, relation: *zijn naaste familieleden* his next of kin
fan [fɛn] *de (~s)* fan
fanaat [f̪an̪a̠t] *de (fanaten)* fanatic
fanatiek [f̪an̪at̪ik̪] *adj, adv* fanatical, crazy: *een* ~ *schaker* a chess fanatic
fanatiekeling [f̪an̪at̪ik̪əlɪŋ] *de (~en) (iron)* fanatic
fanatisme [f̪an̪at̪ɪs̪mə] *het* fanaticism, zealotry
fancy-fair [f̪ɛns̪ifɛ:r] *de (~s)* bazaar, jumble sale
fanfare [f̪ɑnf̪a̠rə] *de (~s)* brass band
¹fantaseren [fɑnt̪az̪e̠rə(n)] *vb* fantasize (about), dream (about)
²fantaseren [fɑnt̪az̪e̠rə(n)] *vb* dream up, make up, imagine, invent
fantasie [fɑnt̪az̪i] *de (~ën)* imagination
fantast [f̪ɑnt̪ɑst] *de (~en)* dreamer, visionary, storyteller, liar
¹fantastisch [f̪ɑnt̪ɑstis] *adj* 1 fantastic, fanciful: ~*e verhalen* fanciful *(or:* wild) stories; 2 fantastic, marvellous
²fantastisch [f̪ɑnt̪ɑstis] *adv* fantastically, terrifically
farao [f̪a̠rao] *de (~'s)* pharaoh
farde [f̪ɑrd̪ə] *de (Belg)* 1 file; 2 carton (of cigarettes)
Farizeeën [farizej̪ə(n)] *de* Pharisees
farmaceutisch [f̪ɑrmas̪œytis̪] *adj* pharmaceutic(al)
fascinatie [f̪ɑsina̠(t̪)si] *de (~s)* fascination
fascineren [f̪ɑsin̪e̠rə(n)] *vb* fascinate, captivate
fascinerend [f̪ɑsin̪e̠rənt̪] *adj* fascinating
fascisme [f̪ɑʃɪsmə] *het* fascism
fascist [f̪ɑʃɪst] *de (~en)* fascist
fascistisch [f̪ɑʃɪstis] *adj, adv* fascist
fase [f̪a̠zə] *de (~s, ~n)* phase: *eerste fase* undergraduate course of studies; *tweede* ~ postgraduate course of studies
faseren [fazere̠(n)] *vb* phase
fataal [fat̪a̠l] *adj, adv* fatal, terminal, lethal, mortal: *dat zou* ~ *zijn voor mijn reputatie* that would ruin my reputation
fata morgana [fatamɔrɣa̠na] *de (~'s)* fata morgana, mirage
fatsoen [f̪ɑts̪un] *het* decorum, decency, propriety: *geen enkel* ~ *hebben* lack all basic sense of propriety *(or:* decency); *zijn* ~ *houden* behave (oneself)
fatsoenlijk [f̪ɑts̪un̪lək] *adj, adv* 1 decent, respectable: *op een* ~*e manier aan de kost komen* make an honest living; 2 decent, respectable, fair
fatsoenshalve [f̪ɑts̪unshɑlvə] *adv* for decency's sake, for the sake of decency
fauna [f̪a̠una] *de* fauna
fauteuil [fot̪œy] *de (~s)* armchair, easy chair
¹favoriet [favorit̪] *de (~en)* favourite
²favoriet [favorit̪] *adj* favourite, *(pers)* favoured
fax [f̪ɑks] *de (~en)* fax
faxen [f̪ɑks̪ə(n)] *vb* fax
faxmodem [f̪ɑks̪modəm] *het (~s)* fax modem
fazant [fazɑnt̪] *de (~en)* pheasant

februari [febrywari] *de* February
federaal [fedəral] *adj* federal
federatie [fedəra(t)si] *de (~s)* federation, confederation
fee [fe] *de (~ën)* fairy
feeks [feks] *de (~en)* shrew, vixen
feest [fest] *het (~en)* **1** party; **2** feast, treat: *dat ~ gaat niet door* you can put that (idea) right out of your head
feestartikelen [festɑrtikələ(n)] *de* party goods (*or*: gadgets)
feestavond [festavɔnt] *de (~en)* gala night; social evening
feestdag [fezdɑχ] *de (~en)* holiday: *op zon- en feestdagen* on Sundays and public holidays; *prettige ~en*: *a)* Merry Christmas; *b)* Happy Easter
feestelijk [festələk] *adj, adv* festive: *een ~e jurk* a party dress
feesten [festə(n)] *vb* celebrate, make merry
feestganger [festχɑŋər] *de (~s)* party-goer, guest
feestmaal [festmal] *het (-malen)* feast, banquet
feestneus [festnøs] *de (-neuzen)* **1** false nose; **2** party-goer
feestvarken [festfɑrkə(n)] *het (~s)* birthday boy (*or*: girl), guest of honour
feestvieren [festfirə(n)] *vb* celebrate
feestzaal [festsal] *de (-zalen)* party, reception room
feilloos [feilos] *adj, adv* infallible; unerring; faultless, flawless: *~ de weg terug vinden* find one's way back unerringly
feit [feit] *het (~en)* fact, circumstance, event: *het is* (*or*: *blijft*) *een ~ dat …* the fact is (*or*: remains) that …; *de ~en spreken voor zichzelf* the facts speak for themselves; *in ~e* in fact, actually
¹feitelijk [feitələk] *adj* actual: *de ~e macht* the de facto (*or*: real, actual) power
²feitelijk [feitələk] *adv* actually, practically
fel [fɛl] *adj, adv* **1** fierce, bitter, sharp, bright, vivid, blazing (*light*), glaring (*light*): *een felroze jurk* a brilliant pink dress; **2** fierce, sharp, keen, violent, bitter: *een ~le brand* a blazing (*or*: raging) fire; **3** fierce, fiery, vehement, spirited (*pers*), scathing, biting: *~ tegen iets zijn* be dead set against sth
felicitatie [felisita(t)si] *de (~s)* congratulation(s)
feliciteren [felisitərə(n)] *vb* congratulate on: *iem ~ met iets* congratulate s.o. on sth; *gefeliciteerd en nog vele jaren* happy birthday and many happy returns (of the day)
feminisme [feminɪsmə] *het* feminism, Women's Liberation
feminist [feminɪst] *de (~en)* feminist
feministisch [feminɪstis] *adj, adv* feminist
fenomeen [fenomen] *het (fenomenen)* phenomenon
fenomenaal [fenomenal] *adj, adv* phenomenal
feodaal [fejodal] *adj, adv* feudal
ferm [fɛrm] *adj, adv* firm, resolute
fermette [fɛrmɛtə] *de (~s) (Belg)* restored farmhouse (as second home)

fertilisatie [fɛrtiliza(t)si] *de* fertilization
fervent [fɛrvɛnt] *adj, adv* fervent, ardent
fes [fɛs] *de (~sen) (mus)* F flat
festijn [fɛstɛin] *het (~en)* feast, fête
festival [fɛstival] *het (~s)* festival
festiviteit [fɛstivitɛit] *de (~en)* festivity, celebration
fetisj [fetiʃ] *de (~en)* fetish
fetisjist [fetiʃɪst] *de (~en)* fetishist
feuilleton [fœyətɔn] *het, de (~s)* serial (story)
fez [fɛs] *de (~zen)* fez
fiasco [fijɑsko] *het (~'s)* fiasco, disaster
fiche [fiʃə] *het, de (~s)* **1** counter, token, chip; **2** index card, filing card
fictie [fɪksi] *de (~s)* fiction
fictief [fɪktif] *adj, adv* fictitious, imaginary: *een ~ bedrag* an imaginary sum
fier [fir] *adj, adv* proud
fiets [fits] *de (~en)* bike, bicycle, cycle: *we gaan op (met) de ~* we're going by bike
fietsen [fitsə(n)] *vb* ride (a bike, bicycle), cycle, bike: *het is een uur ~* it takes an hour (to get there) by bike
fietsenmaker [fitsə(n)makər] *de (~s)* bicycle repairer (*or*: mender)
fietsenstalling [fitsə(n)stɑliŋ] *de* bicycle shed
fietser [fitsər] *de (~s)* (bi)cyclist
fietspad [fitspɑt] *het (~en)* bicycle track (*or*: path)
fietsstrook [fitstrok] *de (-stroken)* bicycle lane
fietstas [fitstɑs] *de (~sen)* saddlebag
fietstocht [fitstɔχt] *de (~en)* bicycle ride (*or*: trip, tour), cycling trip (*or*: tour): *een ~je gaan maken* go for a bicycle ride
figurant [fiɣyrɑnt] *de (~en)* extra, walk-on
figuratief [fiɣyratif] *adj, adv* **1** figurative; **2** decorative, ornamental
figuur [fiɣyr] *het, de (figuren)* figure, character, individual: *een goed ~* a good figure; *geen gek ~ slaan* not come off badly compared with; *wat is hij voor een ~?* what sort of person is he?
figuurlijk [fiɣyrlək] *adj, adv* figurative, metaphorical: *~ gesproken* metaphorically speaking
figuurzaag [fiɣyrzaχ] *de (-zagen)* fretsaw, jigsaw
figuurzagen [fiɣyrzaɣə(n)] *vb* do fretwork, jigsaw
Fiji-eilanden [fidʒiɛilɑndə(n)] *de* Fiji Islands
¹fijn [fɛin] *adj* **1** fine: *~e instrumenten* delicate instruments; *de ~e keuken* fine cooking; **2** delicate; **3** nice, lovely, fine, great, grand: *een ~e tijd* a good time; **4** subtle, fine: *een ~e neus* a fine (*or*: subtle) nose
²fijn [fɛin] *adv* nice: *ons huis is fijn groot* our house is nice and big
³fijn [fɛin] *int* that's nice, lovely: *we gaan op vakantie, ~!* we're going on holiday, great!
fijngevoelig [fɛiŋɣəvuləχ] *adj, adv* **1** sensitive; **2** tactful
fijnproever [fɛimpruvər] *de (~s)* connoisseur, gourmet
fijnsnijden [fɛinsnɛidə(n)] *vb* cut fine(ly), slice

thinly

fijnstampen [fɛinstɑmpə(n)] *vb* crush, pound, pulverize, mash

fik [fɪk] *de (~ken)* fire: *in de ~ steken* set fire to

fikken [fɪkə(n)] *vb* burn

fiks [fɪks] *adj* sturdy, firm

fiksen [fɪksə(n)] *vb* fix (up), manage

filantroop [filɑntrop] *de (filantropen)* philanthropist

filatelist [filatəlɪst] *de (~en)* philatelist

file [filə] *de (~s)* queue, line, row, tailback, traffic jam: *in een ~ staan* (or: *raken)* be in (*or:* get into) a traffic jam

fileparkeren [filəpɑrkərə(n)] *vb* parallel parking

filet [file] *het, de (~s)* fillet

filharmonisch [filhɑrmonis] *adj* philharmonic

filiaal [filijal] *het (filialen)* branch, chain store

filiaalhouder [filijalhɑudər] *de (~s)* branch manager

Filippijn [filipɛin] *de (~en)* Filipino

Filippijnen [filipɛinə(n)] *de* (the) Philippines

Filippijns [filipɛins] *adj* Philippine, Filipino

film [film] *de (~s)* film: *een stomme ~* a silent film (*or:* picture); *welke ~ draait er in die bioscoop?* what's on at that cinema?; *een ~(pje) ontwikkelen* develop a film

filmacademie [filmakademi] *de (~s)* film academy (*or:* school)

filmacteur [filmɑktør] *de (~s)* film actor

filmcamera [filmkɑmərɑ] *de (~'s)* (cine-)camera; (film)camera, motion-picture camera

filmdoek [filmduk] *het (~en)* (film) screen

filmen [filmə(n)] *vb* film, make (a film), shoot (a film)

filmer [filmər] *de (~s)* film-maker

filmkeuring [filmkørɪŋ] *de (~en)* film censorship, film censorship board, board of film censors

filmmuziek [filmyzik] *de* soundtrack

filmopname [filmɔpnamə] *de (~n, ~s)* shot, sequence, take: *een ~ maken van* make (*or:* shoot) a film of

filmploeg [filmpluχ] *de (~en)* film crew

filmproducent [filmprodysɛnt] *de (~en)* film producer

filmregisseur [filmreɣisør] *de (~s)* film director

filmrol [filmrɔl] *de (~len)* **1** role (*or:* part) in a film; **2** reel of film

filmster [filmstɛr] *de (~ren)* (film) star, movie star

filmvoorstelling [filmvorstɛlɪŋ] *de (~en)* film showing

filosoferen [filozofɛrə(n)] *vb* philosophize

filosofie [filozofi] *de (~ën)* philosophy: *de ~ van Plato* Plato's philosophy

filosofisch [filozofis] *adj, adv* philosophic(al)

filosoof [filozof] *de (filosofen)* philosopher

filter [filtər] *het, de (~s)* filter

¹filteren [filtərə(n)] *vb* filter; percolate

²filteren [filtərə(n)] *vb* filter through (*or:* into); percolate (through)

filterzakje [filtərzɑkjə] *het (~s)* (coffee) filter

Fin [fɪn] *de (~nen)* Finn, Finnish woman

finaal [final] *adj, adv* **1** final; **2** complete, total: *ik ben het ~ vergeten* I clean forgot (it)

finale [finalə] *de (~s)* (*mus*) finale; (*sport*) final(s)

finalist [finalɪst] *de (~en)* finalist

financieel [finɑnʃel] *adj, adv* financial

financiën [finɑnsijə(n)] *de* finance; finances, funds

financier [finɑnsir] *de (~s)* financier

financieren [finɑnsirə(n)] *vb* finance, fund, back

fineer [finer] *het* veneer

fingeren [fɪŋɣerə(n)] *vb* **1** feign, sham, stage: *een gefingeerde overval* a staged robbery; **2** invent, make up, dream up: *een gefingeerde naam* a fictitious name, an assumed name

finish [fɪnɪʃ] *de* finish, finishing line

finishen [fɪnɪʃə(n)] *vb* finish: *als tweede ~* finish second, come (in) second

Finland [fɪnlɑnt] *het* Finland

¹Fins [fɪns] *het* Finnish

²Fins [fɪns] *adj* Finnish

FIOD [fijɔt] *de Fiscale Inlichtingen- en Opsporingsdienst* tax inspectors of the Inland Revenue Service

firma [fɪrma] *de (~'s)* firm, partnership, company: *de ~ Smith & Jones* the firm of Smith and Jones

fis [fɪs] *de (~sen)* (*mus*) F sharp

fiscaal [fɪskal] *adj, adv* fiscal, tax(-): *~ aftrekbaar* tax-deductible

fiscus [fɪskʏs] *de* the Inland Revenue, the Treasury, the taxman

fit [fɪt] *adj* fit, fresh: *niet ~ zijn* be out of condition, be under the weather

fitness [fɪtnəs] *de* fitness training, keep-fit exercises: *aan ~ doen* do fitness training, work out

fitnesscentrum [fɪtnəsɛntrʏm] *het (~s, -centra)* fitness club, health club

fitting [fɪtɪŋ] *de (~s, ~en)* socket; screw(cap), fitting

fixeer [fɪkser] *het* fixer, fixative

fixeren [fɪkserə(n)] *vb* fix

fjord [fjɔrt] *de (~en)* fjord, fiord

flacon [flakɔn] *de (~s)* bottle, flask, flagon

fladderen [flɑdərə(n)] *vb* **1** flap about, flutter; **2** flutter, flap, stream

flakkeren [flɑkərə(n)] *vb* flicker

flamberen [flɑmberə(n)] *vb* flambé

flamingo [flamɪŋɡo] *de (~'s)* flamingo

flanel [flanɛl] *het (~len)* flannel, flannelette

flanellen [flanɛlə(n)] *adj* flannel

flaneren [flanerə(n)] *vb* stroll, parade

flank [flɑŋk] *de (~en)* flank, side

flankeren [flɑŋkerə(n)] *vb* flank

flansen [flɑnsə(n)] *vb* (with *in elkaar)* knock together, put together

flap [flɑp] *de (~pen)* **1** flap; **2** turnover; **3** (bank) note; **4** flysheet

flapdrol [flɑbdrɔl] *de (~len)* wally

flapoor [flɑpor] *het* protruding ear, sticking-out ear

flappen [flɑpə(n)] *vb* fling down, bang down,

plonk down || *eruit ~* blab(ber), blurt out

flappentap [flɑpə(n)tɑp] *de (~pen)* hole-in-the-wall (machine)

flapuit [flɑpœyt] *de (~s)* blab, blabber

flard [flɑrt] *de (~en)* **1** shred, tatter: *aan ~en scheuren* tear to shreds; **2** fragment, scrap: *enkele ~en van het gesprek* a few fragments (*or:* snatches) of the conversation

flat [flɛt] *de (~s)* **1** block of flats, block of apartments; **2** flat, *(Am)* apartment: *op een ~* in a flat

flater [flɑtər] *de (~s)* blunder, howler

flauw [flɑu] *adj, adv* **1** bland, tasteless, washy, watery; **2** faint, feeble, weak, dim: *ik heb geen ~ idee* I haven't the faintest idea; **3** feeble: *een ~e grap* a feeble (*or:* corny, silly) joke; **4** silly, chicken(-hearted), unsporting, faint-hearted; **5** gentle, slight

flauwekul [flɑuwəkʏl] *de* rubbish, nonsense

flauwerd [flɑuwərt] *de (~s)* silly person, wet person, coward

flauwte [flɑutə] *de (~s)* faint, fainting fit: *van een ~ bijkomen* come round (*or:* to)

flauwtjes [flɑucəs] *adj, adv* faint, *(light)* dim, bland, dull, silly: *~ glimlachen* smile weakly

flauwvallen [flɑuvɑlə(n)] *vb* faint, pass out: *~ van de pijn* faint with pain

flensje [flɛnʃə] *het (~s)* crêpe, thin pancake

fles [flɛs] *de (~sen)* bottle, jar: *een melkfles* a milk bottle; *de baby krijgt de ~* the baby is bottle-fed

flesopener [flɛsopənər] *de (~s)* bottle-opener

flesvoeding [flɛsfudɪŋ] *de (~en)* **1** bottle-feeding; **2** baby milk, *(Am)* formula

flets [flɛts] *adj, adv* **1** pale, wan: *er ~ uitzien* look pale (*or:* washed-out); **2** pale, dull: *~e kleuren* pale (*or:* faded, dull) colours

fleurig [flørəχ] *adj, adv* colourful, cheerful

flexibel [flɛksibəl] *adj* flexible, pliable, *(fig also)* supple, *(fig also)* elastic: *~e werktijden* flexible hours, flexitime

flexibiliteit [flɛksibilitɛit] *de* flexibility, *(fig also)* elasticity

flexwerker [flɛkswɛrkər] *de (~s)* flexiworker

flik [flɪk] *de (~ken) (Belg: inf)* cop

flikken [flɪkə(n)] *vb* bring off, pull off; get away with: *dat moet je me niet meer ~* don't you dare try that one on me again

flikkeren [flɪkərə(n)] *vb* **1** flicker, blink: *het ~de licht van een kaars* the flickering light of a candle; **2** glitter, sparkle: *de zon flikkert op het water* the sun shimmers on the water; **3** *(inf)* fall, tumble: *van de trap ~* nosedive (*or:* tumble) down the stairs

¹flink [flɪŋk] *adj* **1** robust, stout, sturdy; **2** considerable, substantial: *een ~e dosis* a stiff dose; *een ~e wandeling* a good (long) walk; **3** firm; plucky: *een ~e meid* a big girl; *zich ~ houden* put on a brave front (*or:* face)

²flink [flɪŋk] *adv* considerably, thoroughly, soundly: *~ wat mensen* quite a number of people, quite a few people; *iem er ~ van langs geven* give s.o. what for

flinter [flɪntər] *de (~s)* wafer, thin slice

flipperen [flɪpərə(n)] *vb* play pinball

flipperkast [flɪpərkɑst] *de (~en)* pinball machine

flirt [flʏːrt] *de (~s, ~en)* flirtation

flirten [flʏːrtə(n)] *vb* flirt

flits [flɪts] *de (~en)* **1** *(photography)* flash(bulb), flash(light); **2** flash, streak; **3** flash, split second; **4** clip, flash: *~en van een voetbalwedstrijd* highlights of a football match

flitsend [flɪtsənt] *adj* **1** stylish, snappy, snazzy; **2** brilliant

flitslicht [flɪtslɪχt] *het* flash(light)

flodder [flɔdər] *de (~s)* || *losse ~s* dummy (*or:* blank) cartridges, blanks

flodderig [flɔdərəχ] *adj, adv* **1** baggy, floppy; **2** sloppy, shoddy, messy

flonkeren [flɔŋkərə(n)] *vb* twinkle, sparkle, glitter: *~de ogen* sparkling eyes

flonkering [flɔŋkərɪŋ] *de (~en)* sparkle, sparkling, twinkling

floppen [flɔpə(n)] *vb* flop

floppydisk [flɔpidɪsk] *de (~s)* floppy disk, diskette

floppydrive [flɔpidrɑjf] *de (~s)* disk drive

flora [flɔra] *de* flora

floreren [florerə(n)] *vb* flourish, bloom, thrive

floret [florɛt] *het, de (~ten)* foil

florijn [florɛin] *de (~en)* florin, guilder

florissant [florisɑnt] *adj* flourishing, blooming, thriving, well, healthy: *dat ziet er niet zo ~ uit* that doesn't look so good

flossen [flɔsə(n)] *vb* floss one's teeth

fluctuatie [flʏktywa(t)si] *de (~s)* fluctuation, swing

fluctueren [flʏktywerə(n)] *vb* fluctuate

fluisteren [flœystərə(n)] *vb* whisper

fluit [flœyt] *de (~en)* **1** flute, fife; **2** whistle

fluitconcert [flœytkɔnsɛrt] *het (~en)* **1** flute concerto, concerto for flute, flute recital (*or:* concert); **2** catcalls, hissing: *op een ~ onthaald worden* be catcalled

¹fluiten [flœytə(n)] *vb* **1** whistle, blow a whistle; **2** play the flute; **3** whistle, sing, *(ship)* pipe, hiss

²fluiten [flœytə(n)] *vb* **1** whistle, play, sing: *een deuntje ~* whistle a tune; **2** referee, act as referee in

fluitist [flœytɪst] *de (~en)* flautist, flute(-player)

fluitje [flœycə] *het (~s)* whistle || *een ~ van een cent* a doddle, a piece of cake

fluitketel [flœytketəl] *de (~s)* whistling kettle

fluitspeler [flœytspelər] *de (~s)* flute-player

fluittoon [flœyton] *de (-tonen)* whistle, whistling, whine, b(l)eep

fluor [flywɔr] *het* fluorine

fluwelen [flywelə(n)] *adj* velvet, velvety

FM [ɛfɛm] *de frequentiemodulatie* FM, VHF

FNV [ɛfɛnve] *de Federatie van Nederlandse Vakverenigingen (roughly)* TUC, (Dutch) Trades Union Congress

fobie [fobi] *de (~ën)* phobia: *een ~ voor katten* a phobia about cats

focus [fokʏs] *het, de (~sen)* focal point, focus

foedraal [fudral] *het (foedralen)* case, cover, sheath

foefelen [fufələ(n)] *vb (Belg)* cheat, fiddle

foefje [fufjə] *het (~s)* trick

foei [fuj] *int* naughty naughty!

foeteren [futərə(n)] *vb* grumble, grouse

foetus [føtʏs] *het, de (~sen)* fetus

föhn [føn] *de (~s)* 1 *(meteorology)* föhn; 2 blow-dry-er

föhnen [fønə(n)] *vb* blow-dry

fok [fɔk] *de (~ken)* foresail

fokken [fɔkə(n)] *vb* breed, rear, raise

fokker [fɔkər] *de (~s)* breeder, stockbreeder, cattle-raiser, fancier

fokkerij [fɔkərɛi] *de (~en)* 1 (cattle-)breeding, cattle-raising, (live)stock farming; 2 breeding farm, stock farm, breeding kennel(s), stud farm

fokstier [fɔkstir] *de (~en)* (breeding) bull

fokzeil [fɔkscil] *het* foresail

folder [fɔldər] *de (~s)* leaflet, brochure, folder

folie [foli] *de (~s)* (tin)foil

folk [fok] *de* folk (music)

folklore [fɔlklorə] *de* folklore

folkmuziek [fɔkmyzik] *de* folk music

folteren [fɔltərə(n)] *vb* torture, *(fig also)* rack, *(fig also)* torment

fonds [fɔnts] *het (~en)* 1 fund, capital, resources, funds; 2 fund, trust

fonduen [fɔndywə(n)] *vb* eat fondue, have fondue

fonetisch [fonetis] *adj, adv* phonetic

fonkelen [fɔŋkələ(n)] *vb* 1 sparkle, glitter, twinkle; 2 sparkle, effervesce

fontein [fɔntɛin] *de (~en)* fountain

fooi [foj] *de (~en)* 1 tip, gratuity; 2 *(fig)* pittance, starvation wages

foor [for] *de (foren) (Belg)* fair

foppen [fɔpə(n)] *vb* fool, hoax, trick

fopspeen [fɔpspen] *de (fopspenen)* dummy (teat), soother, *(Am)* pacifier

¹forceren [fɔrsɛrə(n)] *vb* 1 force, enforce: *de zaak ~* force the issue, rush things; 2 force, strain, overtax, overwork: *zijn stem ~* (over)strain one's voice

²forceren [fɔrsɛrə(n)] *ref vb* force oneself, overtax oneself, overwork oneself

forel [fɔrɛl] *de (~len)* trout

forens [fɔrɛns] *de (forenzen)* commuter

forfait [fɔrfɛ] *het (~s) (Belg) ‖ (sport) ~ geven* fail to turn up

formaat [fɔrmat] *het (formaten)* size, format, *(fig)* stature, *(fig)* class

formaliseren [fɔrmalizɛrə(n)] *vb* formalize, standardize

formaliteit [fɔrmalitɛit] *de (~en)* formality, matter of routine: *de nodige ~en vervullen* go through the necessary formalities

formatie [fɔrma(t)si] *de (~s)* 1 formation; 2 band, group

formatteren [fɔrmatɛrə(n)] *vb* format

formeel [fɔrmel] *adj, adv* formal, official: *~ heeft u gelijk* technically speaking you are right

formeren [fɔrmɛrə(n)] *vb* 1 form, create; 2 form, create, make; 3 form, shape

¹formica [fɔrmika] *het* formica

²formica [fɔrmika] *adj* formica

formidabel [fɔrmidabəl] *adj, adv* formidable, tremendous

formule [fɔrmylə] *de (~s)* formula: *de ~ van water is H₂O* the formula for water is H_2O

formuleren [fɔrmylɛrə(n)] *vb* formulate, phrase: *iets anders ~* rephrase sth

formulering [fɔrmylɛrɪŋ] *de (~en)* formulation, phrasing, wording: *de juiste ~ is als volgt* the correct wording is as follows

formulewagen [fɔrmyləwaɣə(n)] *de (~s)* racing car, formula (racing) car

formulier [fɔrmylir] *het (~en)* form: *een ~ invullen* fill in *(or Am:* fill out*)* a form

fornuis [fɔrnœys] *het (fornuizen)* 1 cooker; 2 furnace

fors [fɔrs] *adj, adv* 1 sturdy, robust, loud, vigorous, forceful, massive *(bldg)*, heavy: *een ~e kerel* a big fellow; 2 substantial, considerable: *een ~ bedrag* a substantial sum

fort [fɔrt] *het (~en)* fort(ress)

fortuin [fɔrtœyn] *het (~en)* 1 (good) fortune, (good) luck: *zijn ~ zoeken* seek one's fortune; 2 fortune

forum [forʏm] *het (~s)* 1 forum, panel discussion; 2 panel

fosfaat [fosfat] *het (fosfaten)* phosphate

fosfor [fɔsfɔr] *het, de* phosphorus

fossiel [fɔsil] *adj* fossil; fossilized

foto [foto] *de (~'s)* photograph, picture, photo: *wil je niet op de ~?* don't you want to be in the picture?; *hij wil niet op de ~* he doesn't want his picture taken

fotocamera [fotokaməra] *de (~'s)* camera

fotograaf [fotoɣraf] *de (-grafen)* photographer

fotograferen [fotoɣrafɛrə(n)] *vb* photograph, take a photograph (of)

fotografie [fotoɣrafi] *de (~ën)* photography

fotokopie [fotokopi] *de (~ën)* photocopy, xerox: *een ~ maken van iets* photocopy sth

fotokopiëren [fotokopijɛrə(n)] *vb* photocopy, xerox

fotomodel [fotomodɛl] *het (~len)* model, photographer's model, cover girl

fouilleren [fujɛrə(n)] *vb* search, frisk

fouillering *de* (body) search

fournituren [furnityrə(n)] *de* haberdashery

¹fout [faut] *de (~en)* 1 fault, flaw, defect: *zijn ~ is dat …* the trouble with him is that …; *niemand is zonder ~en* nobody's perfect; 2 mistake, error, foul, fault: *menselijke ~* human error; *in de ~ gaan: a)* make a mistake; *b)* slip up

²fout [faut] *adj, adv* wrong, incorrect, erroneous: *de boel ging ~* everything went wrong; *een ~ antwoord* a wrong answer

foutloos [fautlos] *adj, adv* faultless, perfect

foutparkeren [fautparkərə(n)] *vb* park illegally

foyer [fwajɛ] *de (~s)* foyer

fr. *frank* fr., franc(s)

fraai [fraj] *adj, adv* **1** pretty, fine; **2** fine, splendid

fractie [frɑksi] *de (~s)* fraction: *in een ~ van een seconde* in a fraction of a second

fractieleider [frɑksilɛidər] *de (~s) (roughly)* leader of the *(or:* a) parliamentary party, *(Am; roughly)* floor leader

fractuur [frɑktyr] *de (fracturen)* fracture

fragment [frɑɣmɛnt] *het (~en)* fragment, section

framboos [frɑmbos] *de* raspberry

frame [frem] *het (~s)* frame

Française [frɑsɛːzə] *de (~s)* Frenchwoman

franchise [frɑnʃizə] *de* franchise

franco [frɑŋko] *adv* prepaid, postage paid; *(goods)* carriage paid

frangipane [frɑʒipanə] *de (Belg)* pastry with almond filling

franje [frɑɲə] *de (~s)* **1** fringe, fringing; **2** *(fig)* frill, trimmings: *zonder (overbodige) ~* stripped of all its frills

frank [frɑŋk] *de (~en)* franc ǁ *(Belg) zijn ~ valt* the penny has dropped

frankeren [frɑŋkerə(n)] *vb* stamp; frank, *(Am)* meter, prepay: *onvoldoende gefrankeerd* understamped, postage due

Frankrijk [frɑŋkrɛik] *het* France

¹Frans [frɑns] *het* French: *in het ~* in French

²Frans [frɑns] *adj* French: *de ~en* the French; *twee ~en* two French people, two Frenchmen

Fransman [frɑnsmɑn] *de (Fransen)* Frenchman

frappant [frɑpɑnt] *adj, adv* striking, remarkable

frase [frɑzə] *de (~n)* phrase

frater [frɑtər] *de (~s)* friar, brother

fraude [frɑudə] *de (~s)* fraud, embezzlement

frauderen [frɑudɛrə(n)] *vb* commit fraud

freak [fri:k] *de (~s)* **1** freak, nut, fanatic, buff: *een filmfreak* a film buff; **2** freak, weirdo

freelance [frilɛs] *adj, adv* freelance

freelancer [frilɛsər] *de (~s)* freelance(r)

fregat [frəɣɑt] *het (~ten)* frigate

frequent [frekwɛnt] *adj, adv* frequent

frequentie [frekwɛnsi] *de (~s)* frequency: *de ~ van zijn hartslag* his pulse (rate)

fresco [frɛsko] *het (~'s)* fresco

fresia [frezija] *de (~'s)* freesia

¹fret [frɛt] *het (~ten)* ferret

²fret [frɛt] *de (~ten)* fret

freudiaans [frɔjdijɑns] *adj* Freudian: *een ~e vergissing (verspreking)* a Freudian slip

freule [frœːlə] *de (~s) (roughly)* gentlewoman, lady: *~ Jane A. (roughly)* the Honourable Jane A.

frezen [frezə(n)] *vb* mill

fricandeau [frikɑndo] *de (~s)* fricandeau

frictie [frɪksi] *de (~s)* friction

friemelen [frimələ(n)] *vb* fiddle: *~ aan (met)* fiddle with

Fries [fris] *de* Frisian

Friesland [frislɑnt] *het* Friesland

friet [frit] *de (~en)* chips, *(Am)* French fries: *~je*

oorlog chips with mayonnaise and peanut sauce; *~je zonder* just chips (no sauce)

friettent [fritɛnt] *de (~en)* fish-and-chip stall *(or:* stand); *(roughly)* chippy, *(Am; roughly)* hamburger joint

frigobox [friɣoboks] *de (~en) (Belg)* cool box

frikadel [frikadɛl] *de (~len)* minced-meat hot dog

¹fris [frɪs] *het* soft drink, pop: *een glaasje ~* a soft drink, a glass of pop

²fris [frɪs] *adj* **1** fresh, fit, lively: *met ~se moed* with renewed vigour; **2** fresh, airy, breezy: *het ruikt hier niet ~* it's stuffy (in) here; **3** clean; **4** cool(ish), chilly

frisdrank [frɪzdrɑŋk] *de (~en)* soft drink; pop

frisjes [frɪʃəs] *adj* chilly, nippy

friteuse [fritøzə] *de (~s)* deep fryer, chip pan

frituren [frityrə(n)] *vb* deep-fry

frituur [frityr] *de* chip shop

frituurpan [frityrpɑn] *de (~nen)* deep frying pan, deep fryer, chip pan

frivool [frivol] *adj, adv* frivolous

¹frommelen [frɔmələ(n)] *vb* fiddle, fumble: *aan het tafelkleed ~* fiddle with the tablecloth

²frommelen [frɔmələ(n)] *vb* **1** crumple (up), rumple, crease: *iets in elkaar ~* crumple sth up; **2** stuff away

frons [frɔns] *de (~en)* **1** wrinkle; **2** frown, scowl

fronsen [frɔnsə(n)] *vb* frown, scowl: *de wenkbrauwen ~* frown, knit one's brow(s)

front [frɔnt] *het (~en)* front, façade, forefront: *het vijandelijke* (or: *oostelijke) ~* the enemy (or: eastern) front

frontaal [frɔntal] *adj, adv* frontal, head-on

frou-frou [frufru] *de (Belg)* fringe

fruit [frœyt] *het* fruit ǁ *Turks ~* Turkish delight

fruitautomaat [frœytautomat] *de (-automaten)* fruit machine, *(Am)* slot machine, one-armed bandit

fruiten [frœytə(n)] *vb* fry, sauté

fruithandelaar [frœythɑndəlar] *de (~s, -handelaren)* fruiterer, fruit merchant (or: trader, dealer)

fruitsap [frœytsɑp] *het (~pen) (Belg)* fruit juice

fruitteler [frœytelər] *de* fruit grower, fruit farmer

frunniken [frʏnəkə(n)] *vb* fiddle

frustratie [frʏstra(t)si] *de (~s)* frustration

frustreren [frʏstrerə(n)] *vb* **1** frustrate; **2** thwart

f-sleutel [ɛfsløtəl] *de* F clef

fuga [fyɣa] *de (~'s)* fugue

fuif [fœyf] *de (fuiven)* party, bash: *een ~ geven (houden)* give (or: have) a party

fuiven [fœyvə(n)] *vb* have a party: *we hebben tot diep in de nacht gefuifd* the party went on into the small hours

fulltime [fʊltajm] *adj, adv* full-time

functie [fʏŋksi] *de (~s)* post, position, duties: *een hoge ~ bekleden* hold an important position; *in ~ treden* take up office; *(maths) x is een ~ van y* x is a function of y

functiebeschrijving [fʏŋksibəsxrɛiviŋ] *de (~en)* job description, job specification

functionaris [fʏŋkʃonᴀrıs] *de (~sen)* official
functioneel [fʏŋkʃonel] *adj* functional
functioneren [fʏŋkʃonerə(n)] *vb* **1** act, function, serve; **2** work, function, perform: *niet (or: goed) ~d* out of order, in working order
fundament [fʏndamɛnt] *het (~en)* foundation; *(fig also)* fundamental(s): *de ~en leggen (voor)* lay the foundations (for)
fundamenteel [fʏndamɛntel] *adj, adv* fundamental, basic
funderen [fʏnderə(n)] *vb* **1** found, build; **2** *(fig also)* base, ground
fundering [fʏnderıŋ] *de (~en)* foundation(s), *(fig also)* basis, groundwork: *de ~(en) leggen* lay the foundation(s)
funest [fynɛst] *adj* disastrous, fatal: *de droogte is ~ voor de tuin* (the) drought is disastrous for the garden
fungeren [fʏŋɣerə(n)] *vb* **1** act as, function as; **2** be the present … *(or:* acting …, officiating …)
furie [fyri] *de (~s, furiën)* fury, shrew: *tekeergaan als een ~* go raving mad
furieus [fyrijøs] *adj, adv* furious, enraged
furore [fyrorə] *de* furore
fuseren [fyzerə(n)] *vb* merge (with), incorporate
fusie [fyzi] *de (~s)* merger
fusilleren [fyzijerə(n)] *vb* execute by firing squad
fusioneren [fyzijonerə(n)] *vb (Belg)* merge
fust [fʏst] *het (~en)* cask, barrel
fut [fʏt] *de* go, energy, zip: *de ~ is eruit bij hem* there's no go in him anymore
futiliteit [fytilitɛit] *de (~en)* trifle, futility
futuristisch [fytyrıstis] *adj, adv* futurist(ic)
fuut [fyt] *de (futen)* great crested grebe
fysica [fizika] *de* physics
fysicus [fizikʏs] *de (fysici)* physicist
fysiek [fizik] *adj, adv* physical
fysiologie [fizijoloɣi] *de* physiology
fysiotherapeut [fizijoterapœyt] *de (~en)* physiotherapist
fysiotherapie [fizijoterapi] *de* **1** physiotherapy; **2** *(Belg)* rehabilitation
fysisch [fizis] *adj, adv* physical

g

gaaf [ɣaf] *adj* **1** whole, intact, sound: *een ~ gebit* a perfect set of teeth; **2** great, super: *Sampras speelde een gave partij* Sampras played a great game

¹gaan [ɣan] *vb* **1** go, move: *hé, waar ga jij naar toe?* where are you going?, where do you think you're going?; *het gaat niet zo best (or: slecht) met de patiënt* the patient isn't doing so well (or: so badly); **2** leave, be off: *hoe laat gaat de trein?* what time does the train go?; *ik moet nu ~* I must go now, I must be going (or: off); *ik ga ervandoor* I'm going (or: off); *ga nu maar* off you go now; **3** go, be going to: *~ kijken* go and (have a) look; *~ liggen* lie down; *~ staan* stand up; *ze ~ trouwen* they're getting married; *~ zwemmen* go for a swim, go swimming; *aan het werk ~* set to work; **4** be, run: *de zaken ~ goed* business is going well; *als alles goed gaat* if all goes well; *dat kon toch nooit goed ~* that was bound to go wrong; *hoe is het gegaan?* how was it?, how did it (or: things) go?; **5** (with *over*) run, be in charge (of): *daar ga ik niet over* that's not my responsibility; **6** (with *over*) be (about): *waar gaat die film over?* what's that film about?; *zich laten ~* let oneself go; *(fig) dat gaat mij te ver* I think that is going too far; *eraan ~* have had it, *(pers also)* be (in) for it; *opzij ~* give way to, make way for, go to one side; *vreemd ~* be unfaithful; *daar ~ we weer* (t)here we go again; *we hebben nog twee uur te ~* we've got two hours to go; *aan de kant ~* move aside; *zijn gezin gaat bij hem boven alles* his family comes first (with him)

²gaan [ɣan] *vb* **1** be, happen: *het is toch nog gauw gegaan* things went pretty fast (after all); **2** (with *om*) be (about): *daar gaat het niet om* that's not the point; *daar gaat het juist om* that's the whole point; *het gaat erom of ...* the point is whether ...; *het gaat om het principe* it's the principle that matters; *het gaat om je baan* your job is at stake; *het gaat hier om een nieuw type* we're talking about a new type; *het ga je goed* all the best; *hoe gaat het (met u)?* how are you?, how are things with you?; *hoe gaat het op het werk?* how is your work (going)?, how are things (going) at work?; *het gaat* it's all right, it's OK

gaande [ɣandə] *adj* **1** going, running: *een gesprek ~ houden* keep a conversation going; **2** going on, up: *~ zijn* be going on, be in progress

gaandeweg [ɣandəwɛχ] *adv* gradually

gaap [ɣap] *de (gapen)* yawn

gaar [ɣar] *adj* **1** done; cooked: *de aardappels zijn ~* the potatoes are cooked (or: done); *het vlees is goed ~* (or: *precies ~*) the meat is well done (or: done to a turn); *iets ~ koken* cook sth; *iets ~ koken* overcook sth; **2** done, tired (out)

gaarne [ɣarnə] *adv* gladly, with pleasure

gaas [ɣas] *het (gazen)* **1** gauze, net(ting): *fijn* (or: *grof*) *~* fine-meshed (or: large-meshed) gauze; **2** wire mesh, (wire) netting, (wire) gauze: *het ~ van een hor* the wire gauze of a screen

gaatje [ɣacə] *het (~s)* (little, small) hole, puncture: *~s in de oren laten prikken* have one's ears pierced; *ik had geen ~s* I had no cavities; *ik zal eens kijken of ik voor u nog een ~ kan vinden* I'll see if I can fit (or: squeeze) you in

gabber [ɣɑbər] *de (~s)* mate, pal, chum, buddy

gadeslaan [ɣadəslan] *vb* **1** observe, watch; **2** follow, watch (closely)

gaffel [ɣɑfəl] *de (~s)* (two-pronged) fork

gage [ɣaʒə] *de (~s)* pay, fee, salary

gajes [ɣajəs] *het* rabble, riff-raff

gal [ɣɑl] *de (~len)* bile; gall

gala [ɣala] *het* gala

gala-avond [ɣalaavɔnt] *de (~en)* gala night

galant [ɣalɑnt] *adj, adv* chivalrous, gallant: *~e manieren* elegant manners

galblaas [ɣɑlblas] *de (galblazen)* gall bladder: *een operatie aan de ~* a gall bladder operation

galei [ɣalɛi] *de (~en)* galley

galeislaaf [ɣalɛislaf] *de (-slaven)* galley slave

galerie [ɣaləri] *de (~s)* (art) gallery

galeriehouder [ɣalərihaudər] *de (~s)* gallery owner; manager of a gallery

galerij [ɣalərɛi] *de (~en)* gallery, walkway, (shopping) arcade

galg [ɣɑlχ] *de (~en)* gallows: *aan de ~ ophangen* hang on the gallows; *~je spelen* play hangman; *hij groeit voor ~ en rad op* he'll come to no good

Galilea [ɣalileja] *het* Galilee

galjoen [ɣɑljun] *het (~en)* galleon

galm [ɣɑlm] *de (~en)* sound, peal(ing) ‖ *de luide ~ van zijn stem* his booming voice

¹galmen [ɣɑlmə(n)] *vb* resound, boom, peal: *de klokken ~* the bells peal

²galmen [ɣɑlmə(n)] *vb* bellow

galop [ɣalɔp] *de (~s)* gallop: *in ~* at a gallop; *in ~ overgaan* break into a gallop

galopperen [ɣalɔpərə(n)] *vb* gallop: *een paard laten ~* gallop a horse

game [gem] *de (~s)* game

gameboy [gembɔj] *de* Game Boy

gamma [ɣɑma] *de, het (~'s) (mus)* scale, gamut

gammel [ɣɑməl] *adj* **1** rickety, wobbly, ramshackle: *een ~e constructie* a ramshackle construction; **2** shaky, faint: *ik ben een beetje ~* I don't feel up to much

gang [ɣɑŋ] *de (~en)* **1** passage(way), corridor, hall(way); **2** passage(way); tunnel: *een ondergrondse ~* an underground passage(way); **3** walk, gait:

herkenbaar aan zijn moeizame ~ recognizable by his laboured gait; **4** movement, speed: *er ~ achter zetten* speed it up; *de les was al aan de ~* the lesson had already started (*or:* got going); *een motor aan de ~ krijgen* get an engine going; *goed op ~ komen (also fig)* get into one's stride; *iem op ~ helpen* help s.o. to get going, give s.o. a start; **5** course, run: *de ~ van zaken is als volgt* the procedure is as follows; *de dagelijkse ~ van zaken* the daily routine; *verantwoordelijk zijn voor de goede ~ van zaken* be responsible for the smooth running of things; *het feest is in volle ~* the party is in full swing; *alles gaat weer zijn gewone ~* everything's back to normal; **6** course: *het diner bestond uit vijf ~en* it was a five-course dinner; *ga je ~ maar: a)* (just, do) go ahead; *b)* (just, do) carry on; *c)* after you; *zijn eigen ~ gaan* go one's own way

gangbaar [ɣɑŋbar] *adj* **1** current, contemporary, common: *een gangbare uitdrukking* a common expression; **2** popular: *een gangbare maat* a common size

Ganges [χɑŋəs] *de* the (River) Ganges

gangetje [ɣɑŋəcə] *het (~s)* **1** pace, rate; **2** alley(way), passage(way), narrow corridor (*or:* passage) ‖ *alles gaat z'n ~* things are going all right

gangmaker [ɣɑŋmakər] *de (~s)* (the) life and soul of the party

gangpad [ɣɑŋpɑt] *het (~en)* aisle

gangreen [ɣɑŋɣren] *het* gangrene: *~ krijgen* get gangrene, *(part of the body)* become gangrenous

gangster [ɡɛŋstər] *de (~s)* gangster

gans [ɣɑns] *de (ganzen)* goose: *de sprookjes van Moeder de Gans* the (fairy) tales of Mother Goose

gapen [ɣapə(n)] *vb* **1** yawn: *~ van verveling* yawn with boredom; **2** gape, gawk (at): *naar iets staan ~* stand gaping at sth; **3** yawn, gape: *een ~de afgrond (also fig)* a yawning abyss

gappen [ɣɑpə(n)] *vb* pinch, swipe

garage [ɣara3ə] *de (~s)* garage: *de auto moet naar de ~* the car has to go to the garage

garagedeur [ɣara3ədør] *de* garage door

garagehouder [ɣara3əhaudər] *de (~s)* garage owner; garage manager

garagist [ɣara3ɪst] *de (~en) (Belg)* **1** garage owner; **2** motor mechanic

garanderen [ɣarandɛrə(n)] *vb* guarantee, warrant: *gegarandeerd echt goud* guaranteed solid gold; *ik kan niet ~ dat je slaagt* I cannot guarantee that you will succeed; *dat garandeer ik je* I guarantee you that

garant [ɣarɑnt] *de (~en)* guarantor, guarantee underwriter; *(law)* surety: *~ staan voor de schulden van zijn vrouw* stand surety for one's wife's debts; *zijn aanwezigheid staat ~ voor een gezellige avond* his presence ensures an enjoyable evening

garantie [ɣarɑnsi] *de (~s)* guarantee, warranty: *dat valt niet onder de ~* that is not covered by the guarantee; *drie jaar garantie op iets krijgen* get a three-year guarantee on sth

garantiebewijs [ɣarɑnsibəwɛis] *het* guarantee (card), warranty, certificate of guarantee

garantietermijn [ɣarɑn(t)sitɛrmɛin] *de* period (*or:* term) of guarantee, warranty period: *de ~ is verlopen* the (period, term of) guarantee has expired

garantievoorwaarden [ɣarɑn(t)sivorwardə(n)] *de* guarantee conditions, terms of guarantee

garde [ɣɑrdə] *de (~n)* **1** guard: *de nationale ~* the national guard; **2** whisk, beater

garderobe [ɣardərɔːbə] *de (~s)* **1** wardrobe: *een uitgebreide ~ bezitten* possess an extensive wardrobe; **2** cloakroom

gareel [ɣarel] *het (garelen)* ‖ *iem (weer) in het ~ brengen* bring s.o. to heel, make s.o. toe the line; *in het ~ lopen* toe the line

garen [ɣarə(n)] *het (~s)* thread, yarn: *een klosje ~* a reel of thread

garnaal [ɣɑrnal] *de (garnalen)* shrimp, prawn

garnalencocktail [ɣɑrnalə(n)kɔktel] *de (~s)* shrimp cocktail, prawn cocktail

garneren [ɣɑrnɛrə(n)] *vb* garnish

garnering [ɣɑrnɛrɪŋ] *de (~en)* garnishing

garnituur [ɣɑrnityr] *het (garnituren)* **1** garnishing, trim, trimming(s); **2** accessories *(pl)*, set, ensemble

garnizoen [ɣɑrnizun] *het (~en)* garrison

gas [ɣɑs] *het (~sen)* **1** gas: *~, water en elektra* gas, water and electricity; *vloeibaar ~* liquid gas; *het ~ aansteken* (*or:* uitdraaien) light (*or:* turn) off the gas; *op ~ koken* cook with (*or:* by) gas; **2** mixture, gas: *~ geven* step on the gas; *vol ~ de bocht door* (round the bend) at full speed; *de auto rijdt op ~* the car runs on LPG

gasfabriek [ɣɑsfabrik] *de (~en)* gasworks, gas plant

gasfitter [ɣɑsfitər] *de (~s)* gas fitter; plumber

gasfornuis [ɣɑsfɔrnœys] *het (gasfornuizen)* gas cooker

gaskamer [ɣɑskamər] *de (~s)* gas chamber, gas oven

gasketel [ɣɑsketəl] *de (~s)* gasholder, gasometer

gaskomfoor [ɣɑskɔmfor] *het (gaskomforen)* gas cooker, gas ring

gaskraan [ɣɑskran] *de (gaskranen)* gas tap: *de ~ opendraaien* (*or:* dichtdraaien) turn on (*or:* off) the gas (tap)

gasleiding [ɣɑslɛidɪŋ] *de (~en)* gas pipe(s), service pipe, gas main(s)

gaslicht [ɣɑslɪχt] *het* gaslight

gaslucht [ɣɑslʏχt] *de* smell of gas

gasmasker [ɣɑsmaskər] *het (~s)* gas mask

gasmeter [ɣɑsmetər] *de (~s)* gas meter

gaspedaal [ɣɑspədal] *het, de (gaspedalen)* accelerator (pedal): *het ~ indrukken* (*or:* intrappen) step on (*or:* press down) the accelerator

gaspijp [ɣɑspɛip] *de (~en)* gas pipe(line)

gasrekening [ɣɑsrekənɪŋ] *de* gas bill

gasstel [ɣɑstɛl] *het (~len)* gas ring (*or:* burner)

gast [ɣɑst] *de (~en)* **1** guest, visitor: *~en ontvangen* entertain (guests); *bij iem te ~ zijn* be s.o.'s guest; **2** customer: *vaste ~en: a)* regular guests; *b)* regular customers

gastarbeid [ɣɑstɑrbɛit] *de* foreign labour

gastarbeider [ɣɑstɑrbɛidər] *de (~s)* immigrant worker

gastcollege [ɣɑstkɔleʒə] *het (~s)* guest lecture

gastdocent [ɣɑzdosɛnt] *de (~en)* visiting lecturer

gastgezin [ɣɑstχəzɪn] *het (~nen)* host family

gastheer [ɣɑsther] *de (-heren)* host: *als ~ optreden* act as host

gastoevoer [ɣɑstuvur] *de* gas supply: *de ~ afsluiten* cut (*or:* shut) off the gas supply

gastoptreden [ɣɑstɔptredə(n)] *het* guest appearance (*or:* performance)

gastrol [ɣɑstrɔl] *de (~len)* guest appearance

gastronomisch [ɣɑstronomis] *adj, adv* gastronomic

gastspreker [ɣɑstsprekər] *de (~s)* guest speaker

gastvrij [ɣɑstfrɛi] *adj, adv* hospitable, welcoming: *iem ~ onthalen* entertain s.o. well; *iem ~ ontvangen (opnemen)* extend a warm welcome to s.o.

gastvrijheid [ɣɑstfrɛihɛit] *de* hospitality: *bij iem ~ genieten* enjoy s.o.'s hospitality

gastvrouw [ɣɑstfrɑu] *de (~en)* hostess

gasvormig [ɣɑsfɔrməχ] *adj* gaseous

gat [ɣɑt] *het (~en)* **1** hole, gap: *zwart ~* black hole; *een ~ dichten* stop (*or:* fill) a hole; *een ~ maken in* make a hole in (sth); **2** opening: *(fig) een ~ in de markt ontdekken* discover a gap (*or:* hole) in the market; **3** hole, cavity: *een ~ in je kies* a hole (*or:* cavity) in your tooth; **4** hole, dump; **5** cut, gash: *zij viel een ~ in haar hoofd* she fell and cut her head; *hij heeft een ~ in z'n hand* he spends money like water; *iets in de ~en hebben* realize sth, be aware of sth; *iem (iets) in de ~en houden* keep an eye on s.o. (sth); *niets in de ~en hebben* be quite unaware of anything; *in de ~en lopen* attract (too much) attention

¹gauw [ɣɑu] *adj, adv* quick, fast, hasty: *ga zitten en ~ een beetje* sit down and hurry up about it! (*or:* and make it snappy!); *dat heb je ~ gedaan, dat is ~ that* was quick (work); *ik zou maar ~ een jurk aantrekken* (if I were you) I'd just slip into a dress

²gauw [ɣɑu] *adv* **1** soon, before long: *hij had er al ~ genoeg van* he had soon had enough (of it); *hij zal nu wel ~ hier zijn* he won't be long now; *dat zou ik zo ~ niet weten* I couldn't say offhand; **2** easily: *ik ben niet ~ bang, maar …* I'm not easily scared, but …; *dat kost al ~ €100* that can easily cost 100 euros; *zo ~ ik iets weet, zal ik je bellen* as soon as I hear anything I'll ring you

gave [ɣavə] *de (~n)* **1** gift, donation, endowment; **2** gift, talent

Gazastrook [ɣazastrok] *de* Gaza Strip

gazelle [ɣazɛlə] *de (~n)* gazelle

gazet [χazɛt] *de (~ten) (Belg)* newspaper

gazon [ɣazɔn] *het (~s)* lawn

gazonsproeier [ɣazɔnsprujər] *de (~s)* lawn sprinkler

ge [ɣə] *pers pron* **1** thou; **2** *(Belg)* you: *wat zegt ~? what did you say?

geaard [ɣəart] *adj* **1** earthed: *een ~ stopcontact* an earthed socket; **2** natured, inclined, tempered

geaardheid [ɣəarthɛit] *de (-heden)* disposition, nature, inclination: *seksuele ~* sexual orientation

geabonneerd [ɣəabɔnert] *adj || ~ zijn (op)* have a subscription (to)

geacht [ɣəaχt] *adj* respected, esteemed: *Geachte Heer* (*or: Mevrouw*) Dear Sir (*or:* Madam); *~e luisteraars* Ladies and Gentlemen

geadresseerde [ɣəadrɛserdə] *de (~n)* addressee, consignee

geallieerden [ɣəalijɛrdə(n)] *de* Allies

geamuseerd [ɣəamyzert] *adj, adv* amused: *~ naar iets kijken* watch sth in amusement

geanimeerd [ɣəanimert] *adj* animated, lively, warm: *een ~ gesprek* an animated (*or:* a lively) conversation

geavanceerd [ɣəavɑnsert] *adj* advanced, latest: *~e technieken* advanced techniques

gebaar [ɣəbar] *het (gebaren)* **1** gesture, sign(al): *expressie in woord en ~* expression in word and gesture; *door een ~ beduidde zij hem bij haar te komen* she motioned him to come over; *met gebaren iets duidelijk maken* signal sth (by means of gestures); **2** gesture, move: *een vriendelijk ~ aan zijn adres* a gesture of friendliness towards him

gebak [ɣəbɑk] *het* pastry, confectionery, cake(s): *~ van bladerdeeg* puff (pastry); *vers ~* fresh pastry (*or:* confectionery); *koffie met ~* coffee and cake(s)

gebakje [ɣəbɑkjə] *het (~s)* (fancy) cake, pastry: *op ~s trakteren* treat (s.o.) to cake(s)

gebakken [ɣəbɑkə(n)] *adj* baked; fried: *~ aardappelen* (*or: vis*) fried potatoes (*or:* fish)

gebaren [ɣəbarə(n)] *vb* gesture, gesticulate, signal, motion: *met armen en benen ~* gesticulate wildly

gebarentaal [ɣəbarə(n)tal] *de* sign language

gebed [ɣəbɛt] *het (~en)* prayer, devotions, grace: *mijn ~en werden verhoord* my prayers were answered; *het ~ vóór de maaltijd* (saying) grace

gebedskleedje [ɣəbɛtsklecə] *het* prayer mat

gebedsoproep *de* call (*or:* summons) to prayer

gebedsrichting [ɣəbɛtsrɪχtɪŋ] *de (~en)* kiblah

gebeente [ɣəbentə] *het (~n)* bones: *zwaar van ~* with heavy bones; *wee je ~!* woe betide you!, don't you dare!

gebergte [ɣəbɛrχtə] *het (~n, ~s)* **1** mountains; **2** mountain range, chain of mountains

gebeurde [ɣəbørdə] *het* incident, event: *hij wist zich niets van het ~ te herinneren* he couldn't remember anything of what had happened

¹gebeuren [ɣəbørə(n)] *vb* happen, occur, take place: *er is een ongeluk gebeurd* there's been an accident; *voor ze (goed) wist wat er gebeurde* (the) next thing she knew; *er gebeurt hier nooit iets* nothing ever happens here; *alsof er niets gebeurd was* as if nothing had happened; *een waar gebeurd verhaal* a true story; *wat is er met jou gebeurd?* what's happened to you?; *voor als er iets gebeurt* just in case; *er moet nog heel wat ~, voor het zo ver is* we have a long way to go yet; *het is zó gebeurd* it'll only take a second (*or:* minute); *er moet nog het een en ander aan* – it needs a bit more doing to it; *dat gebeurt wel meer* these things do happen; **2** happen, occur: *dat kan de beste ~* it could happen to anyone; *er kan niets (mee) ~* nothing's can happen (to it)

²gebeuren [ɣəbøːrə(n)] *het (~s)* event, incident, happening: *een eenmalig ~* a unique event

gebeurtenis [ɣəbøːrtənɪs] *de (~sen)* **1** event, occurrence, incident: *dat is een belangrijke ~* that's a major event; *een onvoorziene ~* an unforeseen occurrence (*or:* incident); **2** event: *een eenmalige ~* a unique occasion

gebied [ɣəbiːt] *het (~en)* **1** territory, domain; **2** area, district, region: *onderontwikkelde* (*or: achtergebleven*) *~en* underdeveloped (*or:* depressed) areas/regions; **3** field, department: *op ecologisch ~* in the field of ecology; *vragen op financieel ~* financial problems; *wij verkopen alles op het ~ van …* we sell everything (which has) to do with …; **4** territory, land

gebieden [ɣəbiːdə(n)] *vb* **1** order, dictate: *iem ~ te zwijgen* impose silence on s.o., bind s.o. to secrecy; **2** compel, necessitate

gebiedsdeel [ɣəbiːtsdeːl] *het (-delen)* territory: *de overzeese gebiedsdelen* the overseas territories

gebit [ɣəbɪt] *het (~ten)* **1** (set of) teeth: *een goed ~ hebben* have a good set of teeth; *een regelmatig* (*or: onregelmatig, sterk*) *~* regular (*or:* irregular, strong) teeth; **2** (set of) dentures, (set of) false teeth

gebitsverzorging [ɣəbɪtsfərzɔːrɣɪŋ] *de* dental care

gebladerte [ɣəblaːdərtə] *het* foliage

geblaf [ɣəblɑf] *het* barking; baying

geblesseerd [ɣəblɛseːrt] *adj* injured

geblindeerd [χəblɪndeːrt] *adj* shuttered, blacked out; armoured

gebloemd [ɣəbluːmt] *adj* floral (patterned), flowered: *~ behang* floral (patterned) wallpaper

geblokkeerd [ɣəblɔkeːrt] *adj* **1** blockaded, ice-bound; **2** blocked; **3** blocked, frozen: *een ~e rekening* a frozen account; *de wielen raakten ~* the wheels locked

geblokt [ɣəblɔkt] *adj* chequered

gebocheld [ɣəbɔχəlt] *adj* hunchbacked, humpbacked

gebochelde [ɣəbɔχəldə] *de (~n)* hunchback, humpback: *de ~ van de Notre-Dame* the hunchback of the Notre-Dame

gebod [ɣəbɔt] *het (~en)* order, command: *~en en verboden* do's and don'ts; *een ~ uitvaardigen* issue an order (*or:* injunction); *de tien ~en* the Ten Commandments

gebogen [ɣəboːɣə(n)] *adj* bent, curved: *met ~ hoofd* with bowed head, with head bowed

gebonden [ɣəbɔndə(n)] *adj* **1** bound, tied (up), committed: *niet contractueel ~* not bound by contract; *aan huis ~* housebound; *niet aan regels ~* not

bound by rules; **2** bound: *een ~ boek* a hardback; *~ aspergesoep* cream of asparagus (soup)

geboorte [ɣəbɔːrtə] *de (~n, ~s)* birth, delivery: *bij de ~ woog het kind …* the child weighed … at birth

geboorteakte [ɣəbɔːrtəɑktə] *de (~n, ~s)* birth certificate, certificate of birth

geboortebeperking [ɣəbɔːrtəbəpɛrkɪŋ] *de (~en)* **1** birth control, family planning; **2** contraception, family-planning methods

geboortecijfer [ɣəbɔːrtəsɛifər] *het (~s)* birth rate

geboortedag [ɣəbɔːrtədɑχ] *de (~en)* **1** birthday: *de honderdste* (*or: tweehonderdste*) *~* the centenary (*or:* bicentenary) of s.o.'s birth; **2** day of birth

geboortedatum [ɣəbɔːrtədaːtʏm] *de* date of birth, birth date

geboortegolf [ɣəbɔːrtəɣɔlf] *de (-golven)* baby boom

geboortejaar [ɣəbɔːrtəjaːr] *het (-jaren)* year of birth

geboortekaartje [ɣəbɔːrtəkaːrcə] *het (~s)* birth announcement card

geboorteland [ɣəbɔːrtəlɑnt] *het (~en)* native country, country of origin

geboorteplaats [ɣəbɔːrtəplaːts] *de (~en)* place of birth, birthplace

geboorteregister [ɣəbɔːrtərəɣɪstər] *het (~s)* register of births

geboren [ɣəbɔːrə(n)] *adj* born: *een ~ leraar* a born teacher; *mevrouw Jansen, geboren Smit* Mrs Jansen née Smit; *~ en getogen in Amsterdam* born and bred in Amsterdam; *waar* (*or: wanneer*) *bent u ~?* where (*or:* when) were you born?; *een te vroeg ~ kind* a premature baby

geborgenheid [ɣəbɔrɣənhɛit] *de* security, safety

gebouw [ɣəbɑu] *het (~en)* building, structure, construction: *een groot* (*or: ruim*) *~* a large (*or:* spacious) building; *een houten ~(tje)* a wooden structure

gebouwd [ɣəbɑut] *adj* built, constructed: *hij is fors* (*stevig*) *~* he is well-built; *mooi ~ zijn* have a fine figure, be well-proportioned

gebrabbel [ɣəbrɑbəl] *het* jabber, gibberish, prattle

gebrand [ɣəbrɑnt] *adj* roasted, burnt: *~e amandelen* burnt (*or:* roasted) almonds

gebrek [ɣəbrɛk] *het (~en)* **1** lack, shortage, deficiency: *groot ~ hebben aan* be greatly lacking in, (*stronger*) be in desperate need of; *~ aan personeel hebben* be short-handed, be understaffed; *bij ~ aan beter* for want of anything (*or:* sth) better; **2** want, need: *~ hebben (lijden)* be in want (*or:* need), go short; **3** ailment, infirmity: *de ~en van de ouderdom* the ailments of old age; **4** shortcoming, weakness: *alle mensen hebben hun ~en* we all have our faults, no one is perfect; **5** flaw, fault, defect: *een ~ verhelpen* correct a fault; (*ernstige*) *~en vertonen* be (seriously) defective, show serious flaws; *zonder ~en* flawless, faultless, perfect

¹gebrekkig [ɣəbrɛkəχ] *adj, adv* **1** infirm, ailing, lame: *een ~ mens* an ailing person; **2** faulty, defective, inadequate, poor: *~e huisvesting* poor housing; *een ~e kennis van het Engels* poor (knowledge of) English

²**gebrekkig** [ɣəbrɛkəχ] *adv* poorly, inadequately: *een taal ~ spreken* speak a language poorly

gebroeders [ɣəbrudərs] *de* brothers: *de ~ Jansen, handelaren in wijnen* Jansen Brothers (*or:* Bros.), wine merchants

gebroken [ɣəbrokə(n)] *adj* **1** broken; fractured: *~ lijn* broken line; *een ~ rib* a broken (*or:* fractured) rib; **2** broken: *zich ~ voelen* be a broken man (*or:* woman); **3** broken: *hij sprak haar in ~ Frans aan* he addressed her in broken French

gebruik [ɣəbrœyk] *het (~en)* **1** use, application, consumption, be on, take, taking: *het ~ van sterkedrank* (the) consumption of spirits; *voor algemeen ~* for general use; *voor eigen ~* for personal use; *alleen voor uitwendig ~* for external use (*or:* application) only; *(geen) ~ van iets maken* (not) make use of sth; *van de gelegenheid ~ maken* take (*or:* seize) the opportunity; *iets in ~ nemen* put sth into use; **2** custom, habit: *de ~en van een land* the customs of a country

gebruikelijk [ɣəbrœykələk] *adj* usual, customary, common: *de ~e naam van een plant* the common name of a plant; *op de ~e wijze* in the usual way

¹**gebruiken** [ɣəbrœykə(n)] *vb* use, apply, take: *de auto gebruikt veel brandstof* the car uses (*or:* consumes) a lot of fuel; *slaapmiddelen ~* take sleeping pills (*or:* tablets); *zijn verstand ~* use one's common sense; *dat kan ik net goed ~* I could just use that; *dat kan ik goed ~* that comes in handy; *ik zou best wat extra geld kunnen ~* I could do with some extra money; *zich gebruikt voelen* feel used; *zijn tijd goed ~* make good use of one's time, put one's time to good use

²**gebruiken** [ɣəbrœykə(n)] *vb* be on drugs, take drugs

gebruiker [ɣəbrœykər] *de (~s)* **1** user; consumer: *de ~s van een computer* computer users; **2** drug user, drug addict

gebruikersonvriendelijk [ɣəbrœykərsɔnvrindələk] *adj* user-unfriendly

gebruikersvriendelijk [ɣəbrœykərsfrindələk] *adj, adv* user-friendly, easy to use, convenient

gebruiksaanwijzing [ɣəbrœyksanweizɪŋ] *de (~en)* directions (for use), instructions (for use)

gebruiksgoederen [ɣəbrœyksɣudərə(n)] *de* consumer goods (*or:* durables, commodities)

gebruind [ɣəbrœynt] *adj* tanned, sunburnt

gebukt [ɣəbʏkt] *adj* ‖ *~ gaan onder zorgen* be weighed down (*or:* be burdened) with worries

gecharmeerd [ɣəʃarmert] *adj* ‖ *van iem (iets) ~ zijn* be taken with s.o. (sth)

gecompliceerd [ɣəkɔmplisert] *adj* complicated, involved: *een ~e breuk* a compound fracture; *een ~ geval* a complicated case

geconcentreerd [ɣəkɔnsɛntrert] *adj, adv* **1** concentrated; **2** concentrated, intent, *(as adverb also)*

with concentration: *~ werken* work with (great) concentration

geconserveerd [ɣəkɔnsɛrvɛrt] *adj* preserved; canned: *goed ~ zijn* be well-preserved

gedaagde [ɣədaydə] *de (~n)* defendant, respondent

gedaan [ɣədan] *adj* **1** done, finished, over: *dan is het ~ met de rust* then there won't be any peace and quiet; **2** done, finished, over (with): *ik kan alles van hem ~ krijgen* he'll do anything for me; *iets ~ krijgen* get sth done; *van iem iets ~ krijgen* get sth out of s.o.

gedaante [ɣədantə] *de (~n, ~s)* form, figure, shape, guise: *een andere ~ aannemen* take on another form, change (its) shape; *in menselijke ~* in human form (*or:* shape); *zijn ware ~ tonen* show (oneself in) one's true colours

gedaanteverwisseling [ɣədantəvərwɪsəlɪŋ] *de (~en)* transformation, metamorphosis: *een ~ ondergaan* be(come) transformed

gedachte [ɣədaχtə] *de (~n)* **1** thought: *iemands ~n ergens van afleiden* take s.o.'s mind off sth; *(diep) in ~n zijn* be deep in thought; *iets in ~n doen* do sth absent-mindedly, do sth with one's mind elsewhere; *iets in ~n houden* keep one's mind on sth, bear sth in mind; *er niet bij zijn met zijn ~n* have one's mind on sth else; **2** thought, idea: *de achterliggende ~ is dat …* the underlying idea (*or:* thought) is that …; *zijn ~n bij iets houden* keep one's mind on sth; *de ~ niet kunnen verdragen dat …* not be able to bear the thought (*or:* bear to think) that …; *de ~ alleen al …* the very thought (*or:* idea) …; *(iem) op de ~ brengen* give (s.o.) the idea; *van ~n wisselen over* exchange ideas on, discuss; **3** opinion, view: *iem tot andere ~n brengen* make s.o. change his mind; **4** idea: *van ~n veranderen* change one's mind

gedachtegang [ɣədaχtəɣaŋ] *de (~en)* train of thought; (line of) reasoning

gedachteloos [ɣədaχtəlos] *adj, adv* unthinking, thoughtless

gedachteloosheid [χədaχtəlosheit] *de* thoughtlessness, lack of thought

gedachtewisseling [ɣədaχtəwɪsəlɪŋ] *de (~en)* exchange of ideas (*or:* opinions): *een ~ houden over* exchange ideas on, compose notes on

gedag [ɣədaχ] ‖ *~ zeggen* say hello (*or:* goodbye)

gedagvaarde [ɣədaχfardə] *de (~n)* person summon(s)ed

gedecolleteerd [χədekɔlətert] *adj* low-cut, décolleté: *een ~e jurk* a low-necked dress, a dress with a low neckline

gedeelte [ɣədeltə] *het (~n, ~s)* part, section, instalment: *het bovenste* (or: *onderste*) *~* the top (*or:* bottom) part; *het grootste ~ van het jaar* most of the year; *voor een ~* partly

¹**gedeeltelijk** [ɣədeltələk] *adj* partial: *een ~e vergoeding voor geleden schade* partial compensation for damage sustained

²**gedeeltelijk** [ɣədɛltələk] *adv* partly, partially: *dat is slechts ~ waar* that is only partly (*or:* partially) true

gedegen [ɣədeɣə(n)] *adj* thorough: *een ~ studie* a thorough study

gedegradeerd [ɣədeɣradɛrt] *adj* demoted; *(mil also)* reduced in rank; *(sport)* relegated

gedeisd [ɣədɛist] *adj, adv* quiet, calm: *zich ~ houden* lie low

gedekt [ɣədɛkt] *adj* 1 covered; 2 covered: *een ~e cheque* a covered cheque

gedelegeerde [ɣədeleɣɛrdə] *de (~n)* delegate, representative: *een ~ bij de VN* a delegate to the UN

gedemotiveerd [ɣədemotivɛrt] *adj* demoralized, dispirited: *~ raken* lose one's motivation

gedempt [ɣədɛmpt] *adj* subdued, faint, muffled, hushed: *op ~e toon* in a low (*or:* subdued) voice

gedenken [ɣədɛŋkə(n)] *vb* commemorate; remember: *iem in zijn testament ~* remember s.o. in one's will

gedenksteen [ɣədɛŋksten] *de (-stenen)* memorial stone

gedenkteken [ɣədɛŋktekə(n)] *het (~en, ~s)* memorial: *een ~ voor* a memorial to

gedenkwaardig [ɣədɛŋkwardəɣ] *adj* memorable: *een ~e gebeurtenis* a memorable event

gedeprimeerd [ɣədeprimɛrt] *adj* depressed

gedeputeerd [ɣədepytɛrt] *adj* ‖ *Gedeputeerde Staten (roughly)* the provincial executive

gedeputeerde [ɣədepytɛrdə] *de (~n)* 1 delegate, representative; 2 member of parliament; 3 *(roughly)* member of the provincial executive

gedesillusioneerd [ɣədɛsɪlyʃonɛrt] *adj* disillusioned

¹**gedetailleerd** [ɣədetajɛrt] *adj* detailed: *een ~ verslag* a detailed report

²**gedetailleerd** [ɣədetajɛrt] *adv* in detail

gedetineerde [ɣədetinɛrdə] *de (~n)* prisoner

gedicht [ɣədɪxt] *het (~en)* poem: *een ~ maken* (*or:* *voordragen*) write (*or:* recite) a poem

gedichtenbundel [ɣədɪxtə(n)bʏndəl] *de (~s)* volume of poetry (*or:* verse), collection of poems

gedifferentieerd [ɣədɪfərɛn(t)ʃɛrt] *adj, adv* differentiated

gedijen [ɣədɛiə(n)] *vb* thrive, prosper, do well

geding [ɣədɪŋ] *het (~en)* (law)suit, (legal) action, (legal) proceedings: *in kort ~ behandelen* discuss in summary proceedings; *een ~ aanspannen (beginnen) tegen* institute proceedings against

gediplomeerd [ɣədiplomɛrt] *adj* qualified, certified, registered

gedistilleerd [ɣədɪstilɛrt] *het* spirits; liquor: *handel in ~ en wijnen* trade in wines and spirits

gedistingeerd [ɣədɪstɪŋɣɛrt] *adj, adv* distinguished: *een ~ voorkomen* a distinguished appearance

gedoe [ɣədu] *het* business, stuff, (carry on): *zenuwachtig ~* fuss

gedogen [ɣədoɣə(n)] *vb* tolerate, put up with

gedonder [ɣədɔndər] *het* 1 thunder(ing), rumble: *het ~ weerklonk door het gebergte* the thunder rolled through the mountains; 2 trouble, hassle: *daar kun je een hoop ~ mee krijgen* that can land you in a good deal of trouble

gedrag [ɣədrɑx] *het* behaviour, conduct: *een bewijs van goed ~* evidence of good behaviour, certificate of good character; *wegens slecht ~* for bad behaviour (*or:* misconduct); *iemands ~ goedkeuren* (*or:* *afkeuren*) approve of (*or:* disapprove of) s.o.'s behaviour

gedragen [ɣədraɣə(n)] *ref vb* behave; behave oneself: *hij beloofde zich voortaan beter te zullen ~* he promised to behave better in future; *zich goed* (*or:* *slecht*) *~* behave well (*or:* badly); *zich niet (slecht) ~* misbehave (oneself); *gedraag je!* behave (yourself)!

gedragslijn [ɣədrɑxslɛin] *de (~en)* course (of action), line of conduct: *een ~ volgen* persue a course of action

gedragspatroon [ɣədrɑxspatron] *het (-patronen)* pattern of behaviour

gedragsregel [ɣədrɑxsreɣəl] *de (~s)* rule of conduct (*or:* behaviour)

gedragswetenschappen [ɣədrɑxs-wetənsxɑpə(n)] *de* behavioural sciences

gedrang [ɣədrɑŋ] *het* jostling, pushing: *in het ~ komen: a)* end up (*or:* find oneself) in a crush; *b)* get into a tight corner

gedresseerd [ɣədrɛsɛrt] *adj* trained, performing: *een ~e hond* a performing dog

gedreven [ɣədrevə(n)] *adj* passionate, fanatic(al): *een ~ kunstenaar* s.o. who lives for his art

gedrevenheid [ɣədrevənhɛit] *de* passion, fanaticism

gedrieën [ɣədrijə(n)] *num* (the) three (of): *zij zaten ~ op de bank* the three of them sat on the bench

gedrocht [ɣədrɔxt] *het (~en)* monster, freak

gedrukt [ɣədrʏkt] *adj* 1 printed; 2 *(com)* depressed, dull: *de markt was ~* the market was depressed

geducht [ɣədʏxt] *adj, adv* formidable, fearsome: *een ~e tegenstander* a formidable opponent

geduld [ɣədʏlt] *het* patience: *zijn ~ bewaren* remain patient; *~ hebben met iem* be patient with s.o.; *zijn ~ verliezen* lose (one's) patience; *even ~ a.u.b.* one moment, please; *veel van iemands ~ vergen, iemands ~ op de proef stellen* try s.o.'s patience

geduldig [ɣədʏldəɣ] *adj, adv* patient: *~ afwachten* wait patiently

gedupeerd [xədypɛrt] *adj* duped

gedupeerde [ɣədypɛrdə] *de* victim, dupe

gedurende [ɣədyrəndə] *prep* during, for, over, in the course of: *~ de hele dag* all through the day; *~ het hele jaar* throughout the year; *~ vier maanden* for (a period of) four months; *~ het onderzoek* during the enquiry; *~ de laatste (afgelopen) drie weken* over the past three weeks

gedurfd [ɣədʏrft] *adj* daring, provocative: *een zeer ~ optreden* a highly provocative performance

gedwee [ɣədwe] *adj* meek, submissive

gedwongen [ɣədwɔŋə(n)] *adj, adv* (en)forced, compulsory, involuntary: ~ *ontslag* compulsory redundancy; *een ~ verkoop* a forced sale; ~ *ontslag nemen* be forced to resign

geel [ɣel] *adj* yellow || *(in de Ronde van Frankrijk) in het ~ rijden* be wearing the yellow jersey (in the Tour de France); *de scheidsrechter toonde hem het ~* the referee showed him the yellow card

geelzucht [ɣelzʏɣt] *de* jaundice

geëmancipeerd [ɣəemɑnsipe̞rt] *adj* liberated, emancipated

geëmotioneerd [ɣəemo(t)ʃone̞rt] *adj, adv* emotional, touched, moved

¹geen [ɣen] *num* none; not a, not any; no: *hij heeft ~ auto* he doesn't have a car, he hasn't got a car; *hij heeft ~ geld* he doesn't have any money, he has no money; *er zijn bijna ~ koekjes meer* we're nearly out of cookies; *bijna ~* almost none, hardly any; *~ van die jongens* (or: *beiden)* none of those lads, neither (of them)

²geen [ɣen] *art* **1** not a; no: *nog ~ tien minuten later* not ten minutes later; *nog ~ twee jaar geleden* less than two years ago; *~ enkele reden hebben om te* have no reason whatsoever to; **2** not a(ny); no: *hij kent ~ Engels* he doesn't know (any) English; *~ één* not (a single) one

geenszins [ɣensɪns] *adv* by no means, not at all

geest [ɣest] *de (~en)* **1** mind, consciousness: *iets voor de ~ halen* call sth to mind; **2** soul; **3** spirit, character: *jong van ~ zijn* be young at heart; **4** ghost, spirit: *de Heilige Geest* the Holy Ghost (or: Holy Spirit); *een boze (kwade) ~* an evil spirit, a demon; *in ~en geloven* believe in ghosts; **5** spirit, vein, intention

geestdrift [ɣezdrɪft] *de* enthusiasm, passion, zeal

geestdriftig [ɣezdrɪftəɣ] *adj* enthusiastic

geestelijk [ɣestələk] *adj, adv* **1** mental, intellectual, psychological, spiritual: *~e aftakeling* mental deterioration; *een ~ gehandicapte* a mentally handicapped person; *~e inspanning* mental effort; *~ gestoord* mentally disturbed (or: deranged); **2** spiritual: *~e bijstand verlenen aan iem: a)* give (spiritual) counselling to s.o.; *b)* (rel) minister to s.o.; **3** clerical

geestelijke [ɣestələkə] *de (~n)* clergyman, *(Protestantism)* minister, *(esp Roman Catholicism)* priest

geesteskind [ɣestəskɪnt] *het (~eren)* brainchild

geestestoestand [ɣestəstustɑnt] *de* state of mind, mental state

geestesziek [ɣestəsik] *adj* mentally ill

geestig [ɣestəɣ] *adj, adv* witty, humorous, funny

geestigheid [ɣestəɣhɛit] *de (-heden)* witticism, quip

geestverruimend [ɣestfərœymənt] *adj* mind-expanding, hallucinogenic

geestverschijning [ɣestfərsχɛinɪŋ] *de (~en)* apparition, phantom, spectre, ghost

geestverwant [ɣestfərwɑnt] *de (~en)* kindred spirit, *(pol)* sympathizer

geeuw [ɣew] *de (~en)* yawn

geeuwen [ɣewə(n)] *vb* yawn: ~ *van slaap* yawn with sleepiness

gefingeerd [ɣəfɪŋɣe̞rt] *adj* fictitious, fake(d), feigned

geflatteerd [ɣəflɑte̞rt] *adj* flattering

geflirt [ɣəflɪ̯ːrt] *het* flirtation, flirting

gefluister [ɣəflœystər] *het* whisper(ing)(s), murmur

gefluit [ɣəflœyt] *het* whistling; warbling, singing

geforceerd [ɣəfɔrse̞rt] *adj, adv* forced, contrived, artificial

gefrustreerd [ɣəfrʏstre̞rt] *adj* frustrated

gefundeerd [ɣəfʏnde̞rt] *adj* (well-)founded, (well-)grounded

gegadigde [ɣəɣadəɣdə] *de (~n)* applicant, candidate; prospective buyer; interested party: *een ~ voor iets vinden* find a (potential) buyer for sth

¹gegarandeerd [ɣəɣɑrɑnde̞rt] *adj, adv* guaranteed

²gegarandeerd [ɣəɣɑrɑnde̞rt] *adv (fig)* definitely: *dat gaat ~ mis* that's bound (or: sure) to go wrong

gegeerd [χəχe̞rt] *adj (Belg)* in demand, sought-after

¹gegeven [ɣəɣevə(n)] *het (~s)* **1** data; datum, fact, information; data, entry, item: *nadere ~s* further information; *~s opslaan* (or: *invoeren, opvragen)* store (or: input, retrieve) data; **2** theme, subject

²gegeven [ɣəɣevə(n)] *adj* given, certain: *op een ~ moment begin je je af te vragen … *there comes a time when you begin to wonder …

gegevensverwerking [ɣəɣevənsfərwɛrkɪŋ] *de* data processing

gegiechel [ɣəɣiɣəl] *het* giggle(s), giggling, snigger(ing): *onderdrukt ~* stifled giggling

gegijzelde [ɣəɣɛizəldə] *de (~n)* hostage

gegil [ɣəɣɪl] *het* screaming, screams

gegoochel [ɣəɣoɣəl] *het* juggling

gegoten [ɣəɣotə(n)] *adj* || *die jurk zit als ~* that dress fits you like a glove

gegrinnik [χəχrɪnək] *het* snigger, grinning

gegrond [ɣəɣrɔnt] *adj* (well-)founded, valid, legitimate

gehaaid [ɣəhajt] *adj, adv* smart, sharp

gehaast [ɣəhast] *adj, adv* hurried, hasty, in a hurry

gehaat [ɣəhat] *adj* hated, hateful: *zich (bij iem) ~ maken* incur s.o.'s hatred

gehakt [ɣəhɑkt] *het* minced meat, mince

gehaktbal [ɣəhɑktbɑl] *de (~len)* meatball

gehaktmolen [ɣəhɑktmolə(n)] *de (~s)* mincer

gehalte [ɣəhɑltə] *het (~s)* content, percentage, proportion: *een hoog* (or: *laag) ~ aan* a high (or: low) content of

gehandicapt [ɣəhɛndikɛpt] *adj* handicapped, disabled

gehandicapte [ɣəhɛndikɛptə] *de (~n)* handicapped person, mentally handicapped person: *de (lichamelijk) ~n* the (physically) handicapped, the disabled

gehavend [ɣəhavənt] *adj* battered, tattered

gehecht [ɣəhɛχt] *adj* attached (to), *(stronger)* devoted (to)

¹geheel [ɣəhel] *adv* entirely, fully, completely, totally: *ik voel mij een ~ ander mens* I feel a different person altogether, revised

²geheel [ɣəhel] *het* **1** whole, entity, unit(y); **2** whole, entirety || *over het ~ genomen* on the whole

geheelonthouder [ɣəhelɔnthaudər] *de (~s)* teetotaller

¹geheim [ɣəhɛim] *adj* **1** secret, hidden, concealed, clandestine; undercover: *dat moet ~ blijven* this must remain private (*or:* a secret); *een ~e bijeenkomst* a secret meeting; **2** secret, classified, confidential, private: *uiterst ~e documenten* top-secret documents; *een ~ telefoonnummer* an unlisted telephone number

²geheim [ɣəhɛim] *het (~en)* **1** secret: *een ~ toevertrouwen* (or: *bewaren*) confide (*or:* keep) a secret; **2** secrecy: *in het ~* secretly

geheimhouding [ɣəhɛimhaudɪŋ] *de* secrecy, confidentiality, privacy

geheimschrift [ɣəhɛimsχrɪft] *het (~en)* (secret) code, cipher

¹geheimzinnig [ɣəhɛimzɪnəχ] *adj* mysterious, unexplained, cryptic

²geheimzinnig [ɣəhɛimzɪnəχ] *adv* mysteriously, secretly: *erg ~ doen (over iets)* be very secretive (about sth)

geheimzinnigheid [ɣəhɛimzɪnəχhɛit] *de* **1** secrecy, stealth; **2** mysteriousness, mystery

gehemelte [ɣəheməltə] *het (~s)* palate, roof of the mouth

geheugen [ɣəhøɣə(n)] *het (~s)* **1** memory; mind: *mijn ~ laat me in de steek* my memory is letting me down; **2** memory, storage

geheugencapaciteit [ɣəhøɣə(n)kapasitɛit] *de (~en)* storage capacity, memory space

geheugensteuntje [ɣəhøɣə(n)støncə] *het (~s)* reminder, prompt

geheugenverlies [ɣəhøɣə(n)vərlis] *het* amnesia, loss of memory: *tijdelijk ~* a blackout

gehoor [ɣəhor] *het* (sense of) hearing; ear(s): *bij geen ~* if there's no reply; *geen muzikaal ~ hebben* have no ear for music

gehoorapparaat [ɣəhoraparat] *het (-apparaten)* hearing aid

gehoorbeentje [ɣəhorbencə] *het* auditory ossicle

gehoorgang [ɣəhorɣaŋ] *de (~en)* auditory duct (*or:* passage)

gehoorgestoord [ɣəhorɣəstort] *adj* hearing-impaired, hard of hearing, deaf

gehoororgaan [ɣəhorɔrɣan] *het (-organen)* ear, auditory organ, organ of hearing

gehoorsafstand [ɣəhorsafstant] *de* earshot, hearing

gehoorzaal [ɣəhorzal] *de (-zalen)* auditorium

gehoorzaam [ɣəhorzam] *adj, adv* obedient

gehoorzamen [ɣəhorzamə(n)] *vb* obey, comply (with)

gehorig [ɣəhorəχ] *adj* noisy, thin-walled

gehucht [ɣəhʏχt] *het (~en)* hamlet, settlement

gehuisvest [χəhœysfɛst] *adj* housed, lodged

gehumeurd [ɣəhymørt] *adj* good-tempered, ill-humoured: *slecht* (or: *vrolijk, goed*) *~ zijn* be in a bad (*or:* cheerful, good) mood

gehuwd [ɣəhywt] *adj* married

geil [ɣɛil] *adj, adv* randy, horny

geïmproviseerd [ɣəimprovizert] *adj* improvised, ad lib

gein [ɣɛin] *de* fun, merriment: *~ trappen* make merry

geinig [ɣɛinəχ] *adj, adv* funny, cute

geïnteresseerd [ɣəintərɛsert] *adj, adv* interested

geintje [ɣɛincə] *het (~s)* joke, prank, (wise)crack: *~s uithalen* play jokes

geiser [ɣɛizər] *de (~s)* geyser

geisha [ɡɛiʃa] *de (~'s)* geisha

geit [ɣɛit] *de (~en)* goat

gejaagd [ɣəjaχt] *adj, adv* hurried, agitated

gejank [χəjaŋk] *het* whining, whine, whimper

gejoel [χəjul] *het* shouting, cheering, cheers, jeering

gejuich [ɣəjœyχ] *het* cheer(ing)

¹gek [ɣɛk] *adj* **1** mad, crazy (with), insane: *je lijkt wel ~* you must be mad; **2** mad, silly, stupid, foolish: *dat is geen ~ idee* that's not a bad idea; *je zou wel ~ zijn als je het niet deed* you'd be crazy (*or:* mad) not to (do it); **3** crazy, ridiculous, bad: *op de ~ste plaatsen* in the oddest (*or:* most unlikely) places; *~ genoeg* oddly (*or:* strangely) enough; *niet ~, hè?* not bad, eh?; **4** fond (of), keen (on), mad (about), crazy (about): *hij is ~ op die meid* he's crazy about that girl

²gek [ɣɛk] *adv* silly, badly: *doe niet zo ~* don't act (*or:* be) so silly

³gek [ɣɛk] *de (~ken)* **1** lunatic, loony, nut(case): *rijden als een ~* drive like a maniac; **2** fool, idiot: *iem voor de ~ houden* pull s.o.'s leg, make a fool of s.o.; **3** clown: *voor ~ lopen* look absurd (*or:* ridiculous)

gekarteld [ɣəkɑrtəlt] *adj (bot)* crenated, serrated

gekheid [ɣɛkhɛit] *de (-heden)* joking, banter: *alle ~ op een stokje* (all) joking apart

gekkekoeienziekte [ɣɛkəkujə(n)ziktə] *de* mad cow disease, *(scientific)* BSE

gekkenhuis [ɣɛkə(n)hœys] *het (-huizen)* madhouse, nuthouse: *wat is dat hier voor een ~?* what kind of a madhouse is this?

gekkigheid [ɣɛkəχhɛit] *de (-heden)* folly, foolishness, madness

gekleed [ɣəklet] *adj* dressed: *hij is slecht (slordig) ~* he is badly dressed

geklets [ɣəklɛts] *het* chatter, waffle: *~ in de ruimte* hot air

gekleurd [ɣəklørt] *adj* coloured; *(fig also)* colourful: *iets door een ~e bril zien* have a coloured view of sth

geklungel [χəklʏnəl] *het* fiddling (about), bungling

gekoeld [ɣəkuːlt] *adj* cooled, frozen
gekras [ɣəkrɑs] *het* **1** scratch(ing), scrape, scraping; **2** screech(ing)
gekreukeld [ɣəkrøkəlt] *adj* wrinkled, wrinkly, (c)rumpled, creased
gekreun [ɣəkrøn] *het* groan(s), moan(s), groaning, moaning
gekriebel [ɣəkribəl] *het* tickle, tickling, itch(ing)
gekrijs [ɣəkrɛis] *het* scream(ing), screech(ing)
gekruid [ɣəkrœyt] *adj* spiced, spicy, seasoned
gekruist [ɣəkrœyst] *adj* crossed; cross-bred
gekruld [ɣəkrylt] *adj* curly, crinkly, curled, crimped
gekscherend [ɣɛksxɛrənt] *adj, adv* joking, bantering
gekuist [ɣəkœyst] *adj* expurgated, edited, cut
gekwalificeerd [ɣəkwalifisɛrt] *adj* qualified; skilled
gekweld [ɣəkwɛlt] *adj* tormented, anguished
gekwetst [ɣəkwɛtst] *adj* **1** hurt, wounded, injured; **2** hurt, offended: *zich ~ voelen* take offence
gel [dʒɛl] *het, de (~s)* gel, jelly
gelaat [ɣəlaːt] *het (gelaten)* countenance, face
gelaatskleur [ɣəlaːtsklør] *de* complexion
gelach [ɣəlɑx] *het* laughter: *in luid ~ uitbarsten* burst out laughing
geladen [ɣəlaːdə(n)] *adj* loaded, charged
gelasten [ɣəlɑstə(n)] *vb* order, direct, instruct, charge: *iem ~ het pand te ontruimen* order s.o. to vacate the premises
gelaten [ɣəlaːtə(n)] *adj* resigned, uncomplaining
gelatine [ʒelatiːnə] *de* gelatine, gel, jelly
geld [ɣɛlt] *het (~en)* **1** money, currency, cash: *je ~ of je leven* your money or your life!; *klein ~* (small) change; *vals ~* counterfeit money; *zwart ~* undisclosed income; *bulken van (zwemmen in) het ~* be loaded, be rolling in money (*or:* in it); *het ~ groeit mij niet op de rug* I'm not made of money; *iem ~ uit de zak kloppen* wheedle money out of s.o.; *waar voor zijn ~ krijgen* get value for money; **2** money, cash, funds, resources: *iem ~ afpersen* extort money from s.o.; *zonder ~ zitten* be broke; **3** money, amount, sum, price, rate: *kinderen betalen half ~* children half-price; *voor geen ~ ter wereld* not for love or money
geldautomaat [ɣɛltɑutomaːt] *de (-automaten)* cash dispenser, cashpoint
geldboete [ɣɛldbuːtə] *de (~s)* fine
geldbuidel [ɣɛldbœydəl] *de (~s)* moneybag
geldelijk [ɣɛldələk] *adj, adv* financial
gelden [ɣɛldə(n)] *vb* **1** count; **2** apply, obtain, go for: *hetzelfde geldt voor jou* that goes for you too
geldend [ɣɛldənt] *adj* valid, applicable, current: *een algemeen ~e regel* a universal rule
geldgebrek [ɣɛltxəbrɛk] *het* lack of money, shortage (*or:* want) of money
geldig [ɣɛldəx] *adj* valid, legitimate, current
geldigheid [ɣɛldəxhɛit] *de* validity, legitimacy, currency

geldinzameling [ɣɛltɪnzaməlɪŋ] *de (~en)* fund-raising
geldkas [ɣɛltkɑs] *de (~sen)* cashbox; cash register, till
geldkist [ɣɛltkɪst] *de (~en)* strongbox, coffer, money box
geldkoers [ɣɛltkurs] *de (~en)* rate of exchange
geldlade [ɣɛltlaːdə] *de (~n)* (cash) till, cash-drawer
geldmarkt [ɣɛltmɑrkt] *de (~en)* **1** money-market; **2** stock exchange
geldschieter [ɣɛltsxiːtər] *de (~s)* moneylender, sponsor
geldstroom [ɣɛltstroːm] *de (-stromen)* flow of money
geldstuk [ɣɛltstʏk] *het (~ken)* coin
geldverslindend [ɣɛltfərslɪndənt] *adj, adv* costly, expensive
geldverspilling [ɣɛltfərspɪlɪŋ] *de (~en)* waste of money, extravagance
geldwolf [ɣɛltwɔlf] *de (-wolven)* money-grubber
geldzaak [ɣɛltsak] *de (-zaken)* matter of money, financial matter, money matter
geldzorgen [ɣɛltsɔrɣə(n)] *de* financial worries (*or:* problems), money troubles
geleden [ɣəleːdə(n)] *adj* ago, back, before, previously, earlier: *het is een hele tijd ~, dat …* it has been a long time since …; *ik had het een week ~ nog gezegd* I had said so a week before; *het is donderdag drie weken ~ gebeurd* it happened three weeks ago this (*or:* last Thursday)
geleding [ɣəleːdɪŋ] *de (~en)* section, part
geleed [ɣəleːt] *adj* jointed, articulate(d): *een ~ dier* a segmental animal
geleerd [ɣəleːrt] *adj* learned, scholarly, erudite, academic
geleerde [ɣəleːrdə] *de (~n)* scholar, man of learning, scientist: *daarover zijn de ~n het nog niet eens* the experts are not yet agreed on the matter
gelegen [ɣəleːɣə(n)] *adj* **1** situated, lying: *op het zuiden ~* facing south; **2** convenient, opportune: *kom ik ~?* are you busy?, am I disturbing you?
gelegenheid [ɣəleːɣənhɛit] *de (-heden)* **1** place, site; **2** opportunity, chance, facilities: *een gunstige ~ afwachten* wait for the right moment; *die streek biedt volop ~ voor fietstochten* that area offers ample facilities for cycling; *als de ~ zich voordoet* when the opportunity presents itself; *in de ~ zijn om …* be able to, have the opportunity to …; *ik maak van de ~ gebruik om …* I take this opportunity to …; **3** eating place, (*roughly*) restaurant, eating house: *openbare gelegenheden* public places; **4** occasion: *een feestelijke ~* a festive occasion; *ter ~ van* on the occasion of
gelegenheidskleding [ɣəleːɣənhɛitskledɪŋ] *de* formal dress, full dress
gelei [ʒəlɛi] *de (~en)* jelly, preserve
geleidehond [ɣəlɛidəhɔnt] *de (~en)* guide-dog
geleidelijk [ɣəlɛidələk] *adj, adv* gradual, by degrees, by (*or:* in) (gradual) stages

geleiden [ɣəlɛidə(n)] *vb* **1** guide, conduct, accompany, lead; **2** conduct, transmit: *koper geleidt goed* copper is a good conductor

geleider [ɣəlɛidər] *de (~s)* conductor

gelid [ɣəlɪt] *het (gelederen) (mil)* rank, file, order: *in de voorste gelederen* in the front ranks, in the forefront

geliefd [ɣəlift] *adj* **1** beloved, dear, well-liked; **2** favourite, cherished, pet: *zijn ~ onderwerp* his favourite subject; **3** favourite, popular: *hij is niet erg ~ bij de leerlingen* he is not very popular with the pupils

geliefde [ɣəlivdə] *de (~n)* sweetheart; lover

¹**gelijk** [ɣəlɛik] *het* right: *het grootste ~ van de wereld hebben* be absolutely right; *iem ~ geven* agree with s.o.; *(groot, volkomen) ~ hebben* be (perfectly) right

²**gelijk** [ɣəlɛik] *adj* **1** equal, the same: *twee mensen een ~e behandeling geven* treat two people (in) the same (way); *(sport) ~ spel* a draw; *twee maal twee is ~ aan vier* two times two is four; **2** equal, equivalent: *veertig ~* deuce, forty all; **3** right

³**gelijk** [ɣəlɛik] *adv* **1** likewise, alike, in the same way *(or:* manner), similarly: *zij zijn ~ gekleed* they are dressed alike *(or:* the same); **2** equally: *~ (op)delen* share equally, *(+ direct object)* divide equally; **3** level; **4** simultaneously, at the same time: *de twee treinen kwamen ~ aan* the two trains came in simultaneously *(or:* at the same time); **5** at once, straightaway, immediately, in a minute: *ik kom ~ bij u* I'll be with you in a moment, I'll be right with you

gelijkaardig [ɣəlɛikardəχ] *adj (Belg)* similar

gelijkbenig [ɣəlɛiɡbenəχ] *adj* isosceles

gelijke [ɣəlɛikə] *de (~n)* equal, peer

gelijkelijk [ɣəlɛikələk] *adv* equally, evenly

gelijkenis [ɣəlɛikənɪs] *de (~sen)* resemblance, similarity, likeness: *~ vertonen met* bear (a) resemblance to

gelijkheid [ɣəlɛikhɛit] *de* equality

gelijklopen [ɣəlɛiklopə(n)] *vb* be right, keep (good) time

¹**gelijkmaken** [ɣəlɛikmakə(n)] *vb (sport)* equalize, draw level, tie *(or:* level) the score

²**gelijkmaken** [ɣəlɛikmakə(n)] *vb* **1** level, make even, smooth (out), even (out); **2** equate, make even *(or:* equal), even up, level up, bring into line (with)

gelijkmaker [ɣəlɛikmakər] *de (~s)* equalizer, a game-tying goal

gelijkmatig [ɣəlɛikmatəχ] *adj, adv* even, equal, constant, smooth: *een ~e druk* (a) steady pressure

gelijknamig [ɣəlɛiknaməχ] *adj* of the same name

gelijkschakelen [ɣəlɛiksχakələ(n)] *vb* regard *(or:* treat) as equal(s)

gelijksoortig [ɣəlɛiksortəχ] *adj* similar, alike, analogous

gelijkspel [ɣəlɛikspɛl] *het (gelijke spelen)* draw, tie(d game)

gelijkspelen [ɣəlɛikspelə(n)] *vb* draw, tie, halve:

A. speelde gelijk tegen F. A. drew with F.

gelijkstaan [ɣəlɛikstan] *vb* **1** be equal (to); be tantamount (to); **2** be level (with), be all square (with): *op punten ~* be level(-pegging)

gelijkstellen [ɣəlɛikstɛlə(n)] *vb* equate (with), put on a par *(or:* level) (with), give equal rights (to): *voor de wet ~* make equal before the law

gelijkstroom [ɣəlɛikstrom] *de* direct current, DC

gelijktijdig [ɣəlɛiktɛidəχ] *adj, adv* simultaneous, at the same time: *~ vertrekken* leave at the same time

gelijktijdigheid [χəlɛiktɛidəχhɛit] *de* simultaneity

gelijktrekken [ɣəlɛiktrɛkə(n)] *vb* level (up), equalize

gelijkvloers [ɣəlɛikflurs] *adj, adv* on the ground floor; ground-floor; *(Am also)* first-floor

gelijkwaardig [ɣəlɛikwardəχ] *adj* equal (to, in), equivalent (to), of the same value *(or:* quality) (as), equally matched, evenly matched

gelijkwaardigheid [χəlɛikwardəχhɛit] *de* equivalence, equality, parity

gelijkzetten [ɣəlɛikzɛtə(n)] *vb* set (by): *laten we onze horloges (met elkaar) ~* let's synchronize (our) watches

gelijkzijdig [ɣəlɛikzɛidəχ] *adj* equilateral

gelobd [ɣəlɔpt] *adj (bot)* lobate, lobed

gelofte [ɣəlɔftə] *de (~n, ~s)* vow, oath, pledge

geloof [ɣəlof] *het (geloven)* **1** faith, belief, trust; conviction: *een vurig ~ in God* ardent faith in God; *~ in de mensheid hebben* have faith in humanity; **2** faith, religion, creed, (religious) belief

geloofwaardig [ɣəlofwardəχ] *adj, adv* credible; reliable; plausible, convincing

¹**geloven** [ɣəlovə(n)] *vb* **1** (with *in*) believe (in), have faith (in): *~ in God* believe in God; **2** (with *aan*) believe (in): *ik geloof van wel* I think so

²**geloven** [ɣəlovə(n)] *vb* **1** believe, credit: *je kunt me ~ of niet* believe it or not; *niet te ~!* incredible!; *iem op zijn woord ~* take s.o. at his word; **2** think, believe: *hij is het er, geloof ik, niet mee eens* I don't think he agrees

gelovig [ɣəlovəχ] *adj, adv* religious; pious; faithful: *een ~ christen* a faithful Christian

gelovige [ɣəlovəɣə] *de (~n)* believer

geluid [ɣəlœyt] *het (~en)* **1** sound: *sneller dan het ~* faster than sound, supersonic; **2** sound, noise: *het ~ van krekels* the sound of crickets; *verdachte ~en* suspicious noises; **3** tone, timbre, sound: *er zit een mooi ~ in die viool* that violin has a beautiful tone

geluiddempend [ɣəlœydɛmpənt] *adj* soundproof(ing), muffling

geluiddemper [ɣəlœydɛmpər] *de (~s)* silencer; mute

geluiddicht [ɣəlœydɪχt] *adj* soundproof

geluidsapparatuur [χəlœytsɑparatyr] *de* sound equipment, audio equipment

geluidsbarrière [ɣəlœytsbɑrijɛːrə] *de (~s)* sound barrier

geluidscassette [χɑlœɛytskɑsɛtə] *de (~s)* audio cassette

geluidseffect [γɑlœɛytsɛfɛkt] *het (~en)* sound effect

geluidshinder [γɑlœɛytshɪndər] *de* noise nuisance

geluidsinstallatie [γɑlœɛytsɪnstɑla(t)si] *de (~s)* sound (reproducing) equipment, stereo, public-address system

geluidsisolatie [γɑlœɛytsizola(t)si] *de* sound insulation, soundproofing

geluidsoverlast [γɑlœɛytsovərlɑst] *de* noise nuisance

geluidssterkte [γɑlœɛytstɛrktə] *de (~s)* sound intensity, volume

geluidstechnicus [γɑlœɛytstɛχnikʏs] *de (-technici)* sound engineer (*or:* technician)

geluidswal [γɑlœɛytswɑl] *de (~len)* noise barrier

geluidsweergave [γɑlœɛytsweryɑvə] *de (~n)* sound reproduction

geluk [γɑlʏk] *het* 1 (good) luck, (good) fortune: *dat brengt ~* that will bring (good) luck; *iem ~ toewensen* wish s.o. luck (*or:* happiness); *veel ~!* good luck!; *dat is meer ~ dan wijsheid* that is more (by) good luck than good judgement; 2 happiness, good fortune, *(stronger)* joy; 3 lucky thing, piece (*or:* bit) of luck, lucky break: *wat een ~ dat je thuis was* a lucky thing you were (at) home

¹**gelukkig** [γɑlʏkəχ] *adj* 1 lucky, fortunate: *de ~e eigenaar* the lucky owner; 2 happy, lucky: *een ~e keuze* a happy choice; 3 fortunate, happy, successful, prosperous: *~ kerstfeest* happy (*or:* merry) Christmas; *een ~ paar* a happy couple

²**gelukkig** [γɑlʏkəχ] *adv* 1 well, happily: *zijn woorden ~ kiezen* choose one's words well; 2 luckily, fortunately: *~ was het nog niet te laat* luckily (*or:* fortunately) it wasn't too late

gelukkige [γɑlʏkəyə] *de (~n)* happy man (*or:* woman); lucky one, winner: *tot de ~n behoren* be one of the lucky ones

geluksspel [χɑlʏkspɛl] *het (~en)* game of chance

geluksvogel [γɑlʏksfoyəl] *de (~s)* lucky devil, lucky dog

gelukwens [γɑlʏkwɛns] *de (~en)* congratulation, birthday wish

gelukwensen [γɑlʏkwɛnsə(n)] *vb* (with *met*) congratulate (on), offer one's congratulations (on): *iem met zijn verjaardag ~* wish s.o. many happy returns (of the day)

gelukzoeker [γɑlʏksukər] *de (~s)* fortune-hunter, adventurer

gelul [γɑlʏl] *het* (bull)shit

gemaakt [γəmɑkt] *adj, adv* 1 pretended, sham: *een ~e glimlach* an artificial (*or:* a forced) smile; 2 affected

¹**gemaal** [γəmɑl] *de* consort

²**gemaal** [γəmɑl] *het* 1 pumping-engine; 2 fuss, bother

gemachtigde [γəmɑχtəydə] *de (~n)* deputy; authorized representative, endorsee, *(law)* proxy

gemak [γəmɑk] *het (~ken)* 1 ease, leisure: *zijn ~ (ervan) nemen* take things easy; 2 quiet, calm: *zich niet op zijn ~ voelen* feel ill at ease, feel awkward; 3 ease, facility: *met ~ winnen* win easily, win hands down, have a walkover; *voor het ~* for convenience's sake

¹**gemakkelijk** [γəmɑkələk] *adj, adv* 1 easy, easygoing: *de ~ste weg kiezen* take the line of least resistance; *~ in de omgang* easy to get on with; 2 comfortable, convenient

²**gemakkelijk** [γəmɑkələk] *adv* 1 easily: *dat is ~er gezegd dan gedaan* that's easier said than done; 2 comfortably

gemakshalve [γəmɑkshɑlvə] *adv* for convenience('s sake), for the sake of convenience

gemakzuchtig [γəmɑksʏχtəχ] *adj* lazy, easygoing

gemarineerd [γəmarinɛrt] *adj* marinaded, pickled, soused

gemaskerd [γəmɑskərt] *adj* masked

gematigd [γəmɑtəχt] *adj, adv* moderate, measured

gember [γɛmbər] *de* ginger

gemberbier [γɛmbərbir] *het* ginger ale

¹**gemeen** [γəmen] *adj* 1 nasty, vicious, malicious, low, vile, shabby: *een gemene hond* a vicious dog; *een gemene streek* a dirty trick; *dat was ~ van je* that was a mean (*or:* rotten) thing to do; 2 common, joint: *niets met iem ~ hebben* have nothing in common with s.o.

²**gemeen** [γəmen] *adv* nastily, viciously, maliciously, shabbily: *iem ~ behandelen: a)* treat s.o. badly (*or:* shabbily); *b)* give s.o. a raw deal

gemeend [γəment] *adj* sincere

gemeenschap [γəmensχɑp] *de (~pen)* 1 community: *in ~ van goederen trouwen* have community of property; 2 *(Belg)* federal region; 3 intercourse

gemeenschappelijk [γəmensχɑpələk] *adj* 1 common, communal: *een ~e bankrekening* a joint bank account; *een ~e keuken* a communal kitchen; 2 joint, common, concerted, united: *onze ~e kennissen* our mutual acquaintances

gemeenschapsgeld [γəmensχɑpsχɛlt] *het (~en)* public funds (*or:* money)

gemeenschapshuis [γəmensχɑpshœys] *het (-huizen)* community centre

gemeenschapsonderwijs [γəmensχɑpsɔndərwɛis] *het (Belg)* education controlled by regional authorities

gemeente [γəmentə] *de (~n, ~s)* 1 local authority (*or:* council), metropolitan city (*or:* town, parish) council: *bij de ~ werken* work for the local council; 2 district, borough, city, town, parish: *de ~ Eindhoven* the city of Eindhoven

gemeenteadministratie [γəmentəɑtmɪnistra(t)si] *de* local government

gemeenteambtenaar [γəmentəɑmtənar] *de (-ambtenaren, ~s)* local government official

gemeentebedrijf [γəmentəbədrɛif] *het (-bedrijven)* ‖ *de gemeentebedrijven* public works

gemeentebelasting [ɣəmɛntəbəlɑstɪŋ] *de (~en)*
council tax

gemeentebestuur [ɣəmɛntəbəstyr] *het (-bestu-
ren)* district council, local authority (*or:* authorities)

gemeentegrond [ɣəmɛntəχrɔnt] *de (~en)* council
land

gemeentehuis [ɣəmɛntəhœys] *het (-huizen)* local
government offices, town hall, city hall

gemeentelijk [ɣəmɛntələk] *adj* local authority,
council, community: *het ~ vervoerbedrijf* the municipal (*or:* corporation, city) transport company

gemeenteraad [ɣəmɛntərat] *de (-raden)* council,
town (*or:* city, parish) council: *in de ~ zitten* be on
the council

gemeenteraadslid [ɣəmɛntəratslɪt] *het (-raadsle-
den)* local councillor, member of the (local) council

gemeenteraadsverkiezing [ɣəmɛntəratsfərkizɪŋ]
de (~en) local election(s)

gemeentereiniging [ɣəmɛntərɛinəɣɪŋ] *de* environmental (*or:* public) health department

gemeentesecretaris [ɣəmɛntəsɪkrətarɪs] *de
(~sen) (roughly)* Town Clerk

gemeentewerken [ɣəmɛntəwɛrkə(n)] *de* public
works (department)

gemeentewoning [ɣəmɛntəwonɪŋ] *de* council
house (*or:* flat)

gemenebest [ɣəmenəbɛst] *het (~en)* commonwealth: *het Gemenebest van Onafhankelijke Staten*
the Commonwealth of Independent States; *het
Britse Gemenebest* the (British) Commonwealth (of
Nations)

gemengd [ɣəmɛŋt] *adj, adv* mixed, blended, miscellaneous

gemeubileerd [ɣəməbilert] *adj* furnished

¹**gemiddeld** [ɣəmɪdəlt] *adj* **1** average: *iem van ~e
grootte* s.o. of average (*or:* medium) height; **2** average, mean: *de ~e hoeveelheid regen per jaar* the average (*or:* mean) annual rainfall

²**gemiddeld** [ɣəmɪdəlt] *adv* on average, an average
(of)

gemiddelde [ɣəmɪdəldə] *het* average, mean: *boven
(or: onder) het ~* above (*or:* below) (the) average

gemis [ɣəmɪs] *het* **1** lack, want, absence, deficiency;
2 loss: *zijn dood wordt als een groot ~ gevoeld* his
death is felt as a great loss

gemoed [ɣəmut] *het (~eren)* mind, heart: *de ~eren
raakten verhit* feelings started running high

gemoedelijk [ɣəmudələk] *adj, adv* agreeable,
pleasant, amiable, easygoing

gemoedsrust [ɣəmutsrʏst] *de* peace (*or:* tranquillity) of mind, inner peace (*or:* calm)

gemoeid [ɣəmujt] *adj || alsof haar leven er mee ~
was* as if her life depended on it (*or:* were at stake);
er is een hele dag mee ~ it will take a whole day

gemotiveerd [ɣəmotivert] *adj* **1** reasoned,
well-founded; **2** motivated

gemotoriseerd [ɣəmotorizɛrt] *adj* motorized

gems [ɣɛms] *de (gemzen)* chamois

gemunt [ɣəmʏnt] *adj* coined || *het op iem gemunt
hebben* have it in for s.o.

gemutst [ɣəmʏtst] *adj || goed* (or: *slecht*) *~ zijn* be
in a good (*or:* bad) mood

gen [ɣɛn] *het (~en)* gene

genaamd [ɣənamt] *adj* **1** named, called; **2** (also)
known as, alias, going by the name of

genade [ɣənadə] *de* **1** mercy, grace, quarter: *geen ~
hebben met* have no mercy on; **2** mercy, pardon,
forgiveness

genadeloos [ɣənadəlos] *adj, adv* merciless, ruthless

genadeslag [ɣənadəslɑχ] *de (~en)* death blow

gênant [ʒənɑnt] *adj* embarrassing

gendarme [ʒɑndɑrm(ə)] *de (~s, ~n) (Belg)* member of national police force

gene [ɣenə] *dem pron* that, the other: *deze of ~*
somebody (or other)

genealogie [ɣenejaloɣi] *de (~ën)* genealogy

geneesheer [ɣənesher] *de (-heren)* physician, doctor

geneeskrachtig [ɣəneskrɑχtəχ] *adj* therapeutic,
healing: *~e bronnen* medicinal springs

geneeskunde [ɣəneskʏndə] *de* medicine, medical
science: *een student in de ~* a medical student

geneeskundig [ɣəneskʏndəχ] *adj, adv* medical,
medicinal, therapeutic

geneesmiddel [ɣənesmɪdəl] *het (~en)* medicine,
drug, remedy: *rust is een uitstekend ~* rest is an excellent cure

geneeswijze [ɣənesweizə] *de (~n)* (form of) treatment, therapy

genegenheid [ɣəneɣənhɛit] *de* affection, fondness, attachment

geneigd [ɣənɛiχt] *adj* **1** inclined, apt, prone: *~ tot
luiheid* inclined to be lazy (*or:* to laziness); **2** inclined, disposed: *ik ben ~ je te geloven* I am inclined
to believe you

¹**generaal** [ɣenəral] *de (~s)* general

²**generaal** [ɣenəral] *adj* general: *de generale repetitie* (the) (full) dress-rehearsal

generalisatie [ɣenəraliza(t)si] *de (~s)* generaliza-
tion, sweeping statement

generaliseren [ɣenəralizɛrə(n)] *vb* generalize

generatie [ɣenəra(t)si] *de (~s)* generation

generator [ɣenəratɔr] *de (~en)* generator, dynamo

generen [ʒənerə(n)] *ref vb* be embarrassed, feel
embarrassed, feel shy (*or:* awkward)

genereren [ɣenərerə(n)] *vb* generate

generiek [χenərik] *de (Belg)* credits, credit titles

Genesis [ɣenəzɪs] *de* Genesis

genetica [ɣənɛtika] *de* genetics

genetisch [ɣənɛtis] *adj, adv* genetic: *~e manipulatie* genetic engineering, gene splicing

Genève [ʒənɛːvə] *het* Geneva

¹**genezen** [ɣənezə(n)] *vb* cure; heal

²**genezen** [ɣənezə(n)] *vb* recover, get well again:
van een ziekte ~ recover from an illness

genezing [ɣəne̯zɪŋ] *de (~en)* cure, recovery, healing

geniaal [ɣenijaˑl] *adj, adv* brilliant: *een geniale vondst (zet)* a stroke of genius

¹genie [ʒəniˑ] *de (~ën) (mil)* military engineering

²genie [ʒəniˑ] *het (~ën)* genius: *een groot ~* an absolute genius

geniepig [ɣəniˑpəχ] *adj, adv* sly; sneaky: *op een ~e manier* on the sly

¹genieten [ɣəniˑtə(n)] *vb* enjoy oneself, have a good time, have fun: *van het leven ~* enjoy life; *ik heb genoten!* I really enjoyed myself!

²genieten [ɣəniˑtə(n)] *vb* enjoy, have the advantage of || *hij is vandaag niet te ~* he's unbearable today, he's in a bad mood today

genitaliën [ɣenitaˑlijə(n)] *de* genitals

genocide [ɣenosiˑdə] *de* genocide

genodigde [ɣənoˑdəɣdə] *de (~n)* (invited) guest, invitee

¹genoeg [ɣənuˑχ] *num* enough, plenty, sufficient, adequate: *er is eten ~* there is plenty of food; *ik heb ~ aan een gekookt ei* a boiled egg will do for me; *ik weet ~* I've heard enough; *er is ~ voor allemaal* there is enough to go round; *er zijn al slachtoffers ~* there are too many victims (as it is); *er schoon ~ van hebben* have had it up to here, be heartily sick of it; *zo is het wel ~* that will do

²genoeg [ɣənuˑχ] *adv* enough, sufficiently: *ben ik duidelijk ~ geweest* have I made myself clear; *jammer ~* regrettably, unfortunately; *men kan niet voorzichtig ~ zijn* one can't be too careful; *vreemd ~* strangely enough, strange to say

genoegen [ɣənuˑɣə(n)] *het (~s)* **1** satisfaction, gratification: *~ nemen met iets* put up with sth; **2** pleasure, satisfaction: *iem een ~ doen* do s.o. a favour, oblige s.o.

genoemd [ɣənuˑmt] *adj* (above-)mentioned, said

genootschap [ɣənoˑtsχap] *het (~pen)* society, association, fellowship

genot [ɣənɔˑt] *het (genietingen)* enjoyment, pleasure, delight, benefit, advantage: *onder het ~ van een glas wijn* over a glass of wine

genre [ʒãˑrə] *het (~s)* genre

Gent [ɣɛnt] *het* Ghent

genuanceerd [ɣənywɑnseˑrt] *adj, adv* subtle

geodriehoek [ɣeˑjodrihuk] *de (~en)* combination of a protractor and a setsquare

geoefend [ɣəuˑfənt] *adj* experienced, trained: *een ~ pianist* an accomplished pianist

geografie [ɣejoˑɣrafi] *de* geography

geolied [χəoˑlit] *adj* oiled, lubricated

geologie [ɣejoloˑɣi] *de* geology

geologisch [ɣejoloˑɣis] *adj* geological: *een ~ tijdperk* a geological age

geometrie [ɣejometriˑ] *de* geometry

geoorloofd [ɣəoˑrloft] *adj* permitted, permissible: *een ~ middel* lawful means, a lawful method

geordend [ɣəoˑrdənt] *adj, adv* (well-)ordered, regulated, orderly

georganiseerd [ɣəoˑrɣanize̯rt] *adj* organized: *een ~e reis* a package tour

Georgië [ɣejɔˑrɣija] *het* Georgia

Georgiër [ɣejɔˑrɣijər] *de* Georgian

georiënteerd [ɣəoˑrijɛntert] *adj* oriented, orientated

gepaard [ɣəpaˑrt] *adj* coupled (with), accompanied (by), attendant (on), attached (to): *de risico's die daarmee ~ gaan* the risks involved

gepakt [ɣəpɑˑkt] *adj* || *~ en gezakt* ready for off, all ready to go

gepantserd [ɣəpɑˑntsərt] *adj* armoured, in armour: *een ~e auto* an armour-plated car

geparfumeerd [ɣəpɑˑrfymert] *adj* perfumed, scented

gepast [ɣəpɑˑst] *adj, adv* **1** (be)fitting, becoming, proper: *dat is niet ~* that is not done; **2** exact: *met ~ geld betalen* pay the exact amount

gepeins [ɣəpeˑins] *het* musing(s), meditation(s), pondering

gepensioneerd [ɣəpɛnʃone̯rt] *adj* retired, pensioned-off, superannuated

gepeperd [ɣəpeˑpərt] *adj* peppery, peppered; *(fig also)* spicy: *zijn rekeningen zijn nogal ~* his bills are a bit steep

geperforeerd [ɣəpɛˑrforert] *adj* perforated

gepeuter [ɣəpøˑtər] *het* **1** fiddling, picking: *schei uit met dat ~ in je neus* stop picking your nose; **2** tinkering (at, with), fiddling (with)

gepiep [ɣəpiˑp] *het* **1** squeak(ing); **2** peep(ing), chirp, cheep(ing), squeak(ing), squeal(ing), screech(ing); **3** wheeze, wheezing

gepikeerd [ɣəpikeˑrt] *adj* piqued, nettled: *gauw ~ zijn* be touchy

gepingel [χəpɪˑŋəl] *het* haggling, bargaining

geplaatst [ɣəplaˑtst] *adj* qualified, qualifying

geplaveid [ɣəplaveˑit] *adj* paved

gepraat [ɣəprɑˑt] *het* talk, gossip, chat, (tittle-)tattle: *hun huwelijk leidde tot veel ~* their marriage caused a lot of talk

geprefabriceerd [ɣəprefabrise̯rt] *adj* prefabricated, prefab

geprikkeld [ɣəprɪˑkəlt] *adj* irritated, irritable: *gauw ~ zijn* be huffish (or: huffy)

gepromoveerd [ɣəpromove̯rt] *adj* promoted

geraakt [ɣərɑˑkt] *adj* **1** offended, hurt; **2** moved, touched

geraamte [ɣərɑˑmtə] *het (~n, ~s)* **1** skeleton: *(fig) een wandelend* (or: *levend) ~* a walking (or: living) skeleton; **2** *(fig)* frame(work)

geraas [ɣərɑˑs] *het* din, roar(ing), noise

geradbraakt [ɣərɑˑdbrakt] *adj* shattered, exhausted, *(Am)* bushed

geraden [ɣərɑˑdə(n)] *adj, adv* advisable, expedient || *dat is je ~ ook!* you'd better!

geraffineerd [ɣərɑfineˑrt] *adj, adv* **1** refined; **2** refined, subtle: *een ~ plan* an ingenious plan; **3** crafty, clever

geraken [ɣərɑˑkə(n)] *vb (Belg) see* raken

gerammel [ɣərɑ̆məl] *de* rattle, rattling, clank(ing) jingling, clatter(ing)

geranium [ɣəra̅nijʏm] *de (~s)* geranium

geraspt [ɣərɑ̆spt] *adj* grated

¹gerecht [ɣərɛχt] *het (~en)* dish; course: *als volgende ~ hebben we ...* the next course is ...

²gerecht [ɣərɛχt] *het (~en)* court (of justice), court of law, law court, tribunal: *voor het ~ gedaagd worden* be summoned (to appear in court); *voor het ~ verschijnen* appear in court

¹gerechtelijk [ɣərɛχtələk] *adj* **1** judicial, legal, court: *(Belg) ~e politie* criminal investigation department; *~e stappen ondernemen* take legal action (*or:* proceedings); **2** forensic, legal: *~e geneeskunde* forensic medicine

²gerechtelijk [ɣərɛχtələk] *adv* legally, judicially: *iem ~ vervolgen* take (*or:* institute) (legal) proceedings against s.o., prosecute s.o.

gerechtigd [ɣərɛχtəχt] *adj* authorized, qualified, entitled: *hij is ~ dat te doen* he is authorized to do that

gerechtigheid [ɣərɛχtəχhɛit] *de (-heden)* justice

gerechtsgebouw [ɣərɛχtsχəbɑu] *het (~en)* court(house)

gerechtshof [ɣərɛχtshɔf] *het (-hoven)* court (of justice)

gerechtvaardigd [ɣərɛχtfɑ̅rdəχt] *adj, adv* justified, warranted: *~e eisen* just (*or:* legitimate) claims

gereed [ɣərɛt] *adj* (all) ready, finished

gereedheid [ɣərɛthɛit] *de* readiness: *alles in ~ brengen (maken)* get everything ready (*or:* in readiness)

gereedhouden [ɣərɛthɑudə(n)] *vb* have ready, have in readiness: *plaatsbewijzen ~, s.v.p.* (have your) tickets (ready,) please!

gereedmaken [ɣərɛtmakə(n)] *vb* make ready, get ready, prepare

gereedschap [ɣərɛtsχɑp] *het (~pen)* tools, equipment, apparatus, utensils: *een stuk ~* a tool, a piece of equipment

gereedschapskist [ɣərɛtsχɑpskɪst] *de (~en)* toolbox

gereedstaan [ɣərɛtstan] *vb* be ready, stand ready, be waiting, *(pers also)* stand by

gereformeerd [ɣərefɔrmɛrt] *adj* (Dutch) Reformed

geregeld [ɣərɛɣəlt] *adj* **1** regular, steady: *hij komt ~ te laat* he is often (*or:* nearly always) late; **2** orderly, well-ordered: *een ~ leven gaan leiden* settle down, start keeping regular hours

gerei [ɣərɛi] *het* gear, things, tackle, kit: *keukengerei* kitchen utensils; *scheergerei* shaving things (*or:* kit); *schrijfgerei* writing materials

geremd [ɣərɛmt] *adj, adv* inhibited

gerenommeerd [ɣərenɔmɛrt] *adj* renowned, illustrious, well-established: *een ~ hotel* a reputable hotel

gereserveerd [ɣərezɛrvɛrt] *adj, adv* **1** reserved,

distant: *een ~ houding aannemen* keep one's distance; **2** reserved, booked

gerespecteerd [ɣərɛspɛktɛrt] *adj* respected

geribbeld [χərɪbəlt] *adj see* geribd

geribd [ɣərɪpt] *adj* ribbed; corded; corrugated: *~ katoen* corduroy

gericht [ɣərɪχt] *adj, adv* directed (at, towards), aimed (at, towards), *(fig)* specific: *~e vragen* carefully chosen (*or:* selected) questions

gerief [ɣərif] *het (Belg)* accessories: *school~* school needs

gerieflijk [ɣəriflək] *adj, adv* comfortable

gerimpeld [ɣərɪmpəlt] *adj* wrinkled, wrinkly, shrivelled: *een ~ voorhoofd* a furrowed brow

gering [ɣərɪŋ] *adj* **1** small, little: *een ~e kans* a slim (*or:* remote) chance; *in ~e mate* to a small extent (*or:* degree); **2** petty, slight, minor: *een ~ bedrag* a petty (*or:* trifling) sum

geritsel [ɣərɪtsəl] *het* rustling, rustle

Germanen [ɣɛrma̅nə(n)] *de* Germans, Teutons

¹Germaans [ɣɛrma̅ns] *het* Germanic

²Germaans [ɣɛrma̅ns] *adj* Germanic, Teutonic

geroddel [ɣərɔdəl] *het* gossip(ing), tittle-tattle

geroep [ɣərup] *het* calling, shouting, crying, call(s), shout(s), cries, cry: *hij hoorde hun ~ niet* he did not hear them calling

geroepen [ɣərupə(n)] *adj* called: *je komt als ~* you're just the person we need

geroezemoes [ɣəruzəmus] *het* buzz(ing), hum: *met al dat ~ kan ik jullie niet verstaan* I can't make out what you're saying with all the din

gerommel [ɣərɔməl] *het* **1** rumbling, rumble: *~ in de buik* rumbling in one's stomach; **2** rummaging (about, around); **3** messing, fiddling about

geronk [ɣərɔŋk] *het* drone, droning, roar(ing); snoring

geronnen [ɣərɔnə(n)] *adj* clotted

gerookt [ɣərokt] *adj* smoked

geroutineerd [ɣərutinɛrt] *adj, adv* experienced, practised

gerst [ɣɛrst] *de* barley

gerucht [ɣərʏχt] *het (~en)* rumour: *het ~ gaat dat ...* there is a rumour that ...; *dat zijn maar ~en* it is only hearsay

geruchtmakend [ɣərʏχtma̅kənt] *adj* controversial, sensational

geruim [ɣərœym] *adj* considerable

geruisloos [ɣərœyslos] *adj, adv* noiseless, silent, *(fig)* quietly

geruit [ɣərœyt] *adj* check(ed)

¹gerust [ɣərʏst] *adj* easy, at ease: *een ~ geweten (or: gemoed)* an easy (*or:* a clear) conscience, an easy mind; *met een ~ hart de toekomst tegemoet zien* face the future with confidence; *(Belg) iem ~ laten* leave s.o. alone, let s.o. be

²gerust [ɣərʏst] *adv* safely, with confidence, without any fear (*or:* problem): *ga ~ je gang (do)* go ahead!, feel free to ...; *vraag ~ om hulp* don't hesitate to ask for help

geruststellen [ɣərʏstɛlə(n)] *vb* reassure, put (*or:* set) (s.o.'s) mind at rest

geruststellend [ɣərʏstɛlənt] *adj* reassuring

geruststelling [ɣərʏstɛlɪŋ] *de (~en)* reassurance, comfort, relief

geruzie [ɣərʏzi] *het* arguing, quarrelling, bickering

gescheiden [ɣəsχɛidə(n)] *adj* **1** separated, apart: ~ *leven (van)* live apart (from); **2** divorced: ~ *gezin* broken home

geschenk [ɣəsχɛŋk] *het (~en)* present, gift

geschieden [ɣəsχidə(n)] *vb* occur, take place, happen

geschiedenis [ɣəsχidənɪs] *de (~sen)* **1** history: *de* ~ *herhaalt zich* history repeats itself; **2** tale, story: *dat is een andere* ~ that's another story

geschift [ɣəsχɪft] *adj* **1** crazy, nuts; **2** curdled

geschikt [ɣəsχɪkt] *adj, adv* suitable, fit, appropriate: *is twee uur een* ~*e tijd?* will two o'clock be convenient?; ~ *zijn voor het doel* serve the purpose; *dat boek is niet* ~ *voor kinderen* that book is not suitable for children

geschil [ɣəsχɪl] *het (~len)* dispute, disagreement, quarrel: *een* ~ *bijleggen* settle a dispute (with s.o.)

geschonden [ɣəsχɔndə(n)] *adj* damaged, disfigured

geschoold [ɣəsχolt] *adj* trained, skilled

geschut [ɣəsχʏt] *het* artillery

geselen [ɣesələ(n)] *vb* whip, flog

gesis [χəsɪs] *het* hiss(ing); fizz(le), sizzle

geslaagd [ɣəslaχt] *adj* successful

geslacht [ɣəslaχt] *het (~en)* **1** family, line, house: *uit een nobel* (or: *vorstelijk*) ~ *stammen* be of noble (*or:* royal) descent; **2** sex; **3** generation

geslachtsdaad [ɣəslaχtsdat] *de* sex(ual) act, *(med)* coitus

geslachtsdelen [ɣəslaχtsdelə(n)] *de* genitals, sex organs, genital organs, private parts

geslachtsgemeenschap [ɣəslaχtsχəmensχap] *de* sexual intercourse (*or:* relations), sex

geslachtsnaam [ɣəslaχtsnam] *de (-namen)* family name, surname

geslachtsziekte [ɣəslaχtsiktə] *de (~n, ~s)* venereal disease, V.D.

geslepen [ɣəslepə(n)] *adj, adv* sly, cunning, sharp

gesloten [ɣəslotə(n)] *adj* **1** closed, shut, drawn: *een* ~ *geldkist* (or: *enveloppe, goederenwagon*) a sealed chest (*or:* envelope, goods wagon); *een hoog* ~ *bloes* a high-necked blouse; **2** close(-mouthed), tight-lipped: *dat kind is nogal* ~ that child doesn't say much (for himself, herself); *een* ~ *circuit* a closed circuit

gesmeerd [ɣəsmert] *adj, adv* **1** greased, buttered; **2** smoothly: *ervoor zorgen dat het* ~ *gaat* make sure everything goes smoothly

gesmoord [ɣəsmort] *adj* **1** stifled, smothered; **2** *(culinary)* braised

gesp [ɣɛsp] *de (~en)* buckle, clasp

gespannen [ɣəspɑnə(n)] *adj, adv* **1** tense(d), taut, bent; **2** tense, strained, *(pers also)* nervous, on edge:

te hoog ~ *verwachtingen* exaggerated expectations; ~ *luisteren* listen intently; *tot het uiterste* ~ at full strain

gespecialiseerd [ɣəspeʃalizert] *adj* specialized; specializing

gespen [ɣɛspə(n)] *vb* buckle, strap

gespierd [ɣəspirt] *adj* muscular, brawny, beefy

gespikkeld [ɣəspɪkəlt] *adj* spotted, speckled, dotted

gespitst [ɣəspɪtst] *adj* keen ‖ *met* ~*e oren* with one's ears pricked up, all ears

gespleten [ɣəspletə(n)] *adj* split, cleft, cloven

gesprek [ɣəsprɛk] *het (~ken)* **1** talk, conversation, call: *het* ~ *van de dag zijn* be the talk of the town; *het* ~ *op iets anders brengen* change the subject; *een* ~ *voeren* hold a conversation; *(het nummer is) in* ~ (the number's) engaged; *een* ~ *onder vier ogen* a private discussion; **2** discussion, consultation: *inleidende* ~*ken* introductory talks

gesprekkosten [ɣəsprɛkɔstə(n)] *de* call charge(s)

gespreksstof [ɣəsprɛkstɔf] *de* topic(s) of conversation, subject(s) for discussion

gesproken [ɣəsprokə(n)] *adj* oral, verbal, spoken

gespuis [ɣəspœys] *het* riff-raff, rabble, scum

gestalte [ɣəstɑltə] *de (~n, ~s)* **1** figure, build: *fors van* ~ heavily-built; *een slanke* ~ a slim figure; **2** shape, form: ~ *geven (aan)* give shape (to)

gestampt [χəstɑmt] *adj* crushed, mashed: *gestampte muisjes* aniseed (sugar) crumble

gesteente [ɣəstentə] *het (~n, ~s)* rock, stone

gestel [ɣəstɛl] *het (~len)* **1** constitution; **2** system: *het zenuwgestel* the nervous system

gesteld [ɣəstɛlt] *adj* **1** keen (on), fond (of): *zij zijn erop* ~ *(dat)* they would like it (if), they are set on (…-ing); *erg op comfort* ~ *zijn* like one's comfort; **2** appointed: *binnen de* ~*e tijd* within the time specified

gesteldheid [ɣəstɛlthɛit] *de* state, condition, constitution

gesteriliseerd [ɣəsterilizert] *adj* sterilized

gesticht [ɣəstɪχt] *het (~en)* mental home (*or:* institution)

gesticuleren [ɣɛstikylerə(n)] *vb* gesticulate

gestippeld [ɣəstɪpəlt] *adj* **1** dotted: *een* ~*e lijn* a dotted line; **2** spotted, speckled, dotted

gestoffeerd [ɣəstɔfert] *adj* **1** upholstered; **2** (fitted) with curtains and carpets

gestoomd [ɣəstomt] *adj* steamed

gestoord [ɣəstort] *adj* disturbed: *(fig) ergens* ~ *van worden* be sick to one's back teeth of sth

gestotter [χəstɔtər] *het* stammer(ing), stutter(ing)

gestreept [ɣəstrept] *adj* striped

gestrekt [ɣəstrɛkt] *adj* (out)stretched

gestrest [χəstrɛst] *adj* stressed

getal [ɣətɑl] *het (~len)* number, figure: *een rond* ~ a round number (*or:* figure); *een* ~ *van drie cijfers* a three-digit (*or:* three-figure) number

getalenteerd [ɣətalɛntert] *adj* talented

getand [ɣətɑnt] *adj (bot)* dentate, denticulate

getekend [ɣət.ekənt] *adj* **1** marked, branded: *een fraai ~e kat* a cat with beautiful markings; *voor het leven ~ zijn* be marked for life; **2** lined

getemperd [χətɛmpərt] *adj* moderate, subdued *(light)*

getij [ɣətɛi] *het (~en)* tide

getik [χətɪk] *het* tick(ing); tapping

getikt [ɣətɪkt] *adj* **1** crazy, cracked, nuts: *hij is compleet ~* he's completely off his rocker; **2** typed

getint [ɣətɪnt] *adj* tinted, dark

getiteld [ɣətitəlt] *adj* entitled

getob [χətɔp] *het* worry(ing), brooding

getralied [ɣətralit] *adj* latticed, grated, barred

getroffen [ɣətrɔfə(n)] *adj* **1** hit, struck; **2** stricken, afflicted: *de ~ ouders* the stricken parents, the bereaved parents

getrouw [ɣətrɑu] *adj* faithful, true: *een ~e vertaling* (or: *weergave)* a faithful translation (or: representation)

getrouwd [ɣətrɑut] *adj* married, wed(ded): *hij is ~ met zijn werk* he is married to his work

getto [ɡɛto] *het (~'s)* ghetto

getuige [ɣətœyɣə] *de (~n)* witness

getuige-deskundige [ɣətœyɣədɛskʏndəɣə] *de (~n)* expert witness

¹getuigen [ɣətœyɣə(n)] *vb* **1** give evidence (or: testimony), testify (to); **2** speak: *alles getuigt voor* (or: *tegen)* haar everything speaks in her favour (or: against her); **3** be evidence (or: a sign) (of), show, indicate: *die daad getuigt van moed* that act shows courage

²getuigen [ɣətœyɣə(n)] *vb* testify (to), bear witness (to)

getuigenverklaring [ɣətœyɣə(n)vərklarɪŋ] *de (~en)* testimony, deposition

getuigschrift [ɣətœyχsχrɪft] *het (~en)* certificate, report, reference

geul [ɣøl] *de (~en)* **1** channel; **2** trench, ditch, gully

geur [ɣør] *de (~en)* smell, perfume, scent, aroma: *een onaangename ~ verspreiden (afgeven)* give off an unpleasant smell

geuren [ɣørə(n)] *vb* **1** smell; **2** show off, flaunt

geurig [ɣørəχ] *adj* fragrant, sweet-smelling

gevaar [ɣəvar] *het (gevaren)* danger, risk: *hij is een ~ op de weg* he's a menace on the roads; *~ bespeuren* (or: *ruiken)* sense (or: scent) danger; *~ voor brand* fire hazard; *het is niet zonder ~* it is not without its dangers; *er bestaat (het) ~ dat* there is a risk that; *iem (iets) in ~ brengen* endanger s.o. (sth)

gevaarlijk [ɣəvarlək] *adj* dangerous, hazardous, risky: *zich op ~ terrein begeven* tread on thin ice

gevaarte [ɣəvartə] *het (~n, ~s)* monster, colossus

geval [ɣəvɑl] *het (~len)* **1** case, affair: *een lastig ~* an awkward case; **2** circumstances, position: *in uw ~ zou ik het nooit doen* in your position I'd never do that; **3** case, circumstances: *in het uiterste ~* at worst, if the worst comes to the worst; *in ~ van oorlog* (or: *brand, ziekte)* in the event of war (or: fire, illness); *in negen van de tien ~len* nine times out of

ten; *in enkele ~len* in some cases; *voor het ~ dat* (just) in case; **4** chance, luck: *wat wil nou het ~?* guess what

gevallen [χəvɑlə(n)] *adj* fallen: *de ~en* the dead

gevangen [ɣəvɑŋə(n)] *adj* caught, captive, imprisoned

gevangene [ɣəvɑŋənə] *de (~n)* **1** prisoner, arrested person, captive; **2** prisoner, convict

gevangenis [ɣəvɑŋənɪs] *de (~sen)* prison, jail: *hij heeft tien jaar in de ~ gezeten* he has served ten years in prison (or: jail)

gevangenisstraf [ɣəvɑŋənɪstrɑf] *de (~fen)* imprisonment, prison sentence, jail sentence, prison term: *tot één jaar ~ veroordeeld worden* be sentenced to one year's imprisonment; *levenslange ~* life imprisonment

gevangennemen [ɣəvɑŋənemə(n)] *vb* arrest, capture, take prisoner (or: captive)

gevangenschap [ɣəvɑŋə(n)sχɑp] *de* captivity, imprisonment

gevarendriehoek [ɣəvarə(n)drihuk] *de (~en)* warning triangle, emergency triangle, (Am; roughly) flares

gevarieerd [ɣəvarijert] *adj* varied

gevat [ɣəvɑt] *adj, adv* quick(-witted), sharp; quick, ready: *een ~ antwoord* a ready (or: quick) retort

gevecht [ɣəvɛχt] *het (~en)* **1** (mil) fight(ing), combat: *een ~ van man tegen man* hand-to-hand combat; **2** fight, struggle: *een ~ op leven en dood* a life-or-death struggle

geveinsd [ɣəvɛinst] *adj* pretended, feigned

gevel [ɣevəl] *de (~s)* façade, (house)front; outside wall, outer wall

¹geven [ɣevə(n)] *vb* give, donate, hand: *geschiedenis ~* teach history; *geef mij maar een glaasje wijn* I'll have a glass of wine; *kunt u me de secretaresse even ~?* can I please speak to the secretary?; *kun je me het zout ~?* could you give (or: pass, hand) me the salt?; *(cards) wie moet er ~?* whose deal is it?; *geef op!* (come on,) hand it over!

²geven [ɣevə(n)] *vb* **1** be fond of: *niets (geen cent) om iem ~* not care a thing about s.o.; **2** matter: *dat geeft niks* it doesn't matter a bit (or: at all)

gevestigd [ɣəvɛstəχt] *adj* old-established, long-standing: *de ~e orde* the established order

gevierd [ɣəvirt] *adj* celebrated

gevlekt [ɣəvlɛkt] *adj* spotted, specked, stained, mottled

gevlogen [χəvloχə(n)] *adj* flown, gone

gevoel [ɣəvul] *het (~ens)* **1** touch, feel(ing): *op het ~ af* by feel (or: touch); **2** feeling, sensation: *een brandend ~ in de maag* a burning sensation in one's stomach; *ik vind het wel een lekker ~* I like the feeling; *ik heb geen ~ meer in mijn vinger* my finger's gone numb, I've got no feeling left in my finger; **3** feeling, sense: *het ~ hebben dat …* have a feeling that …, feel that …; **4** feeling(s), emotion(s): *op zijn ~ afgaan* play it by ear; **5** sense (of), feeling (for): *geen ~ voor humor hebben* have no sense of humour

gevoelen [ɣəvulə(n)] *het (~s)* **1** feeling, emotion: *zijn ~s tonen* show one's feelings; **2** feeling, sentiment: *~s van spijt* feelings of regret; **3** feeling, opinion

gevoelig [ɣəvuləχ] *adj* **1** sensitive (to), sore, tender, allergic (to); **2** sensitive (to), susceptible (to), touchy: *een ~ mens* a sensitive person; **3** tender, sore: *een ~e klap* a painful (*or:* nasty) blow

gevoeligheid [χəvuləχhɛit] *de (-heden)* sensitivity (to), susceptibility (to)

gevoelloos [ɣəvulos] *adj* **1** numb; **2** insensitive (to), unfeeling: *een ~ mens* an unfeeling person

gevoelloosheid [χəvuloshɛit] *de* numbness; insensitivity, callousness

gevoelsmatig [ɣəvulsmatəχ] *adj, adv* instinctive

gevogelte [ɣəvoɣəltə] *het* poultry, fowl

gevolg [ɣəvɔlχ] *het (~en)* consequence, result, effect, outcome, success: *met goed ~ examen doen* pass an exam; *~ geven* (*or:* gevend) *aan een opdracht* carry out (*or:* according to) instructions; *(geen) nadelige ~en hebben* have (no) adverse effects; *met alle ~en van dien* with all its consequences; *tot ~ hebben* result in

gevolmachtigd [ɣəvɔlmaχtəχt] *adj* authorized, having (full) power of attorney

gevorderd [ɣəvɔrdərt] *adj* advanced

gevormd [χəvɔrmt] *adj* **1** -formed, (-)shaped: *een stel fraai ~e benen* a pair of shapely legs; *een goed ~e neus* a regular nose; **2** fully formed: *een ~ karakter* a fully developed character

gevraagd [χəvraχt] *adj* in demand: *een ~ boek* a book that is much (*or:* greatly) in demand

gevreesd [ɣəvrest] *adj* dreaded

gevuld [ɣəvʏlt] *adj* **1** full, plump: *een ~ figuur* a full figure; **2** stuffed, filled: *een ~e kies* a filled tooth; *~e tomaten* stuffed tomatoes

gewaad [ɣəwat] *het (gewaden)* garment, attire, robe, gown

gewaagd [ɣəwaχt] *adj* **1** hazardous, risky: *een ~e sprong* a daring leap; **2** daring, suggestive

gewaarwording [ɣəwarwɔrdɪŋ] *de (~en)* perception; sensation

gewapend [ɣəwapənt] *adj* armed; reinforced: *~ beton* reinforced concrete

gewas [ɣəwɑs] *het (~sen)* plant

gewatteerd [ɣəwɑtert] *adj* quilted: *een ~e deken* a quilt, a duvet

geweer [ɣəwer] *het (geweren)* rifle, gun: *een ~ aanleggen* aim a rifle (*or:* gun)

gewei [ɣəwɛi] *het (~en)* antlers

geweld [ɣəwɛlt] *het* violence, force, strength: *grof ~* brute force (*or:* strength); *verbaal ~* verbal violence (*or:* assault); *de waarheid ~ aandoen* stretch the truth; *hij wilde met alle ~ naar huis* he wanted to go home at all costs

gewelddadig [ɣəwɛldadəχ] *adj, adv* violent, forcible

geweldig [ɣəwɛldəχ] *adj, adv* **1** tremendous, enor-

gewonde

mous: *een ~ bedrag* a huge sum; *een ~e eetlust* an enormous appetite; *zich ~ inspannen* go to great lengths; **2** terrific, fantastic, wonderful: *je hebt me ~ geholpen* you've been a great help; *hij is ~* he's a great guy; *die jurk staat haar ~* that dress looks smashing on her; *hij zingt ~* he sings wonderfully; *~!* great!, terrific!; **3** tremendous, terrible

gewelf [ɣəwɛlf] *het (gewelven)* **1** vault(ing), arch; **2** vault

gewend [ɣəwɛnt] *adj* used (to), accustomed (to), in the habit (of), inured (to): *~ raken aan zijn nieuwe huis* settle down in one's new house; *dat zijn we niet van hem ~* that's not like him at all, that's quite unlike him!

gewenst [ɣəwɛnst] *adj* desired, wished for

gewerveld [ɣəwɛrvəlt] *adj* vertebrate

gewest [ɣəwɛst] *het (~en)* **1** district, region; **2** province, county, *(Belg)* region: *overzeese ~en* overseas territories

gewestelijk [ɣəwɛstələk] *adj, adv* regional, provincial

geweten [ɣəwetə(n)] *het* conscience: *veel op zijn ~ hebben* have a lot to answer for

gewetenloos [ɣəwetənlos] *adj, adv* unscrupulous, unprincipled

gewetensvol [ɣəwetənsfɔl] *adj, adv* conscientious, scrupulous, painstaking

gewettigd [ɣəwɛtəχt] *adj* **1** legitimate, justified, well-founded; **2** legitimated

gewezen [ɣəwezə(n)] *adj* former, ex-

gewicht [ɣəwɪχt] *het (~en)* weight, importance: *maten en ~en* weights and measures; *zaken van het grootste ~* matters of the utmost importance; *soortelijk ~* specific gravity; *op zijn ~ letten* watch one's weight; *beneden het ~* underweight

gewichtheffen [ɣəwɪχthɛfə(n)] *vb* weightlifting

¹gewichtig [ɣəwɪχtəχ] *adj* weighty, important, grave: *~e gebeurtenissen* important events; *hij zette een ~ gezicht* he put on a grave face

²gewichtig [ɣəwɪχtəχ] *adv* (self-)importantly, pompously: *~ doen* be important (about sth)

gewichtsklasse [ɣəwɪχtsklɑsə] *de (~n)* weight

gewiekst [ɣəwikst] *adj* sharp, shrewd; fly

gewijd [ɣəwɛit] *adj* **1** consecrated, holy: *~ water* holy water; **2** ordained

gewild [ɣəwɪlt] *adj* sought-after, popular, in demand

¹gewillig [ɣəwɪləχ] *adj* **1** willing, docile, obedient: *zich ~ tonen* show (one's) willingness; **2** willing, ready: *een ~ oor lenen aan iem* lend a ready ear to s.o.

²gewillig [ɣəwɪləχ] *adv* willingly, readily, voluntarily: *hij ging ~ mee* he came along willingly

gewoel [ɣəwul] *het* **1** tossing (and turning), struggling; **2** bustle

gewond [ɣəwɔnt] *adj* injured, wounded, hurt: *~ aan het been* injured (*or:* wounded) in the leg

gewonde [ɣəwɔndə] *de* injured person, wounded person, casualty

gewonnen [ɣəwɔnə(n)] *adj* || *zich ~ geven* admit defeat

¹gewoon [ɣəwo̯on] *adj* **1** usual, regular, customary, ordinary: *in zijn gewone doen zijn* be oneself; *zijn gewone gang gaan* go about one's business, carry on as usual; **2** common: *dat is ~* that's natural; **3** ordinary, common(place), plain: *het gewone leven* everyday life; *de gewone man* the common man; *de gewoonste zaak ter wereld* (something) perfectly normal

²gewoon [ɣəwo̯on] *adv* **1** normally: *doe maar ~* (do) act normal(ly), behave yourself; **2** normally, ordinarily, usually; **3** simply, just: *zij praatte er heel ~ over* she was very casual about it

gewoonlijk [ɣəwo̯onlək] *adv* usually, normally: *zoals ~ kwam ze te laat* as usual, she was late

gewoonte [ɣəwo̯ontə] *de (~n, ~s)* **1** custom, practice; **2** habit, custom: *de macht der ~* the force of habit; *tegen zijn ~* contrary to his usual practice; *hij heeft de ~ om* he has a habit (*or:* way) of

gewoonweg [ɣəwo̯onwɛɣ] *adv* simply, just

gewricht [ɣəvrɪɣt] *het (~en)* joint, articulation

gezaagd [ɣəzaɣt] *adj (bot)* serrate

gezag [ɣəzɑɣ] *het* **1** authority, power, *(mil)* command, rule, dominion: *ouderlijk ~* parental authority; **2** authority, authorities: *het bevoegd ~* the competent authorities; **3** authority, weight: *op ~ van* on the authority of

gezaghebbend [ɣəzɑɣhɛbənt] *adj, adv* authoritative, influential: *iets vernemen uit ~e bron* have sth on good authority

gezaghebber [ɣəzɑɣhɛbər] *de (~s)* person in charge (*or:* authority), authorities

gezagvoerder [ɣəzɑɣfurdər] *de (~s)* captain, skipper

¹gezamenlijk [ɣəzamə(n)lək] *adj* collective, combined, united, joint: *met ~e krachten* with united forces

²gezamenlijk [ɣəzamə(n)lək] *adv* together

gezang [ɣəzɑŋ] *het (~en)* song, singing

gezant [ɣəzɑnt] *de (~en)* envoy, ambassador, representative, delegate

gezapig [ɣəzapəɣ] *adj* lethargic, indolent, complacent

gezegde [ɣəzɛɣdə] *het (~n, ~s)* **1** saying, proverb; **2** *(linguistics)* predicate: *naamwoordelijk ~* nominal predicate

gezegend [ɣəzeɣənt] *adj, adv* blessed, fortunately, luckily

gezellig [ɣəzɛləɣ] *adj, adv* **1** enjoyable, pleasant, sociable, companionable: *het zijn ~e mensen* they are good company (*or:* very sociable); **2** pleasant, comfortable, cosy: *een ~ hoekje* a snug (*or:* cosy) corner

gezelligheid [ɣəzɛləɣhɛit] *de* **1** sociability: *hij houdt van ~* he is fond of company; **2** cosiness, snugness

gezelschap [ɣəzɛlsɣɑp] *het (~pen)* **1** company, companionship: *iem ~ houden* keep s.o. company;

2 company, society; **3** company, party: *zich bij het ~ voegen* join the party

gezelschapsspel [ɣəzɛlsɣɑpspɛl] *het (~en)* party game

gezet [ɣəzɛt] *adj* **1** set, regular; **2** stout, thickset

gezeur [ɣəzø̯r] *het* moaning, nagging, fuss(ing): *hou nu eens op met dat eeuwige ~!* for goodness' sake stop that perpetual moaning!

gezicht [ɣəzɪɣt] *het (~en)* **1** sight: *liefde op het eerste ~* love at first sight; *een vreselijk ~* a gruesome sight; **2** face: *iem in zijn ~ uitlachen* laugh in s.o.'s face; *iem van ~ kennen* know s.o. by sight; **3** face, expression, look(s): *een ~ zetten alsof* look as if; *ik zag aan zijn ~ dat* I could tell by the look on his face that; **4** view, sight: *aan het ~ onttrekken* conceal

gezichtsbedrog [ɣəzɪɣtsbədrɔɣ] *het* optical illusion

gezichtspunt [ɣəzɪɣtspʏnt] *het (~en)* point of view, angle || *een heel nieuw ~* an entirely fresh perspective (*or:* viewpoint, angle)

gezichtsveld [ɣəzɪɣtsfɛlt] *het (~en)* field (*or:* range) of vision, sight

gezichtsverlies [ɣəzɪɣtsfərlis] *het* loss of face

gezichtsvermogen [ɣəzɪɣtsfərmoɣə(n)] *het* (eye)sight

gezien [ɣəzin] *adj* **1** esteemed, respected, popular: *een ~ man* an esteemed man, a respected man; **2** seen (by me), endorsed: *het voor ~ houden* pack it in

gezin [ɣəzɪn] *het (~nen)* family

gezind [ɣəzɪnt] *adj* (pre)disposed (to), inclined (to): *iem vijandig ~ zijn* be hostile toward s.o.

gezinsbijslag [ɣəzɪnzbɛislɑɣ] *de (Belg)* child benefit (*or:* allowance)

gezinshulp [ɣəzɪnshʏlp] *de (~en)* home help

gezinsverpakking [ɣəzɪnsfərpɑkɪŋ] *de (~en)* family(-size(d)) pack(age), king-size(d) pack(age), jumbo pack(age)

gezinsverzorgster [ɣəzɪnsfərzɔrɣstər] *de (~s)* home help

gezinszorg [ɣəzɪnsɔrɣ] *de (~en)* home help

gezocht [ɣəzɔɣt] *adj* strained, contrived, forced, far-fetched

¹gezond [ɣəzɔnt] *adj, adv* **1** healthy, sound, well *(after vb):* zo ~ als een vis* as fit as a fiddle; **2** sound, good: *~ verstand* common sense

²gezond [ɣəzɔnt] *adj* **1** able-bodied, fit: *~ en wel* safe and sound; **2** robust: *~e wangen* rosy cheeks

gezondheid [ɣəzɔnthɛit] *de* health: *naar iemands ~ vragen* inquire after s.o.('s health); *op uw ~!* here's to you!, here's to your health!, cheers!; *zijn ~ gaat achteruit* his health is failing; *~!* (God) bless you!

gezondheidsdienst [χəzɔnthɛitsdinst] *de (~en)* (public) health service

gezondheidstoestand [ɣəzɔnthɛitstustɑnt] *de* health, state of health

gezondheidszorg [ɣəzɔnthɛitsɔrɣ] *de* **1** health care, medical care; **2** health service(s)

gezouten [ɣəzɑutə(n)] *adj* salt(ed), salty

gezusters [ɣəzʏstərs] *de* sisters

gezwam [ɣəzwɑm] *het* drivel, piffle: ~ *in de ruimte* hot air

gezwel [ɣəzwɛl] *het (~len)* swelling; growth, tumour: *een goedaardig* (or: *kwaadaardig*) ~ a benign (or: malignant) tumour

gezwets [ɣəzwɛts] *het* drivel, rubbish

gezwollen [ɣəzwɔlə(n)] *adj* swollen

gezworen [ɣəzwɔrə(n)] *adj* sworn

gft-afval [ɣeeftɡɑfɑl] *het (roughly)* organic waste

gids [ɣɪts] *de (~en)* **1** guide; mentor: *iemands ~ zijn* be s.o.'s guide (or: mentor); **2** guide(book), handbook, manual; **3** (Girl) Guide; (*Am*) Girl Scout; **4** (telephone) directory, telephone book: *de gouden* ~ the yellow pages

giebelen [ɣibələ(n)] *vb* giggle, titter

giechelen [ɣiχələ(n)] *vb* giggle, titter

giek [ɣik] *de (~en)* **1** (*shipp*) boom; **2** jib

¹gier [ɣir] *de (~en)* vulture

²gier [ɣir] *de (~en)* liquid manure, slurry

gieren [ɣirə(n)] *vb* shriek, scream, screech

gierig [ɣirəχ] *adj* miserly, stingy

gierigaard [ɣirəχart] *de (~s)* miser, skinflint

gierigheid [ɣirəχhɛit] *de* miserliness, stinginess

gierst [ɣirst] *de* millet

gieten [ɣitə(n)] *vb* **1** pour; **2** cast; found; mould: *een gegoten kachel* a cast-iron stove; *die kleren zitten* (*hem*) *als gegoten* his clothes fit (him) like a glove; **3** water

gieter [ɣitər] *de (~s)* watering can

gietijzer [ɣitɛizər] *het* cast iron

gif [ɣɪf] *het (~fen)* poison, venom, toxin

gifgas [ɣɪfχɑs] *het (~sen)* poison(ous) gas

gift [ɣɪft] *de (~en)* gift, donation, contribution

giftig [ɣɪftəχ] *adj* **1** poisonous, venomous; **2** venomous, vicious: *toen hij dat hoorde, werd hij ~* when he heard that he was furious

gigabyte [ɣiɣabɑjt] *de (~s)* gigabyte

gigant [ɣiɣɑnt] *de (~en)* giant

gigantisch [ɣiɣɑntis] *adj, adv* gigantic, huge

gigolo [dʒiɣolo] *de (~'s)* gigolo

gij [ɣɛi] *pers pron* thou

gijzelaar [ɣɛizəlar] *de (~s)* hostage

gijzelen [ɣɛizələ(n)] *vb* take hostage, kidnap, hijack

gijzeling [ɣɛizəlɪŋ] *de (~en)* taking of hostages, kidnapping, hijack(ing): *iem in ~ houden* hold s.o. hostage

gil [ɣɪl] *de (~len)* scream, yell, screech, squeal, shriek: *als je me nodig hebt, geef dan even een ~* if you need me just give (me) a shout

gilde [ɣɪldə] *het, de (~n)* guild

gilet [ʒilɛt] *het (~s)* gilet

gillen [ɣɪlə(n)] *vb* **1** scream, screech, squeal, shriek: *het is om te ~* it's a (perfect) scream; ~ *als een mager speenvarken* squeal like a (stuck) pig; **2** scream; screech

ginds [ɣɪns] *adj, adv* over there, up there, down there

gin-tonic [dʒɪntɔnɪk] *de* gin and tonic

gips [ɣɪps] *het* **1** plaster (of Paris): *zijn been zit in het ~* his leg is in plaster; ~ *aanmaken* mix plaster; **2** plaster cast

giraal [ɣiral] *adj* giro

giraffe [ʒirɑf] *de (~n, ~s)* giraffe

gireren [ɣirerə(n)] *vb* pay (or: transfer) by giro

giro [ɣiro] *de* **1** giro; **2** giro account; **3** transfer by bank (or: giro), bank transfer, giro transfer

girobank [ɣirobɑŋk] *de (~en)* transfer bank, clearing bank, Girobank

girobetaalkaart [ɣirobətalkart] *de (~en)* giro cheque

giromaat [ɣiromat] *de (giromaten) (roughly)* cash dispenser, cashpoint, automated teller (machine)

giromaatpas [ɣiromatpɑs] *de (~sen)* cashpoint card

gironummer [ɣironʏmər] *het (~s)* Girobank (account) number

giropas [ɣiropɑs] *de (~sen)* (giro cheque) guarantee card

gissen [ɣɪsə(n)] *vb* guess (at), estimate

gissing [ɣɪsɪŋ] *de (~en)* guess; (*pl also*) guesswork, speculation: *dit zijn allemaal (maar) ~en* this is just (or: mere) guesswork

gist [ɣɪst] *de* yeast

gisten [ɣɪstə(n)] *vb* ferment

gisteren [ɣɪstərə(n)] *adv* yesterday: *de krant van ~* yesterday's paper; ~ *over een week* yesterday week, a week from yesterday

gisternacht [ɣɪstərnɑχt] *adv* last night

gisting [ɣɪstɪŋ] *de (~en)* fermentation, ferment, effervescence

git [ɣɪt] *het, de* jet

gitaar [ɣitar] *de (gitaren)* guitar

gitarist [ɣitarɪst] *de (~en)* guitarist, guitar player

gitzwart [ɣɪtswɑrt] *adj* jet-black

glaasje [χlaʃə] *het (~s)* **1** (small) glass, slide; **2** drop, drink: *(wat) te diep in het ~ gekeken hebben* have had one too many; ~ *op, laat je rijden* don't drink and drive

¹glad [χlɑt] *adj* **1** slippery, icy: *het is ~ op de wegen* the roads are slippery; **2** (*fig*) slippery, slick: *hij heeft een ~de tong* he has a glib tongue; **3** shiny, glossy; polished; **4** smooth, even: *~de banden* bald tyres; *een ~de kin* a clean-shaven chin (or: face)

²glad [χlɑt] *adv* smoothly

gladgeschoren [χlɑtχəsχorə(n)] *adj* clean-shaven

gladheid [χlɑthɛit] *de* slipperiness, iciness: ~ *op de wegen* icy patches on the roads

gladiator [χladijator] *de (~en)* gladiator

gladiool [χladijol] *de (gladiolen)* gladiolus

gladstrijken [χlɑtstrɛikə(n)] *vb* smooth (out, down), iron out: *moeilijkheden ~* iron out difficulties; *zijn veren ~* preen one's feathers

glans [χlɑns] *de (~en, glanzen)* **1** glow; **2** gleam, lustre, gloss; sheen: *P. geeft uw meubelen een fraaie ~* P. gives your furniture a beautiful shine

glansrijk

glansrijk [ɣlɑnsrɛik] *adj, adv* splendid, brilliant, glorious

¹glanzen [ɣlɑnzə(n)] *vb* **1** gleam, shine: *~d papier* glossy (*or:* high-gloss) paper; **2** shine, glow, twinkle: *~d haar* glossy (*or:* sleek) hair

²glanzen [ɣlɑnzə(n)] *vb* polish, glaze, gloss

glas [ɣlɑs] *het (glazen)* glass, (window-)pane: *een ~ bier* a (glass of) beer; *dubbel ~* double glazing; *geslepen ~* cut glass; *laten we het ~ heffen op ...* let's drink to ...; *~ in lood* leaded glass, stained glass

glasbak [ɣlɑzbɑk] *de (~ken)* bottle bank

glasfabriek [ɣlɑsfabrik] *de (~en)* glassworks

glasgordijn [ɣlɑsχɔrdɛin] *het, de (~en)* net curtain, lace curtain

glashandel [χlɑshɑndəl] *de (~s)* glazier's (shop)

glashard [ɣlɑshɑrt] *adj, adv* unfeeling: *hij ontkende ~* he flatly denied

glashelder [ɣlɑshɛldər] *adj, adv* crystal-clear, as clear as a bell

glas-in-loodraam [ɣlɑsɪnlotram] *het (-ramen)* leaded window, stained-glass window

glasplaat [χlɑsplat] *de (-platen)* sheet of glass, glass plate, glass top

glassnijder [ɣlɑsnɛidər] *de (~s)* glass cutter

glasvezel [ɣlɑsfezəl] *de (~s)* glass fibre, fibreglass

glaswerk [ɣlɑswɛrk] *het* glass(ware)

glazen [ɣlazə(n)] *adj* glass

glazenwasser [ɣlazə(n)wɑsər] *de (~s)* window cleaner

glazig [ɣlazəχ] *adj* **1** glassy; **2** waxy

glazuren [ɣlazyrə(n)] *vb* glaze, enamel

glazuur [ɣlazyr] *het* **1** glaze, glazing, enamel; **2** icing

gletsjer [ɡlɛtʃər] *de (~s)* glacier

gleuf [ɣløf] *de (gleuven)* **1** groove, slot, slit; **2** trench, ditch, fissure

glibberen [ɣlɪbərə(n)] *vb* slither, slip, slide

glibberig [ɣlɪbərəχ] *adj* slippery, slithery, slimy, greasy: *(fig) zich op ~ terrein bevinden* have got onto a tricky subject

glijbaan [ɣlɛiban] *de (-banen)* slide, chute

glijden [ɣlɛidə(n)] *vb* **1** slide, glide; **2** slip, slide: *het boek was uit haar handen gegleden* the book had slipped from her hands

glijdend [ɣlɛidənt] *adj* sliding, flexible: *een ~e belastingschaal* a sliding tax scale

glimlach [ɣlɪmlɑχ] *de* smile, grin: *een stralende ~* a radiant smile

glimlachen [ɣlɪmlɑχə(n)] *vb* smile, grin: *blijven ~* keep (on) smiling

glimmen [ɣlɪmə(n)] *vb* **1** glow, shine; **2** shine, gleam: *de tafel glimt als een spiegel* the table is shining like a mirror; **3** shine, glitter: *haar ogen glommen van blijdschap* her eyes shone with pleasure

glimp [ɣlɪmp] *de (~en)* glimpse: *(fig) een ~ van iem opvangen (zien)* catch a glimpse of s.o.

glinsteren [ɣlɪnstərə(n)] *vb* **1** glitter, sparkle, glisten; **2** shine, gleam, sparkle

glippen [ɣlɪpə(n)] *vb* **1** slide: *naar buiten ~* sneak (*or:* steal) out; **2** slip, drop: *hij liet het glas uit de*

handen ~ he let the glass slip from his hands

glitter [ɣlɪtər] *de (~s)* glitter: *een bloes met ~* a sequined blouse

globaal [ɣlobal] *adj, adv* rough, broad

globalisering [ɣlobalizerɪŋ] *de* globalization

globe [ɣlobə] *de (~s)* globe

gloed [ɣlut] *de* **1** glow, blaze: *in ~ zetten* (*or:* staan) set (*or:* be) aglow; **2** glow, glare, blush

gloednieuw [ɣlutniw] *adj* brand new

gloeien [ɣlujə(n)] *vb* **1** glow, shine, burn; **2** smoulder, glow; **3** be red-hot (*or:* white-hot), glow

gloeiend [ɣlujənt] *adj, adv* **1** glowing, red-hot, white-hot; **2** scalding hot, boiling hot, scorching: *het was ~ heet vandaag* today was a scorcher; **3** glowing, fervent: *je bent er ~ bij* you're in for it now, (I) caught you red-handed

gloeilamp [ɣlujlɑmp] *de (~en)* (light) bulb

glooien [ɣlojə(n)] *vb* slope, slant

glooiend [ɣlojənt] *adj* sloping, slanted, rolling

glooiing [ɣlojɪŋ] *de (~en)* slope, slant

gloria [ɣlorija] *de* **1** *(rel)* gloria; **2** glory

glorie [ɣlori] *de (gloriën, ~s)* glory, *(rel)* gloria

glorietijd [ɣloritɛit] *de (~en)* heyday, golden age: *in zijn ~* in his heyday

glucose [ɣlykozə] *de* glucose, grape-sugar

gluiperig [ɣlœypərəχ] *adj, adv* shifty, sneaky

glunderen [ɣlʏndərə(n)] *vb* smile happily

gluren [ɣlyrə(n)] *vb* peep, peek

gluurder [ɣlyrdər] *de (~s)* peeping Tom

glycerine [ɣlisərinə] *de* glycerine

gniffelen [ɣnɪfələ(n)] *vb* snigger, chuckle

gnoe [ɣnu] *de (~s)* gnu

goal [ɡol] *de (~s)* goal: *een ~ maken* score a goal

god [ɣɔt] *de (~en)* god, idol || *een houten ~* a wooden idol (*or:* god)

God [ɣɔt] *de* God: *~s water over ~s akker laten lopen* let things take (*or:* run) their (natural) course; *in ~ geloven* believe in God

goddank [ɣɔdɑŋk] *int* thank God (*or:* goodness)

goddelijk [ɣɔdələk] *adj, adv* divine

godheid [ɣɔthɛit] *de (-heden)* deity, god(head)

godin [ɣodɪn] *de (~nen)* goddess

godlasterend [ɣɔtlɑstərənt] *adj* blasphemous

godloochenaar [ɣɔtloχənar] *de (~s)* atheist

godsdienst [ɣɔtsdinst] *de (~en)* religion

godsdienstig [ɣɔtsdinstəχ] *adj, adv* religious, devout

godsdienstonderwijs [ɣɔtsdinstɔndərwɛis] *het* religious education (*or:* instruction)

godshuis [ɣɔtshœys] *het (-huizen)* house of God, place of worship, church

godslastering [ɣɔtslɑstərɪŋ] *de (~en)* **1** blasphemy; **2** profanity

¹goed [ɣut] *adj, adv* **1** good; well, right, correct: *alle berekeningen zijn ~* all the calculations are correct; *hij bedoelt (meent) het ~* he means well; *begrijp me ~* don't get me wrong; *als je ~ kijkt* if you look closely; *dat zit wel ~* that's all right, don't worry about it; *net ~!* serves you right!; *het is ook nooit ~*

bij hem nothing's ever good enough for him; *precies* ~ just (*or:* exactly) right; **2** well: *hij was* ~ *nijdig* he was really annoyed; *het betaalt* ~ it pays well; *toen ik* ~ *en wel in bed lag* when I finally (*or:* at last) got into bed; ~ *bij zijn* be clever; *we hebben het nog nooit zo* ~ *gehad* we've never had it so good; *(heel)* ~ *Engels spreken* speak English (very) well, speak (very) good English; *die jas staat je* ~ that coat suits you (*or:* looks good on you); *de soep is niet* ~ *meer* the soup has gone off; *dat komt* ~ *uit* that's (very) convenient; *hij maakt het* ~ he is doing well (*or:* all right); *(fig) hij staat er* ~ *voor* his prospects are good; *de rest hou je nog te* ~ I'll owe you the rest; *dat hebben we nog te* ~ that's still in store for us; ~ *zo!* good!, that's right!, well done!, that's the way!; *ook* ~ very well, all right; *de opbrengst komt ten* ~*e van het Rode Kruis* the proceeds go to the Red Cross; *zij is* ~ *in wiskunde* she is good at mathematics; *dat is te veel van het* ~*e* that is too much of a good thing; *het is maar* ~ *dat* … it's a good thing that …; ~ *dat je 't zegt* that reminds me; *dat was maar* ~ *ook* it was just as well; *zo* ~ *als niets* next to nothing, hardly anything

²goed [ɣut] *adj* **1** good, kind, nice: *ik ben wel* ~ *maar niet gek* I'm not as stupid as you think; *ik voel me heel* ~ I feel fine (*or:* great); *zou u zo* ~ *willen zijn* … would (*or:* could) you please …, would you be so kind as to …, do (*or:* would) you mind …; **2** well, fine: *daar word ik niet* ~ *van (also fig)* that makes me (feel) sick; ~ *en kwaad* good and evil, right and wrong

³goed [ɣut] *het (~eren)* **1** goods, ware(s); **2** goods, property, estate: *onroerend* ~ real estate; **3** clothes: *schoon* ~ *aantrekken* put on clean clothes; **4** material, fabric, cloth: *wit (or: bont)* ~ white (*or:* coloured) wash, whites, coloureds

goedaardig [ɣutardəχ] *adj* **1** good-natured, kind-hearted; **2** *(med)* benign

goeddoen [ɣudun] *vb* do good, help

goedemiddag [ɣudəmɪdɑχ] *int* good afternoon

goedemorgen [ɣudəmɔrɣə(n)] *int* good morning

goedenacht [ɣudənɑχt] *int* good night

goedenavond [ɣudə(n)avɔnt] *int* good evening; good night

goederen [ɣudərə(n)] *de* **1** goods, *(economics)* commodities, merchandise: ~ *laden (or: lossen)* load (*or:* unload) goods; **2** goods, property

goederentrein [ɣudərə(n)trɛin] *de (~en)* goods train, *(Am)* freight train

goedgeefs [ɣutχefs] *adj* generous, liberal

goedgelovig [ɣutχəlovəχ] *adj* credulous, gullible

goedgemutst [ɣutχəmʏtst] *adj* good-humoured; good-natured

goedheid [ɣutɦɛit] *de* **1** goodness: *hij is de* ~ *zelf* he is goodness personified; **2** benevolence, indulgence

goedig [ɣudəχ] *adj, adv* gentle, meek

goedje [ɣucə] *het* stuff

goedkeuren [ɣutkørə(n)] *vb* **1** approve (of), pass: *(med) goedgekeurd worden* pass one's medical; **2** approve, adopt

goedkeurend [ɣutkørənt] *adj, adv* approving, favourable: ~ *knikken* (or: *glimlachen*) nod (*or:* smile) (one's) approval

goedkeuring [ɣutkørɪŋ] *de (~en)* approval, consent

¹goedkoop [ɣutkop] *adj* **1** cheap, inexpensive: ~ *tarief* cheap rate, off-peak tariff; **2** *(fig)* cheap

²goedkoop [ɣutkop] *adv* cheaply, at a low price: *er* ~ *afkomen* get off cheap(ly)

goedlachs [ɣutlɑχs] *adj* cheery

goedlopend [ɣutlopənt] *adj* successful

goedmaken [ɣutmakə(n)] *vb* **1** make up (*or:* amends) for: *iets weer* ~ *bij iem* make amends to s.o. for sth; **2** make up for, compensate (for); **3** cover, make good

goedmoedig [ɣutmudəχ] *adj, adv* good-natured; good-humoured

goedpraten [ɣutpratə(n)] *vb* explain away, justify, gloss over

goedschiks [ɣutsχɪks] *adv* willingly: ~ *of kwaadschiks* willing(ly) or unwilling(ly)

¹goedvinden [ɣutfɪndə(n)] *vb* approve (of), consent (to): *als jij het goedvindt* if you agree

²goedvinden [ɣutfɪndə(n)] *het* permission, consent, agreement

goeroe [ɣuru] *de (~s)* guru

goesting [ɣustɪŋ] *de (Belg)* liking, fancy, appetite

gok [ɣɔk] *de* gamble: *zullen we een ~je wagen?* shall we have a go (at it)?

gokhuis [ɣɔkhœys] *het (-huizen)* gambling joint

gokken [ɣɔkə(n)] *vb* gamble, (place a) bet (on): ~ *op een paard* (place a) bet on a horse

gokker [ɣɔkər] *de (~s)* gambler

gokpaleis [ɣɔkpalɛis] *het* casino

gokverslaafde [χɔkfərslavdə] *de (~n)* gambling addict

¹golf [ɣɔlf] *de (golven)* **1** wave: *korte (or: lange)* ~ short (*or:* long) wave; **2** gulf, bay; **3** stream, flood; **4** *(fig)* wave, surge: *een* ~ *van geweld* a wave of violence

²golf [ɡɔlf] *het (golven)* golf

golfbaan [ɡɔlvban] *de (-banen)* golf course (*or:* links)

golfband [ɣɔlvbɑnt] *de (~en)* waveband

golfen [ɡɔlfə(n)] *vb* play golf

golflengte [ɣɔlflɛŋtə] *de (~n, ~s)* wavelength: *(niet) op dezelfde* ~ *zitten (also fig)* (not) be on the same wavelength

golfstok [ɡɔlfstɔk] *de (~ken)* golf club

Golfstroom [ɣɔlfstrom] *de* Gulf Stream

golven [ɣɔlvə(n)] *vb* **1** undulate, wave, heave, surge: *de wind deed het water* ~ the wind ruffled the surface of the water; **2** gush, flow

golvend [ɣɔlvənt] *adj* undulating, wavy ‖ *een* ~ *terrein* rolling terrain

gom [ɣɔm] *het* rubber; *(esp Am)* eraser

gondel [ɣɔndəl] *de (~s)* gondola

gong [ɣɔŋ] *de (~s)* gong

gonorroe [ɣonorø] *de* gonorrhoea
gonzen [ɣɔnzə(n)] *vb* buzz, hum
goochelaar [ɣoːxəlar] *de (~s)* conjurer, magician
goochelen [ɣoːxələ(n)] *vb* **1** conjure, do (conjuring, magic) tricks: ~ *met kaarten* do *(or:* perform) card tricks; **2** juggle (with): ~ *met cijfers* juggle with figures
goocheltruc [ɣoːxəltryk] *de (~s)* conjuring trick, magic trick
goochem [ɣoːxəm] *adj* smart, crafty
gooi [ɣoj] *de (~en)* throw, toss: *(fig) een ~ doen naar het presidentschap* make a bid for the Presidency
gooien [ɣojə(n)] *vb* throw, toss, fling (at), hurl (at): *geld ertegenaan ~* spend a lot of money on (sth); *iem eruit ~* throw s.o. out; *met de deur ~* slam the door
gooi-en-smijtfilm [ɣojɛnsmɛitfɪlm] *de (~s)* slapstick film
goor [ɣor] *adj, adv* **1** filthy, foul; **2** bad, nasty: ~ *smaken (or: ruiken)* taste *(or:* smell) revolting
goot [ɣot] *de (goten)* **1** wastepipe, drain(pipe), gutter; **2** gutter, drain: *(fig) in de ~ terechtkomen* end up in the gutter
gootsteen [ɣotsten] *de (-stenen)* (kitchen) sink: *iets door de ~ spoelen* pour sth down the sink
gordel [ɣɔrdəl] *de (~s)* belt
gordijn [ɣɔrdɛin] *het, de (~en)* curtain
gordijnrail [ɣɔrdɛinrel] *de (~s)* curtain rail *(or:* track)
gorgelen [ɣɔrɣələ(n)] *vb* gargle
gorilla [ɣorɪla] *de (~'s)* gorilla
gort [ɣɔrt] *de* pearl barley; groats
gortig [ɣɔrtəx] *adj* ‖ *dat is (me) al te ~* it's too much (for me), it's more than I can take
gotisch [ɣotis] *adj* Gothic
goud [ɣaut] *het* gold: *zulke kennis is ~ waard* such knowledge is invaluable; *voor geen ~* not for all the tea in China; *ik zou me daar voor geen ~ vertonen* I wouldn't be seen dead there; *het is niet alles ~ wat er blinkt* all that glitters is not gold
goudeerlijk [ɣauterlək] *adj* honest through and through
gouden [ɣaudə(n)] *adj* **1** gold, golden: *een ~ ring* a gold ring; **2** golden
goudmijn [ɣautmɛin] *de (~en)* gold mine: *een ~ ontdekken (fig)* strike oil
goudstuk [ɣautstyk] *het (~ken)* gold coin
goudvis [ɣautfis] *de (~sen)* goldfish
goulash [ɡulaʃ] *de* goulash
gouvernante [ɣuvərnɑntə] *de (~s)* governess, nanny
gouvernement [ɣuvɛrnəmɛnt] *het (~en) (Belg)* provincial government *(or:* administration)
gouverneur [ɣuvərnør] *de (~s)* **1** governor; **2** *(Belg)* provincial governor
graad [ɣrat] *de (graden)* degree, *(mil)* rank: *een academische ~* a university degree; *de vader is eigenwijs, maar de zoon is nog een ~je erger* the father

is conceited, but the son is even worse; *18° Celsius* 18 degrees Celsius; *een draai van 180 graden maken* make a 180-degree turn; *tien graden onder nul* ten degrees below zero
graaf [ɣraf] *de (graven)* count, earl
graafmachine [ɣrafmaʃinə] *de (~s)* excavator
graafschap [ɣrafsxɑp] *het (~pen)* county
graag [ɣrax] *adv* **1** gladly, with pleasure: ~ *gedaan* you're welcome; *ik wil je ~ helpen* I'd be glad to help (you); *hoe ~ ik het ook zou doen* much as I would like to do it; ~ *of niet* take it or leave it; *(heel)* ~*!* (okay) thank you very much!, yes please!; **2** willingly, readily: *zij praat niet ~ over die tijd* she dislikes talking about that time; *dat wil ik ~ geloven* I can quite believe that, I'm not surprised
graaien [ɣrajə(n)] *vb* grabble, rummage
graal [ɣral] *de* the (Holy) Grail
graan [ɣran] *het (granen)* grain; corn ‖ *een ~je meepikken* get one's share, get in on the act
graat [ɣrat] *de (graten)* **1** (fish) bone; **2** bones *(pl)* ‖ *(Belg) ergens geen graten in zien* see nothing wrong with
grabbel [ɣrɑbəl] ‖ *zijn goede naam te ~ gooien* throw away one's reputation
grabbelen [ɣrɑbələ(n)] *vb* rummage (about, around), grope (about, around): *de kinderen ~ naar de pepernoten* the children are scrambling for the ginger nuts
grabbelton [ɣrɑbəltɔn] *de (~nen)* lucky dip, *(Am)* grab bag
gracht [ɣrɑxt] *de (~en)* canal; moat: *aan een ~ wonen* live on a canal
grachtengordel [ɣrɑxtə(n)ɣɔrdəl] *de (~s)* ring of canals
gracieus [ɣraʃøs] *adj, adv* graceful, elegant
gradenboog [xradə(n)box] *de (-bogen)* protractor
gradueel [ɣradywel] *adj, adv* of degree, in degree, gradual
graf [ɣraf] *het (graven)* grave, tomb ‖ *zwijgen als het ~* be quiet *(or:* silent) as the grave
graffiti [ɡrɛfiti] *de* graffiti
grafiek [ɣrafik] *de (~en)* graph, diagram
grafiet [ɣrafit] *het* graphite
grafisch [ɣrafis] *adj, adv* graphic
grafschennis [ɣrɑfsxɛnis] *de* desecration of graves
grafschrift [ɣrɑfsxrift] *het (~en)* epitaph
grafsteen [ɣrɑfsten] *de (-stenen)* gravestone, tombstone
gram [ɣrɑm] *het, de (~men)* gram: *vijf ~ zout* five grams of salt
grammatica [ɣrɑmɑtika] *de* grammar
grammaticaal [ɣrɑmɑtikal] *adj, adv* grammatical
grammofoon [ɣrɑmofon] *de (~s)* gramophone
granaat [ɣranat] *de* grenade, shell
granaatappel [ɣranatɑpəl] *de (~en, ~s)* pomegranate
granaatscherf [ɣranatsxɛrf] *de (-scherven)* piece of shrapnel, shell fragment, *(pl)* shrapnel
grandioos [ɣrɑndijos] *adj, adv* monumental,

mighty

graniet [ɣraniˌt] *het* granite

granieten [ɣraniˌtə(n)] *adj* granite

grap [ɣrɑp] *de (~pen)* joke, gag: *een flauwe ~* a feeble *(or:* poor*)* joke; *~pen vertellen* tell *(or:* crack*)* jokes; *een ~ met iem uithalen* play a joke on s.o.; *ze kan wel tegen een ~* she can take a joke

grapefruit [ɡrɛpfrut] *de (~s)* grapefruit

grapje [ɣrɑpjə] *het (~s)* (little) joke: *iets met een ~ afdoen* shrug sth off with a joke; *kun je niet tegen een ~?* can't you take a joke?

grappenmaker [ɣrɑpə(n)makər] *de (~s)* joker, wag

grappig [ɣrɑpəχ] *adj, adv* **1** funny, amusing: *zij probeerden ~ te zijn* they were trying to be funny; **2** funny, comical, amusing, humorous: *het was een ~ gezicht* it was a funny *(or:* comical*)* sight; *een ~e opmerking* a humorous remark; *wat is daar nou zo ~ aan?* what's so funny about that?; **3** attractive, *(Am)* cute

gras [ɣrɑs] *het (~sen)* grass: *het ~ maaien* mow the lawn

grasduinen [ɣrɑzdœynə(n)] *vb* browse (through)

grasmaaier [ɣrɑsmajər] *de (~s)* (lawn)mower

graspriet [ɣrɑsprit] *de (~en)* blade of grass

grasveld [ɣrɑsfɛlt] *het (~en)* field (of grass)

graszode [ɣrɑsodə] *de (~n)* turf, sod

gratie [ɣra(t)si] *de* **1** grace; **2** favour: *bij iem uit de ~ raken* fall out of favour with s.o.; **3** mercy; **4** pardon: *~ krijgen* be pardoned

gratificatie [ɣratifika(t)si] *de (~s)* gratuity, bonus

gratis [ɣratɪs] *adj, adv* free (of charge): *~ en voor niks* gratis, absolutely free

grauw [ɣrɑu] *adj* grey, ashen

gravel [ɡrɛvəl] *het* gravel

graven [ɣravə(n)] *vb* **1** dig, excavate, delve, mine: *een put ~* sink a well; *een tunnel ~* dig a tunnel, tunnel; **2** dig, burrow

graveren [ɣravɛrə(n)] *vb* engrave

graveur [ɣravør] *de (~s)* engraver

gravin [ɣravɪn] *de (~nen)* countess

gravure [ɣravyrə] *de (~s)* engraving, print

grazen [ɣrazə(n)] *vb* graze, (be at) pasture: *het vee laten ~* let the cattle out to graze; *te ~ genomen worden* be had, be taken in; *iem te ~ nemen* take s.o. for a ride, take s.o. in

greep [ɣrep] *de* **1** grasp, grip, grab: *~ krijgen op iets* get a grip on sth; *vast in zijn ~ hebben* have firmly in one's grasp; **2** random selection *(or:* choice*)*: *doe maar een ~* take your pick

greintje [ɣrɛincə] *het (~s)* (not) a bit (of): *geen ~ hoop* not a ray of hope; *geen ~ gezond verstand* not a grain of common sense

grendel [ɣrɛndəl] *de (~s)* bolt: *achter slot en ~ zitten* be under lock and key

grendelen [ɣrɛndələ(n)] *vb* bolt

grenen [ɣrenə(n)] *adj* pine(wood), deal

grens [ɣrɛns] *de (grenzen)* border; boundary; limit, bounds: *aan de Duitse ~* at the German border; *we*

moeten ergens een ~ trekken we have to draw the line somewhere; *binnen redelijke grenzen* within reason

grensgebied [ɣrɛnsχəbit] *het (~en)* **1** border region; **2** *(fig)* borderline, grey area, fringe (area)

grensgeval [ɣrɛnsχəvɑl] *het (~len)* borderline case

grenslijn [ɣrɛnslɛin] *de (~en)* boundary line, *(fig)* dividing line

grensovergang [ɣrɛnsovərɣɑŋ] *de (~en)* border crossing(-point)

grensrechter [ɣrɛnsrɛχtər] *de (~s)* linesman *(socc)*; line judge

grensstreek [ɣrɛnstrek] *de (-streken)* border region

grenzeloos [ɣrɛnzəlos] *adj, adv* infinite, boundless

grenzen [ɣrɛnzə(n)] *vb* **1** border (on), be adjacent to: *hun tuinen ~ aan elkaar* their gardens border on one another; **2** *(fig)* border (on), verge (on), approach: *dat grenst aan het ongelofelijke* that verges on the incredible

greppel [ɣrɛpəl] *de (~s)* channel, trench, ditch

gretig [ɣretəχ] *adj, adv* eager, greedy

grief [ɣrif] *de (grieven)* objection, grievance, complaint

Griek [ɣrik] *de (~en)* Greek

Griekenland [ɣrikə(n)lɑnt] *het* Greece

Grieks [ɣriks] *adj* Greek

Griekse [ɣriksə] *de (~n)* Greek

grienen [ɣrinə(n)] *vb* snivel, blub(ber)

griep [ɣrip] *de* (the) flu, (a) cold: *~ oplopen* catch the flu

griesmeel [ɣrismel] *het* semolina

griet [ɣrit] *de* bird, chick, doll

grieven [ɣrivə(n)] *vb* hurt, offend

griezel [ɣrizəl] *de (~s)* ogre, terror, *(pers)* creep, *(pers)* weirdo

griezelen [ɣrizələ(n)] *vb* shudder, shiver, get the creeps

griezelfilm [ɣrizəlfɪlm] *de (~s)* horror film

griezelig [ɣrizələχ] *adj, adv* gruesome, creepy

griezelverhaal [ɣrizəlvərhal] *het (-verhalen)* horror story

grif [ɣrɪf] *adj. adv* ready, adept, rapid, prompt: *ik geef ~ toe dat ...* I readily admit to ... (-ing); *~ van de hand gaan* sell like hot cakes

griffel [ɣrɪfəl] *de (~s)* slate-pencil

griffie [ɣrɪfi] *de (~s)* registry, clerk of the court's office

griffier [ɣrɪfir] *de (~s) (roughly)* registrar, clerk

grijns [ɣrɛins] *de* grin, smirk, sneer

grijnzen [ɣrɛinzə(n)] *vb* **1** smirk, sneer; **2** grin: *sta niet zo dom te ~!* wipe that silly grin off your face!

¹grijpen [ɣrɛipə(n)] *vb* grab (hold of), seize, grasp, snatch: *de dief werd gegrepen* the thief was nabbed; *hij greep zijn kans* he grabbed *(or:* seized*)* his chance; *(fig) door iets gegrepen zijn* be affected *(or:* moved*)* by sth; *voor het ~ liggen* be there for the taking

²grijpen [ɣrɛipə(n)] *vb* grab, reach (for): *dat is te*

hoog gegrepen that is aiming too high; *naar de fles* ~ reach for (*or*: turn to) the bottle

¹grijs [ɣrɛis] *het* grey

²grijs [ɣrɛis] *adj* grey: *hij wordt al aardig* ~ he is getting quite grey

grijsaard [ɣrɛisart] *de (~s)* old man

gril [ɣrɪl] *de (~len)* whim, fancy

grill [ɣrɪl] *de (~s)* grill

grillen [ɣrɪlə(n)] *vb* grill

grillig [ɣrɪləχ] *adj, adv* whimsical, fanciful, capricious: ~ *weer* changeable weather

grilligheid [ɣrɪləχɦɛit] *de (-heden)* capriciousness, whimsicality, fickleness

grimas [ɣrimɑs] *de (~sen)* grimace

grime [ɣrim] *de (~s)* make-up, greasepaint

grimeren [ɣrimerə(n)] *vb* make up

grimmig [ɣrɪməχ] *adj, adv* **1** furious, irate; **2** fierce, forbidding: *een ~e kou* a severe cold

grind [ɣrɪnt] *het* gravel, shingle

grindweg [ɣrɪntwɛχ] *de (~en)* gravel(led) road

grinniken [ɣrɪnəkə(n)] *vb* chuckle, snigger: *zit niet zo dom te ~!* stop that silly sniggering!

grip [ɣrɪp] *de* grip, traction: ~ *hebben op (also fig)* have a grip on

grissen [ɣrɪsə(n)] *vb* snatch, grab

grizzlybeer [ɡrɪzliber] *de (-beren)* grizzly (bear)

groef [ɣruf] *de (groeven)* groove, furrow, slot

groei [ɣruj] *de* **1** growth, development: *een broek die op de ~ gemaakt is* trousers which allow for growth; **2** growth, increase, expansion

groeien [ɣrujə(n)] *vb* grow, develop: *zijn baard laten ~* grow a beard; *het geld groeit mij niet op de rug* I am not made of money

groeihormoon [ɣrujhɔrmon] *het (-hormonen)* growth hormone

groeipijn [ɣrujpɛin] *de (~en)* growing pains

groen [ɣrun] *adj* green: *deze aardbeien zijn nog ~* these strawberries are still green; *het signaal sprong op ~* the signal changed to green; *ze was in het ~ (gekleed)* she was (dressed) in green

Groenland [ɣrunlɑnt] *het* Greenland

Groenlander [ɣrunlɑndər] *de (~s)* Greenlander

groenstrook [ɣrunstrok] *de (-stroken)* **1** green belt, green space (*or*: area); **2** grass strip, centre strip

groente [ɣruntə] *de (~n, ~s)* vegetable: *vlees en twee verschillende soorten ~* meat and two vegetables

groenteboer [ɣruntəbur] *de (~en)* greengrocer; greengrocer's (shop)

groentesoep [ɣruntəsup] *de* vegetable soup

groentetuin [ɣruntətœyn] *de (~en)* vegetable garden, kitchen garden

groentje [ɣruncə] *het (~s)* greenhorn, new boy, new girl, fresher, freshman

groep [ɣrup] *de (~en)* group; party: *een grote ~ van de bevolking* a large section of the population; *leeftijdsgroep* age group (*or*: bracket); *in ~jes van vijf of zes* in groups of five or six; *we gingen in een ~ rond de gids staan* we formed a group round the guide

¹groeperen [ɣruperə(n)] *vb* group: *anders (opnieuw) ~* regroup

²groeperen [ɣruperə(n)] *ref vb* **1** cluster (round), gather (round), huddle (round); **2** group (together), form a group

groepering [ɣruperɪŋ] *de (~en)* grouping, faction

groepsgeest [ɣrupsχest] *de* team spirit

groepsreis [ɣrupsrɛis] *de (-reizen)* group travel

groepsverband [ɣrupsfɑrbɑnt] *het* ‖ *in ~* in a group (*or*: team); *werken in ~* work as a team

groepswerk [ɣrupswɛrk] *het* teamwork

groet [ɣrut] *de (~en)* greeting, (*mil*) salute: *een korte ~ tot afscheid* a parting word; *met vriendelijke ~en* yours sincerely; *doe hem de ~en van mij* give him my best wishes, say hello to him for me; *je moet de ~en van haar hebben. O, doe haar de ~en terug* she sends (you) her regards (*or*: love). Oh, the same to her; *de ~en!: a) (greeting)* see you!; *b) (forget it)* not on your life!, no way!

groeten [ɣrutə(n)] *vb* greet, say hello: *wees gegroet Maria* Hail Mary

groeve [ɣruvə] *de (~n)* quarry

grof [ɣrɔf] *adj, adv* **1** coarse, hefty; **2** coarse, rough, crude: *grove gelaatstrekken* coarse features; *iets ~ schetsen: a)* make a (rough) sketch of sth; *b) (fig also)* sketch sth in broad outlines; **3** gross, rude: *een grove fout* a glaring error; *je hoeft niet meteen ~ te worden* there's no need to be rude

grofgebouwd [ɣrɔfχəbɑut] *adj* heavily-built

grofheid [ɣrɔfɦɛit] *de (-heden)* coarseness, rudeness, roughness, grossness

grofweg [ɣrɔfwɛχ] *adv* roughly, about, in the region of

grog [ɣrɔk] *de (~s)* grog, (hot) toddy

grol [ɣrɔl] *de (~len)* joke, gag

¹grommen [ɣrɔmə(n)] *vb* grumble, mutter: *hij gromde iets onduidelijks* he muttered something indistinct

²grommen [ɣrɔmə(n)] *vb* growl, snarl: *de hond begon tegen mij te ~* the dog began to growl at me

grond [ɣrɔnt] *de (~en)* **1** ground, land: *er zit een flink stuk ~ bij het huis* the house has considerable grounds; *een stuk ~* a plot of land; *braakliggende ~* waste land; *iem tegen de ~ slaan* knock s.o. flat; *zij heeft haar bedrijf van de ~ af opgebouwd* she built up her firm from scratch; **2** ground, earth: *schrale (or: onvruchtbare) ~* barren (*or*: poor) soil; *iem nog verder de ~ in trappen* kick s.o. when he is down; **3** ground, floor: *de begane ~* the ground floor, (*Am*) the first floor; *ik had wel door de ~ kunnen gaan* I wanted the ground to open up and swallow me; **4** bottom: *aan de ~ zitten* be on the rocks; **5** ground, foundation, basis: *op ~ van zijn huidskleur* because of (*or*: on account of) his colour; *op ~ van artikel 461* by virtue of section 461; **6** bottom, essence: *dat komt uit de ~ van zijn hart* that comes from the bottom of his heart

grondbeginsel [ɣrɔndbəɣɪnsəl] *het (~en)* (basic, fundamental) principle; (*pl also*) fundamentals, basics

grondbezit [ɣrɔndbəzɪt] *het* **1** landownership, ownership of land; **2** landed property, (landed, real) estate

grondbezitter [ɣrɔndbəzɪtər] *de (~s)* landowner

grondgebied [ɣrɔntχəbit] *het (~en) (also fig)* territory, soil

grondig [ɣrɔndəχ] *adj, adv* thorough, radical: *een ~e hekel aan iets hebben* loathe sth, dislike sth intensely; *iets ~ bespreken* talk sth out (*or:* through); *iets ~ onderzoeken* examine sth thoroughly

grondigheid [χrɔndəχhɛit] *de* thoroughness, soundness, validity

grondlaag [ɣrɔntlaχ] *de (-lagen)* undercoat

grondlegger [ɣrɔntlɛɣər] *de (~s)* founder, (founding) father

grondpersoneel [ɣrɔntpɛrsonel] *het* ground crew

grondprijs [ɣrɔntprɛis] *de (-prijzen)* the price of land

grondslag [ɣrɔntslaχ] *de (~en) (fig)* basis, foundation(s): *de ~ leggen van iets* lay the foundation for sth

grondsoort [ɣrɔntsort] *de (~en)* (type, kind of) soil

grondstewardess [ɣrɔntscuwardɛs] *de (~en)* ground hostess (*or* Am: stewardess)

grondstof [ɣrɔntstɔf] *de (~fen)* raw material, raw produce

grondverf [ɣrɔntfɛrf] *de (-verven)* primer

grondvest [ɣrɔntfɛst] *de (~en)* foundation

grondvlak [ɣrɔntflak] *het (~ken)* base

grondwater [ɣrɔntwatər] *het* groundwater

grondwerk [ɣrɔntwɛrk] *het (~en)* groundwork

grondwet [ɣrɔntwɛt] *de (~ten)* constitution

grondwettelijk [ɣrɔntwɛtələk] *adj* constitutional

groot [ɣrot] *adj* **1** big, large: *een tamelijk grote kamer* quite a big (*or:* large) room; *de kans is ~ dat …* there's a good chance that …; *op één na de grootste* the next to largest; **2** big, tall: *wat ben jij ~ geworden!* how you've grown!; *de grootste van de twee* the bigger of the two; **3** big, grown-up: *zij heeft al grote kinderen* she has (already) got grown-up children; *daar ben je te ~ voor* you're too big for that (sort of thing); **4** in size: *het stuk land is twee hectare ~* the piece of land is two hectares in area; *twee keer zo ~ als deze kamer* twice as big as this room; **5** great, large: *een ~ gezin* a large family; *een steeds groter aantal* an increasing (*or:* a growing) number; *in het ~ inkopen* (*or:* verkopen) buy (*or:* sell) in bulk; *Karel de Grote* Charlemagne; *Alexander de Grote* Alexander the Great; *je hebt ~ gelijk!* you are quite (*or:* perfectly) right!

grootbeeld [χrodbelt] *het* large screen (television)

grootboek [ɣrodbuk] *het (~en)* ledger

grootbrengen [ɣrodbrɛŋə(n)] *vb* bring up, raise: *een kind met de fles ~* bottle-feed a child

Groot-Brittannië [ɣrodbrɪtɑn(i)jə] *het* Great Britain

groothandel [ɣrɔthɑndəl] *de (~s)* wholesaler's,

wholesale business

groothandelaar [ɣrɔthɑndəlar] *de (~s, -handelaren)* wholesaler

grootheid [ɣrɔthɛit] *de* quantity

grootheidswaanzin [ɣrɔthɛitswanzɪn] *de* megalomania

groothertog [ɣrɔthɛrtɔχ] *de (~en)* grand duke

groothoeklens [ɣrɔthuklɛns] *de (-lenzen)* wide-angle lens

groothouden [ɣrɔthaudə(n)] *ref vb* **1** bear up (well, bravely); **2** keep up appearances, keep a stiff upper lip

grootmeester [ɣrɔtmestər] *de (~s)* **1** grandmaster; **2** (great, past) master

grootmoeder [ɣrɔtmudər] *de (~s)* grandmother

grootouders [ɣrɔtaudərs] *de* grandparents

groots [ɣrots] *adj, adv* **1** grand, magnificent, majestic; **2** spectacular, large-scale, ambitious: *het ~ aanpakken: a)* go about it on a grand scale; *b) (inf)* think big

grootschalig [ɣrotsχaləχ] *adj, adv* large-scale, ambitious

grootscheeps [ɣrotsχeps] *adj, adv* large-scale, great, massive, full-scale

grootspraak [ɣrotsprak] *de* **1** boast(ing): *waar blijf je nu met al je ~!* where's all your boasting now?; **2** hyperbole, overstatement

grootte [ɣrotə] *de (~n, ~s)* size: *onder de normale ~* undersize(d); *een model op ware ~* a life-size model; *ter ~ van* the size of

grootvader [ɣrotfadər] *de (~s)* grandfather

grootverbruiker [ɣrotfərbrœykər] *de (~s)* large-scale consumer, bulk consumer

gros [ɣrɔs] *het (~sen)* **1** majority, larger part; **2** gross: *per ~* by the gross

grossier [ɣrɔsir] *de (~s)* wholesaler

grossiersprijs [χrɔsirspreis] *de (-prijzen)* trade price, wholesale price

grot [ɣrɔt] *de (~ten)* cave

grotendeels [ɣrotəndels] *adv* largely

grotesk [ɣrotɛsk] *adj, adv* grotesque

gruis [ɣrœys] *het* grit

grut [ɣryt] *het* toddlers, small fry, young fry

grutto [ɣryto] *de (~'s)* (black, bar-tailed) godwit

gruwel [ɣrywəl] *de (~en)* horror

gruweldaad [ɣrywəldat] *de (-daden)* atrocity: *gruweldaden bedrijven* commit atrocities

gruwelijk [ɣrywələk] *adj, adv* **1** horrible, gruesome: *een ~e misdaad* a horrible crime, an atrocity; **2** terrible, enormous: *een ~e hekel aan iem hebben* hate s.o.'s guts; *zich ~ vervelen* be bored stiff (*or:* to death)

gruwelverhaal [χrywəlvərhal] *het (-verhalen)* horror story

gruwen [ɣrywə(n)] *vb* be horrified (by): *ik gruw bij de gedachte aan al die ellende* I'm horrified by the thought of all this misery

g-sleutel [ɣesløtəl] *de (~s)* G clef, Treble clef

gsm [ɣeesɛm] *de (~'s)* GSM

Guatemala [ɣuwatəmạla] *het* Guatemala

guerrilla [ɡərịlja] *de (~'s)* guer(r)illa (warfare)

guerrillastrijder [ɡərịljastrɛidər] *de (~s)* guer(r)il-la (fighter)

guillotine [ɡijotịnə] *de (~s)* guillotine

Guinees [ɡinẹs] *adj* Guinean

guirlande [ɡirlạ̈də] *de (~s)* festoon, garland

guitig [ɣœ̣ytəχ] *adj, adv* roguish, mischievous

¹gul [ɣʏl] *adj* **1** generous: *met ~le hand (geven)* (give) generously; *~ zijn met iets* be liberal with sth; **2** cordial: *een ~le lach* a hearty laugh

²gul [ɣʏl] *adv* cordially

gulden [ɣʏ̣ldə(n)] *de (~s)* (Dutch) guilder, florin; *(abbr)* Dfl; NLG

gulheid [χʏ̣lhɛit] *de (-heden)* **1** generosity; **2** cordiality

gulp [ɣʏlp] *de (~en)* fly (front), zip: *je ~ staat open* your fly is open

gulzig [ɣʏ̣lzəχ] *adj, adv* greedy: *met ~e blikken* with greedy eyes

gum [ɣʏm] *de, het* rubber, *(Am)* eraser

gummi [ɣʏ̣mi] *het, de* rubber

gummihandschoen [ɣʏ̣mihɑntsχun] *de (~en)* rubber glove

gummiknuppel [ɣʏ̣miknʏpəl] *de (~s)* baton, *(Am)* club

gunnen [ɣʏ̣nə(n)] *vb* **1** grant: *iem een blik op iets ~* let s.o. have a look at sth; *hij gunde zich de tijd niet om te eten* he did not allow himself time to eat; **2** not begrudge: *het is je van harte gegund* you're very welcome to it

gunst [ɣʏnst] *de (~en)* favour: *iem een ~ bewijzen* do s.o. a favour

gunstig [ɣʏ̣nstəχ] *adj, adv* **1** favourable, kind: *~ staan tegenover* sympathize with; **2** favourable, advantageous: *een ~e gelegenheid* a good (*or:* favourable) opportunity; *in het ~ste geval* at best; *met ~e uitslag* with a favourable (*or:* satisfactory) result; *~e voortekenen* favourable (*or:* hopeful) signs; *~ voor …* favourable (*or:* good) for …; **3** favourable, agreeable: *~ bekendstaan* have a good reputation

gunsttarief [ɣʏ̣nstarif] *het (-tarieven) (Belg)* concessionary rate

gutsen [ɣʏ̣tsə(n)] *vb* gush, pour

guur [ɣyr] *adj, adv* bleak, rough, wild, cutting

¹gym [ɣɪm] *de* gym

²gym [ɣɪm] *het (roughly)* grammar school, *(Am)* high school, *(in Netherlands etc)* gymnasium: *Zhanel zit op het ~* Zhanel is at (the) grammar school

gymmen [ɣɪ̣mə(n)] *vb* **1** do gym(nastics); **2** have gym

gymnasium [ɣɪmnạzijʏm] *het (~s, gymnasia)* (roughly) grammar school, *(Am)* high school, *(in Netherlands)* gymnasium

gymnast [ɣɪmnɑ̣st] *de (~en)* gymnast

gymnastiek [ɣɪmnɑstịk] *de* gymnastics: *op ~ zijn* be at gymnastics

gymnastieklokaal [ɣɪmnɑstịklokal] *het* gym

gympje [ɣɪ̣mpjə] *het (~s)* gym shoe

gynaecoloog [ɣinekolọ̈χ] *de (-logen)* gynaecologist

h

haag [haχ] *de (hagen)* hedge(row): *Den Haag* The
Hague

haai [haj] *de (~en)* shark: *naar de ~en gaan* go
down the drain

haaientanden [haja(n)tandə(n)] *de* **1** shark's
teeth; **2** triangular road marking (at junction)

haaienvinnensoep [haja(n)vınə(n)sup] *de*
shark-fin soup

haak [hak] *de (haken)* hook: *er zitten veel haken en
ogen aan* it's a tricky business; *(Belg) met haken en
ogen aan elkaar hangen* be shoddily made; *dat is
niet in de ~* that's not quite right; *de hoorn van de ~
nemen* take the receiver off the hook

haakje [hakjə] *het (~s)* bracket, parenthesis: *~ openen* (or: *sluiten*) open (or: close) (the) brackets;
tussen (twee) ~s: a) in brackets; *b) (fig)* incidentally,
by the way

haaknaald [haknalt] *de (~en)* crochet hook (*or:*
needle)

haaks [haks] *adj, adv* square(d) ‖ *hou je ~* (keep
your) chin up

haakwerk [hakwɛrk] *het (~en)* crochet (work), cro-
cheting

haal [hal] *de (halen)* **1** tug, pull: *met een flinke ~ trok
hij het schip aan de wal* with a good tug he pulled
the boat ashore; **2** stroke: *aan de ~ gaan met* run off
with

haalbaar [halbar] *adj* attainable, feasible

haalbaarheid [halbarhɛit] *de* feasibility

haan [han] *de (hanen)* cock: *daar kraait geen ~
naar* no one will know a thing; *de ~ spannen (overhalen)* cock the gun

haantje [hancə] *het (~s)* young cock; chicken

haantje-de-voorste [hancədəvorstə] *de* ringleader: *~ zijn* be (the) cock-of-the-walk

¹haar [har] *het, de* hair: *iets met de haren erbij slepen*
drag sth in; *geen ~ op m'n hoofd die eraan denkt* I
would not dream of it; *elkaar in de haren vliegen* fly
at each other; *het scheelde maar een ~ of ik had hem
geraakt* I only just missed hitting him; *op een ~ na*
very nearly

²haar [har] *het* hair: *met lang ~, met kort ~*
long-haired, short-haired; *z'n ~ laten knippen* have
a haircut; *z'n ~ verven* dye one's hair; *(Belg) iem
van ~ noch pluim(en) kennen* not know s.o. from
Adam; *(Belg) met het ~ getrokken* utterly implausible

³haar [har] *pers pron* her; it: *vrienden van ~* friends
of hers; *hij gaf het ~* he gave it to her; *die van ~ is
wit* hers is white

⁴haar [har] *pos pron* her; its: *Els ~ schoenen* Elsie's
shoes

haarborstel [harbɔrstəl] *de (~s)* hairbrush

haard [hart] *de (~en)* **1** stove: *eigen ~ is goud waard*
there's no place like home; **2** hearth: *huis en ~*
hearth and home; *een open ~* a fireplace; *bij de ~* by
(*or:* at) the fireside

haardos [hardɔs] *de (~sen)* (head of) hair: *een dichte (volle) ~* a thick head of hair

haardroger [hardroɣər] *de (~s)* hairdryer

haardvuur [hartfyr] *het (-vuren)* open fire

haarlok [harlɔk] *de (~ken)* lock (of hair)

haarscherp [harsχɛrp] *adj, adv* very sharp, exact

haarspeld [harspɛlt] *de (~en)* **1** hairslide, *(Am)* hair
clasp; **2** hairpin

haarspoeling [harspulıŋ] *de* hair colouring

haarstukje [harstʏkjə] *het (~s)* hairpiece

haaruitval [harœytfɑl] *de* hair loss

haarvat [harvɑt] *het (~en)* capillary

haas [has] *de (hazen)* **1** hare; **2** fillet: *een biefstuk
van de ~* fillet steak; **3** *(sport)* pacemaker: *het ~je
zijn* be for it; *mijn naam is ~* I'm saying nothing, I
know nothing about it

haasje-over [haʃoovər] *het* ‖ *~ springen* (play)
leapfrog

¹haast [hast] *adv* almost, nearly, hardly: *men zou ~
denken dat ...* one would almost think that ...; *hij
was ~ gevallen* he nearly fell; *hij zei ~ niets toen hij
wegging* he said hardly anything when he left; *~
niet* hardly; *~ nooit* scarcely ever

²haast [hast] *de* hurry, haste: *in grote ~* in a great
hurry, in haste; *~ hebben* be in a hurry; *waarom
zo'n ~?* what's the rush?

haasten [hastə(n)] *ref vb* hurry, hurry up: *we hoeven ons niet te ~* there's no need to hurry; *haast je
maar niet!* don't hurry!, take your time!

haastig [hastəχ] *adj, adv* hasty, rash: *niet zo ~!*
(take it) easy!

haat [hat] *de* hatred, hate

habijt [habɛit] *het (~en)* habit

hachee [hɑʃe] *het, de* stew, hash

hachelijk [hɑχələk] *adj* precarious

hachje [hɑχjə] *het (~s)* skin: *alleen aan zijn eigen ~
denken* only think of one's own safety

hacken [hɛkə(n)] *vb* hack

hagedis [haɣədıs] *de (~sen)* lizard

hagel [haɣəl] *de (~s)* **1** hail; **2** (lead, ball) shot

hagelbui [haɣəlbœy] *de (~en)* hailstorm

hagelen [haɣələ(n)] *vb* hail: *het hagelt* it hails, it is
hailing

hagelslag [haɣəlslɑχ] *de* chocolate strands

hagelsteen [haɣəlsten] *de (-stenen)* hailstone

hagelwit [haɣəlwıt] *adj* (as) white as snow: *~te tanden* pearly-white teeth

hak [hɑk] *de* **1** heel: *schoenen met hoge* (or: *lage*)

~ken high-heeled (*or:* flat-heeled) shoes; *met de ~ken over de sloot slagen* pass by the skin of one's teeth; **2** cut: *van de ~ op de tak springen* skip from one subject to another

hakblok [hɑgblɔk] *het (~ken)* chopping block, butcher's block

¹**haken** [hakə(n)] *vb* catch: *hij bleef met zijn jas aan een spijker ~* he caught his coat on a nail

²**haken** [hakə(n)] *vb* crochet

hakenkruis [hakə(n)krœys] *het (-kruizen)* swastika

hakkelen [hɑkələ(n)] *vb* stammer (out), stumble (over one's words)

¹**hakken** [hɑkə(n)] *vb* hack (at)

²**hakken** [hɑkə(n)] *vb* **1** chop (up): *in stukjes ~* cut (*or:* chop) (up); **2** cut (off, away); **3** cut (out)

hakmes [hɑkmɛs] *het (~sen)* **1** chopper, machete; **2** chopping knife

hal [hɑl] *de (~len)* (entrance) hall: *in de ~ van het hotel* in the hotel lobby (*or:* lounge, foyer)

halen [halə(n)] *vb* **1** pull, drag: *ervan alles bij ~* drag in everything (but the kitchen sink); *ik kan er mijn kosten niet uit ~* it doesn't cover my expenses; *eruit ~ wat erin zit* get the most out of sth; *overhoop ~* turn upside down; *waar haal ik het geld vandaan?* where shall I find the money?; *zijn zakdoek uit zijn zak ~* pull out one's handkerchief; *iem uit zijn concentratie ~* break s.o.'s concentration; *geld van de bank ~* (with)draw money from the bank; **2** fetch, get: *de post ~* collect the mail; *ik zal het gaan ~* I'll go and get it; *ik zal je morgen komen ~* I'll come for you tomorrow; *iem van de trein ~* meet s.o. at the station; *twee ~ een betalen* two for the price of one; **3** fetch, go for: *de dokter ~* go for the doctor; *iem (iets) laten ~* send for s.o. (sth); **4** get, take, pass: *goede cijfers ~* get good marks; **5** reach, catch, get; make, compare, pull through: *hij heeft de finish niet gehaald* he did not make it to the finish; *daar haalt niets (het) bij* nothing can touch (*or:* beat) it; *je haalt twee zaken door elkaar* you are mixing up two things

¹**half** [hɑlf] *adj* **1** half: *voor ~ geld* (at) half price; *vier en een halve mijl* four and a half miles; *de halve stad spreekt ervan* half the town is talking about it; **2** halfway up/down (*or:* along, through): *ik ga ~ april* I'm going in mid-April; *er is een bus telkens om vier minuten vóór ~* there is a bus every four minutes to the half-hour; *het is ~ elf: a)* it is half past ten; *b)* it is half ten

²**half** [hɑlf] *adv* half, halfway: *een glas ~ vol schenken* pour half a glass; *met het raam ~ dicht* with the window halfway down (*or:* open)

³**half** [hɑlf] *het (halven)* half: *twee halven maken een heel* two halves make a whole

halfbroer [hɑlvbrur] *de (~s)* half-brother

halfdood [hɑlvdot] *adj* half-dead

halfduister [hɑlvdœystər] *het* semi-darkness, twilight

halfgaar [hɑlfxar] *adj* **1** half-done; **2** half-witted

halfgeleider [hɑlfxəlɛidər] *de (~s)* semiconductor

halfjaar [hɑlfjar] *het (-jaren)* six months, half a year

halfpension [hɑlfpɛnʃɔn] *het* half board

halfrond [hɑlfrɔnt] *het (~en)* hemisphere

halfstok [hɑlfstɔk] *adv* half-mast

halfuur [hɑlfyr] *het* half (an) hour

halfvol [hɑlfɔl] *adj* **1** half-full; **2** low-fat, half-fat

halfweg [hɑlfwɛx] *prep* halfway: *~ Utrecht en Amersfoort heeft hij een huis gekocht* he has bought a house halfway between Utrecht and Amersfoort; *ik kwam hem ~ tegen* I met him halfway

halfzacht [hɑlfsɑxt] *adj* **1** soft-boiled; **2** soft-headed, soft (in the head)

halfzuster [hɑlfsʏstər] *de (~s)* half-sister

¹**halfzwaargewicht** [hɑlfswaryəwɪxt] *de (~en) (person)* light heavyweight

²**halfzwaargewicht** [hɑlfswaryəwɪxt] *het* light heavyweight

halleluja [hɑlelyja] *int* alleluia, halleluja(h)

hallo [hɑlo] *int* hello, hallo, hullo

hallucineren [hɑlysinerə(n)] *vb* hallucinate, hear things, see things

halm [hɑlm] *de (~en)* stalk, blade

halo [halo] *de (~'s)* halo; *(around moon)* corona

halogeen [haloɣen] *het (halogenen)* halogen

hals [hɑls] *de (halzen)* **1** neck: *de ~ van een gitaar* the neck of a guitar; *iem om de ~ vallen* throw one's arms round s.o.'s neck; *een japon met laag uitgesneden ~* a low-necked dress; **2** throat; **3** nape

halsband [hɑlzbɑnt] *de (~en)* **1** collar; **2** necklace

halsbrekend [hɑlzbrekənt] *adj* daredevil

halsdoek [hɑlzduk] *de (~en)* scarf

halsketting [hɑlskɛtɪŋ] *de (~en)* **1** necklace; **2** collar

halsoverkop [hɑlsovərkɔp] *adv* in a hurry (*or:* rush), headlong, head over heels: *~ over kop verliefd worden* fall head over heels in love; *~ naar het ziekenhuis gebracht worden* be rushed to hospital; *~ de trap af komen* come tumbling downstairs

halsslagader [hɑlsslaɣadər] *de (~s, ~en)* carotid (artery)

halsstarrig [hɑlstɑrəx] *adj* obstinate, stubborn

halster [hɑlstər] *het, de (~s)* halter

¹**halt** [hɑlt] *het* stop: *iem een ~ toeroepen* stop s.o.; *~ houden* halt

²**halt** [hɑlt] *int* halt!, stop!, wait!

halte [hɑltə] *de (~s)* stop

halter [hɑltər] *de (~s)* dumb-bell; bar bell

halvarine [hɑlvarinə] *de (~s)* low-fat margarine

halvemaan [hɑlvəman] *de (-manen)* **1** half-moon; **2** crescent

halveren [hɑlverə(n)] *vb* **1** divide into halves; **2** halve

halverwege [hɑlvərwɛɣə] *adv* halfway, halfway through || *~ blijven steken in een boek* get stuck halfway through a book

halvezool [hɑlvəzol] *de (-zolen)* nitwit

ham [hɑm] *de (~men)* ham: *een broodje ~* a ham roll

hamburger [hɑmbʏryər] *de (~s)* hamburger, beef-
burger: ~ *met kaas* cheeseburger
hamer [hamər] *de (~s)* hammer
hameren [hamərə(n)] *vb* hammer: *er bij iem op
blijven* ~ keep on at s.o. about sth
hamster [hɑmstər] *de (~s)* hamster
hamsteren [hɑmstərə(n)] *vb* hoard (up)
hamstring [hɛmstrɪŋ] *de (~s)* hamstring
hand [hɑnt] *de (~en)* hand: *blote ~en* bare hands;
in goede (or: *verkeerde*) *~en vallen* fall into the right
(or: wrong) hands; *iem de helpende ~ bieden* lend
s.o. a (helping) hand; *de laatste ~ aan iets leggen*
put the finishing touches to sth; *niet met lege ~en
komen* not come empty-handed; *iem (de) ~en vol
werk geven* give s.o. no end of work (or: trouble); *de
~en vol hebben aan iem (iets)* have one's hands full
with s.o. (sth); *dat kost ~en vol geld* that costs lots
of money; *iem de ~ drukken* (or: *geven, schudden*)
shake hands with s.o., give s.o. one's hand; *iemands ~ lezen* read s.o.'s palm; *de ~ ophouden (fig)*
hold out one's hand for a tip, beg; *zijn ~en uit de
mouwen steken (fig)* roll up one's sleeves, get down
to it; *hij kan zijn ~en niet thuishouden* he can't keep
his hands to himself; *zijn ~ uitsteken* indicate; *~en
omhoog! (of ik schiet)* hands up! (or I'll shoot); *~en
thuis!* hands off!; *niks aan de ~!* there's nothing the
matter; *wat geld achter de ~ houden* keep some
money for a rainy day; *in de ~en klappen* clap one's
hands; *(fig) iets in de ~ hebben* have sth under control; *de macht in ~en hebben* have power, be in control; *in ~en vallen van de politie* fall into the hands
of the police; *met de ~ gemaakt* hand-made; *iets
om ~en hebben* have sth to do; *iem onder ~en nemen* take s.o. in hand (or: to task); *uit de ~ lopen* get
out of hand; *iem het werk uit (de) ~en nemen* take
work off s.o.'s hands; *iets van de ~ doen* sell sth,
part with sth, dispose of sth; *dat ligt voor de ~* that
speaks for itself, is self-evident; *aan de winnende ~
zijn* be winning; *iem op zijn ~ hebben* have s.o. on
one's side; *wat is er daar aan de ~?* what's going on
there?; *er is iets aan de ~* there's sth the matter (or:
up)
handbagage [hɑndbaɣaʒə] *de (~s)* hand-luggage
handbal [hɑndbɑl] *het* handball
handbereik [hɑndbərɛik] *het* reach: *onder (in, binnen)* ~ within reach
handboei [hɑndbuj] *de (~en)* handcuffs
handboek [hɑndbuk] *het (~en)* **1** handbook; **2** reference book
handbreed [hɑndbret] *het* hand('s-)breadth: *geen
~ wijken* not budge, give an inch
handdoek [hɑnduk] *de (~en)* towel
handdruk [hɑndrʏk] *de (~ken)* handshake
handel [hɑndəl] *de* **1** trade, business: *binnenlandse
~* domestic trade; *zwarte ~* black market; *~ in verdovende middelen* drug trafficking; **2** merchandise,
goods; **3** business, shop
handelaar [hɑndəlar] *de (~s, handelaren)* trader,
merchant, dealer; *(depr)* trafficker

handelbaar [hɑndəlbar] *adj* manageable, docile
handelen [hɑndələ(n)] *vb* **1** trade, do business,
transact business, *(depr)* traffic: *hij handelt in
drugs* he traffics in drugs; **2** act: *~d optreden* take
action; *ik zal naar eer en geweten* ~ I shall act in all
conscience; **3** (with *over*) treat (of), deal (with)
handeling [hɑndəlɪŋ] *de (~en)* **1** act, deed; **2** action,
plot: *de plaats van ~* the scene (of the action)
handelsagent [hɑndəlsaɣɛnt] *de (~en)* commercial agent
handelsakkoord [hɑndəlsɑkort] *het (~en)* trade
agreement
handelsartikel [hɑndəlsɑrtikəl] *het (~en)* commodity, *(pl also)* goods, *(pl also)* merchandise
handelsbetrekkingen [hɑndəlzbətrɛkɪŋ] *de* trade
relations, commercial relations
handelskapitaal [hɑndəlskapital] *het (-kapitalen)*
trading capital, business capital
handelskennis [hɑndəlskɛnɪs] *de* knowledge of
commerce (or: business), business studies
handelsmerk [hɑndəlsmɛrk] *het (~en)* trademark,
brand name
handelsonderneming [hɑndəlsɔndərnemɪŋ] *de
(~en)* commercial enterprise, business enterprise
handelspartner [hɑndəlspɑrtnər] *de (~s)* business
partner, trading partner
handelsrecht [hɑndəlsrɛχt] *het* commercial law
handelsverkeer [hɑndəlsfərker] *het* trade, business
handelswaar [hɑndəlswar] *de (-waren)* commodity, article, merchandise, goods
handenarbeid [hɑndə(n)ɑrbɛit] *de* hand(i)craft,
industrial art, manual training
hand- en spandiensten [hɑntɛnspɑndinstə(n)] *de*
|| ~ *verrichten* lend a helping hand, aid and abet
handgebaar [hɑntχəbar] *het (-gebaren)* gesture
handgemeen [hɑntχəmen] *het* (hand-to-hand)
fight
handgranaat [hɑntχranat] *de (-granaten)* (hand)
grenade
handgreep [hɑntχrep] *de* handle, grip
¹handhaven [hɑnthavə(n)] *vb* **1** maintain, keep up,
uphold, enforce: *de orde* ~ maintain (or: keep, preserve) order; **2** maintain, stand by: *zijn bezwaren* ~
stand by one's objections
²handhaven [hɑnthavə(n)] *ref vb* hold one's own
handhaving [hɑnthavɪŋ] *de* maintenance, upholding, enforcement
handicap [hɛndikɛp] *de (~s)* handicap: *speciale
voorzieningen voor mensen met een* ~ special facilities for the disabled
handig [hɑndəχ] *adj, adv* **1** skilful, dexterous,
handy: *een ~ formaat* a handy size; *~ in (met) iets
zijn* be good (or: handy) at sth; **2** clever: *hij legde
het ~ aan* he set about it cleverly
handigheid [hɑndəχɛit] *de (-heden)* **1** skill; **2**
knack
handje [hɑncə] *het (~s)* hand(shake) || *een ~ helpen*
give (or: lend) a (helping) hand

handkar [hɑntkɑr] *de (~ren)* handcart
handlanger [hɑntlɑŋər] *de (~s)* accomplice
handleiding [hɑntlɛidɪŋ] *de (~en)* manual, handbook, directions (*or:* instructions) (for use)
handlezer [hɑntlezər] *de (~s)* palmist, palm reader
handmatig [hɑntmɑtəχ] *adj* manual
handomdraai [hɑntɔmdraj] *de ‖ in een ~* in (less than) no time
handoplegging [hɑntɔplɛχɪŋ] *de (~en)* laying on of hands, faith healing
handpalm [hɑntpɑlm] *de (~en)* palm (of the hand)
handrem [hɑntrɛm] *de (~men)* handbrake
hands [hɛnts] *het* hands, handling (the ball), handball: *aangeschoten ~* unintentional hands
handschoen [hɑntsχun] *de (~en)* glove: *een paar ~en* a pair of gloves
handschrift [hɑntsχrɪft] *het (~en)* 1 handwriting; 2 manuscript
handstand [hɑntstɑnt] *de (~en)* handstand
handtas [hɑntɑs] *de (~sen)* (hand)bag
handtastelijk [hɑntɑstələk] *adj* free, (over)familiar: *~ worden* paw s.o.
handtekening [hɑntekənɪŋ] *de (~en)* signature, autograph
handvaardigheid [hɑntfɑrdəχhɛit] *de (-heden)* (handi)craft(s)
handvat [hɑntfɑt] *het (~ten)* handle, hilt, butt: *het ~ van een koffer* the handle of a suitcase
handvest [hɑntfɛst] *het (~en)* charter
handvol [hɑntfɔl] *de* handful
handwarm [hɑntwɑrm] *adj* lukewarm
handwerk [hɑntwɛrk] *het (~en)* 1 handiwork: *dit tapijt is ~* this carpet is handmade; 2 needlework; embroidery; crochet(ing); 3 manual work, trade
handwerksman [hɑntwɛrksmɑn] *de (handwerkslieden, handwerkslui)* craftsman, artisan
handzaam [hɑntsam] *adj* handy
hanenkam [hɑnə(n)kɑm] *de (~men)* 1 (cocks)comb; 2 Mohawk haircut
hanenpoot [hɑnə(n)pot] *de (-poten)* 1 cock's foot; 2 *(illegible handwriting)* scrawl
hangaar [hɑŋɣar] *de (~s)* hangar
hangbuik [hɑŋbœyk] *de (~en)* pot-belly
¹hangen [hɑŋə(n)] *vb* 1 hang: *de zeilen ~ slap* the sails are slack, the sails are hanging (loose); *het schilderij hangt scheef* the painting is (hanging) crooked; *aan het plafond ~* hang (*or:* swing, be suspended) from the ceiling; *de hond liet zijn staart ~* the dog hung its tail; 2 sag: *het koord hangt slap* the rope is sagging (*or:* slack); 3 lean (over), hang (over), loll, slouch, hang around: *hij hing op zijn stoel* he lay sprawled in a chair, he lolled in his chair; 4 stick (to), cling (to), be (*or:* get) stuck (in): *(fig) blijven ~* linger (*or:* stay, hang) (on), get hung up (*or:* stuck); *(fig) ze ~ erg aan elkaar* they are devoted to (*or:* wrapped up in) each other; *de wolken ~ laag* the clouds are (hanging) low; *de bloemen zijn gaan hangen* the flowers are wilting
²hangen [hɑŋə(n)] *vb* 1 hang (up): *de was buiten ~*

hang out the washing (to dry); *zijn jas aan de kapstok ~* hang (up) one's coat on the peg; 2 hang
hangend [hɑŋənt] *adj* hanging, drooping
hanger [hɑŋər] *de (~s)* 1 (clothes) hanger, coat-hanger; 2 pendant, pendent; pendant earring, drop earring
hangijzer [hɑŋɛizər] *het (~s)* pot-hook: *een heet ~* a controversial issue, hot potato
hangkast [hɑŋkɑst] *de (~en)* wardrobe
hangmap [hɑŋmɑp] *de (~pen)* suspension file
hangmat [hɑŋmɑt] *de (~ten)* hammock
hangslot [hɑŋslɔt] *het (~en)* padlock
Hans [hɑns] ‖ *~ en Grietje* Hansel and Gretel
hanteerbaar [hɑntɛrbar] *adj* manageable
hanteren [hɑntɛrə(n)] *vb* 1 handle, operate, employ, wield: *de botte bijl ~* take heavy-handed, crude measures; *moeilijk te ~* unwieldy, difficult (*or:* awkward) to handle, unmanageable; 2 manage, manoeuvre
hap [hɑp] *de (~pen)* 1 bite, peck: *in één ~ was het op* it was gone in one (*or:* in a single) bite; 2 bite, mouthful: *een ~ nemen* take a bite (*or:* mouthful)
haperen [hɑpərə(n)] *vb* 1 stick, get stuck: *de conversatie haperde* the conversation flagged; 2 have sth wrong (*or:* the matter) with oneself
hapje [hɑpjə] *het (~s)* 1 bite, mouthful: *wil je ook een ~ mee-eten?* would you like to join us (for a bite, meal)?; 2 snack, bite to eat, hors d'oeuvre, appetizer: *voor (lekkere) ~s zorgen* serve refreshments
happen [hɑpə(n)] *vb* 1 bite (at), snap (at): *naar lucht ~* gasp for air; 2 bite (into), take a bite (out of)
happig [hɑpəχ] *adj* (with *op*) keen (on), eager (for)
harakiri [harakiri] *het* hara-kiri
¹hard [hɑrt] *adj* 1 hard, firm, solid: *~e bewijzen* firm proof, hard evidence; *~ worden* harden, become hard, set; 2 stiff, rigid: *~e schijf* hard disk; 3 hard, loud: *~e muziek* loud music; *~e wind* strong (*or:* stiff) wind; 4 hard, harsh: *een ~e politiek* a tough policy; *een ~ vonnis* a severe sentence; 5 harsh, garish: *~e trekken* harsh features
²hard [hɑrt] *adv* 1 hard: *~ lachen* laugh heartily; *een band ~ oppompen* pump a tyre up hard; *hij ging er nogal ~ tegenaan* he went at it rather hard; *zijn rust ~ nodig hebben* be badly in need of a rest; *dit onderdeel is ~ aan vervanging toe* this part is in urgent need of replacement; 2 loudly: *niet zo ~ praten!* keep your voice down!; *de tv ~er zetten* turn up the TV; 3 fast, quickly: *~ achteruitgaan* deteriorate rapidly (*or:* fast); *te ~ rijden* drive (*or:* ride) too fast, speed; 4 hard, harshly: *iem ~ aanpakken* be hard on s.o.
hardboard [hɑːrdbɔːrd] *het* hardboard
harddisk [hɑrdɪsk] *de (~s)* hard disk
¹harden [hɑrdə(n)] *vb* harden, become hard, dry, set
²harden [hɑrdə(n)] *vb* 1 harden, temper; 2 toughen (up): *hij is gehard door weer en wind* he has been hardened (*or:* seasoned) by wind and weather; 3 bear, stand, take, stick: *deze hitte is niet te ~* this

heat is unbearable

hardgebakken [hɑrtχəbɑkə(n)] *adj* crispy, crusty

hardgekookt [hɑrtχəkokt] *adj* hard-boiled

hardhandig [hɑrthɑndəχ] *adj, adv* hard-handed, rough, heavy-handed: ~ *optreden* take hard-handed (*or*: harsh, drastic) action, use strong-arm tactics

hardheid [hɑrthɛit] *de (-heden)* hardness, toughness *(also fig)*, harshness

hardhorig [hɑrthorəχ] *adj* hard of hearing

hardhout [hɑrthɑut] *het* hardwood

hardleers [hɑrtlɛrs] *adj* **1** dense, slow, thick(-skulled); **2** headstrong, stubborn

hardlopen [hɑrtlopə(n)] *vb* run; race, run a race

hardloper [hɑrtlopər] *de (~s)* runner

hardnekkig [hɑrtnɛkəχ] *adj, adv* stubborn, obstinate, persistent: *een ~ gerucht* a persistent rumour

hardnekkigheid [hɑrtnɛkəχhɛit] *de* obstinacy, stubbornness

hardop [hɑrtɔp] *adv* aloud, out loud: ~ *denken* (*or*: *lachen)* think/laugh aloud (*or*: out loud); *iets ~ zeggen* say sth out loud

hardrijden [hɑrtrɛidə(n)] *vb (sport)* race, speed-skate

hardrijder [hɑrtrɛidər] *de (~s)* racer, speedskater, racing cyclist

hardvochtig [hɑrtfɔχtəχ] *adj, adv* hard(-hearted), unfeeling

hardware [hɑːrdwɛːr] *de* hardware

harem [hɑrəm] *de (~s)* harem

haren [hɑrə(n)] *adj* hair

harig [hɑrəχ] *adj* hairy, furry

haring [hɑrɪŋ] *de (~en)* **1** herring, kipper: *een school ~en* a shoal of herring; *nieuwe* (*or*: *zure) ~* new (*or*: pickled) herring; *als ~(en) in een ton* (packed) like sardines; **2** tent peg, tent stake

hark [hɑrk] *de (~en)* rake

harken [hɑrkə(n)] *vb* rake (up, together)

harlekijn [hɑrləkɛin] *de (~s)* **1** harlequin; **2** jumping jack; **3** clown

harmonica [hɑrmonika] *de ('~'s)* **1** accordion; **2** harmonica, mouth-organ

harmonie [hɑrmoni] *de (~ën, ~s)* **1** harmony, concord, agreement: *in* (*or*: *niet in) ~ zijn met* be in (*or*: out of) harmony with; **2** (brass)band

harmoniëren [hɑrmonijɛrə(n)] *vb* harmonize (with), blend (in) (with)

harmonieus [hɑrmonijøs] *adj, adv* harmonious, melodious

harmonisch [hɑrmonis] *adj, adv* **1** harmonic: *een ~ geheel vormen* blend (in), go well (together); **2** harmonious

harnas [hɑrnɑs] *het (~sen)* (suit of) armour: *in het ~ sterven* die in harness; *iem tegen zich in het ~ jagen* put s.o.'s back up

harp [hɑrp] *de (~en)* harp

harpist [hɑrpɪst] *de (~en)* harpist, harp player

harpoen [hɑrpun] *de (~en)* harpoon

hars [hɑrs] *het, de (~en)* resin, rosin

hart [hɑrt] *het (~en)* **1** heart: *uit de grond van zijn ~* from the bottom of one's heart; *hij is een jager in ~ en nieren* he is a hunter in heart and soul; *met ~ en ziel* with all one's heart; *met een gerust ~* with an easy mind; *een zwak ~ hebben* have a weak heart; *iemands ~ breken* break s.o.'s heart; *het ~ op de juiste plaats hebben* have one's heart in the right place; *ik hield mijn ~ vast* my heart missed a beat; *je kunt je ~ ophalen* you can enjoy it to your heart's content; *zijn ~ uitstorten* pour out (*or*: unburden, open) one's heart (to s.o.); *(diep) in zijn hart hield hij nog steeds van haar* in his heart (of hearts) he still loved her; *waar het ~ van vol is, loopt de mond van over* what the heart thinks, the tongue speaks; **2** heart, nerve: *heb het ~ eens!* don't you dare!, just you try it!; *het ~ zonk hem in de schoenen* he lost heart; **3** heart, centre: *iets niet over zijn ~ kunnen verkrijgen* not find it in one's heart to do sth; *van ~e gefeliciteerd* my warmest congratulations

hartaanval [hɑrtanvɑl] *de (~len)* heart attack

hartchirurg [hɑrtʃirvrχ] *de* cardiac surgeon, heart surgeon

¹hartelijk [hɑrtələk] *adj* **1** hearty, warm: ~ *dank voor …* many thanks for …; ~*e groeten aan je vrouw* kind regards to your wife; **2** warm-hearted, open-hearted, cordial: ~ *tegen iem zijn* be friendly towards s.o.

²hartelijk [hɑrtələk] *adv* heartily, warmly: ~ *bedankt voor …* thank you very much for …; ~ *gefeliciteerd* sincere congratulations

hartelijkheid [hɑrtələkhɛit] *de (-heden)* **1** cordiality, warm-heartedness, open-heartedness; **2** cordiality, hospitality

harten [hɑrtə(n)] *de (~)* hearts: *hartenboer* jack (*or*: knave) of hearts

hartenlust [hɑrtə(n)lʏst] || *naar ~* to one's heart's content

hart- en vaatziekten [hɑrtɛnvatsiktə(n)] *de* cardiovascular diseases

hartgrondig [hɑrtχrɔndəχ] *adj* wholehearted, hearty

hartig [hɑrtəχ] *adj, adv* **1** tasty, well-seasoned, hearty; **2** salt(y)

hartinfarct [hɑrtɪnfɑrkt] *het (~en)* coronary (thrombosis)

hartje [hɑrcə] *het (~s)* **1** (little) heart: *hij heeft een grote mond, maar een klein ~* he's not all what he makes out to be; **2** heart, centre: ~ *winter* the dead of winter; ~ *zomer* the height of summer

hartklacht [hɑrtklɑχt] *de (~en)* heart complaint (*or*: condition)

hartklep [hɑrtklɛp] *de (~pen)* heart valve, valve (of the heart)

hartklopping [hɑrtklɔpɪŋ] *de (~en)* palpitation (of the heart)

hartpatiënt [hɑrtpaʃɛnt] *de (~en)* cardiac patient

hartsgeheim [hɑrtsχəhɛim] *het (~en)* (most) intimate secret

hartslag [hɑrtslɑχ] *de (~en)* heartbeat, pulse, heart

rate

hartstikke [hɑrtstɪkə] *adv* awfully, terribly, completely: ~ *gek* stark staring mad, crazy; ~ *goed* fantastic, terrific, smashing; ~ *bedankt!* thanks awfully (*or:* ever so much)

hartstilstand [hɑrtstɪlstɑnt] *de (~en)* cardiac arrest

hartstocht [hɑrtstɔχt] *de (~en)* passion, emotion (*esp pl*)

¹**hartstochtelijk** [hɑrtstɔχtələk] *adj* 1 passionate, emotional, excitable; 2 passionate, ardent, fervent: *hij is een ~ skiër* he is an ardent skier

²**hartstochtelijk** [hɑrtstɔχtələk] *adv* passionately, ardently

hartverscheurend [hɑrtfərsχørənt] *adj, adv* heartbreaking, heart-rending

hartverwarmend [hɑrtfərwɑrmənt] *adj, adv* heart-warming

hasj [hɑʃ] *de* hash

hasjiesj [hɑʃiʃ] *de* hashish

haspel [hɑspəl] *de (~s)* reel, spool

hatelijk [hatələk] *adj, adv* nasty, spiteful, snide

hatelijkheid [hatələkhɛit] *de (-heden)* nasty remark, snide remark, gibe, (nasty) crack

haten [hatə(n)] *vb* hate

hatsjie [hɑtʃi] *int* atishoo

haveloos [havələos] *adj* 1 shabby, scruffy, delapidated: *wat ziet hij er ~ uit* how scruffy he looks; 2 shabby, beggarly, down-and-out

haven [havə(n)] *de (~s)* harbour, port, (safe) haven: (*fig*) *een veilige ~ vinden* find refuge; *een ~ binnenlopen (aandoen)* put into a port

havenarbeider [havə(n)ɑrbɛidər] *de (~s)* dockworker

havenstad [havə(n)stɑt] *de (-steden)* port, seaport (town)

haver [havər] *de* oat, oats

haverklap [havərklɑp] || *om de ~: a)* every other minute, continually; *b)* at the drop of a hat

havermout [havərmɑut] *de* 1 rolled oats, oatmeal; 2 (oatmeal) porridge

havik [havɪk] *de (~en)* 1 goshawk; 2 (*pol*) hawk

havo [havo] *de (~'s) hoger algemeen voortgezet onderwijs* school for higher general secondary education

hazelaar [hazəlar] *de (~s)* hazel

hazelnoot [hazəlnot] *de* 1 hazel; 2 hazelnut

hazenlip [hazə(n)lɪp] *de (~pen)* harelip

hazenpad [hazə(n)pɑt] *het (~en)* || *het ~ kiezen* take to one's heels

hazewind [hazəwɪnt] *de (~en)* greyhound

hbo [habeo] *het, de hoger beroepsonderwijs* (school for) higher vocational education

hé [he] *int* hey!; hello, oh (really)?

hè [hɛ] *int* oh (dear), ah: ~, *dat doet zeer!* oh (*or:* ouch), that hurts!; ~, *blij dat ik zit!* phew, glad I can take the weight off my feet!; *lekker weertje,* ~? nice day, isn't it?

heao [heao] *het, de (~'s) hoger economisch en administratief onderwijs* school (institute) for business

administration and economics

¹**hebben** [hɛbə(n)] *vb* 1 have (got), own: *geduld ~ be* patient; *iets moeten ~* need sth; *iets bij zich ~* be carrying sth, have sth with (*or:* on) one; 2 have: *die pantoffels heb ik van mijn vrouw* I got those slippers from my wife; *van wie heb je dat?* who told (*or:* gave) you that?; 3 (with *aan*) be of use (to): *je weet niet wat je aan hem hebt* you never know where you are with him; *verdriet ~* be sad; *wat heb je?* what's the matter (*or:* wrong) with you?; *wat heb je toch?* what's come over you?; *het koud* (*or:* *warm*) ~ *be* cold (*or:* hot); *hij heeft iets tegen mij* he has a grudge against me; *ik heb nooit Spaans gehad* I've never learned Spanish; *ik moet er niets van ~* I want nothing to do with it; *dat heb je ervan* that's what you get; *daar heb je het al* I told you so; *zo wil ik het ~* that's how I want it; *iets gedaan willen ~* want (to see) sth done; *ik weet niet waar je het over hebt* I don't know what you're talking about; *daar heb ik het straks nog over* I'll come (back) to that later on (*or:* in a moment); *nu we het daar toch over ~* now that you mention it …

²**hebben** [hɛbə(n)] *vb* have: *had ik dat maar geweten* if (only) I had known (that); *had dat maar gezegd* if only you'd told me (that); *ik heb met Marco B. op school gezeten* I was at school with Marco B.

hebberig [hɛbərəχ] *adj* greedy

hebbes [hɛbəs] *int* got you, gotcha!; got it

¹**Hebreeuws** [hebrews] *het* Hebrew

²**Hebreeuws** [hebrews] *adj* Hebrew

Hebriden [hebridə(n)] *de* Hebrides

hebzuchtig [hɛpsχtəχ] *adj* greedy, avaricious

hecht [hɛχt] *adj, adv* solid, (*fig*) strong, tight, tightly-knit, close(ly)-knit: *een ~e vriendschap* a close friendship

¹**hechten** [hɛχtə(n)] *vb* 1 stitch, suture: *een wond ~* sew up, stitch a wound; 2 attach, fasten, (af)fix: *een prijskaartje aan iets ~* put a price tag on sth; 3 attach: *waarde* (*or:* *belang*) *aan iets ~* attach value (*or:* importance) to sth

²**hechten** [hɛχtə(n)] *vb* 1 adhere, stick; 2 be attached (to), devoted (to), adhere (to): *ik hecht niet aan deze dure auto* I'm not very attached to this expensive car

³**hechten** [hɛχtə(n)] *ref vb* (with *aan*) become attached to, cling to: *hij hecht zich gemakkelijk aan mensen* he gets attached to people easily

hechtenis [hɛχtənɪs] *de* 1 custody, detention; 2 imprisonment, prison

hechting [hɛχtɪŋ] *de (~en)* stitches, suture(s): *de ~en verwijderen* take out the stitches

hectare [hɛktarə] *de (~n)* hectare

hectisch [hɛktis] *adj, adv* hectic

¹**heden** [hedə(n)] *het* present (day)

²**heden** [hedə(n)] *adv* today, now(adays), at present: *tot op ~* up to (*or:* up) till/until now; *vanaf ~, met ingang van ~* as from today

hedendaags [hedə(n)daχs] *adj* contemporary, present-day: *woordenboeken voor ~ taalgebruik* dictionaries of current usage

hedonisme [hedonɪsmə] *het (~n)* hedonism

¹heel [hel] *adj* **1** intact: *het ei was nog ~* the egg was unbroken; **2** whole, entire, all: *~ Engeland* all England; *een ~ jaar* a whole year; **3** quite a, quite some: *het is een ~ eind (weg)* it's a good way (off); *een hele tijd* quite some time

²heel [hel] *adv* **1** very (much), really: *dat is ~ gewoon* that's quite normal; *een ~ klein beetje* a tiny bit; *dat kostte ~ wat moeite* that took a great deal of effort; *je weet het ~ goed!* you know perfectly well!; *~ vaak* very often (*or:* frequently); **2** completely, entirely, wholly: *dat is iets ~ anders* that's a different matter altogether

heelal [helɑl] *het* universe

heelhuids [helhœyts] *adv* unharmed, unscathed, whole: *~ terugkomen* return safe and sound

heen [hen] *adv* **1** gone, away: *~ en weer lopen* walk/pace up and down (*or:* back and forth); **2** on the way there, out: *je kunt daar niet ~* you cannot go there; *langs elkaar ~ praten* talk at cross purposes; *je kunt niet om hem ~* you can't ignore him

¹heengaan [heŋɣan] *vb* **1** depart, leave; **2** pass away

²heengaan [heŋɣan] *het* **1** passing away; **2** departure

heenreis [henrɛis] *de* way there, outward journey, journey out

heenweg [henwɛχ] *de* way there, way out

heer [her] *de (heren)* **1** man; **2** Mr; Sir; *(pl)* gentlemen: *(mijne) dames en heren!* ladies and gentlemen!; **3** gentleman: *een echte ~* a real gentleman; **4** Lord: *als de Heer het wil* God (*or:* the Lord) willing; **5** lord, master: *mijn oude ~* my old man; **6** *(cards)* king

heerlijk [herlək] *adj, adv* **1** delicious; **2** delightful, lovely, wonderful, splendid: *het is een ~ gevoel* it feels great

heerschappij [hersχɑpɛi] *de* dominion, mastery, rule

heersen [hersə(n)] *vb* **1** rule (over), reign; **2** dominate; **3** be, be prevalent: *er heerst griep* there's a lot of flu about

heersend [hersənt] *adj* ruling, prevailing: *de ~e klassen* the ruling class(es); *de ~e mode* the current fashion

heerser [hersər] *de (~s)* ruler

hees [hes] *adj* hoarse: *een hese keel* a sore throat

heesheid [hesheit] *de* hoarseness, huskiness

heester [hestər] *de (~s)* shrub

heet [het] *adj* **1** hot: *een hete adem* a fiery breath *(also fig)*; *in het ~st van de strijd* in the thick (*or:* heat) of the battle; **2** *(fig)* hot, heated, fiery; **3** hot, spicy: *hete kost* spicy food; **4** hot, horny

heetgebakerd [hetχəbakərt] *adj* hot-tempered, quick-tempered

hefboom [hɛvbom] *de (hefbomen)* lever

hefbrug [hɛvbrʏχ] *de (~gen)* **1** (vertical) lift bridge; **2** (hydraulic) lift

heffen [hɛfə(n)] *vb* **1** lift, raise: *het glas ~* raise one's

glass (to), drink (to); **2** levy, impose

heffing [hɛfɪŋ] *de (~en)* levy, charge

heft [hɛft] *het (~en)* handle, haft, hilt: *het ~ in handen hebben* be in control, command

heftig [hɛftəχ] *adj, adv* violent, fierce, furious, intense, severe, heated: *~ protesteren* protest vigorously

heftruck [hɛftrʏk] *de (~s)* fork-lift truck

heg [hɛχ] *de (~gen)* hedge

heggenschaar [hɛɣə(n)sχar] *de (-scharen)* garden shears, hedge trimmer

hei [hɛi] *de (~en)* **1** heath(land); **2** *(bot)* heather

heibel [hɛibəl] *de* row, racket

heide [hɛidə] *de* heath

heiden [hɛidə(n)] *de (~en)* heathen, pagan

heidens [hɛidəns] *adj, adv* **1** heathen, pagan; **2** atrocious, abominable; infernal; rotten

heien [hɛiə(n)] *vb* drive (piles)

heiig [hɛiəχ] *adj* hazy

heil [hɛil] *het* good: *ik zie er geen ~ in* I do not see the point of it

Heiland [hɛilɑnt] *de* Saviour

heilbot [hɛilbɔt] *de (~ten)* halibut

heilig [hɛiləχ] *adj* holy; sacred: *heilige koe* (or: *muziek)* sacred cow (*or:* music); *hem is niets ~* nothing is sacred to him

heiligdom [hɛiləɣdɔm] *het (~men)* sanctuary

heilige [hɛiləɣə] *de (~n)* saint

heiligschennis [hɛiləχsχɛnɪs] *de* sacrilege, desecration

heilloos [hɛilos] *adj, adv* fatal, disastrous

heilzaam [hɛilzam] *adj* **1** curative, healing, wholesome, healthful; **2** salutary, beneficial: *een heilzame werking* (or: *invloed) hebben* have a beneficial effect (*or:* influence)

heimelijk [hɛimələk] *adj, adv* secret, clandestine, surreptitious, sneaking

heimwee [hɛimwe] *het* homesickness: *ik kreeg ~ (naar)* I became homesick (for)

Hein [hɛin] || *magere ~* the Grim Reaper

heinde [hɛində] *adv* || *van ~ en verre* from far and near (*or:* wide)

heipaal [hɛipal] *de (heipalen)* pile

hek [hɛk] *het (~ken)* **1** fence, barrier; **2** gate, wicket(-gate)

hekel [hekəl] *de* hackle || *een ~ aan iem (iets) hebben* hate s.o. (sth)

hekje [hɛkjə] *het (~s)* **1** small gate (*or:* door); **2** *(comp, telecommunications)* number sign

heks [hɛks] *de (~en)* **1** witch; **2** shrew; **3** hag

heksenjacht [hɛksə(n)jɑχt] *de (~en)* witch-hunt

heksenketel [hɛksə(n)ketəl] *de (~s)* bedlam, pandemonium

heksenkring [hɛksə(n)krɪŋ] *de (~en)* fairy ring

hekserij [hɛksərɛi] *de (~en)* sorcery, witchcraft

hekwerk [hɛkwɛrk] *het (~en)* fencing, railings

¹hel [hɛl] *de* hell

²hel [hɛl] *adj, adv* vivid, bright

hela [hela] *int* hey

helaas [helạs] *adv* unfortunately: ~ *kunnen wij u niet helpen* I'm afraid (*or:* sorry) we can't help you

held [hɛlt] *de (~en)* hero ‖ *hij is geen ~ in rekenen* he is not much at figures

heldendaad [hɛldǝ(n)dat] *de (-daden)* heroic deed (*or:* feat), act of heroism, exploit

heldendicht [hɛldǝ(n)dɪχt] *het (~en)* heroic poem, epic poem, epic

helder [hɛldǝr] *adj, adv* **1** clear: *een ~e lach* a ringing laugh; **2** clear, bright: ~ *wit* (*or:* *groen*) brilliant white, bright green; **3** clear, lucid: *zo ~ als kristal (glas)* as clear as crystal, crystal-clear

helderheid [hɛldǝrhɛit] *de* **1** clearness; clarity; **2** brightness, vividness; **3** brightness; **4** clarity, lucidity

helderziende [hɛldǝrzɪndǝ] *de (~n)* clairvoyant: *ik ben toch geen ~* I'm not a mind-reader

helderziendheid [hɛldǝrzɪnthɛit] *de* clairvoyance, second sight

heldhaftig [hɛlthɑftǝχ] *adj, adv* heroic, valiant

heldin [hɛldɪn] *de (~nen)* heroine

heleboel [helǝbul] *de* (quite) a lot, a whole lot: ~ *mensen zouden het niet met je eens zijn* an awful lot of people wouldn't agree with you

helemaal [helǝmal] *adv* **1** completely, entirely: *ik heb het ~ alleen gedaan* I did it all by myself; ~ *nat zijn* be wet through; *ben je nu ~ gek geworden?* are you completely out of your mind?; ~ *niets* nothing at all; *het kan mij ~ niets schelen* I couldn't care less; ~ *niet* absolutely not; *niet ~ juist* not quite correct; ~ *in het begin* right at the beginning (*or:* start); **2** right; all the way: ~ *bovenaan* right at the top; ~ *in het noorden* way up in the north

¹helen [helǝ(n)] *vb* heal: *de wond heelt langzaam* the wound is healing slowly

²helen [helǝ(n)] *vb* **1** (*law*) receive; **2** (*med*) heal

heler [helǝr] *de (~s)* receiver, (*fig*) fence

helft [hɛlft] *de (~en)* half: *ieder de ~ betalen* pay half each, go halves, go Dutch; *meer dan de ~* more than half; *de ~ minder* half as much (*or:* many); *de ~ van tien is vijf* half of ten is five; *de tweede ~ van een wedstrijd* the second half of a match

helikopter [helikɔptǝr] *de (~s)* helicopter, chopper

heling [helɪŋ] *de* receiving

helium [helijʏm] *het* helium

hellen [hɛlǝ(n)] *vb* slope, lean (over), slant: *de muur helt naar links* the wall is leaning

hellenisme [hɛlenɪsmǝ] *het* Hellenism

helling [hɛlɪŋ] *de (~en)* **1** slope, incline, ramp; **2** inclination

helm [hɛlm] *de (~en)* helmet, hard hat

helmdraad [hɛlmdrat] *de (-draden)* filament

helmgras [hɛlmɣrɑs] *het* marram (grass)

helmknop [hɛlmknɔp] *de (~pen)* anther

helpdesk [hɛlbdɛsk] *de (~s)* help desk

helpen [hɛlpǝ(n)] *vb* **1** help, aid: *kun je mij aan honderd euro ~?* can you let me have a hundred euros?; *help!* help!; **2** attend to: *welke specialist heeft u geholpen?* which specialist did you see? (*or:* have?);

u wordt morgen geholpen you are having your operation tomorrow; **3** help, assist: *iem een handje ~* give (*or:* lend) s.o. a hand; *help me eraan denken, wil je?* remind me, will you?; **4** help (out): *iem aan een baan ~* get s.o. fixed up with a job; **5** help, serve: *wordt u al geholpen?* are you being served?; *kan ik 't ~ dat hij zich zo gedraagt?* is it my fault if he behaves like that?; *wat helpt het?* what good would it do?, what is the use?; *dat helpt tegen hoofdpijn* that's good for a headache

helper [hɛlpǝr] *de (~s)* helper, assistant

hels [hɛls] *adj, adv* infernal: *een ~ karwei* a (*or:* the) devil of a job

hem [hɛm] *pers pron* him; it: *dit boek is van ~* this book is his; *vrienden van ~* friends of his; *dat is het ~ nu juist* that's just it (*or:* the point)

hemd [hɛmt] *het (~en)* **1** vest, (*Am*) undershirt: *iem het ~ van zijn lijf vragen* want to know everything (from s.o.), pester s.o. (with questions); **2** shirt

hemel [hemǝl] *de (~en)* sky; heaven(s): *hij heeft er ~ en aarde om bewogen* he moved heaven and earth for it; *een heldere* (*or:* *blauwe, bewolkte*) ~ a clear (*or:* blue, cloudy) sky; *Onze Vader die in de ~en zijt* Our Father who (*or:* which) art in heaven; *hij was in de zevende ~* he was in seventh heaven

hemellichaam [hemǝlɪχam] *het (-lichamen)* heavenly body, celestial body

hemelsbreed [hemǝlzbret] *adj, adv* **1** vast, enormous; **2** as the crow flies, in a straight line

hemelvaartsdag [hemǝlvartsdɑχ] *de (~en)* Ascension Day

hemofilie [hemofilị] *de* haemophilia

¹hen [hɛn] *de (~nen)* hen

²hen [hɛn] *pers pron* them: *hij gaf het ~* he gave it to them; *dit boek is van ~* this book is theirs; *vrienden van ~* friends of theirs

hendel [hɛndǝl] *het, de (~s)* handle, lever

hengel [hɛŋǝl] *de (~s)* fishing rod

hengelaar [hɛŋǝlar] *de (~s)* angler

hengelen [hɛŋǝlǝ(n)] *vb* angle, fish

hengsel [hɛŋsǝl] *het (~s)* **1** handle; **2** hinge

hengst [hɛŋst] *de (~en)* stallion, stud (horse)

hennep [hɛnǝp] *de* hemp, cannabis

hens [hɛns] *de* ‖ *alle ~ aan dek!* all hands on deck!

hepatitis [hepatịtɪs] *de* hepatitis

her [hɛr] *adv* hither, here

heraldiek [heraldịk] *de* heraldry

herbenoemen [hɛrbǝnumǝ(n)] *vb* reappoint

herberg [hɛrbɛrχ] *de (~en)* inn, tavern

herbergen [hɛrbɛrɣǝ(n)] *vb* accommodate, house, harbour: *de zaal kan 2000 mensen ~* the hall seats 2000 people

herboren [hɛrborǝ(n)] *adj* reborn, born again

herdenken [hɛrdɛŋkǝ(n)] *vb* commemorate

herdenking [hɛrdɛŋkɪŋ] *de (~en)* commemoration

herder [hɛrdǝr] *de (~s)* **1** cowherd; shepherd; **2** pastor

herdershond [hɛrdǝrshɔnt] *de (~en)* sheepdog;

Alsatian, *(Am)* German shepherd (dog)
herdruk [hɛrdrʏk] *de (~ken)* (new) edition; reprint
herdrukken [hɛrdrʏkə(n)] *vb* reprint
herenafdeling [herə(n)avdelɪŋ] *de (~en)* **1** men's department; **2** menswear department
herenakkoord [herə(n)akort] *het (~en)* gentleman's agreement
herenhuis [herə(n)hœys] *het (-huizen)* mansion, (imposing) town house, (desirable) residence
hereniging [herɛnəɣɪŋ] *de (~en)* reunification, reunion
herenkleding [herə(n)kledɪŋ] *de* menswear, men's clothes (*or:* clothing)
herexamen [hɛrɛksamə(n)] *het (~s)* re-examination, resit
herfst [hɛrfst] *de* autumn: *in de ~* in (the) autumn
herfstvakantie [hɛrfstfakɑnsi] *de (~s)* autumn half-term (holiday), *(Am)* fall break, mid-term break
hergeboorte [hɛrɣəbortə] *de (~n)* rebirth, regeneration
hergebruik [hɛrɣəbrœyk] *het* **1** reuse; **2** recycling
herhaald [hɛrhalt] *adj* repeated: *~e pogingen doen* make repeated attempts
herhaaldelijk [hɛrhaldələk] *adv* repeatedly: *dat komt ~ voor* that happens time and again
¹herhalen [hɛrhalə(n)] *vb* repeat, redo, revise, *(Am)* review: *iets in het kort ~* summarize sth
²herhalen [hɛrhalə(n)] *ref vb* repeat oneself, recur
herhaling [hɛrhalɪŋ] *de (~en)* **1** recurrence, repetition, replay, repeat, rerun: *voor ~ vatbaar zijn* bear repetition (*or:* repeating); **2** repetition, revision, *(Am)* review: *in ~en vervallen* repeat oneself
herhalingscursus [hɛrhalɪŋskʏrzʏs] *de* refresher course
herindelen [hɛrɪndelə(n)] *vb* regroup
¹herinneren [hɛrɪnərə(n)] *vb* remind, recall: *die geur herinnerde mij aan mijn jeugd* that smell reminded me of my youth; *herinner mij eraan dat …* remind me that … (*or:* to …)
²herinneren [hɛrɪnərə(n)] *ref vb* remember, recall: *kun je je die Ier nog ~?* do you remember that Irishman?; *als ik (het) me goed herinner* if I remember correctly (*or:* rightly); *zich iets vaag ~* have a vague recollection of sth; *voor zover ik mij herinner* as far as I can remember
herinnering [hɛrɪnərɪŋ] *de (~en)* **1** recollection, remembrance: *iets in ~ brengen* recall sth; **2** memory: *iets in zijn ~ voor zich zien* see sth before one; **3** memory, reminiscence: *ter ~ aan* in memory of; **4** souvenir, reminder: *een tweede ~ van de bibliotheek* a second reminder from the library
herintreden [hɛrɪntredə(n)] *vb* return to work || *een ~de vrouw* a (woman) returner
herkansing [hɛrkɑnsɪŋ] *de (~en)* repêchage; extra heat
herkauwer [hɛrkɑuwər] *de (~s)* ruminant
herkenbaar [hɛrkɛmbar] *adj* recognizable: *een herkenbare situatie* a familiar situation

herkennen [hɛrkɛnə(n)] *vb* recognize; identify, spot: *ik herkende hem aan zijn manier van lopen* I recognized him by his walk; *iem ~ als de dader* identify s.o. as the culprit
herkenning [hɛrkɛnɪŋ] *de (~en)* recognition, identification
herkenningsmelodie [hɛrkɛnɪŋsmelodi] *de (~ën)* signature tune, theme song
herkeuring [hɛrkørɪŋ] *de (~en)* re-examination, reinspection
herkomst [hɛrkɔmst] *de (~en)* origin, source: *het land van ~* the country of origin
herleiden [hɛrlɛidə(n)] *vb* reduce (to), convert (into): *een breuk ~* reduce (to) a fraction
herleven [hɛrlevə(n)] *vb* revive: *~d fascisme* resurgent fascism
hermafrodiet [hɛrmafrodit] *de (~en)* hermaphrodite
¹hermelijn [hɛrməlɛin] *de (~en) (animal)* ermine
²hermelijn [hɛrməlɛin] *het (fur)* ermine
hermetisch [hɛrmetis] *adj, adv* hermetic: *~ gesloten* hermetically sealed
hernemen [hɛrnemə(n)] *vb* resume, regain
hernia [hɛrnija] *de (~'s)* slipped disc
heroïne [herowinə] *de* heroin
heroïnehoer [herowinəhur] *de (~en)* heroin prostitute, junkie prostitute
heroïnespuit [herowinəspœyt] *de* fix, shot
herontdekken [hɛrɔndɛkə(n)] *vb* rediscover
heropenen [hɛrɔpənə(n)] *vb* reopen
heropvoeding [hɛrɔpfudɪŋ] *de* re-education
heroveren [hɛrovərə(n)] *vb* recapture, recover, retake, regain: *hij wilde zijn oude plaats ~* he wanted to regain his old seat (*or:* place)
herovering [hɛrovərɪŋ] *de* recapture
heroverwegen [hɛrovərweɣə(n)] *vb* reconsider, rethink
herpes [hɛrpɛs] *de* herpes
herrie [hɛri] *de* **1** noise, din, racket: *maak niet zo'n ~* don't make such a racket; **2** bustle, commotion, turmoil, fuss: *~ schoppen* make trouble
herrijzen [hɛrɛizə(n)] *vb* rise again: *hij is als uit de dood herrezen* it is as if he has come back from the dead
herroepen [hɛrupə(n)] *vb* revoke, repeal, retract, reverse
herschrijven [hɛrsχrɛivə(n)] *vb* rewrite
hersenbloeding [hɛrsə(n)bludɪŋ] *de (~en)* cerebral haemorrhage
hersenen [hɛrsənə(n)] *de* brain
hersenhelft [hɛrsə(n)hɛlft] *de (~en)* (cerebral) hemisphere, half of the brain
herseninfarct [hɛrsə(n)ɪnfɑrkt] *het (~en)* cerebral infarction
hersens [hɛrsəns] *de* **1** brain(s): *een goed stel ~ hebben* have a good head on one's shoulders; *hoe haal je het in je ~!* have you gone off your rocker?; **2** skull: *iem de ~ inslaan* beat s.o.'s brains out
hersenschudding [hɛrsə(n)sχʏdɪŋ] *de (~en)* con-

cussion

hersenspoeling [hɛrsə(n)spulıŋ] *de (~en)* brainwashing

hersentumor [hɛrsə(n)tymɔr] *de* brain tumour

hersenvliesontsteking [hɛrsə(n)vlisɔntstekıŋ] *de (~en)* meningitis

herstel [hɛrstɛl] *het* **1** repair, mending, rectification, correction; **2** recovery, convalescence, recuperation: *voor ~ van zijn gezondheid* to recuperate, to convalesce; **3** restoration

¹herstellen [hɛrstɛlə(n)] *vb* **1** repair, mend, restore; **2** restore, re-establish: *de rust ~* restore quiet; **3** right, repair, rectify, correct: *een onrecht ~* right a wrong; *de heer Blaak, herstel: Braak* Mr Blaak, correction: Braak

²herstellen [hɛrstɛlə(n)] *vb* recover, recuperate: *snel (or: goed) ~ van een ziekte* recover quickly (or: well) from an illness

herstelwerkzaamheden [hɛrstɛlwɛrksamhedə(n)] *de* repairs

hert [hɛrt] *het (~en)* deer, red deer

hertenkamp [hɛrtə(n)kɑmp] *de (~en)* deer park, deer forest

hertog [hɛrtɔx] *de (~en)* duke

hertogdom [hɛrtɔxdɔm] *het (~men)* duchy, dukedom

hertogin [hɛrtoɣın] *de (~nen)* duchess

herverdeling [hɛrvərdelıŋ] *de (~en)* redistribution, reorganization, reshuffle

hervormd [hɛrvɔrmt] *adj* **1** reformed; **2** *(rel)* Reformed; Protestant *(as opposed to Catholicism)*: *de hervormde Kerk* the Reformed Church

hervormen [hɛrvɔrmə(n)] *vb* reform

hervormer [hɛrvɔrmər] *de (~s)* reformer

hervorming [hɛrvɔrmıŋ] *de (~en)* **1** reformation; **2** reform

herwaarderen [hɛrwardərə(n)] *vb* revalue; reassess

herwaardering [hɛrwardərıŋ] *de* revaluation, reassessment

herzien [hɛrzin] *vb* revise ‖ *een beslissing ~* reconsider a decision

herziening [hɛrzinıŋ] *de (~en)* revision, review: *een ~ van de grondwet* an amendment to the constitution

hes [hɛs] *de (~sen)* smock, blouse

hesp [hɛsp] *de (~en) (Belg)* ham

¹het [ət] *pron* it: *ik denk (or: hoop) ~* I think *(or:* hope) so; *wie is ~? ben jij ~? ja, ik ben ~* who is it? is that you? yes, it is me; *zij waren ~ die ...* it were they who ...; *als jij ~ zegt* if you say so; *het kind heeft honger; geef ~ een boterham* the child is hungry; give him *(or:* her) a sandwich; *de machine doet ~* the machine works; *hoe gaat ~? ~ gaat* how are you? I'm all right *(or:* O.K.); *wat geeft ~? wat zou ~?* what does it matter? who cares?; *~ regent* it is raining

²het [ət] *art* the: *in ~ zwart gekleed* dressed in black; *Nederland is ~ land van de tulpen* Holland is the country for tulips; *die vind ik ~ leukst* that's the one

I like best; *zij was er ~ eerst* she was there first

¹heten [hetə(n)] *vb* be called *(or:* named): *een jongen, David geheten* a boy by the name of David; *het boek heet ...* the book is called ...; *hoe heet dat?, hoe heet dat in het Arabisch?* what is that called?, what is that in Arabic? *(or:* the Arabic for that?)

²heten [hetə(n)] *vb* bid: *ik heet u welkom* I bid you welcome

heterdaad [hetərdat] *de* ‖ *iem op ~ betrappen* catch s.o. in the act, catch s.o. red-handed

heterogeen [hetəroɣen] *adj* heterogeneous

¹heteroseksueel [hetərosɛksywel] *de (-seksuelen)* heterosexual

²heteroseksueel [hetərosɛksywel] *adj* heterosexual

hetgeen [ətxen] *pron* **1** that which, what: *ik blijf bij ~ ik gezegd heb* I stand by what I said; **2** which: *hij kon niet komen, ~ hij betreurde* he could not come, which he regretted

hetzelfde [ətsɛlvdə] *dem pron* the same: *wie zou niet ~ doen?* who wouldn't (do the same)?; *het is (blijft) mij ~* it's all the same to me; *(van) ~* (the) same to you

hetzij [ətsɛi] *conj* either, whether: *~ warm of koud* either hot or cold

heuglijk [høxlək] *adj* happy, glad, joyful

heup [høp] *de (~en)* hip

heupgewricht [høpxəvrıxt] *het (~en)* hip joint

heus [høs] *adj, adv* real, true: *hij doet het ~ wel* he is sure to do do it

heuvel [høvəl] *de (~s)* hill, *(small)* hillock, mound

heuvelachtig [høvəlɑxtəx] *adj* hilly

¹hevig [hevəx] *adj* **1** violent, intense: *~e angst* acute terror; *een ~e brand* a raging fire; *een ~e koorts* a raging fever; *~e pijnen* severe pains; **2** violent, vehement, fierce: *onder ~ protest* under strong *(or:* vehement) protest; *~e uitvallen* violent outbursts

²hevig [hevəx] *adv* violently, fiercely, intensely: *hij was ~ verontwaardigd* he was highly indignant; *~ bloeden* bleed profusely; *zij snikte ~* she cried her eyes out

hevigheid [hevəxhɛit] *de* violence, vehemence, intensity, fierceness, acuteness

hiel [hil] *de (~en)* heel: *iem op de ~en zitten* be (close) on s.o.'s heels

hier [hir] *adv* **1** here: *dit meisje ~* this girl; *ik ben ~ nieuw* I'm new here; *wie hebben we ~!* look who's here!; *~ is het gebeurd* this is where it happened; *~ is de krant* here's the newspaper; *~ staat dat ...* it says here that ...; *~ of daar vinden wij wel wat* we'll had it up to here; **2** this: *~ moet je het mee doen* you'll have to make do with this

hieraan [hiran] *adv* to this, at/on *(or:* by, from) this: *~ valt niet te twijfelen* there is no doubt about this

hierachter [hirɑxtər] *adv* behind this, after this: *~ ligt een grote tuin* there is a large garden at the back

hiërarchie [hijərarxi] *de (~ën)* hierarchy

hiërarchisch [hijərarɣis] *adj, adv* hierarchic(al)

hierbeneden [hirbənedə(n)] *adv* down here

hierbij [hirbɛi] *adv* at this, with this, herewith, hereby: ~ *bericht ik u, dat …* I hereby inform you that …; ~ *komt nog dat hij …* in addition (to this), he …

hierbinnen [hirbɪnə(n)] *adv* in here, inside

hierboven [hirbovə(n)] *adv* up here, above: ~ *woont een drummer* a drummer lives upstairs

hierbuiten [hirbœytə(n)] *adv* outside

hierdoor [hirdor] *adv* **1** through here, through this, by doing so: ~ *wil hij ervoor zorgen dat …* by doing so he wants to ensure that …; **2** because of this: ~ *werd ik opgehouden* this held me up

hierheen [hirhen] *adv* (over) here, this way: *op de weg* ~ on the way here; *hij kwam helemaal* ~ *om …* he came all this way …

hierin [hirɪn] *adv* in here, within, in this

hierlangs [hirlɑŋs] *adv* past here, along here, by here

hiermee [hirme] *adv* with this, by this: *in verband* ~ in this connection

hierna [hirna] *adv* **1** after this; **2** below

hiernaast [hirnast] *adv* next door, alongside: *de illustratie op de bladzijde* ~ the illustration on the facing page; ~ *hebben ze twee auto's* the next-door neighbours have two cars

hiernamaals [hirnamals] *het* hereafter, next world, (great) beyond

hiëroglief [hijəroɣlif] *de* (~*en*) hieroglyph, (*pl also*) hieroglyphics

hierom [hirɔm] *adv* **1** (a)round this: *dat ringetje moet* ~ that ring belongs around this; **2** because of this, for this reason: ~ *blijf ik thuis* this is why I'm staying at home

hieromheen [hirɔmhen] *adv* (a)round this: ~ *loopt een gracht* there is a canal surrounding this

hieronder [hirɔndər] *adv* **1** under here, underneath, below: *zoals* ~ *aangegeven* as stated below; **2** among these: ~ *zijn veel personen van naam* among them there are many people of note; ~ *versta ik …* by this I understand …

hierop [hirɔp] *adv* **1** (up)on this: *het komt* ~ *neer* it comes down to this; **2** after this, then

hierover [hirovər] *adv* **1** over this; **2** about this, regarding this, on this

hiertegen [hirteɣə(n)] *adv* against this

hiertegenover [hirteɣə(n)ɔvər] *adv* opposite, across the street, over the way

hiertoe [hirtu] *adv* **1** (up to) here: *tot* ~ so far, up to now; **2** to this, for this: *wat heeft u* ~ *gebracht?* what brought you to do this?

hieruit [hirœyt] *adv* **1** out of here: *van* ~ *vertrekken* depart from here; **2** from this: ~ *volgt, dat …* it follows (from this) that …

hiervan [hirvɑn] *adv* of this

hiervandaan [hirvɑndan] *adv* from here, away

hiervoor [hirvor] *adv* **1** in front (of this), before this; **2** of this: ~ *hoeft u niet bang te zijn* you needn't be afraid of this; **3** for this purpose, to this end; **4** (in exchange, return) for this

hifi-installatie [hɑjfɔjɪnstɑla(t)si] *de* (~*s*) hi-fi (set)

hij [hɛi] *pers pron* he, it: *iedereen is trots op het werk dat* ~ *zelf doet* everyone is proud of the work they do themselves; ~ *is het* it's him; ~ *daar* him over there

hijgen [hɛiɣə(n)] *vb* pant, gasp

hijger [hɛiɣər] *de* (~*s*) heavy breather: *ik had weer een* ~ *vandaag* I had another obscene phone-call today

hijsen [hɛisə(n)] *vb* **1** hoist, lift: *de vlag (in top)* ~ hoist (*or:* run up) the flag; **2** haul, heave

hijskraan [hɛiskran] *de* (-*kranen*) crane

hik [hɪk] *de* (~*ken*) hiccup

hikken [hɪkə(n)] *vb* hiccup ‖ *tegen iets aan* ~ shrink from sth

hilariteit [hilaritɛit] *de* hilarity, mirth

Himalaya [himalaja] *de* (the) Himalayas

hinde [hɪndə] *de* (~*n*) hind, doe

hinder [hɪndər] *de* nuisance, bother, hindrance, obstacle: *het verkeer ondervindt veel* ~ *van de sneeuw* traffic is severely disrupted by the snow

hinderen [hɪndərə(n)] *vb* impede, hamper, obstruct: *zijn lange jas hinderde hem bij het lopen* his long coat got in his way as he walked

hinderlaag [hɪndərlaχ] *de* (*hinderlagen*) ambush, (*fig also*) trap: *de vijand in een* ~ *lokken* lure the enemy into an ambush

¹hinderlijk [hɪndərlək] *adj* **1** annoying, irritating; **2** objectionable, disturbing; **3** unpleasant, disagreeable: *ik vind de warmte niet* ~ the heat does not bother me

²hinderlijk [hɪndərlək] *adv* annoyingly, blatantly

hindernis [hɪndərnɪs] *de* (~*sen*) obstacle, barrier, (*fig also*) hindrance, (*fig also*) impediment

hindernisloop [hɪndərnɪslop] *de* (-*lopen*) steeplechase

hinderpaal [hɪndərpal] *de* (-*palen*) obstacle, impediment

hinderwetvergunning [hɪndərwɛtfərɣynɪŋ] *de* (*roughly*) licence under the Nuisance Act

Hindoe [hɪndu] *de* Hindu

hindoeïsme [hɪnduwɪsmə] *het* Hinduism

Hindoestaan [hɪndustan] *de* (*Hindoestanen*) Hindu(stani)

hinkelen [hɪŋkələ(n)] *vb* hop, play hopscotch

hinken [hɪŋkə(n)] *vb* **1** limp, have a limp, walk with a limp, hobble (along); **2** hop

hink-stap-sprong [hɪŋkstɑpsprɔŋ] *de* triple jump, hop, step and jump

hinniken [hɪnəkə(n)] *vb* neigh, whinny

hint [hɪnt] *de* (~*s*) hint, tip(-off): *(iem) een* ~ *geven* drop (s.o.) a hint

hiphop [hɪphɔp] *de* hip hop

hippie [hɪpi] *de* (~*s*) hippie

historicus [hɪstorikʏs] *de* (*historici*) historian

historie [hɪstori] *de* (*historiën*) **1** history; **2** story, anecdote; **3** affair, business

historisch [hɪstoris] *adj* **1** historic: *wij beleven een* ~ *moment* we are witnessing a historic moment; **2**

historical, period: *een ~e roman* a historical novel;
3 historical, true: *dat is ~* that's a historical fact (*or:* a true story)
hit [hɪt] *de (~s)* hit (record)
hitlijst [hɪtlɛist] *de (~en)* chart(s), hit parade
hitsig [hɪtsəχ] *adj, adv* **1** hot-blooded; **2** hot, randy, horny
hitte [hɪtə] *de* heat
hittebestendig [hɪtəbəstɛndəχ] *adj* heat-resistant, heatproof
hittegolf [hɪtəγɔlf] *de (-golven)* heatwave
hiv [haivɛ] *het human immunodeficiency virus* HIV
hm [həm] *int* (a)hem
ho [ho] *int* **1** stop: *zeg maar '~'* say when; **2** come on!, that's not fair!
hobbel [hɔbəl] *de (~s)* bump
hobbelen [hɔbələ(n)] *vb* bump, jolt, lurch
hobbelig [hɔbələχ] *adj* bumpy, irregular
hobbelpaard [hɔbəlpart] *het (~en)* rocking horse
hobby [hɔbi] *de (~'s)* hobby
hobbyruimte [hɔbirœymtə] *de (~n, ~s)* workroom
hobo [hobo] *de (~'s)* oboe
hoboïst [hobowɪst] *de (~en)* oboist
hobu [hoby] *het (Belg) hoger onderwijs buiten de universiteit* non-university higher education
hockey [hɔki] *het* hockey
hockeystick [hɔkistɪk] *de (~s)* hockey stick
hocus-pocus [hokʏspokʏs] *het, de* hocus-pocus, mumbo-jumbo
hoe [hu] *adv* **1** how: *je kunt wel nagaan ~ blij zij was* you can imagine how happy she was; *~ eerder ~ beter* the sooner the better; *het gaat ~ langer ~ beter* it is getting better all the time; *~ ouder ze wordt, ~ minder ze ziet* the older she gets, the less she sees; *~ fietst zij naar school?* which way does she cycle to school?; *~ moet het nu verder?* where do we go from here?; *~ dan ook: a)* anyway, anyhow, no matter how; *b)* by hook or by crook; *c)* no matter what; *~ vreemd het ook lijkt, ~ duur het ook is* strange as it may seem, expensive though it is; *~ kom je erbij?* how can you think such a thing?; *~zo?, ~ dat zo?* how (*or:* what) do you mean?, why do you ask?; *~ vind je mijn kamer?* what do you think of my room?; **2** what: *~ noemen jullie de baby?* what are you going to call the baby?; *Dorine danste, en ~!* Dorine danced, and how!
hoed [hut] *de (~en)* hat: *een hoge ~* a top hat
hoede [hudə] *de* **1** care, protection, custody, charge, (safe) keeping; **2** guard: *op zijn ~ zijn (voor)* be on one's guard (against)
¹hoeden [hudə(n)] *vb* tend, keep watch over, look after
²hoeden [hudə(n)] *ref vb* (with *voor*) guard (against), beware (of), be on one's guard (against)
hoedenmaker [hudə(n)makər] *de* hatter
hoedenplank [hudə(n)plaŋk] *de (~en)* shelf, (car) rear (*or:* parcel, back) shelf
hoederecht [hudərɛχt] *het (~en) (Belg)* child custody

hoedje [hucə] *het (~s)* (little) hat: *onder één ~ spelen met* be in league with
hoef [huf] *de (hoeven)* hoof
hoefijzer [hufɛizər] *het (~s)* (horse)shoe
hoefsmid [hufsmɪt] *de (-smeden)* farrier, blacksmith
hoek [huk] *de (~en)* **1** corner: *in de ~ staan* (or: *zetten*) stand (*or:* put) in the corner; *de ~ omslaan* turn the corner; *(vlak) om de ~ (van de straat)* (just) around the corner; **2** *(maths)* angle: *(fig) iets vanuit een andere ~ bekijken* look at sth from a different angle; *in een rechte ~* at right angles; *een scherpe* (*or: een stompe*) *~* an acute (*or:* obtuse) angle; *die lijnen snijden elkaar onder een ~ van 45°* those lines meet at an angle of 45°; **3** quarter, point of the compass: *dode ~* blind spot
hoekig [hukəχ] *adj, adv* angular, craggy, rugged, jagged
hoekje [hukjə] *het (~s)* corner, nook ‖ *het ~ omgaan* kick the bucket
hoekschop [huksχɔp] *de (~pen)* corner (kick)
hoeksteen [huksten] *de (-stenen)* cornerstone, *(fig)* keystone, linchpin, pillar
hoektand [huktant] *de (~en)* canine tooth, eye-tooth, fang
hoelang [hulaŋ] *adv* how long
hoen [hun] *het (~ders)* hen, chicken, *(pl also)* poultry, (domestic) fowl
hoepel [hupəl] *de (~s)* hoop
hoepla [hupla] *int* whoops, oops(-a-daisy); ups-a-daisy, here we go
hoer [hur] *de (~en)* whore
hoera [hura] *int* hooray, hurray, hurrah
hoes [hus] *de (hoezen)* cover(ing), case
hoest [hust] *de* cough
hoestbui [hustbœy] *de (~en)* fit of coughing, coughing fit
hoestdrank [huzdraŋk] *de (~en)* cough mixture
hoesten [hustə(n)] *vb* cough
hoesttablet [hustablɛt] *het, de (~ten)* cough lozenge, pastille
hoeve [huvə] *de (~n)* farm(stead), farmhouse, homestead
hoeveel [huvel] *num* how much, how many: *~ appelen zijn er?* how many apples are there?; *~ geld heb je bij je?* how much money do you have on you?; *~ is vier plus vier?* what do four and four make?, how much is four plus four?; *met hoevelen waren jullie?* how many of you were there?, how many were you?
hoeveelheid [huvelhɛit] *de (-heden)* amount, quantity, volume, dose
hoeveelste [huvelstə] *num* ‖ *de ~ juli ben je jarig?* when in July is your birthday?; *voor de ~ keer vraag ik het je nu?* how many times have I asked you?; *de ~ is het vandaag?* what day of the month is it today?; *het ~ deel van een liter is 10 cm³?* what fraction of a litre is 10cc?
¹hoeven [huvə(n)] *vb* need (to), have to: *dat had je*

niet ~ (te) doen you shouldn't have (done that); *daar hoef je niet bang voor te zijn* you needn't worry about that

²hoeven [hu̲və(n)] *vb* matter, be necessary: *het had niet gehoeven* you didn't have to do that, you shouldn't have done that; *het mag wel, maar het hoeft niet* you can but you don't have to

hoever [huve̲r] *adv* how far: *in ~re* to what extent

hoewel [huwe̲l] *conj* 1 (al)though, even though: *~ het pas maart is, zijn de bomen al groen* even though it's only March the trees are already in leaf; 2 (al)though, however

hoezeer [hu̲ze̲r] *adv* how much: *ik kan je niet zeggen ~ het mij spijt* I can't tell you how sorry I am

hoezo [hu̲zo̲] *int* what (*or:* how) do you mean?, in what way? (*or:* respect?)

hof [hɔf] *het* 1 *(law)* court; 2 court, royal household

hofdame [hɔ̲vdamə] *de (~s)* lady-in-waiting, maid of honour

hoffelijk [hɔ̲fələk] *adj, adv* courteous, polite

hofhouding [hɔ̲fhaudɪŋ] *de (~en)* (royal) household, court

hofleverancier [hɔ̲flevəransir] *de (~s)* purveyor to the Royal Household, purveyor to His (Her) Majesty the King (Queen), Royal Warrant Holder

hofnar [hɔ̲fnar] *de (~ren)* court jester, fool

hogedrukgebied [hoɣədrx̲kxɔbit] *het (~en)* anticyclone

hogedrukspuit [hoɣədrx̲kspœyt] *de (~en)* high-pressure paint spray; high-pressure spraying pistol

hogepriester [ho̲ɣəpristər] *de (~s)* high priest

hogerhand [ho̲ɣərhant] *de || op bevel van ~* by order of the authorities

Hogerhuis [ho̲ɣərhœys] *het* House of Lords, Upper House

hogerop [ho̲ɣərɔp] *adv* higher up: *hij wil ~* he wants to get on

hogeschool [ho̲ɣəsxol] *de (-scholen)* college (of advanced, higher education), polytechnic, academy: *Economische ~ School* of Economics; *Technische ~ College* (*or:* Institute) of Technology, Polytechnic (College)

hogesnelheidstrein [ho̲ɣəsnɛlhɛitstrɛin] *de (~en)* high-speed train

hoi [hɔj] *int* hi, hello, hurray, whoopee

hok [hɔk] *het (~ken)* 1 shed; storeroom; 2 pen, (dog) kennel, (pig)sty, dovecote, hen house, hen-coop

hokje [hɔ̲kjə] *het (~s)* 1 cabin; (sentry) box; cubicle; booth; 2 compartment, pigeon-hole *(also fig)*; square, box: *het ~ aankruisen (invullen)* put a tick in the box

hokken [hɔ̲kə(n)] *vb* shack up (with)

¹hol [hɔl] *het (~en)* 1 cave, cavern, grotto: *een donker ~* a dark, gloomy hole; 2 hole, lair, den, burrow: *zich in het ~ van de leeuw wagen* beard (*or:* brave) the lion in his den; 3 hole, haunt: *een op ~ geslagen paard* a runaway (horse)

²hol [hɔl] *adj, adv* 1 hollow, female, sunken; gaunt: *een ~ geslepen brillenglas* a concave lens; *het ~le van de hand* (*or:* voet) the hollow of the hand, the arch of the foot; 3 hollow, empty; 4 hollow, cavernous: *in het ~st van de nacht* at dead of night

Holland [hɔ̲lant] *het* the Netherlands; Holland

Hollander [hɔ̲landər] *de (~s)* 1 Dutchman; 2 inhabitant of North or South Holland

Hollands [hɔ̲lants] *adj* 1 from (the province of) North or South Holland; 2 Dutch, Netherlands: *~e nieuwe* Dutch (*or:* salted) herring

Hollandse [hɔ̲lantsə] *de* Dutchwoman

hollen [hɔ̲lə(n)] *vb* 1 bolt, run away; 2 run, race: *het is met hem ~ of stilstaan* it's always all or nothing with him

holocaust [ho̲lokɔ:st] *de (~en)* holocaust

hologram [ho̲loɣram] *het (~men)* hologram

holster [hɔ̲lstər] *de (~s)* holster

holte [hɔ̲ltə] *de (~s, ~n)* 1 cavity, hollow, hole, niche; 2 hollow, socket, pit, crook; 3 draught, depth

homeopathie [homejopati̲] *de* homoeopathy

hometrainer [hɔ̲mtrenər] *de (~s)* home trainer

hommage [ɔmaʒə] *de (~s)* homage

hommel [hɔ̲məl] *de (~s)* bumblebee

homo [ho̲mo] *de (~'s)* gay; fairy, queen

¹homofiel [homofi̲l] *de (~en)* homosexual

²homofiel [homofi̲l] *adj* homosexual

homogeen [homoɣe̲n] *adj* homogeneous, uniform

homoseksualiteit [homosɛksywalitɛit] *de* homosexuality, lesbianism

¹homoseksueel [homosɛksywe̲l] *de (-seksuelen)* homosexual

²homoseksueel [homosɛksywe̲l] *adj* homosexual

homp [hɔmp] *de (~en)* chunk, hunk, lump

hond [hɔnt] *de (~en)* 1 dog, hound: *pas op voor de ~* beware of the dog; *de ~ uitlaten* take the dog (out) for a walk, let the dog out; *~en aan de lijn!* dogs must be kept on the lead (leash)!; *geen ~* not a soul, nobody; *men moet geen slapende ~en wakker maken* let sleeping dogs lie; *blaffende ~en bijten niet (roughly)* his bark is worse than his bite; 2 dog, cur: *ondankbare ~!* ungrateful swine!; *(Belg) welkom zijn als een ~ in een kegelspel* be extremely unwelcome

hondenasiel [hɔ̲ndə(n)azil] *het (~en)* dogs' home

hondenlijn [hɔ̲ndə(n)lɛin] *de (~en)* lead, leash

hondenpoep [hɔ̲ndə(n)pup] *de* dog dirt

hondenras [hɔ̲ndə(n)ras] *het (~sen)* breed of dog

hondenweer [hɔ̲ndə(n)wer] *het* foul weather, filthy weather

¹honderd [hɔ̲ndərt] *het (~en)* hundred; hundred(s): *~en jaren* (*or:* keren) hundreds of years (*or:* times); *zij sneuvelden bij ~en* they died in their hundreds; *alles loopt in het ~* everything is going haywire

²honderd [hɔ̲ndərt] *num* hundred: *een bankbiljet van ~ euro* a hundred-euro (bank)note; *dat heb ik nu al (minstens) ~ keer gezegd* (if I've said it once) I've said it a hundred times; *ik voel me niet helemaal ~ procent* I'm feeling a bit under the weather;

~ procent zeker zijn (van) be absolutely positive; *er zijn er over de ~* there are more than a hundred

honderdduizend [hɔndərdœyzənt] *num* a (*or:* one) hundred thousand: *(enige) ~en (mensen)* hundreds of thousands (of people)

honderdduizendste [hɔndərdœyzəntstə] *num* (one) hundred thousandth

honderdje [hɔndərcə] *het (~s)* hundred-guilder note

honderdste [hɔndərstə] *num* hundredth: *ik probeer het nu al voor de ~ maal* I've tried it a hundred times

hondje [hɔncə] *het (~s)* doggy, little dog, bowow

honds [hɔnts] *adj, adv* despicable, shameful, scandalous

hondsdolheid [hɔntsdɔlhɛit] *de* rabies

Honduras [hɔnduras] *het* Honduras

honen [honə(n)] *vb* jeer

Hongaar [hɔŋɣar] *de (Hongaren)* Hungarian

¹Hongaars [hɔŋɣars] *het* Hungarian

²Hongaars [hɔŋɣars] *adj* Hungarian

Hongarije [hɔŋɣarɛiə] *het* Hungary

honger [hɔŋər] *de* appetite, hunger: *ik heb toch een ~!* I'm starving; *~ hebben* be (*or:* feel) hungry; *van ~ sterven* die of hunger, starve to death

hongerig [hɔŋərəχ] *adj, adv* hungry; famished; peckish

hongerloon [hɔŋərlon] *het (-lonen)* pittance, subsistence wages, starvation wages

hongersnood [hɔŋərsnot] *de (-noden)* famine, starvation, dearth

hongerstaking [hɔŋərstakɪŋ] *de (~en)* hunger strike

honing [honɪŋ] *de* honey

honingdrank [honɪŋdraŋk] *de (~en)* mead

honingraat [honɪŋrat] *de (-raten)* honeycomb

honk [hɔŋk] *het (~en)* base

honkbal [hɔŋgbal] *het* baseball

honkballen [hɔŋgbalə(n)] *vb* play baseball

honorarium [honorarijʏm] *het (honoraria, ~s)* fee; salary; royalty, honorarium

honoreren [honorerə(n)] *vb* **1** pay, remunerate, fee; **2** honour, give due recognition, recognize

hoofd [hoft] *het (~en)* **1** head: *met gebogen ~* with head bowed; *een ~ groter* (or: *kleiner) zijn dan* be a head taller (*or:* shorter) than; *een hard ~ in iets hebben* have grave doubts about sth; *het ~ laten hangen* hang one's head, be downcast; *het werk is hem boven het ~ gegroeid* he can't cope with his work any more; *het succes is hem naar het ~ gestegen* success has gone to his head; *iets over het ~ zien* overlook sth; **2** head, mind, brain(s): *mijn ~ staat er niet naar* I'm not in the mood for it; *hij heeft veel aan zijn ~* he has a lot of things on his mind; *iets uit het ~ kennen* learn sth by heart (*or:* rote); *uit het ~ zingen* sing from memory; *iem het ~ op hol brengen* turn s.o.'s head; *per ~ van de bevolking* per head of (the) population; **3** head; top; **4** head, front, vanguard; **5** head, chief, leader, principal, headmaster,

headmistress; **6** main, chief: *hoofdbureau* head office

hoofdagent [hoftaɣɛnt] *de (~en)* senior police officer

hoofdartikel [hoftartikəl] *het (~en)* editorial, leading article, leader

hoofdcommissaris [hoftkɔmɪsarɪs] *de (~sen)* (chief) superintendent (of police); commissioner

hoofddeksel [hovdɛksəl] *het (~s)* headgear; (*pl also)* headwear

hoofddoek [hovduk] *de (~en)* (head)scarf

hoofdeind [hoftɛint] *het* head

hoofdgerecht [hoftɣərɛχt] *het (~en)* main course

hoofdhuid [hofthœyt] *de* scalp

hoofding [hovdɪŋ] *de (~en)* (*Belg)* letterhead

hoofdinspecteur [hoftɪnspɛktør] *de (~s)* chief inspector, chief medical officer, inspector general

hoofdkantoor [hoftkantor] *het (-kantoren)* head office, headquarters

hoofdkraan [hoftkran] *de (-kranen)* mains (tap)

hoofdkwartier [hoftkwartir] *het (~en)* headquarters

hoofdletter [hoftlɛtər] *de (~s)* capital (letter)

hoofdlijn [hoftlɛin] *de (~en)* outline

hoofdmaaltijd [hoftmaltɛit] *de* main meal

hoofdmoot [hoftmot] *de (-moten)* principal part

hoofdpersoon [hoftpɛrson] *de (-personen)* principal person, leading figure, main character

hoofdpijn [hoftpɛin] *de (~en)* headache: *barstende ~* splitting headache

hoofdprijs [hoftprɛis] *de (-prijzen)* first prize

hoofdredacteur [hoftredaktør] *de (~en)* editor(-in-chief)

hoofdrekenen [hoftrekənə(n)] *het* mental arithmetic

hoofdrol [hoftrɔl] *de (~len)* leading part: *de ~ spelen* play the leading part, be the leading man (*or:* lady)

hoofdrolspeler [hoftrɔlspelər] *de (~s)* leading man, star, (*fig)* main figure

hoofdslagader [hoftslaɣadər] *de* aorta

hoofdstad [hoftstat] *de (-steden)* capital (city), provincial capital

hoofdstel [hoftstɛl] *het (~len)* bridle

hoofdsteun [hoftstøn] *de (~en)* headrest

hoofdstraat [hoftstrat] *de (-straten)* high street; main street

hoofdstuk [hoftstʏk] *het (~ken)* chapter

hoofdtelwoord [hoftɛlwort] *het (~en)* cardinal number

hoofdvak [hoftfak] *het (~ken)* main subject

hoofdverpleegkundige [hoftfərpleɣkʏndəɣə] *de* charge nurse

hoofdvogel [hoftfoɣəl] *de (~s)* (*Belg)* main prize ‖ *de ~ afschieten* make (*or:* commit) a serious blunder

hoofdweg [hoftwɛχ] *de (~en)* main road

hoofdzaak [hoftsak] *de (-zaken)* main point (*or:* thing), essentials: *~ is, dat we slagen* what matters is that we succeed

hoofdzakelijk [hoftsakələk] *adv* mainly

hoofdzin [hoftsɪn] *de (~nen)* main sentence (*or:* clause)

hoofdzonde [hoftsɔndə] *de (~n)* cardinal sin

hoofdzuster [hoftsʏstər] *de (~s)* charge nurse

hoog [hoːχ] *adj, adv* high, tall: *een hoge bal* a high ball; *een hoge C* a high C, a top C; *de ~ste verdieping* the top floor; *het water staat ~* the water is high; *~ in de lucht* high up in the air; *een stapel van drie voet ~* a three-foot high pile; *hij woont drie ~* he lives on the third (*or Am:* second) floor; *een hoge ambtenaar* a senior official; *naar een hogere klas overgaan* move up (*or:* be moved up) to a higher class; *een ~ stemmetje* (or: *geluid*) a high-pitched voice (*or:* sound); *de ruzie liep ~ op* the quarrel became heated; *de verwarming staat ~* the heating is on high; *de temperatuur mag niet hoger zijn dan 60°* the temperature must not go above (*or:* exceed) 60°

hoogachten [hoːχaχtə(n)] *vb* esteem highly, respect highly: *~d* yours faithfully

hoogbegaafd [hoːɣbəɣaft] *adj* highly gifted (*or:* talented): *scholen voor ~e kinderen* schools for highly-gifted children

hoogbouw [hoːɣbau] *de* high-rise building (*or:* flats)

hoogdag [hoːɣdɑχ] *de (~en) (Belg)* feast day

hoogdravend [hoːɣdraːvənt] *adj* high-flown, bombastic

hoogdringend [hoːɣdrɪŋənt] *adj (Belg)* urgent

hooggebergte [hoːχəbɛrχtə] *het (~n, ~s)* high mountains

hooggeëerd [hoːχəərt] *adj* highly honoured: *~ publiek!* Ladies and Gentlemen!

hooggelegen [hoːχəleɣə(n)] *adj* high: *een ~ oord in de Rocky Mountains* a place high up in the Rocky Mountains

hooggerechtshof [hoːχərɛχ(t)shɔf] *het (-hoven)* Supreme Court

hooghartig [hoːχhɑrtəχ] *adj, adv* haughty

hoogheid [hoːχhɛit] *de (-heden)* highness

hoogleraar [hoːχleraːr] *de (-leraren, ~s)* professor

Hooglied [hoːχlit] *het* Song of Songs

hooglopend [hoːχloːpənt] *adj* violent

hoogmis [hoːχmɪs] *de (~sen)* high mass

hoogmoed [hoːχmut] *de* pride: *~ komt ten val* pride goes before a fall

hoognodig [hoːχnoːdəχ] *adj, adv* highly necessary, much needed, urgently needed: *hij moest ~ naar het toilet* he was taken short

hoogoven [hoːχoːvə(n)] *de (~s)* blast furnace

hoogseizoen [hoːχsɛizun] *het (~en)* high season: *buiten het ~* out of season

hoogspanning [hoːχspɑnɪŋ] *de* high tension (*or:* voltage)

hoogspanningsmast [hoːχspɑnɪŋsmɑst] *de* pylon

hoogspringen [hoːχsprɪŋə(n)] *vb* high-jump, high-jumping

¹hoogst [hoːχst] *het* **1** top, highest; **2** utmost: *je krijgt op zijn ~ wat strafwerk* at the very worst you'll be given some lines

²hoogst [hoːχst] *adv* highly, extremely: *~ (on)waarschijnlijk* highly (un)likely

hoogstandje [hoːχstɑncə] *het (~s)* tour de force

hoogstens [hoːχstəns] *adv* **1** at the most, at (the very) most, up to, no(t) more than: *~ twaalf* twelve at the (very) most; **2** at worst: *~ kan hij u de deur wijzen* the worst he can do is show you the door; **3** at best

hoogstnodig [hoːχstnoːdəχ] *adj* absolutely necessary, strictly necessary: *alleen het ~e kopen* buy only the bare necessities

hoogstpersoonlijk [hoːχs(t)pɛrsoːnlək] *adv* in person, personally

hoogstwaarschijnlijk [hoːχstwarsχɛinlək] *adj, adv* most likely (*or:* probable), in all probability

hoogte [hoːχtə] *de (~n, ~s)* **1** height: *de ~ ingaan* go up, rise, ascend; *hij deed erg uit de ~* he was being very superior; *lengte, breedte en ~* length, breadth and height; **2** height, level: *de ~ van de waterspiegel* the water level; *tot op zekere ~ hebt u gelijk* up to a point you're right; **3** level, latitude, elevation, altitude: *er staat een file ter ~ van Woerden* there is a traffic jam near Woerden; *zich van iets op de ~ stellen* acquaint oneself with sth; *op de ~ blijven* keep oneself informed, keep in touch; *indien u verhinderd bent wordt u verzocht ons hiervan op de ~ te stellen* please let us know if you are unable to come; *ik kan geen ~ van hem krijgen* I don't understand him, I can't figure him out

hoogtelijn [hoːχtəlɛin] *de (~en)* altitude

hoogtepunt [hoːχtəpʏnt] *het (~en)* height, peak, highlight: *naar een ~ voeren, een ~ doen bereiken* bring to a climax

hoogtevrees [hoːχtəvres] *de* fear of heights

hoogtezon [hoːχtəzɔn] *de (~nen)* sun lamp

hooguit [hoːχœyt] *adv* at the most, at (the very) most, no(t) more than

hoogverraad [hoːχfəraːt] *het* high treason

hoogvlakte [hoːχflɑktə] *de (~n, ~s)* plateau

hoogwaardig [hoːχwardəχ] *adj* high-quality

hoogwater [hoːχwaːtər] *het* high water; high tide: *bij (met) ~* at high tide

hoogwerker [hoːχwɛrkər] *de (~s)* tower waggon

hooi [hoj] *het* hay: *te veel ~ op zijn vork nemen* bite off more than one can chew

hooiberg [hojbɛrχ] *de (~en)* haystack

hooien [hojə(n)] *vb* make hay

hooikoorts [hojkorts] *de* hay fever

hooimijt [hojmɛit] *de (~en)* haystack

hooivork [hojvɔrk] *de (~en)* pitchfork

hooiwagen [hojwaːɣə(n)] *de (~s)* **1** haycart, hay-wagon; **2** daddy-long-legs

hoongelach [hoːŋɣəlaχ] *het* jeering, jeers

¹hoop [hop] *de (hopen)* **1** heap, pile: *op een ~ leggen* pile up, stack up; *je kunt niet alles* (or: *iedereen*) *op één ~ gooien* you can't lump everything (*or:* everyone) together; **2** great deal, good deal, lot: *een hele ~* a good many; *ik heb nog een ~ te doen* I've still got a lot (*or:* lots) to do; **3** business: *het kind heeft een ~(je) gedaan* the child has done its business

²hoop [hop] *de (hopen)* hope: *goede ~ hebben* have high hopes; *valse ~ wekken* raise false hopes; *zolang er leven is, is er ~* while there's life there's hope; *weer (nieuwe) ~ krijgen* regain hope; *de ~ opgeven (or: verliezen) dat ...* give up (*or:* lose) hope that ...

hoopgevend [hopχevənt] *adj* hopeful

hoopvol [hopfɔl] *adj* hopeful, promising: *de toekomst zag er niet erg ~ uit* the future did not look very promising

hoorapparaat [horaparat] *het (-apparaten)* hearing aid

hoorbaar [horbar] *adj, adv* audible

hoorcollege [horkɔleʒə] *het (~s)* (formal) lecture

hoorn [horn] *de (~s)* **1** horn: *de stier nam hem op zijn ~s* the bull tossed him (on his horns); **2** receiver: *de ~ erop gooien* slam down the receiver; *de ~ van de haak nemen* lift the receiver; **3** horn; **4** conch

hoornist [hornɪst] *de (~en)* horn player

hoornvlies [hornvlis] *het (-vliezen)* cornea

hoorspel [horspɛl] *het (~en)* radio play

hoorzitting [horzɪtɪŋ] *de (~en)* hearing

hop [hɔp] *de (~pen)* hop(plant); hops

hopelijk [hopələk] *adv* I hope, let's hope, hopefully: *~ komt hij morgen* I hope (*or:* let's hope) he is coming tomorrow

hopeloos [hopəlos] *adj, adv* hopeless, desperate: *hij is ~ verliefd op* he's hopelessly (*or:* desperately) in love with

¹hopen [hopə(n)] *vb* **1** hope (for): *dat is niet te ~* I hope (*or:* let's hope) not; *ik hoop van wel* (or: *van niet*) I hope so (*or:* hope not); *ik hoop dat het goed met u gaat* I hope you are well; *tegen beter weten in (blijven) ~* hope against hope; *blijven ~* keep (on) hoping; **2** pile (up): *op elkaar gehoopt* heaped

²hopen [hopə(n)] *vb* hope (for): *~ op betere tijden* hope for better times

hopman [hɔpmɑn] *de (~nen)* Scoutmaster

hor [hɔr] *de (~ren)* screen

horde [hɔrdə] *de (~s)* **1** horde: *de hele ~ komt hierheen* the whole horde is coming here; **2** (*sport*) hurdle

hordeloop [hɔrdəlop] *de* hurdle race

horeca [horəka] *de* (hotel and) catering (industry)

¹horen [horə(n)] *vb* **1** hear: *we hoorden de baby huilen* we heard the baby crying; *nu kun je het me vertellen, hij kan ons niet meer ~* you can tell me now, he is out of earshot; *ik heb het alleen van ~ zeggen* I only have it on hearsay; *ik hoor het hem nog zeggen* I can still hear him saying it; *hij deed alsof hij het niet hoorde* he pretended not to hear (it); *ik kon aan zijn stem ~ dat hij zenuwachtig was* I could tell by his voice that he was nervous; **2** listen to; **3** hear, be told, get to know: *Johan kreeg te ~ dat het zo niet langer kon* Johan was told that it can't go on like that; *wij kregen heel wat te ~* we were given a hard

time of it; *laat eens iets van je ~* keep in touch; *zij wil geen nee ~* she won't take no for an answer; *hij vertelde het aan iedereen die het maar ~ wilde* he told it to anyone who would listen; *toevallig ~* overhear; *hij wilde er niets meer over ~* he didn't want to hear any more about it; *daar heb ik nooit van gehoord* I've never heard of it; *daarna hebben we niets meer van hem gehoord* that was the last we heard from him; *u hoort nog van ons* you'll be hearing from us; *nou hoor je het ook eens van een ander* so I'm not the only one who says so; *ik hoor het nog wel* let me know (about it); **4** listen (to): *moet je ~!* just listen!, listen to this!; *moet je ~ wie het zegt!* look who is talking!; *hoor eens* listen, I say

²horen [horə(n)] *vb* **1** hear: *hij hoort slecht* he is hard of hearing; **2** belong: *wij ~ hier niet* we don't belong here; *de kopjes ~ hier* the cups go here; **3** be done, should be; **4** belong (to): *dit huis hoort aan mijn vader* this house belongs to my father; *dat hoor je te weten* you should (*or:* ought to) know that; *dat hoort niet* it is not done; *dat hoort zo* that's how it should be

horizon [horizɔn] *de (~nen)* horizon: *zijn ~ verruimen (uitbreiden)* broaden one's horizons

horizontaal [horizɔntal] *adj* horizontal; (*crossword puzzle*) across

horloge [hɔrloʒə] *het (~s)* watch

horlogebandje [hɔrloʒəbɑncə] *het (~s)* watchband, watch strap

hormoon [hɔrmon] *het (hormonen)* hormone

horoscoop [horoskop] *de (horoscopen)* horoscope: *een ~ trekken (opmaken)* cast a horoscope

horrorfilm [hɔrorfɪlm] *de (~s)* horror film

hort [hɔrt] *de (~en)* jerk: *met ~en en stoten spreken* speak haltingly

horzel [hɔrzəl] *de (~s)* hornet

hospes [hɔspɛs] *de (~sen)* landlord; host

hospita [hɔspita] *de (~'s)* landlady

hospitaal [hɔspital] *het (hospitalen)* hospital

hospitaliseren [hɔspitalizerə(n)] *vb* hospitalize

hossen [hɔsə(n)] *vb* dance (*or:* leap) about (arm in arm)

hostie [hɔsti] *de (~s)* host

hotdog [hɔdɔɡ] *de (~s)* hotdog

hotel [hotɛl] *het (~s)* hotel

hotelhouder [hotɛlhaudər] *de (~s)* hotelkeeper

hotelschool [hotɛlsχol] *de (-scholen)* hotel and catering school: *hogere ~* hotel management school

houdbaar [haudbar] *adj* **1** not perishable: *ten minste ~ tot* best before; **2** tenable

houdbaarheid [haudbarhɛit] *de* shelf life, storage life (*of foods etc*)

¹houden [haudə(n)] *vb* **1** keep: *je mag het ~* you can keep (*or:* have) it; *kippen* (or: *duiven*) *~* keep hens (*or:* pigeons); *de blik op iets gericht ~* keep looking at sth; *laten we het gezellig ~* let's keep it (*or:* the conversation) pleasant; *ik zal het kort ~* I'll keep it short; *iem aan de praat ~* keep s.o. talking; *hij kon er zijn gedachten niet bij ~* he couldn't keep his mind on it; *iets tegen het licht* ~ hold sth up to the light; *ik kon hun namen niet uit elkaar* ~ I kept getting their names mixed up; *contact met iem* ~ keep in touch with s.o.; *orde* ~ keep order; **2** hold: *(sport) die had hij gemakkelijk kunnen* ~ he could have easily stopped that one; *de balk hield het niet* the beam didn't hold, the beam gave way; **3** hold, organize, give: *een lezing* ~ give *(or:* deliver) a lecture; **4** *(with voor)* take to be, consider to be *(or:* as): *iets voor gezien* ~ leave it at that, call it a day; **5** take, stand: *het was er niet om te* ~ *van de hitte* the heat was unbearable; *ik hou het niet meer* I can't take it any more *(or:* longer); *rechts* ~ keep (to the) right; *William houdt nooit zijn woord (or:* beloften) William never keeps his word *(or:* promises); *we* ~ *het op de 15e* let's make it the 15th, then

²houden [hɑudə(n)] *vb* **1** (with *van*) love: *wij* ~ *van elkaar* we love each other; **2** (with *van*) like, care for: *niet van dansen* ~ not like dancing; *hij houdt wel van een grapje* he can stand a joke; *ik hou meer van bier dan van wijn* I prefer beer to wine; **3** hold, stick: *het ijs houdt nog niet* the ice isn't yet strong enough to hold your weight

³houden [hɑudə(n)] *ref vb* **1** (with *aan*) keep to; adhere to; abide by; comply with, observe; **2** keep: *hij kon zich niet goed* ~ he couldn't help laughing *(or:* crying)

houder [hɑudər] *de (~s)* **1** holder, bearer: *een recordhouder* a record-holder; **2** *(law)* keeper, holder; **3** keeper, manager, proprietor; **4** holder, container

houdgreep [hɑutχrep] *de (-grepen)* hold

houding [hɑudɪŋ] *de (~en)* **1** position, pose: *in een andere* ~ *gaan liggen (zitten)* assume a different position; **2** pose, air: *zich geen* ~ *weten te geven* feel awkward; **3** attitude, manner

house [hɑus] *de* house (music)

houseparty [hɑuspɑ:rti] *de (~'s)* house party

hout [hɑut] *het* wood: ~ *sprokkelen* gather wood *(or:* sticks); *(Belg) niet meer weten van welk* ~ *pijlen te maken* not know which way to turn, be at a complete loss

houten [hɑutə(n)] *adj* wooden

houterig [hɑutərəχ] *adj, adv* wooden: *zich* ~ *bewegen* move woodenly

houthakker [hɑuthɑkər] *de (~s)* lumberjack

houthandel [hɑuthɑndəl] *de (~s)* **1** timber trade; **2** timber yard

houtje [hɑucə] *het (~s)* bit of wood || *iets op eigen* ~ *doen* do sth on one's own (initiative); *op een* ~ *bijten* have difficulty in keeping body and soul together

houtje-touwtjejas [hɑucətɑucəjɑs] *de (~sen)* duffel coat (with toggle fastenings)

houtskool [hɑutskol] *de* charcoal

houtsnede [hɑutsnedə] *de (~n, ~s)* woodcut

houtzagerij [hɑutsaɣərɛi] *de (~en)* sawmill

houvast [hɑuvɑst] *het* hold, grip: *niet veel (or: geen enkel)* ~ *geven* provide little *(or:* no) hold

houweel [hɑuwel] *het (houwelen)* pickaxe

houwen [hɑuwə(n)] *vb* **1** chop, hack, carve, hew: *uit marmer gehouwen* carved out of marble; **2** chop down

hovenier [hovənir] *de (~s)* horticulturist, gardener

hozen [hozə(n)] *vb* bail (out) || *het hoost* it is pouring down *(or:* with rain)

HSL [hɑɛsɛl] *de (~'s)* hogesnelheidslijn high-speed rail link

hso [hɑɛso] *het (Belg) hoger secundair onderwijs* senior general secondary education

hts [hateɛs] *de (~'en) hogere technische school* Technical College

huichelaar [hœyχəlar] *de (~s)* hypocrite

huichelarij [hœyχəlarɛi] *de (~en)* hypocrisy

¹huichelen [hœyχələ(n)] *vb* play the hypocrite, be hypocritical

²huichelen [hœyχələ(n)] *vb* feign, sham

huid [hœyt] *de (~en)* **1** skin: *hij heeft een dikke* ~ he is thick-skinned; *zijn* ~ *duur verkopen* fight to the bitter end; *iem de* ~ *vol schelden* call s.o. everything under the sun; *iem op zijn* ~ *zitten* keep on at s.o.; **2** hide; skin

huidarts [hœytɑrts] *de (~en)* dermatologist

huidig [hœydəχ] *adj* present, current

huiduitslag [hœytœytslɑχ] *de* rash

huidziekte [hœytsiktə] *de (~n, ~s)* skin disease

huifkar [hœyfkɑr] *de (~ren)* covered wagon

huig [hœyχ] *de (~en)* uvula

huilbui [hœylbœy] *de (~en)* crying fit

huilebalk [hœyləbɑlk] *de (~en)* cry-baby

huilen [hœylə(n)] *vb* **1** cry, whine, snivel: *ze kon wel* ~ she could have cried; *half lachend, half* ~*d* between laughing and crying; ~ *om iets* cry about sth; ~ *van blijdschap (or:* pijn) cry with joy *(or:* pain); **2** howl

huis [hœys] *het (huizen)* **1** house, home: ~ *van bewaring* remand centre; ~ *en haard* hearth and home; *halfvrijstaand* ~ semi-detached, *(Am)* duplex; *open* ~ *houden* have an open day *(or* Am: house); *het ouderlijk* ~ *verlaten, uit* ~ *gaan* leave home; *dicht bij* ~ near home; *een* ~ *in een rij* a terraced *(or* Am: row) house; *heel wat in* ~ *hebben (fig)* have a lot going for one; *nu de kinderen het* ~ *uit zijn* now that the children have all left; *een* ~ *van drie verdiepingen* a three-storeyed house; *ik kom van* ~ I have come from home; *dan zijn we nog verder van* ~ then we will be even worse off; *(op kosten) van het* ~ on the house; *het is niet om over naar* ~ *te schrijven* it is nothing to write home about; *van* ~ *uit* originally, by birth; **2** House: *het Koninklijk* ~ the Royal Family; *(Belg) daar komt niets van in* ~: *a)* that's not on; *b)* it won't work, nothing will come of it

huisarts [hœysɑrts] *de (~en)* family doctor

huisbaas [hœyzbas] *de (-bazen)* landlord

huisbezoek [hœyzbəzuk] *het (~en)* house call

huisdier [hœyzdir] *het (~en)* pet

huiselijk [hœysələk] *adj* **1** domestic, home, family; **2** homelike, homey: *een* ~ *type* a home-loving type

huisgenoot [hœysχənot] *de (-genoten)* housemate; member of the family

huishoudelijk [hœyshɑudələk] *adj* domestic, household

¹huishouden [hœyshɑudə(n)] *het (~s)* **1** housekeeping: *het ~ doen* run the house, do the housekeeping; **2** household: *woningen voor een- en tweepersoonshuishoudens* houses for single people and couples

²huishouden [hœyshɑudə(n)] *vb* carry on, cause damage *(or:* havoc)

huishoudgeld [hœyshɑutχɛlt] *het* housekeeping (money)

huishouding [hœyshɑudɪŋ] *de (~en)* housekeeping: *een gemeenschappelijke ~ voeren* have a joint household

huishoudster [hœyshɑutstər] *de (~s)* housekeeper

huisje [hœyʃə] *het (~s)* bungalow, cottage, small house, little house

huiskamer [hœyskamər] *de (~s)* living room

huisman [hœysmɑn] *de (~nen)* househusband

huismerk [hœysmɛrk] *het (~en)* own brand, generic brand

huismiddel [hœysmɪdəl] *het (~en)* home remedy

huismus [hœysmʏs] *de (~sen)* **1** house sparrow; **2** stay-at-home

huisraad [hœysrat] *de* household effects

huisregels [hœysreɣəls] *de* house rules

huissleutel [hœysløtəl] *de (~s)* latchkey, front-door key

huisvader [hœysfadər] *de (~s)* family man, father (of the family)

huisvesting [hœysfɛstɪŋ] *de* **1** housing; **2** accommodation: *ergens ~ vinden* find accommodation somewhere

huisvriend [hœysfrint] *de (~en)* family friend, friend of the family

huisvrouw [hœysfrɑu] *de (~en)* housewife

huisvuil [hœysfœyl] *het* household refuse

huisvuilzak [hœysfœylzɑk] *de* dustbin liner

huiswaarts [hœyswarts] *adv* homeward(s)

huiswerk [hœyswɛrk] *het* homework: *~ maken* do one's homework

huiszoeking [hœysukɪŋ] *de (~en)* (house) search

huiveren [hœyvərə(n)] *vb* **1** shiver; shudder, tremble: *~ van de kou* shiver with cold; **2** recoil (from), shrink (from)

huiverig [hœyvərəχ] *adj* hesitant, wary

huivering [hœyvərɪŋ] *de (~en)* shiver, shudder

huizenhoog [hœyzə(n)hoχ] *adj, adv* towering: *huizenhoge golven* mountainous waves

hulde [hʏldə] *de* homage; tribute

huldigen [hʏldəɣə(n)] *vb* honour, pay tribute (to)

huldiging [hʏldəɣɪŋ] *de (~en)* homage, tribute

¹hullen [hʏlə(n)] *vb* wrap up in, *(fig also)* veil (in), cloak (in)

²hullen [hʏlə(n)] *ref vb* wrap oneself (up), *(fig also)* veil *(or:* cloak, shroud) oneself (in)

hulp [hʏlp] *de (~en)* **1** help, assistance: *om ~ roepen* call (out) for help; *iem te ~ komen* come to s.o.'s aid; *eerste ~ (bij ongelukken)* first aid; **2** helper, assistant: *~ in de huishouding* home help

hulpactie [hʏlpɑksi] *de (~s)* relief action *(or:* measures)

hulpbehoevend [hʏlbəhuvənt] *adj* in need of helps, invalid, infirm, needy

hulpdienst [hʏlbdinst] *de (~en)* auxiliary service(s), emergency service(s): *telefonische ~* helpline

hulpeloos [hʏlpəlos] *adj, adv* helpless

hulpkreet [hʏlpkret] *de (-kreten)* cry for help

hulpmiddel [hʏlpmɪdəl] *het (~en)* aid, help, means

hulppost [hʏlpɔst] *de (~en)* aid station, first-aid post

hulpprogramma [hʏlproɣrama] *het (~'s)* utility

hulpstuk [hʏlpstʏk] *het (~ken)* accessory, attachment

hulptroepen [hʏlptrupə(n)] *de* auxiliary troops *(or:* forces), reinforcements

hulpvaardig [hʏlpfardəχ] *adj* helpful

hulpverlener [hʏlpfərlenər] *de (~s)* social worker

hulpverlening [hʏlpfərlenɪŋ] *de* assistance, aid, relief

huls [hʏls] *de (hulzen)* **1** case, cover, container; **2** cartridge case, shell

hulst [hʏlst] *de* holly

humaniora [hymanijɔra] *de (Belg; roughly)* grammar school education

humanitair [hymanitɛːr] *adj, adv* humanitarian

humeur [hymør] *het (~en)* humour, temper, mood

humeurig [hymørəχ] *adj, adv* moody

hummel [hʏməl] *de (~s)* toddler, (tiny) tot

humor [hymɔr] *de* humour: *gevoel voor ~* sense of humour

humorist [hymorɪst] *de (~en)* humorist, comic

humoristisch [hymorɪstis] *adj, adv* humorous: *een ~e opmerking* a humorous remark

humus [hymʏs] *de* humus

¹hun [hʏn] *pers pron* them: *ik zal het ~ geven* I'll give it (to) them; *heb je ~ al geroepen?* have you already called them?

²hun [hʏn] *pos pron* their: *~ kinderen* their children; *die zoon van hun* that son of theirs

hunebed [hʏnəbɛt] *het (~den)* megalith(ic tomb, monument, grave)

hunkeren [hʏŋkərə(n)] *vb* long for, yearn for

hup [hʏp] *int* **1** come on, go (to it): *~ Henk ~!* come on Henk!; **2** hup, oops-a-daisy: *een, twee, ... ~!* one, two, ... up you go!

huppeldepup [hʏpəldəpʏp] *de* what's-his-name, what's-her-name

huppelen [hʏpələ(n)] *vb* hop, skip, frolic

huren [hyrə(n)] *vb* **1** rent; charter: *een huis ~* rent a house; *kamers ~* live in rooms; **2** hire, take on: *een kok ~* hire *(or:* take on) a cook

hurken [hʏrkə(n)] *vb* squat: *zij zaten gehurkt op de grond* they were squatting on the ground; *op zijn ~ (gaan) zitten* squat (on one's haunches)

hut [hʏt] *de (~ten)* **1** hut: *een lemen ~* a mud hut; **2** cabin

hutkoffer [hʏtkɔfər] *de (~s)* cabin trunk

hutselen [hʏtsələ(n)] *vb* mix (up), shake (up): *dominostenen door elkaar ~* shuffle dominoes

hutspot [hʏtspɔt] *de* hot(ch)-pot(ch)

huur [hyr] *de (huren)* rent; lease: *achterstallige ~* rent in arrears, back rent; *kale ~* basic rent; *iem de ~ opzeggen* give s.o. notice (to leave, quit); *dit huis is te ~* this house is to let (*or Am:* for rent); *hij betaalt* €*800,- ~ voor dit huis* he pays 800 euros rent for this house

huurachterstand [hyraχtərstɑnt] *de (~en)* arrears of rent

huurauto [hyrɑuto] *de (~'s)* rented car, hire(d) car

huurcontract [hyrkɔntrɑkt] *het (~en)* rental agreement, lease: *een ~ aangaan* sign a lease; *een ~ opzeggen* terminate a lease

huurder [hyrdər] *de (~s)* renter, tenant, hirer: *de huidige ~s* the sitting tenants

huurhuis [hyrhœys] *het (-huizen)* rented house

huurkoop [hyrkop] *de* instalment buying, hire purchase (system)

huurling [hyrlɪŋ] *de (~en)* hireling, mercenary

huurmoordenaar [hyrmordənar] *de (~s)* (hired) assassin

huurovereenkomst [hyrovərɛŋkɔmst] *de (~en) see* huurcontract

huurprijs [hyrprɛis] *de (-prijzen)* rent, rental (price)

huurschuld [hyrsχʏlt] *de (~en)* rent arrears, arrears of rent: *de ~ bedraagt* €*5000,-* the rent arrears amount to €5000

huursoldaat [hyrsɔldat] *de (-soldaten)* mercenary

huursubsidie [hyrsʏpsidi] *het, de (~s)* rent subsidy

huurverhoging [hyrvərhoγɪŋ] *de* rent increase

huurverlaging [hyrvərlaγɪŋ] *de* rent reduction

huurwaarde [hyrwardə] *de (~n)* rental value

huurwoning [hyrwonɪŋ] *de (~en)* rented house (*or:* flat)

huwelijk [hywələk] *het (~en)* **1** marriage, wedding: *ontbinding van een ~* dissolution of a marriage; *gemengd ~* mixed marriage; *een wettig ~* a lawful marriage; *een ~ inzegenen* perform a marriage service; *een ~ sluiten (aangaan) met* get married to; *een kind, buiten ~ geboren* a child born out of wedlock; *zijn ~ met* his marriage to; *een meisje ten ~ vragen* propose to a girl; *een ~ uit liefde* a love match; *een burgerlijk ~* a civil wedding; *een kerkelijk ~* a church wedding; *een ~ voltrekken* perform a marriage service, celebrate a marriage; **2** matrimony: *na 25 jaar ~* after 25 years of matrimony

huwelijks [hywələks] *adj* marital, married: *~e voorwaarden* marriage settlement (*or:* articles)

huwelijksaanzoek [hywələksanzuk] *het (~en)* proposal (of marriage): *een ~ doen* propose (to s.o.); *een ~ krijgen* receive a proposal (of marriage)

huwelijksadvertentie [hywələksatfərtɛnsi] *de (~s)* (ad in the) lonely hearts column

huwelijksakte [hywələksɑktə] *de (~n, ~s)* marriage certificate

huwelijksbureau [hywələksbyro] *het (~s)* marriage bureau

huwelijksgeschenk [hywələksχəsχɛŋk] *het (~en)* wedding present (*or:* gift)

huwelijksnacht [hywələksnɑχt] *de (~en)* wedding night: *de eerste ~* the wedding night

huwelijksplechtigheid [hywələksplɛχtəχhɛit] *de (-heden)* wedding, marriage ceremony, wedding ceremony

huwelijksreis [hywələksrɛis] *de (-reizen)* honeymoon (trip): *zij zijn op ~* they are on (their) honeymoon (trip)

huwelijksvoorwaarden [hywələksforwardə(n)] *de* marriage settlement (*or:* articles): *trouwen zonder ~* marry without a marriage settlement (*or:* marriage articles)

huwen [hywə(n)] *vb* marry

huzaar [hyzar] *de (huzaren)* hussar

huzarensalade [hyzarə(n)saladə] *de (~s) (roughly)* Russian salad

hyacint [hijasɪnt] *de (~en)* hyacinth

hybride [hibridə] *de (~n)* hybrid, cross

hydraulisch [hidrɑulis] *adj, adv* hydraulic: *~e pers* (*or: remmen*) hydraulic press (*or:* brakes)

hyena [hijena] *de (~'s)* hy(a)ena

hygiëne [hiγ(i)jenə] *de* hygiene: *persoonlijke (intieme) ~* personal hygiene

¹hygiënisch [hiγ(i)jenis] *adj* hygienic, sanitary: *~e omstandigheden* sanitary conditions; *~e voorschriften* hygienic (*or:* sanitary) regulations

²hygiënisch [hiγ(i)jenis] *adv* hygienically: *~ verpakt* hygienically packed (*or:* wrapped)

hymne [hɪmnə] *de (~n)* hymn

hyper- [hipər-] hyper-, ultra-, super-

hyperactief [hipərɑktif] *adj* hyperactive

hypermarkt [hipərmɑrkt] *de (~en)* hypermarket

hypermodern [hipərmodɛrn] *adj, adv* ultramodern, super-fashionable: *een ~ interieur* an ultramodern interior

hyperventilatie [hipərvɛntila(t)si] *de* hyperventilation

hyperventileren [hipərvɛntilerə] *vb* hyperventilate

hypnose [hipnozə] *de* hypnosis: *iem onder ~ brengen* put s.o. under hypnosis

hypnotisch [hipnotis] *adj, adv* hypnotic: *~e blik* hypnotic gaze

hypnotiseren [hipnotizerə(n)] *vb* hypnotize

hypnotiseur [hipnotizør] *de (~s)* hypnotist, hypnotherapist

¹hypocriet [hipokrit] *de (~en)* hypocrite

²hypocriet [hipokrit] *adj* hypocritical, insincere

hypocrisie [hipokrizi] *de* hypocrisy

hypotheek [hipotek] *de (hypotheken)* mortgage: *een ~ aflossen* pay off a mortgage; *een ~ afsluiten* take out a mortgage; *een ~ nemen op een huis* take out a mortgage on a house

hypotheekrente [hipotɛkrɛntə] *de* mortgage (interest)

hypothese [hipotɛzə] *de (~n, ~s)* hypothesis: *een ~ opstellen* formulate a hypothesis

hypothetisch [hipotɛtis] *adj, adv* hypothetical

hysterie [hɪsteri] *de* hysteria

hysterisch [hɪstɛris] *adj, adv* hysterical: *~ gekrijs* hysterical screams; *~e toevallen (aanvallen) krijgen* have (fits of) hysterics; *doe niet zo ~!* don't be so (*or:* get) hysterical!

i

ibis [íbıs] *de (~sen)* ibis
icoon [ikón] *de (iconen)* icon
ICT [isetè] *de informatie- en communicatietechnologie* ICT
¹ideaal [idejál] *het (idealen)* **1** ideal: *zich iem tot ~ stellen* take s.o. as a model; **2** ideal, ambition: *het ~ van zijn jeugd was arts te worden* the ambition of his youth was to become a doctor
²ideaal [idejál] *adj, adv* ideal, perfect
idealiseren [idejalizèrə(n)] *vb* idealize, glamorize
idealisme [idejalísmə] *het* idealism
idealist [idejalíst] *de (~en)* idealist
idee [idé] *het, de (~ën)* **1** idea: *zich een ~ vormen van iets* form an idea of sth; **2** idea; notion, concept(ion): *ik heb geen (flauw) ~* I haven't the faintest (*or:* foggiest) idea; **3** idea; view: *ik heb een ~* I've got an idea; *op een ~ komen* think of sth, hit upon an idea; *zij kwam op het ~ om* she hit upon the idea of
ideëel [idejél] *adj* idealistic
ideeënbus [idejə(n)bʏs] *de (~sen)* suggestion box
idem [ídɛm] *adv* ditto, idem
identiek [idɛntík] *adj* identical (with, to)
identificatie [idɛntifika(t)sí] *de (~s)* identification
identificeren [idɛntifisèrə(n)] *vb* identify
identiteit [idɛntitéit] *de* identity
identiteitsbewijs [idɛntitéitsbəwɛis] *het (-bewijzen)* identity card, ID card
identiteitspapieren [idɛntitéitspapirə(n)] *de* identity papers, identification papers
ideologie [idejoloɣí] *de (~ën)* ideology
ideologisch [idejolóɣis] *adj, adv* ideological
idioom [idijóm] *het (idiomen)* idiom
¹idioot [idijót] *de (idioten)* idiot, fool: *een volslagen ~* an absolute fool
²idioot [idijót] *adj, adv* idiotic; foolish: *doe niet zo ~* don't be such a fool (*or:* an idiot)
idool [idól] *het (idolen)* idol
idyllisch [idílis] *adj, adv* idyllic
ieder [ídər] *ind pron* **1** every; each; any: *het kan ~e dag afgelopen zijn* it may be over any day (now); *werkelijk ~e dag* every single day; *ze komt ~e dag* she comes every day; **2** everyone, everybody; each (one); anyone, anybody: *tot ~s verbazing* to everyone's surprise; *~ van ons* each of us, every one of us; *~ voor zich* every man for himself

iedereen [idərén] *ind pron* everyone, everybody, all; anybody, anyone: *jij bent niet ~* you're not just anybody
iemand [ímɑnt] *ind pron* someone, somebody, anyone, anybody: *is daar ~?* is anybody there?; *hij is niet zomaar ~* he's not just anybody; *hij wilde niet dat ~ het wist* he didn't want anyone to know; *zij maakte de indruk van ~ die* she gave the impression of being someone (*or:* a woman) who
iep [ip] *de (~en)* elm
Ier [ir] *de (~en)* Irishman: *tien ~en* ten Irishmen
Ierland [írlɑnt] *het* Ireland; Republic of Ireland
¹Iers [irs] *het* Irish
²Iers [irs] *adj* Irish
¹iets [its] *ind pron* **1** anything: *hij heeft ~ wat ik niet begrijp* there is something about him which I don't understand; **2** something, anything: *~ lekkers* (*or:* moois*)* something tasty (*or:* beautiful); *~ dergelijks* something like that; *zo ~ heb ik nog nooit gezien* I have never seen anything like it; *er is ook nog zo ~ als* there is such a thing as; **3** something, a little, a bit: *beter ~ dan niets* something is better than nothing; *een mysterieus ~* something mysterious, a mysterious something
²iets [its] *adv* a bit, a little, slightly: *als zij er ~ om gaf* if she cared at all; *we moeten ~ vroeger weggaan* we must leave a bit (*or:* slightly) earlier
ietwat [ítwɑt] *adv* somewhat, slightly
iglo [íɣlo] *de (~'s)* igloo
ijdel [ɛídəl] *adj, adv* vain, conceited
ijdelheid [ɛídəlhɛit] *de (-heden)* vanity, conceit
ijdeltuit [ɛídəltœyt] *de (~en)* vain person
ijken [ɛíkə(n)] *vb* calibrate
ijkpunt [ɛíkpʏnt] *het (~en)* benchmark (figure)
ijl [ɛil] *adj* rarefied: *~e lucht* thin (*or:* rarefied) air
ijlen [ɛílə(n)] *vb* be delirious, ramble, rave
ijs [ɛis] *het* **1** ice: *zich op glad ~ bevinden (begeven)* skate on thin ice; *het ~ breken* break the ice; *de haven was door ~ gesloten* the port was icebound; **2** ice cream
ijsbaan [ɛízban] *de (ijsbanen)* skating rink, ice(-skating) rink
ijsbeer [ɛízber] *de (ijsberen)* polar bear
ijsberen [ɛízberə(n)] *vb* pace up and down
ijsberg [ɛízbɛrɣ] *de (~en)* iceberg
ijsbergsla [ɛízbɛrɣsla] *de* iceberg lettuce
ijsblokje [ɛízblɔkjə] *het (~s)* ice cube
ijscoman [ɛískoman] *de (~nen)* ice-cream man
ijselijk [ɛísələk] *adj, adv* hideous, dreadful
ijshockey [ɛíshɔki] *het* ice hockey
ijsje [ɛíʃə] *het (~s)* ice (cream)
ijskar [ɛískar] *de* ice-cream cart
ijskast [ɛískɑst] *de (~en)* fridge; refrigerator: *iets in de ~ zetten: a)* put sth in the fridge; *b) (fig)* shelve sth, put sth on ice
ijskoud [ɛískɑut] *adj, adv* **1** ice-cold, icy(-cold); **2** *(fig)* icy, (as) cold as ice: *een ~e ontvangst* an icy welcome
IJsland [ɛíslɑnt] *het* Iceland

IJslands [ɛislɑnts] *adj* Icelandic

ijslolly [ɛislɔli] *de (~'s)* ice lolly, *(Am)* popsicle

ijsmuts [ɛismʏts] *de (~en) (roughly)* woolly hat

ijspegel [ɛispeɣəl] *de (~s)* icicle

ijssalon [ɛisalɔn] *de (~s)* ice-cream parlour

ijsschots [ɛisxɔts] *de (~en)* (ice) floe

ijstijd [ɛistɛit] *de (~en)* ice age, glacial period (*or:* epoch)

ijsvogel [ɛisfoɣəl] *de (~s)* kingfisher

ijver [ɛivər] *de* diligence

ijverig [ɛivərəx] *adj, adv* diligent: *een ~ scholier* an industrious (*or:* a diligent) pupil; *men deed ~ onderzoek* painstaking inquiries were made

ijzel [ɛizəl] *de* black ice

ijzelen [ɛizələ(n)] *vb* freeze over: *het ijzelt* it is freezing over

ijzer [ɛizər] *het (~s)* iron: *~ smeden* (or: *gieten*) forge (*or:* cast) iron; *men moet het ~ smeden als het heet is* strike while the iron is hot

ijzerdraad [ɛizərdrat] *de, het* (iron) wire

ijzeren [ɛizərə(n)] *adj* iron: *een ~ gezondheid* an iron constitution

ijzererts [ɛizərɛrts] *het (~en)* iron ore

ijzerhandel [ɛizərhandəl] *de (~s)* **1** hardware store, ironmonger's shop; **2** hardware trade, ironmongery

ijzersterk [ɛizərstɛrk] *adj* iron, cast-iron: *hij kwam met ~e argumenten* he produced very strong arguments

ijzerwaren [ɛizərwarə(n)] *de* hardware, ironmongery

ijzig [ɛizəx] *adj, adv* icy, freezing: *~e kalmte* steely composure

ik [ɪk] *pers pron* I: *~ ben het* it's me; *als ~ er niet geweest was …* if it hadn't been for me …; *ze is beter dan ~* she's better than I am

illegaal [ileɣal] *adj, adv* **1** illegal; **2** underground: *~ werk* underground work

illusie [ilyzi] *de (~s)* illusion, (pipe)dream, delusion: *een ~ verstoren* (or: *wekken*) shatter (*or:* create) an illusion

illusionist [ilyz(i)jonɪst] *de (~en)* conjurer

illustratie [ɪlʏstra(t)si] *de (~s)* illustration

illustrator [ɪlʏstratɔr] *de (~s, ~en)* illustrator

illustreren [ɪlʏstrerə(n)] *vb* illustrate; exemplify

imago [imaɣo] *het, de (~'s)* image

imam [imɑm] *de (~s)* imam

imbeciel [ɪmbesil] *de (~en)* imbecile

IMF [iɛmɛf] *het Internationaal Monetair Fonds* IMF

imitatie [imita(t)si] *de (~s)* imitation, copy, copying, impersonation: *een slechte ~* a poor (*or:* bad) imitation

imitator [imitatɔr] *de (~s, ~en)* imitator; impersonator

imiteren [imiterə(n)] *vb* imitate, copy, impersonate

imker [ɪmkər] *de (~s)* bee-keeper

immens [ɪmɛns] *adj, adv* immense

immer [ɪmər] *adv* ever, always

immers [ɪmərs] *adv* **1** after all: *hij komt ~ morgen* after all, he is coming tomorrow, he is coming tomorrow, isn't he?; **2** for, since

immigrant [ɪmiɣrɑnt] *de (~en)* immigrant

immigratie [ɪmiɣra(t)si] *de (~s)* immigration

immigreren [ɪmiɣrerə(n)] *vb* immigrate

immobiliën [ɪmobilijə(n)] *de (Belg)* property, real estate

immoreel [ɪmorel] *adj, adv* immoral

immuniteit [imynitɛit] *de (~en)* immunity

immuun [imyn] *adj* immune: *~ voor kritiek* immune to criticism

impasse [ɪmpɑsə] *de (~s, ~n)* impasse, deadlock

imperiaal [ɪmperijal] *het, de (~s)* roof-rack

imperialisme [ɪmperijalɪsmə] *het* imperialism

imperialist [ɪmperijalɪst] *de (~en)* imperialist

imperium [ɪmperijʏm] *het (~s, imperia)* empire

impliceren [ɪmplisɛrə(n)] *vb* imply

impliciet [ɪmplisit] *adj, adv* implicit

imponeren [ɪmponɛrə(n)] *vb* impress, overawe: *laat je niet ~ door die deftige woorden* don't be overawed by those posh words

impopulair [ɪmpopylɛːr] *adj* unpopular

import [ɪmpɔrt] *de* **1** import(ation); **2** import(s)

importeren [ɪmpɔrtɛrə(n)] *vb* import

importeur [ɪmpɔrtøːr] *de (~s)* importer

imposant [ɪmpozɑnt] *adj* impressive, imposing

impotent [ɪmpotɛnt] *adj* impotent

impregneren [ɪmprɛɣnɛrə(n)] *vb* impregnate

impresario [ɪmprɛsarijo] *de (~'s)* impresario

impressie [ɪmprɛsi] *de (~s)* impression

impressionisme [ɪmprɛʃonɪsmə] *het* impressionism

improviseren [ɪmprovizɛrə(n)] *vb* improvise

impuls [ɪmpʏls] *de (~en)* **1** impulse, impetus; **2** impulse, urge: *hij handelde in een ~* he acted on (an) impulse

impulsief [ɪmpʏlsif] *adj, adv* impulsive, impetuous

¹in [ɪn] *prep* **1** in, at: *een vertegenwoordiger ~ het bestuur* a representative on the board; *puistjes ~ het gezicht* pimples on one's face; *~ heel het land* throughout (*or:* all over) the country; *hij is nog nooit ~ Londen geweest* he has never been to London; *hij zat niet ~ dat vliegtuig* he wasn't on that plane; *~ slaap* asleep; **2** into: *~ de hoogte kijken* look up; *~ het Japans vertalen* translate into Japanese; **3** in, at, during: *~ het begin* at the beginning; *een keer ~ de week* once a week; **4** in: *er gaan 100 cm ~ een meter* there are 100 centimetres to a metre; *twee meter ~ omtrek* two metres in circumference; *~ een rustig tempo* at an easy pace; *~ tweeën snijden* cut in two; *professor ~ de natuurkunde* professor of physics; *zij is goed ~ wiskunde* she's good at mathematics; *uitbarsten ~ gelach* burst into laughter

²in [ɪn] *adv* **1** in, into, inside: *dat wil er bij mij niet ~* I find that hard to believe; *dag ~ dag uit* day in (and) day out; **2** in, inside: *tussen twee huizen ~* (in) between two houses; *tegen alle verwachtingen ~* contrary to all expectations

³in [ɪn] *adj* in: *de bal was ~* the ball was in

inacceptabel [ɪnɑksɛptɑbəl] *adj, adv* unacceptable

inademen [ɪnadəmə(n)] *vb* inhale, breathe in

inbeelden [ɪmbeldə(n)] *ref vb* imagine: *dat beeld je je maar in* that's just your imagination

inbeelding [ɪmbeldɪŋ] *de (~en)* imagination

inbegrepen [ɪmbəɣrepə(n)] *adj* included, including

inbegrip [ɪmbəɣrɪp] ‖ *met ~ van* including

inbellen [ɪmbɛlə(n)] *vb* dial up

inbelpunt [ɪmbɛlpʏnt] *het (~en)* dial-up access (account)

inbinden [ɪmbɪndə(n)] *vb* bind

inblazen [ɪmblazə(n)] *vb* blow into, *(fig)* breathe into: *iets nieuw leven ~* breathe new life into sth

inblikken [ɪmblɪkə(n)] *vb* can, tin

inboedel [ɪmbudəl] *de (~s)* moveables, furniture, furnishings: *een ~ verzekeren (roughly)* insure the contents of one's house against fire and theft

inboezemen [ɪmbuzəmə(n)] *vb* inspire

inboorling [ɪmborlɪŋ] *de (~en)* native

inbouwen [ɪmbɑuwə(n)] *vb* build in

inbraak [ɪmbrak] *de (inbraken)* breaking in, burglary: *~ plegen in* break into, burgle

inbreken [ɪmbrekə(n)] *vb* break in(to) (a house), burgle (a house): *~ in een computersysteem* break into a computer system; *er is alweer bij ons ingebroken* our house has been broken into *(or:* burgled) again

inbreker [ɪmbrekər] *de (~s)* burglar; *(in computer)* hacker

inbreng [ɪmbrɛŋ] *de (~en)* contribution

inbrengen [ɪmbrɛŋə(n)] *vb* 1 bring in(to), insert, inject; 2 contribute; 3 bring (forward): *daar valt niets tegen in te brengen* there is nothing to be said against this

inbreuk [ɪmbrøk] *de (~en)* infringement, violation

inburgeren [ɪmbʏrɣərə(n)] *vb* naturalize, settle down, settle in

inburgeringsprogramma *het* integration programme

inbussleutel [ɪmbʏsløtəl] *de (~s)* Allen key

Inca [ɪŋka] *de* Inca

incarnatie [ɪŋkɑrna(t)si] *de (~s)* incarnation

incasseren [ɪŋkɑsɛrə(n)] *vb* 1 collect, cash (in); 2 accept, take

incest [ɪnsɛst] *de* incest

incident [ɪnsidɛnt] *het (~en)* incident

incidenteel [ɪnsidɛntel] *adj, adv* incidental, occasional: *dit verschijnsel doet zich ~ voor* this phenomenon occurs occasionally

inclusief [ɪŋklyzif] *adv* including; *(abbr: incl.)* inclusive (of): *45 euro ~ (bedieningsgeld)* 45 euros, including service

incognito [ɪŋkɔɣnito] *adv* incognito

incompleet [ɪŋkɔmplet] *adj* incomplete

inconsequent [ɪŋkɔnsəkwɛnt] *adj, adv* inconsistent

incontinent [ɪŋkɔntinɛnt] *adj* incontinent

incorrect [ɪŋkɔrɛkt] *adj, adv* incorrect

incubatietijd [ɪŋkyba(t)sitɛit] *de (~en)* incubation period

indekken [ɪndɛkə(n)] *ref vb* cover oneself (against)

indelen [ɪndelə(n)] *vb* 1 divide, order, class(ify): *zijn dag ~* plan one's day; 2 group, class(ify)

indeling [ɪndelɪŋ] *de (~en)* division, arrangement, classification, lay-out: *de ~ van een gebied in districten* the division of a region into districts

indenken [ɪndɛŋkə(n)] *ref vb* imagine: *zich in iemands situatie ~* put oneself in s.o.'s place *(or:* shoes)

inderdaad [ɪndərdat] *adv* indeed, really, sure enough: *ik heb dat ~ gezegd, maar ...* I did say that, but ...; *het lijkt er ~ op dat het helpt* it really does seem to help; *dat is ~ het geval* that is indeed the case; *~, dat dacht ik nu ook!* exactly, that's what I thought, too!

index [ɪndɛks] *de (~en)* index

India [ɪndija] *het* India

indiaan [ɪndijan] *de (indianen)* (American) Indian

indiaans [ɪndijans] *adj* Indian

Indiaas [ɪndijas] *adj* Indian

indianenverhaal [ɪndijanə(n)vərhal] *het (-verhalen)* tall story

indicatie [ɪndika(t)si] *de (~s)* indication

Indië [ɪndijə] *het* the Dutch East Indies; India

indien [ɪndin] *conj* if, in case, supposing

indienen [ɪndinə(n)] *vb* submit

Indiër [ɪndijər] *de (~s)* Indian

indigestie [ɪndiɣesti] *de* indigestion

indikken [ɪndɪkə(n)] *vb* thicken

indirect [ɪndirɛkt] *adj, adv* indirect, roundabout: *op ~e manier* in an indirect way, in a roundabout way; *~e vrije trap* indirect free kick

Indisch [ɪndis] *adj* (East) Indian

individu [ɪndividy] *het, de (~en)* individual, person

individualisme [ɪndividywɑlɪsmə] *het* individualism

individualist [ɪndividywɑlɪst] *de (~en)* individualist

¹individueel [ɪndividywel] *adj* individual; particular

²individueel [ɪndividywel] *adv* individually, singly

indommelen [ɪndɔmələ(n)] *vb* doze off

Indonesië [ɪndonezijə] *het* Indonesia

Indonesiër [ɪndonezijər] *de (~s)* Indonesian

Indonesisch [ɪndonezis] *adj* Indonesian

¹indraaien [ɪndrajə(n)] *vb* turn in(to): *de auto draaide de straat in* the car turned into the street

²indraaien [ɪndrajə(n)] *vb* screw in(to): *een schroef ~ drive (or:* turn) in a screw

indringen [ɪndrɪŋə(n)] *vb* penetrate (into), intrude (into), soak (into)

indringend [ɪndrɪŋənt] *adj* penetrating: *een ~e blik* a penetrating gaze, a piercing look

indringer [ɪndrɪŋər] *de (~s)* intruder, trespasser

indrinken [ɪndrɪŋkə(n)] *vb* drink in

indruisen [ɪndrœysə(n)] *vb* go against, conflict

with

indruk [ɪndrʏk] *de (~ken)* **1** impression, air, idea: *diepe (grote)* ~ *maken* make a deep impression; *ik kon niet aan de ~ ontkomen dat* I could not escape the impression that; *dat geeft* (or: *wekt*) *de* ~ ... that gives (or: creates) the impression that ...; *ik kreeg de ~ dat* I got the impression that; *weinig ~ maken op iem* make little impression on s.o.; **2** impression, (im)print: *op de sneeuw waren ~ken van vogel-pootjes zichtbaar* in the snow the prints (or: imprints) of birds' feet were visible

indrukken [ɪndrʏkə(n)] *vb* push in, press

indrukwekkend [ɪndrʏkwɛkənt] *adj, adv* impressive

induiken [ɪndœykə(n)] *vb* **1** dive in(to): *zijn bed* (or: *de koffer*) ~ turn in, hit the sack; **2** plunge in(to): *ergens dieper* ~ delve deeper into sth

industrialiseren [ɪndʏstrijalizɛrə(n)] *vb* industrialize

industrie [ɪndʏstri] *de (~ën)* (manufacturing) industry

industriebond [ɪndʏstribɔnt] *de (~en)* industrial union

industrieel [ɪndʏstrijel] *adj* industrial

industriegebied [ɪndʏstriɣəbit] *het (~en)* industrial area; industrial estate (or: park), trading estate

industriestad [ɪndʏstristat] *de (-steden)* industrial town, manufacturing town

industrieterrein [ɪndʏstritɛrɛin] *het (~en)* industrial zone (or: estate, park)

indutten [ɪndʏtə(n)] *vb* doze off, nod off

induwen [ɪndywə(n)] *vb* push in(to)

ineengedoken [ɪnɛŋɣədokə(n)] *adj* crouched, hunched (up)

ineenkrimpen [ɪnɛŋkrɪmpə(n)] *vb* curl up, double up, (*fig*) flinch

ineens [ɪnɛns] *adv* **1** (all) at once: *bij betaling ~ krijg je korting* you get a discount for cash payment; **2** all at once, all of a sudden, suddenly: *zomaar ~* just like that

ineenstorten [ɪnɛnstɔrtə(n)] *vb* collapse

ineffectief [ɪnɛfɛktif] *adj, adv* ineffective, inefficient

inefficiënt [ɪnɛfiʃɛnt] *adj, adv* inefficient

inenten [ɪnɛntə(n)] *vb* vaccinate, inoculate

inenting [ɪnɛntɪŋ] *de (~en)* vaccination, inoculation

infanterie [ɪnfɑntəri] *de* infantry

infarct [ɪnfɑrkt] *het (~en)* infarct(ion); heart attack

infecteren [ɪnfɛktɛrə(n)] *vb* infect

infectie [ɪnfɛksi] *de (~s)* infection

infectieziekte [ɪnfɛksiziktə] *de (~n, ~s)* infectious disease

inferieur [ɪnferijør] *adj* inferior, low-grade

infiltratie [ɪnfɪltra(t)si] *de (~s)* infiltration

infiltreren [ɪnfɪltrɛrə(n)] *vb* infiltrate: ~ *in een beweging* infiltrate (into) a movement

inflatie [ɪnfla(t)si] *de (~s)* inflation

influisteren [ɪnflœystərə(n)] *vb* whisper (in s.o.'s ear)

informaliteit [ɪnfɔrmalitɛit] *de (~en)* informality

informant [ɪnfɔrmɑnt] *de (~en)* informant

informatica [ɪnfɔrmatika] *de* computer science, informatics

informatie [ɪnfɔrma(t)si] *de (~s)* **1** information, data; **2** information, intelligence: *om nadere ~ verzoeken* request further information; *~(s) inwinnen (bij ...)* make inquiries (of ...), obtain information (from ...)

informatief [ɪnfɔrmatif] *adj* informative

informeel [ɪnfɔrmel] *adj, adv* informal; unofficial, casual

¹informeren [ɪnfɔrmɛrə(n)] *vb* inquire, enquire, ask: *ik heb ernaar geïnformeerd* I have made inquiries about it; ~ *bij iem* ask s.o.; *naar de aanvangstijden* ~ inquire about opening times

²informeren [ɪnfɔrmɛrə(n)] *vb* inform

infrarood [ɪnfrarot] *adj* infra-red

infrastructuur [ɪnfrastrʏktyr] *de (-structuren)* infrastructure

infuus [ɪnfys] *het (infusen)* drip

ingaan [ɪŋɣan] *vb* **1** go in(to): *een deur ~* go through a door; **2** go in(to), come in(to), enter: *een weg ~* turn into a road; **3** examine, go into: *uitgebreid ~ op* consider at length; **4** agree with, agree to, comply with: *op een aanbod ~* accept an offer; **5** take effect: *de regeling gaat 1 juli in* the regulation is effective as from (or: of) July 1st; ~ *tegen* run counter to

ingang [ɪŋɣɑŋ] *de (~en)* **1** entrance, entry, doorway, acceptance: *de nieuwe ideeën vonden gemakkelijk ~ bij het publiek* the new ideas found a ready reception with the public; **2** commencement: *met ~ van 1 april* as from (or: of) April 1st

ingebeeld [ɪŋɣəbelt] *adj* imaginary

ingebonden [ɪŋɣəbɔndə(n)] *adj* bound

ingebouwd [ɪŋɣəbaut] *adj* built-in

ingeburgerd [ɪŋɣəbʏrɣərt] *adj* **1** naturalized; **2** established: ~ *raken* take hold

ingehouden [ɪŋɣəhaudə(n)] *adj* **1** restrained; **2** subdued; bated

ingelegd [ɪŋɣələxt] *adj* inlaid

ingemaakt [ɪŋɣəmakt] *adj* preserved, bottled

ingenaaid [ɪŋɣənajt] *adj* stitched

ingenieur [ɪnʒenjør] *de (~s)* engineer

ingenieus [ɪŋɣenijøs] *adj, adv* ingenious

ingesloten [ɪŋɣəslotə(n)] *adj, adv* **1** enclosed; **2** surrounded

ingespannen [ɪŋɣəspɑnə(n)] *adj, adv* **1** intensive, intense: ~ *luisteren* listen intently; **2** strenuous: *na drie dagen van ~ arbeid* after three strenuous days

ingetogen [ɪŋɣətoɣə(n)] *adj, adv* modest

ingevallen [ɪŋɣəvɑlə(n)] *adj* hollow, sunken

ingeven [ɪŋɣevə(n)] *vb* inspire: *doe wat uw hart u ingeeft* follow the dictates of your heart

ingeving [ɪŋɣevɪŋ] *de (~en)* inspiration, intuition: *een ~ krijgen* have a flash of inspiration, have a brainwave

ingevroren [ɪnɣəvrorə(n)] *adj* icebound; frozen

ingewanden [ɪnɣəwɑndə(n)] *de* intestines

ingewijde [ɪnɣəwɛidə] *de (~n)* initiate, *(fig also)* insider, adept

ingewikkeld [ɪnɣəwɪkəlt] *adj, adv* complicated

ingeworteld [ɪnɣəwɔrtəlt] *adj* deep-rooted

ingezetene [ɪnɣəzetənə] *de (~n)* resident, inhabitant

ingezonden [ɪnɣəzɔndə(n)] *adj* sent in: *~ brieven* letters to the editor

ingooi [ɪnɣoj] *de (~en)* throw-in

¹**ingooien** [ɪnɣojə(n)] *vb* **1** throw in(to); **2** smash

²**ingooien** [ɪnɣojə(n)] *vb* throw in

ingraven [ɪnɣravə(n)] *vb* bury: *zich (in de grond) ~* dig (oneself) in, burrow

ingrediënt [ɪnɣredijɛnt] *het (~en)* ingredient

ingreep [ɪnɣrep] *de (ingrepen)* intervention

ingrijpen [ɪnɣrɛipə(n)] *vb* **1** interfere; **2** intervene

ingrijpend [ɪnɣrɛipənt] *adj, adv* radical

inhaalrace [ɪnhalres] *de (~s)* race to recover lost ground; race to catch up

inhaalstrook [ɪnhalstrok] *de (-stroken)* fast lane

inhaken [ɪnhakə(n)] *vb (with op)* take up

¹**inhalen** [ɪnhalə(n)] *vb* **1** draw in, take in, haul in; **2** catch up with, outrun; **3** make up (for), recover: *de verloren tijd ~* make up for lost time; **4** bring in

²**inhalen** [ɪnhalə(n)] *vb (traf)* overtake, pass

inhaleren [ɪnhalɛrə(n)] *vb* inhale; *(only with direct object)* draw in

inhalig [ɪnhaləχ] *adj* greedy

inham [ɪnhɑm] *de (~men)* bay, cove, creek

inheems [ɪnhems] *adj* native: *~e planten* indigenous plants

inhoud [ɪnhɑut] *de (~en)* **1** content, capacity; **2** content; **3** contents; **4** import

¹**inhouden** [ɪnhɑudə(n)] *vb* **1** restrain, hold (in, back): *de adem ~* hold one's breath; **2** deduct: *een zeker percentage van het loon ~* withhold a certain percentage of the wages; **3** contain, hold; **4** involve, mean: *wat houdt dit in voor onze klanten?* what does this mean for our customers?; **5** hold in

²**inhouden** [ɪnhɑudə(n)] *ref vb* control oneself: *zich ~ om niet in lachen uit te barsten* keep a straight face

inhouding [ɪnhɑudɪŋ] *de (~en)* deduction, amount withheld

inhoudsmaat [ɪnhɑutsmat] *de (-maten)* measure of capacity *(or:* volume)

inhoudsopgave [ɪnhɑutsɔpχavə] *de (~n)* (table of) contents

inhuldigen [ɪnhɣldəɣə(n)] *vb* inaugurate, install

inhuldiging [ɪnhɣldəɣɪŋ] *de (~en)* inauguration

inhuren [ɪnhɣrə(n)] *vb* engage

initiaal [ini(t)ʃal] *de (initialen)* initial

initiatief [ini(t)ʃatif] *het (initiatieven)* initiative, enterprise

injecteren [ɪnjɛktɛrə(n)] *vb* inject

injectie [ɪnjɛksi] *de (~s)* injection

injectienaald [ɪnjɛksinalt] *de (~en)* (hypodermic) needle

inkapselen [ɪŋkɑpsələ(n)] *vb* encase

inkeer [ɪŋker] *de* repentance

inkeping [ɪŋkepɪŋ] *de (~en)* notch

inkijken [ɪŋkɛikə(n)] *vb* take a look at

inklappen [ɪŋklɑpə(n)] *vb* fold in, fold up

inklaren [ɪŋklarə(n)] *vb* clear (inwards)

inkleden [ɪŋkledə(n)] *vb* frame, express: *hoe zal ik mijn verzoek ~?* how shall I put my request?

inkleuren [ɪŋklørə(n)] *vb* colour

inkom [ɪŋkɔm] *de (Belg)* admission, entrance fee

¹**inkomen** [ɪŋkomə(n)] *het (~s)* income, revenue

²**inkomen** [ɪŋkomə(n)] *vb* enter, come in(to): *ingekomen stukken* (or: *brieven)* incoming correspondence (or: letters); *daar kan ik ~* I (can) appreciate that, I quite understand that; *daar komt niets van in* that's out of the question, no way!

inkomgeld [ɪŋkɔmɣɛlt] *het (~en) (Belg)* admission (charge), entrance fee

inkomsten [ɪŋkɔmstə(n)] *de* income, earnings; revenue(s)

inkomstenbelasting [ɪŋkɔmstə(n)bəlɑstɪŋ] *de (~en)* income tax

inkoop [ɪŋkop] *de (inkopen)* purchase, purchasing, buying

inkoopprijs [ɪŋkopreis] *de (-prijzen)* cost price

inkopen [ɪŋkopə(n)] *vb* buy, purchase

inkoper [ɪŋkopər] *de (~s)* buyer, purchasing agent

inkoppen [ɪŋkɔpə(n)] *vb* head (the ball) in(to the goal)

inkorten [ɪŋkɔrtə(n)] *vb* shorten, cut down

inkrimpen [ɪŋkrɪmpə(n)] *vb* reduce, cut (down)

inkrimping [ɪŋkrɪmpɪŋ] *de (~en)* reduction, cut(s)

inkt [ɪŋkt] *de (~en)* ink: *met ~ schrijven* write in ink

inktvis [ɪŋktfis] *de (~sen)* octopus; squid

inktvlek [ɪŋktflɛk] *de (~ken)* ink blot

inladen [ɪnladə(n)] *vb* load

inlander [ɪnlɑndər] *de (~s)* native

inlands [ɪnlɑnts] *adj* native, internal, domestic, home-grown

inlassen [ɪnlɑsə(n)] *vb* insert

inlaten [ɪnlatə(n)] *ref vb* meddle (with, in), concern oneself (with): *zich ~ met dergelijke mensen* associate with such people

inleg [ɪnlɛχ] *de* **1** deposit(ing); deposit; **2** stake

inleggen [ɪnlɛɣə(n)] *vb* **1** deposit, stake, invest; **2** put, throw in (or: down); **3** preserve

inlegvel [ɪnlɛχfɛl] *het (~len)* insert

inleiden [ɪnlɛidə(n)] *vb* introduce

inleidend [ɪnlɛidənt] *adj* introductory, opening

inleider [ɪnlɛidər] *de (~s)* (opening) speaker

inleiding [ɪnlɛidɪŋ] *de (~en)* **1** introductory remarks, opening remarks, preamble; **2** introduction, preface, foreword

inleven [ɪnlevə(n)] *ref vb* put (or: imagine) oneself (in), empathize (with)

inleveren [ɪnleverə(n)] *vb* hand in, turn in

inlichten [ɪnlɪχtə(n)] *vb* inform

inlichting [ɪnlɪχtɪŋ] *de (~en)* **1** (piece of) information: *~en inwinnen* make inquiries, ask for information; **2** *(pl)* information (office), inquiries, intelligence (service)

inlichtingendienst [ɪnlɪχtɪŋə(n)dinst] *de (~en)* **1** information office, inquiries office; **2** intelligence (service), secret service

inlijsten [ɪnlɛistə(n)] *vb* frame

in-lineskate [ɪnlɑjnsket] *de (~s)* in-line skate

inloggen [ɪnlɔɣə(n)] *vb* log on, log in (on)

¹inlopen [ɪnlopə(n)] *vb* **1** walk into, step into, *(bldg)* enter, turn into; **2** catch up: *op iem* ~ catch up on s.o.

²inlopen [ɪnlopə(n)] *vb* **1** wear in; **2** make up ‖ *zich* ~ warm up

inluiden [ɪnlœydə(n)] *vb* herald

¹inmaken [ɪmakə(n)] *vb* preserve, conserve

²inmaken [ɪmakə(n)] *vb (fig)* slaughter

inmengen [ɪmɛŋə(n)] *ref vb* interfere (in, with)

inmenging [ɪmɛŋɪŋ] *de (~en)* interference (in, with)

inmiddels [ɪmˌdəls] *adv* meanwhile, in the meantime: *dat is* ~ *bevestigd* this has since (*or:* now) been confirmed

in natura [ɪnatyra] *adj* in kind

innemen [ɪnemə(n)] *vb* **1** take; **2** take (up), occupy: *zijn plaats* ~ take one's seat; **3** capture

innemend [ɪnemənt] *adj, adv* captivating, engaging, winning

innen [ɪnə(n)] *vb* collect, cash

¹innerlijk [ɪnərlək] *het (~en)* inner self, inner nature

²innerlijk [ɪnərlək] *adj, adv* inner

¹innig [ɪnəχ] *adj* **1** profound, deep(est); **2** ardent, fervent; **3** close, deep, intimate

²innig [ɪnəχ] *adv* (most) deeply

inning [ɪnɪŋ] *de (~en)* **1** collection, cashing; **2** innings; inning

innovatie [ɪnova(t)si] *de (~s)* innovation

innoveren [ɪnoverə(n)] *vb* innovate

¹inpakken [ɪmpakə(n)] *vb* **1** pack (up); **2** wrap (up)

²inpakken [ɪmpakə(n)] *vb* pack in: ~ *en wegwezen* pack up and go

inpakpapier [ɪmpakpapir] *het* wrapping paper

inpalmen [ɪmpalmə(n)] *vb* charm, win over

inpassen [ɪmpasə(n)] *vb* fit in

inpeperen [ɪmpepərə(n)] *vb (fig)* get even with (s.o.) (for)

inperken [ɪmpɛrkə(n)] *vb* restrict, curtail

in petto [ɪmpɛto] *adv* in reserve, in store

inpikken [ɪmpɪkə(n)] *vb* **1** grab, snap up, pinch; **2** *(Belg)* take up

inplakken [ɪmplakə(n)] *vb* stick (*or:* glue, paste) in

inpolderen [ɪmpɔldərə(n)] *vb* drain, impolder

inpoldering [ɪmpɔldərɪŋ] *de (~en)* (land) reclamation, impoldering

inpompen [ɪmpɔmpə(n)] *vb* pump in(to)

inpraten [ɪmpratə(n)] *vb* talk (s.o.) into (sth): *op iem* ~ work on s.o.

inprenten [ɪmprɛntə(n)] *vb* impress (on), instil (in(to)), imprint

inquisitie [ɪŋkwizi(t)si] *de* inquisition

inramen [ɪnramə(n)] *vb* frame: *dia's* ~ mount slides

inrekenen [ɪnrekənə(n)] *vb* pull in; round up

¹inrichten [ɪnrɪχtə(n)] *vb* equip, furnish: *een compleet ingerichte keuken* a fully-equipped kitchen

²inrichten [ɪnrɪχtə(n)] *het (Belg)* organize: *de ~de macht* the (school) administration (*or:* management)

inrichter [ɪnrɪχtər] *de (Belg)* organizer

inrichting [ɪnrɪχtɪŋ] *de (~en)* **1** design; layout; **2** institution

¹inrijden [ɪnrɛidə(n)] *vb* ride in(to); *(car)* drive in(to)

²inrijden [ɪnrɛidə(n)] *vb* run in; break in

inrit [ɪnrɪt] *de (~ten)* drive(way)

inruil [ɪnrœyl] *de* exchange; trade-in, part exchange: *€2000,- bij ~ van uw oude auto* 2,000 euros in part exchange for your old car

inruilauto [ɪnrœylauto] *de (~'s)* trade-in (car)

inruilen [ɪnrœylə(n)] *vb* **1** exchange; **2** trade in, part-exchange

inruilwaarde [ɪnrœylwardə] *de (~n)* trade-in (*or:* part-exchange) value

inruimen [ɪnrœymə(n)] *vb* clear (out)

inrukken [ɪnrykə(n)] *vb* dismiss, withdraw: *ingerukt mars!* dismiss!

inschakelen [ɪnsχakələ(n)] *vb* **1** switch on, connect; **2** call in, bring in, involve

inschatten [ɪnsχatə(n)] *vb* estimate, assess

inschenken [ɪnsχɛŋkə(n)] *vb* pour (out)

inschepen [ɪnsχepə(n)] *vb* embark

¹inschieten [ɪnsχitə(n)] *vb* **1** lose; **2** shoot into the net

²inschieten [ɪnsχitə(n)] *vb* **1** fall through: *mijn lunch zal er wel bij ~* then I can say goodbye to my lunch; **2** shoot in(to): *een zijstraat ~* shoot into a side street; **3** score

inschoppen [ɪnsχɔpə(n)] *vb* **1** kick in(to); **2** kick in, kick down

inschrijfformulier [ɪnsχreiformylir] *het (~en)* registration form, entry form, enrolment form

inschrijfgeld [ɪnsχreifχɛlt] *het (~en)* registration fee, entry fee, enrolment fee

¹inschrijven [ɪnsχreivə(n)] *vb* bid, submit a bid

²inschrijven [ɪnsχreivə(n)] *vb* register, enter, enrol, sign up: *zich (laten)* ~ sign up, register (oneself); *zich als student* ~ enrol as a student

inschrijving [ɪnsχreivɪŋ] *de (~en)* **1** registration, entry, enrolment; **2** *(com)* subscription, bid: *een ~ openen* call for bids (*or:* tenders)

inschrijvingsformulier [ɪnsχreivɪŋsformylir] *het (~en)* application form, enrolment form

inschuiven [ɪnsχœyvə(n)] *vb* push in, slide in

inscriptie [ɪnskrɪpsi] *de (~s)* inscription, legend

insect [ɪnsɛkt] *het (~en)* insect

insecticide [ɪnsɛktisidə] *het (~n, ~s)* insecticide

inseminatie [ɪnsemina(t)si] *de* insemination: *kunstmatige* ~ artificial insemination

insigne [ɪnsiɲə] *het (~s)* badge

insinuatie [ɪnsinywa̱(t)si] *de (~s)* insinuation

insinueren [ɪnsinywe̱rə(n)] *vb* insinuate

¹**inslaan** [ɪnslan] *vb* **1** smash (in), beat (in); **2** stock (up on, with)

²**inslaan** [ɪnslan] *vb* **1** take, turn into: *(fig) een verkeerde weg* ~ take the wrong path (*or*: turning), go the wrong way; *(fig) nieuwe wegen* ~ break new ground, blaze a (new) trail; **2** strike, hit

inslag [ɪnslɑχ] *de (~en)* **1** impact; **2** streak *(pers)*; slant, bias

inslapen [ɪnslapə(n)] *vb* **1** fall asleep, drop off (*or*: go) to sleep; **2** pass away, pass on

inslikken [ɪnslɪkə(n)] *vb* swallow

insluiper [ɪnslœypər] *de (~s)* sneak-thief, intruder

insluiten [ɪnslœytə(n)] *vb* **1** enclose; surround: *een antwoordformulier* ~ enclose an answer form; **2** shut in, lock in

¹**insmeren** [ɪnsmerə(n)] *vb* rub (with), put … on

²**insmeren** [ɪnsmerə(n)] *ref vb* put oil on: *zich ~ met bodylotion* rub oneself with body lotion

insneeuwen [ɪnsnewə(n)] *vb* snow in

insnijden [ɪnsnɛidə(n)] *vb* cut into, *(med)* lance: *een wond* ~ make an incision in a wound

inspannen [ɪnspɑnə(n)] *vb* use; exert: *zich ~ voor iets* take a lot of trouble about sth; *zich moeten ~ om wakker te blijven* have to struggle to stay awake

inspannend [ɪnspɑ̱nənt] *adj* strenuous, laborious; exacting

inspanning [ɪnspɑnɪŋ] *de (~en)* effort, exertion, strain: *met een laatste ~ van zijn krachten* with a final effort, with one last effort

inspecteren [ɪnspɛkte̱rə(n)] *vb* inspect, examine, survey

inspecteur [ɪnspɛktø̱r] *de (~s)* inspector, examiner

inspectie [ɪnspɛ̱ksi] *de (~s)* **1** inspection, examination, survey; **2** inspectorate

¹**inspelen** [ɪnspelə(n)] *vb* practise, warm up

²**inspelen** [ɪnspelə(n)] *vb* **1** anticipate; **2** go along with, capitalize on, take advantage of, feel for

inspiratie [ɪnspira̱(t)si] *de (~s)* inspiration

inspireren [ɪnspire̱rə(n)] *vb* inspire: *geïnspireerd worden door iets (iem)* be inspired by sth (s.o.)

inspirerend [ɪnspire̱rənt] *adj, adv* inspiring

inspraak [ɪnsprak] *de* participation, involvement, say (in sth)

inspreken [ɪnsprekə(n)] *vb* record: *u kunt nu uw boodschap* ~ you may leave (*or*: record) your message now

inspringen [ɪnsprɪŋə(n)] *vb* **1** stand in: *voor een collega* ~ stand in for a colleague; **2** jump on(to), leap on(to), seize (up)on: *deze regel moet een beetje* ~ this line needs to be indented slightly

inspuiten [ɪnspœytə(n)] *vb* inject, fix

instaan [ɪnstan] *vb* answer, be answerable (*or*: responsible); guarantee, vouch: *voor iem* ~ vouch for s.o.

instabiel [ɪnstabi̱l] *adj* unstable

instabiliteit [ɪnstabilitɛ̱it] *de* instability

installateur [ɪnstɑlatø̱r] *de (~s)* fitter, installer, electrician

installatie [ɪnstɑla̱(t)si] *de (~s)* **1** installation; **2** installation, plant, equipment, machinery, fittings: *een nieuwe stereo-~* a new hifi-set; **3** installation, inauguration

installeren [ɪnstɑle̱rə(n)] *vb* install, inaugurate: *iem als lid* ~ initiate s.o. as a member

instantie [ɪnstɑ̱nsi] *de (~s)* **1** body, authority; **2** *(law)* instance ‖ *in eerste ~ dachten we dat het waar was* initially we thought it was true

instappen [ɪnstɑpə(n)] *vb* get in; get on; board

insteken [ɪnsteka̱(n)] *vb* put in: *de stekker* ~ plug in, put in the plug

instellen [ɪnstɛlə(n)] *vb* **1** establish, create; **2** set up, start; **3** adjust, focus, tune: *een camera (scherp)* ~ focus a camera; *zakelijk ingesteld zijn* have a businesslike attitude (*or*: mentality)

instelling [ɪnstɛlɪŋ] *de (~en)* **1** institute, institution; **2** focus(s)ing; tuning; **3** attitude, mentality: *een negatieve* ~ a negative attitude

instemmen [ɪnstɛmə(n)] *vb* agree (with, to)

instemming [ɪnstɛmɪŋ] *de* approval

instinct [ɪnstɪŋkt] *het (~en)* instinct

instinctief [ɪnstɪŋkti̱f] *adj, adv* instinctive

instinctmatig [ɪnstɪŋktmɑtəχ] *adj, adv* instinctive: *~ handelen* act on one's instinct(s)

instinker [ɪnstɪŋkər] *de* tricky question

institutioneel [ɪnstity(t)ʃone̱l] *adj* institutional

instituut [ɪnstity̱t] *het (instituten)* institution, institute

instoppen [ɪnstɔpə(n)] *vb* **1** put in; **2** tuck in: *iem lekker* ~ tuck s.o. in nice and warm

instorten [ɪnstɔrtə(n)] *vb* **1** collapse, fall down, cave in: *de zaak staat op* ~ the business is at the point of collapse; **2** collapse, break down

instorting [ɪnstɔrtɪŋ] *de (~en)* collapse *(bldg)*, breakdown, caving, cave-in

instructeur [ɪnstrʏktø̱r] *de (~s)* instructor

instructie [ɪnstrʏ̱ksi] *de (~s)* instruction, order, directive

instrueren [ɪnstrywe̱rə(n)] *vb* instruct

instrument [ɪnstrymɛ̱nt] *het (~en)* **1** instrument: *~en aflezen* read instruments (*or*: dials); **2** tool; **3** (musical) instrument: *een ~ bespelen* play an instrument

instrumentaal [ɪnstrymɛnta̱l] *adj* instrumental

instuderen [ɪnstyde̱rə(n)] *vb* practise, learn: *een muziekstuk* ~ practise a piece of music

instuif [ɪnstœyf] *de (instuiven)* **1** (informal) party; **2** youth centre

insturen [ɪnstyrə(n)] *vb* **1** send in, submit; **2** steer into; sail into *(ship)*

insuline [ɪnsyli̱nə] *de* insulin

intact [ɪntɑkt] *adj* intact

intake [ɪntek] *de (~s)* register

inteelt [ɪntelt] *de* inbreeding

integendeel [ɪnteɣə(n)del] *adv* on the contrary: *ik lui? ~!* me lazy? quite the contrary!

integer [ɪnteɣər] *adj, adv* upright, honest

¹integraal [ɪnteɣra̱l] *adj, adv* integral, complete
²integraal [ɪnteɣra̱l] *de (integralen) (maths)* integral
integraalhelm [ɪnteɣra̱lhɛlm] *de (~en)* regulation (crash-)helmet
integratie [ɪnteɣra̱(t)si] *de* integration
integreren [ɪnteɣre̱rə(n)] *vb* integrate
integriteit [ɪnteɣrite̱it] *de* integrity
¹intekenen [ɪ̱ntekənə(n)] *vb* subscribe, sign up
²intekenen [ɪ̱ntekənə(n)] *vb* register, enter
intekenlijst [ɪ̱nteka(n)lɛist] *de (~en)* subscription list
intellect [ɪntɛlɛkt] *het* intellect
intellectueel [ɪntɛlɛktywe̱l] *adj, adv* intellectual
intelligent [ɪntɛliɣɛnt] *adj, adv* intelligent, bright
intelligentie [ɪntɛliɣɛnsi] *de* intelligence
intelligentiequotiënt [ɪntɛliɣɛnsikoʃɛnt] *het (~en)* intelligence quotient, IQ
intelligentietest [ɪntɛliɣɛnsitɛst] *de (~s)* intelligence test
intens [ɪntɛns] *adj, adv* intense: *~ gelukkig* blissfully happy; *~ genieten* enjoy immensely
intensief [ɪntɛnzi̱f] *adj, adv* intensive
intensiteit [ɪntɛnzite̱it] *de* intensity, intenseness
intensive care [ɪntɛnsɪfkɛːr] *de* intensive care: *op de ~ liggen* be in intensive care
intensiveren [ɪntɛnzive̱rə(n)] *vb* intensify
intentie [ɪntɛnsi] *de (~s)* intention, purpose: *de ~ hebben om* intend to
interactie [ɪntɛra̱ksi] *de (~s)* interaction
interactief [ɪntɛraktife̱f] *adj, adv* interactive
intercity [ɪntɛrsɪ̱ti] *de (~'s)* intercity (train): *de ~ nemen* go by intercity (train)
intercitylijn [ɪntɛrsɪ̱tilɛin] *de* intercity line
intercom [ɪ̱ntɛrkɔm] *de (~s)* intercom: *iets over de ~ omroepen* announce sth over (*or:* on) the intercom
interen [ɪ̱ntərə(n)] *vb* eat into (one's capital)
interessant [ɪntərɛsɑ̱nt] *adj, adv* 1 interesting: *~ willen zijn (doen)* show off; 2 advantageous, profitable
interesse [ɪntərɛ̱sə] *het, de (~s)* interest: *een brede ~ hebben* have wide interests
¹interesseren [ɪntərɛse̱rə(n)] *vb* interest: *wie het gedaan heeft interesseert me niet* I am not interested in who did it
²interesseren [ɪntərɛse̱rə(n)] *ref vb* be interested
interieur [ɪntér(i)jø̱r] *het (~s)* interior, inside
interim [ɪ̱ntərɪm] *het (~s)* 1 interim: *de directeur ad ~* the acting manager; 2 (*Belg*) temporary replacement (*or:* job)
interimbureau [ɪ̱ntərɪmbyro] *het (~s) (Belg)* employment agency
interland [ɪ̱ntərlɑnt] *de (~s)* international (match), test match
interlokaal [ɪntərloka̱l] *adj, adv* trunk
intermezzo [ɪntərmɛ̱dzo] *het (~'s)* intermezzo, (*fig*) interlude
intern [ɪntɛrn] *adj, adv* 1 resident: *~e patiënten* in-patients; 2 internal, domestic: *uitsluitend voor ~*

gebruik confidential
internaat [ɪntərna̱t] *het (internaten)* boarding school
internationaal [ɪntərna(t)ʃona̱l] *adj, adv* international
internationaliseren [ɪntərna(t)ʃonalize̱rə(n)] *vb* internationalize
internet [ɪ̱ntərnɛt] *het* Internet
internetten [ɪ̱ntərnɛtə(n)] *vb* surf the Net
internist [ɪntərnɪ̱st] *de (~en)* internist
interpretatie [ɪntərpreta̱(t)si] *de (~s)* interpretation, reading: *foute (verkeerde) ~* misinterpretation
interpreteren [ɪntərprete̱rə(n)] *vb* interpret
interpunctie [ɪntərpʏ̱ŋksi] *de* punctuation
interruptie [ɪntərʏ̱psi] *de (~s)* interruption
interval [ɪ̱ntərvɑl] *het (~len)* interval
interventie [ɪntərvɛ̱nsi] *de (~s)* intervention
interview [ɪ̱ntərvju] *het (~s)* interview
interviewen [ɪntərvjuwə(n)] *vb* interview
intiem [ɪntim] *adj, adv* 1 intimate; 2 cosy: *een ~ gesprek* a cosy chat
intimidatie [ɪntimida̱(t)si] *de (~s)* intimidation
intimideren [ɪntimide̱rə(n)] *vb* intimidate
intimiteit [ɪntimite̱it] *de (~en)* 1 intimacy, familiarity; 2 liberty: *ongewenste ~en* sexual harassment
intocht [ɪ̱ntɔxt] *de (~en)* entry: *zijn ~ houden in* make one's entry into
intoetsen [ɪ̱ntutsə(n)] *vb* key in, enter
intolerant [ɪ̱ntolerɑnt] *adj* intolerant
intomen [ɪ̱ntomə(n)] *vb* curb, restrain, check
intonatie [ɪntona̱(t)si] *de (~s)* intonation
intrappen [ɪ̱ntrɑpə(n)] *vb* kick in (*or:* down)
intraveneus [ɪntravenø̱s] *adj, adv* intravenous
intrede [ɪ̱ntredə] *de* entry: *zijn ~ doen* set in
intreden [ɪ̱ntredə(n)] *vb* 1 enter a convent (*or:* monastery); 2 set in, occur, take effect
intrek [ɪ̱ntrɛk] *de* residence: *bij iem zijn ~ nemen* move in with s.o.
¹intrekken [ɪ̱ntrɛkə(n)] *vb* 1 move in (with): *bij zijn vriendin ~* move in with one's girlfriend; 2 be absorbed, soak in: *de verf moet nog ~* the paint must soak in first
²intrekken [ɪ̱ntrɛkə(n)] *vb* 1 draw in, draw up, retract; 2 withdraw, cancel, abolish, drop, repeal: *een verlof ~* cancel leave
intrekking [ɪ̱ntrɛkɪŋ] *de (~en)* withdrawal, abolition, cancellation, repeal
intrige [ɪntri̱ʒə] *de (~s)* intrigue; plot
intrigeren [ɪntriɣe̱rə(n)] *vb* intrigue, fascinate
intro [ɪ̱ntro] *het, de (~'s)* intro
introducé [ɪntrodyse̱] *de (~s)* guest, friend
introduceren [ɪntrodyse̱rə(n)] *vb* 1 introduce, initiate; 2 introduce, phase in
introductie [ɪntrodʏ̱ksi] *de (~s)* 1 introduction, presentation; 2 launch(ing)
introductieweek [ɪntrodʏ̱ksiwek] *de* orientation week
introvert [ɪ̱ntrovɛrt] *adj* introverted

intuinen [ɪntœynə(n)] *vb* go for, fall for: *er (or: ergens)* ~ fall for it (*or:* sth)

intuïtie [ɪntywi(t)si] *de (~s)* intuition, instinct: *op zijn ~ afgaan* act on one's intuition

intuïtief [ɪntywitɪf] *adj, adv* intuitive, instinctive: ~ *aanvoelen* know intuitively

intussen [ɪntxsə(n)] *adv* meanwhile, in the meantime

intypen [ɪntipə(n)] *vb* type in, enter

inval [ɪnvɑl] *de (~len)* **1** raid, invasion: *een ~ doen in* raid *(bldg)*, invade; **2** (bright) idea

invalide [ɪnvɑlidə] *adj* invalid, handicapped

invallen [ɪnvɑlə(n)] *vb* **1** raid, invade; **2** set in, fall, close in; **3** stand in (for), (act as a) substitute (for); **4** fall down, come down, collapse: *ingevallen wangen* hollow (*or:* sunken) cheeks

invaller [ɪnvɑlər] *de (~s)* substitute, replacement

invalshoek [ɪnvɑlshuk] *de (~en)* **1** angle of incidence; **2** approach, point of view

invasie [ɪnvazi] *de (~s)* invasion

inventaris [ɪnvɛntɑrɪs] *de (~sen)* **1** inventory, list (of contents); **2** stock (in trade), inventory, fittings, furniture

inventarisatie [ɪnvɛntɑriza(t)si] *de (~s)* stocktaking, making (*or:* drawing up) an inventory

inventariseren [ɪnvɛntɑrizerə(n)] *vb* **1** (make an) inventory, take stock (of), draw up a statement of assets and liabilities; **2** list

inventief [ɪnvɛntɪf] *adj* inventive, ingenious

inventiviteit [ɪnvɛntivitɛit] *de* inventiveness, ingenuity

investeerder [ɪnvɛsterdər] *de (~s)* investor

investeren [ɪnvɛsterə(n)] *vb* invest

investering [ɪnvɛsterɪŋ] *de (~en)* investment

investeringsmaatschappij [ɪnvɛsterɪŋsmatsχɑpɛi] *de (~en) (Belg)* organization for state investment in industry

invliegen [ɪnvliɣə(n)] *vb* ‖ *er* ~ be had, be fooled

invloed [ɪnvlut] *de (~en)* influence: *zijn ~ gebruiken* exert (*or:* use) one's influence; *rijden onder* ~ drive under the influence

invloedrijk [ɪnvlutrɛik] *adj* influential

¹**invoegen** [ɪnvuɣə(n)] *vb* insert (into)

²**invoegen** [ɪnvuɣə(n)] *vb* join the (stream of) traffic, merge

invoegstrook [ɪnvuχstrok] *de (-stroken)* acceleration lane

invoer [ɪnvur] *de (~en)* **1** import; *(goods)* imports; **2** input

invoeren [ɪnvurə(n)] *vb* **1** import; **2** introduce; **3** enter, input (to), read in(to)

invoerhandel [ɪnvurhɑndəl] *de* import trade

invoerrecht [ɪnvurɛχt] *het (~en)* import duty

invoerverbod [ɪnvurvərbɔt] *het* import ban

invoervergunning [ɪnvurvərɣynɪŋ] *de (~en)* import licence (*or:* permit)

invriezen [ɪnvrizə(n)] *vb* freeze

invullen [ɪnvylə(n)] *vb* fill in

invulling [ɪnvylɪŋ] *de (~en)* interpretation

inwaaien [ɪnwajə(n)] *vb* be blown in

inweken [ɪnwekə(n)] *vb* soak

inwendig [ɪnwɛndəχ] *adj, adv* internal, inner, inside

¹**inwerken** [ɪnwɛrkə(n)] *vb* show the ropes, break in

²**inwerken** [ɪnwɛrkə(n)] *vb* (with *op*) act on, affect: *op elkaar* ~ interact

inwerking [ɪnwɛrkɪŋ] *de (~en)* action, effect

inwerktijd [ɪnwɛrktɛit] *de (~en)* training period

inwerpen [ɪnwɛrpə(n)] *vb* throw in, insert

inwijden [ɪnwɛidə(n)] *vb* **1** inaugurate, dedicate, consecrate; **2** initiate

inwijding [ɪnwɛidɪŋ] *de (~en)* **1** inauguration, dedication, consecration; **2** initiation

inwijkeling [ɪnwɛikəlɪŋ] *de (~en) (Belg)* immigrant

inwijken [ɪnwɛikə(n)] *het (Belg)* immigrate

inwikkelen [ɪnwɪkələ(n)] *vb* wrap (up)

inwinnen [ɪnwɪnə(n)] *vb* obtain, gather

inwisselbaar [ɪnwɪsəlbar] *adj* exchangeable, convertible, redeemable

inwisselen [ɪnwɪsələ(n)] *vb* exchange, convert, cash, change, redeem

inwonen [ɪnwonə(n)] *vb* live, live in: *Gerard woont nog bij zijn ouders in* Gerard still lives with his parents

inwonend [ɪnwonənt] *adj* resident, living in: *~e kinderen* children living at home

inwoner [ɪnwonər] *de (~s)* inhabitant, resident

inworp [ɪnwɔrp] *de (~en)* throwing in, insertion

inwrijven [ɪnvrɛivə(n)] *vb* rub in(to): *dat zal ik hem eens* ~ I'll rub his nose in it

inzaaien [ɪnzajə(n)] *vb* sow, seed

inzage [ɪnzaɣə] *de* inspection: *een exemplaar ter* ~ an inspection copy

inzakken [ɪnzɑkə(n)] *vb* **1** collapse, give way; **2** *(com)* collapse, slump

inzamelen [ɪnzamələ(n)] *vb* collect, raise

inzameling [ɪnzaməlɪŋ] *de (~en)* collection

inzamelingsactie [ɪnzaməlɪŋsaksi] *de (~s)* collection, (fund-raising) drive

inzegenen [ɪnzeɣənə(n)] *vb* solemnize

inzegening [ɪnzeχənɪŋ] *de (~en)* solemnization

inzenden [ɪnzɛndə(n)] *vb* send in, submit, contribute

inzending [ɪnzɛndɪŋ] *de (~en)* **1** submission, contribution; **2** entry; contribution; exhibit

inzepen [ɪnzepə(n)] *vb* soap; lather

inzet [ɪnzɛt] *de (~ten)* **1** effort: *de spelers vochten met enorme* ~ the players gave it all they'd got; **2** stake, bet

inzetbaar [ɪnzɛdbar] *adj* usable, available

¹**inzetten** [ɪnzɛtə(n)] *vb* **1** put in, set; **2** start, launch: *de aanval* ~ go onto the attack; *de achtervolging* ~ set off in pursuit; **3** bring into action

²**inzetten** [ɪnzɛtə(n)] *vb* **1** stake, bet; **2** start, strike up

³**inzetten** [ɪnzɛtə(n)] *vb* set in

⁴**inzetten** [ɪnzɛtə(n)] *ref vb* do one's best: *zich voor een zaak* ~ devote oneself to a cause

inzicht [ɪnzɪχt] *het (~en)* **1** insight, understanding: *een beter ~ krijgen in* gain an insight into; **2** view, opinion

inzien [ɪnzin] *vb* **1** have a look at: *stukken ~* examine documents; *een boek vluchtig ~* leaf through a book; **2** see, recognize: *de noodzaak gaan ~ van* come to recognize the necessity of; **3** take a ... view of, consider: *ik zie het somber in* I'm pessimistic about it

inzinking [ɪnzɪŋkɪŋ] *de (~en)* breakdown: *ik had een kleine ~* it was one of my off moments

inzitten [ɪnzɪtə(n)] *vb* sit in: *(fig) dat zit er niet in* there's no chance of that

inzittende [ɪnzɪtəndə] *de (~n)* occupant, passenger

i.p.v. *in plaats van* instead of

IQ [iky] *het (~'s) intelligentiequotiënt* I.Q.

Iraaks [iraks] *adj* Iraqi

Iraans [irans] *adj* Iranian

Irak [irɑk] *het* Iraq

Irakees [irakes] *de (Irakezen)* Iraqi

Iran [iran] *het* Iran

Iraniër [iranijər] *de (~s)* Iranian

iris [ɪrɪs] *de (~sen)* iris

ironie [ironi] *de* irony

ironisch [ironis] *adj, adv* ironic(al)

irrationeel [ɪra(t)ʃonel] *adj, adv* irrational

irreëel [ɪrejel] *adj* unreal, imaginary

irrelevant [ɪreləvɑnt] *adj* irrelevant: *dat is ~* that's beside the point

irrigatie [ɪriɣa(t)si] *de (~s)* irrigation

irritant [iritɑnt] *adj, adv* irritating, annoying

irritatie [irita(t)si] *de (~s)* irritation

irriteren [iriterə(n)] *vb* irritate, annoy: *het irriteert mij* it is getting on my nerves

ischias [ɪsχijɑs] *de* sciatica

islam [ɪslɑm] *de* Islam

islamitisch [ɪslamitis] *adj* Islamic

isolatie [izola(t)si] *de (~s)* **1** insulation; **2** isolation

isoleercel [izolersɛl] *de (~len)* isolation cell, padded cell

isolement [izoləmɛnt] *het* isolation

¹isoleren [izolerə(n)] *vb* isolate, quarantine, cut off

²isoleren [izolerə(n)] *vb* insulate (from, against)

Israël [ɪsraɛl] *het* Israel

Israëli [ɪsraeli] *de (~'s)* Israeli

Israëlisch [ɪsraelis] *adj* Israeli

Italiaan [itɑljan] *de (Italianen)* Italian

¹Italiaans [itɑljans] *het* Italian

²Italiaans [itɑljans] *adj* Italian

Italië [itɑlijə] *het* Italy

i.t.t. *in tegenstelling tot* in contrast with; as opposed to

ivbo [ivebeo] *het individueel voorbereidend beroepsonderwijs* individual preparatory vocational education

ivf [ivɛf] *de in-vitrofertilisatie* IVF

i.v.m. *in verband met* in connection with

ivoor [ivor] *het (ivoren)* ivory

Ivoorkust [ivorkʏst] *de* Ivory Coast

ivoren [ivorə(n)] *adj* ivory

Ivriet [ivrit] *het* (modern) Hebrew

j

ja [ja] *int* **1** yes, yeah, all right, OK: ~ *knikken* nod; *en zo* ~ and if so; **2** really, indeed: *o* ~? oh yes?, (oh) really?; *o* ~, *nu ik je toch spreek* ... oh, yes, by the way ...

jaap [jap] *de (japen)* cut, gash, slash

jaar [jar] *het (jaren)* year: *een half* ~ half a year; *het hele* ~ *door* throughout the year; ~ *in,* ~ *uit* year after year; *in de laatste paar* ~, *de laatste jaren* in the last few years, in recent years; *om de twee* ~ every other year; *over vijf* ~ five years from now; *per* ~ yearly, a year; *een kind van zes* ~ a six-year-old (child); *uit het* ~ *nul* from the year dot; *vorige week dinsdag is ze twaalf* ~ *geworden* she was twelve last Tuesday

jaarbalans [jarbalɑns] *de (~en)* annual balance sheet

jaarbeurs [jarbørs] *de (-beurzen)* **1** (annual) fair, trade fair; **2** exhibition centre

jaarboek [jarbuk] *het (~en)* yearbook, annual

jaargang [jarɣɑŋ] *de (~en)* volume, year (of publication)

jaargenoot [jarɣənot] *de (-genoten)* classmate

jaargetijde [jarɣətɛidə] *het (~n)* season

jaarinkomen [jarɪŋkomə(n)] *het (~s)* annual income

jaarkaart [jarkart] *de (~en)* annual season ticket

jaarlijks [jarləks] *adj, adv* annual, yearly: *dit feest wordt* ~ *gevierd* this celebration takes place every year

jaarmarkt [jarmɑrkt] *de (~en)* (annual) fair

jaarring [jarɪŋ] *de (~en)* annual ring, growth (or: tree) ring

jaartal [jartɑl] *het (~len)* year, date

jaartelling [jartɛlɪŋ] *de (~en)* era: *de christelijke* ~ the Christian era

jaarvergadering [jarvərɣadərɪŋ] *de (~en)* annual meeting

jaarwisseling [jarwɪsəlɪŋ] *de (~en)* turn of the year: *goede (prettige)* ~! Happy New Year!

JAC [jɑk] *het Jongerenadviescentrum* young people's advisory centre

¹jacht [jɑχt] *het (~en)* yacht

²jacht [jɑχt] *de (~en)* **1** hunting, shooting: *op* ~ *gaan: a)* go (out) hunting, go (out) shooting; *b)* go hunting, prowl; **2** hunt, shoot; **3** hunt, chase: ~ *maken op oorlogsmisdadigers* hunt down war crimi-

nals

jachten [jɑχtə(n)] *vb* hurry, rush

jachtgebied [jɑχtχəbit] *het (~en)* hunt(ing ground), shoot(ing), shooting ground

jachthaven [jɑχthavə(n)] *de (~s)* yacht basin, marina

jachthond [jɑχthɔnt] *de (~en)* hound

jachtig [jɑχtəχ] *adj, adv* hurried, hectic

jachtluipaard [jɑχtlœypart] *de (~en)* cheetah

jachtopziener [jɑχtɔpsinər] *de (~s)* game-warden

jachtseizoen [jɑχtsɛizun] *het (~en)* hunting season, shooting season

jack [jɛk] *het (~s)* jacket, coat

jacquet [ʒakɛt] *het, de (~ten)* morning coat

jade [jadə] *het, de* jade

¹jagen [jaɣə(n)] *vb* **1** hunt; hunt for; shoot; **2** drive, put, race, rush: *prijzen omhoog* (or: *omlaag*) ~ drive prices up (or: down)

²jagen [jaɣə(n)] *vb* hunt, shoot: *op patrijs* ~ hunt partridge

jager [jaɣər] *de (~s)* hunter

jaguar [dʒɛguwɑr] *de (~s)* jaguar

jakhals [jɑkhɑls] *de (jakhalzen)* jackal

jakkeren [jɑkərə(n)] *vb* ride hard; rush along

jakkes [jɑkəs] *int* ugh!, bah!, pooh!

jaknikken [jaknɪkə(n)] *vb* nod (agreement)

Jakob [jakɔp] *de James, Jacob: de ware* ~ Mr Right

jaloers [jalurs] *adj, adv* jealous (of), envious (of)

jaloezie [ʒaluzi] *de (~ën)* **1** envy; jealousy; **2** (Venetian) blind

jam [ʒɛm] *de (~s)* jam

Jamaica [jamajka] *het* Jamaica

Jamaicaan [jamajkan] *de (Jamaicanen)* Jamaican

jammen [dʒɛmə(n)] *vb* gig, jam

jammer [jɑmər] *adj* a pity, a shame, too bad, bad luck: *het is* ~ *dat* ... : *a)* it's a pity (or: shame) that ...; *b)* too bad that ...; *wat* ~! what a pity! (or: shame!); *het is erg* ~ *voor hem* it's very hard on him; ~, *hij is net weg* (a) pity (or: bad luck), he has just left

jammeren [jɑmərə(n)] *vb* moan

jammerlijk [jɑmərlək] *adj, adv* pitiful, miserable: ~ *mislukken* fail miserably

jampot [ʒɛmpɔt] *de (~ten)* jam jar

Jan [jɑn] *de John:* ~ *Rap en zijn maat* ragtag and bobtail; ~ *en alleman* every Tom, Dick and Harry; ~ *met de pet* the (ordinary) man in the street

janboel [jɑmbul] *de* shambles, mess

janet [ʒanɛt] *de (~ten) (Belg)* homo, poof(ter), pansy

janken [jɑŋkə(n)] *vb* whine, howl, (*inf*) blubber

Janklaassen [jɑŋklasə(n)] *de Punch:* ~ *en Katrijn* Punch and Judy

januari [jɑnywari] *de* January

jap [jɑp] *de (~pen)* Jap

Japan [japɑn] *het* Japan

Japanner [japɑnər] *de (~s)* Japanese

¹Japans [japɑns] *het* Japanese

²Japans [japɑns] *adj* Japanese

japon [jap<u>ɔ</u>n] *de (~nen)* dress; gown

jappenkamp [j<u>ɑ</u>pə(n)kɑmp] *het (~en)* Japanese (POW) camp

¹**jarenlang** [j<u>a</u>rə(n)lɑŋ] *adj* many years': *een ~e vriendschap* a friendship of many years' (standing)

²**jarenlang** [j<u>a</u>rə(n)lɑŋ] *adv* for years and years

jargon [jɑry<u>ɔ</u>n] *het (~s)* jargon: *ambtelijk ~* officialese

jarig [j<u>a</u>rəχ] *adj* || *de ~e Job* (or: *Jet*) the birthday boy (or: girl); *ik ben vandaag ~* it's my birthday today

jarige [j<u>a</u>rəɣə] *de (~n)* person celebrating his (or: her) birthday, birthday boy (or: girl)

jarretelle [ʒɑrɑtɛl] *de (~s)* suspender, *(Am)* garter

jas [jɑs] *de (~sen)* **1** coat; **2** jacket || *in een nieuw ~je steken* give (or: get) a facelift

jasje [j<u>ɑ</u>ʃə] *het (~s)* **1** (short, little) coat; **2** jacket

jasmijn [jɑsm<u>ɛ</u>in] *de (~en)* jasmine

jasses [j<u>ɑ</u>səs] *int* ugh!

jat [jɑt] *de (~ten)* paw

jatten [j<u>ɑ</u>tə(n)] *vb* pinch, nick

Java [j<u>a</u>va] *het* Java

Javaan [jav<u>a</u>n] *de (Javanen)* Javan(ese)

jawel [jaw<u>ɛ</u>l] *int* (oh) yes, certainly: *~ meneer* certainly sir

jawoord [j<u>a</u>wort] *het* consent, *(roughly)* 'I will'

jazz [dʒɛːz] *de* jazz

¹**je** [jə] *pers pron* you: *jullie zouden ~ moeten schamen* you ought to be ashamed of yourselves

²**je** [jə] *ind pron* you: *zoiets doe ~ niet* you don't do things like that

³**je** [jə] *pos pron* your: *één van ~ vrienden* a friend of yours

jeans [dʒiːns] *de* jeans

jee [je] *int* (oh) Lord!, dear me!

jeep [dʒip] *de (~s)* jeep

jegens [j<u>e</u>ɣəns] *prep* towards: *diep wantrouwen koesteren ~ iem* have a deep distrust of s.o.

jekker [j<u>ɛ</u>kər] *de (~s)* pea-jacket, reefer

Jemen [j<u>e</u>mə(n)] *het* (the) Yemen

Jemenitisch [jem<u>ə</u>nitis] *adj* Yemenite

jenever [jən<u>e</u>vər] *de (~s)* Dutch gin, jenever

jeneverbes [jən<u>e</u>vərbɛs] *de (~sen)* juniper berry

jengelen [j<u>ɛ</u>ŋələ(n)] *vb* **1** whine, moan; **2** drone: *~ op een gitaar* twang (away) on a guitar

jennen [j<u>ɛ</u>nə(n)] *vb* badger, pester

jerrycan [dʒ<u>ɛ</u>rikɛn] *de (~s)* jerrycan

Jeruzalem [jer<u>y</u>zalɛm] *het* Jerusalem

jetski [dʒ<u>ɛ</u>tski] *de (~'s)* jet-ski

jeu de boules [ʒødəb<u>u</u>l] *het* boule

jeugd [jøχt] *de* **1** youth; **2** young people: *de ~ van tegenwoordig* young people nowadays

jeugdbende [j<u>ø</u>χtbɛndə] *de* gang of youths

jeugdbescherming [j<u>ø</u>χtbəsχɛrmɪŋ] *de (Belg)* child welfare

jeugdherberg [j<u>ø</u>χthɛrbɛrχ] *de (~en)* youth hostel

jeugdherinnering [j<u>ø</u>χthɛrɪnərɪŋ] *de (~en)* reminiscence of childhood, childhood memory

jeugdig [j<u>ø</u>ɣdəχ] *adj* youthful, young(ish): *een programma voor ~e kijkers* a programme for younger viewers

jeugdjournaal [j<u>ø</u>χtʃurnal] *het (~s)* news broadcast for young people

jeugdliefde [j<u>ø</u>χtlivdə] *de (~s)* youthful love, adolescent love, calf-love, *(pers)* old flame: *zij is een van zijn ~s* she's one of his old loves

jeugdpuistjes [j<u>ø</u>χtpœyʃəs] *de* acne, spots, pimples

jeugdrechter [j<u>ø</u>χtrɛχtər] *de (~s) (Belg)* juvenile court magistrate

jeugdwerk [j<u>ø</u>χtwɛrk] *het (~en)* youth work

jeuk [jøk] *de* itch(ing): *ik heb overal ~* I'm itching all over

jeuken [j<u>ø</u>kə(n)] *vb* itch: *mijn handen ~ om hem een pak slaag te geven* I'm (just) itching to give him a good thrashing

jeukerig [j<u>ø</u>kərəχ] *adj* itchy

je-weet-wel [jəw<u>e</u>twɛl] *de (of pers)* what's-his-name; you know …

jezelf [jəz<u>ɛ</u>lf] *ref pron* yourself: *kijk naar ~* look at yourself

jezuïet [jezyw<u>i</u>t] *de (~en)* Jesuit

Jezus [j<u>e</u>zʏs] *de* Jesus

jicht [jɪχt] *de* gout

¹**Jiddisch** [j<u>ɪ</u>dis] *het* Yiddish

²**Jiddisch** [j<u>ɪ</u>dis] *adj* Yiddish

jij [jɛi] *pers pron* you: *zeg, ~ daar!* hey, you!; *~ hier?* goodness, are you here?

jioe-jitsoe [jiujɪtsu] *het* ju-jitsu

jippie [j<u>ɪ</u>pi] *int* yippee

job [dʒɔp] *de (~s)* job

Job [jɔp] *de* Job: *zo arm als ~* as poor as a church mouse

jobdienst [dʒ<u>ɔ</u>bdinst] *de (~en) (Belg)* (student) employment agency

jobstijding [j<u>ɔ</u>psteidɪŋ] *de (~en)* bad tidings, bad news

jobstudent [dʒ<u>ɔ</u>pstydɛnt] *de (~en) (Belg)* student with part-time job

joch [jɔχ] *het* lad

jochie [j<u>ɔ</u>χi] *het (~s)* (little) lad

jockey [dʒ<u>ɔ</u>ki] *de (~s)* jockey

jodelen [j<u>o</u>dələ(n)] *vb* yodel

jodendom [j<u>o</u>dəndɔm] *het* **1** Jews, Jewry; **2** Judaism

jodin [jodɪn] *de (~nen)* Jewess

jodium [j<u>o</u>dijʏm] *het* iodine

Joegoslaaf [juɣosl<u>a</u>f] *de (Joegoslaven)* Yugoslav(ian)

Joegoslavië [juɣoslavijə] *het* Yugoslavia

Joegoslavisch [juɣosl<u>a</u>vis] *adj* Yugoslav(ian)

joekel [j<u>u</u>kəl] *de (~s)* whopper: *wat een ~ van een huis!* what a whacking great house!

joelen [j<u>u</u>lə(n)] *vb* whoop, roar: *een ~de menigte* a roaring crowd

joetje [j<u>u</u>cə] *het (~s)* tenner

jofel [j<u>o</u>fəl] *adj, adv* great

joggen [dʒ<u>ɔ</u>ɡə(n)] *vb* jog

joggingpak [dʒ<u>ɔ</u>ɡɪŋpɑk] *het (~ken)* tracksuit

joh [jɔ] *int* you: *hé ~, kijk een beetje uit* hey (you), watch out; *kop op, ~* (come on) cheer up, (old boy, girl)

Johannes [johɑnəs] *de* John: *~ de Doper* John the Baptist

joint [dʒɔjnt] *de (~s)* joint, stick

jojo [jojo] *de (~'s)* yo-yo

joker [jokər] *de (~s)* joker

jokkebrok [jɔkəbrɔk] *de (~ken)* (little) fibber

jokken [jɔkə(n)] *vb* fib, tell a fib

jolig [joləχ] *adj, adv* jolly

Jonas [jonɑs] *de* Jonah

jonassen [jonɑsə(n)] *vb* toss in the air *(or:* in a blanket)

¹jong [jɔŋ] *het (~en)* **1** young (one), pup(py); **2** kid, child

²jong [jɔŋ] *adj* **1** young: *op ~e leeftijd* at an early age; *~ en oud* young and old; **2** recent, late: *de ~ste berichten* the latest news; **3** young, new, immature: *~e kaas* unmatured *(or:* green) cheese

jongedame [jɔŋədɑmə] *de (~s)* young lady

jongeheer [jɔŋəher] *de (-heren)* young gentleman

jongelui [jɔŋəlœy] *de* youngsters, young people

¹jongen [jɔŋə(n)] *de (~s)* **1** boy, youth, lad: *is het een ~ of een meisje?* is it a boy or a girl?; **2** boy, lad, guy: *onze ~s hebben zich dapper geweerd* our boys put up a brave defence; **3** *(pl)* kids; lads, chaps; folks, guys: *gaan jullie mee, ~s?* are you coming, you lot?

²jongen [jɔŋə(n)] *vb* give birth, drop (their) young, bear young; litter: *onze kat heeft vandaag gejongd* our cat has had kittens today

jongensachtig [jɔŋənsɑχtəχ] *adj, adv* boyish: *zich ~ gedragen* behave like a boy

jongere [jɔŋərə] *de (~n)* young person, youngster

jongerencentrum [jɔŋərə(n)sɛntrʏm] *het (~s, -centra) (roughly)* youth centre

jongerenpaspoort [jɔŋərə(n)pɑspoort] *het (~en)* ‖ *cultureel ~ (roughly)* youth discount card for cultural events

jongerenwerk [jɔŋərə(n)wɛrk] *het* youth work

jongleren [jɔŋlerə(n)] *vb* juggle

jongleur [jɔŋlør] *de (~s)* juggler, acrobat

jongstleden [jɔŋstledə(n)] *adj* last: *de 14e ~* the 14th of this month

jonkheer [jɔŋkher] *de (-heren)* esquire

jonkvrouw [jɔŋkfrɑu] *de (~en) (roughly)* Lady

jood [jot] *de (joden)* Jew

joods [jots] *adj, adv* Jewish, Judaic

jopper [jɔpər] *de (~s)* pea-jacket, reefer

Jordaan [jɔrdɑn] *de* (the river) Jordan

Jordanië [jɔrdɑnijə] *het* Jordan

Jordaniër [jɔrdɑnijər] *de (~s)* Jordanian

jota [jotɑ] *de (~'s)* iota

jou [jɑu] *pers pron* you: *~ moet ik hebben* you're just the person I need; *is dit boek van ~?* is this book yours?

journaal [ʒurnɑl] *het (journalen)* news, newscast: *het ~ van 8 uur* the 8 o'clock news

journalist [ʒurnɑlɪst] *de (~en)* journalist

journalistiek [ʒurnɑlɪstik] *de* journalism

jouw [jɑu] *pos pron* your: *is dat ~ werk?* is that your work?; *dat potlood is het ~e* that pencil is yours

joviaal [jovijɑl] *adj, adv* jovial

joystick [dʒɔjstɪk] *de (~s)* joystick

jr. *junior* Jr.

jubelen [jybələ(n)] *vb* shout with joy, be jubilant

jubileren [jybilerə(n)] *vb* celebrate one's jubilee *(or:* anniversary)

jubileum [jybilejʏm] *het (jubilea)* anniversary; jubilee: *gouden ~* golden jubilee, 50th anniversary

judo [jydo] *het* judo

juf [jʏf] *de (~s, ~fen)* teacher, *(form of address)* Miss

juffershondje [jʏfərshɔncə] *het (~s)* lapdog

juffrouw [jʏfrɑu] *de (~en)* madam

juichen [jœyχə(n)] *vb* shout with joy, be jubilant: *de menigte juichte toen het doelpunt werd gemaakt* the crowd cheered when the goal was scored

¹juist [jœyst] *adj, adv* **1** right, correct: *de ~e tijd* the right *(or:* correct) time; *is dit de ~e spelling?* is this the right spelling?; **2** right, proper: *precies op het ~e ogenblik* just at the right moment

²juist [jœyst] *adv* **1** just, exactly, of all times *(or:* places, people); no, on the contrary: *ze bedoelde ~ het tegendeel* she meant just the opposite; *gelukkig? ik ben juist diepbedroefd!* happy? no *(or:* on the contrary), I'm terribly sad!; *daarom ~* that's exactly why; *~ op dat ogenblik kwam zij binnen* just at that very moment *(or:* right at that moment) she came in; **2** just

juistheid [jœysthɛit] *de* correctness, accuracy, truth, appropriateness

juk [jʏk] *het (~ken)* yoke

jukbeen [jʏgben] *het (~deren)* cheekbone

juli [jyli] *de* July

¹jullie [jʏli] *pers pron* you: *~ hebben gelijk* you're right

²jullie [jʏli] *pos pron* your: *is die auto van ~?* is that car yours?

jungle [dʒʏŋgəl] *de (~s)* jungle

juni [jyni] *de* June

junior [jynijɔr] *de (~en)* junior

junk [dʒʏŋk] *de (~s)* **1** junkie, junky; **2** junk, smack

junta [χʏntɑ] *de (~'s)* junta

jureren [ʒyrerə(n)] *vb* adjudicate

jurering [ʒyrerɪŋ] *de (~en)* adjudication

juridisch [jyridis] *adj, adv* legal, law

jurisdictie [jyrɪzdɪksi] *de (~s)* jurisdiction, competence

jurisprudentie [jyrɪsprydɛnsi] *de* jurisprudence

jurist [jyrɪst] *de (~en)* jurist, lawyer

jurk [jʏrk] *de (~en)* dress: *een blote ~* a revealing dress

jury [ʒyri] *de (~'s)* jury

jurylid [ʒyrilɪt] *het (-leden)* **1** member of the jury; **2** (panel of) judges

jus [ʒy] *de* gravy

jus d'orange [ʒydorɑ̃ʃ] *de* orange juice

justitie [jʏsti(t)si] *de* **1** justice: *minister van ~* Minister of Justice; *officier van ~* public prosecutor; **2** judiciary, the law, the police: *met ~ in aanra-king komen* come into conflict with the law

justitiepaleis [jʏsti(t)sipalɛis] *het (-paleizen)*
(Belg) Palace of Justice

¹jute [jʏtə] *de* jute

²jute [jʏtə] *adj* jute

Jutland [jʏtlɑnt] *het* Jutland

jutten [jʏtə(n)] *vb* search beaches

jutter [jʏtər] *de (~s)* beachcomber

juweel [jywel] *het (juwelen)* **1** jewel, gem; **2** *(pl)* jewellery

juwelier [jywəlir] *de (~s)* jeweller

k

K [ka] *1024 bytes, kilobyte* K: *een bestand van 2506 ~ a 2506K file*

kaaiman [kajmɑn] *de (~nen)* cayman

kaak [kak] *de (kaken)* jaw

kaakchirurg [kakʃirʏrχ] *de (~en)* oral surgeon, dental surgeon

kaakje [kakjə] *het (~s)* biscuit

kaal [kal] *adj* **1** bald: *zo ~ als een biljartbal zijn* be (as) bald as a coot; **2** (thread)bare: *een kale plek* a (thread)bare spot; *de kale huur* the basic rent; **3** bare: *de bomen worden ~* the trees are losing their leaves

kaalgeknipt [kalɣəknɪpt] *vb* close-cropped

kaalheid [kalhɛit] *de* baldness

kaalslag [kalslɑχ] *de* deforestation

kaap [kap] *de (kapen)* cape: *~ de Goede Hoop* Cape of Good Hope

Kaapstad [kapstɑt] *het* Cape Town

Kaapverdische Eilanden [kapfɛrdisəɣilɑndə(n)] *de* Cape Verde Islands

kaars [kars] *de (~en)* candle

kaarslicht [karslɪχt] *het* candlelight

kaarsrecht [karsrɛχt] *adj, adv* dead straight; bolt upright

kaarsvet [karsfɛt] *het* candle-grease

kaart [kart] *de (~en)* **1** card: *de gele* (or: *rode*) *~ krijgen* be shown the yellow (or: red) card; **2** menu; **3** cards, hand: *een spel ~en* a pack of cards; **4** ticket; **5** map; chart: *dat is geen haalbare ~* it's not a viable proposition; *open ~ spelen* put all one's cards on the table

kaarten [kartə(n)] *vb* play cards

kaartenbak [kartə(n)bɑk] *de (~ken)* card-index box (or: drawer)

kaarting [kartɪŋ] *de (~en) (Belg)* drive, bridge drive, whist drive

kaartje [karcə] *het (~s)* **1** (business) card; **2** ticket

kaartlezen [kartlezə(n)] *vb* read maps

kaartspel [kartspɛl] *het* card playing; card game, cards: *geld verliezen bij het ~* lose money at cards

kaartsysteem [kartsistem] *het (-systemen)* card index

kaas [kas] *de (kazen)* cheese: *belegen ~* matured cheese; *jonge ~* new cheese

kaasboer [kazbur] *de (~en)* cheesemonger

kaasschaaf [kasχaf] *de (-schaven)* cheese slicer

kaatsen [katsə(n)] *vb* bounce

kabaal [kabal] *het* racket, din

kabbelen [kɑbələ(n)] *vb* lap; *(also fig)* ripple, babble, murmur

kabel [kabəl] *de (~s)* **1** cable; **2** wire, cable

kabelaansluiting [kabəlanslœytɪŋ] *de* connection to cable TV

kabelbaan [kabəlban] *de (-banen)* funicular (railway), cable-lift

kabeljauw [kabəljɑu] *de (~en)* cod(fish)

kabelkrant [kabəlkrɑnt] *de (~en)* cable TV information service

kabelnet [kabəlnɛt] *het (~ten)* cable television network: *aangesloten zijn op het ~* receive cable television

kabinet [kabinɛt] *het (~ten)* cabinet, government: *het ~ Kok* the Kok cabinet (or: government)

kabouter [kabɑutər] *de (~s)* **1** gnome, pixie, *(pl also)* little people: *dat hebben de ~tjes gedaan* it must have been the fairies (or: the little people); **2** Brownie

kachel [kɑχəl] *de (~s)* stove; heater; fire; fire

kadaster [kadɑstər] *het* **1** *(roughly)* land register; **2** *(roughly)* land registry

kadaver [kadavər] *het (~s)* (dead) body; corpse

kade [kadə] *de (~n)* quay, wharf: *het schip ligt aan de ~* the ship lies by the quay(side)

kader [kadər] *het (~s)* **1** frame(work): *in het ~ van* within the framework (or: scope) of, as part of; **2** executives

kadetje [kadɛcə] *het (~s)* (bread) roll

kaf [kɑf] *het* chaff

Kaffer [kɑfər] *de* Kaffir

kaft [kɑft] *het, de (~en)* **1** cover; **2** jacket

kaftan [kɑftɑn] *de (~s)* kaftan

kaftpapier [kɑftpapir] *het* wrapping paper, brown paper

KAJ [kaajɛ] *de (Belg) Kristelijke Arbeidersjeugd* (Organization of) Christian workers' children

kajak [kajɑk] *de (~s)* kayak

kajotter [kajɔtər] *de (~s) (Belg)* member of KAJ

kajuit [kajœyt] *de (~en)* saloon

kak [kɑk] *de* **1** shit, crap; **2** la-di-da people, snooty people, snobs || *kale (kouwe) ~* swank, la-di-da behaviour

kakelen [kakələ(n)] *vb* cackle; *(fig also)* chatter

kakelvers [kakəlvɛrs] *adj* farm-fresh

kaketoe [kakətu] *de (~s)* cockatoo

kaki [kaki] *het* khaki

kakken [kɑkə(n)] *vb* crap, shit

kakkerlak [kɑkərlɑk] *de (~ken)* cockroach

kalebas [kaləbɑs] *de (~sen)* gourd, calabash

kalender [kalɛndər] *de (~s)* calendar

kalf [kɑlf] *het (kalveren)* calf: *de put dempen als het ~ verdronken is* lock the stable door after the horse has bolted

kalfsgehakt [kɑlfsχəhɑkt] *het* minced veal

kalfsleer [kɑlfsler] *het* calf, calfskin

kalfsvlees [kɑlfsfles] *het* veal

kaliber [kalibər] *het (~s)* calibre, bore
kalium [kalijʏm] *het* potassium, potash
kalk [kɑlk] *de* **1** lime, (quick)lime, slaked lime; **2** (lime) mortar; **3** plaster, whitewash
kalkaanslag [kɑlkanslɑχ] *de* scale, fur
kalken [kɑlkə(n)] *vb* **1** scribble; **2** chalk
kalkgebrek [kɑlkχəbrɛk] *het* calcium deficiency
kalkoen [kɑlkun] *de (~en)* turkey
kalligraferen [kɑliɣrafərə(n)] *vb* write in calligraphy *(or:* fine handwriting)
kalligrafie [kɑliɣrafi] *de (~ën)* calligraphy, penmanship
kalm [kɑlm] *adj, adv* **1** calm, cool, composed; **2** peaceful, quiet: *~ aan!* take it easy!, easy does it!
kalmeren [kɑlmerə(n)] *vb* calm down; soothe, tranquillize: *een ~d effect* a calming *(or:* soothing, tranquillizing) effect
kalmeringsmiddel [kɑlmerɪŋsmɪdəl] *het (~en)* sedative, tranquillizer
kalmpjes [kɑlmpjəs] *adv* calmly
kalmte [kɑlmtə] *de* **1** calm(ness), composure: *zijn ~ bewaren* keep one's head/composure *(or:* self-control, cool); **2** calm(ness), tranquillity, quietness
kalven [kɑlvə(n)] *vb* calve
kalverliefde [kɑlvərlivdə] *de (~s)* calf love
kam [kɑm] *de (~men)* comb
kameel [kamel] *de (kamelen)* camel
kameleon [kamelejɔn] *het, de (~s)* chameleon
kamer [kamər] *de (~s)* **1** room, chamber; **2** room, apartment: *~s verhuren* take in lodgers; *~ met ontbijt* Bed and Breakfast, B & B; *Renske woont op ~s* Renske is *(or:* lives) in lodgings; *op ~s gaan wonen* move into lodgings; **3** chamber, house: *(Belg) Kamer van Volksvertegenwoordigers* Lower House (of Parliament); *de Eerste Kamer: a)* the Upper Chamber *(or:* Upper House); *b)* the (House of) Lords, the Upper House; *c) (Am)* the Senate; *de Tweede Kamer: a)* the Lower Chamber *(or:* Lower House); *b)* the (House of) Commons; *c) (Am)* the House (of Representatives); **4** chamber, board: *de Kamer van Koophandel en Fabrieken* the Chamber of Commerce
kameraad [kamərat] *de (kameraden)* comrade, companion, mate, pal, buddy
kameraadschap [kaməratsχɑp] *de* companionship, (good-)fellowship, camaraderie
kamerbewoner [kamərbəwonər] *de (~s)* lodger
kamerbreed [kamərbret] *adj* wall-to-wall
kamergenoot [kamərɣənot] *de (-genoten)* room-mate
kamerjas [kamərjɑs] *de (~sen)* dressing gown
kamerlid [kamərlɪt] *het (-leden)* Member of Parliament, M.P.
kamermeisje [kamərmɛiʃə] *het (~s)* chambermaid
Kameroen [kamərun] *het* Cameroon
kamerplant [kamərplɑnt] *de (~en)* house plant, indoor plant
kamerverkiezing [kamərvərkizɪŋ] *de (~en)* parliamentary elections, *(Am)* congressional elections
kamervoorzitter [kamərvorzɪtər] *de (~s)* chairman *(or:* president) of the House (of Parliament), Speaker, Lord Chancellor
kamerzetel [kamərzetəl] *de (~s)* seat
kamfer [kamfər] *de* camphor
kamikaze [kamikazə] *de (~s)* kamikaze, suicide pilot
kamille [kamɪlə] *de* camomile
kammen [kamə(n)] *vb* comb
kamp [kamp] *het (~en)* camp
kampeerboerderij [kampɛrburdərɛi] *de (~en)* farm campsite
kampeerder [kampɛrdər] *de (~s)* camper
kampeerterrein [kampɛrtɛrɛin] *het (~en)* camp(ing) site, caravan park *(or:* site)
kampeerwagen [kampɛrwaɣə(n)] *de (~s)* **1** caravan; **2** camper
kampen [kampə(n)] *vb* contend (with), struggle (with), wrestle (with): *met tegenslag te ~ hebben* have to cope with setbacks
kamperen [kampərə(n)] *vb* camp (out), encamp, pitch (one's) tents, bivouac: *vrij (or: bij de boer) ~* camp wild *(or:* on a farm)
kamperfoelie [kampərfuli] *de (~s)* honeysuckle
kampioen [kampijun] *de (~en)* champion; titleholder
kampioenschap [kampijunsχɑp] *het (~pen)* championship, contest, competition, tournament
kampvuur [kampfyr] *het (-vuren)* campfire
kan [kɑn] *de (~nen)* jug: *de zaak is in ~nen en kruiken* it's in the bag
kanaal [kanal] *het (kanalen)* **1** canal, channel: *Het Kanaal* the (English) Channel; **2** canal, duct
Kanaaleilanden [kanalɛilɑndə(n)] *de* Channel Islands *(or:* Isles)
Kanaaltunnel [kanaltʏnəl] *de* Channel Tunnel; Chunnel
kanaliseren [kanalizərə(n)] *vb (fig)* channel
kanarie [kanari] *de (~s)* canary (bird)
kandelaar [kɑndəlar] *de (~s)* candlestick, candleholder
kandidaat [kɑndidat] *de (kandidaten)* **1** candidate, applicant: *zich ~ stellen (voor)* run (for); **2** candidate, examinee
kandidaatsexamen [kɑndidatsɛksamə(n)] *het (~s, -examina) (roughly)* first university examination *(or:* degree), bachelors degree
kandidatuur [kɑndidatyr] *de (kandidaturen)* candidature, nomination
kandij [kɑndɛi] *de* candy
kaneel [kanel] *het, de* cinnamon
kangoeroe [kɑŋɣəru] *de (~s)* kangaroo
kanjer [kɑɲər] *de (~s)* **1** wizard; humdinger, whizz kid; *(sport)* star (player); **2** whopper, colossus: *een ~ van een vis (or: appel)* a whopping fish *(or:* apple)
kanker [kɑŋkər] *de* cancer, carcinoma: *aan ~ doodgaan* die of cancer
kankerbestrijding [kɑŋkərbəstrɛidɪŋ] *de* fight

against cancer, cancer control, (anti-)cancer campaign

kankeren [kɑŋkərə(n)] *vb* grouse, grumble, gripe: ~ *op de maatschappij* grouse about society

kankerspecialist [kɑŋkərspeʃalɪst] *de (~en)* cancer specialist, oncologist

kankerverwekkend [kɑŋkərvərwɛkənt] *adj* carcinogenic

kannibaal [kɑnibal̠] *de (kannibalen)* cannibal, man-eater

kannibalisme [kɑnibalɪsmə] *het* cannibalism

kano [kan̠o] *de (~'s)* canoe

kanon [kanɔn] *het (~nen)* **1** gun, cannon; **2** big shot, big name

kanonschot [kanɔnsχɔt] *het (~en)* gunshot, cannonshot

kans [kɑns] *de (~en)* **1** chance, possibility, opportunity, liability, risk: *vijftig procent ~* equal chances, even odds; *(een) grote ~ dat ...* a good chance that ...; *hij heeft een goede* (or: *veel*) *~ te winnen* he stands (or: has) a good chance of winning; *de ~en keren* the tide (or: his luck) is turning; *geen ~ maken op* stand no chance of (sth, doing sth); *ik zie er wel ~ toe* I think I can manage it; *~ zien te ontkomen* manage to escape; *de ~ is honderd tegen één* the odds (or: chances) are a hundred to one; *zijn ~en grijpen* seize the opportunity; *zijn ~ afwachten* await one's chances; *een gemiste ~* a lost (or: missed) opportunity; *geen schijn van ~* not a chance in the world

kansarm [kɑnsɑrm] *adj* underprivileged, deprived

kansel [kɑnsəl] *de (~s)* pulpit

kanselier [kɑnsəli̠r] *de (~s)* chancellor

kansloos [kɑnslos] *adj, adv* prospectless: *hij was ~ tegen hem* he didn't stand a chance against him

kansrijk [kɑnsrɛik] *adj* likely (*candidate*), strong

kansspel [kɑnspɛl] *het (~en)* game of chance

kant [kɑnt] *de (~en)* **1** edge, side; margin: *aan de ~ !* out of the way!; *aan de ~ gaan staan* stand (or: step) aside; *zijn auto aan de ~ zetten* pull up (or: over); **2** lace; **3** bank, edge: *op de ~ klimmen* climb ashore; **4** side, face, surface, *(fig)* aspect, *(fig)* facet, *(fig)* angle, *(fig)* view: *zich van zijn goede ~ laten zien* show one's good side; *iemands sterke* (or: *zwakke) ~en* s.o.'s strong (or: weak) points; *deze ~ boven* this side up; **5** side, end, edge: *iets op zijn ~ zetten* put sth on its side; *de scherpe ~en van iets afnemen* tone sth down (a bit); *scherpe ~* (cutting) edge; **6** way, direction: *zij kan nog alle ~en op* she has kept her options open; *deze ~ op, alstublieft* this way, please; *van alle ~en* on all sides; *geen ~ meer op kunnen* have nowhere (left) to go; **7** side, part(y): *familie van vaders* (or: *moeders) ~* relatives on one's father's (or: mother's) side; *ik sta aan jouw ~* I'm on your side; *iem van ~ maken* do s.o. in

¹kantelen [kɑntələ(n)] *vb* tilt, tip (over, to one side), turn over: *niet ~!* this side up!

²kantelen [kɑntələ(n)] *vb* topple over, turn over

kanten [kɑntə(n)] *adj* (of) lace, lacy

kant-en-klaar [kɑntɛnkla̠r] *adj* ready-to-use, ready for use, ready-made, instant, ready-to-wear, off the peg: *geen kant-en-klare oplossing hebben* have no cut-and-dried solution

kantine [kɑntin̠ə] *de (~s)* canteen

kantje [kɑncə] *het (~s)* **1** edge, verge: *dat was op het ~ af* that was a near thing (*or*: close shave); **2** page, side: *een opstel van drie ~s* a three-page essay; *er de ~s aflopen* cut corners

kantlijn [kɑntlɛin] *de (~en)* margin

kanton [kɑntɔn] *het (~s)* canton, district

kantongerecht [kɑntɔnɣərɛχt] *het (~en)* cantonal court, *(England; roughly)* magistrates' court, *(Am; roughly)* municipal (*or*: police, Justice) of the Peace court

kantonrechter [kɑntɔnrɛχtər] *de (~s)* cantonal judge, magistrate, J.P., *(Am)* Justice of the Peace

kantoor [kɑntor̠] *het (kantoren)* office: *na ~ een borrel pakken* have a drink after office hours; *naar ~ gaan* go to the office; *hij is op zijn ~* he is in his office; *overdag ben ik op (mijn) ~* I am at the office in the daytime; *op ~ werken* work in an office

kantoorbaan [kɑntorban] *de (-banen)* office job, clerical job

kantoorboekhandel [kɑntorbukhɑndəl] *de (~s)* (office) stationer's (shop)

kantoorgebouw [kɑntor̠ɣəbau] *het (~en)* office block (*or*: building)

kantoorpersoneel [kɑntorpɛrsonel] *het* office staff (*or*: employees, workers)

kantooruren [kɑntor̠yrə(n)] *de* office hours, working hours, business hours: *tijdens (de) ~* during business hours (*or*: office hours)

kanttekening [kɑntekənɪŋ] *de (~en)* (short, marginal) comment

kap [kɑp] *de (~pen)* **1** hood; **2** cap; **3** hood; bonnet, *(Am)* hood: *het ~je van het brood* the end slice, the crust; *twee (huizen) onder één ~* two semi-detached houses, a semi-detached house; *(Belg) op iemands ~ zitten* pester s.o.

kapbal [kɑbɑl] *de (~len)* cut shot, sliced shot

kapel [kapɛl̠] *de (~len)* **1** chapel; **2** dormer (window); **3** band

kapelaan [kapəlan] *de (~s)* curate, assistant priest

kapen [kapə(n)] *vb* hijack

kaper [kapər] *de (~s)* hijacker: *er zijn ~s op de kust* we've got plenty of competitors (*or*: rivals)

kaping [kapɪŋ] *de (~en)* hijack(ing)

kapitaal [kapital] *het* **1** fortune: *een ~ aan boeken* a (small) fortune in books; **2** capital

kapitaalgoederen [kapital̠yudərə(n)] *de* capital goods, investment goods

kapitaalkrachtig [kapitalkrɑχtəχ] *adj* wealthy, substantial

kapitalisme [kapital̠ɪsmə] *het* capitalism

kapitalist [kapital̠ɪst] *de (~en)* capitalist

kapitein [kapitɛin] *de (~s)* captain; skipper

kaplaars [kɑplars] *de (kaplaarzen)* top boot, jackboot

kapmes [kɑpmɛs] *het (~sen)* chopping-knife; cleaver; machete

kapok [kapɔk] *de* kapok

kapot [kapɔt] *adj* 1 broken, in bits: *die jas is* ~ that coat is torn; 2 broken, broken down *(car): de koffie-automaat is* ~ the coffee machine is out of order; 3 dead beat, worn out: *zich* ~ *werken* work one's fingers to the bone; *hij is niet* ~ *te krijgen* he's a tough one (*or:* cookie); 4 cut up, broken-hearted: *ergens* ~ *van zijn* be (all) cut up about sth

kapotgaan [kapɔtxan] *vb* 1 break, fall apart, break down; 2 pop off, kick the bucket

kapotje [kapɔcə] *het (~s)* rubber, French letter

kapotmaken [kapɔtmakə(n)] *vb* break (up), destroy, wreck, ruin

kapotslaan [kapɔtslan] *vb* smash, break (up)

kapotvallen [kapɔtfɑlə(n)] *vb* fall to pieces, fall and break, smash

¹kappen [kɑpə(n)] *vb* 1 cut down, chop down, fell; 2 do one's (*or:* s.o.'s) hair: *zich laten* ~ have one's hair done; 3 cut, hew

²kappen [kɑpə(n)] *vb* chop, cut || *ik kap er mee* I'm knocking off

kapper [kɑpər] *de (~s)* hairdresser, hairstylist; barber

kapsalon [kɑpsalɔn] *het, de (~s)* hairdresser's, barber's shop

kapseizen [kɑpsɛizə(n)] *vb* capsize, keel over

kapsel [kɑpsəl] *het (~s)* 1 hairstyle, haircut; 2 hairdo

kapsones [kɑpsonəs] *de* || ~ *hebben* be full of oneself

kapstok [kɑpstɔk] *de (~ken)* hallstand, hatstand; hat rack, coat hooks

kapucijner [kapysɛinər] *de (~s) (roughly)* marrowfat (pea)

kar [kɑr] *de (~ren)* 1 cart, barrow: *(fig) de* ~ *trekken* do the dirty work; 2 car

karaat [karat] *het (~s, karaten)* carat

karabijn [karabɛin] *de (~en)* carbine

karaf [karɑf] *de (~fen)* carafe, decanter

karakter [karɑktər] *het (~s)* 1 character, nature: *iem met een sterk* ~ s.o. with (great) strength of character; 2 character, personality, spirit: ~ *tonen* show character (*or:* spirit); *zonder* ~ without character, spineless; 3 character, symbol

karaktereigenschap [karɑktərɛiɣə(n)sxɑp] *de (~pen)* character trait

karakteriseren [karɑkterizɛrə(n)] *vb* characterize

karakteristiek [karɑkteristik] *adj* characteristic (of), typical (of)

karaktertrek [karɑktərtrɛk] *de (~ken)* characteristic, feature, trait

karamel [karamɛl] *de (~s)* caramel; toffee

karaoke [karaokə] *het* karaoke

karate [karatə] *het* karate

karavaan [karavan] *de (karavanen)* caravan, train

karbonade [karbonadə] *de (~s)* chop, cutlet

kardinaal [kardinal] *de (kardinalen)* cardinal

Karel [karəl] *de* Charles: ~ *de Grote* Charlemagne

kariboe [karibu] *de (~s)* caribou

karig [karəx] *adj* 1 sparing, mean, frugal; 2 meagre, scant(y), frugal: *een* ~ *maal* a frugal meal

karikatuur [karikatyr] *de (karikaturen)* caricature

karkas [karkɑs] *het, de (~sen)* carcass

karma [kɑrma] *het* karma

karnemelk [kɑrnəmɛlk] *de* buttermilk

karper [kɑrpər] *de (~s)* carp

karpet [kɑrpɛt] *het (~ten)* rug

karrenspoor [kɑrə(n)spor] *het (-sporen)* cart track

karrenvracht [kɑrə(n)vrɑxt] *de (~en)* cartload

karretje [kɑrəcə] *het (~s)* (little) cart, car, trap; trolley, soapbox

kartel [kɑrtɛl] *het* cartel, trust

kartelen [kɑrtələ(n)] *vb* serrate, notch, mill

karton [kɑrtɔn] *het (~s)* 1 cardboard; 2 carton, cardboard box

kartonnen [kɑrtɔnə(n)] *adj* cardboard: *een* ~ *bekertje* a paper cup

karwats [kɑrwɑts] *de (~en)* (riding) crop, (riding) whip

karwei [kɑrwɛi] *het, de (~en)* 1 job, work: *de loodgieter is op* ~ the plumber is (out) on a job; 2 odd job, chore; 3 job; task, chore

kas [kɑs] *de (~sen)* 1 greenhouse; hothouse; 2 cashdesk, cashier's office; 3 cash, fund(s): *de kleine* ~ petty cash; *de* ~ *beheren* (*or: houden*) manage (*or:* keep) the cash; *krap (slecht) bij* ~ *zitten* be short of cash (*or:* money); 4 socket

kasboek [kɑzbuk] *het (~en)* cash book, account(s) book

kasbon [kɑzbɔn] *de (~nen) (Belg)* (type of) savings certificate

kasjmier [kɑʃmir] *het* cashmere

Kaspische Zee *de* Caspian Sea

kasplant [kɑsplɑnt] *de (~en)* hothouse plant

kassa [kɑsa] *de (~'s)* 1 cash register, till; 2 cash desk; checkout; box office, booking office

kassabon [kɑsabɔn] *de (~nen)* receipt, sales slip, docket

kassaldo [kɑsɑldo] *het (~'s)* cash balance

kassei [kɑsɛi] *de (~en)* cobble(stone), paving stone, sett

kassier [kɑsir] *de (~s)* cashier, teller

kasstelsel [kɑstɛlsəl] *het (~s)* accounts system (*or:* method), accounting

kassucces [kɑsyksɛs] *het (~sen)* box-office success, box-office hit

kast [kɑst] *de (~en)* 1 cupboard, wardrobe, chest of drawers, cabinet: *iem op de* ~ *jagen (krijgen)* get a rise out of s.o.; *alles uit de* ~ *halen* pull out all the stops; 2 barracks, barn: *een* ~ *van een huis* a barn of a house

kastanje [kɑstɑɲə] *de* (Spanish, sweet) chestnut

¹kastanjebruin [kɑstɑɲəbrœyn] *het* chestnut, auburn

²kastanjebruin [kɑstɑɲəbrœyn] *adj* chestnut, auburn

kaste [kɑstə] *de (~n)* caste
kasteel [kɑstel] *het (kastelen)* castle
kastelein [kɑstəlɛin] *de (~s)* innkeeper, publican, landlord
kastestelsel [kɑstəstɛlsəl] *het* caste system
kasticket [kɑstikɛt] *het (~s) (Belg)* receipt
kastijden [kɑstɛidə(n)] *vb* chastise, castigate, punish
kastje [kɑʃə] *het (~s)* **1** cupboard, locker: *van het ~ naar de muur gestuurd worden* be sent (*or:* driven) from pillar to post; **2** box
kat [kɑt] *de (~ten)* **1** cat: *leven als ~ en hond* be like cat and dog; *de Gelaarsde Kat* Puss-in-Boots; **2** snarl: *iem een ~ geven* snarl (*or:* snap) at s.o.; *(Belg) geen ~* not a soul
katachtig [kɑtɑχtəχ] *adj* catlike
katalysator [kɑtalizɑtər] *de (~s, ~en)* (catalytic) converter *(of car)*
katapult [kɑtapʏlt] *de (~en)* catapult
kater [kɑtər] *de (~s)* **1** tomcat; **2** hangover; **3** disillusionment
katern [kɑtɛrn] *het, de (~en)* quire, gathering
katheder [kɑtedər] *de (~s)* lectern
kathedraal [kɑtedral] *de (kathedralen)* cathedral
katholicisme [kɑtolisɪsmə] *het* (Roman) Catholicism
katholiek [kɑtolik] *adj* (Roman) Catholic
katje [kɑcə] *het (~s)* **1** kitten; **2** *(bot)* catkin
katoen [kɑtun] *het, de* cotton
katoenen [kɑtunə(n)] *adj* cotton
katoenplantage [kɑtumplɑntaʒə] *de* cotton plantation
katrol [kɑtrɔl] *de (~len)* **1** (fishing) reel; **2** pulley
kattebelletje [kɑtəbɛləcə] *het (~s)* (scribbled) note, memo
katten [kɑtə(n)] *vb* snap (at), snarl (at)
kattenbak [kɑtə(n)bɑk] *de (~ken)* **1** cat('s) box; **2** dicky seat, *(Am)* rumble seat
kattenbakkorrels [kɑtə(n)bɑkərəls] *de* cat litter
kattenkop [kɑtə(n)kɔp] *de (~pen)* **1** cat's head; **2** cat, bitch
kattenkwaad [kɑtə(n)kwat] *het* mischief: *~ uithalen* get into mischief
kattenoog [kɑtə(n)oχ] *het (-ogen)* cat's eye, cat eye
kattenpis [kɑtə(n)pɪs] *de* || *dat is geen ~* no kidding, that's not to be sneezed at
kattig [kɑtəχ] *adj, adv* catty
kattin [kɑtɪn] *de (~nen) (Belg)* tabby cat
katvis [kɑtfɪs] *de (~sen)* **1** catfish; **2** *(roughly)* tiddler, *(pl also)* fry
kauw [kɑu] *de (~en)* jackdaw
kauwen [kɑuwə(n)] *vb* chew
kauwgom [kɑuɣɔm] *het, de* chewing gum
kavel [kɑvəl] *de (~s)* lot, parcel, share
kavelen [kɑvələ(n)] *vb* parcel (out); divide, apportion
kaviaar [kɑvijɑr] *de* caviar
Kazach [kɑzɑk] *de* Kazakh
Kazachstan [kɑzɑkstɑn] *het* Kazakhstan

kazerne [kazɛrnə] *de (~s)* barrack(s) *(mil);* station
kazuifel [kazœyfəl] *het (~s)* chasuble
kB [kilobɑjt(s)] *de* kilobyte K, KB
KBVB [kabevebe] *de (Belg) Koninklijke Belgische Voetbalbond* Royal Belgian Football Association
kebab [kebɑb] *de* kebab
keel [kel] *de (kelen)* throat: *het hangt me (mijlenver) de ~ uit* I'm fed up with it; *zijn ~ schrapen* clear one's throat
keelarts [kelɑrts] *de (~en)* throat specialist, laryngologist: *keel-, neus- en oorarts* ear, nose and throat *(or:* ENT) specialist
keelgat [kelɣat] *het (~en)* gullet: *in het verkeerde ~ schieten: a)* go down the wrong way; *b) (fig)* not go down very well (with s.o.)
keelontsteking [kelɔntstekɪŋ] *de (~en)* throat infection, laryngitis
keelpijn [kelpɛin] *de* sore throat
keeper [kipər] *de (~s)* (goal)keeper, goalie
keer [ker] *de (keren)* time: *een doodenkele ~* once in a blue moon; *een enkele ~* once or twice; *geen enkele ~* not once; *(op) een andere ~* another time; *nou vooruit, voor deze ~ dan!* all right then, but just this once!; *nog een ~(tje)* (once) again, once more; *(op) een ~* one day; *één enkele ~, slechts één ~* only once; *negen van de tien ~* nine times out of ten; *dat heb ik nu al tien* (or: *honderd) ~ gehoord* I've already heard that dozens of times (*or:* a hundred times); *twee ~* twice; *twee ~ twee is vier* twice two is four
keerkring [kerkrɪŋ] *de (~en)* tropic
keerpunt [kerpʏnt] *het (~en)* turning point
keerzijde [kerzɛidə] *de (~n)* other side, reverse
keet [ket] *de (keten)* **1** hut, shed; **2** racket: *~ trappen/schoppen* horse about (around)
keffen [kɛfə(n)] *vb* yap
keffertje [kɛfərcə] *het (~s)* yapper
kegel [keɣəl] *de (~s)* **1** cone; **2** ninepin, skittle
kegelen [keɣələ(n)] *vb* play skittles (*or:* ninepins)
kei [kɛi] *de (~en)* **1** boulder; **2** cobble(stone); set(t) || *Eric is een ~ in wiskunde* Eric is brilliant at maths
keihard [kɛihɑrt] *adj, adv* **1** rock-hard, hard, as hard as rock *(after vb);* **2** hard, tough || *~ schreeuwen* shout at the top of one's voice; *de radio stond ~ aan* the radio was on full blast (*or:* was blaring away)
keizer [kɛizər] *de (~s)* emperor
keizerin [kɛizərɪn] *de (~nen)* empress
keizerrijk [kɛizərɛik] *het (~en)* empire
keizersnede [kɛizərsnedə] *de (~n)* Caesarean (section)
kelder [kɛldər] *de (~s)* cellar, basement
kelderen [kɛldərə(n)] *vb* plummet, tumble
kelk [kɛlk] *de (~en)* **1** goblet; **2** calyx
kelner [kɛlnər] *de (~s)* waiter
Kelten [kɛltə(n)] *de* Celts
¹Keltisch [kɛltis] *het* Celtic
²Keltisch [kɛltis] *adj* Celtic
kenbaar [kɛmbar] *adj* known

kengetal [kɛŋɣətɑl] *het (~len)* dialling code, *(Am)* area code, prefix

Kenia [kenija] *het* Kenya

Keniaan [kenijaːn] *de (Kenianen)* Kenyan

kenmerk [kɛmɛrk] *het (~en)* (identifying) mark, hallmark *(also fig)*; reference *(abbr: ref)*

kenmerken [kɛmɛrkə(n)] *vb* characterize, mark, typify

kenmerkend [kɛmɛrkənt] *adj, adv* (with *voor*) characteristic (of), typical (of), specific (to): *~e eigenschappen* distinctive characteristics

kennel [kɛnəl] *de (~s)* kennel

¹kennelijk [kɛnələk] *adj* evident, apparent, clear, obvious, unmistakable

²kennelijk [kɛnələk] *adv* evidently, clearly, obviously: *het is ~ zonder opzet gedaan* it was obviously done unintentionally

kennen [kɛnə(n)] *vb* know, be acquainted with: *iem leren ~* get to know s.o.; *elkaar (beter) leren ~* get (better) acquainted; *ken je deze al?* have you heard this one?; *ik ken haar al jaren* I've known her for years; *sinds ik jou ken …* since I met you …; *iem van naam ~* know s.o. by name; *iem door en door ~* know s.o. inside out; *iets van buiten ~, iets uit zijn hoofd ~* know sth by heart

kenner [kɛnər] *de (~s)* 1 connoisseur; 2 authority (on), expert (on)

kennis [kɛnɪs] *de (~sen)* 1 knowledge (of), acquaintance (with): *met ~ van zaken* knowledgeably; *~ is macht* knowledge is power; 2 consciousness: *zij is weer bij ~ gekomen* she has regained consciousness, she has come round; 3 knowledge, information, learning, know-how: *een grondige ~ van het Latijn hebben* have a thorough knowledge of Latin; 4 acquaintance: *hij heeft veel vrienden en ~sen* he has a lot of friends and acquaintances

kennisgeving [kɛnɪsχevɪŋ] *de (~en)* notification, notice

kennismaken [kɛnɪsmakə(n)] *vb* get acquainted (with), meet, get to know, be introduced: *aangenaam kennis te maken!* pleased to meet you

kennismaking [kɛnɪsmakɪŋ] *de (~en)* 1 acquaintance; 2 introduction (to)

kenschetsen [kɛnsχɛtsə(n)] *vb* characterize

kenteken [kɛntekə(n)] *het (~s)* registration number, *(Am)* license number

kentekenbewijs [kɛntekə(n)bəwɛis] *het (-bewijzen)* (roughly) vehicle registration document, logbook

kentekenplaat [kɛntekə(n)plat] *de (-platen)* number plate, *(Am)* license plate

keramiek [keramik] *de* ceramics; pottery

kerel [kerəl] *de (~s)* 1 (big) fellow, (big) guy, (big) chap *(or:* bloke); 2 he-man: *kom naar buiten als je een ~ bent* come outside if you're man enough

¹keren [kerə(n)] *vb* turn (round), shift: *~ verboden* no U-turns

²keren [kerə(n)] *vb* 1 turn; 2 turn (towards); 3 turn (back), stem: *het water ~* stem the (flow of) water

³keren [kerə(n)] *ref vb* 1 turn (round): *zich ergens niet kunnen wenden of ~* not have room to move; 2 turn: *zich ten goede ~: a)* turn out well; *b)* take a turn for the better

kerf [kɛrf] *de (kerven)* notch, nick, groove

kerfstok [kɛrfstɔk] *de (~ken)* ‖ *heel wat op zijn ~ hebben* have a lot to answer for

kerk [kɛrk] *de (~en)* church

kerkbank [kɛrgbɑŋk] *de* pew

kerkdienst [kɛrgdinst] *de (~en)* (divine) service, church, mass

kerkelijk [kɛrkələk] *adj* church, ecclesiastical

kerker [kɛrkər] *de (~s)* dungeon, prison, jail

kerkhof [kɛrkhɔf] *het (-hoven)* churchyard, graveyard

kerkklok [kɛrklɔk] *de (~ken)* 1 church bell; 2 church clock

kerktoren [kɛrktorə(n)] *de (~s)* church tower, steeple, spire

kerkuil [kɛrkœyl] *de (~en)* barn owl

kermen [kɛrmə(n)] *vb* moan, whine, wail

kermis [kɛrməs] *de (~sen)* fair

kern [kɛrn] *de (~en)* 1 core, heart, pith; 2 *(fig)* core, heart, essence: *tot de ~ van een zaak doordringen* get (down) to the (very) heart of the matter; 3 central

kernachtig [kɛrnɑχtəχ] *adj, adv* pithy, concise, terse

kernafval [kɛrnɑfɑl] *het, de* nuclear waste

kernbewapening [kɛrmbəwapənɪŋ] *de* nuclear armament

kerncentrale [kɛrnsɛntralə] *de (~s)* nuclear *(or:* atomic) power station, nuclear plant, atomic plant

kerndoel [kɛrndul] *het (~en)* primary objective, chief aim

kernfysicus [kɛrnfizikʏs] *de (-fysici)* nuclear physicist, atomic physicist

kerngezond [kɛrŋɣəzɔnt] *adj* perfectly healthy, in perfect health, as fit as a fiddle

kernoorlog [kɛrnorlɔχ] *de (~en)* nuclear war

kernproef [kɛrmpruf] *de (-proeven)* nuclear test, atomic test

kernreactie [kɛrnrejaksi] *de (~s)* nuclear reaction

kernreactor [kɛrnrejaktɔr] *de (~s, ~en)* (nuclear, atomic) reactor

kernwapen [kɛrnwapə(n)] *het (~s)* nuclear weapon, atomic weapon

kerosine [kerozinə] *de* kerosene

kerrie [kɛri] *de* curry

kers [kɛrs] *de* cherry

kerst [kɛrst] *de* Christmas

kerstavond [kɛrstavɔnt] *de (~en)* evening of Christmas Eve

kerstboom [kɛrstbom] *de (-bomen)* Christmas tree

kerstdag [kɛrzdɑχ] *de (~en)* Christmas Day: *prettige ~en!* Merry *(or:* Happy) Christmas!; *eerste ~* Christmas Day; *tweede ~* Boxing Day

kerstfeest [kɛrstfest] *het (~en)* (feast, festival of) Christmas: *zalig (gelukkig) ~!* Merry Christmas!

kerstkaart [kɛrstkart] *de* Christmas card
kerstkrans [kɛrstkrɑns] *de (~en)* (almond) pastry ring
kerstlied [kɛrstlit] *het (~eren)* (Christmas) carol
kerstman [kɛrstmɑn] *de (~nen)* Santa (Claus), Father Christmas
Kerstmis [kɛrstmɪs] *de* Christmas
kerstnacht [kɛrstnɑχt] *de (~en)* Christmas night
kerststal [kɛrstɑl] *de (~len)* crib
kerstverhaal [kɛrstfərhal] *het (-verhalen)* Christmas story
kerstviering [kɛrs(t)firɪŋ] *de (~en)* Christmas service
kervel [kɛrvəl] *de* chervil
¹kerven [kɛrvə(n)] *vb* gouge (out), cut
²kerven [kɛrvə(n)] *vb* **1** notch, nick, cut, score; **2** carve (out), cut (out): *zij kerfden hun naam in de boom* they carved their names in the tree
ketchup [kɛtʃʏp] *de* ketchup
ketel [ketəl] *de (~s)* **1** kettle, cauldron; **2** boiler
keten [ketə(n)] *de (~s)* **1** *(pl)* chains; **2** chain; **3** chain, series
ketjap [kɛtjɑp] *de* soy sauce
ketsen [kɛtsə(n)] *vb* **1** glance off, ricochet (off); **2** misfire, fail to go off: *het geweer ketste* the gun misfired
ketter [kɛtər] *de (~s)* heretic ‖ *roken als een ~* smoke like a chimney
ketterij [kɛtərɛi] *de (~en)* heresy
ketting [kɛtɪŋ] *de (~en)* chain: *aan de ~ leggen* chain up
kettingbotsing [kɛtɪŋbɔtsɪŋ] *de (~en)* multiple collision (*or:* crash), pile-up
kettingkast [kɛtɪŋkɑst] *de (~en)* chain guard
kettingzaag [kɛtɪŋzɑχ] *de (-zagen)* chainsaw
keu [kø] *de (~s)* (billiard) cue
keuken [køkə(n)] *de (~s)* **1** kitchen; **2** (art of) cooking; cuisine: *de Franse ~* French cooking (*or:* cuisine)
keukengerei [køkə(n)ɣərɛi] *het* kitchen utensils, cooking utensils
keukenhulp [køkə(n)hʏlp] *de (~en)* food processor
keukenkruid [køkə(n)krœyt] *het* kitchen herb
keukenmachine [køkə(n)maʃinə] *de (~s)* food processor
keukenrol [køkə(n)rɔl] *de (~len)* kitchen roll
keukenschort [køkə(n)sχɔrt] *het* apron
keukentrap [køkə(n)trɑp] *de (~pen)* (household) steps, stepladder
Keulen [kø-lə(n)] *het* Cologne
keur [kør] *de (~en)* **1** hallmark; **2** choice (selection)
keuren [kørə(n)] *vb* test, inspect; sample, taste, examine: *films ~* censor films
¹keurig [kørəχ] *adj* **1** neat, tidy: *er ~ uitzien* look neat (and tidy), look smart; **2** smart, nice: *een ~ handschrift* a neat hand; **3** fine, choice: *een ~ rapport* (or: *opstel*) an excellent report (*or:* essay)
²keurig [kørəχ] *adv* nicely, neatly ‖ *~ netjes gekleed*

properly dressed
keuring [kørɪŋ] *de (~en)* **1** test, inspection, examination: *een medische ~* a medical (examination); **2** testing, inspection, sampling, tasting, examination
keuringsarts [kørɪŋsɑrts] *de* medical examiner
keuringsdienst [kørɪŋzdinst] *de (~en)* inspection service: *~ van waren* commodity inspection department
keurmeester [kørmestər] *de (~s)* inspector, *(gold and silver)* assay-master
keurmerk [kørmɛrk] *het (~en)* hallmark, quality mark
keurslijf [kørslɛif] *het (-lijven)* straitjacket
keus [køs] *de (keuzen)* **1** choice, selection; **2** choice, option, alternative: *er is volop ~* there's a lot to choose from; *aan u de ~* the choice is yours; **3** choice, assortment: *een grote ~* a large choice (*or:* assortment), a wide range
keutel [køtəl] *de (~s)* droppings, pellet
keuvelen [køvələ(n)] *vb* (have a) chat, talk
keuze [køzə] *de (~n) see* keus
keuzemogelijkheid [køzəmoɣələkhɛit] *de (-heden)* option, choice
keuzepakket [køzəpɑkɛt] *het (~ten)* options, choice of subjects (*or:* courses)
keuzevak [køzəvɑk] *het (~ken)* option, optional subject (*or:* course)
kever [kevər] *de (~s)* **1** beetle; **2** Beetle
keyboard [kiːbɔːrd] *het (~s)* keyboard
kg *kilogram* kg
KI [kai] *de kunstmatige inseminatie* artificial insemination
kibbelen [kɪbələ(n)] *vb* bicker, squabble
kibbeling [kɪbəlɪŋ] *de* cod parings
kibboets [kɪbuts] *de (~en, ~im)* kibbutz
kick [kɪk] *de (~s)* kick
kickboksen [kɪgbɔksə(n)] *vb* kickboxing
kidnappen [kɪtnɛpə(n)] *vb* kidnap
kiekeboe [kikəbu] *int* peekaboo!
kiekje [kikjə] *het (~s)* snap(shot)
kiel [kil] *de (~en)* **1** smock; **2** *(shipp)* keel
kielhalen [kilhalə(n)] *vb* keelhaul
kielzog [kilzɔχ] *het* wake, wash
kiem [kim] *de (~en)* germ, seed
kiemen [kimə(n)] *vb* germinate
kien [kin] *adj, adv* sharp, keen
¹kiepen [kipə(n)] *vb* topple, tumble: *het glas is van de tafel gekiept* the glass toppled off the table
²kiepen [kipə(n)] *vb* tip over, tumble (over)
¹kieperen [kipərə(n)] *vb* tumble, topple
²kieperen [kipərə(n)] *vb* dump
kier [kai] *de (~en)* chink, slit, crack: *door een ~ van de schutting* through a crack in the fence; *de deur staat op een ~* the door is ajar
kies [kis] *de (kiezen)* molar, back tooth
kiesbrief [kizbrif] *de (-brieven) (Belg)* polling card
kiesdistrict [kizdɪstrɪkt] *het (~en)* electoral district, constituency
kieskeurig [kiskørəχ] *adj* choosy, fussy

kiespijn [kispεin] *de* toothache
kiesrecht [kisrεχt] *het (~en)* suffrage, right to vote, (the) vote
kiesschijf [kisχεif] *de (-schijven)* dial
kiestoon [kiston] *de* dialling tone
kietelen [kitələ(n)] *vb* tickle
kieuw [kiw] *de (~en)* gill
kieviet [kivit] *de (~en)* lapwing, peewit, plover
kiezel [kizəl] *het (~s)* gravel, shingle
kiezelsteen [kizəlsten] *de (-stenen)* pebble
¹**kiezen** [kizə(n)] *vb* **1** choose, decide: *zorgvuldig ~* pick and choose; *~ tussen* choose between; *je kunt uit drie kandidaten ~* you can choose from three candidates; **2** vote: *voor een vrouwelijke kandidaat ~* vote for a woman candidate
²**kiezen** [kizə(n)] *vb* **1** choose, select, pick (out): *partij ~* take sides; **2** vote (for), elect; **3** choose, elect: *een nummer ~* dial a number
kiezer [kizər] *de (~s)* voter, constituent, *(pl)* electorate
kijk [kεik] *de* view, outlook, insight: *~ op iets hebben* have a good eye for sth
kijkcijfer [kεiksεifər] *het (~s)* rating
¹**kijken** [kεikə(n)] *vb* **1** look, see: *ga eens ~ wie er is* go and see who's there; *daar sta ik van te ~* well I'll be blowed; *kijk eens wie we daar hebben* look who's here!; *goed ~* watch closely; *(fig) naar iets ~* have a look at (or: see) about sth; *zij ~ niet op geld (een paar euro)* money is no object with them; *uit het raam ~* look out (of) the window; *even de andere kant op ~* look the other way; **2** look, search: *we zullen ~ of dat verhaal klopt* we shall see whether that story checks out; **3** look, appear: *laat eens ~, wat hebben we nodig* let's see, what do we need
²**kijken** [kεikə(n)] *vb* look at, watch: *kijk haar eens (lachen)* look at her (laughing)
kijk- en luistergeld [kεikɛnlœystərγɛlt] *het* radio and television licence fee
kijker [kεikər] *de (~s)* **1** spectator, onlooker, viewer; **2** binoculars; opera-glass(es)
kijkje [kεikjə] *het (~s)* (quick) look, glance: *de politie zal een ~ nemen* the police will have a look
kijkwoning [kεikwoniŋ] *de (~en) (Belg)* show house
kijven [kεivə(n)] *vb* quarrel, wrangle, rail (at)
kik [kik] *de* sound || *zonder een ~ te geven* without a sound *(or:* murmur*)*
kikker [kikər] *de (~s)* frog
kikkerbad [kikərbat] *het* paddling pool, wading pool
kikkerdril [kikərdril] *het* frogspawn, frogs' eggs
kikkervisje [kikərviʃə] *het (~s)* tadpole
kikvors [kikfɔrs] *de (~en)* frog
kikvorsman [kikfɔrsman] *de (~nen)* frogman
kil [kil] *adj, adv* chilly, cold
kilo [kilo] *het, de (~'s)* kilo
kilobyte [kilobajt] *de (~s)* kilobyte
kilogram [kiloγram] *het, de (~men)* kilogram(me)
kilometer [kilometər] *de (~s)* kilometre: *op een ~*

afstand at a distance of one kilometre; *90 ~ per uur rijden* drive at 90 kilometres an hour
kilometerteller [kilometərtɛlər] *de (~s)* milometer, *(Am)* odometer
kilowatt [kilowat] *de (~s)* kilowatt
kim [kim] *de (~men)* horizon
kimono [kimono] *de (~'s)* kimono
kin [kin] *de (~nen)* chin || *(Belg) op zijn ~ kloppen* get nothing to eat
kind [kint] *het (~eren)* child, baby: *een ~ hebben van* have a child by; *een ~ krijgen* have a baby; *~eren opvoeden* bring up children; *een ~ van zes jaar* a child of six, a six-year-old (child)
kinderachtig [kindəraχtəχ] *adj, adv* **1** childlike, child(ren)'s; **2** *(depr)* childish, infantile: *doe niet zo ~* grow up!, don't be such a baby!
kinderafdeling [kindəravdeliŋ] *de (~en)* **1** children's department; **2** children's section; paediatric ward
kinderarbeid [kindərarbεit] *de* child labour
kinderarts [kindərarts] *de (~en)* paediatrician
kinderbescherming [kindərbəsχɛrmiŋ] *de* child welfare: *Raad voor de Kinderbescherming* child welfare council
kinderbijslag [kindərbεislaχ] *de* family allowance, child benefit
kinderboerderij [kindərburdərɛi] *de (~en)* children's farm
kinderdagverblijf [kindərdɑχfərblεif] *het (-verblijven)* crèche; day-care centre
kinderjuffrouw [kindərjʏfrɑu] *de (~en)* nurse(maid), nanny
kinderkaartje [kindərkarcə] *het* child's ticket
kinderkamer [kindərkamər] *de (~s)* nursery
kinderkribbe [kindərkribə] *de (~n) (Belg)* crèche; day nursery
kinderlijk [kindərlək] *adj, adv* childlike, childish
kinderloos [kindərlos] *adj* childless
kindermeisje [kindərmεiʃə] *het (~s)* nurse(maid), nanny
kindermishandeling [kindərmishandəliŋ] *de* child abuse
kinderoppas [kindərɔpas] *de (~sen)* babysitter, childminder
kinderopvang [kindərɔpfaŋ] *de* (day) nursery; day-care centre, crèche
kinderporno [kindərpɔrno] *de* child pornography
kinderprogramma [kindərproχrama] *het (~'s)* children's programme
kinderrechter [kindərɛχtər] *de (~s) (roughly)* magistrate of *(or:* in) a juvenile court
kinderrijmpje [kindərɛimpjə] *het (~s)* nursery rhyme
kinderschoen [kindərsχun] *de (~en)* child(ren)'s shoe: *nog in de ~en staan* still be in its infancy
kinderspeelplaats [kindərspelplats] *de (~en)* children's playground
kinderspel [kindərspɛl] *het (~en)* **1** children's games, *(fig)* child's play; **2** children's game

kinderstoel [kɪndərstul] *de (~en)* high chair
kindertelefoon [kɪndərteləfon] *de (~s)* children's helpline, childline
kindertijd [kɪndərtɛit] *de* childhood (days)
kinderverlamming [kɪndərvərlɑmɪŋ] *de* polio
kinderwagen [kɪndərwaɣə(n)] *de (~s)* baby buggy, pram
kinderziekte [kɪndərziktə] *de (~n, ~s)* childhood disease, *(pl; fig)* teething troubles, growing pains: *de ~n (nog niet) te boven zijn* still have teething troubles
kinderzitje [kɪndərzɪcə] *het (~s)* baby seat, child's seat
kinds [kɪnts] *adj* senile, in one's second childhood
kinesist [kinezɪst] *de (~en) (Belg)* physiotherapist
kinesitherapie [kineziterapi] *de (Belg)* physiotherapy
kinine [kininə] *de* quinine
kink [kɪŋk] *de (~en)* kink, hitch
kinkhoest [kɪŋkhust] *de* whooping cough
kiosk [kijɔsk] *de (~en)* kiosk, newspaper stand, book stand
kip [kɪp] *de (~pen)* **1** chicken, hen: *er was geen ~ te zien* (or: *te bekennen)* there wasn't a soul to be seen; **2** *(pl)* chickens, poultry
kipfilet [kɪpfile] *het, de (~s)* chicken breast(s)
kiplekker [kɪplɛkər] *adj* as fit as a fiddle
kippengaas [kɪpə(n)ɣas] *het* chicken wire
kippenren [kɪpə(n)rɛn] *de (~nen)* chicken run
kippenvel [kɪpə(n)vɛl] *het* goose flesh (or: pimples)
kippig [kɪpəɣ] *adj* short-sighted, near-sighted
Kirgizië [kɪrɣizijə] *het* Kirghizistan
kirren [kɪrə(n)] *vb* coo; gurgle
kirsch [kɪrʃ] *de* kirsch
kist [kɪst] *de (~en)* **1** chest; **2** coffin; **3** box, case, crate
kistje [kɪʃə] *het (~s)* **1** box, case; **2** clodhopper
kit [kɪt] *het, de* cement, glue, sealant
kits [kɪts] *adj* || *alles ~?* how's things?, everything O.K.? (or: all right?)
kitsch [kɪtʃ] *de* kitsch
kittelaar [kɪtəlar] *de (~s)* clitoris
kiwi [kiwi] *de (~'s)* kiwi
klaar [klar] *adj, adv* **1** clear; **2** pure; **3** ready: *de boot is ~ voor vertrek* the boat is ready to sail; *~ voor de strijd* ready for action; *~ terwijl u wacht* ready while you wait; *~? af!* ready, get set, go!; **4** finished, done: *ik ben zo ~* I won't be a minute *(or:* second); *we zijn ~ met eten* (or: *opruimen)* we've finished eating (or: clearing up)
klaarkomen [klarkomə(n)] *vb* **1** (be) finish(ed), complete, settle things; **2** come
klaarleggen [klarlɛɣə(n)] *vb* put ready, lay out
klaarlicht [klarlɪɣt] *adj* || *op ~e dag* in broad daylight
klaarliggen [klarlɪɣə(n)] *vb* be ready: *iets hebben ~* have sth ready
klaarmaken [klarmakə(n)] *vb* **1** get ready, prepare; **2** make, get ready, prepare, cook: *het ontbijt ~ get* breakfast ready
klaar-over [klarovər] *de* member of the school crossing patrol, lollipop boy (or: girl)
klaarspelen [klarspelə(n)] *vb* manage (to do), pull off
klaarstaan [klarstan] *vb* be ready, be waiting, stand by: *zij moet altijd voor hem ~* he expects her to be at his beck and call
klaarwakker [klarwɑkər] *adj* wide awake, *(fig)* (on the) alert
klaarzetten [klarzɛtə(n)] *vb* put ready, put out, set out
Klaas [klas] *de* Nick, Nicholas: *~ Vaak* the sandman, Wee Willie Winkie
klacht [klɑɣt] *de (~en)* **1** complaint, symptom: *wat zijn de ~en van de patiënt?* what are the patient's symptoms?; *zijn ~en uiten* air one's grievances; *~en behandelen* deal with complaints; **2** lament, complaint
klad [klɑt] *het (~den)* (rough) draft
kladblaadje [klɑdblacə] *het (~s)* (piece of) scrap paper
kladblok [klɑdblɔk] *het (~ken)* scribbling-pad
kladden [klɑdə(n)] *vb* make stains (or: smudges, blots)
kladderen [klɑdərə(n)] *vb* make blots (or: smudges)
kladje [klɑcə] *het* (rough) draft; (piece of) scrap paper
kladpapier [klɑtpapir] *het (~en)* scrap paper
kladversie [klɑtfɛrzi] *de (~s)* rough version (or: copy)
klagen [klaɣə(n)] *vb* complain
klager [klaɣər] *de (~s)* complainer
klakkeloos [klɑkəlos] *adj, adv* unthinking, indiscriminate, groundless: *iets ~ aannemen* accept sth unthinkingly (or: uncritically)
klam [klɑm] *adj, adv* clammy, damp
klamboe [klɑmbu] *de (~s)* mosquito net
klandizie [klɑndizi] *de* clientele, customers
klank [klɑŋk] *de (~en)* sound
klankbord [klɑŋgbɔrt] *het (~en)* sounding board
klant [klɑnt] *de (~en)* customer, client, *(in catering industry)* guest: *de ~ is koning* the customer is always right
klantenservice [klɑntə(n)sɛrvɪs] *de* after-sales service, *(Am)* customer service, service department
klap [klɑp] *de (~pen)* **1** bang, crash, crack: *met een ~ dichtslaan* slam (shut); **2** slap, smack, *(fig)* blow: *iem een ~ geven* hit s.o.; *iem een ~ om de oren geven* box s.o.'s ears
klapband [klɑbɑnt] *de (~en)* blow-out, flat
klapdeur [klɑbdør] *de (~en)* swing-door, self-closing door
klappen [klɑpə(n)] *vb* **1** clap, flap, slam: *in de handen ~* clap (one's hands); **2** burst: *de voorband is geklapt* the front tyre has burst; *in elkaar ~* collapse; *uit de school ~, (Belg)* uit de biecht ~ tell tales

klapper [klɑpər] *de (~s)* **1** folder, file; **2** smash, hit

klapperen [klɑpərə(n)] *vb* bang, rattle, chatter

klappertanden [klɑpərtɑndə(n)] *vb (roughly)* shiver

klaproos [klɑpros] *de (-rozen)* poppy

klapstoel [klɑpstul] *de (~en)* folding chair, tip-up seat, theatre seat

klarinet [klarinɛt] *de (~ten)* clarinet

klas [klɑs] *de (~sen)* **1** classroom; **2** class; **3** form, *(Am)* grade: *in de vierde ~ zitten* be in the fourth form; **4** class, grade, *(sport)* league, *(sport)* division: *(sport) in de tweede ~ spelen* play in the second division; *(sport) naar een lagere ~ overgaan* be relegated to a lower division

klasgenoot [klɑsχənot] *de (-genoten)* classmate

klaslokaal [klɑslokal] *het (-lokalen)* classroom

klasse [klɑsə] *de (~n)* class; league: *dat is grote ~! that's first-rate!*

klassejustitie [klɑsəjʏsti(t)si] *de* class justice

klassement [klɑsəmɛnt] *het (~en)* list of rankings *(or:* ratings), *(sport)* league table: *hij staat bovenaan (in) het ~* he is (at the) top of the league (table)

klassenboek [klɑsə(n)buk] *het (~en)* class register, form register, *(Am)* roll book

klassenleraar [klɑsə(n)lerar] *de (-leraren)* form teacher, class teacher, *(Am)* homeroom teacher

klassenvertegenwoordiger
[klɑsə(n)vərteɣə(n)wordəɣər] *de (~s)* class representative *(or:* spokesman)

¹klasseren [klɑsɛrə(n)] *vb* **1** classify; **2** *(Belg)* list

²klasseren [klɑsɛrə(n)] *ref vb* qualify, rank: *zich ~ voor de finale* qualify for the final(s)

klassestrijd [klɑsəstrɛit] *de* class struggle

klassiek [klɑsik] *adj* classic(al); traditional: *de ~e Oudheid* classical antiquity; *een ~ voorbeeld* a classic example

klassieker [klɑsikər] *de (~s)* classic

klassikaal [klɑsikal] *adj, adv* class, group: *iets ~ behandelen* deal with sth in class

klastitularis [klɑstitylarıs] *de (~sen) (Belg)* class teacher

klateren [klatərə(n)] *vb* splash, gurgle

klatergoud [klatərɣaut] *het* tinsel, gilt

klauteren [klɑutərə(n)] *vb* clamber, scramble

klauw [klɑu] *de (~en)* claw, clutch(es); talon: *uit de ~en lopen* get out of hand *(or:* control)

klavecimbel [klavəsımbəl] *het, de (~s)* harpsichord, *(clavi)*cembalo

klaver [klavər] *de (~s)* clover

klaverblad [klavərblɑt] *het (~en)* cloverleaf

klaveren [klavərə(n)] *de* clubs

klaverjassen [klavərjɑsə(n)] *vb* play (Klaber)jass

klavertjevier [klavərcəvir] *het (~en)* four-leaf clover

klavier [klavir] *het (~en)* keyboard

kledder [klɛdər] *de (~s)* blob, dollop

kledderen [klɛdərə(n)] *vb* slop

kleddernat [klɛdərnɑt] *adj* soaking (wet); soaked

kleden [kledə(n)] *vb* dress, clothe

klederdracht [kledərdrɑχt] *de (~en)* (traditional, national) costume *(or:* dress)

kleding [kledıŋ] *de* clothing, clothes, garments

kledingstuk [kledıŋstʏk] *het (~ken)* garment, article of clothing

kleed [klet] *het (kleden)* **1** carpet, rug, (table)cloth; **2** *(Belg)* dress

kleedhokje [klethɔkjə] *het (~s)* changing cubicle

kleedkamer [kletkamər] *de (~s)* dressing room; *(sport)* changing room

kleerhanger [klerhɑŋər] *de (~s)* coat-hanger, clothes hanger

kleerkast [klerkɑst] *de (~en)* wardrobe

kleermaker [klermakər] *de (~s)* tailor

kleermakerszit [klermakərzıt] *de || in ~ zitten* sit cross-legged

kleerscheuren [klersχørə(n)] *de || er zonder ~ afkomen* escape unscathed *(or:* unhurt), get off scot-free

klef [klɛf] *adj* **1** sticky, clammy; **2** sticky, gooey, doughy; **3** clinging

klei [klɛi] *de* clay

kleiduif [klɛidœyf] *de (-duiven)* clay pigeon

klein [klɛin] *adj* **1** small, little: *een ~ eindje* a short distance, a little way; *een ~ beetje* a little bit; **2** little, young; **3** small, minor: *hebt u het niet ~er?* have you got nothing smaller?

Klein-Azië [klɛinazijə] *het* Asia Minor

kleinbeeldcamera [klɛimbeltkaməra] *de (~'s)* miniature camera

kleinburgerlijk [klɛimbʏrɣərlək] *adj* lower middle class, petty bourgeois, narrow-minded

kleindochter [klɛindɔχtər] *de (~s)* granddaughter

Kleinduimpje [klɛindœympjə] *het* Tom Thumb

kleineren [klɛinɛrə(n)] *vb* belittle, disparage

kleingeestig [klɛiŋɣɛstəχ] *adj* narrow-minded, petty

kleingeld [klɛiŋɣɛlt] *het* (small) change

kleinigheid [klɛinəχɦɛit] *de (-heden)* **1** little thing: *ik heb een ~je meegebracht* I have brought you a little something; **2** trivial matter, unimportant matter, trifle

kleinkind [klɛiŋkınt] *het (~eren)* grandchild

kleinmaken [klɛimakə(n)] *vb* cut small, cut up

kleinsnijden [klɛinsnɛidə(n)] *vb* cut up (into small pieces)

kleintje [klɛincə] *het (~s)* **1** small one, short one, shorty; **2** little one, baby

kleinzerig [klɛinzɛrəχ] *adj || hij is altijd ~* he always makes a fuss about a little bit of pain

kleinzielig [klɛinziləχ] *adj* petty, narrow-minded

kleinzoon [klɛinzon] *de (~s, -zonen)* grandson

¹klem [klɛm] *de (~men)* **1** grip; **2** emphasis, stress: *met ~ beweren dat …* insist on the fact that …; **3** trap; **4** clip

²klem [klɛm] *adj* jammed, stuck

¹klemmen [klɛmə(n)] *vb* clasp, press

²klemmen [klɛmə(n)] *vb* stick, jam

klemtoon [klɛmton] *de (-tonen)* stress, accent, *(fig)* emphasis: *de ~ ligt op de eerste lettergreep* the stress (*or:* accent) is on the first syllable

klep [klɛp] *de (~pen)* **1** lid, valve, key; **2** flap, ramp; **3** flap, fly; **4** visor

klepel [klɛpəl] *de (~s)* clapper

kleppen [klɛpə(n)] *vb* **1** clack; **2** peal, toll

klepperen [klɛpərə(n)] *vb* clatter, rattle

kleptomaan [klɛptoma̱n] *de (-manen)* kleptomaniac

kleren [kle̱rə(n)] *de* clothes: *andere* (or: *schone*) *~ aantrekken* change (into sth else, into clean clothes); *zijn ~ uittrekken* undress

klerk [klɛrk] *de (~en)* clerk

klets [klɛts] *de* **1** rubbish, twaddle; **2** splash

kletsen [klɛtsə(n)] *vb* **1** chatter; chat; **2** gossip; **3** talk nonsense (*or:* rubbish), babble

kletskoek [klɛtskuk] *de* nonsense, twaddle

kletsmajoor [klɛtsmajor] *de (~s)* twaddler, gossipmonger

kletsnat [klɛtsnɑt] *adj* soaking (wet)

kletteren [klɛtərə(n)] *vb* clash, clang; patter; rattle: *de borden kletterden op de grond* the plates crashed to the floor

kleumen [klømə(n)] *vb* be half frozen

kleur [klør] *de (~en)* **1** colour: *wat voor ~ ogen heeft ze?* what colour are her eyes?; *primaire ~en* primary colours; **2** complexion: *een ~ krijgen* flush, blush; **3** *(cards)* suit

kleurdoos [klørdos] *de (-dozen)* paintbox

kleurecht [klørɛχt] *adj* colour fast

kleuren [klørə(n)] *vb* colour, paint, dye, tint

kleurenblind [klørə(n)blɪnt] *adj* colour-blind

kleurenfoto [klørə(n)foto] *de (~'s)* colour photo(graph), colour picture

kleurig [klørəχ] *adj, adv* colourful

kleurling [klørlɪŋ] *de (~en)* coloured person

kleurloos [klørlos] *adj* **1** colourless; pale; **2** colourless, dull

kleurpotlood [klørpɔtlot] *het (-potloden)* colour pencil, (coloured) crayon

kleurrijk [klørɛik] *adj* colourful

kleurspoeling [klørspulɪŋ] *de (~en)* colour rinse

kleurstof [klørstɔf] *de (~fen)* **1** colour, dye, colouring (matter): *(chemische) ~fen toevoegen* add colouring matters; **2** pigment

kleurtje [klørcə] *het (~s)* colour, flush, blush

kleuter [kløtər] *de (~s)* pre-schooler (in a nursery class), *(Am)* kindergartner

kleuterbad [kløtərbɑt] *het (~en)* paddling pool, wading pool

kleuterleidster [kløtərlɛitstər] *de (~s)* nursery school teacher, *(Am)* kindergarten teacher

kleuteronderwijs [kløtərɔndərwɛis] *het* pre-school education, nursery education

kleuterschool [kløtərsχol] *de (-scholen)* nursery school, *(Am)* kindergarten

kleven [kle̱və(n)] *vb* **1** stick (to), cling (to): *zijn overhemd kleefde aan zijn rug* his shirt stuck (*or:* clung) to his back; **2** be sticky: *mijn handen ~ my* hands are sticky

kleverig [kle̱vərəχ] *adj* sticky

kliederen [kli̱dərə(n)] *vb* make a mess, mess about (*or:* around)

kliek [klik] *de (~en)* clique

kliekje [kli̱kjə] *het (~s)* leftover(s)

klier [klir] *de* **1** gland; **2** pain in the neck

klieven [kli̱və(n)] *vb* cleave

klif [klɪf] *de (~fen)* cliff

klik [klɪk] *de (~ken)* click

klikken [klɪkə(n)] *vb* **1** click; **2** tell (on s.o.), snitch (on), blab: *je mag niet ~* don't tell tales; **3** click, hit it off: *het klikte meteen tussen hen* they hit it off immediately

klikspaan [klɪkspan] *de (-spanen)* tell-tale

klim [klɪm] *de* climb

klimaat [klima̱t] *het (klimaten)* climate

klimaatbeheersing [klima̱dbəhersɪŋ] *de* air conditioning

klimmen [klɪmə(n)] *vb* climb (up, down), clamber (about): *met het ~ der jaren* with advancing years

klimmer [klɪmər] *de (~s)* climber

klimop [klɪmɔp] *het, de* ivy

klimplant [klɪmplɑnt] *de (~en)* climber, climbing plant, creeper

klimrek [klɪmrɛk] *het (~ken)* **1** climbing frame; **2** wall bars

klingelen [klɪŋələ(n)] *vb* tinkle, jingle

kliniek [klini̱k] *de (~en)* clinic

klinisch [kli̱nis] *adj, adv* clinical

klink [klɪŋk] *de (~en)* **1** (door)handle; **2** latch

klinken [klɪŋkə(n)] *vb* sound, resound, clink, ring: *die naam klinkt me bekend (in de oren)* that name sounds familiar to me

klinker [klɪŋkər] *de (~s)* **1** vowel; **2** clinker

klinknagel [klɪŋknaɣəl] *de (~s)* rivet

klip [klɪp] *de (~pen)* rock, cliff

klipper [klɪpər] *de (~s)* clipper

klissen [klɪsə(n)] *het (Belg)* arrest, run in: *een inbreker ~* arrest a burglar

klit [klɪt] *de (~ten)* tangle

klitten [klɪtə(n)] *vb* **1** stick: *aan elkaar ~* hang (*or:* stick) together; **2** become entangled, get entangled

klittenband [klɪtə(n)bɑnt] *het (~en)* Velcro

klodder [klɔdər] *de (~s)* daub; clot; blob: *een ~ mayonaise* a dollop of mayonnaise

klodderen [klɔdərə(n)] *vb* **1** mess (about, around); **2** daub

¹kloek [kluk] *de (~en)* broody hen

²kloek [kluk] *adj* stout, sturdy, robust

klojo [klo̱jo] *de (~'s)* jerk

klok [klɔk] *de (~ken)* **1** clock: *hij kan nog geen ~ kijken* he can't tell (the) time yet; *de ~ loopt voor* (*or:* *achter, gelijk*) the clock is fast (*or:* slow, on time); *met de ~ mee* clockwise; *tegen de ~ in* anticlockwise, *(Am)* counter-clockwise; **2** bell

klokgelui [klɔkχəlœy] *het* (bell-)ringing, chiming, bell tolling

klokhuis [klɔkhœys] *het (-huizen)* core

klokken [klɔkə(n)] *vb (sport)* time, clock
klokkengieterij [klɔkə(n)ɣitərɛi] *de* bell-foundry
klokkenspel [klɔkə(n)spɛl] *het (~len)* 1 carillon, chimes; 2 glockenspiel
klokkentoren [klɔkə(n)torə(n)] *de (~s)* bell tower, belfry
klokslag [klɔkslaɣ] *de (~en)* ‖ ~ *vier uur* on (*or:* at) the stroke of four
klokvast [klɔkfɑst] *adj (Belg)* punctual: ~*e treinen* punctual trains
klomp [klɔmp] *de (~en)* 1 clog, *(Am)* wooden shoe; 2 clod, lump
klompvoet [klɔmpfut] *de (~en)* club-foot
klonen [klonə(n)] *vb* clone
klont [klɔnt] *de (~en)* 1 lump, dab: *de saus zit vol ~en* the sauce is full of lumps (*or:* is lumpy); 2 clot
klonteren [klɔntərə(n)] *vb* become lumpy, get lumpy; clot; curdle
klontje [klɔncə] *het (~s)* 1 lump, dab; 2 sugar lump (*or:* cube)
kloof [klof] *de (kloven)* 1 split; 2 crevice, chasm, cleft; 3 *(fig)* gap, gulf
klooien [klojə(n)] *vb* bungle, mess up
kloon [klon] *de (klonen)* clone
klooster [klostər] *het (~s)* monastery; convent, nunnery; cloister
kloosterling [klostərlɪŋ] *de (~en)* religious, monk, nun
kloot [klot] *de (kloten)* ball ‖ *naar de kloten zijn* be screwed up
klootzak [klotsɑk] *de (~ken)* bastard, son-of-a-bitch
klop [klɔp] *de (~pen)* 1 knock; 2 lick(ing)
klopjacht [klɔpjɑχt] *de (~en)* round-up, drive
¹kloppen [klɔpə(n)] *vb* 1 knock (at, on), tap: *er wordt geklopt* there's a knock at the door; 2 beat, throb: *met ~d hart* with one's heart racing (*or:* pounding); 3 agree: *dat klopt* that's right
²kloppen [klɔpə(n)] *vb* knock, tap; beat: *eieren ~* beat (*or:* whisk) eggs; *iem op de schouder ~* pat s.o. on the back
klopper [klɔpər] *de* knocker
klos [klɔs] *de (~sen)* bobbin, reel ‖ *de ~ zijn* be the fall guy
klossen [klɔsə(n)] *vb* clump, stump
klotsen [klɔtsə(n)] *vb* slosh, splash
kloven [klovə(n)] *vb* split, cleave, cut
klucht [klʏχt] *de (~en)* farce
kluif [klœyf] *de (kluiven)* knuckle(bone); *(fig)* big job, tough job
kluis [klœys] *de (kluizen)* safe, safe-deposit box
kluit [klœyt] *de (~en)* 1 lump, clod: *zich niet met een ~je in het riet laten sturen* not let oneself be fobbed off (*or:* be given the brush-off); 2 ball of earth (*or:* soil)
kluiven [klœyvə(n)] *vb* gnaw
kluizenaar [klœyzənar] *de (~s)* hermit, recluse
klunen [klynə(n)] *vb* walk (on skates)
klungel [klʏŋəl] *de (~s)* clumsy oaf

klungelen [klʏŋələ(n)] *vb* bungle, botch (up)
kluns [klʏns] *de (klunzen)* dimwit, oaf, bungler
klus [klʏs] *de (~sen)* 1 big job, tough job; 2 small job, chore: ~*jes opknappen (klaren)* do odd jobs
klusjesman [klʏʃəsman] *de (~nen)* handyman, odd-job man
klussen [klʏsə(n)] *vb* 1 do odd jobs; 2 moonlight
kluts [klʏts] *de* ‖ *de ~ kwijt zijn (raken)* be lost (*or:* confused), be shaken (*or:* rattled)
klutsen [klʏtsə(n)] *vb* beat (up)
kluwen [klywə(n)] *het (~s)* ball
klysma [klɪsma] *het (~'s)* enema
km *kilometer* km
knaagdier [knaɣdir] *het (~en)* rodent
knaagtand [knaχtɑnt] *de (~en)* (rodent) incisor
knaak [knak] *de (knaken)* two guilders fifty
knaap [knap] *de (knapen)* boy, lad
knabbelen [knɑbələ(n)] *vb* nibble (on), munch (on)
knabbeltje [knɑbɛlcə] *het (~s)* nibble(s), snack
knäckebröd [knɛkəbrøt] *het* crispbread, knäckebröd
knagen [knaɣə(n)] *vb* gnaw, eat: *een ~d geweten* pangs of conscience
knak [knɑk] *de (~ken)* crack, snap
knakken [knɑkə(n)] *vb* snap, break; crack
knakworst [knɑkwɔrst] *de (~en) (roughly)* frankfurter
knal [knɑl] *de (~len)* bang, pop
knallen [knɑlə(n)] *vb* bang, crack, pop
knalpot [knɑlpɔt] *de (~ten)* silencer, *(Am)* muffler
¹knap [knɑp] *adj, adv* 1 good-looking, handsome, pretty; 2 clever, bright: *een ~pe kop* a brain, a whizz kid; 3 smart, capable, clever, handy: *een ~ stuk werk* a clever piece of work
²knap [knɑp] *adv* cleverly, well
knappen [knɑpə(n)] *vb* 1 crackle, crack; 2 crack, snap
knapperd [knɑpərt] *de (~s)* brain, whiz(z) kid
knapperen [knɑpərə(n)] *vb* crackle, crack
knapperig [knɑpərəχ] *adj* crisp, crunchy, brittle, crusty
knapzak [knɑpsɑk] *de (~ken)* knapsack
knarsen [knɑrsə(n)] *vb* crunch: *de deur knarst in haar scharnieren* the door creaks (*or:* squeaks) on its hinges
knarsetanden [knɑrsətɑndə(n)] *vb* grind one's teeth
knauw [knau] *de (~en)* 1 bite; 2 *(fig)* blow
knauwen [knɑuwə(n)] *vb* gnaw (at), chew, crunch (on)
knecht [knɛχt] *de (~en)* servant, farmhand
kneden [knedə(n)] *vb* knead, mould
kneep [knep] *de (knepen)* 1 pinch (mark); 2 *(fig)* knack: *de ~jes van het vak kennen* know the tricks of the trade
¹knel [knɛl] *de (~len)* 1 catch; 2 fix, jam
²knel [knɛl] *adj* stuck, caught: ~ *komen te zitten* get stuck (*or:* caught)

¹knellen [knɛlə(n)] *vb* squeeze, press

²knellen [knɛlə(n)] *vb* squeeze, pinch

knelpunt [knɛlpʏnt] *het (~en)* bottleneck

knetteren [knɛtərə(n)] *vb* crackle; sputter

knettergek [knɛtərɣɛk] *adj* nuts, (stark staring) mad, *(Am)* (raving) mad

kneus [knøs] *de (kneuzen)* **1** old crock (*or:* wreck) *(esp cars);* **2** *(educ)* drop-out

kneuterig [knøtərəχ] *adj, adv* snug, cosy

kneuzen [knøzə(n)] *vb* bruise

kneuzing [knøzɪŋ] *de (~en)* bruise, bruising

knevel [knevəl] *de (~s)* **1** moustache; **2** gag

knevelen [knevələ(n)] *vb* tie down, tie up, gag

knie [kni] *de (~ën)* knee: *iets onder de ~ krijgen* master sth, get the hang (*or:* knack) of sth

knieband [knibɑnt] *de (~en)* **1** knee protector (*or:* supporter); **2** hamstring

kniebeschermer [knibəsχɛrmər] *de (~s)* knee-pad

kniebroek [knibruk] *de (~en)* knee breeches

kniegewricht [kniɣəvrɪχt] *het (~en)* knee joint

knielen [knilə(n)] *vb* kneel

knieschijf [knisχɛif] *de (-schijven)* kneecap

kniezen [knizə(n)] *vb* grumble (about), moan (about), mope

knijpen [knɛipə(n)] *vb* **1** pinch; **2** press, squeeze ‖ *'m ~* have the wind up

knijper [knɛipər] *de (~s)* (clothes) peg, clip

knijpfles [knɛipflɛs] *de (~sen)* squeeze-bottle

knijpkat [knɛipkɑt] *de (~ten)* dynamo torch

knik [knɪk] *de (~ken)* **1** crack, kink; **2** twist, kink; **3** nod

knikkebollen [knɪkəbɔlə(n)] *vb* nod

¹knikken [knɪkə(n)] *vb* **1** crack, snap; **2** bend, buckle; **3** nod

²knikken [knɪkə(n)] *vb* bend; twist

knikker [knɪkər] *de (~s)* marble

knip [knɪp] *de (~pen)* **1** snap, (spring) catch, clasp; **2** catch

knipmes [knɪpmɛs] *het (~sen)* clasp-knife: *buigen als een ~* bow and scrape, grovel

knipoog [knɪpoχ] *de (-ogen)* wink: *hij gaf mij een ~* he winked at me

¹knippen [knɪpə(n)] *vb* cut (off, out): *de heg ~ clip (or:* trim) the hedge; *zijn nagels ~* cut (*or:* clip) one's nails

²knippen [knɪpə(n)] *vb* cut, snip

knipperen [knɪpərə(n)] *vb* **1** blink; **2** flash

knipperlicht [knɪpərlɪχt] *het (~en)* indicator; flashing light

knipsel [knɪpsəl] *het (~s)* cutting

KNMI [kaɛnɛmi] *het Koninklijk Nederlands Meteorologisch Instituut* Royal Dutch Meteorological Institute

KNO-arts [kaɛnoɑrts] *de (~en)* ENT specialist

knobbel [knɔbəl] *de (~s)* **1** knob, knot, bump; **2** *(fig)* gift, talent: *een wiskundeknobbel hebben* have a gift for mathematics

¹knock-out [nɔkɑut] *de (~s)* knock-out

²knock-out [nɔkɑut] *adj* knock-out

knoei [knuj] *de ‖ lelijk in de ~ zitten* be in a terrible mess (*or:* fix)

knoeiboel [knujbul] *de* mess

knoeien [knujə(n)] *vb* **1** make a mess, spill; **2** make a mess (of); **3** tinker (with), monkey about (with); **4** cheat, tamper (with)

knoest [knust] *de (~en)* knot

knoet [knut] *de (~en)* cat-o'-nine-tails

knoflook [knɔflok] *het, de* garlic

knokkel [knɔkəl] *de (~s)* knuckle

knokken [knɔkə(n)] *vb* **1** fight; **2** *(fig)* fight hard

knokpartij [knɔkpɑrtɛi] *de (~en)* fight, scuffle

knokploeg [knɔkpluχ] *de (~en)* (bunch, gang of) thugs, henchmen

knol [knɔl] *de (~len)* **1** tuber; **2** turnip

knolraap [knɔlrap] *de (-rapen)* swede; kohlrabi

knolselderie [knɔlsɛldəri] *de* celeriac

knoop [knop] *de (knopen)* **1** button; **2** knot: *een ~ leggen* (or: *maken*) tie (*or:* make) a knot; *(met zichzelf) in de ~ zitten* be at odds with oneself; *het schip voer negen knopen* the ship was doing nine knots

knooppunt [knopʏnt] *het (~en)* intersection, interchange

knoopsgat [knopsχɑt] *het (~en)* buttonhole

knop [knɔp] *de (~pen)* **1** button, switch; **2** button, handle: *de ~ van een deur* the handle of a door; **3** bud: *de roos is nog in de ~* the rose bush is in bud (*or:* is not fully out yet)

knopen [knopə(n)] *vb* knot, make a knot, tie: *twee touwen aan elkaar ~* tie two ropes together

knorren [knɔrə(n)] *vb* grunt

knot [knɔt] *de (~ten)* knot, ball, tuft

¹knots [knɔts] *de (~en)* **1** club; **2** whopper

²knots [knɔts] *adj, adv* crazy, loony

knotten [knɔtə(n)] *vb* top, head

knotwilg [knɔtwɪlχ] *de (~en)* pollard willow

knudde [knʏdə] *adj* no good at all, rubbishy

knuffel [knʏfəl] *de (~s)* cuddle, hug

knuffeldier [knʏfəldir] *het (~en)* soft toy, cuddly toy, teddy (bear)

knuffelen [knʏfələ(n)] *vb* cuddle

knuist [knœyst] *de (~en)* fist

knul [knʏl] *de (~len)* fellow, guy, chap, bloke

knullig [knʏləχ] *adj, adv* awkward: *dat is ~ gedaan* that has been done clumsily

knuppel [knʏpəl] *de (~s)* **1** club, truncheon; **2** stick, joystick

knus [knʏs] *adj, adv* cosy, homey

knutselaar [knʏtsəlar] *de (~s)* handyman, do-it-yourselfer

knutselen [knʏtsələ(n)] *vb* knock together, knock up

koala [kowala] *de (~'s)* koala (bear)

koe [ku] *de (~ien)* **1** cow: *over ~tjes en kalfjes praten* talk about one thing and another; **2** giant

koeienletters [kujə(n)lɛtərs] *de* giant letters

koek [kuk] *de (~en)* **1** cake: *dat is andere ~!* that is another (*or:* a different) kettle of fish; **2** biscuit,

(Am) cooky, cookie
koekenpan [kukə(n)pɑn] *de (~nen)* frying pan
koekoek [kukuk] *de (~en)* cuckoo
koektrommel [kuktrɔməl] *de (~s)* biscuit tin, *(Am)* cooky tin
koel [kul] *adj* 1 cool; chilly; 2 cool, calm
koelbloedig [kulbludəχ] *adj, adv* cold-blooded, calm, cool
koelbox [kulbɔks] *de (~en)* cool box, cooler
koelen [kulə(n)] *vb* cool (down, off), chill
koeling [kulɪŋ] *de* 1 cold store; 2 cooling; refrigeration
koelkast [kulkɑst] *de (~en)* fridge, refrigerator
koelte [kultə] *de* cool(ness)
koeltjes [kulcəs] *adj* (a bit) chilly || ~ *reageren* respond coolly
koelvloeistof [kulvlujstɔf] *de (~fen)* coolant
koepel [kupəl] *de (~s)* dome
koepokken [kupɔkə(n)] *de* cowpox
koer [kur] *de* (school) playground
Koerd [kurt] *de (~en)* Kurd
koerier [kurir] *de (~s)* courier
koers [kurs] *de* 1 course: *van ~ veranderen* change course *(or:* tack); 2 route; 3 price, (exchange) rate
koersen [kursə(n)] *vb* set course for
koersnotering [kursnoterɪŋ] *de (~en)* (price, market) quotation
koersstijging [kursteiɣɪŋ] *de (~en)* rise *(or:* increase) in prices, rise in the exchange rate
koerswaarde [kurswardə] *de (~n, ~s)* market value *(or:* price), exchange value
koeskoes [kuskus] *de (koeskoezen)* couscous
koest [kust] *adj* || *zich ~ houden* keep quiet, keep a low profile
koesteren [kustərə(n)] *vb* cherish, foster: *hoop ~* nurse hopes
koets [kuts] *de (~en)* coach, carriage
koetsier [kutsir] *de (~s)* coachman
koevoet [kuvut] *de (~en)* crowbar
Koeweit [kuwɛit] *het* Kuwait
koffer [kɔfər] *de (~s)* (suit)case, (hand)bag, trunk
kofferbak [kɔfərbɑk] *de (~ken)* boot, *(Am)* trunk
koffie [kɔfi] *de* coffee: ~ *drinken* have coffee
koffiemelk [kɔfimɛlk] *de* evaporated milk
koffiepot [kɔfipɔt] *de (~ten)* coffeepot
kogel [koɣəl] *de (~s)* 1 bullet, ball: *een verdwaalde ~* a stray bullet; 2 shot
kogelbiefstuk [koɣəlbifstʏk] *de (~ken)* round steak
kogellager [koɣəlaɣər] *het (~s)* ball-bearing
kogelslingeren [koɣəlslɪŋərə(n)] *vb* hammer (throw)
kogelstoten [koɣəlstotə(n)] *vb* shot-put(ting)
kogelvrij [koɣəlvrɛi] *adj* bulletproof
kok [kɔk] *de (~ken)* cook: *de chef-kok* the chef
koken [kokə(n)] *vb* 1 boil: *water kookt bij 100° C* water boils at 100° C; 2 cook, do the cooking: ~ *van woede* boil *(or:* seethe) with rage
kokendheet [kokənthet] *adj* piping *(or:* boiling,

scalding) hot
koker [kokər] *de (~s)* 1 case; 2 cylinder; 3 shaft, chute
koket [kokɛt] *adj* 1 coquettish; 2 smart, stylish
kokhalzen [kɔkhɑlzə(n)] *vb* retch, heave
kokos [kokɔs] *het* 1 coconut; 2 coconut fibre
kokosmat [kokɔsmɑt] *de (~ten)* coconut matting
kokosnoot [kokɔsnot] *de* coconut
kolder [kɔldər] *de* nonsense, rubbish
kolen [kolə(n)] *de* coal: *op hete ~ zitten* be on tenterhooks
kolencentrale [kolə(n)sɛntralə] *de (~s)* coal-fired power station
kolenmijn [kolə(n)mɛin] *de (~en)* coal mine
kolere [kolerə] *de* || *krijg de ~!* get stuffed!, drop dead!
kolf [kɔlf] *de (kolven)* 1 butt; 2 flask; retort; 3 cob
kolibrie [kolibri] *de (~s)* hummingbird
koliek [kolik] *de, het (~en)* colic
kolk [kɔlk] *de (~en)* eddy, whirlpool
kolken [kɔlkə(n)] *vb* swirl, eddy
kolom [kolɔm] *de (~men)* column
kolonel [kolonɛl] *de (~s)* colonel
koloniaal [kolonijal] *adj* colonial
kolonialisme [kolonijalɪsmə] *het* colonialism
kolonie [koloni] *de (~s, koloniën)* colony
kolonist [kolonɪst] *de (~en)* colonist, settler
kolossaal [kolɔsal] *adj, adv* colossal, immense
¹kom [kɔm] *de (~men)* 1 bowl, washbasin; 2 basin, bowl; 3 socket: *haar arm is uit de ~ geschoten* her arm is dislocated; *de bebouwde ~* the built-up area, *(Am)* the city limits
²kom [kɔm] *int* come on!: ~ *nou, dat maak je me niet wijs* come on (now) *(or:* look), don't give me that; ~, *ik stap maar weer eens op* right, I'm off now!; ~ *op!* come on!
kombuis [kɔmbœys] *de (kombuizen)* galley
komediant [komedijɑnt] *de (~en)* comedy actor, comedian
komedie [komedi] *de (~s)* comedy, *(fig also)* (play-)acting
komediespelen [komedispelə(n)] *vb* 1 act; 2 (play-)act, put on an act
komeet [komet] *de (kometen)* comet
komen [komə(n)] *vb* 1 come, get: *er komt regen* it is going to rain; *er kwam bloed uit zijn mond* there was blood coming out of his mouth; *ergens bij kunnen ~* be able to get at sth; *de politie laten ~* send for *(or:* call) the police; *ik kom eraan!* (or: *al!)* (I'm) coming!, I'm on my way!; *kom eens langs!* come round some time!; *ergens achter ~* find out sth, get to know sth; *hoe kom je erbij?* what(ever) gave you that idea?; *ergens overheen ~* get over sth; *(fig) we kwamen er niet uit* we couldn't work it out; *hoe kom je van hier naar het museum?* how do you get to the museum from here?; *hij komt uit Engeland* he's from England; *wie het eerst komt, het eerst maalt* first come, first served; 2 come ((a)round, over), call: *er ~ mensen vanavond* there are *(or:* we've got)

people coming this evening; **3** *(with aan)* touch: *kom nergens aan!* don't touch (anything)!; **4** come (about), happen: *hoe komt het?* how come?, how did that happen?; *daar komt niets van in* that's out of the question; *dat komt ervan als je niet luistert* that's what you get *(or:* what happens) if you don't listen; **5** *(with aan)* come (by), get (hold of): *aan geld zien te ~* get hold of some money; *daar kom ik straks nog op* I'll come round to that in a moment; *daar komt nog bij dat ...* what's more ..., besides ...; *kom nou!* don't be silly!, come off it!

komend [ko̲mənt] *adj* coming, to come, next: *~e week* next week

komiek [komi̲k] *de (~en)* comedian, comic

komijn [komɛi̲n] *de* cumin

komisch [ko̲mis] *adj, adv* comic(al), funny

komkommer [komko̲mər] *de (~s)* cucumber

komma [ko̲ma] *het, de (~'s)* **1** comma; **2** (decimal) point: *tot op vijf cijfers na de ~ uitrekenen* calculate to five decimal places; *nul ~ drie (0,3)* nought *(or Am:* zero) point three (0.3)

kommer [ko̲mər] *de* sorrow: *~ en kwel* sorrow and misery

kompas [kompa̲s] *het (~sen)* compass

kompres [komprɛ̲s] *het (~sen)* compress

komst [komst] *de* coming, arrival: *er is storm op ~* there is a storm brewing

Kongo [ko̲ŋo] *de* Congo

konijn [koni̲n] *het (~en)* rabbit, bunny

konijnenhol [koni̲nə(n)hol] *het (~en)* rabbit hole *(or:* burrow)

koning [ko̲nɪŋ] *de (~en)* king

koningin [konɪŋɪ̲n] *de (~nen)* queen

Koninginnedag [konɪŋɪ̲nədaχ] *de (~en)* Queen's Birthday

koningshuis [ko̲nɪŋshœys] *het (-huizen)* royal family *(or:* house)

koninklijk [ko̲nɪŋklək] *adj* royal, regal

koninkrijk [ko̲nɪŋkrɛik] *het (~en)* kingdom

konkelen [ko̲ŋkələ(n)] *vb* scheme, intrigue

kont [kont] *de (~en)* bottom, behind, bum: *de ~ tegen de krib gooien* dig one's heels in

konvooi [konvo̲j] *het (~en)* convoy

kooi [koj] *de (~en)* **1** cage; **2** pen, coop, fold, sty; **3** berth, bunk

kook [kok] *de* boil: *aan de ~ brengen* bring to the boil; *volkomen van de ~ raken* go to pieces

kookboek [ko̲gbuk] *het (~en)* cookery book

kookkunst [ko̲kʏnst] *de* cookery, (the art of) cooking, culinary art

kookplaat [ko̲kplat] *de (-platen)* hotplate, hob

kookpunt [ko̲kpʏnt] *het (~en)* boiling point: *het ~ bereiken (also fig)* reach boiling point

kookwekker [ko̲kwɛkər] *de (~s)* kitchen timer

kool [kol] *de (kolen)* **1** cabbage; **2** coal

kooldioxide [ko̲ldijɔksidə] *het* carbon dioxide

koolhydraat [ko̲lhidrat] *het (-hydraten)* carbohydrate

koolmees [ko̲lmes] *de (-mezen)* great tit

koolmonoxide [ko̲lmonɔksidə] *het* carbon monoxide

koolraap [ko̲lrap] *de (-rapen)* kohlrabi, turnip cabbage

koolstof [ko̲lstɔf] *de* carbon

koolwitje [ko̲lwɪcə] *het (~s)* cabbage white (butterfly)

koolzaad [ko̲lzat] *het* (rape)seed, colza

koolzuur [ko̲lzyr] *het* carbon dioxide

koop [kop] *de (kopen)* buy, sale, purchase: *~ en verkoop* buying and selling; *de ~ gaat door* the deal *(or:* sale) is going through; *op de ~ toe* into the bargain; *te ~ (zijn, staan)* (be) for sale; *te ~ of te huur* to buy or let; *te ~ gevraagd* wanted

koopavond [ko̲pavɔnt] *de (~en)* late-night shopping, late opening

koopcontract [ko̲pkɔntrakt] *het (~en)* contract *(or:* bill) of sale, purchase deed, title deed, deed of purchase

koophandel [ko̲phandəl] *de* commerce, trade: *Kamer van Koophandel (roughly)* Chamber of Commerce

koopje [ko̲pjə] *het (~s)* bargain, good buy *(or:* deal)

koopkracht [ko̲pkraχt] *de* buying power

koopman [ko̲pman] *de (kooplieden)* merchant, businessman

koopvaardij [kopfardɛi̲] *de* merchant navy

koopwaar [ko̲pwar] *de (-waren)* merchandise, wares

koor [kor] *het (koren)* choir; chorus: *een gemengd ~* a mixed (voice) choir

koord [kort] *het, de (~en)* cord, (thick) string, (light) rope

koorddansen [ko̲rdansə(n)] *vb* walk a tightrope

koorts [korts] *de* fever: *bij iem de ~ opnemen* take s.o.'s temperature

koortsaanval [ko̲rtsanval] *de (~len)* attack of fever

koortsachtig [kortsa̲χtəχ] *adj, adv* feverish: *~e bedrijvigheid* frenzied activity

koortsig [ko̲rtsəχ] *adj* feverish

koorzanger [ko̲rzaŋər] *de (~s)* choir singer, chorus member

kop [kɔp] *de (~pen)* **1** head: *er zit ~ noch staart aan* you can't make head or tail of it; *(Belg) van ~ tot teen* from top to toe; *~ dicht!* shut up!; *een mooie ~ met haar* a beautiful head of hair; *een rooie ~ krijgen* go red, flush; *iem op zijn ~ geven* give s.o. what for; **2** head, brain: *hij is een knappe ~* he is a clever *(or:* smart) fellow; **3** head, top: *de ~ van Overijssel* the north of Overijssel; *de ~ van een spijker* (or: *hamer)* the head of a nail *(or:* hammer); *op ~ liggen* be in the lead; *over de ~ slaan* overturn, somersault; *over de ~ gaan* go broke, fold; **4** cup, mug; **5** headline, heading: *~ of munt* heads or tails; *het is vijf uur op de ~ af* it is exactly five o'clock

kopbal [ko̲bal] *de (~len)* header

¹kopen [ko̲pə(n)] *vb* **1** buy, purchase: *wat koop ik ervoor?* what good will it do me?; **2** buy (off)

²kopen [ko̲pə(n)] *vb* trade (with), deal (with), buy

¹koper [kopər] *het (~s)* **1** copper; **2** brass; **3** brass (section)

²koper [kopər] *de (~s)* buyer

koperen [kopərə(n)] *adj* brass, copper

koperwerk [kopərwɛrk] *het* copper work, brass work, brassware

kopgroep [kopχrup] *de (~en)* leading group; break(away)

kopie [kopi] *de (~ën)* **1** copy, duplicate; **2** (photo)copy

kopieerapparaat [kopijɛraparat] *het (-apparaten)* photocopier

kopiëren [kopijɛrə(n)] *vb* **1** copy, make a copy (of), transcribe; **2** (photo)copy, xerox

kopij [kopɛi] *de (~en)* copy, manuscript

kopje [kopjə] *het (~s)* (small, little) cup ‖ *~ duikelen* turn somersaults; *de poes gaf haar steeds ~s* the cat kept nuzzling (up) against her

kopje-onder [kopjəɔndər] *adv* ‖ *hij ging ~* he got a ducking

koplamp [koplɑmp] *de (~en)* headlight

koploper [koplopər] *de (~s)* leader, front runner, trendsetter

¹koppel [kopəl] *de* (sword) belt

²koppel [kopəl] *het* **1** couple, pair, group, bunch, set; **2** couple: *een aardig ~* a nice couple

koppelaar [kopəlar] *de (~s)* matchmaker, marriage broker

koppelen [kopələ(n)] *vb* **1** couple (with, to); **2** link, relate: *twee mensen proberen te ~* try to pair two people off

koppeling [kopəlɪŋ] *de (~en)* clutch (pedal): *de ~ intrappen* let out the clutch

koppelteken [kopəltekə(n)] *het (~s)* hyphen

koppeltjeduiken [kopəlcədœykə(n)] *vb* (turn, do a) somersault

koppen [kopə(n)] *vb* head

koppensnellen [kopə(n)snɛlə(n)] *vb* headhunt

koppig [kopχ] *adj, adv* **1** stubborn, headstrong: *(zo) ~ als een ezel* (as) stubborn as a mule; **2** heady

koppigaard [kopəχart] *de (~s) (Belg)* stubborn person, obstinate person

koppigheid [kopəχhɛit] *de* stubbornness

koppositie [kopozi(t)si] *de (sport)* lead

koprol [koprɔl] *de (~len)* somersault

kopspijker [kopspɛikər] *de (~s)* clout (nail), tack

kopstem [kopstɛm] *de (~men)* falsetto

kopstoot [kopstot] *de (kopstoten)* butt (of the head): *iem een ~ geven* headbutt s.o.

kopstuk [kopstʏk] *het (~ken)* head man, boss

koptelefoon [kopteləfon] *de (~s)* headphone(s), earphone(s), headset

kopzorg [kopsɔrχ] *de (~en)* worry, headache

koraal [koral] *het (koralen)* coral

koraaleiland [koralɛilɑnt] *het (~en)* coral island

koraalrif [koralrɪf] *het (~fen)* coral reef

koran [koran] *de* Koran

kordaat [kordat] *adj, adv* firm, plucky, bold

kordon [kordɔn] *het (~s)* cordon

Korea [koreja] *het* Korea

Koreaan [korejan] *de (Koreanen)* Korean

koren [korə(n)] *het (~s)* corn, *(Am)* wheat, grain

korenbloem [korə(n)blum] *de (~en)* cornflower

korenhalm [korə(n)hɑlm] *de (~en)* cornstalk, *(Am)* wheat stalk

korenschuur [korə(n)sχyr] *de (-schuren)* granary

korenwolf [korə(n)wɔlf] *de (-wolven)* European hamster

korf [korf] *de (korven)* basket, hive

korfbal [korvbɑl] *het* korfball

korfballen [korvbɑlə(n)] *vb* play korfball

korporaal [korporal] *de (~s)* corporal

korps [korps] *het (~en)* corps, body, staff, force

korpschef [korpʃɛf] *de (~s)* superintendent

korrel [korəl] *de (~s)* granule, grain: *iets met een ~(tje) zout nemen* take sth with a pinch of salt

korrelig [korələχ] *adj* granular

korset [korsɛt] *het (~ten)* corset

korst [korst] *de (~en)* crust, scab, rind

korstmos [korstmɔs] *het (~sen)* lichen

kort [kort] *adj, adv* short; brief: *alles ~ en klein slaan* smash everything to pieces; *een ~ overzicht* a brief *(or:* short) summary; *~ daarvoor* shortly before; *tot voor ~* until recently; *iets in het ~ uiteenzetten* explain sth briefly; *we komen drie man te ~* we're three men short; *te ~ komen* run short (of)

kortademig [kortadəməχ] *adj* short of breath, *(also fig)* short-winded

kortaf [kortɑf] *adj, adv* curt, abrupt

kortegolfband [kortəɣɔlvbɑnt] *de* short-wave band

korten [kortə(n)] *vb* cut (back): *~ op de uitkeringen* cut back on social security

korting [kortɪŋ] *de (~en)* discount, concession, cut: *~ geven op de prijs* give a discount off the price

kortingkaart [kortɪŋkart] *de (~en)* concession *(or:* reduced-fare) card/pass, discount card

kortom [kortɔm] *adv* in short, to put it briefly *(or:* shortly)

kortsluiting [kortslœytɪŋ] *de (~en)* short circuit, short

kortstondig [kortstɔndəχ] *adj* short-lived, brief

kortweg [kortwɛχ] *adv* briefly, shortly

kortwieken [kortwikə(n)] *vb* clip the wings of

kortzichtig [kortsɪχtəχ] *adj, adv* short-sighted

kosmisch [kosmis] *adj* cosmic

kosmonaut [kosmonɑut] *de (~en)* cosmonaut

kosmos [kosmɔs] *de* cosmos

kost [kost] *de (~en)* **1** *(pl)* cost, expense, outlay, charge: *~en van levensonderhoud* cost of living; *op haar eigen ~en* at her own expense; *op ~en van* at the expense of; **2** living: *wat doe jij voor de ~?* what do you do for a living?; **3** board(ing), keep: *~ en inwoning* board and lodging; **4** fare, food: *dagelijkse ~* ordinary food

kostbaar [kostbar] *adj* **1** expensive; **2** valuable, *(stronger)* precious

kostbaarheden [kostbarhedə(n)] *de* valuables

kostelijk [kɔstələk] *adj, adv* precious, exquisite, delicious, excellent

¹kosteloos [kɔstəlos] *adj* free

²kosteloos [kɔstəlos] *adv* free of charge

kosten [kɔstə(n)] *vb* cost, be, take: *het heeft ons maanden gekost om dit te regelen* it took us months to organize this; *het ongeluk kostte (aan) drie kinderen het leven* three children died (*or:* lost their lives) in the accident; *dit karwei zal heel wat tijd ~* this job will take (up) a great deal of time

kostenbesparend [kɔstə(n)bəsparənt] *adj* money-saving, cost-cutting

kostenstijging [kɔstə(n)stɛiɣɪŋ] *de* increase in costs

kostenverhogend [kɔstə(n)vərhoːɣənt] *adj, adv* cost-raising

kostenverlagend *adj* cost-reducing

koster [kɔstər] *de* (~*s*) verger

kostganger [kɔstχɑŋər] *de* (~*s*) boarder, lodger

kostgeld [kɔstχɛlt] *het* (~*en*) board (and lodging)

kostje [kɔʃə] *het* (~*s*) ‖ *zijn ~ is gekocht* he has it made

kostprijs [kɔstprɛis] *de* cost price

kostschool [kɔstsχol] *de* (*-scholen*) boarding school, public school: *op een ~ zitten* attend a boarding school

kostuum [kɔstym] *het* (~*s*) 1 suit; 2 costume, dress

kostwinner [kɔstwɪnər] *de* (~*s*) breadwinner

kostwinning [kɔstwɪnɪŋ] *de* livelihood, living

kot [kɔt] *het* (~*ten*) 1 hovel; 2 (*Belg*) student apartment (*or:* room): *op ~ zitten* be in digs

kotbaas [kɔdbas] *de* (*kotbazen*) (*Belg*) landlord

kotelet [kotəlɛt] *de* (~*ten*) chop, cutlet

kotmadam [kɔtmadam] *de* (~*men*, ~*s*) (*Belg*) landlady

kotsen [kɔtsə(n)] *vb* puke

kou [kɑu] *de* cold(ness), chill: *~ vatten* catch a cold

koud [kɑut] *adj* cold, chilly: *het laat mij ~* it leaves me cold

koudbloedig [kɑudbludəχ] *adj* cold-blooded

koudvuur [kɑutfyr] *het* gangrene

koukleum [kɑukləm] *de* (~*en*) shivery type

kous [kɑus] *de* (~*en*) stocking, sock

kouwelijk [kɑuwələk] *adj, adv* chilly, sensitive to cold

kozak [kozɑk] *de* (~*ken*) Cossack

¹kozijn [kozɛin] *het* (window, door) frame

²kozijn [kozɛin] *de* (*Belg*) cousin

kraag [kraχ] *de* (*kragen*) 1 collar: *iem bij (in) zijn ~ grijpen* grab s.o. by the collar, collar s.o.; 2 head

kraai [krɑj] *de* (~*en*) crow

kraaien [krɑjə(n)] *vb* crow

kraaiennest [krɑjənɛst] *het* (~*en*) crow's-nest

kraaienpootjes [krɑjə(n)pocəs] *de* crow's-feet

kraak [krɑk] *de* (*kraken*) break-in

kraakbeen [krɑɡben] *het* (~*deren*) cartilage

kraal [krɑl] *de* (*kralen*) bead

kraam [krɑm] *het, de* (*kramen*) stall, booth

kraamafdeling [krɑmɑvdelɪŋ] *de* (~*en*) maternity ward

kraambed [krɑmbɛt] *het* childbed: *een lang ~* a long period of lying-in

kraambezoek [krɑmbəzuk] *het* (~*en*) ‖ *op ~ komen* come to see the new mother and her baby

kraamhulp [krɑmhʏlp] *de* (~*en*) maternity assistant

kraamkamer [krɑmkamər] *de* (~*s*) delivery room, *(before delivery)* labour room

kraamkliniek [krɑmklinik] *de* (~*en*) maternity clinic

kraamverzorgster [krɑmvərzɔrχstər] *de* (~*s*) maternity nurse

kraamvrouw [krɑmvrɑu] *de* (~*en*) woman in childbed; mother of newly-born baby

kraamzorg [krɑmzɔrχ] *de* maternity care

kraan [krɑn] *de* (*kranen*) 1 tap, (*Am*) faucet, (stop)cock, valve; 2 crane

kraanvogel [krɑnvoɣəl] *de* (~*s*) (common) crane

krab [krɑp] *de* (~*ben*) crab

krabbel [krɑbəl] *de* (~*s*) 1 scratch (mark); 2 scrawl

¹krabbelen [krɑbələ(n)] *vb* scratch ‖ *(weer) overeind ~* scramble to one's feet

²krabbelen [krɑbələ(n)] *vb* scrawl

krabbeltje [krɑbəlcə] *het* (~*s*) scrawl

¹krabben [krɑbə(n)] *vb* scratch: *zijn hoofd ~* scratch one's head

²krabben [krɑbə(n)] *vb* scratch out, scratch off

krach [krɑχ] *de* (~*s*) crash

kracht [krɑχt] *de* (~*en*) strength, power, force: *drijvende ~ achter* moving force (*or:* spirit) behind; *op eigen ~* on one's own, by oneself; *op volle* (*or:* *halve*) *~ (werken)* operate at full (*or:* half) speed/power; *met zijn laatste ~en* with a final effort; *het vergt veel van mijn ~en* it's a great drain on my energy; *van ~ zijn* be valid (*or:* effective)

krachtbron [krɑχtbrɔn] *de* (~*nen*) source of energy (*or:* power), power station

krachtcentrale [krɑχtsɛntralə] *de* (~*s*) power station

krachteloos [krɑχtəlos] *adj* weak, limp, powerless

krachtens [krɑχtəns] *prep* by virtue of, under

krachtig [krɑχtəχ] *adj, adv* 1 strong, powerful: *een ~e motor* a powerful engine; *matige tot ~e wind* moderate to strong winds; 2 powerful, forceful: *kort maar ~: a)* brief and to the point; *b)* (*fig*) short but (*or:* and) sweet; 3 potent

krachtmeting [krɑχtmetɪŋ] *de* (~*en*) contest, trial of strength

krachtpatser [krɑχtpatsər] *de* (~*s*) muscle-man, bruiser

krachtsinspanning [krɑχtsɪnspanɪŋ] *de* (~*en*) effort

krachtsport [krɑχtspɔrt] *de* (~*en*) strength sport

krakelen [krakələ(n)] *vb* quarrel, row

¹kraken [krakə(n)] *vb* crack, creak, crunch: *een krakende stem* a grating voice

²kraken [krakə(n)] *vb* 1 crack (*also fig*); 2 break into (*bldg*); crack; hack; 3 pan, slate ‖ *het pand is ge-*

kraakt the building has been broken into by squatters

kraker [krakər] *de (~s)* **1** squatter; **2** *(comp)* hacker

kram [krɑm] *de (~men)* clamp, cramp (iron), clasp || *(Belg) uit zijn ~men schieten* blow one's top

kramiek [kramik] *de (~en) (Belg)* currant loaf

kramp [krɑmp] *de (~en)* cramp

krampachtig [krɑmpɑχtəχ] *adj, adv* **1** forced: *met een ~ vertrokken gezicht* grimacing; **2** frenetic: *zich ~ aan iem (iets) vasthouden* cling to s.o. (sth) for dear life; **3** convulsive

kranig [kranəχ] *adj* plucky, brave

krankzinnig [krɑŋksɪnəχ] *adj* **1** mentally ill, insane, mad: *~ worden* go insane, go out of one's mind; **2** crazy, mad

krankzinnige [krɑŋksɪnəχə] *de (~n)* madman, madwoman

krankzinnigheid [krɑŋksɪnəχhɛit] *de* madness, insanity, lunacy

krans [krɑns] *de (~en)* **1** wreath; **2** ring: *een ~ om de zon* (or: *de maan*) a corona round the sun (or: moon)

kransslagader [krɑnslaχadər] *de (~s)* coronary artery

krant [krɑnt] *de (~en)* (news)paper

krantenbericht [krɑntə(n)bərɪχt] *het (~en)* newspaper report

krantenbezorger [krɑntə(n)bəzɔrɣər] *de (~s)* (news)paper boy (or: girl)

krantenknipsel [krɑntə(n)knɪpsəl] *het (~s)* newspaper cutting, press cutting

krantenkop [krɑntə(n)kɔp] *de (~pen)* (newspaper) headline

krantenwijk [krɑntə(n)wɛik] *de (~en)* (news)paper round (or *Am:* route)

krap [krɑp] *adj, adv* **1** tight, narrow; **2** tight, scarce: *een ~pe markt* a small market; *~ (bij kas) zitten* be short of money (or: cash); *met een ~pe meerderheid* with a bare majority

¹kras [krɑs] *de (~sen)* scratch

²kras [krɑs] *adj, adv* **1** strong, vigorous, hale and hearty; **2** strong, drastic: *dat is een nogal ~se opmerking* that is a rather crass remark

kraslot [krɑslɔt] *het (~en)* scratch card

¹krassen [krɑsə(n)] *vb* **1** scrape: *zijn ring kraste over het glas* his ring scraped across the glass; **2** rasp, scrape; croak; hoot, screech

²krassen [krɑsə(n)] *vb* scratch, carve

krat [krɑt] *het (~ten)* crate

krater [kratər] *de (~s)* crater: *een ~ slaan* leave a crater

krediet [krədit] *het (~en)* **1** credit: *veel ~ hebben* enjoy great trust; **2** credit, respect

kredietuur [krədityr] *het (-uren) (Belg) (roughly)* refresher course leave, study leave

kredietwaardig [krəditwardəχ] *adj* creditworthy

kreeft [kreft] *de (~en)* lobster

Kreeft [kreft] *de (~en) (astrology)* Cancer

kreeftskeerkring [kreftskerkrɪŋ] *de* tropic of Cancer

kreek [krek] *de (kreken)* **1** creek; cove; **2** stream

kreet [kret] *de (kreten)* **1** cry; **2** slogan, catchword

krekel [krekəl] *de (~s)* cricket

kreng [krɛŋ] *het (~en)* **1** beast, bastard, bitch; **2** wretched thing; **3** carrion

krenken [krɛŋkə(n)] *vb* offend, hurt

krent [krɛnt] *de* currant: *de ~en uit de pap* the best bits

krentenbol [krɛntə(n)bɔl] *de (~len)* currant bun

krentenbrood [krɛntə(n)brot] *het (-broden)* currant loaf

krenterig [krɛntərəχ] *adj, adv* stingy

Kreta [kreta] *het* Crete

kreukel [krøkəl] *de (~s)* crease

¹kreukelen [krøkələ(n)] *vb* crease: *het zat in gekreukeld papier* it was wrapped in crumpled paper

²kreukelen [krøkələ(n)] *vb* get creased (or: rumpled)

kreukelig [krøkələχ] *adj* crumpled, creased

¹kreuken [krøkə(n)] *vb* crease, crumple

²kreuken [krøkə(n)] *vb* get creased (or: rumpled)

kreunen [krønə(n)] *vb* groan, moan

kreupel [krøpəl] *adj, adv* **1** lame; **2** poor, clumsy

kreupele [krøpələ] *de* cripple

kreupelhout [krøpəlhɑut] *het* undergrowth

krib [krɪp] *de (~ben)* manger, crib

kribbig [krɪbəχ] *adj, adv* grumpy, catty

kriebel [kribəl] *de (~s)* itch, tickle: *ik krijg daar de ~s van* it gets on my nerves

kriebelen [kribələ(n)] *vb* tickle, itch

kriek [krik] *de (~en)* **1** black cherry; **2** *(Belg)* (sour) cherry

krieken [krikə(n)] *vb* || *met (bij) het ~ van de dag* at (the crack of) dawn

krielaardappel [krilardɑpəl] *de (~en, ~s)* (small) new potato

krijgen [krɛiɣə(n)] *vb* get, receive, catch: *aandacht ~ receive* attention; *je krijgt de groeten van … …* sends (you) his regards; *zij kreeg er hoofdpijn van* it gave her a headache; *slaap* (or: *trek*) *~ feel* sleepy (or: hungry); *iets af~* get sth done (or: finished); *dat goed is niet meer te ~* you can't get hold of that stuff any more; *iem te pakken ~* get (hold of) s.o.; *ik krijg nog geld van je* you (still) owe me some money; *iets voor elkaar ~* manage sth

krijger [krɛiɣər] *de (~s)* warrior

krijgsgevangene [krɛiχsχəvɑŋənə] *de (~n)* prisoner of war

krijgshaftig [krɛiχshɑftəχ] *adj, adv* warlike

krijgsmacht [krɛiχsmɑχt] *de (~en)* armed forces, army

krijgsraad [krɛiχsrat] *de (-raden)* court-martial

krijgstucht [krɛiχstyχt] *de* military discipline

krijsen [krɛisə(n)] *vb* **1** shriek, screech; **2** scream

krijt [krɛit] *het* chalk, crayon || *bij iem in het ~ staan* owe s.o. sth

krijten [krɛitə(n)] *vb* chalk

krijtje [krɛicə] *het (~s)* piece of chalk

krik [krɪk] *de* (~s) jack

Krim [krɪm] || *de* ~ the Crimea

krimp [krɪmp] *de* shrinkage || *geen* ~ *geven* not flinch

krimpen [krɪmpə(n)] *vb* shrink, contract

krimpfolie [krɪmpfoli] *de* clingfilm, shrink-wrapping

kring [krɪŋ] *de* (~en) circle, ring, circuit: *in politieke* ~*en* in political circles; *de huiselijke* ~ the family (*or:* domestic) circle; ~*en onder de ogen hebben* have bags under one's eyes; ~*en maken op een tafelblad* make rings on a table top; *in een* ~ *zitten* sit in a ring (*or:* circle)

kringelen [krɪŋələ(n)] *vb* spiral

kringloop [krɪŋlop] *de* cycle, circulation

kringlooppapier [krɪŋlopapir] *het* recycled paper

krioelen [krijulə(n)] *vb* swarm, teem

kriskras [krɪskrɑs] *adv* criss-cross

kristal [krɪstɑl] *het* (~len) crystal

kristalhelder [krɪstɑlhɛldər] *adj* crystal-clear, lucid

kristallen [krɪstɑlə(n)] *adj* crystal

¹kritiek [kritik] *de* (~en) **1** criticism: *opbouwende* (*or: afbrekende*) ~ constructive (*or:* destructive) criticism; **2** (critical) review: *goede* (or: *slechte*) ~*en krijgen* get good (*or:* bad) reviews

²kritiek [kritik] *adj* critical; crucial: *de toestand van de patiënt was* ~ the patient's condition was critical

kritisch [kritis] *adj, adv* **1** critical; **2** fault-finding: *een* ~ *iemand* a fault-finder

kritiseren [kritizerə(n)] *vb* criticize, review

Kroaat [krowat] *de* (*Kroaten*) Croat, Croatian

Kroatië [krowa(t)sijə] *het* Croatia

kroeg [kruχ] *de* (~en) pub: *altijd in de* ~ *zitten* always be in the pub

kroegbaas [kruχbas] *de* (-bazen) publican

kroegloper [kruχlopər] *de* (~s) pub-crawler

kroepoek [krupuk] *de* prawn crackers, shrimp crackers

kroes [krus] *de* (*kroezen*) mug

kroeshaar [krushar] *het* (-haren) frizzy hair, curly hair

krokant [krokɑnt] *adj* crisp(y), crunchy

kroket [krokɛt] *de* croquette

krokodil [krokodɪl] *de* (~len) crocodile

krokus [krokʏs] *de* (~sen) crocus

krokusvakantie [krokʏsfakɑnsi] *de* (*roughly*) spring half-term, (*Am; roughly*) semester break

krols [krɔls] *adj* on heat

krom [krɔm] *adj, adv* **1** bent, crooked, curved: ~*me benen* bow-legs; **2** clumsy: ~ *Nederlands* bad Dutch

krommenaas [krɔmənas] *de* || (*Belg*) *zich van* ~ *gebaren* act dumb, pretend not to hear

kromming [krɔmɪŋ] *de* (~en) bend(ing), curving, curvature

kromtrekken [krɔmtrɛkə(n)] *vb* warp, buckle

kromzwaard [krɔmzwart] *het* (~en) scimitar, sabre

kronen [kronə(n)] *vb* crown

kroning [kronɪŋ] *de* (~en) crowning, coronation

kronkel [krɔŋkəl] *de* (~s) twist(ing), kink

kronkelen [krɔŋkələ(n)] *vb* twist, wind, wriggle: ~ *van pijn* writhe in agony

kronkelweg [krɔŋkəlwɛχ] *de* (~en) twisting road, winding road, crooked path

kroon [kron] *de* (*kronen*) **1** crown; (*of flower*) corolla; **2** Crown: *een benoeming door de* ~ a Crown appointment; *dat is de* ~ *op zijn werk* that is the crowning glory of his work

kroongetuige [kronχətœyɣə] *de* (~n) crown witness

kroonjuwelen [kronjywelə(n)] *de* crown jewels

kroonkurk [kroŋkʏrk] *de* (~en) crown cap

kroonlijst [kronlɛist] *de* (~en) cornice

kroonsteentje [kronstencə] *het* (~s) connector

kroos [kros] *het* duckweed

kroost [krost] *het* offspring

krop [krɔp] *de* (~pen) **1** head: *een* ~ *sla* a head of lettuce; **2** crop, gizzard

krot [krɔt] *het* (~ten) slum (dwelling), hovel

krottenwijk [krɔtə(n)wɛik] *de* (~en) slum(s)

kruid [krœyt] *het* (~en) **1** herb; **2** herb, spice

kruiden [krœydə(n)] *vb* season, flavour, (*fig also*) spice (up)

kruidenbuiltje [krœydə(n)bœylcə] *het* (~s) bouquet garni

kruidenier [krœydənir] *de* (~s) grocer

kruidenierswinkel [krœydənirswɪŋkəl] *de* (~s) grocery (shop)

kruidenrekje [krœydə(n)rɛkjə] *het* (~s) spice rack

kruidenthee [krœydə(n)te] *de* herb(al) tea

kruidnagel [krœytnaɣəl] *de* (~s, ~en) clove

¹kruien [krœyə(n)] *vb* wheel

²kruien [krœyə(n)] *vb* break up; drift

kruier [krœyər] *de* (~s) porter

kruik [krœyk] *de* (~en) **1** jar, pitcher, crock; **2** hot-water bottle

kruim [krœym] *het* (~en) **1** crumb; **2** (*Belg*) the pick of the bunch, the very best

kruimel [krœyməl] *de* (~s) crumb

kruimeldief [krœyməldif] *de* (-dieven) **1** petty thief; **2** crumb-sweeper, dustbuster

kruimelen [krœymələ(n)] *vb* crumble

kruin [krœyn] *de* (~en) crown

kruipen [krœypə(n)] *vb* **1** creep, crawl; **2** crawl (along), drag: *de uren kropen voorbij* time dragged (on)

kruiperig [krœypərəχ] *adj, adv* cringing, slimy, servile

kruippakje [krœypɑkjə] *het* (~s) romper (suit), playsuit

kruis [krœys] *het* (*kruizen*) **1** cross; **2** crotch, seat; **3** crotch, groin; **4** head: ~ *of munt?* heads or tails?; (*Belg; fig*) *een* ~ *over iets maken* put an end to sth; *een* ~ *slaan* cross oneself

kruisbeeld [krœyzbelt] *het* (~en) crucifix

kruisbes [krœyzbɛs] *de* (~sen) gooseberry

kruiselings [krœysəlɪŋs] *adj, adv* crosswise, crossways

kruisen [krœysə(n)] *vb* cross, intersect: *patroon van elkaar ~de lijnen* pattern of intersecting lines
kruiser [krœysər] *de (~s)* **1** cruiser; **2** cabin cruiser
kruisigen [krœysəyə(n)] *vb* crucify
kruisiging [krœysəyɪŋ] *de (~en)* crucifixion
kruising [krœysɪŋ] *de (~en)* **1** crossing, junction, intersection, crossroads; **2** crossing, hybridization, cross-fertilization; **3** cross, hybrid, cross-breed
kruisje [krœyʃə] *het (~s)* **1** cross, mark; **2** sign of the cross
kruiskopschroef [krœyskɔpsχruf] *de (-schroeven)* cross-head screw
kruispunt [krœyspʏnt] *het (~en)* crossing, junction, intersection, crossroad(s)
kruisraket [krœysrakɛt] *de (~ten)* cruise missile
kruisridder [krœysrɪdər] *de (~s)* crusader
kruisteken [krœystekə(n)] *het (~s)* (sign of the) cross
kruistocht [krœystɔχt] *de (~en)* crusade
kruisvaarder [krœysfardər] *de (~s)* crusader
kruisvereniging [krœysfərenəyɪŋ] *de (~en)* (roughly) home nursing service
kruiswoordpuzzel [krœyswortpʏzəl] *de (~s)* crossword (puzzle)
kruit [krœyt] *het* (gun)powder
kruitvat [krœytfat] *het (~en)* powder keg
kruiwagen [krœywaɣə(n)] *de (~s)* **1** (wheel)barrow; **2** *(fig)* connections: *~s gebruiken* pull strings
kruk [krʏk] *de* **1** stool; **2** crutch; **3** (door) handle
krul [krʏl] *de (~len)* curl; ringlet
krullen [krʏlə(n)] *vb* curl
krulspeld [krʏlspɛlt] *de (~en)* curler, roller
krultang [krʏltaŋ] *de (~en)* curling iron
kso [kaɛso] *het (Belg) kunstsecundair onderwijs* secondary fine arts education
kubiek [kybik] *adj* cubic
kubus [kybʏs] *de (~sen)* cube
kuchen [kʏχə(n)] *vb* cough
kudde [kʏdə] *de (~s)* herd; flock
kuieren [kœyərə(n)] *vb* stroll; go for a walk
kuif [kœyf] *de (kuiven)* **1** forelock, quiff; **2** (head of) hair; **3** crest, tuft
kuiken [kœykə(n)] *het (~s)* chick(en)
kuil [kœyl] *de (~en)* pit, hole, hollow, pothole
kuiltje [kœylcə] *het (~s)* dimple, cleft
kuip [kœyp] *de (~en)* tub, barrel
kuipje [kœypjə] *het (~s)* tub
¹kuis [kœys] *adj, adv* chaste, pure
²kuis [kœys] *de (kuizen) (Belg)* (house)cleaning: *grote ~* spring-cleaning
kuisen [kœysə(n)] *vb (Belg)* clean
kuisheid [kœysheit] *de* chastity, purity
kuisvrouw [kœysfrau] *de (~en) (Belg)* cleaning lady *(or:* woman)
kuit [kœyt] *de (~en)* **1** *(anatomy)* calf; **2** spawn
kukeleku [kykələky] *int* cock-a-doodle-doo
kul [kʏl] *de (~len)* rubbish
kunde [kʏndə] *de* knowledge, learning
kundig [kʏndəχ] *adj, adv* able, capable, skilful: *iets*

~ repareren repair sth skilfully
¹kunnen [kʏnə(n)] *vb* can, could, be able to; be possible: *hij kan goed zingen* he's a good singer; *een handige man kan alles* a handy man can do anything; *hij liep wat hij kon* he ran as fast as he could; *hij kan niet meer* he can't go on; *buiten iets ~* do without sth; *het deksel kan er niet af* the lid won't come off; *morgen kan ik niet* tomorrow's impossible for me
²kunnen [kʏnə(n)] *vb* may, might, could, it is possible that ...: *het kan een vergissing zijn* it may be a mistake
³kunnen [kʏnə(n)] *vb* can, be allowed to, may, could, be allowed to, might: *zoiets kun je niet doen* you can't do that sort of thing; *je had het me wel ~ vertellen* you might *(or:* could) have told me; *de gevangene kon ontsnappen* the prisoner was able to *(or:* managed to) escape
⁴kunnen [kʏnə(n)] *vb* be acceptable: *zo kan het niet langer* it *(or:* things) can't go on like this; *die trui kán gewoon niet* that sweater's just impossible
kunst [kʏnst] *de (~en)* **1** art: *een handelaar in ~* an art dealer; **2** art, skill: *zwarte ~* black magic; **3** trick
kunstacademie [kʏnstakademi] *de (~s)* art academy
kunstarm [kʏnstarm] *de (~en)* artificial arm
kunstbloem [kʏnstblum] *de (~en)* artificial flower
kunstenaar [kʏnstənar] *de (~s)* artist
kunstgalerij [kʏns(t)χalərɛi] *de (~en)* (art) gallery
kunstgebit [kʏnstχəbit] *het (~ten)* (set of) false teeth, (set of) dentures, (dental) plate
kunstgeschiedenis [kʏnstχəsχidənɪs] *de (~sen)* history of art, *(subject)* art history
kunstgreep [kʏnstχrep] *de (-grepen)* trick, manoeuvre
kunsthandelaar [kʏnsthandəlar] *de (~s, -handelaren)* art dealer
kunstig [kʏnstəχ] *adj, adv* ingenious, skilful
kunstijs [kʏnstɛis] *het* artificial ice, man-made ice, (ice) rink
kunstijsbaan [kʏnstɛizban] *de (-banen)* ice rink, skating rink
kunstje [kʏnʃə] *het (~s)* **1** knack, trick: *dat is een koud ~* that's child's play, there's nothing to it; **2** trick: *geen ~s!* none of your tricks!
kunstleer [kʏnstler] *het* imitation leather
kunstlicht [kʏnstlɪχt] *het* artificial light
kunstliefhebber [kʏnstlifhebər] *de* art lover
kunstmatig [kʏnstmatəχ] *adj, adv* artificial, synthetic, man-made, imitation
kunstmest [kʏnstmɛst] *de* fertilizer
kunstschaatsen [kʏn(st)sχatsə(n)] *het* figure-skating
kunstschilder [kʏnstsχɪldər] *de (~s)* artist, painter
kunststof [kʏnstɔf] *de (~fen)* synthetic (material, fibre), plastic: *van ~* synthetic, plastic
kunststuk [kʏnstʏk] *het (~ken)* work of art, feat, stunt: *een journalistiek ~je* a masterpiece of journalism; *dat is een ~ dat ik je niet na zou doen* that's

a feat I couldn't match

kunstuitleen [kʏnstœytlen] *de (-lenen)* art library, art-lending centre

kunstverzamelaar [kʏnstfərzaməlar] *de (~s)* art collector

kunstvezel [kʏnstfezəl] *de (~s)* man-made fibre, synthetic fibre

kunstvorm [kʏnstfɔrm] *de (~en)* art form, medium (of art)

kunstwerk [kʏnstwɛrk] *het (~en)* work of art, masterpiece: *dat is een klein ~je* it's a little gem (*or:* masterpiece)

kunstzinnig [kʏnstsɪnəχ] *adj* artistic(ally-minded): *~e vorming* art(istic) training (*or:* education)

kunstzwemmen [kʏnstswɛmə(n)] *vb* synchronized swimming

¹kuren [kʏrə(n)] *de* quirks, moods: *hij heeft altijd van die vreemde ~* he's quirky (*or:* moody); *vol ~: a)* moody; *b)* awkward

²kuren [kʏrə(n)] *vb* take a cure

¹kurk [kʏrk] *de* cork: *doe de ~ goed op de fles* cork the bottle properly

²kurk [kʏrk] *de, het* cork: *wij hebben ~ in de gang* we've got cork flooring in the hall

kurkdroog [kʏrgdroχ] *adj* (as) dry as a bone, bone-dry

kurken [kʏrkə(n)] *adj* cork: *met ~ zolen* cork-soled

kurkentrekker [kʏrkə(n)trɛkər] *de (~s)* corkscrew

kus [kʏs] *de (~sen)* kiss: *geef me eens een ~* give me a kiss, how about a kiss?; *een ~ krijgen van iem* get a kiss from (*or:* be kissed by) s.o.; *iem een ~ toewerpen* blow s.o. a kiss; *~jes!* (lots of) love (and kisses)

kushandje [kʏshɑncə] *het (~s)* a blown kiss: *~s geven* blow kisses (to s.o.)

¹kussen [kʏsə(n)] *het (~s)* cushion, pillow; pad: *de ~s (op)schudden* plump up the pillows

²kussen [kʏsə(n)] *vb* kiss: *iem gedag (vaarwel) ~* kiss s.o. goodbye; *elkaar ~* kiss (each other)

kussensloop [kʏsə(n)slop] *het, de (-slopen)* pillowcase, pillowslip

kust [kʏst] *de (~en)* **1** coast, (sea)shore: *de ~ is veilig* the coast is clear; *een huisje aan de ~* a cottage by the sea; *onder (voor) de ~* off the coast, offshore, inshore; *vijftig kilometer uit de ~* fifty kilometres offshore (*or:* off the coast); **2** seaside

kustgebied [kʏstχəbit] *het (~en)* coastal area (*or:* region)

kustlijn [kʏstlɛin] *de (~en)* coastline, shoreline

kustplaats [kʏstplats] *de (~en)* seaside town, coastal town

kustvaarder [kʏstfardər] *de (~s)* coaster

kut [kʏt] *de (~ten)* cunt

kuub [kyp] *de* cubic metre: *te koop voor een tientje de ~* on sale for ten euros a cubic metre

kuur [kyr] *de (kuren)* cure, course of treatment

kuuroord [kyrort] *het (~en)* health resort; spa

¹kwaad [kwat] *adj, adv* **1** bad, wrong: *het te ~ krijgen* be overcome (by), break down; **2** bad, evil: *ze bedoelde er niets ~s mee* she meant no harm (*or:* of-fence); **3** angry: *zich ~ maken, ~ worden* get angry; *iem ~ maken* make s.o. angry; *~ zijn op iem* be angry at (*or:* with) s.o.; *~ zijn om iets* be angry at (*or:* about) sth

²kwaad [kwat] *adj* bad, vicious: *hij is de ~ste niet* he's not a bad guy

³kwaad [kwat] *het (kwaden)* **1** wrong, harm: *een noodzakelijk ~* a necessary evil; *van ~ tot erger ver-vallen* go from bad to worse; **2** harm, damage: *meer ~ dan goed doen* do more harm than good; *dat kan geen ~* it can't do any harm

kwaadaardig [kwatardəχ] *adj, adv* **1** malicious, vicious; **2** pernicious, malignant

kwaadheid [kwathɛit] *de* anger: *rood worden van ~* turn red with anger (*or:* fury)

kwaadschiks [kwatsχɪks] *adv* unwillingly

kwaadspreken [kwatsprekə(n)] *vb* speak ill (*or:* badly): *~ van (iem)* speak ill (*or:* badly) of (s.o.), slander (s.o.)

kwaadwillig [kwatwɪləχ] *adj* malevolent

kwaal [kwal] *de (kwalen)* **1** complaint, disease, illness: *een hartkwaal* a heart condition; **2** trouble, problem

kwab [kwɑp] *de (~ben)* (roll of) fat (*or:* flab), jowl

kwadraat [kwɑdrat] *het (kwadraten)* square: *drie ~* three squared

kwajongen [kwajɔŋə(n)] *de (~s)* **1** mischievous boy, naughty boy, brat; **2** rascal

kwajongensachtig [kwajɔŋənsɑχtəχ] *adj, adv* boyish, mischievous

kwajongensstreek [kwajɔŋə(n)strek] *de (-stre-ken)* (boyish) prank, practical joke: *een ~ uithalen* play a practical joke

kwak [kwɑk] *de (~ken)* **1** dab; blob; dollop: *een ~ eten* a dollop of food; **2** thud, thump, smack

kwaken [kwakə(n)] *vb* quack, croak

kwakkel [kwɑkəl] *de (~s) (Belg)* canard, unfounded rumour (*or:* story)

kwakkelen [kwɑkələ(n)] *vb* drag on, linger; be fitful

kwakkelweer [kwɑkəlwer] *het* unsteady weather, changeable weather

¹kwakken [kwɑkə(n)] *vb* bump, crash, fall with a thud: *hij kwakte tegen de grond* he landed with a thud on the floor

²kwakken [kwɑkə(n)] *vb* dump, chuck, dab: *zij kwakte haar tas op het bureau* she smacked her bag down on the desk

kwakzalver [kwɑksɑlvər] *de (~s)* quack (doctor)

kwakzalverij [kwɑksɑlvərɛi] *de* quackery

kwal [kwɑl] *de (~len)* **1** jellyfish; **2** jerk

kwalificatie [kwalifika(t)si] *de (~s)* qualification(s)

kwalificatieronde [kwalifika(t)sirɔndə] *de (~n, ~s)* qualifying round

kwalificatiewedstrijd [kwalifika(t)siwɛtstrɛit] *de (~en)* qualifying match

¹kwalificeren [kwalifisɛrə(n)] *vb* **1** call, describe as; **2** qualify

²kwalificeren [kwalifisɛrə(n)] *ref vb* qualify (for)

kwalijk [kwaːlək] *adj, adv* evil, vile, nasty, *(adverb)* vilely, nastily, badly: *de ~e gevolgen van het roken* the bad *(or:* detrimental) effects of smoking; *dat is een ~e zaak* that is a nasty business; *neem me niet ~, dat ik te laat ben* excuse my being late, excuse me for being late; *neem(t) (u) mij niet ~* I beg your pardon; *je kunt hem dat toch niet ~ nemen* you can hardly blame him

kwalitatief [kwaːlitatif] *adj, adv* qualitative: *~ was het verschil groot* there was a large difference in quality

kwaliteit [kwaːlitɛit] *de (~en)* **1** quality: *hout van slechte ~* low-quality wood; *van slechte ~ (of)* poor quality; **2** characteristic

kwaliteitscontrole [kwaːlitɛitskɔntroːlə] *de (~s)* quality control

kwaliteitseisen [kwaːlitɛitsɛisə(n)] *de* quality requirements *(or:* standards), requirements as to quality, specifications

kwaliteitsproduct [kwaːlitɛitsprodʏkt] *het* (high-)quality product

kwantificeren [kwɑntifisɛrə(n)] *vb* quantify

kwantitatief [kwɑntitatif] *adj, adv* quantitative

kwantiteit [kwɑntitɛit] *de (~en)* quantity, amount

kwantumkorting [kwɑntʏmkɔrtɪŋ] *de (~en)* quantity rebate

kwark [kwɑrk] *de* fromage frais, curd cheese

kwarktaart [kwɑrktaːrt] *de (~en) (roughly)* cheesecake

kwart [kwɑrt] *het (~en)* quarter: *voor een ~ leeg* a quarter empty; *het is ~ voor (or:* over) elf* it is a quarter to *(or:* past) eleven, it is ten forty-five *(or:* eleven fifteen)

kwartaal [kwɑrtaːl] *het (kwartalen)* quarter, trimester, *(educ)* term: *(eenmaal) per ~* quarterly

kwartel [kwɑrtəl] *de (~s)* quail: *zo doof als een ~* as deaf as a post

kwartet [kwɑrtɛt] *het (~ten)* quartet: *een ~ voor strijkers* a string quartet

kwartetspel [kwɑrtɛtspɛl] *het (~en)* happy families, *(Am)* old maid

kwartetten [kwɑrtɛtə(n)] *vb* play happy families *(or Am:* old maid)

kwartfinale [kwɑrtfinaːlə] *de (~s)* quarter-finals: *de ~(s) halen* make the quarter-finals

kwartfinalist [kwɑrtfinaːlɪst] *de* quarter-finalist

kwartier [kwɑrtiːr] *het (~en)* quarter (of an hour): *het duurde een ~: a)* it took a quarter of an hour; *b)* it lasted a quarter of an hour; *om het ~* every quarter (of an hour) of an hour; *drie ~* three-quarters of an hour

kwartje [kwɑrcə] *het (~s)* 25-cent piece, *(Am)* quarter: *het kost twee ~s* it costs fifty cents

kwartnoot [kwɑrtnoːt] *de (-noten)* crotchet, *(Am)* quarter note

kwarts [kwɑrts] *het* quartz

kwartshorloge [kwɑrtshɔrloːʒə] *het (~s)* quartz watch

kwast [kwɑst] *de (~en)* **1** brush; **2** tassel, *(small)*

tuft: *met ~en (versierd)* tasselled; **3** (lemon) squash, lemonade

kwatong [kwaːtɔŋ] *de (~en) (Belg)* scandalmonger: *~en beweren … it is rumoured that …*

kwatrijn [kwaːtrɛin] *het (~en)* quatrain

kwebbel [kwɛbəl] *de* chatterbox ‖ *houd je ~ dicht* shut your trap

kwebbelen [kwɛbələ(n)] *vb* chatter

kweek [kwek] *de* **1** cultivation, culture, growing; **2** culture, growth

kweekplaats [kwekplaːts] *de (~en)* **1** nursery, *(fig also)* breeding ground; **2** *(fig)* hotbed

kweekvijver [kwekfɛivər] *de (~s)* fish-breeding pond; *(fig)* breeding ground

kweken [kwekə(n)] *vb* **1** grow, cultivate: *gekweekte planten* cultivated plants; *zelf gekweekte tomaten* home-grown tomatoes; **2** raise, breed: *oesters ~ breed* oysters; **3** *(fig)* breed, foster: *goodwill ~ foster* goodwill

kweker [kwekər] *de (~s)* grower, (market) gardener, nurseryman

kwekerij [kwekərɛi] *de (~en)* nursery, market garden

kwelgeest [kwɛlɣest] *de (~en)* tormentor, teaser, pest

kwellen [kwɛlə(n)] *vb* **1** hurt, *(stronger)* torment, torture; **2** torment: *gekweld worden door geldgebrek* be troubled by lack of money; *een ~de pijn* an excruciating pain; **3** trouble, worry: *die gedachte bleef hem ~* the thought kept troubling him; *gekweld door wroeging (or: een obsessie)* haunted by remorse *(or:* by an obsession)

kwelling [kwɛlɪŋ] *de (~en)* **1** torture, torment; **2** torment, agony: *een brief schrijven is een ware ~ voor hem* writing a letter is sheer torment for him

kwestie [kwɛsti] *de (~s)* question, matter, issue: *een slepende ~* a matter that drags on; *de persoon (or: de zaak) in ~* the person *(or:* matter) in question; *een ~ van smaak* a question *(or:* matter) of taste; *een ~ van vertrouwen* a matter of confidence

kwetsbaar [kwɛtsbaːr] *adj* vulnerable: *dit is zijn kwetsbare plek (or: zijde)* this is his vulnerable spot *(or:* side)

kwetsbaarheid [kwɛtsbaːrhɛit] *de* vulnerability

kwetsen [kwɛtsə(n)] *vb* injure, wound, hurt, bruise: *iemands gevoelens ~* hurt s.o.'s feelings; *gekwetste trots* wounded pride

kwetsuur [kwɛtsyr] *de (kwetsuren)* injury

kwetteren [kwɛtərə(n)] *vb* twitter

kwiek [kwik] *adj, adv* alert, spry

kwijl [kwɛil] *het, de* slobber

kwijlen [kwɛilə(n)] *vb* slobber: *om van te ~* mouth-watering

kwijt [kwɛit] *adj* **1** lost: *ik ben mijn sleutels ~* I have lost my keys; *zijn verstand ~ zijn* have lost one's mind; **2** rid (of): *ik ben mijn kiespijn ~* my toothache is gone *(or:* over); *hij is al die zorgen ~* he is rid of all those troubles; *die zijn we gelukkig ~* we are well rid of him, good riddance to him; **3** deprived

(of): *ik ben zijn naam* ~ I've forgotten his name;
(fig) nu ben ik het ~ it has slipped my memory; *de
weg* ~ *zijn* be lost, have lost one's way; *ik kan mijn
auto nergens* ~ I can't park my car anywhere

kwijtraken [kwɛitrakə(n)] *vb* **1** lose: *zijn evenwicht
~ (also fig)* lose one's balance (*or:* composure); *de
weg* ~ lose one's way; **2** dispose of, sell: *die zul je
makkelijk* ~ you will easily dispose (*or:* get rid) of
those

kwijtschelden [kwɛitsχɛldə(n)] *vb* forgive, let off:
hij heeft mij de rest kwijtgescholden he has let me off
the rest; *van zijn straf is (hem) 2 jaar kwijtgescholden* he had 2 years of his punishment remitted; *iem
een straf* ~ let s.o. off a punishment

kwijtschelding [kwɛitsχɛldɪŋ] *de (~en)* pardon;
absolution: ~ *van straf krijgen* be pardoned

kwik [kwɪk] *het* mercury: *het* ~ *stijgt* (or: *daalt)* the
thermometer is rising (*or:* falling)

kwikzilver [kwɪksɪlvər] *het* mercury

kwinkslag [kwɪŋslɑχ] *de (~en)* witticism

kwintet [kwɪntɛt] *het (~ten)* quintet

kwispelen [kwɪspələ(n)] *vb* wag: *met de staart* ~
wag one's tail

kwistig [kwɪstəχ] *adj, adv* lavish

kwitantie [kwitɑnsi] *de (~s)* receipt ‖ *een* ~ *innen*
collect payment

l

¹**la** [la] *de* (~'s) drawer, till: *de ~ uittrekken* (or: *dicht-schuiven*) open (or: shut) a drawer

²**la** [la] *de* (~'s) *(mus)* la

laadbak [ládbɑk] *de* (~ken) (loading) platform

laadklep [látklɛp] *de* (~pen) tailboard

laadruim [látrœym] *het* (~en) cargo hold, cargo compartment, freight compartment

laadvermogen [látfərmoɣə(n)] *het* carrying capacity

¹**laag** [laɣ] *de* (lagen) **1** layer, coating, film, sheet, coat; **2** stratum: *in brede lagen van de bevolking* in large sections of the population; *de volle ~ krijgen* get the full blast (of s.o.'s disapproval)

²**laag** [laɣ] *adj, adv* **1** low: *een laag bedrag* a small amount; *het gas ~ draaien* turn the gas down; *de barometer staat ~* the barometer is low; **2** low, mean

laag-bij-de-gronds [laɣbɛidəɣrɔnts] *adj, adv* commonplace: *~e opmerkingen* crude remarks

laagseizoen [laɣsɛizun] *het* (~en) low season, off season

laagte [láɣtə] *de* (~n, ~s) depression, hollow

laagvlakte [láɣflɑktə] *de* (~n, ~s) lowland plain, lowland(s)

laagwater [láɣwatər] *het* low tide

laaien [lájə(n)] *vb* blaze

laaiend [lájənt] *adj, adv* **1** wild; **2** furious

laan [lan] *de* (lanen) avenue: *iem de ~ uitsturen* sack s.o., fire s.o., send s.o. packing

laars [lars] *de* (laarzen) boot

laat [lat] *adj, adv* late: *van de vroege morgen tot de late avond* from early in the morning till late at night; *een wat late reactie* a rather belated reaction; *is het nog ~ geworden gisteravond?* did the people stay late last night?; *~ opblijven* stay up late; *gisteravond ~ late last night*; *hoe ~ is het?* what's the time?, what time is it?; *'s avonds ~ late at night*; *te ~ komen (op school, op kantoor, op je werk)* be late (for school, at the office, for work); *een dag te ~ a* day late (or: overdue); *~ in de middag* (or: *het voorjaar*) in the late afternoon (or: spring); *beter ~ dan nooit* better late than never

laatkomer [látkomər] *de* (~s) latecomer

¹**laatst** [latst] *adj* **1** last: *dat zou het ~e zijn wat ik zou doen* that is the last thing I would do; **2** latest, last: *in de ~e jaren* in the last few years, in recent years; *de ~e tijd* recently, lately; **3** final, last: *voor de ~e*

keer optreden make one's last (or: final) appearance; **4** latter: *in de ~e helft van juli* in the latter (or: second) half of July; *ik heb voorkeur voor de ~e* I prefer the latter

²**laatst** [latst] *adv* **1** recently, lately: *ik ben ~ nog bij hem geweest* I visited him recently; **2** last: *morgen op zijn ~* tomorrow at the latest; *op het ~ waren ze allemaal dronken* they all ended up drunk; *voor het ~* for the last time; *toen zag hij haar voor het ~* that was the last time he saw her

laatstgenoemde [latstχənumdə] *de* last (named, mentioned), latter

laattijdig [latɛidəχ] *adj, adv (Belg)* tardy, tardily

lab [lɑp] *het* (~s) lab

label [lébəl] *het, de* (~s) label, sticker, address tag

labelen [lébələ(n)] *vb* label

labeur [labør] *het (Belg)* labour, chore

labeuren [labørə(n)] *vb (Belg)* slave away, toil

labiel [labil] *adj* unstable

labo [lábo] *het* (~'s) *(Belg)* lab

laborant [laborɑnt] *de* (~en) laboratory assistant (or: technician)

laboratorium [laboratórijʏm] *het (laboratoria)* lab(oratory)

labrador [lábrador] *de* labrador

labyrint [labirɪnt] *het* (~en) labyrinth

lach [lɑχ] *de* laugh, (burst of) laughter: *de slappe ~ hebben* have the giggles; *in de ~ schieten* burst out laughing, *(Am also)* crack up

lachbui [lɑχbœy] *de* (~en) fit of laughter

lachen [lɑχə(n)] *vb* **1** laugh; smile: *hij kon zijn ~ niet houden* he couldn't help laughing; *laat me niet ~* don't make me laugh; *er is (valt) niets te ~* this is no laughing matter; *om* (or: *over*) *iets ~* laugh about (or: at); *tegen iem ~* laugh at s.o.; *wie het laatst lacht, lacht het best* he who laughs last laughs longest; **2** (with *om*) laugh at: *daar kun je nu wel om ~, maar …* it's all very well to laugh, but …

lachend [lɑχənt] *adj* laughing, smiling

lacherig [lɑχərəχ] *adj* giggly

lachertje [lɑχərcə] *het* (~s) laugh, joke

lachfilm [lɑχfɪlm] *de* (~s) comedy

lachsalvo [lɑχsɑlvo] *het* (~'s) burst of laughter

lachspiegel [lɑχspiɣəl] *de* (~s) carnival mirror

lachwekkend [lɑχwɛkənt] *adj* laughable, ridiculous

laconiek [lakonik] *adj, adv* laconic

ladder [lɑdər] *de* (~s) ladder; scale ‖ *een ~ in je kous* a run (or: ladder) in your stocking

ladekast [ládəkɑst] *de* (~en) chest (of drawers), filing cabinet

laden [ládə(n)] *vb* **1** load: *koffers uit de auto ~* unload the bags from the car; **2** charge: *een geladen atmosfeer* a charged atmosphere

lading [ládɪŋ] *de* (~en) **1** cargo, *(ship)* load: *te zware ~* overload; **2** charge

laf [lɑf] *adj, adv* cowardly

lafaard [lɑfart] *de* (~s) coward

lafheid [lɑfhɛit] *de* (-heden) cowardice

lagedrukgebied [laɣədrykχəbit] *het (~en)* low-pressure area

lager [laɣər] *het (~s)* bearing

lagerbier [laɣərbir] *het (~en)* lager (beer)

Lagerhuis [laɣərhœys] *het* Lower House, *(Great Britain and Canada)* House of Commons

lagerwal [laχərwɑl] *de* lee shore: *aan ~ geraken* come down in the world

lagune [laɣynə] *de (~s)* lagoon

lak [lɑk] *het, de (~ken)* lacquer, varnish, polish: *de ~ is beschadigd* the paintwork is damaged

lakei [lakɛi] *de (~en)* lackey

laken [lakə(n)] *het (~s)* 1 sheet, tablecloth: *de ~s uitdelen* rule the roost, run the show; 2 cloth, worsted: *het ~ van een biljart* the cloth of a billiard table; *van hetzelfde ~ een pak krijgen, (Belg) van hetzelfde ~ een broek krijgen* have a taste of one's own medicine

lakken [lɑkə(n)] *vb* 1 lacquer, varnish, polish; 2 paint, enamel

laklaag [lɑklaχ] *de (laklagen)* (layer of) lacquer (*or:* varnish, enamel)

laks [lɑks] *adj, adv* lax

lakwerk [lɑkwɛrk] *het* paint(work)

¹lam [lɑm] *het (~meren)* lamb

²lam [lɑm] *adj, adv* 1 paralysed, *(fig also)* out of action; 2 numb

lama [lama] *de (~'s)* llama

lambrisering [lɑmbrizerɪŋ] *de (~en)* wainscot(t)ing, panelling

lamel [lamɛl] *de (~len)* plate, (laminated) layer, strip

laminaat [laminat] *het (laminaten)* laminate

lamlendig [lɑmlɛndəχ] *adj, adv* shiftless

lamp [lɑmp] *de (~en)* lamp; light; bulb: *er gaat een ~je bij mij branden* that rings a bell; *tegen de ~ lopen* get caught

lampion [lɑmpijɔn] *de (~s, ~nen)* Chinese lantern

lamsbout [lɑmzbɑut] *de (~en)* leg of lamb

lamskarbonade [lɑmskarbonadə] *de* lamb chop

lamswol [lɑmswɔl] *de* lambswool

lanceerbasis [lɑnserbazɪs] *de (-bases)* launch site, launch pad

lanceren [lɑnserə(n)] *vb* launch; blast, lift off: *een bericht (or: een gerucht) ~ spread a report (or: a rumour)*

lancering [lɑnserɪŋ] *de (~en)* launch(ing); blast-off, lift-off

lancet [lɑnsɛt] *het (~ten)* lancet

land [lɑnt] *het (~en)* 1 land: *aan ~ gaan* go ashore; *te ~ en ter zee* on land and sea; *~ in zicht!* land ho!; 2 country: *~ van herkomst* country of origin; *in ons ~* in this country

landaanwinning [lɑntanwɪnɪŋ] *de (~en)* land reclamation

landarbeider [lɑntɑrbɛidər] *de (~s)* farm worker, agricultural worker

landbouw [lɑndbɑu] *de* farming: *~ en veeteelt: a)* arable farming and stockbreeding; *b)* arable and dairy farming

landbouwbedrijf [lɑndbɑubədrɛif] *het (-bedrijven)* farm

landbouwer [lɑndbɑuwər] *de (~s)* farmer

landbouwgrond [lɑndbɑuɣrɔnt] *de (~en)* agricultural land, farming land, farmland

landbouwhogeschool [lɑndbɑuhoɣəsχol] *de (-scholen)* agricultural university; *(as a name)* University of Agriculture

landbouwkundig [lɑndbɑukyndəχ] *adj* agricultural

landbouwmachine [lɑndbɑumaʃinə] *de (~s)* agricultural machine, farming machine

landeigenaar [lɑntɛiɣənar] *de (~s, -eigenaren)* landowner

landelijk [lɑndələk] *adj, adv* 1 national; 2 rural, country

landen [lɑndə(n)] *vb* land: *~ op Zaventem* land at Zaventem

landengte [lɑndɛŋtə] *de (~n, ~s)* isthmus, neck of land

landenwedstrijd [lɑndə(n)wɛtstreit] *de (~en)* international match (*or:* contest)

landerig [lɑndərəχ] *adj* down in the dumps, listless

landerijen [lɑndərɛiə(n)] *de* (farm)land(s)

landgenoot [lɑntχənot] *de (-genoten)* (fellow) countryman

landgoed [lɑntχut] *het (~eren)* country estate

landhuis [lɑnthœys] *het (-huizen)* country house

landing [lɑndɪŋ] *de (~en)* landing: *een zachte ~* a smooth landing

landingsbaan [lɑndɪŋzban] *de (-banen)* runway

landingsgestel [lɑndɪŋsχəstɛl] *het (~len)* landing gear; undercart

landinwaarts [lɑntɪnwarts] *adv* inland

landkaart [lɑntkart] *de (~en)* map

landklimaat [lɑntklimat] *het* continental climate

landloper [lɑntlopər] *de (~s)* tramp, vagrant

landmacht [lɑntmaχt] *de* army, land forces

landmijn [lɑntmɛin] *de (~en)* landmine

landschap [lɑntsχap] *het (~pen)* landscape

landsverdediging [lɑntsfərdedəɣɪŋ] *de (Belg)* defence

landtong [lɑntɔŋ] *de (~en)* spit of land, headland

landverraad [lɑntfərat] *het* (high) treason

landweg [lɑntwɛχ] *de (~en)* country road lane; (country) track

¹lang [lɑŋ] *adj* long; tall: *de kamer is zes meter ~* the room is six metres long; *een ~e vent* a tall guy

²lang [lɑŋ] *adv* 1 long, (for) a long time: *ik blijf geen dag ~er* I won't stay another day, I won't stay a day longer; *~ duren* take a long time, last long (*or:* a long time); *ze leefden ~ en gelukkig* they lived happily ever after; *~ zal hij leven!* for he's a jolly good fellow!; *~ meegaan* last (a long time); *~ opblijven* stay up late; *ze kan niet ~er wachten* she can't wait any longer (*or:* more); 2 far (from), (not) nearly: *dat smaakt ~ niet slecht* it doesn't taste at all bad; *hij is nog ~ niet zo ver* he hasn't got nearly as far as that; *wij zijn er nog ~ niet* we've (still got) a long way to go

langdradig [lɑŋdrɑdəχ] *adj, adv* long-winded

langdurig [lɑŋdyrəχ] *adj, adv* long(-lasting), lengthy; long-standing, long-established

langeafstandsloper [lɑŋəɑfstɑntslopər] *de (~s)* long-distance runner

langgerekt [lɑŋɣərɛkt] *adj* long-drawn-out, elongated

langlaufen [lɑŋlaufə(n)] *vb* ski cross-country

langlopend [lɑŋlopənt] *adj* long-term

¹**langs** [lɑŋs] *prep* **1** along: *~ de rivier wandelen* go for a walk along the river; **2** via, by (way, means of): *~ de regenpijp naar omlaag* down the drainpipe; *hier* (or: *daar*) *~* this (or: that) way; **3** past: *~ elkaar heen praten* talk at cross purposes; **4** in at: *wil jij even ~ de bakker rijden?* could you just drop in at the bakery?

²**langs** [lɑŋs] *adv* **1** along: *in een boot de kust ~ varen* sail along the coast, skirt the coast; **2** round, in, by: *ik kom nog wel eens ~* I'll drop in (or: round, by) sometime; **3** past: *hij kwam net ~* he just came past

langsgaan [lɑŋsχan] *vb* **1** pass (by); **2** call in (at)

langskomen [lɑŋskomə(n)] *vb* **1** come past, come by, pass by; **2** come round (or: over), drop by, drop in

langsrijden [lɑŋsrɛidə(n)] *vb* ride past; drive past

langstlevende [lɑŋstlevəndə] *de (~n)* survivor

langszij [lɑŋsɛi] *adv* alongside

languit [lɑŋœyt] *adv* (at) full-length, stretched out

langverwacht [lɑŋvərwɑχt] *adj* long-awaited

langwerpig [lɑŋwɛrpəχ] *adj, adv* elongated, long

langzaam [lɑŋzam] *adj, adv* **1** slow: *een langzame dood sterven* die a slow (or: lingering) death; *~ aan!* slow down!, (take it) easy!; *het ~ aan doen* take things eas(il)y; *~ maar zeker* slowly but surely; **2** gradual, bit by bit, little by little: *~ werd hij wat beter* he gradually got a bit better

langzamerhand [lɑŋzamərhɑnt] *adv* gradually, bit by bit, little by little: *ik krijg er ~ genoeg van* I'm beginning to get tired of it

lans [lɑns] *de (~en)* lance

lantaarn [lɑntarn] *de (~s)* **1** street lamp, street light; **2** lantern; torch; *(Am)* flashlight

lantaarnpaal [lɑntarnpal] *de (-palen)* lamp post

lanterfanten [lɑntərfɑntə(n)] *vb* lounge (about), loaf (about), sit about (or: around)

lap [lɑp] *de (~pen)* piece, length, rag

Lap [lɑp] *de (~pen)* Lapp

lapjeskat [lɑpjəskɑt] *de (~ten)* tabby-and-white cat, *(Am)* calico cat

Lapland [lɑplɑnt] *het* Lapland

Laplander [lɑplɑndər] *de (~s)* Lapp, Laplander

lapmiddel [lɑpmɪdəl] *het (~en)* makeshift (measure), stopgap

lapnaam [lɑpnam] *de (lapnamen) (Belg)* nickname

lappen [lɑpə(n)] *vb* patch, mend, cobble ‖ *ramen ~* cobble the windows; *dat zou jij mij niet moeten ~* don't try that (one) on me; *iem erbij ~* blow the

whistle on s.o.

lappendeken [lɑpə(n)dekə(n)] *de (~s)* patchwork quilt

lariekoek [larikuk] *de* (stuff and) nonsense, rubbish

¹**lariks** [lariks] *de (~en) (tree)* larch

²**lariks** [lariks] *het (wood)* larch

larve [lɑrvə] *de (~n)* larva

las [lɑs] *de (~sen)* weld, joint; *(film)* splice

lasapparaat [lɑsaparat] *het (lasapparaten)* welding apparatus, welder, *(film)* splicer

lasbril [lɑzbril] *de (~len)* welding goggles

laserstraal [lezərstral] *de (-stralen)* laser beam

¹**lassen** [lɑsə(n)] *vb* weld; join; *(film)* splice

²**lassen** [lɑsə(n)] *vb* put in, *(also fig)* insert

lasser [lɑsər] *de (~s)* welder

lasso [lɑso] *de (~'s)* lasso

last [lɑst] *de (~en)* **1** load, burden: *hij bezweek haast onder de ~* he nearly collapsed under the burden; **2** cost(s), expense(s): *sociale ~en* National Insurance contributions, *(Am)* social security premiums; **3** trouble, inconvenience: *iem tot ~ zijn* bother s.o.; *wij hebben veel ~ van onze buren* our neighbours are a great nuisance to us; **4** charge

laster [lɑstər] *de* slander; libel

lastercampagne [lɑstərkɑmpɑɲə] *de (~s)* smear campaign

lasteren [lɑstərə(n)] *vb* slander; libel

lastig [lɑstəχ] *adj, adv* difficult: *een ~ vraagstuk* a tricky problem; *iem ~ vallen* bother (or: trouble) s.o., harass s.o.

lastpost [lɑstpɔst] *de (~en)* nuisance, pest

lat [lɑt] *de (~ten)* slat: *de bal kwam tegen de ~* the ball hit the crossbar; *zo mager als een ~* (as) thin as a rake

¹**laten** [latə(n)] *vb* **1** omit, keep from: *laat dat!* stop that!; *hij kan het niet ~* he can't help (doing) it; *laat maar!* never mind!; **2** leave, let: *waar heb ik dat potlood gelaten?* where did I leave (or: put) that pencil?; *iem ~ halen: a)* send for s.o.; *b)* have s.o. fetched; *daar zullen we het bij ~!* let's leave it at that!; **3** put: *waar moet ik het boek ~?* where shall I put (or: leave) the book?; **4** show (into), let (into): *hij werd in de kamer gelaten* he was shown into the room; **5** let, allow: *laat de kinderen maar* just let the kids do

²**laten** [latə(n)] *vb* let: *~ we niet vergeten, dat ...* don't let us forget that ...

latent [latɛnt] *adj, adv* latent

¹**later** [latər] *adv* later (on), afterwards, presently: *enige tijd ~* after some time (or: a while), a little later (on); *even ~* soon after, presently; *niet ~ dan twee uur* no later than two o'clock; *~ op de dag* later that (same) day, later in the day

²**later** [latər] *adj* later, subsequent, future: *op ~e leeftijd* at an advanced age, late in life

Latijn [latɛin] *het* Latin

Latijns-Amerika [latɛinsamerika] *het* Latin America

Latijns-Amerikaans [latɛinsamerikans] *adj*

Latin-American

laurier [lɑurir] *de (~en)* **1** laurel; **2** bay *(culinary)*

lauw [lɑu] *adj, adv* lukewarm

lauweren [lɑuwərə(n)] *de* laurels: *op zijn ~ rusten* rest on one's laurels

lava [lava] *de (~'s)* lava

lavabo [lavabo] *de (~'s) (Belg)* washbasin

laveloos [lavəlos] *adj* sloshed, loaded

lavendel [lavɛndəl] *de (~s)* lavender

laveren [lavərə(n)] *vb* tack; *(fig)* steer a middle course

lawaai [lawaj] *het* noise, din, *(stronger)* racket

lawaaierig [lawajərəχ] *adj, adv* noisy

lawine [lawinə] *de (~s)* avalanche, *(fig also)* barrage

laxeermiddel [lɑksermɪdəl] *het (~en)* laxative

lbo [ɛlbeo] *het lager beroepsonderwijs* lower vocational education

leao [leao] *het (~'s) lager economisch en administratief onderwijs* lower economic and administrative education *(or: training)*

leaseauto [li:sauto] *de (~'s)* leased car

leasen [li:sə(n)] *vb* lease

lectuur [lɛktyr] *de* reading (matter)

ledematen [ledəmatə(n)] *de* limbs

ledental [ledə(n)tal] *het (~len)* membership (figure)

lederen [ledərə(n)] *adj* leather

lederwaren [ledərwarə(n)] *de* leather goods *(or: articles)*

ledikant [ledikɑnt] *het (~en)* bed(stead)

leed [let] *het* sorrow, grief

leedvermaak [letfərmak] *het* malicious pleasure

leefbaar [levbar] *adj* liveable, bearable, endurable: *een huis ~ maken* make a house inhabitable

leefgemeenschap [lefχəmensχɑp] *de (~pen)* commune; community

leefmilieu [lefmɪljø] *het (~s)* environment

leeftijd [leftɛit] *de (~en)* age: *Gérard is op een moeilijke ~* Gérard is at an awkward age; *hij bereikte de ~ van 65 jaar* he lived to be 65; *op vijftienjarige ~* at the age of *(or:* aged*)* fifteen; *Eric ziet er jong uit voor zijn ~* Eric looks young for his age; *(Belg) de derde ~* the over sixty-fives

leeftijdgenoot [leftɛitχənot] *de (-genoten)* contemporary, peer

leeftijdsgrens [leftɛitsχrɛns] *de (-grenzen)* age limit

leeftijdsgroep [leftɛitsχrup] *de (~en)* age group

leefwijze [lefwɛizə] *de (~n)* lifestyle, way of life, manner of living

leeg [leχ] *adj* **1** empty, vacant, flat, blank: *een lege accu* a flat battery; *met lege handen vertrekken (fig)* leave empty-handed; **2** idle, empty; **3** *(fig)* empty, hollow

leegeten [leχetə(n)] *vb* finish, empty

leeggoed [leχut] *het (Belg)* empties

leeghalen [leχhalə(n)] *vb* empty; clear out *(bldg)*, turn out; ransack

leeglopen [leχlopə(n)] *vb* (become) empty, become deflated, go flat, run down

leegmaken [leχmakə(n)] *vb* empty, finish, clear: *zijn zakken ~* turn out one's pockets

leegstaan [leχstan] *vb* be empty *(or:* vacant*)*

leegte [leχtə] *de (~s, ~n)* emptiness: *hij liet een grote ~ achter* he left a great void (behind him)

leek [lek] *de (leken)* layman

leem [lem] *het, de* loam

leen [len] *het (lenen)* loan: *iets van iem in (te) ~ hebben* have sth on loan from s.o.

leenheer [lenher] *de (-heren)* liege (lord)

leenman [lemɑn] *de (~nen)* vassal

leenstelsel [lenstɛlsəl] *het (~s)* feudal system

¹**leer** [ler] *het* leather

²**leer** [ler] *de* apprenticeship: *in de ~ zijn (bij)* serve one's apprenticeship (with)

leerboek [lerbuk] *het (~en)* textbook

leergang [lerγɑŋ] *de (~en)* (educational) method, methodology

leerjaar [lerjar] *het (-jaren)* (school) year: *beroepsvoorbereidend ~* vocational training year

leerkracht [lerkrɑχt] *de (~en)* teacher, instructor

leerling [lerlɪŋ] *de (~en)* **1** student, pupil; **2** disciple, follower; **3** apprentice, trainee: *leerling-verpleegster* trainee nurse

leerlooierij [lerlojərɛi] *de (~en)* **1** tanning; **2** tannery

leermeester [lermestər] *de (~s)* master

leermethode [lermetodə] *de* teaching method, training method

leermiddelen [lermɪdələ(n)] *het* educational aids

leerplan [lerplɑn] *het (~nen)* syllabus, curriculum

leerplicht [lerplɪχt] *de* compulsory education

leerplichtig [lerplɪχtəχ] *adj* of school age

leerrijk [lerɛik] *adj* instructive, informative

leerschool [lersχol] *de (-scholen)* school

leerstoel [lerstul] *de (~en)* chair

leerstof [lerstɔf] *de* subject matter, (subject) material

leertje [lercə] *het (~s)* washer

leervak [lervak] *het (~ken)* subject

leerweg [lerwɛχ] *de* study option

leerzaam [lerzam] *adj, adv* instructive, informative: *een leerzame ervaring* a valuable experience

leesbaar [lezbar] *adj, adv* **1** legible; **2** readable

leesbaarheid [lezbarhɛit] *de* **1** legibility; **2** readability

leesblind [lezblɪnt] *adj* dyslexic

leesblindheid [lezblɪnthɛit] *de* dyslexia

leesmoeder [lesmudər] *de (~s)* (parent) volunteer reading teacher

leesportefeuille [lespɔrtəfœyə] *de (~s)* portfolio (with magazines)

leest [lest] *de (~en)* last

leesteken [lestekə(n)] *het (~s)* punctuation mark

leesvaardigheid [lesfardəχhɛit] *de* reading proficiency *(or:* skill*)*

leeszaal [lesal] *de (-zalen)* reading room; public library

leeuw [lew] *de (~en)* lion: *zo sterk als een ~* as strong as an ox

Leeuw [lew] *de (~en) (astrology)* Leo

leeuwendeel [lɛwə(n)del] *het* lion's share

leeuwenkooi [lɛwə(n)koj] *de (~en)* lion's cage

leeuwentemmer [lɛwə(n)tɛmər] *de (~s)* lion-tamer

leeuwerik [lɛwərɪk] *de (~en)* lark

leeuwin [lewɪn] *de (~nen)* lioness

lef [lɛf] *het, de* guts, nerve: *heb het ~ niet om dat te doen* don't you dare do that

legaal [leɣal] *adj, adv* legal

legaliseren [leɣalizərə(n)] *vb* legalize

legbatterij [lɛɣbatərɛi] *de (~en)* battery (cage)

legen [leɣə(n)] *vb* empty

legendarisch [leɣɛndaris] *adj* legendary

legende [ləɣɛndə] *de (~n, ~s)* legend

leger [leɣər] *het (~s)* **1** army; armed forces: *een ~ op de been brengen* raise an army; *in het ~ gaan* join the army; **2** lair

legerbasis [leɣərbazɪs] *de (-bases)* army base

legeren [leɣərə(n)] *vb* **1** encamp; **2** quarter; billet

legergroen [leɣərɣrun] *adj* olive drab (*or:* green)

legering [ləɣerɪŋ] *de* alloy

legerkamp [leɣərkamp] *het (~en)* army camp

legerkorps [leɣərkɔrps] *het (~en)* army corps

legermacht [leɣərmaχt] *de (~en)* armed forces; army

leggen [lɛɣə(n)] *vb* **1** lay (down), floor: *te ruste(n) ~* lay to rest; **2** lay; **3** put, put aside: *geld opzij ~* put money aside; *hij legde het boek opzij tot 's avonds* he put the book aside till the evening

legging [lɛgɪŋ] *de (~s)* leggings

legioen [leɣijun] *het (~en)* **1** legion; **2** supporters

legitimatie [leɣitima(t)si] *de (~s)* identification, proof of identity

legitimeren [leɣitimərə(n)] *ref vb* identify oneself, prove one's identity

lego [leɣo] *de, het* Lego

legpuzzel [lɛχpyzəl] *de (~s)* jigsaw (puzzle)

leguaan [leɣywan] *de (leguanen)* iguana

lei [lɛi] *de* slate: *(weer) met een schone ~ beginnen* start again with a clean slate

leiden [lɛidə(n)] *vb* **1** lead; bring, guide: *iem ~ naar* lead (*or:* steer) s.o. towards; *de nieuwe bezuinigingen zullen ertoe ~ dat …* as a result of the new cutbacks, …; *de weg leidde ons door het dorpje* the road took (*or:* led) us through the village; *zij leidde hem door de gangen* she led (*or:* guided) him through the corridors; *tot niets ~* lead nowhere; **2** manage, conduct, direct: *zich laten ~ door* be guided (*or:* ruled) by; **3** *(sport)* (be in the) lead: *een druk leven ~* lead a busy life

leider [lɛidər] *de (~s)* leader; *(com)* director, manager; guide

leiderstrui [lɛidərstrœy] *de (~en)* leader's jersey: *de gele ~* the yellow jersey

leiding [lɛidɪŋ] *de (~en)* **1** guidance, direction: *onder zijn bekwame ~* under his (cap)able leadership;

~ geven (aan) direct, lead, manage, run, govern, preside over, chair; *wie heeft er hier de ~?* who's in charge here?; **2** direction, management, managers, (board of) directors, leadership: *de ~ heeft hier gefaald* the management is at fault here; **3** pipe; wire; cable: *elektrische ~* electric wire (*or:* cable); **4** lead: *Ajax heeft de ~ met 2 tegen 1* Ajax leads 2-1

leidinggevend [lɛidɪŋɣevənt] *adj* executive, managerial, management

leidingwater [lɛidɪŋwatər] *het* tap water

leidraad [lɛidrat] *de (leidraden)* guide(line)

leidsel [lɛitsəl] *het (~s)* rein

leien [lɛiə(n)] *adj* slate

¹lek [lɛk] *het (~ken)* leak(age), puncture, flat: *een ~ dichten* stop a leak

²lek [lɛk] *adj* leaky, punctured, flat: *een ~ke band krijgen* get a puncture

lekkage [lɛkaʒə] *de (~s)* leak(age)

lekken [lɛkə(n)] *vb* **1** leak, be leaking, take in water, drip; **2** leak, seep

¹lekker [lɛkər] *adj* **1** nice, good, tasty, delicious: *ze weet wel wat ~ is* she knows a good thing when she sees it; *is het ~? ja, het heeft me ~ gesmaakt* do you like it? yes, I enjoyed it; **2** nice, sweet; **3** well, fine: *ik ben niet ~* I'm not feeling too well; **4** nice, pleasant; **5** nice, comfortable, lovely: *~ rustig* nice and quiet

²lekker [lɛkər] *adv* **1** well, deliciously: *~ (kunnen) koken* be a good cook; **2** nicely, fine: *slaap ~, droom maar ~* sleep tight, sweet dreams; *het ~ vinden om* like to

lekkerbek [lɛkərbɛk] *de (~ken)* gourmet, foodie

lekkerbekje [lɛkərbɛkjə] *het (~s)* fried fillet of haddock

lekkernij [lɛkərnɛi] *de (~en)* delicacy, sweet

lekkers [lɛkərs] *het* sweet(s); snack

lel [lɛl] *de* clout

lelie [leli] *de (~s)* (madonna) lily

lelietje-van-dalen [lelicəvandalə(n)] *het (lelietjes-van-dalen)* lily of the valley

¹lelijk [lelək] *adj* **1** ugly: *het was een ~ gezicht* it looked awful; **2** bad, nasty

²lelijk [lelək] *adv* badly, nastily: *zich ~ vergissen in iem (iets)* be badly mistaken about s.o. (sth)

lemen [lemə(n)] *adj* loam

lemmet [lɛmət] *het (~en)* blade

lemming [lɛmɪŋ] *de (~s, ~en)* lemming

lende [lɛndə] *de (~nen)* **1** lumbar region, small of the back; **2** loin, haunch

lendebiefstuk [lɛndəbifstʏk] *de (~ken)* sirloin

lenden [lɛndə(n)] *de* loins

lenen [lenə(n)] *vb* **1** lend (to): *ik heb hem geld geleend* I have lent him some money; **2** borrow (of, from): *mag ik je fiets vandaag ~?* can I borrow your bike today?

lener [lenər] *de (~s)* **1** lender; **2** borrower

lengte [lɛŋtə] *de (~n, ~s)* **1** length: *een plank in de ~ doorzagen* saw a board lengthways (*or:* lengthwise); **2** length, height: *hij lag in zijn volle ~ op de grond* he lay full-length on the ground; *over een ~*

van 60 meter for a distance of 60 metres

lengtecirkel [lɛ̃ŋtəsɪrkəl] *de (~s)* meridian

lengterichting [lɛ̃ŋtərɪχtɪŋ] *de* longitudinal direction, linear direction

lenig [lenəχ] *adj, adv* lithe

lenigheid [lenəχhɛit] *de* litheness

lening [lenɪŋ] *de (~en)* loan: *iem een ~ verstrekken* grant s.o. a loan

lens [lɛns] *de (lenzen)* lens, *(contact lenses also)* contacts

lente [lɛntə] *de (~s)* spring: *in de ~* in (the) spring, in springtime

lepel [lepəl] *de (~s)* **1** spoon, ladle, teaspoon: *een baby met een ~ voeren* spoonfeed a baby; **2** spoonful

lepelaar [lepəlar] *de (~s)* spoonbill

lepra [lepra] *de* leprosy

lepralijder [lepralɛidər] *de (~s)* leprosy sufferer; leper

leraar [lerar] *de (leraren)* teacher: *hij is ~ Engels* he's an English teacher

lerarenkamer [lerarə(n)kamər] *de (~s)* teachers' room, staffroom

lerarenopleiding [lerarə(n)ɔplɛidɪŋ] *de (~en)* secondary teacher training (course): *de tweedefaselerarenopleiding* post-graduate teacher training (course)

lerarenvergadering [lerarə(n)vərɣadərɪŋ] *de (~en)* staff meeting

¹leren [lerə(n)] *adj* leather

²leren [lerə(n)] *vb* **1** learn ((how) to do): *een vak ~* learn a trade; *iem ~ kennen* get to know s.o.; *op dat gebied kun je nog heel wat van hem ~* he can still teach you a thing or two; *hij wil ~ schaatsen* he wants to learn (how) to skate; *iets al doende ~* pick sth up as you go along; *iets van buiten ~* learn sth by heart; **2** teach: *de ervaring leert ...* experience teaches ...; **3** study, learn: *haar kinderen kunnen goed* (or: *niet*) ~ her children are good (*or:* no good) at school

³leren [lerə(n)] *vb* **1** teach (s.o. (how) to do sth): *iem ~ lezen en schrijven* teach s.o. to read and write; **2** pick up, learn: *hij leert het al aardig* he is beginning to get the hang of it

les [lɛs] *de (~sen)* **1** lesson, class: *ik heb ~ van 9 tot 12* I have lessons (*or:* classes) from 9 to 12; *een ~ laten uitvallen* drop a class; *~ in tekenen* drawing (*or:* art) classes; **2** (*fig*) lecture, lesson: *dat is een goede ~ voor hem geweest* that's been a good lesson to him; *iem de ~ lezen, (Belg) iem de ~ spellen* give s.o. a talking-to

lesauto [lɛsauto] *de (~'s)* learner car, *(Am)* driver education car

lesbienne [lɛzb(i)jɛnə] *de (~s)* lesbian

lesbisch [lɛzbis] *adj* lesbian

lesgeld [lɛsχɛlt] *het* tuition fee(s)

lesgeven [lɛsχevə(n)] *vb* teach

leslokaal [lɛslokal] *het (leslokalen)* classroom

lesrooster [lɛsrostər] *het, de (~s)* school timetable (*or Am:* schedule)

lessen [lɛsə(n)] *vb* quench

lessenaar [lɛsənar] *de (~s)* (reading, writing) desk, lectern

lesuur [lɛsyr] *het (lesuren)* lesson, period

Letland [lɛtlɑnt] *het* Latvia

¹Lets [lɛts] *het* Latvian

²Lets [lɛts] *adj* Latvian

letsel [lɛtsəl] *het* injury

letten [lɛtə(n)] *vb* **1** pay attention (to): *daar heb ik niet op gelet* I didn't notice; *op zijn gezondheid ~* watch one's health; *let op mijn woorden* mark my words; *let maar niet op haar* don't pay any attention to her; **2** take care of: *goed op iem ~* take good care of s.o.; *er wordt ook op de uitspraak gelet* pronunciation is also taken into consideration (*or:* account)

letter [lɛtər] *de (~s)* letter; *(pl, notice)* lettering: *met grote ~s* in capitals

lettergreep [lɛtərɣrep] *de (-grepen)* syllable

letterkunde [lɛtərkʏndə] *de* literature

letterkundig [lɛtərkʏndəχ] *adj, adv* literary

letterlijk [lɛtərlək] *adj, adv* literal: *iets al te ~ opvatten* take sth too literally

lettertype [lɛtərtipə] *het (~s)* type(face), fount, *(Am)* font

leugen [løɣə(n)] *de (~s)* lie: *een ~tje om bestwil* a white lie

leugenaar [løɣənar] *de (~s)* liar

leugendetector [løɣə(n)detɛktɔr] *de (~s)* lie detector

leuk [løk] *adj, adv* **1** funny, amusing: *hij denkt zeker dat hij ~ is* he seems to think he is funny; *ik zie niet in wat daar voor ~s aan is* I don't see the funny side of it; **2** pretty, nice: *een ~ bedrag* quite a handsome sum; *echt een ~ event (knul)* a really nice guy; *dat staat je ~* that suits you; **3** nice, pleasant: *ik vind het ~ werk* I enjoy the work; *iets ~ vinden* enjoy (*or:* like) sth; *laten we iets ~s gaan doen* let's do sth nice; *~ dat je gebeld hebt* it was nice of you to call

leukemie [løykəmi] *de* leukaemia

leukoplast [løkoplɑst] *de, het* sticking plaster

leunen [lønə(n)] *vb* lean (on, against): *achterover ~* lean back, recline

leuning [lønɪŋ] *de (~en)* **1** (hand)rail; **2** back; arm (rest); **3** rail(ing), guard rail

leunstoel [lønstul] *de (~en)* armchair

leuren [lørə(n)] *vb* peddle

leus [løs] *de (leuzen)* slogan, motto

leut [løt] *de* fun

leuteren [løtərə(n)] *vb* drivel

Leuven [løvə(n)] *het* Leuven, Louvain

¹leven [levə(n)] *het (~s)* **1** life, existence: *de aanslag heeft aan twee mensen het ~ gekost* the attack cost the lives of two people; *het ~ schenken aan* give birth to; *zijn ~ wagen* risk one's life; *nog in ~ zijn* be still alive; *zijn ~ niet (meer) zeker zijn* be not safe here (any more); **2** life, reality: *een organisatie in het ~ roepen* set up an organization; **3** life, lifetime: *zijn hele verdere ~* for the rest of his life; *hun ~ lang* *hebben ze hard gewerkt* they worked hard all their lives; **4** life, living: *het ~ wordt steeds duurder* the cost of living is going up all the time; *zijn ~ beteren* mend one's ways; **5** life, liveliness: *er kwam ~ in de brouwerij* things were beginning to liven up

²leven [le̯və(n)] *vb* **1** live, be alive: *blijven ~* stay alive; *en zij leefden nog lang en gelukkig* and they lived happily ever after; *leef je nog?* are you still alive?; *stil gaan ~* retire; *naar iets toe ~* look forward to sth; **2** *(fig)* live (on); **3** live (on, by), live off: *zij moet ervan ~* she has to live on it

levend [le̯vənt] *adj* living, live, alive

levendig [le̯vəndəχ] *adj, adv* **1** lively; **2** lively, vivacious: *~ van aard zijn* have a vivacious nature; **3** vivid, clear: *ik kan mij die dag nog ~ herinneren* I remember that day clearly; **4** vivid, spirited: *over een ~e fantasie beschikken* have a vivid imagination

levensbedreigend [levənzbədre̯iɣənt] *adj* life-threatening

levensbehoefte [le̯vənzbəhuftə] *de (~n)* **1** necessity of life; **2** *(pl)* necessities (of life)

levensbelang [le̯vənzbəlaŋ] *het (~en)* vital importance

levensbeschrijving [le̯vənzbəsχre̯iviŋ] *de (~en)* biography, curriculum vitae

levensduur [le̯vənzdyr] *de (fig)* **1** lifespan: *de gemiddelde ~ van de Nederlander* the life expectancy of the Dutch; **2** life

¹levensecht [levənse̯χt] *adj* lifelike

²levensecht [levənse̯χt] *adv* in a lifelike way (*or:* manner)

levenservaring [le̯vənservariŋ] *de (~en)* experience of life

levensgevaar [le̯vənsχavar] *het* danger of life, peril to life: *buiten ~ zijn* be out of danger

levensgevaarlijk [levənsχəvarlək] *adj, adv* perilous

levensgezel [le̯vənsχəzɛl] *de (~len)* life partner (*or:* companion)

levensgroot [levənsχro̯t] *adj* **1** life-size(d); **2** huge, enormous

levensjaar [le̯vənsjar] *het (-jaren)* year of (one's) life

¹levenslang [levənslɑŋ] *adj* lifelong: *~e herinneringen* lasting memories; *hij kreeg ~* he was sentenced to life (imprisonment)

²levenslang [levənslɑŋ] *adv* all one's life

levensloop [le̯vənslop] *de* **1** course of life; **2** curriculum vitae

levenslustig [levənsly̯stəχ] *adj* high-spirited

levensmiddelen [le̯vənsmɪdələ(n)] *de* food(s)

levensomstandigheden [le̯vənsɔm-stɑndəχhedə(n)] *de* living conditions, circumstances (*or:* conditions) of life

levensonderhoud [le̯vənsɔndərhaut] *het* support, means of sustaining life: *de kosten van ~ stijgen* (or: *dalen*) living costs are rising (*or:* falling)

levenspartner [le̯vənspɑrtnər] *de (~s)* life partner, life companion

levenssfeer [le̯vənsfer] *de (-sferen)* privacy, private life

levensstandaard [le̯vənstɑndart] *de* standard of living

levensstijl [le̯vənste̯il] *de (~en)* lifestyle, style of living

levensverwachting [le̯vənsfərwɑχtiŋ] *de* **1** expectation of (*or:* from) life; **2** life expectancy

levensverzekering [le̯vənsfərzekəriŋ] *de (~en)* life insurance (policy)

levenswandel [le̯vənswɑndəl] *de* conduct (in life), life

levenswerk [le̯vənswɛrk] *het* life's work, lifework

levenswijze [le̯vənswe̯izə] *de* way of life

lever [le̯vər] *de (~s)* liver: *(Belg) het ligt op zijn ~* it rankles him; *iets op zijn ~ hebben* have sth on one's mind

leverancier [levərɑnsir] *de (~s)* supplier

leverantie [levərɑnsi] *de (~s)* delivery, supply(ing)

leverbaar [le̯vərbar] *adj* available, ready for delivery: *niet meer ~* out of stock

leveren [le̯vərə(n)] *vb* **1** supply, deliver; **2** furnish, provide: *iemand stof ~ voor een verhaal* provide s.o. with material for a story; **3** fix, do, bring off: *ik weet niet hoe hij het het geleverd heeft* I don't know how he pulled it off

levering [le̯vəriŋ] *de (~en)* delivery

leverpastei [le̯vərpaste̯i] *de (~en)* liver paté

levertijd [le̯vərte̯it] *de (~en)* delivery time

lezen [le̯zə(n)] *vb* **1** read: *je handschrift is niet te ~* your (hand)writing is illegible; *veel ~ over een schrijver* (or: *een bepaald onderwerp*) read up on a writer (*or:* on a particular subject); *ik lees hier dat … it says here that …*; **2** read (out, aloud): *de angst stond op zijn gezicht te ~* anxiety was written all over his face

lezer [le̯zər] *de (~s)* reader: *het aantal ~s van deze krant neemt nog steeds toe* the readership of this newspaper is still increasing

lezing [le̯ziŋ] *de (~en)* **1** reading: *bij oppervlakkige* (or: *nauwkeurige*) ~ on a cursory (*or:* a careful reading); **2** lecture

liaan [lijan] *de (lianen)* liana, liane

Libanees [libane̯s] *de* Lebanese

Libanon [li̯banɔn] *het* (the) Lebanon

libel [libɛl] *de (~len)* dragonfly

liberaal [liberal] *adj, adv* **1** liberal; *(in the Netherlands also)* conservative; **2** liberal, broad-minded

liberaliseren [liberalizərə(n)] *vb* liberalize

liberalisme [liberalɪsmə] *het* liberalism

Liberia [libe̯rija] *het* Liberia

libero [li̯bəro] *de (~'s) (sport)* sweeper

libido [li̯bido] *de* libido, sex drive

Libië [li̯bijə] *het* Libya

Libiër [li̯bijər] *de (~s)* Libyan

¹licentiaat [lisɛnsjat] *de (Belg)* licentiate

²licentiaat [lisɛnsjat] *het* licentiate, licence

licentiaatsthesis [lisɛn(t)ʃatstezɪs] *de (~sen, -the-*

ses) (Belg) licentiate's thesis, (roughly) M.A. thesis, M.Sc. thesis

licentie [lisɛnsi] de (~s) **1** licence; **2** permit

lichaam [lɪχam] het (lichamen) **1** body: over zijn hele ~ beven shake all over; **2** trunk

lichaamsbeweging [lɪχamzbəweɣɪŋ] de (~en) (physical) exercise, gymnastics

lichaamsbouw [lɪχamzbɑu] de build, figure

lichaamsdeel [lɪχamzdel] het (-delen) part of the body, limb

lichaamsverzorging [lɪχamsfərzɔrχɪŋ] de personal hygiene

lichamelijk [lɪχaməlǝk] adj, adv physical

¹licht [lɪχt] het (~en) light: tussen ~ en donker in the twilight; waar zit de knop van het ~? where's the light switch?; groot ~ full beam; dat werpt een nieuw ~ op de zaak that puts things in a different light; het ~ aandoen (or: uitdoen) put the light on (or: off); toen ging er een ~je (bij me) op then it dawned on me; het ~ staat op rood the light is red; aan het ~ komen come to light

²licht [lɪχt] adj **1** light, delicate: zij voelde zich ~ in het hoofd she felt light in the head; een kilo te ~ a kilogram underweight; **2** light, bright: het wordt al ~ it is getting light; **3** light, pale; **4** light, easy; **5** light, slight: een ~e afwijking hebben be a bit odd; een ~e blessure a minor injury

³licht [lɪχt] adv **1** lightly, light: ~ slapen sleep light; **2** slightly; **3** easily: ~ verteerbaar (easily) digestible, light; **4** highly: ~ ontvlambare stoffen highly (in)flammable materials

lichtbak [lɪχtbɑk] de (~ken) illuminated sign

lichtelijk [lɪχtǝlǝk] adv slightly

lichten [lɪχtǝ(n)] vb **1** lift, raise; **2** remove: iem van zijn bed ~ arrest s.o. in his bed

lichtend [lɪχtǝnt] adj shining

lichterlaaie [lɪχtǝrlajǝ] ‖ het gebouw stond in ~ the building was in flames (or: ablaze)

lichtgelovig [lɪχtχəlovǝχ] adj gullible

lichtgevend [lɪχtχevǝnt] adj luminous

lichting [lɪχtɪŋ] de (~en) **1** levy, draft; **2** collection

lichtjaar [lɪχtjar] het (-jaren) light year

lichtkrans [lɪχtkrɑns] de (~en) halo, aureole

lichtmast [lɪχtmɑst] de (~en) lamp-post, lamp standard

lichtnet [lɪχtnɛt] het (~ten) (electric) mains, lighting system: een apparaat op het ~ aansluiten connect an appliance to the mains; op het ~ werken run off the mains

lichtpen [lɪχtpɛn] de (~nen) light pen(cil)

lichtpunt [lɪχtpʏnt] het (~en) **1** point (or: spot) of light; **2** (fig) ray of hope

lichtreclame [lɪχtrəklamə] de illuminated advertising, neon signs (or: advertising)

lichtschip [lɪχtsχɪp] het (-schepen) lightship

lichtshow [lɪχtʃo] de (~s) light show

lichtsignaal [lɪχtsɪɲal] het (-signalen) light signal, flash: een ~ geven flash

lichtsnelheid [lɪχtsnɛlhɛit] de speed of light

lichtstraal [lɪχtstral] de (-stralen) ray of light, beam (or: shaft) of light

lichtvaardig [lɪχtfardǝχ] adj, adv rash

lichtzinnig [lɪχtsɪnǝχ] adj, adv **1** frivolous: ~ omspringen met trifle with; **2** light, loose: ~ leven live a loose life

lichtzinnigheid [lɪχtsɪnǝχhɛit] de frivolity

lid [lɪt] het (leden) **1** member: het aantal leden bedraagt ... the membership is ...; ~ van de gemeenteraad (town) councillor; ~ van de Kamer Member of Parliament, M.P.; deze omroep heeft 500.000 leden this broadcasting company has a membership of 500,000; ~ worden van join, become a member of; ~ zijn van de bibliotheek belong to the library; ~ zijn van be a member of, be (or: serve) on; zich als ~ opgeven apply for membership; **2** part, member, limb: recht van lijf en leden straight-limbed; het (mannelijk) ~ the (male) member

lidgeld [lɪtχɛlt] het (Belg) subscription

lidkaart [lɪtkart] de (~en) (Belg) membership card

lidmaatschap [lɪtmatsχɑp] het (~pen) membership: bewijs van ~ membership card; iem van het ~ van een vereniging uitsluiten exclude s.o. from membership of a club; het ~ kost €25,- the membership fee is 25 euros; zijn ~ opzeggen resign one's membership

lidmaatschapskaart [lɪtmatsχɑpskart] de (~en) membership card

lidstaat [lɪtstat] de (lidstaten) member state

lidwoord [lɪtwort] het (~en) article: bepaald en onbepaald ~ definite and indefinite article

lied [lit] het (~eren) song: het hoogste ~ zingen be wild with joy

lieden [lidǝ(n)] de folk, people: dat kun je verwachten bij zulke ~ that's what you can expect from people like that

liedje [licǝ] het (~s) song: het is altijd hetzelfde ~ it's the same old story

liedjesschrijver [licǝsχrɛivǝr] de (~s) songwriter

¹lief [lif] het **1** girlfriend, boyfriend, beloved; **2** joy: ~ en leed met iem delen share life's joys and sorrows with s.o.

²lief [lif] adj **1** dear, beloved: (maar) mijn lieve kind (but) my dear; (in letters) Lieve Maria Dear Maria; **2** nice, sweet: een ~ karakter a sweet nature, a kind heart; zij zijn erg ~ voor elkaar they are very devoted to each other; dat was ~ van haar om jou mee te nemen it was nice of her to take you along; **3** dear, sweet: er ~ uitzien look sweet (or: lovely); **4** dear, treasured: iets voor ~ nemen put up with sth, make do with sth; tegenslagen voor ~ nemen take the rough with the smooth

³lief [lif] adv sweetly, nicely: iem ~ aankijken give s.o. an affectionate look; ik ga net zo ~ niet I'd (just) as soon not go

liefdadig [livdadǝχ] adj charitable: een ~ doel a good cause; het is voor een ~ doel it is for charity; ~e instellingen charitable institutions

liefdadigheid [livdadǝχhɛit] de charity, benevo-

lence, beneficence: ~ *bedrijven* do charitable work
liefdadigheidsconcert *het* charity concert; benefit
concert
liefdadigheidsinstelling [livdadəχhɛitsɪnstɛlɪŋ]
de (~en) charity, charitable institution
liefde [livdə] *de (~s, ~n)* love: *haar grote ~* her great
love; *kinderlijke ~* childish love (*or*: affection), filial
love (*or*: affection); *een ongelukkige ~ achter de rug
hebben* have suffered a disappointment in love;
vrije ~ free love; *de ware ~* true love; *iemands ~ beantwoorden* return s.o.'s love (*or*: affection); *de ~
bedrijven* make love; *geluk hebben in de ~* be fortunate (*or*: successful) in love; *~ op het eerste gezicht*
love at first sight; *hij deed het uit ~* he did it for love;
trouwen uit ~ marry for love; *de ~ voor het vaderland* (the) love of one's country; *~ voor de kunst*
love of art; *~ is blind* love is blind
liefdesbrief [livdəzbrif] *de (-brieven)* love letter
liefdesleven [livdəslevə(n)] *het (~s)* love life
liefdeslied [livdəslit] *het (-liederen)* love song
liefdesverdriet [livdəsfərdrit] *het* pangs of love: *~
hebben* be disappointed in love
liefdevol [livdəvɔl] *adj, adv* loving: *~le verzorging*
tender loving care; *iem ~ aankijken* give s.o. a loving look
liefdewerk [livdəwɛrk] *het (~en)* charity, charitable work: *het is ~ oud papier* it's for love only
liefhebben [lifhɛbə(n)] *vb* love
liefhebber [lifhɛbər] *de (~s)* lover: *een ~ van chocola* a chocolate lover; *een ~ van opera* an opera lover
(*or*: buff); *zijn er nog ~s?* (are there) any takers?;
daar zullen wel ~s voor zijn there are sure to be customers for that
liefhebberij [lifhɛbərɛi] *de (~en)* hobby, pastime:
een dure ~ (*fig*) an expensive hobby; *tuinieren is
zijn grootste ~* gardening is his favourite pastime
liefje [lifjə] *het (~s)* sweetheart
liefkozen [lifkozə(n)] *vb* caress, fondle, cuddle
liefkozing [lifkozɪŋ] *de (~en)* caress
liefst [lifst] *adv* **1** dearest, sweetest: *zij zag er van allen het ~ uit* she looked the sweetest (*or*: prettiest)
of them all; **2** rather, preferably: *men neme een banaan, ~ een rijpe ...* take a banana, preferably a ripe
one ...; *wat zou je het ~ doen?* what would you rather do?, what would you really like to do?; *in welke
auto rijd je het ~?* which car do you prefer to drive?
liefste [lifstə] *de (~n)* sweetheart, darling: *mijn ~*
my dear(est) (*or*: love)
liegen [liɣə(n)] *vb* lie, tell a lie: *hij staat gewoon te
~!* he's a downright liar!; *tegen iem ~* lie to s.o.; *hij
liegt alsof het gedrukt staat, hij liegt dat hij barst* he
is telling barefaced lies; *dat is allemaal gelogen*
that's a pack of lies
lier [lir] *de (~en)* lyre
lies [lis] *de (liezen)* groin
Lieveheer [livəher] *de* Blessed Lord: *onze ~* Our
Lord
lieveheersbeestje [livəherzbeʃə] *het (~s)* ladybird, (*Am*) ladybug

lieveling [livəlɪŋ] *de (~en)* **1** darling, sweetheart: *zij
is de ~ van de familie* she's the darling of the family;
2 favourite, darling: *de ~ van het publiek* the darling (*or*: favourite) of the public
liever [livər] *adv* rather: *ik drink ~ koffie dan thee* I
prefer coffee to tea; *ik zou ~ gaan (dan blijven)* I'd
rather go than stay; *ik weet het, of ~ gezegd, ik denk
het* I know, at least, I think so; *als je ~ hebt dat ik
wegga, hoef je het maar te zeggen* if you'd sooner
(*or*: rather) I'd leave, just say so; *ik zie hem ~ gaan
dan komen* I'm glad to see the back of him; *hoe
meer, hoe ~* the more the better; *hij ~ dan ik* rather
him than me
lieverd [livərt] *de (~s)* darling: (*iron*) *het is me een
~je* he's (*or*: she's) a nice one
lift [lɪft] *de (~en)* **1** lift, (*Am*) elevator: *de ~ nemen*
take the lift; **2** lift, ride: *iem een ~ geven* give s.o. a
lift (*or*: ride); *een ~ krijgen* get (*or*: hitch) a lift; *een
~ vragen* thumb (*or*: hitch) a lift
liften [lɪftə(n)] *vb* hitch(hike)
lifter [lɪftər] *de (~s)* hitchhiker
liftjongen [lɪftjɔŋə(n)] *de (~s)* liftboy
liga [liɣa] *de (~'s)* league
ligbad [lɪɣbat] *het (~en)* bath, (*Am*) (bath)tub
liggen [lɪɣə(n)] *vb* **1** lie, be laid up: *er lag een halve
meter sneeuw* there was half a metre of snow; *lekker
tegen iem aan gaan ~* snuggle up to s.o.; *lig je lekker? (goed?)* are you comfortable?; *ik blijf morgen ~
tot half tien* I'm going to stay in bed till 9.30 tomorrow; *gaan ~* lie down; *hij ligt in (op) bed* he is (lying) in bed; *op sterven ~* lie (*or*: be) dying; **2** (with
aan) depend (on), be caused by, be due to: *dat ligt
eraan* it depends; *ik denk dat het aan je versterker
ligt* I think that it's your amplifier that's causing the
trouble; *aan mij zal het niet ~* it won't be my fault;
is het nu zo koud of ligt het aan mij? is it really so
cold, or is it just me?; *het ligt aan die rotfiets van me*
it's that bloody bike of mine; *als het aan mij ligt
niet* not if I can help it; *waar zou dat aan ~?* what
could be the cause of that?; *het lag misschien ook
een beetje aan mij* I may have had sth to do with it;
het kan aan mij ~, maar ... it may be just me, but
...; *als het aan mij ligt* if it is up to me; **3** die down:
de wind ging ~ the wind died down; *die zaak ligt
nogal gevoelig* the matter is a bit delicate; *dat werk
is voor ons blijven ~* that work has been left for us;
ik heb (nog) een paar flessen wijn ~ I have a few bottles of wine (left); (*Belg*) *iem ~ hebben* take s.o. in;
ik heb dat boek laten ~ I left that book (behind); *dit
bed ligt lekker* (*or*: *hard*) this bed is comfortable (*or*:
hard); *de zaken ~ nu heel anders* things have
changed a lot (since then); *het plan, zoals het er nu
ligt, is onaanvaardbaar* as it stands, the plan is unacceptable; *uw bestelling ligt klaar* your order is
ready (for dispatch, collection); *zo ~ de zaken nu
eenmaal* I'm afraid that's the way things are; *Antwerpen ligt aan de Schelde* Antwerp lies on the
Scheldt; *de schuld ligt bij mij* the fault is mine; *onder het gemiddelde ~* be below average; *de bal ligt*

op de grond the ball is on the ground; *op het zuiden* ~ face (the) south; *ze* ~ *voor het grijpen* they're all over the place

liggend [lɪɣənt] *adj* lying, horizontal: *een ~e houding* a lying (*or:* recumbent) posture

ligging [lɪɣɪŋ] *de (~en)* position, situation, location: *de* ~ *van de heuvels* the lie of the hills; *de schilderachtige* ~ *van dat kasteel* the picturesque location of the castle

ligplaats [lɪχplats] *de (~en)* berth, mooring (place)

ligstoel [lɪχstul] *de (~en)* reclining chair (*or:* seat), deckchair

liguster [liɣystər] *de (~s)* privet

¹**lijden** [lɛidə(n)] *vb* suffer, undergo: *hevige pijn* ~ suffer (*or:* be in) terrible pain

²**lijden** [lɛidə(n)] *vb* suffer: *zij leed het ergst van al* she was (the) hardest hit of all; *aan een kwaal* ~ suffer from a complaint; *zijn gezondheid leed er onder* his health suffered (from it)

³**lijden** [lɛidə(n)] *het* suffering, pain, agony, grief, misery: *nu is hij uit zijn* ~ *verlost: a)* he is now released from his suffering; *b) (fig)* that's put him out of his misery; *een dier uit zijn* ~ *verlossen* put an animal out of its misery

lijdend [lɛidənt] *adj* suffering

lijf [lɛif] *het (lijven)* body: *in levenden lijve: a)* in person; *b)* alive and well; *bijna geen kleren aan zijn* ~ *hebben* have hardly a shirt to one's back; *iets aan den lijve ondervinden* experience (sth) personally; *iem te* ~ *gaan* go for (*or:* attack) s.o.; *iem (toevallig) tegen het* ~ *lopen* run into s.o., stumble upon s.o.; *ik kon hem niet van het* ~ *houden* I couldn't keep him off me; *gezond van* ~ *en leden* able-bodied

lijfrente [lɛifrɛntə] *de (~n, ~s)* annuity

lijfwacht [lɛifwɑχt] *de* bodyguard

lijk [lɛik] *het (~en)* **1** corpse, (dead) body: *over mijn* ~*!* over my dead body!; *over ~en gaan* let nothing (*or:* no one) stand in one's way; **2** *(fig)* carcass: *een levend* ~ a walking corpse

lijkbleek [lɛigblek] *adj* deathly pale, ashen

lijken [lɛikə(n)] *vb* **1** be like; look (a)like, resemble: *je lijkt je vader wel* you act (*or:* sound, are) just like your father; *het lijkt wel wijn* it's almost like wine; *zij lijkt op haar moeder* she looks like her mother; *ze* ~ *helemaal niet op elkaar* they're not a bit alike; *dat lijkt nergens op (naar)* it is absolutely hopeless (*or:* useless); **2** seem, appear, look: *hij lijkt jonger dan hij is* he looks younger than he is; *het lijkt me vreemd* it seems odd to me; *het lijkt maar zo* it only seems that way; **3** suit, fit: *dat lijkt me wel wat* I like the sound (*or:* look) of that; *het lijkt me niets* I don't think much of it

lijkenhuis [lɛikə(n)hœys] *het (-huizen)* mortuary, morgue

lijkschouwer [lɛiksχɑuwər] *de (~s)* autopsist, medical examiner, *(law)* coroner

lijkschouwing [lɛiksχɑuwɪŋ] *de (~en)* autopsy

lijm [lɛim] *de (~en)* glue

lijmen [lɛimə(n)] *vb* glue (together), *(also fig)* patch up, *(also fig)* mend: *(fig) de brokken* ~ pick up the pieces; *de scherven aan elkaar* ~ glue (*or:* stick) the pieces together

lijn [lɛin] *de (~en)* **1** line, rope, leash, lead: *~en trekken* (or: *krassen) op* draw (*or:* scratch) lines on; *een hond aan de* ~ *houden* keep a dog on the leash; **2** line, crease: *de scherpe ~en om de neus* the deep lines around the nose; **3** (out)line, contour: *iets in grote ~en aangeven* sketch sth in broad outlines; *in grote ~en* broadly speaking, on the whole; *aan de (slanke)* ~ *doen* slim, be on a diet; **4** line, rank: *op dezelfde* (or: *op één) ~ zitten* be on the same wavelength; **5** line, route: *de ~ Haarlem-Amsterdam* the Haarlem-Amsterdam line; *die* ~ *bestaat niet meer* that service (*or:* route) no longer exists; *blijft u even aan de* ~ *a.u.b.* hold the line, please; *ik heb je moeder aan de* ~ your mother is on the phone; **6** *(fig)* line, course, trend: *de grote ~en uit het oog verliezen* lose oneself in details; *iem aan het ~tje houden* keep s.o. dangling

lijnbus [lɛimbys] *de (~sen)* regular (*or:* scheduled) service bus

lijndienst [lɛindinst] *de (~en)* regular service, scheduled service, line: *een* ~ *onderhouden op* run a regular service on

lijnen [lɛinə(n)] *vb* slim, diet

lijnkaart [lɛinkart] *de (Belg)* smart card for payment on public transport

lijnolie [lɛinoli] *de* linseed oil

¹**lijnrecht** [lɛinrɛχt] *adj* (dead) straight

²**lijnrecht** [lɛinrɛχt] *adv* **1** straight, right: ~ *naar beneden* straight down; **2** directly, flatly: ~ *staan tegenover* be diametrically (*or:* flatly) opposed to

lijnrechter [lɛinrɛχtər] *de (~s)* linesman

lijntoestel [lɛintustɛl] *het (~len)* airliner, scheduled plane

lijnvlucht [lɛinvlyχt] *de (~en)* scheduled flight

lijp [lɛip] *adj, adv* silly, daft: *doe niet zo* ~*!* don't be silly! (*or:* daft!)

lijst [lɛist] *de (~en)* **1** list, record, inventory, register: *~en bijhouden van de uitgaven* keep records of the costs; *zijn naam staat bovenaan de* ~ he is (at the) top of the list; *iem (iets) op een* ~ *zetten* put s.o. (sth) on a list; **2** frame: *een vergulde* ~ a gilt frame

lijstaanvoerder [lɛistanvurdər] *de (~s)* (league) leader

lijstenmaker [lɛistə(n)makər] *de (~s)* picture framer

lijster [lɛistər] *de (~s)* thrush

lijsterbes [lɛistərbɛs] *de* rowan (tree), mountain ash

lijsttrekker [lɛistrɛkər] *de (~s) (roughly)* party leader (during election campaign)

lijvig [lɛivəχ] *adj* corpulent, hefty

lik [lɪk] *de (~ken)* **1** lick; smack; **2** lick; dab

likeur [likør] *de (~en)* liqueur

likkebaarden [lɪkəbardə(n)] *vb* lick one's lips

likken [lɪkə(n)] *vb* lick

lik-op-stukbeleid [lɪkɔpstYɣbəlɛit] *het* tit-for-tat

policy (or: strategy)

lila [lila] adj lilac, lavender

lilliputter [lilipʏtər] de (~s) midget, dwarf

Limburg [lɪmbʏrχ] Limburg

Limburger [lɪmbʏrɣər] de (~s) Limburger

Limburgs [lɪmbʏrχs] adj Limburg

limiet [limit] de (~en) limit

limiteren [limiterə(n)] vb limit, confine

limonade [limonadə] de (~s) lemonade: priklimonade, ~ gazeuse fizzy (or: aerated, sparkling) lemonade

limonadesiroop [limonadəsirop] de lemon syrup

limousine [limuzinə] de (~s) limousine; limo

linde [lɪndə] de (~n) lime (tree), linden

lineair [linejɛːr] adj linear ‖ ~e hypotheek level repayment mortgage

lingerie [leʒəri] de lingerie, women's underwear, ladies' underwear

linguïst [lɪŋɣwɪst] de (~en) linguist

liniaal [linijal] het, de (linialen) ruler

linie [lini] de (~s) line, rank: door de vijandelijke ~ (heen)breken break through the enemy lines; over de hele ~ on all points, across the board

link [lɪŋk] adj 1 risky, dicey: ~e jongens a nasty bunch; 2 sly, cunning

linker [lɪŋkər] adj left, left-hand, nearside: ~ rijbaan left lane; het ~ voorwiel the nearside wheel

linkerarm [lɪŋkərarm] de left arm

linkerbeen [lɪŋkərben] het (-benen) left leg: hij is met zijn ~ uit bed gestapt he got out of bed on the wrong side

linkerbenedenhoek [lɪŋkərbənedə(n)huk] de bottom left-hand corner

linkerbovenhoek [lɪŋkərbovə(n)huk] de top left-hand corner

linkerhand [lɪŋkərhant] de (~en) left hand: twee ~en hebben be all fingers and thumbs

linkerkant [lɪŋkərkant] de (~en) left(-hand) side, left

linkervleugel [lɪŋkərvløɣəl] de (~s) 1 left wing: de ~ van een gebouw (or: een voetbalelftal) the left wing of a building (or: football team); 2 left (wing), Left

linkervoet [lɪŋkərvut] de left foot

linkerzijde [lɪŋkərzɛidə] de (~n) left(-hand) side, left, nearside: zij zat aan mijn ~ she was sitting on my left

links [lɪŋks] adj, adv 1 left; to (or: on) the left: de tweede straat ~ the second street on the left; ~ en rechts (also fig) right and left, on all sides; ~ houden keep (to the) left; iem ~ laten liggen ignore s.o., pass s.o. over, give s.o. the cold shoulder; iets ~ laten liggen ignore sth, pass sth over; ~ van iem zitten sit to (or: on) s.o.'s left; 2 left, left-handed, anticlockwise: ~ afslaan turn (to the) left; ~ de bocht om rijden take the left-hand bend (or: turn); 3 left-handed, left-footed: ~ schrijven write with one's left hand; 4 left-wing, leftist, socialist

linksachter [lɪŋksaχtər] de (~s) left back

linksaf [lɪŋksaf] adv (to the) left, leftwards: bij de brug moet u ~ (gaan) turn left at the bridge

linksback [lɪŋksbɛk] de (~s) left back

linksbuiten [lɪŋksbœytə(n)] de (~s) outside left, left-wing(er)

linkshandig [lɪŋkshandəχ] adj left-handed

linksom [lɪŋksɔm] adv left: ~ draaien turn (to the) left

linnen [lɪnə(n)] adj linen, flax: ~ ondergoed linen underwear, linen

linnengoed [lɪnə(n)ɣut] het linen

linnenkast [lɪnə(n)kast] de (~en) linen cupboard

¹linoleum [linolejʏm] de, het linoleum

²linoleum [linolejʏm] adj linoleum

linolzuur [linɔlzyr] het (-zuren) linoleic acid

lint [lɪnt] het (~en) ribbon, tape, (bias) binding, band: het ~ van een schrijfmachine a (typewriter) ribbon; door het ~ gaan blow one's top, fly off the handle

lintje [lɪncə] het (~s) decoration: een ~ krijgen be decorated, get a medal

lintmeter [lɪntmetər] de (~s) (Belg) tape measure

lintworm [lɪntwɔrm] de (~en) tapeworm

lintzaag [lɪntsaχ] de (-zagen) bandsaw

linze [lɪnzə] de (~n) lentil

lip [lɪp] de (~pen) lip: dikke ~pen thick (or: full) lips; gesprongen ~pen chapped (or: cracked) lips; zijn ~pen ergens bij aflikken lick (or: smack) one's lips; aan iemands ~pen hangen hang on s.o.'s lips (or: every word)

lipje [lɪpjə] het tab, lip

liplezen [lɪplezə(n)] vb lip-read

liposuctie [liposʏksi] de (~s) liposuction

lippenstift [lɪpə(n)stɪft] de (~en) lipstick

liquidatie [likwida(t)si] de (~s) 1 liquidation, elimination; 2 liquidation, winding-up, break-up, dissolution, settlement

liquide [likidə] adj liquid, fluid: ~ middelen liquid (or: fluid) assets

liquideren [likwidərə(n)] vb 1 (com) wind up, liquidate; 2 eliminate, dispose of

lire [lirə] de (~s) lira

lis [lɪs] de (~sen) (bot) flag, iris

lisdodde [lɪzdɔdə] de (~n) reed mace

lispelen [lɪspələ(n)] vb lisp, speak with a lisp

Lissabon [lɪsabɔn] het Lisbon

list [lɪst] de (~en) trick, ruse, stratagem; cunning, craft, deception: ~ en bedrog double-crossing, double-dealing

listig [lɪstəχ] adj, adv cunning, crafty, wily

liter [litər] de (~s) litre: twee ~ melk two litres of milk

literair [litərɛːr] adj, adv literary: ~ tijdschrift literary journal

literatuur [litəratyr] de literature

literatuurlijst [litəratyrlɛist] de (~en) reading list, bibliography

literatuurprijs [litəratyrprɛis] de (-prijzen) literary prize

literfles [litərflɛs] *de (~sen)* litre bottle

literprijs [litərprɛis] *de (-prijzen)* price per litre

litho [lito] *de (~'s)* litho

Litouwen [litɑuwə(n)] Lithuania

Litouwer [litɑuwər] *de (~s)* Lithuanian

¹Litouws [litɑus] *het* Lithuanian

²Litouws [litɑus] *adj* Lithuanian

lits-jumeaux [liӡymo] *het (~)* twin beds

litteken [litekə(n)] *het (~s)* scar; mark: *met ~s op zijn gezicht* with a scarred face

liturgie [litʏrɣi] *de (~ën)* liturgy, rite

lob [lɔp] *de (~ben, ~s)* **1** seed leaf; **2** *(sport)* lob

lobben [lɔbə(n)] *vb* lob

lobbes [lɔbəs] *de (~en)* **1** big, good-natured dog; **2** kind soul, good-natured fellow, big softy

lobby [lɔbi] *de (~'s)* **1** lobby; **2** lobby; lounge, foyer, hall

lobbyen [lɔbijə(n)] *vb* lobby

loco-burgemeester [lokobʏrɣəmestər] *de (~s)* deputy mayor, acting mayor

locomotief [lokomotif] *de (locomotieven)* engine, locomotive

loden [lodə(n)] *adj* **1** lead, leaden: *~ pijp* lead pipe; **2** *(fig)* leaden, heavy

loei [luj] *de* thump, bash; sizzler, cracker: *een ~ verkopen (uitdelen)* hit (*or*: lash) out (at s.o.)

loeien [lujə(n)] *vb* **1** moo, low; bellow; **2** howl, whine; roar; blare, hoot; wail: *de motor laten ~* race the engine; *met ~de sirenes* with blaring sirens

loempia [lumpija] *de (~'s)* spring roll, egg roll

loensen [lunzə(n)] *vb* squint, be cross-eyed

loep [lup] *de (~en)* magnifying glass, lens: *iets onder de ~ nemen* scrutinize sth, take a close look at sth

loepzuiver [lupsœyvər] *adj, adv* flawless, perfect

loer [lur] *de* **1** lurking: *op de ~ liggen (also fig)* lie in wait (for), lurk, be on the lookout (for); **2** trick: *iem een ~ draaien* play a nasty (*or*: dirty) trick on s.o.

loeren [lurə(n)] *vb* leer (at), peer at, spy on: *het gevaar loert overal* there is danger lurking everywhere; *op iem (iets) ~* lie in wait for s.o. (sth)

¹lof [lɔf] *de* **1** praise, commendation: *iem ~ toezwaaien* give (high) praise to s.o., pay tribute to s.o.; *vol ~ zijn over* speak highly of, be full of praise for; **2** honour, credit

²lof [lɔf] *het* chicory

log [lɔχ] *adj, adv* unwieldy, cumbersome, ponderous, clumsy, heavy, sluggish, lumbering: *een ~ gevaarte* a cumbersome (*or*: an unwieldy) monster; *een ~ge olifant* a ponderous elephant; *met ~ge tred lopen* lumber (along), move with heavy gait

logaritme [loɣarɪtmə] *de (~n)* logarithm

logaritmetafel [loɣarɪtmətafəl] *de (~s)* log table, table of logarithms

logboek [lɔɣbuk] *het (~en)* log(book), journal: *in het ~ opschrijven* log

loge [lo:ӡə] *de (~s)* box, loge

logé [loӡe] *de (~s)* guest, visitor: *we krijgen een ~* we are having a visitor (*or*: someone to stay)

logeerbed [loӡerbɛt] *het (~den)* spare bed

logeerkamer [loӡerkamər] *de (~s)* guest room, spare (bed)room, visitor's room

logeerpartij [loӡerpartɛi] *de (~en)* stay; slumber party, pyjama party

logen [loɣə(n)] *vb* soak in (*or*: treat with) lye

logeren [loӡerə(n)] *vb* stay, put up, board, lodge: *blijven ~* stay the night, stay over; *ik logeer bij een vriend* I'm staying at a friend's (home) (*or*: with a friend); *kan ik bij jou ~?* could you put me up (for the night)?; *in een hotel ~* stay at a hotel; *iem te ~ krijgen* have s.o. staying

logica [loɣika] *de* logic: *er zit geen ~ in wat je zegt* there is no logic in what you're saying

logies [loӡis] *het* accommodation, lodging(s): *~ met ontbijt* bed and breakfast

loginnaam [lɔɣɪnam] *de* log-in name

logisch [loɣis] *adj, adv* logical, rational: *een ~e tegenstrijdigheid* a logical paradox; *~ denken* think logically (*or*: rationally); *dat is nogal ~* that's only logical, that figures

logischerwijs [loɣisərwɛis] *adv* logically

logistiek [loɣɪstik] *de* logistics

logo [loɣo] *het (~'s)* logo

logopedie [loɣopedi] *de* speech therapy

logopedist [loɣopedɪst] *de (~en)* speech therapist

lok [lɔk] *de (~ken)* **1** lock, strand of hair, tress; curl, ringlet; **2** *(pl)* locks, hair, tresses

¹lokaal [lokal] *het (lokalen)* (class)room

²lokaal [lokal] *adj* local, topical: *om 10 uur lokale tijd* at 10 o'clock local time; *lokale verdoving* local anaesthesia

lokaas [lɔkas] *het (lokazen)* bait

lokaliseren [lokalizerə(n)] *vb* locate

lokatie [loka(t)si] *de (~s)* location

loket [lokɛt] *het (~ten)* (office) window, booking office, ticket office, box-office (window), counter

lokettist [lokɛtɪst] *de (~en)* booking-clerk, ticket-clerk, box-office clerk, counter clerk

lokken [lɔkə(n)] *vb* **1** entice, lure: *in de val ~* lure into a trap; **2** tempt, entice, attract

lokkertje [lɔkərcə] *het (~s)* bait, carrot, loss leader, special offer

lol [lɔl] *de* laugh, fun, lark: *zeg, doe me een ~ (en hou op)* do me a favour (and knock it off, will you); *voor de ~* for a laugh, for fun (*or*: a lark); *ik doe dit niet voor de ~* I'm not doing this for the good of my health

lolly [lɔli] *de (~'s)* lollipop, lolly

lom [lɔm] *leer- en opvoedingsmoeilijkheden* learning and educational problems

¹lomp [lɔmp] *de (~en) (esp pl)* rag, *(esp pl)* tatter

²lomp [lɔmp] *adj, adv* **1** ponderous, unwieldy: *~e schoenen* clumsy shoes; *zich ~ bewegen* move clumsily, he got in an ungainly manner; **2** clumsy, awkward, ungainly; **3** rude, unmannerly, uncivil: *iem ~ behandelen* treat s.o. rudely, be uncivil to s.o.

lompweg [lɔmpwɛχ] *adv* bluntly, flatly: *~ iets weigeren* refuse sth point-blank

Londen [lɔndə(n)] *het* London

Londens [lɔndə(n)s] *adj* London

lonen [lonə(n)] *vb* be worth: *dat loont de moeite niet* it is not worth one's while

lonend [lonənt] *adj* paying, rewarding, profitable, remunerative: *dat is niet ~* that doesn't pay

long [lɔŋ] *de (~en)* lung

longarts [lɔŋɑrts] *de (~en)* lung specialist

longontsteking [lɔŋɔntstekɪŋ] *de (~en)* pneumonia

lonken [lɔŋkə(n)] *vb* make eyes at

lont [lɔnt] *de (~en)* fuse, touchpaper

loochenen [loxənə(n)] *vb* deny

lood [lot] *het* **1** lead: *met ~ in de schoenen* with a heavy heart; **2** lead; shot, ammunition: *uit het ~ (geslagen) zijn* be thrown off one's balance

loodgieter [lotxitər] *de (~s)* plumber

loodje [locə] *het (~s)* (lead) seal ‖ *de laatste ~s wegen het zwaarst* the last mile is the longest one

loodlijn [lotlɛin] *de (~en)* perpendicular (line), normal (line)

loodrecht [lotrɛxt] *adj, adv* perpendicular (to), plumb, sheer: *~ op iets staan* be at right angles to sth

¹loods [lots] *de* pilot

²loods [lots] *de* shed, hangar

loodsen [lotsə(n)] *vb* pilot; steer, conduct, shepherd

loodvrij [lotfrɛi] *adj* lead-free, unleaded

loodzwaar [lotswar] *adj, adv* heavy

loof [lof] *het* foliage, leaves, green

loofboom [lovbom] *de (-bomen)* deciduous tree

loog [lox] *het, de (logen)* caustic (solution), lye

looien [lojə(n)] *vb* tan

loom [lom] *adj, adv* **1** heavy, leaden, slow, sluggish: *zich ~ bewegen* move heavily (*or:* sluggishly); **2** languid, listless

loon [lon] *het (lonen)* **1** pay, wage(s): *een hoog ~ verdienen* earn high wages; **2** deserts, reward: *hij gaf hem zijn verdiende ~* he gave him his just deserts

loonadministratie [lonɑtministra(t)si] *de (~s)* wages administration (*or:* records)

loonbelasting [lombəlastɪŋ] *de (~en)* income tax

loondienst [londinst] *de (~en)* paid employment, salaried employment

loonlijst [lonlɛist] *de (~en)* payroll

loonschaal [lonsxal] *de (-schalen)* pay scale, wage scale

loonstrookje [lonstrokjə] *het (~s)* payslip

loonsverhoging [lonsfərhoɣɪŋ] *de (~en)* wage increase, pay increase, increase in wages (*or:* pay), rise, *(Am)* raise

loop [lop] *de (lopen)* **1** course, development: *de ~ van de Rijn* the course of the Rhine; *zijn gedachten de vrije ~ laten* give one's thoughts (*or:* imagination) free rein; *in de ~ der jaren* through the years; **2** barrel; **3** run, flight

loopafstand [lopɑfstɑnt] *de* walking distance

loopbaan [loban] *de (-banen)* career

loopgraaf [lopxraf] *de (-graven)* trench

loopje [lopjə] *het (~s) (mus)* run, roulade

loopjongen [lopjɔŋə(n)] *de (~s)* errand boy, messenger boy

looplamp [loplɑmp] *de (~en)* portable inspection lamp

loopneus [lopnøs] *de (-neuzen)* runny nose, running nose

looppas [lopɑs] *de* jog, run

loopplank [loplɑŋk] *de (~en)* gangplank, gangway

loops [lops] *adj* on heat, in heat, in season

looptijd [loptɛit] *de (~en)* term, (period of) currency, duration

loos [los] *adj* false, empty: *~ alarm* false alarm

loot [lot] *de (loten)* shoot, cutting

lootje [locə] *het (~s)* lottery ticket, raffle ticket, lot: *~s trekken* draw lots

¹lopen [lopə(n)] *vb* **1** walk, go: *iem in de weg ~* get in s.o.'s way; *op handen en voeten ~* walk on one's hands and feet, walk on all fours; **2** run: *het op een ~ zetten* take to one's heels; **3** run, go: *het is anders gelopen* it worked out (*or:* turned out) otherwise; *dit horloge loopt uitstekend* this watch keeps excellent time; *de kraan loopt niet meer* the tap's stopped running; *een motor die loopt op benzine* an engine that runs on petrol

²lopen [lopə(n)] *vb* go to, attend: *college ~* attend lectures

lopend [lopənt] *adj* **1** running, moving: *~e band* conveyor belt, assembly line; *(fig) aan de ~e band* continually, ceaselessly; **2** current, running: *het ~e jaar* the current year; **3** running, streaming; runny

loper [lopər] *de (~s)* **1** walker, courier, messenger; **2** carpet (strip), runner; **3** bishop; **4** pass-key, master key, skeleton key, picklock

lor [lɔr] *het, de (~ren)* rag

los [lɔs] *adj, adv* **1** loose, free, undone; detachable, movable: *er is een schroef ~* a screw has come loose; *~!* let go!; **2** loose, separate, odd, single: *thee wordt bijna niet meer ~ verkocht* tea is hardly sold loose any more; **3** slack, loose: *met ~se handen rijden* ride with no hands; *ze leven er maar op ~* they live from one day to the next

losbandig [lɔzbɑndəx] *adj, adv* lawless, loose, fast, dissipated

losbarsten [lɔzbɑrstə(n)] *vb* break out, burst out, flare up, erupt, blow up

¹losbreken [lɔzbrekə(n)] *vb* break off, tear off (*or:* loose), separate

²losbreken [lɔzbrekə(n)] *vb* **1** break out (*or:* free), escape: *de hond is losgebroken* the dog has torn itself free; **2** burst out, blow up: *een hevig onweer brak los* a heavy thunderstorm broke

losdraaien [lɔzdrajə(n)] *vb* **1** unscrew, untwist; **2** take off, twist off, loosen

losgaan [lɔsxan] *vb* come loose, work loose, become untied (*or:* unstuck, detached)

losgeld [lɔsxɛlt] *het (~en)* ransom (money)

losjes [lɔʃəs] *adv* **1** loosely; **2** airily; casually
loskloppen [lɔsklɔpə(n)] *vb* beat, knock loose (*or:* off)
losknopen [lɔsknopə(n)] *vb* undo, untie
loskomen [lɔskomə(n)] *vb* **1** come loose, come off, break loose (*or:* free), come apart: *hij kan niet ~ van zijn verleden* he cannot forget his past; **2** come out, unbend, relax
loskoppelen [lɔskɔpələ(n)] *vb* detach, uncouple, disconnect, separate
loskrijgen [lɔskrɛiɣə(n)] *vb* **1** get loose, get undone, get free (*or:* released): *een knoop ~* get a knot untied; **2** secure, extract, (manage to) obtain, raise
¹loslaten [lɔslatə(n)] *vb* **1** release, set free, let off, let go, discharge, unleash: *laat me los!* let go of me!, let me go!; **2** reveal, speak, release, leak
²loslaten [lɔslatə(n)] *vb* come off, peel off, come loose (*or:* unstuck, untied), give way
losliggend [lɔslıɣənt] *adj* loose
loslopen [lɔslopə(n)] *vb* walk about (freely), run free, be at large, stray ‖ *het zal wel ~* it will be all right, it'll sort itself out
loslopend [lɔslopənt] *adj* stray, unattached
losmaken [lɔsmakə(n)] *vb* **1** release, set free, untie: *de hond ~* unleash the dog; *een knoop ~* untie a knot, undo a button; **2** loosen (up), rake; **3** stir up: *die tv-film heeft een hoop losgemaakt* that TV film has created quite a stir
losraken [lɔsrakə(n)] *vb* come loose (*or:* off, away), dislodge, become detached
losrukken [lɔsrʏkə(n)] *vb* tear loose, rip off, wrench, yank away (*or:* off)
löss [lʏs] *de* loess
losscheuren [lɔsχørə(n)] *vb* tear loose, rip off (*or:* away)
losschroeven [lɔsχruvə(n)] *vb* unscrew, loosen, screw off, disconnect
lossen [lɔsə(n)] *vb* **1** unload, discharge; **2** discharge, shoot, fire: *een schot op (het) doel ~* shoot at goal
losstaand [lɔstant] *adj* detached, isolated, free-standing, disconnected
lostrekken [lɔstrɛkə(n)] *vb* pull loose, loosen, draw loose
los-vast [lɔsfast] *adj* half-fastened, (*fig*) casual
¹losweken [lɔswekə(n)] *vb* soak off, steam off (*or:* open)
²losweken [lɔswekə(n)] *vb* become unstuck
loswrikken [lɔsvrɪkə(n)] *vb* wrench, dislodge
loswringen [lɔsfrɪŋə(n)] *vb* wring, extricate
loszitten [lɔsɪtə(n)] *vb* be loose, be slack: *die knoop zit los* that button is coming off
lot [lɔt] *het (~en)* **1** lottery ticket; raffle ticket; **2** lot, share: (*fig*) *zij is een ~ uit de loterij* she is one in a thousand; **3** fortune, chance; **4** lot, fate, destiny: *iem aan zijn ~ overlaten* leave s.o. to fend for himself, leave s.o. to his fate
loten [lotə(n)] *vb* draw lots
loterij [lotərɛi] *de (~en)* lottery
loterijbriefje [lotərɛibrifjə] *het (~s)* (lottery) ticket

lotgenoot [lɔtχənot] *de (lotgenoten)* companion (in misfortune, adversity), fellow-sufferer
loting [lotɪŋ] *de (~en)* drawing lots
lotion [loʃɔn] *de (~s)* lotion, wash
lotto [lɔto] *de (~'s)* lottery
lotus [lotʏs] *de (~sen)* lotus
louche [luʃ(ə)] *adj* shady, suspicious(-looking)
¹louter [lautər] *adv* purely, merely, only: *het heeft ~ theoretische waarde* it has only theoretical value
²louter [lautər] *adj* sheer, pure, mere, bare: *uit ~ medelijden* purely out of compassion
loven [lovə(n)] *vb* **1** praise, commend, laud; **2** (*rel*) praise, bless, glorify: *looft de Heer* praise the Lord
lovend [lovənt] *adj, adv* laudatory, approving, full of praise
lovertje [lovərcə] *het (~s)* spangle, sequin
loyaal [lojal] *adj, adv* loyal, faithful, steadfast
loyaliteit [lwajalitɛit] *de* loyalty
¹lozen [lozə(n)] *vb* drain, empty: *~ in (op) de zee* discharge into the sea
²lozen [lozə(n)] *vb* get rid of, send off, dump
lozing [lozɪŋ] *de (~en)* drainage, discharge, dumping
lp [ɛlpe] *de (~'s)* LP
LPG [ɛlpeɣe] *het liquefied petroleum gas* LPG, LP gas
lso [ɛlɛso] *het (Belg) lager secundair onderwijs* junior secondary general education
lts [ɛltɛːs] *de (~'en) lagere technische school* technical school
lucht [lʏχt] *de (~en)* **1** air: *in de open ~ slapen* sleep in the open air; *~ krijgen: a)* breathe; *b) (fig)* get room to breathe; *in de ~ vliegen* blow up, explode; *die bewering is uit de ~ gegrepen* that statement is totally unfounded; *uit de ~ komen vallen* appear out of thin air, be dumbfounded; **2** sky; **3** smell, scent, odour
luchtaanval [lʏχtanvɑl] *de (~len)* air raid
luchtafweergeschut [lʏχtɑfweːrɣəsχʏt] *het* anti-aircraft guns
luchtalarm [lʏχtalɑrm] *het (~en)* air-raid warning (*or:* siren), (air-raid) alert
luchtballon [lʏχtbɑlɔn] *de (~nen)* (hot-air) balloon
luchtbasis [lʏχ(t)bazɪs] *de (~sen, -bases)* airbase
luchtbed [lʏχtbɛt] *het (~den)* air-bed, Lilo, inflatable bed
luchtbel [lʏχtbɛl] *de (~len)* air bubble (*or:* bell)
luchtdicht [lʏɣdɪχt] *adj, adv* airtight, hermetic
luchtdruk [lʏɣdrʏk] *de* (atmospheric) pressure, air pressure
luchtdrukpistool [lʏɣdrʏkpistol] *het (-pistolen)* air pistol
luchten [lʏχtə(n)] *vb* air, ventilate
luchter [lʏχtər] *de (~s)* candelabrum, chandelier
luchtfoto [lʏχtfoto] *de (~'s)* aerial photo(graph), aerial view
luchthartig [lʏχthɑrtəχ] *adj, adv* light-hearted, carefree
luchthaven [lʏχthavə(n)] *de (~s)* airport

luchtig [lʏχtəχ] *adj* **1** light, airy; **2** light, cool, thin; **3** airy, light-hearted: *iets op ~e toon meedelen* announce sth casually; **4** airy, vivacious, light: *~ gekleed* lightly dressed

luchtje [lʏχjə] *het (~s)* smell, scent, odour: *er zit een ~ aan (fig)* there is sth fishy about it

luchtkasteel [lʏχtkɑstel] *het (-kastelen)* castle in the air, daydream

luchtkussen [lʏχtkʏsə(n)] *het (~s)* air cushion (*or:* pillow)

luchtledig [lʏχtledəχ] *adj* exhausted (*or:* void) of air: *een ~e ruimte* a vacuum

luchtmacht [lʏχtmɑχt] *de (~en)* air force

luchtmobiel [lʏχtmobil] *adj* airborne

luchtopname [lʏχtɔpnamə] *de* aerial photo(graph)

luchtpijp [lʏχtpεip] *de (~en)* windpipe, trachea

luchtpost [lʏχtpɔst] *de* airmail

luchtruim [lʏχtrœym] *het* atmosphere; airspace, air

luchtspiegeling [lʏχtspiɣəlıŋ] *de (~en)* mirage

luchtsprong [lʏχtsprɔŋ] *de (~en)* jump in the air, caper

luchtstreek [lʏχtstrek] *de (-streken)* zone, region

luchtstroom [lʏχtstrom] *de (-stromen)* air current, flow of air

luchtvaart [lʏχtfart] *de* aviation, flying

luchtvaartmaatschappij [lʏχtfartmatsχɑpεi] *de (~en)* airline (company): *de Koninklijke Luchtvaartmaatschappij* Royal Dutch Airlines, KLM

luchtvaartverkeer [lʏχtfartfərker] *het* air traffic

luchtverfrisser [lʏχtfərfrısər] *de (~s)* air freshener

luchtvervuiling [lʏχtfərvœylıŋ] *de* air pollution

luchtvochtigheid [lʏχtfɔχtəχhεit] *de* humidity

luchtvracht [lʏχtfrɑχt] *de (~en)* air cargo, airfreight

luchtwegen [lʏχtweɣə(n)] *de* bronchial tubes

luchtziek [lʏχtsik] *adj* airsick

lucifer [lysifɛr] *de (~s)* match

lucifersdoosje [lysifɛrzdoʃə] *het (~s)* matchbox

lucifershoutje [lysifɛrshɑucə] *het (~s)* matchstick

lucratief [lykratif] *adj, adv* lucrative, profitable

luguber [lyɣybər] *adj, adv* lugubrious, sinister

¹lui [lœy] *adj, adv* lazy, idle, indolent, slow, heavy: *een ~e stoel* an easy chair; *liever ~ dan moe zijn* be bone idle

²lui [lœy] *de* people, folk: *zijn ouwe ~* his old folks (*or:* parents)

luiaard [lœyart] *de (~s)* **1** lazybones; **2** sloth

luid [lœyt] *adj, adv* loud: *met ~e stem* in a loud voice

¹luiden [lœydə(n)] *vb* **1** sound, ring, toll: *de klok luidt* the bell is ringing (*or:* tolling); **2** read, run: *het vonnis luidt …* the verdict is …

²luiden [lœydə(n)] *vb* ring, sound

luidkeels [lœytkels] *adv* loudly, at the top of one's voice

luidop [lœytɔp] *adv (Belg)* aloud, out loud

luidruchtig [lœytrʏχtəχ] *adj, adv* noisy, boisterous

luidspreker [lœytsprekər] *de (~s)* (loud)speaker

luier [lœyər] *de (~s)* nappy

luieren [lœyərə(n)] *vb* be idle (*or:* lazy), laze

luifel [lœyfəl] *de (~s)* awning

luiheid [lœyhɛit] *de* laziness, idleness

luik [lœyk] *het (~en)* hatch; trapdoor; shutter

Luik [lœyk] *het* Liège

luilak [lœylɑk] *de (~ken)* lazybones, sluggard

luilekkerland [lœylɛkərlɑnt] *het* (land of) Cockaigne, land of plenty

luipaard [lœypart] *de (~en)* leopard

luis [lœys] *de (luizen)* louse; aphid

luisteraar [lœystərar] *de (~s)* listener

luisteren [lœystərə(n)] *vb* **1** listen: *goed kunnen ~* be a good listener; *luister eens* listen …, say …; **2** eavesdrop, listen (in); **3** listen, respond: *naar hem wordt toch niet geluisterd* nobody pays any attention to (*or:* listens to) him anyway

luisterrijk [lœystərɛik] *adj, adv* splendid, glorious, magnificent

luistervaardigheid [lœystərvardəχhɛit] *de* listening (skill)

luistervaardigheidstoets *de* listening comprehension test

luistervink [lœystərvıŋk] *de (~en)* eavesdropper

luit [lœyt] *de (~en)* lute

luitenant [lœytənɑnt] *de (~s)* lieutenant

luizen [lœyzə(n)] *vb ‖ iem erin ~* take s.o. in, trick s.o. into sth, trip s.o. up

luizenbaan [lœyzə(n)ban] *de (-banen)* soft job, cushy job

luizenleven [lœyzə(n)levə(n)] *het (~s)* cushy life

lukken [lʏkə(n)] *vb* succeed, be successful, work, manage, come off (*or:* through), gel: *het is niet gelukt* it didn't work, it didn't go through, it was no go; *het lukte hem te ontsnappen* he managed to escape; *die foto is goed gelukt* that photo has come out well

lukraak [lʏkrak] *adj, adv* haphazard, random, wild, hit-or-miss

lul [lʏl] *de (~len)* **1** prick, cock; **2** prick, drip

lullen [lʏlə(n)] *vb* (talk) bullshit, drivel

lumineus [lyminøs] *adj* brilliant, bright

lummel [lʏməl] *de (~s)* clodhopper, gawk

lunch [lʏnʃ] *de (~es)* lunch(eon)

lunchconcert [lʏnʃkɔnsɛrt] *het (~en)* lunch concert

lunchen [lʏnʃə(n)] *vb* lunch, have (*or:* eat, take) lunch

lunchpakket [lʏnʃpakɛt] *het (~ten)* packed lunch

lurken [lʏrkə(n)] *vb* suck noisily

lurven [lʏrvə(n)] *de ‖ iem bij zijn ~ pakken* get s.o., grab s.o.

lus [lʏs] *de (~sen)* loop, noose

lust [lʏst] *de (~en)* **1** desire, interest: *tijd en ~ ontbreken me om …* I have neither the time nor the energy to (*or:* for) …; **2** lust, passion, desire; **3** delight, joy: *~en en lasten* joys and burdens; *zwemmen is zijn ~ en zijn leven* swimming is all the world to him, swimming is his ruling passion; *een ~ voor het* *oog* a sight for sore eyes

lusteloos [lʏstəlos] *adj, adv* listless, languid, apathetic

lusten [lʏstə(n)] *vb* like, enjoy, be fond of, have a taste for: *ik zou wel een pilsje* ~ I could do with a beer

lustig [lʏstəχ] *adj, adv* cheerful, gay, merry

lustobject [lʏstɔpjɛkt] *het (~en)* sex object

lustrum [lʏstrʏm] *het (lustra)* lustrum

luttel [lʏtəl] *adj* little, mere, few, inconsiderable

luw [lyw] *adj* sheltered, protected

luwte [lywtə] *de (~n)* lee, shelter

luxaflex [lʏksaflɛks] *de* Venetian blinds

¹**luxe** [lʏksə] *de* luxury: *het zou geen (overbodige)* ~ *zijn* it would certainly be no luxury, it's really necessary

²**luxe** [lʏksə] *adj* luxury, fancy, de luxe: *een* ~ *tent* a posh (*or:* fancy) place

Luxemburg [lʏksəmbʏrχ] *het* Luxemb(o)urg

luxueus [lyksywøs] *adj, adv* luxurious, opulent, plush

lyceum [lisejʏm] *het (lycea) (roughly)* grammarschool, *(Am)* high school

lymf [lɪmf] *de* lymph

lymfklier [lɪmfklir] *de (~en)* lymph node (*or:* gland)

lynchen [lɪnʃə(n)] *vb* lynch

lynx [lɪnks] *de (~en)* lynx

lyrisch [liris] *adj, adv* lyric(al)

m

ma [ma] *de (~'s)* mum, *(Am)* mom: *pa en ~* Mum (*or:* Mom) and Dad

maag [maχ] *de (magen)* stomach: *ergens mee in zijn ~ zitten* be worried about sth, be troubled by sth

maagd [maχt] *de (~en)* virgin

Maagd [maχt] *de (~en) (astrology)* Virgo

maagdelijkheid [maγdələkhɛit] *de* virginity

maagklacht [maχklaχt] *de (~en)* stomach disorder

maagkramp [maχkramp] *de (~en) (pl)* stomach cramps

maagpatiënt [maχpaʃɛnt] *de (~en)* gastric patient

maagpijn [maχpɛin] *de (~en)* stomach-ache

maagzuur [maχsyr] *het* heartburn

maaien [maja(n)] *vb* mow, cut

maaier [majər] *de (~s)* mower

maaimachine [majmaʃinə] *de (~s)* (lawn)mower

¹**maal** [mal] *het, de* **1** time: *een paar ~* once or twice, several times; *anderhalf ~ zoveel* half as much (*or:* many) (again); **2** times: *lengte ~ breedte ~ hoogte* length times width times height; *twee ~ drie is zes* two times three is six

²**maal** [mal] *het* meal: *een feestelijk ~* a festive meal

maalteken [maltekə(n)] *het (~s)* multiplication sign

maaltijd [maltɛit] *de (~en)* meal, dinner

maan [man] *de (manen)* moon

maand [mant] *de (~en)* month: *de ~ januari* the month of January; *een ~ vakantie* a month's holiday; *drie ~en lang* for three months; *binnen een ~* within a month; *een baby van vier ~en* a four-month-old baby

maandabonnement [mantabɔnəmɛnt] *het (~en)* monthly subscription, monthly season ticket

maandag [mandaχ] *de (~en)* Monday: *ik train altijd op ~* I always train on Mondays; *ik doe het ~ wel* I will do it on Monday; *'s maandags* on Mondays, every Monday

¹**maandags** [mandaχs] *adj* Monday

²**maandags** [mandaχs] *adv* on Mondays

maandblad [mandblat] *het (~en)* monthly (magazine)

maandelijks [mandələks] *adj, adv* monthly, once a month, every month: *in ~e termijnen* in monthly instalments

maandenlang [mandə(n)laŋ] *adj, adv* for months, months long

maandloon [mantlon] *het (-lonen)* monthly wages

maandverband [mantfərbant] *het (~en)* sanitary towel (*or Am:* napkin)

maanlander [manlandər] *de (~s)* lunar module

maanlanding [manlandɪŋ] *de (~en)* moon landing

maanlicht [manlɪχt] *het* moonlight

maanmannetje [manmanəcə] *het* Man in the Moon

maansverduistering [mansfərdœystərɪŋ] *de (~en)* eclipse of the moon, lunar eclipse

maanzaad [manzat] *het* poppy seed

¹**maar** [mar] *adv* **1** but; only, just: *zeg het ~: koffie of thee?* which will it be: coffee or tea?; *kom ~ binnen* come on in; *dat komt ~ al te vaak voor* that happens only (*or:* all) too often; *het is ~ goed dat je gebeld hebt* it's a good thing you rang; *als ik ook ~ een minuut te lang wegblijf* if I stay away even a minute too long; *doe het nu ~* just do it; *let ~ niet op hem* don't pay any attention to him; *ik zou ~ uitkijken* you'd better be careful; **2** only, as long as: *als het ~ klaar komt* as long as (*or:* so long as) it is finished; **3** (if) only: *ik hoop ~ dat hij het vindt* I only hope he finds it; *wat je ~ wil* whatever you want; *waarom doe je dat?* zo ~ why do you do that? just for the fun of it; *ik vind het ~ niks* I'm none too happy about it; *zoveel als je ~ wilt* as much (*or:* many) as you like

²**maar** [mar] *conj* but: *klein, ~ dapper* small but tough; *ja ~, als dat nu niet zo is* yes, but what if that isn't true?; *nee ~!* really!

maarschalk [marsχalk] *de (~en)* Field Marshal, *(Am)* General of the Army

maart [mart] *de* March

maas [mas] *de (mazen)* mesh: *door de mazen (van het net) glippen* slip through the net

Maas [mas] *de* Meuse

¹**maat** [mat] *de* **1** size, measure, measurements: *in hoge mate* to a great degree, to a large extent; *in toenemende mate* increasingly, more and more; *welke ~ hebt u?* what size do you take?; **2** measure: *maten en gewichten* weights and measures; **3** moderation; **4** *(mus)* time, beat: *(geen) ~ kunnen houden* be (un)able to keep time; **5** *(mus)* bar, measure: *de eerste maten van het volkslied* the first few bars of the national anthem; *de ~ is vol* that's the limit

²**maat** [mat] *de* **1** pal, mate; **2** (team)mate, *(cards)* partner

maatbeker [madbekər] *de (~s)* measuring cup

maatgevoel [maχəvul] *het* sense of rhythm

maathouden [mathaudə(n)] *vb (mus)* keep time

maatje [maɔə] *het (~s)* chum, pal: *goede ~s zijn met iem* be the best of friends with s.o.; *goede ~s worden met iem* chum up with s.o.

maatkostuum [matkɔstym] *het (~s)* custom-made suit, tailored suit

maatregel [matreγəl] *de (~en)* measure: *~en nemen* (or: *treffen*) take steps

maatschap [matsχap] *de (~pen)* partnership

maatschappelijk [matsχɑpələk] *adj, adv* **1** social: *hij zit in het ~ werk* he's a social worker; **2** joint: *het ~ kapitaal* nominal capital

maatschappij [matsχɑpɛi] *de (~en)* **1** society; association; **2** company

maatschappijleer [matsχɑpɛiler] *de* social studies

maatstaf [mɑtstɑf] *de (-staven)* criterion, standard(s)

maatwerk [mɑtwɛrk] *het* custom-made clothes (*or:* shoes)

macaber [makɑbər] *adj, adv* macabre

Macedonië [mɑsədonijə] *het* Macedonia

Macedoniër [mɑsədonijər] *de* Macedonian

¹machinaal [maʃinɑl] *adj* mechanized, machine

²machinaal [maʃinɑl] *adv* mechanically, by machine

machine [maʃinə] *de (~s)* machine, *(pl also)* machinery

machinebankwerker [maʃinəbɑŋkwɛrkər] *de (~s)* lathe operator

machinefabriek [maʃinəfabrik] *de (~en)* engineering works

machinegeweer [maʃinəɣəwer] *het (-geweren)* machine-gun

machinekamer [maʃinəkɑmər] *de (~s)* engine room

machinist [maʃinɪst] *de (~en)* **1** *(railways)* engine driver, *(Am)* engineer; **2** *(shipp)* engineer

¹macho [mɑtʃo] *de (~'s)* macho

²macho [mɑtʃo] *adj* macho

macht [mɑχt] *de (~en)* **1** power, force: *(naar) de ~ grijpen* (attempt to) seize power; *aan de ~ zijn* be in power; *iem in zijn ~ hebben* have s.o. in one's power; *de ~ over het stuur verliezen* lose control of the wheel; **2** authority: *rechterlijke ~* the judicial branch, the judiciary; *de uitvoerende* (or: *wetgevende) ~* the executive (*or:* legislative) branch; **3** power, force: *dat gaat boven mijn ~* that is beyond my power; *met (uit) alle ~* with all one's strength; *(maths) een getal tot de vierde ~ verheffen* raise a number to the fourth power; *(maths) drie tot de derde ~* three cubed

machteloos [mɑχtəlos] *adj, adv* powerless: *machteloze woede* impotent (*or:* helpless) anger

machteloosheid [mɑχtəlosheit] *de* powerlessness

machthebber [mɑχthɛbər] *de (~s)* ruler, leader

machtig [mɑχtəχ] *adj* **1** powerful, mighty: *haar gevoelens werden haar te ~* she was overcome by her emotions; **2** rich, heavy; **3** competent (in)

machtigen [mɑχtəɣə(n)] *vb* authorize

machtiging [mɑχtəɣɪŋ] *de (~en)* authorization

machtsstrijd [mɑχtstreit] *de (~en)* struggle for power, power struggle

machtsverheffen [mɑχ(t)sfərhɛfə(n)] *vb* raise to the pwoer

machtsverhouding [mɑχtsfərhaudɪŋ] *de (~en)* || *de ~en zijn gewijzigd* the balance of power has shifted

machtsvertoon [mɑχtsfərton] *het* display of pow-

er, show of strength

macramé [makramɛ] *het* macramé

macro [mɑkro] *adv* macro

madam [madɑm] *de (~men)* lady: *de ~ spelen (uithangen)* act the lady

made [mɑdə] *de (~n)* maggot, grub

madeliefje [mɑdəlifjə] *het (~s)* daisy

madonna [madɔna] *de (~'s)* Madonna

maf [mɑf] *adj, adv* crazy, nuts: *doe niet zo ~* don't be so daft, stop goofing around

maffen [mɑfə(n)] *vb* sleep, snooze, kip

maffia [mɑfija] *de* mafia

maffioso [mafijozo] *de (maffiosi)* mafioso

magazijn [maɣazɛin] *het (~en)* **1** warehouse, stockroom, supply room; **2** magazine

magazijnbediende [maɣazɛimbədində] *de (~n, ~s)* warehouseman, supply clerk

magazine [mɛgəzɪn] *het (~s)* **1** magazine; **2** current affairs programme

mager [mɑɣər] *adj, adv* **1** thin, skinny; **2** lean: *~e riblappen* lean beef (ribs); **3** feeble

magie [maɣi] *de* magic

magisch [mɑɣis] *adj* magic(al)

magistraat [maɣistrɑt] *de (magistraten)* magistrate

magma [mɑɣma] *het* magma

magnaat [maɣnɑt] *de (magnaten)* magnate, tycoon

magneet [maɣnet] *de (magneten)* magnet

magnesium [maɣnezijʏm] *het* magnesium

magnetisch [maɣnetis] *adj* magnetic

magnetisme [maɣnetɪsmə] *het* magnetism

magnetron [maɣnetrɔn] *de (~s)* microwave

magnifiek [maɲifɪk] *adj, adv* magnificent

magnolia [maɣnolija] *de (~'s)* magnolia

maharadja [maharɑtja] *de (~'s)* maharaja(h)

¹mahonie [mahoni] *het* mahogany

²mahonie [mahoni] *adj* mahogany

mailen [mɛlə(n)] *vb* **1** e-mail; **2** do a mailshot

maillot [majo] *de (~s)* tights

mainport [mɛnpɔːrt] *de (~s)* transport hub

maïs [mɑjs] *de* maize, *(Am)* corn: *gepofte ~* popcorn

maïskolf [mɑjskɔlf] *de (-kolven)* corn-cob

maïskorrel [mɑjskɔrəl] *de (~s)* kernel of maize (*or: Am:* corn)

maîtresse [mɛːtrɛsə] *de (~s)* mistress

maïzena [majzena] *de* cornflour, *(Am)* cornstarch

majesteit [majəstɛit] *de (~en)* Majesty

majeur [maʒør] *de* major: *in ~ spelen* play in a major key

majoor [major] *de (~s)* major

majorette [majorɛtə] *de (~s)* (drum) majorette

mak [mɑk] *adj, adv* **1** tame(d); **2** *(fig)* meek, gentle

makelaar [mɑkəlar] *de (~s)* **1** estate agent, *(Am)* real estate agent; **2** broker, agent: *~ in assurantiën* insurance broker

makelaardij [mɑkəlardɛi] *de* brokerage, agency, estate agency

makelij [makəlɛi] *de* make, produce: *van eigen ~* home-grown, home-produced

maken [makə(n)] *vb* **1** repair, fix: *zijn auto kan niet meer gemaakt worden* his car is beyond repair; *zijn auto laten ~* have one's car repaired (*or:* fixed); **2** make, produce, manufacture: *fouten ~* make mistakes; *cider wordt van appels gemaakt* cider is made from apples; **3** cause: *je hebt daar niets te ~* you have no business there; *dat heeft er niets mee te ~* that's got nothing to do with it; *ze wil niets meer met hem te ~ hebben* she doesn't want anything more to do with him; *het (helemaal) ~* make it (to the top); *hij zal het niet lang meer ~* he is not long for this world; *je hebt het ernaar gemaakt* you('ve) asked for it; *ik weet het goed gemaakt* I'll tell you what, I'll make you an offer; *hoe maakt u het?* how do you do?; *hoe maakt je broer het?* how is your brother?; *maak dat je wegkomt!* get out of here!

maker [makər] *de* (~s) maker, producer, artist

make-up [mekʏp] *de* make-up

¹makkelijk [makələk] *adj* easy, simple

²makkelijk [makələk] *adv* easily, readily: *jij hebt ~ praten* it's easy (enough) for you to talk

makker [makər] *de* (~s) pal; mate

makkie [maki] *het* (~s) piece of cake, cushy job, easy job

makreel [makrel] *de* (makrelen) mackerel

¹mal [mal] *de* (~len) mould, template ǁ *iem voor de ~ houden* make fun of s.o., pull s.o.'s leg

²mal [mal] *adj, adv* silly; foolish: *nee, ~le meid (jongen)* no, silly!

malaise [malɛːzə] *de* **1** malaise; **2** depression, slump

malaria [malarija] *de* malaria

Malediven [malədivə(n)] *de* Maldive Islands, Maldives

Maleier [malɛiər] *de* (~s) Malay, Malaysian

Maleis [malɛis] *adj* Malay, (*Am*) Malayan

Maleisië [malɛisijə] *het* Malaysia

Maleisiër [malɛisijər] *de* Malaysian

¹malen [malə(n)] *vb* turn, grind

²malen [malə(n)] *vb* grind, crush

maling [malɪŋ] *de* grind ǁ *daar heb ik ~ aan* I don't care two hoots (*or:* give a hoot); *~ aan iets (iem) hebben* not care/give a rap about sth (s.o.); *iem in de ~ nemen* pull s.o.'s leg, fool s.o.

mals [mals] *adj, adv* tender

Maltees [maltes] *adj* Maltese

mama [mama] *de* (~'s) mam(m)a

mammie [mami] *de* (~s) Mum(my), (*Am*) Mom(my)

mammoet [mamut] *de* (~en, ~s) mammoth

man [man] *de* (~nen) **1** man: *op de ~ spelen: a)* go for the man (*or:* player); *b) (fig)* get personal; *een ~ uit duizenden* a man in a million; *een ~ van weinig woorden* a man of few words; *hij is een ~ van zijn woord* he is as good as his word; **2** man, human: *de gewone (kleine) ~* the man in the street, the common man; *vijf ~ sterk* five strong; *met hoeveel ~ zijn we?* how many are we?, how many of us are

there?; **3** husband

management [mɛnədʒmənt] *het* management

manager [mɛnədʒər] *de* (~s) manager

manchet [manʃɛt] *de* (~ten) cuff

manchetknoop [manʃɛtknop] *de* (-knopen) cuff link

manco [maŋko] *het* (~'s) **1** defect, shortcoming; **2** shortage

mand [mant] *de* (~en) basket ǁ *bij een verhoor door de ~ vallen* have to own up (*or:* come clean)

mandarijn [mandarɛin] *de* (~en) mandarin, (*small*) tangerine

mandoline [mandolinə] *de* (~s) mandolin

mandril [mandrɪl] *de* (~s) mandrill

manege [manɛʒə] *de* (~s) riding school, manège

¹manen [manə(n)] *vb* **1** remind, (*stronger*) demand: *iem om geld ~* demand payment from s.o.; **2** urge

²manen [manə(n)] *de* mane

maneschijn [manəsχɛin] *de* moonlight

mangaan [maŋɣan] *het* manganese

mango [maŋɡo] *de* (~'s) mango

maniak [manijak] *de* (~ken) maniac, freak, buff, fan

manicure [manikyrə] *de* (~n) manicurist

manie [mani] *de* (~s) mania

manier [manir] *de* (~en) **1** way, manner: *daar is hij ook niet op een eerlijke ~ aangekomen* he didn't get that by fair means; *hun ~ van leven* their way of life; *(Belg) bij ~ van spreken* in a manner of speaking; *op een fatsoenlijke ~* in a decent manner, decently; *op de een of andere ~* somehow or other; *op de gebruikelijke ~* (in) the usual way; *dat is geen ~ (van doen)* that is no way to behave; **2** (*pl*) manners: *wat zijn dat voor ~en!* what kind of behaviour is that!

manifest [manifɛst] *het* (~en) manifesto

manifestatie [manifɛsta(t)si] *de* (~s) demonstration, happening, event

manifesteren [manifɛstərə(n)] *ref vb* manifest oneself

manipulatie [manipyla(t)si] *de* (~s) manipulation: *genetische ~* genetic engineering

manipuleren [manipylərə(n)] *vb* manipulate

manisch-depressief [manizdeprɛsif] *adj* manic-depressive

manjaar [manjar] *het* (manjaren) man-year

mank [maŋk] *adj, adv* lame: *~ lopen* (walk with a) limp

mankement [maŋkəmɛnt] *het* (~en) defect, bug

manken [maŋkə(n)] *vb* limp

¹mankeren [maŋkərə(n)] *vb* be wrong, be the matter: *wat mankeert je toch?* what's wrong (*or:* the matter) with you?; *er mankeert een schroefje* one screw is missing

²mankeren [maŋkərə(n)] *vb* have sth the matter: *ik mankeer niets* I'm all right, there's nothing wrong with me

mankracht [maŋkraχt] *de* manpower

mannelijk [manələk] *adj, adv* male; masculine: *een ~e stem* a masculine voice

mannenkoor [mɑnə(n)kor] *het (-koren)* male choir, men's chorus

mannequin [mɑnəkɛ] *de (~s)* model

mannetje [mɑnəcə] *het* **1** little fellow, little guy; **2** man: *daar heeft hij zijn ~s voor* he leaves that to his underlings; **3** male

manoeuvre [manœːvrə] *het, de (~s)* manoeuvre

manoeuvreren [manuvrɛrə(n)] *vb* manoeuvre: *iem in een onaangename positie ~* manoeuvre s.o. into an awkward position

mans [mɑns] *adj* ‖ *zij is er ~ genoeg voor* she can handle it

manschappen [mɑnsχɑpə(n)] *de* men

manshoog [mɑnshoχ] *adj* man-size(d), of a man's height

mantel [mɑntəl] *de (~s)* **1** coat, cloak; **2** *(technology)* casing, housing

mantelpak [mɑntəlpɑk] *het (~ken)* suit

mantelzorg [mɑntəlzɔrχ] *de* volunteer aid

manufacturen [manyfaktyrə(n)] *de* drapery

manuscript [manyskrɪpt] *het (~en)* manuscript, typescript

manusje-van-alles [manyʃəvɑnɑləs] *het (manusjes-van-alles)* jack-of-all-trades; (general) dogsbody

manuur [mɑnyr] *het (manuren)* man-hour

map [mɑp] *de (~pen)* file, folder

maquette [mɑkɛtə] *de (~s)* (scale-)model

maraboe [mɑrabu] *de (~s)* marabou

marathon [mɑratɔn] *de (~s)* marathon

marathonloop [mɑratɔnlop] *de (-lopen)* marathon race

marcheren [mɑrʃɛrə(n)] *vb* march

marconist [mɑrkɔnɪst] *de (~en)* radio operator

marechaussee [marəʃosɛ] *de (~s)* military police, MP

maretak [mɑrətɑk] *de (~ken)* mistletoe

margarine [mɑrɣɑrinə] *de (~s)* margarine

marge [mɑːrʒə] *de (~s)* **1** margin: *gerommel in de ~* fiddling about; **2** band

margriet [mɑrɣrit] *de (~en)* marguerite, (ox-eye) daisy

Maria-Hemelvaart [marijahɛmɛlvart] *de* Assumption (of the Virgin Mary)

marihuana [marijuwɑna] *de* marijuana, marihuana

marine [mɑrinə] *de* navy

marinebasis [mɑrinəbazɪs] *de (-bases)* naval base

marinier [mɑrinir] *de* marine: *het Korps Mariniers* the Marine Corps, the Marines

marionet [marijonɛt] *de* puppet

maritiem [maritim] *adj* maritime

marjolein [mɑrjolɛin] *de* marjoram

mark [mɑrk] *de (~en)* mark

markeerstift [mɑrkɛrstɪft] *de (~en)* marker, marking pen

markeren [mɑrkɛrə(n)] *vb* mark

markies [mɑrkis] *de (markiezen)* marquis

markiezin [mɑrkizɪn] *de (~nen)* marquise

markt [mɑrkt] *de (~en)* market: *een dalende* (or: *stijgende*) *~* a bear (or: bull) market; *naar de ~ gaan* go to market; *van alle ~en thuis zijn* be able to turn one's hand to anything; *(Belg) het niet onder de ~ hebben* be having a hard time

marktaandeel [mɑrktandel] *het (-aandelen)* market share, share of the market

marktdag [mɑrɡdɑχ] *de (~en)* market day

markthal [mɑrkthɑl] *de (~len)* market hall, covered market

marktkoopman [mɑrktkopmɑn] *de (~nen, -kooplui)* market vendor, stallholder

marktkraam [mɑrktkram] *het, de (-kramen)* market stall (or: booth)

marmelade [mɑrməladə] *de (~s)* marmalade

marmer [mɑrmər] *het (~s)* marble

marmeren [mɑrmərə(n)] *adj* marble

marmot [mɑrmɔt] *de (~ten)* **1** marmot; **2** guinea pig

Marokkaan [mɑrɔkan] *de (Marokkanen)* Moroccan

Marokko [mɑrɔko] *het* Morocco

mars [mɑrs] *de (~en)* march ‖ *hij heeft niet veel in zijn ~: a)* he hasn't got much about him; *b)* he is pretty ignorant; *c)* he isn't very bright; *d)* he's not up to much; *hij heeft heel wat in zijn ~: a)* he has a lot to offer; *b)* he is pretty knowledgeable; *c)* he's a clever chap; *voorwaarts ~!* forward march!; *ingerukt ~!* dismiss!

Mars [mɑrs] *de* Mars

marsepein [mɑrsəpɛin] *het, de* marzipan

marskramer [mɑrskramər] *de (~s)* hawker, pedlar

marsmannetje [mɑrsmɑnəcə] *het (~s)* Martian

martelaar [mɑrtəlar] *de (martelaren)* martyr

martelen [mɑrtələ(n)] *vb* torture

marteling [mɑrtəlɪŋ] *de (~en)* torture

¹marter [mɑrtər] *de (~s) (animal)* marten

²marter [mɑrtər] *het (fur)* marten

marxisme [mɑrksɪsmə] *het* Marxism

marxist [mɑrksɪst] *de (~en)* Marxist

mascara [mɑskara] *de* mascara

mascotte [mɑskɔtə] *de (~s)* mascot

masker [mɑskər] *het (~s)* mask

maskeren [mɑskɛrə(n)] *vb* mask, disguise

masochisme [mɑsoχɪsmə] *het* masochism

masochist [mɑsoχɪst] *de (~en)* masochist

massa [mɑsa] *de (~'s)* **1** mass, heaps: *hij heeft een ~ vrienden* he has heaps (or: loads) of friends; *~'s mensen* masses (or: swarms) of people; **2** mass, crowd, *(pol)* masses *(pl)*: *met de ~ meedoen* go with (or: follow) the crowd

massaal [mɑsal] *adj, adv* **1** massive: *~ verzet* massive resistance; **2** mass, wholesale, bulk *(goods)*

massabijeenkomst [mɑsabɛiŋkɔmst] *de (~en)* mass meeting

massage [mɑsaʒə] *de* massage

massagraf [mɑsaɣraf] *het (-graven)* mass grave

massamedia [mɑsamedija] *de* mass media

massamoordenaar [mɑsamordənar] *de (~s)* mass

murderer

massasprint [mɑsasprɪnt] *de (~s)* field sprint

masseren [masɛrə(n)] *vb* massage, do a massage on

masseur [masøːr] *de (~s)* masseur

massief [masif] *adj* solid, massive, heavy: *een ring van ~ zilver* a ring of solid silver

mast [mɑst] *de (~en)* **1** mast: *de ~ strijken* lower the mast; **2** pylon

masturberen [mɑstʏrbɛrə(n)] *vb* masturbate

mat! [mɑt] *int* (check)mate!

¹mat [mɑt] *de (~ten)* mat: *~ten kloppen* beat (*or:* shake) mats

²mat [mɑt] *adj, adv* **1** mat(t); dull; dim *(light);* pearl; **2** mat(t), frosted

³mat [mɑt] *adj* checkmate: *~ staan* be checkmated; *iem ~ zetten* checkmate s.o.

matador [matadɔr] *de (~s)* matador

mate [mɑtə] *de (~n)* measure, extent, degree: *in dezelfde ~* equally, to the same extent; *in mindere ~* to a lesser degree; *in grote (or: hoge) ~* to a great (*or:* large) extent, largely

materiaal [mater(i)jɑl] *het (materialen)* material(s)

materialistisch [nater(i)jaḷstis] *adj, adv* materialistic

materie [matɛri] *de (~s)* matter; (subject) matter

¹materieel [materijɛl] *het* material(s), equipment: *rollend ~* rolling stock

²materieel [materijɛl] *adj* material

materniteit [matɛrnitɛit] *de (Belg)* maternity ward

matglas [mɑtχlas] *het* frosted glass

mathematisch [matematis] *adj, adv* mathematical

matig [matəχ] *adj, adv* **1** moderate; **2** moderate, mediocre

matigen [matəɣə(n)] *vb* moderate, restrain: *matig uw snelheid* reduce your speed

matinee [matinɛ] *de (~s)* matinè

matje [mɑcə] *het (~s)* mat: *op het ~ moeten komen: a)* be put on the spot; *b)* be (put) on the carpet

matrak [matrɑk] *de (~ken) (Belg)* truncheon, baton

matras [matrɑs] *het, de (~sen)* mattress

matrijs [matrɛis] *de (matrijzen)* mould, matrix

matrix [matrɪks] *de (matrices)* matrix

matrixprinter [matrɪksprɪntər] *de (~s)* matrix printer, dot printer

matroos [matrɔs] *de (matrozen)* sailor

Mauritanië [mauritanijə] *het* Mauretania

Mauritius [maurɪtsijʏs] *het* (island of) Mauritius

mavo [mavo] *het (~'s) middelbaar algemeen voortgezet onderwijs* lower general secondary education

maxi [mɑksi] *het* maxi

¹maximaal [mɑksimal] *adj* maximum, maximal

²maximaal [mɑksimal] *adv* at (the) most: *dit werk duurt ~ een week* this work takes a week at most

maximum [mɑksimʏm] *het (maxima)* maximum

maximumsnelheid [mɑksimʏmsnɛlhɛit] *de (-heden)* speed limit; maximum speed

mayonaise [majɔnɛːzə] *de* mayonnaise: *patat met ~ chips (or Am:* French fries) with mayonnaise

mazelen [mazələ(n)] *de* measles

mazzel [mɑzəl] *de* (good) luck: *de ~!* see you!

mbo [ɛmbeo] *het middelbaar beroepsonderwijs* intermediate vocational education

m.b.v. *met behulp van* by means of

me [mə] *pers pron* me

ME [ɛmɛ] *de (~'s) mobiele eenheid* anti-riot squad

meander [mejɑndər] *de (~s)* meander

meao [meao] *het (~'s) middelbaar economisch en administratief onderwijs* intermediate business education

mecanicien [mekaniʃɛ] *de (~s)* mechanic

meccano [mɛkano] *de (~'s)* meccano (set)

mechanica [meχanika] *de* mechanics

mechaniek [meχanik] *het, de (~en)* mechanism

mechanisatie [meχanizatsi] *de* mechanization

mechanisch [meχanis] *adj, adv* mechanical: *~ speelgoed* clockwork toys

mechanisme [meχanɪsmə] *het (~n)* mechanism, *(fig also)* machinery

medaille [medɑjə] *de (~s)* medal

medaillon [medajɔn] *het (~s)* medallion, locket

medebewoner [medəbəwonər] *de (~s)* co-occupant, fellow resident

medeburger [medəbʏrɣər] *de (~s)* fellow citizen

mededeling [medədelɪŋ] *de (~en)* announcement, statement

mededelingenbord [medədelɪŋə(n)bɔrt] *het (~en)* notice board

mede-eigenaar [medəɛiɣənar] *de (~s, -eigenaren)* joint owner

medeklinker [medəklɪŋkər] *de (~s)* consonant

medelander [medəlandər] *de (~s)* non-native (inhabitant)

medeleerling [medəlerlɪŋ] *de (~en)* fellow pupil

medeleven [medəlevə(n)] *het* sympathy: *oprecht ~* sincere sympathy; *mijn ~ gaat uit naar* my sympathy lies with; *zijn ~ tonen* express one's sympathy

medelijden [medəlɛidə(n)] *het* pity, compassion: *heb ~ (met)* have mercy (upon); *~ met zichzelf hebben* feel sorry for oneself

medemens [medəmɛns] *de (~en)* fellow man

medeplichtig [medəplɪχtəχ] *adj* accessory

medeplichtige [medəplɪχtəɣə] *de (~n)* accessory (to), accomplice, partner

medereiziger [medərɛizəɣər] *de (~s)* fellow traveller (*or:* passenger)

medestander [medəstandər] *de (~s)* supporter

medewerker [medəwɛrkər] *de (~s)* **1** fellow worker, co-worker, collaborator, contributor, correspondent: *onze juridisch (or: economisch) ~* our legal (*or:* economics) correspondent; **2** employee, staff member

medewerking [medəwɛrkɪŋ] *de* cooperation; assistance: *de politie riep de ~ in van het publiek* the police made an appeal to the public for cooperation

medezeggenschap [medəzɛɣə(n)sχap] *het, de* say, participation

media [medija] *de* media

mediageniek [medijaʒənik] *adj* mediagenic

meekomen [mekomə(n)] *vb* **1** come (also), come along; **2** keep up (with)

mediatheek [medijatɛk] *de (mediatheken)* multimedia centre (*or:* library)

medicament [medikamɛnt] *het (~en)* medicament, medicine

medicijn [medisɛin] *de (~en)* medicine: *een student (in de) ~en* a medical student

medicijnkastje [mediscɛinkɑʃə] *het (~s)* medicine chest (*or:* cabinet)

medio [medijo] *adv* in the middle of: *~ september* in mid-September

medisch [medis] *adj, adv* medical: *op ~ advies* on the advice of one's doctor

meditatie [medita(t)si] *de (~s)* meditation

mediteren [mediterə(n)] *vb* meditate

¹medium [medijʏm] *het (media)* medium

²medium [medijʏm] *adj* medium(-sized)

mee [me] *adv* with, along: *waarom ga je niet ~?* why don't you come along?; *met de klok ~* clockwise; *kan ik ook ~?* can I come too?; *hij heeft zijn uiterlijk ~* he has his looks going for him; *dat kan nog jaren ~* that will last for years; *het kan er ~ door* it's all right, it'll do; *ergens te vroeg* (or: *te laat*) *~ komen* be too early (*or:* late) with sth

meebrengen [mebrɛŋə(n)] *vb* **1** bring (along) (with one): *wat zal ik voor je ~?* what shall I bring you?; **2** involve: *de moeilijkheden die dit met zich heeft meegebracht* the difficulties which resulted from this

¹meedelen [medelə(n)] *vb* share (in), participate (in): *alle erfgenamen delen mee* all heirs are entitled to a share

²meedelen [medelə(n)] *vb* inform (of), let ... know, notify, announce, report: *ik zal het haar voorzichtig ~* I shall break it to her gently; *hierbij deel ik u mee, dat ...* I am writing to inform you that ...

meedingen [medɪŋə(n)] *vb* compete

meedoen [medun] *vb* join (in), take part (in): *mag ik ~?* can I join in? (*or:* you?); *~ aan een wedstrijd* compete in a game; *~ aan een project* (or: *staking*) take part in a project (*or:* strike); *okay, ik doe mee* okay, count me in

meedogenloos [medoɣə(n)los] *adj, adv* merciless

mee-eten [meetə(n)] *vb* eat with (s.o.)

mee-eter [meetər] *de (~s)* blackhead, whitehead

meegaan [meɣan] *vb* **1** go along (*or:* with), accompany, come along (*or:* with): *is er nog iemand die meegaat?* is anyone else coming? (*or:* going?); **2** (*fig*) go (along) with, agree (with): *met de mode ~* keep up with (the) fashion; **3** last: *dit toestel gaat jaren mee* this machine will last for years

¹meegeven [meɣevə(n)] *vb* give: *iem een boodschap ~ send* a message with s.o.

²meegeven [meɣevə(n)] *vb* give (way), yield: *de planken geven niet mee* there is no give in the boards

meehelpen [mehɛlpə(n)] *vb* help (in, with), assist

(with)

meekomen [mekomə(n)] *vb* **1** come (along, with, also): *ik heb er geen bezwaar tegen als hij meekomt* I don't object to his coming (along); **2** keep up (with)

meekrijgen [mekrɛiɣə(n)] *vb* **1** get, receive: *kan ik het geld direct ~?* can I have the money immediately?; **2** win over, get on one's side

meel [mel] *het* flour

meeldraad [meldrat] *de (-draden)* stamen

meeleven [melevə(n)] *vb* sympathize

meelijwekkend [melɛiwɛkənt] *adj* pitiful

meelopen [melopə(n)] *vb* walk along (with), accompany

meeloper [melopər] *de (~s)* hanger-on

meeluisteren [melœystərə(n)] *vb* listen (in)

meemaken [memakə(n)] *vb* experience; go through, live; see; take part (in): *had hij dit nog maar mee mogen maken* if he had only lived to see this; *ze heeft heel wat meegemaakt* she has seen (*or:* been through) a lot

meenemen [menemə(n)] *vb* take along (*or:* with): (*in restaurant*) *~ graag* to take away please

meepraten [mepratə(n)] *vb* take part (*or:* join) in a conversation: *daar kun je niet over ~* you don't know anything about it

¹meer [mer] *het (meren)* lake

²meer [mer] *num* **1** more: *~ dood dan levend* more dead than alive; *des te ~ all* the more (so); *steeds ~* more and more; *hij heeft ~ boeken dan ik* he has got more books than I (have); **2** more, further: *wie waren er nog ~?* who else was there?; *wat kan ik nog ~ doen?* what else can I do?; **3** any more, no more, (any) longer: *zij is geen kind ~* she is no longer a child; *hij had geen appels ~* he had no more apples, he was out of apples; **4** more (often): *we moeten dit ~ doen* we must do this more often; *onder ~* among other things, among others; *zonder ~: a)* naturally, of course; *b)* right away

¹meerdere [merdərə] *de (~n)* superior, superior officer

²meerdere [merdərə] *num* several, a number of

meerderheid [merdərhɛit] *de* majority

meerderjarig [merdərjarəχ] *adj* of age: *~ worden* come of age

meerderjarige [merdərjarəɣə] *de (~n)* adult

meerderjarigheid [merdərjarəχhɛit] *de* adulthood, legal age

meerekenen [merekənə(n)] *vb* count (in)

meerijden [merɛidə(n)] *vb* come (*or:* ride) (along) with: *ik vroeg of ik mee mocht rijden* I asked for a lift

meerkeuzetoets [merkøzətuts] *de (~en)* multiple-choice test

meerkeuzevraag [merkøzəvraχ] *de (-vragen)* multiple-choice question

meerpaal [merpal] *de (-palen)* mooring post

meervoud [mervɑut] *het (~en)* plural: *in het ~* (in the) plural

meerzijdig [merzɛidəχ] *adj* multilateral

mees [mes] *de (mezen)* tit

meesjouwen [meʃɑuwə(n)] *vb* lug, *(Am)* tote

meeslepen [meslepə(n)] *vb* **1** drag (along); **2** carry (with, away): *zich laten ~* get carried away

meeslepend [meslepənt] *adj, adv* compelling, moving

meesleuren [meslørə(n)] *vb* sweep away *(or:* along)

meespelen [mespelə(n)] *vb* take part *(or:* join) in a game, play (along with), be a cast member

¹meest [mest] *adj* **1** most, the majority of: *op zijn ~* at (the) most; **2** most, greatest: *de ~e tijd doet ze niets* most of the time she doesn't do a thing

²meest [mest] *adv* most, best: *de ~ gelezen krant* the most widely read newspaper

meestal [mestɑl] *adv* mostly, usually

meester [mestər] *de (~s)* **1** master: *~ in de rechten (roughly)* Master of Laws; **2** teacher, (school)master

meesterbrein [mestərbrɛin] *het (~en)* mastermind

meesteres [mestorɛs] *de (~sen)* mistress

meesterlijk [mestərlək] *adj, adv* masterly

meesterwerk [mestərwɛrk] *het (~en)* masterpiece, masterwork

meetbaar [medbar] *adj* measurable

¹meetellen [metɛlə(n)] *vb* count also, count in, include

²meetellen [metɛlə(n)] *vb* count: *dat telt niet mee* that doesn't count

meetkunde [metkyndə] *de* geometry

meetlat [metlɑt] *de (~ten)* measuring rod

meetlint [metlɪnt] *het (~en)* tape-measure

meetrekken [metrɛkə(n)] *vb* pull along, drag along

meeuw [mew] *de (~en)* (sea)gull

meevallen [mevɑlə(n)] *vb* turn out *(or:* prove, be) better than expected: *dat zal wel ~* it won't be so bad

meevaller [mevɑlər] *de (~s)* piece *(or:* bit) of luck: *een financiële ~* a windfall

meevoelen [mevulə(n)] *vb* sympathize (with)

meewarig [mewarəχ] *adj, adv* pitying: *met een ~e blik keek ze hem aan* she looked at him pityingly

meewerken [mewɛrkə(n)] *vb* **1** cooperate, work together: *we werkten allemaal een beetje mee* we all pulled together, we all did our little bit; **2** assist: *allen werkten mee om het concert te laten slagen* everyone assisted in making the concert a success; *meewerkend voorwerp* indirect object

meezingen [mezɪŋə(n)] *vb* sing along (with)

meezitten [mezɪtə(n)] *vb* be favourable: *het zat hem niet mee* luck was against him; *als alles meezit* if all goes well, if everything runs smoothly

megabioscoop [meɣabijoskop] *de* multiplex

megafoon [meɣafɔn] *de (~s, -fonen)* megaphone

megahertz [meɣahɛrts] *de (onv.)* megahertz

mei [mɛi] *de* May

meid [mɛit] *de (~en)* girl, (young) woman: *je bent al een hele ~* you're quite a woman *(or:* girl)

meidengroep [mɛidə(n)ɣrup] *de (~en)* female band

meikever [mɛikevər] *de (~s)* May-bug, cockchafer

meiklokje [mɛiklɔkjə] *het (~s)* lily of the valley

meineed [mɛinet] *de (meineden)* perjury

meisje [mɛiʃə] *het (~s)* **1** girl, daughter; **2** girl, young woman *(or:* lady); **3** girlfriend; **4** girl, maid

meisjesnaam [mɛiʃəsnam] *de (-namen)* maiden name

Mej. *Mejuffrouw* Miss

mejuffrouw [məjʏfrɑu] *de (~en)* Miss, Ms

mekaar [məkar] *ref pron (inf)* each other, one another || *komt voor ~* OK, I'll see to it

melaats [melats] *adj* leprous

melaatsheid [melatshɛit] *de* leprosy

melancholie [melɑŋχoli] *de* melancholy

melancholiek [melɑŋχolik] *adj, adv* melancholy

melange [melãʒə] *de (~s)* blend, mélange

¹melden [mɛldə(n)] *vb* report, inform (of), announce: *ze heeft zich ziek gemeld* she has reported (herself) sick, she called in sick; *niets te ~ hebben (fig)* have nothing *(or:* no news) to report

²melden [mɛldə(n)] *ref vb* report, check in

melding [mɛldɪŋ] *de (~en)* mention(ing), report(ing)

meldkamer [mɛltkamər] *de (~s)* centre, emergency room

melig [meləχ] *adj, adv* corny

melk [mɛlk] *de* milk: *koffie met ~* white coffee

melkboer [mɛlgbur] *de (~en)* milkman

melkbus [mɛlgbʏs] *de (~sen)* milk churn

melken [mɛlkə(n)] *vb* milk

melkgebit [mɛlkχəbit] *het (~ten)* milk teeth

melkkoe [mɛlku] *de* **1** dairy cow; **2** *(fig)* milch cow

melkpoeder [mɛlkpudər] *het, de* powdered milk, dehydrated milk

melktand [mɛlktɑnt] *de (~en)* milk tooth

melkvee [mɛlkfe] *het* dairy cattle

melkveehouder [mɛlkfehɑudər] *de (~s)* dairy farmer

melkweg [mɛlkwɛχ] *de (~en)* Milky Way

melodie [melodi] *de (~ën)* melody, tune

melodieus [melod(i)jøs] *adj, adv* melodious

melodrama [melodrama] *het (~'s)* melodrama

meloen [məlun] *de (~en)* melon

membraan [mɛmbran] *het, de (membranen)* membrane

memo [memo] *het, de (~'s)* memo

memoires [memwarəs] *de* memoirs

men [mɛn] *ind pron* **1** one, people, they: *~ zegt* it is said, people *(or:* they) say; *~ zegt dat hij ziek is* he is said to be ill; **2** one, you: *~ kan hen niet laten omkomen* they cannot be allowed to die; *~ zou zeggen dat …* by the look of it …; **3** one, they: *~ had dat kunnen voorzien* that could have been foreseen; *~ hoopt dat …* it is hoped that …

meneer [məner] *de (meneren)* gentleman; *(before surname)* Mr

menen [mɛnə(n)] *vb* **1** mean: *dat meen je niet!* you can't be serious!; *ik meen het!* I mean it!; **2** intend, mean: *het goed met iem ~* mean well towards s.o.; **3** think: *ik meende dat ...* I thought ...

menens [mɛnəns] *adj* ‖ *het is ~* it's serious

mengeling [mɛŋəlɪŋ] *de (~en)* mixture

mengelmoes [mɛŋəlmus] *het* mishmash, jumble

¹mengen [mɛŋə(n)] *vb* **1** mix, blend: *door elkaar ~* mix together; **2** mix, bring in: *mijn naam wordt er ook in gemengd* my name was also brought in (*or:* dragged in)

²mengen [mɛŋə(n)] *ref vb* get (oneself) involved (in), get (oneself) mixed up (in): *zich in de discussie ~* join in the discussion

mengpaneel [mɛŋpanel] *het (-panelen)* mixing console, mixer

mengsel [mɛŋsəl] *het (~s)* mixture, blend

menie [meni] *de* red lead

menig [menəχ] *num* many; many a: *in ~ opzicht* in many respects

menigte [menəχtə] *de (~n, ~s)* crowd

mening [menɪŋ] *de (~en)* opinion, view: *afwijkende ~* dissenting view (*or:* opinion); *naar mijn ~* in my opinion (*or:* view), I think, I feel; *van ~ veranderen* change one's opinion (*or:* view); *voor zijn ~ durven uitkomen* stand up for one's opinion

meningsuiting [menɪŋsœytɪŋ] *de* (expression of) opinion, speech: *vrije ~* freedom of speech

meningsverschil [menɪŋsfərsχɪl] *het (-len)* difference of opinion

meniscus [menɪskʏs] *de* meniscus, kneecap

mennen [mɛnə(n)] *vb* drive

menopauze [menopauzə] *de* menopause

¹mens [mɛns] *de* **1** human (being), man, man(kind): *ik ben ook maar een ~* I'm only human; *dat doet een ~ goed* that does you good; *geen ~* not a soul; **2** *(pl)* people: *de gewone ~en* ordinary people; **3** person: *een onmogelijk ~ zijn* be impossible (to deal with)

²mens [mɛns] *het* thing, creature: *het is een braaf (best) ~* she's a good (old) soul

mensa [mɛnza] *de (~'s)* refectory, (student) cafeteria

mensaap [mɛnsap] *de (-apen)* anthropoid (ape), man ape

menselijk [mɛnsələk] *adj* **1** human: *vergissen is ~* to err is human; **2** humane: *niet ~* inhumane, inhuman

menselijkheid [mɛnsələkhɛit] *de* humanity

menseneter [mɛnsə(n)etər] *de (~s)* cannibal

mensenhandel [mɛnsə(n)hɑndəl] *de* human trafficking

mensenheugenis [mɛnsə(n)høyənɪs] *de* human memory: *sinds ~* from (*or:* since) time immemorial

mensenkennis [mɛnsə(n)kɛnɪs] *de* insight into (human) character (*or:* human nature)

mensenleven [mɛnsə(n)levə(n)] *het (~s)* (human) life

mensenrechten [mɛnsə(n)rɛχtə(n)] *de* human rights

mens-erger-je-niet [mɛnsɛrɣərjənit] *het* ludo, *(Am)* sorry

mensheid [mɛnshɛit] *de* human nature, humanity

menslievend [mɛnslivənt] *adj, adv* charitable, humanitarian, philanthropic

mensonterend [mɛnsɔntərənt] *adj* degrading, disgraceful

menstruatie [mɛnstrywa(t)si] *de* menstruation, period

menstruatiepijn [mɛnstrywa(t)sipɛin] *de (~en)* menstrual pain

menstrueren [mɛnstrywerə(n)] *vb* menstruate

menswaardig [mɛnswardəχ] *adj* decent, dignified

menswetenschappen [mɛnswetə(n)sχɑpə(n)] *de* life sciences; social sciences

menswetenschapper [mɛnswetənsχɑpər] *de* life scientist; social scientist

mentaal [mɛntal] *adj, adv* mental

mentaliteit [mɛntalitɛit] *de* mentality

menthol [mɛntɔl] *de* menthol

mentor [mɛntɔr] *de (~en)* **1** tutor; *(Am)* student adviser; **2** mentor

menu [mənʏ] *het, de (~'s)* menu

menubalk [mənʏbɑlk] *de (~en)* menu bar, button bar

menugestuurd [mənʏɣəstyrt] *adj* menu-driven

menukaart [mənʏkart] *de (~en)* menu

mep [mɛp] *de (~pen)* smack ‖ *de volle ~* the full whack

meppen [mɛpə(n)] *vb* smack

merci [mɛrsi] *int* thanks

Mercurius [mɛrkʏrijʏs] *de* Mercury

merel [merəl] *de (~s)* blackbird

meren [merə(n)] *vb* moor

merendeel [merə(n)del] *het* greater part, majority

merg [mɛrχ] *het* (bone) marrow: *die kreet ging door ~ en been* it was a harrowing (*or:* heart-rending) cry

mergel [mɛrɣəl] *de* marl

meridiaan [meridijan] *de (meridianen)* meridian

merk [mɛrk] *het (~en)* **1** brand (name), trademark; make; **2** mark, hallmark

merkbaar [mɛrgbar] *adj, adv* noticeable

merken [mɛrkə(n)] *vb* **1** notice, see: *dat is (duidelijk) te ~* it shows; *hij liet niets ~* he gave nothing away; *je zult het wel ~* you'll find out; *ik merkte het aan zijn gezicht* I could tell (*or:* see) by the look on his face; **2** mark, brand

merkkleding [mɛrkkledɪŋ] *de* designer wear (*or:* clothes)

merkwaardig [mɛrkwardəχ] *adj, adv* peculiar: *het ~e van de zaak is ...* the curious (*or:* odd) thing (about it) is ...

merrie [mɛri] *de (~s)* mare

mes [mɛs] *het (~sen)* knife, blade: *het ~ snijdt aan twee kanten* it is doubly advantageous

mesjogge [məʃɔɣə] *adj* crazy, nutty

mess [mɛs] *de (~es)* mess (hall), messroom

messcherp [mɛsχɛrp] *adj* razor-sharp

Messias [mɛsijɑs] *de* Messiah

messing [mɛsɪŋ] *het* brass

messteek [mɛstek] *de (messteken)* stab (of a knife)

mest [mɛst] *de* **1** manure; **2** fertilizer

mesten [mɛstə(n)] *vb* fertilize; fatten

mesthoop [mɛsthop] *de (-hopen)* dunghill

mestvee [mɛstfe] *het* beef cattle, store cattle; fatstock

met [mɛt] *prep* **1** (along) with, of: ~ *Janssen (on the telephone)* Janssen speaking (*or:* here); ~ *wie spreek ik? (on the telephone)* who am I speaking to?; *spreken* ~ *iem* speak to s.o.; ~ *(zijn) hoevelen zijn zij?* how many of them are there?; **2** with, and, including: ~ *rente* with interest; ~ *vijf* plus (*or:* and) five; *tot en* ~ *hoofdstuk drie* up to and including chapter three; **3** (mixed) with, and; **4** with, by, through, in: ~ *de trein van acht uur* by the eight o'clock train; **5** with, by, at: *ik kom* ~ *Kerstmis* I'm coming at Christmas; *een zak* ~ *geld* a bag of money

¹metaal [metal] *het* metal

²metaal [metal] *de* metal industry, steel industry

metaalarbeider [metalɑrbɛidər] *de (~s)* metalworker; steelworker

metaalnijverheid [metalnɛivərhɛit] *de* metal industry, metallurgical industry, steel industry

metalen [metalə(n)] *adj* **1** metal, metallic; **2** metallic

metamorfose [metamɔrfozə] *de (~n, ~s)* metamorphosis

meteen [mətẹn] *adv* **1** immediately, at once, right (*or:* straightaway): *ze kwam* ~ *toen ze het hoorde* she came as soon as she heard it; *dat zeg ik u zo* ~ I'll tell you in (just) a minute; *ze was* ~ *dood* she was killed instantly; *nu* ~ (right) now, this (very) minute; **2** at the same time, too: *koop er ook* ~ *eentje voor mij* buy one for me (too) while you're about it

meten [metə(n)] *vb* measure, meter

meteoor [metejọr] *de (meteoren)* meteor

meteoriet [metejorịt] *de (~en)* meteorite

meteorologie [metejoroloɣi] *de* meteorology

meteoroloog [metejoroloɣ] *de (-logen)* meteorologist

¹meter [metər] *de* **1** metre: *méters boeken* yards of books; *vierkante (or: kubieke)* ~ square (*or:* cubic) metre; **2** meter, gauge: *de* ~ *opnemen* read the meter; **3** indicator, (meter) needle

²meter [metər] *de* godmother

meterkast [metərkɑst] *de (~en)* meter cupboard

metgezel [mɛtxəzɛl] *de (~len)* companion

methadon [metadɔn] *het* methadone

methode [metodə] *de (~n, ~s)* method, system

meting [metɪŋ] *de (~en)* measuring, measurement

metro [metro] *de (~'s)* underground (railway), *(Am)* subway, tube, metro

metronoom [metronọm] *de (-nomen)* metronome

metropool [metropọl] *de (-polen)* metropolis

metrostation [metrosta(t)ʃɔn] *het (~s)* undergroundstation, *(Am)* subway station, tube station, metro station

metselaar [mɛtsəlar] *de (~s)* bricklayer

metselen [mɛtsələ(n)] *vb* build (in brick, with bricks), lay bricks

metten [mɛtə(n)] *de || korte* ~ *maken (met)* make short (*or:* quick) work (of)

metterdaad [metərdat] *adv* indeed, in fact

meubel [møbəl] *het (~s, ~en)* piece of furniture, *(pl)* furniture

meubelzaak [møbəlzak] *de (-zaken)* furniture business (*or:* shop)

meubilair [møbilɛːr] *het* furniture, furnishings

meubileren [møbilerə(n)] *vb* furnish

meute [møtə] *de (~s)* gang, crowd

mevrouw [məvrɑu] *de (~en)* **1** madam, ma'am, miss; **2** Mrs; Ms

Mexicaan [mɛksikan] *de (Mexicanen)* Mexican

Mexico [mɛksiko] *het* Mexico

mezelf [məzɛlf] *ref pron* myself, me: *ik vermaak* ~ *wel* I'll look after myself

miauwen [mijɑuwə(n)] *vb* miaow, mew

micro [mikro] *de (~'s) (Belg)* mike

microbe [mikrobə] *de (~n)* microbe

microfoon [mikrofọn] *de (~s)* microphone, mike

microprocessor [mikroprosɛsɔr] *de (~s)* microprocessor

microscoop [mikroskọp] *het, de (microscopen)* microscope

middag [mɪdɑχ] *de (~en)* **1** afternoon: *'s middags* in the afternoon; *om 5 uur 's middags* at 5 o'clock in the afternoon, at 5 p.m.; **2** noon: *tussen de* ~ at lunchtime

middagdutje [mɪdɑɣdʏcə] *het (~s)* afternoon nap

middageten [mɪdɑχetə(n)] *het* lunch(eon)

middagpauze [mɪdɑχpauzə] *de (~s)* lunch hour, lunchtime, lunch-hour break

middagtemperatuur [mɪdɑχtɛmpəratyr] *de* afternoon temperature

middagvoorstelling [mɪdɑχforstɛlɪŋ] *de (~en)* matiné

middel [mɪdəl] *het (~en)* **1** waist; **2** means: *het is een* ~, *geen doel* it's a means to an end; *door* ~ *van* by means of; **3** remedy: *een ~tje tegen hoofdpijn* a headache remedy; *het* ~ *is soms erger dan de kwaal* the remedy may be worse than the disease

middelbaar [mɪdəlbar] *adj* middle; *(educ)* secondary

Middeleeuwen [mɪdəlewə(n)] *de* Middle Ages

middeleeuws [mɪdəlews] *adj* medi(a)eval: *~e geschriften* medi(a)eval documents

middelgroot [mɪdəlɣrot] *adj* medium-size(d)

middellands [mɪdəlɑn(t)s] *adj* Mediterranean: *de Middellandse Zee* the Mediterranean (Sea)

middellijn [mɪdəlɛin] *de (~en)* diameter

middelmaat [mɪdəlmat] *de* average

middelmatig [mɪdəlmatəχ] *adj, adv* average, mediocre: *ik vind het maar* ~ I think it's pretty mediocre

middelmatigheid [mɪdəlmatəχhɛit] *de (-heden)* mediocrity

middelpunt [mɪdəlpʏnt] *het (~en)* centre, middle
middelst [mɪdəlst] *adj* middle(most)
middelvinger [mɪdəlvɪŋər] *de (~s)* middle finger
¹midden [mɪdə(n)] *het (~s)* **1** middle, centre: *dat laat ik in het ~* I won't go into that; *de waarheid ligt in het ~* the truth lies (somewhere) in between; **2** middle, midst: *te ~ van* in the midst of, among
²midden [mɪdə(n)] *adv* in the middle of: *~ in de zomer* in the middle of (the) summer; *hij is ~ (in de) veertig* he is in his middle forties (*or*: mid-forties)
Midden-Amerika [mɪdə(n)amerɪka] *het* Central America
middenbaan [mɪdə(n)ban] *de (-banen)* middle lane, centre lane
middenberm [mɪdə(n)bɛrm] *de (~en)* central reservation
Midden-Europa [mɪdə(n)ørɔpa] *het* Central Europe
Midden-Europees [mɪdə(n)ørɔpes] *adj* Central-European
middengolf [mɪdə(n)ɣɔlf] *de* medium wave
middenklasse [mɪdə(n)klɑsə] *de* medium range (*or*: size)
middenmoot [mɪdə(n)mot] *de* middle bracket (*or*: group): *die sportclub hoort thuis in de ~* that's just an average club
middenoor [mɪdə(n)or] *het (-oren)* middle ear
Midden-Oosten [mɪdə(n)ostə(n)] *het* Middle East
middenpad [mɪdə(n)pɑt] *het* (centre) aisle, gangway
middenrif [mɪdə(n)rɪf] *het* midriff, diaphragm
middenstand [mɪdə(n)stɑnt] *de* (the) self-employed, tradespeople
middenstander [mɪdə(n)stɑndər] *de (~s)* tradesman, shopkeeper
middenstandsdiploma [mɪdə(n)stɑntsdiploma] *het (~'s) (roughly)* retailer's certificate (*or*: diploma)
middenstip [mɪdə(n)stɪp] *de (~pen)* centre spot
middenveld [mɪdə(n)vɛlt] *het* midfield
middenvelder [mɪdə(n)vɛldər] *de (~s)* midfielder, midfield player
middernacht [mɪdərnɑχt] *de* midnight
midgetgolf [mɪdʒətɡɔlf] *het* miniature golf, midget golf
midvoor [mɪtfor] *de* centre forward
mier [mir] *de (~en)* ant
miereneter [mirə(n)etər] *de (~s)* ant-eater
mierenhoop [mirə(n)hop] *de (-hopen)* anthill
mietje [micə] *het (~s)* gay, pansy
miezeren [mizərə(n)] *vb* drizzle
miezerig [mizərəχ] *adj* **1** drizzly; **2** tiny, puny
migraine [miɡrɛːnə] *de* migraine
migratie [miɣra(t)si] *de (~s)* migration
migreren [miɣrerə(n)] *vb* migrate
mij [mɛi] *pers pron* **1** me: *hij had het (aan) ~ gegeven* he had given it to me; *dat is van ~* that's mine; *een vriend van ~* a friend of mine; *dat is ~ te duur* that's too expensive for me; **2** myself: *ik schaam ~ zeer* I

am deeply ashamed
mijl [mɛil] *de (~en)* mile
mijlenver [mɛilə(n)vɛr] *adj, adv* miles (away); *(adverb also)* for miles
mijlpaal [mɛilpal] *de (mijlpalen)* milestone
mijmeren [mɛimərə(n)] *vb* muse (on), (day)dream (about)
¹mijn [mɛin] *de (~en)* mine: *op een ~ lopen* strike (*or*: hit) a mine
²mijn [mɛin] *pos pron* my ‖ *daar moet ik het ~e van weten* I must get to the bottom of this
mijnenveld [mɛinə(n)vɛlt] *het (~en)* minefield
mijnheer [mənɛr] *de (mijnheren)* **1** sir: *~ de voorzitter* Mr chairman; *~ Jansen* Mr Jansen; **2** gentleman: *is ~ thuis?* is Mr X in?
mijnschacht [mɛinsχɑχt] *de (~en)* mine shaft
mijnwerker [mɛinwɛrkər] *de (~s)* miner
mijt [mɛit] *de (~en)* mite
mijter [mɛitər] *de (~s)* mitre
mijzelf [mɛizɛlf] *ref pron* myself
mikken [mɪkə(n)] *vb* (take) aim: *~ op iets* (take) aim at sth
mikmak [mɪkmɑk] *de* caboodle
mikpunt [mɪkpʏnt] *het (~en)* butt, target
Milaan [milan] *het* Milan
mild [mɪlt] *adj, adv* mild, soft, gentle
milicien [miliʃɛ] *de (~s) (Belg; historical)* conscript
milieu [miljø] *het (~s)* **1** milieu: *iem uit een ander ~* s.o. from a different social background (*or*: milieu); **2** environment
milieubeheer [miljøbəher] *het* conservation (of nature), environmental protection
milieubeweging [miljøbəweχɪŋ] *de (~en)* ecology movement, environmental movement
milieubewust [miljøbəwʏst] *adj* environment-minded
milieudeskundige [miljødɛskʏndəχə] *de (~n)* environmentalist, ecologist
milieuvriendelijk [miljøvrɪndələk] *adj, adv* ecologically sound, environmentally friendly (*or*: safe)
¹militair [militɛr] *de (~en)* soldier, serviceman
²militair [militɛr] *adj, adv* military: *in ~e dienst gaan* do one's military service, join the Army
militant [militɑnt] *de (~en) (Belg)* activist
militie [mili(t)si] *de (Belg; historical)* compulsory military service
miljard [mɪljɑrt] *num* billion, (a, one) thousand million: *de schade loopt in de ~en euro* the damage runs into billions of euros
miljardair [mɪljɑrdɛːr] *de (~s)* multimillionaire
miljardennota [mɪljɑrdənota] *de (~'s)* budget
miljardste [mɪljɑrtstə] *num* billionth
miljoen [mɪljun] *het (~en)* million
miljoenste [mɪljunstə] *de* millionth
miljonair [mɪljonɛːr] *de (~s)* millionaire
mille [mɪl] *het* (one) thousand
millennium [mɪlɛnijʏm] *het (millennia)* millennium
millibar [mɪlibar] *de (~en, ~s)* millibar

milligram [mɪliɣrɑm] *het (~men)* milligram

milliliter [mɪlilitər] *de (~s)* millilitre

millimeter [mɪlimetər] *de (~s)* millimetre

milt [mɪlt] *de (~en)* spleen

mime [mɪm] *de* mime

mimespeler [mɪmspelər] *de (~s)* mime artist

mimiek [mimɪk] *de* facial expression

mimosa [mimoza] *de (~'s)* mimosa

¹min [mɪn] *de (~nen)* minus; minus (sign) ǁ *zij heeft op haar rapport een zeven ~* she has a seven minus on her report; *de thermometer staat op ~ 10°* the thermometer is at minus 10°; *tien ~ drie is zeven* ten minus three equals seven; *~ of meer* more or less

²min [mɪn] *adj* **1** poor: *arbeiders waren haar te ~* workmen were beneath her; **2** little, few: *zo ~ mogelijk fouten maken* make as few mistakes as possible

minachten [mɪnɑχtə(n)] *vb* disdain, hold in contempt

minachting [mɪnɑχtɪŋ] *de* contempt, disdain: *uit ~ voor* in contempt of

minaret [minarɛt] *de (~ten)* minaret

minarine [minarinə] *de (Belg)* low-fat margarine

minder [mɪndər] *adj* **1** less; fewer, smaller: *hij heeft niet veel geld, maar nog ~ verstand* he has little money and even less intelligence; *dat was ~ geslaagd* that was less successful; *hoe ~ erover gezegd wordt, hoe beter* the less said about it the better; *vijf minuten meer of ~* give or take five minutes; *groepen van negen en ~* groups of nine and under; **2** worse: *mijn ogen worden ~* my eyes are not what they used to be

mindere [mɪndərə] *de (~n)* inferior

minderheid [mɪndərhɛit] *de (-heden)* minority

mindering [mɪndərɪŋ] *de (~en)* decrease: *iets in ~ brengen (op)* deduct sth (from)

minderjarig [mɪndərjarəχ] *adj* minor: *~ zijn* be a minor

minderjarigheid [mɪndərjarəχhɛit] *de* minority

minderwaardig [mɪndərwardəχ] *adj* inferior (to)

minderwaardigheid [mɪndərwardəχhɛit] *de* inferiority

mineraal [minəral] *adj* mineral ǁ *rijk aan mineralen* rich in minerals

mineraalwater [minəralwatər] *het* mineral water

mineur [minør] *de* minor

mineurstemming [minørstɛmɪŋ] *de* minor key

mini [mini] *het* mini

miniatuur [minijatyr] *de (miniaturen)* miniature

minidisc [minidɪsk] *de (~s)* minidisc

¹miniem [minim] *adj, adv* small, slight, negligible

²miniem [minim] *de (~en) (Belg)* junior member (10, 11 years) of sports club

minigolf [miniɣɔlf] *het* miniature golf

minima [minima] *de* minimum wage earners

minimaal [minimal] *adj, adv* **1** minimal, minimum: *~ presteren* perform very poorly; **2** at least

minimum [minimʏm] *het (minima)* minimum

minimumleeftijd [minimʏmleftɛit] *de (~en)* mini-

mum age

minimumloon [minimʏmlon] *het (-lonen)* minimum wage

minirok [minirɔk] *de (~ken)* miniskirt

minister [minɪstər] *de (~s)* minister, secretary of state, *(Am)* secretary: *~ van Binnenlandse Zaken* Minister of the Interior, Home Secretary, *(Am)* Secretary of the Interior; *~ van Buitenlandse Zaken* Minister for Foreign Affairs, Secretary of State for Foreign and Commonwealth Affairs, Foreign Secretary, *(Am)* Secretary of State; *~ van Defensie* Minister of Defence, Secretary of State for Defence, *(Am)* Secretary of Defense, Defense Secretary; *~ van Economische Zaken* Minister for Economic Affairs, Secretary of State for Trade and Industry, *(Am; roughly)* Secretary for Commerce; *~ van Financiën* Minister of Finance, Chancellor of the Exchequer, *(Am)* Secretary of the Treasury; *~ van Justitie* Minister of Justice, *(roughly)* Lord (High) Chancellor, *(Am; roughly)* Attorney General; *~ van Landbouw en Visserij* Minister of Agriculture and Fisheries; *~ van Onderwijs en Wetenschappen* Minister of Education and Science, *(Am)* Secretary of Education; *~ van Ontwikkelingssamenwerking* Minister for Overseas Development; *~ van Sociale Zaken en Werkgelegenheid* Minister for Social Services and Employment, *(Am; roughly)* Secretary of Labor; *~ van Verkeer en Waterstaat* Minister of Transport and Public Works, *(Am)* Secretary of Transportation; *~ van Volkshuisvesting, Ruimtelijke Ordening en Milieubeheer* Minister for Housing, Regional Development and the Environment, *(Am; roughly)* Secretary for Housing and Urban Development; *~ van Welzijn, Volksgezondheid, en Cultuur* Minister of Welfare, Health and Cultural Affairs, *(Am; roughly)* Secretary of Health and Human Services; *eerste ~* prime minister, premier

ministerie [minɪsteri] *het (~s)* ministry; department: *~ van Buitenlandse Zaken* Ministry of Foreign Affairs, Foreign (and Commonwealth) Office, *(Am)* State Department; *~ van Defensie* Ministry of Defence, *(Am)* Department of Defense, (the) Pentagon; *~ van Financiën* Ministry of Finance, Treasury, *(Am)* Treasury Department; *het Openbaar Ministerie* the Public Prosecutor

minister-president [minɪstərprezidɛnt] *de (~en)* prime minister, premier

ministerraad [minɪstərat] *de (-raden)* council of ministers

minnaar [mɪnar] *de (~s)* lover, mistress

minnetjes [mɪnəɔs] *adj, adv* poor

minst [mɪnst] *adj, adv* **1** slightest, lowest: *niet de (het) ~e ...* not a shadow of ..., not the slightest ...; **2** least: *op z'n ~ at* (the very) least; *bij het ~e of geringste* at the least little thing; **3** least; fewest: *zij verdient het ~e geld* she earns the least money; *de ~e fouten* the fewest mistakes

minstens [mɪnstəns] *adv* at least: *ik moet ~ vijf euro hebben* I need five euros at least

minstreel [mɪnstre̯l] *de (minstrelen)* minstrel
minteken [mɪnteko(n)] *het (~s)* minus (sign)
minus [mi̯nʏs] *prep* minus
minuscuul [minʏsky̯l] *adj, adv* tiny, minuscule, minute
minutenwijzer [minʏto(n)wɛizər] *de (~s)* minute hand
minuut [minʏt] *de (minuten)* **1** minute: *het is tien minuten lopen* it's a ten-minute walk; **2** second, minute: *de situatie verslechterde met de ~* the situation was getting worse by the minute
mirakel [mira̯kəl] *het (~s, ~en)* miracle, wonder
mirre [mi̯rə] *de* myrrh
¹mis [mɪs] *de (~sen)* Mass
²mis [mɪs] *adj, adv* **1** out, off target: *~ poes!* tough (luck)!; *was het ~ of raak?* was it a hit or a miss?; **2** wrong: *het liep ~* it went wrong
misbaar [mɪzba̯r] *het* uproar, hullabaloo
misbaksel [mɪzbɑksəl] *het (~s)* bastard, louse
misbruik [mɪzbrœyk] *het (~en)* abuse, misuse, excess: *~ van iem maken* take advantage of s.o., use s.o., exploit s.o.
misbruiken [mɪzbrœy̯ko(n)] *vb* **1** abuse, misuse, impose upon; **2** violate
misdaad [mɪzdat] *de (misdaden)* crime
misdaadbestrijding [mɪzdadbəstrɛidɪŋ] *de* crime prevention, fight against crime
misdadig [mɪzda̯dəχ] *adj, adv* criminal
misdadiger [mɪzdadəγər] *de (~s)* criminal
misdadigheid [mɪzdadəχhɛit] *de* crime, criminality
misdienaar [mɪzdinar] *de (~s)* acolyte, altar boy
misdoen [mɪzdu̯n] *vb* do wrong
misdragen [mɪzdra̯γə(n)] *ref vb* misbehave, be (a) naughty (boy, girl)
misdrijf [mɪzdrɛif] *het (misdrijven)* criminal offence, criminal act, crime, *(law)* felony
miserabel [mizera̯bəl] *adj, adv* miserable, wretched
misère [mizɛːrə] *de (~s)* misery
misgaan [mɪsχan] *vb* go wrong: *dit plan moet haast wel ~* this plan is almost sure to fail
misgunnen [mɪsχʏnə(n)] *vb* (be)grudge, resent
mishandelen [mɪshɑndələ(n)] *vb* ill-treat, maltreat, batter: *dieren ~ be* cruel to (*or:* maltreat) animals
mishandeling [mɪshɑndəlɪŋ] *de (~en)* ill-treatment, maltreatment, *(law)* battery
miskennen [mɪskɛnə(n)] *vb* misunderstand: *een miskend genie* (or: *talent)* a misunderstood genius (*or:* talent)
miskleun [mɪsklønn] *de (~en)* blunder, boob
miskoop [mɪskop] *de (miskopen)* bad bargain, bad buy
miskraam [mɪskram] *het, de (miskramen)* miscarriage
misleiden [mɪslɛi̯də(n)] *vb* mislead, deceive: *iem ~* lead s.o. up the garden path
misleiding [mɪslɛi̯dɪŋ] *de (~en)* deception

¹mislopen [mɪslopə(n)] *vb* miss (out on)
²mislopen [mɪslopə(n)] *vb* go wrong, miscarry: *het plan liep mis* the plan miscarried (*or:* was a failure)
mislukkeling [mɪslʏ̯kəlɪŋ] *de (~en)* failure
mislukken [mɪslʏ̯kə(n)] *vb* fail, be unsuccessful, go wrong, fall through, break down: *een mislukte advocaat* (or: *schrijver)* a failed lawyer (*or:* writer); *een mislukte poging* an unsuccessful attempt
mislukking [mɪslʏ̯kɪŋ] *de (~en)* failure
mismaakt [mɪsma̯kt] *adj* deformed
mismaaktheid [mɪsma̯ktheit] *de (-heden)* deformity
mispeuteren [mɪspøtərə(n)] *vb (Belg)* do sth wrong, be up to
misplaatst [mɪspla̯tst] *adj* out of place, misplaced, uncalled-for
mispunt [mɪspʏnt] *het (~en)* pain (in the neck), bastard, louse
missaal [mɪsa̯l] *het (missalen)* missal
misschien [mɪsχi̯n] *adv* perhaps, maybe: *bent u ~ mevrouw Hendriks?* are you Mrs Hendriks by any chance?; *heeft u ~ een paperclip voor me?* do you happen to have (*or:* could you possibly let me have) a paper clip?; *het is ~ beter als …* it may be better (*or:* perhaps) it's better if …; *~ vertrek ik morgen, ~ ook niet* maybe I'll leave tomorrow, maybe not; *zoals je ~ weet* as you may know; *wilt u ~ een kopje koffie?* would you care for some coffee?
misselijk [mɪsa̯lək] *adj, adv* **1** sick (in the stomach): *om ~ van te worden* sickening, nauseating, disgusting; **2** nasty, disgusting, revolting: *een ~e grap* a sick joke
misselijkheid [mɪsələkhɛit] *de (-heden)* (feeling of) sickness, nausea
missen [mɪsə(n)] *vb* miss; go without, spare, afford; lack, lose: *zijn doel ~ (fig)* miss the mark; *iem zeer ~* miss s.o. badly; *ik kan mijn bril niet ~* I can't get along without my glasses; *kun je je fiets een paar uurtjes ~?* can you spare your bike for a couple of hours?; *ze kunnen elkaar niet ~* they can't get along without one another; *ik zou het voor geen geld willen ~* I wouldn't part with it (*or:* do without it) for all the world; *dat kan niet ~* that can't go wrong (*or:* fail), that's bound to work/happen
misser [mɪsər] *de (~s)* **1** failure, mistake, flop; **2** miss, bad shot, poor shot, misthrow, bad throw, miscue
missie [mɪsi] *de (~s)* mission, missionary work
missionaris [mɪʃonɑris] *de (~sen)* missionary
misstand [mɪstɑnt] *de (~en)* abuse, wrong
misstap [mɪstɑp] *de (~pen)* **1** false step, wrong step; **2** slip: *een ~ begaan* make a slip, slip up
missverkiezing [mɪsfərkizɪŋ] *de (~en)* beauty contest
mist [mɪst] *de* fog, mist: *dichte ~* (a) thick fog; *de ~ ingaan: a)* go wrong (*or:* fail) completely; *b)* fall flat; *c)* go wrong, be all at sea
mistbank [mɪstbɑŋk] *de (~en)* fog bank
misten [mɪstə(n)] *vb* be foggy, be misty

mistig [mɪstəχ] *adj* foggy, misty
mistlamp [mɪstlɑmp] *de (~en)* fog lamp
misverstand [mɪsfərstɑnt] *het (~en)* misunderstanding: *een ~ uit de weg ruimen* clear up a misunderstanding
misvormd [mɪsfɔrmt] *adj* deformed, disfigured, *(fig)* distorted
misvorming [mɪsfɔrmɪŋ] *de (~en)* **1** deformation, *(fig)* distortion; **2** deformity, *(fig)* distortion
mitella [mitɛla] *de (~'s)* sling
mitrailleur [mitrajør] *de (~s)* machine-gun
mits [mɪts] *conj* if, provided that: *~ goed bewaard, kan het jaren meegaan* (if) stored well, it can last for years
mixen [mɪksə(n)] *vb* mix
mixer [mɪksər] *de (~s)* mixer; liquidizer, blender
ml *milliliter* ml
mlk-school [ɛmɛlkɑsχol] *de* school for children with learning problems
mm *millimeter* mm
m.m.v. *met medewerking van* with the cooperation of
mobiel [mobil] *adj* mobile
mobieltje [mobiltɕə] *het (~s)* mobile (phone)
mobilisatie [mobiliza(t)si] *de (~s)* mobilization
mobiliseren [mobilizerə(n)] *vb* mobilize
mobiliteit [mobilitɕit] *de (~en)* mobility
mobilofoon [mobilofon] *de (~s)* radio-telephone
mocassin [mɔkasɛ] *de (~s)* moccasin
modaal [modal] *adj* average
modder [mɔdər] *de* mud, sludge
modderbad [mɔdərbɑt] *het (~en)* mudbath
modderen [mɔdərə(n)] *vb* muddle (along, through)
modderig [mɔdərəχ] *adj* muddy
modderpoel [mɔdərpul] *de (~en)* quagmire; mire
modderschuit [mɔdərsχœyt] *de (~en)* mud boat *(or:* barge)
moddervet [mɔdərvɛt] *adj* gross(ly fat)
mode [mɔdə] *de (~s)* fashion: *zich naar de laatste ~ kleden* dress after the latest fashion; *(in de) ~ zijn* be fashionable
modebewust [mɔdəbəwyst] *adj, adv* fashion-conscious
model [modɛl] *het (~len)* **1** model; type, style: *~ staan voor* serve as a model *(or:* pattern) for; *als ~ nemen voor iets* model sth *(or:* oneself) on; **2** model, design: *het ~ van een overhemd* the style of a shirt; **3** model, style: *goed in ~ blijven* stay in shape
modelbouw [modɛlbɑu] *de* model making, modelling (to scale)
modellenbureau [modɛlə(n)byro] *het (~s)* modelling agency
modelleren [modɛlerə(n)] *vb* model: *~ naar* fashion after, model on
modem [mɔdəm] *het, de (~s)* modem
modeontwerper [mɔdəɔntwɛrpər] *de (~s)* fashion designer
modern [modɛrn] *adj, adv* modern: *het huis is ~ in-*

gericht the house has a modern interior; *de ~ste technieken* most modern *(or:* state-of-the-art) technology
moderniseren [modɛrnizerə(n)] *vb* modernize
modernisering [modɛrnizerɪŋ] *de (~en)* modernization
modeshow [mɔdəʃow] *de (~s)* fashion show
modewoord [mɔdəwort] *het (~en)* vogue word
modieus [modijøs] *adj, adv* fashionable: *een modieuze dame* a lady of fashion
module [modylə] *de (~s)* module
¹moe [mu] *de* mum(my), *(Am)* mom || *nou ~!* well I say!
²moe [mu] *adj* **1** tired: *~ van het wandelen* tired with walking; **2** tired (of), weary (of): *zij is het warme weer ~* she is (sick and) tired of the hot weather
moed [mut] *de* **1** courage, nerve: *al zijn ~ bijeenrapen (verzamelen)* muster up *(or:* summon up, pluck up) one's courage; **2** courage, heart: *met frisse ~ beginnen* begin with fresh courage, come up smiling; *de ~ opgeven* lose heart; *de ~ zonk hem in de schoenen* his heart sank into his boots
moedeloos [mudəlos] *adj, adv* despondent, dejected
moedeloosheid [mudəlosɦɛit] *de* despondency, dejection
moeder [mudər] *de (~s)* mother: *hij is niet bepaald ~s mooiste* he's no oil-painting; *bij ~s pappot (blijven) zitten* be *(or:* remain) tied to one's mother's apron strings; *vadertje en ~tje spelen* play house
moederdag [mudərdɑχ] *de* Mother's Day
moederhuis [mudərɦœys] *het (-huizen) (Belg)* maternity home
moederkoek [mudərkuk] *de (~en)* placenta
moederlijk [mudərlək] *adj, adv* **1** motherly; **2** maternal
moedermelk [mudərmɛlk] *de* mother's milk
moederskind [mudərskɪnt] *het (~eren)* **1** mother's child; **2** mummy's boy *(or:* girl)
moedertaal [mudərtal] *de (-talen)* mother tongue: *iem met Engels als ~* a native speaker of English
moedertaalspreker [mudərtalsprekər] *de (~s)* native speaker
moedervlek [mudərvlɛk] *de (~ken)* birthmark, mole
moederziel [mudərzil] || *~ alleen* all alone
moedig [mudəχ] *adj, adv* brave, plucky
moeheid [muɦɛit] *de* tiredness, weariness
moeilijk [mujlək] *adj, adv* **1** difficult: *~ opvoedbare kinderen* problem children; *doe niet zo ~* don't make such a fuss; **2** hard, difficult: *het is ~ te geloven* it's hard to believe; *hij maakte het ons ~* he gave us a hard *(or:* difficult) time; **3** hardly: *daar kan ik ~ iets over zeggen* it's hard for me to say; *zij is een ~ persoon* she is hard to please
moeilijkheid [mujləkɦɛit] *de (-heden)* difficulty, trouble, problem: *om moeilijkheden vragen* be asking for trouble; *daar zit (ligt) de ~* there's the catch
moeite [mujtə] *de* **1** effort, trouble: *vergeefse ~*

wasted effort; *bespaar je de* ~ (you can) save yourself the trouble (*or:* bother); ~ *doen* take pains (*or:* trouble); *u hoeft geen extra* ~ *te doen* you need not bother, don't put yourself out; *het is de* ~ *niet (waard)* it's not worth it (*or:* the effort, the bother); *het is de* ~ *waard om het te proberen* it's worth a try (*or:* trying); *het was zeer de* ~ *waard* it was most rewarding; *dank u wel voor de* ~! thank you very much!, sorry to have troubled you!; *dat is me te veel* ~! that's too much trouble; **2** trouble, difficulty, bother: *ik heb* ~ *met zijn gedrag* I find his behaviour hard to take (*or:* accept)

moeiteloos [mµjtəlos] *adj, adv* effortless, easy: *leer* ~ *Engels!* learn English without tears!

moeizaam [mµjzam] *adj* laborious ‖ *zich* ~ *een weg banen (door)* make one's way with difficulty (through)

moer [mur] *de* **1** nut; **2** mother; **3** doe; queen (bee) ‖ *daar schiet je geen* ~ *mee op* that doesn't get you anywhere

moeras [murɑs] *het (~sen)* swamp, marsh

moerasgebied [murɑsχəbit] *het* marshland

moersleutel [mursløtəl] *de (~s)* spanner, *(Am)* wrench

moerstaal [murstal] *de* mother tongue: *spreek je* ~ speak plain English (*or:* Dutch)

moes [mus] *het* purée

moesson [musɔn] *de (~s)* monsoon

moestuin [mustœyn] *de (~en)* kitchen garden, vegetable garden

¹moeten [mµtə(n)] *vb* **1** must, have to, should, ought to: *ik moet zeggen, dat* ... I must say (*or:* have to say) that ...; *ik moest wel lachen* I couldn't help laughing; *het heeft zo* ~ *zijn* it had to be (like that); *als het moet* if I (*or:* we) must; **2** want, need: *ik moet er niet aan denken wat het kost* I hate to think (of) what it costs; ~ *jullie niet eten?* don't you want to eat?; *dat moet ik nog zien* I'll have to see; *wat moet dat?* what's all this about?; *het huis moet nodig eens geschilderd worden* the house badly needs a coat of paint; **3** should, ought to: *dat moet gezegd (worden)* it has to be said; *moet je eens horen* listen (to this); *de trein moet om vier uur vertrekken* the train is due to leave at four o'clock; *je moest eens weten* ... if only you knew ...; *dat moet jij (zelf) weten* it's up to you; *moet je nu al weg?* are you off already?; *ze moet er nodig eens uit* she needs a day out; **4** must, be supposed to, said to: *zij moet vroeger een mooi meisje geweest zijn* she must have been a pretty girl once; **5** *(Belg)* need (to), have (to): *u moet niet komen* you needn't come

²moeten [mµtə(n)] *vb* like

moezelwijn [mµzəlwɛin] *de (~en)* Moselle (wine)

¹mogelijk [moɣələk] *adj* possible, likely, potential: *hoe is het* ~, *dat je je daarin vergist hebt?* how could you possibly have been mistaken about this?; *het is* ~ *dat hij wat later komt* he may come a little later; *het is heel goed* ~ *dat hij het niet gezien heeft* he may very well not have seen it; *het is ons niet* ~ ... it's

impossible for us, we cannot possibly ...; *al het ~e doen* do everything possible

²mogelijk [moɣələk] *adv* possibly, perhaps

mogelijkerwijs [moɣələkərwɛis] *adv* possibly, perhaps, conceivably

mogelijkheid [moɣələkhɛit] *de (-heden)* **1** possibility, chance, eventuality: *zij onderschat haar mogelijkheden* she underestimates herself; **2** *(pl)* possibilities, prospects

¹mogen [moɣə(n)] *vb* **1** can, be allowed to, may, must, should, ought to: *mag ik een kilo peren van u?* (can I have) a kilo of pears, please; *mag ik uw naam even?* could (*or:* may) I have your name, please?; *je mag gaan spelen, maar je mag je niet vuil maken* you can go out and play, but you're not to get dirty; *als ik vragen mag* if you don't mind my asking; *mag ik even?* do you mind?, may I?; *mag ik er even langs?* excuse me (please); **2** should, ought to: *je had me wel eens ~ waarschuwen* you might (*or:* could) have warned me; *hij mag blij zijn dat* ... he ought to (*or:* should) be happy that ...; **3** may, might: *het mocht niet baten* it didn't help, it was to no avail; *dat ik dit nog mag meemaken!* that I should live to see this!; *het heeft niet zo* ~ *zijn* it was not to be; *zo mag ik het horen* (or: *zien*) that's what I like to hear (*or:* see)

²mogen [moɣə(n)] *vb* like: *ik mag hem wel* I quite (*or:* rather) like him

mogendheid [moɣənthɛit] *de (-heden)* power

¹mohair [mohɛːr] *het* mohair

²mohair [mohɛːr] *adj* mohair

mohikanen [mohikanə(n)] *de* Mohicans

mok [mɔk] *de (~ken)* mug

moker [mokər] *de (~s)* sledgehammer

mokka [mɔka] *de* mocha (coffee)

mokken [mɔkə(n)] *vb* grouse, sulk

¹mol [mɔl] *de* mole

²mol [mɔl] *de (mus)* **1** flat; **2** minor

Moldavië [mɔldaviə] *het* Moldavia

Moldaviër [mɔldavijər] *de (~s)* Moldavian

molecule [molekyl] *het, de (~n)* molecule

molen [molə(n)] *de (~s)* **1** (wind)mill; **2** *(angling)* reel ‖ *het zit in de* ~ it is in the pipeline

molenaar [molənar] *de (~s)* miller

molesteren [molɛsterə(n)] *vb* molest

mollen [mɔlə(n)] *vb* wreck, bust (up)

mollig [mɔləχ] *adj* plump, chubby

molm [mɔlm] *het, de* mouldered wood

molshoop [mɔlshop] *de (-hopen)* molehill

Molukken [molykə(n)] *de* Moluccas, Molucca Islands

Molukker [molykər] *de (~s)* Moluccan

Moluks [molyks] *adj* Molucca(n)

mom [mɔm] ‖ *onder het* ~ *van de weg te vragen* on (*or:* under) the pretext of asking the way

moment [momɛnt] *het (~en)* moment, minute: *één* ~, *ik kom zó* one moment please, I'm coming, hang on a minute, I'm coming; *daar heb ik geen* ~ *aan gedacht* it never occurred to me

momenteel [momɛntel] *adv* at present, at the moment, currently

mompelen [mɔmpələ(n)] *vb* mumble, mutter

Monaco [monako] *het* Monaco

monarchie [monarχi] *de (~ën)* monarchy

mond [mɔnt] *de (~en)* mouth, muzzle: *iem een grote ~ geven* talk back at (*or:* to) s.o., give s.o. lip; *hij kan zijn grote ~ niet houden* he can't keep his big mouth shut; *dat is een hele ~ vol* that's quite a mouthful; *zijn ~ houden* keep quiet, shut up; *zijn ~ opendoen* open one's mouth, speak up; *zijn ~ voorbijpraten* spill the beans; *met de ~ vol tanden staan* be at a loss for words, be tongue-tied

mondeling [mɔndəlɪŋ] *adj, adv* oral, verbal, by word of mouth: *een ~ examen* an oral (exam(ination)); *een ~e toezegging* (*or:* afspraak) a verbal agreement (*or:* arrangement)

mond- en klauwzeer [mɔntɛŋklɑuzer] *het* foot-and-mouth disease

mondharmonica [mɔntharmonika] *de (~'s)* harmonica

mondhoek [mɔnthuk] *de (~en)* corner of the mouth

mondig [mɔndəχ] *adj* of age; mature, independent

monding [mɔndɪŋ] *de (~en)* mouth, estuary

mondje [mɔncə] *het (~s)* mouthful, taste: *een ~ Turks spreken* have a smattering of Turkish; *(denk erom,) ~ dicht* mum's the word; *hij is niet op zijn ~ gevallen: a)* he has a ready tongue; *b)* he gives as good as he gets

mond-op-mondbeademing [mɔntɔpmɔndbaadəmɪŋ] *de* mouth-to-mouth (resuscitation, respiration), rescue breathing

mondstuk [mɔntstʏk] *het (~ken)* **1** mouthpiece, nozzle; **2** filter

mond-tot-mondreclame [mɔntɔtmɔntrəklamə] *de* advertisement by word of mouth, word-of-mouth advertising

mondvol [mɔntfɔl] *de* mouthful

mondvoorraad [mɔntforat] *de* provisions, supplies

monetair [monetɛːr] *adj, adv* monetary: *het Internationaal Monetair Fonds* the International Monetary Fund

Mongolië [mɔŋɣolijə] *het* Mongolia

Mongoloïde [mɔŋɣolowɪdə] *adj* Mongoloid

mongool [mɔŋɣol] *de (mongolen)* mongol

Mongool [mɔŋɣol] *de (Mongolen)* Mongol(ian)

monitor [mɔnitɔr] *de (~s)* **1** monitor; **2** *(Belg)* youth leader; **3** *(Belg)* tutor

monitoren [mɔnitorə(n)] *vb* monitor

monnik [mɔnək] *de (~en)* monk

mono [mono] *adv* mono

monocle [monɔklə] *de (~s)* monocle

monogaam [monoɣam] *adj* monogamous

monogamie [monoɣami] *de* monogamy

monogram [monoɣrɑm] *het (~men)* monogram

monoloog [monolɔχ] *de (-logen)* monologue

monopolie [monopoli] *het (~s)* monopoly

monotoon [monoton] *adj, adv* monotonous, in a monotone

monoxide [monɔksidə] *het (~n)* monoxide

monseigneur [mɔnsɛɲør] *de (~s)* Monsignor

monster [mɔnstər] *het (~s)* **1** monster; **2** sample, specimen; **3** monster, giant

monsterlijk [mɔnstərlək] *adj, adv* monstrous, hideous

monsterzege [mɔnstərzeɣə] *de (~s)* mammoth victory

montage [mɔntaʒə] *de* **1** assembly, mounting; **2** *(film)* editing

Montenegro [mɔntəneɣro] *het* Montenegro

monter [mɔntər] *adj, adv* lively, cheerful, vivacious

monteren [mɔnterə(n)] *vb* **1** assemble; install; **2** mount, fix; **3** edit, cut *(film)*; assemble; **4** fix, mount

montessorischool [mɔntɛsorisχol] *de (-scholen)* Montessori school

monteur [mɔntør] *de (~s)* mechanic, serviceman, repairman

montuur [mɔntyr] *het, de (monturen)* frame: *een bril zonder ~* rimless glasses

monument [monymɛnt] *het (~en)* monument: *een ~ ter herinnering aan de doden* a memorial to the dead

monumentaal [monymɛntal] *adj, adv* monumental

monumentenlijst [monymɛntə(n)lɛist] *de (~en)* (*roughly*) list of national monuments and historic buildings

¹mooi [moj] *adj* **1** beautiful: *iets ~ vinden* think sth is nice; **2** good-looking, handsome, pretty, beautiful; **3** lovely, beautiful: *zij ziet er mooi uit* she looks lovely; *deze fiets is er niet ~er op worden* this bicycle isn't what it used to be; **4** smart: *zich ~ maken* dress up; **5** good, excellent: *~e cijfers halen* get good marks (*or Am:* grades); **6** good, fine, nice, handsome: *het kon niet ~er* it couldn't have been better; *te ~ om waar te zijn* too good to be true; **7** good, nice: *een ~ verhaal* a nice (*or:* good) story; *het is ~ (geweest) zo!* that's enough now!, all right, that'll do!

²mooi [moj] *adv* well, nicely: *jij hebt ~ praten* it's all very well for you to talk; *dat is ~ meegenomen* that is so much to the good; *~ zo!* good!, well done!

moois [mojs] *het* fine thing(s), sth beautiful: *(iron) dat is ook wat ~!* a nice state of affairs!

moord [mort] *de (~en)* murder, assassination, *(law)* homicide: *~ en brand schreeuwen* scream blue murder

moorddadig [mordadəχ] *adj* murderous

moorden [mordə(n)] *vb* kill, murder

moordenaar [mordənar] *de (~s)* murderer, killer

moordend [mordənt] *adj* murderous, deadly, fatal: *~e concurrentie* cut-throat competition

moordzaak [mortsak] *de (-zaken)* murder case

moorkop [morkɔp] *de (~pen)* chocolate éclair

moot [mot] *de (moten)* piece

mop [mɔp] *de (~pen)* joke: *een schuine ~* a dirty joke

mopperaar [mɔpərar] *de (~s)* grumbler
mopperen [mɔpərə(n)] *vb* grumble, grouch
moraal [moral] *de* morality; moral(s)
moraliseren [moralizerə(n)] *vb* moralize
Moravië [moravijə] *het* Moravia
morbide [mɔrbidə] *adj* morbid
¹**moreel** [morel] *het* morale: *het ~ hoog houden* keep up morale
²**moreel** [morel] *adj, adv* moral
mores [mɔrəs] *de* mores
morfine [mɔrfinə] *de* morphine
¹**morgen** [mɔrɣə(n)] *de (~s)* morning: *de hele ~* all morning; *'s morgens* in the morning; *(goede) ~!* (good) morning!; *om 8 uur 's morgens* at 8 a.m.
²**morgen** [mɔrɣə(n)] *adv* tomorrow: *vandaag of ~* one of these days; *~ over een week* a week tomorrow; *tot ~!* see you tomorrow!, till tomorrow!; *de krant van ~* tomorrow's (news)paper
morgenavond [mɔrɣə(n)avɔnt] *adv* tomorrow evening
morgenmiddag [mɔrɣə(n)mɪdɑχ] *adv* tomorrow afternoon
morgenochtend [mɔrɣə(n)ɔχtənt] *adv* tomorrow morning
morgenvroeg [mɔrɣə(n)vruχ] *adv* tomorrow morning
mormel [mɔrməl] *het (~s)* mutt: *een verwend ~* a spoilt brat
morrelen [mɔrələ(n)] *vb* fiddle
morren [mɔrə(n)] *vb* grumble
morsdood [mɔrzdot] *adj* (as) dead as a doornail
morse [mɔrsə] *het* Morse (code)
morsen [mɔrsə(n)] *vb* (make a) mess (on, of), spill: *het kind zit te ~ met zijn eten* the child is messing around with his food
mortel [mɔrtəl] *de* mortar
mortier [mɔrtir] *het, de (~en)* mortar
mortuarium [mɔrtywarijʏm] *het (mortuaria)* **1** mortuary; **2** funeral parlour *(or Am:* home)
mos [mɔs] *het (~sen)* moss
moskee [mɔske] *de (~ën)* mosque
Moskou [mɔskɑu] *het* Moscow
moslim [mɔslɪm] *de (~s)* Muslim, Moslem
mossel [mɔsəl] *de (~en)* mussel
mosterd [mɔstərt] *de* mustard: *hij weet waar Abraham de ~ haalt* he knows what's what
mot [mɔt] *de (~ten)* moth
motel [motɛl] *het (~s)* motel
motie [mo(t)si] *de (~s)* motion
motief [motif] *het (motieven)* **1** motive; **2** motif, design
motivatie [motiva(t)si] *de* motivation
motiveren [motiverə(n)] *vb* **1** explain, account for, defend, justify; **2** motivate
motor [motər] *de (~en)* **1** engine, motor: *de ~ starten* (or: *afzetten)* start (or: turn off) the engine; **2** motorcycle; **3** driving force
motoragent [motəraɣɛnt] *de (~en)* motorcycle policeman

motorblok [motərblɔk] *het (~ken)* engine block
motorboot [motərbot] *de (-boten)* motorboat
motorcoureur [motərkurør] *de (~s)* motorcycle racer, rider
motorcross [motərkrɔs] *de (~es)* motocross
motorfiets [motərfits] *de (~en)* motorcycle, motorbike, bike: *~ met zijspan* sidecar motorcycle
motorhelm [motərhɛlm] *de (~en)* crash helmet, safety helmet
motoriek [motorik] *de* (loco)motor system; locomotion
motoriseren [motorizerə(n)] *vb* motorize
motorkap [motərkɑp] *de (~pen)* bonnet, *(Am)* hood
motorpech [motərpɛχ] *de* engine trouble
motorrace [motəres] *de (~s)* motorcycle race
motorrijtuigenbelasting [motərɛitœyɣə(n)bəlɑstɪŋ] *de (roughly)* road tax
motorsport [motərspɔrt] *de* motorcycle racing
motorvoertuig [motərvurtœyχ] *het (~en)* motor vehicle, *(Am)* automobile
motregen [mɔtreɣə(n)] *de (~s)* drizzle
motregenen [mɔtreɣənə(n)] *vb* drizzle
mottenbal [mɔtə(n)bɑl] *de (~len)* mothball
mottig [mɔtəχ] *adj* moth-eaten, scruffy
motto [mɔto] *het (~'s)* motto, slogan
mountainbike [mɑuntənbɑjk] *de (~s)* mountain bike
mousse [mus] *de (~s)* mousse
mousseren [muserə(n)] *vb* sparkle, fizz
mouw [mɑu] *de (~en)* sleeve: *de ~en opstropen* roll up one's sleeves; *ergens een ~ aan weten te passen* find a way (a)round sth
mozaïek [mozɑjk] *het (~en)* mosaic
Mozambique [mozɑmbik] *het* Mozambique
Mozes [mozəs] *de* Moses
MP [ɛmpe] *de* **1** minister-president PM; **2** militaire politie MP
mts [ɛmteɛs] *de (~'en)* middelbare technische school intermediate technical school
muezzin [muwɛdzɪn] *de* muezzin
muf [mʏf] *adj* musty, stale, stuffy
mug [mʏχ] *de (~gen)* mosquito, *(small)* gnat: *ve ~ een olifant maken* make a mountain out of a molehill
muggenbeet [mʏɣə(n)bet] *de (-beten)* mosquito bite
muggenziften [mʏɣə(n)zɪftə(n)] *vb* niggle, split hairs, nit-pick
muggenzifter [mʏɣə(n)zɪftər] *de (~s)* niggler, hairsplitter, nit-picker
muil [mœyl] *de* mouth, muzzle
muildier [mœyldir] *het (~en)* mule
muilezel [mœylezəl] *de (~s)* hinny
muilkorf [mœylkɔrf] *de (-korven)* muzzle
muis [mœys] *de (muizen)* mouse; ball
muisarm [mœysɑrm] *de (~en)* mouse arm
muismatje [mœysmɑcə] *het (~s)* mouse mat
muisstil [mœystɪl] *adj* (as) still (or: quiet) as a

mouse

muiterij [mœytərɛi] *de (~en)* mutiny: *er brak ~ uit* a mutiny broke out

muizenissen [mœyzənɪsə(n)] *de* worries

muizenval [mœyzə(n)vɑl] *de (~len)* mousetrap

mul [mʏl] *adj* loose, sandy

mulat [mylɑt] *de (~ten)* mulatto

multicultureel [mʏltikʏltyrɛl] *adj* multicultural

multimedia [mʏltimedija] *de* multimedia

multimiljonair [mʏltimiljonɛːr] *de (~s)* multimillionaire

multiple [mʏltipəl] *adj* multiple

multiplex [mʏltiplɛks] *het* multi-ply (board)

mum [mʏm] *het ‖ in een ~ (van tijd)* in a jiffy (*or:* trice)

mummie [mʏmi] *de (~s)* mummy

München [mʏnʃə(n)] *het* Munich

munitie [mynɪ(t)si] *de (am)*munition, ammo

munt [mʏnt] *de (~en)* **1** coin: *iem met gelijke ~ terugbetalen* give s.o. a taste of their own medicine; **2** token

munteenheid [mʏntenhɛit] *de (-heden)* monetary unit

muntgeld [mʏntxɛlt] *het* coin, coinage

muntsoort [mʏntsort] *de* currency

muntstuk [mʏntstʏk] *het (~ken)* coin

munttelefoon [mʏnteləfon] *de (~s)* payphone

muntzijde [mʏntsɛidə] *de (~n)* tail

murmelen [mʏrmələ(n)] *vb* mumble, murmur

murw [mʏrf] *adj* tender, soft

mus [mʏs] *de (~sen)* sparrow

museum [myzɛjʏm] *het (musea)* museum, (art) gallery

museumjaarkaart [myzejʏmjɑrkart] *de (~en)* annual museum pass

musical [mjuzəkəl] *de (~s)* musical

musiceren [myzisɛrə(n)] *vb* make music

musicoloog [myzikoloχ] *de (-logen)* musicologist

musicus [myzikʏs] *de (musici)* musician

muskaatwijn [mʏskɑtwɛin] *de* muscatel

musketier [mʏskətir] *de (~s)* musketeer

muskiet [mʏskit] *de (~en)* mosquito

muskusrat [mʏskʏsrɑt] *de (~ten)* muskrat

müsli [mʏsli] *de* muesli

mutant [mytɑnt] *de (~en)* mutant

mutatie [myta(t)si] *de (~s)* **1** mutation; transaction; **2** mutation, turnover

muts [mʏts] *de (~en)* hat, cap

mutualiteit [mytywalitɛit] *de (Belg)* health insurance scheme

muur [myr] *de (muren)* wall: *een blinde ~* a blank wall; *de muren komen op mij af* the walls are closing in on me; *(sport) een ~tje vormen (opstellen)* make a wall; *uit de ~ eten, iets uit de ~ trekken (roughly)* eat from a vending machine

muurbloempje [mʏrblumpjə] *het* wallflower

muurschildering [mʏrsχɪldərɪŋ] *de (~en)* mural

muurvast [mʏrvɑst] *adj, adv* firm, solid, unyielding, unbending: *de besprekingen zitten ~* the talks

have reached total deadlock

muzak [mʏzɑk] *de* muzak

muze [mʏzə] *de (~n)* **1** muse; **2** *(pl)* (the) Muses: *zich aan de muzen wijden* devote oneself to the arts

muziek [myzik] *de* music: *op de maat van de ~ dansen* dance in time to the music; *op ~ dansen* dance to music; *dat klinkt mij als ~ in de oren* it's music to my ears

muziekbalk *de* stave, staff

muziekcassette [myzikɑsɛtə] *de (~s)* musicassette

muziekinstrument [myzikɪnstrymɛnt] *het (~en)* musical instrument

muzieknoot [myziknot] *de (-noten)* (musical) note

muziekschool [myziksχol] *de (-scholen)* school of music

muziekstuk [myzikstʏk] *het (~ken)* piece of music, composition

muziekuitvoering [myzikœytfurɪŋ] *de (~en)* musical performance

muzikaal [myzikal] *adj, adv* musical: *~ gevoel* feel for music

muzikant [myzikɑnt] *de (~en)* musician

mw. *mevrouw of mejuffrouw* Ms

mysterie [mɪstɛri] *het (~s)* mystery

mysterieus [mɪstɛri(j)øs] *adj, adv* mysterious

mystiek [mɪstik] *adj* **1** mystic, mysterious; **2** mystical: *een ~e ervaring* a mystical experience

mythe [mitə] *de (~n)* myth, *(pers)* legend

mythisch [mitis] *adj* mythic(al)

mythologie [mitoloɣi] *de (~ën)* mythology

mythologisch [mitoloɣis] *adj* mythological

n

na [na] *prep* after: *de ene blunder ~ de andere maken* make one blunder after the other (*or:* another); *wat eten we ~?* what's for dessert?; *op een paar uitzonderingen ~* with a few exceptions; *de op één ~ grootste* (*or: sterkste*) the second biggest (*or:* strongest); *het op drie ~ grootste bedrijf* the fourth largest company

naad [nat] *de (naden)* seam; joint || *zich uit de ~ werken* work oneself to death

naadje [naːcə] *het* || *het naadje van de kous willen weten* want to know all the ins and outs

naadloos [naːtlos] *adj* seamless

naaf [naf] *de (naven)* hub

naaidoos [naːjdos] *de (-dozen)* sewing box

naaien [naːjə(n)] *vb* sew

naaigaren [naːjɣarə(n)] *het (~s)* sewing thread (*or:* cotton): *een klosje ~* a reel of thread (*or:* cotton)

naaimachine [naːjmaʃinə] *de (~s)* sewing machine

naakt [nakt] *adj, adv* **1** naked, nude: *~ slapen* sleep in the nude; **2** bare

naaktloper [naːktlopər] *de (~s)* nudist

naaktloperij [naktlopərɛi] *de* nudism

naald [nalt] *de (~en)* needle: *het oog van een ~* the eye of a needle; *dat is zoeken naar een ~ in een hooiberg* that's like looking for a needle in a haystack

naaldboom [naːldbom] *de (-bomen)* conifer

naaldhak [naːlthɑk] *de (~ken)* stiletto(heel), *(Am)* spike heel

naaldhout [naːlthɑut] *het* softwood, coniferous wood

naaldvakken [naːltfɑkə(n)] *de* sewing, needlework

naam [nam] *de (namen)* name, reputation: *een goede* (*or: slechte*) *~ hebben* have a good (*or:* bad) reputation; *zijn ~ eer aandoen* live up to one's reputation (*or:* name); *dat mag geen ~ hebben* that's not worth mentioning; *~ maken* make a name for oneself (with, as); *de dingen bij de ~ noemen* call a spade a spade; *een cheque uitschrijven op ~ van* make out a cheque to; *ten name van, op ~ van* in the name of; *wat was uw ~ ook weer?* what did you say your name was?

naambord [naːmbɔrt] *het (~en)* nameplate

naamkaartje [naːmkarcə] *het (~s)* calling-card, business card

naamloos [naːmlos] *adj, adv* anonymous, unnamed

naamplaatje [naːmplacə] *het* nameplate

naamval [naːmvɑl] *de (~len)* case

naamwoord [naːmwort] *het (~en)* noun: *een bijvoeglijk ~* an adjective; *een zelfstandig ~* a noun

na-apen [naːapə(n)] *vb* ape, mimic

na-aper [naːapər] *de (~s)* mimic, copycat

¹naar [nar] *prep* **1** to, for: *~ huis gaan* go home; *~ de weg vragen* ask the way; *op zoek ~* in search of; *~ iem vragen* ask for (*or:* after) s.o.; **2** (according to): *ruiken* (or: *smaken*) *~* smell (*or:* taste) of

²naar [nar] *adj, adv* nasty, horrible

naargeestig [narɣestəχ] *adj, adv* gloomy, dismal

naarmate [narmatə] *conj* as: *~ je meer verdient, ga je ook meer belasting betalen* the more you earn, the more tax you pay

¹naast [nast] *prep* **1** next to, beside, wide of: *~ iem gaan zitten* sit down next to (*or:* beside) s.o.; **2** alongside, next to: *~ elkaar* side by side, next to one another; **3** after, next to

²naast [nast] *adj* **1** near(est), closest, immediate: *de ~e bloedverwanten* the next of kin; **2** out, off (target): *hij schoot ~* he shot wide

naaste [naːstə] *de (~n)* neighbour

naastenliefde [naːstə(n)livdə] *de* charity

nabespreken [naːbəsprekə(n)] *vb* discuss afterwards

nabestaande [naːbəstandə] *de (~n)* (surviving) relative, *(pl)* next of kin

nabestellen [naːbəstɛlə(n)] *vb* reorder, have copies made of

¹nabij [nabɛi] *adj* close, near: *de ~e omgeving* the immediate surroundings

²nabij [nabɛi] *prep* near (to), close to: *om en ~ de duizend euro* roughly (*or:* around, about) a thousand euros

nabijgelegen [nabɛiɣəleɣə(n)] *adj* nearby

nabijheid [nabɛihɛit] *de* neighbourhood, vicinity

nablijven [naːblɛivə(n)] *vb* stay behind

nabootsen [naːbotsə(n)] *vb* imitate, copy, mimic

nabootsing [naːbotsɪŋ] *de (~en)* imitation, copying; copy

naburig [nabyrəχ] *adj* neighbouring, nearby

nacht [nɑχt] *de (~en)* night: *de afgelopen ~* last night; *de komende ~* tonight; *het werd ~* night (*or:* darkness) fell; *tot laat in de ~* deep into the night; *'s ~s* at night; *om drie uur 's ~s* at three o'clock in the morning, at three a.m.

nachtclub [nɑχtklʏp] *de (~s)* nightclub

nachtdienst [nɑχtdinst] *de (~en)* night shift

nachtdier [nɑχtdir] *het (~en)* nocturnal animal

nachtegaal [nɑχtəɣal] *de (nachtegalen)* nightingale

nachtelijk [nɑχtələk] *adj, adv* **1** night; **2** nocturnal, of night; **3** night(time)

nachtfilm [nɑχtfɪlm] *de (~s)* late-night film

nachtjapon [nɑχtjapɔn] *de (~nen)* nightgown, nightdress, nightie

nachtkastje [nɑχtkɑʃə] *het (~s)* night table, bedside table

nachtkluis [nɑχtklœys] *de (-kluizen)* night safe

nachtlampje [nɑχtlɑmpjə] *het (~s)* nightlight, nightlamp

nachtmerrie [nɑχtmɛri] *de (~s)* nightmare

nachtmis [nɑχtmɪs] *de (~sen)* midnight mass

nachtpon [nɑχtpɔn] *de (~nen)* nightdress, nightgown, nightie

nachtslot [nɑχtslɔt] *het (~en)* double lock

nachtvoorstelling [nɑχtforstɛlɪŋ] *de (~en)* late-night performance

nachtvorst [nɑχtfɔrst] *de* night frost, ground frost

nachtwake [nɑχtwakə] *de (~n)* vigil, night watch

nachtwerk [nɑχtwɛrk] *het* nightwork

nachtzoen [nɑχtsun] *de (~en)* good-night kiss: *iem een ~ geven* kiss s.o. good night

nachtzuster [nɑχtsʏstər] *de (~s)* night nurse

nacompetitie [nakɔmpəti(t)si] *de (~s) (socc)* play-offs

nadarafsluiting [nadɑrɑfslœytɪŋ] *de (~en) (Belg)* crush barrier

nadat [nadɑt] *conj* after: *het moet gebeurd zijn ~ ze vertrokken waren* it must have happened after they left

nadeel [nadel] *het (nadelen)* disadvantage, damage, drawback: *zo zijn voor- en nadelen hebben* have its pros and cons; *al het bewijsmateriaal spreekt in hun ~* all the evidence is against them; *ten nadele van* to the detriment of

nadelig [nadeləχ] *adj, adv* adverse, harmful

nadenken [nadɛŋkə(n)] *vb* **1** think: *even ~* let me think; *ik heb er niet bij nagedacht* I did it without thinking; *ik moet er eens over ~* I'll think about it; **2** think, reflect (on, upon), consider: *zonder erbij na te denken* without (even, so much as) thinking; *stof tot ~* food for think

nader [nadər] *adj, adv* **1** closer, nearer: *partijen ~ tot elkaar proberen te brengen* try to bring parties closer together; **2** closer; further, more detailed (*or:* specific): *bij ~e kennismaking* on further (*or:* closer) acquaintance

naderbij [nadərbɛi] *adv* closer, nearer

naderen [nadərə(n)] *vb* approach

naderhand [nadərhɑnt] *adv* afterwards

nadoen [nadun] *vb* **1** copy; **2** imitate, copy; mimic: *de scholier deed zijn leraar na* the schoolboy mimicked his teacher

nadruk [nadrʏk] *de (~ken)* emphasis, stress

nadrukkelijk [nadrʏkələk] *adj, adv* emphatic; express

nafluiten [naflœytə(n)] *vb* whistle at: *een meisje ~* give a girl a wolf whistle

nagaan [naɣan] *vb* **1** check (up): *we zullen die zaak zorgvuldig ~* we will look carefully into the matter; **2** work out (for oneself), examine: *voor zover we kunnen ~* as far as we can gather (*or:* ascertain); **3** imagine: *kun je ~!* just imagine!

nageboorte [naɣəbortə] *de (~n)* afterbirth

nagedachtenis [naɣədɑχtənɪs] *de* memory: *ter ~ aan mijn moeder* in memory of my mother

nagel [naɣəl] *de (~s)* nail; claw

nagelbijten [naɣəlbɛitə(n)] *vb* bite one's nails

nagellak [naɣəlɑk] *het, de (~ken)* nail polish (*or:* varnish)

nagerecht [naɣərɛχt] *het (~en)* dessert (course)

nageslacht [naɣəslɑχt] *het (~en)* offspring, descendants

naïef [naif] *adj, adv* naive

najaar [najar] *het* autumn

najaarsmode [najarsmodə] *de* autumn fashion(s)

nakijken [nakɛikə(n)] *vb* **1** watch, follow (with one's eyes): *zij keek de wegrijdende auto na* she watched the car drive off; **2** check, have (*or:* take) a look at: *zich laten ~* have a check-up; **3** correct: *veel proefwerken ~* mark (*or* Am: grade) a lot of papers

nakomeling [nakoməlɪŋ] *de (~en)* descendant; *(pl)* offspring

¹**nakomen** [nakomə(n)] *vb* come later, arrive later, come after(wards)

²**nakomen** [nakomə(n)] *vb* observe, perform, fulfil: *een belofte ~* keep a promise

nalaten [nalatə(n)] *vb* **1** leave (behind), bequeath (to); **2** refrain from (-ing): *hij kan het niet ~ een grapje te maken* he cannot resist making a joke

nalatenschap [nalatənsχɑp] *de (~pen)* estate, inheritance

naleven [nalevə(n)] *vb* observe, comply with

nalezen [nalezə(n)] *vb* read again

nalopen [nalopə(n)] *vb* **1** walk after, run after; **2** check

namaak [namak] *de* imitation, copy, fake, counterfeit

namaken [namakə(n)] *vb* **1** imitate, copy; **2** fake, counterfeit

name [namə] || *met ~* especially, particularly; *ze heeft je niet met ~ genoemd* she didn't mention your name (specifically)

namelijk [namələk] *adv* **1** namely; **2** you see, as it happens, it so happens (that): *ik had ~ beloofd dat …* it so happens I had promised that …

namens [naməns] *prep* on behalf of

namiddag [namɪdɑχ] *de (~en)* afternoon

naoorlogs [naorlɔχs] *adj* postwar

napalm [napɑlm] *het* napalm

Napels [napəls] *het* Naples

¹**nappa** [nɑpa] *het* nap(p)a (leather), sheepskin

²**nappa** [nɑpa] *adj* nap(p)a (leather), sheepskin

napraten [napratə(n)] *vb* echo, parrot

nar [nɑr] *de (~ren)* fool, idiot

narcis [nɑrsɪs] *de (~sen) (white)* narcissus; *(yellow)* daffodil

narcose [nɑrkozə] *de* narcosis, anaesthetic

narekenen [narekənə(n)] *vb* go over (*or:* through) (again), check

narigheid [naraχɛit] *de* trouble

naroepen [narupə(n)] *vb* **1** call after; **2** jeer at

nasaal [nazal] *adj, adv* nasal

nascholing [nasχolɪŋ] *de (~en)* refresher course, continuing education

nascholingscursus [nasχolɪŋskʏrzʏs] *de* continuing-education course, refresher course

naschrift [nasχrıft] *het (~en)* postscript

naseizoen [naseizun] *het (~en)* late season

nasi [nɑsi] *de* rice: ~ *goreng* fried rice

naslagwerk [nɑslɑχwɛrk] *het (~en)* reference book (*or:* work)

nasleep [nɑslep] *de* aftermath, (after)effects, consequences

nasmaak [nɑsmak] *de (nasmaken)* aftertaste

naspelen [nɑspelə(n)] *vb (mus)* repeat (by ear), play (sth) after (s.o.); represent, play (out), act (out)

nastreven [nɑstrevə(n)] *vb* aim for, aim at, strive for (*or:* after): *geluk* ~ seek happiness

nasturen [nɑstyrə(n)] *vb* send after: *iemands post* ~ forward s.o.'s mail

nasynchroniseren [nɑsɪŋχronizerə(n)] *vb* dub

¹nat [nɑt] *adj, adv* **1** wet, moist, damp: ~ *worden* get wet; *door en door* ~ drenched (*or:* soaked) (to the skin); **2** wet, rainy

²nat [nɑt] *het* liquid, juice

natekenen [nɑtekənə(n)] *vb* draw

natellen [nɑtɛlə(n)] *vb* count again, check

natie [nɑ(t)si] *de (~s)* nation, country

nationaal [na(t)ʃonal] *adj, adv* national

nationaal-socialisme [na(t)ʃonalsoʃalısmə] *het* National Socialism, Nazism

nationaal-socialist [na(t)ʃonalsoʃalıst] *de (~en)* National Socialist, Nazi

nationalisatie [na(t)ʃonaliza(t)si] *de (~s)* nationalization

nationaliseren [na(t)ʃonalizerə(n)] *vb* nationalize

nationalisme [na(t)ʃonalısmə] *het* nationalism

nationalist [na(t)ʃonalıst] *de (~en)* nationalist

nationalistisch [na(t)ʃonalıstis] *adj, adv* nationalist(ic)

nationaliteit [na(t)ʃonalitɛit] *de (~en)* nationality: *hij is van Britse* ~ he has the British nationality

natmaken [nɑtmakə(n)] *vb* wet; moisten

natrekken [nɑtrɛkə(n)] *vb* check (out); investigate

natrium [nɑtrijʏm] *het* sodium

nattevingerwerk [nɑtəvɪŋərwɛrk] *het* guesswork

nattigheid [nɑtəχhɛit] *de* damp: ~ *voelen* smell a rat, be uneasy (about sth)

natura [natyra] *de || in* ~ in kind

naturalisatie [natyraliza(t)si] *de (~s)* naturalization

naturaliseren [natyralizerə(n)] *vb* naturalize: *zich laten* ~ be naturalized

naturisme [natyrısmə] *het* naturism, nudism

natuur [natyr] *de* **1** nature; country(side), scenery: *wandelen in de vrije* ~ (take a) walk (out) in the country(side); *terug naar de* ~ back to nature; **2** nature, character: *twee tegengestelde naturen* two opposite natures (*or:* characters); *dat is zijn tweede* ~ that's become second nature (to him)

natuurbeheer [natyrbəher] *het* (nature) conservation

natuurbeschermer [natyrbəsχɛrmər] *de (~s)* conservationist

natuurbescherming [natyrbəsχɛrmıŋ] *de* (nature) conservation, protection of nature

natuurgebied [natyrχəbit] *het (~en)* scenic area; nature reserve, wildlife area

natuurgenezer [natyrχənezər] *de (~s)* healer

natuurkunde [natyrkʏndə] *de* physics

natuurkundig [natyrkʏndəχ] *adj* physical, physics

natuurkundige [natyrkʏndəɣə] *de (~n)* physicist

natuurliefhebber [natyrlifhɛbər] *de (~s)* nature lover, lover of nature

natuurlijk [natyrlək] *adj, adv* natural; true to nature (*or:* life): *maar* ~! why, of course! (*or:* naturally!)

natuurmonument [natyrmonymɛnt] *het (~en)* nature reserve

natuurproduct [natyrprodʏkt] *het (~en)* natural product

natuurtalent [natyrtalɛnt] *het (~en)* gift, natural talent, born talent; *(pers)* gifted (*or:* naturally talented) person

natuurverschijnsel [natyrvərsχɛinsəl] *het (~en, ~s)* natural phenomenon

natuurvoeding [natyrvudıŋ] *de (~en)* organic food, natural food, wholefood

natuurwetenschapper [natyrwetənsχapər] *de (~s)* scientist, physicist

¹nauw [nɑu] *adj, adv* **1** narrow; **2** close: *een* ~*e samenhang* a close connection; **3** precise, particular: *wat geld betreft kijkt hij niet zo* ~ he's not so fussy (*or:* strict) when it comes to money; **4** narrow, close-fitting, tight

²nauw [nɑu] *het* (tight) spot (*or:* corner): *iem in het* ~ *drijven* drive s.o. into a corner, put s.o. in a (tight) spot

nauwelijks [nɑuwələks] *adv* hardly, scarcely, barely || *ik was* ~ *thuis, of*... I'd only just got home when ...

nauwgezet [nɑuɣəzɛt] *adj, adv* painstaking; conscientious, scrupulous; punctual

nauwkeurig [nɑukørəχ] *adj, adv* accurate, precise, careful, close: *tot op de millimeter* ~ accurate to (within) a millimetre

nauwkeurigheid [nɑukørəχhɛit] *de* accuracy, precision, exactness: *met de grootste* ~ with clockwork precision

nauwlettend [nɑulɛtənt] *adj, adv* close; conscientious; careful: ~ *toezien op* keep a close watch on

nauwlettendheid [nɑulɛtənthɛit] *de* accuracy, precision, exactness

n.a.v. *naar aanleiding van* in connection with, with reference to

navel [nɑvəl] *de (~s)* navel

navelstreng [nɑvəlstrɛŋ] *de (~en)* umbilical cord, navel string

navertellen [nɑvərtɛlə(n)] *vb* repeat, retell: *hij zal het niet* ~ he won't live to tell the tale

navigatie [naviɣa(t)si] *de* navigation

navigeren [naviɣerə(n)] *vb* navigate

NAVO [nɑvo] *de Noord-Atlantische Verdragsorgani-*

satie NATO

navolger [na̱vɔlɣər] *de (~s)* follower, imitator, copier

navolging [na̱vɔlɣɪŋ] *de (~en)* imitation, following

navraag [na̱vraχ] *de* inquiry: ~ *doen bij* inquire with

navragen [na̱vraɣə(n)] *vb* inquire (about, into)

navulbaar [na̱vɣlbar] *adj* refillable

navulpak [na̱vɣlpɑk] *het (~ken)* refill pack

naweeën [na̱wejə(n)] *de* 1 afterpains, aftereffects; 2 aftereffects, aftermath

nawerking [na̱wɛrkɪŋ] *de (~en)* aftereffect(s)

nawijzen [na̱wɛizə(n)] *vb* point at (*or:* after): *iem met de vinger ~* point the finger at s.o.

nawoord [na̱wort] *het (~en)* afterword, epilogue

nawuiven [na̱wœyvə(n)] *vb* wave at (*or:* after)

nazeggen [na̱zɛɣə(n)] *vb* repeat: *zeg mij na* repeat after me

nazenden [na̱zɛndə(n)] *vb* send on (*or:* after), forward

nazi [na̱tsi] *de (~'s)* Nazi

nazicht [na̱zɪχt] *het (Belg)* check

nazien [na̱zin] *vb* look over (*or:* through), check

nazisme [na̱zɪsmə] *het* Nazi(i)sm

nazitten [na̱zɪtə(n)] *vb* pursue, chase

nazomer [na̱zomər] *de (~s)* late summer

NB [ɛnbe̱] *nota bene* N.B., NB

Neanderthaler [nejɑndərtalər] *de (~s)* Neanderthal (man)

nectar [nɛktɑr] *de* nectar

nectarine [nɛktari̱nə] *de (~s)* nectarine

nederig [ne̱dərəχ] *adj, adv* humble, modest

nederlaag [ne̱dərlaχ] *de (nederlagen)* defeat; setback: *een ~ lijden* suffer a defeat, be defeated

Nederland [ne̱dərlɑnt] *het* the Netherlands, Holland

Nederlander [ne̱dərlɑndər] *de (~s)* Dutchman: *de ~s* the Dutch

Nederlands [ne̱dərlɑnts] *het* Dutch: *het Algemeen Beschaafd ~* Standard Dutch

Nederlandstalig [ne̱dərlɑntstɑləχ] *adj* Dutch-speaking: *een ~ lied* a song in Dutch

nederzetting [ne̱dərzɛtɪŋ] *de (~en)* settlement, post

nee [ne] *int* 1 no: *geen ~ kunnen zeggen* not be able to say no; *daar zeg ik geen ~ tegen* I wouldn't say no (to that); *~ toch* you can't mean it, really?, surely not?; 2 really, you're joking (*or:* kidding)

neef [nef] *de (neven)* 1 nephew; 2 cousin: *zij zijn ~ en nicht* they are cousins

neer [ner] *adv* down

neerbuigend [nerbœyɣənt] *adj* condescending, patronizing

neerdalen [ne̱rdalə(n)] *vb* come down, go down, descend

neerdrukken [ne̱rdrɣkə(n)] *vb* push (*or:* press, weigh) down

neergaan [ne̱rɣan] *vb* ‖ *de straat* (or: *trap) op- en ~* go up and down the street (*or:* stairs)

neergooien [ne̱rɣojə(n)] *vb* throw down, toss down: *het bijltje er bij ~* throw in the towel

neerhalen [ne̱rhalə(n)] *vb* 1 take down, pull down, lower; 2 pull (*or:* take, knock) down, raze; 3 take down, bring down

neerkijken [ne̱rkɛikə(n)] *vb* look down (on), look down one's nose (at)

neerkomen [ne̱rkomə(n)] *vb* 1 come down, descend, fall, land: *waar is het vliegtuig neergekomen?* where did the aeroplane land?; 2 fall (on): *alles komt op mij neer* it all falls on my shoulders; 3 come (*or:* boil) down (to), amount (to): *dat komt op hetzelfde neer* it comes (*or:* boils down) to the same thing

neerlandicus [nerlɑndikʏs] *de (neerlandici)* Dutch specialist, student of (*or:* authority on) Dutch

neerleggen [ne̱rlɛɣə(n)] *vb* 1 put (down), lay (down), set (down): *een bevel naast zich ~* disregard (*or:* ignore) a command; 2 put aside, lay down: *zijn ambt ~* resign (from) one's office

neerploffen [ne̱rplɔfə(n)] *vb* flop down, plump down

neerschieten [ne̱rsχitə(n)] *vb* 1 shoot (down); 2 bring down, down

¹neerslaan [ne̱rslan] *vb* fall down; drop down: *een wolk van stof sloeg neer op het plein* a cloud of dust settled on the square

²neerslaan [ne̱rslan] *vb* 1 turn down, let down, lower: *de ogen ~* lower one's eyes; 2 strike down, knock down, *(sport)* floor

neerslachtig [nerslɑχtəχ] *adj, adv* dejected, depressed

neerslag [ne̱rslɑχ] *de (~en)* 1 precipitation, rain, rainfall, layer, fall: *kans op ~* chance of rain; 2 deposit

neersteken [ne̱rstekə(n)] *vb* stab (to death)

neerstorten [ne̱rstɔrtə(n)] *vb* crash down, thunder down, crash: *~d puin* falling rubble

neerstrijken [ne̱rstrɛikə(n)] *vb* 1 alight, settle (on), perch (on); 2 descend (on); settle (on): *op een terrasje ~* descend on a terrace

neertellen [ne̱rtɛlə(n)] *vb* pay (out), fork out

neervallen [ne̱rvɑlə(n)] *vb* 1 fall down, drop down: *werken tot je erbij neervalt* work till you drop; 2 drop (down), flop (down)

neerwaarts [ne̱rwarts] *adj, adv* downward(s), down

neerzetten [ne̱rzɛtə(n)] *vb* put down, lay down, place, set down, erect: *een goede tijd ~* record a good time

¹negatief [neɣati̱f] *adj, adv* 1 negative, *(esp maths, science)* minus: *een ~ getal* a negative (*or:* minus) (number); 2 negative, critical

²negatief [neɣati̱f] *het (negatieven)* negative (plate, film)

negen [ne̱ɣə(n)] *num* nine: *~ op (van) de tien keer* nine times out of ten

negende [ne̱ɣəndə] *num* ninth

negentien [ne̱ɣə(n)tin] *num* nineteen

negentiende [neɣə(n)tində] *num* nineteenth

negentiende-eeuws [neɣə(n)tindəɣws] *adj* nineteenth-century

negentig [neɣəntəχ] *num* ninety: *hij was in de ~ he* was in his nineties

neger [neɣər] *de* (*~s*) (African, American) black (person), Negro

negeren [nəɣɛrə(n)] *vb* ignore, take no notice of, *(pers also)* give the cold shoulder, disregard, brush aside: *iem volkomen ~* cut s.o. dead

neigen [neiɣə(n)] *vb* incline (to, towards), be inclined (to, towards), tend (to, towards)

neiging [neiɣɪŋ] *de* (*~en*) inclination, tendency

nek [nɛk] *de* (*~ken*) nape (*or:* back) of the neck: *je ~ breken over de rommel* trip over the rubbish; *zijn ~ uitsteken* stick one's neck out; *tot aan zijn ~ in de schulden zitten* be up to one's ears in debt

nek-aan-nekrace [nɛkanɛkres] *de* (*~s*) neck-and-neck race

nekken [nɛkə(n)] *vb* break (*or:* wring) s.o.'s neck

nekkramp [nɛkramp] *de* (*~en*) spotted fever

nekvel [nɛkfɛl] *het* scruff of the neck: *iem* (or: *een hond*) *in zijn ~ pakken* take s.o. (*or:* a dog) by the scruff of the neck

nemen [nemə(n)] *vb* **1** take: *maatregelen ~* take steps (*or:* measures); *de moeite ~ om* take the trouble to; *ontslag ~* resign; *een kortere weg ~* take a short cut; *iem iets kwalijk ~* take sth ill of s.o.; *iem (niet) serieus ~* (not) take s.o. seriously; *strikt genomen* strictly (speaking); *iem (even) apart ~* take s.o. aside; *voor zijn rekening ~* deal with, account for; **2** have: *wat neem jij?* what are you having?; *neem nog een koekje* (do) have another biscuit; **3** take, get, have, take out: *een dag vrij ~* have (*or:* take) a day off; **4** take, use: *de bus ~* catch (*or:* take) the bus, go by bus; **5** take, seize, capture

neofascist [nejofaʃɪst] *de* (*~en*) neo-fascist

neon [nejɔn] *het* neon

neonazi [nejonatsi] *de* (*~'s*) neo-Nazi

neonreclame [nejɔnrəklamə] *de* (*~s*) neon sign(s)

nep [nɛp] *de* sham, fake, swindle, rip-off

Nepal [nepɑl] *het* Nepal

Nepalees [nepɑles] *de* (*Nepalezen*) Nepalese, Nepali

Neptunus [nɛptynʏs] *de* Neptune

nerf [nɛrf] *de* (*nerven*) grain(ing), texture; vein, rib

nergens [nɛrɣəns] *adv* **1** nowhere: *met onbeleefdheid kom je ~* being rude will get you nowhere; *ik kon ~ naar toe* I had nowhere to go; **2** nothing: *~ aan komen!* don't touch!; *ik weet ~ van* I know nothing about it

¹nerts [nɛrts] *de* (*~en*) (*animal*) mink

²nerts [nɛrts] *het* (*fur*) mink

nerveus [nɛrvøs] *adj, adv* nervous, tense, high(ly)-strung

nest [nɛst] *het* (*~en*) **1** nest, eyrie, den, hole; **2** litter, nest, brood; **3** jam, spot, fix: *in de ~en zitten* be in a fix

nestelen [nɛstələ(n)] *vb* nest

¹net [nɛt] *het* (*~ten*) **1** net: *achter het ~ vissen* miss out, miss the boat; **2** network, system, net, mains, grid: *een ~ van telefoonverbindingen* a network of telephone connections

²net [nɛt] *adj* **1** neat, tidy, trim: *iets in het ~ schrijven* copy out sth; **2** respectable, decent: *een ~te buurt* a respectable (*or:* genteel) neighbourhood

³net [nɛt] *adv* just, exactly: *~ goed* serves you/him (*or:* her, them) right; *het gaat maar ~* it's a tight fit; *zij ging ~ vertrekken* she was about to leave; *~ iets voor hem: a)* just the thing for him; *b)* just like him, him all over; *~ wat ik dacht* just as I thought; *dat is ~ wat ik nodig heb* that's exactly what I need; *ze is ~ zo goed als hij* she's every bit as good as he is; *zo is het maar ~* right you are!, just as you say!; *we hadden ~ zo goed niets kunnen doen* we might just as well have done nothing; *we kwamen ~ te laat* we came just too late; *~ echt* just like the real thing; *wij zijn ~ thuis* we've (only) just come home

netbal [nɛdbɑl] *de* (*~len*) netball

netheid [nɛtheit] *de* neatness, tidiness, cleanliness; smartness

netjes [nɛcəs] *adj, adv* **1** neat, tidy, clean; **2** neat, smart: *~ gekleed* all dressed up; **3** decent, respectable, proper: *gedraag je ~* behave yourself

netnummer [nɛtnʏmər] *het* (*~s*) dialling code; *(Am)* area code

netsurfen [nɛtsʏrfə(n)] *vb* surfing (the Net)

nettiquette [nɛtikɛtə] *de* netiquette

netto [nɛto] *adj, adv* net, nett, clear, real: *het ~ maandsalaris* the take-home pay; *de opbrengst bedraagt ~ €2000,-* the net(t) profit is €2,000

nettobedrag [nɛtobədrɑχ] *het* (*~en*) net(t) (amount)

nettogewicht [nɛtoɣəwɪχt] *het* net(t) weight

netvlies [nɛtflis] *het* (*netvliezen*) retina

netwerk [nɛtwɛrk] *het* network, criss-cross pattern, *(fig also)* system: *een ~ van intriges* a web of intrigue

netwerken [nɛtwɛrkə(n)] *vb* network

neuken [nøkə(n)] *vb* screw, fuck

neuraal [nøyrɑl] *adj* neural

neuriën [nørijə(n)] *vb* hum

neurochirurgie [nøroʃirʏrɣi] *de* neurosurgery

neurologie [nøroloɣi] *de* neurology, neuroscience

neuroloog [nøroloχ] *de* (*-logen*) neurologist

neuroot [nørot] *de* (*neuroten*) neurotic, psycho, nutcase

neurose [nørozə] *de* (*~n, ~s*) neurosis

neurotisch [nørotis] *adj* neurotic

neus [nøs] *de* (*neuzen*) **1** nose, scent, *(fig also)* flair: *een fijne ~ voor iets hebben* have a good nose for sth, have an eye for sth; *een frisse ~ halen* get a breath of fresh air; *doen alsof zijn ~ bloedt* play (*or:* act) dumb; *(Belg) van zijn ~ maken* show off, make a fuss; *de ~ voor iem (iets) ophalen* turn up one's nose at s.o. (sth), look down one's nose at s.o. (sth); *zijn ~ snuiten* blow one's nose; *zijn ~ in andermans zaken steken* stick one's nose into other people's affairs; *iem met zijn ~ op de feiten drukken* make s.o. face the facts; *niet verder kijken dan zijn ~ lang is* be unable to see further than (the end of) one's nose; **2** nose, nozzle, (toe)cap, toe: *dat examen is een wassen ~* that exam is just a mere formality

neusdruppels [nøzdrʏpəls] *de* nose drops

neusgat [nøsχɑt] *het (~en)* nostril

neushoorn [nøshorn] *de (~s)* rhinoceros, rhino

neuslengte [nøslɛŋtə] *de (~n, ~s)* nose, hair('s breadth)

neuspeuteren [nøspøtərə(n)] *vb* pick one's nose

neusvleugel [nøsfløɣəl] *de (~s)* nostril

neut [nøt] *de (~en)* drop, snort(er)

neutraal [nøtral] *adj* neutral, impartial

neutralisatie [nøtraliza(t)si] *de* neutralization

neutraliseren [nøtralizerə(n)] *vb* neutralize, counteract

neutronenbom [nœytronə(n)bɔm] *de (~men)* neutron bomb

neuzen [nøzə(n)] *vb* browse, nose around (*or:* about)

nevel [neɣəl] *de (~en)* mist, *(light)* haze, spray

nevelig [neɣələχ] *adj* misty, hazy

nevenactiviteit [neɣə(n)ɑktiviteit] *de* sideline

neveneffect [neɣə(n)ɛfɛkt] *het (~en)* side effect

nevenfunctie [neɣə(n)fʏŋksi] *de (~s)* additional job

neveninkomsten [neɣə(n)ɪŋkɔmstə(n)] *de* additional income

newfoundlander [ɲufɑundlɛndər] *de (~s)* Newfoundland (dog)

Niagara *de* Niagara

Nicaragua [nikaraɣuwa] *het* Nicaragua

nicht [nɪχt] *de* **1** niece; **2** cousin; **4** fairy, queen, poofter, *(Am)* faggot

nichterig [nɪχtərəχ] *adj, adv* fairy, poofy

nicotine [nikotinə] *de* nicotine

niemand [nimɑnt] *ind pron* no one, nobody: *voor ~ onderdoen* be second to none; *~ anders dan* none other than

niemandsland [nimɑntslɑnt] *het* no man's land

nier [nir] *de (~en)* kidney: *gebakken ~(tjes)* fried kidney(s)

niersteen [nirsten] *de (-stenen)* kidney stone

niesbui [nizbœy] *de (~en)* attack (*or:* fit) of sneezing

¹niet [nit] *adv* not: *~ geslaagd* (or: *gereed*) unsuccessful (*or:* unprepared); *ik hoop van ~* I hope not; *hoe vaak heb ik ~ gedacht ...* how often have I thought ...; *geloof jij dat verhaal niet? ik ook ~* don't you believe this story? neither (*or:* nor) do I; *~ alleen ..., maar ook ...* not only ... but also ...; *het betaalt goed, daar ~ van* it's well-paid, that's not the point, but; *helemaal ~* not at all, no way; *denk dat maar ~* don't you believe it!; *ik neem aan van ~* I don't suppose so, I suppose not; *ze is ~ al te slim* she is none too bright

²niet [nit] *ind pron* nothing, nought: *dat is ~ meer dan een suggestie* that's nothing more than a suggestion

niet-bestaand [nidbəstant] *adj* non-existent

nieten [nitə(n)] *vb* staple

nietes [nitəs] *int* it isn't: *het is jouw schuld! ~! welles!* it's your fault! - oh no it isn't! - oh yes it is!

nietig [nitəχ] *adj* **1** invalid, null (and void); **2** puny

nietje [nicə] *de (~s)* staple

nietmachine [nitmaʃinə] *de (~s)* stapler

niet-roken [nitrokə(n)] *adv* non-smoking

niets [nits] *ind pron* **1** not at all: *dat bevalt mij ~* I don't like that at all; **2** nothing, not anything: *weet je ~ beters?* don't you know (of) anything better?; *zij moet ~ van hem hebben* she will have nothing to do with him; *verder ~?* is that all?; *ik geloof er ~ van* I don't believe a word of it; *voor ~: a)* for nothing, gratis, free (of charge); *b)* for nothing; *niet voor ~* not for nothing, for good reason; *dat is ~ voor mij* that's not my cup of tea; *dit is ~ dan opschepperij* that's just (*or:* mere) boasting; *in het ~ verdwijnen* disappear into thin air

nietsvermoedend [nitsfərmudənt] *adj, adv* unsuspecting

niettemin [nitəmɪn] *adv* nevertheless, nonetheless, even so, still: *~ is het waar dat ...* it is nevertheless true that ...

nietwaar [nitwar] *int* is(n't) it?, do(n't) you?, have(n't) we?: *jij kent zijn pa, ~?* you know his dad, don't you?; *dat is mogelijk, ~?* it's possible, isn't it?

nieuw [niw] *adj* **1** new, recent: *het ~ste op het gebied van* the latest thing in; **2** new, unworn, unused: *zo goed als ~* as good as new; **3** fresh; young: *~e haring* early-season herring(s); **4** new, fresh, original, novel: *een ~ begin maken* make a fresh start; *ik ben hier ~* I'm new here; **5** new, modern

nieuwbouwwijk [niwbɑuwɛik] *de (~en)* new housing estate (*or:* development)

nieuweling [niwəlɪŋ] *de (~en)* **1** novice, beginner; **2** new boy (*or:* girl, pupil)

nieuwemaan [niwəman] *de* new moon

Nieuw-Guinea [niwɣineja] *het* New Guinea

nieuwjaar [niwjar] *het* New Year; New Year's Day: *een gelukkig (zalig) ~!* a Happy New Year!

nieuwjaarsdag [niwjarzdɑχ] *de (~en)* New Year's Day

nieuwjaarswens [niwjarswɛns] *de (~en)* New Year's greeting(s)

nieuwkuis [niwkœys] *de (Belg)* dry cleaning

nieuws [niws] *het* news; piece of news: *buitenlands* (*or:* *binnenlands) ~* foreign (*or:* domestic) news; *ik heb goed ~* I have (some) good news; *dat is oud ~* that's stale news, that's ancient history; *het ~ van acht uur* the eight o'clock news; *is er nog ~?* any news?, what's new?

nieuwsbericht [niwzbərɪχt] *het (~en)* news report; news bulletin; news flash

nieuwsbrief [niwzbrif] *de (-brieven)* newsletter

nieuwsdienst [niwzdinst] *de (~en)* news service, press service

nieuwsgierig [niwsχirəχ] *adj, adv* curious (about),

inquisitive, nosy

nieuwsgierigheid [niwsχirəχhɛit] *de* curiosity, inquisitiveness: *branden van ~* be dying from curiosity

nieuwsgroep [niwsχrup] *de (~en)* newsgroup

nieuwslezer [niwslezər] *de (~s)* newsreader

nieuwsoverzicht [niwsovərzɪχt] *het (~en)* news summary: *kort ~* rundown on the news

nieuwsuitzending [niwsœytsɛndɪŋ] *de (~en)* news broadcast, newscast

nieuwszender [niwsɛndər] *de (~s)* news network

nieuwtje [niwcə] *het (~s)* piece (*or:* item, bit) of news

Nieuw-Zeeland [niwzelɑnt] *het* New Zealand

niezen [nizə(n)] *vb* sneeze

Nigeria [niɣerija] *het* Nigeria

Nigeriaan [niɣerijan] *de (Nigerianen)* Nigerian

nihil [nihil] *adj* nil, zero

nijd [nɛit] *de* envy, jealousy: *groen en geel worden van ~ over iets* be green with envy at sth

nijdig [nɛidəχ] *adj, adv* angry, annoyed, cross

Nijl [nɛil] *de* Nile

nijlpaard [nɛilpart] *het (~en)* hippopotamus, hippo

nijpend [nɛipənt] *adj* pinching, biting: *het ~ tekort aan* the acute shortage of

nijptang [nɛiptɑŋ] *de (~en)* (pair of) pincers

nijverheid [nɛivərhɛit] *de* industry

nikkelen [nɪkələ(n)] *adj* 1 nickel; 2 nickel-plated

niks [nɪks] *ind pron* nothing, *(Am)* zilch: *dat wordt ~ that won't work; nou, ik vind het maar ~!* well I don't think much of it

niksen [nɪksə(n)] *vb* sit around, loaf about, laze about, do nothing

niksnut [nɪksnʏt] *de (~ten)* good-for-nothing, layabout

nimf [nɪmf] *de (~en)* nymph

nimmer [nɪmər] *adv* never

nippen [nɪpə(n)] *vb* sip (at), take a sip

nippertje [nɪpərcə] *het* || *op het ~* at the very last moment (*or:* second), in the nick of time; *dat was op het ~* that was a close (*or:* near) thing; *de student haalde op het ~ zijn examen* the student only passed by the skin of his teeth

nirwana [nɪrvɑna] *het* nirvana

nis [nɪs] *de (~sen)* niche, alcove

nitraat [nitrat] *het (nitraten)* nitrate

nitriet [nitrit] *het (~en)* nitrite

niveau [nivo] *het (~s)* level, standard: *rugby op hoog ~* top-class rugby; *het ~ daalt* the tone (of the conversation) is dropping

nivellering [nivɛlerɪŋ] *de (~en)* levelling (out), evening out

nl. *namelijk* viz.

n.m. *namiddag* p.m.

Noach [nowɑχ] *de* Noah: *de ark van ~* Noah's ark

nobel [nobəl] *adj, adv* noble(-minded); generous

Nobelprijs [nobɛlprɛis] *de (-prijzen)* Nobel prize: *de ~ voor de vrede* the Nobel Peace prize

noch [nɔχ] *conj* neither, nor: *~ de een ~ de ander* neither the one nor the other

no-claimkorting [noklɛmkɔrtɪŋ] *de* no claim(s) bonus

¹nodig [nodəχ] *adj, adv* 1 necessary, needful: *zij hadden al hun tijd ~* they had no time to waste (*or:* spare); *iets ~ hebben* need (*or:* require) sth; *er is moed voor ~ om* it takes courage to; *dat is hard (dringend) ~* that is badly needed, that is vital; *zo (waar) ~* if need be, if necessary; 2 usual, customary

²nodig [nodəχ] *adv* necessarily, needfully, urgently || *dat moet jij ~ zeggen* look who's talking

noemen [numə(n)] *vb* 1 call, name: *noem jij dit een gezellige avond?* is this your idea of a pleasant evening?; *dat noem ik nog eens moed* that's what I call courage!; *iem bij zijn voornaam ~* call s.o. by his first name; *een kind naar zijn vader ~* name a child after his father; 2 mention; cite; name: *om maar eens iets te ~* to name (but) a few

noemenswaardig [numənswardəχ] *adj, adv* appreciable, considerable, noticeable, worthy of mention: *niet ~* inappreciable, nothing to speak of

noemer [numər] *de (~s)* denominator

nog [nɔχ] *adv* 1 still, so far: *niemand heeft dit ~ geprobeerd* no one has tried this (as) yet; *zelfs nu ~* even now; *tot ~ toe* so far, up to now; 2 still; 3 even, still: *~ groter* even larger, larger still; 4 from now (on), more: *~ drie nachtjes slapen* three (more) nights; 5 again, (once) more: *~ één woord en ik schiet* one more word and I'll shoot; *neem er ~ eentje!* have another (one)!; *ik zag hem vorige week ~* I saw him only last week; *verder ~ iets?* anything else?; *ze zijn er ~ maar net* they've only just arrived; *~ geen maand geleden* less than a month ago

noga [noɣa] *de* nougat

nogal [nɔχɑl] *adv* rather, fairly, quite, pretty: *ik vind het ~ duur* I think it is rather (*or:* quite) expensive; *er waren er ~ wat* there were quite a few (of them)

nogmaals [nɔχmals] *adv* once again (*or:* more)

nok [nɔk] *de (~ken)* ridge, crest, peak

nomade [nomadə] *de (~n)* nomad

nominaal [nominal] *adj* nominal

nominatie [nomina(t)si] *de (~s)* nomination (list)

nomineren [nomineːrə(n)] *vb* nominate

non [nɔn] *de (~nen)* nun, sister

non-actief [nɔnɑktif] *het* || *(tijdelijk) op ~ staan* be suspended

nonchalance [nɔnʃalɑsə] *de* nonchalance, casualness

nonchalant [nɔnʃalɑnt] *adj, adv* nonchalant, casual

nonnenschool [nɔnə(n)sχol] *de (-scholen)* convent (school)

nonsens [nɔnsɛns] *de* nonsense, rubbish

nood [not] *de (noden)* distress; extremity; (time(s) of) emergency: *uiterste ~* dire need; *mensen in ~* people in distress (*or:* trouble); *in de ~ leert men* *zijn vrienden kennen* a friend in need is a friend indeed

noodgang [nо̠tχɑŋ] *de* breakneck speed

noodgebouw [nо̠tχəbɑu] *het* temporary building, makeshift building

noodgedwongen [nо̠tχədwo̠ŋə(n)] *adv* out of (*or:* from) (sheer) necessity: *wij moeten ~ andere maatregelen treffen* we are forced to take other measures

noodgeval [nо̠tχəvɑl] *het (~len)* (case of) emergency

noodhulp [nо̠thʏlp] *de (~en)* emergency relief, emergency aid

noodklok [nо̠tklɔk] *de (~ken)* alarm (bell)

noodkreet [nо̠tkret] *de (-kreten)* cry of distress, call for help

noodlanding [nо̠tlɑndɪŋ] *de (~en)* forced landing, emergency landing, belly landing, crash landing

noodlot [nо̠tlɔt] *het* fate

noodlottig [nо̠tlɔtəχ] *adj, adv* fatal (to), disastrous (to), ill-fated: *een ~e reis* an ill-fated journey

noodmaatregel [nо̠tmatreɣəl] *de* emergency measure

noodrem [nо̠trɛm] *de (~men)* emergency brake, safety brake

noodsituatie [nо̠tsitywa(t)si] *de (~s)* emergency (situation), difficult position, precarious position

noodsprong [nо̠tsprɔŋ] *de (~en)* desperate move (*or:* measure)

noodstop [nо̠tstɔp] *de (~pen)* emergency stop

noodtoestand [nо̠tustɑnt] *de (~en)* emergency (situation), crisis

nooduitgang [nо̠tœytχɑŋ] *de (~en)* emergency exit; fire-escape

noodvaart [nо̠tfart] *de* breakneck speed

noodverband [nо̠tfərbɑnt] *het* first-aid (*or:* emergency, temporary) dressing

¹noodweer [nо̠twer] *het* heavy weather, storm, filthy weather

²noodweer [nо̠twer] *de* self-defence

noodzaak [nо̠tsak] *de* necessity, need: *ik zie de ~ daarvan niet in* I don't see the need for this

noodzakelijk [nо̠tsakələk] *adj* necessary; imperative, essential, vital: *het hoogst ~e* the bare necessities

noodzakelijkerwijs [nо̠tsakələkərwɛis] *adv* necessarily, inevitably, of necessity

noodzaken [nо̠tsakə(n)] *vb* force, oblige, compel

nooit [nojt] *adv* **1** never: *bijna ~* hardly ever, almost never; *~ van mijn leven* never in my life; *~ van gehoord!* never heard of it (*or:* him); **2** never, certainly not, definitely not, no way: *je moet het ~ doen* you must never do that; *~ ofte nimmer* absolutely not, never ever; *dat ~!* never!

Noor [nor] *de (Noren)* Norwegian

noord [nort] *adj, adv* north(erly), northern

Noord-Afrika [nortafrika] *het* North Africa

Noord-Amerika [nortamerika] *het* North America

Noord-Amerikaans [nortamerikans] *adj* North American

Noord-Atlantisch [nortɑtlɑntis] *adj* North Atlantic

Noord-Brabant [nordbrabɑnt] *het* North Brabant

noordelijk [nordələk] *adj, adv* north(erly); northern, northerly, northward: *de wind is ~* the wind is northerly; *een ~e koers kiezen* steer a northerly course; *het ~ halfrond* the northern hemisphere

noorden [nordə(n)] *het* north; North: *ten ~ van* (to the) north of

noordenwind [nordə(n)wɪnt] *de (~en)* north(erly) wind

noorderbreedte [nordərbretə] *de* north latitude: *Madrid ligt op 40 graden ~* Madrid lies in 40° north latitude

noorderkeerkring [nordərkerkrɪŋ] *de* Tropic of Cancer

noorderlicht [nordərlɪχt] *het* aurora borealis, northern lights

noorderling [nordərlɪŋ] *de (~en)* northerner

noorderzon [nordərzɔn] *de || met de ~ vertrekken* do a moonlight flit, abscond, skeddadle

Noord-Ierland [nortírlɑnt] *het* Northern Ireland

Noordkaap [nо̠rtkap] *de* North Cape, Arctic Cape

noordkust [nо̠rtkʏst] *de* north(ern) coast

noordoosten [nortoo̠stə(n)] *het* north-east

Noordoostpolder [nortoo̠s(t)pо̠ldər] *de* North-east Polder

noordpool [nо̠rtpol] *de* North Pole; Arctic

noordpoolcirkel [nо̠rtpolsɪrkəl] *de* Arctic Circle

noordwaarts [nо̠rtwarts] *adj, adv* northward(s); northward

noordwesten [nortwɛstə(n)] *het* north-west

Noordzee [nо̠rtse] *de* North Sea

Noorman [normɑn] *de (~nen)* Norseman, Viking

Noors [nors] *het* Norwegian

Noorwegen [norweɣə(n)] *het* Norway

noot [not] *de (noten)* **1** nut: *een harde ~ (om te kraken)* a tough (*or:* hard) nut (to crack); **2** (*mus*) note: *hele (*or:* halve) noten spelen* play semibreves (*or:* minims); *een kwart ~* a crotchet; *een valse ~* a wrong note; **3** (foot)note: *ergens een kritische ~ bij plaatsen* comment (critically) on sth

nootmuskaat [notmʏskat] *de* nutmeg

nop [nɔp] *de (~pen)* nix: *voor ~* for nothing, for free

noppes [nɔpəs] *|| je kunt er voor ~ naar binnen* you can go there for nothing (*or:* for free); *heb ik nou alles voor ~ gedaan?* has it all been an utter waste of time?

nor [nɔr] *de (~ren)* clink, nick

noren [norə(n)] *de* racing skates

norm [nɔrm] *de (~en)* standard; norm

normaal [nɔrmal] *adj, adv* normal: *~ ben ik al thuis om deze tijd* I am normally (*or:* usually) home by this time

normaalschool [nɔrmalsχol] *de (-scholen) (Belg)* training college for primary school teachers

normaliter [nɔrmalitər] *adv* normally, usually, as a rule

Normandië [nɔrmɑndijə] *het* Normandy

Normandiër [nɔrmɑndijər] *de (~s)* Norman
Normandisch [nɔrmɑndis] *adj* Norman
normbesef [nɔrmbəsɛf] *het* sense of standards (*or:* values)
normering [nɔrmɛrɪŋ] *de (~en)* standard
normvervaging [nɔrmvərvɑɣɪŋ] *de (~en)* blurring of (moral) standards
nors [nɔrs] *adj, adv* surly, gruff, grumpy
nostalgie [nɔstɑlɣi] *de* nostalgia
nostalgisch [nɔstɑlɣis] *adj, adv* nostalgic
nota [nɔta] *de (~'s)* **1** account, bill; **2** memorandum
notabele [nɔtɑbələ] *de (~n)* dignitary, leading citizen
notariaat [notar(i)jat] *het (notariaten)* **1** office of notary (public); **2** notary's practice
notarieel [notar(i)jel] *adj, adv* notarial: *een notariele akte* a notarial act (*or:* deed)
notaris [notɑrɪs] *de (~sen)* notary (public)
notatie [nɔta(t)si] *de* notation, notation system
notenbalk [nɔtə(n)bɑlk] *de (~en)* staff, stave
notenboom [nɔtə(n)bom] *de (-bomen)* walnut (tree)
notendop [nɔtə(n)dɔp] *de (~pen)* nutshell
notenhout [nɔtə(n)hɑut] *het* walnut
notenschrift [nɔtə(n)sχrɪft] *het (~en)* (musical) notation; staff notation
¹noteren [notɛrə(n)] *vb* **1** note (down), make a note of, record, register, book: *een telefoonnummer ~ jot down* (*or:* make a note) of a telephone number; **2** quote: *aan de beurs genoteerd zijn* be listed on the (stock) market
²noteren [notɛrə(n)] *vb* list; quote
notering [notɛrɪŋ] *de (~en)* quotation; quoted price, rate
notie [nɔ(t)si] *de (~s)* notion, idea: *geen flauwe ~* not the faintest notion
notitie [noti(t)si] *de (~s)* note; memo(randum)
notitieblok [noti(t)siblɔk] *het (~ken)* notepad, memo pad; scribbling pad
notitieboekje [noti(t)sibukjə] *het (~s)* notebook, memorandum book
notulen [nɔtylə(n)] *de* minutes
notuleren [notylɛrə(n)] *vb* take (the) minutes
¹nou [nɑu] *adv* **1** now: *wat moeten we ~ doen?* what do we (have to) do now?; **2** now (that): *~ zij het zegt, geloof ik het* now that she says so I believe it
²nou [nɑu] *int* **1** now, well: *kom je ~?* well, are you coming?; **2** well, really: *meen je dat ~?* do you really mean it?; *hoe kan dat ~?* how on earth can that be? (*or:* have happened?); *~ dan!* exactly, couldn't agree more!; *~, en of!* you bet!; **3** again: *wanneer ga je ~ ook weer weg?* when were you leaving again?; **4** oh (very) well, never mind: *~ ja, zo erg is 't niet* never mind, it's not all that bad; *dat is ~ niet bepaald eenvoudig* well, that's not so easy; **5** oh, now, … on earth, … ever: *waar bleef je ~?* where on earth have you been?; *~ en?* so what?; *~, dat was het dan* well (*or:* so), that was that
Nova Zembla [novazɛmbla] *het* Novaya Zemlya

novelle [novɛlə] *de (~n)* short story, novella
november [novɛmbər] *de* November
NPA *de Nederlandse Politie-academie* Netherlands Police Academy
nu [ny] *adv* **1** now, at the moment: *~ en dan* now and then, at times, occasionally; *ik kan ~ niet* I can't (right, just) now; *~ nog niet* not yet; *tot ~ (toe)* up to now, so far; **2** now(adays), these days: *het hier en het ~* the here and now
nuance [nywãsə] *de (~s)* nuance
nuchter [nyχtər] *adj* **1** fasting; newborn: *voor de operatie moet je ~ zijn* you must have an empty stomach before surgery; **2** sober: *~ worden* sober up; **3** sober, plain: *de ~e waarheid* the plain (*or:* simple) truth; **4** sober(-minded), sensible, level-headed
nucleair [nyklejɛːr] *adj, adv* nuclear
nudist [nydɪst] *de (~en)* nudist, naturist
nuffig [nyfəχ] *adj* prim, prissy
nuk [nʏk] *de (~ken)* mood, quirk
nukkig [nʏkəχ] *adj* quirky, moody, sullen
nul [nʏl] *de (~len)* nought, zero, o: *tien graden onder ~* ten (degrees) below zero; *PSV heeft met 2-0 verloren* PSV lost two-nil
nulmeridiaan [nʏlmeridijan] *de (-meridianen)* prime meridian
nulpunt [nʏlpʏnt] *het* zero (point)
numeriek [nymerik] *adj* numerical, numeric
numero [nymero] *het (~'s)* number
nummer [nʏmər] *het (~s)* **1** number, figure: *~ één van de klas zijn* be top of one's class; **2** number, issue: *een ~ van een tijdschrift* a number (*or:* issue) of a periodical; *een oud ~* a back issue (*or:* number); **3** number, track: *een ~ draaien* play a track; **4** act, routine, number: *een ~ brengen* do a routine (*or:* an act)
nummerbord [nʏmərbɔrt] *het (~en)* number plate; *(Am)* license plate
nummeren [nʏmərə(n)] *vb* number
nummertje [nʏmərcə] *het (~s)* **1** number; **2** screw, fuck
nut [nʏt] *het* use(fulness), benefit, point, value, purpose: *het heeft geen enkel ~ om …* it is useless (*or:* pointless) to …; *ik zie er het ~ niet van in* I don't see the point of it
nutsbedrijf [nʏtsbədrɛif] *het (-bedrijven)* ‖ *openbare nutsbedrijven* public utilities
nutteloos [nʏtəlos] *adj, adv* **1** useless: *een nutteloze vraag* a pointless question; **2** fruitless
nutteloosheid [nʏtəlosɦɛit] *de* uselessness, futility
nuttig [nʏtəχ] *adj, adv* **1** useful: *zich ~ maken* make oneself useful; **2** advantageous: *zijn tijd ~ besteden* make good use of one's time
nuttigen [nʏtəɣə(n)] *vb* consume, take, partake of
NV [ɛnve] *de Naamloze Vennootschap* plc (public limited company), *(Am)* Inc. (incorporated)
n.v.t. *niet van toepassing* n/a
nylon [nɛilɔn] *het, de* nylon
nymfomane [nɪmfomanə] *de (~n, ~s)* nymphoma-

niac

O

o [o] *int* O, oh, ah || ~ *zo verleidelijk* ever so tempting

o.a. *onder andere* among other things, for instance

oase [owaːzə] *de* (~s) oasis

o-benen [obenə(n)] *de* bandy legs, bow-legs: *met* ~ bandy-legged, bow-legged

ober [obər] *de* (~s) waiter

object [ɔpjɛkt] *het* (~en) object

objectief [ɔpjɛktif] *adj, adv* objective

objectiviteit [ɔpjɛktivitɛit] *de* objectiveness, objectivity, impartiality

obligatie [obliɣa(t)si] *de* (~s) bond, debenture

obsceen [ɔpsen] *adj* obscene

obscuur [ɔpskyr] *adj* 1 obscure, dark; 2 shady, obscure: *een* ~ *zaakje* a shady (*or:* doubtful) business

obsederen [ɔpsedeːrə(n)] *vb* obsess

observatie [ɔpsɛrva(t)si] *de* (~s) observation

observatorium [ɔpsɛrvatoːrijʏm] *het* (*observatoria*) observatory

observeren [ɔpsɛrveːrə(n)] *vb* observe, watch

obsessie [ɔpsɛsi] *de* (~s) obsession, hang-up

obstakel [ɔpstaːkəl] *het* (~s) obstacle, obstruction, impediment: *een belangrijk* ~ *vormen* constitute a major obstacle

obus [obʏs] *de* (~sen) (Belg) shell

occasie [ɔkaːzi] *de* (~s) (Belg) bargain

occasion [ɔkeːʒən] *de* (~s) used car

occult [ɔkʏlt] *adj* occult

oceaan [oseːjaːn] *de* (*oceanen*) ocean, sea: *de Stille (Grote) Oceaan* the Pacific (Ocean)

Oceanië [oseːjaːnijə] *het* Oceania

och [ɔχ] *int* oh, o, ah: ~ *kom* oh, go on (with you)

ochtend [ɔχtənt] *de* (~en) morning; dawn, daybreak: *de hele* ~ all morning; *om 7 uur 's* ~*s* at 7 o'clock in the morning, at 7 a.m.

ochtendjas [ɔχtəntjɑs] *de* (~sen) dressing gown, housecoat

ochtendkrant [ɔχtəntkrɑnt] *de* (~en) morning (news)paper

ochtendploeg [ɔχtəntpluχ] *de* (~en) morning shift

octaaf [ɔktaːf] *het, de* (*octaven*) octave, eighth

octaan [ɔktaːn] *het* octane

octopus [ɔktopʏs] *de* (~sen) octopus

octrooi [ɔktroːj] *het* (~en) patent: ~ *aanvragen* apply for a patent

ode [odə] *de* (~n, ~s) ode: *een* ~ *brengen aan iem* pay tribute to s.o.

Oedipuscomplex [œydipʏskɔmplɛks] *het* (~en) Oedipus complex

oef [uf] *int* phew, whew, oof

¹oefenen [ufənə(n)] *vb* train, coach, (*mil*) drill: *zich* ~ *in het zwemmen* practise swimming

²oefenen [ufənə(n)] *vb* train; practise; rehearse; drill (*mil*): ~ *voor een voorstelling* rehearse for a performance

oefening [ufənɪŋ] *de* (~en) 1 exercise: *dat is een goede* ~ *voor je* it is good practice for you; 2 exercise, drill

oefenstuk [ufənstʏk] *het* practice piece

oefenterrein [ufə(n)tɛrɛin] *het* (~en) {practice, training} ground

oefenwedstrijd [ufə(n)wɛtstrɛit] *de* (~en) training (*or:* practice, warm-up) match, sparring match

oeh [u] *int* phew, whew

oei [uj] *int* oops; ouch

¹Oekraïens [ukrains] *het* Ukrainian

²Oekraïens [ukrains] *adj* Ukrainian

Oekraïne [ukrainə] || *de* ~ the Ukraine

Oekraïner [ukrainər] *de* (~s) Ukrainian

oer- [ur-] primal, primitive, primordial, primeval; prehistoric

Oeral [uraːl] || *de* ~ the Urals, the Ural Mountains

oerbos [urbɔs] *het* (~sen) primeval forest

oerknal [urknɑl] *de* Big Bang

oeroud [uraut] *adj* ancient, prehistoric, primeval

oerwoud [urwaut] *het* (~en) 1 primeval forest, virgin forest, jungle; 2 (*fig*) jungle, chaos, hotchpotch

OESO [uzo] *de Organisatie voor Economische Samenwerking en Ontwikkeling* O.E.C.D.

oester [ustər] *de* (~s) oyster

oesterzwam [ustərzwɑm] *de* (~men) oyster mushroom

oestrogeen [œystroɣen] *het* (*oestrogenen*) oestrogen

OETC *het onderwijs in hun eigen taal en cultuur* vernacular education for ethnic minorities

oeuvre [œːvrə] *het* oeuvre, works, body of work

oever [uvər] *de* (~s) bank; shore: *de rivier is buiten haar* ~*s getreden* the river has burst its banks

oeverloos [uvərloːs] *adj* endless, interminable: ~ *gezwets* blather, claptrap

Oezbeek [uzbek] *de* Uzbek

¹Oezbeeks [uzbeks] *het* Uzbek

²Oezbeeks [uzbeks] *adj* Uzbek

Oezbekistan [uzbekistɑn] *het* Uzbekistan

of [ɔf] *conj* 1 (either …) or: *je krijgt* ~ *het een* ~ *het ander* you get either the one or the other; *het is óf het een óf het ander* you can't have it both ways; *Sepke zei weinig* ~ *niets* Sepke said little or nothing; *min* ~ *meer* more or less; *vroeg* ~ *laat* sooner or later, eventually; 2 or: *de influenza* ~ *griep* influenza, or flu; 3 (hardly …) when; (no sooner …) than: *ik weet niet beter* ~ … for all I know …; 4 although, whether … or (not), no matter (how, what, where): ~ *je het nu leuk vindt of niet* whether you like it or not; **5** as if, as though: *hij doet ~ er niets gebeurd is* he is behaving (*or:* acts) as if nothing has happened; *het is net ~ het regent* it looks just as though it were raining; **6** whether, if: *ik vraag me af ~ hij komen zal* I wonder whether (*or:* if) he'll come; *ik weet niet, wie ~ het gedaan heeft* I don't know who did it; *wanneer ~ ze komt, ik weet 't niet* when she is coming I don't know; *een dag ~ tien* about ten days, ten days or so

offensief [ɔfɛnsif] *het (offensieven)* offensive: *in het ~ gaan* go on the offensive

offer [ɔfər] *het (~s)* offering, sacrifice, gift, donation: *zware ~s eisen* take a heavy toll

offeren [ɔfərə(n)] *vb* sacrifice, offer (up)

offerfeest [ɔfərfest] *het (~en)* ceremonial offering

offerte [ɔfɛrtə] *de (~s)* offer, tender, quotation

officieel [ɔfiʃel] *adj, adv* **1** official, formal: *iets ~ meedelen* announce sth officially; **2** formal, ceremonial

officier [ɔfisir] *de (~en)* officer

officieus [ɔfiʃøs] *adj, adv* unofficial, semi-official

ofschoon [ɔfsxon] *conj* (al)though; even though

ofte [ɔftə] *conj* ‖ *nooit ~ nimmer* not ever

oftewel [ɔftəwɛl] *conj see* ofwel

ofwel [ɔfwɛl] *conj* **1** either … or; **2** or, that is, i.e.: *de cobra ~ brilslang* the cobra, or hooded snake

ogenblik [oɣə(n)blɪk] *het (~ken)* **1** moment, instant, minute, second: *een ~ rust* a moment's peace; *in een ~* in a moment; *juist op dat ~* just at that very moment (*or:* instant); *(heeft u) een ~je?* just a moment (*or:* minute), would you mind waiting a moment?; **2** moment, time, minute

ogenblikkelijk [oɣə(n)blɪkələk] *adv* immediately, at once, this instant: *ga ~ de dokter halen* go and fetch the doctor immediately (*or:* at once)

o.g.v. *op grond van* on the basis of

ohm [om] *het, de (~s)* ohm

okay [okɛj] *int* OK

oker [okər] *de (~s)* ochre

oksel [ɔksəl] *de (~s)* armpit

oktober [ɔktobər] *de (~s)* October

olie [oli] *de (oliën)* oil

olielamp [olilamp] *de (~en)* oil lamp

oliemaatschappij [olimatsχapɛi] *de (~en)* oil company

oliën [olijə(n)] *vb* oil, lubricate, grease

olieraffinaderij [olirafinadərɛi] *de (~en)* oil refinery

oliesel [olisəl] *het* anointing, extreme unction, last rites: *het laatste (Heilig) ~ toedienen* administer extreme unction (*or:* the last rites)

olieverfschilderij [oliverfsχɪldərɛi] *het, de (~en)* oil (painting), painting in oils

olifant [olifant] *de (~en)* elephant

olijf [olɛif] *de (olijven)* olive

Olijfberg [olɛivbɛrχ] *de* Mount of Olives

olijfboom [olɛivbom] *de (-bomen)* olive (tree)

olm [ɔlm] *de (~en)* elm (tree)

o.l.v. *onder leiding van* conducted by

olympiade [olɪmpijadə] *de (~s)* Olympiad, Olympics, Olympic Games

olympisch [olɪmpis] *adj* Olympic

¹om [ɔm] *prep* **1** (a)round, about: *~ de hoek* (just) round the corner; **2** at: *ik zie je vanavond ~ acht uur* I'll see you tonight at eight (o'clock); *~ een uur of negen* around nine (o'clock); **3** every: *~ beurten* in turn; *~ de twee uur* every two hours; **4** for (reasons of), on account of, because of: *~ deze reden* for this reason; **5** to, in order to, so as to: *niet ~ te eten* not fit to eat, inedible

²om [ɔm] *adj* **1** roundabout, circuitous: *een straatje (blokje) ~* round the block; **2** over, up, finished: *voor het jaar ~ is* before the year is out; *uw tijd is ~* your time is up

³om [ɔm] *adv* **1** (a)round, about, on: *doe je das ~* put your scarf on; *toen zij de hoek ~ kwamen* when they came (a)round the corner; **2** about: *waar gaat het ~?* what's it about?, what's the matter?

oma [oma] *de (~'s)* gran(ny), grandma, grandmother

ombinden [ɔmbɪndə(n)] *vb* tie on (*or:* round)

ombouwen [ɔmbɑuwə(n)] *vb* convert; reconstruct; rebuild, alter

ombrengen [ɔmbrɛŋə(n)] *vb* kill, murder

ombudsman [ɔmbʏtsman] *de (~nen)* ombudsman

ombuigen [ɔmbœyɣə(n)] *vb* **1** restructure, adjust, change (the direction of); **2** bend (round, down, back)

omcirkelen [ɔmsɪrkələ(n)] *vb* (en)circle, ring, (*fig also*) surround: *de politie omcirkelde het gebouw* the police surrounded the building

omdat [ɔmdɑt] *conj* because, as: *juist ~ …* precisely because …; *waarom ga je niet mee? ~ ik er geen zin in heb* why don't you come along? because I don't feel like it

omdoen [ɔmdun] *vb* put on: *zijn veiligheidsgordel ~ fasten* one's seat belt

¹omdraaien [ɔmdrajə(n)] *vb* **1** turn (round), turn over: *zich ~* roll over (on one's side); **2** reverse, swing round

²omdraaien [ɔmdrajə(n)] *vb* **1** turn (round): *de brandweerauto draaide de hoek om* the fire engine turned the corner; **2** turn back (*or:* round)

omduwen [ɔmdywə(n)] *vb* push over, knock over

omega [omeɣa] *de (~'s)* omega

omelet [ɔməlɛt] *de (~ten)* omelette

omgaan [ɔmɣan] *vb* **1** go round, turn, round: *de hoek ~* turn the corner; *een blokje ~* (go for a) walk around the block; **2** go about (with), associate (with), handle, manage: *zo ga je niet met mensen om* that's no way to treat people

omgang [ɔmɣaŋ] *de* contact, association: *hij is gemakkelijk (or: lastig) in de ~* he is easy (*or:* difficult) to get on with

omgangsvormen [ɔmɣaŋsfɔrmə(n)] *de* manners, etiquette

¹omgekeerd [ɔmɣəkert] *adj* **1** turned round, upside down, inside out, back to front: *~ evenredig* in-

versely proportional (to); **2** opposite, reverse
²omgekeerd [ɔmɣəkert] *adv* the other way round:
het is precies ~ it's just the other way round
omgeving [ɔmɣɛvɪŋ] *de* neighbourhood, vicinity,
surrounding area (*or:* districts)
omgooien [ɔmɣojə(n)] *vb* **1** knock over, upset; **2**
change round
omhakken [ɔmhɑkə(n)] *vb* chop down, cut down,
fell
omhalen [ɔmhalə(n)] *het (Belg)* collect, make a collection
omhaling [ɔmhalɪŋ] *de (~en) (Belg)* collection
omhangen [ɔmhɑŋə(n)] *vb* hang over (*or:* round)
omheen [ɔmhen] *adv* round (about), around: *er-*
gens ~ draaien talk round sth, beat about the bush
omheining [ɔmhɛinɪŋ] *de (~en)* fence, enclosure
omhelzen [ɔmhɛlzə(n)] *vb* embrace, hug: *iem ste-*
*vig ~ give s.o. a good hug
omhelzing [ɔmhɛlzɪŋ] *de (~en)* embrace, hug
omhoog [ɔmhoχ] *adv* **1** up (in the air); **2**
up(wards), in(to) the air: *handen ~!* hands up!
omhoogduwen [ɔmhoχdywə(n)] *vb* push
up(wards)
omhooggaan [ɔmhoχan] *vb* go up(wards), rise: *de*
prijzen gaan omhoog prices are going up (*or:* are
rising)
omhooghouden [ɔmhoχhaudə(n)] *vb* hold up
omhulsel [ɔmhʏlsəl] *het (~s)* covering, casing, envelope, shell, husk, hull, pod
omkadering [ɔmkadərɪŋ] *de (~en) (Belg)* staff-pu-
pil ratio
omkantelen [ɔmkɑntələ(n)] *vb* tip over
omkappen [ɔmkɑpə(n)] *vb* chop down, cut down,
fell
omkeerbaar [ɔmkerbar] *adj* reversible
¹omkeren [ɔmkerə(n)] *vb* **1** turn (round), turn, invert: *zich ~* turn (a)round; **2** switch (round),
change (round), twist (round)
²omkeren [ɔmkerə(n)] *vb* turn back, turn round
omkijken [ɔmkɛikə(n)] *vb* **1** look round: *hij keek*
niet op of om he didn't even look up; **2** look after,
worry about, bother about: *niet naar iem ~* not
worry (*or:* bother) about s.o., leave s.o. to his own
devices; *je hebt er geen ~ naar* it needs no looking
after
omkleden [ɔmkledə(n)] *vb* change, put other
clothes on
omkomen [ɔmkomə(n)] *vb* **1** die, be killed: *~ van*
honger starve to death; **2** come round, turn: *hij zag*
haar juist de hoek ~ he saw her just (as she was)
coming round (*or:* turning) the corner
omkopen [ɔmkopə(n)] *vb* bribe, buy (over), corrupt: *zich laten ~* accept a bribe
omkoperij [ɔmkopərɛi] *de* bribery, corruption
omlaag [ɔmlaχ] *adv* down, below: *naar ~*
down(wards)
omlaaggaan [ɔmlaχan] *vb* go down
omleiden [ɔmlɛidə(n)] *vb* divert, re-route, train
omleiding [ɔmlɛidɪŋ] *de (~en) (traf)* (traffic) diver-

sion, detour, relief route, alternative route
omliggend [ɔmlɪɣənt] *adj* surrounding
omlijnd [ɔmlɛint] *adj* defined, definite: *een vast*
(*or: scherp*) *~ plan* a clear-cut (*or:* well-defined)
plan
omlijsting [ɔmlɛistɪŋ] *de (~en)* frame, *(fig)* setting
omloop [ɔmlop] *de (omlopen)* circulation
¹omlopen [ɔmlopə(n)] *vb* walk round, go round: *ik*
loop wel even om I'll go round the back
²omlopen [ɔmlopə(n)] *vb* (run into and) knock over
ommekeer [ɔməker] *de* turn(about), about-turn,
about-face, U-turn, revolution
ommezien [ɔməzin] *het* || *in een ~ was hij terug* (*or:*
klaar) he was back (*or:* finished) in a jiffy
ommezijde [ɔməzɛidə] *de (~n)* reverse (side),
back, other side: *zie ~* see overleaf
omnibus [ɔmnibʏs] *de (~sen)* omnibus
omnivoor [ɔmnivɔr] *de (omnivoren)* omnivore
omploegen [ɔmpluɣə(n)] *vb* **1** plough (up); **2**
plough in (*or:* under)
ompraten [ɔmpratə(n)] *vb* persuade, bring round,
talk round, talk into, talk out of
omrastering [ɔmrɑstərɪŋ] *de (~en)* fencing,
fence(s)
omrekenen [ɔmrekənə(n)] *vb* convert (to), turn
(into)
¹omrijden [ɔmrɛidə(n)] *vb* make a detour, take a
roundabout route, take the long way round
²omrijden [ɔmrɛidə(n)] *vb* knock down, run down
omringen [ɔmrɪŋə(n)] *vb* surround, enclose
omroep [ɔmrup] *de (~en)* broadcasting corporation (*or:* company), (broadcasting) network
omroepen [ɔmrupə(n)] *vb* **1** broadcast, announce
(over the radio, on TV); **2** call (over the P.A., intercom): *iemands naam laten ~* have s.o. paged
omroeper [ɔmrupər] *de (~s)* announcer
omroeren [ɔmrurə(n)] *vb* stir, churn
omruilen [ɔmrœylə(n)] *vb* exchange, trade (in),
change (over, round, places), swap
omschakelen [ɔmsχakələ(n)] *vb* convert, change
(*or:* switch) over (to)
omschakeling [ɔmsχakəlɪŋ] *de (~en)* switch, shift,
changeover
omscholen [ɔmsχolə(n)] *vb* retrain, re-educate:
waarom laat je je niet ~? why don't you get re-
trained?
omscholing [ɔmsχolɪŋ] *de* retraining, re-education
omschoppen [ɔmsχɔpə(n)] *vb* kick over
omschrijven [ɔmsχrɛivə(n)] *vb* **1** describe, determine; **2** define, specify, state: *iemands bevoegdhe-*
den nader ~ define s.o.'s powers
omschrijving [ɔmsχrɛivɪŋ] *de (~en)* **1** description,
paraphrase; **2** definition, specification, characteri-
zation
omsingelen [ɔmsɪŋələ(n)] *vb* surround, besiege
¹omslaan [ɔmslan] *vb* **1** fold over (*or:* back), turn
down, turn back; **2** turn (over)
²omslaan [ɔmslan] *vb* **1** turn; round; **2** change,

break, swing (round), veer (round): *het weer slaat om* the weather is breaking; **3** overturn, topple, keel (over), capsize *(ship)*

omslachtig [ɔmslɑχtəχ] *adj, adv* laborious, time-consuming, lengthy, wordy, long-winded, roundabout

omslag [ɔmslɑχ] *het, de* **1** cuff; **2** cover, dust jacket

omslagartikel [ɔmslɑχɑrtikəl] *het (~en)* cover story

omslagdoek [ɔmslɑχduk] *de (~en)* shawl, wrap

omsmelten [ɔmsmɛltə(n)] *vb* melt down, re-melt

omspitten [ɔmspɪtə(n)] *vb* dig up, break up, turn over

omspoelen [ɔmspulə(n)] *vb* rinse (out), wash out, wash up

omspringen [ɔmsprɪŋə(n)] *vb* deal (with): *slordig met andermans boeken* ~ be careless with s.o. else's books

omstander [ɔmstɑndər] *de (~s)* bystander, onlooker, spectator: *de ~s* bystanders

omstandigheid [ɔmstɑndəχhɛit] *de (-heden)* circumstance, *(pl also)* situation, condition: *in de gegeven omstandigheden* under *(or:* in) the circumstances

omstoten [ɔmstotə(n)] *vb* knock over

omstreden [ɔmstredə(n)] *adj* controversial, debatable, contentious, contested, disputed: *een ~ boek* a controversial book

omstreeks [ɔmstreks] *prep* (round) about, (a)round, towards, in the region *(or:* neighbourhood) of

omstreken [ɔmstrekə(n)] *de* neighbourhood, district, environs, surroundings: *de stad Brugge en* ~ the city of Bruges and (its) environs

omstrengeling [ɔmstrɛŋəlɪŋ] *de* clasp, grasp, embrace

omtrek [ɔmtrɛk] *de (~ken)* **1** *(maths)* perimeter; circumference, periphery; **2** contour(s), outline(s), silhouette, skyline; **3** surroundings, vicinity, environs, surrounding district *(or:* area): *in de wijde ~* for miles around

¹omtrent [ɔmtrɛnt] *prep* **1** about, (a)round; **2** concerning, with reference to, about

²omtrent [ɔmtrɛnt] *adv* about, approximately

omvallen [ɔmvɑlə(n)] *vb* fall over *(or:* down); turn over *(or:* on its side): *~ van de slaap* be dead tired

omvang [ɔmvɑŋ] *de* **1** girth, circumference, bulk(iness); **2** dimensions, size, volume, magnitude, scope: *de volle ~ van de schade* the full extent of the damage

omvangrijk [ɔmvɑŋrɛik] *adj* sizeable, bulky, extensive

omvatten [ɔmvɑtə(n)] *vb* contain, comprise, include, cover

omver [ɔmvɛr] *adv* over, down

omvergooien [ɔmvɛrɣojə(n)] *vb* knock over, bowl over, upset, overturn

omverlopen [ɔmvɛrlopə(n)] *vb* knock, run down *(or:* over), bowl over: *omvergelopen worden* be

knocked off one's feet

omverrijden [ɔmvɛrɛidə(n)] *vb* run, knock down *(or:* over)

omverwerpen [ɔmvɛrwɛrpə(n)] *vb* **1** knock over *(or:* down), throw down; **2** *(fig)* overthrow

omvliegen [ɔmvliɣə(n)] *vb* **1** fly past, fly by, rush by: *een bocht* ~ tear round a corner; **2** fly round, tear round, race round: *de tijd vloog om* the time flew by

omvouwen [ɔmvɑuwə(n)] *vb* fold down *(or:* over), turn down

omwaaien [ɔmwajə(n)] *vb* be *(or:* get) blown down, blow down, be blown off one's feet

omweg [ɔmwɛχ] *de (~en)* detour, roundabout route, roundabout way: *langs een* ~ indirectly

omwenteling [ɔmwɛntəlɪŋ] *de (~en)* **1** rotation, revolution, turn, orbit; **2** *(pol)* revolution, upheaval

¹omwisselen [ɔmwɪsələ(n)] *vb* exchange (for), swap: *dollars* ~ *in euro* change dollars into euros

²omwisselen [ɔmwɪsələ(n)] *vb* change places, swap places, change seats

omzeilen [ɔmzɛilə(n)] *vb* skirt, get round, by-pass

omzendbrief [ɔmzɛndbrif] *de (-brieven) (Belg)* circular (letter)

omzet [ɔmzɛt] *de (~ten)* **1** turnover, volume of trade *(or:* business); **2** returns, sales, business

omzetbelasting [ɔmzɛdbəlɑstɪŋ] *de* sales tax, turnover tax

omzetten [ɔmzɛtə(n)] *vb* **1** turn over, sell: *goederen* ~ sell goods; **2** convert (into), turn (into): *een terdoodveroordeling in levenslang* ~ commute a sentence from death to life imprisonment

omzichtig [ɔmzɪχtəχ] *adj, adv* cautious, circumspect, prudent

omzien [ɔmzin] *vb* look (after)

onaangekondigd [ɔnaŋɣəkɔndəχt] *adj* unannounced: *een ~ bezoek* a surprise visit

onaangenaam [ɔnaŋɣənam] *adj, adv* unpleasant, disagreeable

onaannemelijk [ɔnanemələk] *adj* implausible, incredible, unbelievable

onaantastbaar [ɔnantɑstbar] *adj* unassailable, impregnable

onaantrekkelijk [ɔnantrɛkələk] *adj* unattractive, unprepossessing, unappealing

onaanvaardbaar [ɔnanvardbar] *adj* unacceptable

onaardig [ɔnardəχ] *adj, adv* unpleasant, unfriendly, unkind

onacceptabel [ɔnakseptɑbəl] *adj* unacceptable

onachtzaam [ɔnɑχtsam] *adj, adv* inattentive, careless, negligent

onaf [ɔnɑf] *adj* unfinished, incomplete

onafgebroken [ɔnɑfχəbrokə(n)] *adj, adv* **1** continuous, sustained: *40 jaar* ~ *dienst* 40 years continuous service; **2** unbroken, uninterrupted: *we hebben drie dagen* ~ *regen gehad* the rain hasn't let up for three days

onafhankelijk [ɔnɑfhɑŋkələk] *adj, adv* independent (of)

onafhankelijkheid [ɔnɑfhɑŋkələkhɛit] *de* independence

onafscheidelijk [ɔnɑfsχɛidələk] *adj, adv* inseparable (from)

onafzienbaar [ɔnɑfsimbar] *adj, adv* immense, vast

onbarmhartig [ɔmbɑrmhɑrtəχ] *adj, adv* merciless, unmerciful, ruthless

onbedachtzaamheid [ɔmbədɑχ(t)samhɛit] *de* thoughtlessness, rashness

onbedekt [ɔmbədɛkt] *adj, adv* uncovered, exposed

onbedoeld [ɔmbədult] *adj, adv* unintentional, inadvertent: *iem ~ kwetsen* hurt s.o. unintentionally

onbedorven [ɔmbədɔrvə(n)] *adj* unspoilt, untainted

onbeduidend [ɔmbədœydənt] *adj* insignificant, trivial, inconsequential

onbegaanbaar [ɔmbəɣambar] *adj* impassable

onbegonnen [ɔmbəɣɔnə(n)] *adj* hopeless, impossible

onbegrensd [ɔmbəɣrɛnst] *adj* unlimited, boundless, infinite

onbegrijpelijk [ɔmbəɣrɛipələk] *adj, adv* incomprehensible, unintelligible

onbeheerd [ɔmbəhɛrt] *adj* abandoned, unattended, ownerless: *laat uw bagage niet ~ achter* do not leave your baggage unattended

onbeheerst [ɔmbəhɛrst] *adj, adv* uncontrolled, unrestrained

onbeholpen [ɔmbəhɔlpə(n)] *adj, adv* awkward, clumsy, inept

onbekend [ɔmbəkɛnt] *adj* unknown, out-of-the-way, unfamiliar: *met ~e bestemming vertrekken* leave for an unknown destination

onbekende [ɔmbəkɛndə] *de (~n)* unknown (person), stranger

onbekwaam [ɔmbəkwam] *adj* incompetent, incapable

onbelangrijk [ɔmbəlɑŋrɛik] *adj, adv* unimportant, insignificant, inconsiderable: *iets ~s* sth trivial

onbeleefd [ɔmbəlɛft] *adj, adv* impolite, rude

onbeleefdheid [ɔmbəlɛfthɛit] *de* impoliteness, rudeness, incivility, discourtesy, insult

onbemand [ɔmbəmɑnt] *adj* unmanned

onbenul [ɔmbənʏl] *de (~len)* fool, idiot

onbenullig [ɔmbənʏləχ] *adj, adv* inane, stupid, fatuous

onbepaald [ɔmbəpalt] *adj* **1** indefinite, unlimited; **2** indefinite, indeterminate, undefined

onbeperkt [ɔmbəpɛrkt] *adj, adv* unlimited, unbounded

onbereikbaar [ɔmbərɛigbar] *adj* **1** inaccessible; **2** unattainable, out of (*or:* beyond) reach: *een ~ ideaal* an unattainable ideal

onberekenbaar [ɔmbərɛkəmbar] *adj, adv* unpredictable

onbeschaafd [ɔmbəsχaft] *adj, adv* **1** uncivilized; **2** uneducated, unrefined

onbeschadigd [ɔmbəsχadəχt] *adj* undamaged, intact

onbescheiden [ɔmbəsχɛidə(n)] *adj, adv* **1** immodest, forward; **2** indiscreet, indelicate; **3** presumptuous, bold: *zo ~ zijn om ...* be so bold as to ...

onbeschoft [ɔmbəsχɔft] *adj, adv* rude, ill-mannered, boorish

onbeschoftheid [ɔmbəsχɔfthɛit] *de* rudeness, boorishness

onbeschrijfelijk [ɔmbəsχrɛifələk] *adj, adv* indescribable, beyond description (*or:* words) *(after vb)*; *(depr)* unspeakable: *het is ~* it defies (*or:* beggars) description

onbeslist [ɔmbəslɪst] *adj* undecided, unresolved: *de wedstrijd eindigde ~* the match ended in a draw

onbespeelbaar [ɔmbəspɛlbar] *adj* unplayable, not fit (*or:* unfit) for play

onbespoten [ɔmbəspotə(n)] *adj* unsprayed

onbesproken [ɔmbəsprokə(n)] *adj* ‖ *van ~ gedrag* of irreproachable (*or:* blameless) conduct

onbestuurbaar [ɔmbəstyrbar] *adj* **1** uncontrollable, out of control, unmanageable; **2** ungovernable

onbetaalbaar [ɔmbətalbar] *adj* **1** prohibitive, impossibly dear; **2** priceless, invaluable; **3** priceless, hilarious

onbetaald [ɔmbətalt] *adj* unpaid (for), outstanding, unsettled, undischarged

onbetrouwbaar [ɔmbətrɑubar] *adj* unreliable, *(pers also)* untrustworthy, shady, shifty

onbetwist [ɔmbətwɪst] *adj* undisputed: *de ~e kampioen* the unrivalled champion

onbevlekt [ɔmbəvlɛkt] *adj* immaculate

onbevoegd [ɔmbəvuχt] *adj* unauthorized, unqualified

onbevoegde [ɔmbəvuɣdə] *de (~n)* unauthorized person, unqualified person

onbevooroordeeld [ɔmbəvɔrordelt] *adj, adv* unprejudiced, open-minded

onbevredigend [ɔmbəvredəɣənt] *adj* unsatisfactory

onbewaakt [ɔmbəwakt] *adj* unguarded, unattended

onbeweeglijk [ɔmbəweχlək] *adj, adv* motionless

onbewerkt [ɔmbəwɛrkt] *adj* unprocessed, raw

onbewogen [ɔmbəwoɣə(n)] *adj, adv* **1** immobile; **2** unmoved

onbewolkt [ɔmbəwɔlkt] *adj* cloudless, clear

onbewoonbaar [ɔmbəwombar] *adj* uninhabitable

onbewoond [ɔmbəwont] *adj* uninhabited: *een ~ eiland* a desert island

onbewust [ɔmbəwʏst] *adj, adv* unconscious (of): *iets ~ doen* do sth unconsciously

onbezoldigd [ɔmbəzɔldəχt] *adj* unpaid

onbezorgd [ɔmbəzɔrχt] *adj, adv* carefree, unconcerned: *een ~e oude dag* a carefree old age

onbillijk [ɔmbɪlək] *adj, adv* unfair, unreasonable

onbrandbaar [ɔmbrɑndbar] *adj* incombustible, non-flammable

onbreekbaar [ɔmbregbar] *adj* unbreakable, non-breakable

onbruikbaar [ɔmbrœygbar] *adj* unusable, useless

onbuigzaam [ɔmbœyxsam] *adj* inflexible

oncomfortabel [ɔnkɔmfɔrtabəl] *adj* uncomfortable

oncontroleerbaar [ɔŋkɔntrolerbar] *adj* unverifiable

onconventioneel [ɔŋkɔnvɛn(t)ʃonel] *adj, adv* unconventional

ondankbaar [ɔndɑŋgbar] *adj, adv* ungrateful: *een ondankbare taak* a thankless (*or:* an unrewarding) task

ondankbaarheid [ɔndɑŋgbarhɛit] *de* ingratitude

ondanks [ɔndɑŋks] *prep* in spite of, contrary to: *~ haar inspanningen lukte het (haar) niet* for (*or:* despite) all her efforts, she didn't succeed

ondenkbaar [ɔndɛŋgbar] *adj* inconceivable, unthinkable

¹onder [ɔndər] *prep* **1** under, below, underneath: *hij zat ~ de prut* he was covered with mud; *de tunnel gaat ~ de rivier door* the tunnel goes (*or:* passes) under(neath) the river; *zes graden ~ nul* six degrees below zero; **2** among(st): *er was ruzie ~ de supporters* there was a fight among the supporters; *~ andere* among other things; *~ ons gezegd (en gezwegen)* between you and me (and the doorpost); *~ toezicht van de politie* under police surveillance; *zij leed erg ~ het verlies* she suffered greatly from the loss

²onder [ɔndər] *adv* below, at the bottom: *~ aan de bladzijde* at the foot (*or:* bottom) of the page

onderaan [ɔndəran] *adv* at the bottom, below: *~ op de bladzijde* at the bottom (*or:* foot) of the page

onderaannemer [ɔndəranemər] *de (~s)* subcontractor

onderaards [ɔndərarts] *adj* subterranean

onderaf [ɔndərɑf] *adv* || *hij heeft zich van ~ opgewerkt* he has worked his way up from the bottom of the ladder

onderarm [ɔndərarm] *de (~en)* forearm

onderbeen [ɔndərben] *het (-benen)* (lower) leg, shin, calf

onderbewuste [ɔndərbəwʏstə] *het* subconscious, unconscious

onderbouw [ɔndərbɑu] *de* the lower classes of secondary school

onderbouwen [ɔndərbɑuwə(n)] *vb* build, found, (*fig also*) substantiate

onderbreken [ɔndərbrekə(n)] *vb* **1** interrupt, break; **2** interrupt, cut short, break in (on)

onderbreking [ɔndərbrekɪŋ] *de (~en)* **1** interruption; **2** break

onderbrengen [ɔndərbrɛŋə(n)] *vb* **1** accommodate, lodge, house, put up: *zijn kinderen bij iem ~* lodge one's children with s.o.; **2** class(ify) (with, under, in)

onderbroek [ɔndərbruk] *de (~en)* underpants; panties

onderbuik [ɔndərbœyk] *de (~en)* abdomen

onderdaan [ɔndərdan] *de (-danen)* subject

onderdak [ɔndərdɑk] *het* accommodation, shelter, lodging: *~ vinden* find accommodation

onderdanig [ɔndərdanəx] *adj* submissive, humble

onderdeel [ɔndərdel] *het (-delen)* part, (sub)division, branch: *het volgend ~ van ons programma* the next item on our programme

onderdirecteur [ɔndərdirɛktør] *de (~en)* assistant manager: *~ van een school* deputy headmaster

onderdoen [ɔndərdun] *vb* be inferior (to): *voor niemand ~* yield/be second to none (*or:* no one)

onderdompelen [ɔndərdɔmpələ(n)] *vb* immerse, submerge

onderdoor [ɔndərdor] *adv* under

onderdrukken [ɔndərdrʏkə(n)] *vb* **1** oppress; **2** suppress, repress: *een glimlach ~* suppress a smile

onderdrukking [ɔndərdrʏkɪŋ] *de (~en)* oppression

onderduiken [ɔndərdœykə(n)] *vb* **1** go into hiding, go underground; **2** dive (in)

onderduiker [ɔndərdœykər] *de (~s)* person in hiding

onderen [ɔndərə(n)] *adv* **1** (with *naar*) down(wards), downstairs; **2** (with *van*) below, underneath; **3** (with *van*) from below, from downstairs: *van ~ af beginnen* start from scratch (*or:* the bottom)

¹ondergaan [ɔndərɣan] *vb* undergo, go through

²ondergaan [ɔndərɣan] *vb* go down, set: *de ~de zon* the setting sun

ondergang [ɔndərɣɑŋ] *de* **1** ruin, (down)fall: *dat was zijn ~* that was his undoing; **2** setting

ondergeschikt [ɔndərɣəsxɪkt] *adj* **1** subordinate; **2** minor, secondary

ondergeschikte [ɔndərɣəsxɪktə] *de (~n)* subordinate

ondergetekende [ɔndərɣətekəndə] *de (~n)* **1** undersigned: *ik, ~* I, the undersigned; **2** yours truly

ondergoed [ɔndərɣut] *het* underwear

ondergrond [ɔndərɣrɔnt] *de (~en)* base, basis, foundation: *witte sterren op een blauwe ~* white stars on a blue background

ondergronds [ɔndərɣrɔnts] *adj* underground

ondergrondse [ɔndərɣrɔntsə] *de (~n, ~s)* **1** underground, (*Am*) subway; **2** underground, resistance

onderhand [ɔndərhɑnt] *adv* meanwhile

onderhandelaar [ɔndərhɑndəlar] *de (~s, -handelaren)* negotiator

onderhandelen [ɔndərhɑndələ(n)] *vb* negotiate, bargain

onderhandeling [ɔndərhɑndəlɪŋ] *de (~en)* **1** negotiation, bargaining; **2** negotiation, (*pl also*) talks

onderhands [ɔndərhɑnts] *adj, adv* **1** underhand(ed), backstairs, underhand: *iets ~ regelen* make hole-and-corner arrangements; **2** private; **3** (*sport*) underhand, underarm: *een bal ~ ingooien* throw in a ball underarm

onderhavig [ɔndərhavəx] *adj* present, in question, in hand

onderhevig [ɔndərhevəx] *adj* liable (to), subject

(to)
onderhoud [ɔndərhɑut] *het* maintenance, upkeep
onderhouden [ɔndərhɑudə(n)] *vb* **1** maintain, keep up, service: *het huis was slecht ~ the house was in bad repair;* **2** maintain, support
onderhoudend [ɔndərhɑudənt] *adj, adv* entertaining, amusing
onderhoudsbeurt [ɔndərhɑutsbørt] *de (~en)* overhaul, service
onderhuurder [ɔndərhyrdər] *de (~s)* subtenant
¹onderin [ɔndərɪn] *adv* below, at the bottom
²onderin [ɔndərɪn] *prep* at the bottom of: *het ligt ~ die kast* it's at the bottom of that cupboard
onderjurk [ɔndərjʏrk] *de (~en)* slip
onderkaak [ɔndərkak] *de (-kaken)* lower jaw, mandible
onderkant [ɔndərkɑnt] *de (~en)* underside, bottom
onderkin [ɔndərkɪn] *de (~nen)* double chin
onderkomen [ɔndərkomə(n)] *het (~s)* somewhere to go (*or:* sleep, stay), accommodation, shelter
onderkruiper [ɔndərkrœypər] *de (~s)* **1** scab; **2** squirt, shrimp
onderlangs [ɔndərlɑŋs] *adv* along the bottom (*or:* foot), underneath
onderlichaam [ɔndərlɪχam] *het (-lichamen)* lower part of the body
onderling [ɔndərlɪŋ] *adj, adv* mutual, among ourselves, among them(selves), together: *de partijen konden de kwestie ~ regelen* the parties were able to arrange the matter between (*or:* among) themselves
onderlip [ɔndərlɪp] *de (~pen)* lower lip: *de ~ laten hangen (roughly)* pout
onderlopen [ɔndərlopə(n)] *vb* be flooded
ondermijnen [ɔndərmɛinə(n)] *vb* undermine, subvert
ondernemen [ɔndərnemə(n)] *vb* undertake, take upon oneself
ondernemend [ɔndərnemənt] *adj* enterprising
ondernemer [ɔndərnemər] *de (~s)* entrepreneur, employer, operator, owner
onderneming [ɔndərnemɪŋ] *de (~en)* **1** undertaking, enterprise, venture: *het is een hele ~* it's quite an undertaking; **2** company, business, *(large)* concern: *een ~ drijven* carry on an enterprise
ondernemingsraad [ɔndərnemɪŋsrat] *de (-raden)* works council, employees council
onderofficier [ɔndərɔfisir] *de (~en)* NCO, non-commissioned officer
onderontwikkeld [ɔndərɔntwɪkəlt] *adj* underdeveloped, backward
onderop [ɔndərɔp] *adv* at the bottom, below
onderpand [ɔndərpɑnt] *het (~en)* pledge, security, collateral: *tegen ~ lenen* borrow on security
onderpastoor [ɔndərpastor] *de (~s) (Belg; Roman Catholicism)* curate, priest in charge
onderricht [ɔndərɪχt] *het* instruction, tuition
onderschatten [ɔndərsχɑtə(n)] *vb* underestimate

onderscheid [ɔndərsχɛit] *het* difference, distinction: *een ~ maken tussen … distinguish … from …* (*or:* between) …
¹onderscheiden [ɔndərsχɛidə(n)] *vb* **1** distinguish; discern: *niet te ~ zijn van* be indistinguishable from; **2** decorate: *~ worden met een medaille* be awarded a medal
²onderscheiden [ɔndərsχɛidə(n)] *ref vb* distinguish oneself (for)
onderscheiding [ɔndərsχɛidɪŋ] *de (~en)* decoration, honour: *(Belg) met ~* with distinction
onderscheppen [ɔndərsχɛpə(n)] *vb* intercept
onderschrift [ɔndərsχrɪft] *het (~en)* caption, legend
onderspit [ɔndərspɪt] *het* || *het ~ delven* get the worst (of it)
onderst [ɔndərst] *adj* bottom(most), under(most)
onderstaand [ɔndərstant] *adj* (mentioned) below
ondersteboven [ɔndərstəbovə(n)] *adv* **1** upside down: *je houdt het ~* you have it the wrong way up; **2** upset
ondersteek [ɔndərstek] *de (-steken)* bedpan
onderstel [ɔndərstɛl] *het (~len)* chassis, undercarriage; landing gear
ondersteunen [ɔndərstønə(n)] *vb* support, back (up)
ondersteuning [ɔndərstønɪŋ] *de* **1** support; **2** support, (public) assistance
onderstrepen [ɔndərstrepə(n)] *vb* underline
onderstuk [ɔndərstʏk] *het (~ken)* base, lower part
ondertekenen [ɔndərtekənə(n)] *vb* sign
ondertekening [ɔndərtekənɪŋ] *de (~en)* **1** signing; **2** signature
ondertitelen [ɔndərtitələ(n)] *vb* subtitle
ondertiteling [ɔndərtitəlɪŋ] *de (~en)* subtitles
ondertussen [ɔndərtʏsə(n)] *adv* meanwhile, in the meantime
onderuit [ɔndərœyt] *adv* **1** (out) from under: *je kunt er niet ~ haar ook te vragen* you can't avoid inviting her, too; **2** down; flat, over; **3** sprawled, sprawling
onderuitgaan [ɔndərœytχan] *vb* topple over, be knocked off one's feet, trip, slip
onderuithalen [ɔndərœythalə(n)] *vb* **1** *(sport)* bring down, take down; **2** trip up, floor: *hij werd volledig onderuitgehaald* they wiped the floor with him
ondervangen [ɔndərvɑŋə(n)] *vb* overcome
onderverdelen [ɔndərvərdelə(n)] *vb* (sub)divide, break down
onderverdeling [ɔndərvərdelɪŋ] *de (~en)* subdivision, breakdown
ondervinden [ɔndərvɪndə(n)] *vb* experience: *medeleven ~* meet with sympathy; *moeilijkheden* (or: *concurrentie*) *~* be faced with difficulties (or: competition)
ondervinding [ɔndərvɪndɪŋ] *de (~en)* experience
ondervoed [ɔndərvut] *adj* undernourished
ondervoeding [ɔndərvudɪŋ] *de* undernourish-

ment, malnutrition

ondervraagde [ɔndərvraɣdə] *de (~n)* interviewee; person heard (*or:* questioned)

ondervragen [ɔndərvraɣə(n)] *vb* **1** interrogate, question, examine, hear; **2** interview

ondervraging [ɔndərvraɣɪŋ] *de (~en)* questioning, interrogation, examination, interview

onderwaarderen [ɔndərwardərə(n)] *vb* underestimate

onderweg [ɔndərwɛχ] *adv* **1** on (*or:* along) the way, in transit, en route: *we zijn het ~ verloren* we lost it on the way; **2** on one's (*or:* its, the) way

onderwereld [ɔndərwɛrəlt] *de* underworld

onderwerp [ɔndərwɛrp] *het (~en)* subject (matter)

onderwerpen [ɔndərwɛrpə(n)] *vb* subject

onderwijl [ɔndərwɛil] *adv* meanwhile

onderwijs [ɔndərwɛis] *het* education, teaching: *academisch ~* university education; *bijzonder ~* private education, *(Belg)* special needs education; *buitengewoon ~* special needs education; *hoger ~* higher education; *lager ~* primary education; *middelbaar (voortgezet) ~* secondary education; *openbaar ~* state education; *algemeen secundair ~* general secondary education; *speciaal ~* special needs education; *(Belg) technisch secundair ~* secondary technical education; *(Belg) vernieuwd secundair ~* comprehensive school system; *voortgezet ~* secondary education

onderwijsinspecteur [ɔndərwɛisɪnspɛktør] *de* school inspector

onderwijsinspectie [ɔndərwɛisɪnspɛksi] *de (~s)* schools inspectorate

onderwijsinstelling [ɔndərwɛisɪnstɛlɪŋ] *de (~en)* educational institution

onderwijskunde [ɔndərwɛiskʏndə] *de* didactics, theory of education

onderwijsprofiel [ɔndərwɛisprofil] *het* educational profile

onderwijzen [ɔndərwɛizə(n)] *vb* teach, instruct: *iem iets ~* instruct s.o. in sth, teach s.o. sth

onderwijzer [ɔndərwɛizər] *de (~s)* (school)teacher, schoolmaster, schoolmistress

onderzeeër [ɔndərzejər] *de (~s)* submarine

onderzetter [ɔndərzɛtər] *de (~s)* **1** mat, coaster; **2** mat, stand

onderzijde [ɔndərzɛidə] *de (~n)* underside

onderzoek [ɔndərzuk] *het* **1** investigation, examination, study, research: *bij nader ~* on closer examination (*or:* inspection); **2** investigation; inquiry; **3** *(med)* examination, check-up

onderzoeken [ɔndərzukə(n)] *vb* **1** examine, inspect, investigate, search, test (for): *de dokter onderzocht zijn ogen* the doctor examined his eyes; **2** investigate, examine, inquire into: *mogelijkheden ~ examine (or:* investigate) possibilities; **3** inquire into, investigate, examine: *het bloed ~* carry out a blood test

onderzoeker [ɔndərzukər] *de (~s)* researcher, research worker (*or:* scientist), investigator

ondeugd [ɔndøχt] *de* vice

ondeugend [ɔndøɣənt] *adj, adv* naughty, mischievous

ondiep [ɔndip] *adj* shallow, superficial: *een ~e tuin* a short garden

ondier [ɔndir] *het (~en)* monster, beast

onding [ɔndɪŋ] *het (~en)* rotten thing, useless thing

ondoenlijk [ɔndunlək] *adj* unfeasible, impracticable

ondoordacht [ɔndordɑχt] *adj, adv* inadequately considered, rash

ondoordringbaar [ɔndordrɪŋbar] *adj* impenetrable, impermeable (to): *ondoordringbare duisternis* (*or: wildernis*) impenetrable darkness (*or:* wilderness)

ondoorzichtig [ɔndorzɪχtəχ] *adj* **1** non-transparent, opaque; **2** *(fig)* obscure

ondraaglijk [ɔndraχlək] *adj, adv* unbearable

ondrinkbaar [ɔndrɪŋbar] *adj* undrinkable

onduidelijk [ɔndœydələk] *adj, adv* indistinct, obscure, unclear: *de situatie is ~* the situation is obscure (*or:* unclear); *~ spreken* speak indistinctly

onduidelijkheid [ɔndœydələkhɛit] *de (-heden)* indistinctness, lack of clarity, *(stronger)* obscurity

onecht [ɔnɛχt] *adj* **1** illegitimate; **2** false; **3** fake(d)

oneens [ɔnens] *adj* in disagreement, at odds: *het met iem ~ zijn* over iets disagree with s.o. about sth

oneerbaar [ɔnɛrbar] *adj, adv* indecent, improper

oneerbiedig [ɔnerbidəχ] *adj, adv* disrespectful

oneerlijk [ɔnerlək] *adj, adv* dishonest, unfair

oneerlijkheid [ɔnerləkhɛit] *de (-heden)* dishonesty, unfairness

oneetbaar [ɔnedbar] *adj* inedible, not fit to eat *(after vb):* dit oude brood is ~ this stale bread is not fit to eat

oneffen [ɔnɛfə(n)] *adj* uneven

oneindig [ɔnɛindəχ] *adj, adv* infinite, endless: *~ groot (or: klein)* infinite(ly large), infinitesimal(ly)

oneindigheid [ɔnɛindəχhɛit] *de* infinity

onenigheid [ɔnenəχhɛit] *de (-heden)* discord, disagreement

onervaren [ɔnɛrvarə(n)] *adj, adv* inexperienced

onervarenheid [ɔnɛrvarənhɛit] *de* inexperience, lack of experience (*or:* skill)

oneven [ɔnevə(n)] *adj, adv* odd, uneven

onevenwichtig [ɔnevə(n)wɪχtəχ] *adj* unbalanced, unstable

onfatsoenlijk [ɔnfɑtsunlək] *adj, adv* ill-mannered, bad-mannered, offensive, improper, indecent

onfeilbaar [ɔnfɛilbar] *adj, adv* infallible

onfris [ɔnfrɪs] *adj, adv* **1** unsavoury, stale, musty, stuffy: *er ~ uitzien* not look fresh, *(of pers)* look unsavoury; **2** unsavoury, shady: *een ~se affaire* an unsavoury (*or:* a shady) business

ongev *ongeveer* approx.

ongeacht [ɔŋɣəɑχt] *prep* irrespective of, regardless of

ongeboren [ɔŋɣəborə(n)] *adj* unborn

ongebruikelijk [ɔŋɣəbrœykələk] *adj* unusual

ongebruikt [ɔŋɣəbrœykt] *adj* unused; new

ongecompliceerd [ɔŋɣəkɔmplisert] *adj, adv* uncomplicated

ongedaan [ɔŋɣədan] *adj* undone: *dat kun je niet meer ~ maken* you can't go back on it now

ongedeerd [ɔŋɣədert] *adj* unhurt, uninjured, unharmed

ongedekt [ɔŋɣədɛkt] *adj, adv* uncovered

ongedierte [ɔŋɣədirtə] *het* vermin

ongeduld [ɔŋɣədʏlt] *het* impatience

ongeduldig [ɔŋɣədʏldəχ] *adj, adv* impatient

ongedurig [ɔŋɣədyrəχ] *adj* restless, restive, fidgety

ongedwongen [ɔŋɣədwɔŋə(n)] *adj, adv* relaxed, informal

ongeëvenaard [ɔŋɣəevənart] *adj, adv* unequalled, unmatched

ongefrankeerd [ɔŋɣəfraŋkert] *adj* unstamped

ongegrond [ɔŋɣəɣrɔnt] *adj, adv* unfounded, groundless: *~e klachten* unfounded complaints

ongehinderd [ɔŋɣəhɪndərt] *adj, adv* unhindered: *~ werken* work undisturbed

ongehoorzaam [ɔŋɣəhorzam] *adj* disobedient

ongehoorzaamheid [ɔŋɣəhorzamhɛit] *de (-heden)* disobedience

ongehuwd [ɔŋɣəhywt] *adj* single, unmarried

ongeïnteresseerd [ɔŋɣəɪntərəsert] *adj, adv* uninterested: *~ toekijken* watch with indifference

ongekend [ɔŋɣəkɛnt] *adj, adv* unprecedented

ongekookt [ɔŋɣəkokt] *adj* raw, uncooked

ongeldig [ɔŋɣɛldəχ] *adj* invalid

ongelegen [ɔŋɣəleɣə(n)] *adj, adv* inconvenient, awkward

¹ongelijk [ɔŋɣəlɛik] *adj, adv* **1** unequal: *het is ~ verdeeld in de wereld* there's a lot of injustice in the world; **2** uneven

²ongelijk [ɔŋɣəlɛik] *het* wrong: *ik geef je geen ~* I don't blame you

ongelijkheid [ɔŋɣəlɛikhɛit] *de* **1** inequality; difference; **2** unevenness

ongelijkmatig [ɔŋɣəlɛikmatəχ] *adj, adv* uneven, unequal, irregular

ongelofelijk [ɔŋɣəlofələk] *adj, adv* incredible, unbelievable

ongelood [ɔŋɣəlot] *adj* unleaded

ongeloof [ɔŋɣəlof] *het* disbelief

ongeloofwaardig [ɔŋɣəlofwardəχ] *adj* incredible, implausible

ongeloofwaardigheid *de* incredibility, implausibility

ongelovig [ɔŋɣəlovəχ] *adj, adv* **1** disbelieving, incredulous; **2** unbelieving

ongeluk [ɔŋɣəlʏk] *het (~ken)* accident: *een ~ krijgen* have an accident; *per ~ iets verklappen* inadvertently let sth slip

ongelukkig [ɔŋɣəlʏkəχ] *adj, adv* **1** unhappy: *iem diep ~ maken* make s.o. deeply unhappy; **2** unlucky; **3** unfortunate: *hij is ~ terechtgekomen* he landed awkwardly

ongeluksgetal [ɔŋɣəlʏksχətal] *het (~len)* unlucky number

ongemak [ɔŋɣəmak] *het (~ken)* inconvenience, discomfort

ongemakkelijk [ɔŋɣəmakələk] *adj, adv* uncomfortable

ongemerkt [ɔŋɣəmɛrkt] *adj, adv* unnoticed: *~ (weten te) ontsnappen* (manage to) escape without being noticed

ongemotiveerd [ɔŋɣəmotivert] *adj, adv* unmotivated; without motivation

ongenade [ɔŋɣənadə] *de* **1** disgrace, disfavour: *in ~ vallen* fall into disfavour; **2** displeasure

ongeneeslijk [ɔŋɣəneslək] *adj, adv* incurable: *~ ziek* incurably ill

ongenoegen [ɔŋɣənuɣə(n)] *het (~s)* displeasure, dissatisfaction

ongeoorloofd [ɔŋɣəorloft] *adj* illegal, illicit, improper

ongepast [ɔŋɣəpɑst] *adj, adv* improper

ongerechtigheid [ɔŋɣərɛχtəχhɛit] *de (-heden)* **1** injustice; **2** flaw

ongeregeld [ɔŋɣəreɣəlt] *adj, adv* **1** disorderly, disorganized; **2** irregular: *op ~e tijden* at odd times

ongeregeldheden [ɔŋɣəreɣəlthedə(n)] *de* disturbances, disorders

ongerept [ɔŋɣərɛpt] *adj* untouched, unspoilt

ongerust [ɔŋɣərʏst] *adj* worried, anxious (for): *ik begin ~ te worden* I'm beginning to get worried

ongerustheid [ɔŋɣərʏsthɛit] *de* concern, worry

ongeschikt [ɔŋɣəsχɪkt] *adj, adv* unsuitable

ongeschiktheid [ɔŋɣəsχɪkthɛit] *de* unsuitability; inaptitude

ongeschonden [ɔŋɣəsχɔndə(n)] *adj* intact, undamaged

ongeschoold [ɔŋɣəsχolt] *adj* unskilled, untrained

ongesteld [ɔŋɣəstɛlt] *adj* || *zij is ~* she is having a period

ongestoord [ɔŋɣəstort] *adj, adv* **1** undisturbed; **2** clear: *~e ontvangst* clear reception

ongestraft [ɔŋɣəstrɑft] *adj, adv* unpunished: *iets ~ doen* get away with sth

ongetrouwd [ɔŋɣətrɑut] *adj* unmarried, single: *~e oom* bachelor uncle; *~e tante* maiden aunt

ongetwijfeld [ɔŋɣətwɛifəlt] *adv* no doubt, without a doubt, undoubtedly

ongevaarlijk [ɔŋɣəvarlək] *adj* harmless, safe

ongeval [ɔŋɣəvɑl] *het (~len)* accident

ongevallenverzekering [ɔŋɣəvalə(n)vərzekərɪŋ] *de (~en)* accident insurance

ongeveer [ɔŋɣəver] *adv* about, roughly, around: *dat is het ~* that's about it

ongevoelig [ɔŋɣəvuləχ] *adj, adv* insensitive (to), insensible (to)

ongevoeligheid [ɔŋχəvuləχhɛit] *de* insensitivity

ongevraagd [ɔŋɣəvraχt] *adj* unasked(-for), uninvited

ongewapend [ɔŋɣəwapənt] *adj* unarmed

ongewenst [ɔŋɣəwɛnst] *adj* unwanted, undesired, undesirable

ongewerveld [ɔŋɣəwɛrvəlt] *adj* invertebrate: *~e dieren* invertebrates

ongewild [ɔŋɣəwɪlt] *adj, adv* **1** unintentional, unintended; **2** unwanted

ongewisse [ɔŋɣəwɪsə] *het* (state of) uncertainty: *iem in het ~ laten* keep s.o. guessing (*or:* in the dark)

ongewoon [ɔŋɣəwon] *adj, adv* unusual

ongezellig [ɔŋɣəzɛləɣ] *adj, adv* **1** unsociable; **2** cheerless, comfortless; **3** unenjoyable, dreary, no fun

ongezien [ɔŋɣəzin] *adj, adv* **1** unseen, unnoticed; **2** (sight) unseen: *hij kocht het huis ~* he bought the house (sight) unseen

ongezond [ɔŋɣəzɔnt] *adj, adv* **1** unhealthy; **2** unsound, unhealthy

ongrijpbaar [ɔŋɣrɛibar] *adj* elusive

ongunstig [ɔŋɣʏnstəɣ] *adj, adv* unfavourable: *in het ~ste geval* at (the) worst; *op een ~ moment* at an awkward moment

onguur [ɔŋɣyr] *adj* **1** unsavoury; **2** rough

onhandig [ɔnhɑndəɣ] *adj, adv* clumsy, awkward: *zij is erg ~* she's all fingers and thumbs

onhandigheid [ɔnhɑndəɣhɛit] *de (-heden)* clumsiness, awkwardness

onheil [ɔnhɛil] *het (~en)* calamity, disaster, doom

onheilspellend [ɔnhɛilspɛlənt] *adj, adv* ominous

onherkenbaar [ɔnhɛrkɛmbar] *adj, adv* unrecognizable

onherroepelijk [ɔnhɛrupələk] *adj, adv* irrevocable

onherstelbaar [ɔnhɛrstɛlbar] *adj, adv* irreparable: *~ beschadigd* damaged beyond repair

onhoorbaar [ɔnhorbar] *adj, adv* inaudible

onhoudbaar [ɔnhɑudbar] *adj* **1** unbearable, intolerable; **2** unstoppable

onhygiënisch [ɔnhiɣ(i)jenis] *adj, adv* unhygienic, insanitary

onjuist [ɔnjœyst] *adj, adv* **1** inaccurate, false; **2** incorrect, mistaken

onkosten [ɔŋkɔstə(n)] *de* **1** expense(s), expenditure: *~ vergoed* (all) expenses covered; **2** extra expense(s)

onkostendeclaratie [ɔŋkɔstə(n)deklara(t)si] *de (~s)* expenses claim

onkostenvergoeding [ɔŋkɔstə(n)vərɣudɪŋ] *de (~en)* payment (*or:* reimbursement) of expenses, mileage allowance

onkruid [ɔŋkrœyt] *het* weed(s): *~ vergaat niet* ill weeds grow apace

onkwetsbaar [ɔŋkwɛtsbar] *adj, adv* invulnerable

onlangs [ɔnlɑŋs] *adv* recently, lately: *ik heb hem ~ nog gezien* I saw him just the other day

onleesbaar [ɔnlezbar] *adj, adv* **1** illegible; **2** unreadable

onlogisch [ɔnloɣis] *adj, adv* illogical

onlusten [ɔnlʏstə(n)] *de* riots, disturbances

onmacht [ɔmɑχt] *de* impotence, powerlessness

onmeetbaar [ɔmedbar] *adj, adv* immeasurable

onmens [ɔmɛns] *de (~en)* brute, beast

onmenselijk [ɔmɛnsələk] *adj, adv* inhuman

onmerkbaar [ɔmɛrgbar] *adj, adv* unnoticeable, imperceptible

onmetelijk [ɔmetələk] *adj* immense, immeasurable

onmiddellijk [ɔmɪdələk] *adj, adv* immediate; immediately, directly, at once, straightaway: *ik kom ~ naar Utrecht* I'm coming to Utrecht straightaway (*or:* at once, immediately)

onmisbaar [ɔmɪzbar] *adj, adv* indispensable, essential

onmogelijk [ɔmoɣələk] *adj, adv* impossible: *een ~ verhaal* a preposterous story; *ik kan ~ langer blijven* I can't possibly stay any longer

onnatuurlijk [ɔnatyrlək] *adj, adv* unnatural

onnauwkeurig [ɔnɑukørəχ] *adj, adv* inaccurate

onnauwkeurigheid [ɔnɑukørəχhɛit] *de* inaccuracy

onnodig [ɔnodəχ] *adj, adv* unnecessary, needless, superfluous: *~ te zeggen dat …* needless to say …

onnozel [ɔnozəl] *adj, adv* foolish, silly: *met een ~e grijns* with a sheepish grin

onnozelaar [ɔnozəlar] *de (~s) (Belg; depr)* Simple Simon, birdbrain

onofficieel [ɔnɔfiʃel] *adj, adv* unofficial

onomstotelijk [ɔnɔmstotələk] *adj* indisputable, conclusive

ononderbroken [ɔnɔndərbrokə(n)] *adj, adv* continuous, uninterrupted

onontbeerlijk [ɔnɔndbɛrlək] *adj* indispensable

onopgemerkt [ɔnɔpχəmɛrkt] *adj, adv* unnoticed, unobserved

onophoudelijk [ɔnɔphɑudələk] *adj, adv* continuous, ceaseless, incessant

onoplettend [ɔnɔplɛtənt] *adj, adv* inattentive, inadvertent

onoplettendheid [ɔnɔplɛtənthɛit] *de* inattention, inadvertence

onoplosbaar [ɔnɔplɔzbar] *adj* **1** insoluble, indissoluble; **2** unsolvable

onopvallend [ɔnɔpfɑlənt] *adj, adv* inconspicuous, nondescript, unobtrusive, discreet: *~ te werk gaan* act discreetly

onopzettelijk [ɔnɔpsɛtələk] *adj, adv* unintentional, inadvertent

onoverkomelijk [ɔnovərkomələk] *adj* insurmountable

onoverwinnelijk [ɔnovərwɪnələk] *adj* invincible

onoverzichtelijk [ɔnovərzɪχtələk] *adj, adv* cluttered; poorly organized (*or:* arranged)

onpaar [ɔmpar] *adj* unpaired, odd

onpartijdig [ɔmpartɛidəχ] *adj, adv* impartial, unbiased

onpartijdigheid [ɔmpartɛidəχhɛit] *de* impartiality

onpasselijk [ɔmpɑsələk] *adj* sick

onpersoonlijk [ɔmpərsonlək] *adj, adv* impersonal

onplezierig [ɔmpləzirəχ] *adj, adv* unpleasant, nasty

onprettig [ɔmprɛtəχ] *adj, adv* unpleasant, disagreeable, nasty

onraad [ɔnrat] *het* trouble, danger: ~ *bespeuren* smell a rat

onrealistisch [ɔnrejalıstis] *adj* unrealistic

onrecht [ɔnrɛχt] *het* injustice, wrong: *iem ~ (aan)doen* do s.o. wrong

onrechtmatig [ɔnrɛχtmatəχ] *adj, adv* unlawful, illegal; wrongful, unjust

onrechtvaardig [ɔnrɛχtfardəχ] *adj, adv* unjust

onrechtvaardigheid [ɔnrɛχtfardəχhɛit] *de (-heden)* injustice, wrong

onredelijk [ɔnredələk] *adj, adv* unreasonable, unfounded

onregelmatig [ɔnreɣəlmatəχ] *adj, adv* irregular

onrijp [ɔnrɛip] *adj* 1 unripe, unseasoned; 2 immature

onroerend [ɔnrurənt] *adj* immovable: *makelaar in ~ goed* estate agent

onroerendgoedbelasting [ɔnrurəntχudbəlastıŋ] *de (~en)* property tax

onrust [ɔnrʏst] *de* restlessness, agitation: ~ *zaaien* stir up trouble

onrustbarend [ɔnrʏstbarənt] *adj, adv* alarming

onrustig [ɔnrʏstəχ] *adj, adv* restless, turbulent

onruststoker [ɔnrʏstokər] *de (~s)* troublemaker, agitator

¹ons [ɔns] *het (~en, onzen)* quarter of a pound, four ounces: *een ~ ham* a quarter of ham

²ons [ɔns] *pers pron* us: *het is ~ een genoegen* (it's) our pleasure; *onder ~ gezegd* (just) between ourselves; *dat is van ~* that's ours, that belongs to us

³ons [ɔns] *pos pron* our: ~ *huis* our house; *uw boeken en die van ~* your books and ours

onsamenhangend [ɔnsamə(n)hɑŋənt] *adj, adv* incoherent, disconnected

onschadelijk [ɔnsχadələk] *adj, adv* harmless, innocent, non-noxious: *een bom ~ maken* defuse a bomb

onschendbaar [ɔnsχɛndbar] *adj* immune

onschendbaarheid [ɔnsχɛndbarhɛit] *de* immunity

onscherp [ɔnsχɛrp] *adj* out of focus, blurred

onschuld [ɔnsχʏlt] *de* innocence

onschuldig [ɔnsχʏldəχ] *adj* 1 innocent, guiltless; 2 innocent, harmless

onsmakelijk [ɔnsmakələk] *adj, adv* 1 distasteful, unpalatable; 2 distasteful, disagreeable, unsavoury

onsportief [ɔnspɔrtif] *adj, adv* unsporting, unsportsmanlike: *hij heeft zich ~ gedragen* he behaved unsportingly

onstabiel [ɔnstabil] *adj, adv* unstable

onsterfelijk [ɔnstɛrfələk] *adj, adv* immortal

onsterfelijkheid [ɔnstɛrfələkhɛit] *de* immortality

onsympathiek [ɔnsımpatik] *adj, adv* uncongenial: *een ~e houding* an unengaging manner

onzelf [ɔnsɛlf] *ref pron* ourselves

ontaarden [ɔntardə(n)] *vb* degenerate (into), deteriorate

ontactisch [ɔntɑktis] *adj* impolitic

ontbering [ɔndberıŋ] *de (~en)* hardship, (de)privation

ontbieden [ɔndbidə(n)] *vb* summon, send for

ontbijt [ɔndbɛit] *het* breakfast: *een kamer met ~* bed and breakfast, B & B

ontbijten [ɔndbɛitə(n)] *vb* (have) breakfast

ontbijtkoek [ɔndbɛitkuk] *de (~en) (roughly)* gingercake, gingerbread

ontbijtspek [ɔndbɛitspɛk] *het (roughly)* bacon

ontbinden [ɔndbındə(n)] *vb* dissolve, disband, annul

ontbinding [ɔndbındıŋ] *de (~en)* 1 annulment; 2 decomposition, decay, corruption *(also fig): tot ~ overgaan* decompose, decay

ontbloot [ɔndblot] *adj* bare, naked

ontbrandbaar [ɔndbrɑndbar] *adj* ignitable, combustible

ontbreken [ɔndbrekə(n)] *vb* 1 be lacking (in): *waar het aan ontbreekt is …* what's lacking is …; *er ontbreekt nog veel aan* there's still much to be desired; 2 be absent, be missing

ontcijferen [ɔntsɛifərə(n)] *vb* decipher

ontdaan [ɔndan] *adj* upset, disconcerted

ontdekken [ɔndɛkə(n)] *vb* discover: *iets bij toeval ~* hit upon (or: stumble on) sth

ontdekker [ɔndɛkər] *de (~s)* discoverer

ontdekking [ɔndɛkıŋ] *de (~en)* discovery, find: *een ~ doen* make a discovery

ontdekkingsreiziger [ɔndɛkıŋsrɛizəɣər] *de (~s)* explorer, discoverer

ontdoen [ɔndun] *ref vb* (with *van*) dispose of, get rid of, remove

ontdooien [ɔndojə(n)] *vb* thaw, defrost, melt

ontduiken [ɔndœykə(n)] *vb* evade, elude, dodge

ontegenzeglijk [ɔnteɣənzɛχlək] *adj* undeniable, incontestable

ontelbaar [ɔntɛlbar] *adj, adv* countless, innumerable

onterecht [ɔntərɛχt] *adj, adv* undeserved, unjust

ontevreden [ɔntəvredə(n)] *adj, adv* dissatisfied (with): *je mag niet ~ zijn* (you) mustn't grumble

ontevredenheid [ɔntəvredənhɛit] *de* dissatisfaction (about, with)

ontfermen [ɔntfɛrmə(n)] *ref vb* (with *over*) take pity on

ontfutselen [ɔntfʏtsələ(n)] *vb* filch, pilfer

ontgaan [ɔntχan] *vb* 1 escape, pass (by): *de overwinning kon ons niet meer ~* victory was ours; 2 escape, miss, fail to notice: *het kon niemand ~ dat* no one could fail to notice that; 3 escape, elude: *de logica daarvan ontgaat mij* the logic of it escapes me

ontginnen [ɔntχınə(n)] *vb* reclaim, cultivate

ontginning [ɔntχınıŋ] *de* exploitation, development; reclamation

ontgroeien [ɔntχrujə(n)] *vb* outgrow: *(fig) de kinderschoenen* (or: *schoolbanken*) *ontgroeid zijn* have left one's childhood (or: schooldays) behind

ontgroening [ɔntχrunɪŋ] *de* ragging, *(Am)* hazing

onthaal [ɔnthal] *het* **1** welcome, reception; **2** *(Belg)* reception

onthaalmoeder [ɔnthalmudər] *de (~s) (Belg)* babysitter, child minder

onthaalouder [ɔnthalɑudər] *de (Belg)* temporary host to (foreign) children

onthaasten [ɔnthastə(n)] *vb* slow down

ontharen [ɔntharə(n)] *vb* depilate

ontheffen [ɔnthɛfə(n)] *vb* exempt, release

ontheffing [ɔnthɛfɪŋ] *de (~en)* exemption; release: *~ hebben van* be released from

onthoofden [ɔnthovdə(n)] *vb* behead, decapitate

onthoofding [ɔnthovdɪŋ] *de (~en)* decapitation, beheading

¹**onthouden** [ɔnthɑudə(n)] *vb* remember: *goed gezichten kunnen ~* have a good memory for faces; *ik zal het je helpen ~* I'll remind you of it

²**onthouden** [ɔnthɑudə(n)] *ref vb* abstain (from), refrain (from)

onthouding [ɔnthɑudɪŋ] *de* **1** abstention; **2** continence, abstinence

onthullen [ɔnthʏlə(n)] *vb* **1** unveil; **2** reveal, disclose, divulge

onthulling [ɔnthʏlɪŋ] *de (~en)* **1** unveiling; **2** revelation, disclosure: *opzienbarende ~en* startling disclosures

onthutst [ɔnthʏtst] *adj, adv* disconcerted, dismayed

¹**ontkennen** [ɔntkɛnə(n)] *vb* deny, negate: *hij ontkende iets met de zaak te maken te hebben* he denied any involvement in the matter

²**ontkennen** [ɔntkɛnə(n)] *vb* plead not guilty

ontkennend [ɔntkɛnənt] *adj, adv* negative

ontkenning [ɔntkɛnɪŋ] *de (~en)* denial, negation

ontketenen [ɔntketənə(n)] *vb* let loose; unchain; unleash

ontkiemen [ɔntkimə(n)] *vb* germinate, *(fig also)* bud

ontkleden [ɔntkledə(n)] *vb* undress: *zich ~* undress

ontknoping [ɔntknopɪŋ] *de (~en)* ending, dénouement: *zijn ~ naderen* reach a climax

ontkomen [ɔntkomə(n)] *vb* **1** escape, get away; **2** evade, get round

ontlading [ɔntladɪŋ] *de (~en)* **1** release; **2** discharge

ontlasting [ɔntlastɪŋ] *de* stools, (human) excrement, faeces

ontleden [ɔntledə(n)] *vb* **1** dissect, anatomize; **2** analyse: *een zin ~* analyse (or: parse) a sentence

ontleding [ɔntledɪŋ] *de (~en)* **1** dissection; **2** analysis

ontlenen [ɔntlenə(n)] *vb* **1** (with *aan*) derive (from), borrow (from), take; **2** (with *aan*) take (from), derive (from)

ontlopen [ɔntlopə(n)] *vb* differ from: *die twee ~ elkaar niet veel* they don't differ greatly

ontmaagden [ɔntmaɣdə(n)] *vb* deflower

ontmantelen [ɔntmɑntələ(n)] *vb* dismantle, strip

ontmaskeren [ɔntmɑskərə(n)] *vb* unmask, expose

ontmoedigen [ɔntmudəɣə(n)] *vb* discourage, demoralize, deter: *we zullen ons niet laten ~ door …* we won't let … get us down

ontmoeten [ɔntmutə(n)] *vb* **1** meet, run into, bump into; **2** meet, see

ontmoeting [ɔntmutɪŋ] *de (~en)* meeting, encounter: *een toevallige ~* a chance meeting (or: encounter)

ontmoetingsplaats [ɔntmutɪŋsplats] *de (~en)* meeting place

ontmoetingspunt [ɔntmutɪŋspʏnt] *het (~en)* meeting point

ontoegankelijk [ɔntuɣɑŋkələk] *adj* inaccessible, impervious (to)

ontoelaatbaar [ɔntuladbar] *adj* inadmissible

ontoerekeningsvatbaar [ɔnturekənɪŋsfɑdbar] *adj* not responsible, *(law)* of unsound mind

ontploffen [ɔntplɔfə(n)] *vb* explode, blow up: *ik dacht dat hij zou ~* I thought he'd explode

ontploffing [ɔntplɔfɪŋ] *de (~en)* explosion

ontrafelen [ɔntrafələ(n)] *vb* unravel, disentangle

ontregeld [ɔntreɣəlt] *adj* unsettled, disordered

ontregelen [ɔntreɣələ(n)] *vb* disorder, disorganize, dislocate

ontroeren [ɔntrurə(n)] *vb* move, touch

ontroerend [ɔntrurənt] *adj* moving, touching, tear-jerking

ontroering [ɔntrurɪŋ] *de (~en)* emotion

ontroostbaar [ɔntrostbar] *adj* inconsolable, broken-hearted

¹**ontrouw** [ɔntrɑu] *adj* **1** disloyal (to), untrue (to); **2** unfaithful

²**ontrouw** [ɔntrɑu] *de* **1** disloyalty, unfaithfulness; **2** unfaithfulness, infidelity

ontruimen [ɔntrœymə(n)] *vb* **1** clear, vacate; **2** clear, evacuate: *de politie moest het pand ~* the police had to clear the building

ontruiming [ɔntrœymɪŋ] *de (~en)* **1** evacuation; **2** eviction

ontschieten [ɔntsχitə(n)] *vb* slip, elude

ontslaan [ɔntslan] *vb* **1** dismiss, discharge: *ontslagen worden* be dismissed; *iem op staande voet ~* dismiss s.o. on the spot; **2** relieve, discharge

ontslag [ɔntslɑχ] *het (~en)* **1** dismissal, discharge: *eervol ~* honourable discharge; **2** resignation, notice; **3** exemption

ontslagbrief [ɔntslɑɣbrif] *de (-brieven)* notice; (letter of) resignation

ontsmetten [ɔntsmɛtə(n)] *vb* disinfect

ontsmetting [ɔntsmɛtɪŋ] *de* disinfection, decontamination

ontsmettingsmiddel [ɔntsmɛtɪŋsmɪdəl] *het (~en)* disinfectant, antiseptic

ontsnappen [ɔntsnɑpə(n)] *vb* **1** escape (from): *aan de dood ~* escape death; **2** escape, get away, get out: *weten te ~* make one's getaway; **3** escape, elude: *aan de aandacht ~* escape notice; **4** pull (or: break) away (from)

ontsnapping [ɔntsnɑpɪŋ] *de (~en)* escape

¹**ontspannen** [ɔntspɑnə(n)] *adj* relaxed, easy: *zich ~ gedragen* have an easy manner

²**ontspannen** [ɔntspɑnə(n)] *vb* 1 slacken, unbend; 2 relax: *zich ~ relax*

ontspanning [ɔntspɑnɪŋ] *de (~en)* relaxation, recreation

ontsporen [ɔntspɔrə(n)] *vb* 1 be derailed; 2 *(fig)* go *(or:* run) off the rails

ontsporing [ɔntspɔrɪŋ] *de (~en)* derailment; *(fig)* lapse

¹**ontstaan** [ɔntstan] *vb* 1 come into being, arise: *door haar vertrek ontstaat een vacature* her departure has created a vacancy; 2 originate, start

²**ontstaan** [ɔntstan] *het* origin, creation, development, coming into existence

ontsteken [ɔntstekə(n)] *vb* be(come) inflamed

ontsteking [ɔntstekɪŋ] *de (~en)* 1 inflammation; 2 ignition

ontstemd [ɔntstɛmt] *adj* untuned, out of tune

ontstoken [ɔntstokə(n)] *adj* inflamed

ontstopper [ɔntstɔpər] *de (~s)* plunger

onttrekken [ɔntrɛkə(n)] *ref vb* withdraw (from), back out of

ontucht [ɔntʏχt] *de* illicit sexual acts, sexual abuse

ontuchtig [ɔntʏχtəχ] *adj, adv* lewd, lecherous

ontvangen [ɔntfɑŋə(n)] *vb* 1 receive, collect, draw: *in dank ~* received with thanks; 2 receive, welcome: *iem hartelijk* (or: *met open armen) ~* receive s.o. with open arms, make s.o. very welcome

ontvanger [ɔntfɑŋər] *de (~s)* 1 receiver, recipient; 2 receiver

ontvangst [ɔntfɑŋst] *de (~en)* 1 receipt: *betalen na ~ van de goederen* pay on receipt of goods; *na ~ van uw brief* on receipt of your letter; *tekenen voor ~* sign for receipt; 2 collection; 3 reception: *een hartelijke* (or: *gunstige) ~* a warm (or: favourable) reception

ontvangstbewijs [ɔntfɑŋstbəwɛis] *het (-bewijzen)* receipt

ontvlambaar [ɔntflɑmbar] *adj* inflammable

ontvluchten [ɔntflʏχtə(n)] *vb* 1 escape (from), run away from; 2 flee

ontvoerder [ɔntfurdər] *de (~s)* kidnapper

ontvoeren [ɔntfurə(n)] *vb* kidnap

ontvoering [ɔntfurɪŋ] *de (~en)* kidnapping

ontvreemden [ɔntfremdə(n)] *vb* steal

ontwaken [ɔntwakə(n)] *vb* awake, (a)rouse

ontwapenen [ɔntwapənə(n)] *vb* disarm: *een ~de glimlach* a disarming smile

ontwennen [ɔntwɛnə(n)] *vb* get out of the habit

ontwenningskuur [ɔntwɛnɪŋskyr] *de (-kuren)* detoxification

ontwerp [ɔntwɛrp] *het (~en)* draft; design

ontwerpen [ɔntwɛrpə(n)] *vb* 1 design, plan; 2 devise, plan, formulate; draft, draw up

ontwerper [ɔntwɛrpər] *de (~s)* designer, planner

ontwijken [ɔntwɛikə(n)] *vb* avoid

ontwijkend [ɔntwɛikənt] *adj, adv* evasive

ontwikkeld [ɔntwɪkəlt] *adj* 1 developed, mature; 2 educated, informed, cultivated, cultured

¹**ontwikkelen** [ɔntwɪkələ(n)] *vb* 1 develop; 2 educate: *zich ~ educate oneself; foto's ~ en afdrukken* process a film

²**ontwikkelen** [ɔntwɪkələ(n)] *ref vb* develop (into): *we zullen zien hoe de zaken zich ~* we'll see how things develop

ontwikkeling [ɔntwɪkəlɪŋ] *de (~en)* 1 development, growth: *tot ~ komen* develop; 2 education: *algemene ~* general knowledge

ontwikkelingshulp [ɔntwɪkəlɪŋshʏlp] *de* foreign aid, development assistance

ontwikkelingsland [ɔntwɪkəlɪŋslɑnt] *het (~en)* developing country

ontwrichten [ɔntwrɪχtə(n)] *vb* 1 disrupt; 2 dislocate

ontzag [ɔntsɑχ] *het* awe, respect

ontzenuwen [ɔntsenywə(n)] *vb* refute, disprove

ontzet [ɔntsɛt] *adj* relief

¹**ontzettend** [ɔntsɛtənt] *adj* 1 appalling; 2 terrific, immense, tremendous

²**ontzettend** [ɔntsɛtənt] *adv* awfully, tremendously: *het spijt me ~* I'm terribly (or: awfully) sorry

ontzien [ɔntsin] *vb* spare: *iem ~* spare s.o.

onuitputtelijk [ɔnœytpʏtələk] *adj, adv* inexhaustible

onuitstaanbaar [ɔnœytstambar] *adj, adv* unbearable, insufferable: *die kerel vind ik ~* I can't stand that guy

onvast [ɔnvɑst] *adj, adv* unsteady, unstable

onveilig [ɔnvɛiləχ] *adj, adv* unsafe, dangerous

onveiligheid [ɔnvɛiləχhɛit] *de* danger(ousness)

onveranderd [ɔnvərɑndərt] *adj* unchanged, unaltered

onverantwoord [ɔnvərɑntwort] *adj, adv* irresponsible

onverantwoordelijk [ɔnvərɑntwordələk] *adj, adv* irresponsible, unjustifiable

onverbeterlijk [ɔnvərbetərlək] *adj* incorrigible

onverbiddelijk [ɔnvərbɪdələk] *adj, adv* unrelenting, implacable

onverdiend [ɔnvərdint] *adj* undeserved

onverdraagzaam [ɔnvərdraχsam] *adj* intolerant (towards)

onverdraagzaamheid [ɔnvərdraχsamhɛit] *de* intolerance

onvergeeflijk [ɔnvərɣeflək] *adj, adv* unforgivable, inexcusable

onvergelijkbaar [ɔnvərɣəlɛigbar] *adj, adv* incomparable

onvergetelijk [ɔnvərɣetələk] *adj, adv* unforgettable

onverhard [ɔnvərhɑrt] *adj* unpaved

onverklaarbaar [ɔnvərklarbar] *adj, adv* inexplicable, unaccountable: *op onverklaarbare wijze* unaccountably

onverlicht [ɔnvərlɪχt] *adj* unlit, unlighted

onvermijdelijk [ɔnvərmɛidələk] *adj, adv* inevitable: *~e fouten* unavoidable mistakes

onvermoeibaar [ɔnvərmujbar] *adj* indefatigable, tireless

onvermogen [ɔnvərmoɣə(n)] *het* impotence, powerlessness, inability

¹**onverschillig** [ɔnvərsχɪləχ] *adj* indifferent (to): *hij zat daar met een ~ gezicht* he sat there looking completely indifferent (*or:* unconcerned)

²**onverschillig** [ɔnvərsχɪləχ] *adv* indifferently: *iem ~ behandelen* treat s.o. with indifference

onverschilligheid [ɔnvərsχɪləχhɛit] *de* indifference

onverslijtbaar [ɔnvərslɛidbar] *adj* indestructible, durable *(goods)*

onverstaanbaar [ɔnvərstambar] *adj, adv* unintelligible; inarticulate; inaudible

onverstandig [ɔnvərstɑndəχ] *adj, adv* foolish, unwise

onverstoorbaar [ɔnvərstorbar] *adj, adv* imperturbable, unflappable

onvervalst [ɔnvərvɑlst] *adj* pure, unadulterated, broad

onvervangbaar [ɔnvərvɑŋbar] *adj* irreplaceable

onverwacht [ɔnvərwɑχt] *adj, adv* unexpected, surprise: *dat soort dingen gebeurt altijd ~* that sort of thing always happens when you least expect it

onverwachts [ɔnvərwɑχts] *adj, adv* unexpected, sudden, surprise

onverwarmd [ɔnvərwɑrmt] *adj* unheated

onverwoestbaar [ɔnvərwustbar] *adj* indestructible; tough, durable

onverzoenlijk [ɔnvərzunlək] *adj, adv* irreconcilable

onverzorgd [ɔnvərzɔrχt] *adj* careless, untidy; uncared-for, untended: *zij ziet er ~ uit* she neglects her appearance

onvindbaar [ɔnvɪndbar] *adj* untraceable, not to be found

¹**onvoldoende** [ɔnvɔldundə] *de (~s)* unsatisfactory mark (*or Am:* grade), fail: *een ~ halen* fail (an exam, a test); *hij had twee ~s* he had two unsatisfactory marks

²**onvoldoende** [ɔnvɔldundə] *adj, adv* insufficient, unsatisfactory: *een ~ hoeveelheid* an insufficient amount

onvolledig [ɔnvɔledəχ] *adj, adv* incomplete

onvolmaaktheid [ɔnvɔlmaktheit] *de (-heden)* imperfection

onvolwassen [ɔnvɔlwɑsə(n)] *adj* immature: *~ reageren* react in an adolescent way

onvolwassenheid [ɔnvɔlwɑsənhɛit] *de* immaturity

¹**onvoorbereid** [ɔnvɔrbərɛit] *adj* unprepared

²**onvoorbereid** [ɔnvɔrbərɛit] *adv* unaware(s), by surprise

onvoordelig [ɔnvɔrdeləχ] *adj, adv* unprofitable, uneconomic(al): *~ uit zijn* pay too high a price

onvoorspelbaar [ɔnvɔrspɛlbar] *adj, adv* unpredictable

onvoorstelbaar [ɔnvɔrstɛlbar] *adj* inconceivable, unimaginable, unthinkable: *het is ~!* it's unbelievable!, it's incredible!

onvoorwaardelijk [ɔnvɔrwardələk] *adj, adv* unconditional, unquestioning: *~e straf* non-suspended sentence

onvoorzichtig [ɔnvɔrzɪχtəχ] *adj, adv* careless, *(stronger)* reckless: *je hebt zeer ~ gehandeld* you have acted most imprudently

onvoorzichtigheid [ɔnvɔrzɪχtəχhɛit] *de (-heden)* carelessness, *(stronger)* recklessness, lack of caution

¹**onvoorzien** [ɔnvɔrzin] *adj* unforeseen: *~e uitgaven* incidental expenditure(s)

²**onvoorzien** [ɔnvɔrzin] *adv* accidentally

onvrede [ɔnvredə] *de* dissatisfaction (with)

onvriendelijk [ɔnvrindələk] *adj, adv* unfriendly, hostile

onvrij [ɔnvrɛi] *adj* unfree

onvrijwillig [ɔnvrɛiwɪləχ] *adj, adv* involuntary

onvruchtbaar [ɔnvrʏχtbar] *adj* infertile, barren

onvruchtbaarheid [ɔnvrʏχ(t)barhɛit] *de* infertility

onwaar [ɔnwar] *adj* untrue, false

onwaarschijnlijk [ɔnwarsχɛinlək] *adj* unlikely, improbable: *het is hoogst ~ dat* it is most (*or:* highly) unlikely that

onwaarschijnlijkheid [ɔnwarsχɛinləkhɛit] *de (-heden)* improbability, unlikelihood

onweer [ɔnwer] *het (onweren)* thunderstorm: *we krijgen ~* we're going to have a thunderstorm

onweersbui [ɔnwerzbœy] *de (~en)* thunder(y) shower

onweerstaanbaar [ɔnwerstambar] *adj, adv* irresistible, compelling

onwel [ɔnwɛl] *adj* unwell, ill, indisposed

onwelkom [ɔnwɛlkɔm] *adj* unwelcome

onwennig [ɔnwɛnəχ] *adj* unaccustomed, ill at ease: *zij staat er nog wat ~ tegenover* she has not quite got used to the idea

onweren [ɔnwerə(n)] *vb* thunder: *het heeft geonweerd* there has been a thunderstorm

onwerkelijk [ɔnwɛrkələk] *adj* unreal

onwetendheid [ɔnwetəntheit] *de* ignorance: *uit (or: door) ~* out of (*or:* through) ignorance

onwetenschappelijk [ɔnwetənsχɑpələk] *adj, adv* unscientific, unscholarly

onwettig [ɔnwɛtəχ] *adj, adv* **1** illegal; illicit; unlawful; **2** illegitimate

onwijs [ɔnwɛis] *adv* awfully, fabulously, terrifically, ever so: *~ gaaf* brill; *~ hard werken* work like mad (*or:* crazy)

onwil [ɔnwɪl] *de* unwillingness

onwillekeurig [ɔnwɪləkører øχ] *adj* **1** involuntary; **2** inadvertently, unconsciously || *~ lachte hij* he laughed in spite of himself

onzakelijk [ɔnzakələk] *adj, adv* unbusinesslike

onzedelijk [ɔnzedələk] *adj, adv* indecent, obscene

onzedelijkheid [ɔnzedələkhɛit] *de (-heden)* immorality, indecency, immodesty

onzedig [ɔnzedəχ] *adj, adv* immodest

onzeker [ɔnzekər] *adj, adv* **1** insecure, unsure; **2** uncertain, unsure, precarious: *het aantal gewonden is nog ~* the number of injured is not yet known; *hij nam het zekere voor het ~e* he decided to play safe

onzekerheid [ɔnzekərhɛit] *de (-heden)* uncertainty, doubt: *in ~ laten* (or: *verkeren)* keep (or: be) in a state of suspense

Onze-Lieve-Heer [ɔnzəlivəhɛr] *de* (the good) God

onzelieveheersbeestje [ɔnzəlivəhɛrzbeʃə] *het (~s)* ladybird

Onze-Lieve-Vrouw [ɔnzəlivəvrɑu] *de* Our Lady

onzevader [ɔnzəvadər] *het (~s)* Lord's Prayer: *het ~ bidden* say the Lord's Prayer

onzichtbaar [ɔnzɪχtbar] *adj* invisible

onzijdig [ɔnzɛidəχ] *adj* neutral

onzin [ɔnzɪn] *de* nonsense: *klinkklare ~* utter nonsense

onzindelijk [ɔnzɪndələk] *adj, adv* not toilet-trained

onzinnig [ɔnzɪnəχ] *adj, adv* absurd, senseless, nonsensical

onzorgvuldig [ɔnzɔrχfʏldəχ] *adj, adv* careless, negligent

¹onzuiver [ɔnzœyvər] *adj* **1** impure; **2** gross; **3** inaccurate, imperfect

²onzuiver [ɔnzœyvər] *adv* out of tune

oog [oχ] *het (ogen)* **1** eye: *een blauw ~* a black eye; *dan kun je het met je eigen ogen zien* then you can see for yourself; *goede ogen hebben* have good eyesight; *geen ~ dichtdoen* not sleep a wink; *zijn ogen geloven* (or: *vertrouwen)* believe (or: trust) one's eyes; *hij had alleen ~ voor haar* he only had eyes for her; *aan één ~ blind* blind in one eye; *iem iets onder vier ogen zeggen* say sth to s.o. in private; *goed uit zijn ogen kijken* keep one's eyes open; *kun je niet uit je ogen kijken?* can't you look where you're going?; *zijn ogen de kost geven* take it all in; *~ om oog, tand om tand* an eye for an eye, a tooth for a tooth; **2** look, glance, eye: *zij kon haar ogen niet van hem afhouden* she couldn't take (or: keep) her eyes off him; *(zo) op het ~* on the face of it; *iem op het ~ hebben* have s.o. in mind, have one's eye on s.o.; *wat mij voor ogen staat* what I have in mind; **3** view, eye: *zo ver het ~ reikt* as far as the eye can see; *in het ~ lopend* conspicuous, noticeable; *iets uit het ~ verliezen* lose sight of sth; *uit het ~, uit het hart* out of sight, out of mind; *in mijn ogen* in my opinion (or: view); *met het ~ op* with a view to, in view of

oogappel [oχapəl] *de (~s)* apple of one's eye: *hij was zijn moeders ~* he was the apple of his mother's eye

oogarts [oχarts] *de (~en)* ophthalmologist, eye specialist

oogbol [oχbɔl] *de (~len)* eyeball

ooggetuige [oχətœyɣə] *de (~n)* eyewitness

ooghoek [oχhuk] *de (~en)* corner of the eye

ooghoogte [oχhoχtə] *de* eye level

oogje [oχjə] *het (~s)* **1** eye: *een ~ dichtknijpen* (or: *dichtdoen)* close (or: shut) one's eyes (to); **2** glance, look, peep: *een ~ in het zeil houden* keep a lookout; *een ~ hebben op* have one's eye on

ooglid [oχlɪt] *het (oogleden)* (eye)lid

oogluikend [oχlœykənt] *adj* ‖ *iets ~ toelaten (toestaan)* turn a blind eye to sth

oogmeting [oχmetɪŋ] *de (~en)* eye test(ing)

oogopslag [oχɔpslɑχ] *de* glance, look, glimpse

oogpunt [oχpʏnt] *het (~en)* viewpoint, point of view

oogschaduw [oχsχadyw] *de* eyeshadow

oogst [oχst] *de (~en)* **1** harvesting, reaping; **2** harvest, crop: *de ~ binnenhalen* bring in the harvest

oogsten [oχstə(n)] *vb* harvest, pick

oogsttijd [oχstɛit] *de (~en)* harvest(ing) time

oogverblindend [oχfərblɪndənt] *adj* blinding, dazzling: *een ~e schoonheid* a raving beauty

oogwit [oχwɪt] *het* white of the eye

ooi [oj] *de (~en)* ewe

ooievaar [ojəvar] *de (~s)* stork

ooit [ojt] *adv* ever, at any time: *Jan, die ~ een vriend van me was* John, who was once a friend of mine; *groter dan ~ tevoren* bigger than ever (before)

ook [ok] *adv* **1** also, too: *zijn er ~ brieven?* are there any letters?; *morgen kan ~ nog* tomorrow will be all right too; *ik hou van tennis en hij ~* I like tennis and so does he; *ik ben er ~ nog* I'm here too; *hij kookte, en heel goed ~* he did the cooking and very well too; *hij heeft niet gewacht, en ik trouwens ~ niet* he didn't wait and neither did I; *zo vreselijk moeilijk is het nu ~ weer niet* it's not all that difficult (after all); *dat hebben we ~ weer gehad* so much for that, that's over and done with; *opa praatte ~ zo* grandpa used to talk like that (too); *dat is waar ~!* that's true, of course!, oh, I almost forgot!; **2** even: *~ al is hij niet rijk* even though he's not rich; **3** anyhow, anyway: *hoe jong ik ~ ben …* (as) young as I may be (or: am) …; *hoe het ~ zij, laten we nu maar gaan* anyway, let's go now; *wat je ~ doet* whatever you do; *wie (dan) ~* whoever; *hoe zeer zij zich ~ inspande* however she tried; **4** again, too: *dat gezanik ~* all that fuss (too); *jij hebt ~ nooit tijd!* you never have any time!; *hoe heet hij ~ weer?* what was his name again?

oom [om] *de (~s)* uncle

oor [or] *het (oren)* **1** ear: *met een half ~ meeluisteren* listen with only an ear; *dat gaat het ene ~ in, het andere uit* it goes (at) in one ear and out (at) the other; *zijn oren (niet) geloven* (not) believe one's ears; *een en al ~ zijn* be all ears; (Belg) *op zijn beide* (or: *twee) oren slapen* have no worries, sleep the sleep of the just; *doof aan één ~* deaf in one ear; *gaatjes in de oren hebben* have pierced ears; *iets in de oren knopen* get sth into one's head; *ik stond wel even met mijn oren te klapperen* I couldn't believe my ears (or: what I was hearing); *iem met iets om de oren slaan* blow s.o. up over sth; *tot over de oren verliefd* *zijn* be head over heels in love; **2** handle, ear: *iem een ~ aannaaien* fool s.o., take s.o. for a ride

oorarts [ọrɑrts] *de (~en)* otologist, ear specialist

oorbel [ọrbɛl] *de (~len)* earring

oordeel [ọrdel] *het (oordelen)* judg(e)ment, verdict, sentence

oordelen [ọrdelə(n)] *vb* **1** judge, pass judgement, sentence; **2** judge, make up one's mind

oordopje [ọrdɔpjə] *het (~s)* earplug

oordruppels [ọrdrʏpəls] *de* eardrops

oorkonde [ọrkɔndə] *de (~n)* document, charter, deed

oorlel [ọrlɛl] *de (~len)* lobe (of the ear)

oorlog [ọrlɔx] *de (~en)* war: *het is ~* there's a war on; *~ voeren* wage war

oorlogsfilm [ọrlɔxsfɪlm] *de (~s)* war film

oorlogsheld [ọrlɔxshɛlt] *de (~en)* war hero

oorlogspad [ọrlɔxspɑt] *het* ‖ *op het ~ zijn* be on the warpath

oorlogstijd [ọrlɔxstɛit] *de (~en)* time(s) of war, wartime

oorlogvoering [ọrlɔxfurɪŋ] *de* conduct (or: waging) of the war, warfare

oorontsteking [ọrɔntstekɪŋ] *de (~en)* inflammation of the ear

oorpijn [ọrpɛin] *de (~en)* earache

oorring [ọrɪŋ] *de (~en)* earring

oorsprong [ọrsprɔŋ] *de (~en)* origin, source: *van ~* originally

¹oorspronkelijk [orsprɔŋkələk] *adj* original; innovative: *een ~ kunstenaar* an original (or: innovative) artist

²oorspronkelijk [orsprɔŋkələk] *adv* originally, initially

oorspronkelijkheid [orsprɔŋkələkhɛit] *de* originality

oorverdovend [orvərdọvənt] *adj, adv* deafening

oorvijg [ọrvɛix] *de (~en)* box on the ear

oorworm [ọrwɔrm] *de* earwig

oorzaak [ọrzak] *de (oorzaken)* cause, origin: *~ en gevolg* cause and effect

oost [ost] *adj* east: *~ west, thuis best* east, west, home's best

oostelijk [ọstələk] *adj, adv* **1** eastern; **2** *(to the east)* easterly, eastward; *(from the east)* easter(ly) *(wind)*: *een ~e wind* an easterly wind

oosten [ọstə(n)] *het* east: *ten ~ van* (to the) east of; *het ~ van Frankrijk* eastern France

Oostende [ostɛndə] *het* Ostend

Oostenrijk [ọstə(n)rɛik] *het* Austria

Oostenrijker [ọstə(n)rɛikər] *de (~s)* Austrian

Oostenrijks [ọstə(n)rɛiks] *adj* Austrian

oostenwind [osta(n)wɪnt] *de (~en)* east wind, easterly

oosterlengte [ọstərlɛŋtə] *de* eastern longitude

oosters [ọstərs] *adj* oriental

Oost-Indisch [ostɪndis] *adj, adv* East Indian ‖ *~ doof zijn* pretend not to hear

oostkust [ọstkʏst] *de (~en)* east(ern) coast

oostwaarts [ọstwarts] *adv* eastward

Oostzee [ọstse] *de* Baltic (Sea)

oostzijde [ọ(st)sɛidə] *de* east side

¹op [ɔp] *prep* **1** in, on, at: *~ een motor rijden* ride a motorcycle; *~ de de hoek wonen* live on the the corner; *later ~ de dag* later in the day; *~ negenjarige leeftijd* at the age of nine; *~ maandag* (on) Monday; *~ een maandag* on a Monday; *~ vakantie* on holiday; *~ zijn vroegst* at the earliest; *~ haar eigen manier* in her own way; *~ zijn minst* at (the very) least; *~ zijn snelst* at the quickest; **2** in, to: *~ de eerste plaats* in the first place, first(ly), in first place; *de auto loopt 1 ~ 8* the car does 8 km to the litre; *één ~ de duizend* one in a thousand; *~ één na de laatste* the last but one

²op [ɔp] *adv* up: *trap ~ en trap af* up and down the stairs; *de straat ~ en neer lopen* walk up and down the street; *zij had een nieuwe hoed ~* she had a new hat on

³op [ɔp] *adj* used up, gone: *het geld* (or: *mijn geduld) is ~* the money (or: my patience) has run out; *hij is ~ van de zenuwen* he is a nervous wreck

opa [ọpa] *de (~'s)* grandpa, grandad

¹opaal [opạl] *de (opalen) (stone)* opal

²opaal [opạl] *het (mineral)* opal

opbellen [ɔbɛlə(n)] *vb* (tele)phone, call, ring (up): *ik zal je nog wel even ~* I'll give you a call (or: ring)

opbergen [ɔbɛrɣə(n)] *vb* put away, store, file (away)

opbeuren [ɔbøːrə(n)] *vb* cheer up

opbiechten [ɔbixtə(n)] *vb* confess: *alles eerlijk ~* make a clean breast of it

opblaasbaar [ɔblazbar] *adj* inflatable

opblazen [ɔblazə(n)] *vb* blow up, inflate

opblijven [ɔblɛivə(n)] *vb* stay up

opbloeien [ɔblujə(n)] *vb* **1** bloom; **2** flourish, prosper

opbod [ɔbɔt] *het* ‖ *iets bij ~ verkopen* sell sth by auction

opboksen [ɔbɔksə(n)] *vb* compete

opbouw [ɔbɑu] *de* **1** construction; **2** structure

opbouwen [ɔbɑuwə(n)] *vb* build up, set up: *het weefsel is uit cellen opgebouwd* the tissue is made up (or: composed) of cells

opbouwend [ɔbɑuwənt] *adj* constructive

opbranden [ɔbrɑndə(n)] *vb* be burned up (or: down)

opbreken [ɔbrekə(n)] *vb* **1** break up, take down (or: apart); **2** break up, tear up: *de straat ~* dig (or: break) up the street

opbrengen [ɔbrɛŋə(n)] *vb* **1** bring in, yield; **2** work up: *begrip* (or: *belangstelling) ~ voor* show understanding for (or: an interest in); **3** apply

opbrengst [ɔbrɛŋst] *de (~en)* yield, profit, revenue

opdagen [ɔbdaɣə(n)] *vb* turn up, show up

opdienen [ɔbdinə(n)] *vb* serve (up), dish up

opdoeken [ɔbdukə(n)] *vb* shut down

opdoemen [ɔbdumə(n)] *vb* loom (up), appear

opdoen [ɔbdun] *vb* **1** gain, get: *kennis ~* acquire

knowledge; **2** apply, put on

opdoffen [ɔbdɔfə(n)] *ref vb* doll oneself up

opdonder [ɔbdɔndər] *de (~s)* punch

opdonderen [ɔbdɔndərə(n)] *vb* get lost

opdraaien [ɔbdrajə(n)] *vb* ‖ *ik wil hier niet voor ~* I don't want to take any blame for this; *voor de kosten ~* foot the bill; *iem voor iets laten ~* land (*or:* saddle) s.o. with sth

opdracht [ɔbdraχt] *de (~en)* assignment, order: *we kregen ~ om ...* we were told to ..., given orders to ...

opdrachtgever [ɔbdraχtχevər] *de (~s)* client, customer

opdragen [ɔbdraɣə(n)] *vb* charge, commission, assign

opdraven [ɔbdravə(n)] *vb* show up, put in an appearance

opdreunen [ɔbdrønə(n)] *vb* rattle off, reel off, drone

opdrijven [ɔbdrɛivə(n)] *vb* force up, drive up

¹**opdringen** [ɔbdrɪŋə(n)] *vb* push forward, press forward; press on, push on

²**opdringen** [ɔbdrɪŋə(n)] *vb* force on, press on, intrude on, impose on: *dat werd ons opgedrongen* that was forced on us

³**opdringen** [ɔbdrɪŋə(n)] *ref vb* force oneself on, impose oneself (on), impose one's company (on): *ik wil me niet ~* I don't want to intrude

opdringerig [ɔbdrɪŋərəχ] *adj, adv* obtrusive; pushy: *~e reclameboodschappen* aggressive advertising

opdrinken [ɔbdrɪŋkə(n)] *vb* drink (up)

opdrogen [ɔbdroɣə(n)] *vb* dry (up), run dry

opdruk [ɔbdrʏk] *de (~ken)* (im)print

opdrukken [ɔbdrʏkə(n)] *vb* **1** print on(to), impress on(to), stamp on(to); **2** push up, press up: *zich ~* do press-ups

opduikelen [ɔbdœykələ(n)] *vb* dig up

opduiken [ɔbdœykə(n)] *vb* **1** surface, rise (*or:* come) to the surface; **2** turn up

opduwen [ɔbdywə(n)] *vb* push up, press up

opdweilen [ɔbdwɛilə(n)] *vb* mop up

opeen [ɔpɛn] *adv* together

opeens [ɔpɛns] *adv* suddenly, all at once, all of a sudden

opeenstapeling [ɔpɛnstapəlɪŋ] *de (~en)* accumulation, build-up

opeenvolgend [ɔpɛnvɔlɣənt] *adj* successive, consecutive

opeenvolging [ɔpɛnvɔlɣɪŋ] *de (~en)* succession

opeisen [ɔpɛisə(n)] *vb* claim, demand: *de aandacht ~* demand (*or:* compel) attention; *een aanslag ~* claim responsibility for an attack

open [ɔpə(n)] *adj, adv* open, unlocked, vacant: *de deur staat ~* the door is ajar (*or:* open); *met ~ ogen* with one's eyes open; *een ~ plek in het bos* a clearing in the woods; *tot hoe laat zijn de winkels ~?* what time do the shops close?; *~ en bloot* openly, for all (the world) to see

openbaar [ɔpə(n)bar] *adj, adv* public, open: *de openbare orde verstoren* disturb the peace; *in het ~* in public, publicly

openbaarheid [ɔpə(n)barhɛit] *de* publicity

openbaarmaking [ɔpə(n)barmakɪŋ] *de* publication, disclosure

openbaarvervoerkaart [ɔpəmbarvərvurkart] *de (~en)* public transport pass; travel card

openbaring [ɔpə(n)barɪŋ] *de (~en)* revelation

openbarsten [ɔpə(n)barstə(n)] *vb* burst open

openbreken [ɔpə(n)brekə(n)] *vb* break (open), force open, prise open: *een slot ~* force a lock

opendeurdag [ɔpə(n)dørdaχ] *de (~en) (Belg)* open day

¹**opendoen** [ɔpə(n)dun] *vb* open

²**opendoen** [ɔpə(n)dun] *vb* open the door, answer the door (*or:* bell, ring): *er werd niet opengedaan* there was no answer

opendraaien [ɔpə(n)drajə(n)] *vb* open, turn on, unscrew

¹**openen** [ɔpənə(n)] *vb* open, begin: *(cards) met schoppen ~* lead spades

²**openen** [ɔpənə(n)] *vb* **1** open, turn on, unscrew; **2** open, start

opener [ɔpənər] *de (~s)* opener

opengaan [ɔpə(n)ɣan] *vb* open

openhalen [ɔpə(n)halə(n)] *vb* tear: *ik heb mijn jas opengehaald aan een spijker* I tore my coat on a nail

openhartig [ɔpənhartəχ] *adj, adv* frank, candid, straightforward: *een ~ gesprek* a heart-to-heart (talk)

openhartigheid [ɔpə(n)hartəχhɛit] *de* frankness, candour

openheid [ɔpənhɛit] *de* openness, sincerity: *in alle ~* in all candour

openhouden [ɔpə(n)haudə(n)] *vb* keep open: *de deur voor iem ~* hold the door (open) for s.o.

opening [ɔpənɪŋ] *de (~en)* opening, gap

openingsplechtigheid [ɔpənɪŋsplɛχtəχhɛit] *de (-heden)* opening ceremony, inauguration

openingstijd [ɔpənɪŋstɛit] *de (~en)* opening hours, business hours

openlaten [ɔpə(n)latə(n)] *vb* **1** leave open, leave on, leave running; **2** leave blank, leave open

openlijk [ɔpə(n)lək] *adj, adv* **1** open, overt: *~ voor iets uitkomen* openly admit sth; **2** public: *iets ~ verkondigen* declare sth in public

openlucht [ɔpə(n)lʏχt] *de* open air

openmaken [ɔpə(n)makə(n)] *vb* open (up)

openscheuren [ɔpə(n)sχørə(n)] *vb* tear open, rip open

openslaan [ɔpə(n)slan] *vb* open

openslaand [ɔpə(n)slant] *adj* ‖ *~e deuren* double doors

opensnijden [ɔpə(n)snɛidə(n)] *vb* cut (open)

openstaan [ɔpə(n)stan] *vb* be open, be unlocked: *mijn huis staat altijd voor jou open* my door will always be open to (*or:* for) you; *de kraan staat open* the tap is on (*or:* is running)

opentrappen [ǫpə(n)trɑpə(n)] *vb* kick open

opentrekken [ǫpə(n)trɛkə(n)] *vb* pull open, open: *een grote bek ~* open one's big mouth

openvallen [ǫpə(n)vɑlə(n)] *vb* fall open, drop open

openvouwen [ǫpə(n)vɑuwə(n)] *vb* unfold, open (out)

openzetten [ǫpə(n)zɛtə(n)] *vb* open, turn on

opera [ǫpera] *de (~'s)* opera

operatie [opəra(t)si] *de (~s)* operation, surgery: *een grote* (or: *kleine*) ~ *ondergaan* undergo major (or: minor) surgery

operatief [operatif] *adj, adv* surgical, operative

operatiekamer [opəra(t)sikamər] *de (~s)* operating room

operatietafel [opəra(t)sitafəl] *de (~s)* operating table

opereren [opərɛrə(n)] *vb* 1 work; use; 2 operate, perform surgery (or: an operation): *iem ~* operate on s.o.; *zij is geopereerd aan de longen* she has had an operation on the lungs

operette [opərɛtə] *de (~s)* light opera

opeten [ǫpetə(n)] *vb* eat (up), finish

opfleuren [ǫpflørə(n)] *vb* cheer up, brighten up

opflikkeren [ǫpflɪkərə(n)] *vb* flare up, flicker

opfokken [ǫpfɔkə(n)] *vb* work up, whip up, stir up

opfrissen [ǫpfrɪsə(n)] *vb* freshen (up): *zijn Engels ~* brush up (on) one's English; *zich ~* freshen up, (*Am*) wash up

opgaan [ǫpχan] *vb* 1 go up, climb; 2 come up, rise; 3 go, be finished; 4 hold good (or: true), apply: *dit gaat niet op voor arme mensen* this doesn't apply to (or: this is not true of) poor people; *als het die kant opgaat met de maatschappij dan …* if that is the way society is going …

opgaand [ǫpχant] *adj* rising

opgave [ǫpχavə] *de (~n)* 1 statement, specification: *zonder ~ van redenen* without reason given; 2 question: *schriftelijke ~n* written assignments; 3 task, assignment

opgeblazen [ǫpχəblazə(n)] *adj* puffy, bloated, swollen

opgebrand [ǫpχəbrɑnt] *adj* burnt-out, worn-out

opgefokt [ǫpχəfɔkt] *adj* worked up

opgekropt [ǫpχəkrɔpt] *adj* pent-up, bottled up

opgelucht [ǫpχəlyχt] *adj* relieved: *~ ademhalen* heave a sigh of relief

opgemaakt [ǫpχəmakt] *adj* 1 made up: *een ~ gezicht* a made-up face; 2 made (up), laid out: *een ~ bed* a made (up) bed

opgeruimd [ǫpχərœymt] *adj* tidy, neat: *~ staat netjes* good riddance (to bad rubbish)

opgescheept [ǫpχəsχept] *adj* || *met iem (iets) ~ zitten* be stuck with s.o. (sth)

opgeschoten [ǫpχəsχotə(n)] *adj* lanky

opgetogen [ǫpχətoγə(n)] *adj* delighted, overjoyed

opgeven [ǫpχevə(n)] *vb* 1 give up, abandon: *(het) niet ~* not give in (or: up), hang on; *je moet nooit (niet te gauw) ~* never say die; 2 give, state: *zijn in-*

komsten ~ aan de belasting declare one's income to the tax inspector; *als reden ~* give (or: state) as one's reason; 3 give, assign; 4 enter: *zich ~ voor een cursus* enrol (or: sign up) for a course; *als vermist ~* report (as) missing; 5 give (up), surrender

opgewassen [ǫpχəwɑsə(n)] *adj* equal (to), up (to): *hij bleek niet ~ tegen die taak* the task proved beyond him (or: too much for him)

opgewekt [ǫpχəwɛkt] *adj, adv* cheerful, good-humoured: *hij is altijd heel ~* he is always in good spirits (or: bright and breezy)

opgewonden [ǫpχəwɔndə(n)] *adj, adv* 1 excited; 2 agitated, in a fluster

opgezet [ǫpχəzɛt] *adj* 1 swollen, bloated; 2 (*Belg*) happy, content: *~ zijn met iets* be pleased about sth

opgooien [ǫpχojə(n)] *vb* throw up, toss up

opgraven [ǫpχravə(n)] *vb* dig up, unearth, excavate, exhume

opgraving [ǫpχravɪŋ] *de (~en)* 1 dig(ging), excavation, exhumation: *opgravingen vonden plaats in …* excavations were carried out in …; 2 excavation, dig, (archaeological) site

opgroeien [ǫpχrujə(n)] *vb* grow (up)

ophaalbrug [ǫphalbryχ] *de (~gen)* lift bridge, drawbridge

ophaaldienst [ǫphaldinst] *de (~en)* collecting service, collection service

ophalen [ǫphalə(n)] *vb* 1 raise, draw up, pull up, hoist; 2 collect: *een bestand ~* download a file; *vuilnis ~* collect refuse (or: rubbish), (*Am*) collect garbage; *kom je me vanavond ~?* are you coming round for me tonight?; 3 bring up, bring back, recall: *herinneringen ~ aan de goede oude tijd* reminisce about the good old days; 4 collect; 5 brush up (on), polish up: *rapportcijfers ~* improve on one's (report) marks

¹ophangen [ǫphɑŋə(n)] *vb* hang (up), post: *de was ~* hang out the wash(ing)

²ophangen [ǫphɑŋə(n)] *vb* hang up, ring off

ophebben [ǫphɛbə(n)] *vb* 1 wear, have on; 2 have finished, have had

ophef [ǫphɛf] *de* fuss, noise, song (and dance): *zonder veel ~* without much ado

opheffen [ǫphɛfə(n)] *vb* 1 raise, lift: *met opgeheven hoofd* with (one's) head held high; 2 cancel (out), neutralize: *het effect ~ van iets* counteract sth; 3 remove, discontinue: *de club werd na een paar maanden opgeheven* the club was disbanded after a couple of months

opheffing [ǫphɛfɪŋ] *de (~en)* removal, discontinuance, adjournment: *de ~ van het faillissement* the annulment of the bankruptcy

ophefmakend [ǫphɛfmakənt] *adj, adv* (*Belg*) sensational

ophelderen [ǫphɛldərə(n)] *vb* clear up, clarify

opheldering [ǫphɛldərɪŋ] *de (~en)* explanation

ophemelen [ǫphemələ(n)] *vb* praise to the skies, extol

ophijsen [ǫphɛisə(n)] *vb* pull up, hoist (up), raise

ophitsen [ɔphɪtsə(n)] *vb* **1** egg on, goad: *een hond ~ tease (or: bait)* a dog; *iem* ~ get s.o.'s hackles up; **2** incite, stir up: *de mensen tegen elkaar ~* set people at one another's throats

ophoepelen [ɔphupələ(n)] *vb* get lost, clear *(or:* push, buzz*)* off

ophopen [ɔphopə(n)] *ref vb* pile up, accumulate: *de sneeuw heeft zich opgehoopt* the snow has banked up

ophoping [ɔphopɪŋ] *de (~en)* accumulation, pile

¹ophouden [ɔphaudə(n)] *vb* stop, quit, (come to an) end: *de straat hield daar op* the street ended there; *dan houdt alles op* then there's nothing more to be said; *plotseling ~* break off; *ze hield maar niet op met huilen* she (just) went on crying (and crying); *~ met roken* give up *(or:* stop*)* smoking; *het is opgehouden met regenen* the rain has stopped; *even ~ met werken* have a short break in one's work; *hou op!* stop it!, cut it out!; *laten we erover ~* let's leave it at that

²ophouden [ɔphaudə(n)] *vb* **1** hold up, delay, *(pers also)* keep, *(pers also)* detain: *iem niet langer ~* not take up any more of s.o.'s time; *dat houdt de zaak alleen maar op* that just slows things down; *ik werd opgehouden* I was delayed *(or:* held up*)*; **2** keep on

opinie [opini] *de (~s)* opinion, view

opinieblad [opiniblɑt] *het (~en) (roughly)* news magazine

opiniepeiling [opinipɛilɪŋ] *de (~en)* (opinion) poll: *(een) ~(en) houden (over)* canvass opinion (on)

opium [opijʏm] *het, de* opium

opjagen [ɔpjaɣə(n)] *vb* hurry, rush, hound

opkalefateren [ɔpkaləfatərə(n)] *vb* patch (up), doctor (up)

opkijken [ɔpkɛikə(n)] *vb* **1** look up: *~ tegen iem* look up to s.o.; **2** sit up, be surprised: *daar kijk ik van op* I'd never have thought it

opklapbed [ɔpklɑbɛt] *het (~den)* foldaway bed

opklappen [ɔpklɑpə(n)] *vb* fold up

opklaren [ɔpklarə(n)] *vb* brighten up, clear up: *de lucht klaart op* the sky's clearing up

opklimmen [ɔpklɪmə(n)] *vb* climb

opknapbeurt [ɔpknɑbørt] *de (~en)* redecoration, facelift

¹opknappen [ɔpknɑpə(n)] *vb* pick up, revive: *het weer is opgeknapt* the weather has brightened up; *hij zal er erg van ~* it'll do him all the good in the world

²opknappen [ɔpknɑpə(n)] *vb* **1** tidy up, do up, redecorate, restore: *het dak moet nodig eens opgeknapt worden* the roof needs repairing *(or:* fixing*)*; **2** fix, carry out: *dat zal zij zelf wel ~* she'll take care of it herself

³opknappen [ɔpknɑpə(n)] *ref vb* freshen (oneself) up

opknopen [ɔpknopə(n)] *vb* string up

opkomen [ɔpkomə(n)] *vb* **1** come up, rise, come in: *spontaan (vanzelf) ~* crop up; **2** rise, ascend; **3** oc-

cur, recur: *het komt niet bij hem op* it doesn't occur to him; *het eerste wat bij je opkomt* the first thing that comes into your mind; **4** come on, set in, rise: *ik voel een verkoudheid ~ (or: de koorts) ~* I can feel a cold *(or:* the fever*)* coming on; **5** enter, come on (stage); **6** fight (for), stand up (for): *steeds voor elkaar ~* stick together; *kom op, we gaan* come on, let's go; *kom maar op als je durft!* come on if you dare!

opkomst [ɔpkɔmst] *de* **1** rise; **2** attendance, turnout; **3** entrance; **4** rise, boom

opkopen [ɔpkopə(n)] *vb* buy up

opkrikken [ɔpkrɪkə(n)] *vb* **1** jack up; **2** hype up, pep up: *het moreel ~* boost morale

opkroppen [ɔpkrɔpə(n)] *vb* bottle up, hold back

opkuisen [ɔpkœysə(n)] *vb (Belg)* clean (up), tidy (up)

oplaadbaar [ɔplɑdbar] *adj* rechargeable

oplaaien [ɔplajə(n)] *vb* flare *(or:* flame, blaze*)* up

opladen [ɔplɑdə(n)] *vb* charge

oplader [ɔplɑdər] *de (~s)* charger

oplage [ɔplaɣə] *de (~n)* edition, issue, circulation: *een krant met een grote ~* a newspaper with a wide circulation

oplappen [ɔplɑpə(n)] *vb* patch up

oplaten [ɔplɑtə(n)] *vb* fly; release; launch

oplawaai [ɔplawaj] *de (~en)* wallop

opleggen [ɔplɛɣə(n)] *vb* enforce; impose: *wetten ~* enforce *(or:* impose, lay down*)* laws

oplegger [ɔplɛɣər] *de (~s)* semi-trailer, trailer: *truck met ~* articulated lorry *(or Am:* truck*)*

opleiden [ɔplɛidə(n)] *vb* educate, instruct: *hij is tot advocaat opgeleid* he has been trained as a lawyer

opleiding [ɔplɛidɪŋ] *de (~en)* **1** education, training: *een wetenschappelijke ~* an academic *(or:* a university*)* education; *een ~ volgen (krijgen)* receive training, train; *zij volgt een ~ voor secretaresse* she is doing a secretarial course; **2** institute; (training) college; academy

opleidingscentrum [ɔplɛidɪŋsɛntrʏm] *het (-centra)* training centre

opletten [ɔplɛtə(n)] *vb* **1** watch, take care: *let op waar je loopt* look where you're going; *let maar eens op* mark my words, wait and see; **2** pay attention: *opgelet!, let op!* attention please!, take care!

oplettend [ɔplɛtənt] *adj, adv* **1** observant, observing: *zij sloeg hem ~ gade* she watched him carefully *(or:* closely*)*; **2** attentive

oplettendheid [ɔplɛtəntheit] *de* attention, attentiveness

opleven [ɔplevə(n)] *vb* revive

opleveren [ɔplevərə(n)] *vb* **1** deliver, surrender: *tijdig ~* deliver on time; **2** yield: *wat levert dat baantje op?* what does *(or:* how much does*)* the job pay?; *voordeel ~* yield profit; *het schrijven van boeken levert weinig op* writing (books) doesn't bring in much; **3** produce: *het heeft me niets dan ellende opgeleverd* it brought me nothing but misery

oplevering [ɔplevərɪŋ] *de (~en)* delivery; *(bldg)*

completion

opleving [ɔplevɪŋ] *de* revival; recovery; upturn, pick-up: *een plotselinge ~* an upsurge

oplezen [ɔplezə(n)] *vb* read (out), call (out, off)

oplichten [ɔplɪχtə(n)] *vb* swindle, cheat, con: *iem ~ voor 2 ton* swindle (*or:* con) s.o. out of 200,000 euros

oplichter [ɔplɪχtər] *de* (*~s*) swindler, crook, con(fidence) man (woman)

oplichterij [ɔplɪχtərɛi] *de* (*~en*) swindle, con(-trick)

oplichting [ɔplɪχtɪŋ] *de* fraud, con(-trick)

oplikken [ɔplɪkə(n)] *vb* lick up, lap up

oploop [ɔplop] *de* 1 crowd; 2 riot, tumult

¹**oplopen** [ɔplopə(n)] *vb* 1 go up, run up, walk up: *de trap ~* run (*or:* go, walk) up the stairs; 2 increase, mount, rise: *de spanning laten ~* build up the tension; 3 bump into, run into: *tegen een mooi huis ~* chance to come upon a nice house

²**oplopen** [ɔplopə(n)] *vb* catch, get: *een verkoudheid ~* catch a cold

oplopend [ɔplopənt] *adj* 1 rising, sloping (upwards); 2 increasing, mounting: *een hoog ~e ruzie* a flaming row

oplosbaar [ɔplɔzbar] *adj* solvable

oploskoffie [ɔplɔskɔfi] *de* instant coffee

oplosmiddel [ɔplɔsmɪdəl] *het* (*~en*) solvent, thinner

¹**oplossen** [ɔplɔsə(n)] *vb* dissolve: *die vlekken lossen op als sneeuw voor de zon* those stains will vanish in no time

²**oplossen** [ɔplɔsə(n)] *vb* 1 solve; 2 (re)solve: *dit zou het probleem moeten ~* this should settle (*or:* solve) the problem

oplossing [ɔplɔsɪŋ] *de* (*~en*) solution; answer

opluchten [ɔplʏχtə(n)] *vb* relieve: *dat lucht op!* what a relief!

opluchting [ɔplʏχtɪŋ] *de* relief: *tot mijn grote ~ to* my great relief, much to my relief

opmaak [ɔpmak] *de* 1 layout, set-out, mock-up, format; 2 embellishment; trimming

opmaken [ɔpmakə(n)] *vb* 1 finish (up), use up: *al zijn geld ~* spend all one's money; 2 make up: *zich ~* make oneself up; 3 draw up: *de balans ~* weigh the pros and cons, take stock; 4 lay out, make up; 5 gather: *moet ik daaruit ~ dat ...* do I gather (*or:* conclude) from it that ...

opmerkelijk [ɔpmɛrkələk] *adj, adv* remarkable, striking

opmerken [ɔpmɛrkə(n)] *vb* 1 observe, note; 2 note, notice; 3 observe, remark: *mag ik misschien even iets ~?* may I make an observation?

opmerking [ɔpmɛrkɪŋ] *de* (*~en*) remark, observation, comment: *hou je brutale ~en voor je* keep your comments to yourself

opmerkzaam [ɔpmɛrksam] *adj, adv* attentive, observant

opname [ɔpnamə] *de* (*~n, ~s*) 1 admission; 2 shot; (*film*) shooting, take; recording; 3 withdrawal

opnamestudio [ɔpnaməstydijo] *de* (*~'s*) recording studio; film studio; sound stage

opnemen [ɔpnemə(n)] *vb* 1 withdraw: *een snipperdag ~* take a day off; 2 take: *iets (te) gemakkelijk ~* be (too) casual about sth; 3 record, (*film*) shoot: *een concert ~* record a concert; 4 measure: *de gasmeter ~* read the (gas)meter; *de tijd ~ (van)* time a person; 5 take down; 6 admit, introduce, include: *laten ~ in een ziekenhuis* hospitalize; *in het ziekenhuis opgenomen worden* be admitted to hospital; 7 admit, receive: *ze werd snel opgenomen in de groep* she was soon accepted as one of the group; 8 answer: *er wordt niet opgenomen* there's no answer; 9 absorb: *het tegen iem ~* take s.o. on; *hij kan het tegen iedereen ~* he can hold his own against anyone; *het voor iem ~* speak (*or:* stick) for s.o.

opnieuw [ɔpniw] *adv* 1 (once) again, once more: *telkens (steeds) ~* again and again, time and (time) again; 2 (once) again, once more: *nu moet ik weer helemaal ~ beginnen* now I'm back to square one

opnoemen [ɔpnumə(n)] *vb* name, call (out), enumerate: *te veel om op te noemen* too much (*or:* many) to mention

opoe [ɔpu] *de* (*~s*) gran(ny), gran(d)ma

opofferen [ɔpɔfərə(n)] *vb* sacrifice

opoffering [ɔpɔfərɪŋ] *de* (*~en*) sacrifice, (*fig*) expense

oponthoud [ɔpɔnthaut] *het* stop(page), delay: *~ hebben* be delayed

oppakken [ɔpakə(n)] *vb* run in, pick up, round up

oppas [ɔpas] *de* (*~sen*) babysitter, childminder

oppassen [ɔpasə(n)] *vb* 1 look out, be careful: *pas op voor zakkenrollers* beware of pickpockets; 2 babysit

oppasser [ɔpasər] *de* (*~s*) keeper

oppeppen [ɔpɛpə(n)] *vb* pep (up)

opperbest [ɔpərbɛst] *adj, adv* splendid, excellent: *in een ~ humeur* in high spirits

opperbevel [ɔpərbəvɛl] *het* supreme command, high command

opperbevelhebber [ɔpərbəvɛlhɛbər] *de* (*~s*) commander-in-chief, supreme commander

opperhoofd [ɔpərhoft] *het* (*~en*) chief, chieftain

oppermachtig [ɔpərmaχtəχ] *adj, adv* supreme

opperman [ɔpərman] *de* (*-lui, -lieden, ~nen*) bricklayer's assistant (*or:* labourer)

opperst [ɔpərst] *adj* supreme, complete

oppervlak [ɔpərvlak] *het* (*~ken*) 1 surface, face; 2 (surface) area

oppervlakkig [ɔpərvlakəχ] *adj, adv* superficial, shallow: *(zo) ~ beschouwd* on the face of it

oppervlakkigheid [ɔpərvlakəχhɛit] *de* (*-heden*) superficiality, shallowness

oppervlakte [ɔpərvlaktə] *de* (*~n, ~s*) 1 surface, face; 2 surface (area)

oppervlaktemaat [ɔpərvlaktəmat] *de* (*-maten*) square measure, area measure

oppiepen [ɔpipə(n)] *vb* bleep

oppikken [ɔpɪkə(n)] *vb* pick up, collect: *ik pik je bij* *het station op* I will pick you up at the station

opplakken [ɔplɑkə(n)] *vb* stick (on), glue (on), paste (on), affix

oppompen [ɔpɔmpə(n)] *vb* pump up, blow up *(socc)*, inflate

oppositie [ɔpozi(t)si] *de (~s)* opposition

oppositieleider [ɔpozi(t)silɛidər] *de (~s)* opposition leader, leader of the opposition

opprikken [ɔprɪkə(n)] *vb* pin up, hang up: *een bericht ~* put up a notice

oppuntstellen [ɔpʏntstɛlə(n)] *vb (Belg)* arrange, fix up

oprapen [ɔprapə(n)] *vb* pick up, gather

oprecht [ɔprɛχt] *adj, adv* sincere, heartfelt

oprennen [ɔprɛnə(n)] *vb* **1** run (onto etc.): *hij rende het veld op* he ran onto the field; **2** run up

oprichten [ɔprɪχtə(n)] *vb* set up, establish, start, found: *een onderneming ~* establish (*or:* start) a company

oprichter [ɔprɪχtər] *de (~s)* founder

oprichting [ɔprɪχtɪŋ] *de (~en)* foundation, establishment, formation

oprijden [ɔprɛidə(n)] *vb* ride along, drive along: *een oprijlaan ~* turn into a drive; *tegen iets ~* crash into (*or:* collide with) sth

oprijlaan [ɔprɛilan] *de (-lanen)* drive(way)

oprit [ɔprɪt] *de (~ten)* **1** drive, access; **2** approach road, slip road

oproep [ɔprup] *de* call, appeal

oproepen [ɔprupə(n)] *vb* **1** summon, call (up), page: *opgeroepen voor militaire dienst* conscripted (*or:* drafted) into military service; **2** call up, evoke, conjure up, arouse

oproepkracht [ɔprupkrɑχt] *de (~en)* stand-by employee (*or:* worker)

oprollen [ɔprɔlə(n)] *vb* **1** roll up, curl up, coil up, wind; **2** round up

opruimen [ɔprœymə(n)] *vb* clean (out), clear (out), tidy (up), clear (up): *de rommel ~* clear (*or:* tidy) away the mess; *opgeruimd staat netjes: a)* that's things nice and tidy again; *b) (iron)* good riddance (to bad rubbish)

opruiming [ɔprœymɪŋ] *de (~en)* clearance, (clearance) sale, clear-out

opruimingsuitverkoop [ɔprœymɪŋsœytfərkop] *de* (stock-)clearance sale

oprukken [ɔprʏkə(n)] *vb* advance

opschepen [ɔpsχepə(n)] *vb* saddle with, palm off on: *iem met iets ~* saddle s.o. with sth, plant sth on s.o.

¹opscheppen [ɔpsχɛpə(n)] *vb* dish up, serve out, spoon out, ladle out: *mag ik je nog eens ~?* may I give you (*or:* will you have) another helping?

²opscheppen [ɔpsχɛpə(n)] *vb* brag, boast: *~ met (over) zijn nieuwe auto* show off one's new car

opschepper [ɔpsχɛpər] *de (~s)* boaster, braggart

opschepperig [ɔpsχɛpərəχ] *adj, adv* boastful

opschepperij [ɔpsχɛpərɛi] *de (~en)* bragging, exhibitionism, show

opschieten [ɔpsχitə(n)] *vb* **1** hurry up, push on (*or:* ahead); **2** get on, make progress (*or:* headway): *daar schiet je niks mee op* that's not going to get you anywhere; **3** get on (*or:* along)

opschrift [ɔpsχrɪft] *het (~en)* **1** legend, inscription; lettering; **2** headline; heading; caption; direction

opschrijven [ɔpsχrɛivə(n)] *vb* write/take/put (*or:* note, jot) down: *schrijf het maar voor mij op* charge it to (*or:* put it on) my account

opschrikken [ɔpsχrɪkə(n)] *vb* start, startle, jump

opschudding [ɔpsχʏdɪŋ] *de (~en)* commotion, disturbance

opschuiven [ɔpsχœyvə(n)] *vb* move up (*or:* over), shift up, shove up

opslaan [ɔpslan] *vb* **1** lay up, store; **2** hit up, serve; **3** lift, raise; **4** save: *bewaren als tekstbestand* save as text file

opslag [ɔpslɑχ] *de (~en)* **1** rise, raise, surcharge: *~ krijgen* get (*or:* receive) a rise; **2** *(sport)* serve, service, ball; **3** storage

opslagplaats [ɔpslɑχplats] *de (~en)* warehouse, (storage) depot, store, depository *(goods)*

opslagtank [ɔpslɑχtɛŋk] *de* storage tank

¹opsluiten [ɔpslœytə(n)] *vb* shut up, lock up, confine, put (*or:* place) under restraint, cage, pound: *opgesloten in zijn kamertje zitten* be cooped up in one's room

²opsluiten [ɔpslœytə(n)] *ref vb* shut oneself in, lock oneself up

opsluiting [ɔpslœytɪŋ] *de* confinement, imprisonment: *eenzame ~* solitary confinement

opsnuiven [ɔpsnœyvə(n)] *vb* sniff (up), snuff, inhale, snort

opsolferen [ɔpsɔlfərə(n)] *het (Belg)* palm off (on): *iem iets ~* palm sth off on s.o.

opsommen [ɔpsɔmə(n)] *vb* enumerate, recount

opsomming [ɔpsɔmɪŋ] *de (~en)* enumeration, list, run-down

opsparen [ɔpsparə(n)] *vb* save up, hoard (up)

opspelen [ɔpspelə(n)] *vb* play up

opsplitsen [ɔpsplɪtsə(n)] *vb* split up (into), break up (into)

opsporen [ɔpsporə(n)] *vb* track, trace, detect, track down, hunt down

opsporing [ɔpsporɪŋ] *de (~en)* location, tracing

opspraak [ɔpsprak] *de* discredit: *in ~ komen* get oneself talked about

opspringen [ɔpsprɪŋə(n)] *vb* jump/leap (*or:* spring, start) up, spring (*or:* jump, start) to one's feet, bounce

opstaan [ɔpstan] *vb* stand up, get up, get (*or:* rise) to one's feet, get on one's feet: *met vallen en ~* with ups and downs; *hij staat altijd vroeg op* he's an early riser (*or:* bird), he is always up early

opstand [ɔpstɑnt] *de (~en)* (up)rising, revolt, rebellion, insurrection

opstandig [ɔpstɑndəχ] *adj* rebellious, mutinous, insurgent

opstanding [ɔpstɑndɪŋ] *de* resurrection: *de ~ van*

Christus the Resurrection of Christ

opstap [ɔpstɑp] *de (~pen)* step: *struikel niet over het ~je* don't stumble over the step, mind the step

¹opstapelen [ɔpstapələ(n)] *vb* pile up, heap up, stack (up), amass, accumulate

²opstapelen [ɔpstapələ(n)] *ref vb* pile up, accumulate, mount up

opstappen [ɔpstapə(n)] *vb* go away, move on; be off; resign

opsteken [ɔpstekə(n)] *vb* **1** put up, hold up, raise; **2** learn, pick up: *zij hebben er niet veel van opgestoken* they have not taken much of it in; **3** gather up, pin up

opsteker [ɔpstekər] *de (~s)* windfall, piece of (good) luck

opstel [ɔpstɛl] *het (~len)* (school) essay, composition: *een ~ maken over* write/do an essay (*or:* a paper) on

¹opstellen [ɔpstɛlə(n)] *vb* **1** set up (*or:* erect); post, place (sth, s.o.); arrange, dispose, line up; deploy: *(sport) opgesteld staan* be lined up; **2** draw up, formulate, draft: *een plan ~* draw up a plan

²opstellen [ɔpstɛlə(n)] *ref vb* **1** take up a position, form, line up, station oneself, post oneself; **2** take up a position (on), adopt an attitude (towards); pose (as): *zich keihard ~* take a hard line

opstelling [ɔpstɛlɪŋ] *de (~en)* **1** placing, erection, deployment; position, arrangement; **2** position, attitude; **3** *(sport)* line-up

opstijgen [ɔpstɛiɣə(n)] *vb* **1** ascend, rise, go up, take off, lift off; **2** mount

opstoken [ɔpstokə(n)] *vb* incite (to), put up (to sth)

opstopping [ɔpstɔpɪŋ] *de (~en)* stoppage, blockage, traffic jam, congestion

opstrijken [ɔpstrɛikə(n)] *vb* pocket, rake in, scoop in, scoop up

opstropen [ɔpstropə(n)] *vb* roll up, turn up

opsturen [ɔpstyrə(n)] *vb* send, post, mail

optellen [ɔptɛlə(n)] *vb* add (up), count up, total up: *twee getallen (bij elkaar) ~* add up two numbers

optelling [ɔptɛlɪŋ] *de (~en)* **1** addition; **2** (addition) sum

opticien [ɔptiʃɛ̃] *de (~s)* optician

optie [ɔpsi] *de (~s)* **1** option, choice, alternative: *een ~ op een huis hebben* have an option on a house; **2** *(Belg)* optional subject

optiebeurs [ɔpsibørs] *de (-beurzen)* options market

optiek [ɔptik] *de* point of view, angle

optillen [ɔptɪlə(n)] *vb* lift (up), raise

¹optimaal [ɔptimaːl] *adj* optimal

²optimaal [ɔptimaːl] *adj* optimum

optimaliseren [ɔptimalizɛrə(n)] *vb* optimize

optimisme [ɔptimɪsmə] *het* optimism

optimist [ɔptimɪst] *de (~en)* optimist

optimistisch [ɔptimɪstis] *adj, adv* optimistic: *de zaak ~ bekijken* look on the bright side

optisch [ɔptis] *adj* optic(al), visual

optocht [ɔptɔχt] *de (~en)* procession, parade, march

¹optreden [ɔptredə(n)] *het (~s)* **1** action; way of acting, behaviour; attitude, manner; bearing, demeanour: *het ~ van de politie werd fel bekritiseerd* the conduct of the police was strongly criticized; **2** appearance, performance, show

²optreden [ɔptredə(n)] *vb* **1** appear, perform: *in een film ~* appear in a film; **2** act (as), serve (as); **3** act, take action: *streng ~* take firm action

¹optrekken [ɔptrɛkə(n)] *vb* **1** accelerate; **2** be busy (with), take care (of); hang around (with); **3** rise, lift

²optrekken [ɔptrɛkə(n)] *vb* pull up, haul up, raise, hoist (up): *met opgetrokken knieën* with one's knees pulled up

optuigen [ɔptœyɣə(n)] *vb* dress up, tart up

opvallen [ɔpfɑlə(n)] *vb* strike, be conspicuous, attract attention (*or:* notice): *~ door zijn kleding* attract attention because of (*or:* on account of) one's clothes

opvallend [ɔpfɑlənt] *adj, adv* striking, conspicuous, marked: *het ~ste kenmerk* the most striking feature

opvang [ɔpfɑŋ] *de* relief, emergency measures

opvangen [ɔpfɑŋə(n)] *vb* **1** catch, receive; **2** overhear, pick up, catch: *flarden van een gesprek ~* overhear scraps of conversation; **3** take care of, receive: *de kinderen ~ als ze uit school komen* take care of (*or:* look after) the children after school; **4** catch, collect

opvanghuis [ɔpfɑŋhœys] *het (-huizen)* reception centre, relief centre

opvatten [ɔpfɑtə(n)] *vb* take, interpret: *iets verkeerd (fout) ~* misinterpret (*or:* misunderstand) sth

opvatting [ɔpfɑtɪŋ] *de (~en)* view, notion, opinion

opvegen [ɔpfeɣə(n)] *vb* sweep up

opvoeden [ɔpfudə(n)] *vb* bring up, raise: *goed (or: slecht) opgevoed* well-bred (*or:* ill-bred), well (*or:* badly) brought up

opvoeder [ɔpfudər] *de (~s)* educator, tutor, governess

opvoeding [ɔpfudɪŋ] *de (~en)* upbringing, education: *een strenge ~* a strict upbringing

opvoedkundig [ɔpfutkʏndəχ] *adj, adv* educational, educative, pedagogic(al)

opvoeren [ɔpfurə(n)] *vb* **1** increase, step up, speed up, accelerate: *een motor ~* tune (up) an engine; **2** perform, put on, present

opvoering [ɔpfurɪŋ] *de (~en)* **1** production, presentation; **2** performance

opvolgen [ɔpfɔlɣə(n)] *vb* **1** succeed; **2** follow up; observe, comply with; obey: *iemands advies ~* follow (*or:* take) s.o.'s advice

opvolger [ɔpfɔlɣər] *de (~s)* successor (to)

opvouwbaar [ɔpfɑubar] *adj* folding, fold-up, foldaway, collapsible

opvouwen [ɔpfɑuwə(n)] *vb* fold up, fold away

opvragen [ɔpfraɣə(n)] *vb* claim, ask for, reclaim,

ask for (sth) back

opvreten [ɔpfretə(n)] *vb* eat up, devour

opvrolijken [ɔpfroləkə(n)] *vb* cheer (s.o.) up, brighten (s.o., sth) up

opvullen [ɔpfʏlə(n)] *vb* stuff, fill

opwaarderen [ɔpwardərə(n)] *vb* revalue, upgrade, uprate

opwaarts [ɔpwarts] *adj, adv* upward, upwards: *~e druk* upward pressure, upthrust, *(of a liquid)* buoyancy

opwachten [ɔpwɑχtə(n)] *vb* lie in wait for

¹**opwarmen** [ɔpwɑrmə(n)] *vb* warm up, heat up, reheat

²**opwarmen** [ɔpwɑrmə(n)] *vb* 1 warm up, heat up; 2 *(sport)* warm up, loosen up, limber up

opwegen [ɔpweɣə(n)] *vb* be equal (to), make up (for), compensate (for)

opwekken [ɔpwɛkə(n)] *vb* 1 arouse, excite, stir: *de eetlust (van iem)* ~ whet (s.o.'s) appetite; 2 generate, create

opwelling [ɔpwɛlɪŋ] *de (~en)* impulse: *in een ~ iets doen* do sth on impulse

opwerken [ɔpwɛrkə(n)] *ref vb* work one's way up, climb the ladder

¹**opwinden** [ɔpwɪndə(n)] *vb* 1 wind up; 2 wind; 3 excite, wind *(or:* key, tense) up

²**opwinden** [ɔpwɪndə(n)] *ref vb* become incensed, get excited, fume: *zich ~ over iets* get worked up about sth

opwindend [ɔpwɪndənt] *adj* 1 exciting, thrilling: *het was heel ~* it was quite a thrill; 2 sexy, suggestive

opwinding [ɔpwɪndɪŋ] *de (~en)* excitement, tension: *voor de nodige ~ zorgen* cause quite a stir

opzeg [ɔpsɛχ] *de (Belg)* cancellation, termination, resignation

opzeggen [ɔpsɛɣə(n)] *vb* 1 cancel, terminate, resign; give notice: *zijn betrekking ~* resign from one's job, resign one's post; 2 read out, recite

opzegtermijn [ɔpsɛχtɛrmɛin] *de (~en)* (period, term of) notice

¹**opzet** [ɔpsɛt] *de* 1 organization; scheme, idea; layout, design, plan; set-up; 2 intention, aim

²**opzet** [ɔpsɛt] *het* intention, purpose: *met ~* on purpose

opzettelijk [ɔpsɛtələk] *adj, adv* deliberate, intentional, on purpose: *hij deed het ~* he did it on purpose

¹**opzetten** [ɔpsɛtə(n)] *vb* blow up, arise; gather; rise; set in

²**opzetten** [ɔpsɛtə(n)] *vb* 1 put up, raise, stand (sth, s.o.) up: *een tent ~* pitch *(or:* put up) a tent; 2 put on: *zijn hoed ~* put one's hat on; *theewater ~* put the kettle on (for tea); 3 set up, start (off): *een zaak ~* set up in business, set up shop; 4 stuff

opzicht [ɔpsɪχt] *het (~en)* respect, aspect: *ten opzichte van: a)* compared with *(or:* to), in relation to; *b)* with respect *(or:* regard) to, as regards; *in geen enkel ~* in no way, not in any sense

opzichter [ɔpsɪχtər] *de (~s)* 1 supervisor, overseer,

superintendent; 2 inspector, (site) foreman

opzichtig [ɔpsɪχtəχ] *adj, adv* showy; blatant

¹**opzien** [ɔpsin] *vb* 1 look up: *daar zullen ze van ~* that'll make them sit up (and take notice); 2 (with *tegen)* not be able to face, shrink from: *ergens als (tegen) een berg tegen ~* dread sth

²**opzien** [ɔpsin] *het* stir, fuss, amazement: *veel ~ baren* cause quite a stir *(or:* fuss)

opzienbarend [ɔpsimbɑrənt] *adj* sensational, spectacular, stunning

opziener [ɔpsinər] *de (~s)* supervisor, inspector

opzij [ɔpsɛi] *adv* 1 aside, out of the way; 2 at *(or:* on) one side

opzitten [ɔpsɪtə(n)] *vb* sit up (and beg) ‖ *hij heeft er 20 jaar tropen ~* he's been in the tropics 20 years

opzoeken [ɔpsukə(n)] *vb* 1 look up, find: *een adres ~* look up an address; 2 look up, call on

opzuigen [ɔpsœyɣə(n)] *vb* suck up, hoover up, vacuum up: *limonade door een rietje ~* drink lemonade through a straw

opzwellen [ɔpswɛlə(n)] *vb* swell (up, out), bulge, billow, balloon

oraal [oral] *adj, adv* oral

orakel [orakəl] *het (~s)* oracle

orang-oetang [orɑŋutɑŋ] *de (~s)* orang-utan

¹**oranje** [orɑɲə] *het (~s) (color)* orange, *(traffic lights)* amber

²**oranje** [orɑɲə] *adj* orange, *(traffic lights)* amber

Oranje-Nassau [orɑɲənɑsɑu] *het* Orange Nassau

orchidee [orχide] *de (~ën)* orchid

orde [ɔrdə] *de (~n, ~s)* 1 order: *voor de goede ~ wijs ik u erop dat ...* for the record, I would like to remind you that ...; *iem tot de ~ roepen* call s.o. to order; 2 order, discipline: *verstoring van de openbare ~* disturbance of the peace; *dat komt (wel) in ~* it will turn out all right *(or:* OK); *in ~!* all right!, fine!, OK!; *iem een ~ verlenen* invest s.o. with a decoration, decorate s.o.

ordelijk [ɔrdələk] *adj, adv* neat, tidy

ordenen [ɔrdənə(n)] *vb* arrange, sort (out)

ordening [ɔrdənɪŋ] *de (~en)* 1 arrangement, organization; 2 regulation, structuring

order [ɔrdər] *het, de (~s)* order; instruction, command: *uitstellen tot nader ~* put off until further notice; *een ~ plaatsen voor twee vrachtauto's bij D.* order two lorries from D.

ordeverstoring [ɔrdəvərstorɪŋ] *de (~en)* disturbance, disturbance *(or:* breach) of the peace

ordinair [ɔrdinɛːr] *adj, adv* 1 common, vulgar, coarse, crude; 2 common, ordinary, normal

ordner [ɔrtnər] *de (~s)* (document) file

orgaan [orɣan] *het (organen)* organ

orgaandonatie [orχandona(t)si] *de (~s)* organ donation

orgaantransplantatie [orɣantrɑnsplɑnta(t)si] *de* organ transplant(ation)

organisatie [orɣaniza(t)si] *de (~s)* 1 organization, arrangement; 2 organization, society, association

organisator [orɣanizatɔr] *de (~en)* organizer

organisatorisch [ɔrɣanizatˈɔris] *adj, adv* organizational

organiseren [ɔrɣanizerə(n)] *vb* **1** organize, arrange; **2** organize, fix up, stage

organisme [ɔrɣanˌsmə] *het (~n)* organism

organist [ɔrɣanˌst] *de (~en)* organist, organ player

orgasme [ɔrɣasmə] *het (~n)* orgasm, climax

orgel [ˈɔrɣəl] *het (~s)* (pipe) organ: *een ~ draaien* grind an organ

orgelman [ˈɔrɣəlman] *de* organ-grinder

orgie [ˈɔrɣi] *de (~ën)* orgy, revelry

Oriënt [orijˌɛnt] *het, de* Orient

oriëntaal [orijɛntal] *adj* oriental

oriëntatie [orijɛntaˈ(t)si] *de* orientation, information: *zijn ~ kwijtraken* lose one's bearings

oriënteren [orijɛnterə(n)] *ref vb* **1** orientate oneself; **2** look around

originaliteit [oriɣinaliteˌit] *de* originality

origine [oriˈʒinə] *de* origin: *zij zijn van Franse ~* they are of French origin (*or:* extraction)

origineel [oriˈʒinel] *adj, adv* original

orkaan [ɔrkan] *de (orkanen)* hurricane

orkest [ɔrkˌɛst] *het (~en)* orchestra

os [ɔs] *de (~sen)* bullock, ox: *slapen als een ~* sleep like a log

ossenstaartsoep [ɔsə(n)startsup] *de* oxtail soup

otter [ˈɔtər] *de (~s)* otter

oubollig [aubɔlˌəɣ] *adj* corny, waggish

oud [aut] *adj* **1** old: *zo'n veertig jaar ~* fortyish; *vijftien jaar ~* fifteen years old (*or:* of age), aged fifteen; *hij werd honderd jaar ~* he lived to (be) a hundred; *de ~ste zoon: a)* the elder son; *b)* the oldest son; *haar ~ere zusje* her elder (*or:* big) sister; *hoe ~ ben je?* how old are you?; *toen zij zo ~ was als jij* when she was your age; *zij zijn even ~* they are the same age; *hij is vier jaar ~er dan ik* he is four years older than me; *kinderen van zes jaar en ~er* children from six upwards; **2** old, aged: *de ~e dag* old age; *men is nooit te ~ om te leren* you are never too old to learn; **3** old, ancient, long-standing: *een ~e mop* a corny joke; *~ papier* waste paper; *~er in dienstjaren* senior; **4** ancient, outdated, archaic: *~ nummer* back issue; **5** ex-, former, old: *~ en jong* young and old; *~ en nieuw vieren* see in the New Year

oudejaarsavond [audəjarsˌavɔnt] *de (~en)* New Year's Eve

ouder [ˈaudər] *de (~s)* parent: *mijn ~s* my parents, my folks

ouderavond [ˈaudəravɔnt] *de (~en)* parents' evening

ouderdom [ˈaudərdɔm] *de* age; (old) age

ouderejaars [audərəjars] *de* older student, senior student

ouderlijk [ˈaudərlək] *adj* parental

ouderling [ˈaudərlɪŋ] *de (~en)* church warden, elder

ouderraad [ˈaudərat] *de (-raden)* parents' council

ouderwets [audərwˌɛts] *adj, adv* old-fashioned, outmoded

oudheid [ˈaudhɛit] *de (-heden)* antiquity, ancient times

oudjaar [autjˌar] *het* New Year's Eve

oudje [ˈauʧə] *het (~s)* old person, old chap, old fellow, old dear, old girl

oud-leerling [ˈautlerlɪŋ] *de (~en)* former pupil

oudoom [ˈautom] *de (~s)* great-uncle

oudsher [ˈautshɛr] *adv* || *van ~* of old, from way back

oudste [ˈautstə] *de (~n)* **1** oldest, eldest: *wie is de ~, jij of je broer?* who is older, you or your brother?; **2** (most) senior

oudtante [ˈautantə] *de (~s)* great-aunt

ouverture [uvɛrtyrə] *de (~s, ~n)* overture, prelude

ouwe [ˈauwə] *de (~n)* **1** chief, boss; **2** old man || *een gouwe ~* a golden oldie

ouwehoer [ˈauwəhur] *de* windbag

ouwel [ˈauwəl] *de* wafer

¹ovaal [oval] *het (ovalen)* oval

²ovaal [oval] *adj* oval

ovatie [ovaˈ(t)si] *de (~s)* ovation

oven [ˈovə(n)] *de (~s)* oven

¹over [ˈovər] *prep* **1** over, above: *~ een periode van …* over a period of …; **2** across, over: *hij werkt ~ de grens* he works across (*or:* over) the border; *~ heuvels* over (*or:* beyond) the hills; *~ straat lopen* walk around; *~ de hele lengte* all along; **3** about: *de winst ~ het vierde kwartaal* the profit over the fourth quarter; **4** by way of, via: *zij communiceren ~ de mobilofoon* they communicate by mobile telephone; *zij reed ~ Nijmegen naar Zwolle* she drove to Zwolle via Nijmegen; *een brug ~ de rivier* a bridge over (*or:* across) the river; **5** about: *verheugd ~* delighted at (*or:* with); **6** over, across, **7** after, in: *zaterdag ~ een week* a week on Saturday; **8** over, past: *zij is twee maanden ~ tijd* she is two months overdue; *tot ~ zijn oren in de problemen zitten* be up to one's neck in trouble; *het is kwart ~ vijf* it is a quarter past five; *het is vijf ~ half zes* it is twenty-five to six

²over [ˈovər] *adj* over, finished: *de pijn is al ~* the pain has gone

³over [ˈovər] *adv* **1** across, over: *zij zijn ~ uit Ankara* they are over from Ankara; *~ en weer* back and forth, from both sides; **2** left, over: *als er genoeg tijd ~ is* if there is enough time left

overal [ˈovəral] *adv* **1** everywhere, anywhere: *~ bekend* widely known; *van ~* from everywhere, from all over the place; **2** everything: *zij weet ~ van* she knows about everything

overall [ˈovərɔːl] *de (~s)* overalls

overbelast [ovərbəlˌast] *adj* overloaded, overburdened

overbelasten [ˌovərbəlastə(n)] *vb* overload, overburden, overtax

overbelasting [ˌovərbəlastɪŋ] *de* stress, strain

overbelichten [ˌovərbəlˌɪχtə(n)] *vb* overexpose

overbevolking [ˌovərbəvɔlkɪŋ] *de* overpopulation

overbezet [ovərbəzˌɛt] *adj* overcrowded: *mijn agenda is al ~* my programme is already overbooked

overblijfsel [ǫvərblɛifsəl] *het (~en)* 1 relic, remnant, *(pl)* remains; 2 *(pl)* remains, leftovers, remnant

overblijven [ǫvərblɛivə(n)] *vb* 1 be left, remain: *van al mijn goede voornemens blijft zo niets over* all my good intentions are coming to nothing now; 2 be left (over)

overblijver [ǫvərblɛivər] *de (~s)* school-luncher

overbodig [ovərbǫdəχ] *adj, adv* superfluous, redundant, unnecessary: *~ te zeggen* needless to say

overboeken [ǫvərbukə(n)] *vb* transfer

overboeking [ǫvərbukiŋ] *de (~en)* transfer (into, to)

overboord [ovərbǫrt] *adv* overboard: *man ~!* man overboard!

overbrengen [ǫvərbrɛŋə(n)] *vb* 1 take (or: bring, carry) (across), move, transfer; 2 convey, communicate: *boodschappen* (or: *iemands groeten) ~* convey messages (or: s.o.'s greetings); 3 pass (on)

overbruggen [ovərbrχʏə(n)] *vb* bridge, tide over

overdaad [ǫvərdat] *de* excess

overdadig [ovərdadəχ] *adj, adv* excessive, profuse, extravagant, lavish, wasteful

overdag [ovərdaχ] *adv* by day, during the daytime

overdekken [ovərdɛkə(n)] *vb* cover

overdekt [ovərdɛkt] *adj* covered: *een ~ zwembad* an indoor swimming pool

overdenken [ovərdɛŋkə(n)] *vb* consider, think over

overdoen [ǫvərdun] *vb* do again: *een examen ~* resit an examination

overdosis [ǫvərdozɪs] *de (-doses)* overdose

overdragen [ǫvərdrayə(n)] *vb* hand over, assign, delegate

overdreven [ovərdrɛvə(n)] *adj, adv* exaggerated: *hij doet (is) wel wat ~* he lays it on a bit thick; *dat is sterk ~* that is highly (or: grossly) exaggerated, that's a bit thick

overdrijven [ovərdrɛivə(n)] *vb* 1 overdo (it, sth), go too far (with sth): *je moet (het) niet ~* you mustn't overdo it (or: things); 2 exaggerate

overdrijving [ovərdrɛiviŋ] *de (~en)* exaggeration; overstatement

overeen [ovərẹn] *adv* 1 to the same thing; 2 crossed || *(Belg) de armen ~* arms crossed

¹**overeenkomen** [ovərẹŋkomə(n)] *vb* 1 correspond (to): *~ met de beschrijving* fit the description; 2 be similar (to): *geheel ~ met* fully correspond to (or: with)

²**overeenkomen** [ovərẹŋkomə(n)] *vb* agree (on), arrange: *zoals overeengekomen* as agreed; *iets met iem ~* arrange sth with s.o.

overeenkomst [ovərẹŋkɔmst] *de (~en)* 1 similarity, resemblance: *~ vertonen met* show similarity to, resemble; 2 agreement

overeenkomstig [ovərẹŋkɔmstəχ] *prep* in accordance with, according to: *~ de verwachtingen* in line with expectations

overeenstemming [ovərẹnstɛmɪŋ] *de* 1 harmony, conformity, agreement: *niet in ~ met* out of line (or: keeping) with, inconsistent with; 2 agreement: *tot (een) ~ komen* come to terms, reach an agreement

overeind [ovərɛint] *adv* 1 upright, on end: *~ gaan staan* stand up (straight), get to one's feet; 2 standing: *~ blijven* keep upright, keep one's footing

overgaan [ǫvəryan] *vb* 1 move over (or: across), go over, cross (over): *de brug ~* go over the bridge, cross (over) the bridge; 2 transfer, pass; 3 move up: *van de vierde naar de vijfde klas ~* move up from the fourth to the fifth form; 4 change, convert, turn: *de kleuren gingen in elkaar over* the colours shaded into one another; 5 move on to, proceed to, turn to; change (over) (to), switch (over) (to): *~ tot de aanschaf van* (or: *het gebruik van*) … start buying (or: using) …; 6 pass (over, away), wear off, blow over: *de pijn zal wel ~* the pain will wear off; 7 ring

overgang [ǫvəryaŋ] *de (~en)* 1 transitional stage, link; 2 transition, change(over); 3 change of life, menopause: *in de ~ zijn* be at the change of life

overgangsperiode [ǫvəryaŋsperijodə] *de (~n, ~s)* transition(al) period

overgangsrapport [ǫvəryaŋsrapɔrt] *het (~en)* end-of-year report

overgave [ǫvəryavə] *de* 1 surrender, capitulation; 2 dedication, devotion, abandon(ment)

¹**overgeven** [ǫvəryevə(n)] *vb* be sick, vomit, throw up

²**overgeven** [ǫvəryevə(n)] *ref vb* surrender

overgevoelig [ovəryəvuləχ] *adj, adv* hypersensitive, oversensitive

overgewicht [ǫvəryəwɪχt] *het* overweight, extra (weight)

¹**overgieten** [ovəryitə(n)] *vb* bathe *(light);* cover

²**overgieten** [ǫvəryitə(n)] *vb* pour (into)

overgooier [ǫvəryojər] *de (~s)* pinafore dress

overgordijn [ǫvəryɔrdɛin] *het (~en)* (long, heavy, lined) curtain

overgroot [ovəryrǫt] *adj* vast, huge: *met overgrote meerderheid* by an overwhelming majority

overgrootmoeder [ǫvəryrotmudər] *de (~s)* great-grandmother

overgrootvader [ǫvəryrotfadər] *de (~s)* great-grandfather

overhaast [ovərhast] *adj, adv* rash, hurried, (over)hasty

overhaasten [ovərhastə(n)] *vb* rush, hurry

overhalen [ǫvərhalə(n)] *vb* 1 persuade, talk (s.o.) into (sth): *iem tot iets ~* talk s.o. into doing sth; 2 pull (on): *de trekker ~* pull the trigger

overhand [ǫvərhɑnt] *de* upper hand, advantage

overhandigen [ovərhɑndəyə(n)] *vb* hand (over), present: *iem iets ~* hand sth over to s.o.

overhangen [ǫvərhɑŋə(n)] *vb* hang over, overhang

overheadsheet [ǫvərhɛːtʃiːt] *de (~s)* overhead sheet, transparency

overhebben [ǫvərhɛbə(n)] *vb* 1 have (for), be prepared to give (for), not begrudge (s.o. sth): *ik zou er alles voor ~* I would do (*or:* give) anything for it; **2** have over, have left: *geen geld meer ~* have no more money left

overheen [ovərhɛn] *adv* **1** over: *daar groeit hij wel ~* he will grow out of it; **2** across, over: *er een doek (or: dweil) ~ halen* run a cloth (*or:* mop) over it; **3** past: *ergens ~ lezen* miss (*or:* overlook) sth

overheersen [ovərhɛrsə(n)] *vb* dominate, predominate

overheersing [ovərhɛrsɪŋ] *de (~en)* rule, oppression

overheid [ovərhɛit] *de (-heden)* **1** government; **2** authority: *de plaatselijke ~* the local authorities

overheidsbedrijf [ovərhɛitsbədrɛif] *het (-bedrijven)* public enterprise, state enterprise, a public utility company

overheidsdienst [ovərhɛitsdinst] *de (~en)* government service, public service, the civil service

overheidsinstelling [ovərhɛitsɪnstɛlɪŋ] *de (~en)* government institution (*or:* agency)

overhellen [ovərhɛlə(n)] *vb* lean (over), tilt (over)

overhemd [ovərhɛmt] *het (~en)* shirt

overhevelen [ovərhevələ(n)] *vb* transfer

overhoop [ovərhop] *adj* in a mess, upside down || *met elkaar ~ liggen* be at odds with each other

overhoophalen [ovərhophalə(n)] *vb* turn upside down

overhoopliggen [ovərhopliɣə(n)] *vb* **1** be in a mess; **2** be at loggerheads (with): *ze liggen altijd met elkaar overhoop* they're always at loggerheads (with one another)

overhoren [ovərhorə(n)] *vb* test

overhoring [ovərhorɪŋ] *de (~en)* test

overhouden [ovərhaudə(n)] *vb* have left, still have

overig [ovərəχ] *adj* remaining, other

overigens [ovərəɣəns] *adv* anyway, for that matter, though

overkant [ovərkɑnt] *de* other side, opposite side: *zij woont aan de ~* she lives across the street

overkijken [ovərkɛikə(n)] *vb* look over: *zijn les ~* look through one's lesson

overkoepelend [ovərkupələnt] *adj, adv* coordinating

overkoken [ovərkokə(n)] *vb* boil over

¹**overkomen** [ovərkomə(n)] *vb* **1** come over: *oma is uit Marokko overgekomen* granny has come over from Morocco; **2** come across, get across

²**overkomen** [ovərkomə(n)] *vb* happen to, come over: *dat kan de beste ~* that could happen to the best of us; *ik wist niet wat mij overkwam* I didn't know what was happening to me

¹**overladen** [ovərladə(n)] *vb* transfer, trans-ship

²**overladen** [ovərladə(n)] *adj* overloaded, overburdened

³**overladen** [ovərladə(n)] *vb* shower, heap on (*or:* upon): *hij werd ~ met werk* he was overloaded with work

overlangs [ovərlɑŋs] *adj, adv* lengthwise, longitu-

dinal: *iets ~ doorsnijden* cut sth lengthwise

overlappen [ovərlɑpə(n)] *vb* overlap

overlast [ovərlɑst] *de* inconvenience, nuisance: *~ veroorzaken* cause trouble (*or:* annoyance)

overlaten [ovərlatə(n)] *vb* **1** leave: *laat dat maar aan mij over!* just leave that to me!; **2** leave (over): *veel* (*or:* niets) *te wensen ~* leave much (*or:* nothing) to be desired

overleden [ovərledə(n)] *adj* dead

overledene [ovərledənə] *de (~n)* deceased

overleg [ovərlɛχ] *het* **1** thought, consideration; **2** consultation, deliberation: *in (nauw) ~ met* in (close) consultation with; *in onderling ~* by mutual agreement

overleggen [ovərlɛɣə(n)] *vb* **1** consider: *hij overlegt wat hem te doen staat* he is considering what he has to do; **2** consult, confer: *iets met iem ~* consult (with) s.o. on sth

overleven [ovərlevə(n)] *vb* survive, outlive

overlevende [ovərlevəndə] *de (~n)* survivor

overleveren [ovərlevərə(n)] *vb* hand over, turn over, turn in

overlezen [ovərlezə(n)] *vb* read over (*or:* through): *een artikel vluchtig ~* skim through an article

overlijden [ovərlɛidə(n)] *vb* die

overlijdensadvertentie [ovərlɛidənsɑtfərtɛnsi] *de (~s)* death announcement (*or:* notice)

overlijdensakte [ovərlɛidənsɑktə] *de (~n, ~s)* death certificate

overloop [ovərlop] *de (-lopen)* landing

overlopen [ovərlopə(n)] *vb* **1** walk over (*or:* across); **2** go over, defect: *~ naar de vijand* desert (*or:* defect) to the enemy; **3** overflow

overloper [ovərlopər] *de (~s)* deserter, defector

overmacht [ovərmɑχt] *de* **1** superior numbers (*or:* strength, forces): *tegenover een geweldige ~ staan* face fearful odds; **2** circumstances beyond one's control; force majeure, Act of God

overmaken [ovərmakə(n)] *vb* transfer, remit

overmeesteren [ovərmɛstərə(n)] *vb* overpower, overcome

overmoed [ovərmut] *de* overconfidence, recklessness

overmoedig [ovərmudəχ] *adj, adv* overconfident, reckless

overmorgen [ovərmɔrɣə(n)] *adv* the day after tomorrow

overnachten [ovərnɑχtə(n)] *vb* stay (*or:* spend) the night, stay (over)

overnachting [ovərnɑχtɪŋ] *de (~en)* **1** stay; **2** night: *het aantal ~en* the number of nights (spent, slept)

overname [ovərnamə] *de* takeover, purchase, taking-over

overnemen [ovərnemə(n)] *vb* **1** receive; **2** take (over): *de macht ~* assume power; **3** adopt: *de gewoonten van een land ~* adopt the customs of a country; **4** take over, buy

overplaatsen [ovərplatsə(n)] *vb* transfer

overplaatsing [ovərplatsɪŋ] *de (~en)* transfer,

move

overplanten [o̱vərplɑntə(n)] *vb* **1** transplant; **2** transplant, graft

overproductie [o̱vərprodyksi] *de* overproduction

¹overrijden [ovərɛi̱də(n)] *vb* run over, knock down

²overrijden [o̱vərɛi̱də(n)] *vb* drive over, ride over

overrijp [ovərɛi̱p] *adj* overripe

overrompelen [ovəro̱mpələ(n)] *vb* (take by) surprise, catch off guard, catch napping

overschakelen [o̱vərsχɑkələ(n)] *vb* **1** switch over; **2** switch (*or:* change, go) over: *op de vierdaagse werkweek* ~ go over to a four-day week

overschakeling [o̱vərsχɑkəlɪŋ] *de* switch-over, changeover

overschatten [ovərsχɑ̱tə(n)] *vb* overestimate, overrate

overschatting [ovərsχɑ̱tɪŋ] *de* (*~en*) overestimation, overrating

overschieten [o̱vərsχi̱tə(n)] *vb* dash over (*or:* across): *het kind was plotseling de weg overgeschoten* the child had suddenly dashed (out) across the road

overschilderen [o̱vərsχi̱ldərə(n)] *vb* repaint

overschot [o̱vərsχɔt] *het* (*~ten*) remainder; remains, residue; remnant(s) ‖ *(Belg)* ~ *van* be absolutely right

¹overschrijven [o̱vərsχrɛi̱və(n)] *vb* overwrite

²overschrijven [o̱vərsχrɛi̱və(n)] *vb* **1** copy; *(depr)* crib: *iets in het net* ~ copy sth out neatly; **2** transfer; put in (s.o.'s) name

overschrijving [o̱vərsχrɛi̱vɪŋ] *de* (*~en*) **1** putting in s.o. (else)'s name; *(sport)* transfer; **2** remittance

¹overslaan [o̱vərslan] *vb* **1** jump (over), be infectious, be catching; **2** break, crack: *met ~de stem* with a catch in one's voice

²overslaan [o̱vərslan] *vb* miss (out), skip, leave out, omit: *één beurt* ~ miss one turn; *een bladzijde* ~ skip a page; *een jaar overslaan* skip a year

overspannen [ovərspɑ̱nə(n)] *adj* **1** overstrained, overtense(d); **2** overwrought: *hij is erg* ~ he is suffering from severe (over)strain

overspel [o̱vərspɛl] *het* adultery

overspelen [o̱vərspelə(n)] *vb* **1** replay: *de wedstrijd moest overgespeeld worden* the match had to be replayed; **2** *(sport)* play on (to), pass the ball on to

overstap [o̱vərstɑp] *de* (*~pen*) changeover, switch-over

overstappen [o̱vərstɑpə(n)] *vb* **1** step over, cross; **2** change, transfer: ~ *op de trein naar Groningen* change to the Groningen train

overste [o̱vərstə] *de* (*~n*) **1** lieutenant-colonel; **2** (father, mother) superior, prior, prioress

oversteek [o̱vərstek] *de* (*-steken*) crossing

oversteekplaats [o̱vərstekplats] *de* (*~en*) crossing(-place), pedestrian crossing

oversteken [o̱vərstekə(n)] *vb* cross (over), go across, come across

overstemmen [ovərstɛ̱mə(n)] *vb* drown (out), shout down

¹overstromen [o̱vərstromə(n)] *vb* **1** flow over, flood; **2** overflow

²overstromen [ovərstro̱mə(n)] *vb* **1** flood, inundate; **2** flood, swamp: *de markt* ~ *met* flood the market with

overstroming [ovərstro̱mɪŋ] *de* (*~en*) flood

overstuur [ovərsty̱r] *adj, adv* upset, shaken

overtocht [o̱vərtɔχt] *de* (*~en*) crossing, voyage

overtollig [ovərtɔ̱ləχ] *adj, adv* **1** surplus, excess; **2** superfluous; redundant

overtreden [ovərtre̱də(n)] *vb* break, violate

overtreder [ovərtre̱dər] *de* (*~s*) offender, wrongdoer

overtreding [ovərtre̱dɪŋ] *de* (*~en*) offence, violation (*or:* breach) (of the rules), *(sport)* foul: *een zware* ~ a bad foul; *een* ~ *begaan tegenover een tegenspeler* foul an opponent

overtreffen [ovərtrɛ̱fə(n)] *vb* exceed, surpass, excel

overtrek [o̱vərtrɛk] *het, de* (*~ken*) cover, case

¹overtrekken [o̱vərtrɛkə(n)] *vb* pass (over)

²overtrekken [o̱vərtrɛkə(n)] *vb* trace: *met inkt* ~ trace in ink

³overtrekken [ovərtrɛ̱kə(n)] *vb* cover, upholster

overtuigd [ovərtœ̱yχt] *adj* confirmed, convinced: *hij was ervan ~ te zullen slagen* he was confident (*or:* sure) that he would succeed; *ik ben er (vast, heilig) van ~ dat* ... I'm (absolutely) convinced that ...

overtuigen [ovərtœ̱yɣə(n)] *vb* convince, persuade

overtuigend [ovərtœ̱yɣənt] *adj, adv* convincing; cogent; persuasive; conclusive

overtuiging [ovərtœ̱yɣɪŋ] *de* (*~en*) conviction, belief, persuasion: *godsdienstige* ~ religious persuasion (*or:* beliefs); *vol (met)* ~ with conviction

overtypen [o̱vərtipə(n)] *vb* retype; type out

overuur [o̱vəryr] *het* (*-uren*) overtime hour; overtime: *overuren maken* work overtime

overval [o̱vərvɑl] *de* (*~len*) surprise attack, raid, hold-up, stick-up

overvallen [ovərvɑ̱lə(n)] *vb* **1** raid, hold up, assault *(pers)*, surprise; **2** surprise, take by surprise, overtake

overvaller [ovərvɑ̱lər] *de* (*~s*) raider, attacker

¹overvaren [o̱vərvarə(n)] *vb* cross (over), sail across

²overvaren [o̱vərvarə(n)] *vb* ferry, take across, put across

oververhit [ovərvərhi̱t] *adj* overheated: *de gemoederen raakten* ~ feelings ran high

oververhitten [ovərvərhi̱tə(n)] *vb* overheat

oververhitting [ovərvərhi̱tɪŋ] *de* overheating

oververmoeid [ovərvərmu̱it] *adj* overtired, exhausted

oververven [o̱vərvɛrvə(n)] *vb* paint over, repaint, redye

overvloed [o̱vərvlut] *de* abundance

overvloedig [ovərvlu̱dəχ] *adj, adv* abundant, plentiful, copious

overvoeren [ovərvu̱rə(n)] *vb* glut, overstock, oversupply, surfeit

overvol [ovərvⱭl] *adj* overfull, overcrowded, packed

overwaaien [ọvərwajə(n)] *vb* blow over *(also fig)*

overwaarderen [ọvərwardərə(n)] *vb* overvalue, overrate

¹**overweg** [ovərwɛχ] *adv* ‖ *met een nieuwe machine ~ kunnen* know how to handle a new machine; *goed met elkaar ~ kunnen* get along well

²**overweg** [ọvərwɛχ] *de* level crossing: *een bewaakte ~* a guarded (*or:* manned) level crossing

overwegen [ovərwẹɣə(n)] *vb* consider, think over, think out: *de nadelen (risico's) ~* count the cost; *wij ~ een nieuwe auto te kopen* we are thinking of (*or:* considering) buying a new car

overwegend [ovərwẹɣənt] *adv* predominantly, mainly, for the most part

overweging [ovərwẹɣɪŋ] *de (~en)* **1** consideration, thought; **2** consideration, ground, reason

overweldigen [ovərwɛldəɣə(n)] *vb* overwhelm, overcome

overweldigend [ovərwɛldəɣənt] *adj* overwhelming, overpowering: *een ~e meerderheid halen* win a landslide victory

overwerk [ọvərwɛrk] *het* overtime (work)

overwerken [ọvərwɛrkə(n)] *vb* work overtime

overwerkt [ovərwɛrkt] *adj* overworked, overstrained

overwicht [ọvərwɪχt] *het* ascendancy, preponderance, authority

overwinnaar [ovərwɪnar] *de (~s)* victor, winner, conqueror

overwinnen [ovərwɪnə(n)] *vb* **1** defeat, overcome; **2** conquer, overcome; **3** conquer, overcome, surmount

overwinning [ovərwɪnɪŋ] *de (~en)* victory, conquest, triumph, win: *een verpletterende ~* a sweeping victory

overwinteren [ovərwɪntərə(n)] *vb* **1** (over)winter; **2** hibernate

overwintering [ovərwɪntərɪŋ] *de (~en)* (over)wintering, hibernation

overwoekeren [ovərwukərə(n)] *vb* overgrow, overrun: *overwoekerd worden door onkruid* become overgrown with weeds

overzees [ovərzẹs] *adj* oversea(s)

overzetten [ọvərzɛtə(n)] *vb* take across (*or:* over); ferry (across, over): *iem de grens ~* deport s.o.

overzicht [ọvərzɪχt] *het (~en)* **1** survey, view: *~ vanuit de lucht* bird's-eye view; *ik heb geen enkel ~ meer* I have lost all track of the situation; **2** survey, (over)view, summary, review

overzichtelijk [ovərzɪχtələk] *adj, adv* well-organized; clearly set out

overzichtelijkheid [ovərzɪχtələkhɛit] *de* clear organization: *ter wille van de ~* for easy reference, for convenience of comparison

overzien [ovərzịn] *vb* survey; overlook, command (a view of); review: *de gevolgen zijn niet te ~* the consequences are incalculable

overzijde [ọvərzɛidə] *de* other side, opposite side: *aan de ~ van het gebouw* opposite the building

overzwemmen [ọvərzwɛmə(n)] *vb* swim (across): *het Kanaal ~* swim the Channel

OV-jaarkaart [ovejarkart] *de (~en)* annual season ticket, travel card

OVSE *de Organisatie voor Veiligheid en Samenwerking in Europa* OSCE

ovulatie [ovyla(t)si] *de (~s)* ovulation

oxidatie [ɔksida(t)si] *de (~s)* oxidation

oxide [ɔksịdə] *het (~n, ~s)* oxide

ozon [ozɔn] *het, de* ozone

ozonlaag [ozɔnlaχ] *de* ozone layer

p

pa [pa] *de (~'s)* dad(dy), pa: *haar ~ en ma* her mum
and dad(dy)

p.a. [pea] *per adres* c/o

paadje [paːcə] *het (~s)* path; trail

paal [paːl] *de (palen)* **1** post, stake, pole, pile; **2**
(goal)post: *hij schoot tegen (op) de ~* he hit the
(goal)post; *voor ~ staan* look foolish (*or:* stupid)

paar [par] *het (paren)* **1** pair, couple: *twee ~ sokken*
two pairs of socks; **2** (a) few, (a) couple of

paard [part] *het (~en)* **1** horse: *op het verkeerde ~
wedden* back the wrong horse; *men moet een gegeven ~ niet in de bek zien* never look a gift horse in
the mouth; **2** (vaulting) horse; **3** knight

paardenbloem [pardə(n)blum] *de (~en)* dandelion

paardenkastanje [pardə(n)kastaɲə] *de (~s)* horse
chestnut

paardenkracht [pardə(n)kraxt] *de (~en)* horsepower

paardenrennen [pardə(n)rɛnə(n)] *de* horse races

paardensport [pardə(n)spɔrt] *de* equestrian
sport(s); horse racing

paardenstaart [pardə(n)start] *de (~en)* **1** horse-
tail; **2** ponytail

paardentram [pardə(n)trɛm] *de (~s)* horse tram

paardrijden [partrɛidə(n)] *vb* ride (horseback): *zij
zit op ~* she is taking riding lessons

paars [pars] *adj* purple

paartijd [partɛit] *de* mating season, rut

paartje [parcə] *het (~s)* couple, pair: *een pas getrouwd ~* a newly wed couple, newly-weds

paasbest [pazbɛst] *adj || op zijn ~ zijn* be all dressed
up

paasdag [pazdax] *de (~en)* Easter Day: *Eerste
paasdag* Easter Sunday

paasfeest [pasfest] *het (~en)* Easter

paashaas [pashas] *de (-hazen)* Easter bunny (*or:*
rabbit)

paasvakantie [pasfakɑnsi] *de (~s)* Easter holidays

paasviering [pasfirɪŋ] *de (~en)* Easter service

paaszaterdag [pasatərdax] *de* Holy Saturday,
Easter Saturday

pabo [pabo] *de (~'s) pedagogische academie voor
het basisonderwijs* teacher training college (for primary education)

pacht [paxt] *de (~en)* lease: *in ~ nemen* lease, take
on lease

pachten [paxtə(n)] *vb* lease, rent

pachter [paxtər] *de (~s)* leaseholder, lessee, tenant
(farmer)

pachtgeld [paxtxɛlt] *het (~en)* rent

pacifisme [pasifɪsmə] *het* pacifism

pacifist [pasifɪst] *de (~en)* pacifist

pacifistisch [pasifɪstis] *adj, adv* pacifist(ic)

pact [pɑkt] *het (~en)* pact, treaty

¹pad [pɑt] *het* **1** path; walk; track; trail; gangway,
aisle: *platgetreden ~en bewandelen* walk the beaten
path (*or:* tracks); **2** path, way: *iem op het slechte ~
brengen* lead s.o. astray; *hij is het slechte ~ opgegaan*
he has taken to crime; *op ~ gaan* set off

²pad [pɑt] *de* toad || *(Belg) een ~ in iemands korf zet-
ten* thwart s.o., set off

paddestoel [pɑdəstul] *de (~en) (general)* fungus;
(poisonous) toadstool; *(edible)* mushroom

padvinder [pɑtfɪndər] *de (~s)* (boy) scout; girl
guide

padvinderij [pɑtfɪndərɛi] *de* scouting

paffen [pɑfə(n)] *vb* puff

pag. *pagina* p.

pagina [paɣina] *de (~'s)* page: *~ 2 en 3* pages 2 and 3

pagode [paɣodə] *de (~n, ~s)* pagoda

pak [pɑk] *het (~ken)* **1** pack(age); packet; parcel;
carton: *een ~ melk* a carton of milk; *een ~ sneeuw* a
layer of snow; **2** suit; **3** bale; batch; bundle; packet:
een ~ oud papier a batch (*or:* bundle) of waste paper; *een kind een ~ slaag geven* spank (*or:* wallop) a
child, give a child a spanking

pakhuis [pɑkhœys] *het (pakhuizen)* warehouse,
storehouse

Pakistaan [pakistan] *de (Pakistani)* Pakistani

Pakistaans [pakistans] *adj* Pakistan(i), of Pakistan,
from Pakistan

Pakistan [pakistan] *het* Pakistan

pakje [pɑkjə] *het (~s)* parcel, present

¹pakken [pɑkə(n)] *vb* **1** get, take, fetch: *een pen ~* get
a pen; *pak een stoel* grab a chair; **2** catch, grasp,
grab, seize: *een kind (eens lekker) ~* hug (*or:* cuddle) a child; *de daders zijn nooit gepakt* the offend-
ers were never caught; *proberen iem te ~ te krijgen*
try to get hold of s.o.; *iets te ~ krijgen* lay one's
hands on sth; *(fig) iem te ~ nemen* have a go at s.o.;
nou heb ik je te ~ got you!; als ik hem te ~ krijg if I
catch him, if I lay hands on him; *iem op iets ~* get
s.o. on sth; *pak me dan, als je kan!* catch me if you
can!; **3** pack, wrap up: *zijn boeltje bij elkaar ~* pack
(one's bags)

²pakken [pɑkə(n)] *vb* hold, grip; bite; take

pakkend [pɑkənt] *adj* catching, catchy; fascinating,
appealing, fetching; arresting; gripping; catching,
attractive: *een ~e titel* a catchy (*or:* an arresting) title

pakkerd [pɑkərt] *de (~s)* hug and a kiss

pakket [pɑkɛt] *het (~ten)* **1** parcel; **2** pack, kit, *(fig)*
package

pakketpost [pɑkɛtpɔst] *de* parcel post

pakkie-an [pɑkiɑn] ‖ *dat is niet mijn* ~ that's not my department

pakking [pɑkɪŋ] *de (~en)* gasket, packing

pakpapier [pɑkpapir] *het* packing paper, wrapping paper

paksoi [pɑksɔj] *de* pak-choi cabbage

pakweg [pɑkwɛχ] *adv* roughly, approximately, about, around

paleis [palɛis] *het (paleizen)* **1** palace, court; **2** hall

Palestijn [palǝstɛin] *de (~en)* Palestinian

Palestijns [palǝstɛins] *adj* Palestinian, Palestine

Palestina [palǝstina] *het* Palestine

palet [palɛt] *het (~ten)* palette

paling [palɪŋ] *de (~en)* eel; eels

pallet [pɛlǝt] *de (~s)* pallet (board)

palm [pɑlm] *de (~en)* palm

palmboom [pɑlmbom] *de (-bomen)* palm

Palmpasen [pɑlmpasǝn] *de* Palm Sunday

pamflet [pɑmflɛt] *het (~ten)* pamphlet, broadsheet

Pampus [pɑmpʏs] *het* ‖ *voor* ~ *liggen* be dead to the world, be out cold

pan [pɑn] *de (~nen)* **1** pan: *(fig) dat swingt de* ~ *uit* that's really far out; **2** (pan)tile: *in de* ~ *hakken* cut to ribbons (*or*: pieces), make mincemeat of

Panama [panama] *het* Panama

Panamees [panames] *de* Panamanian

pand [pɑnt] *het* **1** premises, property, building, house; **2** pawn, pledge, security

panda [pɑnda] *de (~'s)* panda

pandjesjas [pɑncɔsjas] *de (~sen)* tailcoat

paneel [panel] *het (panelen)* panel

paneermeel [panɛrmel] *het* breadcrumbs

panel [pɛnǝl] *het (~s)* panel

panfluit [pɑnflœyt] *de (~en)* pan pipe(s)

pang [pɑŋ] *int* pow, bang

paniek [panik] *de* panic, alarm, terror: *er ontstond* ~ panic broke out; *geen* ~*!* don't panic

panisch [panis] *adj, adv* panic, frantic: *een ~e angst hebben voor iets* (*or*: *om iets te doen*) be terrified (of doing) sth

panne [pɑnǝ] *de* breakdown: ~ *hebben* have a breakdown, have engine trouble

pannenkoek [pɑnǝ(n)kuk] *de (~en)* pancake

pannenkoekmix [pɑnǝ(n)kukmɪks] *de (roughly)* batter mix

pannenlap [pɑnǝ(n)lɑp] *de (~pen)* oven cloth, oven glove

pannenset [pɑnǝ(n)sɛt] *de (~s)* set of (pots and) pans

panorama [panorama] *het (~'s)* panorama

pantalon [pɑntalɔn] *de (~s)* (pair of) trousers, (pair of) slacks: *twee ~s* two pair(s) of trousers

panter [pɑntǝr] *de (~s)* panther, leopard

pantoffel [pɑntɔfǝl] *de (~s)* (carpet) slipper

pantomime [pɑntomim] *de (~s, ~n)* mime, dumb-show

pantser [pɑntsǝr] *het (~s)* **1** (plate) armour, armour-plating; **2** (suit of) armour

pantserauto [pɑn(t)sǝrauto] *de (~'s)* armoured car

pantserdivisie [pɑn(t)sǝrdivizi] *de (~s)* armoured division

pantseren [pɑntsǝrǝ(n)] *vb* armour(-plate)

panty [pɛnti] *de (~'s)* (pair of) tights: *drie panty's* three pairs of tights

pantykous [pɛntikaus] *de (~en)* nylon knee-socks, pop sock

pap [pɑp] *de (~pen)* porridge; pap: *ik lust er wel* ~ *van* this is meat and drink to me; *geen* ~ *meer kunnen zeggen*: *a)* be (dead)beat, be whacked (out), be fagged (out); *b)* be full up

papa [papa] *de (~'s)* papa, dad(dy)

papaver [papavǝr] *de (~s)* poppy

papegaai [papǝɣaj] *de (~en)* parrot

paperassen [papǝrɔsǝ(n)] *de* papers, paperwork, bumf

paperclip [pepǝrklɪp] *de (~s)* paperclip

Papiamento [papijamɛnto] *het* Papiamento

papier [papir] *het (~en)* **1** paper: *zijn gedachten op* ~ *zetten* put one's thoughts down on paper; **2** paper, document

papieren [papirǝ(n)] *adj* paper

papiergeld [papirɣɛlt] *het* paper money: €*100,- in* ~ 100 euros in notes

papiertje [papircǝ] *het (~s)* piece of paper, wrapper

papierversnipperaar [papirvǝrsnɪpǝrar] *de (~s)* (paper) shredder

papil [papɪl] *de (~len)* papilla

paplepel [pɑplepǝl] *de (~s)* ‖ *dat is hem met de* ~ *ingegeven* he learned it at his mother's knee

Papoea [papuwa] *de (~'s)* Papuan

Papoea-Nieuw-Guinea [papuwaniwɣinеja] *het* Papua New Guinea

pappa [pɑpa] *de (~'s)* papa, dad, daddy

pappie [pɑpi] *de (~s)* daddy

paprika [paprika] *de (~'s)* (sweet) pepper

paps [pɑps] *de* dad, daddy

papyrus [papirʏs] *de (~sen)* papyrus

paraaf [paraf] *de (parafen)* initials

paraat [parat] *adj* ready, prepared

parabel [parabǝl] *de (~s, ~en)* parable

parachute [parafyt] *de (~s)* parachute

parachutespringen [parafytsprɪŋǝ(n)] *vb* parachuting

parachutist [parafytɪst] *de (~en)* parachutist

paracommando [parakɔmɑndo] *de (~'s) (Belg)* peacekeeper

parade [parɑdǝ] *de (~s)* parade

paradepaard [parɑdǝpart] *het (~en)* showpiece

paradijs [paradɛis] *het (paradijzen)* paradise

paradox [paradɔks] *de (~en)* paradox

paradoxaal [paradɔksal] *adj, adv* paradoxical

paraferen [parafеrǝ(n)] *vb* initial

paragnost [paraɣnɔst] *de (~en)* psychic

paragraaf [paraɣraf] *de (-grafen)* section

¹parallel [paralɛl] *de (~len)* parallel: *deze* ~ *kan nog verder doorgetrokken worden* this parallel (*or*: analogy) can be carried further

²**parallel** [paralɛl] *adj, adv* **1** parallel (to, with): *die wegen lopen ~ aan (met) elkaar* those roads run parallel to each other; **2** parallel (to), analogous (to, with)

parallellogram [paralɛloɣrɑm] *het (~men)* parallelogram

paranoia [paranɔja] *de* paranoia

paranoïde [paranowidə] *adj* paranoid

paranormaal [paranɔrmal] *adj, adv* paranormal, psychic

paraplu [paraply] *de (~'s)* umbrella

parapsychologie [parapsiχoloɣi] *de* parapsychology, psychic research

parasiet [parasit] *de (~en)* **1** parasite; **2** parasite, sponge(r)

parasiteren [parasiterə(n)] *vb* parasitize, *(fig)* sponge (on, off)

parasol [parasɔl] *de (~s)* sunshade, parasol

paratyfus [paratifʏs] *de* paratyphoid (fever)

parcours [pɑrkur(s)] *het (~en)* track

pardoes [pɑrdus] *adv* bang, slap, smack

¹**pardon** [pɑrdɔn] *het* pardon, mercy

²**pardon** [pɑrdɔn] *int* pardon (me), I beg your pardon, excuse me, (so) sorry: *stond ik op uw tenen? ~!* sorry, did I step on your toe?

parel [parəl] *de (~s)* pearl

¹**paren** [parə(n)] *vb* mate (with)

²**paren** [parə(n)] *vb (fig)* combine (with), couple (with): *gepaard gaan met* go (hand in hand) with

parfum [pɑrfʏm] *het, de (~s)* perfume, scent

paria [parija] *de (~'s)* pariah, outcast

Parijs [parɛis] *het* Paris

Parisienne [pariʒɛnə] *de* Parisian

park [pɑrk] *het (~en)* **1** park; **2** fleet; plant

parka [pɑrka] *de (~'s)* parka

parkeerautomaat [pɑrkerautomat] *de (-automaten)* (car-park) ticket machine (*or:* dispenser), *(Am)* (parking lot) ticket machine

parkeerboete [pɑrkerbutə] *de (~s)* parking fine

parkeerbon [pɑrkerbɔn] *de (~nen)* parking ticket

parkeergarage [pɑrkerɣaraʒə] *de (~s)* (underground) car park, *(Am)* (underground) parking garage

parkeergeld [pɑrkerɣɛlt] *het* parking fee

parkeerplaats [pɑrkerplats] *de (~en)* parking place (*or:* space), car park, *(Am)* parking lot

parkeerschijf [pɑrkersχɛif] *de (-schijven)* (parking) disc

parkeerterrein [pɑrkertɛrɛin] *het (~en)* car park, *(Am)* parking lot

parkeerverbod [pɑrkervɔrbɔt] *het* parking ban, *(on notice)* No Parking: *hier geldt een ~* this is a no-parking zone

parkeren [pɑrkerə(n)] *vb* park, pull in (*or:* over)

parket [pɑrkɛt] *het (~ten)* **1** parquet (floor); **2** public prosecutor

parkiet [pɑrkit] *de (~en)* parakeet

parkinson [pɑrkinsɔn] *de* Parkinson's disease

parlement [pɑrləmɛnt] *het (~en)* parliament: *in het ~* in parliament

parlementair [pɑrləmɛntɛːr] *adj* parliamentary

parlementariër [pɑrləmɛntarijər] *de (~s)* member of (a) parliament, parliamentarian, representative

parlofoon [pɑrlofɔn] *de (~s) (Belg)* intercom

parmantig [pɑrmɑntəχ] *adj, adv* jaunty, dapper

Parmezaans [pɑrmezans] *adj* || *~e kaas* Parmesan cheese

parochiaal [parɔχijal] *adj* parochial

parochiaan [parɔχijan] *de (parochianen)* parishioner

parochie [parɔχi] *de (~s)* parish

parodie [parodi] *de (~ën)* parody (of, on), travesty (of)

parool [parɔl] *het (parolen)* watchword, slogan: *opletten is het ~* pay attention is the motto

part [pɑrt] *het* share, portion || *voor mijn ~* for all I care, as far as I'm concerned

¹**particulier** [pɑrtikylir] *de (~en)* private individual (*or:* person): *geen verkoop aan ~en* trade (sales) only

²**particulier** [pɑrtikylir] *adj, adv* private: *het ~ initiatief* private enterprise

partij [pɑrtɛi] *de (~en)* **1** party, side: *de strijdende ~en* the warring parties; *~ kiezen* take sides; **2** set, batch, lot, consignment, shipment: *bij (in) ~en verkopen* sell in lots; **3** *(mus)* part; **4** game

partijdig [pɑrtɛidəχ] *adj, adv* bias(s)ed, partial

partijleider [pɑrtɛilɛidər] *de (~s)* party leader

partituur [pɑrtityr] *de (partituren)* score

partizaan [pɑrtizan] *de (partizanen)* partisan

partner [pɑrtnər] *de (~s)* **1** partner, companion; **2** (co-)partner, associate

partnerregister [pɑrtnərəɣistər] *het* register in which cohabitation contracts are officially recorded

parttimebaan [pɑːrtajmban] *de* part-time job

¹**pas** [pɑs] *de* **1** step, pace, gait: *iem de ~ afsnijden* cut (*or:* head) s.o. off; **2** pass; **3** pass, passport: *het leger moest er aan te ~ komen* the army had to step in; *goed van ~ komen* come in handy (*or:* useful); *dat komt uitstekend van ~* that's just the thing; *altijd wel van ~ komen* always come in handy

²**pas** [pɑs] *adv* **1** (only) just, recently: *hij begint ~* he is just beginning, he has only just started; *~ geplukt* freshly picked; *een ~ getrouwd stel* a newly-wed couple; *~ geverfd* wet paint; *ik werk hier nog maar ~* I'm new here (*or:* to this job); **2** only, just: *hij is ~ vijftig (jaar)* he's only fifty; **3** only, not until: *~ toen vertelde hij het mij* it was only then that he told me; *~ toen hij weg was, begreep ik ...* it was only after he had left that I understood ...; *~ geleden, ~ een paar dagen terug* only recently, only the other day; **4** really: *dat is ~ een vent* he's (what I call) a real man; *dat is ~ hard werken!* now, that really is hard work!

Pasen [pasə(n)] *de* Easter

pasfoto [pɑsfoto] *de (~'s)* passport photo(graph)

pasgeboren [pɑsχəborə(n)] *adj* newborn, newly born

pasgetrouwd [pɑsχətrɑut] *adj* newly married
pashokje [pɑshɔkjə] *het (~s)* fitting room
pasje [pɑʃə] *het (~s)* **1** step; **2** pass
paskamer [pɑskamər] *de (~s)* fitting room
pasklaar [pɑsklar] *adj* (made) to measure, fitted; *(fig)* ready-made
paspoort [pɑsport] *het (~en)* passport
paspoortcontrole [pɑspoortkɔntroːlə] *de* passport control
passaatwind [pɑsatwɪnt] *de (~en)* trade wind
passage [pɑsaʒə] *de (~s)* passage; extract: *een ~ uit een gedicht voorlezen* read an extract from a poem
passagier [pɑsaʒir] *de (~s)* passenger
passagiersschip [pɑsaʒirsχɪp] *het (-schepen)* passenger ship
passant [pɑsɑnt] || *en ~* in passing; *(chess) en passant slaan* take (a pawn) en passant
¹passen [pɑsə(n)] *vb* **1** fit: *het past precies* it fits like a glove; *deze sleutel past op de meeste sloten* this key fits most locks; **2** *(with bij)* fit, go (with), match: *deze hoed past er goed bij* this hat is a good match; *ze ~ goed (or: slecht) bij elkaar* they are well-matched *(or: ill-matched)*; **3** *(with op)* look after, take care of: *op de kinderen ~* look after the children; *pas op het afstapje (or: je hoofd)* watch/mind the step *(or:* your head); **4** *(cards)* pass
²passen [pɑsə(n)] *vb* **1** fit: *~ en meten* try it in all different ways; *met wat ~ en meten komen we wel rond* with a bit of juggling we'll manage; **2** pay with the exact money: *hebt u het niet gepast?* haven't you got the exact change? *(or:* money?); **3** try on
passend [pɑsənt] *adj, adv* **1** suitable (for), suited (to), appropriate: *niet bij elkaar ~e partners* incompatible partners; *niet bij elkaar ~e sokken* odd socks; *slecht bij elkaar ~* ill-matched; **2** proper, becoming: *een ~ gebruik maken van* make proper use of
passer [pɑsər] *de (~s)* compass
¹passeren [pɑsɛrə(n)] *vb* pass, overtake: *de auto passeerde (de fietser)* the car overtook (the cyclist); *een huis ~* pass (by) a house
²passeren [pɑsɛrə(n)] *vb* **1** pass through; cross: *de grens (or: een brug) ~* cross the border *(or:* a bridge); *de vijftig gepasseerd zijn* have turned fifty; **2** pass over
passie [pɑsi] *de (~s)* passion (for), zeal (for), enthusiasm (for)
passief [pɑsif] *adj, adv* passive
passievrucht [pɑsivrʏχt] *de (~en)* passion fruit
passiva [pɑsiva] *de* liabilities
pasta [pɑsta] *het, de (~'s)* **1** paste; **2** pasta
pastei [pɑstɛi] *de (~en)* pasty, pie
pastel [pɑstɛl] *het (~s)* pastel
pasteltint [pɑstɛltɪnt] *de (~en)* pastel shade *(or:* tone)
pasteuriseren [pɑstørizɛrə(n)] *vb* pasteurize
pastoor [pɑstor] *de (~s)* (parish) priest, padre: *Meneer Pastoor* Father
pastor [pɑstɔr] *de (~s, ~es)* pastor, minister,

(Roman Catholicism) priest
pastorie [pɑstori] *de (~ën)* parsonage; *(Roman Catholicism)* presbytery
pasvorm [pɑsfɔrm] *de (~en)* fit
pat [pɑt] *adj* stalemate: *iem ~ zetten* stalemate s.o.
patat [pɑtɑt] *de* chips, French fries: *een zakje ~* a bag of chips; *~ met* chips with mayonnaise
patatgeneratie [pɑtɑtɣenəra(t)si] *de* couch potato generation
patatje [pɑtɑcə] *het (~s)* (portion of) chips
patattent [pɑtɑtɛnt] *de* chip shop
paté [pate] *de (~s)* pâté
patent [patɛnt] *het (~en)* patent
pater [patər] *de (~s)* father
pathetisch [patetis] *adj, adv* pathetic
patience [paʃɑ̃s] *het* patience, *(Am)* solitaire
patiënt [paʃɛnt] *de (~en)* patient: *zijn ~en bezoeken* do one's rounds
patio [pa(t)s(i)jo] *de (~'s)* patio
patisserie [patisəri] *de (~ën)* **1** pastries; **2** pastry shop
patrijs [patrɛis] *de (patrijzen)* partridge
patrijspoort [patrɛisport] *de (~en)* porthole
patriottisch [patrijɔtis] *adj* patriotic
patronaat [patronat] *het (patronaten) (Belg)* employers
patrones [patronɛs] *de (~sen)* **1** patron (saint); **2** patron(ess)
¹patroon [patron] *de* **1** patron; **2** boss
²patroon [patron] *de* cartridge: *een losse ~* a blank
³patroon [patron] *het* **1** pattern, design: *volgens een vast ~* according to an established pattern; **2** pattern, style
patrouille [patrujə] *de (~s)* patrol
patrouilleren [patrujɛrə(n)] *vb* patrol
pats [pɑts] *int* wham, bang: *pats-boem* wham bam
patser [pɑtsər] *de (~s)* show-off
patserig [pɑtsərəχ] *adj, adv* flashy
pauk [pɑuk] *de (~en)* kettledrum, *(pl)* timpani
pauper [pɑupər] *de (~s)* pauper
paus [pɑus] *de (~en)* pope
pauw [pɑu] *de (~en)* peacock, *(female also)* peahen
pauze [pɑuzə] *de (~s)* interval, break, intermission, *(sport)* (half-)time: *een kwartier ~ houden* take *(or:* have) a fifteen-minute break
pauzeren [pɑuzɛrə(n)] *vb* pause, take a break, have a rest
paviljoen [pavɪljun] *het (~en, ~s)* pavilion
pc [pese] *de personal computer* pc
pech [pɛχ] *de* **1** bad *(or:* hard, tough) luck: *~ gehad* hard *(or:* tough) luck; **2** breakdown: *~ met de auto* car trouble
pechdienst [pɛχdinst] *de (~en) (Belg)* breakdown service
pechstrook [pɛχstrok] *de (-stroken) (Belg)* hard shoulder
pechvogel [pɛχfoɣəl] *de (~s)* unlucky person: *hij is een echte ~* he's a walking disaster area
pedaal [pədal] *het, de (pedalen)* treadle; pedal

pedaalemmer [pədalɛmər] *de (~s)* pedal bin

pedagogiek [pedaɣoɣik] *de* (theory of) education, educational theory (*or:* science), pedagogy

pedagogisch [pedaɣoɣis] *adj, adv* pedagogic(al): *~e academie* teacher(s') training college

pedagoog [pedaɣox] *de (-gogen)* education(al)ist

peddel [pɛdəl] *de (~s)* paddle

peddelen [pɛdələ(n)] *vb* paddle

pedicure [pedikyrə] *de (~s)* chiropodist, pedicure

¹pedofiel [pedofil] *de (~en)* paedophile

²pedofiel [pedofil] *adj* paedophile

peen [pen] *de (penen)* carrot ‖ *~tjes zweten* be in a cold sweat

peer [per] *de (~s)* **1** pear; **2** bulb

pees [pes] *de (pezen)* tendon, sinew

peetmoeder [petmudər] *de (~s)* godmother

peetoom [petom] *de (~s)* godfather

peettante [petantə] *de (~s)* godmother

peetvader [petfadər] *de (~s)* godfather

pegel [peɣəl] *de (~s)* icicle

peignoir [pɛɲwar] *de (~s)* dressing gown, housecoat

peil [pɛil] *het (~en)* **1** level, standard: *het ~ van de conversatie daalde* the level of conversation dropped; **2** mark, level: *zijn conditie op ~ brengen* (*or: houden*) get oneself into condition, keep fit (*or:* in shape)

peilen [pɛilə(n)] *vb* **1** sound; fathom; **2** *(fig)* gauge; sound (out): *ik zal Bernard even ~, kijken wat die ervan vindt* I'll sound Bernard out, see what he thinks

peiling [pɛilɪŋ] *de (~en)* sounding

peinzen [pɛinzə(n)] *vb* (with *over*) think about, contemplate: *hij peinst er niet over* he won't even contemplate (*or:* consider) it; *hij peinst zich suf over een oplossing* he is racking his brains to find a solution

pek [pɛk] *het, de* pitch

pekel [pekəl] *de* salt, grit

pekinees [pekines] *de (pekinezen)* pekinese

pelgrim [pɛlɣrɪm] *de (~s)* pilgrim

pelgrimstocht [pɛlɣrɪmstɔxt] *de (~en)* pilgrimage

pelikaan [pelikan] *de (pelikanen)* pelican

pellen [pɛlə(n)] *vb* peel, skin, blanch, husk, hull, shell

peloton [pelotɔn] *het (~s)* **1** platoon; **2** *(sport)* pack, (main)bunch

pels [pɛls] *de (pelzen)* fleece, fur

pelsdier [pɛlzdir] *het (~en)* furred animal, furbearing animal

pen [pɛn] *de (~nen)* **1** pen; **2** pin, needle

penalty [pɛnəlti] *de (~'s)* penalty (kick, shot): *een ~ nemen* take a penalty

pendelaar [pɛndəlar] *de (~s)* commuter

pendelen [pɛndələ(n)] *vb* commute

pendule [pɛndylə] *de (~s)* (mantel) clock (with pendulum)

penibel [penibəl] *adj* painful, awkward

penicilline [penisilinə] *de* penicillin

penis [penɪs] *de* penis

pennen [pɛnə(n)] *vb* scribble, pen

penning [pɛnɪŋ] *de (~en)* token

penningmeester [pɛnɪŋmestər] *de (~s)* treasurer

pens [pɛns] *de (~en)* paunch, belly, gut

penseel [pɛnsel] *het (penselen)* (paint)brush

pensioen [pɛnʃun] *het (~en)* pension, retirement (pay), superannuation: *~ aanvragen* apply for a pension; *met ~ gaan* retire

pension [pɛnʃɔn] *het (~s)* **1** guest house, boarding house; **2** bed and board: *vol ~* full board; *in ~ zijn* be a lodger; **3** kennel

pensionaat [pɛnʃonat] *het (pensionaten)* boarding school

pensionhouder [pɛnʃɔnhaudər] *de (~s)* landlord

pensionhoudster [pɛnʃɔnhautstər] *de* landlady

peper [pepər] *de (~s)* pepper: *een snufje ~* a dash of pepper

peperduur [pepərdyr] *adj* very expensive, pricey

peperkoek [pepərkuk] *de (~en)* *(roughly)* gingerbread, gingercake

pepermunt [pepərmʏnt] *de (~en)* peppermints: *een rolletje ~* a tube of peppermints

pepernoot [pepərnot] *de (-noten)* *(roughly)* spiced ginger nut

pepmiddel [pɛpmɪdəl] *het (~en)* pep pill

per [pɛr] *prep* **1** per, a, by: *iets ~ post verzenden* send sth by post (*or:* mail); *het aantal inwoners ~ vierkante kilometer* the number of inhabitants per square kilometre; *iets ~ kilo* (*or: paar*) *verkopen* sell sth by the kilo (*or:* in pairs); *ze kosten 3 euro ~ stuk* they cost 3 euros apiece (*or:* each); *~ uur betaald worden* be paid by the hour; **2** from, as of: *de nieuwe tarieven worden ~ 1 februari van kracht* the new rates will take effect on February 1

perceel [pɛrsel] *het (percelen)* **1** property; **2** parcel, lot, section

percent [pɛrsɛnt] *het (~en)* per cent

percentage [pɛrsɛntaʒə] *het (~s)* percentage

percussie [pɛrkʏsi] *de (~s)* percussion

perenboom [perə(n)bom] *de (-bomen)* pear (tree)

perfect [pɛrfɛkt] *adj, adv* perfect: *hij gaf een ~e imitatie van die zangeres* he did a perfect imitation of that singer; *in ~e staat: a)* in mint condition; *b)* in perfect condition; *alles is ~ in orde* everything is perfect

perfectionist [pɛrfɛkʃonɪst] *de (~en)* perfectionist

perfectionistisch [pɛrfɛkʃonɪstis] *adj* perfectionist

perforator [pɛrforatər] *de (~s)* perforator, punch

pergola [pɛrɣola] *de (~'s)* pergola

periode [perijodə] *de (~s)* period, time, phase, episode, chapter: *~n met zon* sunny periods; *verkozen voor een ~ van twee jaar* elected for a two-year term (of office)

periscoop [periskop] *de (periscopen)* periscope

perk [pɛrk] *het (~en)* **1** bed, flower bed; **2** bound, limit: *binnen de ~en houden* limit, contain; *dat gaat alle ~en te buiten* that's the very limit

perkament [pɛrkamɛnt] *het (~en)* parchment

¹**permanent** [pɛrmanɛnt] *adj* **1** permanent, perpetual; **2** permanent, enduring, lasting, standing

²**permanent** [pɛrmanɛnt] *adv* permanently, perpetually, all the time

³**permanent** [pɛrmanɛnt] *de (~s)* permanent (wave)

permanenten [pɛrmanɛntə(n)] *vb* give a permanent wave, perm

permissie [pɛrmɪsi] *de (~s)* permission, leave

permitteren [pɛrmɪtɛrə(n)] *vb* permit, grant permission, allow: *ik kan me niet ~ dat te doen* I can't afford to do that

perplex [pɛrplɛks] *adj* perplexed, baffled, flabbergasted

perron [pɛrɔn] *het (~s)* platform

pers [pɛrs] *de (~en, perzen)* **1** press: *de ~ te woord staan* talk to the press; **2** (printing) press

Pers [pɛrs] *de (Perzen)* Persian

persagent [pɛrsaʝɛnt] *de (~en)* press agent

persbericht [pɛrzbərɪχt] *het (~en)* press report, newspaper report

persbureau [pɛrsbyro] *het (~s)* news agency, press agency, press bureau

perscommuniqué [pɛrskɔmynike] *het (~s)* news release

persconferentie [pɛrskɔnferɛnsi] *de (~s)* press conference, news conference

per se [pɛrsɛ] *adv* at any price, at all costs: *hij wilde haar ~ zien* he was set on seeing (*or:* determined to see) her

¹**persen** [pɛrsə(n)] *vb* press, compress: *je moet harder ~* you must press harder

²**persen** [pɛrsə(n)] *vb* **1** press, stamp (out); **2** press (out), squeeze (out); **3** press, squeeze, push: *zich door een nauwe doorgang ~* squeeze (oneself) through a narrow gap

persfotograaf [pɛrsfotoʝraf] *de (-grafen)* press photographer, newspaper photographer

persiflage [pɛrsiflaʒə] *de (~s)* (with *op*) parody (of)

personage [pɛrsonaʒə] *het, de (~s)* character, role

personeel [pɛrsonel] *het* personnel, staff, employees, workforce, crew, (factory) hands: *tien man ~* a staff of ten; *wij hebben een groot tekort aan ~* we are badly understaffed (*or:* short-staffed); *onderwijzend ~* teaching staff

personeelschef [pɛrsonelʃɛf] *de (~s)* personnel manager, staff manager

personeelslid [pɛrsonelslɪt] *het (-leden)* staff member, member of (the) staff

personeelszaken [pɛrsonelzakə(n)] *de* **1** personnel matters, staff matters; **2** personnel department

personenauto [pɛrsonə(n)auto] *de (~'s)* (private, passenger) car

personenlift [pɛrsonə(n)lɪft] *de (~en)* passenger lift

persoon [pɛrson] *de (personen)* person, individual, (pl mostly) people: *een tafel voor één ~* a table for one; *ze kwam in (hoogst)eigen ~* she came personally (*or:* in person)

¹**persoonlijk** [pɛrsonlək] *adj* **1** personal, private: *om ~e redenen* for personal (*or:* private) reasons, for reasons of one's own; *een ~ onderhoud* a personal talk; **2** personal, individual

²**persoonlijk** [pɛrsonlək] *adv* personally ‖ *~ vind ik hem een kwal* personally, I think he's a pain

persoonlijkheid [pɛrsonləkhɛit] *de (-heden)* personality; character

persoonsbeschrijving [pɛrsonzbəsχrɛiviŋ] *de (~en)* personal description

persoonsbewijs [pɛrsonzbəwɛis] *het (-bewijzen)* identity card

persoonsvorm [pɛrsonsfɔrm] *de (~en)* finite verb

perspectief [pɛrspɛktif] *het (perspectieven)* **1** prospect, perspective; **2** perspective, context: *iets in breder ~ zien* look at (*or:* see) sth in a wider context; *in ~ tekenen* draw in perspective

persvrijheid [pɛrsfrɛihɛit] *de* freedom of the press

pertinent [pɛrtinɛnt] *adj* definite(ly), emphatic(ally)

Peru [peru] *het* Peru

Peruaan [peruwan] *de (Peruanen)* Peruvian

pervers [pɛrvɛrs] *adj, adv* perverted, degenerate, unnatural

Perzië [pɛrzijə] *het* Persia

perzik [pɛrzɪk] *de (~en)* peach

Perzisch [pɛrzis] *adj* Persian

peseta [peseta] *de (~'s)* peseta

pessimisme [pɛsimɪsmə] *het* pessimism

pessimist [pɛsimɪst] *de (~en)* pessimist

pessimistisch [pɛsimɪstis] *adj, adv* pessimistic, gloomy

pest [pɛst] *de* **1** (bubonic) plague, pestilence; **2** miserable ‖ *de ~ in hebben* be in a foul mood; *de ~ aan iets (iem) hebben* loathe/detest sth (s.o.)

pesten [pɛstə(n)] *vb* pester, tease: *hij zit mij altijd te ~* he is always on at me

pet [pɛt] *de (~ten)* **1** cap: *daar neem ik mijn ~je voor af* I take my hat off for that (*or:* you); *met de ~ naar iets gooien* make a half-hearted attempt at sth, have a shot at sth; *met de ~ rondgaan* pass the hat round; **2** (fig) upstairs: *dat gaat boven mijn ~* that is beyond me; *ik kan er met mijn ~ niet bij* it beats me; *geen hoge ~ op hebben van* not think much of, have a low opinion of

petekind [petəkɪnt] *het (~eren)* godchild

peter [petər] *de (~s)* godfather

peterselie [petərseli] *de* parsley

petitie [pəti(t)si] *de (~s)* petition: *een ~ indienen* file a petition

petroleum [petrolejʏm] *de* petroleum, mineral oil

petticoat [pɛtikot] *de (~s)* petticoat

petto [pɛto] ‖ *iets in ~ hebben* have sth in reserve (*or:* in hand)

petunia [petynija] *de (~'s)* petunia

peuk [pøk] *de (~en)* **1** butt, stub; **2** fag

peul [pøl] *de (~en)* pod, capsule

peulenschil [pølə(n)sχɪl] *de (~len)* trifle: *dat is maar een ~(letje) voor hem:* a) that's peanuts (*or:*

chicken feed) to him; *b)* he can do it standing on his head

peuter [pø̯tər] *de (~s)* pre-schooler; toddler

peuteren [pø̯tərə(n)] *vb* pick: *in zijn neus ~* pick one's nose

peuterleidster [pø̯tərlɛitstər] *de (~s)* nursery-school teacher

peuterspeelzaal [pø̯tərspelzal] *de (-zalen)* play-group

peutertuin [pø̯tərtœyn] *de (~en)* day nursery, crèche

pfeiffer [pfɑ̯jfər] *de* glandular fever

pH-waarde [peha̯wardə] *de* pH value

pi [pi] *de (~'s)* pi

pianist [pijanɪst] *de (~en)* pianist, piano player

piano [pija̯no] *de (~'s)* piano

pianoles [pijanolɛs] *de* piano lesson

pias [pija̯s] *de (~sen)* clown, buffoon

piccalilly [pɪkalˌli] *de* piccalilli

piccolo [pi̯kolo] *de (~'s)* **1** bell-boy; **2** piccolo

picknick [pɪknɪk] *de (~s)* picnic

picknicken [pɪknɪkə(n)] *vb* picnic

picknickmand [pɪknɪkmɑnt] *de (~en)* picnic hamper (*or:* basket)

pick-up [pɪkʏp] *de (~s)* record player

picobello [pikobɛ̯lo] *adj, adv* splendid, outstanding

pictogram [pɪktoɣra̯m] *het (~men)* pictogram

piek [pik] *de (~en)* **1** spike: *een ~ haar* a spike of hair; **2** peak, summit; **3** top

pieken [pi̯kə(n)] *vb* be spiky, stand out

piekeren [pi̯kərə(n)] *vb* worry, brood

piekfijn [pi̯kfɛin] *adj, adv* posh; smart

piemel [pi̯məl] *de (~s)* willie

pienter [pɪntər] *adj* bright, sharp, shrewd

piep [pip] *int* squeak; peep, cheep

piepen [pi̯pə(n)] *vb* squeak; peep, cheep; creak; pipe

pieper [pi̯pər] *de (~s)* **1** b(l)eeper; **2** spud

piepjong [pipjɔ̯ŋ] *adj ‖ niet (zo) ~ meer zijn* be no chicken

piepklein [pipklɛ̯in] *adj* teeny(-weeny), teensy

piepschuim [pipsχœym] *het* styrofoam, polystyrene foam

pieptoon [pi̯pton] *de (-tonen)* bleep, beep

pier [pir] *de (~en)* **1** worm, earthworm; **2** pier

pierenbad [pi̯rə(n)bɑt] *het* paddling pool

pies [pis] *de* pee, wee

piesen [pi̯sə(n)] *vb* pee, wee

piespot [pi̯spɔt] *de (~ten)* chamber pot

piet [pit] *de (~en)* geezer, feller: *hij vindt zichzelf een hele ~* he thinks he's really s.o.

Piet [pit] *‖ Jan, ~ en Klaas* Tom, Dick and Harry; *er voor ~ Snot bijzitten* sit there like a fool; *een ~je precies zijn* be a fusspot

pietje [pi̯cə] *het (~s) (roughly)* budgie

pietluttig [pitlʏtəχ] *adj* meticulous, petty, niggling

pigment [pɪɣmɛ̯nt] *het* pigment

pigmentvlek [pɪɣmɛ̯ntflɛk] *de (~ken)* birthmark, mole

pijl [pɛil] *de (~en)* arrow: *nog meer ~en op zijn boog hebben* have more than one string to one's bow

pijler [pɛi̯lər] *de (~s)* pillar

pijlsnel [pɛilsnɛ̯l] *adj, adv* (as) swift as an arrow

pijltje [pɛi̯lcə] *het (~s)* dart

pijn [pɛin] *de (~en)* pain, ache: *~ in de buik hebben* have (a) stomach-ache, have a pain in one's stomach; *~ in de keel hebben* have a sore throat

pijnappel [pɛi̯nɑpəl] *de (~s)* pine cone

pijnbank [pɛi̯mbɑŋk] *de (~en)* rack

pijnboom [pɛi̯mbom] *de (-bomen)* pine (tree)

¹pijnlijk [pɛi̯nlək] *adj* **1** painful; sore: *~ aanvoelen* hurt, be painful; **2** painful, hurtful: *een ~e opmerking* an embarrassing remark; **3** painful, awkward, embarrassing: *er viel een ~e stilte* there was an uncomfortable silence

²pijnlijk [pɛi̯nlək] *adv* painfully: *~ getroffen zijn* be pained

pijnloos [pɛi̯nlos] *adj* painless

pijnstiller [pɛi̯nstɪlər] *de (~s)* painkiller

pijp [pɛip] *de (~en)* **1** pipe, tube; **2** leg

pijpleiding [pɛi̯plɛidɪŋ] *de (~en)* piping, pipeline

pijplijn [pɛi̯plɛin] *de (~en)* pipeline: *dat zit in de ~* that's in the pipeline

pik [pɪk] *de* penis: *een stijve ~* a hard-on

pikant [pika̯nt] *adj* piquant

pikdonker [pɪɡdɔ̯ŋkər] *adj* pitch-dark; pitch-black

¹pikken [pɪ̯kə(n)] *vb* **1** lift, pinch: *zij heeft dat geld gepikt* she stole that money; **2** take, put up with

²pikken [pɪ̯kə(n)] *vb* peck

pikzwart [pɪ̯kswɑrt] *adj* pitch-black: *~ haar* raven(-black) hair

pil [pɪl] *de (~len)* pill: *het is een bittere ~ voor hem* it is a bitter pill for him to swallow; *de ~ slikken* be on the pill

pilaar [pila̯r] *de (pilaren)* pillar

piloot [pilo̯t] *de (piloten)* pilot: *automatische ~* automatic pilot

pils [pɪls] *het, de* beer, lager

pimpelen [pɪmpələ(n)] *vb* tipple, booze

pin [pɪn] *de (~nen)* peg, pin

pincet [pɪnsɛ̯t] *het, de (~ten)* (pair of) tweezers

pincode [pɪ̯ŋkodə] *de (~s)* PIN code

pinda [pɪ̯nda] *de (~'s)* peanut

pindakaas [pɪ̯ndakas] *de* peanut butter

pindasaus [pɪ̯ndasaus] *de (~en, -sauzen)* peanut sauce

pineut [pinø̯t] *de* dupe: *de ~ zijn* be the dupe

pingelaar [pɪ̯ŋəlar] *de (~s)* **1** *(socc)* player who holds on to the ball; **2** haggler

pingelen [pɪ̯ŋələ(n)] *vb* **1** haggle (over, about); **2** hold on to the ball

pingpong [pɪ̯ŋpɔŋ] *het* ping-pong

pingpongen [pɪ̯ŋpɔŋə(n)] *vb* play ping-pong

pinguïn [pɪ̯ŋgwin] *de (~s)* penguin

pink [pɪŋk] *de (~en)* little finger

pinksterbloem [pɪ̯ŋkstərblum] *de (~en)* cuckoo flower, lady's smock

pinksterdag [pɪŋkstərdɑχ] *de (~en)* Whit Sunday, Whit Monday

Pinksteren [pɪŋkstərə(n)] *de* Whitsun(tide)

pinksterfeest [pɪŋkstərfest] *het (~en)* (feast of) Whitsun

pinkstervakantie [pɪŋkstərvakɑnsi] *de (~s)* Whitsun holiday

pinnen [pɪnə(n)] *vb* **1** pay by switch card; **2** withdraw cash from a cashpoint

pinpas [pɪmpɑs] *de (~sen)* cash card; switch card

pint [pɪnt] *de (~en)* pint

pioen [pijun] *de (~en)* peony

pion [pijɔn] *de (~nen)* pawn

pionier [pijonir] *de (~s)* pioneer

pipet [pipɛt] *het, de (~ten)* pipette

piraat [pirat] *de (piraten)* pirate

piramide [piramidə] *de (~n, ~s)* pyramid

piranha [pirɑɲa] *de (~'s)* piranha

piratenzender [piratə(n)zɛndər] *de (~s)* pirate (radio station)

pirouette [piruwɛt(ə)] *de (~n, ~s)* pirouette

pis [pɪs] *de* piss

pisang [pisɑŋ] *de* banana

pissebed [pɪsəbɛt] *de (~den)* woodlouse

pissen [pɪsə(n)] *vb* piss

pissig [pɪsəχ] *adj, adv* pissed off, bloody annoyed

pistache [pistɑʃ] *de (~s)* pistachio (nut)

piste [pistə] *de (~s)* **1** ring; **2** *(cycling)* track; **3** *(skiing)* piste

pistolet [pistolɛt] *de (~s)* bread roll

pistool [pistol] *het (pistolen)* pistol, gun: *nietpistool* staple gun

¹pit [pɪt] *de (~s)* **1** seed, pip, stone; **2** wick; **3** burner

²pit [pɪt] *het, de (~s)* spirit: *er zit ~ in die meid* she's a girl with spirit

pitabroodje [pitabrocə] *het (~s)* pitta (bread)

pitbullterriër [pɪtbultɛrijər] *de (~s)* pit bull (terrier)

pits [pɪts] *de* pit(s)

pitten [pɪtə(n)] *vb* turn in, kip: *gaan ~* hit the sack

pittig [pɪtəχ] *adj, adv* **1** lively, pithy, racy; **2** *(fig)* stiff; **3** spicy, hot, strong; **4** tough

pizza [pidza] *de (~'s)* pizza

pizzakoerier [pitsakurir] *de (~s)* pizza deliverer, pizza delivery boy

pizzeria [pidzərija] *de (~'s)* pizzeria

pk [peka] *de paardenkracht* h.p.

plaag [plaχ] *de (plagen)* plague

plaaster [plastər] *de (Belg)* plaster of Paris

plaat [plat] *de (platen)* **1** plate, sheet, slab; **2** record; **3** plate, print

plaatje [placə] *het (~s)* **1** plate, sheet, slab, identity disc; **2** snapshot, photo; **3** picture

plaats [plats] *de (~en)* **1** place, position: *de ~ van bestemming* the destination; *de juiste man op de juiste ~* the right man in the right place; *op uw ~en! klaar, af* on your marks, get set, go; *in (op) de eerste ~* in the first place; *op de eerste ~ komen* come first, take first place; *op de eerste ~ eindigen* be (placed)

first; **2** room, space, seat: *~ maken (voor iem)* make room (for s.o.); **3** town; **4** place, seat: *neemt u a.u.b. ~* please take your seats; *in ~ van* instead of

plaatsbewijs [platsbəwɛis] *het (-bewijzen)* ticket

¹plaatselijk [platsələk] *adj* local: *een ~e verdoving* a local anaesthetic

²plaatselijk [platsələk] *adv* **1** locally, on the spot: *iets ~ onderzoeken* investigate sth on the spot; **2** in some places: *~ regen* local showers

¹plaatsen [platsə(n)] *vb* **1** place, put: *de ladder tegen het schuurtje ~* lean (*or*: put) the ladder against the shed; **2** rank: *een order ~* place an order

²plaatsen [platsə(n)] *ref vb* qualify (for)

plaatsgebrek [platsχəbrɛk] *het* lack of space

plaatshebben [platshɛbə(n)] *vb* take place

plaatsing [platsɪŋ] *de (~en)* **1** placement, positioning; **2** *(sport)* ranking; qualification

plaatsnaam [platsnam] *de (-namen)* place name

plaatsnemen [platsnemə(n)] *vb* take a seat

plaatsvervanger [platsfərvɑŋər] *de (~s)* substitute, replacement, deputy

plaatsvinden [platsfɪndə(n)] *vb* take place, happen

placemat [plɛsmɛt] *de (~s)* place mat

placenta [plasɛnta] *de (~'s)* placenta

pladijs [pladɛis] *de (pladijzen) (Belg)* plaice

plafond [plafɔn] *het (~s)* ceiling

plag [plɑχ] *de (~gen)* sod, turf

plagen [plaχə(n)] *vb* tease: *iem met iets ~* tease s.o. about sth

plagerig [plaχərəχ] *adj, adv* teasing

plagiaat [plaɣijat] *het (plagiaten)* plagiarism: *~ plegen* plagiarize

plak [plɑk] *de (~ken)* **1** slice: *iets in ~ken snijden* slice sth; **2** (dental) plaque

plakband [plɑgbant] *het* adhesive tape

plakboek [plɑgbuk] *het (~en)* scrapbook

plakbord [plɑgbɔrt] *het (~en)* noticeboard

plakkaatverf [plakatfɛrf] *de* poster paint

¹plakken [plɑkə(n)] *vb* stick, paste

²plakken [plɑkə(n)] *vb* **1** stick (to, on), glue (to, on); **2** repair: *een band ~* repair a puncture

plakker [plɑkər] *de (~s)* billsticker

plakkerig [plɑkərəχ] *adj* sticky

plakplaatje [plɑkplacə] *het (~s)* transfer

plaksel [plɑksəl] *het (~s)* paste

plakwerk [plɑkwɛrk] *het* sticking, glueing

plamuren [plamyrə(n)] *vb* fill

plamuur [plamyr] *de* filler

plan [plɑn] *het (~nen)* **1** plan: *een ~ uitvoeren* carry out a plan; *een ~ maken (voor ...)* draw up a plan for sth, plan sth; *zijn ~ trekken (Belg)* manage, cope; *wat ben je van ~?* what are you going to do?; *we waren net van ~ om ...* we were just about (*or*: going) to ...; **2** plan, design

planeet [planet] *de (planeten)* planet

plank [plɑŋk] *de (~en)* plank; board, shelf: *de ~ misslaan* be wide of the mark

plankenkoorts [plɑŋkə(n)korts] *de* stage fright

plankgas [plɑŋkχas] *het (roughly)* full throttle: *~*

geven step on the gas
plankton [plɑŋktɔn] *de* plankton
plannen [plɛnə(n)] *vb* plan
planning [plɛnɪŋ] *de* plan, planning
plant [plɑnt] *de (~en)* plant
plantaardig [plɑntardəχ] *adj* vegetable
plantage [plɑntaʒə] *de (~s)* plantation
planten [plɑntə(n)] *vb* plant, plant out
planteneter [plɑntə(n)etər] *de (~s)* herbivore
plantenkas [plɑntə(n)kɑs] *de (~sen)* greenhouse
planter [plɑntər] *de (~s)* planter
plantkunde [plɑntkʏndə] *de* botany
plantsoen [plɑntsun] *het (~en)* public garden(s), park
plas [plɑs] *de (~sen)* **1** puddle, pool; **2** water, pee: *een ~je (moeten) doen* (have to) go (to the toilet, loo), (have to) do a wee(-wee); **3** pool, pond
plasma [plɑsma] *het (~'s)* plasma
¹**plassen** [plɑsə(n)] *vb* **1** go (to the toilet, loo), (have a) pee: *ik moet nodig ~* I really have to go; **2** splash
²**plassen** [plɑsə(n)] *vb* pass: *bloed ~* pass blood (in one's urine)
¹**plastic** [plɛstɪk] *het* plastic
²**plastic** [plɛstɪk] *adj* plastic
plasticlijm [plɛstɪklɛim] *de* (a) plastic adhesive, plastic cement
plastificeren [plɑstifisɛrə(n)] *vb* plasticize
plastisch [plɑstis] *adj* plastic
¹**plat** [plɑt] *adj* **1** flat; **2** closed down, shut down: *de haven gaat morgen ~* tomorrow the port will be shut down
²**plat** [plɑt] *adj, adv* broad ‖ *~ uitgedrukt* to put it crudely (*or:* coarsely)
¹**plataan** [platan] *de (platanen) (tree)* plane (tree)
²**plataan** [platan] *het (wood)* plane (tree)
platbranden [plɑdbrɑndə(n)] *vb* burn to the ground
plateau [plato] *het (~s)* **1** dish, platter; **2** plateau
plateauzool [platozol] *de (-zolen)* platform sole
platenmaatschappij [platə(n)matsχapɛi] *de (~en)* record(ing) company
platenspeler [platə(n)spelər] *de (~s)* record player
platenzaak [platə(n)zak] *de (-zaken)* record shop
platform [platfɔrm] *het (~s)* platform
platgaan [plɑtχan] *vb* be bowled over by (s.o.): *de zaal ging plat* the audience was rolling in the aisles
¹**platina** [platina] *het* platinum
²**platina** [platina] *adj* platinum
platleggen [plɑtlɛɣə(n)] *vb* **1** lay flat; **2** bring to a standstill
platliggen [plɑtlɪɣə(n)] *vb* be at a standstill
plattegrond [platəɣrɔnt] *de (~en)* **1** (street) map; **2** floor plan
plattekaas [platəkas] *de (Belg)* cottage cheese, cream cheese
platteland [platəlɑnt] *het* country(side)
platvis [plɑtfis] *de (~sen)* flatfish
platvloers [plɑtflurs] *adj* coarse, crude
platvoet [plɑtfut] *de (~en)* flatfoot

plausibel [plɑuzibəl] *adj* plausible
plaveisel [plavɛisəl] *het (~s)* paving, pavement
plavuis [plavœys] *de (plavuizen)* (floor) tile; flag(stone)
playback [plejbɛk] *de, het (~s)* miming
playbacken [plejbɛkə(n)] *vb* mime (to one's own, another person's voice)
playboy [plɛjbɔj] *de (~s)* playboy
plechtig [plɛχtəχ] *adj, adv* solemn: *~ beloven (te)* solemnly promise (to)
plechtigheid [plɛχtəχɛit] *de (-heden)* ceremony
plectrum [plɛktrʏm] *het (~s, plectra)* plectrum
plee [ple] *de (~s)* loo, (Am) john: *op de ~ zitten* be in the loo
pleegdochter [pleɣdɔχtər] *de (~s)* foster-daughter
pleeggezin [pleɣəzɪn] *het (~nen)* foster home
pleegkind [pleχkɪnt] *het (-kinderen)* foster-child: *(iem) als ~ opnemen* take (s.o.) in as foster-child
pleegmoeder [pleχmudər] *de (~s)* foster-mother
pleegouders [pleχaudərs] *de* foster-parents
pleegvader [pleχfadər] *de (~s)* foster-father
pleegzoon [pleχson] *de (-zonen, ~s)* foster-son
plegen [pleɣə(n)] *vb* commit
pleidooi [plɛidɔj] *het (~en)* **1** plea: *een ~ houden voor* make a plea for; **2** counsel's speech (*or:* argument)
plein [plɛin] *het (~en)* square, plaza: *op (aan) het ~* in the square
¹**pleister** [plɛistər] *de* (sticking) plaster
²**pleister** [plɛistər] *het* plaster
pleisteren [plɛistərə(n)] *vb* **1** plaster; **2** put a plaster on
pleiten [plɛitə(n)] *vb* plead: *dat pleit voor hem* that is to his credit
pleiter [plɛitər] *de (~s)* counsel
plek [plɛk] *de (~ken)* **1** spot: *een blauwe ~* a bruise; *iemands zwakke ~ raken* find s.o.'s weak spot; **2** spot, place
plensbui [plɛnzbœy] *de (~en)* downpour
¹**plenzen** [plɛnzə(n)] *vb* pour
²**plenzen** [plɛnzə(n)] *vb* splash
pleonasme [plejonɑsmə] *het (~n)* pleonasm
pletter [plɛtər] ‖ *te ~ slaan tegen de rotsen* be dashed against the rocks; *zich te ~ vervelen* be bored stiff (*or:* to death)
plevier [pləvir] *de (~en)* plover
plexiglas [plɛksiɣlɑs] *het* plexiglass
plezant [pləzɑnt] *adj (Belg)* pleasant
plezier [pləzir] *het* **1** pleasure, fun: *iem een ~ doen* do s.o. a favour; *veel ~!* enjoy yourself!; **2** pleasure, enjoyment: *met alle ~* with pleasure; *ik heb hier altijd met ~ gewerkt* I have always enjoyed working here
plezierig [pləzirəχ] *adj, adv* pleasant
plezierjacht [pləzirjɑχt] *het (~en)* pleasure yacht
plicht [plɪχt] *de (~en)* duty: *het is niet meer dan je ~ (om ...)* you are in duty bound (to ...); *de ~ roept* duty calls
plichtsbesef [plɪχtsbəsɛf] *het* sense of duty

plichtsgetrouw [plɪχtsχətrɑu] *adj, adv* dutiful
plint [plɪnt] *de (~en)* skirting board, *(Am)* baseboard
ploeg [pluχ] *de (~en)* **1** gang, shift: *in ~en werken* work (in) shifts; **2** *(sport)* team; side; **3** plough
ploegen [pluɣə(n)] *vb* plough: *een akker* (or: *het land) ~* plough a field (*or:* the land)
ploegendienst [pluɣə(n)dinst] *de (~en)* shift work: *in ~ werken* work (in) shifts
ploeggeest [pluχɣeest] *de* team spirit
ploegleider [pluχlɛidər] *de (~s) (sport)* team manager; captain
ploegverband [pluχfərbɑnt] *het (sport)* ‖ *in ~* as a team
ploeteren [plutərə(n)] *vb* plod (away, along)
plof [plɔf] *de (~fen)* thud, bump, plop
ploffen [plɔfə(n)] *vb* **1** thud, flop; **2** pop, bang ‖ *in een stoel ~* plump down (*or:* flop) into a chair
plomp [plɔmp] *adj, adv* plump, squat; cumbersome
plons [plɔns] *de (~en, plonzen)* splash ‖ *~! daar viel de steen in het water* splash! went the stone into the water
plonzen [plɔnzə(n)] *vb* splash
plooi [ploj] *de (~en)* pleat, fold
plooien [plojə(n)] *vb* fold, pleat, crease
¹plotseling [plɔtsəlɪŋ] *adj* sudden, unexpected
²plotseling [plɔtsəlɪŋ] *adv* suddenly, unexpectedly
¹pluche [plyʃ(ə)] *de, het* plush
²pluche [plyʃ(ə)] *adj* plush
plug [plyχ] *de (~gen)* plug
pluim [plœym] *de (~en)* **1** plume, feather; **2** plume, *(small)* tuft: *een ~ van rook* a plume of smoke; *iem een ~ geven* pat s.o. on the back
pluimage [plœymaːʒə] *de (~s)* plumage
pluimvee [plœymveː] *het* poultry
pluimveehouderij [plœymveːhɑudərɛi] *de (~en)* **1** poultry farm; **2** poultry farming
pluis [plœys] *de* bit of fluff ‖ *het is daar niet ~* there's sth fishy there
pluizen [plœyzə(n)] *vb* give off fluff; pill
pluk [plyk] *de (~ken)* **1** tuft, wisp; **2** crop
plukken [plykə(n)] *vb* **1** pick: *pluk de dag* live for the moment; **2** pluck
plumpudding [plʏmpydɪŋ] *de (~en, ~s)* plum pudding
plunderaar [plʏndərar] *de (~s)* plunderer, looter
plunderen [plʏndərə(n)] *vb* **1** plunder, loot; **2** plunder, raid, rifle through: *de koelkast ~* raid the fridge
plundering [plʏndərɪŋ] *de (~en)* plundering, looting
plunjezak [plʏɲəzak] *de (~ken)* kitbag
¹plus [plʏs] *prep* plus: *twee ~ drie is vijf* two plus (*or:* and) three is five; *vijfenzestig ~* over-65
²plus [plʏs] *het, de (~sen)* **1** plus (sign); **2** plus (pole)
plusminus [plʏsmɪnʏs] *adv* approximately, about: *~ duizend euro* approximately (*or:* about) a thousand euros
pluspunt [plʏspʏnt] *het (~en)* plus, asset: *ervaring*

is bij sollicitaties een ~ experience is a plus (*or:* an asset) when applying for a job
plusteken [plʏsteːkə(n)] *het (~s)* plus (sign)
plutonium [plytoːnijʏm] *het* plutonium
pneumatisch [pnøːmatis] *adj, adv* pneumatic
po [poː] *de (~'s)* chamber pot, po
pochen [pɔχə(n)] *vb* boast, brag
pocheren [pɔʃerə(n)] *vb* poach
pochet [pɔʃɛt] *de (~ten)* dress-pocket handkerchief, breast-pocket handkerchief
pocketboek [pɔkədbuk] *het (~en)* paperback
podium [poːdijʏm] *het (podia)* **1** stage, apron; **2** platform, podium
poedel [pudəl] *de (~s)* poodle
poeder [pudər] *het (~s)* powder
poederdoos [pudərdos] *de (-dozen)* compact
poederen [pudərə(n)] *vb* powder: *zich (het gezicht) ~* powder one's face (*or:* nose)
poederkoffie [pudərkɔfi] *de* instant coffee
poedermelk [pudərmɛlk] *de* dried milk, powdered milk
poedersuiker [pudərsœykər] *de* icing sugar
poef [puf] *de (~en)* hassock
poel [pul] *de (~en)* pool, puddle
poelier [pulir] *de (~s)* poulterer('s)
poema [puma] *de (~'s)* puma
poen [pun] *het, de* dough, dosh
poep [pup] *de* crap, shit, dog-do, bird-do
poepen [pupə(n)] *vb* (have a) crap: *in zijn broek ~* do it in one's pants
poes [pus] *de (poezen)* (pussy)cat: *een jong ~je* a kitten; *mis ~!* wrong!
poeslief [puslif] *adj, adv* suave, bland, smooth, honeyed, sugary, silky: *iets ~ vragen* purr a question, ask sth in the silkiest tones
poespas [puspas] *de* hoo-ha, song and dance: *laat die ~ maar achterwege* stop making such a song and dance about it
poëtisch [poweːtis] *adj, adv* poetic
poetsdoek [putsduk] *de (~en)* cleaning cloth, cleaning rag
poetsen [putsə(n)] *vb* clean, polish: *zijn tanden ~* brush one's teeth
poetsvrouw [putsfrɑu] *de (~en)* cleaning woman
poëzie [poweːzi] *de* poetry
pofbroek [pɔvbruk] *de (~en)* knickerbockers
poffen [pɔfə(n)] *vb* roast, pop
poffertje [pɔfərcə] *het (~s)* kind of small pancake
poging [poɣɪŋ] *de (~en)* attempt, try, effort: *een ~ wagen* have a try at sth; *~ tot moord* attempted murder
poken [poːkə(n)] *vb* poke
poker [poːkər] *het* poker
pokeren [poːkərə(n)] *vb* play poker
pokergezicht [poːkərɣəzɪχt] *het (~en)* poker face
pokken [pɔkə(n)] *de* smallpox
pokkenprik [pɔkə(n)prɪk] *de (~ken)* smallpox vaccination
pokkewerk [pɔkəwɛrk] *het* nasty work, unpleasant

work

pol [pɔl] *de (~len)* clump

polariseren [polarizera(n)] *vb* polarize

polaroid [pɔlarɔjt] *de (~s)* polaroid

polder [pɔldər] *de (~s)* polder

poldermodel [pɔldərmodɛl] *het (~len)* polder model

polderpop [pɔldərpɔp] *de* Dutch pop music

polemiek [polemik] *de (~en)* polemic: *een ~ voeren* engage in a polemic (*or*: controversy)

polemist [polemɪst] *de (~en)* polemicist

Polen [pola(n)] *het* Poland

poli [poli] *de (~'s)* outpatients'

polijsten [polɛɪsta(n)] *vb* polish (up), sand(paper)

polikliniek [poliklinɪk] *de (~en)* outpatient clinic

poliklinisch [poliklinɪs] *adj* || *~e patiënt* outpatient

polio [polijo] *de* polio

polis [polɪs] *de (~sen)* (insurance) policy

polishouder [polɪshaudər] *de (~s)* policyholder

polisvoorwaarden [polɪsforwarda(n)] *de* terms (*or*: conditions) of a policy

politicologie [politikoloɣi] *de* political science

politicus [politikʏs] *de (politici)* politician

¹politie [poli(t)si] *de (~s)* see politieagent

²politie [poli(t)si] *de (~s)* police (force)

politieacademie [poli(t)siakademi] *de (~s)* police college (*or Am*: academy)

politieagent [poli(t)siaɣɛnt] *de (~en)* police officer, policeman

politieauto [poli(t)siauto] *de (~'s)* police car, patrol car

politiebureau [poli(t)sibyro] *het (~s)* police station

politiecommissaris [poli(t)sikɔmɪsarɪs] *de (~sen)* Chief of Police

¹politiek [politik] *de* **1** politics: *in de ~ zitten* be in politics, be a politician; **2** policy: *binnenlandse (or: buitenlandse) ~* internal (*or*: foreign) policy

²politiek [politik] *adj, adv* political

politiekordon [poli(t)sikɔrdɔn] *het (~s)* police cordon

politiekorps [poli(t)sikɔrps] *het (~en)* police (force), constabulary

politieman [poli(t)simɑn] *de (~nen)* policeman, police officer

politierechter [poli(t)sirɛɣtər] *de (~s)* magistrate

politieschool [poli(t)sisɣol] *de (-scholen)* police college

politiestaat [poli(t)sistat] *de (-staten)* police state

politieverordening [poli(t)sivarɔrdənɪŋ] *de (~en)* by-law, *(Am)* local ordinance

polka [pɔlka] *de (~'s)* polka

pollen [pɔla(n)] *de* pollen

pollepel [pɔlepəl] *de (~s)* wooden spoon

polo [polo] *het* **1** polo; **2** sports shirt

polonaise [polonɛːzə] *de (~s)* **1** conga: *een ~ houden* do the conga; **2** polonaise

pols [pɔls] *de (~en)* **1** wrist; **2** pulse: *iem de ~ voelen* feel (*or*: take) s.o.'s pulse

polsen [pɔlsə(n)] *vb* || *iem ~ over iets* sound s.o. out on (*or*: about) sth

polsgewricht [pɔlsɣəvrɪɣt] *het* wrist (joint)

polshorloge [pɔlshɔrloʒə] *het (~s)* wristwatch

polsslag [pɔlslaɣ] *de (~en)* pulse

polsstok [pɔlstɔk] *de (~ken)* (jumping) pole

polsstokhoogspringen [pɔlstɔkhoɣsprɪŋə(n)] *vb* pole vaulting

polyester [polijɛstər] *de (~s)* polyester

polyether [polijɛtər] *de* polyether, foam rubber

Polynesisch [polinezis] *adj* Polynesian

pomp [pɔmp] *de (~en)* pump

pompbediende [pɔmbədində] *de (~n, ~s)* service (*or*: petrol) station attendant

pompelmoes [pɔmpəlmus] *de (-moezen)* grapefruit

pompen [pɔmpa(n)] *vb* pump

pomphouder [pɔmphaudər] *de (~s)* petrol (*or Am*: gas) station owner

pompoen [pɔmpun] *de (~en)* pumpkin

pompstation [pɔmpsta(t)ʃɔn] *het (~s)* filling station, service station

poncho [pɔnʃo] *de (~'s)* poncho

pond [pɔnt] *het (~en)* half a kilo(gram), 500 grams, *(approx)* pound; pound: *het weegt een ~* it weighs half a kilo; *het volle ~ moeten betalen* have to pay the full price

ponsen [pɔnsə(n)] *vb* punch

pont [pɔnt] *de (~en)* ferry(boat)

pontonbrug [pɔntɔmbrʏɣ] *de (~gen)* pontoon bridge

pony [poni] *de* **1** pony; **2** fringe

pooier [pojər] *de (~s)* pimp

pook [pok] *de (poken)* **1** poker; **2** gear lever, (gear)stick

pool [pol] *de (polen)* pole

Pool [pol] *de (Polen)* Pole

poolcirkel [polsɪrkəl] *de (~s)* polar circle

poolen [puːlə(n)] *vb (Am)* carpool

poolexpeditie [polɛkspedi(t)si] *de (~s)* polar expedition

poolgebied [polɣəbit] *het (~en)* polar region

¹Pools [pols] *het* Polish

²Pools [pols] *adj* Polish

poolshoogte [polshoɣtə] *de* latitude, altitude of the pole: *~ nemen: a) (shipp)* take one's bearings; *b) (fig)* size up the situation

Poolster [polstɛr] *de (the)* Pole Star, Polaris

poon [pon] *de (ponen)* gurnard

poort [port] *de (~en)* gate, gateway

poos [pos] *de (pozen)* while, time: *een hele ~* a good while, a long time

poot [pot] *de (poten)* paw, leg: *de poten van een tafel* the legs of a table; *(fig) zijn ~ stijf houden* stand firm, stick to one's guns; *geen ~ hebben om op te staan* not have a leg to stand on; *de ~ van een bril* the arms of a pair of glasses; *(fig) alles kwam op zijn ~s terecht* everything turned out all right

pootjebaden [potʃəbadə(n)] *vb* paddle

pop [pɔp] *de (~pen)* **1** doll; **2** puppet: *daar heb je de ~pen al aan het dansen* here we go, now we're in for it; **3** dummy: *zij is net een aangeklede ~* she looks like a dressed-up doll

popconcert [pɔpkɔnsɛrt] *het (~en)* rock concert, pop concert

popcorn [pɔpkɔːrn] *het* popcorn

popelen [pɔpələ(n)] *vb* quiver: *zitten te ~ om weg te mogen* be raring (*or:* itching) to go

popfestival [pɔpfɛstival] *het* pop festival, rock festival

popgroep [pɔpχrup] *de (~en)* pop group, rock group, rock band

popmuziek [pɔpmyzik] *de* rock music, pop music

poppengezicht [pɔpə(n)ɣəzɪχt] *het (~en)* baby face

poppenhuis [pɔpə(n)hœys] *het (-huizen)* doll's house

poppenkast [pɔpə(n)kɑst] *de (~en)* **1** puppet theatre; **2** puppet show

poppenwagen [pɔpə(n)waɣə(n)] *de (~s)* doll's pram, *(Am)* baby carriage

populair [popylɛːr] *adj, adv* popular

populair-wetenschappelijk [popylɛːrwetə(n)sχɑpələk] *adj, adv* popular-science

populariteit [popylaritɛit] *de* popularity

populatie [popyla(t)si] *de (~s)* population

populier [popylir] *de (~en)* poplar

popzanger [pɔpsɑŋər] *de* pop singer, rock singer

por [pɔr] *de (~ren)* jab, prod, dig

poreus [porøs] *adj* porous

porie [pori] *de (poriën)* pore

porno [pɔrno] *de* porn(o)

pornografie [pɔrnoɣrafi] *de* pornography

porren [pɔrə(n)] *vb* prod: *iem in de zij ~* poke s.o. in the ribs

porselein [pɔrsəlɛin] *het* china(ware), porcelain

porseleinen [pɔrsəlɛinə(n)] *adj* china, porcelain

¹port [pɔrt] *het, de (~en)* **1** postage; **2** surcharge

²port [pɔrt] *de (~en)* port (wine)

portaal [pɔrtal] *het (portalen)* porch, hall, portal

portefeuille [pɔrtəfœyə] *de (~s)* wallet

portemonnee [pɔrtəmɔnɛ] *de (~s)* purse, wallet

portfolio [pɔrtfolijo] *het (~'s)* portfolio

portie [pɔrsi] *de (~s)* **1** share, portion: *zijn ~ wel gehad hebben* have had one's fair share; **2** portion, helping: *een grote (flinke) ~ geduld* a good deal of patience

portiek [pɔrtik] *het, de (~en)* porch; doorway

¹portier [pɔrtir] *de* doorkeeper, gatekeeper

²portier [pɔrtir] *het* door

portierraampje [pɔrtirampjə] *het (~s)* car window

porto [pɔrto] *het, de (porti)* postage

portofoon [pɔrtofɔn] *de (~s)* walkie-talkie

portokosten [pɔrtokɔstə(n)] *de* postage charges (*or:* expenses)

portret [pɔrtrɛt] *het (~ten)* portrait

Portugal [pɔrtyɣal] *het* Portugal

Portugees [pɔrtyɣes] *adj* Portuguese

portvrij [pɔrtfrɛi] *adj* post-paid, postage free

pose [pozə] *de (~s)* pose, posture: *een ~ aannemen* assume a pose

poseren [pozerə(n)] *vb* pose, sit

positie [pozi(t)si] *de (~s)* **1** position, posture: *~ kiezen* (or: *innemen*) choose (*or:* take) up a position; **2** position, attitude: *in een conflict ~ nemen* (or: *kiezen*) take (*or:* choose) sides in a conflict; **3** position, situation; **4** position, post; **5** (social) position, status, (social) rank: *een hoge ~* a high position (*or:* rank) (in society)

positief [pozitif] *adj, adv* **1** positive, affirmative; **2** positive, favourable: *positieve kritiek* constructive criticism; *iets ~ benaderen* approach sth positively

positiekleding [pozi(t)sikledɪŋ] *de* maternity clothes

positieven [pozitivə(n)] *de* || *weer bij zijn ~ komen* come to one's senses

post [pɔst] *de (~en)* **1** post office, postal services; **2** post; mail: *aangetekende ~* registered mail; *elektronische ~* electronic mail, e-mail; **3** post, post office, letterbox; **4** post, jamb; **5** item, entry: *de ~ salarissen* the salary item; **6** post, position: *een ~ bekleden* hold a post, occupy a position

postadres [pɔstadrɛs] *het (~sen)* address

postagentschap [pɔstaɣɛntsχɑp] *het (~pen)* sub-post office

postbank [pɔs(t)bɑŋk] *de* (Dutch) Post Office Bank

postbeambte [pɔstbəɑmtə] *de (~n)* postal employee (*or:* worker)

postbestelling [pɔstbəstɛlɪŋ] *de (~en)* postal delivery, *(Am)* mail delivery, delivery of the post (*or Am:* mail)

postbode [pɔstbodə] *de (~s)* postman, *(Am)* mailman

postbus [pɔstbys] *de (~sen)* postoffice box, P.O. Box

postcheque [pɔstʃɛk] *de (~s)* giro cheque

postcode [pɔstkodə] *de (~s)* postal code; *(Am)* ZIP code

postduif [pɔzdœyf] *de (-duiven)* carrier pigeon, homing pigeon

postelein [pɔstəlɛin] *de* purslane

¹posten [pɔstə(n)] *vb* post, *(Am)* mail, send off

²posten [pɔstə(n)] *vb* stand guard

poster [postər] *de (~s)* poster

poste restante [pɔstərɛstɑntə] *adv* poste restante, *(Am)* general delivery: *De heer H. de Vries, ~ Hoofdpostkantoor Brighton* Mr H. de Vries, c/o Main Post Office, Brighton

posterijen [pɔstərɛiə(n)] *de* Post Office, Postal Services

postgiro [pɔstχiro] *de* (Post Office) giro

postkantoor [pɔstkantor] *het (-kantoren)* post office

postkoets [pɔstkuts] *de (~en)* stagecoach

postmeester [pɔstmestər] *de (~s) (Belg)* postmaster

postmodern [pɔstmodɛrn] *adj* postmodern
postnataal [pɔstnatal] *adj* postnatal
postnummer [pɔstnʏmər] *het (~s) (Belg)* postcode, postal code
postorder [pɔstɔrdər] *de (~s)* mail order
postorderbedrijf [pɔstɔrdərbədrɛif] *het (-bedrijven)* mail-order firm (*or:* company), catalogue house
postpakket [pɔstpɑkɛt] *het (~ten)* parcel, parcel-post package
postpapier [pɔstpapir] *het* writing paper, letter paper, notepaper: *~ en enveloppen* stationery
postreclame [pɔstrəklamə] *de* direct mail advertising
postrekening [pɔstrekənɪŋ] *de (~en)* giro bank account
postspaarbank [pɔ(st)sparbɑŋk] *de (~en)* post office savings bank
poststempel [pɔstɛmpəl] *de, het* postmark
postuum [pɔstym] *adj, adv* posthumous
postuur [pɔstyr] *het (posturen)* figure, shape, build, stature
postvak [pɔstfɑk] *het (~ken)* pigeon-hole
postwissel [pɔstwɪsəl] *de (~s)* postal order, money order
postzegel [pɔstseɣəl] *de (~s)* stamp: *voor een euro aan ~s bijplakken* stamp an excess amount of one euro; *voor drie euro aan ~s bijsluiten* enclose three euros in stamps
postzegelverzameling [pɔ(st)seɣəlvərzaməlɪŋ] *de (~en)* stamp collection
¹pot [pɔt] *de* **1** pot, jar: *een ~ jam* a jar of jam; **2** pot, chamber pot: *hij kan (me) de ~ op* he can get stuffed; **3** pot, saucepan: *eten wat de ~ schaft* eat whatever's going; **4** kitty, pool: *dat is één ~ nat* you can't really tell the difference, *(of pers)* they're birds of a feather
²pot [pɔt] *de* dyke, dike, gay
potdicht [pɔdɪxt] *adj* tight, locked, sealed: *de deur is ~* the door is shut tight
poten [pɔtə(n)] *vb* plant, set, put in
potent [potɛnt] *adj* potent, virile
¹potentieel [potɛnʃel] *het* potential, capacity
²potentieel [potɛnʃel] *adj, adv* **1** potential: *potentiele koper* prospective (*or:* would-be) buyer; **2** latent, potential
potentiepil [potɛn(t)sipɪl] *de (~len)* anti-impotence drug
potig [pɔtəx] *adj* burly, sturdy, husky
potje [pɔcə] *het (~s)* **1** (little) pot, terrine: *zijn eigen ~ koken (fig)* fend for oneself; **2** game; **3** fund: *er een ~ van maken* mess (*or:* muck) things up
potlood [pɔtlot] *het (potloden)* pencil: *met ~ tekenen* draw in pencil
potloodventer [pɔtlotfɛntər] *de (~s)* flasher
potplant [pɔtplɑnt] *de (~en)* pot plant, potted plant
potpourri [pɔtpori] *het, de (~'s)* potpourri, medley
potsierlijk [pɔtsirlək] *adj* clownish, ridiculous, grotesque

pottenbakken [pɔtə(n)bɑkə(n)] *vb* pottery(-making), ceramics
pottenbakker [pɔtə(n)bɑkər] *de (~s)* potter
pottenbakkerij [pɔtə(n)bɑkərɛi] *de (~en)* pottery
pottenkijker [pɔtə(n)kɛikər] *de (~s)* Nosy Parker, snooper
potverteren [pɔtfərterə(n)] *vb* squander
potvis [pɔtfɪs] *de (~sen)* sperm whale
poule [pul] *de (~s)* group
pover [poᵛər] *adj, adv* poor, meagre, miserable: *een ~ resultaat* a poor result
pr [peɛr] *de public relations* PR
Praag [prax] *het* Prague
praat [prat] *de* talk: *veel ~(s) hebben* be all talk; *met iem aan de ~ raken* get talking to s.o.; *een auto aan de ~ krijgen* get a car to start
praatgroep [pratxrup] *de (~en)* discussion group
praatje [pracə] *het (~s)* **1** chat, talk; **2** talk, speech: *mooie ~s* fine words; **3** *(pl)* airs: *~s krijgen* put on airs
praatjesmaker [pracəsmakər] *de (~s)* **1** boaster, braggart; **2** windbag, gasbag
praatpaal [pratpal] *de (-palen)* emergency telephone
praatshow [pratʃo] *de (~s)* chat show, talk show
pracht [prɑxt] *de* **1** magnificence, splendour; **2** *(fig)* beauty, gem
prachtig [prɑxtəx] *adj, adv* **1** splendid, magnificent; **2** exquisite, gorgeous || *~!* excellent!
practicum [prɑktikʏm] *het (practica)* practical, lab(oratory): *ik heb vanmiddag ~* I've got a practical this afternoon
prairie [prɛːri] *de (~s)* prairie
prak [prɑk] *de* mash, mush || *een auto in de ~ rijden* smash (up) a car
prakken [prɑkə(n)] *vb* mash
prakkeseren [prɑkəzerə(n)] *vb* **1** muse, think; **2** brood, worry: *zich suf ~* worry oneself sick
prakkiseren [prɑkizerə(n)] *vb* brood (on, over), have a think
praktijk [prɑktɛik] *de (~en)* practice, experience: *echt een man van de ~* a doer (rather than a thinker); *een eigen ~ beginnen* start a practice of one's own; *in de ~* in (actual) practice
praktijkervaring [prɑktɛikɛrvarɪŋ] *de* practical experience
praktijkgericht [prɑktɛikxərɪxt] *adj* practically-oriented
¹praktisch [prɑktis] *adj, adv* **1** practical; handy, useful: *~e kennis* working knowledge; **2** practical, realistic, businesslike
²praktisch [prɑktis] *adv* practically, almost: *de was is ~ droog* the laundry's practically dry
praktiseren [prɑktizerə(n)] *vb* practise
praline [pralinə] *de (~s)* chocolate (praline)
prat [prɑt] *adj, adv* proud: *~ gaan op zijn intelligentie* boast (*or:* brag) about one's intelligence
praten [pratə(n)] *vb* talk, speak: *we ~ er niet meer over* let's forget it, let's leave it at that; *je hebt ge-*

makkelijk ~ it's easy (*or:* it's all right) for you to talk; *daarover valt te* ~ that's a matter for discussion; *iedereen praat erover* it's the talk of the town, everyone is talking about it

prater [pratər] *de* (*~s*) talker: *hij is geen grote* ~ he isn't much of a talker

prauw [prɑu] *de* (*~en*) proa

precedent [presədɛnt] *het* (*~en*) precedent: *een* ~ *scheppen* establish (*or:* create) a precedent

¹**precies** [prəsis] *adj, adv* precise, exact, accurate, specific: ~ *een kilometer* one kilometre exactly; *dat is* ~ *hetzelfde* that is precisely (*or:* exactly) the same (thing); *om* ~ *te zijn* to be precise; ~ *in het midden* right in the middle; ~ *om twaalf uur* at twelve (o'clock) sharp, on the stroke of twelve; ~ *op tijd* right on time; ~ *drie jaar geleden* exactly (*or:* precisely) three years ago

²**precies** [prəsis] *int* precisely, exactly

precisie [presizi] *de* precision, accuracy

predikant [predikɑnt] *de* (*~en*) 1 minister, pastor; vicar, rector, parson (*Anglican Church*); clergyman; 2 (*Roman Catholic church*) preacher

preek [prek] *de* (*preken*) 1 sermon, homily (on): *een* ~ *houden* deliver a sermon; 2 sermon, lecture (on)

preekstoel [prekstul] *de* (*~en*) pulpit

prefabriceren [prefabrisɛrə(n)] *vb* prefabricate

prefereren [prefɛrɛrə(n)] *vb* prefer: *dit is te* ~ *boven dat* this is preferable to that

prehistorie [prehɪstori] *de* prehistory

prehistorisch [prehɪstoris] *adj* prehistoric

prei [prɛi] *de* (*~en*) leek

preken [prekə(n)] *vb* 1 preach, deliver (*or:* preach) a sermon; 2 preach, moralize

premie [premi] *de* (*~s*) 1 premium, bonus, gratuity; 2 premium, (insurance) contribution: *de sociale ~s* social insurance (*or:* security) contributions

premier [prəmjɛ] *de* (*~s*) prime minister, premier

première [prəmjɛːrə] *de* (*~s*) première, first night, opening performance

preminiem [preminim] *de* (*~en*) (*Belg*) junior member (6-10 years) of sports club

prent [prɛnt] *de* (*~en*) print, illustration, cartoon

prentbriefkaart [prɛndbrifkart] *de* (*~en*) (picture) postcard

prepareren [prepɑrɛrə(n)] *vb* prepare

presbyteriaan [prɛzbiterijɑn] *de* (*-rianen*) Presbyterian

preselectie [presəlɛksi] *de* (*Belg*) qualifying round

¹**present** [prezɛnt] *het* (*~en*) present, gift

²**present** [prezɛnt] *adj* present, in attendance: *ze waren allemaal* ~ they were all present; ~*!* present!, here!

presentatie [prezɛnta(t)si] *de* (*~s*) presentation, introduction: *de* ~ *is in handen van Joris* the programme is presented by Joris

presentator [prezɛntɑtɔr] *de* (*~en*) presenter, host, hostess, anchorman

presenteerblaadje [prəzɛntɛrblacə] *het* tray, plat-

ter: *de baan werd hem op een* ~ *aangeboden* the job was handed to him on a silver platter

presenteren [prezɛntɛrə(n)] *vb* 1 present, introduce; 2 present, offer; 3 pass off (as); 4 present, host

presentie [prezɛn(t)si] *de* presence

presentielijst [prezɛnsilɛist] *de* (*~en*) attendance list, (attendance) roll, (attendance) register

president [prezidɛnt] *de* (*~en*) President

president-directeur [prezidɛndirɛktɸr] *de* (*~en*) chairman (of the board)

presidentsverkiezing [prezidɛn(t)sfərkizɪŋ] *de* presidential election

prestatie [prestɑ(t)si] *de* (*~s*) performance, achievement, feat: *een hele* ~ quite an achievement

prestatieloon [prestɑ(t)silon] *het* (*-lonen*) merit pay

presteren [prestɛrə(n)] *vb* achieve, perform: *hij heeft nooit veel gepresteerd* he has never done anything to speak of

prestige [prestiːʒə] *het* prestige

pret [prɛt] *de* 1 fun, hilarity: ~ *hebben* (*or:* maken) have fun, have a good time; *dat mag de* ~ *niet drukken* never mind; 2 fun, enjoyment; 3 fun, entertainment: *(het is) uit met de* ~*!* the party is over

pretje [prɛcə] *het* (*~s*) bit of fun: *dat is geen* ~ that's no picnic

pretogen [prɛtoγə(n)] *de* twinkling eyes

pretpark [prɛtpark] *het* (*~en*) amusement park

prettig [prɛtəχ] *adj, adv* pleasant, nice: ~ *weekend!* have a pleasant (*or:* nice) weekend; *deze krant leest* ~ this paper is nice to read

preuts [prøts] *adj, adv* prudish, prim (and proper)

preutsheid [prøtshɛit] *de* prudishness, primness

prevelen [prevələ(n)] *vb* mumble, murmur

preventie [prevɛnsi] *de* (*~s*) prevention

preventief [prevɛntif] *adj, adv* preven(ta)tive, precautionary

pr-functionaris [peɛrfʏŋkʃonɑrɪs] *de* PR officer

prieel [prijel] *het* (*priëlen*) summerhouse, arbour

priegelen [priγələ(n)] *vb* do fine (*or:* delicate) (needle)work

priegelwerk [priγəlwɛrk] *het* close work, delicate work

priem [prim] *de* (*~en*) awl, bodkin

priemgetal [primγətɑl] *het* (*~len*) prime (number)

priester [pristər] *de* (*~s*) priest

prijken [prɛikə(n)] *vb* be resplendent, adorn

prijs [prɛis] *de* (*prijzen*) 1 price, fare, charge: *voor een zacht ~je* at a bargain price; *tot elke* ~ at any price (*or:* cost), at all costs; 2 price (tag): *het ~je hangt er nog aan* it has still got the price on; 3 prize, award: *een* ~ *uitloven* put up a prize; *in de prijzen vallen* be among the winners; 4 reward, prize

prijsbewust [prɛizbəwʏst] *adj* cost-conscious

prijsdaling [prɛizdalɪŋ] *de* (*~en*) fall (*or:* drop, decrease) in price

prijskaartje [prɛiskarcə] *het* (*~s*) price tag

prijsklasse [prɛisklɑsə] *de* (*~n*) price range, price bracket

prijslijst [prɛislɛist] *de (~en)* price list

prijsopgave [prɛisɔpχavə] *de (~n)* estimate; quotation, tender

prijsuitreiking [prɛisœytrɛikiŋ] *de (~en)* distribution of prizes, prize-giving (ceremony)

prijsverhoging [prɛisfərhoχiŋ] *de* price increase, rise

prijsverlaging [prɛisfərlaχiŋ] *de* price reduction, price cut

prijsvraag [prɛisfraχ] *de (-vragen)* competition, (prize) contest

prijswinnaar [prɛiswinar] *de (~s)* prizewinner

¹prijzen [prɛizə(n)] *vb* praise, commend: *een veelgeprezen boek* a highly-praised book

²prijzen [prɛizə(n)] *vb* price, ticket, mark: *vele artikelen zijn tijdelijk lager geprijsd* many articles have been temporarily marked down

prijzig [prɛizəχ] *adj* expensive, pricey

prik [prɪk] *de (~ken)* **1** prick, prod; **2** injection, shot; **3** pop, fizz: *mineraalwater zonder ~* still mineral water

prikactie [prɪkɑksi] *de (~s)* lightning strike

prikbord [prɪgbɔrt] *het (~en)* noticeboard, *(Am)* bulletin board

prikje [prɪkjə] *het (~s)* ‖ *iets voor een ~ kopen* buy sth dirt cheap *(or:* for next to nothing)

prikkaart [prɪkart] *de (~en)* time card

prikkel [prɪkəl] *de (~s)* incentive, stimulant, stimulus

prikkelbaar [prɪkəlbar] *adj* touchy, irritable

prikkeldraad [prɪkəldrat] *het, de* barbed wire

¹prikkelen [prɪkələ(n)] *vb* irritate, vex

²prikkelen [prɪkələ(n)] *vb* prickle, tingle, sting: *mijn been prikkelt* my leg is tingling

¹prikken [prɪkə(n)] *vb* **1** prick, prod: *een ballon lek ~* pop a balloon; **2** stick (to), affix (to): *een poster op de muur ~* pin a poster on the wall; **3** inject

²prikken [prɪkə(n)] *vb* sting, tingle: *de rook prikt in mijn ogen* the smoke is making my eyes smart

prikklok [prɪklɔk] *de (~ken)* time clock

priklimonade [prɪklimonadə] *de (~s)* pop

pril [prɪl] *adj* early, fresh, young

¹prima [prima] *adj, adv* excellent, great, terrific, fine: *een ~ vent* a nice chap, *(Am)* a great guy

²prima [prima] *int* great

¹primair [primɛːr] *adj, adv* **1** primary, initial, first; **2** primary, principal, essential, chief

²primair [primɛːr] *adj* primary, basic

primeur [primør] *de (~s)* something new, scoop

primitief [primitif] *adj, adv* **1** primitive, elemental; **2** primitive, makeshift: *het ging er heel ~ toe* it was very rough and ready there

principe [prɪnsipə] *het (~s)* principle: *een man met hoogstaande ~s* a man of high principles; *uit ~* on principle, as a matter of principle

principieel [prɪnsipjel] *adj, adv* **1** fundamental, essential, basic; **2** on principle, of principle: *een ~ dienstweigeraar* a conscientious objector (to military service)

prins [prɪns] *de (~en)* prince

prinses [prɪnsɛs] *de (~sen)* princess

prinsjesdag [prɪnʃəzdɑχ] *de (~en) (roughly)* day of the Queen's *(or:* King's) speech

printen [prɪntə(n)] *vb* print

printer [prɪntər] *de (~s)* printer

prior [prijɔr] *de (~s)* prior

prioriteit [prijoritɛit] *de (~en)* priority: *~en stellen* establish priorities, get one's priorities right

prisma [prɪsma] *het (~'s)* prism

privacy [prɑjvəsi] *de* privacy, seclusion

privatiseren [privatizerə(n)] *vb* privatize, denationalize

privé [prive] *adj, adv* private, confidential, personal: *ik zou je graag even ~ willen spreken* I'd like to talk to you privately *(or:* in private) for a minute

privédetective [privedɪtɛktɪf] *de (~s)* private detective

privéleven [privelevə(n)] *het* private life

privérekening [priverekəniŋ] *de (~en)* personal account

privilege [privileʒə] *het (~s)* privilege

pr-man [peɛrmɑn] *de* PR-man, public relations officer

pro [pro] *adj* pro(-) ‖ *het ~ en het contra horen* hear the pros and cons

probeersel [probɛrsəl] *het (~s)* experiment, try-out

proberen [probɛrə(n)] *vb* **1** try (out), test: *het met water en zeep ~* try soap and water; **2** try, attempt: *dat hoef je niet eens te ~* you needn't bother (trying that)

probleem [problem] *het (problemen)* problem, difficulty, trouble: *in de problemen zitten* be in difficulties *(or:* trouble); *geen ~!* no problem!

probleemloos [problemlos] *adj, adv* uncomplicated, smooth, trouble-free: *alles verliep ~* things went very smoothly *(or:* without a hitch)

problematiek [problematik] *de* problem(s), issue

problematisch [problematis] *adj* problematic(al)

procédé [prosede] *het (~s)* process, technique

procederen [prosedɛrə(n)] *vb* litigate, take legal action, proceed (against), prosecute: *gaan ~* go to court

procedure [prosədyrə] *de (~s)* **1** procedure, method; **2** (law)suit, action, legal proceedings *(or:* procedure): *een ~ tegen iem aanspannen* start legal proceedings against s.o.

procedurefout [prosədyrəfɑut] *de (~en)* procedural mistake; mistake in procedure

procent [prosɛnt] *het (~en)* per cent, percent: *honderd ~ zeker* dead certain *(or:* sure)

proces [prosɛs] *het (~sen)* **1** (law)suit, trial, action, legal proceedings: *iem een ~ aandoen* take s.o. to court; **2** process

proceskosten [prosɛskɔstə(n)] *de* (legal) costs

processie [prosɛsi] *de (~s)* procession

proces-verbaal [prosɛsfərbal] *het (processen-verbaal)* charge, summons, ticket: *een ~ aan zijn broek* *krijgen* be booked, get a ticket

pro Deo [prodejo] *adv* free (of charge), for nothing

producent [prodysent] *de (~en)* producer

produceren [prodysera(n)] *vb* produce, make, manufacture, generate

product [prodykt] *het (~en)* product, production, commodity: *het bruto nationaal ~* the gross national product, the G.N.P.

productie [prodyksi] *de (~s)* **1** production: *uit de ~ nemen* stop producing (*or*: production); **2** production, output, yield, produce

productief [prodyktif] *adj* **1** productive, fruitful; **2** productive, prolific: *een ~ dagje* a good day's work

productiekosten [prodyksikɔsta(n)] *de* cost(s) of production

productieleider [prodyksileidər] *de (~s)* production manager, producer

productiemaatschappij [prodyksimatsχapei] *de (~en)* film production company

productieproces [prodyksiprɔsɛs] *het (~sen)* production process, manufacture

productiviteit [prodyktiviteit] *de* productivity, productive capacity

proef [pruf] *de (proeven)* **1** test, examination, trial: *op de ~ stellen* put to the test; *proeven nemen* carry out experiments; **2** test, try, trial, probation: *iets een week op ~ krijgen* have sth on a week's trial; *op ~* on probation; **3** proof

proefdier [pruvdir] *het (~en)* laboratory animal

proefdraaien [pruvdrajə(n)] *vb* trial run, test run

proefkonijn [prufkonein] *het (~en)* guinea pig

proefperiode [prufperijodə] *de (~n, ~s)* trial period, probationary period, probation

proefpersoon [prufpersɔn] *de (-personen)* (experimental, test) subject

proefrit [prufrɪt] *de (~ten)* test drive, trial run: *een ~ maken met de auto* test-drive the car

proefschrift [prufsχrɪft] *het (~en)* (doctoral, Ph.D.) thesis, dissertation

proeftijd [pruftɛit] *de* probation, probationary period, trial period: *(law) voorwaardelijk veroordeeld met een ~ van twee jaar* a suspended sentence with two years' probation

proeftuin [pruftœyn] *de (~en)* experimental garden (*or*: field)

proefwerk [prufwɛrk] *het (~en)* test (paper): *een ~ opgeven* set a test

proesten [prustə(n)] *vb* **1** sneeze; **2** snort, splutter

proeven [pruvə(n)] *vb* taste, try, sample, test: *van het eten ~* try some of the food

prof [prɔf] *de (~s)* **1** prof; **2** pro

profclub [prɔfklyp] *de (~s)* professional club

profeet [profet] *de (profeten)* prophet, prophetess

professionalisme [profɛʃonalɪsmə] *het* professionalism

professioneel [profɛʃonel] *adj* professional ‖ *iets ~ aanpakken* approach sth in a professional way

professor [profɛsɔr] *de (~en)* professor: *~ in de taalwetenschap* a professor of linguistics

profetisch [profetis] *adj, adv* prophetic

proficiat [profisijat] *int* congratulations: *~ met je verjaardag* happy birthday!

profiel [profil] *het (~en)* profile

profielschets [profilsχɛts] *de (~en)* profile

profielzool [profilzol] *de (-zolen)* grip sole, sole with a tread

profijt [profɛit] *het (~en)* profit, benefit

profijtig [profɛitəχ] *adj (Belg)* economical, cheap

profiteren [profiterə(n)] *vb* profit (from, by), take advantage (of), exploit: *zoveel mogelijk ~ van* make the most of

profiteur [profitør] *de (~s)* profiteer

profvoetbal [prɔfudbal] *het* professional football

prognose [prɔɣnozə] *de (~s)* prognosis; forecast

programma [proɣrama] *het (~'s)* **1** programme: *het hele ~ afwerken* go (*or*: get) through the whole programme; **2** *(comp)* program

programmaboekje [proɣramabukjə] *het* programme

programmamaker [proɣramamakər] *de (~s)* programme maker (*or*: writer), producer

programmeertaal [proɣramertal] *de (-talen)* computer language

¹**programmeren** [proɣramerə(n)] *vb (comp)* program

²**programmeren** [proɣramerə(n)] *vb* programme, schedule: *de uitzending is geprogrammeerd voor woensdag* the programme is to be broadcast on Wednesday

programmeur [proɣramør] *de (~s)* programmer

progressief [proɣrɛsif] *adj, adv* progressive, liberal

project [projɛkt] *het (~en)* project

projecteren [projɛkterə(n)] *vb* project

projectie [projɛksi] *de (~s)* projection

projectiel [projɛktil] *het (~en)* missile, projectile

projectonderwijs [projɛktondərwɛis] *het* project learning

projectontwikkelaar [projɛktontwɪkəlar] *de (~s)* property (*or Am:* real estate) developer

projectontwikkeling [projɛktontwɪkəlɪŋ] *de* **1** property (*or Am:* real estate) development; **2** project planning (*or:* development)

projector [projɛktɔr] *de (~s)* projector

promenade [prɔmənadə] *de (~s)* shopping precinct, shopping mall

promillage [promilaʒə] *het (~s)* blood alcohol level

promille [promil] *het (~n)* per thousand, per mil(le): *acht promille* 0.8 percent

prominent [prominɛnt] *adj* prominent

promotie [promo(t)si] *de (~s)* promotion: *~ maken* get promotion

promotieklasse [promo(t)siklasə] *de (~n) (sport)* promotion division

promoveren [promoverə(n)] *vb* **1** take one's doctoral degree (*or:* one's Ph.D.): *hij is gepromoveerd op een onderzoek naar ...* he obtained his doctorate with a thesis on ...; **2** *(sport)* be promoted, go up

prompt [prɔmt] *adj, adv* **1** prompt, speedy; **2** punctual, prompt: ~ *op tijd* right (*or:* dead) on time

pronken [prɔ̯ŋkə(n)] *vb* flaunt (oneself, sth); prance, strut: *zij loopt graag te ~ met haar zoon* she likes to show off her son

prooi [proj] *de (~en)* **1** prey, quarry; **2** prey, victim: *ten ~ vallen aan* become prey to

proost [prost] *int* cheers

proosten [prọstə(n)] *vb* toast, raise one's glass

prop [prɔp] *de (~pen)* ball: *een ~ watten* a wad of cotton wool; *met iets op de ~pen komen* come up with sth

propaganda [propaɣɑ̯nda] *de* propaganda

propedeuse [propədœ̯yzə] *de* foundation course

propedeutisch [propədœ̯ytis] *adj* preliminary, introductory

propeller [propɛ̯lər] *de (~s)* (screw) propeller, (air)screw

proper [prọpər] *adj* neat, tidy; clean

proportie [propɔ̯rsi] *de (~s)* **1** proportion, relation: *iets in (de juiste) ~(s) zien* keep sth in perspective; **2** proportion, dimension

proportioneel [propɔrʃonẹl] *adj, adv* proportional

proppen [prɔ̯pə(n)] *vb* shove, stuff, cram, pack: *iedereen werd in één auto gepropt* everyone was squeezed (*or:* packed) into one car

propvol [prɔ̯pfɔl] *adj* full to the brim (*or:* to bursting), chock-full, crammed, packed (tight): *een ~le bus* an overcrowded bus

prospectus [prɔspɛ̯ktʏs] *het, de (~sen)* prospectus

prostaat [prɔstạt] *de (prostaten)* prostate (gland)

prostaatkanker [prɔstɑ̯tkɑŋkər] *de* cancer of the prostate

prostituee [prɔstitywẹ] *de (~s)* prostitute

prostitutie [prɔstitỵ(t)si] *de* prostitution

proteïne [protejịnə] *het, de* protein

protest [protɛ̯st] *het (~en)* protest: *uit ~ (tegen)* in protest (against)

protestant [protɛstɑ̯nt] *de (~en)* Protestant

protestants [protɛstɑ̯nts] *adj, adv* Protestant, *(non-Anglican)* dissenting, Nonconformist

protesteren [protɛstẹrə(n)] *vb* protest

prothese [protẹzə] *de (~n, ~s)* prothesis, prosthesis, dentures, false teeth

protocol [protokɔ̯l] *het (~len)* **1** protocol; **2** record

protonkaart [protọnkart] *de (~en) (Belg)* rechargeable smart card

prototype [protọtipə] *het (~n, ~s)* prototype

proviand [provijɑ̯nt] *het, de* provisions

provinciaal [provɪnʃạl] *adj, adv* provincial: *een provinciale weg (roughly)* a secondary road

provincie [provɪ̯nsi] *de (~s)* province, region: *de ~ Limburg* the Province of Limburg

provisie [provịzi] *de (~s)* commission, brokerage

provoceren [provosẹrə(n)] *vb* provoke, incite

provocerend [provosẹrənt] *adj, adv* provocative, provoking

proza [prọza] *het* prose

pruik [prœ̯yk] *de (~en)* wig, toupee

pruilen [prœ̯ylə(n)] *vb* pout, sulk

pruim [prœ̯ym] *de* **1** plum, prune; **2** plug, wad

pruimen [prœ̯ymə(n)] *vb* chew tobacco

pruimenboom [prœ̯ymə(n)bom] *de (-bomen)* plum (tree)

Pruisen [prœ̯ysə(n)] *het* Prussia

Pruisisch [prœ̯ysis] *adj, adv* Prussian

prul [prʏl] *het (~len)* **1** piece of waste paper; **2** (piece of) trash, piece of rubbish (*or:* junk)

prullenmand [prʏ̯lə(n)mɑnt] *de (~en)* waste paper basket, wastebasket

prut [prʏt] *de* **1** mud, ooze, sludge; **2** mush; **3** grounds

pruts [prʏts] *de (~en) (Belg)* trinket

prutsen [prʏ̯tsə(n)] *vb* mess about (*or:* around), potter (about), tinker (about): *je moet niet zelf aan je tv gaan zitten ~* you shouldn't mess about with your TV-set yourself

prutser [prʏ̯tsər] *de (~s)* botcher, bungler

prutswerk [prʏ̯tswɛrk] *het* botch(-up)

pruttelen [prʏ̯tələ(n)] *vb* simmer; perk, percolate

PS [peẹs] *het* postscriptum PS

psalm [psɑlm] *de (~en)* psalm

psalmboek [psɑ̯lmbuk] *het (~en)* psalm-book, psalter

pseudoniem [psœydonị̯m] *het (~en)* pseudonym

psoriasis [psorijạzɪs] *de* psoriasis

psyche [psị̯χə] *de* psyche

psychedelisch [psiχədẹlis] *adj* psychedelic

psychiater [psiχijạtər] *de (~s)* psychiatrist: *je moet naar een ~* you should see a psychiatrist

psychiatrie [psiχijatrị] *de* psychiatry

psychiatrisch [psiχijạtris] *adj* psychiatric: *een ~e inrichting* a mental hospital

psychisch [psị̯χis] *adj, adv* psychological, mental: *~ gestoord* emotionally disturbed; *dat is ~, niet lichamelijk* that is psychological, not physical

psychoanalyse [psiχoanalizə] *de (~n, ~s)* psychoanalysis

psychologie [psiχoloɣị] *de* psychology

psychologisch [psiχolọɣis] *adj, adv* psychological

psycholoog [psiχolọχ] *de (-logen)* psychologist

psychoot [psiχọt] *de (psychoten)* psychotic

psychopaat [psiχopạt] *de (-paten)* psychopath

psychose [psiχọzə] *de (~n, ~s)* psychosis

psychosomatisch [psiχosomạtis] *adj, adv* psychosomatic

psychotherapeut [psiχoterapœ̯yt] *de (~en)* psychotherapist

psychotherapie [psiχoterapị] *de* psychotherapy, psychotherapeutics

psychotisch [psiχọtis] *adj* psychotic

PTT [petetẹ] *de* Post, Telegrafie, Telefonie Post Office

puber [pỵbər] *de (~s)* adolescent

puberaal [pybərạl] *adj, adv* adolescent

puberen [pybẹrə(n)] *vb* reach puberty

puberteit [pybərtɛ̯it] *de* puberty, adolescence: *in de ~ zijn* be going through one's adolescence

publicatie [pyblikạ(t)si] *de (~s)* publication

publiceren [pyblisẹrə(n)] *vb* publish

publiciteit [pyblisitɛit] *de* publicity: *~ krijgen* attract attention, get publicity; *iets in de ~ brengen* bring sth to public notice

publiciteitsstunt [pyblisitɛitstʏnt] *de (~s)* publicity stunt

¹publiek [pyblik] *het* **1** public, *(sport)* crowd, audience, readership, clientele, visitors: *een breed ~ proberen te bereiken* try to cater for a broad public; *veel ~ trekken* draw a good crowd; **2** (general) public: *toegankelijk voor (het) ~* open to the (general) public

²publiek [pyblik] *adj, adv* public: *er was veel ~e belangstelling* it was well attended

publiekstrekker [pyblikstrɛkər] *de (~s)* crowd-puller, (good) box-office draw, box-office success, box-office hit

publiekswissel [pyblikswɪsəl] *de (~s)* last-minute substitution

pudding [pʏdɪŋ] *de (~en, ~s)* pudding

puf [pʏf] *de* (get up and) go, energy: *ergens de ~ niet meer voor hebben* not feel up to sth any more

puffen [pʏfə(n)] *vb* pant: *~ van de warmte* pant with the heat

pui [pœy] *de (~en)* (lower) front, (lower) façade; shopfront

puik [pœyk] *adj, adv* **1** choice, top quality; **2** great, first-rate

puilen [pœylə(n)] *vb* bulge

puin [pœyn] *het* rubble: *~ ruimen: a)* clear up the rubble; *b) (fig)* pick up the pieces, sort sth out; *in ~ liggen* lie *(or:* be) in ruins, be smashed (up, to bits)

puinhoop [pœynhop] *de (-hopen)* **1** heap of rubble *(or:* rubbish); **2** mess, shambles: *jij hebt er een ~ van gemaakt* you have made a mess of it

puist [pœyst] *de (~en)* pimple, spot: *~jes uitknijpen* squeeze spots

puit [pœyt] *de (~en)* frog

pukkel [pʏkəl] *de (~s)* pimple, spot

pul [pʏl] *de (~len)* tankard, mug

pulken [pʏlkə(n)] *vb* pick: *zit niet zo in je neus te ~* stop picking your nose

pullover [pʏlovər] *de (~s)* pullover, sweater

pulp [pʏlp] *de* **1** pulp: *tot ~ geslagen* beaten to a pulp; **2** pulp, junk (reading)

pump [pʏmp] *de (~s)* pump

pumpschoen [pʏmpsχun] *de (~en)* court (shoe), *(Am)* pump

punaise [pynɛːzə] *de (~s)* drawing pin, *(Am)* thumbtack

punctueel [pʏŋktywel] *adj, adv* punctual

punk [pʏŋk] *de* punk

punker [pʏŋkər] *de (~s)* punk

¹punt [pʏnt] *het (~en)* **1** point, place: *het laagste ~ bereiken* reach rock-bottom; **2** point, moment: *hij stond op het ~ om te vertrekken* he was (just) about to leave; **3** point, item, count, matter, question, issue: *zijn zwakke ~* his weak point; *tot in de ~jes verzorgd: a)* impeccably dressed; *b)* shipshape; *geen ~!* no problem!

²punt [pʏnt] *het, de (~en)* **1** full stop; decimal (point): *~en en strepen* dots and dashes; *de dubbelepunt* the colon; *ik was gewoon kwaad, ~, uit!* I was just angry, full stop; **2** point: *hoeveel ~en hebben jullie?* what's your score?; *op ~en winnen (verslaan)* win on points; *hij is twee ~en vooruitgegaan* he has gone up (by) two marks; **3** mark

³punt [pʏnt] *de (~en)* **1** point, tip, corner, angle: *het ligt op het ~je van mijn tong* it's on the tip of my tongue; *een ~ aan een potlood slijpen* sharpen a pencil; *op het ~je van zijn stoel zitten* be (sitting) on the edge of his seat; **2** wedge

puntdak [pʏndak] *het (~en)* gable(d) roof, peaked roof

puntendeling [pʏntə(n)delɪŋ] *de (~en)* draw

puntenklassement [pʏntə(n)klasəmɛnt] *het (~en)* points classification

puntenlijst [pʏntə(n)lɛist] *de (~en)* scorecard, scoresheet; report

puntenslijper [pʏntə(n)slɛipər] *de (~s)* (pencil) sharpener

puntensysteem [pʏntə(n)sistem] *het (-systemen)* points system, scoring system

puntentelling [pʏntə(n)tɛlɪŋ] *de (~en)* scoring

puntgaaf [pʏntχaf] *adj, adv* perfect, flawless

punthoofd [pʏnthoft] *het (~en)* ǁ *ik krijg er een een ~ van* it is driving me crazy *(or:* up the wall)

puntig [pʏntəχ] *adj, adv* pointed, sharp: *~e uitsteeksels* sharp points; *~e bladeren* pointed leaves

puntje [pʏncə] *het (~s)* **1** (small, little) point, tip, dot: *de ~s op de i zetten* dot the i's and cross the t's; **2** *(roughly)* roll; **3** dot, spot: *als ~ bij paaltje komt* when it comes to the crunch *(or:* point)

puntkomma [pʏntkɔma] *het, de (~'s)* semicolon

puntmuts [pʏntmʏts] *de (~en)* pointed cap, pointed hat

puntsgewijs [pʏntsχəwɛis] *adj, adv* point by point, step by step

puntzak [pʏntsak] *de (~ken)* cornet, cone

pupil [pypɪl] *de* **1** pupil, student; **2** *(sport; roughly)* junior

puppy [pʏpi] *de (~'s)* puppy

puree [pyre] *de* puree, mashed potatoes ǁ *in de ~ zitten* be in hot water *(or:* the soup)

pureren [pyrerə(n)] *vb* puree, mash

¹purper [pʏrpər] *het* purple

²purper [pʏrpər] *adj* purple

pus [pʏs] *het, de* pus

put [pʏt] *de (~ten)* **1** well: *dat is een bodemloze ~* it's a bottomless pit; *diep in de ~ zitten* be down, feel low; *iem uit de ~ halen* cheer s.o. up; **2** drain: *geld in een bodemloze ~ gooien* pour *(or:* throw) money down the drain

putten [pʏtə(n)] *vb* draw (from, on)

puur [pyr] *adj* **1** pure: *pure chocola* plain chocolate; *~ goud* solid gold; *een whisky ~ graag* a straight whisky, please; **2** pure, absolute, sheer

puzzel [pʏzəl] *de (~s)* puzzle

puzzelen [pʏzələ(n)] *vb* do puzzles; solve crossword, jigsaw puzzles

pvc [peves̬e] *het* PVC

pygmee [pɪɣm̬e] *de (~ën)* pygmy

pyjama [pij̬ama] *de (~'s)* pyjamas: *twee ~'s* two pairs of pyjamas

pyjamabroek [pij̬amabruk] *de (~en)* pyjama trousers

Pyreneeën [pirən̬ejə(n)] *adj* Pyrenees

pyromaan [pirom̬an] *de (pyromanen)* pyromaniac, firebug

Pythagoras [pitaɣorɑs] *de* Pythagoras: *stelling van* ~ Pythagorean theorem

python [pit̬ɔn] *de (~s)* python

q

qua [kwa] *prep* as regards, as far as … goes

quadrafonie [kwadrafoni] *de* quadraphonics, quadraphony

quarantaine [karɑntɛːnə] *de* quarantine: *in ~ gehouden worden* be kept in quarantine

quasi [kwasi] *adv* **1** quasi(-), pseudo-: *een ~ intellectueel* a pseudo-intellectual; **2** *(Belg)* almost, nearly: *het is ~ onmogelijk* it is scarcely (*or:* hardly) possible

quatre-mains [katrɔmɛ] *het* (piano) duet, composition for four hands

quatsch [kwatʃ] *de* nonsense, rubbish: *ach, ~!* nonsense!

quiche [kiʃ] *de (~s)* quiche

quitte [kit] *adj* quits, even: *~ spelen* break even; *~ staan met* be quits with

quiz [kwɪs] *de* quiz

quizleider [kwɪslɛidər] *de (~s)* quizmaster

quota [kwota] *de* quota, share

quotiënt [koʃɛnt] *het* quotient

r

¹**ra** [ra] *de (~'s) (shipp)* yard
²**ra** [ra] *int* ‖ ~, ~, *wie is dat?* guess who?
raad [rat] *de (raden)* **1** advice: *iem ~ geven* advise s.o.; *luister naar mijn ~* take my advice; **2** council, board: *de ~ van bestuur* (or: *van commissarissen*) the board (of directors, of management); *met voorbedachten rade* intentionally, deliberately; *moord met voorbedachten rade* premeditated (or: wilful) murder; *hij weet overal ~ op* he's never at a loss; *geen ~ weten met iets* not know what to do with sth, not know how to cope with sth; *ten einde ~ zijn* be at one's wits' end
raadhuis [rathœys] *het (-huizen)* town hall, city hall
raadplegen [ratpleɣə(n)] *vb* consult, confer with
raadsel [ratsəl] *het (~s)* **1** riddle: *een ~ opgeven* ask a riddle; **2** mystery: *het is mij een ~ hoe dat zo gekomen is* it's a mystery to me how that could have happened
raadselachtig [ratsəlaχtəχ] *adj, adv* mysterious, puzzling
raadsheer [ratsher] *de (-heren) (chess)* bishop
raadslid [ratslɪt] *het (-leden)* councillor
raadsman [ratsman] *de (raadslieden)* legal adviser
raadsverkiezing [ratsfərkizɪŋ] *de (~en)* municipal election
raadzaal [ratsal] *de (-zalen)* council chamber
raadzaam [ratsam] *adj* advisable, wise
raaf [raf] *de (raven)* raven
raak [rak] *adj, adv* home: *~ schieten* hit the mark; *ieder schot was ~* every shot went home; *(iron) het is weer ~* they're at it again; *maar ~* at random; *maar ~ slaan* hit right and left; *klets maar ~* say what you like
raaklijn [raklɛin] *de (~en)* tangent (line)
raam [ram] *het (ramen)* window, casement: *het ~pje omlaag draaien* wind down the car window
raamkozijn [ramkozɛin] *het (~en)* window frame
raamvertelling [ramvərtelɪŋ] *de (~en)* frame story
raap [rap] *de (rapen)* turnip ‖ *recht voor zijn ~* straight from the shoulder
raapstelen [rapstelə(n)] *de* turnip tops (or: greens)
¹**raar** [rar] *adj* odd, funny, strange: *een rare* an odd fish, an oddball
²**raar** [rar] *adv* oddly, strangely: *daar zul je ~ van opkijken* you'll be surprised
raaskallen [raskalə(n)] *vb* rave, talk gibberish, talk

rot
raat [rat] *de (raten)* (honey)comb
rabarber [rabɑrbər] *de* rhubarb
rabbi [rɑbi] *de (~'s)* rabbi
rabbijn [rɑbɛin] *de (~en)* rabbi
rabiës [rɑbijəs] *de* rabies
race [res] *de (~s)* race: *nog in de ~ zijn* still be in the running; *een ~ tegen de klok* a race against time
raceauto [resauto] *de (~'s)* racing car
racebaan [rezban] *de (-banen)* (race)track
racefiets [resfits] *de (~en)* racing bicycle (or: bike)
racen [resə(n)] *vb* race
racepaard [respart] *het (~en)* racehorse
racisme [rasɪsmə] *het* racism
racist [rasɪst] *de (~en)* racist
racistisch [rasɪstis] *adj, adv* racist
rad [rɑt] *het (~eren)* (cog)wheel: *het ~ van avontuur* the wheel of Fortune; *iem een ~ voor (de) ogen draaien* pull the wool over s.o.'s eyes
radar [radɑr] *de (~s)* radar
radeloos [radəlos] *adj* desperate
raden [radə(n)] *vb* guess: *raad eens wie daar komt* guess who's coming; *goed geraden!* you've guessed it; *mis (fout) ~* guess wrong; *je raadt het toch niet* you'll never guess; *je mag driemaal ~ wie het gedaan heeft* you'll never guess who did it; *dat is je geraden* you'd better
radertje [radərcə] *het (~s)* cog(wheel): *een klein ~ in het geheel zijn* be just a cog in the machine
radiaalband [radijalbɑnt] *de (~en)* radial (tyre)
radiator [radijatɔr] *de (~en)* radiator
radicaal [radikal] *adj* radical, drastic: *een ~ geneesmiddel* a radical cure; *een radicale partij* a radical party
radijs [radɛis] *de (radijzen)* radish
radio [radijo] *de (~'s)* radio, radio set: *de ~ uitzetten* switch off (or: turn off) the radio
radioactief [radijoɑktif] *adj* radioactive: *~ afval* radioactive waste
radioactiviteit [radijoɑktivitɛit] *de* radioactivity
radiojournaal [radijoʒurnal] *het (-journalen)* radio news (programme)
radionieuwsdienst [radijoniwzdinst] *de* radio news department (or: service)
radio-omroep [radijoɔmrup] *de (~en)* broadcasting service
radio-omroeper [radijoɔmrupər] *de (~s)* radio announcer
radiotherapie [radijoterapi] *de (~ën)* radiotherapy, radiation therapy
radiotoestel [radijotustɛl] *het (~len)* radio (set)
radio-uitzending [radijoœytsɛndɪŋ] *de (~en)* radio broadcast (or: transmission)
radioverslag [radijovərslaχ] *het (~en)* radio report, commentary
radius [radijys] *de (~sen, radii)* radius
radslag [rɑtslaχ] *de (~en)* cartwheel: *~en maken* turn cartwheels
rafelen [rafələ(n)] *vb* fray: *een gerafeld vloerkleed* a

frayed carpet

raffinaderij [rɑfinadərɛi] *de (~en)* refinery

raffineren [rɑfinɛrə(n)] *vb* refine

rag [rɑχ] *het* cobweb(s)

rage [raʒə] *de (~s)* craze, rage: *de nieuwste* ~ the latest craze

ragebol [raɣəbɔl] *de (~len)* ceiling mop

ragfijn [rɑχfɛin] *adj* as light (*or:* fine, thin) as gossamer

ragout [raɣu] *de (~s)* ragout: ~ *van rundvlees* beef ragout (*or:* stew)

rail [rel] *de (~s)* **1** rail: *iets (iem) weer op de ~s zetten* put sth (s.o.) back on the rails; **2** rail(way): *vervoer per* ~ rail transport

rakelings [rakəlɪŋs] *adv* closely, narrowly: *de steen ging* ~ *langs zijn hoofd* the stone narrowly missed his head

¹raken [rakə(n)] *vb* **1** hit; **2** affect, hit: *dat raakt me totaal niet* that leaves me cold; **3** touch: *de auto raakte heel even het paaltje* the car grazed the post

²raken [rakə(n)] *vb* get, become: *betrokken* ~ *bij* become involved in; *gewend* ~ *aan* get used to; *achterop* ~ get (*or:* fall) behind; *op* ~: *a)* run out (*or:* short, low), be low; *b)* run out; *(sport) uit vorm* ~ lose one's form

raket [rakɛt] *de (~ten)* missile, rocket: *een* ~ *lanceren* launch a missile (*or:* rocket)

raketbasis [rakɛdbazɪs] *de (-bases)* missile base, rocket base

rakker [rakər] *de (~s)* rascal

ram [rɑm] *de (~men)* ram

Ram [rɑm] *de (~men)* Aries, the Ram

ramadan [rɑmadan] *de* Ramadan

rammel [rɑməl] *de (~s)* beating: *een pak* ~ a beating

rammelaar [rɑməlar] *de (~s)* rattle

¹rammelen [rɑmələ(n)] *vb* **1** rattle: *aan de deur* ~ rattle the door; *met z'n sleutels* ~ clink one's keys; **2** be ramshackle: *dit plan rammelt aan alle kanten* this plan is totally unsound; *ik rammelde van de honger* my stomach was rumbling with hunger

²rammelen [rɑmələ(n)] *vb* shake: *een kind door elkaar* ~ give a child a shaking

rammen [rɑmə(n)] *vb* ram, bash in (*or:* down): *de deur* ~ bash the door down; *de auto ramde een muur* the car ran into a wall

ramp [rɑmp] *de (~en)* disaster: *een* ~ *voor het milieu* an environmental disaster; *ik zou het geen* ~ *vinden als hij niet kwam* I wouldn't shed any tears if he didn't come; *tot overmaat van* ~ to make matters worse

rampenfilm [rɑmpə(n)fɪlm] *de (~s)* disaster film

rampenplan [rɑmpə(n)plan] *het (~nen)* contingency plan

rampgebied [rɑmpχəbit] *het (~en)* disaster area

rampzalig [rɑmpsaləχ] *adj, adv* disastrous

rand [rɑnt] *de (~en)* **1** edge, rim: *de* ~ *van een bord* (*or:* *schaal*) the rim of a plate (*or:* dish); *een opstaande* ~ a raised edge; *een brief met een zwarte* ~ a black-edged letter; *aan de* ~ *van de stad* on the outskirts of the town; *aan de* ~ *van de samenleving* on the fringes of society; **2** border, edge: *een* ~ *langs het tafelkleed* a border on the tablecloth; **3** frame, rim: *de* ~ *van een spiegel* the frame of a mirror; *een bril met gouden* ~*en* gold-rimmed glasses; **4** edge, brink, (b)rim, verge: *aan de* ~ *van de afgrond: a)* on the brink of the precipice; *b) (fig)* on the verge of disaster; *tot de* ~ *gevuld* filled to the brim; *zwarte* ~*en onder zijn nagels hebben* have dirt under one's fingernails

randapparatuur [rɑntaparatyr] *de* peripheral equipment

randgemeente [rɑntχəmentə] *de (~n, ~s)* suburb

randgroepjongere [rɑntχrupjɔŋərə] *de (~n)* young drop-out

randje [rɑncə] *het (~s)* edge, border, rim, *(fig)* verge, *(fig)* brink ‖ *op het* ~ *(af)* on the borderline; *dat was op het* ~ that was close (*or:* touch and go)

randstad [rɑntstat] *de* ‖ *de* ~ *(Holland)* the cities (*or:* conurbation) of western Holland

randverschijnsel [rɑntfərsχɛinsəl] *het (~en)* marginal phenomenon

randvoorwaarde [rɑntforwardə] *de (~n)* precondition

rang [rɑŋ] *de (~en)* **1** rank, position: *een* ~ *hoger dan hij* one rank above him; *mensen van alle* ~*en en standen* people from all walks of life; **2** circle: *we zaten op de tweede* ~ we were in the upper circle

rangeerder [rɑnʒerdər] *de (~s)* shunter

rangeerterrein [rɑnʒertɛrɛin] *het (~en)* marshalling yard

rangeren [rɑnʒerə(n)] *vb* shunt: *een trein op een zijspoor* ~ shunt a train into a siding

ranglijst [rɑŋlɛist] *de (~en)* (priority) list, list (of candidates); (league) table: *bovenaan de* ~ *staan* be at the top of the list

rangschikken [rɑŋsχɪkə(n)] *vb* **1** classify, order, class; **2** order, arrange: *alfabetisch* ~ arrange in alphabetical order

rangtelwoord [rɑŋtɛlwort] *het (~en)* ordinal (number)

ranja [rɑna] *de* orange squash, orangeade

rank [rɑŋk] *de (~en)* tendril

ranselen [rɑnsələ(n)] *vb* flog, thrash

rantsoen [rɑntsun] *het (~en)* ration, allowance: *een* ~ *boter* a ration (*or:* an allowance) of butter

ranzig [rɑnzəχ] *adj* rancid

rap [rɑp] *adj, adv* quick, swift: *iets* ~ *doen* do sth quickly

rapen [rapə(n)] *vb* pick up

rapmuziek [rɛpmyzik] *de* rap music

rappen [rɛpə(n)] *vb* rap

rapport [rɑpɔrt] *het (~en)* report, despatch: ~ *uitbrengen* (or: *opmaken*) *over* produce (*or:* make) a report on; *een onvoldoende op zijn* ~ *krijgen* get a fail mark in one's report

rapportcijfer [rɑpɔrtsɛifər] *het (~s)* report mark

rapportenvergadering [rɑpɔrtə(n)vərɣadərɪŋ]

de meeting to discuss pupils' reports

rapporteren [rapɔrtɛrə(n)] *vb* report, cover: *~ aan* report to

rapsodie [rapsodi] *de (~ën)* rhapsody

ras [rɑs] *het (~sen)* race, breed, variety: *van gemengd ~* of mixed race

rasartiest [rɑsɑrtist] *de* born artist

rashond [rɑshɔnt] *de* pedigree dog, pure-bred dog

rasp [rɑsp] *de (~en)* grater

raspaard [rɑspart] *het (~en)* thoroughbred

raspen [rɑspə(n)] *vb* grate: *kaas ~* grate cheese

rassendiscriminatie [rɑsə(n)dɪskrimina(t)si] *de* racial discrimination

rasta [rɑsta] *de* Rasta(farian)

raster [rɑstər] *de* fence, lattice

raszuiver [rɑscœyvər] *adj* pure-blooded, pure-bred

rat [rɑt] *de (~ten)* rat: *hij zat als een ~ in de val* he was caught out

ratel [ratəl] *de (~s)* rattle

ratelen [ratələ(n)] *vb* rattle: *de wekker ratelt* the alarm clock is jangling

ratelslang [ratəlslɑŋ] *de (~en)* rattlesnake

ratio [ra(t)sijo] *de* **1** reason; **2** ratio

rationeel [ra(t)ʃonel] *adj, adv* rational

ratjetoe [rɑcətu] *het, de (~s)* hotchpotch, mishmash

rats [rɑts] *de* ‖ *in de ~ zitten (over)* have the wind up (about)

¹rauw [rɑu] *adj* **1** raw: *~e biefstuk* raw steak; **2** sore: *een ~e plek* a raw spot; **3** rough, tough: *dat viel ~ op mijn dak* that was an unexpected blow

²rauw [rɑu] *adv* rawly, sorely, roughly

rauwkost [rɑukɔst] *de* vegetables eaten raw

ravage [ravaʒə] *de (~s)* **1** ravage(s), havoc: *die hevige storm heeft een ~ aangericht* that violent storm has wreaked havoc; **2** debris

ravijn [ravɛin] *het (~en)* ravine, gorge

ravioli [ravijɔli] *de* ravioli

ravotten [ravɔtə(n)] *vb* romp, horse around

rayon [rɛjɔn] *het (~s)* district, territory: *hij heeft Limburg als zijn ~* he works Limburg

rayonchef [rɛjɔnʃɛf] *de (~s)* area supervisor

razen [razə(n)] *vb* race, tear: *de auto's ~ over de snelweg* the cars are racing along the motorway

razend [razənt] *adj, adv* **1** furious: *iem ~ maken* infuriate s.o.; *als een ~e tekeergaan* rave like a madman; **2** terrific: *hij heeft het ~ druk* he's up to his neck in work; *~ snel, in ~e vaart* at a terrific pace, at breakneck speed

razendsnel [razəntsnɛl] *adj, adv* super-fast, high-speed

razernij [razərnɛi] *de* frenzy, rage: *in blinde ~* in a blind rage; *iem tot ~ brengen* infuriate s.o.

razzia [rɑzija] *de (~'s)* razzia

re [re] *de (~'s)* re, D

reactie [rejɑksi] *de (~s)* reaction, response: *als ~ op* in reaction to; *snelle ~s* sharp reflexes

reactiesnelheid [rejɑksisnɛlhɛit] *de* speed of reaction

reactor [rejɑktɔr] *de (~s)* reactor: *snelle ~* fast reactor

reageerbuis [rejaɣɛrbœys] *de (-buizen)* test tube: *bevruchting in een ~* test-tube (*or:* in vitro) fertilization

reageerbuisbaby [rejaɣɛrbœyzbebi] *de (~'s)* test-tube baby

reageerbuisbevruchting [rejaɣɛrbœyzbəvrʏχtɪŋ] *de (~en)* test-tube (*or:* in vitro) fertilization

reageren [rejaɣɛrə(n)] *vb* react (to), respond: *te sterk ~* overreact; *moet je eens kijken hoe hij daarop reageert* look how he reacts to that; *ze reageerde positief op de behandeling* she responded to the treatment

realiseerbaar [rejalizɛrbar] *adj* realizable, feasible

¹realiseren [rejalizɛrə(n)] *vb* realize: *dat is niet te ~* that is impracticable

²realiseren [rejalizɛrə(n)] *ref vb* realize

realisme [rejalɪsmə] *het* realism

realist [rejalɪst] *de (~en)* realist

realistisch [rejalɪstis] *adj, adv* realistic: *~ beschrijven* (*or:* schilderen) describe (*or:* paint) realistically

realiteit [rejalitɛit] *de (~en)* reality: *we moeten de ~ onder ogen zien* we must face facts (*or:* reality)

reanimatie [reanima(t)si] *de* resuscitation, reanimation

reanimeren [reanimɛrə(n)] *vb* resuscitate, revive

rebel [rəbɛl] *de (~len)* rebel

rebellenleider [rəbɛlə(n)lɛidər] *de (~s)* rebel leader

rebelleren [rəbɛlɛrə(n)] *vb* rebel: *~ tegen ...* rebel against ...

rebels [rəbɛls] *adj, adv* rebellious

rebus [rebʏs] *de (~sen)* rebus

recensent [resɛnsɛnt] *de (~en)* reviewer, critic

recensie [resɛnsi] *de (~s)* review, notice: *lovende (juichende) ~s krijgen* get rave reviews

recent [rəsɛnt] *adj* recent

recept [rəsɛpt] *het (~en)* **1** prescription: *alleen op ~ verkrijgbaar* available only on prescription; **2** recipe

receptie [resɛpsi] *de (~s)* **1** reception: *staande ~* stand-up reception; **2** reception (desk): *melden bij de ~* report to the reception (desk)

receptionist [resɛpʃonɪst] *de (~en)* receptionist

recessie [rəsɛsi] *de* recession

recherche [reʃɛrʒə] *de (~s)* criminal investigation department

rechercheur [reʃɛrʃør] *de (~s)* detective

¹recht [rɛχt] *het (~en)* **1** justice, right: *iem ~ doen* do s.o. justice; *iem (iets) geen ~ doen* be unfair to s.o. (sth); *het ~ handhaven* uphold the law; *het ~ aan zijn kant hebben* be in the right; **2** law: *student (in de) ~en* law student; *burgerlijk ~* civil law; *het ~ in eigen handen nemen* take the law into one's own hands; *~en studeren* read (*or:* study) law; *volgens Engels ~* under English law; **3** right: *~ van bestaan hebben* have a right to exist; *het ~ van de sterkste* the law of the jungle; *dat is mijn goed ~* that is my right; *het volste ~ hebben om ...* have every right to ...; *niet het ~ hebben iets te doen* have no right to do sth; *goed tot zijn ~ komen* show up well; *voor zijn ~(en) opkomen* defend one's right(s); **4** *(pl)* rights: *de ~en van de mens* human rights; **5** right, claim: *~ op uitkering* entitlement to a benefit; *~ hebben op iets* have the right to sth; **6** *(pl)* (copy)right(s): *alle ~en voorbehouden* all rights reserved

²**recht** [rɛχt] *adj, adv* **1** straight: *de auto kwam ~ op ons af* the car was coming straight at us; *iets ~ leggen* put sth straight; *~ op iem (iets) afgaan* go straight for s.o. (sth); *iem ~ in de ogen kijken* look s.o. straight in the eye; *~ voor zich uitkijken* look straight ahead; *hij woont ~ tegenover mij* he lives straight across from me; *~ tegenover elkaar* face-to-face; **2** straight (up), upright: *~ zitten* (or: *staan*) sit (or: stand) up straight; *~ overeind* straight up, bolt upright; **3** right; direct; directly: *de ~e zijde van een voorwerp* the right side of an object; **4** right; true: *op het ~e pad blijven* keep to the straight and narrow; *~e hoek* right angle

rechtbank [rɛχtbɑŋk] *de (~en)* **1** court (of law, justice), lawcourt: *voor de ~ moeten komen* have to appear in court (*or:* before the court); **2** court, law courts, magistrates' court, *(Am)* courthouse

rechtbreien [rɛχ(t)brɛijə(n)] *vb* put right, rectify

rechtbuigen [rɛχ(t)bœyɣə(n)] *vb* straighten (out), bend straight

rechtdoor [rɛχtdor] *adv* straight on (or: ahead)

rechtdoorzee [rɛɣdorzɛ] *adj* straight, honest, sincere

¹**rechter** [rɛχtər] *de (~s)* judge, magistrate: *naar de ~ stappen* go to court; *voor de ~ moeten verschijnen* have to appear in court

²**rechter** [rɛχtər] *adj* right; right(-hand): *de ~ deur* the door on the (or: your) right

rechterarm [rɛχtərɑrm] *de* right arm

rechterbeen [rɛχtərben] *het* right leg

rechter-commissaris [rɛχtərkɔmɪsɑrɪs] *de (rechters-commissarissen)* examining judge (or: magistrate)

rechterhand [rɛχtərhɑnt] *de (~en)* right hand: *de tweede straat aan uw ~* the second street on your right

rechterkant [rɛχtərkɑnt] *de* right(-hand) side: *aan de ~* on the right(-hand) side

rechterlijk [rɛχtərlək] *adj, adv* judicial, court: *de ~e macht* the judiciary

rechtervoet [rɛχtərvut] *de* right foot

rechterzijde [rɛχtərzɛidə] *de* right(-hand) side: *pijn in de ~ hebben* have a pain in one's right side; *aan de ~* on the right(-hand side)

rechthoek [rɛχthuk] *de (~en)* rectangle, oblong

rechthoekig [rɛχthukəχ] *adj, adv* **1** right-angled; at right angles: *een ~e driehoek* a right-angled triangle; **2** rectangular, oblong: *een ~e kamer* a rectangular room

rechtmatig [rɛχtmatəχ] *adj, adv* rightful; lawful; legitimate: *de ~e eigenaars* the rightful (or: legitimate) owners

rechtop [rɛχtɔp] *adv* upright, straight (up), on end: *~ lopen* walk upright; *~ zitten* sit up straight

rechts [rɛχts] *adj, adv* **1** right(-hand): *de eerste deur ~* the first door on (or: to) the right; *~ afslaan* turn (off to the) right; *~ houden* keep (to the) right; *~ rijden* drive on the right; *~ boven* (or: *beneden*) top (or: bottom) right; *hij zat ~ van mij* he sat on my right(-hand side); **2** right-handed: *~ schrijven* write with one's right hand; **3** *(pol)* right-wing

rechtsachter [rɛχtsɑχtər] *de (~s)* right back

rechtsaf [rɛχtsɑf] *adv* (to the, one's) right: *bij de splitsing moet u ~* you have to turn right at the junction

rechtsbescherming [rɛχtsbəsχɛrmɪŋ] *de* legal protection

rechtsbijstand [rɛχtsbɛistɑnt] *de* legal aid

rechtsbuiten [rɛχtsbœytə(n)] *de (~s)* right-winger, outside right

rechtsgebouw [rɛχ(t)sχəbɑu] *het (~en)* law courts, magistrates' court, *(Am)* court-house

rechtsgeldig [rɛχtsχɛldəχ] *adj* (legally) valid, lawful

rechtsgeldigheid [rɛχtsχɛldəχhɛit] *de* legality, legal force (or: validity)

rechtsgelijkheid [rɛχtsχəlɛikhɛit] *de* equality before the law, equality of rights (or: status)

rechtshandig [rɛχtshɑndəχ] *adj* right-handed

rechtshulp [rɛχtshʏlp] *de* legal aid: *bureau voor ~* legal advice centre

rechtsomkeert [rɛχtsɔmkert] *adv* ‖ *~ maken:* a) *(mil)* do an about-turn; b) *(fig)* make a U-turn

rechtsongelijkheid [rɛχtsɔŋəlɛikhɛit] *de* inequality of status, legal inequality

rechtsorde [rɛχtsɔrdə] *de* legal order, system of law(s)

rechtspersoon [rɛχtspɛrsɔn] *de (-personen)* legal body (or: entity, person)

rechtspositie [rɛχtspozi(t)si] *de* legal position

rechtspraak [rɛχtsprak] *de* **1** administration of justice (or: of the law); **2** jurisdiction: *de ~ in strafzaken* criminal jurisdiction

rechtspreken [rɛχtsprekə(n)] *vb* administer justice: *de ~de macht* the judicature, the judiciary; *~ in een zaak* judge a case

rechtsstaat [rɛχtstat] *de (-staten)* constitutional state

rechtstreeks [rɛχtstreks] *adj, adv* **1** direct, straight(forward): *een ~e verbinding* a direct connection; *~ naar huis gaan* go straight (or: right) home; **2** direct, immediate: *een ~e uitzending* a direct broadcast; *hij wendde zich ~ tot de minister* he went straight to the minister

rechtsvervolging [rɛχtsfərvɔlɣɪŋ] *de (~en)* legal proceedings, prosecution: *een ~ tegen iem instellen* institute legal proceedings against s.o.; *ontslaan van ~* acquit

rechtswinkel [rɛχtswɪŋkəl] *de (~s)* law centre (or: clinic)

rechtszaak [rɛχtsak] *de (-zaken)* lawsuit: *ergens een ~ van maken* take a matter to court

rechtszaal [rɛχtsal] *de (-zalen)* courtroom

rechtszitting [rɛχtsɪtɪŋ] *de (~en)* sitting (*or:* session) of the court

rechttoe [rɛχtu] *adv* ‖ *~, rechtaan* straightforward; *het was allemaal ~ rechtaan* it was plain sailing all the way

rechttrekken [rɛχtrɛkə(n)] *vb* set right, put right

rechtuit [rɛχtœyt] *adv* straight on (*or:* ahead): *~ lopen* walk straight on

rechtvaardig [rɛχtfardəχ] *adj, adv* just, fair: *een ~ oordeel* a fair judg(e)ment; *iem ~ behandelen* treat s.o. fairly

rechtvaardigen [rɛχtfardəχə(n)] *vb* justify, warrant: *zich tegenover iem ~* justify oneself to s.o.

rechtvaardigheid [rɛχtfardəχhɛit] *de* justice

rechtvaardiging [rɛχtfardəχɪŋ] *de* justification

rechtzetten [rɛχtsɛtə(n)] *vb* **1** put right, set right, rectify; **2** adjust; **3** set up, put up, raise

recital [risɑjtəl] *het (~s)* recital

reclame [rəklamə] *de (~s)* **1** advertising, publicity: *~ maken (voor iets)* advertise (sth); **2** ad(vertisement), sign

reclameaanbieding [rəklaməambidɪŋ] *de (~en)* special offer

reclameblaadje [rəklaməblacə] *het (~s)* advertising leaflet, pamphlet, free sheet

reclameboodschap [rəklaməbotsχɑp] *de (~pen)* commercial

reclamebord [rəklaməbɔrt] *het (~en)* billboard, *(large)* hoarding, (advertising) sign

reclamebureau [rəklaməbyro] *het* advertising agency

reclamecampagne [rəklaməkɑmpɑɲə] *de (~s)* advertising campaign: *een ~ voeren* run (*or:* conduct) an advertising campaign

reclamedrukwerk [rəklamədrykwɛrk] *het (~en)* advertising leaflets (*or:* brochures): *mijn brievenbus zat vol ~* my letterbox was full of advertisements

reclamefolder [rəklaməfɔldər] *de (~s)* advertising brochure (*or:* pamphlet)

reclameren [reklamerə(n)] *vb* complain, put in a claim

reclamespot [rəklaməspɔt] *de (~s)* commercial, (advertising) spot

reclamestunt [rəklaməstynt] *de (~s)* advertising stunt, publicity stunt

reclassering [reklɑserɪŋ] *de* after-care and rehabilitation

reclasseringsambtenaar [reklɑserɪŋsɑmtənar] *de* probation officer

reclasseringswerk [reklɑserɪŋswɛrk] *het* after-care and resettlement (of discharged prisoners)

reconstructie [rekɔnstrʏksi] *de (~s)* reconstruction

reconstrueren [rekɔnstrywerə(n)] *vb* reconstruct

record [rəkɔːr] *het (~s)* record: *een ~ breken* (*or:*

vestigen) break (*or:* establish) a record

recordhouder [rəkɔːrhaudər] *de (~s)* record-holder

recordpoging [rəkɔːrpoɣɪŋ] *de (~en)* attempt on a record

recreatie [rekreja(t)si] *de (~s)* recreation, leisure

recreatief [rekrejatif] *adj* recreational

rectificatie [rɛktifika(t)si] *de (~s)* rectification

rector [rɛktɔr] *de (~en, ~s)* **1** headmaster, principal; **2** rector

reçu [rəsy] *het (~'s)* receipt

recyclen [risɑjk(ə)lə(n)] *vb* recycle

redacteur [redɑktør] *de (~en, ~s)* editor

redactie [redɑksi] *de (~s)* editors, editorial staff

redactioneel [redɑkʃonel] *adj* editorial: *een ~ artikel* an editorial

¹redden [rɛdə(n)] *vb* **1** save, rescue, salvage: *de ~de hand toesteken* be the saving of a person; *we moeten zien te ~ wat er te ~ valt* we must make the best of a bad job; *gered zijn* be helped; **2** (with *het*) manage: *de zieke zal het niet ~* the patient won't pull through; *Jezus redt* Jesus saves

²redden [rɛdə(n)] *ref vb* manage, cope: *ik red me best!* I can manage all right!

redder [rɛdər] *de (~s)* rescuer, saviour

redding [rɛdɪŋ] *de (~en)* rescue, salvation

reddingsactie [rɛdɪŋsɑksi] *de (~s)* rescue operation

reddingsboot [rɛdɪŋzbot] *de (-boten)* lifeboat

reddingsbrigade [rɛdɪŋzbriɣadə] *de (~s, ~n)* rescue party (*or:* team)

reddingsoperatie [rɛdɪŋsopəra(t)si] *de* rescue operation

reddingsploeg [rɛdɪŋsplux] *de* rescue party (*or:* team), search party

reddingspoging [rɛdɪŋspoɣɪŋ] *de (~en)* rescue attempt (*or:* bid, effort): *hun ~en mochten hem niet baten* their attempts (*or:* efforts) to rescue him were in vain

rede [redə] *de (~s)* **1** reason, sense: *hij is niet voor ~ vatbaar* he won't listen to (*or:* see) reason; **2** speech, address: *een ~ houden* make a speech; **3** reason, intelligence, intellect: *iem in de ~ vallen* interrupt s.o.

¹redelijk [redələk] *adj* **2** rational, sensible; **3** reasonable, fair: *binnen ~e grenzen* within (reasonable) limits; *een ~e prijs* a reasonable price; *een ~e kans maken* stand a reasonable chance

²redelijk [redələk] *adv* **1** rationally: *~ denken* think rationally; **2** reasonably, fairly: *ik ben ~ gezond* I am in reasonably good health

redelijkerwijs [redələkərwɛis] *adv* in fairness: *~ kunt u niet meer verlangen* in all fairness you cannot expect more

redeloos [redəlos] *adj, adv* **1** irrational; **2** unreasonable

reden [redə(n)] *de (~en)* **1** reason, cause, occasion: *om persoonlijke ~en* for personal reasons; *ik heb er mijn ~ voor* I have my reasons; *om die ~ voor* for that reason; *geen ~ tot klagen hebben* have no cause (*or:*

ground) for complaint; *een ~ te meer om ...* all the more reason why ...; **2** reason, motive: *zonder opgaaf van ~en* without reason; *~ geven tot* give cause for

redenaar [rẹdənar] *de (~s)* speaker, orator

redeneren [redənẹrə(n)] *vb* reason, argue (about): *daartegen is (valt) niet te ~* there is no arguing with that

redenering [redənẹrıŋ] *de (~en)* reasoning, argumentation: *een fout in de ~* a flaw in the reasoning

reder [rẹdər] *de (~s)* shipowner

rederij [redərẹi] *de (~en)* shipping company, shipowner(s)

redevoering [rẹdəvurıŋ] *de (~en)* speech, address: *een ~ houden* make (*or:* deliver) a speech

reduceren [redysẹrə(n)] *vb* reduce, decrease: *gereduceerd tarief* reduced rate

reductie [redŷksi] *de (~s)* reduction, decrease, cut, cutback: *~ geven* give a discount

ree [re] *het, de (~ën)* roe(deer)

reebok [rẹbɔk] *de (~ken)* roebuck

reëel [rejẹl] *adj, adv* **1** real, actual: *reële groei van het inkomen* growth of real income; **2** realistic, reasonable: *een reële kijk op het leven hebben* have a realistic outlook on life

reeks [reks] *de (~en)* **1** series, row, string; **2** series, succession, sequence: *een ~ ongelukken* a string (*or:* succession) of accidents

reep [rep] *de (repen)* **1** strip, thong; band, sliver: *de komkommer in ~jes snijden* slice the cucumber thinly; **2** (chocolate) bar

reet [ret] *de (reten)* **1** crack, chink; **2** arse, *(Am)* ass, backside

referentie [refərɛnsi] *de (~s)* reference, *(pers also)* referee: *mag ik u als ~ opgeven?* may I use you as a reference?

reflecteren [reflɛktẹrə(n)] *vb* reflect, mirror

reflectie [reflɛksi] *de (~s)* reflection

reflector [reflɛktɔr] *de (~en)* reflector, Catseye

reflex [reflɛks] *de (~en)* reflex: *een aangeboren ~* an innate reflex

reformartikel [refɔrmartikəl] *het (~en)* health food product, wholefood product

reformwinkel [refɔrmwıŋkəl] *de (~s)* health food shop, wholefood shop

refrein [rəfrɛin] *het (~en)* refrain, chorus: *iedereen zong het ~ mee* everybody joined in the chorus

refter [rɛftər] *de (~s)* refectory

regeerakkoord [rəɣẹrakort] *het (~en)* coalition agreement

regeerperiode [rəɣẹrperijodə] *de* period of office, period of government

regel [rẹɣəl] *de (~s)* **1** line: *een ~ overslaan* skip a line, leave a line blank; *tussen de ~s door lezen* read between the lines; **2** rule: *het is ~ dat ...* it is a (general) rule that ...; *in de ~* as a rule, ordinarily; **3** rule, regulation, law: *tegen alle ~s in* contrary to (*or:* against) all the rules

regelafstand [rẹɣəlafstant] *de (~en)* line space,

spacing: *op enkele ~* single-spaced

regelen [rẹɣələ(n)] *vb* **1** regulate, arrange, fix (up), settle, control *(traf)*; adjust, order: *de geluidssterkte ~* adjust the volume; *de temperatuur ~* regulate (*or:* control) the temperature; *het verkeer ~* direct the traffic; *ik zal dat wel even ~* I'll take care of that; **2** regulate, lay down rules for

regeling [rẹɣəlıŋ] *de (~en)* **1** regulation, arrangement, settlement, ordering, control *(traf)*; adjustment: *de ~ van de geldzaken* the settling of money matters; *een ~ treffen* make an arrangement (*or:* a settlement); **2** arrangement, settlement, scheme

regelmaat [rẹɣəlmat] *de* regularity: *met de ~ van de klok* as regular as clockwork

regelmatig [reɣəlmatəχ] *adj, adv* **1** regular, orderly: *een ~e ademhaling* regular (*or:* even) breathing; *een ~ leven leiden* lead a regular (*or:* an orderly) life; **2** regular, frequent: *~ naar de kerk gaan* be a regular churchgoer; *dat komt ~ voor* that happens regularly

regelrecht [reɣəlrɛχt] *adj, adv* straight, direct, *(adverb also)* right: *de kinderen kwamen ~ naar huis* the children came straight home

regen [rẹɣə(n)] *de (~s)* **1** rain: *aanhoudende ~* persistent rain; *in de stromende ~* in the pouring rain; *zure ~* acid rain; **2** rain, shower

regenachtig [rẹɣənaχtəχ] *adj* rainy, showery: *een ~e dag* a rainy day

regenboog [rẹɣə(n)boχ] *de (-bogen)* rainbow

regenboogtrui [rẹɣə(n)boχtrœy] *de (~en) (sport)* rainbow jersey

regenboogvlies [rẹɣə(n)boχflis] *het (-vliezen)* iris

regenbui [rẹɣə(n)bœy] *de (~en)* shower (of rain), downpour

regendruppel [rẹɣə(n)drypəl] *de (~s, ~en)* raindrop

regenen [rẹɣənə(n)] *vb* rain, *(light)* shower, drizzle: *het heeft flink geregend* there was quite a downpour; *het regent dat het giet* it is pouring

regenjas [rẹɣə(n)jas] *de (~sen)* raincoat, mackintosh

regenkleding [rẹɣə(n)kledıŋ] *de* rainproof clothing, rainwear

regenmeter [rẹɣə(n)metər] *de (~s)* rain gauge

regenpijp [rẹɣə(n)pɛip] *de (~en)* drainpipe

regent [rəɣɛnt] *de (~en)* **1** regent; **2** *(Belg)* teacher for lower classes in secondary school

regentijd [rẹχə(n)tɛit] *de (~en)* rainy season, rains: *in de ~* during the rainy season

regenval [rẹɣə(n)val] *de* rain(fall), shower

regenworm [rẹɣə(n)wɔrm] *de (~en)* earthworm

regenwoud [rẹɣə(n)waut] *het (~en)* rainforest

regeren [rəɣẹrə(n)] *vb* rule (over), reign, govern, control: *de ~de partij* the party in power

regering [rəɣẹrıŋ] *de (~en)* government: *de ~ is afgetreden* the government has resigned

regeringsbeleid [rəɣɛrıŋzbəlɛit] *het* government policy

regeringsleider [rəɣɛrıŋslɛidər] *de (~s)* leader of

the government

regeringspartij [rəɣɛrɪŋspɑrtɛi] *de (~en)* party in office (*or:* power), government party

regie [reʒi] *de (~s)* direction, production

regieassistent [reɣiɑsistɛnt] *de (~en)* assistant to the director

regime [reʒim] *het (~s)* regime

regiment [reʒimɛnt] *het (~en)* regiment

regio [reɣijo] *de (~'s)* region, area

regiokorps [reɣijokɔrps] *het (~en)* regional police force

regionaal [reɣ(i)jonɑl] *adj, adv* regional

regisseren [reɣisɛrə(n)] *vb* direct, produce

regisseur [reɣisør] *de (~s)* director, producer

register [rəɣɪstər] *het (~s)* **1** register, record: *de ~s van de burgerlijke stand* the register of births, deaths and marriages; *een alfabetisch ~* an alphabetical register; **2** index, table of contents

registeraccountant [rəɣɪstərɑkauntənt] *de (~s)* chartered accountant; certified public accountant

registratie [reɣistra(t)si] *de (~s)* registration

registreren [reɣistrɛrə(n)] *vb* register, record

reglement [reɣləmɛnt] *het (~en)* regulation(s), rule(s), rule book, rules and regulations: *huishoudelijk ~* regulations

reguleren [reɣylɛrə(n)] *vb* regulate, control, adjust

regulier [reɣylir] *adj* regular, normal

rehabilitatie [rehabilita(t)si] *de (~s)* rehabilitation, vindication

rehabiliteren [rehabilitɛrə(n)] *vb* rehabilitate, vindicate

rei [rɛi] *de (~en) (Belg)* town canal, city canal

reiger [rɛiɣər] *de (~s)* heron

reiken [rɛikə(n)] *vb* reach, extend: *zo ver het oog reikt* as far as the eye can see

reikwijdte [rɛikwɛitə] *de* range, scope

reïncarnatie [rɛɪŋkɑrna(t)si] *de (~s)* reincarnation

reinigen [rɛinəɣə(n)] *vb* clean (up), wash, cleanse: *chemisch ~* dry-clean

reiniging [rɛinəɣɪŋ] *de* cleaning, cleansing, washing, purification: *chemische ~* dry-cleaning

reinigingsdienst [rɛinəɣɪŋzdinst] *de (~en)* cleansing service (*or:* department)

reinigingsmiddel [rɛinəɣɪŋsmɪdəl] *het (~en)* cleansing agent, clean(s)er, detergent

reis [rɛis] *de (reizen)* **1** trip, journey, voyage, passage, flight: *enkele ~* single (journey), *(Am)* one-way; *goede ~* have a good (*or:* pleasant) journey; *een ~ om de wereld maken* go round the world; *op ~ gaan* go on a journey; **2** trip, tour: *een geheel verzorgde ~* a package tour (*or:* holiday)

reisbureau [rɛizbyro] *het (~s)* travel agency, travel agent's

reischeque [rɛisʃɛk] *de (~s)* traveller's cheque

reisdeclaratie [rɛizdeklara(t)si] *de (~s)* claim for travelling expenses

reis- en kredietbrief [rɛisɛŋkrədidbrif] *de (-brieven)* circular letter of credit

reisgezelschap [rɛisxəzɛlsxɑp] *het (~pen)*

tour(ing) group (*or:* party); coach party

reisgids [rɛisxɪts] *de (~en)* **1** travel brochure (*or:* leaflet); **2** guidebook, (travel) guide; **3** (travel) guide, courier

reiskaart [rɛiskart] *de (~en)* ticket

reiskosten [rɛiskɔstə(n)] *de* travelling expenses: *reis- en verblijfkosten* travel and living expenses

reiskostenvergoeding [rɛiskɔstə(n)vərɣudɪŋ] *de (~en)* travelling allowance

reisleider [rɛislɛidər] *de (~s)* (travel, tour) guide, courier

reisorganisatie [rɛisɔrɣaniza(t)si] *de (~s)* travel organization (*or:* company), tour operator

reisorganisator [rɛisɔrɣanizatɔr] *de (~en)* tour operator

reisverzekering [rɛisfərzekərɪŋ] *de (~en)* travel insurance

reiswieg [rɛiswix] *de (~en)* carrycot, portable crib

reizen [rɛizə(n)] *vb* travel, go on a trip (*or:* journey): *op en neer ~* travel up and down; *per spoor ~* travel by train

reiziger [rɛizəɣər] *de (~s)* **1** traveller, tourist, passenger: *~s naar Londen hier overstappen* passengers for London change here; **2** travelling salesman

¹rek [rɛk] *het* rack, shelves

²rek [rɛk] *de* elasticity, give, flexibility: *de ~ is er uit* the party is over

¹rekenen [rekənə(n)] *vb* **1** calculate, do sums (*or:* figures), reckon: *goed kunnen ~* be good at figures; *in euro ~* reckon in euros; **2** consider, include, take into consideration (*or:* account): *daar had ik niet op gerekend* I hadn't counted on (*or:* expected) that; *daar mag je wel op ~* you'd better allow for that; **3** (with *op*) rely, count on, trust: *kan ik op je ~?* can I count (*or:* depend) on you?; *reken maar niet op ons* count us out; **4** (with *op*) expect: *je kunt op 40 gasten ~* you can expect 40 guests

²rekenen [rekənə(n)] *vb* **1** count: *alles bij elkaar gerekend* all told, in all; **2** charge, ask: *hoeveel rekent u daarvoor?* how much do you charge for that?; **3** count, number: *zich ~ tot* count oneself as (*or:* among); **4** bear in mind, remember, allow for: *reken maar!* you bet!

rekening [rekənɪŋ] *de (~en)* **1** bill; check, invoice: *een hoge ~* a stiff bill; *een ~ betalen* (*or:* voldoen) pay/settle an account (*or:* a bill); *ober, mag ik de ~?* waiter, may I have the bill please?; **2** account: *een ~ openen (bij een bank)* open an account (at a bank); *op ~ van* at the expense of; *dat is voor mijn ~* I'll take care of that, leave that to me; *kosten voor zijn ~ nemen* pay the costs; **3** (with *voor*) expense: *voor eigen ~* at one's own expense; *~ houden met iets* take sth into account; *je moet een beetje ~ houden met je ouders* you should show some consideration for your parents

rekening-courant [rekənɪŋkurɑnt] *de (rekeningen-courant)* current account

rekeninghouder [rekənɪŋhaudər] *de (~s)* account holder

rekeningnummer [rɛkənɪŋnʏmər] *het* account number
Rekenkamer [rɛkə(n)kamər] *de* audit office, auditor's office
rekenkunde [rɛkə(n)kʏndə] *de* arithmetic, maths
rekenkundig [rɛkə(n)kʏndəχ] *adj, adv* arithmetic(al)
rekenliniaal [rɛkə(n)linijal] *de (rekenlinialen)* slide rule
rekenmachine [rɛkə(n)maʃinə] *de (~s)* calculator
rekensom [rɛkə(n)sɔm] *de (~men)* **1** sum; *(pl also)* number work; **2** *(fig)* problem, question: *het is een eenvoudig ~metje* it's just a matter of adding two and two; *een eenvoudige ~ leert dat …* it is easy to calculate that …
¹rekken [rɛkə(n)] *vb* stretch: *dat elastiek rekt niet goed meer* that elastic has lost its stretch
²rekken [rɛkə(n)] *vb* **1** stretch (out); **2** drag out, draw out, prolong: *het leven van een stervende ~* prolong a dying person's life; *(socc) tijd ~* use delaying tactics
rekruut [rekrʏt] *de (rekruten)* recruit
rekstok [rɛkstɔk] *de (~ken)* horizontal bar, high bar
rekwisiet [rekwizit] *het (~en)* (stage-)property, prop
rel [rɛl] *de (~len)* disturbance; riot: *een ~ schoppen* kick up *(or:* cause) a row
relais [rəlɛː] *het* relay
relatie [rela(t)si] *de (~s)* **1** relation(s), connection, relationship, contact: *~s onderhouden (met)* maintain relations (with); *in ~ staan tot* have relations with; **2** affair, relationship: *een ~ hebben met iem* have a relationship with s.o.
relatief [relatif] *adj, adv* relative, comparative
relatiegeschenk [rela(t)siɣəsχɛŋk] *het (~en)* business gift
relativeren [relativerə(n)] *vb* put into perspective
relaxen [rilɛksə(n)] *vb* relax
relevant [reləvɑnt] *adj* relevant: *die vraag is niet ~* that question is irrelevant
relevantie [reləvɑnsi] *de* relevance
reliëf [reljɛf] *het* relief
religie [reliɣi] *de (~s)* religion
religieus [reliɣjøs] *adj, adv* religious
relikwie [relikwi] *de* relic
reling [relɪŋ] *de (~en)* rail
relschopper [rɛlsχɔpər] *de (~s)* rioter, hooligan
rem [rɛm] *de (~men)* brake: *op de ~ gaan staan* slam *(or:* jam) on the brakes
rembekrachtiging [rɛmbəkrɑχtəɣɪŋ] *de* power(-assisted) brakes
rembours [rɑmbʏrs] *het (~en)* cash on delivery, COD: *onder ~ versturen* send (sth) COD
remise [rəmizə] *de (~s)* draw, tie, drawn game
remlicht [rɛmlɪχt] *het (~en)* brake light
remmen [rɛmə(n)] *vb* brake, *(fig also)* curb, check, inhibit: *geremd in zijn ontwikkeling* curbed in its development

remming [rɛmɪŋ] *de (~en)* check, *(fig)* inhibition
rempedaal [rɛmpədal] *het, de (-pedalen)* brake pedal
remspoor [rɛmspor] *het (remsporen)* skid mark
remweg [rɛmwɛχ] *de* braking distance
ren [rɛn] *de* run
renaissance [renɛsɑ̃sə] *de* renaissance
renbaan [rɛmban] *de (renbanen)* (race)track, (race)course
rendabel [rɛndabəl] *adj* profitable, cost-effective
rendement [rɛndəmɛnt] *het (~en)* **1** return, yield, output: *het ~ van obligaties* the return *(or:* yield) on bonds; **2** efficiency, output, performance: *het ~ van een elektrische lamp* the efficiency *(or:* output) of an electric lamp
rendier [rɛndir] *het (~en)* reindeer
rennen [rɛnə(n)] *vb* run, race: *we zijn laat, we moeten ~* we're late; we must dash (off) *(or:* must fly)
renner [rɛnər] *de (~s)* rider
renovatie [renova(t)si] *de (~s)* renovation, redevelopment
renoveren [renoverə(n)] *vb* renovate; redevelop
renpaard [rɛmpart] *het (~en)* racehorse, thoroughbred
rentabiliteit [rɛntabilitɛit] *de* productivity, cost-effectiveness, profitability
rente [rɛntə] *de (~n, ~s)* interest: *~ opbrengen* yield interest; *~ op ~* compound interest; *een lening tegen vijf procent ~* a loan at five per cent interest
rentenieren [rɛntənirə(n)] *vb* **1** live off one's investments; **2** lead a life of leisure
rentepercentage [rɛntəpɛrsɛntaʒə] *het* interest rate
renteverhoging [rɛntəvərhoɣɪŋ] *de* rise in interest rates
renteverlaging [rɛntəvərlaɣɪŋ] *de* fall in interest rates
rentevoet [rɛntəvut] *de* interest rate, rate of interest
reorganisatie [reɔrɣaniza(t)si] *de (~s)* reorganization
reorganiseren [reɔrɣanizerə(n)] *vb* reorganize: *het onderwijs ~* reorganize the educational system
rep [rɛp] ‖ *het hele land was in ~ en roer* the entire country was in (an) uproar
reparateur [reparatør] *de (~s)* repairer; repairman; service engineer
reparatie [repara(t)si] *de (~s)* repair: *mijn horloge is in (de) ~* my watch is being repaired
repareren [reparerə(n)] *vb* repair, mend, fix: *dat is niet meer te ~* it's beyond repair
repertoire [repɛrtwar] *het (~s)* repertoire, repertory: *het klassieke ~* the classics; *zijn ~ afwerken* do one's repertoire
¹repeteren [repəterə(n)] *vb* **1** rehearse; **2** repeat; circulate
²repeteren [repəterə(n)] *vb* rehearse, run through, go through
repetitie [repəti(t)si] *de (~s)* rehearsal,

run-through, practice: *generale ~* dress rehearsal, final (*or:* last) rehearsal

reportage [repɔrtaːʒə] *de (~s)* report, coverage, commentary: *de ~ van een voetbalwedstrijd* the coverage of a football match

reporter [ripɔːrtər] *de (~s)* reporter

reppen [rɛpə(n)] *vb* **1** mention; **2** hurry, rush

represaille [reprɛzɑ̯jə] *de (~s)* reprisal, retaliation: *~s nemen (tegen)* retaliate (*or:* take reprisals) (against)

representatief [reprɛzɛntatiˑf] *adj* **1** representative (of), typical (of): *een representatieve groep van de bevolking* a cross-section of the population; *een representatieve steekproef* a representative sample; **2** representative, presentable

representeren [reprɛzɛnteˑrə(n)] *vb* represent

reproduceren [reprodyseˑrə(n)] *vb* reproduce, copy

reproductie [reprodyˑksi] *de (~s)* reproduction, copy

reptiel [rɛptiˑl] *het (~en)* reptile

republiek [repyblik] *de (~en)* republic

republikein [repyblikɛi̯n] *de (~en)* republican

reputatie [repyta(t)si] *de (~s)* reputation, name, fame: *een goede* (or: *slechte) ~ hebben* have a good (*or:* bad) reputation; *iemands ~ schaden, slecht zijn voor iemands ~* damage s.o.'s reputation

requiem [rɛkwijɛm] *het (~s)* requiem (mass)

research [risʏːrtʃ] *de* research

reservaat [rezɛrvaːt] *het (reservaten)* reserve, preserve: *indianenreservaat* Indian reservation; *natuurreservaat* nature reserve

reserve [rəzɛrvə] *de (~s)* **1** reserve(s): *zijn ~s aanspreken* draw on one's reserves; **2** reserve, reservation: *zonder enige ~* without reservations

reserveband [rəzɛrvəbɑnt] *de* spare tyre

reservebank [rəzɛrvəbɑŋk] *de (~en)* reserve(s') bench; sub bench

reserveonderdeel [rəzɛrvəɔndərdel] *het (-onderdelen)* spare part

reserveren [rezɛrveˑrə(n)] *vb* **1** reserve, put aside (*or:* away, by): *1000 euro ~ voor* set aside 1000 euros for; *een artikel voor iem ~* put aside an article for s.o.; **2** book; reserve: *een tafel ~* reserve (*or:* book) a table

reservering [rezɛrveˑrɪŋ] *de (~en)* booking, reservation

reservesleutel [rəzɛrvəsløtəl] *de (~s)* spare key

reservespeler [rəzɛrvəspelər] *de (~s)* reserve (player), substitute (player)

reservewiel [rəzɛrvəwil] *het (~en)* spare wheel

reservoir [rezɛrvwaːr] *het (~s)* reservoir, tank

resoluut [rezolyˑt] *adj, adv* resolute, determined

resoneren [rezoneˑrə(n)] *vb* resonate

respect [rɛspɛkt] *het* respect, regard, deference: *~ afdwingen* command respect; *voor iets (iem) ~ tonen* show respect for sth (s.o.); *met alle ~* with all (due) respect

respectabel [rɛspɛktaˑbəl] *adj, adv* respectable, considerable

respecteren [rɛspɛkteˑrə(n)] *vb* respect; appreciate: *zichzelf ~d* self-respecting; *iemands opvattingen ~* respect s.o.'s views

respectievelijk [rɛspɛktiˑvələk] *adj, adv* respective: *bedragen van ~ 10, 20 en 30 euro* sums of 10, 20 and 30 euros respectively

respons [rɛspɔns] *de, het* response, reaction

rest [rɛst] *de (~en)* rest, remainder: *de ~ van het materiaal* the remainder of the material; *voor de ~ geen nieuws* otherwise no news

restant [rɛstɑnt] *het (~en)* remainder, remnant

restaurant [rɛstorɑnt] *het (~s)* restaurant

restauratie [rɛstora(t)si] *de (~s)* restoration

restaureren [rɛstoreˑrə(n)] *vb* restore

resten [rɛstə(n)] *vb* remain, be left: *hem restte niets meer dan ...* there was nothing left for him but to ...; *nu rest mij nog te verklaren ...* now it only remains for me to say ...

resteren [rɛsteˑrə(n)] *vb* be left, remain

restje [rɛʃə] *het (~s)* || *ik heb nog een ~ van gisteren* I've got a few scraps (left over) from yesterday

restwarmte [rɛstwɑrmtə] *de* residual heat (*or:* warmth)

resultaat [rezʏltaˑt] *het (resultaten)* **1** result, effect, outcome: *het plan had het beoogde ~* the plan had the desired effect; *resultaten behalen* achieve results; *met het ~ dat ...* with the result that ...; *zonder ~* with no result; **2** result, returns

retorisch [retoˑris] *adj, adv* rhetorical: *een ~e vraag* a rhetorical question

retort [rətɔˑrt] *de (~en)* retort

retoucheren [retuʃeˑrə(n)] *vb* retouch, touch up

¹retour [rətuˑr] *het (~s)* return (ticket), (*Am*) round-trip (ticket): *een ~ eerste klas Utrecht* a first-class return (ticket) to Utrecht; *op zijn ~* past his (*or:* its) best

²retour [rətuˑr] *adv* back || *~ afzender* return to sender; *drie euro ~* three euros change

retourbiljet [rətuˑrbiljɛt] *het (~ten)* return ticket, (*Am*) round-trip ticket

retourenveloppe [rətuˑrɛnvəlɔp] *de (~n)* self-addressed envelope

retourneren [returneˑrə(n)] *vb* return

retourtje [rətuˑrcə] *het*, (*Am*) round-trip

retourvlucht [rətuˑrvlʏxt] *de (~en)* **1** return flight; **2** return flight, (*Am*) round-trip flight

reu [rø] *de (~en)* male dog

reuk [røk] *de (~en)* **1** smell, odour: *een onaangename ~ verspreiden* give off an unpleasant smell; **2** smell, scent: *op de ~ afgaan* hunt by scent

reukloos [røklos] *adj, adv* odourless; scentless

reukzin [røksɪn] *de* (sense of) smell

reuma [røma] *het* rheumatism

reumatisch [romaːtis] *adj* rheumatic

reünie [rejyni] *de (~s)* reunion

reus [røs] *de (reuzen)* giant

reusachtig [røzɑχtəχ] *adj* **1** gigantic, huge; **2** great, terrific

reuze [røzə] *adv* enormously: *~ veel* an awful lot; *~*

bedankt thanks awfully

reuzel [rø̜zəl] *de (~s)* lard

reuzenrad [rø̜zə(n)rɑt] *het (~eren)* Ferris wheel

revalidatie [revalida(t)si] *de* rehabilitation

revalidatiecentrum [revalida(t)sisɛntrʏm] *het (-centra)* rehabilitation centre

revalideren [revalidɛrə(n)] *vb* recover, convalesce

revalueren [revalywɛrə(n)] *vb* revalue

revanche [revɑ̃ʃ] *de* 1 revenge: ~ *nemen op iem* take revenge on s.o.; 2 *(sport)* return (game, match); return bout: *iem ~ geven* give s.o. a return game

revers [rəvɛːr] *de* lapel

reviseren [revizɛrə(n)] *vb* overhaul

revolutie [revoly(t)si] *de (~s)* revolution: *de Amerikaanse Revolutie* the American War of Independence

revolutionair [revoly(t)ʃonɛːr] *adj, adv* revolutionary: *een ~e ontdekking* a revolutionary discovery

revolver [revɔlvər] *de (~s)* revolver

revue [rəvy] *de (~s)* 1 revue, show; 2 review

Rhodos [rodɔs] *het* Rhodes

riant [rijɑnt] *adj, adv* ample, spacious: *een ~e villa* a spacious villa

rib [rɪp] *de (~ben)* rib: *de zwevende ~ben* the floating ribs; *je kunt zijn ~ben tellen* he is a bag of bones

ribbel [rɪbəl] *de (~s)* rib, ridge, ripple

ribbenkast [rɪbə(n)kɑst] *de (~en)* rib cage

ribbroek [rɪbruk] *de (~en)* cord(uroy) trousers

ribfluweel [rɪpflywel] *het* cord(uroy)

ribkarbonade [rɪpkɑrbonadə] *de (~s)* rib chop

richel [rɪχəl] *de (~s)* ledge, ridge

¹**richten** [rɪχtə(n)] *vb* 1 direct, aim, orient: *gericht op* aimed at, directed at, oriented towards; *zijn ogen op iets ~* focus one's eyes on sth; *het geweer op iem ~* aim a gun at s.o.; 2 direct, address, extend: *een brief, aan mij gericht* a letter addressed to me; *een vraag ~ tot de voorzitter* direct a question to the chairman; 3 align: *naar het oosten gericht* facing east

²**richten** [rɪχtə(n)] *ref vb* 1 (with *tot*) address (oneself to): *richt u met klachten tot ons bureau* address any complaints to our office; 2 (with *naar*) conform to: *zich ~ naar de omstandigheden* be guided by circumstances

richting [rɪχtɪŋ] *de (~en)* direction: *zij gingen ~ Amsterdam* they went in the direction of (*or:* they headed for) Amsterdam; *iem een zetje in de goede ~ geven* give s.o. a push in the right direction; *(traf) ~ aangeven* indicate direction, signal; *dat komt aardig in de ~* that's looks something like it; *van ~ veranderen* change direction

richtingaanwijzer [rɪχtɪŋanwɛizər] *de (~s)* (direction) indicator

richtinggevoel [rɪχtɪŋɣəvul] *het* sense of direction

richtlijn [rɪχtlɛin] *de (~en)* guideline, *(pl)* directions: *iets volgens de ~en uitvoeren* do sth in the prescribed way

richtmicrofoon [rɪχtmikrofon] *de (~s, -microfonen)* directional microphone

ridder [rɪdər] *de (~s)* knight: *iem tot ~ slaan* dub s.o. a knight, knight s.o.

ridderlijk [rɪdərlək] *adj* chivalrous ‖ *hij kwam er ~ voor uit* he frankly (*or:* openly) admitted it

ridderorde [rɪdərɔrdə] *de (~n, ~s)* knighthood, order

ridicuul [ridikyl] *adj, adv* ridiculous

riedel [ridəl] *de (~s)* tune, jingle

riek [rik] *de (~en)* (three-pronged) fork

riem [rim] *de (~en)* 1 belt; 2 strap, belt, sling, leash; 3 *(pl)* seat belts

riet [rit] *het* reed, cane

rieten [ritə(n)] *adj* reed; rush; cane; wicker(work): ~ *stoel* cane (*or:* wicker) chair; ~ *dak* thatched roof

rietje [ricə] *het (~s)* 1 straw; 2 *(mus)* reed

rietsuiker [ritsœykər] *de* cane sugar

rif [rɪf] *het (~fen)* reef

rigoureus [riɣorøs] *adj, adv* rigorous

rij [rɛi] *de (~en)* 1 row, line: ~*en auto's* rows of cars, queues of cars; *een ~ bomen* a line of trees; *een ~ mensen: a)* a row of people; *b)* a line (*or:* queue) of people; *in de eerste (or: voorste) ~en* in the front seats (*or:* rows); *in de ~ staan* queue, *(Am)* stand in line; 2 row, string: *een ~ getallen: a)* a column of figures; *b)* a row of figures; *ze niet allemaal op een ~tje hebben* have a screw loose

rijbaan [rɛiban] *de (rijbanen)* roadway, lane: *weg met gescheiden rijbanen* dual carriageway

rijbewijs [rɛibəwɛis] *het (rijbewijzen)* driving licence, *(Am)* driver's license: *z'n ~ halen* pass one's driving test

rijbroek [rɛibruk] *de (~en)* jodhpurs, riding breeches

rijden [rɛidə(n)] *vb* 1 drive; ride: *honderd kilometer per uur ~* drive (*or:* do) a hundred kilometres an hour; *het is twee uur ~* it's a two-hour drive; *hij werd bekeurd omdat hij te hard reed* he was fined for speeding; *door het rode licht ~* go through a red light; *in een auto ~* drive (in) a car; *op een (te) paard ~* ride a horse (*or:* on horseback); 2 drive *(car)*; ride; move, run, do: *hoeveel heeft je auto al gereden?* how many miles (*or:* kilometres) has your car done?; *(te) dicht op elkaar ~* not keep one's distance; *de tractor rijdt op dieselolie* the tractor runs (*or:* operates) on diesel oil; *die auto rijdt lekker* that car is pleasant to drive

rijdend [rɛidənt] *adj* 1 mobile: ~*e bibliotheek* mobile (*or:* travelling) library, *(Am)* bookmobile; 2 moving

rijder [rɛidər] *de (~s)* rider; driver *(car)*; cyclist

rijexamen [rɛiɛksamə(n)] *het (~s)* driving test: ~ *doen* take one's driving test

rijgedrag [rɛiɣədrɑχ] *het* driving (behaviour), motoring performance

rijgen [rɛiɣə(n)] *vb* thread, string

rijglaars [rɛiɣlars] *de (-laarzen)* lace-up boot

rijhoogte [rɛihoχtə] *de (~n, ~s)* maximum vehicle height

rij-instructeur [rɛiɪnstrʏktør] *de (~s)* driving in-

structor

¹rijk [rɛik] *het (~en)* **1** realm: *het ~ der hemelen* the Kingdom of Heaven; *het Britse Rijk* the British Empire; **2** state, kingdom, empire; **3** government, State: *door het Rijk gefinancierd* State-financed

²rijk [rɛik] *adj* **1** rich, wealthy: *stinkend ~ zijn* be filthy rich; **2** rich; fertile; generous: *hij heeft een ~e verbeelding* he has a fertile imagination

rijkdom [rɛigdɔm] *de (~men)* **1** wealth, affluence; **2** resource: *natuurlijke ~men* natural resources

rijkelijk [rɛikələk] *adj, adv* lavish, liberal

rijkelui [rɛikəlœy] *de* rich people

rijksambtenaar [rɛiksɑmtənar] *de (-ambtenaren, ~s)* public servant

rijksbegroting [rɛiksbəɣrotɪŋ] *de (~en)* (national) budget

rijksdaalder [rɛiksdɑldər] *de (~s)* two-and-a-half guilder coin

rijksinstelling [rɛiksɪnstɛlɪŋ] *de* government institution (*or:* institute)

rijksinstituut [rɛiksɪnstityt] *het* national institute

rijksluchtvaartdienst [rɛikslʏχtfardinst] *de* Civil Aviation Authority

Rijksmunt [rɛiksmʏnt] *de* Mint

rijksmuseum [rɛiksmyzejʏm] *het (rijksmusea)* national museum, national gallery

rijksoverheid [rɛiksovərhɛit] *de (-heden)* central government, national government

rijkspolitie [rɛikspoli(t)si] *de* national police (force)

rijksrecherche [rɛiksrəʃɛrʃə] *de* national department of criminal investigation

rijksuniversiteit [rɛiksynivɛrzitɛit] *de (~en)* state university

rijksvoorlichtingsdienst [rɛiksforlɪχtɪŋzdinst] *de* government information service

rijkswacht [rɛikswɑχt] *de (Belg)* state police

rijkswachter [rɛikswɑχtər] *de (~s) (Belg)* state policeman

rijkswaterstaat [rɛikswatərstat] *de (roughly)* Department (*or:* Ministry) of Waterways and Public Works

rijksweg [rɛikswɛχ] *de (~en)* national trunk road, *(Am)* state highway

rijles [rɛilɛs] *de (~sen)* driving lesson; riding lesson: *~ nemen* take driving (*or:* riding) lessons

rijm [rɛim] *het (~en)* rhyme, verse: *op ~* rhyming, in rhyme

rijmen [rɛimə(n)] *vb* **1** be in rhyme (*or:* verse); rhyme (with): *deze woorden ~ op elkaar* these words rhyme (with each other); **2** rhyme, versify

rijmpje [rɛimpjə] *het (~s)* rhyme, short verse

Rijn [rɛin] *de* Rhine

rijnaak [rɛinak] *de (rijnaken)* Rhine barge

¹rijp [rɛip] *adj* **1** ripe: *~ maken (worden)* ripen, mature; **2** mature: *op ~ere leeftijd* at a ripe age; **3** (with *voor*) ripe (for), ready (for): *~ voor de sloop* ready for the scrap heap; **4** serious: *na ~ beraad* after careful consideration

²rijp [rɛip] *de* (white) frost, hoarfrost

rijpen [rɛipə(n)] *vb* ripen; mature

rijpheid [rɛiphɛit] *de* ripeness, maturity: *tot ~ komen* ripen, mature

rijschool [rɛisχol] *de (rijscholen)* driving school; riding school (*or:* academy)

rijst [rɛist] *de* rice

rijstebrij [rɛistəbrɛi] *de* rice pudding

rijstijl [rɛistɛil] *de (~en)* driving style

rijstkorrel [rɛistkɔrəl] *de (~s)* grain of rice

rijstoogst [rɛistoχst] *de* rice crop (*or:* harvest)

rijstrook [rɛistrok] *de* (traffic) lane

rijsttafel [rɛistafəl] *de (~s)* (Indonesian) rice meal

rijtjeshuis [rɛicəshœys] *het (-huizen)* terrace(d) house, *(Am)* row house

rijtuig [rɛitœyχ] *het (~en)* **1** carriage; **2** carriage, *(Am)* car

rijvaardigheid [rɛivardəχhɛit] *de* driving ability (*or:* proficiency)

rijven [rɛivə(n)] *het (Belg)* rake

rijweg [rɛiwɛχ] *de (~en)* road(way)

rijwiel [rɛiwil] *het (~en)* (bi)cycle

rijwielhandel [rɛiwilhɑndəl] *de (~s)* bicycle shop

rijwielhandelaar [rɛiwilhɑndəlar] *de (~s, -handelaren)* bicycle dealer

rijwielpad [rɛiwilpɑt] *het (~en)* cycle path, cycle track

rijwielstalling [rɛiwilstɑlɪŋ] *de (~en)* (bi)cycle lock-up

rijzen [rɛizə(n)] *vb* rise: *laat het deeg ~* leave the dough to rise; *de prijzen ~ de pan uit* prices are soaring

rijzweep [rɛizwep] *de (rijzwepen)* (hunting, riding) crop, riding whip

rikketik [rɪkɑtik] *de (~ken)* ticker

riks [rɪks] *de (~en)* two-and-a-half guilder (coin)

riksja [rɪkʃa] *de (~'s)* rickshaw

rillen [rɪlə(n)] *vb* shiver, shudder, tremble: *hij rilde van de kou* he shivered with cold

rilling [rɪlɪŋ] *de (~en)* shiver, shudder, tremble: *koude ~en hebben* have the shakes (*or:* shivers); *er liep een ~ over mijn rug* a shiver ran down my spine

rimboe [rɪmbu] *de (~s)* jungle

rimpel [rɪmpəl] *de (~s)* wrinkle: *een gezicht vol ~s* a wrinkled face

rimpelen [rɪmpələ(n)] *vb* **1** wrinkle (up): *het voorhoofd ~* wrinkle one's forehead; **2** crinkle (up)

rimpelig [rɪmpələχ] *adj* wrinkled: *een ~e appel* a wizened apple

ring [rɪŋ] *de (~en)* ring

ringbaard [rɪŋbart] *de (~en)* fringe of beard

ringband [rɪŋbɑnt] *de (~en)* ring-binder

ringmap [rɪŋmɑp] *de (~pen)* ring-binder

ringslang [rɪŋslɑŋ] *de (~en)* grass snake, ring(ed) snake

ringvinger [rɪŋvɪŋər] *de (~s)* ring finger

ringweg [rɪŋwɛχ] *de (~en)* ring road

ringworm [rɪŋwɔrm] *de (~en)* ringworm

rinkelen [rɪŋkələ(n)] *vb* jingle, tinkle, ring, chink:

~*de ruiten* rattling panes of glass; *de ~de tamboerijn* the jingling tambourine
rinoceros [rinosərɔs] *de (~sen)* rhinoceros, rhino
riolering [rijolɛrɪŋ] *de (~en)* sewerage, sewer system
riool [rijol] *het, de (riolen)* sewer: *een open ~* an open sewer
rioolbuis [rijolbœys] *de (-buizen)* sewer
rioolwaterzuiveringsinrichting [rijolwatərzœyvərɪŋsɪnrɪχtɪŋ] *de* sewage plant
risico [riziko] *het, de (~'s)* risk: *dat behoort tot de ~'s van het vak* that's an occupational hazard; *het ~ lopen (van)* run the risk (of); *te veel ~'s nemen* run (or: take) too many risks; *op eigen ~* at one's own risk; *voor ~ van de eigenaar* at the owner's risk; *geen ~ willen nemen* not want to take any chances
risicodragend [rizikodrayənt] *adj* risk-bearing
risicogroep [rizikoyrup] *de (~en)* high-risk group
riskant [rɪskɑnt] *adj* risky: *een ~e onderneming* a risky enterprise
riskeren [rɪskɛrə(n)] *vb* risk
rit [rɪt] *de (~ten)* **1** ride, run, drive: *een ~je maken* go for a ride; **2** *(cycling)* stage, ride
ritme [rɪtmə] *het (~s)* rhythm: *uit zijn ~ raken* lose one's rhythm
ritmisch [rɪtmis] *adj, adv* rhythmic(al): *~ bewegen* move rhythmically
rits [rɪts] *de (~en)* **1** zipper, zip; **2** bunch, string, batch, battery: *een ~ kinderen* a whole string of children
ritselen [rɪtsələ(n)] *vb* rustle: *ik hoor een muis ~ achter het behang* I can hear a mouse scuffling behind the wallpaper; *~ met een papiertje* rustle a paper
ritssluiting [rɪtslœytɪŋ] *de (~en)* zipper, zip: *kun je me even helpen met mijn ~?* can you help zip me up? (or: unzip me?)
¹**ritueel** [ritywɛl] *het (rituelen)* ritual
²**ritueel** [ritywɛl] *adj* ritual
ritzege [rɪtseyə] *de (~s)* stage victory: *een ~ behalen* win a stage
rivaal [rival] *de (rivalen)* rival
rivaliteit [rivalitɛit] *de* rivalry
rivier [rivir] *de (~en)* river: *een ~ oversteken* cross a river; *een huis aan de ~* a house on the river
Rivièra [rivjɛːra] *de* Riviera
riviermond [rivirmɔnt] *de (~en)* river mouth, estuary
rivierpolitie [rivirpoli(t)si] *de* river police
rob [rɔp] *de (~ben)* seal
robbenjacht [rɔbə(n)jɑχt] *de* seal hunting
robe [rɔːbə] *de (~s)* gown
¹**robijn** [robɛin] *de (gem)* ruby
²**robijn** [robɛin] *het (mineral)* ruby
robot [rɔbɔt] *de (~s)* robot: *hij lijkt wel een ~* he is like a robot
robuust [robyst] *adj, adv* robust, solid: *een ~e gezondheid* robust health
rochelen [rɔχələ(n)] *vb* hawk (up)

rockzanger [rɔksɑŋər] *de (~s)* rock singer
rococo [rokoko] *het* rococo
roddel [rɔdəl] *de (~s)* gossip: *de nieuwste ~s uit de showwereld* the latest gossip in show business
roddelblad [rɔdəlblɑt] *het (~en)* gossip magazine
roddelen [rɔdələ(n)] *vb* gossip (about)
roddelpers [rɔdəlpɛrs] *de* gutter press, gossip papers
rode [rodə] *de (~n)* **1** redhead; **2** red
rodehond [rodəhɔnt] *de* German measles, rubella
rodekool [rodəkol] *de (-kolen)* red cabbage
Rode Kruis [rodəkrœys] *het* Red Cross
rodeo [rodejo] *de (~'s)* rodeo
roe [ru] *de (~s)* rod
roebel [rubəl] *de (~s)* rouble
roedel [rudəl] *het (~s)* herd; pack
roeiboot [rujbot] *de (-boten)* rowing boat
roeien [rujə(n)] *vb* row: *met grote slagen ~* take big strokes
roeier [rujər] *de (~s)* rower, oarsman
roeispaan [rujspan] *de (-spanen)* oar, scull, paddle
roeister [rujstər] *de* rower, oarswoman
roeivereniging [rujvərenəχɪŋ] *de (~en)* rowing club
roeiwedstrijd [rujwɛtstrɛit] *de (~en)* boat race, rowing race, regatta
roekeloos [rukəlos] *adj, adv* reckless: *~ rijden* drive recklessly
roem [rum] *de* glory, fame, renown: *op zijn ~ teren* rest on one's laurels
Roemeen [rumen] *de (Roemenen)* Romanian
Roemeens [rumens] *het* Romanian
Roemenië [rumenijə] *het* Romania
roemer [rumər] *de (~s)* rummer
roep [rup] *de* call, cry, shout
¹**roepen** [rupə(n)] *vb* call, cry, shout; clamour: *om hulp ~* call (or: cry) out for help; *een ~de in de woestijn* a voice (crying) in the wilderness
²**roepen** [rupə(n)] *vb* call, summon: *de ober ~* call the waiter; *de plicht roept (mij)* duty calls; *je komt als geroepen* (you're) just the person we need; *ik zal je om zeven uur ~* I'll call you at seven
roepia [rupija] *de (~'s)* rupiah
roeping [rupɪŋ] *de (~en)* vocation, mission, calling
roepnaam [rupnam] *de (-namen)* nickname
roer [rur] *het (~en)* **1** rudder; **2** helm, tiller: *het ~ niet uit handen geven* remain at the helm; *het ~ omgooien (fig)* change course (or: tack)
roerbakken [rurbɑkə(n)] *vb* stir-fry
roerei [rurɛi] *het (~eren)* scrambled eggs
roeren [rurə(n)] *vb* stir, mix: *de soep ~* stir the soup; *door elkaar ~* mix together
roerend [rurənt] *adj, adv* moving, touching
roerig [ruraχ] *adj* lively, active, restless
roerloos [rurlos] *adj, adv* motionless, immovable, immobile
roerspaan [rurspan] *de (-spanen)* stirrer
roerstaafje [rurstafjə] *het* coffee stirrer
roes [rus] *de (roezen)* **1** flush, high: *in een ~* in a

whirl (of excitement); **2** fuddle, intoxication, high: *zijn ~ uitslapen* sleep it off

roest [rust] *het, de (~en)* rust: *een laag ~* a layer of rust; *oud ~* scrap iron

roestbruin [rustbrœyn] *adj* rust, rust-coloured

roesten [rustə(n)] *vb* rust, get rusty

roestig [rustəχ] *adj* rusty

roestvrij [rustfrɛi] *adj* rustproof, rust-resistant: *~ staal* stainless steel

roet [rut] *het* soot: *zo zwart als ~* as black as soot

roffel [rɔfəl] *de (~s)* roll; ruffle

rog [rɔχ] *de (~gen)* ray

rogge [rɔɣə] *de* rye: *brood van ~* bread made from rye

roggebrood [rɔɣəbrot] *het (-broden)* rye bread, pumpernickel

rok [rɔk] *de (~ken)* **1** skirt, petticoat: *Schotse ~* kilt; *een wijde ~* a full skirt; **2** tail coat, tails: *de heren waren in ~* the men wore evening dress

rokade [rokadə] *de (~s)* castling: *de korte* (or: *lange) ~* castling on the king's side (or: queen's side)

roken [rokə(n)] *vb* **1** smoke, puff (at): *stoppen met ~* stop (or: give up) smoking; *verboden te ~* no smoking; *minder gaan ~* cut down on smoking; *de schoorsteen rookt* the chimney is smoking; **2** smoke, cure

roker [rokər] *de (~s)* smoker

rokeren [rokerə(n)] *vb* castle: *kort (lang) ~* castle on the king's (or: queen's) side

rokerig [rokərəχ] *adj* smoky

rokkenjager [rɔkə(n)jaɣər] *de (~s)* womanizer

rol [rɔl] *de (~len)* **1** part, role: *zijn ~ instuderen* learn one's part; *de ~len omkeren* reverse roles, turn the tables; **2** cylinder; coil; scroll; reel, spool: *een ~ behang* a roll of wallpaper; *een ~ beschuit* a packet of rusks; **3** roller; rolling pin

rolgordijn [rɔlɣɔrdɛin] *het, de (~en)* (roller) blind: *een ~ ophalen* (or: *laten zakken)* let up (or: down) a blind

rollade [rɔladə] *de (~s)* rolled meat

¹**rollen** [rɔlə(n)] *vb* roll: *er gaan koppen ~* heads will roll; *de zaak aan het ~ brengen* set the ball rolling

²**rollen** [rɔlə(n)] *vb* **1** roll (up): *een sigaret ~* roll a cigarette; **2** wrap, roll (up): *zich in een deken ~* wrap oneself up in a blanket; **3** lift: *zakken ~* pick pockets

rollenspel [rɔlə(n)spɛl] *het* role-playing

roller [rɔlər] *de (~s)* curler, roller

rolletje [rɔləcə] *het (~s)* (small) roll; roller: *een ~ drop* a packet of liquorice; *alles liep op ~s* everything went like clockwork (or: went smoothly)

rolluik [rɔllœyk] *het (~en)* roll-down shutter

rolschaats [rɔlsχats] *de (~en)* roller skate

rolschaatsen [rɔlsχatsə(n)] *vb* roller skate

rolschaatser [rɔlsχatsər] *de (~s)* roller skater

rolstoel [rɔlstul] *de (~en)* wheelchair: *toegankelijk voor ~en* with access for wheelchairs

rolstoelgebruiker [rɔlstulɣəbrœykər] *de (~s)* wheelchair user

roltrap [rɔltrap] *de (~pen)* escalator, moving staircase

rolverdeling [rɔlvərdelɪŋ] *de (~en)* cast(ing), (fig) division of roles

Romaans [romans] *adj* **1** Latin: *de ~e volken* the Latin peoples; **2** Romance, Latin

roman [romɑn] *de (~s)* novel

romance [romɑ̃sə] *de (~s)* romance

romanschrijver [romɑnsχrɛivər] *de (~s)* novelist, fiction writer

romanticus [romɑntikʏs] *de (romantici)* romantic

romantiek [romɑntik] *de* romance: *een vleugje ~* a touch of romance

romantisch [romɑntis] *adj, adv* romantic

romantiseren [romɑntizerə(n)] *vb* romanticize

Rome [romə] *het* Rome: *het oude ~* Ancient Rome; *zo oud als de weg naar ~* as old as the hills

Romein [romɛin] *de (~en)* Roman

Romeins [romɛins] *adj* Roman: *uit de ~e Oudheid* from Ancient Rome; *het ~ recht* Roman law

romig [roməχ] *adj* creamy

rommel [rɔməl] *de* **1** mess, shambles: *~ maken* make a mess; **2** junk, rubbish, trash

rommelen [rɔmələ(n)] *vb* **1** rumble, roll: *de donder rommelt in de verte* the thunder is rumbling in the distance; **2** rummage: *in zijn papieren ~* shuffle one's papers

rommelig [rɔmələχ] *adj, adv* messy, untidy

rommelmarkt [rɔməlmɑrkt] *de (~en)* flea market, jumble sale

romp [rɔmp] *de (~en)* **1** trunk, torso; **2** shell; hull

rompslomp [rɔmpslɔmp] *de* fuss, bother: *ambtelijke ~* red tape, bureaucracy; *papieren ~* paperwork

¹**rond** [rɔnt] *adj, adv* **1** round, circular; **2** arranged, fixed (up): *de zaak is ~* everything is arranged (or: fixed); **3** around, about: *een mooi ~ bedrag* a nice round figure

²**rond** [rɔnt] *prep* **1** round, (fig) surrounding: *in de berichtgeving ~ de affaire* in the reporting of the affair; **2** around, about: *~ de middag* around midday; *~ de 2000 betogers* approximately (or: about, some) 2000 demonstrators

rondbazuinen [rɔntbazœynə(n)] *vb* broadcast, trumpet (around)

rondbrengen [rɔntbrɛŋə(n)] *vb* bring round

ronddraaien [rɔntdrajə(n)] *vb* turn (round), spin (round): *~ in een cirkel, kringetje* go round in circles

ronde [rɔndə] *de (~n)* **1** rounds; beat: *de ~ doen* go on one's rounds; **2** round(s): *de eerste ~ van onderhandelingen* the first round of talks; *de praatjes doen de ~* stories are going around; **3** lap, circuit: *laatste ~* bell lap; *twee ~n voor* (or: *achter) liggen* be two laps ahead (or: behind); **4** tour, race: *de ~ van Frankrijk* the Tour de France

rondetijd [rɔndətɛit] *de (~en)* lap time: *de snelste ~* the fastest lap

rondgaan [rɔntχan] *vb* **1** go round: *~ als een lopend* *vuurtje* spread like wildfire; **2** go round, pass round: *laat de schaal nog maar eens ~* pass the plate round again

rondgang [rɔntχaŋ] *de (~en)* **1** circuit; **2** tour

rondhangen [rɔnthaŋə(n)] *vb* hang around (*or:* about)

ronding [rɔndɪŋ] *de (~en)* curve

rondje [rɔncə] *het (~s)* **1** round: *een ~ van de zaak* (a round of) drinks on the house; *hij gaf een ~* he stood a round (of drinks); **2** *(sport)* lap, circuit

rondkijken [rɔntkɛikə(n)] *vb* look round: *goed ~ voor je iets koopt* shop around

rondkomen [rɔntkomə(n)] *vb* manage, get by, live: *hij kan er net mee ~* he can just manage (*or:* get by) on it

rondleiden [rɔntlɛidə(n)] *vb* **1** lead round; **2** show round, take round: *mensen in een museum ~* show (*or:* take) people round a museum

rondleiding [rɔntlɛidɪŋ] *de (~en)* (guided, conducted) tour

rondlopen [rɔntlopə(n)] *vb* go around, walk around: *je moet daar niet mee blijven ~* you shouldn't let that weigh (*or:* prey) on your mind

rondneuzen [rɔntnøzə(n)] *vb* nose about, prowl

¹**rondom** [rɔntɔm] *adv* all round, on all sides: *het plein met de huizen ~* the square with houses round it

²**rondom** [rɔntɔm] *prep* (a)round

rondpunt [rɔntpʏnt] *het (~en) (Belg)* roundabout

rondreis [rɔntrɛis] *de (-reizen)* tour; circular tour: *op haar ~ door de Verenigde Staten* on her tour of America

rondreizen [rɔntrɛizə(n)] *vb* travel around (*or:* about): *de wereld ~* travel round the globe (*or:* world)

rondrennen [rɔntrɛnə(n)] *vb* run around, chase about

rondrijden [rɔntrɛidə(n)] *vb* go for a drive (*or:* run, ride)

rondrit [rɔntrɪt] *de (~ten)* tour

rondslingeren [rɔntslɪŋərə(n)] *vb* lie about (*or:* around): *zijn boeken laten ~* leave his books lying around (*or:* about)

rondsluipen [rɔntslœypə(n)] *vb* prowl about, prowl (a)round

rondsturen [rɔntstyrə(n)] *vb* send round: *circulaires ~* distribute circulars

rondte [rɔntə] *de (~n, ~s)* circle, round(ness): *in de ~ zitten* sit in a circle

rondtrekken [rɔntrɛkə(n)] *vb* travel (a)round: *~de seizoenarbeiders* migrant seasonal workers

ronduit [rɔntœyt] *adv* plain, straight(forward), frank: *het is ~ belachelijk* absolutely (*or:* simply) ridiculous; *iem ~ de waarheid zeggen* tell s.o. the plain truth

rondvaart [rɔntfart] *de (~en)* round trip, circular trip (*or:* tour), cruise: *een ~ door de grachten maken* make (*or:* go) for a tour of the canals

rondvaartboot [rɔntfardbot] *de (-boten)* boat for

canal trips

rondvliegen [rɔntfliɣə(n)] *vb* fly about (*or:* around): *geraakt worden door ~de kogels* be hit by flying bullets

rondvraag [rɔntfraχ] *de ‖ iets voor de ~ hebben* have sth for any other business

rondweg [rɔntwɛχ] *de (~en)* ring road; bypass; relief road: *een ~ aanleggen om L.* by-pass L.

rondzwerven [rɔntswɛrvə(n)] *vb* roam about, wander about: *op straat ~: a)* hang about the streets; *b)* roam the streets

ronken [rɔŋkə(n)] *vb* **1** snore; **2** throb

röntgen [rʏntχə(n)] *de* roentgen

röntgenafdeling [rʏntχənavdelɪŋ] *de* radiography department, X-ray department

röntgenapparaat [rʏntχə(n)aparat] *het (-apparaten)* X-ray machine

röntgenfoto [rʏntχə(n)foto] *de (~'s)* X-ray, roentgenogram, roentgenograph: *een ~ laten maken* have an X-ray taken

röntgenonderzoek [rʏntχənɔndərzuk] *het* X-ray

röntgenstralen [rʏntχə(n)stralə(n)] *de* X-rays, roentgen rays

rood [rot] *adj* red, ginger, ruddy; copper(y); ginger: *met een ~ hoofd van de inspanning* flushed with exertion; *iem de rode kaart tonen* show s.o. the red card; *door ~ (licht) rijden* jump the lights; *~ worden* go red (*or:* scarlet), flush, blush; *het licht sprong op ~* the light changed to red; *over de rooie gaan* flip one's lid, lose one's cool; *~ staan* be in the red; *in het ~ (gekleed)* dressed in red

roodbont [rodbɔnt] *adj* red and white; skewbald

roodborstje [rodbɔrʃə] *het (~s)* robin (redbreast)

roodbruin [rodbrœyn] *adj* reddish brown, russet, sorrel: *het ~ van herfstbladeren* the russet (colour) of autumn leaves

roodgloeiend [rotχlujənt] *adj* red-hot: *de telefoon staat ~* the telephone hasn't stopped ringing

roodharig [rothaɣrχ] *adj* red-haired, red-headed

roodhuid [rothœyt] *de (~en)* redskin

Roodkapje [rotkapjə] *het* Little Red Riding Hood

roodvonk [rotfɔŋk] *de* scarlet fever

roof [rof] *de (roven)* **1** robbery: *op ~ uitgaan* commit robbery; **2** preying, hunting

roofbouw [rovbau] *de* exhaustion, overuse: *~ plegen op zijn gezondheid* undermine one's health; *~ plegen op zijn lichaam* wear oneself out

roofdier [rovdir] *het (~en)* animal (*or:* beast) of prey, predator

roofmoord [rofmort] *de (~en)* robbery with murder

roofoverval [rofovərval] *de (~len)* robbery, hold-up: *een ~ plegen op een juwelierszaak* rob a jeweller's

roofvogel [rofoɣəl] *de (~s)* bird of prey

rooien [rojə(n)] *vb* dig up; lift; raise; uproot: *een bos ~* clear a wood (*or:* forest)

rook [rok] *de* smoke; fume(s): *men kan er de ~ snijden* it's thick with smoke in here; *in ~ opgaan* go up in smoke; *waar ~ is, is vuur* there's no smoke without fire

rookartikelen [r<u>o</u>kɑrtikələ(n)] *de* smokers' requisites

rookbom [r<u>o</u>gbɔm] *de* (~*men*) smoke bomb

rookgordijn [r<u>o</u>kχɔrdɛin] *het* (~*en*) smokescreen: *een ~ leggen* put up (*or:* lay) a smokescreen

rookkanaal [r<u>o</u>kanal] *het* (*-kanalen*) flue

rooklucht [r<u>o</u>klʏχt] *de* smell of smoke

rookmelder [r<u>o</u>kmɛldər] *de* (~*s*) smoke alarm, smoke detector

rookpauze *de* cigarette break: *een ~ inlassen* take a break for a cigarette

rooksignaal [r<u>o</u>ksıɲal] *het* (*-signalen*) smoke signal

rookverbod [r<u>o</u>kfərbɔt] *het* ban on smoking

rookvlees [r<u>o</u>kfles] *het* (*roughly*) smoke-dried beef (*or:* meat)

rookvrij [rokfr<u>ɛi</u>] *adj* no(n)-smoking

rookwolk [r<u>o</u>kwɔlk] *de* (~*en*) cloud (*or:* pall) of smoke

rookworst [r<u>o</u>kwɔrst] *de* (~*en*) (*roughly*) smoked sausage

room [rom] *de* cream: *dikke ~* double cream; *zure ~* sour cream

roomboter [r<u>o</u>mbotər] *de* butter

roomklopper [r<u>o</u>mklɔpər] *de* (~*s*) cream whipper, whisk

rooms [roms] *adj* Roman Catholic

Rooms [roms] *adj* Roman

roomsaus [r<u>o</u>msɑus] *de* (*-sauzen*) cream sauce

rooms-katholicisme [romskɑtolisısmə] *het* Roman Catholicism

rooms-katholiek [romskɑtol<u>i</u>k] *adj* Roman Catholic

roomsoes [r<u>o</u>msus] *de* (*-soezen*) cream puff

roos [ros] *de* (*rozen*) **1** rose: (*fig*) *op rozen zitten* lie on a bed of roses; **2** bull's-eye: *in de ~ schieten* score a bull's-eye; (*midden*) *in de ~* bang in the middle; **3** dandruff

rooskleurig [rosklørəχ] *adj, adv* rosy, rose-coloured: *een ~e toekomst* a rosy (*or:* bright) future

rooster [r<u>o</u>stər] *het, de* (~*s*) **1** grid, grating, grate, grille, gridiron: *het ~ van de kachel* the stove grate; (*Belg*) *iem op het ~ leggen* grill s.o.; **2** grid; **3** schedule, timetable, roster: *een ~ opstellen* (*opmaken*) draw up a roster (*or:* rota)

roosteren [r<u>o</u>stərə(n)] *vb* **1** grill, roast, broil; **2** toast

ros [rɔs] *het* (~*sen*) steed

rosbief [r<u>ɔ</u>zbif] *de* roast beef

rosé [roz<u>e</u>] *de* rosé (wine)

roskammen [r<u>ɔ</u>skɑmə(n)] *vb* groom, curry(comb)

rossig [r<u>ɔ</u>səχ] *adj* reddish, ruddy, sandy

rot [rɔt] *adj* **1** rotten, bad, decayed, putrid: *door en door ~, zo ~ als een mispel* rotten to the core; **2** rotten, lousy, wretched: *zich ~ lachen* split one's sides laughing; *zich ~ vervelen* be bored to tears

rotanstoel [r<u>ɔ</u>tɑnstul] *de* (~*en*) cane rattan chair

rotbaan [r<u>ɔ</u>dban] *de* lousy job

rotding [r<u>ɔ</u>dıŋ] *het* damn thing, bloody thing

rotgang [r<u>ɔ</u>tχɑŋ] *de* breakneck speed: *met een ~ door de bocht gaan* go round the bend at a breakneck speed

rotje [r<u>ɔ</u>cə] *het* (~*s*) (fire)cracker, squib, banger

rotjong *het* brat, little pest

rotmeid [r<u>ɔ</u>tmɛit] *de* (~*en*) bitch, cow

rotonde [rot<u>ɔ</u>ndə] *de* (~*s*) roundabout

rotopmerking [r<u>ɔ</u>tɔpmɛrkıŋ] *de* (~*en*) nasty remark

rotor [r<u>o</u>tɔr] *de* (~*s*) rotor

rots [rɔts] *de* (~*en*) rock, cliff, crag: *als een ~ in de branding* as steady as a rock; *het schip liep op de ~en* the ship struck the rocks

rotsachtig [r<u>ɔ</u>tsɑχtəχ] *adj* rocky, rugged

rotsblok [r<u>ɔ</u>tsblɔk] *het* (~*ken*) boulder

rotskust [r<u>ɔ</u>tskʏst] *de* rocky coast

rotsschildering [r<u>ɔ</u>tsχıldərıŋ] *de* (~*en*) cave painting, wall painting

rotstreek [r<u>ɔ</u>tstrek] *de* (*rotstreken*) dirty trick, mean trick: *iem een ~ leveren* play a dirty trick on s.o.

rotstuin [r<u>ɔ</u>tstœyn] *de* (~*en*) rock garden, rockery

rotsvast [r<u>ɔ</u>tsfɑst] *adj, adv* rock-solid, rocklike: *~e overtuiging* a deep-rooted conviction

rotswand [r<u>ɔ</u>tswɑnt] *de* (~*en*) rock face, cliff face

rotten [r<u>ɔ</u>tə(n)] *vb* rot, decay: *~d hout* rotting wood

rottig [r<u>ɔ</u>təχ] *adj, adv* rotten, nasty

rottigheid [r<u>ɔ</u>təχɛit] *de* misery, wretchedness

rottweiler [r<u>ɔ</u>twɑjlər] *de* (~*s*) Rottweiler

rotvent [r<u>ɔ</u>tfɛnt] *de* (~*en*) bastard, jerk

rotwerk [r<u>ɔ</u>twɛrk] *het* nasty work

rotwijf [r<u>ɔ</u>twɛif] *de* (*rotwijven*) bitch

rotzak [r<u>ɔ</u>tsɑk] *de* (~*ken*) bastard, jerk

rotzooi [r<u>ɔ</u>tsoj] *de* **1** (piece of) junk, trash; **2** mess, shambles

rotzooien [r<u>ɔ</u>tsojə(n)] *vb* mess about: *~ met de boekhouding* tamper with the accounts

rouge [ru:ʒə] *het, de* rouge, blusher

roulatie [rula(t)si] *de* circulation: *in ~ brengen* bring into circulation (*film*)

roulatiesysteem [rula(t)sisistem] *het* rotation system

rouleren [rul<u>e</u>rə(n)] *vb* **1** circulate, be in circulation; **2** rotate, take turns, work in shifts

roulette [rul<u>ɛ</u>tə] *de* (~*s*) roulette (table)

route [r<u>u</u>tə] *de* (~*s*) route, way, round

routebeschrijving [r<u>u</u>təbəsχrɛivıŋ] *de* (~*en*) itinerary, route description

routine [rut<u>i</u>nə] *de* **1** practice, skill, knack; **2** routine, grind: *de dagelijkse ~* the daily grind

routineklus [rut<u>i</u>nəklʏs] *de* routine job

routinematig [rut<u>i</u>nəmatəχ] *adj* routine

routineonderzoek [rut<u>i</u>nəɔndərzuk] *het* (~*en*) routine check-up

routineus [rutin<u>ø</u>s] *adj* routine

rouw [rɑu] *de* mourning, sorrow, grief: *in de ~ zijn* be in mourning

rouwadvertentie [r<u>ɑu</u>ɑtfərtɛn(t)si] *de* (~*s*) death announcement

rouwen [rɑuwə(n)] *vb* mourn, grieve

rouwig [rɑuwəχ] *adj* regretful, sorry: *ergens niet ~ om zijn* not regret sth

rouwkrans [rɑukrɑns] *de* funeral wreath

rouwproces [rɑuprosɛs] *het* mourning process

rouwstoet [rɑustut] *de (~en)* funeral procession

roven [rovə(n)] *vb* steal, rob

rover [rovər] *de (~s)* robber

royaal [rojal] *adj, adv* 1 generous, open-handed: *een royale beloning* a handsome (*or:* generous) reward; 2 spacious, ample: *een royale meerderheid* a comfortable majority

roze [rɔːzə] *adj* pink, rose

rozemarijn [rozəmarɛin] *de* rosemary

rozenbottel [rozə(n)bɔtəl] *de (~s)* rose hip

rozengeur [rozə(n)ɣør] *de* smell (*or:* scent) of roses: *het is er niet alleen ~ en maneschijn* it's not all sweetness and light there

rozenkrans [rozə(n)krɑns] *de (~en)* rosary: *de ~ bidden* say the rosary

rozenstruik [rozə(n)strœyk] *de (~en)* rose bush

rozijn [rozɛin] *de (~en)* raisin

rozijnenbrood [rozɛinə(n)brot] *het (-broden)* raisin loaf

rubber [rʏbər] *het, de* rubber

rubberboot [rʏbərbot] *de (-boten)* (rubber) dinghy

rubberen [rʏbərə(n)] *adj* rubber

rubberlaars [rʏbərlars] *de* rubber boot, wellington

rubriceren [rybrisɛrə(n)] *vb* class, classify

rubriek [rybrik] *de (~en)* 1 column, feature, section: *de advertentierubriek(en)* the advertising columns; 2 section, group

rug [rʏχ] *de (~gen)* back: *iem de ~ toekeren* turn one's back on s.o.; *achter de ~ van iem kwaadspreken* talk about s.o. behind his back; *ik zal blij zijn als het achter de ~ is* I'll be glad to get it over and done with; *hij heeft een moeilijke tijd achter de ~* he had a difficult time; *het (geld) groeit mij niet op de ~* I am not made of money

rugby [rʏɣbi] *het* rugby

rugbybal [rʏχbibɑl] *de (~len)* rugger ball, rugby (foot)ball

rugbyen [rʏɣbijə(n)] *vb* play rugby (*or:* rugger)

ruggengraat [rʏɣə(n)ɣrat] *de (-graten)* backbone, spine

ruggenmerg [rʏɣə(n)mɛrχ] *het* spinal marrow (*or:* cord)

rugklachten [rʏχklɑχtə(n)] *de* back trouble, backache

rugleuning [rʏχlønɪŋ] *de (~en)* back (of a chair)

rugnummer [rʏχnʏmər] *het (~s)* (player's) number

rugpijn [rʏχpɛin] *de* pain in the back, backache

rugslag [rʏχslɑχ] *de* backstroke, back-crawl

rugvin [rʏχfɪn] *de (~nen)* dorsal fin

rugwind [rʏχwɪnt] *de (~en)* tail wind, following wind

rugzak [rʏχsɑk] *de (~ken)* rucksack; backpack

rui [rœy] *de* 1 moult(ing); 2 *(Belg)* covered canal, roofed-over canal

ruien [rœyə(n)] *vb* moult, shed one's feathers

ruif [rœyf] *de (ruiven)* rack

ruig [rœyχ] *adj* 1 rough: *een ~ feest* a rowdy party; 2 shaggy, hairy

¹**ruiken** [rœykə(n)] *vb* 1 smell: *aan iets ~* have a smell (*or:* sniff) at sth; 2 smell, stink, reek

²**ruiken** [rœykə(n)] *vb (also fig)* smell, scent: *onraad ~* scent (*or:* sense) danger; *hoe kon ik dat nu ~!* how could I possibly know!

ruiker [rœykər] *de (~s)* posy, bouquet

ruil [rœyl] *de (~en)* exchange, swap

¹**ruilen** [rœylə(n)] *vb* exchange, swap

²**ruilen** [rœylə(n)] *vb* change: *ik zou niet met hem willen ~* I would not change places with him

ruilhandel [rœylhɑndəl] *de* barter (trade): *~ drijven* barter

ruilmiddel [rœylmɪdəl] *het (~en)* means (*or:* medium) of exchange

¹**ruim** [rœym] *het (~en)* hold

²**ruim** [rœym] *adj, adv* 1 spacious, large; roomy: *een ~ assortiment* a large assortment; *~ wonen* live spaciously; 2 free: *~ baan maken* make way; *in de ~ste zin* in the broadest sense; 3 wide, roomy, loose: *die jas zit ~* that coat is loose-fitting; 4 ample, liberal: *een ~e meerderheid* a big majority

³**ruim** [rœym] *adv* (rather) more than, something over, well over: *~ een uur* well over an hour; *dat is ~ voldoende* that is amply sufficient

ruimdenkend [rœymdɛnkənt] *adj* broad(-minded)

ruimen [rœymə(n)] *vb* 1 clear out; 2 clear away

ruimschoots [rœymsχots] *adv* amply, plentifully: *~ de tijd* (*or:* *gelegenheid*) *hebben* have ample time (*or:* opportunity); *~ op tijd aankomen* arrive in ample time

ruimte [rœymtə] *de (~n, ~s)* room, space: *wegens gebrek aan ~* for lack of room (*or:* space); *de begrippen ~ en tijd* the concepts of time and space; *te weinig ~ hebben* be cramped for space; *~ uitsparen* save space; *iem de ~ geven* give s.o. elbow room

ruimtegebrek [rœymtəɣəbrɛk] *het* lack (*or:* shortage) of space

ruimtelijk [rœymtələk] *adj, adv* 1 spatial, spacial, space: *~e ordening* environmental (*or:* town and country) planning; 2 three-dimensional

ruimtepak [rœymtəpɑk] *het (~ken)* space suit

ruimtesonde [rœymtəsɔndə] *de (~s)* space probe

ruimtestation [rœymtəsta(t)ʃɔn] *het (~s)* space station

ruimtevaarder [rœymtəvardər] *de (~s)* spaceman, astronaut

ruimtevaart [rœymtəvart] *de* space travel

ruimtevaartuig [rœymtəvartœyχ] *het (~en)* spacecraft

ruimteveer [rœymtəver] *het (-veren)* (space) shuttle

ruïne [rywinə] *de (~s)* ruins; ruin, *(pers)* wreck

ruis [rœys] *de* noise, murmur

ruisen [rœysə(n)] *vb* rustle; gurgle

ruisfilter [rœysfɪltər] *het, de (~s)* noise filter

ruit [rœyt] *de (~en)* **1** (window)pane, window; **2** diamond; check

¹ruiten [rœytə(n)] *de* diamonds: *ruitenvrouw* queen of diamonds; *ruitenboer* jack (*or:* knave) of diamonds; *~ is troef* diamonds are trumps

²ruiten [rœytə(n)] *adj* check(ed), chequered

ruitenwisser [rœytə(n)wɪsər] *de (~s)* windscreen wiper, wiper

ruiter [rœytər] *de (~s)* horseman, rider

ruiterij [rœytərɛi] *de* cavalry, horse

ruiterpad [rœytərpɑt] *het (~en)* bridle path

ruitersport [rœytərspɔrt] *de* equestrian sport(s); riding

ruitjespapier [rœycəspapir] *het* squared paper

ruk [rʏk] *de (~ken)* **1** jerk, tug; **2** gust (of wind); **3** distance, way; **4** time, spell: *in één ~ doorwerken* work on at one stretch

¹rukken [rʏkə(n)] *vb* jerk (at), tug (at)

²rukken [rʏkə(n)] *vb* tear, wrench: *iem de kleren van het lijf ~* tear the clothes from s.o.'s body

rukwind [rʏkwɪnt] *de (~en)* squall, gust (of wind)

rul [rʏl] *adj* loose, sandy

rum [rʏm] *de* rum

rumboon [rʏmbon] *de (rumbonen)* rum bonbon

rum-cola [rʏmkola] *de* rum and coke

rumoer [rymur] *het (~en)* noise; din, racket, row: *~ maken* make a noise

rumoerig [rymurəχ] *adj* noisy

rund [rʏnt] *het (~eren)* **1** cow; *(pl)* cattle, ox; **2** cow; bull; *(pl)* cattle; **3** idiot, fool: *een ~ van een vent* a prize idiot

rundergehakt [rʏndərγəhakt] *het* minced beef, mince

runderhaas [rʏndərhas] *de (-hazen)* tenderloin, fillet of beef

runderlap [rʏndərlɑp] *de (~pen)* braising steak

runderrollade [rʏndərɔladə] *de* collared beef, rolled beef

rundvee [rʏntfe] *het* cattle: *twintig stuks ~* twenty head of cattle

rundvlees [rʏntfles] *het* beef

rune [rynə] *de (~n)* rune

rups [rʏps] *de (~en)* caterpillar

rupsband [rʏpsbɑnt] *de (~en)* caterpillar (track)

Rus [rʏs] *de (~sen)* Russian

Rusland [rʏslɑnt] *het* Russia

Russisch [rʏsis] *adj* Russian || *een ~ ei* egg mayonnaise

rust [rʏst] *de* **1** rest, relaxation; **2** rest; lie-down; **3** quiet: *gun hem wat ~* give him a break; *nooit (geen ogenblik) ~ hebben* never have a moment's peace; *wat ~ nemen* take a break; *laat me met ~!* leave me alone!; *tot ~ komen* settle (*or:* calm) (down); **4** (peace and) quiet; still(ness): *alles was in diepe ~* all was quiet; **5** *(sport)* half-time, interval

rustdag [rʏzdɑχ] *de (~en)* rest day; day off, holiday

rusteloos [rʏstəlos] *adj, adv* restless

rusteloosheid [rʏstəlosheit] *de* restlessness

rusten [rʏstə(n)] *vb* **1** rest, relax, take (*or:* have) a rest: *even ~ have* (*or:* take) a break; **2** rest, sleep: *hij ligt te ~* he is resting; **3** rest, pause; **4** weigh; be burdened (*or:* encumbered) with: *op hem rust een zware verdenking* he is under strong suspicion

rustgevend [rʏstχevənt] *adj* **1** comforting; **2** restful, calming

¹rustig [rʏstəχ] *adj, adv* **1** peaceful, quiet; **2** calm, still: *het water is ~* the water's calm; **3** steady: *een ~e ademhaling* even breathing; **4** calm: *~ weer* calm weather; *~ antwoorden* answer calmly; *zich ~ houden* keep calm; *hij komt ~ een uur te laat* he quite happily (*or:* cheerfully) comes an hour late; *ze zat ~ te lezen* she sat quietly reading; *het ~ aan doen* take it easy; **5** quiet, smooth; uneventful: *daar kan ik ~ studeren* I can study there in peace; *het is hier lekker ~* it's nice and quiet here

²rustig [rʏstəχ] *adv* safely: *je kunt me ~ bellen* feel free to call me; *dat mag je ~ weten* I don't mind if you know that

rustplaats [rʏstplats] *de (~en)* resting place: *de laatste ~* the final resting place; *naar zijn laatste ~ brengen* lay to rest

rustpunt [rʏstpʏnt] *het (~en)* pause, period

ruststand [rʏstɑnt] *de (~en) (sport)* half-time score

ruw [ryw] *adj, adv* **1** rough: *een ~e plank* a rough plank; *een ~e schets* a rough draft; *een ~ spel* a rough game; *iets ~ afbreken* break sth off abruptly; *iem ~ behandelen* treat s.o. roughly; **2** raw, crude, rough-hewn: *~e olie* crude oil

ruwweg [rywɛχ] *adv* roughly: *~ geschat* at a rough estimate (*or:* guess)

ruzie [ryzi] *de (~s)* quarrel, argument: *slaande ~ hebben* have a blazing row; *een ~ bijleggen* patch up a quarrel; *~ krijgen met iem* have an argument with s.o.; *~ zoeken* look for trouble (*or:* a fight); *~ hebben met iem* (*or:* om iets) quarrel with s.o. (*or:* over sth)

ruziën [ryzijə(n)] *vb* quarrel

S

saai [saj] *adj, adv* boring, dull

sabbat [sɑbɑt] *de (~ten)* sabbath

sabbelen [sɑbələ(n)] *vb* suck: *~ aan een lolly* suck a lollipop

sabel [sabəl] *de* sabre

sabotage [sabotaʒə] *de* sabotage

saboteren [saboterə(n)] *vb* 1 commit sabotage (on); 2 sabotage, undermine

saboteur [sabotør] *de (~s)* saboteur

sacrament [sɑkramɛnt] *het (~en)* sacrament

sadisme [sadɪsmə] *het* sadism

sadist [sadɪst] *de (~en)* sadist

sadistisch [sadɪstis] *adj, adv* sadistic

sadomasochisme [sadomasoxɪsmə] *het* sadomasochism

safari [safari] *de (~'s)* safari: *op ~ gaan* go on safari

safaripark [safaripɑrk] *het (~en)* safari park

safe [sef] *de (~s)* safe, safe-deposit box

¹saffier [sɑfir] *de (~en) (gem)* sapphire

²saffier [sɑfir] *het (mineral)* sapphire

sage [saɣə] *de (~n)* legend

Sahara [sahara] *de* Sahara

Saksisch [sɑksis] *adj* Saxon

salade [saladə] *de (~s)* salad

salamander [salamɑndər] *de (~s)* salamander

salami [salami] *de* salami

salaris [salarɪs] *het (~sen)* salary, pay

salarisverhoging [salarɪsfərhoɣɪŋ] *de (~en)* (salary) increase, (pay) rise

saldo [sɑldo] *het (saldi)* balance: *een positief ~* a credit balance; *een negatief ~* a deficit; *per ~* on balance

saldotekort [sɑldotəkɔrt] *het (~en)* deficit, overdraft

Salomo [salomo] *de* Solomon

salon [salɔn] *het, de (~s)* drawing room, salon

salontafel [salɔntafəl] *de (~s)* coffee table

salto [sɑlto] *de (~'s)* somersault: *een ~ maken* turn a somersault

salueren [salywerə(n)] *vb* salute

salvo [sɑlvo] *het (~'s)* salvo, volley

Samaritaan [samaritan] *de (Samaritanen)* Samaritan || *een barmhartige ~* a good Samaritan

sambal [sɑmbɑl] *de* sambal

samen [samə(n)] *adv* 1 together, in chorus: *zij hebben ~ een kamer* they share a room; 2 with each oth-er, with one another: *het ~ goed kunnen vinden* get on well (together); 3 in all, altogether: *~ is dat 21 euro* that makes 21 euros altogether (*or:* in all)

samendoen [samə(n)dun] *vb* be partners, go shares

samengaan [samə(n)ɣan] *vb* go together, go hand in hand: *niet ~ met* not go (together) with

samenhang [samə(n)hɑŋ] *de* connection

samenhangen [samə(n)hɑŋə(n)] *vb* be connected, be linked: *dat hangt samen met het klimaat* that has to do with the climate

samenhangend [samə(n)hɑŋənt] *adj, adv* related, connected: *een hiermee ~ probleem* a related problem

samenknijpen [samə(n)knɛipə(n)] *vb* squeeze together, screw up

samenkomen [samə(n)komə(n)] *vb* come together, meet (together), converge (on)

samenkomst [samə(n)kɔmst] *de (~en)* meeting

samenleven [samə(n)levə(n)] *vb* live together

samenleving [samə(n)levɪŋ] *de* society: *de huidige ~* modern society

samenlevingscontract [samə(n)levɪŋskɔntrɑkt] *het (~en)* cohabitation agreement

samenloop [samə(n)lop] *de* concurrence, conjunction: *een ~ van omstandigheden* a combination of circumstances

samenpersen [samə(n)pɛrsə(n)] *vb* compress, press together

samenraapsel [samə(n)rapsəl] *het (~s)* pack, ragbag

samenscholing [samə(n)sxolɪŋ] *de (~en)* gathering, assembly

samensmelten [samə(n)smɛltə(n)] *vb* fuse (together)

samenspannen [samə(n)spɑnə(n)] *vb* conspire, plot (together)

samenspelen [samə(n)spelə(n)] *vb* play together

samenstellen [samə(n)stɛlə(n)] *vb* 1 put together, make up, compose: *samengesteld zijn uit* be made up (*or:* composed) of; 2 draw up, compose, compile

samensteller [samə(n)stɛlər] *de (~s)* compiler, composer

samenstelling [samə(n)stɛlɪŋ] *de (~en)* composition, make-up

samentrekken [samə(n)trɛkə(n)] *vb* contract, shrink

samenvallen [samə(n)vɑlə(n)] *vb* coincide (with), correspond: *gedeeltelijk ~* overlap

samenvatten [samə(n)vɑtə(n)] *vb* summarize, sum up: *kort samengevat* (to put it) in a nutshell; *iets in een paar woorden ~* sum sth up in a few words

samenvatting [samə(n)vɑtɪŋ] *de (~en)* summary, highlights

samenwerken [samə(n)wɛrkə(n)] *vb* cooperate, work together: *gaan ~* join forces (with); *nauw ~* cooperate closely

samenwerking [samə(n)wɛrkɪŋ] *de* cooperation,

teamwork: *in nauwe ~ met* in close collaboration with

samenwonen [sɑmə(n)wonə(n)] *vb* **1** live together, cohabit; **2** live (together) with, share a house (*or:* flat)

samenzweerder [sɑmə(n)zwerdər] *de (~s)* conspirator

samenzweren [sɑmə(n)zwerə(n)] *vb* conspire, plot: *tegen iem ~* conspire (*or:* plot) against s.o.

samenzwering [sɑmə(n)zwerɪŋ] *de (~en)* conspiracy, plot

samsam [sɑmsɑm] *adv* fifty-fifty: *~ doen* go halves (with s.o.)

sanatorium [sɑnɑtorijʏm] *het (sanatoria)* sanatorium

sanctie [sɑŋksi] *de (~s)* sanction: *~s verbinden aan* apply sanctions to

sandaal [sɑndal] *de (sandalen)* sandal

sandwich [sɛntwɪtʃ] *de (~es)* **1** sandwich; **2** *(Belg)* bridge roll

saneren [sanerə(n)] *vb* **1** put in order, see to: *zijn gebit laten ~* have one's teeth seen to; **2** reorganize, redevelop: *de binnenstad ~* redevelop the town centre

sanering [sanerɪŋ] *de* **1** *(roughly)* course of dental treatment; **2** reorganization, redevelopment, clean-up (operation)

¹**sanitair** [sanitɛːr] *het* sanitary fittings, bathroom fixtures

²**sanitair** [sanitɛːr] *adj* sanitary: *~e artikelen* bathroom equipment; *~e voorzieningen* toilet facilities

Sanskriet [sɑnskrit] *het* Sanskrit: *dat is ~ voor hem* that is Greek to him

Saudi-Arabië [saudiarɑbijə] *het* Saudi Arabia

Saudi-Arabisch [saudiarɑbis] *adj* Saudi (Arabian)

sap [sɑp] *het (~pen)* juice; sap; fluid: *het ~ uit een citroen knijpen* squeeze the juice from a lemon

sapje [sɑpjə] *het (~s)* (fruit) juice

sappig [sɑpəχ] *adj* juicy: *~ vlees* juicy (*or:* succulent) meat

sarcasme [sɑrkɑsmə] *het (~n)* sarcasm

sarcastisch [sɑrkɑstis] *adj, adv* sarcastic: *~e opmerkingen* snide remarks

sarcofaag [sɑrkofaχ] *de (-fagen)* sarcophagus

sardine [sɑrdinə] *de (~s)* sardine

Sardinië [sɑrdinijə] *het* Sardinia

sarong [sarɔŋ] *de (~s)* sarong

sarren [sɑrə(n)] *vb* bait, (deliberately) provoke, needle

satan [satɑn] *de (~s)* devil, fiend

Satan [satɑn] *de (~s)* Satan

satanisch [satanis] *adj, adv* satanic(al), diabolic: *een ~e blik* (*or:* lach) a fiendish look (*or:* laugh)

saté [satɛ] *de* satay

satelliet [satəlit] *de (~en)* satellite

satellietschotel [satəlitsχotəl] *de* satellite dish

satellietverbinding [satəlitfərbɪndɪŋ] *de (~en)* satellite link(-up)

satéstokje [satɛstɔkjə] *het (~s)* skewer

satijn [satɛin] *het (~en)* satin

satire [satirə] *de (~s)* satire: *een ~ schrijven op* satirize, write a satire on

satirisch [satiris] *adj, adv* satiric(al)

Saturnus [satʏrnʏs] *de* Saturn

saucijs [sosɛis] *de (saucijzen)* sausage

saucijzenbroodje [sosɛizə(n)brocə] *het (~s)* sausage roll

sauna [souna] *de (~'s)* sauna (bath)

saus [sɑus] *de (sauzen)* sauce, gravy, (salad) dressing: *zoetzure ~* sweet and sour (sauce)

savanne [savɑnə] *de (~n)* savannah

savooikool [savojkol] *de (-kolen)* savoy (cabbage)

sax [sɑks] *de (~en)* sax(ophone)

saxofoon [sɑksofon] *de (~s)* saxophone

scala [skala] *het (~'s)* scale, range: *een breed ~ van artikelen* a wide range of items

scalp [skɑlp] *de (~en)* scalp

scalpel [skɑlpɛl] *het (~s)* scalpel

scalperen [skɑlperə(n)] *vb* scalp

Scandinavië [skɑndinɑvijə] *het* Scandinavia

Scandinaviër [skɑndinɑvijər] *de (~s)* Scandinavian

Scandinavisch [skɑndinɑvis] *adj* Scandinavian

scannen [skɛnə(n)] *vb* scan

scenario [sənarijo] *het (~'s)* scenario, screenplay *(film)*, script

scène [sɛːnə] *de* scene: *hij had de overval zelf in ~ gezet* he had faked the robbery himself

scepter [sɛptər] *de (~s)* sceptre: *de ~ voeren (zwaaien)* hold sway (over)

sceptisch [sɛptis] *adj, adv* sceptical

schaaf [sχaf] *de (schaven)* **1** plane; **2** slicer

schaafwond [sχafwɔnt] *de (~en)* graze, scrape

¹**schaak** [sχak] *het* chess: *een partij ~* a game of chess

²**schaak** [sχak] *adj* in check: *~ staan* be in check; *iem ~ zetten* put s.o. in check

schaakbord [sχagbɔrt] *het (~en)* chessboard

schaakcomputer [sχakɔmpjutər] *de (~s)* chess computer

schaakmat [sχakmɑt] *adj* checkmate: *~ staan* be checkmated; *iem ~ zetten* checkmate s.o.

schaakpartij [sχakpɑrtɛi] *de (~en)* game of chess

schaakspel [sχakspɛl] *het (~len)* **1** chess; **2** chess set

schaakspelen [sχakspelə(n)] *vb* play chess

schaakstuk [sχakstʏk] *het (~ken)* chessman, piece

schaaktoernooi [sχakturnoj] *het (~en)* chess tournament

schaal [sχal] *de (schalen)* **1** scale: *er wordt op grote ~ misbruik van gemaakt* it is misused on a large scale; *op ~ tekenen* draw to scale; *~ 4:1* a scale of four to one; **2** dish, plate: *een ~ met fruit* a bowl of fruit

schaaldier [sχaldir] *het (~en)* crustacean

schaalmodel [sχalmodɛl] *het (~len)* scale model

schaalverdeling [sχalvərdelɪŋ] *de (~en)* graduation, scale division: *een ~ op iets aanbrengen* graduate sth

schaambeen [sχɑmben] *het (~deren)* pubis, pubic bone

schaamdeel [sχɑmdel] *het (-delen)* genital(s), private part(s): *de vrouwelijke* (or: *mannelijke*) *schaamdelen* the female (or: male) genitals

schaamhaar [sχɑmhar] *het (-haren)* pubic hair

schaamlippen [sχɑmlɪpə(n)] *de* labia: *de grote* (or: *de kleine*) ~ the labia majora (or: minora)

schaamte [sχɑmtə] *de* shame: *blozen* (or: *rood worden*) *van* ~ blush (or: go red) with shame

schaap [sχap] *het (schapen)* sheep: *een kudde schapen* a flock of sheep; *het zwarte* ~ *(van de familie) zijn* be the black sheep (of the family); *~jes tellen* count sheep

schaapachtig [sχapɑχtəχ] *adj, adv* silly: *iem* ~ *aankijken* look stupidly at s.o.; *~ lachen* grin sheepishly

schaapherder [sχaphɛrdər] *de (~s)* shepherd

schaar [sχar] *de (scharen)* **1** (pair of) scissors: *de* ~ *in iets zetten* take the scissors (or: a pair of scissors) to sth; *één* ~ one pair of scissors; *twee scharen* two (pairs of) scissors; **2** pincers, claws

¹**schaars** [sχars] *adv* sparingly, sparsely, scantily: ~ *verlicht* dimly lit

²**schaars** [sχars] *adj* scarce: *mijn ~e vrije ogenblikken* my rare free moments

schaarste [sχarstə] *de* scarcity, shortage

schaats [sχats] *de (~en)* skate: *de ~en aanbinden* put on one's skates

schaatsbaan [sχatsban] *de (-banen)* (skating) rink

schaatsen [sχatsə(n)] *vb* skate

schaatser [sχatsər] *de (~s)* skater

schacht [sχɑχt] *de (~en)* **1** shaft; shank; *(bot)* stem; **2** *(Belg)* fresher, first-year student

schade [sχadə] *de (~n)* **1** loss(es): *de* ~ *inhalen* recoup one's losses; ~ *lijden* suffer a loss; **2** damage, *(pers also)* harm: ~ *aanrichten* damage sth; ~ *aan iets toebrengen* (or: *berokkenen*) do (or: cause) damage to sth; *zijn auto heeft heel wat ~ opgelopen* his car has suffered quite a lot of damage; *de ~ loopt in de miljoenen* the damage runs into millions

schadeclaim [sχadəklem] *de (~s)* insurance claim (for damage): *een ~ afhandelen* settle a claim

schadeformulier [sχadəfɔrmylir] *het (~en)* claim form

schadelijk [sχadələk] *adj, adv* harmful, damaging: *~e dieren* pests, vermin; *~e gewoonten* pernicious habits

schadeloos [sχadəlos] *adj, adv* unharmed, undamaged

schadeloosstellen [sχadəlostɛlə(n)] *vb* compensate, repay, reimburse: *zich ergens voor ~* compensate (oneself) for sth

schadeloosstelling [sχadəlostɛlɪŋ] *de (~en)* compensation: *volledige ~ betalen* pay full damages

schaden [sχadə(n)] *vb* damage, harm: *roken schaadt de gezondheid* smoking damages your health

schadepost [sχadəpɔst] *de (~en)* loss, (financial) setback

schadevergoeding [sχadəvərɣudɪŋ] *de (~en)* compensation; damages: *volledige ~ betalen* pay full damages; ~ *eisen voor* claim compensation (or: damages) for; *€1000,- ~ krijgen* receive 1000 euros in damages

schaduw [sχadyw] *de (~en)* shade, shadow: *in iemands ~ staan* be outshone (or: overshadowed) by s.o.

schaduwen [sχadywə(n)] *vb* shadow, tail: *iem laten ~* have s.o. shadowed (or: tailed)

schaduwkabinet [sχadywkabinɛt] *het (~ten)* shadow cabinet

schaduwzijde [sχadywzɛidə] *de (~n)* **1** shady side; **2** drawback: *de ~ van een overigens nuttige maatregel* the drawback to an otherwise useful measure

schaften [sχɑftə(n)] *vb* break (for lunch, dinner)

schakel [sχakəl] *de (~s)* link: *een belangrijke ~* a vital link; *de ontbrekende ~* the missing link

schakelaar [sχakəlar] *de (~s)* switch

schakelarmband [sχakəlɑrmbɑnt] *de (~en)* chain bracelet

schakelen [sχakələ(n)] *vb* **1** connect: *parallel* (or: *in serie*) ~ connect in parallel (or: in series); **2** change, change gear(s): *naar de tweede versnelling ~* change to second (gear)

schakeling [sχakəlɪŋ] *de (~en)* **1** connection; circuit; **2** gear change: *automatische ~* automatic gear change

schaken [sχakə(n)] *vb* play chess: *een partijtje ~* play a game of chess; *simultaan ~* play simultaneous chess

schaker [sχakər] *de (~s)* chess player

schalks [sχɑlks] *adj* mischievous, sly

schamel [sχaməl] *adj, adv* poor, shabby: *een ~ pensioentje* a meagre (or: miserable) pension

schamen [sχamə(n)] *ref vb* be ashamed (of), be embarrassed: *zich dood* (or: *rot*) ~ die with shame; *daar hoef je je niet voor te ~* there's no need to be ashamed of that; *zich nergens voor ~* not be ashamed of anything

schamper [sχɑmpər] *adj* scornful, sarcastic, sneering

schandaal [sχɑndal] *het (schandalen)* **1** scandal, outrage: *een publiek* (or: *een politiek*) ~ a public outrage, a political scandal; **2** shame, disgrace: *een grof ~* a crying shame

schandalig [sχɑndaləχ] *adj, adv* scandalous, outrageous, disgraceful: *~ duur* outrageously expensive; *het is ~ zoals hij ons behandelt* it's disgraceful the way he treats us

schande [sχɑndə] *de* disgrace, shame: *het is (een) ~* it's a disgrace; ~ *van iets spreken* cry out against sth

schandelijk [sχɑndələk] *adj, adv* scandalous, outrageous: *een ~ boek* an infamous book

schandpaal [sχɑntpal] *de (-palen)* ‖ *iem aan de ~ nagelen* pillory s.o.

schans [sχɑns] *de (~en)* ski jump
schansspringen [sχɑnsprɪŋə(n)] *vb* ski jump
schap [sχɑp] *het, de (~pen)* shelf: *de ~pen bijvullen* re-stock the shelves
schapenfokkerij [sχɑpə(n)fɔkərɛi] *de (~en)* **1** sheep breeding; **2** sheep farm
schapenscheerder [sχɑpə(n)sχerdər] *de (~s)* sheepshearer
schapenvacht [sχɑpə(n)vɑχt] *de (~en)* sheepskin, fleece
schapenvlees [sχɑpə(n)vles] *het* mutton, lamb
schapenwol [sχɑpə(n)wɔl] *de* sheep's wool
schappelijk [sχɑpələk] *adj, adv* reasonable, fair
schar [sχɑr] *de (~ren)* dab; sheepdog
scharminkel [sχɑrmɪŋkəl] *het, de (~s)* scrag(gy person): *een mager ~* a bag of bones
scharnier [sχɑrniͅr] *het (~en)* hinge: *om een ~ draaien* hinge
scharnieren [sχɑrniͅrə(n)] *vb* hinge
scharrelei [sχɑrələɛi] *het (~eren)* free-range egg
scharrelen [sχɑrələ(n)] *vb* **1** rummage (about): *hij scharrelt de hele dag in de tuin* he potters about in the garden all day (long); **2** scratch
scharrelkip [sχɑrəlkɪp] *de (~pen)* free-range chicken
scharrelvlees [sχɑrəlvles] *het* free-range meat
schat [sχɑt] *de (~ten)* **1** treasure: *een verborgen ~* a hidden treasure; **2** treasure, riches: *~ten aan iets verdienen* make a fortune out of sth; *een ~ aan gegevens* (or: *materiaal*) a wealth of data (*or*: material); **3** darling, dear, honey: *zijn het geen ~jes?* aren't they sweet?
schatbewaarder [sχɑdbəwardər] *de (~s) (Belg)* treasurer
schateren [sχɑtərə(n)] *vb* roar (with laughter): *de kinderen ~ van plezier* the children shouted with pleasure
schatkamer [sχɑtkamər] *de (~s)* treasury, treasure house
schatkist [sχɑtkɪst] *de (~en)* **1** treasure chest; **2** treasury, (the) Exchequer
schatrijk [sχɑtrɛik] *adj* wealthy: *ze zijn schat- en schatrijk* they are fabulously wealthy
schatten [sχɑtə(n)] *vb* value, estimate, assess, appraise: *de afstand ~* estimate the distance; *hoe oud schat je hem?* how old do you take him to be?; *de schade ~ op* assess the damage at
schattig [sχɑtəχ] *adj, adv* sweet, lovely: *zij ziet er ~ uit* she looks lovely
schatting [sχɑtɪŋ] *de (~en)* estimate, assessment: *een voorzichtige ~* a conservative estimate; *naar ~ drie miljoen* an estimated three million
schaven [sχavə(n)] *vb* **1** plane: *planken ~* plane boards; **2** graze, scrape; **3** slice, shred: *komkommers ~* slice cucumbers
schavot [sχavɔt] *het (~ten)* scaffold: *iem op het ~ brengen: a)* condemn s.o. to the scaffold; *b) (fig)* cause s.o.'s downfall
schede [sχedə] *de (~n, ~s)* **1** sheath; **2** vagina

schedel [sχedəl] *de (~s)* skull
scheef [sχef] *adj, adv* **1** crooked; oblique, leaning, slanting, sloping: *scheve hoeken* oblique angles; *een ~ gezicht trekken* pull a wry face; *een scheve neus hebben* have a crooked nose; *het schilderij hangt ~* the picture is crooked; **2** wrong, distorted: *de zaak gaat (loopt) ~* things are going wrong
scheel [sχel] *adj, adv* cross-eyed
scheen [sχen] *de (schenen)* shin: *iem tegen de schenen schoppen* tread on s.o.'s toes
scheenbeen [sχemben] *het (-beenderen, -benen)* shinbone
scheenbeschermer [sχembəsχɛrmər] *de (~s)* shinguard
scheepsbouwer [sχepsbɑuwər] *de (~s)* shipbuilder
scheepshut [sχepshʏt] *de (~ten)* (ship's) cabin
scheepslading [sχepsladɪŋ] *de (~en)* shipload, (ship's) cargo
scheepsramp [sχepsrɑmp] *de (~en)* shipping disaster
scheepsruim [sχepsrœym] *het (~en)* (ship's) hold
scheepswerf [sχepswɛrf] *de (-werven)* shipyard
scheepvaart [sχepfart] *de* shipping (traffic), navigation
scheepvaartbericht [sχepfardbərɪχt] *het (~en)* shipping news (*or*: report)
scheepvaartverkeer [sχepfartfərker] *het* shipping (traffic)
scheerapparaat [sχeraparat] *het (-apparaten)* shaver
scheermes [sχermɛs] *het (~sen)* razor
scheermesje [sχermɛʃə] *het (~s)* razor blade
scheerwol [sχerwɔl] *de* (virgin) wool: *zuiver ~* pure new wool
scheet [sχet] *de (scheten)* fart: *een ~ laten* fart
¹scheiden [sχɛidə(n)] *vb* **1** separate, divide: *dooier en eiwit ~* separate the yolk from the (egg) white; *het hoofd van de romp ~* sever the head from the body; *twee vechtende jongens ~* separate two fighting boys; **2** divorce, separate: *zich laten ~* get a divorce
²scheiden [sχɛidə(n)] *vb* **1** part (company), separate: *hier ~ onze wegen* here our ways part; *~ van* part (*or*: separate) from; *als vrienden ~* part (as) friends; **2** divorce, separate: *zij gaan ~* they are getting divorced
scheiding [sχɛidɪŋ] *de (~en)* **1** separation, detachment: *een ~ maken (veroorzaken) (in)* rupture, disrupt; **2** divorce: *~ van tafel en bed* legal separation, separation from bed and board; **3** parting
scheidslijn [sχɛitslɛin] *de (~en)* dividing line, *(fig)* borderline
scheidsrechter [sχɛitsrɛχtər] *de (~s)* umpire; referee: *als ~ optreden bij een wedstrijd* umpire (*or*: referee) a match
scheikunde [sχɛikʏndə] *de* chemistry
scheikundig [sχɛikʏndəχ] *adj, adv* chemical
schel [sχɛl] *adj, adv* shrill: *een ~le stem* a shrill (*or*:

piercing) voice

Schelde [sχɛldə] *de* Scheldt

schelden [sχɛldə(n)] *vb* curse, swear: *vloeken en ~* curse and swear; *op iem ~* scold s.o., call s.o. names

scheldnaam [sχɛltnam] *de (-namen)* term of abuse

scheldwoord [sχɛltwort] *het (~en)* term of abuse

schelen [sχelə(n)] *vb* **1** differ: *ze ~ twee maanden* they are two months apart; **2** concern, matter: *het kan mij niets* (or: *geen bal) ~* I don't give a hoot (or: *care two hoots); het kan me niet ~* I don't care, I don't mind; *kan mij wat ~!* why should I care!; *het scheelde geen haar* it was a close shave; *het scheelde weinig, of hij was verdronken* he narrowly escaped being drowned; *dat scheelt (me) weer een ritje* that saves (me) another trip

schelp [sχɛlp] *de (~en)* **1** shell; **2** auricle

schelpdieren [sχɛlbdirə(n)] *de* shellfish

schelvis [sχɛlvɪs] *de (~sen)* haddock

schema [sχema] *het (~'s)* **1** diagram, plan; **2** plan, outline; **3** schedule: *we liggen weer op ~* we're back on schedule; *achter* (or: *voor) op het ~* behind (or: ahead of) schedule

schematisch [sχematis] *adj, adv* schematic, diagrammatic: *iets ~ voorstellen (aangeven)* represent sth in diagram form

schemeren [sχemərə(n)] *vb* grow dark; become light: *het begint te ~* it is getting dark (or: light), twilight is setting in

schemerig [sχemərəχ] *adj, adv* dusky

schemerlamp [sχemərlɑmp] *de (~en)* floor lamp, standard lamp

schenden [sχɛndə(n)] *vb* **1** damage; **2** break, violate: *een verdrag* (or: *mensenrechten) ~* violate a treaty (or: human rights)

schending [sχɛndɪŋ] *de (~en)* violation; breach

schenken [sχɛŋkə(n)] *vb* **1** pour (out); **2** give: *zijn hart ~ aan* give one's heart to

schenking [sχɛŋkɪŋ] *de (~en)* gift, donation: *een ~ doen* make a gift (or: donation)

schep [sχɛp] *de* **1** scoop, shovel; **2** (table)spoon(ful), scoop(ful): *drie ~pen ijs* three scoops of ice cream

schepen [sχepə(n)] *de (~en) (Belg)* alderman

schepijs [sχɛpɛis] *het* (easy-scoop) ice cream

schepje [sχɛpjə] *het (~'s)* **1** (small) spoon; **2** spoon(ful): *een ~ suiker* a spoonful of sugar

scheppen [sχɛpə(n)] *vb* **1** create: *God schiep de hemel en de aarde* God created heaven and earth; **2** scoop, shovel: *een emmer water ~* draw a bucket of water; *leeg ~* empty; *vol ~* fill; *zand op een kruiwagen ~* shovel sand into a wheelbarrow

schepper [sχɛpər] *de (~s)* creator

schepping [sχɛpɪŋ] *de (~en)* creation

schepsel [sχɛpsəl] *het (~en, ~s)* creature

scheren [sχerə(n)] *vb* shave; shear: *zich ~* shave; *geschoren schapen* shorn sheep

scherf [sχɛrf] *de (scherven)* fragment, splinter: *in scherven (uiteen)vallen* fall to pieces

scherm [sχɛrm] *het (~en)* **1** screen, shade; **2** cur-

tain: *de man achter de ~en* the man behind the scenes; **3** screen, display

schermen [sχɛrmə(n)] *vb* fence

schermutseling [sχɛrmʏtsəlɪŋ] *de (~en)* skirmish, clash

¹scherp [sχɛrp] *het* **1** edge: *op het ~ van de snede balanceren* be on a knife-edge; **2** ball: *met ~ schieten* fire (with) live ammunition; *op ~ staan* be on edge

²scherp [sχɛrp] *adj* **1** sharp, pointed, *(maths)* acute: *een ~e kin* a pointed chin; **2** sharp, pungent, hot, spicy, cutting, biting: *~e mosterd* (or: *kerrie)* hot mustard (or: curry); **3** strict, severe: *~ toezicht* close control; **4** sharp, harsh: *~e kritiek* sharp criticism; **5** sharp, clear-cut: *een ~ contrast vormen* be in sharp contrast with; *~ stellen* focus; **6** live; armed

scherpomlijnd [sχɛrpɔmlɛint] *adj* clear-cut, well-defined

scherpschutter [sχɛrpsχʏtər] *de (~s)* sharpshooter, sniper

scherpte [sχɛrptə] *de (~n, ~s)* sharpness, keenness: *de ~ van het beeld* the sharpness of the picture; *de ~ van een foto* the focus of a picture

scherpzinnig [sχɛrpsɪnəχ] *adj, adv* **1** acute, discerning, sharp(-witted): *een ~e geest* a subtle mind; **2** shrewd, clever: *~ antwoorden* give a shrewd answer

scherpzinnigheid [sχɛrpsɪnəχhɛit] *de (-heden)* **1** acuteness, discernment; **2** shrewdness, wit

scherts [sχɛrts] *de* joke, jest

schertsen [sχɛrtsə(n)] *vb* joke, jest

schertsvertoning [sχɛrtsfərtonɪŋ] *de (~en)* joke

schets [sχɛts] *de (~en)* sketch: *een eerste ~* a first draft; *een ruwe* (or: *korte) ~ van mijn leven* a rough (or: brief) outline of my life

schetsboek [sχɛtsbuk] *het (~en)* sketchbook

schetsen [sχɛtsə(n)] *vb* sketch: *ruw (in grote lijnen) ~* give a rough sketch (of)

schetteren [sχɛtərə(n)] *vb* blare

scheur [sχør] *de (~en)* **1** crack, crevice, split: *een ~ in een muur* a crack in a wall; **2** tear: *hij heeft een ~ in mijn nieuwe boek gemaakt* he has torn my new book

¹scheuren [sχørə(n)] *vb* tear: *zijn kleren ~* tear one's clothes

²scheuren [sχørə(n)] *vb* tear (apart); crack; split: *pas op, het papier zal ~* be careful, the paper will tear; *de auto scheurde door de bocht* the car came screeching round the corner

scheut [sχøt] *de (~en)* **1** shoot, sprout; **2** twinge, stab (of pain); **3** dash, shot: *een ~ melk* a dash of milk

scheutig [sχøtəχ] *adj* generous

schichtig [sχɪχtəχ] *adj, adv* nervous, timid, skittish

schielijk [sχilək] *adv* quickly, rapidly

schiereiland [sχirɛilɑnt] *het (~en)* peninsula

schietbaan [sχidban] *de (-banen)* shooting range

¹schieten [sχitə(n)] *vb* **1** shoot, fire: *op iem ~* shoot (or: take a shot) at s.o.; **2** shoot, dash: *de prijzen ~*

omhoog prices are soaring; **3** (with *laten*) let go, release, drop *(pers)*, forget *(pers)*: *laat hem* ~ forget (about) him; *de tranen schoten haar in de ogen* tears rushed to her eyes; *weer te binnen* ~ come back (to mind)

²schieten [sχitə(n)] *vb* shoot: *hij kon haar wel* ~ he could (cheerfully) have murdered her; *zich een kogel door het hoofd* ~ blow out one's brains; *naast* ~ miss; *in het doel* ~ net (the ball)

schietgebed [sχitχəbɛt] *het (~en)* short prayer, quick prayer: *een ~je doen* say a quick prayer

schietschijf [sχitsχɛif] *de (-schijven)* target

schietstoel [sχitstul] *de (~en)* ejector seat, ejection seat

schiettent [sχitɛnt] *de (~en)* rifle gallery, shooting gallery

schietwedstrijd [sχitwɛtstrɛit] *de* shooting-match, archery contest

¹schiften [sχiftə(n)] *vb* sort (out), sift (through)

²schiften [sχiftə(n)] *vb* curdle, turn

schifting [sχiftɪŋ] *de (~en)* **1** sifting: *Jan is bij de eerste* ~ *afgevallen* Jan was weeded out in the first round; **2** curdling

schijf [sχɛif] *de (schijven)* **1** disc; **2** disc, plate, (potter's) wheel; **3** slice: *een ~je citroen* a slice of lemon; **4** disk

schijn [sχɛin] *de* **1** appearance, semblance: *op de uiterlijke* ~ *afgaan* judge by (outward) appearances; ~ *bedriegt* appearances are deceptive; *de* ~ *ophouden tegenover de familie* keep up appearances in front of the family; **2** show, appearances: *schone* ~ glamour, cosmetics, gloss; **3** shadow, gleam: *geen* ~ *van kans hebben* not have the ghost of a chance

schijnbaar [sχɛimbar] *adj, adv* seeming, apparent: ~ *oprecht* seemingly sincere

schijnbeweging [sχɛimbəweγɪŋ] *de (~en)* feint, dummy (movement, pass): *een* ~ *maken* (make a) feint

¹schijndood [sχɛindot] *de* apparent death, suspended animation

²schijndood [sχɛindot] *adj* apparently dead, in a state of suspended animation

schijnen [sχɛinə(n)] *vb* **1** shine: *de zon schijnt* the sun is shining; *met een zaklantaarn in iemands gezicht* ~ flash a torch in s.o.'s face; **2** seem, appear: *het schijnt zo* it looks like it; *hij schijnt erg rijk te zijn* apparently he is very rich

schijnheilig [sχɛinhɛiləχ] *adj, adv* hypocritical, sanctimonious: *met een* ~ *gezicht* sanctimoniously

schijnheilige [sχɛinhɛiləγə] *de* hypocrite

schijnsel [sχɛinsəl] *het (~s)* shine, light

schijntje [sχɛincə] *het (~s)* ‖ *ik kocht het voor een* ~ I bought it for a song

schijnwerper [sχɛinwɛrpər] *de (~s)* floodlight, spotlight: *iem in de ~s zetten* spotlight s.o.

schijt [sχɛit] *het, de* shit, crap

schijten [sχɛitə(n)] *vb* shit, crap

schijterd [sχɛitərt] *de (~s)* funk, scaredy-cat

schijterig [sχɛitərəχ] *adj, adv* chicken-hearted

schijterij [sχɛitərɛi] *de* shits, trots, runs: *aan de* ~ *zijn* have the shits (*or:* trots, runs)

schik [sχɪk] *de* contentment; fun: ~ *hebben in zijn werk* enjoy one's work

schikken [sχɪkə(n)] *vb* arrange, order: *de boeken in volgorde* ~ put the books in order

schikking [sχɪkɪŋ] *de (~en)* arrangement, ordering ‖ *een* ~ *treffen (met)* reach an understanding (with)

schil [sχɪl] *de (~len)* skin; rind; peel

schild [sχɪlt] *het (~en)* **1** shield; shell; **2** sign

schilder [sχɪldər] *de (~s)* **1** (house-)painter, (house-)decorator; **2** painter

schilderachtig [sχɪldərɑχtəχ] *adj, adv* picturesque, scenic

schilderen [sχɪldərə(n)] *vb* paint, decorate: *zijn huis laten* ~ have one's house painted

schilderij [sχɪldərɛi] *het, de (~en)* painting, picture: *een* ~ *in olieverf* an oil painting

schildering [sχɪldərɪŋ] *de (~en)* painting, picture: *~en op een wand* murals

schilderkunst [sχɪldərkʏnst] *de* (art of) painting

schildersbedrijf [sχɪldərzbədrɛif] *het (-bedrijven)* painter and decorator's business

schildersezel [sχɪldərsezəl] *de (~s)* (painter's) easel

schilderstuk [sχɪldərstʏk] *het (~ken)* painting, picture

schilderwerk [sχɪldərwɛrk] *het* **1** painting: *het* ~ *op de wand* the mural (painting); **2** paintwork: *het* ~ *aanbesteden* give out the paintwork by contract

schildklier [sχɪltklir] *de (~en)* thyroid gland

schildknaap [sχɪltknap] *de (-knapen)* shield-bearer, squire

schildpad [sχɪltpɑt] *de (~den)* tortoise, turtle

schildwacht [sχɪltwɑχt] *de (~en)* sentry, guard: *~en aflossen* change the guard

schilfer [sχɪlfər] *de (~s)* scale, flake, chip, sliver

schilferen [sχɪlfərə(n)] *vb* flake (off), peel (off)

schillen [sχɪlə(n)] *vb* peel: *aardappels* ~ peel potatoes

schim [sχɪm] *de (~men)* shadow: *~men in het donker* shadows in the dark

schimmel [sχɪməl] *de (~s)* **1** mould; mildew: *de* ~ *van kaas afhalen* scrape the mould off cheese; *er zit* ~ *op die muur* there is mildew on the wall; **2** *(bot)* fungus; **3** grey

schimmelen [sχɪmələ(n)] *vb* mould, become mouldy (*or:* mildewed)

schimmelinfectie [sχɪmməlɪnfɛksi] *de (~s)* fungal infection

schimmenspel [sχɪmə(n)spɛl] *het* shadow theatre, shadow play

schimmig [sχɪməχ] *adj* shadowy

schip [sχɪp] *het (schepen)* ship, vessel, barge, boat: *zijn schepen achter zich verbranden* burn one's boats; *het zinkende* ~ *verlaten* leave the sinking ship; *per* ~ by ship (*or:* boat)

schipbreuk [sχɪbrøk] *de (~en)* shipwreck, wreck: ~ *lijden: a)* founder, be wrecked; *b)* be shipwrecked

schipbreukeling [sχɪbrøkəlɪŋ] *de (~en)* ship-wrecked person

schipper [sχɪpər] *de (~s)* **1** master (of a ship), captain, skipper; **2** captain of a barge

schipperen [sχɪpərə(n)] *vb* give and take: *je moet een beetje weten te ~* you've got to give and take (a bit)

schippersjongen [sχɪpərsjɔŋə(n)] *de (~s)* barge-hand, deckhand (on a barge)

schipperstrui [sχɪpərstrœy] *de (~en)* seaman's pullover

schitteren [sχɪtərə(n)] *vb* **1** glitter, shine, twinkle: *zijn ogen schitterden van plezier* his eyes twinkled with amusement; **2** shine (in, at), excel (in, at): *~ in gezelschap* be a social success

schitterend [sχɪtərənt] *adj, adv* **1** brilliant, sparkling: *het weer was ~* the weather was gorgeous; **2** splendid, magnificent: *een ~ doelpunt* a marvellous goal

schittering [sχɪtərɪŋ] *de (~en)* brilliance, radiance

schizofreen [sχidzofren] *adj* schizophrenic

schizofrenie [sχidzofreni] *de* schizophrenia

schlager [ʃlagər] *de (~s)* (schmalzy) pop(ular) song

schlemiel [ʃləmil] *de (~en)* wally

schmink [ʃmɪŋk] *de* greasepaint, make-up

schminken [ʃmɪŋkə(n)] *vb* make (s.o.) up: *zich ~* make (oneself) up

schnabbel [ʃnɑbəl] *de (~s)* (bit of a) job on the side: *daar heb ik een leuke ~ aan* it brings in a bit extra for me

schnabbelaar [ʃnɑbəlar] *de (roughly)* moonlighter

schnabbelen [ʃnɑbələ(n)] *vb* have a (bit of a) job on the side, moonlight

schnitzel [ʃnɪtsəl] *de (~s)* (veal, pork) cutlet, schnitzel

schoeisel [sχujsəl] *het* footwear

schoen [sχun] *de (~en)* shoe: *twee paar ~en* two pairs of shoes; *hoge ~en* boots; *(Belg) in nauwe ~tjes zitten* be in dire straits; *zijn ~en aantrekken* put on one's shoes; *zijn ~en uittrekken* take off one's shoes; *ik zou niet graag in zijn ~en willen staan* I wouldn't like to be in his shoes

schoenenzaak [sχunə(n)zak] *de (-zaken)* shoe shop

schoener [sχunər] *de (~s)* schooner

schoenlepel [sχunlepəl] *de (~s)* shoehorn

schoenmaat [sχumat] *de (-maten)* shoe size

schoenmaker [sχumakər] *de (~s)* cobbler, shoe-maker: *die schoenen moeten naar de ~* those shoes need repairing

schoenpoets [sχumputs] *de* shoe polish

schoenpoetsen [sχumputsə(n)] *vb* cleaning (*or:* polishing) of shoes

schoenpoetser [sχumputsər] *de (~s)* shoeshine boy

schoenveter [sχunvetər] *de (~s)* shoelace: *zijn ~s strikken (or: vastmaken)* lace up (*or:* tie) one's shoes

schoenzool [sχunzol] *de (-zolen)* sole

schoffel [sχɔfəl] *de (~s)* hoe

schoffelen [sχɔfələ(n)] *vb* weed

schoft [sχɔft] *de* **1** bastard; **2** shoulder, withers

schoftenstreek [sχɔftə(n)strek] *de (-streken)* dirty trick, nasty trick

schok [sχɔk] *de (~ken)* **1** shock: *dat nieuws zal een ~ geven* that news will come as quite a shock; *de ~ te boven komen* get over the shock; **2** jolt: *de ~ken van een aardbeving* earthquake tremors; *de ~ was zo hevig dat …* the (force of the) impact was so great that …

schokbreker [sχɔgbrekər] *de (~s)* shock absorber

schokeffect [sχɔkɛfɛkt] *het (~en)* shock, impact: *voor een ~ zorgen* create a shock

¹schokken [sχɔkə(n)] *vb* shake, jolt

²schokken [sχɔkə(n)] *vb* shock: *~de beelden* shocking scenes

¹schol [sχɔl] *de (~len)* plaice

²schol [sχɔl] *int (Belg)* cheers!

scholen [sχɔlə(n)] *vb* school, train

scholengemeenschap [sχɔlə(n)ɣəmensχɑp] *de (~pen) (roughly)* comprehensive school

scholier [sχɔlir] *de (~en)* **1** pupil, *(Am)* student; **2** *(Belg)* junior member (14, 15 years) of sports club

scholing [sχɔlɪŋ] *de* training, schooling: *een man met weinig ~* a man of little schooling (*or:* education)

schommel [sχɔməl] *de (~s)* swing

schommelbeweging [sχɔməlbəweɣɪŋ] *de (~en)* swing, swinging motion, rocking motion

schommelen [sχɔmələ(n)] *vb* **1** swing, rock, roll; **2** swing, rock: *ze zijn aan het ~* they are playing on the swings; **3** fluctuate

schommeling [sχɔmməlɪŋ] *de (~en)* fluctuation, swing

schommelstoel [sχɔməlstul] *de (~en)* rocking chair

schone [sχɔnə] *de (~n)* beauty

schooien [sχɔjə(n)] *vb beg: die hond schooit bij iedereen om een stukje vlees* that dog begs a piece of meat from everybody

schooier [sχɔjər] *de (~s)* tramp, vagrant, *(Am)* bum

school [sχol] *de (scholen)* school: *een ~ haringen* a school of herring; *een bijzondere ~* a denominational school; *hogere ~* college for higher education; *de lagere ~* primary school; *de middelbare ~* secondary (*or Am:* high) school; *een neutrale ~* a non-denominational school; *een openbare ~* a state (*or Am:* public) school; *Vrije School* Rudolf Steiner School; *een witte ~* a predominantly white school; *naar ~ gaan* go to school; *de kinderen zijn naar ~* the children are at school; *op de middelbare ~ zitten* go to (*or:* attend) secondary school; *uit ~ komen* come home from school; *als de kinderen van ~ zijn* when the children have finished school; *zij werd van ~ gestuurd* she was expelled from school; *een ~ voor voortgezet onderwijs* a secondary school

schoolagenda [sχolaɣɛnda] *de (~'s)* school diary

schoolartikelen [sχolɑrtikələ(n)] *de* school supplies

schoolbank [sχolbɑŋk] *de (~en)* school desk: *ik heb met hem in de ~en gezeten* we went to school together, we were schoolmates

schoolbegeleidingsdienst [sχolbəɣəlɛidɪŋzdinst] *de (~en)* education advisory service

schoolbel [sχolbɛl] *de (~len)* school bell

schoolbestuur [sχolbəstyr] *het (-besturen)* board of governors

schoolblijven [sχolblɛivə(n)] *vb* stay in (after school), be kept in (after school)

schoolboek [sχolbuk] *het (~en)* school book, textbook

schoolbord [sχolbɔrt] *het (~en)* blackboard

schoolbus [sχolbʏs] *de (~sen)* school bus

schooldag [sχoldɑχ] *de (~en)* school day: *de eerste ~* the first day of school

schooldiploma [sχoldiploma] *het (~'s)* diploma, school (leaving) certificate

schooldirecteur [sχoldirɛktør] *de* principal, headmaster, headmistress

schoolfeest [sχolfest] *het (~en)* school party

schoolgaand [sχolɣant] *adj* schoolgoing

schoolgebouw [sχolɣəbʌu] *het (~en)* school (building)

schoolgeld [sχolɣɛlt] *het (~en)* tuition, fee(s)

schoolhoofd [sχolhoft] *het (~en)* principal, headmaster, headmistress

schoolinspecteur [sχolɪnspɛktør] *de (~s)* school inspector

schooljaar [sχoljar] *het (-jaren)* school year: *het eerste ~ over moeten doen* have to repeat the first year

schooljongen [sχoljɔŋə(n)] *de (~s)* schoolboy

schooljuf [sχoljʏf] *de (~fen)* schoolmarm

schooljuffrouw [sχoljʏfrau] *de (~en)* (school)teacher

schoolkeuze [sχolkøzə] *de* choice of school

schoolkind [sχolkɪnt] *het (~eren)* schoolchild

schoolklas [sχolklɑs] *de (~sen)* class, form

schoolkrant [sχolkrɑnt] *de (~en)* school (news)paper

schoolleiding [sχolɛidɪŋ] *de (~en)* school management

schoollokaal [sχolokal] *het (-lokalen)* schoolroom

schoolmeester [sχolmestər] *de (~s)* **1** schoolteacher; **2** pedant, prig: *de ~ spelen (uithangen)* be a pedant

schoolmeisje [sχolmɛiʃə] *het (~s)* schoolgirl

schoolonderzoek [sχolɔndərzuk] *het (~en)* exam(ination)

schoolopleiding [sχolopleidɪŋ] *de (~en)* education: *een goede ~ genoten hebben* have had the advantage of a good education

schoolplein [sχolplɛin] *het (~en)* (school) playground: *de kinderen spelen op het ~* the children were playing in the playground

schoolradio [sχolradijo] *de* educational radio

schoolreglement [sχolreɣləmɛnt] *het* school regulations (*or:* rules)

schoolreis [sχolrɛis] *de (-reizen)* school trip

schoolreünie *de* school reunion

schools [sχols] *adj, adv* scholastic

schoolschrift [sχolsχrɪft] *het (~en)* school notebook

schoolslag [sχolslɑχ] *de* breaststroke

schooltas [sχoltɑs] *de (~sen)* schoolbag, satchel

schooltelevisie [sχolteləvizi] *de* educational television

schooltijd [sχoltɛit] *de (~en)* school time (*or:* hours): *de ~en variëren soms van school tot school* school hours can vary from school to school; *buiten* (or: *na*) *~* outside (*or:* after) school; *gedurende de ~, onder ~* during school (time)

schooluitgave [sχolœytχavə] *de* school edition

schoolvak [sχolvak] *het (~ken)* school subject

schoolvakantie [sχolvakɑnsi] *de (~s)* school holidays

schoolverlater [sχolvərlatər] *de (~s)* school leaver, *(Am)* recent graduate, drop-out

schoolverzuim [sχolvərzœym] *het* school absenteeism

schoolvoorbeeld [sχolvorbelt] *het (~en)* classic example: *dit is een ~ van hoe het niet moet* this is a classic example of how it shouldn't be done

schoolziek [sχolzik] *adj* shamming, malingering

¹schoon [sχon] *het* beauty: *het vrouwelijk ~* female beauty

²schoon [sχon] *adj* **1** clean, neat: *~ water* clean (*or:* fresh) water; **2** beautiful, fine: *de schone kunsten* the fine arts; **3** clear, after tax: *50 pond ~ per week verdienen* make 50 pounds a week net (*or:* after tax); **4** *(Belg)* fine, pretty

schoonbroer [sχombrur] *de (~s)* brother-in-law

schoondochter [sχondɔχtər] *de (~s)* daughter-in-law

schoonfamilie [sχonfamili] *de (~s)* in-laws

schoonheid [sχonhɛit] *de (-heden)* beauty

schoonheidsfoutje [sχonhɛitsfautɕə] *de* little slip, flaw

schoonheidssalon [sχonhɛitsalɔn] *het, de (~s)* beauty salon (*or:* parlour)

schoonheidsspecialiste [sχonhɛitspeʃalɪstə] *de (~s)* beautician, cosmetician

schoonheidsvlekje [sχonhɛitsflɛkjə] *het (~s)* beauty spot

schoonheidswedstrijd [sχonhɛitswɛtstrɛit] *de (~en)* beauty contest

schoonhouden [sχonhaudə(n)] *vb* clean: *een kantoor ~* clean an office

schoonmaak [sχomak] *de* (house) cleaning, clean-up: *de grote ~* the spring-cleaning; *grote ~ houden* spring-clean, make a clean sweep

schoonmaakartikelen [sχomakɑrtikələ(n)] *de* cleaning products, cleanser(s)

schoonmaakbedrijf [sχomaɡbədrɛif] *het (-be-*

drijven) cleaning agency (*or:* service), (professional) cleaners

schoonmaken [sxomakə(n)] *vb* clean

schoonmaker [sxomakər] *de (~s)* cleaner

schoonmoeder [sxomudər] *de (~s)* mother-in-law

schoonouders [sxonaudərs] *de* in-laws

schoonschrift [sxonsxrift] *het (~en)* calligraphy

schoonschrijven [sxonsxreivə(n)] *vb* calligraphy

schoonspoelen [sxonspulə(n)] *vb* rinse (out)

schoonspringen [sxonspriŋə(n)] *vb* platform diving

schoonvader [sxonvadər] *de (~s)* father-in-law

schoonzoon [sxonzon] *de (~s, -zonen)* son-in-law

schoonzus [sxonzys] *de (~sen)* sister-in-law

schoonzwemmen [sxonzwɛmə(n)] *vb* synchronized swimming

schoorsteen [sxorsten] *de (-stenen)* chimney: *de ~ trekt niet goed* the chimney doesn't draw well; *de ~ vegen* sweep the chimney

schoorsteenbrand [sxorstembrant] *de (~en)* chimney fire

schoorsteenmantel [sxorstemantəl] *de (~s)* mantelpiece

schoorsteenveger [sxorstenveɣər] *de (~s)* chimney sweep

schoorvoetend [sxorvutənt] *adj* reluctantly

schoot [sxot] *de (schoten)* lap: *bij iem op ~ kruipen* clamber onto s.o.'s lap

schoothondje [sxothɔncə] *het (~s)* lapdog

schop [sxɔp] *de* 1 kick: *een vrije ~* a free kick; *iem een ~ onder zijn kont geven* kick s.o. on (*or:* up) the behind; 2 shovel, spade

¹**schoppen** [sxɔpə(n)] *vb* kick: *tegen een bal ~* kick a ball; *het ver ~* go far (in the world)

²**schoppen** [sxɔpə(n)] *de (~)* spades: *schoppenaas* ace of spades; *~ is troef* spades are trump; *één ~* one spade

schor [sxɔr] *adj, adv* hoarse, husky

schorem [sxorəm] *het* riff-raff, scum

schorpioen [sxɔrpijun] *de (~en)* scorpion

Schorpioen [sxɔrpijun] *de (~en)* Scorpio

schors [sxɔrs] *de (~en)* bark

schorsen [sxɔrsə(n)] *vb* 1 adjourn; 2 suspend: *een speler voor drie wedstrijden ~* suspend a player for three games; *als lid ~* suspend s.o. from membership

schorsing [sxɔrsiŋ] *de (~en)* suspension: *door zijn gedrag een ~ oplopen* be suspended for bad conduct

schort [sxɔrt] *het, de (~en)* apron: *een ~ voordoen* put on an apron

schot [sxɔt] *het (~en)* 1 shot: *een ~ in de roos* a bull's-eye; *een ~ op goal* a shot at goal; 2 range: *buiten ~ blijven, zich buiten ~ houden* keep out of range; *iem (iets) onder ~ hebben* have s.o. (sth) within range; *onder ~ houden* keep covered; *onder ~ nemen* cover; 3 movement: *er komt (zit) ~ in de zaak* things are beginning to get going (*or:* to move); 4 partition

Schot [sxɔt] *de (~ten)* Scot

schotel [sxotəl] *de (~s)* 1 dish, (*small*) saucer: *een vuurvaste ~* an ovenproof dish; 2 dish: *een warme ~* a hot dish; *een vliegende ~* a flying saucer

schotelantenne [sxotəlantɛnə] *de (~s)* satallite dish

Schotland [sxɔtlant] *het* Scotland

schots [sxɔts] *de (~en)* (ice) floe || *~ en scheef* higgledy-piggledy, topsy-turvy

Schots [sxɔts] *adj* Scottish, Scots, Scotch: *~e whisky* Scotch (whisky)

schotwond [sxɔtwɔnt] *de (~en)* bullet wound, gunshot wound

schouder [sxaudər] *de (~s)* shoulder: *de ~s ophalen* shrug one's shoulders; *iem op zijn ~ kloppen* pat s.o. on the back

schouderband [sxaudərbant] *de (~en)* shoulder strap: *zonder ~jes* strapless

schouderblad [sxaudərblat] *het (~en)* shoulder blade (*or:* bone)

schouderklopje [sxaudərklɔpjə] *het (~s)* pat on the back

schouderophalen [sxaudərɔphalə(n)] *het* shrug

schoudervulling [sxaudərvyliŋ] *de (~en)* shoulder pad

schouw [sxau] *de (~en)* mantel(piece)

schouwburg [sxaubyrx] *de (~en)* theatre: *naar de ~ gaan* go to the theatre

schouwspel [sxauspɛl] *het (~en)* spectacle, sight, show: *een aangrijpend ~* a touching sight

schraagtafel [sxraxtafəl] *de (~s)* trestle table

schraal [sxral] *adj, adv* 1 lean; 2 poor, arid; 3 bleak; cutting; 4 dry: *schrale handen* chapped hands

schram [sxram] *de (~men)* scratch, scrape: *vol ~men zitten* be all scratched

schrander [sxrandər] *adj, adv* clever, sharp

schransen [sxransə(n)] *vb* gormandize, stuff oneself

schrap [sxrap] *adv* braced: *zich ~ zetten* brace oneself, dig (one's heels) in

schrapen [sxrapə(n)] *vb* 1 clear: *de keel ~* clear one's throat; 2 scrape: *geld bij elkaar ~* scrape money together

schrappen [sxrapə(n)] *vb* 1 scrape, scale; 2 strike off, strike out, delete: *iem als lid ~* drop s.o. from membership

schrede [sxredə] *de (~n)* pace, step

schreef [sxref] *de (schreven)* || *over de ~ gaan* overstep the mark

schreeuw [sxrew] *de (~en)* shout, cry: *een ~ geven* (let out a) yell, give a cry

¹**schreeuwen** [sxrewə(n)] *vb* shout (out), yell (out): *een bevel ~* shout (*or:* yell) (out) an order

²**schreeuwen** [sxrewə(n)] *vb* 1 scream, cry (out), yell (out); 2 cry out (for): *deze problemen ~ om een snelle oplossing* these problems are crying out for a quick solution; 3 scream, shout: *hij schreeuwt tegen iedereen* he shouts at everyone; 4 cry, screech, squeal

schreeuwlelijk [sxrewlelək] *de (~en)* 1 loudmouth,

bigmouth; **2** squaller, screamer
schreien [sχrɛiə(n)] *vb* weep; cry (out) ‖ *bittere (or: hete) tranen ~* weep bitter (*or:* hot) tears
schriel [sχril] *adj* thin, meagre
schrift [sχrɪft] *het (~en)* **1** writing: *iets op ~ stellen* put sth in writing; *ik heb het op ~* I have it in writing; **2** (hand)writing: *duidelijk leesbaar ~* legible handwriting; **3** exercise book, notebook
Schrift [sχrɪft] *de* Scripture(s): *de Heilige ~* (Holy) Scripture, the Scriptures
schriftelijk [sχrɪftələk] *adj, adv* written; in writing: *een ~e cursus* a correspondence course; *~ bevestigen* confirm in writing; *iets ~ vastleggen* put sth in writing; *voor het ~ zakken* fail one's written exams
schrijden [sχrɛidə(n)] *vb* stride, stalk
schrijfbenodigdheden [sχrɛivbənodəχthedə(n)] *de* stationery, writing materials
schrijfblok [sχrɛivblɔk] *het (~ken)* writing pad, (note)pad
schrijfgerei [sχrɛifχərɛi] *het* stationery
schrijfkramp [sχrɛifkramp] *de (~en)* writer's cramp
schrijfmachine [sχrɛifmaʃinə] *de (~s)* typewriter
schrijfster [sχrɛifstər] *de (~s)* writer
schrijftaal [sχrɛiftal] *de* written language
schrijfvaardigheid [sχrɛifardəχhɛit] *de* writing skill
schrijlings [sχrɛilɪŋs] *adj, adv* straddling; astride: *~ op een paard zitten* sit astride a horse
schrijnen [sχrɛinə(n)] *vb* **1** chafe; **2** smart
schrijven [sχrɛivə(n)] *vb* write: *een vriend ~* write to a friend; *voluit ~* write (out) in full; *op een advertentie ~* answer an advertisement; *op het moment waarop ik dit schrijf* at the time of writing
schrijver [sχrɛivər] *de (~s)* writer, author
schrik [sχrɪk] *de (~ken)* **1** terror, shock, fright: *iem ~ aanjagen* give s.o. a fright; *van de ~ bekomen* get over the shock; *met de ~ vrijkomen* have a lucky escape; *tot mijn ~* to my alarm (*or:* horror); *tot hun grote ~* to their horror; **2** fright, fear; **3** terror: *hij is de ~ van de buurt* he is the terror of the neighbourhood
schrikaanjagend [sχrikaɲaχənt] *adj* terrifying, frightening
schrikbarend [sχrɪgbarənt] *adj, adv* alarming, shocking: *~ hoge prijzen* staggering prices
schrikbeeld [sχrɪgbelt] *het (~en)* phantom, spectre, bogey: *het ~ van de werkloosheid* the spectre of unemployment
schrikdraad [sχrɪgdrat] *de (-draden)* electric fence
schrikkeldag [sχrɪkəldaχ] *de (~en)* leap day
schrikkeljaar [sχrɪkəljar] *het (-jaren)* leap year
schrikkelmaand [sχrɪkəlmant] *de (~en)* February
schrikken [sχrɪkə(n)] *vb* be shocked (*or:* scared, frightened): *ik schrik me kapot (dood)* I'm scared stiff (*or:* to death); *wakker ~* wake with a start; *iem laten ~* frighten s.o.; *hij schrok ervan* it frightened him; *van iets ~* be frightened by sth; *iem aan het ~ maken* give s.o. a fright

schril [sχrɪl] *adj, adv* **1** shrill, squeaky: *een ~le stem* a shrill voice; **2** sharp, glaring
schrobben [sχrɔbə(n)] *vb* scrub
schroef [sχruf] *de (schroeven)* **1** screw: *alles staat weer op losse schroeven* everything's not settled (*or:* up in the air) again; *(fig) de schroeven aandraaien* put the screws on; *een ~ vastdraaien* (or: *losdraaien*) tighten (*or:* loosen) a screw; *er zit een ~je bij hem los* he has a screw loose; **2** screw propeller
schroefdeksel [sχruvdɛksəl] *het (~s)* screw cap, screw-on lid
schroefdop [sχruvdɔp] *de (~pen)* screw cap, screw top: *de ~ van een fles losdraaien* screw the top off a bottle
schroefdraad [sχruvdrat] *de (-draden)* (screw) thread
schroeien [sχrujə(n)] *vb* **1** singe, sear: *zijn kleren ~* singe one's clothes; **2** scorch: *de zon schroeide het gras* the sun scorched the grass
schroeven [sχruvə(n)] *vb* screw: *iets in elkaar ~* screw sth together; *iets uit elkaar ~* unscrew sth
schroevendraaier [sχruvə(n)drajər] *de (~s)* screwdriver
schrokken [sχrɔkə(n)] *vb* cram down, gobble: *zit niet zo te ~* don't bolt your food like that
schromelijk [sχromələk] *adj, adv* gross: *~ overdreven* grossly exaggerated
schromen [sχromə(n)] *vb* hesitate
schrompelen [sχrɔmpələ(n)] *vb* shrivel
schroom [sχrom] *de* hesitation; diffidence
¹schroot [sχrot] *het* **1** scrap (iron, metal); **2** lumps
²schroot [sχrot] *de* lath: *een muur met ~jes betimmeren* lath a wall
schroothandelaar [sχrothandəlar] *de (~s, -handelaren)* scrap (iron, metal) dealer, junk dealer
schroothoop [sχrothop] *de (-hopen)* scrap heap: *deze auto is rijp voor de ~* this car is fit for the scrap heap
schrootjeswand [sχrocəswant] *de (~en)* lathed wall
schub [sχʏp] *de (~ben)* scale
schuchter [sχʏχtər] *adj, adv* shy, timid: *een ~e poging* a timid attempt
schudden [sχʏdə(n)] *vb* shake, shuffle: *~ voor gebruik* shake before use; *iem flink de hand ~* pump s.o.'s hand; *nee ~ (met het hoofd)* shake one's head; *iem van zich af ~* shake s.o. off; *iem door elkaar ~* shake s.o. up; *dat kun je wel ~!* forget it!, nothing doing!
schuier [sχœyər] *de (~s)* brush
schuif [sχœyf] *de (schuiven)* **1** bolt; **2** *(Belg)* drawer
schuifdak [sχœyvdak] *het (~en)* sunroof
schuifdeur [sχœyvdør] *de (~en)* sliding door
schuifelen [sχœyfələ(n)] *vb* shuffle: *met de voeten ~* shuffle one's feet
schuifje [sχœyfjə] *het (~s)* (small) bolt
schuifladder [sχœyfladər] *de (~s)* extension ladder
schuifpui [sχœyfpœy] *de (~en)* sliding French window (*or Am:* door), sliding patio doors

schuiftrombone [sχœyftrɔmbɔːnə] *de (~s)* slide trombone

schuiftrompet [sχœyftrɔmpɛt] *de (~ten)* trombone

schuifwand [sχœyfwɑnt] *de (~en)* sliding wall

schuilen [sχœylə(n)] *vb* **1** hide: *daarin schuilt een groot gevaar* that carries a great risk (with it); **2** shelter (from)

schuilkelder [sχœylkɛldər] *de (~s)* air-raid shelter

schuilnaam [sχœylnam] *de (-namen)* pseudonym, pen-name

schuilplaats [sχœylplats] *de (~en)* **1** hiding place, (place of) shelter, hideout: *iem een ~ verlenen* give shelter to s.o.; **2** shelter: *een ~ zoeken* take shelter

schuim [sχœym] *het* foam, froth, lather

schuimbad [sχœymbɑt] *het (~en)* bubble bath

schuimblusapparaat [sχœymblʏsɑparat] *het (-apparaten)* foam extinguisher

schuimen [sχœymə(n)] *vb* foam, froth, lather: *die zeep schuimt niet* that soap does not lather

schuimkraag [sχœymkraχ] *de (-kragen)* head

schuimpje [sχœympjə] *het (~s)* meringue

¹schuimplastic [sχœymplɛstɪk] *het* foam plastic

²schuimplastic [sχœymplɛstɪk] *adj* foam plastic

¹schuimrubber [sχœymrʏbər] *de* foam rubber

²schuimrubber [sχœymrʏbər] *adj* foam rubber

schuimspaan [sχœymspan] *de (-spanen)* skimmer

schuimwijn [sχœymwɛin] *de (~en)* sparkling wine

schuin [sχœyn] *adj, adv* **1** slanting, sloping: *~e rand* bevelled edge; *een ~e streep* a slash; *een stuk hout ~ afzagen* saw a piece of wood slantwise; *iets ~ houden* slant sth; *~ oversteken* cross diagonally; *~ schrijven* write in italics; *hier ~ tegenover* diagonally across from here; **2** smutty, dirty

schuinschrift [sχœynsχrɪft] *het* sloping handwriting, slanting handwriting

schuit [sχœyt] *de (~en)* barge, boat

schuitje [sχœycə] *het (~s)* boat: *in hetzelfde ~ zitten* be in the same boat

¹schuiven [sχœyvə(n)] *vb* push, shove: *een stoel bij de tafel ~* pull up a chair; *iets (iem) terzijde ~* brush ~~sth (s.o.)~~ aside; *iets voor zich uit ~* put sth off, postpone sth

²schuiven [sχœyvə(n)] *vb* **1** slide: *de lading ging ~* the cargo shifted; *in elkaar ~* slide into one another, telescope; **2** move (*or:* bring) one's chair: *dichterbij ~* bring one's chair closer; *laat hem maar ~* let him get on with it; *met data ~* rearrange dates

schuiver [sχœyvər] *de (~s)* skid, lurch: *een ~ maken* skid, lurch

schuld [sχʏlt] *de (~en)* **1** debt: *zijn ~en afbetalen* pay off (*or:* settle) one's debts; *~en hebben* have debts, be in debt; **2** guilt, blame: *iem de ~ van iets geven* blame s.o. for sth; *het is mijn eigen ~* it is my own fault

schuldbekentenis [sχʏldbəkɛntənɪs] *de (~sen)* **1** bond, IOU; **2** admission (*or:* confession) of guilt: *een volledige ~ afleggen* make a full confession

schuldbelijdenis [sχʏldbəlɛidənɪs] *de (~sen)* (*Roman Catholicism*) confession

schuldeiser [sχʏltɛisər] *de (~s)* creditor

schuldgevoel [sχʏltχəvul] *het (~ens)* feeling of guilt, guilty conscience

schuldig [sχʏldəχ] *adj* **1** owing: *hoeveel ben ik u ~?* how much do I owe you?; **2** guilty: *de rechter heeft hem ~ verklaard* the judge has declared him guilty

schuldige [sχʏldəγə] *de (~n)* culprit, guilty party, offender

schuldvraag [sχʏltfraχ] *de (-vragen)* the question of guilt

schulp [sχʏlp] *de (~en)* shell: *in zijn ~ kruipen* withdraw (*or:* retire) into one's shell

schunnig [sχʏnəχ] *adj* shabby, filthy

schuren [sχγrə(n)] *vb* **1** grate, scour; **2** sand(paper)

schurft [sχʏrft] *het, de* scabies, mange: *de ~ aan iem hebben* hate s.o.'s guts

schurk [sχʏrk] *de (~en)* scoundrel, villain

schut [sχʏt] *het (~ten)* shelter, cover ‖ *iem voor ~ zetten* make s.o. look a fool; *voor ~ staan* look a fool (*or:* an idiot)

schutkleur [sχʏtklør] *de (~en)* camouflage

schutter [sχʏtər] *de (~s)* rifleman, marksman ‖ *hij is een goede ~* he is a crack shot

schutting [sχʏtɪŋ] *de (~en)* fence: *een ~ om een bouwterrein zetten* fence off a construction site

schuttingtaal [sχʏtɪŋtal] *de* foul language, obscene language: *~ uitslaan* use foul (*or:* obscene) language

schuttingwoord [sχʏtɪŋwort] *het (~en)* four-letter word, obscenity

schuur [sχyr] *de (schuren)* shed, barn: *de oogst in de ~ brengen* bring in the harvest

schuurmachine [sχyrmaʃinə] *de (~s)* sander, sanding machine

schuurmiddel [sχyrmɪdəl] *het (~en)* abrasive

schuurpapier [sχyrpapir] *het* sandpaper

schuurpoeder [sχyrpudər] *het, de* scouring powder

schuurspons [sχyrspɔns] *de (-sponzen, ~en)* scourer

schuw [sχyw] *adj, adv* shy, timid

schuwen [sχγwə(n)] *vb* shun, shrink from

sclerose [sklerozə] *de (~n, ~s)* sclerosis: *multiple ~* multiple sclerosis

scooter [skutər] *de (~s)* (motor) scooter

score [skɔrə] *de (~s)* score: *een gelijke ~* a draw (*or:* tie); *een ~ behalen van …* make a score of …

scorebord [skɔrəbɔrt] *het (~en)* scoreboard

scoren [skɔrə(n)] *vb* score: *een doelpunt ~* score (a goal)

scrabbelen [skrɛbələ(n)] *vb* play Scrabble

scriptie [skrɪpsi] *de (~s)* thesis, term paper: *een ~ schrijven over* write a thesis about (*or:* on)

seance [sejɑ̃sə] *de (~s)* seance

sec [sɛk] *adj* seconde sec

seconde [səkɔndə] *de (~n)* **1** second: *in een onderdeel van een ~* in a split second; **2** second, moment: *hij houdt geen ~ zijn mond* he never stops talking

secondewijzer [səkɔ̯ndəwɛizər] *de (~s)* second hand

secretaresse [sɪkrətarɛsə] *de (~s)* secretary

secretariaat [sɪkrətarijɑt] *het (secretariaten)* secretariat, secretary's office

secretarie [sɪkrətari] *de (~ën)* office, town clerk's office

secretaris [sɪkrətɑrɪs] *de (~sen)* secretary, clerk

sectie [sɛksi] *de (~s)* **1** autopsy, post-mortem (examination); dissection: *~ verrichten* carry out a post-mortem (*or:* an autopsy); **2** section, department: *de ~ betaald voetbal* the Football League; *de ~ Frans* the French department

sector [sɛktɔr] *de (~en)* sector: *de agrarische ~* the agricultural sector; *de zachte ~* the social sector

secundair [sekʏndɛ̯ːr] *adj, adv* secondary, minor: *van ~ belang* of minor importance

secuur [səkyr] *adj, adv* precise, meticulous

sedert [se̯dərt] *prep* since; for: *~ enige tijd* for some time

seffens [sɛfə(n)s] *adv (Belg)* at once, straightaway

segment [sɛɣmɛnt] *het (~en)* segment: *de ~en van een tunnel* the sections of a tunnel

sein [sɛin] *het (~en)* **1** signal, sign: *het ~ op veilig stellen* set the sign at clear; **2** tip, hint: *geef me even een ~tje als je hulp nodig hebt* just let me know if you need any help

seinen [se̯inə(n)] *vb* **1** signal, flash; **2** telegraph, radio

seinwachter [sɛinwɑχtər] *de (~s)* signalman

seismisch [sɛismis] *adj* seismic

seismograaf [sɛismoɣraf] *de (-grafen)* seismograph

seizoen [sɛizu̯n] *het (~en)* season: *weer dat past bij het ~* seasonable weather; *buiten het ~* in the off-season, out of season, off-season

seizoenarbeid [sɛizu̯nɑrbɛit] *de* seasonal work (*or:* employment)

seizoenartikel [sɛizu̯nɑrtikəl] *het (~en)* seasonal article

seizoenkaart [sɛizu̯ŋkart] *de (~en)* season ticket

seks [sɛks] *de* sex: *~ bedrijven* have sex

seksblad [sɛksblɑt] *het* sex magazine

sekse [sɛksə] *de (~n)* sex: *iem van de andere ~* s.o. of the opposite sex

seksfilm [sɛksfɪlm] *de (~s)* sex film, skin-flick

seksisme [sɛksɪsmə] *het (~n, ~s)* sexism, male chauvinism

seksist [sɛksɪst] *de (~en)* sexist, male chauvinist

seksistisch [sɛksɪstis] *adj, adv* sexist; like a sexist: *een ~e opmerking* a sexist remark

sekslijn [sɛkslɛin] *de (~en)* sex line

seksmaniak [sɛksmanijɑk] *de (~ken)* sex maniac

seksnummer [sɛksnʏmər] *het* sex line, erotic line

seksualiteit [sɛksywalitɛit] *de* sexuality

seksueel [sɛksywel] *adj, adv* sexual: *seksuele voorlichting* sex education; *~ overdraagbare aandoeningen* sexually transmitted disease(s)

seksuoloog [sɛksywolɔχ] *de (-logen)* sexologist

sekte [sɛktə] *de (~n, ~s)* sect

selderij [sɛldərɛi] *de* celery

selecteren [selɛktɛrə(n)] *vb* select, pick (out): *hij werd niet geselecteerd voor die wedstrijd* he was not picked (*or:* selected) for that match

selectie [selɛksi] *de (~s)* selection: *(sport) de ~ bekendmaken* announce the selection, name the squad

selectief [selɛktif] *adj, adv* selective

selectieprocedure [selɛksiprosedyrə] *de (~s)* selection procedure

selectiewedstrijd [selɛksiwɛtstrɛit] *de (~en)* selection match, preliminary match

semafoon [semafo̯n] *de (~s) (roughly)* radio(tele)phone

semester [semɛstər] *het (~s)* six months, semester, term (of six months)

Semieten [semitə(n)] *de* Semites

seminarie [seminɑri] *het (~s)* seminary: *op het ~ zitten* be at a seminary

semi-overheidsbedrijf [semiovərhɛitsbədrɛif] *het (-bedrijven)* semi state-controlled company

senaat [senɑt] *de (senaten)* senate

senator [senɑtɔr] *de (~en)* senator: *tot ~ gekozen worden* be elected (as) senator

Senegal [se̯neɣɑl] *het* Senegal

seniel [senil] *adj* senile

seniliteit [senilitɛit] *de* senility

senior [se̯nijɔr] *de (~en)* senior

seniorenpas [senijɔrə(n)pɑs] *de (~sen)* pensioner's ticket (*or:* pass), senior citizen's pass (*or:* reduction card)

sensatie [sɛnsa(t)si] *de (~s)* sensation, feeling, thrill, stir: *op ~ belust zijn* be looking for sensation

sensatiepers [sɛnsa(t)sipɛrs] *de* gutter press

sensationeel [sɛnsa(t)ʃonel] *adj, adv* sensational, spectacular

sentiment [sɛntimɛnt] *het (~en)* sentiment: *vals ~* cheap sentiment

sentimenteel [sɛntimentel] *adj, adv* sentimental: *een sentimentele film* a sentimental film, a tear-jerker

seponeren [seponɛrə(n)] *vb* dismiss, drop

september [sɛptɛmbər] *de* September

septisch [sɛptis] *adj* septic

sereen [seren] *adj, adv* serene

serenade [serenɑdə] *de (~s)* serenade: *iem een ~ brengen* serenade s.o.

sergeant [sɛrʒɑnt] *de (~s)* sergeant

sergeant-majoor [sɛrʒɑntmajo̯r] *de (~s)* sergeant major

serie [se̯ri] *de (~s)* series; serial: *een Amerikaanse ~ op de tv* an American serial on TV

seriemoordenaar [se̯rimordənar] *de (~s)* serial killer

serieproductie [se̯riprodʏksi] *de* serial production, series production

serieus [serijøs] *adj, adv* serious, straight: *een serieuze zaak* no laughing matter; *~?* seriously?, really?

sering [sərɪŋ] *de (~en)* lilac: *een boeket ~en* a bouquet of lilac

seropositief [seropozitif] *adj* HIV-positive

serpentine [sɛrpɛntinə] *de (~s)* streamer

serre [sɛːrə] *de (~s)* **1** sunroom; **2** conservatory

serum [seːrʏm] *het (sera)* serum

serveerder [sɛrveːrdər] *de (~s)* waiter; server

serveerster [sɛrveːrstər] *de* waitress

serveren [sɛrveːrə(n)] *vb* serve: *koel ~* serve chilled; *onderhands* (or: *bovenhands*) *~* serve underarm (*or:* overarm)

servet [sɛrvɛt] *het (~ten)* napkin

service [sʏːrvɪs] *de* **1** service: *dat is nog eens ~!* that is what I call service!; **2** service charge: *~ inbegrepen* service charges included

servicebeurt [sʏːrvɪzbørt] *de (~en)* service: *met je auto naar de garage gaan voor een ~* take the car to be serviced

serviceflat [sʏːrvɪsflɛt] *de (~s)* service flat

servicekosten [sʏːrvɪskɔstə(n)] *de* service charge(s)

servicelijn [sʏːrvɪslɛin] *de* service line

servicevak [sʏːrvɪsfɑk] *het (~ken)* service court

Servië [sɛrvijə] *het* Serbia

Serviër [sɛrvijər] *de (~s)* Serb(ian)

servies [sɛrvis] *het (serviezen)* service: *theeservies* tea service (*or:* set); *30-delig ~* 30-piece service

serviesgoed [sɛrvisxut] *het (~eren)* crockery

¹Servisch [sɛrvis] *het* Serbian

²Servisch [sɛrvis] *adj* Serbian

sesamzaad [sezɑmzat] *het (-zaden)* sesame seed(s)

sessie [sɛsi] *de (~s)* session, sitting, jam session

set [sɛt] *de (~s)* set

setter [sɛtər] *de (~s)* setter: *Ierse ~* Irish setter

sexshop [sɛkʃɔp] *de (~s)* sex shop, porn shop

Seychellen [seʃɛlə(n)] *de* the Seychelles

sfeer [sfer] *de (sferen)* **1** atmosphere; **2** atmosphere, character, ambience: *een huis met een heel eigen ~* a house with a distinctive character; **3** sphere: *in hogere sferen zijn* have one's head in the clouds

sfeervol [sfervɔl] *adj* attractive

sfinx [sfiŋks] *de (~en)* sphinx

shag [ʃɛk] *de* hand-rolling tobacco: *~ roken* roll one's own

shampoo [ʃɑmpo] *de (~s)* shampoo

sheriff [ʃɛrɪf] *de (~s)* sheriff

sherry [ʃɛri] *de (~'s)* sherry

Shetlander [ʃɛtlɑndər] *de (~s)* Shetland (pony)

shirt [ʃʏːrt] *het (~s)* shirt, blouse

shirtreclame [ʃʏːrtrəklamə] *de (~s)* shirt advertising

shoarma [ʃwɑrma] *de* doner kebab: *een broodje ~* a doner kebab

shoarmabroodje [ʃwɑrmabrocə] *het (~s)* pitta bread

shock [ʃɔk] *de (~s)* shock

shocktoestand [ʃɔktustɑnt] *de (~en)* state of shock: *hij is in ~* he is in (a state of) shock

short [ʃɔːrt] *de* shorts

shotten [ʃɔtə(n)] *het (Belg)* play football

show [ʃow] *de (~s)* show; display

si [si] *de (~'s) (mus)* ti, si

siamees [sijamɛs] *de (siamezen)* Siamese (cat)

Siamees [sijamɛs] *adj* Siamese

Siberië [siberijə] *het* Siberia

Siberisch [siberis] *adj, adv* Siberian

Siciliaan [sisilijan] *de (Sicilianen)* Sicilian

Sicilië [sisilijə] *het* Sicily

sidderen [sɪdərə(n)] *vb* tremble, shiver: *ik sidderde bij de gedachte alleen al* the very thought of it made me shudder

sieraad [sirat] *het (sieraden)* jewel, *(pl)* jewellery

sieren [sirə(n)] *vb* adorn: *dat siert hem* it is to his credit

sierlijk [sirlək] *adj, adv* elegant, graceful

sierlijkheid [sirləkheit] *de (-heden)* elegance, grace(fulness)

sierplant [sirplɑnt] *de (~en)* ornamental plant

sierstrip [sirstrip] *de (~s)* trim

siësta [sijɛsta] *de (~'s)* siesta: *~ houden* have a siesta

sigaar [siɣar] *de (sigaren)* cigar: *een ~ opsteken* light a cigar; *de ~ zijn* have had it, get the blame

sigarenbandje [siɣarə(n)bɑncə] *het (~s)* cigar band

sigarenboer [siɣarə(n)bur] *de* tobacconist

sigarenwinkel [siɣarə(n)wiŋkəl] *de* cigar shop, tobacconist's

sigaret [siɣarɛt] *de (~ten)* cigarette: *een pakje ~ten* a packet (*or Am:* pack) of cigarettes; *een ~ opsteken* (*or: uitmaken*) light (*or:* put out) a cigarette

sigarettenautomaat [siɣarɛtə(n)automat] *de (-automaten)* cigarette (vending) machine

sigarettenpeuk [siɣarɛtə(n)pøk] *de (~en)* cigarette end (*or:* butt)

sigarettenvloei [siɣarɛtə(n)vluj] *het* cigarette paper

signaal [sɪnal] *het (signalen)* **1** signal, sign: *het ~ voor de aftocht geven* sound the retreat; **2** signal: *het ~ stond op rood* the signal was red

signalement [sɪnaləmɛnt] *het (~en)* description: *hij beantwoordt niet aan het ~* he doesn't fit the description

signaleren [sɪnalerə(n)] *vb* **1** see, spot: *hij was in een nachtclub gesignaleerd* he had been seen in a nightclub; **2** point out: *problemen* (or: *misstanden*) *~* point out problems (*or:* evils)

signalisatie [sɪnaliza(t)si] *de (Belg)* traffic signs, road signs

signeren [sɪnerə(n)] *vb* sign, autograph: *een door de auteur gesigneerd exemplaar* a signed (an autographed) copy

significant [sɪɣnifikɑnt] *adj, adv* significant

sijpelen [sɛipələ(n)] *vb* trickle, ooze, seep

sik [sɪk] *de (~ken)* goatee

sikkel [sɪkəl] *de (~s)* sickle

sikkeneurig [sɪkənørəx] *adj, adv* peevish, grouchy

sikkepit [sɪkəpit] *de* whit, bit

silhouet [siluwɛt] *het, de (~ten)* silhouette

silicium [sil̯isijʏm] *het* silicon
siliconenkit [silikɔnə(n)kɪt] *het, de* silicone paste, fibre-glass paste
silo [sil̯o] *de (~'s)* silo
simpel [sɪmpəl] *adj, adv* simple: *~e kost* simple (*or:* modest) fare; *zo ~ ligt dat!* it's as simple as that!
simuleren [simyl̯erə(n)] *vb* simulate, sham
simultaan [simʏltan] *adj, adv* simultaneous: *(sport) ~ spelen* give a simultaneous display
simultaanpartij [simʏltampɑrtɛi] *de (~en)* simultaneous game
sinaasappel [sinɑsɑpəl] *de (~en, ~s)* orange
sinaasappelkist [sinɑsɑpəlkɪst] *de* orange crate, orange box
sinaasappelsap [sinɑsɑpəlsɑp] *het* orange juice
sinas [sinɑs] *de* orangeade, orange soda
¹sinds [sɪnts] *prep* since; for: *ik ben hier al ~ jaren niet meer geweest* I haven't been here for years; *ik heb hem ~ maandag niet meer gezien* I haven't seen him since Monday; *~ kort* recently, for a short time now
²sinds [sɪnts] *conj* since, ever since: *~ ik Jan ken* since I met (*or:* have known) Jan
singel [sɪŋəl] *de (~s)* **1** canal; **2** webbing
single [sɪŋgəl] *de (~s)* single
singlet [sɪŋglɛt] *de (~s)* singlet, *(Am)* undershirt
sinister [sinɪstər] *adj, adv* sinister: *~e plannen* sinister designs
sint [sɪnt] *de (~en)* **1** saint; **2** St Nicholas
sint-bernardshond [sɪndbɛrnɑrtshɔnt] *de (~en)* St Bernard (dog)
sintel [sɪntəl] *de (~s)* cinder: *gloeiende ~s* glowing embers
Sinterklaas [sɪntərklɑs] *de see* Sint-Nicolaas
sinterklaasavond [sɪntərklɑsɑvɔnt] *de (~en)* St Nicholas' Eve
sinterklaasgedicht [sɪntərklɑsχədɪχt] *het (~en)* St Nicholas' poem
sint-juttemis [sɪntjʏtəmɪs] *de ‖ wachten tot ~* wait till the cows come home
Sint-Nicolaas [sɪntnikolas] *de* **1** St Nicholas; **2** feast of St Nicholas
sinus [sinʏs] *de (~sen)* sine (of angle)
sip [sɪp] *adj* glum, crestfallen
Sire [sirə] *de* your Majesty, Sire
sirene [sirɛnə] *de (~s)* siren: *met loeiende ~* with wailing sirens
Sirius [sirijʏs] *de* Sirius
siroop [sirop] *de (siropen)* syrup: *vruchten op lichte* (or: *zware*) *~ fruit* in light (*or:* heavy) syrup
sisklank [sɪsklɑŋk] *de (~en)* sibilant
sissen [sɪsə(n)] *vb* **1** hiss: *een ~d geluid maken* make a hissing noise; **2** sizzle: *het spek siste in de pan* the bacon was sizzling in the pan
sisser [sɪsər] *de (~s) ‖ met een ~ aflopen* blow over, fizzle out
sitar [sitɑr] *de (~s)* sitar
situatie [sitywa(t)si] *de (~s)* situation, position: *een moeilijke ~* a difficult situation; *in de huidige ~* as things stand, in the present situation
sjaal [ʃal] *de (~s)* scarf: *een ~ omslaan* put on a scarf
sjabloon [ʃablon] *de (sjablonen)* stencil (plate), template; *(fig)* stereotype
sjacheraar [ʃɑχərar] *de (~s)* haggler, horse-trader
sjah [ʃa] *de (~s)* shah
sjalot [ʃalɔt] *de (~ten)* shallot
sjansen [ʃɑnsə(n)] *vb* flirt, make eyes at s.o.: *~ met de buurman* flirt with the neighbour
sjasliek [ʃɑslik] *de* shashlik
sjeik [ʃɛik] *de (~s)* sheik(h)
sjekkie [ʃɛki] *het (~s)* (hand-rolled) cigarette, roll-up: *een ~ draaien* roll a cigarette
sjerp [ʃɛrp] *de (~en)* sash
sjiek [ʃik] *adj see* chic
sjilpen [ʃɪlpə(n)] *vb* cheep, chirp
sjoelen [ʃul̯ə(n)] *vb* play at shovelboard
sjofel [ʃofəl] *adj, adv* shabby
sjokken [ʃɔkə(n)] *vb* trudge
sjonnie [ʃɔni] *de (~s)* greaser
sjorren [ʃɔrə(n)] *vb* lug, heave
sjouwen [ʃɑuwə(n)] *vb* lug, drag: *lopen ~* trudge, traipse
sjouwer [ʃɑuwər] *de (~s)* porter, docker
¹skai [skɑj] *het* imitation leather
²skai [skɑj] *adj* imitation leather
skateboard [skɛdbɔːrd] *het (~s)* skateboard
skaten [skɛtɑ(n)] *vb* skateboard
skeeler [skil̯ər] *de (~s)* skeeler
skeeleren [skil̯ərə(n)] *vb* rollerblade
skelet [skəl̯ɛt] *het (~ten)* skeleton, frame
skelterbaan [skɛltərban] *de (-banen)* go-kart (race)track
skelteren [skɛltərə(n)] *vb* go-kart: *het ~* go-karting
sketch [skɛtʃ] *de (~es)* sketch
ski [ski] *de (~'s)* ski
skicentrum [skisɛntrʏm] *het (skicentra)* ski resort
skiën [skijə(n)] *vb* ski: *gaan ~* go skiing
skiër [skijər] *de (~s)* skier
skigebied [skiɣəbit] *het (~en)* skiing area (*or:* centre)
skileraar [skilerar] *de (skileraren)* ski instructor
skilift [skilɪft] *de (~en)* ski lift
skipiste [skipistə] *de (~s, ~n)* ski run
skischans [skisχɑns] *de (~en)* ski jump
skischoen [skisχun] *de (~en)* ski boot
skistok [skistɔk] *de (~ken)* ski stick (or Am: pole)
sla [sla] *de* lettuce, salad: *een krop ~* a head of lettuce; *de ~ aanmaken* dress the salad
slaaf [slaf] *de (slaven)* slave
slaafs [slafs] *adj, adv* slavish, servile: *~e gehoorzaamheid* servile obedience
slaag [slaχ] *de ‖ (also fig) iem (een pak) ~ geven* give s.o. a beating
slaan [slan] *vb* **1** hit, strike, slap, beat: *de klok slaat ieder kwartier* the clock strikes the quarters; *zich ergens doorheen ~* pull through; *zijn hart ging sneller ~* his heart beat faster; *een paal in de grond ~*

drive a stake into the ground; *met de vleugels ~* flap one's wings; *met de deur ~* slam the door; *iem in elkaar ~* beat s.o. up; *hij is er niet (bij) weg te ~* wild horses couldn't drag him away; **2** take, capture; **3** *(with op)* refer to: *waar slaat dat nu weer op?* what do you mean by that?; *dat slaat op mij* that is meant for *(or:* aimed at) me; *dat slaat nergens op* that makes no sense at all; *over de kop ~* overturn; *een ~ mantel om iem heen ~* wrap a coat round s.o.; *de armen om de hals van iem ~* fling one's arms around s.o.'s neck; *de benen over elkaar ~* cross one's legs

slaap [slap] *de* **1** sleep: *in ~ vallen* fall asleep; **2** sleepiness: *~ hebben* be *(or:* feel) sleepy; *~ krijgen* get sleepy; **3** temple

slaapbank [sla̱baŋk] *de (~en)* sofa bed

slaapgelegenheid [sla̱pχəleχənhɛit] *de (-heden)* sleeping accommodation, place to sleep

slaapje [sla̱pjə] *het (~s)* nap, snooze

slaapkamer [sla̱pkamər] *de (~s)* bedroom

slaapkop [sla̱pkɔp] *de (~pen)* **1** sleepyhead; **2** dope

slaapliedje [sla̱plicə] *het (~s)* lullaby

slaapmiddel [sla̱pmɪdəl] *het (~en)* sleeping pill

slaapmuts [sla̱pmʏts] *de (~en)* nightcap

slaapmutsje [sla̱pmʏtʃə] *het (~s)* nightcap

slaappil [sla̱pɪl] *de (~len)* sleeping pill

slaapplaats [sla̱plats] *de (~en)* place to sleep, bed

slaapstad [sla̱pstat] *de (-steden)* dormitory suburb; dormitory town

slaapster [sla̱pstər] *de (~s)* || *de schone ~* Sleeping Beauty

slaaptrein [sla̱ptrɛin] *de (~en)* sleeper, overnight train

slaapverwekkend [sla̱pfərwɛkənt] *adj* sleep-inducing, *(fig)* soporific: *een ~ boek* a tedious book

slaapwandelaar [sla̱pwɑndəlar] *de (~s)* sleepwalker

slaapwandelen [sla̱pwɑndələ(n)] *vb* walk in one's sleep: *het ~* sleepwalking

slaapzaal [sla̱psal] *de (-zalen)* dormitory, dorm

slaapzak [sla̱psak] *de (~ken)* sleeping bag

slaatje [slacə] *het (~s)* salad || *hij wil overal een ~ uit slaan* he tries to cash in on everything

slab [slɑp] *de (~ben)* bib: *een kind een ~ voordoen* put a child's bib on

slabak [sla̱bak] *de (~ken)* salad bowl

slabakken [sla̱bɑkə(n)] *vb (Belg)* hang fire, do badly: *de ~de economie* the stagnating economy

slacht [slɑχt] *de* slaughter(ing)

slachtafval [sla̱χtafɑl] *het, de* offal

slachtbank [sla̱χtbaŋk] *de (~en)* || *naar de ~ geleid worden* be led to the slaughter

slachten [sla̱χtə(n)] *vb* slaughter, butcher: *geslachte koeien* slaughtered cows

slachthuis [sla̱χthœys] *het (-huizen)* slaughterhouse

slachting [sla̱χtɪŋ] *de (~en)* slaughter(ing), massacre

slachtoffer [sla̱χtɔfər] *het (~s)* victim, casualty: *~ worden van* fall victim *(or:* prey) to

slachtofferhulp [sla̱χtɔfərhʏlp] *de* help *(or:* aid) to victims

slachtpartij [sla̱χtpɑrtɛi] *de (~en)* slaughter, massacre

slachtvee [sla̱χtfe] *het* stock *(or:* cattle) for slaughter(ing), beef cattle

¹slag [slɑχ] *de* **1** blow, punch, lash: *iem een (zware) ~ toebrengen* deal s.o. a heavy blow; **2** stroke, drive: *een ~ in de lucht* a shot in the dark; **3** *(mil)* battle: *in de ~ bij Nieuwpoort* at the Battle of Nieuwpoort; *(Belg) zich uit de ~ trekken* get out of a difficult situation; **4** bang, bump; **5** wave: *hij heeft een mooie ~ in zijn haar* he has a nice wave in his hair; **6** stroke, beat: *(totaal) van ~ zijn* be (completely) thrown out; **7** knack: *de ~ van iets te pakken krijgen* get the knack *(or:* hang) of sth; **8** *(cards)* trick: *iem een ~ voor zijn* be one up on s.o.; **9** take, capture; **10** stroke: *vrije ~* freestyle; *een ~ naar iets slaan* have a shot *(or:* stab) at sth; *een goede ~ slaan* make a good deal; *aan de ~ gaan* get to work; *hij was op ~ dood* he was killed instantly

²slag [slɑχ] *het* sort, kind: *dat is niet voor ons ~ mensen* that's not for the likes of us; *iem van jouw ~* s.o. like you

slagader [sla̱χadər] *de (~s)* artery: *grote ~* aorta

slagboom [sla̱χbom] *de (-bomen)* barrier

slagen [sla̱χə(n)] *vb* **1** (with *in, met*) succeed (in), be successful (in): *ben je erin geslaagd?* did you pull it off, did you manage?; **2** (with *in + vb*) succeed in (-ing), manage (to): *ik slaagde er niet in de top te bereiken* I failed to make it to the top; **3** (with *voor*) pass, qualify (as, for): *hij is voor zijn Frans geslaagd* he has passed (his) French; **4** be successful: *de operatie is geslaagd* the operation was successful; *de tekening is goed geslaagd* the drawing has turned out well

slager [sla̱χər] *de (~s)* butcher

slagerij [sla̱χərɛi] *de (~en)* butcher's (shop)

slaggitaar [sla̱χitar] *de (-gitaren)* rhythm guitar

slaghout [sla̱χhaut] *het (~en)* bat

slaginstrument [sla̱χɪnstrymɛnt] *het (~en)* percussion instrument

slagpen [sla̱χpɛn] *de (~nen)* **1** flight feather; **2** firing pin

slagroom [sla̱χrom] *de* || *aardbeien met ~* strawberries and whipped cream

slagschip [sla̱χsχɪp] *het (-schepen)* battleship

slagtand [sla̱χtant] *de (~en)* **1** tusk; **2** fang

slagveld [sla̱χfɛlt] *het (~en)* battlefield

slagwerk [sla̱χwɛrk] *het (~en)* percussion (section), rhythm section

slagwerker [sla̱χwɛrkər] *de (~s)* percussionist, drummer

slagzij [sla̱χsɛi] *de* list *(ship);* bank: *dat schip maakt zware ~* that ship is listing heavily

slagzin [sla̱χsɪn] *de (~nen)* slogan, catchphrase

slak [slɑk] *de (~ken)* **1** snail; slug; **2** slag, dross

slaken [sla̱kə(n)] *vb* give, utter: *een kreet ~* give a cry, shriek; *een zucht ~* give *(or:* heave) a sigh

slakkengang [slɑkə(n)ɣɑŋ] *de* snail's pace
slakkenhuis [slɑkə(n)hœys] *het (-huizen)* **1** snail's shell; **2** *(med)* cochlea
slalom [slɑlɔm] *de (~s)* slalom
slang [slɑŋ] *de (~en)* **1** snake: *giftige ~en* poisonous snakes; **2** hose
slank [slɑŋk] *adj* slender, slim: *aan de ~e lijn doen* be slimming *(or:* dieting)
slaolie [slɑoli] *de* salad oil
slap [slɑp] *adj* **1** slack: *(fig) een ~pe tijd* a slack season; *het touw hangt ~* the rope is slack; **2** soft, limp; **3** weak, flabby: *~pe spieren* flabby muscles; *we lagen ~ van het lachen* we were in stitches; **4** empty, feeble: *een ~ excuus* a lame *(or:* feeble) excuse
slapeloos [slɑpəlos] *adj, adv* sleepless
slapeloosheid [slɑpəloshɛit] *de* insomnia, sleeplessness: *aan ~ lijden* suffer from insomnia
slapen [slɑpə(n)] *vb* **1** sleep: *gaan ~* go to bed, go to sleep; *hij kon er niet van ~* it kept him awake; *slaap lekker* sleep well; *bij iem blijven ~* spend the night at s.o.'s house *(or:* place), spend the night with s.o.; *ik wil er een nachtje over ~* I'd like to sleep on it; *hij slaapt als een os (een roos)* he sleeps like a log; **2** sleep (with): *mijn been slaapt* I've got pins and needles in my leg
slapend [slɑpənt] *adj* sleeping: *~e rijk worden* make money without any effort
slaperig [slɑpərəχ] *adj, adv* sleepy, drowsy
slapjanus [slɑpjanʏs] *de (~sen)* wimp, weed
slappeling [slɑpəlɪŋ] *de (~en)* weakling, softie
slapte [slɑptə] *de* slackness
slasaus [slasɑus] *de (~en, slasauzen)* salad dressing
slavenarbeid [slavə(n)ɑrbɛit] *de* slave labour
slavenhandel [slavə(n)hɑndəl] *de* slave trade
slavernij [slavərnɛi] *de* slavery: *afschaffing van de ~* abolition of slavery
slavin [slavɪn] *de (~nen)* (female) slave
slecht [slɛχt] *adj, adv* **1** bad, poor: *een ~ gebit* bad teeth; *~ betaald* badly *(or:* low) paid; *~er worden* worsen, deteriorate; *~ ter been zijn* have difficulty (in) walking; **2** bad, unfavourable: *hij heeft het ~ getroffen* he has been unlucky; **3** bad, wrong: *zich op het ~e pad begeven* go astray; **4** bad, ill: *het loopt nog eens ~ met je af* you will come to no good
slechterik [slɛχtərɪk] *de (~en)* baddie, bad guy, villain
slechtgehumeurd [slɛχtχəhymørt] *adj* bad-tempered
slechthorend [slɛχthorənt] *adj* hard of hearing
slechts [slɛχts] *adv* only, merely, just: *in ~ enkele gevallen* in only *(or:* just) a few cases
slechtziend [slɛχtsint] *adj* visually handicapped: *~ zijn* have bad eyesight
slee [sle] *de (~ën)* sledge, *(Am)* sled
sleeën [slejə(n)] *vb* sledge, *(Am)* sled, sleigh
sleep [slep] *de (slepen)* tow: *iem een ~(je) geven, iem op ~ nemen* give s.o. a tow, take s.o. in tow
sleepboot [slebot] *de (-boten)* tug(boat)
sleepkabel [slepkabəl] *de (~s)* tow rope

sleeptouw [sleptɑu] *het (~en)* tow rope: *iem op ~ nemen* take s.o. in tow
sleepwagen [slepwaɣə(n)] *de (~s)* breakdown truck; breakdown van, *(Am)* tow truck
slenteren [slɛntərə(n)] *vb* stroll, amble: *op straat ~* loaf about the streets
slepen [slepə(n)] *vb* **1** drag, haul: *iem door een examen ~* pull s.o. through an exam; *iem voor de rechter ~* take s.o. to court; **2** tow
slepend [slepənt] *adj* **1** dragging: *een ~e gang hebben* drag *(or:* shuffle) one's feet; **2** lingering, long-drawn-out
slet [slɛt] *de (~ten)* slut
sleuf [sløf] *de (sleuven)* **1** slot, slit: *de ~ van een spaarpot* the slot in a piggybank; **2** groove, trench
sleur [slør] *de* rut, grind: *de alledaagse ~* the daily grind
sleuren [slørə(n)] *vb* drag, haul
sleutel [sløtəl] *de (~s)* **1** key; **2** *(fig)* key, clue; **3** spanner, *(Am)* wrench: *een Engelse ~* a monkey wrench; **4** *(mus)* clef
sleutelbeen [sløtəlben] *het (~deren)* collarbone, clavicle
sleutelbos [sløtəlbɔs] *de (~sen)* bunch of keys
sleutelen [sløtələ(n)] *vb* **1** work (on), repair; **2** *(fig)* fiddle (with), tinker (with): *er moet nog wel wat aan de tekst gesleuteld worden* the text needs a certain amount of touching up
sleutelgat [sløtəlɣat] *het (~en)* keyhole: *aan het ~ luisteren* listen *(or:* eavesdrop) at the keyhole; *door het ~ kijken* peep through the keyhole
sleutelhanger [sløtəlhɑŋər] *de (~s)* keyring
sleutelpositie [sløtəlpozi(t)si] *de (~s)* key position
sleutelring [sløtəlrɪŋ] *de (~en)* keyring
sleutelrol [sløtəlrɔl] *de (~len)* key role, central role *(or:* part)
slib [slɪp] *het* silt; sludge
slibberig [slɪbərəχ] *adj* slippery, slimy
sliding [slɑjdɪŋ] *de (~s)* sliding tackle
sliert [slirt] *de (~en)* **1** string, thread, wisp: *~en rook* wisps of smoke; **2** pack, bunch: *een hele ~ a* whole bunch
slijk [slɛik] *het* mud, mire: *iem (or: iemands naam) door het ~ sleuren* drag s.o. *(or:* s.o.'s name) through the mud/mire
slijm [slɛim] *het, de (~en)* mucus, phlegm
slijmbal [slɛimbal] *de (~len)* toady, bootlicker
slijmen [slɛimə(n)] *vb* butter up, soft-soap: *~ tegen iem* butter s.o. up
slijmerig [slɛimərəχ] *adj, adv* slimy
slijmvlies [slɛimvlis] *het (-vliezen)* mucous membrane
slijpen [slɛipə(n)] *vb* **1** sharpen; **2** grind, polish, cut: *diamant ~* cut diamonds; **3** cut
slijpsteen [slɛipsten] *de (-stenen)* grindstone
slijtage [slɛitaʒə] *de* wear (and tear): *tekenen van ~ vertonen* show signs of wear; *aan ~ onderhevig zijn* be subject to wear
slijten [slɛitə(n)] *vb* **1** wear (out): *die jas is kaal ge-*

sleten that coat is worn bare; **2** wear away, wear off, waste (away); **3** spend, pass: *zijn leven in eenzaamheid ~* spend one's days in solitude

slijter [slɛitər] *de (~s)* wine merchant, *(Am)* liquor dealer || *ik ga naar de ~* I'm going to the wine shop

slijterij [slɛitərɛi] *de (~en)* wine shop, *(Am)* liquor store

slijtvast [slɛitfɑst] *adj* hard-wearing, wear-resistant

slikken [slɪkə(n)] *vb* **1** swallow, gulp (down); **2** swallow, put up with: *je hebt het maar te ~* you just have to put up with it

slim [slɪm] *adj, adv* clever, smart: *~me oogjes* shrewd eyes; *een ~me zet* a clever move; *iem te ~ af zijn* be too clever for s.o.

slimheid [slɪmhɛit] *de* cleverness

slimmigheid [slɪməxhɛit] *de* dodge, trick: *hij wist zich door een ~je eruit te redden* he weaseled his way out of it

slinger [slɪŋər] *de (~s)* **1** festoon, streamer, garland; **2** swing, sway; **3** pendulum

slingerbeweging [slɪŋərbəweɣɪŋ] *de (~en)* **1** swing; **2** swerve

¹slingeren [slɪŋərə(n)] *vb* **1** swing, sway: *~ op zijn benen* sway on one's legs; **2** sway, lurch, yaw *(ship)*; **3** lie about *(or:* around*)*: *laat je boeken niet altijd op mijn bureau ~!* don't always leave your books lying around on my desk!; **4** wind

²slingeren [slɪŋərə(n)] *vb* **1** sling, fling: *bij de botsing werd de bestuurder uit de auto geslingerd* in the crash the driver was flung out of the car; **2** swing, sway

³slingeren [slɪŋərə(n)] *ref vb* wind; wind (oneself)

slinken [slɪŋkə(n)] *vb* shrink: *de voorraad slinkt* the supply is dwindling

slinks [slɪŋks] *adj, adv* cunning, devious: *op ~e wijze* by devious means

slip [slɪp] *de* skid: *in een ~ raken* go into a skid

slipje [slɪpjə] *het (~s)* (pair of) briefs *(or:* panties*)*, (pair of) knickers

slippen [slɪpə(n)] *vb* slip; skid

slipper [slɪpər] *de (~s)* mule, slipper

slippertje [slɪpərcə] *het (~s)* || *een ~ maken* have a bit on the side

sliptong [slɪptɔŋ] *de (~en)* slip, sole

slissen [slɪsə(n)] *vb* lisp

slobberen [slɔbərə(n)] *vb* **1** bag, sag: *zijn jasje slobbert om zijn lijf* his baggy coat hangs around his body; **2** slobber, slurp

sloddervos [slɔdərvɔs] *de (~sen)* slob

sloeber [slubər] *de (~s)* || *een arme ~* a poor wretch *(or:* devil*)*

sloep [slup] *de (~en)* cutter: *de ~ strijken* lower the boat

slof [slɔf] *de (~fen)* **1** slipper, mule: *zij kan het op haar ~fen af* she can do it with her eyes shut *(or:* with one hand tied behind her back*)*; **2** carton: *uit zijn ~ schieten* hit the roof

sloffen [slɔfə(n)] *vb* shuffle: *loop niet zo te ~!* don't shuffle *(or:* drag*)* your feet!

slogan [slogən] *de (~s)* slogan

slok [slɔk] *de (~ken)* **1** drink, sip *(small)*: *grote ~ken nemen* gulp; **2** swallow, gulp

slokdarm [slɔgdɑrm] *de (~en)* gullet

slons [slɔns] *de (slonzen)* slattern, sloven, slut

slonzig [slɔnzəχ] *adj, adv* slovenly, sloppy

sloom [slom] *adj, adv* listless, slow: *doe niet zo ~* come on, I haven't got all day

¹sloop [slop] *het, de (slopen)* pillowcase: *lakens en slopen* bedlinen

²sloop [slop] *de (slopen)* **1** demolition; **2** demolition firm; scrapyard

sloopauto [slopɑuto] *de (~'s)* scrap car, wreck

sloopbedrijf [slobədrɛif] *het* demolition firm *(or:* contractors*)*; scrapyard, *(Am)* wrecker

sloot [slot] *de (sloten)* ditch, *(sport)* water jump

slootjespringen [slocəsprɪŋə(n)] *vb* leap (over) ditches

slootwater [slotwatər] *het* ditchwater, *(fig)* dishwater

slop [slɔp] *het (~pen)* alley(way), blind alley: *in het ~ raken* come to a dead end

slopen [slopə(n)] *vb* **1** demolish; **2** break up, scrap; **3** undermine: *~d werk* exhausting *(or:* back-breaking*)* work; *een ~de ziekte* a wasting disease

sloper [slopər] *de (~s)* demolition contractor

sloperij [slopərɛi] *de (~en)* demolition firm *(or:* contractors*)*; scrapyard

sloppenwijk [slɔpə(n)wɛik] *de (~en)* slums, slum area

slordig [slɔrdəχ] *adj, adv* careless, untidy, sloppy: *wat zit je haar ~* how untidy your hair is; *~ schrijven* scribble

slordigheid [slɔrdəχhɛit] *de (-heden)* carelessness, sloppiness

slot [slɔt] *het (~en)* **1** lock, fastening: *iem achter ~ en grendel zetten* put s.o. behind bars; *achter ~ en grendel* under lock and key; *een deur op ~ doen* lock a door; *alles op ~ doen* lock up; **2** end, conclusion: *~ volgt* to be concluded; **3** castle

slotenmaker [slotə(n)makər] *de (~s)* locksmith

slotfase [slɔtfazə] *de (~s, ~n)* final stage

slotgracht [slɔtχrɑχt] *de (~en)* (castle) moat

slotscène [slɔtsɛ:nə] *de* final scene

slotsom [slɔtsɔm] *de* conclusion

Sloveen [slovɛn] *de (Slovenen)* Slovene, Slovenian

sloven [slovə(n)] *vb* drudge

Slovenië [slovɛnijə] *het* Slovenia

Slowaak [slowak] *de* Slovak

Slowakije [slowakɛiə] *het* Slovakia

sluier [slœyər] *de (~s)* veil

sluik [slœyk] *adj* straight, lank

sluikreclame [slœykrəklamə] *de (~s)* clandestine advertising

sluikstorten [slœykstɔrtə(n)] *vb (Belg)* dump (illegally)

sluimeren [slœymərə(n)] *vb* slumber

sluipen [slœypə(n)] *vb* **1** steal, sneak, stalk: *naar boven ~* steal *(or:* sneak*)* upstairs; **2** creep

sluiproute [slœyprutə] *de (~s)* short cut

sluipschutter [slœypsχʏtər] *de (~s)* sniper

sluis [slœys] *de (sluizen)* lock; sluice: *door een ~ varen* pass through a lock

sluiswachter [slœyswaχtər] *de (~s)* lock-keeper

¹**sluiten** [slœytə(n)] *vb* **1** shut, close, close down: *de grenzen ~* close the frontiers; *het raam ~* shut (*or:* close) the window; *het winkel (zaak) ~: a)* close (the shop) down; *b)* shut up shop; *dinsdagmiddag zijn alle winkels gesloten* it is early closing day on Tuesday; **2** conclude, enter into: *een verbond ~ (met)* enter into an alliance (with); *vrede ~* make peace, make up (with s.o.); **3** close, conclude

²**sluiten** [slœytə(n)] *vb* balance: *de begroting ~d maken* balance the budget; *over en ~* over and out

sluiting [slœytɪŋ] *de (~en)* **1** shutting (off); closure; conclusion: *~ van de rekening* balancing of the account; **2** fastening, fastener, lock, clasp: *de ~ van deze jurk zit op de rug* this dress does up at the back

sluitingsdatum [slœytɪŋzdatʏm] *de (-data)* closing date

sluitingstijd [slœytɪŋstɛit] *de (~en)* closing time: *na ~* after hours

sluitspier [slœytspir] *de (~en)* sphincter

sluitstuk [slœytstʏk] *het (~ken)* final piece

sluizen [slœyzə(n)] *vb* channel, transfer

slungel [slʏŋəl] *de (~s)* beanpole

slungelig [slʏŋələχ] *adj, adv* lanky

slurf [slʏrf] *de (slurven)* trunk

slurpen [slʏrpə(n)] *vb* slurp

sluw [slyw] *adj, adv* sly, crafty, cunning: *de ~e vos* the sly (*or:* cunning) old fox

sluwheid [slywhɛit] *de (-heden)* slyness, cunning

smaad [smat] *de* defamation (of character), libel

smaak [smak] *de (smaken)* taste, flavour: *een goede ~ hebben* have good taste; *van goede (or: slechte) ~ getuigen* be in good (*or:* bad) taste; *de ~ van iets te pakken hebben* have acquired a taste for; *in de ~ vallen bij …* appeal to …, find favour with …; *over ~ valt niet te twisten* there is no accounting for taste(s)

smaakje [smakjə] *het (~s)* taste: *er zit een ~ aan dat vlees* that meat has a funny taste

smaakstof [smakstɔf] *de (~fen)* flavour(ing), seasoning

smaakvol [smakfɔl] *adj, adv* tasteful, in good taste: *~ gekleed zijn* be tastefully dressed

smachten [smaχtə(n)] *vb* **1** languish: *iem ~de blikken toewerpen* look longingly at s.o.; **2** (with *naar*) long (for), yearn (for)

smadelijk [smadələk] *adj, adv* humiliating; scornful

smak [smak] *de (~ken)* **1** fall: *een ~ maken* fall with a bang; **2** crash, smack: *met een ~ neerzetten* slam (*or:* slap) down; **3** heap, pile: *dat kost een ~ geld* that costs a load of money

smakelijk [smakələk] *adj, adv* tasty, appetizing: *eet ~!* enjoy your meal

smakeloos [smakəlos] *adj, adv* tasteless, lacking in taste

smaken [smakə(n)] *vb* taste: *hoe smaakt het?* how does it taste?; *heeft het gesmaakt, meneer?* (*or: mevrouw?*) did you enjoy your meal, sir? (*or:* madam?); *naar iets ~* taste of sth

smakken [smakə(n)] *vb* **1** smack one's lips: *smak niet zo!* don't make so much noise (when you're eating); **2** crash: *tegen de grond ~* crash to the ground

smal [smal] *adj* narrow: *~le opening* small opening; *een ~ gezichtje* a pinched face; *de ~le weg (fig)* the straight and narrow (path)

smalend [smalənt] *adj, adv* scornful

smalfilm [smalfɪlm] *de (~s)* cinefilm, *(Am)* movie film

¹**smaragd** [smaraχt] *de (~en) (gem)* emerald

²**smaragd** [smaraχt] *het (mineral)* emerald

smart [smart] *de (~en)* **1** sorrow, grief, pain: *gedeelde ~ is halve smart* a sorrow shared is a sorrow halved; **2** yearning, longing: *met ~ op iets (iem) wachten* wait anxiously for sth (s.o.)

smartengeld [smartəχɛlt] *het (~en)* damages, (financial, monetary) compensation

smartlap [smartlap] *de (~pen)* tear-jerker

smeden [smedə(n)] *vb* forge: *twee stukken ijzer aan elkaar ~* weld two pieces of iron (together); *uit één stuk gesmeed* forged in one piece

smederij [smedərɛi] *de (~en)* forge

smeedijzer [smetɛizər] *het (~s)* wrought iron

smeer [smer] *het, de* grease, oil, polish

smeerbaar [smerbar] *adj* spreadable

smeerbeurt [smerbørt] *de* 2000-mile service

smeerboel [smerbul] *de* mess

smeergeld [smerχɛlt] *het (~en)* bribe(s)

smeerkaas [smerkas] *de (-kazen)* cheese spread

smeerlap [smerlap] *de (~pen)* **1** skunk, bastard; **2** pervert; dirty old man

smeerleverworst [smerlevərwɔrst] *de* liver pâté (*or:* sausage)

smeerolie [smeroli] *de (-oliën)* lubricant

smeerworst [smerwɔrst] *de (~en)* pâté

smeken [smekə(n)] *vb* implore, beg: *iem om hulp ~* beg (for) s.o.'s help

smelten [smɛltə(n)] *vb* melt, melt down: *de sneeuw smelt* the snow is melting (*or:* thawing); *deze reep chocolade smelt op de tong* this bar of chocolate melts in the mouth

smeltpunt [smɛltpʏnt] *het (~en)* melting point, point of fusion

smeren [smerə(n)] *vb* **1** grease, oil, lubricate; **2** smear: *crème op zijn huid ~* rub cream on one's skin; **3** butter: *brood ~* butter bread, make sandwiches

smerig [smerəχ] *adj, adv* dirty, (*stronger*) filthy: *een ~e streek (truc)* a dirty (*or:* shabby) trick

smering [smerɪŋ] *de (~en)* lubrication

smeris [smerɪs] *de (~sen)* cop

smeuïg [smøjəχ] *adj, adv* **1** smooth, creamy; **2** vivid

smeulen [smølə(n)] *vb* smoulder

smid [smɪt] *de (smeden)* smith

smiespelen [smi̯spələ(n)] *vb* whisper

smijten [smɛi̯tə(n)] *vb* throw, fling: *met de deuren* ~ slam the doors; *(fig) iem iets naar het hoofd* ~ throw sth in s.o.'s teeth

smikkelen [smɪkələ(n)] *vb* tuck in

smoel [smul] *de* 1 trap: *houd je* ~! shut your trap!; 2 face: ~*en trekken* pull faces

smoes [smus] *de (smoezen)* excuse: *een* ~*je bedenken* think up a story (*or:* an excuse)

smoezelig [smu̯zələɣ] *adj* grubby, dingy

smoezen [smu̯zə(n)] *vb* 1 invent (*or:* cook up) excuses; 2 whisper

smog [smɔɡ] *de* smog

smoking [smokɪŋ] *de (~s)* dinner jacket

smokkel [smɔkəl] *de* smuggling

smokkelaar [smɔkəlar] *de (~s)* smuggler

smokkelarij [smɔkəlarɛi̯] *de (~en)* smuggling

smokkelen [smɔkələ(n)] *vb* smuggle

smokkelwaar [smɔkəlwar] *de (-waren)* contraband

smoorverliefd [smorvərlift] *adj* smitten (with s.o.)

smoren [smorə(n)] *vb* 1 smother, choke; 2 braise

smout [smɑut] *het (Belg)* lard

smullen [smʏlə(n)] *vb* feast (on): *dat wordt* ~! yum-yum!

snaar [snar] *de (snaren)* string; chord; snare: *een gevoelige* ~ *raken* touch a tender spot; *de snaren spannen* string, snare

snaarinstrument [snarɪnstrymɛnt] *het (~en)* stringed instrument

snack [snɛk] *de (~s)* snack

snackbar [snɛɡbɑr] *de (~s)* snack bar

snakken [snɑkə(n)] *vb* 1 gasp, pant: *naar adem* ~ gasp for breath; 2 crave: ~ *naar aandacht* be craving (for) attention

snappen [snɑpə(n)] *vb* get: *snap je?* (you) see?; *ik snap 'm* I get it; *ik snap niet waar het om gaat* I don't see it; *ik snap er niets van* I don't get it, it beats me

snateren [snatərə(n)] *vb* honk

snauwen [snɑuwə(n)] *vb* snarl, growl, snap

snauwerig [snɑuwərəɣ] *adj, adv* snappish, gruff

snavel [snavəl] *de (~s)* bill; beak: *hou je* ~! shut up!

snee [sne] *de (~ën)* 1 slice: *een dun* ~*tje koek* a thin slice of cake; 2 cut, gash; 3 *(med)* incision

sneeuw [snew] *de* snow: *een dik pak* ~ (a) thick (layer of) snow; *natte* ~ sleet; *(Belg) zwarte* ~ *zien* be destitute, live in poverty; *smeltende* ~ slush; *vastzitten in de* ~ be snowbound

sneeuwbal [snewbɑl] *de (~len)* snowball

sneeuwbui [snewbœy] *de (~en)* snow (shower)

sneeuwen [snewə(n)] *vb* snow: *het sneeuwt hard* (*or: licht*) it is snowing heavily (*or:* lightly)

sneeuwgrens [snewɣrɛns] *de* snowline

sneeuwketting [snewkɛtɪŋ] *de (~en)* (snow) chain

sneeuwklokje [snewklɔkjə] *het (~s)* snowdrop

sneeuwman [snewmɑn] *de (~nen)* snowman

sneeuwruimen [snewrœymə(n)] *vb* clear snow, shovel (away) snow

sneeuwruimer [snewrœymər] *de (~s)* snowplough

sneeuwschuiver [snewsχœyvər] *de (~s)* 1 snow shovel; 2 snowplough

sneeuwstorm [snewstɔrm] *de (~en)* snowstorm

sneeuwval [snewvɑl] *de (~len)* snowfall

sneeuwvlok [snewvlɔk] *de (~ken)* snowflake

sneeuwvrij [snewvrɛi̯] *adj* clear of snow: *de wegen* ~ *maken* clear the roads of snow

Sneeuwwitje [snewi̯cə] *het* Snow White

snel [snɛl] *adj* 1 fast, rapid; 2 quick, swift; fast; speedy: *een* ~ *besluit* a quick decision; ~ *achteruitgaan* decline rapidly; ~ *van begrip zijn* be quick (on the uptake)

snelbinder [snɛlbɪndər] *de (~s)* carrier straps

sneldienst [snɛldinst] *de (~en)* fast service, express service

snelfilter [snɛlfɪltər] *het (~s)* coffee filter

snelheid [snɛlhɛit] *de (-heden)* speed, pace, tempo, velocity: *bij hoge snelheden* at high speeds; *de maximum* ~ the speed limit; *op volle* ~ (at) full speed; ~ *minderen* reduce speed, slow down

snelheidsbegrenzer [snɛlhɛitsbəɣrɛnzər] *de (~s)* governor, speed limiting device

snelheidscontrole [snɛlhɛitskɔntroːlə] *de (~s)* speed(ing) check

snelkookpan [snɛlkokpɑn] *de (~nen)* pressure cooker

snelrecht [snɛlrɛχt] *het* summary justice (*or:* proceedings)

sneltrein [snɛltrɛin] *de (~en)* express (train), intercity (train)

sneltreinvaart [snɛltrɛinvart] *de* tearing rush (*or:* hurry): *hij kwam in een* ~ *de hoek om* he came tearing round the corner

snelweg [snɛlwɛχ] *de (~en)* motorway; *(Am)* freeway || *elektronische* (*or: digitale*) ~ electronic (*or:* digital) highway

snerpen [snɛrpə(n)] *vb* 1 bite, cut: *een* ~*de kou* cutting (*or:* piercing) cold; 2 squeal, shriek

snert [snɛrt] *de* pea soup

sneu [snø] *adj, adv* unfortunate

sneuvelen [snøvələ(n)] *vb* 1 fall (in battle), be killed (in action): ~ *in de strijd* be killed in action; 2 break, get smashed

snibbig [snɪbəɣ] *adj* snappy, snappish

snijbloem [snɛibum] *de (~en)* cut flower

snijboon [snɛibon] *de (-bonen)* French bean, *(Am)* string bean

¹snijden [snɛidə(n)] *vb* 1 cut, carve, slice; 2 *(traf)* cut in (on s.o.)

²snijden [snɛidə(n)] *vb* 1 cut: *uit hout een figuur* ~ carve a figure out of wood; 2 cross, intersect

snijdend [snɛidənt] *adj* cutting: *een* ~*e wind* a piercing (*or:* biting) wind

snijkant [snɛikɑnt] *de (~en)* (cutting) edge

snijmachine [snɛimɑʃinə] *de (~s)* cutter, cutting machine; slicer, shredder

snijmaïs [snɛimɑjs] *de* green maize (fodder)

snijplank [snɛiplɑŋk] *de (~en)* breadboard; chopping board; carving board

snijpunt [snɛipʏnt] *het (~en)* crossing; *(math also)* intersection

snijtand [snɛitɑnt] *de (~en)* incisor

snijwond [snɛiwɔnt] *de (~en)* cut

snik [snɪk] *de (~ken)* gasp: *de laatste ~ geven* breathe one's last; *tot aan zijn laatste ~* to his dying day; *niet goed ~* cracked, off one's rocker

snikheet [snɪkhet] *adj* sizzling (hot), scorching (hot)

snikken [snɪkə(n)] *vb* sob

snipper [snɪpər] *de (~s)* snip, shred; clipping: *in ~s scheuren* tear (in)to shreds

snipperdag [snɪpərdɑχ] *de (~en)* day off

snipverkouden [snɪpfərkɑudə(n)] *adj* (all) stuffed up: *~ zijn* have a streaming cold

snob [snɔp] *de (~s)* snob

snoeien [snujə(n)] *vb* 1 trim; prune; 2 cut back, prune: *in een begroting ~* prune a budget

snoeischaar [snujsχar] *de (-scharen)* pruning shears

snoek [snuk] *de (~en)* pike

snoekbaars [snuɡbars] *de (-baarzen)* pikeperch

snoep [snup] *de* sweets, *(Am)* candy

snoepen [snupə(n)] *vb* eat sweets *(or Am:* candy)

snoepgoed [snupχut] *het* confectionery; sweets; *(Am also)* candy

snoepje [snupjə] *het (~s)* sweet, *(Am)* candy

snoepwinkel [snupwɪŋkəl] *de (~s)* sweetshop, *(Am)* candy store

snoer [snur] *het (~en)* 1 string, rope: *kralen aan een ~ rijgen* string beads; 2 flex, lead, *(Am)* cord

snoes [snus] *de (snoezen)* sweetie, pet, poppet

snoet [snut] *de (~en)* 1 snout; 2 face, mug: *een aardig ~je* a pretty little face

snoezig [snuzəχ] *adj, adv* cute, sweet

snol [snɔl] *de (~len)* tart

snor [snɔr] *de (~ren)* 1 moustache: *zijn ~ laten staan* grow a moustache; 2 whiskers

snorfiets [snɔrfits] *de (~en)* moped

snorhaar [snɔrhar] *het (-haren)* 1 (hair of a) moustache; 2 whisker

snorkel [snɔrkəl] *de (~s)* snorkel

snorkelen [snɔrkələ(n)] *vb* snorkel

snorren [snɔrə(n)] *vb* whirr, buzz, hum: *een ~de kat* a purring cat

snorscooter [snɔrskutər] *de (~s)* (motor) scooter

snot [snɔt] *het, de* (nasal) mucus *(or:* discharge), snot

snotlap [snɔtlɑp] *de (~pen)* nose rag

snotneus [snɔtnøs] *de (-neuzen)* 1 runny nose; 2 (tiny) tot, (little) kid; 3 brat

snotteren [snɔtərə(n)] *vb* 1 sniff(le); 2 blubber

snowboarden [snoboːrdə(n)] *vb* go snowboarding

snuffelen [snʏfələ(n)] *vb* 1 sniff (at); 2 nose (about), pry (into): *in laden ~* rummage in drawers

snuffelhond [snʏfəlhɔnt] *de (~en)* sniffer dog

snufferd [snʏfərt] *de (~s)* hooter ‖ *ik gaf hem een klap op zijn ~* I gave him one on the kisser

snufje [snʏfjə] *het (~s)* 1 novelty, newest device *(or:* gadget): *het nieuwste ~* the latest thing; 2 dash: *een ~ zout* a pinch of salt

snugger [snʏɣər] *adj, adv* bright, clever

snuit [snœyt] *de (~en)* snout: *de ~ van een varken* a pig's snout

snuiten [snœytə(n)] *vb* blow (one's nose)

snuiven [snœyvə(n)] *vb* 1 sniff(le), snort: *cocaïne ~* sniff cocaine; *~ als een paard* snort like a horse; 2 sniff (at)

snurken [snʏrkə(n)] *vb* snore

sober [sobər] *adj, adv* austere, frugal: *in ~e bewoordingen* in plain words *(or:* language); *hij leeft zeer ~* he lives very austerely *(or:* frugally)

soberheid [sobərheit] *de* austerity, frugality

¹sociaal [soʃal] *adj* social: *iemands sociale positie* s.o.'s social position

²sociaal [soʃal] *adv* 1 socially; 2 socially-minded: *~ denkend* humanitarian, socially aware

sociaal-democratisch [soʃaldemokratɪs] *adj* social democratic

socialisatie [soʃaliza(t)si] *de* socialization

socialisme [soʃalɪsmə] *het* socialism

socialist [soʃalɪst] *de (~en)* socialist

socialistisch [soʃalɪstɪs] *adj, adv* socialist(ic)

sociëteit [soʃetɛit] *de (~en)* 1 association, club: *lid van een ~ worden* become a member of *(or:* join) an association; 2 association (building), club(house); 3 society

sociologie [soʃoloɣi] *de* sociology

sociologisch [soʃoloɣɪs] *adj, adv* sociological

socioloog [soʃoloχ] *de (-logen)* sociologist

soda [soda] *de* 1 (washing) soda; 2 soda (water): *een whisky-soda* a whisky and soda

Sudan [sudɑn] *de* (the) Sudan

soenniet [sunit] *de (~en)* Sunni

soep [sup] *de (~en)* soup, consommé: *een ~ laten trekken* make a stock *(or:* broth)

soepballetje [subɑləcə] *het (~s)* meatball

soepbord [subɔrt] *het (~en)* soup bowl

soepel [supəl] *adj, adv* 1 supple, pliable; 2 supple, flexible; (com)pliant: *een ~e regeling* a flexible arrangement; 3 supple: *~e bewegingen* supple *(or:* lithe) movements

soepelheid [supəlheit] *de* suppleness, flexibility

soepgroente [supχruntə] *de (~n)* vegetables for soup

soeplepel [suplepəl] *de (~s)* 1 soup ladle; 2 soup spoon

soesa [suza] *de* fuss, to-do, bother

soeverein [suvərɛin] *adj, adv* sovereign

soevereiniteit [suvərɛinitɛit] *de* sovereignty

soezen [suzə(n)] *vb* doze, drowse

sof [sɔf] *de* flop, washout

sofa [sofa] *de (~'s)* sofa, couch

sofinummer [sofinʏmər] *het (~s) (roughly)* National Insurance Number; *(Am; roughly)* Social Security Number

softballen [sɔf(t)bɑlə(n)] *vb* play softball

softijs [sɔftɛis] *het* soft ice-cream, Mr. Softy
softporno [sɔftpɔrno] *de* soft porn(ography)
software [sɔftwɛːr] *de* software
soigneur [swɑɲør] *de (~s)* helper; *(boxing; roughly)* second
soja [soja] *de* (sweet) soy (sauce)
sojaboon [sojabon] *de (-bonen)* soya bean
sojaolie [sojaoli] *de* soya bean oil
sojasaus [sojasɑus] *de* soy sauce
sojavlees [sojavles] *het* soya meat
sok [sɔk] *de* sock: *hij haalde het op zijn ~ken* he did it effortlessly; *iem van de ~ken rijden* bowl s.o. over, knock s.o. down
sokkel [sɔkəl] *de (~s)* pedestal
sol [sɔl] *de (~len) (mus)* so(h), sol, G
solarium [solɑrijʏm] *het (solaria)* solarium
soldaat [sɔldɑt] *de (soldaten)* **1** (common) soldier, private: *de gewone soldaten* the ranks; **2** soldier, *(pl also)* troops: *de Onbekende Soldaat* the Unknown Soldier
soldaatje [sɔldɑcə] *het (~s)* toy soldier, tin soldier: *~ spelen* play (at) soldiers
soldeer [sɔldɛr] *het, de* solder
soldeerbout [sɔldɛrbɑut] *de (~en)* soldering iron
soldeerpistool [sɔldɛrpistol] *het (-pistolen)* soldering gun
solden [sɔldə(n)] *de (Belg)* sale
solderen [sɔldərə(n)] *vb* solder
soldij [sɔldɛi] *de* pay(ment)
solfège [sɔlfɛːʒə] *de* solfeggio
solidair [solidɛːr] *adj, adv* sympathetic: *~ zijn* show solidarity (with)
solidariteit [solidaritɛit] *de* solidarity: *uit ~ met* in sympathy with
solide [solidə] *adj, adv* **1** solid, hard-wearing; **2** steady
solist [solɪst] *de (~en)* soloist
sollen [sɔlə(n)] *vb* (with *met*) trifle with: *hij laat niet met zich ~* he won't be trifled with
sollicitant [sɔlisitɑnt] *de (~en)* applicant
sollicitatie [sɔlisitɑ(t)si] *de (~s)* application
sollicitatiebrief [sɔlisitɑ(t)sibrif] *de (-brieven)* (letter of) application
sollicitatieformulier [sɔlisitɑ(t)sifɔrmylir] *het (~en)* application form
sollicitatiegesprek [sɔlisitɑ(t)siɣəsprɛk] *het (~ken)* interview (for a position, job)
sollicitatieprocedure [sɔlisitɑ(t)siprosedyrə] *de (~s)* selection procedure
solliciteren [sɔlisitərə(n)] *vb* apply (for)
solo [solo] *de, het (~'s, soli)* solo
solocarrière [solokɑrijɛːrə] *de (~s)* solo career
soloconcert [solokɔnsɛrt] *het* solo concert
solotoer [solotur] *de* ‖ *op de ~ gaan* go it alone
som [sɔm] *de (~men)* sum: *een ~ geld* a sum of money; *~men maken* do sums; *8-5=3* eight minus five equals three; *5+3=8* five plus (*or*: and) three is eight; *3×5=15* three times five is (*or*: makes) fifteen; *15:3=5* fifteen divided by three is five; *3²=9* three

squared equals nine; *3³=27* three to the power of three equals twenty-seven; *√9=3* the square root of nine is three; *3√27=3* the cube root of twenty-seven is three
Somalië [somɑlijə] *het* Somalia
somber [sɔmbər] *adj, adv* **1** dejected, gloomy: *het ~ inzien* take a sombre (*or*: gloomy) view (of things); **2** gloomy, dark: *~ weer* gloomy weather
somma [sɔma] *de* sum
sommige [sɔməɣə] *ind pron* some, certain: *~n* some (people)
soms [sɔms] *adv* **1** sometimes; **2** perhaps, by any chance: *heb je Jan ~ gezien?* have you seen John by any chance?; *dat is toch mijn zaak, of niet ~?* that's my business, or am I mistaken?
sonar [sonɑr] *de (~s)* sonar
sonate [sonɑtə] *de (~s)* sonata
sonde [sɔndə] *de (~s)* **1** probe; **2** *(med)* catheter
sondevoeding [sɔndəvudɪŋ] *de (~en)* drip-feed
songfestival [sɔŋfɛstival] *het (~s)* song contest: *het Eurovisie ~* the Eurovision Song Contest
songtekst [sɔŋtɛkst] *de* lyric(s)
sonnet [sɔnɛt] *het (~ten)* sonnet
¹soort [sort] *de (~en)* species: *de menselijke ~* the human species
²soort [sort] *het, de (~en)* **1** sort, kind, type: *ik ken dat ~* I know the type; *in zijn ~* in its way, of its kind; *in alle ~en en maten* in all shapes and sizes; **2** sort (of), kind (of): *als een ~ vis* (rather) like some kind of a fish
soortelijk [sortələk] *adj, adv* specific
soortgelijk [sortχəlɛik] *adj* similar, of the same kind
soos [sos] *de* club
sop [sɔp] *het (~pen)* (soap)suds
sopje [sɔpjə] *het* (soap)suds: *zal ik de keuken nog een ~ geven?* shall I give the kitchen a(nother) wash?
soppen [sɔpə(n)] *vb* dunk
¹sopraan [soprɑn] *de (singer)* soprano
²sopraan [soprɑn] *de (voice)* soprano
sorbet [sɔrbɛt] *de (~s)* sorbet
sorteren [sɔrterə(n)] *vb* sort (out): *op maat ~* sort according to size
sortering [sɔrterɪŋ] *de (~en)* selection, range, assortment
SOS [ɛsoɛs] *het* Save our Souls SOS: *een ~(-signaal) uitzenden* broadcast an SOS (message)
soufflé [suflɛ] *de (~s)* soufflé
souffleren [suflɛrə(n)] *vb* prompt
souffleur [suflør] *de (~s)* prompter
soulmuziek [solmyzik] *de* soul music
souper [supɛ] *het (~s)* supper, dinner
souteneur [sutənør] *de (~s)* pimp
souterrain [sutərɛ] *het (~s)* basement
souvenir [suvənir] *het (~s)* souvenir
sovjet [sɔvjɛt] *de (~s)* soviet: *de opperste ~* the Supreme Soviet
Sovjet-Unie [sɔvjɛtyni] *de* Soviet Union

sowieso [zowiz<u>o</u>] *adv* in any case, anyhow: *het wordt ~ laat op dat feest* that party will in any case go on until late

spa [spa] *de* **1** mineral water; **2** spade

spaak [spak] *de (spaken)* spoke: *iem een ~ in het wiel steken* put a spoke in s.o.'s wheel

spaan [span] *de (spanen)* **1** chip (of wood): *er bleef geen ~ van heel* there was nothing left of it; **2** skimmer

spaander [sp<u>a</u>ndər] *de (~s)* chip, splinter

spaanplaat [sp<u>a</u>mplat] *de (-platen)* chipboard

Spaans [spans] *adj* Spanish ‖ *zeg het eens op z'n ~* say it in Spanish

spaarbank [sp<u>a</u>rbaŋk] *de (~en)* savings bank: *geld op de ~ hebben* have money in a savings bank (*or:* savings account)

spaarbankboekje [sp<u>a</u>rbaŋgbukjə] *het (~s)* deposit book

spaarcenten [sp<u>a</u>rsɛntə(n)] *de* savings

spaargeld [sp<u>a</u>rɣɛlt] *het (~en)* savings

spaarhypotheek [sp<u>a</u>rhipotek] *de* (type of) endowment mortgage

spaarlamp [sp<u>a</u>rlɑmp] *de (~en)* low-energy light bulb

spaarpot [sp<u>a</u>rpɔt] *de (~ten)* **1** money box, piggy bank; **2** savings, nest egg: *een ~je aanleggen* start saving for a rainy day; *zijn ~ aanspreken* draw on one's savings

spaarrekening [sp<u>a</u>rekənɪŋ] *de (~en)* savings account

spaartegoed [sp<u>a</u>rtəɣut] *het (~en)* savings balance

spaarvarken [sp<u>a</u>rvarkə(n)] *het (~s)* piggy bank

spaarzaam [sp<u>a</u>rzam] *adj, adv* **1** thrifty, economical: *hij is erg ~ met zijn lof* he's very sparing in (*or:* with) his praise; *~ zijn met zijn woorden* not waste words; **2** scanty, sparse: *de doodstraf wordt ~ toegepast* the death penalty is seldom imposed

spaarzegel [sp<u>a</u>rzeɣəl] *de (~s)* trading stamp

spade [sp<u>a</u>də] *de (~n)* spade

spagaat [spaɣ<u>a</u>t] *de (spagaten)* splits

spaghetti [spaɣ<u>ɛ</u>ti] *de (~'s)* spaghetti: *een sliert ~* a strand of spaghetti

spalk [spɑlk] *de (~en)* splint

spalken [sp<u>ɑ</u>lkə(n)] *vb* put in splints

span [spɑn] *het (~nen)* team; (*of pers*) couple: *een ~ paarden* a team of horses

spandoek [sp<u>ɑ</u>nduk] *het, de (~en)* banner: *een ~ met zich meedragen* carry a banner

spaniël [sp<u>ɛ</u>nəl] *de (~s)* spaniel

Spanjaard [sp<u>ɑ</u>nart] *de (~en)* Spaniard

Spanje [sp<u>ɑ</u>ɲə] *het* Spain

¹**spannen** [sp<u>ɑ</u>nə(n)] *vb* **1** stretch, tighten: *een draad ~* stretch (*or:* tighten) a string; *zijn spieren ~* tense (*or:* flex) one's muscles; **2** harness: *een paard voor een wagen ~* harness (*or:* hitch) a horse to a cart

²**spannen** [sp<u>ɑ</u>nə(n)] *vb* be tense: *het zal erom ~ wie er wint* it will be a close match (*or:* race)

spannend [sp<u>ɑ</u>nənt] *adj* exciting, thrilling: *een ~*

ogenblik a tense moment; *een ~ verhaal* an exciting story

spanning [sp<u>ɑ</u>nɪŋ] *de (~en)* **1** tension; (*fig also*) suspense: *~ en sensatie* excitement and suspense; *de ~ stijgt* the tension mounts; *de ~ viel van haar af* that was a load off her shoulders; *ze zaten vol ~ te wachten* they were waiting anxiously; *in ~ zitten* be in suspense; **2** tension: *een ~ van 10.000 volt* a charge of 10,000 volts

spant [spɑnt] *het (~en)* rafter, truss

spanwijdte [sp<u>ɑ</u>nwɛitə] *de (~n, ~s)* wingspan; wingspread

spar [spɑr] *de (~ren)* spruce

sparappel [sp<u>ɑ</u>rɑpəl] *de (~s, ~en)* fir cone

¹**sparen** [sp<u>a</u>rə(n)] *vb* save (up): *voor een nieuwe auto ~* save up for a new car

²**sparen** [sp<u>a</u>rə(n)] *vb* **1** save, spare; **2** collect

sparren [sp<u>ɛ</u>rə(n)] *vb* work out; spar

spartelen [sp<u>ɑ</u>rtələ(n)] *vb* flounder, thrash about: *het kleine kind spartelde in het water* the little child splashed about in the water

spastisch [sp<u>ɑ</u>stis] *adj, adv* spastic

spat [spɑt] *de (~ten)* **1** splash; **2** speck, spot

spatader [sp<u>ɑ</u>tadər] *de (~en)* varicose vein

spatbord [sp<u>ɑ</u>dbɔrt] *het (~en)* mudguard, (*Am*) fender

spatel [sp<u>a</u>təl] *de (~s)* spatula

spatie [spa(t)si] *de (~s)* space, spacing, interspace: *iets typen met een ~* type sth with interspacing

spatiebalk [spa(t)sibɑlk] *de (~en)* space bar

spatlap [sp<u>ɑ</u>tlɑp] *de (~pen)* mud flap

spatten [sp<u>ɑ</u>tə(n)] *vb* splash, sp(l)atter: *vonken ~ in het rond* sparks flew all around; *er is verf op mijn kleren gespat* some paint has splashed on my clothes; *zij spatte (mij) met water in mijn gezicht* she spattered water in my face; *uit elkaar ~* burst

specerij [spesər<u>ɛi</u>] *de (~en)* spice, seasoning

specht [spɛχt] *de (~en)* woodpecker

¹**speciaal** [spe<u>a</u>l] *adj* special: *in dit speciale geval* in this particular case

²**speciaal** [spe<u>a</u>l] *adv* especially, particularly, specially: *ik doel ~ op hem* I mean him in particular; *~ gemaakt* specially made

speciaalzaak [spe<u>a</u>lzak] *de (-zaken)* specialist shop

special [sp<u>ɛ</u>ʃəl] *de (~s)* special (issue): *een ~ over de Kinks* a special on the Kinks

specialisatie [speʃaliza(t)si] *de (~s)* specialization

specialiseren [speʃalizɛrə(n)] *ref vb* (with *in*) specialize (in)

specialisme [speʃal<u>ɪ</u>smə] *het (~n)* specialism

specialist [speʃal<u>ɪ</u>st] *de (~en)* specialist

specialiteit [speʃalitɛit] *de (~en)* speciality

specie [sp<u>e</u>si] *de (~s)* cement, mortar

specificatie [spesifik<u>a</u>(t)si] *de (~s)* specification: *~ van een nota vragen* request an itemized bill

specificeren [spesifisɛrə(n)] *vb* specify, itemize

specifiek [spesif<u>i</u>k] *adj, adv* specific

specimen [sp<u>e</u>simɛn] *het (~s)* specimen, exemplar

spectaculair [spɛktakylɛːr] *adj* spectacular

spectrum [spɛktrəm] *het (spectra)* spectrum

speculaas [spekylɑs] *het, de* || *gevulde ~ (roughly)* spiced cake filled with almond paste

speculaaspop [spekylɑspɔp] *de (~pen) (roughly)* gingerbread man

speculant [spekylɑnt] *de (~en)* speculator

speculatie [spekylɑ(t)si] *de (~s)* speculation

speculeren [spekylɛrə(n)] *vb* **1** *(with op)* speculate (on); **2** speculate

speech [spiːtʃ] *de (~es)* speech: *een ~ afsteken* deliver a speech

speedboot [spiːdbot] *de (-boten)* speedboat

speeksel [speksəl] *het* saliva

speelautomaat [spelɑutomɑt] *de (-automaten)* slot machine

speeldoos [speldos] *de (-dozen)* music box

speelduur [speldyr] *de* playing time

speelfilm [spelfɪlm] *de (~s)* (feature) film

speelgoed [spelɣut] *het* toy(s): *een stuk ~ a* toy

speelgoedafdeling [spelɣutɑvdelɪŋ] *de* toy department

speelgoedtrein [spelɣutrɛin] *de* (toy) train

speelhal [spelɦɑl] *de (~len)* amusement arcade

speelhelft [spelɦɛlft] *de (~en)* half

speelhol [spelɦɔl] *het (~en)* gambling den, gaming den

speelkaart [spelkart] *de (~en)* playing card

speelkamer [spelkɑmər] *de (~s)* playroom

speelkameraad [spelkɑmərɑt] *de (-kameraden)* playfellow, playmate

speelkwartier [spelkwɑrtir] *het (~en)* playtime; break

speelplaats [spelplɑts] *de (~en)* playground, play area: *op de ~* in the playground

speelruimte [spelrœymtə] *de (~n, ~s)* **1** play, latitude: *~ hebben* have some play; *iem ~ geven* leave s.o. a bit of elbow room; **2** play area, room to play

speels [spels] *adj* **1** playful, frisky; **2** playful

speelschuld [spelsχ ylt] *de (~en)* gambling debt

speeltafel [speltɑfəl] *de (~s)* gaming table

speeltuin [speltœyn] *de (~en)* playground

speelveld [spelvɛlt] *het (~en)* (sports, playing) field

speen [spen] *de (spenen)* **1** (rubber) teat, *(Am)* nipple; **2** teat

speer [sper] *de (speren)* spear, javelin || *als een ~* like a rocket

speerpunt [sperpynt] *de (~en)* spearhead

speerwerpen [sperwɛrpə(n)] *vb* throw(ing) the javelin: *het ~ winnen* win the javelin (event)

speerwerper [sperwɛrpər] *de (~s)* javelin thrower

spek [spɛk] *het* bacon; fat

spekken [spɛkə(n)] *vb* lard: *zijn verhaal met anekdotes ~* spice one's story with anecdotes

spekkie [spɛki] *het (~s) (roughly)* marshmallow

speklap [spɛklɑp] *de (~pen)* thick slice of fatty bacon

spektakel [spɛktɑkəl] *het (~s)* **1** spectacle, show:

het ~ is afgelopen the show is over; **2** uproar, fuss: *het was me een ~* it was a tremendous fuss

spel [spɛl] *het (~en, ~len)* **1** game, gambling; **2** game, match: *(cards) een goed (sterk) ~ in handen hebben* have a good hand; *doe je ook een ~letje mee?* do you want to join in? (*or:* play?); *het ~ meespelen* play the game, play along (with s.o.); *zijn ~ slim spelen* play one's cards well; **3** play: *hoog ~ spelen* play for high stakes, play high; *vals ~* cheating; *vuil (onsportief) ~* foul play; **4** acting, performance: *een ~ kaarten* a pack (*or:* deck) of cards; *buiten ~ blijven* stay (*or:* keep) out of it; *in het ~ zijn* be involved, be in question, be at stake; *er is een vergissing in het ~* there is an error somewhere; *zijn leven* (*or: alles*) *op het ~ zetten* risk/stake one's life (*or:* everything)

spelbreker [spɛlbrekər] *de (~s)* spoilsport

speld [spɛlt] *de (~en)* pin: *men kon er een ~ horen vallen* you could have heard a pin drop; *daar is geen ~ tussen te krijgen* there's no flaw in that argument

spelden [spɛldə(n)] *vb* pin

speldenkussen [spɛldə(n)kʏsə(n)] *het (~s)* pincushion

speldje [spɛlcə] *het (~s)* **1** pin; **2** pin, badge

¹spelen [spelə(n)] *vb* **1** play: *al ~d leren* learn through play; *vals ~: a)* cheat; *b) (mus)* play out of tune; *(sport) voor ~* play up front; **2** act, play; **3** play: *piano ~* play the piano; **4** play, perform; **5** be of importance, count: *dat speelt geen rol* that is of no account; *die kwestie speelt nog steeds* that is still an (important) issue

²spelen [spelə(n)] *vb* **1** be set (in), take place (in): *de film speelt in New York* the film is set in New York; **2** play: *de wind speelde met haar haren* the wind played (*or:* was playing) with her hair

spelenderwijs [speləndərwɛis] *adv* without effort, with (the greatest of) ease

speler [spelər] *de (~s)* player, gambler

spelfout [spɛlfɑut] *de (~en)* spelling mistake (*or:* error)

speling [spelɪŋ] *de (~en)* **1** play: *een ~ van de natuur* a freak of nature; **2** play, slack; margin

spellen [spɛlə(n)] *vb* spell: *hoe spelt hij zijn naam?* how does he spell his name?; *een woord verkeerd ~* misspell a word

spelletje [spɛləcə] *het (~s)* game

spelling [spɛlɪŋ] *de (~en)* spelling

spelonk [spelɔŋk] *het (~en)* cave, cavern

spelregel [spɛlreɣəl] *de (~s)* rule of play (*or:* the game): *je moet je aan de ~s houden* you must stick to the rules; *de ~s overtreden* break the rules

spelshow [spɛlʃo] *de* game show

spelverdeler [spɛlvərdelər] *de (~s)* playmaker

spenderen [spɛndərə(n)] *vb* spend

sperma [spɛrma] *het* sperm

spermabank [spɛrmabɑŋk] *de (~en)* sperm bank

spermadonor [spɛrmadonɔr] *de (~s)* sperm donor

sperwer [spɛrwər] *de (~s)* sparrowhawk

sperzieboon [spɛrzibon] *de (-bonen)* green bean

spetter [spɛtər] *de (~s)* **1** spatter; **2** hunk
spetteren [spɛtərə(n)] *vb* sp(l)atter, crackle
speurder [spørdər] *de (~s)* detective, sleuth
speuren [spørə(n)] *vb* investigate, hunt: *naar iets ~* hunt (*or:* search) for sth
speurhond [spørhɔnt] *de (~en)* tracker (dog), bloodhound
speurtocht [spørtɔχt] *de (~en)* search
speurwerk [spørwɛrk] *het* investigation, detective work
spichtig [spɪχtəχ] *adj, adv* lanky, spindly: *een ~ meisje* a skinny girl
spie [spi] *de (~ën)* pin; wedge
spieden [spidə(n)] *vb* || *~d om zich heen kijken* look furtively around
spiegel [spiɣəl] *de (~s)* mirror: *vlakke (or: holle, bolle) ~s* flat (*or:* concave, convex) mirrors; *in de ~ kijken* look at oneself (in the mirror)
spiegelbeeld [spiɣəlbelt] *het (~en)* **1** reflection; **2** mirror image
spiegelei [spiɣəlɛi] *het (~eren)* fried egg
spiegelen [spiɣələ(n)] *vb* reflect, mirror
spiegelglad [spiɣəlɣlɑt] *adj* as smooth as glass, icy, slippery
spiegeling [spiɣəlɪŋ] *de (~en)* reflection
spiegelruit [spiɣəlrœyt] *de (~en)* plate-glass window
spiegelschrift [spiɣəlsχrɪft] *het* mirror writing
spiekbriefje [spigbrifjə] *het (~s)* crib (sheet)
spieken [spikə(n)] *vb* copy, use a crib: *bij iem ~* copy from s.o.
spier [spir] *de (~en)* muscle: *de ~en losmaken* loosen up the muscles, limber up, warm up; *hij vertrok geen ~ (van zijn gezicht)* he didn't bat an eyelid
spierbal [spirbɑl] *de (~len)* || *zijn ~len gebruiken* flex one's muscle(s)
spierkracht [spirkrɑχt] *de* muscle (power), muscular strength
spiernaakt [spirnakt] *adj* stark naked
spierpijn [spirpɛin] *de (~en)* sore muscles, aching muscles, muscular pain
spierweefsel [spirwefsəl] *het (~s)* muscular tissue
spierwit [spirwɪt] *adj* (as) white as a sheet
spies [spis] *de (spiezen)* skewer
spijbelaar [spɛibəlar] *de (~s)* truant
spijbelen [spɛibələ(n)] *vb* play truant
spijker [spɛikər] *de (~s)* nail: *de ~ op de kop slaan* hit the nail on the head; *~s met koppen slaan* get down to business
spijkerbroek [spɛikərbruk] *de (~en)* (pair of) jeans: *ik heb een nieuwe ~* I've got a new pair of jeans; *waar is mijn ~?* where are my jeans?
spijkerhard [spɛikərhɑrt] *adj* (as) hard as a rock; *(fig)* (as) hard as nails: *~e journalisten* hard-boiled journalists
spijkerjasje [spɛikərjɑʃə] *het* denim jacket, jeans jacket
spijkerpak [spɛikərpɑk] *het (~ken)* denim suit
spijkerschrift [spɛikərsχrɪft] *het* cuneiform script

spijkerstof [spɛikərstɔf] *de (~fen)* denim
spijl [spɛil] *de (~en)* bar, rail(ing)
spijs [spɛis] *de (spijzen)* foods, victuals
spijsvertering [spɛisfərterɪŋ] *de* digestion: *een slechte ~ hebben* suffer from indigestion
spijt [spɛit] *de* regret: *daar zul je geen ~ van hebben* you won't regret that; *geen ~ hebben* have no regrets; *daar zul je ~ van krijgen* you'll regret that, you'll be sorry; *tot mijn (grote) ~ (much)* to my regret
spijten [spɛitə(n)] *vb* regret, be sorry: *het spijt me dat ik u stoor* I'm sorry to disturb you; *het spijt me u te moeten zeggen …* I'm sorry (to have) to tell you …
spijtig [spɛitəχ] *adj, adv* regrettable
spike [spɑjk] *de (~s)* spikes
spikkel [spɪkəl] *de (~s)* fleck, speck
spiksplinternieuw [spɪksplɪntərnjw] *adj* spanking new, brand new
spil [spɪl] *de (~len)* **1** pivot: *om een ~ draaien* pivot, swivel; **2** pivot, key figure, playmaker *(socc)*
spillebeen [spɪləben] *de* spindleshanks
spin [spɪn] *de (~nen, ~s)* **1** spider: *nijdig als een ~* furious, absolutely wild; **2** spider; **3** spin: *een bal veel ~ geven* give a ball a lot of spin
spinazie [spinazi] *de* spinach: *~ à la crème* creamed spinach
spinet [spinɛt] *het (~ten)* spinet
spinnen [spɪnə(n)] *vb* **1** spin: *garen ~* spin thread (*or:* yarn); **2** purr
spinnenweb [spɪnə(n)wɛp] *het (~ben)* cobweb, spider('s) web
spinnewiel [spɪnəwil] *het (~en)* spinning wheel
spinrag [spɪnrɑχ] *het* cobweb, spider('s) web: *zo fijn (or: zo dun, zo teer) als ~* as fine (*or:* thin, delicate) as gossamer
spion [spijɔn] *de (~nen)* spy
spionage [spijonaʒə] *de* espionage, spying
spioneren [spijonɛrə(n)] *vb* spy
spiraal [spiral] *de (spiralen)* spiral
spiraalmatras [spiralmatrɑs] *het, de (~sen)* spring mattress
spiraaltje [spiralcə] *het (~s)* IUD, coil
spiritisme [spiritɪsmə] *het* spiritualism
spiritistisch [spiritɪstis] *adj* spiritualist: *een ~e bijeenkomst* a spiritualist gathering, a seance
spiritus [spiritʏs] *de* methylated spirits; alcohol
¹**spit** [spɪt] *het (~ten)* spit: *aan het ~ gebraden* broiled on the spit; *kip van 't ~* barbecued chicken
²**spit** [spɪt] *het, de (~ten)* lumbago
¹**spits** [spɪts] *adj, adv* pointed, sharp: *~ toelopen* taper (off), end in a point
²**spits** [spɪts] *de, het* **1** peak, point: *de ~ van een toren* the spire; **2** rush hour; **3** *(sport)* forward line; **4** striker: *de (het) ~ afbijten* open the batting; *iets op de ~ drijven* bring sth to a head
spitsen [spɪtsə(n)] *vb* prick
spitskool [spɪtskol] *de (-kolen)* pointed cabbage, hearted cabbage

spitstechnologie [spɪtstɛχnoloɣi] *de (~ën) (Belg)* state-of-the-art technology

spitsuur [spɪtsyr] *het (-uren)* rush hour: *buiten de spitsuren* outside the rush hour; *in het ~* during the rush hour

spitten [spɪtə(n)] *vb* dig: *land ~* turn the soil over

spleet [splet] *de (spleten)* crack

splijten [splɛitə(n)] *vb* split

splijtstof [splɛitstɔf] *de (~fen)* nuclear fuel, fissionable material

splinter [splɪntər] *de (~s)* splinter

splinternieuw [splɪntərniw] *adj* brand-new

split [splɪt] *het* slit, placket

spliterwt [splɪtɛrt] *de (~en)* split pea

¹**splitsen** [splɪtsə(n)] *vb* **1** divide, split; **2** separate, split up

²**splitsen** [splɪtsə(n)] *ref vb* split (up), divide: *daar splitst de weg zich* the road forks there

splitsing [splɪtsɪŋ] *de (~en)* **1** splitting (up), division; **2** fork, branch(ing): *bij de ~ links afslaan* turn left at the fork

spoed [sput] *de* speed: *op ~ aandringen* stress the urgency of the matter; *met ~* with haste, urgently; *~! (on letters)* urgent

spoedbehandeling [spudbəhandəlɪŋ] *de (~en)* emergency treatment

spoedbestelling [spudbəstɛlɪŋ] *de (~en)* rush order; express delivery, special delivery

spoedcursus [sputkʏrzʏs] *de (~sen)* intensive course, crash course

spoedgeval [sputχəval] *het (~len)* emergency (case), urgent matter

¹**spoedig** [spudəχ] *adj* **1** near: *~e levering* prompt *(or:* swift*)* delivery; **2** speedy, quick: *een ~ antwoord* a quick answer

²**spoedig** [spudəχ] *adv* shortly, soon: *zo ~ mogelijk* as soon as possible

spoedzending [sputsɛndɪŋ] *de* urgent shipment, express parcel

spoel [spul] *de (~en)* **1** reel, *(Am)* spool, bobbin; **2** shuttle

¹**spoelen** [spulə(n)] *vb* rinse (out): *de mond ~* rinse one's mouth (out)

²**spoelen** [spulə(n)] *vb* wash: *naar zee (or: aan land) ~* wash out to sea *(or:* ashore*)*

spoeling [spulɪŋ] *de (~en)* rinse, rinsing: *een ~ geven* rinse (out)

spoken [spokə(n)] *vb* **1** prowl (round, about): *nog laat door het huis ~* prowl about in the house late at night; **2** be haunted: *in dat bos spookt het* that forest is haunted

spons [spɔns] *de (sponzen)* sponge

sponsor [spɔnsɔr] *de (~s)* sponsor

sponsoren [spɔnsɔrə(n)] *vb* sponsor

spontaan [spɔntan] *adj, adv* spontaneous

spontaniteit [spɔntanitɛit] *de (~en)* spontaneity

spook [spok] *het (spoken)* ghost; phantom: *overal spoken zien* see ghosts everywhere

spookachtig [spokaχtəχ] *adj, adv* ghostly

spookhuis [spokhœys] *het (-huizen)* haunted house

spookrijder [spokrɛidər] *de (~s)* ghostrider

spookverschijning [spokfərsχɛinɪŋ] *de (~en)* spectre, ghost

¹**spoor** [spor] *het* **1** track, trail: *ik ben het ~ bijster (kwijt)* I've lost track of things; *op het goede ~ zijn* be on the right track *(or:* trail*)*; *de politie heeft een ~ gevonden* the police have found a clue; *iem op het ~ komen* track s.o. down, trace s.o.; *iem op het ~ zijn* be on s.o.'s track; **2** track; **3** trace: *sporen van geweld(pleging)* marks of violence; **4** track, trail: *op een dood ~ komen (raken)* get into a blind alley; *uit het ~ raken* run off the rails

²**spoor** [spor] *de* spur: *een paard de sporen geven* spur a horse

spoorboekje [sporbukjə] *het (~s)* (train, railway) timetable

spoorboom [sporbom] *de (-bomen)* level-crossing barrier

spoorlijn [sporlɛin] *de (~en)* railway

spoorloos [sporlos] *adj* without a trace: *mijn bril is ~* my glasses have vanished

spoorweg [sporwɛχ] *de (~en)* railway (line)

spoorwegovergang [sporwɛχovərɣaŋ] *de (~en)* level crossing: *bewaakte ~* guarded level crossing

spoorwegstation [sporwɛχsta(t)ʃɔn] *het (~s)* railway station

spoorzoeken [sporzukə(n)] *vb* tracking

sporadisch [sporadis] *adj, adv* sporadic: *maar ~ voorkomen* be few and far between

sport [spɔrt] *de (~en)* **1** sport(s): *veel (or: weinig) aan ~ doen* go in for *(or:* not go in for*)* sports; **2** rung: *de hoogste ~ bereiken* reach the highest rung (of the ladder)

sportartikelen [spɔrtartikələ(n)] *de* sports equipment

sportarts [spɔrtarts] *de (~en)* sports doctor *(or:* physician*)*

sportbril [spɔrdbrɪl] *de (~len)* protective glasses

sportbroek [spɔrdbruk] *de (~en)* shorts

sportclub [spɔrtklʏp] *de (~s)* sports club

sportdag [spɔrdaχ] *de (~en)* sports day

sporten [spɔrtə(n)] *vb || Jaap sport veel* Jaap does a lot of sport

sporter [spɔrtər] *de (~s)* sportsman

sportfanaat [spɔrtfanat] *de* sports fanatic *(or:* freak*)*

sportfiets [spɔrtfits] *de (~en)* sports bicycle, racing bicycle

sporthal [spɔrthal] *de (~len)* sports hall *(or:* centre*)*

sportief [spɔrtif] *adj, adv* **1** sports, sporty: *een ~ evenement* a sports event; *een ~ jasje* a casual *(or:* sporty*)* jacket; **2** sport(s)-loving, sporty; **3** sportsmanlike: *~ zijn* be sporting *(or:* a good sport*)* (about sth)

sportiviteit [spɔrtivitɛit] *de* sportsmanship

sportkleding [spɔrtkledɪŋ] *de* sportswear

sportliefhebber [spɔrtlifhɛbər] *de (~s)* sports enthusiast

sportman [spɔrtmɑn] *de (~nen)* sportsman

sportpark [spɔrtpɑrk] *het (~en)* sports park

sportprestatie [spɔrtprɛsta(t)si] *de (~s)* sporting achievement

sportschoen [spɔrtsχun] *de (~en)* sport(s) shoe

sporttas [spɔrtɑs] *de (~sen)* sports bag, kitbag

sportterrein [spɔrtɛrɛin] *het (~en)* sports field, playing field

sportuitslagen [spɔrtœytslaɣə(n)] *de* sports results

sportveld [spɔrtfɛlt] *het (~en)* sports field, playing field

sportvereniging [spɔrtfərenəɣɪŋ] *de (~en)* sports club

sportvliegtuig [spɔrtfliχtœyχ] *het (~en)* private pleasure aircraft

sportvrouw [spɔrtfrɑu] *de (~en)* sportswoman

sportwagen [spɔrtwaɣə(n)] *de (~s)* sport(s) car

sportzaak [spɔrtsak] *de (-zaken)* sports shop

sportzaal [spɔrtsal] *de (-zalen)* fitness centre, gym

spot [spɔt] *de (~s)* **1** mockery: *de ~ drijven met* poke fun at, mock; **2** (advertising) spot; **3** spot(light)

spotgoedkoop [spɔtχutkop] *adj, adv* dirt cheap

spotprijs [spɔtprɛis] *de (-prijzen)* bargain price, giveaway price

spotten [spɔtə(n)] *vb* **1** joke, jest; **2** mock: *hij laat niet met zich ~* he is not to be trifled with; *daar moet je niet mee ~* that is no laughing matter

spouwmuur [spɑumyr] *de (-muren)* cavity wall

spraak [sprak] *de* speech

spraakgebrek [sprakχəbrɛk] *het (~en)* speech defect

spraakherkenning [sprakhɛrkɛnɪŋ] *de* speech recognition

spraakles [spraklɛs] *de (~sen)* speech training, speech therapy

spraaksynthese [spraksɪntezə] *de* speech synthesis

spraakverwarring [sprakvərwɑrɪŋ] *de (~en)* babel, confusion of tongues

spraakzaam [spraksam] *adj* talkative

sprake [sprakə] || *er is geen ~ van* that is (absolutely) out of the question; *er is hier ~ van …* it is a matter (*or:* question) of …; *iets ter ~ brengen* bring sth up; *ter ~ komen* come up; *geen ~ van!* certainly not!

sprakeloos [sprakəlos] *adj, adv* speechless: *iem ~ doen staan* leave s.o. speechless

sprankelen [sprɑŋkələ(n)] *vb* sparkle

sprankje [sprɑŋkjə] *het (~s)* spark: *er is nog een ~ hoop* there is still a glimmer of hope

spray [sprej] *de (~s)* spray

spreekbeurt [spregbørt] *de (~en)* talk

spreekkamer [sprekamər] *de (~s)* consulting room, surgery

spreektaal [sprektal] *de* spoken language

spreekuur [sprekyr] *het (-uren)* office hours, (*med*) surgery (hours): *~ houden* have office hours, have surgery; *op het ~ komen* come during office hours

spreekvaardigheid [sprekfardəχhɛit] *de* fluency, speaking ability

spreekwoord [sprɛkwort] *het (~en)* proverb, saying: *zoals het ~ zegt* as the saying goes

spreeuw [sprew] *de (~en)* starling

sprei [sprɛi] *de (~en)* (bed)spread

spreiden [sprɛidə(n)] *vb* **1** spread (out): *het risico ~* spread the risk; *de vakanties ~* stagger holidays; **2** spread (out), space

spreiding [sprɛidɪŋ] *de* **1** spread(ing), dispersal; **2** spacing, spread: *de ~ van de macht* the distribution of power

¹**spreken** [sprekə(n)] *vb* speak, talk: *de feiten ~ voor zich* the facts speak for themselves; *het spreekt vanzelf* it goes without saying; *daar spreekt u mee!* speaking; *spreek ik met Jan?* is that Jan?

²**spreken** [sprekə(n)] *vb* **1** speak, tell: *een vreemde taal ~* speak a foreign language; **2** speak, talk to (*or:* with): *iem niet te ~ krijgen* not be able to get in touch with s.o.; *niet te ~ zijn over iets* be unhappy (*or:* be not too pleased) about sth

¹**sprekend** [sprekənt] *adj* **1** speaking, talking: *een ~e film* a talking film; *een ~e papegaai* a talking parrot; **2** strong, striking: *een ~e gelijkenis* a striking resemblance; **3** expressive

²**sprekend** [sprekənt] *adv* exactly: *zij lijkt ~ op haar moeder* she looks exactly (*or:* just) like her mother; *dat portret lijkt ~ op Karin* that picture captures Karin perfectly

spreker [sprekər] *de (~s)* speaker

spreuk [sprøk] *de (~en)* maxim, saying: *oude ~* old saying

spriet [sprit] *de (~en)* blade

springconcours [sprɪŋkɔŋkur] *het, de (~en)* jumping competition

springen [sprɪŋə(n)] *vb* **1** jump, leap, spring, vault: *hoog* (or: *ver, omlaag*) *~* jump high (*or:* far, down); *over een sloot ~* leap a ditch; *staan te ~ om weg te komen* be dying to leave; *zitten te ~ om iets* be bursting (*or:* dying) for sth; **2** burst, explode, blast, pop: *mijn band is gesprongen* my tyre has burst; *een snaar is gesprongen* a string has snapped; *op ~ staan: a)* be about to explode; *b)* be bursting; *op groen ~* change to green

springlading [sprɪŋladɪŋ] *de (~en)* explosive charge

springlevend [sprɪŋlevənt] *adj* alive (and kicking)

springplank [sprɪŋplɑŋk] *de (~en)* springboard

springstof [sprɪŋstɔf] *de (~fen)* explosive

springtouw [sprɪŋtɑu] *het (~en)* skipping rope

springveer [sprɪŋver] *de (-veren)* box spring

sprinkhaan [sprɪŋkhan] *de (-hanen)* grasshopper, (*Africa and Asia*) locust

sprinklerinstallatie [sprɪŋklərɪnstɑla(t)si] *de (~s)* sprinkler system

sprint [sprɪnt] *de (~s)* sprint

sprinten [sprɪntə(n)] *vb* sprint

sprinter [sprɪntər] *de (~s)* sprinter

sproeien [sprujə(n)] *vb* spray, water, sprinkle, irrigate

sproeier [sprujǝr] *de (~s)* sprinkler, jet, spray nozzle; *(agriculture)* irrigator

sproet [sprut] *de (~en)* freckle: *~en in het gezicht hebben* have a freckled face

sprokkelen [sprɔkǝlǝ(n)] *vb* gather wood (*or:* kindling): *hout ~* gather wood

sprong [sprɔŋ] *de (~en)* leap, jump, vault: *hij gaat met ~en vooruit* he's coming along by leaps and bounds

sprookje [sprokjǝ] *het (~s)* fairy tale || *iem ~s vertellen* lead s.o. up the garden path

sprookjesachtig [sprokjǝsɑχtǝχ] *adj, adv* fairy-tale, *(fig)* fairy-like: *de grachten waren ~ verlicht* the canals were romantically illuminated

sprot [sprɔt] *de (~ten)* sprat

spruit [sprœyt] *de* **1** shoot; **2** sprig, sprout

spruitjes [sprœycǝs] *de* (Brussels) sprouts

spruw [spryw] *de* thrush

spugen [spyɣǝ(n)] *vb* **1** spit; **2** throw up: *de boel onder ~* be sick all over the place

spuien [spœyǝ(n)] *vb* spout, unload: *kritiek ~* pour forth criticism

spuigat [spœyɣɑt] *het (~en)* scupper

spuit [spœyt] *de (~en)* **1** syringe, squirt; **2** needle; shot

spuitbus [spœydbʏs] *de (~sen)* spray (can)

¹spuiten [spœytǝ(n)] *vb* **1** squirt, spurt, erupt: *lak op iets ~* spray lacquer on sth; **2** spray(-paint); **3** inject: *hij spuit* he's a junkie

²spuiten [spœytǝ(n)] *vb* squirt, spurt, gush

spuiter [spœytǝr] *de (~s)* junkie

spuitje [spœycǝ] *het (~s)* **1** needle; **2** shot

spul [spʏl] *het (~len)* **1** gear, things, togs, belongings; **2** stuff, things

spurt [spʏrt] *de (~s)* spurt: *er de ~ in zetten* step on it

sputteren [spʏtǝrǝ(n)] *vb* sputter, cough

spuug [spyχ] *het* spittle, spit

spuugzat [spyχsɑt] *adj* || *iets ~ zijn* be sick and tired of sth

spuwen [spywǝ(n)] *vb* **1** spit, spew; **2** spew (up), throw up

squashbaan [skwɔʒban] *de (-banen)* squash court

squashen [skwɔʃǝ(n)] *vb* play squash

sr. *senior* Sr.

Sri Lanka [srilɑŋka] *het* Sri Lanka

sst [st] *int* (s)sh, hush

staaf [staf] *de (staven)* bar

staafmixer [stafmɪksǝr] *de (~s)* hand blender

staak [stak] *de (staken)* stake, pole, post

staakt-het-vuren [staktǝtfyrǝ(n)] *het* cease-fire

staal [stal] *het* **1** steel: *zo hard als ~* as hard as iron; **2** sample: *een (mooi) ~tje van zijn soort humor* a fine example of his sense of humour

staalborstel [stalbɔrstǝl] *de (~s)* wire brush

staalindustrie [stalɪndʏstri] *de (~ën)* steel industry

staan [stan] *vb* **1** stand: *gaan ~* stand up; *achter (or: naast) elkaar gaan ~* queue (or: line) up; *die ge-*

beurtenis staat geheel op zichzelf that is an isolated incident; **2** stand, be: *hoe ~ de zaken?* how are things?; *er goed voor ~* look good; *zij ~ sterk* they are in a strong position; *buiten iets ~* not be involved in sth; *de snelheidsmeter stond op 80 km/uur* the speedometer showed 80 km/h; *zij staat derde in het algemeen klassement* she is third in the overall ranking; **3** look; **4** say, be written: *er staat niet bij wanneer* it doesn't say when; *in de tekst staat daar niets over* the text doesn't say anything about it; *wat staat er op het programma?* what's on the programme?; **5** stand still: *blijven ~* stand still; **6** leave, stand: *hij kon nauwelijks spreken, laat ~ zingen* he could barely speak, let alone sing; *zijn baard laten ~* grow a beard; **7** insist (on): *er staat hem wat te wachten* there is sth in store for him; *ergens van ~ (te) kijken* be flabbergasted; *ze staat al een uur te wachten* she has been waiting (for) an hour

staanplaats [stamplats] *de (~en)* standing room, terrace

staar [star] *de* cataract, stare, film

staart [start] *de (~en)* **1** tail: *met de ~ kwispelen* wag its tail; **2** pigtail; ponytail

staartbeen [stardben] *het (-beenderen, -benen)* tail-bone, coccyx

staartdeling [stardelɪŋ] *de (~en)* long division

staartster [startstɛr] *de (~ren)* comet

staartvin [startfɪn] *de (~nen)* tail fin

staat [stat] *de (staten)* **1** state, condition, status: *burgerlijke ~* marital status; *in goede ~ verkeren* be in good condition; *in prima ~ van onderhoud* in an excellent state of repair; **2** condition: *tot alles in ~ zijn* be capable of anything; **3** state, country, nation, power, the body politic: *de ~ der Nederlanden* the kingdom of the Netherlands; **4** council, board: *de Provinciale Staten* the Provincial Council; **5** statement, record, report, survey

staatsbezoek [statsbǝzuk] *het (~en)* state visit

Staatsblad [statsblɑt] *het (~en)* law gazette

staatsbosbeheer [statsbɔzbǝher] *het* Forestry Commission

staatsburger [statsbʏrɣǝr] *de (~s)* citizen, subject

staatsexamen [statsɛksamǝ(n)] *het (~s)* state exam(ination); university entrance examination

staatsgeheim [statsχǝhɛim] *het (~en)* official secret, state secret

staatsgreep [statsχrep] *de (-grepen)* coup (d'état)

staatshoofd [statshoft] *het (~en)* head of state

staatsieportret [statsipɔrtrɛt] *het (~ten)* official portrait

staatsinrichting [statsɪnrɪχtɪŋ] *de (~en)* civics

staatsloterij [statslotǝrɛi] *de (~en)* state lottery, national lottery

staatssecretaris [statsɪkrǝtarɪs] *de (~sen)* (Belg) State Secretary

staatsveiligheid [statsfɛilǝχhɛit] *de* state (or: national, public) security

stabiel [stabil] *adj* stable, firm

stabilisatie [stabiliza(t)si] *de* stabilization

stabiliseren [stabilizɛrə(n)] *vb* stabilize, steady, firm (up)

stabiliteit [stabilitɛit] *de* stability, balance, steadiness

stacaravan [stakɛrəvɛn] *de (~s)* caravan

stad [stɑt] *de (steden)* town, city, borough: *~ en land aflopen* search high and low, look everywhere (for); *de ~ uit zijn* be out of town

stadbewoner [stɑdbəwonər] *de (~s)* city dweller, citizen

stadhuis [stɑthœys] *het (-huizen)* town hall, city hall

stadion [stadijɔn] *het (~s)* stadium

stadium [stadijʏm] *het (stadia)* stage, phase

stadsbestuur [stɑtsbəstyr] *het (-besturen)* town council, city council, municipality

stadsbus [stɑtsbʏs] *de (~sen)* local bus

stadsdeel [stɑtsdel] *het (-delen)* quarter, area, part of town, district

stadsmens [stɑtsmɛns] *de (~en)* city dweller, townsman

stadsmuur [stɑtsmyr] *de (-muren)* town wall, city wall

stadsplattegrond [stɑtsplatəɣrɔnt] *de (~en)* town plan, town map, street map *(or:* plan) (of a town, the city)

stadsvernieuwing [stɑtsfərniwɪŋ] *de (~en)* urban renewal

staf [stɑf] *de (staven)* **1** staff, (walking) stick; wand; **2** staff, faculty; **3** *(mil)* staff, corps

stafkaart [stɑfkart] *de (~en)* topographic map, ordnance survey map

stage [staʒə] *de (~s)* work placement; teaching practice; *(med)* housemanship, *(Am)* intern(e)ship: *~ lopen* do a work placement practice

stageperiode [staʒəperijodə] *de (~s, ~n)* traineeship, period of practical training *(or:* work experience)

stageplaats [staʒəplats] *de (~en)* trainee post

stagiair [staʒɛːrə] *de (~s)* student on work placement; student teacher

stagnatie [stɑɣna(t)si] *de (~s)* stagnation

stagneren [stɑɣnerə(n)] *vb* stagnate, come to a standstill

¹staken [stakə(n)] *vb* cease, stop, discontinue, suspend: *zijn pogingen ~* cease one's efforts; *het verzet ~* cease resistance

²staken [stakə(n)] *vb* **1** strike, go on strike: *gaan ~* go *(or:* come out) on strike; **2** tie

staker [stakər] *de (~s)* striker

staking [stakɪŋ] *de (~en)* strike (action), walkout: *in ~ zijn* (or: *gaan)* be *(or:* come out) on strike

stakingsactie [stakɪŋsaksi] *de (~s)* strike action

stakingsbreker [stakɪŋzbrekər] *de (~s)* strike-breaker, *(depr)* scab

stakker [stakər] *de (~s)* wretch, poor soul *(or:* creature, thing): *een arme ~* a poor beggar

stal [stɑl] *de (~len)* stable, cowshed, sty, fold: *iets van ~ halen* dig sth out *(or:* up) (again)

stalactiet [stalɑktit] *de (~en)* stalactite

stalagmiet [stalɑɣmit] *de (~en)* stalagmite

stalen [stalə(n)] *adj* steel, steely: *met een ~ gezicht* stony-faced

stalgeld [stɑlɣɛlt] *het (~en)* storage charge(s); garage charge(s)

stalknecht [stɑlknɛχt] *de (~en, ~s)* stableman, stable hand, groom

stallen [stɑlə(n)] *vb* store, put up *(or:* away), garage

stalletje [stɑləcə] *het (~s)* stall, stand, booth

stalling [stɑlɪŋ] *de (~en)* garage; shelter

stam [stɑm] *de (~men)* **1** trunk, stem, stock; **2** stock, clan; **3** tribe, race

stamboek [stɑmbuk] *het (~en)* pedigree, studbook, herdbook

stamboekvee [stɑmbukfe] *het* pedigree(d) cattle

stamboom [stɑmbom] *de (-bomen)* family tree, genealogical tree; genealogy, pedigree

stamcafé [stɑmkafe] *het (~s)* favourite pub *(or* Am: bar); local; *(Am)* hangout

stamelen [stamələ(n)] *vb* stammer, stutter, sp(l)utter

stamgast [stɑmɣɑst] *de (~en)* regular (customer)

stamhoofd [stɑmhoft] *het (~en)* chieftain, tribal chief, headman

stamhouder [stɑmhaudər] *de (~s)* son and heir, family heir

staminee [stamine] *de (~s) (Belg)* pub

stammen [stɑmə(n)] *vb* descend (from), stem (from), date (back to, from)

stammenstrijd [stɑmə(n)strɛit] *de* (inter)tribal dispute; tribal war

¹stampen [stɑmpə(n)] *vb* stamp: *met zijn voet ~* stamp one's foot

²stampen [stɑmpə(n)] *vb* pound, crush, pulverize: *gestampte aardappelen* mashed potatoes

stamper [stɑmpər] *de (~s)* **1** stamp(er), pounder, masher; **2** *(bot)* pistil

stamppot [stɑmpɔt] *de (~ten) (roughly)* stew, hotchpotch, mashed potatoes and cabbage

stampvol [stɑmpfɔl] *adj* packed; full to the brim; full up

stamtafel [stɑmtafəl] *de (~s)* table (reserved) for regulars

stamvader [stɑmvadər] *de (~s)* ancestor, forefather

stand [stɑnt] *de (~en)* **1** posture, bearing: *een ~ aannemen* assume a position; **2** position: *de ~ van de dollar* the dollar rate; *de ~ van de zon* the position of the sun; **3** state, condition: *de burgerlijke ~* the registry office; **4** score: *de ~ is 2-1* the score is 2-1; **5** estate, class, station, order: *mensen van alle rangen en ~en* people from all walks of life; **6** existence, being: *tot ~ brengen* bring about, achieve; **7** stand

¹standaard [stɑndart] *de (~s)* **1** stand, standard; **2** standard, prototype

²standaard [stɑndart] *adj, adv* standard

standaardisatie [stɑndardiza(t)si] *de* standardization

standaardiseren [stɑndardizɛrə(n)] *vb* standardize: *het gestandaardiseerde type* the standard model

standaarduitvoering [stɑndartœytfurɪŋ] *de (~en)* standard type (*or:* model, design)

standaardvoorbeeld [stɑndartforbelt] *het (~en)* classic example

standaardwerk [stɑndartwɛrk] *het (~en)* standard work (*or:* book)

standbeeld [stɑndbelt] *het (~en)* statue

standhouden [stɑnthɑudə(n)] *vb* hold out, stand up

standje [stɑncə] *het (~s)* 1 position, posture; 2 rebuke

standlicht [stɑntlɪχt] *het (~en) (Belg)* sidelight, parking light

standplaats [stɑntplats] *de (~en)* stand: *~ voor taxi's* taxi rank (*or Am:* stand)

standpunt [stɑntpʏnt] *het (~en)* standpoint, point of view: *bij zijn ~ blijven* hold one's ground

standvastig [stɑntfɑstəχ] *adj, adv* firm, perseverant, persistent

standwerker [stɑntwɛrkər] *de (~s)* hawker, (market, street) vendor

stang [stɑŋ] *de (~en)* stave, bar, rod, crossbar ‖ *iem op ~ jagen* needle s.o.

stank [stɑŋk] *de (~en)* stench, bad (*or:* foul, nasty) smell

stansen [stɑnsə(n)] *vb* punch

stap [stɑp] *de (~pen)* 1 step, footstep, pace, stride: *een ~ in de goede richting doen* take a step in the right direction; *~(je) voor ~(je)* inch by inch, little by little; *een ~(je) terug doen* take a step down (in pay); 2 *(fig)* step, move, grade: *~pen ondernemen tegen* take steps against; 3 step, tread: *op ~ gaan* set out (*or:* off)

stapel [stɑpəl] *de (~s)* 1 pile, heap, stack; 2 stock ‖ *te hard van ~ lopen* go too fast

stapelbed [stɑpəlbɛt] *het (~den)* bunk beds

stapelen [stɑpələ(n)] *vb* pile up, heap up, stack

stapelgek [stɑpəlɣɛk] *adj, adv* 1 crazy, (as) mad as a hatter, (raving) mad; 2 mad, crazy

stapelhuis [stɑpəlhœys] *het (-huizen) (Belg)* warehouse

stappen [stɑpə(n)] *vb* 1 step, walk; 2 go out, go for a drink

stappenplan [stɑpə(n)plɑn] *het (~nen)* step-by-step plan

stapvoets [stɑpfuts] *adv* at a walk, at walking pace

star [stɑr] *adj, adv* 1 frozen, stiff, glassy; 2 rigid, inflexible, uncompromising

staren [stɑrə(n)] *vb* 1 stare, gaze; 2 peer: *zich blind ~ op iets* be fixated on sth

start [stɑrt] *de (~s)* start: *(car) de koude ~* the cold start

startbaan [stɑrdban] *de (-banen)* runway, airstrip

startblok [stɑrdblɔk] *het (~ken)* starting block

starten [stɑrtə(n)] *vb* start, begin, take off, *(sport)* be off

starter [stɑrtər] *de (~s)* starter

startkabel [stɑrtkabəl] *de (~s)* jump lead, *(Am)* jumper cable

startklaar [stɑrtklɑr] *adj* ready to start (*or:* go), ready for take-off

startpunt [stɑrtpʏnt] *het (~en)* starting point

stateloos [stɑtəlos] *adj* stateless

Staten [stɑtə(n)] *de* (Dutch) Provincial Council

Statenbijbel [stɑtə(n)bɛibəl] *de (~s)* (Dutch) Authorized Version (of the Bible)

Staten-Generaal [stɑtə(n)ɣenərɑl] *de* States General, Dutch parliament

statief [stɑtif] *het (statieven)* tripod; stand

statiegeld [stɑ(t)siɣɛlt] *het* deposit: *geen ~* non-returnable

statig [stɑtəχ] *adj, adv* 1 stately, grand: *een ~e dame* a queenly woman, a woman of regal bearing; 2 solemn

station [stɑ(t)ʃɔn] *het (~s)* (railway) station, *(Am)* depot

stationair [stɑʃonɛːr] *adj* stationary: *een motor ~ laten draaien* let an engine idle

stationcar [steʃɑnkɑːr] *de (~s)* estate (car), *(Am)* station wagon

stationeren [stɑ(t)ʃɔnerə(n)] *vb* station, post

stationschef [stɑ(t)ʃɔnʃɛf] *de (~s)* stationmaster

stationsgebouw [stɑ(t)ʃɔnsχəbɑu] *het (~en)* station (building)

stationshal [stɑ(t)ʃɔnshɑl] *de (~len)* station concourse

statisch [stɑtis] *adj* static

statistiek [stɑtɪstik] *de (~en)* statistics

statistisch [stɑtɪstis] *adj, adv* statistical

status [stɑtʏs] *de* 1 (social) status, standing; 2 (legal) status

statusregel [stɑtʏsreɣəl] *de (~s)* status line

statussymbool [stɑtʏsɪmbol] *het (-symbolen)* status symbol

statuut [stɑtyt] *het (statuten)* statute, regulation

stedelijk [stedələk] *adj* municipal, urban: *de ~e volking* the urban population

steeds [stets] *adv* 1 always, constantly: *iem ~ aankijken* keep looking at s.o.; *~ weer* time after time, repeatedly; 2 increasingly, more and more: *~ groter* bigger and bigger; *~ slechter worden* go from bad to worse; *het regent nog ~* it is still raining

steeg [steχ] *de (stegen)* alley(way)

steek [stek] *de (steken)* 1 stab, thrust, prick; stab wound; 2 sting, bite; 3 shooting pain, stabbing pain, twinge: *een ~ in de borst* a twinge in the chest; 4 stitch: *iem in de ~ laten* let s.o. down

steekpartij [stekpɑrtɛi] *de (~en)* knifing

steekpenningen [stekpɛnɪŋə(n)] *de* bribe(s), kickback(s)

steekproef [stekpruf] *de (-proeven)* random check, spot check; (random) sample survey

steekproefsgewijs [stekprufsχəwɛis] *adj* random; at random

steeksleutel [steksløtəl] *de (~s)* (open-end, fork)

spanner (or: wrench)

steekvlam [stɛkflɑm] de (~men) (jet, burst of) flame, flash

steekwond [stɛkwɔnt] de (~en) stab wound

steel [stel] de (stelen) **1** stalk, stem; **2** handle, stem

steelpan [stelpɑn] de (~nen) saucepan

steels [stels] adj stealthy

¹steen [sten] het, de stone || ~ en been klagen complain bitterly

²steen [sten] de **1** stone, (Am) rock, (large) rock, pebble; **2** stone, brick, cobble(stone): ergens een ~tje toe bijdragen do one's bit towards sth, chip in with; **3** (sport) man, piece

steenarend [stenarɔnt] de (~en) golden eagle

steenbok [stembɔk] de (~ken) ibex, wild goat

Steenbok [stembɔk] de (~ken) (astrology) Capricorn

steenbokskeerkring [stembɔkskerkrɪŋ] de tropic of Capricorn

steenfabriek [stenfabrik] de brickyard

steenkolenengels [stenkolɔ(n)ɛŋɔls] het broken English

steenkool [stenkol] de coal

steenpuist [stempœyst] de (~en) boil

steentijd [stentɛit] de Stone Age

steentje [stencɔ] het (~s) small stone, pebble: een ~ bijdragen do one's bit

steenweg [stenwɛχ] de (~en) (Belg) (paved) road

steiger [stɛiɣɔr] de (~s) **1** landing (stage, place); **2** scaffold(ing)

steigeren [stɛiɣɔrɔ(n)] vb rear (up)

steil [stɛil] adj, adv steep, precipitous: een ~e afgrond a sharp drop; ~ haar straight hair; ergens ~ van achterover slaan be flabbergasted by sth

stek [stɛk] de (~ken) **1** cutting, slip; **2** niche, den: dat is zijn liefste ~ that is his favourite spot

stekel [stekɔl] de (~s) prickle, thorn, spine

stekelbaars [stekɔlbars] de (-baarzen) stickleback

stekelhaar [stekɔlhar] het crew-cut, bristle

stekelig [stekɔlɔχ] adj **1** prickly; spiny, bristly; **2** (fig) sharp, cutting

¹steken [stekɔ(n)] vb **1** stab: alle banden waren lek gestoken all the tyres had been punctured; **2** sting, cut; **3** sting, prick; **4** stick; **5** put, place: veel tijd in iets ~ spend a lot of time on sth; zijn geld in een zaak ~ put one's money in(to) an undertaking

²steken [stekɔ(n)] vb **1** stick: ergens in blijven ~ get stuck (or: bogged) (down) in sth; **2** sting: de zon steekt there is a burning sun; **3** thrust, stab: daar steekt iets achter there is sth behind it

stekend [stekɔnt] adj, adv stinging, sharp

stekken [stɛkɔ(n)] vb slip, strike: planten ~ take (or: strike) cuttings of plants

stekker [stɛkɔr] de (~s) plug

stel [stɛl] het (~len) **1** set: ik neem drie ~ kleren mee I'll take three sets of clothes with me; **2** couple: een pasgetrouwd ~ newly-weds; **3** couple, lot

stelen [stelɔ(n)] vb steal: uit stelen gaan go thieving

stellage [stɛlaʒɔ] de (~s) stand, stage, platform

stellen [stɛlɔ(n)] vb **1** put, set: iem iets beschikbaar ~ put sth at s.o.'s disposal; **2** set, adjust: een machine ~ adjust (or: regulate) a machine; **3** suppose: stel het geval van een leraar die … take the case of a teacher who …; **4** manage, (make) do: we zullen het met minder moeten ~ we'll have to make do with less

stelletje [stɛlɔcɔ] het (~s) **1** bunch: een ~ ongeregeld a disorderly bunch; **2** couple, pair

stellig [stɛlɔχ] adj, adv definite, certain

stelling [stɛlɪŋ] de (~en) **1** scaffold(ing); **2** rack; **3** proposition; **4** theorem, proposition: de ~ van Pythagoras the Pythagorean theorem

stelpen [stɛlpɔ(n)] vb staunch, stem

stelplaats [stɛlplats] de (~en) (Belg) depot

stelregel [stɛlreɣɔl] de (~s) principle: een goede ~ a good rule to go by

stelsel [stɛlsɔl] het (~s) system

stelselmatig [stɛlsɔlmatɔχ] adj, adv systematic

stelt [stɛlt] de (~en) stilt || de boel op ~en zetten raise hell

steltloper [stɛltlopɔr] de (~s) grallatorial bird

stem [stɛm] de (~men) **1** voice: zijn ~ verliezen lose one's voice; met luide ~ out loud; een ~ van binnen an inner voice; **2** part, voice; **3** vote: beiden behaalden een gelijk aantal ~men it was a tie between the two; de ~men staken there is a tie; de ~men tellen count the votes; zijn ~ uitbrengen cast one's vote, vote

stemband [stɛmbɑnt] de (~en) vocal cord

stembiljet [stɛmbɪljɛt] het (~ten) ballot (paper)

stembureau [stɛmbyro] het (~'s) **1** polling station (or Am: place); **2** polling committee

stembus [stɛmbʏs] de (~sen) ballot box: naar de ~ gaan go to the polls

stemcomputer [stɛmkɔmpjutɔr] de (~s) voting computer

stemdistrict [stɛmdɪstrɪkt] het (~en) constituency, borough, ward

stemgerechtigd [stɛmɣɔrɛχtɔχt] adj entitled to vote

stemhebbend [stɛmhɛbɔnt] adj voiced

stemhokje [stɛmhɔkjɔ] het (~s) (voting) booth

stemloos [stɛmlos] adj voiceless, unvoiced

stemmen [stɛmɔ(n)] vb **1** vote: ik stem voor (or: tegen) I vote in favour (or: against); **2** (mus) tune, tune up

stemmer [stɛmɔr] de (~s) tuner

stemmig [stɛmɔχ] adj, adv sober, subdued

stemming [stɛmɪŋ] de (~en) **1** mood: in een slechte (or: goede) ~ zijn be in a bad (or: good) mood; de ~ zit erin there's a general mood of cheerfulness; **2** feeling: er heerst een vijandige ~ feelings are hostile; **3** vote: een geheime ~ a secret ballot; een voorstel in ~ brengen put a proposal to the vote; **4** (mus) tuning

stempel [stɛmpɔl] de **1** seal: zijn ~ op iem drukken

leave one's mark on s.o.; **2** stamp, postmark
¹stempelen [stɛmpələ(n)] *vb* stamp, postmark
²stempelen [stɛmpələ(n)] *vb (Belg)* be unemployed (*or:* on the dole)
stempelgeld [stɛmpəlɣɛlt] *het (Belg)* unemployment benefit, the dole
stempelkussen [stɛmpəlkʏsə(n)] *het (~s)* inkpad
stemplicht [stɛmplɪχt] *de* compulsory voting
stemrecht [stɛmrɛχt] *het* (right to) vote, voting right, franchise, suffrage
stemvork [stɛmvɔrk] *de (~en)* tuning fork
stencil [stɛnsəl] *het, de (~s)* stencil, handout
stencilen [stɛnsələ(n)] *vb* duplicate, stencil
stenen [stenə(n)] *adj* stone, brick
stengel [stɛŋəl] *de (~s)* **1** stalk, stem; **2** stick
stenigen [stenəɣə(n)] *vb* stone
steniging [stenəχɪŋ] *de* stoning
steno [steno] *het, de* stenography, shorthand
step [stɛp] *de (~pen)* scooter
steppe [stɛpə] *de (~n)* steppe
ster [stɛr] *de (~ren)* star: *een vallende ~* a shooting star
stereo [sterejo] *de* stereo(phony)
stereotiep [sterejotip] *adj, adv* stock, stereotypic(al): *een ~e uitdrukking* a cliché
stereotoren [sterejotorə(n)] *de (~s)* music centre
sterfbed [stɛrvbɛt] *het (~den)* deathbed: *op zijn ~ zal hij er nog berouw over hebben* he'll regret it to his dying day
sterfelijk [stɛrfələk] *adj* mortal
sterfgeval [stɛrfχəval] *het (~len)* death
sterftecijfer [stɛrftəsɛifər] *het (~s)* mortality rate
steriel [steril] *adj* **1** sterile; **2** sterile, infertile
sterilisatie [steriliza(t)si] *de (~s)* sterilization
steriliseren [sterilizərə(n)] *vb* sterilize, fix
steriliteit [sterilitɛit] *de* sterility
¹sterk [stɛrk] *adj* **1** strong, powerful, tough: *~e thee* strong tea; **2** strong, sharp: *een ~e stijging* a sharp rise; *een ~e wind* a strong wind; *~er nog* indeed, more than that
²sterk [stɛrk] *adv* **1** strongly, greatly, highly: *een ~ vergrote foto* a much enlarged photograph; *iets ~ overdrijven* greatly exaggerate sth; **2** well: *zij staat (nogal) ~* she has a strong case
sterkedrank [stɛrkədraŋk] *de* strong drink, liquor
sterkte [stɛrktə] *de (~n, ~s)* **1** strength, power, intensity, volume, loudness: *de ~ ve geluid (or: van het licht)* the intensity of a noise (*or:* the light); *op volle (or: halve) ~* at full (*or:* half) strength; **2** fortitude, courage: *~ (gewenst)!* all the best!, good luck!; **3** strength, potency
sterrenbeeld [stɛrə(n)belt] *het (~en)* sign of the zodiac
sterrenkijker [stɛrə(n)kɛikər] *de (~s)* telescope
sterrenkunde [stɛrə(n)kʏndə] *de* astronomy
sterrenkundige [stɛrə(n)kʏndəɣə] *de (~n)* astronomer
sterrenstelsel [stɛrə(n)stɛlsəl] *het (~s)* stellar system

sterretje [stɛrəcə] *het (~s)* **1** sparkler; **2** star, asterisk
sterveling [stɛrvəlɪŋ] *de (~en)* mortal: *er was geen ~ te bekennen* there wasn't a (living) soul in sight
sterven [stɛrvə(n)] *vb* die: *~ aan een ziekte* die of an illness; *~ aan zijn verwondingen* die from one's injuries; *op ~ na dood zijn* be as good as dead
stethoscoop [stetoskop] *de (stethoscopen)* stethoscope
steun [støn] *de (~en)* **1** support, prop: *een ~tje in de rug* a bit of encouragement (*or:* support), a helping hand; **2** support, assistance: *dat zal een grote ~ voor ons zijn* that will be a great help to us; **3** support, aid, assistance
steunbeer [stømber] *de (-beren)* buttress
¹steunen [stønə(n)] *vb* **1** support, prop (up): *een muur ~* support (*or:* prop up) a wall; **2** (*fig*) support, back up: *iem ergens in ~* back up s.o. in sth
²steunen [stønə(n)] *vb* lean (on), rest (on)
steunfraude [stønfraudə] *de (~s)* social security fraud
steunzool [stønzol] *de (-zolen)* arch support
steur [stør] *de (~en)* sturgeon
steven [stevə(n)] *de (~s) (shipp)* stem; stern
¹stevig [stevəχ] *adj* **1** substantial, hearty; **2** robust, hefty, (*fig*) stiff, (*fig*) heavy: *een ~e hoofdpijn* a splitting headache; **3** solid, strong, sturdy; **4** tight, firm: *een ~ pak slaag* a good hiding; **5** substantial, considerable
²stevig [stevəχ] *adv* **1** solidly, strongly: *die ladder staat niet ~* that ladder is a bit wobbly; **2** tightly; firmly: *we moeten er ~ tegenaan gaan* we really need to get (*or:* buckle) down to it
stevigheid [stevəχɛit] *de* sturdiness, strength, solidity
stewardess [scuwardɛs] *de (~en)* stewardess, (air) hostess
stichtelijk [stɪχtələk] *adj, adv* devotional, pious
stichten [stɪχtə(n)] *vb* found, establish: *een gezin ~* start a family
stichter [stɪχtər] *de (~s)* founder
stichting [stɪχtɪŋ] *de (~en)* foundation, establishment
sticker [stɪkɛr] *de (~s)* sticker
stickie [stɪki] *het (~s)* joint, stick
stiefbroer [stivbrur] *de (~s)* stepbrother
stiefdochter [stivdɔχtər] *de (~s)* stepdaughter
stiefkind [stifkɪnt] *het (~eren)* stepchild
stiefmoeder [stifmudər] *de (~s)* stepmother
stiefvader [stifadər] *de (~s)* stepfather
stiefzoon [stifson] *de (~s, -zonen)* stepson
stiefzuster [stifsʏstər] *de (~s)* stepsister
¹stiekem [stikəm] *adj* **1** sneaky; **2** secret
²stiekem [stikəm] *adv* **1** in an underhand way, on the sly; **2** in secret: *iets ~ doen* do sth on the sly; *~ weggaan* steal (*or:* sneak) away
stiekemerd [stikəmərt] *de (~s)* sneak, sly dog
stielman [stilman] *de (~nen) (Belg)* craftsman, skilled worker

stier [stir] *de (~en)* bull

Stier [stir] *de (~en) (astrology)* Taurus

stierengevecht [stirə(n)ɣəvɛχt] *het (~en)* bull-fight

stierlijk [stirlək] *adv* ‖ *ik verveel me* ~ I'm bored stiff *(or:* to tears)

stift [stɪft] *de (~en)* 1 cartridge; 2 felt-tip (pen)

stifttand [stɪftɑnt] *de (~en)* crowned tooth

¹**stijf** [stɛif] *adj* 1 stiff, rigid: ~ *van de kou* numb with cold; 2 stiff, wooden

²**stijf** [stɛif] *adv* 1 stiffly, rigidly: *zij hield het pak* ~ *vast* she held on to the package with all her might; 2 stiffly, formally

stijfheid [stɛifhɛit] *de (-heden)* stiffness

stijfjes [stɛifjəs] *adj, adv* stiff, formal

stijfkop [stɛifkɔp] *de (~pen)* stubborn person, pig-headed person

stijfsel [stɛifsəl] *het, de* paste

stijgbeugel [stɛiɣbøɣəl] *de (~s)* stirrup

stijgen [stɛiɣə(n)] *vb* 1 rise, climb: *een ~de lijn* an upward trend; 2 increase, rise: *de prijzen* (or: *lonen*) ~ prices (or: wages) are rising

stijging [stɛiɣɪŋ] *de (~en)* rise, increase

stijl [stɛil] *de (~en)* 1 style, register: *ambtelijke* ~ officialese; *journalistieke* ~ journalese; *het onderwijs nieuwe* ~ the new style of education; *in de* ~ *van* after the fashion of; 2 post: *dat is geen* ~ that's no way to behave

stijldansen [stɛildɑnsə(n)] *het* ballroom dancing

stijlfiguur [stɛilfiɣyr] *de (-figuren)* figure of speech, trope

stijlloos [stɛilos] *adj, adv* 1 tasteless, lacking in style; 2 ill-mannered

stijlvol [stɛilvɔl] *adj, adv* stylish, fashionable

stik [stɪk] *int* oh heck, oh damn; nuts (to you), get lost

stikdonker [stɪɡdɔŋkər] *adj* pitch-dark, pitch-black

stikken [stɪkə(n)] *vb* 1 suffocate, choke, be stifled: *in iets* ~ choke on sth; ~ *van het lachen* be in stitches; 2 (with *in*) be bursting (with), be up to one's ears (in); 3 drop dead: *iem laten* ~ leave s.o. in the lurch, stand s.o. up; 4 stitch; 5 be full (of), swarm (with): *dit opstel stikt van de fouten* this essay is riddled with errors

stikstof [stɪkstɔf] *de* nitrogen

¹**stil** [stɪl] *adj* 1 quiet, silent; 2 still, motionless; 3 quiet, calm: *de ~le tijd* the slack season, the off season; *Stille Nacht* Silent Night

²**stil** [stɪl] *adv* 1 quietly; 2 still; 3 quietly, calmly

stiletto [stilɛto] *de (~'s)* flick knife, *(Am)* switchblade

¹**stilhouden** [stɪlhɑudə(n)] *vb* 1 keep quiet, hold still; 2 keep quiet, hush up: *zij hielden hun huwelijk stil* they got married in secret

²**stilhouden** [stɪlhɑudə(n)] *vb* stop, pull up

stille [stɪlə] *de (~n)* plain-clothes policeman

stilleggen [stɪlɛɣə(n)] *vb* stop, shut down, close down

stilletjes [stɪləɕəs] *adv* 1 quietly; 2 secretly, on the sly

stilleven [stɪlevə(n)] *het (~s)* still life

stilliggen [stɪlɪɣə(n)] *vb* 1 lie still (or: quiet); 2 lie idle, be idle: *het werk ligt stil* work is at a standstill

stilstaan [stɪlstan] *vb* 1 stand still; pause, come to a standstill: *heb je er ooit bij stilgestaan dat …* has it ever occurred to you that …; 2 stand still, stop, be at a standstill

stilstand [stɪlstɑnt] *de* 1 standstill, stagnation; 2 *(Belg)* stop: *deze trein heeft ~en te Lokeren en te Gent* this train stops at Lokeren and Ghent

stilte [stɪltə] *de* 1 silence, quiet: *een minuut* ~ a minute's silence; *de* ~ *verbreken* break the silence; 2 quiet, privacy, secrecy

stilzetten [stɪlzɛtə(n)] *vb* (bring to a) stop

stilzitten [stɪlzɪtə(n)] *vb* sit still, stand still

stilzwijgend [stɪlzwɛiɣənt] *adj, adv* tacit, understood: ~ *aannemen (veronderstellen) dat …* take (it) for granted that …; *een contract* ~ *verlengen* automatically renew a contract

stimulans [stimylɑns] *de (~en)* stimulus

stimuleren [stimylerə(n)] *vb* stimulate, encourage, boost *(com)*

stimulus [stimylʏs] *de (stimuli)* stimulus, incentive

stinkbom [stɪŋgbɔm] *de (~men)* stink bomb

stinkdier [stɪŋgdir] *het (~en)* skunk

stinken [stɪŋkə(n)] *vb* stink, smell: *uit de mond* ~ have bad breath

stinkend [stɪŋkənt] *adj* stinking, smelly

stip [stɪp] *de (~pen)* 1 dot, speck; 2 *(sport)* (penalty) spot (or: mark)

stippelen [stɪpələ(n)] *vb* dot, speckle

stippellijn [stɪpəlɛin] *de (~en)* dotted line

stipt [stɪpt] *adj, adv* exact, punctual, prompt, strict: ~ *om drie uur* at three o'clock sharp; ~ *op tijd* right on time

stiptheid [stɪptɛit] *de* accuracy, punctuality, promptness, strictness

stiptheidsactie [stɪptɛitsɑksi] *de (~s)* work-to-rule, go-slow, *(Am)* slow-down (strike)

stockeren [stɔkerə(n)] *vb (Belg)* stock

stoeien [stujə(n)] *vb* play around: *met het idee* ~ toy with the idea (of)

stoel [stul] *de (~en)* chair, seat: *een luie (gemakkelijke)* ~ an easy chair; *pak een* ~ take a seat; *de poten onder iemands* ~ *wegzagen* cut the ground from under s.o.'s feet, pull the rug from under s.o.

stoelendans [stulə(n)dɑns] *de (~en)* musical chairs

stoelgang [stulɣɑŋ] *de* (bowel) movement; stool(s)

stoeltjeslift [stulɕəslɪft] *de (~en)* chairlift

stoep [stup] *de (~en)* 1 pavement, *(Am)* sidewalk; 2 (door)step: *onverwachts op de* ~ *staan bij iem* turn up on s.o.'s doorstep

stoeprand [stuprɑnt] *de (~en)* kerb, *(Am)* curb

stoeptegel [stupteɣəl] *de* paving stone

stoer [stur] *adj, adv* 1 sturdy, powerful(ly built); 2 tough

stoet [stut] *de (~en)* procession, parade
stoethaspel [stuthɑspəl] *de (~s)* clumsy person, bungler
¹**stof** [stɔf] *het (~fen)* dust: ~ *afnemen* dust; *in het ~ bijten* bite the dust; *iem in het ~ doen bijten* make s.o. grovel, make s.o. eat dirt
²**stof** [stɔf] *de (~fen)* **1** substance, matter; **2** material, cloth, fabric; **3** (subject) matter, material: ~ *tot nadenken hebben* have food for thought
stofdoek [stɔvduk] *de (~en)* duster, (dust)cloth
stoffelijk [stɔfələk] *adj* material
¹**stoffen** [stɔfə(n)] *adj* cloth, fabric
²**stoffen** [stɔfə(n)] *de* dust
stoffer [stɔfər] *de (~s)* brush: ~ *en blik* dustpan and brush
stofferen [stɔferə(n)] *vb* **1** upholster; **2** *(roughly)* decorate, furnish with carpets and curtains
stoffering [stɔferɪŋ] *de (~en)* soft furnishings, *(Am)* fabrics, cloth, upholstery
stofjas [stɔfjɑs] *de (~sen)* dustcoat, duster
stofwisseling [stɔfwɪsəlɪŋ] *de* metabolism
stofzuigen [stɔfsœyɣə(n)] *vb* vacuum, hoover
stofzuiger [stɔfsœyɣər] *de (~s)* vacuum (cleaner), hoover
stok [stɔk] *de (~ken)* stick, cane: *zij kregen het aan de ~ over de prijs* they fell out over the price
stokbrood [stɔgbrot] *het (-broden)* baguette, French bread
stokdoof [stɔgdof] *adj* stone-deaf, (as) deaf as a post
¹**stoken** [stokə(n)] *vb* **1** stoke (up), feed, light, kindle: *het vuur ~* stoke up the fire; **2** burn; **3** stir up: *ruzie ~* stir up strife; **4** distil
²**stoken** [stokə(n)] *vb* **1** heat; **2** make trouble
stoker [stokər] *de (~s)* **1** fireman, stoker; *(fig)* firebrand, troublemaker; **2** distiller
stokje [stɔkjə] *het (~s)* stick, perch: *ergens een ~ voor steken* put a stop to sth; *van zijn ~ gaan* pass out, faint
stokoud [stɔkɑut] *adj* ancient
stokpaardje [stɔkparcə] *het (~s)* hobbyhorse: *iedereen heeft wel zijn ~* everyone has his fads and fancies
stokstijf [stɔkstɛif] *adj, adv* (as) stiff as a rod, stock-still
stokvis [stɔkfɪs] *de (~sen)* stockfish
stollen [stɔlə(n)] *vb* solidify, coagulate, congeal, set, clot
stolp [stɔlp] *de (~en)* (bell-)glass
stolsel [stɔlsəl] *het (~s)* coagulum, clot
stom [stɔm] *adj* **1** dumb, mute; **2** stupid, dumb: *ik voelde me zo ~* I felt such a fool; *iets ~s doen* do sth stupid
stomdronken [stɔmdrɔŋkə(n)] *adj* dead drunk
¹**stomen** [stomə(n)] *vb* steam
²**stomen** [stomə(n)] *vb* dry-clean: *een pak laten ~* have a suit cleaned
stomerij [stomərɛi] *de (~en)* dry cleaner's
stomheid [stɔmhɛit] *de (-heden)* dumbness, muteness, speechlessness: *met ~ geslagen zijn* be dumbfounded
stommelen [stɔmələ(n)] *vb* stumble
stommeling [stɔmɔlɪŋ] *de (~en)* fool, idiot
stommetje [stɔmɔcə] *het* || ~ *spelen* keep one's mouth shut
stommiteit [stɔmitɛit] *de (~en)* stupidity: ~en *begaan* make stupid mistakes
¹**stomp** [stɔmp] *de (~en)* **1** stump, stub; **2** thump, punch
²**stomp** [stɔmp] *adj* blunt: *een ~e neus* a snub nose
stompen [stɔmpə(n)] *vb* thump, punch
stompzinnig [stɔmpsɪnəχ] *adj, adv* obtuse, dense, stupid: ~ *werk* monotonous (or: stupid) work
stompzinnigheid [stɔmpsɪnəχhɛit] *de* stupidity, denseness, obtuseness
stomtoevallig [stɔmtuvɑləχ] *adv* accidentally; by a (mere) fluke
stomverbaasd [stɔmvərbɑst] *adj, adv* astonished, amazed, flabbergasted
stomvervelend [stɔmvərvelənt] *adj* deadly dull, boring, really annoying: ~ *werk moeten doen* have to do deadly boring work
stomweg [stɔmwɛχ] *adv* simply, just
stoned [stont] *adj* high, stoned
stoof [stof] *de (stoven)* footwarmer
stoofpan [stofpɑn] *de (~nen)* stew(ing)-pan
stoofschotel [stofsχotəl] *de (~s)* stew, casserole
stookkosten [stokɔstə(n)] *de* fuel costs, heating costs
stookolie [stokoli] *de (-oliën)* fuel oil
stookplaat [stokplat] *de (-platen)* grate
stoom [stom] *de* steam: ~ *afblazen* let off steam
stoombad [stombɑt] *het (~en)* steam bath, Turkish bath
stoomboot [stombot] *de (-boten)* steamboat, steamer
stoomcursus [stomkʏrzʏs] *de (~sen)* crash course, intensive course
stoornis [stornɪs] *de (~sen)* disturbance, disorder
stoorzender [storzɛndər] *de (~s)* jammer, jamming station
stoot [stot] *de* thrust, punch, stab, gust: *een ~ onder de gordel* a blow below the belt
stootje [stocə] *het (~s)* thrust, push, nudge: *wel tegen een ~ kunnen* stand rough handling (or: hard wear), be thick-skinned
¹**stop** [stɔp] *de (~pen)* **1** fuse: *alle ~pen sloegen bij hem door* he blew a fuse; **2** stop, break: *een sanitaire ~ maken* stop to go to the bathroom
²**stop** [stɔp] *int* **1** stop!; **2** stop (it)
stopbord [stɔbɔrt] *het (~en)* stop sign
stopcontact [stɔpkɔntɑkt] *het (~en)* (plug-)socket, power point, electric point, outlet
stopgaren [stɔpχarə(n)] *het* mending wool, mending cotton, darning cotton
stoplicht [stɔplɪχt] *het (~en)* traffic light(s)
stopnaald [stɔpnalt] *de (~en)* darning needle
stoppel [stɔpəl] *de (~s)* stubble, bristle

¹**stoppen** [stɔpə(n)] *vb* stop: *stop!* stop!

²**stoppen** [stɔpə(n)] *vb* **1** fill (up), stuff: *een gat ~* fill a hole; **2** put (in(to)): *iets in zijn mond ~* put sth in(to) one's mouth; **3** stop: *de keeper kon de bal niet ~* the goalkeeper couldn't save the ball; **4** darn, mend

stopplaats [stɔplats] *de (~en)* stop, stopping place

stopstreep [stɔpstrep] *de (-strepen)* halt line

stoptrein [stɔptrɛin] *de (~en)* slow train

stopverf [stɔpfɛrf] *de* putty

stopwoord [stɔpwort] *het (~en)* stopgap

stopzetten [stɔpsɛtə(n)] *vb* stop, bring to a standstill *(or:* halt), discontinue; suspend

storen [storə(n)] *vb* **1** disturb, intrude, interrupt, interfere: *de lijn is gestoord* there is a breakdown on the line; *stoor ik u?* am I in your way?, am I interrupting (you)?, am I intruding?; *niet ~!* do not disturb!; *iem in zijn werk ~* disturb s.o. at his work; **2** take notice (of), mind: *zij stoorde er zich niet aan* she took no notice of it

storing [storɪŋ] *de (~en)* **1** disturbance, interruption, trouble, failure, breakdown; **2** interference, static; **3** *(meteorology)* disturbance, depression

storm [stɔrm] *de (~en)* gale; storm: *een ~ in een glas water* a storm in a teacup; *het loopt ~* there is a real run on it

stormachtig [stɔrmɑχtəχ] *adj, adv* **1** stormy, blustery; **2** stormy, tumultuous

stormen [stɔrmə(n)] *vb* storm, rush: *naar voren ~* rush forward *(or:* ahead)

stormloop [stɔrmlop] *de* rush, run

stormram [stɔrmrɑm] *de (~men)* battering-ram

stormvloed [stɔrmvlut] *de (~en)* storm tide, storm flood *(or:* surge)

stort [stɔrt] *het (~en)* dump, tip

stortbak [stɔrdbɑk] *de (~ken)* cistern, tank

stortbui [stɔrdbœy] *de (~en)* downpour, cloudburst

¹**storten** [stɔrtə(n)] *vb* fall, crash: *in elkaar ~: a)* collapse, cave in *(bldg); b)* collapse, crack up

²**storten** [stɔrtə(n)] *vb* **1** throw, dump; **2** pay, deposit: *het gestorte bedrag is …* the sum paid is …

³**storten** [stɔrtə(n)] *ref vb* **1** throw oneself: *zich in de politiek ~* dive into politics; **2** (with *op)* throw oneself (into), dive (into), plunge (into)

storting [stɔrtɪŋ] *de (~en)* payment, deposit

stortkoker [stɔrtkokər] *de (~s)* (garbage) chute *(or:* shoot)

stortplaats [stɔrtplats] *de (~en)* dump, dumping ground *(or:* site)

stortregen [stɔrtreɣə(n)] *de (~s)* downpour

stortregenen [stɔrtreɣənə(n)] *vb* pour (with rain, down)

¹**stoten** [stotə(n)] *vb* bump, knock, hit: *pas op, stoot je hoofd niet* mind your head; *op moeilijkheden ~* run into difficulties

²**stoten** [stotə(n)] *vb* **1** thrust, push: *niet ~!* handle with care!; *een vaas van de kast ~* knock a vase off the sideboard; **2** play *(or:* shoot) (a ball)

³**stoten** [stotə(n)] *ref vb* bump (oneself): *we stootten ons aan de tafel* we bumped into the table

stotteraar [stɔtərar] *de (~s)* stutterer, stammerer

stotteren [stɔtərə(n)] *vb* stutter, stammer

stout [stɑut] *adj, adv* naughty: *~ zijn* misbehave

stouwen [stɑuwə(n)] *vb* stow, cram

stoven [stovə(n)] *vb* stew, simmer

stoverij [stovərɛi] *de (~en)* (Belg) stew

straal [stral] *de (stralen)* **1** beam, ray; **2** jet, trickle; **3** radius: *binnen een ~ van 10 kilometer* within a radius of 10 km

straaljager [straljaɣər] *de (~s)* fighter jet

straalkachel [stralkɑχəl] *de (~s)* electric heater

straalvliegtuig [stralvliχtœyχ] *het (~en)* jet

straat [strat] *de (straten)* street: *een doodlopende ~* dead end street; *de volgende ~ rechts* the next turning to the right; *de ~ opbreken* dig up the street; *op ~ staan* be (out) on the street(s); *drie straten verderop* three streets away

straatarm [stratɑrm] *adj* penniless

straatbende [stradbɛndə] *de* street gang

straathandelaar [strathɑndəlar] *de (~s, -handelaren)* street vendor, pusher, dealer

straathond [strathɔnt] *de (~en)* cur, mutt

straatje [stracə] *het (~s)* alley, lane

straatjongen [stratjɔŋə(n)] *de (~s)* street urchin

straatlantaarn [stratlɑntarn] *de (~s)* street lamp

straatorgel [stratɔrɣəl] *het (~s)* barrel organ

Straatsburg [stratsbʏrχ] *het* Strasbourg

straatsteen [stratsten] *de (-stenen)* paving brick

straatventer [stratfɛntər] *de (~s)* vendor

straatvuil [stratfœyl] *het* street refuse *(or Am:* garbage)

¹**straf** [strɑf] *de (~fen)* punishment, penalty: *een zware* (or: *lichte) ~* a heavy *(or:* light) punishment; *een ~ ondergaan* pay the penalty; *zijn ~ ontlopen* get off scot-free; *voor ~* for punishment

²**straf** [strɑf] *adj, adv* stiff, severe: *~fe taal* hard words

strafbaar [strɑvbar] *adj* punishable: *een ~ feit* an offence, a punishable *(or:* penal) act; *dat is ~* that's an offence; *iets ~ stellen* attach a penalty to sth, make sth punishable

strafbank [strɑvbɑŋk] *de* **1** dock: *op het ~je zitten* be in the dock; **2** *(sport)* penalty box *(or:* bench)

strafblad [strɑvblɑt] *het* police record, record of convictions *(or:* offences)

strafcorner [strɑfkɔːrnər] *de (~s)* penalty corner

straffen [strɑfə(n)] *vb* punish, penalize

strafport [strɑfpɔrt] *het, de* surcharge

strafpunt [strɑfpʏnt] *het (~en)* penalty point: *een ~ geven* award a penalty point

strafrecht [strɑfrɛχt] *het* criminal law, criminal justice

strafrechtelijk [strɑfrɛχtələk] *adj, adv* criminal: *iem ~ vervolgen* prosecute s.o.

strafschop [strɑfsχɔp] *de (~pen)* penalty (kick), spot kick

strafschopgebied [strɑfsχɔpχəbit] *het (~en)* penalty area, penalty box

strafwerk [strɑfwɛrk] *het* lines, (school) punishment: ~ *maken* do (*or:* write) lines, do impositions (*or:* an imposition)

strafworp [strɑfwɔrp] *de (~en)* penalty throw; foul shot

strak [strɑk] *adj, adv* **1** tight, taut: *iem* ~ *houden* keep s.o. on a tight rein; ~ *trekken* stretch, pull tight; **2** fixed, set, intent; **3** fixed, set, stern, tense

strakblauw [strɑgblɑu] *adj* clear blue, sheer blue, cloudless

straks [strɑks] *adv* later, soon, next: ~ *meer hierover* I'll return to this later; *tot* ~ so long, see you later (*or:* soon)

stralen [strɑlə(n)] *vb* **1** radiate, beam; **2** shine, beam, radiate

stralend [strɑlənt] *adj, adv* **1** radiant, brilliant, (*stronger*) dazzling; **2** radiant, beaming; **3** glorious, splendid

straling [strɑlɪŋ] *de (~en)* radiation

stram [strɑm] *adj, adv* stiff, rigid

strand [strɑnt] *het (~en)* beach, seaside

stranden [strɑndə(n)] *vb* **1** be cast (*or:* washed) ashore; run aground (*or:* ashore), be stranded; **2** fail: *een plan laten* ~ wreck a project; **3** be stranded

strandhuisje [strɑnthœyʃə] *het (~s)* beach cabin

strandjutter [strɑntjʏtər] *de (~s)* beachcomber, wrecker

strandstoel [strɑntstul] *de (~en)* deck chair

strandwandeling [strɑntwɑndəlɪŋ] *de (~en)* walk on (*or:* along) the beach

strateeg [stratex] *de (strategen)* strategist

strategie [strateɣi] *de (~ën)* strategy

strategisch [strateɣis] *adj, adv* strategic

stratengids [stratə(n)ɣɪts] *de (~en)* street map (*or:* plan), A to Z

stratenmaker [stratə(n)makər] *de (~s)* paviour, road worker, road mender

stratosfeer [stratosfer] *de* stratosphere

streber [strebər] *de (~s)* careerist, (social) climber

streefgetal [strefxətɑl] *het (~len)* target number (*or:* figure)

streek [strek] *de (streken)* **1** trick, prank, antic, caper: *een stomme* ~ *uithalen* do sth silly; **2** region, area: *in deze* ~ in these parts (*or:* this part) of the country; **3** stroke: *van* ~ *zijn: a)* be out of sorts; *b)* be upset, be in a dither; *c)* be upset, be out of order

streekbus [stregbʏs] *de (~sen)* regional (*or:* county, country) bus

streekroman [strekromɑn] *de (~s)* regional novel

streep [strep] *de (strepen)* **1** line, score, mark(ing); **2** stripe, line, band, bar, streak: *iem over de* ~ *trekken* win s.o. over; **3** stripe, chevron

streepje [strepjə] *het (~s)* thin line, narrow line; hyphen; dash; slash

streepjescode [strepjəskodə] *de (~s)* bar code

¹strekken [strɛkə(n)] *vb* **1** extend, stretch, go; **2** last, go

²strekken [strɛkə(n)] *vb* stretch, unbend, extend, straighten

strekking [strɛkɪŋ] *de (~en)* import, tenor, purport, purpose, intent, effect: *de* ~ *van het verhaal* the drift of the story

strelen [strɛlə(n)] *vb* caress, stroke, fondle

streling [strɛlɪŋ] *de (~en)* caress

stremmen [strɛmə(n)] *vb* block, obstruct

¹streng [strɛŋ] *de (~en)* **1** twist, twine, skein, hank; **2** strand

²streng [strɛŋ] *adj, adv* **1** severe, hard: *het vriest* ~ there's a sharp frost; **2** severe, strict, stringent, rigid; harsh: *~e eisen* stern demands; *een ~e onderwijzer* a stern (*or:* strict) teacher

strepen [strepə(n)] *vb* line, streak, stripe

stress [strɛs] *de* stress, strain

stressen [strɛsə(n)] *vb* work under stress

stretch [strɛtʃ] *het* stretchy material (*or:* fabric), elastic

stretcher [strɛtʃər] *de (~s)* stretcher

¹streven [strevə(n)] *het* **1** striving (for), pursuit (of), endeavour: *het* ~ *naar onafhankelijkheid* the pursuit of independence; **2** ambition, aspiration, aim

²streven [strevə(n)] *vb* strive (for, after), aspire (after, to), aim (at): *je doel voorbij* ~ defeat your object

striem [strim] *de (~en)* slash, score, weal, welt

strijd [strɛit] *de* **1** fight, struggle, combat, battle: *hevige (zware)* ~ fierce battle (*or:* struggle, fighting), battle royal; ~ *leveren* wage a fight, put up a fight (*or:* struggle); *de* ~ *om het bestaan* the struggle for life; **2** strife, dispute, controversy, conflict: *innerlijke* ~ inner struggle (*or:* conflict); *in* ~ *met de wet* against the law

strijdbijl [strɛidbɛil] *de (~en)* battle-axe; tomahawk: *de* ~ *begraven* bury the hatchet

strijden [strɛidə(n)] *vb* **1** struggle, fight, wage war (against, on), battle; **2** compete, contend

strijder [strɛidər] *de (~s)* fighter, warrior, combatant

strijdig [strɛidəx] *adj* **1** contrary (to), adverse (to), inconsistent (with); **2** conflicting, incompatible (with)

strijdkrachten [strɛitkrɑxtə(n)] *de* (armed) forces (*or:* services)

strijdkreet [strɛitkret] *de (-kreten)* battle cry, war cry

strijdlustig [strɛitlʏstəx] *adj* pugnacious, combative, militant

strijdperk [strɛitpɛrk] *het (~en)* arena

strijkbout [strɛigbaut] *de (~en)* iron

¹strijken [strɛikə(n)] *vb* brush, sweep ‖ *met de eer gaan* ~ carry off the palm (for), take the credit (for)

²strijken [strɛikə(n)] *vb* **1** smooth, spread, brush; **2** stroke, brush; **3** iron

strijkijzer [strɛikɛizər] *het (~s)* iron, flat-iron

strijkinstrument [strɛikɪnstrymɛnt] *het (~en)* stringed instrument: *de ~en* the strings

strijkorkest [strɛikɔrkɛst] *het (~en)* string orchestra

strijkplank [strɛikplɑŋk] *de (~en)* ironing board

strijkstok [strɛikstɔk] *de (~ken)* bow || *er blijft veel aan de ~ hangen* the rake-off is considerable
strik [strɪk] *de (~ken)* **1** bow; **2** snare, trap
strikje [strɪkjə] *het (~s)* bow tie
strikken [strɪkə(n)] *vb* **1** tie in a bow: *zijn das ~ knot a tie*; **2** snare; **3** trap (into)
strikt [strɪkt] *adj, adv* strict, stringent, rigorous: *~ vertrouwelijk* strictly confidential
strikvraag [strɪkfraχ] *de (-vragen)* catch question, trick question
strip [strɪp] *de (~s, ~pen)* **1** strip, slip, band; **2** comic strip, (strip) cartoon
stripboek [strɪbuk] *het (~en)* comic (book)
stripfiguur [strɪpfiɣyr] *de (-figuren)* comic(-strip) character
stripheld [strɪphɛlt] *de (~en)* comic(-strip) hero
strippen [strɪpə(n)] *vb* strip
strippenkaart [strɪpə(n)kart] *de (~en) (roughly)* bus and tram card
stripteasedanseres [strɪpti:zdɑnsərɛs] *de (~sen)* striptease dancer (*or:* artist), stripper
striptekenaar [strɪptekənar] *de (~s)* strip cartoonist
stripverhaal [strɪpfərhal] *het (-verhalen)* comic (strip)
stro [stro] *het* straw
strobloem [strɔblum] *de (~en)* strawflower, everlasting (flower)
stroef [struf] *adj, adv* **1** rough, uneven; **2** stiff, difficult, awkward, jerky, brusque, tight; **3** stiff, staid, awkward, stern, difficult (to get on with), remote, reserved, stand-offish
strohalm [strɔhɑlm] *de (~en)* (stalk of) straw: *zich aan een (laatste) ~ vastklampen* clutch at a straw (*or:* at straws)
stroman [strɔmɑn] *de (~nen)* straw man, man of straw, puppet, figurehead
stromen [strɔmə(n)] *vb* **1** stream, pour, flow: *een snel ~de rivier* a fast-flowing river; **2** pour, flock
stroming [strɔmɪŋ] *de (~en)* **1** current, flow; **2** movement, trend, tendency
strompelen [strɔmpələ(n)] *vb* stumble, totter, limp
stronk [strɔŋk] *de (~en)* **1** stump, stub; **2** stalk
stront [strɔnt] *de* shit, dung, filth: *er is ~ aan de knikker* the shit has hit the fan, we're in the shit
strooibiljet [strɔjbɪljɛt] *het (~ten)* handbill, pamphlet, leaflet
¹strooien [strɔjə(n)] *vb* scatter; strew; sow; sprinkle; dredge: *zand (pekel) ~ bij gladheid* grit icy roads
²strooien [strɔjə(n)] *adj* straw: *een ~ dak* a thatched roof, a thatch
strooizand [strɔjzɑnt] *het* (road) grit
strook [strok] *de (stroken)* **1** strip, band; **2** strip, slip, label, tag, stub, counterfoil
stroom [strom] *de (stromen)* **1** stream, flow, current, flood: *de zwemmer werd door de ~ meegesleurd* the swimmer was swept away by the current (*or:* tide); **2** stream, flood: *een ~ goederen* a flow of

goods; *er kwam een ~ van klachten binnen* complaints came pouring in; **3** (electric) power, (electric) current: *er staat ~ op die draad* that is a live wire
stroomafwaarts [stromɑfwarts] *adj, adv* downstream, downriver
stroomdraad [stromdrat] *de* live wire, contact wire, electric wire
stroomlijnen [stromlɛinə(n)] *vb* streamline
stroomopwaarts [stromɔpwarts] *adj, adv* upstream, upriver
stroomschema [stromsχema] *het* flow chart (*or:* sheet, diagram)
stroomstoot [stromstot] *de (-stoten)* (current) surge, pulse, transient
stroomstoring [stromstorɪŋ] *de (~en)* electricity failure, power failure
stroomuitval [stromœytfɑl] *de* power failure
stroomverbruik [stromvərbrœyk] *het* electricity consumption, power consumption
stroomversnelling [stromvərsnɛlɪŋ] *de (~en)* rapid: *in een ~ geraken* gain momentum, develop (*or:* move) rapidly, be accelerated
stroop [strop] *de (stropen)* syrup, treacle: *~ (om iemands mond) smeren* butter s.o. up, softsoap s.o.
stroopwafel [strɔpwafəl] *de (~s)* treacle waffle
strop [strɔp] *de (~pen)* **1** halter, (hangman's) rope, noose, snare, trap; **2** bad luck, tough luck, raw deal, financial blow (*or:* setback), loss
stropdas [strɔbdɑs] *de (~sen)* tie
stropen [strɔpə(n)] *vb* **1** skin; **2** poach
stroper [strɔpər] *de (~s)* poacher
stroperij [strɔpərɛi] *de (~en)* poaching
strot [strɔt] *de (~ten)* throat, gullet: *het komt me de ~ uit* I'm sick of it; *ik krijg het niet door mijn ~* I couldn't eat it to save my life, the words stick in my throat
strottenhoofd [strɔtə(n)hoft] *het (~en)* larynx
structureel [strʏktyrel] *adj, adv* structural; constructional
structureren [strʏktyrerə(n)] *vb* structure, structuralize
structuur [strʏktyr] *de (structuren)* structure, texture, fabric
structuurverf [strʏktyrvɛrf] *de (-verven)* cement paint
struif [strœyf] *de (struiven)* (contents of an) egg
struik [strœyk] *de (~en)* **1** bush, shrub; **2** bunch; head
struikelblok [strœykəlblɔk] *het (~ken)* stumbling block, obstacle
struikelen [strœykələ(n)] *vb* stumble (over), trip (over)
struikgewas [strœykχəwɑs] *het (~sen)* bushes, shrubs, brushwood
struikrover [strœykrovər] *de (~s)* highwayman, footpad
struisvogel [strœysfoɣəl] *de (~s)* ostrich
struisvogelpolitiek [strœysfoɣəlpolitik] *de* ostrich

policy: *een ~ volgen* refuse to face facts, bury one's head in the sand

stucwerk [stykwɛrk] *het* stucco(work)

stucwerker [stykwɛrkər] *de (~s)* plasterer

student [stydɛnt] *de (~en)* student, undergraduate, (post)graduate: *~ Turks* student of Turkish

studentenbeweging [stydɛntə(n)bəweɣɪŋ] *de* student movement

studentencorps [stydɛntə(n)kɔːr] *het (-corpora) (roughly)* student(s') union

studentenflat [stydɛntə(n)flɛt] *de (~s)* (block of) student flats, *(roughly)* hall of residence, student apartments

studententijd [stydɛntə(n)tɛit] *de (~en)* college days, student days

studentenvereniging [stydɛntə(n)vərenəɣɪŋ] *de (~en) (roughly)* student union

studeren [stydɛrə(n)] *vb* **1** study, go to *(or:* be at) university/college: *Marijke studeert* Marijke is at university *(or:* college); *oude talen ~* read classics; *hij studeert nog* he is still studying *(or:* at college); *verder ~* continue one's studies; *~ voor een examen* study *(or:* revise) for an exam; **2** practise (music): *piano ~* practise the piano

studie [stydi] *de (~s)* study: *met een ~ beginnen* take up a (course of) study

studiebegeleiding [stydibəɣəlɛidɪŋ] *de (~en)* tutoring, coaching

studiebeurs [stydibørs] *de (-beurzen)* grant

studieboek [stydibuk] *het (~en)* textbook, manual

studiebol [stydibɔl] *de (~len)* bookworm, scholar

studiefinanciering [stydifinɑnsirɪŋ] *de* student grant(s)

studiegids [stydiɣɪts] *de (~en)* prospectus, *(Am)* catalog

studiehuis [stydihœys] *het (-huizen)* **1** space in secondary school for private study; **2** educational reform stimulating private study

studiejaar [stydijar] *het (-jaren)* (school) year, university year, academic year

studiekosten [stydikɔstə(n)] *de* cost(s) of studying, university expenses, college expenses

studiemeester [stydimestər] *de (~s) (Belg) (roughly)* supervisor

studieprogramma [stydiproɣrɑma] *het (~'s)* course programme, study programme, syllabus

studiepunt [stydipynt] *het, de (~en)* credit

studiereis [stydirɛis] *de (-reizen)* study tour *(or:* trip)

studierichting [stydirɪχtɪŋ] *de (~en)* subject, course(s), discipline, branch of study *(or:* studies)

studietoelage [styditulaɣə] *de (~n)* scholarship, (study) grant

studieverlof [stydivərlɔf] *het (-verloven)* study leave, sabbatical (leave)

studiezaal [stydizal] *de (-zalen)* reading room

studio [stydijo] *de (~'s)* studio

stuff [styf] *de* dope, stuff; pot; grass, weed

stug [styχ] *adj, adv* **1** stiff, tough; **2** surly, dour, stiff

|| *~ doorwerken* work *(or:* slog) away

stuifmeel [stœyfmel] *het* pollen

stuip [stœyp] *de (~en)* convulsion, *(small)* twitch; fit, spasm: *iem de ~en op het lijf jagen* scare s.o. stiff, scare the (living) daylights out of s.o.

stuiptrekken [stœyptrɛkə(n)] *vb* convulse, be convulsed, become convulsed

stuiptrekking [stœyptrɛkɪŋ] *de (~en)* convulsion, spasm, *(small)* twitch

stuitbeen [stœydben] *het (~deren)* tailbone, coccyx

stuiten [stœytə(n)] *vb* **1** encounter, happen upon, chance upon, stumble across; **2** meet with, run up against; **3** bounce, bound

stuiter [stœytər] *de (~s)* big marble, taw, bonce

stuiteren [stœytərə(n)] *vb* play at marbles

stuitje [stœycə] *het* tail bone

stuiven [stœyvə(n)] *vb* **1** blow, fly about, fly up; **2** dash, rush, whiz || *(Belg) het zal er ~* there'll be a proper dust-up

stuiver [stœyvər] *de (~s)* five-cent piece

¹stuk [styk] *het (~ken)* **1** piece, part, fragment, lot, length: *iets in ~ken snijden* cut sth up (into pieces); *uit één ~ vervaardigd* made in *(or:* of) one piece; **2** piece, item: *een ~ gereedschap* a piece of equipment, a tool; *per ~ verkopen* sell by the piece, sell singly; *twintig ~s vee* twenty head of cattle; *een ~ of tien appels* about ten apples, ten or so apples; **3** (postal) article, (postal) item; **4** piece, article; **5** document, paper; **6** piece, picture; **7** piece, play; **8** piece, chessman, draughtsman: *iem van zijn ~ brengen* unsettle *(or:* unnerve, disconcert) s.o.; *een ~ in de kraag hebben* be tight *(or:* plastered); *(Belg) op het ~ van ...* as far as ... is concerned, as for ...

²stuk [styk] *adj* **1** apart, to pieces; **2** out of order, broken down, bust: *iets ~ maken* break *(or:* ruin) sth

stukadoor [stykadɔr] *de (~s)* plasterer

stuken [stykə(n)] *vb* plaster

stukgaan [stykχan] *vb* break down, fail, break to pieces

stukje [stykjə] *het (~s)* **1** small piece, little bit: *~ bij beetje* bit by bit, inch by inch; **2** short piece

stukprijs [stykprɛis] *de (-prijzen)* unit price

stulp [stylp] *de (~en)* **1** hovel, hut; **2** bell-glass

stumper [stympər] *de (~s)* wretch

stunt [stynt] *de (~s)* stunt, tour de force, feat

stuntelen [styntələ(n)] *vb* bungle, flounder

stunten [styntə(n)] *vb* stunt

stuntman [styntmɑn] *de (~nen)* stunt man

stuntprijs [styntprɛis] *de (-prijzen)* incredibly *(or:* record) low price, price breakers

stuntvliegen [styntfliɣə(n)] *vb* stunt flying, aerobatics

stuntwerk [styntwɛrk] *het* stuntwork

sturen [styrə(n)] *vb* **1** steer; drive; guide; **2** send, forward *(goods);* dispatch, address: *van school ~* expel (from school)

stut [styt] *de (~ten)* prop, stay, support

stutten [stytə(n)] *vb* prop (up), support

stuur [styr] *het (sturen)* steering wheel, *(car)* wheel, *(shipp)* helm, rudder, controls; handlebars: *aan het ~ zitten* be at (*or:* behind) the wheel; *de macht over het ~ verliezen* lose control (of one's car, bike)

stuurboord [styrbort] *het* starboard

stuurcabine [styrkabinə] *de (~s)* cockpit

stuurknuppel [styrknʏpəl] *de (~s)* control stick (*or:* lever), (joy) stick

stuurloos [styrlos] *adj, adv* out of control, rudderless, adrift

stuurman [styrmɑn] *de (stuurlui)* 1 mate; 2 *(sport)* helmsman, cox(swain)

stuurs [styrs] *adj, adv* surly, sullen

stuurslot [styrslɔt] *het (~en)* steering wheel lock

stuurwiel [styrwil] *het (~en)* (steering) wheel; control wheel, *(shipp)* helm

stuw [styw] *de (~en)* dam, barrage, flood-control dam

stuwadoor [stywadǫr] *de (~s)* stevedore

stuwdam [stywdɑm] *de (~men)* dam, barrage, flood-control dam

stuwen [stywə(n)] *vb* 1 drive, push, force, propel, impel; 2 stow, pack, load

stuwkracht [stywkrɑχt] *de (~en)* force, drive, thrust

stuwmeer [stywmer] *het (-meren)* (storage) reservoir

stylist [stilɪst] *de (~en)* stylist

subcultuur [sʏpkʏltyr] *de (subculturen)* subculture, (the) underground

subjectief [sʏpjɛktif] *adj, adv* subjective, personal

subjectiviteit [sʏpjɛktivitɛit] *de* subjectivity

subliem [syblim] *adj, adv* sublime; fantastic, super

subsidie [sʏpsidi] *het, de (~s)* subsidy, (financial) aid, grant, allowance: *een ~ geven voor* grant a subsidy for

subsidiëren [sʏpsidijerə(n)] *vb* subsidize, grant (an amount)

substantie [sʏpstɑnsi] *de (~s)* substance, matter

subtiel [sʏptil] *adj, adv* subtle, sophisticated, delicate

subtopper [sʏptɔpər] *de (~s)* sub-world-class player

subtotaal [sʏptotal] *het (subtotalen)* subtotal

subtropisch [sʏptropis] *adj* subtropical

succes [sʏksɛs] *het (~sen)* success, luck: *een goedkoop ~je boeken* score a cheap success; *veel ~ toegewenst!* good luck!; *~ met je rijexamen!* good luck with your driving test!; *een groot ~ zijn* be a big success, be a hit

succesnummer [sʏksɛsnʏmər] *het (~s)* hit

succesvol [sʏksɛsfɔl] *adj, adv* successful

sudderen [sʏdərə(n)] *vb* simmer

¹**suède** [sywɛːdə] *de, het* suede

²**suède** [sywɛːdə] *adj* suede

Suezkanaal [sywɛskanal] *het* Suez Canal

suf [sʏf] *adj, adv* drowsy, dozy, dopey, groggy

suffen [sʏfə(n)] *vb* nod, (day)dream

sufferd [sʏfərt] *de (~s)* dope, fathead

suggereren [sʏɣərerə(n)] *vb* suggest, imply

suggestie [sʏɣɛsti] *de (~s)* suggestion, proposal: *een ~ doen* make a suggestion (*or:* proposal)

suiker [sœykər] *de (~s)* sugar: *~ doen in* put sugar in

suikerbiet [sœykərbit] *de (~en)* sugar beet

suikerfabriek [sœykərfabrik] *de (~en)* sugar refinery

suikerklontje [sœykərklɔncə] *het (~s)* lump of sugar, sugar cube

suikeroom [sœykərom] *de (~s)* rich uncle

suikerpatiënt [sœykərpaʃɛnt] *de (~en)* diabetic

suikerpot [sœykərpɔt] *de (~ten)* sugar bowl

suikerriet [sœykərit] *het* sugar cane

suikerspin [sœykərspɪn] *de (~nen)* candy floss, *(Am)* cotton candy

suikertante [sœykərtɑntə] *de (~s)* rich aunt

suikervrij [sœykərvrɛi] *adj* sugarless, diabetic, low-sugar

suikerzakje [sœykərzɑkjə] *het (~s)* sugar bag

suikerziek [sœykərzik] *adj* diabetic

suikerziekte [sœykərziktə] *de* diabetes

suite [switə] *de (~s)* suite (of rooms)

suizen [sœyzə(n)] *vb* rustle, sing, whisper

sukade [sykadə] *de* candied peel

sukkel [sʏkəl] *de (~s)* dope, idiot, twerp

sukkelaar [sʏkəlar] *de (~s)* wretch, poor soul (*or:* beggar)

sukkelen [sʏkələ(n)] *vb* be ailing, be sickly, suffer (from sth): *hij sukkelt met zijn gezondheid* he is in bad health

sukkelgangetje [sʏkəlɣɑŋəcə] *het* jog(trot), shambling gait

sul [sʏl] *de (~len)* softy, sucker

sulky [sʏlki] *de (~'s)* sulky

sultan [sʏltɑn] *de (~s)* sultan

summier [sʏmir] *adj, adv* summary, brief

super [sypər] *adj, adv* super, great, first class

superbenzine [sypərbɛnzinə] *de* 4 star petrol, *(Am)* high octane gas(oline)

superette [sypərɛtə] *de (~s) (Belg)* small self-service shop

supergeleiding [sypərɣəlɛidɪŋ] *de (~en)* superconductivity

superieur [syperijør] *de (~en)* superior

supermacht [sypərmɑχt] *de (~en)* superpower

supermarkt [sypərmɑrkt] *de (~en)* supermarket

supermens [sypərmɛns] *de (~en)* superman, superwoman

supersonisch [sypərsonis] *adj* supersonic

supervisie [sypərvizi] *de* supervision

supplement [sypləmɛnt] *het (~en)* supplement

suppoost [sypǫst] *de (~en)* attendant

supporter [sypɔrtər] *de (~s)* supporter

supportersbus [sypɔrtərzbʏs] *de* supporters' special (bus, coach)

supporterstrein [sypɔrtərstrɛin] *de* supporters' special (train)

surfen [sy:rfə(n)] *vb* 1 be surfing (*or:* surfboard-

ing); windsurfing; **2** *(comp)* surf
surfer [sy̆:rfər] *de (~s)* surfer; windsurfer
surfplank [sy̆:rfplɑŋk] *de (~en)* surfboard; sailboard
Surinaams [syrinɑms] *adj* Surinamese, Surinam (+ *noun*)
Suriname [syrinɑmə] *het* Surinam
Surinamer [syrinɑmər] *de (~s)* Surinamese
surprise [syrpriːzə] *de (~s)* surprise (gift)
surrealisme [syrejalɪsmə] *het* surrealism
surrealistisch [syrejalɪstis] *adj, adv* surrealist(ic)
surrogaat [syroɣɑt] *het (surrogaten)* surrogate
surveillance [syrvɛiɑsə] *de* surveillance, supervision, duty
surveillancewagen [syrvɛiɑsəwaɣə(n)] *de (~s)* patrol car
surveillant [syrvɛiɑnt] *de (~en)* supervisor, observer, invigilator
surveilleren [syrvɛierə(n)] *vb* supervise, invigilate, (be on) patrol
sussen [sysə(n)] *vb* soothe, pacify *(pers)*, ease, hush up
s.v.p. [ɛsfepe] *s'il vous plaît* please
swastika [swɑstika] *de (~'s)* swastika
Swaziland [swɑzilɑnt] *het* Swaziland
sweater [swɛtər] *de (~s)* sweater, jersey
sweatshirt [swɛtʃy̆:rt] *het (~s)* sweatshirt
swingen [swɪŋə(n)] *vb* swing
syfilis [sifɪlɪs] *de* syphilis
symboliek [sɪmbolik] *de (~en)* symbolism
symbolisch [sɪmbolis] *adj, adv* symbolic(al): *een ~ bedrag* a nominal amount
symboliseren [sɪmbolizerə(n)] *vb* symbolize, represent
symbool [sɪmbol] *het (symbolen)* symbol
symfonie [sɪmfoni] *de (~ën)* symphony
symfonieorkest [sɪmfoniɔrkɛst] *het (~en)* symphony orchestra
symmetrie [sɪmetri] *de* symmetry
symmetrisch [sɪmetris] *adj, adv* symmetrical
sympathie [sɪmpati] *de (~ën)* sympathy, feeling: *zijn ~ betuigen* express one's sympathy
sympathiek [sɪmpatik] *adj, adv* sympathetic, likable, congenial: *ik vind hem erg ~* I like him very much; *~ staan tegenover iem (iets)* be sympathetic to(wards) s.o. (sth)
symptomatisch [sɪmtomatis] *adj, adv* symptomatic
symptoom [sɪmtom] *het (symptomen)* symptom, sign: *een ~ zijn van* be symptomatic (*or:* a symptom) of
synagoge [sinaɣoɣə] *de (~n)* synagogue
synchronisatie [sɪŋχroniza(t)si] *de (~s)* synchronization
synchroon [sɪŋχron] *adj, adv* synchronous, synchronic
syndicaat [sɪndikɑt] *het (syndicaten)* syndicate
syndroom [sɪndrom] *het (syndromen)* syndrome
¹**synoniem** [sinonim] *het (~en)* synonym

²**synoniem** [sinonim] *adj* synonymous (with)
syntactisch [sɪntɑktis] *adj, adv* syntactic(al)
syntaxis [sɪntɑksɪs] *de* syntax
synthese [sɪntezə] *de (~n, ~s)* synthesis
synthesizer [sɪntəsɑjzər] *de (~s)* synthesizer
synthetisch [sɪntetis] *adj, adv* synthetic, man-made
Syrië [sirijə] *het* Syria
Syriër [sirijər] *de (~s)* Syrian
¹**Syrisch** [siris] *het* Syrian
²**Syrisch** [siris] *adj* Syrian
systeem [sistem] *het (systemen)* system, method: *daar zit geen ~ in* there is no system (*or:* method) in it; *(socc) spelen volgens het 4-3-3-systeem* play in the 4-3-3 line-up
systeembeheerder [sistembəherdər] *de (~s)* system manager
systematisch [sistematis] *adj, adv* systematic, methodical: *een ~ overzicht* a systematic survey

t

taai [taj] *adj, adv* tough; hardy: *~ vlees* tough meat; *houd je ~: a)* take care (of yourself); *b) (Am)* hang in there; *c)* chin up

taaitaai [tajtaj] *het, de* gingerbread

taak [tak] *de (taken)* **1** task, job, duty, responsibility, assignment: *een zware ~ op zich nemen* undertake an arduous task; *het is niet mijn ~ dat te doen* it is not my place to do that; *iem een ~ opgeven (opleggen)* set s.o. a task; *tot ~ hebben* have as one's duty; *niet voor zijn ~ berekend zijn* be unequal to one's task; **2** *(educ)* assignment

taakleerkracht [taklerkraχt] *de (~en)* remedial teacher

taakleraar [taklerar] *de (-leraren, ~s) (Belg)* remedial teacher

taakomschrijving [takomsχrɛiviŋ] *de (~en)* job description

taakstraf [takstraf] *de (~fen)* community service

taakuur [takyr] *het (-uren)* non-teaching period, free period

taakverdeling [takfərdeliŋ] *de* division of tasks *(or:* labour)

taal [tal] *de (talen)* **1** language, speech, language skills: *vreemde talen* foreign languages; **2** language: *gore ~ uitslaan* use foul language; *de ~ van het lichaam* body language

taalbarrière [talbar(i)jɛːrə] *de (~s)* language barrier

taalfout [talfaut] *de (~en)* language error

taalgebruik [talɣəbrœyk] *het* (linguistic) usage, language

taalkunde [talkyndə] *de* linguistics

taalkundig [talkyndəχ] *adj, adv* linguistic: *~ ontleden* parse

taallab [talap] *het (~s) (Belg)* language laboratory

taalvaardigheid [talvardəχɛit] *de* language proficiency, *(as school subject)* (Dutch) language skills

taalwetenschap [talwetə(n)sχap] *de* linguistics

taart [tart] *de (~en)* cake, pie, tart

taartje [tarcə] *het (~s)* a (piece of) cake; a tart *(or:* pie)

tabak [tabɑk] *de* tobacco

tabaksartikel [tabɑksartikəl] *het (~en)* tobacco product

tabaksrook [tabɑksrok] *de* tobacco smoke, cigar smoke

tabaksvergunning [tabɑksfərɣynɪŋ] *de (~en)* licence to sell tobacco

tabel [tabɛl] *de (~len)* table

tabernakel [tabərnakəl] *het, de (~s)* tabernacle

tablet [tablɛt] *het, de (~ten)* tablet, bar: *een ~je innemen tegen de hoofdpijn* take a pill for one's headache

¹taboe [tabu] *het (~s)* taboo

²taboe [tabu] *adj* taboo: *iets ~ verklaren* pronounce sth taboo

taboeret [taburɛt] *het (~ten)* tabouret

tachtig [tɑχtəχ] *num* eighty: *mijn oma is ~ (jaar oud)* my grandmother is eighty (years old); *de jaren ~* the eighties; *in de ~ zijn* be in one's eighties

tachtigjarig [tɑχtəχjarəχ] *adj* **1** eighty-year-old: *een ~e* an eighty-year-old; **2** eighty years'

tachtigste [tɑχtəχstə] *num* eightieth

tackelen [tɛkələ(n)] *vb (sport)* tackle

tact [tɑkt] *de* tact: *iets met ~ regelen* use tact in dealing with sth

tactiek [tɑktik] *de* tactics, strategy: *dat is niet de juiste ~ om zoiets te regelen* that is not the way to go about such a thing; *van ~ veranderen* change (*or:* alter) one's tactics

tactisch [tɑktis] *adj, adv* tactical; tactful: *iets ~ aanpakken* set about sth tactically (*or:* shrewdly)

tactvol [tɑktfɔl] *adj, adv* tactful

Tadzjikistan [tɑdʒikistɑn] *het* Tadzhikistan

tafel [tafəl] *de (~s)* table: *de ~s van vermenigvuldiging* the multiplication tables; *de ~ afruimen* (*or:* dekken) clear (*or:* lay) the table; *aan ~ gaan* sit down to dinner; *om de ~ gaan zitten* sit down at the table (and start talking); *iem onder ~ drinken* drink s.o. under the table; *het ontbijt staat op ~* breakfast is on the table (*or:* ready); *ter ~ komen* come up (for discussion); *van ~ gaan* leave the table

tafelkleed [tafəlklet] *het (-kleden)* tablecloth

tafelpoot [tafəlpot] *de (-poten)* table-leg

tafeltennissen [tafəltɛnɪsə(n)] *vb* play table tennis

tafeltennisser [tafəltɛnɪsər] *de (~s)* table-tennis player

tafelvoetbal [tafəlvudbal] *het* table football

tafelwijn [tafəlwɛin] *de (~en)* table wine

tafelzilver [tafəlzɪlvər] *het* silver cutlery, silverware

tafereel [tafərel] *het (taferelen)* tableau, scene

taille [tɑjə] *de (~s)* waist: *een dunne ~ hebben* have a slender waist

Taiwan [tajwɑn] *het* Taiwan

tak [tɑk] *de (~ken)* branch, fork, section: *een ~ van sport* a branch of sports; *de wandelende ~* the stick insect, *(Am)* the walking stick

takel [takəl] *het, de (~s)* tackle: *in de ~s hangen* be in the sling

takelen [takələ(n)] *vb* hoist: *een auto uit de sloot ~* hoist a car (up) out of the ditch

takelwagen [takəlwaɣə(n)] *de (~s)* breakdown lorry, *(Am)* tow truck

takenpakket [takə(n)pakɛt] *het* job responsibilities (in a job)

taks [tɑks] *de (~en)* regular (*or:* usual) amount, share

tal [tɑl] *het* number: ~ *van voorbeelden* numbers of (*or:* numerous) examples

talenknobbel [tɑlə(n)knɔbəl] *de* linguistic talent, gift (*or:* feel) for languages

talenpracticum [tɑlə(n)prɑktikʏm] *het (-practica)* language lab(oratory)

talent [tɑlɛnt] *het (~en)* 1 talent, gift, ability: *ze heeft* ~ she is talented; 2 talent(ed) person)

talentenjacht [tɑlɛntə(n)jɑχt] *de (~en)* talent scouting

¹talentvol [tɑlɛntfɔl] *adj* talented, gifted

²talentvol [tɑlɛntfɔl] *adv* ably, with great talent

talenwonder [tɑlə(n)wɔndər] *het (~en)* linguistic genius

talisman [tɑlısmɑn] *de (~s)* talisman

talkpoeder [tɑlkpudər] *het, de* talcum powder

talloos [tɑlos] *adj, adv* innumerable, countless

talrijk [tɑlrɛik] *adj* numerous, many

talud [tɑlʏt] *het* incline, slope; bank

tam [tɑm] *adj* 1 tame, tamed; domestic: *een ~me vos* a tame fox; ~ *maken* domesticate, tame; 2 tame, gentle: *een ~ paard* a gentle (*or:* tame) horse

tamboer [tɑmbur] *de (~s)* drummer

tamboerijn [tɑmburɛin] *de (~en)* tambourine

tamelijk [tɑmələk] *adv* fairly, rather: ~ *veel bezoekers* quite a lot of visitors

Tamil [tɑmil] *de* Tamil

tampon [tɑmpɔn] *de (~s)* tampon

tamtam [tɑmtɑm] *de (~s)* 1 tom-tom; 2 fanfare: ~ *maken over iets* make a fuss about (*or:* a big thing) of sth

tand [tɑnt] *de (~en)* 1 tooth: *er breekt een ~ door* he/she is cutting a tooth (*or:* teething); *een ~ laten vullen* (or: *trekken*) have a tooth filled (*or:* extracted); *zijn ~en laten zien* show (*or:* bare) one's teeth; *zijn ~en poetsen* brush one's teeth; *iem aan de ~ voelen* grill s.o.; *tot de ~en gewapend zijn* be armed to the teeth; 2 tooth, prong, cog: *de ~en van een kam* (or: *hark, zaag*) the teeth of a comb (*or:* rake, saw)

tandarts [tɑndɑrts] *de (~en)* dentist

tandartsassistente [tɑndɑrtsɑsistɛntə] *de (~s)* dentist's assistant

tandeloos [tɑndəlos] *adj* toothless

tandem [tɛndəm] *de (~s)* tandem

tandenborstel [tɑndə(n)bɔrstəl] *de (~s)* toothbrush

tandenknarsen [tɑndə(n)knɑrsə(n)] *vb* gnash (*or:* grind) one's teeth

tandenstoker [tɑndə(n)stokər] *de (~s)* toothpick

tandheelkunde [tɑnthelkʏndə] *de* dentistry

tandheelkundig [tɑnthelkʏndəχ] *adj* dental

tandpasta [tɑntpɑsta] *het, de (~'s)* toothpaste

tandplak [tɑntplɑk] *de* (dental) plaque

tandsteen [tɑntsten] *het, de* tartar

tandvlees [tɑntfles] *het* gums

tandwiel [tɑntwil] *het (~en)* gearwheel, cogwheel, chainwheel, sprocket wheel

tang [tɑŋ] *de (~en)* 1 tongs, (pair of) pliers, (pair of) pincers; 2 shrew, bitch

tangens [tɑŋəns] *de (~en, tangenten)* tangent

tango [tɑŋgo] *de (~'s)* tango

tank [tɛŋk] *de (~s)* tank: *een volle ~ benzine* a full/whole tank of petrol (*or Am:* gas); *de ~ volgooien* fill up (the tank)

tankauto [tɛŋkɑuto] *de (~'s)* tank lorry (*or Am:* truck)

tanken [tɛŋkə(n)] *vb* fill up (with): *ik heb 25 liter getankt* I put 25 litres in (the tank); *ik tank meestal super* I usually take four star (*or Am:* super)

tanker [tɛŋkər] *de (~s)* tanker

tankschip [tɛŋksχɪp] *het (-schepen)* (oil) tanker, tankship

tankstation [tɛŋksta(t)ʃɔn] *het (~s)* filling station

tankwagen [tɛŋkwaɣə(n)] *de (~s)* tank lorry (*or Am:* truck)

tante [tɑntə] *de (~s)* 1 aunt; auntie; 2 woman, female: *een lastige ~, geen gemakkelijke ~* a fussy (*or:* difficult) lady/woman

Tanzania [tɑnzɑnija] *het* Tanzania

tap [tɑp] *de (~pen)* 1 plug, bung, stopper, tap; 2 tap, spigot: *bier uit de ~* beer on tap (*or:* draught); 3 bar: *achter de ~ staan* serve at the bar

tapdansen [tɛbdɑnsə(n)] *vb* tap-dance

tapdanser [tɛbdɑnsər] *de (~s)* tap-dancer

tape [tep] *de (~s)* tape

tapijt [tɑpɛit] *het (~en)* carpet, *(small)* rug: *een vliegend ~* a magic carpet

tapijttegel [tɑpɛiteɣəl] *de (~s)* carpet tile (*or:* square)

tapkraan [tɑpkran] *de (tapkranen)* tap

tappen [tɑpə(n)] *vb* 1 tap, draw (off); serve: *hier wordt bier getapt* they sell beer here; *bier ~* tap beer; 2 crack: *moppen ~* crack (*or:* tell) jokes

tapvergunning [tɑpfərɣʏnɪŋ] *de (~en)* licence to sell spirits, *(Am)* liquor license

tarief [tɑrif] *het (tarieven)* tariff, rate, fare: *het gewone ~ betalen* pay the standard charge (*or:* rate); *vast ~* fixed (*or:* flat) rate; *tegen verlaagd ~* at a reduced tariff (*or:* rate); *het volle ~ berekenen* charge the full rate

tarra [tɑra] *de* tare (weight)

tartaar [tɑrtar] *de* steak tartare

Tartaar [tɑrtar] *de* Tartar

tarten [tɑrtə(n)] *vb* defy, flout: *de dood ~* brave death; *het noodlot ~* tempt fate

tarwe [tɑrwə] *de* wheat

tarwebloem [tɑrwəblum] *de* wheat flour

tarwekorrel [tɑrwəkɔrəl] *de (~s)* grain of wheat

tas [tɑs] *de (~sen)* 1 bag, satchel, (brief)case, (hand)bag: *een plastic ~* a plastic bag; 2 *(Belg)* cup

tasjesdief [tɑʃəzdif] *de (-dieven)* bag snatcher, purse snatcher

Tasmanië [tɑsmɑnijə] *het* Tasmania

tast [tɑst] *de* 1 touch; 2 groping, feeling: *hij greep op* *de ~ naar de lamp* he groped (*or:* felt) for the lamp; *iets op de ~ vinden* find sth by touch

tastbaar [tɑstbar] *adj, adv* tangible

tasten [tɑstə(n)] *vb* **1** grope; **2** dip: *in zijn beurs ~* dip into one's purse

tatoeage [tatuwaʒə] *de (~s)* tattoo

tatoeëren [tatuwerə(n)] *vb* tattoo: *zich laten ~* have oneself tattooed

taugé [tɑuge] *de* bean sprouts

t.a.v. **1** *ten aanzien van* with regard to; **2** *ter attentie van* attn., (for the) attention (of)

taxateur [tɑksatør] *de (~s)* appraiser, assessor

taxatie [tɑksa(t)si] *de (~s)* **1** assessment, appraisal: *een ~ verrichten* make an assessment; **2** estimation; **3** valuation

taxatiekosten [tɑksa(t)sikɔstə(n)] *de* cost(s) of evaluation (*or:* assessment, appraisal)

taxatiewaarde [tɑksa(t)siwardə] *de* assessed value

taxeren [tɑkserə(n)] *vb* evaluate, value (at): *de schade ~* assess the damage

taxi [tɑksi] *de (~'s)* taxi, cab: *een ~ bestellen* call a cab

taxichauffeur [tɑksiʃofør] *de (~s)* taxi driver

taxistandplaats [tɑksistɑntplats] *de (~en)* taxi rank (*or Am:* stand)

taxus [tɑksʏs] *de (~sen)* yew (tree)

tb [tebe] *de tuberculose* TB

tbc [tebese] *de see* tb

T-biljet [tebɪljet] *het (~ten)* tax reclaim form

tbs [tebees] *de terbeschikkingstelling* ‖ *~ krijgen* be detained under a hospital order

t.b.v. **1** *ten behoeve van* on behalf of; **2** *ten bate van* in favour of

¹te [tə] *adv* too: *~ laat* too late, late, overdue; *dat is een beetje te* that's a bit much; *~ veel om op te noemen* too much (*or:* many) to mention

²te [tə] *prep* **1** to: *dreigen ~ vertrekken* threaten to leave; *zij ligt ~ slapen* she is sleeping (*or:* asleep); *een dag om nooit ~ vergeten* a day never to be forgotten; **2** in: *~ Parijs aankomen* arrive in Paris; **3** to, for: *~ huur* to let; *~ voet* on foot

team [tim] *het (~s)* team: *een ~ samenstellen* put together a team; *samen een ~ vormen* team up together

teamgeest [timyest] *de* team spirit

teamverband [timvərbɑnt] *het* team: *in ~ werken* work in (*or:* as) a team

techneut [tɛχnøt] *de (~en)* boffin

technicus [tɛχnikʏs] *de (technici)* engineer, technician

techniek [tɛχnik] *de (~en)* **1** technique, skill: *over onvoldoende ~ beschikken* possess insufficient skills; **2** engineering, technology

technisch [tɛχnis] *adj* technical, technological, engineering: *een Lagere (*or: *Middelbare) Technische School* a junior (*or:* senior) secondary technical school; *een Hogere Technische School* (*or: Technische Universiteit)* a college (*or:* university) of technology; *een ~e term* a technical term; *hij is niet erg*

~ he is not very technical(ly-minded)

technisch-onderwijsassistent *de* school laboratory assistant

technokeuring [tɛχnokørɪŋ] *de (~en)* inspection, AA report

technologie [tɛχnoloyi] *de* technology

technologisch [tɛχnoloyis] *adj, adv* technological

teckel [tɛkkəl] *de (~s)* dachshund

tectyleren [tɛktilerə(n)] *vb* rustproof

teddybeer [tɛdiber] *de (-beren)* teddy bear

teder [tedər] *adj, adv* tender

tederheid [tedərhɛit] *de (-heden)* tenderness

teef [tef] *de (teven)* bitch: *een loopse ~* a bitch on (*or:* in) heat

teek [tek] *de (teken)* tick

teelt [telt] *de (~en)* **1** culture, cultivation, production: *de ~ van druiven* the cultivation of grapes; **2** culture, crop, harvest: *eigen ~* home-grown

teen [ten] *de (tenen)* toe; (*garlic*) clove: *de grote* (*or: kleine*) *~* the big (*or:* little) toe; *op zijn tenen lopen* (*fig*) push oneself to the limit; *van top tot ~* from head to food

¹teer [ter] *adj, adv* delicate: *een tere huid* a delicate skin

²teer [ter] *het* tar

teergehalte [teryəhɑltə] *het* tar content

teevee [teve] *de (~s)* TV, telly: *(naar de) ~ kijken* watch TV

tegel [teyəl] *de (~s)* tile, paving stone: *~s zetten* tile

tegelijk [təyəlɛik] *adv* at the same time (*or:* moment); also, as well: *~ met* at the same time as; *hij is dokter en ~ apotheker* he is a doctor as well as a pharmacist

tegelijkertijd [təyəlɛikərtɛit] *adv* at the same time (*or:* moment), simultaneously

tegelpad [teyəlpɑt] *het* tile, path, flagstone path

tegelvloer [teyəlvlur] *de (~en)* tiled floor

tegelwand [teyəlwɑnt] *de (~en)* tiled wall

tegelzetter [teyəlzɛtər] *de (~s)* tiler

tegemoet [təyəmut] *adv* ‖ *iem ~ gaan* (*or:* komen, lopen) go to meet s.o., go (*or:* come, walk) towards s.o.; *aan iemands wensen ~ komen* meet s.o.'s wishes; *iem een heel eind ~ komen* meet s.o. (more than) half way; *iets ~ zien* await (*or:* face) sth, look forward to sth

tegemoetkomend [təyəmutkomənt] *adj* oncoming, approaching: *~ verkeer* oncoming traffic

tegemoetkoming [təyəmutkomɪŋ] *de (~en)* subsidy, contribution: *een ~ in* a contribution towards, a grant for

¹tegen [teyə(n)] *prep* **1** against: *~ de stroom in* against the current; **2** (up) to, against: *iets ~ iem zeggen* say sth to s.o.; **3** against, to, with: *vriendelijk* (*or: lomp*) *~ iem zijn* be friendly towards (*or:* rude to) s.o.; *daar kun je niets op ~ hebben* you cannot object to that; *zij heeft iets ~ hem* she has a grudge against him; *daar is toch niets op ~?* nothing wrong with that, is there?; *hij kan niet ~ vliegen* flying doesn't agree with him; *ergens niet ~ kunnen* not be able to stand (*or:* take) sth; *er is niets ~ te doen* it can't be helped; *zich ~ brand verzekeren* take out fire insurance; **4** against, counter to, in contravention of: *dat is ~ de wet* that is illegal (*or:* against the law); **5** towards, by, come: *~ elf uur* towards eleven (o'clock), just before eleven o'clock, by eleven; *een man van ~ de zestig* a man getting (*or:* going) on for sixty; **6** (up) against; **7** against, for, at: *~ elke prijs* whatever the cost; *een lening ~ 7,5 % rente* a loan at 7.5 % interest; **8** to, (as) against: *tien ~ één* ten to one

²tegen [tɛɣə(n)] *adv* against: *zijn stem ~ uitbrengen* vote against (*or:* no); *ergens iets (op) ~ hebben* mind sth, have something against sth, be opposed to sth, object to sth; *iedereen was ~* everybody was against it; *hij was fel ~* he was dead set against it

³tegen [tɛɣə(n)] *het (~s)* con(tra), disadvantage: *alles heeft zijn voor en ~* everything has its advantages and disadvantages; *de voors en ~s op een rij zetten* weigh the pros and cons; *de argumenten voor en ~* the arguments for and against

tegenaan [tɛɣə(n)an] *adv* (up) against: *er flink ~ gaan* go hard at it; *ergens (toevallig) ~ lopen* hit (*or:* chance) upon sth, run into sth

tegenaanval [tɛɣə(n)anval] *de (~len)* counter-attack: *in de ~ gaan* counter-attack, strike (*or:* hit) back

tegenargument [tɛɣə(n)arɣymɛnt] *het (~en)* counter-argument

tegenbericht [tɛɣə(n)bərɪɣt] *het (~en)* notice (*or:* message) to the contrary: *zonder ~ reken ik op uw komst* if I don't hear otherwise, I'll be expecting you

tegenbod [tɛɣə(n)bɔt] *het* counter-offer

tegendeel [tɛɣə(n)del] *het* opposite: *het bewijs van het ~ leveren* provide proof (*or:* evidence) to the contrary

tegendoelpunt [tɛɣə(n)dulpʏnt] *het (~en)* goal against one('s team): *twee ~en krijgen* concede two goals; *een ~ maken* score in reply

tegeneffect [tɛχə(n)ɛfɛkt] *het* **1** counter-effect; **2** backspin

tegengas [tɛɣə(n)ɣas] *het* || *~ geven* resist, put up a fight

tegengesteld [tɛɣə(n)ɣəstɛlt] *adj, adv* opposite: *in ~e richting* in the opposite direction

tegengestelde [tɛɣə(n)ɣəstɛldə] *het* opposite

tegengif [tɛɣə(n)ɣɪf] *het* antidote

tegenhanger [tɛɣə(n)haŋər] *de (~s)* counterpart

tegenhouden [tɛɣə(n)haudə(n)] *vb* **1** stop: *ik laat me door niemand ~* I won't be stopped by anyone; **2** prevent, stop

tegenin [tɛɣə(n)ɪn] *adv* opposed to, against: *ergens ~ gaan* oppose sth

tegenkandidaat [tɛɣə(n)kandidat] *de (-kandidaten)* opponent, rival (candidate)

tegenkomen [tɛɣə(n)komə(n)] *vb* **1** meet: *iem op straat ~* run (*or:* bump) into s.o. on the street; **2** stumble across (*or:* upon); run across

tegenlicht [tɛɣə(n)lɪɣt] *het* backlight(ing)

tegenligger [tɛɣə(n)lɪɣər] *de (~s)* oncoming vehicle, approaching vehicle

tegenoffensief [tɛɣə(n)ɔfɛnsif] *het (-offensieven)* counter-offensive

tegenop [tɛɣə(n)ɔp] *adv* up: *er ~ zien om ...* not look forward to ...; *daar kan ik niet ~* that's too much for me; *niemand kon tegen hem op* nobody could match (*or:* beat) him

tegenover [tɛɣə(n)ovər] *prep* **1** across, facing, opposite: *~ elkaar zitten* sit opposite (*or:* facing) each other; *de huizen hier ~* the houses across from here (*or:* opposite); **2** against, as opposed to: *daar staat ~ dat je ...* on the other hand you ...; **3** towards, before: *hoe sta je ~ die kwestie?* how do you feel about that matter?; *staat er nog iets ~?* what's in it (for me)?

tegenovergesteld [tɛɣə(n)ovərɣəstɛlt] *adj* opposite, reverse

tegenoverstellen [tɛɣə(n)ovərstɛlə(n)] *vb* provide (*or:* offer) (sth) in exchange; set (sth) against: *ergens een financiële vergoeding ~* offer compensation for sth

tegenpartij [tɛɣə(n)partɛi] *de (~en)* opposition, (the) other side: *een speler van de ~* a player from the opposing team

tegenpool [tɛɣə(n)pol] *de (-polen)* opposite

tegenprestatie [tɛɣə(n)prɛsta(t)si] *de (~s)* sth done in return (*or:* exchange): *een ~ leveren* do sth in return

tegenslag [tɛɣə(n)slaɣ] *de (~en)* setback, reverse: *~ hebben* (or: *ondervinden*) meet with (*or:* experience) adversity

tegenspel [tɛɣə(n)spɛl] *het (~en)* defence; response: *~ bieden* offer resistance

tegenspeler [tɛɣə(n)spelər] *de (~s)* co-star

tegenspoed [tɛɣə(n)sput] *de* adversity, misfortune

tegenspraak [tɛɣə(n)sprak] *de* **1** objection, protest, argument; **2** contradiction: *dat is in flagrante ~ met* that is in flagrant contradiction to (*or:* with)

tegenspreken [tɛɣə(n)sprekə(n)] *vb* **1** object, protest, argue (with), answer back, talk back; **2** deny, contradict: *dat gerucht is door niemand tegengesproken* nobody disputed (*or:* refuted) the rumour; *zichzelf ~* contradict oneself

tegensputteren [tɛɣə(n)spʏtərə(n)] *vb* protest, grumble

tegenstaan [tɛɣə(n)stan] *vb* || *dat eten staat hem tegen* he can't stomach that food; *zijn manieren staan me tegen* I can't stand his manners

tegenstand [tɛɣə(n)stant] *de* opposition, resistance: *~ bieden (aan)* offer resistance (to)

tegenstander [tɛɣə(n)standər] *de (~s)* opponent: *~ van iets zijn* be opposed to sth

tegenstelling [tɛɣə(n)stɛlɪŋ] *de (~en)* contrast: *in ~ met* (or: *tot*) in contrast with (*or:* to), contrary to

tegenstemmen [tɛɣə(n)stɛmə(n)] *vb* vote against

tegenstoot [tɛɣə(n)stot] *de (-stoten)* countermanoeuvre; countermove

tegenstrever [teɣə(n)strevər] *de (~s)* opponent

tegenstribbelen [teɣə(n)strɪbələ(n)] *vb* struggle (against), resist

tegenstrijdig [teɣə(n)strɛidəχ] *adj, adv* contradictory, conflicting

tegenstrijdigheid [teɣə(n)strɛidəχɛit] *de (-heden)* contradiction, inconsistency

tegenvallen [teɣə(n)vɑlə(n)] *vb* disappoint: *dat valt mij van je tegen* you disappoint me

tegenvaller [teɣə(n)vɑlər] *de (~s)* disappointment: *een financiële ~* a financial setback

tegenvoorstel [teɣə(n)vorstɛl] *het (~len)* counter-proposal

tegenwerken [teɣə(n)wɛrkə(n)] *vb* work against (one, s.o.), cross, oppose

tegenwerking [teɣə(n)wɛrkɪŋ] *de (~en)* opposition

tegenwerping [teɣə(n)wɛrpɪŋ] *de (~en)* objection

tegenwicht [teɣə(n)wɪχt] *het (~en)* counterbalance

tegenwind [teɣə(n)wɪnt] *de (~en)* headwind, *(fig)* opposition: *wij hadden ~* we had the wind against us

¹tegenwoordig [teɣə(n)wordəχ] *adj* present, current

²tegenwoordig [teɣə(n)wordəχ] *adv* now(adays), these days: *de jeugd van ~* today's youth

tegenzet [teɣə(n)zɛt] *de (~ten)* countermove, response

tegenzin [teɣə(n)zɪn] *de* dislike; *(stronger)* aversion: *hij doet alles met ~* he does everything reluctantly

tegenzitten [teɣə(n)zɪtə(n)] *vb* be against, go against

tegoed [təɣut] *het (~en)* balance

tegoedbon [təɣudbɔn] *de (~nen)* credit note

Teheran [teherɑn] *het* Teh(e)ran

tehuis [təhœys] *het (tehuizen)* home, hostel, shelter: *~ voor ouden van dagen* old people's home

teil [tɛil] *de (~en)* (wash)tub; washing-up bowl

teint [tɛːnt] *het, de* complexion

teisteren [tɛistərə(n)] *vb* ravage, sweep: *door de oorlog geteisterd* war-stricken

tekeergaan [təkerɣan] *vb* rant (and rave), storm, carry on (about sth): *tegen iem ~* rant and rave at s.o.

teken [tekə(n)] *het (~s)* **1** sign, indication: *het is een veeg ~* it promises no good; *een ~ van leven* a sign of life; **2** sign, symbol; signal: *een ~ geven om te beginnen* (or: *vertrekken*) give a signal to start (or: leave); *het is een ~ aan de wand* the writing is on the wall; **3** mark

tekenaar [tekənar] *de (~s)* artist; draughtsman

tekenacademie [tekənakademi] *de (~s, -academien)* academy (or: college, school) of art

tekenblok [tekə(n)blɔk] *het (~ken)* drawing pad, sketch pad

tekenbord [tekə(n)bɔrt] *het (~en)* drawing board

tekendoos [tekə(n)dos] *de (-dozen)* set (or: box) of drawing instruments

tekenen [tekənə(n)] *vb* **1** draw, *(fig)* portray, depict: *figuurtjes ~ doodle*; *met potlood* (or: *houtskool, krijt) ~* draw in pencil (or: charcoal, crayon); **2** sign: *hij tekende voor vier jaar* he signed on for four years

tekenfilm [tekə(n)fɪlm] *de (~s)* (animated) cartoon

tekening [tekənɪŋ] *de (~en)* **1** drawing; design, plan: *een ~ op schaal* a scale drawing; **2** pattern, marking

tekenleraar [tekə(n)lerar] *de (-leraren)* art teacher

tekenles [tekənlɛs] *de (~sen)* drawing lesson

tekenlokaal [tekə(n)lokal] *het (-lokalen)* art room

tekentafel [tekə(n)tafəl] *de (~s)* drawing table (or: stand)

tekort [təkɔrt] *het (~en)* **1** deficit, shortfall; **2** shortage, deficiency: *een ~ aan vitamines* a vitamin deficiency

tekortkoming [təkɔrtkomɪŋ] *de (~en)* shortcoming, failing

tekst [tɛkst] *de (~en)* **1** text, *(theatre; pl)* lines; **2** words, lyrics

tekstboekje [tɛkstbukjə] *het (~s)* book (of words), libretto

tekstschrijver [tɛkstsχrɛivər] *de (~s)* scriptwriter, copywriter, songwriter

tekstverklaring [tɛkstfərklarɪŋ] *de (~en)* close reading

tekstverwerker [tɛkstfərwɛrkər] *de (~s)* word processor

tekstverwerking [tɛkstfərwɛrkɪŋ] *de* word processing

tel [tɛl] *de* **1** count: *ik ben de ~ kwijt* I've lost count; **2** moment, second: *in twee ~len ben ik klaar* I'll be ready in two ticks (or: a jiffy); **3** account: *weinig in ~ zijn* not count for much; *op zijn ~len passen* watch one's step, mind one's p's and q's; *(Belg) van geen ~ zijn* be of little (or: no) account

telbaar [tɛlbar] *adj* countable: *~ naamwoord* count(able) noun

telebankieren [teləbɑŋkirə(n)] *vb* computerized banking

telecommunicatie [teləkɔmynika(t)si] *de* telecommunication

telefax [teləfɑks] *de (~en)* **1** (tele)fax; **2** (tele)fax (machine)

telefoneren [teləfonerə(n)] *vb* telephone, phone, call: *hij zit te ~* he's on the phone; *met iem ~* telephone s.o.

telefonisch [teləfonis] *adj, adv* by telephone: *~e antwoorddienst* (telephone) answering service

telefonist [teləfonɪst] *de (~en)* telephonist, (switchboard) operator

telefoon [teləfon] *de (~s)* **1** telephone, phone: *draagbare (draadloze) ~* cellular (tele)phone, cellphone, mobile phone; *de ~ gaat* the phone is ringing; *blijft u even aan de ~?* would you hold on for a moment please?; *per ~* by telephone; **2** receiver: *de ~ neerleggen* put down the receiver (or: phone); *de*

~ **opnemen** answer the phone; **3** (telephone) call: *er is ~ voor u* there's a (phone) call for you

telefoonaansluiting [teləfɔnanslœytɪŋ] *de (~en)* (telephone) connection

telefoonboek [teləfɔmbuk] *het (~en)* (telephone) directory, phone book

telefooncel [teləfɔnsɛl] *de (~len)* telephone box (*or:* booth)

telefooncentrale [teləfɔnsɛntralə] *de (~s)* (telephone) exchange, switchboard

telefoongesprek [teləfɔŋɣəsprɛk] *het (~ken)* **1** telephone conversation; **2** phone call

telefoongids [teləfɔŋɣɪts] *de (~en)* (telephone) directory, phone book

telefoonkaart [teləfɔŋkart] *de (~en)* phonecard

telefoonlijn [teləfɔnlɛin] *de* telephone line

telefoonnummer [teləfɔnʏmər] *het (~s)* (phone) number: *geheim ~* ex-directory number

telefoonrekening [teləfɔnrekənɪŋ] *de (~en)* telephone bill

telefoonseks [teləfɔnsɛks] *de* telephone sex

telefoontik [teləfɔntɪk] *de* (telephone) unit

telefoontoestel [teləfɔntustɛl] *het (~len)* telephone

telegraaf [teləɣraf] *de (-grafen)* telegraph

telegraferen [teləɣraferə(n)] *vb* telegraph: *hij telegrafeerde naar Parijs* he telegraphed (*or:* cabled) Paris

telegrafie [teləɣrafi] *de* telegraphy

telegrafisch [teləɣrafis] *adj, adv* telegraphic

telegrafist [teləɣrafɪst] *de (~en)* telegrapher, telegraph operator

telegram [teləɣrɑm] *het (~men)* telegram: *iem een ~ sturen* telegraph (*or:* cable) s.o.; *per ~* by telegram (*or:* cable)

telegramstijl [teləɣrɑmstɛil] *de* telegram style

telelens [telelɛns] *de (-lenzen)* telephoto lens

telemarketeer [teləmɑːrkəti:r] *de (~s)* telemarketer

telen [telə(n)] *vb* grow, cultivate

teleonthaal [teleɔnthal] *het (Belg)* helpline

telepathie [teləpati] *de* telepathy

telepathisch [teləpatis] *adj, adv* telepathic

telescoop [teləskop] *de (-scopen)* telescope

teleshoppen [teləʃɔpə(n)] *vb* teleshopping

teletekst [telətɛkst] *de* teletext

teleurstellen [tələrstɛlə(n)] *vb* disappoint, let down, be disappointing: *zich teleurgesteld voelen* feel disappointed; *stel mij niet teleur* don't let me down; *teleurgesteld zijn over iets (iem)* be disappointed with sth (in s.o.)

teleurstellend [tələrstɛlənt] *adj* disappointing

teleurstelling [tələrstɛlɪŋ] *de (~en)* disappointment

televergaderen [teləvərɣadərə(n)] *vb* teleconferencing

televisie [teləvizi] *de (~s)* television, television set: *(naar de) ~ kijken* watch television

televisieactie [teləviziɑksi] *de* telethon

televisieantenne [teləviziɑntɛnə] *de (~s)* television aerial

televisiefilm [teləvizifɪlm] *de (~s)* TV film

televisiekijker [teləvizikɛikər] *de (~s)* (television) viewer

televisieomroep [teləviziɔmrup] *de (~en)* television company

televisieopname [teləviziɔpnamə] *de* television recording

televisieprogramma [teləviziproɣramа] *het* television programme

televisieserie [teləviziseri] *de (~s)* television series

televisietoestel [teləvizitustɛl] *het (~len)* television set, TV set

televisie-uitzending [teləviziœytsɛndɪŋ] *de (~en)* television broadcast (*or:* programme)

televisiezender [teləvizizɛndər] *de (~s)* **1** television channel (*or Am:* station); **2** television transmitter (*or:* mast)

telewerken [teləwɛrkə(n)] *het* teleworking

telewerker *de* teleworker

telewinkelen [teləwɪŋkələ(n)] *het* teleshopping

telex [telɛks] *de* telex: *per ~* by telex

telexbericht [telɛksbərɪxt] *het (~en)* telex (message)

telexen [telɛksə(n)] *vb* telex

telg [tɛlx] *de (~en)* descendant

telganger [tɛlɣaŋər] *de (~s)* ambler

telkens [tɛlkəns] *adv* **1** every time, in each case: *~ en ~ weer, ~ maar weer* again and again, time and (time) again; **2** repeatedly

¹tellen [tɛlə(n)] *vb* **1** count: *tot tien ~* count (up) to ten; **3** count, matter: *het enige dat telt bij hem* the only thing that matters to him

²tellen [tɛlə(n)] *vb* **1** count: *wel (goed) geteld zijn er dertig* there are thirty all told; **2** number, have, consist of: *het huis telde 20 kamers* the house had 20 rooms

teller [tɛlər] *de (~s)* **1** *(maths)* numerator: *de ~ en de noemer* the numerator and the denominator; **2** counter, meter

telling [tɛlɪŋ] *de (~en)* count(ing): *de ~ bijhouden* keep count (*or:* score)

telraam [tɛlram] *het (telramen)* abacus

telwoord [tɛlwort] *het (~en)* numeral

temmen [tɛmə(n)] *vb* **1** tame, domesticate: *zijn driften (or: hartstochten) ~* control one's urges (*or:* passions); **2** tame, break

temmer [tɛmər] *de (~s)* tamer

tempel [tɛmpəl] *de (~s)* temple

temperament [tɛmpəramɛnt] *het (~en)* **1** temperament, disposition; **2** spirit

temperatuur [tɛmpəratyr] *de (temperaturen)* temperature: *iemands ~ opnemen* take s.o.'s temperature; *op ~ moeten komen* have to warm up

temperatuurschommeling [tɛmpəratyrsxɔməlɪŋ] *de (~en)* fluctuation in temperature

temperatuurstijging [tɛmpəratyrstɛiɣɪŋ] *de* rise (*or:* increase) in temperature

temperatuurverschil [tɛmpəratyrvərsχɪl] *het* difference in temperature

temperen [tɛmpərə(n)] *vb* temper, mitigate

tempex [tɛmpɛks] *het* expanded polystyrene, styrofoam

tempo [tɛmpo] *het (~'s)* **1** tempo, pace: *het jachtige ~ van het moderne leven* the feverish pace of modern life; *het ~ aangeven* set the pace; *het ~ opvoeren* increase the pace; **2** *(mus)* tempo, time; **3** speed: *~ maken* make good time

tempobeul [tɛmpobøl] *de (~en)* pacer; stayer

tendens [tɛndɛns] *de (~en)* tendency, trend

tendentieus [tɛndɛnʃøs] *adj, adv* tendentious, biased

teneinde [tɛnɛində] *conj* so that, in order to

tengel [tɛŋəl] *de (~s)* paw

tenger [tɛŋər] *adj* slight, delicate: *~ gebouwd* slightly built

tenminste [tɛmɪnstə] *adv* at least: *ik doe het liever niet, ~ niet dadelijk* I'd rather not, at least not right away; *dat is ~ iets* that is sth at any rate

tennis [tɛnɪs] *het* tennis

tennisarm [tɛnɪsɑrm] *de* tennis elbow

tennisbaan [tɛnɪzban] *de (-banen)* tennis court: *verharde ~* hard court

tennishal [tɛnɪshɑl] *de (~len)* indoor tennis court(s)

tennisracket [tɛnɪsrɛkət] *het, de (~s)* tennis racket

tennissen [tɛnɪsə(n)] *vb* play tennis

tennisser [tɛnɪsər] *de (~s)* tennis player

tennistoernooi [tɛnɪsturnoi] *het* tennis tournament

tenor [tənor] *de (~en)* tenor

tenslotte [tɛnslɔtə] *adv* **1** after all: *~ is zij nog maar een kind* after all she's only a child; **2** finally; eventually; at last

tent [tɛnt] *de (~en)* **1** tent; stand: *een ~ opslaan* (or: *opzetten, afbreken*) pitch (or: put up, take down) a tent; *iem uit zijn ~ lokken* draw s.o. out; **2** place, joint: *ze braken de ~ bijna af* you could hardly keep them in their seats

tentakel [tɛntakəl] *de (~s)* tentacle

tentamen [tɛntamə(n)] *het (~s)* exam: *~ doen* take an exam

tentenkamp [tɛntə(n)kɑmp] *het (~en)* (en)camp(ment), campsite

tentharing [tɛnthɑrɪŋ] *de (~en)* tent peg

tentoonstellen [tɛntonstɛlə(n)] *vb* exhibit, display: *tentoongestelde voorwerpen* exhibits, articles on display

tentoonstelling [tɛntonstɛlɪŋ] *de (~en)* exhibition, show, display

tentstok [tɛntstɔk] *de (~ken)* tent pole

tentzeil [tɛntsɛil] *het (~en)* canvas

tenue [tənγ] *het, de (~s)* dress, uniform

tenzij [tɛnzɛi] *conj* unless, except(ing)

tepel [tepəl] *de (~s)* nipple, teat

terdege [tɛrdeγə] *adv* thoroughly, properly

¹terecht [tərɛχt] *adv* **1** found (again): *haar horloge*

is ~ her watch has been found; **2** rightly: *hij is voor zijn examen gezakt, en ~* he failed his examination and rightly so

²terecht [tərɛχt] *adj* correct, appropriate

terechtkomen [tərɛχtkomə(n)] *vb* **1** fall, land, end up (in, on, at): *lelijk ~ have* (or: *take*) a nasty fall; **2** turn out all right: *wat is er van hem terechtgekomen?* what has happened to him?

terechtkunnen [tərɛχtkʏnə(n)] *vb* **1** go into, enter; **2** (get) help (from): *daarmee kun je overal terecht* that will do (or: be acceptable) everywhere; *iedereen kan altijd bij hem ~* everyone can call on him any time

terechtstaan [tərɛχtstan] *vb* stand trial, be tried: *~ wegens diefstal* be tried for theft

terechtstellen [tərɛχtstɛlə(n)] *vb* execute, put to death

terechtstelling [tərɛχtstɛlɪŋ] *de (~en)* execution

teren [tərə(n)] *vb* live (on, off)

tergen [tɛrγə(n)] *vb* provoke (deliberately), badger, bait: *iem zo ~ dat hij iets doet* provoke s.o. into (doing) sth

tergend [tɛrγənt] *adj, adv* provocative: *~ langzaam* exasperatingly slow

tering [terɪŋ] *de (~en)* consumption, tuberculosis

terloops [tɛrlops] *adj, adv* casual, passing

term [tɛrm] *de (~en)* term, expression: *in bedekte ~en iets meedelen* speak about sth in guarded terms

termiet [tɛrmit] *de (~en)* termite, white ant

termijn [tɛrmɛin] *de (~en)* **1** term, period: *op korte* (or: *op lange*) *~* in the short (or: long) term; *op kortst mogelijke ~* as soon as possible; **2** deadline: *een ~ vaststellen* set a deadline; **3** instalment

termijnhandel [tɛrmɛinhɑndəl] *de* futures (dealings): *~ in olie* oil futures

termijnmarkt [tɛrmɛinmɑrkt] *de (~en)* forward market, futures market: *de ~ voor goud* the forward market in gold, gold futures

terminaal [tɛrminal] *adj* terminal, final: *terminale zorg* terminal care

terminal [tʏrmɪnəl] *de (~s)* terminal

terminologie [tɛrminoloγi] *de (~ën)* terminology, jargon

terminus [tɛrminʏs] *de (termini) (Belg)* terminus

ternauwernood [tɛrnɑuwərnot] *adv* hardly, scarcely, barely

terp [tɛrp] *de (~en)* mound, terp

terpentine [tɛrpəntinə] *de* white spirit

terrarium [tɛrarijʏm] *het (~s, terraria)* terrarium

terras [tɛrɑs] *het (~sen)* **1** pavement café, *(Am)* sidewalk café, outdoor café: *op een ~je zitten* sit in an outdoor café; **2** terrace, patio; **3** terrace, sunroof

terrein [tɛrɛin] *het (~en)* **1** ground(s), territory, terrain: *de voetbalclub speelde op eigen ~* the football team played on home turf; *eigen ~* (or: *privé ~*) private property; *het ~ verkennen: a) (literally)* explore the area; *b) (fig)* scout (out) the territory; *~ winnen* gain ground; **2** *(fig)* field, ground: *zich op bekend ~ bevinden* be on familiar ground; *zich op* *gevaarlijk ~ begeven* be on slippery ground, be on thin ice; *onderzoek doen op een bepaald ~* do research in a particular area (*or:* field)

terreur [tɛrøːr] *de* terror

terriër [tɛrijər] *de (~s)* terrier

territoriaal [tɛritor(i)jaːl] *adj* territorial

territorium [tɛritor(i)jʏm] *het (territoria)* territory

terroriseren [tɛrorizɛrə(n)] *vb* terrorize

terrorisme [tɛrorɪsmə] *het* terrorism

terrorist [tɛrorɪst] *de (~en)* terrorist

terroristisch [tɛrorɪstis] *adj, adv* terrorist(ic): *een ~e aanslag* a terrorist attack

terstond [tɛrstɔnt] *adv* **1** at once, immediately; **2** presently, shortly

tertiair [tɛr(t)ʃɛːr] *adj* tertiary: *~ onderwijs* higher education

terts [tɛrts] *de (~en) (mus)* tierce, third

terug [tərʏx] *adv* **1** back: *hij wil zijn fiets ~* he wants his bike back; *ik ben zo ~* I'll be back in a minute; *heb je ~ van 20 euro?* do you have change for 20 euros?; *wij moeten ~* we have to go back; *heen en ~* back and forth; *~ naar af* back to square one; *~ uit het buitenland* back from abroad; *~ van weg geweest: a)* be back again; *b) (fig)* have made a comeback; **2** (*Belg*) again: *daar heeft hij niet van ~* that's too much for him

terugbellen [tərʏxbɛlə(n)] *vb* call back

terugbetalen [tərʏxbətalə(n)] *vb* pay back, refund

terugbetaling [tərʏxbətalɪŋ] *de (~en)* repayment; reimbursement

terugbezorgen [tərʏxbəzɔrɣə(n)] *vb* return: *iem iets ~* return sth to s.o.

terugblik [tərʏxblɪk] *de* review, retrospect(ive)

terugbrengen [tərʏxbrɛŋə(n)] *vb* **1** bring back, take back, return: *een geleend boek ~* return a borrowed book; **2** restore: *iets in de oorspronkelijke staat ~* restore sth to its original state; **3** reduce, cut back: *de werkloosheid* (or: *inflatie*) *~* reduce unemployment (*or:* inflation)

terugdeinzen [tərʏxdɛinzə(n)] *vb* shrink, recoil: *voor niets ~* stop at nothing

terugdenken [tərʏxdɛŋkə(n)] *vb* think back to: *met plezier aan iets ~* remember sth with pleasure

terugdoen [tərʏxdun] *vb* **1** put back; **2** return, do in return: *doe hem de groeten terug* return the compliments to him

terugdraaien [tərʏxdrajə(n)] *vb* reverse, change, undo: *een maatregel ~* reverse a measure

terugeisen [tərʏxɛisə(n)] *vb* demand back, claim back, reclaim

terugfluiten [tərʏxflœytə(n)] *vb* call back

teruggaan [tərʏxaːn] *vb* go back, return: *~ in de geschiedenis* (or: *tijd*) go back in history (*or:* time); *naar huis ~* go back home

teruggang [tərʏxaŋ] *de* decline, decrease: *economische ~* economic recession

teruggave [tərʏxavə] *de* restoration, return, restitution: *~ van de belasting* income tax refund

teruggetrokken [tərʏxətrɔkə(n)] *adj* retired,

withdrawn: *een ~ leven leiden* lead a retired (*or:* secluded) life

teruggeven [tərʏxevə(n)] *vb* **1** give back, return: *ik zal je het boek morgen ~* I'll return the book (to you) tomorrow; **2** give (back), refund: *hij kon niet ~ van vijftig euro* he couldn't change a fifty-euro note

terugkeer [tərʏxker] *de* return, comeback, recurrence

terugkeren [tərʏxkerə(n)] *vb* return, come back, go back; recur: *naar huis ~* return home; *een jaarlijks ~d festival* a recurring yearly festival

terugkijken [tərʏxkɛikə(n)] *vb* look back (on, upon)

terugkomen [tərʏxkomə(n)] *vb* return, come back; recur: *ze kan elk moment ~* she may be back (at) any moment; *weer ~ bij het begin* come full circle; *daar kom ik nog op terug* I'll come back to that; *op een beslissing ~* reconsider a decision; *hij is er van teruggekomen* he changed his mind

terugkomst [tərʏxkɔmst] *de* return: *bij zijn ~* on his return

terugkrabbelen [tərʏxkrɑbələ(n)] *vb* back out, go back on, cop out, opt out

terugkrijgen [tərʏxkrɛiɣə(n)] *vb* **1** get back, recover, regain: *zijn goederen ~* get one's goods (*or:* things) back; **2** get in return: *te weinig (wissel)geld ~* be short-changed

terugleggen [tərʏxlɛɣə(n)] *vb* put back

terugloop [tərʏxlop] *de* fall(ing-off), decrease

teruglopen [tərʏxlopə(n)] *vb* **1** walk back, flow back; **2** drop, fall, decline: *de dollar liep nog verder terug* the dollar suffered a further setback

terugnemen [tərʏxnemə(n)] *vb* take back, retract: *(fig) gas ~* ease up (*or:* off), take things easy; *zijn woorden ~* retract (*or:* take back) one's words

terugreis [tərʏxrɛis] *de (-reizen)* return trip

terugrijden [tərʏxrɛidə(n)] *vb* drive back, ride back

terugroepen [tərʏxrupə(n)] *vb* call back, recall, call off: *de acteurs werden tot driemaal toe teruggeroepen* the actors had three curtain calls

terugschakelen [tərʏxsxakələ(n)] *vb* change down, shift down

terugschieten [tərʏxsxitə(n)] *vb* shoot back

terugschrijven [tərʏxsxrɛivə(n)] *vb* write back

terugschrikken [tərʏxsxrɪkə(n)] *vb* **1** recoil, shy; **2** (*fig*) recoil, baulk: *~ van de hoge bouwkosten* baulk at the high construction costs; *nergens voor ~* be afraid of nothing

¹**terugslaan** [tərʏxslan] *vb* **1** hit back; **2** backfire: *de motor slaat terug* the engine backfires; **3** blow back, move back

²**terugslaan** [tərʏxslan] *vb* hit back, strike back

terugslag [tərʏxslɑx] *de* **1** recoil(ing), backfire: *het geweer had een ontzettende ~* the gun had a terrible kick (*or:* recoil); **2** reaction, backlash: *een ~ krijgen* be set back, experience a backlash

terugspelen [tərʏxspelə(n)] *vb* play back

terugspoelen [tərɣχspulə(n)] *vb* rewind

terugsturen [tərɣχstyrə(n)] *vb* send back, return

terugtraprem [tərɣχtraprɛm] *de (~men)* hub brake, back-pedalling brake

¹terugtrekken [tərɣχtrɛkə(n)] *vb* **1** withdraw: *troepen ~* withdraw (*or:* pull back) troops; **2** draw back, pull back

²terugtrekken [tərɣχtrɛkə(n)] *ref vb* **1** retire, retreat: *zich ~ op het platteland* retreat to the country; **2** withdraw (from): *zich voor een examen ~* withdraw from an exam

terugval [tərɣχfal] *de* reversion, relapse, *(com)* spin

terugvallen [tərɣχfalə(n)] *vb* (with *op*) fall back on

terugverdienen [tərɣχfərdinə(n)] *vb* recover the costs on

terugverlangen [tərɣχfərlaŋə(n)] *vb* recall longingly: *naar huis ~* long to go back home

terugvinden [tərɣχfində(n)] *vb* find again, recover

terugvragen [tərɣχfraɣə(n)] *vb* ask back

terugwedstrijd [tərɣχwɛtstrɛit] *de (~en) (Belg)* return match

terugweg [tərɣχwɛχ] *de (~en)* way back: *op de ~ gaan we bij oma langs* on the way back we shall drop in on grandma

terugwerken [tərɣχwɛrkə(n)] *vb* be retrospective, be retroactive: *met ~de kracht* retrospectively

terugzetten [tərɣχsɛtə(n)] *vb* put back, set back; replace: *de wijzers ~* put (*or:* move) back the hands; *de teller ~ op nul* reset the counter (to zero)

terugzien [tərɣχsin] *vb* see again

terwijl [tərwɛil] *conj* **1** while: *~ hij omkeek, ontsnapte de dief* while he looked round, the thief escaped; **2** whereas, while: *hij werkt over, ~ zijn vrouw vandaag jarig is* he is working overtime even though his wife has her birthday today

test [tɛst] *de (~s)* test: *een schriftelijke ~* a written test

testament [tɛstamɛnt] *het (~en)* **1** will: *een ~ maken (*or:* herroepen)* make (*or:* revoke) a will; **2** Testament

testbeeld [tɛstbelt] *het (~en)* test card

testen [tɛstə(n)] *vb* test

testosteron [tɛstɔsterɔn] *het* testosterone

testpiloot [tɛstpilot] *de (-piloten)* test pilot

tetanus [tɛtanys] *de* tetanus

teug [tøχ] *de (~en)* draught, *(Am)* draft, pull: *met volle ~en van iets genieten* enjoy sth thoroughly (*or:* to the full)

teugel [tøɣəl] *de (~s)* rein (*oft pl*): *de ~s in handen nemen* take (up) the reins, assume control

teut [tøt] *adj* **1** dawdler; **2** bore

teveel [təvel] *het* surplus

tevens [tevəns] *adv* **1** also, besides, as well as; **2** at the same time: *hij was voorzitter en ~ penningmeester* he was chairman and treasurer at the same time

tevergeefs [təvərɣefs] *adj, adv* in vain, vainly

tevoren [təvorə(n)] *adv* before, previously: *van ~* before(hand), in advance

tevreden [təvredə(n)] *adj* satisfied, contented

tevredenheid [təvredənhɛit] *de* satisfaction: *werk naar ~ verrichten* work satisfactorily

tevredenstellen [təvredə(n)stɛlə(n)] *vb* satisfy

teweegbrengen [təweɣbrɛŋə(n)] *vb* bring about, bring on, produce

textiel [tɛkstil] *het, de* textile

textielfabriek [tɛkstilfabrik] *de (~en)* textile factory

Thailand [tɑjlɑnt] *het* Thailand

Thailander [tɑjlɑndər] *de (~s)* Thai

thans [tɑns] *adv* at present, now

theater [tejatər] *het (~s)* **1** theatre: *die film draait in verschillende ~s* that film is running in several cinemas (*or Am:* movie theaters); **2** dramatic arts, performing arts, (the) stage

theaterschool [tejatərsχol] *de (-scholen)* school of dramatic arts

theatervoorstelling [tejatərvorstɛlŋ] *de (~en)* theatre performance

thee [te] *de* tea: *een kopje ~* a cup of tea; *slappe ~* weak tea; *~ drinken* drink (*or:* have) tea; *~ inschenken* pour out tea; *~ zetten* make tea

theedoek [teduk] *de (~en)* tea towel

theedrinken [tedrŋkə(n)] *vb* have tea

theelepel [telepəl] *de (~s)* teaspoon

theelepeltje [telepəlcə] *het (~s)* teaspoon, teaspoonful

theelichtje [telŋçjə] *het (~s)* hot plate (for tea); tea-warmer

Theems [tems] *de* Thames

theemuts [temyts] *de (~en)* (tea-)cosy

theepauze [tepauzə] *de (~s)* tea break

theepot [tepɔt] *de (~ten)* teapot

theeservies [teservis] *het (-serviezen)* tea service

theezakje [tezakjə] *het (~s)* tea bag

theezeefje [tezefjə] *het (~s)* tea strainer

thema [tema] *het (~'s)* theme, subject (matter): *een ~ aansnijden* broach a subject

themapark [temapɑrk] *het (~en)* theme park

theologie [tejoloɣi] *de* theology, divinity

theologisch [tejoloɣis] *adj, adv* theological

theoloog [tejoloχ] *de (-logen)* theologian

theoreticus [tejoretikys] *de (theoretici)* theoretician, theorist

¹theoretisch [tejoretis] *adj* theoretic(al)

²theoretisch [tejoretis] *adv* theoretically, in theory

theorie [tejori] *de (~ën)* theory; hypothesis: *~ en praktijk* theory and practice; *in ~ is dat mogelijk* theoretically (speaking) that's possible

therapeut [terapœyt] *de (~en)* therapist

therapeutisch [terapœytis] *adj, adv* therapeutic(al)

therapie [terapi] *de (~ën)* **1** therapy; **2** (psycho)therapy: *in ~ zijn* be having (*or:* undergoing) therapy

thermometer [tɛrmometər] *de (~s)* thermometer: *de ~ daalt (*or:* stijgt)* the thermometer is falling (*or:* rising); *de ~ stond op twintig graden Celsius* the thermometer read (*or:* stood at) twenty degrees centigrade

thermopane [tɛrmopen] *de* double glazing

thermosfles [tɛrmɔsflɛs] *de (~sen)* thermos (flask)

thermoskan [tɛrmɔskɑn] *de (~nen)* thermos (jug)

thermostaat [tɛrmɔstɑt] *de (-staten)* thermostat

thesis [tezɪs] *de (theses) (Belg)* dissertation, thesis

Thomas [tomɑs] || *een ongelovige* ~ a doubting Thomas

thora [tora] *de* Torah

¹thuis [tœys] *adv* **1** home: *de artikelen worden kosteloos* ~ *bezorgd* the articles are delivered free; *wel* ~! safe journey!; **2** at home: *verzorging* ~ home nursing; *doe maar of je* ~ *bent* make yourself at home; *zich ergens* ~ *gaan voelen* settle down (*or:* in); *(sport) spelen we zondag* ~? are we playing at home this Sunday?; *iem (bij zich)* ~ *uitnodigen* ask s.o. round (*or:* to one's house); *zich ergens* ~ *voelen* feel at home (*or:* ease) somewhere; *hij was niet* ~ he wasn't in (*or:* at home), he was out; *bij ons* ~ at our place, at home, back home; *bij jou* ~ (over) at your place

²thuis [tœys] *het* home, hearth: *hij heeft geen* ~ he has no home; *mijn* ~ my home; *bericht van* ~ *krijgen* receive news from home

thuisbankieren [tœyzbɑŋkirə(n)] *vb* home banking

thuisbezorgen [tœyzbəzɔrɣə(n)] *vb* deliver (to the house, door)

thuisblijven [tœyzblɛivə(n)] *vb* stay at home, stay in

thuisbrengen [tœyzbrɛŋə(n)] *vb* **1** bring home, see home, take home: *de man werd ziek thuisgebracht* the man was brought home sick; **2** place: *iets (iem) niet thuis kunnen brengen* not be able to place sth (s.o.)

thuisclub [tœysklʏp] *de (~s)* home team

thuisfront [tœysfrɔnt] *het* home front

thuishaven [tœyshavə(n)] *de (~s)* home port, port of register (*or:* registry); home base, haven

thuishoren [tœyshorə(n)] *vb* **1** belong, go: *dat speelgoed hoort hier niet thuis* those toys don't belong here; *waar hoort dat thuis?* where does that go?; **2** be from, come from: *waar* (or: *in welke haven) hoort dat schip thuis?* what is that ship's home port? (*or:* port of registry?)

thuishouden [tœyshaudə(n)] *vb* keep at home || *hou je handen thuis!* keep (*or:* lay) off me!, (keep your) hands off (me)!

thuiskomen [tœyskomə(n)] *vb* come home, come back, get back: *je moet* ~ you're wanted at home; *ik kom vanavond niet thuis* I won't be in tonight

thuiskomst [tœyskɔmst] *de* homecoming, return: *behouden* ~ safe return

thuisland [tœyslɑnt] *het (~en)* homeland

thuismoeder [tœysmudər] *de (~s)* baby minder

thuisonderwijs [tœysɔndərwɛis] *het* distance learning

thuisreis [tœysrɛis] *de (-reizen)* homeward journey: *hij is op de* ~ he is bound for home

thuisverpleging [tœysfərplexɪŋ] *de* home nursing, home care

thuiswedstrijd [tœyswɛtstrɛit] *de (~en)* home game (*or:* match)

thuiswerk [tœyswɛrk] *het* outwork, cottage industry: ~ *doen* take in outwork

thuiswerker [tœyswɛrkər] *de (~s)* outworker

thuiszorg [tœysɔrx] *de* home care

ti [ti] *de (~'s) (mus)* te, ti

tic [tɪk] *de (~s)* **1** trick, quirk: *zij heeft een* ~ *om alles te bewaren* she's got a quirk of hoarding things; **2** tic, jerk; **3** *(roughly)* shot: *een tonic met een* ~ a tonic with a shot (of gin), a gin and tonic

ticket [tɪkət] *het (~s)* ticket

tiebreak [tɑjbrek] *de (~s)* tie break(er)

tien [tin] *num* ten; *(in dates)* tenth: *zij is* ~ *jaar* she is ten years old (*or:* of age); *een man of* ~ about ten people; ~ *tegen één dat …* ten to one that …; *een* ~ *voor Engels* top marks for English, an A+ for English

tiende [tində] *adj* tenth, tithe: *een* ~ *gedeelte, een* ~ a tenth (part), a tithe

tienduizend [tindœyzənt] *num* ten thousand || *enige ~en* some tens of thousands

tiener [tinər] *de (~s)* teenager

tienerjaren [tinərjarə(n)] *de* teens

tienjarig [tinjarəx] *adj* decennial, ten-year

tienkamp [tinkɑmp] *de (~en)* decathlon

tiental [tintɑl] *het (~len)* ten: *na enkele ~len jaren* after a few decades

tientallig [tintɑləx] *adj* decimal, denary

tientje [tincə] *het (~s)* ten euros, ten-euro note

tienvoud [tinvɑut] *het (~en)* tenfold

tiet [tit] *de (~en)* boob, knocker

tig [tɪx] *num* umpteen; zillions: *ik heb het al* ~ *keer gezegd* I've already said it umpteen times

tij [tɛi] *het (~en)* tide: *het is hoog* (or: *laag)* ~ it's high (*or:* low) tide, the tide is in (*or:* out)

tijd [tɛit] *de (~en)* **1** time: *in de helft van de* ~ in half the time; *in een jaar* ~ (with)in a year; *na bepaalde* ~ after some (*or:* a) time, eventually; *een hele* ~ *geleden* a long time ago; *een* ~ *lang* for a while (*or:* time); *vrije* ~ spare (*or:* free) time, time off, leisure (time); *het duurde een ~je voor ze eraan gewend was* it took a while before (*or:* until) she got used to it; *ik geef je vijf seconden de* ~ I'm giving you five seconds; *heb je even ~?* have you got a moment? (*or:* a sec?); ~ *genoeg hebben* have plenty of time, have time enough; ~ *kosten* take time; *de* ~ *nemen voor iets* take one's time over sth; ~ *opnemen* record the time; *dat was me nog eens een ~!* those were the days!; ~ *winnen* gain time, play for time; *uw* ~ *is om* your time is up; *binnen de kortst mogelijke* ~ in (next to) no time; *het heeft in ~en niet zo geregend* it hasn't rained like this for ages; *sinds enige* ~ for some time (past); *de* ~ *zal het leren* time will tell; *de* ~ *van aankomst* the time of arrival; *vorig jaar om dezelfde* ~ (at) the same time last year; *het is* ~ it's time, time's up; *zijn ~ uitzitten* serve (*or:* do) one's time; *eindelijk! het werd ~* at last! it was about time (too)!; *het wordt ~ dat ...* it is (high) time that ...; *morgen om deze ~* (about, around) this time tomorrow; *op vaste ~en* at set (*or:* fixed) times; *de brandweer kwam net op ~* the fire brigade arrived just in time; *stipt op ~* punctual, on the dot; *op ~ naar bed gaan* go to bed in good time; *te zijner ~* in due course, when appropriate; *tegen die ~* by that time, by then; *van ~ tot ~* from time to time; *van die ~ af* from that time (on, onwards), ever since, since then; *veel ~ in beslag nemen* take up a lot of time; *~ te kort komen* run out (*or:* run short) of time; **2** time(s), period, age: *de laatste ~* lately, recently; *hij heeft een moeilijke ~ gehad* he has been through (*or:* had) a hard time; *de goede oude ~* the good old days; *zijn (beste) ~ gehad hebben* be past one's best (*or:* prime); *de ~en zijn veranderd* times have changed; *in deze ~ van het jaar* at this time of (the) year; *met zijn ~ meegaan* keep up with (*or:* move with) the times; *dat was voor mijn ~* that was before my time (*or:* day); *dat was voor die ~ heel ongebruikelijk* in (*or:* for) those days it was most unusual; *je moet de eerste ~ nog rustig aandoen* to begin with (*or:* at first) you must take it easy; *een ~je* a while; **3** season, time; **4** tense: *de tegenwoordige* (or: *verleden*) *~* the present (*or:* past) tense; *toekomende ~* future tense

tijdbom [tɛitbɔm] *de (~men)* time bomb

¹tijdelijk [tɛidələk] *adj* temporary; provisional; interim: *~ personeel* temporary staff

²tijdelijk [tɛidələk] *adv* temporarily

tijdens [tɛidəns] *prep* during

tijdgebrek [tɛitχəbrɛk] *het* lack of time

tijdgenoot [tɛitχənot] *de (-genoten)* contemporary

¹tijdig [tɛidəχ] *adj* timely: *~e hulp is veel waard* timely help is of great value

²tijdig [tɛidəχ] *adv* in time; on time

tijdloos [tɛitlos] *adj, adv* timeless, ageless

tijdnood [tɛitnot] *de* lack (*or:* shortage) of time: *in ~ zitten* be pressed for time

tijdperk [tɛitpɛrk] *het (~en)* period; age, era: *het ~ van de computer* the age of the computer; *het stenen ~* the Stone Age

tijdrekken [tɛitrɛkə(n)] *vb* time wasting; playing for time

tijdrit [tɛitrɪt] *de (~ten)* time trial

tijdrovend [tɛitrovənt] *adj* time-consuming: *dit is zeer ~* this takes up a lot of time

tijdsbesparend [tɛitsbəsparənt] *adj* time-saving

tijdschrift [tɛitsχrɪft] *het (~en)* periodical; journal; magazine

tijdsduur [tɛitsdyr] *de* (length of) time

tijdslimiet [tɛitslimit] *de (~en)* time limit, deadline: *de ~ overschrijden* exceed (*or:* go over) the time limit

tijdstip [tɛitstɪp] *het (~pen)* (point of, in) time, moment

tijdsverschil [tɛitsfərsχɪl] *het (~len)* time difference

tijdverdrijf [tɛitfərdrɛif] *het* pastime

tijdverlies [tɛitfərlis] *het* loss of time

tijdverspilling [tɛitfərspɪlɪŋ] *de* waste of time

tijdwaarnemer [tɛitwarnemər] *de (~s)* timekeeper

tijdwinst [tɛitwɪnst] *de* gain in time: *enige ~ boeken* gain some time

tijger [tɛiɣər] *de (~s)* tiger

tijm [tɛim] *de* thyme

tik [tɪk] *de (~ken)* tap, slap, tick: *iem een ~ om de oren* (or: *op de vingers*) *geven* give s.o. a cuff on the ear (*or:* a rap on the knuckles)

tikfout [tɪkfaut] *de (~en)* typing error (*or:* mistake)

tikje [tɪkjə] *het (~s)* **1** touch, clip: *de bal een ~ geven* clip the ball; **2** touch, shade: *zich een ~ beter voelen* feel slightly better

tikkeltje [tɪkəlcə] *het* touch, shade

¹tikken [tɪkə(n)] *vb* **1** tap: *de maat ~* tap (out) the beat; **2** type: *een brief ~* type a letter

²tikken [tɪkə(n)] *vb* tap, tick: *de wekker tikte niet meer* the alarmclock had stopped ticking; *tegen het raam ~* tap at (*or:* on) the window

tikkertje [tɪkərcə] *het* tag: *~ spelen* play tag

til [tɪl] || *er zijn grote veranderingen op ~* there are big changes on the way

¹tillen [tɪlə(n)] *vb* lift (a weight): *ergens niet (zo) zwaar aan ~* not feel strongly about

²tillen [tɪlə(n)] *vb* lift, raise: *iem in de hoogte ~* lift s.o. up (in the air)

tilt [tɪlt] *de* || *op ~ slaan* hit the roof

timbre [tɛbrə] *het (~s) (mus)* timbre

timen [tɑjmə(n)] *vb* time

timide [timidə] *adj* timid, shy

¹timmeren [tɪmərə(n)] *vb* hammer: *goed kunnen ~* be good at carpentry; *de hele boel in elkaar ~* smash the whole place up

²timmeren [tɪmərə(n)] *vb* build, put together: *een boekenkast ~* build a bookcase

timmerman [tɪmərmɑn] *de (timmerlieden, timmerlui)* carpenter

timmerwerk [tɪmərwɛrk] *het* carpentry, woodwork

tin [tɪn] *het* tin

tingelen [tɪŋələ(n)] *vb* tinkle, jingle: *op de piano ~* tinkle away at the piano

tinkelen [tɪŋkələ(n)] *vb* tinkle, jingle

tinnen [tɪnə(n)] *adj* tin, pewter: *~ soldaatjes* tin soldiers

tint [tɪnt] *de (~en)* tint, hue: *iets een feestelijk ~je geven* give sth a festive touch; *Mary had een frisse* (or: *gelige*) *~* Mary had a fresh (*or:* sallow) complexion; *warme ~en* warm tones

tintelen [tɪntələ(n)] *vb* tingle

tinteling [tɪntəlɪŋ] *de (~en)* tingle, tingling

tinten [tɪntə(n)] *vb* tint, tinge

tip [tɪp] *de (~s)* **1** tip, corner: *een ~je van de sluier oplichten* lift (*or:* raise) (a corner of) the veil; **2** tip, lead, clue, tip-off: *iem een ~ geven* tip s.o. off, give s.o. a tip-off

tipgeld [tɪpχɛlt] *het* tip-off money

tipgever [tɪpχevər] *de (~s)* (police) informer, tipster

tippelaarster [tɪpəlarstər] *de (~s)* streetwalker

tippelen [tɪpələ(n)] *vb* be on (*or:* walk) the streets, solicit

tippen [tɪpə(n)] *vb* **1** tip (s.o.) off, *(to police also; Am)* finger; **2** tip (as); **3** tip, touch lightly, finger lightly: *aan iets (iem) niet kunnen ~* have nothing on sth (s.o.)

tiptoets [tɪptuts] *de (~en)* touch control

tiran [tirɑn] *de (~nen)* tyrant

Tiroler [tirolər] *de (~s)* Tyrolean

tissue [tɪʃu] *het (~s)* paper handkerchief

titel [titəl] *de (~s)* **1** title, heading; **2** title, (university) degree: *een ~ behalen* get a degree, win a title; *de ~ veroveren* (or: *verdedigen*) win (*or:* defend) the title

titelhouder [titəlhaudər] *de (~s)* title-holder

titelpagina [titəlpaɣina] *de (~'s)* title-page, title

titelrol [titəlrɔl] *de (~len)* title role

titelsong [titəlsɔŋ] *de (~s)* title track

titelverdediger [titəlvərdedəɣər] *de (~s)* titleholder, defender

titularis [tityLɑrɪs] *de (~sen)* (*Belg*) class teacher

tja [ca] *int* well

tjaptjoi [cɑpcɔj] *de* chop suey

tjilpen [cɪlpə(n)] *vb* chirp, peep, tweet

tjirpen [cɪrpə(n)] *vb* chirp, chirrup; chirr

tjonge [cɔŋə] *int* dear me

T-kruising [tekrœysɪŋ] *de (~en)* T-junction

tl-buis [teɭbœys] *de (tl-buizen)* strip light, neon light (*or:* tube, lamp)

tl-verlichting [teɭvərlɪχtɪŋ] *de (~en)* neon light(ing)

tmt *technologie, media en telecommunicatie* TMT

toast [tost] *de (~s)* **1** toast: *een ~ (op iem) uitbrengen* propose a toast (to s.o.); **2** (piece, slice of) toast

toasten [tostə(n)] *vb* toast: *~ op* drink (a toast) to

tobbe [tɔbə] *de (~s)* (wash)tub

tobben [tɔbə(n)] *vb* **1** worry, fret; **2** struggle: *opa tobt met zijn been* grandpa is troubled by his leg

toch [tɔχ] *adv* **1** nevertheless, still, yet, all the same: *ik doe het (lekker) ~* I'll do it anyway; *maar ~* (but) still, even so; **2** rather, actually; **3** indeed; **4** anyway, anyhow: *het wordt ~ niks* it won't work anyway; *nu je hier ~ bent* since you're here; *dat kunnen ze ~ niet menen?* surely they can't be serious?; *we hebben het ~ al zo moeilijk* it's difficult enough for us as it is

tocht [tɔχt] *de (~en)* **1** draught, breeze: *~ voelen* feel a draught; **2** journey, trip: *een ~ maken met de auto* go for a drive in the car

tochten [tɔχtə(n)] *vb* be draughty

tochtig [tɔχtəχ] *adj* draughty, breezy

tochtje [tɔχjə] *het (~s)* trip, ride, drive

tochtstrip [tɔχtstrɪp] *de (~s)* draught excluder, weather strip(ping)

¹toe [tu] *adv* **1** to(wards): *waar moet dit naar ~?* where will this lead us?; **2** too, as well: *dat doet er niet(s) ~* that doesn't matter; **3** to, for: *aan iets ~ komen* get round to sth; **4** shut, closed: *er slecht aan ~ zijn* be in a bad way; *tot nu ~* so far, up to now

²toe [tu] *int* **1** come on; **2** please, do; **3** come on, go on; **4** there now

¹toebehoren [tubəhorə(n)] *het* accessories, attachments

²toebehoren [tubəhorə(n)] *vb* belong to

toebrengen [tubrɛŋə(n)] *vb* deal, inflict, give: *iem een wond ~* inflict a wound on s.o.

toedekken [tudɛkə(n)] *vb* cover up, tuck in, tuck up: *iem warm ~* tuck s.o. in nice and warm

toedienen [tudinə(n)] *vb* administer, apply: *medicijnen ~* administer medicine

¹toedoen [tudun] *het* agency; doing: *dit is allemaal door jouw ~ gebeurd* this is all your doing

²toedoen [tudun] *vb* add: *wat doet het er toe?* what does it matter?, what difference does it make?; *wat jij vindt, doet er niet toe* your opinion is of no consequence

toedracht [tudrɑχt] *de* facts, circumstances: *de ware ~ van de zaak* what actually happened

toe-eigenen [tuɛiɣənə(n)] *ref vb* appropriate

toef [tuf] *de (~en)* tuft: *een ~ slagroom* a blob of cream

toegaan [tuɣan] *vb* happen, go on: *het gaat er daar ruig aan toe* there are wild goings-on there

toegang [tuɣɑŋ] *de (~en)* **1** entrance, entry, access: *verboden ~* no admittance; **2** access, admittance, admission: *bewijs van ~* ticket (of admission); *~ hebben tot een vergadering* be admitted to a meeting; *zich ~ verschaffen* gain access (to)

toegangskaartje [tuɣɑŋskarcə] *het* (admission) ticket, pass

toegangsprijs [tuɣɑŋsprɛis] *de (-prijzen)* entrance fee, price of admission

toegangsweg [tuɣɑŋswɛχ] *de (~en)* access (road), approach

toegankelijk [tuɣɑŋkələk] *adj* accessible, approachable: *moeilijk* (or: *gemakkelijk*) *~* difficult (*or:* easy) of access; *~ voor het publiek* open to the public

toegankelijkheid [tuɣɑŋkələkhɛit] *de* accessibility, approachability

toegeeflijk [tuɣeflək] *adj* indulgent, lenient: *~ zijn tegenover een kind* indulge a child

toegeeflijkheid [tuɣefləkhɛit] *de* indulgence; lenience

¹toegeven [tuɣevə(n)] *vb* **1** yield, give in, give way: *onder druk ~* submit under pressure; **2** admit, own: *hij wou maar niet ~* he wouldn't own up

²toegeven [tuɣevə(n)] *vb* **1** indulge, humour, pamper, spoil, allow (for), take into account: *over en weer wat ~* give and take; **2** admit, grant: *zijn nederlaag ~* admit defeat; **3** throw in, add: *op de koop ~* include in the bargain

toegevend [tuɣevənt] *adj* indulgent, lenient

toegewijd [tuɣəwɛit] *adj* devoted, dedicated: *een ~e verpleegster* a dedicated nurse

toegift [tuɣɪft] *de (~en)* encore: *een ~ geven* do an encore

toehoorder [tuhordər] *de (~s)* listener

toejuichen [tujœyχə(n)] *vb* **1** cheer, clap, applaud; **2** applaud: *een besluit ~* welcome a decision

toekennen [tukɛnə(n)] *vb* **1** ascribe to, attribute to; **2** award, grant: *macht ~ aan* assign authority to

toekijken [tukɛikə(n)] *vb* **1** look on, watch; **2** sit by (and watch)

toekomen [tukomə(n)] *vb* **1** belong to, be due: *iem de eer geven die hem toekomt* do s.o. justice; **2** approach: *daar ben ik nog niet aan toegekomen* I haven't got round to that yet

toekomend [tukomənt] *adj* future

toekomst [tukɔmst] *de* future: *in de nabije (or: verre) ~* in the near (or: distant) future; *de ~ voorspellen* tell fortunes

toekomstig [tukɔmstəχ] *adj* future, coming ‖ *zijn ~e echtgenote* his bride-to-be; *de ~e eigenaar* the prospective owner

toekomstmuziek [tukɔmstmyzik] *de* ‖ *dat is nog ~* that's still in the future

toelaatbaar [tuladbar] *adj* permissible, permitted

toelage [tulaɣə] *de (~n)* allowance, grant

toelaten [tulatə(n)] *vb* **1** permit, allow: *als het weer het toelaat* weather permitting; **2** admit, receive: *zij werd niet in Nederland toegelaten* she was refused entry to the Netherlands

toelatingsexamen [tulatɪŋsɛksamə(n)] *het (~s)* entrance exam(ination)

toeleggen [tulɛɣə(n)] *vb* add (to)

toeleveringsbedrijf [tulevərɪŋzbədrɛif] *het (-bedrijven)* supplier, supply company

toelichten [tulɪχtə(n)] *vb* explain; throw light on, clarify: *zijn standpunt ~* explain one's point of view; *als ik dat even mag ~* if I may go into that briefly

toelichting [tulɪχtɪŋ] *de (~en)* explanation; clarification: *dat vereist enige ~* that requires some explanation

toelopen [tulopə(n)] *vb* taper (off), come (or: run) to a point

toeluisteren [tulœystərə(n)] *vb* listen (to): *aandachtig ~* listen carefully

toemaatje [tumacə] *het (~s) (Belg)* extra, bonus

¹toen [tun] *adv* **1** then, in those days, at the (or: that) time: *er stond hier ~ een kerk* there used to be a church here; **2** then, next: *en ~?* (and) then what?, what happened next?

²toen [tun] *conj* when, as: *~ hij binnenkwam* when he came in

toenadering [tunadərɪŋ] *de (~en) (oft pl)* advance; approach

toename [tunamə] *de (~n)* increase, growth: *een ~ van het verbruik* an increase in consumption

toendra [tundra] *de (~'s)* tundra

toenemen [tunemə(n)] *vb* increase, grow, expand: *in ~de mate* increasingly, to an increasing extent; *in kracht ~* grow (or: increase) in strength

toenmalig [tumaləχ] *adj* then: *de ~e koning* the king at the (or: that) time

toepasselijk [tupasələk] *adj* appropriate, suitable

toepassen [tupasə(n)] *vb* **1** use, employ; **2** apply, adopt, enforce: *een methode ~* use a method; *in de praktijk ~* use in (actual) practice

toepassing [tupasɪŋ] *de (~en)* **1** use, employment: *niet van ~ (n.v.t.)* not applicable (n/a); *van ~ zijn op* apply to; **2** application: *in ~ brengen* put into practice

toer [tur] *de (~en)* **1** trip, tour, ride, drive; **2** revolution: *op volle ~en draaien* go at full speed, be in top gear; *hij is een beetje over zijn ~en* he's in a bit of a state; **3** job, business: *op de lollige ~ gaan* act the clown

toerbeurt [turbørt] *de (~en)* turn: *bij ~* in rotation, by turns; *we doen dat bij ~* we take turns at it

toerekeningsvatbaar [turekənɪŋsfadbar] *adj* accountable, responsible

toeren [turə(n)] *vb* go for a ride, go for a drive

toerfiets [turfits] *de (~en)* touring bicycle, sports bicycle

toerisme [turɪsmə] *het* tourism

toerist [turɪst] *de (~en)* tourist

toeristenindustrie [turɪstə(n)ɪndystri] *de* tourist industry, tourism

toeristenklasse [turɪstə(n)klasə] *de (~n)* tourist class, economy class

toeristenplaats [turɪstə(n)plats] *de* tourist centre

toeristenseizoen [turɪstə(n)sɛizun] *het (~en)* tourist season

toeristisch [turɪstis] *adj* tourist: *een ~e trekpleister* a tourist attraction

toernooi [turnɔj] *het (~en)* tournament

toerusten [turystə(n)] *vb* equip, furnish: *een leger ~* equip an army; *toegerust met* equipped (or: fitted) (out) with

toeschietelijk [tusχitələk] *adj* accommodating, obliging

toeschouwer [tusχauwər] *de (~s)* **1** spectator, viewer, *(pl also)* audience: *veel ~s trekken* draw a large audience; **2** onlooker, bystander

toeschrijven [tusχrɛivə(n)] *vb* **1** blame, attribute: *een ongeluk ~ aan het slechte weer* blame an accident on the weather; **2** attribute, ascribe: *dit schilderij schrijft men toe aan Vermeer* this painting is attributed to Vermeer

toeslaan [tuslan] *vb* **1** hit home, strike home; **2** strike: *inbreker slaat opnieuw toe!* burglar strikes again!

toeslag [tuslaχ] *de (~en)* **1** surcharge; **2** bonus: *een ~ voor vuil werk* a bonus for dirty work

toespelen [tuspelə(n)] *vb* pass (to), slip (to)

toespeling [tuspelɪŋ] *de (~en)* allusion, reference: *~en maken* drop hints, make insinuations

toespijs [tuspɛis] *de (toespijzen)* **1** dessert, sweet, pudding; **2** side dish

toespitsen [tuspɪtsə(n)] *vb* intensify

toespraak [tusprak] *de (toespraken)* speech, address: *een ~ houden* make a speech

toespreken [tŭsprekə(n)] *vb* speak to, address

toestaan [tŭstan] *vb* allow, permit: *uitstel* (or: *een verzoek*) ~ grant a respite (or: a request)

toestand [tŭstant] *de (~en)* state, condition, situation: *de ~ van de patiënt is kritiek* the patient is in a critical condition; *de ~ in de wereld* the state of world affairs

toesteken [tŭstekə(n)] *vb* extend, put out, hold out: *de helpende hand ~* extend (or: lend) a helping hand

toestel [tŭstɛl] *het (~len)* **1** apparatus, appliance, set: *vraag om ~ 212* ask for extension 212; **2** plane

toestelnummer [tŭstɛlnymər] *het (~s)* extension (number)

toestemming [tŭstɛmɪŋ] *de (~en)* agreement, consent, approval (of), permission: *zijn ~ geven* (or: *verlenen, weigeren) aan iem* give (or: grant, refuse) permission to s.o.

toestoppen [tŭstɔpə(n)] *vb* slip

toestromen [tŭstromə(n)] *vb* stream to(wards), flow (or: flock, crowd) towards

toesturen [tŭstyrə(n)] *vb* send, remit

toet [tut] *de (~en)* face

toetakelen [tŭtakələ(n)] *vb* **1** beat (up), knock about: *hij is lelijk toegetakeld* he has been badly beaten (up); **2** rig out

toeter [tŭtər] *de (~s)* **1** tooter; **2** horn

¹toeteren [tŭtərə(n)] *vb* hoot, honk

²toeteren [tŭtərə(n)] *vb* bellow

toetje [tŭcə] *het (~s)* dessert: *als ~ is er fruit* there is fruit for dessert

toetreding [tŭtredɪŋ] *de (~en)* joining, entry (into)

toets [tuts] *de (~en)* **1** test, check; **2** key: *een ~ aanslaan* strike a key

toetsen [tŭtsə(n)] *vb* test, check: *iets aan de praktijk ~* test sth out in practice

toetsenbord [tŭtsə(n)bɔrt] *het (~en)* keyboard, console

toeval [tŭval] *het* coincidence, accident, chance: *door een ongelukkig ~* by mischance; *stom ~* by sheer accident, (by) a (mere) fluke; *niets aan het ~ overlaten* leave nothing to chance

¹toevallig [tuvɑləχ] *adj* accidental: *een ~e ontmoeting* a chance meeting; *een ~e voorbijganger* a passer-by

²toevallig [tuvɑləχ] *adv* by (any) chance: *elkaar ~ treffen* meet by chance

toevalligheid [tuvɑləχhɛit] *de (-heden)* coincidence

toevalstreffer [tŭvalstrefər] *de (~s)* chance hit, stroke of luck

toevertrouwen [tŭvərtrauwə(n)] *vb* **1** entrust: *dat is hem wel toevertrouwd* leave that to him, trust him for that; **2** confide (to): *iets aan het papier ~* commit sth to paper

toevlucht [tŭvlyχt] *de* refuge, shelter: *dit middel was zijn laatste ~* this (expedient) was his last resort

toevluchtsoord [tŭvlyχtsort] *het (~en)* (port,

house, haven of) refuge

toevoegen [tŭvuɣə(n)] *vb* add: *suiker naar smaak ~* add sugar to taste

toevoeging [tŭvuɣɪŋ] *de (~en)* addition, additive

toevoer [tŭvur] *de* supply

toewensen [tŭwɛnsə(n)] *vb* wish: *iem veel geluk ~* wish s.o. all the best (or: every happiness)

toewijding [tŭwɛidɪŋ] *de* devotion

toewijzen [tŭwɛizə(n)] *vb* assign, grant: *het kind werd aan de vader toegewezen* the father was awarded (or: granted, given) custody of the child; *een prijs ~* award a prize

toezeggen [tŭzɛɣə(n)] *vb* promise

toezegging [tŭzɛɣɪŋ] *de (~en)* promise: *~en doen* make promises

toezenden [tŭzɛndə(n)] *vb* send (to)

toezicht [tŭzɪχt] *het* supervision: *~ houden op* supervise, oversee, look after; *onder ~ staan van* be supervised by

toezichthouder [tŭzɪχthaudər] *de (~s)* supervisor

toezien [tŭzin] *vb* **1** look on, watch: *machteloos ~* stand by helplessly; **2** see, take care: *hij moest er op ~ dat alles goed ging* he had to see to it that everything went all right

tof [tɔf] *adj, adv* **1** decent, O.K.: *een ~fe meid* a decent girl, an O.K. girl; **2** great

toffee [tɔfe] *de (~s)* toffee

toga [toɣa] *de (~'s)* gown, robe: *een advocaat in ~* a robed lawyer

toilet [twalɛt] *het (~ten)* toilet: *een openbaar ~* a public convenience, (Am) a restroom; *naar het ~ gaan* go to the toilet

toiletartikel [twalɛtɑrtikəl] *het (~en)* toiletry, (pl also) toilet requisites (or: things)

toiletjuffrouw [twalɛtjyfrau] *de (~en)* lavatory attendant

toiletpapier [twalɛtpapir] *het* toilet paper (or: tissue)

toiletreiniger [twalɛtrɛinəɣər] *de (~s)* toilet cleaner

toiletrol [twalɛtrɔl] *de (~len)* toilet paper

toilettafel [twalɛtafəl] *de (~s)* dressing table

toilettas [twalɛtas] *de (~sen)* toilet bag

toiletverfrisser [twalɛtfərfrɪsər] *de (~s)* toilet freshener, lavatory freshener

tokkelen [tɔkələ(n)] *vb* strum

tol [tɔl] *de (~len)* **1** top: *mijn hoofd draait als een ~* my head is spinning; **2** toll: *ergens ~ voor moeten betalen* (fig) have to pay the price for sth; *~ heffen* levy (or: take) (a) toll (on)

tolerant [tolerɑnt] *adj, adv* tolerant

tolereren [tolererə(n)] *vb* tolerate, put up with

tolgeld [tɔlɣɛlt] *het (~en)* toll (money)

tolk [tɔlk] *de (~en)* interpreter

tolken [tɔlkə(n)] *vb* interpret

tollen [tɔlə(n)] *vb* **1** play with (or: spin) a top; **2** spin, whirl: *zij stond te ~ van de slaap* she was reeling with sleep

tolweg [tɔlwɛχ] *de (~en)* toll road; turnpike

tomaat [tomat] *de (tomaten)* tomato

tomatenketchup [tomatə(n)kɛtʃʏp] *de (~s)* (tomato) ketchup

tomatenpuree [tomatə(n)pyre] *de* tomato purée

tomatensap [tomatə(n)sɑp] *het* tomato juice

tomatensoep [tomatə(n)sup] *de* tomato soup

tombe [tɔmbə] *de (~s, ~n)* tomb

tompoes [tɔmpus] *de (tompoezen, ~en)* vanilla slice

ton [tɔn] *de (~nen)* **1** cask, barrel; **2** a hundred thousand euros; **3** (metric) ton

tondeuse [tɔndøzə] *de (~s)* (pair of) clippers, trimmers, shears

toneel [tonel] *het (tonelen)* **1** stage: *op het ~ verschijnen* enter the stage, appear on the stage; **2** scene, spectacle; **3** theatre

toneelgezelschap [tonelɣəzɛlsχɑp] *het (~pen)* theatrical company, theatre company

toneelschool [tonelsχol] *de (-scholen)* drama school

toneelschrijver [tonelsχrɛivər] *de (~s)* playwright

toneelspel [tonelspɛl] *het (~en)* **1** play; **2** play-acting

toneelspelen [tonelspelə(n)] *vb* **1** act, play; **2** play-act, dramatize: *wat kun jij ~!* what a play-actor you are!

toneelspeler [tonelspelər] *de (~s)* **1** actor, player; **2** play-actor

toneelstuk [tonelstʏk] *het (~ken)* play: *een ~ opvoeren* perform a play

toneelvereniging [tonelvərenəχɪŋ] *de (~en)* drama club

tonen [tonə(n)] *vb* show, display

toner [tonər] *de (~s)* toner

tong [tɔŋ] *de (~en)* **1** tongue: *met dubbele (dikke) ~ spreken* speak thickly, speak with a thick tongue; *de ~en kwamen los* the tongues were loosened, tongues were wagging; *zijn ~ uitsteken tegen iem* put out one's tongue at s.o.; *het ligt vóór op mijn ~* it's on the tip of my tongue; **2** sole

tongzoen [tɔŋzun] *de (~en)* French kiss

tonijn [tonɛin] *de (~en)* tunny(fish), tuna (fish)

tooi [toj] *de (~en)* decoration(s), ornament(s), plumage

toom [tom] *de (tomen)* bridle, reins: *in ~ houden* (keep in) check, keep under control

toon [ton] *de (tonen)* **1** tone, note: *een halve ~* a semitone, a half step; *de ~ aangeven: a)* give the key; *b) (fig)* lead (*or:* set) the tone; *c)* set the fashion; *een ~tje lager zingen* change one's tune; *uit de ~ vallen* not be in keeping, not be incongruous, be the odd man out; *(fig) de juiste ~ aanslaan* strike the right note; **2** tone (colour), timbre

toonaangevend [tonaŋɣevənt] *adj* authoritative, leading

toonaard [tonart] *de (~en)* ǁ *in alle ~en* in every possible way

toonbank [tombɑŋk] *de (~en)* counter: *illegale cd's (van) onder de ~ verkopen* sell bootleg CDs under the counter

toonder [tondər] *de (~s)* bearer: *een cheque aan ~* a cheque (payable) to bearer

toonhoogte [tonhoχtə] *de (~n, ~s)* pitch: *de juiste ~ hebben* be at the right pitch

toonladder [tonlɑdər] *de (~s)* scale: *~s spelen* play (*or:* practise) scales

toonsoort [tonsort] *de (~en) (mus)* key

toonzaal [tonzal] *de (-zalen)* showroom

toorn [torn] *de* wrath, anger

toorts [torts] *de (~en)* torch

top [tɔp] *de (~pen)* **1** top, tip, peak: *aan (op) de ~ staan* be at the top; *van ~ tot teen* from head to foot; **2** top, peak, height: *(Belg) hoge ~pen scheren* be successful

topaas [topas] *de* topaz

topatleet [tɔpatlet] *de (topatleten)* top-class athlete

topconditie [tɔpkɔndi(t)si] *de* (tip-)top condition (*or:* form)

topconferentie [tɔpkɔnferɛnsi] *de (~s)* summit (conference, meeting), summit talks, top-level talks

topfunctie [tɔpfʏŋksi] *de (~s)* top position, leading position

topje [tɔpjə] *het (~s)* **1** tip: *het ~ van de ijsberg* the tip of the iceberg; **2** top

topklasse [tɔpklɑsə] *de (~n)* top class

topkwaliteit [tɔpkwalitɛit] *de* top quality, (the) highest quality

topman [tɔpmɑn] *de (~nen)* senior man (*or:* executive), top-ranking official, senior official: *~ in het bedrijfsleven* captain of industry

topografie [topoɣrafi] *de (~ën)* topography

topoverleg [tɔpovərlɛχ] *het* top-level talks, summit talks

toppositie [tɔpozi(t)si] *de* top position, leading position

topprestatie [tɔprɛsta(t)si] *de (~s)* top performance, record performance: *een ~ leveren* turn in a top performance

toppunt [tɔpʏnt] *het (~en)* **1** height, top: *dat is het ~!* that's the limit!, that beats everything!; **2** top, highest point, summit

topscorer [tɔpskorər] *de (~s)* top scorer

topsnelheid [tɔpsnɛlhɛit] *de (-heden)* top speed: *op ~ rijden* drive at top speed

topspeler [tɔpspelər] *de (~s)* top(-class) player

topspin [tɔpspɪn] *de* topspin

topsport [tɔpsport] *de* top-class sport

top-tien [tɔptin] *de* top ten

topvorm [tɔpfɔrm] *de* top(-notch) form

topzwaar [tɔpswar] *adj* top-heavy

tor [tɔr] *de (~ren)* beetle

toren [torə(n)] *de (~s)* **1** tower, steeple, spire: *in een ivoren ~ zitten* live in an ivory tower; **2** rook, castle

torenflat [torə(n)flɛt] *de (~s)* high-rise flat(s) (*or Am:* apartment(s))

torenhoog [torə(n)hoχ] *adj* towering, sky-high

torenvalk [torə(n)vɑlk] *de (~en)* kestrel, windhover

tornado [tɔrnado] *de (~'s)* tornado

tornen [tɔrnə(n)] *vb* unsew, unstitch: *er valt aan deze beslissing niet te ~* there's no going back on this decision

torpederen [tɔrpədɛrə(n)] *vb* torpedo

torpedo [tɔrpedo] *de (~'s)* torpedo

tortelduif [tɔrtəldœyf] *de (-duiven)* turtle-dove

tossen [tɔsə(n)] *vb* toss (up, for)

tosti [tɔsti] *de (~'s)* toasted ham and cheese sandwich

tot [tɔt] *prep* **1** (up) to, as far as: *de trein rijdt ~ Amsterdam* the train goes as far as Amsterdam; *~ hoever, ~ waar?* how far?; *~ bladzijde drie* up to page three; **2** to, until: *van dag ~ dag* from day to day; *~ zaterdag!* see you on Saturday!; *~ de volgende keer* until (the) next time; *~ nog (nu) toe* so far; *~ en met 31 december* up to and including 31 December; *van 3 ~ 12 uur* from 3 to (or: till) 12 o'clock; *van maandag ~ en met zaterdag* from Monday to Saturday, *(Am also)* Monday through Saturday; **3** at: *~ elke prijs* at any price; *iem ~ president kiezen* elect s.o. president

totaal [total] *adj, adv* total, complete: *een totale ommekeer (ommezwaai)* an about-turn, an about-face; *totale uitverkoop* clearance sale; *iets ~ anders* sth completely different; *het is €33,- ~ ~* it's 33 euro in all; *in ~* in all (or: total)

totaalbedrag [totalbədraχ] *het (~en)* total (sum, amount)

total loss [totəllɔs] *adj ||* *een auto ~ rijden* smash (up) a car, wreck a car

totdat [tɔdɑt] *conj* until

totempaal [totəmpal] *de (-palen)* totem pole

toto [toto] *de* tote; *(socc)* (football) pools: *in de ~ geld winnen* win money on the pools

toupet [tupɛt] *de (~ten)* toupee

tour [tur] *de (~s)* **1** outing, trip; **2** tour

touringcar [turiŋkaːr] *de (~s)* (motor) coach, *(Am)* bus

tournee [turne] *de (~s)* tour: *op ~ zijn* be on tour

touw [tɑu] *het (~en)* rope; (piece of) string: *ik kan er geen ~ aan vastknopen* I can't make head or tail of it; *iets met een ~ vastbinden (dichtbinden)* tie sth (up)

touwladder [tɑuladər] *de (~s)* rope ladder

touwtje [tɑucə] *het (~s)* (piece of) string: *de ~s in handen hebben* be pulling the strings, be running the show

touwtjespringen [tɑucəspriŋə(n)] *vb* skipping

touwtrekken [tɑutrɛkə(n)] *vb* tug-of-war

tovenaar [tovənar] *de (~s)* magician, sorcerer, wizard

¹toveren [tovərə(n)] *vb* work magic, do conjuring tricks

²toveren [tovərə(n)] *vb* conjure (up): *iets te voorschijn ~* conjure up sth

toverfluit [tovərflœyt] *de (~en)* magic flute

toverheks [tovərhɛks] *de (~en)* sorceress, magician

toverij [tovərɛi] *de (~en)* magic, sorcery

toverspreuk [tovərsprøk] *de (~en)* (magic) spell, (magic) charm

toverstaf [tovərstaf] *de (-staven)* magic wand

traag [traχ] *adj, adv* slow: *hij is nogal ~ van begrip* he isn't very quick in the uptake; *~ op gang komen* get off to a slow start

traagheid [traχhɛit] *de* slowness: *de ~ van geest* slowness (of mind)

traan [tran] *de (tranen)* tear, teardrop: *in tranen uitbarsten* burst into tears, burst out crying

traangas [traŋɡɑs] *het* tear-gas

traanklier [traŋklir] *de (~en)* tear gland

trachten [trɑχtə(n)] *vb* attempt, try

tractor [trɑktɔr] *de (~s)* tractor

traditie [tradi(t)si] *de (~s)* tradition: *een ~ in ere houden* uphold a tradition

traditiegetrouw [tradi(t)siɣətrɑu] *adj, adv* traditional, true to tradition

traditioneel [tradi(t)ʃonel] *adj, adv* traditional

tragedie [traɣedi] *de (~s)* tragedy

tragiek [traɣik] *de* tragedy

tragisch [traɣis] *adj, adv* tragic: *het ~e is* the tragedy of it is …

trailer [trelər] *de (~s)* trailer

¹trainen [trenə(n)] *vb* train, work out: *(weer) gaan ~* go into training (again)

²trainen [trenə(n)] *vb* train: *een elftal ~* train (or: coach) a team; *zijn geheugen ~* train one's memory; *zich ~ in iets* train for sth

trainer [trenər] *de (~s)* trainer, coach

training [treniŋ] *de (~en)* training, practice; workout: *een zware ~* a heavy workout

trainingspak [treniŋspɑk] *het (~ken)* tracksuit, jogging suit

traject [trajɛkt] *het (~en)* route, stretch, section

traktatie [trɑkta(t)si] *de (~s)* treat

trakteren [trɑkterə(n)] *vb* treat: *~ op gebakjes* treat s.o. to cake; *ik trakteer* this is my treat

tralie [trali] *de (~s)* bar: *achter de ~s zitten* be behind bars

tram [trɛm] *de (~s)* tram: *met de ~ gaan* take the (or: go by) tram

tramhalte [trɛmhɑltə] *de (~s)* tramstop

trammelant [trɑmələnt] *het* trouble

trampoline [trɑmpolinə] *de (~s)* trampoline

trampolinespringen [trɑmpolinəspriŋə(n)] *vb* trampolining

trance [trɛs] *de (~s)* trance: *iem in ~ brengen* send s.o. into a trance

tranen [tranə(n)] *vb* run, water: *~de ogen* running (or: watering) eyes

transactie [trɑnsɑksi] *de (~s)* transaction, deal

trans-Atlantisch [trɑnsɑtlɑntis] *adj* transatlantic

transferlijst [trɑnsfɛːrlɛist] *de* transfer list

transfersom [trɑnsfɛːrsɔm] *de (~men)* transfer fee

transformator [trɑnsfɔrmatɔr] *de (~en, ~s)* transformer

transistor [tranzɪstɔr] *de (~s)* transistor
transistorradio [tranzɪstɔradijo] *de (~'s)* transistor (radio)
transit [trɑnzit] *de* transit
transitief [trɑnzitif] *adj* transitive
¹**transparant** [trɑnsparɑnt] *adj* transparent
²**transparant** [trɑnsparɑnt] *het (~en)* transparency, overhead sheet
transpiratie [trɑnspira(t)si] *de (~s)* perspiration
transpiratiegeur [trɑnspira(t)siχør] *de (~en)* body odour
transpireren [trɑnspirɛrə(n)] *vb* perspire
transplantatie [trɑnsplɑnta(t)si] *de (~s)* transplant(ation)
transplanteren [trɑnsplɑntərə(n)] *vb* transplant
transport [trɑnspɔrt] *het (~en)* transport; transportation: *tijdens het ~* in (*or:* during) transit
transportbedrijf [trɑnspɔrdbədrɛif] *het (-bedrijven)* transport company, haulier
¹**transporteren** [trɑnspɔrtərə(n)] *vb* transport
²**transporteren** [trɑnspɔrtərə(n)] *vb* wind (the film) (on)
transporteur [trɑnspɔrtør] *de (~s)* carrier
transportkosten [trɑnspɔrtkɔstə(n)] *de* transport costs (*or:* charges)
transportonderneming [trɑnspɔrtɔndərnemɪŋ] *de (~en) see* transportbedrijf
transportschip [trɑnspɔrtsχɪp] *het (-schepen)* transport (ship)
transportvliegtuig [trɑnspɔrtfliχtœyχ] *het (~en)* transport aircraft
transportwagen [trɑnspɔrtwaχə(n)] *de (~s)* truck; (*small*) van
transseksualiteit [trɑnsɛksywalitɛit] *de* transsexualism
¹**transseksueel** [trɑnsɛksywel] *de (-seksuelen)* transsexual
²**transseksueel** [trɑnsɛksywel] *adj* transsexual
trant [trɑnt] *de* **1** style, manner: *in dezelfde ~* (all) in the same key; **2** kind: *iets in die ~* something of the kind (*or:* sort)
trap [trɑp] *de (~pen)* **1** (flight of) stairs; (flight of) steps: *een steile ~* steep stairs; *de ~ afgaan* go down(stairs); *de ~ opgaan* go upstairs; *boven* (*or: onder, beneden) aan de ~* at the head (*or:* at the foot, at the bottom) of the stairs; **2** kick: *vrije ~* free kick; *iem een ~ nageven* (*fig*) hit s.o. when he is down; **3** step; **4** (*language*) degree: *de ~pen van vergelijking* the degrees of comparison; *overtreffende ~* superlative; *vergrotende ~* comparative
trapeze [trapezə] *de (~s)* trapeze
trapezium [trapezijʏm] *het (~s)* trapezium, (*Am*) trapezoid
trapleuning [trɑplønɪŋ] *de (~en)* (stair) handrail, banister
traploos [trɑplos] *adj* stepless
traploper [trɑplopər] *de (~s)* stair carpet
trappelen [trɑpələ(n)] *vb* stamp: *~de paarden* stamping (and pawing) horses; *~ van ongeduld*

strain at the leash, be dying (to do sth, go somewhere)
¹**trappen** [trɑpə(n)] *vb* step, stamp: *ergens in ~* fall for sth, rise to the bait, buy sth
²**trappen** [trɑpə(n)] *vb* kick, boot: *tegen een bal ~* kick a ball; *eruit getrapt zijn* have got the boot (*or:* sack), have been kicked out
trappenhuis [trɑpə(n)hœys] *het (-huizen)* (stair)well
trapper [trɑpər] *de (~s)* pedal: *op de ~s gaan staan* throw one's weight on the pedals
trappist [trɑpɪst] *de (~en)* Trappist
trappistenbier [trɑpɪstə(n)bir] *het* Trappist beer
trapportaal [trɑpɔrtal] *het (-portalen)* landing
trauma [trɑuma] *het, de (~'s)* trauma
traumateam [trɑumati:m] *het (~s)* medical emergency team
traumatisch [trɑumatis] *adj* traumatic
traumatiseren [trɑumatizɛrə(n)] *vb* traumatize
travestie [travɛsti] *de (~ën)* transvestism
travestiet [travɛstit] *de (~en)* transvestite
trechter [trɛχtər] *de (~s)* funnel
tred [trɛt] *de (~en)* step, pace: *gelijke ~ houden met* keep pace with
trede [tredə] *de (~n)* step; rung
treden [tredə(n)] *vb* step: *in bijzonderheden ~* go into detail(s); *in contact ~ met iem* contact s.o.; *in het huwelijk ~ (met)* get married (to s.o.)
tree [tre] *de (treeën, ~s) see* trede
treeplank [treplɑŋk] *de (~en)* footboard
treffen [trɛfə(n)] *vb* **1** hit: *getroffen door de bliksem* struck by lightning; **2** meet: *niemand thuis ~* find nobody (at) home; **3** hit, strike: *getroffen worden door* meet with, be stricken by; **4** make: *voorbereidingen ~* make preparations; *je treft het (goed)* you're lucky (*or:* in luck)
treffend [trɛfənt] *adj, adv* striking, apt: *een ~e gelijkenis* a striking similarity
treffer [trɛfər] *de (~s)* hit, goal
trefpunt [trɛfpʏnt] *het (~en)* meeting place, crossroads
trefwoord [trɛfwort] *het (~en)* headword, reference
trefwoordenregister [trɛfwordə(n)rəχɪstər] *het (~s)* subject index
trein [trɛin] *de (~en)* train: *per ~ reizen* go by train; *iem van de ~ halen* meet s.o. at the station
treinbestuurder [trɛimbəstyrdər] *de (~s)* train driver
treinbotsing [trɛimbɔtsɪŋ] *de (~en)* train crash
treinconducteur [trɛiŋkɔndʏktør] *de (~s)* guard, (*Am*) conductor
treincoupé [trɛiŋkupe] *de (~s)* (train) compartment
treinkaartje [trɛiŋkarcə] *het (~s)* train ticket
treinongeval [trɛinɔnχəval] *het* train accident
treinramp [trɛinrɑmp] *de (~en)* train disaster
treinreis [trɛinrɛis] *de (-reizen)* train journey
treinreiziger [trɛinrɛizəχər] *de (~s)* rail(way) pas-

senger

treinstel [trɛi̯nstɛl] *het (~len)* train unit

treintaxi [trɛi̯ntɑksi] *de (~'s)* train taxi

treinverkeer [trɛi̯nvərker] *het* train traffic, rail traffic

treiteren [trɛi̯tərə(n)] *vb* torment

trek [trɛk] *de (~ken)* **1** pull; **2** stroke; **3** feature, line; **4** (characteristic) feature, trait: *dat is een akelig ~je van haar* that is a nasty trait of hers; **5** appetite: *~ hebben* feel (*or:* be) hungry; *heeft u ~ in een kopje koffie?* do you feel like a cup of coffee, would you care for a cup of coffee?; **6** popularity: *in ~ zijn* be popular, be in demand; **7** migration: *Boyzone-fans komen vanavond goed aan hun ~ken* Boyzone fans will get their money's worth tonight; *een ~ aan een sigaar doen* take a puff at a cigar

trekhaak [trɛkhak] *de (-haken)* drawbar, tow bar

trekharmonica [trɛkhɑrmonika] *de (~'s)* accordion, concertina

¹trekken [trɛkə(n)] *vb* **1** pull: *aan een sigaar ~* puff at (*or:* draw) a cigar; **2** go, move; travel; migrate: *in een huis ~* move into a house; **3** stretch: *met zijn been ~* walk with a stiff leg; *deze planken zijn krom getrokken* these planks are warped; *thee laten ~* brew tea

²trekken [trɛkə(n)] *vb* **1** draw, extract, pull (out); **2** draw, attract: *publiek* (or: *kopers*) *~* draw an audience (*or:* customers); **3** pull: *iem aan zijn haar ~* pull s.o.'s hair; *iem aan zijn mouw ~* pull (at) s.o.'s sleeve; **4** pull, draw, tow: *de aandacht ~* attract attention; **5** draw, (*maths*) extract: *een conclusie ~* draw a conclusion; *gezichten ~* make (*or:* pull) (silly) faces

trekker [trɛkər] *de (~s)* **1** hiker; **2** trigger: *de ~ overhalen* pull the trigger; **3** truck, lorry: *~ met oplegger* truck and trailer; **4** tractor

trekking [trɛkɪŋ] *de (~en)* draw

trekkracht [trɛkrɑχt] *de (~en)* tractive power, pulling power

trekpleister [trɛkplɛi̯stər] *de (~s)* draw, attraction: *een toeristische ~* a tourist attraction

trekschuit [trɛksχœy̯t] *de (~en)* tow barge

trektocht [trɛktɔχt] *de (~en)* hike, hiking tour

trekvogel [trɛkfoɣəl] *de (~s)* migratory bird; bird of passage

trema [tremɑ] *het (~'s)* diaeresis

tremolo [tremolo] *adv* tremolo

trend [trɛnt] *de (~s)* trend

trendgevoelig [trɛntχəvuləχ] *adj, adv* subject to trends

trendsettend [trɛntsɛtənt] *adj* trendsetting

treuren [trørə(n)] *vb* **1** sorrow, mourn, grieve: *~ om een verlies* mourn a loss; **2** be sorrowful, be mournful

treurig [trørəχ] *adj, adv* sad, tragic, unhappy: *een ~ gezicht* a sorry (*or:* gloomy) sight, a sad (*or:* dejected) face

treurigheid [trørəχhɛi̯t] *de* sorrow, sadness

treurspel [trørspɛl] *het (~en)* tragedy

treuzelen [trøzələ(n)] *vb* dawdle: *~ met zijn werk* dawdle over one's work

triangel [trijɑŋəl] *de (~s)* triangle

triatlon [trijɑtlɔn] *de (~s)* triathlon

tribunaal [tribynal] *het (tribunalen)* tribunal

tribune [tribynə] *de (~s)* stand (*oft pl*); gallery

tricot [triko] *het (~s)* tricot

triest [trist] *adj, adv* **1** sad; **2** melancholy, depressing, dreary

triktrak [trɪktrɑk] *het* backgammon

triktrakken [trɪktrɑkə(n)] *vb* play backgammon

trillen [trɪlə(n)] *vb* vibrate, tremble, shake: *met ~de stem* in a trembling voice

trilling [trɪlɪŋ] *de (~en)* **1** vibration, tremor; **2** trembling, shaking

trilogie [triloɣi] *de (~ën)* trilogy

trimbaan [trɪmban] *de (-banen)* keep-fit trail

trimester [trimɛstər] *het (~s)* trimester; term: *midden in het ~* (in) mid-term

¹trimmen [trɪmə(n)] *vb* do keep-fit (exercises), jog, work out

²trimmen [trɪmə(n)] *vb* trim

trimmer [trɪmər] *de (~s)* jogger

trimoefening [trɪmufənɪŋ] *de* (keep-fit) exercise

trimpak [trɪmpɑk] *het* tracksuit

trimschoen [trɪmsχun] *de (~en)* training shoe, jogging shoe

trimtoestel [trɪmtustɛl] *het (~len)* exerciser

trio [trijo] *het (~'s)* trio

triomf [trijɔmf] *de (~en)* triumph

triomfantelijk [trijɔmfɑntələk] *adj, adv* triumphant

trip [trɪp] *de (~s)* **1** trip; **2** (acid) trip

triphop [trɪphɔp] *de* trip hop

triplex [triplɛks] *het* plywood

triplo [triplo] *|| in ~* in triplicate

trippelen [trɪpələ(n)] *vb* trip, patter

trippen [trɪpə(n)] *vb* trip (out): *hij tript op hardrockmuziek* he gets off on hard rock (music)

triptiek [trɪptik] *de (~en)* triptych

troebel [trubəl] *adj* turbid, cloudy: *in ~ water vissen* fish in troubled waters

troef [truf] *de (troeven)* trumps; trump (card): *welke kleur is ~?* what suit is trumps?; *zijn laatste ~ uitspelen* play one's trump card

troep [trup] *de (~en)* **1** troop, pack; **2** mess: *gooi de hele ~ maar weg* just get rid of the whole lot; *~ maken* make a mess; **3** (*mil*) troop; **4** company

troepenmacht [trupə(n)mɑχt] *de (~en)* (military) force

troeteldier [trutəldir] *het (~en)* cuddly toy, soft toy

troetelkind [trutəlkɪnt] *het (-kinderen)* darling, pet; spoiled child

troetelnaam [trutəlnam] *de (-namen)* pet name

troeven [truvə(n)] *vb (cards)* trump, play trumps

trofee [trofe] *de (~ën)* trophy

troffel [trɔfəl] *de (~s)* trowel

trog [trɔχ] *de (~gen)* trough

Trojaans [trojɑ̃ns] *adj* Trojan

Troje [troːjə] *het* Troy

trol [trɔl] *de (~len)* troll

trolley [trɔli] *de (~s)* (tea) trolley

trolleybus [trɔlibʏs] *de (~sen)* trolleybus

trom [trɔm] *de (~men)* drum

trombone [trɔmbɔːnə] *de (~s)* trombone

trombonist [trɔmbonɪst] *de (~en)* trombonist

trombose [trɔmboːzə] *de* thrombosis

trommel [trɔməl] *de (~s)* **1** drum: *de ~ slaan* beat the drum; **2** box

trommeldroger [trɔməldroːɣər] *de (~s)* tumble-dryer

trommelen [trɔmələ(n)] *vb* drum: *op de tafel ~* drum (on) the table; *een groep mensen bij elkaar ~* drum up a group of people

trommelrem [trɔməlrɛm] *de (~men)* drum brake

trommelvlies [trɔməlvlis] *het (-vliezen)* eardrum, tympanum

trompet [trɔmpɛt] *de (~ten)* trumpet

trompettist [trɔmpɛtɪst] *de (~en)* trumpet player

tronie [troːni] *de (~s)* mug

troon [tron] *de (tronen)* throne: *de ~ beklimmen (bestijgen)* come to (*or:* ascend) the throne

troonopvolger [tronɔpfɔlɣər] *de (~s)* heir (to the throne)

troonopvolgster [tronɔpfɔlχstər] *de* heiress

troonrede [tronredə] *de (~s)* Queen's speech, King's speech

troost [trost] *de* comfort, consolation: *een bakje ~: a)* (in the Netherlands) a cup of coffee; *b)* (in Britain) a cuppa; *een schrale ~* cold (*or:* scant) comfort/consolation

troosteloos [trostəlos] *adj, adv* disconsolate, cheerless: *een ~ landschap* a dreary (*or:* desolate) landscape/scene

troosten [trostə(n)] *vb* comfort, console: *zij was niet te ~* she was beyond (all) consolation

troostprijs [trostprɛis] *de (-prijzen)* consolation prize

tropen [tropə(n)] *de* tropics

tropenuitrusting [tropə(n)œytrʏstɪŋ] *de (~en)* tropical gear, tropical outfit

tropisch [tropis] *adj, adv* tropical: *het is hier ~ (warm)* it is sweltering here

tros [trɔs] *de (~sen)* **1** cluster, bunch; **2** hawser: *~sen losgooien* cast off, unmoor

trostomaat [trɔstomat] *de (-tomaten)* vine tomato

¹**trots** [trɔts] *de* pride; glory: *ze is de ~ van haar ouders* she is her parents' pride and joy

²**trots** [trɔts] *adj, adv* proud

trotseren [trɔtsɛrə(n)] *vb* **1** defy, brave: *de blik(ken) ~ (van)* outface, outstare; **2** stand up (to)

trottoir [trɔtwar] *het (~s)* pavement, (Am) sidewalk

troubadour [trubadur] *de (~s)* troubadour

¹**trouw** [trɑu] *de* fidelity, loyalty, faith(fulness), allegiance: *te goeder ~ zijn* be bona fide, be in good faith; *te kwader ~* mala fide, in bad faith

²**trouw** [trɑu] *adj, adv* faithful: *~e onderdanen* loyal subjects; *elkaar ~ blijven* be (*or:* remain) faithful/true to each other

trouwdag [trɑudɑχ] *de (~en)* wedding day

¹**trouwen** [trɑuwə(n)] *vb* get married: *ik ben er niet mee getrouwd* I'm not wedded (*or:* tied) to it; *ze trouwde met een arts* she married a doctor; *voor de wet ~* get married in a registry office

²**trouwen** [trɑuwə(n)] *vb* marry

trouwens [trɑuwəns] *adv* **1** mind you: *ik vind haar ~ wel heel aardig* mind you, I do think she's very nice; *hij komt niet; ik ~ ook niet* he isn't coming; neither am I for that matter; **2** by the way: *~, was Jan er ook?* by the way, was Jan there as well?

trouwerij [trɑuwɛrɛi] *de (~en)* wedding

trouwjurk [trɑujʏrk] *de (~en)* wedding dress

trouwpartij [trɑupartɛi] *de (~en)* **1** wedding (party); **2** wedding ceremony, marriage ceremony

trouwplannen [trɑuplanə(n)] *de ǁ ~ hebben* be going (*or:* planning) to get married

trouwreportage [trɑurəportaʒə] *de* wedding photos

trouwring [trɑurɪŋ] *de (~en)* wedding ring

truc [tryk] *de (~s)* trick: *een ~ met kaarten* a card trick

trucage [trykaʒə] *de (~s)* trickery

truck [trʏk] *de (~s)* articulated lorry, (Am) trailer truck; truck

trucopname [trʏkɔpnamə] *de (~s, ~n)* special effect

truffel [tryfəl] *de (~s)* truffle

trui [trœy] *de (~en)* **1** jumper, sweater; **2** jersey, shirt: *de gele ~* the yellow jersey

trust [trʏst] *de (~s)* trust, cartel

trut [trʏt] *de (~ten)* cow: *stomme ~!* silly cow!

tsaar [tsar] *de (tsaren)* tsar, czar

T-shirt [tiʃʏːrt] *het, de (~s)* T-, tee shirt

Tsjaad [tʃat] *het* Chad

Tsjech [tʃɛχ] *de (~en)* Czech

Tsjechië [tʃɛχijə] *het* Czech Republic

tso [teːso] *het (Belg) technisch secundair onderwijs* secondary technical education

tuba [tyba] *de (~'s)* tuba

tube [tybə] *de (~s)* tube

tuberculose [tybɛrkyloːzə] *de* tuberculosis

tucht [tʏχt] *de* discipline: *de ~ handhaven* maintain (*or:* keep) discipline

tuchtcollege [tʏχtkɔleʒə] *het (~s)* disciplinary tribunal

tuchtschool [tʏχtsχol] *de (-scholen)* youth custody centre

tuig [tœyχ] *het (~en)* **1** harness; **2** riff-raff: *langharig werkschuw ~* long-haired workshy layabouts; **3** tackle

tuigen [tœyɣə(n)] *vb* harness; tackle (up); bridle

tuigje [tœyχjə] *het (~s)* safety harness

tuimelaar [tœymələr] *de (~s)* tumbler, wobbly clown, wobbly man

tuimelbeker [tœyməlbekər] *de (~s)* training cup

tuimelen [tœymələ(n)] *vb* tumble, topple

tuin [tœyn] *de (~en)* garden ǁ *iem om de ~ leiden*

lead s.o. up the garden path

tuinboon [tœymbon] *de (-bonen)* broad bean

tuinbouw [tœymbɑu] *de* horticulture, market gardening

tuinbouwbedrijf [tœymbɑubədrɛif] *het (-bedrijven)* market garden

tuinbouwschool [tœymbɑusχol] *de (-scholen)* horticultural school (*or:* college)

tuinbroek [tœymbruk] *de (~en)* dungarees, overalls

tuincentrum [tœynsɛntrʏm] *het (-centra)* garden centre

tuinder [tœyndər] *de (~s)* market gardener

tuinfeest [tœynfest] *het (~en)* garden party

tuingereedschap [tœyŋɣəretsχɑp] *het* garden(ing) tools

tuinhuis [tœynhœys] *het (-huizen)* garden house

tuinier [tœynir] *de (~s)* gardener

tuinieren [tœynirə(n)] *vb* garden

tuinkabouter [tœyŋkabɑutər] *de (~s)* garden gnome

tuinman [tœymɑn] *de (tuinlieden)* gardener

tuinslang [tœynslɑŋ] *de (~en)* (garden) hose

tuinstoel [tœynstul] *de (~en)* garden chair

tuit [tœyt] *de (~en)* **1** spout; **2** nozzle

¹tuiten [tœytə(n)] *vb* purse: *de lippen ~* purse one's lips

²tuiten [tœytə(n)] *vb* tingle, ring: *mijn oren ~* my ears are ringing

tuk [tʏk] *adj* keen (on): *daar ben ik ~ op* I'm keen on (*or:* mad about) that; *ik had je lekker ~ gisteren, hè?* I really had you fooled yesterday, didn't I?; *iem ~ hebben* pull s.o.'s leg

tukje [tʏkjə] *het (~s)* nap: *een ~ doen* take a nap

tukken [tʏkə(n)] *vb* nap, doze

tulband [tʏlbɑnt] *de (~en)* turban

tulp [tʏlp] *de (~en)* tulip

tulpenbol [tʏlpə(n)bɔl] *de (~len)* tulip bulb

tulpvakantie [tʏlpfakɑn(t)si] *de (~s)* half-term holiday, spring holiday

tumor [tymɔr] *de (~en)* tumour: *kwaadaardige* (*or: goedaardige*) *~ malignant* (*or:* benign) tumour

tumtum [tʏmtʏm] *het, de* dolly mixture

tumult [tymʏlt] *het (~en)* tumult, uproar

tuner-versterker [cu:nərvərstɛrkər] *de (~s)* tuner-amplifier

Tunesië [tynezijə] *het* Tunisia

Tunesiër [tynezijər] *de (~s)* Tunisian

tunnel [tʏnəl] *de (~s)* tunnel

turbine [tʏrbinə] *de (~s)* turbine

turbo [tʏrbo] *de (~'s)* **1** turbo((super)charger); **2** turbo(-car) ‖ *turbostofzuiger* high-powered vacuum cleaner

tureluurs [tyrəlʏrs] *adj* mad, whacky, crazy: *het is om ~ (van) te worden* it's enough to drive anybody mad (*or:* up the wall)

turen [tyrə(n)] *vb* peer, gaze, stare: *in de verte ~ gaze* into the distance

turf [tʏrf] *de (turven)* **1** peat; **2** tally; **3** tome

Turijn [tyrɛin] *het* Turin

Turk [tʏrk] *de (~en)* Turk

Turkije [tʏrkɛiə] *het* Turkey

Turkmeens [tʏrkmens] *adj* Turkoman, Turkman

Turkmenistan [tʏrkmenistɑn] *het* Turkmenistan

¹turkoois [tʏrkɔjs] *de (gem)* turquoise

²turkoois [tʏrkɔjs] *het (mineral)* turquoise

Turks [tʏrks] *adj* Turkish: *~ bad* Turkish bath

turnen [tʏrnə(n)] *vb* practise gymnastics, perform gymnastics

turner [tʏrnər] *de (~s)* gymnast

turquoise [tʏrkwɑzə] *adj* turquoise

turven [tʏrvə(n)] *vb* tally

tussen [tʏsə(n)] *prep* **1** between: *~ de middag* at lunchtime; *dat blijft ~ ons (tweeën)* that's between you and me; **2** among: *het huis stond ~ de bomen in* the house stood among(st) the trees; *~ vier muren* within four walls; *iem er (mooi) ~ nemen* have s.o. on, take s.o. in; *als er niets ~ komt, dan …* unless something unforeseen should occur

tussenbeide [tʏsə(n)bɛidə] *adv* between, in: *~ komen* interrupt, butt in, step in, intervene, intercede

tussendeur [tʏsə(n)dør] *de (~en)* communicating door, dividing door

tussendoor [tʏsə(n)dor] *adv* **1** through; between them; **2** between times: *proberen ~ wat te slapen* try to snatch some sleep

tussendoortje [tʏsə(n)dorcə] *het (~s)* snack

tussenhandel [tʏsə(n)hɑndəl] *de* distributive trade(s)

tussenhandelaar [tʏsə(n)hɑndəlar] *de (~s, -handelaren)* middleman

tussenin [tʏsə(n)ɪn] *adv* in between, between the two, in the middle

tussenkomst [tʏsə(n)kɔmst] *de* **1** intervention; **2** mediation

tussenlanding [tʏsə(n)lɑndɪŋ] *de (~en)* stop(over)

tussenliggend [tʏsə(n)lɪɣənt] *adj* intervening

tussenmuur [tʏsə(n)myr] *de (-muren)* partition; dividing wall

tussenperiode [tʏsə(n)perijodə] *de (~n, ~s)* intervening period

tussenpersoon [tʏsə(n)pɛrson] *de (-personen)* go-between, intermediary: *als ~ fungeren* act as an intermediary

tussenpoos [tʏsə(n)pos] *de (-pozen)* ‖ *met korte tussenpozen* at short intervals; *met tussenpozen* every so often

tussenruimte [tʏsə(n)rœymtə] *de (~n, ~s)* space: *met gelijke ~n plaatsen* space evenly

tussenstand [tʏsə(n)stɑnt] *de (~en)* (roughly) score (so far), half-time score

tussenstop [tʏsə(n)stɔp] *de (~s)* stop(over)

tussenstuk [tʏsə(n)stʏk] *het* joint, connecting-piece

tussentijd [tʏsə(n)tɛit] *de (~en)* interim: *in de ~* in the meantime, meanwhile

tussentijds [tʏsə(n)tɛits] *adj* interim: *~e verkiezingen* by-elections

tussenuit [tʏsə(n)œʏt] *adv* out (from between two things) ‖ *er ~ knijpen* do a bunk, cut and run

tussenuur [tʏsə(n)yr] *het (-uren)* **1** free hour; **2** free period

tussenvoegen [tʏsə(n)vuɣə(n)] *vb* insert

tussenwand [tʏsə(n)want] *de (~en)* partition

tussenweg [tʏsə(n)wɛɣ] *de (~en)* middle course

tussenwoning [tʏsə(n)wonɪŋ] *de (~en)* terraced house; town house

tut [tʏt] *de (~ten)* frump

tuthola [tʏthola] *de (~'s)* silly old cow (*or*: bitch)

tutoyeren [tytwajerə(n)] *vb* be on first-name terms

tutu [tyty] *de (~'s)* tutu

tv [teve] *de (~'s)* TV, television: *~ kijken* watch TV; *wat komt er vanavond op (de) ~?* what's on (TV) tonight?

tv-serie [teveseri] *de (~s)* TV series

twaalf [twalf] *num* twelve; (*in dates*) twelfth: *~ dozijn* gross; *om ~ uur 's nachts* at midnight; *om ~ uur 's middags* at (twelve) noon; *de grote wijzer staat al bijna op de ~* the big hand is nearly on the twelve

twaalfde [twalvdə] *num* twelfth

twaalfjarig [twalfjarəɣ] *adj* **1** twelve-year-old; **2** twelve-year

twaalftal [twalftal] *het (~len)* dozen, twelve

twaalfuurtje [twalfyrcə] *het (~s)* midday snack, lunch

twee [twe] *num* two; (*in dates*) second: *~ keer per week* twice a week; *een stuk of ~* a couple of; *~ weken* a fortnight, two weeks; *in ~ën delen* divide in two, halve; *zij waren met hun ~ën* there were two of them; *hij eet en drinkt voor ~* he eats and drinks (enough) for two; *~ aan ~* in twos

tweebaansweg [twebanswɛɣ] *de (~en)* **1** two-lane road; **2** dual carriageway, (*Am*) divided highway

tweedaags [twedaɣs] *adj* two-day

¹tweede [twedə] *num* second: *de ~ Kamer* the Lower House (*or*: Chamber); *~ keus* second rate, seconds; *als ~ eindigen: a)* finish second, be runner-up; *b)* (*fig*) come off second best; *ten ~* in the second place

²tweede [twedə] *de (~n)* half: *anderhalf is gelijk aan drie ~n* one and a half is the same as three halves

tweedegraads [twedəɣrats] *adj* second-degree: *tweedegraadsbevoegdheid* lower secondary school teaching qualification; *tweedegraadsverbranding* second-degree burn

tweedehands [twedəhants] *adj, adv* second-hand

tweedejaars [twedəjars] *adj* second-year

Tweede-Kamerlid [twedəkamərlɪt] *het (-leden)* member of the Lower House

tweedekansonderwijs [twedəkansɔndərwɛis] *het* secondary education for adults

tweedelig [twedeləɣ] *adj* two-piece: *een ~ badpak* a two-piece (bathing-suit)

tweederangs [twedərɑŋs] *adj* second-class

tweeduizend [twedœyzənt] *num* two thousand

twee-eiig [tweɛiəɣ] *adj* fraternal

tweehonderd [twehɔndərt] *num* two hundred

tweehonderdste [twehɔndərtstə] *num* two-hundredth

tweehoog [twehoɣ] *adv* on the second (*or* Am: third) floor

tweejarig [twejarəɣ] *adj* **1** two-year(-old); **2** biennial

tweekamerwoning [twekamərwonɪŋ] *de (~en)* two-room flat

tweekamp [twekamp] *de (~en)* twosome

tweekwartsmaat [twekwartsmat] *de (-maten)* two-four time

tweeledig [tweledəɣ] *adj, adv* double, twofold

tweeling [twelɪŋ] *de (~en)* **1** twins: *eeneiige* (*or*: *twee-eiige) ~en* identical (*or*: fraternal) twins; **2** twin

tweelingbroer [twelɪŋbrur] *de (~s)* twin brother

Tweelingen [twelɪŋə(n)] *de (astrology)* Gemini, Twins

tweelingzus [twelɪŋzʏs] *de (~sen)* twin sister

tweemaal [twemal] *adv* twice: *zich wel ~ bedenken* think twice

tweemaandelijks [twemandələks] *adj* **1** bimonthly: *een ~ tijdschrift* a bimonthly; **2** two-month

twee-onder-een-kapwoning [tweɔndəreŋkapwonɪŋ] *de (~en)* semi-detached house, (*Am*) (one side of a) duplex

tweepersoonsbed [twepɛrsonzbɛt] *het (~den)* double bed

tweepersoonskamer [twepɛrsonskamər] *de (~s)* double(-bedded) room; twin-bedded room

tweestrijd [twestrɛit] *de* internal conflict: *in ~ staan* be torn between (two things)

tweetal [twetal] *het (~len)* pair, couple

tweetalig [twetaləɣ] *adj* bilingual

tweetallig [twetaləɣ] *adj* binary

tweetjes [twecəs] *num* ‖ *wij ~* we two; *zij waren met hun ~* there were two of them

tweeverdiener [twevərdinər] *de (~s)* two-earner, (*pl*) two-earner family, double-income family

tweevoud [twevaut] *het (~en)* **1** double, duplicate: *in ~* in duplicate; **2** binary, double (of a number)

tweevoudig [twevaudəɣ] *adj, adv* double, twofold

tweewieler [twewilər] *de (~s)* two-wheeler

tweezitsbank [twezɪtsbaŋk] *de (~en)* two-person settee, two-seater settee

twijfel [twɛifəl] *de (~s)* doubt: *het voordeel van de ~* the benefit of the doubt; *boven (alle) ~ verheven zijn* be beyond all doubt; *iets in ~ trekken* cast doubt on sth, question sth; *zonder ~* no doubt, doubtless, undoubtedly

twijfelachtig [twɛifəlɑχtəɣ] *adj, adv* **1** doubtful; **2** dubious: *de ~e eer hebben om ...* have the dubious honour of (doing sth)

twijfelen [twɛifələ(n)] *vb* doubt: *daar valt niet aan te ~* that is beyond (all) doubt

twijfelgeval [twɛifəlɣəval] *het (~len)* dubious case, doubtful case

twijg [twɛiɣ] *de (~en)* twig

twinkelen [twɪŋkələ(n)] *vb* twinkle

twinkeling [twɪŋkəlɪŋ] *de (~en)* twinkling

twintig [twɪntəχ] *num* twenty; *(in dates)* twentieth: *de jaren ~* the Twenties, the 1920s; *zij was in de ~* she was in her twenties; *er waren er in de ~* there were twenty odd

twintiger [twɪntəɣər] *de (~s)* person in his (*or:* her) twenties

twintigste [twɪntəχstə] *num* twentieth: *een shilling was een ~ pond* a shilling was a twentieth of a pound

twist [twɪst] *de (~en)* quarrel: *een ~ bijleggen* settle a quarrel (*or:* dispute)

twisten [twɪstə(n)] *vb* **1** dispute: *daarover wordt nog getwist* that is still a moot point (*or:* in dispute); *over deze vraag valt te ~* this is a debatable (*or:* an arguable) question; **2** quarrel: *de ~de partijen* the contending parties

tyfoon [tɑjfuːn] *de (~s)* typhoon

tyfus [tɪfʏs] *de* typhoid

type [tipə] *het, de (~s)* type, character: *een onguur ~* a shady customer; *hij is mijn ~ niet* he's not my type

typefout [tipfɑut] *de (~en)* typing error, typo

typekamer [tipkamər] *de (~s)* typing pool

typemachine [tipmaʃinə] *de (~s)* typewriter

typen [tipə(n)] *vb* type: *een getypte brief* a typed (*or:* typewritten) letter; *blind ~* touch-type

typeren [tipɛrə(n)] *vb* typify, characterize: *dat typeert haar* that is typical of her

typerend [tipɛrənt] *adj* typical (of)

typewerk [tipwɛrk] *het* typing

typisch [tipis] *adj, adv* **1** typical: *dat is ~ mijn vader* that's typical of my father; *~ Amerikaans* typically American; *het ~e van de zaak* the curious part of the matter; **2** peculiar

typist [tipɪst] *de (~en)* typist

tyrannosaurus [tirɑnosɑʊrʏs] *de* tyrannosaurus

u

u [y] *pers pron* you: *als ik ~ was* if I were you
ufo [ɣfo] *de (~'s)* unidentified flying object UFO
Uganda [uɣɑnda] *het* Uganda
Ugandees [uɣɑndɛs] *de* Ugandan
ui [œy] *de (~en)* onion
uiensoep [œyə(n)sup] *de* onion soup
uier [œyər] *de (~s)* udder
uil [œyl] *de (~en)* owl
uilenbal [œylə(n)bɑl] *de (~len)* **1** (owl's) pellet; **2** dimwit, nincompoop
uilskuiken [œylskœykə(n)] *het (~s) (fig)* ninny, nitwit
¹uit [œyt] *prep* **1** out (of), from: *~ het raam kijken* look out of the window; *een speler ~ het veld sturen* order a player off (the field); **2** off: *2 km ~ de kust* 2 kilometres off the coast; **3** (out) of: *iets ~ ervaring kennen* know sth from experience; *~ zichzelf* of itself, of one's own accord *(pers); 4* out of, from: *~ bewondering* out of *(or:* in) admiration; *zij trouwden ~ liefde* they married for love
²uit [œyt] *adv* out: *hij liep de kamer ~* he walked out of the room; *Ajax speelt volgende week ~* Ajax are playing away next week; *moet je ook die kant ~?* are you going that way, too?; *voor zich ~ zitten kijken* sit staring into space; *ik zou er graag eens ~ willen* I would like to get away sometime; *de aankoop heb je er na een jaar ~* the purchase will save its cost in a year
³uit [œyt] *adj* **1** out, away: *de bal is ~* the ball is out; *die vlek gaat er niet ~* that stain won't come out; **2** over: *de school gaat ~* school is over, school is out; *het is ~ tussen hen* it is finished between them; *het is ~ met de pret* the game *(or:* party) is over now; **3** (gone) out: *de lamp is ~* the light is out *(or:* off); **4** out, after: *op iets ~ zijn* be out for *(or:* after) sth; *dit boek is pas ~* this book has just been published
uitademen [œytadəmə(n)] *vb* breathe out, exhale
uitademing [œytadəmiŋ] *de* exhalation
uitbalanceren [œytbalɑnserə(n)] *vb* balance
uitbarsten [œytbɑrstə(n)] *vb* **1** burst out: *in lachen ~* burst out laughing; *in tranen ~* burst into tears; **2** erupt
uitbarsting [œytbɑrstiŋ] *de (~en)* **1** outburst, eruption; **2** bursting out: *tot een ~ komen* come to a head
uitbeelden [œydbeldə(n)] *vb* portray, represent:

een verhaal ~ act out a story
uitbeelding [œydbeldiŋ] *de (~en)* portrayal, representation
uitbesteden [œydbəstedə(n)] *vb* **1** board out: *de kinderen een week ~* board the children out for a week; **2** farm out, contract (out)
uitbetalen [œydbətalə(n)] *vb* pay (out), cash
uitbetaling [œydbətaliŋ] *de (~en)* payment
uitbijten [œydbɛitə(n)] *vb* **1** bite (out); **2** eat away: *dat zuur bijt uit* that acid is corrosive
¹uitblazen [œydblazə(n)] *vb* **1** blow (out), breathe out: *de laatste adem ~* breathe one's last; **2** blow out
²uitblazen [œydblazə(n)] *vb* take a breather, catch one's breath
uitblijven [œydblɛivə(n)] *vb* **1** stay away, stay out; **2** fail to occur *(or:* appear, materialize): *de gevolgen bleven niet uit* the consequences (soon) became apparent
uitblinken [œydbliŋkə(n)] *vb* excel: *~ in* excel in
uitblinker [œydbliŋkər] *de (~s)* brilliant person *(or:* student): *in sport was hij geen ~* he did not shine in sports
uitbloeien [œydblujə(n)] *vb* leave off flowering: *de rozen zijn uitgebloeid* the roses have finished flowering
uitbouw [œydbɑu] *de (~en)* extension, addition
uitbouwen [œydbɑuwə(n)] *vb* **1** build out, add on to; **2** develop, expand
uitbraak [œydbrak] *de* break, jailbreak
¹uitbranden [œydbrɑndə(n)] *vb* **1** burn up; **2** be burnt down *(or:* out)
²uitbranden [œydbrɑndə(n)] *vb* burn down, burn out
uitbrander [œydbrɑndər] *de (~s)* dressing down, telling-off
¹uitbreiden [œydbrɛidə(n)] *vb* extend, expand: *zijn kennis ~* extend one's knowledge
²uitbreiden [œydbrɛidə(n)] *ref vb* extend, expand, spread
uitbreiding [œydbrɛidiŋ] *de (~en)* **1** extension, expansion; **2** extension, addition, development
uitbreken [œydbrekə(n)] *vb* break out: *er is brand (or: een epidemie) uitgebroken* a fire *(or:* an epidemic) has broken out; *een muur ~* knock down (a part of) a wall
uitbrengen [œydbrɛŋə(n)] *vb* **1** bring out, say: *een toast ~ op iem* propose a toast to s.o.; **2** make, give: *verslag ~ van een vergadering* give an account of a meeting; **3** bring out, release, publish: *een nieuw merk auto ~* put a new make of car on the market
uitbroeden [œydbrudə(n)] *vb* hatch (out): *eieren ~* hatch (out) eggs; *hij zit een idee uit te broeden* he is brooding over an idea
uitbuiten [œydbœytə(n)] *vb* exploit, use: *een gelegenheid ~* make the most of an opportunity
uitbuiter [œydbœytər] *de (~s)* exploiter
uitbuiting [œydbœytiŋ] *de (~en)* exploitation
uitbundig [œydbʏndəχ] *adj, adv* exuberant
uitdagen [œydaɣə(n)] *vb* challenge: *tot een duel ~*

challenge s.o. to a duel

uitdagend [œydaɣənt] *adj, adv* defiant: ~ *gekleed gaan* dress provocatively

uitdager [œydaɣər] *de (~s)* challenger

uitdaging [œydaɣɪŋ] *de (~en)* challenge, provocation

uitdelen [œydelə(n)] *vb* distribute, hand out

uitdeuken [œydøkə(n)] *vb* beat out (a dent, dents)

uitdijen [œydɛiə(n)] *vb* expand, swell, grow

uitdoen [œydun] *vb* **1** take off, remove: *zijn kleren* ~ take off one's clothes; **2** turn off, switch off

uitdokteren [œydɔktərə(n)] *vb* work out, figure out

uitdossen [œydɔsə(n)] *vb* dress up, deck out

uitdoven [œydovə(n)] *vb* extinguish, stub out

uitdraai [œydraj] *de (~en)* print-out

uitdraaien [œydrajə(n)] *vb* **1** turn off, switch off, turn out, put out; **2** print out

uitdragen [œydraɣə(n)] *vb* propagate, spread

uitdrijven [œydrɛivə(n)] *vb* drive out, expel, exorcize

uitdrogen [œydroɣə(n)] *vb* dry out, dry up

uitdrukkelijk [œydrʏkələk] *adj, adv* express, distinct: *iets ~ verbieden* expressly forbid sth

uitdrukken [œydrʏkə(n)] *vb* **1** express, put: *zijn gedachten* ~ express (*or:* convey, voice) one's thoughts; *om het eenvoudig uit te drukken* in plain terms, to put it plainly (*or:* simply); **2** stub out, put out: *de waarde van iets in geld* ~ express the value of sth in terms of money

uitdrukking [œydrʏkɪŋ] *de (~en)* **1** expression, idiom, term: *een vaste* ~ a fixed expression; **2** expression, look: *een verwilderde ~ in zijn ogen* a wild (*or:* haggard) look in his eyes

uitdunnen [œydʏnə(n)] *vb* thin (out), deplete

uiteenlopen [œytɛnlopə(n)] *vb* vary, differ, diverge: *de meningen liepen zeer uiteen* opinions were sharply (*or:* much) divided; *sterk* ~ vary (*or:* differ) widely

uiteenlopend [œytɛnlopənt] *adj* various, varied

uiteenzetting [œytɛnzɛtɪŋ] *de (~en)* explanation, account: *een ~ houden over een kwestie* give an account of sth

uiteinde [œytɛində] *het (~n)* **1** extremity, tip, (far) end; **2** end, close, end of the year: *iem een zalig ~ wensen* wish s.o. a happy New Year

¹uiteindelijk [œytɛindələk] *adj, adv* final, ultimate, last: *de ~e beslissing* the final decision

²uiteindelijk [œytɛindələk] *adv* finally, eventually, in the end: *~ belandde ik in Rome* eventually I ended (*or:* landed) up in Rome

uiten [œytə(n)] *vb* utter, express, speak

uitentreuren [œytəntrører(n)] *adv* over and over again, continually

uiteraard [œytərart] *adv* of course; naturally

¹uiterlijk [œytərlək] *het* **1** appearance, looks: *hij heeft zijn ~ niet mee* his looks are against him; *mensen op hun ~ beoordelen* judge people by their looks; **2** (outward) appearance, show: *dat is alleen*

maar voor het ~ that's just for appearance's sake (*or:* for show)

²uiterlijk [œytərlək] *adj* outward, external: *op de ~e schijn afgaan* judge by appearances

³uiterlijk [œytərlək] *adv* **1** outwardly, from the outside, externally: *~ scheen hij kalm* outwardly he seemed calm enough; **2** at the (very) latest, not later than: *~ (op) 1 november* not later than November 1; *tot ~ 10 juli* until July 10 at the latest

¹uiterst [œytərst] *adj* **1** far(thest), extreme, utmost: *het ~e puntje* the (extreme) tip, the far end; ~ *rechts* (the) far right; **2** greatest, utmost: *zijn ~e best doen om te helpen* do one's level best to help, bend over backwards to help; **3** final, last: *een ~e poging* a last-ditch effort

²uiterst [œytərst] *adv* extremely, most

uiterste [œytərstə] *het (~n)* **1** extreme, utmost, limit: *tot ~n vervallen* go to extremes; *van het ene ~ in het andere (vervallen)* go from one extreme to the other; **2** utmost, extreme, last: *bereid zijn tot het ~ te gaan* be prepared to go to any length; **3** extremity, end

uitfluiten [œytflœytə(n)] *vb* hiss (at), give (s.o.) the bird: *uitgefloten worden* receive catcalls, get the bird

uitgaan [œytχan] *vb* **1** go out, leave: *het huis (de deur)* ~ leave the house; *een avondje* ~ have a night out; *met een meisje* ~ go out with a girl, take a girl out, date a girl; **2** be over, be out, break up, go out: *de school* (*or: de bioscoop) gaat uit* school (*or:* the film) is over; **3** (with *van*) start (from), depart (from), take for granted, assume: *men is ervan uitgegaan dat …* it has been assumed (*or:* taken for granted) that …; *die vlekken gaan er niet uit* these spots won't come out

uitgaand [œytχant] *adj* outgoing, outward, outbound, outward bound: *~e brieven* (*or: post*) outgoing letters (*or:* post)

uitgaansavond [œytχansavɔnt] *de (~en)* (regular) night out

uitgaansgelegenheid [œytχansχəleɣə(n)hɛit] *de (-heden)* place of entertainment

uitgaansleven [œytχanslevə(n)] *het* nightlife: *een bruisend ~* a bustling nightlife

uitgang [œytχaŋ] *de (~en)* exit, way out

uitgangspositie [œytχaŋspozi(t)si] *de (~s)* point of departure: *zich in een goede* (*or: slechte) ~ bevinden om …* be in a good (*or:* bad) position for sth

uitgangspunt [œytχaŋspʏnt] *het (~en)* point of departure, starting point

uitgave [œytχavə] *de (~n)* **1** outlay; *(pl)* spending, expenditure, costs: *de ~n voor defensie* defence expenditure; **2** edition, issue; **3** publication, production

uitgavepatroon [œytχavəpatron] *het* pattern of spending

uitgeblust [œytχəblʏst] *adj* washed out: *een ~e indruk maken* look washed out

uitgebreid [œytχəbrɛit] *adj, adv* extensive, comprehensive, detailed

uitgehongerd [œytχəhɔŋərt] *adj* famished, starving

uitgekiend [œytχəkint] *adj* sophisticated, cunning

uitgekookt [œytχəkokt] *adj* sly, shrewd

uitgelaten [œytχəlatə(n)] *adj, adv* elated, exuberant

uitgemaakt [œytχəmakt] *adj* established, settled

uitgemergeld [œytχəmɛryəlt] *adj* emaciated, gaunt

uitgeput [œytχəpyt] *adj* **1** exhausted, worn out: ~ *van pijn* exhausted with pain; **2** empty, flat; **3** exhausted, at an end: *onze voorraden zijn* ~ our supplies have run out (*or:* are exhausted)

uitgerekend [œytχərekənt] *adv* precisely, of all (people, things), very: ~ *jij!* you of all people!; ~ *vandaag* today of all days

uitgeslapen [œytχəslapə(n)] *adj* wide awake, rested

uitgesloten [œytχəslotə(n)] *adj* out of the question, impossible

uitgestorven [œytχəstɔrvə(n)] *adj* **1** deserted, desolate; **2** extinct

uitgestrekt [œytχəstrɛkt] *adj* vast, extensive

uitgeteld [œytχətɛlt] *adj* exhausted, deadbeat, *(sport)* (counted) out || *wanneer is zijn vrouw* ~*?* when is their baby due?

uitgeven [œytχevə(n)] *vb* **1** spend, pay: *geld aan boeken* (or: *als water*) ~ spend money on books (*or:* like water); **2** issue, emit: *vals geld* ~ pass counterfeit money; **3** publish; **4** pass off (as): *zich voor iem anders* ~ impersonate s.o., pose as s.o. else

uitgever [œytχevər] *de (~s)* publisher

uitgeverij [œytχevərɛi] *de (~en)* publishing house (*or:* company), publisher('s)

uitgewerkt [œytχəwɛrkt] *adj* elaborate, detailed

uitgewoond [œytχəwont] *adj* run-down, dilapidated

uitgezakt [œytχəzakt] *adj* flopped down: ~ *in een luie stoel zitten* lie slumped in an armchair

¹uitgezonderd [œytχəzɔndərt] *conj* except(ing), apart from, but, except for the fact that: *iedereen ging mee,* ~ *hij* everyone came (along), except for him, everybody but him came (along)

²uitgezonderd [œytχəzɔndərt] *prep* except for, apart from: *niemand* ~ with no exceptions, bar none

uitgifte [œytχɪftə] *de (~n)* issue, distribution

uitgillen [œytχɪlə(n)] *vb* scream (out), shriek (out): *hij gilde het uit van de pijn* he screamed with pain

uitglijden [œytχlɛidə(n)] *vb* **1** slip, slide; **2** slip (and fall): ~ *over een bananenschil* slip on a banana peel

uitgooien [œytχojə(n)] *vb* throw out, eject (from): *een anker* ~ cast (*or:* drop) anchor

uitgraven [œytχravə(n)] *vb* **1** dig up, excavate; **2** dig out: *een sloot* ~ deepen (*or:* dig out) a ditch

uitgroeien [œytχrujə(n)] *vb* grow (into), develop (into)

uithaal [œythal] *de (uithalen)* hard shot, sizzler

uithakken [œythakə(n)] *vb* **1** chop (*or:* cut, hack) away; **2** cut out

¹uithalen [œythalə(n)] *vb* **1** take out, pull out, remove, unpick, undo, extract; **2** empty, clear out, clean out, draw: *een vogelnest* ~ take the eggs from a bird's nest; **3** play, do: *een grap met iem* ~ play a joke on s.o.; *wat heb je nu weer uitgehaald!* what have you been up to now!; **4** be of use, help: *het haalt niets uit* it is no use (*or:* all in vain)

²uithalen [œythalə(n)] *vb* (take a) swing: ~ *in de richting van de bal* take a swing (*or:* swipe) at the ball

uithangbord [œythaŋbɔrt] *het (~en)* sign(board): *mijn arm is geen* ~ I can't hold this forever

¹uithangen [œythaŋə(n)] *vb* **1** hang out; **2** be, hang out

²uithangen [œythaŋə(n)] *vb* **1** hang out, put out; **2** play, act

uitheems [œythems] *adj* exotic, foreign

uithoek [œythuk] *de (~en)* remote corner, outpost: *tot in de verste ~en van het land* to the farthest corners of the country; *in een* ~ *wonen* live in the back of beyond

uithollen [œythɔlə(n)] *vb* **1** scoop out, hollow out; **2** erode: *de democratie* ~ undermine (*or:* erode) democracy

uithongeren [œythɔŋərə(n)] *vb* starve (out): *de vijand* ~ starve the enemy out (*or:* into submission)

uithoren [œythorə(n)] *vb* interrogate, question

uithouden [œythaudə(n)] *vb* **1** stand, endure: *hij kon het niet langer* ~ he could not take (*or:* stand) it any longer; **2** stick (it) out: *het ergens lang* ~ stay (*or:* stick it out) somewhere for a long time

uithoudingsvermogen [œythaudɪŋsfərmoyə(n)] *het* staying power, endurance: *geen* ~ *hebben* lack stamina

uithuilen [œythœylə(n)] *vb* cry to one's heart's content

uithuwelijken [œythywələkə(n)] *vb* marry off, give in marriage

uiting [œytɪŋ] *de (~en)* utterance, expression, word(s): ~ *geven aan zijn gevoelens* express (*or:* vent, air) one's feelings; *tot* ~ *komen in* manifest (*or:* reveal) itself in

uitje [œycə] *het (~s)* **1** outing, (pleasure) trip, excursion; **2** cocktail onion

uitjoelen [œytjulə(n)] *vb see* uitjouwen

uitjouwen [œytjauwə(n)] *vb* boo, hoot at, jeer at

uitkammen [œytkamə(n)] *vb* comb (out), search

uitkauwen [œytkauwə(n)] *vb* chew (up)

uitkeren [œytkerə(n)] *vb* pay (out), remit

uitkering [œytkerɪŋ] *de (~en)* payment, remittance; benefit, allowance, pension: *recht hebben op een* ~ be entitled to benefit; *een maandelijkse* ~ a monthly allowance; *van een* ~ *leven* live on social security, be on the dole

uitkiezen [œytkizə(n)] *vb* choose, select: *je hebt het maar voor het* ~ (you can) take your pick

uitkijk [œytkɛik] *de (~en)* lookout, watch: *op de* ~

staan be on the watch (*or:* lookout) (for), keep watch (for)

uitkijken [œytkεikə(n)] *vb* 1 watch out, look out, be careful: ~ *met oversteken* take care crossing the street; 2 overlook, look out on: *dit raam kijkt uit op de zee* this window overlooks the sea; 3 look out (for), watch (for): *naar een andere baan* ~ watch (*or:* look) out for a new job; 4 look forward (to): *naar de vakantie* ~ look forward to the holidays; 5 tire (of sth): *gauw uitgekeken zijn op iets* quickly tire (*or:* get tired) of sth

uitkijkpost [œytkεikpɔst] *de* (~*en*) lookout, observation post

uitkijktoren [œytkεiktorə(n)] *de* (~*s*) watchtower

uitklapbaar [œytklɑbar] *adj* folding, collapsible: *deze stoel is* ~ *tot een bed* this chair converts into a bed

uitklappen [œytklɑpə(n)] *vb* fold (out)

uitklaren [œytklarə(n)] *vb* clear (through customs)

uitkleden [œytkledə(n)] *vb* undress, strip (off): *zich* ~ undress, strip (off)

uitkloppen [œytklɔpə(n)] *vb* beat (out), shake (out): *een kleed* ~ beat a carpet

uitknijpen [œytknεipə(n)] *vb* squeeze (out, dry): *een puistje* ~ squeeze out a pimple

uitknippen [œytknɪpə(n)] *vb* cut, clip: *prentjes* ~ cut out pictures

uitkomen [œytkomə(n)] *vb* 1 end up, arrive at: *op de hoofdweg* ~ join (onto) the main road; 2 lead (to), give out (into, on to): *die deur komt uit op de straat* ~ this door opens (out) on to the street; 3 come out, sprout; 4 hatch (out); 5 be revealed (*or:* disclosed): *het kwam uit* it was revealed, it transpired; 6 (with *voor*) admit: *voor zijn mening durven* ~ stand up for one's opinion; *eerlijk* ~ *voor* admit openly, be honest about; 7 prove to be true (*or:* correct), come true, come out, work out, be right: *die som komt niet uit* that sum doesn't add up; *mijn voorspelling kwam uit* my prediction proved correct (*or:* came true); 8 (*sport*) play; (*cards*) lead: *met klaveren* (or: *troef*) ~ lead clubs (*or:* trumps); 9 appear, be published: *een nieuw tijdschrift laten* ~ publish a new magazine; 10 turn out, work out: *bedrogen* ~ be deceived; *dat komt (me) goed uit* that suits me fine, that's very timely (*or:* convenient); 11 show up, stand out, come out, be apparent: *iets goed laten* ~ show sth to advantage; *tegen de lichte achtergrond komen de kleuren goed uit* the colours show up (*or:* stand out) well against the light background

uitkomst [œytkɔmst] *de* (~*en*) (final, net) result, outcome

uitkopen [œytkopə(n)] *vb* buy out

uitkotsen [œytkɔtsə(n)] *vb* throw up, spew up

uitkrijgen [œytkrεiɣə(n)] *vb* 1 get off, get out of: *zijn laarzen niet* ~ not be able to get one's boots off; 2 finish, get to the end of

uitlaat [œytlat] *de* (*uitlaten*) exhaust (pipe), (*Am*) muffler; funnel

uitlaatgassen [œytlatχɑsə(n)] *de* exhaust fumes

uitlaatklep [œytlatklεp] *de* (~*pen*) 1 outlet valve; exhaust valve, escape valve; 2 (*fig*) outlet

uitlaatpijp [œytlatpεip] *de* (~*en*) (*car*) exhaust pipe

uitlachen [œytlɑχə(n)] *vb* laugh at, deride, scoff (at), ridicule: *iem in zijn gezicht* ~ laugh in s.o.'s face

uitladen [œytladə(n)] *vb* unload, discharge (*ship*)

uitlaten [œytlatə(n)] *vb* show out (*or:* to the door), see out (*or:* to the door), let out, discharge: *een bezoeker* ~ show a visitor out (*or:* to the door); *de hond* ~ take the dog out (for a walk)

uitleentermijn [œytlentεrmεin] *de* (~*en*) lending period

uitleg [œytlεχ] *de* explanation, account: *haar* ~ *van wat er gebeurd was* her account of what had happened

uitleggen [œytlεɣə(n)] *vb* explain, interpret: *dromen* ~ interpret dreams; *verkeerd* ~ misinterpret, misconstrue

uitlekken [œytlεkə(n)] *vb* 1 drain, drip dry: *groente laten* ~ drain vegetables; 2 get out, leak out

uitlenen [œytlenə(n)] *vb* lend (out), loan

uitleven [œytlevə(n)] *ref vb* live it up, let oneself go

uitleveren [œytlevərə(n)] *vb* extradite, hand over: *iem aan de politie* ~ hand s.o. over (*or:* turn s.o. in) to the police

uitlevering [œytlevərɪŋ] *de* (~*en*) extradition

uitlezen [œytlezə(n)] *vb* 1 read to the end, read through, finish (reading); 2 (*comp*) read out

uitlikken [œytlɪkə(n)] *vb* lick clean, lick out

uitloggen [œytlɔɣə(n)] *vb* log off; log out

uitlokken [œytlɔkə(n)] *vb* provoke, elicit, stimulate: *een discussie* ~ provoke a discussion; *hij lokt het zelf uit* he is asking for it (*or:* trouble)

uitloop [œytlop] *de* extension: *een* ~ *tot vier jaar* an extension to four years

uitlopen [œytlopə(n)] *vb* 1 run out (of), walk out (of), leave: *de straat* ~ walk down the street; 2 sprout, shoot, come out; 3 result in, end in: *dat loopt op niets* (or: *een mislukking*) *uit* that will come to nothing (*or:* end in failure); *die ruzie liep uit op een gevecht* the quarrel ended in a fight; 4 draw ahead (of): *hij is al 20 seconden uitgelopen* he's already in the lead by 20 seconds; 5 overrun its (*or:* one's) time: *de receptie liep uit* the reception went on longer than expected; 6 run: *uitgelopen oogschaduw* smeared (*or:* smudged) eyeshadow; *de verf is uitgelopen* the paint has run

uitloten [œytlotə(n)] *vb* 1 eliminate by lottery; 2 draw, select

uitloven [œytlovə(n)] *vb* offer, put up: *een beloning* ~ offer (*or:* put up) a reward

uitmaken [œytmakə(n)] *vb* 1 break off; finish, terminate: *het* ~ break (*or:* split) up; 2 constitute, make up: *deel* ~ *van* be (a) part of; *een belangrijk deel van de kosten* ~ form (*or:* represent) a large part of the cost; 3 matter, be of importance: *het maakt mij niet(s) uit* it is all the same to me, I don't care; *wat maakt dat uit?* what does that matter?; *weinig* ~ make little difference; **4** determine, establish, make out: *dat maakt hij toch niet uit* that's not for him to decide; *dat maak ik zelf nog wel uit* I'll be the judge of that; **5** *(with voor)* call, brand: *iem voor dief* ~ call s.o. a thief

uitmelken [œytmɛlkə(n)] *vb* bleed dry *(or:* white), strip bare: *een onderwerp* ~ flog a subject to death

uitmergelen [œytmɛrɣələ(n)] *vb* emaciate, starve, exhaust: *een uitgemergeld paard* a wasted horse

uitmesten [œytmɛstə(n)] *vb* **1** clean out, muck out: *een stal* ~ muck out a stable; **2** clean up, tidy up: *een kast* ~ tidy up *(or:* clear out) a cupboard

uitmonden [œytmɔndə(n)] *vb* **1** flow (out), discharge, run into; **2** lead to, end in: *het gesprek mondde uit in een enorme ruzie* the conversation ended in a fierce quarrel

uitmoorden [œytmordə(n)] *vb* massacre, butcher

uitmuntend [œytmʏntənt] *adj, adv* excellent, first-rate

uitnemen [œytnemə(n)] *vb* remove, take out

uitnodigen [œytnodəɣə(n)] *vb* invite, ask: *iem op een feestje* ~ invite *(or:* ask) s.o. to a party

uitnodiging [œytnodəɣɪŋ] *de (~en)* invitation: *een* ~ *voor de lunch* an invitation to lunch

uitoefenen [œytufənə(n)] *vb* **1** practise, pursue, be engaged in; **2** exert, exercise, wield: *kritiek* ~ *op* criticize, censure

uitoefening [œytufənɪŋ] *de* exercise, exertion, practice: *in de* ~ *van zijn ambt* in the performance *(or:* discharge, exercise) of his duties

uitpakken [œytpɑkə(n)] *vb* unwrap, unpack

uitpersen [œytpɛrsə(n)] *vb* squeeze, crush

uitpluizen [œytplœyzə(n)] *vb* unravel, sift (out, through): *iets helemaal* ~ get to the bottom of sth

¹**uitpraten** [œytpratə(n)] *vb* finish (talking), have one's say: *iem laten* ~ let s.o. finish, hear s.o. out

²**uitpraten** [œytpratə(n)] *vb* talk out *(or:* over), have out: *we moeten het* ~ we'll have to talk this out *(or:* over)

uitprinten [œytprɪntə(n)] *vb* print (out)

uitproberen [œytprobərə(n)] *vb* try (out), test

uitpuilen [œytpœylə(n)] *vb* bulge (out), protrude: *~de ogen* bulging *(or:* protruding) eyes

uitputten [œytpʏtə(n)] *vb* **1** exhaust, finish (up): *de voorraad raakt uitgeput* the supply is running out; **2** exhaust, wear out

uitputting [œytpʏtɪŋ] *de (~en)* exhaustion, fatigue: *de* ~ *van de olievoorraden* the exhaustion of oil supplies

uitrangeren [œytrɑnʒerə(n)] *vb* sidetrack, shunt

uitrazen [œytrazə(n)] *vb* let *(or:* blow) off steam, blow out: *de kinderen laten* ~ let the children have their fling

uitreiken [œytrɛikə(n)] *vb* distribute, give out, present: *diploma's* ~ present diplomas; *iem een onderscheiding* ~ confer a distinction on s.o.

uitreiking [œytrɛikɪŋ] *de (~en)* distribution, presentation

uitreisvisum [œytrɛisfizʏm] *het (-visa)* exit visa

uitrekenen [œytrekənə(n)] *vb* calculate, compute ‖ *zij is begin maart uitgerekend* the baby is due at the beginning of March

¹**uitrekken** [œytrɛkə(n)] *vb* stretch (out), elongate: *een elastiek* ~ stretch out a rubber band; *zich* ~ stretch oneself (out)

²**uitrekken** [œytrɛkə(n)] *vb* stretch: *de trui is in de was uitgerekt* the sweater has stretched in the wash

uitrichten [œytrɪχtə(n)] *vb* do, accomplish: *dat zal niet veel* ~ that won't help much

uitrijden [œytrɛidə(n)] *vb* drive to the end (of); ride to the end (of) ‖ *mest* ~ spread manure *(or:* fertilizer)

uitrijstrook [œytrɛistrok] *de (-stroken)* deceleration lane

uitrit [œytrɪt] *de (~ten)* exit: ~ *vrijhouden s.v.p.* please keep (the) exit clear

uitroeien [œytrujə(n)] *vb* exterminate, wipe out

uitroeiing [œytrujɪŋ] *de (~en)* extermination

uitroep [œytrup] *de (~en)* exclamation, cry

uitroepen [œytrupə(n)] *vb* **1** exclaim, shout, cry (out), call (out); **2** call, declare: *een staking* ~ call a strike; *hij werd tot winnaar uitgeroepen* he was declared *(or:* voted) the winner

uitroepteken [œytruptekə(n)] *het (~s)* exclamation mark

uitroken [œytrokə(n)] *vb* smoke out: *vossen* ~ smoke out foxes

uitrollen [œytrɔlə(n)] *vb* unroll: *de tuinslang* ~ unreel the garden hose

uitruimen [œytrœymə(n)] *vb* clear out, tidy out, turn out: *een kast* ~ tidy *(or:* turn) out a cupboard

¹**uitrukken** [œytrʏkə(n)] *vb* tear out, pull out: *planten* ~ root up *(or:* uproot) plants

²**uitrukken** [œytrʏkə(n)] *vb* turn out: *de brandweer rukte uit* the fire brigade turned out

¹**uitrusten** [œytrʏstə(n)] *vb* rest

²**uitrusten** [œytrʏstə(n)] *vb* equip, fit out: *uitgerust met 16 kleppen* fitted with 16 valves

uitrusting [œytrʏstɪŋ] *de (~en)* equipment, kit, outfit, gear: *zijn intellectuele* ~ his intellectual baggage; *ze waren voorzien van de modernste* ~ they were fitted out with the latest equipment

uitschakelen [œytsχakələ(n)] *vb* **1** switch off: *de motor* ~ cut *(or:* stop) the engine; **2** *(fig)* eliminate, knock out: *door ziekte uitgeschakeld zijn* be out of circulation through ill health

uitscheiden [œytsχɛidə(n)] *vb (inf)* (with *met*) stop (-ing), cease (to, -ing): *ik schei uit met werken als ik zestig word* I'll stop working when I turn sixty; *schei uit!* cut it out!, knock it off!

uitschelden [œytsχɛldə(n)] *vb* abuse, call names: *iem* ~ *voor dief* call s.o. a thief

¹**uitscheuren** [œytsχørə(n)] *vb* tear out

²**uitscheuren** [œytsχørə(n)] *vb* tear: *het knoopsgat is uitgescheurd* the buttonhole is torn

uitschieten [œytsχitə(n)] *vb* shoot out, dart out: *het mes schoot uit* the knife slipped

uitschieter [œytsχitər] *de (~s)* peak, highlight
uitschijnen [œytsχɛinə(n)] *vb (Belg)* || *iets laten ~* let it be understood, hint at sth
uitschoppen [œytsχɔpə(n)] *vb* kick out
uitschot [œytsχɔt] *het* **1** refuse; **2** scum, dregs
uitschreeuwen [œytsχrewə(n)] *vb* cry out: *het ~ van pijn* cry out (*or:* yell, bellow) with pain
uitschrijven [œytsχrɛivə(n)] *vb* **1** write out, copy out: *aantekeningen ~* write out notes; **2** call; hold, organize; **3** write out: *een recept ~* write out a prescription; *rekeningen ~* make out accounts; *iem als lid ~* strike s.o.'s name off the membership list
uitschudden [œytsχγdə(n)] *vb* shake (out)
uitschuifbaar [œytsχœyvbar] *adj* extending
uitschuiven [œytsχœyvə(n)] *vb* **1** slide out, pull out; **2** extend: *een tafel ~* extend (*or:* pull out) a table
¹uitslaan [œytslan] *vb* **1** beat out, strike out: *het stof ~* beat (*or:* shake) out the dust; **2** shake out, beat out: *een stofdoek ~* shake out a duster; **3** utter, talk: *onzin ~* talk rot
²uitslaan [œytslan] *vb* grow mouldy, become mouldy, sweat || *een ~de brand* a blaze
uitslag [œytslɑχ] *de (~en)* **1** rash; damp: *daar krijg ik ~ van* that brings out (*or:* gives me) a rash; **2** result, outcome: *de ~ van de verkiezingen* (or: *van het examen)* the results of the elections (*or:* examination)
uitslapen [œytslapə(n)] *vb* have a good lie-in, sleep late: *goed uitgeslapen zijn (fig)* be pretty astute (*or:* shrewd); *tot 10 uur ~* stay in bed until 10 o'clock
uitsloven [œytslovə(n)] *vb* slave away, work oneself to death
uitsluiten [œytslœytə(n)] *vb* **1** shut out, lock out: *zij wordt van verdere deelname uitgesloten* she has been disqualified; **2** exclude, rule out: *die mogelijkheid kunnen we niet ~* that is a possibility we can't rule out (*or:* ignore); *dat is uitgesloten* that is out of the question
uitsluitend [œytslœytənt] *adj, adv* only, exclusively: *~ volwassenen* adults only
uitsluiting [œytslœytɪŋ] *de (~en)* **1** exclusion; *(sport)* disqualification; **2** exception: *met ~ van* exclusive of, to the exclusion of
uitsmijter [œytsmɛitər] *de (~s)* **1** bouncer; **2** fried bacon and eggs served on slices of bread; **3** final number of a show
uitsnijden [œytsnɛidə(n)] *vb* cut (out), carve (out): *een laag uitgesneden japon* a low-cut (*or:* low-necked) dress
uitsparen [œytsparə(n)] *vb* **1** save (on), economize (on): *dertig euro ~* save thirty euros; **2** leave blank (*or:* open): *openingen ~* leave spaces
uitsparing [œytsparɪŋ] *de (~en)* cutaway; notch
uitspatten [œytspɑtə(n)] *vb* live it up
uitspatting [œytspɑtɪŋ] *de (~en)* splurge; extravagance: *zich overgeven aan ~en* indulge in excesses
uitspelen [œytspelə(n)] *vb* **1** finish, play out; **2** play, lead: *mensen tegen elkaar ~* play people off against one another

uitsplitsen [œytsplɪtsə(n)] *vb* itemize, break down
uitsplitsing [œytsplɪtsɪŋ] *de (~en)* itemization, breakdown
uitspoelen [œytspulə(n)] *vb* rinse (out), wash (out)
uitspoken [œytspokə(n)] *vb* be (*or:* get) up to
uitspraak [œytsprak] *de (uitspraken)* **1** pronunciation, accent: *de ~ van het Chinees* the pronunciation of Chinese; **2** pronouncement, judgement; **3** *(law)* judg(e)ment, sentence, verdict: *~ doen* pass judg(e)ment, pass (*or:* pronounce) sentence
uitspreiden [œytsprɛidə(n)] *vb* spread (out), stretch (out)
uitspreken [œytsprekə(n)] *vb* **1** pronounce, articulate: *hoe moet je dit woord ~?* how do you pronounce this word?; **2** say, express: *iem laten ~* let s.o. have his say, hear s.o. out; **3** declare, pronounce: *een vonnis ~* pronounce judgement
uitspringen [œytsprɪŋə(n)] *vb* stand out
uitspugen [œytspyγə(n)] *vb* spit out
uitspuwen [œytspywə(n)] *vb see* uitspugen
¹uitstaan [œytstan] *vb* stand (*or:* stick, jut) out, protrude
²uitstaan [œytstan] *vb* stand, endure, bear: *hitte* (or: *lawaai) niet kunnen ~* not be able to endure the heat (*or:* noise); *iem niet kunnen ~* hate s.o.'s guts; *ik heb nog veel geld ~* I have a lot of money out (at interest)
uitstalkast [œytstɑlkɑst] *de (~en)* show case, display case
uitstallen [œytstɑlə(n)] *vb* display, expose (for sale), *(fig)* show off
uitstalraam [œytstɑlram] *het (-ramen) (Belg)* shop window, display window
uitstapje [œytstapjə] *het (~s)* trip, outing, excursion: *een ~ maken* take (*or:* make) a trip, go on an outing
uitstappen [œytstapə(n)] *vb* get off (*or:* down), step out, get out
uitsteeksel [œytsteksəl] *het (~s)* projection, protuberance
¹uitsteken [œytstekə(n)] *vb* **1** stick out, jut out, project, protrude; **2** stand out: *de toren steekt boven de huizen uit* the tower rises (high) above the houses; *boven alle anderen ~* tower above all the others
²uitsteken [œytstekə(n)] *vb* **1** hold out, put out; **2** reach out, stretch out: *zijn hand naar iem ~* extend one's hand to s.o.
uitstekend [œytstekənt] *adj, adv* excellent, first-rate: *van ~e kwaliteit* of high quality
uitstel [œytstɛl] *het* delay, postponement, deferment: *~ van betaling* postponement (*or:* extension) of payment; *zonder ~* without delay; *(Belg; law) met ~* suspended
uitstellen [œytstɛlə(n)] *vb* put off, postpone, defer: *voor onbepaalde tijd ~* postpone indefinitely
uitsterven [œytstɛrvə(n)] *vb* die (out), become extinct: *het dorp was uitgestorven* the village was deserted

uitstijgen [œytstɛiɣə(n)] *vb* surpass

uitstippelen [œytstɪpələ(n)] *vb* outline, map out, trace out, work out: *een route* ~ map out a route

uitstoot [œytstot] *de (uitstoten)* discharge, emissions

uitstorten [œytstɔrtə(n)] *vb* **1** pour out (*or:* forth), empty (out); **2** pour out: *zijn woede* ~ *over iem* vent one's rage upon s.o.

uitstorting [œytstɔrtɪŋ] *de (~en)* **1** pouring out, outpouring *(fig)*; **2** effusion

uitstoten [œytstotə(n)] *vb* **1** expel, cast out: *iem* ~ *uit de groep* expel (*or:* banish) s.o. from the group; **2** emit, utter: *onverstaanbare klanken* ~ emit (*or:* utter) unintelligible sounds; **3** eject, emit

¹**uitstralen** [œytstralə(n)] *vb (also fig)* radiate, give off, exude: *zelfvertrouwen* ~ radiate (*or:* exude, ooze) self-confidence

²**uitstralen** [œytstralə(n)] *vb* radiate, emanate

uitstraling [œytstralɪŋ] *de (~en)* radiation, emission, *(fig)* aura: *een enorme* ~ *hebben (roughly)* possess charisma, have a certain magic

¹**uitstrekken** [œytstrɛkə(n)] *vb* **1** stretch (out), reach (out), extend: *met uitgestrekte armen* with outstretched arms; **2** extend

²**uitstrekken** [œytstrɛkə(n)] *ref vb* extend, stretch (out): *zich* ~ *over* extend over

uitstrijken [œytstrɛikə(n)] *vb* spread, smear

uitstrijkje [œytstrɛikjə] *het (~s)* (cervical) smear, swab

uitstromen [œytstromə(n)] *vb* **1** stream out, pour out; **2** flow (*or:* discharge, empty) into

uitstrooien [œytstrojə(n)] *vb* scatter, spread

uitsturen [œytstyrə(n)] *vb* send out, *(sport)* send off (the field): *iem op iets* ~ send s.o. for sth

uittekenen [œytekənə(n)] *vb* draw, trace out: *ik kan die plaats wel* ~ I know every detail of that place

uittesten [œytɛstə(n)] *vb* test (out), try (out), put to the test

uittikken [œytɪkə(n)] *vb* type out

uittocht [œytɔχt] *de (~en)* exodus, trek

uittrap [œytrɑp] *de (~pen)* goal kick

uittrappen [œytrɑpə(n)] *vb* **1** kick (the ball) into play, take a goal kick; **2** put out of play (*or:* into touch, over the line); **3** kick off

uittreden [œytredə(n)] *vb* resign (from): *vervroegd* ~ retire early, take early retirement

¹**uittrekken** [œytrɛkə(n)] *vb* **1** take off, pull off: *zijn kleren* ~ take off one's clothes, undress; **2** put aside, set aside, reserve: *een bedrag voor iets* ~ put (*or:* set) aside a sum (of money) for sth

²**uittrekken** [œytrɛkə(n)] *vb* go out, march out: *erop* ~ *om* set out to

uittreksel [œytrɛksəl] *het (~s)* excerpt, extract

uittypen [œytipə(n)] *vb* type out

uitvaardigen [œytfardəɣə(n)] *vb* issue, put out, *(law also)* make

uitvaart [œytfart] *de (~en)* funeral (service), burial (service)

uitvaartcentrum [œytfartsɛntrʏm] *het (-centra)* funeral parlour, mortuary

uitvaartdienst [œytfardinst] *de (~en)* funeral service, burial service

uitvaartmis [œytfartmɪs] *de (~sen)* funeral mass

uitvaartstoet [œytfartstut] *de (~en)* funeral procession

uitval [œytfɑl] *de (~len)* **1** outburst, explosion; **2** (hair) loss

uitvallen [œytfɑlə(n)] *vb* **1** burst out, explode, blow up; **2** fall (*or:* drop, come) out: *zijn haren vallen uit* he is losing his hair; **3** drop out, fall out, break down: *de stroom is uitgevallen* there's a power failure; **4** turn out, work out: *we weten niet hoe de stemming zal* ~ we don't know how (*or:* which way) the vote will go

uitvaller [œytfɑlər] *de (~s)* person who drops out, casualty

uitvalsweg [œytfɑlswɛχ] *de (~en)* main traffic road (out of a town)

uitvaren [œytfarə(n)] *vb* sail, put (out) to sea, leave port

uitvechten [œytfɛχtə(n)] *vb* fight out: *iets met iem* ~ fight (*or:* have) sth out with s.o.

uitvegen [œytfeɣə(n)] *vb* **1** sweep out, clean out; **2** wipe out; erase: *een woord op het schoolbord* ~ wipe (*or:* rub) out a word on the blackboard

uitvergroten [œytfərɣrotə(n)] *vb* enlarge, magnify, blow up

uitvergroting [œytfərɣrotɪŋ] *de (~en)* enlargement, blow-up

uitverkocht [œytfərkɔχt] *adj* **1** sold out: *onze kousen zijn* ~ we have run out of stockings; **2** sold out, booked out, fully booked: *voor een ~e zaal spelen* play to a full house

uitverkoop [œytfərkop] *de* (clearance, bargain) sale

uitverkopen [œytfərkopə(n)] *vb* sell off, clear, sell out

uitvinden [œytfɪndə(n)] *vb* **1** invent; **2** find out, discover

uitvinder [œytfɪndər] *de (~s)* inventor

uitvinding [œytfɪndɪŋ] *de (~en)* invention; gadget: *een* ~ *doen* invent sth

uitvissen [œytfɪsə(n)] *vb* dig (*or:* fish, ferret) out

uitvlucht [œytflʏχt] *de (~en)* excuse, pretext: *~en zoeken* make excuses, dodge (*or:* evade) the question

uitvoegen [œytfuɣə(n)] *vb* exit

uitvoegstrook [œytfuχstrok] *de (-stroken)* deceleration lane

uitvoer [œytfur] *de (~en)* **1** export: *de in- en* ~ *van goederen* the import and export of goods; **2** exports; **3** execution: *een opdracht ten* ~ *brengen* carry out an instruction (*or:* order)

uitvoerartikel [œytfurɑrtikəl] *het (~en, ~s)* export product

uitvoerbaar [œytfurbar] *adj* feasible, workable, practicable

uitvoerder [œytfurdər] *de (~s)* works foreman

382

uitvoeren [œytfurə(n)] *vb* **1** export; **2** do: *hij voert niets uit* he doesn't do a stroke (of work); **3** perform, carry out: *plannen ~* carry out (*or:* execute) plans

uitvoerend [œytfurənt] *adj* executive: *~ personeel* staff carrying out the work

uitvoerhaven [œytfurhavə(n)] *de (~s)* port of export (*or:* shipment), shipping port

uitvoerig [œytfurəχ] *adj, adv* comprehensive, full; elaborate, detailed: *iets ~ beschrijven* (or: *bespreken*) describe/discuss sth at great (*or:* some) length

uitvoering [œytfurıŋ] *de (~en)* **1** carrying out, performance: *werk in ~* road works (ahead), men at work, work in progress; **2** performance, execution; **3** design, construction, workmanship: *wij hebben dit model in twee ~en* we have two versions of this model

uitvoerrecht [œytfurɛχt] *het (~en)* export duty

uitvoerverbod [œytfurvərbɔt] *het (~en)* prohibition of export(s), ban on export(s)

uitvoervergunning [œytfurvərɣynıŋ] *de (~en)* export licence

uitvouwen [œytfɑuwə(n)] *vb* unfold, fold out, spread out

uitvreten [œytfretə(n)] *vb* be up to: *wat heeft hij nou weer uitgevreten?* what has he been up to now?

uitwaaien [œytwajə(n)] *vb* **1** blow out, be blown out; **2** get a breath of (fresh) air

uitwas [œytwas] *het, de (~sen)* excrescence, morbid growth, *(pl)* excesses

uitwasemen [œytwasəmə(n)] *vb* **1** evaporate; **2** steam, perspire

uitwassen [œytwasə(n)] *vb* **1** wash (out); swab (out); **2** wash out (*or:* away)

uitwedstrijd [œytwɛtstrɛit] *de (~en)* away match (*or:* game)

uitweg [œytwɛχ] *de (~en)* way out, answer: *hij zag geen andere ~ meer dan onder te duiken* he had no choice but to go into hiding

uitweiden [œytwɛidə(n)] *vb* expatiate (on), hold forth

uitwendig [œytwɛndəχ] *adj, adv* external, outward, exterior: *een geneesmiddel voor ~ gebruik* a medicine for external use

¹uitwerken [œytwɛrkə(n)] *vb* **1** work out, elaborate: *zijn aantekeningen ~* work up one's notes; *een idee ~* develop an idea; *uitgewerkte plannen* detailed plans; **2** work out, compute: *sommen ~* work out sums

²uitwerken [œytwɛrkə(n)] *vb* wear off, have spent one's force: *de verdoving is uitgewerkt* (the effect of) the anaesthetic has worn off

uitwerking [œytwɛrkıŋ] *de (~en)* **1** effect, result: *de beoogde ~ hebben* have the desired (*or:* intended) effect, be effective; *de medicijnen hadden geen ~* the medicines had no effect (*or:* didn't work); **2** working out, elaboration; **3** working out, computation

uitwerpen [œytwɛrpə(n)] *vb* **1** throw out: *zijn hen-gel ergens ~* cast one's line somewhere; **2** throw out

uitwerpselen [œytwɛrpsələ(n)] *de* excrement; droppings

uitwijkeling [œytwɛikəlıŋ] *de (~en) (Belg)* emigrant

uitwijken [œytwɛikə(n)] *vb* get out of the way (of); make way (for): *rechts ~* swerve to the right; *men liet het luchtverkeer naar Oostende ~* air traffic was diverted to Ostend

uitwijzen [œytwɛizə(n)] *vb* **1** show, reveal: *de tijd zal het ~* time will tell; **2** deport, expel

uitwijzing [œytwɛizıŋ] *de (~en)* deportation, expulsion

uitwisselbaar [œytwısəlbar] *adj* interchangeable, exchangeable

uitwisselen [œytwısələ(n)] *vb* exchange, swap: *ervaringen ~* compare notes

uitwisseling [œytwısəlıŋ] *de (~en)* exchange, swap

uitwissen [œytwısə(n)] *vb* wipe out, erase, efface: *een opname ~* wipe (*or:* erase) a recording; *sporen ~* cover up one's tracks

uitwonend [œytwɔnənt] *adj* (living) away from home: *een ~e dochter* one daughter living away from home

uitworp [œytwɔrp] *de (~en)* throw(-out)

uitwrijven [œytfrɛivə(n)] *vb* **1** rub, polish (up): *zijn ogen ~* rub one's eyes; **2** spread, rub over

uitwringen [œytfrıŋə(n)] *vb* wring out

¹uitzaaien [œytsajə(n)] *vb (med)* sow, disseminate

²uitzaaien [œytsajə(n)] *ref vb (med)* metastasize, spread: *de kanker had zich uitgezaaid* the cancer had spread (*or:* formed secondaries)

uitzaaiing [œytsajıŋ] *de (~en) (med)* spread, dissemination

uitzakken [œytsakə(n)] *vb* sag, give way: *een uitge-zakt lichaam* a sagging body

uitzeilen [œytsɛilə(n)] *vb* sail (away, off), set sail

uitzendbureau [œytsɛndbyro] *het (~s)* (temporary) employment agency, temp(ing) agency: *voor een ~ werken* temp, do temping

uitzenden [œytsɛndə(n)] *vb* broadcast, transmit: *de tv zendt de wedstrijd uit* the match will be televised (*or:* be broadcast)

uitzending [œytsɛndıŋ] *de (~en)* broadcast, transmission: *een rechtstreekse ~* a direct (*or:* live) broadcast; *u bent nu in de ~* you're on the air now

uitzendkracht [œytsɛntkraχt] *de (~en)* temporary worker (*or:* employee); temp

uitzet [œytsɛt] *het, de (~ten)* outfit; trousseau

uitzetten [œytsɛtə(n)] *vb* **1** throw out, put out, expel, deport: *ongewenste vreemdelingen ~* deport (*or:* expel) undesirable aliens; **2** switch off, turn off: *het gas ~* turn the gas off; **3** expand, enlarge, extend

uitzetting [œytsɛtıŋ] *de (~en)* ejection, expulsion, deportation, eviction

uitzicht [œytsıχt] *het (~en)* **1** view, prospect, panorama: *vrij ~* unobstructed view; *met ~ op* with a view of, overlooking, looking (out) onto; **2** prospect, outlook: *~ geven op promotie* hold out prospects (*or:* the prospect) of promotion

uitzichtloos [œytsɪχtlos] *adj* hopeless, dead-end

uitzien [œytsin] *vb* face, front, look out on: *een kamer die op zee uitziet* a room with a view of the sea, a room facing the sea

uitzingen [œytsɪŋə(n)] *vb* hold out, manage

uitzinnig [œytsɪnəχ] *adj, adv* delirious, wild: *een ~e menigte* a frenzied (*or:* hysterical) crowd

uitzitten [œytsɪtə(n)] *vb* sit out, stay until the end of: *zijn tijd ~* sit out (*or:* wait out) one's time

uitzoeken [œytsukə(n)] *vb* **1** select, choose, pick out; **2** sort (out); **3** sort out, figure out

uitzonderen [œytsɔndərə(n)] *vb* except, exclude

uitzondering [œytsɔndərɪŋ] *de (~en)* exception: *een ~ maken voor* make an exception for; *een ~ op de regel* an exception to the rule; *met ~ van* with the exception of, excepting, save

uitzonderlijk [œytsɔndərlək] *adj, adv* exceptional, unique

uitzuigen [œytsœyɣə(n)] *vb* **1** squeeze dry, bleed dry, exploit; **2** vacuum (out)

uitzuiger [œytsœyɣər] *de (~s)* bloodsucker, extortionist

uitzwaaien [œytswajə(n)] *vb* send off, wave goodbye to

uitzweten [œytswetə(n)] *vb* sweat out

uk [ʏk] *de (~ken)* toddler, kiddy

ultiem [ʏltim] *adj* ultimate, last-minute

ultimatum [ʏltimatʏm] *het (~s)* ultimatum: *een ~ stellen* give (s.o.) an ultimatum

ultramodern [ʏltramodɛrn] *adj* ultramodern

ultraviolet [ʏltravijolɛt] *adj* ultraviolet

unaniem [ynanim] *adj, adv* unanimous: *~ aangenomen* adopted unanimously

unie [yni] *de (~s)* union, association: *Europese Unie* European Union

unief [ynif] *de (~s) (Belg)* university

uniek [ynik] *adj, adv* unique

uniform [ynifɔrm] *het (~en)* uniform: *een ~ dragen* wear a uniform

uniseks [yniseks] *adj* unisex

universeel [ynivɛrzel] *adj, adv* universal: *de universele rechten van de mens* the universal rights of man

universitair [ynivɛrzitɛːr] *adj* university: *iem met een ~e opleiding* s.o. with a university education

universiteit [ynivɛrzitɛit] *de (~en)* university: *hoogleraar aan de ~ van Oxford* professor at Oxford University; *naar de ~ gaan* go to the university, go to college

universum [ynivɛrzʏm] *het* universe

unzippen [ʏnzɪpə(n)] *vb* unzip, decompress, unpack

uranium [yranijʏm] *het* uranium: *verrijkt ~* enriched uranium

urgent [ʏrɣɛnt] *adj* urgent

urgentie [ʏrɣɛnsi] *de* urgency

urgentieverklaring [ʏrɣɛnsivərklarɪŋ] *de (~en)* certificate of urgency (*or:* need)

urine [yrinə] *de* urine

urineonderzoek [yrinɔɔndərzuk] *het (~en)* urine analysis

urineren [yrinɛrə(n)] *vb* urinate

urinoir [yrinwar] *het (~s)* urinal

urn [ʏrn] *de (~en)* urn

urologie [yroloɣi] *de* urology

uroloog [yroloχ] *de (urologen)* urologist

Uruguay [urugwaj] *het* Uruguay

utopie [ytopi] *de (~ën)* utopia, utopian dream

utopisch [ytopis] *adj* utopian

uur [yr] *het (uren)* **1** hour: *lange uren maken* put in (*or:* work) long hours; *verloren ~(tje)* spare time (*or:* hour); *het duurde uren* it went on for hours, it took hours; *over een ~* in an hour; *€25 per ~ verdienen* earn 25 euros an hour; *100 kilometer per ~* 100 kilometres per (*or:* an) hour; *per ~ betaald worden* be paid by the hour; *kun je hier binnen twee ~ zijn?* can you be here within two hours?; *het is een ~ rijden* it is an hour's drive; *een ~ in de wind stinken* stink to high heaven; **2** hour, period, lesson: *we hebben het derde uur natuurkunde* we have physics for the third lesson; **3** o'clock: *op het hele ~* on the hour; *op het halve ~* on the half hour; *hij kwam tegen drie ~* he came around three o'clock; *om ongeveer acht ~* round about eight (o'clock); *om negen ~ precies* at nine o'clock sharp; **4** hour, moment: *het ~ van de waarheid is aangebroken* the moment of truth is upon us; *zijn laatste ~ heeft geslagen* his final hour has come, his number is up

uurloon [yrlon] *het (uurlonen)* hourly wage, hourly pay: *zij werkt op ~* she is paid by the hour

uurtarief [yrtarif] *het (-tarieven)* hourly rate

uurtje [yrcə] *het (~s)* hour: *in de kleine ~s thuiskomen* come home in the small hours

uurwerk [yrwɛrk] *het (~en)* clock, timepiece

uurwijzer [yrwɛizər] *de (~s)* hour hand

uw [yw] *pos pron* your: *het ~e* yours

uzelf [yzɛlf] *ref pron* yourself, yourselves

V

vaag [vɑχ] *adj, adv* vague, faint, dim: *ik heb zo'n ~ vermoeden dat …* I have a hunch (*or:* a sneaking suspicion) that …
vaagheid [vɑχhɛit] *de (-heden)* vagueness
vaak [vak] *adv* often, frequently: *dat gebeurt niet ~* that doesn't happen very often; *steeds vaker* more and more (frequently)
vaal [val] *adj* faded
vaan [van] *de (~s)* flag, standard
vaandel [vɑndəl] *het (~s)* banner, flag
vaantje [vɑncə] *het (~s)* (small) flag, pennant
vaarbewijs [vɑrbəwɛis] *het (-bewijzen)* navigation licence
vaardig [vɑrdəχ] *adj* skilful, proficient
vaardigheid [vɑrdəχhɛit] *de (-heden)* skill, skilfulness, proficiency: *sociale vaardigheden* social skills; *~ in het schrijven* writing skill
vaargeul [vɑrɣøl] *de (~en)* channel, waterway
vaarroute [vɑrutə] *de (~s)* sea lane
vaars [vars] *de (vaarzen)* heifer
vaart [vart] *de (~en)* **1** speed, *(also fig)* pace: *in volle ~* at full speed (*or:* tilt); *de ~ erin houden* keep up the pace; *het zal zo'n ~ niet lopen* it won't come to that (*or:* get that bad); *~ minderen* reduce speed, slow down; *ergens ~ achter zetten* hurry (*or:* speed) things up, get a move on; **2** navigation, (sea) trade: *de wilde ~* tramp shipping
vaartijd [vartɛit] *de* sailing time
vaartuig [vartœyχ] *het (~en)* vessel, craft
vaarwater [varwatər] *het (~s, ~en)* water(s): *in rustig ~* in smooth water(s)
vaarwel [varwɛl] *het* farewell: *iem ~ zeggen* bid s.o. farewell
vaas [vas] *de (vazen)* vase
vaat [vat] *de* washing-up, dishes
vaatdoek [vaduk] *de (~en)* dishcloth
vaatwasmachine [vatwɑsmaʃinə] *de (~s)* dishwasher
vaatwasser [vatwɑsər] *de (~s)* dishwasher
vacant [vakɑnt] *adj* vacant, free, open: *een ~e betrekking* a vacancy, an opening
vacature [vakatʏrə] *de (~s)* vacancy, opening: *voorzien in een ~* fill a vacancy
vacaturebank [vakatʏrəbɑŋk] *de (~en)* job vacancy department
vaccin [vɑksɛ̠] *het (~s)* vaccine

vaccinatie [vɑksinɑ̠(t)si] *de (~s)* vaccination
vaccineren [vɑksinerə(n)] *vb* vaccinate
vacht [vɑχt] *de (~en)* **1** fleece; fur, coat; **2** sheepskin; **3** fur, pelt: *de ~ van een beer* a bearskin
vacuüm [vɑkywʏm] *het (~s)* vacuum
vader [vadər] *de (~s)* father: *~tje en moedertje spelen* play house; *het Onze Vader* the Lord's Prayer; *natuurlijke (or: wettelijke) ~* natural (*or:* legal) father; *hij zou haar ~ wel kunnen zijn* he is old enough to be her father; *van ~ op zoon* from father to son; *zo ~, zo zoon* like father, like son
vaderdag [vadərdɑχ] *de* Father's Day
vaderland [vadərlɑnt] *het (~en)* (native) country: *voor het ~ sterven* die for one's country; *een tweede ~* a second home
vaderlands [vadərlɑnts] *adj* national, native: *de ~e geschiedenis* national history
vaderlandsliefde [vadərlɑntslivdə] *de* patriotism, love of (one's) country
¹vaderlijk [vadərlək] *adj* **1** paternal; **2** fatherly
²vaderlijk [vadərlək] *adv* in a fatherly way, like a father
vaderschap [vadərsχɑp] *het* paternity, fatherhood
vaderszijde [vadərsɛidə] *de* father's side, paternal side: *grootvader van ~* paternal grandfather
vadsig [vɑtsəχ] *adj, adv* (fat and) lazy
vagebond [vaɣəbɔnt] *de (~en)* vagabond, tramp
vagelijk [vaɣələk] *adv* vaguely, faintly
vagevuur [vaɣəvyr] *het* purgatory
vagina [vaɣina] *de (~'s)* vagina
vaginaal [vaɣinal] *adj* vaginal
vak [vɑk] *het (~ken)* **1** section, square, space; box; **2** compartment, pigeon-hole, shelf: *de ~ken bijvullen* fill the shelves; **3** trade; profession: *een ~ leren* learn a trade; *een ~ uitoefenen* practise a trade, be in a trade (*or:* business); *zijn ~ verstaan* understand one's business, know what one is about; **4** subject, course: *exacte ~ken* (exact) sciences, science and maths
vakantie [vakɑnsi] *de (~s)* holiday(s), vacation: *een week ~* a week's holiday; *de grote ~* the summer holidays; *prettige ~!* have a nice holiday!; *een geheel verzorgde ~* a package tour; *~ hebben* have a holiday; *~ nemen* take a holiday; *met ~ gaan* go on holiday
vakantieadres [vakɑn(t)siadrɛs] *het (~sen)* holiday address
vakantiebestemming [vakɑnsibəstɛmɪŋ] *de (~en)* holiday destination
vakantiedag [vakɑnsidɑχ] *de (~en)* (day of one's) holiday
vakantieganger [vakɑnsiɣɑŋər] *de (~s)* holidaymaker
vakantiegeld [vakɑnsiɣɛlt] *het (~en)* holiday pay
vakantiehuis [vakɑnsihœys] *het (-huizen)* holiday cottage
vakantietijd [vakɑnsitɛit] *de (~en)* holiday period (*or:* season)
vakantiewerk [vakɑnsiwɛrk] *het* holiday job, sum-

mer job
vakbekwaam [vɑgbəkwa̠m] *adj* skilled
vakbekwaamheid [vɑgbəkwa̠mhɛit] *de* (professional) skill
vakbeurs [va̠gbørs] *de (vakbeurzen)* trade fair
vakbeweging [va̠gbəweɣɪŋ] *de* trade unions
vakblad [va̠gblɑt] *het (~en)* trade journal
vakbond [va̠gbɔnt] *de (~en)* (trade) union
vakbondsleider [va̠gbɔntslɛidər] *de (~s)* (trade) union leader
vakbondslid [va̠gbɔntslɪt] *het* (trade) union member
vakcentrale [va̠ksɛntralə] *de (~s)* trade union federation
vakdidactiek [va̠gdidɑktik] *de* teaching method(ology)
vakdiploma [va̠gdiploma] *het (~'s)* (professional) diploma
vakgebied [va̠kχəbit] *het (~en)* field (of study)
vakjargon [va̠kjarɣɔn] *het (~s)* (technical) jargon
vakje [va̠kjə] *het* **1** compartment; **2** box; **3** pigeon-hole
vakkennis [va̠kɛnɪs] *de* professional knowledge, expert knowledge, know-how
vakkenpakket [va̠kə(n)pɑkɛt] *het (~ten)* chosen set of course options
vakkenvuller [va̠kə(n)vʏlər] *de (~s)* stock clerk, grocery clerk
vakkleding [va̠kledɪŋ] *de* working clothes
¹vakkundig [vɑkʏndəχ] *adj* skilled, competent
²vakkundig [vɑkʏndəχ] *adv* competently, with great skill: *het is ~ gerepareerd* it has been expertly done
vakman [va̠kmɑn] *de (vaklui, vaklieden, ~nen, vakmensen)* expert, professional, skilled worker
vakmanschap [va̠kmɑnsχɑp] *het* skill, craftsmanship: *het ontbreekt hem aan ~* he lacks skill
vakonderwijs [va̠kɔndərwɛis] *het* vocational education *(or:* training*)*
vakopleiding [va̠kɔplɛidɪŋ] *de (~en)* vocational training
vaktechnisch [va̠ktɛχnis] *adj* technical
vakterm [va̠ktɛrm] *de (~en)* technical term
vakwerk [va̠kwɛrk] *het* craftmanship, workmanship: *~ afleveren* produce excellent work
val [vɑl] *de (~len, ~len)* **1** fall (off, from), trip: *een vrije ~ maken* skydive; *hij maakte een lelijke ~* he had a nasty fall; *ten ~ komen* fall (down), have a fall; *iem ten ~ brengen* bring s.o. down; **2** (down)fall, collapse: *de regering ten ~ brengen* overthrow *(or:* bring down) the government; **3** trap, snare: *een ~ opzetten* set *(or:* lay) a trap; **4** trap, frame-up: *in de ~ lopen* walk *(or:* fall) into a trap, rise to *(or:* swallow) the bait
valavond [va̠lavɔnt] *de (Belg)* dusk, twilight
Valentijnsdag [va̠ləntɛinzdɑχ] *de* St Valentine's Day
valhelm [va̠lhɛlm] *de (~en)* (crash) helmet
valies [valis] *het (valiezen)* (suit)case

valium [va̠lijʏm] *het* Valium
valk [vɑlk] *de (~en)* falcon
valkuil [va̠lkœyl] *de (~en)* pitfall, trap
vallei [vɑlɛi] *de (~en)* valley
vallen [vɑlə(n)] *vb* **1** fall, drop: *er valt sneeuw (or: hagel)* it is snowing *(or:* hailing); *uit elkaar ~* fall apart, drop to bits; *zijn blik laten ~ op* let one's eye fall on; **2** fall (over), trip (up): *iem doen ~* make s.o. fall, trip s.o. up; *zij kwam lelijk te ~* she had a bad fall; *met ~ en opstaan* by trial and error; *van de trap ~ fall (or:* tumble) down the stairs; **3** come, fall: *dat valt buiten zijn bevoegdheid* that falls outside his jurisdiction; **4** drop: *iem laten ~* drop *(or:* ditch) s.o.; *hij liet de aanklacht ~* he dropped the charge; **5** go (for), take (to): *zij valt op donkere mannen* she goes for dark men; *Kerstmis valt op een woensdag* Christmas (Day) is on a Wednesday; *het ~ van de avond* nightfall; *er vielen doden (or:* gewonden) there were fatalities *(or:* casualties); *er viel een stilte* there was a hush, silence fell; *met haar valt niet te praten* there is no talking to her; *er valt wel iets voor te zeggen om …* there is sth to be said for …
valling [vɑlɪŋ] *de (~en)* slope, gradient
valluik [va̠lœyk] *het (~en)* trapdoor
valnet [va̠lnɛt] *het (~ten)* safety net
valpartij [va̠lpɑrtɛi] *de (~en)* spill, fall
valreep [va̠lrep] *de (valrepen)* gangway, gangplank ‖ *op de ~* right at the end, at the final *(or:* last) moment
¹vals [vɑls] *adj* **1** false, fake, phoney, (+ *noun)* pseudo-; **2** wrong, false: *een ~ spoor* a false trail; **3** *(mus)* flat; sharp; false; **4** mean, vicious: *een ~ beest* a vicious animal; **5** forged, fake, false, counterfeit: *een ~e Vermeer* a forged *(or:* fake) Vermeer; **6** false, artificial, (+ *noun)* mock, (+ *noun)* imitation: *~ haar* false hair
²vals [vɑls] *adv* falsely: *~ spelen* play out of tune, cheat (at cards); *~ zingen* sing out of tune, sing off key
valsemunter [vɑlsəmʏntər] *de (~s)* counterfeiter, forger
valsemunterij [vɑlsəmʏntərɛi] *de* counterfeiting, forgery
valsheid [va̠lshɛit] *de (-heden)* **1** spuriousness: *overtuigd van de ~ van het schilderij* convinced that the painting is a fake; **2** forgery, fraud, counterfeiting: *~ in geschrifte* forgery
valstrik [va̠lstrɪk] *de (~ken)* snare, trap: *iem in een ~ lokken* lead *(or:* lure) s.o. into a trap
valuta [valyta] *de (~'s)* currency
vampier [va̠mpir] *de (~s)* vampire
¹van [vɑn] *prep* **1** from: *hij is ~ Amsterdam* he's from Amsterdam; *~ dorp tot dorp* from one village to another; *~ een bord eten* eat from *(or:* off) a plate; **2** from: *~ de vroege morgen tot de late avond* from (the) early morning till late at night; *~ tevoren* beforehand, in advance; *~ toen af* from then on, from that day *(or:* time) (on); **3** of: *het hoofd ~ de school* the head(master) of the school; *de trein ~ 9.30 uur*

the 9.30 train; *een foto ~ mijn vader: a)* a picture of my father's; *b)* a picture of my father; *~ wie is dit boek? het is ~ mij* whose book is this? it's mine; **4** (made, out) of: *een tafel ~ hout* a wooden table; **5** by, of: *dat was niet slim ~ Jan* that was not such a clever move of Jan's; *het volgende nummer is ~ Van Morrison* the next number is by Van Morrison; *een plaat ~ de Stones* a Stones record, a record by the Stones; *drie ~ de vier* three out of four; *een jas met ~ die koperen knopen* a coat with those brass buttons; *~ dat geld kon hij een auto kopen* he was able to buy a car with that money; *daar niet ~* that's not the point; *ik geloof ~ niet* I don't think so; *ik verzeker u ~ wel* I assure you I do; *het lijkt ~ wel* it seems (*or:* looks) like it

²van [vɑn] *adv* of, from: *je kunt er wel een paar ~ nemen* you can have some (of those)

vanaf [vɑnɑf] *prep* **1** from; as from, (*Am*) as of, beginning, since: *~ de 16e eeuw* from the 16th century onward(s); *~ vandaag* as from (*or Am:* as of) today; **2** from, over: *prijzen ~ ...* prices (range) from ...

vanavond [vɑnavɔnt] *adv* tonight, this evening

vanbinnen [vɑmbɪnə(n)] *adv* (on the) inside

vanboven [vɑmbovə(n)] *adv* **1** on the top, on the upper surface, above; **2** from above

vanbuiten [vɑmbœytə(n)] *adv* **1** from the outside; **2** on the outside; **3** by heart: *iets ~ kennen* (*or: leren*) know (*or:* learn) sth by heart

vandaag [vɑndaχ] *adv* today: *~ de dag* nowadays, these days, currently; *tot op de dag van ~* to this very day, to date; *~ is het maandag* today is Monday; *~ over een week* a week from today, in a week's time, a week from now; *de krant van ~* today's paper; *liever ~ dan morgen* the sooner the better; *~ of morgen* one of these days, soon

vandaal [vɑndal] *de (vandalen)* vandal

vandaan [vɑndan] *adv* **1** away, from: *we moeten hier ~!* let's go away!; **2** out of, from: *waar heb je die oude klok ~?* where did you pick up (*or:* get) that old clock?; *waar kom (ben) jij ~?* where are you from?, where do you come from?; *hij woont overal ver ~* he lives miles from anywhere

vandaar [vɑndar] *adv* therefore, that's why

vandalisme [vɑndalɪsmə] *het* vandalism

vandoor [vɑndor] *adv* off, away: *ik moet er weer ~* I have to be off; *hij is er met het geld ~* he has run off with the money

vaneen [vɑnen] *adv* separated, split up

vangen [vɑŋə(n)] *vb* **1** catch, capture, (en)trap: *een dief ~* catch a thief; **2** catch; **3** make: *twintig piek per uur ~* make five quid (*or Am:* ten bucks) an hour

vangnet [vɑŋnɛt] *het (~ten)* **1** (trap-)net; **2** safety net

vangrail [vɑŋrel] *de (~s)* crash barrier

vangst [vɑŋst] *de (~en)* catch, capture, haul: *de politie deed een goede ~* the police made a good catch (*or:* haul)

vanille [vɑnɪljə] *de* vanilla

vanilleijs [vɑnɪljɛis] *het* vanilla ice cream

vanillevla [vɑnɪljəvla] *de (roughly)* vanilla custard

vanmiddag [vɑmɪdɑχ] *adv* this afternoon

vanmorgen [vɑmɔrɣə(n)] *adv* this morning, in the morning: *~ vroeg* early this morning

vannacht [vɑnɑχt] *adv* tonight, last night: *je kunt ~ blijven slapen, als je wil* you can stay the night, if you like; *hij kwam ~ om twee uur thuis* he came home at two o'clock in the morning

vanouds [vɑnɑuts] *adv* || *het was weer als ~* it was just like old times again

vanuit [vɑnœyt] *prep* **1** from, out of: *ik keek ~ mijn raam naar beneden* I looked down from (*or:* out of) my window; **2** starting from

vanwaar [vɑnwar] *adv* **1** from where; **2** why: *~ die haast?* what's the hurry?

vanwege [vɑnweɣə] *prep* because of, owing to, due to, on account of

vanzelf [vɑnzɛlf] *adv* **1** by oneself, of oneself, of one's own accord; **2** as a matter of course, automatically: *alles ging (liep) als ~* everything went smoothly; *dat spreekt ~* that goes without saying

¹vanzelfsprekend [vɑnzɛlfsprekənt] *adj* obvious, natural, self-evident

²vanzelfsprekend [vɑnzɛlfsprekənt] *adv* obviously, naturally, of course: *als ~ aannemen* take sth for granted

¹varen [varə(n)] *vb* sail: *het schip vaart 10 knopen* the ship sails at 10 knots; *hij wil gaan ~* he wants to go to sea (*or:* be a sailor)

²varen [varə(n)] *de (~s)* fern

variabel [varijabəl] *adj* variable, flexible: *~e werktijden* flexible working hours

variabele [varijabələ] *de (~n)* variable

variant [varijɑnt] *de (~en)* variant, variation: *een ~ op* a variant of, a variation on

variatie [varija(t)si] *de (~s)* variation, change: *voor de ~* for a change

variëren [varijerə(n)] *vb* vary, differ: *sterk ~de prijzen* widely differing prices

variété [varijete] *het (~s)* variety, music hall

variëteit [varijetɛit] *de (~en)* variety, diversity

varken [vɑrkə(n)] *het (~s)* pig, hog; swine: *zo lui als een ~* bone idle (*or:* lazy)

varkensfokkerij [vɑrkənsfɔkərɛi] *de (~en)* pig farm

varkenshaas [vɑrkənshas] *de (-hazen)* pork tenderloin (*or:* steak)

varkenshok [vɑrkə(n)shɔk] *het (~ken)* pigsty

varkenskotelet [vɑrkə(n)skotəlɛt] *de (~ten)* pork chop

varkensleer [vɑrkənsler] *het* pigskin

varkensstal [vɑrkə(n)stɑl] *de (~len)* pigsty, pig house

varkensvlees [vɑrkənsfles] *het* pork

varkensvoer [vɑrkə(n)sfur] *het* pigfeed, pigfood, (pig)swill

vaseline [vazəlinə] *de* vaseline

¹vast [vɑst] *adj* **1** fixed, immovable: *~e vloerbedekking* wall-to-wall carpet(ing); **2** fixed, stationary: *~*

raken get stuck (*or:* caught, jammed); *~e datum* fixed date; *~e inkomsten* a fixed (*or:* regular) income; *~e kosten* fixed (*or:* standing) charges; *een ~e prijs* a fixed (*or:* set) price; **3** firm, steady: *met ~e hand* with a steady (*or:* sure) hand; *~e overtuiging* firm conviction; **4** permanent, regular, steady: *~ adres* fixed address; *een ~e betrekking* a permanent position; **5** solid: *~ voedsel* solid food; **6** firm: *~e vorm geven* shape; **7** tight, firm; **8** established, standing: *een ~ gebruik* a (set) custom; *een ~e regel* a fixed (*or:* set) rule

²**vast** [vɑst] *adv* **1** fixedly, firmly; **2** certainly, for certain (*or:* sure): *hij is het ~ vergeten* he must have forgotten (it); *~ en zeker* definitely, certainly; **3** for the time being, for the present: *begin maar ~ met eten* go ahead and eat (*or:* start eating)

vastberaden [vɑstbərɑdə(n)] *adj* resolute, firm; determined

vastbesloten [vɑstbəslotə(n)] *adj* determined

vastbinden [vɑstbɪndə(n)] *vb* tie (up, down), bind (up), fasten: *zijn armen werden vastgebonden* his arms were tied (*or:* bound) (up)

vasteland [vɑstəlɑnt] *het* **1** continent; **2** mainland, Continent

¹**vasten** [vɑstə(n)] *de* fast(ing)

²**vasten** [vɑstə(n)] *vb* fast

vastentijd [vɑstə(n)tɛit] *de* **1** Lent; **2** fast, time of fasting

vastgeroest [vɑs(t)χərust] *adj* stuck: *in zijn gewoonten ~* set in his ways

vastgoed [vɑstχut] *het* real estate (*or:* property)

vasthouden [vɑsthaudə(n)] *vb* hold (fast), grip, detain: *iemands hand ~* hold s.o.'s hand; *hou je vast!* brace yourself (for the shock)!

vasthoudend [vɑsthaudənt] *adj* tenacious, persistent, persevering

vastklemmen [vɑstklɛmə(n)] *vb* clip (on), tighten: *de deur zat vastgeklemd* the door was jammed

vastleggen [vɑstlɛɣə(n)] *vb* **1** tie up: *zich niet ~ op iets, zich nergens op ~* refuse to commit oneself, leave one's options open, be non-committal; **2** set down, record: *iets schriftelijk ~* put sth down in writing

vastliggen [vɑstlɪɣə(n)] *vb* be tied up, be fixed: *die voorwaarden liggen vast in het contract* those conditions have been laid down in the contract

vastlijmen [vɑstlɛimə(n)] *vb* glue (together), stick (together)

vastlopen [vɑstlopə(n)] *vb* **1** jam, get jammed: *het schip is vastgelopen* the ship has run aground; **2** (*fig*) get stuck, be bogged down: *de onderhandelingen zijn vastgelopen* negotiations have reached a deadlock

vastmaken [vɑstmakə(n)] *vb* fasten, tie up, do up, button up; secure

vastpakken [vɑstpɑkə(n)] *vb* grip, grasp, grab

vastplakken [vɑstplɑkə(n)] *vb* stick together, glue together

vastroesten [vɑstrustə(n)] *vb* rust

vastspijkeren [vɑ(st)spɛikərə(n)] *vb* nail (down), tack

vaststaan [vɑstan] *vb* **1** be certain: *het staat nu vast, dat* it is now definite (*or:* certain) that; *de datum stond nog niet vast* the date was still uncertain (yet); **2** be fixed: *zijn besluit staat vast* his mind is made up

vaststaand [vɑ(st)stant] *adj* certain, final: *een ~ feit* an established (*or:* a recognized) fact

vaststellen [vɑstɛlə(n)] *vb* **1** fix, determine, settle, arrange: *een datum ~* settle on (*or:* fix) a date; *een prijs ~* fix a price; **2** decide (on), specify, lay down: *op vastgestelde tijden* at stated times (*or:* intervals); **3** find, conclude; **4** determine, establish: *de doodsoorzaak ~* establish (*or:* determine) the cause of death; *de schade ~* assess the damage

vastvriezen [vɑstfrizə(n)] *vb* freeze (in)

vastzetten [vɑstsɛtə(n)] *vb* **1** fix, fasten, secure; **2** tie up, lock up, settle (on): *zijn spaargeld voor vijf jaar ~* tie up one's savings for five years

vastzitten [vɑstsɪtə(n)] *vb* **1** be stuck, be jammed: *~ in de file* be stuck in a tailback; **2** be stuck (*or:* fixed): *daar zit heel wat aan vast* there is (a lot) more to it (than meets the eye); **3** be locked up, be behind bars: *hij heeft een jaar vastgezeten* he has been inside for a year; **4** be in a fix; **5** be tied (down) (to), be committed (to): *hij heeft het beloofd; nu zit hij eraan vast* he made that promise, he can't get out of it now

¹**vat** [vɑt] *het* barrel; cask; drum: *een ~ petroleum* an oil drum; *bier van het ~* draught beer

²**vat** [vɑt] *de* hold, grip, handle: *geen ~ op iem hebben* have no hold over s.o.

vatbaar [vɑdbar] *adj* **1** susceptible to, liable to: *hij is zeer ~ voor kou* he is very prone to catching colds; **2** amenable (to), open to: *hij is niet voor rede ~* he's impervious (*or:* not open) to reason

Vaticaan [vatikan] *het* Vatican

Vaticaanstad [vatikanstɑt] *de* Vatican City

vatten [vɑtə(n)] *vb* catch: *kou ~* catch cold

vbo [vebeo] *het voorbereidend beroepsonderwijs* junior secondary vocational education

v.Chr. *voor Christus* BC

vechten [vɛχtə(n)] *vb* **1** fight, combat: *wij moesten ~ om in de trein te komen* we had to fight our way into the train; **2** fight (for, against): *tegen de slaap ~* fight off sleep

vechter [vɛχtər] *de* (*~s*) fighter, combatant

vechtlustig [vɛχtlʏstəχ] *adj* pugnacious

vechtpartij [vɛχtpɑrtɛi] *de* (*~en*) fight, brawl

vechtsport [vɛχtsport] *de* (*~en*) combat sport

vector [vɛktɔr] *de* (*~en*) vector

¹**vedergewicht** [vedərɣəwɪχt] *de (boxer)* featherweight

²**vedergewicht** [vedərɣəwɪχt] *het* featherweight

vedette [vədɛtə] *de* (*~s, ~n*) star, celebrity

vee [ve] *het* cattle: *een stuk ~* a head of cattle

veearts [vearts] *de* (*~en*) veterinary (surgeon), (*Am*) veterinarian, vet

¹veeg [veχ] *adj* **1** fatal; **2** ominous; fateful: *een ~ te-ken* a bad sign (*or:* omen)

²veeg [veχ] *de (vegen)* **1** wipe, lick; **2** streak, smudge: *er zit een zwarte ~ op je gezicht* there's a black smudge on your face

veehouder [vehaudər] *de (~s)* cattle breeder, cattle farmer, (*Am*) rancher

veehouderij [vehaudərɛi] *de (~en)* cattle farm (*or Am:* ranch)

¹veel [vel] *adv* much, a lot: *hij was kwaad, maar zij was nog ~ kwader* he was angry, but she was even more so; *ze lijken ~ op elkaar* they are very much alike

²veel [vel] *ind pron* much, many, a lot, lots: *~ geluk!* good luck!; *weet ik ~ how* should I know?; *~ te ~ far* too much (*or:* many); *één keer te ~* (just) once too often

³veel [vel] *num* many, a lot ‖ *het zijn er ~* there's a lot of them

veelbelovend [velbəlovənt] *adj, adv* promising: *~ zijn* show great promise

veeleisend [velɛisənt] *adj* demanding, particular (about)

veelvoud [velvaut] *het (~en)* multiple: *zijn salaris bedraagt een ~ van het hare* his salary is many times larger than hers

veelvraat [velvrat] *de (-vraten)* glutton

veelvuldig [velvyldəχ] *adj* frequently, often

veelzijdig [velzɛidəχ] *adj* many-sided, versatile: *haar ~e belangstelling* her varied interests; *een ~e geest* a versatile mind

veelzijdigheid [velzɛidəχhɛit] *de* versatility

veemarkt [vemarkt] *de (~en)* cattle market

veen [ven] *het (venen)* peat

veenbes [vembɛs] *de (~sen)* cranberry

¹veer [ver] *de* **1** feather; **2** spring

²veer [ver] *het* ferry

veerdienst [verdinst] *de (~en)* ferry (service, line)

veerkracht [verkraχt] *de* elasticity, resilience

veerkrachtig [verkraχtəχ] *adj* elastic, springy, resilient

veerpont [verpɔnt] *de (~en)* ferry(boat)

veertien [vertin] *num* fourteen: *vandaag over ~ da-gen* in a fortnight('s time), two weeks from today; *~ dagen* fourteen days, a fortnight; *het zijn er ~* there are fourteen (of them)

veertiendaags [vertindaχs] *adj* **1** biweekly; fort-nightly: *een ~ tijdschrift* a biweekly (magazine); **2** (+ *noun*) two-week, fourteen-day; **3** two weeks (*or:* fourteen days) old

veertiende [vertində] *num* fourteenth

veertiende-eeuws [vertindəews] *adj* four-teenth-century

veertig [fertəχ] *num* forty: *in de jaren ~* in the for-ties; *hij loopt tegen de ~* he is pushing forty; *~ plus* more than 40 % fat

veertiger [fertəɣər] *de (~s)* man of forty: *hij is een goede ~* he is somewhere in his forties

veertigjarig [fertəχjarəχ] *adj* **1** forty years', forti-eth: *~e bruiloft* fortieth wedding anniversary; **2** forty-year-old

veertigplusser *de* over-40

veertigste [fertəχstə] *num* fortieth

veertigurig [fertəχyrəχ] *adj* forty-hour: *de ~e werkweek* the forty-hour week

veestal [vestal] *de (~len)* cowshed

veestapel [vestapəl] *de (~s)* (live)stock

veeteelt [vetelt] *de* stock breeding, cattle breeding

veevervoer [vevərvur] *het* transport of livestock (*or:* cattle)

veevoer [vevur] *het* feed

veewagen [vewaɣə(n)] *de (~s)* cattle truck; cattle lorry

vegen [veɣə(n)] *vb* **1** sweep, brush: *de schoorsteen ~* sweep the chimney; **2** wipe: *voeten ~ a.u.b.* wipe your feet please

veger [veɣər] *de (~s)* (sweeping) brush: *~ en blik* dustpan and brush

vegetariër [veɣetarijər] *de (~s)* vegetarian

vegetarisch [veɣetaris] *adj* vegetarian: *ik eet altijd ~* I'm a vegetarian

vehikel [vehikəl] *het (~s)* vehicle

veilen [vɛilə(n)] *vb* sell by auction: *antiek* (or: *hui-zen*) *~* auction antiques (*or:* houses)

veilig [vɛiləχ] *adj, adv* safe, secure, (all-)clear: *~ verkeer (roughly)* road safety; *iets ~ opbergen* put sth in a safe place; *~ thuiskomen* return home safe(ly); *~ en wel* safe and sound

veiligheid [vɛiləχhɛit] *de (-heden)* safety, security: *de openbare ~* public security; *iets in ~ brengen* bring sth to (a place of) safety

veiligheidsagent [vɛiləχhɛitsaɣɛnt] *de (~en)* se-curity officer

veiligheidsbril [vɛiləχhɛitsbril] *de (~len)* safety goggles, protective goggles

veiligheidsdienst [vɛiləχhɛitsdinst] *de (~en)* se-curity forces: *binnenlandse ~* (counter)intelligence

veiligheidsgordel [vɛiləχhɛitsɣɔrdəl] *de (~s)* safety belt, seat belt

veiligheidshelm [vɛiləχhɛitshɛlm] *de* safety hel-met, hard hat

veiligheidsmaatregel [vɛiləχhɛitsmatreɣəl] *de (~en, ~s)* security measure

Veiligheidsraad [vɛiləχhɛitsrat] *de* Security Council

veiligheidsslot [vɛiləχhɛitslɔt] *het (~en)* safety lock

veiligheidsspeld [vɛiləχhɛitspɛlt] *de (~en)* safety pin

veiling [vɛiliŋ] *de (~en)* auction

veilinghuis [vɛiliŋhœys] *het (-huizen)* auctioneer-ing firm

veilingmeester [vɛiliŋmestər] *de (~s)* auctioneer

vel [vɛl] *het (~len)* **1** skin: *het is om uit je ~ te sprin-gen* it is enough to drive you up the wall; *~ over been zijn* be all skin and bone; **2** sheet

veld [vɛlt] *het (~en)* field, open country (*or:* fields), pitch, square: *in geen ~en of wegen was er iem te* *zien* there was no sign of anyone anywhere; *een speler uit het ~ sturen* send a player off (the field)

veldbed [vɛldbɛt] *het (~den)* camp bed

veldboeket [vɛldbukɛt] *het, de (~ten)* bouquet of wild flowers

veldfles [vɛltflɛs] *de (~sen)* water bottle

veldloop [vɛltlop] *de (-lopen)* cross-country (race)

veldmaarschalk [vɛltmarsχɑlk] *de (~en)* Field Marshal, *(Am)* General of the Army

veldmuis [vɛltmœys] *de (-muizen)* field vole, field mouse

veldrijder [vɛltrɛidər] *de (~s)* cyclo-cross rider

veldsla [vɛltsla] *de* lamb's lettuce

veldslag [vɛltslɑχ] *de (~en)* (pitched) battle

veldspeler [vɛltspelər] *de (~s)* fielder

veldsport [vɛltspɔrt] *de (~en)* outdoor sports

veldwerk [vɛltwɛrk] *het* fieldwork: *het ~ verrichten* do the donkey work, do the spadework

velg [vɛlχ] *de (~en)* rim

vellen [vɛlə(n)] *vb* cut down, fell: *bomen ~* cut down trees

ven [vɛn] *het (~nen)* pool, hollow

Venetië [venɛ(t)sijə] *het* Venice

Venezuela [venezywɛla] *het* Venezuela

venijn [vənɛin] *het* poison, venom: *het ~ zit in de staart* the sting is in the tail

venijnig [vənɛinəχ] *adj, adv* vicious, venomous: *~e blikken* malicious looks

venkel [vɛŋkəl] *de* fennel

vennoot [vɛnot] *de (vennoten)* partner

vennootschap [vɛnotsχɑp] *de (~pen)* 1 partnership, firm, company; 2 trading partnership: *besloten ~* private limited company; *naamloze ~* public limited company

venster [vɛnstər] *het (~s)* window

vensterbank [vɛnstərbɑŋk] *de (~en)* windowsill

vensterenveloppe [vɛnstərɛnvəlɔp] *de (~n)* window envelope

vensterglas [vɛnstərɣlɑs] *het (-glazen)* window glass; window-pane

vent [vɛnt] *de (~en)* 1 fellow, guy, bloke: *een leuke ~* a dishy bloke *(or:* guy); 2 son(ny), lad(die)

venten [vɛntə(n)] *vb* hawk, peddle

venter [vɛntər] *de (~s)* street trader, hawker, pedlar

ventiel [vɛntil] *het (~en)* valve

ventilatie [vɛntila(t)si] *de* ventilation

ventilator [vɛntilatər] *de (~s, ~en)* fan, ventilator

¹ventileren [vɛntilerə(n)] *vb* air

²ventileren [vɛntilerə(n)] *vb* ventilate, air

ventweg [vɛntwɛχ] *de (~en)* service road

¹ver [vɛr] *adv* 1 far; a long way: *hij sprong zeven meter ~* he jumped a distance of seven metres; *~ gevorderd zijn* be well advanced; *het zou te ~ voeren om … it* would be going too far to …; *~ vooruitzien* look well *(or:* way) ahead; *hoe ~ is het nog?* how much further is it?; *hoe ~ ben je met je huiswerk?* how far have you got with your homework?; *dat gaat te ~!* that is the limit!; *~ weg* a long way off, far away; *het is zo ~!* here we go, this is it; *ben je zo ~?*

(are you) ready?; *van ~ komen* come a long way, come from distant parts; 2 (by) far, way: *~ heen zijn* be far gone; *zijn tijd ~ vooruit zijn* be way ahead of one's time

²ver [vɛr] *adj* distant; far, (+ *noun)* far-off, *(after vb)* far off, a long way: *~re landen* distant *(or:* far-off) countries; *de ~re toekomst* the distant future; *in een ~ verleden* in some distant *(or:* remote) past; *een ~re reis* a long journey

verachten [vərɑχtə(n)] *vb* despise, scorn

verademing [vəradəmɪŋ] *de* relief

veraf [vɛrɑf] *adv* far away, far off, a long way away *(or:* off)

verafgelegen [vɛrɑfχəleχə(n)] *adj (+ noun)* far-away; *(after vb)* far away, remote

veranda [vərɑnda] *de (~'s)* veranda

¹veranderen [vərɑndərə(n)] *vb* 1 alter, change: *een jurkje ~* alter a dress; *dat verandert de zaak* that changes things; *daar is niets meer aan te ~* nothing can be done about that; 2 change, turn (into): *Jezus veranderde water in wijn* Jesus turned water into wine

²veranderen [vərɑndərə(n)] *vb* 1 change: *de tijden ~* times are changing; 2 change, switch: *van huisarts ~* change one's doctor; *van onderwerp ~* change the subject

verandering [vərɑndərɪŋ] *de (~en)* 1 change, variation: *~ van omgeving* change of scene(ry); *voor de ~* for a change; 2 alteration: *een ~ aanbrengen in* make an alteration *(or:* a change) to

veranderlijk [vərɑndərlək] *adj* changeable, variable; unsettled, fickle

verantwoord [vərɑntwort] *adj* 1 safe, sensible; 2 well-considered, sound: *~e voeding* a well-balanced *(or:* sensible) diet

verantwoordelijk [vərɑntwordələk] *adj* responsible: *de ~e minister* the minister responsible; *iem voor iets ~ stellen* hold s.o. responsible for sth

verantwoordelijkheid [vərɑntwordələkhɛit] *de (-heden)* responsibility: *de ~ voor iets op zich nemen* take *(or:* assume) responsibility for sth; *de ~ voor een aanslag opeisen* claim responsibility for an attack

verantwoordelijkheidsgevoel [vərɑntwordələkhɛitsχəvul] *het* sense of responsibility

¹verantwoorden [vərɑntwordə(n)] *vb* justify, account for: *ik kan dit niet tegenover mijzelf ~* I cannot square this with my conscience

²verantwoorden [vərɑntwordə(n)] *ref vb* justify, answer (to s.o. for sth)

verantwoording [vərɑntwordɪŋ] *de (~en)* 1 account: *~ afleggen* render account; *een iem ~ verschuldigd zijn* be accountable *(or:* answerable) to s.o.; *iem ter ~ roepen* call s.o. to account; 2 responsibility: *op jouw ~* you take the responsibility

verassen [vərɑsə(n)] *vb* incinerate; cremate

¹verbaal [vɛrbal] *adj* verbal

²verbaal [vɛrbal] *het (verbalen)* booking, ticket

verbaasd [vərbast] *adj* surprised, astonished,

amazed: ~ *zijn over iets* be surprised (*or:* amazed) at sth

verband [vərbɑnt] *het (~en)* **1** bandage: *een ~ aanleggen* put on a bandage; **2** connection; context, relation(ship): *in landelijk* (or: *Europees*) *~* at a national (*or:* European) level; *in ruimer ~* in a wider context; *~ houden met iets* be connected with sth; *dit houdt ~ met het feit dat* this has to do with the fact that; *de woorden uit hun ~ rukken* take words out of context

verbandtrommel [vərbɑntrɔməl] *de (~s)* first-aid kit, first-aid box

verbannen [vərbɑnə(n)] *vb* banish, exile: *~ zijn* be banished, be under a ban

verbanning [vərbɑnɪŋ] *de (~en)* banishment, exile

¹verbazen [vərbazə(n)] *vb* amaze, surprise, astonish: *dat verbaast me niets* that doesn't surprise me in the least

²verbazen [vərbazə(n)] *ref vb* be surprised (*or:* amazed) (at)

verbazing [vərbazɪŋ] *de* surprise, amazement, astonishment: *wie schetst mijn ~* imagine my surprise; *dat wekte ~* that came as a surprise; *tot mijn ~ hoorde ik …* I was surprised to hear …

verbazingwekkend [vərbazɪŋwɛkənt] *adj, adv* astonishing, surprising, amazing

¹verbeelden [vərbɛldə(n)] *ref vb* imagine, fancy: *dat verbeeld je je maar* you are just imagining it (*or:* things); *hij verbeeldt zich heel wat* he has a high opinion of himself; *verbeeld je maar niets!* don't go getting ideas (into your head)!

²verbeelden [vərbɛldə(n)] *vb* represent, be meant (*or:* supposed) to be: *dat moet een badkamer ~!* that is supposed to be a bathroom!

verbeelding [vərbɛldɪŋ] *de* **1** imagination: *dat spreekt tot de ~* that appeals to one's imagination; **2** conceit(edness), vanity: *~ hebben* be conceited, think a lot of oneself

verbergen [vərbɛrɣə(n)] *vb* hide, conceal: *zij hield iets voor hem verborgen* she was holding sth back from him

verbeten [vərbetə(n)] *adj* grim, dogged

¹verbeteren [vərbetərə(n)] *vb* **1** improve: *zijn Engels ~* improve (*or:* brush up) one's English; **2** correct; **3** beat, improve on: *een record ~* break a record

²verbeteren [vərbetərə(n)] *vb* improve, get better: *verbeterde werkomstandigheden* improved working conditions

verbetering [vərbetərɪŋ] *de (~en)* **1** improvement: *het is een hele ~ vergeleken met …* it's a great improvement on …; **2** correction, rectification, marking

verbieden [vərbidə(n)] *vb* forbid, ban, suppress: *verboden toegang* no admittance; *verboden in te rijden* no entry (*or:* access); *verboden te roken* no smoking; *verboden voor onbevoegden* no unauthorized entry, no trespassing

verbijsterd [vərbɛistərt] *adj* bewildered, amazed, baffled

verbijsteren [vərbɛistərə(n)] *vb* bewilder, amaze

verbijstering [vərbɛistərɪŋ] *de* bewilderment, amazement

verbinden [vərbɪndə(n)] *vb* **1** join (together), connect (to, with): *~ met* join to, link up to (*or:* with); **2** connect, link; **3** bandage; **4** connect, attach, join (up): *er zijn geen kosten aan verbonden* there are no expenses involved; **5** connect (with), put through (to): *ik ben verkeerd verbonden* I have got a wrong number; *kunt u mij met de heer Jefferson ~?* could you put me through to Mr Jefferson?

verbinding [vərbɪndɪŋ] *de (~en)* **1** connection, link: *een ~ tot stand brengen* establish (*or:* make) a connection; **2** connection: *een directe ~* a direct connection, a through train; *de ~en met de stad zijn uitstekend* connections with the city are excellent; **3** connection: *geen ~ kunnen krijgen* not be able to get through; *de ~ werd verbroken* the connection was broken, we (*or:* they) were cut off

verbindingsstreepje [vərbɪndɪŋstrepjə] *het (~s)* hyphen

verbitterd [vərbɪtərt] *adj, adv* bitter (at, by), embittered (at, by)

verbittering [vərbɪtərɪŋ] *de* bitterness

verbleken [vərblekə(n)] *vb* **1** (turn, go) pale, turn white, go white; **2** fade

verblijf [vərblɛif] *het (verblijven)* **1** stay; **2** residence, accommodation: *de verblijven voor de bemanning* (or: *het personeel*) the crew's (*or:* servants') quarters

verblijfkosten [vərblɛifkɔstə(n)] *de* accommodation expenses, living expenses

verblijfplaats [vərblɛifplats] *de (~en)* (place of) residence, address: *iem zonder vaste woon- of ~* s.o. with no permanent home or address

verblijfsvergunning [vərblɛifsfərɣynɪŋ] *de (~en)* residence permit

verblijven [vərblɛivə(n)] *vb* **1** stay: *hij verbleef enkele maanden in Japan* he stayed in Japan for several months; **2** live

verblinden [vərblɪndə(n)] *vb* dazzle, blind: *een ~de schoonheid* a dazzling (*or:* stunning) beauty

verbloemen [vərblumə(n)] *vb* disguise, gloss over, cover up

verbluffend [vərblyfənt] *adj, adv* staggering, astounding: *~ snel handelen* act amazingly (*or:* incredibly) quickly

verbluft [vərblyft] *adj* staggered, stunned: *~ staan kijken* be dumbfounded

verbod [vərbɔt] *het (~en)* ban, prohibition, embargo: *een ~ uitvaardigen* impose (*or:* declare) a ban

verboden [vərbodə(n)] *adj* forbidden, banned, prohibited: *tot ~ gebied verklaren* declare (*or:* put) out of bounds; *~ wapenbezit* illegal possession of arms

verbond [vərbɔnt] *het (~en)* **1** treaty, pact: *een ~ sluiten* (or: *aangaan*) *met* make (*or:* enter) into a treaty with; **2** union

verbonden [vərbɔndə(n)] *adj* **1** committed,

bound; **2** allied, joined (together); **3** bandaged, dressed; **4** joined (to), united (with), bound (to), wedded (to): *zich met iem ~ voelen* feel a bond with s.o.; *verkeerd ~* wrong number

verborgen [vərb<u>ɔ</u>rɣə(n)] *adj* hidden, concealed

verbouwen [vərb<u>au</u>wə(n)] *vb* **1** cultivate, grow; **2** carry out alterations, renovate

verbouwereerd [vərb<u>au</u>wər<u>e</u>rt] *adj* dumbfounded, flabbergasted

verbouwing [vərb<u>au</u>wɪŋ] *de (~en)* alteration, renovation: *gesloten wegens ~* closed for repairs (*or:* alterations)

¹**verbranden** [vərbr<u>a</u>ndə(n)] *vb* **1** burn (down), incinerate; **2** burn, scald: *zijn gezicht is door de zon verbrand* his face is sunburnt

²**verbranden** [vərbr<u>a</u>ndə(n)] *vb* **1** burn down, burn up: *hij is bij dat ongeluk levend verbrand* he was burnt alive in that accident; **2** burn, scorch: *het vlees staat te ~* the meat is burning

verbranding [vərbr<u>a</u>ndɪŋ] *de (~en)* **1** burning, incineration; **2** burn, scald

verbrandingsmotor [vərbr<u>a</u>ndɪŋsmotər] *de (~en)* (internal-)combustion engine

¹**verbreden** [vərbr<u>e</u>də(n)] *vb* broaden, widen

²**verbreden** [vərbr<u>e</u>də(n)] *ref vb* broaden (out): *de weg verbreedt zich daar* the road broadens (out) there

verbreken [vərbr<u>e</u>kə(n)] *vb* **1** break (up): *een zegel ~* break a seal; **2** break (off), sever: *een relatie ~* break off a relationship

verbrijzelen [vərbr<u>ɛi</u>zələ(n)] *vb* shatter, crush

verbrodden [vərbr<u>ɔ</u>də(n)] *vb (Belg)* botch (up), mess up

verbrokkelen [vərbr<u>ɔ</u>kələ(n)] *vb* crumble

verbruik [vərbr<u>œy</u>k] *het* consumption

verbruiken [vərbr<u>œy</u>kə(n)] *vb* consume, use up

verbruiker [vərbr<u>œy</u>kər] *de (~s)* consumer, user

verbuigen [vərb<u>œy</u>ɣə(n)] *vb* bend, twist

¹**verdacht** [vərd<u>a</u>χt] *adj* **1** suspected: *iem ~ maken* cast a slur on s.o., smear s.o.; **2** suspicious, questionable: *een ~ zaakje* a questionable (*or:* shady) business

²**verdacht** [vərd<u>a</u>χt] *adv* suspiciously: *dat lijkt ~ veel op ...* that looks suspiciously like ...

verdachte [vərd<u>a</u>χtə] *de (~n)* suspect

verdachtenbank [vərd<u>a</u>χtə(n)baŋk] *de* dock, witness box (*or Am:* stand)

verdachtmaking [vərd<u>a</u>χtmakɪŋ] *de (~en)* imputation, insinuation, slur

verdagen [vərd<u>a</u>ɣə(n)] *vb* adjourn: *een zitting ~* adjourn a session

verdaging [vərd<u>a</u>χɪŋ] *de (~en)* postponement, adjournment

verdampen [vərd<u>a</u>mpə(n)] *vb* evaporate, vaporize

verdamping [vərd<u>a</u>mpɪŋ] *de* evaporation, vaporization

verdedigen [vərd<u>e</u>dəɣə(n)] *vb* **1** defend: *een ~de houding aannemen* be on the defensive; **2** defend, support: *zijn belangen ~* stand up for (*or:* defend)

one's interests; *zich ~ defend (or:* justify) oneself

verdediger [vərd<u>e</u>dəɣər] *de (~s)* **1** defender, advocate; **2** counsel (for the defence); **3** *(sport)* defender, back: *centrale ~* central defender; *vrije ~* libero

verdediging [vərd<u>e</u>dəɣɪŋ] *de (~en)* **1** defence: *(sport) in de ~ gaan* go on the defensive; **2** counsel (for the defence), defence

verdeeld [vərd<u>e</u>lt] *adj* divided: *hierover zijn de meningen ~* opinions are divided on this (problem, issue, question)

verdeeldheid [vərd<u>e</u>ltheit] *de* discord, dissension: *er heerst ~ binnen de partij* the party is divided (*or:* split); *~ zaaien* spread discord

verdekt [vərd<u>ɛ</u>kt] *adj* concealed, hidden: *zich ~ opstellen* conceal oneself, take cover

¹**verdelen** [vərd<u>e</u>lə(n)] *vb* **1** divide, split (up); **2** divide (up), distribute: *de buit ~* divide the loot; **3** spread: *de taken ~* allocate (*or:* share) (out) the tasks

²**verdelen** [vərd<u>e</u>lə(n)] *ref vb* divide, split (up): *de rivier verdeelt zich hier in twee takken* the river divides (*or:* forks) here

verdelgingsmiddel [vərd<u>ɛ</u>lɣɪŋsmɪdəl] *het* pesticide; insecticide; weedkiller

verdeling [vərd<u>e</u>lɪŋ] *de (~en)* **1** division; **2** distribution

verdenken [vərd<u>ɛ</u>ŋkə(n)] *vb* suspect (of): *zij wordt ervan verdacht, dat ...* she is under the suspicion of ...; *iem van diefstal ~* suspect s.o. of theft

verdenking [vərd<u>ɛ</u>ŋkɪŋ] *de (~en)* suspicion: *iem in hechtenis nemen op ~ van moord* arrest s.o. on suspicion of murder

¹**verder** [v<u>ɛ</u>rdər] *adj* **1** (the) rest of; **2** further, subsequent

²**verder** [v<u>ɛ</u>rdər] *adv* **1** farther, further: *twee regels ~* two lines (further) down; *hoe ging het ~?* how did it go on?; *~ lezen* go on (*or:* continue) reading, read on; **2** further, furthermore, in addition, moreover: *~ verklaarde zij ...* she went on (*or:* proceeded) to say ...; **3** for the rest, apart from that: *is er ~ nog iets?* anything else?

verderf [v<u>ɛ</u>rdɛrf] *het* ruin, destruction: *iem in het ~ storten* ruin s.o., bring ruin upon s.o.

verderfelijk [vərd<u>ɛ</u>rfələk] *adj* pernicious: *~e invloeden* baneful influences

verderop [vɛrdər<u>ɔ</u>p] *adv* further on, farther on: *zij woont vier huizen ~* she lives four houses (further) down; *~ in de straat* down (*or:* up) the street

verderven [vərd<u>ɛ</u>rvə(n)] *vb* deprave, corrupt

¹**verdiend** [vərd<u>i</u>nt] *adj* deserved: *volkomen ~* richly deserved

²**verdiend** [vərd<u>i</u>nt] *adv* deservedly: *de thuisclub won ~ met 3-1* the home team won deservedly by 3 to 1

¹**verdienen** [vərd<u>i</u>nə(n)] *vb* **1** earn, make, be paid: *een goed salaris ~* earn a good salary; *zuur verdiend* hard-earned, hard-won; **2** deserve, merit: *dat voorbeeld verdient geen navolging* that example ought not to be followed

²verdienen [vərdinə(n)] *vb* **1** earn, make money: *zij verdient uitstekend* she is very well paid; **2** pay: *dat baantje verdient slecht* that job does not pay well

verdienste [vərdinstə] *de (~n)* **1** wages, pay, earnings; profit: *zonder ~n zijn* be out of a job, earn no money; **2** merit: *een man van ~* a man of (great) merit

verdienstelijk [vərdinstələk] *adj, adv* deserving, (praise)worthy: *zich ~ maken* make oneself useful

¹verdiepen [vərdipə(n)] *ref vb* (with *in*) go (deeply) into, be absorbed in: *verdiept zijn in* be engrossed (*or*: absorbed) in

²verdiepen [vərdipə(n)] *vb* deepen, broaden: *zijn kennis ~* gain more in-depth knowledge

verdieping [vərdipɪŋ] *de (~en)* floor, storey: *een huis met zes ~en* a six-storeyed house; *op de tweede ~* on the second floor, *(Am)* on the third floor

verdikking [vərdɪkɪŋ] *de (~en)* thickening, bulge

verdoemd [vərdumt] *adj* damned

verdoen [vərdun] *vb* waste (away), fritter (away), squander: *ik zit hier mijn tijd te ~* I am wasting my time here

verdoezelen [vərduzələ(n)] *vb* blur, disguise: *de ware toedracht ~* fudge (*or*: disguise) the real facts

verdonkeremanen [vərdɔŋkərəmanə(n)] *vb* embezzle, suppress

verdoofd [vərdoft] *adj* stunned, stupefied, numb

verdord [vərdɔrt] *adj* shrivelled, withered, parched: *~e bladeren* withered leaves

verdorren [vərdɔrə(n)] *vb* shrivel (up), parch, wither (up), wilt

verdorven [vərdɔrvə(n)] *adj* depraved, perverted: *een ~ mens* a wicked person, a pervert

verdoven [vərdovə(n)] *vb* stun, stupefy, benumb: *~de middelen* drugs, narcotic(s); *de patiënt wordt plaatselijk verdoofd* the patient receives a local anaesthetic

verdoving [vərdovɪŋ] *de (~en)* **1** anaesthesia, anaesthetic; **2** stupor

verdovingsmiddel [vərdovɪŋsmɪdəl] *het (~en)* anaesthetic

verdraaglijk [vərdraxlək] *adj* bearable, tolerable

verdraagzaam [vərdraxsam] *adj* tolerant: *~ jegens elkaar zijn* be tolerant of each other

verdraagzaamheid [vərdraxsamhɛit] *de* tolerance

verdraaien [vərdrajə(n)] *vb* **1** turn; **2** distort, twist: *de waarheid ~* distort the truth; **3** disguise: *zijn stem ~* disguise (*or*: mask) one's voice

verdraaiing [vərdrajɪŋ] *de (~en)* distortion, twist

verdrag [vərdrax] *het (~en)* treaty, agreement: *een ~ sluiten* enter into (*or*: make) a treaty

verdragen [vərdrayə(n)] *vb* **1** bear, endure, stand: *hij kan de gedachte niet ~, dat ...* he cannot bear (*or*: stand) the idea that ...; **2** bear, stand, put up with, take: *ik kan veel ~, maar nu is 't genoeg* I can stand (*or*: take) a lot, but enough is enough

verdriet [vərdrit] *het* grief (*or*: distress) (at, over), sorrow (at): *iem ~ doen (aandoen)* distress s.o., give s.o. pain (*or*: sorrow); *~ hebben* be in distress, grieve

verdrietig [vərdritəx] *adj* sad, grieved: *~ maken* sadden

verdrievoudigen [vərdrivɑudəyə(n)] *vb* triple, treble: *de winst is verdrievoudigd* profit has tripled

verdrijven [vərdrɛivə(n)] *vb* drive away, chase away, dispel: *de pijn ~* dispel the pain

¹verdringen [vərdrɪŋə(n)] *vb* **1** push away (*or*: aside); **2** shut out, repress, suppress

²verdringen [vərdrɪŋə(n)] *ref vb* crowd (round): *de menigte verdrong zich voor de etalage* people crowded round the shop window

¹verdrinken [vərdrɪŋkə(n)] *vb* drown: *~ in het huiswerk* be swamped by homework

²verdrinken [vərdrɪŋkə(n)] *vb* drink away; drown

verdrinkingsdood [vərdrɪŋkɪŋzdot] *de* death by drowning

verdrogen [vərdroyə(n)] *vb* **1** dry out, dry up, dehydrate: *dat brood is helemaal verdroogd* that loaf (of bread) has completely dried out; **2** shrivel (up), wither (away, up)

verdrukken [vərdrykə(n)] *vb* oppress, repress

verdrukking [vərdrykɪŋ] *de (~en)* ‖ *in de ~ raken (komen)* get into hot water (*or*: a scrape)

verdubbelen [vərdybələ(n)] *vb* double: *met verdubbelde energie* with redoubled energy

verduidelijken [vərdœydələkə(n)] *vb* explain, make (more) clear, clarify

verduidelijking [vərdœydələkɪŋ] *de (~en)* explanation: *ter ~* by way of illustration

verduisteren [vərdœystərə(n)] *vb* **1** darken, dim: *de zon ~* blot out the sun; **2** embezzle

verduistering [vərdœystərɪŋ] *de (~en)* **1** darkening; **2** eclipse; **3** embezzlement

verdunnen [vərdynə(n)] *vb* **1** thin, dilute: *melk met water ~* dilute milk with water; **2** thin (out)

verdunning [vərdynɪŋ] *de (~en)* thinning, dilution

verduren [vərdyrə(n)] *vb* bear, endure, suffer: *heel wat moeten ~* have to put up with a great deal; *het zwaar te ~ hebben: a)* have a hard (*or*: rough) time of it; *b)* suffer great hardship(s)

verduurzamen [vərdyrzamə(n)] *vb* preserve, cure

verdwaald [vərdwalt] *adj* lost, stray: *een ~e kogel* a stray bullet; *~ raken* lose one's way

verdwaasd [vərdwast] *adj* foolish, groggy: *~ voor zich uit staren* stare vacantly into space

verdwalen [vərdwalə(n)] *vb* lose one's way, get lost, go astray

verdwijnen [vərdwɛinə(n)] *vb* disappear, vanish: *een verdwenen boek* a missing (*or*: lost) book; *mijn kiespijn is verdwenen* my toothache has worn off (*or*: disappeared); *geleidelijk ~* fade out (*or*: away), melt away; *spoorloos ~* vanish without (leaving) a trace

verdwijning [vərdwɛinɪŋ] *de (~en)* disappearance

verdwijntruc [vərdwɛintryk] *de (~s)* disappearing act, vanishing trick

veredelen [vəredələ(n)] *vb* ennoble, elevate, refine

veredeling [vəredəlɪŋ] *de* refinement, improvement, upgrading

vereenvoudigen [vərenvɑudəɣə(n)] *vb* simplify: *de vereenvoudigde spelling* simplified spelling

vereenvoudiging [vərenvɑudəɣɪŋ] *de (~en)* simplification, reduction *(fraction)*

vereenzamen [vərɛnzamə(n)] *vb* grow lonely, become lonely

vereenzaming *de* (social) isolation, (enforced) loneliness

vereenzelvigen [vərenzɛlvəɣə(n)] *vb* identify: *zij vereenzelvigde zich met Julia Roberts* she identified (herself) with Julia Roberts

vereerder [vərɛrdər] *de (~s)* worshipper, admirer

vereffenen [vərɛfənə(n)] *vb* settle, square, smooth out: *iets* (or: *een rekening*) *met iem te ~ hebben* have to settle an account

vereffening [vərɛfənɪŋ] *de (~en)* settlement; payment

vereisen [vərɛisə(n)] *vb* require, demand: *ervaring vereist* experience required; *de vereiste zorg aan iets besteden* give the necessary care (or: attention) to sth

vereiste [vərɛistə] *het, de (~n)* requirement: *aan de ~n voldoen* meet (or: fulfil) the requirements; *dat is een eerste ~* that is a prerequisite (or: a must)

¹**veren** [vɛrə(n)] *adj* feather: *een ~ pen* a quill (pen)

²**veren** [vɛrə(n)] *vb* **1** be springy: *het veert niet meer* it has lost its spring (or: bounce); **2** spring: *overeind ~* spring to one's feet

verend [vɛrənt] *adj* springy, elastic: *een ~ matras* a springy (or: bouncy) mattress

verenigbaar [vərɛnəɣbar] *adj* compatible (with), consistent (with)

verenigd [vərɛnəɣt] *adj* united, allied

Verenigde Arabische Emiraten [vərenəɣdəarabisəemiratə(n)] *de* United Arab Emirates

Verenigde Staten [vərenəɣdəstatə(n)] *de* United States (of America)

Verenigd Koninkrijk [vərenəɣtkonɪŋkrɛik] *het* United Kingdom

verenigen [vərɛnəɣə(n)] *vb* unite (with), combine, join (to, with): *zich ~ in een organisatie* form an organisation; *het nuttige met het aangename ~ mix* (or: combine) business with pleasure

vereniging [vərɛnəɣɪŋ] *de (~en)* club, association, society: *een ~ oprichten* found an association

vereren [vərɛrə(n)] *vb* worship, adore

¹**verergeren** [vərɛrɣərə(n)] *vb* worsen, make worse, aggravate

²**verergeren** [vərɛrɣərə(n)] *vb* worsen, become worse, grow worse, deteriorate: *de toestand verergert* the situation is deteriorating (or: growing worse)

verering [vərɛrɪŋ] *de (~en)* **1** worship, veneration; **2** *(rel)* devotion, cult: *de ~ van Maria* the devotion to Maria, the Maria cult

verf [vɛrf] *de (verven)* paint, dye: *pas op voor de ~!* (watch out,) fresh (or: wet) paint!; *het huis zit nog goed in de ~* the paintwork (on the house) is still

good; *niet uit de ~ komen* not live up to its promise, not come into its own

verfdoos [vɛrvdos] *de (-dozen)* paint box, (box of) paints

verffabriek [vɛrfabrik] *de (~en)* paint factory

verfijnen [vərfɛinə(n)] *vb* refine: *zijn techniek ~* refine (or: polish (up)) one's technique

verfijning [vərfɛinɪŋ] *de (~en)* refinement, sophistication

verfilmen [vərfɪlmə(n)] *vb* film, turn (or: make) into a film: *een roman ~ film* a novel, adapt a novel for the screen

verfilming [vərfɪlmɪŋ] *de (~en)* film version, screen version

verfkwast [vɛrfkwɑst] *de (~en)* paintbrush

verflaag [vɛrflaχ] *de (-lagen)* coat (or: layer) of paint: *bovenste ~* topcoat

verfoeien [vərfujə(n)] *vb* detest, loathe

verfomfaaid [vərfɔmfajt] *adj* dishevelled, tousled

verfomfaaien [vərfɔmfajə(n)] *vb* crumple (up), rumple

verfpot [vɛrfpɔt] *de (~ten)* paint pot

verfraaien [vərfrajə(n)] *vb* embellish (with)

verfraaiing [vərfrajɪŋ] *de (~en)* embellishment

verfrissen [vərfrɪsə(n)] *vb* refresh, freshen up: *zich ~* freshen up, refresh (oneself)

verfrissend [vərfrɪsənt] *adj* refreshing, invigorating

verfrissing [vərfrɪsɪŋ] *de (~en)* refreshment: *enige ~en gebruiken* take (or: have) some refreshments

verfroller [vɛrfrɔlər] *de (~s)* paint roller

verfrommelen [vərfrɔmələ(n)] *vb* crumple (up), rumple (up)

verfspuit [vɛrfspœyt] *de (~en)* paint spray(er), spray gun

verfstof [vɛrfstɔf] *de (~fen)* paint, dye (base), pigment

verfverdunner [vɛrfərdʏnər] *de (~s)* thinner

verfwinkel [vɛrfwɪŋkəl] *de (~s)* paint shop

vergaan [vərɣan] *vb* **1** fare: *vergane glorie* lost (or: faded) glory; **2** perish, pass away: *horen en zien vergaat je erbij* the noise is enough to waken the dead; **3** perish, decay, rot; **4** perish, *(fig)* be consumed with, be wrecked (or: lost), founder: *ik verga van de kou* I am freezing to death; *~ van de honger* be starving to death; *~ van de dorst* be dying of thirst

vergaand [vɛrɣant] *adj* far-reaching, drastic

vergaderen [vərɣadərə(n)] *vb* meet, assemble: *hij heeft al de hele ochtend vergaderd* he has been in conference all morning; *de raad vergaderde twee uur lang* the council sat for two hours

vergadering [vərɣadərɪŋ] *de (~en)* meeting, assembly: *het verslag van een ~* the minutes of a meeting; *gewone (algemene) ~* general meeting (or: assembly); *een ~ bijwonen* (or: *houden*) attend (or: hold) a meeting; *een ~ sluiten* close (or: conclude) the meeting; *een ~ leiden* chair a meeting

vergaderzaal [vərɣadərzal] *de (-zalen)* meeting hall, assembly room, conference room

vergallen [vərɣɑlə(n)] *vb* embitter, spoil

vergankelijk [vərɣɑŋkələk] *adj* transitory, transient, fleeting

vergapen [vərɣɑpə(n)] *ref vb* gaze at, gape at: *zich ~ aan een motor* gape (in admiration) at a motorbike

vergaren [vərɣɑrə(n)] *vb* gather

vergassen [vərɣɑsə(n)] *vb* **1** gas; **2** gasify

vergassing *de* **1** gasification; **2** gassing

¹vergeefs [vərɣefs] *adv* in vain: *~ zoeken* look in vain

²vergeefs [vərɣefs] *adj* vain, futile, in vain: *een ~e reis* a futile (*or:* useless) journey

vergeetachtig [vərɣetɑχtəχ] *adj* forgetful

vergeet-mij-niet [vərχetmɛinit] *de (~en)* forget-me-not

vergelden [vərɣɛldə(n)] *vb* repay, reward, take revenge on: *kwaad met kwaad ~* pay back (*or:* repay) evil with evil

vergelding [vərɣɛldɪŋ] *de (~en)* repayment, reward, revenge, retaliation: *ter ~ werden krijgsgevangenen doodgeschoten* prisoners of war were shot in retaliation (*or:* reprisal)

vergeldingsactie [vərɣɛldɪŋsɑksi] *de (~s)* reprisal (attack, raid)

vergelen [vərɣelə(n)] *vb* yellow, go yellow, turn yellow

vergelijkbaar [vɛrɣəlɛigbar] *adj* comparable: *meel en vergelijkbare producten* flour and similar products; *~ zijn met* be comparable to

vergelijken [vɛrɣəlɛikə(n)] *vb* compare; compare with sth: *vergelijk artikel 12, tweede lid* see (*or:* cf.) article 12, subsection two; *niet te ~ zijn met* be (*or:* bear) no comparison with, not be comparable to

vergelijking [vɛrɣəlɛikɪŋ] *de (~en)* **1** comparison, analogy: *de trappen van ~* the degrees of comparison; *in ~ met* in (*or:* by) comparison with; *ter ~* by way of comparison, for comparison; **2** *(maths)* equation

vergemakkelijken [vɛrɣəmɑkələkə(n)] *vb* simplify, facilitate: *dat dient om het leven te ~* that serves to make life easier

vergemakkelijking *de* simplification, facilitation

vergen [vɛrɣə(n)] *vb* demand, require, tax: *het uiterste ~ van iem* strain (*or:* try) s.o. to the limit

¹vergeten [vərɣetə(n)] *vb* **1** forget, slip one's mind: *alles is ~ en vergeven* everything is forgiven and forgotten, (there are) no hard feelings; *dat ben ik glad ~* clean forgot(ten); *dat kun je wel ~* you can kiss that goodbye!; **2** forget, overlook, leave behind: *ze waren ~ zijn naam op de lijst te zetten* they had forgotten to put his name on the list; *niet te ~* not forgetting (*or:* omitting); **3** forget, put out of one's mind: *zijn zorgen ~* forget one's worries; *vergeet het maar!* forget it!, no way!

²vergeten [vərɣetə(n)] *adj* forgotten, neglected: *~ schrijvers* forgotten (*or:* obscure) writers

vergeven [vərɣevə(n)] *vb* **1** forgive: *ik kan mezelf* *nooit ~, dat ik ...* I can never forgive myself for (...ing); **2** poison: *het huis is ~ van de stank* the house is pervaded by the stench; *~ van de luizen* lice-ridden, crawling with lice; **3** give (away): *zij heeft zes vrijkaartjes te ~* she has six free tickets to give away

vergeving [vərɣevɪŋ] *de* forgiveness, pardon, absolution: *iem om ~ vragen voor iets* ask s.o.'s forgiveness for sth

vergevorderd [vɛrɣəvɔrdərt] *adj* (far) advanced

vergezellen [vɛrɣəzɛlə(n)] *vb* accompany, attend (on): *iem op (de) reis ~* accompany s.o. on a journey

vergezicht [vɛrɣəzɪχt] *het (~en)* (panoramic, wide) view, vista

vergezocht [vɛrɣəzɔχt] *adj* far-fetched

vergiet [vərɣit] *het, de (~en)* colander, strainer: *zo lek als een ~* leak like a sieve

vergif [vərɣɪf] *het (~fen)* poison, venom: *dodelijk ~* lethal (*or:* deadly) poison

vergiffenis [vərɣɪfənɪs] *de* forgiveness, pardon, absolution

vergiftig [vərɣɪftəχ] *adj* poisonous, venomous

vergiftigen [vərɣɪftəɣə(n)] *vb* poison

vergiftiging [vərɣɪftəɣɪŋ] *de (~en)* poisoning: *hij stierf door ~* he died of poisoning

vergissen [vərɣɪsə(n)] *ref vb* be mistaken (*or:* wrong), make a mistake: *zich lelijk ~* be greatly mistaken; *vergis je niet* make no mistake; *als ik mij niet vergis* if I'm not wrong (*or:* mistaken); *zich in de persoon ~* mistake s.o.; *zich in iem ~* be mistaken (*or:* wrong) about s.o.; *als hij dat denkt, vergist hij zich* if he thinks that he'll have to think again; *~ is menselijk* to err is human

vergissing [vərɣɪsɪŋ] *de (~en)* mistake, error: *iets per ~ doen* do sth by mistake (*or:* inadvertently)

vergoeden [vərɣudə(n)] *vb* **1** make good, compensate for, refund: *onkosten ~* pay expenses; *iem de schade ~* compensate (*or:* pay) s.o. for the damage; **2** compensate, make up (for): *dat vergoedt veel* that makes up for a lot

vergoeding [vərɣudɪŋ] *de (~en)* **1** compensation, reimbursement: *~ eisen* claim damages; *een ~ vragen voor charge for; **2** allowance, fee, expenses: *tegen een geringe ~* for a small fee

vergokken [vərɣɔkə(n)] *vb* gamble away

vergooien [vərɣojə(n)] *vb* throw away, waste: *zijn leven ~* throw (*or:* fritter) away one's life

vergrendelen [vərɣrɛndələ(n)] *vb* bolt, (double) lock

vergrijp [vərɣrɛip] *het (~en)* offence: *een licht ~* a minor offence

vergrijpen [vərɣrɛipə(n)] *ref vb* assault, violate: *zich aan iem ~* assault s.o.

vergrijzen [vərɣrɛizə(n)] *vb* age, get old: *Nederland vergrijst* the population of the Netherlands is ageing

vergrijzing [vərɣrɛizɪŋ] *de* ageing

vergroeien [vərɣrujə(n)] *vb* grow crooked, grow

deformed, become deformed

vergroeiing [vərɣrujıŋ] *de (~en)* **1** deformity; **2** crooked growth: ~ *van de ruggengraat* curvature of the spine

vergrootglas [vərɣrotχlɑs] *het (-glazen)* magnifying glass

vergroten [vərɣrotə(n)] *vb* **1** increase: *de kansen (or: risico's)* ~ increase the chances (or: risks); **2** enlarge: *de kamer* ~ extend (or: enlarge) the room; **3** magnify, enlarge, blow up

vergroting [vərɣrotıŋ] *de (~en)* **1** increase: ~ *van de omzet* increase in the turnover; **2** enlargement

vergruizen [vərɣrœyzə(n)] *vb* pulverize, crush

verguld [vərɣʏlt] *adj* **1** gilded, gilt, gold-plated; **2** pleased, flattered: *Laurette was er vreselijk mee* ~ Laurette was absolutely delighted with it

vergulden [vərɣʏldə(n)] *vb* gild, gold-plate

vergunning [vərɣʏnıŋ] *de (~en)* **1** permission; **2** permit, licence: *een restaurant met volledige* ~ a fully licensed restaurant; *een* ~ *verlenen* (or: *intrekken*) grant (or: suspend) a licence

vergunninghouder [vərɣʏnıŋhɑudər] *de (~s)* licensee, licence-holder

verhaal [vərhal] *het (verhalen)* story: *de kern van het* ~ the point of the story; *om een lang* ~ *kort te maken* to cut a long story short; *sterke verhalen* tall stories; *zijn* ~ *doen* tell (or: relate) one's story; *~tjes vertellen* tell tales; *het is weer het bekende* ~ it's the same old story; *iem op* ~ *laten komen* let s.o. get one's breath back

verhalen [vərhalə(n)] *vb* recover, recoup: *de schade op iem* ~ recover the damage from s.o.

verhandelen [vərhɑndələ(n)] *vb* trade (in), sell

verhandeling [vərhɑndəlıŋ] *de (~en) (Belg)* (mini-)dissertation

verhangen [vərhɑŋə(n)] *ref vb* hang oneself

verhard [vərhɑrt] *adj* **1** hard, paved: *~e wegen* metalled (*or Am:* paved) roads; **2** *(fig)* hardened, callous

¹verharden [vərhɑrdə(n)] *vb* harden: *in het kwaad* ~ become set in evil ways

²verharden [vərhɑrdə(n)] *vb* harden, metal, pave: *een tuinpad* ~ pave a garden path

verharding [vərhɑrdıŋ] *de (~en)* hardening, metalling, paving: *een* ~ *van standpunten* a hardening of points of view

verharen [vərharə(n)] *vb* moult, shed (hair): *de kat is aan het* ~ the cat is moulting

¹verheffen [vərhɛfə(n)] *vb* **1** raise, lift; **2** *(fig)* raise, elevate, uplift, lift up: *iets tot regel* ~ make sth the rule

²verheffen [vərhɛfə(n)] *ref vb* rise: *zich hoog* ~ *boven de stad* rise (or: tower) above the city

¹verhelderen [vərhɛldərə(n)] *vb* clear (up): *de lucht verhelderde* the sky cleared (or: brightened up)

²verhelderen [vərhɛldərə(n)] *vb* clarify: *een ~d antwoord* an illuminating answer

verhelpen [vərhɛlpə(n)] *vb* put right, remedy

verhemelte [vərheməltə] *het (~n, ~s)* palate, roof

of the mouth: *een gespleten* ~ a cleft palate

verheugd [vərhøχt] *adj* glad, pleased: *zich bijzonder* ~ *tonen (over iets)* take great pleasure in sth

verheugen [vərhøɣə(n)] *ref vb* be glad, be pleased (or: happy): *zich* ~ *op* look forward to

verheugend [vərhøɣənt] *adj* joyful: ~ *nieuws* good news

verheven [vərhevə(n)] *adj* elevated; *(fig)* above (to), superior (to): *boven iedere verdenking* ~ above (or: beyond) all suspicion

verhevigen [vərhevəɣə(n)] *vb* intensify

verhinderen [vərhındərə(n)] *vb* prevent: *iemands plannen* ~ obstruct (or: foil) s.o.'s plans; *dat zal mij niet* ~ *om tegen dit voorstel te stemmen* that won't prevent me from voting against this proposal; *verhinderd zijn* be unable to come (or: attend)

verhindering [vərhındərıŋ] *de (~en)* absence, inability to come: *bij* ~ in case of absence

verhit [vərhıt] *adj* **1** hot, flushed; **2** heated: *~te discussies* heated discussions

verhitten [vərhıtə(n)] *vb* **1** heat; **2** inflame, stir up: *dat verhitte de gemoederen* that made feelings run high

verhitting [vərhıtıŋ] *de* heating(-up)

verhoeden [vərhudə(n)] *vb* prevent, forbid: *God verhoede dat je ziek wordt* God forbid that you should be ill

verhogen [vərhoɣə(n)] *vb* **1** raise: *een dijk* ~ raise a dike; **2** increase: *de prijzen* ~ raise (or: increase) prices

verhoging [vərhoɣıŋ] *de (~en)* **1** raising; **2** elevation, platform, rise: *de spreker stond op een* ~ the speaker stood on a (raised) platform; **3** increase, rise; **4** temperature, fever: *ik had wat* ~ I had a slight temperature

¹verhongeren [vərhɔŋərə(n)] *vb* **1** starve (to death), die of starvation; **2** starve, go hungry

²verhongeren [vərhɔŋərə(n)] *vb* starve (to death): *de kinderen waren half verhongerd* the children were famished (or: half starved)

verhoogd [vərhoχt] *adj* increased, raised: *~e bloeddruk* high blood pressure

verhoor [vərhor] *het (verhoren)* interrogation, examination

verhoren [vərhorə(n)] *vb* **1** interrogate, question, cross-examine: *getuigen* ~ hear witnesses; **2** hear, answer, grant: *een gebed* ~ answer (or: hear) a prayer

verhouden [vərhɑudə(n)] *ref vb* be as, be in the proportion of: *60 verhoudt zich tot 12 als 5 tot 1* 60 is to 12 as 5 to 1

verhouding [vərhɑudıŋ] *de (~en)* **1** relation(ship), proportion: *in* ~ *tot* in proportion to; *naar* ~ *is dat duur* that is comparatively expensive; **2** affair, relationship; **3** *(pl)* proportions: *gevoel voor ~en bezitten* have a sense of proportion

verhoudingsgewijs [vərhɑudıŋsχəwɛis] *adv* comparatively, relatively

verhuisbedrijf [vərhœyzbədrɛif] *het (-bedrijven)*

removal firm (or: company)

verhuisbericht [vərhœyzbərıχt] *het (~en)* change of address card

verhuiswagen [vərhœyswayə(n)] *de (~s)* removal van

verhuizen [vərhœyzə(n)] *vb* move (house), relocate ‖ *iem ~* move s.o.

verhuizer [vərhœyzər] *de (~s)* remover

verhuizing [vərhœyzıŋ] *de (~en)* move; moving

verhullen [vərhүlə(n)] *vb* veil, conceal (from): *niets ~de foto's* revealing photos

verhuren [vərhүrə(n)] *vb* let; *(Am)* rent, lease out

verhuur [vərhүr] *de* letting, *(Am)* rental

verhuurbedrijf [vərhүrbədreif] *het* leasing company; hire company (or: firm); *(esp Am also)* rental company (or: agency)

verhuurder [vərhүrdər] *de (~s)* letter, *(Am)* renter, landlord, landlady

verifiëren [verifijərə(n)] *vb* verify, examine, audit, prove

verijdelen [vərɛidələ(n)] *vb* frustrate, defeat: *een aanslag ~* foil an attempt on s.o.'s life

vering [vɛrıŋ] *de (~en)* springs, *(car)* suspension

verjaard [vərjaːrt] *adj* time-barred, superannuated

verjaardag [vərjaːrdaχ] *de (~en)* birthday: *vandaag is het mijn ~* today is my birthday

verjaardagscadeau [vərjaːrdaχskado] *het* birthday present

verjaardagsfeest [vərjaːrdaχsfest] *het (~en)* birthday party

verjaardagskaart [vərjaːrdaχskart] *de* birthday card

verjaardagskalender [vərjaːrdaχskalɛndər] *de (~s)* birthday calendar

verjagen [vərjaːɣə(n)] *vb* drive away, chase away

verjaren [vərjaːrə(n)] *vb* become prescribed, become (statute-)barred, become out-of-date

verjaring [vərjaːrıŋ] *de (~en)* prescription; limitation

verjongen [vərjɔŋə(n)] *vb* rejuvenate, make young

verkalking [vərkɑlkıŋ] *de* calcification, hardening

verkassen [vərkɑsə(n)] *vb* move (house)

verkavelen [vərkaːvələ(n)] *vb* parcel out, (sub)divide

verkaveling [vərkaːvəlıŋ] *de (~en)* allotment, subdivision

verkeer [vərkeːr] *het* **1** traffic: *handel en ~* trade (or: traffic) and commerce; *druk ~* heavy traffic; *veilig ~* road safety; *het overige ~ in gevaar brengen* be a danger to other road-users; **2** association: *in het maatschappelijk ~* in society; *in het dagelijks ~* in everyday life; **3** movement: *er bestaat vrij ~ tussen die twee landen* there is freedom of movement between the two countries

verkeerd [vərkeːrt] *adj, adv* **1** wrong: *een verdediger op het ~e been zetten* wrong-foot a defender; *een ~e diagnose* a faulty diagnosis; *de ~e dingen zeggen* say the wrong things; *het eten kwam in mijn ~e keelgat* the food went down the wrong way; *op een ~ spoor zitten* be on the wrong track; *iets ~ aanpakken* go about sth the wrong way; *hij doet alles ~* he can't do a thing right; *pardon, u loopt ~* pardon me, but you're going the wrong way (or: in the wrong direction); *het liep ~ met hem af* he came to grief (or: to a bad end); *iets ~ spellen* (or: *uitspreken, vertalen*) misspell (or: mispronounce, mistranslate) sth; *~ verbonden zijn* have dialled a wrong number; *we zitten ~* we must be wrong; *hij had iets ~s gegeten* sth he had eaten had upset him; *je hebt de ~e voor* you've mistaken your man; **2** wrong; inside out: *zijn handen staan ~* he's all thumbs; *~ om* the other way round, upside down

verkeersagent [vərkeːrsayɛnt] *de* traffic policeman (or: policewoman)

verkeersbord [vərkeːrzbɔrt] *het (~en)* road sign, traffic sign

verkeersbrigadier [vərkeːrzbriɣadir] *de (~s)* lollipop man (or: lady)

verkeerscontrole [vərkeːrskɔntrɔːlə] *de (~s)* (road) traffic surveillance

verkeersdrempel [vərkeːrzdrɛmpəl] *de (~s)* speed ramp

verkeersdrukte [vərkeːrzdrүktə] *de* (amount of) traffic

verkeersleider [vərkeːrsleidər] *de (~s)* air-traffic controller

verkeersleiding [vərkeːrsleidıŋ] *de (~en)* traffic department, *(aviation)* air-traffic control, ground control

verkeerslicht [vərkeːrslıχt] *het (~en)* traffic lights: *het ~ sprong op groen* the traffic lights changed to green

verkeersongeval [vərkeːrsɔŋɣəval] *het (~len)* road accident, traffic accident

verkeersopstopping [vərkeːrsɔpstɔpıŋ] *de (~en)* traffic jam

verkeersovertreding [vərkeːrsovərtredıŋ] *de (~en)* traffic offence

verkeersplein [vərkeːrsplɛin] *het (~en)* roundabout, *(Am)* rotary (intersection)

verkeerspolitie [vərkeːrspoli(t)si] *de* traffic police

verkeersregel [vərkeːrsreɣəl] *de (~s)* traffic rule

verkeerstoren [vərkeːrstorə(n)] *de (~s)* control tower

verkeersveiligheid [vərkeːrsfɛiləχheit] *de* road safety, traffic safety

verkeersweg [vərkeːrswɛχ] *de (~en)* traffic route, thoroughfare

verkeerswisselaar [vərkeːrswısəlar] *de (~s) (Belg)* cloverleaf junction

verkennen [vərkɛnə(n)] *vb* explore, scout (out), *(mil)* reconnoitre: *de boel ~* explore the place; *de markt ~* feel out the market

verkenner [vərkɛnər] *de (~s)* **1** scout; **2** (Boy) Scout; Girl Scout

verkenning [vərkɛnıŋ] *de (~en)* exploration, scout(ing)

verkeren [vərkeːrə(n)] *vb* be (in): *in de hoogste*

kringen ~ move in the best circles

verkering [vərkẹriŋ] *de (~en)* courtship: *vaste ~ hebben* go steady; *~ krijgen met iem* start going out with s.o.

verkiesbaar [vərkịzbar] *adj* eligible (for election): *zich ~ stellen als president* run for president; *zich ~ stellen* stand for office

verkiezen [vərkịzə(n)] *vb* prefer (to): *lopen boven fietsen ~* prefer walking to cycling

verkiezing [vərkịziŋ] *de (~en)* election: *algemene ~en* general elections; *tussentijdse ~en (roughly)* by-elections; *~en uitschrijven* call (for) an election

verkiezingscampagne [vərkịziŋskampaɲə] *de (~s)* election campaign

verkiezingsdebat [vərkịziŋzdəbat] *het (~ten)* election debate

verkiezingsprogramma [vərkịziŋsproɣrama] *het (~'s)* (electoral) platform: *iets als punt in het ~ opnemen* make sth a plank in one's platform

verkiezingsstrijd [vərkịziŋstrɛit] *de* electoral struggle

verkiezingsuitslag [vərkịziŋsœytslaɣ] *de (~en)* election result: *de ~ bekendmaken* declare the poll

¹**verkijken** [vərkɛịkə(n)] *ref vb* make a mistake, be mistaken: *ik heb me op hem verkeken* I have been mistaken in him

²**verkijken** [vərkɛịkə(n)] *vb* give away, let go by: *die kans is verkeken* that chance has gone by

verkikkerd [vərkịkərt] *adj* nuts (on, about), gone (on)

verklaarbaar [vərklarbar] *adj* explicable, explainable, understandable: *om verklaarbare redenen* for obvious reasons

verklappen [vərklạpə(n)] *vb* give away, let out: *een geheim ~* tell a secret

¹**verklaren** [vərklarə(n)] *vb* **1** explain, elucidate: *iemands gedrag ~* account for s.o.'s conduct; **2** declare; certify: *iem krankzinnig ~* certify s.o. insane; *iets ongeldig ~* declare sth invalid; *een huis onbewoonbaar ~* condemn a house

²**verklaren** [vərklarə(n)] *ref vb* explain oneself: *verklaar je nader* explain yourself

verklaring [vərklariŋ] *de (~en)* **1** explanation: *dat behoeft geen nadere ~* that needs no further explanation; **2** statement, testimony: *een beëdigde ~* a sworn statement; *een ~ afleggen* make a statement

verkleden [vərklẹdə(n)] *ref vb* **1** change (one's clothes): *ik ga me ~* I'm going to change (my clothes); *zich ~ voor het eten* dress for dinner; **2** dress up

verkleinen [vərklɛịnə(n)] *vb* **1** reduce, make smaller: *op verkleinde schaal* on a reduced scale; **2** reduce, diminish, lessen

verkleining [vərklɛịniŋ] *de (~en)* reduction

verkleinwoord [vərklɛịnwort] *het (~en)* diminutive

verkleumd [vərklømt] *adj* numb (with cold)

verkleumen [vərklømə(n)] *vb* grow numb: *we staan hier te ~* we are freezing in (*or:* out) here

verkleuren [vərklørə(n)] *vb* discolour, lose colour, fade: *deze trui verkleurt niet* this sweater will keep its colour

verkleuring [vərkløriŋ] *de (~en)* fading; discoloration

verklikken [vərklịkə(n)] *vb* give away, squeal on: *iets ~* blab sth, spill the beans

verklikker [vərklịkər] *de (~s)* telltale, tattler; informer, grass

verknallen [vərknạlə(n)] *vb* blow, spoil: *je hebt het mooi verknald* you've made a hash of it

verknipt [vərknịpt] *adj* hung-up, kooky, nutty: *een ~e figuur* a weirdo, a nut(case)

verknocht [vərknɔχt] *adj* devoted (to), attached (to)

verknoeien [vərknụjə(n)] *vb* botch (up), spoil, mess up: *de boel lelijk ~* make a fine mess of things

verkoelend [vərkụlənt] *adj* cooling, refreshing

verkoeling [vərkụliŋ] *de (~en)* cooling

verkommeren [vərkɔmərə(n)] *vb* sink into poverty, pine away

verkondigen [vərkɔndəɣə(n)] *vb* proclaim, put forward

verkondiging [vərkɔndəɣiŋ] *de (~en)* proclamation, preaching

verkoop [vɛrkop] *de (verkopen)* sale(s): *~ bij opbod* (sale by) auction; *iets in de ~ brengen* put sth up for sale (*or:* on the market)

verkoopafdeling [vɛrkopavdeliŋ] *de (~en)* sales department

verkoopakte [vɛrkopaktə] *de* sales document

verkoopbaar [vərkọbar] *adj* saleable, marketable

verkoopbaarheid *de* saleability, marketability

verkoopcijfers [vɛrkopsɛifərs] *de* sales figures

verkoopdatum [vɛrkobdatym] *de (~s, -data)* date of sale: *uiterste ~* sell-by date

verkoopleider [vɛrkoplɛidər] *de (~s)* sales manager

verkoopovereenkomst [vɛrkopovərenkɔmst] *de* sales agreement

verkooppraatje [vɛrkopracə] *het (~s)* sales pitch

verkoopprijs [vɛrkoprɛis] *de (-prijzen)* selling price

verkooppunt [vɛrkopynt] *het (~en)* (sales) outlet, point of sale

verkoopresultaat [vɛrkoprəzyltat] *het* sales figure (*or:* result)

verkoopster [vɛrkopstər] *de (~s)* saleswoman, shop assistant

verkooptechniek [vɛrkoptɛχnik] *de (~en)* salesmanship

verkoopvoorwaarden *de* terms and conditions of sale

verkoopwaarde [vɛrkopwardə] *de* selling value, market value

verkopen [vərkọpə(n)] *vb* **1** sell: *nee ~* give (s.o.) no for an answer; *met winst* (*or: verlies*) *~* sell at a profit (*or:* loss); *éénmaal! andermaal! verkocht!* going! going! gone!; **2** give: *iem een dreun ~* clobber s.o.

verkoper [vərko̯pər] *de (~s)* salesman, shop assistant

verkoping [vərko̯pɪŋ] *de (~en)* (public) sale, auction: *bij openbare ~* by auction

verkort [vərkɔ̯rt] *adj* shortened, abridged, condensed

verkorten [vərkɔ̯rtə(n)] *vb* shorten, abridge, condense, reduce

verkouden [vərko̯udə(n)] *adj* || *~ worden* catch (a) cold; *~ zijn* have a cold

verkoudheid [vərko̯uthɛit] *de (-heden)* (common) cold: *een ~ opdoen* catch (a) cold

verkrachten [vərkrɑ̯χtə(n)] *vb* rape, (sexually) assault

verkrachter [vərkrɑ̯χtər] *de (~s)* rapist

verkrachting [vərkrɑ̯χtɪŋ] *de (~en)* rape

verkrampt [vərkrɑ̯mt] *adj* contorted, *(fig)* constrained

¹verkreukelen [vərkrøkələ(n)] *vb* crumple: *een verkreukeld pak* a creased suit

²verkreukelen [vərkrøkələ(n)] *vb* rumple (up), crumple (up): *papier ~* crumple up paper

verkrijgbaar [vərkrɛi̯bar] *adj* available: *het formulier is ~ bij de administratie* the form can be obtained from the administration; *zonder recept ~* over-the-counter

verkrijgen [vərkrɛi̯ɣə(n)] *vb* **1** receive, get; **2** obtain, come by, secure: *een betere positie ~* secure a better position; *moeilijk te ~* hard to come by

verkromming [vərkrɔ̯mɪŋ] *de (~en)* bend, twist: *~ van de ruggengraat* curvature of the spine

verkroppen [vərkrɔ̯pə(n)] *vb* || *iets niet kunnen ~* be unable to take sth

verkrotten [vərkrɔ̯tə(n)] *vb* decay, become run-down: *verkrotte huizen* slummy (*or:* dilapidated) houses

verkruimelen [vərkrœ̯ymələ(n)] *vb* crumble

verkwanselen [vərkwɑ̯nsələ(n)] *vb* bargain away, fritter away; squander

verkwikkend [vərkwɪ̯kənt] *adj* refreshing, invigorating, stimulating

verkwisten [vərkwɪ̯stə(n)] *vb* waste, squander

verkwisting [vərkwɪ̯stɪŋ] *de (~en)* waste(fulness), squandering: *het is pure ~* it's an utter waste

verlagen [vərla̯ɣə(n)] *vb* lower, reduce: *(met) 30 % ~* lower (*or:* reduce) by 30 %

verlaging [vərla̯ɣɪŋ] *de (~en)* lowering, reduction

¹verlammen [vərlɑ̯mə(n)] *vb* become paralysed (*or:* numb)

²verlammen [vərlɑ̯mə(n)] *vb* paralyse: *de schrik verlamde mij* I was paralysed with fear

verlammend [vərlɑ̯mənt] *adj, adv* paralysing

verlamming [vərlɑ̯mɪŋ] *de (~en)* paralysis

¹verlangen [vərlɑ̯ŋə(n)] *vb* (with *naar*) long (for), crave: *ik verlang ernaar je te zien* I long to see you, *(stronger)* I'm dying to see you

²verlangen [vərlɑ̯ŋə(n)] *vb* want, wish for, demand: *wat kun je nog meer ~* what more can you ask for?;

dat kunt u niet van mij ~ you can't expect me to do that

³verlangen [vərlɑ̯ŋə(n)] *het (~s)* longing, desire, craving: *aan iemands ~ voldoen* comply with s.o.'s wish

verlanglijst [vərlɑ̯ŋlɛist] *de (~en)* list of gifts wanted

¹verlaten [vərla̯tə(n)] *vb* **1** leave: *het land ~* leave the country; *de school ~* leave school; **2** abandon, leave: *vrouw en kinderen ~* leave (*or:* abandon) one's wife and children

²verlaten [vərla̯tə(n)] *adj* **1** deserted: *een ~ huis* an abandoned house; **2** desolate, lonely; **3** abandoned

verlatenheid [vərla̯tənhɛit] *de* desolation, abandonment: *een gevoel van ~* a feeling of desolation

¹verleden [vərle̯də(n)] *het* past: *het ~ laten rusten* let bygones be bygones; *teruggaan in het ~* go back in time

²verleden [vərle̯də(n)] *adj* past: *het ~ deelwoord* the past (*or:* perfect) participle; *de ~ tijd* the past tense; *voltooid ~ tijd* past perfect (*or:* pluperfect) (tense); *~ week* last week

verlegen [vərle̯ɣə(n)] *adj, adv* **1** shy: *~ zijn tegenover meisjes* be shy with girls; **2** (with *om*) in need of, at a loss for, pressed for: *ik zit niet om werk ~* I have my work cut out as it is

verlegenheid [vərle̯ɣə(n)hɛit] *de* **1** shyness; **2** embarrassment, trouble: *iem in ~ brengen* embarrass s.o.

verleggen [vərlɛ̯ɣə(n)] *vb* move, shift, push back

verleidelijk [vərlɛi̯dələk] *adj, adv* tempting, inviting, seductive: *een ~ aanbod* a tempting offer

verleiden [vərlɛi̯də(n)] *vb* **1** tempt, invite, entice: *iem ertoe ~ om iets te doen* tempt s.o. into doing sth; **2** seduce

verleider [vərlɛi̯dər] *de (~s)* seducer, tempter

verleiding [vərlɛi̯dɪŋ] *de (~en)* temptation, seduction: *de ~ niet kunnen weerstaan* be unable to resist (the) temptation; *in de ~ komen om* feel (*or:* be) tempted to

verleidster [vərlɛi̯tstər] *de* seducer, temptress

verlenen [vərle̯nə(n)] *vb* grant, confer: *iem onderdak ~* take s.o. in, harbour s.o.; *voorrang ~* give way (*or:* priority), *(traf)* give right of way, *(Am)* yield

verlengde [vərlɛ̯ŋdə] *het* extension: *in elkaars ~ liggen* be in line

verlengen [vərlɛ̯ŋə(n)] *vb* **1** extend, lengthen; **2** extend, prolong: *een (huur)contract ~* renew a lease; *zijn verblijf ~* prolong one's stay; *verlengd worden* go into extra (*or:* injury) time, *(Am)* go (into) overtime

verlenging [vərlɛ̯ŋɪŋ] *de (~en)* **1** extension, *(sport)* extra time, injury time, *(Am)* overtime; **2** lengthening, extension

verlengsnoer [vərlɛ̯ŋsnur] *het (~en)* extension lead

verlept [vərlɛ̯pt] *adj* withered, wilted

verleren [vərle̯rə(n)] *vb* forget (how to), unlearn: *je bent het schaken blijkbaar een beetje verleerd* your chess seems a bit rusty; *om het niet (helemaal) te ~* just to keep one's hand in

verlevendigen [vərle̯vəndəɣə(n)] *vb* revive, enliven

verlicht [vərlɪχt] *adj* 1 lit (up), lighted, illuminated: *helder ~* well-lit, brightly lit; 2 relieved, lightened: *met ~ gemoed* with (a) light heart

verlichten [vərlɪχtə(n)] *vb* 1 light, illuminate; 2 relieve, lighten: *dat verlicht de pijn* that relieves (*or:* eases) the pain

verlichting [vərlɪχtɪŋ] *de (~en)* 1 light(ing), illumination; 2 lightening: *~ van straf* mitigation of punishment

verliefd [vərlift] *adj* in love (with); amorous, loving: *zwaar ~ zijn* be madly (*or:* deeply) in love; *hij keek haar ~ aan* he gave her a fond (*or:* loving) look

verliefdheid [vərliftheit] *de (-heden)* being in love; love

verlies [vərlis] *het (verliezen)* loss: *~ lijden* suffer a loss, make a loss; *met ~ verkopen* sell at a loss; *met ~ draaien* make a loss (*or:* losses); *niet tegen (zijn) ~ kunnen* be a bad loser

verliesgevend [vərlisχe̯vənt] *adj* loss-making

verliezen [vərli̯zə(n)] *vb* 1 lose: *zijn bladeren ~* defoliate; *de macht ~* fall from power; *terrein ~* lose ground; 2 lose, miss: *er is geen tijd te ~* there is no time to lose (*or:* to be lost)

verliezer [vərli̯zər] *de (~s)* loser

verlinken [vərlɪŋkə(n)] *vb* tell on; grass on

verloedering [vərlu̯dərɪŋ] *de* corruption

verlof [vərlɔf] *het (verloven)* 1 leave, permission: *~ krijgen om ...* obtain permission to ...; 2 leave (of absence), furlough: *buitengewoon ~* special leave; *met ~ zijn* be on leave

verloofd [vərloft] *adj* engaged (to)

verloofde [vərlofdə] *de (~n, ~s)* fiancé, fiancée

verloop [vərlop] *het* 1 course, passage: *na ~ van tijd* in time, after some time; 2 course, progress, development: *voor een vlot ~ van de besprekingen* for smooth progress in the talks; 3 turnover, wastage: *natuurlijk ~* natural wastage

verlopen [vərlopə(n)] *vb* 1 (e)lapse, go by, pass; 2 expire: *mijn rijbewijs is ~* my driving licence has expired; 3 go (off): *vlot ~* go smoothly; 4 drop off, fall off, go down(hill)

verloren [vərlorə(n)] *adj* lost: *~ moeite* wasted effort; *een ~ ogenblik* an odd moment; *voor een ~ zaak vechten* fight a losing battle

verloskamer [vərlɔskamər] *de (~s)* delivery room

verloskunde [vərlɔskʏndə] *de* obstetrics

verloskundig [vərlɔskʏndəχ] *adj* obstetric

verloskundige [vərlɔskʏndəɣə] *de (~n)* midwife; obstetrician

verlossen [vərlɔsə(n)] *vb* 1 deliver (from), release (from), save (from): *een dier uit zijn lijden ~* put an animal out of its misery; 2 deliver (of)

verlosser [vərlɔsər] *de (~s)* saviour, rescuer: *de Verlosser* our Saviour, the Redeemer

verlossing [vərlɔsɪŋ] *de (~en)* deliverance, release

verloten [vərlotə(n)] *vb* raffle (off)

verloven [vərlovə(n)] *ref vb* get engaged (to)

verloving [vərlovɪŋ] *de (~en)* engagement: *zijn ~ verbreken* break off one's (*or:* the) engagement

verlovingsring [vərlovɪŋsrɪŋ] *de (~en)* engagement ring

verlummelen [vərlʏmələ(n)] *vb* fritter away

vermaak [vərmak] *het (vermaken)* amusement, enjoyment, pleasure: *onschuldig ~* good clean fun

vermaard [vərmart] *adj* renowned (for), celebrated (for), famous (for)

vermageren [vərmaɣərə(n)] *vb* lose weight, become thin(ner), get thin(ner), slim: *sterk vermagerd* emaciated, wasted

vermageringskuur [vərmaɣərɪŋskyr] *de (-kuren)* slimming diet: *een ~ ondergaan* be (*or:* go) on a (slimming, reducing) diet

vermaken [vərmakə(n)] *vb* 1 amuse, entertain: *zich ~* enjoy (*or:* amuse) oneself, have fun; 2 bequeath, make over

vermalen [vərmalə(n)] *vb* grind

vermanen [vərmanə(n)] *vb* admonish, warn

vermannen [vərmɑnə(n)] *ref vb* screw up one's courage, take heart

vermeend [vərment] *adj* supposed, alleged

vermeerderen [vərmerdərə(n)] *vb* increase, enlarge, grow: *~ met 25 %* increase by 25 per cent

vermelden [vərmɛldə(n)] *vb* 1 mention; 2 state, give

vermelding [vərmɛldɪŋ] *de (~en)* mention, statement: *eervolle ~* honourable mention; *onder ~ van ... giving (or:* stating, mentioning) ...

vermengen [vərmɛŋə(n)] *vb* mix, blend

vermenging [vərmɛŋɪŋ] *de (~en)* mix(ture), mixing, blend(ing)

¹**vermenigvuldigen** [vərmenəχfʏldəɣə(n)] *vb* 1 duplicate; 2 *(maths)* multiply: *vermenigvuldig dat getal met 8* multiply that number by 8

²**vermenigvuldigen** [vərmenəχfʏldəɣə] *ref vb* multiply, increase; reproduce

vermenigvuldiging [vərmenəχfʏldəɣɪŋ] *de (~en)* multiplication: *tafel van ~* multiplication table

vermicelli [vɛrmisɛli] *de* vermicelli

vermijden [vərmɛidə(n)] *vb* avoid: *angstvallig ~* shun, fight shy of

verminderd [vərmɪndərt] *adj, adv* diminished, reduced: *~ toerekeningsvatbaar* not fully accountable for one's actions

verminderen [vərmɪndərə(n)] *vb* decrease, reduce: *de uitgaven ~* cut (back on) expenses

vermindering [vərmɪndərɪŋ] *de (~en)* decrease, reduction: *~ van straf* reduction of (a) sentence

verminken [vərmɪŋkə(n)] *vb* mutilate

verminking [vərmɪŋkɪŋ] *de (~en)* mutilation

vermissen [vərmɪsə(n)] *vb* miss: *iem (iets) als vermist opgeven* report s.o. missing, report sth lost

vermissing [vərmɪsɪŋ] *de (~en)* loss, absence

vermiste [vərmɪstə] *de (~n)* missing person

vermits [vərmɪts] *adv (Belg)* since, as, because

vermoedelijk [vərmu̯dələk] *adj, adv* supposed: *de ~e dader* the suspect; *de ~e oorzaak* the probable cause

¹**vermoeden** [vərmu̯də(n)] *vb* suspect, suppose: *dit heb ik nooit kunnen ~* this is the last thing I expected

²**vermoeden** [vərmu̯də(n)] *het (~s)* **1** conjecture, surmise; **2** suspicion: *ik had er geen flauw ~ van* I didn't have the slightest suspicion (*or:* the faintest idea); *ik had al zo'n ~, ik had er al een ~ van* I had my suspicions (all along)

vermoeid [vərmu̯jt] *adj* tired (with), weary (of): *dodelijk ~* dead tired, completely worn-out

vermoeidheid [vərmu̯jthɛit] *de* tiredness, weariness, fatigue: *~ van de ogen* eye strain

vermoeien [vərmu̯jə(n)] *vb* tire (out), weary, fatigue, exhaust

vermoeiend [vərmu̯jənt] *adj* tiring, wearisome, tiresome

vermogen [vərmo̯ɣə(n)] *het (~s)* **1** fortune, property, capital; **2** power, capacity; **3** power, ability: *naar mijn beste ~* to the best of my ability

vermogend [vərmo̯ɣənt] *adj* rich, wealthy: *~e mensen* people of substance

vermolmd [vərmɔlmt] *adj* mouldered, decayed, rotten

vermommen [vərmɔmə(n)] *vb* disguise, dress up: *vermomd als* disguised as

vermomming [vərmɔmɪŋ] *de (~en)* disguise

vermoorden [vərmo̯rdə(n)] *vb* murder, assassinate

vermorzelen [vərmɔrzələ(n)] *vb* crush, smash up

vermout [vɛrmut] *de* vermouth

vernauwen [vərnɑu̯wə(n)] *vb* narrow (down), constrict, contract ‖ *zich ~* narrow

vernauwing [vərnɑu̯wɪŋ] *de (~en)* narrowing, constriction: *~ van de bloedvaten* stricture (*or:* stenosis) of the blood vessels

vernederen [vərnɛdərə(n)] *vb* humble; humiliate

vernederend [vərnɛdərənt] *adj* humiliating, degrading

vernedering [vərnɛdərɪŋ] *de (~en)* humiliation: *een ~ ondergaan* suffer a humiliation (*or:* an indignity)

vernederlandsen [vərnɛdərlɑntsə(n)] *vb* become Dutch, turn Dutch

vernemen [vərnɛmə(n)] *vb* learn, be told (*or:* informed) (of)

vernielen [vərnilə(n)] *vb* destroy, wreck

vernieling [vərnilɪŋ] *de (~en)* destruction, devastation: *~en aanrichten* go on the rampage; *zij ligt helemaal in de ~* she's a complete wreck

vernielzucht [vərnilzʏχt] *de* destructiveness, vandalism

vernietigen [vərnitəɣə(n)] *vb* destroy, ruin, annihilate: *iemands verwachtingen ~* dash s.o.'s expectations

vernietigend [vərnitəɣənt] *adj, adv* destructive, devastating: *een ~ oordeel* a scathing judgment

vernietiging [vərnitəɣɪŋ] *de (~en)* destruction, annihilation

vernietigingskamp [vərnitəɣɪŋskɑmp] *het (~en)* extermination camp

vernieuwen [vərniwə(n)] *vb* **1** renew, modernize, renovate; **2** renew, restore

vernieuwer [vərniwər] *de (~s)* **1** renewer, renovator; **2** innovator

vernieuwing [vərniwɪŋ] *de (~en)* **1** renewal, modernization, renovation, rebuilding; **2** modernization, renovation, reform: *allerlei ~en aanbrengen* carry out all sorts of renovations

vernis [vərnɪs] *het, de (~sen)* varnish

vernissen [vərnɪsə(n)] *vb* varnish

vernuftig [vərnʏftəχ] *adj* ingenious, witty

veronderstellen [vərɔndərstɛlə(n)] *vb* suppose, assume: *ik veronderstel van wel* I suppose so

veronderstelling [vərɔndərstɛlɪŋ] *de (~en)* assumption, supposition: *in de ~ verkeren dat ...* be under the impression that ...

verongelukken [vərɔŋɣəlʏkə(n)] *vb* **1** have an accident, be lost, be killed; **2** (have a) crash, be wrecked, be lost *(ship):* *het vliegtuig verongelukte* the plane crashed

verontreinigen [vərɔntrɛinəɣə(n)] *vb* pollute, contaminate

verontreiniging [vərɔntrɛinəɣɪŋ] *de (~en)* pollution, contamination: *de ~ van het milieu* environmental pollution

verontrust [vərɔntrʏst] *adj* alarmed, worried, concerned

verontrustend [vərɔntrʏstənt] *adj* alarming, worrying, disturbing

¹**verontschuldigen** [vərɔntsχʏldəɣə(n)] *vb* excuse, pardon: *iem ~* excuse s.o.

²**verontschuldigen** [vərɔntsχʏldəɣə(n)] *ref vb* apologize, excuse: *zich laten ~* beg to be excused; *zich vanwege ziekte ~* excuse oneself on account of illness

verontschuldiging [vərɔntsχʏldəɣɪŋ] *de (~en)* **1** excuse, apology: *~en aanbieden* apologize, offer one's apologies; **2** excuse, defence: *hij voerde als ~ aan dat* he offered the excuse that

verontwaardigd [vərɔntwardəχt] *adj, adv* indignant (about, at)

verontwaardiging [vərɔntwardəɣɪŋ] *de* indignation, outrage: *tot grote ~ van* to the great indignation of

veroordeelde [vərordeldə] *de (~n)* condemned man (*or:* woman), convict

veroordelen [vərordelə(n)] *vb* **1** condemn, *(law)* sentence, find guilty: *~ tot de betaling van de kosten* order (s.o.) to pay costs; **2** condemn; denounce

veroordeling [vərordelɪŋ] *de (~en)* **1** *(law)* conviction; sentence: *voorwaardelijke ~* suspended sentence; **2** condemnation, denunciation

veroorloven [vərorlovə(n)] *vb* permit, allow, afford: *zo'n dure auto kunnen wij ons niet ~* we can't afford such an expensive car

veroorzaken [vərο̱rzakə(n)] *vb* cause, bring about: *schade* ~ cause damage

verorberen [vərο̱rbərə(n)] *vb* consume

verordening [vərο̱rdənιŋ] *de (~en)* regulation(s), ordinance, statute

verouderd [vərα̱udərt] *adj* old-fashioned, (out)dated

verouderen [vərα̱udərə(n)] *vb* become obsolete (*or:* antiquated); date, go out of date

veroudering [vərα̱udərιŋ] *de* obsolescence, getting (*or:* becoming) out of date

veroveraar [vərο̱vərar] *de (~s)* conqueror: *Willem de Veroveraar* William the Conqueror

veroveren [vərο̱vərə(n)] *vb* conquer, capture, win: *de eerste plaats* ~ *in de wedstrijd* take the lead

verovering [vərο̱vərιŋ] *de (~en)* conquest, capture

verpachten [vərpα̱xtə(n)] *vb* lease (out): *verpachte grond* land on lease

verpakken [vərpα̱kə(n)] *vb* pack (up), package: *een cadeau in papier* ~ wrap a present in paper

verpakking [vərpα̱kιŋ] *de (~en)* packing, wrapping, paper

verpakkingsmateriaal [vərpα̱kιŋsmaterijal] *het (-materialen)* packing material

verpatsen [vərpα̱tsə(n)] *vb* flog

verpauperen [vərpα̱upərə(n)] *vb* impoverish, go down (in the world), be reduced to poverty: *een verpauperde stad* a run-down town

verpaupering [vərpα̱upərιŋ] *de* deterioration, impoverishment

verpesten [vərpε̱stə(n)] *vb* poison, contaminate, spoil: *de sfeer* ~ spoil the atmosphere

verpinken [vərpιŋkə(n)] *het (Belg)* ‖ *zonder (te)* ~ without batting an eyelid

verplaatsbaar [vərplα̱tsbar] *adj* movable, portable, mobile: *een verplaatsbare barak* a transportable shed

¹**verplaatsen** [vərplα̱tsə(n)] *vb* move, shift: *zijn activiteiten* ~ shift one's activities

²**verplaatsen** [vərplα̱tsə(n)] *ref vb* **1** move, shift, change places; **2** project oneself, put oneself in s.o. else's shoes: *zich in iemands positie* ~ imagine oneself in s.o. else's position

verplanten [vərplα̱ntə(n)] *vb* transplant

verpleeghuis [vərplε̱xhœys] *het (-huizen)* nursing home, convalescent home

verpleeghulp [vərplε̱xhγlp] *de (~en)* nurse's aide, nursing auxiliary, medical orderly

verpleegkundige [vərplε̱xkγndəyə] *de (~n)* nurse: *gediplomeerd* ~ trained (*or:* qualified) nurse

verpleegster [vərplε̱xstər] *de (~s)* nurse

verplegen [vərplε̱yə(n)] *vb* nurse, care for: *~d personeel* nursing staff

verpleger [vərplε̱yər] *de (~s)* (male) nurse

verpleging [vərplε̱yιŋ] *de* nursing, care: *zij gaat in de* ~ she is going into nursing

verpletteren [vərplε̱tərə(n)] *vb* **1** crush, smash; **2** (*fig*) shatter: *dit bericht verpletterde haar* the news shattered her

verpletterend [vərplε̱tərənt] *adj, adv* crushing: *een ~e nederlaag* a crushing defeat

verplicht [vərplιχt] *adj, adv* **1** compelled, obliged: *zich* ~ *voelen om* feel compelled to; **2** compulsory, obligatory: *~e lectuur* required reading (matter); ~ *verzekerd zijn* be compulsorily insured; *iets* ~ *stellen* make sth compulsory

verplichten [vərplιχtə(n)] *vb* oblige, compel: *de wet verplicht ons daartoe* the law obliges us to do that

verplichting [vərplιχtιŋ] *de (~en)* obligation, commitment, liability: *financiële ~en* financial liabilities (*or:* obligations); *sociale ~en* social duties; *~en aangaan* enter into obligations (*or:* a contract); *zijn ~en nakomen* fulfil one's obligations

verpoten [vərpο̱tə(n)] *vb* transplant

verprutsen [vərprγ̱tsə(n)] *vb* bungle, botch

verpulveren [vərpγ̱lvərə(n)] *vb* pulverize, (+ *direct object also*) crush

verraad [vərα̱t] *het* treason, treachery, betrayal: ~ *plegen* commit treason

verraden [vərα̱də(n)] *vb* **1** betray, commit treason: *iem aan de politie* ~ squeak (*or:* rat) on s.o.; **2** betray: *een geheim* ~ betray (*or:* let out) a secret; *niets* ~*, hoor!* don't breathe a word!

verrader [vərα̱dər] *de (~s)* traitor; betrayer; squealer

verraderlijk [vərα̱dərlək] *adj, adv* treacherous

verrassen [vərα̱sə(n)] *vb* (take by) surprise: *door noodweer verrast* caught in a thunderstorm

verrassing [vərα̱sιŋ] *de (~en)* **1** surprise; shock: *voor iem een* ~ *in petto hebben* have a surprise in store for s.o.; *het was voor ons geen* ~ *meer* it didn't come as a surprise to us; **2** surprise, amazement: *tot mijn* ~ *bemerkte ik …* I was surprised to see that …

verrast [vərα̱st] *adj, adv* surprised; amazed: ~ *keek hij op* he looked up in surprise

verregaand [vε̱rəyant] *adj, adv* far-reaching; outrageous; radical: *in ~e staat van ontbinding* in an advanced state of decomposition

verrek [vərε̱k] *int* gosh, (good) gracious

verrekenen [vərε̱kənə(n)] *vb* settle; deduct, adjust; pay out: *iets met iets* ~ balance sth with sth

verrekening [vərε̱kənιŋ] *de (~en)* settlement

verrekijker [vε̱rəkεikər] *de (~s)* binoculars; telescope

¹**verrekken** [vərε̱kə(n)] *vb* strain, pull, twist, wrench, sprain: *een pees* ~ stretch a tendon; *zich* ~ strain oneself

²**verrekken** [vərε̱kə(n)] *vb* die; kick the bucket: ~ *van de honger* starve; ~ *van de pijn* be groaning with pain; ~ *van de kou* perish with cold

verrekt [vərε̱kt] *adj, adv* strained

verreweg [vε̱rəwε̱χ] *adv* (by) far; much, easily: *dat is ~ het beste* that's easily (*or:* much) the best; *hij is ~ de sterkste* he's far and away the strongest

verrichten [vərιχtə(n)] *vb* perform; conduct; carry out: *wonderen* ~ work wonders, perform miracles

verrijden [vərɛidə(n)] *vb* **1** move; wheel; drive; **2** compete in, compete for: *een kampioenschap ~ or-ganize (or: hold) a championship; een wedstrijd la-ten ~* run off a race

verrijken [vərɛikə(n)] *vb* enrich: *zijn kennis ~* im-prove one's knowledge; *zich ~ ten koste van een an-der* get rich at the expense of s.o. else

verrijzen [vərɛizə(n)] *vb* (a)rise, spring up *(bldg)*; shoot up

verrijzenis [vərɛizənis] *de* resurrection

verroeren [vərurə(n)] *ref vb* move: *je kunt je hier nauwelijks ~* you can hardly move in here; *verroer je niet* don't move

verroest [vərust] *adj* rusty

verroesten [vərustə(n)] *vb* rust, get rusty: *verroest ijzer* rusty iron

verrot [vərɔt] *adj* rotten, bad, putrid, wretched: *iem ~ slaan* knock the living daylights out of s.o.; *door en door ~* rotten to the core

verrotten [vərɔtə(n)] *vb* rot, decay: *doen ~ rot (down), decay*

verrotting [vərɔtiŋ] *de* rot(ting), decay: *dit hout is tegen ~ bestand* this wood is treated for rot

verruilen [vərœylə(n)] *vb* (ex)change, swap

verruimen [vərœymə(n)] *vb* widen, broaden, liber-alize: *zijn blik ~* widen *(or:* broaden) one's outlook; *mogelijkheden ~* create more possibilities

verruiming [vərœymiŋ] *de* widening, broadening, liberalization

verrukkelijk [vərʏkələk] *adj, adv* delightful, gor-geous, delicious

verrukt [vərʏkt] *adj* delighted, overjoyed

verruwing [vərywiŋ] *de* coarsening, vulgarization

¹vers [vɛrs] *het (verzen)* **1** verse: *Lucas 6, ~ 10* St Luke, chapter 6, verse 10; **2** verse, stanza, couplet: *dat is ~ twee* that's another story; **3** verse, poem, rhyme

²vers [vɛrs] *adj, adv* fresh, new: *~ bloed* fresh *(or:* young, new) blood; *~e eieren* new-laid eggs; *~e sneeuw* fresh *(or:* new-fallen) snow; *~ blijven* keep fresh *(or:* good); *~ van de pers* hot from the press

verschaffen [vərsχɑfə(n)] *vb* provide (with), sup-ply (with): *het leger verschafte hem een complete uitrusting* the army issued him with a complete kit

verschansen [vərsχɑnsə(n)] *ref vb* entrench one-self, barricade oneself, take cover: *zich in zijn ka-mer ~* barricade oneself in one's room

verscheidene [vərsχɛidənə] *num* several, various

verscheidenheid [vərsχɛidənhɛit] *de (-heden)* va-riety, diversity, assortment, range: *een grote ~ aan gerechten* a wide variety of dishes

verschepen [vərsχepə(n)] *vb* ship (off, out)

verscheping [vərsχepiŋ] *de (~en)* shipping

verscherpen [vərsχɛrpə(n)] *vb* tighten (up): *het toezicht ~* tighten up control

verscheuren [vərsχørə(n)] *vb* **1** tear (up); shred; rip (up); **2** maul, tear to pieces *(or:* apart)

verschieten [vərsχitə(n)] *vb* fade: *de gordijnen zijn verschoten* the curtains are *(or:* have) faded

verschijnen [vərsχɛinə(n)] *vb* **1** appear; surface, emerge; **2** appear, turn up; **3** appear, come out, be published

verschijning [vərsχɛiniŋ] *de (~en)* **1** appearance; publication; **2** figure, presence: *een indrukwekken-de ~* an imposing presence

verschijnsel [vərsχɛinsəl] *het (~en)* phenomenon, symptom, sign: *een eigenaardig ~* a strange phe-nomenon

verschil [vərsχɪl] *het (~len)* **1** difference, dissimi-larity, distinction: *~ van mening* a difference of opinion; *een groot ~ maken* make all the difference; *~ maken tussen* draw a distinction between, differ-entiate between; *~ maken* make a difference; *met dit ~, dat ...* with one difference, namely that ...; *een ~ van dag en nacht* a world of difference; **2** dif-ference, remainder: *het ~ delen* split the difference

verschillen [vərsχɪlə(n)] *vb* differ (from), be differ-ent (from), vary: *van mening ~ met iem* disagree with s.o., differ with s.o.

verschillend [vərsχɪlənt] *adj, adv* **1** different (from), various: *wij denken daar ~ over* we don't see eye to eye on that; **2** several, various, different: *bij ~e gelegenheden* on various occasions

verscholen [vərsχolə(n)] *adj* hidden; secluded: *het huis lag ~ achter de bomen* the house was tucked away behind the trees

verschonen [vərsχonə(n)] *vb* change: *de baby ~* change the baby's nappy; *de bedden ~* put clean sheets on the beds; *zich ~* put on clean clothes

verschoning [vərsχoniŋ] *de (~en)* change of un-derwear

verschoppeling [vərsχɔpəliŋ] *de (~en)* outcast

¹verschrikkelijk [vərsχrɪkələk] *adj* terrible; devas-tating; excruciating: *een ~ e hongersnood* a devas-tating famine; *~e sneeuwman* Abominable Snowman, yeti; *een ~ kabaal* an infernal racket

²verschrikkelijk [vərsχrɪkələk] *adv* terribly, awful-ly, terrifically: *Sander maakte een ~ mooi doelpunt* Sander scored a terrific goal

verschrikking [vərsχrɪkiŋ] *de (~en)* terror, horror: *de ~en van de oorlog* the horrors of war

verschroeien [vərsχrujə(n)] *vb* scorch; singe; sear: *de tactiek van de verschroeide aarde* scorched earth policy

verschrompelen [vərsχrɔmpələ(n)] *vb* shrivel (up), atrophy: *een verschrompeld gezicht* a wizened face

verschuilen [vərsχœylə(n)] *ref vb* hide (oneself); lurk: *zich in een hoek ~* hide (oneself) in a corner

verschuiven [vərsχœyvə(n)] *vb* **1** move, shift, shove aside; **2** postpone

verschuiving [vərsχœyviŋ] *de (~en)* **1** shift; **2** post-ponement

verschuldigd [vərsχʏldəχt] *adj* due, indebted: *het ~e geld* the money due; *iem iets ~ zijn* be indebted to s.o., owe s.o. sth

versheid [vɛrshɛit] *de* freshness

versie [vɛrzi] *de (~s)* version

versierder [vərsi̱rdər] *de (~s)* womanizer, ladykiller

versieren [vərsi̱rə(n)] *vb* **1** decorate: *de kerstboom* ~ trim the Christmas tree; *straten* ~ decorate the streets; **2** pick up; get off with

versiering [vərsi̱rɪŋ] *de (~en)* decoration

versimpelen [vərsi̱mpələ(n)] *vb* (over)simplify

versjouwen [vərʃa̱uwə(n)] *vb* drag away

verslaafd [vərsla̱ft] *adj* addicted (to), hooked (on): ~ *raken aan drugs* contract the drug habit; *aan de drank* (or: *het spel*) ~ *zijn* be addicted to drink (or: gambling)

verslaafde [vərsla̱vdə] *de (~n)* alcoholic; (drug) addict; junkie

verslaafdheid [vərsla̱ftheit] *de* addiction

verslaan [vərsla̱n] *vb* defeat, beat *(sport)*: *iem* ~ *met schaken* defeat s.o. at chess

verslag [vərsla̱x] *het (~en)* report, commentary: *een direct* ~ *van de wedstrijd* a live commentary on the match; ~ *uitbrengen* report on, give an account of

verslagen [vərsla̱yə(n)] *adj* **1** defeated, beaten; **2** dismayed

verslagenheid [vərsla̱yənheit] *de* dismay (at), consternation (at)

verslaggever [vərsla̱xevər] *de (~s)* reporter; commentator

verslaggeving [vərsla̱xevɪŋ] *de (~en)* (press) coverage

verslapen [vərsla̱pə(n)] *ref vb* oversleep: *hij had zich drie uur* ~ he overslept and was three hours late

verslappen [vərsla̱pə(n)] *vb* slacken, flag, wane: *de pols verslapt* the pulse is getting weaker

verslavend [vərsla̱vənt] *adj, adv* addictive

verslaving [vərsla̱vɪŋ] *de* addiction, (drug-)dependence

verslechteren [vərsle̱xtərə(n)] *vb* get worse, worsen, deteriorate

verslepen [vərsle̱pə(n)] *vb* drag (off, away); tow (away)

versleten [vərsle̱tə(n)] *adj* **1** worn(-out), shabby: *tot op de draad* ~ threadbare; **2** worn-out; burnt-out: *een* ~ *paard* an old nag

versleuteling *de (comp)* encryption

verslijten [vərsle̱itə(n)] *vb* wear out: *hij had al drie echtgenotes versleten* he had already got through three wives

verslikken [vərsli̱kə(n)] *ref vb* **1** choke: *pas op, hij verslikt zich* watch out, it has gone down the wrong way; *zich in een graat* ~ choke on a bone; **2** underrate, underestimate

verslinden [vərsli̱ndə(n)] *vb* devour, eat up, eat: *die auto verslindt benzine* that car drinks petrol; *een boek* ~ devour a book

verslingerd [vərsli̱ŋərt] *adj* || *zij is* ~ *aan slagroomgebakjes* she is mad about cream cakes

¹versmallen [vərsma̱lə(n)] *vb* narrow

²versmallen [vərsma̱lə(n)] *ref vb* narrow, become narrow(er): *ginds versmalt de weg zich* the road

gets narrow(er) there

versmelten [vərsme̱ltə(n)] *vb* blend, merge

versnapering [vərsna̱pərɪŋ] *de (~en)* snack, titbit

versnellen [vərsne̱lə(n)] *ref vb* quicken; accelerate, speed up

versnelling [vərsne̱lɪŋ] *de (~en)* **1** acceleration, increase (in); **2** gear: *in de eerste* ~ *zetten* put into first gear; *in een hogere* ~ *schakelen* change up, move into gear; *een auto met automatische* ~ a car with automatic transmission; *een fiets met tien* ~*en* a ten-speed bike

versnellingsbak [vərsne̱lɪŋzbɑk] *de (~ken)* gearbox

versnellingspook [vərsne̱lɪŋspok] *de (-poken)* gear lever, gearstick

versnipperen [vərsni̱pərə(n)] *vb* **1** cut up (into pieces); **2** fragment; fritter away

versoepelen [vərsu̱pələ(n)] *vb* relax; liberalize

verspelen [vərspe̱lə(n)] *vb* forfeit, lose: *een kans* ~ throw away a chance; *zijn rechten* ~ forfeit one's rights

versperren [vərspe̱rə(n)] *vb* block, barricade: *iem de weg* ~ bar s.o.'s way; *de weg* ~ block the road

versperring [vərspe̱rɪŋ] *de (~en)* barrier, barricade

verspillen [vərspi̱lə(n)] *vb* waste, fritter away

verspilling [vərspi̱lɪŋ] *de (~en)* **1** wasting: ~ *van energie* wasting energy; **2** waste: *wat een* ~*!* what a waste!

versplinteren [vərspli̱ntərə(n)] *vb* smash, splinter: *die plank is versplinterd* that plank has splintered

versplintering [vərspli̱ntərɪŋ] *de* smashing; *(also fig)* fragmentation

verspreid [vərspre̱it] *adj, adv* scattered: *een over het hele land* ~ *e organisatie* a nationwide organization; *haar speelgoed lag* ~ *over de vloer* the floor was strewn with her toys; *wijd* ~ widespread, widely (or: commonly) held

¹verspreiden [vərspre̱idə(n)] *vb* **1** spread, disperse, distribute, circulate: *een kwalijke geur* ~ give off a ghastly smell; *licht* ~ shed light; *warmte* ~ give off heat; **2** disperse

²verspreiden [vərspre̱idə(n)] *ref vb* spread (out): *de menigte verspreidde zich* the crowd dispersed

verspreiding [vərspre̱idɪŋ] *de* spread; distribution

verspreken [vərspre̱kə(n)] *ref vb* make a slip (or: mistake)

verspreking [vərspre̱kɪŋ] *de (~en)* slip of the tongue, mistake

¹verspringen [ve̱rsprɪŋə(n)] *vb* do the long jump: *zij sprong zes meter ver* she jumped six metres

²verspringen [vərsprɪŋə(n)] *vb* **1** jump; **2** stagger: ~*de naden* staggered seams

verspringer [ve̱rsprɪŋər] *de* long jumper, *(Am)* broad-jumper

versregel [ve̱rsreyəl] *de (~s)* line (of poetry)

verst [verst] *adj, adv* furthest; farthest: *het* ~*e punt* the farthest point; *dat is in de* ~*e verte niet mijn bedoeling* that's the last thing I intended

verstaan [vərsta̱n] *vb* **1** (be able to) hear: *helaas* *verstond ik zijn naam niet* unfortunately I didn't catch his name; *ik versta geen woord!* I can't hear a word that is being said; *hij kon zichzelf nauwelijks ~* he could hardly hear himself speak; **2** understand: *heb ik goed ~ dat ...* did I hear you right ...; *wel te ~* that is (to say); *te ~ geven* give (s.o.) to understand (that); **3** understand, mean: *wat versta jij daaronder?* what do you understand by that?; **4** know: *zijn vak ~* know one's trade

verstaanbaar [vərstɑmbar] *adj, adv* **1** audible; **2** understandable: *zich ~ maken* make oneself understood

verstand [vərstɑnt] *het* **1** (power of) reason, (powers of) comprehension, brain(s): *gezond ~* common sense; *een goed ~ hebben* have a good head on one's shoulders; *iem iets aan het ~ brengen* drive sth home to s.o.; *bij zijn (volle) ~* in full possession of one's faculties; **2** knowledge, understanding: *~ hebben van* know about, understand, be a good judge of; *daar heb ik geen ~ van* I don't know the first thing about that

¹verstandelijk [vərstɑndələk] *adj* intellectual: *~e vermogens* intellect, intellectual powers

²verstandelijk [vərstɑndələk] *adv* rationally

verstandhouding [vərstɑnthɑudɪŋ] *de (~en)* understanding, relations: *een blik van ~* an understanding look; *een goede ~ hebben met* be on good terms with

verstandig [vərstɑndəχ] *adj, adv* sensible: *iets ~ aanpakken* go about sth in a sensible way

verstandskies [vərstɑntskis] *de (-kiezen)* wisdom tooth

verstandsverbijstering [vərstɑntsfərbɛistərɪŋ] *de* madness: *handelen in een vlaag van ~* act in a fit of madness (*or:* insanity)

verstedelijking [vərstedələkɪŋ] *de* urbanization

versteend [vərstent] *adj* petrified; *(also fig)* fossilized

verstek [vərstɛk] *het (~ken)* default (of appearance): *~ laten gaan* be absent, fail to appear

verstekeling [vərstekəlɪŋ] *de (~en)* stowaway

verstelbaar [vərstɛlbar] *adj* adjustable

versteld [vərstɛlt] *adj* stunned: *iem ~ doen staan* astonish s.o.; *~ staan (van iets)* be dumbfounded

verstellen [vərstɛlə(n)] *vb* **1** adjust; **2** mend, repair

versterken [vərstɛrkə(n)] *vb* **1** strengthen; intensify: *geluid ~* amplify sound; **2** fortify

versterker [vərstɛrkər] *de (~s)* amplifier

versterking [vərstɛrkɪŋ] *de (~en)* strengthening, reinforcement; amplification: *het leger kreeg ~* the army was reinforced

verstevigen [vərstevəχə(n)] *vb* strengthen, consolidate, prop up: *zijn positie ~* consolidate one's position

verstijven [vərstɛivə(n)] *vb* stiffen: *~ van kou* grow numb with cold; *~ van schrik* be petrified with fear

verstikken [vərstɪkə(n)] *vb* smother, choke

verstikkend [vərstɪkənt] *adj* suffocating: *~e hitte* stifling heat

verstikking [vərstɪkɪŋ] *de (~en)* suffocation

¹verstoken [vərstokə(n)] *vb* spend on heating

²verstoken [vərstokə(n)] *adj* deprived (of)

verstokt [vərstɔkt] *adj* hardened, confirmed: *een ~e vrijgezel* a confirmed bachelor

verstomd [vərstɔmt] *adj* || *~ doen staan* strike dumb, astound; *~ staan* be dumbfounded (*or:* flabbergasted)

verstommen [vərstɔmə(n)] *vb* become silent: *het lawaai verstomde* the noise died down

verstoord [vərstort] *adj* annoyed, upset

verstoppen [vərstɔpə(n)] *vb* hide: *zijn geld ~* hide (*or:* stash) away one's money

verstoppertje [vərstɔpərcə] *het* hide-and-seek: *~ spelen* play (at) hide-and-seek

verstopt [vərstɔpt] *adj* blocked (up): *mijn neus is ~* my nose is all stuffed up; *het riool is ~* the sewer is clogged

verstoren [vərstorə(n)] *vb* disturb: *het evenwicht ~* upset the balance; *de stilte ~* break the silence

verstoring [vərstorɪŋ] *de (~en)* disruption: *~ van de openbare orde* disorderly conduct

verstoten [vərstotə(n)] *vb* cast off, cast out: *een kind ~* disown a child

verstrekken [vərstrɛkə(n)] *vb* supply with, provide with; distribute: *de bank zal hem een lening ~* the bank will grant him a loan

verstrekkend [vɛrstrɛkənt] *adj* far-reaching

verstrekking [vərstrɛkɪŋ] *de (~en)* supply, provision

verstrijken [vərstrɛikə(n)] *vb* go by; elapse; expire: *de termijn verstrijkt op 1 juli* the term expires on the 1st of July

verstrikken [vərstrɪkə(n)] *vb* entangle: *in iets verstrikt raken* get entangled in sth

verstrooid [vərstrojt] *adj* absent-minded

verstrooidheid [vərstrojtheit] *de (-heden)* absent-mindedness: *uit ~ iets doen* do sth from absent-mindedness

verstuiken [vərstœykə(n)] *vb* sprain

verstuiver [vərstœyvər] *de (~s)* spray, atomizer

versturen [vərstyrə(n)] *vb* send (off): *iets naar iem ~* send sth to s.o.; *per post ~* mail

versuft [vərsyft] *adj* dizzy; dazed, stunned

vertaalbureau [vərtalbyro] *het (~s)* translation agency

vertakken [vərtɑkə(n)] *ref vb* branch (off)

vertalen [vərtalə(n)] *vb* translate; interpret: *vrij ~* give a free translation; *uit het Engels in het Frans ~* translate from English into French

vertaler [vərtalər] *de (~s)* translator: *beëdigd ~* sworn translator

vertaling [vərtalɪŋ] *de (~en)* translation: *een ~ maken* do a translation

verte [vɛrtə] *de (~n, ~s)* distance: *in de verste ~ niet* not remotely; *het lijkt en in de ~ op* there is a slight resemblance; *uit de ~* from a distance

vertederen [vərtedərə(n)] *vb* soften, move: *zij keek het kind vertederd aan* she gave the child a tender look

verteerbaar [vərtērbar] *adj* digestible, *(fig also)* palatable, acceptable: *licht ~ voedsel* light food

vertegenwoordigen [vərteɣə(n)wǫrdəɣə(n)] *vb* represent

vertegenwoordiger [vərteɣə(n)wǫrdəɣər] *de (~s)* **1** representative; **2** (sales) representative

vertegenwoordiging [vərteɣə(n)wǫrdəɣɪŋ] *de (~en)* **1** representation; **2** delegation

vertekend [vərtekənt] *adj* distorted

vertekenen [vərtekənə(n)] *vb* distort

vertekening [vərtekənɪŋ] *de* distortion

vertellen [vərtɛlə(n)] *vb* tell: *een mop ~* crack a joke; *moet je mij ~!* you're telling me!; *dat wordt verteld* so they say; *zal ik je eens wat ~?* you know what?, let me tell you sth; *wat vertel je me nou?* I can't believe it!; *je kunt me nog meer ~* tell me another (one); *iets verder ~ aan anderen* pass sth on to others; *vertel het maar niet verder* this is just between us

verteller [vərtɛlər] *de (~s)* narrator

¹verteren [vərtɛrə(n)] *vb* digest: *niet te ~* indigestible

²verteren [vərtɛrə(n)] *vb* be consumed (*or:* eaten away): *dat laken verteert door het vocht* that sheet is mouldering away with the damp

verticaal [vɛrtikạl] *adj, adv* vertical: *in verticale stand* in (an) upright position

vertier [vərtịr] *het* entertainment, diversion

vertikken [vərtɪkə(n)] *vb* refuse (flatly)

vertillen [vərtɪlə(n)] *ref vb* strain oneself (in) lifting: *(fig) zich aan iets ~* bite off more than one can chew

vertimmeren [vərtɪmərə(n)] *vb* alter, renovate

vertoeven [vərtụvə(n)] *vb* sojourn, stay

¹vertonen [vərtǫnə(n)] *vb* **1** show: *geen gelijkenis ~ met* bear no resemblance to; *tekenen ~ van* show signs of; **2** show, present: *kunsten ~* do tricks

²vertonen [vərtǫnə(n)] *ref vb* show one's face, turn up: *je kunt je zo niet ~ in het openbaar* you're not fit to be seen in public (like this); *ik durf me daar niet meer te ~* I'm afraid to show my face there now

vertoning [vərtǫnɪŋ] *de (~en)* **1** show(ing), presentation; **2** show, production: *het was een grappige ~* it was a curious spectacle

vertoon [vərtǫn] *het* showing, presentation: *op ~ van een identiteitsbewijs* on presentation of an ID

vertragen [vərtraɣə(n)] *vb* slow down; be delayed: *een vertraagde filmopname* a slow-motion film scene

vertraging [vərtraɣɪŋ] *de (~en)* delay: *~ ondervinden* be delayed

vertrappen [vərtrɑpə(n)] *vb* tread on, trample underfoot

vertrek [vərtrɛk] *het (~ken)* **1** departure; sailing: *bij zijn ~* on his departure; *op het punt van ~ staan* be about to leave; **2** room

vertrekdatum [vərtrɛgdatʏm] *de* departure date, date of departure

vertrekhal [vərtrɛkhɑl] *de (~len)* departure hall

¹vertrekken [vərtrɛkə(n)] *vb* leave: *wij ~ morgen naar Londen* we're off to (*or:* leave for) London tomorrow

²vertrekken [vərtrɛkə(n)] *vb* pull, distort: *zonder een spier te ~* without batting an eyelid

vertrekpunt [vərtrɛkpʏnt] *het (~en)* start(ing point), point of departure *(also fig)*

vertreksein [vərtrɛksɛin] *het* departure signal, green light

vertrektijd [vərtrɛktɛit] *de (~en)* time of departure

¹vertroebelen [vərtrubələ(n)] *vb* cloud, obscure *(also fig)*: *dat vertroebelt de zaak* that confuses (*or:* obscures) the issue

²vertroebelen [vərtrubələ(n)] *vb* become clouded

vertroetelen [vərtrutələ(n)] *vb* pamper

vertrouwd [vərtrạut] *adj* **1** reliable, trustworthy: *een ~ persoon* a trusted person; **2** familiar (with): *zich ~ maken met die technieken* familiarize oneself with those techniques

vertrouwdheid [vərtrạuthɛit] *de* familiarity

vertrouwelijk [vərtrạuwələk] *adj, adv* intimate; confidential: *~ met iem omgaan* be close to s.o.; *~ met elkaar praten* have a heart-to-heart talk; *een ~e mededeling* a confidential communication

vertrouwelijkheid [vərtrạuwələkhɛit] *de (-heden)* confidentiality

¹vertrouwen [vərtrạuwə(n)] *het* confidence, trust: *op goed ~* on trust; *ik heb er weinig ~ in* I'm not very optimistic; *~ hebben in de toekomst* have faith in the future; *vol ~ zijn* be confident; *iem in ~ nemen* take s.o. into one's confidence; *goed van ~ zijn* be (too) trusting

²vertrouwen [vərtrạuwə(n)] *vb* trust: *hij is niet te ~* he is not to be trusted; *ik vertrouw erop dat …* I trust that …; *op God ~* trust in God; *iem voor geen cent ~* not trust s.o. an inch

vertwijfeld [vərtwɛifəlt] *adj, adv* despairing: *~ raken* (be driven to) despair

vertwijfeling [vərtwɛifəlɪŋ] *de (~en)* despair, desperation

veruit [vɛrœyt] *adv* by far: *~ de beste zijn* by far and away the best

vervaardigen [vərvardəɣə(n)] *vb* make: *met de hand vervaardigd* made by hand; *deze tafel is van hout vervaardigd* this table is made of wood

vervaardiging [vərvardəɣɪŋ] *de* manufacture, construction

¹vervagen [vərvaɣə(n)] *vb* become faint (*or:* blurred); dim; fade (away)

²vervagen [vərvaɣə(n)] *vb* blur, dim: *de tijd heeft die herinneringen vervaagd* time has dimmed those memories

verval [vərvɑl] *het* **1** decline: *het ~ van de goede zeden* the deterioration of morals; *dit gebouw is flink in ~ geraakt* this building has fallen into disrepair; **2** fall

vervaldag [vərvɑldɑχ] *de (~en)* expiry date

¹vervallen [vərvɑlə(n)] *adj* **1** dilapidated; **2** bedraggled

²**vervallen** [vərvɑ̯lə(n)] *vb* **1** fall into disrepair; **2** lapse: *in oude fouten ~* relapse into old errors; *tot armoede ~* be reduced to poverty; **3** expire: *400 arbeidsplaatsen komen te ~* 400 jobs are to go (*or:* disappear); *die mogelijkheid vervalt* that possibility is no longer open; *de vergadering vervalt* the meeting has been cancelled

vervalsen [vərvɑ̯lsə(n)] *vb* **1** forge, counterfeit; **2** tamper (with): *een cheque ~* forge a cheque

vervalser [vərvɑ̯lsər] *de (~s)* forger, counterfeiter

vervalsing [vərvɑ̯lsɪŋ] *de (~en)* forgery; counterfeit

vervangen [vərvɑ̯ŋə(n)] *vb* replace, take the place of, substitute: *niet te ~* irreplaceable

vervanger [vərvɑ̯ŋər] *de (~s)* replacement, substitute: *de ~ van de minister* the substitute minister

vervanging [vərvɑ̯ŋɪŋ] *de (~en)* replacement, substitution

verveeld [vərve̯lt] *adj* bored, weary: *(Belg) ~ zitten met iets* not know what to do about sth; *~ toekijken* watch indifferently

verveelvoudigen [vərvelvɑ̯udəɣə(n)] *vb* multiply

¹**vervelen** [vərve̯lə(n)] *vb* bore, annoy: *tot ~s toe* ad nauseam, over and over again

²**vervelen** [vərve̯lə(n)] *ref vb* be(come) bored: *ik verveel me dood* I am bored stiff

vervelend [vərve̯lənt] *adj, adv* **1** boring; **2** annoying: *een ~ karwei* a chore; *wat een ~e vent* what a tiresome fellow; *doe nu niet zo ~* don't be such a nuisance; *wat ~!* what a nuisance!

verveling [vərve̯lɪŋ] *de* boredom: *louter uit ~* out of pure boredom

vervellen [vərvɛ̯lə(n)] *vb* peel

verven [vɛ̯rvə(n)] *vb* **1** paint; **2** dye

verversen [vərvɛ̯rsə(n)] *vb* **1** refresh; **2** change, freshen

verversing [vərvɛ̯rsɪŋ] *de (~en)* replacement

verviervoudigen [vərvirvɑ̯udəχə(n)] *vb* quadruple, multiply by four

vervliegen [vərvli̯ɣə(n)] *vb* **1** fly; **2** evaporate

vervloeken [vərvlu̯kə(n)] *vb* curse: *hij zal die dag ~!* he will rue the day!

vervoer [vərvu̯r] *het* transport, transportation: *met het openbaar ~* by public transport; *tijdens het ~ beschadigde goederen* goods damaged in transit

vervoerbedrijf [vərvu̯rbədrɛif] *het (-bedrijven)* transport company: *het gemeentelijk ~* public transport

vervoerder [vərvu̯rdər] *de (~s)* transporter, carry

vervoeren [vərvu̯rə(n)] *vb* transport

vervoermiddel [vərvu̯rmɪdəl] *het (~en)* (means of) transport: *openbare ~* public service vehicles

vervoersacademie [vərvu̯rsɑkɑdemi] *de* centre for logistics and road transport studies

vervoersbedrijf [vərvu̯rzbədrɛif] *het (-bedrijven)* (goods) haulier, haulage firm; passenger transport company

vervoersonderneming [vərvu̯rsɔndərnemɪŋ] *de (~en)* transport company

vervolg [vərvɔ̯lχ] *het (~en)* **1** future; **2** continuation (of), sequel (to); **3** continuation: *~ op blz. 10* continued on page 10

vervolgcursus [vərvɔ̯lχkʏrzʏs] *de (~sen)* follow-up course

vervolgen [vərvɔ̯lɣə(n)] *vb* **1** continue: *wordt vervolgd* to be continued; **2** pursue, persecute; **3** *(law)* sue; prosecute: *iem gerechtelijk ~* take legal action against s.o.

vervolgens [vərvɔ̯lɣəns] *adv* then: *~ zei hij …* he went on to say …

vervolging [vərvɔ̯lɣɪŋ] *de (~en)* **1** persecution; **2** *(law)* legal action (*or:* proceedings), prosecution: *tot ~ overgaan* (decide to) prosecute

vervolgonderwijs [vərvɔ̯lɣɔndərwɛis] *het* secondary education

vervolgopleiding [vərvɔ̯lɣɔplɛidɪŋ] *de (~en)* continuation course, *(Am)* continuing education (course), advanced training

vervolgverhaal [vərvɔ̯lχfərhal] *het (-verhalen)* serial (story)

vervolledigen [vərvɔle̯dəɣə(n)] *vb* complete, round out

vervormen [vərvɔ̯rmə(n)] *vb* **1** transform; deform, disfigure; **2** distort: *geluid vervormd weergeven* distort a sound

vervorming [vərvɔ̯rmɪŋ] *de (~en)* transformation; disfiguring, deforming

¹**vervreemden** [vərvre̯mdə(n)] *vb* alienate, estrange: *zich ~ van* alienate oneself from

²**vervreemden** [vərvre̯mdə(n)] *vb* become estranged (*or:* alienated): *van zijn werk vervreemd raken* lose touch with one's work; *van elkaar ~* drift apart

vervreemding [vərvre̯mdɪŋ] *de (~en)* alienation, estrangement

vervroegen [vərvru̯ɣə(n)] *vb* advance, (move) forward: *vervroegde uittreding* early retirement

vervuild [vərvœ̯ylt] *adj* polluted, contaminated: *~e rivieren* polluted rivers; *~ water* contaminated water

vervuilen [vərvœ̯ylə(n)] *vb* pollute, make filthy, contaminate

vervuiler [vərvœ̯ylər] *de (~s)* polluter, contaminator: *de ~ betaalt* the polluter pays

vervuiling [vərvœ̯ylɪŋ] *de* pollution, contamination: *de ~ van het milieu* environmental pollution

vervullen [vərvʏ̯lə(n)] *vb* **1** fill: *dat vervult ons met zorg* that fills us with concern; *van iets vervuld zijn* be full of sth; **2** fulfil, perform: *tijdens het ~ van zijn plicht* in the discharge of his duty; **3** fulfil, realize: *iemands wensen ~* comply with s.o.'s wishes

vervulling [vərvʏ̯lɪŋ] *de* fulfilment, discharge, realization: *een droom ging in ~* a dream came true

verwaand [vərwa̯nt] *adj, adv* conceited, stuck-up

verwaandheid [vərwa̯ntheit] *de* conceit(edness), arrogance: *naast zijn schoenen lopen van ~* be too big for one's boots

verwaarloosbaar [vərwa̯rlozbar] *adj* negligible

verwaarloosd [vərwaːrlost] *adj* neglected
verwaarlozen [vərwaːrloːzə(n)] *vb* neglect
verwaarlozing [vərwaːrloːzıŋ] *de* neglect, negligence
verwachten [vərwαχtə(n)] *vb* **1** expect: *daar moet je ook niet alles van ~* don't set your hopes too high; *lang verwacht* long-awaited; *dat had ik wel verwacht* that was just what I had expected; **2** expect, be expecting: *ze verwacht een baby* she is expecting (a baby), she is in the family way
verwachting [vərwαχtıŋ] *de (~en)* **1** anticipation: *in ~ zijn* be expecting, be an expectant mother; **2** expectation, outlook: *de ~en waren hoog gespannen* expectations ran high; *het overtrof haar stoutste ~en* it surpassed her wildest expectations; *~en wekken* arouse (one's) hopes; *beneden de ~en blijven* fall short of expectations, disappoint; *aan de ~ beantwoorden* come up to one's expectations
¹verwant [vərwαnt] *adj* **1** related (to); **2** kindred: *daar voel ik me niet mee ~* I feel no affinity for (*or:* with) that
²verwant [vərwαnt] *de (~en)* relative, relation
verward [vərwαrt] *adj, adv* **1** confused, (en)tangled; **2** confused, muddled, incoherent
verwarmen [vərwαrmə(n)] *vb* warm, heat: *de kamer was niet verwarmd* the room was unheated; *een glas hete melk zal je wat ~* a glass of hot milk will warm you up
verwarming [vərwαrmıŋ] *de (~en)* heating (system): *centrale ~ aanleggen* put in central heating; *de ~ hoger* (or: *lager*) *zetten* turn the heat up (*or:* down)
verwarmingsbuis [vərwαrmıŋzbœys] *de (-buizen)* heating pipe
verwarmingsinstallatie [vərwαrmıŋsınstαla(t)si] *de (~s)* heating system
verwarmingsketel [vərwαrmıŋsketəl] *de (~s)* (central heating) boiler
verwarren [vərwαrə(n)] *vb* **1** tangle (up), confuse: *~d werken* lead to confusion; **2** (with *met*) confuse, mistake: *u verwart hem met zijn broer* you mistake him for his brother; *niet te ~ met* not to be confused with
verwarring [vərwαrıŋ] *de (~en)* entanglement, confusion; muddle: *er ontstond enige ~ over zijn identiteit* some confusion arose concerning (*or:* as to) his identity; *~ stichten* cause confusion; *in ~ raken* become confused
verwateren [vərwaːtərə(n)] *vb* become diluted (*or:* watered down), peter out: *de vriendschap tussen hen is verwaterd* their friendship has cooled off
verwedden [vərwɛdə(n)] *vb* bet: *ik wil er alles om ~ dat …* I'll bet you anything that …
verweerd [vərweːrt] *adj* weather-beaten
verwekken [vərwɛkə(n)] *vb* beget, father: *kinderen ~* beget (*or:* father) children
verwekker [vərwɛkər] *de (~s)* begetter, father: *de ~ van het kind* the child's natural father
verwelken [vərwɛlkə(n)] *vb* **1** wilt, wither; **2** (*fig*)

fade: *~de schoonheid* fading beauty
verwelkomen [vərwɛlkoːmə(n)] *vb* welcome, greet, salute: *iem hartelijk ~* give s.o. a hearty welcome
verwend [vərwɛnt] *adj* **1** spoilt, pampered: *zij is een ~ kreng* she is a spoilt brat; **2** discriminating: *een ~ publiek* a discriminating public (*or:* audience)
verwennen [vərwɛnə(n)] *vb* spoil, indulge: *zichzelf ~* indulge (*or:* pamper) oneself
¹verweren [vərweːrə(n)] *vb* weather, erode, become weather-beaten
²verweren [vərweːrə(n)] *ref vb* defend oneself, put up a fight: *voor hij zich kon ~* before he could defend himself
verwerkelijken [vərwɛrkələkə(n)] *vb* realize: *een droom* (or: *wens*) *~* make a dream (*or:* wish) come true
verwerken [vərwɛrkə(n)] *vb* **1** process, handle, convert: *zijn maag kon het niet ~* his stomach couldn't digest it; *huisvuil tot compost ~* convert household waste into compost; **2** incorporate: *de nieuwste gegevens zijn erin verwerkt* the latest data are incorporated (in it); **3** cope with: *ze heeft haar verdriet nooit echt goed verwerkt* she has never really come to terms with her sorrow; **4** absorb, cope with: *stadscentra kunnen zoveel verkeer niet ~* city centres cannot absorb so much traffic
verwerking [vərwɛrkıŋ] *de* processing, handling, assimilation, incorporation: *bij de ~ van deze gegevens* in processing (*or:* handling) these data
verwerkingseenheid [vərwɛrkıŋsenhɛit] *de (-heden)* ‖ *de centrale ~* the mainframe, the processor
verwerkingstijd [vərwɛrkıŋstɛit] *de* processing time
verwerpen [vərwɛrpə(n)] *vb* reject; vote down, turn down
verwerven [vərwɛrvə(n)] *vb* obtain, acquire, achieve
verweven [vərweːvə(n)] *vb* (inter)weave: *hun belangen zijn nauw ~* their interests are closely knit; *met elkaar ~ zijn* be interwoven
verwezenlijken [vərweːzə(n)ləkə(n)] *vb* realize, fulfil, achieve: *plannen* (or: *voornemens*) *~* realize one's plans (*or:* intentions)
verwezenlijking [vərweːzə(n)ləkıŋ] *de* realization, fulfilment
verwijderd [vərwɛidərt] *adj* remote, distant: *(steeds verder) van elkaar ~ raken* drift (further and further) apart; *een kilometer van het dorp ~* a kilometre out of the village
verwijderen [vərwɛidərə(n)] *vb* remove: *iem uit zijn huis ~* evict s.o.; *iem van het veld ~* send s.o. off (the field)
verwijdering [vərwɛidərıŋ] *de (~en)* **1** removal: *~ van school* expulsion from school; **2** estrangement: *er ontstond een ~ tussen hen* they drifted apart
verwijding [vərwɛidıŋ] *de (~en)* widening, (*med*) dila(ta)tion
verwijfd [vərwɛift] *adj* effeminate, sissy
verwijsbriefje [vərwɛizbrifjə] *het (~s)* (doctor's)

referral (letter)
verwijt [vərwɛit] *het (~en)* reproach, blame: *elkaar ~en maken* blame one another; *iem ~en maken* reproach s.o.
verwijten [vərwɛitə(n)] *vb* reproach, blame: *iem iets ~* reproach s.o. with sth, blame s.o. for sth
verwijtend [vərwɛitənt] *adj, adv* reproachful: *iem ~ aankijken* look at s.o. reproachfully
verwijzen [vərwɛizə(n)] *vb* refer: *een patiënt naar een specialist ~* refer a patient to a specialist
verwikkelen [vərwɪkələ(n)] *vb* involve, implicate, mix up
verwikkeling [vərwɪkəlɪŋ] *de (~en)* complication
verwilderd [vərwɪldərt] *adj* **1** wild, neglected: *~e boomgaard* a neglected (*or:* an overgrown) orchard; **2** wild, unkempt, dishevelled; **3** wild, mad: *er ~ uitzien* look wild (*or:* haggard)
verwisselbaar [vərwɪsəlbar] *adj* exchangeable, convertible: *onderling ~* interchangeable
verwisselen [vərwɪsələ(n)] *vb* **1** (ex)change, swap; **2** mistake, confuse: *ik had u met uw broer verwisseld* I had mistaken you for your brother
verwisseling [vərwɪsəlɪŋ] *de (~en)* (ex)change, interchange, swap
verwittigen [vərwɪtəɣə(n)] *vb* inform, advise, notify
verwoed [vərwut] *adj, adv* passionate, ardent, impassioned: *~e pogingen doen* make frantic efforts
verwoest [vərwust] *adj* destroyed, devastated, ravaged
verwoesten [vərwustə(n)] *vb* destroy, devastate, lay waste
verwoestend [vərwustənt] *adj, adv* devastating, destructive
verwoesting [vərwustɪŋ] *de (~en)* devastation; *(pl also)* ravages; destruction
verwonden [vərwɔndə(n)] *vb* wound; injure
verwonderd [vərwɔndərt] *adj* surprised, *(stronger)* amazed, astonished
verwonderen [vərwɔndərə(n)] *vb* amaze, astonish
verwondering [vərwɔndərɪŋ] *de* surprise, *(stronger)* amazement, astonishment: *het hoeft geen ~ te wekken dat …* it comes as no surprise that …
verwonding [vərwɔndɪŋ] *de (~en)* injury, wounding, wound: *~en oplopen* sustain injuries, be injured
verwringen [vərwrɪŋə(n)] *vb* twist, distort, contort: *een van pijn verwrongen gezicht* a face contorted with pain
verzachten [vərzɑχtə(n)] *vb* soften; ease: *pijn ~* relieve (*or:* alleviate) pain
verzachtend [vərzɑχtənt] *adj* mitigating, extenuating
verzadigd [vərzadəχt] *adj* **1** satisfied, full (up); **2** saturated: *een ~e arbeidsmarkt* a saturated labour market
verzadigen [vərzadəɣə(n)] *vb* saturate
verzadiging [vərzadəɣɪŋ] *de* satisfaction, saturation

verzakken [vərzɑkə(n)] *vb* subside, settle, sink, sag: *de grond verzakt* the ground has subsided (*or:* is subsiding)
verzamelaar [vərzaməlar] *de (~s)* collector
verzamel-cd [vərzaməlsede] *de* compilation CD
¹**verzamelen** [vərzamələ(n)] *vb* **1** collect, gather, compile: *krachten ~* summon up (one's) strength; *de verzamelde werken van …* the collected works of …; **2** collect, save
²**verzamelen** [vərzamələ(n)] *vb* gather (together), assemble, meet: *zich ~* gather, assemble, congregate; *we verzamelden (ons) op het plein* we assembled (*or:* met) in the square
verzameling [vərzaməlɪŋ] *de (~en)* **1** collection, gathering, assembly, compilation: *een bonte ~ aanhangers* a motley collection of followers; *een ~ aanleggen* build up (*or:* put together) a collection; **2** *(maths)* set
verzamelnaam [vərzaməlnam] *de (-namen)* collective term, generic term, umbrella term
verzamelobject [vərzaməlɔpjɛkt] *het (~en)* collector's item
verzamelplaats [vərzaməlplats] *de (~en)* meeting place (*or:* point), assembly point
verzamelwoede [vərzaməlwudə] *de* mania for collecting things
verzanden [vərzɑndə(n)] *vb* get bogged down
verzegelen [vərzeɣələ(n)] *vb* seal, put (*or:* set) a seal on: *een woning ~* put a house under seal
verzegeling [vərzeɣəlɪŋ] *de (~en)* sealing; seal: *een ~ aanbrengen* (or: *verbreken*) affix (*or:* break) a seal
verzeilen [vərzɛilə(n)] *vb* ‖ *hoe kom jij hier verzeild?* what brings you here?; *in moeilijkheden verzeild raken* run into (*or:* hit) trouble, run into difficulties
verzekeraar [vərzekərar] *de (~s)* insurer, assurer
verzekerd [vərzekərt] *adj* **1** assured (of), confident (of): *succes ~!* success guaranteed!; *u kunt ervan ~ zijn dat* you may rest assured that; **2** insured: *het ~e bedrag* the sum insured
verzekerde [vərzekərdə] *de (~n)* policyholder, insured party, assured party
verzekeren [vərzekərə(n)] *vb* **1** ensure, assure: *iem van iets ~* assure s.o. of sth; **2** guarantee, assure; insure, assure: *zich ~ (tegen)* insure oneself (against)
verzekering [vərzekərɪŋ] *de (~en)* **1** assurance, guarantee: *ik kan u de ~ geven, dat …* I can give you an assurance that …; **2** insurance, assurance: *sociale ~* national insurance, social security; *een ~ aangaan (afsluiten)* take out insurance (*or:* an insurance policy); *een all-risk ~* a comprehensive insurance policy; **3** insurance company, assurance company
verzekeringsadviseur [vərzekərɪŋsatfizør] *de (~s)* insurance adviser
verzekeringsagent [vərzekərɪŋsaɣɛnt] *de (~en)* insurance agent
verzekeringsmaatschappij [vərzekərɪŋsmatsχa-

pei] *de (~en)* insurance company, assurance company

verzekeringspolis [vərzɛ̱kərɪŋspolɪs] *de (~sen)* insurance policy

verzekeringspremie [vərzɛ̱kərɪŋspremi] *de (~s)* insurance premium

verzekeringsvoorwaarden *de* policy conditions

verzendadres [vərzɛntadrɛs] *het* dispatch address, address for delivery

verzenden [vərzɛ̱ndə(n)] *vb* send, mail, dispatch, *(goods)* ship: *per schip ~* ship

verzender [vərzɛ̱ndər] *de (~s)* sender, shipper, consignor

verzending [vərzɛ̱ndɪŋ] *de (~en)* dispatch, mailing, shipping, forwarding

verzendkosten [vərzɛ̱ntkɔstə(n)] *de* shipping *(or:* mailing, postage) costs

verzengen [vərzɛ̱ŋə(n)] *vb* scorch: *een ~de hitte* a blistering heat

verzet [vərzɛ̱t] *het* resistance: *in ~ komen (tegen)* offer resistance (to)

verzetje [vərzɛ̱cə] *het (~s)* diversion, distraction: *hij heeft een ~ nodig* he needs a bit of variety *(or:* a break)

verzetsbeweging [vərzɛ̱tsbəweɣɪŋ] *de (~en)* resistance (movement), underground

verzetsgroep [vərzɛ̱tsχrup] *de (~en)* resistance group

verzetsstrijder [vərzɛ̱tstrɛidər] *de (~s)* resistance fighter, member of the resistance *(or:* underground)

¹**verzetten** [vərzɛ̱tə(n)] *vb* move (around), shift: *een vergadering ~* put off *(or:* reschedule) a meeting

²**verzetten** [vərzɛ̱tə(n)] *ref vb* resist, offer resistance *(or:* opposition)

verzieken [vərzi̱kə(n)] *vb* spoil, ruin: *de sfeer ~* spoil the atmosphere

verziend [vɛrzint] *adj* long-sighted

verziendheid [vɛrzinthɛit] *de* long-sightedness

verzilveren [vərzɪ̱lvərə(n)] *vb* **1** (plate with) silver, silver-plate: *verzilverde lepels* plate(d) spoons; **2** cash, convert into *(or:* redeem for) cash

verzinken [vərzɪ̱ŋkə(n)] *vb* sink (down, away), submerge: *in gedachten verzonken zijn* be lost *(or:* deep) in thought

verzinnen [vərzɪ̱nə(n)] *vb* invent, think/make *(or:* dream, cook) up, devise: *een smoesje ~* think up *(or:* cook up) an excuse

verzinsel [vərzɪ̱nsəl] *het (~s)* fabrication, invention, figment of one's imagination

verzoek [vərzu̱k] *het (~en)* **1** request, appeal, petition: *dringend ~* urgent request, entreaty; *aan een ~ voldoen* comply with a request; *op ~ van mijn broer* at my brother's request; **2** petition, appeal: *een ~ indienen* petition, appeal, make a petition *(or:* an appeal)

verzoeken [vərzu̱kə(n)] *vb* request, petition, ask, beg: *mag ik om stilte verzoeken* silence please, may I have a moment's silence

verzoeknummer [vərzu̱knʏmər] *het (~s)* request

verzoenen [vərzu̱nə(n)] *vb* reconcile, appease: *zich met iem ~* become reconciled with s.o.

verzoenend [vərzu̱nənt] *adj, adv* conciliatory, expiatory

verzoening [vərzu̱nɪŋ] *de (~en)* reconciliation

verzorgd [vərzɔ̱rχt] *adj* well cared-for, carefully kept *(or:* tended): *een goed ~ gazon* a well-tended lawn; *er ~ uitzien* be well dressed *(or:* groomed)

verzorgen [vərzɔ̱rɣə(n)] *vb* look after, (at)tend to, care for: *tot in de puntjes verzorgd* taken care of down to the last detail

verzorger [vərzɔ̱rɣər] *de (~s)* attendant, caretaker: *ouders, voogden of ~s* parents or guardians

verzorging [vərzɔ̱rɣɪŋ] *de* care, maintenance, nursing: *medische ~* medical care

verzorgingsflat [vərzɔ̱rɣɪŋsflɛt] *de (~s)* warden-assisted flat, *(Am)* retirement home with nursing care

verzorgingsstaat [vərzɔ̱rɣɪŋstat] *de* welfare state

verzorgingstehuis [vərzɔ̱rɣɪŋstəhœys] *het (-tehuizen)* home, home for the elderly, old people's home, rest home

verzuim [vərzœ̱ym] *het (~en)* omission, non-attendance, absence: *~ wegens ziekte* absence due to illness

verzuimen [vərzœ̱ymə(n)] *vb* be absent, fail to attend: *een les ~* cut *(or:* skip) (a) class

verzuipen [vərzœ̱ypə(n)] *vb* **1** drown, be drowned; **2** be flooded

verzuren [vərzy̱rə(n)] *vb* sour, turn sour, go sour, go off; acidify: *verzuurde grond* acid soil

verzwakken [vərzwɑ̱kə(n)] *vb* weaken, grow weak, enfeeble; impair

verzwaren [vərzwa̱rə(n)] *vb* make heavier; *(fig also)* increase, strengthen: *de dijken ~* strengthen the dykes; *exameneisen ~* make an examination stiffer

verzwarend [vərzwa̱rənt] *adj* aggravating

verzwijgen [vərzwɛi̱ɣə(n)] *vb* keep silent about, withhold, suppress, conceal: *iets voor iem ~* keep *(or:* conceal) sth from s.o.; *een schandaal ~* hush up a scandal

verzwikken [vərzwɪ̱kə(n)] *vb* sprain, twist: *zijn enkel ~* sprain one's ankle

vest [vɛst] *het (~en)* waistcoat, vest, cardigan: *een pak met ~* a three-piece suit

vestibule [vɛstibylə] *de (~s)* hall(way), entrance hall, vestibule

¹**vestigen** [vɛ̱stəɣə(n)] *vb* direct, focus: *ik heb mijn hoop op jou gevestigd* I'm putting (all) my hopes in you

²**vestigen** [vɛ̱stəɣə(n)] *ref vb* settle: *zich ergens ~* establish oneself, settle somewhere

vestiging [vɛ̱stəɣɪŋ] *de (~en)* branch, office, outlet

vestigingsplaats [vɛ̱stəɣɪŋsplats] *de (~en)* place of business, registered office, seat, *(pers)* place of residence

vesting [vɛ̱stɪŋ] *de (~en)* fortress, fort, stronghold

¹**vet** [vɛt] *het (~ten)* fat, oil, grease, dripping, lard:

iets in het ~ zetten grease sth

²**vet** [vɛt] *adj, adv* **1** fat, rich, creamy; **2** fatty, greasy, rich; **3** fat, plum(my): *een ~te buit* rich spoils; **4** greasy, oily: *een ~te huid* a greasy (*or:* an oily) skin; **5** bold: *~te letters* bold (*or:* heavy) type, boldface

vetarm [vɛtɑrm] *adj* low-fat

vete [veːtə] *de (~s)* feud, vendetta

veter [veːtər] *de (~s)* lace: *zijn ~s vastmaken (strikken)* do up (*or:* tie) one's shoelaces; *je ~ zit los!* your shoelace is undone!

veteraan [veːtəraːn] *de (veteranen)* veteran

veteranenziekte [veːtərɑnə(n)ziktə] *de* Legionnaire's disease

vetgedrukt [vɛtxədrʏkt] *adj* in bold (*or:* heavy) type

vetgehalte [vɛtxəhɑltə] *het (~s, ~n)* fat content, percentage of fat

vetkuif [vɛtkœyf] *de (vetkuiven)* greased quiff

vetmesten [vɛtmɛstə(n)] *vb* fatten (up), feed up

veto [veːto] *het (~'s)* veto: *het recht van ~ hebben* have the right (*or:* power) of veto; *zijn ~ over iets uitspreken* veto sth, exercise one's veto against sth

vetplant [vɛtplɑnt] *de (~en)* succulent

vettig [vɛtəx] *adj, adv* **1** fatty, greasy: *een ~e glans* an oily sheen; **2** greasy, oily

vetvlek [vɛtflɛk] *de (~ken)* grease stain, greasy spot (*or:* mark): *vol ~ken* grease-stained

vetvrij [vɛtfrɛi] *adj* **1** greaseproof: *~ papier* greaseproof paper; **2** fat-free, non-fat

vetzak [vɛtsɑk] *de (~ken)* fatso, fatty

veulen [vøːlə(n)] *het (~s)* foal, colt, filly

vezel [veːzəl] *de (~s)* fibre, thread, filament

vezelrijk [veːzəlrɛik] *adj* high-fibre

vgl. *vergelijk* cf., cp.

V-hals [veːhɑls] *de (V-halzen)* V-neck

via [viːja] *prep* via, by way of, by, through, by means of: *~ de snelweg komen* take the motorway (*or* Am: expressway); *ik hoorde ~ mijn zuster, dat …* I heard from (*or:* through) my sister that …; *iets ~ ~ horen* learn (*or:* hear) of sth in a roundabout way, hear sth on the grapevine

viaduct [viːjadʏkt] *het, de (~en)* viaduct, flyover, crossover, *(Am)* overpass

vibrafoon [vibrafoːn] *de (~s)* vibraphone, vibes

vibratie [vibraː(t)si] *de (~s)* vibration

vicaris [vikaːrəs] *de (~sen)* vicar

vice-premier [viːsəprəmje] *de* vice-premier

vice-president [viːsəprezidɛnt] *de* vice-president; vice-chairman

vice versa [visəvɛrza] *adv* vice versa

vice-voorzitter [viːsəvoːrzɪtər] *de* vice-chairman, deputy chairman

Victoriaans [vɪktoːrijans] *adj* Victorian

video [viːdejo] *de (~'s)* video (tape, recorder): *iets op ~ zetten* record sth on video

videoapparatuur [viːdejoɑparatyr] *de* video equipment

videobewaking [viːdejobəwaːkɪŋ] *de* closed circuit TV

videocamera [viːdejokamɘra] *de (~'s)* video camera

videocassette [viːdejokɑsɛtə] *de (~s)* video cassette

videoclip [viːdejoklɪp] *de (~s)* videoclip

videofilm [viːdejofɪlm] *de (~s)* video (film, recording)

videofoon [viːdejofoːn] *de (~s)* video(tele)phone

video-opname [viːdejoɔpnaːmə] *de (~n)* video recording

videorecorder [viːdejorikɔːrdər] *de (~s)* video (recorder), VCR, video cassette recorder

videospel [viːdejospɛl] *het (~en)* video game

videotheek [viːdejotɛk] *de (videotheken)* video shop

vief [vif] *adj, adv* lively, energetic

vier [vir] *num* four; *(in dates)* fourth: *vier mei* the fourth of May; *een gesprek onder ~ ogen* a private conversation, a tête-à-tête; *zo zeker als tweemaal twee ~ is* as sure as I'm standing here; *half ~* half past three; *ze waren met z'n ~en* there were four of them; *hij kreeg een ~ voor wiskunde* he got four out of ten for maths

vierbaansweg [virbanswɛx] *de (~en)* four-lane motorway; dual carriageway, *(Am)* divided highway

vierde [virdə] *num* fourth: *de ~ klas* the fourth form (*or* Am: grade); *ten ~* fourthly, in the fourth place; *het is vandaag de ~* today is the fourth; *drie ~* three fourths, three-quarters; *als ~ eindigen* come in fourth

vierdelig [virdeləx] *adj* four-part; four-piece

vieren [virə(n)] *vb* **1** celebrate, observe; commemorate: *dat gaan we ~* this calls for a celebration; **2** pay out, slacken: *een touw (laten) ~* pay out a rope

vierhoek [virhuk] *de (~en)* quadrangle, rectangle, square

viering [virɪŋ] *de (~en)* celebration, observance; commemoration, *(rel)* service: *ter ~ van* in celebration of

vierjarig [virjarəx] *adj* four-year-old; four-year(s'); four-yearly

¹**vierkant** [virkɑnt] *het (~en)* square, quadrangle

²**vierkant** [virkɑnt] *adj* square: *de kamer meet drie meter in het ~* the room is three metres square, the room is three by three (metres)

vierkleurendruk [virkløːrə(n)drʏk] *de* four-colour printing

vierkwartsmaat [virkwɑrtsmat] *de (-maten)* four-four time, quadruple time, common time (*or:* measure)

vierling [virlɪŋ] *de (~en)* quadruplets, quads

viermaal [virmal] *adv* four times

vierspan [virspɑn] *het (~nen)* four-in-hand

viersprong [virsprɔŋ] *de (~en)* crossroads

viertal [virtɑl] *het (~len)* (set of) four, foursome

vieruurtje [viryrcə] *het (~s) (Belg)* tea break, mid-afternoon snack

viervoeter [virvutər] *de (~s)* quadruped, four-footed animal

viervoetig [virvutəx] *adj* four-footed, quadruped
viervoud [virvɑut] *het (~en)* quadruple
viervoudig [virvɑudəx] *adj* fourfold, quadruple
vierwielaandrijving [virwilandrɛiviŋ] *de* four-wheel drive
vies [vis] *adj, adv* **1** dirty, filthy; **2** nasty, foul: *een ~ drankje* a nasty (*or:* vile) mixture; *bij een ~ zaakje betrokken zijn* be involved in dirty (*or:* funny) business; *ergens niet ~ van zijn* not be averse to sth; *die film viel ~ tegen* that film was a real let-down
viespeuk [vispøk] *de (~en)* pig: *een oude ~* a dirty old man
Vietnam [vjɛtnɑm] *het* Vietnam
Vietnamees [vjɛtnamɛs] *de* Vietnamese
viezerik [vizərɪk] *de (~en)* pig, slob, dirty sod
viezigheid [vizəxhɛit] *de (-heden)* dirt, grime
vignet [vɪɳɛt] *het (~ten)* **1** device, logo, emblem; **2** sticker
vijand [vɛiɑnt] *de (~en)* enemy: *dat zou je je ergste ~ nog niet toewensen* you wouldn't wish that on your worst enemy; *gezworen ~en* sworn (*or:* mortal) enemies
vijandelijk [vɛiɑndələk] *adj, adv* enemy, hostile
vijandelijkheid [vɛiɑndələkhɛit] *de (-heden)* hostility, act of war
vijandig [vɛiɑndəx] *adj, adv* hostile, inimical: *een ~e daad* a hostile act; *iem ~ gezind zijn* be hostile towards s.o.
vijandigheid [vɛiɑndəxhɛit] *de (-heden)* hostility, animosity, enmity
vijandschap [vɛiɑntsxɑp] *de (~pen)* enmity, hostility, animosity: *in ~ leven* be at odds (with)
vijf [vɛif] *num* five; *(in dates)* fifth: *vijf juni* the fifth of June; *om de ~ minuten* every five minutes; *het is over vijven* it is past (*or:* gone) five; *een stuk of ~* about five, five or so, five-odd; *een briefje van ~* a five-pound note
vijfdaags [vɛivdaxs] *adj* five-day-old; five-day: *de ~e werkweek* the five-day (working) week
vijfde [vɛivdə] *num* fifth: *auto met ~ deur* hatchback; *ten ~* fifthly, in the fifth place; *als ~ eindigen* come in fifth
vijfenzestigpluskaart [vɛifə(n)sɛstəxplyskart] *de (~en)* senior citizen's ticket (*or:* pass)
vijfenzestigplusser [vɛifə(n)sɛstəxplysər] *de (~s)* senior citizen, pensioner
vijfhoek [vɛifhuk] *de (~en)* pentagon
vijfjarenplan [vɛifjarə(n)plɑn] *het (~nen)* five-year plan
vijfjarig [vɛifjarəx] *adj* five-year-old; five-year(s'); five-yearly
vijfje [vɛifjə] *het (~s)* five pound note, *(Am)* five dollar bill
vijfkamp [vɛifkɑmp] *de* pentathlon
vijfling [vɛiflɪŋ] *de (~en)* quintuplets, quins: *zij kreeg een ~* she had quintuplets (*or:* quins)
vijftal [vɛiftɑl] *het (~len)* (set of) five: *een ~ jaren* (about) five years, five (or so) years; *een vrolijk ~* a merry fivesome

vijftien [vɛiftin] *num* fifteen; *(in dates)* fifteenth: *vijftien maart* the fifteenth of March; *rugnummer ~* number fifteen; *een man of ~* about fifteen people, fifteen or so people
vijftig [vɛiftəx] *num* fifty: *de jaren ~* the fifties; *hij is in de ~* he is in his fifties; *tegen de ~ lopen* be getting on for (*or:* be pushing) fifty
vijftiger [vɛiftəyər] *de (~s)* s.o. in his fifties
vijg [vɛix] *de* fig (tree) || *(Belg) dat zijn ~en na Pasen* that is (*or:* comes) too late to be of use
vijl [vɛil] *de (~en)* file
vijlen [vɛilə(n)] *vb* file
vijs [vɛis] *de (vijzen) (Belg)* screw
vijver [vɛivər] *de (~s)* pond
vijzel [vɛizəl] *de* **1** jack; **2** Archimedean screw
viking [vikɪŋ] *de (~en)* Viking
villa [vila] *de (~'s)* villa: *halve ~* semi-detached house
villawijk [vilawɛik] *de (~en)* (exclusive) residential area
villen [vilə(n)] *vb* skin, flay
vilt [vɪlt] *het* felt
vilten [vɪltə(n)] *adj* felt
viltje [vɪlcə] *het (~s)* beer mat
viltstift [vɪltstɪft] *de (~en)* felt-tip (pen)
vin [vɪn] *de (~nen)* **1** fin; flipper: *geen ~ verroeren* not raise (*or:* lift) a finger, not move a muscle; **2** fin, vane
vinden [vɪndə(n)] *vb* **1** find, discover, come across, strike: *dat boek is nergens te ~* that book is nowhere to be found; *ergens voor te ~ zijn* be (very) ready to do sth, be game for sth; *iem (iets) toevallig ~* happen/chance upon s.o. (sth); **2** find, think of; **3** think, find: *ik vind het vandaag koud* I think it's (*or:* I find it) cold today; *ik zou het prettig ~ als …* I'd appreciate it if …; *hoe vind je dat?* what do you think of that?; *zou je het erg ~ als …?* would you mind if …?; *ik vind het goed* that's fine by me, it suits me fine; *vind je ook niet?* don't you agree?; *daar vind ik niets aan* it doesn't do a thing for me; *het met iem kunnen ~* get on (*or:* along) with s.o.; *zich ergens in kunnen ~* agree with sth; *zij hebben elkaar gevonden: a)* they have come to terms (over it); *b)* they have found each other
vinder [vɪndər] *de (~s)* finder, discoverer
vinding [vɪndɪŋ] *de (~en)* idea, invention
vindingrijk [vɪndɪŋrɛik] *adj* ingenious, inventive: *een ~e geest* a fertile (*or:* creative) mind
vindingrijkheid [vɪndɪŋrɛikhɛit] *de* ingenuity, inventiveness, resourcefulness
vindplaats [vɪntplats] *de (~en)* place where sth is found, site, location
vinger [vɪŋər] *de (~s)* finger: *groene ~s hebben* have green fingers, *(Am)* have a green thumb; *lange ~s hebben* have sticky fingers; *met een natte ~* roughly, approximately; *als men hem een ~ geeft, neemt hij de hele hand* give him an inch and he'll take a mile; *hij heeft zich in de ~s gesneden (fig)* he got (his fingers) burned; *de ~ opsteken* put up (*or:* raise) one's

hand; *iets door de ~s zien* turn a blind eye to sth;
overlook sth; *iets in de ~s hebben* be a natural at sth;
een ~ in de pap hebben have a finger in the pie; *met
de ~s knippen* snap one's fingers; *hij had haar nog
met geen ~ aangeraakt* he hadn't put (*or:* laid) a finger on her; *op de ~s van één hand te tellen zijn* be
few and far between; *iem op de ~s tikken* rap s.o.
over the knuckles; *iem op de ~s kijken* breathe
down s.o.'s neck; *dat had je op je ~s kunnen natellen* that was to be expected
vingerafdruk [vɪŋərɑvdrʏk] *de (~ken)* fingerprint:
~ken nemen (van) fingerprint s.o., take s.o.'s fin-
gerprints
vingerhoed [vɪŋərhut] *de (~en)* thimble
vingertop [vɪŋərtɔp] *de (~pen)* fingertip
vingerverf [vɪŋərvɛrf] *de (-verven)* finger paint
vingerzetting [vɪŋərzɛtɪŋ] *de (~en)* fingering
vink [vɪŋk] *de (~en)* **1** finch; chaffinch; **2** check
(mark), tick
vinkenslag [vɪŋkə(n)slɑχ] *(Belg)* ‖ *op ~ zitten* lie in
wait
vinnig [vɪnəχ] *adj, adv* sharp, caustic
vinyl [vinil] *het* vinyl
violet [vijolɛt] *adj* violet
violist [vijolɪst] *de (~en)* violinist
viool [vijol] *de (violen)* violin, fiddle: *(op de) ~ spelen* play the violin (*or:* fiddle); *eerste ~* first violin;
hij speelt de eerste ~ he is (*or:* plays) first fiddle
viooiconcert [vijolkɔnsɛrt] *het (~en)* violin concerto
viooltje [vijoltʃə] *het (~s)* violet: *Kaaps ~* African
violet
virtueel [vɪrtywel] *adj, adv* virtual, potential: *een ~
winkelcentrum* a virtual shopping centre
virtuoos [vɪrtywos] *adj, adv* virtuoso
virus [virʏs] *het (~sen)* virus
virusinfectie [virʏsɪnfɛksi] *de (~s)* virus infection,
viral infection
virusscanner [virʏskɛnər] *de (~s)* virus scanner
vis [vɪs] *de (~sen)* fish: *een mand ~* a basket of fish;
er zit hier veel ~ the fishing's good here; *zo gezond
als een ~* fit as a fiddle
Vis [vɪs] *de (~sen)* Pisces, Piscean
visagist [vizaʒɪst] *de (~en)* cosmetician, beauty
specialist, beautician
visakte [vɪsɑktə] *de (~n, ~s)* fishing licence
visboer [vɪzbur] *de (~en)* fishmonger
visgraat [vɪsχrat] *de (visgraten)* fish bone
vishandel [vɪshɑndəl] *de* fish trade, fish shop (*or:
Am:* dealer)
vishandelaar [vɪshɑndəlar] *de (~s, -handelaren)*
fishmonger, *(Am)* fish dealer
visie [vizi] *de (~s)* view, outlook, point of view: *een
man met ~* a man of vision
visioen [vizjun] *het (~en)* vision: *een ~ hebben* see
(*or:* have) a vision
visite [vizitə] *de (~s)* **1** visit, call: *bij iem op ~ gaan*
pay s.o. a visit, call on s.o., visit; **2** visitors, guests,
company

visitekaartje [vizitəkarcə] *het (~s)* visiting card;
(business) card: *zijn ~ achterlaten* make one's
mark, establish one's presence
viskom [vɪskɔm] *de (~men)* fishbowl
vismarkt [vɪsmɑrkt] *de (~en)* fish market
visnet [vɪsnɛt] *het (~ten)* fish net, fishing net
visrestaurant [vɪsrɛstorɑnt] *het (~s)* fish restaurant, seafood restaurant
visschotel [vɪsχotəl] *de (~s)* fish dish
visseizoen [vɪsɛizun] *het* fishing season, angling
season
vissen [vɪsə(n)] *vb* **1** fish, angle: *op haring ~* fish for
herring; *parels ~* dive (*or:* fish) for pearls; **2** drag,
dredge
Vissen [vɪsə(n)] *de* Pisces
visser [vɪsər] *de (~s)* fisherman, angler
visserij [vɪsərɛi] *de (~en)* fishing, fisheries, fishery
vissersboot [vɪsərzbot] *de (-boten)* fishing boat
vissersvloot [vɪsərsflot] *de* fishing fleet
vissoep [vɪsup] *de* fish soup
visstand [vɪstɑnt] *de* fish stock
visstick [vɪstɪk] *de (~s)* fish finger
visueel [vizywel] *adj, adv* visual: *~ gehandicapt* visually handicapped
visum [vizʏm] *het (visa)* visa: *een ~ aanvragen* apply for a visa
visvangst [vɪsfɑŋst] *de* fishing, catching of fish: *van
de ~ leven* fish for one's living
visvergunning [vɪsfərɣʏnɪŋ] *de (~en)* fishing licence (*or:* permit)
visvijver [vɪsfɛivər] *de (~s)* fishpond
viswater [vɪswatər] *het (~s, ~en)* fishing ground(s)
viswinkel [vɪswɪŋkəl] *de (~s)* fish shop (*or Am:*
dealer), fishmonger's (shop)
vitaal [vitɑl] *adj* vital: *hij is nog erg ~ voor zijn leeftijd* he's still very active for his age
vitaliteit [vitalitɛit] *de* vitality, vigour
vitamine [vitaminə] *de (~s)* vitamin: *rijk aan ~*
rich in vitamins, vitamin-rich
vitrage [vitraʒə] *het, de (~s)* net curtain
vitrine [vitrinə] *de (~s)* **1** (glass, display) case,
showcase; **2** shop window, show window
vitten [vɪtə(n)] *vb* find fault, carp
vivisectie [vivisɛksi] *de (~s)* vivisection
vizier [vizir] *het (~s)* **1** sight: *iem in het ~ krijgen*
spot s.o., catch sight of s.o.; **2** visor
vla [vla] *de (~'s)* **1** (roughly) custard; **2** flan, *(Am)*
(open-faced) pie
vlaag [vlaχ] *de (vlagen)* **1** gust, squall; **2** fit, flurry:
in een ~ van verstandsverbijstering in a frenzy, in a
fit of insanity; *bij vlagen* in fits and starts, in spurts
(*or:* bursts)
vlaai [vlaj] *de (~en)* flan, *(Am)* (open-faced) pie
¹Vlaams [vlams] *het* Flemish
²Vlaams [vlams] *adj* Flemish ‖ *~e gaai* jay
Vlaamse [vlamsə] *de* Flemish woman
Vlaanderen [vlandərə(n)] *het* Flanders
vlag [vlaχ] *de (~gen)* flag, colours, ensign: *met ~ en
wimpel slagen* pass with (*or:* come through with)

flying colours; *de Britse* ~ the Union Jack

vlaggenmast [vlɑɣə(n)mɑst] *de (~en)* flagpole, flagstaff

vlaggenstok [vlɑɣə(n)stɔk] *de (~ken)* flagpole, flagstaff

¹**vlak** [vlɑk] *adj* 1 flat, level, even: *iets ~ strijken* level off sth, level sth out; 2 flat, shallow

²**vlak** [vlɑk] *adv* 1 flat, right, immediately, directly: ~ *tegenover elkaar* right (*or:* straight) opposite each other; 3 close: ~ *achter je* right (*or:* just) behind you; ~ *bij de school* close to the school, right by the school; *het is* ~ *bij* it's no distance at all; *het is hier* ~ *in de buurt* it's just round (*or Am:* around) the corner; *het ligt* ~ *voor je neus* it is staring you in the face, it's right under your nose

³**vlak** [vlɑk] *het (~ken)* 1 surface, face, facet: *het voorste* (*or: achterste*) ~ the front (*or:* rear) face; 2 sphere, area, field: *op het menselijke* ~ in the human sphere

vlakaf [vlɑkɑf] *adv (Belg)* plainly, bluntly

vlakbij [vlɑgbɛi] *adv* nearby

vlakgom [vlɑkχɔm] *de* rubber, eraser

vlakte [vlɑktə] *de (~n, ~s)* plain: *een golvende* ~ a rolling plain; *zich op de* ~ *houden* not commit oneself, leave (*or:* keep) one's options open; *na twee klappen ging hij tegen de* ~ a couple of blows laid him flat

vlam [vlɑm] *de (~men)* 1 flame: ~ *vatten* catch fire, burst into flames; *in ~men opgaan* go up in flames; 2 flame

Vlaming [vlɑmɪŋ] *de (~en)* Fleming

vlammend [vlɑmənt] *adj* fiery, burning: *een ~ protest* a burning protest

vlammenwerper [vlɑmə(n)wɛrpər] *de (~s)* flame-thrower

vlammenzee [vlɑmə(n)ze] *de* sea of flame(s)

vlamverdeler [vlɑmvərdelər] *de (~s)* stove mat

vlas [vlɑs] *het* flax

vlecht [vlɛχt] *de (~en)* braid, plait, tress: *een valse* ~ a switch, a tress of false hair

vlechten [vlɛχtə(n)] *vb* braid, plait, twine

vlechtwerk [vlɛχtwɛrk] *het* plaiting

vleermuis [vlermœys] *de (-muizen)* bat

vlees [vles] *het* 1 flesh; meat: *dat is ~ noch vis* that is neither fish, flesh, nor good red herring; *in eigen ~ snijden* queer one's own pitch; *mijn eigen ~ en bloed* my own flesh and blood; 2 flesh, pulp

vleesetend [vlesetənt] *adj* carnivorous

vleeseter [vlesetər] *de (~s)* meat-eater; carnivore

vleesmes [vlesmɛs] *het (~sen)* carving knife

vleesschotel [vlesχotəl] *de (~s)* meat course (*or:* dish)

vleesverwerkend [vlesfərwɛrkənt] *adj* meat-packing

vleeswaren [vleswarə(n)] *de* meat products, meats: *fijne* ~ (assorted) sliced cold meat, cold cuts

vleeswond [vleswɔnt] *de (~en)* flesh wound

vlegel [vleɣəl] *de (~s)* brat, lout

vleien [vlɛiə(n)] *vb* flatter, butter up: *ik voelde me*

gevleid door haar antwoord I was (*or:* felt) flattered by her answer

vleiend [vlɛiənt] *adj, adv* flattering, coaxing

vleierij [vlɛiərɛi] *de (~en)* flattery: *met ~ kom je nergens* flattery will get you nowhere

vlek [vlɛk] *de (~ken)* 1 spot, mark, stain, blemish, blotch: *die ~ gaat er in de was wel uit* that spot will come out in the wash; 2 (*fig*) blot, blemish: *blinde ~ (in het oog)* blind spot (in the eye)

vlekkeloos [vlɛkəlos] *adj* spotless, immaculate

vlerk [vlɛrk] *de* boor, lout

vleugel [vløɣəl] *de (~s)* 1 wing: *de linker* (*or:* rechter) ~ the left (*or:* right) wing; (*sport*) *over de ~s spelen* play up and down the wings; 3 grand piano

vleugelmoer [vløɣəlmur] *de (~en)* wing nut, butterfly nut

vleugelspeler [vløɣəlspelər] *de (~s) (sport)* (left, right) winger

vleugje [vløɣjə] *het (~s)* breath, touch: *een ~ ironie* a tinge of irony; *een ~ romantiek* a romantic touch

vlieg [vliχ] *de (~en)* fly: *twee ~en in één klap (slaan)* kill two birds with one stone; *hij doet geen ~ kwaad* he wouldn't harm (*or:* hurt) a fly

vliegangst [vliχɑŋst] *de* fear of flying

vliegbasis [vliɣbazɪs] *de (-bases)* airbase

vliegbiljet [vliɣbɪljɛt] *het (~ten)* airline ticket

vliegbrevet [vliɣbrəvɛt] *het (~ten)* pilot's licence, flying licence: *zijn ~ halen* qualify as a pilot, get one's wings

vliegdekschip [vliɣdɛksχɪp] *het (-schepen)* (aircraft) carrier

vliegen [vliɣə(n)] *vb* fly, race: *de dagen ~ (om)* the days are simply flying; *hij ziet ze ~* he has got bats in the belfry; *eruit ~* get sacked; *met SakkersAirlines ~* fly SakkersAirlines; *erin ~* fall for sth

vliegenier [vliɣənir] *de (~s)* airman, aviator

vliegenmepper [vliɣə(n)mepər] *de (~s)* (fly) swatter

vliegenraam [vliɣə(n)ram] *het (-ramen) (Belg)* gauze screen against flies

¹**vliegensvlug** [vliɣənsflyχ] *adj* lightning

²**vliegensvlug** [vliɣənsflyχ] *adv* as quick as lightning, like lightning (*or:* a shot)

vliegenzwam [vliɣə(n)zwɑm] *de (~men)* fly agaric

vlieger [vliɣər] *de (~s)* kite: *een ~ oplaten* fly a kite

vliegeren [vliɣərə(n)] *vb* fly kites (*or:* a kite)

vlieghoogte [vliχhoχtə] *de (~n)* altitude

vlieginstructeur [vliχɪnstryktør] *de (~s)* flying instructor

vliegramp [vliχrɑmp] *de (~en)* plane crash

vliegreis [vliχrɛis] *de (-reizen)* flight

vliegroute [vliχrutə] *de (~s, ~n)* flying route, flyway

vliegticket [vliχtɪkət] *het, de* airline ticket

vliegtuig [vliχtœyχ] *het (~en)* aeroplane, (*Am*) airplane, aircraft, plane: *~jes vouwen* make paper aeroplanes (*or:* airplanes); *met het ~ reizen* fly, travel by air (*or:* plane)

vliegtuigbemanning [vliχtœyɣbəmɑnɪŋ] *de*

(~en) aircrew

vliegtuigindustrie [vliːxtœyɣɪndʏstri] *de* aircraft industry

vliegtuigkaper [vliːxtœyɣχapər] *de (~s)* (aircraft) hijacker

vliegtuigkaping [vliːxtœyɣχapɪŋ] *de (~en)* (aircraft) hijack(ing)

vliegveld [vliːxfɛlt] *het (~en)* airport

vlier [vlir] *de (~en)* elder(berry)

vliering [vlirɪŋ] *de (~en)* attic, loft

vlies [vlis] *het (vliezen)* film, skin

vlijen [vlɛiə(n)] *vb* lay down, nestle

vlijmscherp [vlɛimsχɛrp] *adj* razor-sharp

vlijtig [vlɛitəχ] *adj, adv* diligent, industrious

vlinder [vlɪndər] *de (~s)* butterfly: *~s in mijn buik* butterflies in my stomach

vlinderdas [vlɪndərdɑs] *de (~sen)* bow tie

vlinderslag [vlɪndərslɑχ] *de* butterfly stroke

vlo [vlo] *de (vlooien)* flea: *onder de vlooien zitten* be flea-ridden

vloed [vlut] *de (~en)* (high) tide, flood (tide), rising tide: *het is nu ~* the tide is in; *bij vloed* at high tide; *een ~ van klachten* a flood (*or:* deluge) of complaints

vloedgolf [vlutχɔlf] *de (-golven)* **1** groundswell; **2** tidal wave

vloei [vluj] *het* tissue paper: *een pakje shag met ~* (a packet) rolling tobacco and cigarette papers

vloeibaar [vlujbar] *adj* liquid, fluid: *~ voedsel* liquid food

vloeien [vlujə(n)] *vb* **1** flow, stream: *in de kas ~* flow in; **3** blot, smudge

vloeiend [vlujənt] *adj, adv* flowing, liquid: *~e kleuren* blending colours; *een ~e lijn* a flowing line; *hij spreekt ~ Engels* he speaks English fluently

vloeipapier [vlujpapir] *het* **1** blotting paper; **2** tissue paper, cigarette paper

vloeistof [vlujstɔf] *de (~fen)* liquid, fluid

vloek [vluk] *de (~en)* curse: *er ligt een ~ op dat huis* a curse rests on that house; *een ~ uitspreken (over iem, iets)* curse s.o. (sth)

vloeken [vlukə(n)] *vb* curse, swear (at): *op iets ~* curse (*or:* swear) at sth

vloer [vlur] *de (~en)* floor: *planken ~* planking, strip flooring; *met iem de ~ aanvegen* mop (*or:* wipe) the floor with s.o.; *ik dacht dat ik door de ~ ging* I didn't know where to put myself; *veel mensen over de ~ hebben* have a lot of visitors; *hij komt daar over de ~* he is a regular visitor there

vloerbedekking [vlurbədɛkɪŋ] *de (~en)* floor covering: *vaste ~* wall-to-wall carpet(ting)

vloerkleed [vlurklet] *het (-kleden)* carpet, *(small)* rug

vloermat [vlurmɑt] *de (~ten)* floor mat

vloertegel [vlurteɣəl] *de (~s)* (paving) tile (*or:* stone): *~s leggen* pave, lay (paving) tiles

vloerverwarming [vlurvərwɑrmɪŋ] *de (~en)* underfloor heating

vlok [vlɔk] *de (~ken)* **1** flock, tuft: *~ken stof* whirls

of dust; **2** flake: *~ken op brood* bread with chocolate flakes

vlonder [vlɔndər] *de (~s)* **1** (wooden) platform, planking; **2** pallet

vlooienband [vlojə(n)bɑnt] *de (~en)* flea collar

vlooienmarkt [vlojə(n)mɑrkt] *de (~en)* flea market

vloot [vlot] *de (vloten)* fleet

vlos [vlɔs] *het* floss (silk)

¹vlot [vlɔt] *adj, adv* **1** facile; fluent, smooth: *een ~te pen* a ready pen; *~ spreken* speak fluently; **2** smooth, ready, prompt: *een zaak ~ afwikkelen* settle a matter promptly; *het ging heel ~* it went off without a hitch; *~ van begrip zijn* be quick-witted; **3** sociable, easy to talk to: *hij is wat ~ter geworden* he has loosened up a little; **4** easy, comfortable: *hij kleedt zich heel ~* he is a sharp dresser; **5** afloat

²vlot [vlɔt] *het (~ten)* raft: *op een ~ de rivier oversteken* raft across the river

vlotjes [vlɔcəs] *adv* smoothly, easily, promptly: *alles ~ laten verlopen* have things run smoothly

vlotten [vlɔtə(n)] *vb* go smoothly: *het werk wil niet ~* we are not making any progress (*or:* headway)

vlucht [vlʏχt] *de (~en)* flight, escape: *wij wensen u een aangename ~* we wish you a pleasant flight; *iem de ~ beletten* prevent s.o. from escaping; *op de ~ slaan* flee, run (for it); *iem op de ~ jagen (drijven)* put s.o. to flight; *voor de politie op de ~ zijn* be on the run from the police

vluchteling [vlʏχtəlɪŋ] *de (~en)* fugitive, *(pol)* refugee

vluchtelingenhulp [vlʏχtəlɪŋə(n)hʏlp] *de* aid to refugees

vluchtelingenkamp [vlʏχtəlɪŋə(n)kɑmp] *het (~en)* refugee camp

vluchten [vlʏχtə(n)] *vb* flee, escape, run away: *uit het land ~* flee (from) the country; *een bos in ~* take refuge in the woods

vluchtgedrag [vlʏχtχədrɑχ] *het* flight

vluchtheuvel [vlʏχthøvəl] *de (~s)* traffic island

vluchthuis [vlʏχthœys] *het (-huizen) (Belg)* refuge (*or:* shelter) for battered women

vluchtig [vlʏχtəχ] *adj, adv* **1** brief, *(depr)* cursory, quick: *~e kennismaking* casual acquaintance; *iets ~ doorlezen* glance over (*or:* through) sth, skim through sth; **2** volatile

vluchtleider [vlʏχtlɛidər] *de (~s)* flight controller

vluchtleiding [vlʏχtlɛidɪŋ] *de (~en)* flight (*or:* mission) control (team), ground control

vluchtmisdrijf [vlʏχtmɪzdrɛif] *het (Belg)* offence of failing to stop

vluchtpoging [vlʏχtpoɣɪŋ] *de (~en)* attempted escape

vluchtrecorder [vlʏχtrikɔːrdər] *de (~s)* flight recorder, black box

vluchtstrook [vlʏχtstrok] *de (-stroken)* hard shoulder, *(Am)* shoulder

vluchtweg [vlʏχtwɛχ] *de (~en)* escape route

vlug [vlʏχ] *adj, adv* fast, quick: *~ lopen* run fast; *~*

ter been zijn be quick on one's feet; *iem te ~ af zijn* be too quick for s.o.; **2** quick, nimble, agile; **3** quick, fast, prompt: *hij was ~ klaar* he was soon ready; *iets ~ doornemen* (or: *bekijken*) glance over (or: through) sth; *~ iets eten* have a quick snack; **5** quick, sharp: *hij behoort niet tot de ~sten* he's none too quick; *hij was er al ~ bij* he was quick at everything; *~ in rekenen* quick at sums

vmbo *het voorbereidend middelbaar beroepsonderwijs* lower vocational professional education

VN [veːn] *de Verenigde Naties* UN

VN-vredesmacht [veenvredəsmɑχt] *de* UN peace-keeping force

vo. *het voortgezet onderwijs* secondary education

vocaal [vokal] *adj* vocal

vocabulaire [vokabylɛːr(ə)] *het* vocabulary

vocht [vɔχt] *het* **1** liquid, fluid; **2** moisture, damp(ness): *de hoeveelheid ~ in de lucht* the humidity in the air

vochtig [vɔχtəχ] *adj* damp, moist: *een ~ klimaat* a damp climate; *de lucht is ~* the air is damp; *zijn ogen werden ~* his eyes became moist

vochtigheid [vɔχtəχhɛit] *de* **1** moistness, dampness; **2** moisture, humidity

vod [vɔt] *het, de (~den)* **1** rag: *een ~je papier* a scrap of paper; **2** trash, rubbish: *dit is een vod* this is trash; *iem achter de ~den zitten* keep s.o. (hard) at it

voddenboer [vɔdə(n)bur] *de (~en)* rag-and-bone man

¹voeden [vudə(n)] *vb* feed: *die vogels ~ zich met insecten* (or: *met zaden*) these birds feed on insects (or: seeds); *zij voedt haar kind zelf* she breast-feeds her baby

²voeden [vudə(n)] *vb* be nourishing (or: nutritious)

voeder [vudər] *het (~s)* fodder, feed

voeding [vudɪŋ] *de (~en)* **1** feeding, nutrition: *kunstmatige ~* artificial (or: forced) feeding; **2** food, feed: *eenzijdige ~* an unbalanced diet; *gezonde* (or: *natuurlijke*) *~* health (or: natural) food; **3** power supply

voedingsbodem [vudɪŋzbodəm] *de (~s)* breeding ground

voedingsindustrie [vudɪŋsɪndʏstri] *de (~ën)* food industry

voedingsmiddel [vudɪŋsmɪdəl] *het (~en)* food, *(oft pl)* foodstuff: *gezonde ~en* healthy (or: wholesome) foods

voedingsstof [vudɪŋstɔf] *de (~fen)* nutrient

voedsel [vutsəl] *het* food: *plantaardig ~* vegetable food; *~ tot zich nemen* take food (or: nourishment)

voedselhulp [vutsəlhʏlp] *de* food aid

voedselpakket [vutsəlpɑkɛt] *het (~ten)* food parcel

voedselvergiftiging [vutsəlvərχiftəɣɪŋ] *de* food poisoning

voedzaam [vutsam] *adj* nutritious, nourishing

voeg [vuχ] *de (~en)* joint, seam: *de ~en van een muur dichtmaken (aanstrijken)* point (the brick-

work of) a wall; *uit zijn ~en barsten* come apart at the seams

voege [vuɣə] *de (Belg)* ‖ *in ~ treden* take effect, come into force

voegen [vuɣə(n)] *vb* join (up): *hierbij voeg ik een biljet van € 100,-* I enclose a 100-euro note; *zich bij iem ~* join s.o.; **2** add: *stukken bij een dossier ~* add documents to a file; **3** point

voegwoord [vuχwort] *het (~en)* conjunction

voelbaar [vulbar] *adj, adv* tangible, perceptible: *het ijzer wordt ~ warmer* the iron is getting perceptibly hotter

¹voelen [vulə(n)] *vb* **1** feel: *leven ~* feel the baby move; *dat voel ik!* that hurts!; *zijn invloed doen ~* make one's influence felt; *als je niet wil luisteren, moet je maar ~* (you'd better) do it or else!; *voel je (hem)?* get it?; **3** feel (for, after): *laat mij eens ~* let me (have a) feel

²voelen [vulə(n)] *ref vb* feel: *zich lekker ~* feel fine, feel on top of the world

³voelen [vulə(n)] *vb* **1** feel: *het voelt hard* (or: *ruw, zacht*) it feels hard (or: rough, soft); **2** be fond (of), like: *iets gaan ~ voor iem* grow fond of s.o.; **3** feel (like), like the idea (of): *veel voor de verpleging ~* like the idea of nursing; *ik voel wel iets voor dat plan* I rather like that plan; *ik voel er niet veel voor (om) te komen* I don't feel like coming

voeling [vulɪŋ] *de* touch, contact: *~ houden met* maintain contact with, keep in touch with

voelspriet [vulsprit] *de (~en)* feeler, antenna

voer [vur] *het* feed, *(also fig)* food: *~ geven* feed; *~ voor psychologen* a fit subject for a psychologist

voerbak [vurbɑk] *de (~ken)* (feeding) trough, manger

¹voeren [vurə(n)] *vb* lead, guide: *dat zou (mij, ons) te ver ~* that would be getting too far off the subject; *de reis voert naar Rome* the trip goes to Rome

²voeren [vurə(n)] *vb* **1** line; **2** feed ‖ *een harde politiek ~* pursue a tough policy; *een proces ~* go to court (over)

voering [vurɪŋ] *de (~en)* lining

voertaal [vurtal] *de (-talen)* language of instruction *(educ)*; *(at conferences etc)* official language

voertuig [vurtœyχ] *het (~en)* vehicle

voet [vut] *de (~en)* **1** foot: *op blote ~en* barefoot; *iem op staande ~ ontslaan* dismiss s.o. on the spot; *iem op vrije ~en stellen* set s.o. free; *(Belg) met iemands ~en spelen* make a fool of s.o.; *(Belg) ergens zijn ~en aan vegen* drag one's feet; *de ~en vegen* wipe one's feet; *dat heeft heel wat ~en in de aarde* that'll take some doing; *onder de ~ gelopen worden* be overrun; *iem op de ~ volgen* follow in s.o.'s footsteps; *de gebeurtenissen* (or: *de ontwikkelingen*) *op de ~ volgen* keep a close track of events (or: developments); *te ~ gaan* walk, go on foot; *zich uit de ~en maken* take to one's heels; *iem onder de ~en lopen* hamper s.o., get in s.o.'s way (or: under s.o.'s feet); *geen ~ aan de grond krijgen* have no success; *~ bij stuk houden* stick to one's guns; **2** foot, base: *de ~*

van een glas the stem (*or:* base) of a glass; **3** footing;
terms: *zij staan op goede* (or: *vertrouwelijke*) *~ met
elkaar* they are on good (*or:* familiar) terms (with
each other); *op ~ van oorlog leven* be on a war footing

voetafdruk [vụtɑvdrɪk] *de (~ken)* footprint

voetbad [vụdbɑt] *het (~en)* footbath

¹voetbal [vụdbɑl] *de (~len) (ball)* football

²voetbal [vụdbɑl] *het (sport)* football: *Amerikaans
~* American football; *betaald ~* professional football

voetbalbond [vụdbɑlbɔnt] *de* football association

voetbalclub [vụdbɑlklʏp] *de* football club

voetbalcompetitie [vụdbɑlkɔmpəti(t)si] *de (~s)*
football competition

voetbalelftal [vụdbɑlɛlftɑl] *het* football team: *het
~ van Ajax* the Ajax team

voetbalfan [vụdbɑlfɛn] *de (~s)* football fan

voetbalknie [vụdbɑlkni] *de (~ën)* cartilage trouble

voetballen [vụdbɑlə(n)] *vb* play football

voetballer [vụdbɑlər] *de (~s)* football player

voetbalpasje [vụdbɑlpɑʃə] *het (~s)* football identity card

voetbalschoen [vụdbɑlsχun] *de* football boot

voetbalsupporter [vụdbɑlsʏpɔrtər] *de (~s)* football supporter

voetbaluitslagen [vụdbɑlœytslɑɣə(n)] *de* football
results

voetbalvandaal [vụdbɑlvɑndɑl] *de (-vandalen)*
football hooligan

voetbalvandalisme [vụdbɑlvɑndɑlɪsmə] *het* football hooliganism

voetbalveld [vụdbɑlvɛlt] *het* football pitch

voetbalwedstrijd [vụdbɑlwɛtstrɛit] *de* football
match

voeteneind [vụtə(n)ɛint] *het (~en)* foot

voetfout [vụtfɑut] *de (~en)* foot-fault

voetganger [vụtχɑŋər] *de (~s)* pedestrian

voetgangersbrug [vụtχɑŋərzbrʏχ] *de (~gen)*
footbridge, pedestrian bridge

voetgangersgebied [vụtχɑŋərsχəbit] *het (~en)*
pedestrian precinct (*or:* area)

voetgangersoversteekplaats [vụtχɑŋərs-
ovərstekplats] *de (~en)* pedestrian crossing, zebra
crossing

voetje [vụcə] *het (~s)* (little, small) foot: *~ voor ~*
inch by inch

voetlicht [vụtlɪχt] *het (~en)* footlights: *iets voor het
~ brengen* bring sth out into the open

voetnoot [vụtnot] *de (-noten)* **1** footnote; **2** note in
the margin, critical remark (*or:* comment)

voetpad [vụtpɑt] *het (~en)* footpath

voetreis [vụtrɛis] *de (-reizen)* walking-trip; walk-
ing-tour, hike

voetspoor [vụtspor] *het (-sporen)* footprint, (*pl also)* track, trail

voetstap [vụtstɑp] *de (~pen)* (foot)step

voetstuk [vụtstʏk] *het (~ken)* base, pedestal: *iem
op een ~ plaatsen* put (*or:* place) s.o. on a pedestal

voettocht [vụtɔχt] *de (~en)* walking tour, hiking
tour

voetvolk [vụtfɔlk] *het* foot soldiers, infantry

voetzoeker [vụtsukər] *de (~s)* jumping jack,
(roughly) firecracker

voetzool [vụtsol] *de (-zolen)* sole (of the, one's
foot)

vogel [voɣəl] *de (~s)* **1** bird: *(Belg) een ~ voor de kat
zijn* be irretrievably lost; *de ~ is gevlogen* the bird
has flown; **2** customer, character: *het is een rare ~*
he's an odd character; *Joe is een vroege ~* Joe's an
early bird

vogelhandelaar [voɣəlhɑndəlar] *de (~s, -handela-
ren)* bird-seller; bird-dealer

vogelhuis [voɣəlhœys] *het (-huizen)* aviary; nest-
ing box

vogelkooi [voɣəlkoj] *de (~en)* birdcage

vogelnest [voɣəlnɛst] *het (~en)* bird's nest: *~en
uithalen* go (bird-)nesting

vogelpik [voɣəlpɪk] *de (Belg)* darts

vogelpoep [voɣəlpup] *de* bird droppings

vogelverschrikker [voɣəlvərsχrɪkər] *de (~s)*
scarecrow

vogelvlucht [voɣəlvlʏχt] *de (~en)* bird's-eye view:
iets in ~ behandelen sketch sth briefly; *iets in ~ tekenen* draw a bird's-eye view of sth

vogelvrij [voɣəlvrɛi] *adj* outlawed

vol [vɔl] *adj, adv* **1** full (of), filled (with): *~ nieuwe
ideeën* full of new ideas; *een huis ~ mensen* a house
full of people; *met ~le mond praten* talk with one's
mouth full; *iets ~ maken (gieten, stoppen)* fill sth
up; *helemaal ~* full up, packed; *~ van iets zijn* be
full of sth; *een ~ gezicht* a full (*or:* chubby) face; *zij
is een ~le nicht van me* she's my first cousin; **2** full
(of), covered (with, in): *de tafel ligt ~ boeken* the table is covered with books; *de kranten staan er ~ van*
the papers are full of it; **3** complete, whole: *een ~le
dagtaak* a full day's work, *(fig also)* a full-time job;
het kostte hem acht ~le maanden it took him a good
(*or:* all of) eight months; *in het ~ste vertrouwen* in
complete confidence; *een ~le week de tijd hebben*
have a full (*or:* whole) week; *iem voor ~ aanzien*
take s.o. seriously

volautomatisch [vɔlautomɑtis] *adj* fully automatic

¹volbloed [vɔlblut] *de (~s, ~en)* thoroughbred: *Arabische ~* Arab (thoroughbred)

²volbloed [vɔlblut] *adj* **1** full-blood(ed); pedigree: *~
rundvee* pedigree cattle; **2** thoroughbred

voldaan [vɔldan] *adj* **1** satisfied, content(ed): *een ~
gevoel* a sense of satisfaction; *~ zijn over iets* be satisfied (*or:* content) with sth; **2** paid: *voor ~ tekenen*
receipt, sign for receipt

¹voldoen [vɔldun] *vb* pay, settle: *een rekening* (or:
de kosten) *~* pay a bill (*or:* the costs)

²voldoen [vɔldun] *vb* (with *aan*) satisfy; meet, carry
out; comply with: *aan de behoeften van de markt ~*
meet the needs of the market; *niet ~ aan* fall short
of

¹voldoende [vɔldundə] *adj* sufficient, satisfactory:

één blik op hem is ~ *om* ... one look at him is enough to ...; *jouw examen was net* ~ you only just scraped through your exam; *het is niet* ~ *om van te leven* it is not enough to live on; *ruimschoots* ~ ample, more than enough

²voldoende [vɔldundə] *adv* sufficiently, enough: *heb je je* ~ *voorbereid?* have you done enough preparation?

³voldoende [vɔldundə] *de (~s, ~n)* pass (mark), a bare pass: *een* ~ *halen voor wiskunde* pass (one's) maths

voldoening [vɔldunɪŋ] *de* satisfaction

voldongen [vɔldɔŋə(n)] *adj* ‖ *voor een* ~ *feit geplaatst worden* be presented with a fait accompli

voldragen [vɔldraɣə(n)] *adj* full-term

volgeboekt [vɔlɣəbukt] *adj* fully booked, booked up

volgeling [vɔlɣəlɪŋ] *de (~en)* follower, *(rel also)* disciple

¹volgen [vɔlɣə(n)] *vb* **1** follow: *een spoor* (or: *de weg*) ~ follow a trail (*or:* the road); **2** follow, attend; **4** follow, pursue: *zijn hart* ~ follow the dictates of one's heart

²volgen [vɔlɣə(n)] *vb* **1** follow; be next: *nadere instructies* ~ further instructions will follow; *hier* ~ *de namen van de winnaars* the names of the winners are as follows; *op elkaar* ~ follow one another; *als volgt* as follows; **2** follow (on): *daaruit volgt dat* ... it follows that ...

volgend [vɔlɣənt] *adj* following, next: *de* ~*e keer* next time (round); *wie is de* ~*e?* who's next?; *het gaat om het* ~*e* the problem is (*or:* the facts are) as follows

volgens [vɔlɣəns] *prep* according to; in accordance with: ~ *mijn horloge is het drie uur* it's three o'clock by my watch; ~ *mij* ... I think ..., in my opinion ...

volgooien [vɔlɣojə(n)] *vb* fill (up): *de tank* ~ fill (up) the tank, fill her up

volgorde [vɔlɣɔrdə] *de (~n, ~s)* order; sequence: *in de juiste* ~ *leggen* put in the right order; *in willekeurige* ~ at random; *niet op* ~ out of order, not in order

¹volhouden [vɔlhaudə(n)] *vb* **1** carry on, keep up: *dit tempo is niet vol te houden* we can't keep up this pace; **2** maintain, insist: *zijn onschuld* ~ insist on one's innocence; *iets hardnekkig* ~ stubbornly maintain sth

²volhouden [vɔlhaudə(n)] *vb* persevere, keep on: *we zijn ermee begonnen, nu moeten we* ~ now we've started we must see it through; ~*!* keep it up!, keep going!

volhouder [vɔlhaudər] *de (~s)* stayer

volière [voljɛːrə] *de (~s)* aviary; birdhouse

volk [vɔlk] *het (~en, ~eren)* **1** people, nation, race; **3** people, populace, folk: *een man uit het* ~ a working(-class) man; *het gewone* ~ the common people; **4** people: *het circus trekt altijd veel* ~ the circus always draws a crowd

¹volkomen [vɔlkomə(n)] *adv* completely: *dat is* ~

juist that's perfectly true

²volkomen [vɔlkomə(n)] *adj* complete, total

volkorenbrood [vɔlkorə(n)brot] *het* wholemeal bread, *(Am)* whole-wheat bread

volksbuurt [vɔlksbyrt] *de (~en)* working-class area (*or:* district)

volksdans [vɔlksdans] *de (~en)* folk dance

volksdansen [vɔlksdansə(n)] *het* folk dancing

volksgeloof [vɔlksχəlof] *het* popular belief (*or:* superstition)

volksgezondheid [vɔlksχəzɔntheit] *de* public health, national health

volksheld [vɔlkshɛlt] *de (~en)* popular hero, national hero

volkslied [vɔlkslit] *het (~eren)* **1** national anthem; **2** folk song

volksmond [vɔlksmɔnt] *de* ‖ *in de* ~ in popular speech (*or:* parlance); *in de* ~ *heet dit* this is popularly called

volkspartij [vɔlkspartɛi] *de (~en)* people's party

volksrepubliek [vɔlksrepyblik] *de (~en)* people's republic: *de volksrepubliek China* the People's Republic of China

volksstam [vɔlkstam] *de (~men)* crowd, horde

volkstaal [vɔlkstal] *de (-talen)* vernacular, everyday language

volkstelling [vɔlkstɛlɪŋ] *de (~en)* census: *er werd een* ~ *gehouden* a census was taken

volkstuin [vɔlkstœyn] *de (~en)* allotment (garden)

volksuniversiteit [vɔlksyniversitɛit] *de (~en)* (*roughly*) adult education centre

volksvermaak [vɔlksfərmak] *het (-vermaken)* popular amusement (*or:* entertainment)

volksvertegenwoordiger [vɔlksfərteɣə(n)wordəɣər] *de (~s)* representative (of the people), member of parliament, M.P., *(Am)* Congressman

volksvertegenwoordiging [vɔlksfərteɣə(n)wordəɣɪŋ] *de (~en)* house (*or:* chamber) of representatives, parliament

volksverzekering [vɔlksfərzekərɪŋ] *de (~en)* national insurance, social insurance

volksvijand [vɔlksfɛiant] *de (~en)* public enemy, enemy of the people: *roken is* ~ *nummer één* smoking is public enemy number one

volkswoede [vɔlkswudə] *de* popular fury (*or:* anger)

volledig [vɔledəχ] *adj, adv* **1** full, complete: ~*e betaling* payment in full; *het schip is* ~ *uitgebrand* the ship was completely burnt out; *ik lees u de titel* ~ *voor* I'll read you the title in full; **2** full, full-time: ~*e (dienst)betrekking* full-time job

volledigheid [vɔledəχheit] *de* completeness

volledigheidshalve [vɔledəχheitshalvə] *adv* for the sake of completeness

volleerd [vɔlert] *adj* fully-qualified

vollemaan [vɔləman] *de* full moon: *het is* ~ there is a full moon; *bij* ~ when the moon is full, at full moon

¹volleybal [vɔlibɑl] *de (~len) (ball)* volleyball

²volleybal [vɔlibɑl] *het (sport)* volleyball

volleyballen [vɔlibɑlə(n)] *vb* play volleyball

vollopen [vɔlopə(n)] *vb* fill up, be filled: *de zaal begon vol te lopen* the hall was getting crowded; *het bad laten ~* run the bath

¹volmaakt [vɔlmɑkt] *adj* perfect, consummate

²volmaakt [vɔlmɑkt] *adv* perfectly: *ik ben ~ gezond* I am in perfect health

volmacht [vɔlmɑχt] *de (~en)* **1** power (of attorney), mandate, authority; **2** warrant, authorization

volmondig [vɔlmɔndəχ] *adj, adv* wholehearted, frank: *~ iets bekennen* (or: *toegeven*) confess (or: admit) sth frankly

volop [vɔlɔp] *adv* in abundance, plenty, a lot of: *~ ruimte* ample room; *het is ~ zomer* it is the height of summer; *er was ~ te eten* there was food in abundance

volpension [vɔlpɛnʃɔn] *het* full board

volproppen [vɔlprɔpə(n)] *vb* cram, stuff: *volgepropte trams* overcrowded (or: jam-packed) trams; *zich ~* stuff oneself

volslagen [vɔlslaɣə(n)] *adj, adv* complete, utter: *een ~ onbekende* a total stranger; *~ belachelijk* utterly ridiculous

volslank [vɔlslɑŋk] *adj* plump, well-rounded

volstoppen [vɔlstɔpə(n)] *vb* stuff (full), fill to the brim (or: top)

volstrekt [vɔlstrɛkt] *adj, adv* total, complete: *ik ben het ~ niet met hem eens* I disagree entirely with him

volt [vɔlt] *de (~s)* volt

voltage [vɔltaʒə] *het, de (~s)* voltage

voltallig [vɔltɑləχ] *adj* complete, full, entire: *het ~e bestuur* the entire committee; *de ~e vergadering* the plenary assembly (or: meeting)

voltijds [vɔltɛits] *adj* full-time

voorn [vorn] *de (~s)* roach

voltmeter [vɔltmetər] *de (~s)* voltmeter

voltooid [vɔltojt] *adj* complete, finished: *een ~ deelwoord* a past (or: perfect) participle; *de ~ tegenwoordige* (or: *verleden*) *tijd* the perfect (or: pluperfect)

voltooien [vɔltojə(n)] *vb* complete, finish

voltooiing [vɔltojɪŋ] *de (~en)* completion

voltreffer [vɔltrɛfər] *de (~s)* direct hit

voltrekken [vɔltrɛkə(n)] *vb* execute; celebrate, perform

voltrekking [vɔltrɛkɪŋ] *de (~en)* celebration, performing

voluit [vɔlœyt] *adv* in full

volume [volymə] *het (~n, ~s)* volume, loudness

volumeknop [volyməknɔp] *de (~pen)* volume control (or: knob)

volvet [vɔlvɛt] *adj* full-cream

volwaardig [vɔlwardəχ] *adj* full, able(-bodied): *een ~ lid* a full member

¹volwassen [vɔlwɑsə(n)] *adj* adult, grown-up, mature, full-grown, ripe: *~ gedrag* mature (or: adult) behaviour; *ik ben een ~ vrouw!* I'm a grown wom-

an!; *toen zij ~ werd* on reaching womanhood; *~ worden* grow to maturity, grow up

²volwassen [vɔlwɑsə(n)] *adv* in an adult (or: a mature) way: *zich ~ gedragen* behave like an adult

volwassene [vɔlwɑsənə] *de (~n)* adult, grown-up

volwassenenonderwijs [vɔlwɑsənə(n)ɔndərwɛis] *het* adult education

volwassenheid [vɔlwɑsənhɛit] *de* adulthood, maturity

volzet [vɔlzɛt] *adj (Belg)* no vacancy

vondeling [vɔndəlɪŋ] *de (~en)* abandoned child: *een kind te ~ leggen* abandon a child

vondst [vɔnst] *de (~en)* invention, discovery: *een ~ doen* make a (real) find; *een gelukkige ~* a lucky strike

vonk [vɔŋk] *de (~en)* spark || *de ~ sloeg over* the audience caught on

vonken [vɔŋkə(n)] *vb* spark(le), shoot sparks

vonnis [vɔnɪs] *het (~sen)* judgement, sentence, verdict: *een ~ vellen (uitspreken) over* pass (or: pronounce, give) judgement on

vonnissen [vɔnɪsə(n)] *vb* sentence, convict; pass judgement (or: sentence) (on)

voodoo [vudu] *de* voodoo

voogd [voχt] *de (~en)* guardian: *toeziend ~* co-guardian, joint guardian; *~ zijn over iem* be s.o.'s guardian

voogdij [voχdɛi] *de (~en)* guardianship: *onder ~ staan* (or: *plaatsen*) be (or: place) under guardianship

voogdijraad [voχdɛirat] *de (-raden)* guardianship board

voogdijschap [voχdɛisχɑp] *het (~pen)* guardianship

¹voor [vor] *de (~s)* **1** furrow; **2** wrinkle, furrow

²voor [vor] *prep* **1** for: *zij is een goede moeder ~ haar kinderen* she is a good mother to her children; *dat is net iets ~ hem: a)* that is just the thing for him; *b)* that is just like him; *dat is niets ~ mij* that is not my kind of thing (or: my cup of tea); **2** before, in front of: *de dagen die ~ ons liggen* the days (that lie) ahead of us; **3** before, for; **4** before, ahead of: *~ zondag* before Sunday; *tien ~ zeven* ten to seven; **5** for, instead of: *ik zal ~ mijn zoon betalen* I'll pay for my son; **6** for, in favour of: *ik ben ~ FC Utrecht* I'm a supporter of FC Utrecht; *wat zijn het ~ mensen?* what sort of people are they?

³voor [vor] *adv* **1** in (the) front: *een kind met een slab ~* a child wearing a bib; *de auto staat ~* the car is at the door; *hij is ~ in de dertig* he is in his early thirties; *~ in het boek* near the beginning of the book; **2** ahead; in the lead: *vier punten ~* four points ahead; *zij zijn ons ~ geweest* they got (t)here before (or: ahead of) us; **3** for, in favour: *ik ben er niet ~* I'm not in favour of that

⁴voor [vor] *conj* before: *~ hij vertrok, was ik al weg* I was already gone before he left

⁵voor [vor] *het (~s)* pro; advantage: *het ~ en tegen van een voorstel* the pros and cons of a proposition

419

vooraan [vorạn] *adv* in (the) front: ~ *lopen* walk at the front; *iets ~ zetten* put sth (up) in front

vooraanstaand [vorạnstant] *adj* prominent, leading

vooraanzicht [vọranzɪχt] *het* front view

vooraf [vorạf] *adv* beforehand, in advance: *een verklaring ~* an explanation in advance; *je moet ~ goed bedenken wat je gaat doen* you need to think ahead about what you're going to do

voorafgaan [vorạfχan] *vb* precede, go before, go in front (of): *de weken ~de aan het feest* the weeks preceding the celebration

voorafgaand [vorạfχant] *adj* preceding, foregoing: *~e toestemming* prior permission

vooral [vorạl] *adv* especially, particularly: *dat moet je ~ doen* do that (*or:* go ahead) by all means; *ga ~ vroeg naar bed* be sure to go to bed early; *maak haar ~ niet wakker* don't wake her up whatever you do; *vergeet het ~ niet* whatever you do, don't forget it; *~ omdat* especially because

voorarrest [vọrarɛst] *het* remand, custody, detention: *in ~ zitten* be on remand, be in custody; *in ~ gehouden worden* be taken into custody

vooravond [vọravɔnt] *de (~en)* eve

voorbaat [vọrbat] || *bij ~ dank* thank (*or:* thanking) you in advance; *bij ~ kansloos zijn* not stand a chance from the very start

voorbakken [vọrbɑkə(n)] *vb* pre-fry: *voorgebakken friet* pre-fried chips (*or:* French fries)

voorbank [vọrbɑŋk] *de (~en)* front seats

voorbarig [vorbạrəχ] *adj, adv* premature: *~ spreken* (*or:* *antwoorden*) speak (*or:* answer) too soon

voorbeeld [vọrbelt] *het (~en)* example, model; instance: *een afschrikwekkend ~* a warning; *een ~ stellen* make an example of s.o.; *iemands ~ volgen* follow s.o.'s lead (*or:* example); *tot ~ dienen* serve as an example (*or:* a model) for

voorbeeldig [vorbẹldəχ] *adj, adv* exemplary, model: *een ~ gedrag* exemplary conduct

voorbehoedmiddel [vọrbəhutmɪdəl] *het (~en)* contraceptive

voorbehoud [vọrbəhaut] *het* restriction, reservation; condition: *iets onder ~ beloven* make a conditional promise; *zonder ~* without reservations

voorbehouden [vọrbəhaudə(n)] *het* reserve

voorbereiden [vọrbərɛidə(n)] *vb* prepare, get ready: *zich ~ op een examen* prepare for an exam; *op alles voorbereid zijn* be ready for anything

voorbereidend [vọrbərɛidənt] *adj* preparatory: *~ wetenschappelijk onderwijs* pre-university education; *~e werkzaamheden* groundwork

voorbereiding [vọrbərɛidɪŋ] *de (~en)* preparation: *~en treffen* make preparations

voorbespeeld [vọrbəspelt] *adj* pre-recorded

voorbespreking [vọrbəsprekɪŋ] *de (~en)* preliminary talk

voorbestemmen [vọrbəstɛmə(n)] *vb* predestine, predetermine: *voorbestemd zijn om te ... predestined (or: fated) to ...*

¹voorbij [vorbɛi] *prep* beyond, past: *we zijn al ~ Amsterdam* we've already passed Amsterdam; *hij ging ~ het huis* he went past the house

²voorbij [vorbɛi] *adj* past, (*after vb*) over: *die tijd is ~* those days are gone; *~e tijden* bygone times

³voorbij [vorbɛi] *adv* **1** past, by: *wacht tot de trein ~ is* wait until the train has passed; **2** beyond, past: *hij is die leeftijd al lang ~* he is way past that age; *je bent er al ~* you have already passed it

voorbijgaan [vorbɛiɣan] *vb* pass by, go by: *de jaren gingen voorbij* the years passed by; *een kans voorbij laten gaan* pass up a chance; *er gaat praktisch geen week voorbij of ...* hardly a week goes by when (*or:* that) ...

voorbijgaand [vorbɛiɣant] *adj* transitory, passing: *van ~e aard* of a temporary nature

voorbijganger [vorbɛiɣɑŋər] *de (~s)* passer-by

voorbijkomen [vorbɛikomə(n)] *vb* come past, come by, pass (by)

voorbijrijden [vorbɛirɛidə(n)] *vb* drive past, ride past

voorbijschieten [vorbɛisχitə(n)] *vb* whizz by || *zijn doel ~* overshoot the mark

voorbijtrekken [vorbɛitrɛkə(n)] *vb* pass: *hij zag zijn leven aan zijn oog ~* he saw his life pass before his eyes

voorbijvliegen [vorbɛivliɣə(n)] *vb* fly (by): *de weken vlogen voorbij* the weeks just flew (by)

voorbode [vọrbodə] *de (~s)* forerunner, herald; omen: *de zwaluwen zijn de ~n van de lente* swallows are the heralds of spring

voordat [vordạt] *conj* **1** before, until: *alles was gemakkelijker ~ hij kwam* things were easier before he came; *~ ik je brief kreeg, wist ik er niets van* I knew nothing about it until I got your letter; **2** before (that)

voordeel [vọrdel] *het (-delen)* **1** advantage, benefit: *Agassi staat op ~* advantage Agassi; *zijn ~ met iets doen* take advantage of sth; *~ hebben bij profit (or:* benefit) from; *hij is in zijn ~ veranderd* he has changed for the better; *3-0 in het ~ van Nederland* 3-0 for the Dutch side (*or:* team); *iem het ~ van de twijfel gunnen* give s.o. the benefit of the doubt; **2** advantage, plus point: *de voor- en nadelen* the advantages and disadvantages; *een ~ behalen* gain an advantage

voordeelregel [vọrdelreɣəl] *de* advantage rule

voordek [vọrdɛk] *het* foredeck

voordelig [vordẹləχ] *adj, adv* **1** profitable, lucrative: *~ kopen* get a bargain; **2** economical, inexpensive: *~er zijn* be cheaper; *~ in het gebruik* be economical in use, go a long way

voordeur [vọrdør] *de (~en)* front door

¹voordoen [vọrdun] *vb* show, demonstrate

²voordoen [vọrdun] *ref vb* act, appear, pose: *zich flink voordoen* put on a bold front; *zich ~ als politieagent* pose as a policeman

voordracht [vọrdraχt] *de (~en)* lecture: *een ~ houden over* read a paper on, give a lecture on

voordragen [vordraɣə(n)] *vb* **1** recite; **2** nominate, recommend

voordringen [vordrɪŋə(n)] *vb* push forward (*or:* past, ahead), jump the queue

voorfilm [vorfɪlm] *de (~s)* short

voorgaan [vorɣan] *vb* **1** go ahead (*or:* before), lead (the way): *dames gaan voor* ladies first; *iemand laten ~* let s.o. go first; *gaat u voor!* after you!, lead the way; **2** take precedence, come first: *het belangrijkste moet ~* the most important has to come first

voorgaand [vorɣant] *adj* preceding, former, last, previous: *op de ~e bladzijde* on the preceding page

voorganger [vorɣaŋər] *de (~s)* predecessor

voorgekookt [vorɣəkokt] *adj* pre-cooked, parboiled: *~e aardappelen* pre-cooked potatoes; *~e rijst* parboiled rice

voorgeleiden [vorɣəlɛidə(n)] *vb* bring in

voorgenomen [vorɣənomə(n)] *adj* intended, proposed: *de ~ maatregelen* the proposed measures

voorgerecht [vorɣərɛχt] *het (~en)* first course, starter

voorgeschiedenis [vorɣəsχidənɪs] *de* previous history; (*of pers*) ancestry, past history

voorgeschreven [vorɣəsχrevə(n)] *adj* prescribed, required

voorgevel [vorɣevəl] *de (~s)* face

voorgevoel [vorɣəvul] *het (~ens)* premonition, foreboding: *ergens een ~ van hebben* have a premonition about sth

voorgoed [vorɣut] *adv* for good, once and for all: *dat is nu ~ voorbij* that is over and done with now

voorgrond [vorɣront] *de (~en)* foreground: *op de ~ treden, zich op de ~ plaatsen* come into prominence; *iets op de ~ plaatsen* place sth in the forefront; *hij dringt zich altijd op de ~* he always pushes himself forward

voorhamer [vorhamər] *de (~s)* sledge(hammer)

voorhebben [vorhɛbə(n)] *vb* **1** have on, wear: *een schort ~* have on (*or:* wear) an apron; **2** have in front of: *de verkeerde ~* have got the wrong one (in mind)

voorheen [vorhen] *adv* formerly, in the past

voorhoede [vorhudə] *de (~s)* forward line, forwards

voorhoedespeler [vorhudəspelər] *de (~s)* forward

voorhoofd [vorhoft] *het (~en)* forehead

voorhoofdsholteontsteking [vorhoftshɔltəontstekɪŋ] *de (~en)* sinusitis

voorhouden [vorhaudə(n)] *vb* represent, confront: *iem zijn slechte gedrag ~* confront s.o. with his bad conduct

voorhuid [vorhœyt] *de (~en)* foreskin

voorin [vorɪn] *adv* in (the) front; at the beginning

voorjaar [vorjar] *het (-jaren)* spring, springtime

voorjaarsmoeheid [vorjarsmuhɛit] *de* springtime fatigue

voorkamer [vorkamər] *de (~s)* front room

voorkant [vorkant] *de (~en)* front: *de ~ van een auto* the front of a car

voorkauwen [vorkauwə(n)] *vb* repeat over and over

voorkennis [vorkɛnɪs] *de* foreknowledge, inside knowledge: *~ hebben van* have prior knowledge of

voorkeur [vorkør] *de* preference: *mijn ~ gaat uit naar* I (would) prefer; *de ~ geven aan* give preference to; *bij ~* preferably

voorkeurzender [vorkørzɛndər] *de (~s)* pre-set station

¹voorkomen [vorkomə(n)] *het* **1** appearance, bearing: *nu krijgt de zaak een geheel ander ~* things are now looking a lot different; **2** occurrence, incidence: *het regelmatig ~ van ongeregeldheden* the recurrence of disturbances

²voorkomen [vorkomə(n)] *vb* **1** occur, happen; **2** occur, be found: *die planten komen overal voor* those plants grow everywhere; **3** appear: *hij moet ~* he has to appear in court; **4** seem, appear: *dat komt mij bekend voor* that rings a bell, that sounds familiar

³voorkomen [vorkomə(n)] *vb* prevent: *om misverstanden te ~* to prevent (any) misunderstandings; *we moeten ~ dat hij hier weggaat* we must prevent him from leaving; *~ is beter dan genezen* prevention is better than cure

voorkomend [vorkomənt] *adj* occurring: *dagelijks ~e zaken* everyday events, recurrent matters; *een veel ~ probleem* a common problem; *zelden ~* unusual, rare

voorkoming [vorkomɪŋ] *de* prevention: *ter ~ van ongelukken* to prevent accidents

voorland [vorlant] *het (~en)* future: *dat is ook haar ~* that's also in store for her

voorlaten [vorlatə(n)] *vb* allow to go first, give precedence to

voorleggen [vorlɛɣə(n)] *vb* present: *iem een plan ~* present s.o. with a plan; *een zaak aan de rechter ~* bring a case before the court

voorletter [vorlɛtər] *de (~s)* initial (letter): *wat zijn uw ~s?* what are your initials?

voorlezen [vorlezə(n)] *vb* read aloud, read out loud: *iem een brief* (*or:* *de krant*) *~* read aloud a letter (*or:* the newspaper) to s.o.; *kinderen houden van ~* children like to be read to; *~ uit een boek* read aloud from a book

voorlichten [vorlɪχtə(n)] *vb* **1** inform: *zich goed laten ~* seek good advice; *we zijn verkeerd voorgelicht* we were misinformed; **2** tell (s.o.) the facts of life

voorlichter [vorlɪχtər] *de (~s)* press officer, information officer

voorlichting [vorlɪχtɪŋ] *de (~en)* information: *de afdeling ~* public relations department; *seksuele ~* sex education; *goede ~ geven* give good advice

voorlichtingsavond [vorlɪχtɪŋsavɔnt] *de (~en)* open information evening

voorlichtingsdienst [vorlɪχtɪŋzdinst] *de (~en)* (public) information service

voorlichtingsfilm [vorlɪχtɪŋsfɪlm] *de (~s)* information film, publicity film

voorliefde [vorlivdə] *de* predilection, preference,

fondness

voorlopen [vorlopə(n)] *vb* **1** walk (*or:* go) in front; **2** be fast: *de klok loopt vijf minuten voor* the clock is five minutes fast

voorloper [vorlopər] *de* (~*s*) precursor, forerunner

¹voorlopig [vorlopəχ] *adj* temporary, provisional: *een ~e aanstelling* a temporary appointment; ~ *verslag* interim report

²voorlopig [vorlopəχ] *adv* for the time being: *hij zal het ~ accepteren* he will accept it provisionally; ~ *niet* not for the time being; ~ *voor een maand* for a month to begin with

voormalig [vormaləχ] *adj* former

voorman [vormɑn] *de* (~*nen*) foreman

voormiddag [vormɪdɑχ] *de* (~*en*) **1** morning; **2** early afternoon

¹voornaam [vornam] *de* first name: *iem bij zijn ~ noemen* call s.o. by his first name

²voornaam [vornam] *adj* **1** distinguished, prominent: *een ~ voorkomen* a dignified (*or:* distinguished) appearance; **2** main, important: *de ~ste dagbladen* the leading dailies; *de ~ste feiten* the main facts

voornaamwoord [vornamwort] *het* (~*en*) pronoun: *aanwijzend ~* demonstrative pronoun; *bezittelijk ~* possessive pronoun; *betrekkelijk ~* relative pronoun; *persoonlijk ~* personal pronoun

voornamelijk [vornamələk] *adv* mainly, chiefly

¹voornemen [vornemə(n)] *het* (~*s*) intention, resolution: *zij is vol goede ~s* she is full of good intentions; *het vaste ~ iets te bereiken* the determination to achieve sth

²voornemen [vornemə(n)] *ref vb* resolve: *hij had het zich heilig voorgenomen* he had firmly resolved to do so; *zij bereikte wat ze zich voorgenomen had* she achieved what she had set out (*or:* planned) to do

vooronderzoek [vorɔndərzuk] *het* (~*en*) preliminary investigation: *gerechtelijk ~* hearing

vooroordeel [vorordel] *het* (*-oordelen*) prejudice: *een ~ hebben over* be prejudiced against; *zonder vooroordelen* unbiased, unprejudiced

vooroorlogs [vororlɔχs] *adj* pre-war

voorop [vorɔp] *adv* in front, in the lead, first: *het nummer staat ~ het bankbiljet* the number is on the front of the banknote; ~ *staat, dat …* the main thing is that …

vooropleiding [vorɔplɛidɪŋ] *de* (~*en*) (preliminary, preparatory) training

vooroplopen [vorɔplopə(n)] *vb* **1** walk (*or:* run) in front; **2** lead (the way): ~ *in de modewereld* be a trendsetter in the fashion world

vooropstellen [vorɔpstɛlə(n)] *vb* **1** assume: *laten we dit ~:* … let's get one thing straight right away: …; *ik stel voorop dat hij altijd eerlijk is geweest* to begin with, I maintain that he has always been honest; **2** put first (and foremost): *de volksgezondheid ~* put public health first (and foremost)

voorouders [vorɑudərs] *de* ancestors, forefathers

voorover [vorovər] *adv* headfirst, face down: *met het gezicht ~ liggen* lie face down(ward); ~ *tuimelen* tumble headfirst (*or:* forward)

voorpagina [vorpaɣina] *de* (~*'s*) front page: *de ~'s halen* make the front pages

voorpaginanieuws [vorpaɣinaniws] *het* front-page news

voorpoot [vorpot] *de* (*-poten*) foreleg, forepaw

voorpret [vorprɛt] *de* pleasurable anticipation

voorproefje [vorprufjə] *het* (~*s*) (fore)taste

voorprogramma [vorproɣrama] *het* (~*'s*) curtain-raiser, supporting programme: *een concert van Doe Maar met Frans Bauer in het ~* a Doe Maar concert with Frans Bauer as supporting act

voorraad [vorat] *de* (*voorraden*) **1** stock, supply: *de ~ goud* the gold reserve(s); *de ~ opnemen* take stock; *zo lang de ~ strekt* as long as (*or:* while) supplies/stocks last; *niet meer in ~ zijn* not be in stock anymore; *uit ~ leverbaar* available from stock; **2** supplies, stock(s): ~ *inslaan voor de winter* lay in supplies for the winter; *we zijn door onze ~ heen* we have gone through our supplies

voorraadkast [voratkɑst] *de* (~*en*) store cupboard, (*Am*) supply closet

voorradig [voradəχ] *adj* in stock (*or:* store), on hand: *in alle kleuren ~* available in all colours

voorrang [vorɑŋ] *de* right of way, priority: ~ *hebben op* have (the) right of way over; *verkeer van rechts heeft ~* traffic from the right has (the) right of way; *geen ~ verlenen* fail to yield, fail to give (right of) way; ~ *verlenen aan verkeer van rechts* give way (*or:* yield) to the right; (*de*) ~ *hebben (boven)* have (*or:* take) priority (over); *met ~ behandelen* give preferential treatment

voorrangsweg [vorɑŋswɛχ] *de* (~*en*) major road

voorrecht [vorɛχt] *het* (~*en*) privilege: *ik had het ~ hem te verwelkomen* I had the honour (*or:* privilege) of welcoming him

voorrekenen [vorekənə(n)] *vb* figure out, work out

voorrijden [voreidə(n)] *vb* drive up to the front (*or:* entrance, door)

voorrijkosten [voreikɔstə(n)] *de* call-out charge

voorronde [vorɔndə] *de* (~*n*, ~*s*) qualifying round, preliminary round

voorruit [vorœyt] *de* (~*en*) windscreen, (*Am*) windshield

voorschieten [vorsχitə(n)] *vb* advance, lend: *ik zal het even ~* I'll lend you the money

voorschijn [vorsχεin] || *te ~ komen* appear, come out; *te ~ brengen* produce; *zijn zakdoek te ~ halen* take out one's handkerchief

voorschoot [vorsχot] *de* (*-schoten*) apron, pinafore

voorschot [vorsχɔt] *het* (~*ten*) advance, loan

voorschotelen [vorsχotələ(n)] *vb* dish up, serve up

voorschrift [vorsχrɪft] *het* (~*en*) **1** prescription, order: *op ~ van de dokter* on doctor's orders; **2** regulation, rule: *aan de ~en voldoen* satisfy (*or:* meet) the requirements; *volgens ~* as prescribed (*or:* directed)

voorschrijven [vorsχreivə(n)] *vb* prescribe: *rust ~* prescribe rest; *op de voorgeschreven tijd* at the appointed time

voorseizoen [vorseizun] *het (~en)* pre-season

voorselectie [vorseleksi] *de (~s)* pre-selection

voorsorteren [vorsortərə(n)] *vb* get in lane: *rechts ~* get in the right-hand lane

voorspel [vorspɛl] *het (~en)* **1** prelude; prologue: *het ~ van de oorlog* the prelude to the war; **3** foreplay

voorspelbaar [vorspɛlbar] *adj* predictable

voorspelbaarheid [vorspɛlbarhɛit] *de (-heden)* predictability

voorspelen [vorspelə(n)] *vb* play

voorspellen [vorspɛlə(n)] *vb* **1** predict, forecast: *iem een gouden toekomst ~* predict a rosy future for s.o.; *ik heb het u wel voorspeld* I told you so; **2** promise: *dat voorspelt niet veel goeds* that doesn't bode well

voorspelling [vorspɛlɪŋ] *de (~en)* **1** prophecy; **2** prediction: *de ~en voor morgen* the (weather) forecast for tomorrow

voorspoed [vorsput] *de* prosperity: *in voor- en tegenspoed* for better or for worse; *voor- en tegenspoed* ups and downs

voorspoedig [vorspudəχ] *adj, adv* successful, prosperous: *alles verliep ~* it all went off well

voorsprong [vorsproŋ] *de (~en)* (head) start, lead: *hij won met grote ~* he won by a large margin; *iem een ~ geven* give s.o. a head start; *een ~ hebben op iem* have the jump (*or:* lead) on s.o.

voorst [vorst] *adj* first, front: *op de ~e bank zitten* be (*or:* sit) in the front row

voorstaan [vorstan] *vb* stand (*or:* be) in front: *de auto staat voor* the car is (out) at the front

voorstad [vorstat] *de (-steden)* suburb

voorstander [vorstandər] *de (~s)* supporter, advocate: *ik ben er een groot ~ van* I'm all for it

voorsteken [vorstekə(n)] *vb* overtake, pass

voorstel [vorstɛl] *het (~len)* proposal, suggestion: *iem een ~ doen* make s.o. a proposal (*or:* proposition)

voorstelbaar [vorstɛlbar] *adj* imaginable, conceivable

¹voorstellen [vorstɛlə(n)] *vb* **1** introduce: *zich ~ aan* introduce oneself to; **2** suggest, propose; **3** represent, play; **4** represent, depict: *het schilderij stelt een huis voor* the painting depicts a house; *dat stelt niets voor* that doesn't amount to anything

²voorstellen [vorstɛlə(n)] *ref vb* imagine, conceive: *ik kan mij zijn gezicht niet meer ~* I can't recall his face; *dat kan ik me best ~* I can imagine (that); *stel je voor!* just imagine!

voorstelling [vorstɛlɪŋ] *de (~en)* **1** show(ing), performance: *doorlopende ~* non-stop (*or:* continuous) performance; **2** representation, depiction; **3** impression, idea: *dat is een verkeerde ~ van zaken* that is a misrepresentation; *zich een ~ van iets maken* picture sth, form an idea of sth

voorstellingsvermogen [vorstɛlɪŋsfərmoγə(n)] *het* (power(s) of) imagination

voorstemmen [vorstɛmə(n)] *vb* vote for

voorsteven [vorstevə(n)] *de (~s)* stem, prow

voorstopper [vorstopər] *de (~s)* centre back

voortaan [vortan] *adv* from now on

voortand [vortant] *de (~en)* front tooth

voortbestaan [vortbəstan] *het* continued existence (*or:* life), survival

¹voortbewegen [vortbəweγə(n)] *vb* drive, move on (*or:* forward): *het karretje werd door stroom voortbewogen* the buggy was driven by electricity

²voortbewegen [vortbəweγə(n)] *ref vb* move on (*or:* forward)

voortborduren [vortbordyrə(n)] *vb* embroider, elaborate: *op een thema ~* elaborate (*or:* embroider) on a theme

voortbrengen [vortbrɛŋə(n)] *vb* produce, create, bring forth: *kinderen ~* produce children

voortbrengsel [vortbrɛŋsəl] *het (~en)* product

voortduren [vortdyrə(n)] *vb* continue, go on, wear on

voortdurend [vortdyrənt] *adj, adv* constant, continual; continuous: *een ~e dreiging* a constant threat (*or:* menace); *haar naam duikt ~ op in de krant* her name keeps cropping up in the (news)papers

voorteken [vortekə(n)] *het (~s, ~en)* omen, sign

voortent [vortɛnt] *de (~en)* front bell (end), (front) extension; awning

voortgang [vortχaŋ] *de* progress

voortgezet [vortχəzɛt] *adj* continued, further: *~ onderwijs* secondary education

voortijdig [vortɛidəχ] *adj, adv* premature, untimely: *de les werd ~ afgebroken* the lesson was cut short; *~ klaar zijn* be finished ahead of time

voortkomen [vortkomə(n)] *vb* (with *uit*) stem (from), flow (from): *de daaruit ~de misstanden* the resulting (*or:* consequent) abuses

voortleven [vortlevə(n)] *vb* live on: *zij leeft voort in onze herinnering* she lives on in our memory

voortouw [vortau] *het ‖ het ~ nemen* take the lead

voortplanten [vortplantə(n)] *ref vb* **1** reproduce, multiply; **2** propagate, be transmitted: *geluid plant zich voort in golven* sound is transmitted (*or:* travels) in waves

voortplanting [vortplantɪŋ] *de* reproduction, multiplication, breeding: *geslachtelijke ~* sexual reproduction

voortplantingsorgaan [vortplantɪŋsorγan] *het (-organen)* reproductive organ

voortreffelijk [vortrɛfələk] *adj, adv* excellent, superb: *hij danst ~* he dances superbly (*or:* exquisitely)

voortrekken [vortrɛkə(n)] *vb* favour, give preference to: *de een boven de ander ~* favour one person above another

voortrekker [vortrɛkər] *de (~s)* **1** pioneer; **2** Venture Scout, *(Am)* Explorer

voortuin [vɔrtœyn] *de (~en)* front garden (*or Am:* yard)

voortvarend [vortfɑrənt] *adj, adv* energetic, dynamic

voortzetten [vɔrtsɛtə(n)] *vb* continue, carry on (*or:* forward): *de kennismaking ~* pursue the acquaintance; *iemands werk ~* carry on s.o.'s work

¹vooruit [vorœyt] *adv* **1** ahead, further: *hiermee kan ik weer een tijdje ~* this will keep me going for a while; **2** before(hand), in advance: *zijn tijd ~ zijn* be ahead of one's time; *ver ~* well in advance

²vooruit [vorœyt] *int* get going, let's go, come on, go on: *~! aan je werk* come on, time for work

vooruitbetalen [vorœydbətalə(n)] *vb* prepay, pay in advance

vooruitblik [vorœydblɪk] *de (~ken)* preview, look ahead: *een ~ op het volgende seizoen* a preview of (*or:* look ahead at) the coming season

vooruitdenken [vorœydɛŋkə(n)] *vb* think ahead

vooruitgaan [vorœytχan] *vb* progress, improve: *zijn gezondheid gaat vooruit* his health is improving; *er financieel op ~* be better off (financially), profit (financially)

vooruitgang [vorœytχɑŋ] *de (~en)* progress, improvement

vooruitkijken [vorœytkɛikə(n)] *vb* look ahead

vooruitkomen [vorœytkomə(n)] *vb* get on (*or:* ahead), get somewhere, make headway: *moeizaam ~ progress* with difficulty

vooruitlopen [vorœytlopə(n)] *vb* anticipate, be ahead (of): *~d op* in advance of; *op de gebeurtenissen ~* anticipate events

vooruitstrevend [vorœytstrɛvənt] *adj* progressive

vooruitzicht [vorœytsɪχt] *het (~en)* prospect, outlook: *goede ~en hebben* have good prospects

vooruitzien [vorœytsin] *vb* look ahead (*or:* forward): *regeren is ~* foresight is the essence of government

vooruitziend [vorœytsint] *adj* far-sighted, visionary

voorvader [vorvadər] *de (~en)* ancestor, forefather

voorval [vorval] *het (~len)* incident, event

voorvallen [vorvɑlə(n)] *vb* occur, happen

voorverkiezing [vorvərkizɪŋ] *de (~en)* preliminary election, primary (election)

voorverkoop [vorvərkop] *de* advance booking (*or:* sale(s)): *de kaarten in de ~ zijn goedkoper* the tickets are cheaper if you buy them in advance

voorverpakt [vorvərpɑkt] *adj* pre-packed

voorverwarmen [vorvərwɑrmə(n)] *vb* preheat

voorvoegsel [vorvuχsəl] *het (~s)* prefix

voorwaarde [vorwardə] *de (~n)* **1** condition, provision: *onder ~ dat ...* provided that ..., on condition that ...; *onder geen enkele ~* on no account, under no circumstances; *iets als ~ stellen* state (*or:* stipulate) sth as a condition; **2** (*com*) condition, (*pl also*) terms: *wat zijn uw ~n?* what are your terms?

voorwaardelijk [vorwardələk] *adj, adv* conditional, provisional: *~e invrijheidstelling* (release on)

parole; *hij is ~ overgegaan* he has been put in the next class (*or Am:* grade) on probation; *~ veroordelen* give a suspended sentence, put on probation

¹voorwaarts [vorwarts] *adj, adv* forward(s), onward(s): *een stap ~* a step forward(s)

²voorwaarts [vorwarts] *int* forward: *~ mars!* forward march!

voorwas [vorwɑs] *de* pre-wash

voorwasmiddel [vorwɑsmɪdəl] *het (~en)* pre-washer (and soaker)

voorwedstrijd [vorwɛtstrɛit] *de (~en)* preliminary competition (*or:* game)

voorwenden [vorwɛndə(n)] *vb* pretend, feign

voorwendsel [vorwɛntsəl] *het (~s)* pretext, pretence: *onder valse ~s* under false pretences; *onder ~ van* under the pretext of

voorwerk [vorwɛrk] *het (~en)* preliminary work

voorwerp [vorwɛrp] *het (~en)* object: *het lijdend ~* the direct object; *meewerkend ~* indirect object; *gevonden ~en* lost property

voorwetenschap [vorwetənsχɑp] *de (~pen)* foreknowledge, inside knowledge

voorwiel [vorwil] *het (~en)* front wheel

voorwielaandrijving [vorwilandrɛivɪŋ] *de* front-wheel drive

voorwoord [vorwort] *het (~en)* foreword, preface

voorzeggen [vorzɛɣə(n)] *vb* prompt: *het antwoord ~* whisper the answer; *niet ~!* no prompting!

voorzet [vorzɛt] *de (~ten)* cross, centre; ball into the area: *een goede ~ geven* cross the ball well, send in a good cross

voorzetsel [vorzɛtsəl] *het (~s)* preposition

voorzetten [vorzɛtə(n)] *vb* **1** put (*or:* place) in front (of); **2** put forward, set forward, put ahead; **3** cross; hit the ball into the area

voorzichtig [vorzɪχtəχ] *adj, adv* **1** careful, cautious: *~! breekbaar!* fragile! handle with care!; *iem het nieuws ~ vertellen* break the news gently to s.o.; *~ te werk gaan* proceed cautiously (*or:* with caution); **2** cautious, discreet: *~ naar iets informeren* make discreet inquiries (about sth)

voorzichtigheid [vorzɪχtəχɦɛit] *de* caution, care

¹voorzien [vorzin] *vb* **1** foresee, anticipate: *dat was te ~* that was to be expected; **2** (with *in*) provide (for), see to: *in een behoefte ~* fill a need; *in zijn onderhoud kunnen ~* be able to support oneself (*or:* to provide for oneself); **3** (with *van*) provide (with), equip (with): *het huis is ~ van centrale verwarming* the house has central heating

²voorzien [vorzin] *adj* provided: *wij zijn al ~* we have been taken care of (*or:* seen to); *het gebouw is ~ van videobewaking* the buildiing is equipped with CCTV; *de deur is ~ van een slot* the door is fitted with a lock

voorzienigheid [vorzinəχɦɛit] *de* providence: *Gods ~* divine providence

voorziening [vorzinɪŋ] *de (~en)* provision, service: *sociale ~en* social services; *sanitaire ~en* sanitary facilities; *~en treffen* make arrangements

voorzijde [vọrzɛidə] *de (~n)* front (side)

voorzitster [vọrzɪtstər] *de* chairwoman

voorzitten [vọrzɪtə(n)] *vb* chair

voorzitter [vọrzɪtər] *de (~s)* chairman: *mijnheer (or: mevrouw) de ~* Mr Chairman, Madam Chairman *(or:* Chairwoman); *~ zijn* chair a *(or:* the) meeting

voorzorg [vọrzɔrχ] *de (~en)* precaution: *uit ~ iets doen* do sth as a precaution(ary measure)

voorzorgsmaatregel [vọrzɔrχsmatreɣəl] *de (~en)* precaution, precautionary measure: *~en nemen (treffen) tegen* take precautions against

voos [vos] *adj* **1** dried-out; **2** hollow; **3** rotten

¹**vorderen** [vọrdərə(n)] *vb* (make) progress, move forward, make headway: *naarmate de dag vorderde* as the day progressed *(or:* wore on)

²**vorderen** [vọrdərə(n)] *vb* **1** demand, claim: *het te bedrag is …* the amount due is …; *geld ~ van iem* demand money from s.o.; **2** requisition

vordering [vọrdərɪŋ] *de (~en)* **1** progress, headway: *~en maken* (make) progress, make headway; **2** demand, claim: *een ~ instellen tegen iem* put in *(or:* submit) a claim against s.o.; *~ op iem* claim against s.o.

voren [vọrə(n)] *adv* ‖ *kom wat naar ~* come closer *(or:* up here) a bit; *naar ~ komen: a)* come forward; *b) (fig)* come up, come to the fore; *van ~ from (or:* on) the front (side); *van ~ af aan* from the beginning

vorig [vọrəχ] *adj* **1** last, previous: *de ~e avond* the night before, the previous night; *in het ~e hoofdstuk* in the preceding *(or:* last) chapter; *de ~e keer* (the) last time; **2** earlier, former: *haar ~e man* her former husband

vork [vɔrk] *de (~en)* fork

vorkheftruck [vɔrkhɛftryk] *de (~s)* forklift (truck)

vorm [vɔrm] *de (~en)* **1** form, shape, outline: *naar ~ en inhoud* in form and content; *de lijdende ~ van een werkwoord* the passive voice *(or:* form) of a verb; **2** mould, form; **3** (proper) form, shape, build: *in goede ~ zijn* be in good shape *(or:* condition)

vormen [vọrmə(n)] *vb* **1** shape, form, mould; **2** form, make (up), build (up): *die delen ~ een geheel* those parts make up a whole; *zich een oordeel ~* form an opinion

vormend [vọrmənt] *adj* formative: *algemeen ~ onderwijs* general *(or:* non-vocational) education

vormgever [vọrmɣevər] *de (~s)* designer, stylist

vormgeving [vọrmɣevɪŋ] *de* design, style, styling: *een heel eigen ~* a very personal *(or:* individual) style

vorming [vọrmɪŋ] *de (~en)* **1** formation; **2** education, training

vormingswerk [vọrmɪŋswɛrk] *het* work in socio-cultural *(or* Am: sociological) training/education, work in day-release courses *(or* Am: job corps program)

vorst [vɔrst] *de (~en)* **1** frost, freeze: *vier graden ~* four degrees below freezing; *strenge ~* hard *(or:*

sharp) frost; *we krijgen ~* there's (a) frost coming; *bij ~* in frosty weather, in case of frost; **2** sovereign, monarch: *iem als een ~ onthalen* entertain s.o. like a prince

vorstelijk [vɔrstələk] *adj, adv* princely, royal, regal, lordly: *een ~ salaris* a princely salary; *iem ~ belonen* reward s.o. generously

vorstenhuis [vɔrstə(n)hœys] *het (-huizen)* dynasty, royal house

vorstin [vɔrstɪn] *de (~nen)* queen, princess, sovereign's wife, ruler's wife

vos [vɔs] *de (~sen)* fox: *een troep ~sen* a pack of foxes; *een sluwe ~* a sly old fox; *een ~ verliest wel zijn haren, maar niet zijn streken* the leopard cannot change his spots

vossenjacht [vɔsə(n)jaχt] *de (~en)* **1** treasure hunt; **2** fox hunt: *op ~ gaan (zijn)* go foxhunting, ride to *(or:* follow) the hounds

vouw [vau] *de (~en)* crease, fold: *een scherpe ~* a sharp crease; *zo gaat je broek uit de ~* that will take the crease out of your trousers

vouwbaar [vaubar] *adj* foldable

vouwdeur [vaudər] *de (~en)* folding door

vouwen [vauwə(n)] *vb* fold: *de handen ~* fold one's hands (in prayer); *naar binnen ~* fold in(wards), turn in

vouwfiets [vaufits] *de (~en)* folding bike, collapsible bike

voyeur [vwajør] *de (~s)* voyeur, peeping Tom

vraag [vraχ] *de (vragen)* **1** question, request: *een pijnlijke ~ stellen* ask an embarrassing *(or:* a delicate) question; *de ~ brandde mij op de lippen* the question was on the tip of my tongue; *vragen stellen (or:* beantwoorden) ask *(or:* answer) questions; **2** demand, call: *~ en aanbod* supply and demand; *niet aan de ~ kunnen voldoen* be unable to meet the demand; *er is veel ~ naar tulpen* there's great demand *(or:* call) for tulips; **3** question, problem, assignment; **4** question, issue, problem, topic: *dat is zeer de ~* that is highly debatable *(or:* questionable); *het is nog de ~, of …* it remains to be seen whether …

vraaggesprek [vraχəsprɛk] *het (~ken)* interview

vraagprijs [vraχprɛis] *de (-prijzen)* asking price

vraagstuk [vraχstyk] *het (~ken)* problem, question

vraagteken [vraχtekə(n)] *het (~s)* question mark; *(fig also)* mystery: *de toekomst is een groot ~* the future is one big question mark

vraagzin [vraχsɪn] *de (~nen)* interrogative sentence

vraatzucht [vratsyχt] *de* gluttony

vraatzuchtig [vratsyχtəχ] *adj, adv* gluttonous, greedy

vracht [vraχt] *de (~en)* **1** freight(age), cargo, load: *~ innemen* take in cargo *(or:* freight(age)); **2** load, burden, weight: *onder de ~ bezwijken* succumb under the burden; **3** load, shipment; **4** (cart)load, ton(s)

vrachtbrief [vraχtbrif] *de (-brieven)* waybill, consignment note, delivery note, forwarding note

vrachtdienst [vrɑχdinst] *de (~en)* freight service, cargo service

vrachtprijs [vrɑχtprɛis] *de (-prijzen)* freightage, freight (rate), carriage (rate), haulage (rate)

vrachtschip [vrɑχtsχɪp] *het (-schepen)* freighter, cargo ship

vrachtverkeer [vrɑχtfərker] *het* cargo trade, goods transport(ation); lorry (*or Am:* truck) traffic

vrachtvliegtuig [vrɑχtfliχtœyχ] *het (~en)* cargo plane (*or:* aircraft)

vrachtwagen [vrɑχtwaɣə(n)] *de (~s)* lorry, *(Am)* truck, van

vrachtwagenchauffeur [vrɑχtwaɣə(n)ʃofør] *de* lorry driver, *(Am)* truck driver, *(Am)* trucker

¹vragen [vraɣə(n)] *vb* **1** ask (for): *een politieagent de weg* ~ ask a policeman for (*or:* to show one) the way; *zou ik u iets mogen* ~? would you mind if I asked you a question?, can I ask you sth?; ~ *hoe laat het is* ask (for) the time; **2** ask, demand, request: *de rekening* ~ ask (*or:* call) for the bill

²vragen [vraɣə(n)] *vb* **1** ask, invite; **2** ask, request: *hoeveel vraagt hij voor zijn huis?* how much does he want for his house?; *gevraagd: typiste* wanted: typist; *je vraagt te veel van jezelf* you're asking (*or:* demanding) too much of yourself; *veel aandacht* ~ demand a great deal of attention

³vragen [vraɣə(n)] *vb* **1** ask (after, about), inquire (after, about): *daar wordt niet naar gevraagd* that's beside the point; **2** ask (for), call (for): *erom* ~ ask for it; *dat is om moeilijkheden* ~ that's asking for trouble

¹vragend [vraɣənt] *adj, adv* questioning

²vragend [vraɣənt] *adj* interrogative: *een* ~ *voornaamwoord* an interrogative (pronoun)

vragenlijst [vraɣə(n)lɛist] *de (~en)* list of questions; questionnaire, inquiry form

vragensteller [vraɣə(n)stɛlər] *de* questioner, inquirer, interviewer

vrede [vredə] *de* **1** peace: ~ *sluiten met* conclude the peace with; ~ *stichten* make peace; **2** peace, quiet(ude): ~ *met iets hebben* be resigned (*or:* reconciled) to sth, accept sth

vredesactivist [vredəsɑktivɪst] *de (~en)* peace activist

vredesakkoord [vredəsɑkort] *het (~en)* peace agreement (*or:* treaty)

vredesbesprekingen [vredəzbəsprekɪŋə(n)] *de* peace talks (*or:* negotiations)

vredesbeweging [vredəzbəweɣɪŋ] *de (~en)* peace movement

vredesconferentie [vredəskɔnferɛnsi] *de (~s)* peace conference

vredesdemonstratie [vredəzdemɔnstra(t)si] *de (~s)* peace demonstration

vredesduif [vredəzdœyf] *de (-duiven)* dove of peace

vredesmacht [vredəsmɑχt] *de* peacekeeping force

vredesmissie [vredəsmɪsi] *de (~s)* peace mission

vredesoffensief [vredəsɔfɛnsif] *het (-offensieven)* peace offensive (*or:* initiative)

vredesonderhandelingen [vredəsɔndərhɑndəlɪŋə(n)] *de* peace negotiations (*or:* talks)

vredesoverleg [vredəsovərlɛχ] *het* peace talks

Vredespaleis [vredəspalɛis] *het* Peace Palace

vredespijp [vredəspɛip] *de (~en)* pipe of peace: *de* ~ *roken* smoke the pipe of peace, keep the (*or:* make) peace

vredestijd [vredəstɛit] *de* peacetime

vredesverdrag [vredəsfərdrɑχ] *het (~en)* peace treaty

vredig [vredəχ] *adj* peaceful, quiet

vreedzaam [vretsam] *adj, adv* peaceful, non-violent

¹vreemd [vremt] *adj* **1** strange, odd, unfamiliar, unusual: *een* ~ *gewoonte* an odd (*or:* a strange) habit; *het* ~ *e is, dat* ... the odd (*or:* strange, funny) thing is that ...; **2** foreign, strange, imported: *zij is hier* ~ she is a stranger here; **3** foreign, exotic: ~ *geld* foreign currency; ~ *e talen* foreign languages; **4** strange, outside: ~ *gaan* have an (extramarital) affair

²vreemd [vremt] *adv* strangely, oddly, unusually: ~ *doen* behave in an unusual way; ~ *genoeg* strangely enough, strange to say

vreemde [vremdə] *de* **1** foreigner, stranger; **2** stranger, outsider: *dat hebben ze van geen* ~ it's obvious who they got that from (*or:* where they learnt that)

vreemdeling [vremdəlɪŋ] *de (~en)* foreigner, stranger: *ongewenste ~en* undesirable aliens; *hij is een* ~ *in zijn eigen land* he is a stranger in his own country

vreemdelingendienst [vremdəlɪŋə(n)dinst] *de* aliens (registration) office

vreemdelingenlegioen [vremdəlɪŋə(n)leɣijun] *het* foreign legion

vreemdelingenpolitie [vremdəlɪŋə(n)poli(t)si] *de* aliens police, aliens (registration) office

vrees [vres] *de (vrezen)* fear, fright: *hij greep haar vast uit* ~ *dat hij zou vallen* he grabbed hold of her for fear he should fall

vreetpartij [vretpartɛi] *de (~en)* blow-out

vreetzak [vretsɑk] *de (~ken)* glutton, pig

vrek [vrɛk] *de (~ken)* miser, skinflint, Scrooge

¹vreselijk [vresələk] *adj, adv* **1** terrible, awful: ~ *e honger hebben* have a ravenous appetite; *we hebben* ~ *gelachen* we nearly died (of) laughing; **2** terrifying, horrible: *een* ~ *e moord* a shocking (*or:* horrible) murder

²vreselijk [vresələk] *adv* terribly, awfully, frightfully: ~ *gezellig* awfully nice

¹vreten [vretə(n)] *vb* **1** feed: *dat is niet te* ~! that's not fit for pigs!; **2** stuff (*or:* cram, gorge) (oneself): *zich te barsten* ~ stuff oneself to the gullet (*or:* sick); **3** feed, eat; **4** eat (up), devour: *kilometers* ~ burn up the road; *dat toestel vréét stroom* this apparatus simply eats up electricity

²**vreten** [vrẹtə(n)] *vb* eat (away), gnaw (at), prey (on): *het schuldbesef vrat aan haar* the sense of guilt gnawed at her (heart)

³**vreten** [vrẹtə(n)] *het* **1** fodder; food; forage; slops; **2** grub, nosh

vreter [vrẹtər] *de (~s)* glutton, pig

vreugde [vrøɣdə] *de (~n)* joy, delight, pleasure: *tot mijn ~ hoor ik* I am delighted to hear

vreugdekreet [vrøɣdəkret] *de* cry (*or*: shout) of joy

vreugdevuur [vrøɣdəvyr] *het (-vuren)* bonfire

vrezen [vrẹzə(n)] *vb* fear, dread, be afraid (of, that): *ik vrees het ergste* I fear the worst; *God ~* fear God; *ik vrees van niet* (*or*: *wel*) I'm afraid not (*or*: so); *ik vrees dat hij niet komt* I'm afraid he won't come (*or*: show up)

vriend [vrint] *de (~en)* **1** friend: *~en en vriendinnen!* friends!; *dikke ~en zijn* be (very) close friends; *even goede ~en* no hard feelings, no offence; *van je ~en moet je het maar hebben* with friends like that who needs enemies; **2** (boy)friend: *ze heeft een ~(je)* she has a boyfriend; *iem te ~ houden* remain on good terms with s.o.

vriendelijk [vrịndələk] *adj, adv* **1** friendly, kind, amiable: *~ lachen* give a friendly smile; *zou u zo ~ willen zijn om …* would you be kind enough (*or*: so kind) as to …; *dat is erg ~ van u* that's very (*or*: most) kind of you; **2** pleasant

vriendelijkheid [vrịndələkhɛit] *de (-heden)* friendliness, kindness, amiability

vriendendienst [vrịndə(n)dinst] *de (~en)* friendly turn, kind turn, act of friendship

vriendenkring [vrịndə(n)krɪŋ] *de (~en)* circle of friends

vriendenprijsje [vrịndə(n)prɛiʃə] *het (~s)* give-away: *voor een ~* for next to nothing

vriendin [vrịndɪn] *de (~nen)* **1** (girl)friend, (lady) friend: *zij zijn dikke ~nen* they're the best of friends; **2** girl(friend): *een vaste ~ hebben* have a steady girl(friend), go steady

vriendjespolitiek [vrịncəspolitik] *de* favouritism, nepotism

vriendschap [vrịntsχɑp] *de (~pen)* friendship: *~ sluiten* make (*or*: become) friends, strike up a friendship; *uit ~ iets doen* do sth out of friendship

vriendschappelijk [vrịntsχɑpələk] *adj, adv* friendly, amicable; in a friendly way: *~e wedstrijd* friendly match; *~ met elkaar omgaan* be on friendly terms

vriescel [vrịsɛl] *de (~len)* cold-storage room (*or*: chamber), freezer, deep-freeze

vrieskast [vrịskɑst] *de (~en)* (cabinet-type) freezer, deep-freeze

vrieskist [vrịskɪst] *de (~en)* (chest-type) freezer, deep-freeze

vriespunt [vrịspʏnt] *het* freezing (point): *temperaturen boven* (*or*: *onder, rond*) *het ~* temperatures above (*or*: below, about) freezing (point)

vriesvak [vrịsfɑk] *het (~ken)* freezing compartment, freezer

vriezen [vrịzə(n)] *vb* freeze: *het vriest vijf graden* it's five (degrees) below freezing

vriezer [vrịzər] *de (~s)* freezer, deep-freeze

¹**vrij** [vrɛi] *adj* **1** free, open, unrestricted: *~e handel* free trade; *de ~e slag* freestyle; *een ~ uitzicht hebben* have a clear (*or*: an open) view; *de weg is ~* the road is clear; *weer op ~e voeten zijn* be outside again; **2** free, complimentary; **3** free, vacant: *die wc is ~* that lavatory is free (*or*: vacant, unoccupied); *de handen ~ hebben* have a free hand, have one's hands free; *een stoel ~ houden* reserve a seat

²**vrij** [vrɛi] *adv* quite, fairly, rather, pretty: *het komt ~ vaak voor* it occurs quite (*or*: fairly) often

vrijaf [vrɛiɑf] *adj* off: *een halve dag ~* a half-holiday, half a day off; *~ nemen* take a holiday (*or*: some time off)

vrijblijvend [vrɛiblɛivənt] *adj, adv* without (*or*: free of) obligations

vrijbuiter [vrɛibœytər] *de (~s)* freebooter

vrijdag [vrɛidɑχ] *de (~en)* Friday: *Goede Vrijdag* Good Friday

¹**vrijdags** [vrɛidɑχs] *adj* Friday

²**vrijdags** [vrɛidɑχs] *adv* on Fridays

vrijen [vrɛiə(n)] *vb* **1** neck, pet: *die twee zitten lekker te ~* those two are having a nice cuddle; **2** make love, go to bed

vrijer [vrɛiər] *de (~s)* boyfriend, lover, sweetheart, (young) man

vrijetijdsbesteding [vrɛiətɛitsbəstedɪŋ] *de* leisure activities, recreation

vrijetijdskleding [vrɛiətɛitskledɪŋ] *de* casual clothes (*or*: wear)

vrijgeleide [vrɛiɣəlɛidə] *het (~n, ~s)* (letter of) safe-conduct, safeguard, pass(port), permit

¹**vrijgeven** [vrɛiɣevə(n)] *vb* give time off, give a holiday

²**vrijgeven** [vrɛiɣevə(n)] *vb* release: *de handel ~* decontrol the trade; *iets voor publicatie ~* release sth for publication

vrijgevig [vrɛiɣevəχ] *adj, adv* generous, free with, liberal with

vrijgevigheid [vrɛiɣevəχhɛit] *de* generosity, liberality

vrijgezel [vrɛiɣəzɛl] *de (~len)* bachelor, single: *een verstokte ~* a confirmed bachelor

vrijgezellenavond [vrɛiɣəzɛlə(n)avɔnt] *de (~en)* **1** stag-night; hen-party; **2** singles night

vrijhandel [vrɛihɑndəl] *de* free trade

vrijhandelsgebied [vrɛihɑndəlsχəbit] *het (~en)* free-trade zone (*or*: area)

vrijhaven [vrɛihavə(n)] *de (~s)* free port

vrijheid [vrɛihɛit] *de* freedom, liberty: *het is hier ~, blijheid* it's Liberty Hall here; *~ van godsdienst* (*or*: *meningsuiting*) freedom of religion (*or*: speech); *persoonlijke ~* personal freedom (*or*: liberty); *kinderen veel ~ geven* give (*or*: allow) children a lot of freedom; *iem in ~ stellen* set s.o. free (*or*: at liberty), free/release s.o.

vrijheidsbeeld [vrɛiɦɛitsbelt] ‖ *het Vrijheidsbeeld* the Statue of Liberty

vrijheidsberoving [vrɛiɦɛitsbərovɪŋ] *de* deprivation of liberty (*or:* freedom)

vrijheidsstrijder [vrɛiɦɛitstrɛidər] *de* (*~s*) freedom fighter

vrijhouden [vrɛiɦɑudə(n)] *vb* **1** keep (free), reserve, set aside: *een plaats ~* keep a place (*or:* seat) free; *de weg ~* keep the road open (*or:* clear); **2** pay (for), stand (s.o. sth)

vrijkaart [vrɛikɑrt] *de* (*~en*) free (*or:* complimentary) ticket

vrijkomen [vrɛikomə(n)] *vb* **1** come out, be set free, be released; **2** be released, be set free; **3** become free (*or:* available): *zodra er een plaats vrijkomt* as soon as there is a vacancy (*or:* place)

vrijlaten [vrɛilatə(n)] *vb* **1** release, set free (*or:* at liberty), liberate, emancipate; **2** leave free (*or:* vacant), leave clear: *deze ruimte ~ s.v.p.* please leave this space clear

vrijmaken [vrɛimakə(n)] *vb* reserve, keep (free): *tijd ~* make time (for)

vrijmarkt [vrɛimɑrkt] *de* (*~en*) unregulated street market

vrijmetselaar [vrɛimɛtsəlar] *de* (*~s*) freemason, Mason

vrijmetselarij [vrɛimɛtsəlarɛi] *de* Freemasonry, Masonry

vrijmoedig [vrɛimudəχ] *adj* frank, outspoken

vrijplaats [vrɛiplats] *de* (*~en*) refuge

vrijpleiten [vrɛiplɛitə(n)] *vb* clear (of), exonerate (from)

vrijpostig [vrɛipɔstəχ] *adj* impertinent, impudent, saucy

vrijspraak [vrɛisprak] *de* acquittal

vrijspreken [vrɛisprekə(n)] *vb* acquit (from), clear: *vrijgesproken worden van een beschuldiging* be cleared of (*or:* be acquitted on) a charge

vrijstaan [vrɛistan] *vb* be free (to), be allowed (to), be permitted (to), be at liberty (to)

vrijstaand [vrɛistant] *adj* apart, free, detached: *een ~ huis* a detached house

vrijstellen [vrɛistɛlə(n)] *vb* exempt, excuse, release: *vrijgesteld van militaire dienst* exempt from military service

vrijstelling [vrɛistɛlɪŋ] *de* (*~en*) exemption, release, freedom: *~ verlenen van* exempt from; *een ~ hebben voor wiskunde* be exempted from the maths exam

vrijster [vrɛistər] *de* (*~s*) spinster: *een oude ~* an old maid

vrijuit [vrɛiœyt] *adv* freely: *u kunt ~ spreken* you can speak freely; *~ gaan: a)* not be to blame; *b)* get off (*or:* go) scot-free, go clear/free

vrijwel [vrɛiwɛl] *adv* nearly, almost, practically: *dat is ~ hetzelfde* that's nearly (*or:* almost) the same; *~ niets* hardly anything, next to nothing; *~ tegelijk aankomen* arrive almost simultaneously

(*or:* at the same time); *het komt ~ op hetzelfde neer* it boils down to pretty well the same thing

vrijwillig [vrɛiwɪləχ] *adj, adv* voluntary, volunteer, of one's own free will, of one's own volition: *~ iets op zich nemen* volunteer to do sth, take on sth voluntarily

vrijwilliger [vrɛiwɪləγər] *de* (*~s*) volunteer: *er hebben zich nog geen ~s gemeld* so far nobody has volunteered

vrijwilligerswerk [vrɛiwɪləγərswɛrk] *het* voluntary work, volunteer work

vroedvrouw [vrutfrɑu] *de* (*~en*) midwife

vroeg [vruχ] *adj, adv* **1** early: *van ~ tot laat* from dawn till dusk (*or:* dark); *je moet er ~ bij zijn* you've got to get in quickly; *hij toonde al ~ tekentalent* he showed artistic talent at an early age; *volgende week is ~ genoeg* next week is soon enough; *niet ~er dan …* not before …, *…* at the earliest; *het is nog ~: a)* the day is still young; *b)* the night is still young; *'s morgens ~* early in the morning; **2** early, young, premature: *een te ~ geboren kind* a premature baby

¹vroeger [vruγər] *adv* formerly, before, previously: *~ heb ik ook wel gerookt* I used to smoke; *~ stond hier een kerk* there used to be a church here; *het Londen van ~* London as it used to be (*or:* once was)

²vroeger [vruγər] *adj* previous, former: *zijn ~e verloofde* his former (*or:* ex-fiancée)

vroegrijp [vruχrɛip] *adj* precocious, forward, early-ripening: *~e kinderen* precocious (*or:* forward) children

vroegte [vruχtə] *de* ‖ *in alle ~* at (the) crack of dawn, bright and early

vroegtijdig [vruχtɛidəχ] *adj, adv* early, premature

vrolijk [vrolək] *adj, adv* cheerful, merry: *~ behang* cheerful (*or:* bright) wallpaper; *het was er een ~e boel* they were a merry crowd; *~ worden* get (a bit, rather) merry; *een ~ leventje leiden* lead a merry life

vroom [vrom] *adj, adv* pious, devout

vrouw [vrɑu] *de* (*~en*) **1** woman: *een alleenstaande ~* a single (*or:* an unattached) woman; *achter de ~en aanzitten* chase (after) women, womanize; *de werkende ~* working women, career women; *een ~ achter het stuur* a woman driver; *Vrouw Holle* Mother Carey; **2** wife: *man en ~* husband (*or:* man) and wife; *hoe gaat het met je ~?* how's your wife?; *een dochter van zijn eerste ~* a daughter by his first wife; **3** queen; **4** mistress, lady: *de ~ des huizes* lady (*or:* mistress) of the house

vrouwelijk [vrɑuwələk] *adj* **1** female, woman: *een ~e arts* a woman doctor; *de ~e hoofdrol* the leading lady role (*or:* part); **2** feminine, womanly: *~e charme* feminine charm; *de ~e intuïtie* woman's intuition

vrouwenafdeling [vrɑuwə(n)ɑvdelɪŋ] *de* (*~en*) women's section (*or:* branch), women's ward, female ward

vrouwenarts [vrɑuwə(n)ɑrts] *de* (*~en*) gynaecologist

vrouwenbeweging [vrɑ̠u̯wə(n)bəweɣɪŋ] *de* feminist movement, women's (rights) movement

vrouwenblad [vrɑ̠u̯wə(n)blɑt] *het (~en)* women's magazine

vrouwenhandel [vrɑ̠u̯wə(n)hɑndəl] *de* trade (*or:* traffic) in women, white slave trade

vrouwenjager [vrɑ̠u̯wə(n)jaɣər] *de (~s)* womanizer, ladykiller

vrouwenliteratuur [vrɑ̠u̯wə(n)litərɑtyr] *de* women's literature

vrouwenpraatgroep [vrɑ̠u̯wə(n)prɑtχrup] *de (~en)* women's circle, ladies' circle

vrouwenrol [vrɑu̯wə(n)rɔl] *de (~len)* female part

vrouwtje [vrɑ̠u̯cə] *het (~s)* **1** woman, wife(y): *hij kijkt te veel naar de ~s* he's too keen on women (*or:* the ladies); **2** mistress; **3** female

vrouwvijandig [vrɑu̯vɛi̯ɑndəχ] *adj* anti-female, hostile to(wards) women

vrouwvriendelijk [vrɑu̯vrɪndələk] *adj, adv* women-friendly

vrucht [vrγχt] *de (~en)* **1** fruit: *~en op sap* fruit in syrup; *verboden ~en* forbidden fruit; **2** foetus, embryo: *een onvoldragen ~* a foetus that has not been carried to term; **3** (*fig*) fruit(s), reward(s): *zijn werk heeft weinig ~en afgeworpen* he has little to show for his work; *~en afwerpen* bear fruit; *de ~en van iets plukken* reap the fruit(s) (*or:* rewards) of sth

vruchtbaar [vrγχtbar] *adj* **1** fruitful, productive; **2** fertile, fruitful: *de vruchtbare periode van de vrouw* a woman's fertile period; *een vruchtbare bodem vinden* find fertile soil

vruchtbaarheid [vrγχtbarhɛit] *de* fertility, fruitfulness

vruchteloos [vrγχtəlos] *adj, adv* fruitless, futile

vruchtenpers [vrγχtə(n)pɛrs] *de (~en)* fruit press

vruchtensap [vrγχtə(n)sɑp] *het (~pen)* fruit juice

vruchtentaart [vrγχtə(n)tart] *de (~en)* fruit tart

vruchtvlees [vrγχtfles] *het* flesh (of a, the fruit), (fruit) pulp

vruchtwater [vrγχtwatər] *het* amniotic fluid, water(s)

vruchtwateronderzoek [vrγχtwatərɔndərzuk] *de (~en)* amniocentesis

V-snaar [vesnar] *de (V-snaren)* V-belt

vso [veesɔ] *het voortgezet speciaal onderwijs* comprehensive school system

V-teken [vetekə(n)] *het* V-sign

¹vuil [vœyl] *adj, adv* **1** dirty, filthy, polluted: *de ~e kopjes* the dirty (*or:* used) cups; *een ~e rivier* a dirty (*or:* polluted) river; **2** dirty, foul: *iem een ~e streek leveren* play a dirty (*or:* nasty trick) on s.o.; *~e viezerik* (or: *leugenaar*) dirty (*or:* filthy) swine/liar; **3** dirty, nasty: *iem ~ aankijken* give s.o. a dirty (*or:* filthy, nasty) look

²vuil [vœyl] *het* **1** refuse, rubbish; garbage: *iem behandelen als een stuk ~* treat s.o. like dirt; *grof ~* (collection of) bulky refuse; *~ storten* tip (*or:* dump, shoot) rubbish; *verboden ~ te storten* dumping prohibited, no tipping (*or:* dumping); **2** dirt,

filth

vuiligheid [vœyləχhɛit] *de (-heden)* dirt, filth

vuilmaken [vœylmakə(n)] *vb* make dirty, dirty, soil

vuilnis [vœylnɪs] *het, de* refuse, rubbish, garbage

vuilnisauto [vœylnɪsauto] *de (~'s)* dustcart, (*Am*) garbage truck, trash truck

vuilnisbak [vœylnɪzbɑk] *de (~ken)* dustbin, rubbish bin, (*Am*) garbage can, trash can

vuilnisbakkenras [vœylnɪzbɑkə(n)rɑs] *het (~sen)* mongrel

vuilnisbelt [vœylnɪzbɛlt] *de (~en)* rubbish dump

vuilnishoop [vœylnɪshop] *de (-hopen)* rubbish dump, (*Am*) garbage heap

vuilniskoker [vœylnɪskokər] *de (~s)* rubbish chute

vuilnisman [vœylnɪsmɑn] *de (~nen)* binman; garbage collector

vuilniszak [vœylnɪsɑk] *de (~ken)* rubbish bag, refuse bag

vuilophaaldienst [vœylɔphaldinst] *de (~en)* refuse collection

vuilstortplaats [vœylstɔrtplats] *de (~en)* rubbish dump

vuiltje [vœylcə] *het (~s)* smut, speck of dirt (*or:* dust, grit): *een ~ in het oog hebben* have sth (*or:* a smut) in one's eye; *er is geen ~ aan de lucht* everything is absolutely fine (*or Am:* peachy keen)

vuilverbranding [vœylvərbrɑndɪŋ] *de (~en)* (waste, refuse, garbage) incinerator

vuist [vœyst] *de (~en)* fist: *met gebalde ~en* with clenched fists; *een ~ maken* take a stand (*or:* hard line); *met de ~ op tafel slaan* bang one's fist on the table, take a hard line; *op de ~ gaan* come to blows; *uit het ~je eten* eat with one's fingers; *voor de ~ (weg)* off the cuff, ad lib

vuistregel [vœystreɣəl] *de (~s)* rule of thumb

vuistslag [vœystslɑχ] *de (~en)* punch

vuldop [vγldɔp] *de (~pen)* filler cap, (*Am*) fill cap

vulgair [vγlɣɛːr] *adj, adv* vulgar, common, rude

vulkaan [vγlkan] *de (vulkanen)* volcano

vulkaanuitbarsting [vγlkanœydbɑrstɪŋ] *de* volcanic eruption

vulkanisch [vγlkanis] *adj* volcanic: *~e stenen* volcanic rocks

vullen [vγlə(n)] *vb* **1** fill (up), inflate: *het eten vult ontzettend* the meal is very filling; **2** fill (up), stuff, pad: *een gat ~* fill (up) a hole; *een kip met gehakt ~* stuff a chicken with mince

vulling [vγlɪŋ] *de (~en)* **1** filling, stuffing; **2** cartridge, refill

vulpen [vγlpɛn] *de (~nen)* fountain pen

vulpotlood [vγlpɔtlot] *het (vulpotloden)* propelling pencil, (*Am*) refillable lead pencil

vunzig [vγnzəχ] *adj* dirty, filthy

¹vuren [vyrə(n)] *vb* fire: *staakt het ~* cease fire

²vuren [vyrə(n)] *adj* pine, deal

vurenhout [vyrə(n)hɑut] *het* pine(wood), deal

vurenhouten [vyrə(n)hɑutə(n)] *adj* pine, deal

vurig [vyrəχ] *adj, adv* **1** fiery, (red-)hot: *~e kolen* coals of fire; **3** fiery, ardent, fervent, devout, burning: *~e paarden* fiery (*or:* high-spirited) horses; *een ~ voorstander van iets* a strong (*or:* fervent) supporter of sth; *daarmee was zijn ~ste wens vervuld* it fulfilled his most ardent wish

VUT [vʏt] *de vervroegde uittreding* early retirement: *in de ~ gaan* retire early, take early retirement

vut-regeling [vʏtreχəlɪŋ] *de (~en) (roughly)* early-retirement scheme

vuur [vyr] *het (vuren)* **1** fire: *voor iem door het ~ gaan* go through fire (and water) for s.o.; *het huis staat in ~ en vlam* the house is in flames; *ik zou er mijn hand voor in het ~ durven steken* I'd stake my life on it; *in ~ en vlam zetten* set ablaze (*or:* on fire); *met ~ spelen* play with fire; *een ~ aansteken* light a fire; *iem het ~ na aan de schenen leggen* make it (*or:* things) hot for s.o.; *een ~ uitdoven* put out (*or:* extinguish) a fire; *een pan op het ~ zetten* put a pan on the stove; *iem zwaar onder ~ nemen* let fly at s.o.; *tussen twee vuren zitten* get caught in the middle (*or:* in the firing line); **2** fire, ardour, fervour: *in het ~ van zijn betoog* in the heat of his argument

vuurbal [vyrbɑl] *de (~len)* fireball, ball of fire

vuurdoop [vyrdop] *de* baptism of fire

vuurgevecht [vyrɣəveχt] *het (~en)* gunfight

vuurhaard [vyrhart] *de (~en)* seat of the fire

Vuurland [vyrlɑnt] *het* Tierra del Fuego

vuurlinie [vyrlini] *de (~s)* firing line, line of fire

vuurpeloton [vyrpelətɔn] *het (~s)* firing squad

vuurpijl [vyrpɛil] *de (~en)* rocket

vuurproef [vyrpruf] *de (-proeven)* trial by fire; *(fig)* ordeal, acid test: *de ~ doorstaan* stand the test; *de ~ ondergaan* undergo a severe ordeal

vuurrood [vyrot] *adj* crimson, scarlet: *~ aanlopen* turn crimson (*or:* scarlet)

vuurspuwend [vyrspywənt] *adj* erupting; fire-breathing; fire-spitting

vuursteen [vyrsten] *de* flint

vuurtje [vyrcə] *het (~s)* **1** (small) fire: *het nieuws ging als een lopend ~ door de stad* the news spread through the town like wildfire; **2** light: *iem een ~ geven* give s.o. a light

vuurtoren [vyrtorə(n)] *de (~s)* lighthouse

vuurvast [vyrvɑst] *adj* fireproof, flame-resistant, heat-resistant: *een ~ schaaltje* an ovenproof (*or:* a heat-resistant) dish

vuurvliegje [vyrvliχjə] *het (~s)* firefly

vuurvreter [vyrvretər] *de (~s)* fire-eater

vuurwapen [vyrwapə(n)] *het (~s)* firearm, gun, arm

vuurwerk [vyrwɛrk] *het* **1** firework; **2** (display of) fireworks

vuurzee [vyrze] *de (~ën)* blaze, sea of fire (*or:* flame(s))

VVV [veveve] *de Vereniging voor Vreemdelingenverkeer* Tourist Information Office

VVV-kantoor [vevevekɑntor] *het (VVV-kantoren)* tourist (information) office

vwo [veweo] *het voorbereidend wetenschappelijk onderwijs* pre-university education

W

waaien [wajə(n)] *vb* **1** blow; be blown: *er woei een harde storm* a storm was blowing; **2** wave, fly: *laat maar ~* let it rip

waaier [wajər] *de (~s)* fan

waakhond [wakhɔnt] *de (~en)* watchdog

waaks [waks] *adj* watchful

waakvlam [wakflɑm] *de (~men)* pilot light (*or:* flame)

waakzaam [waksam] *adj, adv* watchful

waakzaamheid [waksamhɛit] *de* watchfulness

Waal [wal] *de (Walen) (pers)* Walloon

¹Waals [wals] *het* Walloon

²Waals [wals] *adj* Walloon

waan [wan] *de* delusion: *iem in de ~ laten* not spoil s.o.'s illusions

waanzin [wanzɪn] *de* madness: *dat is je reinste ~* that is pure nonsense (*or:* sheer madness)

waanzinnig [wanzɪnəχ] *adj, adv* mad: *~ populair zijn* be wildly popular

waanzinnige [wanzɪnəɣə] *de (~n)* madman, maniac, madwoman

¹waar [war] *adj* **1** true, real, actual: *de ware oorzaak* the real (*or:* actual) cause; *'t is toch niet ~!* you don't say!, not really!; *het is te mooi om ~ te zijn* it's too good to be true; *echt ~?* is that really true?, really?; *eerlijk ~!* honest!; **2** true, (+ *noun*) actual, real: *een ~ genot* a regular (*or:* real) treat; **3** true, correct: *dat is je ware* it's the real thing; *dat is ~ ook ...* that reminds me ..., by the way ...; *hij moest om acht uur thuis zijn, niet ~?* he had to be home at eight o'clock, didn't he?

²waar [war] *adv* **1** where; what: *~ gaat het nu eigenlijk om?* what is it really all about?; **2** where; that, which: *de boodschap ~ hij niet aan gedacht had* the message (that, which) he hadn't remembered; *het dorp ~ hij geboren is* the village where (*or:* in which) he was born; **3** wherever; everywhere; anywhere: *meer welvaart dan ~ ook* more prosperity than anywhere else; **4** really, actually: *dat is ~ gebeurd* it really (*or:* actually) happened

³waar [war] *de (waren)* goods, ware(s): *iem ~ voor zijn geld geven* give value for money

waaraan [waran] *adv* **1** what ... to: *~ ligt dit?* what is the reason for it?; *~ heb ik dit te danken?* what do I owe this to?, to what do I owe this?; **2** what (*or:* which) ... to/of: *het huis ~ ik dacht* the house

(which) I was thinking of; **3** whatever ... to (*or:* of): *~ je ook denkt* whatever you're thinking of (*or:* about)

waarachter [waraχtər] *adv* **1** behind which; **2** behind what (*or:* which)

waarachtig [waraχtəχ] *adj, adv* truly, really

waarbij [warbɛi] *adv* at (*or:* by, near) ... which: *een ongeluk ~ veel gewonden vielen* an accident in which many people were injured

waarborg [warbɔrχ] *de (~en)* guarantee, security

waarborgen [warbɔrɣə(n)] *vb* guarantee

waarborgsom [warbɔrχsɔm] *de (~men)* deposit, (*law)* bail

¹waard [wart] *adj* worth; worthy (of sth, s.o.): *laten zien wat je ~ bent* show s.o. what you're made of; *hij is haar niet ~* he's not worthy of her; *na een dag werken ben ik 's avonds niets (meer)* work I'm no good for anything; *veel ~ zijn* be worth a lot

²waard [wart] *de (~en)* landlord

waarde [wardə] *de (~n)* **1** value: *ter ~ van ...* at (the value of), worth ...; *voorwerpen van ~* objects of value, valuables; *iem niet op zijn juiste ~ schatten* underestimate s.o.; *(zeer) veel ~ aan iets hechten* value sth highly; *weinig ~ aan iets hechten* attach little value to sth; *van ~ zijn, ~ hebben* be valuable, be of value; **2** value, reading: *de gemiddelde ~n van de zomertemperaturen* the average summer temperature

waardebon [wardəbɔn] *de (~nen)* voucher, coupon, gift voucher (*or:* coupon)

waardeloos [wardəlos] *adj* worthless: *dat is ~* that's useless (*or:* hopeless)

waarderen [warderə(n)] *vb* appreciate, value: *hij weet een goed glas wijn wel te ~* he likes (*or:* appreciates) a good glass of wine

waarderend [warderənt] *adj, adv* appreciative: *zich (zeer) ~ over iem uitlaten* speak (very) highly of s.o.

waardering [wardərɪŋ] *de (~en)* appreciation, esteem: *~ ondervinden (van)* win the esteem (*or:* regard) (of)

waardevol [wardəvɔl] *adj* valuable, useful: *~le voorwerpen* valuables, objects of value

waardig [wardəχ] *adj, adv* dignified, worthy

waardigheid [wardəχhɛit] *de (-heden)* dignity, worth: *iets beneden zijn ~ achten* think sth beneath one's dignity (*or:* beneath one)

waardoor [wardor] *adv* **1** (as a result of) what, how: *~ ben je van gedachten veranderd?* what made you change your mind?; *ik weet ~ het komt* I know how it happened, I know what caused it; **2** through which, by which, (which, that) ... through (*or:* by), (as a result of) which: *de buis ~ het gas stroomt* the tube through which the gas flows; *het begon te regenen, ~ de weg nog gladder werd* it started to rain, which made the road even more slippery

waarheen [warhen] *adv* **1** where, where ... to: *~ zullen wij vandaag gaan?* where shall we go today?;

2 where, to which, (which, that) … to: *de plaats ~ ze me stuurden* the place to which they directed me; **3** wherever: *~ u ook gaat* wherever you (may) go

waarheid [wa̱rhɛit] *de (-heden)* truth; fact: *de ~ achterhalen* get at (or: find out) the truth; *om (u) de ~ te zeggen* to be honest (with you), to tell (you) the truth; *de ~ ligt in het midden* the truth lies (somewhere) in between; *een ~ als een koe* a truism

waarheidsgetrouw [wa̱rhɛitsχətrɑu] *adj, adv* truthful, true

waarin [wari̱n] *adv* **1** where, in what: *~ schuilt de fout?* where's the mistake?; **2** in which, where, (which, that) … in: *de tijd ~ wij leven* the age (that, which) we live in; **3** wherever, in whatever: *~ de fout ook gemaakt is* wherever the mistake was made

waarlangs [warlɑ̱ns] *adv* **1** what … past (or: along); **2** past which, along which; (which, that) … past (or: along): *de weg ~ hij gaat* the way he is going, the road along which he is going; **3** past whatever, along whatever: *~ zij ook kwamen* whatever way they came along

¹waarmaken [wa̱rmakə(n)] *vb* **1** prove; **2** fulfil: *de gewekte verwachtingen (niet) ~* (fail to) live up to expectations

²waarmaken [wa̱rmakə(n)] *ref vb* prove oneself

waarmee [warme̱] *adv* **1** what … with (or: by): *~ sloeg hij je?* what did he hit you with?; **2** with which, by which, which, (which) … with (or: by): *de boot ~ ik vertrek* the boat on which I leave; **3** (with, by) whatever: *~ hij ook dreigde, zij werd niet bang* whatever he threatened her with she didn't get scared

waarmerk [wa̱rmɛrk] *het (~en)* stamp

waarmerken [wa̱rmɛrkə(n)] *vb* stamp: *een gewaarmerkt afschrift* a certified (or: an authenticated) copy

waarna [warna̱] *adv* after which: *~ Paul als spreker optrad* after which Paul spoke (or: took the floor)

waarnaar [warna̱r] *adv* **1** what … at (or: of, for): *~ smaakt dat?* what does it taste of?; **2** to which; after (or: for, according to) which; (which, that) … to (or: after, for): *het hoofdstuk ~ ze verwees* the chapter (that, which) she referred to; **3** whatever … to (or: at, for); wherever: *~ ik hier ook zoek, ik vind nooit wat* whatever I look for here, I never find anything

waarnaast [warna̱st] *adv* **1** what … next to (or: beside); **2** (which, that) … next to (or: beside); **3** whatever … next to (or: beside): *~ je dit schilderij ook hangt* whatever you hang this picture next to

waarneembaar [warne̱mbar] *adj, adv* perceptible: *niet ~* imperceptible

¹waarnemen [wa̱rnemə(n)] *vb* replace (temporarily), fill in, take over (temporarily), act: *de zaken voor iem ~* fill in for (or: replace) s.o.

²waarnemen [wa̱rnemə(n)] *vb* observe, perceive

waarnemend [wa̱rnemənt] *adj* temporary, acting

waarnemer [wa̱rnemər] *de (~s)* **1** observer; **2** representative, deputy, substitute

waarneming [wa̱rnemɪŋ] *de (~en)* **1** observation, perception; **2** substitution

waarom [warɔ̱m] *adv* **1** why, what … for: *~ denk je dat?* why do you (or: what makes you) think so?; *~ in vredesnaam?* why on earth?, why for goodness' sake?; **2** why, (which, that) … for: *de reden ~ hij het deed* the reason (why, that) he did it; **3** for whatever, whatever … for: *~ hij het ook doet, hij moet ermee ophouden!* whatever he does it for, he has to stop it!

waaromheen [warɔmhe̱n] *adv* **1** what … (a)round; **2** (a)round which: *het huis ~ een tuin lag* the house which was surrounded by a garden

waaronder [warɔ̱ndər] *adv* **1** what … under (or: among); among what; **2** under which; among which (*inf*): *de boom ~ wij zaten* the tree under which we were sitting; *hij had een schat aan boeken, ~ heel zeldzame* he had a wealth of books, including some very rare ones; **3** under whatever; whatever … under: *~ hij ook keek, hij vond het niet* whatever he looked under, he couldn't find it

waarop [warɔ̱p] *adv* **1** what … on (or: for), where; **2** (which, that) … on/in (or: by, to): *de dag ~ hij aankwam* the day (on which) he arrived; *de manier ~ beviel me niet* I didn't like the way (in which) it was done; *op het tijdstip ~* at the time that; **3** whatever … on: *~ je nu ook staat, ik wil dat je naar beneden komt* whatever you are standing on now, I want you to get down

waarover [warɔ̱vər] *adv* **1** what … over (or: about, across): *~ gaat het?* what is it about?; **2** (which, that) … over (or: about, across): *de auto ~ ik met je vader gesproken heb* the car of (or: about) which I've spoken with your dad; **3** whatever … about: *~ de discussie dan ook gaat, …* whatever the discussion is about, …

waarschijnlijk [warsχɛ̱inlək] *adj, adv* probable, likely: *dat lijkt mij heel ~* that seems quite likely to me; *~ niet* I suppose not; *meer dan ~* more than likely

waarschijnlijkheid [warsχɛ̱inləkhɛit] *de (-heden)* probability, likelihood, odds: *naar alle ~* in all probability (or: likelihood)

waarschuwen [wa̱rsχywə(n)] *vb* **1** warn, alert: *ik heb je gewaarschuwd* I gave you fair warning, I told you so; **2** warn, notify: *een dokter laten ~* call a doctor; **3** warn, caution: *ik waarschuw je voor de laatste maal* I'm telling you for the last time; *wees gewaarschuwd* you've been warned

waarschuwing [wa̱rsχywɪŋ] *de (~en)* warning, caution; reminder, notice: *(sport) een officiële ~ krijgen* be booked (or: cautioned); *Waarschuwing! Zeer brandbaar!* Caution! Highly flammable!

waartegen [warte̱χə(n)] *adv* **1** what … against (or: to): *~ helpt dit middel?* what is this medicine for?; **2** against which, to which; (which, that) … against (or: to): *de muur ~ een ladder staat* the wall against which a ladder is standing; *een raad ~ niets in te brengen valt* a piece of advice to which no objections can be made; **3** whatever … against (or: to)

waartoe [wɑrtu] *adv* 1 what … for (*or:* to); why; 2 (which, that) … for (*or:* to); 3 whatever … for (*or:* to): ~ *dit ook moge leiden* whatever this may lead to

waartussen [wɑrtʏsə(n)] *adv* 1 what … between (*or:* among, from): ~ *moeten wij kiezen?: a)* what are we (supposed) to choose between; *b)* what are the alternatives?; 2 between (*or:* among, from) which; (which, that) … between (*or:* among, from); 3 whatever … between (*or:* among, from)

waaruit [wɑrœyt] *adv* 1 from what: ~ *bestaat de opdracht?* what does the assignment consist of?; 2 from which: *het boek* ~ *u ons net voorlas* the book from which you read to us just now

waarvan [wɑrvɑn] *adv* 1 what … from (*or:* of): ~ *maakt hij dat?* what does he make that of? (*or:* from?), of (*or:* from) what does he make that?; 2 (which, that) … from; of whom *(of pers);* whose: *100 studenten,* ~ *ongeveer de helft chemici* 100 students, of whom about half are chemists; *op grond* ~ on the basis of which; *dat is een onderwerp* ~ *hij veel verstand heeft* that is a subject he knows a lot about; 3 whatever … from: *klei en hout, of* ~ *die hutten gemaakt zijn* clay and wood, or whatever those huts are made from

waarvandaan [wɑrvɑndɑn] *adv* 1 where … from; 2 (which, that) … from; 3 wherever … from: ~ *je ook belt, draai altijd eerst een o* wherever you call from, always dial an o first

waarvoor [wɑrvor] *adv* 1 what … for (*or:* about): ~ *dient dat?* what's that for?; 2 what … for: ~ *doe je dat?* what are you doing that for?; 3 (which, that) … for: *een gevaar* ~ *ik u gewaarschuwd heb* a danger I warned you about; 4 whatever … for: ~ *hij het ook doet, het is in elk geval niet het geld* whatever he does it for, it's not the money, that's for sure

waarzegster [wɑrzɛχstər] *de* fortune-teller

waas [was] *het* haze, *(fig)* air, aura, film: *een* ~ *van geheimzinnigheid* a shroud of secrecy; *een* ~ *voor de ogen krijgen* get a mist (*or:* haze) before one's eyes

wacht [wɑχt] *de* (~en) 1 watchman; 2 watch, lookout: *(de)* ~ *houden* be on (*or:* stand) guard; *(Belg) van* ~ *zijn* be on night (*or:* weekend) duty, be on call; 3 watch, guard: *iets in de* ~ *slepen* carry off sth, pocket (*or:* bag) sth

wachten [wɑχtə(n)] *vb* 1 wait, stay: *op de bus* ~ wait for the bus; 2 wait, await: *iem laten* ~ keep s.o. waiting; *waar wacht je nog op?* what are you waiting for?; *op zijn beurt* ~ await one's turn; *er zijn nog drie* ~*den voor u* hold the line, there are three callers before you; *je moet er niet te lang mee* ~ don't put it off too long; 3 wait, await (s.o.), be in store for (s.o.): *er wachtte hem een onaangename verrassing* there was an unpleasant surprise in store for him; *er staan ons moeilijke tijden te* ~ difficult times lie ahead of us

wachter [wɑχtər] *de* (~s) guard(sman), watchman

wachtgeld [wɑχtχɛlt] *het* (~en) reduced pay

wachtlijst [wɑχtlɛist] *de* (~en) waiting list

wachtlopen [wɑχtlopə(n)] *vb* be on patrol, be on (guard) duty

wachtpost [wɑχtpɔst] *de* (~en) watch (*or:* sentry, guard) post

wachtstand [wɑχ(t)stɑnt] *de* (~en) suspension mode, suspended mode

wachttijd [wɑχtɛit] *de* (~en) wait, waiting period

wachtwoord [wɑχtwort] *het* (~en) password

wad [wɑt] *het* (~den) (mud) flat(s), shallow(s) ‖ *de Wadden* the (Dutch) Wadden

waden [wɑdə(n)] *vb* wade

waf [wɑf] *int* woof

wafel [wɑfəl] *de* (~s) waffle, wafer

¹wagen [wɑγə(n)] *de* (~s) 1 wagon; cart, van, pram; 2 car: *met de* ~ *komen* come by car

²wagen [wɑγə(n)] *vb* 1 risk: *het erop* ~ chance (*or:* risk) it; *wie niet waagt, die niet wint* nothing ventured, nothing gained; 2 venture, dare: *zijn kans* ~ try one's luck; *waag het eens!* just you dare!

wagenpark [wɑγə(n)pɑrk] *het* (~en) fleet (of cars, vans, taxis, buses)

wagenwijd [wɑγə(n)wɛit] *adv* wide open

wagenziek [wɑγə(n)zik] *adj* carsick

waggelen [wɑγələ(n)] *vb* totter, stagger, waddle, toddle

wagon [wɑγɔn] *de* (~s) (railway) carriage, coach; wagon; van

wagonlading [wɑγɔnladɪŋ] *de* (~en) wagonload

wak [wɑk] *het* (~ken) hole: *hij zakte in een* ~ *en verdronk* he fell through the thin ice and (was) drowned

wake [wɑkə] *de* (~n) watch, wake

waken [wɑkə(n)] *vb* 1 watch, keep watch, stay awake: *bij een zieke* ~ sit up with a sick person; 2 watch, guard

wakker [wɑkər] *adj, adv* awake: *daar lig ik niet van* ~ I'm not going to lose any sleep over it; ~ *schrikken* wake up with a start; *iem* ~ *schudden* shake s.o. awake

wal [wɑl] *de* (~len) 1 bank, embankment, wall; 2 quay(side), waterside: *aan lager* ~ *geraken* come down in the world, go to seed; *aan de* ~ on shore; *van* ~ *steken* push off, go ahead, proceed; 3 shore: *aan* ~ *brengen* land, bring (sth, s.o.) ashore; 4 bag: *de* ~*letjes (in Amsterdam)* the red-light district (in Amsterdam)

walgelijk [wɑlγələk] *adj, adv* disgusting, revolting: *een* ~*e stank* a nauseating stench

walgen [wɑlγə(n)] *vb* be nauseated, be disgusted, be revolted: *ik walg ervan* it turns my stomach

walging [wɑlγɪŋ] *de* disgust, revulsion, nausea

walhalla [wɑlhɑla] *het* Valhalla

walkie-talkie [wɔːkitɔːki] *de* (~s) walkie-talkie

walkman [wɔːkmɛːn] *de* (~s) walkman

Wallonië [wɑlonijə] *het* the Walloon provinces in Belgium

walm [wɑlm] *de* (~en) (thick, dense) smoke

walmen [wɑlmə(n)] *vb* smoke

walnoot [wɑlnot] *de* walnut

walrus [wɑlrʏs] *de (~sen)* walrus
wals [wɑls] *de (~en)* **1** roller; **2** steamroller, road-roller; (rolling) mill; **3** waltz
¹walsen [wɑlsə(n)] *vb* waltz
²walsen [wɑlsə(n)] *vb* roll, steamroller; roll
walvis [wɑlvɪs] *de (~sen)* whale
wanbedrijf [wɑmbədrɛif] *het (-bedrijven) (Belg)* criminal offence
wanbegrip [wɑmbəɣrɪp] *het (~pen)* fallacy, misconception, wrong idea, false idea
wanbeheer [wɑmbəher] *het* mismanagement
wanbetaler [wɑmbətalər] *de (~s)* defaulter
wanbetaling [wɑmbətalɪŋ] *de (~en)* default, non-payment
wand [wɑnt] *de (~en)* wall, face, side, skin: *een buis met dikke ~en* a thick-walled tube
wandel [wɑndəl] *de* walk
wandelaar [wɑndəlar] *de (~s)* walker, hiker
wandelen [wɑndələ(n)] *vb* walk, ramble, hike: *met de kinderen gaan ~* take the children for a walk
wandelend [wɑndələnt] *adj* walking
wandelgang [wɑndəlɣɑŋ] *de (~en)* ‖ *ik hoorde het in de ~en* I just picked up some gossip
wandeling [wɑndəlɪŋ] *de (~en)* walk, ramble, *(sport)* hike
wandelpad [wɑndəlpɑt] *het (~en)* footpath
wandelstok [wɑndəlstɔk] *de (~ken)* walking stick
wandeltocht [wɑndəltɔχt] *de (~en)* walking tour
wandelwagen [wɑndəlwaɣə(n)] *de (~s)* buggy, pushchair, *(Am)* stroller
wandkleed [wɑntklet] *het (-kleden)* tapestry, wall hanging(s)
wandmeubel [wɑntmøbəl] *het (~s)* wall unit
wandrek [wɑntrɛk] *het (~ken) (pl)* wall bars
wang [wɑŋ] *de (~en)* cheek: *bolle ~en* round *(or:* chubby) cheeks
wangedrag [wɑŋɣədrɑχ] *het (~ingen)* misbehaviour, bad conduct
wanhoop [wɑnhop] *de despair,* desperation: *de ~ nabij zijn* be on the verge of despair
wanhoopsdaad [wɑnhopsdat] *de (-daden)* act of despair, desperate act
wanhopen [wɑnhopə(n)] *vb* despair
wanhopig [wɑnhopəχ] *adj, adv* desperate, despondent, despairing: *iem ~ maken* drive s.o. to despair; *zich ergens ~ aan vastklampen* hang on to sth like grim death
wankel [wɑŋkəl] *adj, adv* shaky, unstable: *~ evenwicht* shaky balance; *~e stoelen* rickety chairs
wankelen [wɑŋkələ(n)] *vb* stagger, wobble
¹wanneer [wɑner] *adv* when: *~ dan ook* whenever
²wanneer [wɑner] *conj* **1** when: *~ de zon ondergaat, wordt het koeler* when the sun sets it gets cooler; **2** if: *hij zou beter opschieten, ~ hij meer zijn best deed* he would make more progress if he worked harder; **3** whenever, if: *(altijd) ~ ik oesters eet, word ik ziek* whenever I eat oysters I get ill
wanorde [wɑnɔrdə] *de* disorder, disarray: *de keuken was in de grootste ~* the kitchen was in a colossal mess

wanprestatie [wɑmprɛsta(t)si] *de (~s)* failure
wansmaak [wɑnsmak] *de* bad taste
¹want [wɑnt] *conj* because, as, for
²want [wɑnt] *de (~en)* mitt(en)
wanten [wɑntə(n)] *vb* ‖ *hij weet van ~* he knows the ropes *(or:* what's what)
wantoestand [wɑntustɑnt] *de (~en)* disgraceful state of affairs
¹wantrouwen [wɑntrɑuwə(n)] *vb* distrust, mistrust
²wantrouwen [wɑntrɑuwə(n)] *het* distrust, suspicion
wantrouwend [wɑntrɑuwənt] *adj, adv* suspicious (of), distrustful
wantrouwig [wɑntrɑuwəχ] *adj, adv* suspicious: *~ van aard* have a suspicious nature
WAO [weaʊ] *de Wet op de Arbeidsongeschiktheidsverzekering* disability insurance act
WAO'er [weaʊər] *de* recipient of disablement insurance benefits
wapen [wapə(n)] *het (~s)* **1** weapon, arms: *de ~s neerleggen* lay down arms; **2** (coat of) arms: *een leeuw in zijn ~ voeren* bear a lion in one's coat of arms
wapenbeperking [wapə(n)bəpɛrkɪŋ] *de* arms limitation
wapenbezit [wapə(n)bəzɪt] *het* possession of firearms *(or:* weapons)
wapenen [wapənə(n)] *vb* arm, armour, reinforce
wapenkunde [wapə(n)kʏndə] *de* heraldry
wapenstilstand [wapə(n)stɪlstɑnt] *de (~en)* **1** armistice, suspension of arms *(or:* hostilities), ceasefire; **2** *(fig)* truce
wapenstok [wapə(n)stɔk] *de (~ken) (roughly)* baton
wapenvergunning [wapə(n)vərɣʏnɪŋ] *de (~en)* firearms licence, gun licence
wapenwedloop [wapə(n)wɛtlop] *de* arms race
wapperen [wɑpərə(n)] *vb* blow, fly, stream, flap, flutter: *laten ~* fly, blow, stream, wave
war [wɑr] *de* tangle, muddle, confusion: *in de ~ zijn* be confused; *iem in de ~ brengen* confuse s.o.; *plannen in de ~ sturen* upset s.o.'s plans
warboel [wɑrbul] *de* muddle, mess; tangle
waren [warə(n)] *de* goods, commodities
warenhuis [warə(n)hœys] *het (-huizen)* (department) store
warhoofd [wɑrhoft] *het, de (~en)* scatterbrain
¹warm [wɑrm] *adj* **1** warm, hot: *het ~ hebben* be warm *(or:* hot); *het begon (lekker) ~ te worden in de kamer* the room was warming up; *iets ~s* sth warm *(or:* hot) (to eat, drink); **2** enthusiastically: *~ lopen voor iets* feel enthusiasm for sth; **3** warmly, pleasantly; **4** warm, warm-hearted, ardent: *een ~ voorstander van iets zijn* be an ardent *(or:* a fervent) supporter of sth; **5** warmed up, enthusiastic; **6** warm, pleasant: *je bent ~!* you are (getting) warm! *(or:* hot!)
²warm [wɑrm] *adv* warmly: *iem iets ~ aanbevelen*

recommend sth warmly to s.o.

warmbloedig [wɑrmbludəχ] *adj* warm-blooded

warmen [wɑrmə(n)] *vb* warm (up), heat (up)

warming-up [wɔrmɪŋɣp] *de (~s)* warm-up (exercise)

warmlopen [wɑrmlopə(n)] *vb* **1** have warmed to, feel (great) enthusiasm for (s.o., sth): *hij loopt niet erg warm voor het plan* he has not really warmed to the plan; **2** *(sport)* warm up, limber up

warmte [wɑrmtə] *de* warmth, heat: *~ (af)geven* give off (*or:* emit) heat

warmtebron [wɑrmtəbrɔn] *de (~nen)* source of heat

warmwaterkraan [wɑrmwatərkran] *de (-kranen)* hot(-water) tap

warrig [wɑrəχ] *adj* knotty, tangled, *(fig)* confused, muddled

Warschau [wɑrʃau] *het* Warsaw

wartaal [wɑrtal] *de* gibberish, nonsense: *(er) ~ uitslaan* talk double Dutch (*or:* gibberish)

warwinkel [wɑrwɪŋkəl] *de* mess, muddle

¹was [wɑs] *de (~sen)* wash, washing, laundry, linen: *de fijne ~* the fine (*or:* delicate) fabrics; *de vuile ~ buiten hangen* wash one's dirty linen in public; *iets in de ~ doen* put sth in the wash

²was [wɑs] *het, de (~sen)* wax: *meubels in de ~ zetten* wax furniture; *goed in de slappe ~ zitten* have plenty of dough

wasautomaat [wɑsautomat] *de (wasautomaten)* (automatic) washing machine

wasbaar [wɑzbar] *adj* washable

wasbak [wɑzbɑk] *de (~ken)* washbasin, sink

wasbeer [wɑzber] *de (wasberen)* racoon

wasbenzine [wɑzbɛnzinə] *de* benzine

wasdag [wɑzdɑχ] *de (~en)* wash(ing)-day

wasdroger [wɑzdroɣər] *de (~s)* (tumble-)dryer

wasem [wɑsəm] *de (~s)* steam, vapour

wasgoed [wɑsχut] *het* wash, laundry, linen

wasknijper [wɑsknɛipər] *de (~s)* clothes-peg

waskrijt [wɑskrɛit] *het* grease pencil

waslijn [wɑslɛin] *de (~en)* clothes line

waslijst [wɑslɛist] *de (~en)* shopping list, catalogue

wasmachine [wɑsmaʃinə] *de (~s)* (automatic) washing machine

wasmand [wɑsmɑnt] *de (~en)* (dirty) clothes basket

wasmiddel [wɑsmɪdəl] *het (~en)* detergent

waspoeder [wɑspudər] *het, de (~s)* washing-powder, soap powder

¹wassen [wɑsə(n)] *adj* wax: *een ~ beeld* a wax figure

²wassen [wɑsə(n)] *vb* **1** wash, launder, clean: *waar kan ik hier mijn handen ~?* where can I wash my hands?; *zich ~: a)* wash, have a wash, have (*or:* take) a bath; *b)* wash oneself; *iets op de hand ~* wash sth by hand; **2** wash, do the wash(ing)

wassenbeeldenmuseum [wɑsə(n)beldə(n)myzejɣm] *het* waxworks

wasserette [wɑsərɛtə] *de (~s)* launderette

wasserij [wɑsərɛi] *de (~en)* laundry

wastafel [wɑstafəl] *de (~s)* washbasin

wasverzachter [wɑsfərzɑχtər] *de (~s)* fabric softener

¹wat [wɑt] *adv* **1** somewhat, rather, a little, a bit: *hij is ~ traag* he is a little slow, he is on the slow side; **2** very, extremely: *hij is er ~ blij mee* (*or:* trots op) he is extremely pleased with it (*or:* proud of it); **3** isn't it (*or:* that, he) ..., ..., aren't they (*or:* those) ...: *mooi hè, die bloemen* aren't they beautiful, those flowers; *~ lief van je!* how nice of you!; *(iron) ~ ben je weer vriendelijk* I see you're your usual friendly self again; *~ ze niet verzinnen tegenwoordig* the things they come up with these days; *~ wil je nog meer?* what more do (*or:* can) you want?; *~ zal hij blij zijn!* how happy (*or:* pleased) he will be!

²wat [wɑt] *pron* that; which: *geef hem ~ hij nodig heeft* give him what he needs; *alles ~ je zegt, klopt* everything you say is true; *en ~ nog belangrijker is* and what's (even) more (important); *doe nou maar ~ ik zeg* just do as I say; *je kunt doen en laten ~ je wilt* you can do what (*or:* as you) please; *ze zag eruit als een verpleegster, ~ ze ook was* she looked like a nurse, which in fact she was (too)

³wat [wɑt] *pron* what, which, whatever: *~ bedoel je daar nou mee?* just what do you mean by that?, *(stronger)* just what is that supposed to mean?; *wát ga je doen?* you are going to do what?; *~ heb je 't liefste, koffie of thee?* which do you prefer, coffee or tea?; *~ zeg je?* (I beg your) pardon?; *~ is het voor iem?* what's he (*or:* she) like?

⁴wat [wɑt] *pron* **1** something, anything, *(with ook)* whatever: *ze heeft wel ~* she has got a certain something; *wil je ~ drinken?* would you like something to drink?; *zie jij ~?* do (*or:* can) you see anything?; *het is altijd ~ met hem* there is always something up with him; **2** some, a bit (of), a little, a few: *geef me ~ suiker* (*or:* geld) give me some sugar (*or:* money); *geef mij ook ~* let me have some too; *~ meer* a bit (*or:* little) more; *~ minder* a bit (*or:* little) less; *heel ~ boeken* quite a few books, a whole lot of books; *dat scheelt nogal ~* that makes quite a (bit of) a) difference; *~ kun jij mooi tekenen* how well you draw!; *~ een onzin* what (absolute) nonsense; *~! komt hij niet?* what! isn't he coming?

water [watər] *het (~en)* **1** water: *de bloemen ~ geven* water the flowers; *bij laag ~* at low water (*or:* tide); *stromend ~* running water; *een schip te ~ laten* launch a ship; **2** water; waterway

waterafstotend [watərafstotənt] *adj* water-repellent, waterproof

waterafvoer [watərafur] *de* drainage (of water), sewage disposal

waterbed [watərbɛt] *het (~den)* waterbed

waterbouwkunde [watərbaukɣndə] *de* hydraulic engineering: *weg- en ~* civil engineering

waterbron [watərbrɔn] *de (~nen)* spring

waterdamp [watərdɑmp] *de* (water) vapour

waterdicht [watərdɪχt] *adj* waterproof, watertight: *een ~ alibi* a watertight alibi

waterdoorlatend [waːtərdorlaːtənt] *adj* porous

wateren [waːtərə(n)] *vb* urinate

waterfiets [waːtərfits] *de (~en)* pedalo, pedal boat

waterfietsen [waːtərfitsə(n)] *vb* cycle (along) on a pedal boat

watergladheid [waːtərɣlɑtɦɛit] *de (Belg)* aquaplaning

watergolf [waːtərɣɔlf] *de (-golven)* **1** wave; **2** set

watergolven [waːtərɣɔlvə(n)] *vb* set: *zijn haar laten* ~ have one's hair set

waterhoofd [waːtərɦoft] *het (~en)* hydrocephalus

waterig [waːtərəχ] *adj* **1** watery, slushy: *~e soep* thin soup; **2** watery, *(fig)* wishy-washy

waterijsje [waːtərɛiʃə] *het* ice lolly, *(Am)* popsicle

waterkans [waːtərkɑns] *de (~en) (Belg)* remote chance

waterkant [waːtərkɑnt] *de (~en)* waterside, waterfront: *aan de ~* on the waterfront

waterketel [waːtərketəl] *de (~s)* kettle

waterkoker [waːtərkokər] *de (~s)* electric kettle

waterlanders [waːtərlɑndərs] *de* waterworks

waterleiding [waːtərlɛidɪŋ] *de (~en)* **1** water pipe *(or:* supply): *een huis op de ~ aansluiten* to connect a house to the water main(s); **2** waterworks; water pipes: *een bevroren ~* a frozen water pipe

waterleidingbedrijf [waːtərlɛidɪŋbədrɛif] *het (-bedrijven)* waterworks

waterlelie [waːtərleli] *de (~s)* water lily

Waterman [waːtərmɑn] *de (~nen) (astrology)* Aquarius

watermeloen [waːtərməlun] *de (~en)* watermelon

watermerk [waːtərmɛrk] *het (~en)* watermark

watermolen [waːtərmolə(n)] *de (~s)* watermill

¹**waterpas** [waːtərpɑs] *adj* level

²**waterpas** [waːtərpɑs] *de (~sen)* spirit level, *(Am)* level

waterpeil [waːtərpɛil] *het* water level

waterpijp [waːtərpɛip] *de (~en)* water pipe, hookah

waterpokken [waːtərpɔkə(n)] *de* chickenpox

waterpolitie [waːtərpoli(t)si] *de* river police; harbour police

waterpolo [waːtərpolo] *het* water polo

waterpomp [waːtərpɔmp] *de (~en)* water pump

waterpomptang [waːtərpɔmptɑŋ] *de (~en)* adjustable-joint pliers; *(large)* (adjustable) pipe wrench

waterput [waːtərpʏt] *de (~ten)* well

waterrijk [waːtərɛik] *adj* watery, full of water

waterschade [waːtərsχadə] *de* water damage

waterski [waːtərski] *de (~'s)* water-ski

waterskiër [waːtərskijər] *de (~s)* water-skier

waterslang [waːtərslɑŋ] *de (~en)* hose(pipe)

watersnood [waːtərsnot] *de* flood(ing)

watersnoodramp [waːtərsnotrɑmp] *de (~en)* flood (disaster)

watersport [waːtərspɔrt] *de (~en)* water sport, aquatic sport

waterstaat [waːtərstat] *de see* minister

waterstand [waːtərstɑnt] *de (~en)* water level: *bij hoge (or: lage) ~* at high *(or:* low) water

waterstof [waːtərstɔf] *de* hydrogen

waterstofbom [waːtərstɔvbɔm] *de (~men)* hydrogen bomb, fusion bomb, H-bomb

waterstofperoxide [waːtərstɔfpɛrɔksidə] *het* hydrogen peroxide

waterstraal [waːtərstral] *de (-stralen)* jet of water

watertanden [waːtərtɑndə(n)] *vb* ‖ *deze chocolatjes doen mij* ~ these chocolates make my mouth water

watertoren [waːtərtorə(n)] *de (~s)* water tower

watertrappen [waːtərtrɑpə(n)] *vb* tread water

waterval [waːtərvɑl] *de (~len)* waterfall, fall: *de Niagara ~len* Niagara Falls

waterverf [waːtərvɛrf] *de (-verven)* watercolour

waterverfschilderij [waːtərvɛrfsχɪldərɛi] *het, de (~en)* painting in watercolour, aquarelle

waterverontreiniging [waːtərvərɔntrɛinəχɪŋ] *de* water pollution

watervliegtuig [waːtərvliχtœyχ] *het (~en)* seaplane, water plane

watervogel [waːtərvoɣəl] *de (~s)* waterbird

watervrees [waːtərvres] *de* hydrophobia: *~ hebben* be hydrophobic

waterweg [waːtərwɛχ] *de (~en)* waterway

waterzuivering [waːtərzœyvərɪŋ] *de* water treatment

waterzuiveringsinstallatie [waːtərzœyvərɪŋsɪnstala(t)si] *de (~s)* sewage treatment plant

watje [wɑcə] *het (~s)* **1** wad of cotton wool *(or Am:* absorbent cotton); **2** wally

watt [wɑt] *de (~s)* watt

watten [wɑtə(n)] *de* cotton wadding, cotton wool, *(Am)* absorbent cotton: *een prop (dot)* ~ a plug *(or:* wad) of cottonwool; *iem in de ~ leggen* pamper *(or:* mollycoddle) s.o.

wattenstaafje [wɑtə(n)stafjə] *het (~s)* cotton bud *(or Am:* swab)

wauwelen [wɑuwələ(n)] *vb* chatter, jabber, drone (on)

WA-verzekering [weaːvərzekərɪŋ] *de* third-party insurance

waxinelichtje [wɑksinəlɪχjə] *het (~s)* tealight

wazig [waːzəχ] *adj, adv* **1** hazy, blurred: *alles ~ zien* see everything (as if) through a haze *(or:* in a blur); **2** muzzy, drowsy: *met een ~e blik in de ogen* with a dazed look in the eyes

wc [wese] *de (~'s)* **1** *watercloset* WC, toilet, lavatory: *ik moet naar de ~* I have to go to the toilet; **2** toilet(bowl)

wc-bril [wesebrɪl] *de (~len)* toilet seat

we [wə] *pers pron* we, us: *laten ~ gaan (or: ophouden)* let's go *(or:* stop)

web [wɛp] *het (~ben)* web

website [wɛpsɑjt] *de (~s)* website

websurfen [wɛpsʏrfə(n)] *vb* surf (the web)

wecken [wɛkə(n)] *vb* can, preserve

wedden [wɛdə(n)] *vb* bet (on): *met iem ~ om een tientje dat* bet s.o. ten euros that; *denk jij dat Ron vandaag komt? - ik wed van wel* you think Ron will come today? - I bet he will

weddenschap [wɛdə(n)sχɑp] *de (~pen)* bet: *een ~ verliezen* lose a bet

wedergeboorte [wedərɣəbortə] *de (~n)* rebirth

wederkerend [wedərkerənt] *adj* reflexive

wederkerig [wedərkerəχ] *adj, adv* mutual, reciprocal

¹**wederzijds** [wedərzɛits] *adj* mutual, reciprocal: *de liefde was ~* their love was mutual

²**wederzijds** [wedərzɛits] *adv* mutually

wedijveren [wɛtɛivərə(n)] *vb* strive (for)

wedloop [wɛtlop] *de (wedlopen)* race

wedren [wɛtrɛn] *de (~nen)* race

wedstrijd [wɛtstrɛit] *de (~en)* match, competition, game: *een ~ bijwonen* attend a match; *met nog drie ~en te spelen* with three games (still) to go

wedstrijdbeker [wɛtstrɛidbekər] *de (~s)* (sports) cup

weduwe [wedywə] *de (~n)* widow: *groene ~* housebound wife

weduwenpensioen [wedywə(n)pɛnʃun] *het (~en)* widows' benefit (*or:* pension)

weduwnaar [wedywnar] *de (~s, -naren)* widower

¹**wee** [we] *de* labour pain, contraction: *de ~ën zijn begonnen* labour has started

²**wee** [we] *adj* sickly

³**wee** [we] *int* woe: *o ~ als je het nog eens doet* woe betide you if you do it again

weeffout [wefɑut] *de (~en)* flaw, weaving fault

weefsel [wefsəl] *het (~s)* **1** fabric, textile, weave; **2** tissue, web

weegbrug [weɣbrʏχ] *de (~gen)* weighbridge

weegschaal [weχsχal] *de (-schalen)* (pair of) scales, balance: *twee weegschalen* two pairs of scales, two balances

Weegschaal [weχsχal] *de (Weegschalen)* (astrology) Libra

¹**week** [wek] *de (weken)* week: *een ~ rust* a week's rest; *volgende ~ dinsdag* next Tuesday; *een ~ weggaan* go away for a week; *door de ~* on weekdays; *over een ~* in a week from now; *dinsdag over een ~* Tuesday week, a week from Tuesday; *morgen over twee weken* two weeks from tomorrow; *vandaag een ~ geleden* a week ago today

²**week** [wek] *de (weken)* soak: *de was in de ~ zetten* put the laundry in (to) soak

³**week** [wek] *adj* **1** soft: *~ worden* soften; *een ~ gestel* a weak constitution; **2** weak, soft-hearted

weekblad [weɣblɑt] *het (~en)* weekly, (news) magazine

weekdier [weɣdir] *het (~en)* mollusc

weekeinde [wekɛində] *het (-einden)* weekend: *in het ~* at (*or Am:* on) the weekend

weekenddienst [wikɛndinst] *de (~en)* weekend duty

weekloon [weklon] *het (-lonen)* weekly wage

weelde [weldə] *de* luxury; over-abundance, wealth

weelderig [weldərəχ] *adj, adv* luxuriant, lush, sumptuous

weemoed [wemut] *de* melancholy, sadness

Weens [wens] *adj* Viennese

¹**weer** [wer] *het* **1** weather: *mooi ~ spelen (tegen iem)* put on a show of friendliness; *~ of geen ~* come rain or shine; **2** weathering: *het ~ zit in het tentdoek* the tent is weather-stained; *hij is altijd in de ~* he is always on the go

²**weer** [wer] *adv* **1** again: *morgen komt er ~ een dag* tomorrow is another day; *het komt wel ~ goed* it will all turn out all right; *nu ik ~* now it's my turn; *wat moest hij nu ~?* what did he want now?; *wat nu ~?* now what?; **2** back: *heen en ~ gaan* (*or:* reizen) go (*or:* travel) back and forth; *heen en ~ lopen* pace up and down; *zo moeilijk is het nou ook ~ niet* it's not all that hard

weerbarstig [werbɑrstəχ] *adj, adv* stubborn, unruly

weerbericht [werbərıχt] *het (~en)* weather forecast (*or:* report)

weergalmen [werɣɑlmə(n)] *vb* echo, resound: *de straten weergalmden van het gejuich* the streets resounded with the cheers

weergaloos [werɣalos] *adj, adv* unequalled, unparalleled

weergave [werɣavə] *de (~n)* reproduction, account

weergeven [werɣevə(n)] *vb* **1** reproduce, render, represent, recite, convey; **2** reproduce, repeat, report: *dit onderzoek geeft de feiten juist weer* this study presents the facts accurately; **3** reflect

weerhaak [werhak] *de (-haken)* barb, beard

weerhaan [werhan] *de (-hanen)* weathercock, weathervane

weerhouden [werhɑudə(n)] *vb* **1** hold back, restrain: *iem ervan ~ om iets te doen* stop (*or:* keep) s.o. from doing sth; **2** *(Belg)* retain, keep: *de beslissing is ~* the decision is upheld

weerkaart [werkart] *de (~en)* weather chart, weather map

weerkaatsen [werkatsə(n)] *vb* reflect; reverberate, (re-)echo: *de muur weerkaatst het geluid* the wall echoes the sound; *het geluid weerkaatst tegen de muur* the sound reflects off (*or:* from) the wall

weerklinken [werklıŋkə(n)] *vb* **1** resound, ring out: *een schot weerklonk* a shot rang out; **2** resound, reverberate

weerleggen [werlɛɣə(n)] *vb* refute

weerlicht [werlıχt] *het, de* (heat, sheet) lightning

weerlichten [werlıχtə(n)] *vb* lighten

weerloos [werlos] *adj* defenceless

weerman [wermɑn] *de (~nen)* weatherman

weeroverzicht [werovərzıχt] *het (~en)* weather survey: *en nu het ~* and now for a look at the weather

weerpraatje [werpracə] *het (~s)* (the) weather in brief, weather report

weerskanten [werskɑntə(n)] *de* ‖ *aan ~ van de tafel* (or: *het raam)* on both sides of the table (*or:* window); *van (*or: *aan) ~ from (*or:* on) both sides

weersomstandigheden [wersɔmstandəχhedə(n)] *de* weather conditions

weerspiegelen [werspiɣələ(n)] *vb* reflect

weerspiegeling [werspiɣəlıŋ] *de (~en)* reflection: *een getrouwe ~ van iets* a true reflection (*or:* mirror) of sth

weerstaan [wɛrstan] *vb* resist, stand up to

weerstand [wɛrstɑnt] *de (~en)* **1** resistance, opposition: *~ bieden* offer resistance; **2** aversion

weerstation [wɛrsta(t)ʃɔn] *het (~s)* weather station

weersverwachting [wɛrsfərwaχtıŋ] *de (~en)* weather forecast

weerwoord [wɛrwort] *het (~en)* answer, reply

¹**weerzien** [wɛrzin] *het* reunion, meeting: *tot ~s* goodbye, until the next time

²**weerzien** [wɛrzin] *vb* meet again, see again

weerzin [wɛrzın] *de* disgust, reluctance, aversion, distaste: *iets met ~ doen* do sth with great reluctance

weerzinwekkend [werzınwɛkənt] *adj, adv* disgusting, revolting

wees [wes] *de (wezen)* orphan

weesgegroetje [wesχəχrucə] *het (~s)* Hail Mary: *tien ~s bidden* say ten Hail Marys

weeshuis [weshœys] *het (-huizen)* orphanage

weeskind [weskınt] *het (~eren)* orphan (child)

weetgierig [wetχirəχ] *adj, adv* inquisitive

weetje [wecə] *het (~s)* ǁ *allerlei ~s* all kinds of trivia

¹**weg** [wɛχ] *de (~en)* **1** road, way, track: *zich een ~ banen* work (*or:* edge) one's way through; *(iem) in de ~ staan* stand in s.o.'s (*or:* the) way; *(voor) iem uit de ~ gaan* keep (*or:* get) out of s.o.'s way, avoid s.o.; *een misverstand uit de ~ helpen* clear up a misunderstanding; *een kortere ~ nemen* take a short cut; *op de goede* (or: *verkeerde*) *~ zijn* be on the right (*or:* wrong) track; *op ~ gaan* set off (on a trip), set out (for), go; *iem op ~ helpen* set s.o. up; **2** way, channel, means: *de ~ van de minste weerstand* the line (*or:* road) of least resistance; **3** way, journey: *nog een lange ~ voor zich hebben* have a long way to go

²**weg** [wɛχ] *adv* **1** gone: *een mooie pen is nooit ~* a nice pen always comes in useful; *~ wezen!* (let's) get away from here!, (let's) get out of here!; *~ met …* away (*or:* down) with …; **2** crazy; **3** away: *ze heeft veel ~ van haar zus* she takes after her sister, she is very like her sister

wegbergen [wɛɣbɛrɣə(n)] *vb* stow away, put away

wegblazen [wɛɣblazə(n)] *vb* blow away, blow off

wegblijven [wɛɣblɛivə(n)] *vb* stay away

wegbranden [wɛɣbrandə(n)] *vb* ǁ *die man is niet weg te bránden* there's no getting rid of that man

wegbrengen [wɛɣbrɛŋə(n)] *vb* **1** take (away), deliver; **2** see (off)

wegcode [wɛχkodə] *de (~s) (Belg)* traffic regulations; *(roughly)* Highway Code

wegdek [wɛɣdɛk] *het (~ken)* road (surface)

wegdenken [wɛɣdɛŋkə(n)] *vb* think away: *de computer is niet meer uit onze maatschappij weg te denken* it's impossible to imagine life today without

the computer

wegdoen [wɛɣdun] *vb* **1** dispose of, part with, get rid of; **2** put away

wegdragen [wɛɣdraɣə(n)] *vb* carry away, carry off

wegdrijven [wɛχdrɛivə(n)] *vb* float away, drift away

wegduiken [wɛɣdœykə(n)] *vb* duck (away), dive away

wegen [weɣə(n)] *vb* weigh: *zwaarder ~ dan* outweigh; *zich laten ~* have oneself weighed, be weighed

wegenbelasting [weɣə(n)bəlɑstıŋ] *de* road tax

wegenbouw [weɣə(n)bɑu] *de* road building (*or:* construction)

wegenkaart [weɣə(n)kart] *de (~en)* road map

wegennet [weɣənɛt] *het (~ten)* road network (*or:* system)

wegens [weɣəns] *prep* because of, on account of, due to: *terechtstaan ~ …* be tried on a charge of …

wegenwacht [weɣə(n)waχt] *de (~en)* AA patrol, RAC patrol; *(Am)* AAA road service

weggaan [wɛɣan] *vb* **1** go away, leave: *Joe is bij zijn vrouw weggegaan* Joe has left his wife; *~ zonder te betalen* leave without paying; *ga weg!* go away!, get lost!, get away!, you're kidding!; **2** go away: *de pijn gaat al weg* the pain is already getting less

weggebruiker [wɛχəbrœykər] *de (~s)* road user

weggedrag [wɛχədrɑχ] *het* driving (behaviour, manners), standards of driving

weggeven [wɛχevə(n)] *vb* give away

weggevertje [wɛχevərcə] *het (~s)* giveaway, dead giveaway

wegglijden [wɛχlɛidə(n)] *vb* slip (away): *de auto gleed weg in de modder* the car slipped in the mud

weggooien [wɛχojə(n)] *vb* throw away, throw out, discard: *dat is weggegooid geld* that is money down the drain

weggooiverpakking [wɛχojvərpɑkıŋ] *de* disposable container (*or:* packaging, package)

weghalen [wɛχhalə(n)] *vb* remove, take away: *alle huisraad werd uit het huis weggehaald* the house was stripped (bare)

weghelft [wɛχhɛlft] *de (~en)* side of the road

weghollen [wɛχholə(n)] *vb* run away, run off, dash away, dash off

wegjagen [wɛχjaɣə(n)] *vb* chase away: *klanten ~ door de hoge prijzen* frighten customers off by high prices

wegkijken [wɛχkɛikə(n)] *vb* frown away: *hij werd weggekeken* they stared at him coldly until he left

wegkomen [wɛχkomə(n)] *vb* get away: *de meeste favorieten zijn goed weggekomen bij de start* the favourites got (off to) a good start; *slecht* (or: *goed*) *~ bij iets* come off badly (*or:* well) with sth; *ik maakte dat ik wegkwam* I got out of there

wegkruipen [wɛχkrœypə(n)] *vb* crawl away, creep away

wegkwijnen [wɛχkwɛinə(n)] *vb* pine away, waste away

weglaten [wɛχlatə(n)] *vb* leave out, omit

wegleggen [wɛχlɛɣə(n)] *vb* **1** put aside; put away; **2** lay aside, set aside, save

weglligging [wɛχlɪɣɪŋ] *de* road-holding

weglopen [wɛχlopə(n)] *vb* **1** walk away, walk off: *dat loopt niet weg* that can wait; ~ *voor een hond* run away from a dog; **2** run away, walk out, run off: *een weggelopen kind* a runaway (child); **3** run off, run out

wegmaken [wɛχmakə(n)] *vb* lose

wegmarkering [wɛχmarkerɪŋ] *de* (~en) road marking

wegnemen [wɛχnemə(n)] *vb* remove, take away, dispel ‖ *dat neemt niet weg, dat ik hem aardig vind* all the same I like him; *dat neemt niet weg, dat het geld verdwenen is* that doesn't alter the fact that the money has disappeared

wegomlegging [wɛχɔmlɛɣɪŋ] *de* (~en) diversion, *(Am)* detour

wegparcours [wɛχparkur] *het* (~en) road-racing circuit

wegpesten [wɛχpestə(n)] *vb* harass (*or:* pester) (s.o.) until he leaves

wegpiraat [wɛχpirat] *de* (*wegpiraten*) road hog

wegraken [wɛχrakə(n)] *vb* **1** faint; **2** get lost

wegrennen [wɛχrɛnə(n)] *vb* run off (*or:* away)

wegrestaurant [wɛχrestorant] *het* (~s) transport cafe, wayside restaurant

wegrijden [wɛχrɛidə(n)] *vb* drive off (*or:* away), ride off (*or:* away): *de auto reed met grote vaart weg* the car drove off at high speed

wegroepen [wɛχrupə(n)] *vb* call off (*or:* away)

wegschoppen [wɛχsχɔpə(n)] *vb* kick away

wegslaan [wɛχslan] *vb* knock off (*or:* away): *weggeslagen worden* be swept away

wegslepen [wɛχslepə(n)] *vb* tow away, drag away

wegslikken [wɛχslɪkə(n)] *vb* swallow (down): *ik moest even iets ~* I had to swallow hard

wegsmelten [wɛχsmɛltə(n)] *vb* melt away

¹**wegspoelen** [wɛχspulə(n)] *vb* **1** wash away, carry away, flush down; **2** wash down

²**wegspoelen** [wɛχspulə(n)] *vb* be washed (*or:* carried, swept) away

wegstemmen [wɛχstɛmə(n)] *vb* vote out (of office), vote down

wegsterven [wɛχstɛrvə(n)] *vb* die away (*or:* down), fade away

wegstoppen [wɛχstɔpə(n)] *vb* hide away, stash away: *weggestopt zitten* be hidden (*or:* tucked) away

wegstrepen [wɛχstrepə(n)] *vb* cross off, cross out, delete

wegsturen [wɛχstyrə(n)] *vb* send away

wegtrappen [wɛχtrapə(n)] *vb* kick away

wegtrekken [wɛχtrɛkə(n)] *vb* draw off, move away, withdraw: *mijn hoofdpijn trekt weg* my headache is going (*or:* disappearing)

wegvallen [wɛχfalə(n)] *vb* **1** be omitted (*or:* dropped): *er is een regel* (or: *letter*) *weggevallen* a

line (*or:* letter) has been left out; **2** fall away

wegvegen [wɛχfeɣə(n)] *vb* wipe (*or:* sweep, brush) away

wegverkeer [wɛχfarker] *het* road traffic

wegversmalling [wɛχfarsmalɪŋ] *de* (~en) narrowing of the road, road narrows

wegversperring [wɛχfarspɛrɪŋ] *de* (~en) roadblock

wegvervoer [wɛχfarvur] *het* road transport

wegvliegen [wɛχfliɣə(n)] *vb* **1** fly away (*or:* off, out); **2** sell like hot cakes

wegvoeren [wɛχfurə(n)] *vb* carry away, carry off

wegwaaien [wɛχwajə(n)] *vb* be blown away, fly away, fly off

wegwerken [wɛχwɛrkə(n)] *vb* get rid of, polish off, put away, smoothe away: *iets op een foto ~* block out sth on a photo

wegwerker [wɛχwɛrkər] *de* (~s) roadmender, *(Am)* road worker

wegwerpartikel [wɛχwɛrpartikəl] *het* disposable article, *(pl also)* disposables

wegwerpbeker [wɛχwɛrbekər] *de* disposable cup

wegwerpmaatschappij [wɛχwɛrpmatsχapɛi] *de* consumer society

wegwezen [wɛχwezə(n)] *vb* clear off, clear out, push off, buzz off, scram: *jongens, ~!* let's get out of here!; *hé, jij daar, ~!* buzz off!, scram!

wegwijs [wɛχwɛis] *adj* familiar, informed

wegwijzer [wɛχwɛizər] *de* (~s) signpost

wegzakken [wɛχsakə(n)] *vb* sink

wegzetten [wɛχsɛtə(n)] *vb* set aside, put aside; put away (*or:* aside): *ik kon mijn auto nergens ~* I couldn't find anywhere to park

wegzinken [wɛχsɪŋkə(n)] *vb* sink, go under, subside

wei [wɛi] *de* (*weiden*) see weide

weide [wɛidə] *de* (~n) **1** meadow; pasture, grasslands; **2** playground, playing field

weids [wɛits] *adj* grand

weifelachtig [wɛifəlaχtəχ] *adj* wavering, hesitant

weifelen [wɛifələ(n)] *vb* waver, hesitate, be undecided: *na enig ~ koos ik het groene jasje* after some hesitation I opted for the green jacket

weigeraar [wɛiɣərar] *de* (~s) refuser

¹**weigeren** [wɛiɣərə(n)] *vb* refuse, reject, turn down: *een visum ~* withhold a visa; *iem iets ~* deny s.o. sth

²**weigeren** [wɛiɣərə(n)] *vb* fail; jam, be jammed: *de motor weigert* the engine won't start

weigering [wɛiɣərɪŋ] *de* (~en) refusal, denial

weiland [wɛilant] *het* (~en) pasture (land), grazing (land), meadow

¹**weinig** [wɛinəχ] *adv* **1** little: ~ *bekende feiten* little-known facts; *er ~ om geven* care little about it; *dat scheelt maar ~* it's a close thing; **2** hardly ever: ~ *thuis zijn* not be in often

²**weinig** [wɛinəχ] *ind pron* little, not much, not a lot: ~ *Engels kennen* not know much English; ~ *of (tot) geen geld* little or no money; *er ~ van weten* not

know a lot about it; *dat is veel te ~* that's insufficient (*or:* quite inadequate); *twintig pond te ~ hebben* be twenty pounds short

³**weinig** [wɛ̱inəχ] *num* few, not many: *slechts ~ huizen staan leeg* there are only a few unoccupied houses; *~ of (tot) geen mensen* few if any people

¹**wekelijks** [we̱kələks] *adj* weekly: *onze ~e vergadering* our weekly meeting

²**wekelijks** [we̱kələks] *adv* **1** weekly, once a week, every week: *~ samenkomen* meet once a week; **2** a week, per week: *hij verdient ~ 500 euro* he earns 500 euros a week

weken [we̱kə(n)] *vb* soak

¹**wekenlang** [wekə(n)lɑ̱ŋ] *adj, adv* lasting several weeks

²**wekenlang** [wekə(n)lɑ̱ŋ] *adv* for weeks (on end)

wekken [wɛ̱kə(n)] *vb* **1** wake (up), call: *tot leven ~* bring into being; **2** awaken, arouse, stir, excite, create

wekker [wɛ̱kər] *de (~s)* alarm (clock): *de ~ op zes uur zetten* set the alarm for six (o'clock)

wekkerradio [wɛ̱kəradijo] *de (~'s)* radio alarm (clock), clock radio

¹**wel** [wɛl] *adv* **1** well: *en (dat) nog ~ op zondag* and on a Sunday, too!; **2** rather, quite: *het was ~ aardig* it was all right; *'hoe is het ermee?' 'het gaat ~'* 'how are you?' 'all right'; *ik mag dat ~* I quite like that; *het kan er ~ mee door* it'll do; **3** probably: *het zal ~ lukken* it'll work out (all right); *dat zal ~ niet* I suppose not; *je zult ~ denken* what will you think?; *hij zal het ~ niet geweest zijn* I don't think it was him; *dat kan ~ (zijn)* that may be (so); *hij zal nu ~ in bed liggen* he'll be in bed by now; **4** as much as; as many as; as often as: *dat kost ~ 100 euro* it'll cost as much as 100 euro; *wat moet dat ~ niet kosten* I hate to think (of) what that costs; **5** at least, just as: *dat is ~ zo makkelijk* it would be a lot easier that way; *het lijkt me ~ zo verstandig* it seems sensible to me; **6** completely, all: *we zijn gezond en ~ aangekomen* we arrived safe and sound; *och, ik mag hem ~* oh, I think he's all right; *dat dacht ik ~* I thought as much; *wat zullen de mensen er ~ van zeggen?* what'll people say?; *heeft hij het ~ gedaan?* did he really do it?; *hij komt ~* he will come (all right); *kom jij? misschien ~!* will you come?, I might!; *het is wél waar* but it ís true; *'ik doe het niet', 'je doet het ~!'* 'I won't do it', 'oh yes you will!'; *jij wil niet? ik ~!* you don't want to? well I do!; *liever ~ dan niet* as soon as not; *nietes! wélles!: a)* 'tisn't! 'tis!, *(Am)* it isn't, it is so! (*or:* too!); *b) (depending on verb in previous sentence)* didn't! did!; *~ eens* once in a while, ever; *dat komt ~ eens voor* it happens at times; *heb je ~ eens Japans gegeten?* have you ever eaten Japanese food?; *dát ~* granted, agreed; *hij wou ~ he* was all for it; *wil je ~ eens luisteren!* will you just listen (to me)!

²**wel** [wɛl] *int* well; why: *~? wat zeg je daarvan?* well? what do you say to that?; *~ allemachtig!* well I'll be damned!; *~ nee!* of course not!

³**wel** [wɛl] *het (~len)* welfare, well-being: *zijn ~ en wee* his fortunes

welbekend [wɛlbəke̱nt] *adj* well-known, famous, familiar

welbespraakt [wɛlbəspra̱kt] *adj* eloquent

welbewust [wɛlbəwʏ̱st] *adj, adv* deliberate, well-considered

weldaad [wɛ̱ldat] *de (weldaden)* benefaction, charity

weldadig [wɛldа̱dəχ] *adj* benevolent

weldoener [wɛ̱ldunər] *de (~s)* benefactor

weldra [wɛ̱ldra] *adv* presently

weleer [wɛle̱r] *het* olden days (*or:* times)

welgemanierd [wɛlɣəmani̱rt] *adj, adv* well-mannered

welgemeend [wɛlɣəme̱nt] *adj* well-meaning, well-meant

welgesteld [wɛlɣəste̱lt] *adj* well-to-do, well-off

welgeteld [wɛlɣəte̱lt] *adv* all-in-all, all told

welig [we̱ləχ] *adj* luxuriant, abundant

welingelicht [wɛlɪŋɣəli̱χt] *adj* well-informed

weliswaar [wɛli̱swar] *adv* it's true, to be sure: *ik heb het ~ beloofd, maar ik kan het nu niet doen* I did promise (, it's true), but I cannot do it now

¹**welk** [wɛlk] *pron* which, what, which one: *om ~e reden?, met ~e bedoeling?* what for?; *~e van die twee is van jou?* which of those two is yours?

²**welk** [wɛlk] *pron* **1** who, whom; which: *de man ~e u gezien hebt, is hier* the man (whom) you saw here; **2** which: *wij verkopen koffie en thee, ~e artikelen veel aftrek vinden* we sell coffee and tea, (articles) which are much in demand; *... vanuit ~e overtuiging hij ertoe overging om ... ...* from which conviction he proceeded to ...

³**welk** [wɛlk] *ind pron* (often with *ook*) whatever, any (... what(so)ever); whichever, any: *~e kleur je ook (maar) wilt, om het even ~e kleur je wilt* take any colour whatsoever; *om ~e reden ook* for any reason whatsoever; *~e van de twee je ook kiest* whichever of the two you choose; *(geef me er maar een,) het geeft niet ~e* any (of them) will do, either (of them) will do

welkom [wɛ̱lkɔm] *adj* welcome: *je bent altijd ~* you're always welcome; *iem hartelijk ~ heten* give s.o. a hearty (*or:* cordial) welcome; *~ thuis* welcome home

welles [wɛ̱ləs] *int* yes, it is (*or:* does): *nietes! ~!* it isn't! it is!

welletjes [wɛ̱ləcəs] *adj* quite enough: *'t is zo ~* that will do

wellicht [wɛli̱χt] *adv* perhaps, possibly

wellustig [wɛlʏ̱stəχ] *adj, adv* sensual, voluptuous

welnu [wɛlny̱] *int* well then: *~, laat eens horen* well then, tell me (your story)

welopgevoed [wɛlɔ̱pχəvut] *adj* well-bred: *~e kinderen* well brought up children

weloverwogen [wɛlovərwo̱ɣə(n)] *adj, adv* **1** (well-)considered: *in ~ woorden* in measured words; **2** deliberate: *iets ~ doen* do sth deliberately

welp [wɛlp] *de* 1 cub; 2 Cub Scout

welstand [wɛlstɑnt] *de* 1 good health; 2 well-being

welste [wɛlstə] || *een succes van je ~* a howling success

welterusten [wɛltərɣstə(n)] *int* goodnight, sleep well

welvaart [wɛlvart] *de* prosperity

welvaartsmaatschappij [wɛlvartsmatsχɑpɛi] *de* affluent society

welvaartsstaat [wɛlvartstat] *de* welfare state

welvarend [wɛlvarənt] *adj* thriving; well-to-do

welverdiend [wɛlvərdint] *adj* well-deserved; well-earned; just

welwillend [wɛlwɪlənt] *adj, adv* kind, sympathetic, favourable: *~ staan tegenover iets* be favourably disposed towards sth

welwillendheid [wɛlwɪləntheit] *de* benevolence, kindness: *dank zij de ~ van* by (*or*: through) the courtesy of

welzijn [wɛlzɛin] *het* welfare, well-being

welzijnssector [wɛlzɛinsɛktɔr] *de (~en)* (field of) welfare

welzijnswerk [wɛlzɛinswɛrk] *het* welfare work, social work

wemelen [wemələ(n)] *vb* teem (with), swarm (with): *zijn opstel wemelt van de fouten* his essay is full of mistakes

¹wenden [wɛndə(n)] *vb* turn (about): *hoe je het ook wendt of keert* whichever way you look at it

²wenden [wɛndə(n)] *ref vb* (with *tot*) turn (to), apply (to)

wending [wɛndɪŋ] *de (~en)* turn: *het verhaal een andere ~ geven* give the story a twist

wenen [wenə(n)] *vb* weep

Wenen [wenə(n)] *het* Vienna

wenk [wɛŋk] *de (~en)* sign, wink, nod

wenkbrauw [wɛŋgbrɑu] *de (~en)* (eye)brow: *de ~en fronsen* frown

wenkbrauwpotlood [wɛŋgbrɑupɔtlot] *het* eyebrow pencil

wenken [wɛŋkə(n)] *vb* beckon, signal, motion

wennen [wɛnə(n)] *vb* 1 get (*or*: become) used (to), get (*or*: become) accustomed (to): *dat zal wel ~* you'll get used to it; 2 adjust, settle in (*or*: down)

wens [wɛns] *de (~en)* 1 wish, desire: *zijn laatste ~* his dying wish; *mijn ~ is vervuld* my wish has come true; *het gaat naar ~* it is going as we hoped it would; *is alles naar ~?* is everything to your liking?; 2 wish, greeting: *de beste ~en voor het nieuwe jaar* best wishes for the new year

wenselijk [wɛnsələk] *adj, adv* desirable; advisable: *ik vind het ~ dat …* I find it advisable to …

wensen [wɛnsə(n)] *vb* wish, desire: *dat laat aan duidelijkheid niets te ~ over* that is perfectly clear; *nog veel te ~ overlaten* leave a lot to be desired; *ik wens met rust gelaten te worden* I want to be left alone; *iem goede morgen (or: een prettige vakantie) ~* wish s.o. good morning (*or*: a nice holiday)

wenskaart [wɛnskart] *de (~en)* greetings card

wentelen [wɛntələ(n)] *vb* roll, turn (round), revolve

wenteltrap [wɛntəltrɑp] *de (~pen)* spiral staircase, winding stairs (*or*: staircase)

wereld [werəlt] *de (~en)* world, earth: *zij komen uit alle delen van de ~* they come from the four corners (*or*: from every corner) of the world; *aan het andere eind van de ~* on the other side of the world; *wat is de ~ toch klein!* isn't it a small world!; *de ~ staat op zijn kop* it's a mad (*or*: topsy-turvy) world; *een kind ter ~ brengen (helpen)* bring a child into the world; *de rijkste man ter ~* the richest man in the world; *er ging een ~ voor hem open* a new world opened up for him; *de derde ~* the Third World

Wereldbank [werəldbɑŋk] *de* World Bank

wereldbeeld [werəldbelt] *het* world-view

wereldbeker [werəldbekər] *de (~s)* World Cup

wereldberoemd [werəldbərumt] *adj* world-famous

wereldbevolking [werəldbəvɔlkɪŋ] *de* world population

wereldbol [werəldbɔl] *de (~len)* (terrestrial) globe

werelddeel [werəldel] *het (-delen)* continent

werelddierendag [werəldirə(n)dɑχ] *de* World Animal Day

wereldgeschiedenis [werəltχəsχidənɪs] *de* world history

wereldhandel [werəlthɑndəl] *de* world trade, international trade

wereldhandelscentrum [werəlthɑndəlsɛntrym] *het (-centra, ~s)* world trade centre

wereldkampioen [werəltkɑmpijun] *de (~en)* world champion

wereldkampioenschap [werəltkɑmpijunsχɑp] *het (~pen)* world championship, (*Am*) world's championship

wereldleider [werəltlɛidər] *de* world leader

Wereldnatuurfonds [werəltnatyrfɔn(t)s] *het* World Wildlife Fund

wereldomroep [werəltɔmrup] *de (~en)* world service

wereldontvanger [werəltɔntfɑŋər] *de (~s)* world(-band) receiver, short wave receiver

wereldoorlog [werəltorlɔχ] *de (~en)* world war: *Tweede Wereldoorlog* the second World War, World War II

wereldpremière [werəltprəmjɛːrə] *de (~s)* world première

wereldranglijst [werəltrɑŋlɛist] *de (~en)* world rankings

wereldrecord [werəltrəkɔːr] *het (~s)* world record

wereldrecordhouder [werəltrəkɔːrhɑudər] *de (~s)* world record holder

wereldreis [werəltrɛis] *de (-reizen)* journey around the world, world tour

wereldstad [werəltstat] *de (-steden)* metropolis

wereldtentoonstelling [werəltɛntonstɛlɪŋ] *de (~en)* world fair

wereldvreemd [werəltfremt] *adj* unworldly; oth-

er-worldly
wereldwijd [wer̩əltwɛit] *adj* worldwide
wereldwinkel [wer̩əltwɪŋkəl] *de (~s)* third-world
(aid) shop
wereldwonder [wer̩əltwɔndər] *het (~en)* ‖ *de ze-*
ven ~en the Seven Wonders of the World
weren [wer̩ə(n)] *vb* avert, prevent, keep out
werf [wɛrf] *de (werven)* **1** shipyard; dockyard: *een*
schip van de ~ laten lopen launch a ship; **2** yard; **3**
(Belg) (building) site
werk [wɛrk] *het (~en)* work, job, task: *het verzamel-*
de ~ van W.F. Hermans W.F. Hermans' (collected)
works; *ze houden hier niet van half~* they don't do
things by halves here; *dat is een heel~* it's quite a
job; *het is onbegonnen ~* it's a hopeless task; *aan-*
genomen ~ contract work; *(vast) ~ hebben* have a
regular job; *aan het ~ gaan* set to work; *aan het ~*
houden keep going; *iedereen aan het ~!* everybody
to their work!; *iem aan het ~ zetten* put (*or:* set) s.o.
to work; *er is ~ aan de winkel* there is work to be
done; *~ in uitvoering* roadworks; *ieder ging op zijn*
eigen manier te ~ everyone set about it in their own
way; *ze wilden er geen ~ van maken* they didn't
want to take the matter in hand; *alles in het ~ stellen*
make every effort to
werkbaar [wɛrgbar] *adj* workable, feasible
werkbalk *de* tool bar
werkbank [wɛrgbaŋk] *de (~en)* bench,
(work)bench
werkbespreking [wɛrgbəsprekɪŋ] *de (~en)*
(roughly) discussion of progress
werkbezoek [wɛrgbəzuk] *het (~en)* working visit
werkbij [wɛrgbɛi] *de (~en)* worker (bee)
werkdag [wɛrgdɑχ] *de (~en)* working day, work-
day, weekday
werkdruk [wɛrgdrʏk] *de* pressure of work
werkelijk [wɛrkələk] *adj* real; true
werkelijkheid [wɛrkələkhɛit] *de* reality: *de alle-*
daagse ~ everyday reality; *~ worden* come true; *in*
*~ actually; *dat is in strijd met de ~* that conflicts
with the facts
werkeloos [wɛrkəlos] *adj* **1** idle; **2** unemployed
werken [wɛrkə(n)] *vb* **1** work, operate: *de tijd werkt*
in ons voordeel time is on our side; *iem hard laten*
*~ work s.o. hard; *hard ~* work hard; *aan iets~* work
at (*or:* on) sth; *~ op het land* work the soil (*or:* land);
2 work, function: *dit apparaat werkt heel eenvoudig*
this apparatus is simple to operate; *zo werkt dat*
niet that's not the way it works; **3** work, take effect:
de pillen begonnen te ~ the pills began to take effect;
zich kapot ~ work one's fingers to the bone; *een on-*
gewenst persoon eruit ~ get rid of an unwanted person
werkend [wɛrkənt] *adj* working; employed: *snel ~e*
medicijnen fast-acting medicines
werker [wɛrkər] *de (~s)* worker
werkervaring [wɛrkɛrvarɪŋ] *de* work experience
werkgeheugen [wɛrkχəhøyə(n)] *het (~s)* main
memory

werkgelegenheid [wɛrkχəleyənhɛit] *de* employment
werkgever [wɛrkχevər] *de (~s)* employer
werkgeversorganisatie [wɛrkχevərsɔryа-
niza(t)si] *de (~s)* employers' organization (*or:* federation)
werkgroep [wɛrkχrup] *de (~en)* study group,
working party
werking [wɛrkɪŋ] *de (~en)* **1** working, action, func-
tioning: *buiten ~* out of order; *de wet treedt 1 janu-*
ari in ~ the law will come into force (*or:* effect) on
January 1st; **2** effect(s)
werkje [wɛrkjə] *het (~s)* pattern
werkkamer [wɛrkamər] *de (~s)* study
werkkast [wɛrkast] *de (~en)* broom cupboard
werkkleding [wɛrkledɪŋ] *de* workclothes, working
clothes
werkklimaat [wɛrklimat] *het (-klimaten) see* werk-
sfeer
werkkracht [wɛrkraχt] *de (~en)* worker, employee
werkkring [wɛrkrɪŋ] *de (~en)* post, job, working
environment
werkloos [wɛrklos] *adj* unemployed, out of work
(*or:* a job)
werkloosheid [wɛrklosheit] *de* unemployment
werkloze [wɛrklozə] *de (~n)* unemployed person
werknemer [wɛrknemər] *de (~s)* employee
werknemersorganisatie [wɛrknemərsɔryа-
niza(t)si] *de (~s)* (trade) union
werkonderbreking [wɛrkɔndərbrekɪŋ] *de (~en)*
(work) stoppage, walkout
werkplaats [wɛrkplats] *de (~en)* workshop, workplace
werkruimte [wɛrkrœymtə] *de (~n, ~s)* workroom
werksituatie [wɛrksitywa(t)si] *de (~s)* work situation
werkstation [wɛrksta(t)ʃɔn] *het (~s)* workstation
werkster [wɛrkstər] *de (~s)* **1** (woman, female)
worker; **2** cleaning lady
werkstraf [wɛrkstraf] *de (-fen)* community service
werkstudent [wɛrkstydɛnt] *de (~en)* student
working his way through college with a (part-time)
job
werkstuk [wɛrkstʏk] *het (~ken)* **1** piece of work; **2**
(educ) paper; project
werktafel [wɛrktafəl] *de (~s)* work table, desk
werkterrein [wɛrktɛrɛin] *het (~en)* working space,
work area
werktijd [wɛrktɛit] *de (~en)* working hours, office
hours: *na ~* after hours
werktuig [wɛrktœyχ] *het (~en)* tool (*also fig*), piece
of equipment, machine
werktuigbouwkunde [wɛrktœyɣbaukyndə] *de*
mechanical engineering
werkuur [wɛrkyr] *het (-uren)* working hour, hour
of work
werkvergunning [wɛrkfəryʏnɪŋ] *de (~en)* work
permit
werkvloer [wɛrkflur] *de* shop floor

werkweek [wɛrkwek] *de (-weken)* **1** (working) week; **2** study week, project week: *op ~ zijn* have a study week (*or:* project week)

werkwijze [wɛrkwɛizə] *de (~n)* method (of working), procedure; (manufacturing) process; routine: *dit is de normale ~* this is (the) standard (operating) procedure

werkwillige [wɛrkwɪləɣə] *de (~n)* non-striker

werkwoord [wɛrkwort] *het (~en)* verb: *onregelmatig ~* irregular verb

werkzaam [wɛrksam] *adj, adv* **1** working, active; employed, engaged; **2** active, industrious: *hij blijft als adviseur ~* he will continue to act as (an) adviser

werkzaamheden [wɛrksamhedə(n)] *de* activities, duties, operations, proceedings, business: *~ aan de metro* work on the underground

werkzoekende [wɛrksukəndə] *de (~n)* job-seeker, person in search of employment

werpen [wɛrpə(n)] *vb* have puppies (*or:* kittens): *onze hond heeft (drie jongen) geworpen* our dog has had (three) pups

werper [wɛrpər] *de (~s)* pitcher

werphengel [wɛrphɛŋəl] *de (~s)* casting rod

wervel [wɛrvəl] *de (~s)* vertebra

wervelend [wɛrvələnt] *adj* sparkling

wervelkolom [wɛrvəlkolɔm] *de (~men)* vertebral column, spinal column, spine, backbone

wervelstorm [wɛrvəlstɔrm] *de (~en)* cyclone, tornado, hurricane

wervelwind [wɛrvəlwɪnt] *de (~en)* whirlwind, tornado: *als een ~* like a whirlwind

werven [wɛrvə(n)] *vb* **1** recruit; **2** *(Belg)* appoint

werving [wɛrvɪŋ] *de (~en)* recruitment, enlistment, enrolment: *~ en selectie* recruitment and selection

wesp [wɛsp] *de (~en)* wasp

wespennest [wɛspənɛst] *het (~en)* wasps' nest

west [wɛst] *adj, adv* **1** west(erly), westward, to the west; **2** west(erly), from the west

westelijk [wɛstələk] *adj, adv* west, westerly, western, westward: *~ van* (to the) west of

westen [wɛstə(n)] *het* west: *het ~ van Nederland* the west(ern part) of the Netherlands; *het wilde ~* the (Wild) West, the Frontier; *buiten ~ raken* pass out; *iem buiten ~ slaan* knock s.o. out (cold); *buiten ~ zijn* be out (cold)

westenwind [wɛstə(n)wɪnt] *de (~en)* west(erly) wind

westerlengte [wɛstərlɛŋtə] *de* longitude west: *op 15° ~* at 15° longitude west

westerling [wɛstərlɪŋ] *de (~en)* Westerner; westerner

¹westers [wɛstərs] *adj* western

²westers [wɛstərs] *adv* in a western fashion (*or:* manner)

West-Europa [wɛstøropa] *het* Western Europe

West-Europees [wɛstøropes] *adj* West(ern) European

West-Indië [wɛstɪndijə] *het* (the) West Indies

westkust [wɛstkʏst] *de (~en)* west coast

wet [wɛt] *de (~ten)* **1** law; statute: *een ongeschreven ~* an unwritten rule; *de ~ naleven* (or: *overtreden*) abide by (*or:* break) the law; *de ~ schrijft voor dat ...* the law prescribes that ...; *de ~ toepassen* enforce the law; *volgens de ~ is het een misdaad* it's a crime before the law; *volgens de Engelse ~* under English law; *bij de ~ bepaald* regulated by law; *in strijd met de ~* unlawful, against the law; *voor de ~ trouwen* marry at a registry office; *de ~ van Archimedes* Archimedes' principle; **2** law; rule: *iem de ~ voorschrijven* lay down the law to s.o.

wetboek [wɛdbuk] *het (~en)* code, lawbook

¹weten [wetə(n)] *vb* know; manage: *dat weet zelfs een kind!* even a fool knows that!; *ik had het kunnen ~* I might have known; *ik zal het u laten ~* I'll let you know; *~ te ontkomen* manage to escape; *ik zou wel eens willen ~ waarom hij dat zei* I'd like to know why he said that; *daar weet ik alles van* I know all about it; *ik weet het!* I've got it!; *voor je het weet, ben je er* you're there before you know it; *ze hebben het geweten* they found out (to their cost); *hij wou er niets van ~* he wouldn't hear of it; *nu weet ik nóg niets!* I'm no wiser than I was (before)!; *je weet wie het zegt* look who is talking; *je moet het zelf (maar) ~* it's your decision; *je zou beter moeten ~* you should know better (than that); *hij wist niet hoe gauw hij weg moest komen* he couldn't get away fast enough; *als dat geen zwendel is dan weet ik het niet (meer)* if that isn't a fraud I don't know what is; *ik zou niet ~ waarom (niet)* I don't see why (not); *weet je wel, je weet wel* you know; *iets zeker ~* be sure about sth; *voor zover ik weet* as far as I know; *iets te ~ komen* find out sth; *als je dat maar weet!* keep it in mind!; *niet dat ik weet* not that I know; *weet je nog?* (do you) remember?; *weet ik veel!* search me!; *ik wist niet wat ik zag!* I couldn't believe my eyes!; *je weet ('t) maar nooit* you never know

²weten [wetə(n)] *het* knowledge: *buiten mijn ~* without my knowledge; *naar mijn beste ~* to the best of my knowledge

wetenschap [wetə(n)sχɑp] *de (~pen)* **1** knowledge; **2** learning; science; scholarship, learning

wetenschappelijk [wetə(n)sχɑpələk] *adj, adv* scholarly; scientific: *voorbereidend ~ onderwijs* pre-university education; *~ personeel* academic staff, *(Am)* faculty

wetenschapper [wetənsχɑpər] *de (~s)* scholar; scientist; academic

wetgevend [wɛtχevənt] *adj* legislative

wetgever [wɛtχevər] *de (~s)* legislator

wetgeving [wɛtχevɪŋ] *de (~en)* legislation

wethouder [wɛthaudər] *de (~s)* alderman, (city, town) councillor: *de ~ van volkshuisvesting* the alderman for housing

wetsartikel [wɛtsɑrtikəl] *het (~en, ~s)* section of a (*or:* the) law

wetsdienaar [wɛtsdinar] *de (-dienaren, ~s)* police officer

wetsontwerp [wɛtsɔntwɛrp] *het (~en)* bill: *een ~ aannemen* pass (*or:* adopt) a bill

wetsovertreding [wɛtsovərtredɪŋ] *de (~en)* violation of a (*or:* the) law

wetswinkel [wɛtswɪŋkəl] *de (~s)* law centre

wettelijk [wɛtələk] *adj, adv* legal, statutory: *~e aansprakelijkheid* legal liability; *wettelijke-aansprakelijkheidsverzekering* third-party insurance

wettig [wɛtəχ] *adj, adv* legal, legitimate, valid: *de ~e eigenaar* the rightful owner

weven [wevə(n)] *vb* weave

wever [wevər] *de (~s)* weaver

wezel [wezəl] *de (~s)* weasel: *zo bang als een ~* as timid as a hare

¹**wezen** [wezə(n)] *het (~s)* **1** being, creature: *geen levend ~ te bespeuren* not a living soul in sight; **2** being, nature, essence, substance: *haar hele ~ kwam ertegen in opstand* her whole soul rose against it

²**wezen** [wezə(n)] *vb* be: *dat zal wel waar ~!* I bet!; *kan ~, maar ik mag hem niet* be that as it may, I don't like him; *wij zijn daar ~ kijken* we've been there to have a look; *laten we wel ~* (let's) be fair (*or:* honest) (now); *een studie die er ~ mag* a substantial study; *weg ~!* off with you!

wezenlijk [wezənlək] *adj, adv* essential: *van ~ belang* essential, of vital importance; *een ~ verschil* a substantial difference

wezenloos [wezə(n)los] *adj, adv* vacant: *zich ~ schrijven* write oneself silly; *zich ~ schrikken* be scared out of one's wits

whisky [wɪski] *de* whisky: *Amerikaanse ~* bourbon; *Ierse ~* Irish whiskey; *Schotse ~* Scotch (whisky); *~ puur* a straight (*or:* neat) whisky

wichelroede [wɪχəlrudə] *de (~n)* divining rod, dowsing rod

wicht [wɪχt] *het (~en)* child

wie [wi] *pron* **1** who; whose; which: *van ~ is dit boek?* whose book is this?; *~ heb je gezien?* who have you seen?; *met ~ (spreek ik)?* who is this? (*or:* that?); *~ van jullie?* which of you?; *~ er ook komt, zeg maar dat ik niet thuis ben* whoever comes, tell them I'm out; **2** who; whose: *de man ~ns dood door ieder betreurd wordt* the man whose death is generally mourned; *het meisje (aan) ~ ik het boek gaf* the girl to whom I gave the book; **3** whoever: *~ anders dan Jan?* who (else) but John?; *~ dan ook* anybody, anyone, whoever; *~ niet akkoord gaat ...* anyone who disagrees ...

wiebelen [wibələ(n)] *vb* **1** wobble; **2** rock: *ze zat te ~ op haar stoel* she was wiggling about on her chair

wieden [widə(n)] *vb* weed

wieg [wiχ] *de (~en)* cradle: *van de ~ tot het graf verzorgd* looked after from the cradle to the grave

wiegen [wiχə(n)] *vb* rock

wiek [wik] *de (~en)* **1** sail, vane; **2** wing

wiel [wil] *het (~en)* wheel: *het ~ weer uitvinden* re-invent the wheel; *iem in de ~en rijden* put a spoke in s.o.'s wheel

wieldop [wildɔp] *de (~pen)* hubcap

wielerbaan [wilərban] *de (-banen)* bicycle track, cycling track

wielersport [wilərspɔrt] *de* (bi)cycling

wielklem [wilklɛm] *de (~men)* wheel clamp

wielrennen [wilrɛnə(n)] *vb* (bi)cycle racing

wielrenner [wilrɛnər] *de (~s)* (racing) cyclist, bicyclist, cycler

wieltje [wilcə] *het (~s)* (little) wheel; castor: *dat loopt op ~s* that's running smoothly

wienerschnitzel [winərʃnɪtsəl] *de (~s)* Wiener schnitzel

wiens [wins] *pron* whose

wier [wir] *het* **1** alga; **2** seaweed

wierook [wirok] *de* incense: *~ branden* burn incense

wiet [wit] *de* weed, grass

wig [wɪχ] *de (~gen)* wedge

wigwam [wɪχwɑm] *de (~s)* wigwam

wij [wɛi] *pers pron* we: *(beter) dan ~* (better) than we are; *~ allemaal* all of us, we all

wijd [wɛit] *adj, adv* **1** wide: *een ~e blik* a broad view; *met ~ open ogen* wide-eyed; **2** wide, loose: *~er maken* let out, enlarge; **3** wide, broad: *de ~e zee* the open sea

wijdbeens [wɛidbens] *adv* with legs wide apart

wijden [wɛidə(n)] *vb* **1** devote; **2** (*rel*) consecrate, ordain: *gewijde muziek* sacred music

wijdte [wɛitə] *de (~n, ~s)* breadth, distance: *de ~ tussen de banken* the space between the benches

wijdverspreid [wɛitfərspreit] *adj* widespread, rife, rampant

wijf [wɛif] *het* bitch: *een oud ~* an old bag

wijfje [wɛifjə] *het* female

wijk [wɛik] *de (~en)* district, area: *de deftige ~en* the fashionable areas

wijkagent [wɛikaɣɛnt] *de (~en)* policeman on the beat; local bobby

wijkcentrum [wɛiksɛntrʏm] *het (wijkcentra)* community centre

wijken [wɛikə(n)] *vb* give in (to), give way (to), yield (to): *hij weet van geen ~* he sticks to his guns

wijkverpleegkundige [wɛikfərpleɣkʏndəɣə] *de (~n)* district nurse

wijlen [wɛilə(n)] *adj* late, deceased: *~ de heer Smit* the late Mr Smit

wijn [wɛin] *de (~en)* wine: *oude ~ in nieuwe zakken* old wine in new bottles

wijnfles [wɛinflɛs] *de (~sen)* wine bottle

wijngaard [wɛiŋɣart] *de (~en)* vineyard

wijnhandelaar [wɛinhɑndəlar] *de (~s, -handelaren)* wine merchant

wijnkaart [wɛiŋkart] *de (~en)* wine list

wijnkenner [wɛiŋkɛnər] *de (~s)* connoisseur of wine

wijnstok [wɛinstɔk] *de (~ken)* (grape)vine

wijnstreek [wɛinstrek] *de (-streken)* wine(-growing) region

wijnvlek [wɛinvlɛk] *de (~ken)* birthmark

¹**wijs** [wɛis] *de (wijzen)* **1** way, manner: *bij wijze van*

spreken so to speak, as it were; *bij wijze van uitzondering* as an exception; **2** tune: *hij kan geen ~ houden* he sings (*or:* plays) out of tune; *van de ~ raken* get in a muddle; *iem van de ~ brengen* put s.o. out (*or:* off) his stroke; *hij liet zich niet van de ~ brengen* he kept a level head (*or:* his cool); *onbepaalde ~* infinitive

²**wijs** [wɛis] *adj, adv* wise: *ben je niet (goed) ~?* are you mad? (*or:* crazy?); *ik werd er niet wijzer van* I was none the wiser for it; *ik kan er niet ~ uit worden* I can't make head or tail of it

wijsbegeerte [wɛizbəɣertə] *de (~n)* philosophy

wijsgeer [wɛisχer] *de (-geren)* philosopher

wijsheid [wɛishɛit] *de (-heden)* wisdom; piece of wisdom: *hij meent de ~ in pacht te hebben* he thinks he knows it all

wijsheidstand [wɛishɛitstɑnt] *de (~en) (Belg)* wisdom tooth

wijsje [wɛiʃə] *het (~s)* tune

wijsmaken [wɛismakə(n)] *vb* fool, kid: *laat je niks ~!* don't buy that nonsense!

wijsneus [wɛisnøs] *de (-neuzen)* know(-it)-all

wijsvinger [wɛisfɪŋər] *de (~s)* forefinger

wijten [wɛitə(n)] *vb* blame (s.o. for sth)

wijwater [wɛiwatər] *het* holy water

wijze [wɛizə] *de (~n)* **1** manner, way; **2** wise man (*or:* woman); learned man (*or:* woman)

¹**wijzen** [wɛizə(n)] *vb* **1** point: *naar een punt ~* point to a spot; *(fig) met de vinger naar iem ~* point the finger at s.o.; *er moet op worden gewezen dat ...* it should be pointed out that ...; **2** indicate: *alles wijst erop dat ...* everything seems to indicate that ...

²**wijzen** [wɛizə(n)] *vb* show, point out: *de weg ~* lead (*or:* show) the way

³**wijzen** [wɛizə(n)] *ref vb* show: *dat wijst zich vanzelf* that is self-evident

wijzer [wɛizər] *de (~s)* indicator; hand; pointer: *met de ~s van de klok mee* clockwise

wijzerplaat [wɛizərplat] *de (-platen)* dial

wijzigen [wɛizəɣə(n)] *vb* alter, change

wijziging [wɛizəɣɪŋ] *de (~en)* alteration, change: *~en aanbrengen in* make changes in

wikkel [wɪkəl] *de (~s)* wrapper

wikkelen [wɪkələ(n)] *vb* wind; wrap (up), enfold

wil [wɪl] *de* will, wish: *geen eigen ~ hebben* have no mind of one's own; *met een beetje goeie ~ gaat het best* with a little good will it'll all work out; *een sterke ~ hebben* be strong-willed; *zijn ~ is wet* his word is law; *ter ~le van* for the sake of

¹**wild** [wɪlt] *adj, adv* wild: *~e dieren* wild animals; *~ enthousiast zijn over iets* go overboard about sth; *in het ~e (weg)* at random

²**wild** [wɪlt] *het* **1** game: *~, vis en gevogelte* fish, flesh and fowl; **2** wild: *in het ~ leven* (or: *groeien*) live (*or:* grow) (in the) wild

wilde [wɪldə] *de (~n)* savage

wildernis [wɪldərnɪs] *de (~sen)* wilderness

wildgroei [wɪltχruj] *de* proliferation

wildkamperen [wɪltkɑmpərə(n)] *vb* camp wild

wildpark [wɪltpɑrk] *het (~en)* wildlife park, game park (*or:* reserve)

wildplassen [wɪltplɑsə(n)] *vb* urinate in public

wildvreemd [wɪltfremt] *adj* completely strange, utterly strange: *een ~ iemand* a perfect stranger

wildwestfilm [wɪltwɛstfɪlm] *de (~s)* western

wilg [wɪlχ] *de (~en)* willow (tree)

wilgen [wɪlɣə(n)] *adj* willow

wilgenhout [wɪlɣə(n)haut] *het* willow (wood)

Wilhelmus [wɪlhɛlmʏs] *het* Wilhelmus, Dutch national anthem

willekeur [wɪləkør] *de* **1** will, discretion: *naar ~* at will, at one's (own) discretion; **2** arbitrariness, unfairness, capriciousness

willekeurig [wɪləkørəχ] *adj, adv* **1** arbitrary, random, indiscriminate: *neem een ~e steen* take any stone (you like); **2** arbitrary, high-handed, capricious

¹**willen** [wɪlə(n)] *vb* want, wish, desire: *het is (maar) een kwestie van ~* it's (only) a matter of will; *ik wil wel een pilsje* I wouldn't mind a beer; *wil je wat pinda's?* would you like some peanuts?; *ik wil het niet hebben* I won't have (*or:* allow) it; *niet ~ luisteren* refuse to listen; *ik wil niets meer met hem te maken hebben* I've done with him; *ik wil wel toegeven dat ...* I'm willing to admit that ...; *ik wou net vertrekken toen ...* I was just about (*or:* going) to leave when ...; *dat had ik best eens ~ zien!* I would have liked to have seen it!; *ja, wat wil je?* what else can you expect?; *wat wil je nog meer?* what more do you want?; *wilt u dat ik het raam openzet?* shall I open the window (for you)?; *ik wou dat ik een fiets had* I wish I had a bike; *of je wilt of niet* whether you want to or not; *we moesten wel glimlachen, of we wilden of niet* we could not help but smile (*or:* help smiling); *dat ding wil niet* the thing won't (*or:* refuses to) go; *de motor wil niet starten* the engine won't start; *men wil er niet aan* people are not buying (it), nobody is interested

²**willen** [wɪlə(n)] *vb* will, would: *wil je me de melk even (aan)geven?* could (*or:* would) you pass me the milk, please?; *wil je me even helpen?* would you mind helping me?

wilskracht [wɪlskrɑχt] *de* will-power, will, backbone

wimpel [wɪmpəl] *de (~s)* pennon, pennant

wimper [wɪmpər] *de (~s)* (eye)lash

wind [wɪnt] *de (~en)* wind, breeze, gale: *bestand zijn tegen weer en ~* be wind and weatherproof; *geen zuchtje ~* not a breath of wind, dead calm; *een harde* (or: *krachtige*) *~* a high (*or:* strong) wind; *de ~ gaat liggen* the wind is dropping; *de ~ van voren krijgen* get lectured at; *kijken uit welke hoek de ~ waait* see which way the wind blows; *de ~ mee hebben: a)* have the wind behind one; *b) (fig)* have everything going for one; *(fig) een waarschuwing in de ~ slaan* disregard a warning; *tegen de ~ in* against the wind, into the teeth of the wind; *het gaat hem voor de ~* he is doing well, he is flying high; *~en la-*

windbuks [wɪndbʏks] *de (~en)* air rifle, airgun
windei [wɪntɛi] *het (~eren)* ‖ *dat zal hem geen ~eren leggen* he'll do well out of it
winden [wɪndə(n)] *vb* wind, twist, entwine, wrap
windenergie [wɪntenɛrʒi] *de* wind energy
winderig [wɪndərəχ] *adj* **1** windy, blowy, breezy, stormy, windswept; **2** windy, flatulent
windhaan [wɪnthan] *de (-hanen)* weathercock
windhond [wɪnthɔnt] *de (~en)* greyhound, whippet
windhoos [wɪnthos] *de (-hozen)* whirlwind
windjack [wɪntjɛk] *het (~s)* windcheater
windjak [wɪntjɑk] *het (~ken, ~s)* windcheater
windkracht [wɪntkrɑχt] *de* wind-force: *wind met ~ 7* force 7 wind(s)
windmolen [wɪntmolə(n)] *de (~s)* windmill: *tegen ~s vechten* tilt at windmills, fight windmills
windmolenpark [wɪntmolə(n)pɑrk] *het (~en)* wind park (*or:* farm)
windrichting [wɪntrɪχtɪŋ] *de (~en)* wind direction, (*pl also*) points of the compass
windroos [wɪntros] *de (-rozen)* compass card
windscherm [wɪntsχɛrm] *het (~en)* windbreak
windsnelheid [wɪntsnɛlhɛit] *de (-heden)* wind speed
windstil [wɪntstɪl] *adj* calm, windless, still
windstoot [wɪntstot] *de (-stoten)* gust (of wind), squall
windstreek [wɪntstrek] *de (-streken)* quarter, point of the compass
windsurfen [wɪntsʏrfə(n)] *vb* go windsurfing
windsurfer [wɪntsʏrfər] *de (~s)* windsurfer
windvlaag [wɪntflaχ] *de (-vlagen)* gust (of wind), blast, squall
windwijzer [wɪntwɛizər] *de (~s)* weathercock, weathervane
wingerd [wɪŋərt] *de (~s, ~en)* (grape)vine
winkel [wɪŋkəl] *de (~s)* shop, store: *een ~ in mode-artikelen* a boutique, a fashion store; *~s kijken* go window-shopping
winkelbediende [wɪŋkəlbədində] *de* shop-assistant, counter-assistant, salesman, saleswoman
winkelcentrum [wɪŋkəlsɛntrʏm] *het (-centra)* shopping centre (*or:* precinct)
winkeldief [wɪŋkəldif] *de (-dieven)* shoplifter
winkelen [wɪŋkələ(n)] *vb* shop, go shopping, do some (*or:* the) shopping
winkelgalerij [wɪŋkəlχɑlərɛi] *de (~en)* (shopping-)arcade
winkelhaak [wɪŋkəlhak] *de (-haken)* **1** three-cornered tear, right-angled tear; **2** (carpenter's) square
winkelier [wɪŋkəli̯r] *de (~s)* shopkeeper, retailer, tradesman
winkelketen [wɪŋkəlketə(n)] *de (~s)* chain of shops (*or:* stores), store chain
winkelpersoneel [wɪŋkəlpɛrsonel] *het* shopworkers, shop staff (*or:* personnel)
winkelstraat [wɪŋkəlstrat] *de (-straten)* shopping street

winkelwagen [wɪŋkəlwaχə(n)] *de (~s)* (shopping) trolley
winnaar [wɪnar] *de (~s)* winner, victor, winning team
¹winnen [wɪnə(n)] *vb* win: *het ~de doelpunt* the winning goal; *je kan niet altijd ~* you can't win them all; *~ bij het kaarten* win at cards; *~ met 7-2* win 7-2, win by 7 goals (*or:* points) to 2; *(het) ~ van iem* beat s.o., have the better of s.o.
²winnen [wɪnə(n)] *vb* **1** win, gain, mine, extract: *zout uit zeewater ~* obtain salt from sea water; **2** win, gain, enlist, secure: *iem voor zich ~* win s.o. over
winning [wɪnɪŋ] *de* winning, extraction, reclamation
winst [wɪnst] *de (~en)* **1** profit, return, earning(s), winning: *netto ~* net returns (*or:* gain, profit); *~ behalen* (*or:* opleveren) gain (*or:* make, yield) a profit; *tel uit je ~* it can't go wrong; *op ~ spelen* play to win; **2** gain, benefit, advantage: *een ~ van drie zetels in de Kamer behalen* gain three seats in Parliament
winstdeling [wɪnzdelɪŋ] *de (~en)* profit-sharing, participation
winstgevend [wɪnstχevənt] *adj* profitable, lucrative, remunerative, (*fig*) fruitful, economic
winstmarge [wɪnstmɑːrʒə] *de (~s)* profit margin, margin of profit
winstpunt [wɪnstpʏnt] *het (~en)* point (scored)
winstrekening [wɪnstrekənɪŋ] *de* statement of profits, profit account
winter [wɪntər] *de (~s)* winter: *hartje ~* the dead (*or:* depths) of winter; *we hebben nog niet veel ~ gehad* we haven't had much wintry weather (*or:* much of a winter) yet; *'s ~s in* (the) winter, in (the) wintertime
winteravond [wɪntərɑvɔnt] *de (~en)* winter evening
winterdag [wɪntərdɑχ] *de (~en)* winter('s) day
winterhanden [wɪntərhɑndə(n)] *de* chilblained hands
winterjas [wɪntərjɑs] *de (~sen)* winter coat
winterkoninkje [wɪntərkonɪŋkjə] *het (~s)* wren
wintermaanden [wɪntərmɑndə(n)] *de* winter months
winterpeen [wɪntərpen] *de (-penen)* winter carrot
winters [wɪntərs] *adj, adv* wintery: *zich ~ aankleden* dress for winter
winterslaap [wɪntərslap] *de* hibernation, winter sleep: *een ~ houden* hibernate
winterspelen [wɪntərspelə(n)] *de* winter Olympics
wintersport [wɪntərspɔrt] *de (~en)* winter sports: *met ~ gaan* go skiing, go on a winter sports holiday
wintertijd [wɪntərtɛit] *de* wintertime, winter season
win-winsituatie [wɪnwɪnsitywa(t)si] *de (~s)* win-win situation
wip [wɪp] *de (~pen)* **1** seesaw: *op de ~ zitten* have one's job on the line; **2** skip; hop: *met een ~ was hij*

bij de deur he was at the door in one bound; **3** lay, screw

wipneus [wɪpnøs] *de (wipneuzen)* turned-up nose, snub nose

¹**wippen** [wɪpə(n)] *vb* **1** hop, bound, skip; **2** whip, pop: *er even tussenuit* ~ nip (*or:* pop) out for a while; *zij zat met haar stoel te* ~ *van ongeduld* she sat tilting her chair with impatience; **3** play on a seesaw

²**wippen** [wɪpə(n)] *vb* topple, overthrow, unseat

wirwar [wɪrwɑr] *de* criss-cross, jumble, tangle, snarl, maze: *een* ~ *van steegjes* a rabbit warren

wiskunde [wɪskʏndə] *de* mathematics

wiskundeknobbel [wɪskʏndəknɔbəl] *de* gift (*or:* head) for mathematics

wiskundig [wɪskʏndəχ] *adj, adv* mathematic(al)

wispelturig [wɪspəltʏrəχ] *adj, adv* inconstant, fickle, capricious

¹**wissel** [wɪsəl] *de (~s)* **1** substitute; sub: *een* ~ *inzetten* put in a substitute; **2** change, switch

²**wissel** [wɪsəl] *het, de (~s)* points, switch: *een* ~ *overhalen* (*or: verzetten*) change (*or:* shift) the points

wisselautomaat [wɪsəlɑutomat] *de (-automaten)* (automatic) money changer, change machine

wisselbeker [wɪsəlbekər] *de (~s)* challenge cup

¹**wisselen** [wɪsələ(n)] *vb* **1** change, exchange: *van plaats* ~ change places; **2** change, give change: *kunt u ~?* can you change this?; **3** exchange, bandy: *van gedachten* ~ *over* exchange views (*or:* ideas) about

²**wisselen** [wɪsələ(n)] *vb* change, vary

wisselgeld [wɪsəlɣɛlt] *het* change; (small, loose) change: *te weinig* ~ *terugkrijgen* be short-changed

wisseling [wɪsəlɪŋ] *de (~en)* **1** change, exchange; **2** change, changing, turn(ing)

wisselkoers [wɪsəlkurs] *de (~en)* exchange-rate, rate of exchange

wisselslag [wɪsəlslɑχ] *de* (individual) medley

wisselspeler [wɪsəlspelər] *de (~s)* substitute, reserve; sub

wisselstroom [wɪsəlstrom] *de* alternating current, AC

wisseltrofee [wɪsəltrofe] *de (~ën)* challenge trophy

wisselvallig [wɪsəlvɑləχ] *adj* changeable, unstable, uncertain, precarious

wisselwachter [wɪsəlwɑχtər] *de (~s)* pointsman, signalman

wisselwerking [wɪsəlwɛrkɪŋ] *de (~en)* interaction, interplay

wissen [wɪsə(n)] *vb* **1** wipe; **2** erase, *(comp)* delete

wit [wɪt] *het* **1** white; **2** cut-price

witjes [wɪcəs] *adj* pale, white: ~ *om de neus zien* look white about the gills

witlof [wɪtlɔf] *het* chicory

witregel [wɪtreɣəl] *de (~s)* extra space (between the lines)

Wit-Rus [wɪtrʏs] *de (~sen)* White Russian, Belorussian

Wit-Rusland [wɪtrʏslɑnt] *het* White Russia, Belorussia

witteboordencriminaliteit [wɪtəbɔrdə(n)krimi-naliteit] *de (~en)* white-collar crime

wittebrood [wɪtəbrot] *het (-broden)* white bread

wittebroodsweken [wɪtəbrotswekə(n)] *de* honeymoon

wittekool [wɪtəkol] *de (-kolen)* white cabbage

witten [wɪtə(n)] *vb* whitewash

witwassen [wɪtwɑsə(n)] *vb* launder

wodka [wɔtka] *de* vodka

woede [wudə] *de* **1** rage, fury, anger: *buiten zichzelf van* ~ *zijn* be beside oneself with rage (*or:* anger); **2** mania

woedeaanval [wudəanvɑl] *de (~len)* tantrum, fit (of anger)

woeden [wudə(n)] *vb* rage, rave

woedend [wudənt] *adj, adv* furious, infuriated

woef [wuf] *int* bow-wow, woof

woekeraar [wukərɑr] *de (~s)* usurer, profiteer

woekeren [wukərə(n)] *vb* **1** practise usury, profiteer; **2** make the most (of): *met de ruimte* ~ use (*or:* utilize) every inch of space; **3** grow rank (*or:* rampant)

woekering [wukərɪŋ] *de (~en)* uncontrolled growth, rampant growth

woekerprijs [wukərprɛis] *de (-prijzen)* usurious price, exorbitant price

¹**woelen** [wulə(n)] *vb* **1** toss about: *zij lag maar te* ~ she was tossing and turning; **2** churn (about, around)

²**woelen** [wulə(n)] *vb* **1** turn up (the soil); **2** grub (up), root (out): *de varkens* ~ *de wortels bloot* the pigs are grubbing up the roots

woelig [wuləχ] *adj, adv* restless: ~*e tijden* turbulent times

woensdag [wunzdɑχ] *de (~en)* Wednesday: *'s* ~*s* Wednesday, on Wednesdays

¹**woensdags** [wunzdɑχs] *adj* Wednesday

²**woensdags** [wunzdɑχs] *adv* on Wednesdays

woerd [wurt] *de (~en)* drake

woest [wust] *adj, adv* **1** savage, wild: *een* ~ *voorkomen hebben* have a fierce countenance; **2** rude, rough; **3** furious, infuriated: *in een* ~*e bui* in a fit of rage; **4** waste; desolate

woestijn [wustɛin] *de (~en)* desert

wok [wɔk] *de (~ken)* wok

wol [wɔl] *de* wool: *zuiver* ~ 100 % (*or:* pure) wool

wolf [wɔlf] *de (wolven)* wolf

wolfraam [wɔlfram] *het* tungsten

Wolga [wɔlχa] *de* Volga

wolindustrie [wɔlɪndʏstri] *de* wool industry

wolk [wɔlk] *de (~en)* cloud || *een* ~ *van een baby* a bouncing baby

wolkbreuk [wɔlgbrøk] *de (~en)* cloudburst

wolkenkrabber [wɔlkə(n)krɑbər] *de (~s)* skyscraper

wolkje *het* cloudlet, little cloud, small cloud: *er is geen* ~ *aan de lucht* there isn't a cloud in the sky

wollen [wɔlə(n)] *adj* woollen, wool

wollig [wɔləχ] *adj, adv* woolly: ~ *taalgebruik*

woolly language

wolmerk [wɔlmɛrk] *het* wool mark

wolvin [wɔlvɪn] *de (~nen)* she-wolf

wond [wɔnt] *de (~en)* wound, injury: *een gapende ~* a gaping wound, a gash; *Joris had een ~je aan zijn vinger* Joris had a cut (*or:* scratch) on his finger

wonder [wɔndər] *het (~en)* **1** wonder, miracle: *het is een ~ dat …* it is a miracle that …; *geen ~* no (*or:* small) wonder, not surprising; **2** wonder, marvel: *de ~en van de natuur* the wonders (*or:* marvels) of nature; *~ boven ~* by amazing good fortune

wonderbaarlijk [wɔndərbɑrlək] *adj, adv* miraculous, strange, curious

wonderkind [wɔndərkɪnt] *het (~eren)* (child) prodigy

wonderlijk [wɔndərlək] *adj* strange, surprising

wonderolie [wɔndəroli] *de* castor oil

wonen [wonə(n)] *vb* live: *op zichzelf gaan ~* set up house, go and live on one's own

woning [wonɪŋ] *de (~en)* house, home: *iem uit zijn ~ zetten* evict s.o.

woningbouw [wonɪŋbɑu] *de* house-building; house-construction: *sociale ~* council housing, (*Am*) public housing

woningbouwvereniging [wonɪŋbɑuvərenəɣɪŋ] *de (~en)* housing association (*or:* corporation)

woningbureau [wonɪŋbyro] *het (~s)* housing agent's (*or:* agency)

woninginrichting [wonɪŋɪnrɪχtɪŋ] *de* home furnishing(s)

woningmarkt [wonɪŋmɑrkt] *de (~en)* housing market

woningnood [wonɪŋnot] *de* housing shortage

woonachtig [wonɑχtəχ] *adj* ‖ *hij is ~ in Leiden* he is a resident of Leiden

woonboot [wombot] *de (-boten)* houseboat

woonerf [wonɛrf] *het (-erven)* residential area (with restrictions to slow down traffic)

woongroep [wonɣrup] *de (~en)* commune

woonhuis [wonhœys] *het (-huizen)* (private) house, home

woonkamer [wonkamər] *de (~s)* living room

woonkeuken [wonkøkə(n)] *de (~s)* open kitchen, kitchen-dining room

woonomgeving [wonɔmɣevɪŋ] *de* environment

woonplaats [womplats] *de (~en)* (place of) residence, address, city, town

woonruimte [wonrœymtə] *de (~n, ~s)* (housing, living) accommodation

woonst [wonst] *de (~en)* (*Belg*) **1** house; **2** (place of) residence

woonwagen [wonwaɣə(n)] *de (~s)* caravan, (*Am*) (house) trailer

woonwagenbewoner [wonwaχə(n)bəwonər] *de (~s)* caravan dweller, (*Am*) trailer park resident

woonwagenkamp [wonwaɣə(n)kɑmp] *het* caravan camp, (*Am*) trailer camp

woon-werkverkeer [wonwɛrkfərker] *het* commuter traffic

woonwijk [wonwɛik] *de (~en)* residential area; housing estate; district, quarter

woord [wort] *het (~en)* word: *in ~ en beeld* in pictures and text; *met andere ~en* in other words; *geen goed ~ voor iets over hebben* not have a good word to say about sth; *het hoogste ~ voeren* do most of the talking; *hij moet altijd het laatste ~ hebben* he always has to have the last word; *iem aan zijn ~ houden* keep (*or:* hold) s.o. to his promise; *het ~ geven aan* give the floor to; *zijn ~ geven* give one's word; *het ~ tot iem richten* address (*or:* speak to) s.o.; *iem aan het ~ laten* allow s.o. to finish (speaking); *in één ~* in a word, in sum (*or:* short); *op zijn ~en letten* be careful about what one says; *iem te ~ staan* speak to (*or:* see) s.o.; *niet uit zijn ~en kunnen komen* not be able to express oneself, fumble for words; *met twee ~en spreken (roughly)* be polite

woordblind [wordblɪnt] *adj* dyslexic

woordblindheid [wordblɪnthɛit] *de* dyslexia

woordelijk [wordələk] *adj, adv* word for word, literal(ly)

woordenboek [wordə(n)buk] *het (~en)* dictionary: *een ~ raadplegen* consult a dictionary, refer to a dictionary

woordenlijst [wordə(n)lɛist] *de (~en)* list of words, vocabulary

woordenschat [wordə(n)sχɑt] *de* **1** lexicon; **2** vocabulary

woordenwisseling [wordə(n)wɪsəlɪŋ] *de (~en)* **1** exchange of words, discussion; **2** argument

woordgebruik [wortχəbrœyk] *het* use of words

woordje [wɔrcə] *het (~s)* word: *een hartig ~ met iem spreken* give s.o. a (good) talking-to; *ook een ~ meespreken* say one's piece

woordkeus [wortkøs] *de* choice of words, wording

woordsoort [wortsort] *de (~en)* part of speech

woordspeling [wortspelɪŋ] *de (~en)* pun, play on words

woordvoerder [wortfurdər] *de (~s)* **1** speaker; **2** spokesman

woordvolgorde [wortfɔlχɔrdə] *de* word order

¹worden [wɔrdə(n)] *cop* **1** be, get: *het wordt laat (or: kouder)* it is getting late (*or:* colder); *hij wordt morgen vijftig* he'll be fifty tomorrow; **2** become: *dat wordt niets* it won't work, it'll come to nothing; *wat is er van hem geworden?* whatever became of him?

²worden [wɔrdə(n)] *vb* be: *er werd gedanst* there was dancing; *de bus wordt om zes uur gelicht* the post will be collected at six o'clock

³worden [wɔrdə(n)] *vb* will be, come to, amount to: *dat wordt dan €2,00 per vel* that will be 2.00 euro per sheet

worm [wɔrm] *de (~en)* worm

worp [wɔrp] *de (~en)* throw(ing), shot

worst [wɔrst] *de (~en)* sausage: *dat zal mij ~ wezen* I couldn't care less

worstelaar [wɔrstəlar] *de (~s)* wrestler

worstelen [wɔrstələ(n)] *vb* struggle; wrestle (*sport*): *zich door een lijvig rapport heen ~* struggle (*or:* plough) (one's way) through a bulky report

worsteling [wɔrstəlɪŋ] *de (~en)* struggle, wrestle

worstenbroodje [wɔrstə(n)brocə] *het (~s) (roughly)* sausage roll

wortel [wɔrtəl] *de (~s)* root; carrot: *3 is de ~ van 9* 3 is the square root of 9

wortelteken [wɔrtəltekə(n)] *het (~s)* radical sign

worteltje [wɔrtəlcə] *het* carrot

worteltrekken [wɔrtəltrɛkə(n)] *het* extraction of the root(s)

woud [waut] *het (~en)* forest

woudloper [wautlopər] *de (~s)* trapper

wraak [vrak] *de* revenge, vengeance: *~ nemen op iem* take revenge on s.o.

wraakactie [vrakɑksi] *de (~s)* act of revenge (*or:* vengeance, retaliation)

wrak [vrɑk] *het (~ken)* wreck: *zich een ~ voelen* feel a wreck

wrakhout [vrɑkhaut] *het* (pieces of) wreckage, driftwood

wrakstuk [vrɑkstʏk] *het (~ken)* piece of wreckage, *(pl also)* wreckage

wrang [vrɑŋ] *adj, adv* 1 sour, acid; 2 unpleasant, nasty, wry

wrat [vrɑt] *de (~ten)* wart

wreed [vret] *adj, adv* cruel

wreedheid [vretɛit] *de (-heden)* cruelty

wreef [vref] *de (wreven)* instep

wreken [vrekə(n)] *vb* revenge; avenge: *zich voor iets op iem ~* revenge oneself on s.o. for sth

wreker [vrekər] *de (~s)* avenger, revenger

wrevel [vrevəl] *de* resentment, *(stronger)* rancour

wrevelig [vrevələχ] *adj* 1 peevish, tetchy, grumpy; 2 resentful

wriemelen [vrimələ(n)] *vb* fiddle (with)

wrijven [vrɛivə(n)] *vb* 1 rub: *neuzen tegen elkaar ~* rub noses; 2 polish: *de meubels ~* polish the furniture

wrijving [vrɛivɪŋ] *de (~en)* friction

wrikken [vrɪkə(n)] *vb* lever, prize

¹wringen [vrɪŋə(n)] *vb* 1 wring: *zich in allerlei bochten ~* wriggle, squirm; 2 wring, press

²wringen [vrɪŋə(n)] *vb* pinch

wringer [vrɪŋər] *de (~s)* wringer; mangle

wroeging [vruɣɪŋ] *de (~en)* remorse

¹wroeten [vrutə(n)] *vb* root, rout: *in iemands verleden ~* pry into s.o.'s past

²wroeten [vrutə(n)] *vb* burrow; root (up): *de grond ondersteboven ~* root up the earth

wrok [vrɔk] *de* resentment, grudge, *(stronger)* rancour

wrong [vrɔŋ] *de (~en)* roll, wreath, chignon, bun

wuiven [wœyvə(n)] *vb* wave

wurgen [wʏrɣə(n)] *vb* strangle

wurgslang [wʏrχslɑŋ] *de (~en)* constrictor (snake)

¹wurm [wʏrm] *de* worm

²wurm [wʏrm] *het* mite: *het ~ kan nog niet praten* the poor mite can't talk yet

wurmen [wʏrmə(n)] *vb* squeeze, worm

WVC [wevese] *(ministerie van) Welzijn, Volksgezondheid en Cultuur* (Ministry of) Welfare, Health and Cultural Affairs

WW [wewe] *de Werkloosheidswet* Unemployment Insurance Act: *in de ~ lopen (zitten)* be on unemployment (benefit), be on the dole

WW-uitkering [wewecɛytkerɪŋ] *de (~en)* unemployment benefit(s)

X

xantippe [ksɑntˌɪpə] *de (~s)* Xanthippe
x-as [ˌɪksɑs] *de (~sen)* x-axis
x-benen [ˌɪkzbenə(n)] *het* knock knees: *~ hebben*
be knock-kneed, have knock knees
X-chromosoom [ˌɪksχromozom] *het (X-chromoso-*
men) X chromosome
xylofoon [ksilofo̱n] *de (~s)* xylophone

y

yang [jɑŋ] *het* yang
y-as [ɛias] *de (~sen)* y-axis
Y-chromosoom [ɛiχromozom] *het (Y-chromoso-*
men) Y chromosome
yen [jɛn] *de (~s)* yen
yes [jɛs] *int* ‖ *reken maar van ~!* you bet!
yeti [jeti] *de (~'s)* yeti
yin [jɪn] *het* yin
yoga [joɣa] *de* yoga
yoghurt [jɔɣʏrt] *de* yogurt

Z

zaad [zat] *het (zaden)* 1 seed; 2 sperm, semen
zaadcel [zatsɛl] *de (~len)* germ cell; sperm cell
zaaddodend [zadodənt] *adj* spermicidal
zaaddonor [zadonɔr] *de (~s)* sperm donor
zaaddoos [zados] *de (-dozen)* seedbox, capsule
zaadlozing [zatlozɪŋ] *de (~en)* seminal discharge, ejaculation
zaag [zaχ] *de (zagen)* saw
zaagmachine [zaχmaʃinə] *de (~s)* saw
zaagmeel [zaχmel] *het* sawdust
zaagsel [zaχsəl] *het* sawdust
zaagvormig [zaχfɔrməχ] *adj (bot)* serrate
zaaien [zajə(n)] *vb* sow: *onrust ~* create unrest; *interessante banen zijn dun gezaaid* interesting jobs are few and far between
zaaier [zajər] *de (~s)* sower
zaaigoed [zajɣut] *het* sowing seed
zaak [zak] *de (zaken)* 1 thing, object; 2 matter, affair, business: *de normale gang van zaken* the normal course of events; *zich met zijn eigen zaken bemoeien* mind one's own business; *dat is jouw ~* that is your concern; *de ~ in kwestie* the matter in hand; 3 business, deal: *goede zaken doen (met iem)* do good business (with s.o.); *er worden goede zaken gedaan in ...* trade is good in ...; *zaken zijn zaken* business is business; *hij is hier voor zaken* he is here on business; 4 business, shop: *op kosten van de ~* on the house; *een ~ hebben* run a business; *een auto van de ~* a company car; 5 case, things: *weten hoe de zaken ervoor staan* know how things stand, know what the score is; 6 point, issue: *dat doet hier niet(s) ter zake* that is irrelevant, that is beside the point; *kennis van zaken hebben* know one's facts, be well-informed (on the matter); 7 case, lawsuit: *Maria's ~ komt vanmiddag voor* Maria's case comes up this afternoon; 8 affair: *Binnenlandse Zaken* Home (*or:* Internal) Affairs; *Buitenlandse Zaken* Foreign Affairs; 9 cause
zaakje [zakjə] *het (~s)* little matter/business (*or:* affair, thing); small deal; job: *ik vertrouw het ~ niet* I don't trust the set-up
zaakvoerder [zakfurdər] *de (~s) (Belg)* manager
zaal [zal] *de (zalen)* 1 room, hall; 2 hall, ward, auditorium; 3 hall, house: *een stampvolle ~* a crowded (*or:* packed) hall, a full house; *de ~ lag plat* it brought the house down

zaalsport [zalspɔrt] *de (~en)* indoor sport
zaalvoetbal [zalvudbɑl] *het* indoor football
zacht [zaχt] *adj, adv* 1 soft, smooth: *een ~e landing* a smooth landing; *~e sector* social sector; 2 mild; 3 kind, gentle: *op zijn ~st gezegd* to put it mildly; 4 quiet, soft: *met ~e stem* in a quiet voice
zachtboard [zaχtbɔːrt] *het* softboard
zachtjes [zaχjəs] *adv* softly, quietly, gently: *~ doen* be quiet; *~ rijden* drive slowly; *~ aan!* easy does it!, take it easy!; *~!* hush!, quiet!
zachtzinnig [zaχtsɪnəχ] *adj, adv* 1 good-natured, mild(-mannered); 2 gentle, kind(ly), tender
zadel [zadəl] *het (~s)* saddle
zadelen [zadələ(n)] *vb* saddle (up)
zagen [zaɣə(n)] *vb* 1 saw (up); 2 saw, cut: *planken (or: figuren) ~* saw into planks (*or:* shapes)
zagerij [zaɣərɛi] *de (~en)* sawmill
zak [zɑk] *de (~ken)* 1 bag, *(large)* sack: *een ~ patat* a bag (*or:* packet) of chips; *(fig) iem de ~ geven* give s.o. the sack, sack s.o.; 2 pocket: *geld op ~ hebben* have some money in one's pockets (*or:* on one); 3 purse: *uit eigen ~ betalen* pay out of one's own purse; 4 *(inf)* bore, jerk; *(stronger)* bastard
zakagenda [zɑkaɣɛnda] *de* pocket diary, *(Am)* (small) agenda
zakboekje [zɑgbukjə] *het (~s)* (pocket) notebook
zakcentje [zɑksɛncə] *het (~s)* pocket money
zakdoek [zɑgduk] *de (~en)* handkerchief
zakelijk [zakələk] *adj, adv* 1 business(like), commercial; 2 business(like), objective; 3 compact, concise: *een ~e stijl van schrijven* a terse style of writing; 4 practical, real(istic); down-to-earth
zakenbrief [zakə(n)brif] *de (-brieven)* business letter
zakencentrum [zakə(n)sɛntrʏm] *het (-centra, ~s)* business centre
zakenleven [zakə(n)levə(n)] *het* business (life), commerce
zakenman [zakə(n)mɑn] *de (zakenlui, zakenlieden)* businessman: *een gewiekst ~* a shrewd (*or:* an astute) businessman
zakenreis [zakə(n)rɛis] *de (-reizen)* business trip
zakenrelatie [zakə(n)rela(t)si] *de (~s)* business relation
zakformaat [zɑkfɔrmat] *het (-formaten)* pocket size
zakgeld [zɑkχɛlt] *het* pocket money, spending money, allowance
zakken [zɑkə(n)] *vb* 1 fall, drop, sink: *in elkaar ~* collapse; 2 fall (off), drop, come down, go down, sink: *de hoofdpijn is gezakt* the headache has eased; *het water is gezakt* the water has gone down (*or:* subsided); 3 fail, go down
zakkenrollen [zɑkə(n)rɔlə(n)] *vb* pick pockets
zakkenroller [zɑkə(n)rɔlər] *de (~s)* pickpocket: *pas op voor ~s!* beware of pickpockets!
zaklamp [zɑklɑmp] *de (~en)* (pocket) torch, *(Am)* flashlight
zaklantaarn [zɑklɑntarn] *de (~s)* (pocket) torch,

flashlight

zakloep *de* pocket magnifying glass

zaklopen [zɑklopə(n)] *vb* (run a) sack race

zakmes [zɑkmɛs] *het (~sen)* pocket knife

zakrekenmachientje [zɑkrekə(n)mɑʃincə] *het* pocket calculator

zaktelefoon [zɑkteləfon] *de (~s)* mobile phone, portable phone, cellphone

zalf [zɑlf] *de (zalven)* ointment, salve: *met ~ insmeren* rub ointment (*or:* salve) on

zalig [zaləχ] *adj, adv* gorgeous, glorious, divine

zalm [zɑlm] *de (~en)* salmon

zalven [zɑlvə(n)] *vb* put (*or:* rub) ointment on

zalving [zɑlvɪŋ] *de (~en)* anointment (with)

zand [zɑnt] *het* sand: *~ erover* let's forget it, let bygones be bygones

zandbak [zɑndbɑk] *de (~ken)* sandbox

zandbank [zɑndbɑŋk] *de (~en)* sandbank

zanderig [zɑndərəχ] *adj* sandy

zandkasteel [zɑntkɑstel] *het (-kastelen)* sandcastle

zandkorrel [zɑntkɔrəl] *de (~s)* grain of sand

zandloper [zɑntlopər] *de (~s)* hourglass, egg-timer

zandpad [zɑntpɑt] *het (~en)* sandy path

zandsteen [zɑntsten] *het, de* sandstone

zandstorm [zɑntstɔrm] *de (~en)* sandstorm

zandstralen [zɑntstralə(n)] *vb* sandblast

zandvlakte [zɑntflɑktə] *de (~n, ~s)* sand flat, sand(y) plain

zandweg [zɑntwɛχ] *de (~en)* sand track (*or:* road), dirt track

zandzak [zɑntsɑk] *de (~ken)* sandbag

zang [zɑŋ] *de (~en)* song, singing, warbling

zanger [zɑŋər] *de (~s)* singer, vocalist

zangerig [zɑŋərəχ] *adj* melodious, sing-song

zangkoor [zɑŋkor] *het (-koren)* choir

zangleraar [zɑŋlerar] *de (-leraren, ~s)* singing teacher

zangvereniging [zɑŋvərenəχɪŋ] *de (~en)* choir, choral society

zangvogel [zɑŋvoɣəl] *de (~s)* songbird

zaniken [zanəkə(n)] *vb* nag, moan, whine

zappen [zɛpə(n)] *vb* zap

¹**zat** [zɑt] *adj* **1** (+ *noun*) drunken; *(after vb)* drunk; **2** fed up: *'t ~ zijn* be fed up (with it)

²**zat** [zɑt] *adv* (+ *noun*) plenty; to spare: *zij hebben geld ~* they have plenty (*or:* oodles) of money; *tijd ~* time to spare, plenty of time

zaterdag [zatərdɑχ] *de (~en)* Saturday

¹**zaterdags** [zatərdɑχs] *adj* Saturday

²**zaterdags** [zatərdɑχs] *adv* on Saturdays

zatlap [zɑtlɑp] *de (~pen)* boozer

ze [zə] *pers pron* **1** she; her: *~ komt zo* she is just coming; **2** *(pl)* they; them: *roep ~ eens* just call them; *daar moesten ~ eens iets aan doen* they ought to do sth about that

zebra [zebra] *de (~'s)* zebra

zebrapad [zebrapɑt] *het (~en)* pedestrian crossing, zebra crossing

zede [zedə] *de (~n)* **1** custom, usage: *~n en gewoon-*

ten customs and traditions; **2** *(pl)* morals, manners

zedelijk [zedələk] *adj, adv* moral

zedenleer [zedə(n)ler] *de (Belg; educ)* ethics

zedenpolitie [zedə(n)poli(t)si] *de* vice squad

zedig [zedəχ] *adj, adv* modest

zee [ze] *de (~ën)* sea: *een ~ van tijd* oceans (*or:* heaps) of time; *aan ~* by the sea, on the coast; *met iem in ~ gaan* join in with s.o., throw in one's lot with s.o.

zeebanket [zebɑŋkɛt] *het* seafood

zeebeving [zebevɪŋ] *de (~en)* seaquake

zeebodem [zebodəm] *de (~s)* ocean floor, seabed, bottom of the sea

zeef [zef] *de (zeven)* sieve, strainer: *zo lek als een ~ zijn* leak like a sieve

zeefdruk [zevdrʏk] *de (~ken)* silk-screen (print)

zeegat [zeɣɑt] *het (~en)* tidal inlet (*or:* outlet)

zeehaven [zehavə(n)] *de (~s)* harbour, seaport

zeehond [zehɔnt] *de (~en)* seal

zeekaart [zekart] *de (~en)* sea chart, nautical chart

zeeklimaat [zeklimat] *het* maritime climate, oceanic climate

zeekoe [zeku] *de (~ien)* sea cow

Zeeland [zelɑnt] *het* Zeeland

zeeleeuw [zelew] *de (~en)* sea lion

zeelieden [zelidə(n)] *de* seamen, sailors

zeelucht [zelʏχt] *de* sea air

¹**zeem** [zem] *het* shammy, chamois

²**zeem** [zem] *de, het* shammy, chamois

zeemacht [zemɑχt] *de* navy, *(pl)* naval forces

zeeman [zemɑn] *de (zeelieden, zeelui)* sailor

zeemeermin [zemermɪn] *de (~nen)* mermaid

zeemeeuw [zemew] *de (~en)* (sea)gull

zeemijl [zemɛil] *de (~en)* nautical mile

zeemleer [zemler] *het* chamois (*or:* shammy) leather, washleather

zeemleren [zemlerə(n)] *adj* chamois, shammy

zeep [zep] *de (zepen)* **1** soap; **2** (soap)suds ‖ *iemand om ~ brengen* kill s.o., do s.o. in

zeepaardje [zeparcə] *het (~s)* sea horse

zeepbel [zebɛl] *de (~len)* (soap) bubble

zeepost [zepɔst] *de* overseas surface mail

zeeppoeder [zepudər] *het, de* washing powder, detergent

zeepsop [zepsɔp] *het* (soap)suds

¹**zeer** [zer] *adj* sore, painful, aching: *een ~ hoofd* an aching head

²**zeer** [zer] *het* pain, ache; sore: *dat doet ~* that hurts

³**zeer** [zer] *adv* very, extremely, greatly: *~ tot mijn verbazing* (very) much to my amazement

zeereis [zerɛis] *de (zeereizen)* (sea) voyage, passage

zeerover [zerovər] *de (~s)* pirate

zeeschip [zesχɪp] *het (zeeschepen)* seagoing vessel, ocean-going vessel

zeeslag [zeslɑχ] *de (~en)* sea battle, naval battle; *(game)* battleships

zeespiegel [zespiɣəl] *de (~s)* sea level

Zeeuws [zews] *adj* Zeeland (+ *noun*)

Zeeuws-Vlaanderen [zewsflɑndərə(n)] *het*

Zeeland Flanders

zeevaart [ze̱vart] *de* seagoing; shipping

zeevaartschool [ze̱vartsχol] *de (-scholen)* nautical college

zeevis [ze̱vɪs] *de (~sen)* saltwater fish, sea fish

zeewaardig [zewa̱rdəχ] *adj* seaworthy

zeewater [ze̱watər] *het* seawater, salt water

zeewier [ze̱wir] *het* seaweed

zeeziek [ze̱zik] *adj* seasick

zege [ze̱ɣə] *de (~s)* victory, triumph, win

¹zegel [ze̱ɣəl] *de* stamp

²zegel [ze̱ɣəl] *het* seal: *zijn ~ ergens op drukken, zijn ~ hechten aan iets* set one's seal on sth, give one's blessing to sth

zegelring [ze̱ɣəlrɪŋ] *de (~en)* signet ring

zegen [ze̱ɣə(n)] *de* **1** blessing, benediction: *(iron) mijn ~ heb je (voor wat het waard is)* you've got my blessing(, for what it's worth); **2** blessing, boon: *dat is een ~ voor de mensheid* that is a blessing (*or:* boon) to mankind

zegenen [ze̱ɣənə(n)] *vb* bless

zegevieren [ze̱ɣəvirə(n)] *vb* triumph

zeggen [zɛ̱ɣə(n)] *vb* **1** say, tell: *wat wil je daarmee ~?* what are you trying to say?, what are you driving at?; *wat ik ~ wou* by the way; *wat zegt u?* (I beg your) pardon?, sorry?; *wie zal het ~?* who can say? (*or:* tell?); *zegt u het maar* yes, please?; *zeg dat wel* you can say that again; *men zegt dat hij heel rijk is* he is said (*or:* reputed) to be very rich; *wat zeg je me daarvan!* how about that!, well I never!; *dat is toch zo, zeg nou zelf* it is true, admit it; *hoe zal ik het ~?* how shall I put it?; *nou je het zegt* now (that) you mention it; *zo gezegd, zo gedaan* no sooner said than done; *zonder iets te ~* without (saying) a word; *zeg maar 'Tom'* call me 'Tom'; *niets te ~ hebben* have no authority, have no say; **2** say, mean: *dat wil ~ that* means, i.e., that is (to say); **3** say, prove; **4** say, state: *laten we ~ dat …* let's say that …

zegje [zɛ̱χjə] *het* ‖ *ieder wil zijn ~ doen* everyone wants to have their say

zegswijze [zɛ̱χswɛizə] *de (~n)* phrase, saying

zeik [zɛik] *de* piss

zeiken [zɛi̱kə(n)] *vb* **1** piss; **2** go on, harp (*or:* carry) on

zeikerd [zɛi̱kərt] *de (~s)* bugger

zeikerig [zɛi̱kərəχ] *adj, adv* fretful, whiny

zeiknat [zɛi̱knɑt] *adj* sopping (wet)

zeil [zɛil] *het (~en)* **1** sail: *alle ~en bijzetten* employ full sail, pull out all the stops; *onder ~ gaan: a)* set sail; *b) (fig)* doze off; **2** floor covering; **3** canvas, sail-cloth, tarpaulin

zeilboot [zɛi̱lbot] *de (-boten)* sailing boat

zeilen [zɛi̱lə(n)] *vb* sail

zeiler [zɛi̱lər] *de (~s)* yachtsman, yachtswoman, sailor

zeiljacht [zɛi̱ljɑχt] *het (~en)* yacht

zeilplank [zɛi̱lplɑŋk] *de (~en)* sailboard

zeilsport [zɛi̱lspɔrt] *de* sailing

zeis [zɛis] *de (~en)* scythe

zeker [ze̱kər] *adj, adv* **1** safe: *(op) ~ spelen* play safe; *hij heeft het ~e voor het onzekere genomen* he did it to be on the safe side; **2** sure, certain: *iets ~ weten* know sth for sure; *om ~ te zijn* to be sure; *vast en ~!, (Belg) ~ en vast!* definitely; **3** probably: *je wou haar ~ verrassen* I suppose you wanted to surprise her; *je hebt het ~ al af* you must have finished it by now; *~ niet* certainly not; *op ~e dag* one day; *een ~e meneer Pietersen* a (certain) Mr Pietersen

zekerheid [ze̱kərhɛit] *de (-heden)* **1** safety, safe keeping: *iem een gevoel van ~ geven* give s.o. a sense of security; *voor alle ~* for safety's sake, to make quite sure; **2** certainty, confidence: *sociale ~* social security

zekering [ze̱kərɪŋ] *de (~en)* (safety) fuse: *de ~en zijn doorgeslagen* the fuses have blown

zelden [zɛ̱ldə(n)] *adv* rarely, seldom: *~ of nooit* rarely if ever

zeldzaam [zɛ̱ltsam] *adj, adv* rare

zeldzaamheid [zɛ̱ltsamhɛit] *de (-heden)* rarity

zelf [zɛlf] *dem pron* zelf; myself, yourself, himself, herself, itself, ourselves, yourselves, themselves, oneself: *~ een zaak beginnen* start one's own business; *~ gebakken brood* home-made bread; *ik kook ~* I do my own cooking; *al zeg ik het ~* although I say it myself; *het huis ~ is onbeschadigd* the house itself is undamaged

zelfbediening [zɛ̱lvbədinɪŋ] *de* self-service

zelfbedieningsrestaurant [zɛ̱lvbədinɪŋsrɛstorɑnt] *het (~s)* self-service restaurant

zelfbeheersing [zɛ̱lvbəhersɪŋ] *de* self-control: *zijn ~ verliezen* lose control of oneself

zelfbewust [zɛlvbəwʏst] *adj, adv* self-confident; self-assured

zelfbewustheid [zɛlvbəwʏsthɛit] *de* self-confidence; self-assurance

zelfde [zɛ̱lvdə] *adj* similar; very (same): *in deze ~ kamer* in this very room

zelfdiscipline [zɛ̱lvdisiplinə] *de* self-discipline

zelfdoding [zɛ̱lvdodɪŋ] *de (~en)* suicide

zelfmedelijden [zɛ̱lfmedəlɛidə(n)] *het* self-pity

zelfmoord [zɛ̱lfmort] *de (~en)* suicide: *~ plegen* commit suicide

zelfontplooiing [zɛ̱lfɔntplojɪŋ] *de* self-development, self-realization

zelfontspanner [zɛ̱lfɔntspɑnər] *de (~s)* self-timer

zelfportret [zɛ̱lfpɔrtrɛt] *het (~ten)* self-portrait

zelfrespect [zɛ̱lfrɛspɛkt] *het* self-respect

zelfrijzend [zɛ̱lfrɛizənt] *adj* self-raising

zelfs [zɛlfs] *adv* even: *~ zijn vrienden vertrouwde hij niet* he did not even trust his friends; *~ in dat geval* even then so

zelfstandig [zɛlfstɑ̱ndəχ] *adj, adv* independent, self-employed: *een kleine ~e* a self-employed person

zelfstandigheid [zɛlfstɑ̱ndəχhɛit] *de (-heden)* independence

zelfstudie [zɛ̱lfstydi] *de (~s)* private study, home study

zelfverdediging [zɛlfərdedəɣɪŋ] *de* self-defence: *uit ~ handelen* act in self-defence

zelfvertrouwen [zɛlfərtrɑuwə(n)] *het* (self-)confidence

zelfverzekerd [zɛlfərzɛkərt] *adj, adv* (self-)assured

zelfwerkzaamheid [zɛlfwɛrksɑmhɛit] *de* self-activation; self-motivation, independence

zemelen [zeməlɑ(n)] *de* bran

zemen [zemə(n)] *vb* leather

zenboeddhisme [zɛmbudɪsmə] *het* Zen (Buddhism)

zendamateur [zɛntɑmɑtør] *de* (~s) (radio) ham, amateur radio operator, CB-er

zendeling [zɛndəlɪŋ] *de* (~en) missionary

¹zenden [zɛndə(n)] *vb* broadcast, transmit

²zenden [zɛndə(n)] *vb* send: *iem om de dokter ~* send for the doctor

zender [zɛndər] *de* (~s) 1 broadcasting station, transmitting station; 2 sender; 3 emitter, transmitter

zending [zɛndɪŋ] *de* (~en) supply, parcel, package

zendingswerk [zɛndɪŋswɛrk] *het* missionary work

zendinstallatie [zɛntɪnstɑla(t)si] *de* (~s) transmitting station (*or:* equipment)

zendmast [zɛntmɑst] *de* (~en) (radio, TV) mast; radio tower, TV tower

zendstation [zɛntstɑ(t)ʃɔn] *het* (~s) broadcasting station, transmitting station

zendtijd [zɛntɛit] *de* (~en) broadcast(ing) time

zenuw [zenyw] *de* (~en) nerve; *(pl)* nerves: *stalen ~en* nerves of steel; *de ~en hebben* have the jitters; *ze was óp van de ~en* she was a nervous wreck

zenuwachtig [zenywɑχtəχ] *adj, adv* nervous: *~ zijn voor het examen* be jittery before the exam

zenuwachtigheid [zenywɑχtəχhɛit] *de* nervousness

zenuwcel [zenywsɛl] *de* (~len) neuron

zenuwgestel [zenywɣəstɛl] *het* nervous system

zenuwslopend [zenywslopənt] *adj* nerve-racking

zenuwstelsel [zenywstɛlsəl] *het* (~s) nervous system

zenuwtrek [zenywtrɛk] *de* (~ken) tic: *een ~ in het ooglid* a twitch of the eyelid

zeppelin [zɛpəlɪn] *de* (~s) Zeppelin

zerk [zɛrk] *de* (~en) tombstone

zes [zɛs] *num* six; *(in dates)* sixth: *hoofdstuk ~* chapter six; *iets in ~sen delen* divide sth into six (parts); *wij zijn met z'n ~sen* there are six of us; *met ~ tegelijk* in sixes; *~ min* barely a six; *voor dat proefwerk kreeg hij een ~* he got six for that test; *een zesje* six (out of ten), a mere pass mark

zesde [zɛzdə] *num* sixth

zeshoek [zɛshuk] *de* (~en) hexagon

zeshoekig [zɛshukəχ] *adj* hexagonal

zestal [zɛstɑl] *het* (~len) six

zestien [zɛstin] *num* sixteen; *(in dates)* sixteenth

zestiende [zɛstində] *num* sixteenth

zestig [sɛstəχ] *num* sixty: *in de jaren ~* in the sixties; *voor in de ~ zijn* be just over sixty; *hij loopt te-*

gen de ~ he is close on sixty, he is pushing sixty

zestigplusser [sɛstəχplʏsər] *de* over-60, senior citizen

zet [zɛt] *de* (~ten) 1 move: *een ~ doen* make a move; *jij bent aan ~* (it's) your move; 2 push: *geef me eens een ~je* give me a boost, will you

zetbaas [zɛdbɑs] *de* (zetbazen) manager

zetel [zetəl] *de* (~s) seat; *(Belg)* armchair

zetelen [zetələ(n)] *vb* be established, have one's seat; reside

zetfout [zɛtfɑut] *de* (~en) misprint

zetmeel [zɛtmel] *het* starch

zetpil [zɛtpɪl] *de* (~len) suppository

zetten [zɛtə(n)] *vb* 1 set, put, move: *enkele stappen ~* take a few steps; *iem eruit ~* eject, evict s.o., throw s.o. out; *opzij ~* put (*or:* set) aside, table, discard, scrap; *een apparaat in elkaar ~* fit together, assemble a machine, contrive, think up; 2 make: *zet de muziek harder* (or: *zachter*) turn up (*or:* down) the music

zetter [zɛtər] *de* (~s) compositor

zetting [zɛtɪŋ] *de* (~en) setting

zetwerk [zɛtwɛrk] *het* typesetting

zeug [zøχ] *de* (~en) sow

zeulen [zø:lə(n)] *vb* lug, drag

zeuren [zørə(n)] *vb* nag, harp; whine: *wil je niet zo aan mijn kop ~* stop badgering me; *iem aan het hoofd ~* (om, over) nag s.o. (into, about)

¹zeven [zevə(n)] *vb* sieve, sift, strain

²zeven [zevə(n)] *num* seven; *(in dates)* seventh: *morgen wordt ze ~* tomorrow she'll be seven; *een ~ voor Nederlands* (a) seven for Dutch

zevende [zevəndə] *num* seventh

zeventien [zevə(n)tin] *num* seventeen; *(in dates)* seventeenth

zeventiende [zevəntində] *num* seventeenth

zeventig [sevəntəχ] *num* seventy

zever [zevər] *de* (~s) drivel

zeveren [zevərə(n)] *vb* 1 slobber, slaver; 2 drivel

zgn. *zogenaamd* so-called

zich [zɪχ] *ref pron* 1 himself, herself, itself, oneself, themselves; him(self), her(self), it(self), one(self), them(selves): *geld bij ~ hebben* have money on one; *iem bij ~ hebben* have s.o. with one; 2 yourself, yourselves: *vergist u ~ niet?* aren't you mistaken?

zicht [zɪχt] *het* 1 sight, view: *iem het ~ belemmeren* block s.o.'s view; *uit het ~ verdwijnen* disappear from view; 2 insight

zichtbaar [zɪχtbar] *adj, adv* visible: *~ opgelucht* visibly relieved; *niet ~ met het blote oog* not visible to the naked eye

zichtbaarheid [zɪχtbarhɛit] *de* visibility, visibleness

zichtrekening [zɪχtrekənɪŋ] *de* (~en) *(Belg)* current account

zichzelf [zɪχsɛlf] *ref pron* himself, herself, itself, oneself, themselves, self: *niet ~ zijn* not be oneself; *op ~ wonen* live on one's own; *tot ~ komen* come to oneself; *uit ~* of one's own accord; *voor ~ beginnen*

start a business of one's own
ziedend [zi̯dənt] *adj* seething, furious, livid
ziek [zik] *adj* ill, sick: ~ *van iemands gezeur worden* get sick of s.o.'s moaning; ~ *worden* fall ill (*or:* sick)
ziekbriefje *het* sick note
zieke [zi̯kə] *de* (~*n*) patient, sick person
ziekelijk [zi̯kələk] *adj* 1 sickly; 2 morbid, sick
ziekenauto [zi̯kə(n)ɑuto] *de* (~*'s*) ambulance
ziekenbezoek [zi̯kə(n)bəzuk] *het* (~*en*) visit to a (*or:* the) patient
ziekenbroeder [zi̯kə(n)brudər] *de* (~*s*) male nurse
ziekenfonds [zi̯kə(n)fɔnts] *het* (~*en*) (*roughly*) (Dutch) National Health Service: *ik zit in het* ~ I'm covered by the National Health Service
ziekenfondskaart [zi̯kə(n)fɔn(t)skart] *de* (*roughly*) medical insurance card
ziekenhuis [zi̯kə(n)hœys] *het* (*-huizen*) hospital
ziekenhuisopname [zi̯kə(n)hœysɔpnamə] *de* (~*n*, ~*s*) hospitalization
ziekenverpleger [zi̯kə(n)vərpleɣər] *de* (~*s*) nurse
ziekenzaal [zi̯kə(n)zal] *de* (*-zalen*) ward
ziekte [zi̯ktə] *de* (~*n*, ~*s*) 1 illness, sickness; 2 disease, illness: *de* ~ *van Weil* Weil's disease; *een ernstige* ~ a serious disease (*or:* illness); *een* ~ *oplopen* develop a disease (*or:* an illness)
ziektekiem [zi̯ktəkim] *de* (~*en*) germ (of a, the disease)
ziektekosten [zi̯ktəkɔstə(n)] *de* medical expenses
ziekteverlof [zi̯ktəvərlɔf] *het* (*-verloven*) sick leave
ziektewet [zi̯ktəwɛt] *de* (~*ten*) (Dutch) Health Law: *in de* ~ *lopen* be on sickness benefit (*or:* sick pay), (*Am*) be (out) on sick leave
ziel [zil] *de* (~*en*) soul: *zijn* ~ *en zaligheid voor iets over hebben* sell one's soul for sth; *zijn* ~ *ergens in leggen* put one's heart and soul into sth; *hoe meer* ~*en, hoe meer vreugd* the more the merrier
zielepiet [zi̯ləpit] *de* (~*en*) poor soul
zielig [zi̯ləɣ] *adj, adv* 1 pitiful, pathetic: *ik vind hem echt* ~ I think he's really pathetic; *wat* ~! how sad!; 2 petty
zielsgelukkig [zilsɣəlʏkəɣ] *adj* ecstatic, blissfully happy
zielsveel [zi̯lsfel] *adv* deeply, dearly: ~ *van iem houden* love s.o. (with) heart and soul
¹zien [zin] *vb* 1 see; 2 look: *Bernard zag zo bleek als een doek* Bernard was (*or:* looked) as white as a sheet; 3 look (out)
²zien [zin] *vb* 1 see: (*fig*) *iem niet kunnen* ~ not be able to stand (the sight of) s.o.; *zich ergens laten* ~ show one's face somewhere; *waar zie je dat aan?* how can you tell?; *ik zie aan je gezicht dat je liegt* I can tell by the look on your face that you are lying; *tot* ~*s* goodbye; *het niet meer* ~ *zitten* have had enough (of it), not be able to see one's way out (of a situation); *zie je, ziet u?* you see?, see?; 2 see (to it): *je moet maar* ~ *hoe je het doet* you'll just have to manage; *dat* ~ *we dán wel weer* we'll cross that bridge when we come to it
ziener [zi̯nər] *de* (~*s*) seer

zier [zir] *de* the least bit
ziezo [zizo̯] *int* there (we, you are)
zigeuner [siɣønər] *de* (~*s*) Gypsy
zigzag [zɪχsɑχ] *de* zigzag
zigzaggen [zɪχsɑɣə(n)] *vb* zigzag
¹zij [zɛi] *de* (~*den*) side: ~ *aan* ~ side by side
²zij [zɛi] *het* (~*den*) silk
³zij [zɛi] *pers pron* 1 she; 2 they (*pl*)
zijde [zɛi̯də] *de* (~*n*) 1 side: *op zijn andere* ~ *gaan liggen* turn over; *van vaders* ~ from one's father's side; 2 silk
zijdeachtig [zɛi̯dəɑχtəχ] *adj* silky
zijdelings [zɛi̯dəlɪŋs] *adj, adv* indirect
zijden [zɛi̯də(n)] *adj* silk
zijderups [zɛi̯dərʏps] *de* (~*en*) silkworm
zijdeur [zɛi̯dør] *de* (~*en*) side door
zijkant [zɛi̯kant] *de* (~*en*) side
zijlijn [zɛi̯lɛin] *de* (~*en*) 1 branch (line); 2 sideline, touchline
¹zijn [zɛin] *vb* be: *er* ~ *mensen die* ... there are people who ...; *wat is er?* what's the matter?, what is it?; *we* ~ *er* here we are; *dat* ~ *mijn ouders* those are my parents; *dát is nog eens lopen* (now) that's what I call walking; *die beker is van tin* that cup is made of pewter; *als ik jou was, zou ik* ... if I were you, I would ...; *er was eens een koning* ... once (upon a time) there was a king ...; *Piet is voetballen* Piet is (out) playing football
²zijn [zɛin] *vb* 1 have: *er waren gunstige berichten binnengekomen* favourable reports had come in; 2 be: *hij is ontslagen* he has been fired
³zijn [zɛin] *het* being, existence
⁴zijn [zɛin] *pos pron* his, its, one's: *vader* ~ *hoed* father's hat; *dit is* ~ *huis* this is his house; *ieder het* ~*e geven* give every man his due
zijpad [zɛi̯pat] *het* (~*en*) side path
zijrivier [zɛi̯rivir] *de* (~*en*) tributary
zijspan [zɛi̯span] *het, de* (~*nen*) sidecar
zijspiegel [zɛi̯spiɣəl] *de* (~*s*) wing mirror
zijspoor [zɛi̯spor] *het* (*zijsporen*) siding: *iem op een* ~ *brengen* (*zetten*) put s.o. on the sidelines, sideline s.o.
zijtak [zɛi̯tak] *de* (~*ken*) 1 side branch; 2 branch
zijwaarts [zɛi̯warts] *adj, adv* sideward, sideways
zijweg [zɛi̯wɛχ] *de* (~*en*) side road
zijwind [zɛi̯wɪnt] *de* (~*en*) side wind, crosswind
zilver [zɪlvər] *het* silver
zilveren [zɪlvərə(n)] *adj* 1 silver; 2 silver(y)
zilveruitje [zɪlvərœycə] *het* (~*s*) pearl onion, cocktail onion
zin [zɪn] *de* (~*nen*) 1 sentence; 2 (*pl*) senses: *bij* ~*nen komen* come to, come to one's senses; 3 mind: *zijn eigen* ~ *doen* do as one pleases; *zijn* ~*nen op iets zetten* set one's heart on sth; 4 liking: *ergens (geen)* ~ *in hebben* (not) feel like sth; *het naar de* ~ *hebben* find sth to one's liking; ~ *of geen* ~ whether you like it or not; 5 sense, meaning: *in de letterlijke* ~ *van het woord* in the literal sense of the word; 6 sense, point

zindelijk [zɪndələk] *adj* toilet-trained, clean, house-trained

zingen [zɪŋə(n)] *vb* sing: *zuiver (or: vals)* ~ sing in *(or:* out) of tune

zink [zɪŋk] *het* zinc

¹zinken [zɪŋkə(n)] *vb* sink: *diep gezonken zijn* have fallen low

²zinken [zɪŋkə(n)] *adj* zinc

zinloos [zɪnlos] *adj, adv* **1** meaningless; **2** useless, futile: *het is* ~ *om ...* there's no sense *(or:* point) (in) ...(-ing)

zinloosheid [zɪnlosheit] *de* **1** meaninglessness; **2** uselessness

zinnen [zɪnə(n)] *vb* ‖ *dat zinde haar helemaal niet* she did not like that at all

zinnig [zɪnəχ] *adj* sensible: *het is moeilijk daar iets* ~*s over te zeggen* it's hard to say anything meaningful about that

zinsbouw [zɪnzbɑu] *de* sentence structure

zinsdeel [zɪnzdel] *het (-delen)* part (of a, the sentence); tag

zinsverband [zɪnsfərbɑnt] *het* context

zintuig [zɪntœyχ] *het (~en)* sense

zintuiglijk [zɪntœyχlək] *adj, adv* sensual, sensory

zinvol [zɪnvɔl] *adj* significant, advisable, a good idea

zionisme [zijonɪsmə] *het* Zionism

zippen [zɪpə(n)] *vb* zip, pack, compress

zit [zɪt] *de* sit

zitbank [zɪdbɑŋk] *de (~en)* sofa, settee

zithoek [zɪthuk] *de (~en)* sitting area

zitje [zɪcə] *het (~s)* **1** sit(-down), seat; **2** table and chairs

zitkamer [zɪtkamər] *de (~s)* living room

zitplaats [zɪtplats] *de (~en)* seat

zitten [zɪtə(n)] *vb* **1** sit: *blijf ~: a)* stay sitting (down); *b)* remain seated; ~ *blijven* repeat a year; *gaan ~: a)* sit down; *b)* take a seat; *zit je goed? (lekker?)* are you comfortable?; *aan de koffie* ~ be having coffee; *waar zit hij toch?* where can he be?; *ernaast* ~ be wrong, be out, be off (target); *wij* ~ *nog midden in de examens* we are still in the middle of the exams; *zonder benzine* ~ be out of petrol; *(bijna) zonder geld* ~ have run short of money; *ik zit: op een kantoor* ~ be *(or:* work) in an office; **3** fit: *goed* ~ be a good fit; **4** be *(... -ing),* sit *(... -ing): we* ~ *te eten* we are having dinner *(or:* lunch); *in zijn eentje* ~ *zingen* sit singing to oneself; *met iets blijven* ~ be left *(or:* stuck) with sth; *laat maar* ~ that's all right, (let's) forget it; *hij heeft zijn vrouw laten* ~ he has left his wife (in the lurch); *met iets* ~ be at a loss (what to do) about sth; *hoe zit het (dan) met ...?* what about ... (then)?; *(sport) de bal zit* it's a goal!, it has (gone) in!, it's in the back of the net!; *het blijft niet* ~ it won't stay put; *hoe zit dat in elkaar?* how does it (all) fit together?, how does that work?; *daar zit wat in* you (may) have sth there, there's sth in that; *onder de modder* ~ be covered with mud; *het zit er (dik) in* there's a good chance (of that (hap-

pening)); *eruit halen wat erin zit* make the most (out) of sth; *dat zit wel goed (snor)* that will be all right; *alles zit hem mee (or: tegen)* everything is going his way *(or:* against him); *hij zit overal aan* he cannot leave anything alone; *achter de meisjes aan* ~ *chase* ((around) after) girls; *mijn taak zit er weer op* that's my job out of the way

zittenblijver [zɪtə(n)blɛivər] *de (~s)* repeater, pupil who stays down a class

zittend [zɪtənt] *adj* **1** sitting, seated; **2** sedentary; **3** incumbent

zitting [zɪtɪŋ] *de (~en)* **1** seat; **2** session, meeting

zitvlak [zɪtflɑk] *het (~ken)* seat, bottom

zmlk-school [zɛtɛmɛlkasχol] *de school voor zeer moeilijk lerende kinderen* special school (for children with serious learning problems)

zmok-school [zɛtɛmokasχol] *de school voor zeer moeilijk opvoedbare kinderen* special school (for children with serious behaviour problems)

¹zo [zo] *adv* **1** so, like this *(or:* that), this way, that way: *zó doe je dat!* that's the way you do it!; *zó is het!* that's the way it is!; *als dat* ~ *is ...* if that's the case ...; ~ *zijn er niet veel* there aren't many like that; ~ *iets geks heb ik nog nooit gezien* I've never seen anything so crazy; *zij heeft er toch* ~ *een hekel aan* she really hates it; *een jaar of* ~ a year or so; **2** as, so: *het is allemaal niet* ~ *eenvoudig* it's not as simple as it seems *(or:* as all that); *half* ~ *lang (or: groot)* half as long *(or:* big); *hij is niet* ~ *oud als ik* he is not as old as I am; ~ *goed als ie kon* as well as he could; ~ *maar* just like that, without so much as a by-your-leave; ~ *nu en dan* every now and then; **3** right away: *ik ben* ~ *terug* I'll be back right away; ~ *juist* just now; *het was maar* ~ ~ it was just so-so

²zo [zo] *conj* if: ~ *ja, waarom;* ~ *nee, waarom niet* if so, why; if not, why not; *je zult je huiswerk maken,* ~ *niet, dan krijg je een aantekening* you must do your homework, otherwise you'll get a bad mark

³zo [zo] *int* well, so: *goed* ~*, Jan!* well done, John!; *o* ~! so there; ~*, dat is dat* well (then), that's that; *mijn vrouw heeft een nieuwe computer aangeschaft!* ~! my wife has bought herself a new computer. Really?

zoab [zowɑp] *het zeer open asfaltbeton* porous asphalt

zoals [zoɑls] *conj* **1** like: ~ *gewoonlijk* as usual; **2** as: ~ *je wilt* as *(or:* whatever) you like

zodat [zodɑt] *conj* so (that), (so as) to: *ik zal het eens tekenen,* ~ *je kunt zien wat ik bedoel* I'll draw it so (that) you can see what I mean

zode [zodə] *de (~n)* turf: *dat zet geen ~n aan de dijk* that's no use, that won't get us anywhere

zodoende [zodundə] *adv* (in) this, (in) that way, that's why, that's the reason

zodra [zodrɑ] *conj* as soon as: ~ *ik geld heb, betaal ik u* I'll pay you as soon as I have the money; ~ *hij opdaagt* the moment he shows up

zoek [zuk] *adj* missing, gone: ~ *raken* get lost; *op* ~ *gaan (zijn) naar iets* look for sth; *op* ~ *naar het ge-*

luk in pursuit of happiness

zoekactie [zukɑksi] *de (~s)* search (operation)

zoeken [zukə(n)] *vb* **1** look for, search for: *we moeten een uitweg ~* we've got to find a way out; *zoek je iets?* have you lost sth?; *hij wordt gezocht (wegens diefstal)* he is wanted (for theft); **2** look for, search for, be after: *jij hebt hier niets te ~* you have no business (being) here; *zoiets had ik achter haar niet gezocht* I hadn't expected that of her

zoeklicht [zuklɪχt] *het (~en)* searchlight, spotlight

zoekmachine [zukmɑʃinə] *de (~s)* search engine

zoekmaken [zukmakə(n)] *vb* **1** mislay, lose; **2** waste (on)

zoekplaatje [zukplacə] *het (~s) (roughly)* (picture) puzzle

zoekprogramma [zukproɣrɑma] *het* search engine

zoekraken [zukrakə(n)] *vb* get mislaid, be misplaced

zoektocht [zuktɔχt] *de (~en)* search (for), quest (for)

Zoeloe [zulu] *de (~s)* Zulu

zoemen [zumə(n)] *vb* buzz

zoemer [zumər] *de (~s)* buzzer

zoemtoon [zumton] *de (-tonen)* buzz, hum, tone, signal

zoen [zun] *de (~en)* kiss

zoenen [zunə(n)] *vb* kiss

zoet [zut] *adj* **1** sweet: *lekker ~* nice and sweet; **2** sweet, good: *iem ~ houden* keep s.o. happy *(or:* quiet)

zoethoudertje [zuthaudərcə] *het (~s)* sop

zoethout [zuthaut] *het* liquorice

zoetigheid [zutəχɛit] *de (-heden)* sweet(s)

zoetje [zucə] *het (~s)* sweetener

zoetsappig [zutsɑpəχ] *adj, adv* namby-pamby, sugary

zoetwatervis [zutwatərvɪs] *de (~sen)* freshwater fish

¹zoetzuur [zutsyr] *adj* **1** slightly sour *(or:* sharp); **2** pickled, sweet-and-sour

²zoetzuur [zutsyr] *het* (sweet) pickles

zoëven [zoevə(n)] *adv see* zojuist

zogen [zoɣə(n)] *vb* breastfeed

zogenaamd [zoɣənɑmt] *adj, adv* so-called, would-be: *ze was ~ verhinderd* something supposedly came up (to prevent her from coming)

zojuist [zojœyst] *adv* just (now)

¹zolang [zolɑŋ] *adv* meanwhile, meantime

²zolang [zolɑŋ] *conj* as long as: *(voor) ~ het duurt (iron)* as long as it lasts

zolder [zɔldər] *de (~s)* attic, loft

zolderkamer [zɔldərkamər] *de (~s)* attic room, room in the loft

zoldertrap [zɔldərtrɑp] *de (~pen)* attic stairs *(or:* ladder)

zomaar [zomar] *adv* just (like that), without (any) warning: *~ ineens* suddenly

zombie [zɔmbi] *de (~s)* zombie

zomer [zɔmər] *de (~s)* summer: *van (in) de ~* in the summer

zomeravond [zɔmərɑvɔnt] *de (~en)* summer('s) evening

zomerdag [zɔmərdɑχ] *de (~en)* summer('s) day

zomers [zɔmərs] *adj* summery

zomerspelen [zɔmərspelə(n)] *de* summer games, Summer Olympics

zomertijd [zɔmərtɛit] *de* summer(time); summer time

zomervakantie [zomərvakɑnsi] *de (~s)* summer holiday

zon [zɔn] *de (~nen)* sun: *de ~ gaat op (or:* gaat onder*)* the sun is rising *(or:* setting); *er is niets nieuws onder de ~* there is nothing new under the sun; *af en toe ~* sunny periods

zo'n [zɔn] *dem pron* **1** such (a): *in ~ geval zou ik niet gaan* I wouldn't go if that were the case; **2** such (a): *ik heb ~ slaap* I am so sleepy; **3** just like; **4** about; **5** one of those: *~ beetje* more or less; *ik vind haar ~ meid* I think she's a terrific girl

zondaar [zɔndar] *de (~s)* sinner

zondag [zɔndɑχ] *de (~en)* Sunday

¹zondags [zɔndɑχs] *adj* Sunday

²zondags [zɔndɑχs] *adv* on Sundays

zondagskind [zɔndɑχskɪnt] *het (~eren)* Sunday's child

zonde [zɔndə] *de (~n)* **1** sin; **2** shame: *het zou ~ van je tijd zijn* it would be a waste of time

zondebok [zɔndəbɔk] *de (~ken)* scapegoat, whipping boy

zonder [zɔndər] *prep* without || *~ meer* just like that, of course, without delay

zonderling [zɔndərlɪŋ] *de (~en)* strange character, odd character

zondig [zɔndəχ] *adj, adv* sinful

zondigen [zɔndəɣə(n)] *vb* sin

zondvloed [zɔntflut] *de* Flood

zone [zɔːnə] *de (~s)* zone, belt

zoneclips [zɔːneklɪps] *de (~en)* solar eclipse

zonenummer [zɔːnənʏmər] *het (~s) (Belg)* area code

zonkracht [zɔnkrɑχt] *de* sunpower

zonlicht [zɔnlɪχt] *het* sunlight

zonnebaden [zɔnəbadə(n)] *vb* sunbathe

zonnebank [zɔnəbɑŋk] *de (~en)* sunbed, solarium

zonnebloem [zɔnəblum] *de (~en)* sunflower

zonnebrand [zɔnəbrɑnt] *de* sunburn

zonnebrandolie [zɔnəbrɑntoli] *de* sun(tan) oil

zonnebril [zɔnəbrɪl] *de (~len)* sunglasses

zonnecel [zɔnəsɛl] *de (~len)* solar cell

zonne-energie [zɔnəenɛrʒi] *de* solar energy

zonnehemel [zɔnəheməl] *de (~s)* sunbed

zonneklep [zɔnəklɛp] *de (~pen)* (sun) visor

zonnen [zɔnə(n)] *vb* sunbathe

zonnepaneel [zɔnəpanel] *het (-panelen)* solar panel

zonnescherm [zɔnəsχɛrm] *het (~en)* (sun)blind; parasol

zonneschijn [zɔnəsχɛin] *de* sunshine
zonneslag [zɔnəslɑχ] *de (~en)* sunstroke
zonnesteek [zɔnəstek] *de (-steken)* sunstroke: *een ~ krijgen* get sunstroke
zonnestelsel [zɔnəstɛlsəl] *het (~s)* solar system
zonnestraal [zɔnəstral] *de (-stralen)* ray of sun(shine)
zonnetje [zɔnəcə] *het (~s)* **1** little sun, *(fig)* little sunshine; **2** sun(shine): *iem in het ~ zetten* make s.o. the centre of attention
zonnewende [zɔnəwɛndə] *de* solstice
zonnewijzer [zɔnəwɛizər] *de (~s)* sundial
zonnig [zɔnəχ] *adj* sunny: *een ~e toekomst* a bright future
zonsondergang [zɔnsɔndərɣɑŋ] *de (~en)* sunset
zonsopgang [zɔnsɔpχɑŋ] *de (~en)* sunrise
zonsverduistering [zɔnsfərdœystərɪŋ] *de (~en)* eclipse of the sun
zonwering [zɔnwerɪŋ] *de* awning, sunblind, (venetian) blind
zoogdier [zoɣdir] *het (~en)* mammal
zooi [zoj] *de (~en)* **1** mess; **2** heap, load
zool [zol] *de (zolen)* **1** sole; **2** insole
zoölogie [zooloɣi] *de* zoology
zoölogisch [zooloɣis] *adj* zoological
zoom [zom] *de (zomen)* **1** hem; **2** edge: *aan de ~ van de stad* at the edge (*or:* on the outskirts) of the city
zoomlens [zumlɛns] *de (-lenzen)* zoom lens
zoon [zon] *de (zonen, ~s)* son: *Angelo is de jongste ~* Angelo is the youngest (*or:* younger) son; *de oudste ~: a)* the oldest son; *b)* the elder son; *c)* the eldest son
zootje [zocə] *het (~s)* **1** heap, load: *het hele ~* the whole lot; **2** mess
zorg [zɔrχ] *de (~en)* **1** care, concern: *iets met ~ behandelen* handle sth carefully; **2** concern, worry: *geen ~en hebben* have no worries; *dat is een (hele) ~ minder* that's (quite) a relief; *zich ~en maken over* worry about; *'t zal mij een ~ wezen, mij een ~* I couldn't care less
zorgelijk [zɔrɣələk] *adj* worrisome, alarming
zorgeloos [zɔrɣəlos] *adj, adv* carefree
zorgeloosheid [zɔrɣəloshɛit] *de* freedom from care (*or:* worry)
zorgen [zɔrɣə(n)] *vb* **1** see to, take care of, provide, supply: *voor het eten ~* see to the food; *daar moet jij voor ~* that's your job; **2** care for, look after, take care of; **3** see (to), take care (to)
zorgverlof [zɔrɣfərlɔf] *het* care leave
zorgverzekeraar [zɔrɣfərzekərar] *de (~s)* health insurer, health insurance company
zorgvuldig [zɔrχfʏldəχ] *adj, adv* careful, meticulous, painstaking: *een ~ onderzoek* a careful (*or:* thorough) examination
zorgvuldigheid [zɔrχfʏldəχhɛit] *de* care, carefulness, precision
zorgzaam [zɔrχsam] *adj, adv* careful, considerate: *een ~ huisvader* a caring father
¹zot [zɔt] *adj, adv* crazy, idiotic, silly

²zot [zɔt] *de* fool, idiot
¹zout [zɑut] *het (~en)* (common) salt
²zout [zɑut] *adj* **1** salty; **2** salted
zoutarm [zɑutɑrm] *adj* low-salt
zoutje [zɑucə] *het (~s)* salt(y) biscuit, cocktail biscuit
zoutloos [zɑutlos] *adj* salt-free
zoutzak [zɑutsɑk] *de (~ken)* salt-bag: *hij zakte als een ~ in elkaar* he collapsed (like a burst balloon)
zoveel [zovel] *num* **1** as much, as many: *net ~* just as much (*or:* many); *dat is tweemaal ~* that's twice as much (*or:* many); **2** so, that much (*or:* many): *om de ~ dagen* every so many days; *niet zóveel* not (as much as) that
zoveelste [zovelstə] *num* such-and-such, umpteenth
¹zover [zovɛr] *adv* so far, this far, that far: *ben je ~?* (are you) ready?; *het is ~* the time has come, here we go!
²zover [zovɛr] *conj* as far: *voor ~ ik weet niet* not to my knowledge, not that I know of
zowat [zowɑt] *adv* almost: *ze zijn ~ even groot* they're about the same height
zowel [zowɛl] *adv* both, as well as: *~ de mannen als de vrouwen* both the men and the women, the men as well as the women
z.o.z. [zɛtozɛt] *zie ommezijde* p.t.o., please turn over
zozo [zozo] *adv* so-so
z.s.m. *zo spoedig mogelijk* asap, as soon as possible
zucht [zʏχt] *de (~en)* **1** desire, longing, craving; **2** sigh: *een diepe ~ slaken* heave a deep sigh
zuchten [zʏχtə(n)] *vb* sigh
zuid [zœyt] *adj, adv* south; south(ern), southerly
Zuid-Afrika [zœytɑfrika] *het* South Africa
Zuid-Afrikaan [zœytafrikɑn] *de (Zuid-Afrikanen)* South African
Zuid-Amerika [zœytamerika] *het* South America
Zuid-Amerikaan [zœytamerikɑn] *de (Zuid-Amerikanen)* South American
¹zuidelijk [zœydələk] *adj* **1** southern; **2** south(ern), southerly
²zuidelijk [zœydələk] *adv* (to the) south, southerly, southwards
zuiden [zœydə(n)] *het* south: *ten ~ (van)* (to the) south (of)
zuidenwind [zœydə(n)wɪnt] *de (~en)* south (*or:* southern, southerly) wind
zuiderbreedte [zœydərbretə] *de* southern latitude: *op 4° ~* at a latitude of 4° South
zuiderkeerkring [zœydərkerkrɪŋ] *de* tropic of Capricorn
Zuid-Europa [zœytørɔpa] *het* Southern Europe
Zuid-Europees [zœytørøpes] *adj* Southern European
Zuid-Holland [zœythɔlɑnt] *het* South Holland
Zuid-Hollands [zœythɔlɑnts] *adj* South Holland
Zuid-Korea [zœytkoreja] *het* South Korea
Zuid-Koreaans [zœytkorejɑns] *adj* South Korean
zuidkust [zœytkʏst] *de (~en)* south(ern) coast

¹zuidoost [zœytǫst] *adv* south-east(wards), to the south-east

²zuidoost [zœytǫst] *adj* south-east(ern), south-easterly

Zuidoost-Azië [zœytostazijə] *het* South-East Asia

¹zuidoostelijk [zœytǫstələk] *adv* (to the) south-east, south-easterly

²zuidoostelijk [zœytǫstələk] *adj* south-east(ern), south-easterly

zuidoosten [zœytǫstə(n)] *het* south-east; South-East

zuidooster [zœytǫstər] *de* (~s) southeaster

zuidpool [zœytpol] *de* Antarctic, South Pole

zuidpoolcirkel [zœytpǫlsɪrkəl] *de* Antarctic Circle

zuidpoolgebied [zœytpǫlɣəbit] *het* Antarctic, South Pole

zuidvrucht [zœytfrʏχt] *de* (~en) subtropical fruit

¹zuidwaarts [zœytwarts] *adj* southward, southerly

²zuidwaarts [zœytwarts] *adv* south(wards)

¹zuidwest [zœytwɛst] *adv* south-west(wards), to the south-west

²zuidwest [zœytwɛst] *adj* south-west(ern), south-westerly

¹zuidwestelijk [zœytwɛstələk] *adv* (to the) south-west, south-westerly, south-westwards

²zuidwestelijk [zœytwɛstələk] *adj* south-west(ern), south-westerly

zuidwesten [zœytwɛstə(n)] *het* south-west; South-West

zuidwester [zœytwɛstər] *de* (~s) 1 southwester; 2 sou'wester

zuigeling [zœyɣəlɪŋ] *de* (~en) infant, baby

¹zuigen [zœyɣə(n)] *vb* 1 suck, nurse; 2 vacuum, hoover

²zuigen [zœyɣə(n)] *vb* suck (on, away at)

zuiger [zœyɣər] *de* (~s) piston

zuigfles [zœyχflɛs] *de* (~sen) feeding bottle

zuigtablet [zœyχtablɛt] *het, de* (~ten) lozenge

zuil [zœyl] *de* (~en) pillar, column, pile

zuinig [zœynəχ] *adj, adv* 1 economical, frugal, thrifty, sparing: ~ *op iets zijn* be careful about sth; 2 economical, efficient: *een motor* ~ *afstellen* tune (up) an engine to run efficiently

zuinigheid [zœynəχhɛit] *de* economy, frugality, thrift(iness)

¹zuipen [zœypə(n)] *vb* drink: *die auto zuipt benzine* that car just eats up petrol

²zuipen [zœypə(n)] *vb* booze || *zich zat* ~ get sloshed (*or:* plastered)

zuiplap [zœyplɑp] *de* (~pen) boozer, drunk(ard)

zuippartij [zœypɑrtɛi] *de* (~en) drinking bout (*or:* spree)

zuivel [zœyvəl] *het, de* dairy produce, dairy products

zuivelbedrijf [zœyvəlbədrɛif] *het* (-bedrijven) dairy farm

zuivelfabriek [zœyvəlfabrik] *de* (~en) dairy factory, creamery

zuivelproduct [zœyvəlprodʏkt] *het* (~en) dairy product

¹zuiver [zœyvər] *adj* 1 pure: *van* ~ *leer* genuine leather; 2 clear, clean, pure; 3 correct, true, accurate: *een* ~ *schot* an accurate shot

²zuiver [zœyvər] *adv* 1 purely; 2 *(mus)* in tune

zuiveren [zœyvərə(n)] *vb* clean, purify, clear, cleanse: *de lucht* ~ clear the air; *zich* ~ *van een verdenking* clear oneself of a suspicion

zuiverheid [zœyvərhɛit] *de* purity, soundness, accuracy

zuivering [zœyvərɪŋ] *de* (~en) purification

zuiveringsinstallatie [zœyvərɪŋsɪnstɑla(t)si] *de* (~s) purification plant, sewage-treatment plant

¹zulk [zʏlk] *adv* such: *het zijn* ~*e lieve mensen* they're such nice people

²zulk [zʏlk] *dem pron* such: ~*e zijn er ook* that kind also exists

zullen [zʏlə(n)] *vb* 1 shall; will; should, would: *maar het zou nog erger worden* but worse was yet to come; *dat zul je nu altijd zien!* isn't that (just) typical!; *wat zou dat?* so what?, what's that to you?; 2 will; would, be going (*or:* about) to: *zou je denken?* do you think (so)?; *als ik het kon, zou ik het doen* I would (do it) if I could; *hij zou fraude gepleegd hebben* he is said to have committed fraud; *dat zal vorig jaar geweest zijn* that would be (*or:* must have been) last year; *wie zal het zeggen?* who's to say?, who can say?; *zou hij ziek zijn?* can he be ill? (*or:* sick?); *dat zal wel* I bet it is, I suppose it will, I dare say

zult [zʏlt] *de* brawn, *(Am)* headcheese

zuring [zyrɪŋ] *de* sorrel

¹zus [zʏs] *de* (~sen) sister; sis

²zus [zʏs] *adv* so: *mijnheer* ~ *of zo* Mr so-and-so, Mr something-or-other

zuster [zʏstər] *de* (~s) 1 sister; 2 nurse

¹zuur [zyr] *het* (zuren) 1 acid; 2 *(roughly)* pickles, pickled vegetables (*or:* onions); 3 heartburn, acidity (of the stomach)

²zuur [zyr] *adj, adv* 1 sour: *de melk is* ~ the milk has turned sour; 2 acid

zuurkool [zyrkol] *de* sauerkraut

zuurstof [zyrstɔf] *de* oxygen

zuurstofmasker [zyrstɔfmɑskər] *het* (~s) oxygen mask

zuurstok [zyrstɔk] *de* (~ken) stick of rock

zuurtje [zyrcə] *het* (~s) acid drop

zuurverdiend [zyrvərdint] *adj* hard-earned

zwaai [zwaj] *de* (~en) swing, sweep, sway, wave

zwaaideur [zwajdər] *de* (~en) swing-door

zwaaien [zwajə(n)] *vb* swing, sway, wave, flourish, brandish, wield: *met zijn armen* ~ wave one's arms; *er zal wat* ~ there'll be the devil to pay

zwaailicht [zwajlɪχt] *het* (~en) flashing light

zwaan [zwan] *de* (zwanen) swan

zwaantje [zwɑncə] *het* *(Belg)* motorcycle policeman

¹zwaar [zwar] *adj, adv* 1 heavy; rough, full-bodied, strong: *dat is tien kilo* ~ that weighs ten kilos; ~*der* *worden* put on (*or:* gain) weight; *twee pond te ~* two pounds overweight (*or:* too heavy); **2** difficult, hard: *zware ademhaling* hard breathing, wheezing; *een zware bevalling* a difficult delivery; *een ~ examen* a stiff (*or:* difficult) exam; *hij heeft het ~* he is having a hard time of it; **3** heavy, serious: *~ verlies* a heavy loss; **4** heavy, deep

²zwaar [zwar] *adv* heavily, heavy, hard, seriously, badly: *~ gewond* badly (*or:* seriously, severely) wounded

zwaarbeladen [zwɑrbəladə(n)] *adj* heavy laden, heavily laden

zwaarbewolkt *adj* overcast

zwaard [zwart] *het* (*~en*) sword

zwaardvis [zwɑrtfis] *de* (*~sen*) swordfish

zwaargebouwd [zwarɣəbɑut] *adj* heavily built, heavy-set, large-boned, thickset

zwaargewapend [zwarɣəwapənt] *adj* heavily armed

¹zwaargewicht [zwarɣəwıχt] *de* (*boxer*) heavyweight

²zwaargewicht [zwarɣəwıχt] *het* heavyweight

zwaargewond [zwarɣəwɔnt] *adj* badly, seriously wounded (*or:* injured)

zwaarmoedig [zwarmudəχ] *adj* melancholy, depressed: *~ kijken* look melancholy (*or:* depressed)

zwaarmoedigheid [zwarmudəχhɛit] *de* **1** depressiveness, melancholy; **2** melancholia, depression; **3** melancholy, gloom, dejection

zwaarte [zwartə] *de* **1** heaviness, weight; **2** weight, size, strength

zwaartekracht [zwartəkrɑχt] *de* gravity, gravitation

zwaartepunt [zwartəpʏnt] *het* centre, central point, main point

zwaarwegend [zwarweɣənt] *adj* weighty, important

zwaarwichtig [zwarwıχtəχ] *adj, adv* weighty, ponderous

zwabber [zwɑbər] *de* (*~s*) mop

zwabberen [zwɑbərə(n)] *vb* mop

zwachtel [zwɑχtəl] *de* (*~s*) bandage

zwager [zwaɣər] *de* (*~s*) brother-in-law

zwak [zwɑk] *adj, adv* **1** weak, feeble: *de zieke is nog ~ op zijn benen* the patient is still shaky on his legs; **2** weak, delicate: *een ~ke gezondheid hebben* be in poor health; **3** weak, poor, bad: *~ zijn in iets* be bad (*or:* poor) at sth, be weak in sth; **4** weak, vulnerable; **5** weak, insubstantial, poor; **6** weak, faint

zwakbegaafd [zwɑgbəɣaft] *adj* retarded

zwakheid [zwɑkhɛit] *de* (*-heden*) weakness, failing

zwakkeling [zwɑkəlıŋ] *de* (*~en*) weakling

zwakstroom [zwɑkstrom] *de* low-voltage current, weak current

zwakzinnig [zwɑksɪnəχ] *adj* mentally handicapped

zwakzinnigheid [zwɑksɪnəχhɛit] *de* mental defectiveness (*or:* deficiency)

zwalken [zwɑlkə(n)] *vb* drift about, wander

zwaluw [zwɑlyw] *de* (*~en*) swallow: *één ~ maakt nog geen zomer* one swallow does not make a summer

zwam [zwɑm] *de* (*~men*) fungus

zwanenhals [zwanə(n)hɑls] *de* (*-halzen*) U-trap, gooseneck

zwang [zwɑŋ] || *in ~ zijn* be in vogue, be fashionable, be in fashion

zwanger [zwɑŋər] *adj* pregnant, expecting

zwangerschap [zwɑŋərsχɑp] *de* (*~pen*) pregnancy

zwangerschapstest [zwɑŋərsχɑpstɛst] *de* (*~s*) pregnancy test

zwangerschapsverlof [zwɑŋərsχɑpsfərlɔf] *het* (*-verloven*) maternity leave

zwart [zwart] *adj, adv* **1** black, dark: *een ~e bladzijde in de geschiedenis* a black page in history; *~e goederen* black-market goods; **2** black, dirty: *iem ~ maken* blacken s.o.'s reputation; *~ op wit* in writing, in black and white

zwartboek [zwɑrdbuk] *het* (*~en*) black book

zwartepiet [zwartəpit] *de* (*~en*) knave (*or:* jack) of spades

zwarthandelaar [zwɑrthɑndəlar] *de* (*~s, -handelaren*) black marketeer, profiteer

zwartkijker [zwɑrtkɛikər] *de* (*~s*) **1** pessimist, worrywart; **2** TV licence dodger

zwartmaken [zwɑrtmakə(n)] *vb* || *iem ~ blacken* s.o.'s good name (*or:* s.o.'s character)

zwartrijden [zwɑrtrɛidə(n)] *vb* **1** evade paying road (*or Am:* highway) tax; **2** dodge paying the fare

zwartrijder [zwɑrtrɛidər] *de* (*~s*) **1** road-tax dodger; **2** fare-dodger

zwartwerk [zwɑrtwɛrk] *het* moonlighting

zwartwerken [zwɑrtwɛrkə(n)] *vb* moonlight, work on the side

zwart-wit [zwɑrtwɪt] *adv* black-and-white

zwavel [zwavəl] *de* sulphur

zwaveldioxide [zwavəldijɔksidə] *het* sulphur dioxide

¹zwavelzuur [zwavəlzyr] *het* sulphuric acid

²zwavelzuur [zwavəlzyr] *adj* sulphuric acid

Zweden [zwedə(n)] *het* Sweden

Zweed [zwet] *de* (*Zweden*) Swede, Swedish woman

Zweeds [zwets] *adj* Swedish

zweefduik [zwevdœyk] *de* (*~en*) (*sport*) swallow dive, (*Am*) swan dive

zweefmolen [zwefmolə(n)] *de* (*~s*) whirligig

zweefvliegen [zwefliɣə(n)] *vb* glide

zweefvliegtuig [zwefliχtœyχ] *het* (*~en*) glider

zweem [zwem] *de* trace, hint: *zonder een ~ van twijfel* without a shadow of a doubt

zweep [zwep] *de* (*zwepen*) whip, lash, crop

zweepslag [zwepslɑχ] *de* (*~en*) **1** lash, whip(lash); **2** whiplash (injury)

zweer [zwer] *de* (*zweren*) ulcer, abscess, boil

zweet [zwet] *het* sweat: *het ~ breekt hem uit* he's in a (cold) sweat

zweetband [zwedbɑnt] *de* (*~en*) sweatband

zweetdruppel [zwedrʏpəl] *de* (*~s*) drop (*or:* bead)

of sweat

zweethanden [zwɛthɑndə(n)] *de* sweaty hands

zweetvoeten [zwɛtfutə(n)] *de* sweaty feet

zwellen [zwɛlə(n)] *vb* swell: *doen ~: a)* swell; *b)* belly, billow; *c)* bulge

zwelling [zwɛlɪŋ] *de (~en)* swell(ing)

zwembad [zwɛmbɑt] *het (~en)* (swimming) pool

zwemband [zwɛmbɑnt] *de (~en)* water ring

zwembroek [zwɛmbruk] *de (~en) (pl)* bathing trunks, swimming trunks

zwemdiploma [zwɛmdiploma] *het* swimming certificate

zwemles [zwɛmlɛs] *de* swimming lesson: *op ~ zitten* take swimming lessons

zwemmen [zwɛmə(n)] *vb* swim: *verboden te ~* no swimming allowed; *gaan ~* go for a swim

zwemmer [zwɛmər] *de (~s)* swimmer

zwempak [zwɛmpɑk] *het (~ken)* swimming suit, swimsuit

zwemtas [zwɛmtɑs] *de (~sen)* swimming bag

zwemvest [zwɛmvɛst] *het (~en)* life jacket (*or:* vest)

zwemvlies [zwɛmvlis] *het (-vliezen)* **1** web; **2** flipper

zwemvogel [zwɛmvoɣəl] *de (~s)* web-footed bird

zwemwedstrijd [zwɛmwɛtstrɛit] *de (~en)* swimming competition (*or:* contest)

zwendel [zwɛndəl] *de* swindle, fraud

zwendelaar [zwɛndəlar] *de (~s)* swindler, fraud

zwendelen [zwɛndələ(n)] *vb* swindle

zwengel [zwɛŋəl] *de (~s)* handle, crank

zwenken [zwɛŋkə(n)] *vb* swerve, *(shipp)* sheer: *naar rechts ~* swerve to the right

zwenkwiel [zwɛŋkwil] *het (~en)* castor, roller

zweren [zwɛrə(n)] *vb* **1** swear, vow: *ik zou er niet op durven ~* I wouldn't take an oath on it; *ik zweer het (je)* I swear (to you); **2** ulcerate; fester

zwerfkat [zwɛrfkɑt] *de (~ten)* stray cat

zwerfkind [zwɛrfkɪnt] *het (~eren)* young vagrant, vagrant child, runaway

zwerftocht [zwɛrftɔχt] *de (~en)* ramble, wandering

zwerfvuil [zwɛrfœyl] *het* (street) litter

zwerm [zwɛrm] *de (~en)* swarm, flock

zwerven [zwɛrvə(n)] *vb* **1** wander, roam, rove; **2** tramp (about), knock about; **3** lie about

zwerver [zwɛrvər] *de (~s)* **1** wanderer, drifter; **2** tramp, vagabond

zweten [zwetə(n)] *vb* sweat

zwetsen [zwɛtsə(n)] *vb* blather; boast, brag: *hij kan enorm ~* he talks a lot of hot air

zwetser [zwɛtsər] *de (~s)* boaster, bragger

zweven [zwevə(n)] *vb* **1** be suspended: *boven een afgrond ~* hang over an abyss; **2** float, glide; **3** hover

zweverig [zwevərəχ] *adj* **1** woolly, free-floating; **2** dizzy

zwichten [zwɪχtə(n)] *vb* yield, submit, give in: *voor de verleiding ~* yield to the temptation

zwiepen [zwipə(n)] *vb* bend: *de takken zwiepten in de wind* the branches swayed in the wind

zwier [zwir] *de ‖ aan de ~ gaan* go on a spree

zwieren [zwirə(n)] *vb* sway, reel; whirl

zwierig [zwirəχ] *adj, adv* elegant, graceful, dashing, flamboyant

¹zwijgen [zwɛiɣə(n)] *vb* be silent: *zwijg!* hold your tongue!, be quiet!

²zwijgen [zwɛiɣə(n)] *het* silence: *het ~ verbreken* break the silence

zwijger [zwɛiɣər] *de (~s)* silent person: *Willem de Zwijger* William the Silent

zwijggeld [zwɛiχɛlt] *het (~en)* hush money

zwijgplicht [zwɛiχplɪχt] *de* oath of secrecy

zwijgzaam [zwɛiχsam] *adj* silent, incommunicative, reticent

zwijmelen [zwɛiмələ(n)] *vb* swoon

zwijn [zwɛin] *het (~en)* swine: *een wild ~* a wild boar

zwijnenstal [zwɛinə(n)stɑl] *de (~len)* pigsty

zwikken [zwɪkə(n)] *vb* sprain, wrench

Zwitser [zwɪtsər] *de (~s)* Swiss

Zwitserland [zwɪtsərlɑnt] *het* Switzerland

Zwitsers [zwɪtsərs] *adj* Swiss

zwoegen [zwuɣə(n)] *vb* **1** plod, drudge, slave (away); toil, labour; **2** heave; pant

zwoel [zwul] *adj* sultry, muggy

zwoerd [zwurt] *het (~en)* rind

English-Dutch

a

¹a [ee] *n* 1 a, A; **2** de eerste, de hoogste (rang, graad), eersteklas ‖ *A-1* eersteklas, prima

²a [ə, ee], **an** [ən, æn] *art* **1** een; **2** per: *five times a day* vijf keer per dag; **3** dezelfde, hetzelfde: *all of an age* allemaal even oud

A.A. 1 *Automobile Association (roughly)* ANWB; **2** *(Am) Alcoholics Anonymous* AA

¹abandon [əbændən] *vb* **1** in de steek laten, aan zijn lot overlaten: *~ a baby* een baby te vondeling leggen; *the order to ~ ship* het bevel het schip te verlaten; **2** opgeven, afstand doen van: *~ all hope* alle hoop laten varen; **3** *(sport)* afgelasten

²abandon [əbændən] *n* ongedwongenheid, vrijheid: *with ~* uitbundig

abandoned [əbændənd] **1** verlaten, opgegeven; **2** verdorven, losbandig, schaamteloos; **3** ongedwongen, ongeremd, uitbundig

abate [əbeet] verminderen, afnemen: *the wind ~d* de wind ging liggen

abbey [æbie] **1** abdij; **2** abdijkerk

abbot [æbət] abt

abbreviate [əbrie:vie·eet] **1** inkorten, verkorten; **2** afkorten

abbreviation [əbrie·vie·eesjən] **1** inkorting, verkorting; **2** afkorting

abdicate [æbdikkeet] aftreden: *~ (from) the throne* troonsafstand doen

abduction [æbduksjən] ontvoering, kidnapping

aberrant [æberrənt] afwijkend, abnormaal

abhor [əbho:] verafschuwen, walgen van

abide [əbajd] blijven ‖ *~ by: a)* zich neerleggen bij, zich houden aan; *b)* trouw blijven aan

ability [əbillittie] bekwaamheid, vermogenʰ, bevoegdheid

abject [æbdzjekt] **1** rampzalig, ellendig, miserabel: *~ poverty* trooosteloze armoede; **2** verachtelijk, laag

ablaze [əbleez] **1** in lichterlaaie: *set ~* in vuur en vlam zetten; **2** schitterend, stralend

able [eebl] **1** bekwaam, competent; **2** in staat, de macht (mogelijkheid) hebbend: *be ~ to* kunnen

ably [eeblie] *see* able

abnormal [æbno:məl] **1** abnormaal, afwijkend; **2** uitzonderlijk

¹aboard [əbo:d] *adv* aan boord: *all ~!* instappen!

²aboard [əbo:d] *prep* aan boord van

abolish [əbollisj] afschaffen, een eind maken aan:

~ the death penalty de doodstraf afschaffen

abolition [æbəlisjən] afschaffing

abominable [əbomminnəbl] afschuwelijk, walgelijk

aboriginal [æbəridzjinl] inheems, autochtoon, oorspronkelijk

abort [əbo:t] *(comp)* afbreken

abortion [əbo:sjən] abortus, miskraam

abortive [əbo:tiv] vruchteloos, mislukt

abound [əbaund] overvloedig aanwezig zijn, in overvloed voorkomen, wemelen (van)

¹about [əbaut] *prep* **1** rond, om … heen; **2** rondom, in (de buurt van) *(also fig): there was an air of mystery ~ the boy* de jongen had iets geheimzinnigs over zich; **3** door … heen, over: *travel ~ the country* in het land rondreizen; **4** over, met betrekking tot: *be quick ~ it* schiet eens wat op; **5** omstreeks, omtrent, ongeveer: *~ midnight* rond middernacht; *while you are ~ it* als je (er) toch (mee) bezig bent; *what ~ it?* nou, en …?, so what?, wat wil je nu zeggen?; *what* (of: *how) ~ a cup of coffee?* zin in een kop koffie?

²about [əbaut] *adv* **1** ongeveer, bijna: *that's ~ it* dat moet het zo ongeveer zijn; *~ twenty pence* ongeveer twintig pence; **2** *(indicating place and direction)* rond(om), in het rond (de buurt): *there's a lot of flu ~* er heerst griep; **3** om(gekeerd) *(also fig): the wrong way ~* omgekeerd; *~ turn!, (Am) ~ face!* rechtsomkeert!

¹above [əbuv] *prep* **1** boven; **2** hoger dan, meer dan: *~ fifty* meer dan vijftig; *~ all* vooral

²above [əbuv] *adv* **1** boven, hoger: *from ~* van boven, *(fig)* uit de hemel; *the ~: a)* het bovengenoemde; *b)* de bovengenoemde personen; **2** hoger, meer: *twenty and ~* twintig en meer; *imposed from ~* van hogerhand opgelegd

aboveboard eerlijk, openlijk, rechtuit

¹abrasive [əbreesiv] *adj* **1** schurend, krassend; **2** ruw, kwetsend: *~ character* irritant karakter

²abrasive [əbreesiv] *n* schuurmiddelʰ

abreast [əbrest] **1** zij aan zij, naast elkaar, op een rij: *two ~* twee aan twee; **2** in gelijke tred, gelijk, op dezelfde hoogte: *keep wages ~ of* de lonen gelijke tred doen houden met

abridge [əbridzj] verkorten, inkorten

abroad [əbro:d] in (naar) het buitenland: *(back) from ~* (terug) uit het buitenland

abrupt [əbrupt] **1** abrupt, plots(eling); **2** kortaf

abscess [æbses] abcesʰ, ettergezwelʰ

absence [æbsns] **1** afwezigheid, absentie: *he was condemned in his ~* hij werd bij verstek veroordeeld; **2** gebrekʰ: *in the ~ of proof* bij gebrek aan bewijs

absent [æbsnt] afwezig, absent

absent-minded verstrooid, afwezig

absolute [æbsəloe:t] **1** absoluut, geheel, totaal: *~ proof* onweerlegbaar bewijs; **2** onvoorwaardelijk: *~ promise* onvoorwaardelijke belofte

absolution [æbsəloe:sjən] absolutie, vergiffenis

absolve [əbz_olv] **1** vergeven, de absolutie geven; **2** ontheffen, kwijtschelden: ~ *s.o. from a promise* iem ontslaan van een belofte

absorb [əbzo:b] absorberen, (in zich) opnemen, opzuigen

abstain [əbsteen] *(with from)* zich onthouden (van)

abstinence [æbstinnəns] onthouding

¹abstract [æbstrækt] *adj* abstract, theoretisch, algemeen

²abstract [æbstrækt] *n* **1** samenvatting, uittreksel[h]; **2** abstract kunstwerk[h]

³abstract [æbstrækt] *vb* **1** onttrekken, ontvreemden; **2** afleiden; **3** samenvatten

absurd [əbso:d] absurd, dwaas, belachelijk

abundance [əbundəns] overvloed, weelde, menigte

abundant [əbundənt] **1** overvloedig; **2** rijk: *a river ~ in fish* een rivier rijk aan vis

¹abuse [əbjoe:z] *vb* **1** misbruiken; **2** mishandelen; **3** (uit)schelden

²abuse [əbjoe:s] *n* **1** misbruik[h], verkeerd gebruik[h]; **2** scheldwoorden; **3** mishandeling: *child ~* kindermishandeling

abusive [əbjoe:siv] beledigend: *become ~* beginnen te schelden

abyss [əbis] afgrond, peilloze diepte

A.C. *alternating current* wisselstroom

¹academic [ækədemmik] *adj* academisch, *(fig)* abstract, theoretisch

²academic [ækədemmik] *n* academicus, wetenschapper

academy [əkædəmie] academie, genootschap[h], school voor speciale opleiding

¹accelerate [əkselləreet] *vb* sneller gaan, het tempo opvoeren, optrekken

²accelerate [əkselləreet] *vb* versnellen

accelerator [əkselləreetə] gaspedaal[h]

¹accent [æksnt] *n* accent[h] *(also fig)*, klemtoon, uitspraak: *the ~ is on exotic flowers* de nadruk ligt op exotische bloemen

²accent [əksent] *vb* accentueren *(also fig)*, de klemtoon leggen op, (sterk) doen uitkomen

accept [əksept] **1** aannemen, aanvaarden, accepteren: *an ~ed fact* een (algemeen) aanvaard feit; *be ~ed practice* algemeen gebruikelijk zijn; **2** aanvaarden, tolereren, verdragen; **3** goedvinden, goedkeuren, erkennen: *all members ~ed the proposal* alle leden namen het voorstel aan

acceptable [əkseptəbl] **1** aanvaardbaar, aannemelijk; **2** redelijk

acceptance [əkseptəns] **1** aanvaarding, overneming; **2** gunstige ontvangst, bijval; **3** instemming, goedkeuring; **4** *(com)* accept(atie)

access [ækses] *(with to)* toegang (tot), toegangsrecht[h], toelating: *no (public) ~* verboden toegang

accessibility [əksessəbillittie] toegankelijkheid

accessible [əksessibl] *(with to)* toegankelijk (voor), bereikbaar (voor), *(fig)* begrijpelijk (voor)

accessory [əksessərie] medeplichtige

accident [æksiddənt] **1** toeval[h], toevalligheid, toevallige omstandigheid: *by ~* bij toeval, toevallig; **2** ongeluk[h], ongeval[h]: *by ~* per ongeluk

accidental [æksiddentl] toevallig, onvoorzien, niet bedoeld: *~(ly) on purpose* per ongeluk expres

acclaim [əkleem] toejuiching, bijval, gejuich[h]: *receive (critical) ~* (door de critici) toegejuicht worden

acclimatize [əklajmətajz] acclimatiseren

accommodate [əkommədeet] **1** huisvesten, onderbrengen; **2** plaats hebben voor; **3** aanpassen, (met elkaar) in overeenstemming brengen *(plans, ideas)*: *~ oneself (to)* zich aanpassen (aan)

accommodating [əkommədeeting] inschikkelijk, meegaand, plooibaar

accommodations [əkommədeesjənz] *(Am)* **1** onderdak, (verblijf)plaats, logies; **2** plaats, ruimte

accompany [əkumpənie] **1** begeleiden, vergezellen: *~ing letter* bijgaande brief; **2** *(mus)* begeleiden

accomplice [əkumplis] medeplichtige

accomplish [əkumplisj] **1** volbrengen, voltooien; **2** tot stand brengen, bereiken

accomplishment [əkumplisjmənt] **1** prestatie; **2** bekwaamheid, vaardigheid; **3** voltooiing, vervulling

accord [əko:d] akkoord[h], schikking, overeenkomst, verdrag[h]: *of one's own ~* uit eigen beweging

accordance [əko:dəns]: *in ~ with* overeenkomstig, in overeenstemming met

according to [əko:ding toe] volgens, naar … beweert

account [əkaunt] **1** verslag[h], beschrijving, verklaring, uitleg *(of behaviour)*: *by all ~s* naar alles wat men hoort; *annual ~* jaarverslag; *give (of: render) an ~ of* verslag uitbrengen over; **2** rekening, factuur *(also fig)*: *settle an ~ with s.o.* de rekening vereffenen met iem; **3** rekenschap, verantwoording: *bring (of: call) s.o. to ~ for sth.* iem ter verantwoording roepen voor iets; *give (of: render) ~ of* rekenschap afleggen over; **4** beschouwing, aandacht: *take sth. into ~, take ~ of sth.* rekening houden met iets; **5** belang[h], waarde, gewicht[h]: *of no ~* van geen belang; **6** voordeel[h]: *put (of: turn) sth. to (good) ~* zijn voordeel met iets doen; *do (of: keep) (the) ~s* boekhouden; *on ~ of* wegens; *on no ~* in geen geval

accountability [əkauntəbillittie] verantwoordelijkheid, aansprakelijkheid

accountancy [əkauntənsie] accountancy, boekhouding

accountant [əkauntənt] accountant, (hoofd)boekhouder

account for 1 rekenschap geven van, verslag uitbrengen over; **2** verklaren, uitleggen, veroorzaken: *his disease accounts for his strange behaviour* zijn ziekte verklaart zijn vreemde gedrag; **3** vormen, uitmaken: *computer games accounted for two-thirds of his spending* computerspelletjes vormden tweederde van zijn uitgaven; **4** bekend zijn: *the rest of the passengers still have to be ac-*

counted for de overige passagiers worden nog steeds vermist

accumulate [əkjoe:mjoeleet] (zich) op(een)stapelen, (zich) op(een)hopen: ~ *a fortune* een fortuin vergaren

accumulation [əkjoe:mjoeleesjən] **1** op(een)stapeling, op(een)hoping, accumulatie; **2** aangroei

accuracy [ækjərəsie] nauwkeurigheid, correctheid, exactheid

accurate [ækjərət] nauwkeurig, correct

accusation [ækjoezeesjən] beschuldiging, aanklacht

accuse [əkjoe:z] beschuldigen, aanklagen

accused [əkjoe:zd] beschuldigd, aangeklaagd

accustom [əkustəm] (ge)wennen, gewoon maken: ~*d to* gewend aan

ace [ees] **1** *(cards)* aas[+h], één, *(fig)* troef; **2** *(sport, esp tennis)* ace; **3** *(inf)* uitblinker: *an* ~ *at arithmetic* een hele piet in het rekenen

acerbity [əsə:bittie] wrangheid, zuurheid, bitterheid

¹ache [eek] *vb* **1** (pijn) lijden *(also fig)*; **2** pijn doen, zeer doen; **3** *(inf)* (hevig) verlangen, hunkeren: *be aching to do sth.* staan te popelen om iets te doen; ~ *for* hunkeren naar

²ache [eek] *n* (voortdurende) pijn: ~*s and pains* pijntjes

achieve [ətsjie:v] **1** volbrengen, voltooien, tot stand brengen; **2** bereiken *(goal etc)*, presteren

achievement [ətsjie:vmənt] **1** prestatie; **2** voltooiing; **3** het bereiken

¹acid [æsid] *n* **1** zuur[h], zure stof (drank); **2** *(inf)* acid, LSD

²acid [æsid] *adj* **1** zuur, zuurhoudend: ~ *rain* zure regen; **2** bits, bijtend

acid test vuurproef *(fig)*

acknowledge [əknollidzj] **1** erkennen, accepteren; **2** toegeven: ~ *sth. to s.o.* t.o.v. iem iets toegeven; **3** ontvangst bevestigen van: *I herewith* ~ *(receipt of) your letter* hierbij bevestig ik de ontvangst van uw brief; **4** een teken van herkenning geven aan *(by means of a nod, greeting)*

acknowledg(e)ment [əknollidzjmənt] **1** erkenning, acceptatie; **2** (bewijs[h] van) dank: *in* ~ *of* als dank voor; **3** ontvangstbevestiging, kwitantie

acorn [eeko:n] eikel

acoustic [əkoe:stik] akoestisch

acquaint [əkweent] op de hoogte brengen, in kennis stellen, vertrouwd maken: ~ *s.o. of* (of: *with*) *the facts* iem op de hoogte stellen van de feiten

acquaintance [əkweentəns] **1** kennis, bekende; **2** kennissenkring; **3** bekendheid, vertrouwdheid, kennis: *have a nodding* ~ *with s.o.* iem oppervlakkig kennen; **4** kennismaking: *make s.o.'s* ~ kennis maken met iem

acquiescence [ækwie·esns] instemming, berusting

acquire [əkwajjə] **1** verwerven, verkrijgen, aanleren: ~*d characteristics* aangeleerde eigenschappen; *it's an* ~*d taste* men moet het leren waarderen

(food, drink, etc); **2** aanschaffen, (aan)kopen

acquisition [ækwizzisjən] aanwinst, verworven bezit[h], aankoop

acquisitive [əkwizzittiv] hebzuchtig, hebberig

acquit [əkwit] vrijspreken: *be* ~*ed (on a charge) of murder* vrijgesproken worden van moord; ~ *oneself ill: a)* zich slecht van zijn taak kwijten; *b)* het er slecht van afbrengen

acre [eekə] **1** acre *(4,047 square metres)*; **2** ~*s* landerijen, grondgebied[h], groot gebied[h]

acrid [ækrid] bijtend *(also fig)*, scherp, bitter

acrimonious [ækrimmooniəs] bitter, scherp, venijnig

acrobat [ækrəbæt] acrobaat

acrobatic [ækrəbætik] **1** acrobatisch; **2** soepel, lenig

¹across [əkros] *adv* **1** *(place)* overdwars, gekruist: *it measured fifty yards* ~ het had een doorsnede van vijftig yards; **2** *(place)* aan de overkant; **3** *(direction, also fig)* over, naar de overkant: *the actor came* ~ *well* de acteur kwam goed over (bij het publiek); *put a message* ~ een boodschap overbrengen; **4** *(in crossword)* horizontaal

²across [əkros] *prep* **1** (tegen)over *(also fig)*, dwars, gekruist, aan (naar) de overkant van: *look* ~ *the hedge* kijk over de haag; *from* ~ *the sea* van overzee; *the people* ~ *the street: a)* de overburen; *b)* de mensen aan de overkant (van de straat)

acrylic [əkrillik] acryl

¹act [ækt] *n* **1** handeling, daad, werk[h]; **2** besluit[h], bepaling, wet: ~ *of Parliament* (Am: *Congress*) wet van het Parlement (*Am:* Congres); **3** akte, (proces)stuk[h]; **4** *(theatre)* bedrijf[h], akte; **5** *(circus)* nummer[h], act; **6** *(inf; depr)* komedie: *put on an* ~ komedie spelen; *(rel)* Acts *(of the Apostles)* Handelingen (van de Apostelen); ~ *of God* overmacht, force majeure *(force of nature); catch* (of: *take*) *s.o. in the (very)* ~ iem op heterdaad betrappen; *(inf) get in on the* ~, *get into the* ~ meedoen (om zijn deel van de koek te hebben); *(inf) get one's* ~ *together* orde op zaken stellen, zijn zaakjes voor elkaar krijgen

²act [ækt] *vb* **1** zich voordoen, zich gedragen: *he* ~*s like a madman* hij gedraagt zich als een krankzinnige; **2** handelen, optreden, iets doen; **3** fungeren, optreden: ~ *as chairman* het voorzitterschap waarnemen; **4** werken, functioneren; **5** acteren, spelen; **6** komedie spelen, zich aanstellen

³act [ækt] *vb* **1** uitbeelden, spelen, uitspelen: ~ *out one's emotions* zijn gevoelens naar buiten brengen; **2** *(theatre)* spelen, opvoeren, acteren; **3** spelen, zich voordoen als: ~ *the fool* de idioot uithangen; *she doesn't* ~ *her age* zij gedraagt zich niet naar haar leeftijd

acting [ækting] waarnemend, plaatsvervangend, tijdelijk

action [æksjən] **1** actie, daad, handeling, activiteit: *a man of* ~ een man van de daad; *take* ~ maatregelen nemen, tot handelen overgaan; ~*s speak louder than words* geen woorden maar daden; **2** gevechts-

actie, strijd: *be killed in ~* in de strijd sneuvelen; **3** proces^h, klacht, eis: *the ~ of the novel takes place in London* de roman speelt zich af in Londen
activate [ǽktivveet] activeren, actief maken, in werking brengen
active [ǽktiv] **1** actief, werkend, in werking: *an ~ remedy* een werkzaam middel; *an ~ volcano* een werkende vulkaan; **2** actief, bedrijvig: *lead an ~ life* een actief leven leiden; **3** *(econ)* actief, productief: *be under ~ consideration* (ernstig) overwogen worden; *(com) ~ securities* (of: *stocks*) actieve fondsen, druk verhandelde fondsen; *(mil) on ~ service* aan het front, *(Am)* in actieve (of: feitelijke) dienst
activity [ǽktivvittie] **1** activiteit, bedrijvigheid, drukte: *economic ~* conjunctuur, economische bedrijvigheid; **2** werking, functie
act on 1 inwerken op, beïnvloeden; **2** opvolgen, zich laten leiden door: *she acted on his advice* zij volgde zijn raad op
actor [ǽktə] acteur *(also fig)*, toneelspeler
actress [ǽktris] actrice *(also fig)*, toneelspeelster
actual [ǽktsjoeəl] werkelijk, feitelijk, eigenlijk: *~ figures* reële cijfers; *~ size* ware grootte; *what were his ~ words?* wat zei hij nou precies?
actually [ǽktsjoeəlie] **1** eigenlijk, feitelijk, werkelijk; **2** zowaar, werkelijk, echt: *they've ~ paid me!* ze hebben me zowaar betaald!; *You've met John, haven't you? - Actually, I haven't* Je kent John, hè? - Nee, ik ken hem niet
acute [əkjoe:t] **1** acuut, ernstig, hevig; **2** scherp(zinnig), fijn, gevoelig *(wit, senses)* || *an ~ angle* een scherpe hoek; *~ accent* accent aigu *(on letter: é)*
ad [æd] *advertisement (inf)* advertentie
A.D. *Anno Domini* n. Chr., na Christus || *~ 79* 79 n.Chr.
adamant [ǽdəmənt] vastbesloten, onbuigzaam
¹adapt [ədǽpt] *vb* aanpassen, bewerken, geschikt maken: *~ a novel for TV* een roman voor de tv bewerken
²adapt [ədǽpt] *vb (with to)* zich aanpassen (aan)
adaptable [ədǽptəbl] buigzaam, soepel, flexibel
adaptation [ædəpteesjən] **1** aanpassing(sproces^h); **2** bewerking: *an ~ of a novel by Minette Walters* een bewerking van een roman van Minette Walters
¹add [æd] *vb* **1** toevoegen, erbij doen: *value ~ed tax* belasting op de toegevoegde waarde, btw; **2** optellen: *~ five to three* tel vijf bij drie op
²add [æd] *vb* **1** bijdragen; **2** (op)tellen, (een) optelling maken
adder [ǽdə] adder
addict [ǽdikt] verslaafde, *(fig)* fanaat, enthousiasteling
addiction [ədiksjən] verslaving, verslaafdheid
addictive [ədiktiv] verslavend
addition [ədisjən] **1** toevoeging, aanwinst, bijvoegsel^h; **2** optelling: *in ~* bovendien, daarbij; *in ~ to* behalve, naast
additional [ədisjənəl] bijkomend, aanvullend, extra

¹address [ədres] *n* **1** adres^h *(also comp)*; **2** toespraak; **3** aanspreekvorm, aanspreektitel
²address [ədres] *vb* **1** richten, sturen: *~ complaints to our office* richt u met klachten tot ons bureau; *~ oneself to: a)* zich richten tot; *b)* zich bezighouden met, zich toeleggen op; **2** adresseren; **3** toespreken, een rede houden voor: *the teacher ~ed the pupils* de onderwijzer sprak tegen de leerlingen; **4** aanspreken: *you have to ~ the judge as 'Your Honour'* je moet de rechter met 'Edelachtbare' aanspreken
addressee [ædressie:] geadresseerde
¹add up *vb (inf)* **1** steek houden, kloppen: *the evidence does not ~* het bewijsmateriaal deugt niet; **2** *(with to)* als uitkomst geven, *(fig)* neerkomen (op), inhouden: *this so-called invention does not ~ to much* deze zogenaamde uitvinding stelt weinig voor
²add up *vb* optellen
¹adept [ǽdept] *n* expert
²adept [ǽdept] *adj (with at, in)* bedreven (in), deskundig, ingewijd
adequacy [ǽdikwəsie] geschiktheid, bekwaamheid
adequate [ǽdikwət] **1** voldoende, net (goed) genoeg; **2** geschikt, bekwaam
adhere [ədhiə] **1** kleven, aankleven, vastkleven, hechten; **2** *(with to)* zich houden (aan), vasthouden (aan), blijven bij
adherent [ədhiərənt] aanhanger, voorstander, volgeling
¹adhesive [ədhie:siv] *adj* klevend, plakkend: *~ plaster* hechtpleister; *~ tape* plakband
²adhesive [ədhie:siv] *n* kleefstof, plakmiddel^h, lijm
adjacent [ədzjeesnt] **1** aangrenzend; **2** nabijgelegen
adjective [ǽdzjəktiv] bijvoeglijk naamwoord^h
¹adjoin [ədzjojn] *vb* aaneengrenzen
²adjoin [ədzjojn] *vb* grenzen aan
adjourn [ədzjə:n] **1** verdagen, uitstellen; **2** schorsen, onderbreken
adjudicate [ədzjoe:dikkeet] oordelen, arbitreren, jureren: *~ (up)on a matter* over een zaak oordelen
adjunct [ǽdzjungkt] **1** toevoegsel^h, aanhangsel^h; **2** adjunct *(employee, civil servant)*
adjust [ədzjust] **1** regelen, in orde brengen, rechtzetten; **2** afstellen, instellen, bijstellen: *use button A to ~ the volume* gebruik knop A om de geluidssterkte te stellen; **3** taxeren, vaststellen *(damage)*; **4** (zich) aanpassen, in overeenstemming brengen, harmoniseren: *~ (oneself) to new circumstances* (zich) aan nieuwe omstandigheden aanpassen
adjustable [ədzjustəbl] regelbaar, verstelbaar
¹ad lib [æd lib] *adv* **1** ad libitum, naar believen; **2** onvoorbereid, geïmproviseerd
²ad lib [æd lib] *adj* onvoorbereid, geïmproviseerd
administer [ədministə] **1** beheren, besturen; **2** toepassen, uitvoeren: *~ justice* rechtspreken; *~ to s.o.'s needs* in iemands behoeften voorzien
administration [ədminnistreesjən] **1** beheer^h, administratie, bestuur^h; **2** *Administration (Am)* rege-

ring, bestuur^h, ambtsperiode || ~ *of an oath* afneming van een eed

administrative [ədmɪnnistrətiv] administratief, beheers-, bestuurs-

administrator [ədmɪnnistreetə] bestuurder, beheerder

admirable [ædmrəbl] **1** bewonderenswaard(ig); **2** voortreffelijk, uitstekend

admiral [ædmrəl] admiraal: *Admiral of the Fleet* opperadmiraal *(British Navy)*

admiration [ædmirreesjən] bewondering, eerbied

admire [ədmajjə] bewonderen

admirer [ədmajrə] bewonderaar, aanbidder

admissible [ədmɪssibl] **1** aannemelijk, aanvaardbaar, acceptabel; **2** geoorloofd *(also law)*, toelaatbaar

admission [ədmɪsjən] **1** erkenning, bekentenis, toegeving: *an ~ of guilt* een schuldbekentenis; **2** toegang, toegangsprijs, entree

¹admit [ədmɪt] *vb* **1** toelaten, ruimte laten: *these facts ~ of one interpretation only* deze feiten zijn maar voor één interpretatie vatbaar; **2** toegang geven; **3** erkennen, toegeven, bekennen

²admit [ədmɪt] *vb* **1** binnenlaten, toelaten: *he was ~ted to hospital* hij werd in het ziekenhuis opgenomen; **2** toelaten, mogelijk maken: *his statement ~s more than one interpretation* zijn verklaring is voor meer dan één interpretatie vatbaar; **3** erkennen, toegeven, bekennen: *he ~ted having lied* hij gaf toe dat hij gelogen had

admittance [ədmɪttəns] toegang: *no ~* geen toegang

admonish [ədmɒnnisj] waarschuwen, berispen

admonition [ædmənnisjən] waarschuwing, berisping

adolescence [ædəlɛsns] puberteit, adolescentie

¹adolescent [ædəlɛsnt] *adj* **1** opgroeiend; **2** puberachtig, puberaal, jeugd-

²adolescent [ædəlɛsnt] *n* puber, tiener, adolescent

adopt [ədɒpt] **1** adopteren, aannemen, (uit)kiezen; **2** overnemen, aannemen: *~ an idea* een idee overnemen; **3** aannemen, gebruiken, toepassen: *~ modern techniques* nieuwe technieken in gebruik nemen; **4** aannemen, aanvaarden, goedkeuren: *~ a proposal* een voorstel aanvaarden

adoption [ədɒpsjən] **1** adoptie, aanneming; **2** aanneming, het aannemen; **3** gebruik^h, toepassing; **4** aanvaarding, goedkeuring, aanneming

adoptive [ədɒptiv] adoptief, aangenomen, pleeg-: *an ~ child* een geadopteerd kind; *~ parents* pleegouders, adoptiefouders

adorable [ədɔːrəbl] schattig, lief

adore [ədɔː] **1** aanbidden, bewonderen; **2** *(rel)* aanbidden, vereren; **3** *(inf)* dol zijn op

adorn [ədɔːn] versieren, mooi maken

adrenalin(e) [ədrɛnnəlin] adrenaline

adrift [ədrɪft] **1** op drift; **2** stuurloos, losgeslagen *(also lit)*, hulpeloos, doelloos

adroit [ədrɔjt] handig: *be ~ at* (of: *in*) *carpentering*

goed kunnen timmeren

¹adult [ædult] *adj* **1** volwassen, volgroeid, rijp; **2** voor volwassenen: *~ education* volwassenenonderwijs; *~ movie* pornofilm

²adult [ædult] *n* volwassene *(also animal)*

adulterate [ədultəreet] vervalsen; versnijden

adulterer [ədultrə] overspelige (man)

adultery [ədultərie] overspel^h

¹advance [ədvaːns] *vb* vooruitgaan, voortbewegen, vorderen, vooruitgang boeken: *the troops ~d against* (of: *on*) *the enemy* de troepen naderden de vijand

²advance [ədvaːns] *vb* **1** vooruitbewegen, vooruitbrengen, -schuiven, -zetten; **2** promoveren, bevorderen (in rang): *~ s.o. to a higher position* iem bevorderen; **3** bevorderen, steunen *(plan)*; **4** naar voren brengen, ter sprake brengen: *~ one's opinion* zijn mening naar voren brengen; **5** voorschieten, vooruitbetalen

³advance [ədvaːns] *n* **1** voorschot^h, vooruitbetaling; **2** avance, eerste stappen, toenadering; **3** vooruitgang *(also fig)*, vordering, ontwikkeling, verbetering: *in ~: a)* vooraf, van tevoren *(time); b)* vooruit, voorop *(space); to be paid in ~* vooraf te voldoen

⁴advance [ədvaːns] *adj* vooraf, van tevoren, bij voorbaat: *~ booking* reservering (vooraf); *~ notice* vooraankondiging

advanced [ədvaːnst] **1** (ver)gevorderd; **2** geavanceerd, modern, vooruitstrevend: *~ ideas* progressieve ideeën

advancement [ədvaːnsmənt] **1** vordering; **2** bevordering, verbetering, vooruitgang

advantage [ədvaːntidzj] **1** voordeel^h, gunstige omstandigheid: *have the ~ of* (of: *over*) *s.o.* iets voorhebben op iem; **2** voordeel^h, nut^h, profijt^h: *take (full) ~ of sth.* (gretig) gebruik *(of:* misbruik) maken van iets; **3** overwicht^h: *get the ~* de bovenhand krijgen; **4** *(tennis)* voordeel^h

advantageous [ædvənteedzjəs] **1** voordelig, nuttig, gunstig; **2** winstgevend

advent [ædvent] **1** aankomst, komst, nadering *(of sth or s.o. important)*; **2** *Advent (rel)* advent

adventure [ədventsjə] avontuur^h, riskante onderneming

adventurer [ədventsjərə] avonturier, gelukzoeker, huurling, speculant

adventurous [ədventsjrəs] **1** avontuurlijk, ondernemend; **2** avontuurlijk, gewaagd, gedurfd

adverb [ædvəːb] bijwoord^h

adversary [ædvəsərie] tegenstander, vijand

adverse [ædvəːs] **1** vijandig: *~ criticism* afbrekende kritiek; **2** ongunstig, nadelig

adversity [ədvəːsittie] tegenslag, tegenspoed

advertise [ædvətajz] **1** adverteren, reclame maken (voor), bekendmaken, aankondigen; **2** *(with for)* een advertentie plaatsen (voor)

advertisement [ədvəːtismənt] advertentie: *classified ~s* rubrieksadvertenties

advertising [ædvətajzing] reclame

advice [ədvajs] **1** raad, advies[h]: *give s.o. a piece* (of: *bit*) *of ~* iem een advies geven; *act on* (of: *follow, take*) *s.o.'s ~* iemands advies opvolgen; *on the doctor's ~* op doktersadvies; **2** *(com)* verzendadvies[h], verzendbericht[h]

advisability [ədvajzəbịllittie] raadzaamheid, wenselijkheid

advisable [ədvajzəbl] raadzaam, wenselijk

¹advise [ədvajz] *vb* adviseren, (aan)raden: *~ (s.o.) against sth.* (iem) iets afraden; *~ (s.o.) on sth.* (iem) advies geven omtrent iets; *be well ~ed to ...* er verstandig aan doen om ...

²advise [ədvajz] *vb* informeren, inlichten

adviser [ədvajzə] adviseur, raadsman

¹advocate [ædvəkit] *n* verdediger, voorstander

²advocate [ædvəkeet] *vb* bepleiten, verdedigen, voorstaan: *he ~s strong measures against truants* hij bepleit maatregelen tegen spijbelaars

¹aerial [eəriəl] *n* antenne

²aerial [eəriəl] *adj* lucht-, in de lucht, bovengronds

aerobatics [eərəbætiks] stuntvliegen

aerodrome [eərədroom] vliegveld[h], (kleine) luchthaven

aeronautics [eərənọːtiks] luchtvaart(kunde)

aeroplane [eərəpleen] vliegtuig[h]

aerosol (can) [eəressol] spuitbus

aesthetics [ie:sθettik] esthetica, schoonheidsleer, esthetiek

afar [əfạː] (van) ver(re), veraf, ver weg: *from ~* van verre

affair [əfeə] **1** zaak, aangelegenheid: *current ~s* lopende zaken, actualiteiten; *foreign ~s* buitenlandse zaken; *that is my ~* dat zijn mijn zaken, dat gaat je niets aan; **2** *(inf)* affaire, kwestie, ding[h], zaak(je[h]); **3** verhouding

affect [əfekt] **1** voorwenden, doen alsof; **2** zich voordoen als, spelen: *~ the grieving widow* de diepbedroefde weduwe uithangen; **3** (ont)roeren, aangrijpen: *his death ~ed me deeply* ik was diep getroffen door zijn dood; **4** beïnvloeden, treffen: *how will the new law ~ us?* welke invloed zal de nieuwe wet op ons hebben?; **5** aantasten, aanvallen: *smoking ~s your health* roken is slecht voor de gezondheid

affected [əfektid] **1** voorgewend, hypocriet: *~ politeness* niet gemeende beleefdheid; **2** gemaakt; **3** ontroerd, aangedaan; **4** getroffen, betrokken: *the ~ area* het getroffen gebied; **5** aangetast: *~ by acid rain* door zure regen aangetast

affection [əfeksjən] genegenheid: *~ for* genegenheid tot, liefde tot

affectionate [əfeksjənət] hartelijk, warm, lief(hebbend): *~ly (yours)* veel liefs *(in letters)*

affiliate [əfịllie·eet] (zich) aansluiten, opnemen, aannemen

affinity [əfịnnittie] **1** (aan)verwantschap[h]; **2** affiniteit, overeenkomst, sympathie: *feel ~ with* (of: *for*) sympathie voelen voor

affirm [əfạːm] bevestigen, beamen, verzekeren

affirmation [æfəmeesjən] **1** bevestiging, verzeke-

ring; **2** *(law)* belofte

¹affix [əfịks] *vb* toevoegen, (aan)hechten, kleven, vastmaken *(also fig)*: *~ one's name to a letter* een brief ondertekenen

²affix [æfiks] *n* toevoegsel[h], aanhangsel[h]

afflict [əflịkt] kwellen, treffen, teisteren: *be ~ed with leprosy* lijden aan lepra

affluent [æfloeənt] rijk, overvloedig, welvarend: *the ~ society* de welvaartsstaat

afford [əfọːd] zich veroorloven, zich permitteren, riskeren: *I cannot ~ a holiday* ik kan me geen vakantie veroorloven

¹affront [əfrụnt] *n* belediging

²affront [əfrụnt] *vb* (openlijk) beledigen

afield [əfịeːld] ver (van huis), ver weg *(also fig)*

afloat [əflọot] **1** vlot(tend), drijvend, varend; **2** aan boord, op zee

afoot [əfoet] *(oft depr)* op gang, in voorbereiding, in aantocht: *there is trouble ~* er zijn moeilijkheden op til

aforesaid bovengenoemd

afraid [əfreed] bang, angstig, bezorgd: *she was ~ to wake her grandfather* ze durfde haar grootvader niet wakker te maken; *~ of sth.* bang voor iets; *don't be ~ of asking for help* vraag gerust om hulp; *I'm ~ I'm late* het spijt me, maar ik ben te laat; *I'm ~ not* helaas niet, ik ben bang van niet; *I'm ~ I can't help you* ik kan u helaas niet helpen

afresh [əfresj] opnieuw, andermaal: *start ~* van voren af aan beginnen

¹African [æfrikkən] *adj* Afrikaans

²African [æfrikkən] *n* Afrikaan(se) || *~ violet* Kaaps viooltje

¹after [aːftə] *prep* **1** achter, na: *cloud ~ cloud* de ene wolk na de andere; *Jack ran ~ Jill* Jack liep Jill achterna; *~ you* nu u, ga je gang; **2** *(time)* na: *day ~ day* dag in dag uit; *it's ~ two o'clock* het is over tweeën; *time ~ time* keer op keer; **3** na, met uitzondering van: *the greatest (composer) ~ Beethoven* de grootste (componist) na Beethoven; **4** naar, volgens, in navolging van: *Jack takes ~ his father* Jack lijkt op zijn vader; *~ all* toch, per slot (van rekening); *be ~ sth.* uit zijn op iets, iets najagen

²after [aːftə] *conj* nadat, als, toen, wanneer: *come back ~ finishing that job* kom terug als je met die klus klaar bent

³after [aːftə] *adv* na, nadien, erachter: *five years ~* vijf jaar later; *shortly ~* spoedig daarna; *they lived happily ever ~* zij leefden nog lang en gelukkig

⁴after [aːftə] *adj* later, volgend

aftermath [aːftəmaːθ] nasleep, naspel[h]

afternoon [aːftənoeːn] middag, *(Belg)* namiddag *(also fig)*: *in* (of: *during*) *the ~* 's middags

afterthought 1 latere overweging; **2** latere toevoeging, postscriptum[h]

afterwards [aːftəwədz] later, naderhand

again [əgen] **1** opnieuw, weer, nog eens: *time and (time)* ~ telkens opnieuw; *(the) same ~!* schenk nog eens in!, hetzelfde nog eens!; *be oneself ~* hersteld zijn, er weer bovenop zijn; *back* ~ weer terug; *never* ~ nooit meer; *once* ~ nog een keer, voor de zoveelste keer; *now and* ~ nu en dan; *~ and ~* telkens opnieuw; **2** nogmaals: *what is his name ~?* hoe heet hij ook (al) weer?

against [əgɛnst] **1** *(place or direction; also fig)* tegen, tegen ... aan, in strijd met: *a race ~ the clock* een race tegen de klok; *~ the current* tegen de stroom in; *evidence ~ John* bewijs(materiaal) tegen John; *vaccination ~ the measles* inenting tegen de mazelen; **2** tegenover, in tegenstelling met: *18, as ~ the 30 sold last year* 18, tegenover de 30 die vorig jaar zijn verkocht

¹age [eedzj] *n* **1** leeftijd, ouderdom: *be your ~!* doe niet zo kinderachtig!; *be of ~* meerderjarig zijn; *look one's ~* er zo oud uitzien als men is; *what is your ~?* hoe oud ben je?; *at the ~ of ten* op tienjarige leeftijd; *in his (old) ~* op zijn oude dag; *ten years of ~* tien jaar oud; *under ~* minderjarig, te jong; **2** mensenleven[h], levensduur; **3** eeuw, tijdperk[h]: *the Stone Age* het stenen tijdperk, de steentijd; **4** *~s (inf)* eeuwigheid: *wait for ~s* een eeuwigheid wachten; *you've been ~s* je bent vreselijk lang weggebleven

²age [eedzj] *vb* verouderen, ouder worden: *he has ~d a lot* hij is erg oud geworden

age bracket leeftijdsgroep

¹aged [eedzjd] *adj* oud: *~ ten* tien jaar oud

²aged [eedzjid] *adj* oud, (hoog)bejaard ‖ *the ~* de bejaarden

ageless [eedzjləs] leeftijdloos, nooit verouderend, eeuwig (jong)

agency [eedzjənsie] **1** bureau[h], instantie, instelling: *travel ~* reisbureau; **2** agentuur, agentschap[h], vertegenwoordiging; **3** bemiddeling, tussenkomst, toedoen[h]: *through* (of: *by) the ~ of friends* door toedoen van vrienden

agenda [ədzjɛndə] agenda: *the main point on the ~* het belangrijkste punt op de agenda

agent [eedzjənt] **1** agent, tussenpersoon, bemiddelaar, vertegenwoordiger: *secret ~* geheim agent; **2** middel[h]: *cleansing ~* reinigingsmiddel

agglomeration [əglomməreesjən] opeenhoping, (chaotische) verzameling

aggravate [ægrəveet] **1** verergeren: *~ an illness* een ziekte verergeren; **2** *(inf)* ergeren, irriteren

aggravation [ægrəveesjən] **1** verergering; **2** ergernis

aggregate [ægrigət] totaal[h]: *in (the) ~* alles bij elkaar genomen, opgeteld

aggression [əgrɛsjən] agressie

aggressive [əgrɛssiv] **1** agressief, aanvallend: *~ salesmen* opdringerige verkopers; **2** ondernemend, ambitieus

aggressor [əgrɛssə] aanvaller

aggrieved [əgrie:vd] gekrenkt, gekwetst: *feel (oneself) ~ at* (of: *by, over) sth.* zich gekrenkt voelen door iets

aghast [əgɑːst] (*with at*) ontzet (door), verbijsterd,

verslagen

agile [ædzjajl] lenig, beweeglijk, soepel

agility [ədzjɪllittie] **1** behendigheid, vlugheid; **2** alertheid

agitate [ædzjitteet] optreden, strijden (voor of tegen): *~ for* actie voeren voor

agitation [ædzjitteesjən] **1** actie, strijd; **2** opschudding, opgewondenheid, spanning

agitator [ædzjitteetə] oproerkraaier

ago [əgoo] geleden: *ten years ~* tien jaar geleden; *not long ~* kort geleden

agonize [ægənajz] vreselijk lijden, worstelen *(fig)*: *~ over* zich het hoofd breken over

agonizing [ægənajzing] kwellend, hartverscheurend: *an ~ decision* een moeilijke beslissing

agony [ægənie] (ondraaglijke) pijn, kwelling, foltering

¹agree [əgrie:] *vb* **1** akkoord gaan, het eens zijn, het eens worden, afspreken: *~ to do sth.* afspreken iets te zullen doen; *~ on sth.* het ergens over eens zijn; *~ to sth.* met iets instemmen, in iets toestemmen; *~ with s.o. about sth.* het met iem over iets eens zijn; *~d!* akkoord!; **2** overeenstemmen, goed opschieten, passen: *~ with* kloppen met

²agree [əgrie:] *vb* **1** bepalen, overeenkomen, afspreken: *~ a price* een prijs afspreken; **2** goedkeuren, aanvaarden: *~ a plan* een plan goedkeuren

agreeable [əgrie:əbl] prettig, aangenaam: *the terms are not ~ to us* de voorwaarden staan ons niet aan

agreement [əgrie:mənt] **1** overeenkomst, overeenstemming, afspraak, contract[h]: *be in ~ about* (of: *on, with)* 't eens zijn over, akkoord gaan met; **2** instemming, goedkeuring

agriculture [ægrikkultsjə] landbouw

aground [əgraund] aan de grond, vast

ahead [əhɛd] **1** voorop: *(sport) be ~* leiden, voorstaan; *go ~* voorop gaan; **2** vooruit, voorwaarts, van tevoren, op voorhand: *full speed ~!* met volle kracht vooruit!; *look (of: plan) ~* vooruitzien; *straight ~* rechtdoor

ahead of voor: *the days ~ us* de komende dagen; *~ his time* zijn tijd vooruit; *straight ~ you* recht voor je

ahoy [əhoj] ahoi

¹aid [eed] *n* **1** hulp, bijstand, assistentie: *come* (of: *go) to s.o.'s ~* iem te hulp komen; *in ~ of* ten dienste van; *first ~* eerste hulp (bij ongelukken), EHBO; **2** hulpmiddel[h], apparaat[h], toestel[h]: *audiovisual ~s* audiovisuele hulpmiddelen; **3** helper, assistent

²aid [eed] *vb* helpen, steunen, bijstaan

aide [eed] **1** aide de camp, adjudant; **2** assistent, naaste medewerker, helper

AIDS [eedz] *Acquired Immune Deficiency Syndrome* aids

¹ail [eel] *vb* ziek(elijk) zijn, sukkelen, iets mankeren *(also fig)*

²ail [eel] *vb* schelen, mankeren

ailment [eelmənt] kwaal, ziekte, aandoening

¹aim [eem] *vb* proberen, willen: ~ *to be an artist* kunstenaar willen worden; ~ *at doing sth.* iets willen doen, van plan zijn iets te doen; *what are you ~ing at?* wat wil je nu eigenlijk?

²aim [eem] *vb* richten, mikken, aanleggen: ~ *high* hoog mikken, *(fig)* ambitieus zijn; ~ *(a gun) at* (een vuurwapen) richten op

³aim [eem] *n* **1** (streef)doel^h, bedoeling, plan^h; **2** aanleg: *take* ~ *(at)* aanleggen (op), richten (op)

aimless [eemləs] doelloos, zinloos

¹air [eə] *n* **1** lucht, atmosfeer, dampkring, luchtruim^h, hemel: *in the open* ~ in (de) open lucht; *get some (fresh)* ~ een frisse neus halen; *by* ~ met het vliegtuig, per luchtpost; **2** *(radio, TV)* ether: *be on the* ~ in de ether zijn, uitzenden, uitgezonden worden; **3** bries(je^h), lichte wind; **4** voorkomen^h, sfeer, aanzicht^h: *have an* ~ *of superiority* een superieure indruk maken; **5** houding, manier van doen, aanstellerij: *give oneself ~s, put on ~s* zich aanstellen, indruk proberen te maken; *rumours are in the* ~ het gerucht doet de ronde; *my plans are still (up) in the* ~ mijn plannen staan nog niet vast

²air [eə] *vb* **1** drogen, te drogen hangen; **2** luchten, ventileren; **3** bekendmaken, luchten, ventileren: ~ *one's grievances* uiting geven aan zijn klachten

airborne 1 in de lucht, door de lucht vervoerd; **2** per vliegtuig getransporteerd: ~ *troops* luchtlandingstroepen

aircraft vliegtuig^h

aircraft carrier vliegdekschip^h

airfield vliegveld^h, luchthaven

air force luchtmacht, luchtstrijdkrachten

air hostess stewardess

airlift luchtbrug

airline luchtvaartmaatschappij

airmail luchtpost: *by* ~ per luchtpost

airplane [eəpleen] *(Am)* vliegtuig^h

airport luchthaven, vliegveld^h

air raid luchtaanval

airship luchtschip^h, zeppelin

airspace luchtruim^h *(of country)*

airstrip landingsstrook

airtight luchtdicht, *(fig)* sluitend, onweerlegbaar: *his alibi is* ~ hij heeft een waterdicht alibi

aisle [ajl] **1** zijbeuk *(of church);* **2** gang(pad^h), middenpad^h *(in church, train, theatre, etc)* || *we had them rolling in the ~s* het publiek lag in een deuk

ajar [ədzja:] op een kier

akimbo [əkimboo] (met de handen) in de zij

akin [əkin] *(with to)* verwant (aan), gelijk(soortig)

alabaster [æləba:stə] albast^h: ~ *skin* albasten huid

alacrity [əlækrittie] monterheid, bereidwilligheid, enthousiasme^h

¹alarm [əla:m] *n* **1** alarm^h, schrik, paniek: *take* ~ *at* opschrikken van, in paniek raken bij; **2** alarm^h, waarschuwing, alarmsignaal^h: *raise* (of: *sound) the* ~ alarm geven; **3** wekker; **4** alarmsysteem^h, alarminstallatie

²alarm [əla:m] *vb* alarm slaan

³alarm [əla:m] *vb* alarmeren, opschrikken, verontrusten

alarm clock wekker

alarming [əla:ming] alarmerend, onrustbarend, verontrustend

alas [əlæs] helaas

Albania [ælbeeniə] Albanië

Albanian [ælbeeniən] Albanees

albatross [ælbətros] albatros || *an* ~ *around one's neck* een blok aan zijn been

albeit [o:lbie:it] zij het: *a small difference, ~ an important one* een klein verschil, zij het een belangrijk verschil

album [ælbəm] **1** album^h, fotoalbum^h, poëziealbum^h; **2** grammofoonplaat, cd

alchemy [ælkəmie] alchemie

alcohol [ælkəhol] alcohol

¹alcoholic [ælkəhollik] *n* alcoholicus

²alcoholic [ælkəhollik] *adj* alcoholisch, alcoholhoudend

alder [o:ldə] els, elzenboom

alderman [o:ldəmən] *(roughly)* wethouder, gedeputeerde, *(Belg)* schepen

ale [eel] ale, (licht, sterk gehopt) bier^h

¹alert [ələ:t] *adj* **1** alert, waakzaam, op zijn hoede: ~ *to danger* op gevaar bedacht; **2** levendig, vlug

²alert [ələ:t] *n* alarm(signaal)^h, luchtalarm^h: *on the* ~ *(for)* op zijn hoede (voor)

³alert [ələ:t] *vb* alarmeren, waarschuwen, attent maken: ~ *s.o. to the danger* iem wijzen op het gevaar

A level *advanced level* Brits (examenvak^h op) eindexamenniveau^h

algebra [ældzjəbrə] algebra

algebraic [ældzjəbreeik] algebraïsch

Algeria [ældzjiəriə] Algerije

¹Algerian [ældzjiəriən] *adj* Algerijns

²Algerian [ældzjiəriən] *n* Algerijn

algorithm [ælgəriðm] algoritme^h, handelingsvoorschrift^h

¹alias [eeliəs] *adv* alias, anders genoemd

²alias [eeliəs] *n* alias, bijnaam, schuilnaam

alibi [ælibbaj] **1** alibi^h; **2** *(inf)* excuus^h, uitvlucht

¹alien [eeliən] *adj* **1** vreemd, buitenlands; **2** afwijkend: ~ *to his nature* strijdig met zijn aard

²alien [eeliən] *n* vreemdeling, buitenlander, buitenaards wezen^h

alienate [eeliəneet] vervreemden, doen bekoelen *(friendship)*

¹alight [əlajt] *adj* brandend, in brand: *set* ~ aansteken

²alight [əlajt] *vb* afstappen, uitstappen, afstijgen: ~ *from a horse* van een paard stijgen

align [əlajn] **1** zich richten, op één lijn liggen; **2** *(with with)* zich aansluiten (bij)

alignment [əlajnmənt] het op één lijn brengen; het in één lijn liggen: *out of* ~ ontzet, uit zijn verband

¹alike [əlajk] *adj* gelijk(soortig), gelijkend: *they are very much* ~ ze lijken heel erg op elkaar

²alike [əlajk] *adv* gelijk, op dezelfde manier: *treat all*

children ~ alle kinderen gelijk behandelen

alimony [ǽlimmənie] alimentatie

alive [əlájv] **1** levend, in leven; **2** levendig, actief: ~ *and kicking* springlevend; ~ *to* bewust, op de hoogte van *(a fact etc)*

¹all [o:l] *pron* **1** alle(n), allemaal, iedereen: *(tennis) thirty* ~ dertig gelijk; *one and* ~, ~ *and sundry* alles en iedereen, jan en alleman; *they have* ~ *left*, ~ *of them have left* ze zijn allemaal weg; **2** alles, al, allemaal: *when* ~ *is (said and) done* uiteindelijk; *it's* ~ *one* (of: *the same) to me* het kan me (allemaal) niet schelen; *above* ~ bovenal, voor alles; **3** de grootst mogelijke: *with* ~ *speed* zo snel mogelijk; *(inf) of* ~ ...! nota bene!; *today of* ~ *days* uitgerekend vandaag; **4** enig(e): *beyond* ~ *doubt* zonder enige twijfel; **5** één en al, *(Am)* puur, zuiver: *he was* ~ *ears* hij was één en al oor; *(Am) it's* ~ *wool* het is zuivere wol; **6** al(le), geheel: ~ *(the) angles (taken together) are 180°* alle hoeken van een driehoek (samen) zijn 180°; *with* ~ *my heart* van ganser harte; ~ *(the) morning* de hele morgen; **7** al(le), ieder, elk: ~ *(the) angles are 60°* alle hoeken zijn 60°; *once and for* ~ voorgoed, voor eens en altijd; *after* ~ per slot van rekening, toch, tenslotte; *he can't walk at* ~ hij kan helemaal niet lopen; *if I could do it at* ~ als ik het maar enigszins kon doen; *(after thank you) not at* ~ niets te danken, graag gedaan; *for* ~ *I know* voor zover ik weet; *in* ~ in 't geheel, in totaal; ~ *in* ~ al met al

²all [o:l] *adv* helemaal, geheel, volledig, *(inf)* heel, erg: ~ *right* in orde, okay; *if it's* ~ *the same to you* als het jou niets uitmaakt; *I've known it* ~ *along* ik heb het altijd al geweten; ~ *at once* plotseling; ~ *over again* van voren af aan; *(Am) books lay scattered* ~ *over (the place)* er lagen overal boeken; ~ *round* overal, *(fig)* in alle opzichten; ~ *too soon* (maar) al te gauw; *I'm* ~ *for it* ik ben er helemaal voor; ~ *the same* toch, desondanks; *(inf) it's not* ~ *that difficult* zo (vreselijk) moeilijk is het nu ook weer niet; ~ *out: a)* uit alle macht; *b)* op volle snelheid; *that's Jack* ~ *over: a) (inf)* dat is nou typisch Jack; *b)* hij lijkt precies op Jack

³all [o:l] *n* gehele bezitʰ: *her jewels are her* ~ haar juwelen zijn haar gehele bezit

allay [əlée] *(form)* **1** verminderen, verlichten, verkleinen; **2** kalmeren, (tot) bedaren (brengen): ~ *all fears* alle angst wegnemen

all but bijna, vrijwel: *he was* ~ *dead* hij was bijna dood; ~ *impossible* vrijwel onmogelijk

allegation [æligéesjən] bewering, (onbewezen) beschuldiging

allege [əlédzj] *(form)* beweren, aanvoeren: *the* ~*d thief* de vermeende dief

allegiance [əlíːdzjəns] trouw, loyaliteit

allegory [ǽligərie] symbolische voorstelling

alleluia [ælillóeːjə] hallelujaʰ

allergic [ələ́ːdzjik] *(with to)* allergisch (voor), *(inf; fig)* afkerig

allergy [ǽlədzjie] *(with to)* allergie (voor)

alleviate [əlíːvieˑeet] verlichten, verzachten

alleviation [əliːvieˑéesjən] verlichting, verzachtend middelʰ

alley [ǽlie] **1** steeg(jeʰ), (door)gang; **2** laan(tjeʰ), padʰ; **3** kegelbaan ‖ *blind* ~ doodlopende steeg

alliance [əlájjəns] **1** verdragʰ, overeenkomst, verbintenis; **2** bond, verbondʰ, vereniging, (bond)genootschapʰ

allied [ǽlajd] verbonden *(also fig)*, verenigd: *the Allied Forces* de geallieerden; *(closely)* ~ *to* (nauw) verwant met

alligator [ǽligeetə] alligator

all-in all-inclusive *(inf)* all-in, alles inbegrepen, inclusief

allocate [ǽləkeet] toewijzen, toekennen

allot [əlót] toewijzen, toebedelen

allotment [əlótmənt] **1** toegewezen deelʰ, aandeelʰ; **2** toewijzing, toekenning; **3** perceelʰ *(rented from government)*, volkstuintjeʰ

all-out *(inf)* volledig, intensief: *go* ~ alles op alles zetten

allow [əláu] **1** toestaan, (toe)laten, veroorloven: *no dogs* ~*ed* honden niet toegelaten; ~ *oneself* zich veroorloven; **2** voorzien in, mogelijk maken, zorgen voor: *the plan* ~*s one hour for lunch* het plan voorziet in één uur voor de lunch; **3** toekennen, toestaan, toewijzen: ~ *twenty per cent off (for)* twintig procent korting geven (op); **4** toegeven, erkennen: *we must* ~ *that he is clever* we moeten toegeven dat hij slim is

allowance [əláuəns] **1** toelage, uitkering, subsidie; **2** deelʰ, portie, rantsoenʰ; **3** vergoeding, toeslag; **4** korting, aftrek ‖ *make (an)* ~ *for, make* ~*(s) for* rekening houden met

alloy [ǽloj] legering, metaalmengselʰ

¹all right *adj* **1** gezond, goed, veilig, ongedeerd; **2** goed (genoeg), aanvaardbaar, in orde: *his work is* ~ zijn werk is acceptabel; *it's* ~ *by me* van mij mag je; *if that's all right with you* als jij dat goed vindt

²all right *adv* **1** in orde, voldoende: *he's doing* ~ hij doet het aardig; **2** inderdaad, zonder twijfel: *he's crazy* ~ hij is inderdaad écht gek; **3** begrepen, in orde, (dat is) afgesproken

all-round allround, veelzijdig

All Saints' Day Allerheiligen *(1 November)*

All Souls' Day Allerzielen *(2 November)*

all-time van alle tijden: *an* ~ *record* een (langdurig) ongebroken record; *an* ~ *high* een absoluut hoogtepunt

allude to [əlóeːd toe] zinspelen op, toespelingen maken op

allure [əljóeə] aantrekkingskracht, charme

allusion [əlóeːzjən] *(with to)* zinspeling (op), toespeling

¹ally [ǽlaj] *n* bondgenoot, medestander, geallieerde: *the Allies* de geallieerden

²ally [əláj] *vb* (zich) verenigen, (zich) verbinden: ~ *oneself with* een verbond sluiten met

almanac [óːlmənæk] almanak

almighty [o:lmajtie] **1** almachtig: *the Almighty* de Almachtige; **2** *(inf)* allemachtig, geweldig: *an ~ din* een oorverdovend lawaai

almond [a:mənd] amandel *(fruit)*

almost [o:lmoost] bijna, praktisch, haast: *~ all of them* haast iedereen

alms [a:mz] aalmoes

aloft [əloft] **1** omhoog, opwaarts *(also fig)*: *smoke kept rising ~* er bleef maar rook opstijgen; **2** *(shipp)* in de mast, in 't want

¹**alone** [əloon] *adj* alleen, afzonderlijk, in zijn eentje

²**alone** [əloon] *adv* **1** slechts, enkel, alleen; **2** alleen, in zijn eentje: *go it ~* het op zijn eentje opknappen; *leave* (of: *let*) *~* met rust laten, afblijven van; *he cannot walk, let ~ run* hij kan niet eens lopen, laat staan rennen

¹**along** [əlong] *adv* **1** door, verder, voort: *he brought his dog ~* hij had zijn hond bij zich; *come ~* kom mee; *go ~ (with)* meegaan (met); *I suspected it all ~* ik heb het altijd wel vermoed; *~ with* samen met; **2** langs: *come ~ anytime* (je bent) altijd welkom

²**along** [əlong] *prep* langs, door: *flowers ~ the path* bloemen langs het pad

alongside langszij

¹**aloof** [əloe:f] *adj* afstandelijk, koel

²**aloof** [əloe:f] *adv* op een afstand, ver: *keep* (of: *hold, stand*) *~ (from)* zich afzijdig houden (van)

aloud [əlaud] hardop, hoorbaar

alphabet [ælfəbet] alfabetʰ, abcʰ *(also fig)*

alphabetic(al) [ælfəbettik(l)] alfabetisch

already [o:lreddie] reeds, al (eerder)

¹**Alsatian** [ælseesjən] *adj* Elzassisch

²**Alsatian** [ælseesjən] *n* **1** Elzasser; **2** Duitse herder(shond)

also [o:lsoo] ook, bovendien, eveneens

altar [o:ltə] altaarʰ

alter [o:ltə] **1** (zich) veranderen, (zich) wijzigen; **2** *(Am; inf; euph)* helpen *(pet)*, castreren, steriliseren

alteration [o:ltəreesjən] **1** wijziging, verandering; **2** *(Am; inf; euph)* castratie, sterilisatie

altercation [o:ltəkaisjən] onenigheid, twist, ruzie, geruzieʰ

¹**alternate** [o:ltə:nət] *adj* afwisselend, beurtelings: *on ~ days* om de (andere) dag

²**alternate** [o:ltəneet] *vb* afwisselen, verwisselen: *alternating current* wisselstroom

alternation [o:ltəneesjən] (af)wisseling

¹**alternative** [o:ltə:nətiv] *adj* alternatief

²**alternative** [o:ltə:nətiv] *n* alternatiefʰ, keuze, optie

although [o:lðoo] hoewel; ofschoon

altitude [æltitjoe:d] hoogte

alto [æltoo] **1** altpartij, altinstrumentʰ, altstem; **2** alt, altzanger(es)

altogether [o:ltəgeðə] **1** totaal, geheel, helemaal: *at 50 he stopped working ~* met 50 hield hij helemaal op met werken; **2** in totaal, alles bij elkaar: *there were 30 people ~* er waren in totaal 30 mensen

aluminium [æljoeminniəm] aluminiumʰ

always [o:lweez] **1** altijd, steeds, voorgoed: *he's ~*

complaining hij loopt voortdurend te klagen; **2** in elk geval, altijd nog: *we can ~ sell the boat* we kunnen altijd nog de boot verkopen

a.m. *ante meridiem* vm., voor de middag: *at 5 ~* om vijf uur 's ochtends

Am. *America(n)*

amalgamate [əmælgəmeet] (doen) samensmelten, (zich) verbinden, annexeren, in zich opnemen

amass [əmæs] vergaren, opstapelen

¹**amateur** [æmətə] *n* amateur, liefhebber

²**amateur** [æmətə] *adj (oft depr)* amateur(s)-, amateuristisch

amaze [əmeez] verbazen, verwonderen, versteld doen staan

amazement [əmeezmənt] verbazing, verwondering

amazing [əmeezing] verbazingwekkend, verbazend

ambassador [æmbæsədə] ambassadeur, vertegenwoordiger, (af)gezant

amber [æmbə] **1** amber(steen), barnsteen; **2** amber(kleur); *(traffic light)* geelʰ, oranjeʰ

ambience [æmbiəns] sfeer, stemming, ambiance

ambiguity [æmbigjoe:ittie] dubbelzinnigheid

ambiguous [æmbigjoeəs] dubbelzinnig, onduidelijk

ambition [æmbisjən] ambitie, eerzucht

ambitious [æmbisjəs] ambitieus, eerzuchtig

ambivalent [æmbivvələnt] ambivalent, tegenstrijdig

¹**amble** [æmbl] *n* **1** telgang, pasgang *(of horse)*; **2** kuierpas, kalme gang

²**amble** [æmbl] *vb* **1** in de telgang lopen; **2** kuieren, op zijn gemak wandelen

ambulance [æmbjoeləns] ziekenwagen, ambulance

ambulant [æmbjoelənt] ambulant, in beweging, rondtrekkend

ambush [æmboesj] hinderlaag, val(strik): *lie* (of: *wait*) *in ~* in een hinderlaag liggen

amen [a:men] amen, het zij zo: *(fig) say ~ to sth.* volledig met iets instemmen

amenable [əmie:nəbl] **1** handelbaar, plooibaar; **2** ontvankelijk (voor): *~ to reason* voor rede vatbaar

amend [əmend] verbeteren *(eg text, bill)*, (bij amendement) wijzigen

amendment [əmendmənt] **1** amendementʰ; **2** verbetering, rectificatie

amends [əmendz] genoegdoening, schadeloosstelling, compensatie: *make ~ for sth. to s.o.* iets weer goedmaken bij iem, iem schadevergoeding betalen voor iets

amenity [əmie:nittie] (sociale) voorziening, gemakʰ: *this house has every ~* (of: *all the amenities)* dit huis is van alle gemakken voorzien

America [əmerrikkə] Amerika

¹**American** [əmerrikkən] *n* **1** Amerikaan(se): *Latin ~* iem uit Latijns-Amerika; **2** Amerikaans(-Engels)ʰ

²American [əmɛrrikkən] *adj* Amerikaans: ~ *Indian* (Amerikaanse) indiaan

amethyst [æmiθist] **1** amethist; **2** violet[h], violetkleur, purperviolet[h]

amiable [eemiəbl] beminnelijk, vriendelijk

amicable [æmikkəbl] amicaal, vriend(schapp)elijk: *come to an ~ agreement* een minnelijke schikking treffen

amid(st) [əmid(st)] te midden van, tussen, onder

¹amiss [əmis] *adj* **1** verkeerd, gebrekkig: *there is nothing ~ with her* ze mankeert niets; **2** misplaatst, ongelegen: *an apology would not be ~* een verontschuldiging zou niet misstaan

²amiss [əmis] *adv* verkeerd, gebrekkig, fout(ief): *take sth. ~* iets kwalijk nemen

ammunition [æmjoenisjən] (am)munitie

amnesia [æmnie:ziə] amnesie, geheugenverlies[h]

amnesty [æmnəstie] amnestie, generaal pardon[h]

amoeba [əmie:bə] amoebe

amok [əmok]: *run ~* amok maken, als een bezetene tekeergaan

among(st) [əmung(st)] onder, te midden van, tussen: *customs ~ the Indians* gebruiken bij de indianen; ~ *themselves* onder elkaar; *we have ten copies ~ us* we hebben samen tien exemplaren

amorous [æmərəs] amoureus, verliefd

amount [əmaunt] **1** hoeveelheid, grootte: *any ~ of money* een berg geld; **2** totaal[h], som, waarde: *to the ~ of* ten bedrage van

amount to 1 bedragen, oplopen tot, bereiken: *it does not ~ much* het heeft niet veel te betekenen; **2** neerkomen op, gelijk staan met: *his reply amounted to a refusal* zijn antwoord kwam neer op een weigering

ampersand [æmpəsænd] en-teken[h] *(the & sign)*

ample [æmpl] **1** ruim, groot, uitgestrekt; **2** rijk(elijk), overvloedig: *have ~ resources* bemiddeld zijn

amplifier [æmpliffajjə] versterker

amplify [æmpliffaj] **1** vergroten, vermeerderen; **2** *(electr)* versterken

amputate [æmpjoeteet] amputeren, afzetten

amuse [əmjoe:z] amuseren, vermaken, bezighouden: *be ~d at* (of: *by, with*) *sth.* iets amusant vinden

amusement [əmjoe:zmənt] **1** amusement[h], vermaak[h]; **2** plezier[h], pret, genot[h]: *watch in ~* geamuseerd toekijken

amusing [əmjoe:zing] vermakelijk, amusant

an [ən] *see* a

anaemia [ənie:miə] bloedarmoede

¹anaesthetic [ænisθettik] *n* verdovingsmiddel[h]

²anaesthetic [ænisθettik] *adj* verdovend, narcotisch

anaesthetize [ənie:sθətajz] verdoven, onder narcose brengen

anagram [ænəgræm] anagram[h]

analogous [ənæləgəs] (with *to, with*) analoog (aan), overeenkomstig (met), parallel

analogy [ənælədzjie] analogie, overeenkomst: *on the ~ of, by ~ with* naar analogie van

analyse [ænəlajz] analyseren, ontleden, ontbinden

analysis [ənælissis] analyse *(also maths)*, onderzoek[h], ontleding

analyst [ænəlist] analist(e), scheikundige

anarchy [ænəkie] anarchie

anatomy [ənætəmie] **1** (anatomische) bouw; **2** anatomie, ontleding, analyse

ancestor [ænsestə] **1** voorouder, voorvader; **2** oertype[h], voorloper, prototype[h]

ancestral [ænsestrəl] voorouderlijk, voorvaderlijk

ancestry [ænsestrie] **1** voorgeslacht[h], voorouders, voorvaderen; **2** afkomst, afstamming

anchor [ængkə] anker[h]: ~ *man* vaste presentator *(of news and current affairs programmes)*

anchorage [ængkəridzj] **1** verankering; **2** ankerplaats

anchovy [æntsjəvie] ansjovis

ancient [eensjənt] antiek, klassiek, uit de Oudheid: ~ *history* de oude geschiedenis

ancillary [ænsillərie] **1** ondergeschikt, bijkomstig: ~ *industry* toeleveringsbedrijf; **2** helpend, aanvullend

and [ænd] **1** en, (samen) met, en toen, dan: *children come ~ go* kinderen lopen in en uit; ~ *so forth*, ~ *so on* enzovoort(s); ~/*or* en/of; **2** *(intensifying or repetition)* en (nog), (en) maar: *thousands ~ thousands of people* duizenden en nog eens duizenden mensen; **3** *(between two verbs)* te: *try ~ finish it* probeer het af te maken; *nice ~ quiet* lekker rustig

anecdote [ænikdoot] anekdote

anemone [ənemmənie] anemoon; zeeanemoon

anew [ənjoe:] **1** opnieuw, nogmaals, weer; **2** anders

angel [eendzjəl] **1** engel, beschermengel, engelbewaarder; **2** schat, lieverd

¹anger [ænggə] *n* woede, boosheid: *be filled with ~ at sth.* woedend zijn om iets

²anger [ænggə] *vb* boos maken

¹angle [ænggl] *n* **1** hoek *(also maths)*, kant, uitstekende punt[h]: *at an ~ (with)* schuin (op); **2** gezichtshoek, perspectief[h], *(fig)* gezichtspunt[h], standpunt[h]: *look at sth. from a different* (of: *another*) ~ iets van een andere kant bekijken

²angle [ænggl] *vb* (with *for*) vissen (naar) *(also fig)*, hengelen (naar)

angler [ænggle] visser, hengelaar

Anglican [ænglikkən] anglicaans

angling [ængling] hengelsport

¹Anglo-Saxon [ænglosaxen] *adj* **1** Angelsaksisch; **2** *(Am)* Engels

²Anglo-Saxon *adv* Oud-Engels

³Anglo-Saxon *n* **1** Oud-Engels[h]; **2** Angelsakser; **3** (typische) Engelsman

angry [ænggrie] boos, kwaad: *be ~ about* (of: *at*) *sth.* boos zijn over iets; *be ~ at* (of: *with*) *s.o.* boos zijn op iem

anguish [ænggwisj] leed[h], pijn

angular [ænggjoelə] **1** hoekig, hoekvormig, hoek-; **2** kantig, met scherpe kanten

¹animal [ænimməl] *n* dier[h], beest[h]

²animal [ænimməl] *adj* **1** dierlijk: ~ *husbandry* veeteelt; **2** vleselijk, zinnelijk: ~ *desires* vleselijke lusten

¹animate [ænimmət] *adj* **1** levend; bezield; **2** levendig, opgewekt

²animate [ænimmeet] *vb* **1** leven geven, bezielen; **2** verlevendigen, opwekken; **3** animeren, aanmoedigen, inspireren

animated [ænimmeetid] levend(ig), bezield, geanimeerd || ~ *cartoon* tekenfilm

animation [ænimmeesjən] **1** animatiefilm, tekenfilm, poppenfilm; **2** het maken van animatiefilms, animatie; **3** levendigheid, opgewektheid, animoʰ

animosity [ænimmossittie] vijandigheid, haat, wrok

aniseed [ænissie:d] anijszaad(jeʰ)

ankle [æŋkl] enkel

anklet [æŋklit] **1** enkelring; **2** *(Am)* enkelsok, halve sok

annals [ænlz] annalen *(also fig)*, kronieken, jaarboeken

¹annex [əneks] *vb* **1** aanhechten, (bij)voegen; **2** annexeren, inlijven, *(inf, iron)* zich toe-eigenen

²annex [æneks] *n* **1** aanhangselʰ, addendumʰ, bijlage; **2** aanbouw, bijgebouwʰ, dependance

annexation [ænekseesjən] **1** aanhechting; **2** annexatie, inlijving

annihilate [ənajjəleet] vernietigen, tenietdoen *(also fig)*

annihilation [ənajjəleesjən] vernietiging

anniversary [ænivvə:sərie] **1** verjaardag, jaardag, gedenkdag; **2** verjaarsfeestʰ, jaarfeestʰ

¹annotate [ænəteet] *vb* (with *(up)on*) aantekeningen maken (bij), commentaar schrijven (op)

²annotate [ænəteet] *vb* annoteren

announce [ənauns] **1** aankondigen, bekendmaken, melden; **2** omroepen

announcement [ənaunsmənt] aankondiging, bekendmaking, mededeling

annoy [ənoj] **1** ergeren, kwellen, irriteren: *be ~ed at sth.* zich over iets ergeren; *be ~ed with s.o.* boos zijn op iem; **2** lastig vallen, hinderen, plagen

annoyance [ənojjəns] **1** ergernis, kwelling; **2** last, hinder, plaag

¹annual [ænjoeəl] *adj* **1** jaarlijks: *(bookkeeping)* ~ *accounts* jaarrekening; ~ *income* jaarinkomen; **2** eenjarig

²annual [ænjoeəl] *n* **1** eenjarige plant; **2** jaarboekʰ

annuity [ənjoe:ittie] jaargeldʰ, jaarrente

annul [ənul] **1** vernietigen, tenietdoen, schrappen; **2** ongeldig verklaren, herroepen, annuleren

annunciation [ənunsie-eesjən] **1** aankondiging, afkondiging; **2** *the Annunciation* Maria-Boodschap

anoint [ənojnt] **1** *(rel)* zalven; **2** inwrijven, insmeren

anomaly [ənomməlie] anomalie, onregelmatigheid

anonymous [ənonnimməs] anoniem

anorak [ænəræk] anorak, parka

another [ənuðə] **1** een ander(e), nog één; **2** andere, verschillende: *that's ~ matter* dat is een heel andere

zaak; *for one reason or* ~ om een of andere reden; *in one way or* ~ op een of andere wijze; **3** nog een, een tweede, een andere: *have* ~ *biscuit* neem nog een koekje

¹answer [a:nsə] *n* antwoordʰ, reactie, oplossing, resultaatʰ: *he gave* (of: *made*) *no* ~ hij gaf geen antwoord; *no* ~ er wordt niet opgenomen, ik krijg geen gehoor; *my only* ~ *to that* mijn enige reactie daarop

²answer [a:nsə] *vb* **1** antwoorden, een antwoord geven; **2** voldoende zijn, aan het doel beantwoorden: *one word would* ~ één woord zou volstaan

³answer [a:nsə] *vb* **1** antwoorden (op), beantwoorden, een antwoord geven op: ~ *your father!* geef je vader antwoord!; **2** reageren op: ~ *the telephone* de telefoon opnemen; ~ *the door* de deur opendoen (als er gebeld wordt); **3** beantwoorden aan, voldoen aan: ~ *the description* aan het signalement beantwoorden

answerable [a:nsrəbl] **1** verantwoordelijk, aansprakelijk: *be* ~ *to s.o. for sth.* bij iem voor iets verantwoording moeten afleggen; **2** beantwoordbaar

¹answer back *vb* zich verdedigen

²answer back *vb* brutaal antwoorden, (schaamteloos) wat terugzeggen, tegenspreken

answer for verantwoorden, verantwoordelijk zijn voor: *I can't* ~ *the consequences* ik kan niet voor de gevolgen instaan

ant [ænt] mier

antagonistic [æntægənistik] vijandig

antagonize [æntægənajz] tegen zich in het harnas jagen

¹Antarctic [ænta:ktik] *adj* antarctisch; zuidpool-: ~ *Circle* zuidpoolcirkel

²Antarctic [ænta:ktik] *n* **1** Antarctica, zuidpool(gebiedʰ); **2** Zuidelijke IJszee

antecedent [æntissie:dənt] iets voorafgaands, voorafgaand feitʰ, ~s antecedenten

antelope [æntilloop] antilope

antenatal [æntieneetl] prenataal: ~ *care* zwangerschapszorg

antenna [æntennə] **1** *(Am)* antenne; **2** voelhoorn, (voel)spriet, antenne

anterior [æntiəriə] **1** voorste, eerste, voor-; **2** voorafgaand: ~ *to* vroeger dan, voorafgaand aan

anthem [ænθəm] lofzang: *national* ~ volkslied

anthology [ænθollədzjie] anthologie, bloemlezing

anthracite [ænθrəsajt] antracietʰ

anthropology [ænθrəpollədzjie] antropologie, studie van de mens

anti [æntie] tegen, anti, tegenstander van, strijdig met

¹antibiotic [æntiebajjottik] *n* antibioticumʰ

²antibiotic [æntiebajjottik] *adj* antibiotisch

antic [æntik] capriool, gekke streek

anticipate [æntissippeet] **1** vóór zijn, voorkomen, ondervangen, de wind uit de zeilen nemen; **2** verwachten, tegemoet zien, hopen op: *trouble is ~d* men rekent op moeilijkheden; **3** een voorgevoel hebben van; **4** anticiperen, vooruitlopen (op): *I won't ~* ik wil niet op mijn verhaal vooruitlopen

anticlimax [æntieklajmæks] anticlimax

anticlockwise [æntieklokwajz] linksomdraaiend, tegen de wijzers vd klok (in)

antidote [æntiddoot] tegengif^h

antifreeze [æntifrie:z] antivries(middel)^h

antipathy [æntippəθie] antipathie, vooringenomenheid, afkeer

^1**antiquarian** [æntikwɛəriən] *adj* **1** oudheidkundig; **2** antiquarisch

^2**antiquarian** [æntikwɛəriən] *n* **1** oudheidkundige, oudheidkenner; **2** antiquair; **3** antiquaar, handelaar in oude boeken, prenten, enz.

antiquated [æntikweetid] ouderwets, verouderd, achterhaald

antique [æntie:k] **1** antiek, oud; **2** ouderwets

antiquity [æntikwittie] **1** *-ies* antiquiteit, overblijfsel^h, ruïne, *-ies* oudheden; **2** ouderdom; **3** Oudheid

anti-Semitism [æntiesemmittizm] anti-semitisme^h

antiseptic [æntieseptik] antiseptisch, ontsmettend

antisocial [æntiesoosjl] **1** asociaal; **2** ongezellig

antithesis [æntiθəsis] antithese, tegenstelling, tegenstrijdigheid; tegengestelde^h

antithetic(al) [æntiθetik(l)] tegengesteld, tegenstrijdig

antitoxin [æntittoksin] tegengif^h

antler [æntlə] geweitak, *~s* gewei^h

anus [eenəs] anus, aars

anvil [ænvil] aambeeld^h

anxiety [æng(k)zajjətie] bezorgdheid, ongerustheid, vrees

anxious [æng(k)sjəs] **1** bezorgd, ongerust: *you needn't be ~ about me* je hoeft je over mij geen zorgen te maken; **2** verontrustend, zorgwekkend, beangstigend; **3** *(inf)* verlangend: *he was ~ to leave* hij stond te popelen om te mogen vertrekken

^1**any** [enie] *pron* **1** *(number or amount)* enig(e), enkele, wat: *I cannot see ~ houses* ik zie geen huizen; *have you got ~ paper?* heb je papier?; *~ child can tell you that* elk kind kan je dat vertellen; *I didn't get ~* ik heb er geen enkele gehad; *few, if ~* weinig of geen, zo goed als geen; **2** iemand, iets, om het even wie (wat), wie (wat) ook: *~ will do* geef me er maar een, het geeft niet welke

^2**any** [enie] *adv (in negative and interrogative sentences)* enigszins, in enig opzicht: *are you ~ happier here?* ben je hier gelukkiger?; *I cannot stand it ~ longer* ik kan er niet meer tegen

anybody [enieboddie] om het even wie, wie dan ook, iemand, iedereen: *she 's not just ~* ze is niet de eerste de beste

anyhow [eniehau] **1** toch (maar) *(at the end of a sentence)*: *it's probably not worth it but let me see it ~* het heeft waarschijnlijk geen zin, maar laat me het toch maar zien; **2** hoe dan ook *(at the beginning of a sentence, after a pause)*: *~, I have to go now, sorry* hoe dan ook, ik moet nu gaan, het spijt me; **3** on-

geordend, slordig, kriskras: *he threw his clothes down just ~* hij gooide zijn kleren zomaar ergens neer

anymore [eniemo:] nog, meer, opnieuw, langer: *it's not hurting ~* het doet geen pijn meer

anyone [enniewun] *see* anybody

^1**anything** [ennieθing] *pron* om het even wat, wat dan ook, iets, (van) alles: *she didn't eat ~* ze at niets; *~ but safe* allesbehalve veilig; *if ~ this food is even worse* dit eten is zo mogelijk nog slechter

^2**anything** [ennieθing] *n* alles, wat dan ook, wat het ook zij

^3**anything** [ennieθing] *adv* enigszins, in enige mate, *(+ negation)* bijlange na (niet): *it isn't ~ much* het heeft niet veel om het lijf

anytime [ennietajm] *(inf)* wanneer (dan) ook, om het even wanneer: *he can come ~ now* hij kan nu elk ogenblik komen; *come ~ you like* kom wanneer je maar wilt

anyway [enniewee] **1** toch (maar): *he had no time but helped us ~* hij had geen tijd maar toch hielp hij ons; **2** hoe dan ook, in ieder geval: *~, I must be off now* in ieder geval, ik moet er nu vandoor; **3** eigenlijk: *why did he come ~?* waarom kwam hij eigenlijk?

^1**anywhere** [enniewɛə] *adv* **1** overal, ergens, om het even waar; **2** in enigerlei mate, ergens: *she isn't ~ near as tall as me* ze is lang niet zo groot als ik

^2**anywhere** [enniewɛə] *conj* waar … maar …: *go ~ you like* ga waar je maar naar toe wilt

apart [əpa:t] **1** los, onafhankelijk, op zichzelf; **2** van elkaar (verwijderd), op … afstand, met … verschil: *five miles ~* op vijf mijlen (afstand) van elkaar; **3** uit elkaar, aan stukken, kapot: *take ~* uit elkaar halen, demonteren

apartment [əpa:tmənt] **1** kamer, vertrek^h; **2** *often ~s* appartement^h, appartementen, reeks kamers; **3** *(Am)* flat, etage

apathy [æpəθie] apathie, lusteloosheid, onverschilligheid

^1**ape** [eep] *n* (mens)aap, *(fig)* na-aper

^2**ape** [eep] *vb* na-apen

aperture [æpətsjə] **1** opening, spleet; **2** lensopening

apex [eepeks] top, tip, hoogste punt^h, *(fig)* toppunt^h, hoogtepunt^h

apiarist [eepiərist] imker, bijenhouder

apiculture [eepikkultsjə] bijenteelt

apiece [əpie:s] elk, per stuk: *she gave us £10 ~* ze gaf ons elk £10

aplomb [əplom] aplomb^h, zelfverzekerdheid

apogee [æpədzjie:] hoogste punt^h, toppunt^h

apologetic [əpollədzjettik] verontschuldigend, schuldbewust

apologize [əpollədzjajz] zich verontschuldigen, zijn excuses aanbieden

apology [əpollədzjie] verontschuldiging: *~ for absence* bericht van verhindering; *offer an ~ to s.o. for sth.* zich bij iem voor iets verontschuldigen

apoplexy [æpəpleksie] beroerte

apostle [əpɔsl] apostel

apostrophe [əpɔstrəfie] apostrof, weglatingsteken[h]

appal [əpɔːl] met schrik vervullen: *they were ~led at* (of: *by*) *it* ze waren er ontsteld over

appalling [əpɔːling] verschrikkelijk

apparatus [æpəreetəs] apparaat[h], toestel[h], machine || *the men set up their ~* de mannen stelden hun apparatuur op

apparent [əpærənt] duidelijk, blijkbaar, kennelijk: *~ly he never got your letter* blijkbaar heeft hij je brief nooit ontvangen

apparition [æpərisjən] verschijning, spook[h], geest

¹**appeal** [əpiːl] *vb* 1 verzoeken, smeken; 2 aantrekkelijk zijn voor, aanspreken, aantrekken; 3 in beroep gaan, appelleren: *~ against that decision* tegen die beslissing beroep aantekenen

²**appeal** [əpiːl] *n* 1 verzoek[h], smeekbede; 2 *(law)* appel[h], (recht[h] van) beroep[h]: *lodge an ~* beroep aantekenen; 3 aantrekkingskracht

appealing [əpiːling] 1 smekend, meelijwekkend; 2 aantrekkelijk, aanlokkelijk

appeal to een beroep doen op, appelleren aan *(feelings, common sense)*: *may we ~ your generosity?* mogen wij een beroep doen op uw vrijgevigheid?

¹**appear** [əpiə] *vb* 1 schijnen, lijken: *so it ~s* 't schijnt zo te zijn; 2 blijken: *he ~ed to be honest* hij bleek eerlijk te zijn

²**appear** [əpiə] *vb* 1 verschijnen, voorkomen: *he had to ~ before court* hij moest voorkomen; 2 opdagen; 3 optreden

appearance [əpiərəns] 1 verschijning, optreden[h]: *he put in* (of: *made*) *an ~ at the party* hij liet zich even zien op het feest; 2 uiterlijk[h], voorkomen[h], ~s schijn: *~s are deceptive* schijn bedriegt; *keep up ~s* de schijn ophouden

appease [əpiːz] kalmeren, bedaren, sussen, verzoenen

appendicitis [əpendissajtis] blindedarmontsteking

appetite [æpittajt] 1 eetlust, honger, trek: *lack of ~* gebrek aan eetlust; 2 begeerte, zin: *whet s.o.'s ~* iem lekker maken

appetizer [æpittajzə] 1 aperitief[h]; 2 voorgerecht(je)[h], hapje[h] vooraf

¹**applaud** [əplɔːd] *vb* applaudisseren

²**applaud** [əplɔːd] *vb* toejuichen *(also fig)*, prijzen, loven

applause [əplɔːz] applaus[h], toejuiching

apple [æpl] appel || *~ of the* (of: *one's*) *eye* oogappel *(also fig)*

appliance [əplajjəns] 1 middel[h], hulpmiddel[h]; 2 toestel[h], gereedschap[h], apparaat[h]

applicable [əplikkəbl] 1 toepasselijk, van toepassing, bruikbaar: *not ~* niet van toepassing; 2 geschikt, passend, doelmatig

applicant [æplikkənt] sollicitant, aanvrager

application [æplikkeesjən] 1 sollicitatie: *letter of ~* sollicitatiebrief; 2 aanvraag(formulier[h]); 3 toepas-

sing, gebruik[h]: *for external ~ only* alleen voor uitwendig gebruik; 4 het aanbrengen *(eg unction on wound)*; 5 aanvraag, verzoek[h]: *on ~* op aanvraag; 6 ijver, vlijt, toewijding

¹**apply** [əplaj] *vb* 1 van toepassing zijn, betrekking hebben (op), gelden: *these rules don't ~ to you* dit reglement geldt niet voor u; 2 zich richten, zich wenden: *~ within* hier te bevragen; 3 *(with for)* solliciteren (naar), inschrijven (voor), aanvragen

²**apply** [əplaj] *vb* 1 aanbrengen, (op)leggen, toedienen; 2 toepassen, aanwenden, gebruiken: *~ the brakes* remmen; *~ oneself (to)* zich inspannen (voor), zich toeleggen (op)

appoint [əpɔjnt] 1 vaststellen, bepalen, vastleggen: *at the ~ed time* op de vastgestelde tijd; 2 benoemen, aanstellen

appointment [əpɔjntmənt] 1 afspraak: *by ~* volgens afspraak; 2 aanstelling, benoeming

appraisal [əpreezl] schatting, waardering, evaluatie

appraise [əpreez] schatten, waarderen, evalueren

¹**appreciate** [əpriːsjie-eet] *vb* 1 waarderen, (naar waarde) schatten; 2 zich bewust zijn van, zich realiseren, erkennen: *you should ~ the risks* je moet je bewust zijn van de risico's; 3 dankbaar zijn voor, dankbaarheid tonen voor

²**appreciate** [əpriːsjie-eet] *vb* stijgen *(in price, value)*

appreciation [əpriːsjie-eesjən] 1 waardering, beoordeling; 2 waardering, erkenning

apprehend [æprihend] aanhouden, in hechtenis nemen

apprehension [æprihhensjən] 1 vrees, bezorgdheid; 2 aanhouding, arrestatie

apprehensive [æprihhensiv] ongerust, bezorgd

apprentice [əprentis] leerjongen, leerling

¹**approach** [əprootsj] *vb* naderen, (naderbij) komen

²**approach** [əprootsj] *vb* 1 naderen, komen bij; 2 contact opnemen met, aanspreken, benaderen; 3 aanpakken

³**approach** [əprootsj] *n* 1 toegang(sweg), oprit, aanvliegroute *(of aeroplane)*; 2 aanpak, (wijze van) benadering; 3 contact[h], toenadering: *make ~es to s.o.* bij iem avances maken, met iem contact zoeken; 4 benadering: *it's the nearest ~ to ...* het is bijna ..., het lijkt het meeste op ...

approbation [æprəbeesjən] officiële goedkeuring

¹**appropriate** [əproopriət] *adj* geschikt, passend, toepasselijk: *where ~* waar nodig (of: van toepassing), in voorkomende gevallen; *~ for, ~ to* geschikt voor

²**appropriate** [əprooprie-eet] *vb* 1 bestemmen, toewijzen; 2 (zich) toe-eigenen: *he had ~d large sums to himself* hij had zich grote bedragen toegeëigend

approval [əproeːvl] goedkeuring, toestemming: *on ~* op zicht

¹**approve** [əproeːv] *vb* akkoord gaan, zijn goedkeuring geven

²**approve** [əproeːv] *vb* goedkeuren, toestemmen in,

akkoord gaan met: *an ~d contractor* een erkend aannemer

approximate [əprɔ̯ksimmət] bij benadering (aangegeven), naar schatting: *~ly three hours* ongeveer drie uur

apricot [ee̯prikkot] abrikoos

April [ee̯prəl] april: *~ Fools' Day* één april

a priori [ee prajjo̯:raj] van tevoren, vooraf

apron [ee̯prən] **1** schort[h], voorschoot[h]; **2** platform[h] *(at airport)*

apt [æpt] **1** geschikt, passend; **2** geneigd; **3** begaafd: *~ at* goed in

aptitude [æptitjoe:d] **1** geschiktheid; **2** neiging; **3** aanleg, talent[h], begaafdheid

aquarium [əkwe̯əriəm] aquarium[h]

Aquarius [əkwe̯əriəs] (de) Waterman

aquatic [əkwæ̯tik] water-

aqueduct [æ̯kwədukt] aquaduct[h]

¹Arab [æ̯rəb] *adj* Arabisch

²Arab [æ̯rəb] *n* **1** Arabier; **2** Arabische volbloed

Arabia [əre̯ebiə] Arabië

Arabian [əre̯ebiən] Arabisch

Arabic [æ̯rəbik] Arabisch: *~ numerals* Arabische cijfers

¹arable [æ̯rəbl] *adj* bebouwbaar, akker-

²arable [æ̯rəbl] *n* bouwland[h], landbouwgrond, akkerland[h]

arbiter [a̯:bittə] **1** leidende figuur, toonaangevend iem; **2** scheidsrechter

arbitrary [a̯:bitrərie] **1** willekeurig, grillig; **2** eigenmachtig; **3** scheidsrechterlijk

¹arbitrate [a̯:bitreet] *vb* arbitreren, als bemiddelaar optreden

²arbitrate [a̯:bitreet] *vb* aan arbitrage onderwerpen, scheidsrechterlijk (laten) regelen

arbour [a̯:bə] prieel[h]

arc [a:k] **1** (cirkel)boog; **2** *(electr)* lichtboog, vlamboog

arcade [a:ke̯ed] **1** arcade, zuilengang; **2** winkelgalerij

¹arch [a:tsj] *n* **1** boog, gewelf[h], arcade: *triumphal ~* triomfboog; **2** voetholte

²arch [a:tsj] *vb* **1** (over)welven, overspannen; **2** krommen, buigen: *the cat ~ed its back* de kat zette een hoge rug op

³arch [a:tsj] *vb* (with *across, over*) (zich) welven (over), zich uitspannen

⁴arch [a:tsj] *adj* ondeugend, schalks, guitig: *an ~ glance* een schalkse blik

archaeologist [a:kie·ɔ̯lədzjist] archeoloog, oudheidkundige

archaeology [a:kie·ɔ̯lədzjie] archeologie, oudheidkunde

archaic [a:ke̯eik] verouderd, ouderwets

archangel [a̯:keendzjl] aartsengel

archbishop [a:tsjbi̯sjəp] aartsbisschop

archer [a̯:tsjə] boogschutter

archipelago [a:kippe̯ləgoo] *(also -es)* archipel, eilandengroep

architect [a̯:kittekt] **1** architect; **2** ontwerper; **3** *(fig)* maker, schepper, grondlegger

architecture [a̯:kittektsjə] architectuur, bouwkunst, bouwstijl

archives [a̯:kajvz] **1** archief *(storage location)*; **2** archieven *(documents stored)*

archivist [a̯:kivvist] archivaris

arctic [a̯:ktik] **1** (noord)pool-: *Arctic Circle* noordpoolcirkel; **2** ijskoud

Arctic [a̯:ktik] noordpoolgebied, Arctica

ardent [a̯:dənt] vurig, hevig, hartstochtelijk

ardour [a̯:də] vurigheid, hartstocht

arduous [a̯:djoeəs] moeilijk, zwaar, lastig

area [e̯əriə] **1** oppervlakte: *a farm of 60 square kilometres in ~* een boerderij met een oppervlakte van 60 vierkante kilometer; **2** gebied[h] *(also fig)*, streek, domein[h]; **3** ruimte, plaats

arena [ərie̯:nə] arena, strijdperk[h] *(also fig)*

Argentina [a:dzjntie̯:nə] Argentinië

¹Argentinian [a:dzjnti̯nniən] *adj* Argentijns

²Argentinian [a:dzjnti̯nniən] *n* Argentijn

arguable [a̯:gjoeəbl] **1** betwistbaar, aanvechtbaar; **2** aantoonbaar, aanwijsbaar

¹argue [a̯:gjoe:] *vb* **1** argumenteren, pleiten: *they were ~ing against* zij pleitten tegen; **2** (with *about, over*) redetwisten (over), debatteren; **3** twisten, ruziën, kibbelen: *don't ~ with me!* spreek me niet tegen!

²argue [a̯:gjoe:] *vb* **1** doorpraten, bespreken; **2** stellen, aanvoeren, bepleiten; **3** overreden, overhalen: *I managed to ~ him into coming* ik kon hem overreden om te komen

argument [a̯:gjoemənt] **1** argument[h], bewijs[h], bewijsgrond: *a strong ~ for* een sterk argument voor; **2** ruzie, onenigheid, woordenwisseling; **3** hoofdinhoud, korte inhoud *(of book)*; **4** bewijsvoering, betoog[h], redenering: *let us, for the sake of ~, suppose … stel nu eens (het hypothetische geval) dat …*; **5** discussie, gedachtewisseling

argumentation [a:gjoementee̯sjən] argumentatie, bewijsvoering

arid [æ̯rid] dor, droog, schraal, onvruchtbaar

Aries [e̯ərie:z] (de) Ram

arise [əra̯jz] **1** zich voordoen, gebeuren, optreden: *difficulties have ~n* er zijn moeilijkheden ontstaan; **2** voortkomen, ontstaan: *~ from* voortkomen uit, het gevolg zijn van

aristocracy [æristɔ̯krəsie] *(also fig)* **1** aristocratie; **2** aristocraten, aristocratie, adel

aristocrat [æ̯ristəkræt] aristocraat

arithmetic [əri̯θmmətik] **1** rekenkunde; **2** berekening

ark [a:k] ark: *Noah's ~* ark van Noach

¹arm [a:m] *n* **1** arm *(of human being, animal; also fig)*: *~ in ~* arm in arm, gearmd; *at ~'s length* op een afstand, op gepaste afstand; *within ~'s reach* binnen handbereik; *a list as long as your ~* een ellenlange lijst; *twist s.o.'s ~* iemands arm omdraaien, *(fig)* forceren, het mes op de keel zetten; **2** mouw; **3**

armleuning; **4** afdeling, tak; **5** ~s wapenen, (oorlogs)wapens, bewapening: *lay down (one's) ~s* de
wapens neerleggen; *present ~s* het geweer presenteren; **6** ~s oorlogvoering, strijd; **7** ~s wapen^h, fami-
liewapen^h: *be up in ~s about* (of: *over, against*) *sth.*
verontwaardigd zijn over iets

²**arm** [a:m] *(also fig)*

³**arm** [a:m] *vb* (be)wapenen *(also fig)*, uitrusten: ~*ed
with a lot of information* voorzien van een boel informatie

armada [a:mɑːdə] armada, oorlogsvloot: *the
(Spanish) Armada* de (Spaanse) Armada *(of 1588)*

armament [a:məmənt] **1** wapentuig^h *(of tank, ship,
aeroplane)*; **2** bewapening

armchair leunstoel: ~ *critics* stuurlui aan wal; ~
shopping thuiswinkelen

armistice [a:mistis] wapenstilstand, bestand^h

armour [a:mə] **1** wapenrusting, harnas^h; **2** pantser^h,
pantsering, pantserbekleding; **3** beschutting, dekking, schuilplaats

armoured [a:məd] **1** gepantserd: ~ *car* pantserwagen; **2** gewapend *(glass, concrete etc)*; **3** geharnast

armoury [a:mərie] **1** wapenkamer, wapenmaga-
zijn^h; **2** wapens, wapensysteem^h; **3** arsenaal^h *(also
fig)*

armpit oksel

army [a:mie] leger^h *(also fig)*, massa, menigte

aroma [ərəumə] aroma^h, geur

aromatic [ærəmætik] aromatisch, geurig

¹**around** [əraund] *adv* **1** rond *(also fig)*, in de vorm
van een cirkel: *the other way ~* andersom; *a way ~*
een omweg; *bring ~* tot een andere mening brengen, overreden; *people gathered ~ to see* mensen
verzamelden zich om te kijken; *pass it ~* geef het
rond; *turn ~* (zich) omdraaien; **2** in het rond, aan
alle kanten, verspreid: *news gets ~ fast* nieuws verspreidt zich snel; **3** *(proximity)* in de buurt: *for
miles ~* kilometers in de omtrek; *stay ~* blijf in de
buurt; **4** *(approximation)* ongeveer, omstreeks:
he's ~ sixty hij is rond de zestig; ~ *fifty people* om en
nabij de vijftig mensen

²**around** [əraund] *prep* **1** rond, rondom, om … heen:
~ *the corner* om de hoek; *a chain ~ his neck* een ketting om zijn hals; **2** *(proximity)* in het rond, rondom, om … heen: *only those ~ him* alleen zijn naaste
medewerkers; **3** *(in all directions)* door, rond, her
en der in: *all ~ the country* door het hele land

arousal [ərauzl] **1** opwinding, prikkeling, ophit-
sing; **2** het (op)wekken, uitlokking

arouse [ərauz] **1** wekken *(also fig)*, uitlokken, doen
ontstaan: ~ *suspicion* wantrouwen wekken; **2** opwekken, prikkelen, ophitsen

¹**arrange** [əreendzj] *vb* **1** (rang)schikken, ordenen,
opstellen; **2** bijleggen, rechtzetten, rechttrekken; **3**
regelen, organiseren, arrangeren, zorgen voor: ~ *a
meeting* een vergadering beleggen; **4** *(mus)* arrangeren

²**arrange** [əreendzj] *vb* **1** maatregelen nemen, in
orde brengen: ~ *for sth.* iets regelen, ergens voor

zorgen; **2** overeenkomen, het eens zijn: ~ *with s.o.
about sth.* iets overeenkomen met iem

arrangement [əreendzjmənt] **1** ordening,
(rang)schikking, opstelling; **2** afspraak, regeling,
overeenkomst; **3** maatregel, voorzorg; **4** *(mus)* ar-
rangement^h, bewerking; **5** plan^h

¹**array** [əree] *n* **1** serie, collectie, reeks; **2** gelid^h, mars-
orde, slagorde

²**array** [əree] *vb* (in slagorde) opstellen, verzamelen,
(in het gelid) schikken

arrears [əriəz] **1** achterstand: *in ~ with one's work*
achter met zijn werk; **2** (geld)schuld: *be in ~* ach-
ter(op) zijn *(payment)*

¹**arrest** [ərest] *vb* **1** tegenhouden, bedwingen; **2** arresteren, aanhouden; **3** boeien, fascineren

²**arrest** [ərest] *n* **1** stilstand *(of growth, movement)*:
(med) cardiac ~ hartstilstand; **2** bedwinging, beteugeling *(of disease, decay etc)*; **3** arrestatie, aanhouding, (voorlopige) hechtenis: *place* (of: *put*)
under ~ in arrest nemen; *under ~* in arrest

arresting [ərestɪŋ] boeiend, fascinerend

arrival [ərajvl] **1** (aan)komst: *on ~* bij aankomst; **2**
binnengevaren schip^h, binnengekomen trein
(vliegtuig^h): *(fig) new ~* pasgeborene; **3** nieuwkomer, nieuweling

arrive [ərajv] **1** arriveren, aankomen *(of persons,
things)*; **2** arriveren, het (waar) maken; **3** aanbreken, komen *(of time)*

arrive at bereiken *(also fig)*, komen tot: ~ *a conclusion* tot een besluit komen, een conclusie trekken

arrogant [ærəgənt] arrogant, verwaand

arrow [ærəu] pijl

arse [a:s] *(vulg)* **1** reet; **2** klootzak, lul

arsenal [a:snəl] *(mil)* arsenaal^h, (wapen)arsenaal^h

arsenic [a:snik] **1** arsenicum^h, arseen^h; **2** ratten-
kruit^h

arson [a:sn] brandstichting

art [a:t] **1** kunst, bekwaamheid, vaardigheid: ~*s and
crafts* kunst en ambacht; *work of ~* kunstwerk; *the
black ~* zwarte kunst; **2** kunst(greep), truc, list; **3**
kunst(richting): *the fine ~s* de schone kunsten; **4**
the Arts letteren

artefact [a:tifækt] kunstvoorwerp^h

artery [a:tərie] slagader, *(fig)* verkeersader, han-
delsader

artful [a:tfoel] listig, spitsvondig

arthritis [a:θrajtis] artritis, jicht, gewrichtsontste-
king

artichoke [a:titsjook] artisjok

article [a:tikl] **1** artikel^h, stuk^h, tekstfragment^h: *a
newspaper ~* een krantenartikel; **2** *(law)* (wets)arti-
kel^h, bepaling; **3** *(com)* artikel^h, koopwaar, handelswaar: ~ *of clothing* kledingstuk; **4** *(linguistics)* lid-
woord^h: *definite ~* bepaald lidwoord; **5** ~*s* con-
tract^h, statuten, akten

¹**articulate** [a:tikjoelət] *adj* **1** zich duidelijk uitdruk-
kend *(pers)*; **2** duidelijk, helder (uitgedrukt, ver-
woord) *(thought etc)*

²**articulate** [a:tikjoeleet] *vb* duidelijk spreken, arti-

culeren

³artⁱculate [a:tɪkjoeleet] *vb* **1** articuleren, duidelijk uitspreken; **2** (helder) verwoorden, onder woorden brengen

artⁱfice [a:tɪffɪs] **1** truc, kunstgreep, list; **2** handigheid; **3** listigheid

artⁱficial [a:tɪffɪsjl] **1** kunstmatig: ~ *intelligence* kunstmatige intelligentie; **2** kunst-, namaak-: ~ *flowers* kunstbloemen; **3** gekunsteld, gemaakt: *an ~ smile* een gemaakte glimlach

artⁱllery [a:tɪllərie] *(mil)* **1** artillerie, geschutʰ; **2** artillerie *(part of army)*

artⁱsan [a:tizæn] handwerksman, vakman, ambachtsman

artⁱst [a:tist] artiest, (beeldend) kunstenaar (kunstenares)

artⁱste [a:tie:st] (variété)artiest(e)

artⁱstic [a:tɪstik] artistiek

artless [a:tləs] argeloos, onschuldig

arty [a:tie] *(oft depr)* **1** kitscherig; **2** artistiekerig

¹as [æz] *adv* even, zo: ~ *fast as John* zo snel als John; ~ *well as* zowel … als, niet alleen … maar ook; ~ *from now* van nu af

²as [æz] *prep* **1** *(nature, role, function etc)* als, in de rol van, in de hoedanigheid van: *Mary starring ~ Juliet* Mary in de rol van Julia; **2** *(comparison)* als, gelijk: *as light ~ a feather* vederlicht; ~ *such* als zodanig

³as [æz] *conj* **1** *(agreement or comparison)* (zo)als, naarmate, naargelang: *he lived ~ a hermit (would)* hij leefde als een kluizenaar; *cheap ~ cars go* goedkoop voor een wagen; *it's bad enough ~ it is* het is zo al erg genoeg; ~ *he later realized* zoals hij later besefte; ~ *it were* als het ware, om zo te zeggen; *such ~* zoals; *he was so kind ~ to tell me all about it* hij was zo vriendelijk om mij alles daarover te vertellen; **2** terwijl, toen: *Jim sang ~ he scrubbed* Jim zong onder het schrobben; **3** aangezien, daar, omdat: ~ *he was poor* daar hij arm was; ~ *for*, ~ *to* wat betreft; ~ *from* (Am: *of*) *today* vanaf vandaag, met ingang van heden

⁴as [æz] *pron* die, dat: *the same ~ he had seen* dezelfde die hij gezien had

asap *as soon as possible* z.s.m., zo spoedig mogelijk

asbestos [æzbestos] asbestʰ

¹ascend [əsend] *vb* **1** (op)stijgen, omhooggaan; **2** oplopen *(of slope, terrain)*

²ascend [əsend] *vb* **1** opgaan, naar boven gaan, beklimmen; **2** bestijgen *(throne)*

ascendancy [əsendənsie] overwichtʰ, overhand: *have (the) ~ over* (het) overwicht hebben op

Ascension [əsensjən] Hemelvaart: ~ *Day* hemelvaartsdag

ascent [əsent] bestijging, opstijging, (be)klim(ming), het omhooggaan

ascertain [æsətein] vaststellen, bepalen, te weten komen, ontdekken

¹ascetic [əsettik] *adj* ascetisch, zich onthoudend van weelde en genoegens

²ascetic [əsettik] *n* asceet, iemand die zich onthoudt

van weelde en genoegens

ASCII [æskie] *American Standard Code for Information Interchange* ASCII

ascribe [əskrajb] *(with to)* toeschrijven (aan)

ash [æsj] **1** es, essenhoutʰ; **2** ~*es* as *(after burning of corpse etc)*

ashamed [əsjeemd] beschaamd: *feel ~* zich schamen; *be ~ of* zich schamen over

ashore [əsjo:] **1** kustwaarts, landwaarts; **2** aan land, aan wal, op het strand

ashtray asbak

Ash Wednesday Aswoensdag

Asia [eesjə] Azië: ~ *Minor* Klein-Azië

Asian [eesjən] Aziatisch

¹aside [əsajd] *adv* terzijde, opzij, zijwaarts: *(fig)* brush ~ protests protesten naast zich neerleggen; *set ~: a)* opzijzetten; *b)* sparen *(money); (Am) ~ from* afgezien van, behalve

²aside [əsajd] *n* terloopse opmerking

¹ask [a:sk] *vb* vragen, informeren, navraag doen: ~ *for advice* om raad vragen; *(inf)* ~ *for it* erom vragen, het uitlokken

²ask [a:sk] *vb* **1** vragen, verzoeken: ~ *s.o. a question* iem een vraag stellen; ~ *a favour of s.o.* iem om een gunst vragen; **2** eisen, verlangen: *that's too much to* ~ dat is te veel gevraagd; **3** vragen, uitnodigen: *(inf) if you ~ me* volgens mij, als je het mij vraagt

askance [əska:ns] achterdochtig, wantrouwend: *look ~ at s.o. (sth.)* iem (iets) wantrouwend aankijken (bekijken)

askew [əskjoe:] scheef, schuin

asleep [əslie:p] in slaap, slapend

asparagus [əspærəgəs] asperge

aspect [æspekt] **1** gezichtspuntʰ, oogpuntʰ; **2** zijde, kant, facetʰ

aspen [æspən] esp(enboom), ratelpopulier

asperity [æsperrittie] ruwheid, scherpheid

¹asphalt [æsfælt] *n* asfaltʰ

²asphalt [æsfælt] *vb* asfalteren

asphyxia [æsfiksiə] verstikking(sdood)

aspirant [əspajjərənt] kandidaat

aspirate [æspirreet] **1** opzuigen, door zuigen verwijderen; **2** *(linguistics)* aspireren

aspiration [æspirreesjən] **1** aspiratie, strevenʰ, ambitie; **2** inademing; **3** aspiratie, op-, weg-, afzuiging; **4** *(linguistics)* aspiratie

aspire [əspajjə] sterk verlangen, streven: ~ *after*, ~ *to sth.* naar iets streven

aspirin [æsprin] aspirine, aspirientjeʰ

ass [æs] ezel *(also fig)*, domoor: *make an ~ of oneself* zichzelf belachelijk maken

assail [əseel] *(form)* aanvallen *(also fig)*, overvallen

assassin [əsæsin] moordenaar, sluipmoordenaar, huurmoordenaar

assassinate [əsæsinneet] **1** vermoorden; **2** vernietigen *(character, reputation)*

assassination [ə sæsinneesjən] (sluip)moord

¹assault [əso:lt] *vb* **1** aanvallen *(also fig)*; **2** *(mil)* bestormen

²**assault** [əso:lt] *n* 1 aanval *(also fig);* 2 *(mil)* bestorming; 3 daadwerkelijke bedreiging: ~ *and battery* mishandeling, geweldpleging

assay [əsee] analyseren, keuren *(metal, ore)*

¹**assemble** [əsembl] *vb* 1 assembleren, samenbrengen, verenigen, *(techn)* in elkaar zetten, monteren; 2 ordenen

²**assemble** [əsembl] *vb* zich verzamelen, samenkomen

assembly [əsemblie] 1 samenkomst, vergadering, verzameling; 2 assemblage, samenvoeging, montage; 3 assemblee

¹**assent** [əsent] *vb* toestemmen, aanvaarden: ~ *to sth.* met iets instemmen

²**assent** [əsent] *n* toestemming, aanvaarding

assert [əsə:t] 1 beweren, verklaren; 2 handhaven, laten gelden, opkomen voor *(rights):* ~ *oneself* op zijn recht staan, zich laten gelden

assertive [əsə:tiv] 1 stellig, uitdrukkelijk, beslist; 2 zelfbewust, zelfverzekerd, assertief

assess [əses] 1 bepalen, vaststellen *(value, amount, damage);* 2 belasten, aanslaan *(person, estate);* 3 taxeren, schatten, ramen, beoordelen: ~ *the situation* de situatie beoordelen

assessment [əsesmənt] 1 belasting, aanslag; 2 schatting, taxatie, raming; 3 vaststelling, bepaling; 4 beoordeling

assessor [əsesə] taxateur, schade-expert

asset [æset] 1 goedʰ, bezitʰ, *(fig also)* waardevolle eigenschap, pluspuntʰ, aanwinst: *health is the greatest* ~ gezondheid is het grootste goed; 2 *(econ)* creditpost; 3 ~*s* activa, baten, bedrijfsmiddelen: ~*s and liabilities* activa en passiva, baten en lasten

assiduous [əsidjoeəs] volhardend, vlijtig

assign [əsajn] 1 toewijzen, toekennen, aanwijzen: ~ *s.o. a task* iem een taak toebedelen; 2 bepalen, vaststellen *(day, date),* opgeven, aanwijzen; 3 aanwijzen, aanstellen, benoemen: ~ *s.o. to a post in Berlin* iem voor een functie in Berlijn aanwijzen

assignment [əsajnmənt] 1 taak, opdracht, huiswerkʰ; 2 toewijzing, toekenning, bestemming

assimilate [əsimmilleet] zich assimileren, opgenomen worden, gelijk worden: ~ *into,* ~ *with sth.* opgenomen worden in iets

assist [əsist] helpen, bijstaan, assisteren

assistance [əsistəns] hulp, bijstand, assistentie

¹**assistant** [əsistənt] *n* 1 helper, assistent, adjunct; 2 bediende, hulp

²**assistant** [əsistənt] *adj* assistent-, hulp-, ondergeschikt

¹**associate** [əsoosjie·eet] *vb* 1 zich verenigen, zich associëren; 2 *(with with)* omgaan (met)

²**associate** [əsoosjie·eet] *vb* verenigen, verbinden, *(also fig)* associëren, in verband brengen: *closely* ~*d with* nauw betrokken bij

³**associate** [əsoosjiət] *n* 1 partner, compagnon; 2 (met)gezel, kameraad, makker

⁴**associate** [əsoosjiət] *adj* toegevoegd, bijgevoegd, mede-: ~ *member* buitengewoon lid

association [əsoosjie·eesjən] 1 vereniging, genootschapʰ, gezelschapʰ, bond; 2 associatie, verbandʰ, verbinding; 3 samenwerking, connectie: *in* ~ *with* samen met, in samenwerking met; 4 omgang, vriendschap

assort [əso:t] sorteren, ordenen, classificeren

assortment [əso:tmənt] 1 assortimentʰ, collectie, ruime keuze; 2 sortering, ordening

assuage [əsweedzj] 1 kalmeren, verzachten, verlichten, (tot) bedaren (brengen); 2 bevredigen, stillen *(hunger, desire),* lessen *(thirst)*

assume [əs·joe:m] 1 aannemen, vermoeden, veronderstellen; 2 overnemen, nemen, grijpen; 3 op zich nemen: *he* ~*d the role of benefactor* hij speelde de weldoener; 4 voorwenden: ~*d name* aangenomen naam, schuilnaam

assuming [əs·joe:ming] ervan uitgaande dat

assumption [əsumpsjən] vermoedenʰ, veronderstelling

assurance [əsjoeərəns] 1 zekerheid, vertrouwenʰ; 2 zelfvertrouwenʰ; 3 verzekering, levensverzekering; 4 verzekering, belofte, garantie

assure [əsjoeə] verzekeren: ~ *s.o. of one's support* iem van zijn steun verzekeren

asterisk [æstərisk] asterisk, sterretjeʰ

asteroid [æstərojd] asteroïde, kleine planeet

asthma [æsmə] astma

astonish [əstonnisj] verbazen, versteld doen staan: *be* ~*ed at sth.* zich over iets verbazen, stomverbaasd zijn over iets

astonishment [əstonnisjmənt] verbazing

astound [əstaund] ontzetten, verbazen, schokken

astray [əstree] verdwaald: *go* ~ verdwalen, de verkeerde weg op gaan; *lead s.o.* ~ iem op een dwaalspoor brengen

astride [əstrajd] schrijlings, wijdbeens, dwars ‖ *she sat* ~ *her horse* ze zat schrijlings op haar paard

astrology [əstrollədzjie] astrologie

astronaut [æstrəno:t] astronaut, ruimtevaarder

astronomer [əstronnəmə] astronoom, sterrenkundige

astronomical [æstrənommikl] astronomisch *(also fig),* sterrenkundig

astronomy [əstronnəmie] astronomie, sterrenkunde

astute [əstjoe:t] scherpzinnig, slim, sluw

asylum [əsajləm] 1 asielʰ, toevlucht(soordʰ); 2 (krankzinnigen)inrichting

at [æt] 1 *(place, time, point on a scale)* aan, te, in, op, bij: ~ *my aunt's* bij mijn tante; ~ *Christmas* met Kerstmis; ~ *the corner* op de hoek; *cheap* ~ *10 p.* goedkoop voor 10 pence; ~ *that time* toen, in die tijd; *we'll leave it* ~ *that* we zullen het daarbij laten; 2 *(activity or profession)* bezig met: ~ *work* aan het werk; *they're* ~ *it again* ze zijn weer bezig; 3 *(skill)* op het gebied van: *my mother is an expert* ~ *wallpapering* mijn moeder kan geweldig goed behangen; 4 door, naar aanleiding van, als gevolg van, door middel van, via: ~ *my command* op mijn bevel; ~ *a* *glance* in één oogopslag

atheism [ee̯θie·izm] atheïsme[h], godloochening

atheist [ee̯θie·ist] atheïst, godloochenaar

athlete [æθlie:t] atleet

athletics [æθletiks] atletiek

Atlantic [ətlæntik] Atlantische Oceaan

atlas [ætləs] atlas

atmosphere [ætməsfiə] 1 dampkring; atmosfeer *(also unit of pressure);* 2 (atmo)sfeer, stemming

atmospheric [ætməsferrik] atmosferisch, lucht-, dampkrings-

atoll [ætol] atol[h], ringvormig koraaleiland[h]

atom [ætəm] 1 *(science)* atoom[h]; 2 zeer kleine hoeveelheid, greintje[h]

atomize [ætəmajz] verstuiven, vernevelen

atomizer [ætəmajzə] verstuiver

atone for [ətoo̯n] goedmaken

atonement [ətoo̯nmənt] vergoeding, boetedoening: *make ~ for* goedmaken

atop [ətop] boven op

atrocious [ətroo̯sjəs] 1 wreed, monsterachtig; 2 afschuwelijk slecht

atrocity [ətrossittie] 1 wreedheid; 2 afschuwelijkheid

attach [ətætsj] (aan)hechten, vastmaken, verbinden: *~ too much importance to sth.* ergens te zwaar aan tillen

attaché [ətæsjee] attaché

attaché case diplomatenkoffertje[h]

attachment [ətætsjmənt] 1 hulpstuk[h], ~s toebehoren[h], accessoires; 2 aanhechting, verbinding; 3 gehechtheid, genegenheid, trouw

¹attack [ətæk] *vb* aanvallen *(also fig),* overvallen

²attack [ətæk] *vb* 1 aantasten, aanvreten; 2 aanpakken *(eg a problem)*

³attack [ətæk] *n* 1 aanval, (scherpe) kritiek: *be under ~* aangevallen worden; 2 aanpak

attain [əteen] bereiken, verkrijgen: *~ old age* een hoge leeftijd bereiken

attainment [əteenmənt] 1 verworvenheid, kundigheid; 2 het bereiken, verwerving

¹attempt [ətempt] *vb* proberen, wagen

²attempt [ətempt] *n* 1 (with *to*) poging (tot): *~ at conciliation* toenaderingspoging; 2 aanval, aanslag: *~ on s.o.'s life* aanslag op iemands leven

¹attend [ətend] *vb* 1 bijwonen, aanwezig zijn bij: *will you be ~ing his lecture?* ga je naar zijn lezing?; 2 zorgen voor, verplegen; 3 letten op, bedienen; 4 begeleiden, vergezellen, *(fig)* gepaard gaan met

²attend [ətend] *vb* 1 aanwezig zijn: *~ at church* de dienst bijwonen; 2 opletten, (aandachtig) luisteren

attendance [ətendəns] 1 opkomst, aantal aanwezigen; 2 aanwezigheid: *compulsory ~* verschijningsplicht, verplichte aanwezigheid; 3 dienst, toezicht[h]: *doctor in ~* dienstdoende arts

attendant [ətendənt] 1 bediende, knecht; 2 begeleider, volgeling, ~s gevolg[h]; 3 bewaker, suppoost

attend to 1 aandacht schenken aan, luisteren naar; 2 zich inzetten voor, zorgen voor, bedienen: *~ s.o.'s*

interests iemands belangen behartigen; *are you being attended to?* wordt u al geholpen?

attention [ətensjən] 1 aandacht, zorg: *this plant needs a lot of ~* deze plant vraagt veel zorg; *pay ~* opletten; *for the ~ of* ter attentie van; 2 belangstelling, erkenning; 3 attentie, hoffelijkheid: *be (of: stand) at ~* in de houding staan

attentive [ətentiv] 1 aandachtig, oplettend; 2 attent, hoffelijk

attenuate [ətenjoe·eet] 1 verdunnen, dunner worden, versmallen; 2 verzwakken, verminderen, dempen *(sound): with old age memories ~* met de oude dag vervagen de herinneringen

¹attest [ətest] *vb* (with *to*) getuigen (van), getuigenis afleggen (van)

²attest [ətest] *vb* 1 plechtig verklaren, officieel bevestigen; 2 getuigen van, betuigen

attic [ætik] vliering, zolder(kamer)

attire [ətajjə] gewaad[h], kledij

attitude [ætitjoe:d] 1 houding, stand, attitude; 2 houding, gedrag[h]: *~ of mind* instelling; 3 standpunt[h], opvatting

attorney [ətə:nie] 1 procureur, gevolmachtigde: *power of ~* volmacht; 2 *(Am)* advocaat

Attorney General 1 procureur-generaal; 2 *(Am)* Minister van Justitie

attract [ətrækt] aantrekken *(also fig),* lokken, boeien

attraction [ətræksjən] 1 aantrekkelijkheid; aantrekking(skracht); 2 attractie, bezienswaardigheid

attractive [ətræktiv] aantrekkelijk, attractief

¹attribute [ətribjoe:t] *vb* toeschrijven, toekennen

²attribute [ætribjoe:t] *n* 1 eigenschap, (essentieel) kenmerk[h]; 2 attribuut[h], symbool[h]

attune [ətjoe:n] doen overeenstemmen, afstemmen

aubergine [oo̯bəzjie:n] aubergine

¹auction [o:ksjən] *n* veiling, verkoop bij opbod

²auction [o:ksjən] *vb* veilen, verkopen bij opbod

audacious [o:deesjəs] 1 dapper, moedig; 2 roekeloos; 3 brutaal

audacity [o:dæsittie] 1 dappere daad, waagstuk[h]; 2 dapperheid; 3 roekeloosheid; 4 brutaliteit, onbeschoftheid

audible [o:dibl] hoorbaar, verstaanbaar

audience [o:diəns] 1 publiek[h], toehoorders, toeschouwers; 2 (with *with*) audiëntie (bij)

¹audit [o:dit] *n* 1 accountantsonderzoek[h], -controle; 2 accountantsverslag[h]; 3 balans, afrekening

²audit [o:dit] *vb* (de boeken, rekeningen) controleren

audition [o:disjən] auditie, proefoptreden[h]

auditor [o:dittə] 1 toehoorder, luisteraar; 2 (regist
er)accountant, *(Belg)* bedrijfsrevisor

auditorium [o:ditto:riəm] gehoorzaal, auditorium[h], aula

augment [o:gment] vergroten, (doen) toenemen, vermeerderen

augury [o:gjərie] voorspelling; voorteken[h]: *a hopeful ~* een gunstig voorteken

august [o:gʌst] verheven, groots

August [o:gəst] augustus

aunt [a:nt] tante

aura [o:rə] aura, sfeer, waasʰ: *he has an ~ of respectability* hij heeft iets waardigs over zich

auspices [o:spissiz] auspiciën, bescherming: *under the ~ of Her Majesty* onder de bescherming van Hare Majesteit

auspicious [o:spisjəs] **1** gunstig, voorspoedig; **2** veelbelovend

austere [o:stiə] **1** streng, onvriendelijk, ernstig; **2** matig, sober; eenvoudig

austerity [osterrittie] **1** soberheid, matiging; **2** (strenge) eenvoud, soberheid; **3** beperking, bezuiniging(smaatregel), inlevering: *~ drive* bezuinigingscampagne

¹**Australasian** [ostrəleezjn] *adj* Austraal-Aziatisch

²**Australasian** [ostrəleezjn] *n* bewoner van Austraal-Azië *(Oceania)*

Australia [ostreeliə] Australië

¹**Australian** [ostreeliən] *adj* Australisch

²**Australian** [ostreeliən] *n* Australiër

Austria [ostriə] Oostenrijk

¹**Austrian** [ostriən] *adj* Oostenrijks

²**Austrian** [ostriən] *n* Oostenrijker

authentic [o:θentik] authentiek, onvervalst, origineel

authenticate [o:θentikkeet] (voor) echt verklaren: *~ a will* een testament bekrachtigen

author [o:θə] auteur, schrijver, maker, schepper

¹**authoritarian** [o:θorritteəriən] *adj* autoritair, eigenmachtig

²**authoritarian** [o:θorritteəriən] *n* autoritair iemand, eigenmachtig individuʰ

authority [o:θorrittie] **1** autoriteit, overheidsinstantie, -persoon: *the competent authorities* de bevoegde overheden, het bevoegd gezag; **2** rechtʰ, toestemming; **3** autoriteit, deskundige: *an ~ on the subject* een autoriteit op dit gebied; **4** autoriteit, gezagʰ, wettige macht: *abuse of ~* machtsmisbruik; **5** autoriteit, (moreel) gezagʰ, invloed: *you cannot deny his ~* je kunt niet ontkennen dat hij iemand van aanzien is; **6** volmacht, machtiging

authorization [o:θərəzeesjən] **1** autorisatie, machtiging, volmacht; **2** vergunning, goedkeuring

authorize [o:θərajz] **1** machtigen, recht geven tot, volmacht verlenen: *~d agent* gevolmachtigd vertegenwoordiger, gevolmachtigde; **2** goedkeuren, inwilligen, toelaten

auto [o:too] *(Am; inf)* auto

autobiography [o:toobajjogrəfie] autobiografie

autograph [o:təgra:f] handschriftʰ, handtekening *(of celebrity)*

automate [o:təmeet] automatiseren

¹**automatic** [o:təmætik] *adj* automatisch, zelfwerkend; zonder na te denken: *he ~ally thought of her* hij dacht onwillekeurig aan haar

²**automatic** [o:təmætik] *n* automatisch wapenʰ

automobile [o:təməbie:l] *(Am)* auto

autonomous [o:tonnəməs] autonoom, met zelfbestuur

autonomy [o:tonnəmie] autonomie, zelfbestuurʰ, onafhankelijkheid

autopsy [o:topsie] *(med)* autopsie, lijkschouwing, sectie

autumn [o:təm] *(also fig)* herfst, najaarʰ, nadagen

¹**auxiliary** [o:gzilliərie] *adj* **1** hulp-, behulpzaam, helpend: *~ troops* hulptroepen; *~ verb* hulpwerkwoord; **2** aanvullend, supplementair, reserve-

²**auxiliary** [o:gzilliərie] *n* **1** helper, hulpkracht, assistent; **2** hulpmiddelʰ; **3** hulpwerkwoordʰ

¹**avail** [əveel] *n* nutʰ, voordeelʰ, baat: *to no ~* nutteloos, vergeefs

²**avail** [əveel] *vb* baten, helpen, van nut zijn || *Joe ~ed himself of the opportunity* Joe maakte van de gelegenheid gebruik

availability [əveeləbillittie] beschikbaarheid, verkrijgbaarheid, leverbaarheid, aanwezigheid

available [əveeləbl] beschikbaar, verkrijgbaar, leverbaar; ten dienste staand: *Mr Jones was not ~ for comment* meneer Jones was niet beschikbaar voor commentaar

avalanche [ævəla:ntsj] lawine, *(fig)* vloed(golf), stortvloed

avarice [ævəris] gierigheid, hebzucht

avaricious [ævərisjəs] hebzuchtig, gierig

Ave. *avenue* ln, laan

avenge [əvendzj] wreken, wraak nemen (voor)

avenue [ævənjoe:] **1** avenue, (brede) laan; **2** oprijlaan *(to castle, estate)*; **3** weg *(only fig)*, toegang, middelʰ: *explore every ~* alle middelen proberen

¹**average** [ævridzj] *n* gemiddeldeʰ, middelmaat, *(also fig)* doorsnee: *eight is the ~ of ten and six* acht is het gemiddelde van tien en zes; *above (the) ~* boven het gemiddelde; *below (the) ~* onder het gemiddelde; *on (the) ~* gemiddeld, door de bank genomen

²**average** [ævridzj] *adj* gemiddeld, midden-, doorsnee-: *~ man* de gewone man

³**average** [ævridzj] *vb* het gemiddelde berekenen

¹**average out** *vb (inf)* gemiddeld op hetzelfde neerkomen: *the profits averaged out at fifty pounds a day* de winst kwam gemiddeld neer op vijftig pond per dag

²**average out** *vb (inf)* een gemiddelde berekenen van

averse [əvə:s] *(with to)* afkerig (van), tegen, afwijzend

aversion [əvə:sjən] **1** *(with to)* afkeer (van): *take an ~ to* een afkeer krijgen van; **2** persoon (iets) waar men een hekel aan heeft

avert [əvə:t] **1** *(with from)* afwenden (van) *(eyes)*, afkeren; **2** voorkomen, vermijden, afwenden

aviary [eeviərie] vogelhuisʰ, vogelverblijfʰ

aviation [eevie·eesjən] **1** luchtvaart, vliegkunst; **2** vliegtuigbouw

avid [ævid] **1** gretig, enthousiast: *an ~ reader* een grage lezer; **2** verlangend

avoid [əvojd] (ver)mijden, ontwijken: *they couldn't ~ doing it* zij moesten (het) wel (doen)

avoidance [əvojdəns] vermijding, het vermijden

avow [əva·oe] **1** toegeven, erkennen; **2** (openlijk) bekennen, belijden *(belief etc): they are ~ed enemies* het zijn gezworen vijanden

avuncular [əvungkjoelə] als een (vriendelijke) oom, vaderlijk

await [əweet] opwachten; verwachten, tegemoet zien ‖ *a warm welcome ~s them* er wacht hen een warm welkom

¹**awake** [əweek] *adj* **1** wakker: *wide ~* klaarwakker *(also fig);* **2** waakzaam, alert: *~ to* zich bewust van

²**awake** [əweek] *vb* **1** ontwaken *(also fig),* wakker worden; **2** *(with to)* zich bewust worden (van), gaan beseffen

³**awake** [əweek] *vb* **1** wekken, wakker maken; **2** bewust maken

¹**award** [əwo:d] *vb* **1** toekennen *(prize),* toewijzen; **2** belonen

²**award** [əwo:d] *n* **1** beloning, prijs; **2** toekenning *(of reward, prize, damages)*

aware [əweə] zich bewust, gewaar: *politically ~* politiek bewust; *be ~ of* zich bewust zijn van

¹**away** [əwee] *adj* uit-: *~ match* uitwedstrijd

²**away** [əwee] *adv* **1** weg *(also fig),* afwezig, op (een) afstand, uit: *give ~* weggeven; **2** voortdurend, onophoudelijk: *she was knitting ~* ze zat aan één stuk door te breien; *I'll do it right ~* ik zal het meteen doen

awe [o:] ontzagʰ, eerbied: *hold* (of: *keep) s.o. in ~* ontzag hebben voor iem; *stand in ~ of* groot ontzag hebben voor

awe-inspiring ontzagwekkend

awesome [o:səm] ontzagwekkend, ontzag inboezemend

awful [o:foel] *(inf)* afschuwelijk, enorm: *an ~ lot* ontzettend veel

awfully [o:flie] *(inf)* erg, vreselijk, ontzettend: *thanks ~* reuze bedankt; *~ nice* vreselijk aardig

awhile [əwajl] korte tijd, een tijdje

awkward [o:kwəd] **1** onhandig, onbeholpen; **2** onpraktisch; **3** ongelegen, ongunstig *(date, time);* **4** gênant: *~ situation* pijnlijke situatie; **5** opgelaten, niet op zijn gemak

awry [əraj] scheef *(also fig),* schuin, fout: *go ~* mislukken

¹**axe** [æks] *n* bijl: *(fig) have an ~ to grind* ergens zelf een bijbedoeling mee hebben

²**axe** [æks] *vb* **1** ontslaan, aan de dijk zetten; **2** afschaffen, wegbezuinigen

axis [æksis] *(axes)* as(lijn), spil

axle [æksl] *(techn)* (draag)as, spil

azure [æzjə,æzjjoeə] hemelsblauw, azuurblauw, *(fig)* wolkenloos

b

b. *born* geb., geboren

B.A. *Bachelor of Arts* baccalaureus *(university degree)*

¹**babble** [bæbl] *n* gebabbelʰ; gewauwelʰ, gekletsʰ

²**babble** [bæbl] *vb* babbelen

babe [beeb] **1** kindjeʰ, baby; **2** *(Am; inf)* popjeʰ, liefjeʰ

baboon [bəboe:n] baviaan *(also fig; depr)*, lomperd

baby [beebie] **1** baby, zuigeling, kleuter; **2** jongste, benjamin; **3** *(fig)* klein kindʰ, kinderachtig persoon; **4** jongʰ *(of animal)*; **5** schatjeʰ; **6** *(inf)* persoon, zaak: *that's your ~* dat is jouw zaak; *(fig) be left carrying* (of: *holding) the ~* met de gebakken peren blijven zitten

baby minder babysitter, oppas

baby sit babysitten

babysitter babysitter, oppas

bachelor [bætsjələr] **1** vrijgezel; **2** baccalaureus *(lowest university degree)*: *Bachelor of Arts* baccalaureus in de Letteren; *Bachelor of Science* baccalaureus in de exacte wetenschappen

¹**back** [bæk] *n* **1** rug, achterkant: *behind s.o.'s ~* achter iemands rug *(also fig)*; **2** achter(hoede)speler, verdediger, back; **3** achterkant, -zijde, keerzijde, rug: *~ to ~: a)* ruggelings, rug tegen rug; *b)* achtereenvolgens; **4** (rug)leuning; **5** achterste deelʰ: *(fig) at the ~ of one's mind* in zijn achterhoofd; *at the ~* achterin; **6** *(sport)* achterʰ: *know like the ~ of one's hand* als zijn broekzak kennen; *(fig) with one's ~ to the wall* met zijn rug tegen de muur; *(inf) get* (of: *put) s.o.'s ~ up* iem irriteren; *(inf) get off s.o.'s ~* iem met rust laten; *pat oneself on the ~* tevreden zijn over zichzelf; *put one's ~ into sth.* ergens de schouders onder zetten; *glad to see the ~ of s.o.* iem liever zien gaan dan komen; *stab s.o. in the ~* iem een dolk in de rug steken, iem verraden; *turn one's ~ on* de rug toekeren

²**back** [bæk] *adv* **1** achter(op), aan de achterkant: *(Am) ~ of* achter; **2** achteruit, terug; **3** terug *(also fig)*, weer thuis; **4** *(inf)* in het verleden, geleden, terug: *~ in 1975* al in 1975; **5** op (enige) afstand: *a few miles ~* een paar mijl terug; **6** achterom: *~ and forward* (of: *forth)* heen en weer

³**back** [bæk] *adj* **1** achter(-): *~ room: a)* achterkamer(tje); *b) (also fig)* ergens achteraf; *~ seat: a)* achterbank *(of car); b) (fig)* tweede plaats; **2** terug-;

3 ver (weg), (achter)afgelegen; **4** achterstallig; **5** oud *(of edition)*: *~ issue* (of: *number)* oud nummer *(of magazine)*

⁴**back** [bæk] *vb* krimpen *(of wind)*

⁵**back** [bæk] *vb* achteruit bewegen, achteruitrijden, (doen) achteruitgaan: *~ out* achteruit wegrijden

⁶**back** [bæk] *vb* **1** (onder)steunen *(also fin)*, schragen, bijstaan; **2** *(inf)* wedden (op), gokken op: *(fig) ~ the wrong horse* op het verkeerde paard wedden

backache rugpijn

back away (also with *from)* achteruit weglopen (van), zich terugtrekken

backbencher gewoon Lagerhuislidʰ

backbite kwaadspreken (over), roddelen (over)

backbone ruggengraat *(also fig)*, wervelkolom, wilskracht, pit

backbreaking slopend, zwaar

back down terugkrabbelen, toegeven

backfire 1 terugslaan *(of engine)*, naontsteking hebben; **2** mislopen, verkeerd aflopen

background achtergrond *(also fig)*

backing [bæking] **1** (ruggen)steun, ondersteuning; **2** achterban, medestanders

backlash tegenstroom, verzetʰ, reactie

back off terugdeinzen, achteruitwijken

back out (with *of)* zich terugtrekken (uit), afzien (van)

backpack rugzak

backside 1 *(inf)* achterwerkʰ, zitvlakʰ; **2** achtereindeʰ

backslide 1 terugvallen *(in bad behaviour)*, vervallen; **2** afvallig worden

backstage achter het podium, achter de schermen, in het geheim

backstair(s) 1 privé-, heimelijk: *~ gossip* achterklap; **2** achterbaks, onderhands

back street achterbuurt(en)

backstroke rugslag

¹**back up** *vb* **1** (onder)steunen, staan achter, bijstaan; **2** bevestigen *(story)*

²**back up** *vb* **1** *(Am)* een file vormen; **2** *(Am)* achteruitrijden *(of car)*

back-up *(inf)* (ruggen)steun, ondersteuning; **2** reserve, voorraad; **3** reservekopie (van computerbestandʰ); **4** *(Am)* file

backward [bækwəd] **1** achter(lijk), achtergebleven *(in development)*, traag, niet bij; **2** achteruit(-), ruggelings: *a ~ glance* een blik achterom

backwards [bækwədz] **1** achteruit *(also fig)*, achterwaarts, ruggelings: *~ and forward(s)* heen en weer; **2** naar het verleden, terug

backwater 1 (stil) binnenwaterʰ, *(fig)* gatʰ, afgelegen stadjeʰ, *(fig)* impasse, (geestelijke) stagnatie; **2** achterwaterʰ

backyard 1 plaatsjeʰ, achterplaats, *(fig)* achtertuin: *in one's own ~* in zijn eigen achtertuin; **2** *(Am)* achtertuin

bacon [beekən] baconʰ, spekʰ ‖ *(inf) bring home the*

~ de kost verdienen; *(inf) save one's* ~ zijn hachje redden, er zonder kleerscheuren afkomen

bacterium [bæktjəriəm] bacterie

¹bad [bæd] *adj* **1** slecht, minderwaardig, verkeerd: *a ~ conscience* een slecht geweten; *(inf) make the best of a ~ job* het beste er van (zien te) maken; *go ~* bederven; *bad-mannered* ongemanierd; *not half, not so* ~ niet zo gek; **2** kwaad, kwaadaardig, stout: *in ~ faith* te kwader trouw; *from ~ to worse* van kwaad tot erger; **3** ziek, naar, pijnlijk; **4** erg, ernstig, lelijk: *~ debt* oninbare schuld; *be in a ~ way* er slecht aan toe zijn; **5** ongunstig: *make the best of a ~ bargain* er het beste van maken; *that looks ~* dat voorspelt niet veel goeds; **6** schadelijk: *~ for your liver* slecht voor je lever; **7** vol spijt: *I feel ~ about that* dat spijt me

²bad [bæd] *n* **1** het slechte, het kwade: *go to the* ~ de verkeerde kant opgaan; **2** debet^h, schuld: *be £ 500 to the* ~ voor 500 pond in het krijt staan

badge [bædzj] badge, insigne^h, politiepenning

¹badger [bædzjə] *n* das *(animal)*

²badger [bædzjə] *vb* pesten, lastig vallen

badly [bædlie] **1** slecht: *do* ~ een slecht resultaat behalen, het er slecht van afbrengen; **2** erg, zeer, hard: *I need it* ~ ik heb het hard nodig; *~ wounded* zwaar gewond

baffle [bæfl] verbijsteren, van zijn stuk brengen: *a problem that has ~d biologists for years* een probleem dat biologen al jaren voor raadsels stelt

bafflement [bæflmənt] verbijstering

¹bag [bæg] *n* **1** zak, baal: *~s under the eyes* wallen onder de ogen; **2** zak, tas, koffer; **3** zak vol, *(fig)* grote hoeveelheid: *the whole ~ of tricks* de hele santenkraam; *(inf) ~s of money* hopen geld; **4** vangst *(game): a mixed ~* een allegaartje; *(inf) it's in the ~* het is in kannen en kruiken

²bag [bæg] *vb* vangen, schieten *(game, fowl)*

baggage [bægidzj] bagage

baggy [bægie] zakachtig, flodderig: *~ cheeks* hangwangen

bagpipes doedelzak

¹bail [beel] *n* borg(stelling), borgtocht, borgsom: *out on* ~ vrijgelaten op borgtocht

²bail [beel] *vb* hozen

³bail [beel] *vb* **1** vrijlaten tegen borgstelling; **2** leeghozen

bailiff [beelif] **1** *(law)* deurwaarder; **2** *(Am; law)* gerechtsdienaar

¹bail out *vb* hozen

²bail out *vb* **1** door borgtocht in vrijheid stellen, vrijkopen; **2** *(inf)* uit de penarie helpen; **3** leeghozen

¹bait [beet] *n* aas^h, lokaas^h, *(fig)* verleiding

²bait [beet] *vb* **1** van lokaas voorzien; **2** ophitsen *(animal, esp dogs);* **3** treiteren, boos maken

bake [beek] bakken (in een oven)

baker [beekə] bakker: *(fig) ~'s dozen* dertien

bakery [beekərie] **1** bakkerij; **2** bakkerswinkel

balaclava [bæləkla:və] bivakmuts

¹balance [bæləns] *n* **1** balans, weegschaal: *(fig) his*

fate is *(of: hangs) in the* ~ zijn lot is onbeslist; **2** *(com)* balans: *~ of payments* betalingsbalans; *strike a* ~ *(fig)* een compromis *(of:* het juiste evenwicht) vinden; **3** *(fin, com)* saldo^h, tegoed^h, overschot^h: *~ in hand* kasvoorraad; *~ due* debetsaldo; **4** evenwicht^h, balans: *~ of power* machtsevenwicht; *redress the* ~ het evenwicht herstellen; *on* ~ alles in aanmerking genomen

²balance [bæləns] *vb* **1** schommelen, balanceren, slingeren; **2** *(com)* sluiten *(of balance sheet)*, gelijk uitkomen, kloppen: *the books* ~ de boeken kloppen, de administratie klopt

³balance [bæləns] *vb* **1** wegen, *(fig)* overwegen, tegen elkaar afwegen; **2** in evenwicht brengen, balanceren; **3** *(com)* opmaken, laten kloppen, sluitend maken *(balance sheet):* ~ *the books* het boekjaar afsluiten

balanced [bælənst] evenwichtig, harmonisch: *~ diet* uitgebalanceerd dieet

balcony [bælkənie] balkon^h, galerij

bald [bo:ld] **1** kaal, *(fig also)* sober, saai: *~ as a coot* kaal als een biljartbal; *~ tyre* gladde band; **2** naakt, bloot

baldly [bo:ldlie] gewoonweg, zonder omwegen, regelrecht

bale [beel] baal

baleful [beelfoel] **1** noodlottig; **2** onheilspellend *(eg glance)*

¹bale out *vb* **1** hozen; **2** het vliegtuig uitspringen *(with parachute)*

²bale out *vb* uithozen, leeghozen

¹balk [bo:k] *vb* **1** weigeren, stokken, blijven steken: *the horse ~ed at the fence* het paard weigerde de hindernis; **2** *(with at)* terugschrikken (van, voor), bezwaar maken (tegen)

²balk [bo:k] *vb* verhinderen: *~ s.o.'s plans* iemands plannen in de weg staan

³balk [bo:k] *n* balk

Balkans [bo:lkənz] Balkan

ball [bo:l] **1** bal, *(sport only)* worp, schop, slag: *the* ~ *is in your court* nu is het jouw beurt *(also fig); set (of: start) the ~ rolling* de zaak aan het rollen brengen; **2** bol, bolvormig voorwerp^h, bal; **3** prop, kluwen, bol; **4** rond lichaamsdeel^h, bal *(of foot)*, muis *(of hand)*, oogbol, oogappel; **5** kogel; **6** bal^h, dansfeest^h; **7** *(inf)* plezier^h, leut, lol; **8** balspel^h, *(Am)* honkbal^h: *play* ~ met de bal spelen, *(Am)* honkbal spelen, *(fig)* meewerken

ballad [bæləd] ballade

ballast [bæləst] ballast, *(fig)* bagage

ballet [bælee] **1** ballet^h, balletkunst; **2** stuk balletmuziek

balloon [bəloe:n] **1** (lucht)ballon; **2** ballon(netje^h) *(in cartoon)*

ballot [bælət] **1** stem, stembiljet^h, stembriefje^h: *~ box* stembus; *cast one's* ~ zijn stem uitbrengen; **2** stemming, stemronde: *let's take (of: have) a* ~ laten we erover stemmen

ballroom balzaal, danszaal

balm 488

balm [ba:m] balsem *(also fig)*; troost
Baltic [bo:ltik] Baltisch: ~ *Sea* Oostzee
balustrade [bæləstre:d] balustrade
bamboo [bæmbo:] bamboe⁺ʰ
bamboozle [bæmbo:zl] *(inf)* **1** bedriegen, beetnemen: ~ *s.o. out of his money* iem zijn geld afhandig maken; **2** in de war brengen
ban [bæn] **1** verbieden; verbannen, uitsluiten: *he was banned from driving* hij mocht geen auto meer rijden; **2** verwerpen, afwijzen: ~ *the bomb* weg met de atoombom
banal [bəna:l] *(oft depr)* banaal, gewoon, alledaags
banana [bənɑ:nə] banaan
bananas [bənɑ:nəz] *(inf)* knettergek: *go* ~ stapelgek worden
¹**band** [bænd] *n* **1** band *(also fig)*, riem, ring, (dwars)streep *(on animal)*, reep, rand, boordʰ: *a rubber* ~ een elastiekje; **2** bende, groep, troep; **3** band, (dans)orkestjeʰ, fanfare, popgroep
²**band** [bænd] *vb* zich verenigen: ~ *together against* zich als één man verzetten tegen
¹**bandage** [bændidzj] *n* verbandʰ
²**bandage** [bændidzj] *vb* verbinden
b. and b. *bed and breakfast* logiesʰ met ontbijt
bandit [bændit] bandiet
bandsman [bændzmən] muzikant
bandwagon 1 muziekwagen; **2** *(fig)* iets dat algemene bijval vindt: *climb* (of: *jump*) *on the* ~: *a)* met de massa meedoen; *b)* aan de kant van de winnaar gaan staan
bandy [bændie] heen en weer doen bewegen || ~ *words with s.o.* ruzie maken met iem; ~ *about: a)* te pas en te onpas noemen; *b)* verspreiden, rondbazuinen; *have one's name bandied about* voortdurend genoemd worden
bane [been] **1** last, pest, kruisʰ: *the* ~ *of my existence* (of: *life*) een nagel aan mijn doodskist; **2** vloek, verderfʰ
¹**bang** [bæng] *vb* **1** knallen, dreunen; **2** *(with on)* bonzen (op), kloppen, slaan || ~ *about* lawaai maken
²**bang** [bæng] *vb* **1** stoten, bonzen, botsen; **2** dichtgooien, dichtsmijten; **3** smijten, (neer)smakken
³**bang** [bæng] *n* **1** klap, dreun, slag; **2** knal, ontploffing, schotʰ; **3** plotselinge inspanning: *start off with a* ~ hard aan het werk gaan, hard van stapel lopen; *(inf) go off with a* ~ een reuzesucces oogsten
⁴**bang** [bæng] *adv* **1** precies, pats, vlak: ~ *in the face* precies in zijn gezicht; *(inf)* ~ *on* precies goed, raak; ~ *on time* precies op tijd; **2** plof, boem, paf: *go* ~ uiteenbarsten, in elkaar klappen
⁵**bang** [bæng] *interj* boem!, pats!, pang!
bang away 1 *(inf)* hard werken, ploeteren; **2** ratelen, er op los knallen *(firearms)*
banger [bængə] **1** worstjeʰ; **2** stukʰ (knal)vuurwerk
bangle [bænggl] armband
banish [bænisj] verbannen, uitwijzen; toegang ontzeggen, verwijderen: ~ *those thoughts from your mind* zet die gedachten maar uit je hoofd

banishment [bænisjmənt] ballingschap, verbanning
banister [bænistə] **1** (trap)spijl; **2** (trap)leuning
¹**bank** [bæ ngk] *n* **1** bank, mistbank, wolkenbank, sneeuwbank, zandbank, ophoging, aardwal; **2** oever, glooiing; **3** bank *(money, also in games)*: *break the* ~ de bank doen springen
²**bank** [bæ ngk] *vb* **1** *(also with up)* zich opstapelen, een bank vormen: ~ *up* zich ophopen; **2** (over)hellen *(in a bend)*; **3** een bankrekening hebben: *who(m) do you ~ with?* welke bank heb jij?; *(inf)* ~ *on* vertrouwen op
³**bank** [bæ ngk] *vb* **1** opstapelen, ophopen; **2** doen hellen *(eg an aeroplane, road)*, doen glooien; **3** *(with up)* opbanken, afdekken, inrekenen *(fire)*
banker [bæ ngkə] bankier
banking [bæ ngking] bankwezenʰ
banknote bankbiljetʰ
bankrupt [bæ ngkrupt] failliet
banner [bænə] banier *(also fig)*, vaandelʰ
banquet [bæ ngkwit] banketʰ, feestmaalʰ, smulpartij
¹**banter** [bæntə] *n* geplaagʰ, scherts
²**banter** [bæntə] *vb* schertsen
³**banter** [bæntə] *vb* plagen, pesten
baptism [bæptizm] doop: ~ *of fire* vuurdoop
Baptist [bæptist] **1** doper: *John the* ~ Johannes de Doper; **2** doopsgezinde
baptize [bæptajz] dopen
¹**bar** [ba:] *n* **1** langwerpig stukʰ *(of hard material)*, staaf, stang, baar, reep, *(sport)* lat: ~ *of chocolate* reep chocola; ~ *of gold* baar goud; ~ *of soap* stuk zeep; **2** afgrendelend iets, tralie, grendel, slagboom, afsluitboom, *(fig)* obstakelʰ, hindernis: *put behind* ~*s* achter (de) tralies zetten; **3** streep, balk *(on weapon, as mark of distinction)*; **4** bar *(also as part of pub)*, buffetʰ; **5** balie *(in courthouse)*, gerechtʰ, rechtbank: *be tried at (the)* ~ in openbare terechtzitting berecht worden; **6** *the Bar* advocatuur, balie, advocatenstand, *(Am)* orde der juristen: *read* (of: *study) for the Bar* voor advocaat studeren
²**bar** [ba:] *vb* **1** vergrendelen, afsluiten; opsluiten, insluiten: ~ *oneself in* zichzelf binnensluiten; **2** versperren *(also fig)*, verhinderen; **3** verbieden: ~ *s.o. from participation* iem verbieden deel te nemen
³**bar** [ba:] *prep* behalve, uitgezonderd
barb [ba:b] **1** weerhaak, prikkel; **2** steek *(fig)*, hatelijkheid
¹**barbarian** [ba:beəriən] *n* **1** barbaar *(also hist)*, onbeschaafd iem, primitieveling; **2** woesteling
²**barbarian** [ba:beəriən] *adj* barbaars
barbaric [ba:bærik] barbaars, ruw, onbeschaafd, wreed
barbarous [ba:bərəs] barbaars, onbeschaafd, wreed
barbecue [ba:bikjoe:] barbecue; barbecuefeestʰ
barbed [ba:bd] **1** met weerhaken; **2** *(fig)* scherp, bijtend *(remarks, words)* || ~ *wire* prikkeldraad
barber [ba:bə] herenkapper

bar-code streepjescode, barcode
bard [ba:d] bard; dichter
¹**bare** [beə] *adj* **1** naakt: *in his ~ skin* in zijn blootje; *lay ~ blootleggen*; **2** kaal, leeg: *the ~ facts* de naakte feiten; **3** enkel, zonder meer: *the ~ necessities (of life)* het strikt noodzakelijke
²**bare** [beə] *vb* **1** ontbloten: *~ one's teeth* zijn tanden laten zien; **2** blootleggen, onthullen: *~ one's soul* zijn gevoelens luchten
barefaced onbeschaamd, brutaal
barefoot blootsvoets: *walk ~* op blote voeten lopen
barely [beəlie] nauwelijks, amper: *~ enough to eat* nauwelijks genoeg te eten
¹**bargain** [ba:gin] *n* **1** afspraak, akkoordʰ, transactie: *make (of: strike) a ~* tot een akkoord komen; **2** koopjeʰ: *into the ~* op de koop toe
²**bargain** [ba:gin] *vb* onderhandelen, dingen ‖ *more than he ~ed for* meer dan waar hij op rekende
¹**barge** [ba:dzj] *n* schuit, aak; sloep
²**barge** [ba:dzj] *vb (inf)* stommelen: *~ into (of: against) sth.* ergens tegenaan botsen; *~ in: a)* binnenvallen; *b)* zich bemoeien
¹**bark** [ba:k] *n* **1** blaffend geluidʰ, geblafʰ, ruw stemgeluidʰ: *his ~ is worse than his bite* (het is bij hem) veel geschreeuw en weinig wol; **2** schors, bast
²**bark** [ba:k] *vb (with at)* blaffen (tegen): *(fig) ~ at s.o.* iem afblaffen
³**bark** [ba:k] *vb* (uit)brullen, aanblaffen, luid aanprijzen: *~ (out) an order* een bevel schreeuwen
barley [ba:lie] gerst
barman [ba:mən] barman
barn [ba:n] **1** schuur; **2** *(Am)* stal, loods
barnyard [ba:nja:d] boerenerfʰ, hof
barometer [bəroomittə] barometer *(also fig)*, maatstaf
baron [bærən] **1** baron; **2** *(Am)* magnaat
baronet [bærənit] baronet
baroque [bərok] barok
barrack [bærək] **1** barak, keet; **2** *~s* kazerne
barrage [bæra:zj] **1** stuwdam; **2** versperring; **3** spervuurʰ *(also fig)*, barrage
barrel [bærəl] ton, vatʰ ‖ *scrape the ~* zijn laatste duiten bijeenschrapen, de laatste reserves gebruiken; *over a ~* hulpeloos
barren [bærən] **1** onvruchtbaar, steriel, *(also fig)* nutteloos; **2** dor, bar, kaal
¹**barricade** [bærikeed] *n* barricade, versperring
²**barricade** [bærikeed] *vb* barricaderen, versperren, afzetten: *~ oneself in one's room* zich opsluiten in zijn kamer
barrier [bæriə] barrière, hekʰ, slagboom, hindernis
barring [ba:ring] behalve, uitgezonderd: *~ very bad weather* tenzij het zeer slecht weer is; *he's the greatest singer, ~ none* hij is de allerbeste zanger, niemand uitgezonderd
barrister [bæristə] **1** advocaat; **2** *(Am)* jurist
barrow [bæroo] **1** kruiwagen; **2** draagbaar; **3** handkar
bartender *(Am)* barman

¹**barter** [ba:tə] *vb* **1** ruilhandel drijven; **2** loven en bieden
²**barter** [ba:tə] *vb* **1** (with *for*) ruilen (voor, tegen); **2** opgeven *(in exchange for sth)*: *~ away one's freedom* zijn vrijheid prijsgeven
³**barter** [ba:tə] *n* ruilhandel
¹**base** [bees] *n* **1** basis, voetstukʰ, grondlijn, grondvlakʰ: *the ~ of the mountain* de voet van de berg; **2** grondslag, fundamentʰ, *(fig)* uitgangspuntʰ; **3** hoofdbestanddeelʰ; **4** basiskampʰ, basis, hoofdkwartierʰ; **5** *(sport)* honkʰ: *catch s.o. off ~* iem onverwacht treffen
²**base** [bees] *vb* **1** (with *(up)on*) baseren (op), gronden (op) *(also fig)*: *~ oneself on* uitgaan van; *~d (up)on mere gossip* slechts op roddel berustend; **2** vestigen
³**base** [bees] *adj* **1** laag, minderwaardig: *a ~ action* een laffe daad; **2** onedel *(metal)*, onecht *(coin)*
baseball honkbalʰ
baseless [beesləs] ongegrond, ongefundeerd
basement [beesmənt] souterrainʰ, kelder
¹**bash** [bæsj] *vb* botsen, bonken
²**bash** [bæsj] *vb* slaan, beuken: *~ the door down* de deur inbeuken
³**bash** [bæsj] *n* **1** dreun, stoot, mep; **2** *(inf)* fuif ‖ *(inf) have a ~ (at sth.)* iets eens proberen
bashful [bæsjfoel] verlegen
basic [beesik] basis-, fundamenteel; minimum-: *~ data* hoofdgegevens; *~ pay (of: salary)* basisloon
basically [beesiklie] eigenlijk, voornamelijk
basics [beesiks] *(oft inf)* grondbeginselen, basiskennis
basin [beesn] **1** kom, schaal, schotel; **2** waterbekkenʰ, bak; **3** bekkenʰ, stroomgebiedʰ; **4** wasbak, waskom, fonteintjeʰ; **5** bassinʰ, (haven)dokʰ
basis [beesis] *(bases)* basis, fundamentʰ, *(fig)* grondslag, hoofdbestanddeelʰ: *on the ~ of* op grond van
bask [ba:sk] *(also fig)* zich koesteren
basket [ba:skit] mand, korf, schuitjeʰ, gondel, *(basketball)* basket
basketball basketbalʰ
Basque [bæsk] Bask(isch)
¹**bass** [bees] *n* bas ‖ *~ guitar* basgitaar
²**bass** [bæs] *n* baars; zeebaars
bassoon [bəsoe:n] fagot, basson
bastard [ba:stəd, bæstəd] **1** bastaard, onecht kindʰ; **2** *(inf; depr)* smeerlap, schoft; **3** *(inf)* vent: *you lucky ~!* geluksvogel die je bent!
baste [beest] bedruipen *(with fat)*
bastion [bæstiən] bastionʰ *(also fig)*, bolwerkʰ
¹**bat** [bæt] *n* **1** vleermuis; **2** knuppel, *(cricket, table tennis)* batʰ, slaghoutʰ, racketʰ ‖ *(inf) have ~s in the belfry* een klap van de molen gehad hebben; *(inf) off one's own ~* uit eigen beweging, op eigen houtje; *(Am; inf) (right) off the ~* direct
²**bat** [bæt] *vb* **1** batten; **2** knipp(er)en *(eyes): without ~ting an eye(lid)* zonder een spier te vertrekken
batch [bætsj] partij, groep, troep: *a ~ of letters* een

stapel brieven
¹bath [ba:θ] *n* **1** bad^h: *have (of: take) a ~* een bad nemen; **2** zwembad^h; **3** *~s* badhuis^h; kuuroord^h
²bath [ba:θ] *vb* een bad nemen
¹bathe [beeð] *vb* **1** zich baden, zwemmen; **2** *(Am)* een bad nemen, zich wassen; **3** *(with in)* baden (in) *(fig),* opgaan
²bathe [beeð] *vb* **1** baden, onderdompelen: *~d in sunshine* met zon overgoten; **2** betten *(eg wound)*
³bathe [beeð] *n* bad^h, zwempartij
bathroom **1** badkamer; **2** *(euph)* toilet^h, wc
bathtub badkuip
baton [bæton] stok, wapenstok, gummistok, dirigeerstok, *(sport)* estafettestokje^h
battalion [bətæliən] bataljon^h
¹batten [bætn] *n* lat, plank
²batten [bætn] *vb* **1** *(with (up)on)* zich vetmesten (met); **2** *(with (up)on)* parasiteren (op)
¹batter [bætə] *vb* beuken, timmeren: *~ (away) at* inbeuken op
²batter [bætə] *vb* slaan, timmeren op, havenen
battery [bætərie] **1** batterij *(also mil),* reeks: *a ~ of questions* een spervuur van vragen; **2** (elektrische) batterij; accu(mulator); **3** *(law)* aanranding
¹battle [bætl] *n* **1** (veld)slag, gevecht^h, competitie: *fight a losing ~* een hopeloze strijd voeren; **2** overwinning: *youth is half the ~* als je maar jong bent
²battle [bætl] *vb* slag leveren *(also fig),* strijden: *~ through the crowd* zich een weg banen door de menigte
battlefield slagveld^h *(also fig)*
battleground gevechtsterrein^h *(also fig),* slagveld^h
battleship slagschip^h
batty [bætie] *(inf)* getikt
bauxite [bo:ksajt] bauxiet^h
Bavaria [bəveəriə] Beieren
¹bawdy [bo:die] *adj* schuin; vies
²bawdy [bo:die] *n* schuine praat, schuine grap
bawl [bo:l] schreeuwen: *~ at s.o.* iem toebrullen; *~ out* uitfoeteren
¹bay [bee] *n* **1** baai, zeearm, golf; **2** (muur)vak^h; **3** nis, erker; **4** afdeling, vleugel, ruimte *(in bldg etc)*; **5** laurier(boom); **6** luid geblaf^h || *hold (of: keep) at ~* op een afstand houden
²bay [bee] *adj* voskleurig *(horse)*
³bay [bee] *vb* (aan)blaffen, huilen
bayonet [beeənit] bajonet; bajonetsluiting
bazaar [bəza:] bazaar
B.B.C. *British Broadcasting Corporation* BBC
B.C. *before Christ* v.Chr., voor Christus
¹be [bie:] *vb* **1** zijn, bestaan, voorkomen, plaatshebben; **2** geweest (gekomen) zijn: *has the postman been?* is de postbode al geweest?
²be [bie:] *vb* **1** zijn: *she is a teacher* zij is lerares; *the bride-to-be* de aanstaande bruid; *~ that as it may* hoe het ook zij; **2** (+ *indication of size or quantity*) (waard, groot, oud) zijn, kosten, meten, duren: *it's three pounds* het kost drie pond; *it is three minutes* het duurt drie minuten; **3** zijn, zich bevinden,

plaatshebben *(also fig): it was in 1953* het gebeurde in 1953; *what's behind this?* wat steekt hier achter?; **4** zijn, betekenen: *what's it to you?* wat gaat jou dat aan?; **5** bedoeld zijn, dienen: *an axe is to fell trees with* een bijl dient om bomen om te hakken; *(inf) ~ nowhere* ver achterliggen; *as is* zoals hij is
³be [bie:] *vb* **1** aan het ... zijn: *they were reading* ze waren aan het lezen, ze lazen; **2** worden, zijn: *he has been murdered* hij is vermoord; **3** mocht, zou: *if this were to happen, were this to happen* als dit zou gebeuren
be about 1 rondhangen, rondslingeren; **2** er zijn, beschikbaar zijn: *there is a lot of flu about* er is heel wat griep onder de mensen; **3** op het punt staan: *he was about to leave* hij ging net vertrekken
beach [bie:tsj] strand^h, oever
beachcomber strandjutter
beachhead bruggenhoofd^h *(on beach)*
beacon [bie:kən] **1** (vuur)baken^h, vuurtoren, lichtbaken^h; **2** bakenzender, radiobaken^h
bead [bie:d] **1** kraal; **2** *~s* kralen halssnoer^h; **3** druppel, kraal
beadle [bie:dl] bode, ceremoniemeester, pedel *(at university)*
beagle [bie:gl] brak, kleine jachthond
beak [bie:k] snavel, bek, snuit; mondstuk^h
beaker [bie:kə] beker(glas)
¹beam [bie:m] *n* **1** balk; **2** boom, disselboom, ploegboom; **3** straal, stralenbundel; **4** geleide straal, bakenstraal; **5** stralende blik (glimlach)
²beam [bie:m] *vb* stralen, schijnen
bean [bie:n] **1** boon; **2** *(Am; inf)* knikker, kop, hersens || *(inf) spill the ~s* zijn mond voorbijpraten
¹bear [beə] *n* **1** beer; **2** ongelikte beer, bullebak
²bear *vb* **1** dragen: *~ fruit* vruchten voortbrengen, *(fig)* vruchten afwerpen; *~ away a prize, ~ off a price* een prijs in de wacht slepen; **2** (over)brengen; **3** vertonen, hebben: *~ signs of* tekenen vertonen van; **4** hebben (voelen) voor, toedragen, koesteren; **5** verdragen, uitstaan: *his words won't ~ repeating* zijn woorden zijn niet voor herhaling vatbaar; **6** voortbrengen, baren: *borne by* geboren uit
³bear *vb* **1** houden *(of ice)*; **2** dragen *(of wall)*; **3** vruchten voortbrengen, vruchtbaar zijn; **4** (aan)houden *(of direction),* (voort)gaan, lopen: *~ (to the) left* links afslaan; **5** druk uitoefenen, duwen, leunen: *~ hard (of: heavily, severely) (up)on* zwaar drukken op *(fig)*; **6** *(with (up)on)* invloed hebben (op), van invloed zijn (op), betrekking hebben (op)
bearable [beərəbl] draaglijk, te dragen
beard [biəd] **1** baard; **2** weerhaak
bear down persen, druk uitoefenen || *~ (up)on* zwaar drukken op
bearer [beərə] **1** drager: *the ~ of a passport* de houder van een paspoort; **2** bode, boodschapper: *the ~ of this letter* de brenger dezes; **3** toonder *(of cheque etc): pay to ~* betaal aan toonder
bear-hug *(inf)* houdgreep, onstuimige omhelzing
bearing [beəring] **1** verband^h, betrekking: *have no*

~ *on* los staan van; **2** betekenis, strekking; **3** ~*s* positie, ligging, plaats: *get* (of: *take*) *one's* ~*s* zich oriënteren, poolshoogte nemen; **4** het dragen; **5** houding, voorkomen[h], gedrag[h], optreden[h]

be around even aanlopen, bezoeken

bear out (onder)steunen, bekrachtigen, staven: *bear s.o. out* iemands verklaring bevestigen

bear zich (goed) houden, zich redden: ~ *against sth.* ergens tegen opgewassen zijn

bear with geduld hebben met

beast [bie:st] **1** beest[h] *(also fig)*; **2** rund[h]

beastly [bie:stlie] beestachtig: ~ *stench* walgelijke stank; ~ *drunk* stomdronken

¹beat [bie:t] *vb* **1** slaan, bonzen, beuken, woeden, kloppen *(of heart, blood)*, fladderen *(of wing)*; **2** een klopjacht houden; **3** zich (moeizaam) een weg banen

²beat [bie:t] *vb* **1** slaan (op), klutsen, kloppen *(rug)*, fladderen met *(wing)*: *(inf)* ~ *s.o.'s brains out* iem de hersens inslaan; *the recipe to* ~ *all recipes* het recept dat alles slaat; ~ *back* terugslaan, terugdrijven; **2** (uit)smeden, pletten; **3** banen *(path)*; **4** verslaan, eronder krijgen, breken *(record)*: *(inf) can you* ~ *that?* heb je ooit zoiets gehoord?; **5** uitputten: *he was dead* ~ hij was (dood)op; **6** afzoeken; **7** *(Am; inf)* ontlopen *(punishment)*: *(inf)* ~ *it!* smeer 'm!

³beat [bie:t] *n* **1** slag; **2** (vaste) ronde, (vaste) route: *be on one's* ~ zijn ronde doen; **3** *(mus)* ritme[h], beat

¹beat down *vb* **1** neerslaan; **2** intrappen *(door)*; **3** naar beneden brengen, drukken *(price)*; **4** afdingen (bij, op)

²beat down *vb* branden *(of sun)*

beaten **1** veel betreden, gebaand *(of road, track; also fig)*: *be off the* ~ *track* verafgelegen zijn; **2** gesmeed, geplet: ~ *gold* bladgoud; **3** verslagen

beating [bie:ting] afstraffing *(also fig)*: *take some* (of: *a lot of*) ~ moeilijk te overtreffen zijn

beatitude [bie·ætitjoe:d] **1** zaligverklaring; **2** (geluk)zaligheid

beat off afslaan, terugdrijven, afweren

beat up **1** *(inf)* in elkaar slaan; **2** (op)kloppen, klutsen; **3** *(inf)* optrommelen, werven

beautician [bjoe:tisjən] schoonheidsspecialist(e)

beautiful [bjoe:tifoel] **1** mooi, fraai, prachtig; **2** heerlijk, verrukkelijk *(of weather)*

beautify [bjoe:tiffaj] verfraaien, (ver)sieren, mooi maken

beauty [bjoe:tie] **1** schoonheid: *that is the* ~ *of it* dat is het mooie ervan; **2** *(inf)* pracht(exemplaar[h]), juweeltje[h]

beauty parlour schoonheidssalon

beaver [bie:və] bever

beaver away *(inf)* zwoegen, ploeteren

because [bikkoz] **1** omdat, want; **2** (het feit) dat

because of wegens, vanwege

beck [bek] teken[h], knik, gebaar[h]: *be at s.o.'s* ~ *and call* iem op zijn wenken bedienen

beckon [bekkən] wenken, gebaren, een teken geven

¹become [bikkum] *vb* worden, (ge)raken: ~ *mayor*

burgemeester worden

²become [bikkum] *vb (with of)* gebeuren (met), worden (van), aflopen (met)

³become [bikkum] *vb* **1** passen: *it ill* ~*s you* het siert je niet; **2** eer aandoen; **3** (goed) staan *(of clothes)*

becoming [bikkumming] gepast, behoorlijk: *as is* ~ zoals het hoort

¹bed [bed] *n* **1** bed[h], slaapplaats, huwelijk[h], leger[h] *(of animal)*, bloembed[h], tuinbed[h]: ~ *and board* kost en inwoning; ~ *and breakfast* logies met ontbijt; *double* (of: *single*) ~ tweepersoonsbed, eenpersoonsbed; *spare* ~ logeerbed; *wet one's* ~ bedwateren; **2** (rivier)bedding; **3** bed(ding), grondslag, onderlaag, (bodem)laag

²bed [bed] *vb* **1** *(inf)* naar bed gaan met; **2** planten: ~ *out* uitplanten

bedding [bedding] **1** beddengoed[h]; **2** onderlaag, grondslag, bedding; **3** gelaagdheid

bedevil [biddevl] treiteren, dwarszitten, achtervolgen; (ernstig) bemoeilijken

bedfellow bedgenoot, bedgenote

bedlam [bedləm] gekkenhuis[h] *(also fig)*, gesticht[h], *(inf)* heksenketel

Bed(o)uin [beddoein] bedoeïen

be down **1** beneden zijn, minder, gezakt zijn *(lit and fig)*; **2** uitgeteld zijn, *(fig)* somber zijn: *(inf)* ~ *with the flu* geveld zijn door griep; **3** buiten bedrijf zijn, plat liggen *(of computer)*: *(inf)* ~ *on s.o.* iem aanpakken, iem fel bekritiseren; *he is down to his last pound* hij heeft nog maar één pond over

bedpan (onder)steek

bedraggled [bidrægld] **1** doorweekt; **2** verfomfaaid, toegetakeld, sjofel

bedridden [bedridn] bedlegerig

bedstead ledikant[h]

bee [bie:] **1** bij; **2** *(inf)* gril || *(inf) have a* ~ *in one's bonnet (about sth.)*: *a)* door iets geobsedeerd worden; *b)* niet helemaal normaal zijn (op een bepaald punt)

beech [bie:tsj] beuk; beukenhout[h]

¹beef [bie:f] *n* **1** rundvlees[h]: *corned* ~ cornedbeef; **2** *(inf)* kracht, spierballen

²beef [bie:f] *vb (inf)* kankeren, mopperen, zeuren

beefeater **1** koninklijke lijfwacht; **2** hellebaardier vd Tower; **3** *(Am; inf)* Engelsman

beefsteak biefstuk, runderlap(je[h])

beef up *(inf)* versterken, opvoeren

beehive **1** bijenkorf *(also fig)*; **2** suikerbrood[h] *(hairdo)*

beekeeper bijenhouder, imker

¹beep [bie:p] *n* **1** getoeter[h], toet; **2** fluittoon, pieptoon, piep(je[h]) *(indicating time)*

²beep [bie:p] *vb* **1** toeteren; **2** piepen

beeper [bie:pə] pieper, portofoon, semafoon

beer [biə] bier[h], glas[h] bier

beeswax [bijen)was

beet [bie:t] **1** biet; **2** *(Am)* (bieten)kroot, rode biet

beetle [bie:tl] kever, tor

beetroot **1** (bieten)kroot, rode biet; **2** beetwortel, suikerbiet

befall [biffo:l] *(form)* overkomen, gebeuren (met)

befit [biffit] *(form)* passen

be for zijn voor, voorstander zijn van || *you're for it!* er zwaait wat voor je!

¹before [biffo:] *prep* **1** *(time)* vóór, vroeger dan, alvorens: ~ *Christmas* voor Kerstmis; ~ *long* binnenkort; **2** *(place)* voor, voor ... uit, tegenover: *put a bill* ~ *parliament* een wetsontwerp bij het parlement indienen; *put friendship* ~ *love* vriendschap hoger achten dan liefde; ~ *all else* bovenal

²before [biffo:] *adv* **1** voorop, vooraan, ervoor; **2** vroeger, eerder, vooraf: *three weeks* ~ drie weken geleden

³before [biffo:] *conj* alvorens, voor

beforehand [biffo:hænd] vooraf, van tevoren, vooruit

befriend [bifrend] een vriend zijn voor, bijstaan

¹beg [beg] *vb* **1** opzitten *(of dog);* **2** de vrijheid nemen, zo vrij zijn: *I* ~ *to differ* ik ben zo vrij daar anders over te denken

²beg [beg] *vb* **1** bedelen: ~ *for* bedelen om, smeken om; **2** (dringend, met klem) verzoeken, smeken, (nederig) vragen

¹beggar [begə] *n* bedelaar(ster), schooier || ~*s can't be choosers (roughly)* lieverkoekjes worden niet gebakken

²beggar [begə] *vb* te boven gaan: ~ *(all) description* alle beschrijving tarten

begin [bigin] beginnen, aanvangen, starten: *life* ~*s at sixty* met zestig begint het echte leven; *to* ~ *with* om te beginnen, in de eerste plaats

beginning [biginning] **1** begin[h], aanvang: *from* ~ *to end* van begin tot einde; *in the* ~ aanvankelijk; **2** ~*s* (prille) begin[h]

begrudge [bigrudzj] misgunnen, benijden, niet gunnen

beguile [bigajl] **1** bedriegen, verleiden: ~ *into* ertoe verleiden (te); **2** korten, verdrijven: *we* ~*d the time by playing cards* we kortten de tijd met kaartspelen; **3** charmeren, betoveren

beguiling [bigajling] verleidelijk

behalf [bihha:f] *on* ~ *of my father* namens mijn vader; *in my* ~ voor mij

behave [bihheev] zich gedragen, zich goed gedragen

behaviour [bihheeviə] gedrag[h], houding, optreden[h]: *be on one's best* ~ zichzelf van zijn beste kant laten zien

behead [bihhed] onthoofden

¹behind [bihhajnd] *prep* **1** *(place, direction or time; also fig)* achter, voorbij, verder dan, om: *the house* ~ *the church* het huis achter de kerk; *put one's problems* ~ *one* zijn problemen van zich afzetten; **2** *(delay or arrears)* achter op, later dan, onder: *the bus is* ~ *schedule* de bus heeft vertraging; **3** achter, aan de oorsprong van: *the real reasons* ~ *the quarrel* de echte redenen voor de ruzie; **4** achter, ter ondersteuning van: *we are* (of: *stand*) ~ *you* wij staan

achter je, steunen je

²behind [bihhajnd] *adv* **1** *(movement, place or space)* erachter, achteraan, achterop, achterin, achterom, voorbij; **2** *(delay or arrears)* achterop, achter, achterstallig: *they fell* ~ ze raakten achter *(also fig)*

³behind [bihhajnd] *n (inf, euph)* achterste[h]

behindhand [bihhajndhænd] **1** achter(stallig); **2** achter, achterop: *be* ~ *with one's work* achter zijn met zijn werk

behold [bihhoold] *(form)* aanschouwen

beige [beezj] beige[h]

be in 1 binnen zijn, er zijn, aanwezig zijn: *the new fabrics aren't in yet* de nieuwe stoffen zijn nog niet binnen; **2** geaccepteerd zijn, erbij, aanvaard, opgenomen zijn, in de mode zijn, in zijn *(of things):* ~ *on* meedoen aan; *(inf) we're in for a nasty surprise* er staat ons een onaangename verrassing te wachten

being [bie:ing] **1** wezen[h], schepsel[h], bestaan[h], zijn[h], existentie: *bring* (of: *call*) *into* ~ creëren, doen ontstaan; *come into* ~ ontstaan; **2** wezen[h], essentie, aard, het wezenlijke

belated [billeetid] laat

¹belch [beltsj] *vb* **1** boeren; **2** (uit)braken, uitbarsten: *the volcano* ~*ed out rocks* de vulkaan spuwde stenen (uit)

²belch [beltsj] *n* boer, oprisping

beleaguer [billie:gə] belegeren

¹Belgian [beldzjən] *adj* Belgisch

²Belgian [beldzjən] *n* Belg

Belgium [beldzjəm] België

belie [billaj] **1** een valse indruk geven van, tegenspreken; **2** logenstraffen: *the attack* ~*d our hopes for peace* de aanval logenstrafte onze hoop op vrede; **3** niet nakomen

belief [billie:f] **1** (geloofs)overtuiging; **2** geloof[h], vertrouwen[h]: *beyond* ~ ongelofelijk, niet te geloven; **3** geloof[h], mening: *to the best of my* ~ naar mijn beste weten

believe [billie:v] **1** geloven, gelovig zijn; **2** (with *in*) geloven (in), vertrouwen hebben (in); **3** geloven, menen, veronderstellen; **4** geloven, voor waar aannemen: *I'll* ~ *anything of James* James acht ik tot alles in staat

belittle [billitl] onbelangrijk(er) doen lijken, kleineren

bell [bel] klok, bel, belsignaal[h] || *that rings a* ~ dat komt me ergens bekend voor

bellicose [bellikoos] strijdlustig, oorlogszuchtig, agressief

belligerent [billidzjərənt] **1** oorlogvoerend; **2** strijdlustig, uitdagend, agressief

¹bellow [belloo] *vb* loeien, brullen

²bellow [belloo] *n* gebrul[h], geloei[h]

bellows [bellooz] blaasbalg: *a (pair of)* ~ een blaasbalg

belly [bellie] **1** *(inf)* buik, maag, schoot; **2** ronding *(as of a stomach)*, uitstulping, onderkant: *the* ~ *of an aeroplane* de buik van een vliegtuig

bellyache buikpijn

belong [billong] **1** passen, (thuis)horen: *it doesn't ~ here* dat hoort hier niet (thuis); **2** *(inf)* thuishoren, zich thuis voelen, op z'n plaats zijn: *a sense of ~ing* het gevoel erbij te horen

belongings [billongingz] persoonlijke eigendommen, bagage

belong to 1 toebehoren aan, (eigendom) zijn van; **2** horen bij, lid zijn van: *which group do you ~?* bij welke groep zit jij?

beloved [billuvvid] bemind, geliefd

¹below [billoo] *adv* beneden, eronder, onderaan: *she lives in the flat ~* ze woont in de flat hieronder; *see ~* zie verder

²below [billoo] *prep* **1** onder, beneden, lager (gelegen) dan, *(fig)* (verscholen, verborgen) achter: *the flat ~ ours* de flat onder de onze; **2** ondergeschikt, lager dan, minder dan: *~ average* minderwaardig, slecht; *~ the average* onder het gemiddelde

¹belt [belt] *n* **1** gordel, (broek)riem, ceintuur; **2** drijfriem: *fan ~* ventilatorriem; **3** (transport)band, lopende band; **4** *(esp as second part of compound)* zone, klimaatstreek, klimaatgebiedʰ: *a ~ of low pressure* een lagedrukgebied; *hit below the ~* onder de gordel slaan; *tighten one's ~, (Am also) pull one's ~ in* de buikriem aanhalen; *under one's ~* in zijn bezit, binnen

²belt [belt] *vb* **1** omgorden; **2** een pak slaag geven (met een riem) ‖ *~ out* brullen, bulken

belt up zijn veiligheidsgordel aandoen

bemoan [bimmoon] *(form)* beklagen

bemused [bimjoe:zd] **1** verbijsterd, verdwaasd; **2** verstrooid

bench [bentsj] **1** bank, zitbank; **2** (parlements)zetel, bank *(in House of Commons)*; **3** rechterstoel; **4** werkbank; **5** *(sport)* reservebank, strafbank(jeʰ); **6** rechtbank, de rechters; **7** *(sport)* de reservebank, de reservespelers

bench-mark standaard, maatstaf

¹bend [bend] *n* **1** buiging, kromming, knik; **2** bocht, draai: *a sharp ~ in the road* een scherpe bocht in de weg; *(go) (a)round the ~* knettergek (worden)

²bend [bend] *vb* buigen, zwenken: *~ down* zich bukken, vooroverbuigen; *~ over backwards* zich vreselijk uitsloven

³bend [bend] *vb* **1** buigen, krommen, verbuigen ‖ *(fig) ~ the rules* de regels naar zijn hand zetten; *bend down* naar beneden buigen; **2** onderwerpen, (doen) buigen, plooien: *~ s.o. to one's will* iem naar zijn hand zetten

¹beneath [binnie:θ] *adv* eronder, daaronder, onderaan

²beneath [binnie:θ] *prep* **1** onder, beneden, lager dan; **2** achter, verborgen achter; **3** onder, onder de invloed van: *bent ~ his burden* onder zijn last gebukt; **4** beneden, onder, beneden de waardigheid van: *he thinks manual labour is ~ him* hij vindt zichzelf te goed voor handenarbeid

benediction [benniddiksjən] *(rel)* zegening

benefactor [bennifæktə] weldoener

beneficent [binneffisnt] weldadig

beneficial [benniffisjl] voordelig, nuttig, heilzaam

beneficiary [benniffisjərie] begunstigde

¹benefit [benniffit] *n* **1** voordeelʰ, profijtʰ, hulp: *give s.o. the ~ of the doubt* iem het voordeel van de twijfel geven; **2** uitkering, steun, steungeldʰ; **3** benefietʰ, liefdadigheidsvoorstelling, benefiet-

²benefit [benniffit] *vb* voordeel halen, baat vinden

³benefit [benniffit] *vb* ten goede komen aan, goed doen voor

benevolent [binnevvələnt] **1** welwillend, goedgunstig; **2** liefdadig, vrijgevig

benign [binnajn] **1** vriendelijk; **2** zacht, gunstig, heilzaam: *a ~ climate* een zacht klimaat; **3** goedaardig: *a ~ tumour* een goedaardig gezwel

benignant [binnignənt] **1** beminnelijk, welwillend; **2** goedaardig

¹bent *n* neiging, aanleg, voorliefde, zwakʰ

²bent *adj* **1** afwijkend, krom, illegaal; **2** *(inf)* omkoopbaar; **3** *(vulg)* homoseksueel; **4** vastbesloten: *~ on* uit op

be off 1 *(inf)* ervandoor gaan *(also fig)*, vertrekken, weg zijn, wegwezen, *(sport)* starten, weg zijn, beginnen *(talking): ~ to a bad start* slecht van start gaan; **2** verwijderd zijn *(also fig): Easter was two weeks off* het was nog twee weken vóór Pasen; **3** afgelast zijn, niet doorgaan; **4** *(inf)* bedorven zijn *(of food);* **5** afgesloten zijn *(of water, gas, electricity): (inf) be badly off* er slecht voorstaan

¹be on *vb* **1** aan (de gang) zijn, aan staan *(of light, radio etc): the match is on* de wedstrijd is bezig; **2** gevorderd zijn: *it was well on into the night* het was al diep in de nacht; **3** doorgaan, gehandhaafd worden: *the party is on* het feest gaat door; **4** *(inf)* toegestaan zijn: *that's not on!* dat doe je niet!; **5** op het toneel staan, spelen *(of actor);* **6** op het programma staan *(radio, TV, play): (inf) ~ about sth.* het hebben over iets, *(depr)* altijd maar zeuren over iets; *(inf) ~ to sth.* iets in de gaten hebben

²be on *vb + prep (inf)* op kosten zijn van, betaald worden door: *the drinks are on John* John trakteert

be out 1 (er)uit zijn, (er)buiten zijn, weg zijn, er niet (meer) zijn; **2** *(inf)* uit zijn, voorbij zijn: *before the year is out* voor het jaar voorbij is; **3** uit(gedoofd) zijn; **4** openbaar (gemaakt) zijn, gepubliceerd zijn: *the results are out* de resultaten zijn bekend; **5** *(inf)* onmogelijk zijn, niet mogen: *rough games are out!* geen ruwe spelletjes!; **6** ernaast zitten: *his forecast was well out* zijn voorspelling was er helemaal naast; **7** in staking zijn; **8** laag zijn *(of tide): the tide is out* het is laagtij; **9** *(cricket, baseball)* uit zijn: *(inf) ~ to do sth.* van plan zijn iets te doen; *~ for oneself* zijn eigen belangen dienen

be out of 1 uit zijn, buiten zijn: *~ it* er niet bij horen; **2** zonder zitten: *he is out of a job* hij zit zonder werk; *we're out of sugar* we hebben geen suiker meer; *(inf) be well out of it* er mooi van af (gekomen) zijn

¹be over *vb* **1** voorbij, over zijn: *(inf) that's over and*

done with dat is voor eens en altijd voorbij; **2** overschieten, overblijven: *there's a bit of fabric over* er schiet een beetje stof over; **3** op bezoek zijn *(from a distant country): Henk is over from Australia* Henk is over uit Australië

²be over *vb* + *prep* (with *all*) *(inf)* **1** overal bekend zijn in: *it's all over the office* het hele kantoor weet ervan; **2** niet kunnen afblijven van, (overdreven) enthousiast begroeten

bequeath [bikwie:ð] *(form)* vermaken, nalaten

bereavement [birrie:vmənt] **1** sterfgeval[h], overlijden[h]; **2** verlies[h]: *we sympathize with you in your ~* wij betuigen onze oprechte deelneming met uw verlies

beret [berree] baret

berry [berrie] bes

berserk [bəza:k] woest, razend: *go ~* razend worden

¹berth [bə:θ] *n* **1** kooi, hut; **2** ligplaats, ankerplaats, aanlegplaats

²berth [bə:θ] *vb* aanleggen, ankeren

beseech [bissie:tsj] smeken, dringend verzoeken

beset [bisset] **1** *(esp passive)* belegeren *(also fig)*, overvallen, omsingelen: *young people, ~ by doubts* door twijfel overvallen jongeren; **2** insluiten, versperren, bezetten

beside [bissajd] naast, bij, langs, dichtbij, vergeleken bij: *it's ~ the point* het doet hier niet ter zake; *be ~ oneself with joy* buiten zichzelf van vreugde zijn

¹besides [bissajdz] *adv* **1** bovendien, daarenboven: *Tina bought a new suit and a blouse ~* Tina kocht een nieuw pak en ook nog een bloes; **2** anders, daarnaast, behalve dat; **3** trouwens

²besides [bissajdz] *prep* behalve, buiten, naast: *I can do nothing ~ wait* ik kan alleen maar wachten

besiege [bissie:dzj] **1** belegeren; **2** bestormen: *~ s.o. with questions about* iem bestormen met vragen over

bespatter [bispætə] **1** bespatten; **2** bekladden *(also fig)*, belasteren, uitschelden

¹best [best] *adj* best(e) ‖ *~ man* getuige *(of bridegroom)*, bruidsjonker; *the ~ part of* het merendeel van

²best [best] *adv* **1** (het) best: *~ before* ten minste houdbaar tot; **2** meest: *those ~ able to pay* zij die het gemakkelijkste kunnen betalen

³best [best] *n* (de, het) beste: *with the ~ of intentions* met de beste bedoelingen; *to the ~ of my knowledge (and belief)* voor zover ik weet; *at ~* op z'n best (genomen), hoogstens; *at the ~ of times* onder de gunstigste omstandigheden; *get the ~ of it* de overhand krijgen; *it is (all) for the ~* het komt allemaal wel goed

bestial [bestiəl] *(also fig)* beestachtig, dierlijk

bestow [bistoo] verlenen, schenken

best seller 1 bestseller, succesartikel[h], -product[h]; **2** successchrijver

¹bet [bet] *n* **1** weddenschap: *lay* (of: *make, place) a bet (on sth.)* wedden (op iets); **2** inzet; **3** iets waarop

men wedt, kans, keuze: *your best ~ is* je maakt de meeste kans met

²bet [bet] *vb* **1** wedden, verwedden: *~ on sth.* op iets wedden; **2** *(inf)* wedden, zeker (kunnen) zijn van

be through 1 klaar zijn, er doorheen zijn: *I'm through with my work* ik ben klaar met mijn werk; **2** *(inf)* erdoor zitten, de brui aan geven, afgedaan hebben *(of things): ~ with sth.* iets beu zijn; *I'm through with you* ik trek m'n handen van je af; **3** verbonden zijn, verbinding hebben

be to 1 moeten: *what am I to do* wat moet ik doen?; **2** (+ *negation)* mogen: *visitors are not to feed the animals* bezoekers mogen de dieren niet voeren; **3** gaan, zullen: *we are to be married next year* we gaan volgend jaar trouwen; **4** zijn te: *Molly is nowhere to be found* Molly is nergens te vinden

betray [bitree] **1** verraden, in de steek laten; **2** verraden, uitbrengen, verklappen: *his eyes ~ed his thoughts* zijn ogen verraadden zijn gedachten

betrayal [bitreeəl] (daad van) verraad[h]

betrothal [bitrooðl] verloving

betrothed [bitrooðd] **1** verloofde, aanstaande (bruid, bruidegom); **2** verloofden, aanstaande bruid en bruidegom

¹better [bettə] *adj* **1** beter: *~ luck next time!* volgende keer beter!; *he is little ~ than a thief* hij is nauwelijks beter dan een dief; **2** groter, grootste *(part): the ~ part of the day* het grootste gedeelte van de dag; **3** hersteld, genezen: *I'm none the ~ for it* ik ben er niet beter van geworden

²better [bettə] *adv* **1** beter; **2** meer: *I like prunes ~ than figs* ik hou meer van pruimen dan van vijgen

³better [bettə] *n* **1** *~s* beteren[h], meerderen, superieuren; **2** iets beters; **3** verbetering: *change for the ~* ten goede veranderen; *his emotions got the ~ of him* hij werd door zijn emoties overmand

¹between [bitwie:n] *prep* tussen *(two)*, onder: *~ school, her music and her friends she led a busy life* met de school, haar muziek en haar vrienden, had ze alles bij elkaar een druk leven; *they wrote the book ~ them* ze schreven het boek samen; *~ you and me, ~ ourselves* onder ons (gezegd); *I was sitting ~ my two sisters* ik zat tussen mijn twee zussen in

²between [bitwie:n] *adv* ertussen, tussendoor: *two gardens with a fence ~* twee tuinen met een schutting ertussen

betwixt [bitwikst] (er)tussen

be up 1 in een hoge(re) positie zijn *(also fig): petrol's up again* de benzine is weer duurder geworden; **2** op zijn, opstaan, wakker zijn; **3** op zijn, over zijn: *(inf) it's all up with him* het is met hem gedaan; **4** ter discussie staan, in aanmerking komen: *~ for discussion* ter discussie staan; **5** zijn, wonen, studeren; **6** aan de gang zijn, gaande zijn: *what's up with you?* wat is er met jou aan de hand?; *~ against a problem* op een probleem gestoten zijn; *(inf) ~ against it* in de puree zitten; *be well up in sth.* goed op de hoogte zijn van iets

be up to 1 komen tot: *I'm up to my ears in work* ik

zit tot over m'n oren in het werk; **2** in z'n schild voeren, uit zijn op: *what are you up to now?* wat voer je nu weer in je schild?; **3** *(esp with negation)* voldoen aan, beantwoorden aan: *it wasn't up to our expectations* het beantwoordde niet aan onze verwachtingen; **4** *(with negation or interrogative)* aankunnen, berekend zijn op, aandurven: *he isn't up to this job* hij kan deze klus niet aan; *it's up to you* het is jouw zaak

beverage [bevvəridzj] drank: *alcoholic ~s* alcoholhoudende dranken

bewail [biwweel] betreuren

beware [biwweə] oppassen, op zijn hoede zijn, voorzichtig zijn: *~ of the dog* pas op voor de hond

bewilder [biwwildə] verbijsteren, van zijn stuk brengen

bewitch [biwwitsj] beheksen; betoveren, bekoren

be with *(inf)* **1** (kunnen) volgen, (nog) snappen: *are you still with me?* volg je me nog?; **2** aan de kant staan van, op de hand zijn van, partij kiezen voor; **3** horen bij: *we are with the coach party* wij horen bij het busgezelschap

¹beyond [bijjond] *adv* **1** verder, daarachter, aan de overzijde, daarna; **2** daarenboven, meer, daarbuiten

²beyond [bijjond] *prep* **1** voorbij, achter, verder dan: *the hills ~ the city* de heuvels achter de stad; **2** naast, buiten, behalve, meer dan: *~ hope* er is geen hoop meer; *it is ~ me* dat gaat mijn verstand te boven

³beyond [bijjond] *n* het onbekende, het hiernamaals: *the great ~* het grote onbekende

¹bias [bajjəs] *n* **1** neiging, tendens, vooroordeelʰ, vooringenomenheid: *without ~* onbevooroordeeld; **2** *(one-sided weighting)* eenzijdige verzwaring *(of ball)*, afwijking *(in shape or movement of ball)*, effectʰ

²bias [bajjəs] *vb* bevooroordeeld maken, beïnvloeden: *he was ~ed against foreigners* hij zat vol vooroordelen tegen buitenlanders

biased [bajjəst] **1** vooringenomen, bevooroordeeld; **2** tendentieus, in een bepaalde richting sturend

bib [bib] slab, slabbetjeʰ

bible [bajbl] bijbel *(also fig)*

biblical [biblikl] bijbels

bibliographer [biblie·ogrəfə] bibliograaf

bibliography [biblie·ogrəfie] bibliografie, literatuurlijst

bicarbonate [bajka:bənət] bicarbonaatʰ, zuiveringszoutʰ: *~ of soda* natriumbicarbonaat, zuiveringszout

bicker [bikkə] ruziën

¹bicycle [bajsikl] *n* fiets

²bicycle [bajsikl] *vb* fietsen

¹bid [bid] *vb* **1** bevelen, gelasten; **2** heten, zeggen: *~ s.o. farewell* iem vaarwel zeggen; **3** (uit)nodigen

²bid [bid] *vb* **1** bieden, een bod doen (van); **2** een prijsopgave indienen; **3** dingen: *~ for the public's favour* naar de gunst van het publiek dingen

³bid [bid] *n* **1** bodʰ; **2** prijsopgave, offerte; **3** *(cards)* bodʰ, beurt (om te bieden); **4** poging *(to obtain sth)*, gooi: *a ~ for the presidency* een gooi naar het presidentschap

bidder [biddə] bieder: *the highest ~* de meestbiedende

bidding [bidding] **1** het bieden; **2** gebodʰ, bevelʰ: *do s.o.'s ~* iemands bevelen uitvoeren, *(depr)* naar iemands pijpen dansen

bide [bajd]: *~ one's time* zijn tijd afwachten

biennial [bajjenniəl] tweejarig

bifocals [bajfooklz] dubbelfocusbril

¹big [big] *adj* **1** groot, omvangrijk, dik, zwaar: *~ game* grof wild; *~ money* grof geld, het grote geld; *~ with child* (hoog)zwanger; **2** belangrijk, invloedrijk, voornaam, *(inf)* langverwacht: *~ business* het groot kapitaal, de grote zakenwereld; **3** groot, ouder, volwassen: *my ~ sister* mijn grote zus; **4** *(inf)* groot(s), hoogdravend, ambitieus: *(inf)* have ~ ideas* ambitieus zijn, het hoog in de bol hebben; *be too ~ for one's boots* het hoog in de bol hebben; *(iron)* ~ deal!* reusachtig!, nou, geweldig!; *what's the ~ hurry?* vanwaar die haast?; *what's the ~ idea?* wat is hier aan de hand?

²big [big] *adv (inf)* veel, duur, ruim: *pay ~ for sth.* veel voor iets betalen

bigamy [bigəmie] bigamie, met twee personen gelijktijdig gehuwd zijn

bigheaded *(inf)* verwaand

bigot [bigət] dweper, fanaticus

bigoted [bigətid] onverdraagzaam

bigotry [bigətrie] onverdraagzaamheid

big-time top-, eersteklas(-)

bigwig *(inf; oft iron)* hoge ome, hoge piet

bike [bajk] *(inf)* **1** fiets; **2** *(Am)* motorfiets

bilateral [bajlætərəl] **1** tweezijdig, tweevoudig; **2** bilateraal, wederzijds (bindend), tussen twee landen (partijen)

bilberry [bilbərie] bosbes

bile [bajl] **1** gal; **2** galstoornis; **3** *(fig)* zwartgalligheid, humeurigheid

bilingual [bajlinggwəl] tweetalig

bilious [biliəs] **1** gal-, galachtig, gallig; **2** zwartgallig, humeurig

¹bill [bil] *n* **1** rekening, factuur, nota: *foot the ~ (for)* de hele rekening betalen (voor); **2** lijst, aanplakbiljetʰ, (strooi)biljetʰ, programmaʰ: *~ of fare* menu; *stick no ~s* verboden aan te plakken; **3** certificaatʰ, bewijsʰ, brief, rapportʰ; **4** bek, snavel, neus; **5** *(Am)* (bank)biljetʰ; **6** *(fin)* wissel, schuldbekentenis; **7** wetsvoorstelʰ, wetsontwerpʰ: *fill (of: fit) the ~* geschikt zijn, aan iemands wensen tegemoet komen

²bill [bil] *vb* **1** aankondigen, aanplakken; **2** op de rekening zetten, de rekening sturen

billboard [bilbo:d] *(Am)* aanplakbordʰ, reclamebordʰ

¹billet [billit] *n* **1** kwartierʰ, bestemming, verblijfplaats; **2** inkwartieringsbevelʰ

²billet [billit] *vb* inkwartieren, onderbrengen: *the*

troops were ~ed at our school de troepen werden ondergebracht in onze school

billiards [bɪlliədz] (Engels) biljart^h, het biljartspel

billion [bɪlliən] miljard, duizend miljoen, *(fig)* talloos

¹billow [bɪlloo] *n* **1** (zware) golf, hoge deining; **2** *(fig)* golf, vloedgolf, zee

²billow [bɪlloo] *vb* deinen, golven, bol staan: *the ~ing sea* de golvende zee

billy goat (geiten)bok

bimonthly [bajmʌnθlie] tweemaandelijks

bin [bin] vergaarbak, bak, mand, trommel, vuilnisbak, broodtrommel

binary [bajnərie] binair, tweevoudig, dubbel(-)

¹bind [bajnd] *vb* (aaneen)plakken, zich (ver)binden, vast worden

²bind [bajnd] *vb* **1** (vast)binden, bijeenbinden, boeien; **2** bedwingen, aan banden leggen, hinderen: *be snow-bound* vastzitten in de sneeuw; **3** verplichten, verbinden, dwingen: *she is bound to come* ze moet komen, ze zal zeker komen; *~ s.o. to secrecy* iem tot geheimhouding verplichten; **4** (in)binden *(book),* van een band voorzien: *~ (up) a wound* een wond verbinden; *I'll be bound* ik ben er absoluut zeker van; *he is bound up in his job* hij gaat helemaal op in zijn werk

binder [bajndə] **1** binder *(also agriculture; also machine),* boekbinder; **2** band, snoer^h, touw^h, windsel^h; **3** map, omslag^{+h}, ringband; **4** bindmiddel^h

bindery [bajndərie] (boek)binderij

¹binding [bajnding] *n* band, boekband, verband^h

²binding [bajnding] *adj* bindend

binge [bindzj] *(inf)* feest^h, braspartij: *go on the ~* feesten, gaan stappen

binoculars [binnokjoeləz] (verre)kijker, veldkijker, toneelkijker

biochemistry [bajjookemmistrie] biochemie

biodegradable [bajjoodigreedəbl] (biologisch) afbreekbaar

biographer [bajjogrəfə] biograaf, biografe

biography [bajjogrəfie] biografie, levensbeschrijving

biological [bajjəlodzjikl] biologisch

biologist [bajjollədzjist] bioloog

biology [bajjollədzjie] biologie

bionic [bajjonnik] **1** bionisch; **2** *(inf)* supervlug, supersterk

biosphere [bajjəsfiə] biosfeer

bipartite [bajpa:tajt] tweedelig, tweeledig, tweezijdig: *a ~ contract* een tweezijdig contract

biplane [bajpleen] tweedekker

birch [bə:tsj] **1** berk(enboom); **2** berkenhout^h

bird [bə:d] **1** vogel: *~ of passage* trekvogel, *(fig)* passant, doortrekkend reiziger; *~ of prey* roofvogel; **2** *(inf)* vogel, kerel; **3** *(inf)* stuk^h, meisje^h: *they are ~s of a feather* ze hebben veel gemeen; *kill two ~s with one stone* twee vliegen in één klap slaan; *the ~ is* (of: *has) flown* de vogel is gevlogen; *(inf) give s.o. the ~* iem uitfluiten; *a ~ in the hand (is worth two in the*

bush) beter één vogel in de hand dan tien in de lucht; *~s of a feather flock together* soort zoekt soort

bird's-eye panoramisch, in vogelvlucht: *a ~ view of the town* een panoramisch gezicht op de stad

biro [bajroo] balpen

birth [bə:θ] **1** geboorte, *(fig)* ontstaan^h, begin^h, oorsprong: *give ~ to* het leven schenken aan; **2** afkomst, afstamming: *of noble ~* van adellijke afkomst; *he is French by ~* hij is Fransman van geboorte

birthmark moedervlek

biscuit [biskit] **1** biscuit^h, cracker; **2** *(Am)* zacht rond koekje^h

bisect [bajsekt] in tweeën delen, splitsen, halveren

bishop [bisjəp] **1** bisschop; **2** *(chess)* loper

bit 1 beetje^h, stukje^h, kleinigheid: *~s and pieces, ~s and bobs* stukken en brokken; *not a ~ better* geen haar beter; *not a ~ (of it)* helemaal niet(s), geen zier; **2** ogenblikje^h, momentje^h: *wait a ~!* wacht even!; **3** (ge)bit^h *(mouthpiece for horse);* **4** boorijzer^h; **5** schaafijzer^h, schaafbeitel, schaafmes^h: *take the ~ between its teeth: a)* op hol slaan *(of horse); b)* (te) hard van stapel lopen; **6** bit^h *(smallest unit of information): (inf) do one's ~* zijn steen(tje) bijdragen; *(inf) ~ by ~* bij beetjes, stukje voor stukje

bitch [bitsj] **1** teef, wijfje^h *(of dog, fox);* **2** *(depr)* teef, kreng (ve wijf)

¹bite [bajt] *vb* **1** bijten, toebijten, (toe)happen *(also fig),* zich (gemakkelijk) laten beetnemen, steken, prikken *(of insects): (fig) ~ one's lip(s)* zich verbijten; **2** bijten, inwerken *(of acids; also fig);* **3** voelbaar worden, effect hebben *(esp with sth negative): ~ off more than one can chew* te veel hooi op zijn vork nemen; *once bitten, twice shy (roughly)* door schade en schande wordt men wijs

²bite [bajt] *n* **1** beet, hap; **2** hap(je^h), beetje^h *(food): have a ~ to eat* iets eten; **3** beet *(when fishing);* **4** vinnigheid, bits(ig)heid, scherpte: *there was a ~ in the air* er hing een vinnige kou in de lucht

¹bitter [bittə] *adj* bitter *(also fig),* bijtend, scherp, venijnig, verbitterd

²bitter [bittə] *n* **1** bitter^h (bier); **2** bitterheid, het bittere || *take the ~ with the sweet* het nemen zoals het valt

bivouac [bivvoe·æk] bivak^h

biweekly [bajwie:klie] veertiendaags, tweewekelijks, om de veertien dagen

bizarre [bizza:] bizar, zonderling

¹blab [blæb] *vb* zijn mond voorbij praten, loslippig zijn

²blab [blæb] *vb* (er)uit flappen

blabbermouth *(depr)* kletskous

¹black [blæk] *adj* **1** zwart^h, (zeer) donker, *(fig also)* duister: *be in s.o.'s ~ book(s)* bij iem slecht aangeschreven staan; *Black Death* de Zwarte Dood *(plague epidemic); ~ eye* donker oog, blauw oog *(after blow); ~ market* zwarte markt; *~ sheep* zwart schaap *(fig); ~ spot* zwarte plek, rampenplek *(where many accidents happen);* ~ *tie: a)* zwart strikje; *b)* smoking; **2** zwart, vuil, besmeurd; **3** zwart, (zeer) slecht, somber, onvriendelijk: *give s.o. a ~ look* iem onvriendelijk aankijken; *~ ice* ijzel; *~ and blue* bont en blauw *(beaten)*

²black [blæk] *n* **1** zwart: *~ and white* zwart-wit *(film; also fig);* **2** (roet)zwart^h, zwarte kleurstof; **3** zwarte, neger(in); **4** zwart schaakstuk^h, zwarte damsteen

³black [blæk] *vb* **1** zwart maken, poetsen *((black) shoes);* **2** bevuilen; **3** besmet verklaren *(ship's cargo, by strikers)* || *~ s.o.'s eye* iem een blauw oog slaan

bl_ackberry [blækbərie] **1** braam(struik); **2** braam(bes)

bl_ackbird merel

bl_ackboard (school)bord^h

bl_ackcurrant *(bot)* zwarte bes

bl_acken [blækən] zwart maken, bekladden *(also fig): ~ s.o.'s reputation* iem zwart maken

bl_ackguard [blæga:d] schurk, bandiet

bl_ackhead mee-eter, vetpuistje^h

¹bl_acklist *n* zwarte lijst

¹bl_acklist *vb* op de zwarte lijst plaatsen

¹bl_ackmail *n* afpersing, chantage

²bl_ackmail *vb* chanteren, (geld) afpersen van, afdwingen (onder dreiging): *~ s.o. into sth.* iem iets afdwingen

bl_ackout **1** verduistering; **2** black-out, tijdelijke bewusteloosheid, tijdelijk geheugenverlies^h, tijdelijke blindheid

bl_acksmith smid, hoefsmid

bl_adder [blædə] blaas

blade [bleed] **1** lemmet^h *(of knife),* blad^h *(of axe, saw),* kling *(of sword),* (scheer)mesje^h, dunne snijplaat, ijzer^h *(of skate);* **2** blaadje^h *(eg of grass),* halm

¹blame [bleem] *vb* **1** de schuld geven aan, verwijten, iets kwalijk nemen: *I don't ~ Jane* ik geef Jane geen ongelijk; *he is to ~* het is zijn schuld; **2** afkeuren, veroordelen

²blame [bleem] *n* schuld, blaam, verantwoording *(for sth bad): bear* (of: *take) the ~* de schuld op zich nemen

bl_ameless [bleemləs] onberispelijk, vlekkeloos, onschuldig

bland [blænd] **1** (zacht)aardig, vriendelijk; **2** mild, niet te gekruid, zacht; **3** neutraal, nietszeggend; **4** flauw, saai; **5** nuchter, koel

¹blank [blæŋk] *adj* **1** leeg, blanco, onbeschreven: *a ~ cartridge* een losse patroon; *a ~ cheque* een blanco cheque; **2** uitdrukkingsloos, onbegrijpend, ongeïnteresseerd: *a ~ look* een wezenloze blik; *a ~ refusal* een botte weigering

²blank [blæŋk] *n* **1** leegte, leemte: *his memory is a ~* hij weet zich niets meer te herinneren; **2** blanco formulier^h; **3** losse patroon *(of gun),* losse flodder; **4** niet, niet in de prijzen vallend lot^h: *draw a ~* niet in de prijzen vallen, *(fig)* bot vangen

¹bl_anket [blæŋkit] *n* (wollen) deken, bedekking, *(fig)* (dikke) laag

²bl_anket [blæŋkit] *adj* allesomvattend, algemeen

geldig: *a ~ insurance* een pakketverzekering; *a ~ rule* een algemene regel

blare [bleə] schallen, lawaai maken, luid klinken

bl_asphemy [blæsfəmie] (gods)lastering, blasfemie

¹blast [bla:st] *n* **1** (wind)vlaag, rukwind; **2** sterke luchtstroom *(eg with explosion);* **3** explosie *(also fig),* uitbarsting; **4** stoot *(eg on trumpet),* (claxon)signaal^h || *he was working at full ~* hij werkte op volle toeren

²blast [bla:st] *vb* **1** opblazen, doen exploderen, bombarderen; **2** vernietigen, verijdelen, ruïneren; **3** *(euph)* verwensen, vervloeken: *~ him!* laat hem naar de maan lopen!

bl_asted [bla:stid] *(inf)* **1** getroffen *(by lightning etc);* **2** verschrompeld, verdwenen

bl_ast furnace hoogoven

blast-off lancering *(of rocket)*

bl_atant [bleetənt] **1** schaamteloos, onbeschaamd; **2** overduidelijk, opvallend: *a ~ lie* een regelrechte leugen; **3** hinderlijk, ergerlijk

¹bl_ather [blæðə] *vb* dom kletsen

²bl_ather [blæðə] *n* geklets^h, onzin, nonsens

¹blaze [bleez] *n* **1** vlammen(zee), (verwoestend) vuur^h, brand; **2** uitbarsting, plotselinge uitval: *a ~ of anger* een uitbarsting van woede; **3** felle gloed *(of light, colour),* vol licht^h, schittering

²blaze [bleez] *vb* **1** (fel) branden, gloeien, in lichterlaaie staan, *(also fig)* in vuur en vlam staan *(of rage, excitement): the quarrel ~d up* de ruzie laaide op; **2** (fel) schijnen, verlicht zijn, schitteren

³blaze [bleez] *vb (also fig)* banen *(road, trail),* aangeven, merken: *~ a trail* een pad banen, een nieuwe weg inslaan

blaze away 1 oplaaien *(of fire),* oplichten, opvlammen; **2** erop los schieten

¹bleach [blie:tsj] *vb* bleken, bleek worden (maken), (doen) verbleken

²bleach [blie:tsj] *n* bleekmiddel^h

bleak [blie:k] **1** guur *(eg of weather),* troosteloos, grauw; **2** ontmoedigend, deprimerend, somber: *~ prospects* sombere vooruitzichten; **3** onbeschut, aan weer en wind blootgesteld, kaal

¹bleat [blie:t] *vb* blaten, blèren, mekkeren, *(fig)* zeuren, zaniken

²bleat [blie:t] *n* blatend geluid^h, geblaat^h, *(fig)* gezanik^h

¹bleed [blie:d] *vb* **1** bloeden, bloed verliezen: *(fig) her heart ~s for the poor* ze heeft diep medelijden met de armen; **2** uitlopen, doorlopen *(of colour);* **3** (vloeistof) afgeven, bloeden, afscheiden *(eg of plant);* **4** uitgezogen worden, bloeden, afgezet worden

²bleed [blie:d] *vb* **1** doen bloeden, bloed afnemen van, aderlaten; **2** uitzuigen, laten bloeden; **3** onttrekken *(eg liquid)*

¹bleep [blie:p] *n* piep, hoge pieptoon

²bleep [blie:p] *vb* (op)piepen, oproepen met piepsignaal

bl_eeper [blie:pə] pieper *(of paging system)*

blemish [blemmisj] vlek *(also fig)*, smet, onvolkomenheid

¹blend [blend] *vb* zich vermengen, bij elkaar passen

²blend [blend] *vb* mengen, combineren

³blend [blend] *n* mengsel[h] *(eg of tea, coffee, whisky)*, melange, mengeling

blender [blendə] mengbeker, mixer

bless [bles] **1** zegenen, (in)wijden: ~ *oneself* een kruis slaan, *(fig)* zich gelukkig prijzen; **2** Gods zegen vragen voor; **3** begunstigen, zegenen; **4** vereren *(eg God)*, aanbidden, loven

blessed [blessid] **1** heilig, (door God) gezegend; **2** gelukkig, (geluk)zalig, gezegend: *the whole* ~ *day* de godganse dag; *every* ~ *thing* alles, maar dan ook alles

blessing [blessing] **1** zegen(ing): *a* ~ *in disguise* een geluk bij een ongeluk; *count your* ~*!* wees blij met wat je hebt!; **2** goedkeuring, aanmoediging, zegen

¹blight [blajt] *n* **1** plantenziekte, meeldauw, soort bladluis; **2** afzichtelijkheid, afschuwelijkheid; **3** vloek

²blight [blajt] *vb* **1** aantasten *(with plant disease)*, doen verdorren; **2** een vernietigende uitwerking hebben op, zwaar schaden, verwoesten: *a life ~ed by worries* een leven dat vergald werd door de zorgen

blimey [blajmie] *(vulg)* verdikkeme

¹blind [blajnd] *adj* **1** blind, *(fig)* ondoordacht, roekeloos: ~ *fury* blinde woede; *as* ~ *as a bat* zo blind als een mol, stekeblind; *the* ~ de blinden; **2** blind, zonder begrip, ongevoelig: *be* ~ *to s.o.'s faults* geen oog hebben voor de fouten van iem; **3** doodlopend, *(fig)* zonder vooruitzichten: *turn a* ~ *eye to sth.* iets door de vingers zien, een oogje dichtknijpen voor iets

²blind [blajnd] *vb* **1** verblinden, blind maken; misleiden; **2** verduisteren, overschaduwen; **3** blinddoeken

³blind [blajnd] *n* **1** scherm[h], jaloezie, zonnescherm[h], rolgordijn[h]; **2** voorwendsel[h], uitvlucht, dekmantel

⁴blind [blajnd] *adv* blind(elings), roekeloos ‖ ~ *drunk* stomdronken

¹blindfold *adj* geblinddoekt

²blindfold *vb* blinddoeken, *(fig)* misleiden

¹blink [blingk] *vb* **1** met half toegeknepen ogen kijken, knipogen; **2** knipperen, flikkeren, schitteren

²blink [blingk] *vb* knippe(re)n met

³blink [blingk] *n* **1** knipoog, (oog)wenk; **2** glimp, oogopslag; **3** flikkering, schijnsel[h] ‖ *(inf) on the* ~ niet in orde, defect

blink at een oogje dichtdoen voor: ~ *illegal practices* illegale praktijken door de vingers zien

blinkers [blingkəz] oogkleppen, *(fig)* kortzichtigheid

blip [blip] **1** piep, bliep; **2** *(radar)* echo

bliss [blis] (geluk)zaligheid, het einde, puur genot[h]

¹blister [blistə] *n* **1** (brand)blaar; **2** bladder, blaas

²blister [blistə] *vb* **1** blaren krijgen; **2** (af)bladderen, blazen vormen

³blister [blistə] *vb* doen bladderen, verschroeien, blaren veroorzaken op

blistering [blistəring] **1** verschroeiend, verzengend: *the* ~ *sun* de gloeiendhete zon; **2** vernietigend

blithe [blajð] *(form)* **1** vreugdevol, blij; **2** zorgeloos, onbezorgd

blithering [bliðəring] stom, getikt: *you* ~ *idiot!* stomme idioot die je bent!

blizzard [blizzəd] (hevige) sneeuwstorm

bloated [blootid] opgezwollen, opgezet, opgeblazen

blob [blob] klodder, druppel, spat

bloc [blok] *(pol)* blok[h], groep, coalitie

¹block [blok] *n* **1** blok[h] *(also pol)*, stronk, (hak)blok[h], kapblok[h], steenblok[h], beulsblok[h]; **2** blok[h] *(of buildings)*, huizenblok[h], (groot) gebouw[h]: ~ *of flats* flatgebouw; *walk around the* ~ een straatje omlopen; **3** versperring, stremming, *(psychology, sport)* blokkering, obstructie

²block [blok] *vb (sport)* blokkeren, blokken, obstructie plegen

³block [blok] *vb* **1** versperren, blokkeren: ~ *off* afsluiten, blokkeren; **2** belemmeren, verhinderen, tegenhouden: *he ~ed my plans* hij reed mij in de wielen; **3** *(sport; psychology)* blokkeren, obstructie plegen tegen: ~ *in* (of: *out*) ontwerpen, schetsen

¹blockade [blokeed] *n* blokkade, afsluiting, versperring

²blockade [blokeed] *vb* blokkeren, afsluiten; belemmeren, verhinderen

blockage [blokkidzj] **1** verstopping, opstopping, obstakel[h]; **2** stagnatie, stremming

blockbuster kassucces[h]

blockhead domkop, stommerik

bloke [blook] kerel, gozer, vent

¹blond [blond] *n* **1** blond iem; *(woman)* blondje[h], blondine; **2** iem met een lichte huidkleur; **3** blond[h]

²blond [blond] *adj* **1** blond; **2** met een lichte huidkleur

blood [blud] **1** bloed[h]: *in cold* ~ in koelen bloede; *it makes your* ~ *boil* het maakt je razend; *let* ~ aderlaten; **2** temperament[h], aard, hartstocht; **3** bloedverwantschap[h], afstamming, afkomst: *blue* ~ blauw bloed; *bring in fresh* ~ vers bloed inbrengen; *be* (of: *run) in one's* ~ in het bloed zitten; ~ *is thicker than water* het hemd is nader dan de rok

bloodcurdling [bludkə:dling] ijzingwekkend, huiveringwekkend, bloedstollend

bloodhound bloedhond, *(fig)* speurder, detective

bloodless [bludləs] **1** bloedeloos; **2** bleek, kleurloos; **3** saai, duf

blood relation bloedverwant(e)

bloodshed bloedvergieten[h]

bloodshot bloeddoorlopen

bloodthirsty bloeddorstig, moorddadig

blood vessel bloedvat[h], ader

¹bloody [bluddie] *adj* **1** bloed-, bloedrood, bebloed: ~ *nose* bloedneus; **2** bloed(er)ig; **3** bloeddorstig, wreed; **4** verdraaid: *he's a* ~ *fool* hij is een domme idioot

²bloody [bluddie] *adv (inf)* erg: *you're* ~ *well right* je

hebt nog gelijk ook
bloody-minded *(inf)* dwars, koppig
¹**bloom** [bloe:m] *n* **1** bloem *(esp of cultivated plants)*,
bloesem; **2** bloei(tijd), kracht, hoogste ontwikkeling: *in the ~ of one's youth* in de kracht van zijn
jeugd; **3** waasʰ, dauw; **4** blos, gloed
²**bloom** [bloe:m] *vb* **1** bloeien, in bloei zijn; **2** in volle
bloei komen *(also fig)*, tot volle ontplooiing komen;
3 floreren, gedijen; **4** blozen, stralen *(esp of woman)*; **5** zich ontwikkelen, (op)bloeien, uitgroeien
bloomer [bloe:mə] *(inf)* blunder, flater, miskleun
¹**blossom** [blossəm] *n (also fig)* bloesem, bloei: *be in
~* in bloesem staan
²**blossom** [blossəm] *vb* **1** ontbloeien, tot bloei komen *(of fruit trees)*; **2** zich ontwikkelen, opbloeien,
zich ontpoppen
¹**blot** [blot] *n* vlek *(also fig)*: *the building was a ~ on
the landscape* het gebouw ontsierde het landschap
²**blot** [blot] *vb* vlekken maken, knoeien, kliederen;
vlekken (krijgen), vloeien *(of paper)*
³**blot** [blot] *vb* **1** bevlekken, bekladden; **2** ontsieren; **3**
(af)vloeien, drogen met vloeipapier
blotch [blotsj] vlek, puist, smet
blot out **1** (weg)schrappen, doorhalen; **2** verbergen,
aan het gezicht onttrekken, bedekken: *clouds ~ the
sun* wolken schuiven voor de zon; **3** vernietigen,
uitroeien
blotting paper [blotting peepə] vloei(papier)ʰ
blouse [blauz] bloes *(worn by women)*, blauwe
(werk)kiel
¹**blow** [bloo] *vb* **1** (uit)blazen, fluiten, weerklinken,
(uit)waaien, wapperen: *~ down* neergeblazen worden, omwaaien; *(inf) ~ in: a)* (komen) binnenvallen, (komen) aanwaaien; *b)* inwaaien; *the scandal
will ~ over* het schandaal zal wel overwaaien; **2** hijgen, blazen, puffen; **3** stormen, hard waaien; **4**
(electr) doorsmelten, doorbranden, doorslaan *(of
fuse)*: *(inf) ~ hot and cold (about)* veranderen als
het weer
²**blow** [bloo] *vb* **1** blazen (op, door), aanblazen, afblazen, opblazen, rondblazen, uitblazen, wegblazen, snuiten *(nose)*, doen wapperen, doen dwarrelen: *the door was ~n open* de deur waaide open; *the
wind blew her hair* de wind waaide door haar haar;
~ away wegblazen, wegjagen; *the wind blew the
trees down* de wind blies de bomen om(ver); *~ in:
a)* doen binnenwaaien; *b)* doen springen *(win-
dow-pane)*; *~ off: a)* wegblazen; *b)* laten ontsnappen *(steam)*; *~ over* om(ver)bla-
zen, doen omwaaien; *~ skyhigh* in de lucht laten
vliegen, *(fig)* geen spaan heel laten van; **2** doen
doorslaan, doen doorbranden; **3** bespelen, blazen
op, spelen op; **4** *(inf)* verprutsen, verknoeien; **5**
(vulg) pijpen, afzuigen
³**blow** [bloo] *n* **1** wind(vlaag), rukwind, storm, stevige bries; **2** slag, klap, mep: *come to (of: exchange) ~s*
slaags raken; *~ by ~ account* gedetailleerd verslag;
without (striking) a ~ zonder slag of stoot, zonder
geweld; **3** (tegen)slag, ramp, schok

blow-dryer föhn, haardroger
blower [blooə] **1** aanjager, blower, ventilator; **2**
(inf) telefoon
blowout **1** klapband, lekke band; **2** lek ʰ; **3** uitbarsting *(of oil well, gas well)*, eruptie; **4** *(inf)* eetfes-
tijnʰ, vreetpartij
¹**blow out** *vb* **1** uitwaaien, uitgaan; **2** springen, klappen, barsten; **3** ophouden te werken *(of electr appliances)*, uitvallen, doorbranden
²**blow out** *vb* **1** uitblazen, uitdoen; **2** doen springen,
doen klappen; **3** buiten bedrijf stellen *(electr appliances)*
¹**blow up** *vb* **1** ontploffen, exploderen, springen; **2**
(inf) in rook opgaan, verijdeld worden; **3** opzwellen, opgeblazen worden; **4** (in woede) uitbarsten,
ontploffen; **5** sterker worden *(of wind, storm)*, komen opzetten, *(fig)* uitbreken, losbarsten
²**blow up** *vb* **1** opblazen, laten ontploffen, vullen
(with air); **2** opblazen, overdrijven; **3** aanblazen
(fire), aanwakkeren, (op)stoken; **4** doen opwaaien,
opjagen, opdwarrelen; **5** *(photo)* (uit)vergroten
blow-up **1** explosie, ontploffing; **2** uitbarsting, ruzie, herrie; **3** *(photo)* (uit)vergroting
blowy [blooie] winderig
¹**blubber** [blubbə] *n* **1** blubber; **2** *(inf)* gejankʰ, ge-
grienʰ
²**blubber** [blubbə] *vb* grienen, snotteren, janken
bludgeon [bludzjn] (gummi)knuppel, knots
¹**blue** [bloe:] *adj* **1** blauwʰ, azuur: *~ blooded* van adellijke afkomst; *~ with cold* blauw van de kou; **2** gedeprimeerd, triest, somber; **3** conservatief, Tory; **4**
(inf) obsceen, porno-, gewaagd: *~ film* (of: *movie)*
pornofilm, seksfilm; *wait till one is ~ in the face*
wachten tot je een ons weegt; *once in a ~ moon*
(hoogst) zelden, zelden of nooit; *cry (of: scream,
shout) ~ murder* moord en brand schreeuwen
²**blue** [bloe:] *n* **1** blauw; **2** blauwselʰ *(to dye linen
blue)*; **3** blauwe lucht: *out of the ~* plotseling, als een
donderslag bij heldere hemel; **4** blauwtjeʰ *(butterfly)*; **5** lidʰ (kleur) ve conservatieve politieke partij,
Tory, conservatief
bluebottle aasvlieg, bromvlieg
blue-collar hand-; fabrieks- *(worker(s))*
blueprint blauwdruk, ontwerpʰ, schets
blue ribbon hoogste onderscheiding, eerste prijs
bluestocking *(oft depr)* geleerde vrouw
¹**bluff** [bluf] *vb* **1** bluffen *(also in poker)*, brutaal optreden; **2** doen alsof, voorwenden
²**bluff** [bluf] *vb* **1** overbluffen, overdonderen; **2** misleiden, bedriegen, doen alsof: *~ one's way out of a
situation* zich uit een situatie redden
³**bluff** [bluf] *n* **1** hoge, steile oever, steile rotswand,
klifʰ; **2** bluf: *call one's ~: a)* iem uitdaging; *b)* iemands uitdaging aannemen
⁴**bluff** [bluf] *adj* kortaf maar oprecht, plompverloren
maar eerlijk
¹**blunder** [blundə] *n* blunder, miskleun
²**blunder** [blundə] *vb* **1** blunderen, een stomme fout
maken, een flater slaan; **2** strompelen, (voort)suk-

kelen, zich onhandig voortbewegen
blunt [blʌnt] **1** bot, stomp; **2** afgestompt, ongevoelig, koud; **3** (p)lomp, ongezouten, onomwonden: *tell s.o. sth.* ~*ly* iem iets botweg vertellen
¹blur [blɔ:] *n* onduidelijke plek, wazig beeldʰ, verflauwde indruk
²blur [blɔ:] *vb* **1** vervagen, vaag worden; **2** vlekken
³blur [blɔ:] *vb* **1** bevlekken, besmeren, *(fig)* bekladden; **2** onscherp maken, troebel maken: ~*red photographs* onscherpe foto's
¹blush [blʌsj] *vb* blozen, een kleur krijgen, rood worden
²blush [blʌsj] *n* (schaamte)blos, (rode) kleur, schaamroodʰ
¹bluster [blʌstə] *vb* **1** razen, bulderen, tieren; **2** bulderen, loeien, huilen *(of wind)*; **3** brallen, opscheppen
²bluster [blʌstə] *n* **1** tumultʰ, drukte, geloeiʰ, gebulderʰ *(of storm)*, geraasʰ, getierʰ *(of angry voices)*; **2** gebralʰ, opschepperij
boar [bo:] **1** beer *(male pig)*; **2** wild zwijnʰ, everzwijnʰ
¹board [bo:d] *n* **1** plank, (vloer)deelʰ; **2** (aanplak)bordʰ, scorebordʰ, schildʰ, plaat, bordʰ *(basketball and korfball)*, (schaak)bordʰ, (speel)bordʰ; **3** *(shipp)* boordʰ: *go by the* ~: *a)* overboord slaan; *b)* volledig mislukken *(of plans etc)*; *on* ~ aan boord van; **4** kost, kostgeldʰ, onderhoudʰ, pensionʰ: ~ *and lodging* kost en inwoning; *full* ~ vol pension; **5** raad, bestuur(slichaam)ʰ: ~ *of directors* raad van bestuur; *editorial* ~ redactie; *be on the* ~ in het bestuur zitten, bestuurslid zijn; *sweep the* ~ grote winst(en) boeken, zegevieren; *(inf) take on* ~ begrijpen, accepteren, aannemen *(of new ideas etc)*; *above* ~ open, eerlijk; *across the* ~ over de hele linie, iedereen, niemand uitgezonderd
²board [bo:d] *vb* **1** beplanken, beschieten, betimmeren, bevloeren; **2** in de kost hebben; **3** uit huis doen, in de kost doen; **4** aan boord gaan van, instappen *(aeroplane)*, opstappen *(motorcycle)*: ~ *a ship* zich inschepen; **5** *(shipp)* enteren
³board [bo:d] *vb* in de kost zijn
boarder [bo:də] pensiongast, kostganger; kostleerling, intern
boarding [bo:diŋ] beplanking, betimmering, schutting
boarding card instapkaart
boarding-house kosthuisʰ, pensionʰ
boarding school kostschool, internaatʰ
boardroom bestuurskamer, directiekamer
boardsailing *(sport)* het plankzeilen, het (wind)surfen
¹boast [boost] *n* **1** *(depr)* bluf, grootspraak; **2** trots, roem, glorie
²boast [boost] *vb* opscheppen, overdrijven, sterke verhalen vertellen: ~ *about*, ~ *of* opscheppen over, zich laten voorstaan op
³boast [boost] *vb* **1** in het (trotse) bezit zijn van, (kunnen) bogen op (het bezit van); **2** *(depr)* op-

scheppen
boaster [boostə] opschepper, praatjesmaker
boat [boot] **1** (open) boot, vaartuigʰ, (dek)schuit, sloep: *(fig) be (all) in the same* ~ (allen) in hetzelfde schuitje zitten; **2** *(Am)* (zeewaardig) schipʰ, (stoom)boot *(used esp by non-sailors)*; **3** (jus)kom; sauskom: *burn one's* ~*s* z'n schepen achter zich verbranden; *miss the* ~ de boot missen, zijn kans voorbij laten gaan; *(inf) push the* ~ *out* de bloemetjes buiten zetten; *(inf) rock the* ~ de boel in het honderd sturen, spelbreker zijn
boatswain [boosn] bootsman, boots
¹bob [bob] *n* **1** hangend voorwerpʰ, (slinger)gewichtʰ, lens *(of timepiece)*, gewichtʰ, strik *(of kite)*, loodʰ *(of plumb line)*, dobber, waker; **2** bob(slee); **3** gecoupeerde staart; **4** plotselinge (korte) beweging, sprong, (knie)buiging, knix; **5** bob(bed kapselʰ), kort geknipte kop, jongenskop || *(inf) Bob's your uncle* klaar is Kees, voor mekaar
²bob [bob] *vb* **1** bobben, rodelen, bobsleeën; **2** (zich) op en neer (heen en weer) bewegen, (op)springen, dobberen: ~ *up* (plotseling) te voorschijn komen, komen boven drijven, opduiken; **3** buigen, een (knie)buiging maken
³bob [bob] *vb* **1** (kort) knippen *(hair)*; **2** couperen, kortstaarten; **3** heen en weer (op en neer) bewegen, doen dansen, laten dobberen, knikken
bobbin [bobin] spoel, klos, bobine
bobby [bobie] *(inf)* bobby, oom agent, politieman
¹bobsleigh [bobslee] *n* bob(slee)
²bobsleigh [bobslee] *vb* bobsleeën, bobben
¹bodily [bodillie] *adj* lichamelijk: ~ *harm* lichamelijk letsel
²bodily [bodillie] *adv* **1** met geweld; **2** lichamelijk, in levende lijve; **3** in z'n geheel, met huid en haar
body [boddie] **1** lichaamʰ, romp; lijkʰ: *just enough to keep* ~ *and soul together* net genoeg om je te redden; **2** persoon, *(law)* rechtspersoon, *(inf)* mens, ziel; **3** grote hoeveelheid, massa; **4** voornaamste deelʰ, grootste (centrale) deelʰ, kern, meerderheid, schipʰ *(of church)*, cascoʰ, carrosserie *(of car)*, romp *(of aeroplane)*, klankkast *(of musical instrument)*: *the* ~ *of a letter* de kern van een brief; **5** lichaamʰ, groep, korpsʰ: *the Governing Body is* (of: *are) meeting today* het bestuur vergadert vandaag; *they left in a* ~ ze vertrokken als één man; **6** voorwerpʰ, objectʰ, lichaamʰ: *heavenly bodies* hemellichamen; **7** bodystocking
bodyguard lijfwacht
bog [bog] **1** (veen)moerasʰ; **2** *(inf)* plee, wc
bog down 1 gehinderd worden, vastlopen; **2** vast komen te zitten (in de modder) || *get bogged down in details* in details verzanden
bogey [boogie] **1** boeman, (kwel)duivel, kwade geest; **2** spookbeeldʰ, schrikbeeldʰ; **3** *(golf)* bogey, score van 1 slag boven par voor een hole
boggle [bogl] terugschrikken, terugdeinzen
boggy [bogie] moerassig, drassig
bogus [boogəs] vals, onecht, nep-, vervalst

¹boil [bojl] *vb* **1** (staan te) koken, het kookpunt bereiken, gekookt worden: *~ing hot* kokend heet; *~
down* inkoken; *~ over: a)* overkoken; *b) (fig)* uitbarsten (in woede), tot uitbarsting komen; **2** (inwendig) koken: *~ing with anger* ziedend van woede;
(inf) ~ down to neerkomen op (in het kort, in grote
lijnen)

²boil [bojl] *vb* koken, aan de kook brengen || *(inf) ~
down* kort samenvatten, de hoofdlijnen aangeven

³boil [bojl] *n* **1** steenpuist; **2** kookpunt^h, kook

boiler [bojlə] boiler, stoomketel

boisterous [bojstrəs] **1** onstuimig, luid(ruchtig); **2**
ruw, heftig, stormachtig *(of wind, weather etc)*

bold [boold] **1** (stout)moedig, doortastend; **2** *(oft
depr)* brutaal: *as ~ as brass* (honds)brutaal; **3**
krachtig, goed uitkomend; **4** vet (gedrukt): *put a ~
face on the matter* zich goedhouden

bold-faced **1** brutaal, schaamteloos; **2** vet gedrukt

bollard [bollɑːd] korte paal, bolder, meerpaal
(shipp), verkeerszuiltje^h, -paaltje^h

boloney [bəloonie] *(inf)* onzin, (flauwe)kul, gelul^h

bolster [boolstə] **1** (onder)kussen^h, hoofdmatras^{+h};
2 steun, ondersteuning, stut

bolster up **1** met kussen(s) (onder)steunen; **2**
schragen, ondersteunen, opkrikken *(also fig): ~
s.o.'s morale* iem moed inspreken

¹bolt [boolt] *n* **1** bout; **2** grendel, schuif; **3** bliksemstraal, -flits; **4** sprong, duik: *make a ~ for it* er vandoor gaan; *a ~ from the blue* een complete verrassing

²bolt [boolt] *vb* **1** *(inf)* op de loop gaan, de benen nemen, op hol slaan *(of horse);* **2** (plotseling, ver-
schrikt) op(zij)-, wegspringen; **3** doorschieten,
(vroegtijdig, te vroeg) in het zaad schieten; **4** met
bouten bevestigd zitten; **5** sluiten, een grendel hebben

³bolt [boolt] *vb* **1** (snel) verorberen: *~ down food*
eten opschrokken; **2** vergrendelen, op slot doen; **3**
met bout(en) bevestigen

⁴bolt [boolt] *adv* recht: *~ upright* kaarsrecht

¹bomb [bom] *n* **1** bom; **2** *(inf)* bom geld: *cost a ~* ka-
pitalen kosten; **3** *(inf)* hit, klapper, daverend suc-
ces^h: *go like a ~: a)* als een trein lopen; *b)* scheuren
(of car)

²bomb [bom] *vb* **1** bommen werpen; **2** razen, racen

³bomb [bom] *vb* bombarderen

bombard [bombɑːd] bombarderen, met bommen,
granaten bestoken, *(fig)* bestoken, lastig vallen: *~
s.o. with questions* vragen afvuren op iem

bombardment [bombɑːdmənt] bombardement^h,
bomaanval

bombastic [bombæstik] hoogdravend, gezwollen

bomber [bommə] **1** bommenwerper; **2** bommen-
gooier *(pers)*

bomb scare bommelding

bombshell granaat^h, bom, *(inf; fig)* donderslag,
(onaangename) verrassing

bona fide [boonəfajdie] te goeder trouw, bonafide,
betrouwbaar

bonanza [bənænzə] **1** rijke (erts)vindplaats *(esp of
gold, silver, oil)*, rijke oliebron, mijn, *(fig)* goudmijn; **2** grote (winst)opbrengst

bond [bond] **1** band, verbond^h, verbondenheid,
binding; **2** verbintenis, contract^h, verplichting; **3**
obligatie, schuldbekentenis; **4** verbinding, hechting, *(chem)* verbinding; **5** *~s* boeien, ketenen, gevangenschap

bondage [bondidzj] **1** slavernij; **2** onderworpenheid, het gebonden zijn, gebondenheid

bonded [bondid] **1** in douaneopslag (geplaatst); **2**
aan elkaar gelijmd, gelaagd

¹bone [boon] *n* **1** bot^h, been^h, graat: *I can feel it* (of:
it is) in my ~s ik weet het zeker, ik voel het aankomen; **2** kluif, stuk^h been, bot^h: *~ of contention* twist-
appel; *make no ~s about* niet aarzelen om; *have a ~
to pick with s.o.* met iem een appeltje te schillen
hebben

²bone [boon] *adj* benen, van been, ivoren

³bone [boon] *vb* uitbenen, ontgraten

⁴bone [boon] *adv* extreem, uitermate: *~ dry* kurkdroog; *~ idle* (of: *lazy)* aartslui

boneheaded stom, achterlijk, idioot

bonfire [bonfajjə] vuur^h in de openlucht, vreugde-
vuur^h, vuur^h om dode bladeren (afval) te verbranden

bonkers [bongkəz] gek, maf, getikt

bonnet [bonnit] **1** bonnet, hoed; **2** beschermkap,
schoorsteenkap, motorkap

bonus [boonəs] **1** bonus, premie, gratificatie; **2** bij-
slag, toelage; **3** *(inf)* meevaller, extraatje^h

bony [boonie] benig, met veel botten (graten), mager

¹boo [boe:] *n* boe, kreet van afkeuring, gejouw^h, boe-
geroep^h || *wouldn't* (of: *couldn't) say ~ to a goose: a)*
dodelijk verlegen zijn; *b)* zo bang als een weezel zijn

²boo [boe:] *vb* boe roepen, (weg)joelen, (uit)jouwen

boob [boe:b] *(inf)* **1** flater, blunder; **2** *(inf)* tiet

booby [boe:bie] *(inf)* stommerd, domkop, idioot

booby prize poedelprijs

¹booby trap *n* boobytrap, valstrikbom

²booby trap *vb* een boobytrap plaatsen bij

boodle [boe:dl] **1** omkoopgeld^h, smeergeld^h; **2**
(smak) geld

¹book [boek] *n* **1** boek^h, boekdeel^h, -werk^h, *(inf)* tele-
foonboek^h; **2** *the Book* het Boek (der Boeken), de
Heilige Schrift, de bijbel; **3** boek^h *(chapter of bible,
poem etc)*; **4** tekstboekje^h, libretto^h *(of opera etc)*,
manuscript^h, script *(of play);* **5** (schrijf)boek^h,
schrift, blocnote; **6** boekje^h *(cards, matches,
stamps);* **7** register^h, lijst, boek^h, lijst van aangegane
weddenschappen *(at races):* make (of: *keep) (a) ~*
wedmakelen, bookmaker zijn; **8** *~s* boeken, kas-
boek^h, kantoorboek^h, journaal^h; **9** *~s* boek^h, regis-
ter^h, (leden)lijst: *bring s.o. to ~ for sth.* iem voor iets
rekenschap laten afleggen, iem zijn gerechte straf
doen ondergaan; *read s.o. like a ~* iem volkomen
door hebben; *(inf) throw the ~ (of rules) at s.o.: a)*
iem maximum straf toebedelen; *b)* iem de les lezen;

by the ~ volgens het boekje; *in my* ~ volgens mij, mijns inziens

²book [boek] *vb* **1** boeken, reserveren, bestellen: *~ a passage* passage boeken; *~ed up* volgeboekt, uitverkocht, *(of person)* bezet; **2** inschrijven, registreren, noteren; **3** bekeuren, een proces-verbaal opmaken tegen: *I was ~ed for speeding* ik werd wegens te hard rijden op de bon geslingerd; **4** *(sport)* een gele kaart geven

³book [boek] *vb* een plaats bespreken, een kaartje nemen, reserveren || ~ *in: a)* zich laten inschrijven *(in hotel register); b)* inchecken *(at airport)*

booking [boeking] **1** bespreking, reservering, boeking; **2** verbalisering; **3** *(sport)* gele kaart

booking office bespreekbureauʰ, plaats(kaarten)bureauʰ, loketʰ

bookish [boekisj] **1** leesgraag, verslaafd aan boeken; **2** boekachtig, stijf, onnatuurlijk; **3** theoretisch, schools, saai

bookkeeper boekhouder

bookkeeping boekhouding, het boekhouden

bookmaker *(horse racing)* bookmaker

bookmark boekenlegger

book token boekenbon

book up een plaats bespreken, reserveren

bookworm boekenwurm

¹boom [boe:m] *n* **1** (dof, hol) gedreunʰ, gebulderʰ, gedaverʰ; **2** hausse, (periode van) economische vooruitgang; **3** (hoge) vlucht, grote stijging, bloei, opkomst; **4** *(shipp)* giek, spriet; **5** *(shipp)* (laad)boom; **6** galg, statiefʰ *(of microphone etc);* **7** (haven)boom, versperring *(of harbour entrance)*

²boom [boe:m] *vb* **1** een dof geluid maken, dreunen, bulderen, rollen *(of thunder);* **2** een (hoge) vlucht nemen, zich snel ontwikkelen, bloeien, sterk stijgen *(of price): business is ~ing* het gaat ons voor de wind; **3** (snel) in aanzien stijgen

³boom [boe:m] *vb* (also with *out*) bulderend uiten

¹boomerang [boe:məræng] *n* boemerang *(also fig)*

²boomerang [boe:məræng] *vb* als een boemerang terugkeren, 'n boemerangeffect hebben

boon [boe:n] **1** zegen, weldaad, gemakʰ; **2** gunst, wens

boorish [boeərisj] lomp, boers, onbehouwen

¹boost [boe:st] *n* **1** duw (omhoog), zetjeʰ, (onder)steun(ing); **2** verhoging, (prijs)opdrijving; **3** stimulans, aanmoediging, versterking: *a ~ to one's spirits* een opkikker(tje)

²boost [boe:st] *vb* **1** (omhoog)duwen, een zetje geven, ondersteunen: ~ *s.o. up* iem een duwtje (omhoog) geven; **2** verhogen, opdrijven, opvoeren *(price, production etc);* **3** *(Am)* aanprijzen, reclame maken voor; **4** stimuleren, aanmoedigen, bevorderen: ~ *one's spirits* iem opvrolijken; **5** verhogen *(pressure),* versterken *(radio signal)*

booster [boe:stə] **1** hulpkrachtbron, hulpversterker, aanjager, aanjaagpomp, startmotor; **2** verbetering, opkikker

¹boot [boe:t] *n* **1** laars, hoge schoen; **2** schop, trap; **3**

ontslagʰ; **4** kofferbak, bagageruimte || *put the ~ in* in elkaar trappen, erop inhakken

²boot [boe:t] *vb* **1** schoppen, trappen; **2** (also with *up) (comp)* opstarten, booten

bootee [boe:tie:] kort laarsjeʰ, gebreid babysokjeʰ

booth [boe:ð] **1** kraam, marktkraam, stalletjeʰ, (feest)tent; **2** hokjeʰ, stemhokjeʰ, telefooncel, (luister)cabine *(in record shop etc): polling* ~ stemhokje

bootlace 1 veter voor laars; **2** schoenveter

¹bootleg *vb* smokkelen, clandestien (drank) stoken (verkopen)

²bootleg *adj* illegaal (geproduceerd) *(liquor, records, CDs)*

³bootleg *n* illegale kopie *(of record, CD)*

bootlegger (drank)smokkelaar, illegale drankstoker (drankverkoper)

booty [boe:tie] **1** buit, roof; **2** winst, prijs, beloning

¹booze [boe:z] *vb* zuipen

²booze [boe:z] *n* **1** sterkedrank: *on the* ~ aan de drank; **2** zuippartij

¹border [bo:də] *n* **1** grens, grenslijn, afscheiding; **2** rand, band, bies, lijst

²border [bo:də] *vb* begrenzen, omzomen, omranden

¹borderline *n* grens(lijn), scheidingslijn

²borderline *adj* **1** grens-, twijfelachtig: ~ *case* grensgeval; **2** net (niet) acceptabel, op het kantje

border (up)on grenzen aan, liggen naast, belenden

¹bore [bo:] *n* **1** vervelend persoon; **2** vervelend iets; **3** boorgatʰ; **4** kaliberʰ, diameter, boring *(of a cylinder, firearm);* **5** boor

²bore *vb* vervelen: *I'm ~d stiff* ik verveel mij kapot

³bore *vb* **1** (een gat) boren, drillen, een put slaan; **2** boren, doorboren, uitboren, kalibreren *(weapons),* een gat boren in; **3** doordringen, zich (een weg) banen, moeizaam vooruitkomen

boredom [bo:dəm] verveling

boring [bo:ring] vervelend, saai, langdradig

born [bo:n] **1** geboren, van geboorte: ~ *and bred* geboren en getogen; ~ *again* herboren; *not ~ yesterday* niet op z'n achterhoofd gevallen; **2** geboren, voorbestemd: ~ *to be a leader* voor het leiderschap in de wieg gelegd; **3** geboren, van nature: *he is a ~ actor* hij is een rastoneelspeler; **4** geboren, ontstaan, voortgekomen

borough [burrə] **1** stad, (stedelijke) gemeente: *municipal* ~ (stedelijke) gemeente; **2** kiesdistrictʰ

borrow [borroo] **1** lenen, ontlenen; **2** pikken

bosom [boezəm] **1** borst, boezem; **2** borststukʰ *(of piece of clothing);* **3** ruimte tussen borst en kleding, boezem

¹boss [bos] *n* baas, chef, voorman

²boss [bos] *vb* commanderen, de baas spelen (over)

botanic(al) [bətænik(l)] **1** botanisch, plantkundig; **2** plantaardig, uit planten verkregen

botany [bottənie] plantkunde, botanica

¹botch [botsj] *vb* **1** verknoeien: ~ *it up* het verknallen; **2** oplappen, slecht repareren

²botch [botsj] *n* knoeiwerkʰ, knoeiboel, puinhoop

¹both [booθ] *num* beide(n), allebei, alle twee: *I saw*

them ~ ik heb ze allebei gezien; ~ *of them* alle twee
²**both** [booθ] *conj (with and)* zowel, beide: ~ *Jack and Jill got hurt* Jack en Jill raakten allebei gewond; *he was ~ tall and fat* hij was lang én dik
¹**bother** [boðə] *vb* **1** de moeite nemen, zich de moeite geven: *don't ~ about that* maak je daar nu maar niet druk om; *don't ~* doe maar geen moeite; **2** lastig vallen, dwarszitten, irriteren: *his leg ~s him a lot* hij heeft veel last van zijn been; *I can't be ~ed* dat is me te veel moeite; *that doesn't ~ me* daar zit ik niet mee
²**bother** [boðə] *n* **1** last, lastpost: *I hope I'm not being a ~ to you* ik hoop dat ik u niet tot last ben; **2** moeite, probleem^h, moeilijkheid: *we had a lot of ~ finding the house* het heeft ons veel moeite gekost om het huis te vinden
bothersome [boðəsəm] vervelend, lastig
¹**bottle** [botl] *n* fles, *(fig)* drank: *a ~ of rum* een fles rum; *our baby is brought up on the ~* onze baby wordt met de fles grootgebracht
²**bottle** [botl] *vb* **1** bottelen, in flessen doen; **2** inmaken
bottle bank glasbak
bottleneck flessenhals *(also fig)*, knelpunt^h
bottle up opkroppen
¹**bottom** [botəm] *n* **1** bodem, grond, het diepst: *from the ~ of my heart* uit de grond van mijn hart; **2** onderste deel^h, voet, basis: *from the ~ up* van bij het begin, helemaal (opnieuw); **3** het laagste punt: *the ~ of the garden* achterin de tuin; **4** achterste^h, gat^h; **5** kiel, *(fig)* schip^h, bodem: *I'll get to the ~ of this* ik ga dit helemaal uitzoeken
²**bottom** [botəm] *adj* onderste, laatste, laagste
boulder [booldə] kei, zwerfkei, rotsblok^h
¹**bounce** [bauns] *vb* **1** stuit(er)en, terugkaatsen: ~ *back after a setback* er na een tegenslag weer bovenop komen; **2** (op)springen, wippen; **3** ongedekt zijn, geweigerd worden *(of cheque)*
²**bounce** [bauns] *vb* **1** laten stuit(er)en, kaatsen, stuit(er)en; **2** *(inf)* eruit gooien, ontslaan
³**bounce** [bauns] *n* **1** vermogen tot stuit(er)en; **2** stuit, terugsprong; **3** levendigheid, beweeglijkheid; **4** opschepperij
bouncer [baunsə] **1** uitsmijter; **2** iem die (iets dat) stuit
bouncing [baunsing] gezond, levendig, flink
bouncy [baunsie] **1** levendig, levenslustig; **2** die kan stuiten: *a ~ mattress* een goed verende matras
¹**bound** [baund] *adj* **1** zeker: *he is ~ to pass his exam* hij haalt zijn examen beslist; **2** op weg, onderweg: *this train is ~ for Poland* deze trein gaat naar Polen; **3** gebonden, vast: *she is completely ~ up in her research* ze gaat helemaal op in haar onderzoek
²**bound** *n* **1** ~*s* grens, *(maths)* limiet: *out of ~s* verboden terrein, taboe *(also fig)*; **2** sprong; **3** stuit, terugsprong *(of ball)*: *keep within the ~s of reason* redelijk blijven
³**bound** *vb* **1** springen; **2** stuit(er)en, terugkaatsen
⁴**bound** *vb* begrenzen, beperken
-bound [baund] **1** *(roughly)* gehinderd door, vast-

zittend aan: *be snowbound* vastzitten in de sneeuw; **2** gebonden in: *leather-bound books* in leer gebonden boeken
boundary [baundərie] grens, grenslijn
bountiful [bauntiefoel] **1** vrijgevig, gul, royaal; **2** overvloedig, rijk
bounty [bauntie] **1** gulheid, vrijgevigheid; **2** (gulle) gift, donatie; **3** premie, bonus
bouquet [bookee] **1** boeket^h, bos bloemen, ruiker; **2** bouquet^h, geur en smaak *(of wine)*
bout [baut] **1** vlaag, tijdje^h, periode, aanval *(of illness)*: ~*s of activity* vlagen van activiteit; ~*s of migraine* migraineaanvallen; **2** wedstrijd *(of boxing, wrestling)*
boutique [boe:tie:k] boetiek
bovine [boovajn] runderachtig, runder-
¹**bow** [bau] *vb* **1** buigen, een buiging maken; **2** buigen, zich gewonnen geven: *he ~ed to the inevitable* hij legde zich bij het onvermijdelijke neer
²**bow** [bau] *n* **1** buiging: *take a ~* applaus in ontvangst nemen; **2** boeg *(foremost part of ship)*
³**bow** [boo] *n* **1** boog, kromming; **2** boog, handboog; **3** strijkstok; **4** strik
⁴**bow** [boo] *vb* **1** buigen, krommen; **2** strijken *(of violinist)*
bowel [bauəl] **1** darm, ~*s* ingewanden; **2** binnenste^h: *deep in the ~s of the earth* in de diepste diepten van de aarde
bower [bauə] tuinhuisje^h, prieel(tje)^h
¹**bowl** [bool] *n* **1** kom, schaal, bekken^h; **2** *(Am; geography)* kom, komvormig gebied^h, bekken^h; **3** kop *(of pipe)*; **4** *(Am)* amfitheater^h, stadion^h; **5** *(sport)* bowl
²**bowl** [bool] *vb* **1** *(cricket)* bowlen; **2** voortrollen, rollen ‖ *the batsman was ~ed (out)* de slagman werd uitgegooid
bowl along 1 vlot rijden, rollen *(of car)*; **2** vlotten, lekker gaan *(of work)*
bowlegged [boolegd] met o-benen
bowler (hat) bolhoed
bowling alley kegelbaan, bowlingbaan, -centrum^h
bow out [bau aut] officieel afscheid nemen, zich terugtrekken *(from a high position)*
bow tie [boo taj] strikje^h, vlinderdas
¹**box** [boks] *n* **1** doos, kist, bak, trommel, bus; **2** loge, hokje^h, cel e.d. *(in theatre)*: *telephone ~*, *(Am)* *call ~* telefooncel; *witness ~* getuigenbank; **3** beschermhoes; **4** kader^h, omlijning, omlijnd gebied^h; **5** mep, draai om de oren, oorveeg: *give s.o. a ~ on the ears* iem een draai om de oren geven; **6** buis, tv, televisie
²**box** [boks] *vb* **1** boksen (tegen, met); **2** in dozen doen; **3** een draai om de oren geven: ~ *s.o.'s ears* iem een draai om z'n oren geven
boxer [boksə] **1** bokser; **2** boxer *(dog breed)*
box in opsluiten, insluiten: *feel boxed in* zich gekooid voelen
boxing [boksing] het boksen, bokssport
Boxing Day tweede kerstdag
box number (antwoord)nummer^h

box office bespreekbureau[h], loket[h], kassa *(of cinema)*

¹**boy** [boj] *n* **1** jongen, knul, zoon(tje[h]): *that's my ~* grote jongen, bravo knul; *boys will be boys* zo zijn jongens nu eenmaal; **2** *(Am)* man, jongen, vent: *come on, old ~* vooruit, ouwe jongen; *jobs for the ~s* vriendjespolitiek

²**boy** [boj] *interj (Am)* (t)jonge jonge

¹**boycott** [bojkot] *vb* boycotten

²**boycott** [bojkot] *n* boycot

boyfriend vriend(je[h]), vrijer

boyhood [bojhoed] jongenstijd, jongensjaren

boy scout padvinder

bra [bra:] *brassière* beha

¹**brace** [brees] *n* **1** klamp, (draag)beugel, (muur)anker; **2** steun, stut; **3** booromslag: *~ and bit* boor; **4** band, riem; **5** *(dentistry)* beugel; **6** *~s* bretels; **7** koppel[h], paar[h], stel[h]: *three ~ of partridge* drie koppel patrijzen

²**brace** [brees] *vb* **1** vastbinden, aantrekken, aanhalen; **2** versterken, verstevigen, ondersteunen; **3** schrap zetten: *~ oneself for a shock* zich op een schok voorbereiden

bracelet [breeslit] armband

bracing [breesing] verkwikkend, opwekkend, versterkend

¹**bracket** [brækit] *n* **1** steun, plankdrager; **2** haakje[h], accolade: *in ~s, between ~s* tussen haakjes; **3** klasse, groep: *the lower income ~* de lagere inkomensgroep

²**bracket** [brækit] *vb* **1** tussen haakjes zetten; **2** *(also with together)* koppelen, in een adem noemen, in dezelfde categorie plaatsen; **3** (onder)steunen *(with a brace)*

brag [bræg] (with *about, of*) opscheppen (over)

braggart [brægət] opschepper

braid [breed] **1** vlecht; **2** galon, boordsel[h], tres

¹**brain** [breen] *n* **1** hersenen, hersens, brein[h] *(as organ)*; **2** *(inf)* knappe kop, brein[h], genie[h]; **3** brein[h], intelligentie, hoofd[h]: *she has (a lot of) ~s* ze heeft (een goed stel) hersens; *pick s.o.'s ~(s)* iemands ideeën stelen

²**brain** [breen] *vb* de hersens inslaan

brain drain uittocht vh intellect

brainwash hersenspoelen

brainwave ingeving, (goede) inval, goed idee[h]

brainy [breenie] slim, knap, intelligent

¹**brake** [breek] *n* **1** rem: *apply* (of: *put on) the ~s* remmen, *(fig)* matigen, temperen; **2** stationcar, combi

²**brake** [breek] *vb* (af)remmen

bramble [bræmbl] **1** braamstruik; **2** doornstruik; **3** braam

¹**branch** [bra:ntsj] *n* **1** tak, loot; **2** vertakking, arm *(of river, road etc)*; **3** tak, filiaal[h], bijkantoor[h], plaatselijke afdeling

²**branch** [bra:ntsj] *vb* zich vertakken, zich splitsen: *~ off* zich splitsen, afbuigen

branch out zijn zaken uitbreiden, zich ontwikkelen

¹**brand** [brænd] *n* **1** merk[h], merknaam, soort, type[h];

2 brandmerk[h]

²**brand** [brænd] *vb* **1** (brand)merken, markeren: *~ed goods* merkartikelen; **2** brandmerken

brandish [brændisj] zwaaien met: *~ a sword* (dreigend) zwaaien met een zwaard

brandy [brændie] **1** cognac; **2** brandewijn

¹**brass** [bra:s] *n* **1** messing[h], geelkoper[h]; **2** koper[h], koperen instrumenten; **3** *(inf)* duiten, centen

²**brass** [bra:s] *adj* koperen ‖ *(inf) get down to ~ tacks* spijkers met koppen slaan

brassy [bra:sie] **1** (geel)koperen, koperkleurig; **2** brutaal; **3** blikkerig *(sound)*, schel

brat [bræt] snotaap, rotkind[h]

¹**brave** [breev] *adj* dapper, moedig: *put a ~ face on* zich sterk houden

²**brave** [breev] *vb* trotseren, weerstaan

bravery [breevərie] moed, dapperheid

¹**brawl** [bro:l] *n* vechtpartij, knokpartij

²**brawl** [bro:l] *vb* knokken, op de vuist gaan

brawn [bro:n] spierkracht, spieren

¹**bray** [bree] *vb* balken *(of donkey)*

²**bray** [bree] *n* schreeuw *(of donkey)*, gebalk[h]

Brazil [brəzil] Brazilië

¹**Brazilian** [brəziljən] *adj* Braziliaans

²**Brazilian** [brəziljən] *n* Braziliaan(se)

¹**breach** [brie:tsj] *n* **1** breuk, bres, gat[h]; **2** breuk, schending: *~ of contract* contractbreuk; *~ of the peace* ordeverstoring

²**breach** [brie:tsj] *vb* **1** doorbreken, een gat maken in; **2** verbreken, inbreuk maken op

bread [bred] **1** brood[h]: *~ and butter* boterham(men), *(fig)* dagelijkse levensbehoeften, levensonderhoud; *a loaf of ~* een brood; *slice of ~* boterham; **2** brood[h], kost, levensonderhoud[h]: *daily ~* dagelijks brood, dagelijkse levensbehoeften

breadth [bredθ] **1** breedte *(of dimensions)*; **2** breedte, strook, baan *(of material, wallpaper etc)*; **3** ruimte, uitgestrektheid

¹**break** [breek] *vb* **1** breken, kapot gaan, het begeven: *his voice broke* hij kreeg de baard in zijn keel; *~ with* breken met *(eg tradition, family)*; **2** ontsnappen, uitbreken, *(cycle racing)* demarreren: *~ free (of: loose)* ontsnappen, losbreken; **3** ophouden, tot een einde komen, omslaan *(of weather)*; **4** plotseling beginnen, aanbreken *(of day)*, losbreken, losbarsten *(of storm)*; **5** bekendgemaakt worden *(of news)*; **6** plotseling dalen, kelderen, ineenstorten *(of prices on stock exchange)*: *(inf; also com) ~ even* quitte spelen

²**break** [breek] *vb* **1** breken *(also fig)*, kapot maken, (financieel) ruïneren, laten springen *(bank)*: *~ cover* uit de schuilplaats komen; *~ the law* de wet overtreden; *~ a record* een record verbeteren; **2** onderbreken *(eg trip)*; **3** temmen, dresseren *(horse)*; **4** (voorzichtig) vertellen *((bad) news)*, tactvol vertellen; **5** schaven, bezeren *(skin)*; **6** ontcijferen, breken *(code)*; **7** *(tennis)* doorbreken *(service)*

³**break** [breek] *n* **1** onderbreking, verandering, breuk, stroomstoring: *a ~ for lunch* een lunchpau-

ze; *there was a ~ in the weather* het weer sloeg om; **2** uitbraak, ontsnapping, *(cycle racing)* demarrage: *make a ~ for it* proberen te ontsnappen; **3** *(tennis)* servicedoorbraak; **4** *(inf)* kans, geluk[h]: *lucky ~ geluk*, meevaller; *give s.o. a ~* iem een kans geven, iem een plezier doen; **5** begin[h], het aanbreken *(of day):* *~ of day* dageraad

breakable [br**ee**kǝbl] breekbaar

breakage [br**ee**kidzj] breuk, het breken, barst || *£10 for ~* £10 voor breukschade

¹breakaway *n* **1** afgescheiden groep; **2** uitval, demarrage aanval[h]

²breakaway *adj* afgescheiden

break away *(with from)* wegrennen (van), ontsnappen (aan), *(fig)* zich losmaken (van)

breakdown 1 defect[h], mankement[h]; **2** instorting, zenuwinstorting; **3** uitsplitsing, specificatie: *~ of costs* kostenverdeling, uitsplitsing van de kosten

¹break down *vb* **1** kapot gaan, defect raken *(of machine)*, verbroken raken *(of connections);* **2** mislukken *(of talks, marriage etc);* **3** instorten *(of human being);* **4** zich laten uitsplitsen, verdeeld worden, (with *into)* uiteenvallen (in): *the procedure can be broken down into five easy steps* de werkwijze kan onderverdeeld worden in vijf eenvoudige stappen

²break down *vb* **1** afbreken *(wall; also fig)*, vernietigen, slopen, inslaan, intrappen *(door);* **2** uitsplitsen, analyseren, *(chem)* afbreken

breaker [br**ee**kǝ] **1** sloper; **2** breker, brandingsgolf

break-even break-even, evenwichts-: *~ point* (punt van) evenwicht tussen inkomsten en uitgaven

¹breakfast [br**e**kfǝst] *n* ontbijt[h]

²breakfast [br**e**kfǝst] *vb* ontbijten

¹break in *vb* **1** interrumperen: *~ on* interrumperen, verstoren; **2** inbreken

²break in *vb* **1** africhten, dresseren; **2** inlopen *(shoes)*

break-in inbraak

breakneck halsbrekend: *at (a) ~ speed* in razende vaart

¹break off *vb* **1** afbreken *(eg of branch);* **2** pauzeren; **3** ophouden met praten, zijn mond houden

²break off *vb* **1** afbreken *(eg branch; also fig: negotiations etc);* **2** verbreken *(relationship with s.o.)*, ophouden met

breakout uitbraak, ontsnapping

break out 1 uitbreken; **2** (also with *of)* ontsnappen (uit), uitbreken, ontkomen (aan) || *~ in* bedekt raken met, onder komen te zitten *(eg small stains)*

breakthrough doorbraak

¹break through *vb* doorbreken, *(fig)* een doorbraak maken

²break through *vb + prep* doorbreken *(also fig)*

¹break up *vb* **1** uit elkaar vallen, in stukken breken, *(fig)* ten einde komen, ontbonden worden *(of meeting):* *their marriage broke up* hun huwelijk ging kapot; **2** uit elkaar gaan *(of (marriage) partners, group of people etc)*

²break up *vb* **1** uit elkaar doen vallen, in stukken breken, *(fig)* onderbreken, doorbreken *(routine, part*

of text); **2** kapot maken *(marriage);* **3** verspreiden, uiteenjagen *(group of people);* **4** beëindigen, een eind maken aan *(quarrel, fight, meeting): break it up!* hou ermee op!; **5** doen instorten, in elkaar doen klappen

break-up 1 opheffing, beëindiging *(business);* **2** scheiding *(of lovers)*

breakwater golfbreker

breast [brest] **1** borst, voorzijde, borststuk[h]; **2** hart[h], boezem

breast stroke schoolslag

breath [breθ] **1** adem(haling), lucht, het ademen: *get one's ~ (back) (again)* weer op adem komen; *out of ~* buiten adem; **2** zuchtje[h] (wind), licht briesje[h]; **3** vleugje[h]: *not a ~ of suspicion* geen greintje argwaan; *take one's ~ away* perplex doen staan

breathalyser [br**e**θǝlajzǝ] blaaspijpje[h]

¹breathe [brie:ð] *vb* **1** ademen, ademhalen, *(form)* leven: *~ in* inademen; *~ out* uitademen; **2** op adem komen, uitblazen, bijkomen

²breathe [brie:ð] *vb* **1** inademen; **2** uitblazen, uitademen; **3** inblazen, ingeven: *~ new life into* nieuw leven inblazen

breather [br**ie:**ðǝ] **1** pauze, adempauze; **2** beetje beweging, wandeling

breathless [br**e**θllǝs] **1** buiten adem, hijgend, ademloos; **2** ademloos, gespannen

breeches [brie:tsjǝs] *(pl)* kniebroek, *(inf)* lange broek

¹breed [brie:d] *vb* zich voortplanten, jongen

²breed [brie:d] *vb* **1** kweken, telen, fokken, *(fig)* voortbrengen; **2** kweken, opvoeden, opleiden: *well bred* goed opgevoed, welgemanierd

³breed [brie:d] *n* ras[h], aard, soort

breeding [br**ie:**ding] **1** het fokken, het kweken, fokkerij, kwekerij; **2** voortplanting, het jongen; **3** opvoeding, goede manieren

¹breeze [brie:z] *n* bries, wind

²breeze [brie:z] *vb (inf)* (zich) vlot bewegen: *~ in* (vrolijk) binnen komen waaien

breezy [br**ie:**zie] **1** winderig, tochtig; **2** opgewekt, levendig, vrolijk

brevity [br**e**vvittie] **1** kortheid; **2** beknoptheid, bondigheid

¹brew [broe:] *vb* **1** bierbrouwen; **2** trekken *(of tea);* broeien, dreigen, op komst zijn || *~ up* thee zetten

²brew [broe:] *vb* **1** brouwen *(beer)*, zetten *(tea);* **2** brouwen, uitbroeden

³brew [broe:] *n* brouwsel[h], bier[h]

brewery [br**oe:**ǝrie] brouwerij

¹bribe [brajb] *n* **1** steekpenning, smeergeld[h]; **2** lokmiddel[h]

²bribe [brajb] *vb* (om)kopen, steekpenningen geven, smeergeld betalen

¹brick [brik] *n* **1** baksteen; **2** blok[h] *(toy)* || *drop a ~* iets verkeerds zeggen, een blunder begaan

²brick [brik] *vb* metselen: *~ up, ~ in* dichtmetselen, inmetselen

bricklayer metselaar

brickwork metselwerk^h

bridal [brajdl] bruids-, huwelijks-, bruilofts-

bride [brajd] bruid

bridegroom bruidegom

bridesmaid [brajdzmeed] bruidsmeisje^h

¹bridge [bridzj] *n* **1** brug; **2** neusrug; **3** brug *(of glasses frame)*; **4** kam *(of string instrument)*; **5** bridge^h *(cards)*

²bridge [bridzj] *vb* overbruggen, een brug slaan over

bridgehead bruggenhoofd^h *(also fig)*

¹bridle [brajdl] *n* hoofdstel^h, *(fig)* breidel, toom

²bridle [brajdl] *vb* (verontwaardigd) het hoofd in de nek gooien

³bridle [brajdl] *vb* **1** (een paard) het hoofdstel aandoen; **2** breidelen, in toom houden

¹brief [brie:f] *adj* kort, beknopt, vluchtig: *a ~ look at the newspaper* een vluchtige blik in de krant; *~ and to the point* kort en krachtig; *in ~* om kort te gaan, kortom

²brief [brie:f] *n* **1** stukken, bescheiden, dossier^h; **2** *~s* (dames)slip, herenslip

³brief [brie:f] *vb* instrueren, aanwijzingen geven

briefcase aktetas, diplomatenkoffertje^h

briefing [brie:fing] (laatste) instructies, briefing, instruering

brigade [brigeed] brigade, korps^h

brigadier [brigədjə] brigadegeneraal *(in British army)*, brigadecommandant

brigand [brigənd] (struik)rover, bandiet

bright [brajt] **1** hel(der) *(also fig)*, licht, stralend: *always look on the ~ side of things* de dingen altijd van de zonnige kant bekijken; *~ red* helderrood; **2** opgewekt, vrolijk; **3** slim, pienter: *a ~ idea* een slim idee

brighten [brajtn] **1** (doen) opklaren, ophelderen *(also fig): the sky is ~ing up* de lucht klaart op; **2** oppoetsen, opvrolijken: *she has ~ed up his whole life* dankzij haar is hij helemaal opgeleefd

brill [bril] *(inf)* fantastisch

brilliant [briljənt] **1** stralend, fonkelend, glinsterend: *~ stars* fonkelende sterren; *~ red* hoogrood; **2** briljant, geniaal

¹brim [brim] *n* **1** (boven)rand, boord^h: *full to the ~* tot de rand toe vol, boordevol *(of a glass)*; **2** rand *(of a hat)*

²brim [brim] *vb* boordevol zijn, tot barstens toe gevuld zijn: *her eyes ~med with tears* haar ogen schoten vol tranen

brine [brajn] **1** pekel(nat)^h; **2** het zilte nat

bring [bring] **1** (mee)brengen, (mee)nemen, aandragen: *his cries brought his neighbours running* op zijn kreten kwamen zijn buren aangesneld; *~ a case before the court* een zaak aan de rechter voorleggen; **2** opleveren, opbrengen: *~ a good price* een goede prijs opbrengen; **3** teweegbrengen, leiden tot, voortbrengen: *I can't ~ myself to kill an animal* ik kan me(zelf) er niet toe brengen een dier te doden; *you've brought this problem (up)on yourself* je hebt je dit probleem zelf op de hals gehaald; *~*

home to duidelijk maken, aan het verstand brengen

bring about veroorzaken, teweegbrengen, aanrichten: *~ changes* veranderingen teweegbrengen

bring along 1 meenemen, meebrengen; **2** opkweken, in de ontwikkeling stimuleren; **3** doen gedijen

bring (a)round overhalen, ompraten, overreden

bring back 1 terugbrengen, retourneren, mee terugbrengen; **2** in de herinnering terugbrengen, doen herleven, oproepen: *this song brings back memories* dit liedje brengt (goede) herinneringen boven; **3** herinvoeren, herintroduceren: *~ capital punishment* de doodstraf weer invoeren

bring down 1 neerhalen, neerschieten *(aeroplane, bird)*; **2** aan de grond zetten; **3** *(sport)* neerleggen, onderuithalen, ten val brengen *(opponent)*; **4** ten val brengen, omverwerpen *(government)*; **5** drukken, verlagen, terugschroeven *(costs)*

bring forth *(form)* voortbrengen, *(fig)* veroorzaken, oproepen *(protest, criticism)*

bring in 1 binnenhalen *(harvest)*; **2** opleveren, afwerpen, inbrengen; **3** bijhalen, opnemen in, aanwerven: *~ experts to advise* deskundigen in de arm nemen; **4** inrekenen *(detainee)*; **5** komen aanzetten met, introduceren *(new fashion)*, indienen *(bill)*

bring off 1 in veiligheid brengen, redden uit; **2** *(inf)* voor elkaar krijgen, fiksen: *we've brought it off* we hebben het voor elkaar gekregen

bring on veroorzaken, teweegbrengen

bring out 1 naar buiten brengen, voor de dag komen met, *(fig also)* uitbrengen; **2** op de markt brengen, uitbrengen *(product)*; **3** duidelijk doen uitkomen: *this photo brings out all the details* op deze foto zijn alle details goed te zien

bring round bij bewustzijn brengen, bijbrengen ‖ *~ to* (het gesprek) in de richting sturen van

bring up 1 naar boven brengen; **2** grootbrengen, opvoeden; **3** ter sprake brengen, naar voren brengen; **4** *(inf)* uitbraken, overgeven, uitkotsen

brink [bringk] (steile) rand, (steile) oever: *on (of: to) the ~ of war* op de rand van oorlog

brisk [brisk] **1** kwiek, vlot: *~ trade* levendige handel; **2** verkwikkend, fris *(of wind)*

¹bristle [brisl] *n* stoppel(haar^h)

²bristle [brisl] *vb* recht overeind staan *(of hair): ~ (up)* zijn stekels opzetten, nijdig worden; *~ with anger* opvliegen van woede; *~ with* wemelen van

Brit [brit] *Briton*

Britain [britn] Groot-Brittannië

British [britisj] Brits, Engels: *the ~ Empire* het Britse Rijk; *the ~* de Britten

Briton [britn] Brit(se)

Brittany [britənie] Bretagne

brittle [britl] broos, breekbaar; onbestendig, wankel

broach [broots] **1** aanspreken, openmaken *(bottle etc)*; **2** aansnijden, ter sprake brengen, beginnen over *(topic)*

¹broad [bro:d] *adj* **1** breed, uitgestrekt, in de breedte: *~ bean* tuinboon; *~ shoulders* brede schouders; *~ly* *speaking* in zijn algemeenheid; **2** ruim(denkend); **3** gedurfd, onbekrompen, royaal; **4** duidelijk, direct: *a ~ hint* een overduidelijke wenk; **5** grof, plat, lomp: *~ Scots* met een sterk Schots accent; **6** ruim, globaal, ruw; **7** helder, duidelijk: *in ~ daylight* op klaarlichte dag

²broad [bro:d] *n* **1** brede (ge)deel(te)ʰ; **2** *(Am; inf)* wijfʰ, mokkelʰ ‖ *the Norfolk Broads* de Norfolkse plassen

¹broadcast [bro:dka:st] *n* (radio-)uitzending, tv-uitzending

²broadcast [bro:dka:st] *vb* **1** uitzenden, in de lucht zijn; **2** voor de radio (op de televisie) zijn

³broadcast [bro:dka:st] *vb* **1** breedwerpig zaaien, *(fig)* rondbazuinen, rondstrooien; **2** uitzenden

broaden [bro:dn] (zich) verbreden, breder worden (maken): *reading ~s the mind* lezen verruimt de blik

broad-minded ruimdenkend, tolerant

broccoli [brɔkkəlie] broccoli

brochure [broosjə] brochure, folder, prospectus: *advertising ~s* reclamefolders

¹broil [brojl] *vb* (liggen) bakken

²broil [brojl] *vb (esp Am)* **1** grillen, roosteren; **2** stoven: *~ing hot* smoorheet, bloedheet

broiler [brojlə] **1** grill, braadroosterʰ; **2** braadkuikenʰ, slachtkuikenʰ

broke *(inf)* platzak, blut, aan de grond, bankroet

broken 1 gebroken, kapot, stuk: *~ colours* gebroken kleuren; *~ English* gebrekkig Engels; *~ home* ontwricht gezin; *a ~ marriage* een stukgelopen huwelijk; **2** oneffen *(of terrain)*, ruw, geaccidenteerd; **3** onderbroken, verbrokkeld: *a ~ journey* een reis met veel onderbrekingen

broken-down versleten, vervallen

¹broker [brookə] *n* (effecten)makelaar

²broker [brookə] *vb* als makelaar optreden

³broker [brookə] *vb* (als makelaar) regelen

bronchitis [brongka-ittis] bronchitis

¹bronze [bronz] *n* **1** bronzen (kunst)voorwerpʰ; **2** bronzen medaille, bronsʰ, derde plaats; **3** bronsʰ; bronskleur

²bronze [bronz] *vb* bronsachtig worden, bruinen

³bronze [bronz] *vb* bronzen, bruinen

Bronze Age bronstijd, bronsperiode

brooch [brootsj] broche

¹brood [broe:d] *n* gebroedʰ, broed(selʰ), kroostʰ *(also fig)*

²brood [broe:d] *vb* **1** broeden; **2** tobben, piekeren, peinzen: *she just sits there ~ing* ze zit daar maar te piekeren; *~ about* (of: *on, over*) tobben over, piekeren over; *~ over one's future* inzitten over zijn toekomst

broody [broe:die] **1** broeds; **2** bedrukt, somber

brook [broek] beek, stroompjeʰ

broom [broe:m] **1** bezem, schrobber; **2** *(bot)* brem

Bros. *Brothers* Gebr.: *Jones ~* Gebr. Jones

broth [broθ] bouillon, vleesnatʰ, soep

brothel [broθl] bordeelʰ

brother [bruðə] **1** broer: *he has been like a ~ to me* hij is als een broer voor me geweest; **2** broeder, kloosterbroeder

brotherhood [bruðəhoed] broederschap

brother-in-law zwager

brow [brau] **1** wenkbrauw: *knit one's ~s* (de wenkbrauwen) fronsen; **2** voorhoofdʰ; **3** bovenrand, (overhangende) rotsrand, top, kruin

browbeat overdonderen, intimideren

brown [braun] bruin: *~ bread* bruinbrood, volkorenbrood; *~ paper* pakpapier

brownie [braunie] **1** goede fee, nachtelfjeʰ; **2** *Brownie* padvindster, kabouter *(from 7 to 11 years of age)*

¹browse [brauz] *vb* **1** grasduinen, (in boeken) snuffelen, (rond)neuzen; **2** weiden, (af)grazen

²browse [brauz] *n (esp singular)* het grasduinen, het neuzen: *have a good ~ through* flink grasduinen in; **2** (jonge) scheuten *(as food for animals)*

¹bruise [broe:z] *n* kneuzing *(also of fruit)*, blauwe plek

²bruise [broe:z] *vb* blauwe plek(ken) vertonen, gekneusd zijn

³bruise [broe:z] *vb* kneuzen, bezeren

bruiser [broe:zə] krachtpatser, rouwdouwer

brunt [brunt] eerste stoot, zwaartepuntʰ, toppuntʰ: *she bore the (full) ~ of his anger* zij kreeg de volle laag

¹brush [brusj] *n* **1** borstel, kwast, penseelʰ *(of artist, painter)*, brushes: *(fig) tarred with the same ~* uit hetzelfde (slechte) hout gesneden; **2** (af)borsteling; **3** lichte aanraking, beroering; **4** schermutseling, kort treffenʰ; **5** kreupelhoutʰ, onderhoutʰ; **6** kreupelbosʰ, met dicht struikgewas begroeid gebiedʰ

²brush [brusj] *vb* **1** (af-, op-, uit)borstelen, (af-, weg-, uit)vegen; **2** strijken (langs, over), rakelings gaan (langs): *the cat's whiskers ~ed my cheek* de snorharen van de kat streken langs mijn wang

brush aside 1 opzij-, wegschuiven *(resistance, opposition etc)*, uit de weg ruimen; **2** terzijde schuiven, naast zich neerleggen: *brush complaints aside* klachten wegwuiven

¹brush off *vb* zich laten wegborstelen, (door borstelen) loslaten

²brush off *vb* **1** wegborstelen, afborstelen; **2** (zich van) iem afhouden, afschepen: *I won't be brushed off* ik laat me niet afschepen

brush-off *(inf)* afscheping, afpoeiering, de bons: *give s.o. the ~: a)* iem met een kluitje in het riet sturen; *b)* iem de bons geven

brush up opfrissen, ophalen, bijspijkeren: *~ (on) your English* je Engels ophalen

brushwood onderhoutʰ, kreupelhoutʰ; sprokkelhoutʰ

brusque [broesk] bruusk, abrupt, kort aangebonden

Brussels (sprouts) spruitjes

brutal [broe:tl] bruut, beestachtig, meedogenloos: *~ frankness* genadeloze openhartigheid

brutality [broe:tǽlətie] bruutheid, wreedheid, on-menselijkheid

¹brute [broe:t] *n* 1 beest[h], dier[h]; 2 bruut, woesteling

²brute [broe:t] *adj* bruut, grof: ~ *force* grof geweld

B.Sc. *Bachelor of Science (roughly)* drs., ir.

B.S.I. *British Standards Institution (roughly)* NNI, Nederlands Normalisatie-instituut

B.S.T. *British Summer Time*

¹bubble [bubl] *n* 1 (lucht)bel(letje[h]): *blow ~s* bellen blazen; 2 glaskoepel; 3 *(fig)* zeepbel, ballonnetje[h]

²bubble [bubl] *vb* 1 borrelen, bruisen, pruttelen; 2 glimmen, stralen: ~ *over with enthusiasm* overlopen van enthousiasme

bubble gum klapkauwgom

¹bubbly [bublie] *adj* 1 bruisend, sprankelend; 2 jolig

²bubbly [bublie] *n* champagne

buccaneer [bukkəniə] boekanier, zeerover, vrijbuiter

¹buck [buk] *n* 1 mannetjesdier[h], bok *(of deer)*, ram(melaar) *(of rabbit, hare);* 2 dollar || *(inf) pass the ~ (to s.o.)* de verantwoordelijkheid afschuiven (op iem), (iem) de zwartepiet toespelen

²buck [buk] *vb* bokken *(of horse)*, bokkensprongen maken

³buck [buk] *vb* 1 afwerpen *(horseman, horsewoman)*, afgooien; 2 *(Am; inf)* tegenwerken: *you can't go on ~ing the system* je kunt je niet blijven verzetten tegen het systeem

¹bucket [bukkit] *n* emmer: *(inf; fig) it came down in ~s* het regende dat het goot; *(inf) kick the ~* het hoekje omgaan, de pijp uitgaan

²bucket [bukkit] *vb (inf)* gieten, plenzen, bij bakken neervallen *(of rain also)*

¹buckle [bukl] *n* gesp

²buckle [bukl] *vb* 1 met een gesp sluiten, aangegespt (kunnen) worden; 2 kromtrekken, ontzetten, ontwricht raken; 3 wankelen, wijken, bezwijken

³buckle [bukl] *vb* (vast)gespen: ~ *up a belt* een riem omdoen

¹buck up *vb (inf)* opschieten

²buck up *vb (inf)* opvrolijken

¹bud [bud] *n* knop, kiem: *nip in the ~* in de kiem smoren; *(fig) in the ~* in de dop

²bud [bud] *vb* knoppen, uitlopen

Buddha [boedə] boeddha(beeld)

Buddhism [boedizm] boeddhisme[h]

budding [budding] ontluikend, aankomend, in de dop

buddy [buddie] *(inf)* 1 maat, vriend, kameraad; 2 *(as form of address; Am)* maatje[h], makker

¹budge [budzj] *vb* 1 zich (ver)roeren, (zich) bewegen, zich verplaatsen: *the screw won't ~* ik krijg geen beweging in die schroef; 2 veranderen: *not ~ from one's opinion* aan zijn mening vasthouden

²budge [budzj] *vb* (een klein stukje) verplaatsen, verschuiven, verschikken: *not ~ one inch* geen duimbreed wijken

budgerigar [budzjəriga:] (gras)parkiet

¹budget [budzjit] *n* begroting, budget[h]

²budget [budzjit] *vb* 1 budgetteren, de begroting opstellen; 2 huishouden

³budget [budzjit] *vb* in een begroting opnemen, reserveren, ramen

⁴budget [budzjit] *adj* voordelig, goedkoop: ~ *prices* speciale aanbiedingen

¹buff [buf] *n* 1 *(inf)* enthousiast, liefhebber, fanaat; 2 rundleer[h], buffelleer[h]; 3 vaalgeel[h], bruingeel[h], buff: ~ *yellow* vaalgeel; 4 *(inf)* nakie[h], blootje[h]: *in the ~* naakt

²buff [buf] *vb* polijsten, opwrijven

buffalo [buffəloo] buffel; karbouw; bizon

¹buffer [buffə] *n* buffer, stootkussen[h], -blok[h]

²buffer [buffə] *vb* als buffer optreden voor, beschermen, behoeden

¹buffet [buffit] *vb* 1 meppen, slaan, beuken; 2 teisteren, kwellen, treffen: ~*ed by misfortunes* geteisterd door tegenslag

²buffet [boefee] *n* 1 dressoir[h], buffet[h]; 2 buffet[h], schenktafel; 3 niet-uitgeserveerde maaltijd: *cold ~* koud buffet

³buffet [buffit] *n* slag *(also fig)*, klap, dreun

buffoon [bəfoe:n] hansworst, potsenmaker, clown

¹bug [bug] *n* 1 halfvleugelig insect[h], wants, bedwants; 2 *(Am)* insect[h], beestje[h], ongedierte[h]; 3 *(inf)* virus[h] *(also fig)*, bacil, bacterie; 4 *(inf)* obsessie; 5 *(inf)* mankement[h], storing, defect[h]; 6 *(inf)* afluisterapparaatje[h], verborgen microfoontje[h]

²bug [bug] *vb (inf)* 1 afluisterapparatuur plaatsen in; 2 *(Am)* irriteren, ergeren, lastig vallen: *what is ~ging him?* wat zit hem dwars?

bugger [bugə] 1 *(vulg)* lul(hannes), zak(kenwasser); 2 *(vulg)* pedo(fiel), homo(fiel); 3 (arme) drommel, (arme) donder, kerel || ~ *him!* hij kan de tering krijgen

bugger off ophoepelen

bugger up verpesten, verzieken

buggy [bugie] 1 licht rijtuigje[h], open autootje[h]; 2 *(Am)* kinderwagen; 3 wandelwagen

bugle [bjoe:gl] bugel *(for military signals)*, signaalhoorn

¹build [bild] *vb* 1 (op)bouwen, maken: ~ *a fire* een vuur maken; 2 vormen, ontwikkelen, ontplooien; 3 samenstellen, vormen, opbouwen; 4 *(with on)* baseren (op), grondvesten, onderbouwen: ~ *one's hopes on* zijn hoop vestigen op; 5 inbouwen *(also fig)*, opnemen: *this clause was not built into my contract* deze clausule was niet in mijn contract opgenomen

²build [bild] *vb* 1 bouwen; 2 (in kracht) toenemen, aanwakkeren, verhevigen, groeien, aanzwellen: *tension built within her* de spanning in haar nam toe

³build [bild] *n* (lichaams)bouw, gestalte, vorm

builder [bildə] aannemer, bouwer

building [bilding] 1 gebouw[h], bouwwerk[h], pand[h]; 2 bouw, het bouwen, bouwkunst

¹build up *vb* 1 aangroeien, toenemen, zich opstapelen: *tension was building up* de spanning nam toe;

2 (geleidelijk) toe werken (naar)

²build up *vb* **1** opbouwen, ontwikkelen, tot bloei brengen: *~ a firm from scratch* een bedrijf van de grond af opbouwen; **2** ophemelen, loven, prijzen

build-up 1 opstopping, opeenhoping, opeenstapeling: *a ~ of traffic* een verkeersopstopping; **2** ontwikkeling, opbouw, vorming; **3** (troepen)concentratie

built-in ingebouwd *(also fig)*, aangeboren

built-up 1 samengesteld, geconstrueerd; **2** bebouwd, volgebouwd

bulb [bulb] **1** bol(letjeʰ), bloembol, *(by extension)* bolgewasʰ; **2** (gloei)lamp

Bulgaria [bulgeəriə] Bulgarije

¹Bulgarian [bulgeəriən] *adj* Bulgaars

²Bulgarian [bulgeəriən] *n* **1** Bulgaarsʰ *(language)*; **2** Bulgaar

¹bulge [buldʒj] *n* bobbel

²bulge [buldʒj] *vb* **1** (op)zwellen, uitdijen; **2** bol staan, opbollen, uitpuilen: *~ out* uitpuilen

bulk [bulk] **1** (grote) massa, omvang, volumeʰ: *~ buying* in het groot inkopen; *in ~: a)* onverpakt, los; *b)* in het groot; **2** (scheeps)lading, vracht; **3** grootste deelʰ, merendeelʰ, grosʰ: *the ~ of the books have already been sold* het merendeel van de boeken is al verkocht; **4** kolos, gevaarteʰ, massa; **5** (scheeps)ruimʰ

bulkhead (waterdicht) schotʰ, scheidingswand, afscheiding

bulky [bulkie] lijvig, log, dik, omvangrijk

bull [boel] **1** stier, bul, mannetjeʰ *(of whale, elephant etc): like a ~ in a china shop* als een olifant in een porseleinkast; *take the ~ by the horns* de koe bij de hoorns vatten; **2** (pauselijke) bul; **3** *(vulg)* kletspraat, gekletsʰ, gezeikʰ

bulldog buldog

bulldoze [boeldooz] **1** met een bulldozer bewerken; **2** *(inf)* (plat)walsen, doordrukken, zijn zin doordrijven

bulldozer [boeldoozə] bulldozer

bullet [boelit] (geweer)kogel, patroonʰ ‖ *bite (on) the ~* door de zure appel heen bijten

bulletin [boelətin] (nieuws)bulletinʰ, dienstmededeling

bulletin board *(Am)* mededelingenbordʰ, prikbordʰ

bull market stijgende markt *(at stock exchange)*

bullock [boelək] **1** os; **2** jonge stier, stiertjeʰ

bullring arena *(for bull fights)*

bull's-eye 1 roos *(target)*; **2** schotʰ in de roos *(also fig)*, rake opmerking; **3** *(type)* toverbal *(peppermint)*

bullshit *(vulg)* gekletsʰ, kletspraat, gezeikʰ

bull terrier bulterriër

¹bully [boelie] *n* **1** bullebak, beul, kwelgeest; **2** *(hockey)* afslag

²bully [boelie] *vb* koeioneren, intimideren: *~ s.o. into doing sth.* iem met bedreigingen dwingen tot iets

³bully [boelie] *adj (oft iron)* prima: *~ for you* bravo!, wat geweldig van jou!

bullyboy *(inf)* (gehuurde) zware jongen, vechtersbaas

bully off *(hockey)* de afslag verrichten

bulrush [boelrusj] **1** bies, mattenbies, stoelbies; **2** lisdodde; **3** *(rel)* papyrus(plant)

bulwark [boelwək] **1** (verdedigings)muur, wal, schans; **2** bolwerkʰ *(also fig)*, bastionʰ; **3** *(shipp)* verschansing

¹bum [bum] *n (vulg)* **1** kont, gatʰ, achtersteʰ; **2** *(Am and Austr; depr)* zwerver, schooier, landloper, bedelaar; **3** (kloot)zak, mislukkeling, nietsnut

²bum [bum] *adj (vulg)* waardeloos, rottig

bum along *(inf)* toeren, rustig rijden

bum around *(inf)* lanterfanten, lummelen, rondhangen

bumble [bumbl] **1** mompelen, brabbelen, bazelen: *to keep bumbling on about sth.* blijven doorzeuren over iets; **2** stuntelen, klungelen

bumblebee hommel

bumf [bumf] *(inf) (depr)* papierrommel, papiertroep, papierwinkel

¹bump [bump] *vb* **1** bonzen, stoten, botsen; **2** hobbelen, schokken: *we ~ed along in our old car* we denderden voort in onze oude auto

²bump [bump] *vb* stoten tegen, botsen tegen, rammen: *don't ~ your head* stoot je hoofd niet

³bump [bump] *n* **1** bons, schok, stoot; **2** buil, bult, hobbel *(in road, terrain)*

⁴bump [bump] *adv* pats-boem, pardoes

bumper [bumpə] **1** (auto)bumper, stootkussenʰ, -rand, *(Am)* buffer, stootb(l)okʰ; **2** iets vols, iets groots, overvloed: *~ crop* (of: *harvest*) recordoogst

bumph [bumf] *see* bumf

bump into *(inf)* tegen het lijf lopen, toevallig tegenkomen

bumptious [bumpsjəs] opdringerig, verwaand

bump up *(inf)* opkrikken, opschroeven

bumpy [bumpie] hobbelig, bobbelig

bun [bun] **1** (krenten)bolletjeʰ, broodjeʰ; **2** (haar)knot(jeʰ)

¹bunch [buntsj] *n* **1** bos(je)ʰ, bundel, tros: *a ~ of grapes* een tros(je) druiven; *a ~ of keys* een sleutelbos; **2** *(inf)* troep(jeʰ), groep(jeʰ), stel(letjeʰ): *the best of the ~* de beste van het stel

²bunch [buntsj] *vb* samendringen, samendrommen

¹bundle [bundl] *n* bundel, bosʰ, pak(ket)ʰ, zenuw-, spier-, vezelbundel: *he is a ~ of nerves* hij is één bonk zenuwen

²bundle [bundl] *vb* **1** bundelen, samenbinden, samenpakken, samenvouwen: *~ up old newspapers* een touwtje om oude kranten doen; **2** proppen, (weg)stouwen, (weg)stoppen, induwen, inproppen

¹bung [bung] *n* stop, kurk, afsluiter

²bung [bung] *vb* keilen, gooien, smijten

bungalow [bunggəloo] bungalow

bungee jumping [bundzjie] bungeejumping

bungle [bunggl] (ver)knoeien, (ver)prutsen

bung up *(inf)* verstoppen, dichtstoppen: *my nose is bunged up* mijn neus zit verstopt

bunk [bungk] (stapel)bed^h, kooi ‖ *(inf) do a ~* ertussenuit knijpen, 'm smeren

bunk-bed stapelbed^h

bunk-up duwtje^h

bunny [bunnie] (ko)nijntje^h

bunting [bunting] 1 *(zoology)* gors; vink; 2 dundoek^h, vlaggetjes

¹buoy [boj] *n* 1 boei, ton(boei); 2 redding(s)boei

²buoy [boj] *vb* 1 drijvend houden: *~ed (up) by the sea* drijvend op de zee; 2 schragen, ondersteunen, dragen

buoyant [bojjənt] 1 drijvend; 2 opgewekt, vrolijk, luchthartig

buoy up opvrolijken, opbeuren

bur [bə:] klis, klit

burble [bə:bl] 1 kabbelen; 2 leuteren, ratelen, kwekken

¹burden [bə:dn] *n* 1 last, vracht, verplichting: *beast of ~* lastdier, pakdier, pakezel, pakpaard; *~ of proof* bewijslast; *be a ~ to s.o.* iem tot last zijn; 2 leidmotief^h, grondthema^h, hoofdthema^h, kern

²burden [bə:dn] *vb* belasten, beladen, overladen, (zwaar) drukken op

burdensome [bə:dnsəm] (lood)zwaar, bezwarend, drukkend

bureau [bjoeəroo] 1 schrijftafel; 2 *(Am)* ladekast; 3 dienst, bureau^h, kantoor^h, departement^h, ministerie^h

bureaucracy [bjoerokrəsi] bureaucratie

bureaucrat [bjoeərəkræt] *(oft depr)* bureaucraat

burgh [burrə] 1 stad, (stedelijke) gemeente; 2 kiesdistrict^h

burglar [bə:glə] inbreker

burglary [bə:glərie] inbraak

burgle [bə:gl] inbreken (in), inbraak plegen (bij), stelen (bij)

Burgundy [bə:gəndie] 1 Bourgondië; 2 bourgogne(wijn), Bourgondische wijn; 3 bordeauxrood

burial [berriəl] begrafenis

burlesque [bə:lesk] koddig, kluchtig

burly [bə:lie] potig, zwaar, flink

Burma [bə:mə] Birma

Burmese [bə:mie:z] Birmaans

¹burn [bə:n] *vb* 1 branden, gloeien: *~ low* uitgaan, uitdoven; *~ing for an ideal* in vuur en vlam voor een ideaal; *~ with anger* koken van woede; 2 branden, af-, ver-, ontbranden, in brand staan (steken): *the soup burnt my mouth* ik heb mijn mond aan de soep gebrand; *~ away* opbranden, wegbranden, *(fig)* verteren; *~ off* weg-, afbranden, schoon-, leegbranden; *~ to death* door verbranding om het leven brengen

²burn [bə:n] *vb* 1 verteren; 2 werken op, gebruiken als brandstof; 3 in brand steken

³burn [bə:n] *n* brandwond, brandgaatje^h

burn down (tot de grond toe) afbranden, platbranden

burner [bə:nə] brander, pit *(of cooking apparatus etc)*

burning [bə:ning] brandend, gloeiend, dringend: *a ~ issue* een brandend vraagstuk

burnish [bə:nisj] (op)glanzen, gaan glanzen, polijsten

¹burn out *vb* 1 uitbranden, opbranden *(also fig)*; 2 doorbranden *(of electrical appliance etc)*, doorslaan

²burn out *vb* 1 uitbranden: *the shed was completely burnt out* de schuur was volledig uitgebrand; 2 door brand verdrijven uit, door brand dakloos maken; 3 *(inf)* overwerken, over de kop werken: *burn oneself out* zich over de kop werken; 4 doen doorbranden

burnt gebrand, geschroeid, gebakken: *~ offering* (of: *sacrifice)* brandoffer

burnt-out 1 opgebrand, uitgeblust, versleten; 2 uitgebrand; 3 dakloos *(because of fire)*; 4 *(inf)* doodmoe, uitgeput, afgepeigerd

¹burn up *vb* 1 oplaaien, feller gaan branden; 2 *(inf)* scheuren, jakkeren, hard rijden; 3 *(Am; inf)* laaiend (van woede) zijn

²burn up *vb* verstoken, opbranden

¹burp [bə:p] *n (inf)* boer(tje^h), oprisping

²burp [bə:p] *vb (inf)* (laten) boeren, een boertje laten doen *(baby)*

¹burrow [burroo] *vb* 1 een leger graven, *(fig)* zich nestelen, beschutting zoeken; 2 wroeten, graven, zich (een weg) banen: *(fig) ~ into somebody's secrets* in iemands geheimen wroeten

²burrow [burroo] *n* leger^h *(of rabbit etc)*, hol(letje^h), tunnel(tje^h)

bursar [bə:sə] thesaurier, penningmeester

¹burst [bə:st] *vb* 1 (los-, uit)barsten; doorbreken, uit elkaar springen: *~ forth, ~ out* uitroepen, uitbarsten; *~ out crying* in huilen uitbarsten; *~ into tears* in tranen uitbarsten; 2 op barsten, springen staan, barstensvol zitten: *be ~ing to come* staan te popelen om te komen

²burst [bə:st] *vb* door-, open-, verbreken, forceren, inslaan, intrappen: *the river will ~ its banks* de rivier zal buiten haar oevers treden; *(fig) ~ one's sides (with) laughing* schudden van het lachen

³burst *n* uitbarsting, ontploffing; demarrage: *~ of anger* woede-uitbarsting; *~ of laughter* lachsalvo

burst in komen binnenvallen, binnenstormen, (ruw) onderbreken

bury [berrie] 1 begraven; 2 verbergen, verstoppen: *~ one's hands in one's pockets* zijn handen (diep) in zijn zakken steken; 3 verzinken *(also fig)*: *buried in thoughts* in gedachten verzonken; *~ oneself in one's books* zich in zijn boeken verdiepen

¹bus [bus] *n (Am also ~ses)* 1 (auto)bus: *(fig) miss the ~* de boot missen; *go by ~* de bus nemen; 2 *(inf)* bak, kar; 3 *(inf)* kist, vliegtuig^h

²bus [bus] *vb* met de bus gaan (vervoeren), de bus nemen, per bus reizen, op de bus zetten

busby [buzbie] kolbak, berenmuts

bush [boesj] 1 struik, bosje[h]; 2 struikgewas[h], kreupelhout[h]; 3 rimboe, woestenij, wildernis || *beat about the ~* ergens omheen draaien, niet ter zake komen

bushed [boesjt] *(inf)* bekaf, doodop, uitgeput

business [biznis] 1 handel, zaken: *get down to ~* ter zake komen, spijkers met koppen slaan; *mean ~* het serieus menen; *be in ~* (bezig met) handel drijven, *(fig)* startklaar staan; *on ~* voor zaken; 2 iets afdoends, ruwe behandeling, standje[h]; 3 (ver)plicht(ing), taak, verantwoordelijkheid, werk[h]: *(inf) my affairs are no ~ of yours* (of: *none of your ~)* mijn zaken gaan jou niets aan; *have no ~ to do sth.* ergens niet het recht toe hebben; *I will make it my ~ to see that ...* ik zal het op me nemen ervoor te zorgen dat ...; *(inf) mind your own ~* bemoei je met je eigen (zaken); 4 agenda, programma[h]: *(on agenda of meeting) any other ~* rondvraag, wat verder ter tafel komt; *(inf) like nobody's ~* als geen ander; 5 aangelegenheid, affaire, zaak, kwestie: *I'm sick and tired of this whole ~* ik ben dit hele gedoe meer dan zat; 6 moeilijke taak, hele kluif; 7 zaak, winkel, bedrijf[h]

businessman [biznismən] zakenman

busker [buskə] (bedelend) straatmuzikant

¹**bust** [bust] *n* 1 buste, borstbeeld[h]; 2 boezem, buste, borsten

²**bust** [bust] *adj (inf)* kapot, stuk, naar de knoppen: *go ~* op de fles gaan

³**bust** [bust] *vb (inf)* 1 barsten, breken, kapotgaan; 2 op de fles gaan, bankroet gaan

⁴**bust** [bust] *vb (inf)* 1 breken, mollen, kapotmaken; 2 laten springen, doorbreken, verbreken, bankroet laten gaan, platzak maken; 3 arresteren, aanhouden; 4 een inval doen in, huiszoeking doen bij *(by police)*

¹**bustle** [busl] *vb* druk in de weer zijn, jachten, zich haasten: *~ with* bruisen van

²**bustle** [busl] *n* drukte, bedrijvigheid

bust-up *(inf)* 1 stennis, herrie; 2 *(Am)* mislukking *(of marriage)*, het stuklopen

¹**busy** [bizzie] *adj* 1 bezig, druk bezet, bedrijvig: *she is ~ at* (of: *with) her work* ze is druk aan het werk; 2 *(Am)* bezet, in gesprek *(of telephone)*

²**busy** [bizzie] *vb* bezighouden, zoet houden: *~ oneself with collecting stamps* postzegels verzamelen om iets om handen te hebben

busybody bemoeial

¹**but** [but] *conj* 1 *(exception)* behalve, buiten, uitgezonderd: *what could I do ~ surrender?* wat kon ik doen behalve me overgeven?; 2 *(contrast)* maar (toch), niettemin, desondanks: *not a man ~ an animal* geen mens maar een dier; *~ then (again)* (maar) anderzijds, maar ja; *~ yet* niettemin

²**but** [but] *prep* behalve, buiten, uitgezonderd: *he wanted nothing ~ peace* hij wilde slechts rust; *the last ~ one* op één na de laatste

³**but** [but] *adv* 1 slechts, enkel, alleen, maar, pas: *I could ~ feel sorry for her* ik kon enkel medelijden

hebben met haar; *I know ~ one* ik ken er maar één; 2 (en) toch, echter, anderzijds

butch [boetsj] *(inf)* 1 manwijf[h], pot; 2 ruwe klant, vechtersbaas

¹**butcher** [boetsjə] *n* slager, slachter

²**butcher** [boetsjə] *vb* 1 slachten; 2 afslachten, uitmoorden

but for [but fo:] ware het niet voor, als niet

¹**butt** [but] *n* 1 mikpunt[h] *(of mockery)*; 2 doelwit[h], roos; 3 (dik) uiteinde[h], kolf, handvat[h], restant[h], eindje[h], peuk, *(inf)* achterste[h], krent, *(Am)* romp, tors; 4 *(Am)* sigaret, peuk; 5 (bier)vat[h], wijnvat[h], (regen)ton; 6 ram, kopstoot, stoot *(with head or horns)*

²**butt** [but] *vb* rammen *(with head or horns)*, stoten, een kopstoot geven

butter [butə] boter || *(he looks as if) ~ wouldn't melt in his mouth* hij lijkt van de prins geen kwaad te weten

buttercup boterbloem

butterfly [butəflaj] vlinder

buttermilk karnemelk, botermelk

butter up *(inf)* vleien, stroop om de mond smeren, slijmen

butt in *(inf)* tussenbeide komen, onderbreken

buttock [butlək] 1 bil; 2 *~s* achterste[h], achterwerk[h]

button [butn] 1 knoop(je[h]); 2 (druk)knop, knopje[h]; 3 *(Am)* button, rond insigne[h] || *(Am; inf) on the ~: a)* precies, de spijker op z'n kop; *b)* in de roos

button bar menubalk

¹**buttonhole** *n* knoopsgat[h]

²**buttonhole** *vb* in zijn kraag grijpen, staande houden

¹**button up** *vb* dichtknopen, dichtdoen: *(Am; inf) ~ your lip* hou je kop; *that job is buttoned up* dat is voor elkaar

²**button up** *vb (inf)* zijn kop houden

¹**buttress** [butris] *n* steunbeer, *(fig)* steunpilaar

²**buttress** [butris] *vb (also with up)* versterken met steun(beer), *(fig)* (onder)steunen

¹**buy** [baj] *vb* (aan-, in-, op)kopen, aanschaffen: *peace was dearly bought* de vrede werd duur betaald; *~ time* tijd winnen; *~ back* terugkopen; *~ up* opkopen, overnemen; *(inf) ~ it* gedood worden

²**buy** [baj] *vb (inf)* geloven, accepteren, (voor waar) aannemen: *don't ~ that nonsense* laat je niks wijsmaken

³**buy** [baj] *n* 1 aankoop, aanschaf, koop; 2 koopje[h], voordeeltje[h]

buyer [bajjə] 1 koper, klant; 2 inkoper *(of department store etc)*

¹**buzz** [buz] *vb* 1 zoemen, brommen, gonzen; roezemoezen; 2 druk in de weer zijn; 3 op een zoemer drukken, (aan)bellen || *(Am; inf) ~ along* opstappen *(after visit)*

²**buzz** [buz] *n* 1 brom-, gons-, zoemgeluid[h], geroezemoes[h]; 2 *(inf)* belletje[h], telefoontje[h]: *give mother a ~ bel* moeder even

buzzard [buzzəd] buizerd

¹by [baj] *prep* **1** *(nearness)* bij, dichtbij, vlakbij, naast, *(on compass card)* ten: *sit ~ my side* kom naast mij zitten; *~ oneself* alleen; **2** *(way, medium etc)* door, langs, via, voorbij: *travel ~ air* vliegen; *taught ~ radio* via de radio geleerd; **3** *(time)* tegen, vóór, niet later dan, *(by extension)* op, om *(certain time)*, in *(certain year)*: *finished ~ Sunday* klaar tegen zondag; *~ now* nu (al); **4** *(instrument, means etc)* door, door middel van, per, als gevolg van: *~ accident* per ongeluk; *he missed ~ an inch* hij miste op een paar centimeter; *I did it all ~ myself* ik heb het helemaal alleen gedaan; **5** ten opzichte van, wat … betreft: *paid ~ the hour* per uur betaald; *play ~ the rules* volgens de regels spelen; *that is fine ~ me* ik vind het best, wat mij betreft is het goed; **6** *(time or circumstance)* bij, tijdens: *~ day* overdag; **7** *(sequence)* na, per: *he got worse ~ the hour* hij ging van uur tot uur achteruit; *swear ~ the Bible* op de bijbel zweren

²by [baj] *adv* langs, voorbij: *in years gone ~* in vervlogen jaren; *~ and ~* straks; *~ and large* over 't algemeen

bye [baj] *(inf)* tot ziens, dag

bygone [bajgon] voorbij, vroeger

bygones [bajgonz]: *let ~ be ~* het verleden laten rusten, men moet geen oude koeien uit de sloot halen

by-law 1 (plaatselijke) verordening, gemeenteverordening; **2** *(Am)* (bedrijfs)voorschrift[h], (huis)regel, *~s* huishoudelijk reglement[h]

¹bypass *n* **1** *(traf)* rondweg, ringweg; **2** *(techn)* omloopkanaal[h], omloopleiding, omloopverbinding

²bypass *vb* om … heen gaan, mijden

bystander [bajstændə] omstander, toeschouwer

byte [bajt] byte

byway zijweg ‖ *(fig) the ~s of literature* de minder bekende paden van de letterkunde

byword 1 spreekwoord[h], gezegde[h], zegswijze; **2** belichaming, synoniem[h], prototype[h]: *Joe is a ~ for laziness* Joe is het prototype van de luilak

C

C. 1 *Celsius* **2** *cent* **3** *centigrade* **4** *circa* ca.

cab [kæb] **1** *(Am)* taxi; **2** *(inf; traf)* cabine, bok, cockpit

cabbage [kæbidzj] **1** kool; **2** *(inf)* slome duikelaarʰ, druiloor

cabby [kæbie] *(inf)* taxichauffeur

cabin [kæbin] **1** (houten) optrek, huisjeʰ, hut, kleedhokjeʰ, badhokjeʰ, *(railways)* seinhuisʰ; **2** cabine, (slaap)hut *(on ship)*, laadruimte, bagageruimʰ *(in aeroplane)*

cabin cruiser motorjachtʰ

cabinet [kæbinnət] **1** kast, porseleinkast, televisiemeubelʰ, dossierkast; **2** kabinetʰ, ministerraad; **3** kabinetsberaadʰ, kabinetsvergadering

¹cable [keebl] *n* **1** kabel, sleepkabel, trekkabel; **2** (elektriciteits)kabel, televisiekabel; **3** kabel, kabelvormig ornamentʰ, *(knitting)* kabelsteek

²cable [keebl] *vb* telegraferen

cable car kabelwagen, gondel, cabine ve kabelbaan

caboodle [kəboe:dl] *(inf)* troep, zwik, bups: *the whole ~* de hele bups

cab rank taxistandplaats

cache [kæsj] **1** (geheime) bergplaats; **2** (geheime, verborgen) voorraad

¹cackle [kækl] *vb* **1** kakelen, *(fig)* kwebbelen, kletsen; **2** giechelen, kraaien

²cackle [kækl] *n* **1** kakelgeluidʰ; **2** giechel(lachjeʰ), gekraaiʰ: *~s of excitement* opgewonden gilletjes; **3** gekakelʰ, *(fig)* gekwebbelʰ, gekletsʰ: *(inf) cut the ~* genoeg gekletst

cactus [kæktəs] cactus

cad [kæd] *(depr)* schoft

cadaverous [kədævərəs] lijkachtig, lijkkleurig

caddie [kædie] *(golf)* caddie

caddish [kædisj] schofterig, ploerterig

caddy [kædie] theeblikjeʰ, -busjeʰ

cadence [keedəns] **1** stembuiging, toonval, intonatie; **2** *(mus)* cadens; **3** cadans, vloeiend ritmeʰ

cadet [kədet] cadet

¹cadge [kædzj] *vb (inf; depr)* klaplopen, schooien

²cadge [kædzj] *vb (inf; depr)* bietsen, aftroggelen

C(a)esarean (section) [sizzeəriən] keizersnede

café [kæfee] **1** eethuisjeʰ, café-restaurantʰ, snackbar; **2** theesalon, tearoom; **3** koffiehuisʰ

cafeteria [kæfittjəriə] snelbuffetʰ, zelfbedieningsrestaurantʰ

caff [kæf] *(inf) see* café

¹cage [keedzj] *n* **1** kooi(constructie); **2** liftkooi, liftbak; **3** gevangenis, (krijgs)gevangenkampʰ; **4** *(ice hockey)* kooi, doelʰ

²cage [keedzj] *vb* kooien, in een kooi opsluiten

cag(e)y [keedzjie] *(inf)* **1** gesloten, behoedzaam, teruggetrokken; **2** argwanend, achterdochtig

cajole [kədzjool] (door vleierij) bepraten, ompraten, overhalen: *~ s.o. into giving money* iem geld aftroggelen

cake [keek] **1** cake, taart, (pannen)koek, gebakʰ: *go (of: sell) like hot ~s* verkopen als warme broodjes, lopen als een trein; **2** blokʰ *(of compact material)*, koek: *(inf) you can't have your ~ and eat it* je kunt niet alles willen

calamity [kəlæmittie] onheilʰ, calamiteit, ramp(spoed)

calcium [kælsiəm] calciumʰ

¹calculate [kælkjoeleet] *vb* **1** rekenen, een berekening maken; **2** schatten, een schatting maken

²calculate [kælkjoeleet] *vb* **1** (wiskundig) berekenen, (vooraf) uitrekenen; **2** beramen, bewust plannen: *~d to attract the attention* bedoeld om de aandacht te trekken; **3** incalculeren: *~d risk* ingecalculeerd risico

calculation [kælkjoeleesjən] **1** berekening *(also fig)*; **2** voorspelling, schatting; **3** bedachtzaamheid

calculator [kælkjoeleetə] rekenmachine, calculator

calendar [kælində] **1** kalender; **2** *(Am)* agenda *(of meeting)*

calf [ka:f] *(calves)* kalfʰ

calibre [kælibbə] kaliberʰ, gehalteʰ, niveauʰ, klasse

¹call [ko:l] *vb* **1** afroepen, oplezen, opsommen: *~ out numbers* nummers afroepen; **2** (op)roepen, aanroepen, terugroepen *(actor)*, tot het priesterschap roepen: *~ a witness* een getuige oproepen; **3** afkondigen, bijeenroepen, proclameren: *~ a meeting* een vergadering bijeenroepen; **4** wakker maken, wekken, roepen; **5** (be)noemen, aanduiden als: *~ s.o. a liar* iem uitmaken voor leugenaar; *(inf) what-d'you-call-it* hoe-heet-het-ook-weer?, dinges; *Peter is ~ed after his grandfather* Peter is vernoemd naar zijn grootvader; **6** vinden, beschouwen als: *I ~ it nonsense* ik vind het onzin; **7** het houden op, zeggen, (een bedrag) afmaken op: *let's ~ it ten euros* laten we het op tien euro houden; **8** *(cards)* bieden: *~ into being* in het leven roepen; *~ away* wegroepen; *~ forth* oproepen, (naar) boven brengen

²call [ko:l] *vb* **1** (uit)roepen: *~ for help* om hulp roepen; **2** (op)bellen; **3** *(cards)* bieden

³call [ko:l] *vb* (even) langsgaan (langskomen), (kort) op bezoek gaan, stoppen *(at a station): the ship ~s at numerous ports* het schip doet talrijke havens aan

⁴call [ko:l] *n* **1** kreet, roep van dier, roep van vogel: *we heard a ~ for help* we hoorden hulpgeroep; *within ~* binnen gehoorsafstand; **2** (kort, formeel, zakelijk) bezoekʰ: *pay a ~* een visite afleggen, *(inf; euph)*

naar een zekere plaats (of: nummer 100) gaan; **3** beroep[h], aanspraak, claim; **4** oproep(ing), roep(ing), appel[h], voorlezing van presentielijst, (fin) oproep tot aflossing ve schuld, aanmaning: *the actors received a ~ for eight o'clock* de acteurs moesten om acht uur op; *at ~, on ~* (onmiddellijk) beschikbaar, op afroep; *the doctor was on call* de dokter had bereikbaarheidsdienst; **5** reden, aanleiding, noodzaak, behoefte: *there's no ~ for you to worry* je hoeft je niet ongerust te maken; **6** telefoontje[h], (telefoon)gesprek[h]: *~ to the bar* toelating als advocaat; *(euph) ~ of nature* aandrang *(to go to the toilet)*, natuurlijke behoefte

call-box telefooncel

call charges voorrijkosten

caller [ko:lə] **1** bezoeker; **2** beller, iem die belt

call for 1 komen om, (komen) afhalen; **2** wensen, verlangen, vragen: *~ the bill* de rekening vragen; **3** vereisen: *this situation calls for immediate action* in deze toestand is onmiddellijk handelen geboden

call-girl callgirl

call in 1 laten komen, de hulp inroepen van, consulteren: *~ a specialist* er een specialist bij halen; **2** terugroepen, terugvorderen, uit de circulatie nemen: *some cars had to be called in* een aantal auto's moest terug naar de fabriek

call off afzeggen, afgelasten: *~ one's engagement* het afmaken

callous [kæləs] **1** vereelt, verhard; **2** ongevoelig, gevoelloos

¹call out *vb* **1** uitroepen, een gil geven; **2** roepen, hardop praten

²call out *vb* **1** afroepen, opnoemen; **2** te hulp roepen *(fire bridage etc)*

callow [kæloo] **1** kaal *(of birds)*, zonder veren; **2** groen, jong, onervaren

call up 1 opbellen; **2** in het geheugen roepen, zich (weer) voor de geest halen; **3** *(mil)* oproepen, te hulp roepen, inschakelen: *~ reserves* reserves inzetten

call (up)on 1 (even) langsgaan bij, (kort) bezoeken: *we'll ~ you tomorrow* we komen morgen bij u langs; **2** een beroep doen op, aanspreken

¹calm [ka:m] *n* **1** (wind)stilte *(also fig)*, kalmte; **2** windstilte *(wind-force o)*

²calm [ka:m] *adj* kalm, (wind)stil, vredig, rustig

³calm [ka:m] *vb* kalmeren

calorie [kælərie] calorie

calumny [kæləmnie] laster(praat), roddel, geroddel[h]

camel [kæml] kameel, dromedaris

camera [kæmərə] fototoestel[h], (film)camera || *(law)* in ~ achter gesloten deuren

camisole [kæmissool] (mouwloos) hemdje[h]

camomile [kæməmajl] kamille

¹camouflage [kæməfla:zj] *n* camouflage

²camouflage [kæməfla:zj] *vb* camoufleren, wegmoffelen

¹camp [kæmp] *n* **1** kamp[h], legerplaats, *(fig)* aanhang

van partij: *break* (of: *strike) ~, break up ~* (zijn tenten) opbreken; **2** kitsch

²camp [kæmp] *vb* kamperen, zijn kamp opslaan

³camp [kæmp] *adj* **1** verwijfd; **2** homoseksueel; **3** overdreven, theatraal, bizar; **4** kitscherig

campaign [kæmpeen] campagne, manoeuvre: *advertising ~* reclamecampagne

camphor [kæmfə] kamfer

campsite kampeerterrein[h], camping

campus [kæmpəs] campus *(university or school grounds)*

¹can [kæn] *vb* **1** kunnen, in staat zijn te: *I ~ readily understand that* ik kan dat best begrijpen; **2** kunnen, zou kunnen: *~ this be true?* zou dit waar kunnen zijn?; *I could go to the baker's if you like* ik zou naar de bakker kunnen gaan als je wilt; **3** mogen, kunnen, bevoegd zijn te: *you ~ go now* je mag nu gaan

²can [kæn] *n* **1** houder *(usually of metal)*, kroes, kan; **2** blik[h], conservenblikje[h], filmblik[h]: *in the ~* gereed; **3** *(Am; vulg)* plee; **4** *(inf)* bak, bajes, lik: *(Am; inf) ~ of worms* een moeilijke kwestie; *(inf) carry* (of: *take) the ~ (back)* ergens voor opdraaien

³can [kæn] *vb* inblikken, conserveren, inmaken || *(Am; vulg) ~ it!* hou op!

Canada [kænədə] Canada

¹Canadian [kəneediən] *adj* Canadees, van Canada

²Canadian [kəneediən] *n* Canadees

canal [kənæl] kanaal[h], vaart, gracht, (water)leiding

canalization [kænəlajzeesjən] kanalisatie, het in banen leiden

canary [kənəərie] kanarie(piet)

¹cancel [kænsl] *vb* **1** doorstrepen, doorhalen, (door)schrappen; **2** opheffen, ongedaan maken, vernietigen; **3** annuleren, afzeggen, opzeggen, intrekken *(order)*, herroepen, afgelasten; **4** ongeldig maken, afstempelen *(stamp)*

²cancel [kænsl] *vb* tegen elkaar wegvallen, elkaar compenseren, tegen elkaar opwegen: *the arguments ~ (each other)* de argumenten wegen tegen elkaar op

¹cancel out *vb* elkaar compenseren, tegen elkaar opwegen

²cancel out *vb* compenseren, goedmaken, neutraliseren: *the pros and cons cancel each other out* de voor- en nadelen heffen elkaar op

cancer [kænsə] **1** *Cancer (astrology)* (de) Kreeft: *tropic of Cancer* kreeftskeerkring; **2** kanker, kwaadaardige tumor, *(fig)* (verderfelijk, woekerend) kwaad[h]

candid [kændid] open(hartig), rechtuit, eerlijk

candidate [kændiddit] kandidaat, gegadigde

candidature [kændətsjə] kandidatuur, kandidaatschap[h]

candle [kændl] kaars || *burn the ~ at both ends* te veel hooi op zijn vork nemen; *he can't hold a ~ to her* hij doet voor haar onder

candlestick kandelaar, kaarsenstandaard

candlewick kaarsenpit

candour [kændə] open(hartig)heid, eerlijkheid, oprechtheid

candy [kændie] **1** (stukje^h) kandij^h, suikergoed^h; **2** (Am) snoepje^h, snoepjes, zuurtje^h, zuurtjes, chocola(atje^h)

¹cane [keen] n **1** dikke stengel, rietstengel, bamboestengel, rotan(stok); **2** rotting, wandelstok, plantensteun; **3** (bot) stam, stengel, scheut; **4** riet^h, rotan^h, bamboe^{+h}, suikerriet^h

²cane [keen] vb **1** met het rietje geven, afranselen; **2** matten (of furniture)

canine [keenajn] hondachtig, hondscanister [kænistə] bus, trommel, blik^h

cannabis [kænəbis] (Indische) hennep, cannabis; marihuana, wiet

canned [kænd] ingeblikt, in blik || ~ music ingeblikte muziek, muzak

cannibal [kænibl] kannibaal, menseneter

¹cannon [kænən] n **1** kanon^h, (stuk^h) geschut^h, boordkanon^h; **2** (billiards) carambole

²cannon [kænən] vb (op)botsen: she ~ed into me ze vloog tegen me op

cannonade [kænəneed] kanonnade, bombardement^h

canny [kænie] **1** slim, uitgekookt; **2** zuinig, spaarzaam

¹canoe [kənoe:] n kano

²canoe [kənoe:] vb kanoën, kanovaren

canon [kænən] **1** kerkelijke leerstelling, (algemene) regel (also fig): the Shakespeare ~ (lijst van) aan Shakespeare toegeschreven werken; **2** kanunnik

canonize [kænənajz] heilig verklaren

canoodle [kənoe:dl] (inf) knuffelen, scharrelen

canopy [kænəpie] baldakijn, (fig) gewelf^h, kap, dak^h

cant [kænt] **1** jargon^h, boeventaal; **2** schijnheilige praat

cantankerous [kæntængkərəs] ruzieachtig

canteen [kæntie:n] kantine

¹canter [kæntə] n handgalop^h; rit(je^h) in handgalop

²canter [kæntə] vb in handgalop gaan (brengen)

canvas [kænvəs] **1** canvas, zeildoek, tentdoek; **2** schilderslinnen; **3** borduurgaas; **4** (shipp) zeilvoering: under ~ onder vol zeil; **5** doek^h, stuk^h schilderslinnen, (olieverf)schilderij

canvass [kænvəs] **1** diepgaand (be)discussiëren, grondig onderzoek doen; **2** stemmen werven (in); **3** klanten werven, colporteren: ~ for a magazine colporteren voor een weekblad; **4** opiniepeiling houden (over)

canyon [kænjən] cañon, ravijn^h

¹cap [kæp] n **1** hoofddeksel^h, kapje^h (of nurse, domestic servant etc), muts, pet, baret, (sport) cap (as a sign of selection; also fig), selectie als international: take the ~ round met de pet rondgaan; **2** kapvormig voorwerp^h, hoed (of mushroom), kniekap, (flessen-, vulpen-, afsluit)dop, beschermkapje^h; **3** slaghoedje^h; **4** klappertje^h: ~ in hand onderdanig, nederig; if the ~ fits, wear it wie de schoen past, trekke

hem aan

²cap [kæp] vb **1** een cap opzetten, (sport; fig) in de nationale ploeg opstellen; **2** verbeteren, overtroeven: to ~ it all als klap op de vuurpijl, tot overmaat van ramp

capability [keepəbillittie] **1** vermogen^h, capaciteit, bekwaamheid; **2** vatbaarheid, ontvankelijkheid; **3** -ies talenten, capaciteiten

capable [keepəbl] **1** in staat: he is ~ of anything hij is tot alles in staat; **2** vatbaar: ~ of improvement voor verbetering vatbaar; **3** capabel, bekwaam

capacious [kəpeesjəs] ruim: a ~ memory een goed geheugen

capacity [kəpæsittie] **1** hoedanigheid: in my ~ of chairman als voorzitter; **2** vermogen^h, capaciteit, aanleg; **3** capaciteit, inhoud, volume^h: seating ~ aantal zitplaatsen; filled to ~ tot de laatste plaats bezet

cape [keep] **1** cape; **2** kaap, voorgebergte^h

¹caper [keepə] n **1** (fig) bokkensprong, capriool; **2** (inf) (ondeugende) streek, kwajongensstreek; **3** (inf) karwei^h, klus

²caper [keepə] vb (rond)dartelen, capriolen maken

¹capital [kæpitl] n **1** kapitaal^h: (fig) make ~ (out) of munt slaan uit; **2** (architecture) kapiteel^h; **3** hoofdletter, kapitaal^h; **4** hoofdstad

²capital [kæpitl] adj **1** kapitaal, hoofd-: ~ city (of: town) hoofdstad; ~ letters hoofdletters; **2** dood-, dodelijk: ~ punishment doodstraf

capital gain vermogensaanwas: ~s tax vermogens(aanwas)belasting

capitalism [kæpittəlizm] kapitalisme^h

¹capitalist [kæpittəlist] n kapitalist

²capitalist [kæpittəlist] adj kapitalistisch

capitalize [kæpitlajz] kapitaliseren: (fig) ~ (up)on uitbuiten, munt slaan uit

capitulate [kəpitsjoeleet] capituleren, zich overgeven

capitulation [kəpitsjoeleesjən] overgave

caprice [kəprie:s] gril, kuur, wispelturigheid

Capricorn [kæprikko:n] (astrology) (de) Steenbok

capsize [kæpsajz] (doen) kapseizen, (doen) omslaan

capsule [kæps·joe:l] **1** capsule; **2** neuskegel (of rocket), cabine (of spacecraft)

captain [kæptin] **1** kapitein (also mil), bevelhebber, (scheeps)gezagvoerder, (mil) kapitein-ter-zee: ~ of industry grootindustrieel; **2** (aviation) gezagvoerder; **3** (Am) (korps-, districts)commandant (of police); **4** voorman, ploegbaas; **5** (sport) aanvoerder, captain

caption [kæpsjən] **1** titel, kop, hoofd^h; **2** onderschrift^h, bijschrift^h (of illustration), ondertitel(ing) (film, TV)

captivate [kæptivveet] boeien, fascineren: he was ~d by Geraldine hij was helemaal weg van Geraldine

¹captive [kæptiv] adj **1** (krijgs)gevangen (genomen), (fig) geketend: ~ audience een aan hun stoelen gekluisterd publiek; *be taken ~* gevangengenomen worden; **2** geboeid, gecharmeerd

²**captive** [kæptiv] *n* gevangene *(also fig)*, krijgsgevangene

captivity [kæptivvittie] gevangenschap *(also fig)*, krijgsgevangenschap[h]

¹**capture** [kæptsjə] *vb* **1** vangen, gevangennemen, gevangen houden, *(fig)* boeien, fascineren: *~ the imagination* tot de verbeelding spreken; **2** buitmaken, bemachtigen, veroveren; **3** *(chess, draughts etc)* slaan *(piece, man etc)*

²**capture** [kæptsjə] *n* **1** gevangene, vangst, buit, prijs; **2** vangst, gevangenneming

car [ka:] **1** auto(mobiel), motorrijtuig[h], wagen: *by ~* met de auto; **2** rijtuig[h], *(Am)* (spoorweg)wagon, tram(wagen); **3** gondel *(of airship, cable-lift)*

carafe [kəræf] karaf

caramel [kærəmel] karamel

carat [kærət] karaat[h]

caravan [kærəvæn] **1** karavaan; **2** woonwagen, kermiswagen; **3** caravan, kampeerwagen

carbohydrate [ka:bəhajdreet] koolhydraat[h]

carbon [ka:bən] **1** koolstof[h]; **2** carbon(papier)[h]

carbonated [ka:bəneetid] koolzuurhoudend: *~ water* sodawater, spuitwater

carbon copy 1 doorslag; **2** duplicaat[h], getrouwe kopie

carbon monoxide koolmonoxide[h], kolendamp

carburettor [ka:bjoerettə] carburator

carcass [ka:kəs] **1** karkas[h], romp *(of slaughtered animal)*; **2** geraamte[h], skelet[h]

card [ka:d] **1** kaart: *house of ~s* kaartenhuis; *keep (of: play) one's ~s close to one's chest* zich niet in de kaart laten kijken, terughoudend zijn; **2** *~s* kaartspel[h]: *play ~s* kaarten; **3** programma[h] *(of sport event)*; **4** scorestaat, -kaart *(eg of cricket, golf)*: *have a ~ up one's sleeve* (nog) iets achter de hand hebben; *he played his ~s right (of: well)* hij heeft zijn kansen goed benut; *(inf) it is on the ~s* het zit er in

¹**cardboard** *n* karton[h], bordpapier[h]

²**cardboard** *adj* **1** kartonnen, bordpapieren; **2** onecht, clichématig: *~ characters* stereotiepe figuren

cardiac [ka:die·æk] hart-

cardigan [ka:digən] gebreid vestje[h]

¹**cardinal** [ka:dinnəl] *adj* kardinaal, fundamenteel, vitaal: *~ idea* centrale gedachte; *~ number* hoofdtelwoord

²**cardinal** [ka:dinnəl] *n* **1** hoofdtelwoord[h]; **2** *(Roman Catholicism)* kardinaal

¹**care** [keə] *n* **1** zorg, ongerustheid: *free from ~(s)* zonder zorgen; **2** zorg(vuldigheid), voorzichtigheid: *take ~* oppletten; *handle with ~* (pas op,) breekbaar!; **3** verantwoordelijkheid, zorg, toezicht[h]: *take ~ of* zorgen voor, onder zijn hoede nemen; *take ~ to* ervoor zorgen dat; *~ of* per adres; *under doctor's ~* onder doktersbehandeling; **4** kinderzorg, kleuterzorg: *take into ~* opnemen in een kindertehuis

²**care** [keə] *vb* **1** erom geven, zich erom bekommeren: *well, who ~s?* nou, en?, wat zou het?; *for all I ~* wat mij betreft; **2** bezwaar hebben: *I don't ~ if you do* mij best

³**care** [keə] *vb* **1** (graag) willen, zin hebben (in), bereid zijn te: *if only they would ~ to listen* als ze maar eens de moeite namen om te luisteren; **2** zich bekommeren om, geven om, zich aantrekken van: *I couldn't ~ less* het zal me een zorg zijn; *Paul doesn't seem to ~ very much* zo te zien kan het Paul weinig schelen

¹**career** [kəriə] *n* **1** carrière, (succesvolle) loopbaan; **2** (levens)loop, geschiedenis; **3** beroep[h]: *~s master* (of: *mistress*) schooldecaan; **4** (grote) vaart, (hoge) snelheid: *at* (of: *in) full ~* in volle vaart

²**career** [kəriə] *vb* voortdaveren: *~ about* rondrazen

care for 1 verzorgen, letten op, passen op, onderhouden; **2** zin hebben in, (graag) willen: *would you ~ a cup of coffee?* heb je zin in een kopje koffie?; **3** houden van, belangstelling hebben voor: *more than I ~* meer dan me lief is

carefree 1 onbekommerd, zonder zorgen; **2** *(depr)* onverantwoordelijk, zorgeloos

careful [keəfl] **1** zorgzaam, met veel zorg; **2** angstvallig; **3** voorzichtig, omzichtig, oplettend: *be ~ (about) what you say* let op je woorden; **4** zorgvuldig, nauwkeurig: *~ examination* zorgvuldig onderzoek; **5** nauwgezet

careless [keələs] **1** onverschillig, onvoorzichtig; **2** onoplettend; **3** onzorgvuldig, slordig, nonchalant

carer [keərə] thuisverzorger

¹**caress** [kərẹs] *n* teder gebaar[h], streling

²**caress** [kərẹs] *vb* liefkozen, kussen, aanhalen

caretaker [keəteekə] **1** conciërge, huismeester; **2** huisbewaarder; **3** toezichthouder, zaakwaarnemer

careworn afgetobd, (door zorgen) getekend

car ferry autoveer[h], autoveerboot, autoveerdienst, ferry(boot)

cargo [ka:goo] *(also -es)* lading, vracht, cargo

¹**Caribbean** [kæribbjən] *adj* Caribisch

²**Caribbean** [kæribbjən] *n* Caribisch gebied[h], Caribische zee

caricature [kærikətsjoeə] karikatuur, spotprent

¹**caring** [keəring] *adj* **1** zorgzaam, vol zorg, meelevend, attent: *a ~ society* een zorgzame maatschappij; **2** verzorgend: *a ~ job* een verzorgend beroep

²**caring** [keəring] *n* **1** zorg, verzorging; **2** hartelijkheid, warmte

carnage [ka:nidzj] slachting *(among people)*, bloedbad[h]

carnal [ka:nl] *(oft depr)* vleselijk, lichamelijk

carnation [ka:neesjən] anjer, anjelier

carnival [ka:nivl] **1** carnaval[h], carnavalstijd, -viering; **2** *(Am)* circus; kermis; **3** festival[h], beurs, jaarmarkt

carnivorous [ka:nivvərəs] vleesetend

carol [kærəl] lofzang, kerstlied[h]

¹**carp** [ka:p] *n* karper(achtige)

²**carp** [ka:p] *vb (oft depr)* zeuren, vitten

carpenter [kɑːpintə] timmerman

carpentry [kɑːpintrie] timmerwerk^h, timmerkunst

¹**carpet** [kɑːpit] n (vloer)tapijt^h, (vloer)kleed^h, karpet^h, (trap)loper: ~ *of flowers* bloemenkleed; *fitted* ~ vast tapijt; *sweep under the* ~ in de doofpot stoppen

²**carpet** [kɑːpit] vb 1 tapijt leggen, bekleden: ~ *the stairs* een loper op de trap leggen; 2 *(inf)* een uitbrander geven

carpetbag reistas, valies^h

carping [kɑːping] 1 muggenzifterig, vitterig: ~ *criticism* kinderachtige kritiek; 2 klagerig, zeurderig

carpool carpool, autopool

carport carport

carriage [kærridzj] 1 rijtuig^h, koets, *(railways)* (personen)wagon; 2 slee, onderstel^h *(of carriage)*; 3 (lichaams)houding, gang; 4 vervoer^h, transport^h, verzending; 5 vracht(prijs), vervoerskosten, verzendkosten

carriageway verkeersweg; rijweg, rijbaan

carrier [kæriə] 1 vervoerder van goederen of reizigers, expediteur, transporteur, vrachtvaarder, expeditie-, transport-, vervoerbedrijf^h, luchtvaart-, spoorwegmaatschappij, rederij; 2 *(med, science, chem)* drager; 3 bagagedrager; 4 *(mil)* vervoermiddel^h voor mensen en materieel, vliegdekschip^h; 5 (boodschappen)tas

carrion [kæriən] aas^h *(putrid flesh)*, kadaver^h

carrot [kærət] 1 peen, wortel(tje^h); 2 *(fig; inf)* lokmiddel^h: *hold out* (of: *offer) a ~ to s.o.* iem een worst voorhouden

¹**carry** [kærie] vb 1 dragen, reiken *(eg of voice)*; 2 in verwachting zijn, drachtig zijn; 3 aangenomen worden *(eg of bill)*, erdoor komen

²**carry** [kærie] vb 1 vervoeren, transporteren, (mee)dragen, steunen, (met zich) (mee)voeren, bij zich hebben, afvoeren, *(science)* (ge)leiden, (binnen)halen *(harvest etc)*, drijven: *such a crime carries a severe punishment* op zo'n misdaad staat een strenge straf; *diseases carried by insects* ziekten door insecten overgebracht; ~ *to excess* te ver doordrijven; *the loan carries an interest* de lening is rentedragend; *write 3 and* ~ *2* 3 opschrijven, 2 onthouden; *Joan carries herself like a model* Joan beweegt zich als een mannequin; ~ *into effect* ten uitvoer brengen; 2 in verwachting zijn van; 3 veroveren, in de wacht slepen: ~ *one's motion* zijn motie erdoor krijgen; 4 met zich meebrengen, impliceren; 5 uitzenden, publiceren: ~ *all* (of: *everything) before one* in ieder opzicht slagen; ~ *too far* overdrijven

carryall [kærie·oːl] *(Am)* weekendtas, reistas

carry along stimuleren, aansporen, (voort)drijven

carry away 1 meesleuren, meeslepen, opzwepen; 2 wegdragen

carrycot reiswieg

carry forward 1 *(bookkeeping)* transporteren; 2 vorderen met *(eg work)*, voortzetten; 3 in mindering brengen, overbrengen naar volgend boekjaar

carryings-on [kærie·ingz on] *(inf)* 1 (dolle) streken, handel en wandel; 2 geflirt

carry off 1 winnen, veroveren, in de wacht slepen; 2 wegvoeren, ontvoeren, er vandoor gaan met; 3 trotseren, tarten ‖ *I managed to carry it off* ik heb me eruit weten te redden

¹**carry on** vb 1 doorgaan, zijn gang gaan, doorzetten; 2 *(inf)* tekeergaan, stennis maken, zich aanstellen: *it is a shame how he carried on in there* het is een schande zoals hij daarbinnen tekeer ging; 3 *(inf; oft depr)* scharrelen, het houden met (elkaar)

²**carry on** vb 1 voortzetten, volhouden: ~ *the good work!* hou vol!, ga zo door!; 2 (uit)voeren, drijven, gaande houden; 3 voeren *(war, lawsuit)*

carry out uitvoeren, vervullen, volbrengen

¹**carry through** vb voortbestaan, voortduren

²**carry through** vb erdoor helpen: *his faith carried him through* zijn geloof hield hem op de been

¹**cart** [kɑːt] n kar ‖ *put* (of: *set) the* ~ *before the horse* het paard achter de wagen spannen

²**cart** [kɑːt] vb vervoeren in een kar: ~ *off a prisoner* een gevangene (hardhandig) afvoeren

cartilage [kɑːtillidzj] kraakbeen^h

carton [kɑːtn] kartonnen doos: *a* ~ *of cigarettes* een slof sigaretten; *a* ~ *of milk* een pak melk

cartoon [kɑːtoeːn] 1 (politieke) spotprent, cartoon; 2 strip(verhaal^h): *animated* ~ tekenfilm, animatiefilm; 3 tekenfilm, animatiefilm

cartridge [kɑːtridzj] 1 patroon(huls); 2 (kant-en-klare) vulling, cassette, inktpatroon, gasvulling

cartwheel 1 karrenwiel^h *(also fig)*, wagenwiel^h; 2 radslag: *do* ~s, *turn* ~s radslagen maken

¹**carve** [kɑːv] vb voorsnijden *(meat, poultry etc)*

²**carve** [kɑːv] vb kerven, houwen, beitelen, graveren in: ~ *wood into a figure* uit hout een figuur snijden

³**carve** [kɑːv] vb beeldhouwen

carve out 1 uitsnijden, afsnijden, (uit)houwen; 2 bevechten, zich veroveren: *she has carved out a successful career for herself* zij heeft een succesvolle carrière voor zichzelf opgebouwd

carve up 1 *(inf)* opdelen, aan stukken snijden; 2 *(vulg)* een jaap bezorgen

carving [kɑːving] sculptuur, beeld(houwwerk)^h, houtsnede, gravure, reliëf^h

car-wash autowasserette, carwash

¹**cascade** [kæskeed] n kleine waterval

²**cascade** [kæskeed] vb (doen) vallen (als) in een waterval

¹**case** [kees] n 1 geval^h, kwestie, zaak, stand van zaken, voorbeeld^h, patiënt, ziektegeval^h: *former Yugoslavia is a ~ in point* het voormalige Joegoslavië is een goed voorbeeld (hiervan); *in ~* voor het geval dat, *(Am)* indien; *(just) in ~* voor het geval dat; *in ~ of* in geval van, voor het geval dat; *in the ~ of* met betrekking tot; *in any ~* in elk geval; 2 argumenten, bewijs(materiaal)^h, pleidooi^h: *have a strong ~* er sterk voor staan; *make (out) one's ~* aantonen dat men gelijk heeft; 3 *(law)* (rechts)zaak, geding^h, proces^h; 4 doos, kist, koffer, zak, tas(je^h), schede, ko-

ker, huls, mantel, sloop, overtrek, cassette, etui[h], omslag[+h], band, uitstalkast, vitrine, kast *(of watch, piano; for books etc);* **5** kozijn[h], raamwerk[h], deurlijst; **6** *(linguistics)* naamval

²case [kees] *vb* voorzien ve omhulsel, insluiten, vatten

¹cash [kæsj] *n* contant geld[h], contanten, cash, *(inf)* geld[h], centen: ~ *on delivery* (onder) rembours, betaling bij levering; *hard* ~ munten, *(inf)* contant geld; *ready* ~ baar geld, klinkende munt; *(be) short of* ~ krap (bij kas) (zitten); *pay in* ~ contant betalen; ~ *down* (à) contant

²cash [kæsj] *vb* omwisselen in contanten *(cheques etc),* verzilveren, innen

cashcard betaalpas, pinpas

cash dispenser geldautomaat, flappentap

cashew [kæsjoe:] cashewnoot

cashier [kæsjiə] **1** kassier; **2** caissière, kassabediende

cash in 1 het loodje leggen; **2** zijn slag slaan: ~ *on* profiteren van

cashmere [kæsjmiə] **1** kasjmieren sjaal; **2** kasjmier[h] *(wool)*

cashpoint [kæsjpojnt] geldautomaat, flappentap

cash register kasregister[h], kassa

casing [keesing] **1** omhulsel[h], doos; **2** kozijn[h], raamwerk[h], deurlijst

casino [kəsie:noo] casino[h], gokpaleis[h]

cask [ka:sk] vat[h], fust[h]

casket [ka:skit] **1** (juwelen)kistje[h], cassette, doosje[h]; **2** *(Am)* dood(s)kist

casserole [kæsərool] braadschotel, ovenschotel; stoofschotel, eenpansgerecht[h]

cassette [kəset] cassette

¹cast [ka:st] *vb* **1** zijn hengel uitwerpen; **2** de doorslag geven, beslissend zijn: ~*ing vote* beslissende stem *(of chairman, when votes are equally divided)*

²cast [ka:st] *vb* **1** (be)rekenen, uitrekenen, (be)cijferen, calculeren, optellen, trekken *(horoscope):* ~ *(up) accounts* rekeningen optellen

³cast [ka:st] *vb* **1** werpen, (van zich) afwerpen, uitgooien, laten vallen: *(shipp)* ~ *adrift* losgooien; ~ *ashore* op de kust werpen; **2** kiezen *(actors),* (de) rol(len) toedelen aan, casten; **3** gieten *(metals; also fig),* een afgietsel maken van

⁴cast [ka:st] *n* **1** worp, gooi; **2** iets wat geworpen wordt, lijn *(with a fishing-fly for bait);* **3** gietvorm, model[h], afdruk; **4** gipsverband[h]; **5** hoedanigheid, kwaliteit, aard, uitdrukking, uiterlijk[h] *(of face):* ~ *of mind* geestesgesteldheid; **6** bezetting *(of film, play etc),* cast, rolverdeling

cast about (koortsachtig) zoeken: ~ *for an excuse* koortsachtig naar een excuus zoeken

castanet [kæstənet] castagnet

cast aside afdanken, aan de kant schuiven, laten vallen

castaway [ka:stəwee] **1** schipbreukeling; **2** aan land gezette schepeling

cast away 1 verwerpen, afwijzen; **2** weggooien: ~

one's life zijn leven vergooien

cast down 1 terneerslaan, droevig stemmen: *(past participle)* ~ terneergeslagen; **2** neerslaan *(eyes);* **3** buigen *(head)*

caste [ka:st] kaste

castellated [kæstilleetid] kasteelachtig

castigate [kæstigeet] *(form)* **1** kastijden, tuchtigen; **2** hekelen; **3** corrigeren, herzien *(text)*

casting [ka:sting] gietstuk[h], gietsel[h]

cast iron gietijzer[h]

¹castle [ka:sl] *n* **1** kasteel[h], slot[h], burcht *(also fig);* **2** *(chess)* toren, kasteel[h] || *build* ~*s in the air* luchtkastelen bouwen, dagdromen

²castle [ka:sl] *vb (chess)* || ~ *(the king)* rokeren, de rokade uitvoeren

¹cast off *vb* **1** van zich werpen, weggooien *(clothes);* **2** afdanken, aan de kant zetten

²cast off *vb* **1** *(shipp)* (de trossen) losgooien; **2** *(knitting)* minderen, afhechten

cast-off afgedankt, weggegooid: ~ *clothes* afdankertjes, oude kleren

castor [ka:stə] **1** strooier, strooibus: *a set of* ~*s* peper-en-zoutstelletje, olie-en-azijnstelletje; **2** zwenkwieltje[h], rolletje[h] *(of furniture)*

cast out verstoten, verjagen, uitdrijven

castrate [kæstreet] **1** castreren; **2** ontzielen, beroven van energie; **3** kuisen, zuiveren

cast up 1 doen aanspoelen, aan land werpen; **2** optellen, berekenen

¹casual [kæzjoeəl] *adj* **1** toevallig; **2** ongeregeld, onsystematisch: ~ *labour* tijdelijk werk; ~ *labourer* los werkman; **3** terloops, onwillekeurig: *a* ~ *glance* een vluchtige blik; **4** nonchalant, ongeïnteresseerd; **5** informeel: ~ *clothes* (of: *wear)* vrijetijdskleding, gemakkelijke kleren; **6** oppervlakkig: *a* ~ *acquaintance* een oppervlakkige kennis

²casual [kæzjoeəl] *n* **1** ~*s* gemakkelijk zittende kleding; **2** tijdelijke (arbeids)kracht

casualty [kæzjoeəltie] **1** (dodelijk) ongeval[h], ongeluk[h], ramp: ~ *ward* (afdeling) eerste hulp *(of hospital);* **2** slachtoffer[h], gesneuvelde, gewonde: *suffer heavy casualties* zware verliezen lijden

cat [kæt] kat || *let the* ~ *out of the bag* uit de school klappen *(esp unintentionally); it is raining* ~*s and dogs* het regent bakstenen; *play* ~ *and mouse (with s.o.)* kat en muis (met iem) spelen; *(put) a* ~ *among the pigeons* een knuppel in het hoenderhok (werpen); *like sth. the* ~ *brought in* verfomfaaid; *when the* ~*'s away (the mice will play)* als de kat van huis is, dansen de muizen op tafel

catacomb [kætəkoe:m] catacombe, (graf)kelder

¹catalogue [kætəlog] *n* **1** catalogus; **2** (was)lijst, rits, opsomming: *a whole* ~ *of crimes* een hele rits misdaden

²catalogue [kætəlog] *vb* catalogiseren

catalyst [kætəlist] katalysator *(also fig)*

catamaran [kætəməræn] catamaran

¹catapult [kætəpult] *n* katapult

²catapult [kætəpult] *vb* met een katapult (be)schieten || *the driver was ~ed through the window* de chauffeur werd door de ruit geslingerd

cataract [kǽtərækt] **1** waterval; **2** sterke stroomversnelling *(in river);* **3** grauwe staar, cataract

catastrophe [kətǽstrəfie] catastrofe, ramp

¹catcall *n* fluitconcert^h, (afkeurend) gejoel^h

²catcall *vb* een fluitconcert aanheffen

³catcall *vb* uitfluiten

¹catch [kætsj] *vb* **1** (op)vangen, pakken, grijpen: *~ fish* vis vangen; *I caught my thumb in the car door* ik ben met mijn duim tussen het portier gekomen; **2** (plotseling) stuiten op, tegen het lijf lopen; **3** betrappen, verrassen: *caught in the act* op heterdaad betrapt; *(iron) ~ me!* ik kijk wel uit!; **4** inhalen; **5** halen *(eg train, bus)*, (nog) op tijd zijn voor; **6** oplopen, krijgen, opdoen *(illness): ~ (a) cold* kou vatten; **7** trekken *(attention etc)*, wekken, vangen: *~ s.o.'s attention* iemands aandacht trekken; **8** opvangen: *~ a glimpse of* een glimp opvangen van; **9** stuiten, (plotseling) inhouden: *he caught his breath from fear* van angst stokte zijn adem; **10** bevangen, overweldigen: *(inf) ~ it* de wind van voren krijgen; **11** verstaan, (kunnen) volgen: *I didn't quite ~ what you said* ik verstond je niet goed

²catch [kætsj] *vb* **1** vlam vatten, ontbranden; **2** pakken, aanslaan: *the engine failed to ~* de motor sloeg niet aan; **3** besmettelijk zijn, zich verspreiden *(of disease);* **4** *(baseball)* achtervangen, achtervanger zijn; **5** klem komen te zitten, blijven haken: *~ at any opportunity* iedere gelegenheid aangrijpen

³catch [kætsj] *n* **1** het vangen; vangst, buit, aanwinst, visvangst; **2** houvast^h, greep; **3** het overgooien *(ballgame);* **4** hapering *(of voice, breath, machine etc)*, het stokken; **5** *(inf)* addertje^h onder het gras, luchtje^h, valstrik; **6** vergrendeling, pal, klink

catching [kætsjing] **1** besmettelijk; **2** boeiend

catch on *(inf)* **1** aanslaan, het doen, ingang vinden; **2** doorhebben, snappen *(idea, joke)*

catch out 1 betrappen; **2** vangen, erin laten lopen

¹catch up *vb* inhalen, bijkomen, gelijk komen: *~ to s.o., ~ with s.o.* iem inhalen; *be caught up in* verwikkeld zijn in

²catch up *vb* **1** *(inf)* een achterstand wegwerken: *John had to ~ on* (of: *in*) *geography* John moest zijn aardrijkskunde ophalen; **2** (weer) bij raken, (weer) op de hoogte raken

³catch up *vb* **1** oppakken, opnemen; **2** ophouden, opsteken, omhoog houden

catchword [kætsjwɜːd] kreet, slogan

catchy [kætsjie] **1** pakkend, boeiend; **2** gemakkelijk te onthouden, goed in het gehoor liggend *(of music etc)*

catechism [kǽtikkizm] **1** catechismus; **2** (godsdienst)onderwijs^h *(in the form of question and answer)*, catechese

categorical [kætigɔ́rrikl] categorisch, onvoorwaardelijk, absoluut

category [kǽtigərie] categorie, groep

cater [keetə] maaltijden verzorgen (bij), cateren

caterer [keetərə] **1** cateringbedrijf^h; **2** restaurateur, cateraar, hoteleigenaar, restauranteigenaar

cater for 1 maaltijden verzorgen, cateren: *weddings and parties catered for* wij verzorgen bruiloften en partijen *(of dinners etc);* **2** in aanmerking nemen, overwegen, rekening houden met; **3** zich richten op, bedienen, inspelen op: *a play centre catering for children* een speeltuin die vertier biedt aan kinderen

catering [keetəring] catering, receptieverzorging, dinerverzorging

caterpillar [kætəpillə] **1** rups; **2** rupsband; **3** rupsbaan *(fairground attraction)*

cater to *(depr)* zich richten op, bedienen, inspelen op, tegemoet komen aan: *politicians often ~ the whims of the voters* politici volgen vaak de grillen van de kiezers

cathedral [kəθíːdrəl] kathedraal

catholic [kǽθlik] **1** universeel, algemeen: *a man of ~ tastes* een man met een brede belangstelling; **2** *Catholic* katholiek

Catholicism [kəθɔ́llissizm] katholicisme^h

cat's-eye kat(ten)oog^h *(reflector)*

cat suit jumpsuit, bodystocking

cattle [kætl] (rund)vee^h

catwalk 1 richel, smal looppad^h, *(shipp)* loopbrug; **2** lang, smal podium^h *(for fashion parades etc)*, lichtbrug *(in theatre)*

¹Caucasian [koːkéːzjn] *adj* **1** Kaukasisch; **2** blank, vh Indo-Europese ras

²Caucasian [koːkéːzjn] *n* **1** Kaukasiër; **2** blanke, lid^h vh Indo-Europese ras

cauldron [kɔ́ːldrən] ketel, kookpot

cauliflower [kɔ́lliflauə] bloemkool

causal [kɔ́ːzl] oorzakelijk

¹cause [koːz] *n* **1** oorzaak; reden: *give ~ for* reden geven tot; *there is no ~ for alarm* er is geen reden voor ongerustheid; **2** zaak, doel^h: *make common ~ with s.o.* gemene zaak maken met iem *(in politics etc);* *work for a good ~* voor een goed doel werken

²cause [koːz] *vb* veroorzaken, ertoe brengen

caustic [kɔ́ːstik] **1** brandend; **2** bijtend *(also fig)*, sarcastisch

¹caution [kɔ́ːsjən] *n* **1** waarschuwing; **2** berisping; **3** voorzichtigheid || *throw* (of: *fling) ~ to the winds* alle voorzichtigheid laten varen; *~!* voorzichtig!, *(traf)* let op!

²caution [kɔ́ːsjən] *vb* waarschuwen, tot voorzichtigheid manen

cautionary [kɔ́ːsjənərie] waarschuwend

cautious [kɔ́ːsjəs] voorzichtig, op zijn hoede

cavalier [kævəljə] **1** nonchalant, onnadenkend; **2** hooghartig

cavalry [kǽvlrie] **1** cavalerie, *(originally)* ruiterij; **2** *(Am)* bereden strijdkrachten, lichte pantsers

¹cave [keev] *n* hol^h, grot, spelonk

²cave [keev] *vb* een holte vormen, instorten, inzakken

³cave [keev] *vb* uithollen, uithakken, indeuken

cave-dweller holbewoner

cave in 1 instorten, invallen, inzakken; 2 *(inf)* zwichten, (onder druk) toegeven

caveman holbewoner

cavern [kævən] spelonk, diepe grot, hol^h

cavity [kævittie] 1 holte, gat^h; 2 gaatje^h: *dental ~* gaatje in tand

cavity wall spouwmuur

cc *cubic centimetre(s)* cc, kubieke centimeter

CD 1 *Corps Diplomatique* CD; 2 *compact disc* cd

CD-ROM [sie:die:rom] *compact disc read-only memory* cd-rom

^1**cease** [sie:s] *vb* ophouden, tot een eind komen, stoppen

^2**cease** [sie:s] *vb* beëindigen, uitscheiden met: *~ fire!* staakt het vuren!; *~ to exist* ophouden te bestaan

^3**cease** [sie:s] *n: without ~* onophoudelijk

cease-fire 1 order om het vuren te staken; 2 wapenstilstand

cedar [sie:də] ceder *(tree and wood)*

ceiling [sie:ling] 1 plafond^h; 2 bovengrens *(of wages, prices etc)*, plafond^h: *~ price* maximum prijs; 3 *(aviation)* hoogtegrens *(of aeroplane)*, plafond^h

celebrate [sellibreet] 1 vieren; 2 opdragen: *~ mass* de mis opdragen

celebration [sellibreesjən] viering, festiviteit

celebrity [sillebrittie] 1 beroemdheid, beroemd persoon; 2 roem, faam

celery [sellərie] selderie, bleekselderij

celestial [sillestiəl] 1 goddelijk, hemels mooi; 2 hemels: *~ body* hemellichaam

celibate [sellibbət] ongehuwd

cell [sel] cel; batterijcel || *solar ~* zonnecel

cellar [sellə] 1 kelder; 2 wijnkelder

cellophane [selləfeen] cellofaan^h

cellphone [selfoon] draagbare telefoon

cellular [seljoelə] 1 cellulair, cellig, met cellen: *~ tissue* celweefsel; 2 celvormig; 3 poreus

celluloid [seljoelojd] celluloid^h

Celt [kelt] Kelt *(inhabitant of Ireland, Wales, Cornwall, Scotland, Brittany)*

^1**Celtic** [keltik] *adj* Keltisch

^2**Celtic** [keltik] *n* Keltisch^h *(language)*

^1**cement** [simment] *n* cement^h, mortel *(also fig)*, band, bindende kracht

^2**cement** [simment] *vb* cement(er)en, met cement bestrijken || *~ a union* een verbond versterken

cemetery [semmitrie] begraafplaats, kerkhof^h

^1**censor** [sensə] *n* 1 censor; 2 zedenmeester

^2**censor** [sensə] *vb* 1 censureren; 2 schrappen

^1**censure** [sensjə] *n* afkeuring, terechtwijzing: *a vote of ~* een motie van wantrouwen

^2**censure** [sensjə] *vb* afkeuren, bekritiseren

census [sensəs] 1 volkstelling; 2 (officiële) telling

centenarian [sentinneəriən] honderdjarig

^1**centenary** [sentie:nərie] *n* 1 eeuwfeest^h; 2 periode van honderd jaar

^2**centenary** [sentie:nərie] *adj* honderdjarig

^1**centennial** [sentenniəl] *adj* 1 honderdste, honderd-

jarig: *~ anniversary* eeuwfeest; 2 honderd jaar durend

^2**centennial** [sentenniəl] *n (Am)* eeuwfeest^h

center [sentə] *(Am) see* centre

centigrade [sentigreed] Celsius

centipede [sentippie:d] duizendpoot

central [sentrəl] 1 centraal, midden-: *~ government* centrale regering; 2 belangrijkst, voornaamst: *the ~ issue* de hoofdzaak

^1**centralize** [sentrəlajz] *vb* zich concentreren, samenkomen

^2**centralize** [sentrəlajz] *vb* centraliseren, in één punt samenbrengen

^1**centre** [sentə] *n* 1 midden^h, centrum^h, middelpunt^h *(also fig)*, spil, as, *(pol)* centrumpartij, (zenuw)centrum^h, haard *(of storm, rebellion): ~ of attraction* zwaartepunt, *(fig)* middelpunt van de belangstelling; *~ of gravity* zwaartepunt; 2 centrum^h, instelling, bureau^h

^2**centre** [sentə] *adj* middel-, centraal

^3**centre** [sentə] *vb* zich concentreren, zich richten: *~ (a)round* als middelpunt hebben

^4**centre** [sentə] *vb* 1 in het midden plaatsen; 2 concentreren, (in het midden) samenbrengen; 3 *(techn)* centreren

centrefold (meisje^h op) uitklapplaat *(in magazine)*

centrifugal [sentrifjoe:gl] centrifugaal, middelpuntvliedend

century [sentsjərie] 1 eeuw; 2 honderdtal^h

ceramic [siræmik] keramisch

ceramics [siræmiks] keramiek, pottenbakkerskunst

cereal [siəriəl] 1 graan(gewas)^h *(edible)*; 2 graanproduct^h *(at breakfast)*, cornflakes

cerebral [serribrəl] hersen-

^1**ceremonial** [serrimmooniəl] *adj* ceremonieel, plechtig

^2**ceremonial** [serrimmooniəl] *n* 1 plechtigheid; 2 ritueel^h; 3 ceremonieel^h, het geheel der ceremoniën

ceremony [serrimmənie] 1 ceremonie, *(rel)* rite: *master of ceremonies* ceremoniemeester; 2 formaliteit, vorm: *stand (up)on ~* hechten aan de vormen; *without ~* informeel

certain [sə:tn] 1 zeker, overtuigd: *are you ~?* weet je het zeker?; *make ~ (that)* zich ervan vergewissen (dat); 2 zeker, vaststaand: *he is ~ to come* hij komt beslist; *for ~* (vast en) zeker; 3 zeker, bepaald, een of ander: *a ~ Mr Jones* ene meneer Jones; 4 enig, zeker; 5 sommige(n): *~ of his friends* enkele van zijn vrienden

certainly [sə:tnlie] zeker, ongetwijfeld, beslist || *~ not!* nee!, onder geen beding!

certainty [sə:tntie] zekerheid, (vaststaand) feit^h, vaste overtuiging: *I can't say with any ~ if it will work* ik weet (absoluut) niet zeker of het werkt

certificate [sətiffikkət] certificaat^h *(law)*, getuigschrift^h, legitimatiebewijs^h: *~ of birth* geboorteakte; *Certificate of Secondary Education (CSE)* middelbareschooldiploma, *(roughly)* mavodiploma;

General Certificate of Education (GCE) middelbareschooldiploma, *(roughly)* havodiploma, vwo-diploma; *(since 1987) General Certificate of Secondary Education (GCSE)* middelbareschooldiploma *(roughly combination of diplomas of higher general secondary education and lower general secondary education);* ~ *of marriage* (afschrift van) huwelijksakte, *(roughly)* trouwboekje

certificated [sətiffikkeetid] gediplomeerd, bevoegd

¹certify [sɑːtiffaj] *vb* **1** *(with to)* getuigen (over, betreffende); **2** *(Am)* een diploma uitreiken

²certify [sɑːtiffaj] *vb* **1** (officieel) verklaren: *the bank certified the accounts (as) correct* de bank heeft de rekening gefiatteerd; **2** *(Am)* een certificaat verlenen aan, diplomeren; **3** *(inf)* officieel krankzinnig verklaren: *John should be certified* ze zouden John moeten opbergen

certitude [sɑːtitjoeːd] zekerheid, (vaste) overtuiging

cervical [sɑːvikl] **1** hals-, nek-; **2** baarmoederhals-: ~ *smear* uitstrijkje

cervix [sɑːviks] **1** hals; **2** baarmoederhals

cf. *confer* vergl., vergelijk

ch. *chapter* hfst., hoofdstukʰ

¹chafe [tsjeef] *vb* **1** schuren; **2** zich ergeren, ongeduldig zijn: ~ *at*, ~ *under* zich opwinden over; **3** tekeergaan

²chafe [tsjeef] *vb* **1** warm wrijven; **2** schuren, (open)schaven: *his collar ~d his neck* zijn boord schuurde om zijn nek; **3** ergeren, irriteren

¹chaff [tsjaːf] *n* **1** kafʰ *(also fig)*; **2** namaak, nep, prullaria; **3** (goedmoedige) plagerij

²chaff [tsjaːf] *vb* schertsen, gekheid maken

chaffinch [tsjæfintsj] vink

chagrin [sjægrin] verdrietʰ, boosheid, ergernis

¹chain [tsjeen] *n* **1** ketting, keten *(also chem): a ~ of office* een ambtsketen; **2** reeks, serie: *a ~ of coincidences* een reeks van toevalligheden; **3** groep, maatschappij, keten: *a ~ of hotels* een hotelketen; **4** bergketen; **5** kordonʰ; **6** ~*s* boeien, ketenen: *in ~s* geketend *(also fig)*

²chain [tsjeen] *vb* ketenen, in de boeien slaan

¹chair [tsjeə] *n* **1** stoel, zetel, zitplaats, *(fig)* positie, functie: *take a ~* ga zitten; **2** voorzittersstoel, voorzitter(schap): *be in* (of: *take) the ~* voorzitten; **3** leerstoel; **4** *(inf)* elektrische stoel

²chair [tsjeə] *vb* voorzitten, voorzitter zijn van: ~ *a meeting* een vergadering voorzitten

chairman [tsjeəmən] voorzitter

chairperson voorzitter, voorzitster

¹chalk [tsjoːk] *n* **1** krijt(je)ʰ, kleurkrijt(je)ʰ: *a piece of ~, a stick of ~* een krijtje; *(inf) they are as different as ~ and cheese* ze verschillen als dag en nacht; **2** krijtstreep; **3** krijttekening, crayon

²chalk [tsjoːk] *vb* krijten, met krijt schrijven

chalk up 1 opschrijven *(on blackboard, slate);* **2** optellen (bij de score), noteren: ~ *success* een overwinning boeken; **3** op iemands rekening schrijven:

chalk it up, please! wilt u het op mijn rekening zetten?

¹challenge [tsjælindzj] *vb* **1** uitdagen, tarten, op de proef stellen: ~ *s.o. to a duel* iem uitdagen tot een duel; **2** uitlokken, opwekken: ~ *the imagination* de verbeelding prikkelen; ~ *thought* tot nadenken stemmen; **3** aanroepen, aanhouden: ~ *a stranger* een vreemde staande houden; **4** betwisten, in twijfel trekken; **5** opeisen, vragen: ~ *attention* de aandacht opeisen

²challenge [tsjælindzj] *n* uitdaging, moeilijke taak, test: *rise to the ~* de uitdaging aandurven

challenger [tsjælindzjə] **1** uitdager, *(esp boxing also)* challenger; **2** betwister, bestrijder; **3** eiser, vrager; **4** mededinger *(eg for position)*

chamber [tsjeembə] **1** *(dated)* kamer, vertrekʰ, slaapkamer: ~ *of horrors* gruwelkamer; **2** raad, collegeʰ, groep: *Chamber of Deputies* huis van afgevaardigden; ~ *of commerce* kamer van koophandel; **3** afdeling ve rechtbank, kamer; **4** ~*s* ambtsvertrekken, kantoorʰ, kabinetʰ

chamberlain [tsjeembəlin] **1** kamerheer; **2** penningmeester

chameleon [kəmiːliən] kameleon *(also fig)*

chamois [sjæmwaː] **1** gems; **2** zeemlerenlap

champ [tsjæmp] *champion (inf)* kampioen

champagne [sjæmpeen] champagne

¹champion [tsjæmpiən] *n* **1** kampioen, winnaar; **2** voorvechter

²champion [tsjæmpiən] *vb* verdedigen, pleiten voor, voorstander zijn van

championship [tsjæmpiənsjip] kampioenschapʰ, kampioenswedstrijd

¹chance [tsjaːns] *n* **1** kans, mogelijkheid, waarschijnlijkheid: *fat ~!* weinig kans!; *stand a fair ~* een redelijke kans maken; *are you Mr Buckett by (any) ~?* bent u toevallig de heer Buckett?; *(the) ~s are that* het is waarschijnlijk dat; **2** toevallige gebeurtenis; **3** kans, gelegenheid: *a ~ in a million* een kans van één op duizend; **4** risicoʰ: *take ~s, take a ~* risico's nemen; **5** het lot, de fortuin: *a game of ~* een kansspel; *leave to ~* aan het toeval overlaten

²chance [tsjaːns] *vb* (toevallig) gebeuren: *I ~d to be on the same boat* ik zat toevallig op dezelfde boot; ~ *(up)on* (toevallig) vinden

³chance [tsjaːns] *adj* toevallig: *a ~ meeting* een toevallige ontmoeting

chancellor [tsjaːnsələ] **1** kanselier, hoofd ve kanselarij, hoofd ve universiteit *(in England as title of honour);* **2** *(Am; law)* president, voorzitter *(of some courts of law);* **3** minister van financiën ‖ *Chancellor of the Exchequer* minister van financiën

chancy [tsjaːnsie] *(inf)* gewaagd, riskant, onzeker

chandelier [sjændəliə] kroonluchter

¹change [tsjeendzj] *vb* **1** veranderen, anders worden, wisselen; **2** zich verkleden, andere kleren aantrekken; **3** overstappen; **4** *(techn)* schakelen: ~ *down* terugschakelen; ~ *into second gear* in zijn twee zetten

²change [tsjeendzj] *vb* **1** veranderen, anders maken;

2 (ver)ruilen, omruilen, (ver)wisselen: ~ *one's clothes* zich omkleden; ~ *gear* (over)schakelen; ~ *oil* olie verversen; **3** *(fin)* (om)wisselen; **4** verschonen: ~ *a baby* een baby een schone luier aandoen

³change [tsjeendzj] *n* **1** verandering, afwisseling, variatie: *a ~ for the better* een verandering ten goede; *she has had a ~ of heart* ze is van gedachten veranderd; *for a ~* voor de afwisseling; **2** verversing: *a ~ of oil* nieuwe olie; **3** *(traf)* het overstappen: *you have to ~ at Boxtel* u moet in Boxtel overstappen; **4** wisselgeldʰ: *keep the ~!* laat maar zitten!; **5** kleingeldʰ: *give ~ for a banknote* een briefje wisselen; ~ *of life* overgang(sjaren); *(inf) get no ~ out of s.o.* geen cent wijzer worden van iem

changeover 1 omschakeling, overschakeling, overgang; **2** *(sport)* het wisselen

change over 1 veranderen, overgaan, omschakelen; **2** ruilen (van plaats); **3** omzwaaien: *he changed over from gas to electricity* hij is overgestapt van gas naar elektriciteit

¹channel [tsjænl] *n* **1** kanaalʰ, zee-engte: *the Channel* het Kanaal; **2** (vaar)geul, bedding; **3** kanaalʰ, buis, pijp, goot; **4** *(radio, TV)* kanaalʰ, *(fig)* netʰ, programmaʰ

²channel [tsjænl] *vb* **1** kanaliseren, voorzien van kanalen; **2** leiden, sturen, in bepaalde banen leiden

Channel Islands Kanaaleilanden

¹chant [tsja:nt] *vb* **1** zingen, op één toon zingen; **2** roepen, herhalen

²chant [tsja:nt] *n* **1** liedʰ, (eenvoudige) melodie, psalm; **2** zangerige intonatie

chaos [keeos] chaos, verwarring, wanorde

chaotic [keeottik] chaotisch, verward, ongeordend

¹chap [tsjæp] *n* **1** *(inf)* vent, kerel, knul; **2** kloof(jeʰ), barst(jeʰ) *(in lip or skin)*, scheur *(in soil)*

²chap [tsjæp] *vb* splijten, (doen) barsten, kloven

chapel [tsjæpl] kapel

chaplain [tsjæplin] **1** kapelaan, huisgeestelijke; **2** veldprediker, aalmoezenier

chapter [tsjæptə] **1** hoofdstukʰ: *give ~ and verse (inf; fig)* alle details geven, tekst en uitleg geven; **2** episode, periode: *a whole ~ of accidents* een hele reeks tegenslagen; **3** *(rel)* kapittelʰ, kapittelvergadering

¹char [tsja:] *n* **1** *charlady, charwoman* werkster; **2** klus(jeʰ), taak, (huishoudelijk) karwei(tje)ʰ

²char [tsja:] *vb* werkster zijn

³char [tsja:] *vb* verbranden, verkolen, schroeien

character [kæriktə] **1** (ken)tekenʰ, merktekenʰ, kenmerkʰ, (karakter)trek; **2** tekenʰ, symboolʰ, letter, cijferʰ; **3** persoon, typeʰ, individuʰ *(also depr):* *a suspicious ~* een louche figuur; *he is quite a ~* hij is me d'r eentje; **4** personageʰ, rol, figuur⁺ʰ; **5** *(inf)* excentriek figuur⁺ʰ; **6** karakterʰ, aard, natuur: *out of ~: a)* niet typisch; *b)* ongepast; **7** schriftʰ, handschriftʰ, (druk)letters; **8** moed

¹characteristic [kæriktəristik] *adj* kenmerkend, tekenend

²characteristic [kæriktəristik] *n* kenmerkʰ, (ken-

merkende) eigenschap

characterize [kæriktərajz] kenmerken, typeren

charcoal [tsja:kool] **1** houtskool; **2** donkergrijsʰ, antracietʰ, antracietkleur

¹charge [tsja:dzj] *n* **1** lading *(also electr)*, belasting; **2** lading springstof, bom; **3** prijs, kost(en), schuld; **4** pupil, beschermeling; **5** instructie, opdracht, *(mil)* (bevel tot de) aanval; **6** *(law)* telastlegging, beschuldiging, aanklacht: *face a ~ of theft* terechtstaan wegens diefstal; **7** zorg, hoede, leiding: *officer in ~* dienstdoend officier; *take ~ of* de leiding nemen over, zich belasten met; *in ~ of* verantwoordelijk voor

²charge [tsja:dzj] *vb* **1** (aan)rekenen, in rekening brengen: *he ~d me five pounds* hij rekende mij vijf pond; **2** beschuldigen, aanklagen: ~ *s.o. with theft* iem van diefstal beschuldigen; **3** bevelen, opdragen

³charge [tsja:dzj] *vb* **1** aanvallen, losstormen op; **2** opladen, laden, vullen

charged [tsja:dzjd] **1** emotioneel, sterk voelend; **2** geladen, omstreden: *a ~ atmosphere* een geladen atmosfeer

chariot [tsjæriət] triomfwagen, (strijd)wagen

charismatic [kærizmætik] charismatisch, inspirerend

charitable [tsjærittəbl] **1** menslievend, welwillend; **2** liefdadig, vrijgevig; **3** van een liefdadig doel: ~ *institutions* liefdadige instellingen; **4** mild in zijn oordeel, vergevensgezind

charity [tsjærittie] liefdadigheidsinstelling; liefdadigheid; (naasten)liefde ‖ ~ *begins at home (roughly)* het hemd is nader dan de rok

charlatan [sja:lətən] charlatan, kwakzalver

¹charm [tsja:m] *n* **1** charme, bekoorlijke eigenschap, aantrekkelijkheid; **2** tovermiddelʰ, toverspreuk: *(inf) it works like a ~* het werkt perfect; **3** amulet; **4** bedeltjeʰ *(on bracelet)*

²charm [tsja:m] *vb* **1** betoveren, charmeren; **2** bezweren: ~ *snakes* slangen bezweren

charming [tsja:ming] charmant, aantrekkelijk

¹chart [tsja:t] *n* **1** kaart, zeekaart, weerkaart; **2** grafiek, curve, tabel; **3** ~s hitparade

²chart [tsja:t] *vb* in kaart brengen, een kaart maken van: ~ *a course* een koers uitzetten

¹charter [tsja:tə] *n* **1** oorkonde, (voor)rechtʰ; **2** handvestʰ: *the ~ of the United Nations* het handvest van de Verenigde Naties; **3** (firma)contractʰ, statuten; **4** het charteren, huur

²charter [tsja:tə] *vb* **1** een octrooi verlenen aan: *~ed accountant* (beëdigd) accountant; **2** charteren, (af)huren

charwoman werkster

chary [tsjeərie] **1** voorzichtig; **2** verlegen; **3** zuinig, karig, spaarzaam; **4** kieskeurig

¹chase [tsjees] *vb* **1** achtervolgen, achternazitten, *(fig)* najagen: ~ *up* opsporen; **2** verjagen, verdrijven: ~ *away* (of: *out, off*) wegjagen

²chase [tsjees] *vb* jagen, zich haasten

³chase [tsjees] *n* **1** achtervolging, jacht *(also sport):*

give ~ (to) achternazitten; **2** park[h], jachtveld[h]; **3** (nagejaagde) prooi; **4** steeplechase, wedren met hindernissen

chasm [kæzm] kloof, afgrond, *(fig also)* verschil[h], tegenstelling

chassis [sjæsie] chassis[h], onderstel[h]; landingsgestel[h]

chaste [tsjeest] kuis

chasten [tsjeesn] **1** kuisen, zuiveren; **2** matigen

chastise [tsjæstajz] kastijden, (streng) straffen

¹chat [tsjæt] *vb* babbelen, kletsen, praten: *~ away* erop los kletsen

²chat [tsjæt] *n* **1** babbeltje[h], praatje[h]; **2** geklets[h], gebabbel[h]

chatline babbellijn

¹chatter [tsjætə] *vb* **1** kwebbelen, (druk) praten: *~ away* (erop los) praten; **2** klapperen *(of teeth)*

²chatter [tsjætə] *n* **1** geklets[h]; **2** geklapper[h] *(of teeth)*

chatterbox kletskous

¹cheap [tsjie:p] *adj* **1** goedkoop, voordelig: *on the ~* voor een prikje; **2** gemakkelijk; **3** ordinair, grof: *a ~ kind of humour* flauwe grappen; **4** onoprecht, oppervlakkig

²cheap [tsjie:p] *adv* **1** goedkoop, voordelig; **2** vulgair, ordinair

¹cheapen [tsjie:pən] *vb* **1** goedkoop *(of:* goedkoper) maken, in waarde doen dalen, verlagen, *(fig)* afbreuk doen aan; **2** afdingen op

²cheapen [tsjie:pən] *vb* goedkoop worden, in prijs dalen

¹cheat [tsjie:t] *vb* **1** bedrog plegen, vals spelen; **2** *(inf)* ontrouw zijn

²cheat [tsjie:t] *vb* **1** bedriegen, oplichten, afzetten: *at exams* spieken; *~ s.o. out of sth.* iem iets afhandig maken; **2** ontglippen (aan), ontsnappen aan

³cheat [tsjie:t] *n* **1** bedrog[h], afzetterij; **2** bedrieger, valsspeler

cheater [tsjie:tə] bedrieger, oplichter, afzetter

¹check [tsjek] *(Am) see* cheque

²check *n* **1** belemmering, oponthoud[h]: *keep a ~ on s.o., (Am) have one's ~s upon s.o.* iem in de gaten houden; **2** proef, test, controle; **3** *(Am)* rekening *(in restaurant);* **4** kaartje[h], reçu[h], bonnetje[h]; **5** ruit(je[h]), ruitpatroon[h], geruite stof; **6** controle, bedwang[h]: *without ~* ongehinderd; **7** schaak[h]: *~! schaak; ~!* schaak!

³check *vb* **1** controleren, testen: *~ (up) on sth.* iets controleren; **2** (doen) stoppen, tegenhouden, afremmen; **3** schaak zetten, bedreigen; **4** *(Am)* afgeven *(for safekeeping);* **5** kloppen, punt voor punt overeenstemmen: *~ into a hotel* zich inschrijven in een hotel

checked [tsjekt] geruit, geblokt

checkers [tsjekkəz] *(Am)* damspel[h], dammen

¹check in *vb* zich inschrijven

²check in *vb (Am)* **1** registreren, inschrijven; **2** terugbrengen

checklist checklist, controlelijst

¹checkmate *n* schaakmat[h]

²checkmate *vb* schaakmat zetten

check out vertrekken, zich uitschrijven: *~ of a hotel*

vertrekken uit een hotel

checkroom *(Am)* **1** bagagedepot[h]; **2** garderobe *(in hotel, theatre etc)*

check-up (algemeen medisch) onderzoek[h]

cheddar [tsjeddə] kaas

cheek [tsjie:k] **1** wang: *turn the other ~* de andere wang toekeren; *~ by jowl (with): a)* dicht bijeen; *b)* (als) twee handen op een buik; **2** brutaliteit, lef[h]

cheekbone jukbeen[h]

cheeky [tsjie:kie] brutaal

cheep [tsjie:p] gefluit[h], getjilp[h] *(of birds)*

¹cheer [tsjiə] *n* **1** (juich)kreet, schreeuw, *~s* hoerageroep[h], gejuich[h]; **2** aanmoediging; **3** stemming, humeur[h]: *of (of: with) good ~* welgemoed, vrolijk; **4** vrolijkheid

²cheer [tsjiə] *vb* juichen, schreeuwen, roepen || *~ up!* kop op!

³cheer [tsjiə] *vb* **1** toejuichen, aanmoedigen: *~ on* aanmoedigen; **2** bemoedigen: *~ up* opvrolijken

cheerful [tsjiəfl] vrolijk, blij, opgewekt

cheerio [tsjiərie-oo] *(inf)* **1** dag!, tot ziens!; **2** proost!

cheerleader *(Am)* cheerleader

cheers [tsjiəz] **1** proost!; **2** *(inf)* dag!, tot ziens!; **3** *(inf)* bedankt!

cheese [tsjie:z] kaas

cheeseburger hamburger met kaas

chef [sjef] chef-kok

¹chemical [kemmikl] *adj* chemisch, scheikundig

²chemical [kemmikl] *n* chemisch product[h]

chemist [kemmist] **1** chemicus, scheikundige; **2** apotheker; **3** drogist

chemistry [kemmistrie] **1** scheikunde; **2** scheikundige eigenschappen, *(fig)* geheimzinnige werking: *the ~ of love* de mysterieuze werking van de liefde

cheque [tsjek] *(Am)* cheque

cheque card betaalpas(je[h]), bankkaart

chequer [tsjekkə] schakeren, afwisseling brengen in, *(fig)* kenmerken door wisselend succes: *a ~ed life* een leven met voor- en tegenspoed

cherish [tsjerrisj] koesteren, liefhebben; *~ hopes* hoop koesteren

cherry [tsjerrie] **1** kers; **2** kersenboom; **3** kersenhout[h]; **4** kersrood

chess [tsjes] schaak[h], schaakspel[h]

chessman [tsjesmən] schaakstuk[h]

chest [tsjest] **1** borst(kas): *get sth. off one's ~* over iets zijn hart luchten; **2** kist, kast, bak, doos: *~ of drawers* ladekast

chestnut [tsjesnut] **1** kastanje[h], kastanjeboom; **2** vos(paard[h]); **3** *(inf)* ouwe mop, bekend verhaal[h]; **4** kastanjebruin[h]: *~ mare* kastanjebruine merrie

¹chew [tsjoe:] *vb* **1** kauwen, pruimen; **2** *(inf; also fig)* herkauwen, (over)denken, bepraten: *~ sth. over* er-gens over nadenken; *~ over sth.* iets bespreken; *~ over (of: on) sth.* nadenken over iets

²chew [tsjoe:] *n* (tabaks)pruim[h]: *a ~ of tobacco* een tabakspruim

chewing gum kauwgom

¹chic [sjie:k] *adj* chic, stijlvol, elegant

²**chic** [sjie:k] *n* chic, verfijning, stijl

chick [tsjik] **1** kuiken^h, (jong) vogeltje^h; **2** *(inf)* meisje^h, grietje^h, stuk^h; **3** kind^h

¹**chicken** [tsjikkin] *n* **1** kuiken^h, (jong) vogeltje^h; **2** kip; **3** kind^h: *Mary is no ~* Mary is niet meer zo piep; **4** *(inf; depr)* lafaard, bangerik; **5** *(inf)* lekker stuk^h, grietje^h: *count one's ~s before they are hatched* de huid verkopen voordat men de beer geschoten heeft

²**chicken** [tsjikkin] *adj (inf)* laf, bang

chicken out *(inf)* ertussenuit knijpen, bang worden

chickenpox waterpokken

chicory [tsjikkərie] *(bot)* **1** Brussels lof^h, witlof^h; **2** *(Am)* andijvie

¹**chief** [tsjie:f] *adj* belangrijkst, voornaamst, hoofd-: *~ accountant* hoofdaccountant; *~ constable* hoofd van politie in graafschap

²**chief** [tsjie:f] *n* leider, aanvoerder, opperhoofd^h

chiefly [tsjie:flie] voornamelijk, hoofdzakelijk, vooral

chieftain [tsjie:ftən] **1** hoofdman *(of tribe etc)*; **2** bendeleider

chilblain [tsjilbleen] winterhanden, wintervoeten

child [tsjajld] *(children)* **1** kind^h *(also fig)*; **2** nakomeling; **3** volgeling, aanhanger; **4** (geestes)kind^h, product^h, resultaat^h

childhood [tsjajldhoed] jeugd, kinderjaren

childminding kinderoppas, kinderopvang

Chile [tsjillie] Chili

¹**chill** [tsjil] *n* **1** verkoudheid, koude rilling; **2** kilte, koelte, frisheid, *(fig)* onhartelijkheid: *cast a ~ over sth.* een domper zetten op iets

²**chill** [tsjil] *vb* afkoelen, koud worden ‖ *~ed meat* gekoeld vlees

chilly [tsjillie] **1** koel, kil, koud; **2** huiverig; **3** onvriendelijk, ongevoelig

¹**chime** [tsjajm] *n* **1** klok, klokkenspel^h: *a ~ of bells* een klokkenspel; *ring the ~s* de klokken luiden; **2** klokgelui^h; **3** harmonie, overeenstemming

²**chime** [tsjajm] *vb* **1** luiden, slaan: *~ with* in overeenstemming zijn met; **2** in harmonie zijn, overeenstemmen

chime in 1 overeenstemmen, instemmen: *~ with* overeenstemmen met; **2** opmerken, invallen *(with a remark)*, bijvallen: *~ with* invallen met *(remark)*

chimney [tsjimnie] schoorsteen, rookkanaal^h

chimney-piece schoorsteenmantel

chimney sweep(er) schoorsteenveger

chimpanzee [tsjimpænzie:] chimpansee

chin [tsjin] kin ‖ *(inf) (keep your) ~ up!* kop op!

China [tsjajnə] **1** China; **2** porselein

Chinese [tsjajnie:z] Chinees, uit China ‖ *~ lantern* lampion, papieren lantaarn; *~ wall* Chinese Muur, *(fig)* onoverkomelijke hindernis

¹**chink** [tsjingk] *n* **1** spleet, opening, gat^h: *(fig) that is the ~ in his armour* dat is zijn zwakke plek; **2** lichtstraal *(as if through a crack)*, straaltje^h licht: *a ~ of light* een lichtstraal; **3** kling, het rinkelen

²**chink** [tsjingk] *vb* rinkelen *((as if) of metal, glass)*

³**chink** [tsjingk] *vb* **1** doen rinkelen *((like) metal, glass)*; **2** dichten, (op)vullen

¹**chip** [tsjip] *n* **1** splintertje^h, scherf; **2** fiche^h: *(inf) when the ~s are down* als het erop aankomt, als het menens wordt; **3** friet, patat; **4** *~s (Am, Austr)* chips; **5** *(techn)* chip: *have a ~ on one's shoulder* prikkelbaar zijn, lichtgeraakt zijn

²**chip** [tsjip] *vb* afbrokkelen: *~ away at a piece of wood* hout vorm geven

³**chip** [tsjip] *vb* **1** (af)kappen, afsnijden, onderbreken, in de rede vallen: *~ off* afbikken, afbreken; **2** beitelen, beeldhouwen

chip in 1 (zijn steentje) bijdragen, lappen; **2** opperen, onderbreken

chipping [tsjipping] **1** scherfje^h, stukje^h; **2** bik, losse stukjes steen

chirp [tsjə:p] tjirpen, tjilpen, piepen

chirpy [tsjə:pie] vrolijk, levendig *(inf)*, spraakzaam

chisel [tsjizl] beitel

chit [tsjit] **1** jong kind^h, hummel; **2** *(oft depr; for woman)* jong ding^h; **3** briefje^h, memo^h; **4** rekening, bon(netje^h), cheque

chivalrous [sjivlrəs] ridderlijk, galant

chivalry [sjivlrie] ridderschap^h; ridderlijkheid

chiv(v)y [tsjivvie] achterna zitten, (op)jagen

chlorine [klo:rie:n] chloor^{+h}

chlorophyl(l) [klorrəfil] bladgroen^h

¹**chocolate** [tsjokkələt] *n* **1** chocolaatje^h, bonbon, praline; **2** chocolade

²**chocolate** [tsjokkələt] *adj* **1** chocoladekleurig; **2** chocolade, naar chocolade smakend

¹**choice** [tsjojs] *n* **1** keus, keuze, alternatief^h, voorkeur: *the colour of your ~* de kleur van uw keuze; *John has no ~ but to come* John moet wel komen; *by ~, for ~* bij voorkeur; *from ~* graag, gewillig; **2** keuzemogelijkheid, optie

²**choice** [tsjojs] *adj* **1** uitgelezen: *~ meat* kwaliteitsvlees; **2** zorgvuldig gekozen *(of words)*

choir [kwajjə] koor^h

¹**choke** [tsjook] *vb* (ver)stikken, naar adem snakken, zich verslikken

²**choke** [tsjook] *vb* **1** verstikken, doen stikken: *~ a fire* een vuur doven; **2** verstoppen; **3** onderdrukken, inslikken, bedwingen

³**choke** [tsjook] *n* choke, gasklep

cholera [kollərə] cholera

choleric [kollərik] zwartgallig

cholesterol [kəlestərol] cholesterol

choose [tsjoe:z] **1** (uit)kiezen, selecteren: *a lot to ~ from* veel om uit te kiezen; **2** beslissen, besluiten: *George chose not to come* George besloot niet te komen, kwam liever niet; **3** (ver)kiezen, willen, wensen

choos(e)y [tsjoe:zie] kieskeurig

¹**chop** [tsjop] *vb* **1** hakken, kappen, houwen: *~ down trees* bomen omhakken; **2** fijnhakken, fijnsnijden: *chopped liver* (fijn)gehakte lever

²**chop** [tsjop] *vb* **1** hakken, kappen, houwen; **2** voortdurend veranderen *(also fig)*: *~ and change* erg ver-

anderlijk zijn, vaak van mening veranderen

³chop [tsjop] *n* **1** houw, hak, slag; **2** karbonade, kotelet; **3** (karate)slag; **4** ~*s* kaken, lippen *(of animals)*

chopper [tsjopə] **1** hakker, houwer; **2** hakmes^h, kapmes^h; **3** bijl; **4** *(inf)* helikopter

chopstick (eet)stokje^h

chop suey [tsjop soe:ie] tjaptjoi *(Chinese dish)*

choral [ko:rəl] **1** koor-; **2** gezongen

chord [ko:d] **1** snaar *(also fig):* *(fig) that strikes a* ~ dat herinnert me aan iets; **2** *(mus)* akkoord^h

chore [tsjo:] karwei(tje)^h: *do the* ~*s* het huishouden doen

chorister [korristə] koorknaap

chortle [tsjo:tl] luidruchtig gegrinnik^h

chow [tsjau] **1** chow-chow *(dog);* **2** *(inf)* eten^h, voer^h

chow-chow chow-chow *(dog)*

Christ [krajst] Christus

christen [krisn] **1** dopen; **2** als (doop)naam geven, noemen, dopen

Christendom [krisndəm] christenheid

christening [krisning] doop

¹Christian [kristsjən] *n* christen, christenmens

²Christian [kristsjən] *adj* christelijk

Christianity [kristie·ænittie] **1** christendom^h; **2** christelijkheid

Christian name doopnaam, voornaam

Christmas [krisməs] Kerstmis, kerst(tijd): *the* ~ *season* het kerstseizoen

Christmas Eve kerstavond, avond (dag) voor Kerstmis

chromium [kroomiəm] chromium^h, chroom^h

chromosome [krooməsoom] chromosoom^h

chronic [kronnik] **1** chronisch, slepend, langdurend, *(of disease also)* ongeneeslijk; **2** *(vulg)* erg, slecht, vreselijk

chronicle [kronnikl] kroniek

chronology [krənolladzjie] chronologie

chrysanth(emum) [krisænθimməm] chrysant

chubby [tsjubbie] *(inf)* mollig, gevuld *(of face)*

¹chuck [tsjuk] *vb* **1** *(inf)* gooien; **2** *(inf)* de bons geven, laten zitten; **3** *(inf)* ophouden met, laten, opgeven: ~ *it (in)* er de brui aan geven, ermee ophouden

²chuck [tsjuk] *n* **1** aaitje^h *(under one's chin),* tikje^h, klopje^h; **2** klem *(on a lathe)*

¹chuckle [tsjukl] *vb* **1** grinniken, een binnenpretje hebben; **2** leedvermaak hebben

²chuckle [tsjukl] *n* lachje^h, gegrinnik^h, binnenpretje^h

¹chug [tsjug] *vb* (also with *along*) (voort)puffen

²chug [tsjug] *n* puf, geronk^h

chum [tsjum] **1** makker, gabber, maat *(esp among boys);* **2** *(Am)* kamergenoot

chump [tsjump] *(inf)* sukkel || *go off one's* ~ stapelgek worden

chunk [tsjungk] brok^h, stuk^h, homp *(also fig):* *a* ~ *of cheese* (of: *bread)* een brok kaas, een homp brood

church [tsjə:tsj] **1** kerk(gebouw^h): *established* ~ staatskerk; **2** kerk(genootschap^h): *the Church of England* de anglicaanse kerk; **3** kerk(dienst)

churchyard kerkhof^h, begraafplaats

churlish [tsjə:lisj] boers, lomp

¹churn [tsjə:n] *n* **1** karn(ton); **2** melkbus

²churn [tsjə:n] *vb* **1** roeren *(milk or cream);* **2** karnen; **3** omroeren, laten schuimen || *(inf)* ~ *out* (in grote hoeveelheden tegelijk) produceren, afdraaien *(of text)*

chute [sjoe:t] **1** helling, stortkoker; **2** stroomversnelling; **3** *(inf)* parachute

chutney [tsjutnie] chutney

chutzpah [choetspə] gotspe, schaamteloze brutaliteit

C.I.A. *(Am) Central Intelligence Agency* CIA

cider [sajdə] cider, appelwijn

cigar [siga:] sigaar

cigarette [sigəret] sigaret

C.-in-C. *Commander-in-chief* opperbevelhebber

cinch [sintsj] *(Am) (inf)* makkie^h, kinderspel^h || *it's a* ~ dat is een makkie

cinder [sində] sintel, ~*s* as

Cinderella [sindərellə] **1** Assepoester; **2** stiefkind^h, assepoester

cinefilm smalfilm

cinema [sinnimmə] bioscoop, cinema

cinnamon [sinnəmən] kaneel^h

cipher [sajfə] **1** nul; **2** cijfer^h; **3** sleutel *(of code);* **4** code, geheimschrift^h: *the message was in* ~ de boodschap was in geheimschrift

circa [sə:kə] circa, omstreeks

¹circle [sə:kl] *n* **1** cirkel; **2** kring, ring, *(archeology)* kring stenen, rotonde, ringlijn, rondweg, balkon^h *(in theatre);* (hockey) slagcirkel: *run round in* ~*s* nodeloos druk in de weer zijn; **3** groep, clubje^h, kring: *vicious* ~ vicieuze cirkel

²circle [sə:kl] *vb* rondcirkelen, ronddraaien, rondgaan

³circle [sə:kl] *vb* omcirkelen

circuit [sə:kit] **1** kring, omtrek, ronde; **2** (race)baan, circuit^h; **3** stroomkring, schakeling; **4** *(sport)* circuit^h || *closed* ~ gesloten circuit

¹circular [sə:kjələ] *adj* **1** rond, cirkelvormig: ~ *saw* cirkelzaag; **2** rondlopend, rondgaand, (k)ring-; **3** ontwijkend, indirect: ~ *letter* circulaire, rondschrijven

²circular [sə:kjələ] *n* rondschrijven^h, circulaire

circulate [sə:kjəleet] (laten) circuleren, (zich) verspreiden

circulation [sə:kjəleesjən] **1** oplage; **2** omloop, circulatie, distributie: *in* ~ in de roulatie; **3** bloedsomloop

circumcision [sə:kəmsizjən] besnijdenis

circumference [səkumfrəns] cirkelomtrek

circumflex [sə:kəmfleks] accent^h circonflexe, dakje^h, kapje^h

circumspect [sə:kəmspekt] omzichtig, op zijn hoede, voorzichtig

circumstance [sə:kəmstəns] **1** omstandigheid, (materiële) positie, (financiële) situatie: *straitened* (of: *reduced)* ~*s* behoeftige omstandigheden; *in* (of: *under*) *the* ~*s* onder de gegeven omstandigheden; **2** feit^h, geval^h, gebeurtenis; **3** praal, drukte, omhaal: *pomp and* ~ pracht en praal

circumstantial [sə:kəmstǽnsjl] **1** (afhankelijk) van de omstandigheden: ~ *evidence* indirect bewijs; **2** bijkomstig, niet essentieel; **3** uitvoerig, omstandig

circumvent [sə:kəmvɛnt] ontwijken, omzeilen

circus [sə:kəs] **1** circus; **2** (rond) plein^h

CIS *Commonwealth of Independent States* GOS, Gemenebest van Onafhankelijke Staten

citadel [sittədəl] fort^h, citadel, bolwerk^h

citation [sajteesjən] aanhaling, citaat^h

cite [sajt] aanhalen, citeren: ~ *examples* voorbeelden aanhalen

citizen [sittizzən] **1** burger, stedeling, inwoner; **2** staatsburger, onderdaan: *Jeffrey is a British* ~ Jeffrey is Brits onderdaan; **3** *(Am)* niet-militair, burger

citizenship [sittiznsjip] (staats)burgerschap^h

citrus [sitrəs] citrus-

city [sittie] (grote) stad; *(fig)* financieel centrum^h: *the City* de oude binnenstad van Londen

city council gemeenteraad

city hall *(Am)* **1** gemeentehuis^h, stadhuis^h; **2** stadsbestuur^h

civic [sivvik] **1** burger-, burgerlijk; **2** stedelijk, gemeente-: ~ *centre* bestuurscentrum, openbaar centrum

civics [sivviks] leer van burgerrechten en -plichten, *(educ, roughly)* maatschappijleer

civil [sivl] **1** burger-, burgerlijk, civiel: ~ *disobedience* burgerlijke ongehoorzaamheid; ~ *law* Romeins recht; ~ *marriage* burgerlijk huwelijk; ~ *war* burgeroorlog; **2** beschaafd, beleefd; **3** niet-militair, burger-: ~ *service* civiele dienst, ambtenarij; ~ *engineering* weg- en waterbouwkunde

¹civilian [sivvíljən] *adj* burger-, civiel, burgerlijk

²civilian [sivvíljən] *n* burger, niet-militair

civility [sivvíllittie] beleefde opmerking, beleefdheid

civilization [sivvəlajzéésjən] **1** beschaving, cultuur, ontwikkeling; **2** de beschaafde wereld

civilize [sivvəlajz] **1** beschaven, ontwikkelen, civiliseren; **2** opvoeden

¹claim [kleem] *vb* **1** opeisen, aanspraak maken op: ~ *damages* schadevergoeding eisen; **2** beweren, verkondigen, stellen

²claim [kleem] *vb* een vordering indienen, een eis instellen, schadevergoeding eisen

³claim [kleem] *n* **1** aanspraak, recht^h, claim, eis: *lay* ~ *to, make a* ~ *to* aanspraak maken op; **2** vordering, claim; **3** bewering, stelling

¹clairvoyant [kleəvójjənt] *n* helderziende

²clairvoyant [kleəvójjənt] *adj* helderziend

clamber [klǽmbə] opklimmen tegen, beklimmen

clammy [klǽmie] klam, vochtig

clamorous [klǽmərəs] lawaaierig, luidruchtig

¹clamour [klǽmə] *n* **1** geschreeuw^h, getier^h; **2** herrie, lawaai^h

²clamour [klǽmə] *vb* **1** schreeuwen, lawaai maken; **2** protesteren, zijn stem verheffen, aandringen: ~ *for* aandringen op

¹clamp [klæmp] *n* **1** klem, klamp, (klem)beugel; **2** kram, (muur)anker

²clamp [klæmp] *vb* klampen, vastklemmen

clamp down *(with on)* een eind maken (aan), de kop indrukken: *we're clamping down on overspending* we willen een eind maken aan de te hoge uitgaven

clam up dichtslaan, dichtklappen, weigeren iets te zeggen

clan [klæn] geslacht^h, stam, familie, clan

clandestine [klændéstin] clandestien, geheim

¹clang [klæŋ] *vb* (metalig) (doen) klinken, luiden, rinkelen, (doen) galmen

²clang [klæŋ] *n* metalige klank, galm, luiden *(bell)*, gekletter^h, gerinkel^h

clanger [klǽŋə] miskleun, blunder, flater: *to drop a* ~ een flater slaan, een blunder begaan

¹clap [klæp] *vb* **1** klappen, slaan, kloppen; **2** applaudisseren

²clap [klæp] *vb* **1** (stevig) plaatsen, zetten, planten, poten: ~ *s.o. in jail* iem achter de tralies zetten; **2** slaan: ~ *s.o. on the back* iem op de rug slaan; **3** klappen in, slaan in: ~ *one's hands* in de handen klappen

³clap [klæp] *n* klap, slag, tik, applaus^h: ~ *of thunder* donderslag

clapped-out 1 uitgeteld, afgedraaid; **2** gammel, wrakkig

clapper [klǽpə] **1** klepel; **2** ratel

claptrap 1 holle frasen, goedkope trucs; **2** onzin

clarification [klæriffikkéésjən] **1** zuivering, filtrering *(liquid, air)*; **2** opheldering, verklaring, uitleg

¹clarify [klǽriffaj] *vb* helder worden *(liquid, fat, air)*; *(fig)* verhelderen, duidelijk worden

²clarify [klǽriffaj] *vb* **1** zuiveren, klaren, doen bezinken; **2** ophelderen, duidelijk maken, toelichten

clarinet [klærinnét] klarinet

clarion [klǽriən] **1** klaroen, signaalhoorn; **2** (klaroen)geschal^h

clarity [klǽrittie] helderheid, duidelijkheid

¹clash [klæsj] *vb* **1** slaags raken, botsen; **2** tegenstrijdig zijn, botsen, in conflict zijn (raken) ‖ *the party* ~*es with my exam* het feest valt samen met mijn examen

²clash [klæsj] *n* **1** gevecht^h, botsing, conflict^h; **2** (wapen)gekletter^h

¹clasp [kla:sp] *n* gesp, haak, knip

²clasp [kla:sp] *vb* **1** vastmaken, dichthaken, vastgespen; **2** vastgrijpen, vasthouden: ~ *hands* elkaars hand grijpen; **3** omvatten, omhelzen

clasp knife zakmes^h, knipmes^h

¹class [kla:s] *n* **1** stand, (maatschappelijke) klasse; **2** rang, klas(se), soort, kwaliteit; **3** klas, klasgenoten; **4** les, lesuur^h, college^h, cursus; **5** categorie, groep, verzameling, *(also maths; biology)* klasse: *in a* ~ *of its* (of: *his*) *own* een klasse apart; **6** stijl, distinctie

²**class** [kla:s] *vb* plaatsen, indelen, classificeren: ~ *as* beschouwen als

¹**classic** [klæsik] *adj* 1 klassiek, tijdloos, traditioneel; 2 kenmerkend, typisch, klassiek: *a* ~ *example* een schoolvoorbeeld

²**classic** [klæsik] *n* 1 een van de klassieken: *that film is a real* ~ die film is een echte klassieker; 2 ~*s* klassieke talen

classical [klæsikl] 1 klassiek, traditioneel; 2 antiek, uit de klassieke Oudheid

classification [klæsiffikkeesjǝn] 1 categorie, classificatie, klasse; 2 rangschikking, indeling

classify [klæsiffaj] 1 indelen, rubriceren, classificeren; 2 geheim verklaren, als geheim aanmerken

classmate [kla:smeet] klasgenoot, klasgenote

classy [kla:sie] sjiek, deftig, elegant

¹**clatter** [klætǝ] *vb* kletteren, klepperen

²**clatter** [klætǝ] *n* gekletter^h, gerammel^h, geklepper^h

clause [klo:z] clausule, bepaling, beding^h

¹**claw** [klo:] *n* 1 klauw; 2 poot; 3 schaar *(of crab etc)*

²**claw** [klo:] *vb* klauwen, grissen, graaien

clay [klee] klei, leem^+h, aarde, modder

¹**clean** [klie:n] *adj* 1 schoon, helder, zuiver *(air)*; 2 sierlijk, regelmatig, duidelijk, helder *(style)*; 3 compleet, helemaal: *a* ~ *break* een radicale breuk; 4 oprecht, eerlijk, sportief: *come* ~ voor de draad komen (met), eerlijk bekennen; 5 onschuldig, netjes, fatsoenlijk, kuis: *make a* ~ *breast of sth.* iets bekennen, ergens schoon schip mee maken; *wipe the slate* ~ met een schone lei beginnen

²**clean** [klie:n] *vb* schoonmaken, reinigen, zuiveren: *have a coat* ~*ed* een jas laten stomen; ~ *down* schoonborstelen, schoonwassen

³**clean** [klie:n] *vb* schoon(gemaakt) worden, zich laten reinigen

⁴**clean** [klie:n] *adv* 1 volkomen, helemaal, compleet: ~ *forgotten* glad vergeten; 2 eerlijk, fair

⁵**clean** [klie:n] *n* schoonmaakbeurt: *give the room a* ~ de kamer een (goede) beurt geven

clean-cut duidelijk, helder: *a* ~ *decision* een ondubbelzinnige beslissing

cleaner [klie:nǝ] 1 schoonmaker, schoonmaakster, werkster; 2 schoonmaakmiddel^h, reinigingsmiddel^h; 3 *cleaner's* stomerij || *(fig) take s.o. to the* ~*'s: a)* iem uitkleden; *b)* de vloer met iem aanvegen

cleanly [klenlie] proper, zindelijk, netjes

clean out 1 schoonvegen, uitvegen, uitmesten; 2 *(inf)* kaal plukken, uitschudden, opkopen *(stock)*, afhandig maken *(money)*

cleanse [klenz] reinigen, zuiveren, desinfecteren *(wound)*

¹**clean up** *vb* 1 opruimen; 2 (goed) schoonmaken, opknappen: *clean oneself up* zich opknappen; 3 zuiveren, *(fig)* uitmesten, saneren: ~ *the town* de stad (van misdaad) zuiveren

²**clean up** *vb* de boel opruimen, schoonmaken

clean-up schoonmaakbeurt *(also fig)*, sanering

¹**clear** [kliǝ] *adj* 1 helder, schoon, doorzichtig, klaar; 2 duidelijk, ondubbelzinnig, uitgesproken: *make* oneself ~ duidelijk maken wat je bedoelt; *do I make myself* ~*?* is dat duidelijk begrepen?; 3 netto, schoon *(wages, profit etc)*; 4 compleet, volkomen, absoluut: *a* ~ *majority* een duidelijke meerderheid; 5 vrij, open, op een afstand, veilig, onbelemmerd: *the coast is* ~ de kust is veilig; ~ *conscience* zuiver geweten

²**clear** [kliǝ] *adv* 1 duidelijk, helder: *his voice came through loud and* ~ zijn stem kwam luid en helder door; 2 op voldoende afstand, een eindje, vrij: *keep* (of: *stay, steer)* ~ *of* uit de weg gaan, (proberen te) vermijden

³**clear** [kliǝ] *vb* 1 helder maken, schoonmaken, verhelderen; 2 vrijmaken, ontruimen *(bldg, street):* ~ *the table* de tafel afruimen; 3 verwijderen, opruimen; 4 zuiveren, onschuldig verklaren: ~ *s.o. of suspicion* iem van verdenking zuiveren; 5 (ruim) passeren, springen over *(gate)*, erlangs kunnen; 6 (laten) passeren *(Customs)*, inklaren, klaren, uitklaren; 7 verrekenen, vereffenen *(debt)*, clearen *(cheque)*

⁴**clear** [kliǝ] *vb* 1 helder worden, opklaren *(of air)*; 2 weggaan, wegtrekken, optrekken *(of fog):* ~ *away* optrekken

⁵**clear** [kliǝ] *n: be in the* ~ buiten gevaar zijn, vrijuit gaan

clearance [kliǝrǝns] 1 opheldering, verheldering, verduidelijking; 2 ontruiming, opruiming, uitverkoop; 3 vergunning, toestemming, (akte van) inklaring *(ships); (aviation)* toestemming tot landen (opstijgen); 4 speling, vrije ruimte, tussenruimte: *there was only 2 ft.* ~ *between the two ships* er zat maar twee voet speling tussen de twee schepen

clear-cut scherp omlijnd *(also fig)*, duidelijk, uitgesproken

clear-headed helder denkend, scherpzinnig

clearing [kliǝring] 1 open(gekapte) plek *(in forest)*; 2 verrekening, vereffening

clearly [kliǝlie] 1 duidelijk: *understand sth.* ~ iets goed begrijpen; 2 ongetwijfeld

¹**clear off** *vb (inf)* de benen nemen, 'm smeren, afdruipen: ~*!* opgehoepeld!

²**clear off** *vb* 1 afmaken, een eind maken aan, uit de weg ruimen *(arrears)*; 2 aflossen, afbetalen

¹**clear out** *vb (inf)* de benen nemen, ophoepelen

²**clear out** *vb* 1 uitruimen, leeghalen, uithalen *(cupboard, drain)*, opruimen *(room)*; 2 *(inf)* uitputten, leeghalen *(stocks)*

clear-sighted 1 met scherpe blik *(oft fig)*, scherpzinnig; 2 vooruitziend

¹**clear up** *vb* 1 opklaren *(weather)*; 2 ophouden, bijtrekken *(difficulties)*; 3 (rommel) opruimen

²**clear up** *vb* 1 opruimen, uit de weg ruimen *(mess)*, afmaken *(work)*; 2 verklaren, uitleggen, ophelderen

clearway autoweg *(where there is no stopping)*

cleavage [klie:vidzj] 1 scheiding, kloof, breuk *(also fig)*; 2 gleuf, gootje^h *(between breasts)*, decolleté^h, inkijk

cleave [klie:v] kloven, splijten, hakken, (door)klie-

clef   528

ven
clef [klef] *(mus)* sleutel
¹cleft [kleft] *n* **1** spleet, barst, scheur, kloof *(also fig);*
2 gleuf, kuiltjeʰ *(in chin)*
²cleft *adj* gespleten, gekloofd *(of hoof):* ~ *palate* gespleten gehemelte
clematis [klemmətis] clematis, bosrank
clement [klemmənt] **1** mild, weldadig, zacht; **2** genadig, welwillend
clench [klentsj] **1** dichtklemmen, op elkaar klemmen *(jaws, teeth),* dichtknijpen: *with ~ed fists* met
gebalde vuisten; **2** vastklemmen, vastgrijpen
clergy [klɑ:dzjie] geestelijkheid, geestelijken
clergyman [klɑ:dzjiemən] geestelijke, predikant,
priester
cleric [klerrik] geestelijke
clerical [klerrikl] **1** geestelijk, kerkelijk; **2** administratief, schrijf-: *a ~ job* een kantoorbaan
clerk [klɑ:k] **1** (kantoor)beambte, kantoorbedien-
de, klerk; **2** secretaris, griffier, (hoofd)administra-
teur; **3** *(Am)* (winkel)bediende; **4** *(Am)* receptionist
clever [klevvə] **1** knap, slim, intelligent, vernuftig:
~ *at sth.* goed in iets; **2** handig
¹click [klik] *vb* **1** klikken, tikken, ratelen: *(comp)* ~
on aanklikken; **2** *(inf)* het (samen) kunnen vinden,
bij elkaar passen; **3** *(inf)* op z'n plaats vallen, plotseling duidelijk worden *(joke, remark)*
²click [klik] *vb* klikken met, laten klikken
³click [klik] *n* klik, tik, klak
client [klajjənt] **1** cliënt; **2** klant, afnemer, opdrachtgever
clientele [klie:əntel] **1** klantenkring; **2** praktijk *(of
lawyer);* **3** vaste bezoekers *(of theatre, restaurant
etc)*
cliff [klif] steile rots, klip, klifʰ
cliff-hanger spannende wedstrijd, spannend verhaalʰ
climate [klajmət] **1** klimaatʰ; **2** (lucht)streek; **3**
sfeer, stemming, klimaatʰ: *the present economic* ~
het huidige economische klimaat
climax [klajmæks] **1** hoogtepuntʰ, climax, toppuntʰ; **2** orgasmeʰ
¹climb [klajm] *vb* **1** omhoog gaan, klimmen, stijgen,
toenemen; **2** oplopen, omhooggaan *(of road);* **3**
zich opwerken, opklimmen *(rank, position)*
²climb [klajm] *vb* klimmen in (op), beklimmen, bestijgen
³climb [klajm] *n* **1** klim, beklimming; **2** helling, klim,
weg omhoog
climber [klajmə] **1** klimmer, klauteraar, bergbeklimmer; **2** klimplant
¹clinch [klintsj] *vb* **1** *(boxing)* (met elkaar) in de
clinch gaan, lijf aan lijf staan; **2** *(inf)* elkaar omhelzen
²clinch [klintsj] *vb* beklinken, sluiten, afmaken
(agreement, transaction): that ~ed the matter dat
gaf de doorslag
³clinch [klintsj] *n* **1** vaste greep, omklemming; **2**
(boxing) clinch; **3** omarming, omhelzing

cling [kling] **1** kleven, zich vasthouden, zich vastklemmen; **2** dicht blijven bij, hangen, hechten; **3**
zich vastklampen aan, vasthouden
clinging [klinging] **1** aanhankelijk, plakkerig; **2**
nauwsluitend *(clothing etc)*
clinic [klinnik] **1** kliniek, privékliniek; **2** adviesbu-
reauʰ, consultatiebureauʰ
clinical [klinnikl] klinisch, onbewogen, zakelijk
(attitude)
¹clink [klingk] *n* gerinkelʰ, geklinkʰ
²clink [klingk] *vb* klinken, rinkelen, rammelen
³clink [klingk] *vb* laten rinkelen, klinken met *(eg
glasses)*
¹clip [klip] *vb* **1** (vast)klemmen, vastzetten: ~ *together* samenklemmen; **2** (bij)knippen, afknippen, kort
knippen, trimmen, scheren *(sheep),* uitknippen
(from newspaper, film); **3** afbijten *(words),* inslikken *(letter(s), syllable)*
²clip [klip] *vb* knippen, snoeien
³clip [klip] *n* **1** knippende beweging, scheerbeurt,
trimbeurt; **2** klem, knijper, clip; **3** fragmentʰ, stukʰ,
gedeelteʰ *(from film),* (video)clip
clip out uitknippen
clipper [klippə] **1** knipper, scheerder, (be)snoeier;
2 klipper(schipʰ); **3** ~*s* kniptang *(of guard);* **4** ~*s* na-
gelkniptang; **5** ~*s* tondeuse
clipping [klipping] krantenknipselʰ
clique [klie:k] kliek, club(jeʰ)
¹cloak [klook] *n* **1** cape, mantel; **2** bedekking, laag; **3**
dekmantel, verhulling
²cloak [klook] *vb* verhullen, verbergen, vermommen
cloakroom 1 garderobe; **2** *(euph)* toiletʰ
¹clobber [klobbə] *vb* **1** aftuigen, een pak rammel geven; **2** in de pan hakken
²clobber [klobbə] *n* **1** boeltjeʰ, spullen; **2** plunje,
kloffieʰ
¹clock [klok] *n* **1** klok, uurwerkʰ; **2** *(inf)* meter, teller,
taximeter, prikklok, snelheidsmeter, kilometertel-
ler: *the car had 100,000 miles on the* ~ de auto had
160.000 kilometer op de teller
²clock [klok] *vb* klokken *(time clock):* ~ *in,* ~ *on* inklokken; *we have to* ~ *at 8 o'clock* wij moeten om 8
uur inklokken; ~ *off,* ~ *out* uitklokken
clockwise [klokwajz] met de (wijzers van de) klok
mee
clockwork uurwerkʰ, opwindmechaniekʰ: *like* ~ op
rolletjes, gesmeerd
clockwork orange gerobotiseerde mens, robot
clod [klod] kluit(aarde), klomp(klei), klont
¹clog [klog] *n* klomp
²clog [klog] *vb* **1** verstopt raken, dicht gaan zitten: ~
up: a) verstopt raken *(drain pipe);* b) vastlopen
(machinery); **2** stollen, samenklonteren
³clog [klog] *vb* (doen) verstoppen: ~ *up* doen verstoppen, vast laten draaien *(machines);* ~*ged with
dirt* totaal vervuild
¹clone [kloon] *n* kloon, kopie
²clone [kloon] *vb* klonen
¹close [klooz] *vb* aflopen, eindigen, besluiten *(of*

speaker)

²**close** [klooz] *vb* **1** dichtmaken, (af)sluiten, hechten *(wound)*, dichten *(hole)*; **2** besluiten, beëindigen, (af)sluiten *(argument, plea)*; **3** dichter bij elkaar brengen, aaneensluiten; **4** afmaken, rond maken, sluiten *(agreement, business)*

³**close** [klooz] *n* **1** einde^h, slot^h, besluit^h: *bring to a ~* tot een eind brengen, afsluiten; **2** binnenplaats, hof(je^h); **3** terrein^h *(around church, school etc)*

⁴**close** [kloos] *adj* **1** dicht, gesloten, nauw, benauwd *(space)*, drukkend *(weather, air)*; **2** bedekt, verborgen, geheim, zwijgzaam; **3** beperkt, select, besloten *(partnership)*; **4** nabij, naast *(relative(s))*, intiem, dik *(friend(ship))*, onmiddellijk, direct *(vicinity)*, getrouw, letterlijk *(copy, translation)*, gelijk opgaand *(contest, struggle)*, kort *(hair, grass)*: *~ at hand* bij de hand, dicht in de buurt; *at ~ range* van dichtbij; **5** grondig, diepgaand *(attention)*: *keep a ~ watch on s.o.* iem scherp in de gaten houden; *a ~ shave* (of: *thing, call*) op het nippertje

⁵**close** [kloos] *adv* **1** dicht, stevig; **2** dicht(bij), vlak, tegen: *~ on sixty years* bijna zestig jaar

closed [kloozd] **1** dicht, gesloten; **2** besloten, select, exclusief

closed-circuit [kloozdsə:kit] via een gesloten circuit: *~ television, CCTV* videobewaking, bewaking d.m.v. camera's

close down [klooz daun] **1** sluiten, opheffen, dichtgaan, dichtdoen *(of a business)*; **2** sluiten *(of radio and TV programmes)*

close in [klooz in] **1** korter worden, korten *(of days)*; **2** naderen, dichterbij komen: *~ (up)on* omsingelen, insluiten; **3** (in)vallen *(of darkness)*

close-knit [kloosnit] hecht

¹**closet** [klozzit] *n* **1** (ingebouwde) kast, bergruimte; **2** privévertrek^h

²**closet** [klozzit] *vb* in een privévertrek opsluiten: *(fig) he was ~ed with the headmaster* hij had een privéonderhoud met het schoolhoofd

¹**close up** [klooz up] *vb* dichtgaan *(of flowers)*

²**close up** [klooz up] *vb* afsluiten, blokkeren, sluiten

close-up [kloosup] close-up, *(fig)* indringende beschrijving

closure [kloozjə] **1** het sluiten, sluiting; **2** slot^h, einde^h, besluit^h

¹**clot** [klot] *n* **1** klonter, klont; **2** *(inf)* stommeling, idioot, ezel

²**clot** [klot] *vb* (doen) klonteren, (doen) stollen

cloth [kloθ] **1** stuk^h stof, doek^h, lap; **2** tafellaken^h; **3** stof, materiaal^h, geweven stof; **4** beroepskledij *(of clergymen)*; *(fig)* de geestelijkheid

clothe [klooð] kleden, aankleden, van kleren voorzien

clothes [kloo(ð)z] kleding, kleren, (was)goed

clothing [klooðing] kleding, kledij

¹**cloud** [klaud] *n* **1** wolk, *(fig)* schaduw, probleem^h: *under a ~* uit de gratie; **2** massa, menigte, zwerm *(of insects)*: *every ~ has a silver lining* achter de wolken schijnt de zon

²**cloud** [klaud] *vb* bewolken, verduisteren, betrekken *(also fig): the sky ~ed over* (of: *up*) het werd bewolkt

³**cloud** [klaud] *vb* (zoals) met wolken bedekken, verduisteren, vertroebelen *(also fig): ~ the issue* de zaak vertroebelen

cloudburst wolkbreuk

cloudy [klaudie] bewolkt, betrokken, duister, troebel *(of liquid)*, beslagen, dof *(of glass)*, onduidelijk, verward *(of memory)*

¹**clout** [klaut] *n* **1** *(inf)* mep, klap; **2** (politieke) invloed, (politieke) macht

²**clout** [klaut] *vb* een klap geven

clove [kloov] teen(tje^h): *a ~ of garlic* een teentje knoflook; **2** kruidnagel

clover [kloovə] klaver ‖ *be* (of: *live*) *in ~* leven als God in Frankrijk

cloverleaf klaverblad^h, *(also fig)* verkeersknooppunt^h

clown [klaun] clown, grappenmaker; moppentapper

cloy [kloj] tegenstaan: *cream ~s if you have too much of it* room gaat tegenstaan als je er te veel van eet

¹**club** [klub] *n* **1** knuppel, knots; **2** golfstok; **3** klaveren *(one card)*; **4** clubgebouw^h, clubhuis^h; **5** club, sociëteit, vereniging: *(inf) 'I've lost my money.' 'Join the ~!'* 'Ik heb mijn geld verloren.' 'Jij ook al!'

²**club** [klub] *vb* een bijdrage leveren ‖ *his friends ~bed together to buy a present* zijn vrienden hebben een potje gemaakt om een cadeautje te kopen

³**club** [klub] *vb* knuppelen

club sandwich *(Am)* club sandwich

clue [kloe] aanwijzing, spoor^h, hint: *(inf) I haven't (got) a ~* ik heb geen idee

clueless [kloe:ləs] stom, dom, idioot

¹**clump** [klump] *n* **1** groep, bosje^h *(of trees or plants)*; **2** klont, brok^h: *a ~ of mud* een modderkluit

²**clump** [klump] *vb* stommelen, zwaar lopen

clumsy [klumzie] **1** onhandig, lomp, log; **2** tactloos, lomp

¹**cluster** [klustə] *n* bos(je)^h, groep(je^h)

²**cluster** [klustə] *vb* **1** zich groeperen; **2** in bosjes groeien, in een groep groeien

³**cluster** [klustə] *vb* bundelen, groeperen

¹**clutch** [klutsj] *n* **1** greep, klauw, *(fig also)* macht, controle, bezit^h: *be in the ~es of a blackmailer* in de greep van een chanteur zijn; **2** nest^h *(eieren, kuikens)*, *(fig)* stel^h, groep, reeks; **3** *(techn)* koppeling(spedaal^h): *let the ~ in* koppelen

²**clutch** [klutsj] *vb* grijpen, beetgrijpen, vastgrijpen, stevig vasthouden

¹**clutter** [klutə] *n* rommel, warboel

²**clutter** [klutə] *vb* **1** rommelig maken, onoverzichtelijk maken, in wanorde brengen; **2** (op)vullen, volstoppen: *a sink ~ed (up) with dishes* een aanrecht bedolven onder de borden

c/o *care of* p/a, per adres

Co. 1 *company* **2** *county*

CO *commanding officer* bevelvoerend officier

¹coach [kootsj] *n* **1** koets, staatsiekoets; **2** diligence; **3** spoorrijtuigʰ, spoorwagon; **4** bus, reisbus: *go (of: travel) by* ~ met de bus reizen; **5** trainer, coach

²coach [kootsj] *vb* **1** in een koets vervoeren; **2** trainen, coachen

coachwork koetswerkʰ, carrosserie

coal [kool] **1** steenkool; **2** houtskool || *carry* (of: *take*) *~s to Newcastle* water naar de zee dragen; *haul s.o. over the ~s* iem de les lezen

coalescence [kooəlesns] samensmelting, samenvoeging

coalition [kooəlisjən] *(pol)* coalitie, unie, verbondʰ

coalmine kolenmijn

coal pit kolenmijn

coarse [ko:s] grof, ruw, ordinair, plat

¹coast [koost] *n* kust

²coast [koost] *vb* **1** freewheelen, met de motor in de vrijloop rijden; **2** *(fig)* zonder inspanning vooruitkomen, zich (doelloos) laten voortdrijven, zich niet inspannen: *~ to victory* op zijn sloffen winnen

coastal [koostl] kust-

coaster [koostə] **1** kustbewoner; **2** kustvaarder, coaster; **3** onderzetter, bierviltjeʰ

coastguard 1 kustwachter; **2** kustwacht

¹coat [koot] *n* **1** (over)jas, mantel, jasjeʰ; **2** vacht, beharing, verenkleedʰ; **3** schil, dop, rok; **4** laag, deklaag: *~ of paint* (of: *dust*) verflaag, stoflaag; *~ of arms* wapenschild, familiewapen; *~ of mail* maliënkolder

²coat [koot] *vb* een laag geven, met een laag bedekken

coating [kooting] laag, deklaag

co-author [kooo:θə] medeauteur

coax [kooks] vleien, overreden, overhalen

cob [kob] **1** mannetjeszwaan; **2** maïskolf *(without the corn)*

cobalt [koobo:lt] **1** kobaltʰ; **2** kobaltblauwʰ, ultramarijnʰ

¹cobble [kobl] *n* kei, kinderkopjeʰ, kassei

²cobble [kobl] *vb* bestraten (met keien), plaveien || *~ together* in elkaar flansen

cobbler [koblə] schoenmaker

cobra [koobrə] cobra, brilslang

cobweb [kobweb] **1** spinnenwebʰ, webʰ *(also fig)*; **2** spinragʰ; **3** ragfijn weefselʰ *(also fig)* || *blow the ~s away* de dufheid verdrijven

cochineal [kotsjinnie:l] cochenille *(red paint)*

¹cock [kok] *n* **1** haan, *(fig)* kemphaan; **2** mannetjeʰ *(of birds),* mannetjes-; **3** *(inf)* makker, maat, ouwe jongen; **4** kraan, tap; **5** *(vulg)* lul, pik; **6** haan *(of firearms): go off at half ~: a)* voortijdig beginnen; *b)* mislukken (door overijld handelen)

²cock [kok] *vb* **1** overeind (doen) staan: *~ the ears* de oren spitsen; **2** spannen *(cock of firearm);* **3** scheef (op)zetten

cock-a-doodle-doo [kokkədoe:dldoe:] kukelekuʰ

cock-and-bull story sterk verhaalʰ, kletsverhaalʰ

Cockney [koknie] inwoner van Londen, vnl. East End

cockpit 1 cockpit, stuurhut; **2** vechtplaats voor hanen, *(fig)* slagveldʰ; **3** *(shipp)* kuip

cockroach [kokrootsj] kakkerlak

cocktail [kokteel] cocktail

cock up 1 oprichten, spitsen: *~ one's ears* de oren spitsen; **2** *(vulg)* in de war sturen, in het honderd laten lopen

cock-up *(vulg)* puinhoop, klerezooi

cocky [kokkie] brutaal en verwaand

cocoa [kookoo] **1** warme chocola; **2** cacao(poederʰ)

coconut [kookənut] **1** kokosnoot; **2** kokos(vleesʰ)

cocoon [kəkoe:n] **1** cocon, pop; **2** overtrek, (beschermend) omhulselʰ

cod [kod] kabeljauw

coddle [kodl] **1** zacht koken; **2** vertroetelen, verwennen

code 1 code; **2** gedragslijn: *~ of honour* erecode; **3** wetboekʰ

codify [koodiffaj] codificeren, schriftelijk vastleggen

coed [kooed] *(Am, inf)* studente

coeducation [kooedzjoekeesjən] gemengd onderwijsʰ

coerce [kooə:s] **1** dwingen: *~ s.o. into doing sth.* iem dwingen iets te doen; **2** afdwingen; **3** onderdrukken

coercion [kooə:sjən] dwang

coexistence [kooigzjistəns] coëxistentie, het (vreedzaam) naast elkaar bestaan

C. of E. *Church of England* anglicaanse kerk

coffee [koffie] koffie

coffer [koffə] **1** koffer, (geld)kist, brandkast; **2** ~*s* schatkist, *(inf)* fondsen

coffin [koffin] (dood)kist

cog [kog] tand(jeʰ) *(of wheel)* || *(fig; inf) a ~ in the machine* (of: *wheel)* een klein radertje in een grote onderneming

cogent [koodzjənt] overtuigend

cognac [konjæk] cognac

cognizance [kognizzəns] **1** kennis(neming), nota; **2** gerechtelijk onderzoekʰ

cogwheel tandradʰ

cohabit [koohæbit] samenwonen

coherence [koohjərəns] samenhang

coherent [koohjərənt] samenhangend, begrijpelijk

cohesion [koohie:zjən] (onderlinge) samenhang

¹coil [kojl] *vb* (zich) kronkelen, (op)rollen

²coil [kojl] *n* **1** kronkel *(of rope, cable);* **2** winding, wikkeling; **3** vlecht; **4** *(electr)* spoel; **5** *(med)* spiraaltjeʰ

¹coin [kojn] *n* **1** munt(stukʰ), geldstukʰ: *toss* (of: *flip) a ~* kruis of munt gooien, tossen; **2** gemunt geldʰ

²coin [kojn] *vb* **1** munten, slaan *(money);* **2** verzinnen, uitvinden: *~ a word* een woord verzinnen

coincide [kooinsajd] **1** (with *with*) samenvallen (met); **2** (with *with*) overeenstemmen (met), identiek zijn

coincidence [kooinsiddəns] **1** het samenvallen, samenloop (van omstandigheden): *a mere ~* puur toeval; **2** overeenstemming

coke [kook] **1** cokes; **2** Coca-Cola; **3** *(inf)* cocaïne
Col. *Colonel* kol.
colander [kʌlləndə] vergiet[h]
¹cold [koold] *adj* koud, koel, *(fig)* onvriendelijk: *a ~ fish* een kouwe kikker; *(inf) ~ sweat* het angstzweet; *it leaves me ~* het laat me koud; *~ comfort* schrale troost; *get ~ feet* bang worden; *(fig) put sth. in(to) ~ storage* iets in de ijskast zetten; *make s.o.'s blood run ~* iem het bloed in de aderen doen stollen
²cold [koold] *n* **1** verkoudheid: *catch (a) ~* kou vatten; **2** kou: *she was left out in the ~* ze was aan haar lot overgelaten
³cold [koold] *adv* **1** in koude toestand; **2** *(inf)* volledig, compleet: *~ sober* broodnuchter; *be turned down ~* zonder meer afgewezen worden
coleslaw [koolslo:] koolsalade
colic [kɔllik] koliek
collaborate [kəlæbəreet] **1** samenwerken, medewerken; **2** collaboreren, heulen *(with enemy)*
collaboration [kəlæbəreesjən] **1** samenwerking; **2** collaboratie *(with the occupier(s))*
¹collapse [kəlæps] *vb* **1** in(een)storten, in(een)vallen, in elkaar zakken; **2** opvouwbaar zijn; **3** bezwijken; **4** mislukken
²collapse [kəlæps] *vb* **1** in(een) doen storten, in(een) doen vallen, in elkaar doen zakken; **2** opvouwen, samenvouwen
³collapse [kəlæps] *n* **1** in(een)storting, in(een)zakking; **2** val, ondergang; **3** inzinking, verval[h] van krachten; **4** mislukking, fiasco[h]
collapsible [kəlæpsibl] opvouwbaar, inschuifbaar, inklapbaar, opklapbaar
¹collar [kɔllə] *n* **1** kraag, halskraag; **2** boord(je[h]), halsboord[h]; **3** halsband, halsring; **4** halsketting, halssnoer[h]; **5** gareel[h], haam *(of horse)*
²collar [kɔllə] *vb (inf)* in de kraag grijpen, inrekenen
collarbone sleutelbeen[h]
colleague [kɔllie:g] collega
¹collect [kəlekt] *vb* **1** zich verzamelen; **2** *(inf)* geld ontvangen
²collect [kəlekt] *vb* **1** verzamelen; **2** innen, incasseren, collecteren; **3** (weer) onder controle krijgen: *~ one's thoughts (of: ideas)* zijn gedachten bijeenrapen; *~ oneself* zijn zelfbeheersing terugkrijgen; **4** afhalen, ophalen
³collect [kəlekt] *adj (Am)* te betalen door opgeroepene *(telephone): a ~ call* een telefoongesprek voor rekening van de opgeroepene; *call me ~* bel me maar op mijn kosten
collectable [kəlektəbl] verzamelobject[h]
collected [kəlektid] kalm, bedaard, beheerst
collection [kəleksjən] **1** verzameling, collectie; **2** collecte, inzameling; **3** buslichting; **4** het verzamelen, het inzamelen, de incassering; **5** incasso[h], inning
¹collective [kəlektiv] *adj* gezamenlijk, gemeenschappelijk, collectief
²collective [kəlektiv] *n* **1** groep, gemeenschap, collectief[h]; **2** gemeenschappelijke onderneming, col-

lectief landbouwbedrijf[h]
collector [kəlektə] **1** verzamelaar; **2** collecteur *(of public funds)*, ontvanger (der belasting), inzamelaar; **3** collectant
college [kɔllidzj] **1** hogere beroepsschool, academie, instituut[h]; **2** college[h]; **3** *(Am)* (kleine) universiteit; **4** grote kostschool; **5** universiteitsgebouw[h], universiteitsgebouwen, schoolgebouw[h], schoolgebouwen; **6** raad
collegiate [kəlie:dzjiət] **1** behorend tot een college, universiteit; **2** bestaande uit verschillende autonome afdelingen *(of university)*
collide [kəlajd] botsen, aanrijden, aanvaren, *(fig)* in botsing komen
collision [kəlizjən] botsing, aanrijding, aanvaring, *(fig also)* conflict[h]
colloquial [kəlookwiəl] tot de spreektaal behorend, informeel
colloquialism [kəlookwiəlizm] **1** alledaagse uitdrukking; **2** informele stijl
Cologne [kəloon] Keulen
colon [koolən] **1** dubbelepunt; **2** karteldarm
colonel [kə:nl] kolonel
¹colonial [kəlooniəl] *adj* koloniaal, vd koloniën
²colonial [kəlooniəl] *n* koloniaal
colonialism [kəlooniəlizm] kolonialisme[h], koloniaal stelsel[h]
¹colonize [kɔllənajz] *vb* een kolonie vormen
²colonize [kɔllənajz] *vb* koloniseren
colony [kɔllənie] kolonie *(also biology)*
colossal [kəlɔsl] kolossaal, reusachtig, enorm; **2** *(inf)* geweldig, prachtig, groots
¹colour [kʌllə] *n* **1** kleur, *(fig)* schilderachtigheid, levendigheid, bloemrijke stijl: *(fig) paint in glowing ~s* zeer enthousiast beschrijven; **2** verf(stof), kleurstof, pigment[h]; **3** kleurtje[h], gelaatskleur: *have little ~* er bleekjes uitzien; **4** donkere huidkleur; **5** schijn (van werkelijkheid), uiterlijk[h]: *give (of: lend) ~ to* geloofwaardiger maken; **6** soort, aard, slag; **7** ~s nationale vlag, vaandel[h]; **8** clubkleuren, insigne[h], lint[h]; **9** gevoelens, positie, opvatting: *(inf) show one's (true) ~s* zijn ware gedaante tonen; *with flying ~s* met vlag en wimpel; *feel (of: look) off ~* zich niet lekker voelen
²colour [kʌllə] *vb* **1** kleuren, verven; **2** vermommen; **3** verkeerd voorstellen, verdraaien; **4** beïnvloeden
³colour [kʌllə] *vb* **1** kleur krijgen, kleuren; **2** blozen, rood worden: *~ up* blozen
colour-blind kleurenblind
coloured [kʌlləd] **1** gekleurd; **2** niet-blank, zwart
colouring [kʌlləring] **1** verf(stof), kleur(stof); **2** kleuring; **3** (gezonde) gelaatskleur
colt [koolt] **1** veulen[h], jonge hengst; **2** *(inf; sport)* beginneling, jonge speler
column [kɔlləm] **1** zuil, pilaar, pijler: *~ of smoke* rookzuil; **2** kolom: *the advertising ~s* de advertentiekolommen; **3** *(mil)* colonne
columnist [kɔlləmnist] columnist(e)
¹comb [koom] *n* **1** kam *(also of cock etc)*; **2** honing-

raat

²comb [koom] *vb* **1** kammen; **2** *(inf)* doorzoeken, uitkammen

¹combat [kombæt] *n* strijd, gevecht[h]

²combat [kombæt] *vb* vechten (tegen), (be)strijden

combination [kombinneesjən] **1** combinatie, vereniging, verbinding: *in ~ with* samen met, in combinatie met; **2** (geheime letter)combinatie; **3** samenstelling

¹combine [kəmbajn] *vb* **1** zich verenigen, zich verbinden; **2** samenwerken; **3** *(chem)* zich verbinden

²combine [kəmbajn] *vb* **1** combineren, verenigen, verbinden, samenvoegen: *~d operations* (of: *exercises)* legeroefeningen waarbij land-, lucht- en zeemacht samenwerken; **2** in zich verenigen

³combine [kombajn] *n* maaidorser, combine

comb out *(inf)* **1** uitkammen, doorzoeken; **2** zuiveren, schiften; **3** verwijderen, afvoeren *(redundant staff)*

¹combustible [kəmbustibl] *adj* **1** (ver)brandbaar, ontvlambaar; **2** opvliegend, lichtgeraakt

²combustible [kəmbustibl] *n* brandstof, brandbare stof

combustion [kəmbustsjən] verbranding

come [kum] **1** komen, naderen: *in the years to ~* in de komende jaren; *she came running* ze kwam aanrennen; *~ and go* heen en weer lopen, *(fig)* komen en gaan; **2** aankomen, arriveren: *the goods have ~* de goederen zijn aangekomen; *the train is coming* de trein komt eraan; *I'm coming!* ik kom eraan!; *first ~, first served* die eerst komt, eerst maalt; **3** beschikbaar zijn, verkrijgbaar zijn, aangeboden worden: *this suit ~s in two sizes* dit pak is verkrijgbaar in twee maten; **4** verschijnen: *that news came as a surprise* dat nieuws kwam als een verrassing; **5** meegaan: *are you coming?* kom je mee?; **6** gebeuren: *~ what may* wat er ook moge gebeuren; *(now that I) ~ to think of it* nu ik eraan denk; *(inf) how ~?* hoe komt dat?, waarom?; **7** staan, komen, gaan: *my job ~s before everything else* mijn baan gaat vóór alles; **8** zijn: *it ~s cheaper by the dozen* het is goedkoper per dozijn; **9** beginnen, gaan, worden: *the buttons came unfastened* de knopen raakten los; *~ to believe* tot de overtuiging komen; *~ to know s.o. better* iem beter leren kennen; **10** (een bepaalde) vorm aannemen: *the life to ~* het leven in het hiernamaals; *(inf) he'll be eighteen ~ September* hij wordt achttien in september; *she doesn't know whether she is coming or going* ze is de kluts kwijt; *~ now!* kom, kom!, zachtjes aan!

come about gebeuren: *how did the accident ~?* hoe is het ongeluk gebeurd?

¹come across *vb* aantreffen, vinden, stoten op: *I came across an old friend* ik liep een oude vriend tegen het lijf

²come across *vb* **1** overkomen *(of intention, joke etc)*, begrepen worden: *his speech didn't ~ very well* zijn toespraak sloeg niet erg aan; **2** *(inf)* lijken te zijn, overkomen (als): *he comes across to me as quite a*

nice fellow hij lijkt me wel een aardige kerel

come after 1 volgen, komen na, later komen; **2** *(inf)* (achter iem) aanzitten

come again 1 terugkomen, teruggaan; **2** *(inf)* iets herhalen, iets nog eens zeggen: *~?* zeg 't nog eens

come along 1 meekomen, meegaan; **2** opschieten, vooruitkomen: *how is your work coming along?* schiet je op met je werk?; *~!* vooruit! schiet op!; **3** zich voordoen, gebeuren: *take every opportunity that comes along* elke kans grijpen die zich voordoet; **4** zijn best doen: *~!* komaan!

come apart uit elkaar vallen, losgaan, uit elkaar gaan

come at 1 komen bij, er bij kunnen, te pakken krijgen; **2** bereiken, toegang krijgen tot: *the truth is often difficult to ~* het is vaak moeilijk de waarheid te achterhalen; **3** er op losgaan, aanvallen: *he came at me with a knife* hij viel me aan met een mes

come away 1 losgaan, loslaten; **2** heengaan, weggaan, ervandaan komen

comeback comeback, terugkeer: *stage* (of: *make, try, attempt) a ~* een comeback (proberen te) maken

come back 1 terugkomen, terugkeren, een comeback maken; **2** weer in de mode komen, weer populair worden; **3** weer te binnen schieten: *it'll ~ to me in a minute* het schiet me zo wel weer te binnen

come between tussenbeide komen, zich bemoeien met

come by 1 krijgen, komen aan: *jobs are hard to ~* werk is moeilijk te vinden; **2** oplopen *(disease, wound etc)*, vinden, tegen het lijf lopen; **3** voorbijkomen, passeren

comedian [kəmiediən] **1** (blijspel)acteur, komediant *(also fig);* **2** blijspelauteur; **3** komiek

comedown *(inf)* **1** val, vernedering, achteruitgang; **2** tegenvaller

come down 1 neerkomen, naar beneden komen: *(fig) ~ in the world* aan lagerwal raken; **2** overgeleverd worden *(of tradition etc);* **3** dalen *(also of aeroplane)*, zakken, lager worden *(of price);* **4** overkomen

come down on 1 neerkomen op, toespringen (op), overvallen; **2** straffen; **3** *(inf)* krachtig eisen; **4** *(inf)* berispen, uitschelden, uitvaren tegen: *he came down on me like a ton of bricks* hij verpletterde me onder zijn kritiek

come down to *(inf; fig)* neerkomen op: *the problem comes down to this* het probleem komt hierop neer

comedy [kommədie] **1** blijspel, komedie; **2** humor

come from 1 komen uit: *that's what comes from lying to people* dat komt ervan als je liegt tegen mensen

come in 1 binnenkomen; **2** aankomen: *he came in second* hij kwam als tweede binnen; **3** in de mode komen, de mode worden; **4** deelnemen, een plaats vinden: *this is where you ~* hier kom jij aan de beurt, hier begint jouw rol; **5** voordeel hebben: *where do I ~?* wat levert het voor mij op?; **6** beginnen, aan de beurt komen: *this is where we* ~ hier begint voor ons het verhaal; **7** opkomen, rijzen *(of tide);* **8** binnenkomen, in ontvangst genomen worden, verkregen worden *(of money);* **9** dienen, nut hebben: ~ *handy* (of: *useful)* goed van pas komen

come in for 1 krijgen, ontvangen: ~ *a fortune* een fortuin krijgen; **2** het voorwerp zijn van, uitlokken: ~ *a great deal of criticism* heel wat kritiek uitlokken

come into 1 (ver)krijgen, verwerven, in het bezit komen van: ~ *a fortune* een fortuin erven; ~ *s.o.'s possession* in iemands bezit komen; **2** komen in: ~ *blossom* (of: *flower)* beginnen te bloeien; ~ *fashion* in de mode komen; **3** binnenkomen

comely [ˈkʌmlie] aantrekkelijk, knap

come of 1 komen uit, afstammen van: *he comes of noble ancestors* hij stamt uit een nobel geslacht; **2** het resultaat zijn van: *that's what comes of being late* dat komt ervan als je te laat bent; *nothing came of it* er kwam niets van terecht, het is nooit iets geworden

come off 1 loslaten *(eg of wallpaper from the wall),* losgaan; **2** er afkomen, (het) er afbrengen: ~ *badly* het er slecht van afbrengen; **3** lukken, goed aflopen; **4** plaatshebben: *Henry's birthday party didn't* ~ Henry's verjaardagsfeestje ging niet door; **5** afkomen van, loslaten, verlaten: *has this button* ~ *your coat?* komt deze knoop van jouw jas?; **6** afgaan *(of price): that'll* ~ *your paycheck* dat zal van jouw salaris worden afgetrokken; *(inf)* oh, ~ *it!* schei uit!

come on 1 naderbij komen, oprukken, (blijven) komen: *I'll* ~ *later* ik kom je wel achterna; **2** opschieten, vooruitkomen; **3** beginnen, opkomen *(of thunderstorm),* vallen *(of night),* aangaan *(of light),* beginnen (te ontstaan) *(of disease etc): I've got a cold coming on* ik heb een opkomende verkoudheid; **4** op de tv komen; **5** opkomen *(of actor);* **6** beter worden, herstellen, opknappen *(of disease);* **7** *(Am)* een grote indruk maken, overkomen *(on TV, radio);* **8** aantreffen, stoten op; **9** treffen *(of sth undesirable),* overvallen: *the disease came on her suddenly* de ziekte trof haar plotseling

come-on *(inf)* **1** lokmiddelₕ, verlokking; **2** *(Am; inf)* uitnodiging, invitatie

come out 1 uitkomen, naar buiten komen: *Lucy came out in the top three* Lucy eindigde bij de eerste drie; **2** staken, in staking gaan; **3** verschijnen, te voorschijn komen, gepubliceerd worden *(of book),* uitlopen, bloeien *(of plants, trees),* doorkomen *(of sun):* ~ *with the truth* met de waarheid voor de dag komen; **4** ontdekt worden; **5** duidelijk worden, goed uitkomen, er goed op staan *(photo);* **6** verdwijnen, verschieten, verbleken *(of colour),* uitvallen *(of hair, teeth);* **7** zich voor (tegen) iets verklaren: *the Government came out strong(ly) against the invasion* de regering protesteerde krachtig tegen de invasie; **8** verwijderd worden, er uitgaan *(of stain);* **9** uitkomen, kloppen, juist zijn *(of bill);* **10** openlijk uitkomen voor *(sexual inclination):* ~ *badly* het er slecht afbrengen; ~ *right* goed aflopen; ~ *for s.o.*

(sth.) iem (iets) zijn steun toezeggen

come over 1 overkomen, komen over, oversteken; **2** (naar een andere partij) overlopen; **3** langskomen, bezoeken; **4** inslaan, overkomen, aanslaan; **5** worden, zich voelen: ~ *dizzy* zich duizelig voelen; **6** overkomen, bekruipen: *a strange feeling came over her* een vreemd gevoel bekroop haar; *what has* ~ *you?* wat bezielt je?

come round *(Am)* **1** aanlopen, langskomen, bezoeken; **2** bijkomen, weer bij zijn positieven komen; **3** overgaan, bijdraaien: *Jim has* ~ Jim heeft het geaccepteerd; **4** terugkomen, (regelmatig) terugkeren; **5** een geschil bijleggen; **6** een omweg maken; **7** bijtrekken *(after angry mood): Sue'll soon* ~ Sue komt vast gauw in een beter humeur

comestible [kəˈmestibl] eetbaar

comet [ˈkɒmit] komeet

come through 1 doorkomen, overkomen: *the message isn't coming through clearly* het bericht komt niet goed door; **2** overleven, te boven komen, doorstaan *(disease etc);* **3** *(Am)* slagen, lukken, de bestemming bereiken; **4** *(inf)* doen als verwacht, over de brug komen

come to 1 bijkomen, weer bij zijn positieven komen; **2** betreffen, aankomen op: *when it comes to speaking clearly* wat duidelijk spreken betreft; **3** komen tot (aan), komen bij: ~ *an agreement* het eens worden; ~ *s.o.'s aid* iem te hulp komen; **4** bedragen, (neer)komen op: ~ *the same thing* op hetzelfde neerkomen; **5** te binnen schieten, komen op; **6** toekomen, ten deel vallen, gegeven worden: *it comes naturally to him, (inf) it comes natural to him* het gaat hem makkelijk af; **7** overkomen: *I hope no harm will* ~ *you* ik hoop dat je niets kwaads overkomt; *he'll never* ~ *anything* er zal nooit iets van hem worden; *he had it coming to him* hij kreeg zijn verdiende loon; ~ *nothing* op niets uitdraaien; *we never thought things would* ~ *this!* we hadden nooit gedacht dat het zo ver zou komen!

come up 1 uitkomen, kiemen; **2** aan de orde komen, ter sprake komen; **3** gebeuren, voorkomen, zich voordoen; **4** vooruitkomen: ~ *in the world* vooruitkomen in de wereld; **5** *(inf)* uitkomen, getrokken worden: *I hope my number will* ~ *this time* ik hoop dat mijn lotnummer deze keer wint; ~ *against* in conflict komen met; *our holiday didn't* ~ *to our expectations* onze vakantie viel tegen; *(inf) you'll have to* ~ *with something better* je zult met iets beters moeten komen

come upon 1 overvallen, overrompelen, komen over; **2** aantreffen, stoten op, tegen het lijf lopen

¹comfort [ˈkʌmfət] *n* **1** troost, steun, bemoediging: *derive (of: take)* ~ *from sth.* troost putten uit iets; **2** comfortₕ, gemakₕ; **3** welstand, welgesteldheid: *live in* ~ welgesteld zijn

²comfort [ˈkʌmfət] *vb* troosten, bemoedigen

comfortable [ˈkʌmfətibl] **1** aangenaam, gemakkelijk: *feel* ~ zich goed voelen; **2** royaal, vorstelijk; **3** rustig, zonder pijn: *have a* ~ *night* een rustige nacht hebben; **4** welgesteld: *live in ~ circumstances* in goeden doen zijn

comforter [kʌmfətə] **1** trooster, steun; **2** fopspeen

¹**comic** [kɔmmik] *adj* **1** grappig, komisch: *~ relief* vrolijke noot; **2** blijspel-

²**comic** [kɔmmik] *n* **1** komiek, grappenmaker; **2** *~s* stripboek[h], strippagina

comical [kɔmmikl] *(inf)* **1** grappig, komisch; **2** blijspel-

comic strip strip(verhaal[h])

¹**coming** [kʌmming] *adj* **1** toekomstig, komend, aanstaand: *the ~ week* volgende week; **2** *(inf)* veelbelovend, in opkomst

²**coming** [kʌmming] *n* komst: *the ~s and goings* het komen en gaan

comma [kɔmmə] **1** komma; **2** cesuur || *inverted ~s* aanhalingstekens

¹**command** [kəma:nd] *vb* **1** bevelen geven; **2** het bevel voeren

²**command** [kəma:nd] *vb* **1** bevelen, commanderen; **2** het bevel voeren over; **3** beheersen: *~ oneself* zich beheersen; **4** bestrijken, overzien: *this hill ~s a fine view* vanaf deze heuvel heeft men een prachtig uitzicht; **5** afdwingen: *~ respect* eerbied afdwingen

³**command** [kəma:nd] *n* **1** commando[h]; leiding, militair gezag[h]: *be in ~ of the situation* de zaak onder controle hebben; **2** bevel[h], order, gebod[h], opdracht; **3** legeronderdeel[h], commando[h], legerdistrict[h]; **4** beheersing, controle, meesterschap[h]: *have (a) good ~ of a language* een taal goed beheersen

commandant [kɔmməndænt] commandant, bevelvoerend officier

commander [kəma:ndə] **1** bevelhebber, commandant, *(shipp)* gezagvoerder: *~ in chief* opperbevelhebber; **2** *(shipp)* kapitein-luitenant-ter-zee; **3** commandeur *(of knighthood)*

commanding [kəma:nding] **1** bevelvoerend, bevelend; **2** indrukwekkend, imponerend

commandment [kəma:n(d)mənt] **1** bevel[h], order, gebod[h]; **2** bevelschrift[h]; **3** *(rel)* gebod[h]: *the Ten Commandments* de Tien Geboden

commando [kəma:ndoo] *(also ~es) (mil)* commando[h], stoottroep, stoottroeper

commemorate [kəmemməreet] herdenken, gedenken, vieren

commence [kəmens] beginnen

commencement [kəmensmənt] begin[h], aanvang

commend [kəmend] **1** toevertrouwen, opdragen: *~ sth. to s.o.'s care* iets aan iemands zorg toevertrouwen; **2** prijzen: *highly ~ed* met eervolle vermelding; **3** aanbevelen

commendation [kɔmməndeesjən] **1** prijs, eerbewijs[h], eervolle vermelding; **2** lof, bijval; **3** aanbeveling

¹**comment** [kɔmment] *n* **1** (verklarende, kritische) aantekening, commentaar[h], toelichting: *(inf) no ~* geen commentaar; **2** bemerking, opmerking; **3** gepraat[h], praatjes

²**comment** [kɔmment] *vb* **1** (with *(up)on*) commen-

taar leveren (op); **2** opmerkingen maken, kritiek leveren

commentary [kɔmməntərie] **1** commentaar[h], opmerking; **2** uitleg, verklaring; **3** reportage: *a running ~* een doorlopende reportage

commentator [kɔmmənteetə] **1** commentator; **2** verslaggever

commerce [kɔmmə:s] handel, (handels)verkeer[h]

¹**commercial** [kəmə:sjl] *adj* commercieel *(also depr):* *~ traveller* vertegenwoordiger, handelsreiziger

²**commercial** [kəmə:sjl] *n* reclame, spot

commiserate [kəmizzəreet] *(with with)* medelijden hebben (met), medeleven betuigen

¹**commission** [kəmisjən] *n* **1** opdracht; **2** benoeming, aanstelling *(of officer)*, benoemingsbrief; **3** commissie, comité[h]; **4** commissie, verlening *(of power, position etc)*, machtiging, instructie; **5** provisie, commissieloon[h]; **6** het begaan *(of crime, sin)*

²**commission** [kəmisjən] *vb* **1** opdragen; **2** bestellen

commissioner [kəmisjənə] **1** commissaris; **2** (hoofd)commissaris *(of police)*; **3** (hoofd)ambtenaar

commit [kəmit] **1** toevertrouwen: *~ to memory* uit het hoofd leren; **2** in (voorlopige) hechtenis nemen, opsluiten: *~ to prison* in hechtenis nemen; **3** plegen, begaan, bedrijven: *~ murder* een moord plegen; **4** beschikbaar stellen, toewijzen: *~ money to a new project* geld uittrekken voor een nieuw project; *~ oneself: a)* zich verplichten; *b)* zich uitspreken

commitment [kəmitmənt] **1** verplichting, belofte; **2** overtuiging; **3** inzet, betrokkenheid; **4** (bevel[h] tot) inhechtenisneming, aanhouding

committal [kəmitl] **1** inhechtenisneming, opsluiting, opname; **2** toezegging, belofte; **3** verwijzing, toewijzing

committed [kəmittid] **1** toegewijd, overtuigd; **2** betrokken

committee [kəmittie] commissie, bestuur[h], comité[h]: *~ of inquiry* onderzoekscommissie

commode [kəmood] **1** ladekast, commode; **2** toilet[h]

commodity [kəmoddittie] **1** (handels)artikel[h], product[h], nuttig voorwerp[h]; **2** basisproduct[h], *(roughly)* grondstof

¹**common** [kɔmmən] *adj* **1** gemeenschappelijk, gemeen: *by ~ consent* met algemene instemming; *it is very ~* het komt heel vaak voor; **2** openbaar, publiek: *for the ~ good* in het algemeen belang; **3** gewoon, algemeen, gebruikelijk, gangbaar: *the ~ man* de gewone man, Jan met de pet; **4** ordinair: *as ~ as muck* (of: *dirt*) vreselijk ordinair; *make ~ cause with* onder één hoedje spelen met; *~ law* gewoonterecht, ongeschreven recht; *~ sense* gezond verstand

²**common** [kɔmmən] *n* **1** gemeenschapsgrond; **2** het gewone: *out of the ~* ongewoon, ongebruikelijk; **3** *~s* gemeenschappelijk, (gewone) burgerij; **4** *the Commons* (leden vh) Lagerhuis: *in ~* gemeenschappelijk, gezamenlijk; *in ~ with* evenals, op dezelfde manier

als

commoner [kommənə] burger, gewone man

common-law (volgens het) gewoonterecht: *they are ~ husband and wife* ze zijn zonder boterbriefje getrouwd

¹**commonplace** [kommənplees] *adj* **1** afgezaagd, clichématig; **2** alledaags, gewoon, doorsnee

²**commonplace** [kommənplees] *n* **1** cliché^h; **2** alledaags iets

common-room 1 docentenkamer; **2** studentenvertrek^h, leerlingenkamer

Commonwealth [kommənwelθ] Britse Gemenebest

commotion [kəmoosjən] **1** beroering, onrust, opschudding; **2** rumoer^h, láwaai^h, herrie

communal [komjoenl] gemeenschappelijk: *~ life* gemeenschapsleven

commune [kəmjoe:n] in nauw contact staan, gevoelens uitwisselen, zich één voelen: *~ with friends* een intiem gesprek met vrienden hebben; *~ with nature* zich één voelen met de natuur

communicable [kəmjoe:nikkəbl] **1** besmettelijk; **2** overdraagbaar *(of ideas)*

¹**communicate** [kəmjoe:nikkeet] *vb* **1** communiceren, contact hebben; **2** in verbinding staan: *our living room ~s with the kitchen* onze woonkamer staat in verbinding met de keuken

²**communicate** [kəmjoe:nikkeet] *vb* overbrengen, bekendmaken, doorgeven

communication [kəmjoe:nikkeesjən] **1** mededeling, boodschap, bericht^h; **2** verbinding, contact^h, communicatie; **3** het overbrengen *(of ideas, diseases)*; **4** *~s* verbindingen, communicatiemiddelen

communion [kəmjoe:niən] **1** kerkgenootschap^h, gemeente, gemeenschap; **2** *Communion (Roman Catholicism)* communie; *(Protestant)* Avondmaal^h; **3** gemeenschappelijkheid

communiqué [kəmjoe:nikkee] bekendmaking, bericht^h

communism [komjoenizm] communisme^h

¹**communist** [komjoenist] *adj* communistisch

²**communist** [komjoenist] *n* communist

community [kəmjoe:nittie] **1** gemeenschap, bevolkingsgroep; **2** overeenkomst(igheid), gemeenschappelijkheid: *a ~ of interests* gemeenschappelijke belangen; **3** *(Roman Catholicism)* congregatie, broederschap; **4** bevolking, publiek^h, gemeenschap

commutation [komjoeteesjən] **1** omzetting *(of punishment)*, vermindering; **2** afkoopsom; het afkopen; **3** het pendelen

¹**commute** [kəmjoe:t] *vb* pendelen

²**commute** [kəmjoe:t] *vb* **1** verlichten, verminderen, omzetten: *~ a sentence from death to life imprisonment* een vonnis van doodstraf in levenslang omzetten; **2** veranderen, omzetten, afkopen: *~ an insurance policy into (of: for) a lump sum* een verzekeringspolis afkopen voor een uitkering ineens

commuter [kəmjoe:tə] forens, pendelaar

¹**compact** [kəmpækt] *adj* **1** compact, samengeperst;

2 compact, bondig, beknopt

²**compact** [kəmpækt] *vb* een overeenkomst aangaan

³**compact** [kəmpækt] *vb* samenpakken, samenpersen

⁴**compact** [kompækt] *n* **1** overeenkomst, verbond^h, verdrag^h; **2** poederdoos; **3** *(Am)* middelgrote auto, compact car

companion [kəmpæniən] **1** metgezel, kameraad; **2** vennoot, partner; **3** handboek^h, gids, wegwijzer; **4** één van twee bij elkaar horende exemplaren

company [kumpənie] **1** gezelschap^h: *in ~ with* samen met; *request the ~ of* uitnodigen; *keep ~ with* omgaan met, verkering hebben met; **2** bezoek^h, gasten: *have ~* bezoek hebben; **3** compagnonschap^h, compagnon(s); **4** gezelschap^h: *theatre ~* toneelgezelschap; **5** onderneming, firma, bedrijf^h: *(econ) limited ~* naamloze vennootschap; **6** gilde^h, genootschap^h; **7** *(mil)* compagnie; **8** *(shipp)* (gehele) bemanning

¹**comparative** [kəmpærətiv] *adj* betrekkelijk, relatief

²**comparative** [kəmpærətiv] *n* vergrotende trap

¹**compare** [kəmpeə] *vb* vergelijkbaar zijn, de vergelijking kunnen doorstaan: *our results ~ poorly with theirs* onze resultaten steken mager bij de hunne af

²**compare** [kəmpeə] *vb* vergelijken: *I'm tall ~d to him* bij hem vergeleken ben ik (nog) lang

³**compare** [kəmpeə] *n (form)* ‖ *beyond* (of: *past, without*) *~* onvergelijkbaar, weergaloos

comparison [kəmpærisn] vergelijking: *bear* (of: *stand*) *~ with* de vergelijking kunnen doorstaan met; *by* (of: *in*) *~ with* in vergelijking met

compartment [kəmpa:tmənt] compartiment^h, vakje^h, (trein)coupé, (gescheiden) ruimte

compass [kumpəs] **1** kompas^h: *the points of the ~* de kompasrichtingen, de windstreken; **2** *~es* passer: *a pair of ~es* een passer

compassion [kəmpæsjən] medelijden^h

compassionate [kəmpæsjənət] medelevend, medelijdend: *~ leave* verlof wegens familieomstandigheden

compatible [kəmpætibl] verenigbaar, bij elkaar passend, aansluitbaar, bruikbaar in combinatie *(of technical appliances)*: *~ systems* onderling verenigbare systemen; *~ with* aangepast aan; *drinking is not ~ with driving* drinken en autorijden verdragen elkaar niet

compatriot [kəmpætriət] landgenoot, landgenote

compel [kəmpel] (af)dwingen, verplichten, noodzaken

compelling [kəmpelling] fascinerend, onweerstaanbaar, meeslepend

¹**compensate** [kompənseet] *vb* vergoeden, vereffenen, goedmaken

²**compensate** [kompənseet] *vb* **1** *(with for)* dienen als tegenwicht (voor), opwegen (tegen); **2** compenseren, goedmaken

compensation [kompənseesjən] compensatie, (onkosten)vergoeding, schadevergoeding, schadeloosstelling

compere [kompeə] conferencier, ceremoniemeester, presentator

compete [kəmpie:t] concurreren

competence [kompətəns] (vak)bekwaamheid, vaardigheid, (des)kundigheid

competent [kompətənt] **1** competent, (vak)bekwaam, (des)kundig; **2** voldoende, toereikend, adequaat

competition [kompətisjən] **1** wedstrijd, toernooi[h], concours[h], competitie; **2** rivaliteit, concurrentie

competitive [kəmpettittiv] concurrerend: ~ *examination* vergelijkend examen

competitor [kəmpettittə] concurrent, (wedstrijd)deelnemer, rivaal

compilation [kompilleesjən] samenstelling, bundel(ing), verzameling

compile [kəmpajl] samenstellen, bijeenbrengen, bijeengaren, verzamelen

complacent [kəmpleesnt] *(oft depr)* zelfvoldaan, zelfingenomen

complain [kəmpleen] klagen, zich beklagen, een klacht indienen

complaint [kəmpleent] **1** klacht *(also law)*, grief, kwaal: *lodge a ~ against s.o.* een aanklacht tegen iem indienen; **2** beklag[h], het klagen: *no cause* (of: *ground) for ~* geen reden tot klagen

¹complement [komplimmənt] *n* **1** aanvulling; **2** vereiste hoeveelheid, voltallige bemanning

²complement [komplimment] *vb* aanvullen, afronden

complementary [komplimmentərie] aanvullend

¹complete [kəmplie:t] *adj* **1** compleet, volkomen, totaal; **2** klaar, voltooid

²complete [kəmplie:t] *vb* vervolledigen, afmaken, invullen *(a form)*

completion [kəmplie:sjən] voltooiing, afwerking, afronding

¹complex [kompleks] *adj* gecompliceerd, samengesteld, ingewikkeld

²complex [kompleks] *n* **1** complex[h] *(eg for sports)*, samengesteld geheel[h]; **2** *(psychology)* complex[h], *(inf; fig)* obsessie

complexion [kəmpleksjən] **1** huidskleur, uiterlijk[h]; **2** aanzien[h], voorkomen[h], aard: *that changed the ~ of the matter* dat gaf de kwestie een heel ander aanzien

complexity [kəmpleksittie] **1** complicatie, moeilijkheid, probleem[h]; **2** gecompliceerdheid; complexiteit

compliance [kəmplajjəns] **1** volgzaamheid, meegaandheid: *in ~ with your wish* overeenkomstig uw wens; *~ with the law* naleving van de wet; **2** onderdanigheid, onderworpenheid

compliant [kəmplajjənt] volgzaam; onderdanig

complicate [komplikkeet] **1** ingewikkeld(er) worden (maken); **2** verergeren

complication [komplikkeesjən] complicatie, (extra, onvoorziene) moeilijkheid

complicity [kəmplissittie] medeplichtigheid: *~ in* medeplichtigheid aan

¹compliment [komplimmənt] *n* compliment[h]: *the ~s of the season* prettige feestdagen *(at Christmas, New Year); pay s.o. a ~, pay a ~ to s.o. (on sth.)* iem een complimentje (over iets) maken; *my ~s to your wife* de groeten aan uw vrouw

²compliment [komplimment] *vb* (with *on*) complimenteren (met, over), een compliment maken, gelukwensen

complimentary [komplimmentərie] **1** vleiend; **2** gratis, bij wijze van geste gegeven: *~ copy* presentexemplaar; *~ tickets* vrijkaartjes

comply [kəmplaj] zich schikken, gehoorzamen: *refuse to ~* weigeren mee te werken; *~ with: a)* zich neerleggen bij, gehoor geven aan; *b)* naleven *(law)*

¹component [kəmpoonənt] *adj* samenstellend

²component [kəmpoonənt] *n* component, onderdeel[h], element[h]

compose [kəmpooz] **1** schrijven *(literary or musical work)*, componeren; **2** zetten *(printed matter);* **3** samenstellen, vormen, in elkaar zetten: *~d of* bestaande uit; **4** tot bedaren brengen, bedaren, kalmeren: *~ yourself* kalm nou maar; **5** bijleggen *(difference of opinion)*

composed [kəmpoozd] kalm, rustig, beheerst

composer [kəmpoozə] **1** componist; **2** auteur, schrijver *(of letter, poem)*

¹composite [kompəzit] *adj* samengesteld: *~ photograph* montagefoto, compositiefoto

²composite [kompəzit] *n* samengesteld geheel[h], samenstelling

composition [kompəzisjən] **1** samenstelling, compositie, opbouw: *a piece of his own ~* een stuk van eigen hand; **2** het componeren, het (op)stellen; **3** kunstwerk[h], muziekstuk[h], compositie, dichtwerk[h], tekst; **4** opstel[h], verhandeling; **5** mengsel[h], samengesteld materiaal[h], kunststof: *chemical ~s* chemische mengsels; **6** het letterzetten

compost [kompost] compost

composure [kəmpoozjə] (zelf)beheersing

¹compound [kompaund] *n* **1** samenstel[h], mengsel[h], (chemische) verbinding; **2** omheinde groep gebouwen, (krijgs)gevangenkamp[h], omheind gebied[h] *(for cattle)*

²compound [kompaund] *adj* samengesteld, gemengd, vermengd, gecombineerd: *~ fracture* gecompliceerde breuk; *~ interest* samengestelde interest, rente op rente

³compound [kəmpaund] *vb* **1** dooreenmengen, vermengen, samenstellen, opbouwen: *~ a recipe* een recept klaarmaken; **2** vergroten, verergeren: *the situation was ~ed by his absence* door zijn afwezigheid werd de zaak bemoeilijkt

comprehend [komprihhend] **1** (be)vatten, begrijpen, doorgronden; **2** omvatten

comprehension [komprihhensjən] **1** begrip[h], bevattingsvermogen[h]; **2** *(educ)* begripstest, leestoets, luistertoets, tekstbegrip[h]; **3** (toepassings)bereik[h]

¹**comprehensive** [komprihhensiv] *adj* allesomvattend, veelomvattend, uitvoerig, uitgebreid: ~ *insurance* all-risk verzekering; ~ *school* middenschool

²**comprehensive** [komprihhensiv] *n* scholengemeenschap

¹**compress** [kompres] *vb* samendrukken, samenpersen: ~*ed air* perslucht

²**compress** [kompres] *n* kompres^h, drukverband^h

compression [kompresjən] 1 samenpersing; 2 dichtheid, compactheid

compressor [kompressə] compressor, perspomp

comprise [komprajz] bestaan uit, bevatten: *the house* ~*s five rooms* het huis telt vijf kamers

¹**compromise** [komprəmajz] *n* compromis^h, tussenoplossing, middenweg, tussenweg

²**compromise** [komprəmajz] *vb* een compromis sluiten

³**compromise** [komprəmajz] *vb* 1 door een compromis regelen; 2 in opspraak brengen, de goede naam aantasten van: *you* ~*d yourself by accepting that money* door dat geld aan te nemen heb je je gecompromitteerd; 3 in gevaar brengen

compulsion [kompulsjən] dwang, verplichting, druk

compulsive [kompulsiv] dwingend, gedwongen, verplicht: *a* ~ *smoker* een verslaafd roker

compulsory [kompulsərie] 1 verplicht: ~ *military service* dienstplicht; *(educ)* ~ *subject* verplicht vak; 2 noodzakelijk

compunction [kompungksjən] schuldgevoel^h, (gewetens)bezwaar^h, wroeging

compute [kompjoe:t] berekenen, uitrekenen

computer [kompjoe:tə] computer

¹**computerize** [kompjoe:tərajz] *vb* computeriseren, overschakelen op computers

²**computerize** [kompjoe:tərajz] *vb* verwerken met een computer *(information)*, opslaan in een computer

computer-literate vaardig in het gebruik van de computer, goed overweg kunnend met computers

computing [kompjoe:ting] computerisering, het werken met computers, computerwerk^h

comrade [komreed] kameraad, vriend, makker: ~*s in arms* wapenbroeders

comradeship [komreedsjip] kameraadschap(pelijkheid), vriendschap

¹**con** [kon] *vb* 1 *(inf)* oplichten, afzetten, bezwendelen: ~ *s.o. out of his money* iem zijn geld afhandig maken; 2 *(inf)* ompraten, bewerken, overhalen: *he* ~*ned me into signing* hij heeft me mijn handtekening weten te ontfutselen

²**con** [kon] *n* 1 *contra* tegenargument^h, nadeel^h, bezwaar^h: *the pros and* ~*s of this proposal* de voors en tegens van dit voorstel; 2 tegenstem(mer); 3 *(inf)* oplichterij; 4 *convict (inf)* veroordeelde, (oud-)gevangene

concave [konkeev] hol(rond)

conceal [konsie:l] verbergen, verstoppen, achter-

houden, geheimhouden: ~*ed turning* let op, bocht *(as a traffic sign)*

concealment [konsie:lmənt] geheimhouding, verzwijging

¹**concede** [konsie:d] *vb* 1 toegeven: ~ *defeat* zijn nederlaag erkennen; 2 opgeven, prijsgeven

²**concede** [konsie:d] *vb* zich gewonnen geven, opgeven

conceit [konsie:t] verwaandheid, ijdelheid, verbeelding

conceited [konsie:tid] verwaand, ijdel, zelfingenomen

conceivable [konsie:vəbl] voorstelbaar, denkbaar, mogelijk

¹**conceive** [konsie:v] *vb* 1 bedenken, ontwerpen: *she* ~*d a dislike for me* ze kreeg een hekel aan mij; 2 opvatten, begrijpen

²**conceive** [konsie:v] *vb* ontvangen *(child)*, zwanger worden (van)

conceive of zich voorstellen, zich indenken

¹**concentrate** [konsntreet] *vb (with (up)on)* zich concentreren (op), zich toeleggen

²**concentrate** [konsntreet] *vb* concentreren: ~ *one's attention on* zijn aandacht richten op

concentrated [konsntreetid] 1 geconcentreerd, van sterk gehalte; 2 krachtig, intens

concentration [konsntreesjən] concentratie: *power of* ~ concentratievermogen

concept [konsept] idee^h, voorstelling, denkbeeld^h

conception [konsepsjən] 1 ontstaan^h *(of idea etc)*, ontwerp^h, vinding; 2 voorstelling, opvatting, begrip^h: *I have no* ~ *of what he meant* ik heb er geen idee van wat hij bedoelde; 3 bevruchting *(also fig)*

¹**concern** [konsə:n] *vb* 1 aangaan, van belang zijn voor: *where money is* ~*ed* als het om geld gaat; *to whom it may* ~ aan wie dit leest *(salutation of open letter)*; *as far as I'm* ~*ed* wat mij betreft, voor mijn part; 2 betreffen, gaan over; 3 zich aantrekken, zich interesseren: ~ *oneself about (of: with) sth.* zich ergens voor inzetten, zorgen om maken

²**concern** [konsə:n] *n* 1 aangelegenheid, belang^h, interesse: *your drinking habits are no* ~ *of mine* uw drinkgewoonten zijn mijn zaak niet; 2 (be)zorg(dheid), begaanheid, (gevoel^h van) betrokkenheid: *no cause for* ~ geen reden tot ongerustheid; 3 bedrijf^h, onderneming, firma: *going* ~ bloeiende onderneming; 4 (aan)deel^h, belang^h

concerned [konsə:nd] 1 bezorgd, ongerust; 2 geïnteresseerd, betrokken: *all the people* ~ alle (erbij) betrokkenen, alle geïnteresseerden; ~ *in* betrokken bij; *be* ~ *with* betreffen, gaan over

concerning [konsə:ning] betreffende, in verband met, over

concert [konsət] concert^h, muziekuitvoering ‖ *in* ~ in onderlinge samenwerking, in harmonie

concerted [konsə:tid] gecombineerd, gezamenlijk

concession [konsesjən] 1 concessie(verlening), vergunning, tegemoetkoming; 2 korting, (prijs)reductie *(with discount card)*

conciliate [kǝnsɪllie·eet] **1** tot bedaren brengen, kalmeren; **2** verzoenen, in overeenstemming brengen

concise [kǝnsajs] beknopt, kort maar krachtig

¹conclude [kǝnkloe:d] *vb* **1** eindigen, aflopen; **2** tot een conclusie (besluit, akkoord) komen

²conclude [kǝnkloe:d] *vb* **1** beëindigen, (af)sluiten, afronden; **2** (af)sluiten, tot stand brengen: *~ an agreement* een overeenkomst sluiten; **3** concluderen, vaststellen

conclusion [kǝnkloe:zjǝn] **1** besluit[h], beëindiging, slot[h]: *in ~* samenvattend, tot besluit; **2** conclusie, gevolgtrekking: *come to* (of: *draw, reach*) *~s* conclusies trekken; *a foregone ~* een bij voorbaat uitgemaakte zaak; *jump to ~s* (of: *to a ~*) te snel conclusies trekken

conclusive [kǝnkloe:siv] afdoend, overtuigend, beslissend: *~ evidence* overtuigend bewijs

concoct [kǝnkokt] **1** samenstellen, bereiden, brouwen; **2** *(depr)* verzinnen, bedenken, bekokstoven: *~ an excuse* een smoes verzinnen

concord [kongko:d] **1** verdrag[h], overeenkomst, akkoord[h]; **2** harmonie, eendracht, overeenstemming; **3** *(linguistics)* congruentie, overeenkomst

concourse [kongko:s] **1** menigte; **2** samenkomst, samenloop, bijeenkomst: *a fortunate ~ of circumstances* een gelukkige samenloop van omstandigheden; **3** plein[h], promenade, (stations)hal

¹concrete [kongkrie:t] *adj* **1** concreet, echt, tastbaar; **2** betonnen, beton-

²concrete [kongkrie:t] *n* beton[h]

concubine [kongkjoebajn] concubine, bijzit

concur [kǝnkǝ:] samenvallen, overeenstemmen || *~ with s.o.* (of: *in sth.*) het eens zijn met iem (iets)

concussion [kǝnkusjǝn] **1** schok, stoot, klap; **2** hersenschudding

condemn [kǝndem] **1** veroordelen, schuldig verklaren: *~ed to spend one's life in poverty* gedoemd zijn leven lang armoede te lijden; **2** afkeuren, verwerpen

condemnation [kondemneesjǝn] veroordeling, afkeuring, verwerping

condensation [kondenseesjǝn] condensatie; condens, condenswater[h]

condense [kǝndens] condenseren *(also fig)*, indampen, be-, in-, verkorten: *~d milk* gecondenseerde melk

condescend [kondissend] **1** zich verlagen, zich verwaardigen; **2** neerbuigend doen, neerkijken

condiment [kondimmǝnt] kruiderij, specerij

¹condition [kǝndisjǝn] *n* **1** (lichamelijke) toestand, staat, conditie: *she is in no ~ to work* ze is niet in staat om te werken; *in ~* in conditie; **2** voorwaarde, conditie, beding[h]: *on ~ that* op voorwaarde dat; **3** omstandigheid: *favourable ~s* gunstige omstandigheden; **4** *(med)* afwijking, aandoening, kwaal

²condition [kǝndisjǝn] *vb* bepalen, vaststellen, afhangen (van): *a nation's expenditure is ~ed by its income* de bestedingsmogelijkheden van een land

worden bepaald door het nationale inkomen

conditional [kǝndisjǝnǝl] voorwaardelijk, conditioneel

conditioner [kǝndisjǝnǝ] crèmespoeling

condolence [kǝndoolǝns] **1** deelneming, sympathie, medeleven[h]; **2** *~s* condoleantie, rouwbeklag[h]: *please accept my ~s on ...* mag ik mijn deelneming betuigen met ...

condom [kondǝm] condoom[h], kapotje[h]

condone [kǝndoon] vergeven

¹conduct [kondukt] *n* gedrag[h], houding, handelwijze

²conduct [kǝndukt] *vb* **1** leiden, rondleiden, begeleiden: *~ed tour* verzorgde reis, rondleiding; **2** *(mus)* dirigeren, dirigent zijn (van); **3** (zich) gedragen: *~ oneself* zich gedragen; **4** *(science, electr)* geleiden

conduction [kǝnduksjǝn] *(science)* geleiding, conductie

conductor [kǝnduktǝ] **1** conducteur; **2** *(mus)* dirigent, orkestleider; **3** *(science, electr)* geleider

cone [koon] **1** kegel; **2** (ijs)hoorntje[h]; **3** dennenappel

confectionery [kǝnfeksjǝnǝrie] **1** banketbakkerij, banketbakkerswinkel; **2** gebak[h], zoetigheid, suikergoed[h]

confederation [kǝnfeddǝreesjǝn] (con)federatie, bond, verbond[h]

¹confer [kǝnfǝ:] *vb* confereren, beraadslagen

²confer [kǝnfǝ:] *vb* verlenen, uitreiken, schenken: *~ a knighthood on s.o.* iem een ridderorde verlenen

conference [konfǝrǝns] conferentie, congres[h]

confess [kǝnfes] **1** bekennen, erkennen, toegeven; **2** *(rel)* (op)biechten, belijden

confession [kǝnfesjǝn] **1** bekentenis, erkenning, toegeving: *on his own ~* naar hij zelf toegeeft; **2** *(rel)* biecht; **3** *(rel)* (geloofs)belijdenis

confessor [kǝnfessǝ] *(rel)* **1** biechtvader; **2** belijder

confetti [kǝnfettie] confetti

confidant [konfidænt] vertrouweling, vertrouwensman

confide [kǝnfajd] toevertrouwen, in vertrouwen mededelen

confide in vertrouwen, in vertrouwen nemen

confidence [konfiddǝns] **1** (zelf)vertrouwen[h], geloof[h]: *in ~* in vertrouwen, vertrouwelijk; **2** vertrouwelijke mededeling, geheim[h]

confident [konfiddǝnt] (tref)zeker, zelfverzekerd, overtuigd

confidential [konfiddensjl] **1** vertrouwelijk; **2** vertrouwens-, privé-, vertrouwd

confine [kǝnfajn] **1** beperken; **2** opsluiten, insluiten: *be ~d to bed* het bed moeten houden

confinement [kǝnfajnmǝnt] opsluiting: *solitary ~* eenzame opsluiting

confirm [kǝnfǝ:m] **1** bevestigen, bekrachtigen: *~ by letter* (of: *in writing*) schriftelijk bevestigen; **2** bevestigen, goedkeuren: *he hasn't been ~ed in office yet* zijn benoeming moet nog bevestigd worden; **3** *(Protestantism)* confirmeren, (als lidmaat) aannemen; **4** *(Roman Catholicism)* vormen, het vormsel toedienen

confirmation [konfəmeesjən] 1 bevestiging, bekrachtiging, goedkeuring: *evidence in ~ of your statement* bewijzen die uw bewering staven; 2 *(Protestantism)* confirmatie, bevestiging als lidmaat; 3 *(Roman Catholicism)* (heilig) vormsel[h]

confiscate [konfiskeet] in beslag nemen, verbeurd verklaren, afnemen

conflagration [konfləgreesjən] grote brand *(of forests, buildings)*, vuurzee

¹conflict [konflikt] *n* strijd, conflict(situatie), onenigheid

²conflict [kənflikt] *vb* 1 onverenigbaar zijn, in tegenspraak zijn, botsen: *~ing interests* (tegen)strijdige belangen; 2 strijden, botsen, in conflict komen

confluence [konfloeəns] 1 toeloop, menigte; 2 samenvloeiing

conform [kənfo:m] zich conformeren, zich aanpassen

conformity [kənfo:mittie] 1 overeenkomst, gelijkvormigheid: *in ~ with* in overeenstemming met, overeenkomstig; 2 aanpassing, naleving

confound [kənfaund] 1 verbazen, in verwarring brengen, versteld doen staan; 2 verwarren, door elkaar halen

confront [kənfrunt] confronteren, tegenover elkaar plaatsen, *(fig)* het hoofd bieden aan

confrontation [konfrunteesjən] 1 confrontatie; 2 het tegenover (elkaar) stellen

confuse [kənfjoe:z] in de war brengen; door elkaar halen, verwarren

confused [kənfjoe:zd] verward; wanordelijk, rommelig

confusion [kənfjoe:zjən] verwarring, wanorde

congeal [kəndzjie:l] (doen) stollen

congenial [kəndzjie:niəl] 1 (geest)verwant, gelijkgestemd, sympathiek; 2 passend, geschikt, aangenaam

congestion [kəndzjestsjən] op(een)hoping, opstopping, verstopping

conglomeration [kənglomməreesjən] bundeling, verzameling

congratulate [kəngrætjoeleet] gelukwensen, feliciteren: *~ oneself on* zichzelf gelukkig prijzen met

congratulation [kəngrætjoeleesjən] gelukwens, felicitatie; *~s!* gefeliciteerd!

congregation [konggrigeesjən] 1 bijeenkomst, verzameling; 2 verzamelde groep mensen, menigte, groep; 3 *(rel)* gemeente, congregatie

congress [konggres] 1 congres[h], vergadering, bijeenkomst; 2 *Congress (Am)* Het Congres

congruity [kəngroe:ittie] gepastheid, overeenstemming, overeenkomst

conic(al) [konnik(l)] mbt een kegel, kegelvormig, conisch

conifer [konniffə] naaldboom; conifeer

conjecture [kəndzjektsjə] 1 gis(sing), (vage) schatting, vermoeden[h]; 2 giswerk[h], speculatie, gokwerk[h]

conjugation [kondzjoegeesjən] 1 *(linguistics)* ver-

voeging; 2 vereniging, verbinding, koppeling

conjuncture [kəndzjungktsjə] (kritieke) toestand, samenloop van omstandigheden, (crisis)situatie

¹conjure [kundzjə] *vb* toveren, goochelen, manipuleren

²conjure [kundzjə] *vb* (te voorschijn) toveren, oproepen, voor de geest roepen

conjurer [kundzjərə] goochelaar, illusionist

conk [kongk] *(inf)* een oplawaai geven

¹connect [kənekt] *vb* 1 in verbinding komen, in verband staan: *~ up* in verbinding komen; 2 aansluiten, aansluiting hebben

²connect [kənekt] *vb* 1 verbinden, aaneensluiten, aaneenschakelen, doorverbinden *(telephone)*: *the islands are ~ed by a bridge* de eilanden staan via een brug met elkaar in verbinding; *~ up* verbinden; 2 (*with with*) in verband brengen (met), een verbinding leggen tussen

connection [kəneksjən] 1 verbinding, verband[h], aansluiting: *miss one's ~* zijn aansluiting missen *(of bus, train)*; *in ~ with* in verband met; 2 samenhang, coherentie; 3 connectie, betrekking, relatie; 4 verwant, familielid[h]; 5 verbindingsstuk[h]; 6 *(electr)* lichtpunt[h], stopcontact[h], (wand)contactdoos

connive [kənajv] 1 oogluikend toelaten, (even) de andere kant opkijken: *~ at* oogluikend toelaten, door de vingers zien; 2 samenspannen, samenzweren

connotation [konnəteesjən] (bij)betekenis, connotatie

¹conquer [kongkə] *vb* 1 veroveren, innemen, bemachtigen *(also fig)*; 2 verslaan, overwinnen, bedwingen: *~ mountains* bergen bedwingen

²conquer [kongkə] *vb* overwinnen, de (over)winnaar zijn

conqueror [kongkərə] veroveraar, overwinnaar: *William the Conqueror* Willem de Veroveraar

conquest [kongkwest] verovering, overwinning, het bedwingen *(of a mountain)*

conscience [konsjəns] geweten[h]

conscientious [konsjie-ensjəs] plichtsgetrouw, zorgvuldig: *~ objector* gewetensbezwaarde, principiële dienstweigeraar

conscious [konsjəs] 1 bewust, denkend; 2 welbewust, opzettelijk; 3 (zich) bewust; 4 bewust, bij kennis

consciousness [konsjəsnəs] 1 bewustzijn[h]: *lose ~* het bewustzijn verliezen; 2 gevoel[h], besef[h]

conscript [konskript] dienstplichtige

conscription [kənskripsjən] dienstplicht

consecutive [kənsekjoetiv] opeenvolgend: *on two ~ days* twee dagen achter elkaar

consensus [kənsensəs] algemene opvatting, overeenstemming

¹consent [kənsent] *vb* toestemmen, zijn goedkeuring geven, zich bereid verklaren: *~ to sth.* iets toestaan

²consent [kənsent] *n* toestemming, instemming, goedkeuring: *by common* (of: *general*) *~* met alge-

mene stemmen
consequence [ˈkɒnsikwəns] **1** consequentie, gevolgʰ, gevolgtrekking, resultaatʰ; **2** belangʰ, gewichtʰ: *of no ~* van geen belang
conservation [kɒnsəˈveesjən] **1** behoudʰ, instandhouding: *~ of energy* behoud van energie; **2** milieubeheerʰ; milieubescherming, natuurbescherming, monumentenzorg
conservationist [kɒnsəˈveesjənist] milieubeschermer, natuurbeschermer
conservatism [kənˈsɜːvətizm] conservatismeʰ, behoudzucht
¹**conservative** [kənˈsɜːvətiv] *adj* **1** conservatief, behoudend, traditioneel (ingesteld); **2** voorzichtig, gematigd, bescheiden: *a ~ estimate* een voorzichtige schatting
²**conservative** [kənˈsɜːvətiv] *n* conservatief, behoudend persoon, *(pol)* lidʰ vd Conservatieve Partij
conservatory [kənˈsɜːvətəri] **1** serre, (planten)kas, broeikas; **2** conservatoriumʰ, muziekacademie, toneelschool
¹**conserve** [kənˈsɜːv] *vb* **1** behouden, bewaren, goed houden; **2** inmaken
²**conserve** [kənˈsɜːv] *n* jam, ingemaakte vruchten
consider [kənˈsidə] **1** overwegen, nadenken over; **2** beschouwen, zien: *we ~ him (to be) a man of genius* we beschouwen hem als een genie; **3** in aanmerking nemen, rekening houden met, letten op
considerable [kənˈsidərəbl] aanzienlijk, behoorlijk: *a ~ time* geruime tijd
considerate [kənˈsidərət] attent, voorkomend, vriendelijk
consideration [kənsidəˈreesjən] **1** overweging, aandacht: *take sth. into ~* ergens rekening mee houden; **2** (puntʰ van) overweging, (beweeg)reden; **3** voorkomendheid, attentheid, begripʰ
¹**considering** [kənˈsidəring] *prep* gezien, rekening houdend met
²**considering** [kənˈsidəring] *adv (at the end of a sentence)* alles bij elkaar (genomen): *she has been very successful, ~* eigenlijk heeft ze het ver gebracht
consign [kənˈsain] **1** *(com)* verzenden, versturen, leveren; **2** overdragen, toevertrouwen, in handen stellen: *~ one's child to s.o.'s care* zijn kind aan iemands zorg toevertrouwen
consignment [kənˈsainmənt] (ver)zending
consistency [kənˈsistənsi] **1** consequentheid, samenhang; **2** dikte, stroperigheid
consistent [kənˈsistənt] **1** consequent, samenhangend; **2** overeenkomend, kloppend, verenigbaar: *be ~ with* kloppen met
consist in [kənˈsist in] bestaan in, gevormd worden door: *my duties mainly ~ word processing and filing* mijn werkzaamheden bestaan voornamelijk in tekstverwerken en archiveren
consist of bestaan uit, opgebouwd zijn uit: *the convoy consisted of sixteen ships* het konvooi bestond uit zestien schepen
consolation [kɒnsəˈleesjən] troost, troostrijke gedachte

¹**console** [kənˈsool] *vb* troosten, bemoedigen(d toespreken), opbeuren
²**console** [ˈkɒnsool] *n* **1** steunstukʰ, draagsteen; **2** toetsenbordʰ; (bedienings)paneelʰ, controle-, schakelbordʰ, *(comp)* console; **3** radio-, televisie-, grammofoonmeubelʰ
¹**consolidate** [kənˈsɒlideet] *vb* **1** hechter, steviger worden; **2** zich aaneensluiten, samengaan, fuseren
²**consolidate** [kənˈsɒlideet] *vb* **1** verstevigen, stabiliseren; **2** (tot een geheel) verenigen
consonant [ˈkɒnsənənt] medeklinker
¹**consort** [ˈkɒnsɔːt] *n* gade, gemaalʰ, gemalin
²**consort** [kənˈsɔːt] *vb* omgaan, optrekken: *~ with criminals* omgaan met misdadigers
conspicuous [kənˈspikjoeəs] opvallend, in het oog lopend, opmerkelijk: *be ~ by one's absence* schitteren door afwezigheid
conspiracy [kənˈspirrəsie] samenzwering, complotʰ, *(law)* samenspanning
conspirator [kənˈspirrətə] samenzweerder
constable [ˈkunstəbl] **1** agent, politieman; **2** *(Am)* (ongeüniformeerde) politiefunctionaris onder sheriff, *(roughly)* vrederechter
constabulary [kənˈstæbjoelərie] politie(korpsʰ); politiemacht
constancy [ˈkɒnstənsie] **1** standvastigheid, onveranderlijkheid; **2** trouw
constant [ˈkɒnstənt] **1** constant, voortdurend, onveranderlijk; **2** trouw, loyaal
constellation [kɒnstiˈleesjən] sterrenbeeldʰ, constellatie *(also fig)*
consternation [kɒnstəˈneesjən] opschudding
constipation [kɒnstiˈpeesjən] constipatie, verstopping
constituency [kənˈstitjoeənsie] **1** kiesdistrictʰ; **2** achterban, kiezers
constituent [kənˈstitjoeənt] **1** kiezer, ingezetene ve kiesdistrict; **2** onderdeelʰ, bestanddeelʰ
constitute [ˈkɒnstitjoeːt] vormen, (samen) uitmaken, vertegenwoordigen
constitution [kɒnstiˈtjoeːsjən] **1** grondwet; **2** conditie; gesteldheid
constitutional [kɒnstiˈtjoeːsjənəl] grondwettig, grondwettelijk
constrain [kənˈstreen] (af)dwingen, verplichten, noodzaken: *feel ~ed to do sth.* zich ergens toe verplicht voelen
constraint [kənˈstreent] **1** beperking, restrictie; **2** dwang, verplichting; **3** gedwongenheid, geforceerde stemming, geremdheid
constrict [kənˈstrikt] vernauwen, versmallen, beperken
construct [kənˈstrukt] construeren, in elkaar zetten, bouwen
construction [kənˈstruksjən] **1** interpretatie, voorstelling van zaken, uitleg; **2** constructie, aanbouw, aanleg, (huizen)bouw, bouwwerkʰ: *under ~* in aanbouw

constructive [kənstrúktiv] constructief, opbouwend, positief

construe [kənstroe:] interpreteren, opvatten, verklaren: *giving in now will be ~d as a weakness* nu toegeven zal als zwakheid worden uitgelegd

consul [kónsl] consul

consular [kóns·joelə] consulair

consulate [kóns·joelət] consulaat[h]

¹**consult** [kənsúlt] *vb* raadplegen

²**consult** [kənsúlt] *vb* overleggen, beraadslagen: *~ about* (of: *upon*) beraadslagen over

consultancy [kənsúltənsie] **1** baan als consulterend geneesheer; **2** baan als (bedrijfs)adviseur

consultant [kənsúltənt] **1** consulterend geneesheer; **2** consulent, (bedrijfs)adviseur, deskundige

consultation [konsltéesjən] **1** vergadering, bespreking; **2** overleg[h], raadpleging, consult[h]: *in ~ with* in overleg met

consume [kəns·jóe:m] **1** consumeren, verorberen; **2** verbruiken, gebruiken; **3** verteren, wegvreten, verwoesten: *~d by* (of: *with*) *hate* verteerd door haat

consumer [kəns·jóe:mə] consument, verbruiker, koper

consumer goods consumptiegoederen

consummation [konsəméesjən] **1** (eind)doel[h]; **2** voltooiing, bekroning; **3** huwelijksgemeenschap

consumption [kənsúmpsjən] **1** consumptie, verbruik[h], (ver)tering: *these oranges are unfit for ~* deze sinaasappelen zijn niet geschikt voor consumptie; **2** verwoesting, aantasting

¹**contact** [kóntækt] *n* **1** contact[h], contactpersoon; **2** contact[h] *(also electr)*, aanraking

²**contact** [kóntækt] *vb* **1** in contact brengen, een contact leggen tussen; **2** contact opnemen met

contagious [kəntéedzjəs] besmet(telijk), *(fig)* aanstekelijk

contain [kəntéen] **1** bevatten, tellen, inhouden; **2** beheersen, onder controle houden, bedwingen

container [kəntéenə] **1** houder, vat[h], bak, doosje[h], bus, verpakking; **2** container

contamination [kəntæminnéesjən] vervuiling, besmetting

¹**contemplate** [kóntəmpleet] *vb* nadenken, peinzen, in gedachten verzonken zijn

²**contemplate** [kóntəmpleet] *vb* **1** beschouwen; **2** nadenken over, overdenken, zich verdiepen in; **3** overwegen, zich bezinnen op

contemplation [kontəmpléesjən] overpeinzing, bezinning, overdenking: *lost in ~* in gepeins verzonken

contemplative [kóntəmpleetiv] bedachtzaam, beschouwend

contemporaneous [kəntempəréeniəs] gelijktijdig, in de tijd samenvallend

¹**contemporary** [kəntémpərərie] *adj* **1** gelijktijdig, uit dezelfde tijd; **2** even oud; **3** eigentijds, hedendaags

²**contemporary** [kəntémpərərie] *n* **1** tijdgenoot; **2** leeftijdgenoot, jaargenoot

contempt [kəntémpt] minachting, verachting: *beneath ~* beneden alle peil

contemptuous [kəntémptjoeəs] minachtend, verachtend

¹**contend** [kənténd] *vb* wedijveren, strijden: *~ with difficulties* met problemen (te) kampen (hebben)

²**contend** [kənténd] *vb* betogen, (met klem) beweren

¹**content** [kəntént] *adj* tevreden, blij, content

²**content** [kóntent] *n* **1** capaciteit, volume[h], omvang, inhoud(smaat); **2** inhoud, onderwerp[h]; **3** gehalte[h]: *sugar ~* suikergehalte, hoeveelheid suiker; *nutritional ~* voedingswaarde; **4** *~s* inhoud *(of bottle, bag)*; **5** *~s* inhoud(sopgave) *(of book): table of ~s* inhoudsopgave

contented [kənténtid] tevreden, blij

contention [kənténsjən] **1** standpunt[h], stellingname, opvatting; **2** geschil[h], conflict[h]

contentment [kənténtmənt] tevredenheid, voldoening

¹**contest** [kóntest] *n* **1** krachtmeting, strijd, (kracht)proef; **2** (wed)strijd, prijsvraag, concours[h]

²**contest** [kəntést] *vb* twisten, strijden: *~ against* (of: *with*) strijden met

³**contest** [kəntést] *vb* betwisten, aanvechten

contestant [kəntéstənt] **1** kandidaat, deelnemer (aan wedstrijd), strijdende partij; **2** betwister, aanvechter

context [kóntekst] context *(also fig)*, verband[h], samenhang

contiguity [kontigjóe:ittie] **1** aangrenzing, naburigheid; **2** opeenvolging, aan(een)sluiting

continence [kóntinnəns] zelfbeheersing, matigheid

continent [kóntinnənt] **1** continent[h], werelddeel[h]; **2** *the Continent* vasteland[h] (van Europa) *(opposite Great Britain)*

¹**continental** [kontinnéntl] *adj* continentaal; het vasteland van Europa betreffende: *~ breakfast* ontbijt met koffie en croissants enz.

²**continental** [kontinnéntl] *n* vastelander, bewoner vh Europese vasteland, *(Am also)* Europeaan

contingency [kəntíndzjənsie] eventualiteit, onvoorziene gebeurtenis (uitgave)

¹**contingent** [kəntíndzjənt] *adj* **1** toevallig, onvoorzien; **2** mogelijk, eventueel; **3** bijkomend, incidenteel; **4** voorwaardelijk, afhankelijk: *our success is ~ (up)on his cooperation* ons slagen hangt van zijn medewerking af

²**contingent** [kəntíndzjənt] *n* **1** afvaardiging, vertegenwoordiging; **2** *(mil)* (troepen)contingent[h]

continual [kəntínjoeəl] *(depr)* aanhoudend, voortdurend, onophoudelijk

continuation [kəntinjoe:éesjən] voortzetting, vervolg[h], continuering

¹**continue** [kəntínjoe:] *vb* **1** doorgaan, voortgaan, verder gaan, volhouden, zich voortzetten; **2** (in stand) blijven, voortduren, continueren: *the*

weather ~s fine het mooie weer houdt aan; **3** vervolgen, verder gaan: *~d on page 106* lees verder op blz. 106

²**continue** [kəntinjoe:] *vb* **1** voortzetten, (weer) door-, voortgaan, verder gaan met, volhouden, vervolgen: *to be ~d* wordt vervolgd; **2** handhaven, aanhouden, continueren; **3** verlengen

continuity [kontinjoe:ittie] **1** tijdsmatig verloop, samenhang; **2** *(film)* draaiboek^h; **3** *(radio, TV)* tekstboek^h, draaiboek^h, verbindende teksten

continuous [kəntinjoeəs] ononderbroken, continu: *~ performance* doorlopende voorstelling

contort [kənto:t] verwringen

contortion [kənto:sjən] **1** kronkeling, bocht; **2** verwringing, ontwrichting

contour [kontoeə] contour *(also fig)*, omtrek(lijn), vorm

contraband [kontrəbænd] **1** smokkelwaar, smokkelgoed^h; **2** smokkel(handel)

contraception [kontrəsepsjən] anticonceptie

contraceptive [kontrəseptiv] voorbehoed(s)middel^h

¹**contract** [kontrækt] *n* contract^h, (bindende) overeenkomst, verdrag^h

²**contract** [kəntrækt] *vb* een overeenkomst, verdrag sluiten, een verbintenis aangaan, contracteren: *~ing parties* contracterende partijen; *~ out* zich terugtrekken

³**contract** [kəntrækt] *vb* samentrekken, inkrimpen, slinken

⁴**contract** [kəntrækt] *vb* bij contract regelen, contracteren, aangaan: *~ out* uitbesteden

contraction [kəntræksjən] samentrekking, inkorting, verkorting, (barens)wee

contractor [kəntræktə] **1** aannemer, aannemersbedrijf^h, handelaar in bouwmaterialen; **2** contractant, iemand die een contract aangaat

contradict [kontrədikt] tegenspreken, in tegenspraak zijn met, ontkennen

contradiction [kontrədiksjən] **1** tegenspraak, tegenstrijdigheid; **2** weerlegging

contradictory [kontrədiktərie] **1** tegenstrijdig, in tegenspraak: *~ to* strijdig met; **2** ontkennend

contralto [kəntræltoo] alt

contraption [kəntræpsjən] geval^h, toestand, ding^h, apparaat^h

¹**contrary** [kontrərie] *n* tegendeel^h, tegen(over)gestelde^h: *on the ~* integendeel, juist niet; *if I don't hear anything to the ~ ...* zonder tegenbericht ...

²**contrary** [kontrərie] *adj* **1** tegen(over)gesteld, strijdig: *~ to* tegen ... in, ondanks; **2** ongunstig, tegenwerkend, averechts: *~ winds* tegenwind

³**contrary** [kəntreərie] *adj* tegendraads, weerbarstig, eigenwijs

¹**contrast** [kontra:st] *n* contrast^h, contrastwerking, *(fig also)* tegenbeeld^h, verschil^h: *in ~ to* (of: *with*) in tegenstelling tot

²**contrast** [kəntra:st] *vb* contrasteren, (tegen elkaar) afsteken, (een) verschil(len) vertonen: *~ with* afste-

ken bij

³**contrast** [kəntra:st] *vb* tegenover elkaar stellen, vergelijken

contribute [kəntribjoe:t] een bijdrage leveren, bevorderen: *~ to* bijdragen tot, medewerken aan

contribution [kontribjoe:sjən] bijdrage, inbreng, contributie

contrite [kəntrajt] berouwvol, schuldbewust

contrivance [kəntrajvəns] **1** apparaat^h, toestel^h, (handig) ding^h; **2** *~s* list, truc, slimmigheid(je^h); **3** vernuft^h, vernuftigheid, vindingrijkheid

contrive [kəntrajv] **1** voor elkaar boksen, kans zien om te: *he had ~d to meet her* hij had het zo gepland dat hij haar zou ontmoeten; **2** bedenken, uitvinden, ontwerpen; **3** beramen, smeden

contrived [kəntrajvd] geforceerd, onnatuurlijk, gemaakt

¹**control** [kəntrool] *n* **1** *~s* bedieningspaneel^h, controlepaneel^h; **2** *~s* controlemiddel^h, beheersingsmechanisme^h; **3** beheersing, controle, zeggenschap: *keep under ~* bedwingen, in toom houden; *get (of: go) out of ~* uit de hand lopen; **4** bestuur^h, opzicht^h, toezicht^h, leiding: *be in ~* de leiding hebben, het voor het zeggen hebben

²**control** [kəntrool] *vb* **1** controleren, leiden, toezicht uitoefenen op, beheren; **2** besturen, aan het roer zitten; **3** in toom houden, beheersen, onder controle houden

controller [kəntroolə] **1** controleur, controlemechanisme^h; **2** afdelingschef; afdelingshoofd^h

controversial [kontrəvə:sjl] **1** controversieel, aanvechtbaar, omstreden; **2** tegendraads

controversy [kontrəvə:sie] **1** strijdpunt^h; **2** onenigheid, verdeeldheid

convalesce [konvəles] herstellen, herstellende zijn *(from a disease)*, genezen

convalescence [konvəlesns] herstel(periode), genezing(speriode)

convalescent [konvəlesnt] herstellend, genezend, herstellings-: *~ hospital* (of: *nursing home)* herstellingsoord

convector [kənvektə] warmtewisselaar, kachel

¹**convene** [kənvie:n] *vb* **1** bijeenroepen, samenroepen; **2** (voor het gerecht) dagen, dagvaarden

²**convene** [kənvie:n] *vb* bijeenkomen, samenkomen, (zich) vergaderen

convenience [kənvie:niəns] **1** (openbaar) toilet^h, wc, urinoir^h: *public ~s* openbare toiletten; **2** gemak^h, comfort^h: *his house has all the modern ~s* zijn huis is van alle moderne gemakken voorzien; *at your earliest ~* zodra het u gelegen komt

convenient [kənvie:niənt] **1** geschikt, handig: *they were ~ly forgotten* zij werden gemakshalve vergeten; **2** gunstig gelegen, gemakkelijk bereikbaar

convent [konvent] (nonnen)klooster^h, kloostergebouw^h, kloostergemeenschap

convention [kənvensjən] **1** overeenkomst, verdrag^h; **2** bijeenkomst, congres^h, conferentie; **3** gewoonte, gebruik^h

conventional [kənvɛnsjənəl] gebruikelijk, traditioneel: ~ *wisdom* algemene opinie

¹**converge** [kənvɔːdzj] *vb* samenkomen, samenlopen, samenvallen

²**converge** [kənvɔːdzj] *vb* naar één punt leiden, doen samenkomen

conversation [konvəseesjən] gesprekʰ, conversatie, praatjeʰ

¹**converse** [kənvɔːs] *vb* spreken, converseren

²**converse** [kɔnvɔːs] *n* tegendeelʰ, omgekeerde

³**converse** [kɔnvɔːs] *adj* tegenovergesteld, omgekeerd

conversion [kənvɔːsjən] 1 omzetting, overschakeling, omschakeling, omrekening, verbouwing; 2 *(rel)* bekering; 3 *(rugby, American football)* conversie

¹**convert** [kənvɔːt] *vb* (een) verandering(en) ondergaan, veranderen, overgaan

²**convert** [kənvɔːt] *vb* 1 bekeren *(also fig)*, overhalen; 2 om-, overschakelen, omzetten, veranderen, om-, verbouwen, om-, inwisselen, omrekenen: ~ *a loan* een lening converteren

³**convert** [kɔnvɔːt] *n* bekeerling

¹**convertible** [kənvɔːtibl] *n* cabriolet

²**convertible** [kənvɔːtibl] *adj* 1 inwisselbaar, omwisselbaar; 2 met vouwdak, met open dak

convex [kɔnveks] convex, bol(rond)

convey [kənvee] 1 (ver)voeren, transporteren, (ge)leiden; 2 meedelen, duidelijk maken, uitdrukken: *his tone ~ed his real intention* uit zijn toon bleek zijn werkelijke bedoeling

conveyor [kənveeə] vervoerder, transporteur: ~ *belt* transportband, lopende band

¹**convict** [kɔnvikt] *n* 1 veroordeelde; 2 gedetineerde, gevangene

²**convict** [kənvikt] *vb* veroordelen, schuldig bevinden: *~ed of murder* wegens moord veroordeeld

conviction [kənviksjən] 1 veroordeling; 2 (innerlijke) overtuiging, overtuigdheid, (vaste) mening

convince [kənvins] overtuigen, overreden, overhalen

convivial [kənvivviəl] 1 (levens)lustig, joviaal, uitgelaten; 2 vrolijk

convocation [konvəkeesjən] 1 vergadering; 2 bijeenroeping

convoy [kɔnvoj] 1 konvooiʰ, geleideʰ, escorteʰ; 2 escortering

convulsion [kənvulsjən] 1 ~*s* stuip(trekking), convulsie; 2 uitbarsting, verstoring; 3 lachsalvoʰ, onbedaarlijk gelachʰ

¹**coo** [koeː] *vb* koeren, kirren, lispelen

²**coo** [koeː] *n* roekoe(geluid)ʰ, gekoerʰ

¹**cook** [koek] *vb* op het vuur staan, (af)koken, sudderen

²**cook** [koek] *vb* koken, (eten) bereiden

³**cook** [koek] *vb (inf)* knoeien met, vervalsen ‖ ~ *up* verzinnen

⁴**cook** [koek] *n* kok(kin)

cooker [koekə] kooktoestelʰ, kookplaat, kookstelʰ

cooky [koekie] 1 *(Am)* koekjeʰ, biskwietjeʰ; 2 *(Am; inf)* figuur⁺ʰ, typeʰ, persoon

¹**cool** [koeːl] *adj* 1 koel, fris; 2 koel, luchtig, licht *(of clothing)*; 3 kalm, rustig, beheerst: *(as) ~ as a cucumber* ijskoud, doodbedaard; 4 kil, koel, afstandelijk; 5 *(inf)* koel, ongeëmotioneerd: *a ~ card* (of: *customer, hand)* een gehaaid figuur, sluwe vos

²**cool** [koeːl] *vb* (af)koelen *(also fig)*, verkoelen ‖ ~ *it* rustig maar, kalm aan

³**cool** [koeːl] *n* 1 koelte, koelheid; 2 kalmte, zelfbeheersing, onverstoorbaarheid: *keep your ~* hou je in

cooler [koeːlə] koeler, koelcel, koeltas, *(Am)* ijskast

¹**coop** [koeːp] *n* kippenren, kippenhokʰ

²**coop** [koeːp] *vb* opsluiten (in een hok), kooien *(of chickens):* ~ *up* (of: *in)* opsluiten, kooien

co-op [kɔoop] *co-operative* coöperatieve onderneming

co-operate [kooɔppəreet] samenwerken, meewerken

co-operation [koooppəreesjən] 1 coöperatie, samenwerkingsverbandʰ; 2 medewerking, samenwerking, hulp

¹**co-operative** [kooɔppərətiv] *adj* 1 behulpzaam, meewerkend, bereidwillig; 2 coöperatief, op coöperatieve grondslag

²**co-operative** [kooɔppərətiv] *n* coöperatie, collectiefʰ, coöperatief bedrijfʰ

¹**co-ordinate** [koooːdinneet] *vb* (harmonieus) samenwerken

²**co-ordinate** [koooːdinneet] *vb* coördineren, rangschikken (in onderling verband), ordenen

³**co-ordinate** [koooːdinnət] *n* 1 stand-, klasse-, soortgenoot, gelijke; 2 *(maths)* coördinaat, waarde, grootheid

⁴**co-ordinate** [koooːdinnət] *adj* gelijkwaardig, gelijk in rang

¹**cop** [kɔp] *n* 1 *(inf)* smeris; 2 *(inf)* arrestatie, vangst

²**cop** [kɔp] *vb (inf)* 1 betrappen, grijpen, vangen; 2 raken, treffen ‖ ~ *it* last krijgen

cope [koop] het aankunnen, zich weten te redden: ~ *with* het hoofd bieden (aan), bestrijden

copier [kɔppiə] kopieerapparaatʰ

copious [koopiəs] 1 overvloedig; 2 productief, vruchtbaar *(author etc)*

copper [kɔppə] 1 (rood) koperʰ; 2 koperkleur; 3 koperen muntjeʰ, koper(geld)ʰ; 4 *(inf)* smeris

copulation [kopjoeleesjən] geslachtsgemeenschap

¹**copy** [kɔppie] *n* 1 kopie, reproductie, imitatie, fotokopie; 2 exemplaarʰ, nummerʰ; 3 kopij, (reclame)tekst

²**copy** [kɔppie] *vb* een kopie maken, overschrijven

³**copy** [kɔppie] *vb* 1 kopiëren, een afdruk maken van, overschrijven; 2 navolgen, imiteren, overnemen

¹**copybook** *adj* perfect, (helemaal) volgens het boekje

²**copybook** *n* voorbeeldenboekʰ, schrijfboekʰ ‖ *(inf) blot one's ~* zijn reputatie verspelen, een slechte beurt maken

copycat *(inf)* 1 na-aper, navolger; 2 afkijker, spieker
copyright [kǫppierajt] auteursrecht[h]
coral [kǫrrǝl] 1 koraal[h], kraal(tje[h]); 2 koraalrood[h], koraalkleur[h]
cord [ko:d] 1 *(anatomy)* streng, band: *umbilical* ~ navelstreng; 2 koord[h], streng, touw[h], snaar; 3 (elektrisch) snoer[h], kabel, draad; 4 ribfluweel[h], corduroy[h]
cordial [kǫ:diǝl] hartelijk
cordiality [kǫ:die·ælittie] hartelijkheid, vriendelijkheid
cordon [kǫ:dn] kordon[h], ring
corduroy [kǫ:djǝroj] (fijn) ribfluweel[h]
core [ko:] binnenste[h], kern, klokhuis[h], *(nuclear energy)* reactorkern, *(fig)* wezen[h], essentie, hart[h]: *rotten to the* ~ door en door rot
cork [ko:k] kurk, drijver *(of fishnet, fishing line)*, flessenkurk, (rubber) stop
corkscrew kurkentrekker
corm [ko:m] (stengel)knol
cormorant [kǫ:mǝrǝnt] aalscholver
corn [ko:n] 1 likdoorn, eksteroog[h]; 2 korrel, graan-, maïs-, tarwekorrel, zaadje[h], graantje[h]; 3 graan[h], koren[h], tarwe; *(Am)* maïs: ~ *on the cob* maïskolf, maïs aan de kolf *(as cooked food)*; 4 *(inf)* sentimenteel gedoe[h]
¹corner [kǫ:nǝ] *n* 1 hoek, bocht, hoekje[h]: *in a remote* ~ *of the country* in een uithoek van het land; *cut* ~*s: a)* bochten afsnijden; *b)* het niet zo nauw (meer) nemen; 2 *(sport)* hoekschop: *cut* ~*s: a)* de uitgaven besnoeien; *b)* formaliteiten omzeilen
²corner [kǫ:nǝ] *vb* in het nauw drijven, insluiten, klemzetten
³corner [kǫ:nǝ] *vb* een bocht nemen, door de bocht gaan, de hoek omgaan
cornet [kǫ:nit] 1 *(mus)* kornet; 2 (ijsco)hoorn, cornet
cornflour maïzena, maïsmeel[h]
corny [kǫ:nie] *(inf)* afgezaagd, clichématig, flauw
¹coronary [kǫrrǝnǝrie] *adj* mbt de krans(slag)ader: ~ *arteries* krans(slag)aderen
²coronary [kǫrrǝnǝrie] *n* hartinfarct, hartaanval
coronation [korrǝneesjǝn] kroning
coroner [kǫrrǝnǝ] 1 lijkschouwer; 2 rechter van instructie
coronet [kǫrrǝnit] 1 (adellijk) kroontje[h], prinsenkroon, prinsessenkroon; 2 diadeem[+h], (haar)kransje[h]
¹corporal [kǫ:pǝrǝl] *n* korporaal
²corporal [kǫ:pǝrǝl] *adj* lichamelijk, lijfelijk, lichaams-: ~ *punishment* lijfstraf
corporate [kǫ:pǝrǝt] 1 gezamenlijk, collectief, verenigd: ~ *body, body* ~ lichaam, rechtspersoon; 2 mbt een gemeentebestuur, gemeente-, gemeentelijk; 3 mbt een naamloze vennootschap, bedrijfs-, ondernemings-: ~ *identity* bedrijfsidentiteit, huisstijl; ~ *lawyer* bedrijfsjurist
corporation [ko:pǝreesjǝn] 1 gemeenteraad; gemeentebestuur[h]; 2 rechtspersoon, lichaam[h], *(Am)*

naamloze vennootschap, onderneming: ~ *tax* vennootschapsbelasting
corps [ko:] 1 *(mil)* (leger)korps[h], wapen[h], staf; 2 korps[h], staf
corpse [ko:ps] lijk[h]
corral [kǝra:l] *(Am)* (vee)kraal, omheining voor paarden
¹correct [kǝrekt] *adj* 1 correct, juist: *politically* ~ politiek correct; 2 onberispelijk, beleefd
²correct [kǝrekt] *vb* 1 verbeteren, corrigeren, nakijken; 2 terechtwijzen; 3 rechtzetten, rectificeren; 4 verhelpen, repareren, tegengaan
correction [kǝreksjǝn] correctie, verbetering, rectificatie: ~ *fluid* correctievloeistof, blunderlak
correlation [korrilleesjǝn] correlatie *(also statistics)*, wisselwerking, wederzijdse betrekking
correspond [korrispǫnd] 1 (with *to, with)* overeenkomen, overeenstemmen (met), kloppen, corresponderen; 2 corresponderen, een briefwisseling voeren, schrijven
correspondence [korrispǫndǝns] 1 overeenkomst, overeenstemming, gelijkenis; 2 correspondentie, briefwisseling: *commercial* ~ handelscorrespondentie
corridor [kǫrriddo:] 1 gang *(also pol)*, corridor, galerij; 2 luchtweg, corridor, luchtvaartroute, vliegtuigroute
corroborate [kǝrobbǝreesjǝn] bevestiging, bekrachtiging
¹corrode [kǝrood] *vb* vergaan, verteren, verroesten, (weg)roesten
²corrode [kǝrood] *vb* aantasten, aanvreten, wegvreten
corrosion [kǝroozjǝn] verroesting, aantasting; roest
corrugate [kǫrrǝgeet] plooien, golven: ~*d (card)board* golfkarton; *sheets of* ~*d iron* golfplaten
¹corrupt [kǝrupt] *adj* 1 verdorven, immoreel; 2 corrupt, omkoopbaar; 3 verbasterd, onbetrouwbaar: *a* ~ *form of Latin* verbasterd Latijn
²corrupt [kǝrupt] *vb* slecht worden, (zeden)bederf veroorzaken
³corrupt [kǝrupt] *vb* 1 omkopen, corrupt maken; 2 verbasteren, vervalsen, verknoeien
corruption [kǝrupsjǝn] 1 corruptie, omkoperij; 2 verbastering; 3 bederf[h], verderf[h]
corset [kǫ:sit] korset[h], keurslijfje[h], rijglijfje[h]
¹cosh [kosj] *n* (gummi)knuppel, ploertendoder
²cosh [kosj] *vb* slaan met een gummiknuppel, aftuigen, neerknuppelen
cosine [koosajn] cosinus
¹cosmetic [kozmettik] *n* cosmetisch middel[h], schoonheidsmiddel[h], ~*s* cosmetica
²cosmetic [kozmettik] *adj* 1 cosmetisch, schoonheids-: ~ *surgery* cosmetische chirurgie; 2 *(depr)* verfraaiend, voor de schone schijn, oppervlakkig
cosmic [kozmik] kosmisch, van het heelal
cosmonaut [kozmǝno:t] kosmonaut
cosmopolitan [kozmǝpǫllittǝn] kosmopolitisch

cosset [kossit] vertroetelen, verwennen

¹cost [kost] *n* kost(en), prijs, uitgave: *the ~ of living* de kosten van (het) levensonderhoud; *at all ~s, at any ~* koste wat het kost, tot elke prijs; *at the ~ of* ten koste van; *charged at ~* in rekening gebracht; *count the ~* de nadelen overwegen *(before acting)*

²cost [kost] *vb* kosten, komen (te staan) op, vergen

³cost [kost] *vb* kostbaar zijn, in de papieren lopen

costly [kostlie] kostbaar, duur

costume [kostjoe:m] kostuum[h], pak[h]; (kleder)dracht

¹cosy [koozie] *n* 1 theemuts; 2 eierwarmer

²cosy [koozie] *adj* knus, behaaglijk, gezellig

cosy up *(Am)* dicht(er) aankruipen *(to s.o.); (fig)* in de gunst proberen te komen *(with s.o.)*

cot [kot] 1 ledikantje[h], kinderbed(je[h]), wieg; 2 *(Am)* veldbed[h], stretcher

cottage [kottidzj] 1 (plattelands)huisje[h]; 2 vakantiehuisje[h], zomerhuisje[h]

cottage cheese *(roughly)* kwark, *(Belg)* plattekaas

cotton [kotn] 1 katoen[h], katoenplant; katoendraad, katoenvezel; 2 katoenen stof, katoenweefsel[h]

¹couch [kautsj] *n* (rust)bank, sofa, divan

²couch [kautsj] *vb* 1 inkleden, formuleren, verwoorden: *the instructions were ~ in simple language* de instructies waren in eenvoudige bewoordingen gesteld; 2 vellen *(spear, lance)*

¹cough [kof] *n* 1 hoest: *have a bad ~* erg hoesten; 2 kuch(je[h]); hoestbui, hoestaanval

²cough [kof] *vb* 1 hoesten, kuchen; 2 sputteren, blaffen *(of firearm): the engine ~s and misfires* de motor sputtert en hapert

cough up 1 opbiechten, bekennen; 2 dokken, ophoesten *(money)*

council [kaunsl] 1 raad, (advies)college[h], bestuur[h]: *municipal ~* gemeenteraad; 2 kerkvergadering

councillor [kaunsələ] raadslid[h]

¹counsel [kaunsl] *vb* advies geven, adviseren, aanraden

²counsel [kaunsl] *n* 1 raad, (deskundig) advies[h]; 2 overleg[h]; 3 raadslieden, advocaat, verdediging

counselling [kaunsəling] het adviseren, adviseurschap[h]

counsellor [kaunsələ] 1 adviseur, consulent(e), *(Am)* (studenten)decaan, beroepskeuzeadviseur; 2 *(Am)* raadsman, raadsvrouw, advocaat

¹count [kaunt] *vb* tellen, optellen, tellen tot: *~ down* aftellen

²count [kaunt] *vb* tellen, meetellen, gelden: *~ for little* weinig voorstellen; *~ against* pleiten tegen

³count [kaunt] *vb* 1 meetellen, meerekenen: *there were 80 victims, not ~ing (in) the crew* er waren 80 slachtoffers, de bemanning niet meegerekend; 2 rekenen tot, beschouwen (als), achten: *~ oneself lucky* zich gelukkig prijzen; *they'll ~ it against you …* ze zullen het je kwalijk nemen …

⁴count [kaunt] *n* 1 het uittellen *(of a boxer): be out for the ~* uitgeteld zijn *(also fig)*; 2 (niet-Engelse) graaf; 3 telling, tel, getal[h]: *keep ~* de tel(ling) bijhouden, (mee)tellen; *lose ~* de tel kwijtraken

countdown het aftellen

¹countenance [kauntənəns] *n* 1 gelaat[h], gelaatstrekken, gelaatsuitdrukking; 2 aanzicht[h], aanzien[h]; 3 welwillende blik; 4 kalmte, gemoedsrust, zelfbeheersing: *lose ~* van zijn stuk raken; 5 (morele) steun, instemming, goedkeuring: *we won't give (of: lend) ~ to such plans* we zullen dergelijke plannen niet steunen

²countenance [kauntənəns] *vb* goedkeuren, (stilzwijgend) toestaan, oogluikend toelaten, dulden

¹counter [kauntə] *n* 1 toonbank, balie, bar, loket[h], kassa; 2 fiche[h]; 3 tegenzet, tegenmaatregel, tegenwicht[h] || *over the ~* zonder recept (verkrijgbaar) *(of drugs); under the ~* onder de toonbank

²counter [kauntə] *adj* 1 tegen(over)gesteld, tegenwerkend, contra-; 2 duplicaat-, dubbel

³counter [kauntə] *vb* 1 zich verzetten tegen, tegenwerken, (ver)hinderen; 2 beantwoorden, reageren op; 3 tenietdoen, weerleggen

⁴counter [kauntə] *vb* een tegenzet doen, zich verweren, terugvechten, *(boxing)* counteren

⁵counter [kauntə] *adv* 1 in tegenovergestelde richting; 2 op tegengestelde wijze: *act (of: go) ~ to* niet opvolgen, ingaan tegen

counteract tegengaan, neutraliseren, tenietdoen

¹counter-attack *n* tegenaanval

²counter-attack *vb* in de tegenaanval gaan

³counter-attack *vb* een tegenaanval uitvoeren op

counterbalance tegenwicht[h]

counter-clockwise [kauntəklokwajz] *(Am)* linksdraaiend, tegen de wijzers vd klok in (draaiend)

¹counterfeit [kauntəfit] *vb* 1 vervalsen, namaken; 2 doen alsof

²counterfeit [kauntəfit] *adj* 1 vals, vervalst, onecht; 2 voorgewend, niet gemeend

³counterfeit [kauntəfit] *n* vervalsing, falsificatie

counterfeiter [kauntəfittə] vervalser, valsemunter

counterfoil controlestrookje[h], kwitantiestrook

counterpart tegenhanger

¹counterpoise *n* 1 tegenwicht[h], tegendruk; 2 evenwicht[h]

²counterpoise *vb* in evenwicht brengen, opwegen tegen, compenseren

countersign medeondertekenen

counterweight tegen(ge)wicht[h], contragewicht[h]

countess [kauntis] gravin, echtgenote ve graaf

countless [kauntləs] talloos, ontelbaar

count out *(inf)* 1 niet meetellen, afschrijven, terzijde schuiven: *if it rains tonight you can count me out* als het vanavond regent moet je niet op me rekenen; 2 *(sport)* uittellen *(boxer)*; 3 neertellen

country [kuntrie] 1 land[h], geboorteland[h], vaderland[h]; 2 volk[h], natie: *the ~ doesn't support this decision* het land staat niet achter deze beslissing; 3 (land)streek, terrein[h]; 4 platteland[h], provincie: *go for a day in the ~* een dagje naar buiten gaan

countryfolk plattelanders, buitenlui

country house landhuis[h], buitenverblijf[h]

countryman [kʌntriemən] **1** landgenoot; **2** platte-lander

countryside platteland[h]

count (up)on rekenen (vertrouwen) op

county [kauntie] graafschap[h], provincie

county council graafschapsbestuur[h], provinciaal bestuur[h], *(roughly)* Provinciale Staten

county court districtsrechtbank, *(roughly)* kanton-gerecht[h]

county hall provinciehuis[h]

coup [koe:] **1** slimme zet, prestatie, succes[h]: *make (of: pull off) a ~* zijn slag slaan; **2** staatsgreep, coup

¹couple [kʌpl] *n* **1** koppel[h], paar[h], span[h]: *a ~ of: a)* twee; *b) (inf)* een paar, een stuk of twee *(not more than three);* **2** (echt)paar[h], stel[h]: *a married ~* een ge-trouwd stel, een echtpaar

²couple [kʌpl] *vb* **1** (aaneen)koppelen, verbinden, aanhaken: *~ up* aan elkaar koppelen; **2** (met elkaar) in verband brengen, gepaard laten gaan

³couple [kʌpl] *vb* **1** paren vormen; **2** paren, ge-slachtsgemeenschap hebben

coupling [kʌpling] koppeling, verbinding, koppel-stuk[h]

coupon [koe:pon] **1** bon, kaartje[h], zegel, kortings-bon; **2** (toto)formulier[h]

courage [kʌrridzj] moed, dapperheid, durf: *mus-ter up (of: pluck up, summon up) ~* moed vatten

courageous [kəreedzjəs] moedig, dapper, onver-schrokken

courier [koeriə] **1** koerier, bode; **2** reisgids, reislei-der

course [ko:s] **1** loop, (voort)gang, duur: *the ~ of events* de loop der gebeurtenissen; *run (of: take) its ~* zijn beloop hebben, (natuurlijk) verlopen; **2** koers, richting, route: *stay the ~* tot het eind toe volhouden; *on ~* op koers; **3** manier, weg, (ge-drags)lijn; **4** cursus, curriculum[h]: *an English ~* een cursus Engels; **5** cyclus, reeks, serie: *~ of lectures* le-zingencyclus; **6** *(sport)* baan; **7** *(culinary)* gang: *a three-~ dinner* een diner van drie gangen; *the main ~* het hoofdgerecht; *of ~* natuurlijk, vanzelfspre-kend

¹court [ko:t] *n* **1** rechtbank, gerechtsgebouw[h], ge-rechtszaal, (gerechts)hof[h]: *Court of Appeal(s)* hof van beroep; *Court of Claims* bestuursrechtelijk hof *(Am);* *~ of inquiry* gerechtelijke commissie van on-derzoek; *go to ~* naar de rechter stappen; *settle out of ~* buiten de rechter om schikken; **2** hof[h], konink-lijk paleis[h], hofhouding; **3** *(sport)* (tennis)baan; **4** omsloten ruimte, (licht)hal, binnenhof[h], binnen-plaats: *laugh s.o. (sth.) out of ~* iem (iets) wegho-nen; *rule (of: put) out of ~: a)* uitsluiten *(witness, evidence; also fig); b)* (iets, iem) totaal geen kans ge-ven

²court [ko:t] *vb* **1** vleien, in de gunst trachten te ko-men bij; **2** flirten met; het hof maken, dingen naar de hand van; vragen om, uitlokken: *~ disaster* om moeilijkheden vragen; **3** (trachten te) winnen, stre-ven naar

³court [ko:t] *vb* verkering hebben

courteous [kə:tiəs] beleefd, welgemanierd

courtesy [kə:təsie] beleefdheid, welgemanierd-heid, beleefdheidsbetuiging: *(by) ~ of* welwillend ter beschikking gesteld door, met toestemming van

court-house gerechtsgebouw[h]

courtly [ko:tlie] **1** hoofs, verfijnd, elegant; **2** welge-manierd, beleefd, hoffelijk

¹court martial [ko:tma:sjl] *n* krijgsraad, (hoog) mi-litair gerechtshof[h]

²court martial [ko:tma:sjl] *vb* voor een krijgsraad brengen

courtship [ko:tsjip] **1** verkering(stijd); **2** het hof maken; **3** *(zoology)* balts

courtyard binnenhof, binnenplaats, plein[h]

cousin [kʌzn] neef, nicht, dochter of zoon van tante of oom

cove [koov] **1** inham, kleine baai, kreek; **2** beschutte plek, (beschutte) inham

covenant [kʌvvənənt] **1** overeenkomst; **2** *(rel)* ver-bond[h]

¹cover [kʌvvə] *vb (inf)* (with *for)* invallen (voor), vervangen

²cover [kʌvvə] *vb* **1** bedekken, overtrekken: *he was ~ed in* (of: *with) blood* hij zat onder het bloed; *~ over* bedekken; **2** beslaan, omvatten, bestrijken; **3** afleggen *(distance);* **4** bewaken *(eg access roads);* **5** verslaan, verslag uitbrengen over; **6** dekken, verze-keren: *we aren't ~ed against fire* we zijn niet tegen brand verzekerd; **7** onder schot houden, in be-dwang houden; **8** beheersen, controleren, bestrij-ken; **9** *(sport)* dekken, bewaken: *a ~ing letter* (of: *note)* een begeleidend schrijven

³cover [kʌvvə] *n* **1** bedekking, hoes, (verf)laag, dek-bed[h]; **2** deksel[+h], klep; **3** omslag[+h], stofomslag[+h], boekband: *read a book from ~ to ~* een boek van be-gin tot eind lezen; **4** enveloppe; **5** mes en vork; **6** in-valler, vervanger; **7** dekmantel, voorwendsel[h]: *un-der ~ of friendship* onder het mom van vriend-schap; **8** dekking *(also sport)*, beschutting, schuil-plaats: *take ~* dekking zoeken, (gaan) schuilen; *un-der ~* heimelijk, in het geheim, verborgen; **9** dek-king *(insurance)*

coverage [kʌvvəridzj] **1** dekking *(also insurance)*, verzekerd bedrag (risico); **2** berichtgeving, ver-slag[h], verslaggeving, publiciteit; **3** bereik[h]

covering [kʌvvəring] bedekking, dekzeil[h]

¹covert [kʌvvət] *adj* bedekt, heimelijk, illegaal

²covert [kʌvvət] *n* **1** beschutte plaats, schuilplaats; **2** kreupelhout[h]

¹cover up *vb* **1** verdoezelen, wegmoffelen, verhullen: *~ one's tracks* zijn sporen uitwissen; **2** toedekken, inwikkelen

²cover up *vb* dekking geven, een alibi verstrekken

cover-up 1 doofpotaffaire; **2** dekmantel, alibi[h]

covet [kʌvvit] begeren

cow [kau] koe, wijfje[h]: *(fig) sacred ~* heilige koe; *till the ~s come home* tot je een ons weegt, eindeloos

coward [kauəd] lafaard

cowardice [kauədis] lafheid

cowboy 1 (Am) cowboy, veedrijver; 2 beunhaas, knoeier; 3 (inf) gewetenloos zakenman: ~ employers gewetenloze werkgevers

cower [kauə] in elkaar duiken, ineenkrimpen

cowl [kaul] 1 monnikskap, kap; 2 monnikspij; 3 schoorsteenkap

cowslip 1 sleutelbloem; 2 (Am) dotterbloem

cox [koks] stuurman; stuurʰ (of rowing boat)

coxcomb [kokskoom] ijdeltuit

cozy [koozie] see cosy

¹crab [kræb] n 1 krab; 2 (inf) schaamluis

²crab [kræb] vb 1 krabben vangen; 2 (inf) kankeren, mopperen

crabbed [kræbid] 1 chagrijnig, prikkelbaar; 2 kriebelig, gekrabbeld, onduidelijk (of handwriting); 3 ingewikkeld

¹crack [kræk] n 1 barst(jeʰ), breuk, scheur(tjeʰ); 2 kier, spleet; 3 knal(geluidʰ), knak, kraak; 4 klap, pets; 5 (inf) gooi, poging: have a ~ at een gooi doen naar, proberen; 6 grap(jeʰ), geintjeʰ; 7 (inf) kraan, kei, uitblinker; 8 (inf) (zuivere vorm van) cocaïne: at the ~ of dawn bij het krieken van de dag

²crack [kræk] vb 1 in(een)storten, het begeven, knakken; 2 knallen, kraken; 3 barsten, splijten, scheuren; 4 breken, schor worden, overslaan (of voice)

³crack [kræk] vb 1 (open)breken, stukbreken, knappen: ~ a safe een kluis openbreken; 2 (chem) kraken

⁴crack [kræk] vb 1 laten knallen, laten kraken: ~ a whip klappen met een zweep; 2 doen barsten, splijten, scheuren; 3 meppen, slaan; 4 de oplossing vinden van: ~ a code een code ontcijferen; 5 (inf) vertellen: ~ a joke een mop vertellen

⁵crack [kræk] adj (inf) prima, keur-, uitgelezen: a ~ shot (of: marksman) een eersteklas schutter

crack-brained onzinnig, getikt, dwaas

crackdown (straf)campagne, (politie)optredenʰ, actie

cracker [krækə] cracker(tjeʰ), knäckebrödʰ

crackers [krækəz] (inf) gek

cracking [kræking] (inf) 1 schitterend, uitstekend; 2 snel: ~ pace stevige vaart; get ~ aan de slag gaan

¹crackle [krækl] vb knapp(er)en, knetteren, knisperen, kraken (of telephone)

²crackle [krækl] n geknetterʰ, geknap(per)ʰ, geknisperʰ

¹crack up vb (inf) bezwijken, instorten, eronderdoor gaan

²crack up vb (inf) 1 ophemelen, roemen, prijzen: he isn't everything he's cracked up to be hij is niet zo goed als iedereen zegt; 2 in de lach schieten, in een deuk liggen

crack-up (inf) in(een)storting, inzinking

¹cradle [kreedl] n 1 wieg (also fig), bakermat: from the ~ to the grave van de wieg tot het graf; 2 stellage, (shipp) (constructie)bok, haak (of telephone)

²cradle [kreedl] vb 1 wiegen, vasthouden; 2 in een wieg leggen; 3 op de haak leggen (telephone)

¹craft [kra:ft] n 1 vakʰ, ambachtʰ; 2 (kunst)vaardigheid, kunstnijverheid; 3 bedrijfstak, branche, (ambachts)gildeʰ

²craft n (craft) 1 boot(jeʰ), vaartuigʰ; 2 vliegtuigʰ; 3 ruimtevaartuigʰ

craftsman [kra:ftsmən] handwerksman, vakman (also fig)

crafty [kra:ftie] geslepen, doortrapt, geraffineerd

crag [kræg] steile rots

¹cram [kræm] vb 1 (vol)proppen, aanstampen, (vol)stouwen; 2 klaarstomen (pupil); 3 erin stampen (subject matter)

²cram [kræm] vb 1 zich volproppen, schrokken; 2 blokken, stampen

cramp [kræmp] kramp(scheut), ~s maagkramp, buikkramp

cramped [kræmpt] 1 benauwd, krap, kleinbehuisd; 2 kriebelig (of handwriting); 3 gewrongen

¹crane [kreen] n 1 kraanvogel; 2 kraan, hijskraan

²crane [kreen] vb de hals uitstrekken, reikhalzen

³crane [kreen] vb (reikhalzend) uitstrekken, vooruitsteken

¹crank [krængk] n 1 krukas, autoslinger, crank (of bicycle); 2 (inf) zonderling, excentriekeling; 3 (Am; inf) mopperkont

²crank [krængk] vb aanzwengelen, aanslingeren: ~ up a car een auto aanslingeren

crankshaft krukas, trapas

cranky [krængkie] 1 (inf) zonderling, bizar; 2 (Am; inf) chagrijnig

¹crap [kræp] n (vulg) 1 stront: have a ~ een drol leggen; 2 kletspraat, gekletsʰ: a load of ~ een hoop gezever; 3 (vulg) troep, rotzooi

²crap [kræp] vb (vulg) schijten, kakken

¹crash [kræsj] vb 1 te pletter slaan, verongelukken, botsen, (neer)storten: the plates ~ed to the floor de borden kletterden op de grond; 2 stormen; 3 dreunen, knallen; 4 ineenstorten, failliet gaan, (comp) crashen, down gaan; 5 (inf) (blijven) pitten, de nacht doorbrengen

²crash [kræsj] vb te pletter laten vallen

³crash [kræsj] n 1 klap, dreun; 2 botsing, neerstorting, ongelukʰ; 3 krach, ineenstorting

⁴crash [kræsj] adj spoed-: ~ course stoomcursus, spoedcursus

crash landing buiklanding, noodlanding

crass [kræs] bot, onbehouwen, lomp: ~ stupidity peilloze domheid

crate [kreet] 1 kratʰ, kist; 2 (inf) brik, bak; 3 (inf) kist, wrakkig vliegtuigʰ

crater [kreetə] krater

crave [kreev] hunkeren (naar), smachten (naar)

¹crawl [kro:l] vb 1 kruipen, sluipen, moeizaam vooruitkomen; 2 krioelen, wemelen: the place was ~ing with vermin het krioelde er van ongedierte; 3 kruipen, kruiperig doen, slijmen: ~ to one's boss de hielen likken van zijn baas

²crawl [kro:l] n 1 slakkengang; 2 crawl(slag)

craze [kreez] rage, manie, gril

crazy [kr<u>ee</u>zie] **1** gek, krankzinnig, dol, waanzinnig: *go* ~ gek worden; *(inf)* ~ *about fishing* gek van vissen; **2** *(inf)* te gek, fantastisch

creak [krie:k] geknars^h, gekraak^h

¹cream [krie:m] *n* **1** (slag)room^h; **2** crème *(for use on skin)*; **3** crème(kleurig)

²cream [krie:m] *vb* romen, afromen *(also fig)*: ~ *off* afromen

³cream [krie:m] *vb* **1** room toevoegen aan, in room e.d. bereiden: ~*ed potatoes* aardappelpuree; **2** inwrijven, insmeren *(skin)*

¹crease [krie:s] *n* vouw, plooi, kreukel: ~ *resistant* kreukvrij

²crease [krie:s] *vb* kreuke(le)n, vouwen, plooien

³crease [krie:s] *vb* persen, een vouw maken in

¹create [krie·<u>ee</u>t] *vb* *(inf)* tekeergaan, leven maken

²create [krie·<u>ee</u>t] *vb* **1** scheppen, creëren, ontwerpen; **2** veroorzaken, teweegbrengen

creation [krie·<u>ee</u>sjǝn] **1** schepping, instelling, oprichting: *the Creation* de schepping; **2** creatie, (mode)ontwerp^h

creative [krie·<u>ee</u>tiv] creatief, scheppend, vindingrijk

creativity [krie:ǝtivvittie] creativiteit, scheppingsdrang, scheppingsvermogen^h

creator [krie·<u>ee</u>tǝ] schepper

creature [kr<u>ie:</u>tsjǝ] **1** schepsel^h, schepping, voortbrengsel^h: ~ *of habit* gewoontedier, gewoontemens; **2** dier^h, beest^h; **3** (levend) wezen^h; **4** stakker, mens(je^h), creatuur^h

crèche [kreesj] **1** crèche, kinderdagverblijf^h; **2** *(Am)* kerststal, krib

credence [kr<u>ie:</u>dǝns] geloof^h: *attach/give no ~ to* geen geloof hechten aan

credentials [kriddǝnsjɔlz] introductiebrieven, geloofsbrieven, legitimatiebewijs

credibility [kreddibbillittie] geloofwaardigheid

credible [kreddibl] **1** geloofwaardig, betrouwbaar; **2** overtuigend

¹credit [kreddit] *n* **1** krediet^h: *buy on* ~ op krediet kopen; **2** credit^h, creditzijde, creditpost; **3** tegoed^h, spaarbanktegoed^h, positief saldo^h; **4** geloof^h, vertrouwen^h: *lend* ~ *to* bevestigen, geloofwaardig maken; **5** krediet^h, kredietwaardigheid, goede naam; **6** krediet^h, krediettermijn; **7** eer, lof, verdienste: *it does you* ~, *it is to your* ~, *it reflects* ~ *on you* het siert je, het strekt je tot eer; **8** *(Am)* studiepunt^h, examenbriefje^h, tentamenbriefje^h; **9** sieraad^h: *she's a* ~ *to our family* ze is een sieraad voor onze familie; **10** ~*s* titelrol, aftiteling

²credit [kreddit] *vb* **1** geloven, geloof hechten aan; **2** crediteren, op iemands tegoed bijschrijven; **3** toedenken, toeschrijven: *he is* ~*ed with the invention* de uitvinding staat op zijn naam

creditable [kreddittǝbl] **1** loffelijk, eervol, prijzenswaardig; **2** te geloven

credit card credit card, *(roughly)* betaalkaart

creditor [kreddittǝ] crediteur, schuldeiser

credulity [kridj<u>oe:</u>littie] lichtgelovigheid, goedgelovigheid

creed [krie:d] **1** geloofsbelijdenis, credo^h *(also fig)*; **2** (geloofs)overtuiging, gezindte

creek [krie:k] kreek, inham, bocht; kleine rivier || *(inf) up the* ~ in een lastig parket, in de penarie

¹creep [krie:p] *vb* kruipen, sluipen: ~ *in* binnensluipen; ~ *up on* bekruipen, besluipen

²creep [krie:p] *n* **1** *(inf)* gluiperd, griezel, engerd, slijmerd; **2** *the* ~*s* kriebels, kippenvel^h, koude rillingen

creeper [kr<u>ie:</u>pǝ] **1** kruiper; **2** kruipend gewas^h, klimplant; **3** ~*s (Am)* kruippak^h; **4** ~*s* bordeelsluipers, schoenen met crêpe zolen

creepy [kr<u>ie:</u>pie] griezelig, eng, huiveringwekkend

creepy-crawly *(inf)* beestje^h, (kruipend) insect (ongedierte)

cremate [krimm<u>ee</u>t] cremeren, verassen

cremation [krimm<u>ee</u>sjǝn] crematie

crematorium [kremmǝt<u>o:</u>riǝm] crematorium(gebouw)^h

crescent [kresnt] **1** halvemaan, afnemende maan; **2** halvemaanvormig iets, halvemaantje^h

cress [kres] kers, gewone kers, tuinkers, sterrenkers

¹crest [krest] *n* **1** kam, pluim, kuif; **2** helmbos, helmpluim, verderbos; **3** top, berg-, heuveltop, golfkam: *(fig) he is riding the* ~ *(of the waves)* hij is op het hoogtepunt van zijn carrière, succes

²crest [krest] *vb* de top bereiken van, bedwingen *(mountain)*

crestfallen terneergeslagen, teleurgesteld

crew [kroe:] **1** bemanning; **2** personeel^h; **3** ploeg, roeibootbemanning, roeiploeg

¹crib [krib] *n* **1** *(Am)* ledikantje^h, bedje^h, wieg; **2** krib, voederbak, ruif; **3** kerststal; **4** *(inf)* afgekeken antwoord, spiekwerk^h, plagiaat^h; **5** *(inf)* spiekbriefje^h

²crib [krib] *vb* *(inf)* **1** spieken; afkijken, overschrijven; **2** jatten, pikken

¹crick [krik] *n* stijfheid, spit^h: *a* ~ *in the neck* een stijve nek

²crick [krik] *vb* verrekken, verdraaien, ontwrichten

cricket [krikkit] **1** cricket^h || *that's not* ~ dat is onsportief, zoiets doe je niet; **2** krekel

crime [krajm] **1** misdaad, misdrijf^h; **2** criminaliteit, (de) misdaad; **3** schandaal^h, schande: *it's a* ~ *the way he treats us* het is schandalig zoals hij ons behandelt

¹criminal [krimminl] *adj* **1** misdadig, crimineel: ~ *act* misdrijf, strafbare handeling; **2** *(inf)* schandalig; **3** strafrechtelijk, crimineel: ~ *libel* smaad

²criminal [krimminl] *n* misdadiger

crimson [krimzn] karmozijn(rood)

cringe [krindzj] **1** ineenkrimpen, terugdeinzen, terugschrikken; **2** (with to) kruipen (voor), door het stof gaan (voor), zich vernederen; **3** *(inf)* de kriebel(s) krijgen: *his foolish talk makes me* ~ zijn gezwets hangt me mijlenver de keel uit

¹crinkle [kringkl] *vb* (doen) kreuke(le)n, (doen) rimpelen, verfrommelen

²**crinkle** [kriŋkl] *n* kreuk, (valse, ongewenste) vouw

¹**cripple** [kripl] *vb* verlammen, invalide maken, *(fig)* (ernstig) beschadigen: *~d with gout* krom van de jicht

²**cripple** [kripl] *n* invalide, (gedeeltelijk) verlamde, kreupele

crisis [krajsis] *(crises)* crisis, kritiek stadiumʰ, keerpuntʰ

¹**crisp** [krisp] *n* (aardappel)chip

²**crisp** [krisp] *adj* 1 knapperig, krokant: *a ~ pound note* een kraaknieuw biljet van een pond; 2 stevig, vers *(vegetable etc);* 3 fris, helder, verfrissend: *the ~ autumn wind* de frisse herfstwind; 4 helder, ter zake, kernachtig

crispbread knäckebrödʰ

crisper [krispə] groentelade, groentevakʰ *(in refrigerator)*

crispy [krispie] knapperig, krokant

¹**criss-cross** [kriskros] *adj* kruiselings, kruis-

²**criss-cross** [kriskros] *vb* 1 (kriskras) (door)kruisen; 2 doorsnijden: *train tracks ~ the country* spoorlijnen doorsnijden het land; 3 krassen maken op, bekrassen

³**criss-cross** [kriskros] *adv* kriskras, door elkaar

criterion [krajtiəriən] criteriumʰ

critic [krittik] criticus, recensent

criticism [krittissizm] 1 kritiek, recensie, bespreking; 2 afkeuring, afwijzing

criticize [krittissajz] 1 kritiek hebben (op); 2 (be)kritiseren, beoordelen, recenseren; 3 afkeuren

croak [krook] 1 kwaken *(of frogs),* krassen *(of ravens and crows),* hees zijn, (ontevreden) grommen, brommen; 2 *(vulg)* het loodje leggen

crochet [kroosjee] haakwerkʰ

crock [krok] 1 aardewerk(en) pot, kruik; 2 potscherf; 3 *(inf)* (oud) wrakʰ, kneusjeʰ, ouwe knol

crockery [krokkərie] aardewerkʰ, vaatwerkʰ, serviesgoedʰ

crock up *(inf)* in elkaar klappen, instorten

crocodile [krokkədajl] krokodil: *~ tears* krokodillentranen

crocus [krookəs] krokus

crony [kroonie] makker, maat(jeʰ), gabber

crook [kroek] 1 herdersstaf; 2 bisschopsstaf, kromstaf; 3 bocht, kronkel, buiging; 4 haak, hoek, luikʰ; 5 *(inf)* oplichter, zwendelaar, flessentrekker

crooked [kroekid] 1 bochtig, slingerend, kronkelig; 2 misvormd, krom(gegroeid) *(also with age),* gebocheld; 3 oneerlijk, onbetrouwbaar, achterbaks

crop [krop] 1 krop *(of bird);* 2 rijzweep(jeʰ), karwats, rijstokjeʰ; 3 gewasʰ, landbouwproductʰ, landbouwproducten; 4 oogst *(also fig),* graanoogst, lading, lichting: *a whole new ~ of students* een hele nieuwe lichting studenten; *a fine ~ of hair* een mooie bos haar

cropper [kroppə] *(inf)* smak: *come a ~* een (dood)smak maken, *(fig)* op z'n bek vallen, afgaan

crop up *(inf)* opduiken, de kop opsteken, plotseling ter sprake komen: *her name keeps cropping up in the papers* haar naam duikt voortdurend op in de krant

¹**cross** [kros] *n* 1 the Cross (Heilige) Kruisʰ, kruisiging *(of Christ),* christendomʰ; 2 kruis(jeʰ), crucifixʰ, kruistekenʰ: *make the sign of the ~* een kruisje slaan *(of:* maken); 3 kruisʰ, beproeving, lijdenʰ; 4 kruising, bastaard; 5 *(socc)* voorzet

²**cross** [kros] *vb* (elkaar) kruisen

³**cross** [kros] *vb* 1 oversteken, overtrekken, doortrekken; 2 kruisen, (elkaar) passeren

⁴**cross** [kros] *vb* 1 kruisen, over elkaar slaan: *~ one's arms* zijn armen over elkaar slaan; 2 een kruisteken maken boven: *~ oneself* een kruis slaan; 3 (door)strepen, een streep trekken door: *~ out (of: off)* doorstrepen, doorhalen, schrappen *(also fig);* 4 dwarsbomen, doorkruisen *(plan);* 5 *(biology)* kruisen

⁵**cross** [kros] *adj* boos, kwaad, uit zijn humeur: *be ~ with s.o.* kwaad op iem zijn

crossbreed 1 kruising, bastaard; 2 gekruist rasʰ, bastaardrasʰ

¹**cross-country** *adj* 1 terrein-; 2 over het hele land, van kust tot kust: *~ concert tour* landelijke concerttournee

²**cross-country** *n* cross(-country), terreinwedstrijd, *(athletics)* veldloop, *(cycle racing)* veldrit

cross-examine aan een kruisverhoor onderwerpen *(also fig),* scherp ondervragen

cross-eyed scheel(ogig): *he is slightly ~* hij loenst een beetje

crossing [krossiŋ] 1 oversteek, overtocht, overvaart; 2 kruising, snijpuntʰ, kruispuntʰ; 3 oversteekplaats, zebra, overweg

cross-reference verwijzing, referentie

crossroads wegkruising, twee-, drie-, viersprong, kruispunt, *(fig)* tweesprong, beslissend moment, keerpunt

cross section dwarsdoorsnede *(also fig),* kenmerkende steekproef

crossword kruiswoord(raadsel)ʰ

crotch [krotsj] 1 vertakking, vork; 2 kruisʰ *(of person or article of clothing)*

crotchet [krotsjit] *(mus)* kwartʰ, kwartnoot

crouch [krautsj] zich (laag) bukken, ineenduiken, zich buigen: *~ down* ineengehurkt zitten

¹**crow** [kroo] *n* 1 kraai, roek; 2 gekraaiʰ *(of cock);* 3 kreetjeʰ, geluidjeʰ, gekraaiʰ *(of baby)* || *as the ~ flies* hemelsbreed

²**crow** [kroo] *vb* 1 kraaien *(of cock, child): the baby ~ed with pleasure* het kindje kraaide van plezier; 2 *(inf)* opscheppen, snoeven: *~ over* (triomfantelijk) juichen over, uitbundig leedvermaak hebben over

crowbar koevoet; breekijzerʰ

¹**crowd** [kraud] *n* 1 (mensen)menigte, massa; 2 *(inf)* volkjeʰ, kliek(jeʰ) || *follow (of: move with, go with) the ~* in de pas lopen, zich conformeren aan de massa

²**crowd** [kraud] *vb* elkaar verdringen: *people ~ed round* mensen dromden samen

³**crowd** [kraud] *vb* **1** (over)bevolken, (meer dan) volledig vullen: *shoppers ~ed the stores* de winkels waren vol winkelende mensen; **2** proppen, persen, (dicht) op elkaar drukken: *~ out* buitensluiten, verdringen

crowded [kraudid] vol, druk

¹**crown** [kraun] *n* **1** krans; **2** kroon, *(fig)* vorstelijke macht, regering, *(law)* openbare aanklager: *minister of the Crown* zittend minister *(in England);* **3** hoogste punt^h, bovenste gedeelte^h, (hoofd)kruin, boomkruin, kroon *(of tooth, molar);* **4** *(sport)* kampioen(schap)stitel

²**crown** [kraun] *vb* **1** kronen: *~ed heads* gekroonde hoofden, regerende vorsten; **2** bekronen, belonen, eren; **3** kronen, de top vormen van, sieren; **4** voltooien, (met succes) bekronen, de kroon op het werk vormen: *to ~ (it) all* als klap op de vuurpijl, *(iron)* tot overmaat van ramp

crow's-foot kraaienpootje^h *(wrinkle near corner of the eye)*

crucial [kroe:sjl] **1** cruciaal, (alles)beslissend, *(inf)* zeer belangrijk: *~ point* keerpunt; **2** kritiek

crucifix [kroe:siffiks] kruisbeeld^h

crucify [kroe:siffaj] **1** kruisigen; **2** tuchtigen

crude [kroe:d] **1** ruw, onbewerkt, ongezuiverd; primitief: *~ oil* ruwe olie, aardolie; *a ~ log cabin* een primitieve blokhut; **2** rauw, bot, onbehouwen: *~ behaviour* lomp gedrag

cruel [kroe:əl] wreed, hard(vochtig), gemeen, *(fig)* guur, bar

cruise [kroe:z] **1** een cruise maken; **2** kruisen *(of aeroplane, car etc)*, zich met kruissnelheid voortbewegen, (langzaam) rondrijden, patrouilleren, surveilleren

crumb [krum] **1** kruimel, kruim(pje^h); **2** klein beetje^h, fractie, zweem(pje^h)

crumble [krumbl] ten onder gaan, vergaan, vervallen, afbrokkelen: *crumbling walls* bouwvallige muren; *~ away: a)* afbrokkelen; *b)* verschrompelen

¹**crumple** [krumpl] *vb* (also with *up*) verschrompelen, ineenstorten, ineenklappen

²**crumple** [krumpl] *vb* (also with *up*) kreuk(el)en, rimpelen, verfrommelen

¹**crunch** [kruntsj] *vb* **1** (doen) knarsen; **2** knauwen (op), (luidruchtig) kluiven, knagen (aan)

²**crunch** [kruntsj] *n* **1** knerpend geluid^h, geknars^h; **2** beslissend moment^h, beslissende confrontatie: *if (of: when) it comes to the ~* als puntje bij paaltje komt

crusade [kroe:seed] kruistocht, felle campagne

¹**crush** [krusj] *vb* dringen, (zich) persen

²**crush** [krusj] *vb* **1** in elkaar drukken, indeuken: *be ~ed to death in a crowd* doodgedrukt worden in een mensenmenigte; **2** vernietigen, de kop indrukken

³**crush** [krusj] *n* **1** drom, (samengepakte) mensenmenigte; **2** *(always singular)* gedrang^h: *avoid the ~* de drukte vermijden; **3** *(inf)* overmatig drukke bijeenkomst; **4** *(inf)* (hevige) verliefdheid: *have a ~ on* smoorverliefd zijn op

crushing [krusjing] vernietigend, verpletterend

¹**crust** [krust] *n* **1** korst, broodkorst, kapje^h, korstdeeg^h, bladerdeeg^h: *the earth's ~* de aardkorst; **2** aardkorst; **3** (wond)korst; **4** *(inf)* lef^h, brutaliteit: *(inf) off one's ~* getikt

²**crust** [krust] *vb* met een korst bedekt worden

crutch [krutsj] kruk *(for disabled person)*

crux [kruks] essentie, kern(punt^h)

¹**cry** [kraj] *n* **1** kreet, (uit)roep, geschreeuw^h, schreeuw, strijdkreet; **2** huilpartij, gehuil^h; **3** diergeluid^h, schreeuw, (vogel)roep; **4** roep, smeekbede, appel^h

²**cry** [kraj] *vb* **1** huilen, janken: *~ for sth.* om iets jengelen, om iets huilen; *~ for joy* huilen van blijdschap; **2** roepen, schreeuwen: *the fields are ~ing out for rain* het land schreeuwt om regen; *~ sth. down* iets kleineren, iets afbreken; *~ off* terugkrabbelen, er(gens) van afzien

³**cry** [kraj] *vb* **1** schreeuwen, jammeren: *he cried (out) with pain* hij schreeuwde het uit van de pijn; **2** een geluid geven *(of animals, esp birds)*, roepen

crybaby huilebalk

crying [krajjing] hemeltergend, schreeuwend: *a ~ shame* een grof schandaal

crypt [kript] crypt(e), grafkelder, ondergrondse kapel

cryptic [kriptik] cryptisch, verborgen, geheimzinnig: *~ crossword* cryptogram

¹**crystal** [kristl] *n* **1** kristal^h; **2** *(Am)* horlogeglas^h

²**crystal** [kristl] *adj* **1** kristal(len): *~ ball* kristallen bol *(of fortune-teller);* **2** (kristal)helder

ct. cent c

cub [kub] welp, jong^h, vossenjong^h

¹**cube** [kjoe:b] *n* **1** kubus, klontje^h, blokje^h: *(Am) a ~ of sugar* een suikerklontje; **2** derdemacht: *~ root* derdemachtswortel

²**cube** [kjoe:b] *vb* tot de derdemacht verheffen: *two ~d is eight* twee tot de derde is acht

cubic [kjoe:bik] **1** kubiek, driedimensionaal: *~ metre* kubieke meter; **2** kubusvormig, rechthoekig; **3** kubisch; derdemachts-

cubicle [kjoe:bikl] **1** kleedhokje^h; **2** slaapho(e)kje^h

¹**cuckoo** [koekoe:] *n* **1** koekoek; **2** koekoeksroep; **3** *(fig)* uilskuiken^h, sul || *~ in the nest* ongewenste indringer

²**cuckoo** [koekoe:] *adj (inf)* achterlijk, idioot

cucumber [kjoe:kumbə] komkommer

cud [kud] herkauwmassa *(from rumen):* *chew the ~* herkauwen, *(fig)* prakkeseren, tobben

¹**cuddle** [kudl] *vb* knuffelen, liefkozen

²**cuddle** [kudl] *vb* dicht tegen elkaar aan (genesteld) liggen: *~ up* dicht tegen elkaar aankruipen; *~ up to s.o.* dicht bij iem nestelen

cuddly [kudlie] snoezig, aanhalig: *a ~ toy* een knuffelbeest

cue [kjoe:] **1** aansporing, wenk, hint; **2** richtsnoer^h, voorbeeld^h, leidraad: *take one's ~ from* een voorbeeld nemen aan; **3** (biljart)keu

¹**cuff** [kuf] *n* **1** manchet; **2** *(Am)* (broek)omslag^h; **3**

klap *(with a flat hand)*, draai om de oren, pets ‖
(inf) off the ~ voor de vuist (weg)
²**cuff** [kuf] *vb* een draai om de oren geven
cuff link manchetknoop
cul-de-sac [kul də sæk] **1** doodlopende straat; **2**
dood punt^h
¹**cull** [kul] *vb* **1** plukken *(flowers etc)*; **2** verzamelen,
vergaren; **3** selecteren, uitkammen, uitziften: ~
from selecteren uit
²**cull** [kul] *n* selectie
culminate [kulminneet] culmineren, zijn hoogtepunt bereiken
culpable [kulpəbl] **1** afkeurenswaardig, verwerpelijk; **2** verwijtbaar: ~ *homicide* dood door schuld; **3**
aansprakelijk, schuldig
culprit [kulprit] **1** beklaagde, verdachte, beschuldigde; **2** schuldige, dader, boosdoener
cult [kult] **1** cultus, eredienst, *(depr)* ziekelijke verering, rage; **2** sekte, kliek
cultivate [kultivveet] **1** cultiveren, aanbouwen, bebouwen, ontginnen; **2** kweken *(eg bacteria)*; **3** voor
zich proberen te winnen, vleien
cultivation [kultivveesjən] **1** *(agriculture)* cultuur,
ontginning, verbouw: *under* ~ in cultuur; **2** be-
schaafdheid, welgemanierdheid
cultural [kultsjərəl] cultureel, cultuur-
culture [kultsjə] **1** cultuur, beschaving(stoestand),
ontwikkeling(sniveau^h); **2** (bacterie)kweek; **3** algemene ontwikkeling; **4** kweek, cultuur, teelt
cum [kum] met, plus, inclusief, annex, zowel als, tevens: *bed-cum-sitting room* zit-slaapkamer
cumbersome [kumbəsəm] **1** onhandelbaar, log,
(p)lomp; **2** hinderlijk, lastig, zwaar
cumulus [kjoe:mjoeləs] stapelwolk
¹**cunning** [kunning] *adj* sluw, listig, slim
²**cunning** [kunning] *n* sluwheid, listigheid, slimheid
cunt [kunt] *(vulg)* kut
cup [kup] **1** kop(je^h), mok, beker; **2** *(sport)* (wissel)beker, cup, bokaal ‖ *between* ~ *and lip* op de valreep; *my* ~ *of tea* (echt) iets voor mij
cupboard [kubbəd] kast
cup final *(sport)* bekerfinale
cup-tie *(sport)* bekerwedstrijd
curable [kjoeərəbl] geneesbaar
curate [kjoeərət] hulppredikant, *(Roman
Catholicism)* kapelaan
curator [kjoereetə] beheerder, curator, conservator
¹**curb** [kə:b] *n* rem, beteugeling
²**curb** [kə:b] *vb* intomen *(also fig)*, beteugelen, in bedwang houden
curdle [kə:dl] stremmen, (doen) stollen: *her blood
~d at the spectacle* het schouwspel deed haar bloed
stollen
¹**cure** [kjoeə] *vb* genezen, beter maken, (doen) herstellen: ~ *oneself of bad habits* zijn slechte gewoonten afleren
²**cure** [kjoeə] *vb* **1** kuren, een kuur doen; **2** een heilzame werking hebben; **3** verduurzaamd worden,
roken, drogen

³**cure** [kjoeə] *vb* verduurzamen, conserveren, zou-
ten, roken *(fish, meat)*, drogen *(tobacco)*
⁴**cure** [kjoeə] *n* **1** (medische) behandeling, kuur; **2**
(genees)middel^h, medicament^h, remedie *(also fig)*;
3 genezing, herstel^h
curfew [kə:fjoe:] **1** avondklok, uitgaansverbod^h; **2**
spertijd
curiosity [kjoeərie·ossittie] **1** curiositeit, rariteit; **2**
nieuwsgierigheid, benieuwdheid; **3** leergierigheid
curious [kjoeəriəs] **1** nieuwsgierig, benieuwd; **2**
leergierig; **3** curieus, merkwaardig: ~*ly (enough)*
merkwaardigerwijs, vreemd genoeg
¹**curl** [kə:l] *vb* **1** spiralen, zich winden *(of plant)*; **2**
(om)krullen
²**curl** [kə:l] *vb* krullen *(of hair)*, in de krul zetten,
kroezen
³**curl** [kə:l] *vb* **1** met krullen versieren; **2** doen
(om)krullen; **3** kronkelen om, winden om
⁴**curl** [kə:l] *n* **1** (haar)krul, pijpenkrul; **2** krul, spiraal;
3 (het) krul(len), krulling
curler [kə:lə] krulspeld, roller, kruller
curl up 1 *(inf)* (doen) ineenkrimpen *(in horror, of
shame, with joy etc)*; **2** omkrullen; **3** *(inf)* neergaan,
neerhalen, in elkaar (doen) klappen, tegen de vlakte (doen) gaan; **4** zich (behaaglijk) oprollen, in elkaar kruipen
currant [kurrənt] **1** krent; **2** aalbes: *red* ~ rode bes
currency [kurrənsie] **1** valuta, munt, (papier)geld^h:
foreign currencies vreemde valuta's; **2** munt-, geld-
stelsel^h; **3** (geld)circulatie, (geld)omloop; **4** gang-
baarheid: *gain* ~ ingang vinden, zich verspreiden
¹**current** [kurrənt] *adj* **1** huidig, actueel; **2** gangbaar,
geldend, heersend; **3** *(fin)* in omloop
²**current** [kurrənt] *n* **1** stroom, stroming *(in gas, liquid)*; **2** loop, gang, tendens; **3** (elektrische) stroom:
alternate ~ wisselstroom; *direct* ~ gelijkstroom
current account rekening-courant, (bank)girore-
kening, lopende rekening
currently momenteel, tegenwoordig
curriculum [kərikjoeləm] onderwijsprogramma^h,
leerplan^h
curry [kurrie] kerrie(poeder^h)
¹**curse** [kə:s] *vb* (uit)vloeken, vloeken (op),
(uit)schelden
²**curse** [kə:s] *vb* **1** vervloeken, verwensen, een vloek
uitspreken over: *(inf)* ~ *it!* (of: *you!*) verdraaid!;
(esp passive) straffen, bezoeken, kwellen: *be ~d
with* gebukt gaan onder
³**curse** [kə:s] *n* **1** vloek(woord^h), verwensing, doem:
lay s.o. under a ~ een vloek op iem leggen; **2** bezoeking, ramp, plaag
cursive [kə:siv] aaneengeschreven
cursory [kə:sərie] vluchtig, oppervlakkig
curt [kə:t] kortaf, kortaangebonden: *a* ~ *manner*
een botte manier van doen
curtail [kə:teel] **1** inkorten, bekorten, verkorten; **2**
verkleinen, verminderen; beperken
¹**curtain** [kə:tən] *n* **1** gordijn^h, voorhang(sel^h), *(fig)*
barrière: ~ *of smoke* rookgordijn; **2** *(theatre)* doek^h,

(toneel)gordijn^h, scherm^h

²curtain [kə:tən] *vb* voorzien van gordijn: ~ *off* afschermen *(by means of a curtain)*

curts(e)y [kə:tsie] revérence, korte buiging

¹curve [kə:v] *n* 1 gebogen lijn, kromme, curve, boog; 2 bocht *(in road)*; 3 ronding, welving *(of woman)*

²curve [kə:v] *vb* buigen, een bocht (doen) maken, (zich) krommen

¹cushion [koesjən] *n* 1 kussen^h; (lucht)kussen^h; 2 stootkussen^h, buffer, schokdemper; 3 *(billiards)* band

²cushion [koesjən] *vb* 1 voorzien van kussen(s); 2 dempen, verzachten, opvangen *(bang, shock, effect)*; 3 in de watten leggen, beschermen: *a ~ed life* een beschermd leventje

cushy [koesjie] *(inf)* makkelijk, comfortabel: *a ~ job* een luizenbaantje, een makkie

custodian [kustoodiən] 1 beheerder, conservator, bewaarder; 2 voogd; 3 *(Am)* conciërge, beheerder

custody [kustədie] 1 voogdij, zorg; 2 beheer^h, hoede, bewaring; 3 hechtenis, voorarrest^h, verzekerde bewaring: *take s.o. into ~* iem aanhouden

custom [kustəm] 1 gewoonte, gebruik^h; 2 klandizie; 3 ~s douaneheffing, invoerrechten; 4 ~s douane(dienst)

customary [kustəmərie] 1 gebruikelijk, gewoonlijk, normaal; 2 gewoonte-, gebruik(s)-

custom-built op bestelling gebouwd, gebouwd (gemaakt) volgens de wensen vd koper

customer [kustəmə] 1 klant, (regelmatige) afnemer; 2 *(inf)* klant, gast: *awkward ~* rare snijboon, vreemde vogel; *he is a tough ~* het is een taaie

¹cut [kut] *vb* 1 snijden, kruisen; 2 *(cards)* couperen, afnemen; 3 *(inf)* verzuimen, spijbelen, overslaan

²cut [kut] *vb* 1 snijden in, verwonden, stuksnijden: ~ *one's finger* zich in zijn vinger snijden; 2 (af-, door-, los-, weg)snijden, (af)knippen, (om)hakken, (om)kappen, (om)zagen: ~ *open* openhalen; ~ *away* wegsnijden, weghakken, wegknippen, snoeien; ~ *in half* doormidden snijden, knippen; 3 maken met scherp voorwerp, kerven, slijpen, bijsnijden, bijknippen, bijhakken, boren, graveren, opnemen, maken *(CD, record)*: ~ *one's initials into sth.* zijn initialen ergens in kerven; 4 maaien, oogsten, binnenhalen *(crop)*; 5 inkorten, snijden (in) *(book, film etc)*, afsnijden *(route, corner)*, besnoeien (op), inkrimpen, bezuinigen: ~ *the travelling time by a third* de reistijd tot tweederde terugbrengen; 6 stopzetten, ophouden met, afsluiten, afsnijden *(water, energy)*, uitschakelen, afzetten; 7 krijgen *(tooth)*: *I'm ~ting my wisdom tooth* mijn verstandskies komt door; 8 (diep) raken, pijn doen *(of remark etc)*; 9 negeren, veronachtzamen, links laten liggen: ~ *s.o. dead* (of: *cold*) iem niet zien staan, iem straal negeren

³cut [kut] *vb* 1 (zich laten) snijden, knippen: *the butter ~s easily* de boter snijdt gemakkelijk; 2 een inkeping (scheiding) maken, snijden, knippen, hakken, kappen, kerven, maaien: ~ *and run* de benen ne-

men, 'm smeren; ~ *both ways: a)* tweesnijdend zijn; *b)* voor- en nadelen hebben

⁴cut *n* 1 slag (snee) met scherp voorwerp, (mes)sne(d)e, snijwond, houw, (zweep)slag; 2 afgesneden, afgehakt, afgeknipt stuk^h, lap, bout *(meat)*; 3 (haar)knipbeurt; 4 vermindering, verlaging; 5 coupure, weglating, verkorting; 6 snit, coupe; 7 doorsnijding, geul, kloof, kanaal^h, doorgraving, kortere weg: *take a short* ~ een kortere weg nemen; 8 *(inf)* (aan)deel^h, provisie, commissie; 9 *(film)* scherpe overgang: ~ *and thrust* (woorden)steekspel, vinnig debat; *(inf) be a ~ above* beter zijn dan

cut across 1 afsnijden, doorsteken, een kortere weg nemen; 2 strijdig zijn met, ingaan tegen; 3 doorbreken, uitstijgen boven: ~ *traditional party loyalties* de aloude partijbindingen doorbreken

¹cut back *vb* inkrimpen, besnoeien, bezuinigen

²cut back *vb* snoeien *(plants)*

¹cut down *vb* 1 kappen, omhakken, omhouwen, vellen; 2 inperken, beperken, verminderen: ~ *one's expenses* zijn bestedingen beperken; 3 inkorten, korter maken: ~ *an article* een artikel inkorten

²cut down *vb* minderen: *you work too much, try to ~ a bit* je werkt te veel, probeer wat te minderen

cut down on minderen met, het verbruik beperken van: ~ *smoking* minder gaan roken

cute [kjoe:t] schattig, snoezig, leuk

cuticle [kjoe:tikl] 1 opperhuid; 2 nagelriem

cutie [kjoe:tie] leuk iemand, mooie meid (jongen)

cut in 1 er(gens) tussen komen, in de rede vallen, onderbreken; 2 gevaarlijk invoegen *(with a vehicle)*, snijden

cut into 1 aansnijden: ~ *a cake* een taart aansnijden; 2 onderbreken, tussenbeide komen, in de rede vallen: ~ *a conversation* zich (plotseling) mengen in een gesprek; 3 storend werken op, een aanslag doen op: *this job cuts into my evenings off* deze baan kost me een groot deel van mijn vrije avonden

cutlery [kutlərie] bestek^h, eetgerei^h, couvert^h

cutlet [kutlit] *(culinary)* lapje vlees^h, (lams)koteletje^h, kalfskoteletje^h

cut off 1 afsnijden, afhakken, afknippen; 2 afsluiten, stopzetten, blokkeren; 3 (van de buitenwereld) afsluiten, isoleren: *villages ~ by floods* door overstromingen geïsoleerde dorpen; 4 onderbreken, verbreken *(telephone connection)*

cut-off scheiding, grens, afsluiting: ~ *date* sluitingsdatum

¹cut out *vb* 1 uitsnijden, uitknippen, uithakken, modelleren, vormen; 2 knippen *(dress, pattern)*: *cut it out!* hou ermee op!; 3 *(inf)* weglaten, verwijderen, schrappen; 4 uitschakelen, elimineren, *(inf)* het nakijken geven; 5 uitschakelen, afzetten: *(inf) be ~ for* geknipt zijn voor

²cut out *vb* 1 uitvallen, defect raken, het begeven: *the engine ~* de motor sloeg af; 2 afslaan: *the boiler cuts out at 90 degrees* de boiler slaat af bij 90 graden

cut-out 1 uitgeknipte, uitgesneden, uitgehakte fi-

guur⁺ʰ, knipselʰ; **2** *(techn)* afslag, (stroom)onder-
breker: *automatic* ~ automatische afslag, thermostaat

cutter [kʌttə] **1** iem die snijdt; goedkoper, gebruiker van scherp voorwerp, knipper, snijder, hakker,
houwer, slijper; **2** snijwerktuigʰ, snijmachine,
schaar, tang, mesʰ, *(in butcher's shop)* cutter; **3**
sloep (van oorlogsschipʰ); **4** (motor)barkasʰ *(for
transport between ship and coast);* **5** kotter; **6** kustwachter, kustbewakingsschipʰ; **7** *(film)* filmmon-
teerder

cut through zich worstelen door, doorbreken, zich
heen werken door

¹cutting [kʌtting] *n* **1** (afgesneden, afgeknipt, uitge-
knipt) stuk(je)ʰ; **2** stek *(of plant);* **3** (kranten)knip-
selʰ

²cutting [kʌtting] *adj* **1** scherp, bijtend: ~ *remark*
grievende opmerking; **2** bijtend, snijdend, guur *(of
wind)*

¹cut up *vb* **1** (in stukken) snijden, knippen; **2** in de
pan hakken, (vernietigend) verslaan; **3** *(inf)* niets
heel laten van, afkraken; **4** *(inf)* (ernstig) aangrijpen: *be* ~ *about sth.* zich iets vreselijk aantrekken,
ergens ondersteboven van zijn

²cut up *vb* zich (in stukken) laten snijden, knippen ||
(inf) ~ *rough* tekeergaan

cyclamen [sikləmən] cyclaam

¹cycle [sajkl] *n* **1** cyclus; **2** kringloop, *(fig also)* spiraal; **3** *(electr)* trilling, trilling per seconde, hertz; **4**
bicycle fiets

²cycle [sajkl] *vb* **1** cirkelen, ronddraaien, kringen beschrijven; **2** fietsen

cyclist [sajklist] fietser, wielrenner

cyclone [sajkloon] cycloon, wervelstorm, tyfoon,
tornado

cyder [sajdə] *see* cider

cygnet [signit] jonge zwaan

cylinder [sillində] **1** cilinder; **2** magazijnʰ *(of revolver),* rol, wals, trommel, buis, pijp, (gas)fles

cynical [sinnikl] cynisch

cynicism [sinnissizm] cynisme, cynische uitlating

czar [za:] tsaar, *(Am; inf)* koning

d

d. *died* gest., gestorven

¹dab [dæb] *n* 1 tik(je[h]), klopje[h]; 2 lik(je[h]), kwast(je[h]), hoopje[h]: *a ~ of paint* een likje verf; 3 veegje[h]: *a ~ with a sponge* (even) een sponsje eroverheen; 4 kei, kraan: *he is a ~ (hand) at squash* hij kan ontzettend goed squashen; 5 *~s* vingerafdrukken

²dab [dæb] *vb* 1 (aan)tikken, (be)kloppen; 2 betten, deppen

³dab [dæb] *vb* opbrengen *(paint):* ~ *on* (zachtjes) aanbrengen

dabble [dæbl] 1 plassen, ploeteren; 2 liefhebberen: ~ *at* (of: *in) arts* (wat) rommelen in de kunst; 3 (in water) rondscharrelen *(across bottom)*

dabbler [dæblə] liefhebber, amateur

dachshund [dæksənd] teckel, taks, dashond

daddy [dædie] papa, pappie

daddy longlegs [dædie lɔnglegz] langpoot(mug); *(Am)* hooiwagen(achtige), langbeen

daffodil [dæfədil] (gele) narcis

daft [da:ft] 1 halfgaar, niet goed snik; 2 idioot, belachelijk, maf

dagger [dægə] dolk || *at ~s drawn with s.o.* op voet van oorlog met iem

¹daily [deelie] *adj* 1 dagelijks: ~ *newspaper* dagblad; 2 geregeld, vaak, constant: *the ~ grind* de dagelijkse sleur

²daily [deelie] *adv* dagelijks, per dag

³daily [deelie] *n* 1 dagblad[h], krant; 2 werkster, schoonmaakster

dainty [deentie] 1 sierlijk, verfijnd; 2 teer, gevoelig; 3 kostelijk, verrukkelijk; 4 kieskeurig, veeleisend

dairy [deərie] 1 zuivelbedrijf[h], zuivelproducent; 2 melkboer, melkman; 3 melkvee(stapel)[h]

dais [deeis] podium[h], verhoging

daisy [deezie] 1 madelief(je[h]); 2 margriet, grote madelief || *be pushing up the daisies* onder de groene zoden liggen

dally [dælie] 1 lanterfanten, (rond)lummelen, klungelen; 2 treuzelen || ~ *with: a)* flirten met; *b)* spelen *(of:* stoeien) met *(an idea)*

¹dam [dæm] *n* 1 (stuw)dam; 2 barrière, belemmering, hinderpaal; 3 moederdier[h] *(quadruped)*

²dam [dæm] *vb* 1 van een dam voorzien, afdammen; 2 indammen, beteugelen

¹damage [dæmidzj] *n* 1 schade, beschadiging, averij; 2 ~*s* schadevergoeding, schadeloosstelling: *we will claim ~ from them* we zullen schadevergoeding van hen eisen

²damage [dæmidzj] *vb* beschadigen, schade toebrengen, aantasten

¹damn [dæm] *vb* 1 *(inf)* vervloeken, verwensen: *I'll be ~ed if I go* ik vertik het (mooi) om te gaan; 2 te gronde richten, ruïneren; 3 (af)kraken, afbreken: *the play was ~ed by the critics* het stuk werd door de recensenten de grond in geboord; 4 vloeken (tegen), uitvloeken

²damn [dæm] *n (vulg)* zak, (malle)moer: *not be worth a (tuppenny)* ~ geen ene moer waard zijn; *not give a* ~ het geen (ene) moer kunnen schelen

³damn [dæm] *adj* godvergeten: *a ~ fool* een stomme idioot

damning [dæming] belastend, (ernstig) bezwarend, vernietigend

¹damp [dæmp] *adj* vochtig, nattig, klam || ~ *squib* sof, fiasco

²damp [dæmp] *n* 1 vocht[h], vochtigheid; 2 nevel, damp

³damp [dæmp] *vb* 1 bevochtigen; 2 smoren, doven, temperen: ~ *down* afdekken; 3 temperen, doen bekoelen: ~ *down s.o.'s enthusiasm* iemands enthousiasme temperen

dampen [dæmpən] 1 bevochtigen; 2 temperen, ontmoedigen

damper [dæmpə] 1 sleutel *(of stove),* regelschuif, demper; 2 schokdemper, schokbreker; 3 (trillings)demper; 4 domper, teleurstelling

¹dance [da:ns] *vb* 1 (doen, laten) dansen, springen, (staan te) trappelen: *the leaves were dancing in the wind* de blaren dwarrelden in de wind; *her eyes ~d for* (of: *with) joy* haar ogen tintelden van vreugde; ~ *a baby on one's knee* een kindje op zijn knie laten rijden

²dance [da:ns] *n* 1 dans, dansnummer[h]; 2 dansfeest[h], bal[h], dansavond || *lead s.o. a pretty* ~ iem het leven zuur maken

dancer [da:nsə] danser(es), ballerina

dandelion [dændillajjən] paardenbloem

dandle [dændl] wiege(le)n *(child),* laten dansen: ~ *a baby on one's knee* een kindje op zijn knie laten rijden

dandruff [dændruf] (hoofd)roos

¹dandy [dændie] *n* 1 fat, dandy, modegek; 2 juweel(tje)[h], prachtstuk[h], prachtfiguur[h]

²dandy [dændie] *adj* 1 fatterig, dandyachtig; 2 *(Am)* tiptop, puik, prima

Dane [deen] Deen

danger [deendzjə] gevaar[h], risico[h]: *be in ~ of* het gevaar lopen te; *out of* ~ buiten (levens)gevaar

dangerous [deendzjərəs] gevaarlijk, riskant

¹dangle [dænggl] *vb* bengelen, bungelen, slingeren

²dangle [dænggl] *vb* laten bengelen, slingeren: *(fig)* ~ *sth. before* (of: *in front of) s.o.* iem met iets trachten te paaien

¹Danish [deenisj] *adj* Deens

²Danish [deenisj] *n* Deens[h]

dank [dængk] klam

Danube [dænjoe:b] Donau

dapper [dæpə] **1** keurig, netjes, goed verzorgd; **2** zwierig

dapple [dæpl] (be)spikkelen, met vlekken bedekken

¹**dare** [deə] *vb* (aan)durven, het wagen, het lef hebben te: *he does not ~ to answer back, he ~ not answer back* hij durft niet tegen te spreken; *how ~ (you say such things)?* hoe durf je zoiets te zeggen?; *I ~ say* ik veronderstel, ik neem aan, misschien

²**dare** [deə] *vb* uitdagen, tarten: *she ~d Bill to hit her* ze daagde Bill uit haar te slaan

³**dare** [deə] *n* **1** uitdaging: *do sth. for a ~* iets doen omdat men wordt uitgedaagd; **2** gedurfde handeling, moedige daad

daredevil waaghals, durfal

¹**daring** [deəring] *adj* **1** brutaal, moedig, gedurfd; **2** gewaagd

²**daring** [deəring] *n* **1** moed, durf, lefʰ; **2** gedurfdheid

¹**dark** [da:k] *adj* **1** donker, duister, onverlicht: *~ brown* donkerbruin; **2** somber: *the ~ side of things* de schaduwzijde der dingen; **3** verborgen, geheimzinnig; **4** donker, laag en vol *(of voice)*: *~ horse: a)* outsider *(in race); b)* onbekende mededinger *(at elections)*

²**dark** [da:k] *n* **1** donkere kleur; **2** donkere plaats; **3** duisterⁿ, duisternis: *in the ~* in het donker, *(fig)* in het geniep; **4** vallen vd avond: *after ~* na het donker; *keep s.o. in the ~ about sth.* iem ergens niets over laten weten; *be in the ~ (about sth.)* in het duister tasten (omtrent iets)

darkness [da:knəs] duisternis, verdorvenheid: *powers of ~* kwade machten

¹**darling** [da:ling] *n* schat(jeʰ), lieveling

²**darling** [da:ling] *adj* geliefd, (aller)lief(st)

¹**darn** [da:n] *vb* stoppen, mazen

²**darn** [da:n] *n* stop, gestopt gatʰ, stopselʰ

³**darn** *vb* (ver)vloeken, verwensen

darned [da:nd] *(inf)* verdraaid, vervloekt

¹**dart** [da:t] *n* **1** pijl(tjeʰ); **2** (plotselinge, scherpe) uitval *(also fig)*, steek, sprong: *make a ~ for the door* naar de deur springen

²**dart** [da:t] *vb* (toe-, weg)snellen, (toe-, weg)schieten, (toe-, weg)stuiven

darts [da:ts] dartsʰ, vogelpik

¹**dash** [dæsj] *vb* **1** (vooruit)stormen, (zich) storten, denderen: *I'm afraid I must ~ now* en nu moet ik er als de bliksem vandoor; *~ away* wegstormen; *~ off* er (als de gesmeerde bliksem) vandoor gaan; **2** (rond)banjeren, (met veel vertoon) rondspringen: *~ about* rondbanjeren

²**dash** [dæsj] *vb* (met grote kracht) slaan, smijten, beuken: *~ down* neersmijten; *the waves ~ed against the rocks* de golven beukten tegen de rotsen

³**dash** [dæsj] *vb* **1** verbrijzelen; verpletteren, *(fig)* verijdelen: *all my expectations were ~ed* al mijn verwachtingen werden de bodem ingeslagen; **2** snel doen: *~ sth. down* (of: *off*) iets nog even gauw op-

schrijven; **3** vervloeken, verwensen: *(inf)* ~ *it (all)!* verdraaid!; **4** doorspekken, larderen

⁴**dash** [dæsj] *n* **1** ietsjeʰ, tik(kelt)jeʰ, scheutjeʰ: *~ of brandy* scheutje cognac; **2** (snelle, krachtige) slag, dreun; **3** spurt, sprint, uitval; **4** streep *(in Morse code)*: *dots and ~es* punten en strepen; **5** kastlijn, gedachtestreep(jeʰ)

dashboard dashboardʰ

dashed [dæsjt] verdraaid, verduiveld

dashing [dæsjing] **1** levendig, wilskrachtig, vlot; **2** opzichtig

database database

¹**date** [deet] *n* **1** dadel; **2** datum, dagtekening; **3** afspraak(jeʰ); **4** *(Am)* vriend(innet)jeʰ, partner, 'afspraakjeʰ'; **5** tijd(perkʰ), periode: *of early ~, of an early ~* uit een vroege periode; *out of ~* verouderd, ouderwets; *to ~* tot op heden; *up to ~: a)* bij (de tijd), modern, geavanceerd; *b)* volledig bijgewerkt; *bring up to ~* bijwerken, moderniseren

²**date** [deet] *vb* **1** verouderen, uit de tijd raken; **2** dateren: *~ back to* stammen uit; **3** *(Am)* afspraakjes hebben, uitgaan

³**date** [deet] *vb* **1** dateren, dagtekenen; **2** dateren, de ouderdom vaststellen van: *~ a painting* een schilderij dateren; **3** uitgaan met, afspraakjes hebben met, vrijen met

dated [deetid] ouderwets, gedateerd, verouderd

dative [deetiv] derde naamval

datum [deetəm] *(data)* **1** feitʰ, gegevenʰ; **2** nulpuntʰ *(of scale etc)*, (gemiddeld laag)waterpeilʰ; **3** *data* gegevens, data, informatie: *insufficient data* onvoldoende gegevens; *the data is* (of: *are*) *being prepared for processing* de informatie wordt gereedgemaakt voor verwerking

¹**daub** [do:b] *vb* besmeren, bekladden, besmeuren

²**daub** [do:b] *n* **1** lik, klodder, smeerʰ; **2** kladschilderij, kladderwerkʰ; **3** (muur)pleister, pleisterkalk

daughter [do:tə] dochter

daughter-in-law schoondochter

daunt [do:nt] ontmoedigen, intimideren, afschrikken: *a ~ing prospect* een afschrikwekkend vooruitzicht

dauntless [do:ntləs] **1** onbevreesd; **2** volhardend, vasthoudend

dawdle [do:dl] treuzelen, teuten || *~ over one's food* met lange tanden eten

¹**dawn** [do:n] *n* dageraad *(also fig)*, zonsopgang: *the ~ of civilization* de ochtendstond der beschaving; *at ~* bij het krieken van de dag

²**dawn** [do:n] *vb* dagen *(also fig)*, licht worden, aanbreken, duidelijk worden: *it ~ed on me* het drong tot me door

day [dee] **1** dag, etmaalʰ: *this ~ fortnight* vandaag over veertien dagen; *~ and night, night and ~* dag en nacht; *the ~ after tomorrow* overmorgen; *from ~ one* meteen, vanaf de eerste dag; *~ in, ~ out* dag in, dag uit; *~ after ~* dag in, dag uit; *~ by ~, from ~ to ~* dagelijks, van dag tot dag; **2** werkdag: *an 8-hour ~* een achturige werkdag; *~ off* vrije dag; **3** *(in com-*

pounds) (hoogtij)dag; **4** tijdstip[h], gelegenheid: *some* ~: *a)* eens, eenmaal, op een keer; *b)* bij gelegenheid; **5** dag, daglicht[h]: *(form) by* ~ overdag; **6** tijd, periode, dag(en): *(in)* ~*s of old* (of: *yore)* (in) vroeger tijden; *he has had his* ~ hij heeft zijn tijd gehad; *those were the* ~*s* dat waren nog eens tijden; *these* ~*s* tegenwoordig, vandaag de dag; *(in) this* ~ *and age* vandaag de dag; **7** slag, strijd: *carry* (of: *save, win) the* ~ de slag winnen; **8** ~*s* levensdagen, leven[h]: *that will be the* ~ dat wil ik zien; *all in a* ~*'s work* de normale gang van zaken; *call it a* ~: *a)* het voor gezien houden; *b)* sterven; *make s.o.'s* ~ iemands dag goedmaken; *one of those* ~*s* zo'n dag waarop alles tegenzit; *to the* ~ op de dag af; *to this* ~ tot op de dag van vandaag, tot op heden; *from one* ~ *to the next* van vandaag op morgen; *(inf) every other* ~ om de haverklap; *the other* ~ onlangs, pas geleden; *she is thirty if she is a* ~ ze is op zijn minst dertig

daybreak dageraad, zonsopgang

day-care dagopvang, kinderopvang: ~ *centre* crèche, kinderdagverblijf

[1]**daze** [deez] *vb* verbijsteren, verbluffen

[2]**daze** [deez] *n* verbijstering: *in a* ~ verbluft, ontsteld

[1]**dazzle** [dæzl] *vb* **1** verblinden; **2** verbijsteren

[2]**dazzle** [dæzl] *vb* imponeren, indruk maken (op)

D.C. *direct current* gelijkstroom

D-day [die:dee] *Decision day* D-day, Dag D, kritische begindag

[1]**dead** [ded] *adj* **1** dood, overleden, gestorven: *over my* ~ *body* over mijn lijk; *rise from the* ~ uit de dood opstaan; **2** verouderd; **3** onwerkzaam, leeg, uit, op: ~ *battery* lege accu; *cut out (the)* ~ *wood* verwijderen van overbodige franje; ~ *and gone* dood (en begraven), *(fig)* voorgoed voorbij; **4** uitgestorven: *the place is* ~ het is er een dooie boel; **5** gevoelloos, ongevoelig; **6** *(sport)* uit (het spel) *(of ball);* **7** volkomen, absoluut: ~ *certainty* absolute zekerheid; ~ *loss: a)* puur verlies; *b)* tijdverspilling; *c) (inf)* miskleun, fiasco; **8** abrupt, plotseling: *come to a* ~ *stop* (plotseling) stokstijf stil (blijven) staan; **9** exact, precies: ~ *centre* precieze midden; ~ *as a doornail* morsdood; ~ *duck* mislukk(el)ing, verliezer; ~ *end: a)* doodlopende straat; *b)* impasse, dood punt; *come to a* ~ *end* op niets uitlopen; *(sport)* ~ *heat* gedeelde eerste (tweede enz.) plaats; *flog a* ~ *horse* achter de feiten aanlopen; ~ *letter: a)* dode letter *(of law); b)* onbestelbare brief; *wait for a* ~ *man's shoes* op iemands bezit azen; *make a* ~ *set at: a)* te lijf gaan *(fig); b)* (vastberaden) avances maken; ~ *to the world: a)* in diepe slaap; *b)* bewusteloos; *I wouldn't be seen* ~ *in that dress* voor geen goud zou ik me in die jurk vertonen

[2]**dead** [ded] *adv* **1** volkomen, absoluut: ~ *straight* kaarsrecht; *stop* ~ stokstijf blijven staan; ~ *tired* (of: *exhausted)* doodop, bekaf; **2** pal, onmiddellijk: ~ *ahead of you* pal voor je; ~ *against: a)* pal tegen *(of wind); b)* fel tegen *(plan etc)*

[3]**dead** [ded] *n* hoogte-, dieptepunt[h]: *in the* (of: *at)* ~

of night in het holst van de nacht

deadbeat nietsnut

dead beat doodop, bekaf

[1]**deaden** [dedn] *vb* **1** verzwakken, dempen *(sound),* verzachten, dof maken *(colour);* **2** ongevoelig maken, verdoven: *drugs to* ~ *the pain* medicijnen om de pijn te stillen

[2]**deaden** [dedn] *vb* de kracht, helderheid verliezen, verflauwen, verzwakken

dead-end 1 doodlopend; **2** uitzichtloos

deadline (tijds)limiet, uiterste (in)leverdatum: *meet the* ~ binnen de tijdslimiet blijven; *miss the* ~ de tijdslimiet overschrijden

deadlock patstelling

deadly [dedlie] **1** dodelijk *(also fig),* fataal; **2** *(depr)* doods, dodelijk (saai); **3** doods-, aarts-; **4** *(inf)* enorm; **5** oer-, uiterst: ~ *dull* oersaai; *the seven* ~ *sins* de zeven hoofdzonden

deaf [def] doof *(also fig)* || *as* ~ *as a (door)post* stokdoof; *fall on* ~ *ears* geen gehoor vinden; *turn a* ~ *ear to* doof zijn voor

deaf-aid (ge)hoorapparaat[h]

deafen [defːn] verdoven, doof maken, overstemmen

[1]**deal** [die:l] *n* **1** transactie, overeenkomst, handel; **2** (grote) hoeveelheid, mate: *a great* ~ *of money* heel wat geld; **3** *(depr)* (koe)handeltje[h], deal; **4** *(cards)* gift, het geven, beurt om te geven: *it's your* ~ jij moet geven; *it's a* ~! afgesproken!, akkoord!

[2]**deal** [die:l] *vb* zaken doen, handelen

[3]**deal** [die:l] *vb* geven, (uit)delen: ~ *(out) fairly* eerlijk verdelen

dealer [die:lɔ] **1** handelaar, koopman, dealer; **2** effectenhandelaar

dealing [die:ling] **1** manier van zaken doen, aanpak; **2** ~*s* transacties, affaires, relaties *(business);* **3** ~*s* betrekkingen, omgang

deal with 1 zaken doen met, handel drijven met, kopen bij; **2** behandelen, afhandelen: ~ *complaints* klachten behandelen; **3** aanpakken, een oplossing zoeken voor; **4** optreden tegen; **5** behandelen, omgaan met: *be impossible to* ~ onmogelijk in de omgang zijn; **6** gaan over: *the book deals with racism* het boek gaat over racisme

dean [die:n] **1** deken; **2** oudste, overste; **3** *(university)* decaan, faculteitsvoorzitter; (studenten)decaan

[1]**dear** [diɔ] *adj* **1** dierbaar, lief; **2** lief, schattig; **3** duur, prijzig; **4** beste, lieve, geachte *(eg in salutation):* ~ *Julia* beste Julia; *my* ~ *lady* mevrouw; ~ *sir* geachte heer; ~ *sirs* mijne heren, geachte heren; **5** dierbaar, lief: *I hold her very* ~ ze ligt me na aan het hart; *for* ~ *life* of zijn leven ervan afhangt

[2]**dear** [diɔ] *n* schat, lieverd

[3]**dear** [diɔ] *adv* **1** duur (betaald) *(also fig);* **2** innig, vurig

dearest [diɔrist] liefste

dearly [diɔlie] **1** innig, vurig: *wish* ~ vurig wensen; **2** duur(betaald) *(also fig): pay* ~ *for sth.* iets duur betalen; **3** vurig

dearth [dɔ:θ] schaarste, tekort[h]: *a ~ of talent* te weinig talent

death [deθ] **1** sterfgeval[h], slachtoffer[h]; **2** dood, overlijden[h], *(fig)* einde[h]: *(fig) be in at the ~* een onderneming zien stranden; *be the ~ of s.o.* iemands dood zijn *(also fig); bore s.o. to ~* iem stierlijk vervelen; *war to the ~* oorlog op leven en dood; **3** de Dood, magere Hein: *at ~'s door* op sterven, de dood nabij; *dice with ~* met vuur spelen; *flog to ~* uitentreuren herhalen; *worked to ~* afgezaagd, uitgemolken

death duty successierecht[h]

deathly [deθllie] doods, lijk-: *~ pale* doodsbleek

debase [dibbees] **1** degraderen; **2** vervalsen; **3** verlagen, vernederen

¹**debate** [dibbeet] *vb* **1** *(with about, upon)* debatteren (over), discussiëren, een debat houden; **2** beraadslagen

²**debate** [dibbeet] *vb* bespreken, beraadslagen over, in debat treden over

³**debate** [dibbeet] *n* **1** *(with on, about)* debat[h] (over), discussie, dispuut[h]; **2** twist, conflict[h], strijd; **3** overweging, beraad[h]

¹**debit** [debbit] *n* **1** schuldpost, debitering, debetboeking; **2** debetsaldo[h]

²**debit** [debbit] *vb* debiteren, als debet boeken

debris [debrie:] puin[h], brokstukken

debt [det] schuld, (terugbetalings)verplichting: *owe s.o. a ~ of gratitude* iem dank verschuldigd zijn; *get* (of: *run) into ~* schulden maken

debtor [detta] **1** schuldenaar; **2** debiteur

debug [die:bug] **1** *(roughly)* ontluizen, van insecten ontdoen; **2** *(van mankementen)* zuiveren, kinderziekten verhelpen bij; **3** *(van fouten)* zuiveren, debuggen

debut [debjoe:] debuut[h]

decade [dekkeed] decennium[h], periode van tien jaar

decadence [dekkadans] decadentie, verval[h] *(in art)*

decadent [dekkadant] decadent, genotzuchtig

decaf [die:kæf] *decaffeinated coffee* cafeïnevrij(e koffie)

decapitate [dikæpitteet] onthoofden

decathlon [dikæθlon] *(athletics)* tienkamp

¹**decay** [dikkee] *vb* **1** vervallen, in verval raken; **2** (ver)rotten, bederven, verteren

²**decay** [dikkee] *n* **1** verval[h], (geleidelijke) achteruitgang; **2** bederf[h], rotting

deceased [dissie:st] overleden, pas gestorven

deceit [dissie:t] bedrog[h]; oneerlijkheid

deceive [dissie:v] bedriegen, misleiden, om de tuin leiden: *if my ears do not ~ me* als mijn oren me niet bedriegen

decelerate [die:sellareet] vertragen, afremmen, vaart minderen

December [dissemba] december

decency [die:sansie] fatsoen[h], fatsoenlijkheid

decent [die:snt] **1** fatsoenlijk; **2** wellevend; **3** be-

hoorlijk: *a ~ wage* een redelijk loon; **4** geschikt: *a ~ guy* een geschikte kerel

deception [dissepsjan] **1** misleiding, list, bedrog[h]; **2** (valse) kunstgreep, (smerige) truc, kunstje[h]

deceptive [disseptiv] bedrieglijk, misleidend: *appearances are often ~* schijn bedriegt

¹**decide** [dissajd] *vb* **1** beslissen, een beslissing nemen, een keuze maken; **2** besluiten, een besluit nemen: *~ against* afzien van; *we have decided against it* we hebben besloten het niet te doen

²**decide** [dissajd] *vb* **1** beslissen, uitmaken: *~ a question* een knoop doorhakken; **2** een uitspraak doen in

¹**decimal** [dessimmal] *adj* decimaal: *~ point* decimaalteken, komma

²**decimal** [dessimmal] *n* **1** decimale breuk: *recurring ~* repeterende breuk; **2** decimaal getal[h]

decipher [dissajfa] ontcijferen, decoderen

decision [dissizjan] beslissing, besluit[h], uitspraak: *arrive at* (of: *take) a ~* een beslissing nemen

decisive [dissajsiv] **1** beslissend, doorslaggevend; **2** beslist, gedecideerd, zelfverzekerd

deck [dek] **1** (scheeps)dek[h], tussendekse ruimte: *clear the ~s (for action) (fig)* zich opmaken voor de strijd; *below ~(s)* benedendeks; *on ~* aan dek; **2** verdieping van bus; **3** *(Am)* spel[h] (kaarten); **4** (tape)deck[h], cassettedeck[h]: *hit the ~* op je bek vallen, *(boxing)* neergaan

deck-chair ligstoel, dekstoel

¹**declaim** [dikleem] *vb* **1** uitvaren, schelden: *~ against* uitvaren tegen; **2** retorisch spreken

²**declaim** [dikleem] *vb* declameren, voordragen

declaration [deklareesjan] **1** (openbare, formele) verklaring, afkondiging; **2** geschreven verklaring

¹**declare** [diklea] *vb* **1** bekendmaken, aankondigen, afkondigen; **2** bestempelen als, uitroepen tot: *~ s.o. the winner* iem tot winnaar uitroepen; **3** aangeven *(goods at Customs, income etc): nothing to ~* niets te geven

²**declare** [diklea] *vb* **1** een verklaring afleggen, een aankondiging doen; **2** *(with against, for)* stelling nemen (tegen, voor), zich (openlijk) uitspreken (tegen, voor)

declination [deklinneesjan] **1** (voorover)helling; **2** buiging; **3** verval[h], achteruitgang; **4** *(Am)* afwijzing; **5** declinatie, *(compass)* afwijking(shoek)

¹**decline** [diklajn] *vb* **1** (af)hellen, aflopen, dalen; **2** ten einde lopen, aftakelen: *declining years* oude dag, laatste jaren; **3** afnemen, achteruitgaan

²**decline** [diklajn] *vb* (beleefd) weigeren, afslaan, van de hand wijzen: *~ an invitation* niet op een uitnodiging ingaan

³**decline** [diklajn] *n* **1** verval[h], achteruitgang, aftakeling: *fall* (of: *go) into a ~* beginnen af te takelen, in verval raken; **2** daling, afname, vermindering: *on the ~* tanend; **3** slotfase, ondergang

decode [die:kood] decoderen, ontcijferen

¹**decompose** [die:kampooz] *vb* **1** desintegreren, uiteenvallen; **2** (ver)rotten, bederven

²**decompose** [die:kəmpooz] *vb* 1 ontleden, ontbinden, afbreken; 2 doen rotten

decontaminate [die:kəntæminneet] ontsmetten, desinfecteren

decorate [dekkəreet] 1 afwerken, verven, schilderen, behangen; 2 versieren, verfraaien: *~ the Christmas tree* de kerstboom optuigen; 3 decoreren, onderscheiden, een onderscheiding geven

decoration [dekkəreesjən] 1 versiering, decoratie, opsmuk; 2 inrichting (en stoffering), aankleding; 3 onderscheiding(steken^h), decoratie, ordeteken^h

decorator [dekkəreetə] afwerker (van huis), (huis)schilder, stukadoor, behanger

decorous [dekkərəs] correct, fatsoenlijk

decoy [die:koj] 1 lokvogel, lokeend; 2 lokaas^h, lokmiddel^h

¹**decrease** [dikrie:s] *vb* (geleidelijk) afnemen, teruglopen, achteruitgaan

²**decrease** [dikrie:s] *vb* verminderen, beperken, verkleinen

³**decrease** [die:krie:s] *n* vermindering, afneming, daling

¹**decree** [dikrie:] *n* verordening, besluit^h: *by ~* bij decreet

²**decree** [dikrie:] *vb* verordenen, bevelen

decrepit [dikreppit] 1 versleten, afgeleefd, op; 2 vervallen, bouwvallig, uitgewoond

decry [dikraj] 1 kleineren, openlijk afkeuren; 2 kwaadspreken over, afgeven op

dedicate [deddikkeet] 1 wijden, toewijden, in dienst stellen van; 2 opdragen, toewijden: *~ a book to s.o.* een boek aan iem opdragen

dedicated [deddikkeetid] toegewijd, trouw

dedication [deddikkeesjən] 1 opdracht; 2 (in)wijding, inzegening; 3 *(singular)* toewijding, trouw, toegedaanheid

deduce [didjoe:s] (logisch) afleiden: *and what do you ~ from that?* en wat maak je daaruit op?

deduct [diddukt] *(with from)* aftrekken (van), in mindering brengen (op)

deduction [didduksjən] 1 conclusie, gevolgtrekking, slotsom; 2 inhouding, korting, (ver)mindering

deed [die:d] 1 daad, handeling: *in word and in ~* met woord en daad; 2 wapenfeit^h, (helden)daad; 3 akte, document^h

¹**deep** [die:p] *adj* 1 diep, diepgelegen, ver(afgelegen): *the ~ end* het diepe *(in swimming pool)*; *~ in the forest* diep in het bos; 2 diep(zinnig), moeilijk, duister, ontoegankelijk; 3 diep(gaand), intens *(of feelings)*, donker *(of colours)*: *~ in conversation* diep in gesprek; 4 dik, achter elkaar: *the people were standing ten ~* de mensen stonden tien rijen dik; *thrown in at the ~ end* in het diepe gegooid, meteen met het moeilijkste (moeten) beginnen; *in ~ water(s)* in grote moeilijkheden

²**deep** [die:p] *adv* diep, tot op grote diepte: *~ into the night* tot diep in de nacht

³**deep** [die:p] *n* diepte, afgrond

deep-freeze diepvriezen

deer [diə] hert^h

deface [diffees] 1 beschadigen, verminken; 2 onleesbaar maken, bekladden

defamation [deffəmeesjən] laster

default [diffo:lt] 1 afwezigheid: *by ~* bij gebrek aan beter; *in ~ of* bij gebrek aan, bij ontstentenis van; 2 verzuim^h, niet-nakoming *(of obligation to pay)*, wanbetaling

¹**defeat** [diffie:t] *vb* 1 verslaan, overwinnen, winnen van; 2 verijdelen, dwarsbomen: *be ~ed in an attempt* een poging zien mislukken; 3 verwerpen, afstemmen; 4 tenietdoen, vernietigen: *her expectations were ~ed* haar verwachtingen werden de bodem ingeslagen

²**defeat** [diffie:t] *n* 1 nederlaag; 2 mislukking; 3 verijdeling, dwarsboming

defeatism [diffie:tizm] moedeloosheid

¹**defect** [die:fekt] *n* mankement^h, gebrek^h

²**defect** [diffekt] *vb* 1 overlopen, afvallig worden; 2 uitwijken *(by seeking asylum)*

defective [diffektiv] 1 onvolkomen, gebrekkig, onvolmaakt; 2 te kort komend, onvolledig

defector [diffektə] overloper, afvallige

defence [diffens] 1 verdediging, afweer, defensief^h, bescherming, *(law)* verweer^h, ~s verdedigingswerken: *in ~ of* ter verdediging van; 2 verdediging(srede), verweer^h; 3 *(sport; also chess)* verdediging; 4 defensie, (lands)verdediging

defend [diffend] 1 verdedigen, afweren, verweren, als verdediger optreden (voor); 2 beschermen, beveiligen

defendant [diffendənt] gedaagde, beschuldigde

defender [diffendə] 1 verdediger, *(sport)* achterspeler; 2 titelverdediger

defensive [diffensiv] defensief, verdedigend, afwerend: *be on the ~* een defensieve houding aannemen

¹**defer** [diffə:] *vb* opschorten, uitstellen: *~red payment* uitgestelde betaling

²**defer** [diffə:] *vb* zich onderwerpen, het hoofd buigen: *~ to* eerbiedigen, respecteren, in acht nemen

deference [deffərəns] achting, eerbied, respect^h

defiance [diffajjəns] 1 trotsering, uitdagende houding: *in ~ of* in weerwil van, ondanks; 2 openlijk verzet^h, opstandigheid: *in ~ of: a)* met minachting voor; *b)* in strijd met

deficient [diffisjənt] 1 incompleet, onvolledig; 2 ontoereikend, onvoldoende: *~ in iron* ijzerarm; 3 onvolwaardig, zwakzinnig

deficit [deffissit] 1 tekort^h, nadelig saldo^h; 2 tekort^h, gebrek^h

defile [diffajl] 1 bevuilen, verontreinigen, vervuilen; 2 schenden, ontheiligen

define [diffajn] 1 definiëren, een definitie geven (van); 2 afbakenen, bepalen, begrenzen

definite [deffinnit] 1 welomlijnd, scherp begrensd; 2 ondubbelzinnig, duidelijk; 3 uitgesproken, onbetwistbaar; 4 beslist, vastberaden; 5 *(linguistics)* bepaald: ~ *article* bepaald lidwoord

definitely [d<u>e</u>ffinnitlie] absoluut, beslist: ~ *not* geen sprake van

definition [deffinn<u>i</u>sjən] **1** definitie, omschrijving; **2** afbakening, bepaling, begrenzing; **3** karakteristiek; **4** scherpte, beeldscherpte

definitive [diff<u>i</u>nnittiv] **1** definitief, blijvend, onherroepelijk; **2** beslissend, afdoend; **3** (meest) gezaghebbend, onbetwist; **4** ondubbelzinnig

deflate [die:fl<u>ee</u>t] **1** leeg laten lopen, *(fig)* doorprikken *(conceitedness);* **2** kleineren, minder belangrijk maken

deflation [die:fl<u>ee</u>sjən] deflatie, waardevermeerdering van geld

deflect [difl<u>e</u>kt] **1** (doen) afbuigen, (doen) afwijken, uitwijken; **2** (*with from*) afbrengen (van), afleiden (van)

deforest [die:f<u>o</u>rrist] *(Am)* ontbossen

deformed [diff<u>o</u>:md] **1** misvormd, mismaakt; **2** verknipt, pervers

defraud [difr<u>o</u>:d] bedriegen, bezwendelen

defray [difr<u>ee</u>] financieren, betalen, voor zijn rekening nemen: ~ *the cost(s)* de kosten dragen

defrost [die:fr<u>o</u>st] ontdooien

deft [deft] behendig, handig, bedreven

defunct [diff<u>u</u>ngkt] **1** overleden, dood; **2** verdwenen, in onbruik: ~ *ideas* achterhaalde ideeën

defuse [die:fj<u>oe</u>:z] onschadelijk maken *(also fig),* demonteren *(explosives):* ~ *a crisis* een crisis bezweren

defy [diff<u>aj</u>] **1** tarten, uitdagen: *I* ~ *anyone to prove I'm wrong* ik daag iedereen uit om te bewijzen dat ik ongelijk heb; **2** trotseren, weerstaan: ~ *definition* (of: *description)* elke beschrijving tarten

degenerate [didzj<u>e</u>nnəreet] **1** degenereren, ontaarden, verloederen; **2** verslechteren, achteruitgaan

degrade [digr<u>ee</u>d] **1** degraderen, achteruitzetten, terugzetten: ~ *oneself* zich verlagen; **2** vernederen, onteren

degree [digr<u>ie</u>:] **1** graad: *an angle of 45* ~*s* een hoek van 45 graden; ~ *of latitude* (of: *longitude)* breedtegraad, lengtegraad; **2** (universitaire) graad, academische titel, *(also)* lesbevoegdheid; **3** mate, hoogte, graad, trap: *to a high* ~ tot op grote hoogte; *by* ~*s* stukje bij beetje, gaandeweg

¹dehydrate [die:h<u>a</u>jdreet] *vb* **1** vocht verliezen; **2** (op-, uit-, ver)drogen, verdorren

²dehydrate [die:h<u>a</u>jdreet] *vb* vocht onttrekken aan

deify [d<u>ie</u>:iffaj] vergoddelijken

deign [deen] zich verwaardigen, zich niet te goed achten: *not* ~ *to look at* geen blik waardig keuren

deity [d<u>e</u>:ittie] **1** god(in), godheid; **2** (af)god, verafgode figuur

dejected [didzj<u>e</u>ktid] **1** terneergeslagen, somber; **2** bedroefd, verdrietig

dejection [didzj<u>e</u>ksjən] **1** neerslachtigheid; **2** bedroefdheid, verdriet[h]

¹delay [dill<u>ee</u>] *n* **1** vertraging, oponthoud[h]; **2** uitstel[h], verschuiving: *without (any)* ~ zonder uitstel

²delay [dill<u>ee</u>] *vb* treuzelen, tijd rekken (winnen)

³delay [dill<u>ee</u>] *vb* **1** uitstellen, verschuiven; **2** ophouden, vertragen, hinderen

¹delegate [d<u>e</u>lligət] *n* afgevaardigde, gedelegeerde, ge(vol)machtigde

²delegate [d<u>e</u>lligeet] *vb* **1** afvaardigen, delegeren; **2** machtigen; **3** delegeren, overdragen

delegation [delligeesjən] **1** delegatie, afvaardiging; **2** machtiging

delete [dill<u>ie</u>:t] verwijderen, wissen, doorhalen, wegstrepen: ~ *from* schrappen uit; ~ *as applicable* doorhalen wat niet van toepassing is

deletion [dill<u>ie</u>:sjən] **1** (weg)schrapping, doorhaling; **2** verwijderde passage

deli [d<u>e</u>llie] delicatessen delicatessewinkel

¹deliberate [dill<u>i</u>bbərət] *adj* **1** doelbewust, opzettelijk; **2** voorzichtig, weloverwogen, bedachtzaam

²deliberate [dill<u>i</u>bbəreet] *vb* **1** wikken en wegen, beraadslagen; **2** raad inwinnen, te rade gaan

³deliberate [dill<u>i</u>bbəreet] *vb* **1** (zorgvuldig) afwegen; **2** beraadslagen, zich beraden over

deliberation [dillibbər<u>ee</u>sjən] **1** (zorgvuldige) afweging, overleg[h]: *after much* ~ na lang wikken en wegen; **2** omzichtigheid; bedachtzaamheid

delicacy [d<u>e</u>llikkəsie] **1** delicatesse, lekkernij; **2** (fijn)gevoeligheid, verfijndheid; **3** tact

delicate [d<u>e</u>llikkət] **1** fijn, verfijnd; **2** lekker *(of foods);* **3** teer, zwak, tenger: *a* ~ *constitution* een teer gestel; **4** (fijn)gevoelig; **5** tactvol; **6** kieskeurig, kritisch; **7** netelig

delicious [dill<u>i</u>sjəs] (over)heerlijk, verrukkelijk, kostelijk

¹delight [dill<u>a</u>jt] *n* **1** verrukking, groot genoegen[h]; **2** genot[h], vreugde: *take* ~ *in* genot vinden in

²delight [dill<u>a</u>jt] *vb* genot vinden

³delight [dill<u>a</u>jt] *vb* in verrukking brengen: *she* ~*ed them with her play* haar spel bracht hen in verrukking

delighted [dill<u>a</u>jtid] verrukt, opgetogen: *I shall be* ~ het zal me een groot genoegen zijn; ~ *at* (of: *with)* opgetogen over

delineate [dill<u>i</u>nnie-eet] **1** omlijnen, afbakenen; **2** schetsen, tekenen, afbeelden

delinquency [dill<u>i</u>ngkwənsie] **1** vergrijp[h], delict[h]; **2** criminaliteit, misdadigheid, misdaad

delinquent [dill<u>i</u>ngkwənt] wetsovertreder, jeugdige misdadiger

delirious [dill<u>i</u>rriəs] **1** ijlend: *become* ~ gaan ijlen; **2** dol(zinnig): ~ *with joy* dol(zinnig) van vreugde

¹deliver [dill<u>i</u>vvə] *vb* **1** verlossen, bevrijden: *be* ~*ed of* verlost worden van, bevallen van; **2** ter wereld helpen: ~ *a child* een kind ter wereld helpen; **3** bezorgen, (af)leveren; **4** voordragen, uitspreken: ~ *a lecture* (of: *paper)* een lezing houden

²deliver [dill<u>i</u>vvə] *vb* afkomen, over de brug komen: *he will* ~ *on his promise* hij zal doen wat hij beloofd heeft

deliverance [dill<u>i</u>vvərəns] verlossing, bevrijding, redding

delivery [dill̲ivvərie] 1 bevalling, verlossing, geboorte; 2 bestelling, levering; 3 bevrijding, verlossing, redding; 4 bezorging, (post)bestelling; 5 voordracht, redevoering ‖ *take ~ of* in ontvangst nemen

delude [dill̲oe:d] misleiden, op een dwaalspoor brengen, bedriegen

deluge [d̲eljoe:dzj] 1 zondvloed; 2 overstroming, watervloed; 3 wolkbreuk, stortbui; 4 stortvloed, stroom, waterval *(of words etc)*

delusion [dill̲oe:zjən] waanidee^h, waanvoorstelling

demagogue [d̲emməgog] demagoog, oproerstoker

¹demand [dimm̲a:nd] *n* 1 eis, verzoek^h, verlangen^h; 2 aanspraak, claim, vordering: *make great (of: many) ~s on* veel vergen van; 3 vraag, behoefte: *supply and ~* vraag en aanbod; *meet the ~* aan de vraag voldoen; *be in great ~* erg in trek zijn

²demand [dimm̲a:nd] *vb* 1 eisen, verlangen, vorderen: *I ~ a written apology* ik eis een schriftelijke verontschuldiging; 2 vergen, vragen, (ver)eisen: *this job will ~ much of you* deze baan zal veel van u vragen

demarcation [die:ma:k̲eesjən] afbakening, grens(lijn)

demean [dimm̲ie:n] verlagen, vernederen: *~ oneself* zich verlagen; *such language ~s you* dergelijke taal is beneden je waardigheid

demeanour [dimm̲ie:nə] gedrag^h, houding, optreden^h

demented [dimm̲entid] 1 krankzinnig, gek, gestoord; 2 dement, kinds

demo [d̲emmoo] *demonstration* 1 betoging, demonstratie, protestmars; 2 proefopname

demobilize [die:m̲oobillajz] demobiliseren, uit de krijgsdienst ontslaan

democracy [dimm̲okrəsie] 1 democratie; 2 medezeggenschap

democrat [d̲emməkræt] democraat

democratic [demməkr̲ætik] democratisch

demolish [dimm̲ollisj] 1 slopen, vernielen, afbreken, vernietigen; 2 omverwerpen, te gronde richten; 3 ontzenuwen, weerleggen

demolition [demməl̲isjən] vernieling, afbraak, sloop

demon [d̲ie:mən] 1 demon, boze geest, duivel, *(fig)* duivel(s mens); 2 bezetene, fanaat: *he is a ~ chessplayer* hij schaakt als een bezetene

¹demonstrate [d̲emmənstreet] *vb* demonstreren, betogen

²demonstrate [d̲emmənstreet] *vb* 1 demonstreren, een demonstratie geven van; 2 aantonen, bewijzen; 3 uiten, openbaren

demonstration [demmənstr̲eesjən] 1 demonstratie, betoging, manifestatie; 2 demonstratie, vertoning vd werking; 3 bewijs^h; 4 uiting, manifestatie, vertoon^h

demonstrative [dimm̲onstrətiv] 1 (aan)tonend; 2 open, extravert; 3 *(linguistics)* aanwijzend: *~ pro-*

noun aanwijzend voornaamwoord

demonstrator [d̲emmənstreetə] 1 demonstrateur; 2 demonstrant, betoger

demoralization [dimmorrəlajz̲eesjən] 1 demoralisatie, ontmoediging; 2 zedelijk bederf^h

demoralize [dimm̲orrəlajz] demoraliseren, ontmoedigen

demote [die:m̲oot] degraderen, in rang verlagen

demotivate [die:m̲ootivveet] demotiveren, ontmoedigen

demystification [die:mistiffikk̲eesjən] ontsluiering, opheldering

den [den] 1 hol^h, schuilplaats, leger^h *(of animal)*; 2 hol^h, (misdadigers)verblijf^h; 3 kamertje^h, hok^h

denial [dinn̲ajjəl] 1 ontzegging, weigering; 2 ontkenning; 3 verwerping

denigrate [d̲ennigreet] kleineren, belasteren

denim [d̲ennim] 1 spijkerstof; 2 *~s* spijkerbroek

Denmark [d̲enma:k] Denemarken

denomination [dinnomminn̲eesjən] 1 (eenheids)klasse, munteenheid, muntsoort, getalsoort, gewichtsklasse: *coin of the lowest ~* kleinste munteenheid; 2 noemer: *reduce fractions to the same ~* breuken onder een noemer brengen; 3 gezindte, kerk(genootschap^h)

denominator [dinn̲omminneetə] noemer, deler

denote [dinn̲oot] 1 aanduiden, verwijzen naar, omschrijven; 2 aangeven, duiden op; 3 betekenen, als naam dienen voor

denounce [dinn̲auns] 1 hekelen, afkeuren; 2 aan de kaak stellen, openlijk beschuldigen

dense [dens] 1 dicht, compact, samengepakt: *~ly populated* dichtbevolkt; 2 dom, hersenloos

density [d̲ensittie] 1 dichtheid, compactheid, concentratie; 2 bevolkingsdichtheid

¹dent [dent] *n* 1 deuk; 2 *(fig)* deuk, knauw ‖ *that made a big ~ in our savings* dat kostte ons flink wat van ons spaargeld

²dent [dent] *vb* 1 deuken, een deuk maken (krijgen) in; 2 *(fig)* deuken, een knauw geven

dental [d̲entl] 1 dentaal, mbt het gebit, tand-; 2 tandheelkundig: *~ floss* tandzijde

dentist [d̲entist] tandarts

denture [d̲entsjə] 1 gebit^h; 2 *~s* kunstgebit^h, vals gebit^h

denunciation [dinnunsie·̲eesjən] 1 openlijke veroordeling; 2 beschuldiging, aangifte, aanklacht; 3 opzegging *(of pact etc)*

deny [dinn̲aj] 1 ontkennen: *there is no ~ing that* het valt niet te ontkennen dat; 2 ontzeggen, weigeren

deodorant [die:̲oodərənt] deodorant

¹depart [dipp̲a:t] *vb* heengaan, weggaan, vertrekken: *~ for* vertrekken naar, afreizen naar

²depart [dipp̲a:t] *vb* verlaten: *~ this life* sterven

department [dipp̲a:tmənt] 1 afdeling, departement^h, *(education)* vakgroep, sectie, instituut^h *(at university)*; 2 ministerie^h, departement^h: *Department of Environment (roughly)* Ministerie van Milieuzaken

department store warenhuis[h]
departure [dippa:tsjə] **1** vertrek[h], vertrektijd; **2** afwijking: *new ~* nieuwe koers; *a ~ from the agreed policy* een afwijking van het afgesproken beleid
depend [dippend] afhangen: *it all ~s* het hangt er nog maar van af
dependable [dippendəbl] betrouwbaar
dependant [dippendənt] afhankelijke *(eg for sustenance)*
dependence [dippendəns] **1** afhankelijkheid: *~ on luxury* afhankelijkheid van luxe; **2** vertrouwen[h]; **3** verslaving
dependent [dippendənt] afhankelijk
depend (up)on 1 afhangen van, afhankelijk zijn van; **2** vertrouwen op, bouwen op, zich verlaten op: *can I ~ on that?* kan ik daar op rekenen?
depict [dippikt] (af)schilderen, beschrijven, afbeelden: *in that book his father is ~ed as an alcoholic* in dat boek wordt zijn vader afgeschilderd als een alcoholist
deplete [dipli:t] leeghalen, uitputten
deplorable [diplo:rəbl] betreurenswaardig, zeer slecht
deplore [diplo:] betreuren, bedroefd zijn over
depopulate [die:popjoeleet] ontvolken
deport [dippo:t] **1** (zich) gedragen, (zich) houden: *~ oneself* zich gedragen; **2** verbannen, uitzetten
deportee [die:po:tie:] gedeporteerde, banneling
deportment [dippo:tmənt] **1** (lichaams)houding, postuur[h]; **2** gedrag[h], manieren, houding
depose [dippooz] **1** afzetten, onttronen; **2** getuigen, onder ede verklaren *(in writing)*
[1]**deposit** [dippozzit] *vb* **1** afzetten, bezinken; **2** neerleggen, plaatsen; **3** deponeren, in bewaring geven, storten
[2]**deposit** [dippozzit] *n* **1** onderpand[h], waarborgsom, aanbetaling, statiegeld[h]; **2** storting; **3** deposito[h], depositogeld[h] *(with period of notice)*; **4** afzetting, ertslaag, bezinksel[h]
depository [dippozzittərie] opslagruimte, bewaarplaats
depot [deppoo] **1** depot[h], magazijn[h], opslagruimte; **2** (leger)depot[h], militair magazijn[h]; **3** *(Am)* spoorwegstation[h], busstation[h]
depravation [deprəveesjən] verdorvenheid, bederf[h]
deprave [dipreev] bederven, doen ontaarden
deprecation [deprikkeesjən] **1** afkeuring, protest[h]; **2** geringschatting
depreciate [diprie:sjie:eet] **1** (doen) devalueren, in waarde (doen) dalen; **2** kleineren
depreciation [diprie:sjie:eesjən] **1** devaluatie, waardevermindering, afschrijving; **2** geringschatting
depredation [depriddeesjən] plundering
depressed [diprest] **1** gedeprimeerd, ontmoedigd; **2** noodlijdend, onderdrukt: *~ area: a)* noodlijdend gebied; *b)* streek met aanhoudend hoge werkloosheid

depressing [dipressing] deprimerend, ontmoedigend
depression [dipresjən] **1** laagte, holte, indruk; **2** depressie, lagedrukgebied[h], lage luchtdruk; **3** depressie, crisis(tijd); **4** depressiviteit, neerslachtigheid
deprivation [deprivveesjən] **1** ontbering, verlies[h], gemis[h]; **2** beroving, ontneming
deprive [diprajv] beroven: *the old man was ~d of his wallet* de oude man werd beroofd van zijn portefeuille; *they ~ those people of clean water* ze onthouden deze mensen schoon water
deprived [diprajvd] misdeeld, achtergesteld, arm: *~ children* kansarme kinderen
dept. 1 *department* Dep.; **2** *deputy*
depth [depθ] **1** diepte: *he was beyond* (of: *out of) his ~* hij verloor de grond onder z'n voeten; *in ~* diepgaand, grondig; **2** diepzinnigheid, scherpzinnigheid; **3** het diepst, het holst: *in the ~s of Asia* in het hart van Azië; *in the ~(s) of winter* midden in de winter
deputation [depjoeteesjən] afvaardiging, delegatie
[1]**deputy** [depjoetie] *n* **1** (plaats)vervanger, waarnemer; **2** afgevaardigde, kamerlid[h]; **3** hulpsheriff, *(roughly)* plaatsvervangend commissaris
[2]**deputy** [depjoetie] *adj* onder-, vice-, plaatsvervangend: *~ director* vice-directeur
derail [die:reel] (doen) ontsporen
derange [dirreendzj] verwarren, krankzinnig maken: *mentally ~d* geestelijk gestoord, krankzinnig
derelict [derrillikt] verwaarloosd, verlaten
deride [dirrajd] uitlachen, bespotten, belachelijk maken: *~ as* uitmaken voor
derision [dirrizjən] spot
derivation [derrivveesjən] afleiding, afkomst, etymologie
[1]**derivative** [dirrivvətiv] *adj* afgeleid, niet oorspronkelijk
[2]**derivative** [dirrivvətiv] *n* afleiding
[1]**derive** [dirrajv] *vb* afstammen: *~ from* ontleend zijn aan, (voort)komen uit
[2]**derive** [dirrajv] *vb* afleiden, krijgen, halen: *~ pleasure from* plezier ontlenen aan
derogatory [dirrogətərie] geringschattend, minachtend, kleinerend
[1]**descend** [dissend] *vb* **1** (af)dalen, naar beneden gaan, neerkomen; **2** afstammen: *be ~ed from* afstammen van
[2]**descend** [dissend] *vb* afdalen, naar beneden gaan langs, afzakken *(river)*
descendant [dissendənt] afstammeling, nakomeling
descent [dissent] **1** afkomst, afstamming: *Charles claims ~ from a Scottish king* Charles beweert af te stammen van een Schotse koning; **2** overdracht, overerving; **3** afdaling, landing, val; **4** helling
describe [diskrajb] **1** beschrijven, karakteriseren: *you can hardly ~ his ideas as original* je kunt zijn ideeën toch moeilijk oorspronkelijk noemen; **2** beschrijven, trekken: *~ a circle* een cirkel tekenen

description [diskrịpsjən] **1** beschrijving, omschrijving: *fit the ~* aan de beschrijving voldoen; **2** soort, type[h]: *weapons of all ~s* (of: *every ~*) allerlei (soorten) wapens

¹desert [dẹzzət] *n* woestijn

²desert [dizzạːt] *vb* deserteren

³desert [dizzạːt] *vb* verlaten, in de steek laten: *~ed streets* uitgestorven straten

desertion [dizzạːsjən] desertie

deserve [dizzạːv] verdienen, recht hebben op

¹design [dizzạjn] *vb* **1** ontwerpen; **2** uitdenken, bedenken, beramen: *who ~ed this bank-robbery?* wie beraamde deze bankroof?; **3** bedoelen, ontwikkelen, bestemmen: *~ed for children* bedoeld voor kinderen

²design [dizzạjn] *n* **1** ontwerp[h], tekening, blauwdruk, constructie, vormgeving; **2** dessin[h], patroon[h]; **3** opzet, bedoeling, doel[h]: *have ~s against* boze plannen hebben met; *by ~* met opzet

designer [dizzạjnə] designer, ontwerper, tekenaar: *~ clothes* designerkleding

designing [dizzạjning] listig, berekenend, sluw

desirable [dizzajjərəbl] **1** wenselijk; **2** aantrekkelijk

¹desire [dizzajjə] *vb* wensen, verlangen, begeren

²desire [dizzajjə] *n* **1** (with *for*) wens, verlangen (naar), wil; **2** begeerte, hartstocht

desist [dissịst] (with *from*) ophouden (met), uitscheiden (met), afzien (van)

desk [desk] **1** werktafel, (schrijf)bureau[h]; **2** balie, receptie, kas

desolate [dẹssələt] **1** verlaten, uitgestorven, troosteloos; **2** diepbedroefd, eenzaam: *at 30 he was already ~ and helpless* op zijn dertigste was hij al zo eenzaam en hulpeloos

desolation [dessəlẹẹsjən] **1** verwoesting, ontvolking; **2** verlatenheid; **3** eenzaamheid

¹despair [dispẹə] *n* wanhoop, vertwijfeling: *drive s.o. to ~, fill s.o. with ~* iem tot wanhoop drijven; *be the ~ of s.o.* iem wanhopig maken

²despair [dispẹə] *vb* wanhopen

desperate [dẹspərət] wanhopig, hopeloos, uitzichtloos (of *situation*), vertwijfeld, radeloos (of *deeds, people*): *a ~ action* een wanhoopsactie; *she was ~ for a cup of tea* ze verlangde verschrikkelijk naar een kopje thee

despicable [dispịkkəbl] verachtelijk

despise [dispạjz] verachten, versmaden

despite [dispạjt] ondanks

dessert [dizzạːt] dessert[h]

destination [destinnẹẹsjən] (plaats van) bestemming, doel[h], eindpunt[h]

destine [dẹstin] bestemmen, (voor)beschikken: *be ~d for* bestemd zijn voor

destiny [dẹstinnie] **1** lot[h], bestemming, beschikking; **2** *Destiny* (nood)lot[h]

destitute [dẹstitjoeːt] arm; behoeftig

destroy [distrọj] afmaken, vernietigen, ruïneren: *thousands of houses were ~ed by the earthquakes* door de aardbevingen zijn duizenden huizen ver-

nield

destruction [distrụksjən] **1** vernietiging, afbraak; **2** ondergang

detach [ditạetsj] (with *from*) losmaken (van), scheiden, uit elkaar halen

detached [ditạetsjt] **1** los, vrijstaand (of *house*), niet verbonden, geïsoleerd; **2** onbevooroordeeld: *~ view of sth.* objectieve kijk op iets; **3** afstandelijk, gereserveerd

detachment [ditạetsjmənt] **1** detachering, detachement[h]; **2** scheiding; **3** afstandelijkheid, gereserveerdheid; **4** onpartijdigheid

detail [dịeːteel] **1** detail[h], bijzonderheid, kleinigheid: *enter* (of: *go*) *into ~(s)* op bijzonderheden ingaan; **2** kleine versiering

detailed [dịeːteeld] uitvoerig: *~ information available on request* uitgebreide informatie op aanvraag verkrijgbaar

detain [ditteẹn] **1** aanhouden, laten nablijven, gevangen houden; **2** laten schoolblijven: *Henry was ~ed for half an hour* Henry moest een halfuur nablijven; **3** ophouden, vertragen: *I don't want to ~ you any longer* ik wil u niet langer ophouden

detainee [die:teenịẹ:] (politieke) gevangene, gedetineerde

detect [dittẹkt] ontdekken, bespeuren

detective [dittẹktiv] detective, speurder, rechercheur

detention [dittẹnsjən] **1** opsluiting, (militaire) detentie, hechtenis; **2** het schoolblijven; **3** vertraging, oponthoud[h]

deter [dittạː] (with *from*) afschrikken (van), ontmoedigen, afhouden (van)

detergent [dittạːdzjənt] wasmiddel[h], afwasmiddel[h], reinigingsmiddel[h]

deteriorate [dittịəriəreet] verslechteren, achteruitgaan

determination [dittəːminnẹẹsjən] **1** vast voornemen[h], bedoeling, plan[h]; **2** vastberadenheid, vastbeslotenheid

determine [dittạːmin] **1** besluiten, beslissen: *Sheila ~ed to dye her hair green* Sheila besloot haar haar groen te verven; **2** doen besluiten, drijven tot

determined [dittạːmind] beslist, vastberaden, vastbesloten

deterrence [dittẹrrəns] afschrikking

deterrent [dittẹrrənt] afschrikwekkend middel[h], afschrikmiddel[h], atoombom: *the cameras are a ~ for shoplifters* de camera's hebben een preventieve werking tegen winkeldieven

detest [dittẹst] verafschuwen, walgen van

dethrone [die:θrọọn] afzetten, onttronen

¹detonate [dẹttəneet] *vb* ontploffen, exploderen

²detonate [dẹttəneet] *vb* tot ontploffing brengen, laten exploderen

detour [dịeːtoeə] **1** omweg, bocht, (rivier)kronkel; **2** omleiding

detract [ditrạekt]: *~ from* kleineren, afbreuk doen aan, verminderen

detriment [dɛtrimmənt] (oorzaak van) schade, kwaadʰ, nadeelʰ: *to the ~ of* ten nadele van

deuce [djoe:s] **1** twee *(on dice)*; **2** *(tennis)* veertig gelijk || *a ~ of a fight* een vreselijke knokpartij

devaluation [die:væljoe·ees̬jən] devaluatie, waardevermindering

devalue [die:væljoe:] devalueren, in waarde (doen) dalen

devastate [dɛvvəsteet] verwoesten, ruïneren, vernietigen

devastation [dɛvvəsteesjən] verwoesting

¹develop [divvɛlləp] *vb* (zich) ontwikkelen, (doen) ontstaan, (doen) uitbreiden

²develop [divvɛlləp] *vb* **1** ontwikkelen, uitwerken, ontginnen: *~ing country* ontwikkelingsland; *~ a film* een film(pje) ontwikkelen; **2** ontvouwen, uiteenzetten

developer [divvɛlləpə] **1** projectontwikkelaar; **2** *(photo)* ontwikkelaar

development [divvɛlləpmənt] **1** ontwikkeling, verloopʰ, evolutie, ontplooiing, groei, verdere uitwerking: *await further ~s* afwachten wat er verder komt; **2** gebeurtenis; **3** (nieuw)bouwprojectʰ

deviant [die:viənt] **1** afwijkend, tegen de norm; **2** abnormaal

deviate [die:vie·eet] *(with from)* afwijken (van), afdwalen

deviation [die:vie·ees̬jən] afwijking *(from current norm)*, deviatie: *~ from* afwijking van

device [divvajs] **1** apparaatʰ, toestelʰ: *a new ~ for squeezing lemons* een nieuw apparaat om citroenen te persen; **2** middelʰ, kunstgreep, truc; **3** deviesʰ, mottoʰ, leus; **4** embleemʰ *(on coat of arms): left to his own ~s* op zichzelf aangewezen

devil [dɛvl] **1** duivel; **2** man, jongen, donder, kerel || *give the ~ his due* ere wie ere toekomt, het iem nageven; *~ take the hindmost* ieder voor zich en God voor ons allen; *be a ~* kom op, spring eens uit de band; *there'll be the ~ to pay* dan krijgen we de poppen aan het dansen; *the ~ of an undertaking* een helse klus

devious [die:viəs] **1** kronkelend, slingerend, *(fig)* omslachtig: *~ route* omweg; **2** onoprecht, ontrouwbaar, sluw

devise [divvajz] bedenken, beramen

devoid [divvojd] *(with of)* verstoken (van), ontbloot (van), gespeend (van)

devote [divvoot] *(with to)* (toe)wijden (aan), besteden (aan): *~ oneself to* zich overgeven aan

devotee [dɛvvootie:] **1** *(with of)* liefhebber (van), aanbidder, enthousiast; **2** aanhanger, volgeling *(of religious sect)*; **3** dweper, fanaticus

devotion [divvoos̬jən] **1** toewijding, liefde, overgave: *~ to duty* plichtsbetrachting; **2** het besteden; **3** vroomheid

devour [divvauə] **1** verslinden *(also fig)*, verzwelgen; **2** verteren: *(be) ~ed by jealousy* verteerd (worden) door jaloezie

devout [divvaut] **1** vroom; **2** vurig, oprecht

dew [djoe:] dauw

dexterity [dekstɛrrittie] handigheid, behendigheid, (hand)vaardigheid

diabetes [dajjəbie:tie:z] diabetes, suikerziekte

¹diabetic [dajjəbɛttik] *adj* voor suikerzieken, diabetes-

²diabetic [dajjəbɛttik] *n* suikerzieke

diabolic(al) [dajjəbɔllik(l)] afschuwelijk, afgrijselijk, ontzettend

diagnose [dajjəgnooz] een diagnose stellen (van)

diagnosis [dajjəgnoosis] diagnose

diagonal [dajæɡənl] diagonaal

diagram [dajjəɡræm] diagramʰ, schets, schemaʰ, grafiek

¹dial [dajjəl] *n* **1** schaal(verdeling), wijzerplaat, (afstem)schaal *(of radio etc)*, zonnewijzer; **2** kiesschijf *(of telephone)*; **3** afstemknop *(of radio etc)*

²dial [dajjəl] *vb* draaien, bellen *(of telephone)*

dialect [dajjəlekt] dialectʰ

dialogue [dajjəlog] dialoog

diameter [dajæmittə] diameter, middellijn, doorsne(d)e

diamond [dajjəmənd] **1** diamant, diamanten sieraadʰ; **2** ruit(vormige figuur); **3** ruiten(kaart); **4** *~s* ruiten *(cards): Queen of ~s* ruitenvrouw; *it was ~ cut ~* het ging hard tegen hard

diaper [dajjəpə] *(Am)* luier

diaphragm [dajjəfræm] diafragmaʰ, middenrifʰ

diarrhoea [dajjəriə] diarree *(also fig)*, buikloop

diary [dajjərie] **1** dagboekʰ; **2** agenda

¹dice [dajs] *n (only dice)* **1** dobbelsteen, *(also fig)* kans, gelukʰ: *the dice are loaded against him* het lot is hem niet gunstig gezind; **2** *~s* dobbelspelʰ: *(Am; inf) no dice* tevergeefs

²dice [dajs] *vb* dobbelen

³dice [dajs] *vb* in dobbelsteentjes snijden

dicey [dajsie] link, riskant

dickhead idioot, stommeling

dicky wankel, wiebelig: *a ~ heart* een zwak hart

¹dictate [diktee t] *vb* **1** dicteren; **2** commanderen, opleggen

²dictate [diktee t] *n* ingeving, bevelʰ

dictator [diktee tə] dictator

diction [diksjən] **1** voordracht; **2** taalgebruikʰ, woordkeus

dictionary [diksjənərie] woordenboekʰ

didactic [dajdæktik] didactisch

diddle [didl] ontfutselen, bedriegen: *he ~d me out of £5* hij heeft me voor £5 afgezet

¹die [daj] *vb* **1** sterven, overlijden, omkomen: *~ from (of: of) an illness* sterven aan een ziekte; **2** ophouden te bestaan, verloren gaan: *the mystery ~d with him* hij nam het geheim mee in zijn graf; **3** uitsterven, wegsterven; **4** verzwakken, verminderen, bedaren: *~ away: a)* wegsterven *(of sound); b)* uitgaan *(of fire); c)* gaan liggen *(of wind); ~ down: a)* bedaren, afnemen *(of wind); b)* uitgaan *(of fire); ~ off: a)* een voor een sterven; *b)* uitsterven; *be dying for a cigarette* snakken naar een sigaret; *~ of anxiety*

doodsangsten uitstaan

²die *n* matrijs, stempel[h], gietvorm

diehard 1 taaie[h], volhouder; **2** aartsconservatief; **3** onverzoenlijke

diesel [di̯e:zl] diesel

¹diet [dai̯jət] *n* **1** dieet[h], leefregel: *on a ~* op dieet; **2** voedsel[h], voeding, kost: *her ~ consisted of bread and lentils* haar voedsel bestond uit brood en linzen

²diet [dai̯jət] *vb* op dieet zijn, *(fig)* lijnen

dietician [dai̯jətisjən] diëtist(e), voedingsspecialist(e)

differ [difə] **1** (van elkaar) verschillen, afwijken: *those twin sisters ~ from one another* die tweelingzusjes verschillen van elkaar; **2** van mening verschillen: *~ from s.o.* het met iem oneens zijn

difference [difərəns] **1** verschil[h], onderscheid[h]: *that makes all the ~* dat maakt veel uit; **2** verschil[h], rest: *split the ~* het verschil (samen) delen; **3** meningsverschil[h], geschil(punt)[h]

different [difərənt] **1** verschillend, ongelijk, afwijkend: *as ~ as chalk and* (of: *from) cheese* verschillend als dag en nacht; *(fig) strike a ~ note* een ander geluid laten horen; *~ from*, *~ to* anders dan; **2** ongewoon, speciaal: *a horse of a ~ colour* een geheel andere kwestie

¹differential [difərensjl] *adj* onderscheidend

²differential [difərensjl] *n* **1** loonklasseverschil[h]; **2** koersverschil[h]; **3** *(techn)* differentieel[h]

¹differentiate [difərensjie·eet] *vb* **1** zich onderscheiden; **2** een verschil maken: *~ between* ongelijk behandelen

²differentiate [difərensjie·eet] *vb* onderscheiden, onderkennen

difficult [difikkəlt] moeilijk *(also of character),* lastig

difficulty [difikkəltie] **1** moeilijkheid, probleem[h]; **2** moeite: *with ~* met moeite

diffident [difiddənt] bedeesd, terughoudend

¹diffuse [difjoe:s] *adj* diffuus, wijdlopig *(also style)*

²diffuse [difjoe:z] *vb* zich verspreiden, verstrooid worden *(of light)*

¹dig [dig] *vb* **1** doordringen; **2** zwoegen, ploeteren; **3** graven, delven, opgraven; **4** uitgraven, rooien; **5** uitzoeken, voor de dag halen; **6** porren; **7** vatten, snappen

²dig [dig] *n* **1** por; *(fig)* steek (onder water); **2** (archeologische) opgraving; **3** *~s* kamer(s)

¹digest [dai̯dzjest] *vb* verteren

²digest [dai̯dzjest] *vb* verteren *(also fig),* slikken, verwerken, in zich opnemen

³digest [dai̯dzjest] *n* samenvatting, (periodiek) overzicht[h]

digestion [dai̯dzjestsjən] spijsvertering, digestie

¹digestive [dai̯dzjestiv] *adj* **1** spijsverterings-; **2** goed voor de spijsvertering

²digestive [dai̯dzjestiv] *n* **1** digestief[h]; **2** volkorenbiscuit[h]

digger [digə] **1** graver, gouddelver; **2** graafmachine;

3 Australiër

¹dig in *vb* **1** zich ingraven; **2** aanvallen *(food);* **3** van geen wijken weten

²dig in *vb* **1** ingraven: *dig oneself in* zich ingraven, *(fig)* zijn positie verstevigen; **2** onderspitten

dig into 1 graven in: *dig sth. into the soil* iets ondergraven, iets onderspitten; **2** prikken, slaan, boren in; **3** zijn tanden zetten in; diepgaand onderzoeken: *the journalist dug into the scandal* de journalist beet zich vast in het schandaal

digit [didzjit] cijfer[h], getal[h] *(o up to and including 9)*

digital [didzjitl] digitaal

dignified [digniffajd] waardig, deftig, statig

dignitary [dignittərie] (kerkelijk) hoogwaardigheidsbekleder: *the local dignitaries* de dorpsnotabelen/

dignity [dignittie] waardigheid: *that is beneath his ~* dat is beneden zijn waardigheid

dig out 1 uitgraven; **2** opdiepen, voor de dag halen; **3** blootleggen

digress [dai̯gres] uitweiden: *~ from one's subject* afdwalen van zijn onderwerp

digression [dai̯gresjən] *(with on)* uitweiding (over)

¹dig up *vb* **1** opgraven, uitgraven, omspitten *(road);* **2** blootleggen, opsporen; **3** bij elkaar scharrelen; **4** opscharrelen

²dig up *vb (Am)* bijdrage leveren, betalen

dilapidated [dilæpiddeetid] vervallen, bouwvallig

dilatory [dilətərie] **1** traag, langzaam, laks; **2** vertragend

dilemma [dilemmə] dilemma[h], netelig vraagstuk[h]

diligence [dilidzjəns] ijver, vlijt, toewijding

diligent [dilidzjənt] ijverig, vlijtig

dilute [dai̯ljoe:t] **1** verdunnen, aanlengen: *~ the syrup with water or milk* de siroop met water of melk aanlengen; **2** doen verbleken, doen vervalen; **3** afzwakken, doen verwateren

¹dim [dim] *adj* **1** schemerig, (half)duister; **2** vaag, flauw: *I have a ~ understanding of botany* ik heb een beetje verstand van plantkunde; **3** stom: *take a ~ view of sth.* iets afkeuren, niets ophebben met iets

²dim [dim] *vb* **1** verduisteren, versomberen; **2** temperen, dimmen: *~ the headlights* dimmen

dime [dai̯m] dime, 10-centstuk[h] *(Am),* cent, stuiver ‖ *a ~ a dozen* dertien in een dozijn

dimension [dimmensjən] **1** afmeting, grootte, omvang, *(fig)* kaliber[h], formaat[h]; **2** dimensie, aspect[h], kwaliteit

diminish [dimminnisj] verminderen, verkleinen, afnemen, z'n waarde verliezen, aantasten

diminutive [dimminjoetiv] **1** verklein-; **2** nietig: *a ~ kitten* een piepklein poesje

dimple [dimpl] kuiltje[h]

dimwit [dimwit] sufferd, onbenul[h]

¹din [din] *n* kabaal[h], lawaai[h]: *kick up* (of: *make) a ~* herrie schoppen

²din [din] *vb* **1** verdoven *(of noise);* **2** inprenten: *~ sth. into s.o.* iets er bij iem in stampen

dine [dai̯n] dineren: *~ out* buitenshuis dineren

diner [dajnə] **1** iem die dineert, eter, gast; **2** restauratiewagen; **3** *(Am)* klein (weg)restaurant[h]

dinghy [dinggie] **1** jol; **2** kleine boot, (opblaasbaar) reddingsvlot[h], rubberboot

dingy [dingdzjie] **1** smerig, smoezelig; **2** sjofel, armoedig

dinky [dinkie] **1** snoezig; **2** *(Am)* armzalig

dinner [dinnə] eten[h], avondeten[h], (warm) middagmaal[h]

dinosaur [dajnəsɔ:] dinosaurus

dint [dint] deuk, indruk *(also fig)*

¹dip [dip] *vb* **1** duiken, plonzen, kopje-onder gaan; **2** ondergaan, vallen, zinken; **3** hellen, dalen; **4** tasten, reiken, grijpen: ~ *in* toetasten; ~ *into one's financial resources* aanspraak doen op zijn geldelijke middelen; ~ *into* vluchtig bekijken

²dip [dip] *vb* **1** (onder)dompelen, (in)dopen, galvaniseren *(in bath)*, wassen *(animals in a bathtub with insecticide)*; **2** verven, in verfbad dopen; **3** dimmen *(headlights)*

³dip [dip] *n* **1** indoping, onderdompeling, wasbeurt, *(inf)* duik; **2** schepje[h]; **3** helling, daling, dal[h] *(landscape)*; **4** (kleine) daling, vermindering; **5** dipsaus

diploma [diploomə] diploma[h]

diplomacy [diplooməsie] diplomatie *(also fig)*, (politieke) tact, diplomatiek optreden[h]

diplomat [dipləmæt] diplomaat

diplomatic [dipləmætik] **1** diplomatiek, mbt diplomatieke dienst, *(fig)* met diplomatie: ~ *bag* diplomatieke post(zak) *(for embassy etc)*; **2** subtiel, berekend, sluw

dipsomaniac [dipsəmeenie·æk] (periodiek) alcoholist, kwartaaldrinker

dipstick peilstok, meetstok

dire [dajjə] ijselijk, uiterst (dringend): *be in* ~ *need of water* snakken naar water; ~ *poverty* bittere armoede

¹direct [dirrekt] *vb* **1** richten: *these measures are ~ed against abuse* deze maatregelen zijn gericht tegen misbruik; **2** de weg wijzen, leiden: ~ *s.o. to the post office* iem de weg wijzen naar het postkantoor; **3** bestemmen, toewijzen; **4** leiden, de leiding hebben over, besturen; **5** geleiden, als richtlijn dienen voor; **6** opdracht geven, bevelen, *(law)* instrueren

²direct [dirrekt] *vb* regisseren; dirigeren

³direct [dirrekt] *adj* **1** direct, rechtstreeks, onmiddellijk, openhartig: *be a* ~ *descendant* in een rechte lijn van iem afstammen; *a* ~ *hit* een voltreffer; **2** absoluut, exact, precies: ~ *opposites* absolute tegenpolen; ~ *current* gelijkstroom; ~ *object* lijdend voorwerp

⁴direct [dirrekt] *adv* rechtstreeks: *broadcast* ~ rechtstreeks uitzenden

direction [dirreksjən] **1** opzicht[h], kant, tendens, richting, *(fig also)* gebied[h], terrein[h]: *progress in all* ~*s* vooruitgang op alle gebieden; **2** instructie, bevel[h], aanwijzing: *at the* ~ *of, by* ~ *of* op last van; **3** oogmerk[h], doel[h]; **4** leiding, directie, supervisie: *in the* ~ *of London* in de richting van Londen; **5** geleiding, het geleiden; **6** directie; regie

directive [dirrektiv] instructie, bevel[h]

directly [dirrektli] **1** rechtstreeks, openhartig; **2** dadelijk, zo; **3** precies, direct: ~ *opposite the door* precies tegenover de deur

director [dirrektə] **1** directeur, manager, directielid[h]: *the board of* ~*s* de raad van bestuur; **2** *(Am)* dirigent; **3** regisseur, spelleider

directory [dirrektərie] **1** adresboek[h], gids, adressenbestand[h]; **2** telefoonboek[h]

dirge [də:dzj] lijkzang, treurzang, klaagzang

dirt [də:t] **1** vuil[h], modder, drek, viezigheid: *treat s.o. like* ~ iem als oud vuil behandelen; **2** lasterpraat, geroddel[h]; **3** grond, aarde

dirty [də:tie] **1** vies, vuil, smerig; **2** laag, gemeen: *give s.o. a* ~ *look* iem vuil aankijken; *play a* ~ *trick on s.o.* iem een gemene streek leveren; **3** *(inf)* slecht, ruw *(of weather)*: *wash one's* ~ *linen in public* de vuile was buiten hangen

disability [dissəbillittie] **1** onbekwaamheid, onvermogen[h]; **2** belemmering, nadeel[h], handicap; **3** invaliditeit, lichamelijke ongeschiktheid

disable [disseebl] **1** onmogelijk maken, onbruikbaar, ongeschikt maken; **2** invalide maken, arbeidsongeschikt maken: ~*d persons* (lichamelijk) gehandicapte mensen; *the* ~*d* de invaliden

disadvantage [dissədva:ntidzj] nadeel[h], ongunstige situatie: *at a* ~ in het nadeel

disagree [dissəgrie:] **1** het oneens zijn, verschillen van mening, ruziën; **2** verschillen, niet kloppen, niet overeenkomen: *the two statements* ~ de twee beweringen stemmen niet overeen

disagreeable [dissəgrie:əbl] **1** onaangenaam; **2** slecht gehumeurd, onvriendelijk

disagreement [dissəgrie:mənt] **1** onenigheid, meningsverschil[h], ruzie; **2** verschil[h], afwijking

disallow [dissəlau] **1** niet toestaan, verbieden; **2** ongeldig verklaren, verwerpen, afkeuren: ~ *a goal* een doelpunt afkeuren

disappear [dissəpiə] verdwijnen

disappoint [dissəpojnt] **1** teleurstellen, niet aan de verwachtingen voldoen, tegenvallen; **2** verijdelen *(plan)*, doen mislukken, tenietdoen

disappointed [dissəpojntid] teleurgesteld: *she was* ~ *in him* hij viel haar tegen

disappointment [dissəpojntmənt] teleurstelling

disapprove [dissəproe:v] afkeuren, veroordelen: *he wanted to stay on but his parents* ~*d* hij wilde nog even blijven, maar zijn ouders vonden dat niet goed

¹disarm [dissa:m] *vb* ontwapenen, onschadelijk maken

²disarm [dissa:m] *vb* de kracht ontnemen, vriendelijk stemmen: *his quiet manners* ~*ed all opposition* zijn rustige manier van doen nam alle tegenstand weg; *a* ~*ing smile* een ontwapenende glimlach

disarmament [dissa:məmənt] ontwapening

disarrange [dissəreendzj] in de war brengen, verstoren

disarray [dissərᴇᴇ] wanorde, verwarring

disaster [dizzɑːstə] ramp, catastrofe, *(fig)* totale mislukking: *court ~* om moeilijkheden vragen

disastrous [dizzɑːstrəs] rampzalig, noodlottig

disavowal [dissəvauəl] **1** ontkenning, loochening; **2** afwijzing

disband [disbǽnd] uiteengaan, ontbonden worden

disbelief [disbilliːf] ongeloof[h]: *he stared at us in ~* hij keek ons vol ongeloof aan

disbelieve [disbilliːv] niet geloven, betwijfelen, verwerpen

disc [disk] **1** schijf, parkeerschijf; **2** discus; **3** (grammofoon)plaat, cd; **4** *(med)* schijf, tussenwervelschijf: *a slipped ~* een hernia; **5** *(comp)* schijf

¹discard [diskɑːd] *vb (cards)* afgooien, ecarteren, niet bekennen

²discard [diskɑːd] *vb* zich ontdoen van, weggooien, afdanken

discern [dissəːn] **1** waarnemen, onderscheiden, bespeuren: *I could hardly ~ the words on the traffic sign* ik kon de woorden op het verkeersbord nauwelijks onderscheiden; **2** onderscheiden, verschil zien, onderscheid maken

discerning [dissəːning] scherpzinnig, opmerkzaam, kritisch

¹discharge [distsjɑːdzj] *vb* **1** ontladen, uitladen, lossen; **2** afvuren, afschieten, lossen; **3** ontladen, van elektrische lading ontdoen; **4** wegsturen, ontslaan, ontheffen van, vrijspreken, in vrijheid stellen: *~ the jury* de jury van zijn plichten ontslaan; *~ a patient* een patiënt ontslaan; **5** uitstorten, uitstoten, afgeven; **6** vervullen, voldoen, zich kwijten van: *~ one's duties* zijn taak vervullen

²discharge [distsjɑːdzj] *vb* **1** zich ontladen, zich uitstorten, etteren *(of wound): the river ~s into the sea* de rivier mondt in zee uit; **2** *(electr)* zich ontladen

³discharge [distsjɑːdzj] *n* **1** bewijs[h] van ontslag; **2** lossing, ontlading, het uitladen; **3** uitstorting, afvoer, uitstroming, *(of gas etc; also fig)* uiting; **4** schot[h], het afvuren; **5** aflossing, vervulling; **6** ontslag[h] van rechtsvervolging, vrijspraak

disciple [dissájpl] discipel, leerling, volgeling

¹discipline [dissiplin] *n* **1** methode, systeem[h]; **2** vak[h], discipline, tak van wetenschap; **3** discipline, tucht, orde, controle: *maintain ~* orde houden

²discipline [dissiplin] *vb* **1** disciplineren, onder tucht brengen, drillen; **2** straffen, disciplinaire maatregelen nemen tegen

disc jockey diskjockey

disclaim [disklᴇᴇm] ontkennen, afwijzen, verwerpen, van de hand wijzen

disclose [disklooz] onthullen *(also fig)*, bekendmaken, tonen

disco [diskoo] disco, discotheek

discomfort [diskumfət] **1** ongemak[h], ontbering, moeilijkheid; **2** ongemakkelijkheid, gebrek[h] aan comfort

disconcert [diskənsəːt] **1** verontrusten, in verlegenheid brengen; **2** verijdelen *(plans)*

disconnect [diskənᴇkt] losmaken, scheiden, loskoppelen, afsluiten *(s.o., from gas supply etc)*

¹discontent [diskəntᴇnt] *n* **1** grief, bezwaar[h]; **2** ontevredenheid

²discontent [diskəntᴇnt] *adj (with with)* ontevreden (over, met), teleurgesteld

¹discontinue [diskəntinjoe:] *vb* **1** beëindigen, een eind maken aan, ophouden met; **2** opzeggen *(newspaper etc)*

²discontinue [diskəntinjoe:] *vb* tot een einde komen, ophouden

discord [diskoːd] **1** onenigheid, twist, ruzie; **2** lawaai[h]

discotheque [diskətek] disco, discotheek

¹discount [diskaunt] *n* **1** reductie, korting: *at a ~ of £3* met een korting van drie pond; **2** disconto[h], wisseldisconto[h]

²discount [diskaunt] *vb* **1** disconto geven (nemen), disconteren *(Bill of Exchange);* **2** korting geven (op); **3** buiten beschouwing laten, niet serieus nemen

discourage [diskurridzj] **1** ontmoedigen, de moed ontnemen; **2** weerhouden, afhouden, afbrengen

discourse [diskoːs] **1** gesprek[h], dialoog, conversatie; **2** verhandeling, lezing

discourteous [diskəːtiəs] onbeleefd, onhoffelijk

discover [diskuvvə] **1** ontdekken, (uit)vinden: *Tasman ~ed New Zealand* Tasman heeft Nieuw-Zeeland ontdekt; **2** onthullen, blootleggen, *(fig)* aan het licht brengen, bekendmaken; **3** aantreffen, bemerken, te weten komen

discovery [diskuvvərie] ontdekking: *a voyage of ~* een ontdekkingsreis

¹discredit [diskrᴇddit] *n* schande, diskrediet[h], opspraak: *bring ~ (up)on oneself, bring oneself into ~* zich te schande maken

²discredit [diskrᴇddit] *vb* **1** te schande maken, in diskrediet brengen; **2** wantrouwen, verdenken

discreditable [diskrᴇddittəbl] schandelijk, verwerpelijk

discreet [diskriːt] **1** discreet; **2** bescheiden, onopvallend

discrepancy [diskrᴇppənsie] discrepantie, afwijking, verschil[h]

discretion [diskrᴇsjən] **1** oordeelkundigheid, tact, verstand[h]: *the age (of: years) of ~* de jaren des onderscheids; **2** discretie, oordeel[h], vrijheid (van handelen): *use one's ~* naar eigen goeddunken handelen

¹discriminate [diskrimminneet] *vb* **1** onderscheid maken: *~ between* verschil maken tussen; **2** discrimineren: *~ against* discrimineren; *she felt ~d against in pay* zij voelde zich qua salaris gediscrimineerd

²discriminate [diskrimminneet] *vb* onderscheiden, herkennen

discriminating [diskrimminneeting] **1** opmerkzaam, scherpzinnig; **2** onderscheidend, kenmerkend; **3** kieskeurig, overkritisch; **4** discriminerend

discrimination [diskrimminneesjən] **1** onderscheid[h], het maken van onderscheid; **2** discriminatie; **3** oordeelsvermogen[h], kritische smaak

discus [diskəs] discus

discuss [diskus] bespreken, behandelen, praten over: *okay, let's now ~ my pay rise* goed, laten we het nu eens over mijn loonsverhoging hebben

discussion [diskusjən] **1** bespreking, discussie, gesprek[h]: *be under ~* in behandeling zijn; **2** uiteenzetting, verhandeling, bespreking

disdain [disdeen] minachting

disease [dizzie:z] ziekte, aandoening, kwaal

¹disembark [dissimba:k] *vb* van boord gaan, aan wal gaan, uitstappen

²disembark [dissimba:k] *vb* ontschepen, aan land brengen, lossen

disenchant [dissintsja:nt] ontgoochelen, ontnuchteren, uit de droom helpen

¹disengage [dissinggeedzj] *vb* losraken, zich losmaken

²disengage [dissinggeedzj] *vb* losmaken, vrij maken, bevrijden

¹disentangle [dissintænggl] *vb* ontwarren, ontrafelen, oplossen

²disentangle [dissintænggl] *vb* zich ontwarren

disfavour [disfeevə] **1** afkeuring, lage dunk: *look upon* (of: *regard, view*) *s.o. with ~* iem niet mogen; **2** ongenade, ongunst

disfigurement [disfigəmənt] misvorming, wanstaltigheid

¹disgorge [disgo:dzj] *vb* leegstromen, zich legen, zich uitstorten

²disgorge [disgo:dzj] *vb* **1** uitbraken, uitstoten; **2** uitstorten, uitstromen

¹disgrace [disgrees] *n* schande, ongenade: *be in ~* uit de gratie zijn

²disgrace [disgrees] *vb* te schande maken, een slechte naam bezorgen

disgruntled [disgruntld] ontevreden: *~ at sth.* (of: *with s.o.*) ontstemd over iets

¹disguise [disgajz] *vb* **1** vermommen; **2** een valse voorstelling geven van; **3** verbergen, maskeren, verhullen

²disguise [disgajz] *n* **1** vermomming: *in ~* vermomd, in het verborgene; *a blessing in ~* een geluk bij een ongeluk; **2** voorwendsel[h], schijn, dekmantel

¹disgust [disgust] *n* afschuw, afkeer, walging

²disgust [disgust] *vb* doen walgen, afkeer opwekken: *she was suddenly ~ed at* (of: *by, with*) *him* plotseling vond ze hem weerzinwekkend

disgusting [disgusting] weerzinwekkend, walgelijk

¹dish [disj] *n* **1** schaal, schotel; **2** gerecht[h], schotel; **3** schotelvormig voorwerp[h], schotelantenne: *~ aerial* schotelantenne; **4** lekker stuk[h], lekkere meid

²dish [disj] *vb* ruïneren, naar de maan helpen, verknallen ǁ *~ out: a)* uitdelen *(papers, presents etc); b)* rondgeven, rondstrooien *(advice)*

dishcloth vaatdoek

dishearten [disha:tn] ontmoedigen

dishevelled [disjevld] slonzig, slordig, onverzorgd

dishonest [dissonnist] oneerlijk, bedrieglijk, vals

dishonour [dissonnə] schande, eerverlies[h], smaad

dish up 1 opdienen, serveren, *(fig)* presenteren, opdissen *(facts etc);* **2** het eten opdienen

dishwasher 1 afwasser, bordenwasser; **2** afwasmachine, vaatwasmachine

disillusion [dissilloe:zjən] desillusioneren, uit de droom helpen: *be ~ed at* (of: *about, with*) teleurgesteld zijn over

disinclination [dissingklinneesjən] tegenzin, onwil, afkeer: *feel a ~ to meet s.o.* geen (echte) zin hebben om iem te ontmoeten

disinfect [dissinfekt] desinfecteren, ontsmetten

¹disinfectant [dissinfektənt] *n* desinfecterend middel[h], ontsmettingsmiddel[h]

²disinfectant [dissinfektənt] *adj* desinfecterend, ontsmettend

disinherit [dissinherrit] onterven

disintegrate [dissintigreet] **1** uiteenvallen, uit elkaar vallen, vergaan; **2** *(chem)* afbreken

disinterested [dissintristid] **1** belangeloos; **2** *(fig)* ongeïnteresseerd, onverschillig

disjointed [disdzjojntid] onsamenhangend, verward *(of story, ideas)*

disk [disk] *see* disc

diskette [disket] diskette, floppy(disk)

¹dislike [dislajk] *vb* niet houden van, een afkeer hebben van, een hekel hebben aan

²dislike [dislajk] *n* afkeer, tegenzin: *likes and ~s* sympathieën en antipathieën

dislocate [disləkeet] **1** verplaatsen; **2** onklaar maken, ontregelen, *(fig)* verstoren, in de war brengen; **3** *(med)* ontwrichten

disloyal [dislojjəl] ontrouw, trouweloos, niet loyaal

dismal [dizml] **1** ellendig, troosteloos, somber; **2** zwak, armzalig

¹dismantle [dismæntl] *vb* **1** ontmantelen, van de bedekking ontdoen; **2** leeghalen, van meubilair (uitrusting) ontdoen, onttakelen; **3** slopen, afbreken, uit elkaar halen

²dismantle [dismæntl] *vb* uitneembaar zijn *(eg of appliance)*

¹dismay [dismee] *n* wanhoop, verbijstering, ontzetting

²dismay [dismee] *vb* verbijsteren, ontzetten, met wanhoop vervullen: *be ~ed at* (of: *by*) *the sight* de moed verliezen door de aanblik

dismiss [dismis] **1** laten gaan, wegsturen; **2** ontslaan, opzeggen; **3** van zich afzetten, uit zijn gedachten zetten; **4** afdoen, zich (kort) afmaken van, verwerpen: *they ~ed the suggestion* ze verwierpen het voorstel; **5** afdanken, laten inrukken

dismissal [dismisl] **1** verlof[h] om te gaan; **2** ontslag[h]; **3** verdringing, het uit zijn gedachten zetten; **4** het terzijde schuiven, verwerping, het afdoen

dismissive [dismissiv] minachtend, afwijzend

disobedient [dissəbie:diənt] ongehoorzaam, opstandig

disobey [dissəbee] niet gehoorzamen, ongehoorzaam zijn, negeren *(order)*, overtreden *(rules)*

disorder [disso:də] **1** oproer[h], opstootje[h], ordeverstoring; **2** stoornis, kwaal, ziekte, aandoening: *Boris suffered from a kidney ~* Boris leed aan een nierkwaal; **3** wanorde, verwarring, ordeloosheid

disown [dissoon] **1** verwerpen, afwijzen, ontkennen; **2** verstoten, niet meer willen kennen

disparage [dispæridzj] **1** kleineren, geringschatten; **2** in diskrediet brengen, verdacht maken, vernederen

disparity [dispærittie] ongelijkheid, ongelijksoortigheid, ongelijkwaardigheid: *(a) great ~ of* (of: *in) age between them* een groot leeftijdsverschil tussen hen

[1]dispatch [dispætsj] *vb* **1** (ver)zenden, (weg)sturen; **2** de genadeslag geven, doden; **3** doeltreffend afhandelen; **4** wegwerken *(food etc)*, soldaat maken

[2]dispatch [dispætsj] *n* **1** bericht[h]; **2** het wegsturen; **3** doeltreffendheid, snelle afhandeling: *with great ~* met grote doeltreffendheid

dispel [dispel] verjagen, verdrijven

dispensary [dispensərie] **1** apotheek, huisapotheek *(in school etc);* **2** consultatiebureau[h], medische hulppost

[1]dispense [dispens] *vb* **1** uitreiken, distribueren, geven: *~ justice* het recht toepassen, gerechtigheid doen geschieden; **2** klaarmaken en leveren *(drugs): dispensing chemist* apotheker

[2]dispense [dispens] *vb* ontheffing geven, vrijstelling verlenen

dispenser [dispensə] **1** apotheker; **2** automaat, houder

dispense with 1 afzien van, het zonder stellen, niet nodig hebben; **2** overbodig maken, terzijde zetten

[1]disperse [dispə:s] *vb* zich verspreiden, uiteengaan

[2]disperse [dispə:s] *vb* **1** uiteen drijven, verspreiden, spreiden, uiteenplaatsen; **2** verspreiden, overal bekendmaken; **3** verjagen

dispirited [dispirritid] moedeloos, somber, mistroostig

displace [displees] **1** verplaatsen, verschuiven; **2** vervangen, verdringen

[1]display [displee] *vb* **1** tonen, exposeren, uitstallen; **2** tentoonspreiden, tonen, aan de dag leggen: *a touching ~ of friendship and affection* een ontroerende blijk van vriendschap en genegenheid; **3** te koop lopen met, demonstreren

[2]display [displee] *n* **1** tentoonstelling, uitstalling, weergave: *the more expensive models are on ~ in our showroom* de duurdere modellen zijn uitgestald in onze toonzaal; **2** vertoning, tentoonspreiding; **3** demonstratie, vertoon[h], druktemakerij

displease [displie:z] ergeren, irriteren: *be ~d at sth.* boos zijn over iets

disposable [dispoozəbl] **1** beschikbaar: *~ income* besteedbaar inkomen; **2** wegwerp-, weggooi-

disposal [dispoozl] **1** het wegdoen, verwijdering; **2** overdracht, verkoop, schenking; **3** beschikking: *I am entirely at your ~* ik sta geheel tot uw beschikking

dispose [dispooz] **1** plaatsen, ordenen, rangschikken, regelen; **2** brengen tot, bewegen: *~ s.o. to do sth.* iem er toe brengen iets te doen

disposed [dispoozd] geneigd, bereid: *they seemed favourably ~ to(wards) that idea* zij schenen welwillend tegenover dat idee te staan

dispose of 1 van de hand doen, verkopen, wegdoen; **2** afhandelen, uit de weg ruimen *(questions, problems etc)*

disposition [dispəzisjən] **1** plaatsing, rangschikking, opstelling; **2** aard, karakter[h], neiging: *she has a (*of: *is of a) happy ~* zij heeft een opgewekt karakter

dispossess [dispəzes] onteigenen, ontnemen: *~ s.o. of sth.* iem iets ontnemen

disproportionate [disprəpo:sjənət] onevenredig, niet naar verhouding

disprove [disproe:v] weerleggen, de onjuistheid aantonen van

[1]dispute [dispjoe:t] *vb* redetwisten, discussiëren

[2]dispute [dispjoe:t] *vb* **1** heftig bespreken, heftig discussiëren over; **2** aanvechten, in twijfel trekken; **3** betwisten, strijd voeren over; **4** weerstand bieden aan

[3]dispute [dispjoe:t] *n* **1** twistgesprek[h], discussie, woordenstrijd: *the matter in ~* de zaak in kwestie; **2** geschil[h], twist: *beyond* (of: *past, without) ~* buiten kijf

disqualify [diskwolliffaj] **1** ongeschikt maken; **2** onbevoegd verklaren; **3** diskwalificeren, uitsluiten

disregard [disriga:d] **1** geen acht slaan op, negeren: *~ a warning* een waarschuwing in de wind slaan; **2** geringschatten

disrepair [disrippeə] verval[h], bouwvalligheid: *the house had fallen into ~* (of: *was in ~)* het huis was vervallen

disrepute [disripjoe:t] slechte naam, diskrediet[h]: *bring into ~* in diskrediet brengen

disrupt [disrupt] **1** uiteen doen vallen, verscheuren; **2** ontwrichten, verstoren: *communications were ~ed* de verbindingen waren verbroken

diss [dis] *(Am, inf)* beledigen

dissatisfaction [disætisfæksjən] ontevredenheid

dissect [dissekt] **1** in stukken snijden, verdelen; **2** ontleden, grondig analyseren

dissection [disseksjən] **1** ontleed deel[h] van dier of plant; **2** ontleding, analyse

disseminate [dissemminneet] uitzaaien, verspreiden

dissension [dissensjən] **1** meningsverschil[h]; **2** tweedracht, verdeeldheid, onenigheid

dissent [dissent] verschil[h] van mening

dissertation [dissəteesjən] **1** verhandeling, dissertatie, proefschrift[h]; **2** scriptie

dissident [dissiddənt] **1** dissident, andersdenkend; **2** dissident, andersdenkende

dissimilar [dissimmillə] ongelijk, verschillend: *~*

in character verschillend van aard

dissimulation [dissimjoeleesjǝn] veinzerij

dissipate [dissippeet] **1** verdrijven, verjagen, doen verdwijnen; **2** verspillen, verkwisten

dissociate [dissoosjie·eet] scheiden, afscheiden: *it is very hard to ~ the man from what he did* het is erg moeilijk om de man los te zien van wat hij heeft gedaan; *~ oneself from* zich distantiëren van

dissolute [dissǝloe:t] **1** losbandig; **2** verdorven

¹dissolve [dizzolv] *vb* oplossen, smelten: *(fig) ~ in(to) tears* in tranen wegsmelten

²dissolve [dizzolv] *vb* **1** oplossen; **2** ontbinden *(of parliament)*, opheffen

dissonance [dissǝnǝns] **1** wanklank; **2** onenigheid

dissuade [disweed] ontraden, afraden

distance [distǝns] **1** afstand, tussenruimte, eind(je)ʰ, *(fig)* afstand(elijkheid), terughoudendheid: *keep one's ~* afstand bewaren; *within walking ~* op loopafstand; *in the ~* in de verte; **2** (tijds)afstand, tijdsverloopʰ, tijdruimte

distant [distǝnt] **1** ver, afgelegen, verwijderd: *~ relations* verre bloedverwanten; **2** afstandelijk: *a ~ smile* een gereserveerde glimlach

distaste [disteest] *(with for)* afkeer (van), aversie (van), weerzin: *for once he managed to overcome his ~ hard work* eenmaal wist hij zijn afkeer van hard werken te overwinnen

¹distil [distil] *vb* **1** distilleren; **2** via distillatie vervaardigen, branden, stoken

²distil [distil] *vb* **1** afdruppelen, (neer)druppelen, sijpelen; **2** gedistilleerd worden

distillery [distillǝrie] distilleerderij, stokerij

distinct [distingkt] **1** onderscheiden, verschillend, apart: *four ~ meanings* vier afzonderlijke betekenissen; **2** duidelijk, goed waarneembaar; onmiskenbaar: *a ~ possibility* een stellige mogelijkheid

distinction [distingksjǝn] **1** onderscheiding, eretekenʰ; **2** onderscheidʰ, onderscheiding, verschilʰ: *draw a sharp ~ between* een scherp onderscheid maken tussen; **3** voortreffelijkheid, aanzienʰ, gedistingeerdheid

distinctive [distingktiv] onderscheidend, kenmerkend

distinguish [distinggwisj] **1** indelen, rangschikken; **2** onderscheiden, onderkennen: *~ cause and effect* oorzaak en gevolg onderscheiden; **3** zien, onderscheiden: *I could ~ the tower in the distance* in de verte kon ik de toren onderscheiden; **4** kenmerken, karakteriseren: *~ between* onderscheid maken tussen, uit elkaar houden

distinguished [distinggwisjt] **1** voornaam, aanzienlijk; **2** beroemd, befaamd; **3** gedistingeerd

distort [disto:t] **1** vervormen, verwringen: *the frame of my bike was completely ~ed* het frame van mijn fiets was helemaal vervormd; **2** verdraaien, vertekenen: *a ~ed version of the facts* een verdraaide versie van de feiten

distract [distrækt] **1** afleiden; **2** verwarren, verbijsteren

---

distraction [distræksjǝn] **1** vermakelijkheid, ontspanning, vermaakʰ; **2** afleiding, ontspanning, vermaakʰ; **3** gebrekʰ aan aandacht; **4** verwarring, gekheid: *those children are driving me to ~* ik word stapelgek van die kinderen

distress [distres] **1** leedʰ, verdrietʰ, zorg; **2** nood, armoede; **3** gevaarʰ, nood: *a ship in ~* een schip in nood

distressed [distrest] **1** (diep) bedroefd; **2** bang; **3** overstuur, van streek; **4** noodlijdend, behoeftig

distribute [distribjoe:t] distribueren, verdelen: *the rainfall is evenly ~d throughout the year* de regenval is gelijkmatig over het jaar verdeeld

distribution [distribjoe:sjǝn] verdeling, (ver)spreiding, distributie

district [distrikt] **1** districtʰ, regio; **2** streek, gebiedʰ; **3** wijk, buurt: *a residential ~* een woonwijk

¹distrust [distrust] *vb* wantrouwen, geen vertrouwen stellen in

²distrust [distrust] *n* wantrouwenʰ, argwaan, achterdocht

disturb [distǝ:b] **1** in beroering brengen *(also fig)*, verontrusten: *~ing facts* verontrustende feiten; **2** storen: *be mentally ~ed* geestelijk gestoord zijn; *please do not ~!* a.u.b. niet storen!; **3** verstoren: *~ the peace* de openbare orde verstoren

disturbance [distǝ:bǝns] **1** opschudding, relletjeʰ; **2** stoornis, verstoring: *a ~ of the peace* een ordeverstoring; **3** storing

disunity [disjoe:nittie] verdeeldheid, onenigheid

disuse [disjoe:s] onbruikʰ: *fall into ~* in onbruik (ge)raken

ditch [ditsj] sloot, greppel

¹dither [diðǝ] *vb* **1** aarzelen; **2** zenuwachtig doen

²dither [diðǝ] *n* zenuwachtigheid, nerveuze opwinding: *all of a ~* zenuwachtig, opgewonden

ditto [dittoo] **1** ditoʰ, idem, hetzelfde; **2** duplicaatʰ

ditty [dittie] liedjeʰ, deuntjeʰ

¹dive [dajv] *vb* **1** duiken *(also fig)*, onderduiken, een duikvlucht maken: *~ into one's studies* zich werpen op zijn studie; **2** wegduiken; **3** tasten, de hand steken (in): *she ~d into her handbag* zij stak haar hand diep in haar tasje

²dive [dajv] *n* **1** duik, duikvlucht; **2** plotselinge snelle beweging, greep, duik: *he made a ~ for the ball* hij dook naar de bal; **3** kroeg, tent

diver [dajvǝ] duiker

diverge [dajvǝ:dzj] **1** uiteenlopen, uiteenwijken; **2** afwijken, verschillen: *his account ~s from the official version* zijn verslag wijkt af van de officiële versie; **3** afdwalen

diverse [dajvǝ:s] **1** divers, verschillend; **2** afwisselend, gevarieerd

diversion [dajvǝ:sjǝn] **1** afleidingsactie, schijnbeweging; **2** afleiding, ontspanning; **3** omleiding

diversity [dajvǝ:sittie] **1** ongelijkheid: *their ~ of interests* hun uiteenlopende belangen; **2** verscheidenheid, diversiteit

divert [dajvǝ:t] **1** een andere richting geven, verleggen, omleiden: *why was their plane ~ed to Vienna?* waarom moest hun toestel uitwijken naar Wenen?; **2** afleiden *(attention);* **3** amuseren, vermaken

¹divide [divvajd] *vb* **1** delen, in delen splitsen, indelen; **2** scheiden: *~d highway* weg met gescheiden dubbele rijbanen; **3** onderling verdelen *(also fig)*, distribueren, verkavelen: *~d against itself* onderling verdeeld; **4** delen: *how much is 18 ~d by 3?* hoeveel is 18 gedeeld door 3?

²divide [divvajd] *vb* **1** verdeeld worden; **2** onenigheid krijgen; **3** zich delen, zich vertakken

³divide [divvajd] *n* **1** waterscheiding; **2** scheidslijn

dividend [divviddand] dividend[h], winstaandeel[h], uitkering (van winst)

divination [divvinneesjan] **1** profetie, voorspelling; **2** waarzeggerij

¹divine [divvajn] *adj* **1** goddelijk; **2** aan God gewijd: *~ service* godsdienstoefening; **3** hemels, verrukkelijk

²divine [divvajn] *vb* gissen, raden, inzien, een voorgevoel hebben van

³divine [divvajn] *vb* **1** waarzeggen; **2** (met wichelroede) vaststellen

diviner [divvajna] **1** waarzegger; **2** (wichel)roedeloper

divining rod wichelroede

divinity [divvinnittie] **1** godheid; goddelijkheid, god, goddelijk wezen[h]: *the Divinity* de Godheid; **2** theologie

divisible [divvizzibl] deelbaar

division [divvizjan] **1** (ver)deling, het delen: *a ~ of labour* een arbeidsverdeling; **2** afdeling *(organisation, bureau);* **3** *(mil)* divisie; **4** scheiding, scheidslijn, afscheiding; **5** verschil[h], ongelijkheid, onenigheid: *a ~ of opinion* uiteenlopende meningen

divisive [divvajsiv] tot ongelijkheid leidend, onenigheid brengend

¹divorce [divvo:s] *n* (echt)scheiding

²divorce [divvo:s] *vb* scheiden (van), zich laten scheiden van

divorcee [divvo:sie:] gescheiden vrouw

divulge [dajvuldzj] onthullen, openbaar maken, bekendmaken

D.I.Y. *do-it-yourself* d.h.z., doe-het-zelf

dizzy [dizzie] **1** duizelig, draaierig; **2** verward, versuft; **3** duizelingwekkend *(of height, speed etc)*

D.J. [die:dzjee] *disc jockey* deejay, dj

¹do [doe:] *vb* **1** doen *(sth abstract):* *~ one's best* zijn best doen; *it isn't done* zoiets doet men niet; *what can I ~ for you?* wat kan ik voor je doen?, *(in shop)* wat mag het zijn?; **2** bezig zijn met *(sth concrete, existing)*, doen, opknappen, in orde brengen, herstellen, oplossen *(puzzles etc)*, studeren: *~ one's duty* zijn plicht doen; *~ psychology* psychologie studeren; *have one's teeth done* zijn tanden laten nakijken; *~ up the kitchen* de keuken opknappen; **3** maken, doen ontstaan: *the storm did a lot of damage* de storm richtte heel wat schade aan; *~ wonders* wonderen verrichten; **4** (aan)doen, geven, veroor-

zaken: *~ s.o. a favour* iem een dienst bewijzen; **5** beëindigen, afhandelen, afmaken, *(inf; fig)* uitputten, kapotmaken: *I have done cleaning, (inf) I am done cleaning* ik ben klaar met de schoonmaak; *done in* bekaf, afgepeigerd; *(inf) ~ s.o. in* iem van kant maken; **6** *(culinary)* bereiden, klaarmaken: *well done* goed doorbakken *(of meat);* **7** rijden, afleggen: *~ 50 mph.* 80 km/u rijden; **8** *(inf)* beetnemen, afzetten, neppen: *~ s.o. for $100* iem voor honderd dollar afzetten; **9** ontvangen, onthalen: *he does himself well* hij zorgt wel dat hij niets te kort komt; **10** *(inf)* uitzitten *(a sentence): he has done time in Attica* hij zat vast in Attica; *I've done it again* ik heb het weer verknoeid; *a boiled egg will ~ me* ik heb genoeg aan een gekookt ei; *over and done with* voltooid verleden tijd; *~ up a zip* een rits dichtdoen

²do [doe:] *vb* **1** doen, handelen, zich gedragen: *he did well to refuse that offer* hij deed er goed aan dat aanbod te weigeren; *she was hard done by* zij was oneerlijk behandeld; **2** het stellen, maken, zich voelen: *how do you ~* hoe maakt u het?; *he is ~ing well* het gaat goed met hem; **3** aan de hand zijn, gebeuren: *nothing ~ing: a)* er gebeurt (hier) niets; *b)* daar komt niets van in; **4** klaar zijn, opgehouden zijn (hebben): *be done with s.o.* niets meer te maken (willen) hebben met iem; *have done with sth.* ergens een punt achter zetten; **5** geschikt zijn, voldoen, volstaan: *this copy won't ~* deze kopie is niet goed genoeg; *it doesn't ~ to say such things* zoiets hoor je niet te zeggen; *that will ~!* en nou is 't uit!; **6** het (moeten) doen, het (moeten) stellen met: *they'll have to ~ with what they've got* ze zullen het moeten doen met wat ze hebben; *~ away with: a)* wegdoen, weggooien, een eind maken aan; *b)* afschaffen *(death penalty, institution etc); ~ for s.o.* het huishouden doen voor iem, werkster zijn bij iem; *I could ~ with a few quid* ik zou best een paar pond kunnen gebruiken; *it has got nothing to ~ with you* jij staat erbuiten

³do [doe:] *vb (oft untranslated)* ‖ *(in interrogative sentence) ~ you know him?* ken je hem?; *(in negative sentence) I don't know him* ik ken hem niet; *(replacing verb) he laughed and so did she* hij lachte, en zij ook; *I treat my friends as he does his enemies:* badly ik behandel mijn vrienden zoals hij zijn vijanden: slecht; *(to ask for consent) he writes well, doesn't he?* hij schrijft goed, niet waar?; *(with emphasis, in imperative mood) ~ come in!* kom toch binnen!; *oh, ~ be quiet!* o, houd alsjeblieft eens je mond!

⁴do [doe:] *n* partij, feest[h] ‖ *~'s and don'ts* wat wel en wat niet mag

doc [dok] *doctor* dokter

docile [doosajl] meegaand, volgzaam

¹dock [dok] *n* **1** dok[h], droogdok[h], havendok[h], kade: *floating ~* drijvend dok; **2** *~s* haven(s); **3** werf; **4** beklaagdenbank: *be in the ~* terechtstaan; *in ~: a)* in reparatie; *b)* in het ziekenhuis; *c)* op de helling

²dock [dok] *vb* **1** dokken, de haven binnenlopen, in het dok gaan; **2** gekoppeld worden *(spacecraft)*

³dock [dok] *vb* **1** couperen *(tail etc)*, afsnijden, afknippen; **2** korten, (gedeeltelijk) inhouden, achterhouden; **3** dokken, in het dok brengen; **4** koppelen *(spacecraft)*

docker [dokkə] dokwerker, havenarbeider, stuwadoor

docket [dokkit] **1** bon, kassabon, bewijsstukʰ, reçuʰ; **2** korte inhoud *(of document, report)*

dockyard werf

¹doctor [doktə] *n* **1** dokter, arts, *(Am)* tandarts, veearts: *that is just what the ~ ordered* dat is net wat je nodig hebt; **2** doctor *(somebody holding the highest university degree)*

²doctor [doktə] *vb* **1** *(euph)* helpen, steriliseren, castreren; **2** knoeien met, rommelen met, vervalsen: *~ the accounts* de boeken vervalsen

doctrine [doktrin] **1** doctrine, leer; **2** dogmaʰ, beginselʰ

document [dokjoemənt] documentʰ, bewijsstukʰ

documentary [dokjoementərie] documentaire

documentation [dokjoemənteesjən] **1** documentatie; **2** bewijsmateriaalʰ

dodder [doddə] **1** beven *(with old age, weakness)*; **2** schuifelen, strompelen

¹dodge [dodzj] *vb* ontwijken, vermijden, ontduiken: *he kept dodging the question* hij bleef de vraag ontwijken

²dodge [dodzj] *vb* **1** (opzij) springen, snel bewegen, rennen: *the woman ~d behind the chair* de vrouw dook weg achter de stoel; **2** uitvluchten zoeken, (eromheen) draaien

³dodge [dodzj] *n* **1** (zij)sprong, ontwijkende beweging; **2** foefjeʰ, trucjeʰ, slimmigheidjeʰ: *a tax ~* een belastingtruc

dodgem [dodzjəm] botsautootjeʰ

dodgy [dodzjie] **1** slim, gewiekst; **2** netelig: *~ situation* netelige situatie

doe [doo] wijfjeʰ ve konijn

¹dog [dog] *n* **1** hond; **2** *(inf)* kerel: *lucky ~* geluksvogel, mazzelaar; *not a ~'s chance* geen schijn van kans; *he is a ~ in the manger* hij kan de zon niet in het water zien schijnen; *go to the ~s* naar de bliksem gaan; *the ~s* (wind)hondenrennen

²dog [dog] *vb* (achter)volgen, (achter)nazitten

dog-eared met ezelsoren

dogged [dogid] vasthoudend, volhardend

doggy [dogie] hondjeʰ

dogmatic [dogmætik] **1** dogmatisch; **2** autoritair

dogsbody [dogzboddie] duivelstoejager, sloof: *a general ~* een manusje-van-alles

doing [doeing] **1** handeling, het handelen, het (toe)doen: *it is all their ~* het is allemaal hun schuld; **2** *~s* daden, handelingen

doldrums [doldrəmz] **1** neerslachtigheid: *be in the ~* in de put zitten; **2** het stilliggen ve schip; **3** *(fig)* stilstand

dole [dool] werkloosheidsuitkering, steun: *be on the ~* steun trekken

doll [dol] **1** pop; **2** meisjeʰ, meid

dollar [dollə] dollar

dollop [dolləp] (klein) beetjeʰ, kwak, scheut

doll up zich optutten: *doll oneself up* zich uitdossen

dolly [dollie] *(child language)* pop(jeʰ)

dolphin [dolfin] dolfijn

dolt [doolt] domoor, uilskuikenʰ

domain [dəmeen] **1** domeinʰ, (land)goedʰ; **2** gebiedʰ *(fig)*, veldʰ, terreinʰ: *the garden is my wife's ~* de tuin is het domein van mijn vrouw

dome [doom] **1** koepel; **2** gewelfʰ; **3** ronde top: *the ~ of a hill* de ronde top van een heuvel

¹domestic [dəmestik] *adj* **1** huishoudelijk, het huishouden betreffend: *~ economy* (of: *science*) huishoudkunde; **2** huiselijk; **3** binnenlands: *~ trade* binnenlandse handel; **4** tam: *~ animals* huisdieren

²domestic [dəmestik] *n* bediende, dienstbode

domesticate [dəmestikkeet] **1** aan het huiselijk leven doen wennen; **2** aan zich onderwerpen, temmen, beteugelen, tot huisdier maken

domicile [dommissail] verblijfplaats, woning

dominance [domminnəns] overheersing

dominant [domminnənt] dominant *(also biology)*, (over)heersend

dominate [domminneet] domineren, overheersen: *~ the conversation* het hoogste woord voeren

domination [domminneesjən] overheersing, heerschappij

dominion [dəminniən] **1** domeinʰ, (grond)gebiedʰ, rijkʰ; **2** heerschappij, macht

domino [domminnoo] *(~es)* **1** dominosteen; **2** *~es* domino(spel)ʰ

donate [dooneet] schenken, geven: *~ money towards sth.* geld schenken voor iets

done 1 netjes, gepast: *it is not ~* zoiets doet men niet; **2** klaar, gereed, af: *be ~ with* klaar zijn met; *have ~ with* niets meer te maken (willen) hebben met; **3** doodmoe, uitgeput: *hard ~ by* oneerlijk behandeld; *she seemed completely ~ in* (of: *up*) zij leek volkomen uitgeteld; *done!* akkoord!, afgesproken!

donkey [dongkie] ezel *(also fig)*, domoor, sufferd

donor [doonə] **1** gever, schenker; **2** donor

don't [doont] verbodʰ: *do's and ~s* wat wel en niet mag, geboden en verboden

donut *(Am) see* doughnut

¹doodle [doe:dl] *n* krabbel, figuurtjeʰ, poppetjeʰ

²doodle [doe:dl] *vb* krabbelen, figuurtjes tekenen

¹doom [doe:m] *n* **1** noodlotʰ, lotʰ: *a sense of ~ and foreboding* een gevoel van naderend onheil; **2** ondergang, verderfʰ: *meet one's ~* de ondergang vinden; **3** laatste oordeelʰ

²doom [doe:m] *vb* **1** veroordelen, (ver)doemen; **2** *(esp as part participle)* ten ondergang doemen: *the undertaking was ~ed from the start* de onderneming was vanaf het begin tot mislukken gedoemd

doomsday [doe:mzdee] dag des oordeels *(also fig)*, doemdag: *till ~* eeuwig

door [do:] **1** deur, (auto)portierʰ: *answer the ~* (de deur) opendoen (voor iem die aangebeld heeft); *show s.o. the ~* iem de deur wijzen; *show s.o. to the*

~ iem uitlaten; *out of ~s* buiten(shuis); **2** toegang, mogelijkheid: *leave the ~ open* de mogelijkheid openlaten; *lay the blame at s.o.'s ~* iem de schuld geven

doorway deuropening, ingang, deurgat[h]

¹dope [doop] *n* **1** sufferd, domoor; **2** drugs, verdovende middelen; **3** doping, stimulerende middelen; **4** info(rmatie), nieuws[h]; **5** smeermiddel[h], smeersel[h]

²dope [doop] *vb* verdovende middelen, doping toedienen aan

dormant [do:mənt] **1** slapend, sluimerend, *(biology)* in winterslaap; **2** latent, verborgen; **3** inactief: *a ~ volcano* een slapende vulkaan

dormitory [do:mittərie] **1** slaapzaal; **2** *(Am)* studentenhuis[h]

dormouse [do:maus] slaapmuis

dosage [doosidzj] dosering, dosis

¹dose [doos] *n* dosis *(also fig)*, hoeveelheid, stralingsdosis ‖ *like a ~ of salts* razend vlug

²dose [doos] *vb* doseren, medicijn toedienen aan

dosshouse logement[h], goedkoop hotelletje[h]

¹dot [dot] *n* punt[h] *(also music, Morse; on letter)*, spikkel, stip ‖ *on the ~* stipt (op tijd)

²dot [dot] *vb* **1** een punt zetten op *(also music): (fig)* ~ *the i's (and cross the t's)* de puntjes op de i zetten; **2** stippelen, (be)spikkelen: *~ted line* stippellijn; *sign on the ~ted line* (een contract) ondertekenen

dote (up)on dol zijn op, verzot zijn op, *(fig)* aanbidden, verafgoden

dotty [dottie] **1** gespikkeld, gestippeld; **2** getikt, niet goed snik; **3** *(with about)* dol (op), gek (op)

¹double [dubl] *adj* **1** dubbel, tweemaal (zo groot, veel): *~ the amount* tweemaal zo veel; *~ bed* tweepersoonsbed; *~ chin* onderkin, dubbele kin; *~ cream* dikke room; *~ entry (bookkeeping)* dubbele boekhouding; *~ exposure* dubbele belichting; *~ glazing* dubbele beglazing; *~ standard* het meten met twee maten *(fig);* **2** oneerlijk, dubbelhartig, vals: *~ agent* dubbelagent, dubbelspion; *~ Dutch* koeterwaals, onzin

²double [dubl] *n* **1** dubbel, doublet[h]: *~ or quits* quitte of dubbel; **2** het dubbele, dubbele (hoeveelheid, snelheid e.d.); **3** dubbelganger; **4** *(film etc)* doublure, vervanger, stuntman; **5** verdubbeling *(of score, board, stake etc in various sports);* **6** *~s (tennis)* dubbel(spel)[h]: *mixed ~s* gemengd dubbel; *at (of: on) the ~* in looppas, *(fig)* meteen, onmiddellijk

³double [dubl] *adv* dubbel, tweemaal (zoveel als), samen

⁴double [dubl] *vb* **1** (zich) verdubbelen, doubleren; **2** terugkeren, plotseling omkeren: *~ (back) on one's tracks* op zijn schreden terugkeren; **3** een dubbele rol spelen; **4** *(film etc)* als vervanger optreden: *~ for an actor* een (toneel)speler vervangen

⁵double [dubl] *vb* **1** verdubbelen, doubleren, tweemaal zo groot maken; **2** *(film etc)* als vervanger optreden van; **3** *(bridge)* doubleren

¹double back *vb* terugkeren

²double back *vb* terugslaan, terugvouwen

double-bass contrabas

double-breasted met twee rijen knopen, dubbelrijs

double-cross bedriegen, dubbel spel spelen met, oplichten

¹double-dealing *adj* oneerlijk, vals

²double-dealing *n* oplichterij, bedrog[h]

double-edged tweesnijdend *(also fig): a ~ argument* een argument dat zowel vóór als tegen kan worden gebruikt

double-quick vliegensvlug, razendsnel, zo snel je kunt

double-talk 1 onzin; **2** dubbelzinnigheid, dubbelzinnige opmerking(en)

double-time 1 looppas; **2** overwerkgeld[h], onregelmatigheidstoeslag *(of employee)*

¹double up *vb* ineenkrimpen *(with laughter, in pain)*

²double up *vb* **1** buigen, doen ineenkrimpen: *~ one's legs* zijn benen intrekken; **2** opvouwen, omslaan, terugslaan

doubly [dublie] dubbel (zo), tweemaal (zo): *~ careful* extra voorzichtig

¹doubt [daut] *vb* twijfelen (aan), onzeker zijn, betwijfelen: *~ that* (of: *whether)* (be)twijfelen of

²doubt [daut] *n* twijfel, onzekerheid, aarzeling: *the benefit of the ~* het voordeel van de twijfel; *be in no ~ about sth.* ergens zeker van zijn; *have one's ~s about sth.* ergens aan twijfelen; *without (a) ~* ongetwijfeld; *no ~* ongetwijfeld, zonder (enige) twijfel

dough [doo] **1** deeg[h]; **2** *(inf)* poen, centen

doughnut [doonut] donut

dour [doeə] streng, stug

dove [duv] duif *(also fig)*, aanhanger van vredespolitiek

dovecot(e) [duvkot] duiventil

dovetail precies passen *(also fig)*, overeenkomen: *my plans ~ed with his* mijn plannen sloten aan bij de zijne

dowdy [daudie] slonzig, slordig gekleed

¹down [daun] *adv* neer, (naar) beneden, omlaag, onder: *bend ~* bukken, vooroverbuigen; *the sun goes ~* de zon gaat onder; *up and ~* op en neer; *~ with the president!* weg met de president!; *come (of: go) ~* de universiteit verlaten *(because of holidays or graduation); be sent ~* weggezonden worden van de universiteit; *eight ~ and two to go* acht gespeeld, nog twee te spelen; *~ under* in Australië en Nieuw-Zeeland

²down [daun] *adj* **1** neergaand, naar onder leidend; **2** beneden; **3** depressief, verdrietig ‖ *cash ~* contante betaling, handje contantje; *~ payment* contante betaling

³down [daun] *prep* **1** vanaf, langs: *~ the coast* langs de kust; *~ (the) river* de rivier af, verder stroomafwaarts; *he went ~ the street* hij liep de straat door; **2** neer, af: *~ town* de stad in, in het centrum

⁴down [daun] *n* dons[h], haartjes, veertjes ‖ *have a ~ on s.o.* een hekel hebben aan iem

downcast terneergeslagen, somber, neerslachtig

downgrade 1 degraderen, in rang verlagen; **2** de waarde naar beneden halen van

downhearted ontmoedigd, terneergeslagen, in de put

¹**downhill** *adv* bergafwaarts, naar beneden: *go ~* verslechteren

²**downhill** *adj* **1** (af)hellend, neerwaarts; **2** gemakkelijk: *it's all ~ from here* het is een makkie vanaf hier

download downloaden

downpour stortbui, plensbui

¹**downright** *adv* volkomen, door en door

²**downright** *adj* **1** uitgesproken, overduidelijk: *a ~ liar* iem die liegt dat het gedrukt staat; **2** eerlijk, oprecht

downsizing [daunsajzing] inkrimping, bezuiniging

¹**downstairs** *adv* (naar) beneden, de trap af

²**downstairs** *adj* beneden, op de begane grond

downstream stroomafwaarts

down-to-earth nuchter, met beide benen op de grond

downtown naar de binnenstad, de stad in

downward [daunwəd] naar beneden gaand, neerwaarts, aflopend

downwind met de wind mee (gaand)

downy [daunie] donzig, zacht

dowry [daurie] bruidsschat

dowse [dauz] (met een wichelroede) wateraders (mineralen) opsporen, wichelroede lopen

dowsing-rod wichelroede

¹**doze** [dooz] *vb* sluimeren, dutten, soezen: *~ off* indutten, in slaap sukkelen

²**doze** [dooz] *vb* (with *away*) verdutten, versuffen

³**doze** [dooz] *n* sluimering, dutjeʰ

dozen [duzn] **1** dozijnʰ, twaalftalʰ; **2** groot aantalʰ, heleboel: *~s (and ~s) of people* een heleboel mensen; *by the ~* bij tientallen, bij bosjes; *it's six of one and half a ~ of the other* het is lood om oud ijzer

dozy [doozie] slaperig, soezerig

¹**drab** [dræb] *adj* **1** (inf) vaalbruin; **2** kleurloos, saai

²**drab** [dræb] *n* (vulg) slons, slet, hoer

¹**draft** [dra:ft] *n* **1** klad(jeʰ), conceptʰ, schets: *in ~* in het klad; **2** (Am) dienstplicht

²**draft** [dra:ft] *vb* **1** ontwerpen, schetsen, een klad(je) maken van; **2** (Am) indelen, detacheren; **3** (Am) oproepen (voor militaire dienst)

draftsman [dra:ftsmən] **1** tekenaar, ontwerper; **2** opsteller (van documenten)

¹**drag** [dræg] *vb* (mee)slepen, (voort)trekken, (voort)sleuren, (voort)zeulen: *~ through the mire* (of: mud) door het slijk halen (also fig); *don't ~ my name in* laat mijn naam erbuiten

²**drag** [dræg] *vb* afdreggen, afzoeken (river)

³**drag** [dræg] *vb* **1** dreggen: *~ for* dreggen naar; **2** zich voortslepen, kruipen (of time), lang duren, langdradig zijn: *~ on* eindeloos duren; **3** achterblijven

⁴**drag** [dræg] *n* **1** het slepen, het trekken; **2** het dreggen; **3** dreg, dregnetʰ, dregankerʰ; **4** rem (fig), belemmering, vertraging, blok aan het been: *it was a*

~ on the proceedings het belemmerde de werkzaamheden; **5** saai gedoeʰ, saai figuurʰ, vervelend iets (iem): *it was such a ~* het was stomvervelend; **6** trekjeʰ (of a cigarette), haaltjeʰ; **7** door een man gedragen vrouwenkleding: *in ~* in travestie, als man verkleed

drag down 1 slopen, uitputten, ontmoedigen; **2** neerhalen (also fig), verlagen

draggy [drægie] (inf) duf, saai, vervelend

dragon [drægən] draak

dragonfly libel, waterjuffer

¹**dragoon** [drəgoe:n] *n* dragonder (also fig)

²**dragoon** [drəgoe:n] *vb* (with *into*) (met geweld) dwingen tot

drag out 1 eruit trekken (truth etc); **2** rekken (meeting, story etc), uitspinnen

¹**drain** [dreen] *vb* **1** weglopen, wegstromen, (uit)lekken: *~ away* wegvloeien, (fig) wegebben, afnemen; **2** leeglopen, afdruipen; **3** afwateren, lozen

²**drain** [dreen] *vb* **1** afvoeren, doen afvloeien, afgieten, (fig) doen verdwijnen; **2** leegmaken, leegdrinken: *~ off* afvoeren, leegmaken; **3** droogleggen: *a face ~ed of all colour* een doodsbleek gezicht

³**drain** [dreen] *n* **1** afvoerkanaalʰ, afvoerbuis, rioolʰ: *down the ~* naar de knoppen, verloren; **2** afvloeiing, onttrekking, (fig) druk, belasting: *it is a great ~ on his strength* het vergt veel van zijn krachten

drainpipe regenpijp, afvoerpijp

drake [dreek] woerd, mannetjeseend

dram [dræm] **1** drachme, dram; **2** neutjeʰ

drama [dra:mə] toneelstukʰ, dramaʰ

dramatic [drəmætik] **1** dramatisch, toneel-: *~ irony* tragische ironie; **2** indrukwekkend, aangrijpend

¹**dramatize** [dræmətajz] *vb* zich aanstellen, dramatisch doen, overdrijven

²**dramatize** [dræmətajz] *vb* dramatiseren, als drama bewerken, aanschouwelijk voorstellen

¹**drape** [dreep] *vb* **1** bekleden, omhullen, versieren; **2** draperen (also fig)

²**drape** [dreep] *n* **1** draperie; **2** (Am) gordijnʰ

drapery [dreepərie] **1** stoffen; **2** manufacturenhandel; **3** (Am) gordijnʰ

drastic [dræstik] drastisch, ingrijpend

drat [dræt] verwensen, vervloeken: (inf) *that ~ted animal!* dat vervelende beest!

draught [dra:ft] **1** tocht, trek, luchtstroom: (inf) *feel the ~* op de tocht zitten, (fig) in geldnood verkeren; **2** teug, slok (of medicine); **3** drankjeʰ, medicijnʰ, dosis; **4** het aftappen: *beer on ~* bier van het vat; **5** schets, conceptʰ, kladʰ; **6** damschijf: (game of) *~s* damspel, het dammen

draughtboard dambordʰ

draught-proof tochtdicht, tochtvrij (of windows etc)

draughtsman [dra:ftsmən] **1** tekenaar, ontwerper; **2** opsteller (of documents); **3** damschijf

¹**draw** [dro:] *vb* **1** trekken, slepen, te voorschijn halen (weapon), dichtdoen (curtain): *~ the blinds* de jaloezieën neerlaten; *~ back the curtains* de gordij-

nen opentrekken; ~ *s.o. into a conversation* iem in
een gesprek betrekken; **2** tekenen, schetsen: *(fig)*
one has to ~ the line somewhere je moet ergens een
grens trekken; **3** loten, door loting verkrijgen; **4**
putten *(also fig): ~ inspiration from* inspiratie opdoen uit; *I'll have to ~ upon my savings* ik zal mijn
spaargeld moeten aanspreken; *~ a conclusion* een
conclusie trekken
²draw [dro:] *vb* **1** (aan)trekken, (aan)lokken: *~ at-*
tention to de aandacht vestigen op; **2** (in)halen: *~ a*
deep breath diep inademen, diep ademhalen; **3** ertoe brengen, overhalen; **4** (te voorschijn) halen, uittrekken, *(fig)* ontlokken, naar buiten brengen,
(af)tappen *(beer etc): ~ blood* bloed doen vloeien,
(fig) iem gevoelig raken; *he refused to be ~n* hij liet
zich niet uit zijn tent lokken; **5** van de ingewanden
ontdoen; **6** opstellen, formuleren,
uitschrijven *(cheque);* **7** trekken *(money, wages),*
opnemen, ontvangen; **8** *(sport, game)* in gelijkspel
doen eindigen: *~ off: a)* afleiden *(attention); b)*
weglokken; *c)* aftappen
³draw [dro:] *vb* **1** komen, gaan: *~ to an end* (of: *a*
close) ten einde lopen; *~ level* gelijk komen *(in*
race); **2** aantrekkingskracht uitoefenen, publiek
trekken; **3** *(sport, game)* gelijkspelen, in gelijkspel
eindigen, remise maken; **4** trekken *(of tea)*
⁴draw [dro:] *n* **1** trek, het trekken: *he is quick on the*
~ hij kan snel zijn revolver trekken, *(fig)* hij reageert snel; **2** aantrekkingskracht, attractie, trekpleister; **3** *(lottery)* trekking, (uit)loting, verloting;
4 gelijkspelʰ, remise
draw apart uit elkaar gaan, uit elkaar groeien
draw away 1 *(with from)* wegtrekken (van), (zich)
terugtrekken (van); **2** *(with from)* uitlopen (op),
een voorsprong nemen (op)
drawback nadeelʰ, bezwaarʰ
draw back *(with from)* (zich) terugtrekken (van),
terugwijken (van, voor)
drawbridge ophaalbrug
drawer [dro:] **1** lade: *a chest of ~s* een ladekast; **2** *~s*
(lange) onderbroek
draw in 1 binnenrijden, komen aanrijden; **2** aan de
kant gaan rijden; **3** ten einde lopen *(of day)*, schemerig worden, korter worden *(of days)*
drawing [dro:ing] **1** tekening; **2** het tekenen, teken-
kunst: *Yvonne is good at ~* Yvonne is goed in tekenen
drawing-pin punaise
drawing-room salon, zitkamer
¹drawl [dro:l] *vb* lijzig praten
²drawl [dro:l] *n* lijzige manier van praten
drawn 1 vertrokken, strak, afgetobd *(face);* **2** onbeslist *(match)*
¹draw out *vb* **1** langer worden *(of days);* **2** wegrijden
(of train etc)
²draw out *vb* **1** (uit)rekken, uitspinnen; **2** aan de
praat krijgen, eruit halen, uithoren
¹draw up *vb* **1** opstellen, plaatsen *(soldiers);* **2** opmaken, opstellen, formuleren; **3** aanschuiven *(chair),*

bijtrekken ‖ *draw oneself up* zich oprichten, zich
lang maken
²draw up *vb* stoppen, tot stilstand komen: *~ to* naderen, dichter komen bij
¹dread [dred] *vb* vrezen, erg opzien tegen, doodsbang zijn (voor): *I ~ to think (of) what will happen*
to him ik moet er niet aan denken wat hem allemaal
zal overkomen
²dread [dred] *n* (doods)angst, vrees, schrik
dreadful [dredfoel] vreselijk, ontzettend
dreadlocks [dredloks] rastakapsel, rastavlechten
¹dream [drie:m] *n* droom, *(fig)* ideaalʰ: *a ~ of a dress*
een beeldige jurk
²dream [drie:m] *vb* dromen, zich verbeelden, zich
indenken: *~ up* verzinnen; *she wouldn't ~ of mov-*
ing zij piekerde er niet over om te verhuizen
dreary [driarie] **1** somber, treurig; **2** saai
dredge [dredzj] (op)dreggen, (uit)baggeren: *(fig) ~*
up old memories herinneringen ophalen
dregs [dregz] **1** bezinksel, droesem: *drink (of:*
drain) to the ~ tot op de bodem ledigen; **2** *(depr)* iets
waardeloos, uitvaagsel: *~ of society* uitschot van de
maatschappij
drench [drentsj] doordrenken, doorweken, kletsnat maken: *sun-~ed beaches* zonovergoten stranden
¹dress [dres] *vb* **1** zich (aan)kleden, gekleed gaan; **2**
zich verkleden: *~ for dinner* zich verkleden voor
het eten
²dress [dres] *vb* **1** (aan)kleden, van kleding voorzien,
kleren aantrekken: *~ed to kill* opvallend gekleed; *~*
up verkleden, vermommen; **2** versieren, opsieren,
optuigen: *~ up: a)* opdoffen; *b) (also fig)* mooi doen
lijken, aanvaardbaar laten klinken *(of:* maken),
leuk brengen; **3** *(med)* verbinden, verzorgen
(wound), verband aanleggen op; **4** opmaken, kammen en borstelen, kappen: *~ down: a)* roskammen
(horse); b) een pak slaag geven, op z'n donder geven
³dress [dres] *n* **1** jurk, japon; **2** kleding, dracht
dressing [dressing] **1** het (aan)kleden; **2** *(med)* ver-
band(materiaal)ʰ; **3** slasaus; **4** *(Am; culinary)* vulling
dressing-gown 1 badjas; **2** ochtendjas
dressmaker naaister, kleermaker
dress rehearsal generale repetitie
¹dribble [dribl] *vb* **1** (weg)druppelen, langzaam
wegstromen, *(fig)* haast ongemerkt verdwijnen:
the answers ~d in de antwoorden kwamen binnendruppelen; **2** kwijlen; **3** *(sport)* dribbelen
²dribble [dribl] *vb* (laten) druppelen, langzaam laten vloeien
³dribble [dribl] *n* **1** stroompjeʰ, *(fig)* vleugjeʰ, drup-
peltjeʰ, beetjeʰ; **2** *(sport)* dribbel; **3** kwijlʰ, speekselʰ
dried [drajd] droog, gedroogd: *~ milk* melkpoeder
drier [drajjə] droger, haardroger, wasdroger,
droogmolen
¹drift [drift] *vb* **1** (af)drijven, uiteendrijven *(also fig),*
(zich laten) meedrijven, (rond)zwalken: *~ away*
(of: off) geleidelijk verdwijnen; **2** opwaaien, (zich)

ophopen *(of snow)*

²drift [drift] *vb* **1** meevoeren, voortdrijven; **2** bedekken *(with snow, leaves)*

³drift [drift] *n* **1** afwijking, afdrijving, het zwerven; **2** vlaag, sneeuwvlaag, regenvlaag, stofwolk; **3** opeenhoping, berg, massa; **4** ongeorganiseerde beweging, gang, trek: *the ~ from the country to the city* de trek van het platteland naar de stad; **5** strekking, tendens, bedoeling: *the general ~ of the story* de algemene strekking van het verhaal

¹drill [dril] *vb* **1** boren, gaten boren; **2** stampen, (mechanisch) leren; **3** oefenen, exerceren

²drill [dril] *vb* **1** doorboren; **2** aanboren; **3** drillen, africhten, trainen; **4** erin stampen, erin heien

³drill [dril] *n* **1** boor(machine), drilboor; **2** het drillen, exercitie, oefening; **3** driloefening, het opdreunen, het erin stampen; **4** gebruikelijke procedure, normale gang van zaken

drily [drajlie] droog(jes)

¹drink [dringk] *vb* drinken, leegdrinken, opdrinken: *he ~s like a fish* hij zuipt als een ketter; *~ up* opdrinken, (het glas) leegdrinken

²drink [dringk] *vb* **1** in zich opnemen, (in)drinken: *~ in s.o.'s words* iemands woorden in zich opnemen; **2** drinken op, het glas heffen op: *they drank (to) his health* zij dronken op zijn gezondheid

³drink [dringk] *n* **1** (iets te) drinken, slok, teug: *would you like a ~?* wilt u misschien iets drinken?; **2** drank, sterkedrank, alcohol: *food and ~* eten en drinken

drink to toasten op, een dronk uitbrengen op

¹drip [drip] *vb* druipen, druppelen: *~ping wet* drijfnat, doornat

²drip [drip] *vb* laten druppelen

³drip [drip] *n* **1** gedruppel^h, druppel, het druppelen; **2** infuus^h, infusievloeistof; **3** sukkel, slome (duikelaar)

drippy [drippie] flauw, onnozel

¹drive [drajv] *vb* **1** drijven *(also fig)*, opjagen, bijeendrijven: *~ out* verdrijven, uitdrijven, verdringen; **2** rijden, (be)sturen, vervoeren: *~ in* binnenrijden; *~ off* wegrijden; *~ up* voorrijden; **3** voortdrijven, duwen, slaan *(also sport): ~ home: a)* vastslaan, inhameren; *b)* volkomen duidelijk maken; *~ in: a)* inslaan *(nail etc); b)* inhameren *(fig)*

²drive [drajv] *vb* **1** dwingen, brengen tot: *~ s.o. to despair* iem wanhopig maken; **2** aandrijven

³drive [drajv] *vb* **1** snellen, (voort)stormen, (blijven) doorgaan; **2** gooien, schieten, lanceren

⁴drive [drajv] *n* **1** rit(je^h), rijtoer: *let's go for a ~* laten we een eindje gaan rijden; **2** *(psychology)* drift, drang; **3** actie, campagne; **4** laan, oprijlaan, oprit; **5** (groot) offensief^h, (zware) aanval; **6** aandrijving, overbrenging: *front-wheel ~* voorwielaandrijving; **7** drijfkracht, stuwkracht; **8** energie, doorzettingsvermogen^h; **9** diskdrive: *right-hand ~* met het stuur rechts, (met) rechtse besturing

drive at doelen op, bedoelen: *what is he driving at?* wat bedoelt hij?

¹drive-in *adj* drive-in, inrij-

²drive-in *n* drive-in, bioscoop, cafetaria

¹drivel [drivl] *n* gezwam^h, kletskoek

²drivel [drivl] *vb* zwammen, (onzin) kletsen, zeveren

driver [drajvə] **1** bestuurder, chauffeur, machinist; **2** (vee)drijver

driveway oprijlaan, oprit

driving [drajving] **1** aandrijvend, stuwend *(also fig)*; **2** krachtig, energiek: *~ rain* slagregen

driving licence rijbewijs^h

¹drizzle [drizl] *vb* motregenen, miezeren

²drizzle [drizl] *n* motregen

droll [drool] komiek, humoristisch

¹drone [droon] *n* **1** hommel, dar; **2** gegons^h, gezoem^h, gebrom^h; **3** dreun, eentonige manier van praten

²drone [droon] *vb* **1** gonzen, zoemen, brommen; **2** (op)dreunen *(also fig)*, monotoon spreken

drool [droe:l] **1** kwijlen: *(inf; fig) ~ about (of: over)* dwepen met, weglopen met; **2** *(inf)* zwammen, leuteren

¹droop [droe:p] *vb* **1** neerhangen, (af)hangen, slap worden, krom staan; **2** verflauwen, afnemen, verslappen

²droop [droe:p] *n* hangende houding, het (laten) hangen

¹drop [drop] *vb* **1** druppelen, druipen; **2** vallen, omvallen, neervallen, zich laten vallen, *(fig)* terloops geuit worden: *~ dead!* val dood!; **3** ophouden, verlopen, uitvallen: *let the matter ~* zij lieten de zaak verder rusten; **4** dalen, afnemen, zakken: *the wind has ~ped* de wind is gaan liggen; *~ back (of: behind)* achterblijven, achtergelaten worden; *~ behind* achter raken bij

²drop [drop] *vb* **1** laten druppelen, laten druipen; **2** laten vallen, laten zakken, neerlaten; **3** laten varen, laten schieten, opgeven: *~ (the) charges* een aanklacht intrekken; **4** laten dalen, verminderen, verlagen: *~ one's voice* zachter praten; **5** terloops zeggen, laten vallen: *~ s.o. a hint* iem een wenk geven; *~ me a line* schrijf me maar een paar regeltjes; **6** afleveren, afgeven, afzetten: *he ~ped me at the corner* hij zette mij bij de hoek af

³drop [drop] *n* **1** druppel, drupje^h, neutje^h, *(fig)* greintje^h, spoor(tje)^h: *he has had a ~ too much* hij heeft te diep in het glaasje gekeken; **2** zuurtje^h; **3** *~s* druppels, medicijn^h: *(inf) knock-out ~s* bedwelmingsmiddel; *a ~ in a bucket (of: in the ocean)* een druppel op een gloeiende plaat; *at the ~ of a hat* meteen, bij de minste aanleiding, zonder te aarzelen

drop in langskomen, binnenvallen: *drop in on s.o.* even aanlopen bij iem

¹drop off *vb* **1** geleidelijk afnemen, teruglopen; **2** *(inf)* in slaap vallen

²drop off *vb* afzetten, laten uitstappen

drop out 1 opgeven, zich terugtrekken; **2** *(Am)* vroegtijdig verlaten

drop-out drop-out, voortijdige schoolverlater; ver-

stotene
droppings [dr<u>o</u>ppingz] uitwerpselen *(of animals)*, keutels
drought [draut] (periode van) droogte
drove horde, kudde *(cattle)*, menigte *(people)*: *people came in ~s* de mensen kwamen in drommen
drown [draun] 1 (doen) verdrinken, (doen) verzuipen: *~ one's sorrows (in drink)* zijn verdriet verdrinken; 2 (doen) overstromen, onder water zetten, (rijkelijk) overspoelen, *(fig)* overstemmen, overstelpen
¹**drowse** [drauz] *vb* slaperig zijn, dommelen, loom zijn
²**drowse** [drauz] *vb* slaperig maken, suf maken, sloom maken
drubbing [dr<u>u</u>bbing] 1 pak[h] slaag, aframmeling; 2 (zware) nederlaag
¹**drudge** [drudzj] *n* sloof, zwoeger, werkezel
²**drudge** [drudzj] *vb* zwoegen, zich afbeulen, eentonig werk doen
drudgery [dr<u>u</u>dzjərie] eentonig werk[h], slaafs werk[h]
¹**drug** [drug] *n* 1 geneesmiddel[h], medicijn[h]; 2 drug, verdovend middel[h]
²**drug** [drug] *vb* medicijn(en) e.d. toedienen, bedwelmen, drogeren, verdoven
drug addict drugsverslaafde
drugstore *(Am)* klein warenhuis[h]; apotheek, drogisterij
¹**drum** [drum] *n* 1 trom, trommel; 2 getrommel[h], geroffel[h], roffel, het trommelen; 3 *~s* slagwerk[h], drumstel[h], drums; 4 drum, ton, vat[h]
²**drum** [drum] *vb* trommelen, drummen, slagwerker zijn, roffelen, ritmisch tikken ‖ *~ up* optrommelen, bijeenroepen; *~ up trade* een markt creëren, klanten werven; *~ sth. into s.o.* (of: *s.o.'s head*) iets bij iem erin hameren
drum major tamboer-majoor
drummer [dr<u>u</u>mmə] slagwerker, drummer, tamboer
drumstick 1 trommelstok; 2 (gebraden) kippenpootje[h], drumstick
¹**drunk** *adj* 1 dronken: *~ and disorderly* in kennelijke staat; *blind* (of: *dead*) *~* stomdronken; 2 door het dolle heen, (brood)dronken: *~ with power* tiranniek, machtswellustig
²**drunk** *n* dronkaard, zuiplap
drunken [dr<u>u</u>ngkən] dronken, dronkenmans-
¹**dry** [draj] *adj* 1 droog: *~ land* vaste grond; 2 droog, (op)gedroogd, zonder beleg *(bread)*, drooggelegd *(land; also fig)*: *run ~* opdrogen, droog komen te staan; 3 *(inf)* dorstig; 4 droog, op droge toon (gezegd), ironisch: *~ cleaner('s)* stomerij; *(as) ~ as dust, bone-~* gortdroog, kurkdroog; *~ run* repetitie, het proefdraaien
²**dry** [draj] *vb* (op)drogen, droog worden, uitdrogen: *dried milk* melkpoeder; *~ out: a)* uitdrogen, grondig droog worden; *b)* afkicken *(alcoholics)*; *~ up: a)* opdrogen; *b) (also fig)* afnemen tot niets
³**dry** [draj] *vb* (af)drogen, laten drogen ‖ *~ out: a)*

grondig droog laten worden; *b)* laten afkicken *(alcoholics)*
dry-cleaning 1 het chemisch reinigen; 2 chemisch gereinigde kleding
dryer [dr<u>a</u>jjə:] *see* drier
dual [dj<u>oe</u>:əl] tweevoudig, tweeledig: *~ carriageway* dubbele rijbaan; *~-purpose* voor twee doeleinden geschikt
dub [dub] 1 tot ridder slaan, ridderen; 2 noemen, (om)dopen (tot), de bijnaam geven van; 3 (na)synchroniseren, dubben
dubbing [d<u>u</u>bbing] het bijmixen *(sound)*, (na)synchronisatie
dubious [dj<u>oe</u>:biəs] 1 twijfelend, aarzelend, onzeker; 2 onbetrouwbaar, twijfelachtig
duchy [d<u>u</u>tsjie] hertogdom[h]
¹**duck** [duk] *n* eend, eendvogel ‖ *play ~s and drakes with, make ~s and drakes of* verkwanselen; *take to sth. like a ~ to water* in z'n element zijn
²**duck** [duk] *vb* buigen, (zich) bukken, wegduiken
³**duck** [duk] *vb* 1 plotseling (onder)dompelen, kopje-onder duwen; 2 ontwijken, vermijden; 3 snel intrekken *(head)*
duckboard loopplank *(across ditch or mud)*
duckling [d<u>u</u>kling] jonge eend, eendje[h]
duct [dukt] buis *(also biology)*, kanaal[h], goot, leiding
dud [dud] 1 prul[h], nepding[h]; 2 blindganger *(bomb, grenade)*
dude [djoe:d] 1 kerel, vent; 2 stadsmens *(as a holidaymaker on farm)*
¹**due** [djoe:] *adj* 1 gepast, juist, terecht: *with ~ care* met gepaste zorgvuldigheid; *in ~ time, in ~ course (of time)* te zijner tijd; 2 schuldig, verschuldigd, invorderbaar, verplicht: *postage ~* ongefrankeerd; *the amount ~* het verschuldigde bedrag; *fall* (of: *become*) *~* vervallen, verschijnen *(instalment); our thanks are ~ to you* wij zijn u dank verschuldigd; 3 verwacht: *the aircraft is ~ at 4.50 p.m.* het toestel wordt om 16 uur 50 verwacht; *~ to* toe te schrijven aan
²**due** [djoe:] *n* 1 datgene wat iem toekomt: *give s.o. his ~* iem niet te kort doen, iem geven wat hem toekomt; 2 *~s* schuld(en), rechten, contributie
³**due** [djoe:] *adv* precies *(only for points of the compass)*: *~ south* pal naar het zuiden
duel [dj<u>oe</u>:əl] duel[h]
duet [djoe:<u>e</u>t] duet[h]
due to wegens, vanwege, door
duff [duf] waardeloos, slecht, kapot
dugout 1 (boomstam)kano; 2 schuilhol[h], uitgegraven schuilplaats; 3 *(sport)* dug-out
duke [djoe:k] hertog
dull [dul] 1 saai, vervelend; 2 dom, sloom; 3 mat *(of colour, sound, pain)*, dof; 4 bot, stomp; 5 bewolkt, betrokken; 6 *(com)* flauw: *the ~ season* de slappe tijd; *as ~ as ditchwater* (of: *dishwater*) oersaai
duly [dj<u>oe</u>:lie] 1 behoorlijk, naar behoren, terecht; 2 stipt, prompt

dumb [dum] **1** stom, niet kunnen spreken, zwijg-zaam: *to be struck ~* met stomheid geslagen zijn, sprakeloos zijn; **2** dom, stom, suf

dumbo [dumboo] dombo, stomkop

dumb show gebarenspel[h], pantomime

¹dummy [dummie] *n* **1** dummy, blinde *(cards)*, pop, model[h] *(of book)*, proefpagina, stroman, figurant; **2** nepartikel[h]; **3** fopspeen; **4** *(inf)* sufferd, uilskuiken[h]

²dummy [dummie] *adj* **1** namaak, schijn, nep; **2** proef-: *~ run* het proefdraaien, militaire oefening

¹dump [dump] *n* **1** hoop, (vuilnis)belt, (vuil)stort-plaats; **2** dump, tijdelijk depot[h] van legergoederen; **3** *(inf)* puinhoop, vervallen woning, desolate stad, desolaat dorp[h] || *(inf) (down) in the ~s* in de put, somber

²dump [dump] *vb* **1** dumpen, storten, lozen, neer-smijten; **2** dumpen *(goods on foreign market)*; **3** achterlaten, in de steek laten

dumpy [dumpie] kort en dik

dune [djoe:n] duin

dung [dung] mest, drek, gier

dungarees [dunggərie:z] overall, jeans, tuinbroek

dungeon [dundzjən] kerker

dunghill 1 mesthoop; **2** puinhoop

dunk [dungk] onderdompelen *(also fig)*, (in)dopen, soppen *(bread in tea etc)*

¹dupe [djoe:p] *n* dupe, slachtoffer[h] *(van bedrog)*, be-drogene

²dupe [djoe:p] *vb* bedriegen, benadelen, duperen

¹duplicate [djoe:plikkət] *adj* **1** dubbel, tweevoudig; **2** gelijkluidend, identiek

²duplicate [djoe:plikkət] *n* **1** duplicaat[h], kopie; **2** du-plo[h]: *in ~* in duplo, in tweevoud

³duplicate [djoe:plikkeet] *vb* **1** verdubbelen, kopië-ren, verveelvuldigen; **2** herhalen

duplicity [djoe:plissittie] dubbelhartigheid, be-drog[h]

durable [djoeərəbl] duurzaam, bestendig, onver-slijtbaar

duration [djoeree:sjən] duur

during [djoeəring] tijdens, gedurende, onder: *~ the afternoon* in de loop van de middag

dusk [dusk] schemer(ing), duister[h], duisternis

¹dust [dust] *n* **1** stof[h], poeder; **2** stofwolk: *(fig) when the ~ had settled* toen de gemoederen bedaard wa-ren

²dust [dust] *vb* (af)stoffen, stof afnemen

³dust [dust] *vb* **1** bestuiven, bestrooien: *~ crops* ge-was besproeien *(from aeroplane)*; **2** afstoffen

dustbin vuilnisbak

duster [dustə] **1** stoffer, plumeau; **2** stofdoek

dust jacket stofomslag[h]

dustman [dustmən] vuilnisman

dust off afstoffen, *(fig)* opfrissen, ophalen *(old knowledge)*

dustpan blik[h] *(dustpan and brush)*

dust-up 1 handgemeen[h]; **2** rel, oproer[h]

dusty [dustie] **1** stoffig, bestoft, droog; **2** als stof || *not so ~* lang niet gek

¹Dutch [dutsj] *n* **1** Nederlands; Hollands; **2** Neder-landers, het Nederlandse volk || *(Am; inf) beat the ~* een bijzondere prestatie leveren

²Dutch [dutsj] *adj* Nederlands, Hollands || *~ auction* veiling bij afslag; *~ bargain* overeenkomst die met een dronk bezegeld wordt; *~ comfort* schrale troost; *~ courage* jenevermoed; *~ door* boerderij-deur, onder- en bovendeur; *~ treat* feest waarbij ie-der voor zich betaalt; *talk like a ~ uncle* duidelijk zeggen waar het op staat; *go ~* ieder voor zich beta-len

Dutchman [dutsjmən] Nederlander, Hollander || *… or I am a ~, I am a ~ if …* ik ben een boon als ik …

dutiful [djoe:tiffoel] **1** plicht(s)getrouw; **2** gehoor-zaam, eerbiedigend

duty [djoe:tie] **1** plicht, verplichting, taak, functie, dienst: *do ~ for* dienst doen als, vervangen; *off ~* buiten (de) dienst(tijd), in vrije tijd; *on ~* in func-tie, in diensttijd; **2** belasting, accijns, (invoer-, uit-voer)recht(en); **3** mechanisch arbeidsvermogen[h]: *a heavy ~ drilling machine* een boormachine voor zwaar werk; **4** *-ies* functie, werkzaamheden; **5** be-lasting, accijns, (invoer-, uitvoer)rechten

duty-free belastingvrij

¹dwarf [dwo:f] *n (also dwarves)* dwerg

²dwarf [dwo:f] *adj* dwerg-, dwergachtig

³dwarf [dwo:f] *vb* **1** in z'n groei belemmeren, klein(er) maken, klein houden: *~ plants* minia-tuurplanten kweken; **2** klein(er) doen lijken: *the skyscraper ~ed all the other buildings* bij de wolken-krabber verzonken alle andere gebouwen in het niet

dwell [dwel] **1** wonen, verblijven, zich ophouden; **2** blijven stilstaan, uitweiden: *~ (up)on* (lang) blijven stilstaan bij, (lang) doorgaan over

dwelling [dwelling] woning

dwindle [dwindl] afnemen, achteruitgaan

¹dye [daj] *n* verf(stof), kleurstof

²dye [daj] *vb* verven, kleuren

dyke [dajk] **1** dijk, (keer)dam; **2** kanaaltje[h], sloot, (natuurlijke) waterloop; **3** pot, lesbienne

dynamic [dajnæmik] **1** dynamisch, bewegend; **2** voortvarend, actief, energiek

dynamite [dajnəmajt] dynamiet[h]

dynamo [dajnəmoo] dynamo

dynasty [dinnəstie] dynastie, (vorsten)huis[h]

dysentery [disntrie] bloeddiarree

dyslexia [disleksiə] leesblindheid, dyslexie

e

E 1 *(electr) earth* aarde; 2 *east(ern)* O., Oost(elijk)
each [ie:tsj] 1 elk, ieder afzonderlijk: *~ year he
grows weaker* ieder jaar wordt hij zwakker; 2 elk, ieder *(of a group): they are a dollar ~* ze kosten een
dollar per stuk
each other elkaar, mekaar: *they hate ~'s guts* ze
kunnen elkaars bloed wel drinken
eager [ie:gə] 1 vurig, onstuimig; 2 *(with for)* (hevig) verlangend (naar), begerig ‖ *(inf) ~ beaver*
(overdreven) harde werker
eagle [ie:gl] adelaar, arend
ear [iə] 1 oorʰ: *(fig) play it by ~* improviseren, op z'n
gevoel afgaan; *up to one's ~s* tot over zijn oren; 2 gehoorʰ, oorʰ: *have an ~ for* een gevoel hebben voor;
3 (koren)aar; 4 oorʰ, lus, oogʰ, handvatʰ: *keep an ~
(of: one's ~(s)) (close) to the ground: a)* (goed) op de
hoogte blijven *(of trends, gossip); b)* de boel goed in
de gaten houden; *prick up one's ~s* de oren spitsen;
be out on one's ~ ontslagen worden; *be all ~s* een en
al oor zijn
eardrum trommelvliesʰ
earl [ɔ:l] (Engelse) graaf
¹**early** [ə:lie] adj 1 vroeg, vroegtijdig: *~ bird* vroege
vogel; *~ retirement* VUT, vervroegd pensioen; *the
~ bird catches the worm* vroeg begonnen, veel gewonnen; *in the ~ 1960s* in het begin van de jaren
zestig; 2 spoedig: *an ~ reply* een spoedig antwoord;
3 oud, van lang geleden: *the ~ Celts* de oude Kelten
²**early** [ə:lie] adv 1 vroeg, (in het) begin, tijdig: *~ on
(in)* al vroeg, al in het begin; 2 te vroeg: *we were an
hour ~* we kwamen een uur te vroeg
earmark reserveren *(funds etc): ~ for* opzijleggen
om (… te)
earn [ə:n] 1 verdienen, (ver)krijgen; 2 verwerven,
(terecht) krijgen: *his behaviour ~ed him his nickname* zijn gedrag bezorgde hem zijn bijnaam
¹**earnest** [ə:nist] adj ernstig, serieus, gemeend
²**earnest** [ə:nist] n ernst: *in (real) ~* menens; *I am in
(real) ~* ik méén het
earnings [ə:ningz] 1 inkomen, inkomsten, verdiensten; 2 winst *(of business)*
earphones koptelefoon
earshot gehoorsafstand: *out of ~* buiten gehoorsafstand
earth [ɔ:θ] 1 aarde; 2 *(zoology)* holʰ: *go (of: run) to
~: a)* zijn hol invluchten; *b)* onderduiken; *promise*

the ~ gouden bergen beloven; *down to ~* met beide
benen op de grond, nuchter, eerlijk; *why on ~* waarom in vredesnaam
earthenware [ə:θənweə] aardewerkʰ
earthly [ə:θlie] aards, werelds
earthquake [ə:θkweek] aardbeving
earthworm pier, regenworm
earthy [ə:θie] 1 vuil (van aarde); 2 materialistisch,
aards, grof
earwax oorsmeerʰ
earwig oorwurm
¹**ease** [ie:z] n 1 gemakʰ, gemakkelijkheid; 2 ongedwongenheid, gemakʰ, comfortʰ: *(mil) stand at ~*
op de plaats rust; *at one's ~* op zijn gemak, rustig; 3
welbehagenʰ: *ill at ~* niet op z'n gemak
²**ease** [ie:z] vb 1 verlichten, doen afnemen: *~ back the
throttle* gas terugnemen; 2 gemakkelijk(er) maken:
(fig) ~ s.o.'s mind iem geruststellen; 3 voorzichtig
bewegen: *~ off the lid* voorzichtig het deksel eraf
halen
³**ease** [ie:z] vb afnemen, minder worden, (vaart)
minderen: *~ off (of: up)* afnemen, verminderen,
rustiger aan gaan doen
easel [ie:zl] (schilders)ezel
easily [ie:zillie] 1 moeiteloos, rustig, met gemak; 2
ongetwijfeld, zonder meer, beslist
¹**east** [ie:st] n het oosten *(point of the compass),* oost:
the East het oostelijk gedeelte, de Oost, de Oriënt
²**east** [ie:st] adj oostelijk: *~ wind* oostenwind
³**east** [ie:st] adv in, uit, naar het oosten: *sail due ~*
recht naar het oosten varen
Easter [ie:stə] Pasen
¹**easterly** [ie:stəlie] n oostenwind
²**easterly** [ie:stəlie] adj oostelijk
eastern [ie:stən] 1 oostelijk, oost(en)-; 2 oosters
¹**easy** [ie:zie] adj 1 (ge)makkelijk, eenvoudig, moeiteloos: *have ~ access to sth.* makkelijk toegang hebben tot iets; 2 ongedwongen: *have an ~ manner*
ontspannen manier van doen; 3 comfortabel, gemakkelijk: *~ chair* leunstoel, luie stoel; 4 welgesteld, bemiddeld: *in ~ circumstances* in goede
doen; *have an ~ time (of it)* een gemakkelijk leventje hebben; *by ~ stages* stap voor stap; *on ~ terms*
op gemakkelijke condities, op afbetaling
²**easy** [ie:zie] adv 1 gemakkelijk, eenvoudig: *easier
said than done* gemakkelijker gezegd dan gedaan; 2
kalm, rustig: *take it ~* het rustig aan doen; *~ does
it!* voorzichtig! (dan breekt het lijntje niet)
easygoing [ie:ziegooing] 1 laconiek, makkelijk; 2
gemakzuchtig, laks
¹**eat** [ie:t] vb eten: *~ out* buitenshuis eten
²**eat** [ie:t] vb 1 (op)eten, vreten; 2 verslinden, opvreten: *~en up with curiosity* verteerd door nieuwsgierigheid; 3 aantasten, wegvreten: *what's ~ing you?*
wat zit je zo dwars?
eavesdrop [ie:vzdrop] afluisteren, luistervinkje
spelen
¹**ebb** [eb] n eb, laag waterʰ: *(fig) be at a low ~* in de
put zitten

²**ebb** [eb] *vb* afnemen, wegebben

ebony [ebbənie] ebbenhout^h

ebullient [ibboeliənt] uitbundig, uitgelaten

¹**eccentric** [iksentrik] *adj* zonderling, excentriek

²**eccentric** [iksentrik] *n* zonderling, excentriekeling

ecclesiastical [iklie:zie·æstikl] geestelijk, kerkelijk, kerk-

¹**echo** [ekkoo] *n (~es)* echo, weerklank

²**echo** [ekkoo] *vb* weerklinken, resoneren

³**echo** [ekkoo] *vb* 1 echoën, herhalen, nazeggen; 2 weerkaatsen

¹**eclipse** [iklips] *n* eclips, verduistering: *a total ~ of the sun* een volledige zonsverduistering

²**eclipse** [iklips] *vb* 1 verduisteren; 2 overschaduwen, in glans overtreffen

ecology [ikkollədzjie] ecologie

economic [ekkənommik] 1 economisch; 2 rendabel, lonend, winstgevend

economical [ekkənommikl] 1 zuinig, spaarzaam; 2 economisch, voordelig

economics [ekkənommiks] economie (als wetenschap)

economize [ikkonnəmajz] *(with on)* bezuinigen (op), spaarzaam zijn

economy [ikkonnəmi] 1 economie, economisch stelsel^h: *all those strikes are damaging the French economy* al die stakingen brengen de Franse economie veel schade toe; 2 besparing, bezuiniging; zuinig gebruik: *we bought a smaller house for reasons of ~* we hebben een kleiner huis gekocht om redenen van bezuiniging

economy size voordeelverpakking, voordeelpak^h

ecstasy [ekstəsie] extase, vervoering

ecumenical [ie:kjoemennikl] oecumenisch

eczema [eksimmə] eczeem^h

ed. *edition* uitg, uitgave

¹**eddy** [eddie] *n* werveling, draaikolk

²**eddy** [eddie] *vb* (doen) dwarrelen, (doen) kolken

¹**edge** [edzj] *n* 1 snede, snijkant, scherpte *(also fig)*, effectiviteit, kracht: *her voice had an ~ to it* haar stem klonk scherp; *take the ~ off* het ergste wegnemen; 2 kant, richel; 3 rand, boord^h, oever, grens: *on the ~ of* op het punt van; *(inf) have an ~ over* een voorsprong hebben op; *be on ~* gespannen zijn

²**edge** [edzj] *vb* (langzaam, voorzichtig) bewegen: *~ away* (of: *off)* voorzichtig wegsluipen; *~ up* dichterbij schuiven

³**edge** [edzj] *vb* omranden: *~d with lace* met een randje kant

edging [edzjing] rand, boord^h, bies

edgy [edzjie] 1 scherp; 2 gespannen, prikkelbaar

edible [eddibl] eetbaar, niet giftig

edification [eddiffikkeesjən] stichting, zedelijke en godsdienstige opbouw

edifice [eddiffis] gebouw^h, bouwwerk^h, bouwsel^h

edit [eddit] bewerken, herschrijven: *an ~ed version* een gekuiste versie; *~ed by* onder redactie van *(magazines etc)*

edition [iddisjən] uitgave, editie, oplage, *(fig)* versie

editor [eddittə] 1 bewerker, samensteller; 2 redacteur; 3 uitgever

¹**editorial** [edditto:riəl] *adj* redactioneel, redactie-, redacteurs-

²**editorial** [edditto:riəl] *n* hoofdartikel^h, redactioneel artikel^h

educate [edjoekeet] 1 opvoeden, vormen; 2 opleiden, onderwijzen: *an ~d person* een gestudeerd iem, intellectueel; 3 scholen, trainen

education [edjoekeesjən] 1 onderwijs^h, scholing, opleiding; 2 opvoeding, vorming; 3 pedagogie, opvoedkunde

eel [ie:l] paling || *be as slippery as an ~* zo glad als een aal zijn

eerie [iərie] angstaanjagend, griezelig

¹**effect** [ifekt] *n* 1 resultaat^h, effect^h, gevolg^h; uitwerking: *take ~* resultaat hebben; *to no ~* vruchteloos, tevergeefs; 2 uitvoering, voltrekking: *put plans into ~* plannen uitvoeren; 3 inhoud, strekking: *words to that ~* woorden van die strekking; 4 werking, (rechts)geldigheid: *come into ~, take ~* van kracht worden; 5 *~s* bezittingen, eigendommen: *in ~* in feite, eigenlijk

²**effect** [ifekt] *vb* bewerkstelligen, teweegbrengen, veroorzaken: *~ a cure for s.o.* iem genezen

effective [ifektiv] 1 effectief, doeltreffend; 2 indrukwekkend, treffend: *~ speeches* indrukwekkende toespraken; 3 van kracht *(law etc)*

effeminate [ifemminnət] verwijfd

effervescence [effəvesns] 1 levendigheid, uitgelatenheid; 2 het bruisen

effete [iffie:t] verzwakt, slap, afgeleefd

efficacy [effikkəsie] werkzaamheid, doeltreffendheid

efficiency [iffisjənsie] 1 efficiëntie, doeltreffendheid, doelmatigheid; 2 bekwaamheid; 3 productiviteit

efficient [iffisjənt] 1 efficiënt, doeltreffend, doelmatig; 2 bekwaam; 3 productief

effigy [effidzjie] beeltenis

effluent [efloeənt] 1 afvalwater^h, rioolwater^h; 2 aftakking, zijrivier, afvoer

effort [effət] 1 moeite, inspanning, poging: *make an ~ (to do sth.)* zich inspannen iets te doen; 2 prestatie: *he has made a jolly good ~* hij heeft geweldig zijn best gedaan

effrontery [ifruntərie] brutaliteit

effusion [ifjoe:zjən] ontboezeming

effusive [ifjoe:siv] overdadig *(of utterances)*, uitbundig

e.g. [ie:dzjie:] *exempli gratia* bijv.

egalitarian [igælitteəriən] gelijkheids-, gelijkheid voorstaand

egg [eg] 1 ei^h: *fried ~* gebakken ei; *poached ~* gepocheerd ei; *scrambled ~s* roerei; *~ whisk* eierklopper; 2 eierstruif; 3 eicel: *have (of: put) all one's ~s in one basket* alles op één kaart zetten; *(inf) have ~ on one's face* voor schut staan

eggcup eierdopje^h

egghead *(inf)* intellectueel, gestudeerde

eggplant aubergine

egocentric [egoosentrik] **1** egocentrisch; **2** egoïstisch, zelfzuchtig

egoism [egooizm] egoïsme^h

egotism [egətizm] eigenwaan

eiderdown 1 (donzen) dekbed^h; **2** eiderdons^h

eight [eet] acht

eighteen [eetie:n] achttien

eighth [eetθ] achtste, achtste deel^h: *the ~ fastest runner* de op zeven na snelste loper

eightieth [eetieiθ] tachtigste, tachtigste deel^h

eighty [eetie] tachtig: *in the eighties* in de jaren tachtig

¹either [ajðə] *pron* **1** één van beide(n): *use ~ hand* gebruik een van je (twee) handen; *choose ~ of the colours* kies één van de twee kleuren; **2** beide(n), alle twee, allebei: *in ~ case, ~ way* in beide gevallen, in elk geval; *on ~ side* aan beide kanten

²either [ajðə] *adv* evenmin, ook niet, bovendien niet: *he can't sing, and I can't ~* hij kan niet zingen en ik ook niet

³either [ajðə] *conj* (with *or*) of, ofwel, hetzij: *have ~ cheese or a dessert* neem kaas of een toetje

ejaculation [idzjækjoeleesjən] **1** zaadlozing, ejaculatie; **2** uitroep

eject [idzjekt] uitgooien, uitzetten, uitstoten, uitwerpen

ejection [idzjeksjən] **1** verdrijving, (ambts)ontzetting, uitzetting; **2** uitwerping

eke out 1 rekken *(also supplies)*, aanvullen; **2** bijeenscharrelen: *~ a living* (met moeite) zijn kostje bijeen scharrelen

¹elaborate [ilæbərət] *adj* **1** gedetailleerd, uitgebreid, uitvoerig; **2** ingewikkeld

²elaborate [ilæbəreet] *vb* (with *(up)on*) uitweiden (over)

³elaborate [ilæbəreet] *vb* **1** in detail uitwerken, uitvoerig behandelen, uitweiden over; **2** (moeizaam) voortbrengen, ontwikkelen

elapse [ilæps] verstrijken, voorbijgaan

¹elastic [ilæstik] *adj* **1** elastieken: *~ band* elastiekje; **2** elastisch, rekbaar; **3** flexibel, soepel

²elastic [ilæstik] *n* elastiek(je^h)

elate [ilee̯t] verrukken, in vervoering brengen: *be ~d at* (of: *by*) *sth.* met iets verguld zijn

¹elbow [elboo] *n* **1** elleboog; (scherpe) bocht; **2** *(techn)* elleboog, knie(stuk^h) || *give s.o. the ~* iem de bons geven; *at s.o.'s ~* naast iem, bij iem in de buurt

²elbow [elboo] *vb* zich (een weg) banen, met de ellebogen duwen, werken

elbow-grease zwaar werk^h, poetswerk^h, schoonmaakwerk^h

elbow-room bewegingsvrijheid, armslag

¹elder [eldə] *adj* oudste *(of two)*, oudere

²elder [eldə] *n* **1** oudere: *he is my ~ by four years* hij is vier jaar ouder dan ik; **2** oudste *(of two)*; **3** voorganger, ouderling

elderly [eldəlie] op leeftijd, bejaard

eldest [eldist] oudste *(of three or more)*

¹elect [ilekt] *vb* **1** kiezen, verkiezen (als); **2** besluiten: *~ to become a lawyer* jurist te worden

²elect [ilekt] *adj* gekozen *(but not yet in office): the president ~* de nieuwgekozen president

election [ileksjən] verkiezing, keus: *municipal* (of: *local*) *~(s)* gemeenteraadsverkiezingen

electoral [ilektərəl] **1** kies-, kiezers-: *~ register* (of: *roll*) kiesregister; **2** electoraal, verkiezings-: *~ campaign* verkiezingscampagne

electorate [ilektərət] electoraat^h, de kiezers

electric [ilektrik] **1** elektrisch: *~ chair* elektrische stoel; *~ storm* onweer; **2** opwindend, opzwepend; **3** gespannen *(eg of atmosphere)*

electrical [ilektrikl] elektrisch, elektro-

electrician [ilektrisjən] elektricien, elektromonteur

electricity [ilektrissittie] elektriciteit, elektrische stroom

electrify [ilektriffaj] **1** onder spanning zetten; **2** elektrificeren, voorzien van elektrische installaties; **3** opwinden, geestdriftig maken

electrocute [ilektrəkjoe:t] electrocuteren, op de elektrische stoel ter dood brengen

electronic [ilektronnik] elektronisch

electronics [ilektronniks] elektronica

elegant [elligənt] elegant, sierlijk

elegy [ellidzjie] treurdicht^h, klaaglied^h

element [ellimmənt] **1** element^h, onderdeel^h, (hoofd)bestanddeel^h: *out of one's ~* als een vis op het droge; **2** iets, wat: *there is an ~ of truth in it* er zit wel wat waars in; **3** *(chem, maths)* element^h; **4** *~s* de elementen *(of weather)*; **5** *~s* (grond)beginselen

elementary [ellimmentərie] **1** eenvoudig, simpel: *~ question* eenvoudige vraag; **2** inleidend, elementair: *~ school* lagere school, basisschool; **3** *(science, chem)* elementair

elephant [elliffənt] olifant || *white ~* overbodig luxeartikel

elevate [ellivveet] **1** opheffen, omhoogbrengen, verhogen; **2** verheffen *(only fig)*, op een hoger plan brengen; **3** promoveren, bevorderen: *~d to the presidency* tot president verheven

elevation [ellivveesjən] **1** hoogte, heuvel, ophoging; **2** bevordering, promotie; **3** verhevenheid

elevator [ellivveetə] *(Am)* lift

eleven [ilevn] elf, *(sport)* elftal, ploeg

eleventh [ilevnθ] elfde, elfde deel^h: *(fig) at the ~ hour* ter elfder ure, op het laatste ogenblik

elf [elf] *(elves)* elf, fee

elicit [ilissit] **1** ontlokken, loskrijgen: *~ an answer from s.o.* een antwoord uit iem krijgen; *~ a response* een reactie ontlokken; **2** teweegbrengen, veroorzaken

eligible [ellidzjibl] in aanmerking komend, geschikt, bevoegd: *~ for (a) pension* pensioengerechtigd

eliminate [illimminneet] **1** verwijderen; **2** uitsluiten, buiten beschouwing laten: *~ the possibility of*

murder de mogelijkheid van moord uitsluiten; **3**
uitschakelen *(in match etc)*; **4** *(inf)* van kant maken,
uit de weg ruimen

elimination [illimminn<u>ee</u>sjən] **1** verwijdering, eliminatie; **2** uitschakeling *(in match etc)*; **3** uitsluiting, het schrappen *(of options)*

elk [elk] eland

ellipse [ill<u>i</u>ps] ellips, ovaal[h]

elm [elm] **1** iep, olm; **2** iepenhout[h], olmenhout[h]

elocution [elləkj<u>oe</u>:sjən] voordrachtskunst, welbe-
spraaktheid

elongate [<u>ie</u>:longgeet] langer worden (maken),
(zich) verlengen, in de lengte (doen) groeien

elope [ill<u>oo</u>p] er vandoor gaan *(with lover, or to get
married in secret)*

eloquence [<u>e</u>lləkwəns] welsprekendheid, welbe-
spraaktheid

eloquent [<u>e</u>lləkwənt] welsprekend *(of person, argument)*

else [els] anders, nog meer: *anything ~?* verder nog
iets?; *little ~* niet veel meer; *what ~ did you expect?*
wat had jij anders verwacht?

elsewhere [elsw<u>e</u>ə] elders, ergens anders

elucidate [ill<u>oe</u>:siddeet] (nader) toelichten, licht
werpen op, ophelderen

elude [ill<u>oe</u>:d] **1** ontwijken, ontschieten, ontsnappen aan, *(fig)* ontduiken, zich onttrekken aan *(duties)*, uit de weg gaan: *~ capture* weten te ontkomen;
2 ontgaan *(of fact, name)*, ontschieten: *his name ~s
me* ik ben zijn naam even kwijt

elusive [ill<u>oe</u>:siv] **1** ontwijkend: *~ answer* ontwijkend antwoord; **2** moeilijk te vangen; **3** onvatbaar,
ongrijpbaar: *an ~ name* een moeilijk te onthouden
naam

'em [əm] *see* them

e-mail *electronic mail* elektronische post, e-mail

emancipate [im<u>æ</u>nsippeet] **1** vrijmaken *(slaves
etc)*, emanciperen, zelfstandig maken: *~d women*
geëmancipeerde vrouwen; **2** gelijkstellen voor de
wet, emanciperen

emancipation [imænsipp<u>ee</u>sjən] **1** bevrijding *(of
slaves)*, emancipatie; **2** emancipatie, gelijkstelling
voor de wet: *the ~ of women* de emancipatie van de
vrouw

embalm [imb<u>a</u>:m] balsemen

embankment [imb<u>æ</u>ngkmənt] **1** dijk, dam, wal; **2**
opgehoogde baan, spoordijk; **3** kade

embargo [imb<u>a</u>:goo] embargo[h] *(of ships, trade)*,
blokkade, beslag[h], beslaglegging, verbod[h], belemmering, uitvoerverbod[h]

embark [imb<u>a</u>:k] **1** aan boord gaan (nemen), (zich)
inschepen; **2** beginnen, van start gaan: *~ (up)on*
zich begeven in, beginnen (aan)

embarkation [emba:k<u>ee</u>sjən] **1** inscheping, inla-
ding, het aan boord gaan (brengen); **2** het beginnen

embarrass [imb<u>æ</u>rəs] **1** in verlegenheid brengen; **2**
in geldverlegenheid brengen, in financiële moeilijkheden brengen

embarrassment [imb<u>æ</u>rəsmənt] **1** verlegenheid,

onbehagen[h]; **2** (geld)verlegenheid, (geld)pro-
bleem[h]

embassy [<u>e</u>mbəsie] ambassade, diplomatieke ver-
tegenwoordigers

embed [imb<u>e</u>d] **1** (vast)zetten, vastleggen: *the arrow ~ded itself in his leg* de pijl zette zich vast in zijn
been; *be ~ded in* vastzitten in; **2** omsluiten, insluiten, omringen, omgeven; **3** inbedden

embellish [imb<u>e</u>llisj] verfraaien, versieren: *~ a story* een verhaal opsmukken

ember [<u>e</u>mbə] **1** gloeiend stukje[h] kool; **2** *~s* gloeiende as, smeulend vuur[h], *(fig)* laatste vonken, resten

embezzle [imb<u>e</u>zl] verduisteren, achterhouden

embitter [imb<u>i</u>ttə] verbitteren, bitter(der) maken

emblem [<u>e</u>mbləm] embleem[h], symbool[h]

embody [imb<u>o</u>ddie] **1** vorm geven (aan), uitdrukken: *~ one's principles in actions* zijn principes tot
uiting laten komen in daden; **2** inlijven: *his points
of view were embodied in the article* zijn standpunten waren verwerkt in het artikel

¹embrace [imbr<u>ee</u>s] *vb* elkaar omhelzen, elkaar omarmen

²embrace [imbr<u>ee</u>s] *vb* **1** omhelzen, omarmen, omvatten; **2** gebruik maken van, aangrijpen: *~ an offer*
gebruik maken van een aanbod

³embrace [imbr<u>ee</u>s] *n* omhelzing, omarming

embroider [imbr<u>o</u>jdə] **1** borduren; **2** opsmukken,
verfraaien

embryo [<u>e</u>mbrie·oo] embryo[h]

emend [imm<u>e</u>nd] corrigeren, verbeteringen aanbrengen *(in text)*

emendation [ie:mend<u>ee</u>sjən] correctie, verbetering

emerald [<u>e</u>mmərəld] **1** smaragd(groen); **2** smarag-
den, van smaragd

emerge [imm<u>ə</u>:dzj] **1** verschijnen, te voorschijn komen: *~ from* (of: *out of)* te voorschijn komen uit; **2**
bovenkomen, opduiken; **3** blijken, uitkomen: *after
a long investigation it ~ed that* een langdurig onderzoek wees uit dat

emergence [imm<u>ə</u>:dzjəns] **1** het bovenkomen; **2**
het uitkomen; **3** het optreden

emergency [imm<u>ə</u>:dzjənsie] **1** onverwachte gebeurtenis, onvoorzien voorval[h]; **2** noodsituatie,
noodtoestand, noodgeval[h]: *state of ~* noodtoestand; *~ exit* nooduitgang, nooddeur; *in case of ~*
in geval van nood

emigrant [<u>e</u>mmigrənt] emigrant(e)

emigrate [<u>e</u>mmigreet] emigreren, het land verlaten

eminence [<u>e</u>mminnəns] **1** heuvel, hoogte; **2** emi-
nentie *(also as title)*, verhevenheid

eminent [<u>e</u>mminnənt] **1** uitstekend; **2** hoog, verheven *(also lit)*, aanzienlijk

emission [imm<u>i</u>sjən] afgifte, uitzending, afscheiding *(of body)*; *(science)* emissie, uitstoot *(of (poisonous) gases)*

emit [imm<u>i</u>t] **1** uitstralen, uitzenden; **2** afscheiden,
afgeven, uitstoten *((poisonous) gases)*: *~ a smell*
stank afgeven

¹emollient [imm<u>o</u>lliənt] *adj* verzachtend, zachtmakend

²emollient [imm<u>o</u>lliənt] *n* verzachtend middelʰ

emotion [imm<u>oo</u>sjən] **1** (gevoels)aandoening, emotie, gevoelenʰ, ontroering: *mixed ~s* gemengde gevoelens; **2** het gevoel, de gevoelswereld; **3** bewogenheid

emotional [imm<u>oo</u>sjənəl] **1** emotioneel, gevoels-, gemoeds-; **2** ontroerend

emperor [<u>e</u>mpərə] keizer

emphasis [<u>e</u>mfəsis] **1** accentʰ, klemtoon *(also fig): lay (of: place, put) an ~ on sth.* het accent leggen op iets; **2** nadruk, klem, kracht

emphasize [<u>e</u>mfəsajz] benadrukken, de nadruk leggen op

empire [<u>e</u>mpajjə] (keizer)rijkʰ, imperiumʰ *(also fig)*, wereldrijkʰ

empirical [empi̯rrikl] gebaseerd op ervaring

¹employ [impl<u>o</u>j] *vb* **1** in dienst nemen, tewerkstellen; **2** gebruiken, aanwenden; **3** bezighouden: *be ~ed in* bezig zijn, zich bezighouden met

²employ [impl<u>o</u>j] *n* (loon)dienst: *in the ~ of* in dienst van

employable [impl<u>o</u>jjəbl] bruikbaar, inzetbaar

employee [impl<u>o</u>jjie:] werknemer

employer [impl<u>o</u>jjə] werkgever

employment [impl<u>o</u>jmənt] **1** beroepʰ, werkʰ, baan; **2** bezigheid; **3** werkgelegenheid: *full ~* volledige werkgelegenheid; **4** gebruikʰ, het gebruiken

empower [imp<u>au</u>ə] **1** machtigen; **2** in staat stellen

empress [<u>e</u>mprəs] keizerin

¹empty [<u>e</u>mptie] *adj* **1** leeg, ledig; **2** nietszeggend, hol; **3** onbewoond, leegstaand; **4** leeghoofdig, oppervlakkig

²empty [<u>e</u>mptie] *vb* leeg raken, (zich) legen

³empty [<u>e</u>mptie] *vb* legen, leegmaken

enable [inn<u>ee</u>bl] **1** in staat stellen, (de) gelegenheid geven; **2** mogelijk maken

enact [in<u>æ</u>kt] **1** bepalen, vaststellen; **2** tot wet verheffen

enamel [in<u>æ</u>ml] **1** (email)lak⁺ʰ, glazuurʰ, vernisʰ; **2** emailʰ; (tand)glazuurʰ

encampment [ink<u>æ</u>mpmənt] kamp(ement)ʰ, legerplaats, veldverblijfʰ

encapsulate [ink<u>æ</u>ps·joeleet] **1** (zich) inkapselen; **2** samenvatten

enchant [intsja<u>:</u>nt] **1** betoveren, beheksen; **2** bekoren, verrukken: *be ~ ed by* (of: *with*) verrukt zijn over

encircle [ins<u>ə:</u>kl] omcirkelen, omsingelen, insluiten

encl. *enclosed, enclosure* bijl., bijlage

enclose [inkl<u>oo</u>z] **1** omheinen, insluiten; **2** insluiten, bijsluiten *(enclosure etc)*

enclosure [inkl<u>oo</u>zjə] **1** (om)heining, schutting; **2** omheind stuk land; **3** vakʰ, afdeling; **4** bijlage

encode [ink<u>oo</u>d] coderen

encompass [ink<u>u</u>mpəs] **1** omringen, omgeven; **2** bevatten, omvatten

encore [<u>o</u>ngko:] toegift, encoreʰ

¹encounter [ink<u>au</u>ntə] *vb* **1** ontmoeten, (onverwacht) tegenkomen; **2** ontmoeten, geconfronteerd worden met: *~ difficulties* moeilijkheden moeten overwinnen

²encounter [ink<u>au</u>ntə] *n* **1** (onverwachte) ontmoeting; **2** krachtmeting, confrontatie, treffenʰ

encourage [ink<u>u</u>rridzj] **1** bemoedigen, hoop geven; **2** aanmoedigen, stimuleren, in de hand werken

encroach [inkr<u>oo</u>tsj] opdringen, oprukken: *the sea ~es further (up)on the land* de zee tast de kust steeds verder aan

encrust [inkr<u>u</u>st] **1** met een korst bedekken; **2** bedekken, bezetten: *~ed with precious stones* bezet met edelstenen

encrypt [inkri̯pt] coderen, in code weergeven, versleutelen *(message, data)*

encumber [inku̯mbə] **1** beladen, (over)belasten: *~ed with parcels* met boodschappen beladen; **2** hinderen, belemmeren: *~ oneself with financial responsibilities* zich financiële verplichtingen op de hals halen

encyclop(a)edia [insajklɔpi̯e̯:diə] encyclopedie

¹end [end] *n* **1** eindeʰ, afsluiting, besluitʰ: *come (of: draw) to an ~* ten einde lopen, ophouden; *put an ~ to* een eind maken aan, afschaffen; *in the ~* ten slotte, op het laatst, uiteindelijk; *for weeks on ~* weken achtereen; **2** eindeʰ, uiteindeʰ: *~ to ~* in de lengte; **3** eindeʰ, verste puntʰ, grens, *(also fig)* uitersteʰ; **4** kant, onderkant, bovenkant, zijde, *(also fig)* afdeling, partʰ: *place on ~* rechtop zetten; **5** eindeʰ, vernietiging, dood; **6** doelʰ, bedoeling, (beoogd) resultaatʰ: *the ~ justifies the means* het doel heiligt de middelen; *at the ~ of the day* uiteindelijk, als puntje bij paaltje komt; *be at the ~ of one's tether* aan het eind van zijn krachten zijn; *make (both) ~s meet* de eindjes aan elkaar knopen; *that irritates me no ~* dat irriteert me heel erg

²end [end] *vb* **1** eindigen, aflopen: *our efforts ~ed in a total failure* onze pogingen liepen op niets uit; **2** zijn einde vinden, sterven

³end [end] *vb* **1** beëindigen, een eind maken aan, ophouden met; **2** conclusie vormen van; **3** vernietigen, een eind maken aan: *~ it (all)* er een eind aan maken, zelfmoord plegen

endanger [ind<u>ee</u>ndzjə] in gevaar brengen, een gevaar vormen voor, bedreigen: *~ed species* bedreigde diersoorten

endear [ind<u>i</u>ə] geliefd maken

endearment [ind<u>i</u>əmənt] **1** uiting van genegenheid; **2** innemendheid: *terms of ~* lieve woordjes

¹endeavour [ind<u>e</u>vvə] *vb* pogen, trachten, zich inspannen

²endeavour [ind<u>e</u>vvə] *n* poging, moeite, inspanning

ending [<u>e</u>nding] **1** eindeʰ, beëindiging, afronding, eindspelʰ; **2** eindeʰ, slotʰ, afloop: *happy ~* goede afloop

endive [<u>e</u>ndiv] andijvie

endorse [ind<u>o:</u>s] bevestigen, bekrachtigen, beamen

endow [indau̯] **1** begiftigen, subsidiëren, bekostigen; **2** schenken, geven aan: *~ed with great musical talent* begiftigd met grote muzikaliteit

endowment [indau̯mənt] **1** gave, begaafdheid, talentʰ; **2** gift; **3** het schenken

endue [indjoe:] begiftigen, schenken

endurance [indjoeərəns] **1** uithoudingsvermogenʰ, weerstand; **2** duurzaamheid ‖ *beyond (of: past)* ~ onverdraaglijk, niet uit te houden

¹**endure** [indjoeə] *vb* **1** duren, blijven; **2** het uithouden

²**endure** [indjoeə] *vb* **1** doorstaan, uithouden, verdragen; **2** ondergaan, lijden

enduring [indjoeəring] blijvend, (voort)durend

enemy [ennəmie] vijand; vijandelijke troepen

energetic [ennədzjettik] **1** energiek, vurig, actief; **2** krachtig, sterk *(protest etc)*

energy [ennədzjie] kracht, energie: *nuclear* ~ kernenergie

enervate [ennəveet] ontkrachten, slap maken, verzwakken

enfeeble [infie:bl] verzwakken, uitputten

enforce [info:s] **1** uitvoeren, op de naleving toezien van, de hand houden aan *(rule, law);* **2** (af)dwingen; **3** versterken, benadrukken

enforcement [info:smənt] **1** handhaving, uitvoering; **2** dwang

¹**engage** [ingeedzj] *vb* **1** aannemen, in dienst nemen, contracteren; **2** bezetten, in beslag nemen *(also fig): ~ s.o. in conversation* een gesprek met iem aanknopen; **3** beloven, verplichten: *~ oneself to do sth.* beloven iets te doen; **4** *(mil)* aanvallen; **5** *(techn)* koppelen, inschakelen

²**engage** [ingeedzj] *vb* **1** *(with in)* zich bezighouden (met), zich inlaten (met), doen (aan); **2** zich verplichten, beloven, aangaan; **3** *(techn)* in elkaar grijpen, gekoppeld worden; **4** *(with with) (mil)* de strijd aanbinden (met)

engaged [ingeedzjd] **1** verloofd: *~ to* verloofd met; **2** bezet, bezig, druk; gereserveerd: *I'm ~* ik heb een afspraak; *the telephone is* ~ de telefoon is in gesprek; **3** gecontracteerd

engagement [ingeedzjmənt] **1** verloving; **2** afspraak; **3** belofte, verplichting, *~s* financiële verplichting; **4** gevechtʰ; **5** contractʰ

engaging [ingeedzjing] innemend, aantrekkelijk

engender [indzjendə] veroorzaken, voortbrengen

engine [endzjin] motor; machine; locomotief

¹**engineer** [endzjinniə] *n* **1** ingenieur; **2** machinebouwer; **3** genieofficier, geniesoldaat: *the (Royal) Engineers* de Genie; **4** technicus, mecanicien, *(ship)* werktuigkundige; **5** *(Am)* (trein)machinist

²**engineer** [endzjinniə] *vb* **1** bouwen, maken, construeren; **2** bewerkstelligen, op touw zetten

engineering [endzjinniəring] **1** techniek; **2** bouw, constructie

England [ingglənd] Engeland

¹**English** [ingglisj] *n* Engels, de Engelse taal: *the*

²**English** [ingglisj] *adj* Engels, in het Engels: *~ breakfast* Engels ontbijt, ontbijt met spek en eieren

Englishman [ingglisjmən] Engelsman

engrave [ingreev] graveren

engraving [ingreeving] **1** gravure; **2** graveerkunst

engross [ingroos] geheel in beslag nemen, overheersen: *I was so ~ed in my book that* ik was zo in mijn boek verdiept, dat

enhance [inha:ns] verhogen, versterken, verbeteren

enigma [innigmə] mysterieʰ, raadselʰ

enjoy [indzjoj] genieten van, plezier beleven aan: *Dick ~s a good health* Dick geniet een goede gezondheid; *~ oneself* zich vermaken

enjoyable [indzjojjəbl] plezierig, prettig, fijn

enkindle [inkindl] aansteken *(fig)*, doen oplaaien, opwekken *(anger, passion)*

¹**enlarge** [inla:dzj] *vb* vergroten, groter maken

²**enlarge** [inla:dzj] *vb* **1** groeien, groter worden, zich uitbreiden; **2** uitgebreid spreken, uitweiden: *~ (up)on a subject* uitweiden over een onderwerp; **3** uitvergroot worden

enlighten [inlajtn] onderrichten, onderwijzen

enlightened [inlajtnd] verlicht, rationeel, redelijk: *~ ideas* verlichte opvattingen

enlightenment [inlajtnmənt] opheldering, verduidelijking

¹**enlist** [inlist] *vb* werven, mobiliseren, in dienst nemen: *~ s.o. in an enterprise* iem bij een onderneming te hulp roepen

²**enlist** [inlist] *vb* dienst nemen, vrijwillig in het leger gaan

enmity [enmittie] vijandschap, haat(gevoelʰ), onmin

enormity [inno:mittie] **1** gruweldaad, wandaad; **2** gruwelijkheid, misdadigheid; **3** enorme omvang, immense grootte *(of problem etc)*

enormous [inno:məs] enorm, geweldig groot

¹**enough** [innuf] *pron* genoeg; voldoende: *beer* ~ genoeg bier; *be ~ of a man to* wel zo flink zijn om te

²**enough** [innuf] *adv* **1** genoeg: *~ said* genoeg daarover; *oddly (of: strangely)* ~ merkwaardig genoeg; **2** zeer, heel: *I'm having enough problems with my own children* ik heb al genoeg problemen met mijn eigen kinderen; **3** tamelijk, redelijk: *she paints well* ~ ze schildert vrij behoorlijk

enquire [inkwajjə] *see* inquire

enquiry [inkwajjərie] *see* inquiry

enrage [inreedzj] woedend maken, tot razernij brengen

enrich [inritsj] **1** verrijken, rijk(er) maken, uitbreiden; **2** verrijken, de kwaliteit verhogen: *~ed uranium* verrijkt uranium

¹**enrol** [inrool] *vb* zich inschrijven, zich opgeven

²**enrol** [inrool] *vb* **1** inschrijven, opnemen; **2** werven, aanwerven, in dienst nemen

ensign [ensajn] **1** insigneʰ, embleemʰ; **2** vlag, nationale vlag

enslave [insleev] knechten, tot slaaf maken, onderwerpen

ensnare [insnɛə] vangen, verstrikken, *(also fig)* in de val laten lopen

ensue [ins·joe:] **1** volgen: *the ensuing month* de volgende maand, de maand daarna; **2** *(with from)* voortvloeien (uit), voortkomen (uit)

ensure [insjoeə] **1** veilig stellen, beschermen; **2** garanderen, instaan voor: *~ the safety of our guests* de veiligheid van onze gasten waarborgen; **3** verzekeren van

entail [inteel] met zich meebrengen, noodzakelijk maken, inhouden

entangle [intænggl] verwarren, onontwarbaar maken, *(also fig)* verstrikken, vast laten lopen

¹enter [entə] *vb* binnengaan, binnenlopen *(of ship)*, binnendringen

²enter [entə] *vb* **1** gaan in, op, bij, zich begeven in, zijn intrede doen in: *~ the Church* priester worden; **2** inschrijven, bijschrijven, opschrijven, noteren, boeken, invoeren; **3** opgeven, inschrijven; **4** toelaten, binnenlaten *(as member);* **6** inzenden: *~ sth. in the competition* iets inzenden voor de wedstrijd

³enter [entə] *vb* **1** zich laten inschrijven, zich opgeven; **2** *(theatre)* opkomen

enter into 1 beginnen, aanknopen *(conversation);* **2** zich verplaatsen in, zich inleven in; **3** deel uitmaken van, onderdeel vormen van; **4** ingaan op, onder de loep nemen; **5** aangaan, sluiten *(contract, treaty)*

enterprise [entəprajz] **1** onderneming; **2** firma, zaak; **3** ondernemingsgeest, ondernemingszin

enterprising [entəprajzing] ondernemend

¹entertain [entəteen] *vb* **1** gastvrij ontvangen, aanbieden; **2** onderhouden, amuseren; **3** koesteren, erop nahouden: *~ doubts* twijfels hebben; **4** overdenken, in overweging nemen: *~ a proposal* over een voorstel nadenken

²entertain [entəteen] *vb* **1** een feestje (etentje) geven, gasten hebben; **2** vermaak bieden

entertainer [entəteenə] iem die het publiek vermaakt, zanger, conferencier, cabaretier, goochelaar

entertaining [entəteening] onderhoudend, vermakelijk, amusant

entertainment [entəteenmənt] **1** iets dat amusement biedt, opvoering, uitvoering, show, conference; **2** feestʰ, partij, feestmaalʰ; **3** gastvrijheid, gastvrij onthaalʰ; **4** vermaakʰ, plezierʰ, amusementʰ: *greatly (of: much) to our ~* tot onze grote pret; **5** amusementswereld(jeʰ), amusementsbedrijfʰ

enthralling [inθro:ling] betoverend, boeiend

enthrone [inθroon] op de troon zetten, kronen

¹enthuse [inθjoe:z] *vb (with about, over)* enthousiast zijn (over)

²enthuse [inθjoe:z] *vb* enthousiast maken

enthusiasm [inθjoe:zie·æzm] **1** *(with about, for)* enthousiasmeʰ (voor), geestdrift (voor, over), ver-

rukking, vervoering; **2** vurige interesse, passie

enthusiast [inθjoe:zie·æst] **1** *(with about, for)* enthousiasteling (in), fan (van), liefhebber (van); **2** dweper

entice [intajs] (ver)lokken, verleiden

entire [intajjə] **1** compleet, volledig; **2** geheel, totaal; **3** gaaf, heel, onbeschadigd

entirely [intajjəlie] **1** helemaal, geheel (en al), volkomen; **2** alleen, enkel, slechts

entitle [intajtl] **1** betitelen, noemen: *a novel ~d 'Enduring love'* een roman met als titel 'Enduring love'; **2** recht geven op: *be ~d to compensation* recht hebben op schadevergoeding

entity [entittie] bestaanʰ, wezenʰ, het zijn

entrails [entreelz] ingewanden, darmen

¹entrance [entrəns] *n* **1** ingang, toegang, entree; **2** binnenkomst; **3** opkomst *(on stage);* **4** entree, toelating, *(by extension)* toegangsgeldʰ: *no ~* verboden toegang

²entrance [intra:ns] *vb* in verrukking brengen, meeslepen

entreat [intrie:t] smeken (om), bidden (om), dringend verzoeken

¹entrench [intrentsj] *vb* **1** zich verschansen, zich ingraven; **2** *(with on, upon)* inbreuk maken (op)

²entrench [intrentsj] *vb* stevig vastleggen, verankeren *(right, habit etc)*

entrepreneur [ontrəpronə:] **1** ondernemer; **2** impresario *(stage)*

entrust [intrust] toevertrouwen: *~ sth. to s.o., ~ s.o. with sth.* iem iets toevertrouwen

entry [entrie] **1** intrede, entree, toetreding, intocht, binnenkomst, *(theatre)* opkomst; **2** toegang: *no ~* verboden in te rijden; **3** ingang, toegang, halʰ; **4** notitie, inschrijving, boeking

enumerate [injoe:məreet] **1** opsommen; **2** (op)tellen

enunciate [innunsie·eet] (goed) articuleren, (duidelijk) uitspreken

envelop [invelləp] inwikkelen, inpakken, *(fig)* omhullen, omgeven

envelope [envəloop] **1** omhulling *(also fig);* **2** envelop: *padded ~* luchtkussenenvelop

enviable [enviəbl] benijdenswaardig, begerenswaardig

envious [enviəs] *(with of)* jaloers (op), afgunstig

environment [invajrənmənt] **1** omgeving; **2** milieuʰ, omgeving

environmentalist [invajrənmentəlist] **1** milieudeskundige, milieubeheerder; **2** milieuactivist, milieubewust iem

envisage [invizzidzj] voorzien, zich voorstellen *(in future)*

envoy [envoj] (af)gezant, diplomatiek vertegenwoordiger

¹envy [envie] *n* afgunst: *he was filled with ~ at my new car* hij benijdde me mijn nieuwe wagen

²envy [envie] *vb* benijden

enzyme [enzajm] enzymʰ

¹**epic** [eppik] *n* epos^h, heldendicht^h

²**epic** [eppik] *adj* **1** episch, verhalend; **2** heldhaftig

epidemic [eppiddemmik] epidemie

epilepsy [eppillepsie] epilepsie, vallende ziekte

¹**epileptic** [eppilleptik] *adj* epileptisch

²**epileptic** [eppilleptik] *n* epilepticus

epilogue [eppillog] **1** epiloog, slotrede; **2** naschrift^h, nawoord^h

episcopal [ippiskəpl] bisschoppelijk

episode [eppissood] episode, (belangrijke) gebeurtenis, voorval^h, aflevering *(of serial)*

epitaph [eppitta:f] grafschrift^h

epoch [ie:pok] **1** keerpunt^h, mijlpaal; **2** tijdvak^h, tijdperk^h

equable [ekwəbl] gelijkmatig, gelijkmoedig

¹**equal** [ie:kwəl] *adj* **1** gelijk, overeenkomstig, hetzelfde: *on ~ terms* op voet van gelijkheid; *~ to* gelijk aan; **2** onpartijdig, eerlijk, rechtvaardig: *~ opportunity* gelijkberechtiging; **3** gelijkmatig, effen

²**equal** [ie:kwəl] *vb* evenaren, gelijk zijn aan: *two and four ~s six* twee en vier is zes

³**equal** [ie:kwəl] *n* gelijke, weerga

equality [ikwollittie] gelijkheid, overeenkomst

¹**equalize** [ie:kwəlajz] *vb* **1** gelijk worden; **2** *(sport)* gelijkmaken

²**equalize** [ie:kwəlajz] *vb* gelijkmaken, gelijkstellen

equally [ie:kwəlie] **1** eerlijk, evenzeer; gelijkmatig; **2** in dezelfde mate

equate [ikweet] **1** *(with to, with)* vergelijken (met); **2** *(with with)* gelijkstellen (aan); **3** gelijkmaken, met elkaar in evenwicht brengen

equation [ikweesjən] vergelijking

equator [ikweetə] evenaar, equator

equestrian [ikwestriən] ruiter

equilibrium [ie:kwilliibriəm] evenwicht^h

equip [ikwip] *(with with)* uitrusten (met), toerusten (met)

equipment [ikwipmənt] uitrusting, installatie, benodigdheden

equity [ekwittie] **1** billijkheid, rechtvaardigheid; **2** *-ies* aandelen

¹**equivalent** [ikwivvələnt] *adj (with to)* equivalent (aan), gelijkwaardig (aan)

²**equivalent** [ikwivvələnt] *n* equivalent^h

equivocal [ikwivvəkl] **1** dubbelzinnig; **2** twijfelachtig

equivocate [ikwivvəkeet] **1** eromheen draaien, een ontwijkend antwoord geven; **2** een slag om de arm houden

er [ə:] eh *(hesitation)*

era [iərə] era, tijdperk^h, jaartelling, hoofdtijdperk^h

eradicate [irædikeet] met wortel en al uittrekken, *(fig)* uitroeien, verdelgen

erase [irreez] uitvegen, uitwissen

eraser [irreezə] **1** stukje vlakgom, gummetje^h; **2** bordenwisser

¹**erect** [irrekt] *adj* recht, rechtop (gaand), opgericht

²**erect** [irrekt] *vb* **1** oprichten, bouwen, neerzetten; **2** stichten, vestigen, instellen

erection [irreksjən] **1** erectie; **2** gebouw^h; **3** het oprichten, het bouwen, het optrekken; **4** het instellen

¹**erode** [irrood] *vb* **1** (also with *away*) uitbijten *(of acid)*; **2** (also with *away*) uithollen *(of water)*, afslijpen, eroderen

²**erode** [irrood] *vb* wegspoelen

erosion [irroozjən] erosie *(also fig)*

erotic [irrottik] erotisch

err [ə:] **1** zich vergissen; **2** afwijken: *~ on the side of caution* het zekere voor het onzekere nemen; **3** zondigen

errand [errənd] **1** boodschap: *go on* (of: *run*) *~s for s.o.* boodschappen doen voor iem; **2** doel^h *(of message)*

erratic [irætik] **1** onregelmatig, ongeregeld, grillig; **2** excentriek, onconventioneel; **3** veranderlijk, wispelturig

error [errə] vergissing: *~ of judgement* beoordelingsfout; *human ~* menselijke fout; *be in ~* zich vergissen

erupt [irrupt] **1** uitbarsten *(of volcano, geyser etc)*, (vuur)spuwen, spuiten; **2** barsten *(also fig)*, uitbreken

¹**escalate** [eskəleet] *vb* stijgen *(of prices, wages)*, escaleren

²**escalate** [eskəleet] *vb* verhevigen, doen escaleren

escalator [eskəleetə] roltrap

escapade [eskəpeed] **1** escapade; **2** dolle streek, wild avontuur^h

¹**escape** [iskeep] *vb* **1** *(with from, out of)* ontsnappen (uit, aan), ontvluchten: *~ with one's life* het er levend afbrengen; **2** naar buiten komen, ontsnappen *(of gas, steam)*; **3** verdwijnen, vervagen, vergeten raken

²**escape** [iskeep] *vb* **1** vermijden, ontkomen aan: *~ death* de dood ontlopen; **2** ontschieten, (even) vergeten zijn *(of name, etc)*; **3** ontgaan: *~ one's attention* aan iemands aandacht ontsnappen; **4** ontglippen, ontvallen

³**escape** [iskeep] *n* ontsnapping, vlucht: *make one's ~* ontsnappen

¹**escort** [esko:t] *n* **1** escorte^h, (gewapende) geleide^h; **2** begeleider, metgezel

²**escort** [isko:t] *vb* escorteren; begeleiden, uitgeleide doen

esp. *especially* i.h.b., in het bijzonder

especial [ispesjl] speciaal, bijzonder

especially [ispesjəlie] **1** speciaal: *bought ~ for you* speciaal voor jou gekocht; **2** vooral, in het bijzonder, voornamelijk

espionage [espiəna:zj] spionage

Esq. *esquire* Dhr.

esquire [iskwajjə] de (Weledelgeboren) Heer

essay [essee] essay^h, opstel^h, (korte) verhandeling

essence [esns] **1** essentie, kern; **2** wezen^h, geest: *he's the ~ of kindness* hij is de vriendelijkheid zelf

¹**essential** [issensjl] *adj (with for, to)* **1** essentieel (voor), wezenlijk; **2** onmisbaar (voor), noodzakelijk (voor)

²essential [issensjl] *n* **1** het essentiële, essentie, wezen^h; **2** essentieel punt^h, hoofdzaak; **3** noodzakelijk iets, onontbeerlijke zaak: *the basic ~s* de allernoodzakelijkste dingen

establish [istæblisj] **1** vestigen *(also fig)*, oprichten, stichten: *~ed custom* ingeburgerd gebruik; *~ oneself* zich vestigen; **2** (vast) benoemen, aanstellen; **3** vaststellen *(facts)*, bewijzen: *~ed church* staatskerk

establishment [istæblisjmənt] vestiging, oprichting, instelling

estate [isteet] **1** landgoed^h, buiten(verblijf)^h; **2** (land)bezit^h, vastgoed^h; **3** woonwijk; **4** stand, klasse; **5** *(law)* boedel; **6** plantage ‖ *industrial ~* industrieterrein, industriegebied, industriewijk

estate agent makelaar in onroerend goed

¹esteem [istie:m] *vb* **1** (hoog)achten, waarderen, respecteren; **2** beschouwen: *~ sth. a duty* iets als een plicht zien

²esteem [istie:m] *n* achting, respect^h, waardering: *hold s.o. in high ~* iem hoogachten

esthet- *see* aesthet-

estimable [estimməbl] **1** achtenswaardig; **2** schatbaar, taxeerbaar

¹estimate [estimmeet] *vb* **1** schatten, berekenen: *~ sth. at £100* iets op 100 pond schatten; **2** beoordelen *(pers)*

²estimate [estimmət] *n* **1** schatting: *at a rough ~* ruwweg; **2** (kosten)raming, begroting, prijsopgave; **3** oordeel^h

estimation [estimmeesjən] **1** (hoog)achting: *hold s.o. in ~* iem (hoog)achten; **2** schatting, taxatie

estrangement [istreendzjmənt] vervreemding, verwijdering

etc. *et cetera* enz.; etc., enzovoort

etch [etsj] etsen

eternal [ittə:nl] eeuwig *(also inf)*

eternity [ittə:nittie] **1** eeuwigheid *(also inf); 2* onsterfelijkheid; het eeuwige leven

ethical [eθikl] ethisch

ethics [eθiks] **1** ethiek, zedenleer; **2** gedragsnormen, gedragscode

ethnic [eθnnik] etnisch

EU *European Union* EU, Europese Unie

eulogy [joe:lədzjie] (with *of, on*) lofprijzing (over)

euphemism [joe:fəmizm] eufemisme^h

euphony [joe:fənie] welluidendheid

euphoria [joe:fo:riə] euforie, gevoel^h van welbevinden, opgewektheid

Euro [joeəroo] euro

Europe [joeərəp] Europa

¹European [joeərəpiən] *adj* Europees: *~ Union* Europese Unie, EU

²European [joeərəpiən] *n* Europeaan

euthanasia [joe:θəneeziə] euthanasie

evacuate [ivækjoe·eet] evacueren, ontruimen, *(mil)* terugtrekken uit

evacuation [ivækjoe·eesjən] ontruiming, evacuatie

evade [ivveed] vermijden, (proberen te) ontkomen

aan, ontwijken: *~ one's responsibilities* zijn verantwoordelijkheden uit de weg gaan

evaluate [ivæljoe·eet] **1** de waarde bepalen van, evalueren; **2** berekenen

evaluation [ivæljoe·eesjən] **1** waardebepaling, beoordeling, evaluatie; **2** berekening

evangelical [ie:vændzjellikl] evangelisch

evangelist [ivændzjəlist] evangelist: *the four ~s* de vier evangelisten

evaporate [ivæpəreet] verdampen, (doen) vervliegen, *(fig)* in het niets (doen) verdwijnen: *my hope has ~d* ik heb de hoop verloren

evasion [ivveezjən] ontwijking, uitvlucht: *~ of taxes* belastingontduiking

eve [ie:v] **1** vooravond: *on the ~ of* aan de vooravond van; *on the ~ of the race* de dag voor de wedstrijd; **2** avond

¹even [ie:vn] *adv* **1** zelfs: *~ now* zelfs nu; *~ so* maar toch; *~ if* (of: *though*) zelfs al; **2** *(before comparative)* nog: *that's ~ better* dat is zelfs (nog) beter

²even [ie:vn] *adj* **1** vlak, gelijk, glad; **2** gelijkmatig, kalm, onveranderlijk: *an ~ temper* een evenwichtig humeur; **3** even: *~ and odd numbers* even en oneven getallen; **4** gelijk, quitte: *get ~ with s.o.* 't iem betaald zetten; *now we're ~ again* nu staan we weer quitte; **5** eerlijk: *an ~ exchange* een eerlijke ruil

³even [ie:vn] *vb* gelijk worden, glad worden

⁴even [ie:vn] *vb* gelijk maken

evening [ie:vning] avond, *(fig)* einde^h: *good ~!* goedenavond!; *in* (of: *during*) *the ~* 's avonds; *on Tuesday ~* op dinsdagavond

even out (gelijkmatig) spreiden, gelijk verdelen, uitsmeren

event [ivvent] **1** gebeurtenis, evenement^h, manifestatie: *the normal* (of: *usual*) *course of ~s* de gewone gang van zaken; *happy ~* blijde gebeurtenis *(birth)*; **2** geval^h: *at all ~s* in elk geval; *in the ~ of his death* in het geval dat hij komt te overlijden; **3** uitkomst, afloop: *in the ~, he decided to withdraw from the race* uiteindelijk besloot hij zich uit de wedstrijd terug te trekken; **4** *(sport)* nummer^h, onderdeel^h

eventual [ivventsjoeəl] uiteindelijk

eventuality [ivventsjoe·ælittie] eventualiteit, mogelijke gebeurtenis

eventually [ivventsjoeəlie] ten slotte, uiteindelijk

even up gelijk worden, gelijkmaken, gelijkschakelen, evenwicht herstellen

ever [evvə] **1** ooit: *faster than ~* sneller dan ooit; **2** toch, in 's hemelsnaam: *how ~ could I do that?* hoe zou ik dat in 's hemelsnaam kunnen?; **3** echt, erg, verschrikkelijk, zo ... als het maar kan: *it is ~ so cold* het is verschrikkelijk koud; **4** immer, altijd, voortdurend: *an ~-growing fear* een steeds groeiende angst; *they lived happily ~ after* daarna leefden ze nog lang en gelukkig; *~ since* van toen af, sindsdien

¹evergreen [evvəgrie:n] *adj* altijdgroen, groenblijvend, *(fig)* onsterfelijk, altijd jeugdig

²evergreen [evvəgrie:n] *n* altijd jeugdig iem (iets),

onsterfelijke melodie *(etc)*, evergreen

everlasting [evvəla:sting] **1** eeuwig(durend); eindeloos; **2** onsterfelijk, *(fig)* onverwoestbaar

every [evrie] **1** elk(e), ieder(e), alle: *(inf)* ~ *bit as good* in elk opzicht even goed; ~ *which way* in alle richtingen; ~ *(single) one of them is wrong* ze zijn stuk voor stuk verkeerd; *three out of* ~ *seven* drie op zeven; ~ *other week* om de andere week, eens in de twee weken; **2** alle, alle mogelijke: *she was given* ~ *opportunity* ze kreeg alle kansen; ~ *now and again* (of: *then*), ~ *so often* (zo) nu en dan, af en toe

everybody [evrieboddie] iedereen: ~ *despises her* iedereen kijkt op haar neer

everyday [evriedee] (alle)daags, gewoon, doordeweeks

everyone [evriewun] *see* everybody

everything [evrieθing] **1** alles, alle dingen: ~ *but a success* allesbehalve een succes, bepaald geen succes; **2** (with *and*) van alles, dergelijke, zo, dat (alles), nog van die dingen: *with exams, holidays and* ~ *she had plenty to think of* met examens, vakantie en zo had ze genoeg om over te denken

everywhere [evriewea] **1** overal; **2** overal waar, waar ook: ~ *he looked he saw decay* waar hij ook keek zag hij verval

evict [ivvikt] uitzetten, verdrijven

evidence [evviddəns] **1** aanduiding, spoor[h], teken[h]: *bear* (of: *show*) ~ *of* sporen dragen van, getuigen van; **2** bewijs[h], bewijsstuk[h], bewijsmateriaal[h]: *conclusive* ~ afdoend bewijs; *on the* ~ *of* op grond van; **3** getuigenis, getuigenverklaring: *call s.o. in* ~ iem als getuige oproepen; **4** duidelijkheid, zichtbaarheid, opvallendheid: *be in* ~ zichtbaar zijn, opvallen

evident [evviddənt] duidelijk, zichtbaar, klaarblijkelijk

¹**evil** [ie:vl] *adj* **1** kwaad, slecht, boos: *put off the* ~ *day* (of: *hour*) iets onaangenaams op de lange baan schuiven; **2** kwaad, zondig

²**evil** [ie:vl] *n* **1** kwaad[h], onheil[h], ongeluk[h]: *choose the least* (of: *lesser*) *of two* ~s van twee kwaden het minste kiezen; **2** kwaad[h], zonde: *speak* ~ *of* kwaadspreken over; **3** kwaal

evince [ivvins] tonen, aan de dag leggen

evoke [ivvook] oproepen, te voorschijn roepen, (op)wekken

evolution [ie:vəloe:sjən] evolutie, ontwikkeling, groei

¹**evolve** [ivvolv] *vb* zich ontwikkelen, zich ontvouwen, geleidelijk ontstaan

²**evolve** [ivvolv] *vb* ontwikkelen, afleiden, uitdenken

ewe [joe:] ooi, wijfjesschaap[h]

ex [eks] ex, ex-man, ex-vrouw, ex-verloofde

¹**exact** [igzækt] *adj* **1** nauwkeurig, accuraat; **2** exact, precies: *the* ~ *time* de juiste tijd

²**exact** [igzækt] *vb* **1** vorderen *(money, payment)*, afdwingen, afpersen; **2** eisen, vereisen

exacting [igzækting] veeleisend

exactly [igzæktlie] precies, helemaal, juist; nauwkeurig: *not* ~ eigenlijk niet, *(iron)* niet bepaald

exaggerate [igzædzjəreet] **1** overdrijven, aandikken; **2** versterken

exalt [igzo:lt] **1** verheffen, verhogen, adelen; **2** loven, prijzen; **3** in vervoering brengen

exam [igzæm] *examination* examen[h]

examination [igzæminneesjən] **1** examen[h]: *sit for* (of: *take*) *an* ~ examen doen; **2** onderzoek[h], inspectie, analyse: *a medical* ~ een medisch onderzoek; *on closer* ~ bij nader onderzoek; *under* ~ nog in onderzoek

examine [igzæmin] **1** onderzoeken, onder de loep nemen, nagaan; **2** examineren: ~ *s.o. in* (of: *on*) iem examineren in

examiner [igzæminnə] **1** examinator; **2** inspecteur

example [igza:mpl] voorbeeld[h]: *give* (of: *set*) *a good* ~ een goed voorbeeld geven; *make an* ~ *of s.o.* een voorbeeld stellen; *for* ~ bijvoorbeeld

exasperate [igza:spəreet] **1** erger maken; **2** boos maken, ergeren

exasperation [igza:spəreesjən] ergernis, ergerlijkheid, kwaadheid

excavate [ekskəveet] **1** uitgraven, blootleggen, delven; **2** uithollen

exceed [iksie:d] **1** overschrijden; **2** overtreffen, te boven gaan: *they* ~*ed us in number* zij overtroffen ons in aantal

exceedingly [iksie:dienglie] buitengewoon, bijzonder

¹**excel** [iksel] *vb* uitblinken, knap zijn

²**excel** [iksel] *vb* overtreffen, uitsteken boven

excellence [eksələns] **1** voortreffelijkheid, uitmuntendheid; **2** uitmuntende eigenschap

Excellency [eksələnsie] excellentie: *His* ~ Zijne Excellentie

excellent [eksələnt] uitstekend, voortreffelijk

¹**except** [iksept] *prep* behalve, uitgezonderd, tenzij, op ... na: ~ *for Sheila* behalve Sheila

²**except** [iksept] *conj* ware het niet dat, maar, echter, alleen: *I'd buy that ring for you,* ~ *I've got no money* ik zou die ring best voor je willen kopen, alleen heb ik geen geld

³**except** [iksept] *vb* uitzonderen, uitsluiten, buiten beschouwing laten

exception [iksepsjən] uitzondering, uitsluiting: *with the* ~ *of* met uitzondering van; *an* ~ *to the rule* een uitzondering op de regel; *take* ~ *to* bezwaar maken tegen, aanstoot nemen aan

exceptionable [iksepsjənəbl] **1** verwerpelijk; **2** aanvechtbaar

exceptional [iksepsjənəl] uitzonderlijk, buitengewoon

excerpt [eksə:pt] **1** uittreksel[h]; **2** stukje[h], fragment[h], passage

¹**excess** [ikses] *n* **1** overmaat, overdaad: *in* (of: *to*) ~ overmatig; **2** exces[h], buitensporigheid, uitspatting; **3** overschot[h], surplus[h], rest; **4** eigen risico[h] *(of insurance)*: *in* ~ *of* meer dan, boven; *drink to* ~ (veel te)

veel drinken

²**excess** [ekses] *adj* **1** bovenmatig, buitenmatig; **2** extra-: ~ *baggage* (of: *luggage*) overvracht, overgewicht; ~ *postage* strafport

excessive [iksessiv] **1** buitensporig; **2** overdadig, overmatig

¹**exchange** [ikstsjeendzj] *vb* **1** ruilen, uitwisselen, verwisselen: ~ *words with* een woordenwisseling hebben met; **2** wisselen, inwisselen

²**exchange** [ikstsjeendzj] *n* **1** ruil, (uit)wisseling, woordenwisseling, gedachtewisseling; **2** beurs, beursgebouwʰ; **3** telefooncentrale; **4** het (om)ruilen, het (uit)wisselen: *in* ~ *for* in ruil voor; **5** het wisselen *(of money)*

exchequer [ikstsjekkə] **1** schatkist, staatskas; **2** *the Exchequer* ministerieʰ van Financiën

¹**excise** [eksajz] *n* accijns

²**excise** [eksajz] *vb* uitsnijden, wegnemen

excite [iksajt] **1** opwekken, uitlokken, oproepen; **2** opwinden: *do not get ~d about it!* wind je er niet over op!; **3** prikkelen, stimuleren *(also sexually)*

excited [iksajtid] opgewonden, geprikkeld

excitement [iksajtmənt] **1** opwindende gebeurtenis, sensatie; **2** opwinding, opschudding, drukte

exclamation [ekskləmeesjən] **1** uitroep, schreeuw, kreet: ~ *mark* uitroepteken; **2** geroepʰ, geschreeuwʰ, luidruchtig commentaarʰ

exclude [ikskloe:d] uitsluiten, weren, uitzonderen, verwerpen

exclusion [ikskloe:zjən] uitsluiting, uitzetting, verwerping, uitzondering

exclusive [ikskloe:siv] exclusief: *mutually* ~ *duties* onverenigbare functies; ~ *rights* alleenrecht, monopolie; ~ *of* exclusief, niet inbegrepen

exclusively [ikskloe:sivlie] uitsluitend, enkel, alleen

excrement [ekskrimmənt] uitwerpselʰ, uitwerpselen, ontlasting

excursion [ikskə:sjən] **1** excursie, uitstapjeʰ, pleziertochtjeʰ; **2** uitweiding: *the teacher made a brief* ~ *into politics* de leraar hield een korte uitweiding over politiek

¹**excuse** [ikskjoe:z] *vb* **1** excuseren, verontschuldigen, vergeven: ~ *my being late* neem me niet kwalijk dat ik te laat ben; ~ *me, can you tell me …?* pardon, kunt u me zeggen …?; ~ *me!* sorry!, pardon!; **2** vrijstellen, ontheffen; **3** laten weggaan, niet langer ophouden: *may I be ~d?* mag ik van tafel af?, mag ik even naar buiten? *(to go to the toilet);* ~ *oneself* zich excuseren *(also for absence)*

²**excuse** [ikskjoe:s] *n* **1** excuusʰ, verontschuldiging: *make one's* (of: *s.o.'s*) ~*s* zich excuseren (voor afwezigheid); **2** uitvlucht, voorwendselʰ

execute [eksikjoe:t] **1** uitvoeren *(sentence),* afwikkelen *(testament);* **2** executeren, terechtstellen

execution [eksikjoe:sjən] **1** executie, terechtstelling; **2** uitvoering, volbrenging *(of sentence),* afwikkeling *(of testament);* **3** spelʰ, (muzikale) voordracht, vertolking

executioner [eksikjoe:sjənə] beul

¹**executive** [igzekjoetiv] *adj* **1** leidinggevend: ~ *director* lid van de raad van bestuur, directeur *(who is member of the Board of Directors);* **2** uitvoerend *(also pol)*

²**executive** [igzekjoetiv] *n* **1** leidinggevend persoon, hoofdʰ, directeur; **2** uitvoerend orgaanʰ, administratie, dagelijks bestuurʰ

executor [igzekjoetə] executeur(-testamentair)

exemplary [igzemplərie] voorbeeldig *(of behaviour etc)*

exemplification [igzempliffikkeesjən] **1** voorbeeldʰ, illustratie; **2** toelichting

exemplify [igzemplifaj] toelichten, illustreren *(with an example)*

¹**exempt** [igzempt] *adj* vrij(gesteld), ontheven

²**exempt** [igzempt] *vb* (with *from*) vrijstellen (van), ontheffen, excuseren

¹**exercise** [eksəsajz] *vb* **1** (zich) oefenen, lichaamsoefeningen doen, trainen; **2** (uit)oefenen, gebruiken, toepassen: ~ *patience* geduld oefenen; ~ *power* macht uitoefenen; **3** uitoefenen, waarnemen, bekleden *(office, position);* **4** *(mil)* laten exerceren, drillen

²**exercise** [eksəsajz] *n* **1** (uit)oefening, gebruikʰ, toepassing; **2** lichaamsoefening, training; **3** ~*s* militaire oefeningen, manoeuvres

exercise book schoolschriftʰ

exert [igzə:t] uitoefenen, aanwenden, doen gelden: ~ *pressure* pressie uitoefenen; ~ *oneself* zich inspannen

exertion [igzə:sjən] **1** (zware) inspanning; **2** uitoefening, aanwending

exhale [eksheel] uitademen

¹**exhaust** [igzo:st] *vb* **1** opgebruiken, opmaken; **2** uitputten, afmatten, *(fig)* uitputtend behandelen: ~ *a subject* een onderwerp uitputten; *feel ~ed* zich uitgeput voelen

²**exhaust** [igzo:st] *n* **1** uitlaat(buis, -pijp); **2** afzuigapparaatʰ; **3** uitlaatstoffen, uitlaatgassen

exhaustion [igzo:stsjən] **1** het opgebruiken; **2** uitputting

¹**exhibit** [igzibbit] *vb* **1** tentoonstellen, uitstallen; **2** vertonen, tonen, blijk geven van

²**exhibit** [igzibbit] *n* **1** geëxposeerd stukʰ; **2** geëxposeerde collectie

exhibition [eksibbisjən] **1** tentoonstelling, expositie; **2** vertoning ‖ *make an* ~ *of oneself* zich belachelijk aanstellen

exhilarate [igzilləreet] **1** opwekken, opvrolijken; **2** versterken, stimuleren

exhilarating [igzilləreeting] **1** opwekkend, opbeurend; **2** versterkend, stimulerend

exhort [igzo:t] aanmanen, oproepen

exhume [ekshjoe:m] opgraven, *(fig)* aan het licht brengen

exile [eksajl] **1** balling, banneling; **2** ballingschap: *send into* ~ in ballingschap zenden

exist [igzist] **1** bestaan, zijn, voorkomen, gebeuren;

2 (over)leven, bestaan, voortbestaan: *how can they ~ in these conditions?* hoe kunnen zij in deze omstandigheden overleven?

existence [igzįstəns] **1** bestaanswijze, levenswijze; **2** het bestaan, het zijn: *come into ~* ontstaan

existent [igzįstənt] **1** bestaand; **2** levend, in leven; **3** huidig, actueel

¹**exit** [ẹksit] *n* **1** uitgang; **2** afslag, uitrit *(of motorway)*; **3** vertrekʰ: *make one's ~* van het toneel verdwijnen

²**exit** [ẹksit] *vb* afgaan, van het toneel verdwijnen *(also fig)*

exonerate [igzọnnerreet] **1** zuiveren, vrijspreken; **2** vrijstellen, ontlasten

exorbitant [igzọːbittənt] buitensporig, overdreven

exorcism [ẹkso:sizm] uitdrijving, (geesten)bezwering

exotic [igzọttik] exotisch, uitheems, vreemd

expand [ikspạend] **1** opengaan, (zich) ontplooien; spreiden; **2** (doen) uitzetten, (op)zwellen, (in omvang) doen toenemen; **3** (zich) uitbreiden, (zich) ontwikkelen, uitgroeien: *she owns a rapidly ~ing chain of fast-food restaurants* zij bezit een snelgroeiende keten van fastfoodrestaurants; **4** uitwerken, uitschrijven: *~ on sth.* over iets uitweiden

expansion [ikspạensjən] uitbreiding, uitgezet deelʰ, vergroting: *sudden industrial ~* plotselinge industriële groei

expatriate [ekspạetriət] (ver)banneling, iem die in het buitenland woont

expect [ikspẹkt] **1** verwachten, wachten op, voorzien: *I did not ~ this* ik had dit niet verwacht; **2** rekenen op, verlangen: *~ too much of s.o.* te veel van iem verlangen; **3** *(inf)* aannemen, vermoeden: *I ~ you're coming too* jij komt zeker ook?; *be ~ing (a baby)* in (blijde) verwachting zijn

expectancy [ikspẹktənsie] verwachting, afwachting

expectant [ikspẹktənt] **1** verwachtend, (af)wachtend, vol vertrouwen: *~ crowds* menigte vol verwachting; **2** toekomstige: *~ mother* aanstaande moeder

expectation [ekspekteesjən] verwachting, afwachting, (voor)uitzichtʰ, vooruitzichten *(of inheritance, money):* *~ of life* vermoedelijke levensduur; *against* (of: *contrary to*) *(all) ~(s)* tegen alle verwachting in

expedient [ikspieːdiənt] geschikt, passend

expedite [ẹkspiddajt] **1** bevorderen, bespoedigen; **2** (snel) afhandelen, afwerken

expedition [ekspiddisjən] expeditie, onderzoekingstocht, *(by extension)* plezierreis, excursie

expeditious [ekspiddisjəs] snel, prompt

expel [ikspẹl] **1** verdrijven, verjagen; **2** wegzenden, wegsturen, deporteren

expend [ikspẹnd] **1** besteden, uitgeven, spenderen; **2** (op)gebruiken, verbruiken, uitputten

expenditure [ikspẹnditsjə] uitgave(n), kosten, verbruikʰ

expense [ikspẹns] **1** uitgave(post); **2** kosten, uitgave(n), prijs, *(fig)* moeite, opoffering: *at the ~ of* op kosten van, *(fig)* ten koste van; **3** *~s* onkosten; **4** onkostenvergoeding: *spare no ~* geen kosten sparen

expensive [ikspẹnsiv] duur, kostbaar

¹**experience** [ikspiəriəns] *n* ervaring, belevenis, ondervinding, praktijk

²**experience** [ikspiəriəns] *vb* ervaren, beleven, ondervinden: *~ difficulties* op moeilijkheden stoten

experienced [ikspiəriənst] ervaren, geschikt, geroutineerd

¹**experiment** [ikspẹrrimmənt] *n* experimentʰ, proef(neming), test

²**experiment** [ikspẹrrimmənt] *vb* experimenteren, proeven nemen

¹**expert** [ẹkspɔːt] *adj* bedreven, deskundig, bekwaam: *~ job: a)* vakkundig uitgevoerde klus; *b)* werkje voor een expert

²**expert** [ẹkspɔːt] *n* expert, deskundige

expiration [ekspirreesjən] **1** uitademing; **2** vervaltijd, expiratie; **3** dood

expire [ikspạjjə] verlopen, verstrijken, aflopen, vervallen

expiry [ikspạjjərie] eindeʰ, vervalʰ, vervaldag, afloop: *~ date* vervaldatum

explain [iksplẹen] (nader) verklaren, uitleggen, uiteenzetten, toelichten, verantwoorden, rechtvaardigen: *~ one's conduct* zijn gedrag verantwoorden; *~ away* wegredeneren, goedpraten

explanation [eksplənẹesjən] verklaring, uitleg, toelichting

expletive [ikspliːtiv] krachtterm, vloek, verwensing

explicable [ẹksplikkəbl] verklaarbaar

explicit [iksplịssit] expliciet, duidelijk, uitvoerig, uitgesproken, uitdrukkelijk

¹**explode** [iksplọọd] *vb* **1** exploderen, ontploffen, (uiteen)barsten; **2** uitbarsten, uitvallen: *~ with laughter* in lachen uitbarsten

²**explode** [iksplọọd] *vb* **1** tot ontploffing brengen, opblazen; **2** ontzenuwen, verwerpen: *~d ideas* achterhaalde ideeën

¹**exploit** [ẹksplojt] *n* (helden)daad, prestatie, wapenfeitʰ

²**exploit** [iksplọjt] *vb* **1** benutten, gebruik maken van; **2** uitbuiten: *~ poor children* arme kinderen uitbuiten

exploitation [eksplojtẹesjən] **1** exploitatie, gebruikʰ, ontginning; **2** uitbuiting

exploration [eksplərẹesjən] onderzoekʰ, studie

explore [iksplọː] **1** een onderzoek instellen; **2** onderzoeken, bestuderen: *~ all possibilities* alle mogelijkheden onderzoeken; **3** verkennen

explorer [iksplọːrə] ontdekkingsreiziger, onderzoeker

explosion [iksplọọzjən] **1** explosie, ontploffing, uitbarsting; **2** uitbarsting, losbarsting, uitval: *~ of anger* uitval van woede

¹**explosive** [iksplọọsiv] *n* explosiefʰ, ontplofbare

stof, springstof

²explosive [iksploosiv] *adj* **1** explosief, (gemakkelijk) ontploffend: ~ *population increase* enorme bevolkingsgroei; **2** opvliegend, driftig

¹export [ikspo:t] *vb* exporteren, uitvoeren

²export [ekspo:t] *n* **1** export, uitvoer(handel); **2** exportartikel[h]

expose [ikspooz] **1** blootstellen, blootgeven, introduceren aan; **2** tentoonstellen, uitstallen, (ver)tonen: ~ *the goods* de waren uitstallen; **3** onthullen, ontmaskeren, bekendmaken; **4** *(photo)* belichten

exposed [ikspoozd] blootgesteld, onbeschut, kwetsbaar: ~ *pipes* slecht geïsoleerde leidingen; *be* ~ *to* blootstaan aan

exposure [ikspoozjə] **1** blootstelling *(to weather, danger, light);* **2** bekendmaking, uiteenzetting, onthulling: *the* ~ *of his crimes* de onthulling van zijn misdaden; **3** *(photo)* belichting

¹express [ikspres] *vb* uitdrukken, laten zien, betuigen: *he* ~*ed his concern* hij toonde zijn bezorgdheid

²express [ikspres] *n* sneltrein, snelbus, exprestrein

³express [ikspres] *adv* **1** met grote snelheid, met spoed; **2** per expresse, met snelpost; **3** speciaal

⁴express [ikspres] *adj* **1** uitdrukkelijk, duidelijk (kenbaar gemaakt), nadrukkelijk: *it was his* ~ *wish it should be done* het was zijn uitdrukkelijke wens dat het gedaan werd; **2** snel(gaand), expres-, ijl-: *an* ~ *train* een sneltrein

expression [ikspresjən] **1** uitdrukking, zegswijze; **2** (gelaats)uitdrukking, blik; **3** *(maths)* (hoeveelheids)uitdrukking, symbool[h], symbolen(verzameling); **4** het uitdrukken: *that's beyond* (of: *past)* ~ daar zijn geen woorden voor; **5** expressie, uitdrukkingskracht

expressive [ikspressiv] expressief, betekenisvol, veelzeggend

expressway snelweg

expulsion [ikspulsjən] verdrijving, verbanning, uitwijzing

exquisite [ekskwizzit] **1** uitstekend, prachtig, voortreffelijk; **2** fijn, subtiel

¹extend [ikstend] *vb* **1** (uitt)rekken, langer (groter) maken, uitbreiden: *an* ~*ing ladder* schuifladder; **2** uitstrekken, uitsteken, aanreiken; **3** (aan)bieden, verlenen, betuigen, bewijzen: ~ *a warm welcome to s.o.* iem hartelijk welkom heten

²extend [ikstend] *vb* zich uitstrekken *(of land, time),* voortduren

extension [ikstensjən] **1** aanvulling, verlenging, toevoeging; **2** (extra) toestel(nummer)[h]: *ask for* ~ *212* vraag om toestel 212; **3** uitstel[h], langer tijdvak[h]; **4** uitbreiding, vergroting, verlenging: *the* ~ *of a contract* de verlenging van een contract

extensive [ikstensiv] uitgestrekt, groot, uitgebreid: *an* ~ *library* een veelomvattende bibliotheek

extent [ikstent] **1** omvang, grootte, uitgestrektheid: *the full* ~ *of his knowledge* de volle omvang van zijn kennis; **2** mate, graad, hoogte: *to a certain* ~ tot op zekere hoogte; *to a great* (of: *large)* ~ in belangrijke

mate, grotendeels; *to what* ~ in hoeverre

extenuate [ikstenjoe·eet] verzachten, afzwakken: *extenuating circumstances* verzachtende omstandigheden

exterior [ikstiəriə] **1** buitenkant, oppervlakte, uiterlijk; **2** buiten-, aan buitenkant

exterminate [iksta:minneet] uitroeien, verdelgen

external [iksta:nl] **1** uiterlijk, extern; **2** (voor) uitwendig (gebruik) || ~ *examination* examen van buiten de school

extinct [ikstingkt] **1** uitgestorven; **2** niet meer bestaand, afgeschaft; **3** uitgedoofd, (uit)geblust *(also fig),* dood: *an* ~ *volcano* een uitgedoofde vulkaan

extinction [ikstingksjən] **1** ondergang, uitroeiing: *be threatened by* (of: *with)* *complete* ~ bedreigd worden door totale uitroeiing; **2** het doven

extinguish [ikstinggwisj] **1** doven, (uit)blussen; **2** vernietigen, beëindigen

extinguisher [ikstinggwisjə] **1** (brand)blusapparaat[h], brandblusser; **2** domper, kaarsendover

extol [ikstool] hoog prijzen, ophemelen, verheerlijken: ~ *s.o.'s talents to the skies* iemands talent hemelhoog prijzen

extort [iksto:t] afpersen: ~ *a confession from s.o.* iem een bekentenis afdwingen

¹extra [ekstrə] *adj* extra, bijkomend || ~ *buses for football-supporters* speciaal ingezette bussen voor voetbalsupporters

²extra [ekstrə] *adv* **1** extra, buitengewoon, bijzonder (veel): ~ *good quality* speciale kwaliteit; **2** buiten het gewone tarief: *pay* ~ *for postage* bijbetalen voor portokosten

³extra [ekstrə] *n* **1** niet (in de prijs) inbegrepen zaak, bijkomend tarief[h]; **2** figurant, dummy

¹extract [ekstrækt] *n* **1** passage, fragment[h], uittreksel[h]; **2** extract[h], aftreksel[h], afkooksel[h]

²extract [ikstrækt] *vb* **1** (uit)trekken, (uit)halen, verwijderen, *(fig)* afpersen, weten te ontlokken: ~ *a confession* een bekentenis afdwingen; **2** (uit)halen *(minerals etc),* onttrekken, winnen

extraction [ikstræksjən] **1** het winnen *(of minerals etc);* **2** afkomst, oorsprong: *Americans of Polish and Irish* ~ Amerikanen van Poolse en Ierse afkomst

extradite [ekstrədajt] **1** uitleveren *(criminal);* **2** uitgeleverd krijgen

extramarital [ekstrəmæritl] buitenechtelijk

extraneous [ikstreeniəs] **1** van buitenaf, buiten-, extern; **2** onbelangrijk

extraordinary [ikstro:dənərie] **1** extra: *an* ~ *session* een extra zitting; **2** buitengewoon, bijzonder

extraterrestrial [ekstrətərestriəl] buitenaards

extravagant [ikstrævəgənt] **1** buitensporig, mateloos; **2** verkwistend, verspillend: *she is rather* ~ zij smijt met geld

¹extreme [ikstrie:m] *adj* **1** extreem, buitengewoon; **2** uiterst, verst; **3** grootst, hoogst: ~ *danger* het grootste gevaar

²extreme [ikstrie:m] *n* uiterste[h], extreme[h]: *go from one* ~ *to the other* van het ene uiterste in het andere (ver)vallen; *in the* ~ uitermate, uiterst

extremely [ikstrie:mlie] uitermate, uiterst, buitengewoon

extremity [ikstremmittie] **1** uiteinde^h; **2** *(always singular)* uiterste^h; **3** lidmaat: *the upper and lower extremities* armen en benen; **4** *extremities* handen en voeten; **5** uiterste nood

extricate [ekstrikkeet] halen uit, bevrijden, losmaken: ~ *oneself from difficulties* zich uit de nesten redden

exuberant [igzjoe:bərənt] **1** uitbundig, vol enthousiasme, geestdriftig; **2** overdadig, overvloedig: ~ *growth* weelderige groei

exude [igzjoe:d] **1** (zich) afscheiden, afgeven: ~ *sweat* zweet afscheiden; **2** (uit)stralen, duidelijk tonen: ~ *happiness* geluk uitstralen

exultation [egzulteesjən] uitgelatenheid, verrukking

¹eye [aj] *n* **1** oog^h, ~*s* gezichtsvermogen^h, blik, kijk: *as far as the* ~ *can see* zo ver het oog reikt; *catch s.o.'s* ~ iemands aandacht trekken; *close* (of: *shut*) *one's* ~*s to* oogluikend toestaan; *cry* (of: *weep) one's* ~*s out* hevig huilen; *have an* ~ *for* kijk hebben op; *keep an* ~ *on* in de gaten houden; *keep your* ~*s open* let goed op!; *there is more to it* (of: *in it) than meets the* ~ er zit meer achter (dan je zo zou zeggen); *open s.o.'s* ~*s (to)* iem de ogen openen (voor); *set* (of: *lay) ~s on* onder ogen krijgen; *under his very* ~*s* vlak voor zijn ogen; *with an* ~ *to* met het oog op; *all* ~*s* een en al aandacht; **2** oog^h, opening *(of needle)*, oog^h, ringetje^h *(for fastener);* **3** centrum^h, oog^h, middelpunt^h *(of storm);* **4** *(bot)* kiem, oog^h: *do s.o. in the* ~ iem een kool stoven; *make* ~*s at* lonken naar; *see* ~ *to* ~ *(with s.o.)* het eens zijn (met iem); *with one's* ~*s shut* met het grootste gemak; *(inf) that was one in the* ~ *for him* dat was een hele klap voor hem

²eye [aj] *vb* bekijken, aankijken, kijken naar

eyeball oogappel, oogbal, oogbol: *(inf)* ~ *to* ~ (vlak) tegenover elkaar

eyebrow wenkbrauw: *raise an* ~ (of: *one's) ~s* de wenkbrauwen optrekken; *(be) up to one's* ~*s (in work)* tot over de oren (in het werk zitten)

eyeful [ajfoel] **1** goede blik: *get* (of: *have) an* ~ *(of)* een goede blik kunnen werpen (op); **2** lust voor het oog: *Deborah is quite an* ~ Deborah ziet er heel erg goed uit

eyelash wimper, ooghaartje^h

eye-opener openbaring, verrassing: *it was an* ~ *to him* daar keek hij van op

eyesight gezicht(svermogen)^h

eyesore ontsiering: *be a real* ~ vreselijk lelijk zijn

eyewitness ooggetuige

f

fable [fee̱bl] *n* **1** fabel; mythe, legende; **2** verzinsel[h], verzinsels, fabeltje[h], praatje[h]

fabric [fæbrik] **1** stof, materiaal[h], weefsel[h]; **2** bouw, constructie

fabricate [fæbrikkeet] **1** bouwen, vervaardigen, fabriceren; **2** verzinnen, uit de duim zuigen

fabulous [fæbjələs] **1** legendarisch, verzonnen; **2** fantastisch

façade [fəsa̱:d] gevel, front[h], voorzijde

¹face [fees] *n* **1** gezicht[h], gelaat[h]: *look s.o. in the ~* iem recht aankijken *(also fig)*; *meet s.o. ~ to ~* iem onder ogen komen; *show one's ~* zijn gezicht laten zien; *in (the) ~ of* ondanks, tegenover; **2** (gezichts)uitdrukking: *fall on one's ~* (plat) op zijn gezicht vallen, *(also fig)* zijn neus stoten; **3** aanzien[h], reputatie, goede naam: *lose ~* zijn gezicht verliezen, afgaan; *save (one's) ~* zijn figuur redden; **4** (belangrijkste) zijde, oppervlak[h], bodem, gevel, voorzijde, wijzerplaat, kant, wand: *fly in the ~ of sth.* tegen iets in gaan; *on the ~ of it* op het eerste gezicht

²face [fees] *vb* uitzien, het gezicht (de voorkant) toekeren, uitzicht hebben

³face [fees] *vb* **1** onder ogen zien, (moedig) tegemoet treden: *let's ~ it, ...* laten we wel wezen, ...; **2** confronteren: *Joe was ~d with many difficulties* Joe werd met vele moeilijkheden geconfronteerd; **3** staan tegenover, uitzien op: *the picture facing the title page* de illustratie tegenover het titelblad; *~ s.o. down* iem overbluffen

face-cloth washandje[h]

faceless [fee̱sləs] gezichtloos, grauw, anoniem

face-lift facelift *(also fig)*, opknapbeurt

facer [fee̱sə] **1** klap in het gezicht; **2** onverwachte moeilijkheid, kink in de kabel, probleem[h]

face value 1 nominale waarde; **2** ogenschijnlijke betekenis, eerste indruk: *take sth. at (its) ~* iets kritiekloos accepteren

facile [fæsajl] **1** oppervlakkig, luchtig; **2** makkelijk, vlot; **3** vlot, vaardig, vloeiend

facilitate [fəsi̱llitteet] vergemakkelijken, verlichten

facility [fəsi̱llittie] **1** voorziening, gelegenheid: *research facilities* onderzoeksfaciliteiten; **2** vaardigheid, handigheid, talent[h]; **3** simpelheid, gemakkelijkheid

fact [fækt] **1** feit[h], waarheid, zekerheid: *the ~s of life* de bloemetjes en de bijtjes; *know for a ~* zeker weten; **2** werkelijkheid, realiteit: *in ~* in feite; *in ~* bovendien, zelfs, en niet te vergeten

faction [fæksjən] **1** (pressie)groep; **2** partijruzie, interne onenigheid

factor [fæktə] **1** factor, omstandigheid; **2** agent, vertegenwoordiger, zaakgelastigde

factory [fæktərie] fabriek, werkplaats

factual [fæktsjoeəl] feitelijk, werkelijk

faculty [fækəltie] **1** (geest)vermogen[h], functie, zin, zintuig[h], *-ies* verstandelijke vermogens: *the ~ of hearing* (of: *speech*) de gehoorzin, het spraakvermogen; **2** (leden van) faculteit, wetenschappelijk personeel[h], staf: *the Faculty of Law* de Juridische Faculteit

fad [fæd] bevlieging, rage, gril

¹fade [feed] *vb* langzaam verdwijnen, afnemen, verflauwen, vervagen, verbleken, verschieten, verwelken: *(film) ~ in* (in)faden, invloeien

²fade [feed] *vb* doen verdwijnen, laten wegsterven, laten vervagen: *~ in* (of: *up): a)* het volume (geleidelijk) laten opkomen; *b) (film)* (in)faden, invloeien

fade away (geleidelijk) verdwijnen, afnemen, vervagen, wegsterven

fade out 1 langzaam (doen) wegsterven, wegdraaien; **2** *(film)* geleidelijk (doen) vervagen, langzaam uitfaden

fag [fæg] **1** saai werk[h]; **2** *(inf)* peuk, sigaret

fagged (out) [fægd (au̱t)] *(inf)* afgepeigerd, kapot

faggot [fægət] **1** takkenbos, bundel (aanmaak)houtjes; **2** bal gehakt; **3** vervelend mens, (oude) zak

¹fail [feel] *vb* **1** tekortschieten, ontbreken, het begeven: *words ~ed me* ik kon geen woorden vinden; **2** afnemen, op raken, verzwakken; **3** zakken, een onvoldoende halen; **4** mislukken, het niet halen, het laten afweten; **5** failliet gaan

²fail [feel] *vb* **1** nalaten, niet in staat zijn, er niet in slagen: *I ~ to see your point* ik begrijp niet wat u bedoelt; **2** in de steek laten, teleurstellen; **3** zakken voor, niet halen; **4** laten zakken, als onvoldoende beoordelen

³fail [feel] *n* onvoldoende || *without ~* zonder mankeren

¹failing [fee̱ling] *n* tekortkoming, zwakheid, fout

²failing [fee̱ling] *prep* bij gebrek aan

failure [fee̱ljə] **1** het falen, het zakken, afgang: *power ~* stroomstoring, stroomuitval; **2** mislukking, fiasco[h], mislukkeling; **3** nalatigheid, verzuim[h], onvermogen[h]; **4** het uitblijven, mislukking; **5** storing, ontregeling

¹faint [feent] *adj* **1** flauw, leeg, wee: *~ with hunger* flauw van de honger; **2** halfgemeend, zwak: *damn with ~ praise* het graf in prijzen; **3** laf; **4** nauwelijks waarneembaar, vaag, onduidelijk; **5** gering, vaag, zwak: *I haven't the ~est idea* ik heb geen flauw idee

²faint [feent] *vb* flauwvallen

³faint [feent] *n* flauwte, onmacht: *to fall down in a ~* flauwvallen

¹fair [feə] *n* **1** markt, bazaar; **2** beurs, (jaar)markt, tentoonstelling; **3** kermis

²fair *adj* **1** eerlijk, redelijk, geoorloofd: *get a ~ hearing* een eerlijk proces krijgen; *by ~ means or foul* met alle middelen; *~ play* fair play, eerlijk spel; *(inf) ~ enough!* dat is niet onredelijk!, okay!; **2** behoorlijk, bevredigend, redelijk; **3** mooi, helder; **4** gunstig, veelbelovend: *(shipp) ~ wind* gunstige wind; **5** blank, licht(gekleurd), blond: *the ~ sex* het schone geslacht

³fair *adv* **1** eerlijk, rechtvaardig: *play ~* eerlijk spelen, integer zijn; **2** precies, pal, net: *~ and square: a)* precies; *b)* rechtuit, open(hartig)

fairground kermisterreinʰ

fairly [fɛəlie] **1** eerlijk, billijk; **2** volkomen, helemaal: *I was ~ stunned* ik stond compleet paf; **3** tamelijk, redelijk

fair-minded rechtvaardig, eerlijk

fairy [fɛərie] **1** (tover)fee, elf(jeʰ); **2** *(vulg)* homo, nicht

fairyland sprookjeswereld, sprookjeslandʰ

fairy tale 1 sprookjeʰ; **2** verzinselʰ

faith [feeθ] **1** geloofʰ, geloofsovertuiging, vertrouwenʰ: *pin one's ~ on, put one's ~ in* vertrouwen stellen in; **2** (ere)woordʰ, gelofte; **3** trouw, oprechtheid: *act in good ~* te goeder trouw handelen

faithful [fɛeθfoel] **1** gelovig, godsdienstig; **2** trouw, loyaal; **3** getrouw; **4** betrouwbaar

faithfully [fɛeθfəlie] **1** trouw; **2** met de hand op het hart || *yours ~* hoogachtend

faithless [fɛeθləs] **1** ontrouw; **2** onbetrouwbaar, vals

¹fake [feek] *vb* **1** voorwenden, doen alsof: *a ~d robbery* een in scène gezette overval; **2** namaken, vervalsen

²fake [feek] *adj* namaak-, vals, vervalst

³fake [feek] *n* **1** vervalsing, kopie; **2** oplichter, bedrieger

falcon [fo:lkən] valk

¹fall [fo:l] *vb* **1** vallen, omvallen, invallen, afnemen, dalen, aflopen, afhellen: *~ to pieces* in stukken vallen *(also fig)*; *the wind fell* de wind nam af, de wind ging liggen; *~ apart* uiteenvallen, *(inf)* instorten; *sth. to ~ back on* iets om op terug te vallen; *~ over* omvallen, *(inf) ~ over backwards* zich uitsloven, zich in allerlei bochten wringen; *~ through* mislukken; **2** ten onder gaan, vallen, sneuvelen, ingenomen worden, zijn (hoge) positie verliezen: *~ from power* de macht verliezen; **3** betrekken; **4** terechtkomen, neerkomen, *(fig)* ten deel vallen: *it fell to me to put the question* het was aan mij de vraag te stellen; **5** raken: *~ behind with* achterop raken met; *Easter always ~s on a Sunday* Pasen valt altijd op zondag; *~ asleep* in slaap vallen; *~ flat* niet inslaan, mislukken; *~ short (of)* tekortschieten (voor), niet voldoen (aan)

²fall [fo:l] *vb* worden: *~ ill* ziek worden; *~ silent* stil worden

³fall [fo:l] *n* **1** val, smak, het vallen, *(fig)* ondergang,

verderfʰ: *the Fall (of man)* de zondeval; **2** afname, daling, vervalʰ, het zakken; *~s* waterval; **4** *(Am)* herfst, najaarʰ

fallacy [fæləsie] **1** denkfout, drogreden; **2** vergissing

fall down 1 (neer)vallen, instorten, ten val komen; **2** *(inf)* mislukken, tekortschieten: *~ on sth.* (of: *the job)* er niets van bakken

fallen 1 gevallen; **2** zondig: *~ angel* gevallen engel; **3** gesneuveld

fall in 1 instorten, invallen; **2** *(mil)* aantreden, zich in het gelid opstellen

fall out 1 *(with with)* ruzie maken (met); **2** gebeuren, terechtkomen, uitkomen

fall-out 1 radioactieve neerslag; **2** het uitvallen, het ophouden

fallow [fæloo] braak, onbewerkt: *lie ~* braak liggen *(also fig)*

fallow deer damhertʰ

false [fo:ls] **1** onjuist, fout, verkeerd: *~ pride* onrechtvaardigde trots; *true or ~?* waar of onwaar?; **2** onecht, kunstmatig: *~ teeth* kunstgebit; *a ~ beard* een valse baard; **3** bedrieglijk, onbetrouwbaar: *~ alarm* loos alarm; *~ bottom* dubbele bodem; *under ~ pretences* onder valse voorwendsels

falsify [fo:lsiffaj] **1** vervalsen, falsificeren; **2** verkeerd voorstellen; **3** weerleggen

falter [fo:ltə] **1** wankelen, waggelen; **2** aarzelen, weifelen; **3** stotteren, stamelen

fame [feem] **1** roem, bekendheid; **2** (goede) naam, reputatie: *of ill ~* berucht

familiar [fəmilliə] **1** vertrouwd, bekend, gewoon; **2** *(with with)* op de hoogte (van), bekend (met); **3** informeel, ongedwongen; **4** vrijpostig

familiarity [fəmillie·ærittie] **1** vertrouwdheid, bekendheid: *~ breeds contempt* wat vertrouwd is wordt gemakkelijk doodgewoon; **2** ongedwongenheid; **3** vrijpostigheid, vrijheid

family [fæmillie] **1** (huis)gezinʰ, kinderen, gezinsleden; **2** familie(leden), geslachtʰ: *run in the ~* in de familie zitten; **3** afkomst, afstamming, familie

famine [fæmin] **1** hongersnood; **2** tekortʰ, schaarste, gebrekʰ

famish [fæmisj] (laten) verhongeren, uitgehongerd zijn: *the men were ~ed* de mannen waren uitgehongerd

famous [feeməs] *(with for)* beroemd (om), (wel)bekend

¹fan [fæn] *n* **1** waaier; **2** ventilator, fan; **3** bewonderaar(ster), enthousiast, fan

²fan [fæn] *vb* **1** (toe)waaien, blazen, toewuiven; **2** aanblazen, aanwakkeren *(also fig)*: *~ the flames* het vuur aanwakkeren, olie op het vuur gooien

fanatic [fənætik] fanatiekeling(e)

fanciful [fænsiefoel] **1** fantasievol, rijk aan fantasie; **2** denkbeeldig, verzonnen, ingebeeld

¹fancy [fænsie] *n* **1** fantasie, verbeelding(skracht), inbeelding; **2** voorkeur, voorliefde, zin: *a passing ~* een bevlieging; **3** veronderstelling, ideeʰ, fantasie

²**fancy** [fænsie] *vb* **1** zich voorstellen, zich indenken; **2** vermoeden, geloven: *~ that!* stel je voor!, niet te geloven!; **3** leuk vinden, zin hebben in: *~ a girl* op een meisje vallen; *~ some peanuts?* wil je wat pinda's?; *~ oneself* een hoge dunk van zichzelf hebben

³**fancy** [fænsie] *adj* **1** versierd, decoratief, elegant: *~ cakes* taartjes; *~ dress* kostuum; *~ goods* fantasiegoed, snuisterijen; **2** grillig, buitensporig; **3** verzonnen, denkbeeldig

fang [fæng] hoektand, snijtand, giftand, slagtand

fantasize [fæntəsajz] fantaseren

fantastic [fæntæstik] **1** grillig, bizar; **2** denkbeeldig; **3** enorm, fantastisch, geweldig

fantasy [fæntəsie] **1** verbeelding, fantasie; **2** illusie, fantasie

¹**far** [fa:] *adv* **1** ver: *~ and near* overal; *so ~* (tot) zó ver, in zoverre; *~ from easy* verre van makkelijk; *in so ~ as, as ~ as* voor zover; *as ~ as I can see* volgens mij; **2** lang, ver: *so ~* tot nu toe; *so ~ so good* tot nu toe is alles nog goed gegaan; **3** veel, verreweg: *~ too easy* veel te makkelijk

²**far** [fa:] *adj* ver, (ver)afgelegen: *at the ~ end of the room* aan het andere eind van de kamer

faraway [fa:rəwee] **1** (ver)afgelegen, ver; **2** afwezig, dromerig, ver

farce [fa:s] **1** klucht; **2** schijnvertoning, zinloos gedoeʰ

¹**fare** [feə] *n* **1** vervoerprijs, ritprijs, vervoerkosten, tariefʰ, *(roughly)* kaartjeʰ; **2** kost, voedselʰ, voerʰ: *simple ~* eenvoudige kost

²**fare** [feə] *vb* (ver)gaan || *how did you ~?* hoe is het gegaan?; *~ well* succes hebben, het goed maken

¹**farewell** *interj* vaarwel, adieu, tot ziens

²**farewell** *n* afscheidʰ, vaarwelʰ

far-fetched vergezocht

¹**farm** [fa:m] *n* boerderij, landbouwbedrijfʰ

²**farm** [fa:m] *vb* boer zijn, boeren, een boerderij hebben

³**farm** [fa:m] *vb* bewerken, bebouwen, cultiveren || *~ out: a)* uitbesteden; *b)* overdragen, afschuiven

farmer [fa:mə] boer, landbouwer, agrariër

farm-hand boerenknecht, landarbeider

farmstead boerenhoeve

far-off ver(afgelegen), ver weg, lang geleden

far-out 1 afgelegen, ver weg; **2** *(inf)* uitzonderlijk, uitheems, bizar; **3** *(inf)* fantastisch

far-reaching verstrekkend, verreikend

far-sighted 1 vooruitziend; **2** verziend

¹**fart** [fa:t] *n (vulg)* **1** scheet, wind; **2** lul, klootzak

²**fart** [fa:t] *vb (vulg)* een scheet laten || *~ about (of: around)* klooien, rotzooien

¹**farther** [fa:ðə] *adj* verder (weg)

²**farther** [fa:ðə] *adv* verder, door, vooruit

farthest [fa:ðist] verst (weg)

fascinate [fæsinneet] boeien, fascineren

fascination [fæsinneesjən] **1** aantrekkingskracht, charme, bekoring; **2** geboeidheid

¹**fashion** [fæsjən] *n* **1** gebruikʰ, mode, gewoonte: *set a ~* de toon aangeven; *come into ~* in de mode ra-

ken; **2** manier, stijl, trant: *did he change the nappies? yes, after a ~* heeft hij de baby verschoond? ja, op zijn manier

²**fashion** [fæsjən] *vb* vormen, modelleren, maken

fashionable [fæsjənəbl] modieus, in (de mode), populair

¹**fast** [fa:st] *adj* **1** vast, stevig, hecht: *~ colours* wasechte kleuren; **2** snel, vlug, gevoelig *(film)*: *~ food* gemaksvoedsel; *~ lane* linker rijbaan, inhaalstrook; **3** vóór: *(inf) make a ~ buck* snel geld verdienen; *(inf) pull a ~ one on s.o.* met iem een vuile streek uithalen, iem afzetten

²**fast** [fa:st] *adv* **1** stevig, vast: *~ asleep* in diepe slaap; *play ~ and loose (with)* het niet zo nauw nemen (met), spelen (met); **2** snel, vlug, hard

³**fast** [fa:st] *n* vasten(tijd)

⁴**fast** [fa:st] *vb* vasten

fasten [fa:sn] vastmaken, bevestigen, dichtmaken: *~ up one's coat* zijn jas dichtdoen

fastener [fa:sənə] (rits)sluiting, haakjeʰ

fastening [fa:səning] sluiting, slotʰ, bevestiging

fastidious [fæstiddiəs] veeleisend, pietluttig, kieskeurig

¹**fat** [fæt] *adj* **1** dik, vet(gemest), weldoorvoed; **2** vettig, zwaar, vet; **3** rijk, vruchtbaar, vet; **4** groot, dik, lijvig: *(iron) a ~ lot of good that'll do you* daar schiet je geen moer mee op, nou, daar heb je veel aan; *(inf) a ~ cat: a)* rijke pief; *b)* (stille) financier, geldschieter

²**fat** [fæt] *n* vetʰ, bakvetʰ, lichaamsvetʰ || *the ~ is in the fire* de poppen zijn aan het dansen; *chew the ~* kletsen

fatal [feetl] **1** *(with to)* noodlottig (voor), dodelijk, fataal; **2** rampzalig

fatality [fətælittie] **1** slachtofferʰ, dodelijk ongelukʰ; **2** noodlottigheid

fate [feet] lotʰ, noodlotʰ, bestemming: *as sure as ~* daar kun je donder op zeggen

fateful [feetfoel] noodlottig, rampzalig, belangrijk

fathead sufferd

¹**father** [fa:ðə] *n* **1** vader, huisvader; **2** grondlegger, stichter; **3** *Father* pater, priester: *Father Christmas* de kerstman

²**father** [fa:ðə] *vb* **1** vader zijn van, voor; **2** produceren, de geestelijke vader zijn van

fatherhood [fa:ðəhoed] vaderschapʰ

father-in-law [fa:ðərinlo:] schoonvader

fatherly [fa:ðəlie] vaderlijk

fathom [fæðəm] vadem, vaam

¹**fatigue** [fətie:g] *n* **1** vermoeidheid, moeheid; **2** *(mil)* corvee

²**fatigue** [fətie:g] *vb* afmatten, vermoeien

fatten [fætn] dik(ker) maken: *~ up* (vet)mesten

¹**fatty** [fætie] *n (inf)* vetzak, dikke(rd)

²**fatty** [fætie] *adj* vettig, vet(houdend)

fatuous [fætjoeəs] dom, dwaas, stompzinnig

faucet [fo:sit] *(Am)* kraan

¹**fault** [fo:lt] *n* **1** fout, defectʰ, gebrekʰ; **2** overtreding, misstap; **3** foute service, fout; **4** schuld, oorzaak: *at*

~ schuldig; **5** breuk, verschuiving

²**fault** [fo:lt] *vb* aanmerkingen maken op, bekritiseren

faulty [fo:ltie] **1** defect, onklaar; **2** onjuist, verkeerd, gebrekkig

¹**favour** [feevə] *n* **1** genegenheid, sympathie, goedkeuring: *be in ~ with* in de gunst zijn bij; **2** partijdigheid, voorkeur, voortrekkerij; **3** gunst, attentie, begunstiging: *do s.o. a ~* iem een plezier doen; *do me a ~!* zeg, doe me een lol!

²**favour** [feevə] *vb* **1** gunstig gezind zijn, positief staan tegenover, een voorstander zijn van; **2** begunstigen, prefereren, bevoorrechten

favourable [feevərəbl] **1** welwillend, goedgunstig: *the weather is ~ to us* het weer zit ons mee; **2** gunstig, veelbelovend, positief

¹**favourite** [feevərit] *n* **1** favoriet(e); **2** lieveling(e)

²**favourite** [feevərit] *adj* favoriet, lievelings-

favouritism [feevərittizm] voortrekkerij, vriendjespolitiek

fawn [fo:n] kwispelstaarten || *(fig) ~ (up)on* vleien, kruipen voor

¹**fax** [fæks] *n* **1** fax(apparaat^h); **2** fax(bericht^h)

²**fax** [fæks] *vb* faxen, per fax verzenden

faze [feez] van streek maken, in de war doen geraken

¹**fear** [fiə] *n* vrees, angst(gevoel^h): *in ~ and trembling* met angst en beven; *go in ~ of* bang zijn voor; *(inf) no ~* beslist niet, geen sprake van

²**fear** [fiə] *vb* **1** vrezen, bang zijn voor; **2** vermoeden, een voorgevoel hebben van, vrezen: *~ the worst* het ergste vrezen

fearful [fiəfoel] **1** vreselijk, afschuwelijk, ontzettend; **2** bang, angstig

fearsome [fiəsəm] afschrikwekkend, ontzaglijk

feasible [fie:zibl] **1** uitvoerbaar, haalbaar, doenlijk; **2** aannemelijk, waarschijnlijk, geloofwaardig

¹**feast** [fie:st] *n* **1** feest^h; **2** feestmaal^h, banket^h

²**feast** [fie:st] *vb* feesten, feestvieren

³**feast** [fie:st] *vb* onthalen, trakteren *(also fig)*

feat [fie:t] **1** heldendaad; **2** prestatie, knap stuk werk^h

feather [feðə] veer, pluim || *a ~ in one's cap* iets om trots op te zijn, een eer

¹**feature** [fie:tsjə] *n* **1** (gelaats)trek, ~s gezicht^h; **2** (hoofd)kenmerk^h, hoofdtrek; **3** hoogtepunt^h, specialiteit, hoofdnummer^h; **4** speciaal onderwerp^h, hoofdartikel^h

²**feature** [fie:tsjə] *vb* een (belangrijke) plaats innemen, opvallen

feature film speelfilm, hoofdfilm

February [febroeərie] februari

feckless [feklǝs] lamlendig, futloos

Federal [feddərəl] **1** federaal, bonds-; **2** *(Am)* nationaal, lands-, regerings-

federation [feddəreesjən] **1** federatie, statenbond; **2** bond, federatie, overkoepelend orgaan^h

fed up *(inf)* (het) zat, ontevreden, (het) beu: *be ~ with sth.* van iets balen

fee [fie:] **1** honorarium^h; **2** inschrijfgeld^h, lidmaatschapsgeld^h; **3** ~s schoolgeld^h, collegegeld^h

feeble [fie:bl] **1** zwak, teer, krachteloos; **2** flauw, slap, zwak: *a ~ effort* een halfhartige poging

feeble-minded 1 zwakzinnig, zwak begaafd; **2** dom

¹**feed** [fie:d] *vb* eten, zich voeden, grazen, weiden: *~ on* leven van, zich voeden met *(also fig)*

²**feed** [fie:d] *vb* **1** voeren, (te) eten geven, voederen: *~ up* vetmesten, volstoppen; **2** voedsel geven aan, *(fig)* stimuleren; **3** aanvoeren, toevoeren: *~ coins into the pay phone* munten in de telefoon stoppen

³**feed** [fie:d] *n* **1** voeding, voedering; **2** (vee)voer^h, groenvoer^h

feedback terugkoppeling; antwoord^h, reactie, feedback

¹**feel** [fie:l] *vb* **1** (rond)tasten, (rond)zoeken; **2** voelen; **3** gevoelens hebben, een mening hebben

²**feel** [fie:l] *vb* **1** voelen, gewaarworden; **2** voelen (aan), betasten: *~ s.o.'s pulse* iem de pols voelen *(also fig)*; *~ one's way* op de tast gaan *(also fig)*; **3** voelen, gewaarworden: *~ the effects of* lijden onder de gevolgen van; **4** voelen, aanvoelen, de indruk krijgen: *I ~ it necessary to deny that* ik vind het nodig dat te ontkennen; **5** vinden, menen: *it was felt that … men was de mening toegedaan dat …*

³**feel** [fie:l] *vb* **1** zich voelen: *I felt such a fool* ik voelde me zo stom; *~ cold* het koud hebben; *~ small* zich klein voelen; *I ~ like sleeping* ik heb zin om te slapen; *I ~ like a walk* ik heb zin in een wandelingetje; **2** aanvoelen, een gevoel geven, voelen

⁴**feel** [fie:l] *n* **1** het voelen, betasting; **2** aanleg, gevoel^h, feeling; **3** routine: *get the ~ of sth.* iets in zijn vingers krijgen

feeler [fie:lə] tastorgaan^h, voelhoorn, voelspriet, *(fig)* proefballonnetje: *put (of: throw) out ~s* een balletje opgooien

feeling [fie:ling] **1** gevoel^h, gewaarwording: *a sinking ~* een benauwd gevoel; **2** emotie, gevoel^h, ~s gevoelens: *hurt s.o.'s ~s* iem kwetsen; *mixed ~s* gemengde gevoelens; **3** idee^h, gevoel^h, indruk; **4** aanleg, gevoel^h: *a ~ for colour* een gevoel voor kleur; **5** opinie, mening, gevoel^h; **6** opwinding, ontstemming, wrok: *~s ran high* de gemoederen raakten verhit; **7** gevoel^h: *have lost all ~ in one's fingers* alle gevoel in zijn vingers kwijt zijn

feign [feen] veinzen, simuleren: *~ed indifference* gespeelde onverschilligheid

felicity [fillissittie] geluk^h, gelukzaligheid || *express oneself with ~* zijn woorden goed weten te kiezen

feline [fie:lajn] **1** katachtig; **2** katten-

fell omhakken, kappen

¹**fellow** [felloo] *n* **1** kerel, vent; **2** maat, kameraad; **3** wederhelft, andere helft: *a sock and its ~* een sok en de bijbehorende (sok); **4** lid^h van universiteitsbestuur

²**fellow** [felloo] *adj* mede-, collega, -genoot

fellowship [felloosjip] **1** genootschap^h; **2** broederschap, verbond^h; **3** omgang, gezelschap^h; **4** vriendschap, kameraadschap(pelijkheid)

felony [fɛllənie] (ernstig) misdrijfʰ, zware misdaad
felt viltʰ
fem. *feminine* vrl., vrouwelijkʰ
¹female [fie:meel] *adj* vrouwelijk, wijfjes-
²female [fie:meel] *n* 1 vrouwelijk persoon, vrouw; 2 wijfjeʰ, vrouwtjeʰ; 3 vrouwspersoon
¹feminine [femminnin] *adj* vrouwen-, vrouwelijk
²feminine [femminnin] *n* vrouwelijkʰ
feminism [femminnizm] feminismeʰ
fen [fen] moeras(land)ʰ
¹fence [fens] *n* 1 hekʰ, omheining, afscheiding: *(fig)* be *(of: sit) on the ~* geen partij kiezen; 2 heler
²fence [fens] *vb (sport)* schermen
³fence [fens] *vb* omheinen: *~ in* afrasteren, *(fig)* inperken
fend [fend]: *~ off* afweren, ontwijken; *~ for oneself* voor zichzelf zorgen
fender [fendə] 1 stootrand, stootkussenʰ, *(Am)* bumper; 2 *(Am)* spatbordʰ; 3 haardschermʰ
fennel [fenl] venkel
¹ferment [fa:ment] *n* 1 gist(middelʰ); 2 onrust, opwinding
²ferment [fəment] *vb* 1 (ver)gisten, (doen) fermenteren; 2 in beroering zijn (brengen), onrustig zijn (maken)
fern [fə:n] varen
ferocious [fəroosjəs] woest, ruw, wild, meedogenloos
ferocity [fərossittie] woestheid, ruwheid, gewelddadigheid
¹ferret [ferrit] *n* fret
²ferret [ferrit] *vb* rommelen, snuffelen: *~ about (of: around) among s.o.'s papers* in iemands papieren rondsnuffelen; *~ out* uitvissen, uitzoeken
Ferris wheel [ferris wie:l] reuzenradʰ
¹ferry [ferrie] *n* 1 veerʰ, veerboot, pont; 2 veerdienst, veer
²ferry [ferrie] *vb* 1 overzetten, overvaren; 2 vervoeren: *~ children to and from a party* kinderen naar een feestje brengen en ophalen
ferryboat veerboot
fertile [fa:tajl] 1 vruchtbaar; 2 rijk (voorzien), overvloedig: *~ imagination* rijke verbeelding
fertilize [fa:tillajz] 1 bevruchten, insemineren; 2 vruchtbaar maken, bemesten
fertilizer [fa:tillajzə] (kunst)mest
fervent [fa:vənt] vurig, hartstochtelijk, fervent
fervour [fa:və] heftigheid, hartstocht, vurigheid
fester [festə] 1 zweren, etteren; 2 knagen, irriteren
festival [festivvəl] 1 feestʰ, feestelijkheid; 2 muziekfeestʰ, festivalʰ
festive [festiv] feestelijk: *the ~ season* de feestdagen
festivity [festivvittie] feestelijkheid, festiviteit
festoon [festoe:n] met slingers versieren
fetch [fetsj] 1 halen, brengen, afhalen; 2 te voorschijn brengen, trekken; 3 opbrengen: *the painting ~ed £100* het schilderij ging voor 100 pond weg
fetching [fetsjing] leuk, aantrekkelijk, aardig
fete [feet] feestʰ, festijnʰ

fetish [fettisj] fetisj
fetter [fettə] keten, boei, ketting
feud [fjoe:d] vete, onenigheid, ruzie
feudal [fjoe:dl] feodaal, leen-
feudalism [fjoe:dəlizm] leenstelselʰ
fever [fie:və] 1 opwinding, agitatie, spanning; 2 koorts, verhoging
few [fjoe:] 1 weinige(n), weinig, enkele(n), een paar: *holidays are ~ and far between* feestdagen zijn er maar weinig; *a ~* een paar, enkele(n); 2 weinig, een paar: *a ~ words* een paar woorden; *every ~ days* om de zoveel dagen; *(inf) there were a good ~* er waren er nogal wat; *quite a ~* vrij veel; *quite a ~ books* nogal wat boeken
ff. *following* e.v., en volgende(n)
fiancé [fi-onsee] verloofde
fiasco [fie-æskoo] mislukking, fiascoʰ
fib [fib] leugentjeʰ: *tell ~s* jokken
fibre [fajbə] 1 vezel; 2 draad; 3 kwaliteit, sterkte, karakterʰ: *moral ~* ruggengraat
fibreglass fiberglasʰ, glasvezel
fickle [fikl] wispelturig, grillig
fiction [fiksjən] verzinselʰ, verdichtselʰ, fictie
fictional [fiksjənəl] roman-: *~ character* romanfiguur
fictitious [fiktisjəs] 1 onecht; 2 verzonnen, bedacht, gefingeerd; 3 denkbeeldig, fictief
¹fiddle [fidl] *vb (inf)* 1 vioolspelen, fiedelen; 2 lummelen: *~ about (of: around)* rondlummelen; 3 friemelen, spelen: *~ with* morrelen aan, spelen met
²fiddle [fidl] *vb* 1 spelen; 2 *(inf)* foezelen met, vervalsen, bedrog plegen met: *~ one's taxes* met zijn belastingaangifte knoeien
³fiddle [fidl] *n* viool, fiedel || *play second ~ (to)* in de schaduw staan (van)
fiddlesticks lariekoek, kletskoek
fiddling [fidling] onbeduidend, nietig: *~ little screws* pietepeuterige schroefjes
fidelity [fiddellittie] 1 (natuur)getrouwheid, precisie; 2 (with *to*) trouw (aan, jegens), loyaliteit
¹fidget [fidzjit] *vb* de kriebels hebben, niet stil kunnen zitten
²fidget [fidzjit] *n* zenuwlijer, iem die niet stil kan zitten
¹field [fie:ld] *n* 1 veldʰ, landʰ, weide, akker, vlakte, sportveldʰ, sportterreinʰ, gebiedʰ; 2 arbeidsveldʰ, gebiedʰ, branche: *~ of study* onderwerp (van studie); 3 (kracht)veldʰ, draagwijdte, invloedssfeer, reikwijdte: *magnetic ~* magnetisch veld; 4 bezetting, veldʰ, alle deelnemers, jachtpartij, jachtstoet; 5 concurrentie, veldʰ, andere deelnemers: *play the ~* fladderen, van de een naar de ander lopen
²field [fie:ld] *vb (sport)* in het veld brengen, uitkomen met
field day grote dag
field glasses veldkijker, verrekijker
Field Marshal *(mil)* veldmaarschalk
fiend [fie:nd] 1 duivel, demon, kwade geest; 2 fanaat, maniak

fierce [fiəs] **1** woest, wreed; **2** hevig: ~ *dislike* intense afkeer

fiery [fajjərie] **1** brandend, vurig; **2** onstuimig, vurig, opvliegend: ~ *temperament* fel temperament

fifteen [fiftie:n] vijftien

fifteenth [fiftie:nθ] vijftiende, vijftiende deel[h]

fifth [fifθ] vijfde, vijfde deel[h], *(mus)* kwint

fifty [fiftie] vijftig: *a man in his fifties* een man van in de vijftig

fifty-fifty half om half, fifty-fifty: *go ~ with s.o.* met iem samsam doen

fig [fig] **1** vijg; **2** vijgenboom ‖ *not care* (of: *give*) *a ~ (for)* geen bal geven (om)

[1]fight [fajt] *n* **1** gevecht[h], strijd, vechtpartij: *a ~ to the finish* een gevecht tot het bittere einde; **2** vechtlust, strijdlust: *(still) have plenty of ~ in one* zijn vechtlust (nog lang) niet kwijt zijn

[2]fight [fajt] *vb* **1** vechten, strijden: *~ to a finish* tot het bittere eind doorvechten; **2** ruziën

[3]fight [fajt] *vb* bestrijden, strijden tegen: *~ off sth.* ergens weerstand tegen bieden; *~ it out* het uitvechten

fighter [fajtə] vechter, strijder, vechtersbaas

[1]fighting [fajting] *n* het vechten, gevechten

[2]fighting [fajting] *adj* strijdbaar, uitgerust voor de strijd: *~ spirit* vechtlust; *he has a ~ chance* als hij alles op alles zet lukt het hem misschien

figment [figmənt] verzinsel[h]: *~ of the imagination* hersenspinsel

figurative [figərətiv] figuurlijk

[1]figure [figə] *n* **1** vorm, contour, omtrek, gedaante, gestalte, figuur[h]; **2** afbeelding, *(maths)* figuur[h], motief[h]: *(maths) solid ~* lichaam; **3** personage[h]: *~ of fun* mikpunt van plagerij; **4** cijfer[h]: *double ~s* getal van twee cijfers; **5** bedrag[h], waarde, prijs

[2]figure [figə] *vb* **1** voorkomen, een rol spelen, gezien worden: *~ in a book* in een boek voorkomen; **2** vanzelf spreken, logisch zijn: *that ~s* dat ligt voor de hand, dat zit er wel in

[3]figure [figə] *vb* denken, menen, geloven

figure out 1 berekenen, becijferen, uitwerken; **2** *(Am)* uitpuzzelen, doorkrijgen: *be unable to figure a person out* geen hoogte kunnen krijgen van iem

filch [filtsj] jatten, gappen

[1]file [fajl] *n* **1** vijl; **2** dossier[h], register[h], legger; **3** (dossier)map, ordner, klapper; **4** *(comp)* bestand[h]; **5** rij, file: *in single ~* in ganzenmars

[2]file [fajl] *vb* in een rij lopen, achter elkaar lopen

[3]file [fajl] *vb* **1** vijlen, bijvijlen, bijschaven *(also fig)*: *~ sth. smooth* iets gladvijlen; **2** opslaan, archiveren: *~ away* opbergen

filibuster [fillibbustə] vertragingstactiek

[1]fill [fil] *vb* **1** (op)vullen, vol maken: *~ a gap* een leemte opvullen; **2** vervullen, bezetten, bekleden: *~ a vacancy* een vacature bezetten

[2]fill [fil] *n* vulling, hele portie: *eat one's ~* zich rond eten

filler [fillə] vulling, vulsel[h], vulstof, plamuur[h]

fillet [fillit] filet[+h], lendestuk[h], haas: *~ of pork* var-kenshaas

fill in 1 invullen; **2** passeren: *~ time* de tijd doden; **3** (*with on*) *(inf)* op de hoogte brengen (van), briefen (over); **4** dichtgooien, dempen

filling [filling] vulling, vulsel[h]

filling station benzinestation[h], tankstation[h]

fill out 1 opvullen, groter (dikker) maken: *~ a story* een verhaaltje uitbouwen; **2** *(Am)* invullen

[1]fill up *vb* **1** zich vullen, vollopen, dichtslibben; **2** benzine tanken

[2]fill up *vb* **1** (op)vullen, vol doen, bijvullen; **2** invullen

filly [fillie] merrieveulen[h], jonge merrie

[1]film [film] *n* **1** dunne laag, vlies[h]: *a ~ of dust* een dun laagje stof; **2** rolfilm, film; **3** (speel)film

[2]film [film] *vb* **1** filmen, opnemen; **2** verfilmen, een film maken van

filmy [filmie] dun, doorzichtig

[1]filter [filtə] *n* filter[h], filtertoestel[h], filtreertoestel[h]

[2]filter [filtə] *vb* uitlekken, doorsijpelen, doorschemeren: *the news ~ed out* het nieuws lekte uit

[3]filter [filtə] *vb* filtreren, zeven, zuiveren

filth [filθ] **1** vuiligheid, vuil[h], viezigheid; **2** vuile taal, smerige taal

filthy [filθie] **1** vies, vuil, smerig; **2** schunnig ‖ *~ lucre* vuil gewin, poen

fin [fin] **1** vin; **2** vinvormig voorwerp[h], zwemvlies[h], kielvlak[h], stabilisatievlak[h]

[1]final [fajnl] *adj* **1** definitief, finaal, beslissend; **2** laatste, eind-, slot-

[2]final [fajnl] *n* **1** finale, eindwedstrijd; **2** *~s* (laatste) eindexamen[h]

finalize [fajnəlajz] tot een einde brengen, de laatste hand leggen aan, afronden

finally [fajnəlie] **1** ten slotte, uiteindelijk; **2** afdoend, definitief, beslissend: *it was ~ decided* er werd definitief besloten

[1]finance [fajnæns] *n* **1** financieel beheer[h], geldwezen[h], financiën; **2** *~s* geldmiddelen, fondsen

[2]finance [fajnæns] *vb* financieren, bekostigen

financial [finænsjl] financieel: *~ year* boekjaar

finch [fintsj] vink

[1]find [fajnd] *vb* **1** vinden, ontdekken, terugvinden: *he was found dead* hij werd dood aangetroffen; **2** (be)vinden, (be)oordelen (als), ontdekken; blijken, *(law)* oordelen, verklaren, uitspreken: *it was found that all the vases were broken* alle vazen bleken gebroken te zijn; *be found wanting* niet voldoen, tekortschieten, te licht bevonden worden; *the jury found him not guilty* de gezworenen spraken het onschuldig over hem uit

[2]find [fajnd] *vb (law)* oordelen

[3]find [fajnd] *n* (goede) vondst

find out 1 ontdekken, erachter komen; **2** betrappen ‖ *be found out* door de mand vallen

[1]fine [fajn] *adj* **1** fijn, dun, scherp: *the ~ print* de kleine lettertjes; **2** voortreffelijk, fijn: *that's all very ~* allemaal goed en wel; **3** fijn, goed: *~ workmanship* goed vakmanschap; **4** in orde, gezond: *I'm ~,* *thanks* met mij gaat het goed, dank je; ~ *arts* beeldende kunst(en); *one of these ~ days* vandaag of morgen; *not to put too ~ a point (of: an edge) on it* zonder er doekjes om te winden

²**fine** [fajn] *adv* **1** fijn, in orde: *it suits me ~* ik vind het prima; **2** fijn, dun: *cut up onions ~* uien fijn snipperen

³**fine** [fajn] *n* (geld)boete

⁴**fine** [fajn] *vb* beboeten

finery [fajnərie] opschik, opsmuk, mooie kleren

finger [finggə] vinger ‖ *(inf) work one's ~s to the bone* zich kapot werken; *(inf) have a ~ in every pie* overal een vinger in de pap hebben; *be all ~s and thumbs* twee linkerhanden hebben, erg onhandig zijn; *burn one's ~s* zijn vingers branden; *(inf) cross one's ~s, keep one's ~s crossed* duimen; *have one's ~s in the till* geld stelen uit de kas (van de winkel waar men werkt); *not be able to put (of: lay) one's ~ on sth.* iets niet kunnen plaatsen; *not lift (of: move, raise, stir) a ~* geen vinger uitsteken; *let slip through one's ~s* door de vingers laten glippen; *twist (of: wind) s.o. round one's (little) ~* iem om zijn vinger winden

fingermark (vuile) vinger(afdruk)

fingerprint vingerafdruk

fingertip vingertop ‖ *have sth. at one's ~s* iets heel goed kennen

¹**finish** [finnisj] *vb* **1** eindigen, tot een einde komen, uit zijn: *the film ~es at 11 p.m.* de film is om 11 uur afgelopen; *~ off with* eindigen met; *we used to ~ up with a glass of port* we namen altijd een glas port om de maaltijd af te ronden; **2** uiteindelijk terechtkomen, belanden: *he will ~ up in jail* hij zal nog in de gevangenis belanden

²**finish** [finnisj] *vb* **1** beëindigen, afmaken, een einde maken aan: *~ a book* een boek uitlezen; **2** opgebruiken, opeten, opdrinken; **3** afwerken, voltooien, de laatste hand leggen aan: *~ (up) cleaning* ophouden met schoonmaken

³**finish** [finnisj] *n* beëindiging, eindeʰ, voltooiing: *be in at the ~ (fig)* bij het einde aanwezig zijn; *(fight) to the ~* tot het bittere einde (doorvechten)

finished [finnisjt] **1** (goed) afgewerkt, verzorgd, kunstig; **2** klaar, af: *those days are ~* die tijden zijn voorbij; **3** geruïneerd, uitgeput: *he is ~ as a politician* als politicus is hij er geweest

finishing touch laatste hand: *put the ~es to* de laatste hand leggen aan

finite [fajnajt] eindig, begrensd, beperkt

Finn [fin] Fin(se)

Finnish [finnisj] Fins

fir [fə:] **1** spar(renboom); **2** sparrenhoutʰ, vurenhoutʰ

¹**fire** [fajjə] *n* **1** vuurʰ, haard(vuurʰ): *catch ~* vlam vatten; **2** brand: *set on ~, set ~ to* in brand steken; *on ~* in brand, *(fig)* in vuur (en vlam); **3** het vuren, vuurʰ, schotʰ: *be (of: come) under ~* onder vuur genomen worden *(also fig)*; **4** kachel: *play with ~* met vuur spelen; *~!* brand!

²**fire** [fajjə] *vb* **1** stoken, brandend houden: *oil-~d furnace* oliekachel, petroleumkachel; **2** bakken; **3** schieten, (af)vuren *(also fig)*: *~ questions* vragen afvuren

³**fire** [fajjə] *vb* **1** in brand steken, doen ontvlammen *(also fig)*: *it ~d him with enthusiasm* het zette hem in vuur en vlam; **2** *(inf)* de laan uitsturen, ontslaan: *~ up* bezielen, stimuleren

firearm vuurwapenʰ

firebrand brandhoutʰ

fire brigade brandweer(korpsʰ)

fire exit nooduitgang, branddeur

firefighter brandbestrijder, brandweerman

firefly glimworm

fireman [fajjəmən] **1** brandweerman; **2** stoker

fireplace 1 open haard; **2** schoorsteen, schouw

fireworks vuurwerk

¹**firm** [fə:m] *adj* **1** vast, stevig, hard: *be on ~ ground* vaste grond onder de voeten hebben *(also fig)*; **2** standvastig, resoluut: *~ decision* definitieve beslissing; *take a ~ line* zich (kei)hard opstellen

²**firm** [fə:m] *adv* stevig, standvastig: *stand ~* op zijn stuk blijven

³**firm** *n* firma

¹**first** [fə:st] *num* eerste deel; begin: *at ~* aanvankelijk, eerst; *she came out ~* ze behaalde de eerste plaats; *~ form* eerste klas; *I'll take the ~ train* ik neem de eerstvolgende trein

²**first** [fə:st] *adv* **1** eerst: *he told her ~* hij vertelde het eerst aan haar; *~ and foremost* in de eerste plaats, bovenal; *~ of all* in de eerste plaats, om te beginnen; **2** liever, eerder: *she'd die ~ rather than give in* ze zou eerder sterven dan toe te geven

first-aid eerstehulp-, EHBO-

first name voornaam

first-rate prima, eersterangs

first school *(roughly)* onderbouw

fiscal [fiskl] fiscaal, belasting(s)-: *~ year* belastingjaar

¹**fish** [fisj] *n* vis, zeedierʰ: *~ and chips* (gebakken) vis met patat; *like a ~ out of water* als een vis op het droge; *(inf) drink like a ~* drinken als een tempelier; *have other ~ to fry* wel wat anders te doen hebben

²**fish** [fisj] *vb* vissen *(also fig)*, hengelen, raden

³**fish** [fisj] *vb* (be)vissen: *~ out a piece of paper from a bag* een papiertje uit een tas opdiepen

fisherman [fisjəmən] visser, sportvisser

fishing rod hengel

fishing tackle vistuigʰ, visbenodigdheden

fishmonger vishandelaar, visboer

fishwife visvrouw, *(depr)* viswijfʰ

fishy [fisjie] **1** visachtig; **2** *(inf)* verdacht: *a ~ story* een verhaal met een luchtje eraan

fission [fisjən] splijting, deling, (cel)deling, (kern)splitsing

fist [fist] vuist

¹**fit** [fit] *n* **1** vlaag, opwelling, inval: *by (of: in) ~s (and starts)* bij vlagen; **2** aanval, stuip, toevalʰ *(also fig)*:

a ~ *of coughing* een hoestbui; *give s.o. a* ~ iem de stuipen op het lijf jagen

²**fit** *adj* **1** geschikt, passend: *a* ~ *person to do sth.* de juiste persoon om iets te doen; **2** gezond, fit, in (goede) conditie: *as* ~ *as a fiddle* kiplekker, zo gezond als een vis; **3** gepast: *think* (of: *see*) ~ *to do sth.* het juist achten (om) iets te doen

³**fit** *vb* geschikt zijn, passen, goed zitten: *it* ~*s like a glove* het zit als gegoten

⁴**fit** *vb* **1** passen, voegen; **2** aanbrengen, monteren: *have a new lock* ~*ted* een nieuw slot laten aanbrengen

¹**fit in** *vb* (goed) aangepast zijn, zich aanpassen aan: ~ *with your ideas* in overeenstemming zijn met jouw ideeën; ~ *with our plans* stroken met onze plannen

²**fit in** *vb* **1** inpassen, plaats (tijd) vinden voor; **2** aanpassen: *fit sth. in with sth.* iets ergens bij aanpassen

fitness [fɪtnəs] **1** het passend zijn: ~ *for a job* geschiktheid voor een baan; **2** fitheid, goede conditie

fitted [fɪttid] **1** (volledig) uitgerust, compleet: ~ *kitchen* volledig uitgeruste keuken; ~ *with* (uitgerust) met, voorzien van; **2** vast: ~ *carpet* vast tapijt; ~ *sheet* hoeslaken

fitter [fɪttə] monteur, installateur

fitting [fɪtting] **1** hulpstukʰ, accessoireʰ; **2** maat

fit up *(inf)* onderdak verlenen: *fit s.o. up with a bed* iem onderdak verlenen

five [fajv] vijf

fivefold vijfvoudig

fiver [fajvə] *(inf)* briefjeʰ van vijf

¹**fix** [fiks] *vb* **1** vastmaken, bevestigen, monteren: ~ *sth. in the mind* iets in de geest prenten; **2** vasthouden, trekken, fixeren: ~ *one's eyes (up)on sth.* de blik vestigen op iets; **3** vastleggen, bepalen, afspreken; **4** regelen, schikken: *(depr) the whole thing was* ~*ed* het was allemaal doorgestoken kaart; **5** opknappen, repareren, in orde brengen; **6** *(Am)* bereiden, maken: ~ *sth. up* iets klaarmaken

²**fix** [fiks] *n* **1** moeilijke situatie, knel: *be in a* ~ in de knel zitten; **2** doorgestoken kaart, afgesproken werkʰ: *the election was a* ~ de verkiezingen waren doorgestoken kaart; **3** shot, dosis

fixation [fikseesjən] **1** bevestiging, bepaling; **2** fixatie

fixed [fikst] **1** vast: ~ *idea* idee-fixe; **2** voorzien van: *how are you* ~ *for beer?* hoe staat het met je voorraad bier?

fixer [fiksə] tussenpersoon

fixings [fiksingz] **1** uitrusting, toebehoren; **2** garnering, versiering

fix up regelen, organiseren, voorzien van: *fix s.o. up with a job* iem aan een baan(tje) helpen

¹**fizz** [fiz] *vb* sissen, (op)bruisen, mousseren

²**fizz** [fiz] *n* **1** gebruisʰ, gesisʰ, geschuimʰ; **2** *(inf)* mousserende drank, champagne

fizzle [fizl] (zachtjes) sissen, (zachtjes) bruisen || *(inf)* ~ *out* met een sisser aflopen

fizzy [fizzie] bruisend, sissend, mousserend

flabbergast [flæbəga:st] *(inf)* verstomd doen staan, verbijsteren, overdonderen: *be* ~*ed at* (of: *by)* verstomd staan door

flabby [flæbie] slap, zwak

flaccid [flæksid] slap, zwak, zacht

¹**flag** [flæg] *n* **1** vlag, vaandelʰ, vlaggetjeʰ: ~ *of convenience* goedkope vlag; *show the* ~ *(fig)* je gezicht laten zien; **2** lisbloem: *keep the* ~ *flying* doorgaan met de strijd, volharden

²**flag** [flæg] *vb* verslappen, verflauwen

³**flag** [flæg] *vb* **1** met vlaggen versieren (markeren); **2** doen stoppen (met zwaaibewegingen), aanhouden, aanroepen: ~ *(down) a taxi* een taxi aanroepen

flag-day collectedag, speldjesdag

flagon [flægən] **1** schenkkan, flacon; **2** kan, fles

flagpole vlaggenstok, vlaggenmast

flagrant [fleegrənt] flagrant, in het oog springend

flagship vlaggenschipʰ, *(fig also)* paradepaardjeʰ

flagstaff vlaggenstok, vlaggenmast

¹**flail** [fleel] *n* (dors)vlegel

²**flail** [fleel] *vb* **1** dorsen; **2** wild zwaaien (met): *the boy* ~*ed his arms in the air* de jongen maaide met zijn armen in de lucht

flair [fleə] flair, feeling, fijne neus, bijzondere handigheid

¹**flake** [fleek] *n* vlok, sneeuwvlok, schilfer, bladder

²**flake** [fleek] *vb* (doen) (af)schilferen, (doen) pellen || *(inf)* ~ *out: a)* omvallen van vermoeidheid; *b)* gaan slapen; *c)* flauwvallen

flamboyant [flæmbojjənt] **1** bloemrijk; **2** schitterend, vlammend; **3** opzichtig, zwierig

¹**flame** [fleem] *n* **1** vlam, gloed, ~*s* vuurʰ, hitte: *burst into* ~*(s)* in brand vliegen; **2** geliefde, liefde, passie

²**flame** [fleem] *vb* vlammen, ontvlammen, opvlammen || ~ *out* (of: *up)* (razend) opvliegen, opstuiven

flammable [flæməbl] brandbaar, explosief

flan [flæn] *(roughly)* kleine vla(ai)

Flanders [fla:ndəz] Vlaanderen

flank [flæŋk] zijkant, flank

flannel [flænl] **1** flanelʰ; **2** (flanellen) doekjeʰ, washandjeʰ; **3** *(inf)* mooi praatjeʰ, vleierij, smoesjes

¹**flap** [flæp] *n* **1** geflapperʰ, geklapʰ; **2** klep, flap, (afhangende) rand, (neerslaand) bladʰ; **3** *(inf)* staat van opwinding, paniek, consternatie

²**flap** [flæp] *vb* flapp(er)en, klepp(er)en, slaan

³**flap** [flæp] *vb* op en neer bewegen, slaan met

¹**flare** [fleə] *n* **1** flakkerend lichtʰ, flikkering; **2** signaalvlam, vuursignaalʰ

²**flare** [fleə] *vb* (op)flakkeren, (op)vlammen, *(fig)* opstuiven: ~ *up: a)* opflakkeren; *b) (also fig)* woest worden

flare-up opflakkering, uitbarsting, hevige ruzie

¹**flash** [flæsj] *n* **1** (licht)flits, vlam, (op)flikkering: ~*es of lightning* bliksemschichten; *quick as a* ~ razend snel; *in a* ~ in een flits; **2** flits(lichtʰ); flitsapparaatʰ; **3** lichtseinʰ, vlagseinʰ; **4** kort (nieuws)berichtʰ, nieuwsflits; **5** opwelling, vlaag: *a* ~ *of inspiration* een flits van inspiratie

²**flash** [flæsj] *adj* **1** plotseling (opkomend): ~ *flood*

plotselinge overstroming; 2 *(inf)* opzichtig, poenig

³flash [flæsj] *vb* 1 opvlammen, (plotseling) ontvlammen *(also fig);* 2 plotseling opkomen: ~ *into view* (of: *sight)* plotseling in het gezichtsveld verschijnen; 3 snel voorbijflitsen, (voorbij)schieten: ~ *past* (of: *by)* voorbijvliegen, voorbijflitsen

⁴flash [flæsj] *vb* 1 (doen) flitsen, (doen) flikkeren: ~ *the headlights (of a car)* met de koplampen flitsen; 2 pronken met: ~ *money around* te koop lopen met zijn geld

flashback terugblik

flasher [flæsjə] 1 flitser, knipperlicht[h]; 2 potloodventer

flashlight 1 flitslicht[h], lichtflits, signaallicht[h]; 2 *(Am)* zaklantaarn

flask [fla:sk] 1 fles, flacon, kolf; 2 veldfles; 3 thermosfles

¹flat [flæt] *adj* 1 vlak, plat; 2 laag, niet hoog, plat *(also of feet);* 3 zonder prik, *(Belg)* plat *(water),* verschaald *(beer);* 4 effen, gelijkmatig *(colour, paint);* 5 bot, vierkant, absoluut *(negation, refusal);* 6 leeg, plat *(tyre);* 7 saai, oninteressant, mat, smaakloos, flauw *(food): fall* ~ mislukken, geen effect hebben; 8 *(mus)* te laag; 9 *(mus)* mol, mineur

²flat [flæt] *adv* 1 *(inf)* helemaal: ~ *broke* helemaal platzak; ~ *out* (op) volle kracht, met alle kracht *(advance, work);* 2 *(inf)* botweg, ronduit: *tell s.o. sth.* ~ iem botweg iets zeggen; 3 *(mus)* (een halve toon) lager, te laag; 4 rond, op de kop af, exact: *ten seconds* ~ op de kop af tien seconden

³flat [flæt] *n* 1 vlakte, vlak terrein[h]; 2 flat, etage, appartement[h]: *a block of ~s* een flatgebouw; 3 platte kant, vlak[h], hand(palm); 4 *(Am)* lekke band; 5 *(mus)* mol(teken[h]), *(Belg)* b-molteken[h]

flat-bottomed platboomd, met een platte bodem

flatfish platvis

flat-iron strijkijzer[h], strijkbout

flatly [flætlie] 1 uitdrukkingsloos, mat, dof *(say, speak etc);* 2 botweg, kortaf *(eg refuse): Simon* ~ *refused to say where he had been* Simon vertikte het gewoon om te zeggen waar hij had gezeten; 3 helemaal

flatten [flætn] 1 afplatten, effenen: ~ *out* afvlakken, effenen; 2 flauw(er) maken, dof maken

flatter [flætə] 1 vleien: ~ *oneself* zich vleien, zichzelf te hoog aanslaan; *I flatter myself that I'm a good judge of character* ik vlei mezelf met de hoop dat ik mensenkennis bezit; 2 strelen *(ears, eyes);* 3 flatteren, mooier afschilderen

flattery [flætərie] 1 vleierij, *(teasingly)* slijm, slijm; 2 gevlei[h], vleiende woorden

flaunt [flo:nt] 1 pronken met, pralen met, tentoonspreiden; 2 doen opvallen, (zich) zeer opvallend uitdossen (gedragen)

flautist [flo:tist] fluitist, fluitspeler

flavour [fleevə] 1 smaak, aroma[h], geur, *(fig)* bijsmaak; 2 het karakteristieke, het eigene, het typische: *Camden has its own peculiar* ~ Camden heeft iets heel eigens

flavouring [fleevəring] smaakstof, aroma[h], kruid[h], kruiderij

flaw [flo:] 1 barst, breuk, scheur; 2 gebrek[h], fout *(in jewel, stone, character)*

flax [flæks] vlas[h] *(plant, fibre)*

flay [flee] 1 villen, (af)stropen; 2 afranselen, *(fig)* hekelen

flea [flie:] 1 vlo; 2 watervlo || *go off with a* ~ *in his ear* van een koude kermis thuiskomen; ~ *market* vlooienmarkt, rommelmarkt

fleabite vlooienbeet, *(fig)* iets onbelangrijks, kleinigheid

¹fleck [flek] *n* vlek(je[h]), plek(je[h]), spikkel(tje[h])

²fleck [flek] *vb* (be)spikkelen, vlekken, stippen

flee [flie:] (ont)vluchten

¹fleece [flie:s] *n* 1 (schaaps)vacht; 2 vlies[h]

²fleece [flie:s] *vb* 1 scheren *(sheep);* 2 *(inf)* afzetten, het vel over de oren halen *(pers)*

fleet [flie:t] 1 vloot, marine, luchtvloot; 2 schare, verzameling, groep: *a* ~ *of cars* (of: *taxis)* een wagenpark

fleeting [flie:ting] 1 vluchtig, vergankelijk; 2 kortstondig: *a* ~ *glance* een vluchtige blik

Fleming [flemming] Vlaming

Flemish [flemmisj] Vlaams

flesh [flesj] vlees[h]: ~ *and blood* het lichaam, een mens(elijk wezen); *one's own* ~ *and blood* je eigen vlees en bloed, je naaste verwanten

¹flex [fleks] *vb* buigen, samentrekken

²flex [fleks] *n* (elektrisch) snoer[h]

flexible [fleksibl] 1 buigzaam *(also fig),* soepel, flexibel: ~ *working hours* variabele werktijd; 2 meegaand, plooibaar

flexitime [fleksittajm] variabele werktijd(en)

flexiworker [fleksiwwə:kə] flexwerker

¹flick [flik] *n* 1 tik, mep, slag; 2 ruk, schok: *a* ~ *of the wrist* een snelle polsbeweging; 3 *(inf)* film; 4 *the flicks* bios

²flick [flik] *vb* even aanraken, aantikken, afschudden, aanknippen *(switch):* ~ *crumbs from* (of: *off) the table* kruimels van de tafel vegen; ~ *through a newspaper* een krant doorbladeren

¹flicker [flikkə] *vb* 1 trillen, fladderen, wapperen, flikkeren; 2 heen en weer bewegen, heen en weer schieten

²flicker [flikkə] *n* 1 trilling, (op)flikkering, flikkerend licht[h]; 2 sprankje[h]: *a* ~ *of hope* een sprankje hoop

flier [flajjə] see flyer

flight [flajt] 1 vlucht, het vliegen, baan *(of projectile, ball);* *(fig)* opwelling, uitbarsting: *put to* ~ op de vlucht jagen; 2 zwerm, vlucht, troep; 3 trap: *a* ~ *of stairs* een trap

flight path 1 vliegroute; 2 baan *(of satellite)*

flight recorder vluchtrecorder, zwarte doos

flighty [flajtie] grillig, wispelturig

¹flimsy [flimzie] *adj* 1 broos, kwetsbaar, dun; 2 onbenullig, onnozel

²flimsy [flimzie] *n* doorslag(papier[h]), kopie

flinch [flintsj] *(also fig)* terugdeinzen, terugschrikken *(with fear, pain): without ~ing* zonder een spier te vertrekken

¹fling [fling] *vb* **1** gooien, (weg)smijten, (af)werpen; **2** wegstormen, (boos) weglopen

²fling [fling] *n* **1** worp, gooi; **2** uitspatting, korte, hevige affaire ‖ *have one's ~* uitspatten

flint [flint] vuursteen(tje^h)

¹flip [flip] *vb* **1** wegtikken, wegschieten (met de vingers): *~ a coin* kruis of munt gooien; **2** omdraaien

²flip [flip] *vb (inf)* **1** flippen, maf worden; **2** boos worden, door het lint gaan

³flip [flip] *n* tik, mep, (vinger)knip

⁴flip [flip] *adj* glad, ongepast, brutaal

flip-chart flip-over, flap-over

flippant [flippənt] oneerbiedig, spottend

flipper [flippə] **1** vin, zwempoot; **2** zwemvlies^h

flip side B-kant (van grammofoonplaat)

flip through doorbladeren, snel doorlezen

¹flirt [flə:t] *n* flirt

²flirt [flə:t] *vb* flirten, koketteren

flirt with *vb* **1** flirten met, *(fig)* spelen met, overwegen: *we ~ the idea of* we spelen met de gedachte om; **2** uitdagen, flirten met: *~ danger* een gevaarlijk spel spelen

¹float [floot] *n* **1** drijvend voorwerp^h, vlot^h, boei, dobber; **2** drijver; **3** kar, (praal)wagen; **4** contanten, kleingeld^h

²float [floot] *vb* **1** drijven, dobberen; **2** vlot komen *(of ship)*; **3** zweven

³float [floot] *vb* **1** doen drijven; **2** vlot maken *(ship etc)*; **3** over water vervoeren; **4** in omloop brengen, voorstellen, rondvertellen: *~ an idea* met een idee naar voren komen

floating [flooting] **1** drijvend: *~ bridge: a)* pontonbrug; *b)* kettingpont; **2** veranderlijk: *~ kidney* wandelende nier; *~ voter* zwevende kiezer

¹flock [flok] *n* **1** bosje^h, vlokje^h; **2** troep, zwerm, kudde

²flock [flok] *vb* bijeenkomen, samenstromen: *people ~ed to the cities* men trok in grote groepen naar de steden

flog [flog] slaan, ervan langs geven

¹flood [flud] *n* **1** vloed; **2** uitstorting, stroom, vloed: *~ of reactions* stortvloed van reacties; **3** overstroming

²flood [flud] *vb* (doen) overstromen, overspoelen, buiten zijn oevers doen treden: *we were ~ed (out) with letters* we werden bedolven onder de brieven

floodgate sluisdeur *(fig)*, sluis: *open the ~s* de sluizen openzetten

flooding [fluddieng] overstroming

floodlight 1 schijnwerper; **2** strijklicht^h, spotlicht^h

¹floor [flo:] *n* **1** vloer, grond: *first ~* eerste verdieping, *(Am)* begane grond; **2** verdieping, etage; **3** vergaderzaal *(of parliament): a motion from the ~* een motie uit de zaal; *wipe the ~ with s.o.* de vloer met iem aanvegen

²floor [flo:] *vb* **1** vloeren *(also fig)*, knock-out slaan,

verslaan: *his arguments ~ed me* tegen zijn argumenten kon ik niet op; **2** van de wijs brengen

floorboard 1 vloerplank; **2** bodemplank

floor show floorshow, striptease

¹flop [flop] *vb* **1** zwaaien, klappen, spartelen: *~ about in the water* rondspartelen in het water; **2** smakken, ploffen: *~ down in a chair* neerploffen in een stoel; **3** *(inf)* mislukken, floppen, zakken *(at examination)*

²flop [flop] *n* **1** smak, plof; **2** flop, mislukking

¹floppy [floppie] *n* floppy (disk), diskette, flop

²floppy [floppie] *adj* **1** slap(hangend); **2** *(inf)* zwak

floral [flo:rəl] **1** gebloemd: *~ tribute* bloemenhulde; **2** mbt flora, plant-

florid [florrid] **1** bloemrijk, (overdreven) sierlijk; **2** in het oog lopend, opzichtig; **3** blozend, hoogrood

florin [florrin] florijn, gulden

florist [florrist] **1** bloemist; **2** bloemkweker

flotilla [flətillə] **1** flottielje, smaldeel^h; **2** vloot *(of small ships)*

flotsam [flotsəm] **1** drijfhout^h, wrakhout^h: *(fig) ~ and jetsam* uitgestotenen; **2** rommel, rotzooi

¹flounce [flauns] *n* **1** zwaai, ruk, schok; **2** (gerimpelde) strook *(on article of clothing, curtain)*

²flounce [flauns] *vb* **1** zwaaien *(of body)*, schokken, schudden; **2** ongeduldig lopen: *~ about the room* opgewonden door de kamer ijsberen

flounder [flaundə] **1** ploeteren; **2** stuntelen, van zijn stuk gebracht worden; **3** de draad kwijtraken, hakkelen

flour [flauə] meel^h, (meel)bloem

¹flourish [flurrisj] *vb* **1** gedijen, bloeien; **2** floreren, succes hebben: *his family were ~ing* het ging goed met zijn gezin

²flourish [flurrisj] *vb* tonen, zwaaien met: *he ~ed a letter in my face* hij zwaaide een brief onder mijn neus heen en weer

³flourish [flurrisj] *n* **1** krul, krulletter; **2** bloemrijke uitdrukking, stijlbloempje^h; **3** zwierig gebaar^h; **4** fanfare, geschal^h

flout [flaut] **1** beledigen, bespotten; **2** afwijzen, in de wind slaan

¹flow [floo] *vb* **1** (toe)vloeien, (toe)stromen; **2** golven, loshangen *(of hair, article of clothing)*; **3** opkomen *(of high tide): swim with the ~ing tide* met de stroom meegaan

²flow [floo] *n* **1** stroom, stroming, het stromen; **2** vloed; overvloed: *ebb and ~* eb en vloed

¹flower [flauə] *n* **1** bloem, bloesem; **2** bloei: *the orchids are in ~* de orchideeën staan in bloei

²flower [flauə] *vb* bloeien, tot bloei (ge)komen (zijn)

flowing [flooing] **1** vloeiend; **2** loshangend, golvend

flu [floe:] *influenza* griep

flub [flub] *(Am)* verknoeien

fluctuate [fluktjoe-eet] fluctueren, schommelen, variëren

flue [floe:] schoorsteenpijp, rookkanaal^h

fluency [floe:ənsie] spreekvaardigheid

fluent [floe:ənt] vloeiend: *be ~ in English* vloeiend

fluff 602

Engels spreken

¹fluff [fluf] *n* pluis(jes), dons^h

²fluff [fluf] *vb* blunderen

¹fluid [floeid] *adj* **1** vloeibaar, niet vast, vloeiend; **2** instabiel, veranderlijk: *our plans are still ~* onze plannen staan nog niet vast

²fluid [floeid] *n* vloeistof

fluke [floe:k] bof, meevaller, mazzel: *by a ~* door stom geluk

flummox [flumməks] in verwarring brengen, perplex doen staan

flunk [flungk] *(Am; inf)* (doen) zakken *(examination)*, afwijzen *(at examination)*

flunkey [flungkie] *(oft depr)* **1** lakei; **2** strooplikker

fluorescent [floeərəsnt] fluorescerend: *~ lamp* tl-buis

fluoride [floeərajd] fluoride^h, fluorwaterstofzout^h

flurry [flurrie] vlaag *(also fig)*, windvlaag, windstoot, (korte) bui: *in a ~ of excitement* in een vlaag van opwinding

¹flush [flusj] *vb* **1** doorspoelen, doortrekken *(toilet)*; **2** kleuren, blozen

²flush [flusj] *vb* **1** (schoon)spoelen: *~ sth. away* (of: *down)* iets wegspoelen; **2** opwinden, aanvuren: *~ed with happiness* dolgelukkig; **3** doen wegvliegen: *~ s.o. out of* (of: *from) his hiding place* iem uit zijn schuilplaats verjagen

³flush [flusj] *adj* **1** goed voorzien, goed bij kas: *~ with money* goed bij kas; **2** gelijk, vlak: *~ with the wall* gelijk met de muur

⁴flush [flusj] *n* **1** vloed, (plotselinge) stroom, vloedgolf; **2** (water)spoeling; **3** opwinding: *in the first ~ of victory* in de overwinningsroes; **4** blos; **5** flush, serie kaarten van dezelfde kleur

¹fluster [flustə] *vb* van de wijs brengen, zenuwachtig maken

²fluster [flustə] *n* opwinding, verwarring: *be in a ~* opgewonden zijn

flute [floe:t] fluit

flutist [floe:tist] *(Am)* fluitist

¹flutter [fluttə] *vb* **1** fladderen, klapwieken; **2** dwarrelen *(of leaf)*; **3** wapperen *(of flag)*; **4** zenuwachtig rondlopen, ijsberen; **5** snel slaan, (snel) kloppen

²flutter [fluttə] *n* **1** gefladder^h, geklapper^h; **2** opwinding, drukte: *be in a ~* opgewonden zijn; **3** *(inf)* gokje^h, speculatie

flux [fluks] **1** vloed, het vloeien, stroom; **2** voortdurende beweging, veranderlijkheid: *everything was in a state of ~* er waren steeds nieuwe ontwikkelingen

¹fly [flaj] *vb* **1** vliegen *(of bird, aeroplane etc)*: *~ away* wegvliegen, *(fig)* verdwijnen; *~ in* aankomen per vliegtuig; *~ past* (in formatie) over vliegen; *~ at: a)* aanvallen, zich storten op *(of bird)*; *b) (fig)* uitvallen tegen; *~ into* landen op *(airport)*; **2** wapperen *(of flag, hair)*, fladderen, vliegen; **3** zich snel voortbewegen, vliegen, vluchten, omvliegen *(of time)*, wegvliegen *(of money)*: *let ~: a)* (af)schieten, afvuren; *b)* laten schieten; *~ into a rage* (of: *passion,*

temper) in woede ontsteken; *~ high* hoog vliegen *(fig)*, ambitieus zijn

²fly [flaj] *vb* **1** vliegen, besturen: *~ a plane in* een vliegtuig aan de grond zetten; **2** vliegen (met) *(airline company)*; **3** laten vliegen *(pigeon)*, oplaten *(kite)*: *~ a kite* vliegeren, *(fig)* een balletje opgooien; **4** voeren, laten wapperen *(flag)*; **5** ontvluchten, vermijden

³fly [flaj] *n* **1** vlieg: *die like flies* in groten getale omkomen; *not harm* (of: *hurt) a ~* geen vlieg kwaad doen; **2** gulp: *a ~ in the ointment* een kleinigheid die het geheel bederft; *a ~ on the wall* een spion; *(inf) there are no flies on her* ze is niet op haar achterhoofd gevallen

flyer [flajjə] **1** vlugschrift^h, folder; **2** piloot

flying [flajjing] **1** vliegend: *~ jump* (of: *leap)* sprong met aanloop; *~ saucer* vliegende schotel; **2** (zeer) snel, zich snel verplaatsend (ontwikkelend), vliegend: *~ start* vliegende start *(also fig)*; **3** kortstondig, van korte duur, tijdelijk

flying squad vliegende brigade, mobiele eenheid

flyover viaduct^h *(across motorway)*

flysheet **1** (reclame)blaadje^h, folder, circulaire; **2** informatieblad^h, gebruiksaanwijzing *(of catalogue, book)*

fly swatter vliegenmepper

flyweight *(boxing, wrestling)* **1** worstelaar (bokser) in de vlieggewichtklasse, vlieggewicht; **2** vlieggewicht^h

foal [fool] veulen^h

¹foam [foom] *n* **1** schuim^h; **2** schuimrubber

²foam [foom] *vb* **1** schuimen; **2** schuimbekken: *~ at the mouth* schuimbekken *(also fig)*

fob off 1 wegwuiven, geen aandacht besteden aan; **2** afschepen, zich afmaken van: *we won't be fobbed off this time* deze keer laten we ons niet met een kluitje in het riet sturen

focal point brandpunt^h *(also fig)*, middelpunt^h

¹focus [fookəs] *n* **1** brandpunt^h, focus, *(fig)* middelpunt^h, centrum^h; **2** scherpte: *out of ~* onscherp

²focus [fookəs] *vb* **1** in een brandpunt (doen) samenkomen; **2** (zich) concentreren: *~ on* zich concentreren op

fodder [foddə] (droog) veevoeder^h, voer^h *(also fig)*

foe [foo] *(form)* vijand, tegenstander

foetus [fie:təs] foetus

fog [fog] mist, nevel *(also fig)*, onduidelijkheid, verwarring

fogey [foogie] ouderwets figuur^h, ouwe zeur

foggy [fogie] mistig, (zeer) nevelig, *(also fig)* onduidelijk, vaag: *(inf) I haven't the foggiest (idea)* (ik heb) geen flauw idee

foible [fojbl] **1** zwak^h, zwakheid, zwak punt^h; **2** gril

¹foil [fojl] *n* **1** bladmetaal^h, folie, zilverpapier^h; **2** folie *(packaging material for foodstuffs)*

²foil [fojl] *vb* verijdelen, verhinderen, voorkomen

¹fold [foold] *vb (inf)* **1** op de fles gaan, over de kop gaan; **2** het begeven, bezwijken

²fold [foold] *vb* **1** (op)vouwen: *~ away* opvouwen,

opklappen; ~ *back* terugslaan, omslaan; **2**
(om)wikkelen, (in)pakken; **3** (om)sluiten, omhelzen: ~ *s.o. in one's arms* iem in zijn armen sluiten;
4 hullen *(in fog);* **5** over elkaar leggen, kruisen
(arms), intrekken *(wings)*
³**fold** [foold] *n* **1** vouw, plooi, kronkel(ing), kreuk; **2**
schaapskooi; **3** het vouwen; **4** kudde, *(fig)* kerk, gemeente: *return to the* ~ in de schoot van zijn familie
terugkeren
folder [fooldə] **1** folder, (reclame)blaadjeʰ; **2**
map(jeʰ)
folding [foolding] vouw-, opvouwbaar, opklapbaar, klap-
¹**fold up** *vb* opvouwen, opklappen
²**fold up** *vb* **1** bezwijken, het begeven, het opgeven; **2**
failliet gaan, over de kop gaan
foliage [foolie·idzj] gebladerteʰ, bladʰ, loofʰ
folk [fook] *(inf)* **1** familie, gezin, oude lui: *her ~s*
were from New Jersey haar familie kwam uit New
Jersey; **2** luitjes, jongens, mensen; **3** mensen, lieden,
lui: *some ~ never learn* sommige mensen leren het
nooit
folklore [fooklo:] **1** folklore; **2** volkskunde
folk-tale volksverhaalʰ, sage, sprookjeʰ
follow [folloo] volgen, achternalopen, aanhouden,
gaan langs *(road, direction, river),* achternazitten,
vergezellen, bijwonen, komen na, opvolgen, aandacht schenken aan, in de gaten houden, begrijpen,
bijhouden *(news),* zich laten leiden door, uitvoeren
(order, advice), nadoen *(example),* voortvloeien
uit: ~ *the rules* zich aan de regels houden; ~ *s.o.*
about (of: *around)* iem overal volgen; ~ *on* verder
gaan, volgen *(after interruption);* ~ *up: a)* (op korte
afstand) volgen, in de buurt blijven van; *b)* vervolgen, een vervolg maken op; *c)* gebruik maken van;
d) nagaan; *the outcome is as ~s* het resultaat is als
volgt; *to* ~ als volgend gerecht; *would you like any-*
thing to ~? wilt u nog iets toe?
¹**following** [follooing] *adj* **1** volgend; **2** mee, in de
rug, gunstig *(wind)*
²**following** [follooing] *n* aanhang, volgelingen
³**following** [follooing] *prep* na, volgende op: ~ *the*
meeting na de vergadering
follow-up vervolgʰ, voortzetting, vervolgbrief,
tweede bezoekʰ
folly [follie] **1** (buitensporig) duur en nutteloos iets;
2 dwaasheid, dwaas gedragʰ
foment [fooment] aanstoken, aanmoedigen, stimuleren
fond [fond] **1** liefhebbend, teder, innig; **2** dierbaar,
lief: *his ~est wish was fulfilled* zijn liefste wens ging
in vervulling; **3** al te lief, al te toegeeflijk: *be ~ of* gek
zijn op, *(inf)* er een handje van hebben te
fondle [fondl] liefkozen, strelen, aaien
fondness [fondnəs] **1** tederheid, genegenheid,
warmte; **2** voorliefde, hang: *his ~ for old proverbs is*
quite irritating at times zijn voorliefde voor oude
spreekwoorden is soms heel irritant
font [font] (doop)vontʰ

food [foe:d] **1** voedingsmiddelʰ, voedingsartikelʰ,
levensmiddelʰ, eetwaar: *frozen ~s* diepvriespro-
ducten; **2** voedselʰ, etenʰ, voeding *(also fig):* ~ *for*
thought (of: *reflection)* stof tot nadenken
foodstuff levensmiddelʰ, voedingsmiddelʰ, voedingsartikelʰ
¹**fool** [foe:l] *n* **1** dwaas, gek, zot(skap), stommeling:
more ~ him hij had beter kunnen weten; *make a ~*
of s.o. iem voor de gek houden; **2** nar, zot: *act* (of:
play) the ~ gek doen; **3** dessert van stijf geklopte
room, ei, suiker en vruchten: *he's nobody's* (of: *no)*
~ hij is niet van gisteren
²**fool** [foe:l] *vb* **1** gek doen: ~ *(about, around)* with
spelen, flirten met; **2** lummelen, lanterfanten:
~ *about* (of: *around)* rondlummelen, aanrommelen
³**fool** [foe:l] *vb* voor de gek houden, ertussen nemen:
he ~ed her into believing he's a guitarist hij maakte
haar wijs dat hij gitarist is
foolhardy onbezonnen, roekeloos
foolish [foe:lisj] **1** dwaas, dom, stom; **2** verbouwereerd, beteuterd
¹**foot** [foet] *n (feet)* **1** voet *(also of mountain, stock-*
ing): *put one's feet up* (even) gaan liggen; *stand on*
one's own feet op eigen benen staan; *on* ~ te voet,
op handen; **2** (vers)voet; **3** poot *(of table);* **4** voeten-
eindeʰ *(of bed);* **5** onderste, laatste deelʰ, (uit)ein-
deʰ; **6** *(measure of length)* voet *(0.3048 metre):* have
a ~ in both camps geen partij kiezen; *(fig) feet of*
clay fundamentele zwakte; *carry* (of: *sweep) s.o. off*
his feet iem meeslepen; *(inf) fall* (of: *land) on one's*
feet mazzel hebben; *find one's feet: a)* beginnen te
staan *(of child); b)* op eigen benen kunnen staan;
get to one's feet opstaan; *put one's ~ down* streng
optreden, *(inf)* plankgas rijden; *(inf) put one's ~ in*
it (of: *one's mouth)* een blunder begaan; *(inf) be*
rushed off one's feet zich uit de naad werken; *my ~!*
kom nou!
²**foot** [foet] *vb (inf):* ~ *it: a)* dansen; *b)* de benenwagen nemen, te voet gaan
³**foot** [foet] *vb* betalen, vereffenen, dokken voor
football 1 voetbal *(ball);* **2** rugbybal; **3** speelbal *(fig);*
4 *(Am)* Amerikaans footballʰ
foothill uitloper *(of mountains)*
foothold 1 steun(puntʰ) voor de voet, plaats om te
staan; **2** vaste voet, steunpuntʰ, zekere positie
footing [foeting] **1** steun (voor de voet), steunpuntʰ, houvastʰ, *(fig)* vaste voet: *lose one's ~* wegglijden; **2** voet, niveauʰ, sterkte; **3** voet, verstandhouding, omgang: *on the same* ~ op gelijke voet
footlights voetlicht, *(by extension)* (toneel)carrière
footling [foe:tling] **1** dwaas, stom; **2** onbeduidend,
waardeloos
footloose vrij, ongebonden
footman [foetmən] lakei, livreiknecht
footnote voetnoot, *(fig)* kanttekening
footprint voetafdruk, voetspoorʰ, voetstap
footstep 1 voetstap, voetafdruk, voetspoorʰ *(also*
fig): *follow* (of: *tread) in s.o.'s ~s* in iemands voet-
sporen treden; **2** pas, stap

foppish [fɔppisj] fatterig, dandyachtig

for [fo:] **1** voor, om, met het oog op, wegens, bedoeld om, ten behoeve van: *act ~ the best* handelen om bestwil; *long ~ home* verlangen naar huis; *write ~ information* schrijven om informatie; *thank you ~ coming* bedankt dat je gekomen bent; *now ~ it* en nu erop los; **2** voor, wat betreft, gezien, in verhouding met: *an ear ~ music* een muzikaal gehoor; *it's not ~ me to* het is niet aan mij om te; *so much ~ that* dat is dat; *I ~ one will not do it* ik zal het in elk geval niet doen; *~ all I care* voor mijn part; **3** ten voordele van, ten gunste van, vóór: *~ and against* voor en tegen; **4** in de plaats van, tegenover, in ruil voor; **5** als (zijnde): *left ~ dead* als dood achterlaten; **6** over, gedurende, sinds, ver, met een omvang: *it was not ~ long* het duurde niet lang; **7** dat … zou …, dat … moet …: *~ her to leave us is impossible* het is onmogelijk dat zij ons zou verlaten; **8** opdat: *~ this to work it is necessary to* wil dit lukken, dan is het nodig te; *anyone ~ coffee?* wil er iem koffie?; *and now ~ something completely different* en nu iets anders

forbear [fo:bɛə] zich onthouden, zich inhouden, afzien: *he should ~ from quarrels* hij moet zich verre houden van ruzies

forbid [fəbid] **1** verbieden, ontzeggen; **2** voorkomen, verhoeden, buitensluiten: *God ~!* God verhoede!

forbidden [fəbidn] verboden, niet toegestaan

forbidding [fəbidding] afstotelijk, afschrikwekkend

¹force [fo:s] *n* **1** kracht, geweldʰ, macht: *by ~ of circumstances* door omstandigheden gedwongen; *join ~s (with)* de krachten bundelen (met); *by (of: from, out of) ~ of habit* uit gewoonte; **2** (rechts)geldigheid, het van kracht zijn: *a new law has come into ~* (of: *has been put into ~*) een nieuwe wet is van kracht geworden; **3** macht, krijgsmacht, legerʰ; **4** *the Forces* strijdkrachten

²force [fo:s] *vb* **1** dwingen, (door)drijven, forceren: *~ back* terugdrijven; *Government will ~ the prices up* de regering zal de prijzen opdrijven; **2** forceren, open-, doorbreken: *the burglar ~d an entry* de inbreker verschafte zich met geweld toegang

forced [fo:st] gedwongen, onvrijwillig, geforceerd: *~ labour* dwangarbeid; *~ landing* noodlanding

forcemeat gehaktʰ

forcible [fo:sibl] **1** gewelddadig, gedwongen, krachtig; **2** indrukwekkend, overtuigend

fore [fo:] het voorste gedeelte: *(fig) come to the ~* op de voorgrond treden

forearm onderarm, voorarm

forebear [fo:bɛə] voorvader, voorouder

foreboding [fo:bo̱o̱ding] **1** voortekenʰ, voorspelling; **2** (akelig) voorgevoelʰ

¹forecast [fo̱:ka:st] *n* voorspelling, verwachting *(of weather)*

²forecast [fo̱:ka:st] *vb* voorspellen, verwachten, aankondigen

forecourt voorpleinʰ

forefather voorvader, stamvader

forefinger wijsvinger

forefront voorste deelʰ, voorste gelid, frontʰ, voorgevel: *in the ~ of the fight* aan het (gevechts)front

foregather [fo:gæ̱ðə] samenkomen, (zich) verzamelen

forego [fo:go̱o̱] voorafgaan

foregoing [fo̱:gooing] voorafgaand, voornoemd, vorig

forehead [fo̱rrid] voorhoofdʰ

foreign [fo̱rrən] **1** buitenlands: *~ aid* ontwikkelingshulp; *~ exchange* deviezen; *Foreign Office* Ministerie van Buitenlandse Zaken; **2** vreemd, ongewoon

foreigner [fo̱rrənə] buitenlander, vreemdeling

foreman [fo̱:mən] **1** voorzitter van jury; **2** voorman, ploegbaas

¹foremost [fo̱:moost] *adj* **1** voorst(e), eerst(e), aan het hoofd: *head ~* met het hoofd naar voren; **2** opmerkelijkst, belangrijkst

²foremost [fo̱:moost] *adv* vooraan

forename vo̱o̱rnaam

forensic [fərensik] gerechtelijk, (ge)rechts-, forensisch

forerunner 1 voortekenʰ, *(fig)* voorbode; **2** voorloper

foresee voorzien, verwachten, vooraf zien

foreseeable [fo:si̱e̱:əbl] **1** te verwachten, te voorzien; **2** afzienbaar, nabij: *in the ~ future* in de nabije toekomst

foreshadow aankondigen, voorspellen

foresight 1 vooruitziende blik, het vooruitzien; **2** toekomstplanning, voorzorg

forest [fo̱rrist] woudʰ *(also fig)*, bosʰ

forestall [fo:sto̱:l] **1** vóór zijn; **2** vooruitlopen op; **3** (ver)hinderen, dwarsbomen, voorkomen

forester [fo̱rristə] boswachter, houtvester

foretaste voorproef(jeʰ)

foretell [fo:te̱l] voorspellen, voorzeggen

forethought toekomstplanning, voorzorg, vooruitziende blik

forever [fərevvə] **1** (voor) eeuwig, voorgoed, (voor) altijd; **2** onophoudelijk, aldoor: *I was ~ dragging David away from the fireplace* ik moest David aldoor bij de open haard wegslepen

¹forfeit [fo̱:fit] *vb* verbeuren, verspelen, verbeurd verklaren

²forfeit [fo̱:fit] *n* het verbeurde, boete, straf

¹forge [fo:dzj] *n* **1** smidse, smederij; **2** smidsvuurʰ

²forge [fo:dzj] *vb* **1** vervalsing(en) maken, valsheid in geschrifte plegen; **2** vooruitschieten: *~ ahead* gestaag vorderingen maken

³forge [fo:dzj] *vb* **1** smeden *(also fig)*, bedenken, beramen; **2** vervalsen: *a ~d passport* een vals paspoort

forger [fo̱:dzjə] vervalser, valsemunter

forgery [fo̱:dzjərie] **1** vervalsing, namaak; **2** het vervalsen, oplichterij

¹forget [fəge̱t] *vb* vergeten, niet denken aan, niet

meer weten: *(inf)* ~ *(about)* it laat maar, denk er maar niet meer aan; *(inf)* So you want to borrow my car? ~ it! Dus jij wil mijn auto lenen? Vergeet het maar!; *not ~ting* en niet te vergeten, en ook

²forget [fəg**e**t] *vb* vergeten, nalaten, verwaarlozen: ~ *to do sth.* iets nalaten te doen

forget-me-not vergeet-mij-nietjeʰ

forgive [fəg**i**v] vergeven

forgo [fo:g**oo**] zich onthouden van, afstand doen van, het zonder (iets) doen

¹fork [fo:k] *n* **1** vork, hooivork, mestvork; **2** tweesprong, splitsing

²fork [fo:k] *vb* **1** zich vertakken, zich splitsen, uiteengaan; **2** afslaan, een richting opgaan: ~ *right* rechtsaf slaan

fork out (geld) dokken

forlorn [fəl**o**:n] **1** verlaten, eenzaam; **2** hopeloos, troosteloos || ~ *hope* hopeloze onderneming, laatste hoop

¹form [fo:m] *n* **1** (verschijnings)vorm, gedaante, silhouetʰ; **2** vorm, soort, systeemʰ; **3** vorm(geving), opzet, presentatiewijze; **4** formulierʰ, voorgedrukt velʰ; **5** formaliteit, vast gebruikʰ, gewoonte: *true to* ~ geheel in stijl, zoals gebruikelijk; **6** *(sport)* conditie, vorm: *be on* ~, *be in great* ~ goed op dreef zijn; **7** manier, wijze, vorm; **8** (school)klas: *first* ~ eerste klas

²form [fo:m] *vb* **1** vormen, modelleren, vorm geven; **2** maken, opvatten *(plan)*, construeren, samenstellen: ~ *(a) part of* deel uitmaken van

³form [fo:m] *vb* zich vormen, verschijnen, zich ontwikkelen

formal [f**o**:ml] formeel, officieel, volgens de regels

formality [fo:mæl**i**ttie] **1** vormelijkheid, stijfheid; **2** formaliteit

¹format [f**o**:mæt] *n* **1** (boek)formaatʰ, afmeting, grootte, uitvoering; **2** manier van samenstellen, opzet; **3** (beschrijving van) opmaak, indeling *(of data)*

²format [f**o**:mæt] *vb* formatteren, opmaken, indelen *(data etc)*

formation [fo:m**ee**sjən] **1** vorming; **2** formatie, opstelling, verbandʰ

formative [f**o**:mətiv] vormend, vormings-: *the* ~ *years of his career* de beginjaren van zijn loopbaan

formatting [f**o**:mæting] het formatteren, opmaak

¹former [f**o**:mə] *n* leerling *(of certain form)*: *second-* ~ tweedeklasser

²former [f**o**:mə] *pron* **1** eerste, eerstgenoemde *(of two)*; **2** vroeger, voorafgaand, vorig: *in* ~ *days* in vroeger dagen

formerly [f**o**:məlie] vroeger, eertijds, voorheen

formidable [f**o**:midəbl] **1** ontzagwekkend, gevreesd; **2** formidabel, geweldig, indrukwekkend

formula [f**o**:mjoelə] **1** formule, formulering, formulierʰ, *(fig)* clichéʰ; **2** formule, samenstelling, receptʰ

formulate [f**o**:mjoeleet] **1** formuleren; **2** opstellen, ontwerpen, samenstellen

forsake [fəs**ee**k] verlaten, in de steek laten, opgeven

fort [fo:t] fortʰ, vesting, sterkte || *hold the* ~ de zaken waarnemen, op de winkel letten

forth [fo:θ] voort, te voorschijn: *bring* ~: *a)* voortbrengen, veroorzaken; *b)* baren; *hold* ~ uitweiden; *and so* ~ enzovoort(s)

forthcoming [fo:θk**u**mming] **1** aanstaand, verwacht, aangekondigd: *her* ~ *album* haar binnenkort te verschijnen album; **2** tegemoetkomend, behulpzaam; **3** *(also with negation)* beschikbaar, ter beschikking: *an explanation was not* ~ een verklaring bleef uit

forthright [f**o**:θrajt] rechtuit, openhartig, direct

fortieth [f**o**:tiəθ] veertigste, veerstigste deelʰ

fortification [fo:tiffikk**ee**sjən] versterking, fortificatie

fortify [f**o**:tiffaj] versterken, verstevigen

fortitude [f**o**:titjoe:d] standvastigheid, vastberadenheid

fortnight [f**o**:tnajt] veertien dagen, twee weken: *a* ~ *on Monday: a)* maandag over veertien dagen; *b)* maandag veertien dagen geleden; *Tuesday* ~ dinsdag over veertien dagen

fortress [f**o**:tris] vesting, versterkte stad, fortʰ

fortuitous [fo:tj**oe**:ittəs] **1** toevallig, onvoorzien; **2** *(inf)* gelukkig

fortunate [f**o**:tsjənət] gelukkig, fortuinlijk, gunstig

fortune [f**o**:tsjoe:n] **1** fortuinʰ, voorspoed, gelukʰ; **2** lotgevalʰ, (toekomstige) belevenis: *tell* ~ de toekomst voorspellen; **3** fortuinʰ, vermogenʰ, rijkdom: *she spends a* ~ *on clothes* ze geeft een vermogen uit aan kleren

fortune-teller waarzegger

forty [f**o**:tie] veertig

¹forward [f**o**:wəd] *adj* **1** voorwaarts, naar voren (gericht); **2** vroegrijp: *a* ~ *girl* een vroegrijp meisje; **3** arrogant, brutaal; **4** voorst, vooraan gelegen; **5** gevorderd, opgeschoten; **6** vooruitstrevend, modern, geavanceerd; **7** termijn-, op termijn: ~ *planning* toekomstplanning

²forward [f**o**:wəd] *n* *(sport)* voorspeler: *centre* ~ middenvoor

³forward [f**o**:wəd] *vb* **1** doorzenden, nazenden *(mail)*; **2** zenden, (ver)sturen, verzenden

⁴forward [f**o**:wəd] *adv* **1** voorwaarts, vooruit, naar voren *(in space; also fig)*: *backward(s) and* ~ vooruit en achteruit, heen en weer; **2** vooruit, vooraf, op termijn *(in time)*: *from today* ~ vanaf heden

forwards [f**o**:wədz] voorwaarts, vooruit, naar voren

fossil [f**o**sl] fossielʰ

foster [f**o**stə] **1** koesteren, aanmoedigen, *(fig)* voeden; **2** opnemen in het gezin, als pleegkind opnemen *(without adoption)*: ~ *parent* pleegouder

¹foul [faul] *adj* **1** vuil, stinkend, smerig, vies: ~ *weather* smerig weer; **2** vuil, vulgair: *a* ~ *temper* een vreselijk humeur; ~ *language* vuile taal; **3** *(sport)* onsportief, gemeen, vals: *(oft fig)* ~ *play* onsportief spel, boze opzet, misdaad; *fall* ~ *(of)* in aanvaring komen (met)

²foul [faul] *n (sport)* overtreding, fout

³foul [faul] *vb (sport)* een overtreding begaan, in de fout gaan

⁴foul [faul] *vb* **1** bevuilen, bekladden; **2** *(sport)* een overtreding begaan tegenover

foul-mouthed ruw in de mond, vulgair

foul-up 1 verwarring, onderbreking; **2** blokkering, mechanisch defectʰ

found 1 grondvesten, funderen *(also fig)*; **2** stichten, oprichten, tot stand brengen: *this bakery was ~ed in 1793* deze bakkerij is in 1793 opgericht

foundation [faundeesjən] **1** stichting, fondsʰ, oprichting; **2** fundering *(also fig)*, fundamentʰ, basis: *the story is completely without ~* het verhaal is totaal ongegrond

¹founder [faundə] *n* stichter, oprichter, grondlegger

²founder [faundə] *vb* **1** invallen, instorten, mislukken: *the project ~ed on the ill will of the government* het project mislukte door de onwil van de regering; **2** zinken, vergaan, schipbreuk lijden

foundling [faundling] vondeling

foundry [faundrie] (metaal)gieterij

fountain [fauntin] **1** fontein: *~ pen* vulpen; **2** bron *(also fig)*

four [fo:] vier, viertal, vierspan || *be on all ~s* op handen en knieën lopen, kruipen

four-leaved clover klavertjevierʰ

foursome [fo:səm] viertalʰ, kwartetʰ

foursquare 1 vierkant, vierhoekig; **2** resoluut, open en eerlijk, vastbesloten

fourteen [fo:tie:n] veertien

fourteenth [fo:tie:nθ] veertiende, veertiende deelʰ

fourth [fo:θ] vierde, vierde deelʰ, kwart

fowl [faul] kip, hoenʰ, haan

¹fox [foks] *n* vos *(also fig)*

²fox [foks] *vb* doen alsof

³fox [foks] *vb* **1** beetnemen, bedriegen, te slim af zijn; **2** in de war brengen

fraction [fræksjən] **1** breuk, gebroken getalʰ: *decimal ~* tiendelige breuk; *vulgar ~* (gewone) breuk; **2** fractie, (zeer) klein onderdeelʰ

fractious [fræksjəs] **1** onhandelbaar, dwars, lastig; **2** humeurig, prikkelbaar

fracture [fræktsjə] **1** fractuur, (bot)breuk, beenbreuk; **2** scheur, barst, breuk

fragile [frædzjajl] breekbaar, broos

fragment [frægmənt] fragmentʰ, deelʰ, (brok)stuk

fragmentation [frægmənteesjən] versplintering

fragrance [freegrəns] geur, (zoete) geurigheid

frail [freel] breekbaar, zwak, tenger, teer

¹frame [freem] *n* **1** (het dragende) geraamte *(of construction)*, skeletʰ *(wood construction)*, frameʰ *(of bicycle)*, raamwerkʰ, chassisʰ; **2** omlijsting, kaderʰ, kozijnʰ, montuur *(of glasses)*, raamʰ *(of window etc)*; **3** *(oft fig)* (gestructureerd) geheelʰ, structuur, opzet: *~(s) of reference* referentiekader; *~ of mind* gemoedsgesteldheid

²frame [freem] *vb* **1** vorm geven aan, ontwerpen, uit-

denken, formuleren, uitdrukken, vormen, vervaardigen, verzinnen, zich inbeelden; **2** inlijsten, omlijsten, als achtergrond dienen voor; **3** *(inf)* erin luizen, in de val laten lopen, (opzettelijk) vals beschuldigen: *the swindlers were ~d* de zwendelaars werden in de val gelokt

frame-up complotʰ, gearrangeerde beschuldiging, valstrik

France [fra:ns] Frankrijk

franchise [fræntsjajz] **1** stemrechtʰ, burgerrechtʰ; **2** concessie; **3** franchise, systeemlicentie

¹frank [frængk] *adj (with with)* openhartig (tegen), oprecht, eerlijk

²frank [frængk] *vb* **1** frankeren; **2** stempelen, automatisch frankeren

frankly [frængklie] eerlijk gezegd: *~, I don't like it* eerlijk gezegd vind ik het niet leuk

frantic [fræntik] **1** dol, buiten zichzelf, uitzinnig: *the noise drove me ~* het lawaai maakte me hoorndol; **2** *(inf)* verwoed, extreem: *~ efforts* verwoede pogingen

fraternal [frətə:nl] broederlijk *(also fig)*, vriendelijk

fraternity [frətə:nittie] **1** broederlijkheid; **2** genootschapʰ, broederschap, vereniging: *the medical ~* de medische stand; **3** *(Am)* studentencorpsʰ, studentenclub *(for men)*

fraud [fro:d] **1** bedrogʰ, fraude, zwendel; **2** bedrieger, oplichter; **3** vervalsing, bedriegerij, oplichterij: *the newly-discovered Rembrandt was a ~* de pas ontdekte Rembrandt was een vervalsing

fraudulence [fro:djoeləns] bedrogʰ, bedrieglijkheid

fraught [fro:t] vol, beladen: *the journey was ~ with danger* het was een reis vol gevaren

¹fray [free] *vb* (uit)rafelen, verslijten

²fray [free] *vb* verzwakken, uitputten: *~ed nerves* overbelaste zenuwen

³fray [free] *n* strijd, gevechtʰ, twist: *eager for the ~* strijdlustig

¹freak [frie:k] *n* **1** gril, kuur, nuk; **2** uitzonderlijk verschijnselʰ; **3** *(inf)* fanaticus, freak, fanaat

²freak [frie:k] *adj* abnormaal, uitzonderlijk, ongewoon: *a ~ accident* een bizar ongeval; *~ weather* typisch weer

freckle [frekl] (zomer)sproet

¹free [frie:] *adj* **1** vrij, onafhankelijk, onbelemmerd: *a ~ agent* iem die vrij kan handelen; *~ fight* algemeen gevecht; *give (of: allow) s.o. a ~ hand* iem de vrije hand laten; *(socc) ~ kick* vrije schop; *~ speech* vrijheid van meningsuiting; *set ~* vrijlaten, in vrijheid stellen; *~ from care* vrij van zorgen, onbekommerd; *~ of charge* gratis, kosteloos; **2** vrij, gratis, belastingvrij: *(inf) for ~* gratis, voor niets; **3** vrij, zonder staatsinmenging: *~ enterprise* (de) vrije onderneming; *~ trade* vrije handel, vrijhandel; **4** vrij, niet bezet, niet in gebruik, *(science)* ongebonden: *is this seat ~?* is deze plaats vrij?; **5** vrijmoedig, vrijpostig: *~ and easy* ongedwongen, zorgeloos; *~*

pardon gratie(verlening)

²free [frie:] *adv* **1** vrij, los, ongehinderd: *the dogs ran ~ de honden liepen los;* **2** gratis

³free [frie:] *vb* **1** bevrijden, vrijlaten; **2** verlossen, losmaken, vrijstellen

freebie [frie:bie] *(inf)* weggevertje[h], iets dat je gratis krijgt

freebooter [frie:boe:tə] vrijbuiter *(oft fig)*, kaper

freedom [frie:dəm] **1** vrijheid, onafhankelijkheid: *~ of the press* persvrijheid; *~ of speech* vrijheid van meningsuiting; **2** vrijstelling, ontheffing, vrijwaring

¹freelance [frie:la:ns] *adj* freelance, onafhankelijk, zelfstandig

²freelance [frie:la:ns] *vb* freelance werken, als freelancer werken

freeload [frie:lood] klaplopen, profiteren, bietsen

freeman [frie:mən] **1** vrij man; **2** ereburger

freemason vrijmetselaar

freephone [frie:foon] het gratis bellen *(eg an 0800 number)*

freepost antwoordnummer[h] || *~ no. 1111* antwoordnummer 1111

free-range scharrel-: *~ eggs* scharreleieren

freesia [frie:ziə] fresia

freestyle 1 *(swimming)* vrije slag, (borst)crawl; **2** *(wrestling etc)* vrije stijl

freeway *(Am)* snelweg, autoweg

freewheel rustig aandoen *(also fig)*

¹freeze [frie:z] *vb* bevriezen *(also fig)*, verstijven; ijzig behandelen, opschorten: *make one's blood ~ het bloed in de aderen doen stollen; ~ out (inf)* uitsluiten; *frozen with fear* verstijfd van angst

²freeze [frie:z] *vb* vriezen: *it is freezing in here* het is hier om te bevriezen; *the government froze all contracts* de regering bevroor alle contracten

³freeze [frie:z] *n* **1** vorst, vorstperiode; **2** bevriezing, blokkering, opschorting: *a wage ~* een loonstop

freezer [frie:zə] **1** diepvries, diepvriezer; **2** vriesvak[h]

freight [freet] vracht(goederen)

¹French [frentsj] *n* Frans, de Franse taal

²French [frentsj] *adj* Frans: *~ bread* (of: *loaf)* stokbrood; *~ bean* sperzieboon; *~ fries* patat, friet; *~ kiss* tongzoen; *take ~ leave* er tussenuit knijpen; *~ windows* openslaande (balkon-, terras)deuren

Frenchman [frentsjmən] Fransman

Frenchwoman Française, Franse

frenzy [frenzie] (vlaag van) waanzin, razernij, staat van opwinding

frequency [frie:kwənsie] **1** frequentie, (herhaald) voorkomen[h]; **2** *(science)* frequentie, trillingsgetal[h], periodetal[h]; **3** *(radio)* frequentie, golflengte

¹frequent [frie:kwənt] *adj* frequent, veelvuldig: *a ~ caller* een regelmatig bezoeker

²frequent [friekwent] *vb* regelmatig bezoeken

fresh [fresj] **1** vers, pas gebakken, vers geplukt: *~ from the oven* zo uit de oven, ovenvers; **2** nieuw, ander, recent: *a ~ attempt* een hernieuwde poging; **3** zoet *(of water)*, niet brak; **4** zuiver, helder, levendig: *~ air* frisse lucht; **5** fris, koel, nogal koud: *a ~ breeze* een frisse bries *(wind force 5);* **6** *(inf)* brutaal, flirterig

freshen [fresjən] in kracht toenemen, aanwakkeren

freshen up 1 opfrissen, verfrissen; **2** zich opfrissen, zich verfrissen

freshman [fresjmən] eerstejaars(student), groene

freshwater zoetwater-

fret [fret] zich ergeren, zich opvreten (van ergernis), zich zorgen maken: *the child is ~ting for its mother* het kind zit om z'n moeder te zeuren

fretful [fretfoel] geïrriteerd, zeurderig

fretsaw [fretso:] figuurzaag

friar [frajjə] monnik, broeder

friction [friksjən] wrijving *(also fig)*, frictie, onenigheid

Friday [frajdee] vrijdag

fridge [fridzj] *refrigerator (inf)* koelkast, ijskast

fried gebakken: *~ egg* spiegelei

friend [frend] **1** vriend(in), kameraad, kennis, collega: *make ~s with s.o.* bevriend raken met; *can be still be ~?* kunnen we vrienden blijven?; *a ~ in need (is a friend indeed)* in nood leert men zijn vrienden kennen; **2** vriend(in), voorstander, liefhebber

friendly [frendlie] **1** vriendelijk, welwillend, aardig; **2** vriendschappelijk, bevriend, gunstig gezind: *~ nations* bevriende naties

friendship [frendsjip] vriendschap

Friesian [frie:zjən] *see* Frisian

frieze [frie:z] fries+[h], sierlijst

frigate [frigət] fregat[h]

fright [frajt] angst, vrees, schrik: *give a ~* de schrik op 't lijf jagen; *he took ~ at the sight of the knife* de schrik sloeg hem om 't hart toen hij het mes zag

frighten [frajtn] bang maken, doen schrikken, afschrikken: *we were ~ed to death* we schrokken ons dood; *~ s.o. to death* iem de stuipen op het lijf jagen; *be ~ed of snakes* bang voor slangen zijn

frigid [fridzjid] **1** koud *(also fig)*, koel, onvriendelijk; **2** frigide

frill [fril] **1** (sier)strook; **2** *~s* franje *(also fig)*, fraaiigheden, kouwe drukte

fringe [frindzj] **1** franje; **2** randgroepering, randverschijnsel[h]: *the ~s of society* de zelfkant van de maatschappij; **3** pony(haar[h])

frisbee [frizbie] frisbee

Frisian [frizziən] Fries

¹frisk [frisk] *vb* huppelen, springen

²frisk [frisk] *vb* fouilleren

frisky [friskie] vrolijk, speels

fritter away verkwisten, verspillen

frivolous [frivvələs] **1** onbelangrijk, pietluttig, onnozel; **2** frivool, lichtzinnig

frizz [friz] kroeskop, kroeshaar[h], krul(len)

¹frizzle [frizl] *vb* **1** krullen, kroezen; **2** sissen, knetteren *(in pan)*

²frizzle [frizl] *vb* **1** kroezend maken, doen krullen: *~ up* friseren; **2** laten sissen, laten knetteren *(in pan)*, braden, bakken

fro [froo] *see* to

frock [frok] jurk, japon

frog [frog] kikker, kikvors

frogman [frogmən] kikvorsman

¹frolic [frollik] *n* pret, lol, gekheid: *the little boys were having a* ~ de jongetjes waren aan het stoeien

²frolic [frollik] *vb* **1** (rond)dartelen, rondhossen; **2** pret maken

from [from] van, vanaf, vanuit: ~ *one day to the next* van de ene dag op de andere; *judge* ~ *the facts* oordelen naar de feiten; *I heard* ~ *Mary* ik heb bericht gekregen van Mary; *recite* ~ *memory* uit het geheugen opzeggen; ~ *bad to worse* van kwaad tot erger; *(in) a week* ~ *now* over een week

¹front [frunt] *n* **1** voorkant, voorste gedeelteʰ: *the driver sits in (the)* ~ de bestuurder zit voorin; *in* ~ *of* voor, in aanwezigheid van; **2** *(mil)* frontʰ *(also fig)*, gevechtslinie; **3** façade *(also fig)*, schijn, dekmantel: *show (of: put on) a bold* ~ zich moedig voordoen; **4** (strand)boulevard, promenade langs de rivier; **5** *(meteorology)* frontʰ

²front [frunt] *adj* **1** voorst, eerst: ~ *garden* voortuin; ~ *runner* koploper; **2** façade-, camouflage-: ~ *organisation* mantelorganisatie; *up* ~ eerlijk, rechtdoorzee

frontal [fruntl] frontaal, voor-: ~ *attack* frontale aanval

frontier [fruntiə] grens(gebiedʰ): *the ~s of knowledge* de onontgonnen gebieden der wetenschap

front page voorpagina *(of newspaper)*

front runner *(athletics)* koploper

¹frost [frost] *n* vorst, bevriezing: *there was five degrees of* ~ het vroor vijf graden

²frost [frost] *vb* **1** bevriezen *(plant etc)*; **2** glaceren *(cake)*; **3** matteren *(glas, metal)*: ~ed glass matglas

frostbite bevriezing

frosty [frostie] vriezend, (vries)koud, *(fig)* ijzig, afstandelijk: ~ *welcome* koele verwelkoming

¹froth [froθ] *n* **1** schuimʰ; **2** oppervlakkigheid, zeepbel; **3** gebazelʰ

²froth [froθ] *vb* schuimen, schuimbekken

¹frown [fraun] *vb* de wenkbrauwen fronsen, streng kijken, turen: *(fig)* ~ *at (of: on)* afkeuren(d staan tegenover)

²frown [fraun] *n* frons, fronsende blik, afkeuring

frozen **1** bevroren, vastgevroren, doodgevroren: ~ *over* dichtgevroren; **2** (ijs)koud *(also fig)*, ijzig, hard; **3** diepvries-, ingevroren: ~ *food* diepvriesvoedsel; **4** *(econ)* bevroren, geblokkeerd: ~ *assets* bevroren tegoeden

frugal [froe:gl] **1** *(with of)* zuinig (met), spaarzaam (met); **2** schraal, karig, sober

fruit [froe:t] **1** vrucht, stukʰ fruit; **2** fruitʰ, vruchten; **3** ~s opbrengst, resultaatʰ

fruiterer [froe:tərə] fruithandelaar, fruitkoopman

fruitful [froe:tfoel] vruchtbaar *(also fig)*, productief, lonend

fruition [froe:isjən] vervulling, verwezenlijking, re-

alisatie: *bring (of: come) to* ~ in vervulling doen gaan

fruit machine fruitautomaat, gokautomaat

frustrate [frustreet] frustreren, verijdelen: ~ *s.o. in his plans*, ~ *s.o.'s plans* iemands plannen dwarsbomen

frustration [frustreesjən] **1** frustratie, teleurstelling; **2** verijdeling, dwarsboming

¹fry [fraj] *vb* braden, bakken, frituren: *fried egg* spiegelei

²fry [fraj] *n* jong(e vis), broed(selʰ), *(fig)* kleintje ᵃ, jonkieʰ

ft. *foot, feet* ft, voet

fuck [fuk] *(vulg)* neuken, naaien, wippen

fuddled [fudld] verward, in de war, beneveld, dronken

¹fudge [fudzj] *n* **1** onzin, larie; **2** zachte karamel

²fudge [fudzj] *vb* **1** knoeien (met), vervalsen; **2** er omheen draaien, ontwijken; **3** in elkaar flansen

fuel [fjoeəl] brandstof, *(fig)* voedselʰ: ~ *for dissension* stof tot onenigheid

fug [fug] bedomptheid, mufheid

fugitive [fjoe:dzjittiv] vluchteling, voortvluchtige

fugue [fjoe:g] fuga

fulfil [foelfil] volbrengen, vervullen, uitvoeren, voltooien: ~ *a condition* aan een voorwaarde voldoen; ~ *a purpose* aan een doel beantwoorden

¹full [foel] *adj* vol, volledig: ~ *board* vol(ledig) pension; ~ *to the brim* boordevol; *come* ~ *circle* weer terugkomen bij het begin; *(fig) give* ~ *marks for sth.* iets hoog aanslaan, iets erkennen; ~ *moon* vollemaan; *(at)* ~ *speed* (in) volle vaart; ~ *stop* punt *(punctuation mark); come to a* ~ *stop* (plotseling) tot stilstand komen; *in* ~ *swing* in volle gang; ~ *of oneself* vol van zichzelf; *he was* ~ *of it* hij was er vol van

²full [foel] *adv* **1** volledig, ten volle: ~ *ripe* helemaal rijp; **2** zeer, heel: *know sth.* ~ *well* iets zeer goed weten; **3** vlak, recht: *hit s.o.* ~ *on the nose* iem recht op zijn neus slaan

³full [foel] *n* totaalʰ, geheelʰ: *in* ~ volledig, voluit

full-blooded 1 volbloed, raszuiver; **2** volbloedig, energiek

full-blown 1 in volle bloei; **2** goed ontwikkeld, volledig: ~ *war* regelrechte oorlog

full-grown volwassen, volgroeid

full-scale volledig, totaal, levensgroot

full-time fulltime, met volledige dagtaak

fully [foelie] **1** volledig, geheel: ~ *automatic* volautomatisch; **2** minstens, ten minste: ~ *an hour* minstens een uur

fully-fledged 1 geheel bevederd *(of bird)*; **2** volwassen, ten volle ontwikkeld; **3** (ras)echt, volslagen

fulsome [foelsəm] overdreven

¹fumble [fumbl] *vb* struikelen, hakkelen, klunzen

²fumble [fumbl] *vb* **1** tasten, morrelen (aan), rommelen (in): ~ *about* rondtasten; **2** *(ballgame)* fumbelen

¹fume [fjoe:m] *vb* **1** roken, dampen; **2** opstijgen *(of*

fume); 3 (fig) koken *(with rage),* branden

²fume [fjoe:m] *n* (onwelriekende, giftige) damp, rook

fumigate [fjoe:migeet] uitroken, zuiveren

¹fun [fun] *n* pret, vermaakʰ, plezierʰ: *figure of ~* groteske figuur, schertsfiguur; *~ and games* pretmakerij, iets leuks; *make ~ of, poke ~ at* voor de gek houden, de draak steken met; *for ~, for the ~ of it* (of: *the thing*) voor de aardigheid; *for ~, in ~* voor de grap

²fun [fun] *adj* prettig, amusant, gezellig: *a ~ guy* een leuke kerel; *a ~ game* een leuk spelletje

¹function [fungksjən] *n* **1** functie, taak, werking; **2** plechtigheid, ceremonie

²function [fungksjən] *vb* functioneren, werken: *~ as* fungeren als

functional [fungksjənəl] functioneel, doelmatig, bruikbaar

functionary [fungksjənərie] functionaris, beambte

fund [fund] **1** fondsʰ; **2** voorraad, bron, schat: *a ~ of knowledge* een schat aan kennis; **3** *~s* fondsen, geldʰ, kapitaalʰ: *short of ~s* slecht bij kas

¹fundamental [fundəmentl] *adj* fundamenteel, grond-, basis-

²fundamental [fundəmentl] *n* (grond)beginselʰ, grondslag, fundamentʰ

funeral [fjoe:nərəl] **1** begrafenis(plechtigheid); *(Am)* rouwdienst; **2** *(Am)* begrafenisstoet; **3** *(inf)* zorg, zaak: *it's is your ~* het is jouw zorg

funereal [fjoenjəriəl] akelig, droevig, triest: *a ~ expression* begrafenisgezicht

funfair 1 pretparkʰ, amusementsparkʰ; **2** reizende kermis

fungus [funggəs] fungus, paddestoel, schimmel

funicular [fjoenikjoelə] kabelbaan

funk [fungk] *(inf)* schrik, angst: *be in a (blue) ~* in de rats zitten

funky [fungkie] *(Am; inf)* funky, eenvoudig, gevoelsmatig *(of music)*

¹funnel [funl] *n* **1** trechter; **2** koker, pijp, schoorsteen(pijp) *(of steamship)*

²funnel [funl] *vb* afvoeren (als) door een trechter: *~ off* doen afvloeien

funny [funnie] **1** grappig, leuk; **2** vreemd, gek; **3** niet in orde, niet pluis: *there is sth. ~ about* er is iets niet pluis met; **4** misselijk, onwel: *feel ~* zich onwel voelen; *~ bone* telefoonbotje *(in elbow)*

fur [fə:] **1** vacht; **2** bontʰ, pels(werkʰ), bontjas; **3** aanslag, beslagʰ

furious [fjoeəriəs] **1** woedend, razend; **2** fel, verwoed, heftig: *a ~ quarrel* een felle twist

furnace [fə:nis] oven, verwarmingsketel, hoogoven

furnish [fə:nisj] **1** verschaffen, leveren, voorzien van; **2** uitrusten, meubileren, inrichten: *a ~ed house* een gemeubileerd huis

furniture [fə:nitsjə] meubilairʰ, meubels

furrow [furroo] **1** voorʰ, gleuf, groef, rimpel; **2** zogʰ, spoorʰ *(of ship)*

¹further [fə:ðə] *adj* verder, nader: *on ~ consideration* bij nader inzien; *~ education* voortgezet onderwijs voor volwassenen

²further [fə:ðə] *adv* verder, nader, elders: *inquire ~* nadere inlichtingen inwinnen

³further [fə:ðə] *vb* bevorderen, stimuleren: *~ s.o.'s interests* iemands belangen behartigen

furthermore [fə:ðəmo:] verder, bovendien

furthermost [fə:ðəmoost] verst (verwijderd)

furthest [fə:ðist] verst, laatst, meest

furtive [fə:tiv] heimelijk

fury [fjoeərie] woede(aanval), razernij

¹fuse [fjoe:z] *n* **1** lont; **2** (schok)buis, ontsteker; **3** zekering, stop

²fuse [fjoe:z] *vb* **1** (doen) fuseren *(of businesses etc)*; **2** (doen) uitvallen *(of electrical appliance)*

fusion [fjoe:zjən] fusie(procesʰ), (samen)smelting, mengeling, coalitie, kernfusie

¹fuss [fus] *n* (nodeloze) drukte, omhaal, ophef: *I don't understand what all the ~ is about* ik snap niet waar al die heisa om gemaakt wordt; *kick up* (of: *make*) *a ~* heibel maken, luidruchtig protesteren; *make a ~ of* (of: *over*) overdreven aandacht schenken aan

²fuss [fus] *vb (with about)* zich druk maken (om), drukte maken, zich opwinden: *~ about* zenuwachtig rondlopen

fussy [fussie] **1** (overdreven) druk, zenuwachtig, bemoeieziek; **2** pietluttig, moeilijk: *(inf) I'm not ~* het is mij om het even

futile [fjoe:tajl] vergeefs, doelloos

futility [fjoe:tillitie] nutteloosheid, doelloosheid

¹future [fjoe:tsjə] *n* toekomst: *in the distant ~* in de verre toekomst; *for the* (of: *in*) *~* voortaan, in 't vervolg

²future [fjoe:tsjə] *adj* toekomstig, aanstaande: *~ tense* toekomende tijd

fuzz [fuz] **1** donsʰ, pluis, donzig haarʰ; **2** *(inf)* smeris *(policeman)*; de smerissen *(the police)*

fuzzy [fuzzie] **1** donzig, pluizig; **2** kroes, krullig; **3** vaag; **4** verward

g

g *gram(s)* g, gram
gabble [gæbl] kakelen, kwebbelen: ~ *away* erop los kletsen
gable [geebl] gevelspits, geveltop
gabled [geebld] met gevelspits
gadfly paardenvlieg, horzel
gadget [gædzjit] (handig) dingetjeʰ, apparaatjeʰ, snufjeʰ
gadgetry [gædzjitrie] snufjes
Gaelic [geelik] Gaelisch
gaffer [gæfə] chef-technicus *(at TV or film shootings)*
¹gag [gæg] *n* **1** (mond)prop; **2** (zorgvuldig voorbereid) komisch effectʰ; **3** grap
²gag [gæg] *vb* kokhalzen, braken: ~ *on sth.* zich in iets verslikken
³gag [gæg] *vb* een prop in de mond stoppen
gaga [ga:ga:] **1** kierewiet: *go* ~ kinds worden; **2** stapel: *be* ~ *about* stapel zijn op
gaiety [geeətie] vrolijkheid, pret, opgewektheid
¹gain [geen] *vb* **1** winst maken; **2** winnen: ~ *(up)on* terrein winnen op, inhalen; **3** groeien; **4** voorlopen *(of timepiece): my watch ~s (three minutes a day)* mijn horloge loopt (elke dag drie minuten meer) voor
²gain [geen] *vb* winnen, verkrijgen, behalen: ~ *the victory (of: the day)* de overwinning behalen; ~ *weight* aankomen
³gain [geen] *n* **1** aanwinst; **2** groei, stijging, verhoging; **3** ~*s* winst, opbrengst
gait [geet] gang, pas, loop
gal [gæl] meid, meisjeʰ
gal. *gallon(s)*
galaxy [gæləksie] melkweg
gale [geel] storm, harde wind
¹gall [go:l] *n* **1** gal(blaas); **2** bitterheid, rancune; **3** galnoot, galappel; **4** brutaliteit
²gall [go:l] *vb* (mateloos) irriteren, razend maken
gallant [gælənt] dapper, moedig, indrukwekkend *(of ship, horse)*
gallantry [gæləntrie] **1** moedige daad; **2** moed, dapperheid; **3** hoffelijkheid
gall bladder galblaas
galleon [gæliən] galjoenʰ
gallery [gælərie] **1** galerij, portiek, (zuilen)gang; **2** galerij, balkonʰ; **3** museumʰ, museumzaal; **4**

(kunst)galerie; **5** engelenbak
galley [gælie] **1** galei; **2** kombuis
Gallic [gælik] Gallisch, Frans
gallicize [gælissajz] verfransen
gallon [gælən] gallon *(measure of capacity)*
¹gallop [go:l] *n* galop: *at a* ~ in galop, op een galop, *(fig)* op een holletje
²gallop [go:l] *vb* galopperen, *(fig)* zich haasten, vliegen
gallows [gælooz] galg
gallows humour galgenhumor
gallstone galsteen
galore [gəlo:] in overvloed, genoeg: *examples* ~ voorbeelden te over
galvanic [gælvænik] opwindend, opzienbarend
galvanize [gælvənajz] prikkelen, opzwepen: ~ *s.o. into action* (of: *activity*) iem tot actie aansporen
¹gamble [gæmbl] *vb* **1** gokken, spelen, dobbelen: ~ *on* gokken op; **2** speculeren
²gamble [gæmbl] *vb* op het spel zetten, inzetten: ~ *away* vergokken
³gamble [gæmbl] *n* gok(jeʰ) *(also fig)*, riskante zaak, speculatie: *take a* ~ *(on)* een gokje wagen (op); *it is a* ~ het is een gok
gambler [gæmblə] gokker
gambling [gæmbling] gokkerij
¹game [geem] *n* **1** spelʰ *(also fig)*, wedstrijd, partij: ~ *of chance* kansspel; *play the* ~ eerlijk (spel) spelen, zich aan de regels houden; *it is all in the* ~ het hoort er (allemaal) bij; **2** spelletjeʰ, tijdverdrijfʰ; **3** tennis game: *(one)* ~ *all* gelijk(e stand); ~ *and (set)* game en set; **4** plannetjeʰ: *two can play (at) that* ~ dat spelletje kan ik ook spelen; *none of your (little)* ~*s!* geen kunstjes!; *the* ~ *is up* het spel is uit, nu hangen jullie; **5** jachtdierʰ, prooi *(also fig)*; **6** ~*s* spelenʰ, (atletiek)wedstrijden; **7** ~*s* gym(nastiek), sport *(at school): beat* (of: *play*) *s.o. at his own* ~ iem een koekje van eigen deeg geven
²game [geem] *adj* **1** dapper, kranig, flink; **2** bereid(willig), enthousiast: *be* ~ *to do sth.* bereid zijn om iets te doen; *I am* ~ ik doe mee; **3** lam, kreupel *(of arm, leg)*
gamekeeper jachtopziener
games computer spelcomputer
game show spelshow
gammon [gæmən] **1** (gekookte) achterham; **2** gerookte ham
gander [gændə] mannetjesgans
gang [gæng] groep mensen, (boeven)bende, troep, ploeg *(workers): violent street* ~*s* gewelddadige straatbendes; *a* ~ *of labourers removing graffiti* een ploeg werklui die graffiti verwijderen
gangling [gængling] slungelig
gangplank loopplank
gangrene [gænggrie:n] **1** koudvuurʰ; **2** verrotting
gangster [gængstə] gangster, bendelidʰ
gang up een bende vormen, (samen)klieken, zich verenigen: ~ *against* (of: *on*) samenspannen tegen, aanvallen; ~ *with* zich aansluiten bij, samenspan-

nen met

gangway [gǽngwee] **1** doorgang; **2** (gang)pad^h *(in theatre etc)*; **3** loopplank

gaol [dzjeel] *see* jail

gap [gæp] (tussen)ruimte, opening, gat^h, kloof, barst, ravijn^h, tekort^h: *bridge* (of: *close, fill, stop) a* ~ een kloof overbruggen, een tekort aanvullen; *some developing countries are quickly closing the* ~ sommige ontwikkelingslanden lopen snel de achterstand in

gape [geep] **1** gapen, geeuwen; **2** geopend zijn, gapen: *gaping wound* gapende wond; **3** staren: ~ *at* aangapen, aanstaren

garage [gǽra:zj] garage, garagebedrijf^h, benzinestation^h

garb [ga:b] dracht, kledij

garbage [gá:bidzj] **1** afval^h, huisvuil^h; **2** rommel

garble [gá:bl] onvolledige voorstelling geven van, verkeerd voorstellen, verdraaien: ~*d account* verdraaide voorstelling

¹garden [gá:dn] *n* tuin *(also fig)*, groenten, bloementuin: *the* ~ *of Eden* de hof van Eden, het Aards Paradijs; *lead up the* ~ *(path)* om de tuin leiden

²garden [gá:dn] *vb* tuinieren

gardener [gá:dənə] tuinman, hovenier, tuinier

gardening [gá:dəning] het tuinieren, tuinbouw

garden party tuinfeest^h

gargle [gá:gl] gorgelen

gargoyle [gá:gojl] waterspuwer (als versiering op kerken e.d.)

garish [géərisj] **1** fel, schel; **2** bont, opzichtig

garland [gá:lənd] **1** slinger; **2** lauwer(krans)

garlic [gá:lik] knoflook^h

garment [gá:mənt] kledingstuk^h, ~*s* kleren

¹garnish [gá:nisj] *vb* garneren, verfraaien, opkloppen

²garnish [gá:nisj] *n* garnering, versiering

garret [gǽrət] zolderkamertje^h

garrison [gǽrisn] garnizoen^h, garnizoensplaats

garter [gá:tə] kousenband, jarretelle

gas [gæs] *(Am also* ~*ses)* **1** gas^h, gifgas^h, lachgas^h, mijngas^h: *natural* ~ aardgas; **2** benzine: *step on the* ~ gas geven, er vaart achter zetten; **3** *(vulg)* gezwam^h, kletspraat, geklets^h

gasbag kletsmeier

gas chamber gaskamer

gas fitter gasfitter

gash [gæsj] **1** jaap, gapende wond; **2** kloof, breuk

gasket [gǽskit] pakking

gaslight **1** gaslamp; **2** gaslicht^h

gas lighter gasaansteker, gasontsteker

gas main hoofd(gas)leiding

gasman meteropnemer

gasoline [gǽsəlie:n] **1** gasoline; **2** benzine

¹gasp [ga:sp] *vb* **1** (naar adem) snakken, naar lucht happen: ~ *for breath* naar adem snakken; **2** hijgen, puffen, snuiven

²gasp [ga:sp] *vb* haperend uitbrengen, hijgend uitbrengen: *'call an ambulance!' she* ~*ed* 'bel een zie-kenwagen!' hijgde ze

³gasp [ga:sp] *n* snik: *at one's last* ~ bij de laatste ademtocht

gas ring gaspit

gas station benzinestation^h, tankstation^h

gastric [gǽstrik] maag-

gastronome [gǽstrənoom] fijnproever

gastronomy [gæstrónnəmie] fijnproeverij

gasworks gasfabriek(en)

gate [geet] **1** poort(je^h), deur, hek^h, ingang, afsluitboom, slagboom, sluis(deur), schuif, uitgang *(at airport)*, perron^h: *anti-theft* ~*s* antidiefstalpoortjes; **2** *(sport)* publiek^h *(number of paying spectators)*: *a* ~ *of 2000* 2000 man publiek; **3** entreegelden

gatecrash (onuitgenodigd) binnenvallen *(at party etc)*

gatecrasher onuitgenodigde gast, indringer

gatekeeper portier^h

gatepost deurpost || *between you and me and the* ~ onder ons gezegd en gezwegen

gateway poort: *the* ~ *to success* de poort tot succes; *the* ~ *to Europe* de toegangspoort tot Europa

¹gather [gǽðə] *vb* **1** zich verzamelen, samenkomen: ~ *round* bijeenkomen; ~ *round s.o. (sth.)* zich rond iem (iets) scharen; **2** zich op(een)hopen, zich op(een)stapelen

²gather [gǽðə] *vb* **1** verzamelen, samenbrengen, bijeenroepen, op(een)hopen, op(een)stapelen, vergaren, inzamelen, plukken, oogsten, oprapen: ~ *(one's) strength* op krachten komen; ~ *wood* hout sprokkelen; ~ *speed* op snelheid komen; **2** opmaken, afleiden, concluderen: *your husband is not in I* ~ uw echtgenoot is niet thuis, begrijp ik; ~ *from* afleiden uit

gathering [gǽðəring] **1** bijeenkomst, vergadering; **2** verzameling, op(een)stapeling, op(een)hoping

gauche [goosj] onhandig, onbeholpen

gaudy [gó:die] opzichtig, schel, bont

¹gauge [geedzj] *n* **1** standaardmaat, ijkmaat; vermogen^h, capaciteit, inhoud, kaliber^h *(also of firearms)*: *narrow-~film* smalfilm; **2** meetinstrument^h, meter, kaliber^h

²gauge [geedzj] *vb* meten, uit-, af-, opmeten, peilen

gaunt [go:nt] **1** uitgemergeld, vel over been; **2** somber

gauntlet [gó:ntlit] kaphandschoen, sporthandschoen, werkhandschoen: *fling* (of: *throw) down the* ~ iem uitdagen; *pick* (of: *take) up the* ~ de uitdaging aanvaarden; *run the* ~ spitsroeden (moeten) lopen

gauze [go:z] gaas^h, verbandgaas^h, muggengaas^h

gavel [gǽvəl] voorzittershamer

gawky [gó:kie] klungelig, onhandig

¹gay [gee] *n* homo(seksueel); nicht; lesbienne

²gay [gee] *adj* **1** homoseksueel: ~ *marriage* (of: *blessing)* homohuwelijk; **2** vrolijk, opgeruimd; **3** fleurig, bont: ~ *colours* bonte kleuren

gaze [geez] staren, aangapen: ~ *at* (of: *on)* aanstaren

gazelle [gəzɛl] gazel(le), antilope
gazette [gəzɛt] krant, dagblad[h]
G.B. *Great Britain* Groot-Brittannië
G.C.E. *General Certificate of Education* middelbare-schooldiploma, havodiploma, vwo-diploma
GCSE *General Certificate of Secondary Education* eindexamen
¹gear [giə] *n* **1** toestel[h], mechanisme[h], apparaat[h], inrichting: *landing* ~ landingsgestel; **2** transmissie, koppeling, versnelling: *bottom* ~ eerste versnelling; *reverse* ~ achteruit; *top* ~ hoogste versnelling; *change* ~ (over)schakelen; **3** uitrusting, gereedschap[h], kledij, spullen: *hunting* ~ jagersuitrusting
²gear [giə] *vb* (over)schakelen, in (een) versnelling zetten: ~ *down* terugschakelen, vertragen; ~ *up* opschakelen, overschakelen
gearbox versnellingsbak
gearlever (versnellings)pook
gear to afstemmen op, instellen, afstellen op: *be geared to* ingesteld zijn op, berekend zijn op
gearwheel tandwiel[h], tandrad[h]
gee [dzjie:] jee(tje)!
geezer [gie:zə] (ouwe) vent
¹gel [dzjel] *n* gel
²gel [dzjel] *vb* **1** gel(ei)achtig worden, stollen; **2** vorm krijgen *(of ideas etc)*; goed kunnen samenwerken *(of people)*, lukken
gelatin [dzjɛlətin] gelatine(achtige stof)
geld [geld] castreren
gelding [gelding] castraat, gecastreerd paard[h], ruin
gem [dzjem] **1** edelsteen, juweel[h]; **2** kleinood[h], juweeltje[h]
Gemini [dzjemminnaj] (de) Tweelingen
gemstone (half)edelsteen
gender [dzjendə] (grammaticaal) geslacht[h]
gene [dzjie:n] gen[h]
genealogy [dzjie:nie·ælədzjie] genealogie, familiekunde
¹general [dzjennərəl] *adj* algemeen: ~ *anaesthetic* algehele verdoving; ~ *election* algemene, landelijke verkiezingen; *in the* ~ *interest* in het algemeen belang; *the* ~*public* het grote publiek; *as a* ~ *rule* in 't algemeen, doorgaans; ~ *delivery* poste restante; ~ *practitioner* huisarts
²general [dzjennərəl] *n* **1** algemeenheid, het algemeen: *in* ~ in het algemeen; **2** generaal, veldheer
generality [dzjennərælittie] algemeenheid
generalize [dzjennərəlajz] generaliseren, veralgemenen, (zich) vaag uitdrukken
generally [dzjennərəlie] **1** gewoonlijk, meestal; **2** algemeen: ~ *known* algemeen bekend; **3** in het algemeen, ruwweg: ~ *speaking* in 't algemeen
generate [dzjennəreet] genereren, doen ontstaan, voortbrengen: ~ *electricity* elektriciteit opwekken; ~ *heat* warmte ontwikkelen
generation [dzjennəreesjən] **1** generatie, (mensen)geslacht[h], mensenleven[h]; **2** generatie, voortplanting, ontwikkeling
generator [dzjennəreetə] generator

generic [dzjinnɛrrik] **1** de soort betreffende, generiek; **2** algemeen, verzamel-
generosity [dzjennərossittie] vrijgevigheid, gulheid
generous [dzjennərəs] **1** grootmoedig, edel(moedig); **2** vrijgevig, royaal, gul; **3** overvloedig, rijk(elijk)
genesis [dzjennissis] **1** *Genesis* (het bijbelboek) Genesis; **2** ontstaan[h], wording
genetic [dzjinnɛttik] genetisch: ~ *engineering* genetische manipulatie; ~ *fingerprint* genenprint
geneticist [dzjinnɛttissist] geneticus
genetics [dzjinnɛttiks] genetica, erfelijkheidsleer
Geneva [dzjinnie:və] Genève
genial [dzjie:niəl] **1** mild, zacht, aangenaam, warm *(of weather, climate etc)*; **2** vriendelijk, sympathiek
geniality [dzjie:nie·ælittie] hartelijkheid, sympathie, vriendelijkheid
genital [dzjennitl] genitaal, geslachts-, voortplantings-
genitalia [dzjennitteeliə] genitaliën, geslachtsorganen
genitive [dzjennittiv] genitief, tweede naamval
genius [dzjie:niəs] **1** genie[h] *(pers)*: *be a* ~ *at* geniaal zijn in; **2** genialiteit, begaafdheid: *a woman of* ~ een geniale vrouw; **3** geest: *evil* ~ kwade genius
Genoa [dzjennooə] Genua
genocide [dzjennəsajd] genocide, volkerenmoord
genre [zjonrə] genre[h], soort, type[h]
gent [dzjent] gentleman, heer || *(inf) the Gents* het herentoilet
genteel [dzjentie:l] **1** *(oft iron)* chic, elegant; **2** aanstellerig
¹gentile [dzjentajl] *adj* niet-joods; christelijk; ongelovig
²gentile [dzjentajl] *n* niet-jood; christen; heiden
gentility [dzjentillittie] deftigheid, voornaamheid
gentle [dzjentl] **1** voornaam, van goede afkomst; **2** zacht, licht, (ge)matig(d): ~ *pressure* lichte dwang; *hold it gently* hou het voorzichtig vast; **3** zacht(aardig), teder, vriendelijk: *the* ~ *sex* het zwakke geslacht; **4** kalm, bedaard, rustig
gentleman [dzjentlmən] **1** (echte) heer: *Ladies and Gentlemen!* Dames en Heren!; **2** edelman
gentleman's agreement herenakkoord[h]
gentry [dzjentrie] lage(re) adel, voorname stand: *landed* ~ (groot)grondbezitters, lage landadel
genuine [dzjenjoein] **1** echt, zuiver, onvervalst: ~ *parts* oorspronkelijke onderdelen; **2** oprecht, eerlijk
genus [dzjie:nəs] **1** soort, genre[h], klasse; **2** genus[h], geslacht[h]
geographer [dzjie·ogrəfə] aardrijkskundige, geograaf
geographic(al) [dzjiəgræfik(l)] aardrijkskundig, geografisch
geography [dzjie·ogrəfie] aardrijkskunde, geografie
geological [dzjiələdzjikl] geologisch

geologist [dzjie·<u>o</u>llədzjist] geoloog
geology [dzjie·<u>o</u>llədzjie] geologie
geometric(al) [dzjiəmetrik(l)] meetkundig
geometry [dzjie·<u>o</u>mmitrie] meetkunde
Georgia [dzj<u>o:</u>dzjiə] Georgië
Georgian [dzj<u>o:</u>dzjiən] **1** Georgisch *(of Georgia);* **2** Georgian *(of or characteristic of the time of King George)*
gerbil [dzj<u>ə:</u>bil] woestijnrat
geriatric [dzjerrie·ætrik] ouderdoms-, *(depr)* aftands, oud
geriatrics [dzjerrie·ætriks] geriatrie, ouderdomszorg
germ [dzjə:m] **1** *(biology)* kiem, geslachtscel, *(fig)* oorsprong, begin[h]; **2** *(med)* ziektekiem, bacil
¹German [dzj<u>ə:</u>mən] *adj* Duits: ~ *shepherd* Duitse herder(shond); ~ *measles* rodehond
²German [dzj<u>ə:</u>mən] *n* Duitse(r)
Germanic [dzjə:mænik] **1** Germaans; **2** Duits
Germany [dzj<u>ə:</u>mənie] Duitsland
germ carrier bacillendrager, kiemdrager
germinate [dzj<u>ə:</u>minneet] *(also fig)* ontkiemen, ontspruiten: *the idea ~d with him* het idee kwam bij hem op
germ warfare biologische oorlogvoering
gerontology [dzjerront<u>o</u>llədzjie] ouderdomskunde
gestation [dzjesteesjən] dracht(tijd), zwangerschap(speriode)
gesticulate [dzjestikjoeleet] gebaren
¹gesture [dzjestsjə] *n* gebaar[h], geste, teken[h]: *a ~ of friendship* een vriendschappelijk gebaar
²gesture [dzjestsjə] *vb* gebaren, (met gebaren) te kennen geven
¹get [get] *vb* **1** (ge)raken, (ertoe) komen, gaan, bereiken: ~ *rid of sth.* zich van iets ontdoen; *he is ~ting to be an old man* hij is een oude man aan het worden; *he never ~s to drive the car* hij krijgt nooit de kans om met de auto te rijden; ~ *lost* verdwalen; ~ *lost!* loop naar de maan!; ~ *to see s.o.* iem te zien krijgen; ~ *ahead* vooruitkomen, succes boeken; ~ *behind* achterop raken; *(fig)* ~ *nowhere* niets bereiken; ~ *there* er komen, succes boeken; ~ *above oneself* heel wat van zichzelf denken; ~ *at: a)* bereiken, te pakken krijgen, komen aan, achter; *b) (inf)* bedoelen; *c)* bekritiseren; *d)* knoeien met; *e)* omkopen; *f)* ertussen nemen; ~ *at the truth* de waarheid achterhalen; *what are you ~ting at?* wat bedoel je daarmee?; ~ *in contact* (of: *touch*) with contact opnemen met; ~ *into the car* in de auto stappen; *what has got into you?* wat bezielt je?, wat heb je?; ~ *off: a)* afstappen van *(bicycle, pavement, lawn); b)* ontheven worden van *(obligation);* ~ *onto s.o.* iem te pakken krijgen; ~ *on(to) one's bike* op zijn fiets stappen; ~ *out of sth.* ergens uitraken, zich ergens uit redden; ~ *out of the way* uit de weg gaan, plaats maken; ~ *over* te boven komen, overwinnen; ~ *over an illness* genezen van een ziekte; *I still can't ~ over the fact that ...* ik heb nog steeds moeite met het feit

dat ..., ik kan er niet over uit dat ...; ~ *through* heen raken door *(time, money, clothing, work);* ~ *through an exam* slagen voor een examen; ~ *to* bereiken, kunnen beginnen aan, toekomen aan; *where has he got to?* waar is hij naar toe?; ~ *to the top of the ladder* (of: *tree)* de top bereiken; **2** beginnen, aanvangen: ~ *going!* (of: *moving!)* vooruit!, begin (nu eindelijk)!; ~ *going: a)* op dreef komen *(of person); b)* op gang komen *(of party, project, machine etc);* ~ *to like sth.* ergens de smaak van te pakken krijgen; ~ *off the ground* van de grond raken; *(inf)* ~ *stuffed!* stik!, val dood!
²get [get] *vb* **1** (ver)krijgen, verwerven: ~ *a glimpse of* vluchtig te zien krijgen; ~ *one's hands on* te pakken krijgen; ~ *what is coming to one* krijgen wat men verdient; ~ *sth. out of s.o.* iets van iem loskrijgen; **2** (zich) aanschaffen, kopen: *my car was stolen, so I had to ~ a new one* mijn auto was gestolen, dus moest ik een nieuwe kopen; **3** bezorgen, verschaffen, voorzien: ~ *s.o. some food* iem te eten geven; ~ *sth. for s.o.* iem iets bezorgen, iets voor iem halen; **4** doen geraken, doen komen, gaan, brengen, krijgen, doen: ~ *sth. going* iets op gang krijgen, iets op dreef helpen; ~ *s.o. talking* iem aan de praat krijgen; *(inf; fig)* ~ *s you nowhere* je bereikt er niets mee; ~ *sth. into one's head* zich iets in het hoofd halen; ~ *sth. into s.o.'s head* iets aan iem duidelijk maken; ~ *s.o. out of sth.* iem aan iets helpen ontsnappen; **5** maken, doen worden, bereiden, klaarmaken: ~ *dinner (ready)* het avondmaal bereiden; *let me ~ this clear* (of: *straight)* laat me dit even duidelijk stellen; ~ *ready* klaarmaken; **6** *sth. done* iets gedaan krijgen; **6** nemen, (op-, ont)vangen, grijpen, (binnen)halen: *go and ~ your breakfast!* ga maar ontbijten!; **7** overhalen, zover krijgen: ~ *s.o. to talk* iem aan de praat krijgen; **8** *(inf)* hebben, krijgen: *he got a mobile phone for his birthday* hij kreeg een gsm voor zijn verjaardag; **9** vervelen, ergeren: *it really ~s me when* ik erger me dood wanneer; **10** snappen, begrijpen, verstaan: *he has finally got the message* (of: *got it)* hij heeft het eindelijk door; ~ *sth. wrong* iets verkeerd begrijpen
³get [get] *vb* (ge)raken, worden: ~ *better* beter worden; ~ *used to* wennen aan; ~ *even with s.o.* het iem betaald zetten
⁴get [get] *vb* worden: ~ *killed (in an accident)* omkomen (bij een ongeluk); ~ *married* trouwen; ~ *punished* gestraft worden
get across 1 oversteken, aan de overkant komen; **2** begrepen worden, aanslaan *(of idea etc),* succes hebben; **3** overkomen *(of person),* bereiken, begrepen worden: ~ *to the audience* zijn gehoor weten te boeien
get along 1 vertrekken, voortmaken, weggaan; **2** opschieten, vorderen: *is your work getting along?* schiet het al op met je werk?; **3** (zich) redden, het stellen, het maken: *we can ~ without your help* we kunnen je hulp best missen; **4** (with *with)* (kunnen) opschieten (met), overweg kunnen (met): *they ~*

very well ze kunnen het goed met elkaar vinden
get (a)round 1 op de been zijn, rondlopen *(of person, after illness);* **2** rondtrekken, rondreizen, overal komen; **3** zich verspreiden, de ronde doen *(of news):* ~ *to s.o.* iem ter ore komen; **4** gelegenheid hebben, toekomen: ~ *to sth.: a)* aan iets kunnen beginnen; *b)* ergens de tijd voor vinden
getaway ontsnapping: *make one's* ~ ontsnappen
get away 1 wegkomen, weggaan: *did you manage to* ~ *this summer?* heb je deze zomer wat vakantie kunnen nemen?; **2** ontsnappen, ontkomen: ~ *from* ontsnappen aan; *you can't* ~ *from this* hier kun je niet (meer) onderuit; ~ *from it all* even alles achterlaten, er tussenuit gaan; *he'll never* ~ *with it* dat lukt hem nooit; *some students* ~ *with murder* sommige studenten mogen echt alles en niemand die er wat van zegt; *commit a crime and* ~ *with it* ongestraft een misdaad bedrijven
¹get back *vb* terugkomen, teruggaan, thuiskomen: ~*!* terug!, naar buiten!; ~ *at* (of: *on) s.o.* het iem betaald zetten
²get back *vb* **1** terugkrijgen, terugvinden; **2** terugbrengen, terughalen, naar huis brengen ‖ *get one's own back (on s.o.)* het iem betaald zetten
get by 1 zich er doorheen slaan, zich redden, het stellen: ~ *without sth.* het zonder iets kunnen stellen; **2** (net) voldoen, er (net) mee door kunnen
¹get in *vb* **1** binnenkomen, toegelaten worden *(to school, university):* ~ *on sth.* aan iets meedoen; *(inf)* ~ *on the act* mogen meedoen; **2** instappen *(into vehicle)*
²get in *vb* binnenbrengen, binnenhalen *(harvest)*, inzamelen *(money): get the doctor in* de dokter er bij halen; *I couldn't get a word in (edgeways)* ik kon er geen speld tussen krijgen, ik kreeg geen kans om ook maar iets te zeggen
¹get on *vb* **1** vooruitkomen, voortmaken, opschieten: ~ *with one's work* goed opschieten met zijn werk; **2** bloeien, floreren; **3** (with *with*) (kunnen) opschieten met, overweg kunnen met; **4** oud (laat) worden: *he is getting on (in years)* hij wordt oud, hij wordt een dagje ouder; **5** opstappen *(horse, bicycle)*, opstijgen, instappen *(bus, aeroplane): he is getting on for fifty* hij loopt tegen de vijftig; ~ *to sth.: a)* iets door hebben; *b)* iets op het spoor komen
²get on *vb* **1** aantrekken, opzetten: *get one's hat and coat on* zijn hoed opzetten en zijn jas aantrekken; **2** erop krijgen: *I can't get the lid on* ik krijg het deksel er niet op
¹get out *vb* **1** uitlekken, bekend worden; **2** naar buiten gaan, weggaan, eruit komen; **3** ontkomen, maken dat je weg komt, ontsnappen: *no-one here gets out alive* niemand komt hier levend vandaan; **4** afstappen, uitstappen
²get out *vb* eruit halen (krijgen) *(splinter, stains; also fig)*
¹get over *vb* overbrengen *(meaning etc)*, duidelijk maken, doen begrijpen
²get over *vb* begrepen worden *(of joke, comedian)*

¹get through *vb* (er) doorkomen, zijn bestemming bereiken, goedgekeurd worden *(of bill)*, aansluiting krijgen *(by telephone etc)*, begrepen worden: ~ *to: a)* bereiken, doordringen tot, contact krijgen met; *b)* begrepen worden door
²get through *vb* **1** zijn bestemming doen bereiken, laten goedkeuren, erdoor krijgen *(also at exams);* **2** duidelijk maken, aan zijn verstand brengen
¹get down *vb* dalen: ~ *on one's knees* op zijn knieën gaan (zitten); ~ *to sth.* aan iets kunnen beginnen, aan iets toekomen; ~ *to business* ter zake komen; ~ *to work* aan het werk gaan
²get down *vb* **1** doen dalen, naar beneden brengen; **2** naar binnen krijgen *(food);* **2** deprimeren, ontmoedigen: *it is not just the work that gets you down* het is niet alleen het werk waar je depressief van wordt
¹get off *vb* **1** ontsnappen, ontkomen; **2** afstappen, uitstappen: *you should* ~ *at Denmark Street* je moet bij Denmark Street uitstappen; **3** vertrekken, beginnen: ~ *to a good start* flink van start gaan, goed beginnen; **4** in slaap vallen; **5** vrijkomen, er goed afkomen: ~ *lightly* er licht van afkomen; ~ *with* het aanleggen met, aanpappen met
²get off *vb* **1** doen vertrekken, doen beginnen; **2** doen vrijkomen, er goed doen afkomen, vrijspraak krijgen voor: *he got me off with a fine* hij zorgde ervoor dat ik er met een boot af kwam; **3** (op)sturen *(letter)*, wegsturen: *get s.o. off to school* iem naar school sturen; **4** eraf krijgen: *I can't get the lid off* ik krijg het deksel er niet af; **5** uittrekken *(clothing, shoes)*, afnemen; **6** leren, instuderen: *get sth. off by heart* iets uit het hoofd leren
get-together bijeenkomst
¹get up *vb* **1** opstaan, recht (gaan) staan; **2** opsteken *(of wind, storm etc)* ‖ ~ *to: a)* bereiken; *b)* gaan naar, benaderen; *what is he getting up to now?* wat voert hij nu weer in zijn schild?
²get up *vb* **1** organiseren, op touw zetten *(party, play);* **2** maken, ontwikkelen, produceren: ~ *speed* versnellen; **3** instuderen, bestuderen: *get one up on s.o.* iem de loef afsteken; ~ *to* doen bereiken
get-up 1 uitrusting, kostuum[h]; **2** uitvoering, formaat[h]; **3** aankleding, decor[h]
geyser [gie:zə] **1** geiser; **2** (gas)geiser
ghastly [ga:stlie] verschrikkelijk, afgrijselijk
gherkin [gə:kin] augurk
ghetto [gettoo] getto[h]
ghost [goost] **1** geest, spook[h], spookverschijning; **2** spook(beeld)[h], fata morgana; **3** spoor[h], greintje[h]: *not have the* ~ *of a chance* geen schijn van kans hebben; *a* ~ *of a smile* een zweem van een glimlach; *give up the* ~ de geest geven, sterven
ghostly [goostlie] spookachtig
ghost town spookstad
ghost-writer spookschrijver
G.H.Q. *General Headquarters* hoofdkwartier[h]
GI [dzjie:aj] dienstplichtige
giant [dzjajjənt] reus; kolos, *(fig)* uitblinker: *Shakespeare is one of the* ~*s of English literature*

Shakespeare is een van de allergrootsten in de Engelse literatuur

giant killer reuzendoder *(person who beats a favourite)*

gibberish [dzjibbərisj] gebrabbel[h]

gibbon [gibbən] gibbon

¹**gibe** [dzjajb] *vb* (be)spotten, schimpen: ~ *at* de draak steken met

²**gibe** [dzjajb] *n* spottende opmerking

giddy [giddie] **1** duizelig, draaierig, misselijk; **2** duizelingwekkend; **3** frivool, wispelturig, lichtzinnig

gift [gift] **1** cadeau[h], geschenk[h], gift: *free* ~ gratis geschenk *(by way of promotion);* **2** gave, talent[h], aanleg: *have the* ~ *of (the) gab: a)* welbespraakt zijn; *b)* praatziek zijn

gifted [giftid] begaafd, talentvol, intelligent

gift-horse gegeven paard[h] *(fig)*, geschenk[h]: *don't look a* ~ *in the mouth* je moet een gegeven paard niet in de bek zien

gift shop cadeauwinkel(tje[h])

giftwrap als cadeautje inpakken, in cadeaupapier inpakken

gift-wrapping [giftræping] geschenkverpakking

gig [gig] optreden[h], concert[h]

gigantic [dzjajgæntik] gigantisch, reusachtig (groot)

¹**giggle** [gigl] *vb* giechelen (van)

²**giggle** [gigl] *n* gegiechel[h]: *have the* ~*s* de slappe lach hebben

gild [gild] vergulden, *(fig)* versieren, opsmukken

gilded [gildid] verguld, *(fig)* versierd, sierlijk

gill [gil] kieuw

gilt [gilt] **1** goudgerande schuldbrief *(with government guarantee);* **2** verguldsel[h]

gilt-edged 1 goudgerand; **2** met rijksgarantie: ~ *shares* goudgerande aandelen

gimmick [gimmik] truc(je[h]), vondst

gimmicky [gimmikkie] op effect gericht *(of products)*

gin [dzjin] gin, jenever

ginger [dzjindzjə] **1** gember(plant); **2** roodachtig bruin[h], rossig, *(of person)* rooie

ginger ale gemberbier[h]

gingerbread gembercake, gemberkoek, peperkoek

gingerly [dzjindzjəlie] (uiterst) voorzichtig

ginger up stimuleren, opvrolijken, oppeppen

ginseng [dzjinseng] ginseng(plant)

gipsy [dzjipsie] zigeuner(in)

giraffe [dzjirra:f] giraf(fe)

girder [gə:də] steunbalk, draagbalk, dwarsbalk

girdle [gə:dl] gordel, (buik)riem, korset[h]

girl [gə:l] **1** meisje[h], dochter, *(inf)* vrouw(tje[h]); **2** dienstmeisje[h]; **3** liefje[h], vriendinnetje[h]

girlfriend vriendin(netje[h]), meisje[h]

Girl Guide padvindster

Girl Scout padvindster

giro [dzjajjəroo] **1** giro(dienst): *National Giro* postgiro; **2** girocheque

gist [dzjist] hoofdgedachte, essentie, kern

give [giv] **1** geven, schenken, overhandigen: ~ *him my best wishes* doe hem de groeten van mij; ~ *a dinner* een diner aanbieden; **2** geven, verlenen, verschaffen, gunnen: ~ *a prize* een prijs toekennen; *we were* ~*n three hours' rest* we kregen drie uur rust; *he has been* ~*n two years* hij heeft twee jaar (gevangenisstraf) gekregen; ~ *s.o. to understand* iem te verstaan geven; **3** geven, opofferen, wijden: ~ *one's life for one's country* zijn leven geven voor zijn vaderland; **4** (+ *noun)* doen: ~ *a beating* een pak slaag geven; ~ *a cry* een kreet slaken; ~ *s.o. a sly look* iem een sluwe blik toewerpen; **5** (op)geven, meedelen: *the teacher gave us three exercises (to do)* de onderwijzer heeft ons drie oefeningen opgegeven (als huiswerk); ~ *information* informatie verstrekken; **6** produceren, voortbrengen: ~ *off* (af)geven, verspreiden, maken; ~ *or take 5 minutes* 5 minuten meer of minder; ~ *as good as one gets* met gelijke munt betalen; *don't* ~ *me that* (hou op met die) onzin; ~ *s.o. what for* iem flink op zijn donder geven

give away 1 weggeven, cadeau doen; **2** verraden, verklappen

give-away 1 cadeautje[h]; **2** onthulling, (ongewild) verraad[h]

give in (with *to)* toegeven (aan), zich gewonnen geven, zwichten (voor)

¹**given** *adj* **1** gegeven, gekregen, verleend; **2** gegeven *(also maths),* (wel) bepaald, vastgesteld: *under the* ~ *conditions* in de gegeven omstandigheden; *at any* ~ *time* om het even wanneer, op elk moment; **3** geneigd: ~ *to drinking* verslaafd aan de drank

²**given** *prep* gezien: ~ *the present situation* in het licht van de huidige situatie

³**given** *conj* aangezien: ~ *(that) you don't like it* aangezien je het niet leuk vindt

given name voornaam, doopnaam

¹**give out** *vb* **1** afgeven, verspreiden, maken; **2** verdelen, uitdelen, uitreiken

²**give out** *vb* uitgeput raken, op raken

¹**give over** *vb* ophouden, stoppen

²**give over** *vb* afzien van, stoppen, opgeven: *I asked the students to* ~ *chewing gum in class* ik verzocht de studenten om geen kauwgom meer te kauwen tijdens de les

¹**give up** *vb* (het) opgeven, zich gewonnen geven: ~ *on* geen hoop meer hebben voor; *I* ~ *on you* je bent hopeloos

²**give up** *vb* **1** opgeven, afstand doen van, niet langer verwachten, alle hoop opgeven voor, *(inf)* laten zitten: ~ *one's seat* zijn zitplaats afstaan; ~ *for dead* als dood beschouwen *(also fig);* ~ *smoking* stoppen met roken; **2** ophouden; **3** overgeven, overleveren, (toe)wijden: *give oneself up* zich gevangen geven, zich melden

glacial [gleesjl] ijs- *(also fig),* ijzig, ijskoud

glacier [glæsiə] gletsjer

glad [glæd] blij, gelukkig, verheugd: *be* ~ *to see the back of s.o.* iem gaarne zien vertrekken; *I'd be* ~ *to!*

met plezier!; *I'll be ~ to help* ik wil je graag helpen *(also iron); ~ about* (of: *at, of)* blij om, verheugd over

gladden [glædn] blij maken

gladiator [glædie·eetə] gladiator

gladiolus [glædie- ooləs] gladiool

gladly [glædlie] graag, met plezier

glamorous [glæmərəs] (zeer) aantrekkelijk, bekoorlijk, betoverend (mooi), prachtig, glitter-

glamour [glæmə] betovering, schone schijn

¹**glance** [gla:ns] *n* (vluchtige) blik, oogopslag, kijkje[h]: *at a ~* met één oogopslag, onmiddellijk

²**glance** [gla:ns] *vb* (vluchtig) kijken, een (vluchtige) blik werpen: *~ at* even bekijken, een blik werpen op

gland [glænd] klier: *sweat ~s* zweetklieren

¹**glare** [gleə] *n* **1** woeste (dreigende) blik; **2** verblindend licht[h] *(also fig)*, (felle) glans

²**glare** [gleə] *vb* **1** fel schijnen, blinken, schitteren: *the sun ~d down on our backs* de zon brandde (fel) op onze rug; **2** boos kijken, woest kijken

glaring [gleəring] **1** verblindend, schitterend, fel: *~ colours* schreeuwende kleuren; **2** dreigend, woest: *~ eyes* vlammende ogen

glass [gla:s] **1** glas[h], (drink)glas[h], brillenglas[h], spiegel; **2** lens; **3** glas[h], glaasje[h] *(drink);* **4** glas(werk)[h]; **5** *~es* bril: *two pairs of ~es* twee brillen; **6** *~es* verrekijker, toneelkijker: *people who live in ~ houses should not throw stones* wie in een glazen huisje zit, moet niet met stenen gooien

glass fibre glasvezel, glasdraad

glasshouse (broei)kas

glassworks glasfabriek, glasblazerij

glassy [gla:sie] glasachtig, glazig, (spiegel)glad

¹**glaze** [gleez] *vb* (also with *over*) glazig worden, breken *(of eyes)*

²**glaze** [gleez] *vb* in glas zetten: *double-glazed windows* dubbele ramen

³**glaze** [gleez] *n* glazuur[h], glazuurlaag

glazing [gleezing] **1** glazuur[h], glazuurlaag; **2** beglazing, ruiten, ramen[h]: *double ~* dubbel glas, dubbele ramen

¹**gleam** [glie:m] *n* (zwak) schijnsel[h], glans, schittering, straal(tje[h]) *(also fig): not a ~ of hope* geen sprankje hoop

²**gleam** [glie:m] *vb* (zwak) schijnen, glanzen, schitteren

glean [glie:n] **1** verzamelen, oprapen, vergaren *(ears);* **2** moeizaam vergaren, (bijeen) sprokkelen *(information): ~ ideas from everywhere* overal ideeën vandaan halen

glee [glie:] leedvermaak[h]; vreugde, opgewektheid

glib [glib] welbespraakt, vlot, rad van tong, glad, handig

glide [glajd] **1** glijden, sluipen, zweven; **2** *(aviation)* zweven

glider [glajdə] **1** zweefvliegtuig[h]; **2** zweefvlieger

glimmer [glimmə] **1** zwak licht[h], glinstering, flikkering; **2** straaltje[h] *(fig): ~ of hope* sprankje hoop

glimpse [glimps] glimp: *catch* (of: *get) a ~ of* eventjes zien, een glimp opvangen van

glisten [glisn] schitteren, glinsteren, glimmen: *~ with* schitteren van, fonkelen van

¹**glitter** [glittə] *vb* schitteren, blinken, glinsteren: *~ with* blinken van; *all that ~s is not gold* het is niet al goud wat er blinkt

²**glitter** [glittə] *n* geschitter[h], glans, glinstering

glitz [glits] glitter

glitzy [glitsie] opzichtig, opvallend

gloat [gloot] **1** wellustig staren, begerig kijken; **2** zich verlustigen, zich vergenoegen: *~ over* (of: *on)* zich verkneukelen in

global [gloobl] **1** wereldomvattend, wereld-: *~ warming* opwarming van de aarde ten gevolge van het broeikaseffect; **2** algemeen, allesomvattend, globaal

globe [gloob] globe, aarde, wereldbol

globetrotter globetrotter, wereldreiziger

gloom [gloe:m] **1** duisternis, halfduister[h]: *cast a ~ over sth.* een schaduw over iets werpen; **2** zwaarmoedigheid, somberheid

glorify [glo:riffaj] **1** verheerlijken, vereren; **2** ophemelen, loven, prijzen: *(inf) this isn't a country house but a glorified hut* dit is geen landhuis, maar een veredeld soort hut; **3** mooier voorstellen, verfraaien

glorious [glo:riəs] **1** roemrijk, glorierijk, glorieus, luisterrijk; **2** prachtig, schitterend

glory [glo:rie] **1** glorie, eer, roem: *I wrote that book for my own personal ~* ik heb dat boek geschreven voor mijn eigen roem; **2** lof, dankzegging

gloss [glos] **1** lippenglans; **2** glans; **3** glamour, schone schijn

glossy [glossie] glanzend, blinkend, glad: *~ print* glanzende foto; *~ magazine* duur blad, glossy

glove [gluv] handschoen: *fit like a ~* als gegoten zitten; *throw down the ~* de handschoen toewerpen

¹**glow** [gloo] *n* gloed, *(fig)* bezieling, enthousiasme[h]

²**glow** [gloo] *vb* **1** gloeien, glimmen, *(fig)* bezield zijn, enthousiast zijn; **2** blozen || *~ with pride* zo trots als een pauw zijn

glowworm glimworm

glucose [gloe:koos] glucose, druivensuiker

¹**glue** [gloe:] *n* lijm

²**glue** [gloe:] *vb* lijmen, plakken: *(fig) his eyes were ~d to the girl* hij kon zijn ogen niet van het meisje afhouden

glum [glum] mistroostig

¹**glut** [glut] *vb* **1** volstoppen: *~ oneself with* zich volstoppen met; **2** (over)verzadigen, overladen, overvoeren

²**glut** [glut] *n* **1** overvloed; **2** overschot[h]

glutton [glutn] slokop, gulzigaard, (veel)vraat

gm. *gram* g(r)

G.M.T. *Greenwich Mean Time* GT, Greenwichtijd

gnarled [na:ld] knoestig, ruw, verweerd

gnash [næsj] knarsetanden, tandenknarsen: *~ one's teeth* tandenknarsen

gnat [næt] mug, muskiet

¹gnaw [no:] *vb* knagen *(also fig)*, knabbelen, smart veroorzaken, pijn doen

²gnaw [no:] *vb* **1** knagen aan *(also fig)*, kwellen; **2** (uit)knagen, afknagen: *the mice have ~n a small hole* de muizen hebben een holletje uitgeknaagd

gnome [noom] gnoom, aardmannetjeʰ, kabouter

G.N.P. *gross national product* bnp, bruto nationaal product

gnu [noe:] gnoe

¹go [goo] *vb* **1** gaan, starten, vertrekken, beginnen: *(right) from the word ~* vanaf het begin; *~ to find s.o.* iem gaan zoeken; *get ~ing: a)* aan de slag gaan; *b)* op gang komen; *let ~* laten gaan, loslaten; *(fig) I wouldn't ~ so far as to say that* dat zou ik niet durven zeggen; *~ about sth.: a)* iets aanpakken; *b)* zich bezighouden met; *~ by sth.* zich baseren op, zich laten leiden door; *nothing to ~ by* niets om op af te gaan; *~ off* afgaan van, afstappen van; *~ on the pill* aan de pil gaan; *~ over: a)* doornemen, doorlezen *(text); b)* herhalen *(explanation); c)* repeteren *(part, lesson); ~ through: a)* nauwkeurig onderzoeken, doorzoeken; *b)* nagaan, checken *(assertion etc); c)* doornemen *(text); we ~ through a difficult time* we maken een moeilijke periode door; *ready, steady, ~!* klaar voor de start? af!; **2** gaan, voortgaan, lopen, reizen: *~ by air* met het vliegtuig reizen; *~ for a walk* een wandeling maken; *~ abroad* naar het buitenland gaan; *~ along that way* die weg nemen; **3** gaan (naar), wijzen (naar, op), voeren (naar) *(also fig)*, reiken, zich uitstrekken: *~ from bad to worse* van kwaad tot erger vervallen; *the difference goes deep* het verschil is erg groot; **4** gaan, (voortdurend) zijn *(in a particular condition): as things ~* in het algemeen; *~ armed* gewapend zijn; *how are things ~ing?* hoe gaat het ermee?; **5** gaan, lopen, draaien, werken *(of appliance, system, factory etc): the clock won't ~* de klok doet het niet; *~ slow* een langzaam-aan-actie houden; **6** gaan, afgaan *(of gun)*, aflopen, luiden *(of bell etc)*; **7** verstrijken, (voorbij)gaan, verlopen *(of time): ten days to ~ to (of: before) Easter* nog tien dagen (te gaan) en dan is het Pasen; **8** gaan, afleggen *(distance): five miles to ~* nog vijf mijl af te leggen; **9** gaan, luiden *(of poem, story)*, klinken *(of tune): the tune goes like this* het wijsje klinkt als volgt; **10** aflopen, gaan, uitvallen: *how did the exam ~?* hoe ging het examen?; *~ well* goed aflopen, goed komen; **11** doorgaan, gebeuren, doorgang vinden: *what he says goes* wat hij zegt, gebeurt ook; **12** vooruitgaan, opschieten: *how is the work going?* hoe vordert het (met het) werk?; **13** gelden, gangbaar zijn *(of money)*, gezaghebbend zijn, gezag hebben *(of judgement, person): that goes for all of us* dat geldt voor ons allemaal; **14** wegkomen, er onderuitkomen, er vanaf komen: *~ unpunished* ongestraft wegkomen; **15** (weg)gaan, verkocht worden *(of merchandise): ~ cheap* goedkoop verkocht worden; *~ing!, ~ing!, ~ne!* eenmaal! andermaal! verkocht!; **16** gaan, besteed worden *(of money, time);* **17** verdwijnen, verloren gaan *(also fig): my complaints went unnoticed* mijn klachten werden niet gehoord; **18** verdwijnen, wijken, afgeschaft worden, afgevoerd worden: *my car must ~* mijn auto moet weg; **19** weggaan, vertrekken, heengaan *(also fig)*, sterven, doodgaan: *we must be ~ing* we moeten ervandoor; **20** gaan, passen, thuishoren: *the forks ~ in the top drawer* de vorken horen in de bovenste la; *where do you want this cupboard to ~?* waar wil je deze kast hebben?; **21** dienen, helpen, nuttig zijn, bijdragen: *this goes to prove I'm right* dit bewijst dat ik gelijk heb; *it only goes to show* zo zie je maar; *~ by the book* volgens het boekje handelen; *~ and get sth.* iets gaan halen; *let oneself ~: a)* zich laten gaan, zich ontspannen; *b)* zich verwaarlozen; *anything goes* alles is toegestaan, alles mag; *~ before* voorafgaan *(in time); ~ one better* (één) meer bieden, *(fig)* het beter doen, overtreffen; *~ easy on* geen druk uitoefenen op, matig *(of: voorzichtig)* zijn met; *~ easy with* aardig zijn tegen; *here goes!* daar gaat ie (dan)!; *there you ~: a)* alsjeblieft; *b)* daar heb je het (al); *~ west* het hoekje omgaan, de pijp uitgaan; *~ wrong: a)* een fout maken, zich vergissen; *b)* fout *(of: mis)* gaan, de mist in gaan; *not much evidence to ~ on* niet veel bewijs om op af te gaan; *to ~* om mee te nemen *(of hot dishes)*

²go [goo] *vb* **1** maken, gaan maken *(trip etc);* **2** afleggen, gaan: *~ the shortest way* de kortste weg nemen; *~ it alone* iets helemaal alleen doen

³go [goo] *vb* worden, gaan: *~ bad* slecht worden, bederven; *~ blind* blind worden; *~ broke* al zijn geld kwijtraken; *we'll have to ~ hungry* we moeten het zonder eten stellen; *the milk went sour* de melk werd zuur; *~ing fifteen* bijna vijftien (jaar), naar de vijftien toe

⁴go [goo] *n (~es)* **1** poging: *have a ~ at sth.* eens iets proberen; **2** beurt, keer: *at (of: in) one ~* in één klap, in één keer; **3** aanval: *make a ~ of it* er een succes van maken; *(it's) no ~* het kan niet, het lukt nooit

⁵go [goo] *adj* goed functionerend, in orde, klaar: *all systems (are) ~* (we zijn) startklaar

go about 1 rondlopen; **2** (rond)reizen; **3** de ronde doen, rondgaan *(of rumour, gossip);* **4** omgang hebben, verkering hebben: *~ with s.o.* omgaan met iem

go across oversteken, overgaan, gaan over

goad [good] drijven, *(fig)* aanzetten, prikkelen, opstoken: *she ~ed him on to take revenge* ze stookte hem op wraak te nemen

go against 1 ingaan tegen, zich verzetten tegen; **2** indruisen tegen, in strijd zijn met, onverenigbaar zijn met

go ahead 1 voorafgaan, voorgaan, vooruitgaan: *Peter went ahead of the procession* Peter liep voor de stoet uit; **2** beginnen, aanvangen: *we went ahead with our task* we begonnen aan onze taak; *~!* ga je gang!, begin maar!; **3** verder gaan, voortgaan, vervolgen: *we went ahead with our homework* we gingen verder met ons huiswerk

goal [gool] **1** doelʰ: *one's ~ in life* iemands levensdoel; **2** (eind)bestemming; **3** doel[h], goal: *keep ~ het doel verdedigen*, keepen; **4** doelpunt[h], goal: *kick (of: make) a ~* een doelpunt maken

goal area doelgebied[h]

goalie [goo:lie] *(inf)* keeper, doelman

goalkeeper [goolkie:pə] *(sport)* keeper, doelman, doelverdediger

goal kick doeltrap, uittrap, doelschop

go along 1 meegaan: *she decided to ~ with the children* ze besloot om met de kinderen mee te gaan; **2** vorderen, vooruitgaan: *the work was going along nicely* het werk schoot lekker op

go along with 1 meegaan met *(also fig)*, akkoord gaan met, bijvallen; **2** samenwerken met, terzijde staan; **3** deel uitmaken van, behoren tot, horen bij

go (a)round 1 rondgaan (in), rondlopen, de ronde doen *(of rumour etc)*, zich verspreiden *(of disease)*: *his words kept going round my head* zijn woorden bleven mij door het hoofd spelen; *you can't ~ complaining all of the time!* je kan toch niet de hele tijd lopen klagen!; **2** voldoende zijn (voor): *there are enough chairs to ~* er zijn genoeg stoelen voor iedereen

goat [goot] **1** geit; **2** ezel, stomkop ‖ *get s.o.'s ~* iem ergeren

go at 1 aanvallen, te lijf gaan, *(fig)* van leer trekken tegen, tekeergaan tegen; **2** verkocht worden voor

go away weggaan, vertrekken: *~ with s.o. (sth.)* ervandoor gaan met iem (iets)

gob [gob] **1** rochel, fluim; **2** smoel, mond, bek: *shut your ~!* houd je waffel!, kop dicht!

go back 1 teruggaan, terugkeren; **2** teruggaan, zijn oorsprong vinden, dateren: *Louis and I ~ a long time* Louis en ik kennen elkaar al heel lang; *this tradition goes back to the Middle Ages* deze traditie gaat terug tot de Middeleeuwen; **3** teruggrijpen, terugkeren; **4** teruggedraaid worden, teruggezet worden *(of clock, watch)*

go back on 1 terugnemen, terugkomen op *(word(s) etc)*; **2** ontrouw worden, verraden

gobble [gobl] (op)schrokken: *~ down* (of: *up*) naar binnen schrokken

go-between tussenpersoon, bemiddelaar

go beyond gaan boven, overschrijden, overtreffen, te buiten gaan: *~ one's duty* buiten zijn boekje gaan, zijn bevoegdheid overschrijden; *their teasing is going beyond a joke* hun geplaag is geen grapje meer

gobsmacked met de mond vol tanden, stomverbaasd

go by 1 voorbijgaan *(also fig)*, passeren; **2** verstrijken, verlopen, aflopen

god [god] (af)god, *(fig)* invloedrijk persoon, idool[h]

God [god] God: *in God's name!, for God's sake!* in godsnaam!; *God bless you!* God zegene u!; *thank God!* goddank!

godchild petekind[h]

goddaughter peetdochter

goddess [goddis] godin

godfather *(also fig)* peetvader, peter, peetoom

godforsaken 1 (van) godverlaten; **2** triest, ellendig, hopeloos

godmother meter, peettante

go down 1 naar beneden gaan: *~ to the Mediterranean* naar de Middellandse Zee afzakken; **2** dalen *(of price, temperature)*; **3** zinken, ondergaan *(ship, person)*; **4** in de smaak vallen, ingang vinden: *~ like a bomb* enthousiast ontvangen worden; *~ with* in de smaak vallen bij, gehoor vinden bij; **5** te boek gesteld worden: *~ in history* de geschiedenis ingaan; *~ on one's knees* op de knieën vallen *(also fig)*; *~ with measles* de mazelen krijgen

godson peetzoon

go far 1 het ver schoppen, het ver brengen; **2** toereiken(d zijn), veruit volstaan, lang meegaan ‖ *far gone* ver heen

go for 1 gaan om, (gaan) halen, gaan naar: *Rob went for some more coffee* Rob ging nog wat koffie halen; *~ a walk* een wandeling maken; **2** gelden voor, van toepassing zijn op; **3** verkocht worden voor, gaan voor: *~ a song* voor een prikje van de hand gaan; **4** aanvallen, te lijf gaan, *(also fig; with words)* van leer trekken tegen

go forward 1 vooruitgaan *(also fig)*, vorderen, vooruitgang boeken; **2** zijn gang gaan, voortgaan, vervolgen

go-getter doorzetter

goggle [gogl] staren, turen: *~ at* aangapen

goggles [goglz] veiligheidsbril, sneeuwbril, stofbril

go in 1 erin gaan, (erin) passen; **2** naar binnen gaan

go in for 1 (gaan) deelnemen aan, opgaan voor, zich aanmelden voor *(an exam, competition etc)*; **2** (gaan) doen aan, een gewoonte maken van *(hobby, sport etc)*

¹going [gooing] *n* **1** vertrek[h]: *comings and ~s* komen en gaan *(also fig)*; **2** gang, tempo[h]: *be heavy ~* moeilijk zijn, een hele klus zijn; *while the ~ is good* nu het nog kan

²going [gooing] *adj* **1** voorhanden, in omloop: *there is a good job ~* er is een goede betrekking vacant; *I've got some fresh coffee ~* ik heb nog verse koffie staan; **2** (goed) werkend; **3** gangbaar, geldend: *the ~ rate* het gangbare tarief

go into 1 binnengaan (in), ingaan; **2** gaan in, zich aansluiten bij, deelnemen aan: *~ business* zakenman worden; **3** (nader) ingaan op, zich verdiepen in, onderzoeken: *~ (the) details* in detail treden

gold [goold] **1** goud *(also fig)*; **2** goud[h], goudstukken, rijkdom; **3** goud[h], goudkleur: *~ card* creditcard met speciale voordelen voor de houder; **4** goud(en medaille): *~ medallist* goudenmedaillewinnaar

golden [gooldən] gouden, goudkleurig *(also fig)*: *the Golden Age* de Gouden Eeuw; *~ handshake* gouden handdruk; *~ rule* gulden regel; *~ wedding (anniversary)* gouden bruiloft; *~ oldie* gouwe ouwe

goldfinch putter, distelvink

goldfish goudvis
gold rush goudkoorts
golf [golf] golf^h *(game)*
golfer [gɔlfə] golfspeler
goliath [gəlajjəθ] goliath, reus, krachtpatser
golly [gɔllie] gossie(mijne)
gondola [gɔndələ] 1 gondel *(Venetian boat);* 2 gondola, open (hang)bak *(for displaying articles)*
gondolier [gɔndəliə] gondelier
¹**gone** *adj* 1 verloren *(also fig);* 2 voorbij, vertrokken || *be three months* ~ in de derde maand zijn *(of pregnancy); far* ~ ver heen
²**gone** *prep* over: *he is* ~ *fifty* hij is over de vijftig, hij is de vijftig voorbij; *it's* ~ *three* het is over drieën
gong [gong] 1 gong; 2 medaille, lintje^h
goo [goe:] kleverig goedje^h
¹**good** [goed] *adj* 1 goed, knap, kundig: ~ *looks* knapheid; ~ *for* (of: *on) you* goed zo, knap (van je); 2 goed, correct, juist: ~ *English* goed Engels; *my watch keeps* ~ *time* mijn horloge loopt gelijk; *all in* ~ *time* alles op zijn tijd; 3 goed, fatsoenlijk, betrouwbaar: *(in)* ~ *faith* (te) goede(r) trouw; 4 aardig, lief, gehoorzaam: ~ *humour* opgewektheid; *put in a* ~ *word for, say a* ~ *word for* een goed woordje doen voor, aanbevelen; *be so* ~ *as to* wees zo vriendelijk, gelieve; *it's* ~ *of you to help him* het is aardig van u om hem te helpen; 5 goed, aangenaam, voordelig, lekker, smakelijk, gezond: ~ *buy* koopje, voordeeltje; ~ *afternoon* goedemiddag; *feel* ~: *a)* zich lekker voelen; *b)* lekker aanvoelen; *too* ~ *to be true* te mooi om waar te zijn; 6 afdoend, geldig: *this rule holds* ~ deze regel geldt; 7 aanzienlijk, aardig groot, lang: *stand a* ~ *chance* een goede kans maken; *a* ~ *deal, a* ~ *many* heel wat; *a* ~ *hour* ruim een uur; *all* ~ *things come to an end* aan alle goede dingen komt een einde; *one* ~ *turn deserves another* de ene dienst is de andere waard; *be in s.o.'s* ~ *books* bij iem in een goed blaadje staan; *as* ~ *as gold* erg braaf, erg lief *(of child); stroke of* ~ *luck* buitenkansje; *it's a* ~ *thing that* het is maar goed dat; *it's a* ~ *thing to* … het is verstandig om …; *a* ~ *thing too!* maar goed ook!; *too much of a* ~ *thing* te veel van het goede; *make* ~ *time* lekker opschieten; *as* ~ *as* zo goed als, nagenoeg; *be* ~ *at* goed zijn in; *be* ~ *for another couple of years* nog wel een paar jaar meekunnen; *goodies and baddies* de goeien en de slechteriken
²**good** [goed] *n* 1 goed^h, welzijn^h, voorspoed: *for the common* ~ voor het algemeen welzijn; *he will come to no* ~ het zal slecht met hem aflopen; *for his (own)* ~ om zijn eigen bestwil; 2 nut^h, voordeel^h: *it's no* ~ *(my) talking to her* het heeft geen zin met haar te praten; 3 goed werk^h, dienst: *be after* (of: *up to) no* ~ niets goeds in de zin hebben; 4 goedheid, verdienste, deugd(zaamheid): ~ *and evil* goed en kwaad; 5 ~s goederen, (koop)waar, handelsartikelen: *deliver the* ~s de goederen (af)leveren, *(fig)* volledig aan de verwachtingen voldoen; 6 ~s bezittingen: *for* ~ *(and all)* voorgoed, voor eeuwig (en al-

tijd)
¹**goodbye** [goedbaj] *interj* tot ziens
²**goodbye** [goedbaj] *n* afscheid^h, afscheidsgroet
goodish [goedisj] 1 tamelijk goed; 2 behoorlijk, tamelijk groot: *a* ~ *number of people* een vrij groot aantal mensen
good-looking knap, mooi
good-tempered goedgehumeurd, opgewekt
good-time op amusement belust, gezelligheids-
good will 1 welwillendheid; 2 goodwill, (goede) reputatie *(part of assets);* 3 klantenkring *(commercial value of a business),* klanten, zakenrelaties
¹**goody** [goedie] *n* -*ies* lekkernij, zoetigheid
²**goody** [goedie] *interj (child language)* jippie!, leuk!
goody-goody schijnheilige
¹**goof** [goe:f] *n* 1 sufkop, stommeling; 2 blunder, flater
²**goof** [goe:f] *vb* miskleunen, een flater slaan
go off 1 weggaan *(also fig),* (vh toneel) afgaan: ~ *with* ertussenuit knijpen met, ervandoor gaan met; 2 afgaan *(of alarm, gun),* ontploffen *(of bomb),* aflopen *(of alarm-clock),* losbarsten *(also fig);* 3 slechter worden, achteruit gaan, verwelken *(of flowers),* zuur worden, bederven *(of food): the veal has gone off* het kalfsvlees is niet goed meer
¹**go on** *vb* 1 voortduren *(also fig),* doorgaan (met), aanhouden: *he went on to say that* hij zei vervolgens dat; 2 verstrijken, verlopen, voorbijgaan; 3 (door)zaniken, (door)zagen: ~ *about* doorzeuren over; 4 gebeuren, plaatsvinden, doorgang vinden: *what is going on?* wat is er aan de hand?; *enough to be going* (of: *go) on with* genoeg om mee rond te komen
²**go on** *vb* + *prep* zich baseren op, afgaan op, zich laten leiden door
goose [goe:s] *(geese)* 1 gans; 2 onbenul^h
gooseberry [goezbərie] kruisbes(senstruik)
goose-flesh kippenvel^h
goose pimples *(fig)* kippenvel
go out 1 uitgaan, van huis gaan, afreizen: ~ *with* uitgaan met, verkering hebben met; 2 uitgaan *(of fire, light);* 3 uit de mode raken; 4 teruglopen, eb worden *(of sea): the tide is going out* het is eb; *go (all) out for sth.* zich volledig inzetten voor iets
go out of 1 verlaten, uitgaan *(a room):* ~ *play* 'uit' gaan *(of ball);* 2 verdwijnen uit: ~ *fashion* uit de mode raken; ~ *sight* (of: *view)* uit het zicht verdwijnen; ~ *use* in onbruik raken, buiten gebruik raken
go over 1 (with *to)* overlopen (naar), overschakelen (op), overgaan (tot) *(other party etc): we now* ~ *to our reporter on the spot* we schakelen nu over naar onze verslaggever ter plaatse; 2 aanslaan, overkomen
gorge [go:dzj] kloof, bergengte
gorgeous [go:dzjəs] schitterend, grandioos, prachtig *(also of pers)*
gorilla [gərillə] gorilla
gormless [go:mləs] stom, dom, onnozel
go round 1 (with *to)* langsgaan (bij) *(s.o.);* 2

(rond)draaien

gorse [go:s] brem

gory [go:rie] bloederig, bloedig: *a ~ film* een film met veel bloed en geweld

gospel [gospl] evangelie[h]: *take sth. for ~* iets zonder meer aannemen

gossamer [gossəmə] 1 herfstdraad, spinrag[h]; 2 gaas[h], fijn en licht weefsel[h]

¹gossip [gossip] *n* 1 roddel, kletspraat, praatjes; 2 roddelaar(ster), kletskous

²gossip [gossip] *vb* roddelen

gotcha [gotsjə] hebbes!, nou heb ik je!, gelukt!

Gothic [goθik] 1 *(linguistics)* Gotisch; 2 *(architecture)* gotisch

go through aangenomen worden *(of proposal, bill etc)*, erdoor komen ‖ *~ with* doorgaan met

go to 1 gaan naar *(also fig)*; 2 zich getroosten: *~ great* (of: *considerable) expense* er heel wat geld tegenaan gooien; *~ great lengths* zich de grootste moeite getroosten, alle mogelijke moeite doen

gouge [gaudzj] (uit)gutsen, uitsteken: *~ out s.o.'s eyes* iem de ogen uitsteken

goulash [goe:læsj] goulash

go under 1 ondergaan, zinken, *(fig)* er onder door gaan, bezwijken; 2 failliet gaan, bankroet gaan

go up 1 opgaan, naar boven gaan: *~ in the world* in de wereld vooruitkomen; 2 stijgen, omhooggaan *(of price, temperature)*; 3 ontploffen, in de lucht vliegen: *~ in smoke* in rook opgaan

gourmet [goeəmee] lekkerbek

gout [gaut] jicht

govern [guvvən] 1 regeren, besturen; *~ing body* bestuurslichaam, raad van beheer; 2 bepalen, beheersen, beïnvloeden

governess [guvvənis] gouvernante

government [guvvənmənt] regering(svorm), (staats)bestuur[h], kabinet[h], leiding: *the Government has* (of: *have) accepted the proposal* de regering heeft het voorstel aanvaard

governor [guvvənə] 1 gouverneur; 2 bestuurder, president *(of bank)*, directeur *(of prison)*, commandant *(of garrison)*; 3 *(inf)* ouwe, ouwe heer, baas

go with 1 meegaan met *(also fig)*, het eens zijn met: *~ the times* met de tijd meegaan; 2 gepaard gaan met, passen bij: *your socks don't ~ with your shirt* jouw sokken passen niet bij je overhemd

go without het stellen zonder ‖ *it goes without saying* het spreekt vanzelf

gown [gaun] 1 toga, tabbaard; 2 nachthemd[h], ochtendjas; 3 lange jurk, avondjapon

G.P. *General Practitioner* huisarts

G.P.O. *General Post Office* hoofdpostkantoor

gr. 1 *gram* gr; 2 *gross* gros[h]

¹grab [græb] *vb* 1 grijpen, vastpakken; 2 bemachtigen, in de wacht slepen: *~ s.o.'s seat* iemands plaats inpikken; *try to ~ the attention* proberen de aandacht op zich te vestigen

²grab [græb] *vb* graaien, grijpen, pakken

³grab [græb] *n* greep, graai: *make a ~ at* (of: *for) sth.*

ergens naar grijpen; *up for ~s* voor het grijpen

grace [grees] 1 gratie, charme; 2 *(goodness)* vriendelijkheid, fatsoen[h]: *with bad ~* onvriendelijk, met tegenzin; 3 uitstel[h], genade: *a day's ~* een dag uitstel *(of payment)*; 4 (dank)gebed[h]: *say ~* dank zeggen, bidden (bij maaltijd); 5 genade, goedertierenheid, gunst *(of God)*: *fall from ~* tot zonde vervallen, *(fig)* uit de gratie raken, in ongenade vallen; *his smile is his saving ~* zijn glimlach maakt al het overige goed

graceful [greesfoel] 1 gracieus, bevallig, elegant; 2 aangenaam, correct, charmant

gracious [greesjəs] hoffelijk ‖ *good ~!* goeie genade!

gradation [grədeesjən] 1 (geleidelijke) overgang, verloop[h], gradatie; 2 nuance(ring), stap, trede: *many ~s of red* vele tinten rood

¹grade [greed] *n* 1 rang, niveau[h], kwaliteit; 2 klas *(at elementary school)*; 3 cijfer[h] *(as a mark for work handed in at school)*: *make the ~* slagen, aan de eisen voldoen, carrière maken

²grade [greed] *vb* 1 kwalificeren, rangschikken, sorteren *(size, quality etc)*: *~d eggs* gesorteerde eieren; 2 een cijfer geven, beoordelen: *graded reader* voor een bepaald niveau bewerkt boek

grader [greedə] 1 *(Am; educ)* leerling uit de ... klas, ... jaars: *fourth ~* leerling uit de vierde klas; 2 iem die cijfers geeft

grade school basisschool

gradient [greediənt] helling, stijging, hellingshoek: *on a ~* op een helling

gradual [grædzjoeəl] geleidelijk, trapsgewijs

¹graduate [grædzjoeət] *n* 1 afgestudeerde; 2 gediplomeerde

²graduate [grædzjoe·eet] *vb* een diploma behalen, afstuderen, een getuigschrift behalen: *he has ~d in law from Yale* hij heeft aan Yale een titel in de rechten behaald

graduate student postdoctoraal student *(at graduate school)*, doctorandus

graduation [grædzjoe·eesjən] 1 schaalverdeling, maatstreep; 2 uitreiking van diploma, het afstuderen

graffiti [grəfie:tie] graffiti, opschriften, muurtekeningen

¹graft [gra:ft] *n* 1 ent, griffel; 2 (politiek) geknoei[h], omkoperij; smeergeld[h]; 3 zwaar werk[h]

²graft [gra:ft] *vb* 1 enten, samenbinden, inplanten; 2 verenigen, aan elkaar voegen

grain [green] 1 graankorrel; 2 graan[h], koren[h]; 3 korrel(tje[h]), *(fig)* greintje[h], zier: *take his words with a ~ of salt* neem wat hij zegt met een korreltje zout; 4 textuur, vleug, draad *(of fabric)*, vlam, nerf *(in wood)*, korrel *(of film, metal)*, structuur *(of rock)*: *go against the ~* tegen de draad in gaan *(also fig)*

gram [græm] gram

grammar [græmə] 1 spraakkunst, grammatica; 2 (correct) taalgebruik[h]

grammar school 1 atheneum[h], gymnasium[h] *(with Latin and Greek)*; 2 voortgezet lagere school, *(roughly)* mavo

grammatical [grəmætikl] grammaticaal

gramme [græm] *see* gram

gramophone [græməfoon] grammofoon, platenspeler

gran [græn] oma

¹**grand** [grænd] *adj* **1** voornaam, gewichtig, groots: *live in ~ style* op grote voet leven; **2** grootmoedig: *a ~ gesture* een grootmoedig gebaar; **3** prachtig, indrukwekkend; **4** reusachtig, fantastisch; **5** hoofd-, belangrijkste, *(in titles)* groot-: *~ duke* groothertog; *~ piano* vleugel(piano); *grand jury* jury van 12-23 personen die onderzoekt of het bewijsmateriaal voldoende is om arrestaties te verrichten

²**grand** [grænd] *n* **1** vleugel(piano); **2** duizend pondʰ (dollar), *(roughly)* milleʰ: *it cost me two ~* het kostte me twee mille

grandad [grændæd] opa, grootvader

grandchild [grændtsjajld] kleinkindʰ

granddaughter [grændo:tə] kleindochter

grandfather [grændfa:ðə] grootvader

grandiose [grændie·oos] grandioos, groots, prachtig

grandma [grænma:] oma, grootmoeder

grandmaster *(chess, draughts, bridge)* grootmeester

grandmother grootmoeder

grandpa [grænpa:] opa, grootvader

grandparent grootouder

grandson [grændsun] kleinzoon

grandstand (hoofd-, ere)tribune

granite [grænit] granietʰ

granny [grænie] oma, opoe, grootjeʰ

¹**grant** [gra:nt] *vb* **1** toekennen, inwilligen, verlenen, toestaan: *~ a request* een verzoek inwilligen; *~ a discount* korting verlenen; **2** toegeven, erkennen: *I must ~ you that you've are a better driver than I* ik moet toegeven dat je beter rijdt dan ik; *take sth. for ~ed* iets als (te) vanzelfsprekend beschouwen

²**grant** [gra:nt] *n* subsidie, toelage, beurs

grape [greep] druif: *a bunch of ~s* een tros druiven

grapefruit grapefruit, pompelmoes

grape sugar druivensuiker

grapevine 1 wijnstok, wingerd; **2** geruchtʰ; **3** geruchtencircuitʰ: *I heard it on the ~* het is me ter ore gekomen

graph [gra:f] grafiek, diagramʰ, grafische voorstelling

graphic(al) [græfik(l)] **1** grafisch, mbt tekenen, schrijven, drukken: *the ~ arts* de grafische kunsten; **2** treffend, levendig: *a ~ description* een levendige beschrijving; *~ designer* grafisch ontwerper

graphics [græfiks] grafiek, grafische kunst, grafische media

graphite [græfajt] grafietʰ

graphology [grəfollədzjie] handschriftkunde

graph paper millimeterpapierʰ

grapple [græpl] *(with with)* worstelen (met) *(also fig)*, slaags raken (met): *~ with a problem* met een probleem worstelen

¹**grasp** [gra:sp] *vb* **1** grijpen, vastpakken; **2** vatten, begrijpen: *I ~ed half of what he said* de helft van wat hij zei heb ik begrepen

²**grasp** [gra:sp] *vb* grijpen, graaien

³**grasp** [gra:sp] *n* **1** greep *(also fig)*, macht; **2** begripʰ, bevatting, beheersing: *that is beyond my ~* dat gaat mijn pet te boven

grasping [gra:sping] hebberig, inhalig

¹**grass** [gra:s] *n* **1** grasʰ; **2** tipgever, verklikker; **3** *(inf)* marihuana, weed || *cut the ~ from under s.o.'s feet* iem het gras voor de voeten wegmaaien

²**grass** [gra:s] *vb* klikken *(to police):* *~ on s.o.* iem verraden, iem aangeven

grasshopper [gra:shoppə] sprinkhaan

grassroots 1 van gewone mensen, aan de basis: *the ~ opinion* de publieke opinie; **2** fundamenteel

grass widow onbestorven weduwe, groene weduwe

grassy [gra:sie] **1** grazig, grasrijk; **2** grasachtig

¹**grate** [greet] *n* **1** roosterʰ, haardroosterʰ; **2** traliewerkʰ; **3** haard

²**grate** [greet] *vb* raspen: *~d cheese* geraspte kaas

³**grate** [greet] *vb* **1** knarsen; **2** irriterend werken: *the noise ~d on my nerves* het lawaai werkte op mijn zenuwen

grateful [greetfoel] dankbaar

grater [greetə] rasp

gratification [grætiffikkeesjən] voldoening, bevrediging

gratify [grætiffaj] **1** behagen, genoegen doen; **2** voldoen, bevredigen

grating [greeting] **1** roosterʰ, traliewerkʰ; **2** rasterʰ

gratis [grætis] gratis, kosteloos

gratitude [grætitjoe:d] dankbaarheid, dank

gratuitous [grətjoe:ittəs] **1** ongegrond, nodeloos; **2** gratis, kosteloos

¹**grave** [greev] *n* grafʰ, grafkuil, *(fig)* dood, ondergang: *from the cradle to the ~* van de wieg tot het graf; *dig one's own ~* zichzelf te gronde richten; *rise from the ~* uit de dood opstaan

²**grave** *adj* **1** belangrijk, gewichtig: *~ issue* ernstige zaak; **2** ernstig, plechtig: *a ~ look on his face* een ernstige uitdrukking op zijn gezicht

gravel [grævl] **1** grindʰ, kiezelʰ; **2** kiezelzandʰ, grof zandʰ

graveyard kerkhofʰ, begraafplaats

gravitation [grævitteesjən] zwaartekracht: *law of ~* wet van de zwaartekracht

gravity [grævittie] **1** ernst, serieusheid; **2** zwaarte, gewichtʰ, dichtheid: *centre of ~* zwaartepunt *(also fig);* **3** zwaartekracht

gravy [greevie] **1** jus, vleessaus; **2** gemakkelijk verdiend geldʰ, voordeeltjeʰ

gravy boat juskom *(with spout)*

gray [gree] *see* grey

¹**graze** [greez] *vb* **1** grazen, weiden; **2** schampen, schuren

²**graze** [greez] *vb* **1** laten grazen, weiden, hoeden; **2** licht(jes) aanraken, schampen, schuren: *he ~d his*

arm against the wall hij schaafde zijn arm tegen de muur

³**graze** [greez] *n* 1 schampschot^h; 2 schaafwond, schram

¹**grease** [grie:s] *n* vet^h, smeer^h

²**grease** [grie:z] *vb* invetten, oliën, smeren

¹**great** [greet] *adj* 1 groot, nobel *(persons):* a ~ *man* een groot man; 2 geweldig, fantastisch: *a* ~ *idea* een geweldig idee; 3 groot, belangrijk, vooraanstaand: *Great Britain* Groot-Brittannië; *the Great Wall of China* de Chinese Muur; 4 buitengewoon, groot, zwaar *(emotions, situations etc);* 5 groot, aanzienlijk, hoog *(number):* a ~ *deal* heel wat; *a* ~ *many* heel wat, een heleboel; 6 lang, hoog *(age, time):* live *to a* ~ *age* een hoge leeftijd bereiken; 7 groot, ijverig, enthousiast: *a* ~ *reader* een verwoed lezer; 8 *(inf)* omvangrijk, dik, reuze-, enorm: *a* ~ *big tree* een kanjer van een boom; 9 goed, bedreven: *he is* ~ *at golf* hij is een geweldige golfer; *Great Dane* Deense dog; *at* ~ *length* uitvoerig; *be in* ~ *spirits* opgewekt zijn; *set* ~ *store by* (of: *on)* grote waarde hechten aan; *the* ~*est thing since sliced bread* iets fantastisch; *the Great War* de Eerste Wereldoorlog

²**great** [greet] *n* groten, vooraanstaande figuren: *Hermans is one of the* ~ *of Dutch literature* Hermans is een van de groten van de Nederlandse literatuur

greatly [greetlie] zeer, buitengewoon: ~ *moved* zeer ontroerd

Grecian [grie:sjən] Grieks *(in style etc)*

Greece [grie:s] Griekenland

greed [grie:d] 1 hebzucht, hebberigheid, gulzigheid; 2 gierigheid

¹**Greek** [grie:k] *n* Griek(se)

²**Greek** [grie:k] *adj* Grieks: *(fig) that is* ~ *to me* daar snap ik niks van

¹**green** [grie:n] *adj* 1 groen, met gras begroeid; 2 groen, plantaardig: ~ *vegetables* bladgroenten; 3 groen, onrijp, *(fig)* onervaren, naïef; 4 groen, milieu-: *the* ~ *party* de Groenen; 5 jaloers, afgunstig: ~ *with envy* scheel van afgunst

²**green** [grie:n] *n* 1 grasveld^h, brink, dorpsplein^h; 2 *(golf)* green; 3 groen^h; 4 loof^h, groen gewas^h; 5 ~*s* (blad)groenten; 6 (de) Groenen, (de) milieupartij

greenery [grie:nərie] groen^h, bladeren en groene takken

greengrocer groenteboer, groenteman

greenhorn groentje^h, beginneling

greenhouse broeikas: ~ *effect* broeikaseffect

Greenland Groenland

Greenwich Mean Time [grinnidzj mie:n tajm] Greenwichtijd

greet [grie:t] 1 begroeten, groeten; 2 onthalen, begroeten || *a cold air* ~*ed us* een vlaag koude lucht kwam ons tegemoet

greeting [grie:ting] 1 groet, begroeting, wens: *exchange* ~*s* elkaar begroeten; 2 aanhef *(of letter)*

gregarious [grigəəriəs] 1 in kudde(n) levend: *a* ~ *animal* een kuddedier; 2 van gezelschap houdend, graag met anderen zijnd

Gregorian [grigo:riən] gregoriaans: ~ *calendar* gregoriaanse kalender

gremlin [gremlin] 1 pechduiveltje^h, zetduivel; 2 kwelgeest, lastpak

grenade [grinneed] (hand)granaat

¹**grey** [gree] *adj* 1 grijs(kleurig): ~ *cells* grijze cellen, hersenen; *his face turned* ~ zijn gezicht werd (as)grauw; 2 grijs, bewolkt, grauw; 3 somber, treurig, triest: ~ *with age* grijs van de ouderdom, *(fig)* verouderd

²**grey** [gree] *n* 1 schimmel *(horse);* 2 grijs^h

greyhound 1 hazewind(hond); 2 greyhoundbus *(large coach for long-distance travel)*

grid [grid] 1 rooster^h, traliewerk^h; 2 raster^h, coördinatenstelsel^h *(of map);* 3 netwerk^h, hoogspanningsnet^h

grief [grie:f] leed^h, verdriet^h, smart: *come to* ~: *a)* verongelukken; *b)* vallen; *c) (also fig)* mislukken, falen

grievance [grie:vəns] 1 grief, klacht; 2 bitter gevoel^h: *nurse a* ~ *against s.o.* wrok tegen iem koesteren

¹**grieve** [grie:v] *vb* treuren, verdriet hebben: ~ *for s.o.,* ~ *over s.o.'s death* treuren om iemands dood

²**grieve** [grie:v] *vb* bedroeven, verdriet veroorzaken: *it* ~*s me to hear that* het spijt mij dat te horen

griffin [griffin] griffioen

¹**grill** [gril] *n* 1 grill, rooster^h; 2 geroosterd (vlees)gerecht^h

²**grill** [gril] *vb* roosteren, grilleren, *(fig)* bakken: ~*ing on the beach* op het strand liggen bakken

³**grill** [gril] *vb* verhoren, aan een kruisverhoor onderwerpen

grille [gril] 1 traliewerk^h, rooster^h, rasterwerk^h; 2 traliehek(je^h), kijkraampje^h; 3 radiatorscherm^h *(of car),* sierscherm^h, grille

grim [grim] 1 onverbiddelijk, meedogenloos: ~ *determination* onwrikbare vastberadenheid; 2 akelig, beroerd: ~ *prospects* ongunstige vooruitzichten

grimace [grimmees] grimas, gezicht^h, grijns: *make* ~*s* smoelen trekken

grime [grajm] vuil^h, roet^h

¹**grin** [grin] *n* 1 brede glimlach; 2 grijns, grimas: *take that (silly)* ~ *off your face!* sta niet (zo dom) te grijnzen!

²**grin** [grin] *vb* grijnzen, grinniken, glimlachen: ~ *and bear it* zich flink houden, op zijn tanden bijten

¹**grind** [grajnd] *vb* 1 blokken, ploeteren: *he is* ~*ing away at his maths* hij zit op zijn wiskunde te blokken; 2 knarsen, schuren, krassen: ~ *one's teeth* tandenknarsen; ~ *to a halt* tot stilstand komen *(also fig);* 3 verbrijzelen, (ver)malen, verpletteren, *(fig)* onderdrukken: ~ *coffee* koffie malen; ~*ing poverty* schrijnende armoede; 4 (uit)trappen *(also fig): Joe* ~*ed his cigarette into the rug* Joe trapte zijn sigaret in het tapijt (uit); 5 (doen) draaien *((coffee) grinder, barrel organ etc)*

²**grind** [grajnd] *n* 1 geknars^h, schurend geluid; 2 inspanning, (vervelend) karwei^h

grinder [grajndə] **1** molen; **2** slijper, slijpmachine; **3** maalsteen; **4** kies

grind out uitbrengen, voortbrengen, opdreunen *(continuously and mechanically): the pupil first had to ~ ten irregular verbs* de leerling moest eerst tien onregelmatige werkwoorden opdreunen

gringo [gringgoo] vreemdeling

¹grip [grip] *vb* vastpakken, grijpen, vasthouden, *(fig)* pakken, boeien: *a ~ping story* een boeiend verhaal

²grip [grip] *vb* pakken *(of brake etc)*, grijpen *(of anchor)*

³grip [grip] *n* **1** greep, houvastʰ: *keep a tight ~ on* stevig vasthouden; **2** beheersing, macht, meesterschapʰ, *(fig)* begripʰ, vatʰ: *come to ~s with a problem* een probleem aanpakken; *keep* (of: *take) a ~ on oneself* zich beheersen, zichzelf in de hand houden; **3** greep, handvatʰ; **4** toneelknecht

gripe [grajp] klacht, bezwaarʰ, kritiek

grip fastening klittenbandsluiting

grisly [grizlie] **1** griezelig, akelig; **2** weerzinwekkend, verschrikkelijk

gristle [grisl] kraakbeenʰ *(in meat)*

¹grit [grit] *n* **1** gruisʰ, zandʰ; **2** lefʰ, durf

²grit [grit] *vb* **1** knarsen: *~ one's teeth* knarsetanden *(also fig);* **2** met zand bestrooien: *~ the icy roads* de gladde wegen met zand bestrooien

gritty [grittie] **1** zanderig, korrelig; **2** kranig, moedig, flink

grizzled [grizld] **1** grijs, grauw; **2** grijsharig

grizzly [grizlie] grizzly(beer)

¹groan [groon] *vb* **1** kreunen, kermen, steunen: *~ with pain* kreunen van de pijn; **2** grommen, brommen

²groan [groon] *n* gekreunʰ, gekermʰ, gesteunʰ

grocer [groosə] kruidenier

grocery [groosərie] **1** kruidenierswinkel; **2** kruideniersbedrijfʰ, kruideniersvakʰ; **3** *-ies* kruidenierswaren, levensmiddelen

grog [grog] grog, (warme) drank bestaande uit cognac, wijn e.d. verdund met water

groggy [grogie] **1** onvast op de benen, wankel; **2** suf, versuft, verdoofd: *I feel ~* ik voel me suf

groin [grojn] lies

¹groom [groe:m] *n* **1** bruidegom; **2** stalknecht

²groom [groe:m] *vb* **1** verzorgen *(horses)*, roskammen; **2** een keurig uiterlijk geven, uiterlijk verzorgen *(pers)*

groove [groe:v] **1** groef, gleuf, sponning; **2** routine, sleur: *find one's ~, get into the ~* zijn draai vinden; *be stuck in the ~* in een sleur zitten

¹grope [groop] *vb* tasten, rondtasten, *(fig)* zoeken: *~ for an answer* onzeker naar een antwoord zoeken

²grope [groop] *vb* **1** al tastend zoeken: *~ one's way* zijn weg op de tast zoeken; **2** betasten *(esp with sexual intentions)*

¹gross [groos] *adj* **1** grof *(also fig)*, dik, lomp: *~ injustice* uitgesproken onrechtvaardigheid; *~ language* ruwe taal; **2** bruto, totaal: *~ national product*

bruto nationaal product

²gross [groos] *n* grosʰ, 12 dozijn, 144: *by the ~* bij dozijnen, bij het gros

³gross [groos] *vb* een bruto winst hebben van, in totaal verdienen

grotesque [grootesk] zonderling, belachelijk

grotto [grottoo] *(also ~es)* grot

grotty [grottie] *(inf)* rottig, vies, waardeloos

grouch [grautsj] mopperen, mokken: *he is always ~ing about his students* hij loopt altijd te mopperen over zijn studenten

¹ground *n* **1** terreinʰ; **2** grond, reden, basis *(of action, reasoning): on religious ~s* uit godsdienstige overwegingen; **3** grond, aarde, bodem *(also fig): go to ~: a)* zich in een hol verschuilen *(of animal); b)* onderduiken *(of person); get off the ~* van de grond komen; **4** gebiedʰ *(fig)*, grondgebiedʰ, afstand: *break new* (of: *fresh) ~* nieuw terrein betreden, pionierswerk verrichten; *gain* (of: *make) ~: a)* veld winnen; *b)* erop vooruit gaan; *give* (of: *lose) ~* terrein verliezen, wijken; *hold* (of: *keep, stand) one's ~* standhouden, voet bij stuk houden; **5** *~s* gronden, domeinʰ, parkʰ *(around bldg): a house standing in its own ~s* een huis, geheel door eigen grond omgeven; *cut the ~ from under s.o.'s feet* iem het gras voor de voeten wegmaaien; *it suits him down to the ~* dat komt hem uitstekend van pas

²ground *vb* **1** op de grond terecht komen, de grond raken; **2** aan de grond lopen, stranden

³ground *vb* **1** aan de grond houden *(aeroplane, pilot): the planes have been ~ed by the fog* de vliegtuigen moeten door mist aan de grond blijven; **2** laten stranden *(ship)*

ground control vluchtleiding

ground-floor benedenverdieping, parterre

grounding [graunding] scholing, training, basisvorming

ground plan plattegrond, grondplanʰ, *(fig)* ontwerpʰ, blauwdruk

groundsman [graundzmən] **1** terreinknecht; **2** tuinman

groundswell vloedgolf *(also fig);* zware golving, nadeining *(of sea, after storm or earthquake)*

¹group [groe:p] *n* groep, geheelʰ, verzameling, klasse, familie, afdeling, onderdeelʰ

²group [groe:p] *vb* zich groeperen

³group [groe:p] *vb* groeperen, in groepen plaatsen: *we ~ed ourselves round the guide* we gingen in een groep rond de gids staan

¹grouse [graus] *n* korhoenʰ, Schotse sneeuwhoen

²grouse [graus] *vb* mopperen, klagen

grovel [grovl] kruipen *(fig)*, zich vernederen, zich verlagen: *~ before s.o.* voor iem kruipen

¹grow [groo] *vb* **1** groeien, opgroeien, ontstaan: *~ wild* in het wild groeien; *~ up: a)* opgroeien, volwassen worden; *b) ~ up into* opgroeien tot, zich ontwikkelen tot, worden; *~ out of: a)* ontstaan uit; *b)* ontgroeien *(bad habit, friends); ~ out of one's clothes* uit zijn kleren groeien; **2** aangroeien, zich ontwikkelen, gedijen: ~ *to become* uit-groeien tot; ~ *into sth. big* tot iets groots uitgroeien; ~ *up!* doe niet zo kinderachtig!

²**grow** [groo] *vb* **1** kweken, verbouwen, telen: ~ *vegetables* groenten kweken; **2** laten staan (groeien) *(beard)*; **3** laten begroeien, bedekken

³**grow** [groo] *vb* worden, gaan: *she has ~n (into) a woman* ze is een volwassen vrouw geworden

grower [grooə] kweker, teler, verbouwer

growing pains 1 groeistuipen, groeipijnen; **2** kinderziekten *(fig)*

growl [graul] **1** grommen, brommen; **2** snauwen, grauwen

grown 1 gekweekt, geteeld; **2** volgroeid, rijp, volwassen

grown-up volwassen

growth [grooθ] **1** gewasʰ, productʰ; **2** gezwelʰ, uitwas, tumor; **3** groei, (volle) ontwikkeling: *reach full* ~ volgroeid zijn; **4** toename, uitbreiding; **5** kweek, productie

growth area groeisector, (snel) groeiende bedrijfstak

grub [grub] **1** larve, made, rups; **2** etenʰ, voerʰ, hap

grubby [grubbie] vuil, vies, smerig

¹**grudge** [grudzj] *n* wrok, grief

²**grudge** [grudzj] *vb* misgunnen, niet gunnen, benijden

grudgingly [grudzjinglie] met tegenzin, niet van harte

gruelling [groe:əling] afmattend, slopend

gruesome [groe:səm] gruwelijk, afschuwelijk

gruff [gruf] nors, bars

¹**grumble** [grumbl] *vb* morren, mopperen, brommen: ~ *at s.o. about sth.* tegen iem over iets mopperen

²**grumble** [grumbl] *vb* rommelen *(of thunder)*

grumpy [grumpie] knorrig, humeurig

grunt [grunt] knorren, brommen, grommen

G-string [dzjie:string] tangaslipjeʰ

¹**guarantee** [gærəntie:] *n* waarborg, garantie(bewijsʰ), zekerheid, belofte

²**guarantee** [gærəntie:] *vb* **1** garanderen, waarborgen, borg staan voor; **2** verzekeren

¹**guard** [ga:d] *n* **1** bewaker, cipier, gevangenbewaarder; **2** conducteur *(on train)*; **3** beveiliging, beschterming(smiddelʰ), schermʰ, kap; **4** wacht, bewaking, waakzaamheid: *be on* (of: *keep, stand*) ~ de wacht houden, op wacht staan; *the changing of the* ~ het aflossen van de wacht; *catch s.o. off (his)* ~ iem overrompelen; *be on (one's)* ~ *against* bedacht zijn op; **5** garde, (lijf)wacht, escorteʰ

²**guard** [ga:d] *vb* **1** (zich) verdedigen, zich dekken; **2** zich hoeden, zijn voorzorgen nemen: ~ *against sth.* zich voor iets hoeden; **3** op wacht staan

³**guard** [ga:d] *vb* **1** bewaken, beveiligen, bewaren *(secret)*; **2** beschermen

guarded [ga:did] voorzichtig, bedekt *(terms)*

guardian [ga:diən] **1** bewaker, beschermer, oppasser; **2** voogd(es), curator

guardian angel beschermengel, engelbewaarder

guard rail 1 leuning, reling; **2** vangrail

guava [gwa:və] guave

gue(r)rilla [gərilla] guerrilla(strijder)

¹**guess** [ges] *vb* **1** raden, schatten, gissen: *keep s.o.* ~*ing* iem in het ongewisse laten; ~ *at sth.* naar iets raden; **2** denken, aannemen: *What is that? - That is his new car, I* ~ Wat is dat nou? - Dat is zijn nieuwe auto, neem ik aan

²**guess** [ges] *n* gis(sing), ruwe schatting: *your* ~ *is as good as mine* ik weet het net zo min als jij; *make* (of: *have) a* ~ *(at sth.)* (naar iets) raden; *it is anybody's* (of: *anyone's) ~* dat is niet te zeggen; *at a* ~ naar schatting

guest [gest] **1** gast, logé: ~ *of honour* eregast; **2** genodigde, introducé: *be my* ~*!* ga je gang!

guidance [gajdəns] **1** leiding; **2** raad, adviesʰ, hulp, begeleiding: *vocational* ~ beroepsvoorlichting

¹**guide** [gajd] *n* **1** gids; **2** leidraad; **3** padvindster, gids

²**guide** [gajd] *vb* **1** leiden, gidsen, de weg wijzen, (be)geleiden: *a* ~*d tour of the head office* een rondleiding in het hoofdkantoor; **2** als leidraad dienen voor: *he was* ~*d by his feelings* hij liet zich leiden door zijn gevoelens

guild [gild] gildeʰ

guilder [gildə] gulden

guildhall 1 gildehuisʰ; **2** raadhuisʰ, stadhuisʰ

guile [gajl] slinksheid, bedrogʰ, valsheid: *he is full of* ~ hij is niet te vertrouwen

guillotine [gillətie:n] **1** guillotine, valbijl; **2** papiersnijmachine

guilt [gilt] schuld, schuldgevoelʰ

guilty [giltie] schuldig, schuldbewust: *a* ~ *conscience* een slecht geweten; *plead not* ~ schuld ontkennen

guinea [ginnie] gienjeʰ *(old gold coin with a value of 21 shillings)*

guinea pig 1 cavia; **2** proefkonijnʰ

guitar [gitta:] gitaar

gulf [gulf] golf, (wijde) baai

Gulf stream Golfstroom

gull [gul] meeuw

gullet [gullit] keel(gatʰ), strot ‖ *stick in s.o.'s* ~ onverteerbaar zijn voor iem

gullible [gullibl] makkelijk beet te nemen, lichtgelovig, onnozel

gully [gullie] geul, ravijnʰ, greppel

¹**gulp** [gulp] *vb* schrokken, slokken, slikken: *he* ~*ed down his drink* hij sloeg zijn borrel achterover

²**gulp** [gulp] *n* **1** teug, slok; **2** slikbeweging

gum [gum] **1** ~*s* tandvleesʰ; **2** gom(harsʰ); **3** kauwgom

gumdrop gombal

gumption [gumpsjən] *(inf)* **1** initiatiefʰ, ondernemingslust, vindingrijkheid; **2** gewiekstheid, pienterheid

¹**gun** [gun] *n* **1** stukʰ geschut, kanonʰ; **2** vuurwapenʰ, (jacht)geweerʰ, pistoolʰ; **3** spuitpistoolʰ ‖ *beat* (of: *jump) the* ~ te vroeg van start gaan, *(fig)* op de zaak

vooruitlopen; *stick to one's ~s* voet bij stuk houden

²gun [gʌn] *vb* jagen, op jacht zijn (gaan)

³gun [gʌn] *vb (also with down)* neerschieten, neerknallen: *he was gunned down from an ambush* hij
werd vanuit een hinderlaag neergeknald

gunge [gʌndzj] smurrie

gunman [gʌnmən] gangster, (beroeps)moorde-
naar

gunmetal staalgrijs[h]

gunner [gʌnnə] **1** artillerist, kanonnier; **2** boord-
schutter

gunpoint: *at ~* onder bedreiging van een vuurwapen, onder schot

gun-runner wapensmokkelaar

¹gurgle [gɔːgl] *vb* kirren, klokken, murmelen

²gurgle [gɔːgl] *vb* kirrend zeggen

³gurgle [gɔːgl] *n* gekir[h] *(of baby)*, geklok[h], gemurmel[h]

guru [goeroe:] goeroe

¹gush [gʌsj] *vb* **1** stromen, gutsen; **2** dwepen (met),
overdreven doen (over)

²gush [gʌsj] *vb* spuiten, uitstorten, doen stromen

³gush [gʌsj] *n* **1** stroom *(also fig)*, vloed, uitbarsting;
2 uitbundigheid, overdrevenheid; **3** sentimentaliteit

gust [gʌst] (wind)vlaag, windstoot

gusto [gʌstoo] animo[h]: *with (great) ~* enthousiast

¹gut [gʌt] *n* **1** darm; **2** *~s* ingewanden; **3** *~s* lef[h], durf,
moed || *hate s.o.'s ~s* grondig de pest hebben aan
iem; *sweat (of: work) one's ~s out* zich een ongeluk
werken

²gut [gʌt] *adj* instinctief, onberedeneerd: *a ~ reaction* een (zuiver) gevoelsmatige reactie

³gut [gʌt] *vb* uitbranden *(of bldg)*

¹gutter [gʌttə] *n* goot *(also fig)*, geul, greppel, dakgoot: *he'll end up in the ~* hij belandt nog in de goot

²gutter [gʌttə] *vb* druipen *(of candle)*

guv [gʌv] **1** baas *(employer);* **2** ouwe heer *(father);* **3**
meneer

guy [gɑj] **1** kerel, vent, man; **2** mens, *~s* lui, jongens,
mensen: *where are you ~s going?* waar gaan jullie
naar toe?

guzzler [gʌzlə] zwelger, brasser, zuiper

gym [dzjim] **1** gymlokaal[h], fitnesscentrum[h], sport-
school; **2** gymnastiek(les)

gymnasium [dzjimneeziəm] gymnastieklokaal[h]

gymnast [dzjimnæst] gymnast, turner

gymnastics [dzjimnæstiks] gymnastiek, lichamelijke oefening, turnen[h]

gynaecologist [gajnikkɔllədzjist] gynaecoloog,
vrouwenarts

gypsy [dzjipsie] zigeuner(in)

h

haberdashery [hæbədæsjɔrie] **1** fournituren, garen[h], band; fourniturenwinkel; **2** *(Am)* herenmode(artikelen); herenmodezaak

habit [hæbit] **1** habijt[h], ordekleed[h]; **2** rijkleding: *riding* ~ rijkleding; **3** gewoonte, hebbelijkheid, aanwensel[h]: *fall (of: get) into the* ~ de gewoonte aannemen; *he has a habit of changing the lyrics in mid-song* hij heeft de gewoonte om midden in het lied de tekst de veranderen; *get out of (of: kick) the* ~ *of doing sth.* (de gewoonte) afleren om iets te doen; *be in the* ~ *of doing sth.* gewoon zijn iets te doen

habitable [hæbittəbl] bewoonbaar

habitat [hæbitæt] natuurlijke omgeving *(of plant, animal)*, habitat, woongebied[h]

habitation [hæbitteesjən] woning; bewoning

habitual [həbitsjoeəl] **1** gewoon(lijk), gebruikelijk; **2** gewoonte-

¹hack [hæk] *n* **1** huurpaard[h], knol; **2** broodschrijver; **3** houw, snee, jaap, trap(wond)

²hack [hæk] *vb* **1** hakken, houwen, een jaap geven: ~ *off a branch* een tak afkappen; ~ *at sth.* in iets hakken, op iets in houwen; **2** fijnhakken, bewerken *(soil)*; **3** kraken, een computerkraak plegen, hacken

hacker [hækə] **1** (computer)kraker, hacker; **2** computermaniak

hackneyed [hæknid] afgezaagd, banaal *(of saying)*

hacksaw ijzerzaag, metaalzaag

haddock [hædək] schelvis

haemophilia [hie:məfillìə] hemofilie, bloederziekte

haemorrhage [hemməridzj] bloeding: *massive ~s* zware bloedingen

haemorrhoids [hemmərojdz] aambeien

hag [hæg] (lelijke oude) heks

haggard [hægəd] verwilderd uitziend, wild *(of look)*, met holle ogen, afgetobd

haggle [hægl] **1** kibbelen; **2** pingelen, afdingen: ~ *with s.o. about (of: over) sth.* met iem over iets marchanderen

Hague [heeg]: *The* ~ Den Haag, 's-Gravenhage

¹hail [heel] *n* hagel(steen), *(fig)* regen, stortvloed: *a* ~ *of bullets* een regen van kogels

²hail [heel] *vb* hagelen *(also fig)*, neerkomen (als hagel)

³hail *n* (welkomst)groet

⁴hail *vb* **1** erkennen, begroeten als: *the people ~ed him (as) king* het volk haalde hem als koning in; **2** aanroepen: ~ *a taxi* een taxi (aan)roepen

hailstorm hagelbui

hair [heə] haar[h], haren, hoofdhaar[h]: *let one's ~ down* het haar los dragen, *(fig)* zich laten gaan; *hang by a* ~ aan een zijden draadje hangen; *not harm a ~ on s.o.'s head* iem geen haar krenken; *(inf) keep your ~ on!* maak je niet dik!; *split ~s* haarkloven; *tear one's ~ (out)* zich de haren uit het hoofd trekken; *without turning a* ~ zonder een spier te vertrekken

hairdresser kapper, *(Am)* dameskapper

hairgrip (haar)speld(je[h])

hairpin haarspeld: ~ *bend* haarspeldbocht

hair-splitting haarkloverij

hairstyle kapsel[h], coiffure

hairy [heərie] **1** harig, behaard; **2** riskant

halcyon [hælsiən] kalm, vredig, gelukkig

hale [heel] gezond, kras: ~ *and hearty* fris en gezond

¹half [ha:f] *n* helft, half(je[h]), de helft van: ~ *an hour, a ~ hour* een half uur; *two and a* ~ tweeëneenhalf; *one* ~ een helft; *(inf) go halves with s.o. in sth.* de kosten van iets met iem samsam delen; *he's too clever by* ~ hij is veel te sluw; *(inf) that was a game and a* ~ dat was me een wedstrijd

²half [ha:f] *pron* de helft: ~ *of six is three* de helft van zes is drie

³half [ha:f] *adv* half, *(inf)* bijna: *only* ~ *cooked* maar half gaar; *I* ~ *wish ik zou bijna willen*; ~ *as much (of: many) again* anderhalf maal zoveel; *(inf)* ~ *seven* half acht; *he didn't do* ~ *as badly as we'd thought* hij deed het lang zo slecht niet als we gedacht hadden; ~ *past (of: after) one* half twee; ~ *and* ~ half om half *(also fig)*; *(inf) he didn't* ~ *get mad* hij werd me daar toch razend; *(inf) not* ~ *bad* lang niet kwaad, schitterend; *not* ~ *strong enough* lang niet sterk genoeg

half-breed halfbloed, bastaard-

half holiday vrije middag *(at schools)*

half-life halveringstijd: *some radioactive materials have a* ~ *of thousands of years* sommige radioactieve stoffen hebben een halveringstijd van duizenden jaren

half-term *(school)* korte vakantie

half-time **1** *(sport)* rust: *at* ~ tijdens de rust; **2** halve werktijd, deeltijdarbeid, halve dagen: *be on* ~ halve dagen werken, een deeltijdbaan *(of:* halve baan) hebben

halfway house **1** rehabilitatiecentrum[h], reclasseringscentrum[h]; **2** compromis[h]

halibut [hælibbət] heilbot

hall [ho:l] **1** zaal, ridderzaal; **2** openbaar gebouw[h], paleis[h]; **3** groot herenhuis[h]; **4** vestibule, hal[h], gang; **5** studentenhuis[h]: ~ *of residence* studentenhuis

hallelujah [hælilloe:jə] halleluja[h]

hallmark stempel[h] *(also fig)*, gehaltemerk[h], waarmerk[h], kenmerk[h]

hallo [həl<u>oo</u>] hallo!, hé!

hallowed [hælood] gewijd, heilig

Hallowe′en [hælo<u>ie:</u>n] avond voor Allerheiligen

hallucination [həloe:sinn<u>ee</u>sjən] hallucinatie, zinsbegoocheling

hallway portaal^h, hal^h, vestibule

halo [h<u>ee</u>loo] *(also ~es)* **1** halo; **2** stralenkrans, *(fig)* glans

¹halt [ho:lt] *n* **1** *(inf)* (bus)halte, stopplaats, stationnetje^h; **2** halt, stilstand, rust: *call a ~ to* een halt toeroepen; *come to a ~* tot stilstand komen

²halt [ho:lt] *vb* halt (doen) houden, stoppen, pauzeren

halter [h<u>o:</u>ltə] **1** halster^h; **2** strop

halting [h<u>o:</u>lting] weifelend, aarzelend, onzeker: *a ~ voice* een stokkende stem

halve [ha:v] halveren, in tweeën delen, tot de helft reduceren

¹ham [hæm] *n* **1** ham; **2** dij, bil, ~s achterste^h; **3** *(inf)* amateur

²ham [hæm] *vb* overacteren, overdrijven: *~ up* zich aanstellen

ham-fisted onhandig

hamlet [hæmlət] gehucht^h

¹hammer [hæmə] *n* hamer: *go (of: come) under the ~* geveild worden; *go at it ~ and tongs* er uit alle macht tegenaan gaan

²hammer [hæmə] *vb* **1** hameren: *~ (away) at* er op losbeuken; **2** *(inf)* zwoegen: *~ (away) at sth.* op iets zwoegen

³hammer [hæmə] *vb* **1** hameren, smeden; **2** *(inf)* verslaan, inmaken, een zware nederlaag toebrengen; **3** *(inf)* scherp bekritiseren, afkraken || *~ out a compromise solution* (moeizaam) een compromis uitwerken

hammock [hæmək] hangmat

¹hamper [hæmpə] *n* **1** (grote) sluitmand, pakmand *(for foodstuffs)*: *Christmas ~* kerstpakket; **2** *(Am)* wasmand

²hamper [hæmpə] *vb* belemmeren, storen, *(fig)* hinderen

¹hamstring [hæmstring] *vb* de achillespees doorsnijden bij, kreupel maken, *(fig)* verlammen, frustreren

²hamstring [hæmstring] *n* **1** kniepees; **2** hakpees, achillespees

¹hand [hænd] *n* **1** hand; voorpoot *(of animals)*: *bind (of: tie) s.o. ~ and foot* iem aan handen en voeten binden *(also fig)*; *hold (of: join) ~s* (elkaar) de hand geven; *shake s.o.'s ~, shake ~s with s.o.* iem de hand drukken; *wring one's ~s* ten einde raad zijn; *~s off!* bemoei je er niet mee!; *at ~* dichtbij, *(fig)* op handen; *close (of: near) at ~* heel dichtbij; *by ~: a)* met de hand (geschreven); *b)* in handen, per bode *(letter)*; *make (of: earn) money ~ over fist* geld als water verdienen; **2** arbeider, werkman, bemanningslid^h: *~s needed* arbeidskrachten gevraagd; *all ~s on deck!* alle hens aan dek!; **3** vakman, specialist: *be a poor ~ at sth.* geen slag van iets hebben; **4** wijzer *(of clock)*, naald *(of meter)*; **5** kaart(en) *(assigned to a player)*, hand: *overplay one's ~* te veel wagen, te ver gaan, zijn hand overspelen; *show (of: reveal) one's ~* zijn kaarten op tafel leggen; **6** handbreed(te) *(approximately 10 cm)*; **7** kant, zijde, richting: *at my left ~* aan mijn linkerhand; *on the one ~* aan de ene kant; **8** handschrift^h, handtekening: *set (of: put) one's ~ to a document* zijn hand(tekening) onder een document plaatsen; **9** hulp, steun, bijstand: *give (of: lend) s.o. a (helping) ~* iem een handje helpen; **10** controle, beheersing, bedwang^h: *have the situation well in ~* de toestand goed in handen hebben; *take in ~* onder handen nemen; *get out of ~* uit de hand lopen; **11** ~s macht, beschikking, gezag^h: *change ~s* in andere handen overgaan, van eigenaar veranderen; *put (of: lay) (one's) ~s on sth.* de hand leggen op iets; *the children are off my ~s* de kinderen zijn de deur uit; *have time on one's ~s: a)* tijd zat hebben; *b)* uit de hand lopen; **12** toestemming, (huwelijks)belofte, (handels)akkoord^h *(with handshake)*: *ask for s.o.'s ~* iem ten huwelijk vragen; **13** invloed, aandeel^h: *have a ~ in sth.* bij iets betrokken zijn; **14** applaus^h, bijval: *the actress got a big (of: good) ~* de actrice kreeg een daverend applaus; *try one's ~ at (doing) sth.* iets proberen; *get one's ~ in at sth.* iets onder de knie krijgen; **15** ~s *(sport)* hands^h, handsbal: *wait on (of: serve) s.o. ~ and foot* iem op zijn wenken bedienen; *they are ~ in glove* ze zijn twee handen op één buik; *go ~ in ~* samengaan; *force s.o.'s ~* iem tot handelen dwingen; *lay (of: put) one's ~ on* de hand weten te leggen op; *strengthen one's ~* zijn positie verbeteren; *my ~s are tied* ik ben machteloos; *turn one's ~ to sth.* iets ondernemen; *(euph) where can I wash my ~s?* waar is het toilet?; *wash one's ~s of sth.* zijn handen van iets aftrekken; *win ~s down* op één been winnen; *at the ~s of s.o., at s.o.'s ~s* van(wege) iem, door iem; *live from ~ to mouth* van de hand in de tand leven; *cash in ~* contanten in kas; *we have plenty of time in ~* we hebben nog tijd genoeg; *out of ~: a)* voor de vuist weg; *b)* tactloos; *have s.o. eating out of one's ~* iem volledig in zijn macht hebben; *to ~* bij de hand, dichtbij; *a ~-to-mouth existence* een leven van dag tot dag, *(roughly)* te veel om dood te gaan, te weinig om van te leven; *with one ~ (tied) behind one's back* zonder enige moeite; *(at) first ~* uit de eerste hand

²hand [hænd] *vb* **1** overhandigen, aanreiken, (aan)geven: *~ back* teruggeven; *~ round* ronddelen; **2** helpen, een handje helpen, leiden: *(inf) you have to ~ it to her* dat moet je haar nageven

handcuffs handboeien

hand down 1 overleveren *(tradition etc)*, overgaan *(possession)*: *this watch has been handed down in our family for 130 years* dit horloge gaat in onze familie al 130 jaar over van generatie op generatie; **2** aangeven

handicap [hændiekæp] **1** handicap, nadeel^h; **2** *(sport)* handicap, (wedren met) voorgift

handicapped [hændiekæpt] gehandicapt, invalide

handicraft [hændiekra:ft] handvaardigheid, handenarbeid, handwerk[h]

hand in 1 inleveren: *please ~ your paper to your own teacher* lever alsjeblieft je proefwerk in bij je eigen docent; **2** voorleggen, aanbieden, indienen: *~ one's resignation* zijn ontslag indienen

handkerchief [hæŋgkətsjie:f] *(also handchieves)* zakdoek

¹handle [hændl] *n* **1** handvat[h], hendel, steel; **2** knop, kruk, klink; **3** heft[h], greep; **4** oor[h], hengsel[h] || *(inf) fly off the ~* opvliegen, z'n zelfbeheersing verliezen

²handle [hændl] *vb* **1** aanraken, betasten, bevoelen *(with one's hands)*; **2** hanteren, bedienen, manipuleren: *~ with care!* voorzichtig (behandelen)!; **3** behandelen, omgaan met; **4** verwerken, afhandelen; **5** aanpakken, bespreken *(problem)*: *can he ~ that situation?* kan hij die situatie aan?; **6** verhandelen, handelen in

handlebar stuur[h] *(of bicycle)*

handout 1 gift, aalmoes; **2** stencil[h], folder

hand out ronddelen, uitdelen

hand over overhandigen *(esp money)*, overdragen

handrail leuning

handsome [hænsəm] **1** mooi, schoon, knap *(man)*, elegant, statig *(woman)*; **2** royaal, gul *(reward, prize)*, overvloedig, ruim || *come down ~(ly)* flink over de brug komen

hands-on praktisch, praktijk-: *~ training* praktijkgerichte training

handwriting (hand)schrift[h]

handy [hændie] **1** bij de hand, binnen bereik; **2** handig, praktisch: *come in ~* van pas komen

handyman klusjesman, manusje-van-alles[h]

¹hang [hæŋ] *vb* **1** hangen: *~ loose: a)* loshangen; *b)* kalm blijven; **2** hangen, opgehangen worden; **3** zweven, blijven hangen; **4** aanhangen, zich vastklemmen, vast (blijven) zitten; **5** onbeslist zijn: *~ in the balance* (nog) onbeslist zijn; *~ behind* achterblijven; *(Am) ~ in (there)* volhouden; *she hung on(to) his every word* zij was één en al oor; *~ onto sth.* proberen te (be)houden; *~ over one's head* iem boven het hoofd hangen

²hang [hæŋ] *vb* **1** (op)hangen *(also as punishment)*: *he ~ed himself* hij verhing zich; **2** laten hangen: *~ one's head in shame* het hoofd schuldbewust laten hangen; **3** tentoonstellen *(painting)*: *(inf) ~ it (all)!* ze kunnen van mij allemaal in elkaar storten!; *~ sth. on s.o.* iem de schuld van iets geven

³hang [hæŋ] *n* het vallen, val *(of material)*, het zitten *(of cloting)* || *(inf) get the ~ of sth.* de slag van iets krijgen

hangar [hæŋgə] hanga(a)r, vliegtuigloods

hang (a)round 1 rondhangen, rondlummelen; **2** wachten, treuzelen

hanger-on (slaafse) volgeling, parasiet, handlanger

hang-glider deltavlieger *(appliance as well as user)*, zeilvlieger, hangglider

hangman [hæŋmən] beul

hang on 1 zich (stevig) vasthouden, niet loslaten,

blijven (hangen): *~ tight!* hou (je) stevig vast!; *~ to* zich vasthouden aan; **2** volhouden, het niet opgeven, doorzetten; **3** even wachten, aan de lijn blijven *(telephone)*: *~ (a minute)!* ogenblikje!

hangout verblijf[h], stamkroeg, ontmoetingsplaats

¹hang out *vb (inf)* uithangen, zich ophouden: *where were you hanging out?* waar heb jij uitgehangen?; *I used to ~ with him* vroeger ben ik veel met hem opgetrokken

²hang out *vb* uithangen, ophangen *(laundry)*, uitsteken *(flag)*

hangover [hæŋgoovə] **1** kater, houten kop; **2** overblijfsel[h]: *his style of driving is a ~ from his racing days* zijn rijstijl heeft hij overgehouden aan zijn tijd als autocoureur; **3** ontnuchtering, ontgoocheling

¹hang up *vb* **1** ophangen *(telephone)*: *and then she hung up on me* en toen gooide ze de hoorn op de haak; **2** vastlopen

²hang up *vb* **1** ophangen; **2** uitstellen, ophouden, doen vastlopen || *(inf) be hung up on* (of: *about*) *sth.* complexen hebben over iets

hang-up complex[h], obsessie, frustratie

hank [hæŋk] streng *(yarn)*

hanker [hæŋkə] (with *after, for*) hunkeren (naar)

hanky [hæŋkie] zakdoek

hanky-panky [hæŋkiepæŋkie] **1** hocus-pocus, bedriegerij; **2** gescharrel[h], overspel[h]

haphazard [hæphæzəd] toevallig, op goed geluk (af), lukraak

hapless [hæpləs] ongelukkig, onfortuinlijk

happen [hæpən] **1** (toevallig) gebeuren: *as it ~s* (of: *~ed*) toevallig, zoals het nu eenmaal gaat; *should anything ~ to him* mocht hem iets overkomen; **2** toevallig verschijnen, toevallig komen, gaan: *if you ~ to see him* mocht u hem zien; *I ~ed to notice it* ik zag het toevallig; *I ~ed (up)on it* ik trof het toevallig aan

happening [hæpəning] gebeurtenis

happy [hæpie] **1** gelukkig, blij; **2** gepast, passend, gelukkig *(language, behaviour, suggestion)*; **3** voorspoedig, gelukkig: *Happy Birthday* hartelijk gefeliciteerd met je verjaardag; *Happy New Year* Gelukkig nieuwjaar; **4** blij, verheugd *(in polite phrases)*: *I'll be ~ to accept your kind invitation* ik neem uw uitnodiging graag aan; *(strike) the ~ medium* de gulden middenweg (inslaan); *(euph) ~ event* blijde gebeurtenis, geboorte; *many ~ returns (of the day)!* nog vele jaren!

harass [hærəs] **1** treiteren, pesten, kwellen; **2** teisteren, voortdurend bestoken

¹harbour [ha:bə] *n* **1** haven; **2** schuilplaats

²harbour [ha:bə] *vb* **1** herbergen, onderdak verlenen *(criminal)*; **2** koesteren *(emotions, ideas)*

¹hard [ha:d] *adj* **1** hard, vast(staand), krachtig, taai, robuust: *~ cover* (boek)band, gebonden editie; *~ currency* harde valuta; *a ~ winter* een strenge winter; *~ and fast rule* (of: *line*) vaste regel, ijzeren wet; **2** hard, hardvochtig: *drive a ~ bargain* keihard onderhandelen; *be ~ on s.o.* onvriendelijk zijn tegen iem; **3** moeilijk, hard, lastig: ~ *labour* dwangarbeid; *she gave him a ~ time* hij kreeg het zwaar te verduren van haar; ~ *of hearing* slechthorend, hardhorend; **4** hard, ijverig, energiek: *a ~ drinker* een stevige drinker; *a ~ worker* een harde werker; ~ *cash* baar geld, klinkende munt; *they preferred ~ copy to soft copy* zij verkozen uitdraai boven beeldschermtekst; ~ *feelings* wrok(gevoelens), rancune; ~ *luck* pech, tegenslag; *as ~ as nails* ongevoelig, onverzoenlijk; ~ *shoulder* vluchtstrook; *play ~ to get* moeilijk doen, zich ongenaakbaar opstellen; ~ *by* vlakbij

²hard [ha:d] *adv* **1** hard, krachtig, inspannend, zwaar: *be ~ hit* zwaar getroffen zijn; *think ~* diep nadenken; *be ~ on s.o.'s heels* (of: *trail*) iem op de hielen zitten; **2** met moeite, moeizaam: *be ~ put (to it) to (do sth.)* het moeilijk vinden (om iets te doen); *old habits die ~* vaste gewoonten verdwijnen niet gauw; *take sth. ~* iets zwaar opnemen, zwaar lijden onder iets

hardback (in)gebonden *(book)*

hardboard (hard)board^h, houtvezelplaat

hard-boiled 1 hardgekookt; **2** hard, ongevoelig

hard copy (computer)uitdraai, afdruk

hard disk harde schijf, vaste schijf, harddisk

harden [ha:dn] **1** (ver)harden, ongevoelig worden, maken: *a ~ed criminal* een gewetenloze misdadiger; **2** gewennen: *become ~ed to sth.* aan iets wennen

hard-headed praktisch, nuchter, zakelijk

hard-hearted hardvochtig

hardline keihard, een politiek vd harde lijn voerend

hardly [ha:dlie] nauwelijks, amper: *we had ~ arrived when it began to rain* we waren er nog maar net toen het begon te regenen; *I could ~ move* ik kon me haast niet bewegen; ~ *anything* bijna niets; ~ *anybody* vrijwel niemand; ~ *ever* bijna nooit

hardship [ha:dsjip] ontbering, tegenspoed

hard up slecht bij kas || *be ~ for sth.* grote behoefte aan iets hebben

hardware 1 ijzerwaren, (huis)gereedschap^h; **2** apparatuur *(also of computer)*, hardware, bouwelementen

hardy [ha:die] **1** sterk, robuust; **2** wintervast, winterhard

hare [heə] haas

harelip hazenlip

harem [haa:ri:m] harem

haricot [hærikoo] snijboon

¹harm [ha:m] *n* kwaad^h, schade: *be* (of: *do*) *no ~* geen kwaad kunnen; *she came to no ~* er overkwam haar geen kwaad; *out of ~'s way* in veiligheid

²harm [ha:m] *vb* kwaad doen, schade berokkenen

harmful [ha:mfoel] schadelijk, nadelig

harmless [ha:mləs] **1** onschadelijk, ongevaarlijk; **2** onschuldig

¹harmonic [ha:monnik] *adj* harmonisch

²harmonic [ha:monnik] *n* harmonische (toon), boventoon

harmonious [ha:mooniəs] **1** harmonieus; **2** eensgezind

harmony [ha:mənie] **1** harmonie, eensgezindheid, overeenstemming: *be in ~ with* in overeenstemming zijn met; **2** goede verstandhouding, eendracht: *live in ~* in goede verstandhouding leven

¹harness [ha:nis] *n* gareel^h, (paarden)tuig^h || *get back into ~* weer aan het werk gaan

²harness [ha:nis] *vb* **1** optuigen, inspannen *(horse)*, in het gareel brengen; **2** aanwenden, gebruiken, benutten *((natural) energy sources)*

harp [ha:p] harp

harp on [ha:p on] zaniken, zeuren: ~ *about sth.* doorzeuren over iets

harpoon [ha:poe:n] harpoen

harpsichord [ha:psikko:d] klavecimbel^h

harrow [hæroo] eg

harrowing [hærooing] aangrijpend

harsh [ha:sj] **1** ruw, wrang, verblindend *(light)*, krassend *(sound)*; **2** wreed, hardvochtig

¹harvest [ha:vist] *n* oogst(tijd)

²harvest [ha:vist] *vb* **1** oogsten, vergaren; **2** verkrijgen, behalen (wat men verdient)

hash [hæsj] **1** hachee; **2** mengelmoes^h; **3** hasj(iesj) || *make a ~ of it* de boel verknoeien

hashish [hæsjisj] hasjiesj

¹hassle [hæsl] *n* **1** gedoe^h: *a real ~* een zware opgave, een heel gedoe; **2** ruzie

²hassle [hæsl] *vb* moeilijk maken, dwars zitten, lastig vallen

haste [heest] **1** haast, spoed: *make ~* zich haasten; **2** overhaasting

¹hasten [heesn] *vb* zich haasten

²hasten [heesn] *vb* versnellen, bespoedigen

hat [hæt] hoed: *at the drop of a ~* bij de minste aanleiding, plotseling, zonder aarzeling; *knock into a cocked ~*: *a)* gehakt maken van, helemaal inmaken; *b)* in duigen doen vallen; *I'll eat my ~ if …* ik mag doodvallen als …; *keep sth. under one's ~* iets geheim houden, iets onder de pet houden; *pass* (of: *send, take*) *the ~ (round)* met de pet rondgaan; *(fig) take off one's ~* (of: *take one's ~ off) to s.o.* zijn pet(je) afnemen voor iem; *(inf) talk through one's ~* bluffen, nonsens verkopen; *throw* (of: *toss*) *one's ~ in(to) the ring* zich in de (verkiezings)strijd werpen

¹hatch [hætsj] *n* **1** onderdeur; **2** luik^h; **3** sluisdeur || *down the ~!* proost!

²hatch [hætsj] *vb (also with out)* uit het ei komen *(of chick)*, openbreken *(of egg(shell))*

³hatch [hætsj] *vb* **1** *(also with out)* uitbroeden, broeden; **2** beramen *(plan)*

hatchback [hætsjbæk] **1** (opklapbare) vijfde deur; **2** vijfdeursauto

hatchet [hætsjit] **1** bijltje^h, (hand)bijl; **2** tomahawk, strijdbijl || *(inf) bury the ~* de strijdbijl begraven, vrede sluiten

hatchet man 1 huurmoordenaar, gangster; **2** *(depr)* handlanger, trawant, *(by extension)* waakhond, ordehandhaver

¹hate [heet] *vb* **1** haten, grondig verafschuwen, een hekel hebben aan; **2** *(inf)* het jammer vinden: *I ~ having to tell you … het spijt me u te moeten zeggen …; I ~ to say this, but … ik zeg het niet graag, maar …*

²hate [heet] *n* **1** gehate persoon, gehaat iets; **2** haat

hateful [heetfoel] **1** gehaat, weerzinwekkend; **2** hatelijk *(remark);* **3** onsympathiek, onaangenaam, onuitstaanbaar

hatred [heetrid] haat, afschuw

haughty [ho:tie] trots, arrogant

¹haul [ho:l] *vb* **1** halen, ophalen, inhalen *(with effort): ~ down one's flag* (of: *colours)* de vlag strijken, *(fig)* zich overgeven; *~ in the net* het net binnenhalen; **2** vervoeren; **3** slepen *(take somebody to court)*

²haul [ho:l] *n* **1** haal, trek, het trekken; **2** vangst, buit; **3** afstand, traject[h]: *in* (of: *over) the long ~* op lange termijn; **4** lading, vracht

haulage [ho:lidzj] **1** het slepen, het trekken; **2** vervoer[h], transport[h]; **3** transportkosten, vervoerkosten: *all prices include ~* bij alle prijzen zijn de vervoerkosten inbegrepen

haulier [ho:liə] vrachtrijder, vervoerder, expediteur

haunch [ho:ntsj] lende, heup, bil, dij: *on one's ~es* op zijn hurken

¹haunt [ho:nt] *vb* **1** vaak aanwezig zijn in, zich altijd ophouden in, regelmatig bezoeken: *he ~s that place* daar is hij altijd te vinden; **2** rondspoken in, rondwaren in: *~ed castle* spookkasteel; **3** achtervolgen, niet loslaten, (steeds) lastig vallen: *that tune has been ~ing me all afternoon* dat deuntje speelt de hele middag al door mijn kop

²haunt [ho:nt] *n* **1** trefpunt[h]: *we went for a drink at one of his favourite ~s* we gingen iets drinken in een van de plaatsen waar hij graag kwam; **2** hol[h], schuilplaats *(of animals)*

have [hæv] **1** hebben, bezitten, beschikken over, houden: *he has (got) an excellent memory* hij beschikt over een voortreffelijk geheugen; *~ mercy on us* heb medelijden met ons; *I've got it* ik heb het, ik weet het (weer); *you ~ sth. there* daar zeg je (me) wat, daar zit wat in; *~ sth. about* (of: *on, with) one* iets bij zich hebben; *what does she ~ against me?* wat heeft ze tegen mij?; **2** *(as part of a whole)* bevatten, bestaan uit: *the book has six chapters* het boek telt zes hoofdstukken; **3** krijgen, ontvangen: *we've had no news* we hebben geen nieuws (ontvangen); *you can ~ it back tomorrow* je kunt het morgen terugkrijgen; **4** nemen, pakken, gebruiken *(food, drink etc): ~ breakfast* ontbijten; *~ a drink* iets drinken, een drankje nemen; **5** hebben, genieten van, lijden aan: *~ a good time* het naar zijn zin hebben; **6** hebben, laten liggen, leggen, zetten: *let's ~ the rug in the hall* laten we het tapijt in de hal leggen; **7** hebben, maken, nemen: *~ a bath* een bad nemen; *~ a try* (het) proberen; **8** toelaten, accepteren:

I won't ~ such conduct ik accepteer zulk gedrag niet; *I'm not having any* ik pik het niet, ik pieker er niet over; **9** hebben te: *I still ~ quite a bit of work to do* ik heb nog heel wat te doen; **10** laten, doen, opdracht geven te: *~ one's hair cut* zijn haar laten knippen; **11** krijgen *(child): ~ a child by* een kind hebben van; **12** zorgen voor: *can you ~ the children tonight?* kun jij vanavond voor de kinderen zorgen?; **13** *(inf)* te pakken hebben *(lit and fig),* het winnen van: *you've got me there: a)* jij wint; *b)* geen idee, daar vraag je me wat; **14** *(inf)* bedriegen, bij de neus nemen: *John's been had* ze hebben John beetgenomen; **15** hebben, zijn: *I ~ worked* ik heb gewerkt; *he has died* hij is gestorven; *I had better* (of: *best) forget it* ik moest dat maar vergeten; *I'd just as soon die* ik zou net zo lief doodgaan; *he had it coming to him* hij kreeg zijn verdiende loon; *rumour has it that …* het gerucht gaat dat …; *~ it (from s.o.)* het (van iem) gehoord hebben; *(inf) ~ had it: a)* hangen, de klos zijn; *b)* niet meer de oude zijn, dood zijn; *c)* het beu zijn, er de brui aan geven; *~ it in for s.o.* een hekel hebben aan iem, het op iemand gemunt hebben; *~ it in for s.o.* de pik hebben op iem; *~ it (of: the matter) out with s.o.* het (probleem) uitpraten met iem; *~ s.o. up (for sth.)* iem voor de rechtbank brengen (wegens iets); *~ nothing on* niet kunnen tippen aan

haven [heevn] (beschutte, veilige) haven *(also fig),* toevluchtsoord[h]

have on 1 aanhebben, dragen *(clothes),* ophebben *(hat);* **2** gepland hebben, op zijn agenda hebben: *I've got nothing on tonight* vanavond ben ik vrij; **3** *(inf)* voor de gek houden, een loopje nemen met: *are you having me on?* zit je mij nou voor de gek te houden?

have to moeten, verplicht zijn om te, (be)hoeven: *we have (got) to go now* we moeten nu weg; *he didn't ~ do that* dat had hij niet hoeven doen

havoc [hævok] verwoesting, vernieling, ravage, *(fig)* verwarring: *play ~ among* (of: *with),* make *~ of, wreak ~ on: a)* totaal verwoesten; *b)* grondig in de war sturen, een puinhoop maken van

hawk [ho:k] havik, *(fig)* oorlogszuchtig persoon

hawker [ho:kə] (straat)venter, marskramer

hawthorn [ho:θo:n] haagdoorn, meidoorn

hay [hee] hooi[h] || *hit the ~* gaan pitten; *make ~ while the sun shines* men moet het ijzer smeden als het heet is

hay fever hooikoorts

haywire in de war, door elkaar: *my plans went ~* mijn plannen liepen in het honderd

¹hazard [hæzəd] *n* **1** gevaar[h], risico[h]: *smoking and drinking are health ~s* roken en drinken zijn een gevaar voor de gezondheid; **2** kans, mogelijkheid, toeval[h]; **3** *(golf)* (terrein)hindernis

²hazard [hæzəd] *vb* **1** in de waagschaal stellen, wagen, riskeren; **2** zich wagen aan, wagen: *~ a guess* een gok wagen

hazardous [hæzədəs] gevaarlijk, gewaagd, riskant

¹haze [heez] *n* nevel, damp, waas^h, *(fig)* vaagheid, verwardheid

²haze [heez] *vb* (with *over*) nevelig worden (maken)

hazel [heezl] hazelaar, hazelnotenstruik

hazy [heezie] nevelig, wazig, *(fig)* vaag: *a ~ idea* een vaag idee

he [hie:] hij, die, dat, het: *'Who is he?' 'He's John' 'Wie is dat?' 'Dat is John'*

¹head [hed] *n* **1** hoofd^h, kop, hoofdlengte: *~ and shoulders above* met kop en schouders erbovenuit, *(fig)* verreweg de beste; *~s or tails?* kruis of munt?; *~ first* (of: *foremost*) voorover; **2** hoofd^h, verstand^h: *it never entered* (of: *came into*) *his ~* het kwam niet bij hem op; *get* (of: *take*) *sth. into one's ~* zich iets in het hoofd zetten; *the success has gone to* (of: *turned*) *his ~* het succes is hem naar het hoofd gestegen; *put one's ~s together* de koppen bij elkaar steken; *a ~ for mathematics* een wiskundeknobbel; **3** persoon, hoofd^h: *£1 a ~* £1 per persoon; **4** uiteinde^h, kop; **5** hoofdje^h, korfje^h, kruin; **6** top, bovenkant; **7** breekpunt^h, crisis: *that brought the matter to a ~* daarmee werd de zaak op de spits gedreven; **8** boveneinde^h, hoofd(einde)^h; **9** voorkant, kop, spits, hoofd^h *(also of team);* **10** meerdere, leider, hoofd^h: *~ of state* staatshoofd; *£1 stuk^h* (vee), kudde, aantal^h dieren: *50 ~ of cattle* 50 stuks vee; *have one's ~ in the clouds* met het hoofd in de wolken lopen; *from ~ to foot* van top tot teen; *bury one's ~ in the sand* de kop in het zand steken; *I could not make ~ or tail of it* ik kon er geen touw aan vastknopen; *keep one's ~ above water* het hoofd boven water houden; *keep one's ~* zijn kalmte bewaren; *laugh one's ~ off* zich een ongeluk lachen; *lose one's ~* het hoofd verliezen; *scream* (of: *shout*) *one's ~ off* vreselijk tekeergaan; *have one's ~ screwed on straight* (of: *right*) verstandig zijn, niet gek zijn

²head [hed] *vb* gaan, gericht zijn, koers zetten: *the plane ~ed north* het vliegtuig zette koers naar het noorden

³head [hed] *vb* **1** aan het hoofd staan van, voorop lopen: *the general ~ed the revolt* de generaal leidde de opstand; **2** bovenaan plaatsen, bovenaan staan op; **3** overtreffen, voorbijstreven; **4** *(socc)* koppen; **5** richten, sturen

headache 1 hoofdpijn; **2** probleem^h, vervelende kwestie: *finding reliable staff has become a major ~* het vinden van betrouwbaar is een groot probleem geworden

header [hedde] **1** *(socc)* kopbal; **2** duik(eling): *take a ~* een duikeling maken

head for afgaan op, koers zetten naar: *he was already heading for the bar* hij liep al in de richting van de bar; *you are heading for trouble* als jij zo doorgaat krijg je narigheid

headhunting 1 het koppensnellen; **2** headhunting

heading [hedding] opschrift^h, titel, kop

headlight koplamp

headline (kranten)kop, opschrift^h: *make* (of: *hit*) *the ~s* volop in het nieuws komen; *the ~s* hoofd-punten van het nieuws

headlong 1 voorover, met het hoofd voorover; **2** haastig, halsoverkop

headmaster schoolhoofd^h, rector

head off 1 onderscheppen, van richting doen veranderen; **2** voorkomen

head-on frontaal, van voren: *a ~ collision* een frontale botsing

headphones koptelefoon

headquarters hoofdbureau, hoofdkantoor, hoofd-kwartier

headrest hoofdsteun *(eg in car)*

headset koptelefoon

head start (with *on, over*) voorsprong (op) *(also fig)*, goede uitgangspositie

headstone grafsteen

headstrong koppig, eigenzinnig

headway voortgang, vaart *(of ship):* *(fig) make ~* vooruitgang boeken

headwind tegenwind

heady [heddie] **1** opwindend, wild; **2** bedwelmend, dronken makend *(wine)*

heal [hie:l] *(also with over)* genezen, (doen) herstellen, dichtgaan *(of wound); (fig)* bijleggen, vereffenen

health [helθ] gezondheid, gezondheidstoestand: *have* (of: *be in, enjoy*) *good ~* een goede gezondheid genieten; *drink* (to) *s.o.'s ~* op iemands gezondheid drinken

health food gezonde (natuurlijke) voeding

healthy [helθie] gezond, heilzaam: *he has a ~ respect for my father* hij heeft een groot ontzag voor mijn vader

¹heap [hie:p] *n* **1** hoop, stapel, berg; **2** boel, massa, hoop: *we've got ~s of time* we hebben nog zeeën van tijd

²heap [hie:p] *vb* **1** (with *up*) ophopen, (op)stapelen, samenhopen; **2** (with *on, with*) vol laden (met), opladen (met); **3** overladen, overstelpen: *she ~ed reproaches (up)on her mother* zij overstelpte haar moeder met verwijten

¹hear [hie] *vb* horen: *~ from* bericht krijgen van, horen van; *~ of* horen van; *~! ~!* bravo!

²hear [hie] *vb* **1** luisteren naar, (ver)horen, behandelen, verhoren *(prayer)*, overhoren, gehoor geven aan: *please ~ me out* laat mij uitspreken; **2** vernemen, kennis nemen van, horen: *we are sorry to ~ that* het spijt ons te (moeten) horen dat

hearing [hiering] **1** gehoor^h, hearing, hoorzitting: *he would not even give us a ~* hij wilde zelfs niet eens naar ons luisteren; **2** behandeling *(of a case);* **3** *(Am; law)* verhoor^h; **4** gehoor^h: *she is hard of ~* zij is hardhorend; **5** gehoorsafstand: *out of ~ distance* buiten gehoorsafstand

hearing aid (ge)hoorapparaat^h

hearsay praatjes, geruchten: *I know it from ~* ik weet het van horen zeggen

hearse [hə:s] lijkwagen

heart [ha:t] **1** hart^h, hartspier; binnenste^h, gemoed^h:

from (of: to) the bottom of my ~ uit de grond van mijn hart; *they have their own interests at ~* zij hebben hun eigen belangen voor ogen; *set one's ~ on sth.* zijn zinnen op iets zetten, iets dolgraag willen; *she took it to ~* zij trok het zich aan, zij nam het ter harte; *in one's ~ of ~s* in het diepst van zijn hart; *with all one's ~* van ganser harte; **2** boezem, borst; **3** geest, gedachten, herinnering: *a change of ~* verandering van gedachten; *(learn) by ~* uit het hoofd (leren); **4** kern, hart^h, essentie; **5** moed, durf: *not have the ~* de moed niet hebben; *lose ~* de moed verliezen; *take ~* moed vatten, zich vermannen; *my ~ bleeds* ik ben diepbedroefd, *(iron)* oh jee, wat heb ik een medelijden; *cry (of: weep) one's ~ out* tranen met tuiten huilen; *eat one's ~ out* wegkwijnen (van verdriet, verlangen)

heartbreaking 1 hartbrekend, hartverscheurend; **2** frustrerend *(work)*

heart condition hartkwaal

hearten [ha:tn] bemoedigen, moed geven

heartfelt hartgrondig, oprecht

hearth [ha:θ] haard(stede), *(fig)* huis^h, woning: *~ and home* huis en haard

heartily [ha:tillie] **1** van harte, oprecht, vriendelijk; **2** flink, hartig: *eat ~* stevig eten; **3** hartgrondig: *I ~ dislike that fellow* ik heb een hartgrondige hekel aan die vent

heart-rending hartverscheurend

heartstrings diepste gevoelens, *(iron)* sentimentele gevoelens: *tug at s.o.'s ~* iem zeer (ont)roeren

hearty [ha:tie] **1** hartelijk, vriendelijk; **2** gezond, flink, hartig: *a ~ meal* een stevig maal; *hale and ~* kerngezond; **3** *(inf)* (al te) joviaal

¹heat [hie:t] *n* **1** warmte, hitte; **2** vuur^h, drift, heftigheid: *in the ~ of the conversation* in het vuur van het gesprek; **3** *(inf)* druk, dwang, moeilijkheden: *turn (of: put) the ~ on s.o.* iem onder druk zetten; **4** loopsheid: *on ~* loops, tochtig; **5** voorwedstrijd, serie, voorronde

²heat [hie:t] *vb* warm worden: *~ up* heet worden

³heat [hie:t] *vb* verhitten, verwarmen: *~ up* opwarmen

heater [hie:tə] kachel, verwarming(stoestel^h)

heath [hie:θ] **1** heideveld^h, open veld^h; **2** dopheide, erica

heathen [hie:ðən] **1** heiden, ongelovige; **2** barbaar

heather [heðə] heide(kruid^h), struikheide

heating [hie:ting] verwarming(ssysteem^h)

¹heave [hie:v] *vb* **1** opheffen, (op)hijsen; **2** slaken: *she ~d a sigh* ze zuchtte diep, ze liet een diepe zucht; **3** *(inf)* gooien, smijten; **4** *(shipp)* hijsen, takelen

²heave [hie:v] *vb* **1** (op)zwellen, rijzen, omhooggaan: *his stomach ~d* zijn maag draaide ervan om; **2** op en neer gaan; **3** trekken, sjorren: *~ at (of: on)* trekken aan

³heave [hie:v] *n* **1** hijs, het op en neer gaan: *the ~ of the sea* de deining van de zee; **2** ruk: *he gave a mighty ~* hij gaf een enorme ruk

heaven [hevn] hemel, *(fig)* gelukzaligheid, Voor-

zienigheid: *in Heaven's name, for Heaven's sake* in hemelsnaam; *thank ~(s)!* de hemel zij dank!

heavy [hevvie] **1** zwaar: *~ industry* zware industrie; *~ with zwaar beladen met; ~ with the smell of roses* doortrokken van de geur van rozen; **2** zwaar, hevig, aanzienlijk: *~ traffic* druk verkeer, vrachtverkeer; **3** moeilijk te verteren *(also fig): I find it ~ going* ik schiet slecht op; **4** serieus *(newspaper, part in play)*, zwaar op de hand; **5** streng; **6** zwaar, drukkend; **7** zwaarmoedig: *play the ~ father* een (donder)preek houden; *make ~ weather of sth.* moeilijk maken wat makkelijk is; *(inf) be ~ on* veel gebruiken *(petrol, makeup); time hung ~ on her hands* de tijd viel haar lang

heavyweight 1 zwaar iem; **2** worstelaar (bokser) in de zwaargewichtklasse; **3** kopstuk^h, zwaargewicht

Hebrew [hie:broe:] Hebreeuws, joods

heckle [hekl] steeds onderbreken *(speaker)*

hectic [hektik] koortsachtig *(also fig)*, jachtig, druk, hectisch

¹hedge [hedzj] *n* heg, haag

²hedge [hedzj] *vb* **1** omheinen: *~ about (of: around, in) with* omringen met; **2** dekken *(bets, speculations)*

³hedge [hedzj] *vb* een slag om de arm houden, ergens omheen draaien

hedgehog [hedzjhog] egel

hedge in omheinen, *(fig)* omringen, belemmeren: *hedged in by rules and regulations* door regels en voorschriften omringd

hedgerow haag

heed [hie:d] aandacht, zorg; *give (of: pay) ~ to* aandacht schenken aan; *take ~ of* nota nemen van, letten op

heedless [hie:dləs] **1** achteloos, onoplettend: *be ~ of* niet letten op, in de wind slaan; **2** onvoorzichtig

heel [hie:l] **1** hiel *(also of stocking)*, hak *(also of shoe)*; **2** uiteinde^h, onderkant, korst *(of cheese)*, kapje^h *(of bread)* || *bring to ~* kleinkrijgen, in het gareel brengen; *dig one's ~s in* het been stijf houden; *he took to his ~s* hij koos het hazenpad; *turn on one's ~* zich plotseling omdraaien; *down at ~* met scheve hakken, afgetrapt, *(fig)* haveloos; *at (of: on) the ~s* op de hielen, vlak achter

hefty [heftie] **1** fors, potig; **2** zwaar, lijvig

heifer [heffə] vaars(kalf^h)

height [hajt] **1** hoogte, lengte, peil^h, niveau^h: *it is only 4 feet in ~* het is maar 4 voet hoog; **2** hoogtepunt^h, toppunt^h: *the ~ of summer* hartje zomer; *at its ~* op zijn hoogtepunt; **3** top, piek; **4** terreinverheffing, hoogte

heighten [hajtn] **1** hoger (doen) worden, verhogen; **2** (doen) toenemen, verhevigen

heinous [heenəs] gruwelijk

heir [eə] **1** erfgenaam, *~s* erven: *sole ~* enige erfgenaam; **2** opvolger: *~ to the throne* troonopvolger

heiress [eəris] erfgename *(of fortune)*

heirloom [eəloe:m] erfstuk^h, familiestuk^h

helicopter [hellikkoptə] helikopter

hell [hel] hel *(also fig): she drove ~ for leather* zij reed in vliegende vaart; *come ~ and* (of: *or) high water* wat er zich ook voordoet

hell-bent (with *on, for)* vastbesloten (om)

hello [hǝloo] **1** hallo; **2** hé *(to express surprise)*

helm [helm] helmstok, *(also fig)* stuurrad^h, roer^h

helmet [helmǝt] helm

helmsman [helmzmǝn] roerganger, stuurman

¹help [help] *vb* **1** helpen, bijstaan, (onder)steunen, baten: *~ along* (of: *forward)* vooruithelpen, bevorderen; *~ out: a)* bijspringen; *b)* aanvullen; **2** opscheppen, bedienen: *~ yourself* ga je gang, tast toe; **3** verhelpen, helpen tegen: *it can't be ~ed* er is niets aan te doen; **4** voorkomen, verhinderen: *if I can ~ it* als het aan mij ligt; **5** *(+ negation)* nalaten, zich weerhouden van: *we could not ~ but smile* wij moesten wel glimlachen, of we wilden of niet

²help [help] *n* **1** hulp, steun, bijstand: *that's a big ~!* nou, daar hebben we wat aan!, daar schieten we mee op, zeg!; *can we be of any ~?* kunnen wij ergens mee helpen?; **2** help(st)er, dienstmeisje^h, werkster; **3** huishoudelijk personeel^h; **4** remedie: *there is no ~ for it* er is niets aan te doen

helping [helping] portie *(food)*

helpless [helplǝs] **1** hulpeloos: *~ with laughter* slap van de lach; **2** onbeholpen

helter-skelter holderdebolder, halsoverkop, kriskras

¹hem [hem] *n* boord^h, zoom: *take the ~ up (of sth.)* (iets) korter maken

²hem [hem] *vb* (om)zomen: *~ about* (of: *around)* omringen; *feel ~med in* zich ingekapseld voelen

he-man [hie:mæn] mannetjesputter

hemisphere [hemmisfiǝ] halve bol, *(geography)* halfrond^h: *the northern ~* het noordelijk halfrond

hemp [hemp] hennep, cannabis

hen [hen] **1** hoen^h, hen, kip; **2** pop *(of bird)*

hence [hens] **1** van nu (af): *five years ~* over vijf jaar; **2** vandaar

henceforth van nu af aan, voortaan

henchman [hentsjmǝn] **1** volgeling, aanhanger; **2** trawant

¹her [hǝ:] *pron* **1** haar, aan haar: *he gave ~ a watch* hij gaf haar een horloge; **2** zij: *that's ~* dat is ze

²her [hǝ:] *pron* haar: *it's ~ day* het is haar grote dag

¹herald [herrǝld] *n* **1** heraut, gezant; **2** (voor)bode

²herald [herrǝld] *vb* aankondigen: *~ in* inluiden

heraldry [herrǝldrie] heraldiek, wapenkunde

herb [hǝ:b] kruid^h: *~ and spices* kruiden en specerijen

¹herd [hǝ:d] *n* kudde, troep, horde, *(depr)* massa: *the (common, vulgar) ~* de massa

²herd [hǝ:d] *vb* samendrommen, bij elkaar hokken: *~ with* omgaan met

³herd [hǝ:d] *vb* hoeden: *~ together* samendrijven

here [hiǝ] hier, op deze plaats, hierheen: *where do we go from ~?* hoe gaan we nu verder?; *near ~* hier in de buurt; *(inf) ~ we are* daar zijn we dan, (zie)zo; *~ you are*, alsjeblieft; *~ and now* nu meteen;

over ~ hier(heen); *~, there and everywhere* overal; *that's is neither ~ nor there* dat slaat nergens op, dat heeft er niets mee te maken

hereditary [hirreddittǝrie] erfelijk, erf-

heredity [hirreddittie] **1** erfelijkheid; **2** overerving

heresy [herrǝsie] ketterij

heretic [herrǝtik] ketter

herewith hierbij, bij deze(n)

heritage [herrittidzj] **1** erfenis, erfgoed^h *(also fig)*; **2** erfdeel^h

hermit [hǝ:mit] kluizenaar

hernia [hǝ:niǝ] hernia, (lies)breuk

hero [hiǝroo] *(~es)* **1** held; **2** hoofdpersoon, hoofdrolspeler

heroic [hirrooik] **1** heroïsch, heldhaftig; **2** helden-: *~ age* heldentijd; **3** groots, gedurfd

heroin [herrooin] heroïne

heroine [herrooin] **1** heldin; **2** hoofdrolspeelster

heron [herrǝn] reiger

herring [herring] haring

hers [hǝ:z] van haar, de (het) hare: *my books and ~* mijn boeken en die van haar; *a friend of ~* een vriend van haar

hesitate [hezzitteet] aarzelen, weifelen: *~ about* (of: *over)* aarzelen over

hesitation [hezzitteesjǝn] aarzeling

heterogeneous [hettǝrooedzjie:niǝs] heterogeen, ongelijksoortig

hew [hjoe:] houwen, sabelen, (be)kappen: *~ down: a)* kappen, omhakken *(trees); b)* neermaaien *(people)*

hexagon [heksǝgǝn] regelmatige zeshoek

heyday [heedee] hoogtijdagen, bloei, beste tijd

hi [haj] **1** hé; **2** hallo, hoi

hibernate [hajbǝneet] een winterslaap houden *(also fig)*

hiccup [hikkup] hik

hidden verborgen, geheim

¹hide [hajd] *vb* zich verbergen: *~ away* (of: *out)* zich schuil houden

²hide [hajd] *vb* verbergen, verschuilen: *~ from view* aan het oog onttrekken

³hide [hajd] *n* (dieren)huid, vel^h

hide-and-seek verstoppertje^h: *play ~* verstoppertje spelen

hidebound [hajdbaund] bekrompen

hideous [hiddiǝs] afschuwelijk, afzichtelijk

hideout schuilplaats

hiding [hajding] **1** het verbergen; **2** het verborgen zijn: *come out of ~* te voorschijn komen; *go into ~* zich verbergen; **3** *(inf)* pak^h rammel: *(inf) be on a ~ to nothing* voor een onmogelijke taak staan, geen schijn van kans maken

hiding place schuilplaats, geheime bergplaats

hierarchy [hajjǝra:kie] hiërarchie

hieroglyph [hajrǝglif] hiëroglief

hi-fi [hajfaj] *high fidelity* hifi-geluidsinstallatie, stereo

¹high [haj] *adj* **1** hoog, hooggeplaatst, verheven: *~*

command opperbevel; *a ~ opinion of* een hoge dunk van; *have friends in ~ places* een goede kruiwagen hebben; *~ pressure: a) (meteorology)* hoge druk; *b) (inf)* agressiviteit *(of salesmanship); ~ society* de hogere kringen; *~ tide* hoogwater, vloed, *(fig)* hoogtepunt; *~ water* hoogwater; **2** intens, sterk, groot: *~ hopes* hoge verwachtingen; **3** belangrijk: *~ treason* hoogverraad; **4** vrolijk: *in ~ spirits* vrolijk; **5** gevorderd, hoog, op een hoogtepunt: *~ season* hoogseizoen; *it's ~ time we went* het is de hoogste tijd om te gaan; **6** aangeschoten, zat: *get on one's ~ horse* een hoge toon aanslaan; *the ~ sea(s)* de volle zee; *~ tea* vroeg warm eten, vaak met thee; *~ and dry* gestrand, *(fig)* zonder middelen; *~ and mighty* uit de hoogte

²high [haj] *adv* **1** hoog, zeer; **2** schel || *hold one's head ~* zijn hoofd niet laten hangen; *feelings ran ~* de emoties liepen hoog op; *ride ~* succes hebben; *search ~ and low* in alle hoeken zoeken

³high [haj] *n* **1** (hoogte)record^h, hoogtepunt^h, toppunt^h: *hit a ~* een hoogtepunt bereiken; *an all-time ~* een absoluut hoogtepunt, een absolute topper; **2** hogedrukgebied^h: *from on ~* uit de hemel

¹highbrow *n* (semi-)intellectueel

²highbrow *adj* geleerd

high-class 1 eersteklas, prima, eerlijk; **2** hooggeplaatst, voornaam

high-flyer hoogvlieger, ambitieus persoon

high-grade hoogwaardig

high-handed eigenmachtig, aanmatigend, autoritair

highland [hajlənd] hoogland^h

high-level op hoog niveau

¹highlight *n* **1** lichtste deel^h, *(fig)* opvallend kenmerk^h; **2** hoogtepunt^h; **3** *~s* coupe soleil

²highlight *vb* naar voren halen, doen uitkomen: *use this pen to ~ the relevant passages* gebruik deze pen maar om de relevant passages te markeren

highly [hajlie] **1** hoog: *~ paid officials* goed betaalde ambtenaren; **2** zeer, erg, in hoge mate; **3** met lof: *speak ~ of* loven, roemen

high-minded hoogstaand, verheven

highness [hajnəs] **1** hoogheid: *His Royal Highness* Zijne Koninklijke Hoogheid; **2** hoogte, verhevenheid

high-pitched 1 hoog, schel; **2** steil *(roof)*

high-rise *(Am)* hoog: *~ flats* torenflats

high road hoofdweg, grote weg, *(fig)* (directe) weg

high school *(Am)* middelbare school

high-strung nerveus, overgevoelig

high-tech [hajtek] geavanceerd technisch

highway grote weg, verkeersweg, *(fig)* (directe) weg

highwayman [hajweemən] struikrover

¹hijack [hajdzjæk] *vb* kapen

²hijack [hajdzjæk] *n* kaping

hijacker [hajdzjækə] kaper

¹hike [hajk] *n* lange wandeling, trektocht

²hike [hajk] *vb* lopen, wandelen, trekken

³hike [hajk] *vb* **1** (with *up*) ophijsen, optrekken; **2**

(Am) verhogen

hiker [hajkə] wandelaar

hilarious [hilleəriəs] **1** heel grappig, dolkomisch; **2** vrolijk, uitgelaten

hilarity [hilærittie] hilariteit, vrolijkheid

hill [hil] heuvel || *it is up ~ and down dale* het gaat heuvelop, heuvelaf; *over the ~* over zijn hoogtepunt heen

hillock [hillək] **1** heuveltje^h; **2** bergje^h *(earth)*

hillside helling

hilt [hilt] gevest^h, handvat^h || *(up)to the ~* volkomen, tot over de oren

him [him] **1** hem, aan hem; **2** hij: *~ and his jokes* hij met zijn grapjes

¹hind [hajnd] *n* hinde

²hind [hajnd] *adj* achterst || *talk the ~ leg(s) off a donkey* iem de oren van het hoofd kletsen

hinder [hində] **1** belemmeren, hinderen; **2** (with *from*) beletten (te), verhinderen, tegenhouden

hindquarters achterdeel, achterlijf *(of horse)*

hindrance [hindrəns] belemmering, beletsel^h, hindernis

hindsight [hajndsajt] kennis, inzicht^h achteraf: *with ~* achteraf gezien

¹Hindu [hindoe:] *adj* Hindoes

²Hindu [hindoe:] *n* Hindoe

hinge [hindzj] scharnier^h, *(fig)* spil

¹hint [hint] *n* **1** wenk, hint, tip: *drop a ~* een hint geven; *take a ~* een wenk ter harte nemen; **2** vleugje^h, tikje^h

²hint [hint] *vb* aanwijzingen geven: *~ at* zinspelen op

³hint [hint] *vb* laten doorschemeren

¹hip [hip] *n* heup

²hip [hip] *adj* hip, modern || *~, ~, hurrah!* hiep, hiep, hoera!

hippie [hippie] hippie

hippo [hippoo] nijlpaard^h

hippopotamus [hippəpottəməs] nijlpaard^h

¹hire [hajjə] *n* huur, (dienst)loon^h: *for (of: on) ~* te huur

²hire [hajjə] *vb* **1** huren: *~ out* verhuren; **2** inhuren, (tijdelijk) in dienst nemen

hireling [hajjəling] huurling

hire purchase huurkoop: *on ~* op afbetaling

his [hiz] zijn; van hem; het zijne, de zijne: *these boots are ~* deze laarzen zijn van hem; *a hobby of ~* een hobby van hem; *it was ~ day* het was zijn grote dag

hiss [his] **1** sissen; **2** uitfluiten: *~ off* (of: *away, down*) van het podium fluiten

historian [histo:riən] historicus

historic [historrik] historisch, beroemd

historical [historrikl] historisch, geschiedkundig

history [histərie] **1** geschiedenis: *ancient* (of: *past*) *~* verleden tijd; **2** historisch verhaal^h

¹hit [hit] *vb* **1** aanvallen; **2** hard aankomen || *~ home* doel treffen

²hit [hit] *vb* **1** slaan, geven *(a blow):* *(fig) ~ a man when he is down* iem een trap nageven; *~ and run*

doorrijden na aanrijding; ~ back (at) terugslaan, (fig) van repliek dienen; 2 stoten (op), botsen (tegen)

³hit [hit] vb treffen (also fig), raken: be hard hit zwaar getroffen zijn; (inf) ~ it off (with) het (samen) goed kunnen vinden (met)

⁴hit [hit] n 1 klap, slag; 2 treffer; 3 hit, succes(nummer)ʰ; 4 buitenkansjeʰ, treffer; 5 goede zet: make a ~ (with) succes hebben (bij)

¹hitch [hitsj] vb 1 vastmaken, vasthaken: ~ a horse to a cart een paard voor een wagen spannen; 2 liften: (inf) ~ a ride liften; get ~ed trouwen; ~ up optrekken

²hitch [hitsj] n 1 ruk, zet, duw; 2 storing: go off without a ~ vlot verlopen

hitchhiker [hitsjhajkə] lifter

hither [hiðə] herwaarts: ~ and thither her en der

hitherto [hiðətoe:] tot nu toe, tot dusver

hit man (Am; inf) huurmoordenaar

hit out 1 krachtig slaan; 2 aanvallen ‖ ~ at uithalen naar

hit (up)on bedenken, komen op (an idea), bij toeval ontdekken

HIV human immunodeficiency virus hiv-virusʰ

hive [hajv] 1 bijenkorf (also fig); 2 zwerm, (fig) menigte; 3 ~s netelroos

H.M. 1 Her Majesty H.M., Hare Majesteit; 2 His Majesty Z.M., Zijne Majesteit

¹hoard [ho:d] n 1 (geheime) voorraad, schat; 2 opeenhoping

²hoard [ho:d] vb hamsteren: ~ up oppotten

hoarding [ho:ding] 1 (tijdelijke) schutting; 2 reclamebordʰ

hoarfrost rijp

hoarse [ho:s] 1 hees, schor; 2 met een hese stem

hoary [ho:rie] 1 grijs; 2 grijsharig, witharig; 3 (al)oud, eerbiedwaardig: a ~ joke een ouwe bak

¹hoax [hooks] n bedrogʰ: the bomb scare turned out to be a ~ de bommelding bleek vals (alarm)

²hoax [hooks] vb om de tuin leiden: ~ s.o. into believing that iem laten geloven dat …

hob [hob] kookplaat (of cooker)

hobble [hobl] (doen) strompelen, (fig) moeizaam (doen) voortgaan

hobby [hobbie] hobby, liefhebberij

hobby-horse 1 hobbelpaardʰ; 2 stokpaardjeʰ (also fig)

hobnob [hobnob] (also with with) vriendschappelijk omgaan (met): he is always ~bing with the manager hij papt altijd met de directeur aan

hockey [hokkie] 1 hockeyʰ; 2 (Am) ijshockeyʰ

hocus-pocus [hookəs pookəs] hocus-pocus, gegoochelʰ, bedriegerij

hoe [hoo] schoffel

hog [hog] 1 varkenʰ; 2 zwijnʰ (also fig), veelvraat ‖ (inf) go the whole ~ iets grondig doen

hoist [hojst] hijsen, takelen: ~ one's flag zijn vlag in top hijsen

¹hold [hoold] vb 1 houden, het uithouden, stand-

houden: ~ by (of: to) zich houden aan; 2 van kracht zijn, gelden, waar zijn: ~ good (of: true) for gelden voor, van toepassing zijn op; 3 doorgaan, aanhouden, goed blijven (of weather)

²hold [hoold] vb 1 vasthouden (aan), beethouden, (fig) boeien: will you ~ the line? wilt u even aan het toestel blijven?; ~ together bijeenhouden; ~ s.o. to his promise iem aan zijn belofte houden; 2 hebben: ~ a title een titel dragen; 3 bekleden (eg position); ~ a conversation een gesprek voeren; 5 in bedwang houden, weerhouden: there is no ~ing her zij is niet te stuiten; 6 (inf) ophouden met, stilleggen, stoppen: ~ everything! stop!; 7 menen, beschouwen als: ~ sth. cheap weinig waarde aan iets hechten; ~ sth. against s.o. iem iets verwijten; 8 in hechtenis houden, vasthouden: ~ it! houen zo!, stop!; ~ one's own: a) het (alleen) aankunnen; b) zich handhaven, niet achteruitgaan (of a sick person); ~ one's own with opgewassen zijn tegen

³hold [hoold] n 1 greep, houvastʰ, (fig) invloed: catch (of: get, grab, take) ~ of (vast)grijpen, (vast)pakken; get a ~ on vat krijgen op; have a ~ over s.o. macht over iem hebben; keep (of: leave) ~ of vasthouden, loslaten; take ~ vastgrijpen, (fig) aanslaan; 2 (scheeps)ruimʰ: on ~ uitgesteld, vertraagd, in afwachting; put a project on ~ een project opschorten; no ~s barred alle middelen zijn toegestaan, alles mag

holdall reistas

¹hold back vb aarzelen, schromen, iets verzwijgen: ~ from zich weerhouden van

²hold back vb 1 tegenhouden, inhouden, in de weg staan; 2 achterhouden, voor zich houden

holder [hooldə] 1 houder, bezitter, drager (of a title); 2 bekleder (of an office)

holding [hoolding] 1 pachtgoedʰ; 2 bezitʰ (of shares etc), eigendomʰ

¹hold off vb uitblijven, wegblijven

²hold off vb 1 uitstellen; 2 weerstaan, tegenstand bieden aan

hold on 1 volhouden; 2 zich vasthouden; 3 aanhouden; 4 (inf) wachten, niet ophangen (telephone) ‖ (inf) ~! stop!, wacht eens even!

hold on to 1 vasthouden, niet loslaten: whatever you do, ~ your dreams wat je ook doet, geef nooit je dromen op; 2 (inf) houden

¹hold out vb 1 standhouden, volhouden, het uithouden; 2 weigeren toe te geven ‖ ~ for blijven eisen; ~ on: a) weigeren toe te geven aan; b) iets geheim houden voor

²hold out vb uitsteken (hand)

hold over 1 aanhouden; 2 verdagen, uitstellen

¹hold up vb standhouden, het uithouden

²hold up vb 1 (onder)steunen; 2 omhoog houden, opsteken (hand): ~ as an example tot voorbeeld stellen; ~ to ridicule (of: scorn) bespotten; 3 ophouden, tegenhouden, vertragen; 4 overvallen

hold-up 1 oponthoudʰ; 2 roofoverval, (fig) overval

hole [hool] **1** gat[h], holte, kuil; **2** gat[h], opening, bres: *make a ~ in* een gat slaan in, *(fig)* duchtig aanspreken; *(fig)* pick *~s in* ondergraven *(eg argument);* **3** hol[h] *(of animal),* leger[h]; **4** hok[h], krot[h], *(Am)* isoleercel; **5** penibele situatie: *in a ~ in* het nauw, in de knel; **6** kuiltje[h] *(in ballgames),* knikkerpotje[h], *(billiards)* zak; **7** *(golf)* hole

[1]holiday [holliddee] *n* **1** feestdag: *public ~* officiële feestdag; **2** vakantiedag, *also ~s* vakantie, vrije tijd: *take a ~* vrijaf nemen; *on ~, on one's ~s* op vakantie

[2]holiday [holliddee] *vb* met vakantie zijn

[1]hollow [holloo] *adj* **1** hol; **2** zonder inhoud, leeg, onoprecht; **3** hol *(of sound)* ‖ *beat s.o. ~ iem* totaal verslaan

[2]hollow [holloo] *n* **1** holte, kuil; **2** leegte

holly [hollie] hulst

holocaust [holləko:st] holocaust, vernietiging

holster [hoolstə] holster

holy [hoolie] heilig, gewijd, vroom, godsdienstig: *the Holy Ghost* (of: *Spirit)* de Heilige Geest; *Holy Writ* de Heilige Schrift; *(Roman Catholicism)* the *Holy See* de Heilige Stoel; *~ water* wijwater; *Holy Week* de Goede Week

homage [hommidzj] hulde: *pay* (of: *do) ~ to* eer bewijzen aan

[1]home [hoom] *n* **1** huis[h], woning, verblijf[h], woonhuis[h]; **2** thuis[h]; geboortegrond: *arrive* (of: *get) ~* thuiskomen; *leave ~* het ouderlijk huis verlaten; *at* (of: *back) ~* bij ons thuis, in mijn geboortestreek, geboorteplaats; *be at ~: a)* thuis zijn; *b)* ontvangen; *make yourself at ~* doe alsof je thuis bent; *(away) from ~* van huis; *it's a ~ from ~* het is er zo goed als thuis; **3** bakermat, zetel, haard: *strike ~* doel treffen; **4** (te)huis[h], inrichting; **5** *(sport, game)* eindstreep, finish, (thuis)honk[h]: *drive a nail ~* een spijker er helemaal inslaan; *~ (in) on: a)* zich richten op *(of aeroplane etc); b)* koersen op *(a beacon)*

[2]home [hoom] *adj* **1** huis-, thuis-: *~ base* (thuis)basis, *(sport, game)* doel, honk; *~ brew* zelf gebrouwen bier; *~ help* gezinshulp; *~ movie* zelf genomen film; *~ remedy* huismiddel(tje); **2** huiselijk: *~ life* het huiselijk leven; **3** lokaal: *the Home Counties* de graafschappen rondom Londen; **4** *Home* binnenlands, uit eigen land: *the Home Office* het Ministerie van Binnenlandse Zaken; *the Home Secretary* de Minister van Binnenlandse Zaken

homely [hoomlie] **1** eenvoudig; **2** alledaags; **3** *(Am)* lelijk *(of persons)*

homemaker *(Am) (roughly)* huismoeder, huisvrouw

homesick: *be* (of: *feel) ~* heimwee hebben

homespun 1 zelfgesponnen; **2** eenvoudig

homestead [hoomsted] hofstede, boerderij

homeward(s) [hoomwəd(z)] (op weg) naar huis, terugkerend; huiswaarts: *homeward bound* op weg naar huis

homework huiswerk[h], *(fig)* voorbereiding: *do ~* huiswerk maken; *do one's ~* zich (grondig) voorbereiden

homey [hoomie] huiselijk, gezellig, knus

homicide [hommissajd] doodslag, moord

homoeopathy [hoomie·oppəθie] homeopathie

homogeneity [hoomədzjinnie:ittie] homogeniteit, gelijksoortigheid

homogeneous [hommədzjie:niəs] homogeen, gelijksoortig

homosexual [homməseksjoeəl] homoseksueel

Hon. 1 *Honorary* Ere-; **2** *Hono(u)rable* Hoog(wel)geboren *(title for noblemen)*

hone [hoon] slijpen, wetten, *(fig)* verbeteren

honest [onnist] **1** eerlijk, oprecht: *earn* (of: *turn) an ~ penny* een eerlijk stuk brood verdienen; **2** braaf

honesty [onnistie] eerlijkheid, oprechtheid: *~ is the best policy* eerlijk duurt het langst

honey [hunnie] **1** honing, *(fig)* zoetheid, liefelijkheid; **2** *(Am)* schat, liefje[h] *(as form of address)*

[1]honeycomb *n* **1** honingraat; **2** honingraatmotief[h]

[2]honeycomb *vb* doorboren, doorzeven: *~ed with* doorzeefd met, doortrokken van

honeymoon 1 huwelijksreis; **2** wittebroodsdagen

[1]honk [hongk] *vb* schreeuwen *(of goose)*

[2]honk [hongk] *vb* (doen) toeteren, (doen) claxonneren: *he ~ed the horn* hij toeterde

honorary [onnərərie] honorair, ere-, onbezoldigd

[1]honour [onnə] *n* eer(bewijs[h]); hulde, aanzien[h], reputatie: *code of ~* erecode; *it does him ~, it is to his ~* het strekt hem tot eer; *in ~ bound, on one's ~* moreel verplicht; *do the ~s* als gastheer optreden; *Your* (of: *His) Honour* Edelachtbare *(form of address for judges)*

[2]honour [onnə] *vb* eren, in ere houden, eer bewijzen: *~ with* vereren met; **2** honoreren

honourable [onnərəbl] **1** eerzaam, respectabel; **2** eervol: *~ mention* eervolle vermelding; **3** eerbaar; **4** hooggeboren, edelachtbaar: *Most* (of: *Right) Honourable* edel(hoog)achtbaar *(in titles)*

hooch [hoe:tsj] sterkedrank

hood [hoed] **1** kap, capuchon; **2** overkapping, huif, vouwkap[h] *(of car),* kap *(of carriage, pram);* **3** beschermkap, wasemkap

hoodwink [hoedwingk] bedriegen, voor de gek houden

hooey [hoe:ie] onzin, nonsens, kletskoek

hoof [hoe:f] *(also hooves)* hoef

[1]hook [hoek] *n* **1** (telefoon)haak: *~ and eye* haak en oog; *off the ~* van de haak *(telephone);* **2** vishoek, vishaak; **3** hoek, kaap, landtong: *~, line and sinker* helemaal, van a tot z; *by ~ or by crook* hoe dan ook, op eerlijke of oneerlijke wijze; *get* (of: *let) s.o. off the ~ iem* uit de puree halen

[2]hook [hoek] *vb* **1** vasthaken, aanhaken: *~ on* vasthaken; **2** aan de haak slaan *(also fig),* strikken, bemachtigen

[3]hook [hoek] *vb* vastgehaakt worden

hooked [hoekt] **1** haakvormig: *a ~ nose* een haakneus, haviksneus; **2** met een haak; **3** vast(gehaakt), verstrikt: *her skirt got ~ on a nail* ze bleef met haar rok achter een spijker haken; **4** *(with on)* verslaafd (aan) *(drugs)*: *(fig)* he is completely ~ on that girl hij is helemaal bezeten van dat meisje

hook up 1 (with *with*) aansluiten (op), verbinden (met); **2** aanhaken, vasthaken

hooligan [ho͟ːliɡən] *(jonge)* vandaal, herrieschopper, hooligan

hoop [hoːp] **1** hoepel, ring; **2** *(sport)* hoepel, *(croquet)* hoop, ijzeren poortje[h] ‖ *put s.o. through the ~(s)* iem het vuur na aan de schenen leggen

¹hoot [hoːt] *vb* **1** krassen, schreeuwen; **2** toeteren (met); **3** schateren, bulderen vh lachen

²hoot [hoːt] *vb* uitjouwen: *~ at s.o., ~ s.o. off the stage* iem uitjouwen, iem wegjouwen

³hoot [hoːt] *n* **1** gekras[h] *(of owl)*; **2** getoet[h]; **3** (ge)boe[h], gejouw[h]; **4** *(inf)* giller ‖ *(inf) he doesn't give (of: care) a ~* het kan hem geen zier schelen

hooter [ho͟ːtə] sirene, fabrieksfluit, fabriekssirene

¹hop [hop] *vb* hinkelen, huppen, wippen: *~ in (of: out)* instappen, uitstappen

²hop [hop] *vb* **1** overheen springen; **2** springen in *(on bus, train)* ‖ *(inf) ~ it!* smeer 'em!, donder op!

³hop [hop] *n* **1** hink(el)sprong(etje[h]), huppelsprong(etje[h]); **2** dansje[h], dansfeest[h]; **3** reisje[h]; **4** *~s* hop(plant); hopbel ‖ *catch s.o. on the ~* iem verrassen, bij iem binnenvallen; *on the ~* druk in de weer

¹hope [hoʊp] *n* hoop(volle verwachting), vertrouwen[h], *(Belg)* betrouwen[h]: *hope against ~* tegen beter weten in blijven hopen; *lay (of: set, pin, put) one's ~s on* zijn hoop vestigen op; *live in ~(s)* (blijven) hopen

²hope [hoʊp] *vb* (with *for*) hopen (op): *~ for the best* er het beste (maar) van hopen

¹hopeful [ho͟ʊpfoel] *adj* hoopvol, hoopgevend, veelbelovend, optimistisch: *I'm not very ~ of success* ik heb niet veel hoop op een geslaagde afloop

²hopeful [ho͟ʊpfoel] *n* veelbelovend persoon, belofte

hopeless [ho͟ʊpləs] hopeloos, wanhopig, uitzichtloos: *~ at* hopeloos slecht in

horizon [həra͟ɪzən] horizon *(also fig)*

horizontal [horrizzo͟ntl] horizontaal, vlak

hormone [ho͟ːmoʊn] hormoon[h]

horn [hoːn] **1** hoorn, gewei[h], (voel)hoorn; **2** toeter, claxon, trompet: *blow (of: sound) the ~* toeteren; *draw (of: pull) in one's ~s: a)* terugkrabbelen; *b)* de buikriem aanhalen

hornet [ho͟ːnit] horzel

hornet's nest wespennest[h] ‖ *stir up a ~* zich in een wespennest steken

horrendous [hərendəs] afgrijselijk, afschuwelijk

horrible [ho͟rribl] afschuwelijk, vreselijk, verschrikkelijk

horrid [ho͟rrid] **1** vreselijk, verschrikkelijk; **2** akelig

horrific [həri͟ffik] weerzinwekkend, afschuwelijk

horrify [ho͟rriffaj] met afschuw vervullen, schokken, ontstellen

horror [ho͟rrə] **1** (ver)schrik(king), gruwel, ontzetting; **2** *~s* kriebels ‖ *you little ~!* klein kreng dat je bent!

horse [hoːs] **1** paard[h]: *eat like a ~* eten als een paard;

2 (droog)rek[h], schraag, ezel; **3** bok *(gymnastic apparatus)*, paard[h]; **4** heroïne: *a ~ of another* (of: *a different) colour* een geheel andere kwestie; *(straight) from the ~'s mouth* uit de eerste hand; *hold your ~s!* rustig aan!, niet te overhaast!

horseback paardenrug: *three men on ~* drie mannen te paard

horseman [ho͟ːsmən] ruiter, paardrijder

horseplay stoeipartij, lolbroekerij

horsepower paardenkracht

horseradish 1 mierik(swortel); **2** mierikswortelsaus

horseshoe [ho͟ːsʃoeː] (hoef)ijzer[h]

horticulture [ho͟ːtikkultsjə] **1** tuinbouw; **2** hovenierskunst

¹hose [hoʊz] *n* **1** brandslang, tuinslang; **2** kousen, panty's, sokken

²hose [hoʊz] *vb* (met een slang) bespuiten, schoonspuiten: *~ down a car* een auto schoonspuiten

hospice [ho͟spis] **1** verpleeghuis[h] voor terminale patiënten; **2** *(Am)* wijkverpleger, -verpleegster; **3** gastenverblijf[h] *(in monastery)*

hospitable [ho͟spittəbl] gastvrij, hartelijk

hospital [ho͟spitl] ziekenhuis[h]: *in ~, (Am) in the ~* in het ziekenhuis

hospitality [ho͟spitælittie] gastvrijheid

hospitalize [ho͟spittəlajz] (laten) opnemen in een ziekenhuis

¹host [hoʊst] *n* **1** gastheer; **2** waard; **3** massa, menigte: *~s of tourists* horden toeristen

²host [hoʊst] *vb* ontvangen, optreden als gastheer bij, op: *~ a television programme* een televisieprogramma presenteren

hostage [ho͟stidzj] gijzelaar

hostel [ho͟stl] **1** tehuis[h], studentenhuis[h], pension[h]; **2** jeugdherberg

hostess [ho͟stis] **1** gastvrouw; **2** hostess; **3** stewardess

hostile [ho͟stajl] **1** vijandelijk; **2** vijandig, onvriendelijk

hostilities [hosti͟llittiez] vijandelijkheden, oorlog(shandelingen)

hostility [hosti͟llittie] **1** vijandschap; **2** vijandelijkheid, vijandige daad

hot [hot] **1** heet, warm, gloeiend, scherp, pikant, vurig, hartstochtelijk, heetgebakerd, *(inf)* geil, opgewonden, *(inf; techn)* radioactief: *~ flushes* opvlieger, opvlieging; *with two policemen in ~ pursuit* met twee agenten op zijn hielen; *am I getting ~?* word ik warm? *(while guessing)*; **2** vers *(of track)*, recent, heet (vd naald) *(of news)*: *~ off the press* vers van de pers; *~ air* blabla, gezwets; *like a cat on ~ bricks* (Am: on a ~ tin roof) benauwd, niet op zijn gemak; *sell like ~ cakes* als warme broodjes de winkel uitvliegen; *strike while the iron is ~* het ijzer smeden als het heet is; *a ~ potato* een heet hangijzer; *~ stuff: a)* bink; *b)* prima spul; *c)* (harde) porno; *d)* buit, gestolen goed; *be ~ on s.o.'s track (of: trail)* iem na op het spoor zijn; *be in ~ water* in de problemen zitten; *make it (of: the place, things) (too)* ~ *for s.o.* iem het vuur na aan de schenen leggen; *not so* ~ niet zo goed; ~ *on astrology* gek op astrologie; *blow* ~ *and cold* nu eens voor dan weer tegen zijn

hotbed 1 broeikas; **2** broeinest[h]

hotchpotch [hotsjpotsj] hutspot, ratjetoe[h], *(fig)* mengelmoes[h], allegaartje[h]

hotel [hootel] hotel[h]

hotplate kookplaat(je[h]), warmhoudplaat(je[h])

¹hot up *vb (inf)* warm(er) worden; hevig(er) worden

²hot up *vb (inf)* verhevigen, intensiveren

hound [haund] (jacht)hond, windhond

hour [auə] **1** uur[h]: *after* ~s na sluitingstijd, na kantoortijd; *on the* ~ op het hele uur; *out of* ~s buiten de normale uren; *at the eleventh* ~ ter elfder ure, op het allerlaatste ogenblik; **2** moment[h], huidige tijd: *the* ~ *has come* de tijd is gekomen, het is zover

¹house [haus] *n* **1** huis[h], woning, behuizing, (handels)huis[h]: ~ *of cards* kaartenhuis *(also fig)*; ~ *of God* godshuis, huis des Heren; *eat s.o. out of* ~ *and home* iem de oren van het hoofd eten; *move* ~ verhuizen; *(fig) put (of: set) one's* ~ *in order* orde op zaken stellen; *set up* ~ op zichzelf gaan wonen; *on the* ~ van het huis, (rondje) van de zaak; **2** *House* (gebouw[h] van) volksvertegenwoordiging, kamer: *the House of Commons* het Lagerhuis; *the House of Lords* het Hogerhuis; *the Houses of Parliament* het parlement, de parlementsgebouwen; *the House of Representatives* het Huis van Afgevaardigden; **3** (vorstelijk, adellijk) geslacht[h], koningshuis[h], vorstenhuis[h], adellijke familie; **4** bioscoopzaal, schouwburgzaal, voorstelling: *(fig) bring the* ~ *down* staande ovaties oogsten; *like a* ~ *on fire: a)* krachtig; *b)* (vliegens)vlug; *c)* prima, uitstekend; *keep* ~ (het) huishouden (doen)

²house [hauz] *vb* huisvesten, onderdak bieden aan

household [haushoold] (de gezamenlijke) huisbewoners, huisgenoten, huisgezin[h]

housekeeper huishoudster

housekeeping huishouding, huishouden[h]

houseman [hausmən] **1** (intern) assistent-arts *(in hospital)*; **2** (huis)knecht

houseroom onderdak[h], (berg)ruimte: *(fig) I wouldn't give such a chair* ~ ik zou zo'n stoel niet eens gratis willen hebben

housewarming inwijdingsfeest[h] *(of house)*

housewife huisvrouw

housing [hauzing] **1** huisvesting, woonruimte; **2** *(techn)* huis[h], omhulsel[h]

hovel [hovl] krot[h], bouwval

hover [hovvə] **1** hangen (boven), (blijven) zweven *(of birds etc)*; **2** rondhangen, blijven hangen ‖ *(fig)* ~ *between life and death* tussen leven en dood zweven

hovercraft hovercraft

¹how [hau] *adv* **1** hoe, hoeveel, hoever: ~ *are things?* hoe gaat het ermee?; *(inf)* ~ *idiotic can you get?* kan het nog gekker?; *she knows* ~ *to cook* ze kan koken;

~ *do you like my hat?* wat vind je van mijn hoed?; ~ *do you do?* aangenaam, hoe maakt u het?; ~ *is she (off) for clothes?* heeft ze genoeg kleren?; ~ *about John?* wat doe je (dan) met John?; **2** hoe, waardoor, waarom: ~ *come she is late?* hoe komt het dat ze te laat is?; ~ *about going home?* zouden we niet naar huis gaan?; ~ *about an ice-cream?* wat vind je van een ijsje?

²how [hau] *conj* zoals: *colour it* ~ *you like* kleur het zoals je wilt

¹however [hauevvə] *adv* **1** hoe … ook, hoe dan ook, op welke wijze ook: ~ *you travel, you will be tired* hoe je ook reist, je zult moe zijn; **2** echter, nochtans, desondanks: *this time,* ~*, he meant what he said* deze keer echter meende hij het; **3** hoe in 's hemelsnaam: ~ *did you manage to come?* hoe ben je erin geslaagd te komen?

²however [hauevvə] *conj* hoe … maar, zoals … maar: ~ *he tried, it wouldn't go in* hoe hij het ook probeerde, het wilde er niet in

¹howl [haul] *vb* huilen, jammeren, krijsen: *the wind* ~*ed* de wind gierde; ~ *with laughter* gieren van het lachen; *the speaker was* ~*ed down* de spreker werd weggehoond

²howl [haul] *n* gehuil[h], brul, gil: ~*s of derision* spotgelach, hoongelach

howler [haulə] giller, flater, blunder

howling [hauling] gigantisch, enorm

howsoever *see* however

h.p. 1 *horsepower* pk, paardenkracht; **2** *hire purchase* huurkoop: *on (the)* ~ op huurkoopbasis, *(roughly)* op afbetaling

H.Q. *headquarters* hoofdbureau; hoofdkwartier

H.R.H. *Her Royal Highness* H.K.H., Z.K.H., Hare (Zijne) Koninklijke Hoogheid

hr(s). *hour(s)* uur; uren

hub [hub] **1** naaf; **2** centrum[h], middelpunt[h]

¹huddle [hudl] *vb* bijeenkruipen: ~ *together* bij elkaar kruipen; *the singers* ~*d together around the microphone* de zangeressen stonden dicht bijeen rond de microfoon

²huddle [hudl] *n* **1** (dicht opeengepakte) groep, kluwen, menigte; **2** samenraapsel[h], bos[h], troep ‖ *go into a* ~ de koppen bij elkaar steken

huff [huf] boze bui: *in a* ~ nijdig, beledigd

¹hug [hug] *vb* **1** omarmen, omhelzen, tegen zich aandrukken; **2** (zich) vasthouden aan

²hug [hug] *n* omhelzing, knuffel

huge [hjoe:dzj] reusachtig, kolossaal, enorm: ~*ly overrated* zwaar overschat

hulk [hulk] **1** (scheeps)casco[h], scheepsromp, hulk; **2** vleesklomp, kolos

hull [hul] **1** (scheeps)romp; **2** (peulen)schil, *(fig)* omhulsel[h]

hullo [həloo] hallo

¹hum [hum] *vb* **1** zoemen, brommen; **2** bruisen, (op volle toeren) draaien: *things are beginning to* ~ er komt schot in; ~ *with activity* gonzen van de bedrijvigheid

²**hum** [hum] *vb* neuriën: *he was just ~ming a tune to himself* hij zat in zichzelf een deuntje te neuriën

³**hum** [hum] *n* zoemgeluid[h], bromgeluid[h], brom, gebrom[h], gezoem[h]

¹**human** [hjoe:mən] *adj* menselijk, mensen-: *~ being* mens; *~ interest* het menselijk element, de gevoelsinbreng *(in newspaper articles etc)*; *~ nature* de menselijke natuur; *the ~ race* de mensheid; *~ rights* mensenrechten; *I'm only ~* ik ben (ook) maar een mens

²**human** [hjoe:mən] *n* mens

humane [hjoe:meen] humaan, menselijk

humanistic [hjoe:mənistik] humanistisch

humanitarian [hjoe:mænitteəriən] humanitair, menslievend

humanity [hjoe:mænittie] **1** mensdom[h]; **2** menselijkheid; mensheid, mens-zijn[h]; menslievendheid; **3** *-ies* geesteswetenschappen

¹**humble** [humbl] *adj* bescheiden, onderdanig; nederig, eenvoudig: *my ~ apologies* mijn nederige excuses; *eat ~ pie* een toontje lager zingen, inbinden

²**humble** [humbl] *vb* vernederen

humbug [humbug] **1** bedrieger, oplichter; **2** pepermuntballetje[h], kussentje[h]; **3** onzin, nonsens, larie; **4** bluf

humdrum [humdrum] saai, vervelend, eentonig

humid [hjoe:mid] vochtig

humiliate [hjoe:millie·eet] vernederen, krenken

humiliation [hjoe:millie·eesjən] vernedering

humility [hjoe:millittie] nederigheid, bescheidenheid

humorous [hjoe:mərəs] humoristisch, grappig, komisch

¹**humour** [hjoe:mə] *n* **1** humor, geestigheid: *sense of ~* gevoel voor humor; **2** humeur[h], stemming: *in a bad ~* slechtgeluimd, in een slechte bui

²**humour** [hjoe:mə] *vb* tegemoet komen (aan), paaien, toegeven: *~ a child* een kind zijn zin geven

¹**hump** [hump] *n* **1** bult, bochel; **2** *(inf)* landerigheid: *it gives me the ~* ik baal ervan; *be over the ~* het ergste achter de rug hebben

²**hump** [hump] *vb* **1** welven, bol maken, ronden; **2** *(inf)* torsen, (mee)zeulen

¹**hunch** [huntsj] *n* voorgevoel[h], vaag idee

²**hunch** [huntsj] *vb* krommen, optrekken *(shoulders)*, (krom)buigen

hunchback gebochelde, bultenaar

hundred [hundrəd] honderd, *(fig)* talloos: *one ~ per cent* honderd procent, helemaal, *(fig; esp after negation)* helemaal de oude, weer helemaal opgeknapt

hundredth [hundrədθ] honderdste, honderdste deel[h]

¹**Hungarian** [hunggeəriən] *adj* Hongaars

²**Hungarian** [hunggeəriən] *n* Hongaar(se)

Hungary [hunggərie] Hongarije

¹**hunger** [hunggə] *n* honger, trek, *(fig)* hunkering, dorst: *a ~ for sth.* een hevig verlangen naar iets

²**hunger** [hunggə] *vb* hongeren, honger hebben,

(fig) hunkeren, dorsten

hungry [hunggrie] hongerig, uitgehongerd, *(fig)* (with *for*) hunkerend (naar): *feel ~* honger hebben

hunk [hungk] homp, brok[h]

¹**hunt** [hunt] *vb* **1** jagen (op), jacht maken (op); **2** zoeken, speuren: *~ high and low for sth.* overal zoeken naar iets; **3** opjagen: *a ~ed look* een (op)gejaagde blik

²**hunt** [hunt] *n* jacht(partij), vossenjacht, *(fig)* speurtocht, zoektocht

hunt down opsporen, najagen

hunter [huntə] **1** jager *(also fig)*; **2** jachtpaard[h]

hunting [hunting] jacht, vossenjacht

hunt out opdiepen, opsporen

huntsman [huntsmən] **1** jager; **2** jachtmeester

hunt up opzoeken, natrekken

hurdle [hə:dl] **1** horde, hindernis, obstakel[h] *(also fig)*; **2** schot[h], horde; **3** *~s* horde(loop)

hurl [hə:l] smijten, slingeren: *~ reproaches at one another* elkaar verwijten naar het hoofd slingeren; *the dog ~ed itself at* (of: on) *the postman* de hond stortte zich op de postbode

hurray [hoeree] hoera(atje[h]), hoezee[h], hoerageroep[h] || *hip, hip, ~!* hiep, hiep, hoera!

hurricane [hurrikkən] orkaan, cycloon

hurried [hurried] haastig, gehaast, gejaagd

¹**hurry** [hurrie] *n* haast: *I'm rather in a ~* ik heb nogal haast

²**hurry** [hurrie] *vb* zich haasten, haast maken, opschieten: *he hurried along* hij snelde voort; *~ up!* schiet op! vooruit!

³**hurry** [hurrie] *vb* **1** tot haast aanzetten, opjagen; **2** verhaasten, bespoedigen: *~ up a job* haast maken met een klus; **3** haastig vervoeren

¹**hurt** [hə:t] *vb* pijn doen: *my feet ~* mijn voeten doen pijn; *it won't ~ to cut down on spending* het kan geen kwaad om te bezuinigen

²**hurt** [hə:t] *vb* **1** bezeren, verwonden, blesseren: *I ~ my knee* ik heb mijn knie bezeerd; **2** krenken, kwetsen, beledigen: *feel ~* zich gekrenkt voelen

³**hurt** [hə:t] *n* **1** pijn(lijke zaak); **2** letsel[h], wond

hurtful [hə:tfoel] **1** schadelijk; **2** kwetsend

hurtle [hə:tl] kletteren, razen, suizen

husband [huzbənd] man, echtgenoot: *~ and wife* man en vrouw

husbandry [huzbəndrie] landbouw en veeteelt, het boerenbedrijf: *animal ~* veehouderij, veeteelt

¹**hush** [husj] *n* stilte

²**hush** [husj] *vb* verstommen, tot rust komen || *~!* stil!, sst!

³**hush** [husj] *vb* tot zwijgen brengen, doen verstommen: *~ up* verzwijgen, doodzwijgen

hush-hush *(inf)* (diep) geheim

husk [husk] **1** schil(letje[h]), (maïs)vlies[h]; **2** (waardeloos) omhulsel[h], lege dop

husky [huskie] eskimohond

hussy [hussie] brutaaltje[h]: *brazen* (of: *shameless*) *~* brutaal nest

¹**hustle** [husl] *vb* **1** dringen, duwen; **2** zich haasten,

hard werken, druk in de weer zijn
²**hustle** [hŭsl] *vb* 1 (op)jagen, duwen: *she ~d him out of the house* ze werkte hem het huis uit; 2 *(Am; inf)* bewerken *(eg customers)*
³**hustle** [hŭsl] *n* gedrangʰ, bedrijvigheid, drukte: *~ and bustle* drukte, bedrijvigheid
hut [hut] 1 hut(jeʰ), huisjeʰ, keet; 2 *(mil)* barak
hyacinth [hajjəsinθ] hyacint
hybrid [hajbrid] kruising
hydrant [hajdrənt] brandkraan
hydraulic [hajdrɒllik] hydraulisch: *~ engineering* waterbouw(kunde)
hydroelectric [hajdrooillektrik] hydro-elektrisch
hydrofoil [hajdroofojl] draagvleugel; (draag)vleugelboot
hydrogen [hajdrədzjən] waterstofʰ
hyena [hajjie:nə] hyena
hygiene [hajdzjie:n] hygiëne, gezondheidsleer, gezondheidszorg
hygienic [hajdzjie:nik] hygiënisch
hymn [him] hymne, lofzang, kerkgezangʰ
hype [hajp] 1 kunstjeʰ, truc, list; 2 opgeblazen zaak *(by media, advertising);* schreeuwerige reclame, aanprijzing
hyperbole [hajpɔ:bəlie] *(form)* hyperbool, overdrijving
hypermarket [hajpəma:kit] hypermarkt, weidewinkel
hyphen [hajfən] verbindingsstreepjeʰ, afbrekingstekenʰ, koppeltekenʰ
hyphenate [hajfəneet] afbreken, door een koppelteken verbinden
hypnotism [hipnətizm] hypnotismeʰ
hypnotize [hipnətajz] hypnotiseren *(also fig),* biologeren, fascineren
¹**hypochondriac** [hajpookondrie·æk] *adj* hypochondrisch, zwaarmoedig
²**hypochondriac** [hajpookondrie·æk] *n* hypochonder, zwaarmoedig mens
hypocrite [hippəkrit] hypocriet, huichelaar
hypodermic [hajpoodɔ:mik] onderhuids: *~ needle* injectienaald
hypothesis [hajpoθissis] hypothese, veronderstelling
hypothetical [hajpəθettikl] hypothetisch, verondersteld
hysteria [histiəriə] hysterie

i

I [aj] ik, zelf, eigen persoon

Iberian [ajbi̯əriən] Iberisch

¹**ice** [ajs] *n* **1** ijsʰ: *(fig) put sth. on ~* iets in de ijskast zetten, iets uitstellen; **2** vruchtenijsʰ, waterijs(je)ʰ; **3** ijs(je)ʰ: *break the ~* het ijs breken; *cut no ~ (with s.o.)* geen indruk maken (op iem)

²**ice** [ajs] *vb* bevriezen, dichtvriezen: *~ over* dichtvriezen; *~d drinks* (ijs)gekoelde dranken

ice age ijstijd

icebound ingevroren, door ijs ingesloten

icebreaker ijsbreker

ice cream ijs(je)ʰ, roomijs(je)ʰ

ice cube ijsblokjeʰ

Iceland [ajslənd] IJsland

ice rink (overdekte) ijsbaan

icicle [ajsikl] ijskegel, ijspegel

icing [ajsing] suikerglazuurʰ, glaceerselʰ || *(the) ~ on the cake* tierelantijntje(s)

icing sugar poedersuiker

icky [ikkie] goor, vies, smerig

icon [ajkon] ico(o)nʰ, *(comp)* pictogramʰ, icoon

iconoclast [ajkonnəklæst] beeldenstormer

icy [ajsie] **1** ijzig, ijskoud, ijsachtig: *an ~ look* een ijzige blik; **2** met ijs bedekt, bevroren, glad

ID card [ajdie: ka:d] *see* identity card

idea [ajdiə] idee⁺ʰ, denkbeeldʰ, begripʰ, gedachte: *is this your ~ of a pleasant evening?* noem jij dit een gezellige avond?

¹**ideal** [ajdiəl] *adj* **1** ideaal; **2** ideëel, denkbeeldig; **3** idealistisch

²**ideal** [ajdiəl] *n* ideaalʰ

idealism [ajdiəlizm] idealismeʰ

idealize [ajdiəlajz] idealiseren

identical [ajdentikl] identiek, gelijk(luidend), gelijkwaardig: *~ twins* eeneiige tweeling

¹**identify** [ajdentiffaj] *vb (with with)* zich identificeren (met), zich vereenzelvigen (met)

²**identify** [ajdentiffaj] *vb* **1** identificeren, de identiteit vaststellen van, in verband brengen: *I can't ~ your accent* ik kan uw accent niet thuisbrengen; *s.o. who is identified with a fascist party* iem die in verband gebracht wordt met een fascistische partij; **2** erkennen, vaststellen

identity [ajdentittie] **1** identiteit, persoon(lijkheid): *a case of mistaken ~* een geval van persoonsverwisseling; **2** volmaakte gelijkenis

ideology [ajdie·ollədzjie] ideologie

idiocy [iddiəsie] idiotie, dwaasheid

idiom [iddiəm] **1** idiomatische uitdrukking; **2** idioomʰ, taaleigenʰ, taaleigenaardigheid

idiosyncrasy [iddiəsingkrəsie] eigenaardigheid, typerend kenmerkʰ

idiot [iddiət] idioot

¹**idle** [ajdl] *adj* **1** werkloos, inactief: *he has been ~ all day* hij heeft de hele dag niets uitgevoerd; **2** lui, laks; **3** doelloos, zinloos, vruchteloos: *an ~ attempt* een vergeefse poging; *~ gossip* loze kletspraat; **4** ongebruikt, onbenut: *~ machines only cost money* stilstaande machines kosten alleen maar geld

²**idle** [ajdl] *vb* **1** nietsdoen, luieren: *~ about* luieren, rondhangen; **2** stationair draaien *(of engine)*

idle away verdoen, verlummelen *(time)*

idly *see* idle

idol [ajdl] **1** afgod(sbeeldʰ), idoolʰ; **2** favoriet

idyl(l) [iddil] idylle

i.e. id est d.w.z., dat wil zeggen

¹**if** [if] *conj* **1** indien, als, zo, op voorwaarde dat: *~ anything this is even worse* dit is zo mogelijk nog slechter; *~ not* zo niet; *~ so* zo ja; **2** telkens als, telkens wanneer; **3** of: *I wonder ~ she is happy* ik vraag mij af of ze gelukkig is; **4** zij het, (al)hoewel, al: *a talented ~ arrogant young man* een begaafde, zij het arrogante, jongeman; *protest, ~ only to pester them* protesteer, al was het maar om hen te pesten; *~ we failed we did all we could* we hebben wel gefaald maar we hebben gedaan wat we konden; **5** warempel, zowaar: *~ that isn't Mr Smith!* als dat niet meneer Smith is!; *~ only* als … maar, ik wou dat

²**if** [if] *n* onzekere factor, voorwaarde, mogelijkheid || *~s and buts* maren, bedenkingen

iffy [iffie] onzeker, dubieus

igloo [igloe:] iglo, eskimohut, sneeuwhut

¹**ignite** [ignajt] *vb* aansteken

²**ignite** [ignajt] *vb* ontbranden, vlam vatten

ignition [ignisjən] **1** ontsteking(sinrichting) *(of car): turn the ~, switch the ~ on* het contactsleuteltje omdraaien, starten; **2** ontbranding, ontsteking

ignition key contactsleuteltjeʰ

ignoble [ignoobl] laag(hartig), onwaardig

ignominious [ignəminniəs] schandelijk, oneervol

ignorance [ignərəns] onwetendheid, onkunde, onkundigheid: *keep in ~* in het ongewisse laten

ignorant [ignərənt] **1** onwetend, onkundig: *~ of* onkundig van; *I'm very ~ of politics* ik heb helemaal geen verstand van politiek; **2** dom, onontwikkeld

ignore [ignoː] negeren

¹**ill** [il] *adj* **1** ziek, beroerd, ongezond: *fall (of: be taken) ~* ziek worden; **2** slecht, kwalijk: *~ fame* slechte naam; *~ health* slechte gezondheid; **3** schadelijk, nadelig, ongunstig: *~ effects* nadelige gevolgen; **4** vijandig, onvriendelijk: *~ feeling* haatdragendheid

²**ill** [il] *adv* **1** slecht, kwalijk, verkeerd: *~ at ease* slecht op zijn gemak; **2** nauwelijks, amper, onvoldoende: *I can ~ afford the money* ik kan het geld eigenlijk

niet missen
³ill [il] *n* **1** tegenslag; **2** kwaad^h, onheil^h, vloek: *speak ~ of* kwaadspreken van
ill-advised onverstandig
ill-bred onopgevoed, ongemanierd
ill-disposed **1** kwaadgezind, kwaadwillig; **2** afkerig, onwillig: *~ towards a plan* gekant tegen een plan
illegal [illie:gl] onwettig, illegaal, onrechtmatig
illegality [illigælittie] onwettigheid, onrechtmatigheid
illegible [illedzjibl] onleesbaar
illegitimate [illidzjittimmət] **1** onrechtmatig, illegaal; **2** onwettig *(of child)*, buitenechtelijk; **3** ongewettigd, ongeldig
illicit [illissit] onwettig, illegaal, ongeoorloofd
illiteracy [illittərəsie] analfabetisme^h, ongeletterdheid
illiterate [illittərət] ongeletterd, analfabeet
ill-mannered ongemanierd
ill-natured onvriendelijk
illness [ilnəs] ziekte, kwaal
illogical [illodzjikl] onlogisch, ongerijmd, tegenstrijdig
ill-tempered slecht gehumeurd, humeurig
ill-timed misplaatst, op een ongeschikt ogenblik
illuminate [illoe:minneet] **1** *(also fig)* verlichten, licht werpen op; **2** met feestverlichting versieren
illumination [illoe:minneesjən] **1** verlichting, *(fig)* geestelijke verlichting; **2** opheldering, verduidelijking; **3** *~s* feestverlichting
illusion [illoe:zjən] **1** illusie, waandenkbeeld^h: *optical ~* gezichtsbedrog; *cherish the ~ that* de illusie koesteren dat; *be under an ~* misleid zijn; **2** (zins)begoocheling, zelfbedrog^h
illusory [illoe:sərie] denkbeeldig, bedrieglijk
illustrate [illəstreet] illustreren, verduidelijken, toelichten
illustration [illəstreesjən] illustratie, toelichting, afbeelding
illustrious [illustriəs] illuster, vermaard, gerenommeerd
image [immidzj] **1** beeld^h, afbeelding, voorstelling; **2** imago^h, reputatie: *corporate ~* bedrijfsimago
imaginable [imædzjinnəbl] voorstelbaar, denkbaar, mogelijk
imagination [imædzjinneesjən] verbeelding(skracht), voorstelling(svermogen^h), fantasie
imagine [imædzjin] **1** zich verbeelden, zich indenken, fantaseren: *just ~ that!* stel je voor!; **2** veronderstellen, aannemen
imam [imma:m] imam
imbalance [imbæləns] onevenwichtigheid, wanverhouding
¹imbecile [imbəsie:l] *adj* imbeciel, zwakzinnig, dwaas
²imbecile [imbəsie:l] *n* imbeciel, zwakzinnige, stommeling
imbue [imbjoe:] (door)drenken *(also fig)*, verzadigen, doordringen: *~d with hatred* van haat vervuld

imitate [immitteet] **1** nadoen, imiteren: *you should ~ your brother* neem een voorbeeld aan je broer; **2** lijken op: *it is wood, made to ~ marble* het is hout dat eruitziet als marmer
imitation [immitteesjən] imitatie, navolging, namaak: *~ leather* kunstleer
immaculate [imækjoelət] **1** vlekkeloos, onbevlekt, zuiver: *(Roman Catholicism) Immaculate Conception* Onbevlekte Ontvangenis; **2** onberispelijk
immaterial [immətjəriəl] **1** onstoffelijk, immaterieel; **2** onbelangrijk, irrelevant: *all that is ~ to me* dat is mij allemaal om het even
immature [immətsjoeə] onvolgroeid, onrijp, onvolwassen
immeasurable [immezjərəbl] onmetelijk, immens, oneindig
immediacy [immie:diəsie] **1** nabijheid; **2** dringendheid, urgentie, directheid
immediate [immie:diət] **1** direct, onmiddellijk, rechtstreeks: *an ~ reply* een onmiddellijk antwoord; **2** nabij, dichtstbijzijnd, naast: *my ~ family* mijn naaste familie
¹immediately [immie:diətlie] *adv* meteen, onmiddellijk
²immediately [immie:diətlie] *conj* zodra
immemorial [immimmo:riəl] onheuglijk, eeuwenoud, oeroud: *from time ~* sinds mensenheugenis
immense [immens] immens, oneindig, oneindig: *enjoy oneself ~ly* zich kostelijk amuseren
immerse [imma:s] **1** (onder)dompelen; **2** verdiepen, absorberen, verzinken: *he ~s himself completely in his work* hij gaat helemaal op in zijn werk
immigrant [immigrənt] immigrant
immigrate [immigreet] immigreren
immigration [immigreesjən] immigratie
imminence [imminnəns] dreiging, nabijheid, nadering *(of danger)*
imminent [imminnənt] dreigend, op handen zijnd: *a storm is ~* er dreigt onweer
immobile [immoobail] onbeweeglijk, roerloos
immobilize [immoobillajz] onbeweeglijk maken, stilleggen, lamleggen, inactiveren
immoderate [immoddərət] onmatig, overmatig, buitensporig
immodest [immoddist] **1** onbescheiden, arrogant; **2** onfatsoenlijk, onbeschaamd
immoral [immorrəl] immoreel, onzedelijk, verdorven
immortal [immo:tl] onsterfelijk
immortalize [immo:təlajz] vereeuwigen
immune [imjoe:n] immuun, onvatbaar, bestand: *~ against (of: from, to)* immuun voor; *~ from punishment* vrijgesteld van straf
immune system immuunsysteem^h, natuurlijk afweersysteem^h
immunity [imjoe:nittie] onschendbaarheid: *~ from taxation* vrijstelling van belasting
immutable [imjoe:təbl] onveranderbaar, onveran-

derlijk

imp [imp] **1** duiveltje^h; **2** deugniet

impact [impækt] **1** schok, botsing, inslag: *on* ~ *op het moment van* een botsing; **2** schokeffect^h, (krachtige) invloed, impact

impair [impeə] schaden, benadelen, verslechteren: ~ *one's health* zijn gezondheid schaden

impaired [impeəd] beschadigd, verzwakt: *visually* ~ visueel gehandicapt

impart [impa:t] **1** verlenen, verschaffen; **2** meedelen, onthullen

impartial [impa:sjl] onpartijdig, neutraal, onbevooroordeeld

impassable [impa:səbl] onbegaanbaar

impassioned [impæsjənd] bezield, hartstochtelijk

impassive [impæsiv] ongevoelig, gevoelloos, onbewogen, *(sometimes depr)* hardvochtig, kil

impatient [impeesjənt] **1** ongeduldig, geërgerd, onlijdzaam; **2** begerig: *the child is* ~ *to see his mother* het kind popelt van ongeduld om zijn moeder te zien

impeachment [impie:tsjmənt] beschuldiging, aanklagingsprocedure

impeccable [impekkəbl] **1** foutloos, feilloos, vlekeloos; **2** onberispelijk, smetteloos

impede [impie:d] belemmeren, (ver)hinderen

impediment [impeddimmənt] **1** beletsel^h, belemmering; **2** (spraak)gebrek^h

impel [impel] **1** aanzetten, aanmoedigen; **2** voortdrijven, voortstuwen

impending [impending] dreigend, aanstaand

impenetrable [impennitrəbl] ondoordringbaar, ontoegankelijk, *(fig)* ondoorgrondelijk, onpeilbaar

^1**imperative** [imperrətiv] *n* gebiedende wijs

^2**imperative** [imperrətiv] *adj* **1** noodzakelijk, vereist; **2** verplicht, dwingend; **3** gebiedend, autoritair

imperceptible [impəseptibl] onwaarneembaar, onmerkbaar, onzichtbaar

imperfect [impə:fikt] onvolmaakt, onvolkomen, gebrekkig

imperfection [impəfeksjən] onvolkomenheid, gebrek^h, gebrekkigheid, onvolmaaktheid

imperial [impiəriəl] imperiaal, mbt een keizer(rijk), keizerlijk, rijks-, mbt het Britse rijk

imperialism [impiəriəlizm] imperialisme^h, expansiedrang

impermeable [impə:miəbl] ondoordringbaar, waterdicht

impersonal [impə:sənl] **1** onpersoonlijk, zakelijk; **2** niet menselijk

impersonate [impə:səneet] **1** vertolken, (de rol) spelen (van), imiteren; **2** zich uitgeven voor

impertinent [impə:tinnənt] onbeschaamd, brutaal

imperturbable [impətə:bəbl] onverstoorbaar, onwankelbaar

impervious [impə:viəs] **1** ondoordringbaar; **2** onontvankelijk, ongevoelig: ~ *to* ongevoelig voor

impetuous [impetjoeəs] onstuimig, impulsief, heetgebakerd

impetus [impittəs] **1** impuls, stimulans; **2** drijvende kracht, drijfkracht, stuwkracht, drijfveer

impinge (up)on [impindzj] **1** treffen, raken, inslaan in; **2** beroeren, van invloed zijn op; **3** inbreuk maken op

impish [impisj] ondeugend, schelms

implacable [implækəbl] onverbiddelijk, onvermurwbaar

implant [impla:nt] **1** (in)planten, (in de grond) steken; **2** inprenten, inhameren

implausible [implo:zibl] onaannemelijk, onwaarschijnlijk

^1**implement** [implimmənt] *n* werktuig^h, gereedschap^h, instrument^h

^2**implement** [implimment] *vb* ten uitvoer brengen, toepassen, verwezenlijken: ~ *a new computer network* een nieuw computernetwerk in gebruik nemen

implicate [implikkeet] betrekken, verwikkelen

implication [implikkeesjən] **1** implicatie, (onuitgesproken) suggestie: *by* ~ bij implicatie; **2** verwikkeling, betrokkenheid

implicit [implissit] **1** impliciet, onuitgesproken, stilzwijgend; **2** onvoorwaardelijk: ~ *faith* onvoorwaardelijk geloof

implore [implo:] smeken, dringend verzoeken

imply [implaj] **1** impliceren, met zich meebrengen: *his refusal implies that* … uit zijn weigering blijkt dat …; **2** suggereren, duiden op: *are you ~ing that you're going to resign?* wil je daarmee zeggen dat je ontslag gaat nemen?

impolite [impəlajt] onbeleefd, onhoffelijk

imponderable [impondərəbl] onvoorspelbaar

^1**import** [impo:t] *n* **1** invoerartikel^h; **2** invoer, import

^2**import** [impo:t] *vb* invoeren, importeren: ~ *cars from Japan into Europe* auto's uit Japan invoeren in Europa

important [impo:tənt] belangrijk, gewichtig: ~ *to* belangrijk voor

importation [impo:teesjən] invoer(artikel^h), import(goederen)

impose [impooz] **1** opleggen, heffen, afdwingen: ~ *a task* een taak opleggen; **2** opdringen: ~ *oneself* (of: *one's company*) *(up)on* zich opdringen aan

impose (up)on [impooz] gebruik maken van, tot last zijn, een beroep doen op

imposing [impoozing] imponerend, indrukwekkend, ontzagwekkend

imposition [impəzisjən] **1** heffing, belasting; **2** (opgelegde) last, (zware) taak, druk; **3** straf(taak), strafwerk^h

impossibility [impossibbillittie] onmogelijkheid

impossible [impossibl] onmogelijk: *an* ~ *situation* een hopeloze situatie; *that chap is* ~ *to get along with* die gozer is onmogelijk om mee om te gaan

impostor [impostə] bedrieger, oplichter

impotent [impətənt] **1** machteloos, onmachtig; **2** impotent

impoverish [impovvərisj] verarmen, verpauperen

impracticable [impræktikkəbl] onuitvoerbaar, onrealiseerbaar

impractical [impræktikl] onpraktisch, onhandig

imprecise [imprissajs] onnauwkeurig

impregnable [impregnəbl] onneembaar, onaantastbaar

impregnate [impregneet] 1 zwanger maken; 2 bevruchten

impress [impres] 1 bedrukken, afdrukken, indrukken, opdrukken; 2 (een) indruk maken op, imponeren: *your boyfriend ~es us unfavourably* je vriendje maakt geen beste indruk op ons; *~ed at (of: by, with)* geïmponeerd door, onder de indruk van; 3 inprenten

impression [impresjən] 1 afdruk, indruk; 2 indruk, impressie: *make an ~ (on)* indruk maken (op); *under the ~ that ...* in de veronderstelling dat ...

impressive [impressiv] indrukwekkend, ontzagwekkend

imprint [imprint] (af)drukken, indrukken, stempelen, *(fig)* griffen, inprenten

imprisonment [imprizzənmənt] gevangenneming, gevangenschap

improbability [improbbəbillittie] onwaarschijnlijkheid

improbable [improbbəbl] onwaarschijnlijk, onaannemelijk

¹**impromptu** [impromptjoe:] *adj* onvoorbereid, geëmproviseerd

²**impromptu** [impromptjoe:] *adv* voor de vuist (weg), spontaan

improper [improppə] 1 ongepast, misplaatst; 2 onfatsoenlijk, oneerbaar

impropriety [imprəprajjətie] 1 ongepastheid; 2 onfatsoenlijkheid

improve [improe:v] vooruitgaan, beter worden: *his health is improving* zijn gezondheid gaat vooruit

improvement [improe:vmənt] verbetering, vooruitgang: *that is quite an ~* dat is een stuk beter; *an ~ in the weather* een weersverbetering

improve (up)on overtreffen: *~ a previous performance* een eerdere prestatie overtreffen

improvident [improvviddənt] zorgeloos, verkwistend

improvisation [imprəvajzeesjən] improvisatie

improvise [imprəvajz] improviseren, in elkaar flansen

impudent [impjoedənt] schaamteloos, brutaal

impulse [impuls] 1 impuls, puls, stroomstoot; 2 opwelling, inval, impuls(iviteit): *act on ~* impulsief handelen

impulsive [impulsiv] impulsief

impunity [impjoe:nittie] straffeloosheid: *with ~* straffeloos, ongestraft

impure [impjoeə] onzuiver, verontreinigd

impute [impjoe:t] toeschrijven, wijten, aanwijzen

¹**in** [in] *prep* 1 in: *~ my opinion* naar mijn mening; *play ~ the street* op straat spelen; 2 *(direction; also fig)* in, naar, ter: *~ aid of* ten voordele van; 3 *(time)*

in, binnen: *~ a few minutes* over enkele minuten; *~ all those years* gedurende al die jaren; 4 *(activity, profession)* wat betreft, in: *the latest thing ~ computers* het laatste snufje op het gebied van computers; 5 *(proportion, size, degree)* in, op, uit: *sell ~ ones* per stuk verkopen; *one ~ twenty* één op twintig; 6 *(in the shape of)* als: *buy ~ instalments* op afbetaling kopen; 7 in zover dat, in, met betrekking tot, doordat, omdat: *he resembles you ~ being very practical* hij lijkt op jou in zoverre dat hij heel praktisch is; *he was ~ charge of* hij was verantwoordelijk voor; *~ honour of* ter ere van

²**in** [in] *adv* binnen, naar binnen, erheen: *built-~* ingebouwd; *fit sth. ~* iets (er)in passen; *the police moved ~* de politie kwam tussenbeide

³**in** [in] *adj* 1 intern, inwonend, binnen-; 2 populair, modieus, in; 3 exclusief: *in-crowd* kliekje, wereldje

inability [innəbillittie] onvermogenʰ, onmacht

inaccessible [innəksessibl] ontoegankelijk, onbereikbaar

inaccurate [inækjoerət] 1 onnauwkeurig; 2 foutief

inadequacy [inædikwəsie] ontoereikendheid, tekortʰ, tekortkoming, gebrekʰ

inadequate [inædikwət] ontoereikend, onvoldoende, ongeschikt

inadmissible [innədmissibl] ontoelaatbaar, ongeoorloofd: *~ evidence* ontoelaatbaar bewijs

inadvertent [innədvəːtənt] 1 onoplettend, nonchalant; 2 onopzettelijk: *I dropped it ~ly* ik heb het per ongeluk laten vallen

inane [inneen] leeg, inhoudloos, zinloos

inanimate [inænimmət] levenloos, dood

inapplicable [inæplikkəbl] ontoepasselijk, ontoepasbaar, onbruikbaar

inappropriate [innəproopriət] ongepast, onbehoorlijk, misplaatst

inapt [inæpt] 1 ontoepasselijk, ongeschikt; 2 onbekwaam, on(des)kundig, onhandig

inarticulate [inna:tikjoelət] 1 onduidelijk (uitgesproken), onverstaanbaar, onsamenhangend; 2 onduidelijk sprekend

inasmuch as aangezien, omdat

inattentive [innətentiv] onoplettend, achteloos

inaudible [innoːdibl] onhoorbaar

inaugurate [innoːgjoereet] installeren, inaugureren, (in een ambt, functie) bevestigen

inauguration [inno:gjoereesjən] installatie(plechtigheid), inauguratie, inhuldiging

inborn [inbo:n] aangeboren

inbound [inbaund] *(Am)* binnenkomend, thuiskomend, inkomend, binnenlopend

inbreeding [inbrie:ding] inteelt

Inc. *(Am) Incorporated* NV, Naamloze Vennootschap

incalculable [inkælkjoeləbl] 1 onberekenbaar; 2 onvoorspelbaar

incandescent [inkændesnt] 1 gloeiend: *~ lamp* gloeilamp; 2 kwaad, woedend

incapable [inkeepəbl] onbekwaam, machteloos:

drunk and ~ dronken en onbekwaam; *be ~ of* niet in staat zijn tot, niet kunnen

incapacity [inkəpæsittie] onvermogen[h], onmacht: ~ *for work* arbeidsongeschiktheid

incarnate [inka:nət] vleesgeworden, lijfelijk: *the devil* ~ de duivel in eigen persoon

incautious [inko:sjəs] onvoorzichtig

¹incendiary [insendiərie] *adj* **1** brandgevaarlijk, (licht) ontvlambaar: ~ *bomb* brandbom; **2** opruiend

²incendiary [insendiərie] *n* **1** brandstichter; **2** opruier

¹incense [insens] *vb* kwaad, boos maken: ~*d at* (of: *by*) zeer boos over

²incense [insens] *n* wierook(geur)

incentive [insentiv] **1** stimulans, aansporing, motief[h]; **2** (prestatie)premie, toeslag, aanmoedigingspremie

incessant [insesnt] onophoudelijk, voortdurend, aanhoudend

incest [insest] incest, bloedschande

¹inch [intsj] *n* (Engelse) duim *(24.5 mm)*, inch: *not budge* (of: *give, yield*) *an* ~ geen duimbreed wijken; *every* ~ *a gentleman* op-en-top een heer; *give him an* ~ *and he'll take a mile* als je hem een vinger geeft neemt hij de hele hand; ~ *by* ~ beetje bij beetje; *we came within an* ~ *of death* het scheelde maar een haar of we waren dood geweest

²inch [intsj] *vb* schuifelen, langzaam voortgaan: ~ *forward through a crowd* zich moeizaam een weg banen door een menigte

incidence [insiddəns] (mate van) optreden, frequentie: *a high* ~ *of disease* een hoog ziektecijfer

incident [insiddənt] incident[h], voorval[h], gebeurtenis

incidental [insiddentl] bijkomend, begeleidend, bijkomstig: ~ *expenses* onvoorziene uitgaven; ~ *to* samenhangend met, gepaard gaande met

incidentally [insiddentəlie] **1** terloops; **2** overigens, trouwens, tussen twee haakjes

incinerate [insinnəreet] (tot as) verbranden, verassen

incipient [insippiənt] beginnend, begin-

incision [insizjən] insnijding, inkerving, snee, *(med)* incisie

incisive [insajsiv] **1** scherp(zinnig); **2** doortastend

incisor [insajzə] snijtand

incite [insajt] **1** opwekken, aanzetten, aansporen; **2** bezielen, opstoken, ophitsen

inclemency [inklemmənsie] guurheid

inclination [inklinneesjən] **1** neiging, voorkeur: *have an* ~ *to get fat* aanleg hebben om dik te worden; **2** geneigdheid, zin

¹incline [inklajn] *vb* neigen, geneigd zijn, een neiging hebben: *I* ~ *to think so* ik neig tot die gedachte

²incline [inklajn] *vb* **1** (neer)buigen, neigen: ~ *one's head* het hoofd neigen; **2** beïnvloeden, aanleiding geven: *I am* ~*d to think so* ik neig tot die gedachte

³incline [inklajn] *n* helling, glooiing

inclose [inklooz] *see* enclose

include [inkloe:d] **1** omvatten, bevatten, insluiten: *the price* ~*s freight* de prijs is inclusief vracht; *(mockingly)* ~ *out* uitsluiten, niet meerekenen; **2** (mede) opnemen, bijvoegen, toevoegen

including [inkloe:ding] inclusief: *10 days* ~ *today* 10 dagen, vandaag meegerekend; *up to and* ~ tot en met

inclusive [inkloe:siv] inclusief: *pages 60 to 100* ~ pagina 60 tot en met 100

incoherent [inkoohiərənt] incoherent, onsamenhangend

income [ingkum] inkomen[h], inkomsten: *live within one's* ~ niet te veel uitgeven, rondkomen

incoming [inkumming] **1** inkomend, aankomend, binnenkomend: ~ *tide* opkomend tij; **2** opvolgend, komend: *the* ~ *tenants* de nieuwe huurders

incomparable [inkompərəbl] onvergelijkelijke, onvergelijkbaar

incompatible [inkəmpætibl] onverenigbaar, (tegen)strijdig, tegengesteld

incompetent [inkompittənt] onbevoegd, onbekwaam

incomplete [inkəmplie:t] **1** onvolledig, incompleet; **2** onvolkomen, onvoltooid

incomprehensible [inkomprihhensibl] onbegrijpelijk, ondoorgrondelijk

inconceivable [inkənsie:vəbl] onvoorstelbaar, ondenkbaar

inconclusive [inkənkloe:siv] **1** niet doorslaggevend, onovertuigend; **2** onbeslist

incongruity [inkəngroe:ittie] ongerijmdheid

incongruous [inkonggroeəs] **1** ongerijmd, strijdig; **2** ongelijksoortig

inconsiderable [inkənsiddərəbl] onaanzienlijk, onbetekenend

inconsiderate [inkənsiddərət] onattent, onnadenkend

inconsistent [inkənsistənt] **1** inconsistent, onlogisch; **2** onverenigbaar, strijdig

inconsolable [inkənsooləbl] ontroostbaar

incontrovertible [inkontrəvə:tibl] onweerlegbaar, onomstotelijk

¹inconvenience [inkənvie:niəns] *n* ongemak[h], ongerief[h]

²inconvenience [inkənvie:niəns] *vb* overlast bezorgen, ongelegen komen

inconvenient [inkənvie:niənt] storend, ongelegen

incorporate [inko:pəreet] **1** opnemen, verenigen, incorporeren; **2** omvatten, bevatten: *this theory* ~*s new ideas* deze theorie omvat nieuwe ideeën

incorrect [inkərekt] incorrect, onjuist, verkeerd, ongepast

¹increase [inkrie:s] *vb* toenemen, (aan)groeien, stijgen

²increase [inkrie:s] *vb* vergroten, verhogen

³increase [ingkrie:s] *n* **1** toename, groei, aanwas: *be on the* ~ toenemen; **2** verhoging, stijging

incredible [inkreddibl] ongelofelijk, ongeloofwaardig, *(inf)* verbluffend (goed)

incredulity [inkridjoe:littie] ongelovigheid

incredulous [inkredjoeləs] ongelovig

increment [ingkrimmənt] **1** toename, (waarde)vermeerdering; **2** periodiek[h] *(of salary)*, periodieke verhoging

incriminate [inkrimminneet] **1** beschuldigen, aanklagen; **2** bezwaren, als de schuldige aanwijzen: *incriminating statements* bezwarende verklaringen

incubation [ingkjoebeesjən] **1** uitbroeding; **2** broedperiode; **3** incubatie(tijd)

[1]**incumbent** [inkumbənt] *n* bekleder ve kerkelijk ambt

[2]**incumbent** [inkumbənt] *adj* zittend, in functie zijnd: *(Am)* the ~ *governor* de zittende gouverneur

incur [inkə:] oplopen, zich op de hals halen: ~ *large debts* zich diep in de schulden steken; ~ *expenses* onkosten maken

incurable [inkjoeərəbl] ongeneeslijk: ~ *pessimism* onuitroeibaar pessimisme

incursion [inkə:sjən] inval, invasie, strooptocht: *(fig) an* ~ *upon s.o.'s privacy* een inbreuk op iemands privacy

indebted [indettid] schuldig, verschuldigd: *be ~ to s.o. for …* iem dank verschuldigd zijn voor …

indecency [indie:sənsie] onfatsoenlijkheid

indecent [indie:snt] onfatsoenlijk, onbehoorlijk, indecent

indecision [indissizjən] **1** besluiteloosheid; **2** aarzeling

indecisive [indissajsiv] **1** niet afdoend: *the battle was ~* de slag was niet beslissend; **2** besluiteloos, weifelend

indeed [indie:d] **1** inderdaad: *is it blue?* ~ *it is* is het blauw? inderdaad; **2** in feite, sterker nog: *I don't mind. ~, I would be pleased* ik vind het best. Sterker nog, ik zou het leuk vinden; **3** *(after a word to be emphasised)* echt: *that's a surprise* ~ dat is echt een verrassing; *very kind* ~ werkelijk zeer vriendelijk

indefinite [indeffinnit] **1** onduidelijk, onbestemd, vaag: *postponed ~ly* voor onbepaalde tijd uitgesteld; **2** onbepaald *(also linguistics)*: ~ *article* onbepaald lidwoord; ~ *pronoun* onbepaald voornaamwoord; **3** onzeker, onbeslist

indelible [indellibl] onuitwisbaar

indelicate [indellikkət] **1** onbehoorlijk; **2** smakeloos, grof; **3** tactloos

indemnity [indemnittie] **1** schadeloosstelling, herstelbetaling(en); **2** garantie, (aansprakelijkheids)verzekering; **3** vrijstelling *(of punishment)*, vrijwaring

[1]**indent** [indent] *vb* een schriftelijke bestelling doen

[2]**indent** [indent] *vb* (laten) inspringen *(line)*

[3]**indent** [indent] *vb* kartelen, kerven, inkepen: *an ~ed coastline* een grillige kustlijn

[4]**indent** [indent] *n* **1** inspringing; **2** orderbrief

indentation [indenteesjən] **1** keep, snee; **2** inspringing; **3** inham, fjord; **4** karteling, insnijding

independence [indippendəns] onafhankelijkheid

independent [indippendənt] **1** onafhankelijk, partijloos: *of ~ means* financieel onafhankelijk; ~ *school* particuliere school; **2** vrijstaand

indescribable [indiskrajbəbl] onbeschrijfelijk, niet te beschrijven

indeterminate [inditta:minnət] **1** onbepaald, onbeslist; **2** onbepaalbaar; **3** onduidelijk, vaag

index [indeks] **1** index *(also science)*, indexcijfer[h], verhoudingscijfer[h]; **2** (bibliotheek)catalogus; **3** register[h], index || ~ *finger* wijsvinger

[1]**Indian** [indiən] *n* **1** Indiër; **2** indiaan: *American ~* indiaan; *Red ~* indiaan

[2]**Indian** [indiən] *adj* **1** Indiaas, Indisch; **2** indiaans || ~ *corn* maïs; *in ~ file* in ganzenmars; ~ *ink* Oost-Indische inkt; ~ *summer* Indian summer

indicate [indikkeet] **1** duiden op, een teken zijn van, voor; **2** te kennen geven; **3** de noodzaak aantonen van

indication [indikkeesjən] aanwijzing, indicatie, teken[h]: *there is little ~ of improvement* er is weinig dat op een verbetering duidt

indictment [indajtmənt] **1** (aan)klacht; **2** (staat van) beschuldiging

indifferent [indiffərənt] **1** onverschillig: ~ *to hardship* ongevoelig voor tegenspoed; **2** (middel)matig

indigenous [indidzjinnəs] **1** inheems: *plants ~ to this island* op dit eiland thuishorende planten; **2** aangeboren, geboren

indigestion [indidzjestsjən] indigestie

indignation [indigneesjən] verontwaardiging

indignity [indignittie] vernedering, belediging, hoon

indirect [indirrekt] indirect, niet rechtstreeks: *(linguistics)* ~ *object* meewerkend voorwerp

indiscretion [indiskresjən] indiscretie, onbescheidenheid: *an ~ of his youth* een misstap uit zijn jeugd

indiscriminate [indiskrimminnət] **1** kritiekloos, onzorgvuldig; **2** lukraak: *deal out ~ blows* in het wilde weg om zich heen slaan

indispensable [indispensəbl] onmisbaar, essentieel

indisposition [indispəzisjən] **1** ongesteldheid, onpasselijkheid; **2** ongenegenheid, onwil(ligheid)

indisputable [indispjoe:təbl] onbetwistbaar

indistinct [indistingkt] onduidelijk, vaag

[1]**individual** [indivvidjoeəl] *adj* **1** individueel, persoonlijk, eigen: *I can't thank you all ~ly* ik kan u niet ieder afzonderlijk bedanken; **2** afzonderlijk: *give ~ attention to* persoonlijke aandacht besteden aan

[2]**individual** [indivvidjoeəl] *n* individu[h], *(inf)* figuur[+h], type[h]

indivisible [indivvizzibl] ondeelbaar

indocility [indoosillittie] hardleersheid

indoctrinate [indoktrinneet] indoctrineren

indolence [indələns] traagheid, sloomheid

indomitable [indommittəbl] ontembaar, onbedwingbaar

Indonesia [indoonie:ziǝ] Indonesië

¹**Indonesian** [indǝnie:zjǝn] adj Indonesisch

²**Indonesian** [indǝnie:zjǝn] n Indonesiër

indoor [indo:] binnen-: ~ aerial kamerantenne; ~ sports zaalsporten

induce [indjoe:s] 1 bewegen tot, brengen tot: our reduced prices will ~ people to buy onze verlaagde prijzen zullen de mensen tot kopen bewegen; nothing will ~ me to give in nooit zal ik toegeven; 2 teweegbrengen, veroorzaken, leiden tot, opwekken (contractions)

induction [induksjǝn] 1 installatie, inhuldiging, bevestiging; 2 opwekking (of contractions); 3 opgewekte geboorte; 4 introductie(cursus)

inductive [induktiv] 1 aanleiding gevend, veroorzakend; 2 inductief

¹**indulge** [induldzj] vb zich laten gaan, zich te goed doen, (inf) zich te buiten gaan aan drank (eten): ~ in zich (de luxe) permitteren (van)

²**indulge** [induldzj] vb 1 toegeven aan; 2 (zich) uitleven (in)

indulgence [induldzjǝns] 1 mateloosheid: ~ in strong drink overmatig drankgebruik; 2 toegeeflijkheid

indulgent [induldzjǝnt] toegeeflijk, inschikkelijk

industrial [industriǝl] 1 industrieel; 2 geïndustrialiseerd: the ~ nations de industrielanden; 3 de industriearbeid(ers) betreffende: ~ dispute arbeidsconflict

industrialization [industriǝlajzeesjǝn] industrialisatie

industrious [industriǝs] vlijtig, arbeidzaam

industry [indǝstrie] 1 industrie; 2 bedrijfslevenʰ; 3 vlijt, (werk)ijver

inedible [inneddibl] oneetbaar

ineffective [inniffektiv] 1 ineffectief; 2 inefficiënt, ondoelmatig, onbekwaam

ineffectual [inniffektsjoeǝl] 1 vruchteloos, vergeefs; 2 ongeschikt

inefficient [inniffisjǝnt] inefficiënt, ondoelmatig, onpraktisch

ineligible [innellidzjibl] ongeschikt: ~ to vote niet stemgerechtigd

inept [innept] 1 absurd, dwaas; 2 onbeholpen, onbekwaam

inequality [innikwollittie] ongelijkheid, verschilʰ

inequitable [innekwittǝbl] onrechtvaardig

ineradicable [innirædikkǝbl] onuitroeibaar, onuitwisbaar

inert [inna:t] inert, traag, mat: ~ gas edel gas

inestimable [innestimmǝbl] onschatbaar

inevitable [innevvittǝbl] onvermijdelijk, onontkoombaar, onafwendbaar

inexact [innigzækt] onnauwkeurig

inexhaustible [innigzo:stibl] 1 onuitputtelijk; 2 onvermoeibaar

inexorable [inneksǝrǝbl] onverbiddelijk

inexpensive [innikspensiv] voordelig, goedkoop

inexperienced [innikspiǝriǝnst] onervaren

inexplicable [inniksplikkǝbl] onverklaarbaar

inform [info:m] 1 informeren, op de hoogte stellen: ~ s.o. about (of: of) iem inlichten over; 2 berichten, meedelen

infallible [infælibl] 1 onfeilbaar; 2 feilloos: infallibly, she makes the wrong choice ze doet steevast de verkeerde keus

infamous [infǝmǝs] 1 berucht; 2 schandelijk

infamy [infǝmie] 1 beruchtheid; 2 schanddaad

infancy [infǝnsie] 1 kindsheid, eerste jeugd; 2 beginstadiumʰ: in its ~ in de kinderschoenen

¹**infant** [infǝnt] n jong kindʰ

²**infant** [infǝnt] adj kinder-: ~ prodigy wonderkind

infantile [infǝntajl] 1 infantiel, kinderachtig, onvolwassen; 2 kinder-: ~ paralysis kinderverlamming

infantry [infǝntrie] infanterie, voetvolkʰ

infant school kleuterschool

infatuated [infætjoe-eetid] gek, dol, (smoor)verliefd: be ~ with s.o. (sth.) gek zijn op iem (iets)

infect [infekt] 1 besmetten (also fig), infecteren; 2 vervuilen, bederven

infection [infeksjǝn] infectie, infectieziekte

infectious [infeksjǝs] 1 besmettelijk; 2 aanstekelijk

infer [infa:] 1 (with from) concluderen (uit), afleiden, opmaken; 2 impliceren, inhouden

¹**inferior** [infiǝriǝ] adj 1 lager, minder, ondergeschikt; 2 inferieur, minderwaardig: ~ goods goederen van mindere kwaliteit; be ~ to onderdoen voor

²**inferior** [infiǝriǝ] n ondergeschikte

inferiority [infiǝrie-orrittie] minderwaardigheid

infernal [infa:nl] 1 hels, duivels; 2 afschuwelijk, vervloekt

infest [infest] teisteren, onveilig maken: be ~ed with vergeven zijn van

infidel [infidl] ongelovige

infiltrate [infiltreet] (with into) infiltreren (in), tersluiks binnendringen

¹**infinite** [infinnit] adj 1 oneindig, onbegrensd; 2 buitengemeen groot

²**infinite** [infinnit] n oneindigheid: the ~ het heelal; the Infinite God

infinitesimal [infinnittessiml] oneindig klein ‖ calculus infinitesimaalrekening

infinitive [infinnittiv] infinitief

infinity [infinnittie] oneindigheid, grenzeloosheid

infirm [infa:m] zwak: ~ of purpose besluiteloos

infirmary [infa:mǝrie] ziekenhuisʰ, ziekenafdeling, ziekenzaal

infirmity [infa:mittie] 1 zwakheid; 2 gebrekʰ, kwaal

¹**inflame** [infleem] vb ontsteken, ontstoken raken: an ~d eye een ontstoken oog

²**inflame** [infleem] vb opwinden, kwaad maken: ~d with rage in woede ontsteken

inflammable [inflæmǝbl] ontvlambaar, zeer brandbaar, (fig) opvliegend

inflammation [inflǝmeesjǝn] ontsteking, ontbranding

inflate [infleet] 1 opblazen, doen zwellen; 2 inflateren, kunstmatig opdrijven (eg prices)

inflation [infleesjən] **1** het opblazen; **2** *(econ)* inflatie: *galloping* ~ wilde inflatie
inflect [inflɛkt] *(linguistics)* verbuigen, vervoegen
inflexible [inflɛksibl] onbuigbaar *(also fig)*, onbuigzaam
inflict [inflikt] **1** opleggen, opdringen: ~ *a penalty (up)on s.o.* iem een straf opleggen; **2** toedienen, toebrengen: ~ *a blow (up)on s.o.* iem een klap geven; **3** teisteren
¹**influence** [infloeəns] *n* **1** invloed, inwerking, macht: ~ *on* (of: *upon*) (onbewuste) invloed op; **2** protectie, *(inf)* kruiwagen: *(inf) under the* ~ onder invloed
²**influence** [infloeəns] *vb* beïnvloeden, invloed hebben op
influential [infloe·ɛnsjl] invloedrijk
influenza [infloe·ɛnzə] influenza, griep
influx [influks] toevloed, instroming
info [infoo] *information* info, informatie
informal [info:ml] **1** informeel, niet officieel; **2** ongedwongen: ~ *speech* spreektaal
informant [info:mənt] informant, zegsman
informatics [infəmætiks] informatica
information [infəmeesjən] informatie, inlichting(en), voorlichting: *obtain* ~ informatie inwinnen
informative [info:mətiv] informatief, leerzaam
informed [info:md] ingelicht: *ill-*~ slecht op de hoogte
informer [info:mə] geheim agent, politiespion
infrastructure [infrəstruktsjə] infrastructuur
infrequent [infrie:kwənt] zeldzaam
¹**infringe** [infrindzj] *vb* schenden, overtreden *(agreement etc)*
²**infringe** [infrindzj] *vb (with (up)on)* inbreuk maken (op)
infuriate [infjoeərie·eet] razend maken
infuse [infjoe:z] **1** (in)gieten, ingeven; **2** bezielen, inprenten, storten: ~ *courage into s.o.*, ~ *s.o. with courage* iem moed inblazen
ingenious [indzjie:niəs] ingenieus, vernuftig
ingenuity [indzjinjoe:ittie] **1** vindingrijkheid, vernuftʰ; **2** ingenieuze uitvinding
ingenuous [indzjenjoeəs] **1** argeloos, naïef, onschuldig, ongekunsteld; **2** eerlijk, openhartig
ingot [inggət] baar, (goud)staaf, ingot
ingrained [ingreend] **1** ingeworteld; **2** verstokt, doortrapt
ingratiate [ingreesjie·eet] bemind maken: ~ *oneself with s.o.* bij iem in de gunst trachten te komen
ingratitude [ingrætitjoe:d] ondankbaarheid
ingredient [ingrie:diənt] ingrediëntʰ
ingrown [ingroon] ingegroeid *(of nails): (fig)* ~ *habit* vaste gewoonte
inhabit [inhæbit] bewonen, wonen in
inhabitant [inhæbittənt] bewoner, inwoner
inhale [inheel] inademen, inhaleren
inherent [inhiərənt] inherent, intrinsiek, eigen: *violence is inherent in a dictatorship* geweld is inhe-

rent aan een dictatuur
inherit [inhɛrrit] erven, erfgenaam zijn, meekrijgen *(vices and virtues etc)*
inheritance [inhɛrrittəns] **1** erfenis, nalatenschap; **2** (over)erving
inhibit [inhibbit] **1** verbieden, ontzeggen; **2** hinderen, onderdrukken: ~ *s.o. from doing sth.* iem beletten iets te doen
inhospitable [inhospittəbl] ongastvrij
inhumanity [inhjoe:mænittie] wreedheid
inimical [inimmikl] **1** vijandig; **2** *(with to)* schadelijk (voor)
inimitable [inimmittəbl] onnavolgbaar, weergaloos
iniquity [inikwittie] onrechtvaardigheid, ongerechtigheid, zonde
¹**initial** [innisjl] *adj* begin-, eerste, initiaal: ~ *capital* grondkapitaal; ~ *stage* beginstadium
²**initial** [innisjl] *n* initiaal, beginletter, hoofdletter, voorletter, ~*s* paraaf
initially [innisjəlie] aanvankelijk, eerst, in het begin
initiate [innisjie·eet] **1** beginnen, in werking stellen; **2** *(with into)* inwijden (in)
initiative [innisjiətiv] initiatiefʰ: *on one's own* ~ op eigen initiatief
inject [indzjɛkt] **1** injecteren; **2** inbrengen, introduceren: ~ *a little life into a community* een gemeenschap wat leven inblazen
injection [indzjɛksjən] injectie *(also fig)*, stimulans
injure [indzjə] **1** (ver)wonden, kwetsen, blesseren: *twelve people were* ~*d* er vielen twaalf gewonden; **2** kwaad doen, benadelen, beledigen
injury [indzjərie] **1** verwonding, letselʰ, blessure: *suffer minor injuries* lichte verwondingen oplopen; **2** mishandeling; **3** schade, onrechtʰ
injustice [indzjustis] onrechtvaardigheid: *do s.o. an* ~ iem onrecht doen
ink [ingk] inkt *(also of octopus)*, drukinkt
inkling [ingkling] flauw vermoedenʰ, vaag ideeʰ: *he hasn't an* ~ *of what goes on* hij heeft geen idee van wat er gebeurt
¹**inland** [inlænd] *adj* binnenlands: ~ *navigation* binnen(scheep)vaart
²**inland** [inlænd] *adv* landinwaarts
Inland Revenue 1 staatsbelastinginkomsten; **2** belastingdienst
in-law [inlo:] aangetrouwd familielidʰ: *my* ~*s* mijn schoonouders, schoonfamilie
inlay [inlee] **1** inlegselʰ, inlegwerkʰ, mozaïekʰ; **2** informatiebladʰ; informatieboekjeʰ bij cd
inlet [inlet] **1** inham, kreek; **2** inlaat *(for liquids)*, toegang
inmate [inmeet] (mede)bewoner, kamergenoot, huisgenoot, patiënt, gevangene
inmost [inmoost] **1** binnenst; **2** diepst, geheimst
inn [in] **1** herberg; **2** taveerne, kroeg
innards [innədz] ingewanden
innate [inneet] aangeboren, ingeboren
inner [innə] **1** binnenst, innerlijk: ~ *city: a)* binnen-

649

insouciance

stad; *b*) verpauperde stadskern; ~ *tube* binnenband; **2** verborgen, intiem: ~ *life* gemoedsleven; *the* ~ *meaning* de diepere betekenis

innings [inningz] *(cricket)* slagbeurt, innings

innkeeper waard

innocence [innəsns] onschuld

innocent [innəsnt] onschuldig, schuldeloos

innocuous [innokjoeəs] onschadelijk

innovate [innəveet] vernieuwen

innovation [innəveesjən] vernieuwing, innovatie

innuendo [injoe·endoo] *(also ~es)* (bedekte) toespeling

innumerable [injoe:mərəbl] ontelbaar, talloos

inoculation [innokjoeleesjən] inenting *(with vaccine)*

inoffensive [innəfensiv] onschuldig, onschadelijk, geen ergernis wekkend

inopportune [innoppətjoe:n] ongelegen (komend)

inorganic [inno:gænik] anorganisch

in-patient (intern verpleegd) patiënt

input [inpoet] **1** toevoer, invoer, inbreng; **2** invoer, input

inquest [ingkwest] **1** gerechtelijk onderzoek[h], lijkschouwing; **2** jury voor lijkschouwing

¹inquire [inkwajjə] *vb* (with *into*) een onderzoek instellen (naar)

²inquire [inkwajjə] *vb* (na)vragen, onderzoeken: ~ *after* (of: *for*) *s.o.* naar iemands gezondheid informeren; ~ *of s.o.* bij iem informeren

inquiry [inkwajjərie] *(with into)* onderzoek[h] (naar), (na)vraag, enquête, informatie: *make inquiries* inlichtingen inwinnen; *on* ~ bij navraag

inquisition [ingkwizzisjən] (gerechtelijk) onderzoek[h], ondervraging: *the Inquisition* de inquisitie

inquisitive [inkwizzittiv] nieuwsgierig, benieuwd

ins [inz]: *the* ~ *and outs* de fijne kneepjes (van het vak), de details

insane [inseen] krankzinnig *(also fig)*, onzinnig

insanitary [insænittərie] **1** ongezond; **2** smerig, besmet

insanity [insænittie] krankzinnigheid, waanzin

insatiable [inseesjəbl] onverzadigbaar

inscribe [inskrajb] **1** (with *in(to), on)* (in)schrijven (in), (in)graveren, *(fig)* (in)prenten; **2** opdragen, van een opdracht voorzien *(book etc)*

inscription [inskripsjən] **1** inscriptie, opschrift[h]; **2** opdracht *(in book etc)*

inscrutable [inskroe:təbl] ondoorgrondelijk, raadselachtig

insect [insekt] **1** insect[h]; **2** (nietig) beestje[h], *(fig)* onderkruiper

insecticide [insektissajd] insecticide[h], insectenvergif[h]

insecure [insikjoeə] **1** onveilig, instabiel, wankel; **2** onzeker, bang

insemination [insemminneesjən] bevruchting, inseminatie: *artificial* ~ kunstmatige inseminatie

insensible [insensibl] **1** onwaarneembaar, onmerkbaar; **2** gevoelloos, bewusteloos; **3** ongevoelig, onbewust: *be* ~ *of the danger* zich niet van het gevaar bewust zijn

insensitive [insensittiv] ongevoelig, gevoelloos: ~ *to the feelings of others* onverschillig voor de gevoelens van anderen

inseparable [inseppərəbl] on(af)scheidbaar, onafscheidelijk

¹insert [insə:t] *vb* inzetten, inbrengen, *(comp)* invoegen: ~ *a coin* een muntstuk inwerpen

²insert [insə:t] *n* tussenvoegsel[h], bijlage, inzetstuk[h]

insertion [insə:sjən] **1** insertie, inplanting; **2** tussenvoeging, plaatsing *(in newspaper)*; **3** tussenzetsel[h], inzetstuk[h]

inset [inset] **1** bijvoegsel[h], (losse) bijlage, inlegvel[h], inlegvellen; **2** inzetsel[h], tussenzetsel[h]

¹inside [insajd] *n* binnenkant, binnenste[h], huizenkant *(of pavement)*

²inside *adj* **1** binnen-: *the* ~ *track* de binnenbaan, *(Am)* voordelige positie, voordeel; **2** van ingewijden, uit de eerste hand: ~ *information* inlichtingen van ingewijden; ~ *job* inbraak door bekenden

³inside *adv* **1** *(place and direction; also fig)* (naar) binnen, aan de binnenkant: *turn sth.* ~ *out* iets binnenstebuiten keren; **2** *(inf)* in de bak

⁴inside *prep* **1** *(place)* (binnen)in; **2** *(time)* binnen, (in) minder dan: ~ *an hour* binnen een uur

insider [insajdə] ingewijde

insidious [insiddiəs] verraderlijk, geniepig, bedrieglijk

insight [insajt] *(with into)* inzicht (in), begrip[h] (van)

insignia [insignia] insignes, onderscheidingstekenen

insignificant [insigniffikkənt] onbeduidend, onbelangrijk, gering

insincere [insinsiə] onoprecht, hypocriet

insinuate [insinjoe·eet] insinueren, toespelingen maken, indirect suggereren: *what are you insinuating?* wat wil je daarmee zeggen?; *he was trying to* ~ *himself into the minister's favour* hij probeerde bij de minister in de gunst te komen

insipid [insippid] **1** smakeloos, flauw; **2** zouteloos, banaal, nietszeggend

insist [insist] *(with (up)on)* (erop) aandringen, volhouden, erop staan: *I* ~ *(up)on an apology* ik eis een verontschuldiging

insistence [insistəns] **1** aandrang, eis; **2** volharding, vasthoudendheid

insistent [insistənt] vasthoudend, dringend, hardnekkig

insofar as voor zover

insolent [insələnt] onbeschaamd, schaamteloos, brutaal

insoluble [insoljoebl] onoplosbaar

insolvent [insolvənt] insolvent, niet in staat om geldelijke verplichtingen na te komen

insomnia [insomnia] slapeloosheid

insomuch as zodanig dat, aangezien, daar

insouciance [insoe:siəns] zorgeloosheid, onverschilligheid

inspect [inspɛkt] inspecteren, onderzoeken, keuren

inspection [inspɛksjən] inspectie, onderzoek[h], controle: *on ~: a)* ter inzage; *b)* bij nader onderzoek

inspector [inspɛktə] inspecteur, opzichter, controleur

inspiration [inspirreesjən] 1 inspiratie; 2 *(inf)* inval, ingeving

inspire [inspajjə] 1 inspireren, bezielen; 2 opwekken, doen ontstaan

instability [instəbillittie] onvastheid, instabiliteit

install [instoːl] 1 installeren, plechtig bevestigen *(in office, dignity)*; 2 installeren, aanbrengen, plaatsen: ~ *central heating* centrale verwarming aanleggen; ~ *oneself* zich installeren, zich nestelen

installation [instəleesjən] 1 toestel[h], installatie, apparaat[h]; 2 installatie, plechtige bevestiging *(in office, dignity)*; 3 installering, vestiging; 4 aanleg, installering, montage

instalment [instoːlmənt] 1 (afbetalings)termijn; 2 aflevering *(of story, TV programme etc)*

instance [instəns] geval[h], voorbeeld[h]: *for ~* bijvoorbeeld; *in the first ~* in eerste instantie, in de eerste plaats

¹instant [instənt] *adj* 1 onmiddellijk, ogenblikkelijk: *an ~ replay* een herhaling *(of television recordings)*; 2 kant-en-klaar, instant

²instant [instənt] *n* moment[h], ogenblik(je[h]): *the ~ (that) I saw her* zodra ik haar zag

instantaneous [instənteeniəs] onmiddellijk, ogenblikkelijk

instantly [instəntlie] onmiddellijk, dadelijk

instead [instɛd] in plaats daarvan: ~ *of* in plaats van

instep [instep] 1 wreef *(of foot)*; 2 instap *(of shoes)*

instigate [instigeet] 1 aansporen, aanstichten, teweegbrengen; 2 aanzetten, uitlokken, ophitsen: ~ *s.o. to steal* iem aanzetten tot diefstal

instigation [instigeesjən] aandrang, instigatie: *at Peter's ~* op aandrang van Peter

instil [instil] geleidelijk doen doordringen, bijbrengen, langzaam aan inprenten

instinct [instingkt] instinct[h], intuïtie

instinctive [instingktiv] instinctief, intuïtief

¹institute [institjoeːt] *n* instituut[h], instelling

²institute [institjoeːt] *vb* stichten, invoeren, op gang brengen, instellen || ~ *proceedings against s.o.* een rechtszaak tegen iem aanspannen

institution [institjoeːsjən] 1 instelling, stichting, invoering; 2 gevestigde gewoonte, (sociale) institutie, regel; 3 instituut[h], instelling, genootschap[h]; 4 inrichting, gesticht[h]

instruct [instrukt] 1 onderwijzen, onderrichten, instrueren; 2 opdragen, bevelen

instruction [instruksjən] 1 onderricht[h], instructie, les; 2 voorschrift[h]; order; opdracht: ~*s for use* handleiding

instructive [instruktiv] instructief, leerzaam

instrument [instrəmənt] instrument[h], gereedschap[h], werktuig[h] *(also fig)*

instrumental [instrəmɛntl] 1 (with *in)* behulpzaam (bij), hulpvaardig: *be ~ in* een cruciale rol spelen bij; 2 instrumentaal

insubordinate [insəboːdinnət] ongehoorzaam, opstandig

insufferable [insuffərəbl] on(ver)draaglijk, onuitstaanbaar

insufficient [insəfisjənt] ontoereikend, onvoldoende, te weinig

insular [insˑjoelə] 1 eiland-, geïsoleerd; 2 bekrompen, kortzichtig

insulate [insˑjoeleet] 1 (with *from)* isoleren (van), afschermen (van), beschermen (tegen); 2 isoleren *(heat, sound)*

insulation [insˑjoeleesjən] 1 isolatie, afzondering; 2 isolatiemateriaal[h]

¹insult [insult] *n* belediging: *add ~ to injury* de zaak nog erger maken

²insult [insult] *vb* beledigen

insuperable [insoeːpərəbl] onoverkomelijk, onoverwinnelijk

insupportable [insəpoːtəbl] on(ver)draaglijk, onuitstaanbaar

insurance [insjoeərəns] 1 verzekering, assurantie, verzekeringspolis; 2 *(Am)* zekerheid, bescherming

insure [insjoeə] 1 (laten) verzekeren; 2 *(Am)* garanderen, veilig stellen

insurer [insjoeərə] verzekeraar

insurgence [insəːdzjəns] oproer[h], opstand

insurmountable [insəmoontəbl] onoverkomelijk, onoverwinnelijk

insurrection [insərɛksjən] oproer[h], opstand

intact [intækt] intact, ongeschonden, gaaf

intake [inteek] 1 inlaat, toevoer(opening), toegevoerde, opgenomen hoeveelheid, voeding; 2 opneming, opname, toegelaten aantal[h]

integer [intidzjə] *(maths)* geheel getal[h]

integral [intigrəl] 1 wezenlijk; 2 geheel, volledig, integraal

¹integrate [intigreet] *vb* geïntegreerd worden, integreren, deel gaan uitmaken (van)

²integrate [intigreet] *vb* 1 integreren, tot een geheel samenvoegen; 2 als gelijkwaardig opnemen *(eg minorities)*, integreren

integrity [integrittie] 1 integriteit, rechtschapenheid: *a man of ~* een integer man; 2 ongeschonden toestand, eenheid

intellect [intəlekt] intellect[h], verstand(elijk vermogen)[h]

intelligence [intɛllidzjəns] 1 intelligentie, verstand(elijk vermogen)[h]; 2 informatie, nieuws[h], inlichtingen; 3 (geheime) informatie, inlichtingendienst

intelligent [intɛllidzjənt] intelligent, slim

intelligible [intɛllidzjibl] begrijpelijk, verstaanbaar

intemperate [intɛmpərət] 1 onmatig, buitensporig, heftig, drankzuchtig; **2** guur *(of climate, wind)*, extreem

intend [intend] **1** van plan zijn, bedoelen, in de zin hebben: *I intend to cancel the order* ik ben van plan de order te annuleren; *we ~ them to repair it* we willen dat zij het repareren; **2** (voor)bestemmen, bedoelen: *their son was ~ed for the Church* hun zoon was voorbestemd om priester te worden

intense [intens] intens, sterk, zeer hevig

¹intensify [intensiffaj] *vb* intens(er) worden, versterken, toenemen

²intensify [intensiffaj] *vb* verhevigen, versterken, intensiveren

intensity [intensittie] intensiteit, sterkte, (mate van) hevigheid

intensive [intensiv] intensief, heftig, (in)gespannen

¹intent [intent] *n* bedoeling, intentie, voornemen^h || *to all ~s and purposes* feitelijk, in (praktisch) alle opzichten

²intent [intent] *adj* **1** (in)gespannen, aandachtig; **2** vastbesloten, vastberaden: *be ~ on revenge* zinnen op wraak

intention [intensjən] **1** bedoeling, oogmerk^h, voornemen^h; **2** *~s (inf)* bedoelingen, (huwelijks)plannen

inter [intə:] ter aarde bestellen, begraven

interact [intərækt] op elkaar inwerken, met elkaar reageren

interactive [intəræktiv] interactief

intercede [intəsie:d] **1** ten gunste spreken, een goed woordje doen; **2** bemiddelen, tussenbeide komen

intercept [intəsept] onderscheppen, afsnijden

intercession [intəsesjən] tussenkomst, bemiddeling, voorspraak

¹interchange [intətsjeendzj] *vb* **1** uitwisselen, ruilen; **2** (onderling) verwisselen, afwisselen

²interchange [intətsjeendzj] *n* **1** uitwisseling, ruil(ing), verwisseling; **2** knooppunt^h *(of motorways)*, verkeersplein^h

interchangeable [intətsjeendzjəbl] **1** uitwisselbaar, ruilbaar; **2** (onderling) verwisselbaar

intercom [intəkom] intercom

intercourse [intəko:s] **1** omgang, sociaal verkeer^h, betrekking(en); **2** (geslachts)gemeenschap^h

interdependent [intədippendənt] onderling afhankelijk, afhankelijk van elkaar

interest [intrəst] **1** interesse, (voorwerp^h van) belangstelling: *show an ~ in* belangstelling tonen voor; *take a great ~ in* zich sterk interesseren voor; **2** (eigen)belang^h, interesse, voordeel^h: *it's in the ~ of the community* het is in het belang van de gemeenschap; **3** rente *(also fig)*, interest: *the rate of ~*, *the ~ rate* de rentevoet; *lend money at 7% ~* geld lenen tegen 7% rente

interested [intrəstid] **1** belangstellend, geïnteresseerd, vol interesse; **2** belanghebbend, betrokken: *the ~ party* de betrokken partij

interesting [intrəsting] interessant, belangwek-

kend

interface [intəfees] raakvlak^h *(also fig)*, grensvlak^h, scheidingsvlak^h

interfere [intəfiə] hinderen, in de weg staan: *don't ~ hou je erbuiten*

interference [intəfiərəns] **1** (ver)storing, belemmering; **2** inmenging, tussenkomst, bemoeienis

interfere with 1 aankomen, betasten, knoeien met: *don't ~ that bike* blijf met je handen van die fiets af; **2** zich bemoeien met; **3** *(euph)* aanranden, zich vergrijpen aan

¹interim [intərim] *n* interim, tussentijd: *in the ~* intussen, ondertussen

²interim [intərim] *adj* tijdelijk, voorlopig: *an ~ report* een tussentijds rapport

interior [intiəriə] **1** inwendig, binnenst, binnen-; **2** binnenshuis, interieur-; **3** innerlijk; **4** binnenlands

interject [intədzjekt] (zich) ertussen werpen, tussenbeide komen, opmerken

interjection [intədzjeksjən] **1** tussenwerpsel^h, interjectie; **2** uitroep, kreet

¹interlock [intəlok] *vb* in elkaar grijpen, nauw met elkaar verbonden zijn: *these problems ~* deze problemen hangen nauw met elkaar samen

²interlock [intəlok] *vb* met elkaar verbinden, aaneenkoppelen

interloper [intəloopə] indringer

interlude [intəloe:d] **1** onderbreking, pauze; **2** tussenstuk^h, tussenspel^h

intermarry [intəmærie] **1** een gemengd huwelijk aangaan; **2** onderling trouwen, binnen de eigen familie trouwen

¹intermediary [intəmie:diərie] *adj* bemiddelend, optredend als tussenpersoon

²intermediary [intəmie:diərie] *n* tussenpersoon, bemiddelaar, contactpersoon

intermediate [intəmie:dieət] tussenliggend, tussengelegen, tussentijds

interminable [intə:minnəbl] oneindig (lang), eindeloos

intermingle [intəminggl] (zich) (ver)mengen, (vrijelijk) met elkaar omgaan

intermission [intəmisjən] onderbreking *(also in play etc)*, pauze, rust: *without ~* ononderbroken

intermittent [intəmittənt] met tussenpozen (verschijnend, werkend), onderbroken, met onderbrekingen

¹intern [intə:n] *n (Am)* **1** intern, inwonend (co)assistent; **2** hospitant(e), stagiair(e)

²intern [intə:n] *vb* interneren, gevangen zetten, vastzetten *(during wartime)*

internal [intə:nl] **1** inwendig, innerlijk, binnen-; **2** binnenlands, inwendig

¹international [intənæsjənəl] *adj* internationaal

²international [intənæsjənəl] *n* **1** interland(wedstrijd); **2** international, interlandspeler

internment [intə:nmənt] internering

interplay [intəplee] interactie, wisselwerking

interpose [intəpooz] **1** tussenplaatsen, invoegen; **2**

interrumperen, onderbreken; **3** naar voren brengen, aanvoeren

¹interpret [intə:prit] *vb* **1** interpreteren, uitleggen, opvatten; **2** vertolken, interpreteren; **3** (mondeling) vertalen

²interpret [intə:prit] *vb* als tolk optreden, tolken

interpretation [intə:prəteesjən] **1** interpretatie, uitleg; **2** het tolken; **3** vertolking, interpretatie

interpreter [intə:prittə] tolk

interracial [intəreesjl] tussen (verschillende) rassen, voor verschillende rassen

interregnum [intəregnəm] tussenregering

¹interrelate [intərilleet] *vb* met elkaar in verband staan, met elkaar verbonden zijn

²interrelate [intərilleet] *vb* met elkaar in verband brengen

interrogation [interrəgeesjən] ondervraging, verhoor[h]

¹interrogative [intərogətiv] *n* vragend (voornaam)woord[h]

²interrogative [intərogətiv] *adj* vragend, vraag- *(also linguistics)*

¹interrupt [intərupt] *vb* **1** onderbreken, afbreken, belemmeren; **2** interrumperen, in de rede vallen, storen

²interrupt [intərupt] *vb* storen, onderbreken, in de rede vallen

interruption [intərupsjən] **1** onderbreking, afbreking; **2** interruptie, het storen

intersection [intəseksjən] **1** (weg)kruising, kruispunt[h], snijpunt[h]; **2** doorsnijding, kruising

intersperse [intəspə:s] **1** verspreid zetten, (hier en daar) strooien: *a speech ~d with posh words* een met deftige woorden doorspekte toespraak; **2** afwisselen, variëren, van tijd tot tijd onderbreken

interstice [intə:stis] nauwe tussenruimte, spleet, reet

¹intertwine [intətwajn] *vb* zich in elkaar strengelen, (met elkaar) verweven zijn

²intertwine [intətwajn] *vb* ineenstrengelen, dooreenvlechten

interval [intəvl] **1** tussenruimte, interval, tussentijd: *trams go at 15-minute ~s* er rijdt iedere 15 minuten een tram; **2** pauze, rust; **3** interval, toonsafstand

intervene [intəvie:n] **1** tussenbeide komen, zich erin mengen, ertussen komen; **2** ertussen liggen: *in the intervening months* in de tussenliggende maanden

intervention [intəvensjən] tussenkomst, inmenging, ingreep *(also med)*

¹interview [intəvjoe:] *n* **1** (persoonlijk) onderhoud[h], sollicitatiegesprek[h]; **2** interview[h], vraaggesprek[h]

²interview [intəvjoe:] *vb* interviewen, een vraaggesprek houden met, een sollicitatiegesprek voeren met

intestine [intestin] darm(kanaal[h]), (buik)ingewanden: *large ~* dikke darm; *small ~* dunne darm

intimacy [intimməsie] **1** intimiteit, vertrouwelijk-

heid, intieme mededeling; **2** innige verbondenheid, vertrouwdheid: *they were on terms of ~* er bestond een sterke vriendschapsband tussen hen; **3** intimiteit, intieme omgang, geslachtsverkeer[h]

¹intimate [intimmət] *adj* **1** intiem *(also sexually)*, innig (verbonden); **2** vertrouwelijk, privé: *~ secrets* hartsgeheimen; *they are on ~ terms* zij zijn goede vrienden

²intimate [intimmeet] *vb* suggereren, een hint geven, laten doorschemeren

intimation [intimmeesjən] aanduiding, suggestie, hint

intimidate [intimmiddeet] intimideren, bang maken

into [intoe:] **1** in, binnen-: *look ~ the matter* de zaak bestuderen; *(inf) he's ~ Zen these days* tegenwoordig interesseert hij zich voor zen; **2** *(change of circumstance)* tot, in: *translate ~ Japanese* in het Japans vertalen; **3** *(duration or distance)* tot ... in: *far ~ the night* tot diep in de nacht; *run ~ an old friend* een oude vriend tegen het lijf lopen; *talk somebody ~ leaving* iem ompraten om te gaan

intolerable [intollerrəbl] on(ver)draaglijk, onuitstaanbaar

intolerant [intollərənt] *(with of)* onverdraagzaam (tegenover), intolerant

intonation [intəneesjən] intonatie, stembuiging

¹intoxicant [intoksikkənt] *adj* bedwelmend, alcoholisch

²intoxicant [intoksikkənt] *n* bedwelmend middel[h], alcoholische drank, sterkedrank

intoxication [intoksikkeesjən] **1** bedwelming, dronkenschap; **2** vervoering

intransigent [intrænsidzjənt] onbuigzaam, onverzoenlijk, onverzettelijk

intransitive [intrænsittiv] onovergankelijk

intrepid [intreppid] onverschrokken, dapper

intricate [intrikkət] ingewikkeld, complex, moeilijk

¹intrigue [intrie:g] *n* intrige, gekonkel[h], samenzwering

²intrigue [intrie:g] *vb* intrigeren, nieuwsgierig maken, boeien

³intrigue [intrie:g] *vb* intrigeren, samenzweren

intrinsic [intrinsik] intrinsiek, innerlijk, wezenlijk

introduce [intrədjoe:s] **1** introduceren, voorstellen, inleiden: *~ to: a)* voorstellen aan *(s.o.); b)* kennis laten maken met *(sth);* **2** invoeren, introduceren, naar voren brengen: *~ a new subject* een nieuw onderwerp aansnijden

introduction [intrəduksjən] **1** inleiding, introductie, voorwoord[h]: *an ~ to the Chinese language* een inleiding tot de Chinese taal; **2** introductie, voorstelling, inleiding

introductory [intrəduktərie] inleidend: *~ offer* introductieaanbieding; *~ remarks* inleidende opmerkingen

¹intrude [introe:d] *vb* **1** (zich) binnendringen, zich opdringen: *intruding into conversations* zich ongevraagd in gesprekken mengen; **2** zich opdringen, ongelegen komen, storen: *let's not ~ on his time any longer* laten wij niet langer onnodig beslag leggen op zijn tijd

²**intrude** [intr̯oe:d] *vb* **1** binnendringen, indringen, opdringen; **2** opdringen, lastig vallen, storen

intruder [intr̯oe:də] indringer, insluiper

intrusion [intr̯oe:zjən] binnendringing, indringing, inbreuk: *an ~ (up)on my privacy* een inbreuk op mijn privacy

intuition [intjoe·isjən] intuïtie, ingeving: *she had an ~ that things were wrong* ze had een plotselinge ingeving dat de zaak fout zat

inundate [in̯nəndeet] onder water zetten, overstelpen

inure [inj̯oeə] gewennen, harden

invade [inv̯eed] **1** binnenvallen, een inval doen in, binnendringen; **2** overstromen: *hundreds of people ~d the newly-opened shopping centre* honderden mensen overstroomden het pas geopende winkelcentrum; **3** inbreuk maken op, schenden *(privacy)*

¹**invalid** [inv̯ælid] *adj* **1** ongerechtvaardigd, ongegrond, zwak; **2** ongeldig, onwettig, nietig: *this will is ~* dit testament is ongeldig

²**invalid** [in̯vəlid] *n* invalide

³**invalid** [in̯vəlid] *adj* **1** invalide, gebrekkig; **2** invaliden-, zieken-: *~ chair* rolstoel

invalidate [inv̯æliddeet] ongeldig maken (verklaren), nietig maken: *this automatically ~s the guarantee* hierdoor komt de garantie automatisch te vervallen; *his arguments were ~d* zijn argumenten werden ontzenuwd

invaluable [inv̯æljoeəbl] onschatbaar

invariable [inv̯əəriəbl] onveranderlijk, constant, vast

invasion [inv̯eezjən] **1** invasie *(also fig)*, inval, het binnenvallen; **2** inbreuk, schending

invective [inv̯ektiv] scheldwoord[h], scheldwoorden, getier[h]

inveigh [inv̯ee] krachtig protesteren, uitvaren, tieren

inveigle [inv̯eegl] verleiden, overhalen: *~ s.o. into stealing* iem ertoe brengen om te stelen

invent [inv̯ent] **1** uitvinden, uitdenken; **2** bedenken, verzinnen

invention [inv̯ensjən] **1** uitvinding, vinding; **2** bedenksel[h], verzinsel[h]

inventive [inv̯entiv] inventief, vindingrijk, creatief

inventor [inv̯entə] uitvinder

inventory [in̯vəntərie] **1** inventaris(lijst), inventarisatie, boedelbeschrijving; **2** overzicht[h], lijst

inverse [in̯və:s] omgekeerd, tegenovergesteld, invert: *~ ratio* omgekeerd evenredigheid

invert [inv̯ə:t] omkeren, inverteren: *~ed commas* aanhalingstekens

¹**invertebrate** [inv̯ə:tibrət] *adj* ongewerveld

²**invertebrate** [inv̯ə:tibrət] *n* ongewerveld dier[h]

¹**invest** [inv̯est] *vb* geld beleggen, (geld) investeren

²**invest** [inv̯est] *vb* investeren, beleggen: *they ~ed all*

their spare time in the car ze staken al hun vrije tijd in de auto

¹**investigate** [inv̯estigeet] *vb* onderzoeken, nasporen

²**investigate** [inv̯estigeet] *vb* een onderzoek instellen

investigation [investigeesjən] onderzoek[h]

investment [inv̯estmənt] investering, (geld)belegging

inveterate [inv̯ettərət] **1** ingeworteld, diep verankerd; **2** verstokt, aarts-: *~ liars* onverbeterlijke leugenaars

invidious [inv̯iddiəs] **1** aanstootgevend, ergerlijk; **2** hatelijk, beledigend

invigilate [inv̯idzjilleet] surveilleren *(at an examination)*

invigorate [inv̯igəreet] (ver)sterken, kracht geven

invincible [inv̯insibl] onoverwinnelijk, onomstotelijk || *~ belief* onwankelbaar geloof

invisible [inv̯izzibl] onzichtbaar *(also fig)*, verborgen

invitation [invitteesjən] uitnodiging, invitatie: *an ~ to a party* een uitnodiging voor een feest

invite [inv̯ajt] **1** uitnodigen, inviteren: *~ s.o. over* (of: *round*) iem vragen langs te komen; **2** uitnodigen, verzoeken; **3** vragen om, uitlokken

invoice [in̯vojs] factuur

invoke [inv̯ook] **1** aanroepen, inroepen; **2** zich beroepen op, een beroep doen op

involuntary [inv̯olləntərie] onwillekeurig, onopzettelijk, onbewust: *an ~ movement* een reflexbeweging

involve [inv̯olv] **1** betrekken, verwikkelen: *whose interests are ~d?* om wiens belangen gaat het?; *the persons ~d* de betrokkenen; **2** (met zich) meebrengen, betekenen: *large sums of money are ~d* er zijn grote bedragen mee gemoeid; *this job always ~s a lot of paperwork* dit werk brengt altijd veel administratieve rompslomp met zich mee

invulnerable [inv̯ulnərəbl] onkwetsbaar *(also fig)*, onaantastbaar

¹**inward** [in̯wəd] *adj* **1** innerlijk, inwendig; **2** binnenwaarts, naar binnen gericht

²**inward** [in̯wəd] *adv* **1** binnenwaarts, naar binnen; **2** innerlijk, in de geest

iodine [ajjədie:n] jodium(tinctuur[h])

IOU [aj oo joe:] *I owe you* schuldbekentenis

I.Q. [ajkjoe:] *Intelligence Quotient* IQ[h], intelligentiequotiënt[h]

irascible [ir̯æsibl] prikkelbaar, opvliegend

irate [ajr̯eet] ziedend, woedend

Ireland [ajjələnd] Ierland

iris [ajjəris] **1** iris, regenboogvlies[h] *(of eye)*; **2** lis, iris

¹**Irish** [ajjərisj] *n* Iers, de Ierse taal, (Iers-)Gaelisch

²**Irish** [ajjərisj] *adj* Iers, van Ierland

irk [ə:k] ergeren, hinderen: *it ~s me to do this job* deze klus staat me tegen

¹**iron** [ajjən] *n* ijzer[h], strijkijzer[h], brandijzer[h]: *rule with a rod of ~* met ijzeren vuist regeren; *cast ~*

gietijzer; *wrought* ~ smeedijzer; *have too many ~s in the fire* te veel hooi op z'n vork genomen hebben

²**iron** [ajjən] *adj* **1** ijzeren; **2** ijzersterk: ~ *constitution* ijzeren gestel; *the Iron Curtain* het IJzeren Gordijn

³**iron** [ajjən] *vb* strijken: *(fig)* ~ *out problems* problemen gladstrijken

Iron Age ijzertijd

ironic(al) [ajrọnnik(l)] ironisch, spottend

ironmonger ijzerhandelaar

irony [ajrənie] ironie, spot

irradiate [irreedie·eet] **1** schijnen op, verlichten: *their faces were ~d with happiness* hun gezicht straalde van geluk; **2** bestralen *(also with x-rays etc)*; **3** doen stralen, doen schitteren

¹**irrational** [iræsjənəl] *adj* irrationeel, onredelijk: ~ *behaviour* onberekenbaar gedrag

²**irrational** [iræsjənəl] *n* onmeetbaar getal[h]

irreconcilable [irrekkənsajləbl] **1** onverzoenlijk; **2** onverenigbaar, onoverbrugbaar

irrecoverable [irrikkuvvərəbl] **1** onherstelbaar, hopeloos; **2** onherroepelijk; **3** oninbaar, oninvorderbaar

irrefutable [irrifjoe:təbl] onweerlegbaar, onbetwistbaar

¹**irregular** [irregjoelə] *adj* **1** onregelmatig, abnormaal, afwijkend: *in spite of his* ~ *passport* hoewel zijn paspoort niet in orde was; **2** ongeregeld, ongeordend: *she studies very ~ly* ze studeert zeer onregelmatig; ~ *verbs* onregelmatige werkwoorden

²**irregular** [irregjoelə] *n* lid[h] van ongeregelde troepen, partizaan, guerrillastrijder

irrelevant [irrẹlləvənt] irrelevant, niet ter zake (doend)

irremediable [irrimmie:diəbl] onherstelbaar

irreparable [irrẹppərəbl] onherstelbaar, niet te verhelpen

irreplaceable [irriplẹẹsəbl] onvervangbaar

irrepressible [irriprẹssəbl] onbedwingbaar, ontembaar, onstuitbaar: ~ *laughter* onbedaarlijk gelach

irresistible [irrizzịstibl] onweerstaanbaar, onbedwingbaar, onweerlegbaar

irresolute [irrẹzzəloe:t] besluiteloos, weifelend, aarzelend

irrespective [irrispẹktiv] toch, sowieso: ~ *of* ongeacht; ~ *of whether it was necessary or not* of het nu noodzakelijk was of niet

irresponsible [irrispọnsibl] **1** onverantwoord(elijk); **2** ontoerekenbaar, niet aansprakelijk

irretrievable [irritrie:vəbl] onherstelbaar, niet meer ongedaan te maken, reddeloos (verloren)

irreverent [irrẹvvərənt] oneerbiedig, zonder respect

irreversible [irrivvə:sibl] onomkeerbaar, onherroepelijk, onveranderlijk

irrevocable [irrẹvvəkəbl] onherroepelijk, onomkeerbaar

irrigate [irrịgeet] irrigeren, bevloeien, begieten

irrigation [irrigẹẹsjən] irrigatie, bevloeiing, besproeiing

irritable [irrittəbl] lichtgeraakt, prikkelbaar, opvliegend

irritate [irritteet] **1** irriteren, ergeren, boos maken: *be ~d at* (of: *by, with*) geërgerd zijn door; **2** irriteren, prikkelen *(skin etc)*

irritation [irrittẹẹsjən] **1** irritatie, ergernis; **2** irritatie, branderigheid, branderige plek

Is. *Island(s), Isle(s)* Eiland(en)

Isaiah [ajzajjə] Jesaja, Isaias

Islam [izla:m] islam; islamitische wereld

Islamic [izlæmik] islamitisch

island [ajlənd] **1** eiland[h] *(also fig)*; **2** vluchtheuvel

islander [ajləndə] eilander, eilandbewoner

isle [ajl] *(in specific combinations)* eiland[h]

isolate [ajsəleet] isoleren, afzonderen, afsluiten

isolation [ajsəlẹẹsjən] isolatie, afzondering, isolement[h]: *in* ~ in afzondering, op zichzelf

¹**Israeli** [izrẹẹlie] *adj* Israëlisch

²**Israeli** [izrẹẹlie] *n* Israëli, bewoner van Israël

¹**Israelite** [izrəlajt] *adj* Israëlitisch

²**Israelite** [izrəlajt] *n* Israëliet, nakomeling van Israël

¹**issue** [isjoe:] *n* **1** uitgave, aflevering, nummer[h] *(of magazine)*; **2** kwestie, (belangrijk) punt[h], probleem[h]: *force the* ~ een beslissing forceren; *make an* ~ *of sth.* ergens een punt van maken; **3** publicatie, uitgave, emissie: *the day of* ~ de dag van publicatie

²**issue** [isjoe] *vb* **1** uitbrengen, publiceren, in circulatie brengen, uitvaardigen: *they ~d a new series of stamps* ze gaven een nieuwe serie postzegels uit; **2** uitlenen *(books)*; **3** uitstorten, uitspuwen: *a volcano issuing dangerous gases* een vulkaan die gevaarlijke gassen uitspuwt

³**issue** [isjoe:] *vb* uitkomen, verschijnen: ~ *forth (of: out)* te voorschijn komen

isthmus [ismǝs] istmus, nauwe verbinding, landengte

it [it] **1** het: *I dreamt* ~ ik heb het gedroomd; ~ *is getting on* het wordt laat; ~ *says in this book that ...* er staat in dit boek dat ...; ~ *is reported that* volgens de berichten; *I've got* ~ ik heb een idee; *she let him have* ~ ze gaf hem ervan langs; *who is* ~? wie is het?; **2** hét, het neusje vd zalm, het probleem: *that is* ~, *I've finished* dat was het dan, klaar is Kees; *that is* ~ dat is 't hem nu juist

IT *information technology* IT, informatietechnologie

¹**Italian** [itæliən] *adj* Italiaans

²**Italian** [itæliən] *n* Italiaan(se)

italic [itælik] **1** cursief, cursieve drukletter: *the words in* ~ de schuingedrukte woorden; **2** schuinschrift[h], lopend schrift[h]

Italy [ittəlie] Italië

¹**itch** [itsj] *vb* **1** jeuken, kriebelen: *the wound keeps ~ing* de wond blijft maar jeuken; **2** jeuk hebben; **3** graag willen: *she was ~ing to tell her* ze zat te popelen om het haar te vertellen

²**itch** [itsj] *n* **1** jeuk, kriebel; **2** verlangen[h], hang

item [ajtəm] **1** item[h], punt[h], nummer[h]; **2** onderdeel^h, bestanddeel^h; **3** artikel^h, (nieuws)bericht^h

itinerant [ittinnərənt] rondreizend, (rond)trekkend: ~ *preacher* rondtrekkend prediker

itinerary [ittinnərərie] **1** routebeschrijving, reisbeschrijving; **2** reisroute

its [its] zijn, haar, ervan: *this coat has had ~ day* deze mantel heeft zijn tijd gehad; *the government has lost ~ majority* de regering is haar meerderheid kwijt; ~ *strength frightens me* de kracht ervan maakt mij bang

itself [itself] **1** zich, zichzelf: *the animal hurt ~* het dier bezeerde zich; *by ~* alleen, op eigen kracht; *in ~* op zichzelf; **2** zelf: *the watch ~ was not in the box* het horloge zelf zat niet in de doos

ivory [ajvərie] ivoor^h

ivy [ajvie] klimop

j

¹jab [dzjæb] *vb* porren, stoten, stompen: *he ~bed his elbow into my side* hij gaf me een por in de ribben

²jab [dzjæb] *n* **1** por, steek; **2** *(inf)* prik, injectie

jabber [dzjæbǝ] brabbelen, kwebbelen: *~ away erop los kwebbelen*

jack [dzjæk] **1** toestel^h, hefboom, vijzel, krik, stut, stellage, (zaag)bok; **2** dier^h, mannetje^h; **3** *(cards)* boer: *~ of hearts* hartenboer

jackal [dzjæko:l] jakhals

jackass [dzjækæs] ezel *(also fig)*

jackdaw kauw, torenkraai

jacket [dzjækit] **1** jas(je^h), colbert(je)^h; **2** omhulsel^h, bekleding, mantel, huls; **3** stofomslag^h *(of book)*

¹jackknife *n* (groot) knipmes^h

²jackknife *vb* scharen *(of articulated vehicles)*

jack-of-all-trades manusje-van-alles^h

jackpot pot *(at games of hazard)*, jackpot: *hit the ~: a)* (de pot) winnen *(at poker etc); b) (fig)* een klapper maken, het helemaal maken

jack up opkrikken, *(inf, fig also)* opvijzelen, opdrijven *(prices etc)*

jade [dzjeed] **1** knol *(old horse);* **2** jade; bleekgroen

jaded [dzjeedid] **1** afgemat, uitgeput; **2** afgestompt

jagged [dzjægid] getand, gekarteld, puntig: *~ edge* scherpe rand

¹jail [dzjeel] *n* gevangenis; huis^h van bewaring

²jail [dzjeel] *vb* gevangen zetten

jailbird bajesklant

jailer [dzjeelǝ] cipier, gevangenbewaarder

¹jam [dzjæm] *n* **1** opstopping, blokkering, stremming; **2** knel, knoei, moeilijkheden: *be in a ~* in de nesten zitten

²jam [dzjæm] *vb* vast (blijven) zitten, klemmen, blokkeren, vastraken: *the door ~med* de deur raakte klem

³jam [dzjæm] *vb* **1** vastzetten, klemmen, knellen; **2** (met kracht) drijven, dringen, duwen: *~ the brakes on* op de rem gaan staan; **3** (vol)proppen: *he ~med all his clothes into a tiny case* hij propte al zijn kleren in een piepklein koffertje; **4** blokkeren, verstoppen, versperren: *the crowds ~med the streets* de massa versperde de straten; **5** *(radio)* storen

jam-packed [dzjæmpækt] propvol, barstensvol

¹jangle [dzjæŋgl] *vb* **1** kletteren, rinkelen, rammelen; **2** vals klinken, wanklank geven: *the music ~d on my ears* de muziek schetterde in mijn oren

²jangle [dzjæŋgl] *vb* irriteren, van streek maken: *it ~d his nerves* het vrat aan zijn zenuwen

³jangle [dzjæŋgl] *n* **1** metaalklank, gerinkel^h; **2** wanklank

janitor [dzjænittǝ] **1** portier^h, deurwachter; **2** *(Am)* conciërge, huisbewaarder

January [dzjænjoeǝrie] januari

¹Japanese [dzjæpǝnie:z] *adj* Japans

²Japanese [dzjæpǝnie:z] *n* Japanner, Japanse

¹jar [dzja:] *n* **1** (zenuw)schok, onaangename verrassing, ontnuchtering: *suffer a nasty ~* flink ontnuchterd worden; **2** pot, (stop)fles, kruik, *(inf)* glas^h *(beer etc)*

²jar [dzja:] *vb* **1** knarsen, vals klinken: *(also fig) ~ring note* valse noot, dissonant; **2** botsen, in strijd zijn: *~ring opinions* botsende meningen

jargon [dzja:gǝn] jargon^h, vaktaal, *(depr)* koeterwaals^h, taaltje^h

jasmin(e) [dzjæzmin] jasmijn

¹jaundice [dzjo:ndis] *n* geelzucht

²jaundice [dzjo:ndis] *vb* afgunstig maken, verbitteren: *take a ~d view of the matter* een scheve kijk op de zaak hebben

jaunt [dzjo:nt] uitstapje^h, tochtje^h, snoepreisje^h

jaunty [dzjo:ntie] **1** zwierig, elegant; **2** vrolijk, zelfverzekerd: *a ~ step* een kwieke tred

javelin [dzjævlin] **1** speer, werpspies; **2** *(athletics)* speerwerpen^h

¹jaw [dzjo:] *n* **1** kaak: *lower (of: upper) ~* onderkaak, bovenkaak; **2** praat, geklets^h, gezwam^h, geroddel^h; **3** tegenspraak, brutale praat: *don't give me any ~!* hou je gedeisd!; **4** *~s* bek, muil *(of animal)*

²jaw [dzjo:] *vb* **1** kletsen, zwammen, roddelen; **2** preken: *~ at s.o.* iem de les lezen

jay [dzjee] Vlaamse gaai

jazz [dzjæz] **1** jazz; **2** gesnoef^h; **3** onzin, larie || *and all that ~* en nog meer van die dingen

jazz up opvrolijken, opfleuren, verfraaien: *they jazzed it up* ze brachten wat leven in de brouwerij

jealous [dzjellǝs] **1** jaloers, afgunstig: *~ of* jaloers op; **2** (overdreven) waakzaam, nauwlettend: *guard ~ly* angstvallig bewaken

jealousy [dzjellǝsie] jaloersheid, afgunst, jaloezie

jeans [dzjie:nz] spijkerbroek, jeans

¹jeer [dzjiǝ] *vb* jouwen: *~ at s.o.* iem uitlachen

²jeer [dzjiǝ] *vb* uitjouwen

³jeer [dzjiǝ] *n* hatelijke opmerking, *~s* gejouw^h, hoon

jell [dzjel] **1** (doen) opstijven, geleiachtig (doen) worden; **2** vorm krijgen (geven), kristalliseren: *my ideas are beginning to ~* mijn ideeën beginnen vorm te krijgen

jelly [dzjellie] gelei, gelatine(pudding), jam: *beat s.o. to ~* iem tot moes slaan

jellyfish [dzjelliefisj] kwal

jemmy [dzjemmie] koevoet, breekijzer^h

jeopardize [dzjeppǝdajz] in gevaar brengen, riskeren, op het spel zetten: *~ one's life* zijn leven wagen

jeopardy [dzjeppǝdie] gevaar^h: *put one's future in ~* zijn toekomst op het spel zetten

¹jerk [dzjə:k] *n* **1** ruk, schok, trek; **2** *(vulg)* lul, zak

²jerk [dzjə:k] *vb* schokken, beven: ~ *to a halt* met een ruk stoppen

³jerk [dzjə:k] *vb* rukken aan, stoten, trekken aan: *he ~ed the fish out of the water* hij haalde de vis met een ruk uit het water

jerky [dzjə:kie] schokkerig, spastisch, hortend: *move along jerkily* zich met horten en stoten voortbewegen

jest [dzjest] **1** grap, mop; **2** scherts, gekheid: *in ~* voor de grap

jester [dzjestə] nar

Jesus [dzjie:zəs] Jezus

¹jet [dzjet] *n* **1** straal *(of water etc)*; **2** (gas)vlam, pit; **3** *(inf)* jet, straalvliegtuigʰ, straalmotor

²jet [dzjet] *vb* **1** spuiten, uitspuiten, uitwerpen: ~ *(out) flames* vlammen werpen; ~ *out* eruit spuiten; **2** *(inf)* per jet reizen: ~ *out* vooruitspringen

jet-black gitzwart

jetfoil draagvleugelboot

jetsam [dzjetsəm] strandgoedʰ

jettison [dzjettisn] werpen *(ship's cargo); (fig)* overboord gooien; prijsgeven

jetty [dzjettie] pier, havendam, havenhoofdʰ, golfbreker

Jew [dzjoe:] joodʰ

jewel [dzjoe:əl] **1** juweelʰ *(also fig)*, edelsteen, sieraadʰ; **2** steen *(in timepiece)*

jeweller [dzjoe:ələ] juwelier

jewellery [dzjoe:əlrie] juwelen, sieraden

Jewess [dzjoe:es] jodin

Jewish [dzjoe:isj] joods

Jewry [dzjoe:ərie] jodendomʰ, de joden

jib [dzjib] **1** weigeren (verder te gaan) *(of horse)*; **2** terugkrabbelen: ~ *at* terugdeinzen voor, zich afkerig tonen van

jiffy [dzjiffie] momentjeʰ: *I won't be a* ~ ik kom zo; *in a* ~ in een mum van tijd, in een wip

¹jig [dzjig] *n* sprongetjeʰ

²jig [dzjig] *vb* op en neer (doen) wippen, (doen) huppelen, (doen) hossen

¹jiggle [dzjigl] *vb* schommelen, wiegen

²jiggle [dzjigl] *vb* doen schommelen, (zacht) rukken aan, wrikken

jigsaw (puzzle) (leg)puzzel

jilt [dzjilt] afwijzen, de bons geven *(lover)*

¹jingle [dzjinggl] *vb* (laten) klingelen, (doen) rinkelen

²jingle [dzjinggl] *n* **1** geklingelʰ, gerinkelʰ, getinkelʰ; **2** *(depr)* rijmelarij, rijmpjeʰ; **3** jingle *(on radio)*

jinks [dzjingks] pretmakerij: *high* ~ dolle pret

jinx [dzjingks] **1** onheilsbrenger; **2** doem, vloek: *put a* ~ *on s.o.* iem beheksen

jitters [dzjittəz] kriebels, zenuwen: *give s.o. the* ~ iem nerveus maken

jnr. *junior* jr.

job [dzjob] **1** karweiʰ, klus, (stukʰ) werkʰ, job: *have a* ~ *to get sth. done* aan iets de handen vol hebben; *make a (good)* ~ *of sth.* iets goed afwerken; *on the* ~

aan het werk, bezig; **2** baan(tjeʰ), vakʰ, job, taak: ~*s for the boys* vriendjespolitiek; **3** *(inf)* gevalʰ, dingʰ: *that new car of yours is a beautiful* ~ die nieuwe wagen van je is een prachtslee; **4** *(inf)* toestand: *make the best of a bad* ~ ergens nog het beste van maken; *he has gone, and a good* ~ *too* hij is weg, en maar goed ook; *that should do the* ~ zo moet het lukken

jobbery [dzjobbərie] ambtsmisbruikʰ, (ambtelijke) corruptie

jobbing [dzjobbing] klusjes-: *a* ~ *gardener* een klusjesman voor de tuin

jobless [dzjobləs] zonder werk, werkloos

job-sharing het werken met deeltijdbanen

¹jockey [dzjokkie] *n* jockey

²jockey [dzjokkie] *vb* manoeuvreren: ~ *for position* met de ellebogen werken

jocular [dzjokjoelə] schertsend, grappig

¹jog [dzjog] *vb* **1** joggen, trimmen; **2** op een sukkeldraf(je) lopen, sukkelen: ~ *along* (of: *on*) voortsukkelen

²jog [dzjog] *vb* hotsen, op en neer (doen) gaan, schudden

³jog [dzjog] *vb* (aan)stoten, een duw(tje) geven, (aan)porren by ~ *s.o.'s memory* iemands geheugen opfrissen

⁴jog [dzjog] *n* **1** duw(tjeʰ), schok, stootjeʰ; **2** sukkeldraf(jeʰ); **3** een stukje joggen

joggle [dzjogl] hotsen, heen en weer (op en neer) (doen) gaan, schudden

jogtrot sukkeldraf(jeʰ), lichte draf

john [dzjon] **1** *(Am; inf)* wc; **2** *(Am; vulg)* klant *(of whore)*, hoerenloper

johnny [dzjonnie] kerel, man, vent

¹join [dzjojn] *vb* **1** samenkomen, zich verenigen, verenigd worden, elkaar ontmoeten, uitkomen op: ~ *up (with)* samensmelten (met); **2** zich aansluiten, meedoen, deelnemen: *can I* ~ *in?* mag ik meedoen?; ~ *up* dienst nemen (bij het leger), lid worden, zich aansluiten (bij)

²join [dzjojn] *vb* **1** verenigen, verbinden, vastmaken: ~ *the main road* op de hoofdweg uitkomen; ~ *up (with)* samenvoegen (met); **2** zich aansluiten bij, meedoen met deelnemen aan: ~ *the army* dienst nemen (bij het leger); *will you* ~ *us?* doe je mee?, kom je bij ons zitten?

³join [dzjojn] *n* verbinding(sstukʰ), voeg, las, naad

joiner [dzjojnə] schrijnwerker, meubelmaker

¹joint [dzjojnt] *n* **1** verbinding(sstukʰ), voeg, las, naad; **2** gewrichtʰ, geleding, scharnierʰ: *out of* ~ *(also fig)* ontwricht, uit het lid, uit de voegen; **3** braadstukʰ, gebraadʰ, (groot) stukʰ vlees; **4** *(inf)* tent, kroeg; **5** *(inf)* joint, stickieʰ

²joint [dzjojnt] *adj* gezamenlijk, gemeenschappelijk: ~ *account* gezamenlijke rekening; ~ *owners* mede-eigenaars; ~ *responsibility* gedeelde verantwoordelijkheid

joist [dzjojst] (dwars)balk, bintʰ, (horizontale) steunbalk

¹joke [dzjook] *n* **1** grap(jeʰ), mop: *practical* ~ poets, practical joke; *crack (of: tell) ~s* moppen tappen; *be (of: go) beyond a ~* te ver gaan, niet leuk zijn; *(inf) no ~* geen grapje; **2** mikpunt^h *(of mockery, wittiness)*, spot

²joke [dzjook] *vb* grappen maken, schertsen: *you must be joking!* dat meen je niet!; *joking apart* in alle ernst, nee, nou even serieus

joker [dzjookə] **1** grapjas, grappenmaker; **2** *(cards)* joker, *(fig)* (laatste) troef; **3** kerel, (rot)vent

jollity [dzjollittie] uitgelatenheid, joligheid

¹jolly [dzjollie] *adj* **1** plezierig, prettig; **2** *(also iron)* vrolijk, jolig: *a ~ fellow* een lollige vent; **3** *(inf; euph)* (lichtelijk) aangeschoten, dronken: *(inf) it's a ~ shame* het is een grote schande; *Jolly Roger* piratenvlag

²jolly [dzjollie] *adv (inf)* heel, zeer: *you ~ well will!* en nou en of je het doet!

³jolly [dzjollie] *vb* vleien, bepraten: *~ along (of: up)* zoet houden, bepraten; *~ s.o. into sth.* iem tot iets overhalen

¹jolt [dzjoolt] *vb (with along)* (voort)schokken, horten, botsen, stoten

²jolt [dzjoolt] *vb* schokken, *(fig)* verwarren: *~ s.o. out of a false belief* iem plotseling tot een beter inzicht brengen

³jolt [dzjoolt] *n* schok, ruk, stoot, *(fig also)* verrassing, ontnuchtering

josh [dzjosj] plagen, voor de gek houden

jostle [dzjosl] (ver)dringen, (weg)duwen, (weg)stoten

¹jot [dzjot] *n* jota *(only fig): I don't care a ~* het kan me geen moer schelen

²jot [dzjot] *vb (with down)* (vlug) noteren, neerpennen, opkrabbelen

jotter [dzjottə] blocnote, notitieboekje^h

journal [dzjə:nl] **1** dagboek^h, journaal^h, kasboek^h; **2** dagblad^h, krant; **3** tijdschrift^h

journalese [dzjə:nəlie:z] journalistieke stijl, krantentaal, sensatiestijl

journalism [dzjə:nəlizm] journalistiek

¹journey [dzjə:nie] *n* (dag)reis, tocht *(over land)*

²journey [dzjə:nie] *vb* reizen, trekken

joust [dzjaust] aan een steekspel deelnemen, een steekspel houden *(also fig): ~ with s.o.* met iem in het krijt treden

Jove [dzjoov] Jupiter

jovial [dzjooviəl] joviaal, vrolijk

jowl [dzjaul] kaak, kaaksbeen^h, wang

joy [dzjoj] **1** bron van vreugde: *she's a great ~ to her parents* ze is de vreugde van haar ouders; **2** vreugde, genot^h, blijdschap: *be filled with ~* overlopen van vreugde

joyride joyride

joystick 1 knuppel, stuurstang *(of aeroplane);* **2** bedieningspookje^h, joystick *(of videogames, computer etc)*

JP *Justice of the Peace* politierechter

Jr. *Junior* jr.

jubilant [dzjoo:billənt] **1** uitbundig, triomfantelijk:

~ shout vreugdekreet; *~ at* in de wolken over; **2** jubelend, juichend

jubilee [dzjoo:billie:] jubileum^h: *diamond ~* diamanten jubileum

judder [dzjuddə] (heftig) vibreren, trillen, schudden

¹judge [dzjudzj] *vb* **1** rechtspreken over, berechten; **2** beoordelen, achten, schatten: *~ s.o. by his actions* iem naar zijn daden beoordelen

²judge [dzjudzj] *vb* **1** rechtspreken, vonnis vellen; **2** arbitreren, als scheidsrechter optreden, *(at match)* punten toekennen; **3** oordelen, een oordeel vellen: *judging by (of: from) his manner* naar zijn houding te oordelen

³judge [dzjudzj] *n* **1** rechter; **2** scheidsrechter, arbiter, jurylid^h, beoordelaar *(at competition etc);* **3** kenner, expert: *good ~ of character* mensenkenner, iemand met veel mensenkennis

judg(e)ment [dzjudzjmənt] **1** oordeel^h, uitspraak, vonnis^h, schatting: *sit in ~ on* rechter spelen over; *in my ~* naar mijn mening; **2** inzicht^h: *use one's ~* zijn (gezond) verstand gebruiken; *against one's better ~* tegen beter weten in

Judg(e)ment Day Laatste Oordeel

judicial [dzjoe:disjl] gerechtelijk, rechterlijk, rechter(s)-

judiciary [dzjoe:disjiərie] **1** rechtswezen^h; **2** rechterlijke macht

judicious [dzjoe:disjəs] verstandig, voorzichtig

¹jug [dzjug] *n* **1** kan(netje^h); **2** *(Am)* kruik

²jug [dzjug] *vb* stoven *(hare, rabbit): ~ged hare* gestoofde haas, hazenpeper

juggernaut [dzjugəno:t] grote vrachtwagen, bakbeest^h

juggle [dzjugl] **1** *(with with)* jongleren (met); **2** goochelen, toveren; **3** *(with with)* knoeien (met), frauderen

juggler [dzjuglə] **1** jongleur; **2** goochelaar

Jugoslav *see* Yugoslav

juice [dzjoe:s] sap^h, levenssap^h || *let s.o. stew in their own ~* iem in zijn eigen vet gaar laten koken

July [dzjoelaj] juli

¹jumble [dzjumbl] *vb* dooreengooien, dooreenhaspelen, samenflansen

²jumble [dzjumbl] *n* **1** warboel, janboel, troep; **2** mengelmoes^h, allegaartje^h

jumble sale liefdadigheidsbazaar, rommelmarkt

¹jumbo [dzjumboo] *n* **1** kolos, reus; **2** jumbo(jet)

²jumbo [dzjumboo] *adj* kolossaal, jumbo-, reuze-

¹jump [dzjump] *vb* **1** springen, *(bicycle racing)* wegspringen, demarreren: *~ in* naar binnen springen, vlug instappen, *(fig)* tussenbeide komen; *(fig) he ~ed at the offer* hij greep het aanbod met beide handen aan; *~ on s.o.* iem te lijf gaan, *(fig)* uitvaren tegen iem; **2** opspringen, opschrikken, een schok krijgen: *he ~ed at the noise* hij schrok op van het lawaai; *~ to one's feet* opspringen; **3** zich haasten, overhaast komen (tot): *~ to conclusions* overhaaste conclusies trekken

²jump [dzjump] *n* sprong, *(fig)* (plotselinge, snelle) stijging, schok, ruk: *(fig) stay one ~ ahead* één stap vóór blijven

jumper [dzjumpə] **1** springer; **2** pullover, (dames)trui, jumper; **3** *(Am)* overgooier

jumping jack hansworst, trekpop *(toy)*

jumpy [dzjumpie] **1** gespannen; **2** lichtgeraakt, prikkelbaar

junction [dzjungksjən] verbinding(spunt^h); kruispunt^h, knooppunt^h *(of motorways, railways)*

juncture [dzjungktsjə] tijdsgewricht^h, toestand: *at this ~* onder de huidige omstandigheden

June [dzjoe:n] juni

jungle [dzjunggl] **1** jungle, oerwoud^h; **2** warboel, warwinkel, chaos: *a ~ of tax laws* een doolhof van belastingwetten

¹junior [dzjoe:niə] *n* **1** junior; **2** jongere, kleinere: *he's my ~ by two years, he's two years my ~* hij is twee jaar jonger dan ik; **3** mindere, ondergeschikte

²junior [dzjoe:niə] *adj* **1** jonger, klein(er), junior *(after names);* **2** lager geplaatst, ondergeschikt, jonger: *~ clerk* jongste bediende

junior college *(Am)* universiteit *(with only the first two years of the course)*

junior high (school) *(Am)* middenschool, brugschool

juniper [dzjoe:nippə] jeneverbes(struik)

junk [dzjungk] **1** (oude) rommel, rotzooi, schroot^h; **2** jonk

junk food junkfood^h, ongezonde kost

junkie [dzjungkie] junkie, (drugs)verslaafde

junk mail huis-aan-huispost, ongevraagde post, reclamedrukwerk^h

jurisdiction [dzjoeərisdiksjən] **1** rechtspraak; **2** (rechts)bevoegdheid, jurisdictie, competentie: *have ~ of* (of: *over*) bevoegd zijn over

juror [dzjoeərə] jurylid^h

jury [dzjoeərie] jury

¹just [dzjust] *adv* **1** precies, juist, net: *~ about* zowat, wel zo'n beetje, zo ongeveer; *~ now* net op dit moment, daarnet; **2** amper, ternauwernood, (maar) net: *~ a little* een tikkeltje (maar); **3** net, zoëven, daarnet: *they've (only) ~ arrived* ze zijn er (nog maar) net; **4** gewoon, (alleen) maar, (nu) eens, nu eenmaal: *it ~ doesn't make sense* het slaat gewoon nergens op; *~ wait and see* wacht maar, dan zul je eens zien; **5** gewoonweg, in één woord, (toch) even: *~ the same* toch, niettemin

²just [dzjust] *adj* **1** billijk, rechtvaardig, fair; **2** (wel)verdiend: *get* (of: *receive*) *one's ~ deserts* zijn verdiende loon krijgen; **3** gegrond, gerechtvaardigd

justice [dzjustis] **1** rechter: *Justice of the Peace* kantonrechter, politierechter, *(Belg)* vrederechter; **2** gerechtigheid, rechtmatigheid, recht^h, rechtvaardigheid, Justitia: *do ~ (to)* recht laten wedervaren; *do ~ to oneself, do oneself ~* zich (weer) waarmaken, aan de verwachtingen voldoen; *to do him ~* ere wie ere toekomt; **3** gerecht^h, rechtspleging, justitie:

bring s.o. to ~ iem voor het gerecht brengen

justifiable [dzjustiffajjəbl] **1** gerechtvaardigd, verantwoord, rechtmatig; **2** te rechtvaardigen, verdedigbaar

justify [dzjustiffaj] **1** rechtvaardigen, bevestigen: *we were clearly justified in sacking him* we hebben hem terecht ontslagen; **2** *(esp in passive voice)* in het gelijk stellen, rechtvaardigen, staven: *am I justified in thinking that ...* heb ik gelijk als ik denk dat ...

jut [dzjut] *(also with out)* uitsteken, (voor)uitspringen

¹juvenile [dzjoe:vənajl] *adj* jeugdig, kinderlijk: *~ court* kinderrechter; *~ delinquency* jeugdcriminaliteit

²juvenile [dzjoe:vənajl] *n* jongere, jeugdig persoon

k

kale [keel] (boeren)kool
kaleidoscope [kəlajdəskoop] caleidoscoop
kangaroo [kænggəroe:] kangoeroe
kapok [keepok] kapok
karaoke [kærie·ookie] karaoke
karting [ka:ting] karting[h], go-karting
kayak [kajæk] kajak (of Eskimos), kano
¹Kazakh [kəza:k] adj Kazaks
²Kazakh [kəza:k] n Kazak
Kazakhstan [kæzəksta:n] Kazachstan
keel [kie:l] (shipp) kiel
keelhaul 1 kielhalen, kielen; 2 op z'n nummer zetten, op z'n donder geven: Julian was ~ed by his boss Julian kreeg flink op z'n donder van zijn baas
keen [kie:n] 1 scherp (also fig), bijtend, fel, hevig (of wind, frost, etc; also of fight): we're facing ~ competition from small businesses we kampen met felle concurrentie van kleine ondernemingen; 2 scherp, helder (of senses, intelligence etc): ~ sight scherp gezichtsvermogen; 3 vurig, enthousiast: a ~ golfer een hartstochtelijk golfer; ~ on gespitst op, gebrand op; 4 spotgoedkoop
¹keep [kie:p] vb 1 blijven, doorgaan met: ~ left links houden; will you please ~ still! blijf nou toch eens stil zitten!; how is Richard ~ing? hoe gaat het met Richard?; ~ abreast of (lit) bijhouden, (fig) op de hoogte blijven van; ~ back op een afstand blijven; ~ indoors in huis blijven; if the rain ~s off als het droog blijft; ~ off! (of: out!) verboden toegang!; ~ off uit de buurt blijven van, vermijden; ~ out of: a) zich niet bemoeien met; b) niet betreden; c) zich niet blootstellen aan; 2 goed blijven, vers blijven (of food): (fig) your news will have to ~ a bit dat nieuwtje van jou moet maar even wachten
²keep [kie:p] vb 1 houden, zich houden aan, bewaren: ~ a promise een belofte nakomen; ~ a secret een geheim bewaren; 2 houden, onderhouden, er opna houden, (in dienst) hebben: ~ chickens kippen houden; 3 (in bezit) hebben, bewaren, in voorraad hebben, verkopen: ~ the change laat maar zitten; 4 houden, ophouden, vasthouden, tegenhouden: ~ within bounds binnen de perken houden; ~ it clean houd het netjes; ~ sth. going iets aan de gang houden; ~ s.o. waiting iem laten wachten; what kept you (so long)? wat heeft je zo (lang) opgehouden?, waar bleef je (nou)?; ~ back: a) tegenhou-

den, op een afstand houden; b) achterhouden, geheimhouden; ~ down: a) binnenhouden (food); b) omlaaghouden, laag houden; c) onder de duim houden; d) onderdrukken, inhouden (rage); ~ one's weight down z'n gewicht binnen de perken houden; ~ your head down! bukken!; ~ off op een afstand houden; ~ s.o. out iem buitensluiten; he tried to ~ the bad news from his father hij probeerde het slechte nieuws voor z'n vader verborgen te houden; he couldn't ~ his eyes off the girl hij kon z'n ogen niet van het meisje afhouden; ~ your hands off me! blijf met je poten van me af!; ~ them out of harm's way zorg dat ze geen gevaar lopen; he kept it to himself hij hield het voor zich; 5 bijhouden (book, diary etc), houden: Mary used to ~ (the) accounts Mary hield de boeken bij; 6 houden, aanhouden, blijven in: ~ your seat! blijf (toch) zitten!
³keep [kie:p] n 1 (hoofd)toren; 2 bolwerk[h], bastion[h]; 3 (levens)onderhoud[h], kost, voedsel[h]: earn your ~ de kost verdienen; for ~s voor altijd, voorgoed
keep at door blijven gaan met: ~ it! ga zo door!
keeper [kie:pə] 1 bewaarder; 2 keeper, doelverdediger, (cricket) wicketkeeper
¹keep in vb binnen blijven
²keep in vb na laten blijven
keeping [kie:ping] 1 bewaring, hoede: in safe ~ in veilige bewaring; 2 overeenstemming, harmonie: in ~ with in overeenstemming met
keep in with (proberen) op goede voet (te) blijven met: now that she's old she wishes she had kept in with her children nu dat ze oud is, wilde ze dat ze op goede voet was gebleven met haar kinderen
¹keep on vb 1 volhouden, doorgaan: he keeps on telling me these awful jokes hij blijft me maar van die vreselijke grappen vertellen; 2 doorgaan, doorrijden, doorlopen, verder gaan; 3 blijven praten, doorkletsen
²keep on vb 1 aanhouden, ophouden, blijven dragen (clothing, hat): please ~ your safety helmet throughout the tour houd u alstublieft tijdens de rondleiding uw veiligheidshelm op; 2 aanlaten (light)
keepsake [kie:pseek] aandenken[h], souvenir[h]: for a ~ als aandenken
keep to 1 blijven bij, (zich) beperken tot, (zich) houden (aan): ~ the point bij het onderwerp blijven; she always keeps (herself) to herself ze is erg op zichzelf; 2 houden, rijden: ~ the left links houden
¹keep up vb 1 overeind blijven, blijven staan; 2 hoog blijven (of price, standard; also fig); 3 (in dezelfde, goede staat) blijven, aanhouden: I do hope that the weather keeps up ik hoop wel dat het weer mooi blijft; 4 opblijven; 5 bijblijven, bijhouden: ~ with one's neighbours niet bij de buren achterblijven; ~ with the Joneses z'n stand ophouden; ~ with the times bij de tijd blijven
²keep up vb 1 omhooghouden, ophouden; 2 hoog houden: ~ the costs de kosten hoog houden; keep morale up het moreel hoog houden; 3 doorgaan met, handhaven, volhouden: ~ the conversation de

conversatie gaande houden; ~ *the good work!* ga zo door!

keg [keg] vaatje^h

ken [ken] kennis, bevattingsvermogen^h, begrip^h: *that is beyond* (of: *outside*) *my* ~ dat gaat boven mijn pet

kennel [kenl] **1** hondenhok^h; **2** kennel, hondenfokkerij

kerb [kə:b] stoeprand, trottoirband

kerfuffle [kəfufl] opschudding

kernel [kə:nl] **1** pit, korrel; **2** kern, essentie

kerosene [kerrəsie:n] kerosine; (lampen)petroleum^h, lampolie, paraffineolie

kettle [ketl] ketel: *put the* ~ *on* theewater opzetten

kettledrum keteltrom(mel), pauk

¹**key** [kie:] *n* **1** sleutel, *(fig)* toegang, oplossing, verklaring: ~ *to the mystery* sleutel van het raadsel; **2** toon, *(mus)* toonaard, toonsoort, tonaliteit, stijl: *out of* ~, *off* ~ vals; **3** toets *(of piano, typewriter etc)*, klep *(of wind instrument)*

²**key** [kie:] *adj* sleutel-, hoofd-, voornaamste: ~ *figure* sleutelfiguur; ~ *question* hamvraag; ~ *witness* hoofdgetuige, voornaamste getuige

³**key** [kie:] *vb* (with *in*) invoeren *(by means of keyboard)*, intikken

keyboard 1 toetsenbord^h; **2** klavierinstrument^h, toetsinstrument^h

keyhole sleutelgat^h || ~ *surgery* kijkoperatie

keynote 1 grondtoon, hoofdtoon; **2** hoofdgedachte, grondgedachte

keypad (druk)toetsenpaneel(tje)^h *(of remote control unit, pocket calculator etc)*

keystone 1 sluitsteen *(of arch)*; **2** hoeksteen, fundament^h

key up opwinden, gespannen maken: *the boy looked keyed up* de jongen zag er gespannen uit

kg. *kilogram(s)* kg

khaki [ka:kie] kaki(kleur), kakistof

kibbutz [kibboets] kibboets

¹**kick** [kik] *vb* **1** schoppen, trappen: *(socc)* ~ *off* aftrappen; **2** terugslag hebben *(of gun)*; **3** er tegenaan schoppen, protesteren: ~ *against* (of: *at*) protesteren tegen; ~ *off* sterven

²**kick** [kik] *vb* **1** schoppen, trappen, wegtrappen: ~ *oneself* zich voor zijn kop slaan; ~ *out* eruit schoppen, ontslaan; **2** stoppen met *(addiction etc)*: ~ *a person when he is down* iem nog verder de grond in trappen; ~ *upstairs* wegpromoveren

³**kick** [kik] *n* **1** schop, trap; **2** terugslag *(of gun)*; **3** kick, stimulans, impuls: *do sth. for* ~s iets voor de lol doen; **4** kracht, fut, energie: *a* ~ *in the pants* een schop onder zijn kont *(fig)*; *a* ~ *in the teeth* een slag in het gezicht *(fig)*

¹**kick around** *vb* **1** rondslingeren: *his old bicycle has been kicking around in the garden for weeks now* zijn oude fiets slingert al weken rond in de tuin; **2** in leven zijn, bestaan, rondhollen

²**kick around** *vb* **1** sollen met, grof behandelen; **2** commanderen, bazen

kickback smeergeld^h

kick in in werking treden, beginnen (te werken), (plotseling) beginnen mee te spelen *(eg of fear)*: *but when she saw the rhino at close range, fear kicked in* maar toen ze de neushoorn van dichtbij zag, werd ze ineens bang

kick-off 1 *(socc)* aftrap; **2** begin^h

kick-start 1 snel op gang brengen, een impuls geven aan; **2** aantrappen, starten *(engine)*

kickstart(er) trapstarter

¹**kid** [kid] *n* **1** jong geitje^h, bokje^h; **2** kind^h, joch^h; **3** geitenleer^h

²**kid** [kid] *adj* **1** jonger: ~ *brother* jonger broertje; **2** van geitenleer, glacé: *handle* (of: *treat*) *(s.o.) with* ~ *gloves* (iem) met fluwelen handschoentjes aanpakken

³**kid** [kid] *vb* plagen, in de maling nemen: *no* ~*ding? meen je dat?; no* ~*ding!* echt waar!

kiddie [kiddie] jong^h, joch^h, knul

kidnap [kidnæp] ontvoeren, kidnappen

kidney [kidnie] nier

¹**kill** [kil] *vb* **1** *(also fig)* doden, moorden, ombrengen: *my feet are* ~*ing me* ik verga van de pijn in mijn voeten; ~ *oneself laughing* (of: *with laughter*) zich een ongeluk lachen; ~ *off* afmaken, uit de weg ruimen, uitroeien; *be* ~*ed* om het leven komen; **2** *(socc)* doodmaken, doodleggen, stoppen: *dressed to* ~ er piekfijn uitzien

²**kill** [kil] *n* buit, vangst, (gedode) prooi || *be in at the* ~ erbij zijn als de vos gedood wordt, *(fig)* er (op het beslissende moment) bij zijn

killer [killə] moordenaar

¹**killing** [killing] *n* **1** moord, doodslag; **2** groot (financieel) succes^h: *make a* ~ zijn slag slaan, groot succes hebben

²**killing** [killing] *adj* **1** dodelijk, fataal; **2** slopend, uitputtend

killjoy spelbreker

kiln [kiln] oven

kilo [kie:loo] **1** kilo(gram); **2** kilometer

kilobyte [killəbajt] kilobyte *(1024 (=2¹⁰) bytes)*

kilogramme [killəgræm] kilogram

kilometre [killommittə] kilometer

kilowatt [killəwot] kilowatt

kilt [kilt] kilt

kin [kin] familie, verwanten: *kith and* ~ vrienden en verwanten; *next of* ~ naaste verwanten

¹**kind** [kajnd] *n* **1** soort, type^h, aard: *nothing of the* ~ niets van dien aard, geen sprake van; *three of a* ~ drie gelijke(n), drie dezelfde(n); *a* ~ *of* een soort; *all* ~*s of* allerlei; *I haven't got that* ~ *of money* zulke bedragen heb ik niet; **2** wijze, manier van doen; **3** wezen^h, karakter^h, soort: *pay in* ~ in natura betalen, *(fig)* met gelijke munt terugbetalen

²**kind** [kajnd] *adj* vriendelijk, aardig: *with* ~ *regards* met vriendelijke groeten; *would you be* ~ *enough to* (of: *so* ~ *as to*) *open the window* zou u zo vriendelijk willen zijn het raam open te doen

kindergarten [kindəga:tn] kleuterschool

¹kindle [kɪndl] *vb* **1** ontsteken; **2** opwekken, doen stralen, gloeien: *I don't know what ~d their hatred of him* ik weet niet waardoor ze hem zijn gaan haten

²kindle [kɪndl] *vb* ontbranden, (op)vlammen, vlam vatten: *such dry wood ~s easily* zo'n droog hout vat gemakkelijk vlam

kindling [kɪndlɪŋ] aanmaakhout^h

¹kindly [kajndlie] *adv* alstublieft: *~ move your car* zet u a.u.b. uw auto ergens anders neer; *he did not take ~ to all those rules* hij kon niet zo goed tegen al die regels

²kindly [kajndlie] *adj* vriendelijk, (goed)aardig: *in a ~ fashion* vriendelijk

kindness [kajndnəs] **1** vriendelijke daad, iets aardigs, gunst; **2** vriendelijkheid: *out of ~* uit goedheid

¹kindred [kɪndrɪd] *n* **1** verwantschap; **2** verwanten, familie(leden)

²kindred [kɪndrɪd] *adj* verwant: *a ~ spirit* een verwante geest

king [kɪŋ] koning, *(card game also)* heer

kingcup boterbloem

kingdom [kɪŋdəm] koninkrijk^h, rijk^h, domein^h

kingpin 1 *(bowling)* koning; **2** spil *(fig)*, leidende figuur

King's English standaard Engels, BBC-Engels

king-size(d) extra lang, extra groot

kink [kɪŋk] **1** kink, knik *(in wire etc)*; **2** kronkel, eigenaardigheid

kinky [kɪŋkie] **1** pervers; **2** sexy, opwindend *(of clothes)*

kinship [kɪnsjip] verwantschap, *(also fig)* overeenkomst, verbondenheid: *she felt a deep ~ with the other students in her group* ze voelde een diepe verbondenheid met de andere studenten in haar groep

kinsman [kɪnzmən] (bloed)verwant

kiosk [kie:osk] **1** kiosk, stalletje^h; **2** reclamezuil; **3** telefooncel

¹kip [kɪp] *n* **1** slaapplaats, bed^h; **2** dutje^h, slaap(je^h)

²kip [kɪp] *vb* (also with *down)* (gaan) pitten, (gaan) slapen

¹Kirghiz [kə:giz] *adj* Kirgizisch

²Kirghiz [kə:giz] *n* Kirgies

Kirghizstan [kə:gizsta:n] Kirgizië

¹kiss [kɪs] *n* kus(je^h), zoen(tje^h): *blow a ~* een kushandje geven, een kus toewerpen; *~ of life* mond-op-mondbeademing

²kiss [kɪs] *vb* **1** kussen, elkaar kussen, (elkaar) zoenen: *~ and be friends* het afzoenen, het weer goedmaken; **2** (even, licht) raken, *(billiards)* klotsen (tegen), een klos maken

kisser [kɪssə] snoet, waffel: *he smacked the thief in the ~* hij gaf de dief een klap voor zijn kanis

kissing disease knuffelziekte, ziekte van Pfeiffer

kit [kɪt] **1** (gereedschaps)kist, doos, (plunje)zak; **2** bouwdoos, bouwpakket^h; **3** uitrusting, spullen: *did you remember to bring your squash ~?* heb je eraan gedacht je squashspullen mee te brengen?

kitbag plunjezak

kitchen [kɪtsjin] keuken

kitchen garden moestuin, groentetuin

kite [kajt] **1** vlieger: *fly a ~* vliegeren, een vlieger oplaten, *(fig)* een balletje opgooien; **2** wouw: *go fly a ~* maak dat je weg komt

kitten [kɪtn] katje^h, poesje^h || *have ~s* de zenuwen hebben, op tilt slaan

kitty [kɪttie] **1** katje^h, poesje^h; **2** pot, inzet *(in card game)*, kas

kiwi [kie:wie:] **1** kiwi(vrucht); **2** Nieuw-Zeelander

klaxon [klæksən] claxon

km *kilometre(s)* km

knack [næk] **1** vaardigheid, handigheid, slag: *get the ~ of sth.* de slag te pakken krijgen van iets; **2** truc, handigheidje^h: *there's a ~ in it* je moet de truc even doorhebben

knacker [nækə] sloper

knackered [nækəd] bekaf, doodop

knapsack knapzak, plunjezak

knave [neev] **1** *(cards)* boer; **2** schurk

knead [nie:d] **1** (dooreen)kneden: *make sure you ~ the dough properly* zorg ervoor dat je het deeg goed kneedt; **2** kneden, masseren *(eg muscle)*

knee [nie:] **1** knie: *bring s.o. to his ~s* iem op de knieen krijgen; **2** kniestuk^h: *his ~s were knocking together* hij stond te trillen op zijn benen

kneecap 1 knieschijf; **2** kniebeschermer

kneel [nie:l] (also with *down)* knielen, geknield zitten

knees-up knalfuif, feest^h

knickers [nɪkkəz] slipje, onderbroek *(of woman)*

knick-knack [nɪknæk] prul(letje^h), snuisterij

¹knife [najf] *n (knives)* mes^h || *turn* (of: *twist) the ~* nog een trap nageven

²knife [najf] *vb* (door)steken, aan het mes rijgen

knight [najt] **1** ridder; **2** *(chess)* paard^h

knighthood [najthoed] ridderorde: *confer a ~ on s.o.* iem tot ridder slaan

¹knit [nɪt] *vb* **1** breien; **2** fronsen, samentrekken; **3** verweven, verbinden: *(their interests are) closely ~* (hun belangen zijn) nauw verweven

²knit [nɪt] *vb* één worden, vergroeien: *the broken bones ~ readily* de gebroken botten groeien weer snel aan elkaar

knitting [nɪttɪŋ] breiwerk^h

knob [nob] **1** knop, hendel, handvat^h, schakelaar; **2** knobbel, bult: *the ~ on her leg was quite visible* de bult op haar been was goed te zien; **3** brok(je^h), klontje^h

knobbly [noblie] knobbelig

knobby [nobie] knobbelig

¹knock [nok] *vb* kloppen, tikken: *~ at* (of: *on) a door* op een deur kloppen; *~ against sth.* tegen iets (op) botsen; *~ into s.o.* iem tegen het lijf lopen

²knock [nok] *vb* **1** (hard) slaan, meppen, stoten (tegen): *~ a hole in* een gat slaan in; **2** (af)kraken; **3** met stomheid slaan, versteld doen staan

³knock [nok] *n* **1** slag, klap, klop, tik; **2** oplazer: *take a lot of ~s* heel wat te verduren krijgen

knockabout 1 gooi-en-smijt- *(of films)*; **2** rouw-

douw
knock about 1 rondhangen, lanterfanten; **2** (rond)slingeren; **3** rondzwerven, rondscharrelen, vd hand in de tand leven: *~ with* optrekken met, scharrelen *(of:* rotzooien) met
knockdown 1 verpletterend, vernietigend; **2** afbraak-, spotgoedkoop
knock down 1 neerhalen, tegen de grond slaan, *(fig)* vloeren; **2** slopen, tegen de grond gooien; **3** aanrijden, omverrijden, overrijden; **4** naar beneden krijgen, afdingen, afpingelen: *knock s.o. down a pound* een pond bij iem afdingen; **5** verkopen *(at auction): the chair was knocked down at three pounds* de stoel ging weg voor drie pond
knock-kneed [nokni:d] met x-benen
knock off 1 (af)nokken (met), kappen, stoppen *(work);* **2** goedkoper geven, korting geven; **3** in elkaar draaien; **4** afmaken, nog doen; **5** *(inf)* jatten, beroven
knockout 1 *(boxing)* knock-out; **2** *(sport)* eliminatietoernooi[h], *(roughly)* voorronde; **3** spetter, juweel[h]: *you look a ~* je ziet eruit om te stelen
knock out 1 vloeren, knock-out slaan; **2** verdoven, bedwelmen *(of drug);* **3** *(sport)* uitschakelen, elimineren; **4** in elkaar flansen: *we knocked out a programme for the festivities* we flansten snel een programma voor de festiviteiten in elkaar
knock over 1 omgooien, neervellen, aan-, over-, omverrijden; **2** versteld doen staan; **3** overvallen, beroven
knock together in elkaar flansen, (slordig, haastig) in elkaar zetten
¹knock up *vb (tennis)* inslaan
²knock up *vb* **1** afbeulen, slopen; **2** bij elkaar verdienen *(money);* **3** zwanger maken
¹knot [not] *n* **1** knoop, strik *(as decoration);* **2** knoop *(fig),* moeilijkheid; **3** kwast, (k)noest; **4** kluitje mensen; **5** band, verbinding, huwelijksband; **6** knoop, zeemijl per uur, zeemijl || *get tied (up) into ~s (over)* van de kook raken door, de kluts kwijtraken (van, over)
²knot [not] *vb* **1** (vast)knopen, (vast)binden, een knoop leggen in; **2** dichtknopen, dichtbinden
knotty [nottie] **1** vol knopen, in de knoop (geraakt); **2** kwastig, knoestig *(of wood);* **3** ingewikkeld, lastig
¹know [noo] *vb* **1** weten, kennis hebben (van), beseffen: *if you ~ what I mean* als je begrijpt wat ik bedoel; *for all I ~ he may be in China* misschien zit hij in China, wie weet; *you ~* weet je (wel), je weet wel; *not that I ~ of* niet dat ik weet; **2** kennen, bekend zijn met: *~ one's way* de weg weten; **3** herkennen, (kunnen) thuisbrengen: *I knew Jane by her walk* ik herkende Jane aan haar manier van lopen; *don't I ~ it* moet je mij vertellen; *~ backwards (and forwards)* kennen als zijn broekzak, kunnen dromen; *~ better than to do sth.* (wel) zo verstandig zijn iets te laten
²know [noo] *n: in the ~* ingewijd, (goed) op de hoogte

know-how handigheid, praktische vaardigheid, technische kennis
knowledge [nollidzj] kennis, wetenschap, informatie, geleerdheid: *to the best of one's ~ (and belief)* naar (zijn) beste weten; *without s.o.'s ~* buiten iemands (mede)weten; *be common ~* algemeen bekend zijn
knowledgeable [nollidzjəbl] goed geïnformeerd, goed op de hoogte: *be ~ about* verstand hebben van
known 1 bekend, algemeen beschouwd, erkend; **2** gegeven, bekend || *make oneself ~ to* zich voorstellen aan
knuckle [nukl] knokkel || *rap on (of: over) the ~s* op de vingers tikken; *near the ~* op het randje *(of joke)*
knuckle down *(with to)* zich serieus wijden (aan) *(job, chore),* aanpakken, aanvatten: *it's high time you knuckled down to some hard study* het wordt hoog tijd dat je eens flink gaat studeren
knuckle under *(with to)* buigen (voor), zwichten (voor)
koala [kooa:lə] koala(beer)
kooky [koe:kie] verknipt, geschift
Koran [ko:ra:n] koran
kosher [koosjə] koosjer, jofel, in orde
kowtow [kautau] *(with to)* door het stof gaan (voor), zich verwederen
k.p.h. *kilometres per hour* km/u, kilometer per uur
Kurd [kə:d] Koerd
Kurdish [kə:disj] Koerdisch
kW *kilowatt(s)* kW

I. 1 *left* links; 2 *litre(s)* l; liter(s)
L. *learner driver*
¹**label** [leebl] *n* 1 etiket^h, label^h; 2 label^h *(of CD)*, platenmaatschappij; 3 etiket^h
²**label** [leebl] *vb* 1 etiketteren, labelen, merken; 2 een etiket opplakken, bestempelen als
laboratory [labo̱rratərie] laboratorium^h, proefruimte
laborious [labo̱ːriəs] 1 afmattend, bewerkelijk; 2 moeizaam
¹**labour** [leebə] *n* 1 arbeid, werk^h *(in employment)*; 2 (krachts)inspanning, moeite; 3 arbeidersklasse, arbeidskrachten; 4 (barens)weeën; 5 bevalling: *be in ~* bevallen
²**labour** [leebə] *vb* 1 arbeiden, werken; 2 zich inspannen, ploeteren: *~ at* (of: *over) sth.* op iets zwoegen; 3 moeizaam vooruitkomen, zich voortslepen
labourer [leebərə] (hand)arbeider, ongeschoolde arbeider: *agricultural ~* landarbeider
labour under te kampen hebben met, last hebben van
labyrinth [læbərinθ] doolhof, labyrint^h *(also fig)*
¹**lace** [lees] *n* 1 veter, koord^h; 2 kant(werk^h)
²**lace** [lees] *vb* 1 rijgen, dichtmaken met veter; 2 (door)vlechten, (door)weven; 3 een scheutje sterkedrank toevoegen aan: *~ tea with rum* een scheutje rum in de thee doen
lacerate [læsəreet] (ver)scheuren
¹**lack** [læk] *n* 1 gebrek^h, tekort^h: *die for* (of: *through) ~ of food* sterven door voedselgebrek; 2 behoefte
²**lack** [læk] *vb* 1 missen, niet hebben: *he simply ~s courage* het ontbreekt hem gewoon aan moed; 2 gebrek hebben aan, te kort komen
lackey [lækie] 1 lakei, livreiknecht; 2 kruiper
lacking [læking] afwezig, ontbrekend: *be ~ in* gebrek hebben aan
lacklustre dof, glansloos, mat *(of eyes)*
laconic [ləko̱nnik] kort en krachtig, laconiek
lacquer [lækə] 1 lak; 2 (blanke) lak, vernis^h; 3 (haar)lak
lactation [læktee̱sjən] 1 het zogen, melkvoeding; 2 lactatie(periode), zoogperiode
lad [læd] jongen, knul, jongeman || *be one of the ~s* erbij horen
ladder [lædə] 1 ladder *(also fig)*, trap(leer), touwladder; 2 ladder *(in stocking)*; 3 *(sport)* ladder,

ranglijst
Ladies(') [leediez] dames(toilet^h)
¹**ladle** [leedl] *n* soeplepel
²**ladle** [leedl] *vb* 1 opscheppen, oplepelen; 2 *(with out)* rondstrooien, smijten met
lady [leedie] 1 dame: *ladies and gentlemen* dames en heren; *(Am) First Lady* presidentsvrouw; 2 lady: *~ doctor* vrouwelijke arts
ladybird lieveheersbeestje^h
ladybug *(Am)* lieveheersbeestje^h
ladykiller vrouwenjager, (ras)versierder
ladylike [leedielajk] 1 ladylike, zoals een dame past, beschaafd; 2 elegant
¹**lag** [læg] *vb (with behind)* achterblijven, achteraan komen
²**lag** [læg] *vb* bekleden, betimmeren, isoleren *(pipes etc)*
lager [la̱ːgə] (blond) bier^h, *(fig)* pils^h
laggard [lægəd] treuzelaar, laatkomer, slome duikelaar^h
lagging [læging] bekleding(smateriaal^h), isolatie(materiaal^h), het bekleden
lagoon [ləgoo̱ːn] lagune
la(h)-di-da(h) [la:dieda̱ː] bekakt
laid-back relaxed, ontspannen
lair [leə] 1 hol^h, leger^h *(of wild animal)*; 2 hol^h *(fig)*, schuilplaats
laity [leeittie] 1 leken(dom^h), de leken; 2 leken(publiek^h), de leken
lake [leek] meer^h, vijver
lamb [læm] 1 lam(metje)^h, lamsvlees^h; 2 lammetje^h, lief kind^h, schatje^h
lame [leem] 1 mank, kreupel; 2 onbevredigend, nietszeggend: *~ excuse* zwak excuus; *~ duck* slappeling, zielige *(of:* behoeftige) figuur
¹**lament** [ləme̱nt] *vb* 1 *(with over)* klagen (over), jammeren (over); 2 treuren: *~ for a brother* treuren om een broer
²**lament** [ləme̱nt] *vb* (diep) betreuren, treuren om, bewenen
³**lament** [ləme̱nt] *n* 1 jammerklacht; 2 klaaglied^h
lamentable [læməntəbl] 1 betreurenswaardig, beklagenswaard(ig); 2 erbarmelijk (slecht), bedroevend (slecht)
laminate [læminneet] 1 in dunne lagen splijten; 2 lamineren, tot dunne platen pletten, bedekken met (metalen) platen: *~d wood* triplex, multiplex
lamp [læmp] lamp
¹**lampoon** [læmpoo̱ːn] *n* satire, schotschrift^h
²**lampoon** [læmpoo̱ːn] *vb* hekelen
lamp-post lantaarnpaal
lampshade lampenkap
lance [la:ns] lans, spies, speer
lancet [la̱ːnsit] lancet^h *(surgical knife)*
¹**land** [lænd] *n* 1 (vaste)land^h; 2 landstreek, staat, gebied^h: *native ~* vaderland; 3 bouwland^h, aarde, grond; grondgebied^h, lap grond, weiland^h: *the promised ~* het beloofde land
²**land** [lænd] *vb* 1 landen, aan land gaan; 2 (be)lan-

den, neerkomen, terechtkomen: ~ *in a mess* in de knoei raken; *(inf) I ~ed up in Rome* uiteindelijk belandde ik in Rome

³land [lænd] *vb* **1** aan wal zetten; **2** doen landen, aan de grond zetten *(aeroplane);* **3** doen belanden, brengen: ~ *s.o. in a mess* iem in de knoei brengen; **4** vangen, binnenhalen, binnenbrengen *(fish);* **5** in de wacht slepen, bemachtigen

landed [lændid] **1** land-, grond-, uit land bestaand: ~ *property* grondbezit; **2** land bezittend: ~ *gentry* (of: *nobility)* landadel

land forces landstrijdkrachten, landmacht

landing [lænding] **1** landingsplaats, steiger, aanlegplaats; **2** landing *(of aeroplane),* het aan wal gaan, aankomst *(of ship);* **3** overloop, (trap)portaalʰ

landing craft landingsvaartuigʰ, landingsschipʰ

landing gear landingsgestelʰ, onderstelʰ

landing net schepnetʰ

landing stage (aanleg)steiger, aanlegplaats, losplaats

landlady 1 hospita, pensionhoudster, waardin; **2** huisbazin, vrouw vd huisbaas

landlord 1 landheer; **2** huisbaas, pensionhouder, waard

landmark 1 grenspaal; **2** oriëntatiepuntʰ *(also fig),* markering, bakenʰ; **3** mijlpaal, keerpuntʰ

landscape [læn(d)skeep] landschapʰ, panoramaʰ

landslide [læn(d)slajd] aardverschuiving *(also fig):* *win by a ~* een verpletterende overwinning behalen

lane [leen] **1** (land)weggetjeʰ, laantjeʰ, paadjeʰ; **2** (voorgeschreven) vaarweg, vaargeul; **3** luchtcorridor, luchtweg, (aan)vliegroute; **4** *(traf)* rijstrook; **5** *(sport)* baan

language [længgwidzj] **1** taal: *foreign ~s* vreemde talen; **2** taalgebruikʰ, woordgebruikʰ, stijl; **3** (groeps)taal, vaktaal, jargonʰ; **4** communicatiesysteemʰ, gebarentaal, (programmeer)taal, computertaal; **5** taalbeheersing, spraak(vermogenʰ)

languid [længgwid] lusteloos, (s)loom, slap

languish [længgwisj] (weg)kwijnen, verslappen, verzwakken

languor [længgə] **1** apathie, lusteloosheid, matheid; **2** lome stilte, zwoelheid, drukkendheid

lank [længk] **1** schraal, (brood)mager, dun; **2** krachteloos, slap, sluik *(of hair);* **3** lang en buigzaam *(eg of hair)*

lantern [læntən] lantaarn

¹lap [læp] *n* **1** schoot *(also of article of clothing);* **2** overlap(ping), overlappend deelʰ, overslag; **3** *(sport)* baan, ronde; **4** etappe *(of trip)*

²lap [læp] *vb* (with *against)* kabbelen (tegen), klotsen (tegen)

³lap [læp] *vb* likken, oplikken: ~ *up* oplikken, opslorpen, *(fig)* verslinden

¹lapse [læps] *n* **1** kleine vergissing, fout(jeʰ); **2** misstap; **3** (tijds)verloopʰ, verstrijken van tijd; **4** periode, tijd(jeʰ), poos(jeʰ) *(in past)*

²lapse [læps] *vb* **1** (gaandeweg) verdwijnen, achteruitgaan, afnemen: *my anger had soon ~d* mijn

boosheid was weldra weggeëbd; **2** vervallen, terugvallen, afglijden: ~ *into silence* in stilzwijgen verzinken; **3** verstrijken, verlopen

lapsed [læpst] **1** afvallig, ontrouw; **2** *(law)* verlopen, vervallen

laptop (computer) schootcomputer

larceny [la:sənie] diefstal

¹lard [la:d] *n* varkensvetʰ, (varkens)reuzel

²lard [la:d] *vb* larderen *(also fig),* doorspekken, doorrijgen met spek

larder [la:də] provisiekamer, provisiekast

large [la:dzj] **1** groot, omvangrijk, ruim; **2** veelomvattend, ver(re)gaand; **3** onbevangen, gedurfd; **4** edelmoedig, vrijgevig || *as ~ as life: a)* in levenden lijve, hoogstpersoonlijk; *b)* onmiskenbaar; ~*r than life* overdreven, buiten proporties; *the murderer is still at ~* de moordenaar is nog steeds op vrije voeten

largely [la:dzjlie] grotendeels, hoofdzakelijk, voornamelijk

lark [la:k] **1** grap: *for a ~* voor de gein; **2** leeuwerik

larva [la:və] larve, larf

larynx [læringks] strottenhoofdʰ

lascivious [ləsjvviəs] wellustig, geil

laser [leezə] laser: ~ *beams* laserstralen

¹lash [læsj] *vb* **1** een plotselinge beweging maken (met), slaan, zwiepen *(eg of tail);* **2** met kracht slaan (tegen), geselen, teisteren, striemen *(of rain),* beuken *(of waves)*

²lash [læsj] *vb* **1** opzwepen, ophitsen: ~ *s.o. into a fury* iemand woedend maken; **2** vastsnoeren, (stevig) vastbinden, *(shipp)* sjorren

³lash [læsj] *n* **1** zweepkoordʰ, zweepeindeʰ; **2** zweepslag; **3** wimper

lash out 1 (with *at)* (heftig) slaan, schoppen (naar), uithalen (naar), een uitval doen (naar); **2** (with *at, against)* uitvallen (tegen); **3** met geld smijten

lassie [læsie] meisjeʰ

lassitude [læsitjoe:d] vermoeidheid, uitputting

¹lasso [læsoe:] *n* lasso, werpkoordʰ

²lasso [læsoe:] *vb* met een lasso vangen

¹last [la:st] *num* laatste *(also fig),* vorige, verleden: *at the ~ minute* (of: *moment)* op het laatste ogenblik; ~ *night* gister(en)avond, vannacht; ~ *Tuesday* vorige week dinsdag; *the ~ but one* de voorlaatste; *the ~ few days* de laatste paar dagen; *that's the ~ straw* dat doet de deur dicht; *the ~ word in cars* het nieuwste snufje op het gebied van auto's; *down to every ~ detail* tot in de kleinste details

²last [la:st] *vb* **1** duren, aanhouden; **2** meegaan, intact blijven, houdbaar zijn: *his irritation won't ~* zijn ergernis gaat wel over; ~ *out: a)* niet op raken; *b)* het volhouden; **3** toereikend zijn

³last [la:st] *vb* toereikend zijn voor, voldoende zijn voor

⁴last [la:st] *adv* **1** als laatste, *(in compounds)* laatst-: *come in* ~ als laatste binnenkomen; *last-mentioned* laatstgenoemde; ~ *but not least* (als) laatstgenoemde, maar daarom niet minder belangrijk; **2** (voor)

het laatst, (voor) de laatste keer: *when did you see her ~?* (of: *~ see her?*) wanneer heb je haar voor het laatst gezien?

⁵last [la:st] *num* laatste *(of a series)*, laatstgenoemde: *breathe one's ~* zijn laatste adem uitblazen; *fight to* (of: *till*) *the ~* vechten tot het uiterste; *I don't think we have seen the ~ of him* ik denk dat we nog wel terugzien; *at (long) ~* (uit)eindelijk, ten slotte

⁶last [la:st] *n* (schoenmakers)leest ‖ *stick to one's ~* zich bij zijn leest houden

lasting [la:sting] blijvend, aanhoudend, duurzaam: *a ~ solution* een definitieve oplossing

lastly [la:stlie] ten slotte, in de laatste plaats, tot slot

last-minute allerlaatst, uiterst

latch [lætsj] klink *(of door, gate): on the ~* op de klink *(not locked)*

latchkey huissleutel

latch on to 1 snappen, (kunnen) volgen; 2 hangen aan, zich vastklampen aan

¹late [leet] *adj* 1 te laat, verlaat, vertraagd: *five minutes ~* vijf minuten te laat; 2 laat, gevorderd: *in the ~ afternoon* laat in de middag; *at a ~ hour* laat (op de dag), diep in de nacht; *at the ~st* uiterlijk, op zijn laatst; 3 recent, vd laatste tijd, nieuw: *her ~st album* haar nieuwste album; 4 voormalig, vorig; 5 (onlangs) overleden, wijlen: *his ~ wife* zijn (onlangs) overleden vrouw

²late [leet] *adv* 1 te laat, verlaat, vertraagd: *better ~ than never* beter laat dan nooit; 2 laat, op een laat tijdstip, gevorderd: *~ in (one's) life* op gevorderde leeftijd; *~r on: a)* later, naderhand; *b)* verderop; *of ~* onlangs, kort geleden

lately [leetlie] onlangs, kort geleden

late-night laat(st), nacht-: *~ shopping* koopavond

lateral [lætrəl] zij-, aan, vanaf, naar de zijkant

lath [la:θ] 1 tengel(lat), latwerkʰ; 2 lat

lather [la:ðə] (zeep)schuimʰ, scheerschuimʰ

¹Latin [lætin] *n* 1 Latijn *(language);* 2 Romaan, (een) Romaans(e taal) sprekende

²Latin [lætin] *adj* Latijns: *~ America* Latijns-Amerika

latitude [lætitjoe:d] 1 hemelstreek, luchtstreek, zone; 2 (geografische) breedte, poolshoogte; 3 speelruimte, (geestelijke) vrijheid

latrine [lətrie:n] latrine, (kamp, kazerne) wc

latter [lætə] 1 laatstgenoemde *(of two);* 2 laatst(genoemd) *(of two): the ~ part of the year* het tweede halfjaar; *in his ~ years* in zijn laatste jaren

lattice [lætis] raster(werk)ʰ, vak-, raam-, traliewerkʰ, roosterʰ: *lattice window* glas-in-loodraam

Latvia [lætviə] Letland

laudable [lo:dəbl] prijzenswaardig

¹laugh [la:f] *vb* 1 lachen: *~ to oneself* inwendig lachen; 2 in de lach schieten, moeten lachen

²laugh [la:f] *vb* 1 lachend zeggen; 2 belachelijk maken, uitlachen, weglachen: *~ off* met een grapje afdoen

³laugh [la:f] *n* 1 lach, gelachʰ, lachjeʰ; 2 geintjeʰ, lolletjeʰ, lachertjeʰ: *for ~s* voor de lol; *have the last ~*

het laatst lachen

laughable [la:fəbl] lachwekkend, belachelijk

laugh at 1 uitlachen, belachelijk maken; 2 lachen om, maling hebben aan

laughing [la:fing] 1 lachend, vrolijk, opgewekt; 2 om te lachen: *no ~ matter* een serieuze zaak, geen gekheid

laughing stock mikpuntʰ (van spot) *(also of things)*

laughter [la:ftə] 1 gelachʰ; 2 plezierʰ, pret, lol

¹launch [lo:ntsj] *vb* (also with *out*) (energiek) iets (nieuws) beginnen: *~ out into business for oneself* voor zichzelf beginnen; *~ into* zich storten op

²launch [lo:ntsj] *vb* 1 lanceren, afvuren, (weg)werpen, (weg)smijten; 2 te water laten; 3 op gang brengen, (doen) beginnen, op touw zetten

³launch [lo:ntsj] *n* 1 motorsloep; 2 rondvaartboot, plezierboot; 3 tewaterlating; 4 lancering

launching pad lanceerplatformʰ, *(fig)* springplank

launder [lo:ndə] 1 wassen (en strijken); 2 witmaken *(black money)*

launderette [lo:ndərɛt] wasserette

laundry [lo:ndrie] 1 wasserij, wasinrichting; 2 was, wasgoedʰ

laurel [lorrəl] 1 laurier; 2 lauwerkrans, erepalm; 3 *~s* lauweren, roem, eer: *rest on one's ~s* op zijn lauweren rusten

lavatory [lævətərie] 1 toiletʰ, wc, openbaar toiletʰ; 2 toiletpot

lavender [lævəndə] lavendel

¹lavish [lævisj] *adj* 1 kwistig, gul, verkwistend; 2 overvloedig, overdadig: *~ praise* overdadige lof

²lavish [lævisj] *vb* kwistig schenken

law [lo:] 1 wet, rechtʰ, rechtsregel, wetmatigheid, natuurwet: *~ and order* orde en gezag, recht en orde; *be a ~ unto oneself* zijn eigen wetten stellen, eigenmachtig optreden; 2 wet(geving), rechtsstelselʰ; 3 rechten(studie), rechtsgeleerdheid; 4 rechtʰ, rechtsgang, justitie, gerechtʰ: *go to ~* naar de rechter stappen, een proces aanspannen; 5 (gedrags)code, (spel)regel, norm, beroeps-, sport-, kunstcode; 6 *(inf)* politie, sterke arm: *take the ~ into one's own hands* het recht in eigen hand nemen; *~ of the jungle* recht van de sterkste; *lay down the ~: a)* de wet voorschrijven; *b)* snauwen, blaffen

law-abiding gezagsgetrouw, gehoorzaam aan de wet

law centre wetswinkel

law court rechtscollegeʰ, rechtbank, gerechtshofʰ

lawful [lo:foel] 1 wettig, legaal, rechtsgeldig; 2 rechtmatig, geoorloofd, legitiem

lawless [lo:ləs] 1 wetteloos; 2 onstuimig, losbandig, wild

lawn [lo:n] 1 gazonʰ, grasveldʰ; 2 batistʰ, linnenʰ

lawnmower grasmaaier, gras(maai)machine

lawsuit procesʰ, (rechts)gedingʰ, (rechts)zaak

lawyer [lo:jə] 1 advocaat, (juridisch) raadsman; 2 jurist, rechtsgeleerde

lax [læks] laks, nalatig: *~ about keeping appointments* laks in het nakomen van afspraken

¹laxative [læksətiv] *adj* laxerend

²laxative [læksətiv] *n* laxeermiddelʰ

¹lay *vb* **1** leggen, neerleggen (= neervlijen); **2** installeren, leggen, plaatsen, zetten, dekken *(table): the scene of the story is laid in Oxford* het verhaal speelt zich af in Oxford; **3** (eieren) leggen; **4** in een bepaalde toestand brengen, leggen, zetten, brengen: *~ bare* blootleggen, *(fig)* aan het licht brengen; *~ low: a)* tegen de grond werken; *b)* (vernietigend) verslaan; *c) (fig)* vellen *(eg of disease)*; *~ waste* verwoesten; **5** riskeren, op het spel zetten, (ver)wedden: *~ a wager* een weddenschap aangaan; *~ in: a)* inslaan; *b)* opslaan

²lay *vb* wedden ‖ *~ into* ervan langs geven *(also fig)*

³lay *adj* leken-, niet-priesterlijk, wereldlijk

⁴lay *n* ligging, positie: *(Am) the ~ of the land* de natuurlijke ligging van het gebied, *(fig also)* de stand van zaken

layabout nietsnut

lay about wild (om zich heen) slaan, te lijf gaan, ervan langs geven *(also fig)*

lay aside 1 opzijleggen, sparen, wegleggen, bewaren; **2** laten varen, opgeven *(plan, hope)*

lay down 1 neerleggen: *~ one's tools* staken; **2** vastleggen, voorschrijven, bepalen: *~ a procedure* een procedure uitstippelen; **3** opgeven, laten varen, neerleggen *(office)*

layer [leeə] **1** laag: *~ of sand* laag zand; **2** legger *(chicken)*, leghen

layman [leemən] leek, amateur, niet-deskundige

¹lay off *vb* stoppen, ophouden, opgeven: *~, will you?* laat dat, ja?

²lay off *vb* (tijdelijk) ontslaan, op non-actief stellen, laten afvloeien

lay on zorgen voor, regelen, organiseren: *~ a car* een auto regelen; *lay it on (thick): a)* (sterk, flink) overdrijven, het er dik opleggen; *b)* slijmen

layout indeling, ontwerpʰ, bouwplanʰ

lay out 1 uitgeven, investeren; **2** uitspreiden, etaleren, klaarleggen *(clothing);* **3** afleggen, opbaren *(corpse)*

lay up 1 opslaan, een voorraad aanleggen van, inslaan; **2** uit de roulatie halen, het bed doen houden: *he was laid up with the flu* hij moest in bed blijven met de griep

laze [leez] luieren, niksen: *~ about* (of: *around)* aanklooien, rondlummelen

lazy [leezie] **1** lui; **2** loom, drukkend: *~ day* lome dag

lb. *libra* lb., Engels pond, 454 gram

L-driver *learner-driver* leerling-automobilist

¹lead [lie:d] *vb* **1** leiden, voorgaan, de weg wijzen, begeleiden; **2** aan de leiding gaan, aanvoeren, op kop liggen, *(sport)* voorstaan, een voorsprong hebben op, *(fig)* de toon aangeven: *Liverpool ~s with sixty points* Liverpool staat bovenaan met zestig punten; **3** voeren, leiden *(of road, route); (fig)* resulteren in: *~ to disaster* tot rampspoed leiden; **4** leiden, aanvoeren, het bevel hebben (over): *~ off (with)* begin-

nen (met)

²lead [lie:d] *vb* **1** (weg)leiden, (mee)voeren *(by the hand, on a rope etc);* **2** brengen tot, overhalen, aanzetten tot: *~ s.o. to think that* iem in de waan brengen dat; **3** leiden *(existence, life): ~ a life of luxury* een weelderig leven leiden; *~ away* meeslepen, blind(elings) doen volgen; *~ (s.o.) on: a)* (iem) overhalen (tot); *b)* iem iets wijsmaken; *~ up to: a)* (uiteindelijk) resulteren in; *b)* een inleiding *(of:* voorbereiding) zijn tot

³lead [lie:d] *n* **1** leiding, het leiden: *take the ~* de leiding nemen, het initiatief nemen; **2** aanknopingspuntʰ, aanwijzing, suggestie: *give s.o. a ~* iem op weg helpen, iem een hint geven; **3** leiding, koppositie, eerste plaats; **4** voorsprong; **5** hoofdrol, *(by extension)* hoofdrolspeler; **6** (honden)lijn, hondenriem

⁴lead [led] *n* **1** loodʰ; **2** (diep)loodʰ, peilloodʰ, pasloodʰ; **3** (potlood)stift, grafietʰ ‖ *swing the ~* zich drukken, lijntrekken

leaden [ledn] **1** loden, van lood; **2** loodgrijs, loodkleurig

leader [lie:də] **1** leider, aanvoerder, gids; **2** eerste man, partijleider, voorman, *(mus)* concertmeester, eerste violist, *(Am; music)* dirigent; **3** *(journalism)* hoofdcommentaarʰ

leading [lie:ding] **1** voornaam(st), hoofd-, toonaangevend: *~ actor* hoofdrolspeler; **2** leidend, (be)sturend: *~ question* suggestieve vraag

lead singer [lie:d singə] leadzanger

¹leaf [lie:f] *n (leaves)* **1** bladʰ *(of tree, plant),* (bloem)bladʰ; **2** bladʰ, bladzijde *(of book);* **3** uitklapbare klep, insteek-, uitschuifbladʰ *(of table);* **4** *(as second part in compounds)* folie, blad- *(of metal): gold ~* bladgoud

²leaf [lie:v] *vb* bladeren: *~ through* (snel) doorbladeren

leaflet [lie:flit] **1** blaadjeʰ; **2** foldertjeʰ, brochure

league [lie:g] **1** *(sport)* bond, competitie, divisie; **2** klasse, niveauʰ: *she's not in my ~* ik kan niet aan haar tippen; *in ~ with* in samenwerking met, samenspannend met

¹leak [lie:k] *n* **1** lekʰ, lekkage, ongewenste ontsnapping: *spring a ~* lek raken; *(inf) take a ~* pissen; **2** uitlekking, ruchtbaarheid *(of secret data)*

²leak [lie:k] *vb* lekken, lek zijn, (lekkend) doorlaten, *(information)* onthullen: *~ information (out) to the papers* gegevens aan de kranten doorspelen; *(fig) ~ out* (laten) uitlekken, (onbedoeld) bekend worden

leakage [lie:kidzj] lekkage, lekʰ

¹lean [lie:n] *adj* mager, schraal, karig

²lean [lie:n] *vb* **1** leunen; **2** steunen, staan (tegen); **3** zich buigen: *~ down* zich bukken; *~ over to s.o.* zich naar iem overbuigen; **4** hellen, scheef staan: *~ over backwards* zich in (de gekste) bochten wringen, alle mogelijke moeite doen; *~ on* onder druk zetten; *~ to (of: towards): a)* neigen tot; *b)* prefereren; *~ (up)on* steunen op, afhankelijk zijn van

³lean [lie:n] *vb* **1** laten steunen, zetten (tegen); **2** buigen, doen hellen: *the Leaning Tower of Pisa* de scheve toren van Pisa; ~ *one's head back* zijn hoofd achteroverbuigen; **3** mager, schraal; **4** arm(zalig), weinig opleverend: ~ *years* magere jaren

¹leap [lie:p] *vb* (op)springen, vooruitspringen: ~ *for joy* dansen van vreugde; *her heart ~ed up* haar hart maakte een sprongetje; ~ *at* met beide handen aangrijpen *(chance etc)*

²leap [lie:p] *n* sprong, gesprongen afstand, plotselinge toename, hindernis, obstakel^h || *by ~s and bounds* halsoverkop; *(fig)* a ~ *in the dark* een sprong in het duister

¹leapfrog *n* haasje-over^h, bokspringen^h

²leapfrog *vb* sprongsgewijs vorderen

³leapfrog *vb* haasje-over spelen, bokspringen

leap year schrikkeljaar^h

¹learn [lɜ:n] *vb* **1** leren, studeren: ~ *how to play the piano* piano leren spelen; ~ *from experience* door ervaring wijzer worden; **2** horen, vernemen, te weten komen: ~ *about* (of: *of*) *sth. from the papers* iets uit de krant te weten komen

²learn [lɜ:n] *vb* **1** leren, zich eigen maken, bestuderen; **2** vernemen, horen van, ontdekken: *I learnt it from the papers* ik heb het uit de krant

learned [lɜ:nid] **1** onderlegd, ontwikkeld, geleerd; **2** belezen; **3** wetenschappelijk, academisch: ~ *periodical* wetenschappelijk tijdschrift

learner [lɜ:nə] **1** leerling; **2** beginner, beginneling; **3** leerling-automobilist

¹lease [lie:s] *n* **1** pacht, pachtcontract^h; **2** (ver)huur, (ver)huurcontract^h, -overeenkomst; **3** pachttermijn, huurtermijn, pachtduur

²lease [lie:s] *vb* **1** (ver)pachten; **2** (ver)huren, leasen

leash [lie:sj] (honden)lijn, riem: *always keep Sarah on the* ~ houd Sarah altijd aangelijnd; *strain at the* ~ trappelen van ongeduld

¹least [lie:st] *adv, pron* minst(e): *the ~ popular leader* de minst populaire leider; *to say the* ~ *(of it)* om het zachtjes uit te drukken; *at (the)* ~ *seven* ten minste zeven; *it didn't bother me in the* ~ het stoorde mij helemaal niet

²least [lie:st] *adj* kleinste, geringste: *I haven't the* ~ *idea* ik heb er geen flauw idee van; *the line of* ~ *resistance* de weg van de minste weerstand

¹leather [leðə] *n* leer^h

²leather [leðə] *adj* leren, van leer

¹leave [lie:v] *vb* weggaan (bij, van), verlaten, vertrekken (bij, van): *it's time for you to* ~, *it's time you left* het wordt tijd dat je weggaat

²leave [lie:v] *vb* **1** laten liggen, laten staan, achterlaten, vergeten: ~ *about* (of: *around*) laten (rond)slingeren; **2** laten staan, onaangeroerd laten: ~ *(sth.) undone* (iets) ongedaan laten; *be left with* (blijven) zitten met, opgescheept worden met; **3** overlaten, doen overblijven: *four from six ~s two* zes min vier is twee; **4** afgeven, achterlaten: ~ *a note for s.o.* een boodschap voor iem achterlaten; **5** toevertrouwen, in bewaring geven; **6** nalaten, achterlaten: ~ *it at that* het er (maar) bij laten; ~ *(people) to* themselves zich niet bemoeien met (mensen)

³leave [lie:v] *n* **1** toestemming, permissie, verlof^h: ~ *of absence* verlof, vakantie; *by* (of: *with*) *your* ~ met uw permissie; **2** verlof^h, vrij, vakantie: *on* ~ met verlof; *take one's* ~ *of s.o.: a)* iem gedag zeggen; *b)* afscheid nemen van iem

leave behind 1 thuis laten, vertrekken zonder, vergeten (mee te nemen); **2** (alleen) achterlaten, in de steek laten: *John was left behind* John werd (alleen) achtergelaten; **3** achter zich laten, passeren

¹leave off *vb* ophouden, stoppen

²leave off *vb* **1** uit laten *(not wear any longer)*, niet meer dragen; **2** staken, stoppen met

leave out 1 buiten laten (liggen, staan); **2** weglaten, overslaan, niet opnemen; **3** buitensluiten: *feel left out* zich buitengesloten voelen

leavings [lie:vingz] overschot, overblijfsel(en), etensresten

lecherous [letsjərəs] **1** wellustig, liederlijk; **2** geil, hitsig

¹lecture [lektsjə] *n* **1** lezing, verhandeling, voordracht; **2** (hoor)college^h, (openbare) les; **3** preek, berisping: *read s.o. a* ~ iem de les lezen

²lecture [lektsjə] *vb* **1** spreken (voor), lezing(en) geven (voor); **2** college geven (aan), onderrichten

³lecture [lektsjə] *vb* de les lezen

lecturer [lektsjərə] **1** spreker, houder van lezing; **2** docent *(in higher educ)*

LED *light-emitting diode* LED

ledge [ledzj] richel, (uitstekende) rand

ledger [ledzjə] *(bookkeeping)* grootboek^h, *(Am also)* register^h

lee [lie:] **1** luwte, beschutting, beschutte plek; **2** *(shipp)* lij(zijde)

leech [lie:tsj] bloedzuiger, *(fig)* uitzuiger, parasiet || *cling* (of: *stick*) *like a* ~ *(to)* niet weg te branden zijn (bij)

leek [lie:k] prei

¹leer [liə] *n* **1** wellustige blik; **2** wrede grijns, vuile blik

²leer [liə] *vb* **1** loeren, grijnzen; **2** verlekkerd kijken, wellustige blikken werpen

leeway (extra) speelruimte, speling, *(Am)* veiligheidsmarge

¹left *adj* **1** linker, links; **2** *(pol)* links

²left *n* **1** linkerkant, links^h, linkerhand: *keep to the* ~ links (aan)houden; *turn to the* ~ links afslaan; **2** *(pol)* links^h, de progressieve

³left *adv* **1** links, aan de linkerzijde; **2** naar links, linksaf, linksom: *turn* ~ links afslaan

left-back linksachter

left-hand links, linker: ~ *bend* bocht naar links; ~ *drive* linkse besturing *(of car)*

left-handed 1 links(handig); **2** links, onhandig; **3** dubbelzinnig, dubieus: ~ *compliment* twijfelachtig compliment

leftovers [leftoovəz] **1** (etens)restjes, kliekje(s); **2** kliekjesmaaltijd

leg [leg] **1** been^h; **2** poot *(of animal)*, achterpoot; **3**

beengedeelte^h van kledingstuk, been^h *(of stocking),* (broeks)pijp; **4** poot *(of furniture etc);* **5** gedeelte^h (van groter geheel^h), etappe *(of trip, competition etc),* estafetteonderdeel^h, manche *(of competition);* **6** bout *(of calf, lam):* ~ *of mutton* schapenbout; **7** schenkel: ~ *of veal* kalfsschenkel; *give s.o. a* ~ *up* iem een voetje geven, *(fig)* iem een handje helpen; *pull s.o.'s* ~ iem voor de gek houden; *run s.o. off his* ~*s: a)* iem geen seconde met rust laten; *b)* iem uitputten; *shake a* ~ opschieten; *not have a* ~ *to stand on* geen poot hebben om op te staan; *stretch one's* ~*s* de benen strekken *(by means of a walk);* walk *s.o. off his* ~*s* iem laten lopen tot hij erbij neervalt

legacy [legəsie] erfenis *(also fig),* nalatenschap

legal [lie:gl] **1** wettig, legaal, rechtsgeldig: ~ *tender* wettig betaalmiddel; **2** wettelijk, volgens de wet; **3** juridisch: *(free)* ~ *aid* kosteloze rechtsbijstand

legality [ligælittie] rechtsgeldigheid, rechtmatigheid

legalize [lie:gəlajz] legaliseren, wettig maken

legend [ledzjənd] **1** (volks)overlevering, legende(n); **2** onderschrift^h, opschrift^h

legendary [ledzjəndərie] legendarisch *(also fig)*

legging [leging] beenkap, beenbeschermer, scheenbeschermer

legible [ledzjibl] leesbaar

legion [lie:dzjən] legioen^h

¹legionary [lie:dzjənərie] *n* legionair, legioensoldaat

²legionary [lie:dzjənərie] *adj* legioens-

legislation [ledzjisleesjən] wetgeving

legislative [ledzjislətiv] **1** wetgevend, bevoegd tot wetgeving; **2** wets-, mbt wetgeving

legislator [ledzjisleetə] wetgever, lid^h ve wetgevend lichaam

legit [lidzjit] *legitimate* wettig, legaal, okay

legitimate [lidzjittimmət] **1** wettig, rechtmatig, legitiem; **2** geldig: ~ *purpose* gerechtvaardigd doel

leg-pull plagerij, beetnemerij

leg-up steuntje^h, duwtje^h, zetje^h *(in the right direction)*

¹leisure [lezjə] *n* (vrije) tijd, gelegenheid: *at* ~ vrij, zonder verplichtingen, ontspannen; *at one's* ~ in zijn vrije tijd, als men tijd heeft, als het schikt

²leisure [lezjə] *adj* **1** vrij: ~ *hours* vrije uren; **2** vrijetijds-

leisurely [lezjəlie] zonder haast (te maken), ontspannen, op zijn gemak

lemon [lemmən] **1** citroen; **2** *(inf)* idioot; **3** miskoop, maandagochtendexemplaar^h

lemonade [lemməneed] (citroen)limonade

lemon squash 1 citroensiroop; **2** citroenlimonade

lend [lend] **1** (uit)lenen: ~ *s.o. a book* iem een boek lenen; **2** verlenen, schenken, geven: ~ *assistance to* steun verlenen aan; ~ *itself to: a)* zich (goed) lenen tot; *b)* vatbaar zijn voor

length [lengθ] **1** lengte, omvang, (lichaams)lengte, grootte, gestalte: ~ *of a book* omvang van een boek; *three centimetres in* ~ drie centimeter lang; **2** lengte,

duur: *for the* ~ *of our stay* voor de duur van ons verblijf; **3** eind(je)^h, stuk(je)^h: ~ *of rope* eindje touw; *go to considerable* (of: *great*) ~*s* erg z'n best doen, zich veel moeite getroosten; *at* ~: *a)* langdurig; *b)* uitvoerig; *c)* ten slotte; *go to* (of: *all*) ~*s/any* ~*(s)* er alles voor over hebben; *at some* ~ uitvoerig

lengthen [lengθən] verlengen, langer maken: ~ *a dress* een jurk langer maken

lengthy [lengθie] **1** langdurig; **2** langdradig

lenience [lie:niəns] toegevendheid, mildheid

lenient [lie:niənt] **1** tolerant, toegevend; **2** mild, genadig: ~ *verdict* mild vonnis

lens [lenz] lens

lentil [lentl] linze

leopard [leppəd] luipaard, panter

leotard [lie:əta:d] tricot^h, balletpakje^h, gympakje^h

leper [leppə] lepralijder, melaatse

leprosy [leprəsie] lepra, melaatsheid

¹lesbian [lezbiən] *adj* lesbisch

²lesbian [lezbiən] *n* lesbienne

¹less [les] *adv, pron* minder: ~ *money* minder geld; *he couldn't care* ~ het kon hem geen barst schelen; *more or* ~ min of meer; *none the* ~ niettemin

²less [les] *adj* kleiner: *no* ~ *a person than* niemand minder dan

³less [les] *prep* zonder, verminderd met, op … na: *a year* ~ *one month* een jaar min één maand

lessen [lesn] (ver)minderen, (doen) afnemen

lesser [lessə] minder, kleiner, onbelangrijker: *to a* ~ *extent* in mindere mate

lesson [lesn] **1** les, leerzame ervaring: *let this be a* ~ *to you* laat dit een les voor je zijn; **2** leerstof; **3** lesuur^h; **4** schriftlezing, bijbellezing: *teach s.o. a* ~ iem een lesje leren

lest [lest] (voor het geval, uit vrees) dat, opdat niet: *she was afraid* ~ *he leave her* ze vreesde dat hij haar zou verlaten

¹let [let] *vb* **1** laten, toestaan: ~ *sth. be known* iets laten weten; *please,* ~ *me buy this round* laat mij nou toch dit rondje aanbieden; **2** laten: ~ *me hear* (of: *know)* hou me op de hoogte; ~ *me see* eens kijken; ~*'s not talk about it* laten we er niet over praten; **3** *(maths)* stellen, geven: ~ *x be y+ z* stel x is y+ z, geven x is y+ z; **4** verhuren, in huur geven; **5** aanbesteden: ~ *s.o. be* iem met rust laten; ~ *fly (at)* uithalen (naar); ~ *s.o. get on with it* iem zijn gang laten gaan; ~ *go (of)* loslaten, uit zijn hoofd zetten, ophouden (over); ~ *oneself go* zich laten gaan; ~ *s.o. have it* iem de volle laag geven, iem ervan langs geven; ~ *slip: a)* laten uitlekken; *b)* missen, voorbij laten gaan *(chance);* ~ *through* laten passeren, doorlaten; ~ *into: a)* binnenlaten in, toelaten tot; *b)* in vertrouwen nemen over, vertellen

²let [let] *vb* **1** verhuurd worden; **2** uitbesteed worden || *(inf)* ~ *on (about, that)* verklappen, doorvertellen (dat); *(inf)* ~ *on (that)* net doen (alsof)

³let [let] *n* **1** *(sport, esp tennis)* let(bal), overgespeelde bal; **2** beletsel^h, belemmering: *without* ~ *or hindrance* vrijelijk, zonder (enig) beletsel

let down 1 neerlaten, laten zakken, laten vallen; **2** teleurstellen, in de steek laten: *don't let me down* laat me niet in de steek; **3** leeg laten lopen *(tyre)*
let-down afknapper, teleurstelling
lethal [li:θl] dodelijk, fataal
lethargy [leθədzjie] lethargie, (s)loomheid
let in binnenlaten, toelaten: *let oneself in* zich toegang verschaffen; ~ *for* opschepen met, laten opdraaien voor; *let oneself in for* zich op de hals halen; ~ *on: a)* in vertrouwen nemen over, inlichten over; *b)* laten meedoen met
let off 1 afvuren, afsteken, af laten gaan: ~ *fireworks* vuurwerk afsteken; **2** excuseren, vrijuit laten gaan, vrijstellen van: *the judge let him off* de rechter liet hem vrijuit gaan; *be ~ with* er afkomen met
¹let out *vb* **1** uithalen, van leer trekken: ~ *at s.o.* naar iem uithalen, tegen iem uitvaren; **2** dichtgaan, sluiten, uitgaan *(of school etc)*
²let out *vb* **1** uitnemen, wijder maken *(clothing);* **2** laten uitlekken, verklappen, openbaar maken, bekendmaken; **3** laten ontsnappen, vrijlaten, laten gaan: *let the air out of a balloon* een ballon laten leeglopen; **4** geven *(scream);* **5** de laan uitsturen, ontslaan, (van school) sturen
letter [letə] **1** letter; **2** brief: ~ *to the editor* ingezonden brief; ~ *of introduction* aanbevelingsbrief; *covering* ~ begeleidend schrijven; *by* ~ per brief, schriftelijk; *to the* ~ naar de letter, tot in detail, tot de kleinste bijzonderheden; **3** ~*s* letteren, literatuur
letterhead 1 briefhoofd[h]; **2** postpapier[h] met briefhoofd
lettuce [lettis] sla, salade: *a head of* ~ een krop sla
let up 1 minder worden, afnemen, gaan liggen: *I hope the wind's going to* ~ *a little* ik hoop dat de wind wat gaat liggen; **2** het kalm aan doen, gas terugnemen; **3** pauzeren, ophouden (met werken)
leukaemia [loe:ki:miə] leukemie, bloedkanker
¹level [levl] *adj* **1** waterpas, horizontaal; **2** vlak, egaal, zonder oneffenheden: ~ *teaspoon* afgestreken theelepel; **3** (op) gelijk(e hoogte), even hoog: ~ *crossing* gelijkvloerse kruising, overweg; *draw* ~ *with* op gelijke hoogte komen met; **4** gelijkmatig, evenwichtig, regelmatig: *in a* ~ *voice* zonder stemverheffing; **5** bedaard, kalm: *keep a* ~ *head* zijn verstand erbij houden; **6** gelijkwaardig, op gelijke voet; **7** strak *(of look),* doordringend: *give s.o. a* ~ *look* iem strak aankijken; *(do) one's* ~ *best* zijn uiterste best (doen)
²level [levl] *n* **1** peil[h], niveau[h], hoogte, natuurlijke plaats: ~ *of achievement* (of: *production)* prestatiepeil, productiepeil; *find one's* ~ zijn plaats vinden; **2** vlak[h], (vlak) oppervlak[h], vlakte, vlak land[h]; **3** horizontaal; **4** *(Am)* waterpas: *(inf) on the* ~ rechtdoorzee, goudeerlijk; **5** niveau[h]: *at ministerial* ~ op ministerieel niveau
³level [levl] *vb* (horizontaal) richten, aanleggen, afvuren, uitbrengen *(cricism etc):* ~ *a charge against* (of: *at) s.o.* een beschuldiging tegen iem uitbrengen
⁴level [levl] *vb* **1** egaliseren, effenen; **2** nivelleren, op

gelijk niveau brengen, opheffen *(distinction):* ~ *down* tot hetzelfde niveau omlaag brengen; ~ *up* tot hetzelfde niveau omhoog brengen
⁵level [levl] *adv* vlak, horizontaal, waterpas
level-headed nuchter, afgewogen
¹lever [li:və] *n* **1** hefboom, koevoet, breekijzer[h]; **2** werktuig[h] *(only fig),* pressiemiddel[h], instrument[h]; **3** hendel, handgreep, handvat[h]
²lever [li:və] *vb* opheffen d.m.v. hefboom, tillen, (los)wrikken: ~ *s.o. out of his job* iem wegmanoeuvreren
leverage [li:vəridzj] **1** hefboomwerking, hefboomkracht; **2** macht, invloed, pressie: *even small groups can exert enormous political* ~ zelfs kleine groeperingen kunnen enorme politieke pressie uitoefenen
levity [levvitie] lichtzinnigheid, lichtvaardigheid, oneerbiedigheid
¹levy [levvie] *n* heffing, vordering, belastingheffing: *make a* ~ *on* een heffing instellen op
²levy [levvie] *vb* **1** heffen, opleggen: ~ *a fine* een boete opleggen; **2** vorderen, innen; **3** (aan)werven, rekruteren
lewd [ljoe:d] **1** wellustig; **2** obsceen, schunnig
lexicography [leksikkogrəfie] lexicografie, het samenstellen van woordenboeken
lexicology [leksikkollədzjie] lexicologie *(study of words)*
lexicon [leksikkən] woordenboek[h]
liability [lajjəbillittie] **1** (wettelijke ver)plicht(ing): ~ *to pay taxes* belastingplichtigheid; **2** *-ies* passiva, lasten, schulden; **3** blok aan het been
liable [lajjəbl] **1** (wettelijk) verplicht: ~ *for tax* belastingplichtig; **2** *(with for)* aansprakelijk (voor), (wettelijk) verantwoordelijk (voor); **3** vatbaar, vaak lijdend: ~ *to colds* vaak verkouden; **4** de neiging hebbend, het risico lopend: *it isn't* ~ *to happen* dat zal niet zo gauw gebeuren
liaison [lie:eezn] **1** liaison *(also mil),* verbinding, *(by extension)* samenwerkingsverband[h]; **2** buitenechtelijke verhouding
liana [lie:annə] liaan
liar [lajjə] leugenaar
¹libel [lajbl] *n* **1** smaadschrift[h]; **2** smaad, laster, belastering
²libel [lajbl] *vb* **1** belasteren, valselijk beschuldigen; **2** een smaadschrift publiceren tegen
¹liberal [libbərəl] *adj* **1** ruimdenkend, onbevooroordeeld, liberaal; **2** royaal, vrijgevig; **3** overvloedig, welvoorzien ‖ ~ *arts* vrije kunsten
²liberal [libbərəl] *n* liberaal, ruimdenkend iem
liberate [libbəreet] bevrijden
liberated [libbəreetid] bevrijd, geëmancipeerd *(socially, sexually)*
liberation [libbəreesjən] bevrijding, vrijlating
libero [libbəroo] *(socc)* vrije verdediger
liberty [libbətie] **1** vrijheid, onafhankelijkheid: ~ *of conscience* gewetensvrijheid; *at* ~*: a)* in vrijheid, op vrije voeten; *b)* vrij, onbezet; *c)* ongebruikt, werk-

loos; **2** vrijheid, vrijmoedigheid: *take liberties with s.o.* zich vrijheden veroorloven tegen iem
librarian [lajbrɛəriən] bibliotecaris
library [lajbrərie] bibliotheek, (openbare) leeszaal, uitleenverzameling *(of films, CDs etc)*
Libya [libbiə] Libië
¹licence [lajsns] *n* **1** vergunning, licentie, verlofʰ; **2** verlofʰ, permissie, toestemming; **3** vrijheid; **4** losbandigheid, ongebondenheid; **5** (artistieke) vrijheid
²licence [lajsns] *vb* (een) vergunning verlenen (aan), een drankvergunning verlenen (aan), (officieel) toestemming geven voor: *he will only stay at ~d hotels* hij logeert alleen in hotels met een drankvergunning; *~d to sell tobacco* met tabaksvergunning
licensee [lajsnsie:] vergunninghouder, licentiehouder *(of liquor licence, tobacco licence)*
license plate *(Am)* nummerbordʰ
licentious [lajsensjəs] wellustig
¹lick [lik] *vb* **1** likken; **2** *(inf)* een pak slaag geven *(also fig)*, ervan langs geven, overwinnen: *~ a problem* een probleem uit de wereld helpen
²lick [lik] *vb* lekken, (licht) spelen (langs) *(of waves, flames)*: *the flames ~ed (at) the walls* de vlammen lekten (aan) de muren
³lick [lik] *n* **1** lik, veeg, *(by extension)* ietsjeʰ, klein beetjeʰ: *a ~ of paint* een kwastje (verf); **2** (vliegende) vaart: *(at) full ~, at a great ~* met een noodgang
licking [likking] pakʰ rammel: *the team got a ~* het team werd ingemaakt
lid [lid] **1** dekselʰ, klep; **2** (oog)lidʰ ‖ *take the ~ off* onthullingen doen; *that puts the ~ on* dat doet de deur dicht
¹lie [laj] *vb* **1** (plat, uitgestrekt, vlak) liggen, rusten; **2** (begraven) liggen, rusten: *here ~s ... hier ligt ...*; **3** gaan liggen, zich neerleggen; **4** zich bevinden *(in a place, situation)*, liggen, gelegen zijn: *~ fallow* braak liggen; *my sympathy ~s with ...* mijn medeleven gaat uit naar ...; *I don't know what ~s in store for me* ik weet niet wat me te wachten staat
²lie *vb* liegen, jokken
³lie *n* **1** leugen: *tell a ~* liegen; **2** ligging, situering, positie: *the ~ of the land* de natuurlijke ligging van het gebied, *(fig)* de stand van zaken; *give the ~ to* weerleggen
lie about 1 luieren, niksen; **2** (slordig) in het rond liggen, rondslingeren *(of objects)*
lie down (gaan) liggen: *(fig) we won't take this lying down* we laten dit niet over onze kant gaan
liege [lie:dʒ] **1** leenheer; **2** leenman, vazal
lie in *(inf)* uitslapen, lang in bed blijven liggen
lie over overstaan, blijven liggen, uitgesteld worden: *let sth. ~* iets uitstellen
lieu [ljoe:]: *in ~ of* in plaats van
lie up 1 zich schuilhouden, onderduiken; **2** het bed houden, platliggen
lieutenant [leftɛnnənt] *(mil)* luitenant
lie with zijn aan, de verantwoordelijkheid zijn van, afhangen van: *the choice lies with her* de keuze is aan haar

life [lajf] *(lives)* **1** levend wezenʰ, levenʰ: *several lives were lost* verscheidene mensen kwamen om het leven; **2** levenʰ, bestaanʰ, levendigheid, bedrijvigheid, levensduur, levensbeschrijving: *a matter of ~ and death* een zaak van leven of dood; *make ~ easy* niet moeilijk doen; *you (can) bet your ~* nou en of!, wat dacht je!; *bring to ~* (weer) bijbrengen, *(fig)* tot leven wekken; *come to ~: a)* bijkomen, tot leven komen; *b) (fig)* geïnteresseerd raken; *save s.o.'s ~* iemands leven redden; *take one's (own) ~* zelfmoord plegen; *for ~* voor het leven, levenslang; *for the ~ of me I couldn't remember it* al sla je me dood, ik weet het echt niet meer; *this is the ~!* dit noem ik nog eens leven!; **3** levenslang(e gevangenisstraf): *take one's ~ in one's (own) hands* zijn leven in de waagschaal stellen; *the ~ (and soul) of the party* de gangmaker van het feest; *start ~* zijn carrière beginnen; *not on your ~* nooit van zijn leven
lifebelt redding(s)gordel
lifebuoy redding(s)boei
lifeguard 1 badmeester, strandmeester; **2** lijfwacht
life jacket redding(s)vestʰ
lifeline 1 redding(s)lijn; **2** vitale verbindingslijn, navelstreng *(fig)*
life-raft redding(s)vlotʰ
lifespan (potentiële) levensduur
lifestyle levensstijl
lifetime levensduur, mensenlevenʰ: *the chance of a ~* een unieke kans
¹lift [lift] *vb* **1** (omhoog-, op)tillen, omhoog-, optrekken, (op)hijsen: *not ~ a hand* geen hand uitsteken; **2** opheffen, afschaffen: *~ a blockade* een blokkade opheffen; **3** verheffen, op een hoger plan brengen: *this news will ~ his spirits* dit nieuws zal hem opbeuren; **4** rooien, uit de grond halen; **5** verheffen, luider doen klinken: *~ up one's voice* zijn stem verheffen
²lift [lift] *vb* **1** (op)stijgen, opgaan, opkomen, omhooggaan, omhoogkomen: *~ off* opstijgen, starten; **2** optrekken *(of mist etc)*
³lift [lift] *n* **1** lift; **2** lift, gratis (auto)rit; **3** (ver)heffing
ligament [ligəmənt] gewrichtsband
¹light [lajt] *n* **1** lichtʰ, verlichting, openbaarheid: *bring to ~* aan het licht brengen; *reversing ~* achteruitrijlicht; *see the ~* het licht zien, tot inzicht komen; *shed (of: throw) ~ (up)on* licht werpen op, klaarheid brengen in; **2** vuurtjeʰ, vlammetjeʰ: *can you give me a ~, please?* heeft u misschien een vuurtje voor me?; *set (a) ~ to sth.* iets in de fik steken; *see the ~ at the end of the tunnel* licht in de duisternis zien; *a shining ~* een lichtend voorbeeld; *in (the) ~ of this statement* gezien deze verklaring
²light [lajt] *adj* **1** licht, niet zwaar: *~ clothing* lichte kleding; *~ food* licht (verteerbaar) voedsel; *~ of heart* licht-, luchthartig; *(sport) ~ heavyweight* halfzwaargewicht; *~ opera* operette; *make ~ work of* zijn hand niet omdraaien voor; *make ~ of* niet zwaar tillen aan; **2** licht, verlicht, helder
³light [lajt] *vb* **1** aansteken: *~ a fire* een vuur aanste-

ken; **2** verlichten, beschijnen: *~ed* (of: *lit*) *by electricity* elektrisch verlicht

⁴light [lajt] *vb* **1** ontbranden, vlam vatten; **2** aan gaan, gaan branden *(of lamp etc);* **3** opklaren, oplichten *(also of face, eyes)*

⁵light [lajt] *adv* licht: *sleep ~* licht slapen; *travel ~* weinig bagage bij zich hebben

¹lighten [lajtn] *vb* **1** verlichten, ontlasten, *(fig)* opbeuren; **2** verlichten, verhelderen

²lighten [lajtn] *vb* **1** lichter worden, afnemen in gewicht; **2** opleven, opfleuren; **3** ophelderen, opklaren; **4** klaren, dagen; **5** bliksemen, (weer)lichten

lighter [lajtə] aansteker

light-headed licht-, warhoofdig

light-hearted luchthartig

lighthouse vuurtoren

lighting [lajting] verlichting

lightly [lajtlie] **1** licht(jes), een ietsje; **2** licht(jes), gemakkelijk; **3** luchtig, lichtvaardig

lightning [lajtning] bliksem, weerlichtʰ: *forked ~* vertakte bliksem(straal); *like (greased) ~* als de (gesmeerde) bliksem; *~ conductor* bliksemafleider

¹light up *vb* **1** (ver)licht(ing) aansteken, de lamp(en) aandoen; **2** *(inf)* (een sigaar, sigaret, pijp) opsteken

²light up *vb* **1** aansteken, ontsteken; **2** verlichten

¹like [lajk] *vb* houden van, (prettig) vinden, (graag) willen: *would you ~ a cup of tea?* wilt u een kopje thee?; *I'd ~ to do that* dat zou ik best willen; *how do you ~ your egg?* hoe wilt u uw ei?

²like [lajk] *vb* willen, wensen: *if you ~* zo u wilt, als je wilt

³like [lajk] *n* **1** *~s* voorkeuren: *~s and dislikes* sympathieën en antipathieën; **2** soortgenoot, (soort)gelijke: *(inf) the ~s of us* mensen als wij, ons soort (mensen); *I've never seen the ~ of it* zo iets heb ik nog nooit meegemaakt

⁴like [lajk] *prep* **1** als, zoals, gelijk aan: *cry ~ a baby* huilen als een kind; *it is just ~ John to forget it* echt iets voor John om het te vergeten; *~ that* zo, op die wijze; *just ~ that* zo maar (even); *what is he ~?* wat voor iemand is hij?; *what is it ~?* hoe voelt dat nou?; *more ~ ten pounds than nine* eerder tien pond dan negen; **2** (zo)als: *take a science ~ chemistry* neem nou scheikunde; *it hurts ~ anything* het doet erg veel pijn; *that's more ~ it* dat begint er op te lijken; *there's nothing ~ a holiday* er gaat niets boven een vakantie; *something ~ five days* om en nabij vijf dagen

⁵like [lajk] *adj* soortgelijk, (soort)verwant: *they are as ~ as two peas (in a pod)* ze lijken op elkaar als twee druppels water

⁶like [lajk] *conj* **1** (zo)als, op dezelfde wijze als: *(inf) they ran ~ crazy* ze liepen zo hard zij konden; *it was ~ in the old days* het was zoals vroeger; **2** *(inf)* alsof: *it looks ~ he will win* het ziet ernaar uit dat hij zal winnen

⁷like [lajk] *adv* **1** *(inf)* weet je, wel: *he thinks he's clever ~* hij vindt zichzelf best wel slim; **2** *(inf)* nou, zo-iets als: *her request was … ~ … unusual, you know*

haar verzoek was … nou ja … ongebruikelijk, weet je

likeable [lajkəbl] innemend, aardig, sympathiek

¹likely [lajklie] *adj* waarschijnlijk, aannemelijk, *(by extension)* kansrijk: *he is the most ~ candidate for the job* hij komt het meest in aanmerking voor de baan; *he is ~ to become suspicious* hij wordt allicht achterdochtig

²likely [lajklie] *adv* waarschijnlijk: *not ~!* kun je net denken!; *as ~ as not* eerder wel dan niet

like-minded gelijkgestemd

likeness [lajknəs] gelijkenis, overeenkomst: *it's a good ~* het lijkt er goed op *(eg of photo)*

likewise [lajkwajz] **1** evenzo, insgelijks; **2** evenzeer

liking [lajking] voorkeur, voorliefde: *have a ~ for* houden van, gek zijn op; *is your room to your ~?* is uw kamer naar wens?

lilac [lajlək] **1** sering; **2** lilaʰ

lily [lillie] lelie

limb [lim] **1** lid(maat) *(plural: ledematen)*, arm, beenʰ; **2** (dikke, grote) tak || *out on a ~* op zichzelf aangewezen

limbo [limboo] **1** voorportaalʰ (der hel); **2** vergetelheid; **3** opsluiting; **4** onzekerheid, twijfel: *be in ~* in onzekerheid verkeren

lime [lajm] **1** limoen; **2** linde; **3** gebrande kalk

limelight kalklichtʰ: *in the ~* in de schijnwerpers

limestone kalksteen⁺ʰ

limey [lajmie] *(Am; inf)* Brit, Engelsman

¹limit [limmit] *n* limiet, (uiterste) grens: *(Am) go the ~* tot het uiterste gaan; *(Am; esp mil) off ~s (to)* verboden terrein (voor); *within ~s* binnen bepaalde grenzen; *you're the ~* je bent onmogelijk

²limit [limmit] *vb* begrenzen, beperken: *~ing factors* beperkende factoren; *~ to* beperken tot

limitation [limmiteesjən] beperking, begrenzing: *he has his ~s* hij heeft zijn beperkingen

limited [limmitid] beperkt, gelimiteerd || *~ (liability) company* naamloze vennootschap

¹limp [limp] *vb* **1** mank lopen, slecht ter been zijn; **2** haperen, horten

²limp [limp] *n* kreupele (slepende) gang, mankheid: *he walks with a ~* hij trekt met zijn been

³limp [limp] *adj* (ver)slap(t)

limpid [limpid] (glas)helder

¹line [lajn] *n* **1** lijn, snoerʰ, koordʰ: *the ~ is bad* de verbinding is slecht *(telephone);* **2** smalle streep, lijn: *we must draw the ~ somewhere* we moeten ergens een grens trekken; *in ~ with* het verlengde van, *(fig)* in overeenstemming met; **3** rij (naast, achter elkaar), *(mil)* linie, stelling: *come* (of: *fall) into ~* op één lijn gaan zitten, zich schikken; *read between the ~s* tussen de regels door lezen; *all along the ~: a)* over de (ge)hele linie; *b) (also fig)* van begin tot eind; **4** kort briefjeʰ, krabbeltjeʰ: *drop s.o. a ~* iem een briefje schrijven; **5** beleidslijn, gedragslijn: *~ of thought* zienswijze, denkwijze; **6** koers, route, weg *(also fig): ~ of least resistance* weg van de minste weerstand; **7** lijndienst; **8** spoorweglijn, spoor^h; **9** terrein^h *(fig)*, vlak^h, branche: *banking is his ~* hij zit in het bankwezen; **10** assortiment^h, soort artikel^h; **11** lint^h, lont, band; **12** *~s* (straf)regels, strafwerk^h; **13** *~s* trouwakte; **14** *~s* methode, aanpak: *do sth. along* (of: *on) the wrong ~s* iets verkeerd aanpakken; *lay* (of: *put) it on the ~:* a) betalen; *b)* open kaart spelen; *sign on the dotted ~:* a) (een contract) ondertekenen; *b)* *(inf)* niet tegenstribbelen; *c)* in het huwelijksbootje stappen; *toe the ~* in het gareel blijven; *on ~* aan het werk, functionerend; *out of ~* uit de pas, over de schreef

²line [lajn] *vb* **1** liniëren: *~d paper* gelinieerd papier; **2** flankeren: *a road ~d with trees* een weg met (rijen) bomen erlangs; **3** voeren, (van binnen) bekleden: *~d with fur* met bont gevoerd; *~ one's nest* (of: *pocket, purse)* zijn zakken vullen, zijn beurs spekken

lineage [linnie·idzj] **1** geslacht^h, nageslacht^h; **2** afkomst

linear [linniə] lineair, lengte-, recht(lijnig): *~ measure* lengtemaat

linen [linnin] **1** linnen^h, lijnwaad^h; **2** linnengoed^h

liner [lajnə] **1** lijnboot; **2** lijntoestel^h

linesman [lajnzmən] **1** *(sport)* grensrechter, lijnrechter; **2** lijnwerker

¹line up *vb* in de rij gaan staan: *(fig) ~ alongside* (of: *with)* zich opstellen naast

²line up *vb* **1** opstellen in (een) rij(en); **2** op een rij zetten, samenbrengen

linger [linggə] **1** treuzelen, dralen: *~ over details* lang stilstaan bij details; **2** (zwakjes) voortleven: *the memory ~s on* de herinnering leeft voort

lingo [linggoo] *(~es)* taal(tje)^h, (vak)jargon^h: *at least I master the commercial ~ they use over there* in elk geval beheers ik het handelstaaltje dat ze daar spreken

linguist [linggwist] **1** talenkenner, talenwonder^h; **2** taalkundige, linguïst

linguistic [linggwistik] taalkundig, linguïstisch

linguistics [linggwistiks] taalkunde, linguïstiek: *applied ~* toegepaste taalkunde

lining [lajning] voering(stof), (binnen)bekleding

¹link [lingk] *n* **1** schakel *(also fig)*, verbinding, verband^h: *missing ~* ontbrekende schakel; **2** presentator; **3** *~s (sport)* (golf)links, golfbaan

²link [lingk] *vb* een verbinding vormen, zich verbinden, samenkomen: *~ up* zich aaneensluiten

³link [lingk] *vb* verbinden, koppelen: *~ hands* de handen ineenslaan

linkman [lingkmæn] **1** presentator; **2** middenvelder; **3** bemiddelaar, tussenpersoon

link-up verbinding, koppeling

linoleum [linnooliəm] linoleum^h

lion [lajjən] **1** leeuw; **2** idool^h

lioness [lajjənis] leeuwin

lip [lip] **1** lip: *(fig) hang on s.o.'s ~s* aan iemands lippen hangen; *my ~s are sealed* ik zwijg als het graf; **2** rand; **3** praatjes, grote mond: *we don't want any of your ~* hou jij je praatjes maar voor je

lip-service lippendienst: *give* (of: *pay) ~ to* lippendienst bewijzen aan

lipstick lippenstift

liquefy [likwiffaj] smelten, vloeibaar worden (maken)

liqueur [likjoeə] likeur(tje^h)

¹liquid [likwid] *n* vloeistof, vocht^h

²liquid [likwid] *adj* **1** vloeibaar; **2** *(com)* liquide, vlottend: *~ assets* liquide middelen

liquidate [likwiddeet] elimineren, uit de weg ruimen

liquidity [likwiddittie] **1** vloeibaarheid; **2** *(com)* liquiditeit

liquidizer [likwiddajzə] mengbeker, sapcentrifuge

liquor [likkə] alcoholische drank, alcohol, *(Am)* sterkedrank

liquorice [likkəris] **1** zoethout^h, zoethoutwortel; **2** drop

¹lisp [lisp] *vb* **1** brabbelen, krompraten *(of child);* **2** lispelen, slissen

²lisp [lisp] *n* slissende uitspraak, geslis^h: *he speaks with a ~* hij slist

¹list [list] *n* **1** lijst, tabel; **2** *(shipp)* slagzij; **3** *~s* strijdperk^h, ring: *enter the ~s (against)* in het krijt treden (tegen)

²list [list] *vb* **1** een lijst maken van, rangschikken in een lijst; **2** op een lijst zetten: *~ed buildings* op de monumentenlijst geplaatste gebouwen

³list [list] *vb (shipp)* slagzij maken

listen [lisn] luisteren: *~ in (to)* (mee)luisteren (naar), afluisteren; *~ to* luisteren naar

listener [lissənə] luisteraar

listless [listləs] lusteloos, futloos

lit 1 aan(gestoken), brandend; **2** verlicht, beschenen

literacy [littərəsie] alfabetisme^h, het kunnen lezen en schrijven

literal [littrəl] letterlijk, letter-

literary [littrərie] **1** literair, letterkundig; **2** geletterd: *~ man* gelettered man, letterkundige

literate [littrət] geletterd: *only half the children in this group are ~* niet meer dan de helft van de kinderen in deze groep kan lezen en schrijven

literature [littrətsjə] **1** literatuur, letterkunde: *the ~ of* (of: *on) a subject* de literatuur over een onderwerp; **2** *(inf)* voorlichtingsmateriaal^h

Lithuania [liθjjoe·eeniə] Litouwen

litigation [littigeesjən] proces^h, procesvoering, rechtszaak

litmus paper lakmoespapier(tje)^h

litre [lie:tə] liter

litter [littə] **1** rommel, rotzooi, troep; **2** (stal)stro^h, afdekstro^h *(for plants);* stalmest; **3** nest^h (jongen), worp: *have a ~ of kittens* jongen, jongen krijgen

litterbin afvalbak, prullenmand

¹little [litl] *adj* **1** klein: *a ~ bit* een (klein) beetje; *~ finger* pink; *his ~ sister* zijn jongere zusje; *her ~ ones* haar kinderen; *its ~ ones* haar jongen; *a ~ klein(zielig), kleintjes: ~ minds* kleingeestigen: *things please little little minds* kleine mensen, kleine wensen

²little [lɪtl] *pron* weinig, beetje: *he got ~ out of it* het bracht hem maar weinig op; *make ~ of sth.* ergens weinig van begrijpen; *~ or nothing* weinig of niets; *~ by ~* beetje bij beetje; *every ~ helps* alle beetjes helpen

³little [lɪtl] *adv* **1** weinig, amper, gering: *~ more than an hour* iets meer dan een uur; **2** volstrekt niet: *~ did he know that ...* hij had er geen flauw benul van dat ...

liturgy [lɪttədzjie] liturgie

¹live [liv] *vb* **1** leven, bestaan: *~ and let ~* leven en laten leven; *long ~ the Queen!* (lang) leve de koningin!; *~ together* samenleven, samenwonen; *~ above* (of: *beyond*) *one's means* boven zijn stand leven; *~ for: a*) leven voor; *b*) toeleven naar; *~ with a situation* (hebben leren) leven met een situatie; **2** wonen: *~ in* inwonen, intern zijn; *~ on one's own* op zichzelf wonen; **3** voortleven: *you haven't ~d yet!* je hebt nog helemaal niet van het leven genoten!

²live [liv] *vb* **1** leven: *~ a double life* een dubbelleven leiden; **2** beleven, doormaken, meemaken: *~ it up* het ervan nemen, de bloemetjes buiten zetten

³live [lajv] *adj* **1** levend, in leven (zijnd): *~ bait* levend aas; *a real ~ horse!* een heus paard!; **2** direct, rechtstreeks: *~ broadcast* directe uitzending; **3** levendig, actief: *a ~ topic* een actueel onderwerp; **4** onder spanning staand: *~ wire* onder spanning staande draad, *(fig)* energieke figuur; *~ ammunition* scherpe munitie

liveable [lɪvvəbl] **1** bewoonbaar; **2** leefbaar

livelihood [lajvliehoed] levensonderhoud[h]: *earn* (of: *gain*) *one's ~* de kost verdienen

lively [lajvlie] levendig: *~ colours* sprekende kleuren

liven [lajvn] verlevendigen, opfleuren: *~ up* opfleuren, opvrolijken

liver [lɪvvə] lever

livery [lɪvvərie] livrei, uniform[h]

livestock [lajvstok] vee[h], levende have

live up to naleven, waarmaken: *~ one's reputation* zijn naam eer aan doen

livid [lɪvvid] **1** hels, des duivels: *~ at* razend op; **2** lijkbleek, asgrauw; **3** loodgrijs, blauwgrijs

¹living [lɪvving] *adj* **1** levend, bestaand: *(with)in ~ memory* bij mensenheugenis; **2** levendig: *he's the ~ image of his father* hij is het evenbeeld van zijn vader

²living [lɪvving] *n* **1** inkomen[h], kostwinning: *earn* (of: *gain, get, make*) *a ~ (as, out of, by)* de kost verdienen (als); **2** leven[h], levensonderhoud[h]

lizard [lɪzzəd] hagedis

llama [la:mə] lama(wol)

¹load [lood] *n* **1** lading, last *(also fig)*: *that takes a ~ off my mind* dat is een pak van mijn hart; **2** belasting, massa; **3** (elektrisch) vermogen[h], kracht; **4** *(inf)* hoop, massa's: *they have ~s of money* ze barsten van het geld

²load [lood] *vb* laden, geladen worden, bevrachten:

the table was ~ed with presents de tafel stond vol met cadeaus

³load [lood] *vb* laden *(firearms, camera)*

loaded [loodid] **1** geladen, emotioneel geladen; **2** *(inf)* stomdronken; **3** *(Am; inf)* stoned; **4** venijnig, geniepig: *a ~ question* een strikvraag

loaf [loof] *(loaves)* **1** brood[h]: *a ~ of brown bread* een bruin brood; **2** brood(suiker)[h]; **3** kop, hersens: *use your ~ for once* denk nu eens een keer na

loaf about rondhangen, lummelen

loafer [loofə] **1** leegloper, lanterfanter; **2** *(Am)* lage schoen, loafer

loam [loom] leem[+h]

¹loan [loon] *n* **1** lening: *apply for a ~ with a bank* een lening bij een bank aanvragen; **2** leen[h], tijdelijk gebruik[h]: *have sth. on ~ from s.o.* iets van iem te leen hebben; *thank you for the ~ of your car* bedankt voor het lenen van je auto

²loan [loon] *vb* (uit)lenen: *~ money to a friend* geld aan een vriend lenen

loanword leenwoord[h]

loath [looθ] ongenegen, afkerig: *the elderly couple were ~ to leave the house at night* het oudere echtpaar ging 's avonds niet graag de deur uit

loathe [looð] verafschuwen

loathing [looðing] afkeer

loathsome [looðsəm] walgelijk, weerzinwekkend

lob [lob] **1** *(tennis)* lobben; **2** *(inf)* gooien, smijten

¹lobby [lobbie] *n* **1** hal[h], portaal[h]; **2** foyer; **3** lobby, pressiegroep

²lobby [lobbie] *vb* lobbyen, druk uitoefenen op de politieke besluitvorming

³lobby [lobbie] *vb* in de wandelgangen bewerken, onder druk zetten *(MPs)*

lobe [loob] **1** (oor)lel; **2** kwab, lob *(of brain, lung)*

lobster [lobstə] zeekreeft

¹local [lookl] *adj* plaatselijk, lokaal, buurt-, streek-: *~ authority* plaatselijke overheid; *~ call* lokaal gesprek; *~ government* plaatselijk bestuur

²local [lookl] *n* **1** plaatselijke bewoner, inboorling; **2** *(inf)* stamcafé[h], stamkroeg

locality [lookælittie] plaats, district[h], buurt

localize [lookəlajz] lokaliseren, tot een bepaalde plaats beperken, een plaats toekennen: *they hoped to ~ the outbreak of polio* ze hoopten de uitbarsting van polio tot een klein gebied te beperken

¹locate [lookeet] *vb* **1** de positie bepalen van, opsporen: *I can't ~ that village anywhere* ik kan dat dorp nergens vinden; **2** vestigen, plaatsen, stationeren: *the estate was ~d on the bank of a river* het landgoed was gelegen aan de oever van een rivier

²locate [lookeet] *vb (Am)* zich vestigen, gaan wonen, een zaak opzetten

location [lookeesjən] **1** plaats, ligging, positie; **2** terrein[h], afgebakend land[h]; **3** lokatie: *filmed on ~ in Australia* op lokatie gefilmd in Australië

loch [loch] **1** meer[h]; **2** smalle (ingesloten) zeearm

¹lock [lok] *n* **1** (haar)lok; **2** slot[h] *(also of firearms)*, sluiting: *under ~ and key* achter slot en grendel, *(fig)* in de gevangenis; **3** vergrendeling; **4** (schut)sluis; **5** houdgreep: ~, *stock, and barrel* in zijn geheel, alles inbegrepen

²lock [lok] *vb* **1** (af)sluiten, op slot doen; **2** wegsluiten, opsluiten *(also fig): don't forget to ~ away your valuables* vergeet niet je kostbaarheden op te bergen

³lock [lok] *vb* sluiten, vergrendeld (kunnen) worden: *the doors wouldn't ~* de deuren wilden niet sluiten

locker [lokkə] kast(je[h]), kluis *(eg for clothing, luggage)*

locksmith slotenmaker

¹lock up *vb* **1** op slot doen, afsluiten; **2** opbergen, wegsluiten: *~ one's gold and silver* zijn goud en zilver veilig opbergen; **3** opsluiten, wegstoppen *(in prison, madhouse)*

²lock up *vb* afsluiten, alles op slot doen

lock-up 1 arrestantenhok[h], cachot[h], nor, bajes; **2** afsluitbare ruimte, kiosk, dagwinkel, opbergbox

locomotion [lookəmoosjən] (voort)beweging(svermogen[h])

locomotive [lookəmootiv] locomotief

locust [lookəst] **1** sprinkhaan; **2** *(Am)* cicade

lodestar leidster *(also fig)*, poolster

¹lodge [lodzj] *vb* **1** verblijven, (tijdelijk) wonen, logeren: *~ at a friend's, ~ with a friend* bij een vriend wonen; **2** vast komen te zitten, blijven steken: *the bullet ~d in the ceiling* de kogel bleef in het plafond steken

²lodge [lodzj] *vb* **1** onderdak geven, logeren, (tijdelijk) huisvesten; **2** indienen, voorleggen: *~ a complaint* een aanklacht indienen

³lodge [lodzj] *n* **1** (schuil)hut; **2** personeelswoning, portierswoning; **3** afdeling, (vrijmetselaars)loge

lodger [lodzjə] kamerbewoner, (kamer)huurder

lodgings [lodzjiŋgz] (gehuurde) kamer(s)

loft [loft] zolder(kamer), vliering, hooizolder

lofty [loftie] **1** torenhoog; **2** verheven, edel: *~ ideals* hooggestemde idealen; **3** hooghartig, arrogant: *behave loftily to s.o.* (erg) uit de hoogte doen tegen iem

¹log [log] *n* **1** blok(hout)[h], boomstronk, boomstam; **2** logboek[h], scheepsjournaal[h] || *sleep like a ~* slapen als een os

²log [log] *vb* in het logboek opschrijven || *the truck driver had ~ged up 700 miles* de vrachtrijder had er 700 mijl op zitten; *~ into a computer system* inloggen

logarithm [logəriðm] logaritme

logbook 1 logboek[h], scheepsjournaal[h], journaal[h] ve vliegtuig, werkverslag[h], dagboek[h], reisjournaal[h]; **2** registratiebewijs[h] *(of car)*

log cabin blokhut

logger [logə] *(Am)* houthakker

loggerhead: *they are always at ~s with each other* ze liggen altijd met elkaar overhoop

logic [lodzjik] logica, redeneerkunde

logical [lodzjikl] logisch, steekhoudend, vanzelfsprekend (volgend uit)

logistics [lədzjistiks] logistiek

logo [loogoo] **1** logotype[h], woordmerk[h]; **2** logo[h], beeldmerk[h], firma-embleem[h]

loin [lojn] lende

¹loiter [lojtə] *vb* treuzelen: *~ about* (of: *around*) rondhangen; *~ with intent* zich verdacht ophouden

²loiter [lojtə] *vb* verdoen, verlummelen: *~ away one's time* zijn tijd verdoen

loll [lol] (rond)hangen, lummelen, leunen

lollipop [lolliepop] (ijs)lolly: *~ man* klaar-over

lolly [lollie] **1** lolly; **2** *(vulg)* poen

lone [loon] alleen, verlaten, eenzaam: *be (of: play) a ~ hand (fig)* met niemand rekening houden; *~ wolf* iem die zijn eigen weg gaat

lonely [loonlie] eenzaam, verlaten, alleen

loner [loonə] eenzame, eenling

lonesome [loonsəm] eenzaam, alleen: *by (of: on) his ~* in zijn (dooie) eentje

¹long [loŋ] *adj* lang, langgerekt, langdurig, ver, langlopend: *a ~ haul: a)* een hele ruk *(eg a long trip); b)* een lange tijd *(of:* termijn); *to cut a ~ story short* om kort te gaan, samengevat; *in the ~ term* op den duur, op de lange duur; *~ vacation* zomervakantie; *it won't take ~* het zal niet lang duren; *before ~* binnenkort, spoedig; *he won't stay for ~* hij zal niet (voor) lang blijven; *the ~ arm of the law* de lange arm der wet; *not by a ~ chalk* op geen stukken na, bijlange (na) niet; *make (of: pull) a ~ face* ongelukkig kijken, *(roughly)* een lang gezicht trekken; *in the ~ run* uiteindelijk; *~ shot: a)* kansloos deelnemer; *b)* gok, waagstuk; *(Am) by a ~ shot* veruit, met gemak; *(Am) not by a ~ shot* op geen stukken na, bijlange na niet; *~ in the tooth* lang in de mond, aftands; *take a ~ view* dingen op de lange termijn bekijken; *go a ~ way (towards)* voordelig (in het gebruik) zijn, veel helpen, het ver schoppen

²long [loŋ] *adv* lang, lange tijd: *all night ~* de hele nacht; *be ~ in doing sth.* lang over iets doen

³long [loŋ] *vb (also with for)* hevig verlangen (naar), hunkeren: *after two weeks we were longing for the city again* na twee weken verlangden we al weer naar de stad

longevity [londzjevvittie] lang leven[h], lange levensduur

¹longing [loŋiŋ] *n* verlangen[h], hunkering

²longing [loŋiŋ] *adj* vol verlangen, smachtend

longitude [londzjitjoe:d] (geografische) lengte, longitude

long-life 1 met een lange levensduur; **2** langer houdbaar || *~ batteries* batterijen met een lange levensduur

long-lived van lange duur, hardnekkig

long-sighted 1 verziend; **2** vooruitziend

long-term langlopend, op lange termijn

long-winded langdradig

loo [loe:] wc, plee

¹look [loek] *vb* **1** kijken, (proberen te) zien, aandachtig kijken: *~ about* (of: *around*) om zich heen kijken, rondkijken; *~ ahead* vooruitzien *(also fig)*; ~

on toekijken; ~ *at* kijken naar, beschouwen, onderzoeken; *not* ~ *at* niet in overweging nemen, niets willen weten van; ~ *beyond* verder kijken dan; ~ *down the road* de weg af kijken; ~ *round the town* een kijkje in de stad nemen; ~ *before you leap* bezint eer gij begint; **2** uitkijken, uitzien, liggen: ~ *to the south* op het zuiden liggen; **3** wijzen *(in particular direction)*, (bepaalde kant) uitgaan: ~ *down (up)on* neerkijken op; ~ *forward to* tegemoet zien, verlangen naar; ~ *here!* kijk eens (even hier)!, luister eens!; ~ *in* aanlopen, aanwippen, *(inf)* tv kijken; ~ *in on* s.o. bij iem langskomen; ~ *after* passen op, toezien op; ~ *after oneself*, ~ *after one's own interests* voor zichzelf zorgen; ~ *for* zoeken (naar); ~ *for trouble* om moeilijkheden vragen; ~ *into: a)* even bezoeken; *b)* onderzoeken; ~ *(up)on* s.o. as iem beschouwen als

²**look** [loek] *vb* **1** zijn blik richten op, kijken (naar), zien: ~ *what you've done* kijk nou (eens) wat je gedaan hebt; **2** eruitzien als: ~ *one's age* aan iem zijn leeftijd afzien

³**look** [loek] *vb* lijken (te zijn), uitzien, de indruk wekken te zijn: *(Am)* ~ *good* goed lijken te gaan, er goed uitzien; *it* ~*s like snow* er is sneeuw op komst; *he* ~*s as if he has a hangover* hij ziet eruit alsof hij een kater heeft

⁴**look** [loek] *n* **1** blik, kijkjeʰ: *let's have a* ~ laten we even een kijkje nemen; **2** (gelaats)uitdrukking, blik; **3** uiterlijkʰ, (knap) voorkomenʰ, aanzienʰ: *by the* ~ *of it (of: things)* zo te zien; **4** mode; **5** uitzichtʰ; **6** ~*s* uiterlijkʰ, schoonheid: *lose one's* ~*s* minder mooi worden

lookalike evenbeeldʰ, dubbelganger

looker-on toeschouwer, kijker

looking-glass spiegel

lookout [loek] *n* **1** het uitkijken: *keep a* ~ een oogje in het zeil houden; *be on the* ~ *for* op zoek zijn naar; **2** uitkijkpost; **3** uitzichtʰ

look over doornemen *(eg letters)*, doorkijken

look through goed bekijken, (grondig, een voor een, helemaal) doornemen *(eg documents)*

look to **1** zorgen voor, bekommeren over: ~ *it that ... zorg ervoor, dat ...;* **2** vertrouwen op, rekenen op: *don't* ~ *her for help (of: to help you)* verwacht van haar geen hulp

¹**look up** *vb* **1** opkijken, de ogen opslaan; **2** beter worden *(eg of business)*, vooruitgaan: *prices are looking up* de prijzen stijgen; ~ *to* opkijken naar, bewonderen

²**look up** *vb* **1** opzoeken, naslaan; **2** raadplegen; **3** (kort) bezoeken, opzoeken

¹**loom** [loe:m] *n* weefgetouwʰ

²**loom** [loe:m] *vb* opdoemen *(also fig)*, dreigend verschijnen, zich flauw aftekenen: ~ *large* onevenredig belangrijk lijken, nadrukkelijk aanwezig zijn

¹**loony** [loe:nie] *adj* geschift, gek, getikt

²**loony** [loe:nie] *n* gek, dwaas

loony-bin gekkenhuisʰ

¹**loop** [loe:p] *n* **1** lus, strop, bocht; **2** beugel, handvatʰ;

3 spiraaltjeʰ

²**loop** [loe:p] *vb* **1** een lus maken in, met een lus vastmaken; **2** door een lus halen

³**loop** [loe:p] *vb* een lus vormen

loophole uitvlucht, uitweg: ~*s in the law* mazen in de wet(geving)

¹**loose** [loe:s] *adj* **1** los, slap, open: ~ *ends* losse eindjes, *(fig)* onvolkomenheden, onafgewerkte zaken; **2** vrij, bevrijd, ongehinderd: *break (of: get)* ~ uitbreken, ontsnappen; *cut* ~: *a)* (met moeite) weggaan, zich losmaken; *b)* op gang komen; *let* ~ vrij laten, de vrije hand laten, ontketenen; **3** wijd, ruim, soepel; **4** ongedisciplineerd, lichtzinnig: *have a* ~ *tongue* loslippig zijn; *be at a* ~ *end* niets om handen hebben; *have a screw* ~ ze zien vliegen, een beetje geschift zijn

²**loose** [loe:s] *vb* losmaken, bevrijden

³**loose** [loe:s] *adv* losjes

⁴**loose** [loe:s] *n* (staat van) vrijheid, losbandigheid: *there's a killer on the* ~ er loopt een moordenaar vrij rond

loosely [loe:slie] losjes, vaag, in het wilde weg

¹**loosen** [loe:sn] *vb* los(ser) maken, laten verslappen: *drink* ~*s the tongue* drank maakt spraakzaam; ~ *up* doen ontspannen

²**loosen** [loe:sn] *vb* losgaan, ontspannen, verslappen: ~ *up* een warming-up doen, de spieren losmaken

¹**loot** [loe:t] *n* **1** (oorlogs)buit, gestolen goedʰ, prooi; **2** poet, poen, geldʰ

²**loot** [loe:t] *vb* plunderen, roven

lop [lop] afsnoeien, afkappen

lopsided **1** scheef, overhellend; **2** ongebalanceerd, eenzijdig

¹**lord** [lo:d] *n* **1** heer, vorst, koning; **2** lord, edelachtbare, excellentie: *live like a* ~ als een vorst leven; *My Lord* edelachtbare, heer; **3** *Lord* (de) Heer, God: *the Lord's Prayer* het Onze Vader; **4** *the Lords* het Hogerhuis, de leden vh Hogerhuis

²**lord** [lo:d] *vb* de baas spelen: ~ *it over s.o.* over iem de baas spelen

lordship [lo:dsjip] Lord *(form of address for lord and judge)*, edele heer, edelachtbare

lore [lo:] traditionele kennis, overlevering

lorry [lorrie] vrachtauto

¹**lose** [loe:z] *vb* **1** verliezen, kwijtraken, verspelen: *(inf)* ~ *one's cool* z'n kalmte verliezen; ~ *count* de tel kwijtraken; ~ *sight of* uit het oog verliezen; ~ *one's temper* boos worden; ~ *no time in (doing sth.)* geen tijd verspillen met (iets); ~ *oneself in* geheel opgaan in; **2** doen verliezen, kosten: *her stupid mistake lost us a major customer* haar stomme fout kostte ons een grote klant; **3** missen, niet winnen

²**lose** [loe:z] *vb* **1** verliezen, verlies lijden, er op achteruit gaan: *you can't* ~ daar heb je niets bij te verliezen; ~ *out on sth.* er (geld) bij inschieten; **2** achterlopen *(of watch etc)*

loser [loe:zə] verliezer: *born* ~ geboren verliezer; *a good* ~ een goede verliezer

loss [los] **1** verlies[h]; **2** nadeel[h], schade; **3** achteruitgang, teruggang ‖ *be at a ~ (what to do)* niet weten wat men doen moet; *be at a ~ for words* met de mond vol tanden staan

lost 1 verloren, weg, kwijt: *~ property (department, office)* (afdeling, bureau) gevonden voorwerpen; **2** gemist: *~ chance* gemiste kans; **3** in gedachten verzonken, afwezig, er niet bij: *~ in thought* in gedachten verzonken; **4** verspild: *sarcasm is ~ (up)on him* sarcasme raakt hem niet; *get ~!* donder op!

lot [lot] **1** portie, aandeel[h]; **2** kavel, perceel[h], partij, (veiling)nummer[h]; **3** lot[h], loterijbriefje[h]: *cast (of: draw) ~s* loten; **4** (nood)lot[h], levenslot[h]: *cast (of: throw) in one's ~ with* mee gaan doen met; **5** *(Am)* stuk grond, terrein[h]: *parking ~* parkeerterrein; **6** groep, aantal dingen (mensen), een hoop, een heleboel: *~s and ~s* ontzettend veel, hopen; *a ~ of books, ~s of books* een heleboel boeken; *that's the ~* dat is alles; *things have changed quite a ~* er is nogal wat veranderd

lotion [loosjən] lotion, haarwater[h], gezichtswater[h]

lottery [lottərie] loterij

¹loud [laud] *adj* **1** luid(ruchtig), hard; **2** opzichtig, schreeuwend *(of colour)*

²loud [laud] *adv* luid(ruchtig), hard, schreeuwerig: *~ and clear* erg duidelijk, overduidelijk; *out ~* hardop

loudspeaker luidspreker, box

¹lounge [laundzj] *n* **1** lounge, hal[h], foyer; **2** zitkamer, conversatiezaal

²lounge [laundzj] *vb* **1** luieren, (rond)hangen: *~ about (of: around)* rondhangen; **2** slenteren, kuieren

louse [laus] *(lice)* luis

louse up grondig bederven, verpesten

lousy [lauzie] **1** vol luizen; **2** *(inf)* waardeloos, vuil, beroerd; **3** *(inf)* armzalig *(of amount, number etc)*

lout [laut] lummel, hufter

¹love [luv] *n* **1** liefde, verliefdheid: *mother sends her ~* moeder laat je groeten; *fall in ~ with s.o.* verliefd worden op iem; **2** plezier[h], genoegen[h]: *music is a great ~ of his* muziek is een van zijn grote liefdes; **3** liefje[h]; **4** *(inf)* snoes, geliefd persoon *(also man)*; **5** groeten; **6** *(tennis)* love, nul: *~ all* nul-nul; *not for ~ or money* niet voor geld of goeie woorden; *there is no ~ lost between them* ze kunnen elkaar niet luchten of zien

²love [luv] *vb* **1** houden van, liefhebben, graag mogen: *~ dearly* innig houden van; **2** dol zijn op, heerlijk vinden: *he ~s (to go) swimming* hij is dol op zwemmen

³love [luv] *vb* liefde voelen, verliefd zijn

lovely [luvlie] **1** mooi, lieftallig, aantrekkelijk; **2** *(inf)* leuk, prettig, fijn, lekker

love potion liefdesdrank(je[h])

lover [luvvə] **1** (be)minnaar; **2** liefhebber, enthousiast; **3** *~s* verliefd paar[h]; **4** *~s* minnaars, stel[h]

lovesick [luvsik] smachtend van liefde, smoorverliefd

lovey [luvvie] liefje[h], schatje[h]

¹low [loo] *adj* **1** laag, niet hoog, niet intensief: *the Low Countries* de Lage Landen; *~est common denominator* kleinste gemene deler; *~est common multiple* kleinste gemene veelvoud; *~ point* minimum, dieptepunt; *~ tide* laagwater, eb; **2** laag(hartig): *~ trick* rotstreek; **3** plat, ordinair: *~ expression* ordinaire uitdrukking; **4** zacht, stil, niet luid, laag *(tone)*: *speak in a ~ voice* zacht praten; **5** ongelukkig, depressief: *~ spirits* neerslachtigheid; **6** verborgen, onopvallend: *lie ~* zich gedeisd houden; **7** zwak, slap, futloos: *keep a ~ profile* zich gedeisd houden; *bring ~: a)* aan lagerwal brengen; *b)* uitputten; *c)* plat maken

²low [loo] *adv* **1** laag, diep: *aim ~* laag mikken; **2** zacht, stil; **3** diep *(of sound)*, laag; **4** bijna uitgeput: *run ~* op raken, bijna op zijn

³low [loo] *n* **1** laag terrein[h], laagte; **2** dieptepunt[h], laag punt[h]: *an all-time ~* een absoluut dieptepunt; **3** geloei[h], gebulk[h]; **4** lagedrukgebied[h]

⁴low [loo] *vb* loeien

¹low-down *n* fijne[h] vd zaak, feiten, inzicht[h]: *have the ~ on* het fijne weten over

²low-down *adj* laag, gemeen

¹lower [looə] *adj* **1** lager (gelegen), onder-, van lage(r) orde: *~ classes* lagere stand(en); *~ deck* benedendek; **2** neder-, beneden-: *the Lower Rhine* de Neder-Rijn; *Lower Chamber (of: House)* Lagerhuis

²lower [looə] *vb* **1** verlagen, doen zakken; **2** neerlaten, laten zakken: *~ one's eyes* de ogen neerslaan; **3** verminderen, doen afnemen: *~ one's voice* zachter praten

³lower [looə] *vb* afnemen, minder worden, dalen, zakken

low-fat met laag vetgehalte, mager, halva-, halfvol: *~ margarine* halvarine; *~ milk* magere melk

low-key rustig, ingehouden

lowland [loolənd] **1** mbt (het) laagland; **2** *Lowland* mbt de Schotse Laaglanden

lowly [loolie] **1** bescheiden, laag *(in rank)*; **2** eenvoudig, nederig

loyal [lojjəl] trouw, loyaal

loyalist [lojjəlist] (regerings)getrouwe, loyalist

loyalty [lojjəltie] **1** loyaliteit, trouw: *customer ~* klantentrouw; *~ card* klantenpas; **2** *-ies* banden, binding

lozenge [lozzindzj] **1** ruit, ruitvormig iets; **2** (hoest)tablet[h]

L.P. *long-playing record* lp; elpee

Lt *Lieutenant* lt., luitenant

Ltd *limited (roughly)* NV, Naamloze Vennootschap

lubricant [loe:brikkənt] **1** smeermiddel[h]; **2** glijmiddel[h]

lubricate [loe:brikkeet] (door)smeren, oliën

lucid [loe:sid] **1** helder, duidelijk *(also fig)*; **2** bij zijn verstand

luck [luk] geluk[h], toeval[h], succes[h]: *bad (of: hard) ~* pech; *good ~* succes; *push one's ~* te veel risico's nemen, overmoedig worden; *try one's ~* zijn geluk be-

proeven; *let's do it once more for* ~ laten we het nog
een keer doen, misschien brengt dat geluk; *be out
of* ~, *be down on one's* ~ pech hebben; *with* ~ als alles goed gaat; *no such* ~ helaas niet; *as* ~ *would have
it* (on)gelukkig, toevallig

luckily [lʊkkillie] gelukkig: ~ *for you, I found your
keys* je hebt geluk dat ik je sleutels heb gevonden

lucky [lʊkkie] **1** gelukkig, fortuinlijk, toevallig juist:
a ~ *thing no-one got hurt* gelukkig raakte er niemand gewond; **2** gelukbrengend, geluks-: ~ *charm*
talisman; ~ *dip* grabbelton, *(fig)* loterij; ~ *star* geluksster; *strike* ~ boffen

lucrative [loe:krativ] winstgevend, lucratief

lucre [loe:kə] gewinʰ: *filthy* ~ vuil gewin

ludicrous [loe:dikrəs] belachelijk, bespottelijk

¹**lug** [lug] *vb* (voort)trekken, (voort)zeulen: ~ *sth.
along* iets meesleuren

²**lug** [lug] *n* uitsteekselʰ, handvatʰ, oorʰ

luggage [lʊgidzj] bagage: *left* ~ afgegeven bagage,
bagage in depot

lugubrious [loe:goe:briəs] luguber, naargeestig,
treurig

lukewarm [loe:kwo:m] **1** lauw; **2** niet erg enthousiast

¹**lull** [lul] *n* korte rust: *a* ~ *in the storm* een korte
windstilte tijdens de storm

²**lull** [lul] *vb* **1** sussen, kalmeren: ~ *to sleep* in slaap
sussen; **2** in slaap brengen

lullaby [lʊlləbaj] slaapliedjeʰ

¹**lumber** [lʊmbə] *n* **1** rommel, afgedankt meubilairʰ;
2 *(Am)* half bewerkt houtʰ, timmerhoutʰ, planken

²**lumber** [lʊmbə] *vb* sjokken, zich log voortbewegen:
~ *along* voortsjokken

³**lumber** [lʊmbə] *vb (inf)* (met iets vervelends, moeilijks) opzadelen: ~ (*up) with* opzadelen met

lumberjack *(Am)* bosbouwer, houthakker

lumber-room rommelkamer

luminous [loe:minnəs] lichtgevend, *(fig)* helder,
duidelijk

¹**lump** [lump] *n* **1** klont, klomp, brokʰ: *(fig) with a* ~
in my throat met een brok in mijn keel; **2** bult,
knobbel

²**lump** [lump] *vb* **1** tot een geheel samenvoegen, bij
elkaar gooien: ~ *together* onder één noemer brengen; **2** slikken: *you'll have to like it or* ~ *it* je hebt het
maar te slikken

³**lump** [lump] *vb* klonteren

lump sum bedragʰ ineens, ronde som

lunacy [loe:nəsie] waanzin

lunar [loe:nə] van de maan, maan-: ~ *eclipse*
maansverduistering

¹**lunatic** [loe:nətik] *n* krankzinnige

²**lunatic** [loe:nətik] *adj* krankzinnig, gestoord || *the* ~
fringe het extremistische deel *(of a group)*

¹**lunch** [luntsj] *n* lunch

²**lunch** [luntsj] *vb* lunchen

luncheon [luntsjən] **1** lunch; **2** *(Am)* lichte maaltijd

lung [lung] long

¹**lunge** [lundzj] *vb (with at)* uitvallen (naar), een uit-

val doen

²**lunge** [lundzj] *vb* stoten

³**lunge** [lundzj] *n* stoot, uitval

¹**lurch** [lə:tsj] *vb* slingeren, strompelen

²**lurch** [lə:tsj] *n* ruk, plotselinge slingerbeweging ||
(inf) leave s.o. in the ~ iem in de steek laten

¹**lure** [ljoeə] *vb* (ver)lokken, meetronen: ~ *away
(from)* weglokken (van); ~ *into* verlokken tot

²**lure** [ljoeə] *n* **1** lokmiddelʰ, lokaasʰ; **2** aantrekking,
verleiding, aantrekkelijkheid

lurid [ljoerid] **1** schril, zeer fel (gekleurd), vlammend; **2** luguber, choquerend

lurk [lə:k] **1** op de loer liggen, zich schuilhouden; **2**
latent (aanwezig) zijn, verborgen zijn

luscious [lʊsjəs] **1** heerlijk: *a* ~ *peach* een overheerlijke perzik; **2** weelderig

lust [lust] **1** sterk verlangenʰ, lust, aandrift: *a* ~ *for
power* een verlangen naar macht; **2** wellust(igheid),
(zinnelijke) lust: *his eyes, full of* ~ zijn ogen, vol
wellust

lustre [lʊstə] glans, schittering, luister, roem: *add* ~
to glans geven aan

lustrous [lʊstrəs] glanzend, schitterend: ~ *eyes*
stralende ogen

lusty [lʊstie] **1** krachtig, flink, gezond; **2** wellustig

lute [loe:t] luit

luxuriance [lugzjoeəriəns] overvloed, weelderigheid

luxuriant [lugzjoeəriənt] **1** weelderig, overdadig: ~
flora weelderige flora; **2** vruchtbaar *(also fig):* ~ *imagination* rijke verbeelding

luxurious [lugzjoeəriəs] luxueus, weelderig, duur
(eg of habits)

luxury [lʊksjərie] **1** weelde, luxe, overvloed: *a life of*
~ een luxueus leven; **2** luxe(artikelʰ); **3** weelderigheid

lymph [limf] lymfe, weefselvochtʰ

lynch [lintsj] lynchen

¹**lyric** [lirrik] *n* **1** lyrisch gedichtʰ; **2** ~*s* tekst *(of song)*

²**lyric** [lirrik] *adj* lyrisch *(of poem, poet)*

lyrical [lirrikl] lyrisch

m

m. 1 *married* geh., gehuwd; **2** *masculine* m., mannelijk; **3** *metre(s)* m, meter(s); **4** *mile(s)* mijl(en); **5** *million(s)* mln, miljoen(en); **6** *minute(s)* min., minuut, minuten

ma [ma:] ma

M.A. *Master of Arts* drs.

ma'am [mæm, ma:m] *madam* mevrouw

mac [mæk] *mackintosh* regenjas

macabre [məka:brə] macaber, griezelig

macaroon [mækəroe:n] bitterkoekje[h]

mace [mees] **1** goedendag, strijdknots, knuppel; **2** scepter, staf *(of speaker in House of Commons);* **3** foelie

machine [məsjie:n] **1** machine *(also fig)*, werktuig[h], apparaat[h]; **2** aandrijfmechanisme[h]

machinery [məsjie:nərie] machinerie *(also fig)*, machinepark[h], systeem[h], apparaat[h]

machinist [məsjie:nist] monteur, werktuigkundige, machinebankwerker; vakman voor werktuigmachines

mackerel [mækərəl] makreel

mackintosh [mækintosj] regenjas

macrobiotic [mækroobajjottik] macrobiotisch

mad [mæd] **1** gek, krankzinnig: *go ~* gek worden; *drive s.o. ~* iem gek maken; **2** dwaas, onzinnig: *~ project* dwaze onderneming; **3** wild, razend, hevig *(eg of wind): make a ~ run for …* als een gek rennen naar …; **4** hondsdol; **5** *(with about, after, for, on)* verzot (op); **6** *(with at, about sth.; at, with s.o.)* boos (op), woedend (op, om): *~ as a hatter, ~ as a March hare* stapelgek

madam [mædəm] mevrouw, juffrouw: *excuse me, ~, can I help you?* pardon, mevrouw, kan ik u van dienst zijn?

mad cow disease gekkekoeienziekte

madden [mædn] gek worden (maken); woedend worden (maken), irriteren

maddening [mædəning] erg vervelend: *~ waste of time* ergerlijk tijdverlies

madhouse gekkenhuis[h] *(also fig)*

madly [mædlie] **1** als een bezetene; **2** heel (erg): *~ in love* waanzinnig verliefd

madman [mædmən] gek

madness [mædnəs] **1** krankzinnigheid, waanzin(nigheid); **2** dwaasheid, gekte: *millennium ~* millenniumgekte; **3** enthousiasme[h]

maelstrom [meelstrəm] **1** (enorme) draaikolk; **2** maalstroom *(also fig)*

mafia [mæfiə] maffia

mag [mæg] *magazine* tijdschrift[h]

magazine [mægəzie:n] **1** magazine[h], tijdschrift[h], radio-, tv-magazine[h] *(section);* **2** magazijn[h] *(of gun)*

maggot [mægət] made

¹magic [mædzjik] *n* magie *(also fig)*, toverkunst, betovering: *as if by ~, like ~* als bij toverslag

²magic [mædzjik] *adj* **1** magisch, tover-; **2** betoverend ǁ *~ carpet* vliegend tapijt

magical [mædzjikl] wonderbaarlijk; magisch

magician [mədzjisjən] **1** tovenaar; **2** goochelaar *(also fig)*, kunstenaar

magisterial [mædzjistiəriəl] **1** gezaghebbend *(also fig);* **2** autoritair; **3** magistraal

magistrate [mædzjistreet] **1** magistraat, (rechterlijk) ambtenaar; **2** politierechter, vrederechter

magnanimity [mægnənimmittie] grootmoedigheid

magnate [mægneet] magnaat

magnet [mægnit] magneet *(also fig)*

magnetism [mægnətizm] **1** magnetisme[h]; **2** aantrekkingskracht

magnificence [mægniffisns] **1** pracht, weelde; **2** grootsheid

magnificent [mægniffisnt] **1** prachtig, groots; **2** weelderig; **3** prima

¹magnify [mægniffaj] *vb* **1** vergroten *(of lens etc)*, uitvergroten; **2** versterken *(sound)*

²magnify [mægniffaj] *vb* overdrijven, opblazen

magnitude [mægnitjoe:d] **1** belang[h], belangrijkheid; **2** omvang, grootte; **3** *(astronomy)* helderheid

magnum [mægnəm] anderhalveliterfles

magpie [mægpaj] **1** ekster; **2** verzamelaar, hamsteraar

mahogany [məhogənie] mahonie[h]

maid [meed] **1** hulp, dienstmeisje[h]; **2** meisje[h], juffrouw; **3** maagd ǁ *~ of honour* (ongehuwde) hofdame

¹maiden [meedn] *n* **1** meisje[h], juffrouw; **2** maagd

²maiden [meedn] *adj* **1** maagdelijk, ve meisje; **2** ongetrouwd *(of woman): ~ name* meisjesnaam; **3** eerste *(eg of trip, flight): the Titanic sank on her ~ voyage* de Titanic zonk tijdens haar eerste reis

¹mail [meel] *n* **1** post, brieven; **2** maliënkolder

²mail [meel] *vb* **1** posten, per post versturen; **2** (be)pantseren

mailman *(Am)* postbode

maim [meem] verminken *(also fig)*, kreupel maken

¹main [meen] *adj* hoofd-, belangrijkste, voornaamste: *~ course* hoofdgerecht; *~ line: a)* hoofdlijn *(of railways); b) (Am)* hoofdstraat; *~ street* hoofdstraat

²main [meen] *n* **1** hoofdleiding, hoofdbuis, hoofdkabel; **2** *~s* (elektriciteits)net[h], elektriciteit, lichtnet[h]: *connected to the ~s* (op het elektriciteitsnet) aangesloten; **3** (open) zee: *in the ~* voor het grootste gedeelte, in het algemeen

mainland [meenlənd] vasteland[h]

mainstay steunpilaar, pijler

mainstream 1 heersende stroming; **2** hoofdstroom *(of river);* **3** mainstream *(jazz)*

maintain [meenteen] **1** handhaven, in stand houden: *he ~ed his calm attitude* hij bleef rustig; *~ order* de orde bewaren; **2** onderhouden *(eg house, family),* zorgen voor, een onderhoudsbeurt geven; **3** beweren, stellen: *the suspect ~s his innocence* de verdachte zegt dat hij onschuldig is; **4** verdedigen, opkomen voor: *~ an opinion* een mening verdedigen

maintenance [meentənəns] **1** handhaving *(eg of law);* **2** onderhoudʰ *(of house, machine);* **3** levensonderhoudʰ, levensbehoeften; **4** toelage *(of woman, child),* alimentatie

maisonette [meezɔnɛt] **1** huisjeʰ, flatjeʰ; **2** maisonnette

maize [meez] maïs

majestic [mədzjɛstik] majestueus, verheven

Majesty [mædzjistie] Majesteit, Koninklijke Hoogheid ‖ *on Her (of: His) Majesty's service* dienst *(on envelope)*

¹major [meedzjə] *adj* **1** groot, groter, voornaamste: *a ~ breakthrough* een belangrijke doorbraak; *the ~ part of* de meerderheid van; *~ road* hoofdweg; **2** ernstig, zwaar: *~ operation* zware operatie; **3** meerderjarig, volwassen; **4** *(mus)* in majeur: *C ~ C* grote terts; **5** senior, de oudere: *Rowland ~* Rowland senior

²major [meedzjə] *n* **1** meerderjarige; **2** majoor; **3** *(Am)* hoofdvakʰ *(of study);* **4** *(Am)* hoofdvakstudent

major in *(Am)* als hoofdvak(ken) hebben, (als hoofdvak) studeren

majority [mədzjɔrritie] **1** meerderheid: *the ~ of people* de meeste mensen; **2** meeste: *in the ~* in de meerderheid

¹make [meek] *vb* **1** maken, bouwen, fabriceren, scheppen, veroorzaken, bereiden, opstellen *(law, testament):* *~ coffee* koffie zetten; *God made man* God schiep de mens; *~ over a dress* een jurk vermaken; *show them what you are made of* toon wat je waard bent; **2** maken, vormen; maken tot, benoemen tot: *the workers made him their spokesman* de arbeiders maakten hem tot hun woordvoerder; **3** (ver)krijgen, (be)halen, binnenhalen *(profit),* hebben *(success),* lijden *(loss),* verdienen, scoren, maken *(point etc):* *~ a lot of money* veel geld verdienen; *(cards) ~ a trick* een slag maken; *he made a lot on this deal* hij verdiende een hoop aan deze transactie; **4** laten, ertoe brengen, doen, maken dat: *don't ~ me laugh* laat me niet lachen; *she made the food go round* ze zorgde ervoor dat er genoeg eten was voor iedereen; *you can't ~ me* je kunt me niet dwingen; **5** schatten (op), komen op: *what time do you ~ it?* hoe laat heeft u het?; **6** worden, maken, zijn: *three and four ~ seven* drie en vier is zeven; **7** (geschikt) zijn (voor), (op)leveren, worden: *this student will never ~ a good doctor* deze student zal

nooit een goede arts worden; *the man is made for this job* de man is perfect voor deze baan; **8** bereiken, komen tot, halen *(speed),* gaan, pakken *(train),* zien, in zicht krijgen *(land),* worden, komen in: *~ an appointment* op tijd zijn voor een afspraak; *~ the front pages* de voorpagina's halen; *~ it* op tijd zijn, het halen, *(fig)* succes hebben, slagen; *have it made* geslaagd zijn, op rozen zitten; **9** doen, verrichten, uitvoeren *(research),* geven *(promise),* nemen *(test),* houden *(speech):* *~ an effort* een poging doen, pogen; *~ a phone call* opbellen; **10** opmaken *(bed);* **11** tot een succes maken, het hem doen, de finishing touch geven: *~ sth. of oneself* succes hebben *(in life);* *this fool can ~ or break the project* deze gek kan het project maken of breken; *~ sth. do* zich met iets behelpen; *let's ~ it next week* laten we (voor) volgende week afspreken; *~ the most of: a)* er het beste van maken; *b)* zoveel mogelijk profiteren van; *~ much of: a)* belangrijk vinden; *b)* veel hebben aan; *c)* veel begrijpen van; *~ nothing of: a)* gemakkelijk doen (over), geen probleem maken van; *b)* niets begrijpen van; *they couldn't ~ anything of my notes* ze konden niets met mijn aantekeningen beginnen

²make [meek] *vb* **1** doen, zich gedragen, handelen: *~ as if (of: though): a)* doen alsof; *b)* op het punt staan; **2** gaan, zich begeven: *we were making toward(s) the woods* wij gingen naar de bossen; *you'll have to ~ do with this old pair of trousers* je zult het met deze oude broek moeten doen; *~ away (of: off)* 'm smeren, ervandoor gaan; *~ away with oneself* zich van kant maken; *~ off with* wegnemen, meenemen, jatten

³make [meek] *n* **1** merkʰ; **2** fabricage, vervaardiging ‖ *on the ~:* a) op (eigen) voordeel uit, op winst uit; b) op de versiertoer

make-believe schijn, fantasie, het doen alsof: *this fight is just ~* dit gevecht is maar spel

make for 1 gaan naar, zich begeven naar: *we made for the nearest pub* we gingen naar de dichtstbijzijnde kroeg; **2** bevorderen, bijdragen tot, zorgen voor

¹make out *vb* **1** uitschrijven, invullen: *~ a cheque to* een cheque uitschrijven op naam van; **2** beweren, verkondigen: *she makes herself out to be very rich* zij beweert dat ze erg rijk is; **3** onderscheiden, zien; **4** ontcijferen *(eg handwriting);* **5** begrijpen, snappen, hoogte krijgen van: *I can't ~ this message* ik snap dit bericht niet

²make out *vb* klaarspelen, het maken, zich redden: *the European industry is not making out as bad as everybody says* met de Europese industrie gaat het niet zo slecht als iedereen zegt

maker [meekə] maker, fabrikant ‖ *meet one's ~* sterven, dood gaan

¹makeshift *adj* voorlopig, tijdelijk, nood-

²makeshift *n* tijdelijke vervanging, noodoplossing

¹make up *vb* **1** zich opmaken, zich schminken; **2** zich verzoenen, weer goedmaken ‖ *~ for* weer goedmaken, vergoeden; *~ to s.o.* bij iem in de gunst zien te komen; ~ *to s.o. for sth.*: *a)* iem iets vergoeden; *b)* iets goedmaken met (of: bij) iem

²**make up** *vb* **1** opmaken, schminken; **2** bijleggen, goedmaken *(quarrel): make it up (with s.o.)* het weer goedmaken (met iem); **3** volledig maken, aanvullen: *father made up the difference of three pounds* vader legde de ontbrekende drie pond bij; **4** vergoeden, goedmaken, teruggeven, terugbetalen: ~ *lost ground* de schade inhalen; **5** verzinnen: ~ *an excuse* een excuus verzinnen; **6** vormen, samenstellen: *the group was made up of four musicians* de groep bestond uit vier muzikanten; **7** maken, opstellen, klaarmaken *(medicine)*, bereiden, maken tot (pakje), (kleren) maken (van), naaien; **8** opmaken *(bed)*

m**ake-up** [m**ee**kup] **1** make-up, schmink; **2** aard, karakterʰ, natuur; **3** samenstelling, opbouw

m**aking** [m**ee**king] **1** ~s verdiensten; **2** ~s ingrediënten *(also fig)*, (juiste) kwaliteiten: *have the* ~s *of a surgeon* het in zich hebben om chirurg te worden; *in the* ~ in de maak, in voorbereiding

m**alady** [m**æ**lədie] kwaal, ziekte: *a social* ~ een sociale plaag

mal**aria** [məl**eə**riə] malaria

m**alcontent** [m**æ**lkəntent] ontevredene, ontevreden mens

¹**male** [meel] *adj* **1** mannelijk *(also fig)*: ~ *chauvinism* (mannelijk) seksisme; ~ *choir* mannenkoor; **2** mannetjes-

²**male** [meel] *n* **1** mannelijk persoon; **2** mannetjeʰ *(animal)*

m**alefactor** [m**æ**lifæktə] boosdoener

mal**evolence** [məl**e**vvələns] kwaadwilligheid, boosaardigheid

mal**formed** [mælf**o:**md] misvormd

mal**function** [mælf**u**ngksjən] storing, defectʰ

m**alice** [m**æ**lis] **1** kwaadwilligheid, boosaardigheid: *bear* ~ *towards* (of: *to, against*) *s.o.* (een) wrok tegen iem koesteren; **2** boos opzet

mal**ignant** [məl**i**gnənt] **1** schadelijk, verderfelijk; **2** kwaadwillig, boosaardig; **3** kwaadaardig *(of disease): a* ~*tumour* een kwaadaardig gezwel

mall [mo:l] **1** wandelgalerij, promenade; **2** winkelpromenade, groot winkelcentrumʰ; **3** *(Am)* middenberm

m**alleable** [m**æ**liəbl] *(fig)* kneedbaar

malnu**trition** [mælnjoetr**i**sjən] slechte voeding, ondervoeding

malt [mo:lt] mout, malt

mal**treatment** [mæltr**ie:**tmənt] mishandeling

malver**sation** [mælvəs**ee**sjən] malversatie, verduistering, wanbeheerʰ

mam [mæm] *mammy* mam(s)

m**ammal** [m**æ**ml] zoogdierʰ

m**ammoth** [m**æ**məθ] mammoet

¹**man** [mæn] *n (men)* **1** man, de man, echtgenoot, minnaar, partner: ~ *of letters* schrijver, geleerde; ~ *of means* bemiddeld man; *the* ~ *in the street* de gewone man, jan met de pet; ~ *about town* man van

de wereld, playboy; ~ *and wife* man en vrouw; ~ *of the world* iem met mensenkennis; *the very* ~ de persoon die men nodig heeft, net wie men zocht; *be* ~ *enough to* mans genoeg zijn om; **2** mens, het mensdom: *the rights of Man* de mensenrechten; *to the last* ~ tot op de laatste man; *every* ~ *for himself* ieder voor zich; *as a* ~ als één man; *one* ~, one vote enkelvoudig stemrecht; **3** ondergeschikte, soldaat, *men* manschappen: *officers and men* officieren en manschappen; *I'm your* ~ op mij mag (of: kan) je rekenen; *be enough of a* ~ *to* wel zo flink zijn om te; *(all) to a* ~ eensgezind

²**man** [mæn] *vb* **1** bemannen, bezetten; ~*ned crossing* bewaakte overweg; **2** vermannen: ~ *oneself* zich vermannen

³**man** [mæn] *interj (Am)* sjonge!

¹**manacle** [m**æ**nəkl] *n* **1** handboei; **2** belemmering

²**manacle** [m**æ**nəkl] *vb* in de boeien slaan, aan elkaar vastketenen

¹**manage** [m**æ**nidzj] *vb* **1** slagen in, weten te, kunnen, kans zien te: *the* ~*d to escape* hij wist te ontsnappen; **2** leiden, besturen, beheren *(business)*, hoeden *(cattle)*; **3** beheersen, weten aan te pakken, manipuleren; **4** hanteren; **5** aankunnen, aandurven, in staat zijn tot: *I cannot* ~ *another mouthful* ik krijg er geen hap meer in

²**manage** [m**æ**nidzj] *vb* **1** rondkomen, zich behelpen; **2** slagen, het klaarspelen: *can you* ~? gaat het?, lukt het (zo)?; *I'll* ~ het lukt me wel; **3** als beheerder optreden

m**anagement** [m**æ**nidzjmənt] **1** beheerʰ, managementʰ, bestuurʰ, administratie; **2** overlegʰ, beleidʰ: *more luck than (good)* ~ meer geluk dan wijsheid; **3** werkgevers

m**anager** [m**æ**nidzjə] **1** bestuurder, chef, directeur *(of business)*, manager *(of sports team)*, impresario *(of singer)*; **2** manager, bedrijfsleider

m**andarin** [m**æ**ndərin] **1** *Mandarin* Mandarijnsʰ *(language)*, Chinees; **2** mandarijntjeʰ; **3** bureaucraat

m**andate** [m**æ**ndeet] mandaatʰ, machtiging om namens anderen te handelen

m**andatory** [m**æ**ndətəri] **1** bevel-: ~ *sign* gebodsbord; **2** verplicht: ~ *subject* verplicht (school)vak

m**andolin** [m**æ**ndəlin] mandoline

m**ane** [meen] manen

man**ège** [mæn**ee**zj] **1** manege, (paard)rijschool; **2** rijkunst

m**anger** [m**ee**ndzjə] trog, krib

m**ange-tout** [mânzjt**oe**:] peul(tjeʰ)

¹**mangle** [m**æ**nggl] *vb* **1** mangelen, door de mangel draaien; **2** verscheuren, verminken, havenen, *(fig)* verknoeien: ~*d bodies* verminkte lichamen

²**mangle** [m**æ**nggl] *n* **1** mangel; **2** wringer

m**ango** [m**æ**nggoo] *(also* ~es*)* mango

m**angy** [m**ee**ndzjie] **1** schurftig; **2** sjofel

man**handle** [mænh**æ**ndl] **1** toetakelen, afranselen; **2** door mankracht verplaatsen

m**anhood** [m**æ**nhoed] **1** mannelijkheid; **2** volwassenheid

mania [meeniə] **1** manie, waanzin; zucht: *Beatle ~* Beatlemania, Beatlegekte; **2** (*with for*) rage (om, voor)

maniac [meenie·æk] maniak, waanzinnige

manic [mænik] **1** manisch; **2** erg opgewonden, bezeten

¹**manicure** [mænikjoeə] *n* manicure

²**manicure** [mænikjoeə] *vb* manicuren

¹**manifest** [mæniffest] *adj* zichtbaar; duidelijk, klaarblijkelijk

²**manifest** [mæniffest] *vb* zichtbaar maken; vertonen: *~ one's interest* blijk geven van belangstelling

manifestation [mæniffesteesjən] **1** manifestatie; **2** verkondiging, openbaring; **3** uiting

manifesto [mæniffestoo] (*also ~es*) manifest[h]

manifold [mæniffoold] veelvuldig, verscheiden

manipulate [mənipjoeleet] **1** hanteren (*appliance*); **2** manipuleren (*also med*); **3** knoeien met (*text, figures*)

manipulation [mənipjoeleesjən] manipulatie

mankind [mænkajnd] het mensdom, de mensheid

manly [mænlie] mannelijk, manhaftig

mannequin [mænikkin] **1** mannequin; **2** etalage-pop

manner [mænə] **1** manier, wijze: *in a ~* in zekere zin; *in a ~ of speaking* bij wijze van spreken; **2** houding, gedrag[h]; **3** stijl, trant; **4** soort, slag: *all ~ of* allerlei; **5** *~s* manieren, goed gedrag[h]: *bad ~s* slechte manieren; *it's bad ~s* dat is onbeleefd; **6** *~s* zeden, sociale gewoonten

mannerism [mænərizm] **1** aanwensel[h]; **2** gekunsteldheid

mannish [mænisj] manachtig, mannelijk (*of women*)

¹**manoeuvre** [mənoe:və] *n* manoeuvre

²**manoeuvre** [mənoe:və] *vb* manoeuvreren, (*fig*) slinks handelen: *~ s.o. into a good job* een goed baantje voor iem versieren

manor [mænə] manor, groot (heren)huis[h] met omliggende gronden

manpower [mænpauə] **1** arbeidskrachten; **2** beschikbare strijdkrachten

mansion [mænsjən] herenhuis[h]

manslaughter [mænslo:tə] doodslag

mantelpiece schoorsteenmantel

¹**manual** [mænjoeəl] *adj* hand-: *~ labour* handenarbeid; *~ worker* handarbeider

²**manual** [mænjoeəl] *n* **1** handboek[h], handleiding; **2** (*mus*) manuaal[h]

¹**manufacture** [mænjoefæktsjə] *vb* **1** vervaardigen, verwerken; produceren; **2** verzinnen

²**manufacture** [mænjoefæktsjə] *n* **1** fabrikaat[h], product[h], goederen; **2** vervaardiging, fabricage, productie(proces[h]), makelij

manufacturer [mænjoefæktsjərə] fabrikant

¹**manure** [mənjoeə] *n* mest

²**manure** [mənjoeə] *vb* bemesten, gieren

manuscript [mænjoeskript] manuscript[h], hand-

schrift[h]

many [mennie] **1** vele(n), menigeen: *~'s the time* menigmaal; *a good* (of: *great*) *~* vele(n), menigeen; *and as ~ again* (of: *more*) en nog eens zoveel; *have had one too ~* een glaasje te veel op hebben; *~ of the pages were torn* veel bladzijden waren gescheurd; *as ~ as thirty* wel dertig; **2** veel, een groot aantal: *a good ~ raisins* een flinke hoeveelheid rozijnen; *ten mistakes in as ~ lines* tien fouten in tien regels; **3** (*with a(n)*) menig(e): *~ a time* menigmaal

¹**map** [mæp] *n* **1** kaart; **2** plan[h], grafische voorstelling || *put on the ~* de aandacht vestigen op

²**map** [mæp] *vb* in kaart brengen: *~ out* in kaart brengen, (*fig*) plannen, indelen; *I've got my future ~ped out for me* mijn toekomst is al uitgestippeld

maple [meepl] esdoorn

mar [ma:] bederven, verstoren: *make* (of: *mend*) *or ~ a plan* een plan doen slagen of mislukken

¹**marathon** [mærəθən] *n* marathon(loop)

²**marathon** [mærəθən] *adj* marathon, ellenlang

maraud [məro:d] plunderen, roven

¹**marble** [ma:bl] *n* **1** marmer[h]; **2** knikker: *play* (*at*) *~s* knikkeren; *he has lost his ~s* er zit bij hem een steekje los

²**marble** [ma:bl] *adj* marmeren; gemarmerd

¹**march** [ma:tsj] *vb* (op)marcheren, aanrukken: *quick ~!* voorwaarts mars!

²**march** [ma:tsj] *vb* **1** doen marcheren; **2** leiden, voeren (*on foot*): *be ~ed away* (of: *off*) weggeleid worden

³**march** [ma:tsj] *n* **1** mars; **2** opmars: *on the ~* in opmars; *steal a ~ on s.o.* iem te vlug af zijn

March [ma:tsj] maart

march past defilé[h], parade

mare [meə] merrie

margarine [ma:dzjərie:n] margarine

margin [ma:dzjin] **1** marge, (*Stock Exchange*) surplus[h]: *~ of error* foutenmarge; **2** kantlijn

marginal [ma:dzjinl] **1** in de kantlijn geschreven: *~ notes* kanttekeningen; **2** miniem, onbeduidend, bijkomstig: *of ~ importance* van ondergeschikt belang

marguerite [ma:gərie:t] margriet

marigold [mærigoold] **1** goudsbloem; **2** afrikaan-tje[h]

marijuana [mæriwwa:nə] marihuana

marina [mərie:nə] jachthaven

¹**marine** [mərie:n] *adj* zee-: *~ biology* mariene biologie

²**marine** [mərie:n] *n* **1** marine, vloot; **2** marinier

mariner [mærinnə] zeeman, matroos

marionette [mæriənet] marionet

marital [mæritl] echtelijk, huwelijks-: *~ status* burgerlijke staat

maritime [mærittajm] maritiem: *~ law* zeerecht

marjoram [ma:dzjərəm] marjolein

¹**mark** [ma:k] *n* **1** teken[h], leesteken[h], (*fig*) blijk: *as a ~ of my esteem* als blijk van mijn achting; **2** teken[h], spoor[h], vlek, (*fig*) indruk: *bear the ~s of* de sporen dragen van; *make one's ~* zich onderscheiden; **3**

(rapport)cijfer^h, punt^h; **4** peil^h, niveau^h: *above the ~* boven peil; *I don't feel quite up to the ~* ik voel me niet helemaal fit; **5** *Mark* model^h, type^h, rangnummer^h; **6** start(streep): *not quick off the ~* niet vlug (van begrip); *on your ~s, get set, go!* op uw plaatsen! klaar? af!; **7** doel^h, doelwit^h: *(fig) hit the ~* in de roos schieten; *(fig) miss (of: overshoot) the ~* het doel missen, te ver gaan, de plank misslaan; *keep s.o. up to the ~* zorgen dat iem zijn uiterste best doet; *overstep the ~* over de schreef gaan

²**mark** [ma:k] *vb* **1** merken, tekenen, onderscheiden: *~ the occasion* de gelegenheid luister bijzetten; **2** beoordelen, nakijken, cijfers geven voor *(schoolwork);* **3** letten op *(words etc):* *~ how it is done* let op hoe het gedaan wordt; **4** te kennen geven, vertonen; **5** bestemmen, opzijzetten; **6** vlekken, tekenen *(animal);* **7** *(sport)* dekken

³**mark** [ma:k] *vb* **1** vlekken (maken, krijgen); **2** cijfers geven

mark down **1** noteren, opschrijven; **2** afprijzen; **3** een lager cijfer geven

marked [ma:kt] **1** duidelijk: *a ~ preference* een uitgesproken voorkeur; **2** gemarkeerd, gemerkt *(eg money);* **3** bestemd, uitgekozen

marker [ma:kə] **1** teller; **2** teken^h, merk^h, kenteken^h, mijlpaal, kilometerpaal, baken^h, boekenlegger, scorebord^h; **3** markeerstift

¹**market** [ma:kit] *n* **1** markt, handel, afzetgebied^h: *be in the ~ for sth.* iets willen kopen; *price oneself out of the ~* zich uit de markt prijzen; **2** marktprijs; **3** markt, beurs

²**market** [ma:kit] *vb* **1** op de markt brengen; **2** verkopen, verhandelen

³**market** [ma:kit] *vb* inkopen doen, winkelen

marketing [ma:kəting] **1** markthandel; **2** marketing, marktonderzoek^h

marking [ma:king] **1** tekening *(of animal etc);* **2** (ken)teken^h

mark out **1** afbakenen, markeren; **2** uitkiezen, bestemmen: *marked out as a candidate for promotion* uitgekozen als promotiekandidaat

marksman [ma:ksmən] scherpschutter

mark up in prijs verhogen

marmalade [ma:məleed] marmelade

marmot [ma:mət] marmot

¹**maroon** [məroe:n] *n* **1** vuurpijl, lichtsein^h; **2** kastanjebruin^h

²**maroon** [məroe:n] *vb* **1** achterlaten, *(fig)* aan zijn lot overlaten; **2** isoleren, afsnijden: *~ed by the floods* door de overstromingen ingesloten

marquis [ma:kwis] markies

marriage [mæridzj] huwelijk^h, echt(verbintenis): *~ of convenience* verstandshuwelijk; *her ~ to* haar huwelijk met; *~ settlement* huwelijksvoorwaarden

marriageable [mæridzjəbl] huwbaar

married [mæried] gehuwd: *a ~ couple* een echtpaar

marrow [mæroo] **1** (eetbare) pompoen: *vegetable ~* eetbare pompoen; **2** merg^h; **3** kern, pit

marry [mærie] trouwen (met), in het huwelijk treden (met): *~ money (of: wealth)* een rijk huwelijk sluiten; *get married* trouwen; *married to* verknocht aan; *he is married to his work* hij is met zijn werk getrouwd

marsh [ma:sj] moeras^h

¹**marshal** [ma:sjl] *n* **1** (veld)maarschalk; **2** hofmaarschalk; **3** hoofd^h van ordedienst; **4** *(Am)* hoofd^h van politie, *(roughly)* sheriff; **5** *(Am)* brandweercommandant

²**marshal** [ma:sjl] *vb* **1** (zich) opstellen; **2** leiden, (be)geleiden

¹**marsupial** [ma:s·joe:piəl] *adj* buideldragend

²**marsupial** [ma:s·joe:piəl] *n* buideldier^h

mart [ma:t] handelscentrum^h

marten [ma:tin] **1** *(animal)* marter; **2** *(fur)* marter(bont)^h

martial [ma:sjl] **1** krijgs-: *~ arts* (oosterse) vechtkunsten *(karate, judo etc);* **2** krijgshaftig

¹**martyr** [ma:tə] *n* martelaar *(also fig):* *make a ~ of oneself* zich als martelaar opwerpen

²**martyr** [ma:tə] *vb* de marteldood doen sterven; martelen *(also fig),* kwellen

martyrdom [ma:tədəm] **1** martelaarschap^h; **2** marteldood; **3** marteling, lijdensweg

¹**marvel** [ma:vl] *n* wonder^h: *do (of: work) ~s* wonderen verrichten

²**marvel** [ma:vl] *vb* (with *at*) zich verwonderen (over), zich verbazen (over)

marvellous [ma:vələs] prachtig, fantastisch

marzipan [ma:zipæn] marsepein(tje)^h

masc. *masculine* mnl., mannelijk

mascot [mæskət] mascotte

masculine [mæskjoelin] **1** mannelijk; **2** manachtig

¹**mash** [mæsj] *vb* **1** fijnstampen, fijnmaken: *~ed potatoes* (aardappel)puree; **2** mengen, hutselen

²**mash** [mæsj] *n* (warm) mengvoer^h

¹**mask** [ma:sk] *n* masker^h *(also fig),* mom^h

²**mask** [ma:sk] *vb* zich vermommen, een masker opzetten, *(fig)* zijn (ware) gelaat verbergen

³**mask** [ma:sk] *vb* **1** maskeren, vermommen; **2** verbergen, verhullen

masked [ma:skt] gemaskerd

masking tape [ma:sking teep] afplakband^h

mason [meesn] **1** metselaar; **2** vrijmetselaar

¹**masquerade** [mæskəreed] *vb* (with *as*) zich vermommen (als), zich voordoen (als)

²**masquerade** [mæskəreed] *n* **1** maskerade; **2** vermomming

¹**mass** [mæs] *n* massa, hoop, menigte: *in the ~* in massa; *a ~ of* één en al; *the ~es* de massa

²**mass** [mæs] *vb* (zich) verzamelen: *~ troops* troepen concentreren

³**mass** *n (Roman Catholicism)* mis

¹**massacre** [mæsəkə] *n* **1** bloedbad^h; **2** *(fig)* afslachting

²**massacre** [mæsəkə] *vb* **1** uitmoorden; **2** in de pan hakken

¹**massage** [mæsa:zj] *n* massage

²**massage** [mæsa:zj] *vb* **1** masseren; **2** manipuleren,

knoeien met *(data etc)*

massive [mæsiv] **1** massief, zwaar; **2** groots, indrukwekkend; **3** massaal; **4** aanzienlijk, enorm

mast [ma:st] mast

¹master [ma:stə] *n* **1** meester, heer, baas, schoolmeester: ~ *of the house* heer des huizes; **2** origineel[h], matrijs, master(tape): *Master of Arts (roughly)* doctorandus in de letteren; *Master of Ceremonies* ceremoniemeester

²master [ma:stə] *adj* hoofd-, voornaamste

³master [ma:stə] *vb* overmeesteren, de baas worden *(also fig)*, te boven komen

masterful [ma:stəfoel] **1** meesterachtig; **2** meesterlijk

mastermind uitdenken: *he ~ed the project* hij was het brein achter het project

masterpiece meesterstuk[h], meesterwerk[h]

mastery [ma:stərie] **1** meesterschap[h]: *the ~ over* de overhand op; **2** beheersing, kennis

masticate [mæstikkeet] kauwen

masturbate [mæstəbeet] masturberen

¹mat [mæt] *n* **1** mat(je[h]) *(also fig; sport)*, deurmat; **2** tafelmatje[h], onderzettertje[h]; **3** klit: *a ~ of hair* een wirwar van haren

²mat [mæt] *vb* klitten, in de war raken

³mat [mæt] *vb* verwarren, doen samenklitten

⁴mat *adj* mat, dof

¹match [mætsj] *n* **1** gelijke: *find* (of: *meet*) *one's ~* zijns gelijke vinden; *be more than a ~ for s.o.* iem de baas zijn; **2** wedstrijd; **3** lucifer; **4** huwelijk[h]

²match [mætsj] *vb* **1** evenaren, niet onderdoen voor: *can you ~ that?* kan je dat net zo goed doen?; *they are well ~ed* zij zijn aan elkaar gewaagd; **2** passen bij: *they are well ~ed* ze passen goed bij elkaar; **3** doen passen, aanpassen *(colour):* ~ *jobs and applicants* het juiste werk voor de juiste kandidaten uitzoeken

³match [mætsj] *vb* (bij elkaar) passen: *~ing clothes* bij elkaar passende kleren

matchbox lucifersdoosje[h]

matchless [mætsjləs] weergaloos, niet te evenaren

matchmaking het koppelen, het tot stand brengen van huwelijken

¹mate [meet] *n* **1** maat, kameraad; **2** (huwelijks)partner, gezel(lin), mannetje[h], wijfje[h] *(of birds)*; **3** helper *(of craftsman)*, gezel; **4** stuurman; **5** *(chess)* mat[h]

²mate [meet] *vb* paren, huwen, zich voortplanten

³mate [meet] *vb* **1** koppelen, doen paren; **2** schaken, mat zetten

¹material [mətjəriəl] *adj* **1** materieel, lichamelijk: *~ damage* materiële schade; **2** belangrijk, wezenlijk: *a ~ witness* een belangrijke getuige

²material [mətjəriəl] *n* **1** materiaal[h], grondstof, *(fig)* gegevens, stof; **2** soort

materialist(ic) [mətjəriəlist(iek)] materialistisch

¹materialize [mətjəriəlajz] *vb* **1** werkelijkheid worden: *his dreams never ~d* zijn dromen werden nooit werkelijkheid; **2** te voorschijn komen *(of ghost)*

²materialize [mətjəriəlajz] *vb* **1** verwezenlijken, realiseren, uitvoeren; **2** materialiseren

maternal [mətə:nl] moeder-: ~ *love* moederliefde; ~ *grandfather* grootvader van moederszijde

maternity [mətə:nittie] moederschap[h]: ~ *home* kraamkliniek

matey [meetie] vriendschappelijk: *be ~ with s.o.* beste maatjes met iem zijn

mathematical [mæθəmætikl] **1** wiskundig; **2** precies, exact

mathematics [mæθəmætiks] wiskunde

maths [mæθs] *mathematics* wiskunde

mating season paartijd, bronst

matricide [mætrissajd] moedermoord(enaar)

matriculation [mətrikjoeleesjən] inschrijving, toegang tot universiteit

matrimony [mætrimmənie] huwelijk[h], echt(elijke staat)

matrix [meetriks] **1** matrijs, gietvorm; **2** matrix

matron [meetrən] **1** matrone; **2** directrice, hoofdverpleegster || ~ *of honour* getrouwd bruidsmeisje

matt [mæt] mat, niet glanzend

¹matter [mætə] *n* **1** materie, stof; **2** stof, materiaal[h], inhoud; **3** stof *(in, of body);* **4** belang[h]: *no ~* (het) maakt niet uit, laat maar; **5** kwestie: *just a ~ of time* slechts een kwestie van tijd; *no laughing ~* niets om te lachen; *for that ~,* for the ~ *of that* wat dat betreft; *as a ~ of course* vanzelfsprekend; *as a ~ of fact* eigenlijk; *what is the ~ with him?* wat scheelt hem?

²matter [mætə] *vb* van belang zijn, betekenen: *it doesn't ~* het geeft niet, het doet er niet toe; *what does it ~?* wat zou het?

matter-of-fact zakelijk, nuchter

matting [mæting] matwerk[h], matten *(as floor covering etc)*

mattress [mætrəs] matras[+h]

¹mature [mətsjoeə] *adj* **1** rijp, volgroeid; **2** volwassen: *behave ~ly* zich gedragen als een volwassene; **3** weloverwogen; **4** belegen *(cheese, wine)*

²mature [mətsjoeə] *vb* **1** rijpen, tot rijpheid komen: *~d cheese* belegen kaas; **2** volgroeien, zich volledig ontwikkelen; volwassen worden; **3** vervallen *(of Bill of Exchange etc)*

maturity [mətsjoeərittie] **1** rijpheid; **2** volgroeidheid; volwassenheid

maul [mo:l] **1** verscheuren, aan stukken scheuren *(also fig);* **2** ruw behandelen

maw [mo:] **1** pens, maag *(of animal);* **2** krop *(of bird);* **3** muil, bek *(fig)*

mawkish [mo:kisj] **1** walgelijk, flauw *(of taste);* **2** overdreven sentimenteel

maxim [mæksim] spreuk

maximally [mæksimməlie] hoogstens, maximaal

¹maximum [mæksimməm] *n* maximum[h]: *at its ~* op het hoogste punt

²maximum [mæksimməm] *adj* maximaal, hoogste: *~ speed* topsnelheid

may [mee] **1** mogen: ~ *I ask why you think so?* mag ik vragen waarom je dat denkt?; *you ~ not leave yet* je mag nog niet vertrekken; **2** *(possibility)* kunnen: they ~ *arrive later* ze komen misschien later; *come what* ~ wat er ook gebeurt; ~ *I help you?* kan ik u helpen?; *I hope he* ~ *recover, but I fear he* ~ *not* ik hoop dat hij beter wordt, maar ik vrees van niet; **3** *(in wishes)* mogen: ~ *you stay forever young* moge jij altijd jong blijven

May [mee] mei

maybe [meebie] misschien, wellicht: *as soon as* ~ zo vlug mogelijk

mayday mayday, noodsignaal[h]

May Day 1 mei, dag vd arbeid

mayfly eendagsvlieg

mayhem [meehem] rotzooi: *cause* (of: *create*) ~ herrie schoppen

mayonnaise [meeəneez] mayonaise

mayor [meə] burgemeester

maze [meez] doolhof *(also fig)*

me [mie] mij, voor mij; ik: *he liked her better than* ~ hij vond haar aardiger dan mij; *poor* ~ arme ik; *it is* ~ ik ben het

meadow [meddoo] wei(de), grasland[h]

meagre [mie:gə] schraal *(meal, result etc)*

meal [mie:l] **1** maal[h], maaltijd; **2** meel[h]

mealy [mie:lie] **1** melig; **2** bleek *(complexion)*

¹mean [mie:n] *adj* **1** gemeen, laag, ongemanierd: ~ *tricks* ordinaire trucs; **2** gierig; **3** armzalig, armoedig; **4** *(Am)* kwaadaardig, vals; **5** gemiddeld, doorsnee-; **6** gebrekkig, beperkt: *no* ~ *cook* een buitengewone kok, geen doorsneekok; **7** laag, gering *(origin)*

²mean [mie:n] *n* **1** ~s middel[h]: *by* ~*s of* door middel van; *by no* ~*s, not by any (manner of)* ~*s* in geen geval; *a* ~*s to an end* een middel om een doel te bereiken; **2** ~*s* middelen (van bestaan): *live beyond one's* ~*s* boven zijn stand leven; **3** middelmaat, *(fig)* middenweg; **4** gemiddelde (waarde)

³mean [mie:n] *vb* **1** betekenen, willen zeggen: *it* ~*s nothing to me* het zegt me niets; **2** bedoelen: *what do you* ~ *by that?* wat bedoel je daarmee?; **3** de bedoeling hebben: ~ *business* vastberaden zijn, zeer serieus zijn; *I* ~ *to leave tomorrow* ik ben van plan morgen te vertrekken; **4** menen; **5** bestemmen; **6** betekenen, neerkomen op: *those clouds* ~ *rain* die wolken voorspellen regen

⁴mean [mie:n] *vb* het bedoelen: ~ *ill (to, towards, by s.o.)* het slecht menen (met iem)

meander [mie·ændə] **1** zich (in bochten) slingeren, kronkelen *(of river);* **2** (rond)dolen *(also fig)*

meanderings [mie·ændəringz] slingerpad, kronkelpad, gekronkel

¹meaning [mie:ning] *n* **1** betekenis, zin, inhoud: *(disapprovingly) what's the* ~ *of this?* wat heeft dit te betekenen?; **2** bedoeling, strekking

²meaning [mie:ning] *adj* veelbetekenend, veelzeggend

meaningful [mie:ningfoel] **1** van (grote) betekenis, gewichtig; **2** zinvol

means test inkomensonderzoek[h]

meantime tussentijd: *in the* ~ ondertussen

meanwhile ondertussen

measles [mie:zlz] **1** mazelen; **2** rodehond

¹measure [mezjə] *vb* meten, af-, op-, toe-, uitmeten, de maat nemen: *the room* ~*s three metres by four* de kamer is drie bij vier (meter); ~ *off* (of: *out*) afmeten *(material etc);* ~ *out* toemeten

²measure [mezjə] *vb* **1** beoordelen, taxeren; **2** opnemen, met de ogen afmeten; **3** letten op, overdenken: ~ *one's words* zijn woorden wegen

³measure [mezjə] *n* **1** maatregel, stap: *take strong* ~*s* geen halve maatregelen nemen; **2** maat *(also music)*, maateenheid; maat(beker); maat(streep) *(mus);* mate, gematigdheid: *a* ~ *of wheat* een maat tarwe; *in (a) great* ~ in hoge mate; *made to* ~ op maat gemaakt; **3** maatstaf; **4** maatstok, maatlat, maatlint[h]; **5** ritme[h], melodie

measured [mezjəd] weloverwogen, zorgvuldig

measurement [mezjəmənt] **1** afmeting, maat; **2** meting

measure up voldoen: ~ *to:* a) voldoen aan; b) berekend zijn op *(of:* voor), opgewassen zijn tegen

meat [mie:t] **1** vlees[h]: *white* ~ wit vlees *(eg poultry);* **2** *(Am)* eetbaar gedeelte[h] *(of fruit, crustacean, egg),* (vrucht)vlees[h]; **3** essentie: *there is no real* ~ *in the story* het verhaal heeft weinig om het lijf; **4** fort[h], sterke kant: *one man's* ~ *is another man's poison* de een traag, de ander graag

meatball gehaktbal

meaty [mie:tie] **1** lijvig; **2** vleesachtig; **3** stevig: *a* ~ *discussion* een pittige discussie

mechanic [mikænik] mecanicien, technicus, monteur

mechanical [mikænikl] **1** mechanisch, machinaal, *(fig)* ongeïnspireerd; **2** ambachtelijk, handwerk-; **3** werktuig(bouw)kundig: ~ *engineering* werktuig(bouw)kunde

mechanics [mikæniks] **1** mechanica, werktuigkunde; **2** mechanisme; **3** techniek

mechanism [mekkənizm] **1** mechanisme[h], mechaniek[h]; **2** werking; **3** techniek

mechanization [mekkənajzeesjən] mechanisering

medal [medl] medaille

medallion [midæliən] **1** (grote) medaille; **2** medaillon[h]

meddle in [medl in] zich bemoeien met, zich inlaten met: *don't* ~ *my affairs* bemoei je met je eigen zaken

meddlesome [medlsəm] bemoeiziek

media [mie:diə] media

median [mie:diən] middel-, midden-, middelst-: ~ *point* zwaartepunt

¹mediate [mie:die·eet] *vb* bemiddelen, bijleggen: ~ *between* bemiddelen tussen

²mediate [mie:die·eet] *vb* overbrengen

mediator [mie:die·eetə] bemiddelaar, tussenpersoon

¹medical [meddikl] *adj* medisch: ~ *certificate* doktersverklaring

²**medical** [mɛddikl] *n* (medisch) onderzoekʰ, keuring

medicament [middikkəmənt] medicijnʰ

medication [meddikkeesjən] **1** medicamentʰ, medicijnʰ, medicijnen; **2** medicatie

medicine [mɛdsin] **1** geneesmiddelʰ: *she takes too much ~* ze slikt te veel medicijnen; **2** tovermiddelʰ; **3** geneeskunde, medicijnen

medieval [meddie·ie:vl] middeleeuws

mediocre [mie:die·ookə] middelmatig

¹**meditate** [mɛdditteet] *vb* **1** diep nadenken, in gedachten verzonken zijn: *~ (up)on* overpeinzen; **2** mediteren

²**meditate** [mɛdditteet] *vb* van plan zijn: *~ revenge* zinnen op wraak

Mediterranean [meddittəreeniən] mbt de Middellandse Zee, mbt het Middellandse-Zeegebied

¹**medium** [mie:diəm] *adj* gemiddeld, doorsnee-: *in the ~ term* op middellange termijn; *(radio) ~ wave* middengolf

²**medium** [mie:diəm] *n* **1** middenweg, compromisʰ; **2** gemiddeldeʰ, middenʰ; **3** mediumʰ, middelʰ: *through the ~ of* door middel van; **4** tussenpersoon; **5** (natuurlijke) omgeving, milieuʰ; **6** uitingsvorm, kunstvorm; **7** *(spiritism)* mediumʰ

medlar [mɛdlə] mispel

medley [mɛdlie] **1** mengelmoes(je)ʰ; **2** *(mus)* potpourri, medley

meek [mie:k] **1** gedwee; **2** bescheiden; **3** zachtmoedig

¹**meet** [mie:t] *vb* **1** elkaar ontmoeten, elkaar tegenkomen: *~ up* elkaar (toevallig) treffen; *~ up with* tegen het lijf lopen; **2** samenkomen, bijeenkomen; **3** kennismaken; **4** sluiten, dicht gaan *(of article of clothing)*

²**meet** [mie:t] *vb* **1** ontmoeten, treffen, tegenkomen: *run to ~ s.o.* iem tegemoet rennen; *(fig) ~ s.o. halfway: a)* iem tegemoet komen; *b)* het verschil (samen) delen; **2** (aan)raken; **3** kennismaken met: *pleased to ~ you* aangenaam; **4** afhalen: *I'll ~ your train* ik kom je van de trein afhalen; **5** behandelen, het hoofd bieden: *~ criticism* kritiek weerleggen; **6** tegemoet komen (aan), voldoen (aan), vervullen: *~ the bill* de rekening voldoen; **7** beantwoorden, (onvriendelijk) bejegenen; **8** ondervinden, ondergaan, dragen: *~ one's death* de dood vinden

³**meet** [mie:t] *n* **1** samenkomst, trefpuntʰ *(for hunt)*; **2** jachtgezelschapʰ; **3** *(Am; athletics)* ontmoeting, wedstrijd

meeting [mie:ting] **1** ontmoeting *(also sport)*, wedstrijd; **2** bijeenkomst, vergadering, bespreking: *~-house* kerk

meet with 1 ondervinden, ondergaan: *~ approval* instemming vinden; **2** tegen het lijf lopen; **3** *(Am)* een ontmoeting hebben met

megabyte [mɛgəbajt] megabyte *(1 million bytes)*

megalomania [megəloomeeniə] grootheidswaanzin

megaphone [mɛgəfoon] megafoon

¹**melancholy** [mɛllənkəlie] *adj* **1** melancholisch, zwaarmoedig; **2** droevig, triest

²**melancholy** [mɛllənkəlie] *n* melancholie, zwaarmoedigheid

mellow [mɛlloo] **1** rijp, sappig *(of fruit);* **2** zacht, warm, vol *(of sound, colour, taste);* **3** gerijpt, zacht(moedig), mild

melodious [milloodiəs] melodieus, welluidend

melodrama [mɛllədra:mə] melodramaʰ *(also fig)*

melody [mɛllədie] melodie

melon [mɛllən] meloen

melt [melt] smelten: *~ in the mouth* smelten op de tong; *~ down* omsmelten

meltdown het afsmelten *(at nuclear power plant)*

melting pot smeltkroes *(also fig):* *in the ~* onstabiel

member [mɛmbə] lidʰ, lidmaat, (onder)deelʰ, elementʰ, zinsdeelʰ, lichaamsdeelʰ: *~ of Parliament* parlementslid; *~ state* lidstaat

membership [mɛmbəsjip] **1** lidmaatschapʰ; **2** ledentalʰ, de leden

membrane [mɛmbreen] membraanʰ

memo [mɛmmoo] *memorandum* memoʰ

memoir [mɛmwa:] **1** biografie; **2** verhandeling

memorable [mɛmmərəbl] gedenkwaardig

memorial [mimmo:riəl] gedenktekenʰ, monumentʰ

memorize [mɛmmərajz] **1** uit het hoofd leren; **2** onthouden

memory [mɛmmərie] **1** geheugenʰ, herinnering: *to the best of my ~* voor zover ik mij kan herinneren; *within living ~* bij mensenheugenis; *from ~* van buiten, uit het hoofd; **2** herinnering, aandenkenʰ: *in ~ of, to the ~ of* ter (na)gedachtenis aan

¹**menace** [mɛnnəs] *n* **1** (be)dreiging: *filled with ~* vol dreiging; **2** lastpost, gevaarʰ

²**menace** [mɛnnəs] *vb* (be)dreigen

¹**mend** [mend] *vb* **1** herstellen, repareren: *~ stockings* kousen stoppen; **2** goedmaken; **3** verbeteren

²**mend** [mend] *vb* er weer bovenop komen, herstellen; zich (ver)beteren

³**mend** [mend] *n* herstelling, reparatie ‖ *he's on the ~* hij is aan de beterende hand

mendicant [mɛndikkənt] **1** bedelmonnik; **2** bedelaar

¹**menial** [mie:niəl] *adj (oft depr)* ondergeschikt, oninteressant: *a ~ job* een min baantje

²**menial** [mie:niəl] *n (oft depr)* dienstbode, knecht, meid

menopause [mɛnnəpo:z] menopauze

men's room *(Am)* herentoiletʰ

menstruation [menstroe·eesjən] menstruatie, ongesteldheid

mental [mɛntl] **1** geestelijk, mentaal, psychisch: *~ illness* zenuwziekte; *~ly defective* (of: *deficient, handicapped)* geestelijk gehandicapt; *~ly retarded* achterlijk; **2** hoofd-, met het hoofd: *~ arithmetic* hoofdrekenen; *~ gymnastics* hersengymnastiek; *make a ~ note of sth.* iets in zijn oren knopen; **3** psychiatrisch: *~ hospital* psychiatrische inrichting

mentality [mentælittie] mentaliteit
¹mention [mensjən] *n* vermelding, opgave: *honourable* ~ eervolle vermelding; *make* ~ *of* vermelden
²mention [mensjən] *vb* vermelden: *not to* ~ om (nog maar) niet te spreken van; *don't* ~ *it* geen dank
mentor [mentο:] mentor
menu [menjoe:] menuʰ, (menu)kaart, maaltijd
mercantile [mα:kəntajl] handels-, koopmans-
¹mercenary [mα:sənərie] *adj* **1** op geld belust; **2** gehuurd: ~ *troops* huurtroepen
²mercenary [mα:sənərie] *n* huurling
merchandise [mα:tsjəndajz] koopwaar, artikelen, producten
¹merchant [mα:tsjənt] *n* groothandelaar, koopman
²merchant [mα:tsjənt] *adj* **1** koopvaardij-: ~ *shipping* koopvaardij; **2** handels-, koopmans-
merciful [mα:siefoel] genadig
mercury [mα:kjoerie] kwik(zilver)ʰ
mercy [mα:sie] **1** genade, barmhartigheid; **2** daad van barmhartigheid, weldaad: *be thankful for small mercies* wees maar blij dat het niet erger is; **3** vergevensgezindheid: *throw oneself on a person's* ~ een beroep doen op iemands goedheid; *(oft iron) left to the (tender)* ~ *of* overgeleverd aan de goedheid van; *at the* ~ *of* in de macht van
mere [miə] louter, puur: *by the* ~*st chance* door stom toeval; *at the* ~ *thought of it* alleen al de gedachte eraan
merely [miəlie] slechts, enkel, alleen
merge [mα:dzj] **1** (with *with*) opgaan (in), samengaan (met), fuseren (met); **2** (geleidelijk) overgaan (in elkaar): *the place where the rivers* ~ de plaats waar de rivieren samenvloeien
merger [mα:dzjə] **1** samensmelting; **2** *(econ)* fusie
meridian [məriddiən] meridiaan, middaglijn
¹merit [merrit] *n* **1** verdienste, waarde: *the* ~*s and demerits of sth.* de voors en tegens van iets; *reward each according to his* ~*s* elk naar eigen verdienste belonen; *judge sth. on its (own)* ~*s* iets op zijn eigen waarde beoordelen; **2** ~*s* intrinsieke waarde
²merit [merrit] *vb* verdienen, waard zijn
mermaid [mα:meed] (zee)meermin
merriment [merriəmənt] **1** vrolijkheid; **2** pret, plezierʰ, hilariteit
merry [merrie] **1** vrolijk, opgewekt: *Merry Christmas* Vrolijk kerstfeest; **2** aangeschoten: *lead s.o. a* ~ *dance: a)* iem het leven zuur maken; *b)* iem voor de gek houden; *make* ~ pret maken; *make* ~ *over* zich vrolijk maken over
merry-go-round draaimolen, carrousel, *(fig)* maalstroom, roes
merrymaking 1 pret(makerij), feestvreugde; **2** feestelijkheid
¹mesh [mesj] *n* **1** maas, steek, *(fig also)* strik; **2** net(werk)ʰ: *a* ~ *of lies* een netwerk van leugens
²mesh [mesj] *vb* **1** (with *with*) ineengrijpen, ingeschakeld zijn, *(fig)* harmoniëren (met); **2** verstrikt geraken
mesmerize [mezmərajz] *(esp past participle)* mag-

netiseren, (als) verlammen: ~*d at his appearance* gebiologeerd door zijn verschijning
¹mess [mes] *n* **1** puinhoop, troep, (war)boel, knoeiboel: *his life was a* ~ zijn leven was een mislukking; *clear up the* ~ de rotzooi opruimen; **2** vuile boel; **3** moeilijkheid: *get oneself into a* ~ zichzelf in moeilijkheden brengen; **4** mess, kantine
²mess [mes] *vb* zich bemoeien met iets, tussenkomen: ~ *in other people's business* z'n neus in andermans zaken steken; *no* ~*ing* echt waar
¹mess about *vb* prutsen, (lui) rondhangen: *don't* ~ *with people like him* laat je niet met mensen zoals hij niet in; *he spent the weekend messing about* hij lummelde wat rond tijdens het weekend
²mess about *vb* **1** rotzooien met: *stop messing my daughter about* blijf met je poten van mijn dochter af; **2** belazeren
message [messidzj] **1** boodschap: *the* ~ *of a book* de kerngedachte van een boek; *(I) got the* ~ begrepen, ik snap het al; *send s.o. on a* ~ iem om een boodschap sturen; **2** berichtʰ
messenger [messindzjə] boodschapper, bode, koerier
Messrs. [messəz] **1** (de) Heren; **2** Fa., Firma: ~ *Smith & Jones* de Firma Smith & Jones
mess up 1 in de war sturen, verknoeien: *mess things up* ergens een potje van maken; **2** smerig maken; **3** ruw aanpakken, toetakelen; **4** in moeilijkheden brengen
mess with lastig vallen: *don't* ~ *me* laat me met rust
messy [messie] **1** vuil, vies; **2** slordig, verward
metabolism [mitæbəlizm] metabolismeʰ, stofwisseling
¹metal [metl] *n* **1** metaalʰ; **2** steenslag *(for road)*
²metal [metl] *adj* metalen
metallic [mitælik] **1** metalen: ~ *lustre* metaalglans; **2** metaalhoudend
metamorphosis [mettəmο:fəsis] metamorfose, gedaanteverwisseling
metaphor [mettəfə] metafoor, beeldʰ, beeldspraak
metaphysical [mettəfizzikl] **1** metafysisch, bovennatuurlijk; **2** *(oft depr)* abstract, te subtiel
meteor [mie:tiə] meteoor
meteorite [mie:tiərajt] meteoriet
meteorologist [mie:tiərollədzjist] weerkundige
mete out [mie:t aut] toedienen: ~ *rewards and punishments* beloningen en straffen uitdelen
meter [mie:tə] meter, meettoestelʰ
method [meθəd] methode, procedure: ~*s of payment* wijzen van betaling
methodical [miθodikl] methodisch, zorgvuldig
meticulous [mittikjoeləs] uiterst nauwgezet, pietepeuterig
metre [mie:tə] **1** meter; **2** metrumʰ
metric [metrik] metriek: ~ *system* metriek stelsel
metrical [metrikl] metrisch, ritmisch
metropolis [mitroppəlis] metropool
¹metropolitan [metrəpollittən] *adj* hoofdstedelijk
²metropolitan [metrəpollittən] *n* bewoner ve me-

tropool

mettle [metl] **1** moed, kracht: *a man of ~* een man met pit; *show* (of: *prove*) *one's ~* zijn karakter tonen; **2** temperament[h], aard

mg *milligram(s)*

microbe [majkroob] microbe

microfilm [majkrəfilm] microfilm

micrometer [majkrommittə] micrometer

micron [majkron] micron, micrometer

microphone [majkrəfoon] microfoon

microprocessor [majkrooproosessə] microprocessor *(central processing unit of computer)*

microscope [majkrəskoop] microscoop: *put* (of: *examine*) *under the ~* onder de loep nemen *(also fig)*

microscopic [majkrəskoppik] microscopisch (klein)

microwave [majkrooweev] microgolf

mid(-) [mid] midden, het midden van: *in mid-air* in de lucht; *from mid-June to mid-August* van half juni tot half augustus; *in mid-ocean* in volle zee

midday [middee] middag

midden [midn] mesthoop, afvalhoop

¹middle [midl] *adj* middelst, midden, tussen-: *~ age* middelbare leeftijd; *Middle Ages* Middeleeuwen; *~ class: a)* bourgeoisie; *b)* kleinburgerlijk; *~ finger* middelvinger; *~ distance (athletics)* middenafstand; *Middle East* Midden-Oosten

²middle [midl] *n* **1** midden[h], middelpunt[h], middellijn, middelvlak[h]: *in the ~ (of)* middenin; *be caught in the ~* tussen twee vuren zitten; **2** middel[h], taille: *keep to the ~ of the road* de (gulden) middenweg nemen

middle-class kleinburgerlijk

middleman tussenpersoon, bemiddelaar, makelaar

middle-of-the-road gematigd

middling [midling] middelmatig, tamelijk (goed), redelijk, *(inf)* tamelijk gezond

midge [midzj] mug

¹midget [midzjit] *adj* lilliputachtig, mini-: *~ golf* midgetgolf

²midget [midzjit] *n* dwerg, lilliputter

midland [midlənd] binnenland[h], centraal gewest[h]

Midlands [midləndz] Midden-Engeland: *a ~ town* een stad in Midden-Engeland

midlife middelbare leeftijd: *a ~ crisis* een crisis op middelbare leeftijd

midnight middernacht: *at ~* om middernacht

midriff [midrif] **1** middenrif[h]; **2** maagstreek

midst [midst] midden[h]: *in the ~ of the fight* in het heetst van de strijd

midway halverwege: *stand ~ between* het midden houden tussen

midwife vroedvrouw

miffed [mift] op de tenen getrapt

¹might *vb* **1** mocht(en), zou(den) mogen: *~ I ask you a question?* zou ik u een vraag mogen stellen?; **2** *(possibility)* kon(den), zou(den) (misschien) kun-

nen: *he told her he ~ arrive later* hij zei dat hij misschien later kwam; *it ~ be a good idea to ...* het zou misschien goed zijn te ...; *you ~ have warned us* je had ons wel even kunnen waarschuwen

²might *n* macht, kracht: *with ~ and main* met man en macht

mighty [majtie] **1** machtig, krachtig; **2** indrukwekkend, kolossaal; **3** geweldig

migraine [mie:green] migraine(aanval)

¹migrant [majgrənt] *adj* migrerend, trek-: *~ seasonal workers* rondtrekkende seizoenarbeiders

²migrant [majgrənt] *n* seizoenarbeider

migrate [majgreet] trekken, verhuizen

migration [majgreesjən] migratie, volksverhuizing

migratory [majgrətərie] zwervend: *~ bird* trekvogel

¹mild [majld] *adj* **1** mild, zacht(aardig), welwillend: *only ~ly interested* maar matig geïnteresseerd; *to put it ~ly* om het zachtjes uit te drukken; **2** zwak, licht, flauw: *~ flavoured tobacco* tabak met een zacht aroma

²mild [majld] *n* licht bier[h]

mildew [mildjoe:] **1** schimmel(vorming); **2** meeldauw(schimmel)

mile [majl] mijl *(1,609.34 metres); (fig)* grote afstand: *she is feeling ~s better* ze voelt zich stukken beter; *stick out a ~* in het oog springen; *my thoughts were ~s away* ik was met mijn gedachten heel ergens anders; *recognize s.o. a ~ off* iem van een kilometer afstand herkennen; *run a ~ from s.o.* met een boog om iem heenlopen

mileage [majlidzj] **1** totaal aantal afgelegde mijlen; **2** profijt[h]: *he has got a lot of political ~ out of his proposal* met dat voorstel heeft hij heel wat politiek voordeel gehaald

milestone mijlpaal

milieu [mie:ljə:] milieu[h], sociale omgeving

militant [millittənt] militant, strijdlustig

militarism [millittərizm] militarisme[h]

¹military [millittərie] *adj* militair, krijgs- || *~ service* (leger)dienst; *~ tribunal* krijgsraad

²military [millittərie] *n* leger[h], soldaten, strijdkrachten

militate [millitteet] pleiten: *~ against* pleiten tegen; *~ for* pleiten voor

militia [millisjə] militie(leger[h]), burgerleger

¹milk [milk] *n* melk, *(bot)* melk(sap[h]): *attested ~* kiemvrije melk; *skim(med) ~* magere, afgeroomde melk; *~ run* routineklus, makkie; *~ and honey* melk en honing *(abundance); (it's no use) cry(ing) over spilt ~* gedane zaken nemen geen keer

²milk [milk] *vb* **1** melken; **2** (ont)trekken, sap aftappen van *(tree, snake etc)*; **3** exploiteren, uitbuiten; **4** ontlokken *(information)*, (uit)melken

milkman [milkmən] melkboer

milksop bangerik, huilebalk

milky [milkie] **1** melkachtig, troebel; **2** melkhoudend || *the Milky Way* de melkweg

¹mill [mil] *n* **1** molen, pers; **2** fabriek || *put s.o. through*

the ~ iem flink onder handen nemen; *have been through the ~* het klappen van de zweep kennen

²**mill** [mil] *vb* **1** malen; **2** (metaal) pletten, walsen

mill about krioelen, wemelen

millennium [millenniəm] millennium[h], periode van duizend jaar

miller [millə] molenaar

milligram(me) [milligræm] milligram

millimetre [millimmie:tə] millimeter

million [milliən] miljoen, *(fig)* talloos: *(Am) thanks a ~* reuze bedankt; *a chance in a ~* een kans van één op duizend; *feel like a ~ (dollars)* zich kiplekker voelen

millionaire [milliəneə] miljonair

millionth [milliənθ] miljoenste, miljoenste deel[h]

millipede [millippi:d] duizendpoot

millstone molensteen *(also fig)*

milometer [majlommittə] mijlenteller, kilometerteller

¹**mime** [majm] *n* **1** mime, (panto)mimespeler, mimekunst; **2** nabootsing

²**mime** [majm] *vb* mimen, optreden in mimespel

¹**mimic** [mimmik] *n* **1** mime, mimespeler; **2** na-aper *(also animals)*

²**mimic** [mimmik] *vb* nabootsen, na-apen

³**mimic** [mimmik] *adj* **1** mimisch: *~ art* mimiek; **2** nabootsend, na-apend

mimicry [mimmikrie] **1** nabootsing; **2** mimiek

min. **1** *minimum* **2** *Ministry* Min., ministerie[h]; **3** *minute(s)* min.

minaret [minnəret] minaret

¹**mince** [mins] *vb* **1** aanstellerig spreken; **2** trippelen

²**mince** [mins] *vb* **1** fijnhakken: *~d meat* gehakt (vlees); **2** aanstellerig uitspreken: *she didn't ~ her words* zij nam geen blad voor de mond, ze zei waar het op stond; **3** vergoelijken: *not the matter* er geen doekjes om winden

³**mince** [mins] *n* **1** gehakt[h], gehakt vlees[h]; **2** *(Am)* gehakt voedsel[h]

mincemeat pasteivulling ‖ *make ~ of* in de pan hakken, geen stukje heel laten van *(an argument)*

mincer [minsə] gehaktmolen

¹**mind** [majnd] *n* **1** geest, gemoed[h]: *set s.o.'s ~ at ease* iem geruststellen; *have sth. on one's ~* iets op zijn hart hebben; **2** verstand[h]: *be clear in one's ~ about sth.* iets ten volle beseffen; **3** mening, opinie: *have a ~ of one's own* er zijn eigen ideeën op na houden; *speak one's ~* zijn mening zeggen, zeggen wat je op je hart hebt; *be in two ~s (about)* het met zichzelf oneens zijn over; *to my ~* volgens mij; **4** bedoeling: *nothing is further from my ~!: a)* ik denk er niet aan!, ik pieker er niet over!; *b)* dat is helemaal niet mijn bedoeling; *have half a ~ to* min of meer geneigd zijn om, *(iron)* veel zin hebben om; *change one's ~* zich bedenken; *make up one's ~* tot een besluit komen, een beslissing nemen; **5** wil, zin(nen): *have sth. in ~: a)* iets van plan zijn; *b)* iets in gedachten hebben; **6** aandacht, gedachte(n): *bear in ~* in gedachten houden; *cross* (of: *enter*) *one's ~* bij iem

opkomen; *give* (of: *put, turn*) *one's ~ to* zijn aandacht richten op; *set one's ~ to sth.* zich ergens op concentreren; *it'll take my ~ off things* het zal mij wat afleiden; **7** denkwijze; **8** herinnering: *bring* (of: *call*) *sth. to ~:* a) zich iets herinneren; *b)* doen denken aan; *come* (of: *spring*) *to ~, come into one's ~* te binnen schieten; *keep in ~* niet vergeten; *it slipped my ~* het is mij ontschoten; *who do you have in ~?* aan wie denk je?

²**mind** [majnd] *vb* **1** bezwaren hebben (tegen), erop tegen zijn, zich storen aan: *he doesn't ~ the cold weather* het koude weer deert hem niet; *would you ~?* zou je 't erg vinden?, vindt u het erg?; **2** gehoorzamen

³**mind** [majnd] *vb* **1** denken aan, bedenken, letten op: *~ one's own business* zich met zijn eigen zaken bemoeien; *never ~* maak je geen zorgen, het geeft niet; *never ~ the expense* de kosten spelen geen rol; *never ~ what your father said* ongeacht wat je vader zei; *(when leaving) ~ how you go* wees voorzichtig; **2** zorgen voor, oppassen, bedienen: *he couldn't walk, never ~ run* hij kon niet lopen, laat staan rennen; *~ you go to the dentist* denk erom dat je nog naar de tandarts moet

⁴**mind** [majnd] *vb* opletten, oppassen: *~ (you), I would prefer not to* maar ik zou het liever niet doen

mind-blowing fantastisch, duizelingwekkend

mind-boggling verbijsterend

minded [majndid] geneigd: *he could do it if he were so ~* hij zou het kunnen doen als hij er (maar) zin in had

minder [majndə] **1** kinderoppas; **2** bodyguard

mindful [majndfoel] **1** bedachtzaam; **2** opmerkzaam; **3** denkend aan: *~ of one's duties* zijn plichten indachtig

mindless [majndləs] **1** dwaas, dom; **2** niet lettend op: *~ of danger* zonder oog voor gevaar; *~ violence* zinloos geweld

mind out (with *for*) oppassen (voor)

mind's eye 1 geestesoog[h], verbeelding; **2** herinnering

¹**mine** [majn] *pron* **1** van mij: *that box is ~* die doos is van mij; **2** de mijne(n), het mijne: *a friend of ~* een vriend van me

²**mine** [majn] *n* mijn, *(fig)* goudmijn: *a ~ of information* een rijke bron van informatie

³**mine** [majn] *vb* **1** in een mijn werken, een mijn aanleggen: *~ for gold* naar goud zoeken; **2** mijnen leggen

⁴**mine** [majn] *vb* uitgraven

minefield mijnenveld[h] *(also fig)*

miner [majnə] mijnwerker

¹**mineral** [minnərəl] *adj* delfstoffen-, mineraal-: *~ ores* mineraalertsen

²**mineral** [minnərəl] *n* **1** mineraal[h]; **2** *~s* mineraalwater[h]

mineralogy [minnərælədzjie] mineralogie

minesweeper mijnenveger

mingle [minggl] **1** zich (ver)mengen; **2** zich mengen onder: *they didn't feel like mingling* ze hadden geen zin om met de anderen te gaan praten *(at party)*

mingy [mɪndzjie] krenterig

miniature [mɪnnətsjə] miniatuur

minibar minibar

minimal [mɪnniml] minimaal

minimize [mɪnnimmajz] minimaliseren, zo klein mogelijk maken, vergoelijken

minimum [mɪnnimməm] minimum[h]: *keep sth. to a* ~ iets tot het minimum beperkt houden; ~ *wage* minimumloon

mining [majning] mijnbouw

minion [mɪnniən] gunsteling, slaafs volgeling, hielenlikker

minister [mɪnnistə] 1 minister: *Minister of the Crown* minister (van het Britse kabinet); *Minister of State* onderminister; 2 geestelijke, predikant; 3 gezant

ministerial [minnistiəriəl] 1 ministerieel; 2 geestelijk

ministry [mɪnnistrie] 1 ministerie[h]; 2 dienst, verzorging; 3 geestelijke ambt[h] *(priest, vicar): enter the* ~ geestelijke worden

mink [mingk] 1 nertsbont[h]; 2 nertsmantel

¹minor [majnə] *adj* 1 minder, kleiner, vrij klein; 2 minder belangrijk, lager, ondergeschikt: ~ *poet* minder belangrijke dichter; ~ *road* secundaire weg; 3 minderjarig; 4 *(mus)* mineur: *in a* ~ *key* in mineur *(also fig)*

²minor [majnə] *n* 1 minderjarige; 2 bijvak[h] *(at Am university)*

minority [majnorrittie] 1 minderheid; 2 minderjarigheid

minstrel [mɪnstrəl] minstreel

¹mint [mint] *n* 1 munt *(bldg); (inf)* bom duiten; smak geld; *(fig)* bron; 2 pepermuntje[h]; 3 *(bot)* munt

²mint [mint] *vb* munten, tot geld slaan, *(fig)* smeden: ~ *a new expression* een nieuwe uitdrukking creëren

mint condition perfecte staat: *in* ~ puntgaaf

minuet [minjoe·ɛt] menuet[h]

¹minus [majnəs] *prep* 1 min(us), min, onder nul: *wages* ~ *taxes* loon na aftrekking van belastingen; ~ *six (degrees centigrade)* zes graden onder nul; 2 minder dan: ~ *two cm in diameter* minder dan twee cm doorsnede; 3 *(inf)* zonder: *a teapot* ~ *a spout* een theepot zonder tuit

²minus [majnəs] *n* 1 minteken[h]; 2 minus[h], tekort[h], *(fig)* nadeel[h]

³minus [majnəs] *adj* 1 negatief *(maths, science);* 2 *(educ)* -min, iets minder goed dan: *a B-*~ *(roughly)* een 8 min

¹minute [mɪnnit] *n* 1 minuut, ogenblik[h]: ~ *hand* grote wijzer; *wait a* ~ wacht eens even; *I won't be a* ~ ik ben zo klaar, ik ben zo terug; *just a* ~*!* moment!, ogenblik(je)!; *in a* ~ zo dadelijk; *the* ~ *(that) I saw him* zodra ik hem zag; 2 aantekening, notitie; 3 nota, memorandum[h]; 4 ~*s* notulen

²minute [majnjoe·t] *adj* 1 onbeduidend; 2 minutieus, gedetailleerd

minx [mingks] brutale meid

miracle [mɪrrəkl] mirakel[h], wonder[h]

miraculous [mɪrækjoeləs] miraculeus, wonderbaarlijk

mirage [mɪrra:zj] 1 luchtspiegeling, fata morgana; 2 droombeeld[h], hersenschim

¹mirror [mɪrrə] *n* spiegel, *(fig)* weerspiegeling

²mirror [mɪrrə] *vb* (weer)spiegelen, afspiegelen, weerkaatsen

misadventure tegenspoed, ongeluk[h]: *death by* ~ dood door ongeluk

misanthrope [mɪznθroop] misantroop, mensenhater

misapply 1 verkeerd toepassen; 2 verduisteren *(money)*

misapprehension misverstand[h], misvatting: *under the* ~ *that ...* in de waan dat ...

misbehave zich misdragen, zich slecht gedragen

¹miscalculate *vb* zich misrekenen

²miscalculate *vb* verkeerd schatten, onjuist berekenen: *I had* ~*d the distance* ik had de afstand fout geschat

miscarriage [miskærridzj] 1 mislukking *(of plan):* ~ *of justice* rechterlijke dwaling; 2 miskraam

miscellaneous [missəleeniəs] 1 gemengd, gevarieerd: ~ *articles* artikelen over uiteenlopende onderwerpen; 2 veelzijdig

miscellany [missɛllənie] mengeling; mengelwerk[h]

mischance ongeluk[h], tegenslag: *by* ~, *through a* ~ bij ongeluk

mischief [mistsjif] 1 kattenkwaad[h]: *her eyes were full of* ~ haar ogen straalden ondeugd uit; *get into* ~ kattenkwaad uithalen; 2 ondeugendheid; 3 onheil[h], schade: *the* ~ *had been done* het kwaad was al geschied

misconception verkeerde opvatting

misconduct 1 wangedrag[h], onfatsoenlijkheid; 2 ambtsmisdrijf[h], ambtsovertreding

misconstrue verkeerd interpreteren

misdemeanour misdrijf[h]

miser [majzə] vrek

miserable [mɪzzərəbl] 1 beroerd, ellendig; 2 armzalig: *live on a* ~ *pension* van een schamel pensioentje rondkomen; 3 waardeloos

misery [mɪzzərie] 1 ellende, nood: *put an animal out of its* ~ een dier uit zijn lijden helpen; 2 tegenslag, beproeving; 3 pijn, ziekte

misfortune [misfo:tsjoe:n] ongeluk[h], tegenspoed

misgiving onzekerheid, bang vermoeden[h]: *they had serious* ~*s about employing him* ze twijfelden er ernstig aan of ze hem in dienst konden nemen

misguided [misgajdid] 1 misleid, verblind; 2 ondoordacht

mishandle verkeerd behandelen, slecht regelen

mishap [mɪshæp] ongeluk(je)[h], tegenvaller(tje[h]): *a journey without* ~ een reis zonder incidenten

mishmash [mɪsjmæsj] mengelmoes[h], rommeltje[h]

misinterpret [missɪntə:prit] verkeerd interpreteren, verkeerd begrijpen

misinterpretation [missintə:pritteesjən] verkeerde interpretatie: *open to* ~ voor verkeerde uitleg vatbaar

misjudge [misdzjudzj] verkeerd (be)oordelen: ~ *s.o.* zich in iem vergissen

mislay [mislee] zoekmaken, verliezen: *I've mislaid my glasses* ik kan mijn bril niet vinden

mislead [mislie:d] misleiden, bedriegen, op 't verkeerde spoor brengen

misleading [mislie:ding] misleidend, bedrieglijk

mismanagement [mismænidzjmənt] wanbeheer^h, wanbestuur^h, -beleid^h

mismatch [mismætsj] verkeerde combinatie, verkeerd huwelijk^h

misplace [misplees] misplaatsen: *a ~d remark* een misplaatste opmerking

misread [misrie:d] verkeerd lezen: ~ *s.o.'s feelings* zich in iemands gevoelens vergissen

misrepresent [misreprizzent] **1** verkeerd voorstellen; **2** slecht vertegenwoordigen

¹miss [mis] *vb* **1** missen: *his shots all ~ed* hij schoot er telkens naast; **2** *(in ing-form)* ontbreken: *the book is ~ing* het boek is zoek; **3** mislopen, falen

²miss [mis] *vb* **1** missen, niet raken; **2** mislopen, te laat komen voor: ~ *s.o.* een afspraak mislopen; **3** ontsnappen aan: *he narrowly ~ed the accident* hij ontsnapte ternauwernood aan het ongeluk; **4** vermissen, afwezigheid opmerken: *they'll never ~ it* ze zullen nooit merken dat het verdwenen is

³miss [mis] *n* misser, misslag: *give sth. a ~* iets laten voorbijgaan; *I think I'll give it a ~ this year* ik denk dat ik het dit jaar maar eens oversla

Miss [mis] **1** Mejuffrouw, Juffrouw: *the ~es Brown* de (jonge)dames Brown; **2** *miss* jongedame

missile [missajl] **1** raket; **2** projectiel^h

missing [missing] **1** ontbrekend: *the ~ link* de ontbrekende schakel; **2** vermist: *killed, wounded or ~* gesneuveld, gewond of vermist; **3** verloren, weg

mission [misjən] **1** afvaardiging, legatie: *(Am) foreign ~* gezantschap; **2** roeping, zending: *her ~ in life* haar levenstaak; **3** opdracht: ~ *accomplished* taak volbracht, opdracht uitgevoerd

¹missionary [misjənərie] *n* missionaris, zendeling

²missionary [misjənərie] *adj* **1** zendings-; **2** zendelings-

¹miss out *vb* over het hoofd gezien worden: *she always misses out* ze vist altijd achter het net; ~ *on the fun* de pret mislopen

²miss out *vb* **1** vergeten; **2** overslaan

¹mist [mist] *n* **1** mist *(also fig)*, nevel: *lost in the ~ of antiquity* verloren in de nevelen der oudheid; **2** waas^h: *see things through a ~* alles in een waas zien

²mist [mist] *vb* **1** misten; **2** *(with over, up)* beslaan; **3** beneveld worden; wazig worden

¹mistake [misteek] *n* fout; dwaling: *and make no ~:* *a)* en vergis je niet; *b)* en houd jezelf niet voor de gek; *my ~* ik vergis me, mijn fout; *by ~* per ongeluk; *and no ~, there's no ~ about it* daar kun je van op aan, en dat is zeker

²mistake [misteek] *vb* **1** verkeerd begrijpen; **2** verkeerd kiezen; **3** niet herkennen: *there's no mistaking him with his orange hat* je kunt hem eenvoudig niet mislopen met zijn oranje hoed; **4** *(with for)* verwarren (met)

mistaken verkeerd (begrepen), mis: ~ *identity* persoonsverwisseling; *be ~ about* zich vergissen omtrent

mister [mistə] *(without surname)* meneer: *what's the time, ~?* hoe laat is het, meneer?

mistletoe [misltoo] maretak

mistress [mistris] **1** meesteres, bazin *(eg of dog, shop): she is her own ~* zij is haar eigen baas; ~ *of the house* vrouw des huizes; **2** lerares; **3** maîtresse

¹mistrust [mistrust] *vb* wantrouwig zijn (over), wantrouwen

²mistrust [mistrust] *n* wantrouwen^h

misty [mistie] mistig; nevelig

misunderstand [missundəstænd] **1** niet begrijpen: *a misunderstood artist* een onbegrepen kunstenaar; **2** verkeerd begrijpen

¹misuse [misjoe:s] *n* **1** misbruik^h: ~ *of funds* verduistering van gelden; **2** verkeerd gebruik^h

²misuse [misjoe:z] *vb* **1** misbruiken; **2** verkeerd gebruiken

mitigate [mittigeet] **1** lenigen, verlichten; **2** tot bedaren brengen

mitt [mit] **1** want; **2** *(baseball)* (vang)handschoen

¹mix [miks] *vb* **1** (ver)mengen; **2** bereiden, mixen: *he was ~ing a salad* hij was een slaatje aan het klaarmaken; **3** mixen *(sound):* ~ *it (up)* elkaar in de haren zitten, knokken

²mix [miks] *vb* zich (laten) (ver)mengen: ~ *with* omgaan met

³mix [miks] *n* **1** mengeling, mix; **2** mengsel^h

mixed [mikst] gemengd, vermengd: ~ *bag* allegaartje, ratjetoe, een bonte verzameling; *technology is a ~ blessing* de technologie heeft voor- en nadelen; *(tennis)* ~ *doubles* gemengd dubbel

mixed up 1 in de war, versuft; **2** betrokken, verwikkeld

mixer [miksə] mengtoestel^h, (keuken)mixer || *a good ~* een gezellig mens

mixture [mikstsjə] mengsel^h, mengeling

mix up 1 verwarren: *I kept mixing up the names of those twins* ik haalde steeds de namen van die tweeling door elkaar; **2** in de war brengen

mm *millimetre(s)* mm

mnemonic [nimmonnik] ezelsbruggetje^h, geheugensteuntje^h

¹moan [moon] *vb* **1** kermen, kreunen; **2** klagen, jammeren: *what's he ~ing about now?* waarover zit ie nu weer te zeuren?

²moan [moon] *n* **1** gekreun^h, gekerm^h; **2** geklaag^h, gejammer^h

¹mob [mob] *n* **1** gepeupel^h; **2** menigte; **3** bende

²mob [mob] *vb* **1** in bende aanvallen, lastig vallen; **2** omstuwen, drommen rondom

³mob [mob] *vb* samenscholen

¹mobile [mo͞obajl] adj **1** beweeglijk, mobiel, los, levendig; **2** rondtrekkend (of vehicle, shop): a ~ home een stacaravan

²mobile [mo͞obajl] n **1** mobile; **2** draadloze telefoon || ~ phone draadloze telefoon, gsm

mobility [mo͞obillittie] beweeglijkheid, mobiliteit

mobilize [mo͞obillajz] mobiliseren: he ~d all his forces hij verzamelde al zijn krachten

¹mock [mok] vb spotten, zich vrolijk maken

²mock [mok] vb **1** bespotten; **2** (minachtend) trotseren, tarten

³mock [mok] adj onecht, nagemaakt: ~ trial schijnproces

mode [mood] **1** wijze, manier, methode; **2** gebruikʰ, procedure

¹model [modl] n **1** modelʰ, maquette, evenbeeldʰ; **2** typeʰ (eg of car); **3** exclusief modelʰ (article of clothing); **4** toonbeeldʰ, voorbeeldʰ

²model [modl] adj **1** model-; **2** perfect: a ~ husband een modelechtgenoot

³model [modl] vb mannequin zijn

⁴model [modl] vb **1** modelleren, boetseren; **2** vormen naar een voorbeeld: he ~led his main character on one of his teachers voor de hoofdpersoon gebruikte hij een van zijn leraren als voorbeeld

modem [mo͞odem] modulator-demodulator modemʰ

¹moderate [moddərət] adj gematigd, matig: ~ prices redelijke prijzen

²moderate [moddərət] n gematigde

³moderate [moddəreet] vb **1** (zich) matigen: the strikers have ~d their demands de stakers hebben hun eisen bijgesteld; **2** afnemen, verminderen

modern [moddən] modern: ~ history nieuwe geschiedenis; ~ languages levende talen

modernize [moddənajz] moderniseren, (zich) vernieuwen

modest [moddist] **1** bescheiden; **2** niet groot; **3** redelijk

modification [moddiffikke͞esjən] **1** wijziging; **2** verzachting

modify [moddiffaj] **1** wijzigen; **2** verzachten

module [modjoe:l] **1** module, (archeology) bouwelementʰ; **2** modulus, maat(staf)

moist [mojst] vochtig, klam

moisten [mojsn] bevochtigen, natmaken

moisture [mojstsjə] vochtʰ, vochtigheid

molar [mo͞olə] kies

mole [mool] **1** mol; **2** (kleine) moedervlek, vlekjeʰ; **3** pier, golfbreker; **4** spion, mol

molecule [mollikjoe:l] molecule⁺ʰ

molehill molshoop

molest [məlest] lastig vallen, molesteren

mollify [molliffaj] **1** bedaren; **2** vertederen, vermurwen: be mollified by s.o.'s flatteries zich laten vermurwen door iemands vleierij; **3** matigen, verzachten

mollusc [molləsk] weekdierʰ

molten [mo͞oltən] gesmolten

mom [mom] mamma

moment [mo͞omənt] **1** (geschikt) ogenblikʰ, momentʰ: for the ~ voorlopig; in a ~ ogenblikkelijk; just a ~, please een ogenblikje alstublieft; **2** tijdstipʰ: at the ~ op het ogenblik; **3** belangʰ, gewichtʰ: of (great) ~ van (groot) belang

momentary [mo͞oməntərie] kortstondig, vluchtig

momentous [mo͞omentəs] gewichtig, ernstig

momentum [mo͞omentəm] **1** impuls, hoeveelheid van beweging; **2** vaart (also fig), (stuw)kracht: gain (of: gather) ~ aan stootkracht winnen

monarchy [monnəkie] monarchie

monastery [monnəstrie] (mannen)kloosterʰ

Monday [mundee] maandag

monetary [munnittərie] monetair

money [munnie] **1** geldʰ: one's ~'s worth waar voor je geld; made of ~ stinkend rijk; I'm not made of ~ het geld groeit me niet op de rug; there is ~ in it er valt geld aan te verdienen; **2** welstand, rijkdom: ~ talks met geld open je (alle) deuren; for my ~ wat mij betreft

money-grubber geldwolf

moneylender financier, geldschieter

mongrel [munggrəl] **1** bastaard(hond); **2** mengvorm

¹monitor [monnittə] n **1** monitor, leraarshulpjeʰ; **2** controleapparaatʰ, monitor

²monitor [monnittə] vb controleren, meekijken (meeluisteren) met, afluisteren, toezicht houden op

monk [mungk] (klooster)monnik

monkey [mungkie] **1** aap; **2** deugniet

monkey-nut apennoot(jeʰ)

monkey-puzzle apenboom

monogamous [mənogəməs] monogaam

monogram [monnəgræm] monogramʰ, naamtekenʰ

monologue [monnəlog] monoloog, alleenspraak

monopolize [mənoppəlajz] monopoliseren

monopoly [mənoppəlie] monopolieʰ, alleenrechtʰ

monosyllable [monnoosilləbl] eenlettergrepig woordʰ: speak in ~s kortaf spreken

monotonous [mənotnəs] monotoon, eentonig, slaapverwekkend

monsoon [monso͞e:n] **1** moesson(wind), passaatwind; **2** (natte) moesson, regenseizoenʰ

monster [monstə] **1** monsterʰ, gedrochtʰ; **2** onmens, beestʰ; **3** bakbeestʰ, kanjer: ~ potatoes enorme aardappelen

monstrosity [monstrossittie] monstruositeit, wanproductʰ

monstrous [monstrəs] **1** monsterlijk; **2** enorm

month [munθ] maand || I won't do it in a ~ of Sundays ik doe het in geen honderd jaar

¹monthly [munθlie] adj, adv maandelijks

²monthly [munθlie] n maandbladʰ

monument [monjoemənt] monumentʰ, gedenktekenʰ

monumental [monjoementl] **1** monumentaal; **2**

kolossaal

¹**moo** [moe:] *n* boe(geluid)ʰ *(of cow)*

²**moo** [moe:] *vb* loeien

mooch [moe:tsj] **1** jatten, gappen; **2** *(Am)* bietsen, schooien

mood [moe:d] **1** stemming, bui: *in no ~ for* niet in de stemming voor; **2** wijs: *imperative ~* gebiedende wijs

moody [moe:die] **1** humeurig, wispelturig; **2** slechtgehumeurd

moon [moe:n] maan, satelliet (van andere planeten) ‖ *promise s.o. the ~* iem gouden bergen beloven; *be over the ~* in de wolken zijn, in de zevende hemel zijn

moonbeam manestraal

¹**moonlight** *n* maanlichtʰ

²**moonlight** *vb* **1** een bijbaantje hebben, bijverdienen, klussen; **2** zwartwerken

moonlighter iem die een bijbaantje heeft, schnabbelaar

moonlit [moe:nlit] maanbeschenen, met maanlicht overgoten

moon over dagdromen over, mijmeren

moonshine 1 maneschijn; **2** gekletsʰ, dromerij; **3** *(esp Am)* illegaal gestookte sterkedrank

moonstruck 1 maanziek; **2** warhoofdig, geschift

¹**moor** [moeə] *n* **1** hei(de), woeste grond; **2** *(Am)* veenmoerasʰ

²**moor** [moeə] *vb* (aan-, af-, vast)meren, vastleggen

mooring [moeəring] ligplaats, ankerplaats ‖ *lose one's ~s* zijn houvast verliezen

Moorish [moeərisj] Moors, Saraceens

moorland [moeələnd] heide(landschapʰ)

moose [moe:s] *(moose)* eland *(North America)*

moot [moe:t] onbeslist, onuitgemaakt: *a ~ point* (of: *question*) een onopgeloste kwestie

¹**mop** [mop] *n* **1** zwabber, stokdweil; **2** haarbos, ragebol

²**mop** [mop] *vb* **1** (aan)dweilen, zwabberen; **2** droogwrijven, (af)vegen: *~ one's brow* zich het zweet van het voorhoofd wissen; **3** betten, opnemen

¹**mope** [moop] *vb* kniezen, chagrijnen: *~ about, ~ (a)round* lusteloos rondhangen

²**mope** [moop] *n* **1** kniesoor, brompot; **2** kniesbui: *have a ~* klagerig zeuren; **3** *the ~s* neerslachtigheid

moped [mooped] bromfiets, brommertjeʰ

mop up 1 opdweilen, opnemen; **2** opslokken; **3** zuiveren, verzetshaarden opruimen: *mopping-up operations* zuiveringsacties

¹**moral** [morrəl] *adj* **1** moreel, zedelijk, ethisch: *it's a ~ certainty* het is zo goed als zeker; **2** deugdzaam, kuis

²**moral** [morrəl] *n* **1** moraal, (zeden)les: *the ~ of the story* de moraal van het verhaal; **2** stelregel, principeʰ; **3** *~s* zeden

morale [məra:l] moreelʰ, mentale veerkracht: *the ~ of the troops was excellent* het moreel van de soldaten was uitstekend

morality [mərælittie] zedenleer, moraal

morass [məræs] moerasʰ, *(fig)* poel, *(fig)* uitzichtloze situatie

morbid [mo:bid] **1** morbide, ziekelijk: *a ~ imagination* een ziekelijke fantasie; **2** zwartgallig, somber

¹**more** [mo:] *pron* meer: *$50, ~ or less* ongeveer vijftig dollar; *a few ~* nog een paar; *there was much ~* er was nog veel meer; *there were many ~* er waren er nog veel meer; *one ~ try* nog een poging; *the ~ people there are the happier he feels* hoe meer mensen er zijn, hoe gelukkiger hij zich voelt; *I was just one ~ candidate* ik was niet meer dan de zoveelste kandidaat; *and what's ~* en daarbij komt nog dat

²**more** [mo:] *adv* **1** meer, veeleer, eerder: *~ or less* min of meer, zo ongeveer; *once ~* nog eens, nog een keer; *that's ~ like it* dat begint er al op te lijken, dat is al beter; *I will be ~ than happy to help you* ik zal je met alle liefde en plezier helpen; **2** -er, meer: *~ difficult* moeilijker; *~ easily* makkelijker; **3** bovendien

moreover [mo:roovə] bovendien, daarnaast

morning [mo:ning] ochtend, morgen, *(fig)* beginʰ: *good ~* goedemorgen; *he works ~s* hij werkt 's morgens; *in the ~: a)* 's morgens; *b)* morgenochtend; *at two o'clock in the ~* 's nachts om twee uur; *~!* morgen!

moron [mo:ron] *(inf)* **1** zwakzinnige, debiel; **2** imbeciel, zakkenwasser

morose [məroos] **1** chagrijnig; **2** somber

morphine [mo:fie:n] morfine

morsel [mo:sl] hap, mondvol, stuk(je)ʰ: *he hasn't got a ~ of sense* hij heeft geen greintje hersens

mortal [mo:tl] **1** sterfelijk: *the ~ remains* het stoffelijk overschot; **2** dodelijk, moordend, fataal *(also fig)*; **3** doods-, dodelijk, zeer hevig (groot): *~ enemy* aartsvijand, doodsvijand; *it's a ~ shame* het is een grof schandaal; **4** (op aarde) voorstelbaar: *she did every ~ thing to please him* ze wrong zich in de gekste bochten om het hem naar de zin te maken

mortality [mo:tælittie] **1** sterftecijferʰ; **2** sterfelijkheid

mortally [mo:təlie] **1** dodelijk; **2** doods-, enorm: *~ wounded* dodelijk gewond

¹**mortar** [mo:tə] *n* **1** vijzel; **2** mortier⁺ʰ; **3** mortel, (metsel)specie

²**mortar** [mo:tə] *vb* (vast)metselen

¹**mortgage** [mo:gidzj] *n* hypotheek(bedragʰ)

²**mortgage** [mo:gidzj] *vb* (ver)hypothekeren, *(also fig)* verpanden

mortification [mo:tiffikkeesjən] **1** zelfkastijding, versterving; **2** gekwetstheid: *to his ~* tot zijn schande

mortify [mo:tiffaj] **1** tuchtigen, kastijden: *~ the flesh* het vlees doden; **2** krenken, kwetsen

mortuary [mo:tjoeərie] lijkenhuisʰ, mortuariumʰ

mosaic [moozeeik] mozaïekʰ

mosque [mosk] moskee

mosquito [məskie:too] mug, muskiet: *~ net* klamboe, muskietennet

moss [mos] mosʰ

¹most [moost] *pron* meeste(n), grootste gedeelte van: *twelve at (the)* ~ (of: *at the very* ~) hoogstens twaalf; *this is the* ~ *I can do* meer kan ik niet doen; *for the* ~ *part* grotendeels

²most [moost] *adv* 1 meest, hoogst, zeer: ~ *complicated* zeer ingewikkeld; ~ *of all I like music* voor alles houd ik van muziek; 2 -st(e), meest: *the* ~ *difficult problem* het moeilijkste probleem; 3 *(Am)* bijna, haast: ~ *every evening* bijna elke avond

mostly [moostlie] grotendeels, voornamelijk, meestal

motel [mootel] motel^h

moth [moθ] 1 mot: *this sweater has got the* ~ *in it* de mot zit in deze trui; 2 nachtvlinder

¹mother [muðə] *n* 1 moeder *(also fig)*, bron, oorsprong: *expectant* (of: *pregnant*) ~ aanstaande moeder; 2 moeder(-overste): *shall I be* ~? zal ik (even) opscheppen?

²mother [muðə] *vb* (be)moederen, betuttelen

mother-in-law schoonmoeder

mother tongue moedertaal

motif [mootie:f] (leid)motief^h, (grond)thema^h

¹motion [moosjən] *n* 1 beweging, gebaar^h, wenk; 2 beweging(swijze), gang, loop: *the film was shown in slow* ~ de film werd vertraagd afgedraaid; *put* (of: *set*) *sth. in* ~ iets in beweging zetten; 3 motie; 4 mechaniek^h, bewegend mechanisme^h: *go through the* ~*s* plichtmatig verrichten, net doen alsof

²motion [moosjən] *vb* wenken, door een gebaar te kennen geven: *the policeman* ~*ed the crowd to keep moving* de agent gebaarde de mensen door te lopen

motivate [mootivveet] motiveren

motivation [mootivveesjən] 1 motivering; 2 motivatie

motive [mootiv] 1 motief^h, beweegreden: *without* ~ ongegrond, zonder reden(en); 2 leidmotief^h

motley [motlie] 1 samengeraapt; 2 bont, (veel)kleurig: *a* ~ *collection* een bonte verzameling

motor [mootə] 1 motor; 2 auto

motorbike 1 motor(fiets); 2 *(Am)* bromfiets, brommer

motorcycle motor(fiets)

motor home kampeerauto, camper

motorist [mootərist] automobilist

motorman [mootəmən] 1 wagenbestuurder; 2 chauffeur

motor scooter scooter

motortruck *(Am)* vrachtwagen

motorway autosnelweg

MOT-test verplichte jaarlijkse keuring *(for cars over 3 years old)*, APK

mottled [motld] gevlekt, gespikkeld

motto [mottoo] *(also* ~*es)* lijfspreuk

¹mould [moold] *n* 1 vorm, mal, matrijs, pudding(vorm), *(fig)* aard, karakter^h: *cast in one* (of: *the same*) ~ uit hetzelfde hout gesneden; 2 afgietsel^h; 3 schimmel; 4 teelaarde, bladaarde

²mould [moold] *vb* vormen, kneden: ~ *a person's character* iemands karakter vormen

moulder [mooldə] (tot stof) vergaan, vermolmen, verrotten

moulding [moolding] 1 afgietsel^h, afdruk; 2 lijstwerk^h, profiel^h

mouldy [mooldie] 1 beschimmeld, schimmelig; 2 muf; 3 afgezaagd

¹moult [moolt] *n* rui

²moult [moolt] *vb* ruien, verharen, vervellen

mound [maund] 1 hoop aarde, (graf)heuvel, *(fig)* berg, hoop; 2 wal, dam, dijk

¹mount [maunt] *vb* 1 bestijgen, beklimmen, opgaan: *he* ~*ed the stairs* hij liep de trap op; 2 te paard zetten, laten rijden: ~*ed police* bereden politie; 3 zetten op, opplakken *(photos);* 4 organiseren, in stelling brengen: ~ *an exhibition* een tentoonstelling organiseren

²mount [maunt] *vb* 1 (op)stijgen, (op)klimmen: *the expenses kept* ~*ing up* de uitgaven liepen steeds hoger op; 2 een paard bestijgen

³mount [maunt] *n* 1 berg, heuvel; 2 rijdier^h; 3 plateautje^h, zetting *(of jewels)*, opplakkarton^h, opzetkarton^h *(of photo, picture)*

mountain [mauntin] berg, heuvel, hoop: ~ *bike* terreinfiets, klimfiets; ~ *range* bergketen; *make a* ~ *out of a molehill* van een mug een olifant maken

mountaineer [mauntinnjə] 1 bergbeklimmer; 2 bergbewoner

mountainous [mauntinnəs] 1 bergachtig, berg-; 2 gigantisch, reusachtig

mountebank [mauntibæŋk] 1 kwakzalver; 2 charlatan

¹mourn [mo:n] *vb* 1 (with *for, over*) rouwen (om), in de rouw zijn, treuren; 2 rouw dragen

²mourn [mo:n] *vb* betreuren, bedroefd zijn over

mournful [mo:nfoel] bedroefd, triest

mourning [mo:ning] 1 rouw, rouwdracht; 2 rouwtijd

mouse [maus] *(mice)* muis

moustache [məsta:sj] snor

¹mouth [mauθ] *n* 1 mond, muil, bek: *a big* ~ een grote bek; *keep one's* ~ *shut* niets verklappen; *it makes my* ~ *water* het is om van te watertanden; *out of s.o.'s own* ~ met iemands eigen woorden; ~*-to*-~ mond op mond; 2 opening, ingang, toegang, (uit)monding *(of river)*, mond *(of port etc):* *shoot one's* ~ *off* zijn mond voorbijpraten; *down in the* ~ terneergeslagen, ontmoedigd

²mouth [mauð] *vb* declameren, geaffecteerd (uit)spreken; 2 (voor zich uit) mompelen

mouthpiece [mauθpie:s] 1 mondstuk^h; 2 spreekbuis, woordvoerder

mouthwash [mauθwosj] mondspoeling

movable [moe:vəbl] 1 beweegbaar, beweeglijk, los: ~ *scene* coulisse; 2 verplaatsbaar, verstelbaar: ~ *property* roerend goed

¹move [moe:v] *vb* 1 (zich) bewegen, zich verplaatsen, van positie veranderen: *it's time to be moving* het is tijd om te vertrekken; ~ *along* doorlopen, opschieten; ~ *over* inschikken, opschuiven; 2 vooruitkomen, opschieten: *suddenly things began to ~* plotseling kwam er leven in de brouwerij; *keep moving!* blijf doorgaan!, doorlopen!; **3** *(board game)* een zet doen, zetten, aan zet zijn; **4** verkeren, zich bewegen: *he ~s in the highest circles* hij beweegt zich in de hoogste kringen; **5** verhuizen, (weg)trekken, zich verzetten: *they ~d into a flat* ze betrokken een flat; **6** een voorstel doen: *~ for adjournment* verdaging voorstellen

²**move** [moe:v] *vb* **1** bewegen, (ver)roeren, in beweging brengen: *the police ~d them along* de politie dwong hen door te lopen; **2** verplaatsen, *(board game)* zetten, verschuiven; **3** opwekken, (ont)roeren, raken, aangrijpen: *he is ~d to tears* hij is tot tranen toe geroerd; **4** aanzetten, aansporen: *be ~d to* zich geroepen voelen om te

³**move** [moe:v] *n* **1** beweging: *get a ~ on: a)* in beweging komen, aanpakken; *b)* opschieten; *large forces were on the ~* grote strijdkrachten waren op de been; **2** verhuizing, trek: *be on the ~* op reis zijn, aan het zwerven zijn, op trek zijn *(of birds)*; **3** zet, beurt, slag: *make a ~* een zet doen; *it's your ~* jij bent aan zet; **4** stap, maatregel, manoeuvre: *make a ~: a)* opstaan *(from table); b)* opstappen, het initiatief nemen; *c)* maatregelen treffen, in actie komen

¹**move about** *vb* **1** zich (voortdurend) bewegen, rondlopen, ronddrentelen; **2** dikwijls verhuizen

²**move about** *vb* **1** vaak laten verhuizen, vaak verplanten; **2** vaak verplaatsen, rondsjouwen

move in 1 intrekken, gaan wonen, betrekken *(house, flat etc): ~ with s.o.* bij iem intrekken; **2** binnenvallen, optrekken, aanvallen, tussenbeide komen: *the police moved in on the crowd* de politie reed op de menigte in

movement [moe:vmənt] **1** beweging, voortgang, ontwikkeling, impuls, trend, tendens, *(med)* stoelgang, ontlasting; **2** beweging, organisatie: *the feminist ~* de vrouwenbeweging; **3** mechaniekʰ; **4** *(mus)* beweging, deelʰ *(of symphony etc)*

¹**move on** *vb* **1** verder gaan, opschieten, doorgaan; **2** vooruitkomen, promotie maken

²**move on** *vb* iem gebieden door te gaan

move out verhuizen, vertrekken

move up 1 in een hogere klas komen, in rang opklimmen; **2** stijgen, toenemen

movie [moe:vie] **1** film: *go to the ~s* naar de film gaan; **2** bioscoop; **3** *the ~s* filmindustrie

moving [moe:ving] **1** ontroerend; **2** bewegend: *(Am) ~ picture* film

mow [moo] maaien: *~ down soldiers* soldaten neermaaien

mower [mooə] **1** maaier; **2** maaimachine, grasmaaier

M.P. *Member of Parliament, military police(man)*

m.p.g. *miles per gallon* mijlen per gallon

m.p.h. *miles per hour* mijlen per uur

Mr [mistə] *(Messrs)* mister dhr., de heer

Mrs [missiz] *(Mmes)* Mevr.

Ms [miz] *(Mses, Mss)* Mw. *(instead of Miss or Mrs)*

Mt *Mount* Berg

¹**much** [mutsj] *pron* veel: *how ~ is it?* hoeveel kost het?; *it's not up to ~* het is niet veel soeps; *her contribution didn't amount to ~* haar bijdrage stelde niet veel voor; *that's not ~ use to me now* daar heb ik nu niet veel aan; *there isn't ~ in it* het maakt niet veel uit; *I thought as ~* zoiets dacht ik al; *it was as ~ as I could do to keep from laughing* ik had de grootst mogelijke moeite om niet te lachen; *he's not ~ of a singer* als zanger stelt hij niet veel voor; *well, so ~ for that* dat was dan dat

²**much** [mutsj] *adv* **1** *(degree)* veel, zeer, erg: *she was ~ the oldest* zij was verreweg de oudste; *as ~ as $2 million* (maar) liefst 2 miljoen dollar; *~ as he would have liked to go* hoe graag hij ook was gegaan; *~ to my surprise* tot mijn grote verrassing; **2** veel, vaak, dikwijls, lang: *she didn't stay ~* ze bleef niet lang; **3** ongeveer, bijna: *they were ~ the same size* ze waren ongeveer even groot

muchness [mutsjnəs] hoeveelheid, grootte

¹**muck** [muk] *n* **1** troep, rommel, rotzooi: *make a ~ of a job* niets terecht brengen van een klus, er niets van bakken; **2** (natte) mest, drek; **3** slijkʰ, viezigheid *(also fig)*

²**muck** [muk] *vb* bemesten || *~ out* uitmesten; *~ up* verknoeien

¹**muck about** *vb* **1** niksen, lummelen; **2** vervelen, klieren: *~ with* knoeien met

²**muck about** *vb* **1** pesten; **2** knoeien met

muckraking vuilspuiterij

mud [mud] modder, slijkʰ, *(fig)* roddel, laster: *drag s.o.'s name through the ~* iem door het slijk halen; *fling* (of: *sling, throw) ~ at s.o.* iem door de modder sleuren

¹**muddle** [mudl] *n* verwarring, warboel: *in a ~* in de war

²**muddle** [mudl] *vb* wat aanknoeien, wat aanmodderen: *~ along* (of: *on)* voortmodderen; *~ through* met vallen en opstaan het einde halen

³**muddle** [mudl] *vb* **1** (also with *up)* door elkaar gooien, verwarren; **2** in de war brengen: *a bit ~d* een beetje in de war

muddle-headed warrig, dom

muddy [mudie] **1** modderig; **2** troebel, ondoorzichtig; **3** vaal, dof

muesli [mjoe:zlie] müsli

¹**muff** [muf] *vb* **1** *(sport)* missen: *~ an easy catch* een makkelijke bal missen; **2** verknoeien: *I know I'll ~ it* ik weet zeker dat ik het verpest

²**muff** [muf] *n* **1** mof; **2** misser *(originally at ballgame)*, fiascoʰ

muffle [mufl] **1** warm inpakken, warm toedekken: *~ up* goed inpakken; **2** dempen *(sound): ~d curse* gedempte vloek

muffler [muflə] **1** das, sjaal; **2** geluiddemper, *(Am)* knalpot

¹**mug** [mug] *n* **1** mok, beker; **2** kop, smoel; **3** sufferd, sul

²**mug** [mug] *vb* aanvallen en beroven

mugger [mugə] straatrover

muggins [muginz] sul, sufferd

muggy [mugie] benauwd, drukkend

mugshot portretfoto *(for police file)*

mug up uit je hoofd leren, erin stampen

mule [mjoe:l] **1** muildier[h], muilezel: *obstinate* (of: *stubborn) as a* ~ koppig als een ezel; **2** stijfkop, dwarskop

multicultural [moeltikkultsjrəl] multicultureel

multidimensional [moeltiddajmensjənəl] gecompliceerd, met veel kanten *(eg problem)*

multilateral [moeltilætrəl] **1** veelzijdig; **2** multilateraal

multinational [moeltinæsjənəl] multinationaal

¹**multiple** [multipl] *adj* **1** veelvoudig: ~ *choice* meerkeuze-; ~ *shop* (of: *store*) grootwinkelbedrijf; **2** divers, veelsoortig; **3** *(bot)* samengesteld

²**multiple** [multipl] *n (maths)* veelvoud[h]: *least* (of: *lowest*) *common* ~ kleinste gemene veelvoud

multiplex [multipleks] megabioscoop

multiplication [multiplikkeesjən] vermenigvuldiging

multiplicity [multiplissittie] **1** veelheid, massa; **2** veelsoortigheid: *a* ~ *of ideas* een grote verscheidenheid aan ideeën

¹**multiply** [multiplaj] *vb* **1** vermenigvuldigen: ~ *three by four* drie maal vier vermenigvuldigen; **2** vergroten: ~ *one's chances* zijn kansen doen stijgen

²**multiply** [multiplaj] *vb* **1** zich vermeerderen, aangroeien; **2** zich vermenigvuldigen; **3** een vermenigvuldiging uitvoeren

multipurpose [moeltippə:pəs] veelzijdig, voor meerdere doeleinden geschikt

multiracial [moeltirreesjl] multiraciaal

multitude [multitjoe:d] **1** massa: *a* ~ *of ideas* een grote hoeveelheid ideeën; **2** menigte

¹**mum** [mum] *n* mamma

²**mum** [mum] *adj* stil: *keep* ~ zijn mondje dicht houden

³**mum** [mum] *interj* mondje dicht!, sst!, niets zeggen!: ~*'s the word!* mondje dicht!, niks zeggen!

mumble [mumbl] **1** mompelen; **2** knauwen op, mummelen op

mummify [mummiffaj] mummificeren, balsemen

mummy [mummie] **1** mummie; **2** mammie, mam(s)

mumps [mumps] de bof

munch [muntsj] kauwen (op): ~ *(away at) an apple* aan een appel knagen

mundane [mundeen] gewoon: ~ *matters* routinezaken

Munich [mjoe:nik] München

municipal [mjoe:nissipl] gemeentelijk

municipality [mjoe:nissipælittie] **1** gemeente; **2** gemeentebestuur[h]

¹**mural** [mjoeərəl] *n* muurschildering, fresco[h]

²**mural** [mjoeərəl] *adj* muur-, wand-: ~ *painting* muurschildering

¹**murder** [mə:də] *n* **1** moord: *get away with* ~: *a)* alles

kunnen maken; *b)* precies kunnen doen wat men wil; **2** beroerde toestand

²**murder** [mə:də] *vb* **1** vermoorden, ombrengen; **2** verknoeien, ruïneren

murderer [mə:drə] moordenaar

murky [mə:kie] **1** duister, donker; **2** vunzig, kwalijk: ~ *affairs* weinig verheffende zaken

¹**murmur** [mə:mə] *vb* **1** mompelen; **2** ruisen, suizen; **3** mopperen: ~ *against* (of: *at*) mopperen op, klagen over

²**murmur** [mə:mə] *n* **1** gemurmel[h], geruis[h] *(of brook)*; **2** gemopper[h]; **3** gemompel[h]

muscle [musl] **1** spier: *flex one's* ~*s* de spieren losmaken; **2** (spier)kracht, macht

muscular [muskjoelə] **1** spier-: ~ *dystrophy* spierdystrofie; **2** gespierd, krachtig

¹**muse** [mjoe:z] *vb (with about, over, on)* peinzen (over), mijmeren

²**muse** [mjoe:z] *n* muze, *(fig also)* inspiratie: *The Muses* de (negen) muzen, kunsten en wetenschappen

museum [mjoe:zjəm] museum[h]

mush [musj] **1** moes[h], brij; **2** sentimenteel gekluts[h], kletspraat; **3** *(advertising)* geruis[h]

¹**mushroom** [musjroe:m] *n* **1** champignon; **2** (eetbare) paddestoel

²**mushroom** [musjroe:m] *vb* **1** zich snel ontwikkelen, als paddestoelen uit de grond schieten; **2** paddestoelvormig uitwaaieren *(of smoke)*

music [mjoe:zik] **1** muziek: ~ *hall* variété(theater); **2** bladmuziek, partituur: *face the* ~ de consequenties aanvaarden; *piped* ~ ingeblikte muziek *(in restaurant etc)*

¹**musical** [mjoe:zikl] *adj* **1** muzikaal; **2** welluidend; **3** muziek-: ~ *sound* klank *(as opposed to noise)*; ~ *chairs* stoelendans

²**musical** [mjoe:zikl] *n* musical

musician [mjoe:zisjən] musicus, muzikant

musk [musk] **1** muskus; **2** muskusdier[h]; **3** muskusplant

muskrat muskusrat

Muslim [muzlim] **1** moslim; **2** moslim

¹**muss** [mus] *vb (Am)* in de war maken, verknoeien *(hair, clothing)*: ~ *up one's suit* zijn pak ruïneren

²**muss** [mus] *n (Am)* wanorde

mussel [musl] mossel

¹**must** [must] *vb* **1** *(command, obligation and necessity)* moeten, *(in indirect speech also)* moest(en), *(condition)* zou(den) zeker: *you* ~ *come and see us* je moet ons beslist eens komen opzoeken; *if you* ~ *have your way, then do* als je per se je eigen gang wil gaan, doe dat dan; ~ *you have your way again?* moet je nu weer met alle geweld je zin krijgen?; **2** *(prohibition; with negation)* mogen: *you* ~ *not go near the water* je mag niet dichtbij het water komen; **3** *(supposition)* moeten, *(Am also, with negation)* kunnen: *you* ~ *be out of your mind to say such things* je moet wel gek zijn om zulke dingen te zeggen; *someone* ~ *have seen something, surely?* er moet

toch iemand iets gezien hebben?

²must [must] *n* noodzaak, vereiste^h, must: *the Millennium Dome is a ~* je moet beslist naar de Millennium Dome toe

mustard [mustəd] mosterd

¹muster [mustə] *vb* zich verzamelen, bijeenkomen *(for inspection)*

²muster [mustə] *vb* 1 verzamelen, bijeenroepen; 2 bijeenrapen, verzamelen *(courage, powers): ~ up one's courage* al zijn moed bijeenrapen

³muster [mustə] *n* 1 inspectie: *pass ~* ermee door kunnen; 2 verzameling

musty [mustie] 1 muf: *~ air* bedompte lucht; 2 schimmelig

mutation [mjoe:teesjən] 1 verandering, wijziging; 2 mutatie

¹mute [mjoe:t] *adj* 1 stom; 2 zwijgend, stil, sprakeloos || *~ swan* knobbelzwaan

²mute [mjoe:t] *n* (doof)stomme

mutilate [mjoe:tilleet] verminken, toetakelen *(also fig)*

mutilation [mjoe:tilleesjən] verminking

mutineer [mjoe:tinniə] muiter

¹mutiny [mjoe:tinnie] *n* muiterij, opstand

²mutiny [mjoe:tinnie] *vb* muiten

mutt [mut] halvegare, idioot

¹mutter [mutə] *vb* 1 mompelen: *he ~ed an oath* hij vloekte zachtjes; 2 mopperen: *~ against* (of: *at*) mopperen over

²mutter [mutə] *n* 1 gemompel^h; 2 gemopper^h

mutton [mutn] schapenvlees^h

muttonhead stomkop

mutual [mjoe:tsjoeəl] 1 wederzijds, wederkerig: *~ consent* wederzijds goedvinden; 2 gemeenschappelijk, onderling: *~ interests* gemeenschappelijke belangen

muzak [mjoe:zæk] achtergrondmuziek, muzak

¹muzzle [muzl] *n* 1 snuit, muil *(of animal);* 2 mond, tromp *(of gun);* 3 muilkorf

²muzzle [muzl] *vb* muilkorven *(also fig)*, de mond snoeren

muzzy [muzzie] 1 duf, saai, dof; 2 wazig, vaag; 3 beneveld, verward

¹my [maj] *pron* mijn: *~ dear boy* beste jongen; *he disapproved of ~ going out* hij vond het niet goed dat ik uitging

²my [maj] *interj* 1 o jee; 2 wel: *~, ~ wel*, wel

myopic [majjoppik] 1 bijziend, kippig; 2 kortzichtig

myself [majself] 1 mij, me, mezelf: *I am not ~ today* ik voel me niet al te best vandaag; 2 zelf: *I'll go ~* ik zal zelf gaan

mysterious [mistiəriəs] geheimzinnig, mysterieus

mystery [mistrie] 1 geheim^h, mysterie^h, raadsel^h; 2 geheimzinnigheid

¹mystic [mistik] *n* mysticus

²mystic [mistik] *adj* 1 mystiek; 2 occult, esoterisch, alleen voor ingewijden; 3 raadselachtig

mystification [mistiffikkeesjən] mystificatie, misleiding

mystify [mistiffaj] verbijsteren, verwarren, voor een raadsel stellen: *her behaviour mystified me* ik begreep niets van haar gedrag

myth [miθ] 1 mythe, mythologie; 2 fabel, allegorie; 3 verzinsel^h, fictie

mythological [miθəlodzjikl] 1 mythologisch; 2 mythisch

mythology [miθolədzjie] mythologie

n

N *North* N., Noord(en)
n/a *not applicable* n.v.t., niet van toepassing
nab [næb] (op)pakken, inrekenen
naff [næf] niks waard, waardeloos
¹nag [næg] *vb* **1** zeuren: *a ~ging headache* een zeurende hoofdpijn; *~ (at) s.o.* iem aan het hoofd zeuren; **2** treiteren
²nag [næg] *n* **1** klein paard(je^h), pony; **2** knol, slecht renpaard^h; **3** zeurpiet
¹nail [neel] *n* **1** nagel; **2** spijker: *hit the ~ on the head* de spijker op de kop slaan; *pay on the ~* contant betalen
²nail [neel] *vb* **1** (vast)spijkeren; **2** vastnagelen: *he was ~ed to his seat* hij zat als vastgenageld op zijn stoel; **3** te pakken krijgen: *he ~ed me as soon as I came in* hij schoot me direct aan toen ik binnenkwam; **4** betrappen
nail-biter razend spannende film, razend spannend boek^h
nail up 1 dichtspijkeren; **2** (op)hangen
naïve [najjie:v] naïef; onnozel, dom
naivety [najjie:vətie] naïviteit, onschuld; onnozelheid
naked [neekid] **1** naakt, bloot; **2** onbedekt, kaal ‖ *the ~ eye* het blote oog; *~ truth* naakte waarheid
¹name [neem] *n* **1** naam, benaming: *enter (of: put down) one's ~ for* zich opgeven voor; *what's-his-name?* hoe heet hij ook al weer?, dinges; *I only know him by ~* ik ken hem alleen van naam; *a man by (of: of) the ~ of Jones* iem die Jones heet, een zekere Jones; *he hasn't a penny to his ~* hij heeft geen cent; *I can't put a ~ to it* ik weet niet precies hoe ik het moet zeggen; *first ~* voornaam; *second ~* achternaam; **2** reputatie, naam: *make (of: win) a ~ for oneself, win oneself a ~* naam maken; *the ~ of the game is ...* waar het om gaat is ...; *call s.o. ~s* iem uitschelden; *lend one's ~ to* zijn naam lenen aan; *in the ~ of* in (de) naam van
²name [neem] *vb* **1** noemen, benoemen, een naam geven: *she was ~d after her mother, (Am also) she was ~d for her mother* ze was naar haar moeder genoemd; **2** dopen *(ship);* **3** (op)noemen: *~ your price* noem je prijs; **4** benoemen, aanstellen; **5** vaststellen: *~ the day* de trouwdag vaststellen; *you ~ it* noem maar op
namedropping opschepperij, indruk willen ma-

ken door met namen te strooien
namely [neemlie] namelijk
namesake [neemseek] naamgenoot
nan [næn] *(child language)* oma
nanny [nænie] kinderjuffrouw
¹nap [næp] *n* **1** dutje^h, tukje^h; **2** vleug *(of fabric)*
²nap [næp] *vb* dutten, dommelen: *catch s.o. ~ping* iem betrappen
nape [neep] (achterkant vd) nek
napkin [næpkin] **1** servet^h; doekje^h; **2** luier
nappy [næpie] luier
narcissus [na:sissəs] (witte) narcis
¹narcotic [na:kottik] *adj* verdovend, slaapverwekkend
²narcotic [na:kottik] *n* verdovend middel^h; slaapmiddel^h
¹nark [na:k] *vb* kwaad maken, irriteren: *she felt ~ed at (of: by) his words* zijn woorden ergerden haar
²nark [na:k] *n* verklikker, tipgever
narrate [nəreet] vertellen, beschrijven
narration [nəreesjən] verhaal^h, vertelling, verslag^h
narrator [nəreetə] verteller
¹narrow [næroo] *adj* **1** smal, nauw, eng: *by a ~ margin* nog net, op het nippertje; **2** beperkt, krap: *a ~ majority* een kleine meerderheid; **3** bekrompen; **4** nauwgezet, precies: *a ~ examination* een zorgvuldig onderzoek; *it was a ~ escape* het was op het nippertje; *in the ~est sense* strikt genomen
²narrow [næroo] *n* engte, zee-engte, bergengte
narrow down beperken, terugbrengen: *it narrowed down to this* het kwam (ten slotte) hierop neer
narrowly [næroolie] **1** net, juist: *the sailor ~ escaped drowning* de zeeman ontkwam maar net aan de verdrinkingsdood; **2** zorgvuldig
nasal [neezl] neus-, nasaal: *~ spray* neusspray
nasality [neezælittie] neusgeluid^h, nasaliteit
nasturtium [nəsta:sjm] Oost-Indische kers
nasty [na:stie] **1** smerig, vuil, vies; **2** onaangenaam, onprettig: *the bill was a ~ shock* de rekening zorgde voor een onaangename verrassing; **3** lastig, hinderlijk, vervelend; **4** gemeen, hatelijk: *a ~ look* een boze blik; *he turned ~ when I refused to leave* hij werd giftig toen ik niet wilde weggaan; **5** ernstig, hevig: *a ~ accident* een ernstig ongeluk; *a ~ blow: a)* een flinke klap; *b)* een tegenvaller
nation [neesjən] **1** natie, volk^h; **2** land^h, staat
¹national [næsjənəl] *adj* **1** nationaal, rijks-, staats-, volks-: *~ anthem* volkslied; *~ debt* staatsschuld; *~ monument* historisch monument; *~ service* militaire dienst; *National Trust (roughly)* monumentenzorg; **2** landelijk, nationaal
²national [næsjənəl] *n* **1** landgenoot; **2** staatsburger, onderdaan
nationalism [næsjənəlizm] nationalisme^h
nationalist(ic) [næsjənəlist(ik)] nationalistisch
nationality [næsjənælittie] nationaliteit
nationalize [næsjənəlajz] **1** nationaliseren; **2** naturaliseren; **3** tot een natie maken
nationwide landelijk, door het hele land

¹native [neetiv] *adj* **1** geboorte-: *Native American* indiaan; *a ~ speaker of English* iem met Engels als moedertaal; **2** natuurlijk; **3** autochtoon, inheems, binnenlands, *(oft depr)* inlands: *go ~ zich* aanpassen aan de plaatselijke bevolking

²native [neetiv] *n* **1** inwoner, bewoner: *a ~ of Dublin* een geboren Dubliner; **2** *(oft depr)* inboorling, inlander; **3** inheemse diersoort, plantensoort

nativity [nativvittie] **1** *the Nativity* geboorte(feest^h) van Christus, Kerstmis; **2** geboorte

nativity play kerstspel^h

NATO [neetoo] *North Atlantic Treaty Organization* NAVO, Noord-Atlantische Verdragsorganisatie

natty [nætie] **1** sjiek, netjes, keurig; **2** handig, bedreven

¹natural [nætsjərəl] *adj* **1** natuurlijk, natuur-: *~ forces* natuurkrachten; *~ gas* aardgas; *~ history* natuurlijke historie, biologie; **2** aangeboren, van nature: *he's a ~ linguist* hij heeft een talenknobbel; **3** aangeboren; **4** normaal; **5** ongedwongen

²natural [nætsjərəl] *n* natuurtalent^h, favoriet, meest geschikte persoon: *John's a ~ for the job* John is geknipt voor die baan

naturalist [nætsjərəlist] **1** naturalist; **2** natuurkenner

naturalization [nætsjərəlajzeesjən] **1** naturalisatie; **2** inburgering; **3** het inheems maken *(plants, animals)*

naturalize [nætsjərəlajz] **1** naturaliseren; **2** doen inburgeren, overnemen; **3** inheems maken, uitzetten *(plants, animals): rabbits have become ~d in Australia* konijnen zijn in Australië een inheemse diersoort geworden

naturally [nætsjərəlie] **1** natuurlijk, vanzelfsprekend, uiteraard; **2** van nature || *it comes ~ to her* het gaat haar gemakkelijk af

nature [neetsjə] **1** wezen^h, natuur, karakter^h: *he is stubborn by ~* hij is koppig van aard; *in the (very) ~ of things* uit de aard der zaak; **2** soort, aard: *sth. of that ~* iets van dien aard; **3** de natuur: *~ reserve* natuurreservaat; *(fig) let ~ take its course* de zaken op hun beloop laten; *contrary to ~* wonderbaarlijk, onnatuurlijk

naturism [neetsjərizm] naturisme^h, nudisme^h

naught [no:t] nul, niets: *come to ~* op niets uitlopen

naughty [no:tie] **1** ondeugend, stout; **2** slecht, onfatsoenlijk

nausea [no:ziə] **1** misselijkheid; **2** walging, afkeer

nautical [no:tikl] nautisch, zee(vaart)-: *~ mile: a)* (Engelse) zeemijl *(1,853.18 metres); b)* internationale zeemijl *(1,852 metres)*

naval [neevl] **1** zee-, scheeps-: *~ architect* scheepsbouwkundig ingenieur; **2** marine-, vloot-: *~ battle* zeeslag; *~ officer* marineofficier; *~ power* zeemacht

nave [neev] **1** schip^h *(of church);* **2** naaf *(of wheel)*

navel [neevl] **1** navel; **2** middelpunt^h

navigable [nævigəbl] **1** bevaarbaar; **2** zeewaardig; **3** bestuurbaar

¹navigate [nævigeet] *vb* navigeren, een schip (vliegtuig) besturen

²navigate [nævigeet] *vb* **1** bevaren; **2** oversteken, vliegen over; **3** besturen; **4** loodsen *(fig),* (ge)leiden

navigation [nævigeesjən] navigatie, stuurmanskunst, scheepvaart: *inland ~* binnen(scheep)vaart

navvy [nævie] **1** grondwerker; **2** graafmachine

navy [neevie] **1** marine; **2** oorlogsvloot, zeemacht

nay [nee] **1** nee(n); **2** tegenstemmer, stem tegen; **3** weigering

NE *north-east* N.O.; noordoost

¹near [niə] *adj* **1** dichtbij(gelegen): *Near East* Nabije Oosten; **2** kort *(road);* **3** nauw verwant; **4** intiem, persoonlijk *(friend);* **5** krenterig, gierig: *he had a ~ escape, (inf) it was a ~ thing* het was maar op het nippertje; *it was a ~ miss* het was bijna raak *(also fig)*

²near [niə] *adv* dichtbij, nabij: *from far and ~* van heinde en ver; *nowhere ~ as clever* lang niet zo slim; *she was ~ to tears* het huilen stond haar nader dan het lachen

³near [niə] *vb* naderen

⁴near [niə] *prep* dichtbij, nabij, naast: *he lived ~ his sister* hij woonde niet ver van zijn zuster; *go* (of: *come) ~ to doing sth.* iets bijna doen, op het punt staan iets te doen

nearby dichtbij, nabij gelegen

nearly [niəlie] **1** bijna, vrijwel: *is his book ~ finished?* is zijn boek nu al bijna af?; **2** nauw, na, van nabij: *~ related* nauw verwant; *not ~ (nog)* lang niet, op geen stukken na

nearside linker: *the ~ wheel* het linker wiel

near-sighted bijziend

neat [nie:t] **1** net(jes), keurig; proper; **2** puur, zonder ijs *(of drink);* **3** handig, vaardig, slim; **4** sierlijk, smaakvol; **5** *(Am)* schoon, netto; **6** *(Am)* gaaf, prima; **7** kernachtig

nebulous [nebjoeləs] nevelig *(also fig),* troebel, vaag

¹necessary [nessəserrie] *adj* noodzakelijk, nodig, vereist, essentieel: *~ evil* noodzakelijk kwaad

²necessary [nessəserrie] *n* **1** behoefte: *the ~: a)* het benodigde; *b)* geld; **2** *-ies* benodigdheden, vereisten; **3** *-ies* (levens)behoeften

necessitate [nissessitteet] **1** noodzaken; **2** vereisen, dwingen tot

necessity [nissessittie] **1** noodzaak, dwang: *in case of ~* in geval van nood; **2** noodzakelijkheid; **3** behoefte, vereiste^h; **4** nood, armoede

¹neck [nek] *n* **1** hals, nek: *(sport) ~ and ~* nek aan nek; **2** hals(vormig voorwerp^h), *(eg)* flessenhals; **3** (zee-, land-, berg)engte: *a ~ of land* een landengte; *(Am) ~ of the woods* buurt, omgeving; *breathe down s.o.'s ~: a)* iem op de hielen zitten; *b)* iem op de vingers kijken; *get it in the ~* het voor zijn kiezen krijgen; *risk one's ~* zijn leven wagen; *stick one's ~ out* zijn nek uitsteken; *up to one's ~ in (debt)* tot zijn nek in (de schuld)

²neck [nek] *vb* vrijen (met), kussen

necklace [neklis] halsband^h, halssnoer^h, (hals)ketting

nectar [nɛktə] nectar, godendrank

née [nee] geboren

¹need [nie:d] *n* **1** noodzaak: *there's no ~ for you to leave yet* je hoeft nog niet weg (te gaan); **2** behoefte, nood: *as* (of: *if, when) the ~ arises* als de behoefte zich voordoet; *have ~ of* behoefte hebben aan; *people in ~ of help* hulpbehoevenden; **3** armoede: *a friend in ~* een echte vriend; *if ~ be* desnoods, als het moet

²need [nie:d] *vb* nodig hebben, behoefte hebben aan, vereisen: *they ~ more room to play* ze hebben meer speelruimte nodig; *this ~s to be done urgently* dit moet dringend gedaan worden

³need [nie:d] *vb* hoeven, moeten, (+ *negation*) had (niet) hoeven: *all he ~ do is ...* al wat hij moet doen is ...; *we ~ not have worried* we hadden ons geen zorgen hoeven te maken

needful [nie:dfoel] noodzakelijk

¹needle [nie:dl] *n* **1** naald, breinaald, magneetnaald, injectienaald, dennennaald: *look for a ~ in a haystack* een speld in een hooiberg zoeken; **2** sterke rivaliteit: *~ match* wedstrijd op het scherp van de snede; *(vulg) get the ~* pissig worden

²needle [nie:dl] *vb* **1** naaien, een naald halen door, (door)prikken; **2** zieken, pesten

needless [nie:dləs] onnodig: *~ to say ...* overbodig te zeggen ...

needlework naaiwerkʰ, handwerk(en)

needs [nie:dz] noodzakelijkerwijs: *he ~ must* hij kan niet anders; *at a moment like this, he must ~ go* uitgerekend op een moment als dit moet hij zo nodig weg

needy [nie:die] arm, noodlijdend

nefarious [niffeəriəs] misdadig, schandelijk

negate [nigeet] **1** tenietdoen; **2** ontkennen

negation [nigeesjən] ontkenning

¹negative [negətiv] *adj* **1** negatief: *the ~ sign* het minteken; **2** ontkennend, afwijzend: *~ criticism* afbrekende kritiek

²negative [negətiv] *n* **1** afwijzing; ontkenning: *the answer is in the ~* het antwoord luidt nee; **2** weigering; **3** *(photo)* negatiefʰ

¹neglect [niglɛkt] *vb* **1** verwaarlozen; **2** verzuimen, nalaten

²neglect [niglɛkt] *n* **1** verwaarlozing; **2** verzuimʰ: *~ of duty* plichtsverzuim

negligence [neglidzjəns] nalatigheid, slordigheid

negligible [neglidzjibl] verwaarloosbaar, niet noemenswaardig

¹negotiate [nigoosjie·eet] *vb* onderhandelen

²negotiate [nigoosjie·eet] *vb* **1** (na onderhandeling) sluiten, afsluiten; **2** nemen, passeren, doorkomen, tot een goed einde brengen: *~ a sharp bend* een scherpe bocht nemen

negotiation [nigoosjie·eesjən] **1** onderhandeling, bespreking: *enter into* (of: *open, start) ~s with* in onderhandeling gaan met; **2** (af)sluiting

negress [nie:grəs] negerin

negro [nie:groo] *(~es)* neger

¹neigh [nee] *vb* hinniken

²neigh [nee] *n* (ge)hinnikʰ

neighbour [neebə] **1** buurman, buurvrouw: *my ~ at dinner* mijn tafelgenoot; **2** medemens, naaste: *duty to one's ~* (ver)plicht(ing) t.o.v. zijn naaste

neighbourhood [neebəhoed] **1** buurt, wijk; **2** nabijheid, omgeving || *I paid a sum in the ~ of 150 dollars* ik heb rond de 150 dollar betaald

¹neither [najðə] *pron* geen van beide(n): *~ of us wanted him to come* we wilden geen van beiden dat hij kwam; *~ candidate* geen van beide kandidaten

²neither [najðə] *adv* evenmin, ook niet: *she cannot play and ~ can I* zij kan niet spelen en ik ook niet

³neither [najðə] *conj* noch: *she could ~ laugh nor cry* ze kon (noch) lachen noch huilen

neon [nie:on] neonʰ

nephew [nevjoe:] neef(jeʰ), zoon van broer of zus

nepotism [neppətizm] nepotismeʰ, begunstiging van familieleden en vrienden

nerd [nə:d] sul, klungel, nerd

nerve [nə:v] **1** zenuw: *(fig) hit* (of: *touch) a ~* een zenuw raken; **2** moed, durf, lefʰ, brutaliteit: *you've got a ~!* jij durft, zeg!; *lose one's ~* de moed verliezen; **3** *~s* zenuwen, zelfbeheersing: *get on s.o.'s ~s* op iemands zenuwen werken

nervous [nə:vəs] **1** zenuwachtig, gejaagd; **2** nerveus, zenuw-: *~ breakdown* zenuwinstorting, zenuwinzinking; *(central) ~ system* (centraal) zenuwstelsel; **3** angstig, bang: *~ of* bang voor

nervy [nə:vie] **1** *(inf)* zenuwachtig, schrikkerig; **2** *(Am; inf)* koel(bloedig), onverschillig

nest [nest] **1** nestʰ: *a ~ of robbers* een roversnest; **2** broeinestʰ, haard: *feather one's ~* zijn zakken vullen

¹nestle [nesl] *vb* **1** zich nestelen, lekker (gaan) zitten (liggen); **2** (half) verscholen liggen; **3** schurken, (dicht) aankruipen: *~ up against* (of: *to) s.o.* dicht tegen iem aankruipen

²nestle [nesl] *vb* **1** neerleggen; **2** tegen zich aan drukken, in zijn armen nemen

¹net [net] *n* **1** netʰ, *(fig)* webʰ, (val)strik; **2** netmateriaalʰ, mousseline, tule || *surf the Net* internetten, surfen op internet

²net [net] *vb* (in een net) vangen, *(also fig)* (ver)strikken

³net *adj* netto, schoon, zuiver: *~ profit* nettowinst

⁴net *vb* **1** (als winst) opleveren, (netto) opbrengen; **2** winnen, opstrijken, (netto) verdienen

⁵net *n* nettobedragʰ

Netherlands [neðələndz] Nederland

netting [netting] net(werk)ʰ

¹nettle [netl] *n* (brand)netel || *grasp the ~* de koe bij de hoorns vatten

²nettle [netl] *vb* irriteren, ergeren

network 1 net(werk)ʰ; **2** radio- en televisiemaatschappij, omroep; **3** computernetwerkʰ

networking [netwə:king] **1** het werken met een netwerk(systeem); **2** *(Am)* het netwerken

neurology [njoeərollədzjie] neurologie

¹neurotic [njoeərottik] adj neurotisch

²neurotic [njoeərottik] n neuroot, zenuwlijder

¹neuter [njoe:tə] adj onzijdig (of word, plant, animal)

²neuter [njoe:tə] vb helpen, castreren, steriliseren (animal)

neutral [njoe:trəl] **1** neutraal (also chem), onpartijdig; **2** onzijdig, geslachtloos || in ~ gear in z'n vrij

neutralize [njoe:trəlajz] neutraliseren

never [nevvə] nooit: ~-ending altijddurend, oneindig (lang); ~-to-be-forgotten onvergetelijk; this'll ~ do dit is niks, hier kun je niks mee; he ~ so looked! hij keek niet eens!

nevermore [nevvəmo:] nooit meer

nevertheless [nevvəðələs] niettemin, desondanks, toch

new [njoe:] nieuw, ongebruikt, recent: ~ bread vers brood; ~ moon (eerste fase van de) wassende maan, nieuwemaan; ~ town nieuwbouwstad; the New World de Nieuwe Wereld, Noord- en Zuid-Amerika; ~ year: a) jaarwisseling; b) nieuw jaar; ~ broom frisse wind; turn over a ~ leaf met een schone lei beginnen; break ~ ground (fig) nieuwe wegen banen; that's ~ to me dat is nieuw voor me; I'm ~ to the job ik werk hier nog maar pas

newborn 1 pasgeboren; **2** herboren

newcomer [njoe:kummə] nieuwkomer, beginner

news [njoe:z] **1** nieuwsʰ: break the ~ to s.o. (als eerste) iem het (slechte) nieuws vertellen; that is ~ to me dat is nieuw voor mij; **2** nieuwsʰ, nieuwsberichten, journaalʰ, journaaluitzending

newsagent krantenverkoper, tijdschriftenverkoper

newscast nieuwsuitzending, journaalʰ

newsletter nieuwsbrief, mededelingenbladʰ

newspaper [njoe:speepə] krant, dagbladʰ

newsprint krantenpapierʰ

newsreader nieuwslezer

newsstand kiosk

New Year's Day nieuwjaarsdag

New Year's Eve oudejaarsdag, oudejaarsavond

New Zealand [njoe: zie:lənd] Nieuw-Zeeland

¹next [nekst] adj **1** volgend (of place), na, naast, dichtstbijzijnd: she lives ~ door ze woont hiernaast; the ~ turn past the traffic lights de eerste afslag na de verkeerslichten; the ~ best het beste op één na, de tweede keus; the ~ but one de volgende op één na; **2** volgend (of time), aanstaand: the ~ day de volgende dag, de dag daarop; ~ Monday aanstaande maandag; the ~ few weeks de komende weken

²next [nekst] pron (eerst)volgende: ~, please volgende graag; ~ of kin (naaste) bloedverwant(en), nabestaande(n)

³next [nekst] adv **1** daarnaast: what ~?: a) wat (krijgen we) nu?; b) (depr) kan het nog gekker?; **2** (time; also fig) daarna, daaropvolgend, de volgende keer: the ~ best thing op één na het beste; ~ to impossible bijna onmogelijk; for ~ to nothing bijna voor niks

next-door aangrenzend: we are ~ neighbours we wonen naast elkaar

N.H.S. National Health Service nationaal ziekenfonds

nib [nib] pen, kroontjespen

¹nibble [nibl] vb knabbelen (aan), knagen (aan): ~ away (of: off) weg-, afknabbelen, weg-, afknagen

²nibble [nibl] n hapjeʰ

nice [najs] **1** aardig, vriendelijk: you're a ~ friend! mooie vriend ben jij!; **2** mooi, goed: ~ work! goed zo!; **3** leuk, prettig: have a ~ day nog een prettige dag, tot ziens; **4** genuanceerd, verfijnd; **5** kies(keurig), precies: ~ and warm lekker warm

nicety [najsətie] **1** detailʰ, subtiliteit, nuance; **2** nauwkeurigheid, precisie || to a ~ precies, tot in de puntjes

niche [nie:sj] **1** nis; **2** stek, plek(jeʰ), hoekjeʰ: he has found his ~ hij heeft zijn draai gevonden

¹nick [nik] n **1** kerf, keep; **2** snee(tjeʰ), kras; **3** bajes, nor; **4** politiebureauʰ || in the ~ of time op het nippertje; **5** staat, vorm: in good ~ in prima conditie, in goede staat

²nick [nik] vb **1** inkepen, inkerven, krassen; **2** jatten; **3** in de kraag grijpen, arresteren

nickel [nikl] **1** vijfcentstuk (in Canada and Am), stuiver; **2** nikkel

¹nickname [nikneem] n **1** bijnaam; **2** roepnaam

²nickname [nikneem] vb een bijnaam geven (aan)

nicotine [nikkətie:n] nicotine

niece [nie:s] nicht(jeʰ), oom-, tantezegster, dochter van broer of zus

niff [nif] lucht, stank

nifty [niftie] **1** jofel, tof; **2** handig

niggard [nigəd] vrek

nigger [nigə] (depr) nikker, neger

¹niggle [nigl] vb muggenziften, vitten

²niggle [nigl] vb **1** knagen aan, irriteren; **2** vitten op

night [najt] nacht, avond: ~ and day dag en nacht; stay the ~ blijven logeren; at (of: by) ~ 's nachts, 's avonds; first ~ première(avond); last ~ gisteravond, vannacht; ~ owl nachtbraker, nachtmens; make a ~ of it nachtbraken, doorhalen

nightcap slaapmuts(jeʰ) (also drink)

nightclub nachtclub

nightingale [najtingeel] nachtegaal

nightly [najtlie] nachtelijk, elke nacht (avond), 's nachts, 's avonds

nightmare nachtmerrie

night shift 1 nachtdienst; **2** nachtploeg

night-time nacht(elijk uurʰ)

nightwear nachtkleding, nachtgoedʰ

nighty [najtie] nachthemdʰ, -japon

nil [nil] niﬅl, nietsʰ, nul: three-~ drie-nul

nimble [nimbl] **1** behendig, vlug; **2** alert, gevat, spits

nine [najn] negen || he was dressed (up) to the ~s hij was piekfijn gekleed

ninepins kegelenʰ, kegelspelʰ

nineteen [najntie:n] negentien

nineteenth [najntie:nθ] negentiende, negentiende deelʰ

ninetieth [najntieəθ] negentigste, negentigste deel[h]

ninety [najntie] negentig

ninny [ninnie] imbeciel, sukkel

ninth [najnθ] negende, negende deel[h]

¹nip [nip] vb (with out) eventjes (weg)gaan, vliegen, rennen: ~ in: a) binnenwippen; b) naar links (of: rechts) schieten (in traf)

²nip [nip] vb 1 knijpen, beknellen, bijten (also of animal); 2 in de groei stuiten: ~ in the bud in de kiem smoren

³nip n 1 stokje[h], borreltje[h]; 2 kneep; 3 (bijtende) kou: there was a ~ in the air het was nogal fris(jes)

⁴nip vb nippen, in kleine teugjes nemen

nipper [nippə] 1 peuter; 2 ~s tang, nijptang, buigtang

nipple [nipl] 1 tepel; 2 (Am) speen (of feeding bottle); 3 (smeer)nippel

nippy [nippie] 1 vlug, rap; 2 fris(jes), koud

nit [nit] 1 neet, luizenei[h]; 2 stommeling

¹nitpicking [nitpikking] adj muggenzifterig

²nitpicking [nitpikking] n muggenzifterij

nitrogen [najtrədzjən] stikstof[h]

nitwit [nitwit] idioot, stommeling

¹nix [niks] n niks, niets[h], nop

²nix [niks] vb een streep halen door, niet toestaan

¹no [noo] adv 1 nee(n): oh ~! 't is niet waar!; did you tell her? ~ I didn't heb je het tegen haar gezegd? neen; ~! neen toch!; 2 niet, in geen enkel opzicht: he told her in ~ uncertain terms hij zei het haar in duidelijke bewoordingen; let me know whether or ~ you are coming laat me even weten of je komt of niet; the mayor himself, ~ less niemand minder dan de burgemeester zelf

²no [noo] pron 1 geen, geen enkele, helemaal geen: on ~ account onder geen enkele voorwaarde; there's ~ milk er is geen melk in huis; I'm ~ expert ik ben geen deskundige; 2 haast geen, bijna geen, heel weinig, een minimum van: it's ~ distance het is vlakbij; in ~ time in een mum van tijd

³no [noo] n (~es) 1 neen[h], weigering; 2 tegenstemmer: I won't take ~ for an answer ik sta erop, je kunt niet weigeren, ik wil geen nee horen

nob [nob] 1 kop, hoofd[h]; 2 hoge ome

nobble [nobl] 1 (sport) uitschakelen (horse, dog; esp through doping); 2 omkopen, bepraten (pers); 3 (weg)kapen, jatten (money, prize)

nobility [noobillittie] 1 adel, adelstand; 2 adeldom; 3 edelmoedigheid, nobelheid

¹noble [noobl] adj 1 adellijk, van adel; 2 edel, nobel

²noble [noobl] n edele, edelman, edelvrouw

nobleman [nooblmən] edelman, lid[h] vd adel

nobody [noobədie] niemand, onbelangrijk persoon, nul

nocturnal [noktə:nl] nachtelijk, nacht-

¹nod [nod] vb 1 knikken (as greeting, order), ja knikken (indicating approval): have a ~ding acquaintance with s.o. (sth.) iem (iets) oppervlakkig kennen; 2 (with off) indutten, in slaap vallen; 3 (zitten te) suffen, niet opletten, een fout maken

²nod [nod] vb 1 knikken met (head); 2 door knikken te kennen geven (approval, greeting, permission): ~ approval goedkeurend knikken

³nod [nod] n knik(je[h]), wenk(je[h]): give (s.o.) a ~ (iem toe)knikken; on the ~: a) op de lat, op krediet; b) zonder discussie (of: formele) stemming

no-frill(s) zonder franje, eenvoudig

nohow op geen enkele manier, helemaal niet, van geen kant: we couldn't find it ~ we konden het helemaal nergens vinden

noise [nojz] 1 geluid[h]; 2 lawaai[h], rumoer[h]; 3 (techn) geruis[h], ruis, storing

noisy [nojzie] lawaaierig, luidruchtig, gehorig

nomad [noomæd] 1 nomade; 2 zwerver (also fig)

nominal [nomminl] 1 in naam (alléén), theoretisch, niet echt; 2 zo goed als geen, niet noemenswaardig, symbolisch (eg amount): at (a) ~ price voor een spotprijs

nominate [nomminneet] 1 (with as, for) kandidaat stellen (als, voor), (als kandidaat) voordragen; 2 benoemen: ~ s.o. to be (of: as) iem benoemen tot

nomination [nomminneesjən] 1 kandidaatstelling, voordracht, nominatie; 2 benoeming

nominee [nomminnie:] 1 kandidaat; 2 benoemde

non-aggression [nonnəgresjən] non-agressie, (belofte van) het niet aanvallen: ~ pact (of: agreement) niet-aanvalsverdrag

non-aligned [nonnəlajnd] niet-gebonden, neutraal (country, politics)

nonchalant [nonsjələnt] nonchalant, onverschillig

non-commissioned [nonkəmisjənd] zonder officiersaanstelling: ~ officer onderofficier

non-committal [nonkəmitl] neutraal, vrijblijvend (reply)

¹none [nun] pron geen (enkele), niemand, niets: I'll have ~ of your tricks ik pik die streken van jou niet; there is ~ left er is niets meer over; ~ other than the President niemand anders dan de president; ~ of the students niemand van de studenten

²none [nun] adv helemaal niet, niet erg, niet veel: she was ~ the wiser ze was er niets wijzer op geworden; she is ~ too bright ze is niet al te slim

nonentity [nonnentittie] onbelangrijk persoon (ding[h])

nonetheless [nunðəles] niettemin, echter, toch

non-event [nonnivvent] afknapper

non-existent [nonnigzistənt] niet-bestaand

non-iron [nonnajjən] zelfstrijkend

no-nonsense 1 zakelijk, no-nonsense; 2 zonder franjes (eg dress)

nonplussed [nonplust] verbijsterd

nonproliferation [nonprəliffəreesjən] non-proliferatie

non-returnable [nonrittə:nəbl] zonder statiegeld

nonsense [nonsns] onzin, nonsens, flauwekul: make (a) ~ of tenietdoen, het effect bederven van; stand no ~ geen flauwekul dulden; what ~ wat een flauwekul

nonsensical [nonsensikl] onzinnig, absurd

non-stick [nonstik] antiaanbak-, met een antiaan-
baklaag

non-stop [nonstop] non-stop, zonder te stoppen,
doorgaand *(train)*, zonder tussenlandingen
(flight), direct *(connection)*, doorlopend *(perform-ance)*

noodles [noe:dlz] (soort eier)vermicelli, (soort)
mi, noedels

nook [noek] (rustig) hoekje[h], veilige plek: *search
every ~ and cranny* in elk hoekje en gaatje zoeken,
overal zoeken

noon [noe:n] middag(uur[h]), twaalf uur 's middags

no-one [noowun] niemand

noose [noe:s] lus, strik, strop

nor [no:] **1** evenmin, ook niet: *you don't like melon?
~ do I* je houdt niet van meloen? ik ook niet; **2** *(often
after neither)* noch, en ook niet, en evenmin: *nei-ther Jill ~ Sheila* noch Jill noch Sheila; *she neither
spoke ~ smiled* ze sprak noch lachte

Nordic [no:dik] noords, Noord-Europees, Scandi-navisch

¹normal [no:ml] *adj* normaal, gewoon, standaard

²normal [no:ml] *n* het normale, gemiddelde[h], nor-male toestand: *above ~* boven normaal

normalization [no:məlajzeesjən] **1** normalisatie; **2**
het normaal worden

normalize [no:məlajz] normaal worden (maken),
herstellen, normaliseren

Norman [no:mən] Normandisch

Norseman [no:smən] Noorman

¹north [no:θ] *n* het noorden *(point of the compass)*,
noord: *face (the) ~* op het noorden liggen; *the
North* het Noordelijk gedeelte

²north [no:θ] *adj* noordelijk: *the North Pole* de
noordpool; *the North Sea* de Noordzee

³north [no:θ] *adv* van, naar, in het noorden: *face ~*
op het noorden liggen

northbound iem die, iets dat naar het noorden gaat
(traf, road)

north-east noordoostelijk

northeastern uit het noordoosten, noordoostelijk

¹northerly [no:ðəlie] *n* noordenwind

²northerly [no:ðəlie] *adj* noordelijk

northern [no:ðən] noordelijk, noorden-, noord(-):
the ~ lights het noorderlicht

northward [no:θwəd] noord(waarts), noordelijk

north-west noordwestelijk

northwestern noordwest(elijk)

Norway [no:wee] Noorwegen

¹Norwegian [no:wie:dzjən] *adj* Noors

²Norwegian [no:wie:dzjən] *n* Noor, Noorse

nos *numbers* nummers

¹nose [nooz] *n* **1** neus, reukorgaan[h], *(fig)* reukzin,
speurzin: *(right) under s.o.'s (very) ~* vlak voor zijn
neus; **2** punt[h], neus *(of aeroplane, car, shoe)*: *cut off
one's ~ to spite one's face* woedend zijn eigen glazen
ingooien; *follow one's ~* zijn instinct volgen; *have
a ~ for sth.* ergens een fijne neus voor hebben; *keep
one's ~ to the grindstone* zwoegen, voortdurend

hard werken; *keep one's ~ out of s.o.'s affairs* zich
met zijn eigen zaken bemoeien; *look down one's ~
at s.o.* de neus voor iem ophalen, neerkijken op
iem; *pay through the ~ (for)* zich laten afzetten
(voor); *poke one's ~ into s.o.'s affairs* zijn neus in
andermans zaken steken; *put s.o.'s ~ out of joint: a)*
iem voor het hoofd stoten; *b)* iem jaloers maken;
rub s.o.'s ~ in it (of: *the dirt*) iem iets onder de neus
wrijven; *turn up one's ~ at sth.* zijn neus ophalen
voor iets; *(win) by a ~* een neuslengte vóór zijn

²nose [nooz] *vb* zich (voorzichtig) een weg banen *(of
ship, car)*

nose about rondneuzen (in), rondsnuffelen (in)

nosebleed bloedneus

¹nosedive *n* **1** duikvlucht; **2** plotselinge (prijs)daling

²nosedive *vb* **1** een duikvlucht maken; **2** plotseling
dalen, vallen

nosegay ruiker(tje[h]), boeketje[h]

nose out ontdekken, erachter komen

¹nosh [nosj] *n* eten[h]

²nosh [nosj] *vb* bikken, eten

nosiness [noozienəs] bemoeizucht, nieuwsgierig-heid

nostalgia [nostældzjiə] nostalgie, verlangen[h] (naar
het verleden)

nostril [nostril] **1** neusgat[h]; **2** neusvleugel

nosy [noozie] nieuwsgierig: *Nosey Parker* bemoei-al, nieuwsgierig Aagje

not [not] niet, geen, helemaal niet: *~ a thing* hele-maal niets; *I hope ~* ik hoop van niet; *~ to say* mis-schien zelfs, om niet te zeggen; *~ at all* helemaal
niet; *~ least* vooral; *as likely as ~* waarschijnlijk; *~
only … but (also)* niet alleen …, maar (ook); *~ a
bus but a tram* geen bus maar een tram; *~ that I
care* niet (om)dat het mij iets kan schelen

¹notable [nootəbl] *adj* opmerkelijk, merkwaardig,
opvallend

²notable [nootəbl] *n* belangrijk persoon

notary [nootərie] notaris: *~ public* notaris

notation [nooteesjən] **1** notatie *(music, chess etc)*,
schrijfwijze: *chemical ~* chemische symbolen; **2**
(Am) aantekening, noot

¹notch [notsj] *n* keep *(also fig)*, kerf, inkeping

²notch [notsj] *vb* **1** (in)kepen, (in)kerven, insnijden;
2 *(also with up)* (be)halen *(victory, points)*, binnen-halen

¹note [noot] *n* **1** aantekening, notitie: *make ~s* aan-tekeningen maken; *make a ~ of your expenses* houd
bij wat voor onkosten je maakt; **2** briefje[h], bericht-je[h], (diplomatieke) nota, memorandum[h]; **3**
(voet)noot, annotatie; **4** (bank)biljet[h], briefje[h]; **5**
(mus) toon, noot; **6** (onder)toon, klank: *sound* (of:
strike) *a ~ of warning* een waarschuwend geluid la-ten horen; **7** aanzien[h], belang[h], gewicht[h]: *of ~* van
belang, met een reputatie, algemeen bekend; **8** aan-dacht, nota: *take ~ of* notitie nemen van; *compare
~s* ervaringen uitwisselen

²note [noot] *vb* **1** nota nemen van, aandacht schen-ken aan, letten op; **2** (op)merken, waarnemen; **3**

aandacht vestigen op, opmerken; **4** *(with down)* opschrijven, noteren

notebook 1 notitieboekje[h]; **2** notebook

noted [n<u>oo</u>tid] *(with for)* beroemd (om, wegens), bekend

notepaper postpapier[h]

noteworthy vermeldenswaardig, opmerkelijk

¹nothing [n<u>u</u>θing] *pron* niets, *(pers)* nul, waardeloos iem, *(matter)* kleinigheid, niemendalletje: *she did ~ but grumble* ze zat alleen maar te mopperen; *there was ~ for it but to call a doctor* er zat niets anders op dan een dokter te bellen; *for ~: a)* tevergeefs; *b)* gratis, voor niets; *there's ~ to it* er is niets aan, het is een makkie; *(sport) there's ~ in it* zij zijn gelijk

²nothing [n<u>u</u>θing] *adv* helemaal niet, lang niet: *my painting is ~ like* (of: *near) as good as yours* mijn schilderij is bij lange na niet zo goed als het jouwe

¹notice [n<u>oo</u>tis] *n* **1** aankondiging, waarschuwing, opzegging *(of contract): give one's ~* zijn ontslag indienen; *we received three month's ~* de huur is ons met drie maanden opgezegd; *at a moment's ~* direct, zonder bericht vooraf; **2** aandacht, belangstelling, attentie: *I'd like to bring this book to your ~* ik zou dit boek onder uw aandacht willen brengen; *take (no) ~ of* (geen) acht slaan op; **3** mededeling, bericht[h]

²notice [n<u>oo</u>tis] *vb* (op)merken, zien, waarnemen: *she didn't ~ her friend in the crowd* zij zag haar vriendin niet in de menigte

noticeable [n<u>oo</u>tissəbl] **1** merkbaar, zichtbaar, waarneembaar; **2** opmerkelijk, opvallend, duidelijk

notification [nootiffikk<u>ee</u>sjən] **1** aangifte; **2** informatie, mededeling

notify [n<u>oo</u>tiffaj] informeren, bekendmaken, op de hoogte stellen

notion [n<u>oo</u>sjən] **1** begrip[h]; **2** idee[h], mening, veronderstelling: *she had no ~ of what I was talking about* ze had geen benul waar ik het over had; *the ~ that the earth is flat* het denkbeeld dat de aarde plat is

notoriety [nootər<u>a</u>jjətie] beruchtheid

notorious [noot<u>o:</u>riəs] algemeen (ongunstig) bekend, berucht

¹notwithstanding [notwiθst<u>æ</u>nding] *prep* ondanks, in weerwil van: *the road was built ~ fierce opposition* de verkeersweg werd gebouwd ondanks de felle tegenstand

²notwithstanding [notwiθst<u>æ</u>nding] *adv* desondanks, ondanks dat, toch

nougat [n<u>oo</u>ga:] noga

nought [no:t] nul || *~s and crosses* boter, kaas en eieren, kruisje nulletje

noun [naun] zelfstandig naamwoord[h]

nourish [n<u>u</u>rrisj] **1** voeden *(also fig): ~ing food* voedzaam eten; **2** koesteren: *~ the hope to* de hoop koesteren om te

nourishment [n<u>u</u>rrisjmənt] **1** voeding *(also fig)*, het voeden, het gevoed worden; **2** voedsel[h], eten[h]

¹novel [n<u>o</u>vl] *n* roman

²novel [n<u>o</u>vl] *adj* nieuw, onbekend: *~ ideas* verrassende ideeën

novelist [n<u>o</u>vvəlist] romanschrijver, schrijver

novelty [n<u>o</u>vvəltie] nieuwigheid, nieuws[h], iets onbekends: *the ~ soon wore off* het nieuwe, de nieuwigheid was er al gauw af

November [noov<u>e</u>mbə] november

novice [n<u>o</u>vvis] **1** novice; **2** beginneling, nieuweling

¹now [nau] *adv* **1** nu, tegenwoordig, onder deze omstandigheden: *they'll be here any minute ~* ze kunnen nu elk ogenblik aankomen; *~ what do you mean?* maar wat bedoel je nu eigenlijk?; *(every) ~ and again* (of: *then)* zo nu en dan, af en toe, van tijd tot tijd; *just ~: a)* zoëven, daarnet; *b)* nu, op dit ogenblik; *~ then, where do you think you're going?* zo, en waar dacht jij heen te gaan?; **2** nu (dat), gezien (dat): *~ you are here I will show you* nu je hier (toch) bent zal ik het je laten zien

²now [nau] *n* nu[h], dit moment[h]: *before ~* vroeger, tot nu toe; *by ~* ondertussen, inmiddels; *for ~* voorlopig; *as from ~, from ~ on* van nu af aan; *until ~, up till ~, up to ~* tot nu toe

nowadays [n<u>au</u>ədeez] tegenwoordig, vandaag de dag

nowhere [n<u>oo</u>weə] nergens *(also fig)*, nergens heen: *it got him ~* het leverde hem niets op; *she is ~ near as bright as him* ze is lang niet zo intelligent als hij; *he started from ~ but became famous* hij kwam uit het niets maar werd beroemd

noxious [n<u>o</u>ksjəs] *(also fig)* schadelijk, ongezond

nozzle [n<u>o</u>zl] **1** tuit, pijp; **2** (straal)pijp, mondstuk[h], straalbuis

nub [nub] **1** brok[h], klompje[h], stomp(je[h]); **2** *(singular)* kern(punt[h]), essentie: *the ~ of the matter* de kern van de zaak

nuclear [nj<u>oe:</u>kliə] **1** mbt de kern(en), kern-; **2** nucleair, kern-, atoom-: *~ disarmament* nucleaire ontwapening; *~ waste* kernafval

nucleus [nj<u>oe:</u>kliəs] kern *(also fig)*

¹nude [njoe:d] *adj* naakt

²nude [njoe:d] *n* naakt iem: *in the ~* naakt, in zijn nakie

¹nudge [nudzj] *vb* **1** (zachtjes) aanstoten *(with elbow)*; **2** zachtjes duwen, schuiven

²nudge [nudzj] *n* stoot(je[h]), por, duwtje[h]

nudist [nj<u>oe:</u>dist] nudist, naturist

nudity [nj<u>oe:</u>dittie] naaktheid

nugget [n<u>u</u>git] **1** (goud)klompje[h]; **2** juweel(tje)[h] *(only fig): ~ of information* informatie die goud waard is

nuisance [nj<u>oe:</u>səns] **1** lastig iem (iets), lastpost, lastpak: *make a ~ of oneself* vervelend zijn; **2** (over)last, hinder: *what a ~* wat vervelend

null [nul]: *~ and void* van nul en gener waarde

nullify [n<u>u</u>lliffaj] **1** nietig verklaren, ongeldig verklaren; **2** opheffen, tenietdoen

¹numb [num] *adj* (with *with)* verstijfd (van), verdoofd, verkleumd

²**numb** [num] *vb* **1** verlammen *(also fig),* doen verstijven; **2** verdoven: *medicines ~ed the pain* medicijnen verzachtten de pijn

¹**number** [numbə] *n* **1** getalʰ; **2** aantalʰ: *a ~ of problems* een aantal problemen; *in ~* in aantal, in getal;
any ~ of ontelbaar veel; **3** nummerʰ: *published in ~s*
in afleveringen verschenen; **4** gezelschapʰ, groep; **5**
~s aantallen, hoeveelheid, grote aantallen: *win by
~s* winnen door getalsterkte; *have s.o.'s ~* iem doorhebben; *always think of ~ one* altijd alleen maar
aan zichzelf denken; *my ~ one problem* mijn grootste probleem

²**number** [numbə] *vb* **1** tellen; **2** vormen *(number),*
bedragen: *we ~ed eleven* we waren met ons elven; **3**
tellen, behoren tot: *I ~ him among my best friends*
hij behoort tot mijn beste vrienden; *his days are
~ed* zijn dagen zijn geteld

³**number** [numbə] *vb* nummeren, nummers geven

numberless [numbələs] ontelbaar, talloos

num(b)skull [numskul] sufferd, stomkop

¹**numeral** [njoe:mərəl] *n* **1** cijferʰ: *Roman ~s* Romeinse cijfers; **2** telwoordʰ

²**numeral** [njoe:mərəl] *adj* getal(s)-, van getallen

numerate [njoe:mərət] met een wiskundige basiskennis, gecijferd: *some of my students are hardly ~*
enkele van mijn studenten kunnen nauwelijks rekenen

numerical [njoe:merrikl] **1** getallen-, rekenkundig;
2 numeriek, in aantal, getals-

numerous [njoe:mərəs] talrijk(e), groot, vele

nun [nun] non

nuptial [nupsjl] huwelijks-

¹**nurse** [nə:s] *n* **1** verpleegster, verpleger, verpleegkundige: *male ~* verpleger, ziekenbroeder; *~!* zuster!; **2** kindermeisjeʰ; **3** voedster

²**nurse** [nə:s] *vb* **1** verplegen; verzorgen; **2** zogen,
borstvoeding geven: *nursing mother* zogende moeder; **3** behandelen, genezen: *~ s.o. back to health*
door verpleging iem weer gezond krijgen; **4** bevorderen, koesteren: *~ a grievance against s.o.* een
grief tegen iem koesteren

³**nurse** [nə:s] *vb* zuigen, aan de borst zijn: *be nursing
at one's mother's breast* de borst krijgen

nursemaid kindermeisjeʰ; **2** verzorgster

nursery [nə:sərie] **1** kinderkamer; **2** crèche, kinder-
dagverblijfʰ; **3** kwekerij

nurseryman [nə:səriemən] kweker

nursery rhyme kinderversjeʰ

nursery school peuterklas

nursing [nə:sing] verpleging, verzorging; verpleeg-
kunde

nursing home 1 verpleegtehuisʰ; **2** particulier ziekenhuisʰ

nut [nut] **1** noot; **2** moer; **3** fanaat, gek ‖ *~s and bolts*
grondbeginselen, hoofdzaken; *do one's ~* woedend
zijn; *she can't sing for ~s* ze kan totaal niet zingen;
off one's ~ niet goed bij zijn hoofd

nutcase mafkees

nutcracker notenkraker: *(a pair of) ~s* een noten-

kraker

nutmeg [nutmeg] **1** muskaatnoot; **2** nootmuskaat

¹**nutrient** [njoe:triənt] *adj* voedend, voedings-

²**nutrient** [njoe:triənt] *n* voedingsstof, bouwstof

nutrition [njoe:trisjən] **1** voeding; **2** voedingsleer

nutritious [njoe:trisjəs] voedzaam

nuts [nuts] gek, getikt: *go ~* gek worden

nutshell notendop *(also fig)*

nutty [nuttie] **1** met (veel) noten, vol noten; **2** naar
noten smakend; **3** gek, getikt, gestoord

nuzzle [nuzl] **1** (be)snuffelen; **2** (zich) nestelen

nylon [najlon] nylon⁺ʰ, *~s* nylonkousen

nymph [nimf] nimf

O

o' [ə] *of* van: *five o'clock* vijf uur

oaf [oof] klungel, lomperd

¹oak [ook] *n* eik

²oak [ook] *adj* eiken, eikenhout

oak-apple galappel, galnoot

O.A.P. *old age pension* AOW, Algemene Ouderdomswet

oar [o:] roeispaan, (roei)riem ‖ *put* (of: *shove) one's ~ in* zich ermee bemoeien, zijn neus erin steken

oarsman [o:zmən] roeier

oasis [ooeesis] oase *(also fig)*

oat [oot] haver, haverkorrel ‖ *feel one's ~s* bruisen van energie, *(Am also)* zelfgenoegzaam doen; *off one's ~s* zonder eetlust

oath [ooθ] **1** eed: *make* (of: *take, swear) an ~* een eed afleggen; *under ~* onder ede; **2** vloek

oatmeal 1 havermeel[h], havervlokken; **2** havermout(pap)

obdurate [obdjoerət] **1** onverbeterlijk; **2** onverzettelijk

obedient [əbie:diənt] **1** gehoorzaam; **2** onderworpen

obeisance [oobeesns] **1** buiging; **2** eerbied, respect[h]

obese [oobie:s] zwaarlijvig

obey [əbee] gehoorzamen (aan), opvolgen, toegeven aan

obituary [əbitjoeərie] overlijdensbericht[h] *(with short biography)*

¹object [obdzjikt] *n* **1** voorwerp[h], object[h]; **2** doel[h]; **3** *(linguistics)* voorwerp[h]: *direct ~ (of a verb)* lijdend voorwerp; *indirect ~ (of a verb)* meewerkend voorwerp; *money is no ~* geld speelt geen rol

²object [əbdzjekt] *vb* bezwaar hebben (maken): *he ~ed to being called a coward* hij wou niet voor lafaard doorgaan

objection [əbdzjeksjən] bezwaar[h]: *raise ~s* bezwaren maken

objectionable [əbdzjeksjnəbl] **1** bedenkelijk; **2** ongewenst, onaangenaam

¹objective [əbdzjektiv] *adj* objectief, onpartijdig

²objective [əbdzjektiv] *n* doel[h], doelstelling, doelwit[h], operatiedoel[h]

obligation [obligeesjən] **1** plicht, (zware) taak; **2** verplichting, verbintenis: *lay* (of: *place, put) s.o. under an ~* iem aan zich verplichten

obligatory [əbligətərie] verplicht

¹oblige [əblajdzj] *vb* **1** aan zich verplichten: *(I'm) much ~d (to you)* dank u zeer; **2** verplichten, (ver)binden *(by promise, contract): I feel ~d to say that ...* ik voel me verplicht te zeggen dat ...

²oblige [əblajdzj] *vb* het genoegen doen, ten beste geven: *~ with a song* een lied ten beste geven

obliging [əblajdzjing] attent, voorkomend, behulpzaam

oblique [əblie:k] **1** schuin, scheef: *~ stroke* schuine streep; **2** indirect, ontwijkend

obliterate [əblittəreet] uitwissen, verwijderen

obliteration [əblittəreesjən] **1** uitroeiing, vernietiging; **2** uitwissing, verwijdering; **3** afstempeling *(of stamps)*

oblivion [əblivviən] vergetelheid: *fall* (of: *sink) into ~* in vergetelheid raken

¹oblong [oblong] *adj* rechthoekig

²oblong [oblong] *n* rechthoek, langwerpige figuur

oboe [ooboo] hobo

obscene [əbsie:n] obsceen, onzedelijk

¹obscure [əbskjoeə] *adj* **1** obscuur, onduidelijk, onbekend; **2** verborgen, onopgemerkt

²obscure [əbskjoeə] *vb* **1** verduisteren; **2** overschaduwen; **3** verbergen

obscurity [əbskjoeərittie] **1** duister[h], duisternis; **2** onbekendheid: *live in ~* een obscuur leven leiden; **3** onduidelijkheid, onbegrijpelijkheid

obsequious [əbsie:kwiəs] kruiperig, onderdanig

observable [əbza:vbl] waarneembaar, merkbaar

observant [əbza:vənt] opmerkzaam, oplettend

observation [əbzəveesjən] **1** waarneming, observatie: *keep s.o. under ~* iem in de gaten (blijven) houden; **2** opmerking, commentaar[h]

observatory [əbza:vətərie] sterrenwacht

observe [əbza:v] **1** opmerken, zeggen; **2** naleven, in acht nemen; **3** waarnemen, observeren

observer [əbza:və] **1** toeschouwer; **2** waarnemer *(also aviation)*, observeerder, observator

obsession [əbsesjən] obsessie, dwanggedachte: *have an ~ about sth.* bezeten zijn door iets; **2** bezetenheid, het bezeten-zijn

obsolete [obsəlie:t] verouderd, in onbruik (geraakt), achterhaald

obstacle [obstəkl] obstakel[h], belemmering: *form an ~ to sth.* een beletsel vormen voor iets

obstetrics [əbstetriks] obstetrie, verloskunde

obstinate [obstinnət] **1** halsstarrig; **2** hardnekkig

obstruct [əbstrukt] **1** versperren, blokkeren; **2** belemmeren, hinderen; **3** *(sport, esp football)* obstructie plegen tegen

obstruction [əbstruksjən] **1** belemmering, hindernis; **2** versperring, obstakel[h]; **3** obstructie *(also sport, med)*

obtain [əbteen] (ver)krijgen, behalen

¹obtrude [əbtroe:d] *vb* opdringerig zijn, zich opdringen

²obtrude [əbtroe:d] *vb* (with *(up)on)* opdringen (aan), ongevraagd naar voren brengen

obtuse [əbtjoe:s] **1** stomp: *an ~ angle* een stompe

hoek; **2** traag van begrip

obviate [obvie·eet] ondervangen, voorkomen: ~ *the necessity* (of: *need*) *of sth.* iets overbodig maken

obvious [obviəs] **1** duidelijk, zonneklaar: *an ~ lie* een aperte leugen; **2** voor de hand liggend, doorzichtig; **3** aangewezen, juist: *the ~ man for the job* de aangewezen man voor het karweitje

obviously [obviəslie] duidelijk, kennelijk

¹occasion [əkeezjən] *n* **1** gebeurtenis, voorval[h]; **2** evenement[h], gelegenheid, feest[h]: *he seemed to be equal to the ~* hij leek tegen de situatie opgewassen te zijn; *we'll make an ~ of it* we zullen het vieren; *on the ~ of your birthday* ter gelegenheid van je verjaardag; **3** aanleiding; reden: *give ~ to* aanleiding geven tot; *you have no ~ to leave* jij hebt geen reden om weg te gaan

²occasion [əkeezjən] *vb* veroorzaken, aanleiding geven tot

occasional [əkeezjnəl] **1** incidenteel, nu en dan voorkomend: *~ showers* verspreide buien; **2** gelegenheids-

occidental [oksiddentl] westers

occult [əkult] occult, geheim, verborgen

occupant [okjoepənt] **1** bezitter, landbezitter; **2** bewoner; **3** inzittende *(of car)*; **4** bekleder *(of office)*

occupation [okjoepeesjən] **1** beroep[h]; **2** bezigheid, activiteit; **3** bezetting *(door vijand)*

occupational [okjoepeesjənəl] mbt een beroep, beroeps-: *~ hazard* beroepsrisico

occupy [okjoepaj] **1** bezetten, bezit nemen van: *~ a building* een gebouw bezetten; **2** in beslag nemen: *it will ~ a lot of his time* het zal veel van zijn tijd in beslag nemen; **3** bezighouden: *~ oneself with* zich bezighouden met; **4** bewonen, betrekken

occur [əkə:] **1** voorkomen, aangetroffen worden; **2** opkomen, invallen: *it simply did not ~ to him* het kwam eenvoudigweg niet bij hem op; **3** gebeuren

occurrence [əkurrəns] **1** voorval[h], gebeurtenis; **2** het voorkomen

ocean [oosjn] oceaan: *Pacific Ocean* Stille Zuidzee; *~s of time* zeeën van tijd

ochre [ookə] oker

o'clock [əklok] uur: *ten ~* tien uur

octagon [oktəgən] achthoek

octave [oktiv] octaaf

October [oktoobə] oktober

octogenarian [oktoodzjinneəriən] tachtigjarige

octopus [oktəpəs] inktvis

oculist [okjoelist] oogarts

odd [od] **1** oneven: *~ and even numbers* oneven en even getallen; **2** vreemd, ongewoon: *an ~ habit* een gekke gewoonte; **3** overblijvend: *the ~ man at the table* de man die aan tafel overschiet *(after the others have formed pairs)*; **4** toevallig, onverwacht: *he drops in at ~ times* hij komt zo nu en dan eens langs; **5** los, niet behorend tot een reeks: *an ~ glove* een losse handschoen; *~ job* klusje; **6** *(after noun, cardinal number)* iets meer dan: *five pounds ~* iets meer dan vijf pond; *60-odd persons* ruim 60 perso-

nen; *~ man out* vreemde eend; *which is the ~ man out in the following list?* welke hoort in het volgende rijtje niet thuis?

oddball *(Am)* gekke vent, rare

oddity [oddittie] **1** eigenaardigheid, vreemde eigenschap; **2** gekke vent; **3** iets vreemds, vreemd voorwerp[h], vreemde gebeurtenis; **4** curiositeit

odd-job man manusje-van-alles[h], klusjesman

oddment [odmənt] overschot[h], overblijfsel[h], restant[h]

odds [odz] **1** ongelijkheid, verschil: *that makes no ~* dat maakt niets uit; *what's the ~?* wat doet dat ertoe?; **2** onenigheid: *be at ~ with* in onenigheid leven met; **3** (grote) kans, waarschijnlijkheid: *the ~ are that she will do it* de kans is groot dat ze het doet; **4** verhouding tussen de inzetten bij weddenschap: *take ~ of one to ten* een inzet accepteren van één tegen tien; *~ and ends* prullen; *~ and sods* rommel; *against all (the) ~* tegen alle verwachtingen in; *over the ~* meer dan verwacht

odious [oodiəs] hatelijk, weerzinwekkend

odour [oodə] **1** geur, stank, lucht(je[h]): *an ~ of sanctity* een geur van heiligheid; **2** reputatie, naam: *be in good ~ with* goed aangeschreven staan bij

of [ov] **1** van, van … vandaan: *go wide ~ the mark* ver naast het doel schieten; **2** (afkomstig) van, uit, (veroorzaakt, gemaakt) door: *a colour ~ your own choice* een kleur die u zelf kunt kiezen; *that's too much to ask ~ Jane* dat is te veel van Jane gevraagd; *~ necessity* uit noodzaak; **3** *(composition, contents, amount)* bestaande uit, van: *a box ~ chocolates* een doos chocola; **4** over, van, met betrekking tot: *quick ~ understanding* snel van begrip; **5** van, te, bij, met: *men ~ courage* mannen met moed; *be ~ importance* van belang zijn; **6** van, behorend tot: *it's that dog ~ hers again* het is die hond van haar weer; **7** van, tot, naar, voor: *fear ~ spiders* angst voor spinnen; **8** van, onder: *a pound ~ flour* een pond bloem; *five ~ us* vijf mensen van onze groep; *the month ~ May* de maand mei; *an angel ~ a husband* een engel van een man

¹off [of] *adv* **1** verwijderd, weg, (er)af, ver, hiervandaan: *three miles ~* drie mijl daarvandaan; *send ~ a letter* een brief versturen; **2** af, uit, helemaal, ten einde: *a day ~* een dagje vrij; *kill ~* uitroeien; *turn ~ the radio* zet de radio af; **3** ondergeschikt, minder belangrijk: *5% ~* met 5% korting; *~ and on* af en toe, nu en dan; *be well ~* rijk zijn

²off [of] *prep* **1** van, van af: *he got ~ the bus* hij stapte uit de bus; **2** van de baan, van … af, afgestapt van: *~ duty* vrij (van dienst), buiten dienst; *I've gone ~ fish* ik kan geen vis meer; **3** van … af, naast, opzij van, uit: *it was ~ the mark* het miste zijn doel *(also fig)*; *an alley ~ the square* een steegje dat op het plein uitkomt; **4** onder, beneden, achter zijn, minder dan: *a year or two ~ sixty* een jaar of wat onder de zestig

³off [of] *adj* **1** vrij: *my husband is ~ today* mijn man heeft vandaag vrij; **2** minder (goed), slecht(er): *her*

singing was a bit ~ tonight ze zong niet zo best van-avond; **3** verder (gelegen), ver(ste); **4** rechter(-) *(of side of horse, vehicle)*, rechts; **5** rustig, stil: *during the ~ season* buiten het (hoog)seizoen; **6** (hoogst) onwaarschijnlijk: *~ chance* kleine kans; **7** bedorven *(of food)*, zuur: *this sausage is ~* dit worstje is be-dorven; **8** vd baan, afgelast, uitgesteld: *the meeting is ~* de bijeenkomst gaat niet door; **9** weg, vertrok-ken, gestart: *get ~ to a good start* goed beginnen; **10** uit(geschakeld), buiten werking, niet aan: *the wa-ter is ~* het water is afgesloten; **11** mis, naast: *his guess was slightly ~* hij zat er enigszins naast

offal [ofl] afval[h], vuil[h], vuilnis, slachtafval[h], *(fig)* uit-schot[h]

off-colour onwel, niet lekker

off day ongeluksdag

offence [əfɛns] **1** overtreding, misdrijf[h], delict[h], misdaad: *commit an ~* een overtreding begaan; **2** belediging: *cause* (of: *give*) *~ to s.o.* iem beledigen; *take ~ at* aanstoot nemen aan, zich ergeren aan; *he is quick to take ~* hij is gauw op z'n teentjes getrapt

¹offend [əfɛnd] *vb* beledigen *(also fig)*, boos maken

²offend [əfɛnd] *vb* kwaad doen: *the verdict ~s against all principles of justice* het vonnis is een aan-fluiting van alle rechtsprincipes

offender [əfɛndə] overtreder, zondaar

¹offensive [əfɛnsiv] *adj* **1** offensief, aanvallend; **2** be-ledigend, aanstootgevend

²offensive [əfɛnsiv] *n* aanval, offensief[h], *(fig)* cam-pagne, beweging: *take* (of: *go into*) *the ~* aanvallen, in het offensief gaan

¹offer [ofə] *vb* **1** (aan)bieden, geven, schenken: *~ one's hand* zijn hand uitsteken; *he ~ed to drive me home* hij bood aan me naar huis te brengen; **2** te koop aanbieden, tonen, laten zien

²offer [ofə] *vb* voorkomen, gebeuren, optreden: *as occasion ~s* wanneer de gelegenheid zich voordoet

³offer [ofə] *n* aanbod[h], aanbieding, offerte, voor-stel[h]: *be on ~* in de aanbieding zijn, te koop zijn; *this house is under ~* op dit huis is een bod gedaan

offhand 1 onvoorbereid, geïmproviseerd: *avoid making ~ remarks* maak geen ondoordachte op-merkingen; **2** nonchalant

office [ofis] **1** ambt[h], openbare betrekking, functie: *hold ~* een ambt bekleden; **2** dienst, hulp, zorg: *good ~s* goede diensten; **3** kantoor[h], bureau[h]: *the Foreign ~* het ministerie van Buitenlandse Zaken

officer [ofisə] **1** ambtenaar, functionaris; **2** iem die een belangrijke functie bekleedt, directeur, voorzitter: *clerical* (of: *executive*) *~* (hoge) rege-ringsfunctionaris; **3** politieagent; **4** officier

¹official [əfiʃl] *adj* **1** officieel, ambtelijk; **2** officieel, ambtelijk

²official [əfiʃl] *n* beambte, functionaris, (staats)ambtenaar, *(sport)* official, wedstrijdcom-missaris

officialese [əfiʃəli:z] stadhuistaal, ambtenarenla-tijn[h]

officiate [əfisjie·eet] **1** officieel optreden: *~ as*

chairman (officieel) als voorzitter dienst doen; **2** *(sport)* arbitreren

officious [əfiʃəs] bemoeiziek, opdringerig

off-key vals, uit de toon *(also fig)*

off-licence 1 slijtvergunning; **2** slijterij, drankzaak

off-line off line, niet-gekoppeld

offload 1 lossen *(vehicle, esp aeroplane)*; **2** dumpen

off-peak buiten het hoogseizoen, de spits *(of use, traf)*, goedkoop, rustig: *in the ~ hours* tijdens de daluren

offprint overdruk

off-putting ontmoedigend

offset [ofset] compenseren, opwegen tegen, teniet-doen: *~ against* zetten tegenover

offshoot uitloper *(also fig)*, scheut, zijtak

offshore 1 in zee, voor de kust, buitengaats: *~ fish-ing* zeevisserij; **2** aflandig: *~ wind* aflandige wind

¹offside *n* **1** *(sport)* buitenspel[h], buitenspelpositie; **2** rechterkant *(of car, horse, road etc)*; **3** verste kant

²offside *adj (sport)* buitenspel-: *the ~ rule* de buiten-spelregel

offspring kroost[h], nakomeling(en)

offstage 1 achter (de schermen); **2** onzichtbaar

off-the-record onofficieel, binnenskamers

often [of(t)ən] vaak: *as ~ as not* de helft van de ke-ren, vaak; *he was late once too ~* hij kwam één keer te veel te laat; *every so ~* nu en dan

ogre [oogə] menseneter

oh [oo] o!, och! ach!: *~ no!* dat niet!, o nee!; *~ yes!* o ja!, ja zeker!; *~ yes?* zo?, o ja?; *~ well* och, och kom

¹oil [ojl] *n* **1** (aard)olie, *(Belg)* petroleum; **2** petrole-um, kerosine, stookolie, diesel(brandstof), smeer-olie; **3** olieverf ‖ *~ and vinegar* (of: *water*) water en vuur; *strike ~* olie aanboren, *(fig)* plotseling rijk worden

²oil [ojl] *vb* smeren, oliën, insmeren, invetten

oilcake lijnkoek(en), oliekoek(en)

oilcloth wasdoek[h]

oil-fired met olie gestookt

oil rig booreiland[h]

oilskin 1 oliejas; **2** *~s* oliepak[h]; **3** geolied doek[h], was-doek[h]

oil slick olievlek *(on water)*

oily [ojlie] **1** olieachtig, geolied, vettig; **2** kruiperig, vleiend

ointment [ojntmənt] zalf, smeersel[h]

¹OK [ookee] *adj, adv* okay, o.k., in orde, voldoende, akkoord, afgesproken: *it looks ~ now* nu ziet het er goed uit

²OK [ookee] *n* goedkeuring, akkoord[h], fiat[h]

³OK [ookee] *vb* goedkeuren, akkoord gaan met

¹old [oold] *adj* **1** oud, bejaard, antiek, verouderd, ou-derwets, in onbruik geraakt: *~ age* ouderdom, hoge leeftijd; *~ maid* oude vrijster; *as ~ as the hills* zo oud als de weg naar Rome; **2** voormalig, ex-: *the good ~ days* (of: *times*) de goede oude tijd; *pay off ~ scores* een oude rekening vereffenen; **3** lang bekend: *good ~ John* die beste Jan; **4** oud, vd leeftijd van: *a 17-year-~ girl* een zeventienjarig meisje; **5** ervaren, bekwaam: *an ~ hand at shoplifter* een doorgewinterde winkeldief; *a chip off the ~ block* helemaal haar moeder; *money for ~ rope* iets voor niets, gauw verdiend geld; *~ country: a)* land in de Oude Wereld; *b)* moederland, geboorteland; *the ~ man: a)* de ouwe *(also ship's captain); b)* de baas *(also husband); c)* mijn ouweheer; *in any ~ place* waar je maar kan denken; *any ~ thing will do* alles is goed; *the Old World* de Oude Wereld, *(Am)* (continentaal) Europa, de Oude Wereld

²**old** [oold] *n* vroeger tijden, het verleden: *heroes of ~* helden uit het verleden

old-fashioned ouderwets, verouderd, conservatief

oldie [ooldie] **1** oude grap (grammofoonplaat): *a golden ~* een gouwe ouwe; **2** oudjeʰ *(pers)*

oldish [ooldisj] ouwelijk, nogal oud

oldster [ooldstə] oudjeʰ, ouder lidʰ

old-time [ooltajm] oud, van vroeger, ouderwets

old-timer *(Am)* **1** oudgediende, oude rot; **2** oude bewoner; **3** iets ouds, oude auto

old-world 1 ouderwets, verouderd, van vroeger; **2** *Old World* vd Oude Wereld

O level *ordinary level* Brits (examenvakʰ op) eindexamenniveauʰ

¹**olive** [olliv] *n* olijf(boom); olijfhoutʰ

²**olive** [olliv] *adj* **1** olijfkleurig; **2** olijfgroen; olijfbruin *(complexion)*

Olympic [əlimpik] Olympisch: *the ~ Games* de Olympische Spelen

ombudsman [omboedzmən] ombudsman

omelet(te) [omlit] omelet

omen [oomən] voortekenʰ

ominous [omminnəs] **1** veelbetekenend; **2** onheilspellend, dreigend

omission [əmisjən] weglating, verzuimʰ

omit [əmit] **1** weglaten, overslaan; **2** verzuimen, nalaten, verwaarlozen

omnibus [omnibbəs] **1** (auto)bus; **2** omnibus(uitgave)

omnipotent [omnippətənt] almachtig

omniscient [omnisjənt] alwetend

omnivorous [omnivvərəs] allesetend: *an ~ reader* iem die alles wat los en vast zit leest

¹**on** [on] *prep* **1** *(place or direction; also fig)* op, in, aan, bovenop: *I have it ~ good authority* ik heb het uit betrouwbare bron; *hang ~ the wall* aan de muur hangen; **2** bij, nabij, aan, verbonden aan: *~ your right* aan de rechterkant; *just ~ sixty people* amper zestig mensen; **3** *(time)* op, bij: *arrive ~ the hour* op het hele uur aankomen; *come ~ Tuesday* kom dinsdag; *~ opening the door* bij het openen van de deur; **4** *(condition)* in, met: *the patient is ~ antibiotics* de patiënt krijgt antibiotica; *be ~ duty* dienst hebben; *~ trial* op proef; **5** over: *take pity ~ the poor* medelijden hebben met de armen; **6** ten koste van, op kosten van: *this round is ~ me* dit rondje is voor mij, ik betaal dit rondje

²**on** [on] *adv* **1** in werking, aan, in functie: *the music came ~* de muziek begon; *have you anything ~ to-*

night? heb je plannen voor vanavond?; *leave the light ~* het licht aan laten; **2** *(of clothes)* aan: *put ~ your new dress* trek je nieuwe jurk aan; **3** verder, later, door: *five years ~* vijf jaar later; *send ~* doorsturen, nazenden; *later ~* later; *and so ~* enzovoort; *(talk) ~ and ~* zonder onderbreking (praten); *from that moment ~* vanaf dat ogenblik; **4** *(indicating place or direction; also fig)* op, tegen, aan, toe: *they collided head ~* ze botsten frontaal

³**on** [on] *adj* **1** aan(gesloten), ingeschakeld, open *(appliance, tap etc)*; **2** aan de gang, gaande: *the match is ~* de wedstrijd is aan de gang; **3** op *(stage)*: *you're ~ in five minutes* je moet over vijf minuten op; **4** aan de beurt, dienstdoend: *I'm ~!* okay, ik doe mee; *the wedding is ~* het huwelijk gaat door

on-board aan boord: *~ computer* boordcomputer

¹**once** [wuns] *adv* **1** eenmaal, eens, één keer: *~ again* (of: *more)* opnieuw, nog eens; *~ too often* een keer te veel; *~ or twice* zo nu en dan, van tijd tot tijd; *(all) at ~* tegelijk(ertijd), samen; *(just) for (this) ~* (voor) deze ene keer; *~ and for all* voorgoed, definitief, voor de laatste keer; *~ in a while* een enkele keer; *he only said it the ~* hij zei het maar één keer; **2** vroeger, (ooit) eens: *the ~ popular singer* de eens zo populaire zanger; *~ upon a time there was ...* er was eens ...; *at ~* onmiddellijk, meteen; *all at ~* plots(eling), ineens, opeens

²**once** [wuns] *conj* eens (dat), als eenmaal, zodra: *~ you are ready, we'll leave* zodra je klaar bent, zullen we gaan

once-over kijkjeʰ, vluchtig overzichtʰ: *give s.o. the ~* iem globaal opnemen, iem vluchtig bekijken

oncoming [ongkumming] **1** naderend, aanstaand; **2** tegemoetkomend *(also fig)*: *~ traffic* tegenliggers

¹**one** [wun] *n* één: *the figure ~* het cijfer één; *by ~s and twos* alleen of in groepjes van twee, *(fig)* heel geleidelijk

²**one** [wun] *pron* **1** (er) een, (er) eentje: *the best ~s* de beste(n); *you are a fine ~* jij bent me d'r eentje; *give him ~* geef hem er een van, geef hem een knal; *let's have (a quick) ~* laten we er (gauw) eentje gaan drinken; *the ~ that I like best* degene die ik het leukst vind; *he was ~ up on me* hij was me net de baas; *this ~'s on me* ik trakteer!; *this ~* deze hier; **2** men: *~ must never pride oneself on one's achievements* men mag nooit prat gaan op zijn prestaties; **3** een zeker(e), één of ander(e), ene: *~ day he left* op een goede dag vertrok hij; *~ Mr. Smith called for you* een zekere meneer Smith heeft voor jou gebeld; **4** één, enig, *(fig)* dezelfde, hetzelfde, *(as intensifier)* hartstikke: *this is ~ good book* dit is een hartstikke goed boek; *from ~ chore to another* van het ene klusje naar het andere; *they are all ~ colour* ze hebben allemaal dezelfde kleur; *~ day out of six* één op de zes dagen, om de zes dagen; *my ~ and only friend* mijn enige echte vriend; *for ~ thing: a)* ten eerste; *b)* (al was het) alleen maar omdat; *neither ~ thing nor the other* vlees noch vis, halfslachtig

³**one** [wun] *num* één: *~ after another* een voor een, de

een na de andere; ~ *by* ~ een voor een, de een na de ander; ~ *to* ~ één op één, één tegen één; ~ *and all* iedereen, jan en alleman; *I was* ~ *too many for him* ik was hem te slim af; *like* ~ *o'clock* als een gek, energiek; *I, for* ~, *will refuse* ik zal in ieder geval weigeren

one another elkaar, mekaar: *they loved* ~ ze hielden van elkaar

one-armed eenarmig: ~ *bandit* eenarmige bandiet *(gambling machine)*

one-horse 1 met één paard *(carriage etc)*; **2** derderangs, slecht (toegerust): ~ *town* gat

one-man eenmans-: ~ *show* solovoorstelling

one-off exclusief, uniek; eenmalig

one-on-one 1 *(sport)* één tegen één; **2** *(Am)* individueel *(eg of education)*

one-parent family eenoudergezin^h

onerous [ˈɒnnərəs] lastig, moeilijk

oneself [wunˈsɛlf] **1** zich(zelf): *be* ~ zichzelf zijn; *by* ~ in z'n eentje, alleen; **2** zelf: *one should do it* ~ men zou het zelf moeten doen

one-sided 1 eenzijdig; **2** bevooroordeeld, partijdig

one-time voormalig, vroeger, oud-

one-track beperkt *(fig)*, eenzijdig: *he has a* ~ *mind* hij denkt altijd maar aan één ding

one-upmanship slagvaardigheid, kunst de ander steeds een slag voor te zijn

one-way in één richting: ~ *street* straat met eenrichtingsverkeer

ongoing voortdurend, doorgaand: ~ *research* lopend onderzoek

onion [ˈunjən] ui ‖ *know one's* ~*s* zijn vak verstaan, van wanten weten

on-line gekoppeld

onlooker toeschouwer, (toe)kijker

¹only [ˈoonlie] *adj* **1** enig: *an* ~ *child* een enig kind; *we were the* ~ *people wearing hats* we waren de enigen met een hoed (op); **2** best, (meest) geschikt, juist

²only [ˈoonlie] *adv* **1** slechts, alleen (maar): *she was* ~ *too glad* ze was maar al te blij; ~ *five minutes more* nog vijf minuten, niet meer; *if* ~ als … maar, ik wou dat …; *if* ~ *to, if* ~ *because* al was het alleen maar om; **2** *(with expressions of time)* pas, (maar) eerst, nog: *the train has* ~ *just left* de trein is nog maar net weg; *he arrived* ~ *yesterday* hij is gisteren pas aangekomen; *I like it,* ~ *I cannot afford it* ik vind het mooi, maar ik kan het niet betalen

onrush [ˈɒnrusj] **1** toeloop, toestroming; **2** aanval, bestorming

onset [ˈɒnset] **1** aanval, (plotselinge) bestorming; **2** begin^h, aanvang, aanzet: *the* ~ *of scarlet fever* de eerste symptomen van roodvonk

¹onshore *adj* **1** aanlandig, zee-: ~ *breeze* zeebries; **2** kust-, aan, op de kust gelegen, binnenlands: ~ *fishing* kustvisserij

²onshore *adv* **1** land(in)waarts, langs de kust; **2** aan land

onside *(sport)* niet buitenspel

on-site plaatselijk, ter plekke

onslaught [ˈɒnsloːt] (hevige) aanval, (scherpe) uitval, aanslag

onus [ˈoonəs] **1** last, plicht: *the* ~ *of proof rests with the plaintiff* de bewijslast ligt bij de eiser; **2** blaam, schuld: *put* (of: *shift*) *the* ~ *onto* de blaam werpen op

onward [ˈɒnwəd] voorwaarts, voortgaand: *the* ~ *course of events* het verdere verloop van de gebeurtenissen

onwards [ˈɒnwədz] voorwaarts, vooruit: *move* ~ voortgaan, verder gaan

oompah [ˈoeːmpaː] hoempageluid^h, (eentonig) gehoempapa

oops [oeps] oei, jee(tje), nee maar, pardon

oops-a-daisy hup(sakee), hoepla(la), hop

¹ooze [oeːz] *vb* **1** (binnen-, door-, in)sijpelen, druipen, druppelen: ~ *out of* (of: *from*) sijpelen uit; **2** (uit)zweten, vocht afscheiden, lekken, bloed opgeven: *his courage* ~*d away* de moed zonk hem in de schoenen

²ooze [oeːz] *vb* **1** afscheiden, uitwasemen, *(fig)* druipen van, doortrokken zijn van, uitstralen: *her voice* ~*d sarcasm* er klonk sarcasme in haar stem

³ooze [oeːz] *n* modder, slijk^h, drab

op [ɒp] *operation* operatie

opacity [oˈpæsittie] **1** onduidelijkheid, ondoorgrondelijkheid; **2** ondoorschijnendheid

opal [ˈoopl] **1** opaal^{+h}, opaalsteen; **2** opaalglas^h, melkglas^h

opaque [oˈpeek] **1** ondoorschijnend, ondoorzichtig, dekkend *(of paint, colour)*; **2** onduidelijk, onbegrijpelijk; **3** *(fig)* stompzinnig, dom, traag van begrip

¹open [ˈoopən] *adj* **1** open, geopend, met openingen, onbedekt, niet (af)gesloten, vrij: *keep one's eyes* ~ goed opletten; *(fig) with one's eyes* ~ bij zijn volle verstand, weloverwogen; ~ *prison* open gevangenis; ~ *to the public* toegankelijk voor het publiek; **2** open(staand), beschikbaar, onbeslist, onbepaald: ~ *cheque* ongekruiste cheque; *it is* ~ *to you to* het staat je vrij te; *lay oneself (wide)* ~ *to* zich (helemaal) blootstellen aan; **3** openbaar, (algemeen) bekend, duidelijk, openlijk: ~ *hostilities* openlijke vijandigheden; ~ *secret* publiek geheim; ~ *and* (of: *hearty*), oprecht, mededeelzaam: *admit* ~*ly* eerlijk uitkomen voor; *be* ~ *with* open kaart spelen met; **5** open(baar), vrij toegankelijk: *keep* ~ *house* erg gastvrij zijn; *have* (of: *keep*) *an* ~ *mind on* openstaan voor; *lay oneself* ~ *to ridicule* zich belachelijk maken

²open [ˈoopən] *n* (de) open ruimte, open lucht, veld, zee, *(fig)* openbaarheid: *bring into the* ~ aan het licht brengen, bekendmaken; *come (out) into the* ~: *a)* open kaart spelen *(of s.o.)*; *b)* aan het licht komen, ruchtbaarheid krijgen *(of sth)*

³open [ˈoopən] *vb* **1** openen: ~ *a tin* een blik opendraaien; **2** openen, voor geopend verklaren, starten: ~ *the bidding* het eerste bod doen *(at auction,* at cardgame); ~ fire at (of: on) het vuur openen op

⁴open [oopən] *vb* **1** opengaan, (zich) openen, geopend worden: ~ *into the garden* uitkomen in de tuin; **2** openen, beginnen, van wal steken *(of speaker);* **3** opendoen, (een boek) openslaan

open-air openlucht-, buiten-, in de open lucht

open-and-shut (dood)eenvoudig: *an ~ case* een uitgemaakte zaak

opencast bovengronds, in dagbouw: ~ *mining* dagbouw

open-ended open, met een open einde: ~ *discussion* vrije discussie

openhanded gul, vrijgevig

open-hearted 1 openhartig, eerlijk; **2** hartelijk, open

opening [oopəning] **1** opening, begin(fase), inleiding, *(chess, draughts)* opening(szet), beginspel[h]; **2** opening, kans, (gunstige) gelegenheid: *new ~s for trade* nieuwe afzetgebieden; **3** vacature; **4** opening, het opengaan, geopend worden, bres, gat[h], uitweg: *hours of ~ are Tuesdays 1 to 5* openingsuren dinsdag van 1 tot 5

open-minded onbevooroordeeld, ruimdenkend

open-mouthed met de mond wijd open(gesperd), *(also fig)* sprakeloos *(with surprise)*

¹open out *vb* **1** verbreden, breder worden, zich uitbreiden: ~ *into* uitmonden in *(of river);* **2** opengaan, (naar buiten) openslaan

²open out *vb* openvouwen, openleggen

open-plan met weinig tussenmuren: *an ~ office* een kantoortuin

open season open seizoen[h], jachtseizoen[h], hengelseizoen[h]

¹open up *vb* openen, openmaken, toegankelijk maken, opensnijden

²open up *vb* **1** opengaan, zich openen, zich ontplooien, *(fig)* loskomen, vrijuit (gaan) spreken: *in the second half the game opened up* in de tweede helft werd er aantrekkelijker gespeeld; **2** (de deur) opendoen

opera [oprə] opera

operable [oprəbl] **1** opereerbaar; **2** uitvoerbaar, realiseerbaar

opera glasses toneelkijker

opera house opera(gebouw[h])

¹operate [oppəreet] *vb* **1** in werking zijn, functioneren, lopen *(also of train),* draaien *(of engine),* te werk gaan; **2** (de juiste) uitwerking hebben, werken, (het gewenste) resultaat geven *(of tariff, treaty, law): the new cutbacks will not ~ till next month* de nieuwe bezuinigingsmaatregelen gaan pas volgende maand in; **3** te werk gaan, opereren, *(med also)* een operatie doen, ingrijpen

²operate [oppəreet] *vb* **1** bewerken; **2** bedienen *(machine, appliance),* besturen *(also car, ship): be ~d by* werken op, (aan)gedreven worden door *(steam, electricity);* **3** *(Am; med)* opereren

operating theatre operatiezaal

operation [oppəreesjən] **1** operatie, handeling, on-

derneming, campagne, militaire actie; chirurgische ingreep; **2** werking: *bring sth. into ~* iets in werking brengen; *come into ~* in werking treden, ingaan *(of law);* **3** bediening

operational [oppəreesjənəl] operationeel, gebruiksklaar, bedrijfsklaar, gevechtsklaar: ~ *costs* bedrijfskosten

operations room controlekamer *(at manoeuvres),* commandopost, hoofdkwartier[h]

operative [oprətiv] **1** werkzaam, in werking, van kracht: *the ~ force* de drijvende kracht; *become ~* in werking treden, ingaan *(of law);* **2** meest relevant, voornaamste

operator [oppəreetə] **1** iem die een machine bedient, operateur, telefonist(e), telegrafist(e), bestuurder; **2** gladjanus

operetta [oppərettə] operette

ophthalmic [ofθælmik] oogheelkundig

ophthalmologist [ofθælmol. lədzjist] oogheelkundige, oogarts

ophthalmology [ofθælmol. lədzjie] oogheelkunde

opiate [oopiət] opiaat[h], slaapmiddel[h], pijnstiller

opinion [əpinjən] **1** mening, oordeel[h], opinie, opvatting: *a matter of ~* een kwestie van opvatting; *in the ~ of most people* naar het oordeel van de meeste mensen; *in my ~* naar mijn mening; *be of (the) ~ that* van oordeel zijn dat; **2** (hoge) dunk, waardering, (gunstig) denkbeeld[h]: *have a high ~ of* een hoge dunk hebben van; **3** advies[h], oordeel[h], mening *(of expert): have a second ~* advies van een tweede deskundige inwinnen

opinionated [əpinjəneetid] koppig, eigenwijs

opinion poll opinieonderzoek[h], opiniepeiling

opium [oopiəm] opium[h]

opponent [əpoonənt] opponent, tegenstander, tegenspeler

opportune [oppətjoe:n] geschikt, gunstig (gekozen)

opportunism [oppətjoe:nizm] opportunisme[h], het steeds handelen naar de omstandigheden

¹opportunist [oppətjoe:nist] *adj* opportunistisch

²opportunist [oppətjoe:nist] *n* opportunist, iem die steeds van gunstige gelegenheden gebruik probeert te maken

opportunity [oppətjoe:nittie] (gunstige, geschikte) gelegenheid, kans: *take (of: seize) the ~ to* van de gelegenheid gebruik maken om; *she had ample ~ for doing that* ze had ruimschoots de gelegenheid (om) dat te doen

oppose [əpooz] **1** tegen(over)stellen, contrasteren, tegenover elkaar stellen; **2** zich verzetten tegen, bestrijden

opposed [əpoozd] **1** tegen(over)gesteld: *be ~ to* tegen(over)gesteld zijn aan; **2** tegen, afkerig: *be ~ to* (gekant) zijn tegen, afkeuren; *as ~ to* in tegenstelling met

opposing [əpoozing] **1** tegenoverliggend; **2** tegenwerkend, *(sport)* vijandig: *the ~ team* de tegenpartij

¹opposite [oppəzit] *adj* **1** tegen(over)gesteld, tegenover elkaar gelegen, tegen-: ~ *number* ambtgenoot, collega; **2** *(after noun)* tegenover, aan de overkant: *the houses* ~ de huizen hier tegenover

²opposite [oppəzit] *n* tegen(over)gesteldeʰ, tegendeelʰ: *be ~s* elkaars tegenpolen zijn

³opposite [oppəzit] *adv* tegenover (elkaar), aan de overkant: *she lives* ~ ze woont hiertegenover; ~ *to* tegenover

⁴opposite [oppəzit] *prep* tegenover: *she sat* ~ *a fat boy* ze zat tegenover een dikke jongen

opposition [oppəzisjən] **1** oppositie, het tegen(over)stellen: *in* ~ *to* tegen(over), verschillend van, in strijd met; **2** oppositie, verzetʰ: *meet with strong* ~ op hevig verzet stuiten; **3** oppositie(groep), oppositiepartij

oppress [əprɛs] **1** onderdrukken; **2** benauwen: *~ed by anxiety* doodsbenauwd

oppression [əprɛsjən] **1** benauwing, neerslachtigheid; **2** onderdrukking(smaatregel), verdrukking

oppressive [əprɛssiv] **1** onderdrukkend, tiranniek; **2** benauwend, deprimerend

oppressor [əprɛssə] onderdrukker, tiran

opt [opt] *(with for)* opteren (voor), kiezen, besluiten

optic [optik] gezichts-, oog-, optisch

optical [optikl] **1** optisch: ~ *illusion* optisch bedrog, gezichtsbedrog; **2** gezichtkundig: ~ *fibre* glasvezel

optician [optisjən] opticien

optics [optiks] optica

optimal [optiml] optimaal, best, gunstigst

optimism [optimmizm] optimismeʰ

optimist [optimmist] optimist

optimistic [optimmistik] optimistisch

optimum [optimməm] optimumʰ

option [opsjən] keus, keuze, alternatiefʰ: *have no* ~ *but to go* geen andere keus hebben dan te gaan

optional [opsjənəl] keuze-, facultatief, vrij

opt out niet meer (willen) meedoen, zich terugtrekken: ~ *of: a)* niet meer (willen) meedoen aan *(idea, plan); b)* afschuiven *(responsibility); c)* opzeggen *(contract)*

opulence [opjoeləns] (enorme) rijkdom, overvloed, weelde

opulent [opjoelənt] overvloedig, (schat)rijk

or [o:] **1** of, en, ofwel, anders gezegd, of misschien, nog, ook: *would you like tea* ~ *coffee* wil je thee of koffie; **2** of (anders): *tell me* ~ *I'll kill you!* vertel het mij of ik vermoord je!

oracle [orrəkl] orakelʰ

¹oral [o:rəl] *adj* mondeling, oraal, gesproken: ~ *agreement* mondelinge overeenkomst; ~ *tradition* mondelinge overlevering

²oral [o:rəl] *n* mondelingʰ, mondeling examenʰ

¹orange [orrindzj] *n* sinaasappel

²orange [orrindzj] *adj* oranje(kleurig)

orang-utan [o:ræŋoe:tæn] orang-oetan(g)

oration [o:reesjən] (hoogdravende) rede(voering): *a funeral* ~ een grafrede

orator [orrətə] (begaafd) redenaar

oratorical [orrətorrikl] retorisch, *(sometimes depr)* hoogdravend

oratory [orrətərie] **1** oratoriumʰ; **2** redenaarskunst

orb [o:b] bolvormig iets, globe, hemellichaamʰ

¹orbit [o:bit] *n* **1** kring *(only fig)*, (invloeds)sfeer, interessesfeer; **2** baan *(of planet etc)*, omloop, kring(loop)

²orbit [o:bit] *vb* een (cirkel)baan beschrijven (rond)

orchard [o:tsjəd] boomgaard

orchestra [o:kistrə] orkestʰ

orchestral [o:kestrəl] orkestraal

orchestrate [o:kistreet] orkestreren, voor orkest arrangeren, *(fig)* (harmonieus, ordelijk) samenbrengen, organiseren

orchestration [o:kəstreesjən] orkestratie

orchid [o:kid] orchidee

ordain [o:deen] **1** (tot geestelijke of priester) wijden; **2** (voor)beschikken *(by God, fate);* **3** verordenen

ordeal [o:die:l] **1** beproeving, bezoeking, *(fig)* vuurproef, pijnlijke ervaring; **2** godsoordeelʰ: ~ *by fire* vuurproef

¹order [o:də] *n* **1** orde, stand, rang, (sociale) klasse, soort, aard: ~ *of magnitude* orde (van grootte); *in the* ~ *of* in de orde (van grootte) van, ongeveer, om en (na)bij; **2** (rang)orde, volgorde, op(een)volging: *in alphabetical* ~ alfabetisch gerangschikt; *in* ~ *of importance* in volgorde van belangrijkheid; **3** ordelijke inrichting, orde(lijkheid), ordening, geregeldheid, netheid, *(mil)* opstelling, stelselʰ, (maatschappij)structuur: *in good* ~ piekfijn in orde; *out of* ~ defect, buiten gebruik; **4** (dag)orde, agenda, reglementʰ *(of meeting etc):* call *s.o. to* ~ iem tot de orde roepen; *be out of ~: a)* buiten de orde gaan *(of speaker); b)* (nog) niet aan de orde zijn; **5** orde, tucht, gehoorzaamheid: *keep* ~ de orde bewaren; **6** (klooster)orde, ridderorde; **7** bevelʰ, order, opdracht, instructie: *on doctor's ~s* op doktersvoorschrift; **8** bedoeling, doelʰ: *in* ~ *to* om, teneinde; **9** bestelling, order: *be on* ~ in bestelling zijn, besteld zijn; **10** *(fin)* (betalings)opdracht, order(briefjeʰ): *postal* ~ postwissel; ~*s are* ~*s* (een) bevel is (een) bevel; *made to* ~ op bestelling gemaakt, *(fig)* perfect

²order [o:də] *vb* **1** bevelen, het bevel hebben; **2** bestellen, een order plaatsen

³order [o:də] *vb* **1** ordenen, in orde brengen, (rang)schikken; **2** (een) opdracht geven (om), het bevel geven (tot), verzoeken om, voorschrijven *(of doctor):* he ~*ed the troops to open fire* hij gaf de troepen bevel het vuur te openen; **3** bestellen, een order plaatsen voor: ~ *s.o. about (of: around)* iem (steeds) commanderen, iem voortdurend de wet voorschrijven

order book orderboekʰ, bestel(lingen)boekʰ

ordered [o:dəd] geordend, ordelijk

order form bestelformulierʰ

¹orderly [o:dəlie] *n* **1** ordonnans; **2** (zieken)oppasser, hospitaalsoldaat

²orderly [o:dəlie] *adj* ordelijk, geordend, geregeld

order out wegsturen, de deur wijzen

¹ordinal [o:dinl] *adj* rang-: ~ *numbers* rangtelwoorden

²ordinal [o:dinl] *n* rangtelwoordʰ

ordinance [o:dinnəns] verordening, bepaling, voorschriftʰ

¹ordinary [o:dnərie] *adj* 1 gewoon, gebruikelijk, normaal, vertrouwd; 2 ordinair, middelmatig

²ordinary [o:dnərie] *n* het gewone: *out of the* ~ ongewoon, bijzonder

ordination [o:dinneesjən] *(rel)* wijding

ordnance [o:dnəns] 1 (zwaar) geschutʰ; 2 militaire voorraden en materieel, oorlogsmateriaalʰ

ordnance survey map topografische kaart, stafkaart

ore [o:] ertsʰ

organ [o:gən] 1 orgelʰ; 2 orgaanʰ: *~s of speech* spraakorganen; 3 orgaanʰ, instrumentʰ, instelling

organ grinder orgeldraaier

organic [o:gænik] 1 wezenlijk, essentieel; 2 (organisch-)biologisch, natuurlijk: ~ *food* natuurvoeding; ~ *waste (roughly)* gft-afval

organism [o:gənizm] organismeʰ

organist [o:gənist] organist, orgelspeler

organization [o:gənajzeesjən] organisatie, structuur, vereniging

¹organize [o:gənajz] *vb* 1 organiseren, regelen, tot stand brengen, oprichten; 2 lid worden van *(trade union)*, zich verenigen in

²organize [o:gənajz] *vb* zich organiseren, zich verenigen

orgasm [o:gæzm] orgasmeʰ

orgy [o:dzjie] orgie, uitspatting, *(fig)* overdaad

oriel (window) [o:riəl] erker, erkervensterʰ

orient [o:ri·ent] 1 richten; 2 oriënteren, situeren: ~ *oneself* zich oriënteren

Orient [o:riənt] Oriënt, Oostenʰ

oriental [o:rie-entl] oosters, oostelijk, oriëntaal: ~ *rug* (of: *carpet*) oosters tapijt

orientation [o:riənteesjən] 1 oriëntatie; 2 oriënteringsvermogenʰ

origin [orridzjin] oorsprong, origine, ontstaanʰ, bron, afkomst, herkomst, oorzaak: *country of* ~ land van herkomst

¹original [ərïdzjinnəl] *adj* origineel, oorspronkelijk, authentiek

²original [ərïdzjinnəl] *n* (het) origineel, oorspronkelijke versie

originality [əridzjinælittie] originaliteit, oorspronkelijkheid

originate [əridzjinneet] ontstaan, beginnen, voortkomen: ~ *from* (of: *in*) *sth.* voortkomen uit iets

¹ornament [o:nəmənt] *n* 1 ornamentʰ, sieraadʰ; 2 versiering, decoratie

²ornament [o:nəmənt] *vb* (ver)sieren

ornate [o:neet] sierlijk

ornithology [o:niθolədzjie] vogelkunde

¹orphan [o:fən] *n* wees

²orphan [o:fən] *vb* tot wees maken

orphanage [o:fənidzj] weeshuisʰ

orthodontics [o:θədontiks] orthodontie

orthodox [o:θədoks] 1 orthodox, rechtgelovig; 2 conservatief, ouderwets

orthography [o:θogrəfie] spellingleer

orthopaedic [o:θəpie:dik] orthopedisch

oscillate [ossilleet] 1 trillen, (heen en weer) slingeren: *oscillating current* wisselstroom; 2 weifelen

oscillation [ossilleesjən] 1 schommeling, trilling; 2 besluiteloosheid

ossify [ossiffaj] (doen) verbenen, *(fig)* verharden, afstompen

ostentation [ostənteesjən] vertoonʰ

osteopath [ostiəpæθ] orthopedist

ostracize [ostrəsajz] verbannen, *(fig)* uitstoten

ostrich [ostritsj] struisvogel *(also fig)*

other [uðə] 1 ander(e), nog een, verschillend(e): *every* ~ *week* om de (andere) week, eens in de twee weken; *on the* ~ *hand* daarentegen; 2 (nog, weer) andere(n), overige(n), nieuwe: *someone or* ~ iemand; *one after the* ~ na elkaar; *among* ~s onder andere; 3 anders, verschillend: *none* ~ *than John* niemand anders dan John; *the* ~ *week* een paar weken geleden

other than behalve, buiten: *there was no-one else* ~ *his sister* er was niemand behalve zijn zuster

¹otherwise [uðəwajz] *adv* anders, overigens: *be* ~ *engaged* andere dingen te doen hebben; *go now;* ~ *it'll be too late* ga nu, anders wordt het te laat

²otherwise [uðəwajz] *adj* anders, verschillend, tegengesteld: *mothers, married and* (of: *or*) ~ moeders, al dan niet gehuwd

otter [ottə] (vis)otter

ought to [o:t toe:] 1 *(command, prohibition, obligation)* (eigenlijk) moeten, zou (eigenlijk) moeten: *you* ~ *be grateful* je zou dankbaar moeten zijn; 2 *(supposition)* moeten, zullen, zou moeten: *this* ~ *do the trick* dit zou het probleem moeten oplossen, hiermee zou het moeten lukken

ounce [auns] (Engels, Amerikaans) onsʰ, *(fig)* klein beetjeʰ: *an* ~ *of common sense* een greintje gezond verstand

our [auə] ons, onze, van ons

ours [auəz] van ons, de (het) onze: *the decision is* ~ de beslissing ligt bij ons; *a friend of* ~ een vriend van ons

ourselves [auəselvz] 1 ons, onszelf: *we busied* ~ *with organizing the party* we hielden ons bezig met het organiseren van het feestje; 2 zelf, wij zelf, ons zelf: *we went* ~ we gingen zelf

oust [aust] 1 verdrijven, uitdrijven, ontzetten, afzetten: ~ *s.o. from* (of: *of*) iem ontheffen van; 2 verdringen, vervangen

¹out [aut] *adv* 1 *(place, direction; also fig; also sport)* uit, buiten, weg: *inside* ~ binnen buiten; ~ *in Canada* daarginds in Canada; 2 buiten bewustzijn, buiten gevecht, in slaap, dronken; 3 niet (meer) in werking, uit; **4** uit, openbaar, te voorschijn: *the sun is* ~ de zon schijnt; ~ *with it!* vertel op!, zeg het maar!, voor de dag ermee!; **5** ernaast *(of estimates):* ~ *and about* (weer) op de been, in de weer; ~ *and away* veruit; *she is* ~ *for trouble* ze zoekt moeilijkheden

²**out** [aut] *prep* uit, naar buiten: *from* ~ *the window* vanuit het raam

³**out** [aut] *adj* **1** uit *(of equipment);* **2** voor uitgaande post: ~ *box* (of: *tray)* brievenbak voor uitgaande post

outback [autbæk] *(Austr)* binnenland[h]

outbalance zwaarder wegen dan, belangrijker zijn dan

outbreak [autbreek] uitbarsting, het uitbreken

outburst [autbɔ:st] uitbarsting, uitval

outcast [autka:st] verschoppeling, verworpene

outclass overtreffen

outcome [autkum] resultaat[h], gevolg[h], uitslag

outcry [autkraj] **1** schreeuw, kreet; **2** (publiek) protest[h], tegenwerping: *public* ~ *against* (of: *over)* publiek protest tegen

outdated achterhaald, ouderwets

outdo **1** overtreffen; **2** overwinnen, de loef afsteken

outdoors [autdo:z] buiten(shuis), in (de) open lucht

outer [autə] buitenste: ~ *garments* (of: *wear)* bovenkleding; ~ *space* de ruimte; *the* ~ *world* de buitenwereld

outermost [autəmoost] buitenste, uiterste

outfit [autfit] **1** uitrusting, toerusting; **2** groep, (reis)gezelschap[h], team[h], ploeg

outflow **1** uitloop, afvoer; **2** uitstroming, uitvloeiing, afvloeiing

outgoing [autgooing] **1** hartelijk, vlot; **2** vertrekkend, uitgaand: ~ *tide* aflopend tij; **3** uittredend, ontslag nemend

outgoings [autgooingz] uitgaven, onkosten

outgrow **1** ontgroeien (aan), afleren, te boven komen: ~ *one's strength* uit zijn krachten groeien; **2** boven het hoofd groeien, groter worden dan

outing [auting] **1** uitstapje[h], excursie; **2** wandeling, ommetje[h]

outlast langer duren (meegaan) dan, overleven

¹**outlaw** [autlo:] *n* vogelvrijverklaarde, bandiet

²**outlaw** *vb* verbieden, buiten de wet stellen, vogelvrij verklaren

outlet [autlet] **1** uitlaat(klep), afvoerkanaal[h]; **2** afzetgebied[h], markt; **3** vestiging, verkooppunt[h]; **4** *(Am)* (wand)contactdoos, stopcontact[h]

¹**outline** [autlajn] *n* **1** omtrek(lijn), contour; **2** schets, samenvatting, overzicht[h], ontwerp[h]: *in broad* ~ in grote trekken; **3** ~*s* (hoofd)trekken, hoofdpunten

²**outline** [autlajn] *vb* **1** schetsen, samenvatten; **2** omlijnen, de contouren tekenen van

outlive overleven, langer leven dan

outlook [autloek] **1** uitkijk(post): *be on the* ~ *for* uitzien, uitkijken naar; **2** uitzicht[h], gezicht[h]; **3** vooruitzicht[h], verwachting; **4** kijk, oordeel[h]: *a narrow* ~

on life een bekrompen levensopvatting

outmatch overtreffen

outmoded [autmoodid] **1** uit de mode; **2** verouderd

outnumber in aantal overtreffen, talrijker zijn dan: *be* ~*ed* in de minderheid zijn

out of 1 *(place and direction; also fig)* buiten, uit (... weg): *turned* ~ *doors* de straat opgejaagd, op straat gezet; ~ *the ordinary* ongewoon; *feel* ~ *it* zich buitengesloten voelen; *one* ~ *four* een op vier; **2** uit, vanuit, komende uit: *act* ~ *pity* uit medelijden handelen; **3** zonder, -loos: ~ *breath* buiten adem

out-of-date achterhaald, ouderwets

outperform overtreffen, beter doen dan

outpost [autposst] **1** voorpost; **2** buitenpost

output [autpoet] opbrengst, productie, prestatie, nuttig effect[h], vermogen[h], uitgangsvermogen[h], uitgangsspanning, uitvoer, output

¹**outrage** [autreedzj] *n* **1** geweld(daad), wandaad, misdaad, misdrijf[h], aanslag, belediging, schandaal[h]; **2** *(Am)* verontwaardiging

²**outrage** [autreedzj] *vb* **1** geweld aandoen, zich vergrijpen aan, schenden, overtreden, beledigen; **2** *(Am)* verontwaardigd maken

outrageous [autreedzjəs] **1** buitensporig; **2** gewelddadig; **3** schandelijk, schaamteloos, afschuwelijk

¹**outright** [autrajt] *adv* **1** helemaal, voor eens en altijd; **2** ineens: *kill* ~ ter plaatse afmaken; **3** openlijk

²**outright** *adj* **1** totaal, volledig, grondig; **2** volstrekt: ~ *nonsense* volslagen onzin; **3** onverdeeld, onvoorwaardelijk; **4** direct

outrun **1** harder (verder) lopen dan, inhalen; **2** ontlopen, ontsnappen aan

outset [autset] begin[h], aanvang: *from the (very)* ~ van meet af aan, vanaf het (allereerste) begin

¹**outside** [autsajd] *n* **1** buitenkant, buitenste[h], uiterlijk[h]; **2** buitenwereld; **3** uiterste[h], grens: *at the (very)* ~ uiterlijk, op zijn laatst

²**outside** *adj* **1** buiten-, van buiten(af), buitenstaand; **2** gering, klein: *an* ~ *chance* een hele kleine kans

³**outside** *adv* buiten, buitenshuis

outsider [autsajdə] **1** buitenstaander; **2** zonderling; **3** *(sport)* outsider *(horse)*

outsize extra groot

outskirts [autskɔ:ts] buitenwijken, randgebied: *on the* ~ *of town* aan de rand van de stad

outsmart te slim af zijn

outspoken open(hartig), ronduit

outstanding [autstænding] **1** opmerkelijk, voortreffelijk; **2** onbeslist, onbetaald

outstay langer blijven dan: ~ *one's welcome* langer blijven dan men welkom is

outstrip **1** achter zich laten, inhalen; **2** overtreffen

outward [autwəd] **1** buitenwaarts, naar buiten (gekeerd), uitgaand: ~ *passage* (of: *journey)* heenreis; **2** uitwendig, lichamelijk: *to all* ~ *appearances* ogenschijnlijk

outwardly [autwədlie] klaarblijkelijk, ogenschijnlijk

outwards [autwədz] naar buiten, buitenwaarts: ~

bound uitgaand, op de uitreis
outweigh 1 zwaarder wegen dan; **2** belangrijker zijn dan
outwit te slim af zijn, beetnemen
outwork 1 thuiswerk^h; **2** buitenwerk^h
outworn 1 versleten, uitgeput; **2** verouderd, afgezaagd
¹oval [oovl] *n* ovaal^h
²oval [oovl] *adj* ovaal(vormig), eivormig
ovary [oovərie] eierstok, *(bot)* vruchtbeginsel^h
ovation [ooveesjən] ovatie, hulde(betoon^h)
oven [uvn] (bak)oven, fornuis^h: *like an ~* snikheet
¹over [oovə] *prep* **1** *(place)* over, op, boven ... uit: *chat ~ a cup of tea* (even) (bij)kletsen bij een kopje thee; *buy nothing ~ fifty francs* koop niets boven de vijftig frank; *~ and above these problems there are others* behalve deze problemen zijn er nog andere; **2** *(length, surface etc)* doorheen, door, over: *speak ~ the phone* over de telefoon spreken; *~ the past five weeks* gedurende de afgelopen vijf weken; **3** *(direction)* naar de overkant van, over; **4** *(place)* aan de overkant van, aan de andere kant van; **5** betreffende, met betrekking tot, over, om: *all this fuss ~ a trifle* zo'n drukte om een kleinigheid; **6** *(maths)* gedeeld door: *eight ~ four equals two* acht gedeeld door vier is twee
²over [oovə] *adv* **1** *(direction; also fig)* over-, naar de overkant, omver: *he called her ~* hij riep haar bij zich; **2** *(place)* daarover, aan de overkant, voorbij: *~ in France* (daarginds) in Frankrijk; *~ here* hier, in dit land; *~ there* daarginds; *~ against* tegenover; *~ (to you) (fig)* jouw beurt; **3** *(degree)* boven, meer, te: *some apples were left ~* er bleven enkele appelen over; **4** *(place)* boven, bedekt: *he's mud all ~* hij zit onder de modder; **5** ten einde, af, over; **6** ten einde, helemaal, volledig: *they talked the matter ~* de zaak werd grondig besproken; **7** opnieuw: *~ and ~ again* telkens weer; *that's him all ~* dat is typisch voor hem
overact overdrijven, overacteren
¹overall [oovəro:l] *n* **1** *~s* overal; **2** (werk)kiel
²overall [oovəro:l] *adj* **1** totaal, geheel, alles omvattend: *~ efficiency* totaal rendement; **2** globaal, algemeen
³overall [oovəro:l] *adv* **1** in totaal, van kop tot teen; **2** globaal
¹overbalance *vb* het evenwicht verliezen, kapseizen, omslaan
²overbalance *vb* uit het evenwicht brengen
overboard overboord: *throw ~* overboord gooien *(also fig)*
overburden *(also fig)* overbelasten, overladen
¹overcharge *vb* overvragen, te veel vragen
²overcharge *vb* **1** overdrijven: *~ed with emotion* te emotioneel geladen; **2** overvragen, te veel in rekening brengen (voor): *~ a person* iem te veel laten betalen
overcoat overjas
¹overcome [oovəkum] *vb* overwinnen, zegevieren

(over), te boven komen: *~ a temptation* een verleiding weerstaan
²overcome [oovəkum] *adj* overwonnen, overmand: *~ by the heat* door de warmte bevangen; *~ by (of: with) grief* door leed overmand
overcrowded 1 overvol, stampvol; **2** overbevolkt
overdo 1 overdrijven, te veel gebruiken: *~ things* (of: *it*) te hard werken, overdrijven; **2** te gaar koken, overbakken: *~ne meat* overgaar vlees
overdress (zich) te netjes kleden, (zich) opzichtig kleden
overdrive oversnelling, overdrive
overdue te laat, over (zijn) tijd, achterstallig
overestimate overschatten
¹overflow *vb* overstromen, (doen) overlopen: *full to ~ing* boordevol
²overflow *n* **1** overstroming; **2** overschot^h, overvloed
¹overhang *vb* overhangen, uitsteken
²overhang *vb* boven het hoofd hangen, voor de deur staan, dreigen
³overhang *n* overhang(end gedeelte^h), uitsteeksel^h
¹overhaul *vb* **1** grondig nazien, reviseren, *(by extension)* repareren; **2** *(shipp)* inhalen, voorbijsteken, voorbijvaren
²overhaul *n* revisie, controlebeurt
overhead 1 hoog (aangebracht), in de lucht: *~ railway* luchtspoorweg; **2** algemeen, vast: *~ charges* (of: *expenses*) vaste bedrijfsuitgaven
overheads algemene onkosten
overhear 1 toevallig horen; **2** afluisteren
overjoyed (with *at*) in de wolken (over)
¹overlap *vb* elkaar overlappen, gedeeltelijk samenvallen
²overlap *vb* overlappen, gedeeltelijk bedekken
³overlap *n* overlap(ping)
overlay 1 bekleding, bedekking, (bedden)overtrek; **2** deklaagje^h
overleaf aan ommezijde
overload te zwaar (be)laden, overbelasten
overlook 1 overzien, uitkijken op; **2** over het hoofd zien, voorbijzien; **3** door de vingers zien
overly [oovəlie] *(Am, Scotland)* (al) te, overdreven: *~ protective* overdreven beschermend
¹overnight *adj* **1** van de vorige avond; **2** nachtelijk: *~ journey* nachtelijke reis; **3** plotseling *(eg success)*
²overnight *adv* **1** de avond tevoren; **2** tijdens de nacht: *stay ~* overnachten; **3** in één nacht, zomaar ineens: *become famous ~* van de ene dag op de andere beroemd worden
overpass viaduct^h
overpower 1 bedwingen, onderwerpen; **2** overweldigen; **3** bevangen
overrate overschatten, overwaarderen
¹overreach *vb* verder reiken dan, voorbijschieten, voorbijstreven: *~ oneself* te veel hooi op zijn vork nemen
²overreach *vb* te ver reiken
overreaction te sterke reactie
overriding doorslaggevend, allergrootst

overrule 1 verwerpen, afwijzen, terzijde schuiven *(eg objection);* **2** herroepen, intrekken, nietig verklaren: *~ a decision* een beslissing herroepen

¹overrun *vb* **1** overstromen; **2** *(fig)* uitlopen

²overrun *vb* **1** overstromen *(also fig);* **2** onder de voet lopen, veroveren; **3** overschrijden *(time limit);* **4** overgroeien

¹overseas *adj* overzees, buitenlands

²overseas *adv* overzee, in (de) overzeese gebieden

oversee toezicht houden (op)

overseer opzichter, voorman

overshadow overschaduwen, *(fig)* domineren

overshoot voorbijschieten, verder gaan dan: *~ the runway* doorschieten op de landingsbaan

oversight 1 onoplettendheid, vergissing; **2** supervisie

oversize(d) bovenmaats, te groot

oversleep (zich) verslapen, te lang slapen

overspill 1 overloop, gemorst water[h]; **2** surplus[h]; **3** overloop, migratie *(of surplus of population)*

overstay langer blijven dan: *~ one's welcome* langer blijven dan de gastvrouw of gastheer lief is

overstep overschrijden

overt [oovə:t] open(lijk): *~ hostility* openlijke vijandigheid

overtake inhalen

overthrow 1 om(ver)werpen, omgooien; **2** omverwerpen, ten val brengen

¹overtime *n* **1** (loon[h] voor) overuren, overwerk(geld)[h]; **2** *(Am; sport)* (extra) verlenging: *go into ~* verlengd worden

²overtime *adv* over-: *work ~* overuren maken

overtone 1 *(mus)* boventoon; **2** *(fig)* ondertoon, suggestie

overture [oovətsjoeə] *(mus)* ouverture, inleiding, voorstel[h]: *(fig) make ~s (to)* toenadering zoeken (tot)

¹overturn *vb* doen omslaan, ten val brengen

²overturn *vb* omslaan, verslagen worden

overview overzicht[h], samenvatting

¹overweight *adj* te zwaar, te dik

²overweight *n* over(ge)wicht[h], te zware last *(also fig)*

³overweight *vb* **1** overladen; **2** te zeer benadrukken

overwhelm [oovəwelm] bedelven, verpletteren: *~ed with grief* door leed overmand

overwhelming [oovəwelming] overweldigend, verpletterend: *~ majority* overgrote meerderheid

¹overwork *vb* te hard werken

²overwork *vb* **1** te hard laten werken, uitputten; **2** te vaak gebruiken, tot cliché maken: *an ~ed expression* een afgesleten uitdrukking

ovulate [ovjoeleet] ovuleren

¹owe [oo] *vb* **1** schuldig zijn, verplicht zijn, verschuldigd zijn; **2** *(with to)* te danken hebben (aan), toeschrijven (aan)

²owe [oo] *vb* schuld(en) hebben: *~ for everything one has* voor alles wat men heeft nog (ten dele) moeten betalen

owing [ooing] **1** verschuldigd, schuldig, onbetaald:

how much is ~ to you? hoeveel heeft u nog tegoed?; **2** *(with to)* te danken (aan), te wijten (aan)

owing to wegens, tengevolge van

owl [aul] uil *(also fig)*

¹own [oon] *adj* eigen, van … zelf, eigen bezit (familie): *an ~ goal* een doelpunt in eigen doel; *be one's ~ man* (of: *master)* heer en meester zijn, onafhankelijk zijn; *not have a moment* (of: *minute, second) to call one's ~* geen moment voor zichzelf hebben; *you'll have a room of your ~* je krijgt een eigen kamer; *beat s.o. at his ~ game* iem met zijn eigen wapens verslaan; *in his ~ (good) time* wanneer het hem zo uitkomt; *hold one's ~: a)* standhouden; *b)* niet achteruitgaan *(of health); on one's ~* in zijn eentje, op eigen houtje

²own [oon] *vb* bezitten, eigenaar zijn van

³own [oon] *vb* bekennen, toegeven: *~ up (to)* opbiechten

owner [oonə] eigenaar

ox [oks] *(oxen)* os; rund[h]

oxidation [oksiddeesjən] oxidatie

oxygen [oksidzjən] zuurstof[h]

oyster [ojstə] oester

oz *ounce(s)* ons

ozone [oozoon] **1** ozon; **2** frisse lucht

p

p [pie:] p, P ‖ *mind one's p's and q's* op zijn woorden passen

p. **1** *page* p.; blz., pagina, bladzijde; **2** *penny, pence* penny: *the apples are 12~ each* de appels kosten 12 pence per stuk

pa [pa:] pa

p.a. *per annum* p.j., per jaar

¹pace [pees] *n* **1** pas, stap, schrede; gang; **2** tempo^h, gang, tred: *force the ~* het tempo opdrijven; *keep ~ (with)* gelijke tred houden (met); *put s.o. through his ~s* iem uittesten, iem laten tonen wat hij kan

²pace [pees] *vb* stappen, kuieren: *~ up and down* ijsberen

³pace [pees] *vb* (*also with off, out*) afstappen, afpassen, met stappen afmeten

pacemaker (*sport*) haas

pacific [pəsiffik] vreedzaam, vredelievend ‖ *the Pacific Ocean* de Grote Oceaan

pacifist [pæsiffist] pacifist

pacify [pæsiffaj] kalmeren, de rust herstellen in

¹pack [pæk] *n* **1** pak^h, (rug)zak, last, verpakking, pakket^h; **2** pak^h, hoop, pak^h kaarten, (*Am*) pakje^h (*cigarettes*): *~ of lies* pak leugens; *~ of nonsense* hoop onzin; **3** (veld^h van) pakijs^h; **4** kompres^h; **5** troep, bende, horde, meute, (*sport*) peloton^h (*rugby*)

²pack [pæk] *vb* **1** (in)pakken, verpakken, inmaken (*fruit etc*): (*fig*) *~ one's bags* zijn biezen pakken; *~ed lunch* lunchpakket; **2** samenpakken, samenpersen: *the theatre was ~ed with people* het theater was afgeladen; **3** wegsturen: *~ s.o. off* iem (ver) wegsturen; **4** bepakken, volproppen: *~ed out* propvol; **5** (*Am*) op zak hebben (*eg pistol*), bij de hand hebben: *~ it in* (of: *up*) ermee ophouden

³pack [pæk] *vb* **1** (in)pakken, zijn koffer pakken; **2** inpakken, zich laten inpakken ‖ *~ into* zich verdringen in; *~ up* ermee uitscheiden

¹package [pækidzj] *n* **1** pakket^h, pak(je^h), bundel, (*comp*) programmapakket^h, standaardprogramma^h; **2** verpakking

²package [pækidzj] *vb* **1** verpakken, inpakken; **2** groeperen, ordenen

packet [pækit] **1** pak(je^h), stapeltje^h: *a ~ of cigarettes* een pakje sigaretten; *~ soup* soep uit een pakje; **2** bom geld

packing [pæking] **1** verpakking; **2** pakking, dich-

tingsmiddel^h

pact [pækt] verdrag^h

¹pad [pæd] *n* **1** kussen(tje)^h, vulkussen^h, opvulsel^h, stootkussen^h, onderlegger, stempelkussen^h, (*sport*) beenbeschermer; **2** schrijfblok, blocnote; **3** (lanceer)platform^h; **4** bed^h, verblijf^h, huis^h

²pad [pæd] *vb* **1** draven, trippelen; **2** lopen, stappen

³pad [pæd] *vb* (*also with out*) (op)vullen: *~ded envelope* luchtkussenenveloppe

padding [pæding] opvulling, (op)vulsel^h

¹paddle [pædl] *n* **1** peddel, roeispaan, schoep; **2** vin (*eg of seal*), zwempoot

²paddle [pædl] *vb* **1** pootje baden; **2** (voort)peddelen

paddle boat rader(stoom)boot

paddling pool pierenbad^h, kinder(zwem)bad^h

paddock [pædɔk] kraal, omheinde weide (*near stable or racecourse*)

paddy [pædie] **1** *Paddy* Ier; **2** woedeaanval

paddy field rijstveld^h

padlock [pædlok] hangslot^h

padre [pa:drie] aal(moezenier)

¹pagan [peegən] *n* heiden

²pagan [peegən] *adj* heidens

¹page [peedzj] *n* **1** pagina, bladzijde; **2** page, (schild)knaap

²page [peedzj] *vb* oproepen; oppiepen

pageant [pædzjənt] **1** vertoning, spektakelstuk^h; **2** historisch schouwspel^h

pager [peedzjə] pieper, semafoon

paid betaald, voldaan ‖ *put ~ to* afrekenen met, een eind maken aan

¹pain [peen] *n* **1** pijn, leed^h, lijden^h: *be in ~* pijn hebben; **2** lastpost: *he's a real ~ (in the neck)* hij is werkelijk onuitstaanbaar; **3** *~s* (barens)weeën, pijnen; **4** *~s* moeite, last: *be at ~s (to do sth.)* zich tot het uiterste inspannen (om iets te doen)

²pain [peen] *vb* pijn doen, leed doen

pained [peend] pijnlijk, bedroefd

painstaking [peenzteeking] nauwgezet, ijverig

¹paint [peent] *n* kleurstof, verf: *wet ~!* pas geverfd!

²paint [peent] *vb* **1** verven, (be)schilderen; **2** (af)schilderen, beschrijven, portretteren; **3** (zich) verven, (zich) opmaken: *~ a picture of* een beeld schetsen van

painter [peentə] **1** (kunst)schilder, huisschilder; **2** vanglijn, meertouw^h

painting [peenting] **1** schilderij; **2** schilderkunst; schilderwerk^h

¹pair [peə] *n* **1** paar^h, twee(tal^h): *a ~ of gloves* een paar handschoenen; *the ~ of them* allebei; *in ~s* twee aan twee; **2** tweespan^h: *~ of scissors* schaar; *~ of spectacles* bril; *~ of trousers* broek

²pair [peə] *vb* een paar (doen) vormen, (zich) verenigen, koppelen, huwen, in paren rangschikken: *~ off* in paren plaatsen, koppelen; *~ up* paren (doen) vormen (*work, sport etc*)

pal [pæl] makker

palace [pælis] **1** paleis[h]; **2** het hof
palatable [pælətəbl] **1** smakelijk, eetbaar; **2** aangenaam, aanvaardbaar: *a ~ solution* een bevredigende oplossing
palate [pælət] **1** gehemelte[h], verhemelte[h]; **2** smaak, tong
palatial [pəleesjl] paleisachtig, schitterend
palaver [pəla:və] gewauwel[h]
¹pale [peel] *adj* **1** (ziekelijk) bleek, licht-, flets: *~ blue* lichtblauw; **2** zwak, minderwaardig
²pale [peel] *vb* (doen) bleek worden, (doen) verbleken
³pale [peel] *n* **1** (schutting)paal, staak; **2** (omheind) gebied[h], omsloten ruimte, grenzen *(also fig)*
¹Palestinian [pælistinniən] *adj* Palestijns
²Palestinian [pælistinniən] *n* Palestijn
palette [pælit] (schilders)palet[h]
palisade [pælisseed] **1** palissade, (paal)heining; **2** *~s* (steile) kliffen
¹pall [po:l] *vb* vervelend worden, zijn aantrekkelijkheid verliezen: *his stories began to ~ on us* zijn verhaaltjes begonnen ons te vervelen
²pall [po:l] *n* **1** lijkkleed[h]; **2** *(Am)* doodkist; **3** mantel *(only fig)*, sluier: *~ of smoke* rooksluier
pall-bearer slippendrager
pallet [pælit] **1** strozak; **2** spatel, strijkmes[h] *(of potter)*; **3** pallet, laadbord[h], stapelbord[h]
¹palliative [pæliətiv] *adj* **1** verzachtend, pijnstillend; **2** vergoelijkend
²palliative [pæliətiv] *n* pijnstiller
pallid [pælid] **1** (ziekelijk) bleek, flets; **2** mat, flauw
pallor [pælə] (ziekelijke) bleekheid, bleke gelaatskleur
pally [pælie] vriendschappelijk, vertrouwelijk: *be ~ with* beste maatjes zijn met
¹palm [pa:m] *n* **1** palm(boom); palm(tak), *(by extension)* overwinning, verdienste; **2** (hand)palm ‖ *have* (of: *hold*) *s.o. in the ~ of one's hand* iem geheel in zijn macht hebben; *grease* (of: *oil*) *s.o.'s ~* iem omkopen
²palm [pa:m] *vb* (in de hand) verbergen, wegpikken, achteroverdrukken
palmistry [pa:mistrie] handlijnkunde, handleeskunst
palm off 1 aansmeren, aanpraten: *palm sth. off on s.o.* iem iets aansmeren; **2** afschepen, zoet houden: *~ s.o. with some story* iem zoet houden met een verhaaltje
palmy [pa:mie] **1** palmachtig, vol palmbomen; **2** voorspoedig, bloeiend: *(fig) ~ days* bloeitijd
palpable [pælpəbl] tastbaar, voelbaar, *(fig)* duidelijk
palpitation [pælpitteesjən] hartklopping; klopping, het bonzen *(of heart)*
paltry [po:ltrie] **1** waardeloos, onbetekenend: *two ~ dollars* twee armzalige dollars; **2** verachtelijk, walgelijk: *~ trick* goedkoop trucje
pal up vriendjes worden: *~ with s.o.* goede maatjes worden met iem

pamper [pæmpə] (al te veel) toegeven aan, verwennen
pamphlet [pæmflit] pamflet[h], folder, boekje[h]
¹pan [pæn] *n* pan, braadpan, koekenpan; vat[h], ketel, schaal *(of scales)*, toiletpot
²pan [pæn] *vb* **1** (goud)erts wassen; **2** *(film)* pannen, laten meedraaien *(camera)*
³pan [pæn] *vb* **1** wassen in goudzeef; **2** afkammen, (af)kraken; **3** *(film)* pannen, doen meedraaien *(camera)*
panacea [pænəsie:ə] wondermiddel[h]
pancake [pænkeek] pannenkoek, flensje[h]: *as flat as a ~* zo plat als een dubbeltje
pandemonium [pændimmooniəm] **1** hel, hels spektakel[h]; **2** heksenketel, chaos, tumult[h]
pane [peen] (venster)ruit, glasruit
panel [pænəl] **1** paneel[h], vlak[h], (muur)vak[h], (wand)plaat; **2** (gekleurd) inzetstuk[h] *(of carpet)*; **3** controlebord[h], controlepaneel[h]; **4** naamlijst; **5** paneel[h], comité[h]; jury
panelling [pænəling] lambrisering, paneelwerk[h]
pang [pæng] plotselinge pijn, steek, scheut: *~s of remorse* hevige gewetenswroeging
¹panic [pænik] *n* paniek: *get into a ~ (about)* in paniek raken (over)
²panic [pænik] *vb* in paniek raken (brengen), angstig worden (maken)
pannier [pæniə] **1** (draag)mand, (draag)korf; **2** fietstas
panorama [pænəra:mə] panorama[h], vergezicht[h]
¹pant [pænt] *vb* **1** hijgen; **2** snakken, hunkeren; **3** snuiven, blazen, puffen *(of steam train)*
²pant [pænt] *vb* hijgend uitbrengen, uitstoten: *~ out a few words* enkele woorden uitbrengen
³pant [pænt] *n* hijgende beweging, snak
panther [pænθə] panter, luipaard; poema
panties [pæntiz] slipje, (dames)broekje: *a pair of ~* een (dames)slipje
pantomime [pæntəmajm] **1** (panto)mime[h], gebarenspel[h]; **2** (humoristische) kindermusical, sprookjesvoorstelling
pantry [pæntrie] provisiekast, voorraadkamer
pants [pænts] **1** *(Am)* (lange) broek: *(fig) wear the ~* de broek aanhebben; *wet one's ~* het in zijn broek doen, doodsbenauwd zijn; **2** damesonderbroek; kinderbroek(je), panty's: *scare s.o.'s ~ off* iem de stuipen op het lijf jagen; *with one's ~ down* onverhoeds, met de broek op de enkels
pap [pæp] **1** pap, brij, moes[h]; **2** leesvoer[h]
papa [pəpa:] papa, vader
papal [peepl] **1** pauselijk, vd paus: *~ bull* pauselijke bul; **2** rooms-katholiek
¹paper [peepə] *n* **1** (blad[h], vel[h]) papier[h], papiertje[h]: *on ~* op papier, in theorie; **2** dagblad[h], krant(je[h]); **3** (schriftelijke) test: *set a ~* een test opgeven; **4** verhandeling, voordracht: *read* (of: *deliver*) *a ~* een lezing houden; **5** document[h]: *your ~s, please* uw papieren, alstublieft
²paper [peepə] *vb* behangen, met papier beplakken:

~ *over: a)* (met papier) overplakken; *b)* verdoezelen

paperback paperback, pocket(boek^h)

paperclip paperclip

paperhanger behanger

paperweight presse-papier

papist [peepist] pausgezinde

pappy [pæpie] pappie

paprika [pæprikkə] paprika

par [pa:] **1** gelijkheid, gelijkwaardigheid: *be on* (of: *to) a ~ (with)* gelijk zijn (aan), op één lijn staan (met); *put (up)on a ~* gelijkstellen, op één lijn stellen; **2** gemiddelde toestand: *be up to ~* zich goed voelen, voldoende zijn; ~ *for the course* de gebruikelijke procedure, wat je kunt verwachten

parable [pærəbl] parabel, gelijkenis

parabola [pərǽbələ] parabool

¹**parachute** [pærəsjoe:t] *n* parachute

²**parachute** [pærəsjoe:t] *vb* aan een parachute neerkomen; parachuteren, aan een parachute neerlaten

¹**parade** [pəreed] *n* **1** parade, (uiterlijk) vertoon^h, show: *make a ~ of* paraderen met; **2** stoet, optocht, defilé^h, modeshow; **3** paradeplaats

²**parade** [pəreed] *vb* **1** paraderen, een optocht houden; **2** *(fig)* paraderen: *old ideas parading as new ones* verouderde ideeën opgepoetst tot nieuwe; **3** aantreden, parade houden

paradigm [pærədajm] voorbeeld^h, model^h

paradise [pærədajs] paradijs^h

paradox [pærədoks] paradox, (schijnbare) tegenstrijdigheid

paragon [pærəgən] toonbeeld^h, voorbeeld^h, model^h: ~ *of virtue* toonbeeld van deugd

paragraph [pærəgra:f] **1** paragraaf, alinea, *(law)* lid^h; **2** krantenbericht(je)^h

parakeet [pærəkie:t] parkiet

¹**parallel** [pærəlel] *adj* parallel, evenwijdig, *(fig)* overeenkomend, vergelijkbaar: *(gymnastics)* ~ *bars* brug met gelijke leggers; ~ *to* (of: *with): a)* parallel met, evenwijdig aan; *b)* vergelijkbaar met

²**parallel** [pærəlel] *n* **1** parallel, evenwijdige lijn, *(fig)* gelijkenis, overeenkomst: *draw a ~ (between)* een vergelijking maken (tussen); *without (a) ~* zonder weerga; **2** parallel, breedtecirkel

paralyse [pærəlajz] verlammen *(also fig)*, lamleggen

paralysis [pərǽlissis] verlamming, *(fig)* machteloosheid, onmacht

paramedic [pærəmeddik] paramedicus

paramount [pærəmaunt] opperst, voornaamst: *of ~ importance* van het grootste belang

paranoia [pærənojjə] *(med)* paranoia, vervolgingswaanzin, (abnormale) achterdochtigheid

paranoid [pærənojd] paranoïde

parapet [pærəpit] balustrade, (brug)leuning, muurtje^h

paraphernalia [pærəfəneeliə] uitrusting, toebehoren, accessoires: *photographic ~* fotospullen

¹**paraphrase** [pærəfreez] *n* omschrijving, parafrase

²**paraphrase** [pærəfreez] *vb* omschrijven, in eigen woorden weergeven

¹**paraplegic** [pærəplie:dzjik] *adj* verlamd in de onderste ledematen

²**paraplegic** [pærəplie:dzjik] *n* iem die gedeeltelijk verlamd is

parasite [pærəsajt] **1** parasiet, woekerdier^h, woekerplant, woekerkruid^h; **2** klaploper, profiteur

parasol [pærəsol] parasol, zonnescherm^h

paratroops [pærətroe:ps] para(chute)troepen, parachutisten

parcel [pa:sl] **1** pak(je^h), pakket^h, bundel; **2** perceel^h, lap grond: *a ~ of land* een lap grond

parcel up inpakken

parch [pa:tsj] verdorren, uitdrogen: ~*ed with thirst* uitgedroogd (van de dorst)

parchment [pa:tsjmənt] perkament(papier)^h

¹**pardon** [pa:dn] *n* **1** vergeving, pardon^h; **2** kwijtschelding (van straf), gratie(verlening), amnestie: *free ~* gratie(verlening); *general ~* amnestie; *(I) beg (your) ~* neemt u mij niet kwalijk *(also iron);* ~ pardon, wat zei u?

²**pardon** [pa:dn] *vb* **1** vergeven, genade schenken, een straf kwijtschelden; **2** verontschuldigen: ~ *me for coming too late* neemt u mij niet kwalijk dat ik te laat kom

pare [peə] **1** (af)knippen, schillen; afsnijden; **2** reduceren, besnoeien: ~ *down the expenses* de uitgaven beperken

parent [peərənt] **1** ouder, vader, moeder; **2** moederdier^h, moederplant

parental [pərentl] ouderlijk, ouder-

parenthesis [pərenθissis] **1** uitweiding, tussenzin; **2** ronde haak, haakje(s): *in ~* tussen (twee) haakjes *(also fig)*

pariah [pərajjə] **1** paria *(member of the lowest class in India);* **2** verschoppeling

parish [pærisj] **1** parochie, kerkelijke gemeente; **2** gemeente, dorp^h, district^h

parishioner [pərisjənə] parochiaan, gemeentelid^h

¹**Parisian** [pərizziən] *adj* Parijs, mbt Parijs

²**Parisian** [pərizziən] *n* Parijzenaar, Parisienne

parity [pærittie] **1** gelijkheid, gelijkwaardigheid; **2** overeenkomst, gelijkenis; **3** pari(teit), omrekeningskoers, wisselkoers

¹**park** [pa:k] *n* **1** (natuur)park^h, domein^h, natuurreservaat^h: *national ~* nationaal park, natuurreservaat; **2** parkeerplaats

²**park** [pa:k] *vb* **1** parkeren; **2** (tijdelijk) plaatsen, deponeren, (achter)laten: ~ *oneself* gaan zitten

parka [pa:kə] parka, anorak

parking [pa:king] het parkeren, parkeergelegenheid: *no ~* verboden te parkeren

parking lot parkeerterrein^h

parkland **1** open grasland^h *(full of trees);* **2** parkgrond

parkway *(Am)* snelweg *(through beautiful landscape)*

parley [pa:lie] onderhandelen

parliament [pa:ləmənt] parlement, volksvertegenwoordiging

parliamentary [pa:ləmɛntərie] parlementair, parlements-: ~ *party* kamerfractie

parlour [pa:lə] salon, woonkamer, zitkamer

parlour game gezelschapsspel[h], woordspel[h]

parlous [pa:ləs] gevaarlijk, hachelijk

parochial [pərookiəl] **1** parochiaal, parochie-, gemeentelijk, dorps-; **2** bekrompen, provinciaal

¹parody [pærədie] *n* parodie, karikatuur, nabootsing: *this trial is a ~ of justice* dit proces is een karikatuur van rechtvaardigheid

²parody [pærədie] *vb* imiteren, nadoen, navolgen

parole [pərool] **1** erewoord[h], parool[h], woord[h]; **2** voorwaardelijke vrijlating, parooltijd: *on ~* voorwaardelijk vrijgelaten

paroxysm [pærəksizm] (gevoels)uitbarsting, uitval: *~ of anger* woedeaanval; *~ of laughter* hevige lachbui

parquet [pa:kee] parket[h], parketvloer

parricide [pærissajd] **1** vadermoordenaar, moedermoordenaar; **2** vadermoord, moedermoord

¹parrot [pærət] *n* papegaai *(also fig)*, naprater

²parrot [pærət] *vb* papegaaien, napraten: *~ the teacher's explanation* als een papegaai de uitleg van de leraar opzeggen

¹parry [pærie] *vb* een aanval afwenden *(also fig)*

²parry [pærie] *vb* **1** afwenden, (af)weren: *~ a blow* een stoot afwenden; **2** ontwijken, (ver)mijden: *~ a question* zich van een vraag afmaken

¹parse [pa:z] *vb* taalkundig ontleden *(word, sentence)*

²parse [pa:z] *vb* (zich laten) ontleden, (zich laten) analyseren: *the sentence did not ~ easily* de zin was niet makkelijk te ontleden

parsimonious [pa:simmooniəs] spaarzaam, krenterig

parsley [pa:slie] peterselie

parson [pa:sn] predikant *(in Church of England)*, dominee, pastoor

¹part [pa:t] *n* **1** (onder)deel[h], aflevering, gedeelte[h], stuk[h], deel[h], verzameling: *two ~s of flour* twee delen bloem; **2** rol: *play a ~* een rol spelen, doen alsof; **3** aandeel[h], part[h], functie: *have a ~ in* iets te maken hebben met, een rol spelen in; **4** houding, gedragslijn; **5** zijde, kant: *take the ~ of* de zijde kiezen van; **6** ~*s* streek, gebied[h], gewest[h]; **7** ~*s* bekwaamheid, talent[h], talenten: *~ and parcel of* een essentieel onderdeel van; *in ~(s)* gedeeltelijk, ten dele; *for the most ~: a)* meestal, in de meeste gevallen; *b)* vooral

²part [pa:t] *adv* deels, gedeeltelijk, voor een deel

³part [pa:t] *vb* van elkaar gaan, scheiden: *~ (as) friends* als vrienden uit elkaar gaan

⁴part [pa:t] *vb* **1** scheiden, (ver)delen, breken; **2** scheiden, afzonderen: *he wouldn't be ~ed from his money* hij wilde niet betalen

partake [pa:teek] *(with of)* deelnemen (aan), deel hebben (aan): *~ in the festivities* aan de festiviteiten deelnemen

partial [pa:sjl] **1** partijdig, bevooroordeeld; **2** gedeeltelijk, deel-, partieel; **3** *(with to)* verzot (op), gesteld (op)

participant [pa:tissippənt] deelnemer

participate [pa:tissippeet] *(with in)* deelnemen (aan), betrokken zijn (bij)

participle [pa:tissipl] deelwoord[h]: *past ~* voltooid deelwoord; *present ~* onvoltooid deelwoord

particle [pa:tikl] **1** deeltje[h], partikel[h]; **2** beetje[h], greintje[h]

¹particular [pətikjoelə] *adj* **1** bijzonder, afzonderlijk, individueel: *this ~ case* dit specifieke geval; **2** *(with about, over)* nauwgezet (in), kieskeurig (in, op): *he's not over ~* hij neemt het niet zo nauw; **3** bijzonder, uitzonderlijk: *of ~ importance* van uitzonderlijk belang; *for no ~ reason* zomaar, zonder een bepaalde reden; **4** intiem, persoonlijk: *~ friend* intieme vriend

²particular [pətikjoelə] *n* **1** bijzonderheid, detail[h]: *in ~* in het bijzonder, vooral; **2** ~*s* feiten, (volledig) verslag[h]; **3** ~*s* personalia, persoonlijke gegevens

particularly [pətikjoeləlie] (in het) bijzonder, vooral, voornamelijk: *not ~ smart* niet bepaald slim

parting [pa:ting] scheiding *(also: in hair)*

partisan [pa:tizæn] **1** partijganger, aanhanger; **2** partizaan

¹partition [pa:tisjən] *n* **1** (ver)deling, scheiding; **2** scheid(ing)smuur, tussenmuur

²partition [pa:tisjən] *vb* (ver)delen, indelen: *~ off* afscheiden *(by means of dividing wall)*

partly [pa:tlie] gedeeltelijk: *~ ..., ~ ...* *(also)* enerzijds ..., anderzijds ...

partner [pa:tnə] partner, huwelijkspartner; vennoot, compagnon: *silent* (of: *sleeping*) *~* stille vennoot; *~ in crime* medeplichtige

partnership [pa:tnəsjip] **1** partnerschap[h]: *enter into ~ with* met iem in zaken gaan; **2** vennootschap

partridge [pa:tridzj] patrijs

part-time [pa:t-] in deeltijd

part with 1 afstand doen van, opgeven; **2** verlaten

party [pa:tie] **1** partij, medeplichtige: *be a ~ to* deelnemen aan, medeplichtig zijn aan; *third ~* derde; **2** (politieke) partij; **3** gezelschap[h], groep: *a coach ~* een busgezelschap; **4** feestje[h], partijtje[h]

party piece vast nummer[h] *(at parties etc)*

¹pass [pa:s] *vb* **1** (verder) gaan, (door)lopen, voortgaan: *~ along* doorlopen; *~ to other matters* overgaan naar andere zaken; **2** voorbijgaan, passeren, voorbijkomen, overgaan, eindigen: *~ unnoticed* niet opgemerkt worden; **3** passeren, er door(heen) raken; **4** circuleren, gangbaar zijn *(eg of coins)*, algemeen bekend staan als: *~ by* (of: *under*) *the name of* bekend staan als; *~ as* (of: *for*) doorgaan voor, dienen als; **5** aanvaard worden, slagen *((part of) examination)*, door de beugel kunnen *(eg rude language)*; **6** gebeuren, plaatsvinden: *come to ~* gebeuren; **7** *(cards)* passen; **8** overgemaakt worden: *the estate ~ed to the son* het landgoed werd aan de zoon vermaakt; **9** *(sport)* passeren, een pass geven, *(tennis)* een passeerslag geven

²pass [pa:s] *vb* **1** passeren, voorbijlopen: ~ *a car* een auto inhalen; **2** (door)geven, overhandigen, uitgeven *(money): could you pass me ~ that book, please?* kun je mij even dat boek aangeven?; ~ *in* inleveren; **3** slagen in: ~ *an exam* voor een examen slagen; **4** komen door, aanvaard worden door: *the bill ~ed the senate* het wetsvoorstel werd door de senaat bekrachtigd; **5** overschrijden, te boven gaan, overtreffen *(eg expectations): this ~es my comprehension* dit gaat mijn petje te boven; **6** laten glijden, (doorheen) laten gaan: ~ *one's hand across* (of: *over) one's forehead* met zijn hand over zijn voorhoofd strijken; **7** *(sport)* passeren, toespelen, doorspelen; **8** uiten, leveren *(criticism): ~ judgement (up)on* een oordeel vellen over; **9** vermaken, overdragen; **10** doorbrengen *(eg time)*, spenderen

³pass [pa:s] *n* **1** passage, (berg)pas, doorgang, vaargeul; **2** geslaagd examenʰ, voldoende; **3** (kritische) toestand: *it* (of: *things) had come to such a ~ that ...* het was zo ver gekomen dat ...; **4** pas, toegangsbewijsʰ; **5** *(socc)* pass; **6** *(baseball)* vrije loop; **7** *(tennis)* passeerslag; **8** *(cards)* pas: *make a ~ at a girl* een meisje trachten te versieren

passable [pa:səbl] **1** passabel, begaanbaar, doorwaadbaar; **2** redelijk, tamelijk, vrij goed

passage [pæsidzj] **1** (het) voorbijgaan, doortocht, verloopʰ; **2** (rechtʰ op) doortocht, vrije doorgang; **3** passage, kanaalʰ, doorgang, (zee)reis, overtocht; **4** gang, corridor; **5** passage, plaats *(eg in book)*

passageway gang, corridor

¹pass away *vb* **1** sterven, heengaan; **2** voorbijgaan, eindigen: *the storm passed away* het onweer luwde

²pass away *vb* verdrijven *(time)*

¹pass by *vb* voorbijgaan, voorbijvliegen *(time)*

²pass by *vb* over het hoofd zien, geen aandacht schenken aan: *life passes her by* het leven gaat aan haar voorbij

pass down overleveren, doorgeven

passenger [pæsindzjə] **1** passagier, reiziger; **2** profiteur *(in group)*, klaploper

passer-by (toevallige) voorbijganger

¹passing [pa:sing] *n* het voorbijgaan, het verdwijnen: *in ~* terloops

²passing [pa:sing] *adj* **1** voorbijgaand, voorbijtrekkend; **2** vluchtig, oppervlakkig, terloops

passion [pæsjən] **1** passie, (hartstochtelijke) liefde, enthousiasmeʰ; **2** (hevige) gevoelsuitbarsting, woedeaanval; **3** *the Passion* passie(verhaalʰ)

passionate [pæsjənət] **1** hartstochtelijk, vurig: ~ *plea* vurig pleidooi; **2** begerig; **3** opvliegend

passive [pæsiv] **1** passief: ~ *resistance* lijdelijk verzet; ~ *smoker* meeroker, passieve roker; **2** *(linguistics)* passief, lijdend: *the active and ~ voices* de bedrijvende en lijdende vorm

passkey **1** privésleutel, huissleutel; **2** loper

¹pass off *vb* (geleidelijk) voorbijgaan, weggaan, verlopen ‖ ~ *as* doorgaan voor

²pass off *vb* **1** negeren; **2** uitgeven: *pass s.o. off as* (of:

for) iem laten doorgaan voor

¹pass on *vb* doorgeven, (verder)geven: ~ *the decreased costs to the consumer* de verlaagde prijzen ten goede laten komen aan de consument; *pass it on* zegt het voort

²pass on *vb* **1** verder lopen, doorlopen: ~ *to* overgaan tot; **2** sterven, heengaan

¹pass out *vb* **1** flauw vallen, van zijn stokje gaan; **2** promoveren *(at mil academy)*, zijn diploma behalen

²pass out *vb* verdelen, uitdelen, verspreiden

¹pass over *vb* **1** laten voorbijgaan, overslaan: ~ *an opportunity* een kans laten schieten; **2** voorbijgaan aan, over het hoofd zien; **3** overhandigen, aanreiken

²pass over *vb* sterven, heengaan

Passover [pa:soovə] Pascha *(jewish Easter)*

passport [pa:spo:t] **1** paspoortʰ; **2** vrijgeleideʰ

pass through **1** ervaren, doormaken: ~ *police training* de politieopleiding doorlopen; **2** passeren, reizen door

pass up **1** laten voorbijgaan, laten schieten; **2** (naar boven) aangeven

password wachtwoordʰ

¹past [pa:st] *adj* **1** voorbij(gegaan), over, gepasseerd; **2** vroeger, gewezen; **3** verleden: ~ *participle* verleden deelwoord; ~ *tense* verleden tijd; **4** voorbij(gegaan), geleden: *in times ~* in vroegere tijden; **5** voorbij, vorig, laatst: *for some time ~* al enige tijd; *that is all ~ history now* dat is nu allemaal voltooid verleden tijd

²past [pa:st] *prep* voorbij, verder dan, later dan: *he cycled ~ our house* hij fietste voorbij ons huis; *it is ~ my understanding* het gaat mijn begrip te boven; *he is ~ it* hij is er te oud voor, hij kan het niet meer; *half ~ three* half vier

³past [pa:st] *adv* voorbij, langs: *a man rushed ~* een man kwam voorbijstormen

⁴past [pa:st] *n* verleden (tijd): *in the ~* in het verleden, vroeger

¹paste [peest] *n* **1** deegʰ *(for pastry)*; **2** pastei, paté, puree; **3** stijfselʰ, stijfselpap, plakselʰ; **4** pasta, brij(achtige massa)

²paste [peest] *vb* **1** kleven, plakken *(also comp)*; **2** uitsmeren; **3** pasta maken van

pastel [pæstl] pastelʰ; pastelkleur

paste up aanplakken; dichtplakken

pasteurize [pæstsjərajz] pasteuriseren

pastille [pæstil] pastille

pastime [pa:stajm] tijdverdrijfʰ

pastor [pa:stə] predikant, dominee, pastoor

pastoral [pa:strəl] **1** herders-; **2** uiterst lieflijk; **3** pastoraal, herderlijk: ~ *care* zielzorg, geestelijke (gezondheids)zorg

pastry [peestrie] **1** (korst)deegʰ; **2** gebakʰ, gebakjes, taart; **3** gebakjeʰ

pasture [pa:stsjə] weilandʰ, graslandʰ

¹pat [pæt] *n* **1** klopjeʰ; **2** stukjeʰ, klontjeʰ *(butter)*; **3** geklopʰ, getikʰ ‖ ~ *on the back* (goedkeurend)

722

(schouder)klopje, *(fig)* aanmoedigend woordje

²pat [pæt] *adj* **1** passend: *a ~ solution* een pasklare oplossing; **2** ingestudeerd, (al te) gemakkelijk

³pat [pæt] *vb* **1** tikken op, (zachtjes) kloppen op, aaien; **2** (zacht) platslaan

⁴pat [pæt] *vb* tikken

⁵pat [pæt] *adv* **1** paraat, gereed: *have one's answer ~* zijn antwoord klaar hebben; **2** perfect (aangeleerd), exact (juist): *have* (of: *know) sth. (off) ~* iets uit het hoofd kennen

patch [pætsj] **1** lap(jeʰ), stuk (stof), ooglap, (hecht)pleister; schoonheidspleister(tjeʰ); **2** vlek; **3** lapjeʰ grond, veldjeʰ; **4** stuk(je)ʰ, flard: *~es of fog* mistbanken, flarden mist; *not a ~ on* helemaal niet te vergelijken met

patch pocket opgenaaide zak

patch up 1 (op)lappen, verstellen; **2** (haastig) bijleggen *(quarrel etc)*; **3** in elkaar flansen, aan elkaar lappen

patchwork 1 lapjeswerkʰ: *a ~ of fields* een bonte lappendeken van velden; **2** lapwerkʰ, knoeiwerkʰ

pate [peet] kop, hersens: *bald ~* kale knikker

¹patent [peetnt] *n* patentʰ, octrooiʰ: *~ law* octrooiwet, octrooirecht; *~ medicine: a)* patentgeneesmiddel(en); *b)* wondermiddel

²patent [peetnt] *adj* **1** open(baar); **2** duidelijk || *~ leather* lakleer

patentee [peetntie:] patenthouder

paternal [pətə:nl] **1** vaderlijk *(also fig)*; **2** van vaderszijde: *~ grandmother* grootmoeder van vaders kant

paternity [pətə:nittie] vaderschapʰ

path [pa:θ] **1** padʰ, weg, paadjeʰ: *beat* (of: *clear) a ~* zich een weg banen *(also fig)*; **2** baan *(eg of bullet, comet)*, route, *(fig)* weg, padʰ

pathetic [pəθettik] zielig, erbarmelijk: *~ sight* treurig gezicht

pathfinder 1 verkenner, padvinder; **2** pionier, baanbreker

pathological [pæθəlodzjikl] pathologisch, ziekelijk *(also fig)*

pathos [peeθos] aandoenlijkheid

pathway padʰ

patience [peesjəns] geduldʰ: *~ of Job* jobsgeduld; *lose one's ~* zijn geduld verliezen

¹patient [peesjənt] *n* patiënt

²patient [peesjənt] *adj* geduldig, verdraagzaam

patio [pætie-oo] patio, terrasʰ

patriarch [peetrie·a:k] patriarch, *(fig)* grondlegger

¹patrician [pətrisjən] *adj* patricisch, aanzienlijk, vooraanstaand

²patrician [pətrisjən] *n* patriciër, aanzienlijk burger

patricide [pætrissajd] **1** vadermoordenaar; **2** vadermoord

patrimony [pætrimmənie] patrimoniumʰ, erfdeelʰ

patriot [pætriət] patriot

patriotism [pætriətizm] patriottismeʰ, vaderlandsliefde

¹patrol [pətrool] *n* **1** (verkennings)patrouille: *A.A. ~* wegenwacht; **2** patrouille, (inspectie)ronde

²patrol [pətrool] *vb* patrouilleren, de ronde doen

³patrol [pətrool] *vb* afpatrouilleren, de ronde doen van

patrolman [pətroolmən] **1** wegenwachter; **2** *(Am)* politieagent

patron [peetrən] **1** patroonʰ: *~ of the arts* iemand die kunst of kunstenaars ondersteunt; **2** (vaste) klant

patronage [pætrənidzj] **1** steun, bescherming; **2** klandizie, clientèle

patronize [pætrənajz] **1** beschermen; **2** klant zijn van, vaak bezoeken; **3** uit de hoogte behandelen, kleineren

patronizing [pætrənajzing] neerbuigend

¹patter [pætə] *vb* **1** kletsen; **2** kletteren; **3** trippelen

²patter [pætə] *n* **1** jargonʰ, taaltjeʰ: *salesman's ~* verkoperspraat; **2** gekletsʰ, gekakelʰ; **3** gekletterʰ, getrippelʰ *(of feet)*

¹pattern [pætn] *n* **1** modelʰ, prototypeʰ; **2** patroonʰ, dessinʰ, (giet)modelʰ, mal, planʰ, schemaʰ: *geometric(al) ~s* geometrische figuren; **3** staalʰ, monsterʰ

²pattern [pætn] *vb* vormen, maken, modelleren: *~ after* (of: *on)* modelleren naar; *~ oneself on s.o.* iem tot voorbeeld nemen

³pattern [pætn] *vb* een patroon vormen

paucity [po:sittie] geringheid, schaarste

paunch [po:ntsj] **1** buik(je)ʰ, maag; **2** pens

pauper [po:pə] arme

¹pause [po:z] *n* pauze, onderbreking, rust(puntʰ), weifeling: *~ to take a breath* adempauze

²pause [po:z] *vb* **1** pauzeren, pauze houden; **2** talmen, blijven hangen; **3** aarzelen, nadenken over

paved [peevd] **1** bestraat, geplaveid; **2** vol (van), vergemakkelijkt (door)

pavement [peevmənt] **1** bestrating, wegdekʰ, plaveiselʰ; **2** trottoirʰ, voetpadʰ, stoep; **3** *(Am)* rijweg, straat

pavilion [pəvilliən] paviljoenʰ, cricketpaviljoenʰ, clubhuisʰ

¹paw [po:] *n* **1** poot, klauw; **2** *(inf)* hand

²paw [po:] *vb* **1** ruw aanpakken, betasten; **2** bekrabben

³paw [po:] *vb* **1** krabben; **2** onhandig rondtasten

¹pawn [po:n] *n* **1** (onder)pandʰ: *at* (of: *in) ~* verpand; **2** *(chess)* pion, *(fig)* marionet: *he was only a ~ in their game* hij was niet meer dan een pion in hun spel

²pawn [po:n] *vb* verpanden, in pand geven, *(fig)* op het spel zetten *(life)*: *~ one's word* (of: *honour)* plechtig beloven op zijn woord van eer

pawnbroker pandjesbaas

pawnshop pandjeshuisʰ, bank van lening

¹pay [pee] *vb* **1** betalen, afbetalen, vergoeden: *~ cash* contant betalen; *~ over* (uit)betalen; **2** belonen *(fig)*, vergoeden, schadeloosstellen, betaald zetten: *~ s.o. for his loyalty* iem voor zijn trouw belonen; **3** schenken, verlenen: *~ attention* opletten, aandacht schenken; **4** lonend zijn (voor): *it didn't ~ him at all* het bracht hem niets op; *~ as you earn* loonbelasting

²pay [pee] *vb* **1** betalen, *(fig)* boeten: *make s.o. ~ iem laten boeten; ~ down* contant betalen; **2** lonend zijn: *it ~s to be honest* eerlijk duurt het langst

³pay [pee] *n* **1** betaling; **2** loonʰ, salarisʰ: *on full ~* met behoud van salaris

payable [peeəbl] betaalbaar, verschuldigd: *make ~* betaalbaar stellen *(Bill of Exchange); ~ to* ten gunste van

pay back terugbetalen, vergoeden, *(fig)* betaald zetten: *she paid him back his infidelities* ze zette hem zijn avontuurtjes betaald

paycheck *(Am)* looncheque, salarisʰ

P.A.Y.E. *pay as you earn* loonbelasting

payee [peeie:] begunstigde, ontvanger *(of Bill of Exchange etc)*

payer [peeə] betaler

pay for betalen (voor), de kosten betalen van, *(fig)* boeten voor

paying [peeing] lonend, rendabel

payload 1 betalende vracht *(in ship, aeroplane);* **2** nuttige last, springlading *(in bomb, rocket);* **3** netto lading

payment [peemənt] **1** (uit)betaling, honorering, loonʰ; (af)betaling; **2** vergoeding, beloning, (verdiende) loonʰ; **3** betaalde som, bedragʰ, storting: *make monthly ~s on the car* de auto maandelijks afbetalen; *deferred ~, ~ on deferred terms* betaling in termijnen, afbetaling

¹pay off *vb* renderen, (de moeite) lonen

²pay off *vb* **1** betalen en ontslaan; **2** (af)betalen, vereffenen, aflossen

pay-off 1 *(fig)* afrekening, vergelding; **2** resultaatʰ, inkomsten, winst; **3** climax, ontknoping

payola [peeoolə] *(Am)* **1** omkoperij; **2** steekpenning(en)

¹pay out *vb* **1** uitbetalen; **2** (with *on*) (geld) uitgeven (voor)

²pay out *vb* **1** terugbetalen, met gelijke munt betalen; **2** vieren *(rope, cable)*

payroll 1 loonlijst; **2** loonkosten

payslip loonstrookjeʰ

pay station *(Am)* (publieke) telefooncel

pay train trein met kaartverkoop (en onbemande stations)

pay up betalen, (helemaal) afbetalen, volstorten *(shares): paid-up capital* gestort kapitaal

P.C. 1 *Personal Computer* pc; **2** *police constable* politieagent

P.E. *physical education* gymnastiek

pea [pie:] erwt: *green ~s* erwtjes; *as like as two ~s (in a pod)* (op elkaar lijkend) als twee druppels water

peace [pie:s] **1** vrede, periode van vrede; **2** openbare orde: *keep the ~* de openbare orde handhaven; **3** rust, kalmte, tevredenheid; harmonie: *~ of mind* gemoedsrust; *hold* (of: *keep*) *one's ~* zich koest

houden; *make one's ~ with* zich verzoenen met; *be at ~* de eeuwige rust genieten

peaceful [pie:sfoel] **1** vredig; **2** vreedzaam

peacemaker vredestichter

¹peach [pie:tsj] *n* **1** perzik *(also colour);* **2** perzikboom; **3** prachtexemplaarʰ; prachtmeid: *a ~ of a dress* een schattig jurkje

²peach [pie:tsj] *vb* klikken, een klikspaan zijn: *~ against* (of: *on) an accomplice* een medeplichtige verraden

peacock [pie:kok] (mannetjes)pauw *(also fig)*, dikdoener

peak [pie:k] **1** piek, spits, puntʰ, *(fig)* hoogtepuntʰ, toppuntʰ; **2** (berg)piek, (hoge) berg, top; **3** klep *(of hat)*

peak hour spitsuurʰ

peaky [pie:kie] ziekelijk

¹peal [pie:l] *n* **1** klokkengeluiʰ; klokkenspelʰ, carillonʰ; **2** luide klank: *~s of laughter* lachsalvo's; *a ~ of thunder* een donderslag

²peal [pie:l] *vb* **1** luiden; **2** galmen, (doen) klinken, luid verkondigen: *~ out* weergalmen

peanut [pie:nut] **1** pinda, *(also)* pindaplant; **2** *~s* onbeduidend iets, kleinigheid, een schijntje

peanut butter pindakaas

pear [peə] peer

pearl [pə:l] **1** parel; **2** paarlemoerʰ ‖ *cast ~s before swine* paarlen voor de zwijnen werpen

peasant [pezt] **1** (kleine) boer; **2** plattelander; **3** lomperik, (boeren)kinkel

peasantry [pezntrie] **1** plattelandsbevolking; **2** boerenstand

pea souper erwtensoep

peat [pie:t] turf, (laag)veenʰ

pebble [pebl] kiezelsteen, grindʰ

pebble-dash grindpleister, grindsteen

¹peck [pek] *n* **1** pik (met snavel); **2** vluchtige zoen

²peck [pek] *vb* (with *at*) pikken (in, naar): *~ at: a)* vitten op; *b)* met lange tanden eten van

³peck [pek] *vb* **1** oppikken, wegpikken; **2** vluchtig zoenen

pecking order pikorde; hiërarchie: *be at the bottom of the ~* niets in te brengen hebben

peckish [pekkisj] **1** hongerig; **2** *(Am)* vitterig

peculiar [pikjoe:liə] **1** vreemd, eigenaardig; excentriek, raar: *I feel rather ~* ik voel me niet zo lekker; **2** bijzonder: *of ~ interest* van bijzonder belang; **3** (with *to*) eigen (aan), typisch (voor): *a habit ~ to the Dutch* een gewoonte die Nederlanders eigen is

peculiarity [pikjoe:lie·ærittie] **1** eigenaardigheid, bijzonderheid, merkwaardigheid; **2** eigenheid, (typisch) kenmerkʰ

pedagogic(al) [peddəgodzjik(l)] **1** opvoedkundig, pedagogisch; **2** schoolmeesterachtig

¹pedal [pedl] *n* pedaalʰ, trapper

²pedal [pedl] *vb* **1** peddelen, fietsen; **2** trappen, treden

pedant [peddənt] **1** muggenzifter, betweter; **2** boekengeleerde; **3** geleerddoener

pedantic [pidæntik] pedant, schoolmeesterachtig, frikkerig

¹peddle [pɛdl] *vb* **1** (uit)venten, aan de man brengen: ~ *dope* (of: *drugs*) drugs verkopen; **2** verspreiden, verkondigen: ~ *gossip* roddel(praatjes) verkopen

²peddle [pɛdl] *vb* leuren, venten

pedestal [pɛddistl] voetstuk[h], sokkel: *(fig) knock s.o. off his* ~ iem van zijn voetstuk stoten

pedestrian [piddɛstriən] voetganger: ~ *crossing* voetgangersoversteekplaats; ~ *precinct* autovrij gebied

pediatrician [pie:diətrɪsjən] kinderarts

pedicure [pɛddikjoeə] pedicure

pedigree [pɛddigrie:] **1** stamboom; afstamming, goede komaf; **2** stamboek[h] *(of animals):* ~ *cattle* stamboekvee

pedlar [pɛdlə] **1** venter, straathandelaar; **2** drugsdealer; **3** verspreider *(of gossip)*

¹pee [pie:] *vb* plassen, een plas(je) doen

²pee [pie:] *n* plas, urine: *go for* (of: *have*) *a* ~ een plasje gaan doen

¹peek [pie:k] *n* (vluchtige) blik, kijkje[h]: *have a* ~ *at* een (vlugge) blik werpen op

²peek [pie:k] *vb* **1** gluren; **2** (with *at*) vluchtig kijken (naar)

¹peel [pie:l] *n* schil

²peel [pie:l] *vb* schillen, pellen: ~ *off:* a) lostrekken, losmaken; b) uittrekken *(clothes);* ~ *the skin off a banana* de schil van een banaan afhalen

³peel [pie:l] *vb* **1** (also with *off)* afpellen, afbladderen *(of paint)*, vervellen: *my nose* ~*ed* mijn neus vervelde; ~ *off* afschilferen van; **2** (with *off)* zich uitkleden

peeling [pie:ling] (aardappel)schil

¹peep [pie:p] *vb* **1** (with *at)* gluren (naar), loeren (naar), (be)spieden; **2** (with *at)* vluchtig kijken (naar), een kijkje nemen (bij); **3** te voorschijn komen: ~ *out* opduiken; *the flowers are already* ~*ing through the soil* de bloemen steken hun kopjes al boven de grond uit; **4** piepen, tjirpen: ~*ing Tom* voyeur, gluurder

²peep [pie:p] *n* **1** piep, tjilp(geluid[h]); **2** *(child language)* toeter, claxon; **3** kik, woord[h], nieuws[h]; **4** (vluchtige) blik, kijkje[h]: *take a* ~ *at* vluchtig bekijken

peephole kijkgaatje[h]

¹peer [piə] *n* **1** gelijke, collega; **2** edelman || ~ *of the realm* edelman die lid is van het Hogerhuis

²peer [piə] *vb* turen, staren, spieden

peerage [piəridzj] **1** adel, adeldom[h]; **2** adelstand

peer group (groep van) gelijken, leeftijdgenoten, collega's

peerless [piələs] weergaloos, ongeëvenaard

peeve [pie:v] ergeren, irriteren

peevish [pie:visj] **1** chagrijnig, slechtgehumeurd; **2** weerbarstig, dwars

¹peg [peg] *n* **1** pin, pen, plug; **2** schroef *(of string instrument);* **3** (tent)haring; **4** kapstok *(also fig): buy clothes off the* ~ confectiekleding kopen; **5** wasknij-

per: *take s.o. down a* ~ *(or two)* iem een toontje lager laten zingen

²peg [peg] *vb* **1** vastpennen, vastpinnen: *he is hard to* ~ *down* je krijgt moeilijk vat op hem; **2** stabiliseren, bevriezen

¹peg out *vb* zijn laatste adem uitblazen, het hoekje omgaan

²peg out *vb* afbakenen: ~ *a claim* (een stuk land) afbakenen

pelican [pɛllikkən] pelikaan

pellet [pɛllit] **1** balletje[h], bolletje[h], prop(je[h]); **2** kogeltje[h], hagelkorrel, ~*s* hagel

pellucid [pilloe:sid] doorzichtig, helder *(also fig)*

¹pelt [pelt] *vb* **1** (neer)kletteren, (neer)plenzen: ~*ing rain* kletterende regen; *it is* ~*ing (down) with rain* het regent dat het giet; **2** hollen: ~ *down a hill* een heuvel afrennen

²pelt [pelt] *vb* bekogelen, beschieten, bestoken *(also fig)*

³pelt [pelt] *n* vacht, huid, vel[h]

pelvis [pɛlvis] bekken[h], pelvis[h]

¹pen [pen] *n* **1** pen, balpen, vulpen; **2** hok[h], kooi, cel

²pen [pen] *vb* **1** op papier zetten, (neer)pennen; **2** opsluiten *(also fig)*, afzonderen

penal [pie:nl] **1** strafbaar: ~ *offence* strafbaar feit; **2** zwaar, (heel) ernstig: ~ *taxes* zware belastingen; **3** straf-: ~ *code* wetboek van strafrecht; ~ *servitude* dwangarbeid

penalize [pie:nəlajz] **1** straffen; **2** een achterstand geven, benadelen; **3** een strafschop toekennen; **4** strafbaar stellen, verbieden

penalty [pɛnltie] **1** (geld-, gevangenis)straf, (geld)boete: *on* (of: *under*) ~ *of* op straffe van; **2** (nadelig) gevolg[h], nadeel[h], schade: *pay the* ~ *of* de gevolgen dragen van; **3** handicap, achterstand, strafpunt[h]; **4** strafschop

penalty area *(socc)* strafschopgebied[h]

penalty box *(ice hockey)* strafbank, strafhok(je[h])

penalty kick *(socc)* strafschop

penance [pɛnnəns] boete(doening), straf

¹pencil [pɛnsl] *n* **1** potlood[h], vulpotlood[h], stift; **2** (maquilleer)stift

²pencil [pɛnsl] *vb* **1** (met potlood) kleuren, met potlood merken: ~*led eyebrows* zwartgemaakte wenkbrauwen; **2** schetsen, tekenen *(also fig)*

pendant [pɛndənt] hanger(tje[h]), oorhanger

pendent [pɛndənt] **1** (neer)hangend; **2** overhangend, uitstekend

¹pending [pɛnding] *adj* hangend, onbeslist, in behandeling: *patent* ~ octrooi aangevraagd

²pending [pɛnding] *prep* in afwachting van *(eg arrival)*

pendulum [pɛndjoeləm] slinger, slingerbeweging: *a clock with a* ~ een slingeruurwerk

¹penetrate [pɛnnitreet] *vb* **1** doordringen, dringen door, zich boren in, (ver)vullen; **2** doorgronden, penetreren; **3** dringen door, zien door: *our eyes couldn't* ~ *the darkness* onze ogen konden niet door de duisternis heendringen

²**penetrate** [pennitreet] *vb* doordringen, penetreren; binnendringen, indringen

penetrating [pennitreeting] doordringend, scherp(zinnig), snijdend *(of wind)*, scherp, luid *(of sound)*

penguin [penggwin] pinguïn

penicillin [pennissillin] penicilline

peninsula [pinnins·joelə] schiereiland^h

penis [pie:nis] penis

penitence [pennittəns] 1 boete(doening); 2 berouw^h

penitent [pennittənt] berouwvol || *be* ~ boete doen

¹**penitentiary** [pennittensjərie] *n* federale gevangenis

²**penitentiary** [pennittensjərie] *adj* 1 straf-, boet(e)-; 2 heropvoedings-, verbeterings-

penknife zak(knip)mes^h

penmanship [penmənsjip] kalligrafie, schoonschrijfkunst

pen-name schrijversnaam, pseudoniem^h

penniless [pennieləs] 1 zonder geld, blut, platzak; 2 arm, behoeftig

penny [pennie] *(also pence)* penny, stuiver, cent, duit: *it costs 30 pence* het kost 30 penny; *not have* (of: *be without*) *a* ~ *to one's name* geen rooie duit bezitten; *a* ~ *for your thoughts* waar zit jij met je gedachten?; *the* ~ *has dropped* het kwartje is gevallen, ik snap 't; *spend a* ~ een kleine boodschap doen *(to the toilet)*; *ten a* ~ dertien in een dozijn; *in for a* ~, *in for a pound* wie A zegt, moet ook B zeggen

penny-wise op de kleintjes lettend || ~ *and pound-foolish* zuinig met muntjes maar kwistig met briefjes

pension [pensjən] pensioen^h: *retire on a* ~ met pensioen gaan

pensioner [pensjənə] gepensioneerde

pension off 1 pensioneren, met pensioen sturen; 2 afdanken, afschaffen

pensive [pensiv] 1 peinzend, (diep) in gedachten; 2 droefgeestig, zwaarmoedig

pentagon [pentəgon] 1 vijfhoek; 2 *the Pentagon* ministerie^h van defensie vd USA

pentathlon [pentæθlən] vijfkamp

Pentecost [pentikost] 1 *(Am)* pinksterzondag, Pinksteren; 2 *(Judaism)* pinksterfeest, Wekenfeest

penthouse [pentaus] dakappartement^h, penthouse^h

pent-up 1 opgesloten, ingesloten, vastzittend; 2 opgekropt, onderdrukt: ~ *emotions* opgekropte gevoelens

penultimate [pinnultimmət] voorlaatst, op één na laatst

penury [penjoerie] grote armoede, (geld)nood

¹**people** [pie:pl] *n* 1 volk^h, gemeenschap, ras^h, stam: *nomadic* ~*s* nomadische volken; 2 staat, natie; 3 mensen, personen, volk^h, lui; 4 de mensen, ze, men: ~ *say* … men zegt …; 5 (gewone) volk^h, massa; 6 huisgenoten, ouwelui, (naaste) familie

²**people** [pie:pl] *vb* bevolken *(also fig)*, voorzien van (inwoners), bewonen

pep [pep] *(inf)* fut, vuur^h, energie

¹**pepper** [peppə] *n* 1 peper *(powder, plant, fruit)*; 2 paprika *(plant, fruit)*

²**pepper** [peppə] *vb* 1 (in)peperen; flink kruiden: ~ *a speech with witty remarks* een toespraak doorspekken met grappige opmerkingen; 2 bezaaien, bespikkelen: ~*ed with* bezaaid met; 3 bekogelen, bestoken *(also fig)*

peppercorn peperkorrel, peperbol

peppermint pepermunt(je)^h

pep up oppeppen, opkikkeren, doen opleven, pikanter maken *(dish)*

per [pə] 1 via, per, door; 2 per, voor, elk(e): *60 km* ~ *hour* zestig km per uur

perceive [pəsie:v] 1 waarnemen, bespeuren, (be)merken; 2 bemerken, beseffen

per cent [pəsent] procent^h, percent^h || *I'm one hundred* ~ *in agreement with you* ik ben het volledig met je eens

percentage [pəsentidzj] 1 percentage^h; 2 procent^h, commissie(loon^h)

perceptible [pəseptibl] waarneembaar, merkbaar: *he worsened perceptibly* hij ging zienderogen achteruit

perception [pəsepsjən] 1 waarneming, gewaarwording; 2 voorstelling; 3 (in)zicht^h, besef^h, visie: *a clear* ~ *of* een duidelijk inzicht in

perceptive [pəseptiv] 1 opmerkzaam, oplettend; 2 scherp(zinnig), verstandig

¹**perch** [pə:tsj] *n* 1 stok(je^h), stang, staaf *(for bird)*; 2 baars || *knock s.o. off his* ~ iem op zijn nummer zetten

²**perch** [pə:tsj] *vb* 1 neerstrijken, neerkomen *(of birds)*, plaatsnemen, zich neerzetten; 2 (neer)zetten, (neer)plaatsen, (neer)leggen: *the boy was* ~*ed on the wall* de jongen zat (hoog) bovenop de muur

percolator [pə:kəleetə] koffiezetapparaat^h

percussion [pəkusjən] slagwerk^h, percussie, slaginstrumenten

perdition [pədisjən] verdoemenis; hel

¹**perennial** [pərenniəl] *adj* 1 het hele jaar durend; 2 vele jaren durend, langdurig; eeuwig, blijvend; 3 *(bot)* overblijvend

²**perennial** [pərenniəl] *n* overblijvende plant

¹**perfect** [pə:fikt] *adj* 1 perfect, volmaakt, uitstekend, volledig, (ge)heel, onberispelijk: *have a* ~ *set of teeth* een volkomen gaaf gebit hebben; ~*ly capable of* heel goed in staat om; 2 zuiver, puur: ~ *blue* zuiver blauw; 3 *(linguistics)* voltooid: ~ *participle* voltooid deelwoord; ~ *tense* (werkwoord in de) voltooide tijd; 4 volslagen, volledig, totaal: *a* ~ *stranger* een volslagen onbekende; *have a* ~ *right (to do sth.)* het volste recht hebben (om iets te doen)

²**perfect** [pəfekt] *vb* 1 perfectioneren, vervolmaken; 2 voltooien, beëindigen; 3 verbeteren: ~ *one's English* zijn Engels verbeteren

perfection [pəfeksjən] 1 perfectie, volmaaktheid: *the dish was cooked to* ~ het gerecht was voortreffe-

lijk klaargemaakt; **2** hoogtepunt^h, toonbeeld^h
perfidious [pəfɪdiəs] trouweloos, verraderlijk
perforate [pɔ:fəreet] doorprikken: *stamps with ~d edges* postzegels met tandjes
¹perform [pəfɔːm] *vb* **1** optreden, een uitvoering geven, spelen; **2** presteren, werken, functioneren *(of machines): the car ~s well* de auto loopt goed; **3** presteren, het goed doen; **4** doen, handelen
²perform [pəfɔːm] *vb* **1** uitvoeren, volbrengen, ten uitvoer brengen: *~ miracles* wonderen doen; **2** uitvoeren, opvoeren, (ver)tonen, presenteren
performance [pəfɔːməns] **1** voorstelling, opvoering, uitvoering, tentoonstelling: *theatrical ~* toneelopvoering; **2** prestatie, succes^h: *a peak ~* een topprestatie; **3** uitvoering, volbrenging, vervulling; **4** prestaties, werking: *a car's ~* de prestaties van een auto
performer [pəfɔːmə] **1** uitvoerder; **2** artiest
¹perfume [pɔ:fjoeːm] *n* parfum^h, (aangename) geur
²perfume [pəfjoeːm] *vb* parfumeren
perfunctory [pəfʌŋktərie] plichtmatig (handelend): *a ~ visit* een routinebezoek, een verplicht bezoekje
perhaps [pəhæps] misschien, mogelijk(erwijs), wellicht
peril [perril] (groot) gevaar^h, risico^h: *you do it at your ~* je doet het op eigen verantwoordelijkheid
perilous [perrilləs] (levens)gevaarlijk, riskant
perimeter [pərimmittə] omtrek
¹period [pɪəriəd] *n* **1** periode, tijdperk^h, fase: *bright ~s* opklaringen; **2** lestijd, les(uur^h); **3** (menstruatie)periode, ongesteldheid: *she is having her ~* ze is ongesteld; **4** punt^h *(punctuation mark): I won't do it, ~!* ik doe het niet, punt uit!
²period [pɪəriəd] *adj* historisch, stijl-: *~ costumes* historische klederdrachten; *~ furniture* stijlmeubelen
periodical [pɪərie-ɔddikl] tijdschrift^h
periodic(al) [pɪərie-ɔddik(l)] periodiek, regelmatig terugkerend, cyclisch, kring-
peripatetic [perrippətettik] rondreizend, rondzwervend, (rond)trekkend
periphery [pərɪffərie] (cirkel)omtrek, buitenkant, rand
periscope [perriskoop] periscoop
perish [perrisj] **1** omkomen; **2** vergaan, verteren
¹perishable [perrisjəbl] *adj* **1** kortstondig; **2** (licht) bederfelijk, beperkt houdbaar
²perishable [perrisjəbl] *n* beperkt houdbaar (voedsel)product^h, *~s* snel bedervende goederen
perishing [perrisjing] beestachtig, moordend: *~ cold* beestachtige kou
perjury [pɔ:dzjərie] meineed
perk [pɔːk] extra verdienste, *~s* extraatjes; (extra) voordeel^h
perk up opleven, herleven, opfleuren
perky [pɔ:kie] **1** levendig, opgewekt, geestdriftig; **2** verwaand
perm [pɔːm] **1** permanent; **2** combinatie, selectie

(football pools)
permanence [pɔːmənəns] **1** duurzaamheid; **2** permanent iem (iets), vast element^h: *is your new address a ~ or merely temporary?* is je nieuwe adres permanent of slechts tijdelijk?
permanent [pɔːmənənt] blijvend, duurzaam: *~ address* vast adres; *~ wave* permanent
permeate [pɔːmie-eet] (door)dringen, (door)trekken, zich (ver)spreiden (over): *a revolt ~d the country* een opstand verspreidde zich over het land
permission [pəmɪsjən] toestemming, vergunning, goedkeuring: *without my ~* zonder mijn toestemming
permissive [pəmɪssiv] verdraagzaam, tolerant: *the ~ society* de tolerante maatschappij
¹permit [pəmɪt] *vb* toestaan, toelaten, veroorloven: *weather ~ting* als het weer het toelaat
²permit [pɔːmɪt] *n* **1** verlofbrief, pasje^h, permissiebriefje^h, geleidebiljet^h *(of goods);* **2** (schriftelijke) vergunning, toestemming, machtiging
pernicious [pənɪsjəs] **1** schadelijk, kwaadaardig; **2** dodelijk, fataal
¹perpendicular [pə:pəndɪkjoelə] *adj* loodrecht, heel steil: *~ to* loodrecht op
²perpendicular [pə:pəndɪkjoelə] *n* loodlijn, verticaal, loodrechte lijn: *be out of (the) ~* niet in het lood staan
perpetrate [pɔːpitreet] plegen, begaan: *~ a crime* een misdaad plegen
perpetration [pə:pitreesjən] het plegen, het uitvoeren
perpetual [pəpetsjoeəl] eeuwig(durend), blijvend, permanent, langdurig, onafgebroken: *~ check* eeuwig schaak
perplex [pəpleks] **1** verwarren, van zijn stuk brengen, van streek brengen; **2** ingewikkeld(er) maken, bemoeilijken, compliceren: *a ~ing task* een hoofdbrekend karwei
perquisite [pɔːkwizzit] **1** faciliteit, (extra, meegenomen) voordeel^h; **2** extra verdienste
persecute [pɔːsikjoeːt] vervolgen, achtervolgen, *(fig)* kwellen, vervelen: *~ s.o. with questions* iem voortdurend lastig vallen met vragen
persecution [pə:sikjoeːsjən] vervolging, *(fig)* kwelling
perseverance [pə:sivvɪərəns] volharding, doorzettingsvermogen^h
persevere [pə:sivvɪə] volhouden, doorzetten: *~ at (of: in, with)* volharden in; *~ in doing sth.* volharden in iets, iets doorzetten
Persian [pɔːzjən] Perzisch, Iraans: *~ cat* Perzische kat, pers
persist [pəsɪst] **1** (koppig) volhouden, (hardnekkig) doorzetten: *~ in (of: with)* (koppig) volharden in, (hardnekkig) doorgaan met; **2** (blijven) duren, voortduren, standhouden: *the rain will ~ all day* de regen zal de hele dag aanhouden
persistence [pəsɪstəns] **1** volharding, vasthoudendheid; **2** hardnekkigheid

persistent [pəsistənt] **1** vasthoudend; **2** voortdurend, blijvend, aanhoudend: ~ *rain* aanhoudende regen

person [pə:sn] **1** persoon, individu[h], mens: *you are the ~ I am looking for* jij bent degene die ik zoek; *in ~* in eigen persoon; **2** persoonlijkheid, karakter[h], persoon

personable [pə:sənəbl] knap, voorkomend

personage [pə:sənidzj] **1** personage[h], belangrijk persoon; **2** personage[h], rol, karakter[h]

personal [pə:sənəl] **1** persoonlijk, individueel: *from ~ experience* uit eigen ervaring; **2** persoonlijk, vertrouwelijk, beledigend: ~ *remarks* persoonlijke opmerkingen

personality [pə:sənælittie] **1** persoonlijkheid, karakter[h], sterk karakter[h]; **2** persoonlijkheid, bekende figuur, beroemdheid

personalize [pə:sənəlajz] **1** verpersoonlijken; **2** merken *(with a sign):* ~*d stationery* postpapier voorzien van de naam van de eigenaar

personally [pə:sənəlie] **1** persoonlijk, in (eigen) persoon, zelf; **2** voor mijn part, wat mij betreft; **3** van persoon tot persoon: *speak ~ to s.o. about sth.* iets onder vier ogen met iem bespreken

personification [pəsonniffikkeesjən] verpersoonlijking, personificatie

personify [pəsonniffaj] verpersoonlijken; belichamen, symboliseren

personnel [pə:sənel] **1** personeel[h], staf, werknemers: *most of the ~ work* (of: *works*) *from 9 to 6* het meeste personeel werkt van 9 tot 6; **2** personele hulpmiddelen, troepen, manschappen

perspective [pəspektiv] **1** perspectief[h] *(also fig)*, verhouding, dimensie; **2** vergezicht[h], uitzicht[h], perspectief[h]; **3** gezichtspunt[h] *(also fig)*, standpunt[h]: *see* (of: *look*) *at sth. in its/the right ~* een juiste kijk op iets hebben; **4** toekomstperspectief[h], vooruitzicht[h]; **5** perspectief[h], perspectivisch tekenen, dieptezicht[h] *(also fig): see* (of: *look*) *at sth. in ~* iets relativeren, iets in het juiste perspectief zien

perspex [pə:speks] plexiglas[h]

perspicuous [pəspikjoeəs] doorzichtig, helder, duidelijk

perspiration [pə:spəreesjən] transpiratie; zweet[h]

perspire [pəspajjə] transpireren, zweten

persuade [pəsweed] overreden; overtuigen, bepraten: ~ *s.o. to do sth.* iem tot iets overhalen; ~ *oneself of sth.: a)* zich met eigen ogen van iets overtuigen; *b)* zichzelf iets wijsmaken

persuasion [pəsweezjən] **1** overtuiging, mening, geloof[h]: *people of different ~s* mensen met verschillende (geloofs)overtuiging; **2** overtuiging(skracht), overreding(skracht)

persuasive [pəsweesiv] overtuigend

pert [pə:t] vrijpostig, brutaal

pertain to 1 behoren tot, deel uitmaken van; **2** eigen zijn aan, passend zijn voor; **3** betrekking hebben op, verband houden met

pertinent [pə:tinnənt] relevant, toepasselijk: ~ *to* betrekking hebbend op

perturb [pətə:b] in de war brengen *(also fig)*, van streek brengen

peruse [pəroe:z] **1** doorlezen, nalezen, (grondig) doornemen; **2** bestuderen, analyseren

Peruvian [pəroe:vieən] Peruaans

pervade [pəveed] doordringen *(also fig)*, zich verspreiden in, vervullen: *the author ~s the entire book* de auteur is in het hele boek aanwezig

perverse [pəvə:s] **1** pervers, verdorven, tegennatuurlijk; **2** eigenzinnig, koppig, dwars

[1]**pervert** [pəvə:t] *vb* **1** verkeerd gebruiken, misbruiken: ~ *the course of justice* verhinderen dat het recht zijn loop heeft; **2** verdraaien, vervormen: *his ideas had been ~ed* zijn opvattingen waren verkeerd voorgesteld; **3** perverteren, corrumperen, bederven

[2]**pervert** [pə:və:t] *n* pervers persoon *(sexually)*, viezerik

pessimism [pessimmizm] pessimisme[h], zwartkijkerij

pessimist [pessimmist] pessimist, zwartkijker

pest [pest] **1** lastpost; **2** schadelijk dier[h], schadelijke plant, ~*s* ongedierte[h]: ~ *control* ongediertebestrijding

pester [pestə] kwellen, lastig vallen, pesten: ~ *s.o. into doing sth.* iem door te blijven zeuren dwingen tot het doen van iets

pesticide [pestissajd] pesticide[h], verdelgingsmiddel[h], bestrijdingsmiddel[h]

pestiferous [pestiffərəs] **1** schadelijk; **2** verderfelijk; **3** vervelend, irriterend

pestilence [pestilləns] pest, (pest)epidemie

pestilent [pestillənt] (dood)vervelend, irriterend

pestle [pesl] stamper

[1]**pet** [pet] *n* **1** huisdier[h], troeteldier[h]; **2** lieveling, favoriet

[2]**pet** [pet] *adj* **1** tam, huis-: ~ *snake* huisslang; **2** favoriet, lievelings-: *politicians are my ~ aversion* (of: *hate*) aan politici heb ik een hartgrondige hekel; ~ *topic* stokpaardje

[3]**pet** [pet] *vb* vrijen: *heavy ~ting* stevige vrijpartij

petal [petl] bloemblad[h], kroonblad[h]

peter out [pie:təraut] **1** afnemen, slinken; **2** uitgeput raken, op raken, uitgaan, doven

petite [pətie:t] klein en tenger, fijn, sierlijk *(of woman)*

[1]**petition** [pittisjən] *n* **1** verzoek[h], smeekbede; **2** petitie, smeekschrift[h], verzoek(schrift)[h]; **3** verzoek(schrift)[h], aanvraag

[2]**petition** [pittisjən] *vb* een verzoek richten tot

[1]**petrify** [petriffaj] *vb* verstenen, tot steen worden *(also fig)*

[2]**petrify** [petriffaj] *vb* **1** (doen) verstenen, tot steen maken; **2** doen verstijven, verlammen: *be petrified by* (of: *with*) *terror* verstijfd zijn van schrik

petrol [petrəl] benzine

petroleum [pitrooliəm] aardolie

petticoat [pettiekoot] onderrok

pettifogging [pɛttiefoging] 1 muggenzifterig; 2 nietig, onbelangrijk

pettish [pɛttisj] humeurig

petty [pɛttie] 1 onbetekenend, onbelangrijk: ~ *details* onbelangrijke details; 2 klein, tweederangs, ondergeschikt: *the ~ bourgeoisie* de lagere middenstand; *(shipp)* ~ *officer* onderofficier; 3 klein, gering: ~ *larceny* gewone diefstal, kruimeldiefstal

petulant [pɛtsjoelənt] prikkelbaar, humeurig

petunia [pitjoe:niə] petunia

pew [pjoe:] kerkbank

pewit [pie:wit] kieviet

¹pewter [pjoe:tə] *n* tin[h], tinnegoed[h]

²pewter [pjoe:tə] *adj* tinnen: ~ *mugs* tinnen kroezen

¹phantom [fæntəm] *n* spook[h] *(also fig)*, geest(verschijning)

²phantom [fæntəm] *adj* 1 spook-, spookachtig, schimmig: ~ *ship* spookschip; 2 schijn-, denkbeeldig: ~ *withdrawals* spookopnames

pharisee [færissie:] 1 een vd Farizeeën; 2 farizeeër, schijnheilige

pharmaceutical [fa:məs·joe:tikl] farmaceutisch: ~ *chemist* apotheker

pharmacy [fa:məsie] apotheek

phase [feez] fase, stadium[h], tijdperk[h]: *the most productive ~ in the artist's life* de meest productieve periode in het leven van de kunstenaar; *in ~: a)* in fase; *b)* corresponderend; *out of ~* niet in fase

phase in geleidelijk introduceren

phase out geleidelijk uit de productie nemen, geleidelijk opheffen

Ph.D. *Doctor of Philosophy* dr., doctor in de menswetenschappen

pheasant [fɛzzənt] fazant

phenomenon [finnɔmminnən] fenomeen[h], (natuur)verschijnsel[h]

philanthropist [filænθrəpist] mensenvriend

philatelist [filætəlist] postzegelverzamelaar

philharmonic [filha:mɔnnik] filharmonisch

¹philistine [fillistajn] *adj* acultureel

²philistine [fillistajn] *n* cultuurbarbaar

philosopher [fillossəfə] filosoof, wijsgeer

philosophy [fillossəfie] filosofie; levensbeschouwing, opvatting

phlegm [flem] 1 slijm[h], fluim; 2 flegma[h], onverstoorbaarheid; 3 onverschilligheid, apathie

phlegmatic [flegmætik] flegmatisch, onverstoorbaar

phobia [foobiə] fobie, (ziekelijke) vrees

phoenix [fie:niks] feniks

¹phone [foon] *n* telefoon: *on the ~* aan de telefoon

²phone [foon] *vb* (op)bellen: ~ *back* terugbellen; ~ *up* opbellen

phonetics [fənɛttiks] fonetiek

¹phoney [foonie] *adj* vals, onecht, nep

²phoney [foonie] *n (inf)* 1 onecht persoon, bedrieger; 2 namaak(sel[h]), nep, bedrog[h]

phosphorus [fosfərəs] fosfor[h]

photo [footoo] foto

photocopier [footookoppiə] fotokopieerapparaat[h]

photocopy [footookoppie] fotokopie

photogenic [footoodzjɛnnik] fotogeniek

¹photograph [footəgra:f] *n* foto

²photograph [footəgra:f] *vb* fotograferen, foto's maken, een foto nemen van

photographer [fətogrəfə] fotograaf

photography [fətogrəfie] fotografie

¹phrase [freez] *n* 1 gezegde[h], uitdrukking, woordgroep, zinsdeel[h]; 2 uitdrukkingswijze, bewoordingen: *a turn of* ~ een uitdrukking; *he has quite a turn of* ~ hij kan zich heel goed uitdrukken; *coin a* ~ een uitdrukking bedenken

²phrase [freez] *vb* uitdrukken, formuleren, onder woorden brengen

phraseology [freezie·ollədzjie] idioom[h], woordkeus: *scientific* ~ wetenschappelijk jargon

physical [fizzikl] 1 fysiek, natuurlijk, lichamelijk: ~ *education* lichamelijke oefening, gymnastiek; ~ *exercise* lichaamsbeweging; 2 materieel; 3 natuurkundig, fysisch: *a ~ impossibility* absolute onmogelijkheid

physician [fizzisjən] arts, geneesheer *(oft as opposed to surgeon)*, internist

physicist [fizzissist] natuurkundige

physics [fizziks] natuurkunde

physio [fizzie·oo] 1 fysiotherapeut(e); 2 fysio(therapie)

physiognomy [fizzie·ɔnnəmie] 1 gezicht[h]; 2 kenmerk[h], kenteken[h]

physiology [fizzi·ollədzjie] 1 fysiologie, leer van de lichaamsfuncties van mensen en dieren; 2 levensfuncties

physiotherapist [fizzie·ooθɛrrəpist] fysiotherapeut(e)

physique [fizzie:k] lichaamsbouw

pi [paj] pi *(also maths)*

pianist [piənist] pianist(e)

piano [pie·ænoo] piano

pic [pik] *picture* 1 foto, plaatje[h], illustratie; 2 film

¹pick [pik] *vb* 1 (zorgvuldig) kiezen, selecteren, uitzoeken: ~ *one's words* zijn woorden zorgvuldig kiezen; ~ *and choose* kieskeurig zijn; 2 plukken, oogsten; 3 pikken *(of birds)*; 4 met kleine hapjes eten, peuzelen (aan): ~ *at a meal* zitten te kieskauwen; ~ *over: a)* de beste halen uit; *b)* doorzeuren; ~ *at: a)* plukken aan; *b)* vitten *(of:* hakken) op; ~ *on* vitten op

²pick [pik] *vb* 1 hakken (in), prikken, opensteken *(lock):* ~ *a hole in* een gat maken in; 2 peuteren in *(eg teeth)*, wroeten in, pulken in *(nose)*; 3 afkluiven, kluiven op, ontdoen van *(meat):* ~ *off* één voor één neerslachten

³pick [pik] *n* 1 pikhouweel[h]; 2 keus: *take your* ~ zoek maar uit, kies maar welke je wilt; *the* ~ het beste, het puikje; *the* ~ *of the bunch* het neusje van de zalm

¹picket [pikkit] *n* 1 paal, staak; 2 post(er), een staker die werkwilligen tegenhoudt

²picket [pikkit] *vb* posten, postend bewaken: *~ a factory* een bedrijf posten

picket line groep posters *(at strike)*

pickle [pikl] **1** pekel *(also fig)*, moeilijk parket^h, knoei: *be in a sorry (of: fine) ~* zich in een moeilijk parket bevinden; **2** zuur^h, azijn: *vegetables in ~* groenten in het zuur; **3** *~s* tafelzuur^h, zoetzuur^h

pickled [pikld] **1** ingelegd (in zuur, zout); **2** in de olie, lazarus

pick out 1 (uit)kiezen, eruit halen, uitpikken; **2** onderscheiden, zien, ontdekken; **3** doen uitkomen, afsteken

pickpocket zakkenroller

¹pick up *vb* **1** oppakken, opnemen, oprapen: *~ your feet* til je voeten op; *pick oneself up* overeind krabbelen; **2** opdoen, oplopen, oppikken: *~ speed* vaart vermeerderen; *he picked her up in a bar* hij heeft haar in een bar opgepikt; *where did you pick that up?* waar heb je dat geleerd?; **3** ontvangen; opvangen *(radio or light signals)*; **4** ophalen, een lift geven, meenemen: *I'll pick you up at seven* ik kom je om zeven uur ophalen; **5** (terug)vinden, terugkrijgen: *~ the trail* het spoor terugvinden; **6** (bereid zijn te) betalen *(account)*; **7** weer beginnen, hervatten: *~ the threads* de draad weer opvatten; **8** beter worden, opknappen, er bovenop komen, *(econ)* opleven, aantrekken: *the weather is picking up* het weer wordt weer beter

²pick up *vb* vaart krijgen, aanwakkeren *(of wind)*

pick-up 1 (taxi)passagier, lifter, *(inf)* scharreltje^h; **2** open bestelauto

pick-up truck open bestelauto

picky [pikkie] kieskeurig

¹picnic [piknik] *n* picknick || *it is no ~* het valt niet mee, het is geen pretje

²picnic [piknik] *vb* picknicken

¹picture [piktsjə] *n* **1** afbeelding, schilderij, plaat, prent, schets, foto; **2** plaatje^h, iets beeldschoons; **3** toonbeeld^h: *he is the (very) ~ of health* hij blaakt van gezondheid; **4** (speel)film: *go to the ~s* naar de bioscoop gaan; **5** beeld^h *(on TV)*: *come into the ~* een rol gaan spelen; *put s.o. in the ~* iem op de hoogte brengen

²picture [piktsjə] *vb* **1** afbeelden, schilderen, beschrijven: *~ to oneself* zich voorstellen; **2** zich voorstellen, zich inbeelden

picture gallery schilderijenkabinet^h, galerie voor schilderijen

picturesque [piktsjərɛsk] schilderachtig

piddle [pidl] een plasje doen || *stop piddling around* schiet toch eens op

piddling [pidling] belachelijk (klein), onbenullig, te verwaarlozen

pidgin [pidzjin] mengtaal *(on basis of English)*

pie [paj] **1** pastei; **2** taart

¹piebald [pajbo:ld] *adj* gevlekt *(esp black and white)*, bont

²piebald [pajbo:ld] *n* gevlekt dier^h, bont paard^h

¹piece [pie:s] *n* **1** stuk^h, portie, brok^h, onderdeel^h,

deel^h *(also techn)*, stukje^h (land), lapje^h, eindje^h, schaakstuk^h, damschijf, muntstuk^h, geldstuk^h, artikel^h, muziekstuk^h, toneelstuk^h, *(mil)* kanon^h, geweer^h: *five cents a ~* vijf cent per stuk; *a good ~ of advice* een goede raad; *~ of (good) luck* buitenkansje; *that is a fine ~ of work* dat ziet er prachtig uit; *come (all) to ~s* (helemaal) kapot gaan, instorten, in elkaar vallen; *say (of: speak, state) one's ~* zijn zegje doen, zeggen wat men te zeggen heeft; *in ~s* in stukken; *be all of a ~ with ...* helemaal van hetzelfde slag zijn als ..., uit hetzelfde hout gesneden zijn als ...; *of a ~ in* één stuk; **2** staaltje^h, voorbeeld^h: *(nasty) ~ of work* (gemene) vent *(of: griet)*; *give s.o. a ~ of one's mind* iem flink de waarheid zeggen; *pick up the ~s* de stukken lijmen

²piece [pie:s] *vb* samenvoegen, in elkaar zetten: *~ together* aaneenhechten, aaneenvoegen, in elkaar zetten *(story)*

piecemeal [pie:smie:l] stuksgewijs, geleidelijk, bij stukjes en beetjes

pie chart cirkeldiagram^h, taartdiagram^h

pied [pajd] bont, gevlekt || *the Pied Piper (of Hamelin)* de rattenvanger van Hameln

pier [piə] **1** pier, havenhoofd^h; **2** pijler, brugpijler

pierce [piəs] doordringen, doorboren: *~d ears* gaatjes in de oren

piercing [piəsing] **1** doordringend, onderzoekend *(also of look)*; **2** scherp, snijdend *(wind, cold)*, stekend *(pain)*, snerpend *(sound)*

piety [pajjətie] vroomheid, trouw *(to parents, relatives)*

piffling [pifling] belachelijk (klein), waardeloos, onbenullig

pig [pig] **1** varken^h, (wild) zwijn^h; **2** *(inf)* varken^h *(term of abuse)*, gulzigaard, hufter; **3** *(Am)* big; **4** smeris || *be ~(gy) in the middle* tussen twee vuren zitten; *bleed like a (stuck) ~* bloeden als een rund; *buy a ~ in a poke* een kat in de zak kopen; *and ~s might fly!* ja, je kan me nog meer vertellen!; *make a ~ of oneself* overdadig eten (en drinken), schransen

pigeon [pidzjin] **1** duif; **2** kleiduif || *it is not my ~* het zijn mijn zaken niet

¹pigeon-hole *n* loket^h, hokje^h, (post)vakje^h

²pigeon-hole *vb* **1** in een vakje leggen *(document)*, opbergen; **2** in de ijskast stoppen, opzijleggen, op de lange baan schuiven; **3** in een hokje stoppen, een etiket opplakken

piggery [pigərie] **1** varkensfokkerij; **2** varkensstal; zwijnerij

piggy [pigie] big, varkentje^h || *be ~ in the middle* tussen twee vuren zitten

piggyback [pigiebæk] ritje^h op de rug

pig-headed koppig, eigenwijs

pigment [pigmənt] pigment^h

pigmentation [pigməntee:sjən] **1** huidkleuring; **2** kleuring

pigtail (haar)vlecht, staartje^h

pike [pajk] **1** piek, spies; **2** snoek

¹pile [pajl] *n* **1** (hei)paal, staak, pijler; **2** stapel, hoop:

~ *of books* stapels boeken; **3** hoop geld, fortuin^h: *he has made his* ~ hij is binnen; **4** aambei; **5** (kern)reactor; **6** pool *(on velvet, carpet)*, pluis^h

²pile [pajl] *vb* zich ophopen: ~ *in* binnenstromen, binnendrommen; ~ *up* zich opstapelen

³pile [pajl] *vb* (op)stapelen, beladen ‖ ~ *it on (thick)* overdrijven

pile driver 1 heimachine; **2** harde slag *(in boxing)*, (harde) trap

pile-up 1 opeenstapeling, op(een)hoping; **2** kettingbotsing

pilfer [pilfə] stelen, pikken

pilferer [pilfərə] kruimeldief

pilgrim [pilgrim] pelgrim

pilgrimage [pilgrimmidzj] bedevaart, pelgrimstocht

pill [pil] **1** pil *(also fig)*, bittere pil: *sweeten the* ~ de pil vergulden; **2** (anticonceptie)pil: *be on the* ~ aan de pil zijn; **3** bal

¹pillage [pillidzj] *n* **1** plundering, roof; **2** buit

²pillage [pillidzj] *vb* plunderen, (be)roven

pillar [pillə] **1** (steun)pilaar, zuil *(also fig)*; **2** zuil, kolom *(smoke, water, air)* ‖ *driven from* ~ *to post* van het kastje naar de muur gestuurd

pillar box brievenbus *(of Post Office)*

pillbox 1 pillendoosje^h; **2** klein rond (dames)hoedje^h; **3** *(mil)* bunker

¹pillory [pillərie] *n* blok^h, schandpaal: *in the* ~ aan de schandpaal

²pillory [pillərie] *vb* aan de kaak stellen, hekelen

pillow [pilloo] (hoofd)kussen^h

pillowcase kussensloop

¹pilot [pajlət] *n* **1** loods; **2** piloot, vlieger: *on automatic* ~ op de automatische piloot; **3** gids, leider

²pilot [pajlət] *vb* loodsen, (be)sturen, vliegen, (ge)leiden *(also fig)*: ~ *a bill through Parliament* een wetsontwerp door het parlement loodsen

pilot light 1 waakvlam(metje^h); **2** controlelamp(je^h)

pilot project proefproject^h

pimp [pimp] pooier

pimple [pimpl] puist(je^h), pukkel

¹pin [pin] *n* **1** speld, sierspeld, broche; **2** pin, pen, stift, *(techn)* splitpen, bout, spie, nagel; **3** kegel *(bowling)*; **4** vlaggenstok *(in a hole at golf)* ‖ *I have* ~*s and needles in my arm* mijn arm slaapt

²pin [pin] *vb* **1** (vast)spelden, vastmaken *(with pin)*; **2** doorboren, doorsteken; **3** vasthouden, knellen, drukken: ~ *s.o. down* iem neerdrukken, iem op de grond houden; ~ *s.o. down on sth.* iem ergens op vastpinnen, iem ergens op ophangen

PIN [pin] *personal identification number* persoonlijk identificatienummer^h, pincode

pinball flipper(spel^h)

pincers [pinsəz] **1** (nijp)tang: *a pair of* ~ een nijptang; **2** schaar *(of lobster)*

¹pinch [pintsj] *vb* **1** knijpen, dichtknijpen, knellen, klemmen: ~*ed with anxiety* door zorgen gekweld; **2** verkleumen, verschrompelen: ~*ed with cold* verkleumd van de kou; **3** jatten, pikken, achterover

drukken; **4** inrekenen, in de kraag grijpen; **5** knellen, pijn doen: *these shoes* ~ *my toes* mijn tenen doen pijn in deze schoenen; **6** krenterig zijn, gierig zijn: ~ *and save (of: scrape)* kromliggen

²pinch [pintsj] *n* **1** kneep; **2** klem, nood(situatie): *feel the* ~ de nood voelen; **3** snuifje^h, klein beetje^h: *take sth. with a* ~ *of salt* iets met een korreltje zout nemen; *at a* ~ desnoods, in geval van nood

¹pine [pajn] *n* **1** pijn(boom); **2** vurenhout^h, grenenhout^h, dennenhout^h

²pine [pajn] *vb* **1** kwijnen, treuren: ~ *away (from sth.)* wegkwijnen (van iets); **2** (with *after*) smachten (naar), verlangen, hunkeren: ~ *to do sth.* ernaar hunkeren iets te doen

pineapple ananas

pine cone dennenappel, pijnappel

¹ping [ping] *n* ping, kort tinkelend geluid^h

²ping [ping] *vb* 'ping' doen *(make a short jingling sound)*

ping-pong pingpong^h, tafeltennis^h

pinhead 1 speldenkop; **2** kleinigheid; **3** sufferd

¹pinion [pinniən] *vb* **1** kortwieken; **2** binden, vastbinden *(arms)*, boeien *(hands)*

²pinion [pinniən] *n* **1** vleugelpunt^h; **2** *(techn)* rondsel^h, klein(ste) tandwiel^h

¹pink [pingk] *n* **1** anjelier, anjer; **2** roze(rood)^h; **3** puikje^h, toppunt^h, toonbeeld^h: *in the* ~ *(of health)* in blakende gezondheid

²pink [pingk] *adj* **1** roze: ~ *elephants* witte muizen, roze olifanten *(a drunk's hallucinations)*; **2** gematigd links: *be tickled* ~ bijzonder in zijn schik zijn

pinnacle [pinnəkl] **1** pinakel, siertorentje^h; **2** (berg)top, spits, piek, *(fig)* toppunt^h

pinny [pinnie] schort^h

¹pinpoint *n* **1** speldenpunt; **2** stipje^h, kleinigheid, puntje^h

²pinpoint *vb* uiterst nauwkeurig aanduiden

pinstripe(d) met dunne streepjes *(on material, suit)*, krijtstreep

pint [pajnt] **1** pint *(for liquid 0.568 litre, (Am) 0.473 litre)*; **2** pint, grote pils

pint-size(d) nietig, klein, minuscuul

pin-up pin-up, *(Belg)* prikkelpop

¹pioneer [pajjəniə] *n* pionier, voortrekker

²pioneer [pajjəniə] *vb* pionieren, pionierswerk verrichten (voor), de weg bereiden (voor)

pious [pajjəs] **1** vroom; **2** hypocriet, braaf; **3** vroom, onvervulbaar, ijdel: ~ *hope (of: wish)* ijdele hoop, vrome wens

¹pip [pip] *n* **1** oog^h *(on dice etc)*; **2** pit *(of fruit)*; **3** b(l)iep, tikje^h, toontje^h; **4** ster *(on uniform)*; **5** aanval van neerslachtigheid, humeurigheid: *she gives me the* ~ ze werkt op mijn zenuwen

²pip [pip] *vb* **1** neerknallen, raken; **2** verslaan

¹pipe [pajp] *n* **1** pijp, buis, leiding(buis), orgelpijp, tabakspijp: ~ *of peace* vredespijp; **2** ~*s* doedelzak(ken): *put that in your* ~ *and smoke it* die kun je in je zak steken

²pipe [pajp] *vb* **1** fluiten, op de doedelzak spelen; **2**

door buizen leiden; **3** door kabelverbinding overbrengen *(music, radio programme):* ~*d music* muziek in blik; ~ *down* zijn mond houden; ~ *up* beginnen te zingen

pipe dream droombeeldʰ, luchtkasteelʰ

pipeline 1 pijpleiding, oliepijpleiding; **2** toevoerkanaalʰ, informatiebron || *in the* ~ onderweg, op komst

piper [pajpə] fluitspeler, doedelzakspeler || *pay the* ~ het gelag betalen

¹**piping** [pajpiŋ] *n* **1** pijpleiding, buizennetʰ; **2** het fluitspelen, fluitspelʰ

²**piping** [pajpiŋ] *adj* schril *(voice)* || ~ *hot* kokend heet

piquant [pie:kənt] pikant, prikkelend

¹**pique** [pie:k] *n* gepikeerdheid, wrevel: *in a fit of* ~ in een kwaaie bui

²**pique** [pie:k] *vb* kwetsen *(pride),* irriteren || ~ *oneself (up)on sth.* op iets prat gaan

piracy [pajjərəsie] zeeroverij, piraterij *(also fig)*

¹**pirate** [pajjərət] *n* **1** piraat *(also fig),* zeerover; **2** zeeroversschipʰ

²**pirate** [pajjərət] *vb* **1** plunderen; **2** plagiëren, nadrukken, illegale kopieën maken van: ~*d edition* roofdruk

³**pirate** [pajjərət] *vb* aan zeeroverij doen

Pisces [pajsie:z] *(astrology)* (de) Vissen

¹**piss** [pis] *n (vulg)* pis || *take the* ~ *out of s.o.* iem voor de gek houden; *are you taking the* ~? zit je mij nou in de maling te nemen?

²**piss** [pis] *vb (vulg)* (be)pissen || ~ *about* (of: *around)* rotzooien; *it is* ~*ing (down)* het stortregent; ~ *off* oprotten

pissed [pist] **1** bezopen; **2** kwaad: *be* ~ *off at s.o.* woest zijn op iem

pistil [pistil] *(bot)* stamper

pistol [pistl] pistoolʰ

piston [pistən] *(techn)* zuiger

¹**pit** [pit] *n* **1** kuil, put, (kolen)mijn(schacht); **2** dierenkuil; **3** kuiltjeʰ, putjeʰ; **4** werkkuil, pits *(at racetrack);* **5** orkestbak, parterre *(theatre);* **6** nestʰ *(bed);* **7** *(Am)* pit, steen *(of fruit);* **8** *the* ~*s* (een) ramp, (een) verschrikking: *do you know that town? it's the* ~*s!* ken je die stad? erger kan niet!

²**pit** [pit] *vb* als tegenstander opstellen, uitspelen: ~ *one's strength against s.o.* zijn krachten met iem meten

¹**pitch** [pitsj] *n* **1** worp: *(fig) make a* ~ *for sth.* een gooi naar iets doen; **2** hoogte, intensiteit, top(puntʰ), *(mus)* toon(hoogte); **3** *(sport)* (sport)terreinʰ, veldʰ, *(cricket)* grasmat; **4** (slim) verkoopverhaalʰ, verkooppraat(jeʰ); **5** standplaats, stalletjeʰ, stek; **6** schuinte, (dak)helling; **7** pekᵗʰ

²**pitch** [pitsj] *vb* **1** afhellen, aflopen *(of roof);* **2** strompelen, slingeren || ~ *in(to)* aan het werk gaan

³**pitch** [pitsj] *vb* **1** opslaan *(tent, camp);* **2** doen afhellen *(roof):* ~*ed roof* schuin dak; **3** op toon stemmen, (toon) aangeven

pitch-dark pikdonker

pitcher [pitsjə] **1** grote (aarden) kruik, *(Am)* kan; **2** *(baseball)* werper

pitchfork hooivork

piteous [pittiəs] meelijwekkend, zielig

pitfall valkuil, *(fig)* valstrik

pitiful [pittiffoel] **1** zielig; **2** armzalig

pittance [pittəns] hongerloonʰ: *a mere* ~ een bedroevend klein beetje

¹**pity** [pittie] *n* **1** medelijdenʰ; **2** betreurenswaardig feitʰ: *it is a thousand pities* het is ontzettend jammer; *what a* ~! wat jammer!; *more's the* ~ jammer genoeg

²**pity** [pittie] *vb* medelijden hebben met: *she is much to be pitied* zij is zeer te beklagen

¹**pivot** [pivvət] *n* spil, draaipuntʰ, *(fig)* centrale figuur

²**pivot** [pivvət] *vb* om een spil draaien, *(fig)* draaien: ~ *(up)on sth.* om iets draaien

pix [piks] **1** foto's; **2** film, de filmindustrie

pixie [piksie] fee, elf

pizza [pie:tsə] pizza

pizzazz [pizæz] pit, lefʰ

pl. 1 *place* plaats; **2** *plural* mv., meervoud

placard [plæka:d] plakkaatʰ, aanplakbiljetʰ, protestbordʰ *(of protester)*

placate [pləkeet] tot bedaren brengen, gunstig stemmen

¹**place** [plees] *n* **1** plaats, ruimte: *change* ~*s with s.o.* met iem van plaats verwisselen; *fall into* ~ duidelijk zijn; *lay* (of: *set) a* ~ *for s.o.* voor iem dekken; *put s.o. in his* ~ iem op zijn plaats zetten; *take* ~ plaatsvinden; *take s.o.'s* ~ iemands plaats innemen; *out of* ~ misplaatst, niet passend (of: geschikt); *all over the* ~ overal (rondslingerend); *in the first* ~ in de eerste plaats; **2** (woon)plaats, woning, pleinʰ: *come round to my* ~ *some time* kom eens (bij mij) langs; **3** gelegenheid *(pub etc):* ~ *of worship* kerk, kapel, e.d.; **4** passage *(in book);* **5** stand, rang, positie: *know one's* ~ zijn plaats kennen; **6** taak, functie

²**place** [plees] *vb* **1** plaatsen, zetten: ~ *an order for goods* goederen bestellen; **2** aanstellen, een betrekking geven; **3** thuisbrengen, identificeren

placebo [pləsie:boo] *(also* ~*es)* nepgeneesmiddelʰ, zoethoudertjeʰ

placement [pleesmənt] plaatsing

placid [plæsid] vreedzaam, kalm

plagiarism [pleedzjiərizm] plagiaatʰ

¹**plague** [pleeg] *n* **1** plaag, teistering; **2** pest: *avoid s.o. (sth.) like the* ~ iem (iets) schuwen als de pest; **3** lastpost

²**plague** [pleeg] *vb* **1** teisteren, treffen; **2** *(with with)* lastig vallen (met), pesten

plaice [plees] **1** schol; **2** *(Am)* platvis

¹**plaid** [plæd] *n* plaid

²**plaid** [plæd] *adj* plaid-, met Schots patroon

¹**plain** [pleen] *adj* **1** duidelijk: *in* ~ *language* in duidelijke taal; **2** simpel, onvermengd, puur *(water, whisky etc):* ~ *flour* bloem *(without baking powder);* **3** ronduit, oprecht: ~ *dealing* eerlijk(heid); **4** vlak, ef-

plain

fen; **5** recht *(knitting stitch);* **6** volslagen, totaal *(nonsense): it's ~ foolishness* het is je reinste dwaasheid; *it was ~ sailing all the way* het liep allemaal van een leien dakje

²**plain** [pleen] *n* vlakte, prairie

³**plain** [pleen] *adv* **1** duidelijk; **2** ronduit

plain-clothes in burger(kleren)

plainly [ple̲enlie] **1** ronduit: *speak ~* ronduit spreken; **2** zonder meer: *it is ~ clear* het is zonder meer duidelijk

plaintiff [ple̲entif] aanklager, eiser

plaintive [ple̲entiv] **1** klagend; **2** treurig, triest

¹**plait** [plæt] *n* vlecht

²**plait** [plæt] *vb* vlechten

¹**plan** [plæn] *n* **1** plan[h]: *what are your ~s for tonight?* wat ga je vanavond doen?; **2** plattegrond; **3** ontwerp[h], opzet: *~ of action* (of: *campaign, battle)* plan de campagne; **4** schema[h], ontwerp[h]

²**plan** [plæn] *vb* plannen maken: *he hadn't ~ned for* (of: *on) so many guests* hij had niet op zoveel gasten gerekend; *~ on doing sth.* er op rekenen iets te (kunnen) doen

³**plan** [plæn] *vb* **1** in kaart brengen, schetsen, ontwerpen; **2** plannen, van plan zijn: *he had it all ~ned out* hij had alles tot in de details geregeld

¹**plane** [pleen] *n* **1** plataan[h]; **2** schaaf; **3** vlak[h], draagvlak[h], vleugel *(of aeroplane);* **4** niveau[h], plan[h] *(also fig);* **5** vliegtuig[h]

²**plane** [pleen] *adj* vlak, plat: *~ geometry* vlakke meetkunde

³**plane** [pleen] *vb* **1** glijden, zweven *(of aeroplane);* **2** schaven, effen maken

planet [plænit] planeet

planetarium [plænitte̲əriəm] planetarium[h]

plank [plængk] (zware) plank

plankton [plængktən] plankton[h]

planner [plænə] ontwerper; *(urban development)* planoloog

planning [plæning] planning, ordening

¹**plant** [pla:nt] *n* **1** plant, gewas[h]; **2** fabriek, bedrijf[h], *(electr)* centrale; **3** machinerie, uitrusting, installatie; **4** doorgestoken kaart, vals bewijsmateriaal[h]

²**plant** [pla:nt] *vb* **1** planten, poten *(also fish),* aanplanten; **2** (met kracht) neerzetten *(feet),* plaatsen: *with one's feet ~ed (firmly) on the ground* met beide voeten (stevig) op de grond; **3** zaaien *(only fig);* **4** onderschuiven, verbergen *(stolen goods),* laten opdraaien voor: *~ false evidence* vals bewijsmateriaal onderschuiven

plantain [plæntin] weegbree

plantation [plænte̲esjən] **1** beplanting, aanplant; **2** plantage

planter [pla:ntə] **1** planter, plantagebezitter; **2** bloembak, bloempot

plaque [pla:k] **1** plaat, gedenkplaat; **2** vlek *(on skin);* **3** tandaanslag

plasma [plæzmə] plasma[h]

¹**plaster** [pla:stə] *n* **1** (hecht)pleister; **2** pleister(kalk); **3** gips[h]: *~ of Paris* (gebrande) gips

²**plaster** [pla:stə] *vb* **1** (be)pleisteren, bedekken: *~ make-up on one's face* zich zwaar opmaken, z'n gezicht plamuren; *~ over* (of: *up)* dichtpleisteren; **2** verpletteren, inmaken

plasterer [pla:stərə] stukadoor

¹**plastic** [plæstik] *n* plastic[h], kunststof

²**plastic** [plæstik] *adj* **1** plastisch; **2** plastic, synthetisch; **3** kunstmatig || *~ money* plastic geld *(with cheque card, credit card);* *~ surgery* plastische chirurgie

plate [pleet] **1** plaat(je[h]), naambordje[h], nummerbord[h], nummerplaat, *(geology)* plaat *(large piece of the earth's crust);* **2** bord[h], bordvol[h] *(food);* **3** collecteschaal; **4** zilveren (gouden) bestek[h], verzilverd bestek[h], pleet[h] || *give s.o. sth. on a ~* iem iets in de schoot werpen; *have enough on one's ~* genoeg om handen hebben

plateau [plætoo] plateau[h], tafelland[h], *(fig also)* stilstand *(in growth)*

plateful [ple̲etfoel] bordvol[h]

platform [plætfo:m] **1** platform[h]; **2** podium[h]; **3** balkon[h] *(of bus, tram);* **4** perron[h]; **5** partijprogramma[h], politiek programma[h]

platinum [plætinnəm] platina[h]

platitude [plætitjoe:d] open deur, afgezaagde waarheid

platoon [plətoe̲:n] peloton[h]

platter [plætə] plat bord[h], platte schotel || *on a ~* op een gouden schotel

plausible [plo̲:zibl] **1** plausibel, aannemelijk; **2** bedrieglijk overtuigend

¹**play** [plee] *vb* **1** spelen: *a smile ~ed on her lips* een glimlach speelde om haar lippen; *~ hide-and-seek, ~ at soldiers* verstoppertje (of: soldaatje) spelen; *~ by ear* op het gehoor spelen, *(fig)* op zijn gevoel afgaan; **2** werken, spuiten *(fountain);* **3** zich vermaken; **4** aan zet zijn *(chess);* **5** glinsteren, flikkeren *(light):* *~ about* (of: *around)* stoeien, aanklooien; *what on earth are you ~ing at?* wat heeft dit allemaal te betekenen?; *~ (up)on s.o.'s feelings* op iemands gevoelens werken

²**play** [plee] *vb* **1** spelen, bespelen, opvoeren *(play),* draaien *(gramophone record, CD):* *~ back a tape* een band afspelen; **2** richten, spuiten *(water);* **3** uitvoeren, uithalen *(joke):* *~ s.o. a trick* iem een streek leveren; **4** verwedden, inzetten; **5** *(sport)* opstellen *(player):* *~ s.o. along* iem aan het lijntje houden; *~ sth. down* iets als minder belangrijk voorstellen

³**play** [plee] *n* **1** spel[h]: *~ (up)on words* woordspeling; *allow full* (of: *free) ~ to sth.* iets vrij spel laten; **2** toneelstuk[h]: *the ~s of Shakespeare* de stukken van Shakespeare; **3** beurt, zet, *(Am; esp sport)* manoeuvre: *make a ~ for sth.* iets proberen te krijgen; **4** actie, activiteit, beweging: *bring (of: call) into ~* erbij betrekken; **5** *(techn)* speling: *make great ~ of* erg de nadruk leggen op, sterk benadrukken

play-act doen alsof, toneelspelen

playback 1 opname op tape; **2** weergavetoets

playbill affiche[h] *(for theatre performance)*

playboy playboy

player [pleeə] speler

playful [pleefoel] speels, vrolijk

playgoer [pleegooə] schouwburgbezoeker

playground speelplaats

playgroup peuterklasjeʰ

playhouse 1 schouwburg; **2** poppenhuisʰ

playmate 1 speelkameraad; **2** pin-up

¹play off vb de beslissingsmatch spelen

²play off vb uitspelen: *he played his parents off (against each other)* hij speelde zijn ouders tegen elkaar uit

play-off beslissingsmatch

play out 1 beëindigen *(game; also fig)*: ~ *time* op veilig spelen, geen risico's nemen; **2** helemaal uitspelen; **3** uitbeelden: *played out* afgedaan, uitgeput

playpen box *(for small children)*

play up 1 last bezorgen: *my leg is playing up again* ik heb weer last van mijn been; **2** benadrukken: ~ *to s.o.* iem vleien, iem naar de mond praten

playwright toneelschrijver

PLC *Public Limited Company* NV, Naamloze Vennootschap

plea [plie:] **1** smeekbede; **2** verweerʰ, pleidooiʰ

¹plead [plie:d] vb **1** pleiten, zich verdedigen: ~ *guilty* schuld bekennen; **2** smeken, dringend verzoeken: ~ *with s.o. for sth.* (of: *to do sth.*) iem dringend verzoeken iets te doen

²plead [plie:d] vb **1** bepleiten; **2** aanvoeren *(as defence, apology)*, zich beroepen op: ~ *ignorance* onwetendheid voorwenden

pleasant [pleznt] **1** aangenaam: ~ *room* prettige kamer; **2** aardig, sympathiek; **3** mooi *(weather)*

¹please [plie:z] vb **1** naar de zin maken, tevredenstellen; **2** wensen: *do as you* ~! doe zoals je wilt!; ~ *yourself!* ga je gang!

²please [plie:z] *interj* **1** alstublieft: *may I come in,* ~? mag ik alstublieft binnenkomen?; **2** alstublieft, wees zo goed: *do come in,* ~! komt u toch binnen, alstublieft!; **3** graag *(dank u)*: '*A beer?*' '*Yes,* ~' '*Een biertje?*' 'Ja, graag'

pleased [plie:zd] tevreden, blij: *he was* ~ *as Punch* hij was de koning te rijk

pleasing [plie:zing] **1** aangenaam, innemend; **2** bevredigend

pleasure [pleʒə] genoegenʰ, plezierʰ: *take great* ~ *in sth.* plezier hebben in iets; *with* ~ met genoegen, graag

¹pleat [plie:t] n platte plooi, vouw

²pleat [plie:t] vb plooien: ~*ed skirt* plooirok

¹plebeian [plibbie:ən] adj proleterig, onbeschaafd

²plebeian [plibbie:ən] n proleet

¹pledge [pledzj] n **1** pandʰ, onderpandʰ; **2** plechtige belofte, gelofte

²pledge [pledzj] vb **1** verpanden, belenen; **2** een toast uitbrengen op, toasten op; **3** plechtig beloven, (ver)binden: ~ *allegiance to* trouw zweren aan; ~ *oneself* zich (op erewoord) verbinden

plenary [plie:nərie] **1** volkomen, volledig: *with* ~

powers met volmacht(en); **2** plenair, voltallig: ~ *assembly* plenaire vergadering

plentiful [plentiffoel] overvloedig

¹plenty [plentie] n overvloed || *he has* ~ *going for him* alles loopt hem mee

²plenty [plentie] adj overvloedig, genoeg

³plenty [plentie] adv ruimschoots

pliable [plajjəbl] buigzaam, plooibaar, *(fig)* gedwee

pliant [plajjənt] buigzaam, soepel, *(fig)* gedwee

pliers [plajjəz] buigtang, combinatietang: *a pair of* ~ een buigtang

plight [plajt] (benarde) toestand: *a sorry* (of: *hopeless*) ~ een hopeloze toestand

plimsoll [plimsl] gymschoen, gympieʰ

¹plod [plod] vb ploeteren, zwoegen: ~ *away all night* de hele nacht door zwoegen

²plod [plod] vb afsjokken: ~ *one's way* zich voortslepen

plodding [plodding] moeizaam

¹plop [plop] n plons, floep, plof *(in water)*

²plop [plop] vb met een plons (doen) neervallen, (laten) plonzen

³plop [plop] adv met een plons

¹plot [plot] n **1** stukʰ grond, perceelʰ; **2** intrige, plot *(of play, novel)*, complotʰ; **3** *(Am)* plattegrond, kaart, diagramʰ

²plot [plot] vb samenzweren, plannen smeden

³plot [plot] vb **1** in kaart brengen, intekenen, uitzetten *(graph, diagram)*; **2** (also with *out*) in percelen indelen *(land)*; **3** beramen, smeden *(conspiracy)*

¹plough [plau] n ploeg

²plough [plau] vb ploegen, *(fig)* ploeteren, zwoegen: ~ *through the snow* zich door de sneeuw heen worstelen

³plough [plau] vb (om)ploegen: ~ *one's way through sth.* zich (moeizaam) een weg banen door iets; ~ *back profits into equipment* winsten in apparatuur (her)investeren

plow [plau] *(Am)* ploeg

ploy [ploj] truc(jeʰ), list

¹pluck [pluk] vb **1** (with *at*) rukken (aan), trekken (aan); **2** tokkelen

²pluck [pluk] vb **1** plukken *(chicken etc; also flowers)*, trekken; **2** tokkelen op

³pluck [pluk] n **1** moed, durf, lefʰ; **2** het plukken *(of chicken etc)*

plucky [plukkie] dapper, moedig

¹plug [plug] n **1** stop, prop, pen; **2** stekker; **3** pruim, pluk tabak; **4** aanbeveling, reclame, spot, gunstige publiciteit *(on radio, TV)* || *pull the* ~ *on sth.* iets niet laten doorgaan, een eind maken aan iets

²plug [plug] vb **1** (also with *up*) (op)vullen, dichtstoppen; **2** neerknallen, neerschieten, beschieten; **3** pluggen, reclame maken voor, populair maken *(on radio, TV)*, voortdurend draaien *(gramophone records)* || ~ *in* aansluiten, de stekker insteken

plughole afvoer, gootsteengatʰ

plum [plum] **1** pruim; **2** pruimenboom; **3** donkerroodʰ, donkerpaarsʰ; **4** iets heel goeds, iets begerenswaardigs, het neusje van de zalm

plumage [ploe:midzj] veren(kleed[h]) *(of bird)*

[1]**plumb** [plum] *vb* **1** loden, peilen met dieplood, meten met schietlood; **2** verticaal zetten, loodrecht maken; **3** (trachten te) doorgronden, peilen

[2]**plumb** [plum] *adj* **1** loodrecht; **2** *(Am)* uiterst: *~ nonsense* je reinste onzin

[3]**plumb** [plum] *adv* **1** loodrecht, precies in het lood: *~ in the middle* precies in het midden; **2** *(Am)* volkomen

[4]**plumb** [plum] *n* (loodje[h] van) schietlood[h], paslood[h]: *off* (of: *out*) *of ~* niet loodrecht, niet in het lood

plumber [plummə] loodgieter, gas- en waterfitter

plumbing [plumming] loodgieterswerk[h], (het aanleggen ve) systeem van afvoerbuizen

plumcake rozijnencake, krentencake

plume [ploe:m] **1** pluim, (sier)veer, vederbos; **2** pluim, sliert, wolkje[h]: *a ~ of smoke* een rookpluim

[1]**plummet** [plummit] *vb* (also with *down*) pijlsnel vallen, scherp dalen, instorten, neerstorten: *prices ~ed* de prijzen kelderden

[2]**plummet** [plummit] *n* (loodje[h] van) loodlijn, (gewicht[h] van) dieplood[h], schietlood[h]

plummy [plummie] **1** (zeer) goed, begerenswaardig: *a ~ job* een vet baantje; **2** vol *(of voice)*, te vol, geaffecteerd

plump stevig *(oft euph)*, rond, mollig

[1]**plump down** *vb* neerploffen, neervallen, neerzakken

[2]**plump down** *vb* (plotseling) neergooien, neerploffen, neerkwakken, laten vallen

[1]**plunder** [plundə] *vb* (be)stelen, (be)roven, plunderen

[2]**plunder** [plundə] *n* **1** plundering, roof, beroving; **2** buit

[1]**plunge** [plundzj] *vb* **1** zich werpen, duiken, zich storten; **2** (plotseling) neergaan, dalen, steil aflopen; **3** (with *into*) binnenvallen

[2]**plunge** [plundzj] *vb* werpen, (onder)dompelen, storten: *he was ~d into grief* hij werd door verdriet overmand

[3]**plunge** [plundzj] *n* duik, sprong || *take the ~* de knoop doorhakken, de sprong wagen

[1]**plunk** [plungk] *vb* neerploffen, luidruchtig (laten) vallen: *~ down* neersmijten, neergooien

[2]**plunk** [plungk] *adv* **1** met een plof; **2** precies, juist: *~ in the middle* precies in het midden

[1]**plural** [ploeərəl] *adj* meervoudig, meervouds-

[2]**plural** [ploeərəl] *n* meervoud[h], meervoudsvorm

[1]**plus** [plus] *prep* plus, (vermeerderd) met, en, boven nul: *he paid back the loan ~ interest* hij betaalde de lening terug met de rente; *~ six (degrees centigrade)* zes graden boven nul

[2]**plus** [plus] *n (Am also ~ses)* **1** plus, plusteken[h]; **2** pluspunt[h], voordeel[h]

[3]**plus** [plus] *adj* **1** *(maths)* plus, groter dan nul; **2** *(electr)* plus, positief; **3** ten minste, minimaal, meer (ouder) dan: *she has got beauty ~* ze is meer dan

knap; *you have to be twelve ~ for this* hier moet je twaalf of ouder voor zijn

[1]**plush** [plusj] *adj* **1** pluchen, van pluche; **2** sjiek, luxueus

[2]**plush** [plusj] *n* pluche[h]

plus sign plus, plusteken[h], het symbool +

[1]**ply** [plaj] *n* **1** *(oft in compounds)* laag *(of wood or double material)*, vel[h] *(of thin wood)*: *three-ply wood* triplex; **2** streng, draad *(of rope, wool)*

[2]**ply** [plaj] *vb* (with *between*) een bepaalde route regelmatig afleggen *(of bus, ship etc)*, pendelen (tussen), geregeld heen en weer rijden (varen) (tussen) || *~ for hire* passagiers opzoeken *(of taxi)*

[3]**ply** [plaj] *vb* geregeld bevaren, pendelen over

ply with (voortdurend) volstoppen met *(food, drink)*, (doorlopend) voorzien van || *they plied the M.P. with questions* ze bestookten het kamerlid met vragen

plywood triplex[+h], multiplex[+h]

p.m. *post meridiem* n.m., 's middags

P.M. *Prime Minister* MP, minister-president

pneumatic [njoe:mætik] pneumatisch, lucht(druk)-: *~ drill* lucht(druk)boor

pneumonia [njoe:mooniə] longontsteking

po [poo] po

[1]**poach** [pootsj] *vb* stropen, illegaal vissen (jagen): *~ on s.o.'s preserve(s)* zich op andermans gebied begeven, *(fig)* aan iemands bezit *(of:* zaken, werk) komen

[2]**poach** [pootsj] *vb* **1** pocheren *(egg, fish)*; **2** stropen *(game, fish)*; **3** *(sport)* afpakken *(ball)*

P.O. Box *Post Office Box* postbus

[1]**pocket** [pokkit] *n* **1** zak; **2** (opberg)vak[h], voorvakje[h], map; **3** financiële middelen, portemonnee, inkomen[h]; **4** ertsader, olieader; **5** klein afgesloten gebied[h], *(mil)* haard; **6** zakformaat[h] || *have s.o. in one's ~* iem volledig in zijn macht hebben; *have sth. in one's ~* ergens (bijna) in geslaagd zijn; *I was twenty dollars out of ~* ik ben twintig dollar kwijtgeraakt

[2]**pocket** [pokkit] *vb* **1** in zijn zak steken, in eigen zak steken; **2** opstrijken, (op oneerlijke wijze) ontvangen *(money)*

pocketbook 1 zakboekje[h], notitieboekje[h]; **2** portefeuille; **3** *(Am)* pocket(boek[h]), paperback; **4** *(Am)* (dames)handtas

pockmark [pokma:k] **1** pokput; **2** put, gat[h], holte

pockmarked [pokma:kt] **1** pokdalig; **2** vol gaten, met kuilen of holen

pod [pod] peul(enschil), (peul)dop, huls

podgy [podzjie] rond, klein en dik, propperig

podium [poodiəm] podium[h], (voor)toneel[h]

poem [pooim] gedicht[h], vers[h]

poet [pooit] dichter

poetess [pooittes] dichteres

poetic(al) [pooëttik(l)] dichterlijk, poëtisch: *poetic licence* dichterlijke vrijheid

poetry [pooitrie] poëzie, dichtkunst

poignant [pojnjənt] **1** scherp *(of taste, emotions)*, schrijnend; **2** aangrijpend, ontroerend, gevoelig

¹**point** [pojnt] *n* **1** punt^h, stip, plek, decimaalteken^h, komma: *in English a decimal ~ is used to indicate a fraction*: 8.5 in het Engels wordt een decimaalpunt gebruikt om een breuk aan te geven: 8.5; **2** (waarderings)punt^h, cijfer^h: *be beaten on ~s* op punten verliezen; **3** (puntig) uiteinde^h, (land)punt, tak *(antlers)*, uitsteeksel^h; **4** punt^h, kwestie: *the main ~* de hoofdzaak; **5** karakteristiek, eigenschap: *that's his strong ~* dat is zijn sterke kant; **6** zin, bedoeling, effect^h: *get* (of: *see*) *the ~ of sth.* iets snappen; **7** (kompas)streek; **8** punt^h *(exact location, time etc)*, kern, essentie: *the ~ of the joke* de clou van de grap; *~ of view* gezichtspunt, standpunt; *come* (of: *get*) *to the ~* ter zake komen; *you have a ~ there* daar heb je gelijk in, daar zit iets in; *I always make a ~ of being in time* ik zorg er altijd voor op tijd te zijn; *I take your ~, ~ taken* ik begrijp wat je bedoelt; *that's beside the ~* dat heeft er niets mee te maken, dat staat er buiten; *on the ~ of* op het punt van; *that's (not) to the ~* dat is (niet) relevant; *up to a (certain) ~* tot op zekere hoogte; **9** *~s (railways)* wissel; **10** contactpunt^h, stopcontact^h: *in ~ of fact: a)* in werkelijkheid; *b)* bovendien, zelfs; *stretch a ~* niet al te nauw kijken, van de regel afwijken

²**point** [pojnt] *vb* **1** *(with at, towards)* gericht zijn (op), aandachtig zijn (op); **2** *(with at, to)* wijzen (naar), bewijzen: *~ to sth.* ergens naar wijzen, iets suggereren, iets bewijzen

³**point** [pojnt] *vb* **1** scherp maken; **2** *(with at, towards)* richten (op), (aan)wijzen: *~ out a mistake* een fout aanwijzen, een fout onder de aandacht brengen; **3** voegen *(brickwork)*

point-blank 1 van vlakbij, korte afstands-, regelrecht: *fire ~ at s.o.* van dichtbij op iem schieten; **2** rechtstreeks, (te) direct, bot: *a ~ refusal* een botte weigering

pointed [pojntid] **1** puntig, puntvormig; **2** scherp, venijnig: *a ~ answer* een bits antwoord; **3** nadrukkelijk, duidelijk, opvallend

pointer [pojntə] **1** wijzer *(on scales etc)*; **2** aanwijsstok; **3** aanwijzing, suggestie, advies^h; **4** pointer, staande hond

pointless [pojntləs] zinloos, onnodig, onbelangrijk

point out 1 wijzen naar: *~ sth. to s.o.* iem op iets attenderen; **2** naar voren brengen, in het midden ter sprake brengen: *~ s.o.'s responsibilities* iem zijn plichten voorhouden

poise [pojz] evenwicht^h, *(fig)* zelfverzekerdheid, zelfvertrouwen^h

poised [pojzd] **1** evenwichtig, stabiel, verstandig; **2** zwevend, *(fig)* in onzekerheid, balancerend: *he was ~ between life and death* hij zweefde tussen leven en dood; **3** stil (in de lucht hangend); **4** klaar, gereed: *be ~ for victory* op het punt staan om te winnen

¹**poison** [pojzn] *n* vergif^h, gif^h, *(fig)* schadelijke invloed

²**poison** [pojzn] *vb* **1** vergiftigen; **2** bederven *(atmosphere, mentality)*, verzieken: *their good relationship was ~ed by jealousy* hun goede verhouding

werd door jaloezie verpest

¹**poke** [pook] *vb* **1** porren, prikken, stoten: *~ one's nose into sth.* zijn neus ergens insteken; **2** (op)poken, (op)porren *(fire)*

²**poke** [pook] *vb* **1** *(with out, through)* te voorschijn komen, uitsteken; **2** *(with about)* (rond)lummelen; **3** *(with about)* zoeken, snuffelen, (rond)neuzen, zich bemoeien met iets

³**poke** [pook] *n* **1** por, prik, duw; **2** vuistslag

poker [pookə] **1** kachelpook, pook; **2** poker^h *(cards)*

poky [pookie] benauwd, klein

Poland [poolənd] Polen

polar [poolə] pool-, van de poolstreken: *~ bear* ijsbeer

pole [pool] **1** *Pole* Pool, iem van Poolse afkomst; **2** pool, *(fig)* tegenpool; **3** paal, mast, stok, vaarboom ‖ *drive s.o. up the ~* iem razend maken; *be ~s apart* onverzoenlijk zijn

polecat 1 bunzing *(in Europe)*; **2** stinkdier^h, skunk *(in America)*

polemic [pəlemmik] woordenstrijd, pennenstrijd, twist

pole star Poolster

pole vault polsstoksprong, het polsstok(hoog)springen

¹**police** [pəli:s] *n* politie, politiekorps^h, politieapparaat^h

²**police** [pəli:s] *vb* **1** onder politiebewaking stellen; **2** controleren, toezicht uitoefenen op

policeman [pəli:smən] politieagent ‖ *sleeping ~* verkeersdrempel

police station politiebureau^h

policy [pollissie] **1** beleid^h, gedragslijn, politiek; **2** polis, verzekeringspolis; **3** tactiek, verstand^h

polio [poolie-oo] polio, kinderverlamming

¹**polish** [pollisj] *vb* gaan glanzen, glanzend worden

²**polish** [pollisj] *vb* (also with *up*) (op)poetsen, polijsten *(also fig)*, bijschaven: *a ~ed performance* een perfecte voorstelling

³**polish** [pollisj] *n* **1** poetsmiddel^h; **2** glans, glimmend oppervlak^h; **3** beschaving, verfijning

polish off wegwerken, afraffelen

polite [pəlajt] **1** beleefd, goed gemanierd; **2** verfijnd, elegant

politic [pollittik] diplomatiek, verstandig

political [pəlittikl] **1** politiek, staatkundig; **2** overheids-, rijks-, staats-

politician [pollittisjən] (partij)politicus

politics [pollittiks] **1** politiek; **2** politieke wetenschappen, politicologie; **3** politieke overtuiging

¹**poll** [pool] *n* **1** stemming, het stemmen: *go to the ~s* stemmen; **2** aantal (uitgebrachte) stemmen, opkomst; **3** opiniepeiling; **4** *~s* stembureau^h

²**poll** [pool] *vb* zijn stem uitbrengen

³**poll** [pool] *vb* **1** krijgen, behalen *((preference) vote)*: *he ~ed thirty per cent of the votes* hij kreeg dertig procent van de stemmen; **2** ondervragen, een opiniepeiling houden

pollard [polləd] **1** geknotte boom; **2** *(cattle breed-*

pollen

ing) hoornloos dier[h]

pollen [pollən] stuifmeel[h]

pollination [pollinneesjən] bestuiving

polling booth stemhokje[h]

pollster [poolstə] enquêteur

poll tax personele belasting

pollute [pəloe:t] 1 vervuilen, verontreinigen; 2 verderven *(fig)*, verpesten *(atmosphere)*

pollution [pəloe:sjən] 1 vervuiling, (milieu)verontreiniging; 2 bederf[h], verderf[h]

polo [pooloo] *(sport)* polo[h]

poltergeist [poltəgajst] klopgeest

poly [pollie] *(~s)*, *polytechnic* school voor hoger beroepsonderwijs

polygamy [pəligəmie] veelwijverij

polygon [polliegən] veelhoek, polygoon

polysyllabic [polliesilæbik] veellettergrepig

polytechnic [pollieteknik] hogeschool voor de technische vakken

polythene [polliθie:n] polyethyleen[h], plastic[h]: *~ bag* plastic tasje

pomegranate [pommigrænit] granaatappel(boom)

pomp [pomp] prachtvertoon[h], praal: *~ and circumstance* pracht en praal

pomposity [pompossittie] gewichtigdoenerij, hoogdravendheid

pompous [pompəs] gewichtig, hoogdravend

ponce [pons] 1 pooier, souteneur; 2 verwijfd type[h]

pond [pond] vijver

¹**ponder** [pondə] *vb (with on, over)* nadenken (over), piekeren (over)

²**ponder** [pondə] *vb* overdenken, overwegen

ponderous [pondərəs] 1 zwaar, massief, log; 2 zwaar op de hand, moeizaam, langdradig

¹**pong** [pong] *n* stank, ruft

²**pong** [pong] *vb* stinken, ruften

pontiff [pontif] paus

pontifical [pontiffikl] 1 pauselijk; 2 *(fig)* autoritair, plechtig

pontoon [pontoe:n] 1 ponton, brugschip[h]; 2 eenentwintigen[h]

pony [poonie] 1 pony, ponypaardje[h]; 2 renpaard[h]; 3 *(Am)* klein model[h]

ponytail paardenstaart

¹**poo** [poe:] *n (vulg)* poep

²**poo** [poe:] *vb (vulg)* poepen

poodle [poe:dl] poedel(hond)

poof(ter) [poe:f(tə)] *(vulg, term of abuse)* 1 nicht, flikker, poot; 2 slappeling, zijig ventje[h]

¹**pool** [poe:l] *n* 1 poel, plas; 2 (zwem)bassin[h], zwembad[h]; 3 pot *(at games of chance)*, (gezamenlijke) inzet; 4 poulespel[h] *(American form of billiards)*; 5 the *~s* (voetbal)toto, voetbalpool

²**pool** [poe:l] *vb* samenvoegen, bij elkaar leggen, verenigen *(money, ideas, means)*

pool room biljartgelegenheid, biljartlokaal[h], goklokaal[h]

poop [poe:p] achtersteven, achterdek[h]

pooped [poe:pt] uitgeput, vermoeid: *~ out* uitgeteld, uitgeput

poor [poeə] 1 arm; 2 slecht, schraal, matig: *~ results* slechte resultaten; 3 armzalig, bedroevend: *cut a ~ figure* een armzalig figuur slaan; 4 zielig, ongelukkig: *~ fellow!* arme kerel!

¹**poorly** [poeəlie] *adv* 1 arm, armoedig; 2 slecht, matig, onvoldoende: *think ~ of* geen hoge pet ophebben van

²**poorly** [poeəlie] *adj* niet lekker, ziek || *~ off: a)* in slechte doen; *b)* slecht voorzien

¹**pop** [pop] *vb* 1 knallen, klappen, ploffen; 2 plotseling, onverwacht bewegen, snel komen, gaan: *~ off* opstappen *(also inf, in sense of dying)*; *~ open* uitpuilen *(of eyes)*; *~ out: a)* te voorschijn schieten; *b)* uitpuilen; *~ up* opduiken, (weer) boven water komen, omhoog komen *(of illustrations, greetings cards etc)*; 3 (neer)schieten, (af)vuren: *~ off: a)* afschieten; *b)* afgeschoten worden; 4 laten knallen, laten klappen; 5 snel zetten, leggen, brengen, steken: *I'll just ~ this letter into the post* ik gooi deze brief even op de bus; 6 plotseling stellen, afvuren *(questions)*; 7 slikken, spuiten *(drugs, pills)*

²**pop** [pop] *n* 1 knal, plof; 2 pop(muziek): *top of the ~s* (tophit) nummer één; 3 pap, pa, papa; 4 prik(limonade), frisdrank

popcorn popcorn, gepofte maïs

pope [poop] paus

pop-eyed met uitpuilende ogen, met grote ogen, verbaasd

popgun speelgoedpistooltje[h]

poplar [poplə] populier; populierenhout[h]

popper [poppə] drukknoop(je[h])

poppet [poppit] schatje[h]

poppy [poppie] papaver, klaproos

poppycock klets(praat)

popsy [popsie] liefje[h], schatje[h]

populace [popjoeləs] (gewone) volk[h], massa

popular [popjoelə] 1 geliefd, populair, gezien: *~ with* geliefd bij; 2 algemeen, veel verbreid; 3 volks-, van, voor het volk: *~ belief* volksgeloof; *~ front* volksfront

popularity [popjoelærittie] populariteit, geliefdheid

popularization [popjoelərajzeesjən] popularisering

popularly [popjoeləlie] 1 geliefd; 2 algemeen, gewoon(lijk): *~ known as* in de wandeling bekend als

populate [popjoeleet] bevolken, bewonen: *densely ~d* dichtbevolkt

population [popjoeleesjən] 1 bevolking, inwoners, bewoners; 2 bevolkingsdichtheid

porcelain [po:səlin] porselein[h]

porch [po:tsj] 1 portaal[h], portiek; 2 *(Am)* veranda

porcupine [po:kjoepajn] stekelvarken[h]

pore [po:] porie

pore over zich verdiepen in, aandachtig bestuderen

pork [po:k] varkensvlees[h]

porn [po:n] *pornography* porno

pornography [po:nɔgrɔfie] porno(grafie)
porous [pɔ:rəs] poreus, waterdoorlatend
porpoise [pɔ:pəs] 1 bruinvis; 2 dolfijn
porridge [pɔrridzj] 1 (havermout)pap; 2 bajes: *do ~ in de bak zitten*
port [po:t] 1 haven, havenstad, *(fig)* veilige haven, toevluchtsoordʰ; 2 bakboordʰ, links; 3 port(wijn) || *any ~ in a storm* nood breekt wet(ten)
portable [pɔ:təbl] 1 draagbaar; 2 overdraagbaar: *~ pension* meeneempensioen
portal [pɔ:tl] (ingangs)poort, portaalʰ, ingang
portent [pɔ:tent] voortekenʰ, voorbode || *a matter of great ~* een gewichtige zaak
porter [pɔ:tə] 1 kruier, sjouwer, drager; 2 portierʰ
portfolio [po:tfoolie·oo] portefeuille
porthole patrijspoort
portico [pɔ:tikkoo] *(also ~es)* portiek, zuilengang
portion [pɔ:sjən] gedeelteʰ, (aan)deelʰ, portie
portion out verdelen, uitdelen
portrait [pɔ:trit] portretʰ, foto, schildering *(also in words)*
portray [po:tree] portretteren, (af)schilderen, beschrijven
portrayal [po:treeəl] portrettering, afbeelding, beschrijving
Portugal [pɔ:tsjoegəl] Portugal
Portuguese [po:tsjoegie:z] Portugees
¹**pose** [pooz] *vb* poseren, doen alsof, een pose aannemen: *~ as* zich voordoen als, zich uitgeven voor
²**pose** [pooz] *vb* 1 stellen, voorleggen: *~ a question* een vraag stellen; 2 vormen: *~ a threat* een bedreiging vormen
³**pose** [pooz] *n* houding, vertoonʰ
poser [poozə] moeilijke vraag, lastig vraagstukʰ
¹**posh** [posj] *adj* chic, modieus
²**posh** [posj] *adv* bekakt, kakkineus: *talk ~* bekakt
position [pəzisjən] 1 positie, plaats(ing), ligging, situatie: *be in a ~ to do sth.* in staat zijn iets te doen; 2 positie, juiste plaats; 3 standpuntʰ, houding, mening: *define one's ~* zijn standpunt bepalen; 4 rang, (maatschappelijke) positie, stand; 5 betrekking, baan
¹**positive** [pozzitiv] *adj* 1 positief; 2 duidelijk, nadrukkelijk: *a ~ assertion* een uitspraak die niets aan duidelijkheid te wensen overlaat; 3 overtuigd, absoluut zeker: *'Are you sure?' 'Positive'* 'Weet je het zeker?' 'Absoluut'; 4 echt, volslagen, compleet: *a ~ nuisance* een ware plaag; 5 zelfbewust, (te) zelfverzekerd; 6 wezenlijk, (duidelijk) waarneembaar: *a ~ change for the better* een wezenlijke verbetering; *~ sign* plusteken
²**positive** [pozzitiv] *n* 1 positiefʰ *(of photo);* 2 positief getalʰ
posse [possie] troep, (politie)macht, groep *(with common purpose)*
possess [pəzes] 1 bezitten, hebben, beschikken (over); 2 beheersen, meester zijn van, zich meester maken van: *what could have ~ed him?* wat kan hem toch bezield hebben?

possession [pəzesjən] 1 bezitʰ, eigendomʰ, bezitting: *take ~ of* in bezit nemen, betrekken; 2 (bal)bezitʰ; 3 bezetenheid
possessive [pəzessiv] 1 bezitterig, hebberig; 2 dominerend, alle aandacht opeisend || *~ (pronoun)* bezittelijk voornaamwoord
possessor [pəzessə] eigenaar, bezitter
possibility [possibbillittie] mogelijkheid, kans, vooruitzichtʰ: *there is no ~ of his coming* het is uitgesloten dat hij komt
possible [possibl] 1 mogelijk, denkbaar, eventueel: *do everything ~* al het mogelijke doen; *if ~* zo mogelijk; 2 acceptabel, aanvaardbaar, redelijk
possibly [possiblie] 1 mogelijk, denkbaar, eventueel: *I cannot ~ come* ik kan onmogelijk komen; 2 misschien, mogelijk(erwijs), wellicht: *'Are you coming too?' 'Possibly'* 'Ga jij ook mee?' 'Misschien'
possum [possəm] opossum, buidelrat || *play ~* doen alsof je slaapt
¹**post** [poost] *n* 1 paal, stijl, post; 2 *(equestrian sports)* start-, finishpaal, vertrekpuntʰ, eindpuntʰ; 3 (doel)paal; 4 post(bestelling), postkantoorʰ, brievenbus: *by return of ~* per kerende post, per omgaande; 5 post, (stand)plaats, (leger)kampʰ: *be at one's ~* op zijn post zijn; 6 betrekking, baan, ambtʰ
²**post** [poost] *vb* 1 (also with *up*) aanplakken, beplakken; 2 posteren, plaatsen, uitzetten; 3 (over)plaatsen, stationeren, aanstellen tot; 4 (also with *off*) posten, op de post doen, (ver)sturen; 5 op de hoogte brengen, inlichten: *keep s.o. ~ed* iem op de hoogte houden
poster [poostə] afficheʰ, aanplakbiljetʰ; poster
posterior [postjəriə] later, volgend: *~ to* komend na, volgend op, later dan
posterity [posterrittie] nageslachtʰ
¹**postgraduate** [poostgrædjoeət] *adj* postuniversitair, na de universitaire opleiding komend, postdoctoraal
²**postgraduate** [poostgrædjoeət] *n* afgestudeerde *(continues studies at university)*
posthumous [postjoeməs] postuum, (komend, verschijnend) na de dood
posting [poosting] stationering, (over)plaatsing
postman [poostmən] postbode
postmark poststempelʰ, postmerkʰ
post-mortem [poostmo:təm] 1 lijkschouwing, sectie; 2 nabespreking *(esp to find out what went wrong)*
post office 1 postkantoorʰ; 2 post, posterijen, PTT
postpone [poostpoon] (with *until, to*) uitstellen (tot), opschorten (tot)
postscript [poostskript] postscriptumʰ; naschriftʰ *(in letter)*
postulate [postjoeleet] (zonder bewijs) als waar aannemen, vooronderstellen
¹**posture** [postjə] *n* 1 (lichaams)houding, postuurʰ, pose; 2 houding, standpuntʰ
²**posture** [postjə] *vb* 1 poseren, een gemaakte houding aannemen; 2 (with *as*) zich uitgeven (voor)

posy [poozie] boeket(je)^h

¹pot [pot] *n* **1** pot; (nacht)po, potvormig voorwerp^h (van aardewerk); (gemeenschappelijke) pot, gezamenlijk (gespaard) bedrag^h; **2** hoop *(money)*, bom; **3** hasj(iesj), marihuana; **4** aardewerk^h ‖ *keep the ~ boiling* de kost verdienen, het zaakje draaiende houden; *go (all) to ~* op de fles gaan, in de vernieling zijn

²pot [pot] *vb* schieten: *~ at* (zonder mikken) schieten op

³pot [pot] *vb* **1** *(with up)* potten, in een bloempot planten; **2** in de zak stoten *(billiard ball)*; **3** op het potje zetten *(child)*

potato [pəteetoo] *(~es)* aardappel(plant): *mashed ~(es)* aardappelpuree

potato crisp chips

pot-belly dikke buik, buikje^h, dikzak

potency [pootənsie] invloed, kracht

potent [pootənt] **1** krachtig, sterk, effectief; **2** (seksueel) potent; **3** machtig, invloedrijk

potentate [pootənteet] absoluut heerser, *(fig)* iem die zich zeer laat gelden

¹potential [pətensjl] *adj* potentieel, mogelijk, in aanleg aanwezig

²potential [pətensjl] *n* mogelijkheid: *he hasn't realized his full ~ yet* hij heeft de grens van zijn kunnen nog niet bereikt

pothole 1 gat^h, put, kuil *(in road surface)*; **2** grot

potion [poosjən] drankje^h *(medicine, magic potion, poison)*

pot-roast smoren, stoven, braden

pot-shot schot^h op goed geluk af, schot in het wilde weg, *(fig)* schot in het duister

potted [pottid] **1** pot-: *~ plant* kamerplant, potplant; **2** ingemaakt, in een pot bewaard; **3** (erg) kort samengevat

¹potter [pottə] *n* pottenbakker

²potter [pottə] *vb* **1** *(with about)* rondscharrelen, rondslenteren, aanrommelen, prutsen; **2** *(with away)* je tijd verdoen, rondlummelen, lanterfanten

pottery [pottərie] **1** pottenbakkerij; **2** aardewerk^h, keramiek

¹potty [pottie] *n* (kinder)po, potje^h

²potty [pottie] *adj* **1** knetter, niet goed snik, dwaas: *~ about* helemaal wég van; **2** onbenullig, pietluttig

pouch [pautsj] **1** zak(je^h); **2** (zakvormige) huidplooi, buidel, wangzak: *she had ~es under her eyes* zij had wallen onder haar ogen

pouf [poe:f] **1** poef, zitkussen^h; **2** *(vulg)* flikker, homo

poulterer [pooltərə] poelier

poultry [pooltrie] gevogelte^h, pluimvee^h

¹pounce [pauns] *vb* **1** zich naar beneden storten, (op)springen *(to seize sth)*; **2** plotseling aanvallen, *(fig)* kritiek uitbrengen

²pounce [pauns] *n* het stoten *(of bird of prey)*, het zich plotseling (neer)storten, *(fig)* plotselinge aanval: *make a ~ at* (of: *on*) zich storten op

pounce (up)on 1 (weg)graaien, inpikken, begerig grijpen; **2** plotseling aanvallen, zich storten op *(also fig)*

¹pound [paund] *n* **1** pond^h *(of weight, currency)*; **2** depot^h, *(for seized goods, towed-away cars etc)* asiel^h, omheinde ruimte

²pound [paund] *vb* **1** hard (toe)slaan, flinke klappen uitdelen; **2** (herhaaldelijk) zwaar bombarderen, een spervuur aanleggen; **3** bonzen *(of heart)*

³pound [paund] *vb* **1** (fijn)stampen, verpulveren; **2** beuken op, stompen op

¹pour [po:r] *vb* **1** stromen, (rijkelijk) vloeien *(also fig)*: *the money kept ~ing in* het geld bleef binnenstromen; **2** stortregenen, gieten; **3** (thee, koffie) inschenken

²pour [po:r] *vb* (uit)gieten, doen (neer)stromen

pout [paut] (de lippen) tuiten, pruilen (over)

poverty [povvətie] armoede, behoeftigheid

poverty-stricken straatarm

powder [paudə] **1** poeder, (kool)stof; **2** talkpoeder^h, gezichtspoeder^h; **3** (bus)kruit^h

powdered [paudəd] **1** gepoederd, met poeder bedekt; **2** in poedervorm (gemaakt, gedroogd): *~ milk* melkpoeder; *~ sugar* poedersuiker

powder keg kruitvat^h *(also fig)*, tijdbom, explosieve situatie

powder puff poederdonsje^h, poederkwastje^h

powdery [paudərie] **1** poederachtig, kruimelig, brokkelig; **2** (als) met poeder bedekt, gepoederd

power [pauə] **1** macht, vermogen^h, mogelijkheid; **2** kracht, sterkte; **3** invloed, macht, controle: *come in* (of: *into*) *~* aan het bewind komen; **4** (vol)macht, recht^h, bevoegdheid: *~ of attorney* volmacht; **5** invloedrijk iem (iets), mogendheid, autoriteit: *the Great Powers* de grote mogendheden; **6** *~s* (boze) macht(en), (hemelse) kracht(en); **7** (drijf)kracht, (elektrische) energie, stroom: *electric ~* elektrische stroom; **8** macht: *to the ~ (of)* tot de … macht; **9** grote hoeveelheid, groot aantal^h, hoop: *it did me a ~ of good* het heeft me ontzettend goed gedaan; *a ~ behind the throne* een man achter de schermen; *more ~ to your elbow* veel geluk, succes

powerboat motorboot

power brakes rembekrachtiging

power cut stroomonderbreking, stroomuitval

powerful [pauəfoel] **1** krachtig, machtig, invloedrijk; **2** effectief, met een sterke (uit)werking: *a ~ speech* een indrukwekkende toespraak

power point stopcontact^h

powwow [pauwau] **1** indianenbijeenkomst; **2** *(inf)* lange conferentie, rumoerige bespreking, overleg^h

pp. 1 pianissimo pp; **2** pages pp., bladzijden

p.p. *per pro(curatione)* p.p., bij volmacht, namens

PR *public relations* pr

practicable [præktikkəbl] **1** uitvoerbaar, haalbaar; **2** bruikbaar, begaanbaar *(of road)*

¹practical [præktikl] *adj* **1** praktisch, in de praktijk, handig; **2** haalbaar, uitvoerbaar; **3** zinnig, verstandig ‖ *for all ~ purposes* feitelijk, alles welbeschouwd

²practical [præktikl] *n* practicum^h, praktijkles,

praktijkexamen[h]

practically [præktikkəlie] **1** bijna, praktisch, zo goed als; **2** in de praktijk, praktisch gesproken

practice [præktis] **1** praktijk, toepassing: *put sth. in(to)* ~ iets in praktijk brengen; **2** oefening, training, ervaring: *be out of* ~ uit vorm zijn, het verleerd zijn; **3** gewoonte, gebruik[h], normale gang van zaken: *make a* ~ *of sth.* ergens een gewoonte van maken; **4** uitoefening, beoefening, het praktiseren, praktijk *(of lawyer, doctor etc)*

practise [præktis] **1** praktiseren, uitoefenen, beoefenen: ~ *black magic* zwarte magie bedrijven; *he* ~*s as a lawyer* hij werkt als advocaat; **2** in de praktijk toepassen, uitvoeren; **3** oefenen, instuderen, repeteren

practitioner [præktisjənə] beoefenaar, beroeps(kracht): *medical* ~*s* de artsen

pragmatic [prægmætik] zakelijk, praktisch

Prague [pra:g] Praag

prairie [preərie] prairie, grasvlakte

¹praise [preez] *vb* prijzen, vereren

²praise [preez] *n* **1** lof, het prijzen, aanbeveling; **2** glorie, eer, lof || ~ *be (to God)!* God zij geloofd!

praiseworthy [preezwə:ðie] loffelijk, prijzenswaardig

pram [præm] kinderwagen

prance [pra:ns] **1** steigeren; **2** (vrolijk) springen, huppelen, dansen: ~ *about* (of: *around)* rondspringen, rondlopen

prank [prængk] streek, grap

prat [præt] *(inf)* idioot, zak, eikel

¹prattle [prætl] *vb* babbelen, kleppen, keuvelen

²prattle [prætl] *n* kinderpraat, gebabbel[h]

prawn [pro:n] garnaal

pray [pree] **1** bidden, (God) aanroepen; **2** hopen, wensen: *we're* ~*ing for a peaceful day* we hopen op een rustige dag; *he is past* ~*ing for* hij is niet meer te redden

prayer [preə] **1** gebed[h], het bidden; **2** (smeek)bede, verzoek[h] || *he doesn't have a* ~ hij heeft geen schijn van kans

preach [prie:tsj] preken, *(fig)* een zedenpreek houden

preacher [prie:tsjə] predikant

preamble [prie-æmbl] inleiding, voorwoord[h]

pre-arrange [prie:əreendzj] vooraf regelen, vooraf overeenkomen

precarious [prikkeəriəs] **1** onzeker, onbestendig: *he made a* ~ *living* hij had een ongewis inkomen; **2** onveilig, gevaarlijk; **3** twijfelachtig, niet op feiten gebaseerd

precaution [prikko:sjən] voorzorgsmaatregel, voorzorg: *take* ~*s* voorzorgsmaatregelen treffen

precede [prissie:d] voorgaan, vooraf (laten) gaan, de voorrang hebben: *the years preceding his marriage* de jaren voor zijn huwelijk

precedence [pressiddəns] voorrang, prioriteit, het voorgaan: *give* ~ *to* laten voorgaan, voorrang verlenen aan

precedent [pressiddənt] **1** precedent[h], vroegere beslissing waarom men zich kan beroepen: *create* (of: *establish, set) a* ~ een precedent scheppen; *without* ~ zonder precedent, ongekend; **2** traditie, gewoonte, gebruik[h]

preceding [prissie:ding] voorafgaand

precept [prie:sept] **1** voorschrift[h], principe[h], grondregel; **2** het voorschrijven

precinct [prie:singkt] **1** ~*s* omsloten ruimte *(around church, university)*, (grond)gebied[h], terrein[h]; **2** stadsgebied[h]: *pedestrian* ~ voetgangersgebied; *shopping* ~ winkelcentrum; **3** *(Am)* district[h]

¹precious [presjəs] *adj* **1** kostbaar, waardevol: ~ *metals* edele metalen; **2** dierbaar: *her family is very* ~ *to her* haar familie is haar zeer dierbaar; **3** gekunsteld, gemaakt; **4** kostbaar, waardeloos

²precious [presjəs] *adv* bar: *he had* ~ *little money* hij had nauwelijks een rooie cent

precipice [pressippis] steile rotswand, afgrond

¹precipitate [prissippitteet] *adj* overhaast, plotseling

²precipitate [prissippitteet] *vb* **1** (neer)storten *(also fig)*, (neer)werpen; **2** versnellen, bespoedigen

precipitous [prissippittəs] **1** (vreselijk) steil; **2** als een afgrond, duizelingwekkend hoog

precise [prissajs] nauwkeurig, precies: *at the* ~ *moment that* juist op het moment dat

precisely [prissajslie] **1** precies: *we'll arrive at 10.30* ~ we komen precies om half elf aan; **2** inderdaad, juist, precies

precision [prissizjən] nauwkeurigheid, juistheid

preclude [prikloe:d] uitsluiten, voorkomen, (with *from)* verhinderen, beletten

precocious [prikkoosjəs] vroeg(rijp), vroeg wijs

preconceived [prie:kənsie:vd] vooraf gevormd, zich vooraf voorgesteld: *a* ~ *opinion* een vooropgezette mening

precondition [prie:kəndisjən] eerste vereiste[h], allereerste voorwaarde

precursor [prikkə:sə] voorloper, voorganger

predator [preddətə] roofdier[h]

predecessor [prie:dissessə] **1** voorloper, voorganger; **2** voorvader

predestination [priddestinneesjən] voorbeschikking

predetermine [prie:ditta:min] vooraf bepalen, voorbeschikken: *the colour of s.o.'s eyes is* ~*d by that of his parents* de kleur van iemands ogen wordt bepaald door die van zijn ouders

predicament [priddikkəmənt] hachelijke situatie, kritieke toestand

predicate [preddikkət] *(linguistics)* gezegde[h]

predict [priddikt] voorspellen, als verwachting opgeven

predictable [priddiktəbl] voorspelbaar, zonder verrassing, saai

predisposition [prie:dispəzisjən] neiging, vatbaarheid, aanleg

predominant [priddomminnənt] overheersend,

belangrijkst

predominate [priddɔmminneet] heersen, regeren; overheersen, de overhand hebben, beheersen

pre-eminent [prie:emminnənt] uitstekend, superieur

pre-empt [prie:empt] 1 beslag leggen op, zich toe-eigenen, de plaats innemen van; 2 overbodig maken, ontkrachten

pre-emptive [prie:emptiv] preventief, voorkomend

preen [prie:n] 1 gladstrijken *(feathers)*; 2 (zich) opknappen, (zich) mooi maken || *he ~ed himself on his intelligence* hij ging prat op zijn intelligentie

prefab [prie:fæb] montagewoning, geprefabriceerd gebouw

prefabricate [prie:fæbrikkeet] in onderdelen gereedmaken, volgens systeembouw maken

¹**preface** [preffəs] *n* voorwoord[h], inleiding

²**preface** [preffəs] *vb* 1 van een voorwoord voorzien, inleiden; 2 leiden tot, het begin zijn van

prefect [prie:fekt] *(English educ)* oudere leerling als ordehandhaver

prefer [priffə:] 1 *(with to)* verkiezen (boven), de voorkeur geven (aan), prefereren: *she ~s tea to coffee* ze drinkt liever thee dan koffie; *he ~red to leave rather than to wait* hij wilde liever weggaan dan nog wachten; 2 promoveren, bevorderen

preferable [preffərəbl] verkieslijk, te prefereren: *everything is ~ to* alles is beter dan

preference [preffərəns] voorkeur, voorliefde: *in ~ to* liever dan

preferment [priffə:mənt] bevordering, promotie

prefix [prie:fiks] voorvoegsel[h]

pregnancy [pregnənsie] zwangerschap

pregnant [pregnənt] 1 zwanger, drachtig *(of animals)*; 2 vindingrijk, vol ideeën; 3 vruchtbaar, vol; 4 veelbetekenend: *a ~ silence* een veelbetekenende stilte

prehistoric [prie:historrik] prehistorisch

prejudge [prie:dzjudzj] veroordelen *(without trail or interrogation)*, vooraf beoordelen

¹**prejudice** [predzjoedis] *n* 1 vooroordeel[h], vooringenomenheid: *without ~* onbevooroordeeld; 2 nadeel[h]

²**prejudice** [predzjoedis] *vb* 1 schaden, benadelen: *~ a good cause* afbreuk doen aan een goede zaak; 2 innemen, voorinnemen

prelate [prellət] kerkvorst, prelaat

prelim [prillim] *preliminary examination* tentamen[h]

¹**preliminary** [prillimminnərie] *n* voorbereiding, inleiding: *the preliminaries* de voorronde(s)

²**preliminary** [prillimminnərie] *adj* inleidend, voorbereidend

prelude [preljoe:d] 1 voorspel[h], inleiding; 2 prelude, ouverture *(of opera)*

premarital [prie:mæritl] voorechtelijk, voordat het huwelijk gesloten is: *~ sex* seks voor het huwelijk

premature [premmətsjoeə] 1 te vroeg, voortijdig:

a ~ baby een te vroeg geboren baby; *his ~ death* zijn vroegtijdige dood; 2 voorbarig, overhaast

premeditated [prie:medditteetid] opzettelijk, beraamd: *~ murder* moord met voorbedachten rade

premeditation [primmedditteesjən] opzet

¹**premier** [premmiə] *n* eerste minister, minister-president, premier

²**premier** [premmiə] *adj* eerste, voornaamste

premise [premmis] 1 vooronderstelling; 2 *~s* huis[h] (en erf), zaak: *licensed ~s* café; *the shopkeeper lives on the ~s* de winkelier woont in het pand

premium [prie:miəm] 1 beloning, prijs; 2 (verzekerings)premie; 3 toeslag, extra[h], meerprijs; 4 *(fig)* hoge waarde: *put s.o.'s work at a ~* iemands werk hoog aanslaan

premonition [premmənisjən] voorgevoel[h]

prenatal [prie:neetl] prenataal, voor de geboorte

preoccupation [prie·okjoepeesjən] 1 hoofdbezigheid, (voornaamste) zorg; 2 het volledig in beslag genomen zijn

preoccupied [prie·okjoepajd] in gedachten verzonken, volledig in beslag genomen

¹**prep** [prep] *n* huiswerk[h], voorbereiding(stijd)

²**prep** [prep] *adj* voorbereidend: *~ school* voorbereidingsschool

preparation [preppəreesjən] 1 voorbereiding: *make ~s for* voorbereidingen treffen voor; 2 preparaat[h]; 3 voorbereiding(stijd), huiswerk[h], studie

¹**prepare** [prippeə] *vb* voorbereidingen treffen

²**prepare** [prippeə] *vb* 1 voorbereiden, gereedmaken, prepareren, bestuderen, instuderen; 2 klaarmaken, (toe)bereiden

prepared [prippeəd] 1 voorbereid, gereed; 2 bereid: *be ~ to do sth.* bereid zijn iets te doen

prepay [prie:pee] vooruitbetalen

preponderant [prippondərənt] overwegend; overheersend, belangrijkst

preposition [preppəzisjən] voorzetsel[h]

prepossess [prie:pozes] 1 inspireren; 2 in beslag nemen, bezighouden; 3 bevooroordeeld maken, gunstig stemmen

preposterous [prippostərəs] onredelijk, absurd

prerequisite [prie:rekwizzit] eerste vereiste[h]: *a ~ of* (of: *for, to*) een noodzakelijke voorwaarde voor

¹**Presbyterian** [prezbittjəriən] *adj* presbyteriaans

²**Presbyterian** [prezbittjəriən] *n* presbyteriaan

presbytery [prezbittərie] 1 priesterkoor[h]; 2 (gebied bestuurd door) raad van ouderlingen *(Presbyterian Church)*; 3 pastorie

pre-schooler [prie:skoe:lə] peuter, kleuter, (nog) niet schoolgaand kind[h]

¹**prescribe** [priskrajb] *vb* voorschrijven, opleggen, bevelen

²**prescribe** [priskrajb] *vb* 1 voorschriften geven, richtlijnen geven; 2 *(with for)* een advies geven (over), een remedie voorschrijven (tegen)

prescription [priskripsjən] 1 voorschrift[h] *(also fig)*; 2 recept[h], geneesmiddel[h]

presence [prezns] 1 aanwezigheid, tegenwoordigheid: ~ of mind tegenwoordigheid van geest; **2** nabijheid, omgeving: in the ~ of in tegenwoordigheid van; **3** presentie, (indrukwekkende) verschijning, bovennatuurlijk iem (iets); **4** persoonlijkheid

¹**present** [preznt] adj **1** onderhavig, in kwestie: in the ~ case in dit geval; **2** huidig, tegenwoordig; **3** (linguistics) tegenwoordig: ~ participle onvoltooid deelwoord; ~ tense tegenwoordige tijd; **4** tegenwoordig, aanwezig

²**present** [preznt] n **1** geschenkʰ, cadeauʰ, gift; **2** het heden: at ~ op dit ogenblik, tegenwoordig; for the ~ voorlopig

³**present** [prizzent] vb **1** voorstellen, introduceren, voordragen; **2** opvoeren, vertonen: ~ a show een show presenteren; **3** (ver)tonen: ~ no difficulties geen problemen bieden; **4** aanbieden, schenken, uitreiken: ~ s.o. with a prize iem een prijs uitreiken; **5** presenteren: ~ arms! presenteer geweer!

presentable [prizzentəbl] toonbaar, fatsoenlijk

presentation [preznteesjən] **1** voorstelling; **2** schenking, gift, geschenkʰ: make a ~ of aanbieden

present-day huidig, modern, gangbaar

presenter [prizzentə] presentator

presentiment [prizzentimmənt] (angstig) voorgevoelʰ

presently [prezntlie] **1** dadelijk, binnenkort; **2** (Am) nu, op dit ogenblik

preservation [prezzəveesjən] **1** behoudʰ, bewaring; **2** staat

preservationist [prezzəveesjənist] milieubeschermer, natuurbeschermer

preservative [prizza:vətiv] **1** bewaarmiddelʰ, conserveringsmiddelʰ; **2** voorbehoedmiddelʰ

¹**preserve** [prizza:v] vb **1** bewaren, levend houden (for future generations): only two copies have been ~d slechts twee exemplaren zijn bewaard gebleven; **2** behouden, in stand houden: well ~d goed geconserveerd; **3** inmaken: ~d fruits gekonfijt fruit; **4** in leven houden, redden

²**preserve** [prizza:v] n **1** also ~s jam; **2** (natuur)reservaatʰ, wildparkʰ ‖ poach on another's ~ in iemands vaarwater zitten

pre-set [prie:set] vooraf instellen, afstellen

preside [prizzajd] **1** als voorzitter optreden; **2** (with over) de leiding hebben (van)

presidency [prezziddənsie] presidentschapʰ, presidentstermijn

president [prezziddənt] **1** voorzitter; **2** president; **3** (Am) leidinggevende, directeur

¹**press** [pres] n **1** pers, het drukken, journalisten: freedom (of: liberty) of the ~ persvrijheid; get a good ~ een goede pers krijgen; **2** drukpers: at (of: in) (the) ~ ter perse; **3** drukkerij; **4** Press uitgeverij; **5** pers(toestelʰ); **6** menigte, gedrangʰ

²**press** [pres] vb **1** druk uitoefenen: ~ ahead with onverbiddelijk doorgaan met; **2** persen, strijken; **3** dringen, haast hebben: time ~es de tijd dringt; **4** zich verdringen

³**press** [pres] vb **1** drukken, duwen, klemmen; **2** plat-drukken; **3** bestoken (also fig), op de hielen zitten: ~ s.o. hard iemand het vuur na aan de schenen leggen; **4** druk uitoefenen op, aanzetten: ~ for an answer aandringen op een antwoord; be ~ed for money in geldnood zitten; **5** persen, strijken: ~ home one's point of view zijn zienswijze doordrijven

press gallery perstribune

pressie [prezzie] cadeau(tje)ʰ, geschenkʰ

pressing [pressing] **1** dringend, urgent; **2** (aan)dringend, opdringerig

pressman [presmən] journalist

¹**pressure** [presjə] n **1** druk, gewichtʰ: the ~ of taxation de belastingdruk; **2** stress, spanning: work under ~ werken onder druk; **3** dwang: a promise made under ~ een afgedwongen belofte

²**pressure** [presjə] vb onder druk zetten

pressurize [presjərajz] **1** onder druk zetten (also fig); **2** de (lucht)druk regelen van: ~d cabin drukcabine

prestige [prestie:zj] prestigeʰ, aanzienʰ

presto [prestoo] presto, onmiddellijk: hey ~! hocus pocus pas!

presumable [prizjoe:məbl] aannemelijk, vermoedelijk

¹**presume** [prizjoe:m] vb **1** zich veroorloven, de vrijheid nemen; **2** veronderstellen, vermoeden, aannemen

²**presume** [prizjoe:m] vb zich vrijheden veroorloven

presume (up)on misbruik maken van: ~ s.o.'s kindness misbruik maken van iemands vriendelijkheid

presumption [prizzumpsjən] **1** (redelijke) veronderstelling; **2** reden om te veronderstellen; **3** arrogantie, verwaandheid

presumptuous [prizzumptsjoeəs] aanmatigend, arrogant

presupposition [prie:suppəzisjən] vooronderstelling, voorwaarde, vereisteʰ

pretence [prittens] **1** aanspraak, pretentie: ~ to aanspraak op; **2** valse indruk, schijn: she made a ~ of laughing ze deed alsof ze lachte; **3** uiterlijk vertoonʰ, aanstellerij: devoid of all ~ zonder enige pretentie; **4** huichelarij

¹**pretend** [prittend] vb doen alsof, komedie spelen

²**pretend** [prittend] vb **1** voorgeven, (ten onrechte) beweren; **2** voorwenden

pretender [prittendə] **1** (troon)pretendent; **2** huichelaar, schijnheilige

pretension [prittensjən] **1** aanspraak; **2** pretentie, aanmatiging

pretentious [prittensjəs] **1** pretentieus, aanmatigend; **2** opzichtig

pretext [prie:tekst] voorwendselʰ, excuusʰ: under the ~ of onder voorwendsel van

¹**pretty** [prittie] adj **1** aardig (also iron), mooi, aantrekkelijk: a ~ mess een mooie boel; **2** groot, aanzienlijk, veel: it cost him a ~ penny het heeft hem een flinke duit gekost; a ~ kettle of fish een mooie boel

²**pretty** [prittie] *adv* **1** nogal, vrij: ~ *nearly* zo goed als; *I have ~ well finished my essay* ik heb mijn opstel bijna af; **2** erg, zeer; **3** *(Am)* aardig, behoorlijk

prevail [privveel] **1** de overhand krijgen, zegevieren; **2** wijd verspreid zijn, heersen, gelden

prevailing [privveeling] gangbaar, heersend

prevalent [prevvələnt] **1** heersend, gangbaar, wijd verspreid; **2** (over)heersend

prevarication [priværikkeesjən] draaierij, uitvlucht

¹**prevent** [privvent] *vb* voorkomen, verhinderen

²**prevent** [privvent] *vb* in de weg staan

¹**preventive** [privventiv] *adj* preventief, voorkomend: ~ *detention* voorlopige hechtenis

²**preventive** [privventiv] *n* **1** obstakel[h], hindernis; **2** voorbehoedmiddel[h]

preview [prie:vjoe:] voorvertoning

previous [prie:viəs] voorafgaand, vorig, vroeger

pre-war [prie:wo:] vooroorlogs

¹**prey** [pree] *n* prooi *(also fig)*, slachtoffer[h]: *beast* (of: *bird*) *of* ~ roofdier, roofvogel; *become* (of: *fall*) *(a)* ~ *to* ten prooi vallen aan

²**prey** [pree] *vb*: ~ *(up)on: a)* uitzuigen; *b)* aantasten; *c)* jagen op; *it ~s on his mind* hij wordt erdoor gekweld

¹**price** [prajs] *n* **1** prijs *(also fig)*, som: *set a ~ on* een prijs vaststellen voor; *at a low* ~ voor weinig geld; *at any* ~ tot elke prijs; **2** notering; **3** waarde: *every man has his* ~ iedereen is te koop

²**price** [prajs] *vb* prijzen, de prijs vaststellen van: ~ *oneself out of the market* zich uit de markt prijzen

priceless [prajsləs] onbetaalbaar, onschatbaar, *(fig)* kostelijk

pricey [prajsie] prijzig, duur

¹**prick** [prik] *n* **1** prik; **2** *(inf)* lul, eikel; schoft

²**prick** [prik] *vb* prikken, steken

³**prick** [prik] *vb* prikken, (door)steken, prikkelen *(also fig)*

¹**prickle** [prikl] *n* stekel, doorn, prikkel

²**prickle** [prikl] *vb* prikkelen, steken, kriebelen

pride [prajd] **1** trots, verwaandheid, hoogmoed: *take (a)* ~ *in* fier zijn op; **2** eergevoel[h]: *false* ~ misplaatste trots, ijdelheid; **3** troep *(lions)*

pride (up)on prat gaan op, trots zijn op

priest [prie:st] priester, pastoor

prig [prig] verwaande kwast

prim [prim] **1** keurig: ~ *and proper* keurig netjes; **2** preuts

primacy [prajməsie] voorrang, vooraanstaande plaats

prim(a)eval [prajmie:vl] **1** oorspronkelijk, oer-: ~ *forest* ongerept woud; **2** oeroud

primarily [prajmərəlie] hoofdzakelijk, voornamelijk

¹**primary** [prajmərie] *adj* **1** voornaamste: *of* ~ *importance* van het allergrootste belang; **2** primair, eerst; **3** elementair, grond-: ~ *care* eerstelijnsgezondheidszorg; ~ *colour* primaire kleur; ~ *education* (of: *school*) basisonderwijs, basisschool

²**primary** [prajmərie] *n* **1** hoofdzaak; **2** *(Am)* voorverkiezing

primate [prajmeet] primaat[h]

Primate [prajmət] aartsbisschop

¹**prime** [prajm] *adj* **1** eerst, voornaamst: ~ *suspect* hoofdverdachte; **2** uitstekend, prima: *(radio, TV)* ~ *time* prime time; ~ *quality* topkwaliteit; **3** oorspronkelijk, fundamenteel: ~ *number* priemgetal

²**prime** [prajm] *n* **1** hoogste volmaaktheid, bloei, hoogtepunt[h], puikje[h]: *in the* ~ *of life* in de kracht van zijn leven; *she is well past her* ~ ze is niet meer zo jong, ze heeft haar beste jaren achter de rug; **2** priemgetal[h]

³**prime** [prajm] *vb* **1** klaarmaken, prepareren; **2** laden *(firearm)*; **3** op gang brengen *(by pouring water or oil)*, injecteren *(engine)*

¹**primer** [prajmə] *n* grondverf

²**primer** [prajmə] *n* **1** eerste leesboek[h], abc[h]; **2** beknopte handleiding, inleiding

primitive [primmətiv] **1** primitief; **2** niet comfortabel, ouderwets

primrose [primrooz] **1** sleutelbloem; **2** lichtgeel[h]

primula [primjoelə] primula, sleutelbloem

prince [prins] **1** prins; **2** vorst *(also fig)*, heerser

princedom [prinsdəm] **1** prinsdom[h], vorstendom[h]; **2** prinselijke waardigheid

princess [prinses] prinses

¹**principal** [prinsipl] *adj* voornaamste

²**principal** [prinsipl] *n* **1** directeur, directrice; **2** hoofd[h], hoofdpersoon, ~s hoofdrolspelers; **3** schoolhoofd[h]; **4** *(fin)* kapitaal[h], hoofdsom, geleende som

principality [prinsipælittie] **1** prinsdom[h], vorstendom[h]; **2** *the Principality* Wales

principally [prinsippəlie] voornamelijk, hoofdzakelijk

principle [prinsipl] **1** (grond)beginsel[h], uitgangspunt[h]: *in* ~ in principe; **2** principe[h], beginsel[h]: *live up to* (of: *stick to*) *one's* ~s aan zijn principes vasthouden

prink [pringk] (zich) mooi maken, (zich) optutten: ~ *up* zich chic kleden

¹**print** [print] *vb* **1** (af)drukken: ~*ed papers* drukwerk; ~ *out* een uitdraai maken (van); **2** publiceren; **3** in blokletters (op)schrijven; **4** (be)stempelen

²**print** [print] *vb* **1** (with *off*) een afdruk maken van, afdrukken *(also photo)*; **2** inprenten ‖ ~*ed circuit* gedrukte bedrading

³**print** [print] *n* **1** afdruk, *(fig)* spoor[h]: *a* ~ *of a tyre* een bandenspoor; **2** *(art)* prent; **3** *(foto)*afdruk; druk: *in* ~ gedrukt, verkrijgbaar; **4** stempel; **5** gedrukt exemplaar[h], krant, blad[h]; **6** patroon[h]

printer [printə] **1** (boek)drukker; **2** printer

printing [printing] oplage, druk

printout uitdraai

print preview *(comp)* afdrukvoorbeeld[h]

prior [prajjə] vroeger, voorafgaand

priority [prajjorrittie] prioriteit, voorrang: *get one's priorities right* de juiste prioriteiten stellen

prior to vóór, voorafgaande aan

prism [prizm] prisma[h]

prison [prizn] **1** gevangenis; **2** gevangenisstraf

prisoner [prizzənə] gevangene, gedetineerde: ~ *of war* krijgsgevangene

prissy [prissie] preuts, stijf

privacy [privvəsie] **1** persoonlijke levenssfeer; **2** geheimhouding, stilte, beslotenheid; **3** afzondering

¹private [prajvət] *adj* **1** besloten, afgezonderd: ~ *celebration* viering in familiekring; ~ *hotel* familiehotel; **2** vertrouwelijk, geheim: ~ *conversation* gesprek onder vier ogen; *in* ~ in het geheim; **3** particulier, niet openbaar: ~ *enterprise* particuliere onderneming, *(fig)* ondernemingslust; ~ *life* privéleven; ~ *property* privé-eigendom, particulier eigendom; ~ *school* particuliere school; **4** persoonlijk, eigen: ~ *detective* privédetective; ~ *eye* privédetective; ~ *means: a)* inkomsten anders dan uit loon; *b)* eigen middelen; ~ *practice* particuliere praktijk; ~ *parts* geslachtsdelen

²private [prajvət] *n* soldaat, militair

privation [prajveesjən] ontbering, gebrek[h]

privatize [prajvətajz] privatiseren

¹privilege [privvillidzj] *n* **1** voorrecht[h], privilege[h]; **2** onschendbaarheid, immuniteit: *breach of* ~ inbreuk op de parlementaire gedragsregels; **3** bevoorrechting

²privilege [privvillidzj] *vb* **1** bevoorrechten, een privilege verlenen; **2** machtigen, toestaan; **3** vrijstellen

¹prize [prajz] *n* **1** prijs, beloning; **2** prijs(schip[h]), (oorlogs)buit

²prize [prajz] *vb* **1** waarderen, op prijs stellen; **2** openen *(with instrument):* ~ *a crate open* een krat openbreken

¹pro [proo] *n* **1** *professional* prof, beroeps; **2** argument[h], stem vóór iets: *the ~s and cons* de voor- en nadelen

²pro [proo] *adj* **1** pro, voor; **2** beroeps-

³pro [proo] *adv* (er)vóór, pro

⁴pro [proo] *prep* vóór, ter verdediging van

probable [probbəbl] waarschijnlijk, aannemelijk

probably [probbəblie] **1** waarschijnlijk; **2** ongetwijfeld, vast wel: ~ *the greatest singer of all* misschien wel de grootste zanger van allemaal

probation [prəbeesjən] proef(tijd), onderzoek[h], onderzoeksperiode: *on* ~: *a)* op proef; *b)* voorwaardelijk in vrijheid gesteld

¹probe [proob] *n* **1** sonde; **2** ruimtesonde; **3** (diepgaand) onderzoek[h]

²probe [proob] *vb* **1** (met een sonde) onderzoeken; **2** (goed) onderzoeken, diep graven (in): ~ *into* graven naar

problem [probləm] **1** probleem[h], vraagstuk[h], kwestie; **2** opgave, vraag

problematic(al) [probləmætik(l)] **1** problematisch; **2** twijfelachtig

procedure [prəsie:dzjə] procedure, methode, werkwijze

proceed [prəsie:d] **1** beginnen, van start gaan; **2** verder gaan, doorgaan: *work is ~ing steadily* het werk vordert gestaag; **3** te werk gaan, handelen: *how shall we* ~ welke procedure zullen we volgen?; **4** plaatsvinden, aan de gang zijn; **5** zich bewegen, gaan, rijden; **6** ontstaan: ~ *from* voortkomen uit

proceeding [prəsie:ding] **1** handeling, maatregel; **2** optreden[h], handelwijze; **3** ~*s* gebeurtenissen, voorvallen; **4** ~*s* notulen, handelingen *(of society etc)*, verslag[h]; **5** ~*s* gerechtelijke actie: *take* (of: *start) legal* ~*s* gerechtelijke stappen ondernemen

proceeds [proosie:dz] opbrengst

proceed to overgaan tot, verder gaan met

¹process [prooses] *n* **1** proces[h], ontwikkeling; **2** methode; **3** (serie) verrichting(en), handelwijze, werkwijze; **4** (voort)gang, loop, verloop[h]: *in the* ~ en passant; *in (the)* ~ *of* doende met

²process [prooses] *vb* **1** bewerken, verwerken; **2** ontwikkelen (en afdrukken)

³process [prəses] *vb* (als) in processie gaan, een optocht houden

procession [prəsesjən] **1** stoet, optocht, processie: *walk in* ~ in optocht lopen; **2** opeenvolging

proclaim [prəkleem] **1** afkondigen, verklaren; **2** kenmerken: *his behaviour ~ed him a liar* uit zijn gedrag bleek duidelijk dat hij loog

proclamation [prokləmeesjən] afkondiging

procrastination [prəkræstinneesjən] uitstel[h], aarzeling

procurable [prəkjoeərəbl] verkrijgbaar, beschikbaar

¹procure [prəkjoeə] *vb* verkrijgen, verwerven

²procure [prəkjoeə] *vb* koppelen, tot ontucht overhalen

¹prod [prod] *vb* **1** porren, prikken, duwen; **2** aansporen, opporren

²prod [prod] *n* **1** por, steek; **2** zet *(also fig)*, duwtje[h]

¹prodigal [proddigl] *adj* **1** verkwistend: *the* ~ *son* de verloren zoon; **2** vrijgevig

²prodigal [proddigl] *n* verkwister: *the* ~ *has returned* de verloren zoon is teruggekeerd

prodigious [prədidzjəs] wonderbaarlijk

prodigy [proddidzjie] **1** wonder[h], bovennatuurlijk verschijnsel[h]; **2** wonderkind[h]

¹produce [prədjoe:s] *vb* **1** produceren, voortbrengen, opbrengen; **2** produceren, vervaardigen; **3** tonen, produceren, te voorschijn halen, voor de dag komen met: ~ *evidence* bewijzen aanvoeren; **4** uitbrengen, het licht doen zien: ~ *a play* een toneelstuk op de planken brengen; **5** veroorzaken, teweegbrengen

²produce [prodjoe:s] *n* opbrengst, productie: *agricultural* ~ landbouwproducten

producer [prədjoe:sə] **1** producent, fabrikant; **2** *(film; TV)* producer, productieleider; **3** regisseur; **4** *(radio, TV)* samensteller

product [proddukt] **1** product[h], voortbrengsel[h]: *agricultural* ~*s* landbouwproducten; **2** resultaat[h], gevolg[h]; **3** product[h], uitkomst ve vermenigvuldiging

production [prəd**u**ksjən] 1 product[h], schepping; 2 *(theatre; film)* productie; 3 productie, vervaardiging, opbrengst; 4 het tonen: *on ~ of your tickets* op vertoon van uw kaartje

productive [prəd**u**ktiv] productief, vruchtbaar

prof [prof] *professor* prof, professor

¹profane [prəf**ee**n] *adj* niet kerkelijk, werelds

²profane [prəf**ee**n] *vb* ontheiligen

profess [prəf**e**s] 1 beweren, voorwenden; 2 verklaren, betuigen: *he ~ed his ignorance on the subject* hij verklaarde dat hij niets van het onderwerp afwist; 3 aanhangen

professed [prəf**e**st] 1 voorgevend, zogenaamd; 2 openlijk, verklaard, naar eigen zeggen

profession [prəf**e**sjən] 1 verklaring, uiting; 2 beroep[h], vak[h], alle beoefenaren vh vak

¹professional [prəf**e**sjənəl] *adj* 1 professioneel, beroeps-, prof-: *~ jealousy* broodnijd; 2 vakkundig, bekwaam; 3 met een hogere opleiding; 4 professioneel, opzettelijk *(of foul)*

²professional [prəf**e**sjənəl] *n* 1 beroeps, deskundige; 2 professional, prof: *turn ~* beroeps worden

professor [prəf**e**ssə] professor, hoogleraar: *~ of chemistry* hoogleraar in de scheikunde

proffer [pr**o**ffə] aanbieden, aanreiken

proficiency [prəf**i**sjənsie] vakkundigheid, bekwaamheid

proficient [prəf**i**sjənt] vakkundig, bekwaam

¹profile [pr**oo**fajl] *n* 1 profiel[h], zijaanzicht[h]; 2 silhouet[h], doorsnede; 3 profiel[h], karakterschets

²profile [pr**oo**fajl] *vb* 1 van opzij weergeven; aftekenen, in silhouet weergeven, een dwarsdoorsnede geven van; 2 een karakterschets geven van

¹profit [pr**o**ffit] *n* 1 winst, opbrengst; 2 rente; 3 nut[h], voordeel[h], profijt[h]: *I read the book much to my ~* ik heb veel aan het boek gehad

²profit [pr**o**ffit] *vb* 1 nuttig zijn; 2 *(with by, from)* profiteren (van), profijt trekken

profitable [pr**o**ffittəbl] 1 nuttig, voordelig; 2 winstgevend

¹profiteer [proffitt**ie**ə] *n* woekeraar

²profiteer [proffitt**ie**ə] *vb* woekerwinst maken

profligacy [pr**o**fligəsie] 1 losbandigheid; 2 verkwisting

¹profligate [pr**o**fligət] *adj* 1 losbandig, lichtzinnig; 2 verkwistend

²profligate [pr**o**fligət] *n* 1 losbol; 2 verkwister

profound [prəf**au**nd] 1 wijs, wijsgerig, diepzinnig: *a ~ thinker* een groot denker; 2 diepgaand, moeilijk te doorgronden; 3 diep, grondig: *silence* diepe stilte

profundity [prəf**u**ndittie] 1 diepzinnigheid, wijsgerigheid; 2 ondoorgrondelijkheid

profuse [prəf**joe**:s] 1 gul, kwistig: *be ~ in one's apologies* zich uitputten in verontschuldigingen; 2 overvloedig, overdadig: *bleed ~ly* hevig bloeden

progenitor [prood**j**enittə] voorvader

progeny [pr**o**dzjənie] 1 nageslacht[h], kinderen; 2 volgelingen

prognosis [progn**oo**sis] prognose, voorspelling

¹program [pr**oo**græm] *n* (computer)programma[h]

²program [pr**oo**græm] *vb* programmeren

¹programme [pr**oo**græm] *n* programma[h]

²programme [pr**oo**græm] *vb* programmeren, een schema opstellen voor

programmer [pr**oo**græmə] programmeur

¹progress [pr**oo**gres] *n* voortgang, vooruitgang, *(fig)* vordering: *the patient is making ~* de patiënt gaat vooruit; *in ~* in wording, aan de gang, in uitvoering

²progress [prəgr**e**s] *vb* vorderen, vooruitgaan, vooruitkomen, *(fig also)* zich ontwikkelen

progression [prəgr**e**sjən] 1 opeenvolging, aaneenschakeling; 2 voortgang, vooruitgang

¹progressive [prəgr**e**ssiv] *adj* 1 toenemend, voortschrijdend, voorwaarts, progressief *(tax)*; 2 progressief, vooruitstrevend; 3 *(linguistics)* progressief, duratief: *the ~ (form)* de duurvorm, de bezigheidsvorm

²progressive [prəgr**e**ssiv] *n* vooruitstrevend persoon

prohibit [prooh**i**bbit] verbieden: *smoking ~ed* verboden te roken

prohibition [prooh**i**bbisjən] verbod[h], drankverbod[h]

¹project [pr**o**dzjekt] *n* 1 plan[h], ontwerp[h]; 2 project[h], onderneming; 3 project[h], onderzoek[h]

²project [prədzj**e**kt] *vb* vooruitspringen, uitsteken: *~ing shoulder blades* uitstekende schouderbladen

³project [prədzj**e**kt] *vb* 1 ontwerpen, uitstippelen; 2 werpen, projecteren: *~ slides* dia's projecteren; 3 afbeelden, tonen; 4 schatten

projectile [prədzj**e**ktajl] projectiel[h]; raket

projection [prədzj**e**ksjən] 1 uitstekend deel[h], uitsprong; 2 projectie, beeld[h]; 3 raming, plan[h]; projectie

projector [prədzj**e**ktə] projector, filmprojector, diaprojector

¹proletarian [proolitt**ea**riən] *adj* proletarisch

²proletarian [proolitt**ea**riən] *n* proletariër

proliferation [prəliffər**ee**sjən] 1 woekering, snelle groei; 2 verspreiding

prolific [prəl**i**ffik] vruchtbaar, *(fig)* met overvloedige resultaten, rijk: *a ~ writer* een productief schrijver

prologue [pr**oo**log] proloog, voorwoord[h], inleiding

prolong [prəl**o**ng] 1 verlengen, langer maken; 2 verlengen, aanhouden: *a ~ed silence* langdurige stilte

prom [prom] 1 promenadeconcert[h]; *(Am)* schoolbal[h], universiteitsbal[h], dansfeest[h]; 2 promenade, boulevard

¹promenade [prommən**a**:d] *n* 1 wandeling, het flaneren; 2 promenade, boulevard

²promenade [prommən**a**:d] *vb* 1 wandelen (langs), flaneren; 2 wandelen met, lopen te pronken met

prominence [pr**o**mminnəns] 1 verhoging, uitsteeksel[h]; 2 het uitsteken; 3 opvallendheid; bekendheid, belang^h: *bring sth. into* ~ iets bekendheid geven

prominent [pr<u>o</u>mminnənt] **1** uitstekend, uitspringend: ~ *teeth* vooruitstekende tanden; **2** opvallend; **3** vooraanstaand, prominent: *a ~ scholar* een eminent geleerde

promiscuity [prommiskj<u>oe:</u>ittie] **1** willekeurige vermenging; **2** onzorgvuldigheid; **3** vrij seksueel verkeer^h, promiscuïteit

¹promise [pr<u>o</u>mmis] *n* belofte, toezegging: *break one's* ~ zich niet aan zijn belofte houden

²promise [pr<u>o</u>mmis] *vb* **1** een belofte doen, (iets) beloven; **2** verwachtingen wekken, veelbelovend zijn

³promise [pr<u>o</u>mmis] *vb* **1** beloven, toezeggen, *(inf)* verzekeren: *the ~d land* het Beloofde Land; **2** beloven, doen verwachten: *it ~d to be a severe winter* het beloofde een strenge winter te worden

promising [pr<u>o</u>mmissing] veelbelovend

promontory [pr<u>o</u>mməntərie] kaap, klip, voorgebergte^h

promote [prəm<u>oo</u>t] **1** bevorderen, in rang verhogen; **2** bevorderen, stimuleren; **3** steunen *(eg bill)*; **4** ondernemen, in gang zetten; **5** reclame maken voor

promoter [prəm<u>oo</u>tə] **1** begunstiger, bevorderaar; **2** organisator, financie've manifestatie

promotion [prəm<u>oo</u>osjən] **1** bevordering, promotie; **2** aanbieding, reclame

¹prompt [prompt] *adj* prompt, onmiddellijk, vlug, alert: ~ *payment* prompte betaling

²prompt [prompt] *adv* precies, stipt: *at twelve o'clock* ~ om twaalf uur precies

³prompt [prompt] *vb* **1** bewegen, drijven: *what ~ed you to do that?* hoe kwam je erbij dat te doen?; **2** opwekken, oproepen; **3** herinneren, voorzeggen, souffleren

⁴prompt [prompt] *n* geheugensteuntje^h, het voorzeggen, hulp vd souffleur

prone [proon] **1** voorover, voorovergebogen; **2** vooroverliggend, uitgestrekt; **3** geneigd, vatbaar: *he is ~ to tactlessness* hij is geneigd tot tactloosheid

prong [prong] **1** punt^h, piek, vorktand; **2** tak, vertakking

pronoun [pr<u>oo</u>naun] *(linguistics)* voornaamwoord^h

¹pronounce [prən<u>au</u>ns] *vb* **1** uitspreken; **2** verklaren, verkondigen: ~ *judgement* (of: *verdict*) uitspraak doen

²pronounce [prən<u>au</u>ns] *vb* **1** spreken, articuleren; **2** oordelen, zijn mening verkondigen: ~ *(up)on* uitspraken doen over, commentaar leveren op

pronounced [prən<u>au</u>nst] **1** uitgesproken; **2** uitgesproken, onmiskenbaar

pronto [pr<u>o</u>ntoo] meteen, onmiddellijk

pronunciation [prənunsie·<u>ee</u>sjən] uitspraak

¹proof [proe:f] *n* **1** toets, proefneming: *bring* (of: *put*) *to the* ~ op de proef stellen; **2** bewijs^h: *in* ~ *of his claim* om zijn stelling te bewijzen; **3** drukproef; **4** proefafdruk

²proof [proe:f] *adj* bestand *(also fig)*, opgewassen: ~

against water waterdicht, waterbestendig

-proof [proe:f] -bestendig, -vast, -dicht: *bulletproof* kogelvrij; *childproof* onverwoestbaar *(of toys)*

¹prop [prop] *n* **1** stut, pijler; steun, steunpilaar; **2** rekwisiet^h, benodigd voorwerp^h bij toneelvoorstelling

²prop [prop] *vb* ondersteunen *(also fig)*, stutten

propaganda [proppəgændə] propaganda, propagandamateriaal^h, propagandacampagne

¹propagate [pr<u>o</u>ppəgeet] *vb* (zich) voortplanten

²propagate [pr<u>o</u>ppəgeet] *vb* **1** verspreiden, bekendmaken; **2** voortzetten, doorgeven *(to next generation)*; **3** fokken, telen

propel [prəp<u>e</u>l] voortbewegen, aandrijven ‖ ~*ling pencil* vulpotlood

¹propellant [prəp<u>e</u>llənt] *adj* voortdrijvend *(also fig)*, stuwend

²propellant [prəp<u>e</u>llənt] *n* **1** drijfgas^h; **2** *(space travel)* aandrijfbrandstof

propeller [prəp<u>e</u>llə] propeller

propensity [prəp<u>e</u>nsittie] neiging

proper [pr<u>o</u>ppə] **1** gepast, fatsoenlijk; **2** juist, passend: *the ~ treatment* de juiste behandeling; **3** juist, precies: *the ~ time* de juiste tijd; **4** geweldig, eersteklas: *a ~ spanking* een geweldig pak slaag; **5** behorend *(to)*, eigen *(to)*: ~ *to* behorend tot, eigen aan; **6** eigenlijk, strikt: *London* ~ het eigenlijke Londen; ~ *noun* (of: *name*) eigennaam

properly [pr<u>o</u>ppəlie] **1** goed, zoals het moet; **2** eigenlijk, strikt genomen; **3** correct, fatsoenlijk; **4** volkomen, volslagen

property [pr<u>o</u>ppətie] **1** eigenschap, kenmerk^h; **2** perceel^h, onroerend goed^h; **3** rekwisiet^h, benodigd voorwerp^h bij een toneelvoorstelling; **4** bezit^h, eigendom^h: *lost* ~ gevonden voorwerpen; **5** bezit^h, vermogen^h, onroerend goed^h

prophecy [pr<u>o</u>ffəsie] **1** voorspelling; **2** profetie

¹prophesy [pr<u>o</u>ffəsaj] *vb* **1** voorspellingen doen; **2** als een profeet spreken

²prophesy [pr<u>o</u>ffəsaj] *vb* **1** voorspellen, voorzeggen; **2** aankondigen

prophet [pr<u>o</u>ffit] profeet

proponent [prəp<u>oo</u>nənt] voorstander, verdediger

¹proportion [prəp<u>o:</u>sjən] *n* **1** deel^h, gedeelte^h, aandeel^h; **2** verhouding, relatie: *bear no* ~ *to* in geen verhouding staan tot; **3** proportie, evenredigheid: *out of all* ~ buiten alle verhoudingen

²proportion [prəp<u>o:</u>sjən] *vb* **1** aanpassen, in de juiste verhouding brengen; **2** proportioneren: *well ~ed* goed geproportioneerd

proportional [prəp<u>o:</u>sjənəl] verhoudingsgewijs, proportioneel, evenredig

proposal [prəp<u>oo</u>zl] **1** voorstel^h; **2** huwelijksaanzoek^h

¹propose [prəp<u>oo</u>z] *vb* **1** voorstellen, voorleggen: ~ *a motion* een motie indienen; **2** van plan zijn, zich voornemen; **3** een dronk uitbrengen (op)

²propose [prəp<u>oo</u>z] *vb* **1** een voorstel doen; **2** een huwelijksaanzoek doen

¹proposition [proppəzisjən] *n* **1** bewering; **2** voorstel[h], plan[h]; **3** probleem[h], moeilijk geval[h]: *he's a tough* ~ hij is moeilijk te hanteren
²proposition [proppəzisjən] *vb* oneerbare voorstellen doen aan
propound [prəpaund] voorstellen
proprietary [prəprajjətərie] **1** eigendoms-, vd eigenaar, particulier: ~ *name* (of: *term*) gedeponeerd handelsmerk; **2** bezittend, met bezittingen; **3** als een eigenaar, bezittend: *he always has this* ~ *air* hij gedraagt zich altijd alsof alles van hem is
proprietor [prəprajjətə] eigenaar
propriety [prəprajjətie] **1** juistheid, geschiktheid; **2** correctheid, fatsoen[h], gepastheid
propulsion [prəpulsjən] **1** drijfkracht; **2** voortdrijving, voortstuwing
prop up overeind houden, ondersteunen
prosaic [proozeeik] **1** zakelijk; **2** alledaags
proscribe [prooskrajb] **1** verbieden, als gevaarlijk verwerpen; **2** verbannen *(also fig)*, verstoten
prose [prooz] proza[h]
prosecute [prossikjoe:t] **1** voortzetten, volhouden; **2** (gerechtelijk) vervolgen, procederen tegen: *trespassers will be* ~*d* verboden voor onbevoegden
prosecutor [prossikjoe:tə] **1** eiser, eisende partij; **2** *(Am)* openbare aanklager: *public* ~ openbare aanklager
¹prospect [prospekt] *n* **1** vergezicht[h], panorama[h]; **2** idee[h], denkbeeld[h]; **3** ligging, uitzicht[h]; **4** hoop, verwachting, kans, vooruitzicht[h]; **5** potentiële klant, prospect[h]
²prospect [prəspekt] *vb* naar bodemschatten zoeken
prospective [prəspektiv] **1** voor de toekomst, nog niet in werking; **2** toekomstig: *a* ~ *buyer* een gegadigde, een mogelijke koper
prospector [prəspektə] goudzoeker
prosper [prospə] bloeien, slagen, succes hebben
prosperity [prosperrittie] voorspoed, succes[h]
¹prostitute [prostitjoe:t] *n* prostitué *(man)*, prostituee
²prostitute [prostitjoe:t] *vb* **1** prostitueren, tot prostitué (prostituee) maken: ~ *oneself* zich prostitueren; **2** vergooien, verlagen, misbruiken: ~ *one's honour* zich verlagen, z'n eer te grabbel gooien
prostitution [prostitjoe:sjən] prostitutie
¹prostrate [prostreet] *adj* **1** ter aarde geworpen; **2** liggend, uitgestrekt, languit; **3** verslagen, gebroken: ~ *with grief* gebroken van verdriet
²prostrate [prostreet] *vb* neerwerpen, neerslaan: ~ *oneself* zich ter aarde werpen, in het stof knielen
prosy [proozie] saai, vervelend
protect [prətekt] **1** beschermen; **2** beveiligen, beveiligingen aanbrengen
protection [prəteksjən] **1** beschermer, bescherming, beschutting; **2** vrijgeleide[h]
protective [prətektiv] beschermend, beschermings-: ~ *colouring* schutkleur; ~ *sheath* condoom
protector [prətektə] **1** beschermer, beschermheer;

2 beschermend middel[h]
protectorate [prətektərət] protectoraat[h], land dat onder bescherming ve ander land staat
protein [prootie:n] proteïne, eiwit[h]
¹protest [prootest] *n* protest[h], bezwaar[h]: *enter* (of: *lodge, make) a* ~ *against sth.* ergens protest tegen aantekenen
²protest [prətest] *vb* protesteren, bezwaar maken
³protest [prətest] *vb* **1** bezweren, betuigen: ~ *one's innocence* zijn onschuld betuigen; **2** *(Am)* protesteren tegen: *they are* ~*ing nuclear weapons* ze protesteren tegen kernwapens
Protestant [prottistənt] protestant(s)
protocol [prootəkol] **1** protocol[h]; **2** officieel verslag[h], akte, verslag[h] van internationale onderhandelingen
prototype [prootətajp] prototype[h], oorspronkelijk model[h]
protract [prətrækt] voortzetten, verlengen, rekken
protractor [prətræktə] gradenboog, hoekmeter
protrude [prətroe:d] uitpuilen, uitsteken: *protruding eyes* uitpuilende ogen
protuberant [prətjoe:bərənt] gezwollen, uitpuilend
proud [praud] **1** trots, fier, zelfverzekerd, hoogmoedig, arrogant; **2** trots, vereerd: *I'm* ~ *to know thing*
¹prove [proe:v] *vb* bewijzen, (aan)tonen: *of proven authenticity* waarvan de echtheid is bewezen
²prove [proe:v] *vb* **1** blijken: *our calculations* ~*d incorrect* onze berekeningen bleken onjuist te zijn; **2** *(culinary)* rijzen
provenance [provvənəns] herkomst
proverb [provvə:b] gezegde[h], spreekwoord[h], spreuk
¹provide [prəvajd] *vb* **1** bepalen, eisen, vaststellen: ~ *that ...* bepalen dat ...; **2** voorzien, uitrusten, verschaffen: *they* ~*d us with blankets and food* zij voorzagen ons van dekens en voedsel
²provide [prəvajd] *vb* **1** voorzieningen treffen: ~ *against flooding* maatregelen nemen tegen overstromingen; **2** in het onderhoud voorzien, verzorgen: ~ *for children* kinderen onderhouden
provided [prəvajdid] op voorwaarde dat, (alleen) indien, mits: ~ *that* op voorwaarde dat, mits
providence [provviddəns] **1** *Providence* de Voorzienigheid, God; **2** voorzorg, zorg voor de toekomst, spaarzaamheid
provident [provviddənt] **1** vooruitziend; **2** zuinig, spaarzaam
providential [provviddensjl] wonderbaarlijk
provider [prəvajdə] **1** leverancier; **2** kostwinner
providing [prəvajding] op voorwaarde dat, (alleen) indien, mits: ~ *(that) it is done properly* mits het goed gebeurt
province [provvins] **1** provincie, gewest[h]; **2** vakgebied[h], terrein[h]: *outside one's* ~ buiten zijn vakgebied; **3** ~*s* platteland[h], provincie

¹provincial [prəvinsjl] *adj* provinciaal, van de provincie, *(depr)* bekrompen

²provincial [prəvinsjl] *n* **1** provinciaal, iem uit de provincie; **2** provinciaaltje^h, bekrompen mens

provision [prəvizjən] **1** bepaling, voorwaarde; **2** voorraad, hoeveelheid, rantsoen^h; **3** levering, toevoer, voorziening; **4** voorzorg, voorbereiding, maatregelen: *make ~ for the future* voor zijn toekomst zorgen; **5** *~s* levensmiddelen, provisie, proviand^h

provisional [prəvizjənəl] tijdelijk, voorlopig

proviso [prəvajzoo] voorwaarde, beperkende bepaling

provocation [provvəkeesjən] provocatie, uitdaging: *he did it under ~* hij is ertoe gedreven

provoke [prəvook] **1** tergen, prikkelen: *his behaviour ~d me into beating him* door zijn gedrag werd ik zo kwaad dat ik hem een pak slaag gaf; **2** uitdagen, provoceren, ophitsen; **3** veroorzaken, uitlokken

prow [prau] voorsteven

prowess [prauis] **1** dapperheid; **2** bekwaamheid

¹prowl [praul] *vb* **1** jagen, op roof uit zijn; **2** lopen loeren, rondsluipen, rondsnuffelen: *s.o. is ~ing about* (of: *around*) *on the staircase* er sluipt iem rond in het trappenhuis

²prowl [praul] *n* jacht, roof(tocht), het rondsluipen

prowl car *(Am)* surveillancewagen *(of police)*

proximity [proksimmittie] nabijheid: *in the ~* in de nabijheid, in de nabije toekomst

proxy [proksie] **1** gevolmachtigde, afgevaardigde: *stand ~ for s.o.* als iemands gemachtigde optreden; **2** (bewijs van) volmacht, volmachtbrief: *marry by ~* bij volmacht trouwen

prude [proe:d] preuts mens

prudence [proe:dəns] **1** voorzichtigheid, omzichtigheid: *fling* (of: *throw*) *~ to the winds* alle voorzichtigheid overboord gooien; **2** beleid^h, wijsheid

prudent [proe:dənt] voorzichtig; met inzicht, verstandig

¹prune [proe:n] *n* pruimedant, gedroogde pruim

²prune [proe:n] *vb* (be)snoeien *(also fig)*, korten, reduceren

prurient [proeəriənt] **1** wellustig; **2** obsceen, pornografisch

¹pry [praj] *vb* **1** gluren: *~ about* rondneuzen; **2** nieuwsgierig zijn: *I wish you wouldn't ~ into my affairs* ik wou dat je je niet met mijn zaken bemoeide

²pry [praj] *vb (Am)* (open)wrikken: *~ open a chest* een kist openbreken

P.S. *postscript* PS, post scriptum

psalm [sa:m] psalm, hymne, kerkgezang^h

psyche [sajkie] psyche, ziel

psychiatrist [sajkajjətrist] psychiater

psychiatry [sajkajjətrie] psychiatrie

psychic [sajkik] **1** psychisch, geestelijk; **2** paranormaal, bovennatuurlijk; **3** paranormaal begaafd

psychologist [sajkollədzjist] psycholoog

psychology [sajkollədzjie] **1** karakter^h, aard, psy-

che; **2** (wetenschap der) psychologie; **3** mensenkennis

psychopath [sajkəpæθ] psychopaat, geestelijk gestoorde

psychosis [sajkoosis] psychose

¹psych out *vb (Am)* in de war raken

²psych out *vb (Am)* **1** analyseren, hoogte krijgen van; **2** doorkrijgen, begrijpen: *I couldn't psych him out* ik kon er niet achter komen wat voor iem hij was; **3** intimideren *(opponent)*

P.T.O. *please turn over* z.o.z., zie ommezijde

pub [pub] *public house* café^h, bar, pub, kroeg

puberty [pjoe:bətie] puberteit

pubescence [pjoe:besns] **1** beharing; **2** begin^h van de puberteit

pubic [pjoe:bik] van de schaamstreek, schaam-

¹public [publik] *adj* **1** openbaar, publiek, voor iedereen toegankelijk, algemeen bekend: *~ bar* zaaltje in Brits café met goedkoop bier; *~ conveniences* openbare toiletten; *~ footpath* voetpad, wandelpad; *~ house* café, bar, pub; *~ transport* openbaar vervoer; *~ utility* nutsbedrijf; **2** algemeen, gemeenschaps-, nationaal, maatschappelijk: *~ holiday* nationale feestdag; *~ interest* het algemeen belang; *~ opinion* publieke opinie; *~ school* particuliere kostschool, *(Scotland, Am)* gesubsidieerde lagere school; **3** overheids-, regerings-, publiek-, staats-: *~ assistance* sociale steun, uitkering; *~ spending* overheidsuitgaven

²public [publik] *n* publiek^h, mensen, geïnteresseerden: *in ~* in het openbaar

publication [publikkeesjən] **1** uitgave, publicatie, boek^h, artikel^h; **2** publicatie, bekendmaking

publicity [publissittie] **1** publiciteit, bekendheid, openbaarheid; **2** publiciteit, reclame

publicize [publissajz] bekendmaken, adverteren

publish [publisj] **1** publiceren, schrijven; **2** uitgeven, publiceren; **3** bekendmaken, aankondigen, afkondigen

publisher [publisjə] uitgever(ij)

puck [puk] **1** kwelduivel; **2** ondeugend kind^h; **3** *(ice hockey)* puck

¹pucker [pukkə] *vb* samentrekken, rimpelen

²pucker [pukkə] *n* vouw, plooi, rimpel

pudding [poeding] **1** pudding *(also fig);* **2** dessert^h, toetje^h

puddle [pudl] plas, (modder)poel

pudgy [pudzjie] kort en dik, mollig

puerile [pjoeərajl] **1** kinder-, kinderlijk; **2** kinderachtig

¹puff [puf] *n* **1** ademstoot, puf; **2** rookwolk; **3** trek, haal, puf *(on cigarette etc)*; **4** puf, puffend geluid^h; **5** (poeder)dons^h

²puff [puf] *vb* **1** puffen, hijgen, blazen; **2** roken, dampen: *~ (away) at* (of: *on*) *a cigarette* een sigaret roken; **3** puffen, in wolkjes uitgestoten worden; **4** *(also with out)* opzwellen, zich opblazen

³puff [puf] *vb* **1** uitblazen, uitstoten: *~ smoke into s.o.'s eyes* iem rook in de ogen blazen; **2** roken, trekken *(on cigarette etc)*; **3** *(also with out)* opblazen, doen opzwellen: *~ed up with pride* verwaand, opgeblazen

puffy [puffie] opgezet, gezwollen, opgeblazen

pug [pug] **1** mopshond; **2** klei(mengsel[h])

pugnacious [pugneesjǝs] strijdlustig

puke [pjoe:k] overgeven, (uit)braken: *it makes me ~* ik word er kotsmisselijk van

¹pull [poel] *vb* **1** trekken, getrokken worden, plukken, rukken: *~ at* (of: *on) a pipe* aan een pijp trekken; **2** zich moeizaam voortbewegen: *~ away from* achter zich laten; **3** gaan *(of vehicle, rowing boat)*, gedreven worden, roeien, rijden: *the car ~ed ahead of us* de auto ging voor ons rijden; *the train ~ed into Bristol* de trein liep Bristol binnen

²pull [poel] *vb* **1** trekken (aan), (uit)rukken, naar zich toetrekken, uit de grond trekken, tappen, zich verzekeren van, (eruit) halen: *~ customers* klandizie trekken; *he ~ed a gun on her* hij richtte een geweer op haar; *the current ~ed him under* de stroming sleurde hem mee; **2** doen voortgaan, voortbewegen; **3** verrekken *(muscle)*; **4** (be)roven: *~ the other one* maak dat een ander wijs

³pull [poel] *n* **1** ruk, trek, stoot, *(fig)* klim, inspanning, moeite: *a long ~ across the hills* een hele klim over de heuvels; **2** trekkracht; **3** teug, slok *(drink)*, trek *(on cigar)*; **4** (trek)knop, trekker, handvat[h]; **5** invloed, macht: *have a ~ on s.o.* invloed over iem hebben; **6** het trekken, het rukken

pulley [poelie] **1** katrol; **2** riemschijf

¹pull-in *vb* **1** aankomen, binnenlopen, binnenvaren; **2** naar de kant gaan (en stoppen) *(of vehicle)*

²pull-in *vb* **1** binnenhalen *(money)*, opstrijken; **2** aantrekken, lokken: *Paul Simon always pulls in many people* Paul Simon trekt altijd veel mensen; **3** inhouden: *~ your stomach* houd je buik in; **4** in zijn kraag grijpen *(eg thief)*, inrekenen

pull off 1 uittrekken, uitdoen; **2** bereiken, slagen in: *~ a deal* in een transactie slagen; *he has pulled it off again* het is hem weer gelukt, hij heeft het weer klaargespeeld

¹pull out *vb* **1** (zich) terugtrekken, *(fig)* terugkrabbelen: *~ of politics* uit de politiek gaan; **2** vertrekken, wegrijden; **3** gaan inhalen, uithalen: *the driver who pulled out had not seen the oncoming lorry* de bestuurder die zijn baan verliet had de naderende vrachtauto niet gezien

²pull out *vb* verwijderen, uitdoen, uittrekken: *~ a tooth* een kies trekken

pullover pullover

¹pull over *vb* **1** opzijgaan, uit de weg gaan; **2** *(Am)* (naar de kant rijden en) stoppen

²pull over *vb* **1** naar de kant rijden; **2** stoppen *(vehicle)*

pull round 1 bij bewustzijn komen; **2** zich herstellen

pull through erdoor getrokken worden, erdoor komen: *the patient pulls through* de patiënt komt er doorheen

pull together 1 samentrekken; **2** samenwerken ‖

pull yourself together beheers je

¹pull up *vb* stoppen: *the car pulled up* de auto stopte

²pull up *vb* **1** uittrekken; **2** (doen) stoppen: *~ your car at the side* zet je auto aan de kant; **3** tot de orde roepen, op zijn plaats zetten

pull-up 1 rustplaats, wegrestaurant[h]; **2** optrekoefening *(on bar)*

pulp [pulp] **1** moes[h], pap; **2** vruchtvlees[h]; **3** pulp, houtpap; **4** rommel; **5** sensatieblad[h], sensatieboek[h], sensatieverhaal[h] ‖ *beat s.o. to a ~* iem tot moes slaan

pulpit [poelpit] preekstoel, kansel

pulp magazine sensatieblad[h], pulpblad[h]

pulsate [pulseet] kloppen, ritmisch bewegen, trillen

pulse [puls] **1** hartslag, pols(slag): *feel* (of: *take) s.o.'s ~* iemands hartslag opnemen, *(fig)* iem polsen; **2** (afzonderlijke) slag, stoot, trilling; **3** ritme[h] *(eg in music)*; **4** peul(vrucht); **5** peulen[h], peulvruchten

¹pulverize [pulvǝrajz] *vb* verpulveren, verpulverd worden

²pulverize [pulvǝrajz] *vb* verpulveren, *(fig)* vernietigen, niets heel laten van

puma [pjoe:mǝ] poema

¹pump [pump] *n* **1** pomp; **2** dansschoen, *(Am)* galaschoen

²pump [pump] *vb* **1** pompen, pompend bewegen; **2** bonzen *(of heart)*

³pump [pump] *vb* **1** pompen: *~ money into an industry* geld investeren in een industrie; **2** (krachtig) schudden *(hand)*; **3** met moeite gedaan krijgen, (erin) pompen, (eruit) stampen: *~ a witness* een getuige uithoren

pumpkin [pumpkin] pompoen

pun [pun] *n* woordspeling

pun [pun] *vb* woordspelingen maken

¹punch [puntsj] *n* **1** *Punch* Janklaassen: *Punch and Judy* Janklaassen en Katrijn; **2** werktuig[h] om gaten te slaan, ponsmachine, ponstang, perforator, kniptang; **3** (vuist)slag: *(boxing) pull one's ~es* zich inhouden *(also fig)*; **4** slagvaardigheid, kracht, pit: *his speech lacks ~* er zit geen pit in zijn toespraak; **5** punch, bowl(drank)

²punch [puntsj] *vb* **1** ponsen; **2** slaan: *~ up* op de vuist gaan; **3** *(Am)* klokken, een prikklok gebruiken: *~ in* klokken bij binnenkomst

³punch [puntsj] *vb* **1** slaan, een vuistslag geven; **2** gaten maken in, perforeren, knippen *(ticket)*, ponsen

punchbag *(boxing)* stootzak, zandzak, stootkussen[h]

punchball boksbal

punch-drunk versuft, *(fig)* verward

punch-up knokpartij

punchy [puntsjie] *(inf)* versuft, bedwelmd

punctilious [pungktilliǝs] zeer precies, plichtsgetrouw, nauwgezet

punctual [pungktjoeǝl] punctueel, stipt, nauwgezet

¹punctuate [pungktjoe·eet] *vb* leestekens aanbrengen

²**punctuate** [pungktsjoe·eet] *vb* onderbreken: *a speech ~d by* (of: *with*) *jokes* een toespraak doorspekt met grappen

punctuation [pungktsjoe·eesjən] interpunctie(tekens)

punctuation mark leesteken[h]

¹**puncture** [pungktsjə] *n* gaatje[h] *(eg in tyre)*, lek[h], lekke band

²**puncture** [pungktsjə] *vb* lek maken, doorboren, *(fig)* vernietigen

pungent [pundzjənt] **1** scherp: *~ remarks* stekelige opmerkingen; **2** prikkelend, pikant: *a ~ smell* een doordringende geur

punish [punnisj] **1** (be)straffen; **2** zijn voordeel doen met *(somebody's weakness)*, afstraffen

punishing [punnisjing] slopend, erg zwaar: *a ~ climb* een dodelijk vermoeiende beklimming

punishment [punnisjmənt] **1** straf, bestraffing: *corporal ~* lijfstraf; **2** ruwe behandeling, afstraffing

punitive [pjoe:nittiv] **1** straf-; **2** zeer hoog *(eg of tax)*

¹**punk** [pungk] *n* **1** punk(er); **2** (jonge) boef, relschopper

²**punk** [pungk] *adj* **1** waardeloos; **2** punk-, van (een) punk(s)

punnet [punnit] (spanen) mand(je[h]) *(for fruit, vegetables)*, (plastic) doosje[h]

¹**punt** [punt] *n* punter, platte rivierschuit

²**punt** [punt] *vb* **1** bomen, varen in een punter; **2** gokken *(eg at horce races)*

puny [pjoe:nie] nietig, miezerig, onbetekenend

¹**pup** [pup] *n* **1** pup(py), jong hondje[h]; **2** jong[h] *(eg of otter, seal)*

²**pup** [pup] *vb* jongen, werpen *(of dog)*

pupil [pjoe:pil] **1** leerling; **2** pupil *(of eye)*

puppet [puppit] marionet *(also fig)*, (houten) pop

puppy [puppie] **1** puppy, jong hondje[h]; **2** snotneus

¹**purchase** [pə:tsjəs] *vb* zich aanschaffen, (in)kopen

²**purchase** [pə:tsjəs] *n* **1** (aan)koop, ~s inkoop, aanschaf: *make ~s* inkopen doen; **2** vat[h], greep: *get a ~ on a rock* houvast vinden aan een rots

pure [pjoeə] **1** puur, zuiver, onvervalst: *a ~ Arab horse* een rasechte arabier; *~ and simple* niets dan, eenvoudigweg; **2** volkomen, zuiver, puur

purebred rasecht *(of animals)*, volbloed-

purée [pjoeəree] moes[h], puree

purely [pjoeəlie] uitsluitend, volledig, zonder meer: *a ~ personal matter* een zuiver persoonlijke aangelegenheid

purgation [pə:geesjən] zuivering, reiniging

purgatory [pə:gətərie] vagevuur[h]; (tijdelijke) kwelling

¹**purge** [pə:dzj] *vb* zuiveren, louteren, verlossen

²**purge** [pə:dzj] *n* **1** zuivering; **2** laxeermiddel[h]

purification [pjoeəriffikkeesjən] zuivering, verlossing, bevrijding

¹**purify** [pjoeəriffaj] *vb* zuiver worden

²**purify** [pjoeəriffaj] *vb* zuiveren, louteren

purism [pjoeərizm] purisme[h], (taal)zuivering

¹**puritan** [pjoeərittən] *adj* puriteins, moraliserend, streng van zeden

²**puritan** [pjoeərittən] *n* puritein, streng godsdienstig persoon

purity [pjoeərittie] zuiverheid, puurheid, onschuld

purler [pə:lə] smak, harde val: *come* (of: *take*) *a ~* een flinke smak maken

purple [pə:pl] **1** purper, donkerrood, paarsrood: *he became ~ with rage* hij liep rood aan van woede; **2** (te) sierlijk, bombastisch: *a ~ passage* (of: *patch*) een briljant gedeelte *(in tedious text)*

purport [pə:po:t] strekking, bedoeling

purpose [pə:pəs] **1** doel[h], bedoeling, plan[h], voornemen[h]: *accidentally on ~* per ongeluk expres; *he did it on ~* hij deed het met opzet; **2** zin, (beoogd) effect[h], resultaat[h], nut[h]: *all your help will be to no ~* al je hulp zal tevergeefs zijn; **3** de zaak waarom het gaat: *his remark is (not) to the ~* zijn opmerking is (niet) ter zake; **4** vastberadenheid

purposeful [pə:pəsfoel] **1** vastberaden; **2** met een doel, opzettelijk

¹**purr** [pə:] *n* **1** spinnend geluid[h], gespin[h] *(of cat)*; **2** zoemend geluid[h], gesnor[h] *(of machine)*

²**purr** [pə:] *vb* **1** spinnen *(of cat)*; **2** gonzen, zoemen *(of machine)*

¹**purse** [pə:s] *n* **1** portemonnee; **2** *(Am)* damestas(je[h])

²**purse** [pə:s] *vb* samentrekken, rimpelen, tuiten: *indignantly, she ~d her lips* ze tuitte verontwaardigd de lippen

pursuance [pəs·joe:əns] uitvoering, voortzetting: *in (the) ~ of his duty* tijdens het vervullen van zijn plicht

pursue [pəs·joe:] **1** jacht maken op, achtervolgen; **2** volgen, achternalopen *(also fig)*, lastig vallen: *this memory ~d him* deze herinnering liet hem niet los; **3** doorgaan met, vervolgen: *it is wiser not to ~ the matter* het is verstandiger de zaak verder te laten rusten

pursuit [pəs·joe:t] **1** achtervolging, jacht *(also fig)*: *in ~ of happiness* op zoek naar het geluk; **2** bezigheid, hobby

purvey [pə:vee] bevoorraden met, leveren *(food)*

pus [pus] pus, etter

¹**push** [poesj] *vb* **1** duwen, stoten, dringen; **2** vorderingen maken, vooruitgaan, verder gaan: *~ ahead* (of: *forward, on*) (rustig) doorgaan; *~ ahead* (of: *along, forward, on*) *with* vooruitgang boeken met; **3** pushen, dealen

²**push** [poesj] *vb* **1** (weg)duwen, een zet geven, voortduwen, *(fig)* beïnvloeden, dwingen: *~ the button* op de knop drukken; *he ~es the matter too far* hij drijft de zaak te ver door; *~ s.o. about* (of: *around*) iem ruw behandelen, iem commanderen, iem met minachting behandelen; *~ back the enemy* de vijand terugdringen; *~ oneself forward* zich op de voorgrond dringen; *that ~ed prices up* dat joeg de prijzen omhoog; **2** druk uitoefenen op, lastig vallen, aandringen bij: *don't ~ your luck (too far)!* stel je

geluk niet te veel op de proef!; *he ~ed his luck and fell* hij werd overmoedig en viel; **3** pushen *(drugs)*

³push [poesj] *n* **1** duw, stoot, zet, ruk: *give that door a ~* geef die deur even een zetje; **2** grootscheepse aanval *(of army)*, offensiefʰ, *(fig)* energieke poging; **3** energie, doorzettingsvermogenʰ, fut; **4** druk, nood, crisis: *if* (of: *when*) *it comes to the ~* als het erop aankomt; *give s.o. the ~: a)* iem ontslaan; *b)* iem de bons geven; *at a ~* als het echt nodig is, in geval van nood

pusher [poesjə] **1** (te) ambitieus iem, streber; **2** (illegale) drugsverkoper, (drugs)dealer

push in 1 een gesprek ruw onderbreken, ertussen komen, iem in de rede vallen; **2** voordringen

pushing [poesjing] **1** opdringerig; **2** vol energie, ondernemend

push off 1 ervandoor gaan, weggaan, ophoepelen: *now ~, will you* hoepel nu alsjeblieft eens op; **2** uitvaren, van wal steken

push through doordrukken, er doorheen slepen: *we'll push this matter through* we zullen deze zaak erdoor krijgen

pushy [poesjie] opdringerig

puss [poes] **1** poes *(esp used to call animal)*: *Puss in boots* de Gelaarsde Kat; **2** poesjeʰ, liefjeʰ, schatjeʰ

pussy [poesie] poes(jeʰ), kat(jeʰ)

¹put [poet] *vb* **1** zetten, plaatsen, leggen, steken, stellen *(also fig)*, brengen *(in a situation)*: *~ pressure (up)on* pressie uitoefenen op; *~ a price on sth.* een prijskaartje hangen aan; *~ sth. behind oneself* zich over iets heen zetten, met iets breken; *~ the children to bed* de kinderen naar bed brengen; *~ to good use* goed gebruik maken van; **2** onderwerpen, dwingen, drijven: *~ s.o. through it* iem een zware test afnemen, iem zwaar op de proef stellen; **3** (in)zetten, verwedden: *~ money on* geld zetten op, *(fig)* zeker zijn van; **4** voorleggen, ter sprake brengen: *~ a proposal before* (of: *to*) *a meeting* een vergadering een voorstel voorleggen; **5** uitdrukken, zeggen, stellen: *how shall I ~ it?* hoe zal ik het zeggen; *you'll be hard ~ to think of a second example* het zal je niet meevallen om een tweede voorbeeld te bedenken; *~ it* (of: *one, sth.*) *across s.o.* het iem flikken, iem beetnemen; *not ~ it past s.o. to do sth.* iem ertoe in staat achten iets te doen; *stay ~* blijven waar je bent, op zijn plaats blijven

²put [poet] *vb* varen, koers zetten: *the ship ~ into the port* het schip voer de haven binnen; *his sickness ~ paid to his plans* zijn ziekte maakte een eind aan zijn plannen; *~ (up)on s.o.* iem last bezorgen

¹put about *vb* **1** van richting doen veranderen *(ship)*; **2** verspreiden *(rumour, lies)*

²put about *vb* laveren, van richting veranderen

put across overbrengen *(also fig)*, aanvaardbaar maken, aan de man brengen: *know how to put one's ideas across* zijn ideeën weten over te brengen

put aside opzijzetten, wegzetten, opzijleggen *(also of money)*, sparen

put back 1 terugzetten, terugdraaien: *put the clock back* de klok terugzetten *(also fig)*; **2** vertragen, tegenhouden: *production has been ~ by a strike* de productie is door een staking vertraagd

put by opzijzetten, wegzetten *(money)*

¹put down *vb* **1** neerzetten, neerleggen; **2** onderdrukken *(rebellion, crime etc)*; **3** opschrijven, noteren: *put sth. down to ignorance* iets toeschrijven aan onwetendheid; **4** een spuitje geven *(sick animal)*, uit zijn lijden helpen; **5** afzetten, uit laten stappen *(passengers)*; **6** aanbetalen; **7** kleineren, vernederen, *(fig)* op zijn plaats zetten

²put down *vb* landen *(of aeroplane)*

¹put in *vb* **1** (erin) plaatsen, zetten, inlassen, invoegen: *~ an appearance* zich (eens) laten zien; **2** opwerpen: *~ a (good) word for s.o.* een goed woordje voor iem doen; **3** besteden *(time, work, money)*, doorbrengen *(time)*: *he ~ a lot of hard work on the project* hij heeft een boel werk in het project gestopt; **4** indienen, klacht, document: *~ a claim for damages* een eis tot schadevergoeding indienen

²put in *vb* **1** een verzoek indienen, solliciteren: *~ for* zich kandidaat stellen voor; *~ for leave* verlof (aan)vragen; **2** binnenlopen: *~ at a port* een haven binnenlopen

put off 1 uitstellen, afzeggen; **2** afzetten, uit laten stappen *(passengers)*; **3** afschrikken, (van zich) afstoten: *the smell of that food put me off* de reuk van dat eten deed me walgen; **4** afschepen, ontmoedigen; **5** van de wijs brengen: *the speaker was ~ by the noise* de spreker werd door het lawaai van zijn stuk gebracht; **6** uitdoen, uitdraaien, afzetten *(light, gas, radio etc)*

put on 1 voorwenden, aannemen *(attitude)*: *~ a brave face* flink zijn; **2** toevoegen, verhogen: *~ weight* aankomen, zwaarder worden; *put it on: a)* aankomen *(weight); b)* overdrijven; **3** opvoeren, op de planken brengen: *~ a play* een toneelstuk op de planken brengen; *put it on* doen alsof; **4** aantrekken *(clothing)*, opzetten *(glasses, hat)*; **5** inzetten, inleggen *(extra train etc)*; **6** in werking stellen, aandoen *(light)*, aanzetten *(radio etc)*, opzetten *(record, kettle)*: *~ a brake* (of: *the brakes*) afremmen *(fig)*; **7** in contact brengen, doorverbinden: *who put the police on to me?* wie heeft de politie op mijn spoor gezet?

¹put out *vb* **1** uitsteken, tonen: *~ feelers* zijn voelhoorns uitsteken; **2** aanwenden, inzetten, gebruiken; **3** uitdoen, doven, blussen: *~ the fire* het vuur doven; **4** van zijn stuk brengen; **5** storen: *put oneself out* zich moeite getroosten, moeite doen; **6** buiten zetten *(garbage)*, eruit gooien, de deur wijzen; **7** uitvaardigen, uitgeven, uitzenden *(message)*: *~ an official statement* een communiqué uitgeven; **8** uitbesteden *(work)*: *~ a job to a subcontractor* een werk aan een onderaannemer uitbesteden

²put out *vb* uitvaren: *~ to sea* zee kiezen

¹put over *vb* **1** overbrengen *(also fig)*, aan de man brengen: *put (a fast) one* (of: *sth.*) *over on s.o.* iem iets wijsmaken; **2** *(Am)* uitstellen

²**put over** *vb* overvaren

putrefy [pjoe:triffaj] (doen) (ver)rotten, (doen) bederven

putrid [pjoe:trid] (ver)rot, vergaan, verpest

put through (door)verbinden *(telephone call)*

put together 1 samenvoegen, samenstellen, combineren: *more than all the others* ~ meer dan alle anderen bij elkaar; **2** verzamelen, verenigen: *put two and two together: a)* zijn conclusies trekken; *b)* logisch nadenken

putty [puttie] **1** stopverf; **2** plamuurʰ ‖ *be* ~ *in s.o.'s hands* als was in iemands handen zijn

¹**put up** *vb* logeren: ~ *at an inn* in een herberg logeren; *I wouldn't* ~ *with it any longer* ik zou het niet langer meer slikken

²**put up** *vb* **1** opzetten, oprichten, bouwen *(tent, statue etc):* ~ *a smokescreen* een rookgordijn leggen; **2** opsteken, hijsen, ophangen: *put one's hands up* de handen opsteken *(indicating surrender);* **3** bekendmaken, ophangen: ~ *a notice* een bericht ophangen; **4** verhogen, opslaan: ~ *the rent* de huurprijs verhogen; **5** huisvesten, logeren; **6** beschikbaar stellen *(funds),* voorschieten: *who will* ~ *money for new research?* wie stelt geld beschikbaar voor nieuw onderzoek?; **7** bieden, tonen: *the rebels* ~ *strong resistance* de rebellen boden hevig weerstand; **8** (te koop) aanbieden: *they* ~ *their house for sale* zij boden hun huis te koop aan; **9** kandidaat stellen, voordragen: *they put him up for chairman* zij droegen hem als voorzitter voor; *put s.o. up to sth.: a)* iem opstoken tot iets; *b)* iem op de hoogte brengen van iets

put-up afgesproken: *it's a* ~ *job* het is een doorgestoken kaart

¹**puzzle** [puzl] *n* **1** raadselʰ, probleemʰ; **2** puzzel: *crossword* ~ kruiswoordraadsel

²**puzzle** [puzl] *vb* **1** voor een raadsel zetten, verbazen, verbijsteren; **2** in verwarring brengen; **3** overpeinzen: ~ *one's brains (about, over)* zich het hoofd breken (over); ~ *sth. out* iets uitpluizen

³**puzzle** [puzl] *vb* peinzen, piekeren

puzzled [puzld] in de war, perplex

puzzler [puzlə] **1** puzzelaar(ster); **2** probleemʰ, moeilijke vraag

¹**pygmy** [pigmie] *n* pygmee, dwerg, *(fig)* nietig persoon

²**pygmy** [pigmie] *adj* heel klein, dwerg-

pyjamas [pədzja:məz] pyjama: *four pairs of* ~ vier pyjama's

pyramid [pirrəmid] piramide

pyromaniac [pajjəroomeenie·æk] pyromaan

pyrotechnic [pajjərooteknik] vuurwerk-: *a* ~ *display* een vuurwerk(show)

python [pajθn] python

q

¹**quack** [kwæk] *n* **1** kwakzalver, charlatan; **2** kwak *(of duck)*, gekwaak^h

²**quack** [kwæk] *vb* **1** kwaken *(of duck)*; **2** zwetsen, kletsen

quadrangle [kwodrænggl] **1** vierhoek, vierkant^h, rechthoek; **2** (vierhoekige) binnenplaats, vierkant plein^h (met de gebouwen eromheen)

¹**quadrilateral** [kwodrilætərəl] *adj* vierzijdig

²**quadrilateral** [kwodrilætərəl] *n* vierhoek

quadruped [kwodroeped] viervoeter, (als) ve viervoeter

¹**quadruple** [kwodroe:pl] *adj* vierdelig; viervoudig

²**quadruple** [kwodroe:pl] *n* viervoud^h

quadruplet [kwodroeplit] één ve vierling, ~s vierling

quagmire [kwægmajjə] moeras^h *(also fig)*, poel

¹**quail** [kweel] *n* kwartel

²**quail** [kweel] *vb* (terug)schrikken, bang worden

quaint [kweent] **1** apart, curieus, ongewoon: *a ~ old building* een bijzonder, oud gebouw; **2** vreemd, grillig

¹**quake** [kweek] *vb* schokken, trillen, bibberen

²**quake** [kweek] *n* **1** schok; **2** aardbeving

qualification [kwolliffikkeesjən] **1** beperking, voorbehoud^h: *a statement with many ~s* een verklaring met veel kanttekeningen; **2** kwaliteit, verdienste, kwalificatie; **3** (bewijs^h van) geschiktheid: *a medical ~* een medische bevoegdheid; **4** beschrijving, kenmerking

qualified [kwolliffajd] **1** beperkt, voorwaardelijk, voorlopig: *~ optimism* gematigd optimisme; **2** bevoegd, geschikt: *a ~ nurse* een gediplomeerde verpleegster

¹**qualify** [kwolliffaj] *vb* zich kwalificeren, zich bekwamen, geschikt zijn, worden: *~ for membership* in aanmerking komen voor lidmaatschap

²**qualify** [kwolliffaj] *vb* **1** beperken, kwalificeren, (verder) bepalen: *a ~ing exam* een akte-examen; **2** geschikt maken, het recht geven; **3** verzachten, matigen

qualitative [kwollittətiv] kwalitatief

quality [kwollittie] **1** kwaliteit, deugd, capaciteit: *~ of life* leefbaarheid, kwaliteit van het bestaan; **2** eigenschap, kenmerk^h, karakteristiek; **3** kwaliteit, waarde, gehalte^h: *~ newspaper* kwaliteitskrant; *~ time* kwaliteitstijd

qualm [kwa:m] **1** (gevoel van) onzekerheid, ongemakkelijk gevoel^h: *she had no ~s about going on her own* ze zag er niet tegenop om alleen te gaan; **2** (gewetens)wroeging

quandary [kwondərie] moeilijke situatie, dilemma^h, onzekerheid: *we were in a ~ about how to react* we wisten niet goed hoe we moesten reageren

quantify [kwontiffaj] kwantificeren, in getallen uitdrukken, meten, bepalen

quantity [kwontittie] **1** hoeveelheid, aantal^h, som, portie; **2** grootheid, *(fig)* persoon, ding^h: *an unknown ~* een onbekende (grootheid), een nog niet doorgronde *(of:* berekenbare) persoon; **3** kwantiteit, hoeveelheid, omvang

¹**quantum** [kwontəm] *n* kwantum^h, (benodigde, wenselijke) hoeveelheid

²**quantum** [kwontəm] *adj* spectaculair: *~ leap* spectaculaire stap vooruit, doorbraak, omwenteling

¹**quarantine** [kworrəntie:n] *n* quarantaine, isolatie

²**quarantine** [kworrəntie:n] *vb* in quarantaine plaatsen, *(fig also)* isoleren

¹**quarrel** [kworrəl] *n* **1** ruzie, ónenigheid: *start* (of: *pick*) *a ~ (with s.o.)* ruzie zoeken (met iem); **2** kritiek, reden tot ruzie: *I have no ~ with him* ik heb niets tegen hem

²**quarrel** [kworrəl] *vb* **1** ruzie maken, onenigheid hebben; **2** kritiek hebben, aanmerkingen hebben

quarrelsome [kworrəlsəm] ruziezoekend

quarry [kworrie] **1** (nagejaagde) prooi, wild^h; **2** (steen)groeve

quart [kwo:t] quart^h, kwart gallon, twee pints *(measure of capacity)* ‖ *put a ~ into a pint pot* het onmogelijke proberen

quarter [kwo:tə] **1** kwart^h, vierde deel^h: *a ~ of an hour* een kwartier; *three ~s of the people voted* driekwart van de mensen stemde; **2** kwart dollar, kwartje^h; **3** kwartaal^h, *(Am)* collegeperiode, academisch kwartaal^h; **4** kwartier^h *(of time, moon)*: *for an hour and a ~* een uur en een kwartier (lang); *it's a ~ past eight* het is kwart over acht; **5** quarter, kwart^h *(weight, size, measure)*; **6** (wind)richting, windstreek *(of compass)*, hoek, kant: *I expect no help from that ~* ik verwacht geen hulp uit die hoek; **7** (stads)deel^h, wijk, gewest^h; **8** genade, clementie: *ask for* (of: *cry) ~* om genade smeken; **9** *~s (oft mil)* kwartier^h, verblijf^h, woonplaats, legerplaats, kamer(s), *(fig)* kring: *this information comes from the highest ~s* deze inlichtingen komen uit de hoogste kringen

quarterdeck *(shipp)* **1** (officiers)halfdek^h; **2** (marine)officieren

quarter-final kwartfinale

¹**quarterly** [kwo:təlie] *adj* driemaandelijks, viermaal per jaar, kwartaalsgewijs

²**quarterly** [kwo:təlie] *n* driemaandelijks tijdschrift^h, kwartaalblad^h

quartet [kwo:tet] kwartet^h, viertal^h

quarto [kwo:too] kwarto^h

quartz [kwo:ts] kwarts^h

quasi [kw_eezaj] quasi, zogenaamd

¹quaver [kw_eevə] *n* **1** trilling; **2** *(mus)* achtste (noot)

²quaver [kw_eevə] *vb* trillen, beven, sidderen: *in a ~ing voice* met bevende stem

quay [kie:] kade

queasy [kw_ie:zie] **1** misselijk, onpasselijk; **2** overgevoelig, kieskeurig: *he has a ~ conscience* hij neemt het erg nauw

¹queen [kwie:n] *n* **1** koningin; **2** *(chess)* koningin, dame; **3** *(cards)* vrouw, dame: *~ of hearts* hartenvrouw; **4** nicht, verwijfde flikker

²queen [kwie:n] *vb: ~ it over s.o.* de mevrouw spelen t.o.v. iem

Queen's English standaard Engels, BBC-Engels

¹queer [kwiə] *adj* **1** vreemd, raar, zonderling: *a ~ customer* een rare snuiter; **2** verdacht, onbetrouwbaar; **3** onwel, niet lekker; **4** homoseksueel: *be in Queer Street: a)* in moeilijkheden zitten; *b)* schulden hebben

²queer [kwiə] *n* homo, flikker

quell [kwel] onderdrukken, een eind maken aan, onderwerpen

quench [kwentsj] **1** doven, blussen; **2** lessen *(thirst)*

querulous [kw_erroeləs] **1** klagend; **2** klagerig

¹query [kw_iərie] *n* vraag, vraagteken[h]

²query [kw_iərie] *vb* **1** vragen (naar), informeren (naar); **2** in twijfel trekken, een vraagteken plaatsen bij *(also lit)*, betwijfelen

quest [kwest] zoektocht: *the ~ for the Holy Grail* de zoektocht naar de Heilige Graal

¹question [kw_estsjən] *n* **1** vraag: *a leading ~* een suggestieve vraag; **2** vraagstuk[h], probleem[h], kwestie: *that is out of the ~* er is geen sprake van, daar komt niets van in; *that is not the ~* daar gaat het niet om; **3** twijfel, onzekerheid, bezwaar[h]: *call sth. into ~* iets in twijfel trekken; *beyond (all)* (of: *without) ~* ongetwijfeld, stellig; *beg the ~* het punt in kwestie als bewezen aannvaarden; *pop the ~ (to her)* (haar) ten huwelijk vragen

²question [kw_estsjən] *vb* **1** vragen, ondervragen, uithoren: *~ s.o. about* (of: *on) his plans* iem over zijn plannen ondervragen; **2** onderzoeken; **3** betwijfelen, zich afvragen: *I ~ whether* (of: *if) ...* ik betwijfel het of ...

questionable [kw_estsjənəbl] **1** twijfelachtig; **2** verdacht

question mark vraagteken[h] *(also fig)*, mysterie[h], onzekerheid

questionnaire [kwestsjən_eə] vragenlijst

¹queue [kjoe:] *n* rij, file || *jump the ~* voordringen, voor je beurt gaan

²queue [kjoe:] *vb* een rij vormen, in de rij (gaan) staan

¹quibble [kw_ibl] *n* spitsvondigheid, haarkloverij

²quibble [kw_ibl] *vb* uitvluchten zoeken, bekvechten: *we don't have to ~ about the details* we hoeven niet over de details te harrewarren

¹quick [kwik] *adj* **1** snel, gauw, vlug: *be as ~ as lightning* bliksemsnel zijn; *quick march!* voorwaarts

mars!; *in ~ succession* snel achter elkaar; *he is ~ to take offence* hij is gauw beledigd; **2** gevoelig, vlug (van begrip), scherp; **3** levendig, opgewekt

²quick [kwik] *n* **1** levend vlees[h] *(under skin, nail);* **2** hart[h], kern, essentie: *cut s.o. to the ~* iemands gevoelens diep kwetsen; **3** *(Am)* kwik[h]

quicken [kw_ikən] **1** levend worden, (weer) tot leven komen: *his pulse ~ed* zijn polsslag werd weer ¹sterker; **2** leven beginnen te vertonen, tekenen van leven geven *(of child in womb)*

quickie [kw_ikkie] vluggertje[h], haastwerk[h], prutswerk[h]

quicksand drijfzand[h]

quicksilver kwik(zilver)[h], *(fig)* levendig temperament[h]

quickstep quickstep, snelle foxtrot

quick-witted vlug van begrip, gevat, scherp

quid [kwid] **1** pond[h] *(sterling);* **2** (tabaks)pruim[h]

quiescence [kwaj_esns] rust, stilte

¹quiet [kwaj_ət] *adj* **1** stil, rustig: *~ as a mouse* muisstil; **2** heimelijk, geheim: *keep ~ about last night* hou je mond over vannacht; **3** zonder drukte, ongedwongen: *a ~ dinner party* een informeel etentje

²quiet [kwaj_ət] *n* **1** stilte; **2** rust, kalmte: *they lived in peace and ~* zij leefden in rust en vrede

¹quieten [kwaj_jətn] *vb (also with down)* rustig worden, bedaren, kalmeren

²quieten [kwaj_jətn] *vb (also with down)* tot bedaren brengen, kalmeren, tot rust brengen: *my reassurance didn't ~ her fear* mijn geruststelling verminderde haar angst niet

quietude [kwaj_jətjoe:d] kalmte, (gemoeds)rust, vrede

quilt [kwilt] **1** gewatteerde deken, dekbed[h]: *a continental ~* een dekbed; **2** sprei

quinine [kw_inie:n] kinine

quintessence [kwint_esns] **1** kern, hoofdzaak; **2** het beste, het fijnste

quintet [kwint_et] vijftal[h], (groep van) vijf musici, kwintet[h]

quip [kwip] **1** schimpscheut, steek; **2** geestigheid, woordspeling

quirk [kwə:k] **1** spitsvondigheid, uitvlucht; **2** geestigheid, spotternij; **3** gril, nuk: *a ~ of fate* een gril van het lot; **4** (rare) kronkel, eigenaardigheid

¹quit [kwit] *vb* **1** ophouden, stoppen: *I've had enough, I ~* ik heb er genoeg van, ik kap ermee; **2** opgeven; **3** vertrekken, ervandoor gaan, zijn baan opgeven: *the neighbours have already had notice to ~* de buren is de huur al opgezegd

²quit [kwit] *vb* **1** ophouden met, stoppen met: *~ complaining about the cold!* hou op met klagen over de kou!; **2** verlaten, vertrekken van, heengaan van

³quit [kwit] *adj* vrij, verlost, bevrijd: *we are well ~ of those difficulties* goed, dat we van die moeilijkheden af zijn

quite [kwajt] **1** helemaal, geheel, volledig, absoluut: *~ possible* best mogelijk; *you're ~ right* je hebt volkomen gelijk; *that's ~ another matter* dat is een heel andere zaak; **2** nogal, enigszins, tamelijk: *it's ~ cold today* het is nogal koud vandaag; **3** werkelijk, echt, in feite: *they seem ~ happy together* zij lijken echt gelukkig samen; **4** erg, veel: *there were ~ a few people* er waren flink wat mensen; *that was ~ a (*Am: *some) party* dat was me het feestje wel

quits [kwits] quitte: *now we are ~* nu staan we quitte

¹quiver [kwɪvvə] *n* **1** pijlkoker; **2** trilling, siddering, beving

²quiver [kwɪvvə] *vb* (doen) trillen, (doen) beven, sidderen

¹quiz [kwiz] *n (~zes)* **1** ondervraging, verhoor^h; **2** test, kort examen^h; **3** quiz

²quiz [kwiz] *vb* **1** ondervragen, uithoren; **2** mondeling examineren

quizzical [kwɪzzikl] **1** komisch, grappig; **2** spottend, plagerig; **3** vorsend, vragend: *she gave me a ~ look* ze keek me met een onderzoekende blik aan

quota [kwoːtə] **1** quota, evenredig deel^h, aandeel^h; **2** (maximum) aantal^h

quotation [kwoːteesjən] **1** citaat^h, aanhaling, het citeren; **2** notering *(of Stock Exchange, exchange rate, price);* **3** prijsopgave

quotation mark aanhalingsteken^h

¹quote [kwoot] *vb* **1** citeren, aanhalen; **2** opgeven *(price)*

²quote [kwoot] *n* **1** citaat^h, aanhaling; **2** notering *(of Stock Exchange etc);* **3** aanhalingsteken^h: *in ~s* tussen aanhalingstekens

quotient [kwoːsjənt] quotiënt^h

r

rabbi [rǽbaj] rabbi, rabbijn

¹rabbit [rǽbit] *n* konijn^h, konijnenbont^h, konijnenvlees^h

²rabbit [rǽbit] *vb* 1 op konijnen jagen; 2 kletsen, zeuren

rabbit warren 1 konijnenveld^h; 2 doolhof, wirwar van straatjes

rabble [rǽbl] kluwen, troep, bende: *the ~* het gepeupel

rabid [rǽbid] 1 razend, woest; 2 fanatiek; 3 dol, hondsdol

rabies [réebie:z] hondsdolheid

¹race [rees] *n* 1 wedren, wedloop, race: *~ against time* race tegen de klok; *the ~s* de (honden)rennen, de paardenrennen; 2 sterke stroom; 3 ras^h; 4 volk^h, natie, stam, slag, klasse

²race [rees] *vb* 1 wedlopen, aan een wedloop deelnemen, een wedstrijd houden; 2 rennen, hollen, snellen; 3 doorslaan *(of screw, wheel)*, doordraaien *(of engine)*

³race [rees] *vb* 1 een wedren houden met, om het hardst lopen met: *I'll ~ you to that tree* laten we doen wie het eerst bij die boom is; 2 (zeer) snel vervoeren: *they ~d the child to hospital* ze vlogen met het kind naar het ziekenhuis; 3 laten doordraaien *(engine)*

racecourse renbaan

racehorse renpaard^h

racer [réesə] 1 renner, hardloper; 2 renpaard^h; 3 racefiets; 4 renwagen; 5 raceboot; 6 wedstrijdjacht^h; 7 renschaats, *~s* noren

racetrack (ovale) renbaan, circuit^h

racial [réesjl] raciaal: *~ discrimination* ras(sen)discriminatie

racing [réesing] 1 het wedrennen, het deelnemen aan wedstrijden; 2 rensport

racism [réesizm] 1 racisme^h; 2 rassenhaat

¹racist [réesist] *adj* racistisch

²racist [réesist] *n* racist

¹rack [rǽk] *n* 1 rek^h; (bagage)rek^h; 2 ruif; 3 pijnbank: *(fig) be on the ~* op de pijnbank liggen, in grote spanning *(of:* onzekerheid) verkeren; 4 kwelling, marteling; 5 verwoesting, afbraak, ondergang: *go to ~ and ruin* geheel vervallen, instorten

²rack [rǽk] *vb* kwellen, pijnigen, teisteren: *~ one's brains* zijn hersens pijnigen; *~ed with jealousy* verteerd door jaloezie

racket [rǽkit] 1 *(sport)* racket^h; 2 sneeuwschoen; 3 lawaai^h, herrie, kabaal^h: *kick up a ~* een rel *(of:* herrie) schoppen; 4 bedriegerij, bedrog^h, zwendel; 5 *(inf)* gangsterpraktijken, misdadige organisatie, afpersing, intimidatie

racketeer [rækittíə] gangster, misdadiger, afperser

racoon [rəkoo:n] 1 wasbeer; 2 wasberenbont^h

racy [réesie] 1 markant, krachtig *(style, person(ality))*; 2 pittig, kruidig, geurig; 3 pikant, gewaagd *(story)*

radar [réeda:] radar

radial [réediəl] radiaal, stervormig, straal-: *~ tyre* radiaalband

radiance [réediəns] straling, schittering, pracht

radiant [réediənt] 1 stralend, schitterend: *he was ~ with joy* hij straalde van vreugde; 2 stervormig; 3 stralings-: *~ heat* stralingswarmte

¹radiate [réedie·eet] *vb* 1 stralen, schijnen; 2 een ster vormen: *streets radiating from a square* straten die straalsgewijs vanaf een plein lopen

²radiate [réedie·eet] *vb* 1 uitstralen, (naar alle kanten) verspreiden: *~ confidence* vertrouwen uitstralen; 2 bestralen

radiation [reedie·éesjən] 1 straling; 2 bestraling

radiator [réedie·eetə] radiator, radiatorkachel, radiateur, koeler *(of engine)*

¹radical [rǽdikl] *adj* 1 radicaal, drastisch; 2 fundamenteel, wezenlijk, essentieel; 3 wortel-: *~ sign* wortelteken

²radical [rǽdikl] *n* 1 basis(principe^h); 2 wortel(teken^h); 3 radicaal

radio [réedie·oo] radio(toestel^h)

radioactive [reedie·oo·ǽktiv] radioactief

radiogram [réedie·oogræm] röntgenfoto

radiography [reedie·ógrəfie] radiografie

radiologist [reedie·óllədzjist] radioloog

radish [rǽdisj] radijs

radium [réediəm] radium^h

radius [réediəs] straal, radius, halve middellijn *(of circle)*: *within a ~ of four miles* binnen een straal van vier mijl

raffish [rǽfisj] liederlijk, losbandig, wild

¹raffle [rǽfl] *n* loterij, verloting

²raffle [rǽfl] *vb (also with off)* verloten

raft [ra:ft] 1 vlot^h, drijvende steiger; 2 reddingvlot^h; 3 grote verzameling: *he worked his way through a whole ~ of letters* hij werkte zich door een hele berg brieven heen

rafter [ra:ftə] dakspant^h

¹rag [rǽg] *n* 1 versleten kledingstuk^h, lomp, vod^h: *from ~s to riches* van armoede naar rijkdom; 2 lap(je^h), vodje^h, flard: *I haven't a ~ to put on* ik heb niets om aan te trekken; 3 vlag, gordijn^h, krant, blaadje^h: *the local ~* het plaatselijke blaadje; 4 herrie, keet, (studenten)lol: *chew the ~* mopperen, kankeren

²rag [rǽg] *vb* 1 pesten, plagen: *they ~ged the teacher* zij schopten keet bij de leraar; 2 te grazen nemen, een poets bakken

ragamuffin [rægǝmuffin] schooiertje[h]

ragbag allegaartje[h]

¹rage [reedzj] *n* **1** manie, passie, bevlieging: *short hair is (all) the ~ now* kort haar is nu een rage; **2** woede(-uitbarsting), razernij: *be in a ~* woedend zijn

²rage [reedzj] *vb* woeden, tieren, razen, *(fig)* tekeergaan: *a raging fire* een felle brand

ragged [rægid] **1** haveloos, gescheurd, gerafeld: *~ trousers* een kapotte broek; **2** ruig, onverzorgd: *a ~ beard* een ruige baard; **3** ongelijk, getand, knoestig: *~ rocks* scherpe rotsen

ragtag [rægtæg] gepeupel[h], grauw[h] || *~ and bobtail* uitschot, schorem

¹raid [reed] *n* **1** inval, (verrassings)overval; **2** rooftocht, roofoverval: *a ~ on a bank* een bankoverval; **3** politieoverval, razzia

²raid [reed] *vb* **1** overvallen, binnenvallen; **2** (be)roven, plunderen, leegroven: *they have been ~ing the fridge as usual* ze hebben zoals gewoonlijk de koelkast geplunderd

raider [reedǝ] **1** overvaller; **2** kaper(schip[h]); **3** rover

¹rail [reel] *n* **1** lat, balk, stang; **2** leuning; **3** omheining, hek(werk)[h], slagboom; **4** rail, spoorstaaf, *(fig)* trein, spoorwegen: *travel by ~* sporen, per trein reizen; **5** reling: *run off the ~s* uit de band springen, ontsporen

²rail [reel] *vb* (with *against, at*) schelden (op), uitvaren (tegen), tekeergaan (tegen)

railcard treinabonnement[h]

railing [reeling] **1** traliewerk[h], spijlen *(of gate)*; **2** leuning, reling, hek[h], balustrade; **3** gescheld[h]

raillery [reelǝrie] scherts, grap(pen), gekheid

railroad 1 *(Am)* per trein vervoeren; **2** jagen, haasten, drijven: *~ a bill through Congress* een wetsvoorstel erdoor jagen in het Congres

railway 1 spoorweg, spoorlijn; **2** spoorwegmaatschappij, de spoorwegen

¹rain [reen] *n* **1** regen, regenbui, regenval: *it looks like ~* het ziet er naar uit dat het gaat regenen; **2** (stort)vloed, stroom: *a ~ of blows* een reeks klappen; **3** *the ~s* regentijd, regenseizoen[h]

²rain [reen] *vb* **1** regenen; **2** neerstromen; **3** doen neerdalen, laten neerkomen: *the father ~ed presents upon his only daughter* de vader overstelpte zijn enige dochter met cadeaus; *it ~s invitations* het regent uitnodigingen

rainbow [reenboo] regenboog

raincoat regenjas

rain down neerkomen, neerdalen (in groten getale): *blows rained down (up)on his head* een regen van klappen kwam neer op zijn hoofd

rainfall regen(val), neerslag

rain forest regenwoud[h]

rainproof regendicht, tegen regen bestand

rainstorm stortbui

rainy [reenie] regenachtig, regen-: *save (up) (of: provide, put away, keep) sth. for a ~ day* een appeltje

voor de dorst bewaren

raise [reez] **1** wekken, opwekken *(from death)*, wakker maken: *~ expectations* verwachtingen wekken; **2** opzetten, tot opstand bewegen; **3** opwekken, opbeuren: *the news of her arrival ~d his hopes* het nieuws van haar aankomst gaf hem weer hoop; **4** bouwen, opzetten, stichten; **5** kweken, produceren, verbouwen; **6** grootbrengen, opvoeden: *~ a family* kinderen grootbrengen; **7** uiten, aanheffen, ter sprake brengen, opperen: *~ objections to sth.* bezwaren tegen iets naar voren brengen; **8** doen ontstaan, beginnen, in het leven roepen: *his behaviour ~s doubts* zijn gedrag roept twijfels op; **9** (op)heffen, opnemen, opslaan *(eyes)*, omhoog doen; **10** bevorderen, promoveren; **11** versterken, vergroten, verheffen *(voice)*, vermeerderen, verhogen: *~ the temperature* de verwarming hoger zetten, *(fig)* de spanning laten oplopen; **12** heffen, innen *(money)*, bijeenbrengen, inzamelen: *~ taxes* belastingen heffen; **13** op de been brengen, werven *(eg army)*; **14** opheffen, beëindigen: *~ a blockade* een blokkade opheffen; **15** *(maths)* verheffen tot *(power)*

raisin [reezn] rozijn

¹rake [reek] *n* **1** hark, riek: *as lean as a ~* zo mager als een lat; **2** losbol; **3** schuinte, val *(of mast,)*, helling; **4** hellingshoek

²rake [reek] *vb* **1** (bijeen)harken *(also fig)*, vergaren, bijeenhalen: *you must be raking it in* je moet wel scheppen geld verdienen; **2** rakelen, poken, *(fig)* oprakelen: *~ over old ashes* oprakelen, oude koeien uit de sloot halen; **3** doorzoeken, uitkammen: *~ one's memory* zijn geheugen pijnigen

³rake [reek] *vb* **1** harken; **2** zoeken, snuffelen: *the customs officers ~d through my luggage* de douanebeambten doorzochten mijn bagage van onder tot boven; **3** oplopen, hellen

rake up 1 bijeenharken, aanharken; **2** *(inf)* optrommelen, opscharrelen; **3** oprakelen *(also fig)*: *~ old stories* oude koeien uit de sloot halen

rakish [reekisj] **1** liederlijk, losbandig; **2** zwierig, vlot; **3** smalgebouwd, snel, snelvarend

¹rally [rælie] *n* **1** bijeenkomst, vergadering; **2** opleving, herstel[h]; **3** *(tennis)* rally; **4** rally, sterrit; **5** herstel[h] *(of share prices)*

²rally [rælie] *vb* **1** bijeenkomen, zich verzamelen; **2** zich aansluiten: *~ round the flag* zich om de vlag scharen; **3** (zich) herstellen, opleven, weer bijkomen; **4** weer omhooggaan, zich herstellen *(of share prices)*

³rally [rælie] *vb* **1** verzamelen, ordenen, herenigen; **2** bijeenbrengen, verenigen, op de been brengen; **3** doen opleven, nieuw leven inblazen; **4** plagen, voor de gek houden

rally (a)round te hulp komen, helpen, bijspringen

¹ram [ræm] *n* **1** ram *(male sheep)*; **2** stormram

²ram [ræm] *vb* **1** aanstampen, vaststampen; **2** heien; **3** doordringen, overduidelijk maken; **4** persen, proppen; **5** rammen, bonken, beuken, botsen op

¹ramble [ræmbl] *vb* **1** dwalen, zwerven, trekken; **2**

afdwalen, bazelen; **3** wild groeien, woekeren *(of plants)*; **4** kronkelen *(of path, river)*

²**ramble** [ræmbl] *n* zwerftocht, wandeltocht, uitstapjeʰ

rambler [ræmblə] **1** wandelaar, trekker, zwerver; **2** klimroos

rambling [ræmbling] **1** rondtrekkend, ronddolend; **2** onsamenhangend, verward: *he made a few ~ remarks* hij maakte een paar vage opmerkingen; **3** wild groeiend, kruipend *(of plants)*; **4** onregelmatig, grillig: *~ passages* gangetjes die alle kanten op gaan

rambunctious [ræmbungksjəs] *(Am; inf)* **1** onstuimig, onbesuisd, luidruchtig; **2** (lekker) eigenzinnig

ramification [ræmiffikkeesjən] afsplitsing, vertakking, onderverdeling: *all ~s of the plot were not yet known* alle vertakkingen van de samenzwering waren nog niet bekend

ramp [ræmp] **1** helling, glooiing; **2** oprit, afrit *(also of lorries etc)*, hellingbaan; **3** verkeersdrempel

¹**rampage** [ræmpeedzj] *vb* (uitzinnig) tekeergaan, razen

²**rampage** [ræmpeedzj] *n* dolheid, uitzinnigheid: *be on the ~* uitzinnig tekeergaan

rampant [ræmpənt] **1** wild, woest, verwoed; **2** (te) weelderig, welig tierend

rampart [ræmpa:t] **1** borstwering, wal; **2** verdediging, bolwerkʰ

ramrod [ræmrod] laadstok *(to tamp down gunpowder)*: *as stiff as a ~* kaarsrecht

ramshackle [ræmsjækl] bouwvallig, vervallen

ranch [ra:ntsj] boerderij, ranch

rancid [rænsid] ranzig

rancour [rængkə] wrok, haat

¹**random** [rændəm] *adj* willekeurig, toevallig, op goed geluk: *~ check* steekproef

²**random** [rændəm] *n*: *at ~* op goed geluk af; *fill in answers at ~* zomaar wat antwoorden invullen

random-access *(comp)* directe toegang *(of memory)*: *~ file* direct toegankelijk bestand

randy [rændie] *(vulg)* geil, wellustig

¹**range** [reendzj] *n* **1** rij, reeks, keten: *a ~ of mountains* een bergketen; **2** woeste (weide)grond; **3** schietterreinʰ, testgebiedʰ *(of rockets, projectiles)*; **4** gebiedʰ, kring, terreinʰ; **5** sortering, collectie, assortimentʰ; **6** groot keukenfornuisʰ; **7** bereikʰ, draagkracht, draagwijdte: *the man had been shot at close ~* de man was van dichtbij neergeschoten; *(with)in ~* binnen schootsafstand, binnen bereik

²**range** [reendzj] *vb* **1** zich uitstrekken; **2** voorkomen *(of plant, animal)*, aangetroffen worden; **3** verschillen, variëren: *ticket prices ~ from three to eight pound* de prijzen van de kaartjes liggen tussen de drie en acht pond; **4** zwerven, zich bewegen, gaan: *his new book ~s over too many subjects* zijn nieuwe boek omvat te veel onderwerpen

³**range** [reendzj] *vb* **1** rangschikken, ordenen, (op)stellen; **2** doorkruisen, zwerven over, aflopen, *(fig)* afzoeken, gaan over: *his eyes ~d the mountains*

zijn ogen zochten de bergen af; **3** weiden, hoeden, houden

ranger [reendzjə] **1** boswachter; **2** gids, padvindster *(14-17 years old)*; **3** *(Am)* commandoʰ *(soldier)*

¹**rank** [rængk] *n* **1** rij, lijn, reeks; **2** gelidʰ, rij: *the ~ and file* de manschappen, *(fig)* de gewone man; *close (the) ~s* de gelederen sluiten; **3** taxistandplaats; **4** rang, positie, graad, de hogere stand: *raised to the ~ of major* tot (de rang van) majoor bevorderd; *pull ~* op zijn strepen gaan staan; *pull ~ on s.o.* misbruik maken van zijn macht ten opzichte van iem

²**rank** [rængk] *vb* **1** zich bevinden *(in a certain position)*, staan, behoren: *this book ~s among* (of: *with*) *the best* dit boek behoort tot de beste; *~ as* gelden als; **2** *(Am)* de hoogste positie bekleden

³**rank** [rængk] *vb* **1** opstellen, in het gelid plaatsen; **2** plaatsen, neerzetten, rangschikken: *~ s.o. with Stan Laurel* iem op één lijn stellen met Stan Laurel

⁴**rank** [rængk] *adj* **1** (te) weelderig, (te) welig: *~ weeds* welig tierend onkruid; **2** te vet *(of soil)*; **3** stinkend; **4** absoluut: *(fig) ~ injustice* schreeuwende onrechtvaardigheid

ranking [rængking] classificatie, (positie in een) rangorde

rankle [rængkl] steken, knagen, woekeren

ransack [rænsæk] **1** doorzoeken, doorsnuffelen; **2** plunderen, leegroven, beroven

¹**ransom** [rænsəm] *n* **1** losgeldʰ, losprijs, afkoopsom; **2** vrijlating *(for ransom money)* || *hold s.o. to ~* een losgeld voor iem eisen *(under threat of violence)*

²**ransom** [rænsəm] *vb* **1** vrijkopen; **2** vrijlaten *(for ransom money)*; **3** losgeld voor iem eisen

¹**rant** [rænt] *vb* **1** bombast uitslaan; **2** tieren, tekeergaan

²**rant** [rænt] *n* bombast, holle frasen

¹**rap** [ræp] *n* **1** tik, slag: *get a ~ over the knuckles* een tik op de vingers krijgen, *(fig)* op de vingers getikt worden; **2** geklopʰ, klop; **3** zier, beetjeʰ: *he doesn't give a ~ for her* hij geeft helemaal niets om haar; **4** schuld, straf: *I don't want to take the ~ for this* ik wil hier niet voor opdraaien; **5** *(inf; music)* rap *(rhythmic lyrics to music)*

²**rap** [ræp] *vb* **1** kloppen, tikken: *~ at a door* op een deur kloppen; **2** praten, erop los kletsen

³**rap** [ræp] *vb* **1** slaan, een tik geven; **2** bekritiseren, op de vingers tikken

rapacity [rəpæsittie] hebzucht, roofzucht

¹**rape** [reep] *vb* verkrachten, onteren

²**rape** [reep] *n* **1** verkrachting; **2** koolzaadʰ, raapzaadʰ

¹**rapid** [ræpid] *adj* snel, vlug: *~ fire* snelvuur; *in ~ succession* snel achter elkaar; *(Am) ~ transit* snelverkeer *(train, tram, underground)*

²**rapid** [ræpid] *n* stroomversnelling

rapidity [ræpiddittie] vlugheid

rapist [reepist] verkrachter

rap out 1 eruit gooien, eruit flappen; **2** door kloppen meedelen, door kloppen te kennen geven: *~ an*

758

S.O.S. met klopsignalen een SOS doorgeven

rapt [ræpt] **1** verrukt, in vervoering; **2** verdiept, verzonken

rapture [ræptʃə] **1** vervoering, verrukking, extase; **2** ~s extase, vervoering: *she was in ~s about* (of: *over*) *her meeting with the poet* zij was lyrisch over haar ontmoeting met de dichter

rapturous [ræptʃərəs] hartstochtelijk, meeslepend

rare [reə] **1** ongewoon, ongebruikelijk, vreemd; **2** zeldzaam; **3** halfrauw, niet gaar, kort gebakken (of *meat*)

rarefied [reəriffajd] ijl, dun

rarely [reəlie] **1** zelden: *he rarely comes home before eight* hij komt zelden voor achten thuis; **2** zeldzaam, ongewoon, uitzonderlijk: *we caught a very ~ specimen* wij vingen een zeer zeldzaam exemplaar

raring [reəring] dolgraag, enthousiast

rarity [reərittie] zeldzaamheid, rariteit, schaarsheid

rascal [ra:skl] **1** schoft, schurk; **2** schavuit, deugniet, rakker

¹rash [ræsj] *adj* **1** overhaast, te snel; **2** onstuimig; **3** ondoordacht: *in a ~ moment* op een onbewaakt ogenblik

²rash [ræsj] *n* (huid)uitslag

¹rasp [ra:sp] *n* **1** rasp; **2** raspgeluidʰ, geraspʰ

²rasp [ra:sp] *vb* schrapen, krassen: *with ~ing voice* met krakende stem

³rasp [ra:sp] *vb* raspen, vijlen, schuren

raspberry [ra:zbərie] **1** frambozenstruik; **2** framboos; **3** (inf) afkeurend pf!

rat [ræt] **1** rat; **2** deserteur, overloper; **3** (Am) verrader, klikspaan || *smell a ~* lont ruiken, iets in de smiezen hebben

¹rate [reet] *n* **1** snelheid, vaart, tempoʰ; **2** prijs, tariefʰ, koers: *~ of exchange* wisselkoers; *~ of interest* rentevoet; **3** (sterfte)cijferʰ, geboortecijferʰ; **4** (kwaliteits)klasse, rang, graad; **5** ~s gemeentebelasting, onroerendgoedbelasting: *at any ~* in ieder geval, ten minste; *at this ~* in dit geval, op deze manier

²rate [reet] *vb* gerekend worden, behoren, gelden: *he ~s as one of the best writers* hij geldt als een van de beste schrijvers

³rate [reet] *vb* **1** schatten, bepalen, waarderen (also *fig*): *~ s.o.'s income at* iemands inkomen schatten op; **2** beschouwen, tellen, rekenen: *~ among* rekenen onder

rateable [reetəbl] **1** te schatten, taxeerbaar; **2** belastbaar, schatbaar

ratepayer 1 belastingbetaler; **2** huiseigenaar

rather [ra:ðə] **1** liever, eerder: *I would ~ not invite your brother* ik nodig je broer liever niet uit; **2** juister (uitgedrukt), liever gezegd: *she is my girlfriend, or ~ she was my girlfriend* zij is mijn vriendin, of liever: ze was mijn vriendin; **3** enigszins, tamelijk, nogal, wel: *a ~ shocking experience, ~ a shocking experience* een nogal schokkende ervaring; **4** meer, sterker, in hogere mate: *they depend ~ on Paul's*

than on their own income zij zijn meer van Pauls inkomen afhankelijk dan van het hunne; **5** (inf) ja zeker, nou en of

ratify [rætiffaj] bekrachtigen, goedkeuren (treaty)

rating [reeting] **1** taxering (rated value, assessment); **2** waarderingscijferʰ (of TV programme), kijkcijferʰ; **3** naam, positie, status

ratio [reesjie·oo] (evenredige) verhouding

¹ration [ræsjən] *n* **1** rantsoenʰ, portie (also *fig*); **2** ~s proviandʰ, voedselʰ, rantsoenen

²ration [ræsjən] *vb* rantsoeneren, op rantsoen stellen, distribueren, uitdelen: *petrol is ~ed* de benzine is op de bon

rational [ræsjənəl] **1** rationeel, redelijk; **2** (wel)doordacht, logisch; **3** verstandig: *man is a ~ being* de mens is een redelijk wezen

rationale [ræsjəna:l] grond(reden), grondgedachte(n), beweegreden(en)

¹rationalist [ræsjənəlist] *adj* rationalistisch

²rationalist [ræsjənəlist] *n* rationalist

¹rationalize [ræsjənəlajz] *vb* rationaliseren, aannemelijk maken, verklaren, achteraf beredeneren

²rationalize [ræsjənəlajz] *vb* rationaliseren, efficiënter inrichten (business etc)

rat on laten vallen, verraden, in de steek laten

rat race moordende competitie, carrièrejacht

rattan [rətæn] **1** rotanʰ, Spaans rietʰ; **2** rotting, wandelstok

¹rattle [rætl] *vb* **1** rammelen, ratelen, kletteren; **2** (with *away, on*) (door)ratelen, (blijven) kletsen || *~ through sth.* iets afraffelen, iets gauw afmaken

²rattle [rætl] *vb* **1** heen en weer rammelen, schudden, rinkelen met; **2** (inf) op stang jagen, opjagen, van streek maken

³rattle [rætl] *n* **1** geratelʰ, gerammelʰ, gerinkelʰ; **2** rammelaar, ratel

rattlesnake ratelslang

¹rattling [rætling] *adv* uitzonderlijk, uitstekend: *a ~ good match* een zeldzaam mooie wedstrijd

²rattling [rætling] *adj* levendig, stevig, krachtig: *a ~ trade* een levendige handel

ratty [rætie] **1** ratachtig, vol ratten, rat(ten)-; **2** geïrriteerd

raucous [ro:kəs] rauw, schor

raunchy [ro:ntsjie] (inf) **1** geil, wellustig; **2** rauw, ruig, ordinair; **3** (Am) vies, smerig, goor

¹ravage [rævidzj] *vb* **1** verwoesten, vernietigen, teisteren: *she came from a country ~d by war* zij kwam uit een door oorlog verwoest land; **2** leegplunderen, leegroven

²ravage [rævidzj] *n* **1** verwoesting(en), vernietiging; **2** ~s vernietigende werking: *the ~s of time* de tand des tijds

¹rave [reev] *vb* **1** (with *against, at*) razen (tegen, op), ijlen, (als een gek) tekeergaan (tegen); **2** (with *about*) opgetogen zijn, raken (over), lyrisch worden (over), dwepen (met)

²rave [reev] *vb* wild uiting geven aan, zich gek maken

³rave [reev] *n* **1** juichende bespreking; **2** wild feestʰ,

dansfeest[h] || *be in a* ~ *about* helemaal weg zijn van
raven [reevn] raaf
ravenous [rævənəs] uitgehongerd, begerig, roof-
zuchtig
ravine [rəvie:n] ravijn[h]
¹**raving** [reeving] *adj* malend, raaskallend
²**raving** [reeving] *adv* stapel-: *stark* ~ *mad* knots-
knettergek
ravish [rævisj] 1 verrukken, in vervoering brengen,
betoveren; 2 verkrachten, onteren
ravishing [rævisjing] verrukkelijk, betoverend
raw [ro:] 1 rauw, ongekookt *(of vegetables, meat)*; 2
onuitgewerkt *(figures etc)*, grof, onaf(gewerkt), onrijp: ~ *material* grondstof; ~ *silk* ruwe zijde; 3
groen, onervaren, ongetraind; 4 ontveld, rauw,
open; 5 guur, ruw, rauw *(of weather)*: ~ *deal* oneerlijke behandeling; *touch s.o. on the* ~ iem tegen het
zere been schoppen; *in the* ~ ongeciviliseerd, primitief, naakt
rawboned broodmager, vel over been
rawhide 1 ongelooide huid; 2 zweep
ray [ree] 1 straal *(of light etc)*; 2 sprankje[h], glimp,
lichtpuntje[h]: *a* ~ *of hope* een sprankje hoop; 3 *(zoology)* rog, vleet
raze [reez] met de grond gelijk maken, volledig verwoesten
razor [reezə] (elektrisch) scheerapparaat[h], scheermes[h]
razor-billed auk alk
razor blade (veiligheids)scheermesje[h]
razzle [ræzl] braspartij, lol, stappen: *go on the
razzle* aan de rol gaan, de bloemetjes buiten zetten
R.C. 1 *Red Cross* Rode Kruis; 2 *Roman Catholic* r.-k.
Rd [rood] *road* str., straat
¹**reach** [rie:tsj] *vb* 1 reiken, (zich) (uit)strekken, (een
hand) uitsteken, bereiken, dragen *(of sound)*, halen: *the forests* ~ *down to the sea* de bossen strekken
zich uit tot aan de zee; 2 pakken, (ergens) bij kunnen, grijpen: ~ *down sth. from a shelf* iets van een
plank afpakken; 3 aanreiken, geven, overhandigen;
4 komen tot *(also fig)*, bereiken, arriveren: ~ *a decision* tot een beslissing komen
²**reach** [rie:tsj] *n* 1 bereik[h] *(of arm, power etc; also
fig)*, reikwijdte: *above* (of: *beyond, out of*) ~ buiten
bereik, onbereikbaar, onhaalbaar, niet te realiseren; *within easy* ~ *of* gemakkelijk bereikbaar
van(af); 2 recht stuk rivier *(between two bends)*
react [rie-ækt] 1 reageren *(also fig)*, ingaan (op); 2
(with *(up)on*) uitwerking hebben (op), z'n weerslag
hebben (op), veranderen
reaction [rie-æksjən] 1 reactie, antwoord[h], reflex; 2
terugslag, weerslag, terugkeer
¹**reactionary** [rie-æksjənərie] *adj* reactionair, behoudend
²**reactionary** [rie-æksjənərie] *n* reactionair, behoudend persoon
reactor [rie-æktə] 1 atoomreactor, kernreactor; 2
reactievat[h], reactor
¹**read** [red] *vb* 1 lezen, kunnen lezen; begrijpen, we-

ten te gebruiken: ~ *over* (of: *through*) doorlezen,
overlezen; ~ *up on sth.: a)* zijn kennis over iets opvijzelen; *b)* zich op de hoogte stellen van iets; *widely* ~ zeer belezen; ~ *up* bestuderen; 2 oplezen, voorlezen: ~ *out the instructions* de instructies voorlezen; 3 uitleggen, interpreteren, voorspellen *(future)*; *(fig)* doorgronden, doorzien; 4 aangeven, tonen, laten zien: *the thermometer* ~*s twenty degrees*
de thermometer geeft twintig graden aan
²**read** [red] *vb* 1 studeren, leren: ~ *for a degree in Law*
rechten studeren; 2 zich laten lezen, lezen, klinken:
your essay ~*s like a translation* je opstel klinkt als
een vertaling; *he* ~ *more into her words than she'd
ever meant* hij had meer in haar woorden gelegd
dan zij ooit had bedoeld
readability [rie:dəbillittie] leesbaarheid
readable [rie:dəbl] 1 lezenswaard(ig), leesbaar; 2
leesbaar, te lezen
reader [rie:də] 1 lezer *(also fig)*; 2 leesboek[h], bloemlezing; 3 lector *(at university)*, *(in Belgium roughly)*
docent
readership [rie:dəsjip] lezerspubliek[h], aantal lezers
(of newspaper etc): *a newspaper with a* ~ *of ten million* een krant met tien miljoen lezers
readily [reddillie] 1 graag, bereidwillig; 2 gemakkelijk, vlug, dadelijk: *his motives will be* ~ *understood*
zijn motivatie is zonder meer duidelijk
readiness [reddienəs] 1 bereid(willig)heid, gewil-
ligheid; 2 vlugheid, vaardigheid, gemak[h]: ~ *of
tongue* rapheid van tong; 3 gereedheid: *all is in* ~ alles staat klaar
reading [rie:ding] 1 het (voor)lezen; 2 belezenheid;
3 (voor)lezing, voordracht; 4 stand, waarde *(as
read on instrucment)*: *the* ~*s on the thermometer* de
afgelezen temperaturen; 5 lectuur, leesstof: *these
novels are required* ~ deze romans zijn verplichte
lectuur
¹**readjust** [rie:ədzjust] *vb* zich weer aanpassen, weer
wennen
²**readjust** [rie:ədzjust] *vb* weer aanpassen, opnieuw
instellen, bijstellen
¹**ready** [reddie] *adj* 1 klaar, gereed, af: ~, *steady, go!*
klaar? af!; 2 bereid(willig), graag: *I am* ~ *to pay for
it* ik wil er best voor betalen; 3 vlug, gevat: ~ *cash*
(of: *money*) baar geld, klinkende munt; *find a* ~
sale goed verkocht worden
²**ready** [reddie] *n: at the* ~ klaar om te vuren *(of firearm)*
ready-made kant-en-klaar, confectie-
¹**real** [riəl] *adj* echt, werkelijk, onvervalst: *(inf) the* ~
thing het echte, je ware; *in* ~ *terms* in concrete termen, in de praktijk
²**real** [riəl] *n: for* ~ in werkelijkheid, echt, gemeend
real estate 1 onroerend goed[h]; 2 *(Am)* huizen in
verkoop
realism [riəlizm] realisme[h], werkelijkheidszin
realist [riəlist] realist
realistic [riəlistik] 1 realistisch, mbt realisme, natuurgetrouw; 2 realistisch, praktisch, werkelijk-

heidsbewust

reality [rie·ǽlittie] werkelijkheid, realiteit, werkelijk bestaan[h]: *in ~* in werkelijkheid, in feite

realization [riəlajzeesjən] **1** bewustwording, besef[h], begrip[h]; **2** realisatie, realisering, verwezenlijking

realize [riəlajz] **1** beseffen, zich bewust zijn of worden, zich realiseren: *don't you ~ that …?* zie je niet in dat …?; **2** realiseren, verwezenlijken, uitvoeren; **3** realiseren, verkopen, te gelde maken

¹really [riəlie] *adv* **1** werkelijk, echt, eigenlijk: *I don't ~ feel like it* ik heb er eigenlijk geen zin in; *(O) really?* O ja?, Echt (waar)?; **2** werkelijk, echt, zeer: *it is ~ cold today* het is ontzettend koud vandaag

²really [riəlie] *interj* waarachtig!, nou, zeg!: *~, Mike! Mind your manners!* Mike toch! Wat zijn dat voor manieren!; *well ~!* nee maar!

realm [relm] **1** koninkrijk[h], rijk[h]; **2** rijk[h], sfeer, gebied[h] *(fig): the ~ of science* het domein van de wetenschap

reanimation [rie·ænimmeesjən] reanimatie

reap [rie:p] maaien, oogsten, verwerven, opstrijken *(profit)*

reappear [rie·əpiə] weer verschijnen, opnieuw te voorschijn komen, weer komen opdagen

¹rear [riə] *n* achtergedeelte[h], achterstuk[h], *(fig)* achtergrond ‖ *at (Am: in) the ~* achteraan, aan de achterkant

²rear [riə] *adj* achter-, achterste: *~ door* achterdeur

³rear [riə] *vb* (also with *up*) steigeren

⁴rear [riə] *vb* grootbrengen, fokken, kweken

rear-admiral schout-bij-nacht

rearguard achterhoede

rearmament [rie:a:məmənt] herbewapening

rearmost [riəmoost] achterste, allerlaatste

rearrange [rie·əreendzj] herschikken, herordenen, anders rangschikken

¹reason [rie:zən] *n* **1** reden, beweegreden, oorzaak: *by ~ of* wegens; *with (good) ~* terecht; **2** redelijkheid, gezond verstand[h]: *it stands to ~ that* het spreekt vanzelf dat; *anything (with)in ~* alles wat redelijk is

²reason [rie:zən] *vb* **1** redeneren, logisch denken; **2** (with *with*) redeneren (met), argumenteren (met)

³reason [rie:zən] *vb* door redenering afleiden, beredeneren, veronderstellen: *~ sth. out* iets beargumenteren

reasonable [rie:zənəbl] **1** redelijk, verstandig; **2** redelijk, schappelijk, billijk

reasonably [rie:znəblie] vrij, tamelijk, nogal: *it is in a ~ good state* het is in vrij behoorlijke staat

reassure [rie:əsjoeə] geruststellen, weer (zelf)vertrouwen geven

reassuring [rie:əsjoeəring] geruststellend

rebate [rie:beet] korting: *tax ~* belastingteruggave

¹rebel [rebl] *n* rebel, opstandeling

²rebel [ribbel] *vb* (with *against*) rebelleren (tegen), zich verzetten (tegen), in opstand komen (tegen)

rebellion [ribbelliən] opstand, opstandigheid, rebellie

rebellious [ribbelliəs] opstandig

rebirth [rie:bə:θ] **1** wedergeboorte; **2** herleving, wederopleving

¹rebound [ribbaund] *vb* terugkaatsen, terugspringen, terugstuiten

²rebound [rie:baund] *n* **1** terugkaatsing *(of ball);* **2** terugwerking, reactie: *on the ~* van de weeromstuit, als reactie

¹rebuff [ribbuf] *n* afwijzing, weigering *(of help, proposal etc): he met with (of: suffered) a ~* hij kwam van een koude kermis thuis

²rebuff [ribbuf] *vb* afwijzen, weigeren, afschepen

rebuild [rie:bild] opnieuw bouwen, verbouwen, opknappen

¹rebuke [ribjoe:k] *vb* (with *for*) berispen (om, voor), een standje geven (voor)

²rebuke [ribjoe:k] *n* berisping, standje[h]

¹recalcitrant [rikælsitrənt] *adj* opstandig, weerspannig

²recalcitrant [rikælsitrənt] *n* weerspannige, tegenstribbelaar, ongehoorzame

¹recall [rikko:l] *vb* zich herinneren

²recall [rikko:l] *vb* **1** terugroepen, rappelleren *(envoy);* **2** terugnemen *(present, merchandise etc),* terugroepen *(product, by manufacturer): millions of cans of soft drink have been ~ed* er zijn miljoenen blikjes frisdrank teruggehaald

³recall [rikko:l] *n* **1** rappel[h], terugroeping *(of officers, envoy etc);* **2** herinnering, geheugen[h]: *total ~* absoluut geheugen; *beyond (of: past) ~* onmogelijk te herinneren

¹recap [rie:kæp] *vb* recapituleren, kort samenvatten, samenvattend herhalen

²recap [rie:kæp] *n* recapitulatie, korte opsomming

recapitulate [rie:kəpitjoeleet] recapituleren, kort samenvatten

recede [rissie:d] achteruitgaan, zich terugtrekken, terugwijken, *(also fig)* teruglopen *(of value etc): a receding forehead* een terugwijkend voorhoofd; *a receding hairline* een kalend hoofd

¹receipt [rissie:t] *n* reçu[h], ontvangstbewijs[h], kwitantie

²receipt [rissie:t] *vb* kwiteren, voor ontvangst tekenen *(bill etc)*

receive [rissie:v] **1** ontvangen, verwelkomen, gasten ontvangen; **2** ontvangen, krijgen, in ontvangst nemen; **3** opvangen, toelaten, opnemen: *be at (of: on) the receiving end* al de klappen krijgen

received [rissie:vd] algemeen aanvaard, standaard-: *Received Standard English* Algemeen Beschaafd Engels

receiver [rissie:və] **1** ontvanger *(person, appliance);* **2** hoorn *(of telephone);* **3** bewindvoerder; **4** heler

recent [rie:sənt] **1** recent, van de laatste tijd: *in ~ years* de laatste jaren; *a ~ book* een onlangs verschenen boek; **2** nieuw, modern: *~ fashion* nieuwe mode

recently [rie:sntlie] **1** onlangs, kort geleden; **2** de laatste tijd: *he has been moody, ~* hij is de laatste tijd humeurig (geweest)

receptacle [risseptəkl] vergaarbak, container, vat^h, kom

reception [rissepsjən] **1** ontvangst *(also fig)*, onthaal^h, welkom^h: *the ~ of his book was mixed* zijn boek werd met gemengde gevoelens ontvangen; **2** receptie *(at party; in hotel etc)*; **3** opname

reception centre opvangcentrum^h

reception desk balie *(of hotel, library etc)*

receptionist [rissepsjənist] **1** receptionist(e) *(eg in hotel)*; **2** assistent(e) *(of doctor etc)*

receptive [risseptiv] ontvankelijk, vatbaar, open

recess [rissés] **1** vakantie, onderbreking *(parliament etc)*; **2** *(Am)* (school)vakantie; **3** *(Am)* pauze *(between classes)*; **4** nis, uitsparing, holte

recession [rissesjən] **1** recessie, economische teruggang; **2** terugtrekking, terugtreding

recharge [rie:tsja:dzj] herladen, weer opladen *(battery etc)*

recipe [ressippie] recept^h, keukenrecept^h

reciprocal [rissiprəkl] wederkerig, wederzijds: *~ action* wisselwerking

reciprocate [rissiprəkeet] **1** beantwoorden *(feelings)*, vergelden, op gelijke manier behandelen; **2** uitwisselen

recital [rissajtl] **1** relaas^h, verhaal^h; **2** recital *(music)*; **3** voordracht *(poem, text)*

recite [rissajt] **1** reciteren, opzeggen: *Simon can already ~ the alphabet* Simon kan het alfabet al opzeggen; **2** opsommen

reckless [reklǝs] **1** roekeloos; **2** zorgeloos: *~ of danger* zonder zich zorgen te maken over gevaar

¹reckon [rekkən] *vb* **1** berekenen, (op)tellen; **2** meerekenen, meetellen, rekening houden met; **3** beschouwen, aanzien (voor), houden (voor): *I ~ him among my friends* ik beschouw hem als één van mijn vrienden; **4** aannemen, vermoeden, gissen: *I ~ that he'll be home soon* ik neem aan dat hij gauw thuiskomt

²reckon [rekkən] *vb* **1** (with *on*) rekenen (op), afgaan (op); **2** (with *with*) rekening houden (met): *she is a woman to be ~ed with* dat is een vrouw met wie je rekening moet houden; **3** (with *with*) afrekenen (met)

reckoner [rekkənə] rekenaar: *ready ~* rekentabel

reckoning [rekkəning] **1** berekening, schatting; **2** afrekening: *day of ~* dag van de afrekening, *(fig)* dag des oordeels

¹reclaim [rikleem] *vb* **1** terugwinnen, recupereren, regenereren: *~ed paper* kringlooppapier; **2** droogleggen *(land)*: *land ~ed from the sea* op de zee teruggewonnen land; **3** terugvorderen

²reclaim [rikleem] *n*: *he is beyond ~* hij is onverbeterlijk

reclamation [rekləmeesjən] **1** terugwinning; **2** terugvordering

¹recline [riklajn] *vb* achterover leunen, (uit)rusten, op de rug liggen

²recline [riklajn] *vb* doen leunen, doen rusten

recluse [riklóe:s] kluizenaar

recognition [rekkəgnisjən] **1** erkenning; **2** waardering, erkentelijkheid; **3** herkenning: *change beyond* (of: *out of*) *all ~* onherkenbaar worden

recognizable [rekkəgnajzəbl] herkenbaar

recognize [rekkəgnajz] **1** herkennen; **2** erkennen; **3** inzien

¹recoil [rikkojl] *vb* **1** (with *from*) terugdeinzen (voor), terugschrikken (voor), zich terugtrekken; **2** terugslaan, teruglopen, terugspringen, terugstoten *(of firearm)*

²recoil [rie:kojl] *n* terugslag, terugloop, terugsprong, terugstoot *(of firearm)*

recollect [rekkəlekt] zich (moeizaam) herinneren, zich voor de geest halen

recollection [rekkəleksjən] herinnering: *to the best of my ~* voor zover ik mij herinner

recommend [rekkəmend] **1** aanbevelen, aanraden, adviseren: *I can ~ the self-service in this hotel* ik kan u de zelfbediening in dit hotel aanbevelen; *~ed price* adviesprijs; **2** tot aanbeveling strekken; **3** toevertrouwen, overgeven, (aan)bevelen

recommendation [rekkəmendeesjən] **1** aanbeveling, aanprijzing, advies^h; **2** aanbevelingsbrief

¹recompense [rekkəmpens] *vb* vergoeden, schadeloosstellen: *~ s.o. for sth.* iem iets vergoeden

²recompense [rekkəmpens] *n* vergoeding, schadeloosstelling, beloning: *in ~ for* als vergoeding voor

reconcile [rekkənsajl] verzoenen, in overeenstemming brengen, verenigen: *become ~d to sth.* zich bij iets neerleggen

reconciliation [rekkənsillie·eesjən] verzoening, vereniging

reconnaissance [rikkonnissəns] verkenning

reconnoitre [rekkə:nojtə] op verkenning uitgaan, verkennen

reconsider [rie:kənsiddə] **1** opnieuw bekijken, opnieuw in overweging nemen: *may I ask you to ~ the matter?* mag ik u vragen er nog eens over na te denken?; **2** herroepen, herzien, terugkomen op

reconstruct [rie:kənstrukt] **1** opnieuw opbouwen, herbouwen; **2** reconstrueren *(events)*

¹record [rikko:d] *vb* **1** zich laten opnemen, opnamen maken; **2** optekenen, noteren, te boek stellen: *~ed delivery* aangetekend *(mail)*; **3** vastleggen, opnemen *(on tape, record)*

²record [rekko:d] *n* **1** verslag^h, rapport^h, aantekening: *for the ~* openbaar, officieel; *off the ~* vertrouwelijk, onofficieel; *all this is off the ~* dit alles blijft tussen ons; **2** document^h, archiefstuk^h, officieel afschrift^h; **3** vastgelegd feit^h, het opgetekend zijn; **4** staat van dienst, antecedenten, verleden^h; **5** plaat, opname

³record [rekko:d] *adj* record-: *a ~ amount* een recordbedrag

recorder [rikko:də] **1** rechter, voorzitter van Crown Court; **2** (tape)recorder; **3** blokfluit

recording [rikko:ding] opname, opgenomen programmaʰ: *a studio* ~ een studio-opname

record-player platenspeler, grammofoon

recount [rikkaunt] (uitvoerig) vertellen, weergeven

recoup [rikkoe:p] **1** vergoeden, compenseren, schadeloosstellen; **2** terugwinnen, inhalen: ~ *expenses from a company* onkosten verhalen op een maatschappij

recourse [rikko:s] toevlucht, hulp: *have* ~ *to* zijn toevlucht nemen tot

¹recover [rikkuvvə] *vb* herstellen, genezen, er weer bovenop komen

²recover [rikkuvvə] *vb* terugkrijgen, terugvinden: ~ *consciousness* weer bijkomen

recovery [rikkuvvərie] **1** herstelʰ, recuperatie, genezing: *make a quick* ~ *from an illness* vlug van een ziekte herstellen; **2** het terugvinden, het terugwinnen, het terugkrijgen, herwinning

recreation [rekrie-eesjən] recreatie, ontspanning, hobby

recreational [rekrie-eesjənl] recreatief, recreatie-, ontspannings-

recreation ground speelterreinʰ, recreatieterreinʰ

recrimination [rikrimminneesjən] tegenbeschuldiging, recriminatie, tegeneis: *mutual ~s* beschuldigingen over en weer

¹recruit [rikroe:t] *n* **1** rekruut; **2** nieuw lidʰ

²recruit [rikroe:t] *vb* rekruten (aan)werven

³recruit [rikroe:t] *vb* rekruteren, (aan)werven, aantrekken

rectangle [rektænggl] rechthoek

rectification [rektiffikkeesjən] rectificatie

rectify [rektiffaj] rectificeren, rechtzetten, verbeteren

rectitude [rektitjoe:d] **1** rechtschapenheid; **2** oprechtheid, eerlijkheid

rector [rektə] **1** *(Anglican Church)* predikant, dominee; **2** rector *(head of university)*

recuperate [rikjoe:pəreet] herstellen, opknappen, er weer bovenop komen

recur [rikka:] terugkomen, terugkeren, zich herhalen: *a ~ring dream* een steeds terugkerende droom; ~*ring decimal* repeterende breuk

recurrent [rikkurrənt] terugkomend, terugkerend

recycle [rie:sajkl] recyclen, weer bruikbaar maken: ~*d paper* kringlooppapier

¹red [red] *adj* **1** rood: ~ *currant* rode aalbes; *like a* ~ *rag to a bull* als een rode lap op een stier; **2** rood, communistisch: ~ *herring* bokking, *(fig)* vals spoor, afleidingsmanoeuvre; *Red Indian* indiaan, roodhuid; ~ *lead* (rode) menie; ~ *tape* bureaucratie, ambtenarij, papierwinkel; *paint the town* ~ de bloemetjes buiten zetten; *see* ~ buiten zichzelf raken (van woede)

²red [red] *n* **1** roodʰ, rode kleur; **2** iets roods; **3** rode, communist ‖ *be in the* ~ rood staan

redden [redn] rood worden (maken), (doen) blozen

reddish [reddisj] roodachtig, rossig

redeem [riddie:m] **1** terugkopen, afkopen, inlossen, *(fig)* terugwinnen: ~ *a mortgage* een hypotheek aflossen; **2** vrijkopen, loskopen; **3** goedmaken, vergoeden: ~ *-ing feature* een verzoenende trek; **4** verlossen, bevrijden, redden

Redeemer [riddie:mə] Verlosser, Heiland

redemption [riddempsjən] **1** redding, verlossing, bevrijding: *beyond* (of: *past*) ~ reddeloos (verloren); **2** afkoop, aflossing

redevelop [rie:divvelləp] renoveren: ~ *a slum district* een krottenwijk renoveren

redevelopment [rie:divvelləpmənt] **1** nieuwe ontwikkeling; **2** renovatie

red-handed op heterdaad

redhead roodharige, rooie

red-hot 1 roodgloeiend, *(fig)* enthousiast; **2** heet van de naald, zeer actueel: ~ *news* allerlaatste nieuws

redo [rie:doe:] **1** overdoen, opnieuw doen; **2** opknappen

redouble [rie:dubl] verdubbelen

redress [ridres] herstellen, vergoeden, goedmaken: ~ *the balance* het evenwicht herstellen

redskin roodhuid

reduce [ridjoe:s] **1** verminderen, beperken, verkleinen, verlagen, reduceren; **2** herleiden, reduceren, omzetten, omsmelten; **3** (with *to*) terugbrengen (tot), degraderen (tot): *be ~d to tears* alleen nog maar kunnen huilen; **4** (with *to*) verpulveren (tot), fijnmalen, klein maken *(also fig)*: *his accusations were ~d to nothing* van zijn beschuldigingen bleef niets overeind

reduction [ridduksjən] reductie, vermindering, korting

redundancy [riddundənsie] **1** overtolligheid, overbodigheid; **2** ontslagʰ, *(by extension)* werkloosheid

redundant [riddundənt] **1** overtollig, overbodig; **2** werkloos: *all the workers were made* ~ al de werknemers moesten afvloeien

reduplicate [ridjoe:plikkeet] **1** verdubbelen; **2** (steeds) herhalen

reduplication [ridjoe:plikkeesjən] **1** verdubbeling; **2** herhaling

reed [rie:d] **1** rietʰ, rietsoort; **2** rietʰ, tong *(in wind instrument or organ pipe)*

¹reef [rie:f] *n* **1** rifʰ; **2** klip; **3** *(sailing)* reefʰ, rifʰ

²reef [rie:f] *vb* *(sailing)* reven, inhalen, inbinden

reefer [rie:fə] **1** jekker; **2** marihuanasigaret

¹reek [rie:k] *n* stank

²reek [rie:k] *vb* **1** (slecht) ruiken, *(fig)* stinken: *his statement ~s of corruption* zijn verklaring riekt naar corruptie; **2** roken, dampen, wasemen

¹reel [rie:l] *n* **1** haspel, klos, spoel; (garen)klosjeʰ; **2** (film)rol

²reel [rie:l] *vb* **1** duizelen, draaien; **2** wervelen, warrelen; **3** wankelen, waggelen: ~ *back* terugdeinzen, terugwijken

re-entry [rie:entrie] terugkeer, terugkomst: *the ~ of a spacecraft into the atmosphere* de terugkeer van een ruimtevaartuig in de atmosfeer

refer [riffə:] **1** (with *to*) verwijzen (naar), doorsturen (naar); **2** (with *to*) toeschrijven (aan), terugvoeren (tot)

¹referee [reffərie:] *n* **1** scheidsrechter, *(fig)* bemiddelaar; **2** (vak)referent, expert; **3** referentie *(person giving the reference)*

²referee [reffərie:] *vb* als scheidsrechter optreden (bij)

reference [reffərəns] **1** referentie, getuigschrift[h], pers die referentie geeft; **2** verwijzing: *be outside our terms of* ~ buiten onze competentie vallen; **3** zinspeling: *make no* ~ *to* geen toespeling maken op; **4** raadpleging: *make* ~ *to a dictionary* een woordenboek naslaan; **5** betrekking, verband[h]: *in* (of: *with*) ~ *to* in verband met

reference work naslagwerk[h]

referendum [reffərendəm] referendum[h], volksstemming

refer to 1 verwijzen naar, betrekking hebben op, van toepassing zijn op; **2** zinspelen op, refereren aan, vermelden; **3** raadplegen, naslaan: ~ *a dictionary* iets opzoeken in een woordenboek; *she kept* ~*ring to her home town* ze had het steeds weer over haar geboorteplaats

¹refill [rie:fil] *vb* opnieuw vullen, (opnieuw) aan-, bij-, opvullen

²refill [rie:fil] *n* (nieuwe) vulling, (nieuw) (op)vulsel[h], inktpatroon: *would you like a* ~*?* zal ik je nog eens inschenken?

refine [riffajn] zuiveren, raffineren, *(fig)* verfijnen, verbeteren

refined [riffajnd] verfijnd, geraffineerd, *(fig)* verzorgd, beschaafd: ~ *manners* goede manieren; ~ *sugar* geraffineerde suiker

refinement [riffajnmənt] **1** verbetering, uitwerking; **2** raffinage; **3** verfijning, raffinement[h], (over)beschaafdheid

refinery [riffajnərie] raffinaderij

¹refit [rie:fit] *vb* hersteld worden, opnieuw uitgerust worden

²refit [rie:fit] *vb* herstellen, opnieuw uitrusten

³refit [rie:fit] *n* herstel[h], nieuwe uitrusting

reflect [riflekt] **1** nadenken, overwegen: *he* ~*ed that* … hij bedacht dat …; **2** weerspiegelen, weerkaatsen, reflecteren, *(fig)* weergeven, getuigen van

reflection [rifleksjən] **1** weerspiegeling, weerkaatsing, reflectie; **2** overdenking, overweging: *on* ~ bij nader inzien

reflective [riflektiv] **1** weerspiegelend, reflecterend; **2** bedachtzaam

reflector [riflektə] reflector

reflect (up)on 1 nadenken over, overdenken; **2** zich ongunstig uitlaten over, een ongunstig licht werpen op: *your impudent behaviour reflects only on yourself* je brutale gedrag werkt alleen maar in je eigen nadeel

¹reflex [rie:fleks] *n* **1** weerspiegeling, ~*es* afspiegeling; **2** reflex[h], reflexbeweging, ~*es* reactievermogen[h]

²reflex [rie:fleks] *adj* weerkaatst, gereflecteerd: ~ *camera* spiegelreflexcamera; ~ *action* reflexbeweging

reflexive [rifleksiv] *(linguistics)* reflexief, wederkerend: ~ *pronoun* wederkerend voornaamwoord

¹refloat [rie:floot] *vb* vlot krijgen

²refloat [rie:floot] *vb* weer vlot raken

¹reform [riffo:m] *vb* verbeteren, hervormen: *Reformed Church* hervormde Kerk

²reform [riffo:m] *n* hervorming, verbetering

reformation [reffəmeesjən] **1** hervorming, verbetering; **2** *the Reformation* de Reformatie

reformer [riffo:mə] hervormer

refract [rifrækt] breken *(beams, rays)*

refraction [rifræksjən] (straal)breking: *angle of* ~ brekingshoek

refractory [rifræktərie] (stijf)koppig, halsstarrig

¹refrain [rifreen] *vb* (with *from*) zich onthouden (van), ervan afzien, het nalaten: *kindly* ~ *from smoking* gelieve niet te roken

²refrain [rifreen] *n* refrein[h]

¹refresh [rifresj] *vb* **1** verfrissen: ~ *s.o.'s memory* iemands geheugen opfrissen; **2** aanvullen, herbevoorraden

²refresh [rifresj] *vb* zich verfrissen, zich opfrissen

refresher course herhalingscursus, bijscholingscursus

refreshing [rifresjing] **1** verfrissend, verkwikkend: *a* ~ *breeze* een lekker koel briesje; **2** aangenaam, verrassend

refreshment [rifresjmənt] **1** verfrissing *(also fig)*, verkwikking, verademing; **2** ~*s* iets te drinken met een hapje daarbij

¹refrigerate [rifridzjəreet] *vb* koelen

²refrigerate [rifridzjəreet] *vb* invriezen

refrigeration [rifridzjəreesjən] **1** invriezing, het diepvriezen; **2** afkoeling

refrigerator [rifridzjəreetə] **1** koelruimte, koelkast, ijskast; **2** koeler

refuge [refjoe:dzj] **1** toevlucht(soord[h]) *(also fig)*, schuilplaats, toeverlaat: ~ *from* bescherming tegen; **2** vluchtheuvel

refugee [refjoedzjie:] vluchteling

¹refund [riffund] *vb* terugbetalen, restitueren: ~ *the cost of postage* de verzendkosten vergoeden

²refund [rie:fund] *n* terugbetaling, geld[h] terug

refurbish [rie:fə:bisj] opknappen, *(fig)* opfrissen: ~ *the office* het kantoor opknappen

refusal [rifjoe:zl] **1** weigering, afwijzing; **2** optie, (recht[h] van) voorkeur: *have (the) first* ~ *of a house* een optie op een huis hebben

¹refuse [rifjoe:z] *vb* weigeren, afslaan, afwijzen: ~ *a request* op een verzoek niet ingaan

²refuse [refjoe:s] *n* afval[h], vuil[h], vuilnis

refuse collector vuilnisophaler, vuilnisman

refutation [refjoeteesjən] weerlegging

refute [rifjoe:t] weerleggen

regain [rigeen] **1** herwinnen, terugwinnen: ~ *consciousness* weer tot bewustzijn komen; **2** opnieuw bereiken: *I helped him ~ his footing* ik hielp hem weer op de been *(also fig)*

regal [rie:gl] koninklijk

regale [rigeel] *(with on, with)* vergasten (op), onthalen (op), trakteren (op): *~ oneself on* (of: *with*) zich te goed doen aan

regalia [rigeeliə] **1** rijksinsigniën, regalia; **2** onderscheidingstekenen: *the mayor in full ~* de burgemeester in vol ornaat; **3** staatsiegewaad

¹regard [riga:d] *vb* **1** beschouwen, aanzien: *~ s.o. as* iem aanzien voor; **2** betreffen, betrekking hebben op, aangaan: *as ~s* met betrekking tot

²regard [riga:d] *n* **1** achting, respect[h]: *hold s.o. in high ~* iem hoogachten; **2** betrekking, verband[h], opzicht[h]: *in this ~* op dit punt; **3** aandacht, zorg: *give* (of: *pay) no ~ to* zich niet bekommeren om; *have little ~ for* weinig rekening houden met; **4** *~s* groeten, wensen[h]: *kind ~s to you all* ik wens jullie allemaal het beste

regarding [riga:ding] betreffende, aangaande

regardless [riga:dləs] hoe dan ook || *they did it ~* ze hebben het toch gedaan

regardless of ongeacht, zonder rekening te houden met: *~ expense* zonder op een cent te letten

regency [rie:dzjənsie] regentschap[h]

¹regenerate [ridzjennəreet] *vb* **1** verbeteren, bekeren, vernieuwen; **2** nieuw leven inblazen, doen herleven

²regenerate [ridzjennərət] *adj* **1** herboren, bekeerd; **2** geregenereerd, hernieuwd

regent [rie:dzjənt] **1** regent(es); **2** *(Am)* curator, bestuurslid[h] *(of university)*

reggae [regee] reggae

regicide [redzjissajd] **1** koningsmoord; **2** koningsmoordenaar

regime [reezjie:m] regime[h]

regimen [redzjimmən] **1** regime[h], verloop[h]; **2** regime[h], kuur

regiment [redzjimmənt] regiment[h], *(fig)* groot aantal[h]

region [rie:dzjən] **1** streek, gebied[h], *~s* sfeer, terrein[h]: *the Arctic ~s* de Arctica; *in the ~ of* in de buurt van *(also fig)*; **2** gewest[h], *~s* provincie, regio

regional [rie:dzjənəl] vd streek, regionaal

¹register [redzjistə] *n* **1** register[h], (naam)lijst, rol, gastenboek[h], kiezerslijst: *the Parliamentary Register* de kiezerslijst; **2** (kas)register[h]

²register [redzjistə] *vb* **1** zich (laten) inschrijven: *~ at a hotel* inchecken; *~ with the police* zich aanmelden bij de politie; **2** doordringen tot, (in zich) opnemen

³register [redzjistə] *vb* **1** (laten) registreren, (laten) inschrijven, *(fig)* nota nemen van: *~ a protest against* protest aantekenen tegen; **2** registreren, aanwijzen *(eg degrees);* **3** uitdrukken, tonen: *her face ~ed surprise* op haar gezicht viel verwondering af te lezen; **4** (laten) aantekenen, aangetekend versturen *(mail)*

registered [redzjistəd] **1** geregistreerd, ingeschre-

ven: *~ trademark* (wettig) gedeponeerd handelsmerk; **2** gediplomeerd, erkend, bevoegd: *(Am) ~ nurse* gediplomeerd verpleegkundige; *State Registered nurse* gediplomeerd verpleegkundige; **3** aangetekend *(of letter)*

register office 1 registratiebureau[h]; **2** (bureau vd) burgerlijke stand

registrar [redzjistra:] **1** registrator, ambtenaar vd burgerlijke stand; **2** archivaris; **3** administratief hoofd[h] *(of university);* **4** *(law)* gerechtssecretaris, griffier; **5** *(med)* stagelopend specialist

registration [redzjistreesjən] registratie, inschrijving, aangifte

registry [redzjistrie] **1** archief[h], registratiekantoor[h]; **2** (bureau vd) burgerlijke stand; **3** register[h]; **4** registratie

registry office (bureau vd) burgerlijke stand: *married at a ~* getrouwd voor de wet

regress [rigres] achteruitgaan, teruggaan

regressive [rigressiv] regressief, teruglopend

¹regret [rigret] *vb* betreuren, spijt hebben van, berouw hebben over: *we ~ to inform you* tot onze spijt moeten wij u meedelen

²regret [rigret] *n* **1** spijt, leed(wezen)[h], berouw[h]: *greatly (of: much) to my ~* tot mijn grote spijt; **2** *~s* (betuigingen van) spijt, verontschuldigingen: *have no ~s* geen spijt hebben

regretful [rigretfoel] bedroefd, vol spijt

regrettable [rigrettəbl] betreurenswaardig, te betreuren

regrettably [rigrettəblie] **1** bedroevend, teleurstellend: *~ little response* bedroevend weinig respons; **2** helaas, jammer genoeg

¹regular [regjoelə] *adj* **1** regelmatig: *a ~ customer* een vaste klant; *a ~ job* vast werk; *keep ~ hours* zich aan vaste uren houden; **2** *(Am)* gewoon, standaard-: *the ~ size* het gewone formaat; **3** professioneel: *the ~ army* het beroepsleger; **4** echt, onvervalst: *a ~ fool* een volslagen idioot

²regular [regjoelə] *n* **1** beroeps(militair): *the ~s* de geregelde troepen; **2** vaste klant, stamgast

regularity [regjoelærittie] regelmatigheid

regularize [regjoelərajz] regulariseren, regelen

regulate [regjoeleet] regelen, reglementeren, ordenen

regulation [regjoeleesjən] regeling, reglement[h], reglementering, (wettelijk) voorschrift[h], bepaling: *rules and ~s* regels en voorschriften

regulator [regjoeleetə] regelaar, kompassleutel *(of timepiece)*

rehabilitation [rie:həbillitteesjən] **1** rehabilitatie, eerherstel[h]; **2** herstelling: *economic ~* economisch herstel

¹rehash [rie:hæsj] *n* herbewerking, *(fig)* opgewarmde kost: *his latest book is a ~ of one of his earlier ones* zijn jongste boek is een herbewerking van een van zijn eerdere boeken

²rehash [rie:hæsj] *vb* herwerken, opnieuw bewerken

rehearsal [rihhə:sl] repetitie: *dress ~* generale repe-

titie
¹rehearse [rihh<u>a</u>:s] *vb* herhalen
²rehearse [rihh<u>a</u>:s] *vb* repeteren, (een) repetitie houden
¹reign [reen] *n* regering: *~ of terror* schrikbewind; *in the ~ of Henry* toen Hendrik koning was
²reign [reen] *vb* regeren, heersen *(also fig): the ~ing champion* de huidige kampioen
reimburse [rie:imb<u>a</u>:s] terugbetalen, vergoeden
¹rein [reen] *n* teugel: *(fig) give free ~ to s.o. (sth.)* iem (iets) de vrije teugel laten; *(fig) keep a tight ~ on s.o.* bij iem de teugels stevig aanhalen
²rein [reen] *vb* inhouden *(also fig)*, beteugelen, in bedwang houden: *~ back* (of: *in, up)* halt doen houden
reincarnation [rie:inka:n<u>ee</u>sjən] reïncarnatie, wedergeboorte
reindeer [r<u>ee</u>ndiə] rendier^h
reinforce [rie:inf<u>o</u>:s] versterken: *~d concrete* gewapend beton
reinforcement [rie:inf<u>o</u>:smənt] versterking
reinstate [rie:inst<u>ee</u>t] herstellen
reiterate [rie:<u>i</u>ttəreet] herhalen
reiteration [rie:ittər<u>ee</u>sjən] herhaling
¹reject [ridzj<u>e</u>kt] *vb* **1** verwerpen, afwijzen, weigeren; **2** uitwerpen
²reject [r<u>ie</u>:dzjekt] *n* afgekeurd persoon (voorwerp^h), afgekeurde *(for military service)*, uitschot^h: *~s are sold at a discount* tweedekeusartikelen worden met korting verkocht
rejection [ridzj<u>e</u>ksjən] **1** verwerping, afkeuring, afwijzing; **2** uitwerping
reject shop winkel met tweedekeusartikelen
rejoice [ridzj<u>oi</u>s] *(with at, over)* zich verheugen (over): *I ~ to hear* het verheugt me te vernemen
rejoicing [ridzj<u>oi</u>sing] vreugde, feestviering
¹rejoin [ridzj<u>oi</u>n] *vb* antwoorden
²rejoin [rie:dzj<u>oi</u>n] *vb* **1** (zich) weer verenigen; **2** weer lid worden (van); **3** zich weer voegen bij: *I thought he would ~ his friends, but he went to sit by himself* ik dacht dat hij weer bij zijn vrienden zou gaan staan, maar hij ging apart zitten
rejoinder [ridzj<u>oi</u>ndə] repliek, (vinnig) antwoord^h
rekindle [rie:k<u>i</u>ndl] opnieuw ontsteken, opnieuw aanwakkeren
¹relapse [ril<u>æ</u>ps] *vb* terugvallen, weer vervallen *(into evil)*, (weer) instorten: *~ into poverty* weer tot armoede vervallen
²relapse [ril<u>æ</u>ps] *n* instorting, terugval *(into evil)*: *have a ~* opnieuw achteruitgaan
¹relate [ril<u>ee</u>t] *vb* **1** verhalen, berichten: *strange to ~ ... hoe onwaarschijnlijk het ook moge klinken, maar ... (at beginning of incredible story)*; **2** (met elkaar) in verband brengen, relateren
²relate [ril<u>ee</u>t] *vb (with to)* in verband staan (met), betrekking hebben (op)
related [ril<u>ee</u>tid] verwant, samenhangend, verbonden: *drug-~ crime* misdaad waarbij drugs een rol spelen; *I'm ~ to her by marriage* zij is aangetrouwde familie van me

relation [ril<u>ee</u>sjən] **1** bloedverwant, familielid^h; **2** bloedverwantschap^h, verwantschap; **3** betrekking, relatie, verband^h: *bear no ~ to* geen verband houden met, geen betrekking hebben op; *in (of: with) ~ to* met betrekking tot, in verhouding tot
relationship [ril<u>ee</u>sjənsjip] **1** betrekking, verhouding; **2** bloedverwantschap^h, verwantschap
¹relative [r<u>e</u>llətiv] *adj* **1** betrekkelijk, relatief: *~ pronoun* betrekkelijk voornaamwoord; **2** toepasselijk, relevant
²relative [r<u>e</u>llətiv] *n* familielid^h, (bloed)verwant(e)
relativity [rellət<u>i</u>vvittie] betrekkelijkheid, relativiteit
¹relax [ril<u>æ</u>ks] *vb* **1** verslappen, verminderen, *(fig)* ontdooien; **2** zich ontspannen, relaxen
²relax [ril<u>æ</u>ks] *vb* ontspannen, verslappen, verminderen: *~ one's efforts* zich minder inspannen
relaxation [rie:læks<u>ee</u>sjən] ontspanning(svorm)
relaxing [ril<u>æ</u>ksing] rustgevend, ontspannend
¹relay [r<u>ie</u>:lee] *n* **1** aflossing, verse paarden, nieuwe ploeg, verse voorraad; **2** estafettewedstrijd
²relay [r<u>ie</u>:lee] *vb* heruitzenden, doorgeven *(information)*
relay race estafettewedstrijd
¹release [ril<u>ie</u>:s] *vb* **1** *(with from)* bevrijden (uit), vrijlaten, vrijgeven; **2** *(with from)* ontslaan (van), vrijstellen, ontheffen (van) *(obligation)*; **3** uitbrengen *(film, video)*, in de handel brengen *(CD)*
²release [ril<u>ie</u>:s] *n* **1** bevrijding, vrijgeving, verlossing; **2** ontslag^h, ontheffing *(of obligation)*, vrijspreking; **3** nieuwe film, video, cd, release; het uitbrengen *(of film, video, CD): on general ~* in alle bioscopen (te zien); **4** (artikel^h voor) publicatie
relegate [r<u>e</u>lligeet] **1** *(with to)* verwijzen (naar); **2** overplaatsen; **3** *(sport)* degraderen
relent [ril<u>e</u>nt] minder streng worden, toegeven, *(fig)* afnemen, verbeteren
relentless [ril<u>e</u>ntləs] **1** meedogenloos, zonder medelijden; **2** gestaag, aanhoudend
relevance [r<u>e</u>lləvəns] relevantie
relevant [r<u>e</u>lləvənt] *(with to)* relevant (voor): *I've marked the ~ passages* ik heb de desbetreffende passages aangegeven
reliability [rillajjəb<u>i</u>llittie] betrouwbaarheid
reliable [ril<u>a</u>jjəbl] betrouwbaar, te vertrouwen, geloofwaardig
reliance [ril<u>a</u>jjəns] vertrouwen^h
reliant [ril<u>a</u>jjənt] vertrouwend: *be ~ on s.o.* vertrouwen stellen in iem
relic [r<u>e</u>llik] **1** relikwie; **2** overblijfsel^h, souvenir^h
relief [ril<u>ie</u>:f] reliëf^h, *(fig)* levendigheid, contrast^h: *bring (of: throw) into ~* doen contrasteren *(also fig)*; **2** verlichting, opluchting, ontlasting: *it was a great ~* het was een pak van mijn hart; **3** afwisseling, onderbreking: *provide a little light ~* voor wat afwisseling zorgen; **4** ondersteuning, steun, hulp; **5** ontzet^h, bevrijding *(of city under siege)*
relief fund ondersteuningsfonds^h, hulpfonds^h

relief map reliëfkaart
relieve [rilli:v] **1** verlichten, opluchten, ontlasten: ~ *one's feelings* zijn hart luchten; ~ *oneself* zijn behoefte doen; ~ *of: a)* ontlasten van, afhelpen van; *b) (inf)* afhandig maken; *c)* ontslaan uit, ontheffen van; **2** afwisselen, onderbreken: *a dress ~d with lace* een jurk met kant afgezet; **3** ondersteunen, helpen, troosten, bemoedigen; **4** aflossen, vervangen; **5** *(mil)* ontzetten, bevrijden
relieved [rilli:vd] opgelucht
religion [rillidzjən] **1** godsdienst; **2** vroomheid; **3** gewetenszaak, heilige plicht: *make a ~ of sth.* van iets een erezaak maken
religious [rillidzjəs] godsdienstig, religieus, vroom
religiously [rillidzjəslie] **1** godsdienstig; **2** gewetensvol, nauwgezet
relinquish [rillingkwisj] **1** opgeven, prijsgeven *(eg religion)*; **2** afstand doen van *(claim, right)*; **3** loslaten
¹**relish** [rellisj] *n* **1** genoegen[h], lust, plezier[h], zin: *read with great ~* met veel plezier lezen; **2** smaak *(also fig)*, trek: *add* (of: *give*) *(a)* ~ *to* prikkelen; *eat with (a)* ~ met smaak eten; **3** saus; **4** pikant smaakje[h]
²**relish** [rellisj] *vb* **1** smakelijk maken, kruiden; **2** genieten van, genoegen scheppen in, zich laten smaken; **3** tegemoet zien, verlangen naar: ~ *the prospect* het een prettig vooruitzicht vinden; *I do not exactly* ~ *the idea of going on my own* ik kijk er niet echt naar uit om alleen te gaan
relocation [rie:lookeesjən] vestiging elders, verhuizing naar elders
reluctance [rilluktəns] tegenzin, weerzin, onwil: *with great ~* met grote tegenzin
reluctant [rilluktənt] onwillig, aarzelend
rely (up)on [rillaj (əp)on] vertrouwen (op), zich verlaten op, steunen op: *can he be relied upon?* kun je op hem rekenen?
remain [rimmeen] **1** blijven, overblijven: *it ~s to be seen* het staat te bezien; ~ *behind* achterblijven, nablijven; **2** verblijven, zich ophouden; **3** voortduren, blijven bestaan
¹**remainder** [rimmeendə] *n* **1** rest, overblijfsel[h], restant[h]; **2** ramsj *(of books)*; **3** verschil[h] *(of subtraction)*
²**remainder** [rimmeendə] *vb* opruimen, uitverkopen *(books at reduced prices)*
remains [rimmeenz] **1** overblijfselen, ruïnes, resten; **2** stoffelijk overschot
¹**remake** [rie:meek] *vb* opnieuw maken, omwerken, een nieuwe versie maken
²**remake** [rie:meek] *n* remake, nieuwe versie
¹**remand** [rimma:nd] *vb* **1** terugzenden; **2** terugzenden in voorlopige hechtenis: ~ *into custody* terugzenden in voorlopige hechtenis
²**remand** [rimma:nd] *n* **1** terugzending *(in preventive custody)*; **2** voorarrest[h]: *on ~* in voorarrest
remand centre observatiehuis[h], *(roughly)* huis[h] van bewaring *(for preventive custody)*
¹**remark** [rimma:k] *vb* (with *(up)on*) opmerkingen maken (over)

²**remark** [rimma:k] *vb* opmerken, bemerken
³**remark** [rimma:k] *n* opmerking: *make a ~* een opmerking maken
remarkable [rimma:kəbl] **1** merkwaardig, opmerkelijk; **2** opvallend
remedial [rimmie:diəl] beter makend, genezend, herstellend, verbeterend
¹**remedy** [remmədie] *n* remedie, (genees)middel[h], hulpmiddel[h]
²**remedy** [remmədie] *vb* verhelpen *(also fig)*, voorzien in, genezen
¹**remember** [rimmembə] *vb* (zich) herinneren, onthouden, van buiten kennen, denken aan
²**remember** [rimmembə] *vb* **1** bedenken *(in testament; by tipping)*; **2** gedenken *(the dead; in prayers)*; **3** (with *to*) de groeten doen (aan)
remembrance [rimmembrəns] **1** herinnering: *in ~ of* ter herinnering aan; **2** herinnering, aandenken[h], souvenir[h]; **3** ~*s* groet
remind [rimmajnd] herinneren, doen denken: *will you ~ me?* help me eraan denken, wil je?
reminder [rimmajndə] **1** herinnering; **2** betalingsherinnering; **3** geheugensteuntje[h]
reminisce [remminnis] herinneringen ophalen
reminiscence [remminnisns] herinnering, ~*s* memoires
remiss [rimmis] nalatig: *be ~ in one's duties* in zijn plichten tekortschieten
remission [rimmisjən] **1** vergeving; **2** kwijtschelding; **3** vermindering *(eg of sentence)*
¹**remit** [rimmit] *vb* **1** vergeven *(sins)*; **2** kwijtschelden, schenken *(debt, sentence)*, vrijstellen van; **3** doen afnemen, verminderen, laten verslappen *(attention)*, verzachten, verlichten *(pain)*; **4** terugzenden, zenden, sturen; **5** overmaken, doen overschrijven *(money)*
²**remit** [rimmit] *vb* afnemen
remittance [rimmittəns] overschrijving *(of money)*, overmaking, betalingsopdracht, overgemaakt bedrag[h]
remnant [remnənt] **1** restant[h], rest, overblijfsel[h]; **2** coupon *(material)*
remorse [rimmo:s] **1** wroeging; **2** medelijden[h]
remorseless [rimmo:sləs] meedogenloos
remote [rimmoot] **1** ver (weg), ver uiteen: ~ *control* afstandsbediening; *the ~ past* het verre verleden; **2** afgelegen; **3** gereserveerd, terughoudend; **4** gering, flauw: *I haven't the ~st idea* ik heb er geen flauw benul van
removal [rimmoo:vl] **1** verwijdering; **2** verplaatsing; **3** afzetting, overplaatsing; **4** verhuizing
¹**remove** [rimmoe:v] *vb* **1** verwijderen, wegnemen, opheffen *(doubt, fear)*, afnemen *(hat)*, uitwissen *(traces)*, schrappen, afvoeren *(from list)*, uitnemen, uittrekken; **2** afzetten, ontslaan, wegzenden: ~ *s.o. from office* iem uit zijn ambt ontslaan; **3** verhuizen, verplaatsen, overplaatsen
²**remove** [rimmoe:v] *vb* verhuizen, vertrekken
removed [rimmoe:vd] verwijderd, afgelegen, ver:

far ~ from the truth ver bezijden de waarheid; *a first cousin once ~* een achterneef

rem**o**ver [rimm**oe**:və] verhuizer

remuner**a**tion [rimjoe:nər**ee**sjən] 1 beloning; 2 vergoeding

rem**u**nerative [rimj**oe**:nərətiv] winstgevend

ren**ai**ssance [rinn**ee**səns] renaissance; herleving

ren**a**me [rie:n**ee**m] herdopen, een andere naam geven

rend [rend] 1 scheuren, verscheuren: ~ *apart* vaneenscheuren; 2 doorklieven, kloven, splijten: *(fig) a cry rent the skies* (of: *air*) een gil doorkliefde de lucht; 3 kwellen, verdriet doen *(heart)*

r**e**nder [r**e**ndə] 1 (terug)geven, geven, vergelden, verlenen, verschaffen *(assistance)*, bewijzen *(service)*, betuigen *(thanks)*, uitbrengen *(report)*, uitspreken *(verdict)*: ~ *good for evil* kwaad met goed vergelden; *services ~ed* bewezen diensten; 2 overgeven, overleveren; 3 vertalen, omzetten, overzetten: ~ *into German* in het Duits vertalen; 4 maken, veranderen in

r**e**ndering [r**e**ndəring] 1 vertolking, weergave; 2 vertaling

r**e**negade [r**e**nnigeed] afvallige, overloper

ren**e**ge [rinn**ie**:g] 1 een belofte verbreken: ~ *on one's word* zijn woord breken; 2 *(cards)* verzaken

ren**e**w [rinj**oe**:] 1 vernieuwen, hernieuwen, oplappen *(coat)*, verversen, bijvullen *(water)*, vervangen *(tyres)*; 2 doen herleven, verjongen; 3 hervatten, weer opnemen *(conversation)*, herhalen; 4 verlengen *(contract)*

ren**e**wable [rinj**oe**:əbl] 1 vernieuwbaar, herwinbaar, recycleerbaar: ~ *energy* zonne- en windenergie; 2 verlengbaar

ren**e**wal [rinj**oe**:əl] 1 vernieuwing, vervanging; 2 verlenging

ren**ou**nce [rinn**au**ns] afstand doen van, opgeven, laten varen

r**e**novate [r**e**nnəveet] 1 vernieuwen, opknappen, renoveren, verbouwen; 2 doen herleven

renov**a**tion [rennəv**ee**sjən] vernieuwing, renovatie

ren**ow**n [rinn**au**n] faam, roem

¹rent *n* 1 huur, pacht: *(Am) for ~* te huur; 2 (meer)opbrengst van landbouwgrond; 3 scheur(ing), kloof, barst

²rent *vb* 1 huren; 2 *(also with out)* verhuren

r**e**ntal [r**e**ntl] 1 huuropbrengst; 2 huur(penningen), pacht(geld); 3 *(Am)* het gehuurde, het verhuurde *(eg rented house)*

renunci**a**tion [rinnunsie·**ee**sjən] 1 afstand, verwerping, verstoting; 2 zelfverloochening

re**o**pen [rie:**oo**pən] 1 opnieuw opengaan, opnieuw openen, weer beginnen, heropenen *(of shop etc)*; 2 hervatten *(discussion)*

reorganize [rie:**o**:gənajz] reorganiseren

¹rep**ai**r [ripp**e**ə] *n* herstelling, reparatie, herstel*h*: *in (a) good (state of)* ~ in goede toestand, goed onderhouden; *under* ~ in reparatie

²rep**ai**r [ripp**e**ə] *vb* 1 herstellen, repareren; 2 vergoe-

den, (weer) goedmaken

rep**ai**rer [ripp**e**ərə] hersteller, reparateur

repar**a**tion [reppər**ee**sjən] 1 herstel*h*, herstelling, reparatie; 2 vergoeding, schadeloosstelling, ~s herstelbetaling

repatri**a**tion [rie:pætrie·**ee**sjən] repatriëring

rep**a**y [ripp**ee**] 1 terugbetalen, aflossen; 2 beantwoorden: ~ *kindness by* (of: *with*) *ingratitude* goedheid met ondankbaarheid beantwoorden; 3 vergoeden, goedmaken; 4 betaald zetten

rep**a**yment [ripp**ee**mənt] 1 terugbetaling, aflossing; 2 vergoeding, vergelding, beloning

¹rep**ea**l [ripp**ie**:l] *vb* herroepen, afschaffen, intrekken

²rep**ea**l [ripp**ie**:l] *n* herroeping, afschaffing, intrekking

¹rep**ea**t [ripp**ie**:t] *vb* 1 herhalen: ~ *a course* (of: *year*) blijven zitten *(at school)*; 2 nazeggen, navertellen: *his words will not bear ~ing* zijn woorden laten zich niet herhalen

²rep**ea**t [ripp**ie**:t] *vb* 1 zich herhalen, terugkeren: *history ~s itself* de geschiedenis herhaalt zich; 2 repeteren *(eg timepiece, firearm)*: ~*ing decimal* repeterende breuk

³rep**ea**t [ripp**ie**:t] *n* 1 herhaling; 2 heruitzending: *in summer there are endless ~s of American soaps* in de zomer krijg je eindeloze herhalingen van Amerikaanse soaps

rep**ea**tedly [ripp**ie**:tidlie] herhaaldelijk, steeds weer, telkens

¹rep**e**l [ripp**e**l] *vb* afweren, terugdrijven, afslaan *(offer, attack(er))*, afstoten *(damp)*

²rep**e**l [ripp**e**l] *vb* afkeer opwekken

¹rep**e**llent [ripp**e**lənt] *adj* 1 afwerend, afstotend; 2 weerzinwekkend, walgelijk; 3 onaantrekkelijk

²rep**e**llent [ripp**e**lənt] *n* 1 afweermiddel*h*, insectenwerend middel*h*; 2 waterafstotend middel*h*

rep**e**nt [ripp**e**nt] berouw hebben (over), berouwen

rep**e**ntance [ripp**e**ntəns] berouw*h*

reperc**u**ssion [rie:pək**u**sjən] 1 terugslag, (onaangename) reactie, repercussie; 2 weerkaatsing, echo; 3 terugstoot

repet**i**tion [reppitt**i**sjən] herhaling, repetitie

rep**e**titive [ripp**e**ttitiv] (zich) herhalend, herhaald, herhalings-

rep**i**ne [ripp**ai**n] morren, klagen

repl**a**ce [ripl**ee**s] 1 terugplaatsen, terugleggen, terugzetten; 2 vervangen, in de plaats stellen; 3 de plaats innemen van, verdringen

repl**a**cement [ripl**ee**smənt] 1 vervanging; 2 vervanger, plaatsvervanger, opvolger; 3 vervangstuk*h*, nieuwe aanvoer, versterking *(mil)*

repl**a**y [rie:pl**ee**] 1 opnieuw spelen, overspelen; 2 terugspelen, herhalen

repl**e**nish [ripl**e**nnisj] weer vullen, aanvullen, bijvullen

repl**e**te [ripl**ie**:t] *(with with)* vol (van), gevuld, volgepropt

r**e**plica [r**e**plikkə] 1 replica, kopie; 2 reproductie,

(fig) evenbeeld[h]

¹reply [riplaj] *n* antwoord[h], repliek

²reply [riplaj] *vb* antwoorden: ~ *to* antwoorden op, beantwoorden

¹report [rippo:t] *vb* **1** rapporteren, berichten, melden: ~ *progress* over de stand van zaken berichten; **2** opschrijven, noteren, samenvatten *(reports, proceedings)*; **3** rapporteren, doorvertellen: ~ *s.o. to the police* iem bij de politie aangeven; **4** verslag uitbrengen, verslag doen, rapport opstellen: ~ *back* verslag komen uitbrengen; ~ *(up)on sth.* over iets verslag uitbrengen; **5** zich aanmelden, verantwoording afleggen: ~ *to s.o. for duty* zich bij iem voor de dienst aanmelden

²report [rippo:t] *n* **1** rapport[h], verslag[h], bericht[h]; schoolrapport[h]; **2** knal, slag, schot[h]; **3** gerucht[h], praatje[h], praatjes: *the ~ goes that …, ~ has it that …* het gerucht doet de ronde dat …

reportedly [rippo:tidlie] naar verluidt, naar men zegt

reporter [rippo:tə] reporter, verslaggever

¹repose [rippooz] *vb* **1** rusten, uitrusten; **2** *(with on)* berusten (op), steunen

²repose [rippooz] *vb* stellen, vestigen *(faith, hope)*: ~ *confidence* (of: *trust*) *in sth.* vertrouwen stellen in iets

³repose [rippooz] *n* **1** rust, slaap, ontspanning; **2** kalmte

repository [rippozzittərie] **1** magazijn[h], pakhuis[h], opslagplaats; **2** schatkamer *(fig)*, bron, centrum[h] *(of information)*

represent [reprizzent] **1** voorstellen, weergeven, afbeelden; **2** voorhouden, onder het oog brengen; **3** aanvoeren, beweren: ~ *oneself as* zich uitgeven voor; **4** verklaren, uitleggen, duidelijk maken; **5** symboliseren, staan voor, betekenen; **6** vertegenwoordigen

representation [reprizzenteesjən] **1** voorstelling, af-, uitbeelding, opvoering; **2** vertegenwoordiging; **3** protest[h]

¹representative [reprizzentətiv] *adj* **1** representatief, typisch; **2** voorstellend, symboliserend || *be ~ of* typisch zijn voor

²representative [reprizzentətiv] *n* **1** vertegenwoordiger, agent; **2** afgevaardigde, gedelegeerde, gemachtigde; **3** volksvertegenwoordiger: *(Am) House of Representatives* Huis van Afgevaardigden

repress [ripres] **1** onderdrukken *(also fig)*, verdrukken, in bedwang houden, smoren; **2** verdringen

repression [ripresjən] **1** onderdrukking, verdrukking; **2** verdringing

repressive [ripressiv] onderdrukkend, hardvochtig en wreed *(of regime)*

¹reprieve [riprie:v] *vb* **1** uitstel, gratie verlenen *(death penalty)*; **2** respijt geven *(fig)*, een adempauze geven

²reprieve [riprie:v] *n* **1** (bevel[h] tot) uitstel[h], opschorting *(of death penalty)*; **2** kwijtschelding, gratie, omzetting *(of death penalty)*; **3** respijt[h], verlichting,

verademing: *temporary ~* (voorlopig) uitstel van executie

¹reprimand [reprimma:nd] *vb* (officieel) berispen

²reprimand [reprimma:nd] *n* (officiële) berisping, uitbrander

¹reprint [rie:print] *vb* herdrukken

²reprint [rie:print] *n* **1** overdruk(je[h]); **2** herdruk

reprisal [riprajzl] represaille, vergelding(smaatregel)

¹reproach [riprootsj] *vb* verwijten, berispen, afkeuren: *I have nothing to ~ myself with* ik heb mezelf niets te verwijten

²reproach [riprootsj] *n* **1** schande, smaad, blaam: *above* (of: *beyond*) ~ onberispelijk, perfect; **2** verwijt[h], uitbrander, berisping: *a look of ~* een verwijtende blik

reprocess [rie:prooses] recyclen, terugwinnen, opwerken *(nuclear fuel)*

¹reproduce [rie:prədjoe:s] *vb* **1** weergeven, reproduceren, vermenigvuldigen; **2** voortbrengen; **3** opnieuw voortbrengen, herscheppen, *(biology)* regenereren

²reproduce [rie:prədjoe:s] *vb* zich voortplanten, zich vermenigvuldigen

reproduction [rie:prəduksjən] **1** reproductie, weergave, afbeelding; **2** voortplanting

reprove [riproe:v] berispen, terechtwijzen

reptile [reptajl] **1** reptiel[h]; **2** (lage) kruiper *(fig)*

republic [rippublik] republiek *(also fig)*

¹republican [rippublikkən] *adj* republikeins

²republican [rippublikkən] *n* republikein

repudiate [ripjoe:die-eet] **1** verstoten *(woman, child)*; **2** verwerpen, niet erkennen *(debt etc)*, afwijzen, ontkennen *(accusation)*

repudiation [ripjoe:die-eesjən] **1** verstoting; **2** verwerping, (ver)loochening

repugnant [rippugnənt] weerzinwekkend

repulse [rippuls] **1** terugdrijven, terugslaan *(enemy)*, afslaan *(attack)*; *(fig)* verijdelen; **2** afslaan, afwijzen *(assistance, offer)*

repulsive [rippulsiv] afstotend, weerzinwekkend, walgelijk

reputable [repjoetəbl] achtenswaardig, fatsoenlijk

reputation [repjoeteesjən] reputatie, (goede) naam, faam: *have the ~ for* (of: *of*) *being corrupt* de naam hebben corrupt te zijn

¹repute [ripjoe:t] *n* reputatie, (goede) naam, faam: *know s.o. by ~* iem kennen van horen zeggen

²repute [ripjoe:t] *vb* beschouwen (als), houden voor: *be highly ~d* een zeer goede naam hebben

reputed [ripjoe:tid] **1** befaamd; **2** vermeend

reputedly [ripjoe:tidlie] naar men zegt, naar het heet

¹request [rikwest] *n* verzoek[h], (aan)vraag, verzoeknummer[h]: *at the ~ of* op verzoek van; *on ~* op verzoek

²request [rikwest] *vb* verzoeken, vragen (om)

request programme verzoekprogramma[h]

require [rikwajjə] **1** nodig hebben, behoeven; **2** vereisen, eisen, vorderen: *two signatures are ~d* er zijn twee handtekeningen nodig; *~ sth. from* (of: *s.o.*) *s.o.* iets van iem vereisen

requirement [rikw**a**jjəmənt] **1** eis, (eerste) vereiste: *meet* (of: *fulfil) the ~s* aan de voorwaarden voldoen; **2** behoefte, benodigdheid

¹**requisite** [r**e**kwizzit] *adj* vereist, essentieel, nodig

²**requisite** [r**e**kwizzit] *n* **1** vereiste[h]; **2** rekwisiet[h], benodigdheid

requisition [rekwizz**i**sjən] (op)vorderen

requite [rikw**a**jt] **1** vergelden, betaald zetten, wreken; **2** belonen; **3** beantwoorden: *~ s.o.'s love* iemands liefde beantwoorden

¹**rerun** [rie:r**u**n] *vb* opnieuw (laten) spelen, herhalen *(film, TV programme)*

²**rerun** [rie:run] *n* herhaling *(of film, play etc)*

¹**rescue** [r**e**skjoe:] *vb* redden, verlossen, bevrijden

²**rescue** [r**e**skjoe:] *n* **1** redding, verlossing, bevrijding; **2** hulp, bijstand, steun

rescuer [r**e**skjoe:ə] redder

¹**research** [riss**a**:tsj] *n* (wetenschappelijk) onderzoek[h]

²**research** [riss**a**:tsj] *vb* onderzoekingen doen, wetenschappelijk werk verrichten, wetenschappelijk onderzoeken: *this book has been well ~ed* dit boek berust op gedegen onderzoek

researcher [riss**a**:tsjə] onderzoeker

resemblance [rizz**e**mbləns] gelijkenis, overeenkomst: *show great ~ to s.o.* een grote gelijkenis met iem vertonen

resemble [rizz**e**mbl] lijken op

resent [rizz**e**nt] kwalijk nemen, verontwaardigd zijn over, zich storen aan: *I ~ that remark* ik neem je die opmerking wel kwalijk

resentful [rizz**e**ntfoel] **1** boos, verontwaardigd, ontstemd; **2** wrokkig, haatdragend

resentment [rizz**e**ntmənt] **1** verontwaardiging; **2** wrok, haat

reservation [rezzəv**ee**sjən] **1** middenberm, middenstrook *(of motorway): central ~* middenberm; **2** *(Am)* reservaat[h] *(for indians);* **3** gereserveerde plaats; **4** reserve, voorbehoud[h], bedenking: *without ~(s)* zonder voorbehoud; **5** reservering, plaatsbespreking: *do you have a ~?* heeft u gereserveerd?

¹**reserve** [rizz**a**:v] *n* **1** reserve, (nood)voorraad: *have sth. in ~* iets in reserve hebben; **2** reservaat[h]: *nature ~* natuurreservaat; **3** reservespeler, invaller; **4** reservist; **5** reserve, voorbehoud[h], bedenking: *without ~* zonder enig voorbehoud; **6** gereserveerdheid, reserve, terughoudendheid

²**reserve** [rizz**a**:v] *vb* **1** reserveren, achterhouden, in reserve houden; **2** (zich) voorbehouden *(right): all rights ~d* alle rechten voorbehouden; **3** bespreken *(seat),* openhouden, laten vrijhouden

reserved [rizz**a**:vd] **1** gereserveerd, terughoudend, gesloten; **2** gereserveerd, besproken *(of seat)*

reservoir [r**e**zzəvwa:] (water)reservoir[h], stuwmeer[h]

reshape [rie:sj**ee**p] een nieuwe vorm geven

reside [rizz**a**jd] wonen, zetelen

residence [r**e**zziddəns] **1** residentie, verblijf[h], verblijfplaats, woonplaats: *take up ~ in* gaan wonen in; **2** (voorname) woning, villa, herenhuis[h]; **3** ambtswoning *(of governor)*

residence permit verblijfsvergunning

¹**resident** [r**e**zziddənt] *adj* **1** woonachtig, inwonend, intern: *(Am) ~ alien* vreemdeling met een verblijfsvergunning; **2** vast *(on inhabitant)*

²**resident** [r**e**zziddənt] *n* ingezetene, (vaste) inwoner, bewoner

residential [rezzidd**e**nsjl] woon-, ve woonwijk: *~ area* (of: *district, quarter)* (deftige, betere) woonwijk; *~ hotel* familiehotel

residue [r**e**zzidjoe:] residu[h], overblijfsel[h], rest(ant[h])

¹**resign** [rizz**a**jn] *vb* **1** berusten, zich schikken; **2** afstand doen ve ambt, aftreden, ontslag nemen, bedanken *(for position),* opgeven *(chess)*

²**resign** [rizz**a**jn] *vb* **1** berusten in, zich schikken in, zich neerleggen bij: *~ oneself to sth., be ~ed to sth.* zich bij iets neerleggen; **2** afstaan, afstand doen van *(right, claim, ownership),* overgeven; **3** opgeven *(hope)*

resignation [rezzign**ee**sjən] **1** ontslag[h], ontslagbrief, aftreding, ontslagneming: *hand in* (of: *offer, send in, tender) one's ~* zijn ontslag indienen; **2** afstand; **3** berusting, overgave

resigned [rizz**a**jnd] gelaten, berustend

resilience [rizz**i**lliəns] veerkracht *(also fig),* herstellingsvermogen[h]

resin [r**e**zzin] (kunst)hars[h]: *synthetic ~* kunsthars

resist [rizz**i**st] **1** weerstaan, weerstand bieden (aan), tegenhouden, bestand zijn tegen *(cold, heat, damp),* resistent zijn tegen *(disease, infection): ~ temptation* de verleiding weerstaan; **2** zich verzetten (tegen), bestrijden: *this novel ~s interpretation* deze roman laat zich niet interpreteren

resistance [rizz**i**stəns] **1** weerstand, tegenstand, verzet[h]: *make* (of: *offer) no ~* geen weerstand bieden; *(fig) take the line of least ~* de weg van de minste weerstand kiezen; **2** weerstandsvermogen[h]; **3** *the Resistance* verzetsbeweging, verzet[h]

resistant [rizz**i**stənt] weerstand biedend, resistent, bestand: *heat~* hittebestendig

¹**resit** [rie:s**i**t] *vb* opnieuw afleggen *(examination)*

²**resit** [r**ie**:sit] *n* herexamen[h]

resolute [r**e**zzəloe:t] resoluut, vastberaden, beslist

resolution [rezzəl**oe**:sjən] **1** resolutie, motie, voorstel[h], plan[h]; **2** besluit[h], beslissing, voornemen[h]: *good ~s* goede voornemens; **3** oplossing, ontbinding, ontleding; **4** vastberadenheid, beslistheid, vastbeslotenheid

¹**resolve** [rizz**o**lv] *vb* **1** een besluit nemen, besluiten, zich voornemen: *they ~d (up)on doing sth.* zij besloten iets te doen; **2** zich oplossen, zich ontbinden, uiteenvallen

²**resolve** [rizz**o**lv] *vb* **1** beslissen, besluiten: *he ~d to leave* hij besloot weg te gaan; **2** oplossen, een oplossing vinden voor; **3** opheffen, wegnemen *(doubt);* **4** ontbinden, (doen) oplossen; **5** ertoe brengen, doen

beslissen: *that ~d us to* ... dat deed ons besluiten om ...; **6** besluiten, beëindigen, bijleggen *(dispute)*
³**resolve** [rizzɔlv] *n* **1** besluitʰ, beslissing, voornemenʰ: *a firm ~ to stay* een vast voornemen om te blijven; **2** *(Am)* resolutie, motie, voorstelʰ; **3** vastberadenheid, beslistheid

resolved [rizzɔlvd] vastbesloten, beslist

resonance [rɛzzənəns] resonantie, weerklank, weergalm

resonant [rɛzzənənt] **1** resonerend, weerklinkend, weergalmend; **2** vol, diep *(of voice)*

resort [rizzɔːt] **1** hulpmiddelʰ, redmiddelʰ, toevlucht: *in the last ~, as a last ~* in laatste instantie, in geval van nood; **2** druk bezochte plaats, (vakantie)oordʰ: *without ~ to* zonder zijn toevlucht te nemen tot

resort to zijn toevlucht nemen tot: *~ violence* zijn toevlucht nemen tot geweld

resound [rizzaund] weerklinken *(also fig)*, weergalmen

resounding [rizzaunding] **1** (weer)klinkend; **2** zeer groot, onmiskenbaar: *a ~ success* een daverend succes

resource [rizzɔːs] **1** hulpbron, redmiddelʰ: *left to one's own ~s* aan zijn lot overgelaten; **2** toevlucht, uitweg; **3** vindingrijkheid: *he is full of ~* (of: *a man of ~*) hij is (zeer) vindingrijk; **4** *~s* rijkdommen, (geld)middelen, voorraden: *natural ~s* natuurlijke rijkdommen

resourceful [rizzɔːsfoel] vindingrijk

¹**respect** [rispɛkt] *n* **1** opzichtʰ, detailʰ, (oog)puntʰ: *in all ~s* in alle opzichten; *in some ~* in zeker opzicht, enigermate; **2** betrekking, relatie: *with ~ to* met betrekking tot, wat betreft; **3** aandacht, zorg, inachtneming: *without ~ to* zonder te letten op, ongeacht; **4** eerbied, achting, ontzagʰ: *be held in the greatest ~* zeer in aanzien zijn; *with (all due) ~* als u mij toestaat; **5** *~s* eerbetuigingen, groeten, complimenten: *give her my ~s* doe haar de groeten; *pay one's last ~s to s.o.* iem de laatste eer bewijzen *(at someone's death)*

²**respect** [rispɛkt] *vb* **1** respecteren, eerbiedigen, (hoog)achten; **2** ontzien, ongemoeid laten

respectability [rispɛktəbjllittie] fatsoenʰ, fatsoenlijkheid

respectable [rispɛktəbl] **1** achtenswaardig, eerbiedwaardig; **2** respectabel, (tamelijk) groot, behoorlijk: *a ~ income* een behoorlijk inkomen; **3** fatsoenlijk *(also iron)*

respectful [rispɛktfoel] eerbiedig

respectively [rispɛktivlie] respectievelijk

respiration [respirreesjən] ademhaling

respirator [respirreetə] **1** ademhalingstoestelʰ; **2** gasmaskerʰ, rookmaskerʰ, stofmaskerʰ

respiratory [rispirrətərie] ademhalings-

respite [respajt] respijtʰ, uitstelʰ, opschorting

resplendent [risplɛndənt] schitterend, prachtig

respond [rispɔnd] **1** antwoorden; **2** *(with to)* reageren (op), gehoor geven (aan), gevoelig zijn (voor)

respondent [rispɔndənt] **1** gedaagde *(in appeal of divorce proceedings)*; **2** ondervraagde, geënquêteerde

response [rispɔns] **1** antwoordʰ, repliek, tegenzet; **2** reactie, gehoorʰ, weerklank, respons: *meet with no ~* geen weerklank vinden

responsibility [risponsibbjllittie] verantwoordelijkheid, aansprakelijkheid: *on one's own ~* op eigen verantwoordelijkheid

responsible [rispɔnsibl] **1** betrouwbaar, degelijk, solide; **2** verantwoordelijk, belangrijk *(of job)*; **3** *(with for)* verantwoordelijk (voor), aansprakelijk (voor): *be ~ to* verantwoording verschuldigd zijn aan

responsive [rispɔnsiv] *(with to)* ontvankelijk (voor), gevoelig (voor), vlug reagerend (op)

¹**rest** [rest] *n* **1** rustplaats, verblijfʰ, tehuisʰ; **2** steun, standaard, houder, statiefʰ, *(billiards)* bok; **3** *(mus)* rust(tekenʰ); **4** rust, slaap, pauze: *come to ~* tot stilstand komen; *set s.o.'s mind at ~* iem geruststellen; **5** de rest, het overige, de overigen: *and the ~ of it, all the ~ of it* en de rest

²**rest** [rest] *vb* **1** rusten, stil staan, slapen, pauzeren: *I feel completely ~ed* ik voel me helemaal uitgerust; **2** blijven *(in a certain condition)*: *~ assured* wees gerust, wees ervan verzekerd; **3** braak liggen

³**rest** [rest] *vb* **1** laten (uit)rusten, rust geven; **2** doen rusten, leunen, steunen

restaurant [restərõ] restaurantʰ

restful [restfoel] **1** rustig, kalm, vredig; **2** rustgevend, kalmerend

restitution [restitjoe:sjən] restitutie, teruggave, schadeloosstelling

restive [restiv] **1** weerspannig, onhandelbaar, dwars, koppig *(of horse)*; **2** ongedurig, onrustig, rusteloos *(of person)*

restless [restləs] rusteloos, onrustig, ongedurig

restoration [restəreesjən] **1** restauratie(werkʰ), reconstructie; **2** herstelʰ, herinvoering, rehabilitatie; **3** teruggave

restore [ristɔː] **1** teruggeven, terugbetalen, terugbrengen; **2** restaureren; **3** reconstrueren; **4** in ere herstellen, rehabiliteren; **5** herstellen, weer invoeren, vernieuwen

restrain [ristreen] **1** tegenhouden, weerhouden: *~ from* weerhouden van; **2** aan banden leggen, beteugelen, beperken, in toom houden

restrained [ristreend] **1** beheerst, kalm; **2** ingetogen, sober, gematigd *(of colour)*

restraint [ristreent] **1** terughoudendheid, gereserveerdheid, zelfbeheersing: *without ~* vrijelijk, in onbeperkte mate; **2** ingetogenheid, soberheid

restrict [ristrikt] beperken, begrenzen, aan banden leggen: *~ to* beperken tot

restriction [ristriksjən] beperking, (beperkende) bepaling, restrictie, voorbehoudʰ

restrictive [ristriktiv] beperkend: *~ trade practices* beperkende handelspraktijken

rest room *(Am)* toiletʰ *(in restaurant, office etc)*

rest (up)on (be)rusten op, steunen op

¹result [rizzʌlt] *vb* **1** volgen, het gevolg zijn: ~ *from* voortvloeien uit; **2** aflopen, uitpakken: ~ *in* tot gevolg hebben

²result [rizzʌlt] *n* **1** resultaatʰ, uitkomst, uitslag *(of sporting events);* **2** gevolgʰ, effectʰ, uitvloeiselʰ: *as a* ~ dientengevolge, als gevolg waarvan; *as a* ~ *of* tengevolge van; **3** uitkomst *(of sum)*, antwoordʰ

resultant [rizzʌltənt] resulterend, eruit voortvloeiend

resume [rizjoe:m] **1** opnieuw beginnen, hervatten, hernemen; **2** terugnemen, terugkrijgen; **3** voortzetten, vervolgen, doorgaan

resumption [rizzʌmpsjən] hervatting, voortzetting

resurgence [rissə:dzjəns] heropleving, opstanding

resurrect [rezzərekt] **1** (doen) herleven, (doen) herrijzen; **2** opgraven, weer voor de dag halen

resurrection [rezzəreksjən] **1** *the Resurrection* de verrijzenis, de opstanding; **2** herleving, opleving, opstanding

resuscitate [rissʌssitteet] **1** weer bijbrengen, reanimeren; **2** doen herleven

¹retail [rie:teel] *n* kleinhandel, detailhandel

²retail [rie:teel] *vb* in een winkel verkocht worden: ~ *at* (of: *for) fifty cents* in de winkel voor vijftig cent te koop zijn

³retail [rie:teel] *vb* in een winkel verkopen

⁴retail [ritteel] *vb* omstandig vertellen

retailer [rie:teelə] **1** winkelier, kleinhandelaar; **2** slijter

retain [ritteen] **1** vasthouden, binnenhouden: *a ~ing wall* steunmuur; **2** houden, handhaven, bewaren: *we* ~ *happy memories of those days* wij bewaren goede herinneringen aan die dagen

retainer [ritteenə] **1** voorschotʰ *(of fee);* **2** volgeling, bediende: *an old* ~ een oude getrouwe

retaliate [ritælie·eet] wraak nemen

retard [ritta:d] ophouden, tegenhouden, vertragen

retarded [ritta:did] achtergebleven, achterlijk, geestelijk gehandicapt

retch [retsj] kokhalzen

retention [rittensjən] **1** het vasthouden, het binnenhouden; **2** handhaving, behoudʰ

¹rethink [rie:θingk] *vb* heroverwegen, opnieuw bezien

²rethink [rie:θingk] *n* heroverweging, het opnieuw doordenken

reticence [rettisns] **1** terughoudendheid, gereserveerdheid; **2** het verzwijgen, het achterhouden; **3** zwijgzaamheid, geslotenheid

reticent [rettisnt] **1** terughoudend, gereserveerd; **2** zwijgzaam, gesloten

retinue [rettinjoe:] gevolgʰ, hofstoet

retire [rittajjə] **1** zich terugtrekken, weggaan, heengaan, zich ter ruste begeven: ~ *for the night* zich ter ruste begeven; **2** met pensioen gaan

retired [rittajjəd] **1** teruggetrokken, afgezonderd, afgelegen; **2** gepensioneerd, stil levend, rentenie-

rend

retirement [rittajjəmənt] **1** pensionering, het gepensioneerd worden, met pensioen gaan: *to take early* ~ met de vut gaan, *(Belg)* op brugpensioen gaan; **2** afzondering, eenzaamheid

retiring [rittajjəring] **1** teruggetrokken, niet opdringerig; **2** pensioen-: ~ *age* de pensioengerechtigde leeftijd

¹retort [ritto:t] *vb* een weerwoord geven, antwoorden

²retort [ritto:t] *vb* (vinnig) antwoorden, *(fig)* de bal terugkaatsen

³retort [ritto:t] *n* **1** weerwoordʰ, repliek, antwoordʰ: *say (sth.) in* ~ (iets) als weerwoord gebruiken; **2** distilleerkolf

retrace [ritrees] **1** herleiden, terugvoeren tot; **2** weer nagaan *(in memory);* **3** terugkeren: ~ *one's steps* (of: *way)* op zijn schreden terugkeren

retract [ritrækt] intrekken *(also fig)*, herroepen, afstand nemen van

¹retreat [ritrie:t] *vb* teruggaan, zich terugtrekken

²retreat [ritrie:t] *n* **1** toevluchtsoordʰ, schuilplaats; **2** tehuisʰ, asielʰ; **3** terugtocht, aftocht: *beat a (hasty)* ~ zich (snel) terugtrekken, *(fig)* (snel) de aftocht blazen; **4** retraite

¹retrench [ritrentsj] *vb* bezuinigen

²retrench [ritrentsj] *vb* besnoeien, inkorten, bekorten

retribution [retribjoe:sjən] vergelding, straf

retrieval [ritrie:vl] **1** herwinning, het terugvinden; **2** herstelling, het verhelpen; **3** het ophalen *(data from files)* || *beyond* (of: *past)* ~: *a)* voorgoed verloren; *b)* onherstelbaar

retrieve [ritrie:v] **1** terugwinnen, terugvinden, terugkrijgen; **2** herstellen, weer goedmaken, verhelpen; **3** ophalen *(data from files)*

retrospect [retrəspekt] terugblik: *in* ~ achteraf gezien

retrospective [retrəspektiv] **1** retrospectief, terugblikkend; **2** met terugwerkende kracht

¹return [rittə:n] *vb* terugkeren, terugkomen, teruggaan: ~ *to: a)* terugkeren op; *b)* vervallen in

²return [rittə:n] *vb* antwoorden

³return [rittə:n] *vb* **1** retourneren, terugbrengen, teruggeven; **2** opleveren, opbrengen; **3** beantwoorden, terugbetalen: ~ *like for like* met gelijke munt terugbetalen; **4** *(sport)* terugslaan, retourneren, terugspelen; **5** kiezen, verkiezen, afvaardigen

⁴return [rittə:n] *n* **1** terugkeer, terugkomst, thuiskomst, terugreis: *the point of no* ~ punt waarna er geen weg terug is; **2** retourtjeʰ; **3** teruggave *(also of tax)*, teruggezonden artikelʰ: *on sale and* ~ op commissie; **4** opbrengst, winst, rendementʰ: ~ *on capital* (of: *investment)* kapitaalopbrengst, resultaat van de investering; **5** aangifte, officieel rapportʰ; **6** verkiezing, afvaardiging; **7** terugslag, return, terugspeelbal; **8** return(wedstrijd), revanche: *by* ~ *(of post)* per omgaande, per kerende post; *in* ~ *for* in ruil voor

⁵return [rittə:n] *adj* **1** retour-: ~ *ticket* retour(tje); **2** tegen-, terug-: *a ~ visit* een tegenbezoek

reunion [rie:joe:niən] reünie, hereniging, samenkomst

reunite [rie:joe:najt] (zich) herenigen, weer bij elkaar komen

reusable [rie:joe:zəbl] geschikt voor hergebruik

reuse [rie:joe:z] opnieuw gebruiken

rev. *Reverend* Eerw.

revaluation [rivæljoe:eesjən] herwaardering, revaluatie *(also fin)*

revamp [rie:væmp] opknappen, vernieuwen

reveal [rivvie:l] openbaren, onthullen, bekendmaken

revealing [rivvie:ling] onthullend, veelzeggend

revel [revl] pret maken, feestvieren: ~ *in* erg genieten van, zich te buiten gaan aan

revelation [revvəleesjən] bekendmaking, openbaring, onthulling: *it was quite a ~ to me* dat was een hele openbaring voor mij

revelry [revvəlrie] pret(makerij), uitgelatenheid

¹revenge [rivvendzj] *n* **1** wraak(neming), vergelding; **2** *(sport, game)* revanche(partij)

²revenge [rivvendzj] *vb* wreken, vergelden, wraak nemen

revenue [revvənjoe:] **1** inkomen[h], opbrengst, inkomsten *(from property, investment etc)*; **2** inkomsten

reverberate [rivvə:bəreet] weerkaatsen *(sound, light, heat)*, terugkaatsen, echoën, weerklinken: ~ *upon* terugwerken op *(also fig)*

reverberation [rivvə:bəreesjən] weerklank, weerkaatsing

revere [rivviə] (ver)eren, respecteren, eerbied hebben voor

reverence [revvərəns] verering, respect[h], (diepe) eerbied, ontzag[h]: *hold s.o. (sth.) in* ~ eerbied koesteren voor iem (iets)

¹reverend [revvərənd] *adj* eerwaard(ig)

²reverend [revvərənd] *n the Reverend* Eerwaarde

reverent [revvərənt] eerbiedig, respectvol

reversal [rivvə:sl] omkering, om(me)keer

¹reverse [rivvə:s] *adj* tegen(over)gesteld, omgekeerd, achteraan: ~ *gear* achteruit *(of car); in ~ order* in omgekeerde volgorde

²reverse [rivvə:s] *n* **1** tegenslag, nederlaag; **2** keerzijde *(of coins; also fig)*, rugzijde, achterkant; **3** achteruit *(of car): put a car into ~* een auto in zijn achteruit zetten; **4** tegendeel[h], omgekeerde, tegengestelde[h]: *but the ~ is also true* maar het omgekeerde is ook waar; *in ~* omgekeerd, in omgekeerde volgorde

³reverse [rivvə:s] *vb* achteruitrijden *(of car)*, achteruitgaan

⁴reverse [rivvə:s] *vb* **1** (om)keren, omdraaien, omschakelen, achteruitrijden *(car)*: ~ *one's policy* radicaal van politiek veranderen; **2** herroepen *(decision)*, intrekken, *(law)* herzien

revert [rivvə:t] **1** (with *to*) terugkeren (tot) *(previous condition)*, terugvallen (in) *(habit)*; **2** (with *to*)

terugkomen (op) *(earlier topic of conversation)*; **3** terugkeren *(of property to owner)*

¹review [rivjoe:] *n* **1** terugblik, overzicht[h], bezinning: *be under ~* opnieuw bekeken worden; **2** parade, inspectie; **3** recensie, (boek)bespreking; **4** tijdschrift[h]

²review [rivjoe:] *vb* **1** opnieuw bekijken; herzien; **2** terugblikken op, overzien; **3** parade houden, inspecteren; **4** recenseren, bespreken, recensies schrijven

reviewer [rivjoe:ə] recensent

revile [rivvajl] (uit)schelden

revise [rivvajz] **1** herzien, verbeteren, corrigeren: ~*d edition* herziene uitgave *(of book); enclosed you will find our ~d invoice* bijgesloten vindt u onze gecorrigeerde factuur; **2** repeteren *(lesson)*, herhalen, studeren *(for examination)*

revision [rivvizjən] **1** revisie, herziening, wijziging; **2** herhaling *(of lesson)*, het studeren *(for examination)*

revitalize [rivvajtəlajz] nieuwe kracht geven, nieuw leven geven

revival [rivvajvl] **1** reveil[h]; **2** (her)opleving, wedergeboorte, hernieuwde belangstelling; **3** herstel[h] *(of strengths)*

¹revive [rivvajv] *vb* **1** herleven, bijkomen, weer tot leven (op krachten) komen; **2** weer in gebruik komen, opnieuw ingevoerd worden

²revive [rivvajv] *vb* **1** doen herleven, vernieuwen, weer tot leven brengen; **2** opnieuw invoeren *(old custom)*

¹revoke [rivvook] *vb* herroepen, intrekken *(order, promise, licence)*

²revoke [rivvook] *vb (cards)* verzaken

¹revolt [rivvoolt] *vb* **1** (with *against*) in opstand komen (tegen), rebelleren, muiten; **2** walgen: ~ *at* (of: *against, from*) walgen van

²revolt [rivvoolt] *vb* doen walgen, afstoten, afkerig maken van *(also fig): be ~ed by sth.* van iets walgen

³revolt [rivvoolt] *n* opstand, oproer[h]: *stir people to ~* mensen opruien

revolting [rivvoolting] walg(e)lijk, onsmakelijk, weerzinwekkend

revolution [revvəloe:sjən] **1** (om)wenteling, draaiing *(around centre)*; **2** rotatie, draai(ing) *(around axis)*, toer, slag; **3** revolutie, (staats)omwenteling; **4** ommekeer, omkering: *a ~ in thought* algehele verandering in denkbeelden

revolutionary [revvəloe:sjənərie] revolutionair

revolve [rivvolv] (rond)draaien, (doen) (rond)wentelen: *the discussion always ~s around* (of: *about) money* de discussie draait altijd om geld

revolver [rivvolvə] revolver

revolving [rivvolving] draaiend, roterend: ~ *door* draaideur

revulsion [rivvulsjən] walging, afkeer, weerzin: *a ~ against* (of: *from*) een afkeer van, een weerzin tegen

¹reward [riwwo:d] *n* beloning, compensatie, loon[h]

²reward [riwwo:d] *vb* belonen

rewarding [riwwo:ding] lonend, de moeite waard, dankbaar *(of work, task)*

rewind [rie:wajnd] opnieuw opwinden, terugspoelen

rhapsody [ræpsədie] verhalend gedicht[h]

rhetoric [rettərik] 1 redekunst, retoriek, retorica; 2 welsprekendheid, bombast, holle frasen

rhetorical [rittorrikl] retorisch, gekunsteld || ~ *question* retorische vraag

rheumatism [roe:mətizm] reuma(tiek), reumatisme[h], gewrichtsreumatiek

Rhine [rajn] Rijn

rhinoceros [rajnossərəs] neushoorn

rhododendron [roodədendrən] rododendron

rhubarb [roe:ba:b] rabarber

¹rhyme [rajm] *n* 1 rijm(woord)[h]; 2 (berijmd) gedicht[h], vers[h] || *without ~ or reason* zonder enige betekenis, onzinnig

²rhyme [rajm] *vb* 1 rijmen, rijm hebben: *~d verses* rijmende verzen; 2 dichten, rijmen

³rhyme [rajm] *vb* 1 laten rijmen; 2 berijmen

rhyming [rajming] rijmend, op rijm

rhythm [riðm] ritme[h], maat

rhythmic(al) [riðmik(l)] ritmisch, regelmatig

¹rib [rib] *n* 1 rib; 2 balein *(of umbrella);* 3 bladnerf; 4 ribstuk[h]; 5 ribbelpatroon[h] *(in knitting)*

²rib [rib] *vb* plagen, voor de gek houden

ribaldry [ribldrie] schunnige taal

ribbon [ribbən] 1 lint(je)[h], onderscheiding; 2 ~*s* flard: *(fig) cut to ~s* in de pan hakken; 3 (schrijfmachine)lint[h]

rice [rajs] rijst

rich [ritsj] 1 rijk: *~ in* rijk aan; *the ~* de rijken; 2 kostbaar, luxueus; 3 rijkelijk, overvloedig; 4 vruchtbaar: *~ soil* vruchtbare aarde; 5 machtig *(of food);* 6 vol *(of sounds),* warm *(of colour);* 7 *(inf; oft iron)* kostelijk *(of joke): that's (pretty) ~!: a)* dat is een goeie!; *b)* wat een flater!; *strike it ~* een goudmijn ontdekken, fortuin maken

riches [ritsjiz] 1 rijkdom, het rijk-zijn; 2 kostbaarheden, weelde

richly [ritsjlie] volledig, dubbel en dwars: *~ deserve* volkomen verdienen

¹rick [rik] *n* hooimijt

²rick [rik] *vb* 1 ophopen; 2 verdraaien, verstuiken

rickety [rikkətie] gammel, wankel

rickshaw [riksjo:] riksja

ricochet [rikkəsjee] (doen) ricocheren, (laten) afketsen: *the bullet ~ted off the wall* de kogel ketste af op de muur

rid [rid] bevrijden, ontdoen van: *be well ~ of s.o.* goed van iem af zijn; *get ~ of* kwijtraken, van de hand doen

riddance [riddəns] bevrijding, verwijdering: *they've just left. Good ~!* ze zijn net weg. Mooi zo, opgeruimd staat netjes!

-ridden [ridn] 1 gedomineerd door, beheerst door: *conscience-ridden* gewetensbezwaard; 2 vergeven van: *this place is vermin-ridden* het wemelt hier

van het ongedierte

¹riddle [ridl] *n* 1 raadsel[h], mysterie[h]; 2 (grove) zeef

²riddle [ridl] *vb* 1 zeven *(also fig),* schiften, natrekken; 2 doorzeven: *the body was ~d with bullets* het lichaam was met kogels doorzeefd

riddled [ridld] gevuld, vol, bezaaid: *the translation was ~ with errors* de vertaling stond vol fouten

¹ride [rajd] *vb* 1 rijden, paardrijden; 2 rijden, voor anker liggen || *~ roughshod over s.o. (sth.)* nergens naar kijken, niet al te zachtzinnig te werk gaan; *~ up* omhoogkruipen, opkruipen

²ride [rajd] *vb* 1 berijden, doorrijden; 2 (be)rijden, rijden met: *~ a bicycle* (of: *bike*) op de fiets rijden, fietsen; 3 beheersen, tiranniseren: *the robber was ridden by fears* de dief werd door schrik bevangen; 4 *(Am)* jennen, kwellen

³ride [rajd] *n* 1 rit(je)[h], tocht(je)[h]; 2 rijpad[h], ruiterpad[h] || *take s.o. for a ~* iem voor de gek houden, iem in de maling nemen

ride out overleven *(also fig),* heelhuids doorkomen: *the ship rode out the storm* het schip doorstond de storm

rider [rajdə] (be)rijder, ruiter

ridge [ridzj] 1 (berg)kam, richel; bergketen; 2 nok *(of roof);* 3 ribbel; 4 golftop; 5 rug, (uitgerekt) hogedrukgebied[h]

¹ridicule [riddikjoe:l] *n* spot, hoon

²ridicule [riddikjoe:l] *vb* ridiculiseren, bespotten

ridiculous [riddikjoeləs] ridicuul, belachelijk

rife [rajf] 1 wijdverbreid, vaak voorkomend: *violence is ~ in westerns* er is veel geweld in cowboyfilms; 2 (with *with)* goed voorzien (van), legio

riffle through vluchtig doorbladeren

riff-raff [rifræf] uitschot[h], schorem[h]

¹rifle [rajfl] *n* geweer[h], karabijn

²rifle [rajfl] *vb* doorzoeken, leeghalen: *the burglar had ~d every cupboard* de dief had iedere kast overhoop gehaald

rifle range 1 schietbaan; 2 schootsafstand, draagwijdte: *within ~* binnen schot(bereik)

rift [rift] 1 spleet, kloof; 2 onenigheid, tweedracht

¹rig [rig] *n* 1 tuig[h], tuigage, takelage; 2 uitrusting, (olie)booruitrusting; 3 plunje, uitrusting: *in full ~* in vol ornaat

²rig [rig] *vb* 1 (op)tuigen, optakelen; 2 uitrusten, uitdossen; 3 knoeien met, sjoemelen met: *the elections were ~ged* de verkiezingen waren doorgestoken kaart

rigging [riging] tuig[h], tuigage, takelage, het optuigen

¹right [rajt] *adj* 1 juist, correct, rechtmatig: *you were ~ to tell her* je deed er goed aan het haar te vertellen; *put (of: set) the clock ~* de klok juist zetten; 2 juist, gepast, recht: *strike the ~ note* de juiste toon aanslaan; *on the ~ side of fifty* nog geen vijftig (jaar oud); *keep on the ~ side of the law* zich (keurig) aan de wet houden; *(fig) be on the ~ track* op het goede spoor zitten; 3 in goede staat, in orde: *let me see if I've got this ~* even kijken of ik het goed begrijp; 4

rechts, conservatief; **5** eerlijk, betrouwbaar: *the ~ sort* het goede soort (mensen); *Mister Right* de ware Jakob; *(as) ~ as rain* perfect in orde, kerngezond; *~ angle* rechte hoek; *put (of: set) s.o. ~ iem terechtwijzen; see s.o. ~* zorgen dat iem aan zijn trekken komt; *~ enough* bevredigend, ja hoor; **6** waar, echt, heus: *it's a ~ mess* het is een puinzooi; *~ arm (of: hand)* rechterhand, assistent; *keep on the ~ side* rechts houden; **7** gelijk: *you are ~* je hebt gelijk; **8** rechtvaardig, gerechtvaardigd: *it seemed only ~ to tell you this* ik vond dat je dit moest weten

²**right** [rajt] *n* **1** rechterkant: *keep to the ~* rechts houden; *on (of: to) your ~* aan je rechterkant; **2** rechterhand, rechtse *(in boxing)*; rechter(hand)schoen; **3** rechtsʰ, de conservatieven; **4** rechtʰ, voorrechtʰ, (gerechtvaardigde) eis: *the ~ of free speech* het recht op vrije meningsuiting; *~ of way* recht van overpad, *(traf)* voorrang(srecht); *all ~s reserved* alle rechten voorbehouden; *he has a ~ to the money* hij heeft recht op het geld; *within one's ~s* in zijn recht; **5** rechtʰ, gerechtigheid: *he is in the ~* hij heeft gelijk, hij heeft het recht aan zijn kant; *put (of: set) to ~s* in orde brengen, rechtzetten

³**right** [rajt] *adv* **1** naar rechts, aan de rechterzijde: *~ and left* aan alle kanten, overal, links en rechts; *~, left and centre, left, ~, and centre* aan alle kanten; **2** juist, vlak, regelrecht: *~ ahead* recht vooruit; *~ behind you* vlak achter je; **3** onmiddellijk, direct: *I'll be ~ back* ik ben zó terug; **4** juist, correct: *nothing seems to go ~ for her* niets wil haar lukken; **5** helemaal, volledig: *she turned ~ round* zij maakte volledig rechtsomkeert; **6** zeer, heel, recht; **7** *Right* Zeer *(in forms of address): ~ away* onmiddellijk; *~ off* onmiddellijk; *~ on* zo mogen wij het horen

⁴**right** [rajt] *vb* **1** rechtmaken, recht(op) zetten: *the yacht ~ed itself* het jacht kwam weer recht te liggen; **2** genoegdoening geven, rehabiliteren; **3** verbeteren, rechtzetten *(mistakes): ~ a wrong* een onrecht herstellen; *~ oneself* zich herstellen

right-about in tegenovergestelde richting ‖ *(do a) ~ turn (of: face)* rechtsomkeert (maken) *(also fig)*

right-angled rechthoekig, met rechte hoek(en)

righteous [rajtsjəs] **1** rechtvaardig, deugdzaam; **2** gerechtvaardigd, gewettigd: *~ indignation* gerechtvaardigde verontwaardiging

rightful [rajtfoel] **1** wettelijk, rechtmatig: *the ~ owner* de rechtmatige eigenaar; **2** gerechtvaardigd, rechtvaardig

right-hand rechts, mbt de rechterhand: *~ man* rechterhand, onmisbare helper; *~ turn* bocht naar rechts

right-handed 1 rechtshandig; **2** met de rechterhand toegebracht; **3** voor rechtshandigen

rightly [rajtlie] **1** terecht; **2** rechtvaardig, oprecht

right-minded weldenkend

right-wing vd rechterzijde, conservatief

right-winger 1 lidʰ vd rechterzijde, conservatief; **2** rechtsbuiten, rechtervleugelspeler

rigid [ridzjid] **1** onbuigzaam, stijf, stug, strak; **2** star, verstard

rigidity [ridzjiddittie] **1** onbuigzaamheid; **2** starheid

rigmarole [rigmərool] **1** onzin, gewauwelʰ; **2** rompslomp

rigorous [rigərəs] **1** onbuigzaam, streng, ongenadig; **2** rigoureus, nauwgezet, zorgvuldig

rigour [rigə] **1** gestrengheid, strikte toepassing: *with the utmost ~ of the law* met strenge toepassing van de wet; **2** hardheid, meedogenloosheid; **3** accuratesse, uiterste nauwkeurigheid

rig out 1 uitrusten, ve uitrusting voorzien; **2** uitdossen: *he had rigged himself out as a general* hij had zich als generaal uitgedost

rig-out plunje, (apen)pakʰ

rile [rajl] op stang jagen, nijdig maken, irriteren

rim [rim] rand, boordʰ, velg, montuur *(of glasses)*

rime [rajm] rijp, aangevroren mist

rind [rajnd] schil, korst, zwoerdʰ

¹**ring** [ring] *n* **1** ring, kring, piste, arena; **2** groepering, bende; **3** gerinkelʰ, klank, *(inf)* telefoontjeʰ: *give s.o. a ~* iem opbellen; **4** bijklank, ondertoon: *her offer has a suspicious ~* er zit een luchtje aan haar aanbod; **5** het boksen, bokswereld, ring; **6** circus, circuswereld, piste: *make (of: run) ~s round s.o.* iem de loef afsteken

²**ring** [ring] *vb* **1** rinkelen, klinken, (over)gaan *(of bell)*, bellen: *~ true* oprecht klinken; **2** bellen, de klok luiden, aanbellen; **3** tuiten *(of ears)*, weerklinken; **4** telefoneren, bellen: *~ off* opleggen, ophangen *(telephone);* **5** (with *with*) weergalmen (van), gonzen

³**ring** [ring] *vb* **1** doen rinkelen, luiden; **2** opbellen, telefoneren naar: *I'll ~ you back in a minute* ik bel je dadelijk terug

⁴**ring** [ring] *vb* **1** omringen, omcirkelen; **2** ringelen, ringen *(animals)*

ring-binder ringband

ringleader leider *(of group of agitators)*

ringlet [ringlit] lange krul

ringmaster circusdirecteur

¹**ring up** *vb* opbellen, telefoneren

²**ring up** *vb* **1** (al luidend) optrekken *(bell);* **2** registreren, aanslaan *(on cash register)*

rink [ringk] **1** (kunst)ijsbaan; **2** rolschaatsbaan

¹**rinse** [rins] *vb* **1** spoelen; **2** een kleurspoeling geven aan

²**rinse** [rins] *n* (kleur)spoeling

¹**riot** [rajjət] *n* **1** ordeverstoring, ongeregeldheid; **2** braspartij, uitbundig feestʰ; **3** overvloed, weelde: *a ~ of colour* een bonte kleurenpracht; **4** oproerʰ, tumultʰ; **5** dolle pret, pretmakerij: *run ~: a)* relletjes trappen, uit de band springen; *b)* woekeren *(of plants)*

²**riot** [rajjət] *vb* **1** relletjes trappen; **2** er ongebreideld op los leven, uitspatten

riotous [rajjətəs] **1** oproerig, wanordelijk; **2** luidruchtig, uitgelaten; **3** denderend

¹**rip** [rip] *vb* **1** scheuren, splijten; **2** vooruitsnellen,

scheuren *(fig)*: *let it* (of: *her)* ~ plankgas geven; *let sth.* ~ iets op zijn beloop laten

²rip [rɪp] *vb* **1** openrijten, los-, af-, wegscheuren: *the bag had been ~ped open* de zak was opengereten; ~ *up* aan stukken rijten; **2** jatten, pikken: ~ *off: a)* te veel doen betalen, afzetten; *b)* stelen

³rip [rɪp] *n* **1** (lange) scheur, snee; **2** losbol, snoeper

ripe [rajp] **1** rijp *(also fig)*, volgroeid, belegen *(of cheese, wine)*; **2** wijs, verstandig: *of ~ age* volwassen, ervaren; *a ~ judgement* een doordacht oordeel; **3** op het kantje af, plat; **4** klaar, geschikt: *the time is ~ for action* de tijd is rijp voor actie

ripen [rajpən] rijpen, rijp worden, wijs worden, doen rijpen

rip-off 1 afzetterij; **2** diefstal, roof

¹ripple [rɪpl] *n* **1** rimpeling, golfjeʰ, deining; **2** gekabbelʰ, geruisʰ: *a ~ of laughter* een kabbelend gelach

²ripple [rɪpl] *vb* kabbelen, ruisen

³ripple [rɪpl] *vb* rimpelen, (doen) golven

rip-roaring lawaaierig, totaal uitgelaten

¹rise [rajz] *vb* **1** opstaan *(also from bed)*: ~ *to one's feet* opstaan; **2** (op)stijgen *(also fig)*, (op)klimmen: *(fig)* ~ *to the occasion* zich tegen de moeilijkheden opgewassen tonen; **3** opkomen, opgaan, rijzen *(of celestial body)*; **4** promotie maken, bevorderd worden: ~ *in the world* vooruitkomen in de wereld; **5** opdoemen, verschijnen; **6** toenemen *(also fig)*, stijgen *(of prices)*; **7** in opstand komen, rebelleren: ~ *in arms* de wapens opnemen; **8** ontstaan, ontspringen

²rise [rajz] *n* **1** helling, verhoging, hoogte; **2** stijging *(also fig)*, verhoging, *(Stock Exchange)* **3** loonsverhoging; **4** het rijzen, het omhooggaan; **5** het opgaan, opgang, opkomst *(of celestial body)*: *the ~ of fascism* de opkomst van het fascisme; **6** oorsprong, beginʰ: *give ~ to* aanleiding geven tot; **7** opkomst, groei: *get a ~ out of s.o.* iem op de kast jagen

riser [rajzə] **1** stootbordʰ; **2** iem die opstaat: *a late ~* een langslaper; *an early ~* een vroege vogel, iem die vroeg opstaat

risible [rɪzzibl] **1** lacherig, lachziek; **2** lachwekkend

¹rising [rajzɪng] *adj* **1** opkomend, aankomend: *a ~ politician* een opkomend politicus; **2** stijgend, oplopend: ~ *damp* opstijgend grondwater; **3** opstaand, rijzend: *the land of the ~ sun* het land van de rijzende zon

²rising [rajzɪng] *n* opstand, revolte

¹risk [rɪsk] *n* **1** verzekerd bedragʰ; **2** risicoʰ, kans, gevaarʰ: *at ~* in gevaar; *I don't want to run the ~ of losing my job* ik wil mijn baan niet op het spel zetten

²risk [rɪsk] *vb* **1** wagen, op het spel zetten; **2** riskeren, gevaar lopen

risky [rɪskie] **1** gewaagd, gevaarlijk; **2** gedurfd, gewaagd

rite [rajt] rite *(also fig)*, ritus, (kerkelijke) ceremonie

ritual [rɪtjoeəl] ritueelʰ *(also fig)*, ritus, riten, kerkelijke plechtigheid

¹rival [rajvl] *adj* rivaliserend, mededingend

²rival [rajvl] *n* rivaal

³rival [rajvl] *vb* **1** naar de kroon steken, wedijveren met; **2** evenaren

rivalry [rajvlrie] rivaliteit

river [rɪvvə] rivier *(also fig)*, stroom: ~*s of blood* stromen bloed; *the river Thames* de (rivier de) Theems; *sell s.o. down the ~* iem bedriegen

river bank rivieroever

¹riverside *n* rivieroever, waterkant

²riverside *adj* aan de oever(s) (vd rivier)

¹rivet [rɪvvit] *n* klinknagel

²rivet [rɪvvit] *vb* **1** vastnagelen *(also fig)*: *he stood ~ed to the ground* hij stond als aan de grond genageld; **2** vastleggen, fixeren; **3** boeien *(also fig)*, richten, concentreren *(attention, eyes)*

riveting [rɪvvitting] geweldig, meeslepend, opwindend: *a ~ story* een pakkend verhaal

rivulet [rɪvjoelit] riviertjeʰ, beek(jeʰ)

roach [rootsj] voorn, witvis

road [rood] **1** weg, straat, baan: *on the ~ to recovery* aan de beterende hand, herstellende; *rule(s) of the ~* verkeersregels, scheepvaartreglement; *the main ~* de hoofdweg; *subsidiary ~s* secundaire wegen; *hit the ~: a)* gaan reizen; *b)* weer vertrekken; *one for the ~* een afzakkertje, eentje voor onderweg; **2** ~*s (shipp)* rede

roadblock wegversperring

road hog wegpiraat, snelheidsmaniak

roadhouse pleisterplaats, wegrestaurant

road rage agressie in het verkeer, *(Belg)* verkeersagressie

roadshow 1 drive-inshow *(of radio broadcasting company)*; **2** (hit)teamʰ *(providing the drive-in show)*; **3** (band, theatergroep op) tournee; **4** promotietour

roadside kant vd weg: ~ *restaurant* wegrestaurant

roadsign verkeersbordʰ, verkeerstekenʰ

road tax wegenbelasting

roadworks wegwerkzaamheden, werk in uitvoering

roam [room] ronddolen, zwerven (in): ~ *about* (of: *around)* ronddwalen

¹roar [ro:] *vb* **1** brullen, bulderen, schreeuwen, rollen *(of thunder)*, ronken *(of machine)*, weergalmen; **2** schateren, gieren: ~ *with laughter* brullen van het lachen

²roar [ro:] *n* **1** gebrulʰ, gebulderʰ, geronkʰ *(of machine)*, het rollen *(of thunder)*; **2** schaterlach, gegierʰ

¹roaring [ro:ring] *adj* **1** luidruchtig, stormachtig; **2** voorspoedig, gezond: *a ~ success* een denderend succes; *do a ~ trade* gouden zaken doen

²roaring [ro:ring] *adv* zeer, erg: ~ *drunk* straalbezopen

¹roast [roost] *vb* **1** roosteren, grill(er)en, poffen *(potatoes)*; **2** branden *(coffee)*

²roast [roost] *vb* de mantel uitvegen, een uitbrander geven

³roast [roost] *adj* geroosterd, gegril(leer)d, gebraden: ~ *beef* rosbief, roastbeef

⁴roast [roost] *n* braadstukʰ

776

roasting [rooosting] uitbrander: *give s.o. a good (of: real)* ~ iem een flinke uitbrander geven
rob [rob] (be)roven *(also fig)*, (be)stelen
robber [robbǝ] rover, dief
robbery [robbǝrie] diefstal, roof, beroving
robe [roob] **1** robe, gewaad^h; **2** ambtsgewaad^h, toga; **3** kamerjas, badjas; **4** *(Am)* plaid, reisdeken
robin [robbin] roodborstje^h
robot [roobot] robot *(also fig)*
robust [roobust] **1** krachtig, robuust, fors, gezond; **2** onstuimig, ruw
¹rock [rok] *n* **1** rots, klip; rotsblok^h; vast gesteente^h, mineraal gesteente^h: *as firm as a ~: a)* muurvast; *b)* betrouwbaar; *c)* kerngezond; **2** steun, toeverlaat; **3** rock(muziek), rock-'n-roll; **4** zuurstok, kaneelstok: *be on the ~s: a)* op de klippen gelopen zijn, gestrand zijn; *b)* naar de knoppen zijn; *c)* (financieel) aan de grond (zitten)
²rock [rok] *vb* **1** schommelen, wieg(el)en, deinen; **2** (hevig) slingeren, schudden; **3** rocken, op rock-'n-roll muziek dansen
³rock [rok] *vb* **1** (doen) heen en weer schommelen, wiegen; **2** heen en weer slingeren, doen wankelen; **3** schokken, doen opschrikken
rock-bottom (absoluut) dieptepunt^h: *fall to* ~ een dieptepunt bereiken
rocker [rokkǝ] schommelstoel || *off one's* ~ knetter(gek)
¹rocket [rokkit] *n* **1** raket, vuurpijl; **2** raket *(self-propelling missile)*; **3** *(inf)* uitbrander: *give s.o. a* ~ iem een uitbrander geven
²rocket [rokkit] *vb* omhoog schieten, flitsen: *prices* ~ *up* de prijzen vliegen omhoog
rocking chair schommelstoel
rocky [rokkie] **1** rotsachtig; **2** steenhard, keihard; **3** wankel, onvast
rod [rod] **1** stok, scepter *(also fig)*, heerschappij; **2** roe(de), gesel; **3** stang; **4** stok, hengel, maatstok; **5** *(Am; inf)* blaffer || *rule with a* ~ *of iron* met ijzeren vuist regeren
rodent [roodǝnt] knaagdier^h
rodeo [roodie-oo] rodeo
roe [roo] **1** ree; **2** kuit: *hard* ~ kuit; *soft* ~ hom
roebuck [roobuck] reebok, mannetjesree
rogue [roog] **1** schurk, bandiet; **2** *(mockingly)* snuiter, deugniet; **3** solitair: *a* ~ *elephant* een solitaire olifant
roguery [roogǝrie] schurkenstreek, gemene streek
roguish [roogisj] **1** schurkachtig, gemeen; **2** kwajongensachtig
roisterer [rojstǝrǝ] lawaaimaker, drukmaker
role [rool] **1** rol, toneelrol; **2** rol, functie, taak
roleplay rollenspel^h
¹roll [rool] *n* **1** rol, rolletje^h: *a* ~ *of paper* een rol papier; **2** rol, perkament(rol); **3** rol, register^h, (naam)lijst: *the* ~ *of honour* de lijst der gesneuvelden; **4** broodje^h; **5** buiteling, duikeling; **6** schommelgang, waggelgang; **7** wals, rol; **8** rollende beweging, geslinger^h *(of ship)*, deining *(of water)*; *(fig)*

golving *(of landscape)*; **9** geroffel^h, roffel *(eg on drum)*, gerommel^h, gedreun^h *(of thunder, guns)*
²roll [rool] *vb* **1** rollen, rijden, lopen, draaien *(of press, camera etc)*: *(fig) the years ~ed by* de jaren gingen voorbij; ~ *on the day this work is finished!* leve de dag waarop dit werk af is!; **2** zich rollend bewegen, buitelen, slingeren *(of ship)*; *(fig)* rondtrekken, zwerven: *(inf) be ~ing in it* (of: *money*) bulken van het geld, zwemmen in het geld; **3** dreunen, roffelen *(of drum)*
³roll [rool] *vb* **1** rollen, laten rollen: ~ *on one's stockings* zijn kousen aantrekken; **2** een rollende beweging doen maken, rollen *(with eyes)*, doen slingeren *(ship)*, gooien *(dice)*, laten lopen *(camera)*; **3** een rollend geluid doen maken, roffelen *(drum)*, rollen *(r sound)*: ~ *one's r's* de r rollend uitspreken; **4** oprollen, draaien: *(inf)* ~ *one's own shag roken*; **5** rollen, walsen, pletten; **6** *(Am; inf)* rollen, beroven
roll back 1 terugrollen, terugdrijven, terugdringen: ~ *the hood of a car* de kap van een wagen achteruitschuiven; **2** weer oproepen, weer voor de geest brengen; **3** *(Am)* terugschroeven *(prices)*
roll-call appel^h, naamafroeping
roller [roolǝ] **1** rol(letje^h), wals, cilinder, krulspeld; **2** roller, breker *(heavy wave)*
rollerblade skeeleren
roller coaster roetsjbaan, achtbaan
¹roller skate *n* rolschaats
²roller skate *vb* rolschaatsen
rollicking [rolliekieng] uitgelaten, vrolijk, onstuimig
rolling [rooling] rollend, golvend
rolling pin deegrol(ler)
roll-neck rolkraag
roll-on 1 licht korset^h; **2** (deodorant)roller
roll-on roll-off [roolon roolof] rij-op-rij-af-, roll-on-roll-off-, roro-: *a ~ ferry* een rij-op-rij-af-veerboot *(carrying loaded lorries)*
¹roll over *vb* zich omdraaien
²roll over *vb* **1** over de grond doen rollen; **2** verlengen *(loan, debt)*
¹roll up *vb* **1** zich oprollen; **2** (komen) aanrijden, *(fig)* opdagen || ~*!~! The best show in London!* Komt binnen, komt dat zien! De beste show in Londen!
²roll up *vb* oprollen, opstropen: *roll one's sleeves up* zijn mouwen opstropen, *(fig)* de handen uit de mouwen steken
¹roly-poly [rooliepoolie] *n* kort en dik persoon, propje^h
²roly-poly [rooliepoolie] *adj* kort en dik
ROM [rom] *read-only memory* ROM
roman [roomǝn] romeins, niet cursief
¹Roman [roomǝn] *n* **1** Romein; **2** rooms-katholiek || *when in Rome do as the ~s do* 's lands wijs, 's lands eer
²Roman [roomǝn] *adj* **1** Romeins: ~ *numerals* Romeinse cijfers; **2** rooms-katholiek: ~ *Catholic* rooms-katholiek
¹romance [roomæns] *n* **1** middeleeuws ridderver-

haal^h; romantisch verhaal^h, avonturenroman; (romantisch) liefdesverhaal^h; geromantiseerd verhaal^h, (fig) romantische overdrijving; **2** romance, liefdesavontuur^h; **3** romantisch literatuur

²**romance** [roomæns] *vb* avonturen vertellen, (fig) fantaseren: ~ *about one's love-affairs* sterke verhalen vertellen over zijn liefdesavonturen

Romance [roomæns] Romaans

Romania [roomeeniǝ] Roemenië

Romanian [roomeeniǝn] Roemeens

romantic [rǝmæntik] romantisch

romanticism [rǝmæntissizm] romantiek *(as trend in art)*

romanticize [rǝmæntissajz] romantiseren: *a heavily ~d version of the early years of Hollywood* een sterk geromantiseerde versie van de beginjaren van Hollywood

Romany [rommǝnie] zigeuner-, vd zigeuners

¹**romp** [romp] *vb* **1** stoeien; **2** flitsen, (voorbij)schieten ‖ ~ *through an exam* met gemak voor een examen slagen

²**romp** [romp] *n* stoeipartij

romper [rompǝ] kruippakje, speelpakje: *a pair of ~s* een kruippakje

roof [roe:f] dak^h, (fig) dak^h, hoogste punt^h: ~ *of the mouth* gehemelte, verhemelte; *go through* (of: *hit*) *the ~: a)* ontploffen, woedend worden; *b)* de pan uit rijzen, omhoogschieten *(of prices)*

roofing [roe:fing] dakwerk^h; dakbedekking

roof-rack imperiaal

rooftop 1 top vh dak; **2** dak^h *(flat): shout sth. from the ~s* iets van de daken schreeuwen

¹**rook** [roek] *n* **1** valsspeler, bedrieger; **2** roek; **3** *(chess)* toren

²**rook** [roek] *vb* **1** bedriegen, afzetten; **2** bedriegen door vals spel

rookie [roekie] *(mil)* rekruut; nieuweling, groentje^h, *(Am)* nieuwe speler *(at baseball etc)*

¹**room** [roe:m] *n* **1** kamer, vertrek^h, zaal, ~s appartement^h, flat; **2** ruimte, plaats: *make* ~ plaats maken; **3** ruimte, gelegenheid, kans: *there is still ample* ~ *for improvement* er kan nog een heel wat aan verbeterd worden

²**room** [roe:m] *vb (Am)* een kamer bewonen, inwonen, op kamers wonen: *she ~ed with us for six months* ze heeft een half jaar bij ons (in)gewoond

roomer [roe:mǝ] *(Am)* kamerbewoner, huurder

room-mate kamergenoot

room service bediening op de kamer *(in hotel),* room service

roomy [roe:mie] ruim, groot, wijd

roost [roe:st] **1** roest, stok, kippenhok^h; **2** nest^h, bed^h, slaapplaats *(of birds)* ‖ *it will come home to* ~ je zult er zelf de wrange vruchten van plukken, het zal zich wreken; *rule the* ~ de baas zijn, de lakens uitdelen

rooster [roe:stǝ] *(Am)* haan

¹**root** [roe:t] *n* **1** oorsprong, wortel, basis: *money is the* ~ *of all evil* geld is de wortel van alle kwaad; **2** kern, het wezenlijke: *get to the* ~ *of the problem* tot de kern van het probleem doordringen; *strike* ~, *take* ~: *a)* wortel schieten; *b)* (fig) ingeburgerd raken *(of ideas)*; ~ *and branch* met wortel en tak, grondig; *strike at the ~s of* een vernietigende aanval doen op

²**root** [roe:t] *vb* **1** wortelschieten, wortelen, (fig) zich vestigen; zijn oorsprong hebben; **2** wroeten, graven, woelen: *the pigs were ~ing about in the earth* de varkens wroetten rond in de aarde; ~ *for the team* het team toejuichen

³**root** [roe:t] *vb* vestigen, doen wortelen: *a deeply ~ed love* een diepgewortelde liefde; *she stood ~ed to the ground* (of: *spot*) ze stond als aan de grond genageld

rootless [roe:tlǝs] ontworteld, ontheemd

root out 1 uitwroeten, uitgraven, (fig) te voorschijn brengen; **2** vernietigen, uitroeien

¹**rope** [roop] *n* **1** (stuk^h) touw^h, koord^h, kabel: *(boxing) on the ~s* in de touwen; **2** snoer^h, streng: *a ~ of garlic* een streng knoflook; *money for old* ~ een fluitje van een cent; *know the ~s* de kneepjes van het vak kennen

²**rope** [roop] *vb* **1** vastbinden; **2** met touwen afzetten; **3** *(Am)* vangen *(with a lasso)* ‖ ~ *s.o. in to help* iem zo ver krijgen dat hij komt helpen

ropy [roopie] armzalig, miezerig, beroerd

rosary [roozǝrie] **1** rozentuin; **2** rozenkrans

rose 1 roos, rozenstruik; **2** roos, rozet; **3** sproeidop, sproeier; **4** rozerood^h, dieproze^h ‖ *it is not all ~s* het is niet allemaal rozengeur en maneschijn; *under the* ~ onder geheimhouding

rose-coloured rooskleurig *(also fig),* optimistisch: ~ *spectacles* (fig) een optimistische kijk, een roze bril

rose-hip rozenbottel

rosemary [roozmǝrie] rozemarijn

rosette [roozet] rozet

rosewater rozenwater^h

rosin [rozzin] hars^h, *(mus)* snarenhars^h

roster [rostǝ] rooster^h, werkschema^h, dienstrooster^h

rostrum [rostrǝm] podium^h, spreekgestoelte^h

rosy [roozie] **1** rooskleurig, rozig, blozend, gezond; **2** rooskleurig, optimistisch

¹**rot** [rot] *n* **1** verrotting, bederf^h, ontbinding, (fig) verval^h, de klad: *then the* ~ *set in* toen ging alles mis, toen kwam de klad in; **2** vuur^h *(in wood)*; **3** onzin, flauwekul: *talk* ~ onzin uitkramen

²**rot** [rot] *vb* **1** rotten, ontbinden, bederven; **2** vervallen, ten onder gaan; **3** wegkwijnen, wegteren

³**rot** [rot] *vb* **1** laten rotten, doen wegrotten; **2** aantasten, bederven

rota [rootǝ] rooster^h, aflossingsschema^h

rotary [rootǝrie] roterend: ~ *press* rotatiepers

¹**rotate** [rooteet] *vb* **1** roteren, om een as draaien; **2** elkaar aflossen; **3** rouleren

²**rotate** [rooteet] *vb* **1** ronddraaien, laten rondwentelen; **2** afwisselen

rotation [rooteesjǝn] **1** omwenteling, rotatie; **2** het omwentelen, rotatie; **3** het afwisselen, het aflossen: *the ~ of crops* de wisselbouw; *by* (of: *in*) *~* bij toerbeurt

rotatory [rooteetǝrie] **1** rotatie-, omwentelings-, ronddraaiend; **2** afwisselend, beurtelings

rote [root] het mechanisch leren (herhalen), het opdreunen, stampwerk[h]: *learn sth. by ~* iets uit het hoofd leren

rotten [rotn] **1** rot, verrot, bedorven; **2** vergaan, verteerd; **3** verdorven, gedegenereerd; **4** waardeloos, slecht; **5** ellendig, beroerd: *she felt ~* ze voelde zich ellendig

rotund [rootund] **1** rond, cirkelvormig; **2** diep, vol; **3** breedsprakig, pompeus; **4** dik, rond, mollig

rouble [roe:bl] roebel

¹rough [ruf] *adj* **1** ruw, ruig, oneffen; **2** wild, woest: *~ behaviour* wild gedrag; *(fig) give s.o. a ~ passage* (of: *ride*) het iem moeilijk maken; **3** ruw, scherp, naar: *~ luck* pech, tegenslag; *a ~ time* een zware tijd; *it is ~ on him* het is heel naar voor hem; **4** ruw, schetsmatig, niet uitgewerkt: *a ~ diamond* een ruwe diamant, *(fig)* een ruwe bolster; *~ copy* eerste schets; *~ justice* min of meer rechtvaardige behandeling; *live ~* zwerven, in de open lucht leven

²rough [ruf] *n* **1** gewelddadige kerel, agressieveling; **2** ruw terrein[h]; **3** tegenslag, onaangename kanten: *(fig) take the ~ with the smooth* tegenslagen voor lief nemen; **4** ruwe staat: *write sth. in ~* iets in het klad schrijven

³rough [ruf] *vb: ~ it* zich behelpen, op een primitieve manier leven

rough-and-tumble **1** knokpartij; **2** ruwe ordeloosheid

¹roughen [rufn] *vb* ruw maken

²roughen [rufn] *vb* ruw worden

rough-hewn **1** ruw (uit)gehakt, ruw (uit)gesneden; **2** onbehouwen, lomp

rough-house **1** een rel schoppen, geweld plegen; **2** ruw aanpakken

roughly [ruflie] ruwweg, ongeveer, zo'n beetje: *~ speaking* ongeveer

roughneck *(Am; inf)* gewelddadig iem, ruwe klant

rough out een ruwe schets maken van, (in grote lijnen) schetsen

roughshod onmenselijk, wreed || *ride ~ over s.o.* over iem heen lopen

rough up **1** ruw maken *(hair etc)*; **2** aftuigen, afrossen

¹round [raund] *adj* **1** rond, bol, bolvormig: *~ cheeks* bolle wangen; **2** rond, gebogen, cirkelvormig: *~ trip* rondreis, *(Am)* retour; **3** rond, compleet, afgerond *(of number)*: *in ~ figures* in afgeronde getallen; *~ robin* petitie

²round [raund] *adv* **1** *(direction; also fig)* rond, om: *next time ~* de volgende keer; *he talked her ~* hij praatte haar om; **2** *(place; also fig)* rondom, in het rond: *all ~: a)* rondom; *b)* voor alles en iedereen; *c)* in alle opzichten; **3** bij, bij zich: *they asked us ~ for tea* ze nodigden ons bij hen uit voor de thee; *they*

brought her ~ ze brachten haar weer bij (bewustzijn); **4** *(time)* doorheen: *all (the) year ~* het hele jaar door

³round [raund] *prep* **1** om, rondom, om ... heen: *~ the corner* om de hoek; **2** omstreeks: *~ 8 o'clock* omstreeks acht uur

⁴round [raund] *n* **1** bol, ronding; **2** ronde, rondgang, toer: *go the ~s* de ronde doen, doorverteld worden; **3** schot[h], geweerschot[h]; **4** kring, groep mensen; **5** *(mus)* driestemmige (vierstemmige) canon[h]; **6** rondheid; **7** volledigheid; **8** rondte: *in the ~: a)* losstaand, vrijstaand *(of statue); b)* alles welbeschouwd: *a ~ of applause* een applaus

⁵round [raund] *vb* **1** ronden, rond maken, *(also fig)* afronden: *~ down* naar beneden afronden; *~ off sharp edges* scherpe randen rond afwerken; *~ off* besluiten, afsluiten *(evening etc);* **2** ronden, om(heen) gaan: *~ a corner* een hoek omgaan; *~ out* afronden *(story, study); ~ (up)on s.o.* tegen iem van leer trekken, zich woedend tot iem keren

¹roundabout [raundǝbaut] *n* **1** draaimolen; **2** rotonde, verkeersplein[h]

²roundabout [raundǝbaut] *adj* indirect, omslachtig: *we heard of it in a ~ way* we hebben het via via gehoord

roundly [raundlie] **1** ronduit, onomwonden; **2** volkomen, volslagen

round-the-clock de klok rond, dag en nacht

round-trip *(Am)* retour-: *~ ticket* retourtje, retourbiljet

round up **1** bijeenjagen, bijeendrijven; **2** grijpen, aanhouden *(criminals),* oprollen *(gang);* **3** naar boven toe afronden

¹rouse [rauz] *vb* **1** wakker maken, wekken, *(fig)* opwekken: *~ oneself to action* zichzelf tot actie aanzetten; **2** prikkelen; **3** oproepen, te voorschijn roepen: *his conduct ~d suspicion* zijn gedrag wekte argwaan

²rouse [rauz] *vb* **1** ontwaken, wakker worden; **2** in actie komen

rousing [rauzing] **1** opwindend, bezielend; **2** levendig, krachtig: *a ~ cheer* luid gejuich

¹rout [raut] *n* totale nederlaag, aftocht, vlucht: *put to ~* een verpletterende nederlaag toebrengen

²rout [raut] *vb* **1** verslaan, verpletteren; **2** *(with out)* eruit jagen, wegjagen: *~ out of bed* uit bed jagen; **3** *(with out)* opduike(le)n, opsnorren

route [roe:t] **1** route, weg: *en ~* onderweg; **2** *(Am)* ronde, dagelijkse route

routine [roe:tie:n] routine, gebruikelijke procedure

¹rove [roov] *vb* zwerven, dolen, dwalen: *he has a roving eye* hij kijkt steeds naar andere vrouwen

²rove [roov] *vb* doorzwerven, dolen, dwalen

rover [roovǝ] zwerver

¹row [roo] *n* **1** rij, reeks: *three days in a ~* drie dagen achtereen; **2** huizenrij, straat met (aan weerszijden) huizen, Straat *(in street name);* **3** roeitochtje[h]

²row [roo] *vb* roeien, in een roeiboot varen, per roeiboot vervoeren

³row [rau] *n* **1** rel, ruzie; **2** herrie, kabaal[h]: *kick up* (of:

make) a ~ luidkeels protesteren

⁴row [rau] *vb* **1** ruzie maken; **2** vechten, een rel schoppen

rowan(berry) [rooən] lijsterbes

¹rowdy [raudie] *n* lawaaischopper

²rowdy [raudie] *adj* ruw, wild, ordeloos

rower [rooə] roeier

rowing-boat roeiboot

¹royal [rojjəl] *adj* **1** koninklijk, vd koning(in): *Royal Highness* Koninklijke Hoogheid; **2** koninklijk, vorstelijk: *treat s.o.* ~*ly* iem als een vorst behandelen

²royal [rojjəl] *n* lidʰ vd koninklijke familie

royalist [rojjəlist] royalist, monarchist

royalty [rojjəltie] **1** iem van koninklijken bloede, koning(in), prins(es); **2** royalty, aandeelʰ in de opbrengst; **3** koningschapʰ; **4** leden vh koninklijk huis

r.p.m. *revolutions per minute* omwentelingen per minuut; -toeren

¹rub [rub] *vb* **1** schuren langs, wrijven; **2** slijten, dun, ruw, kaal worden ‖ ~ *up against s.o.* tegen iem aanlopen

²rub [rub] *vb* **1** wrijven, af-, inwrijven, doorheen wrijven, poetsen, boenen: ~ *one's hands* zich in de handen wrijven; **2** schuren; **3** beschadigen, afslijten: ~ *away* wegslijten, afslijten

³rub [rub] *n* **1** poetsbeurt, wrijfbeurt; **2** hindernis, moeilijkheid: *there's the* ~ daar zit de moeilijkheid, dat is het hem juist

rub along 1 zich staande houden, het net klaarspelen; **2** het goed samen kunnen vinden

rubber [rubbə] **1** rubberʰ; synthetisch rubberʰ, rubberachtig materiaalʰ; **2** wrijver, wisser; gum; **3** *(Am)* overschoen; **4** *(sport, game)* robber, reeks van drie partijen

rubberneck *(Am)* nieuwsgierige, zich vergapende toerist

rubber stamp 1 stempel; **2** marionet *(fig)*

rubber-stamp automatisch goedkeuren, gedachteloos instemmen met

rubbery [rubbərie] rubberachtig, taai

¹rubbish [rubbisj] *n* **1** vuilnis, afvalʰ; **2** nonsens, onzin: *talk* ~ zwetsen, kletsen

²rubbish [rubbisj] *vb* afbrekende kritiek leveren op, afkraken

rubbishy [rubbisjie] waardeloos, onzinnig

rubble [rubl] puinʰ, steengruisʰ, steenbrokken

rubella [roebellə] rodehond

rub in inwrijven, (in)masseren ‖ *there's no need to rub it in* je hoeft er niet steeds op terug te komen

¹rub off *vb* **1** weggewreven worden; **2** overgaan op, overgenomen worden: *his stinginess has rubbed off on you* je hebt zijn krenterigheid overgenomen; **3** afslijten, minder worden: *the novelty has rubbed off a bit* de nieuwigheid is er een beetje af

²rub off *vb* **1** wegvegen, afwrijven; **2** afslijten, afschuren

rubric [roebrik] **1** rubriek, titel *(of (chapter in) code)*; **2** rubriek, categorie

rub up 1 oppoetsen, opwrijven; **2** ophalen, bijvijlen:

~ *one's Italian* zijn Italiaans ophalen; *rub s.o. up the wrong way* iem tegen de haren instrijken, iem irriteren

ruby [roebie] **1** robijn⁺ʰ; **2** robijnroodʰ

ruck [ruk] **1** de massa; **2** de gewone dingen, dagelijkse dingen; **3** vouw, kreukel, plooi

rucksack rugzak

ruck up in elkaar kreuke(le)n

ruckus [rukkəs] tumultʰ, ordeverstoring

ruction [ruksjən] kabaalʰ, luid protestʰ

rudder [ruddə] roerʰ

ruddy [ruddie] **1** blozend, gezond; **2** rossig, rood(achtig); **3** verdraaide

rude [roe:d] **1** primitief *(people)*, onbeschaafd; **2** ruw, primitief, eenvoudig; **3** ongemanierd, grof: *be* ~ *to s.o.* onbeleefd tegen iem zijn; *(fig) a* ~ *awakening* een ruwe teleurstelling; ~ *health* onverwoestbare gezondheid

rudiment [roedimmənt] **1** *(biology)* rudimentʰ; **2** ~s beginselen, grondslagen

rudimentary [roedimmentərie] **1** rudimentair, elementair, wat de grondslagen betreft; **2** in een beginstadium

rue [roe:] spijt hebben van, berouw hebben van: *you'll* ~ *the day you said this* je zal de dag berouwen dat je dit gezegd hebt

rueful [roefoel] berouwvol, treurig, bedroefd

¹ruff [ruf] *n* **1** plooikraag; **2** kraag, verenkraag, kraag van haar

²ruff [ruf] *vb (cards)* troeven

ruffian [ruffiən] bruut, woesteling, bandiet

¹ruffle [rufl] *vb* **1** verstoren, doen rimpelen, verwarren: ~ *s.o.'s hair* iemands haar in de war maken; **2** *(with up)* opzetten *(feathers)*; **3** ergeren, kwaad maken, opwinden

²ruffle [rufl] *n* ruche *(along collar, cuff)*, geplooide rand

rug [rug] **1** tapijtʰ, vloerkleedʰ; **2** deken, plaid

rugged [rugid] **1** ruw, ruig, grof; **2** onregelmatig van trekken, doorploegd

rugger [rugə] rugbyʰ

¹ruin [roe:in] *n* **1** ruïne, vervallen bouwwerkʰ; **2** ondergang, vervalʰ: *this will be the* ~ *of him* dit zal hem nog kapot maken; **3** ~s ruïne, bouwval, overblijfselʰ: *in* ~s vervallen, tot een ruïne geworden

²ruin [roe:in] *vb* **1** verwoesten, vernietigen; **2** ruïneren, bederven: *his story has* ~ed *my appetite* zijn verhaal heeft me mijn eetlust ontnomen; **3** ruïneren, tot de ondergang brengen

ruinous [roe:innəs] **1** vervallen, ingestort, bouwvallig; **2** rampzalig, ruïneus

¹rule [roe:l] *n* **1** regel, voorschriftʰ: ~s *of the road* verkeersregels, verkeerscode; *according to* ~ volgens de regels, stipt; **2** gewoonte, gebruikʰ, regel: *as a* ~ gewoonlijk, in het algemeen; **3** duimstok, meetlat; **4** regering, bewindʰ, bestuurʰ: *under British* ~ onder Britse heerschappij; ~ *of thumb* vuistregel, nattevingerwerk

²rule [roe:l] *vb* **1** beheersen *(also fig)*, heersen over, regeren: *be ~d by* zich laten leiden door; **2** beslissen, bepalen, bevelen: **~** *sth. out* iets uitsluiten, iets voor onmogelijk verklaren; **3** trekken *(line): ~d paper* gelinieerd papier

³rule [roe:l] *vb* **1** heersen, regeren, de zeggenschap hebben; **2** een bevel uitvaardigen, bepalen, verordenen

ruler [roe:lə] **1** heerser, vorst; **2** liniaal

¹ruling [roe:ling] *adj* (over)heersend, dominant

²ruling [roe:ling] *n* regel, bepaling: *give a ~* uitspraak doen

¹rum [rum] *n* rum

²rum [rum] *adj* vreemd, eigenaardig

¹rumble [rumbl] *vb* **1** rommelen, donderen: *my stomach is rumbling* mijn maag knort; **2** voortdonderen, voortrollen, ratelen

²rumble [rumbl] *vb* **1** mompelen, mopperen, grommen; **2** doorhebben, doorzien, in de gaten hebben

³rumble [rumbl] *n* **1** gerommelh, rommelend geluidh; **2** *(Am)* tip, informatie; **3** *(Am)* knokpartij, straatgevechth

rumbustious [rumbustiəs] onstuimig, onbesuisd, uitgelaten

¹ruminant [roe:minnənt] *adj* herkauwend

²ruminant [roe:minnənt] *n* herkauwer

ruminate [roe:minneet] **1** herkauwen; **2** peinzen, nadenken, piekeren

¹rummage [rummidzj] *vb* (with *about, through, among*) rondrommelen (in), snuffelen (in), (door)zoeken

²rummage [rummidzj] *n* **1** onderzoekh, het doorzoeken: *I'll have a ~ in the attic* ik zal eens op zolder gaan zoeken; **2** *(Am)* rommel, oude spullen, troep

¹rumour [roe:mə] *n* geruchth, geruchten, praatjes, verhalen: *~ has it that you'll be fired* er gaan geruchten dat je ontslagen zult worden

²rumour [roe:mə] *vb* geruchten verspreiden, praatjes rondstrooien

rump [rump] **1** achterdeelh, bout *(of animal)*, stuit *(of bird);* **2** achtersteh; **3** rest(anth), armzalig overblijfselh *(of parliament, administration)*

rumple [rumpl] kreuken, door de war maken, verfrommelen

rump steak lendebiefstuk

rumpus [rumpəs] tumulth, ruzie, geschreeuwh: *cause* (of: *kick up, make) a ~* ruzie maken

¹run [run] *vb* **1** rennen, hollen, hardlopen; **2** gaan, (voort)bewegen, lopen, (hard) rijden, pendelen, heen en weer rijden (varen) *(of bus, ferry etc)*, voorbijgaan, aflopen *(of time)*, lopen, werken *(of machines)*, (uit)lopen, (weg)stromen, druipen, *(fig)* (voort)duren, zich uitstrekken, gelden: *~ afoul* (of: *foul) of (fig)* stuiten op, in botsing komen met; *(shipp) ~ aground* aan de grond lopen; *feelings run high* de gemoederen raakten verhit; **3** rennen, vliegen, zich haasten; **4** lopen, zich uitstrekken, gaan *(also fig): prices are running high* de prijzen zijn over het algemeen hoog; **5** wegrennen, vluchten; **6** luiden, klin-

ken: *the third line ~s as follows* de derde regel luidt als volgt; **7** kandidaat zijn; **8** *(Am)* laddderen *(of stocking): ~ along!* vooruit!, laat me eens met rust!; *~ across s.o. (sth.)* iem tegen het lijf lopen, ergens tegen aan lopen; *~ for it* op de vlucht slaan, het op een lopen zetten; *~ through the minutes* de notulen doornemen

²run [run] *vb* **1** rijden (lopen) over, volgen *(road)*, afleggen *(a race* een wedstrijd lopen; *~ s.o. over* iem overrijden; **2** doen bewegen, laten gaan, varen, rijden, doen stromen, gieten, in werking stellen, laten lopen, *(fig)* doen voortgaan, leiden, runnen: *~ a business* een zaak hebben; *~ s.o. close* (of: *hard)* iem (dicht) op de hielen zitten, *(fig)* weinig voor iem onderdoen; **3** smokkelen; **4** ontvluchten, weglopen van; **5** kandidaat stellen: *~ a (traffic-)light* door rood rijden

³run *n* **1** looppas, het rennen: *make a ~ for it* het op een lopen zetten; *on the ~: a)* op de vlucht; *b)* druk in de weer; **2** tocht, afstand, eindje hollen, vlucht, rit, trajecth, route, uitstapjeh *(of train, boat); (skiing)* baan, helling, *(cricket, baseball)* run *(a score of 1 point)*; **3** opeenvolging, reeks, serie, *(theatre)* looptijd, *(mus)* loopjeh: *a ~ of success* een succesvolle periode; **4** (with *on)* vraag (naar), stormloop (op): *(com) a ~ on copper* een plotselinge grote vraag naar koper; **5** terreinh, veldh, ren *(for animals);* **6** eindh, stukh, lengte *(of material);* **7** *(Am)* ladder *(in stocking): we'll give them a (good) ~ for their money* we zullen ze het niet makkelijk maken; *give s.o. the ~ of* iem de (vrije) beschikking geven over; *a ~ on the bank* een run op de bank

runabout wagentjeh, (open) autootjeh

run-around het iem afschepen, het iem een rad voor ogen draaien: *give s.o. the ~* een spelletje spelen met iem, iem bedriegen

runaway [runnəwee] vluchteling, ontsnapte || *~ inflation* galopperende inflatie

run away weglopen, vluchten, op de loop gaan || *don't ~ with the idea* geloof dat nu maar niet te snel

rundown 1 vermindering, afname; **2** opsomming, zeer gedetailleerd verslagh

run down 1 reduceren, verminderen in capaciteit; **2** aanrijden; **3** opsporen, vinden, te pakken krijgen: *run a criminal down* een misdadiger opsporen; **4** kritiseren, naar beneden halen, afkraken: *how dare you run her down?* hoe durf je haar te kleineren?

run-down 1 vervallen, verwaarloosd *(of things);* **2** uitgeput, verzwakt, doodmoe

rung [rung] sport, trede

¹run in *vb* binnen (komen) lopen

²run in *vb* **1** oppakken, aanhouden, inrekenen; **2** inrijden *(car)*

run-in 1 aanloop; **2** ruzie, twist, woordenwisseling

run into 1 stoten op, in botsing komen met, botsen tegen; **2** terechtkomen in: *~ difficulties* in de problemen raken; **3** tegen het lijf lopen, onverwacht ontmoeten; **4** bedragen, oplopen: *the costs ~ thousands of pounds* de kosten lopen in de duizenden

runner [rʌnnə] **1** agent, vertegenwoordiger, loopjongen, bezorger; **2** glij-ijzer[h] *(of skate, sleigh)*, glijgoot, glijplank; **3** loper, tafel-, trap-, vloerloper; **4** slingerplant; **5** uitloper; **6** deelnemer *(eg runner, racehorse)*

runner-up tweede, wie op de tweede plaats eindigt, *runners-up* de overige medaillewinnaars

¹**running** [rʌnnɪŋ] *adj* **1** hardlopend, rennend, hollend; **2** lopend: ~ *water* stromend water; **3** (door)lopend, continu, opeenvolgend: ~ *commentary* direct verslag; *(Am; pol)* ~ *mate* kandidaat voor de tweede plaats; *in* ~ *order* goed werkend

²**running** [rʌnnɪŋ] *n* het rennen, *(sport)* hardlopen[h]: *out of the* ~ kansloos (om te winnen); *make the* ~ het tempo bepalen, *(fig)* de toon aangeven, de leiding hebben

runny [rʌnnie] vloeibaar, dun, gesmolten: ~ *nose* loopneus

¹**run off** *vb* weglopen, wegvluchten: ~ *with s.o.* er vandoor gaan met iem

²**run off** *vb* **1** laten weglopen, laten wegstromen, aftappen; **2** reproduceren, afdraaien, fotokopiëren

run-of-the-mill doodgewoon, niet bijzonder, alledaags

run on doorgaan, doorlopen, voortgaan: *time ran on* de tijd ging voorbij

¹**run out** *vb* **1** op raken, aflopen: *our supplies have run out* onze voorraden zijn uitgeput; **2** niets meer hebben, te weinig hebben: *we are running out of time* we komen tijd te kort; **3** weglopen, wegstromen

²**run out** *vb* uitrollen, afwikkelen, laten aflopen *(rope)*

¹**run over** *vb* overlopen, overstromen || ~ *with energy* overlopen van energie

²**run over** *vb* **1** overrijden, aanrijden: *Marco ran over an old lady* Marco reed een oude dame aan; **2** doornemen, nakijken, repeteren

run through 1 doorboren, doorsteken; **2** repeteren, doorlopen

¹**run up** *vb (with against)* (toevallig) tegenkomen: ~ *against difficulties* op moeilijkheden stuiten

²**run up** *vb* (doen) oplopen, snel (doen) toenemen, opjagen: *her debts ran up, she ran up debts* ze maakte steeds meer schulden

run-up voorbereiding(stijd), vooravond: ~ *to an election* verkiezingsperiode

runway start-, landingsbaan

rupee [roeːpiːʔ] *(fin)* roepie *(Asian coin, esp of India and Pakistan)*

¹**rupture** [rʌptsjə] *n* **1** breuk, scheiding, onenigheid; **2** breuk, hernia, ingewandsbreuk

²**rupture** [rʌptsjə] *vb* **1** verbreken, verbroken worden; **2** scheuren *(of muscle etc)*; **3** een breuk krijgen: ~ *oneself lifting sth.* zich een breuk tillen

rural [roeərəl] landelijk, plattelands, dorps

ruse [roeːz] list, truc

¹**rush** [rʌsj] *n* **1** heftige beweging, snelle beweging, stormloop, grote vraag, toevloed; **2** haast, haastige

activiteiten; **3** ~*es (film)* eerste afdruk *(before editing)*; **4** rus, bies; **5** ~*es* biezen *(for twining baskets, mats etc)*

²**rush** [rʌsj] *vb* **1** stormen, vliegen, zich haasten; **2** ondoordacht handelen, overijld doen: ~ *into marriage* zich overhaast in een huwelijk storten

³**rush** [rʌsj] *vb* **1** meeslepen, haastig vervoeren, meesleuren; **2** opjagen, tot haast dwingen; **3** haastig behandelen, afraffelen: ~ *out* massaal produceren

rush-hour spitsuur[h]

rusk [rʌsk] (harde) beschuit, scheepsbeschuit

¹**russet** [rʌssit] *adj* roodbruin

²**russet** [rʌssit] *n* **1** roodbruin[h]; **2** winterappel

Russia [rʌsjə] Rusland

¹**Russian** [rʌsjən] *adj* Russisch

²**Russian** [rʌsjən] *n* **1** Russisch[h] *(language)*; **2** Rus(sin)

¹**rust** [rʌst] *n* **1** roest, oxidatie; **2** roestkleur, roestbruin[h]

²**rust** [rʌst] *vb* roesten, oxideren

¹**rustic** [rʌstik] *adj* **1** boers, simpel, niet beschaafd; **2** rustiek, uit grof materiaal gemaakt: ~ *bridge* rustieke brug *(of unprocessed wood)*; **3** landelijk, dorps, provinciaal

²**rustic** [rʌstik] *n* plattelander, buitenman, boer

¹**rustle** [rʌsl] *vb* ruisen, ritselen, een ritselend geluid maken

²**rustle** [rʌsl] *vb* **1** *(Am)* roven *(cattle, horses)*; **2** weten te bemachtigen, bij elkaar weten te krijgen: ~ *up a meal* een maaltijd in elkaar draaien

³**rustle** [rʌsl] *n* geruis[h], geritsel[h]

rustler [rʌslə] *(Am)* veedief

¹**rustproof** *adj* roestvrij

²**rustproof** *vb* roestvrij maken

rusty [rʌstie] **1** roestig, verroest; **2** verwaarloosd, *(fig)* verstoft, niet meer paraat: *my French is a bit* ~ mijn Frans is niet meer zo goed

rut [rʌt] **1** voor[h], groef, spoor[h]; **2** vaste gang van zaken, sleur: *get into a* ~ vastroesten in de dagelijkse routine; **3** bronst, paartijd

ruthless [roeːθləs] meedogenloos, wreed, hard

rutting [rʌtɪŋ] bronstig, in de bronsttijd, paartijd

rye [raj] **1** rogge; **2** whisky, roggewhisky

S

s. *second* sec., seconde

S *South* Z., Zuid(en)

sabbath [sæbəθ] sabbat, rustdag: *keep the* ~ de sabbat houden

sabbatical [səbætikl] sabbatsverlof^h, verlof^h *(at university)*

¹sabotage [sæbəta:zj] *n* sabotage

²sabotage [sæbəta:zj] *vb* saboteren, sabotage plegen (op)

sabre [seebə] sabel

sabre-rattling sabelgekletter^h, (het dreigen met) militair geweld^h

saccharine [sækərie:n] **1** suikerachtig, sacharine-, mierzoet; **2** *(fig)* suikerzoet, zoet(sappig)

sachet [sæsjee] **1** reukzakje^h; **2** (plastic) ampul *(for shampoo)*

¹sack [sæk] *n* **1** zak, baal, jutezak; **2** zak, ontslag^h: *get the* ~ ontslagen worden; *give s.o. the* ~ iem de laan uitsturen; **3** bed^h: *hit the* ~ gaan pitten, onder de wol kruipen

²sack [sæk] *vb* **1** plunderen; **2** de laan uitsturen, ontslaan

sackcloth jute ‖ *in* ~ *and ashes* in zak en as, in rouw

sacrament [sækrəmənt] sacrament^h

sacramental [sækrəmentl] tot het sacrament behorend, offer-: ~ *wine* miswijn

sacred [seekrid] **1** gewijd, heilig: ~ *cow* heilige koe; **2** plechtig, heilig, oprecht: *a* ~ *promise* een plechtige belofte; **3** veilig, onschendbaar

¹sacrifice [sækriffajs] *n* **1** offer^h, het offeren; **2** opoffering, offer^h, het opgeven, prijsgeven

²sacrifice [sækriffajs] *vb* offeren, een offer brengen

³sacrifice [sækriffajs] *vb* **1** offeren, aanbieden, opdragen; **2** opofferen, opgeven, zich ontzeggen: *he* ~*d his life to save her children* hij gaf zijn leven om haar kinderen te redden

sacrilege [sækrillidzj] heiligschennis

sacrilegious [sækrillidzjəs] heiligschennend, onterend

sacristan [sækristən] koster

sacristy [sækristie] sacristie

sacrosanct [sækroosængkt] heilig, onaantastbaar: *his spare time is* ~ *to him* zijn vrije tijd is hem heilig

sad [sæd] **1** droevig, verdrietig, ongelukkig: *to be* ~*ly mistaken* er totaal naast zitten; **2** schandelijk, bedroevend (slecht)

sadden [sædn] bedroeven, verdrietig maken, somber stemmen

¹saddle [sædl] *n* **1** zadel^h: *be in the* ~ te paard zitten, *(fig)* de baas zijn, het voor het zeggen hebben; **2** lendestuk^h, rugstuk^h: ~ *of lamb* lamszadel

²saddle [sædl] *vb* **1** *(with up)* zadelen, opzadelen: ~ *up one's horse* zijn paard zadelen; **2** *(with with, (up)on)* opzadelen (met), opschepen (met), afschuiven op: *he* ~*d all responsibility on her* hij schoof alle verantwoordelijkheid op haar af

saddlebag zadeltas(je^h)

saddle-sore doorgereden, met zadelpijn

sadism [seedizm] sadisme^h

sadist [seedist] sadist(e)

sadistic [sədjstik] sadistisch

sadly [sædlie] helaas

safari [səfa:rie] safari, jachtexpeditie, filmexpeditie: *on* ~ op safari

¹safe [seef] *adj* **1** veilig, beschermd: ~ *from attack* beveiligd tegen aanvallen; **2** veilig, zeker, gevrijwaard: *as* ~ *as houses* zo veilig als een huis; *be on the* ~ *side* het zekere voor het onzekere nemen; *better (to be)* ~ *than sorry* je kunt beter het zekere voor het onzekere nemen; *play it* ~ op veilig spelen, geen risico nemen; **3** betrouwbaar, gegarandeerd: *the party has twenty* ~ *seats* de partij kan zeker rekenen op twintig zetels; **4** behouden, ongedeerd: *she arrived* ~ *and sound* ze kwam heelhuids aan

²safe [seef] *n* brandkast, (bewaar)kluis, safe(loket^h)

safe conduct vrijgeleide^h, vrije doorgang

safe deposit (brand)kluis, bankkluis

¹safeguard [seefga:d] *n* waarborg, bescherming, voorzorg(smaatregel)

²safeguard [seefga:d] *vb* beveiligen, beschermen, waarborgen

safe-keeping (veilige) bewaring

safety [seeftie] veiligheid, zekerheid

safety belt veiligheidsgordel, veiligheidsriem

safety catch veiligheidspal

safety island vluchtheuvel

safety pin veiligheidsspeld

saffron [sæfrən] saffraan, oranjegeel

¹sag [sæg] *vb* **1** *(also with down)* verzakken, doorzakken, doorbuigen; **2** dalen, afnemen, teruglopen: *her spirits sagged* de moed zonk haar in de schoenen

²sag [sæg] *n* verzakking, doorzakking, doorbuiging

saga [sa:gə] **1** familiekroniek; **2** (lang) verhaal^h

sagacious [səgeesjəs] scherpzinnig, verstandig

sagacity [səgæsittie] scherpzinnigheid, wijsheid, inzicht^h

¹sage [seedzj] *adj* wijs(gerig), verstandig

²sage [seedzj] *n* **1** wijze (man), wijsgeer; **2** salie

said (boven)genoemd, voornoemd

¹sail [seel] *n* **1** zeil^h, de zeilen: *set* ~ de zeilen hijsen, onder zeil gaan; **2** zeiltocht(je^h), boottocht(je^h): *take s.o. for a* ~ met iem gaan zeilen; **3** molenwiek, zeil^h

²sail [seel] *vb* **1** varen, zeilen, per schip reizen: ~ *close* to (of: *near*) *the wind* scherp bij de wind zeilen, *(fig)* bijna zijn boekje te buiten gaan; **2** afvaren, vertrekken, uitvaren: *we're ~ing for England tomorrow* we vertrekken morgen naar Engeland; **3** glijden, zweven, zeilen: *she ~ed through her finals* ze haalde haar eindexamen op haar sloffen

³sail [seel] *vb* **1** bevaren; **2** besturen *(ship)*

sailing [seeling] **1** bootreis; **2** afvaart, vertrek^h, vertrektijd; **3** navigatie, het besturen ve schip; **4** zeilsport

sailor [seelə] zeeman, matroos: *Andy is a good ~* Andy heeft nooit last van zeeziekte

¹saint [seent] *n* **1** heilige, sint: *All Saints' Day* Allerheiligen; **2** engel, *(fig)* iem met engelengeduld

²saint [sənt] *adj*: *Saint* sint, heilig

saint's day [seentsdee] heiligendag, naamdag

sake [seek] **1** belang^h, (best)wil: *for the ~ of the company* in het belang van het bedrijf; *we're only doing this for your ~* we doen dit alleen maar ter wille van jou; **2** doel^h, oogmerk^h: *I'm not driving around here for the ~ of driving* ik rijd hier niet rond voor de lol

salaam [səla:m] oosterse groet *(low bow with right hand on forehead)*

salacious [səleesjəs] **1** geil; **2** obsceen, schunnig

salad [sæləd] **1** salade, slaatje^h; **2** sla

salad cream slasaus

salamander [sæləmændə] salamander

salaried [sæləried] per maand betaald, gesalarieerd

salary [sælərie] salaris^h

sale [seel] **1** verkoop, afzet(markt); *for ~* te koop; **2** verkoping, veiling, bazaar; **3** uitverkoop, opruiming

saleroom veilinglokaal^h

salesclerk winkelbediende

salesgirl winkelmeisje^h, verkoopster

saleslady verkoopster

salesman [seelzmən] **1** verkoper, winkelbediende; **2** vertegenwoordiger, agent, handelsreiziger || *traveling ~* handelsreiziger

salesmanship [seelzmənsjip] verkoopkunde, verkooptechniek

sales representative vertegenwoordiger

sales tax omzetbelasting

saleswoman 1 verkoopster, winkelbediende; **2** vertegenwoordigster, agente, handelsreizigster

salient [seeliənt] opvallend, belangrijkste

saline [seelajn] zout(houdend), zoutachtig, zilt

saliva [səlajvə] speeksel^h

salivate [sælivveet] kwijlen *(also fig)*, speeksel produceren

¹sallow [sæloo] *adj* vaal(geel)

²sallow [sæloo] *n* wilg

sally [sælie] **1** uitval: *the army made a successful ~* het leger deed een succesvolle uitval; **2** uitbarsting, opwelling; **3** kwinkslag, (geestige) inval

sally forth 1 een uitval doen; **2** erop uit gaan, op stap gaan, naar buiten rennen

salmon [sæmən] **1** zalm; **2** zalmkleur

saloon [səloe:n] **1** zaal, salon; **2** bar, café^h; **3** sedan,

gesloten vierdeursauto

¹salt [so:lt] *n* **1** (keuken)zout^h; **2** zoutvaatje^h || *the ~ of the earth* het zout der aarde; *he's not worth his ~* hij is het zout in de pap niet waard

²salt [so:lt] *adj* **1** zout, zilt; **2** gepekeld, gezouten: *~ fish* gezouten vis

³salt [so:lt] *vb* **1** zouten, pekelen, inmaken; **2** pekelen *(roads)*, met zout bestrooien; **3** *(fig)* kruiden || *he's got quite some money ~ed away* (of: *down*) hij heeft aardig wat geld opgepot

saltpetre [so:ltpie:tə] salpeter^{+h}

saltshaker zoutvaatje^h, zoutstrooier

salty [so:ltie] **1** zout(achtig); **2** gezouten, gekruid, pikant *(of language)*

salubrious [səloe:briəs] heilzaam, gezond

salutary [sæljoetərie] weldadig, heilzaam, gunstig, gezond

salutation [sæljoeteesjən] **1** aanhef *(in letter)*; **2** begroeting, groet, begroetingskus

¹salute [səloe:t] *vb* **1** groeten, begroeten, verwelkomen; **2** salueren, een saluutschot lossen (voor)

²salute [səloe:t] *vb* eer bewijzen aan, huldigen: *there were several festivals to ~ the country's 50 years of independence* er waren verschillende festivals om de vijftigjarige onafhankelijkheid van het land eer te bewijzen

³salute [səloe:t] *n* **1** saluut^h, militaire groet, saluutschot^h: *take the ~* de parade afnemen; **2** begroeting, groet

¹salvage [sælvidzj] *n* **1** berging, redding, het in veiligheid brengen; **2** geborgen goed^h, het geborgene: *the divers were not entitled to a share in the ~* de duikers hadden geen recht op een aandeel in de geborgen goederen; **3** bruikbaar afval^h, recycling, hergebruik^h

²salvage [sælvidzj] *vb* **1** bergen, redden, in veiligheid brengen; **2** terugwinnen, verzamelen voor hergebruik

salvation [sælveesjən] **1** redding: *that was my ~* dat was mijn redding; **2** verlossing

Salvation Army Leger des Heils

¹salve [sælv] *n* zalf *(also fig)*, smeersel^h, balsem

²salve [sælv] *vb* sussen, kalmeren, tevreden stellen: *~ one's conscience* zijn geweten sussen

salvia [sælviə] salie

salvo [sælvoo] *(also ~es)* salvo^h, plotselinge uitbarsting: *a ~ of applause* een daverend applaus

¹same [seem] *pron* zelfde, hetzelfde: *the ~ applies to you* hetzelfde geldt voor jou; *~ here* ik ook (niet), met mij precies zo, idem dito; *they are much the ~* ze lijken (vrij) sterk op elkaar; *it's all the ~ to me* het is mij om het even, het maakt me niet uit; *(the) ~ to you* insgelijks, van 't zelfde; *at the ~ time* tegelijkertijd; *much the ~ problem* vrijwel hetzelfde probleem

²same [seem] *adv* net zo, precies hetzelfde: *he found nothing, (the) ~ as my own dentist* hij vond niets, net als mijn eigen tandarts

sameness [seemnəs] **1** gelijkheid, overeenkomst; **2**

eentonigheid, monotonie

¹sample [sɑːmpl] *n* **1** (proef)monster\
h, staal\
h, voorbeeld\
h: *take a ~ of blood* een bloedmonster nemen; **2** steekproef

²sample [sɑːmpl] *vb* **1** een steekproef nemen uit, monsters trekken uit; **2** (be)proeven, testen, keuren

sanatorium [sænətɔːriəm] sanatorium\
h, herstellingsoord\
h

sanctify [sæŋktifaj] **1** heiligen; **2** rechtvaardigen, heiligen; **3** heilig maken, verlossen van zonde(schuld)

sanctimonious [sæŋktimmooniəs] schijnheilig

¹sanction [sæŋksjən] *n* **1** toestemming, goedkeuring; **2** sanctie, dwang(middel\
h), strafmaatregel: *apply ~s against racist regimes* sancties instellen tegen racistische regimes

²sanction [sæŋksjən] *vb* **1** sanctioneren, bekrachtigen, bevestigen; **2** goedkeuren, toestaan, instemmen met

sanctity [sæŋktittie] heiligheid, vroomheid

sanctuary [sæŋktsjoeərie] **1** omtrek van (hoog)altaar, priesterkoor\
h; **2** vogelreservaat\
h, wildreservaat\
h; **3** asiel\
h, vrijplaats, wijkplaats, toevlucht(soord\
h): *he got up and took ~ in his study* hij stond op en zocht zijn toevlucht in zijn studeerkamer

¹sand [sænd] *n* **1** zand\
h; **2** *~s* zandvlakte, strand\
h, woestijn

²sand [sænd] *vb* **1** met zand bestrooien: *~ slippery roads* gladde wegen met zand bestrooien; **2** (with down) (glad)schuren, polijsten

sandal [sændl] sandaal

sandbank zandbank, ondiepte

sandblast zandstralen

sander [sændə] schuurmachine

sandman zandmannetje\
h, Klaas Vaak

¹sandpaper *n* schuurpapier\
h

²sandpaper *vb* schuren

sandpit 1 zandgraverij, zandgroeve; **2** zandbak

sandstone zandsteen\
+h

¹sandwich [sænwidzj] *n* sandwich, dubbele boterham

²sandwich [sænwidzj] *vb* klemmen, vastzetten, plaatsen: *I'll ~ her in between two other appointments* ik ontvang haar wel tussen twee andere afspraken door

sandwich-board advertentiebord\
h, reclamebord\
h *(carried on chest and back)*

sandy [sændie] **1** zand(er)ig, zandachtig; **2** ros(sig) *(of hair)*, roodachtig

sane [seen] **1** (geestelijk) gezond, bij zijn volle verstand; **2** verstandig *(of ideas etc)*, redelijk

sanguine [sæŋgwin] **1** optimistisch, hoopvol, opgewekt; **2** blozend, met een gezonde kleur

sanitarium [sænitteəriəm] sanatorium\
h, herstellingsoord\
h

sanitary [sænittərie] **1** sanitair, mbt de gezondheid; **2** hygiënisch, schoon: *~ fittings* het sanitair; *~ stop* sanitaire stop

sanitary towel maandverband\
h

sanitation [sænitteesjən] **1** bevordering vd volksgezondheid; **2** afvalverwerking, rioolzuivering

sanity [sænittie] **1** (geestelijke) gezondheid; **2** verstandigheid, gezond verstand\
h

Santa Claus [sæntə klɔːz] kerstman(netje)

¹sap [sæp] *n* **1** (planten)sap\
h; **2** levenskracht, energie, vitaliteit: *the ~ of youth* jeugdige levenskracht; **3** slagwapen\
h, knuppel; **4** sul, sukkel, oen

²sap [sæp] *vb* aftappen *(also fig)*, sap onttrekken aan, *(fig)* levenskracht onttrekken aan, uitputten: *the tension at the office was ~ping my energy* de spanning op kantoor vrat al mijn energie

sapphire [sæfajjə] **1** saffier\
+h; **2** saffierblauw\
h

sarcasm [sɑːkæzm] sarcasme\
h, bijtende spot

sarcastic [sɑːkæstik] sarcastisch, bijtend

sarcophagus [sɑːkɔffəgəs] sarcofaag, stenen doodskist

sardine [sɑːdiːn] sardine: *(packed) like ~s* als haringen in een ton

sardonic [sɑːdɔnnik] boosaardig spottend, cynisch

sarky [sɑːkie] sarcastisch

sash [sæsj] **1** sjerp; **2** raam\
h, schuifraam\
h

sashay [sæsjee] nonchalant lopen, paraderen: *the models ~ed down the catwalk* de modellen paradeerden over het podium

¹sass [sæs] *n* tegenspraak, brutaliteit: *I'm not accepting such ~ from anybody* ik accepteer zulke brutale opmerkingen van niemand

²sass [sæs] *vb* brutaal zijn tegen, brutaliseren

¹Sassenach [sæsənæk] *adj* Engels

²Sassenach [sæsənæk] *n* Engelsman

satanic [sətænik] **1** van de duivel; **2** satanisch, duivels, hels

satchel [sætsjl] (school)tas *(oft with shoulder strap)*, pukkel

satellite [sætəlajt] **1** satelliet; **2** voorstad, randgemeente: *New Malden is one of the many ~s of London* New Malden is een van de vele voorsteden van Londen; **3** satellietstaat, vazalstaat

satellite town satellietstad

satiate [seesjie·eet] (over)verzadigen, bevredigen, overvoeden, overladen: *be ~d with: a)* verzadigd zijn van; *b)* zijn buik vol hebben van

¹satin [sætin] *adj* satijnachtig, satijnen, satijnzacht

²satin [sætin] *n* satijn\
h

satire [sætajjə] **1** satire, hekeldicht\
h, hekelroman; **2** satire, bespotting

satiric(al) [sətirrik(l)] satirisch

satirize [sætirrajz] **1** hekelen, bespotten; **2** een satire schrijven op

satisfaction [sætisfæksjən] **1** genoegen\
h, plezier\
h, tevredenheid; **2** voldoening, bevrediging, zekerheid: *prove sth. to s.o.'s ~* iets tot iemands volle tevredenheid bewijzen; **3** genoegdoening, eerherstel\
h, voldoening: *demand ~* genoegdoening eisen; **4** (af)betaling, terugbetaling; voldoening

satisfactory [sætisfæktərie] **1** voldoende, (goed) genoeg; **2** voldoening schenkend, bevredigend; **3**

geschikt

¹satisfy [sætisfaj] *vb* **1** voldoen, toereikend zijn, (goed) genoeg zijn); **2** voldoen, genoegen schenken, tevreden stemmen

²satisfy [sætisfaj] *vb* **1** tevredenstellen, genoegen schenken, bevredigen: *be satisfied with* tevreden zijn over; **2** vervullen, voldoen aan, beantwoorden aan: ~ *the conditions* aan de voorwaarden voldoen; **3** nakomen *(an obligation)*, vervullen; **4** bevredigen, verzadigen: ~ *one's curiosity* zijn nieuwsgierigheid bevredigen; **5** overtuigen, verzekeren: *be satisfied that* ervan overtuigd zijn dat, de zekerheid (verkregen) hebben dat

saturate [sætsjəreet] **1** doordrenken *(also fig)*, doordringen, onderdompelen; **2** (over)verzadigen, volledig vullen: *the computer market will soon be* ~*d* de afzetmarkt voor computers zal weldra verzadigd zijn; **3** *(science, chem)* verzadigen; ~*d fats* verzadigde vetten

Saturday [sætədee] zaterdag

Saturn [sætə:n] Saturnus

satyr [sætə] halfgod

¹sauce [so:s] *n* **1** saus *(also fig)*, sausje^h; **2** brutaliteit, tegenspraak, vrijpostigheid

²sauce [so:s] *vb* brutaal zijn tegen, een brutale mond opzetten tegen: *don't you ~ me, young man* niet zo'n grote mond tegen mij opzetten, jongeman

saucer [so:sə] **1** (thee)schoteltje^h; **2** schotelantenne

saucy [so:sie] **1** brutaal, (lichtjes) uitdagend *(also sexually)*: *don't be ~ with me* wees niet zo brutaal tegen mij; **2** vlot, knap, tof: *a ~ hat* een vlot hoedje

sauna [so:nə] sauna

¹saunter [so:ntə] *vb* drentelen, slenteren: *we spent the afternoon ~ing up and down the pier* de hele middag slenterden we heen en weer op de pier

²saunter [so:ntə] *n* **1** wandeling(etje^h); **2** slentergang

sausage [sossidzj] worst, saucijs

¹savage [sævidzj] *adj* **1** primitief, onbeschaafd; **2** wreed(aardig), woest: *a ~ dog* een valse hond; **3** heftig, fel: ~ *criticism* meedogenloze kritiek; **4** lomp, ongemanierd

²savage [sævidzj] *n* **1** wilde, primitieve (mens); **2** woesteling, wildeman; **3** barbaar

savagery [sævidzjərie] wreedheid, ruwheid, gewelddadigheid

savanna(h) [səvænə] savanne

¹save [seev] *vb* **1** sparen (voor), geld opzijleggen, zuinig zijn; **2** *(sport)* een doelpunt (weten te) voorkomen; **3** verlossing brengen, redden, verlossen

²save [seev] *vb* **1** redden, bevrijden, verlossen: ~ *the situation* de situatie redden, een fiasco voorkomen; **2** (be)sparen, bewaren, opslaan: ~ *time* tijd (uit)sparen; **3** overbodig maken, voorkomen, besparen: *I've been ~d a lot of trouble* er werd me heel wat moeite bespaard; **4** *(sport)* redden; **5** *(sport)* voorkomen *(goal)*, stoppen *(penalty, kick)*: *God ~ the Queen* God behoede de koningin

³save [seev] *n* redding: *the goalkeeper made a brilliant* ~ de doelverdediger wist met een prachtige

actie de bal uit het doel te houden

⁴save [seev] *prep* behalve, met uitzondering van: *everyone ~ Gill* allemaal behalve Gill

saving [seeving] **1** redding, verlossing; **2** besparing: *a ~ of ten dollars* een besparing van tien dollar

savings [seevingz] spaargeld

savings bank spaarbank, spaarkas

saviour [seevjə] **1** redder, bevrijder; **2** (de) Verlosser, (de) Heiland *(Jesus Christ)*

¹savour [seevə] *vb* met smaak proeven, genieten (van)

²savour [seevə] *n* **1** bijsmaak *(also fig)*, zweem: *I detected a certain ~ of garlic* ik bespeurde een bijsmaak van knoflook; **2** smaak *(also fig)*, aroma^h, geur: *the ~ of local life* de eigenheid van het plaatselijke leven

savour of geuren naar *(also fig)*, rieken naar, iets weg hebben van

¹savoury [seevrie] *adj* **1** smakelijk, lekker; **2** hartig, pikant; **3** eerbaar, respectabel, aanvaardbaar: *I'll spare you the less ~ details* ik zal je de minder fraaie bijzonderheden besparen

²savoury [seevrie] *n* hartig voorgerecht^h (nagerecht^h), hartig hapje^h

savvy [sævie] (gezond) verstand^h

¹saw *n* zaag(machine): *circular ~* cirkelzaag

²saw *vb* zagen, gezaagd worden, zich laten zagen

³saw *vb* zagen, in stukken zagen: ~ *down a tree* een boom omzagen

sawdust zaagsel^h

sax [sæks] *saxophone* sax

Saxon [sæksən] **1** Angelsaksisch, Oud-Engels; **2** Saksisch

saxophone [sæksəfoon] saxofoon

¹say [see] *vb* zeggen, praten, vertellen: *I couldn't ~* ik zou het niet kunnen zeggen; *so to ~* bij wijze van spreken; *I'd rather not ~* dat zeg ik liever niet, dat houd ik liever voor me; *a man, they ~, of bad reputation* een man, (zo) zegt men, met een slechte reputatie

²say [see] *vb* **1** (op)zeggen, uiten, (uit)spreken: ~ *grace* (of: *one's) prayers* dank zeggen, bidden; *I dare ~ that* het zou zelfs heel goed kunnen dat; ~ *no more!* geen woord meer!, praat er mij niet van!, dat zegt al genoeg!; *to ~ nothing of* om nog maar te zwijgen over; ~ *to oneself* bij zichzelf denken; *that is to ~* met andere woorden, dat wil zeggen, tenminste; **2** zeggen, vermelden, verkondigen: *to ~ the least* op zijn zachtst uitgedrukt; *she is said to be very rich* men zegt dat ze heel rijk is; *it ~s on the bottle* op de fles staat; **3** zeggen, aanvoeren, te kennen geven: *what do you ~ to this?* wat zou je hiervan vinden?; **4** zeggen, aannemen, veronderstellen: *let's ~, shall we ~* laten we zeggen; ~ *seven a.m.* pakweg zeven uur ('s ochtends); **5** aangeven, tonen, zeggen: *what time does your watch ~?* hoe laat is het op jouw horloge?; *when all is said and done* alles bij elkaar genomen, al met al; *no sooner said than done* zo gezegd, zo gedaan; *it goes without ~ing* het spreekt vanzelf; *you can ~ that again, you said it* zeg dat wel, daar zeg je zo iets, en of!; *~ when* zeg het als 't genoeg is, zeg maar ho

³say [see] *n* **1** invloed, zeggen[h], zeggenschap: *have a ~ in the matter* iets in de melk te brokkelen hebben, een vinger in de pap hebben; **2** zegje[h], mening: *have* (of: *say*) *one's ~* zijn zegje doen

saying [seeing] gezegde[h], spreekwoord[h], spreuk

say-so 1 bewering, woord[h]: *why should he believe you on your ~?* waarom zou hij je op je woord geloven?; **2** toestemming, permissie

scab [skæb] **1** onderkruiper, werkwillige, stakingsbreker; **2** zwartwerker *(non-union member)*; **3** korst(je[h]): *a ~ had formed on her knee* er had zich een korstje gevormd op haar knie

scabbard [skæbəd] **1** schede *(for sword, knife)*; **2** holster

scabies [skeebie:z] schurft

scads [skædz] massa's, hopen: *~s of people* massa's mensen

scaffold [skæfoold] **1** schavot[h]; **2** (bouw)steiger, stellage

scaffolding [skæfəlding] steiger(constructie), stelling(en), stellage

¹scald [sko:ld] *vb* zich branden *(by hot water, steam)*

²scald [sko:ld] *vb* **1** branden, (doen) branden; **2** (uit)wassen, (uit)koken, steriliseren; **3** bijna tot kookpunt verhitten *(milk)*

³scald [sko:ld] *n* brandwond, brandblaar, brandvlek

scalding [sko:lding] *(also adverb)* kokend(heet)

¹scale [skeel] *n* **1** schub, schaal, (huid)schilfer: *(fig) the ~s fell from her eyes* de schellen vielen haar van de ogen; **2** (weeg)schaal: *a pair of ~s* een weegschaal; **3** aanslag, ketelsteen; **4** schaal(verdeling), schaalaanduiding, maatstok, meetlat: *the ~ of the problem* de omvang van het probleem; *(fig) on a large ~* op grote schaal; *draw to ~* op schaal tekenen; **5** *(mus)* toonladder; **6** *(maths)* schaal

²scale [skeel] *vb* (be)klimmen, (op)klauteren, opgaan *(ladder)* || *~ back* (of: *down*) verlagen, verkleinen, terugschroeven; *~ up* verhogen, vergroten, opschroeven

³scale [skeel] *vb* (af)schilferen, (af)bladderen

scale model schaalmodel[h]

scalene [skeelie:n] ongelijkzijdig *(of triangle)*

scallywag [skæliewæg] deugniet, rakker, schavuit

¹scalp [skælp] *n* hoofdhuid

²scalp [skælp] *vb* scalperen

scalpel [skælpl] scalpel, ontleedmes[h], operatiemes[h]

scamp [skæmp] boef(je[h]), rakker, deugniet: *you ~!* (jij) boef!

scamper [skæmpə] hollen, rennen, draven

¹scan [skæn] *vb* **1** scanderen; in versvoeten verdelen: *the audience were ~ning his name: 'John-son, John-son'* het publiek scandeerde zijn naam: 'John-son, John-son'; **2** nauwkeurig onderzoeken, afspeuren, afzoeken; **3** snel, vluchtig doorlezen; **4** aftasten, scannen *(with radar)*

²scan [skæn] *vb* zich laten scanderen *(of poem)*, me-

trisch juist zijn: *some of the lines of this song don't scan* sommige regels van dat liedje kloppen metrisch niet

³scan [skæn] *n* **1** onderzoekende blik; **2** scan, het aftasten, het onderzoeken

scandal [skændl] **1** schandaal[h], schande; **2** achterklap, laster(praat)

scandalize [skændəlajz] choqueren, ergernis geven: *he didn't know whether to laugh or be ~d* hij wist niet of hij nou moest lachen of zich moest ergeren

scandalmonger [skændlmunggə] kwaadspreker, lasteraar(ster)

scandalous [skændələs] schandelijk, schandalig, aanstootgevend

¹Scandinavian [skændinneeviən] *adj* Scandinavisch

²Scandinavian [skændinneeviən] *n* Scandinaviër

scanner [skænə] aftaster, scanner, (draaiende) radarantenne

scant [skænt] weinig, spaarzaam, gering: *do ~ justice to sth.* iets weinig recht doen

scanty [skæntie] karig, krap, gering

scapegoat zondebok

scar [ska:] litteken[h], schram, kras

scarce [skeəs] schaars *(of food, money, etc)*, zeldzaam: *make oneself ~* zich uit de voeten maken

scarcely [skeəslie] **1** nauwelijks, met moeite: *~ ever* haast nooit; **2** *(iron)* zeker niet: *that's ~ the point here* dat is nou niet helemaal waar het hier om gaat

scarcity [skeəsittie] schaarste, gebrek[h]

¹scare [skeə] *vb* **1** doen schrikken, bang maken: *~d out of one's wits* buiten zichzelf van schrik, doodsbang; **2** *(with off, away)* wegjagen, afschrikken

²scare [skeə] *n* schrik, vrees, paniek: *give s.o. a ~* iem de stuipen op het lijf jagen

scarecrow [skeəkroo] vogelverschrikker *(also fig)*

scare up 1 optrommelen, bij elkaar scharrelen; **2** klaarmaken, vervaardigen: *~ a meal from leftovers* uit restjes een maaltijd in elkaar flansen

scarf [ska:f] *(also scarves)* sjaal(tje[h]), sjerp

scarlatina [ska:lətie:nə] roodvonk

scarlet [ska:lət] scharlaken(rood)[h] || *~ fever* roodvonk

scarper [ska:pə] 'm smeren

scary [skeərie] **1** eng, schrikaanjagend; **2** *(snel)* bang, schrikachtig

scat [skæt] snel vertrekken: *~!* ga weg!

scathing [skeeðing] vernietigend, bijtend *(eg sarcasm)*

¹scatter [skætə] *vb* verstrooid raken, zich verspreiden

²scatter [skætə] *vb* verstrooien *(also science)*, verspreiden *(also fig)*: *all his CDs were ~ed through the room* al zijn cd's lagen verspreid door de kamer; *~ about* (of: *around*) rondstrooien

³scatter [skætə] *n* (ver)spreiding, verstrooiing: *a ~ of houses* een paar huizen hier en daar

scatterbrain warhoofd[h]

scattered [skǽtəd] verspreid (liggend), ver uiteen: ~ *showers* hier en daar een bui

scattering [skǽtəring] verspreiding

scatty [skǽtie] gek, warrig

scavenge [skǽvindzj] **1** afval doorzoeken; **2** aas eten

scenario [sinnɑ:rie·oo] scenario[h], draaiboek[h] *(also fig)*, (film)script[h]

scene [sie:n] **1** plaats van handeling, lokatie, toneel[h]: *change of* ~ verandering van omgeving; **2** scène *(also theatre)*, ophef, misbaar[h]; **3** decor[h], coulisse(n): *behind the ~s* achter de schermen *(also fig)*; **4** landschap[h]: *set the* ~ *(for sth.)* (iets) voorbereiden; *steal the* ~ de show stelen

scenery [sie:nərie] **1** decors, coulissen; **2** landschap[h]

scenic [sie:nik] **1** schilderachtig; **2** vd natuur, landschap(s)- || ~ *railway* miniatuurspoorbaan

¹scent [sent] *vb* **1** ruiken *(also fig)*, geuren, lucht krijgen van; **2** parfumeren: ~ *soap* geparfumeerde zeep

²scent [sent] *n* **1** geur, lucht *(also hunt)*; **2** spoor[h] *(also fig)*: *on a false* ~ (of: *wrong*) ~ op een verkeerd spoor; **3** parfum[h], luchtje[h], geurtje[h]; **4** reuk(zin), neus *(also fig)*

sceptic [skeptik] twijfelaar

sceptical [skeptikl] *(with about, of)* sceptisch (over), twijfelend

scepticism [skeptissizm] kritische houding

sceptre [septə] scepter

schedule [sjedjoe:l] **1** programma[h]: *be behind* ~ achter liggen op het schema, vertraging hebben; *on* ~ op tijd; **2** (inventaris)lijst; **3** dienstregeling, rooster[h]

scheduled [sjedjoe:ld] **1** gepland, in het rooster opgenomen; **2** op een lijst gezet; **3** lijn- *(service, flight)*

¹scheme [skie:m] *n* **1** stelsel[h], ordening, systeem[h]; **2** programma[h]; **3** oogmerk[h], project[h]; **4** plan[h], complot[h]; **5** ontwerp[h]

²scheme [skie:m] *vb* plannen maken, plannen smeden: ~ *for sth.* iets plannen

³scheme [skie:m] *vb* **1** beramen *(plans)*, smeden; **2** intrigeren: *he was always scheming against her* hij was altijd bezig complotten tegen haar te smeden

schemer [skie:mə] **1** plannenmaker; **2** intrigant, samenzweerder

scheming [skie:ming] sluw

schism [skizm] scheuring *(in church)*, afscheiding

schizophrenia [skitsəfrie:niə] schizofrenie

schmalzy [sjmo:ltsie] sentimenteel

scholar [skollə] **1** geleerde: *not much of a* ~ geen studiehoofd; **2** beursstudent

scholarly [skolləlie] wetenschappelijk; geleerd

scholarship [skolləsjip] **1** (studie)beurs; **2** wetenschappelijkheid; **3** wetenschap; geleerdheid

scholastic [skəlæstik] **1** school-; **2** schools

¹school [skoe:l] *n* **1** school *(also of fish etc)*, *(of thoughts)* richting: ~ *of thought* denkwijze, (filosofische) school; **2** school, *(fig)* leerschool: *lower* (of: *upper)* ~ onderbouw, bovenbouw; *modern* ~ (roughly) mavo; *keep in after* ~ na laten blijven; *quit* ~ van school gaan; *after* ~ na school(tijd); *at* ~ op school; **3** collegeruimte, examengebouw[h], leslokaal[h]; **4** studierichting; **5** (universitair) instituut[h], faculteit: *medical* ~ faculteit (der) geneeskunde; **6** scholing, (school)opleiding

²school [skoe:l] *vb* scholen, trainen, africhten *(horse)*: ~*ed in* opgeleid tot

schoolboy schooljongen, scholier

schooldays schooltijd

schoolgirl schoolmeisje[h]

schooling [skoe:ling] **1** scholing, onderwijs[h]; **2** dressuur

school-marm [skoe:lma:m] **1** schooljuffrouw; **2** schoolfrik

schoolmaster schoolmeester

schoolmate schoolkameraad

schoolmistress schooljuffrouw

schoolteacher **1** onderwijzer(es); **2** leraar

schooner [skoe:nə] **1** schoener; **2** groot bierglas[h]; **3** groot sherryglas[h] (portglas[h])

science [sajjəns] **1** (natuur)wetenschap: *applied* ~ toegepaste wetenschap; **2** techniek, vaardigheid

science fiction sciencefiction

scientific [sajjəntiffik] **1** wetenschappelijk; **2** vakkundig: *a* ~ *boxer* een bokser met een goede techniek

scientist [sajjəntist] natuurwetenschapper

scintillate [sintilleet] **1** schitteren, fonkelen; **2** vonken; **3** sprankelen, geestig zijn: *scintillating humour* tintelende humor

scissors [sizzəz] schaar: *a pair of* ~ een schaar

¹scoff [skof] *vb* schrokken, vreten

²scoff [skof] *vb (with at)* spotten (met): *they ~ed the idea* ze maakten spottende opmerkingen over het idee

³scoff [skof] *n* **1** spottende opmerking: *he was used to ~s about his appearance* hij was gewend aan spottende opmerkingen over zijn uiterlijk; **2** mikpunt[h] van spotternij; **3** vreten[h]

¹scold [skoold] *vb (with at)* schelden (op)

²scold [skoold] *vb* uitvaren tegen: ~ *s.o. for sth.* iem om iets berispen

scolding [skoolding] standje[h], uitbrander

scone [skon] scone *(small, solid cake)*

¹scoop [skoe:p] *n* **1** schep, lepel, bak: *three ~s of ice cream* drie scheppen ijs; **2** primeur *(in newspaper)*, sensationeel nieuwtje[h]

²scoop [skoe:p] *vb* **1** scheppen, lepelen: ~ *out* opscheppen; ~ *up* opscheppen *(with hands, spoon)*; **2** uithollen, (uit)graven; **3** binnenhalen, grijpen *(money)*, in de wacht slepen

scoot [skoe:t] rennen, vliegen: *is that the time? I'd better* ~ is het al zo laat? Ik moet rennen

scooter [skoe:tə] **1** autoped; **2** scooter

scope [skoop] **1** bereik[h], gebied[h], omvang: *that is beyond* (of: *outside) the* ~ *of this book* dat valt buiten het bestek van dit boek; **2** ruimte, armslag, gelegenheid: *this job gives you* ~ *for your abilities* deze baan geeft je de kans je talenten te ontplooien

¹scorch [sko:tsj] *vb* **1** (ver)schroeien, (ver)zengen, verbranden; **2** verdorren

²scorch [sko:tsj] *vb* razendsnel rijden, vliegen, scheuren

scorcher [skɔ:tsjə] **1** snikhete dag; **2** scherpe kritiek, scherpe uithaal; **3** snelheidsduivel

scorching [skɔ:tsjing] **1** verschroeiend, verzengend: *a ~ summer afternoon* op een snikhete zomermiddag; **2** vernietigend, bijtend

¹score [sko:] *n* **1** stand, puntentotaalʰ, score: *level the ~* gelijkmaken; **2** (doel)puntʰ *(also fig)*, rake opmerking, succesʰ: *(fig) ~ off one's opponent* een punt scoren tegen zijn tegenstander; **3** getrokken lijn, kerf, kras, striem, schram, lijn; **4** reden, grond: *on the ~ of* vanwege; **5** grief: *pay off* (of: *settle*) *old ~s* een oude rekening vereffenen; **6** onderwerpʰ, themaʰ, puntʰ: *on that ~* wat dat betreft; **7** *(mus)* partituur, *(by extension)* muziek *(for musical etc): know the ~* weten hoe de zaken er voorstaan

²score [sko:] *vb* **1** scoren, (doel)punt maken, puntentotaal halen *(eg in test);* **2** de score noteren; **3** succes hebben; **4** geluk hebben ‖ *~ off s.o.* iem aftroeven

³score [sko:] *vb* **1** lijn(en) trekken, (in)kerven, schrammen: *~ out* (of: *through*) doorstrepen; **2** scoren, maken *(point); (fig)* behalen, boeken *(success),* winnen; **3** tellen voor, waard zijn *(of point, run);* **4** toekennen *(points),* geven; **5** een score halen van *(eg in test);* **6** fel bekritiseren, hekelen

scorer [skɔ:rə] **1** scoreteller; **2** (doel)puntenmaker

¹scorn [sko:n] *n* (voorwerpʰ van) minachting, geringschatting: *pour ~ on* verachten

²scorn [sko:n] *vb* **1** minachten, verachten; **2** versmaden, beneden zich achten

scornful [skɔ:nfoel] minachtend: *~ of sth.* met minachting voor iets

scorpion [skɔ:piən] schorpioen

Scot [skot] Schot

scotch [skotsj] **1** een eind maken aan, ontzenuwen *(theory),* de kop indrukken *(rumour);* **2** verijdelen *(plan)*

¹Scotch [skotsj] *adj* Schots: *~ whisky* Schotse whisky; *~ broth* Schotse maaltijdsoep

²Scotch [skotsj] *n* **1** Schotse whisky; **2** de Schotten

scot-free 1 ongedeerd; **2** ongestraft

Scotland [skotlənd] Schotland

Scotland Yard Scotland Yard, opsporingsdienst

Scots [skots] Schots

Scotsman [skotsmən] Schot

Scotswoman Schotse

¹Scottish [skottisj] *adj* Schots

²Scottish [skottisj] *n* de Schotten

scoundrel [skaundrəl] schoft

¹scour [skauə] *vb* **1** (door)spoelen, uitspoelen; **2** (with *out*) uitschuren, uithollen; **3** doorkruisen; **4** afzoeken, doorzoeken, afstropen: *~ the shops for a CD* de winkels aflopen voor een cd

²scour [skauə] *vb* schuren, schrobben

³scour [skauə] *vb* rennen: *~ about after* (of: *for*) *sth.*

rondrennen op zoek naar iets

¹scourge [skɔ:dzj] *n* gesel

²scourge [skɔ:dzj] *vb* **1** geselen; **2** teisteren: *for seven years the country was ~d by war* zeven jaar lang werd het land door oorlog geteisterd

¹scout [skaut] *n* **1** verkenner; **2** talentenjager, scout *(in the world of football, film);* **3** verkenner, padvinder, gids

²scout [skaut] *vb* **1** zoeken: *~ (about, around) for sth.* naar iets op zoek zijn; **2** terrein verkennen

³scout [skaut] *vb* **1** verkennen; **2** minachtend afwijzen: *every offer of help was ~ed* elk aanbod om te helpen werd met minachting van de hand gewezen

scoutmaster hopman

¹scowl [skaul] *vb* (with *at*) het voorhoofd fronsen (tegen), stuurs kijken (naar)

²scowl [skaul] *n* norse blik

¹scrabble [skræbl] *vb* graaien, grabbelen, scharrelen: *~ about for sth.* naar iets graaien

²scrabble [skræbl] *n* gegraaiʰ

scrag [skræg] **1** hals; **2** halsstukʰ

scram [skræm]: *~!* maak dat je wegkomt!

¹scramble [skræmbl] *vb* **1** klauteren, klimmen; **2** (with *for*) vechten (om), zich verdringen; **3** zich haasten: *~ to one's feet* overeind krabbelen

²scramble [skræmbl] *vb* **1** door elkaar gooien, in de war brengen; **2** roeren *(egg);* **3** afraffelen; **4** vervormen *(to encode radio or telephone message),* verdraaien

³scramble [skræmbl] *n* **1** klauterpartij: *it was a bit of a ~ to reach the top* het was een hele toer om de top te bereiken; **2** gedrangʰ, gevechtʰ; **3** motorcross

¹scrap [skræp] *n* **1** stukjeʰ, beetjeʰ, fragmentʰ: *there's not a ~ of truth in what they've told you* er is niets waar van wat ze je verteld hebben; **2** knipselʰ; **3** vechtpartij(tjeʰ), ruzie; **4** afvalʰ, schrootʰ; **5** *~s* restjes

²scrap [skræp] *vb* ruziën, bakkeleien

³scrap [skræp] *vb* **1** afdanken, dumpen, laten varen *(ideas, plans);* **2** slopen, tot schroot verwerken

scrapbook plakboekʰ

¹scrape [skreep] *vb* **1** schuren, strijken; krassen: *the sound of chairs scraping on a tiled floor* het geluid van stoelen die over een tegelvloer schrapen; **2** schrapen, zagen *(eg on violin);* **3** met weinig rondkomen, sober leven; **4** het op het kantje af halen *(also examination): ~ through* in maar net een voldoende halen voor; *~ along on money from friends* het uit weten te zingen met geld van vrienden

²scrape [skreep] *vb* **1** (af)schrapen, (af)krabben, uitschrapen; **2** schaven *(eg knee): ~ the paintwork* de verf beschadigen; *~ together* (of: *up*) bij elkaar schrapen *(money)*

³scrape [skreep] *n* **1** geschraapʰ, geschuurʰ; **2** gekrasʰ, kras; **3** schaafwond; **4** netelige situatie: *get into ~s* in moeilijkheden verzeild raken

scrap heap vuilnisbelt, schroothoop: *(fig) throw s.o. (sth.) on the ~* iem (iets) afdanken

scrap iron schrootʰ, oud ijzerʰ

scrappy [skræpie] fragmentarisch

¹scratch [skrætsj] *vb* krassen, (zich) krabben

²scratch [skrætsj] *vb* **1** (zich) schrammen; **2** krabbelen *(letter);* **3** schrappen, doorhalen; **4** terugtrekken; **5** (with *together, up*) bijeenschrapen *(money; information)*

³scratch [skrætsj] *vb* scharrelen, wroeten ‖ ~ *along* het hoofd boven water weten te houden

⁴scratch [skrætsj] *n* **1** krasjeʰ, schram: *without a* ~ ongedeerd; **2** startstreep: *start from* ~: *a) (fig)* bij het begin beginnen; *b)* met niets beginnen; *up to* ~ in vorm, op het vereiste niveau; *come up to* ~ het halen

⁵scratch [skrætsj] *adj* samengeraapt: *a* ~ *meal* een restjesmaaltijd

scratch card kraslotʰ

scratch paper kladpapierʰ

¹scrawl [skro:l] *vb* krabbelen, slordig schrijven

²scrawl [skro:l] *n* **1** krabbeltjeʰ; **2** poot, onbeholpen handschriftʰ

scrawny [skro:nie] broodmager

¹scream [skrie:m] *vb* gillen, schreeuwen: ~ *for water* om water schreeuwen; ~ *with laughter* gieren van het lachen

²scream [skrie:m] *vb* tieren, razen, tekeergaan

³scream [skrie:m] *n* **1** gil, krijs; **2** giller, dolkomisch iets (iem): *do you know Ernest? He's a* ~ ken jij Ernest? Je lacht je gek

¹screech [skrie:tsj] *vb* knarsen, kraken, piepen

²screech [skrie:tsj] *vb* gillen, gieren

³screech [skrie:tsj] *n* gil, krijs, schreeuw: *a* ~ *of brakes* gierende remmen

¹screen [skrie:n] *n* **1** schermʰ, koorhekʰ *(in church);* **2** beschutting, bescherming, afscherming *(of electrical equipment etc),* muur: *under* ~ *of night* onder dekking van de nacht; **3** doekʰ, projectieschermʰ, beeldschermʰ; **4** het witte doek, de film; **5** hor, venstergaasʰ; **6** zeef, roosterʰ, *(fig)* selectie(procedure)

²screen [skrie:n] *vb* **1** afschermen *(also from radiation),* afschutten, beschermen, dekken *(soldier):* ~ *off one corner of the room* een hoek van de kamer afschermen; **2** beschermen, de hand boven het hoofd houden; **3** doorlichten, op geschiktheid testen, screenen; **4** vertonen, projecteren: *the feature film will be* ~*ed at 8.25* de hoofdfilm wordt om 8.25 uur vertoond; **5** verfilmen

screening [skrie:ning] **1** filmvertoning; **2** doorlichting; **3** afscherming

screenplay scenarioʰ, script

screen print zeefdruk

¹screw [skroe:] *n* **1** schroef; **2** propeller, scheepsschroef; **3** vrek; **4** cipier

²screw [skroe:] *vb* **1** schroeven, aandraaien: *I could* ~ *his neck* ik zou hem zijn nek wel kunnen omdraaien; ~ *down* vastschroeven; ~ *on* vastschroeven; **2** verfrommelen; **3** afzetten: *he's so stupid, no wonder he gets* ~*ed all the time* hij is zo stom, geen wonder dat hij iedere keer wordt afgezet; **4** belazeren; **5** *(vulg)* neuken: ~ *you!* val dood!

³screw [skroe:] *vb* zich spiraalsgewijs bewegen

screwball 1 idioot; **2** *(baseball)* omgekeerde curve

screwdriver schroevendraaier

screwed [skroe:d] *(inf)* dronken

screwed-up 1 verpest; **2** verknipt, opgefokt

screw out of afpersen, uitzuigen: *screw money out of s.o.* iem geld afhandig maken; *screw s.o. out of sth.* zorgen dat iem iets niet krijgt

screw up 1 verwringen, verdraaien, verfrommelen: *she screwed up her eyes* zij kneep haar ogen dicht; **2** verzieken, verknoeien; **3** bij elkaar rapen, verzamelen *(courage);* **4** nerveus maken

screwy [skroe:ie] excentriek, zonderling

¹scribble [skribl] *vb* krabbelen

²scribble [skribl] *n* **1** gekrabbelʰ; **2** briefjeʰ, kladjeʰ

scribe [skrajb] **1** schrijver, klerk; **2** schriftgeleerde

scrimmage [skrimmidzj] schermutseling

¹scrimp [skrimp] *vb* zich bekrimpen: ~ *and save* heel zuinig aan doen

²scrimp [skrimp] *vb* beknibbelen op

script [skript] **1** geschriftʰ; **2** script, manuscriptʰ, draaiboekʰ, tekst; **3** schrijfletters, handschriftʰ

scripture [skriptsjə] heilig geschriftʰ: *the (Holy) Scripture* de Heilige Schrift

scriptwriter scenarioschrijver

scroll [skrool] **1** rol, perkamentrol, geschriftʰ; **2** krul

scrolling [skrooling] het (ver)rollen *(moving text on computer screen)*

¹scrounge [skraundzj] *vb* schooien, bietsen

²scrounge [skraundzj] *vb* **1** in de wacht slepen, achteroverdrukken; **2** bietsen

scrounger [skraundzjə] klaploper, bietser, profiteur

¹scrub [skrub] *n* **1** met struikgewas bedekt gebiedʰ; **2** struikgewasʰ, kreupelhoutʰ; **3** het boenen

²scrub [skrub] *vb* een boender gebruiken, boenen

³scrub [skrub] *vb* **1** schrobben, boenen; **2** (also with *out*) schrappen, afgelasten, vergeten

scrubby [skrubbie] **1** miezerig; **2** met struikgewas bedekt

scruff [skruf] nekvelʰ: *take by the* ~ *of the neck* bij het nekvel grijpen

scruffy [skruffie] smerig, vuil, slordig

¹scruple [skroe:pl] *n* scrupule, gewetensbezwaarʰ: *make no* ~ *about doing sth.* er geen been in zien om iets te doen

²scruple [skroe:pl] *vb* aarzelen

scrupulous [skroe:pjoeləs] nauwgezet: ~*ly clean* kraakhelder

scrutinize [skroe:tinnajz] in detail onderzoeken, nauwkeurig bekijken

scrutiny [skroe:tinnie] **1** nauwkeurig toezichtʰ; **2** kritische blik

scud [skud] voortscheren, ijlen, snellen: *the children were* ~*ding downhill on their sledges* de kinderen raasden van de heuvel af op hun sleeën

¹scuff [skuf] *vb* schuren, slepen

²scuff [skuf] *vb* **1** sloffen; **2** versleten zijn *(of shoe, floor)*

³**scuff** [skuf] *n* slijtplek

¹**scuffle** [sk<u>u</u>fl] *n* knokpartij, schermutseling

²**scuffle** [sk<u>u</u>fl] *vb* bakkeleien, knokken

¹**scull** [skul] *n* **1** korte (roei)riem; **2** sculler, éénpersoonsroeiboot met twee korte riemen

²**scull** [skul] *vb* roeien

sculptor [sk<u>u</u>lptə] beeldhouwer

¹**sculpture** [sk<u>u</u>lptsjə] *n* beeldhouwwerkʰ; plastiekʰ; beeldhouwkunst

²**sculpture** [sk<u>u</u>lptsjə] *vb* **1** beeldhouwen; **2** met sculptuur versieren, bewerken

scum [skum] **1** schuimʰ *(on water);* **2** uitschotʰ *(also fig),* afvalʰ: *the ~ of humanity* (of: *the earth)* het schorem, uitschot

¹**scupper** [sk<u>u</u>ppə] *vb* **1** tot zinken brengen; **2** (overvallen en) in de pan hakken, afmaken: *be ~ed* eraan gaan

²**scupper** [sk<u>u</u>ppə] *n* spuigatʰ

scurf [skə:f] roos *(of skin)*

scurrility [skurr<u>i</u>llittie] **1** grofheid; **2** grove taal

scurrilous [sk<u>u</u>rrilləs] grof

scurry [sk<u>u</u>rrie] dribbelen, zich haasten: *~ for shelter* haastig een onderdak zoeken

¹**scurvy** [sk<u>ə:</u>vie] *n* scheurbuik

²**scurvy** [sk<u>ə:</u>vie] *adj* gemeen

¹**scuttle** [sk<u>u</u>tl] *n* **1** luik(gat)ʰ, ventilatieopening; **2** kolenbak; **3** overhaaste vlucht

²**scuttle** [sk<u>u</u>tl] *vb* zich wegscheren: *~ off* (of: *away)* zich uit de voeten maken

³**scuttle** [sk<u>u</u>tl] *vb* doen zinken *(by making holes)*

¹**scythe** [sajð] *n* zeis

²**scythe** [sajð] *vb* (af)maaien *(also fig)*

SE *southeast* Z.O., zuidoost

sea [sie:] **1** zee, oceaan, *(fig)* massa, overvloed: *put (out) to ~* uitvaren; *at ~* op zee; *the seven ~s* de zeven (wereld)zeeën; **2** zeegolf, sterke golfslag: *heavy ~* zware zee; **3** kust, strandʰ: *be (all) at ~: a)* verbijsterd zijn; *b)* geen notie hebben

seabed zeebedding, zeebodem

seabird zeevogel

seaborne over zee (vervoerd, aangevoerd): *~ supplies* bevoorrading overzee

sea breeze 1 zeebries; **2** wind op zee

sea change ommekeer

sea dog zeebonk, zeerob

seafaring zeevarend

seafood eetbare zeevis en schaal- en schelpdieren

seafront strandboulevard, zeekant *(of town)*

seagoing zeevarend

seagull zeemeeuw

¹**seal** [sie:l] *n* **1** zegelʰ, stempelʰ *(also fig),* lakzegelʰ, (plak)zegel, *(fig)* kenmerkʰ, *(fig)* bezegeling: *set the ~ on: a)* bezegelen; *b) (also fig)* afsluiten; *under ~ of secrecy* onder het zegel van geheimhouding; **2** dichting, dichtingsmateriaalʰ, (luchtdichte, waterdichte) afsluiting, stankafsluiting; **3** (zee)rob, zeehond, zeeleeuw

²**seal** [sie:l] *vb* **1** zegelen, verzegelen *(verdict, orders etc);* *(fig)* opsluiten; **2** dichten, verzegelen, (wa-

ter)dicht maken, dichtschroeien *(meat): my lips are ~ed* ik zal er niets over zeggen; *~ off an area* een gebied afgrendelen; **3** bezegelen, bevestigen: *~ s.o.'s doom* (of: *fate)* iemands (nood)lot bezegelen

sea lane vaarroute

sea legs zeebenen: *get* (of: *find) one's ~* zeebenen krijgen

sea level zeeniveauʰ, zeespiegel

sealing wax zegelwas

sea lion zeeleeuw

seal ring zegelring

sealskin robbenvelʰ, sealskin

seam [sie:m] **1** naad, voeg; **2** scheurtjeʰ *(in metal);* **3** (steenkool)laag || *burst at the ~s* tot barstens toe vol zitten

seaman [s<u>ie:</u>mən] zeeman, matroos

seamanship [s<u>ie:</u>mənsjip] zeemanschapʰ, zeevaartkunde

sea mile zeemijl *(international: 1,852 metres, British: 1,853.18 metres)*

seamless [s<u>ie:</u>mləs] naadloos

seamstress [s<u>e</u>mstris] naaister

seamy [s<u>ie:</u>mie] **1** met een naad; **2** minder mooi: *the ~ side of life* de zelfkant van het leven

seaport zeehaven

sear [siə] **1** schroeien, verschroeien, (dicht)branden; **2** (doen) verdorren, opdrogen, uitdrogen, *(fig)* verharden

¹**search** [sə:tsj] *vb* (with *for)* grondig zoeken (naar), speuren

²**search** [sə:tsj] *vb* grondig onderzoeken, fouilleren, naspeuren || *~ me!* weet ik veel!

³**search** [sə:tsj] *n* grondig onderzoekʰ, opsporing, speurwerkʰ, *(comp)* zoekbewerking, zoekfunctie: *in ~ of* op zoek naar

search engine zoekmachine *(on the Internet)*

searching [s<u>ə:</u>tsjing] **1** onderzoekend *(glance);* **2** grondig

searchlight zoeklichtʰ, schijnwerper

search warrant bevel(schrift)ʰ tot huiszoeking

seascape zeegezichtʰ *(painting)*

seashore zeekust

seasick zeeziek

seaside kust, zee(kust)

¹**season** [s<u>ie:</u>zən] *n* **1** seizoenʰ, *(fig)* jaarʰ: *rainy ~* regentijd; **2** geschikte tijd, seizoenʰ, jachtseizoenʰ, vakantieperiode: *cherries are in ~* het is kersentijd; *a word in ~* een woord op het passende moment, een gepast woord; *in and out of ~* te pas en te onpas; **3** feesttijd, kerst- en nieuwjaarstijd: *the ~ of good cheer* de gezellige kerst- en nieuwjaarstijd

²**season** [s<u>ie:</u>zən] *vb* **1** kruiden *(also fig);* **2** (ge)wennen, harden: *~ed troops* doorgewinterde troepen; **3** laten liggen *(wood)*

seasonable [s<u>ie:</u>zənəbl] **1** passend bij het seizoen; **2** tijdig; **3** passend

seasonal [s<u>ie:</u>zənəl] volgens het seizoen, seizoengevoelig *(com): ~ employment* seizoenarbeid

seasoning [s<u>ie:</u>zəning] **1** het kruiden; **2** specerij

season ticket seizoenkaart, abonnement^h

¹**seat** [si:t] *n* 1 (zit)plaats, stoel: *the back ~ of a car* de achterbank van een auto; *have (of: take) a ~* neem plaats; 2 zitting *(of chair);* wc-bril; 3 zitvlak^h; 4 zetel *(fig),* centrum^h, haard *(of disease, fire): a ~ of learning* een zetel van wetenschap; 5 landgoed^h; 6 zetel, lidmaatschap^h: *have a ~ on a board* zitting hebben in een commissie; 7 kiesdistrict^h

²**seat** [si:t] *vb* zetten, doen zitten, zetelen: *be ~ed* ga zitten; *be deeply ~ed* diep ingeworteld zijn *(of feeling, illness etc)*

seat belt veiligheidsgordel

seating [si:tiŋ] 1 plaatsing, het geven ve plaats; 2 plaatsruimte, zitplaatsen

seawall zeedijk

seaward [si:wəd] zeewaarts

seawater zeewater^h

seaweed 1 zeewier^h; 2 zeegras^h

seaworthy zeewaardig

sec [sek] *second* seconde: *just a ~* een ogenblikje

secateurs [sekətə:z] snoeischaar, tuinschaar

secession [sisesjən] afscheiding, het afscheiden

secluded [siklo̱e:did] afgezonderd, teruggetrokken, stil: *a ~ life* een teruggetrokken leven; *a ~ house* een afgelegen huis

seclusion [siklo̱e:zjən] afzondering, eenzaamheid, rust

¹**second** [sekənd] *num* tweede, ander(e), *(fig)* tweederangs, minderwaardig: *~ class* tweede klas *(also of mail); ~ nature* tweede natuur; *in the ~ place* ten tweede, bovendien; *he was ~ to none* hij was van niemand de mindere; *every ~ day* om de andere dag

²**second** [sekənd] *adv* 1 op één na: *~ best* op één na de beste; 2 ten tweede

³**second** [sekənd] *n* 1 seconde, *(fig)* momentje^h, ogenblikje^h: *I'll be back in a ~* ik ben zo terug; 2 secondant, getuige *(at boxing, duel);* 3 *~s* tweede kwaliteitsgoederen, tweede keus (klas); 4 *~s* tweede keer *(at meal): who would like ~s?* wie wil er nog?

⁴**second** [sekənd] *vb* 1 steunen, bijstaan, meewerken; 2 ondersteunen, goedkeuren, bijvallen *(proposal etc)*

⁵**second** [sikkənd] *vb* tijdelijk overplaatsen, detacheren

secondary [sekəndərie] 1 secundair, bijkomend, bijkomstig, ondergeschikt: *~ to* ondergeschikt aan; 2 secundair, tweederangs: *~ to* inferieur aan; 3 *(school)* secundair, middelbaar: *~ education* middelbaar onderwijs; *~ school* middelbare school; *~ modern (school), (inf) ~ mod* middelbare school, *(roughly)* mavo; *~ technical school* middelbare technische school

second-class 1 tweedeklas-: *~ mail* tweedeklaspost; 2 tweederangs, inferieur, minderwaardig

second hand secondewijzer

second-hand 1 tweedehands: *a ~ car* een tweedehands auto; 2 uit de tweede hand: *a ~ report* een verslag uit de tweede hand

secondly [sekəndlie] ten tweede, op de tweede plaats

second-rate tweederangs, inferieur, middelmatig

secrecy [si:krəsie] geheimhouding, geheimzinnigheid

¹**secret** [si:krət] *adj* 1 geheim, verborgen, vertrouwelijk: *a ~ admirer* een stille aanbidder; *~ ballot* geheime stemming; *~ service* geheime dienst; *keep sth. ~ from s.o.* iets voor iem geheim houden; 2 gesloten, discreet; 3 verborgen, afgezonderd

²**secret** [si:krət] *n* geheim^h, mysterie^h, sleutel: *in ~* in het geheim; *let s.o. into a ~* iem in een geheim inwijden

secretarial [sekrətɛəriəl] ve secretaresse, secretariaats-

secretariat [sekrətɛəriət] secretariaat^h

secretary [sekrətərie] 1 secretaresse; 2 secretaris, secretaris-generaal *(of department);* 3 *Secretary* minister; *Secretary of State* Minister

secretary-general secretaris-generaal

secrete [sikri:t] 1 verbergen, verstoppen, wegstoppen: *~ sth. about one's person* iets op zijn lichaam verstoppen; 2 afscheiden *(of organs, glands)*

secretion [sikri:sjən] afscheiding(sproduct^h)

secretive [si:krətiv] geheimzinnig, gesloten, gereserveerd

sect [sekt] sekte, geloofsgemeenschap

¹**sectarian** [sektɛəriən] *adj* sekte-: *a ~ killing* een sektemoord

²**sectarian** [sektɛəriən] *n* sektariër, lid van een sekte

section [seksjən] 1 sectie, (onder)deel^h, afdeling, lid^h, stuk^h, segment^h, partje^h, wijk, district^h, stadsdeel^h, landsdeel^h, baanvak^h *(of railway): all ~s of the population* alle lagen van de bevolking; 2 groep *(within society);* 3 (onder)afdeling, paragraaf, lid^h, sectie, katern^h *(of newspaper, book);* 4 (dwars)doorsnede *(also in maths),* profiel^h; 5 een vierkante mijl *(640 acres);* 6 (chirurgische) snee, incisie, (in)snijding, sectie: *c(a)esarean ~* keizersnede; *in ~* in profiel

sectional [seksjənəl] 1 uitneembaar, demonteerbaar: *~ furniture* aanbouwmeubilair; 2 sectioneel, mbt een bepaalde bevolkingsgroep: *~ interests* (tegenstrijdige) groepsbelangen

sector [sektə] sector, (bedrijfs)tak, afdeling, terrein^h, branche

secular [sekjoelə] 1 wereldlijk, niet-kerkelijk: *~ music* wereldlijke muziek; 2 vrijzinnig, niet aan vaste leerstellingen gebonden

secularize [sekjoelərajz] verwereldlijken

¹**secure** [sikjo̱eə] *adj* 1 veilig, beschut, beveiligd: *~ against (of: from)* veilig voor; 2 veilig, stevig, zeker: *a ~ method of payment* een veilige manier van betalen; 3 vol vertrouwen

²**secure** [sikjo̱eə] *vb* 1 beveiligen, in veiligheid brengen; 2 bemachtigen, zorgen voor: *~ the biggest number of orders* het grootste aantal orders in de wacht slepen; 3 stevig vastmaken, vastleggen, afsluiten

security [sikjoeǝrittie] **1** veiligheid(sgevoel^h); **2** veiligheidsvoorziening, verzekering; **3** beveiliging, (openbare) veiligheid: *tight ~ is in force* er zijn strenge veiligheidsmaatregelen getroffen; **4** obligatie(certificaat^h), effect^h, aandeel^h; **5** borg *(pers): be s.o.'s ~* zich voor iem borg stellen; **6** (waar)borg, onderpand^h: *give as (a) ~ in onderpand geven*
security check veiligheidscontrole
Security Council Veiligheidsraad *(of United Nations)*
security forces politietroepen
¹sedate [siddeet] *adj* bezadigd, onverstoorbaar, kalm
²sedate [siddeet] *vb* kalmeren, tot rust brengen, een kalmerend middel toedienen aan
¹sedative [seddǝtiv] *adj* kalmerend, pijnstillend
²sedative [seddǝtiv] *n* kalmerend middel^h
sedentary [seddǝntǝrie] (stil)zittend
sediment [seddimmǝnt] sediment^h, neerslag, bezinksel^h, afzetting(smateriaal^h) *(by water, wind etc)*
sedimentation [seddimmǝnteesjǝn] het neerslaan, afzetting, sedimentatie
sedition [siddisjǝn] ongehoorzaamheid, ordeverstoring
seditious [siddisjǝs] opruiend, oproerig, opstandig
seduce [sidjoe:s] verleiden *(also fig)*, overhalen: *~ s.o. into sth.* iem tot iets overhalen
seducer [sidjoe:sǝ] verleider
seduction [sidduksjǝn] verleiding(spoging)
seductive [sidduktiv] verleidelijk
¹see [sie:] *n* **1** (aarts)bisdom^h; **2** (aarts)bisschopszetel: *the Holy See* de Heilige Stoel
²see *vb* **1** zien, kijken (naar), aankijken tegen: *worth ~ing* de moeite waard, opmerkelijk; *I cannot ~ him doing it* ik zie het hem nog niet doen; *we shall ~* we zullen wel zien, wie weet; *~ through s.o. (sth.)* iem (iets) doorhebben; **2** zien, (het) begrijpen, (het) inzien: *I don't ~ the fun of doing that* ik zie daar de lol niet van in; *as far as I can ~* volgens mij; *as I ~ it* volgens mij; **3** toezien (op), opletten, ervoor zorgen, zorgen voor: *~ to it that* ervoor zorgen dat
³see *vb* nadenken, bekijken, zien: *let me ~* wacht eens, even denken; *we will ~ about that* dat zullen we nog wel (eens) zien
⁴see *vb* **1** voor zich zien, zich voorstellen; **2** lezen *(newspaper etc)*, zien: *have you ~n today's papers?* heb je de kranten van vandaag gezien?; **3** tegenkomen, ontmoeten: *~ you (later)!, (I'll) be ~ing you!* tot ziens!, tot kijk!; *~ a lot of s.o.* iem vaak zien; **4** ontvangen, spreken met: *Mrs Richards can ~ you now* Mevr. Richards kan u nu even ontvangen; *can I ~ you for a minute?* kan ik u even spreken?; **5** bezoeken, opzoeken, langs gaan bij: *~ the town* de stad bezichtigen; *~ over (of: round) a house* een huis bezichtigen; **6** raadplegen, bezoeken: *~ a doctor* een arts raadplegen; **7** meemaken, ervaren, getuige zijn van: *have ~n better days* betere tijden gekend hebben; **8** begeleiden, (weg)brengen: *~ a girl home* een meisje naar huis brengen; *~ s.o. out* iem

uitlaten; *I'll ~ you through* ik help je er wel doorheen; *~ sth. out (of: through)* iets tot het einde volhouden
¹seed [sie:d] *n* **1** zaad(je)^h, kiem *(fig)*, zaad^h, begin^h: *go (of: run) to ~* uitbloeien, doorschieten, *(fig)* verlopen, aftakelen; **2** korreltje^h, bolletje^h; **3** *(sport, esp tennis)* geplaatste speler
²seed [sie:d] *vb* **1** zaaien, zaad uitstrooien; **2** bezaaien *(also fig)*, bestrooien; **3** *(sport, esp tennis)* plaatsen
³seed [sie:d] *vb* zaad vormen, uitbloeien, doorschieten
seedbed **1** zaaibed^h; **2** *(fig)* voedingsbodem
seedless [sie:dlǝs] zonder zaad
seedling [sie:dling] zaailing
seedsman [sie:dzmǝn] zaadhandelaar
seedy [sie:die] **1** slonzig, verwaarloosd, vervallen; **2** niet lekker, een beetje ziek, slap
seeing [sie:ing] aangezien, in aanmerking genomen dat: *~ (that) there is nothing I can do* aangezien ik niets kan doen
¹seek [sie:k] *vb* (with *after, for)* zoeken (naar): *~ for a solution* een oplossing zoeken
²seek [sie:k] *vb* **1** nastreven, proberen te bereiken, zoeken; **2** vragen, wensen, verlangen; **3** opzoeken: *~ s.o. out* naar iem toekomen, iem opzoeken; **4** proberen (te), trachten (te): *~ to escape* proberen te ontsnappen
seem [sie:m] (toe)schijnen, lijken, eruitzien: *he ~s (to be) the leader* hij schijnt de leider te zijn; *he ~s to have done it* het ziet ernaar uit dat hij het gedaan heeft; *it would ~ to me that* het lijkt mij dat; *he is not satisfied, it would ~* hij is niet tevreden, naar het schijnt; *it ~s to me* mij dunkt
seeming [sie:ming] schijnbaar, ogenschijnlijk, onoprecht: *in ~ friendship* onder schijn van vriendschap
seep [sie:p] (weg)sijpelen, lekken, doorsijpelen, *(fig)* doordringen: *the water ~s into the ground* het water sijpelt weg in de grond
seer [siǝ] **1** ziener, profeet; **2** helderziende
¹seesaw [sie:so:] *n* wip
²seesaw [sie:so:] *vb* **1** (op en neer) wippen, op en neer wippen, op de wip spelen; **2** schommelen, zigzaggen, veranderlijk zijn: *~ing prices* schommelende prijzen
seethe [sie:ð] koken, zieden, kolken: *he was seething with rage* hij was witheet van woede
segment [segmǝnt] deel^h, segment^h, part(je)^h
segregate [sjegriegeet] afzonderen, scheiden, rassenscheiding toepassen op
segregation [segrigeesjǝn] afzondering, scheiding, rassenscheiding, apartheid
seismic [sajzmik] seismisch, aardbevings-
seismograph [sajzmǝgra:f] seismograaf
seize [sie:z] **1** grijpen, pakken, nemen: *~ the occasion with both hands* de kans met beide handen aangrijpen; *~d with fear* door angst bevangen; **2** in beslag nemen, afnemen; **3** bevatten, begrijpen, inzien: *she never seemed to ~ the point* ze scheen he-

seize **up** vastlopen *(of machine)*, blijven hangen, *(fig also)* blijven steken, niet verder kunnen

s**ei**ze (up)on aangrijpen *(chance, cause)*

s**ei**zure [si:zjə] **1** confiscatie, inbeslagneming, beslaglegging; **2** aanval

s**e**ldom [seldəm] zelden, haast nooit: ~ *if ever*, ~ *or never* zelden of nooit

¹s**e**lect [sillekt] *vb* een keuze maken

²s**e**lect [sillekt] *vb* (uit)kiezen, uitzoeken, selecteren

³s**e**lect [sillekt] *adj* **1** uitgezocht, zorgvuldig gekozen, geselecteerd; **2** exclusief

s**e**lection [silleksjən] keuze, selectie, verzameling

s**e**lective [sillektiv] selectief, uitkiezend

s**e**lector [sillektə] **1** lid[h] van selectiecommissie, benoemingscommissie; **2** kiezer, keuzeschakelaar

s**e**lf [self] *(selves)* **1** (het) zelf, het eigen wezen, het ik; **2** persoonlijkheid, karakter[h]: *he is still not quite his old* ~ hij is nog steeds niet helemaal de oude; **3** de eigen persoon, zichzelf, het eigenbelang: *he never thinks of anything but* ~ hij denkt altijd alleen maar aan zichzelf

-**self** [self] *(-selves)* **1** -zelf: *oneself* zichzelf; **2** *(with emphasis)* zelf: *I did it myself* ik heb het zelf gedaan

self-addr**e**ssed aan zichzelf geadresseerd: ~ *envelope* antwoordenvelop

self-app**oi**nted opgedrongen, zichzelf ongevraagd opwerpend (als): *a* ~ *critic* iem die zich een oordeel aanmatigt

self-ass**u**red zelfverzekerd, vol zelfvertrouwen

self-c**a**tering zelf voor eten zorgend, maaltijden niet inbegrepen: ~ *flat* flat, appartement *(where one has to cook one's own meals)*

self-c**e**ntred egocentrisch, zelfzuchtig

self-c**o**nfidence zelfvertrouwen[h], zelfverzekerdheid

self-c**o**nscious **1** bewust, zich van zichzelf bewust; **2** verlegen, niet op zijn gemak

self-cont**ai**ned **1** onafhankelijk; **2** vrij, met eigen keuken en badkamer

self-contrad**i**ctory tegenstrijdig

self-def**ea**ting zichzelf hinderend, zijn doel voorbijstrevend

self-def**e**nce zelfverdediging: *in* ~ uit zelfverdediging

self-den**i**al zelfopoffering, zelfverloochening

self-destr**u**ct [selfdistrukt] zichzelf vernietigen

self-determin**a**tion zelfbeschikking(srecht[h])

self-**e**ducated autodidactisch: *a* ~ *man* een autodidact

self-empl**o**yed zelfstandig, met een eigen onderneming, eigen baas

self-est**ee**m gevoel[h] van eigenwaarde, trots

self-**e**vident vanzelfsprekend

self-expl**a**natory duidelijk, onmiskenbaar, wat voor zichzelf spreekt

self-fulf**i**lling zichzelf vervullend: *a* ~ *prophecy* een zichzelf vervullende voorspelling

self-imp**o**rtance gewichtigheid, eigendunk

self-imp**o**sed (aan) zichzelf opgelegd

s**e**lfish [selfisj] zelfzuchtig, egoïstisch

s**e**lfless [selfləs] onbaatzuchtig, onzelfzuchtig

self-m**a**de **1** zelfgemaakt; **2** opgewerkt, opgeklommen: *a* ~ *man* een man die alles op eigen kracht bereikt heeft

self-r**ai**sing zelfrijzend

self-rel**i**ant onafhankelijk, zelfstandig

self-r**i**ghteous vol eigendunk, intolerant

self-r**i**ghting zichzelf oprichtend *(after capsizing)*

self-s**a**crifice zelfopoffering

s**e**lfsame precies dezelfde (hetzelfde), identiek

self-s**e**rvice zelfbediening: ~ *restaurant* zelfbedieningsrestaurant

self-s**e**rving uit eigenbelang

self-st**y**led zogenaamd, zichzelf noemend: ~ *professor* iem die zich voor professor uitgeeft

self-suff**i**cient onafhankelijk

self-supp**o**rting zelfstandig

self-t**au**ght **1** zelf geleerd, zichzelf aangeleerd; **2** autodidactisch, zichzelf opgeleid

¹s**e**ll [sel] *vb* **1** verkopen, in voorraad hebben, handelen in, verkwanselen: ~ *off* uitverkopen; ~ *at five pounds* voor vijf pond verkopen; **2** aanprijzen: ~ *oneself* zichzelf goed verkopen; **3** overhalen, warm maken voor, aanpraten: *be sold on sth.* ergens helemaal weg van zijn; **4** misleiden, bedriegen, bezwendelen: ~ *s.o. short* iem te kort doen

²s**e**ll [sel] *vb* **1** verkocht worden, verkopen, kosten, in de handel zijn; **2** handel drijven, verkopen || ~ *up* zijn zaak sluiten

³s**e**ll [sel] *n* bedrog[h], verlakkerij, zwendel

s**e**ll-by date uiterste verkoopdatum

s**e**ller [sellə] **1** verkoper; **2** succes[h], artikel[h] dat goed verkoopt

s**e**lling point *(com)* verkoopargument[h], voordeel[h], aanbeveling

s**e**llotape [selləteep] plakband[h]

sell **out 1** door de voorraad heen raken; **2** verkocht worden, uitverkocht raken; **3** zijn aandeel in een zaak verkopen; **4** verraad plegen: ~ *to the enemy* samenwerken met de vijand

s**e**ll-out **1** volle zaal, uitverkochte voorstelling; **2** verraad[h]

s**e**mblance [sembləns] **1** schijn, uiterlijk[h], vorm: *put on a* ~ *of enthusiasm* geestdriftig doen; **2** gelijkenis; **3** afbeelding, beeld[h], kopie: *without a* ~ *of guilt* zonder ook maar een zweem van schuldgevoel

s**e**men [si:mən] sperma[h], zaad[h]

sem**e**ster [simmestə] semester[h] *(university)*

s**e**micircle [semmiesə:kl] **1** halve cirkel; **2** halve kring

semic**i**rcular [semmiesə:kjoelə] halfrond

s**e**micolon [semmiekoolən] puntkomma

semicond**u**ctor [semmiekənduktə] halfgeleider

semi-c**o**nscious [semmiekonsjəs] halfbewust

¹semi-det**a**ched [semmieditætsjt] *adj* halfvrijstaand

²semi-det**a**ched [semmieditætsjt] *n* halfvrijstaand

lemaal niet te begrijpen waar het om ging

huis[h], huis[h] van twee onder een kap

semi-final [semmiefajnl] halve finale

seminar [semminna:] 1 werkgroep, cursus; 2 congres[h]

seminary [semminnərie] seminarie[h], kweekschool voor priesters

semi-precious [semmiepresjəs] halfedel-

senate [sennət] 1 senaat, Amerikaanse Senaat; 2 senaat, universitaire bestuursraad

senator [sennətə] senator, senaatslid[h], lid[h] vd Amerikaanse Senaat

¹send [send] vb (uit)zenden: ~ s.o. after her stuur iem achter haar aan; ~ s.o. off the field iem uit het veld sturen

²send [send] vb bericht sturen, laten weten: I sent to warn her ik heb haar laten waarschuwen

³send [send] vb 1 (ver)sturen, (ver)zenden; 2 sturen, zenden, (doen) overbrengen (by extension), dwingen tot: ~ to bed naar bed sturen; she ~s her love je moet de groeten van haar hebben; ~ ahead vooruit sturen; ~ in: a) inzenden, insturen (for evaluation); b) indienen; 3 teweegbrengen, veroorzaken: the news sent us into deep distress het nieuws bracht diepe droefenis bij ons teweeg; 4 maken, doen worden: this rattle ~s me crazy ik word gek van dat geratel; 5 opwinden, meeslepen: this music really ~s me ik vind die muziek helemaal te gek; ~ packing de laan uit sturen, afschepen

send down 1 naar beneden sturen, doen dalen (prices, temperature); 2 verwijderen (wegens wangedrag) (from university); 3 opsluiten (in prison)

sender [sendə] afzender, verzender: return to ~ retour afzender

send for 1 (schriftelijk) bestellen; 2 (laten) waarschuwen, laten komen: ~ help hulp laten halen

¹send off vb een bestelbon opsturen: ~ for schriftelijk bestellen

²send off vb 1 versturen, op de post doen; 2 op pad sturen, de deur uit laten gaan; 3 wegsturen, (sport) uit het veld sturen

send-off uitgeleide[h], afscheid[h], het uitzwaaien: give s.o. a ~ iem uitzwaaien

send on 1 vooruitsturen, (alvast) doorsturen; 2 doorsturen (mail)

send out 1 weg sturen, eruit sturen; 2 uitstralen, afgeven, uitzenden (signal)

send up 1 opdrijven, omhoogstuwen, doen stijgen: ~ prices de prijzen opdrijven; 2 parodiëren, de draak steken met; 3 opsluiten (in prison)

send-up parodie, persiflage

senile [sie:najl] 1 ouderdoms-; 2 seniel, afgetakeld

senility [sinnillittie] seniliteit

¹senior [sie:niə] adj 1 oud, op leeftijd, bejaard, oudst(e): a ~ citizen een 65-plusser, bejaarde; 2 hooggeplaatst, hoofd-: a ~ position een leidinggevende positie; 3 hoger geplaatst, ouder in dienstjaren; 4 hoogst in rang; 5 laatstejaars; 6 ouderejaars; 7 senior: Jack Jones Senior Jack Jones senior; ~ service marine

²senior [sie:niə] n 1 oudere, iem met meer dienstjaren: she is four years my ~, she is my ~ by four years ze is vier jaar ouder dan ik; 2 oudgediende, senior; 3 laatstejaars; 4 oudere leerling

senior high (school) laatste vier jaar vd middelbare school

seniority [sie:nie-orrittie] 1 (hogere) leeftijd; 2 anciënniteit, aantal dienstjaren, voorrang op grond van dienstjaren (leeftijd): their names were listed in the order of ~ hun namen waren gerangschikt op volgorde van het aantal dienstjaren

senior school middelbare school (for children of 14-17 years old)

sensation [senseesjən] 1 gevoel[h], (zintuiglijke) gewaarwording, sensatie; 2 sensatie, beroering: cause (of: create) a ~ voor grote opschudding zorgen

sensational [senseesjənəl] 1 sensationeel, opzienbarend, te gek, fantastisch; 2 sensatie-, sensatiebelust

¹sense [sens] n 1 bedoeling, strekking; 2 betekenis, zin: in a ~ in zekere zin; 3 (vaag) gevoel[h], begrip[h], (instinctief) besef[h]: ~ of duty plichtsbesef, plichtsgevoel; ~ of humour gevoel voor humor; 4 (zintuiglijk) vermogen[h], zin, zintuig[h]: ~ of smell reuk(zinvermogen); 5 (gezond) verstand[h], benul[h]: there was a lot of ~ in her words er stak heel wat zinnigs in haar woorden; 6 zin, nut[h]: what's the ~? wat heeft het voor zin?; 7 (groeps)mening, (algemene) stemming; 8 ~s positieven, gezond verstand[h]: bring s.o. to his ~s: a) iem tot bezinning brengen; b) iem weer bij bewustzijn brengen; make ~: a) zinnig zijn; b) ergens op slaan, steekhoudend zijn; it just doesn't make ~ het klopt gewoon niet, het slaat gewoon nergens op; make ~ of sth. ergens uit wijs kunnen (worden); talk ~ verstandig praten

²sense [sens] vb 1 (zintuiglijk) waarnemen, gewaar worden; 2 zich (vaag) bewust zijn, voelen; 3 begrijpen, door hebben: at last he was beginning to ~ what the trouble was eindelijk begon hij door te krijgen wat het probleem was

senseless [senslas] 1 bewusteloos; 2 gevoelloos; 3 onzinnig, idioot

sense-organ zintuig[h]

sensibility [sensibbillittie] 1 (over)gevoeligheid (for impressions, art): offend s.o.'s sensibilities iemands gevoelens kwetsen; 2 lichtgeraaktheid; 3 gevoel[h], gevoeligheid, waarnemingsvermogen[h], bewustzijn[h], erkenning (of problem)

sensible [sensibl] 1 verstandig, zinnig; 2 praktisch, functioneel (of clothes etc); 3 merkbaar, waarneembaar; 4 (with to) gevoelig (voor), ontvankelijk (voor)

sensitive [sensittiv] 1 gevoelig, ontvankelijk; 2 precies, gevoelig (of instrument); 3 (fijn)gevoelig, smaakvol; 4 lichtgeraakt; 5 (photo) (licht)gevoelig; 6 gevoelig, geheim: ~ post vertrouwenspost; ~ plant: a) gevoelige plant; b) kruidje-roer-mij-niet

sensitivity [sensittjvvittie] 1 gevoeligheid; 2 (fijn)gevoeligheid, smaak

sensor [sensə] aftaster, sensor, verklikker

sensory [sensərie] zintuiglijk

sensual [sensjoeəl] sensueel, zinnelijk, wellustig

sensualism [sensjoeəlizm] genotzucht, wellust

sensuous [sensjoeəs] **1** zinnelijk, zintuiglijk; **2** aangenaam, behaaglijk: *with ~ pleasure* vol behagen, behaaglijk

¹sentence [sentəns] *n* **1** (vol)zin: *complex* (of: *compound*) ~ samengestelde zin; **2** vonnisʰ, vonnissing, (rechterlijke) uitspraak, veroordeling, straf: *under ~ of death* ter dood veroordeeld

²sentence [sentəns] *vb* veroordelen, vonnissen: *be ~d to pay a fine* veroordeeld worden tot een geldboete

sententious [sentensjəs] moraliserend, prekerig

sentient [sensjənt] *(with of)* bewust (van)

sentiment [sentimmənt] **1** gevoelʰ, mening, opvatting: *(those are) my ~s exactly* zo denk ik er ook over, precies wat ik wou zeggen; **2** (geluk)wens; **3** gevoelʰ, gevoelens, stemming *(also on Stock Exchange, market)*, emotie, voorkeur: *be swayed by ~* zich laten leiden door zijn gevoel

sentimental [sentimmentl] sentimenteel, (over)gevoelig: *~ value* gevoelswaarde

sentimentality [sentimməntælittie] sentimentaliteit

sentry [sentrie] schildwacht

sepal [sepl] blaadje van een bloemkelk

separable [seppərəbl] (af)scheidbaar, verdeelbaar: *in his poems form is not ~ from content* in zijn gedichten is de vorm niet los te zien van de inhoud

¹separate [seppərət] *adj* afzonderlijk, (af)gescheiden, apart, verschillend, alleenstaand: *~ ownership* particulier eigendom(srecht); *keep ~ from* afgezonderd houden van

²separate [seppəreet] *vb* **1** zich (van elkaar) afscheiden, zich afzonderen, zich verdelen, uiteenvallen: *~ from* zich afscheiden van; **2** scheiden, uit elkaar gaan

³separate [seppəreet] *vb* afzonderen, losmaken, verdelen: *legally ~d* gescheiden van tafel en bed; *widely ~d* ver uit elkaar gelegen

separation [seppəreesjən] (af)scheiding, afzondering, afscheuring, verschilʰ, onderscheidʰ, het uiteengaan, vertrekʰ, (tussen)ruimte, afstand: *judicial* (of: *legal*) ~ scheiding van tafel en bed

separatist [seppərətist] separatist, iem die zich afscheidt, *(pol)* autonomist, nationalist

September [septembə] september

septic [septik] **1** (ver)rottings-: *~ matter* etter; **2** ontstoken, geïnfecteerd

sepulchral [sippulkrəl] graf-, begrafenis-, *(fig)* somber, akelig: *in a ~ voice* met een grafstem

sepulchre [seppəlkə] grafʰ, graftombe

sequel [sie:kwəl] **1** gevolgʰ, resultaatʰ, afloop: *as a ~ to* als gevolg van; **2** vervolgʰ *(to a book)*, voortzetting

sequence [sie:kwəns] **1** reeks *(poems, plays)*; opeenvolging, rij, volgorde: *the ~ of events* de loop der

gebeurtenissen; *in ~* op volgorde, de een na de ander; **2** episode, fragmentʰ, (onder)deelʰ, (film)opname, scène

sequester [sikwestə] **1** afzonderen, verborgen houden; **2** in bewaring stellen, beslag leggen op

seraglio [sirra:li·oo] harem

¹Serb [sə:b] *adj* Servisch

²Serb [sə:b] *n* Serviër

¹Serbian [sə:biən] *adj* Servisch

²Serbian [sə:biən] *n* Serviër

serenade [serrəneed] serenade(muziek)

serene [sərie:n] sereen, helder: *a ~ summer night* een kalme zomeravond

serenity [sərennittie] helderheid, kalmte, rust

serf [sə:f] lijfeigene, slaaf

serfdom [sə:fdəm] lijfeigenschapʰ, slavernij

sergeant [sa:dzjənt] **1** sergeant, wachtmeester; **2** brigadier (van politie)

¹serial [siəriəl] *adj* serieel, in serie, opeenvolgend: *~ number* volgnummer, serienummer

²serial [siəriəl] *n* **1** feuilletonʰ, vervolgverhaalʰ, (televisie)serie; **2** seriepublicatie

serialize [siəriəlajz] **1** als feuilleton publiceren; **2** rangschikken, ordenen in reeksen

serial killer seriemoordenaar

series [siərie:z] **1** reeks, serie, rij, verzameling, groep: *arithmetical ~* rekenkundige reeks; **2** *(electr)* serie(schakeling): *in ~* in serie (geschakeld)

serious [siəriəs] **1** ernstig, serieus: *~ damage* aanzienlijke schade; *after ~ thought* na rijp beraad; **2** oprecht, gemeend

seriously [siəriəslie] **1** ernstig, serieus, belangrijk, aanzienlijk: *~ ill* ernstig ziek; **2** echt, heus, zonder gekheid: *but ~, are you really thinking of moving?* maar serieus, ben je echt van plan te verhuizen?

sermon [sə:mən] preek *(also fig)*, vermaning

serpent [sə:pənt] **1** slang, serpentʰ; **2** onderkruiper

serpentine [sə:pəntajn] **1** slangachtig, slangen-; **2** kronkelig

serrated [serreetid] zaagvormig, getand, gezaagd: *a ~ knife* een kartelmes

serum [siərəm] serumʰ

servant [sə:vənt] **1** dienaar, bediende, (huis)knecht, dienstbode; **2** *~s* personeelʰ

¹serve [sə:v] *vb* **1** dienen (bij), in dienst zijn van: *(fig) ~ two masters* twee heren dienen; **2** serveren, opdienen: *~ dinner* het eten opdienen; *~ at table* bedienen, opdienen; **3** dienen, dienst doen, helpen, baten: *that excuse ~d him well* dat smoesje is hem goed van pas gekomen; *are you being ~d?* wordt u al geholpen?; **4** *(sport)* serveren, opslaan

²serve [sə:v] *vb* **1** dienen, voorzien in, volstaan, vervullen: *~ a purpose* een bepaald doel dienen; *~ the purpose of* dienst doen als; **2** behandelen, bejegenen: *that ~s him right!* dat is zijn verdiende loon!, net goed!; **3** ondergaan, vervullen, (uit)zitten: *he ~d ten years in prison* hij heeft tien jaar in de gevangenis gezeten; **4** dagvaarden, betekenen: *~ a writ on s.o.*, *~ s.o. with a writ* iem dagvaarden

serve out 1 verdelen, ronddelen; **2** uitdienen, uitzitten

servery [sɔːvərie] **1** buffet^h *(in self-service restaurant);* **2** doorgeefluik^h *(between kitchen and dining room)*

¹service [sɔːvis] *n* **1** dienst, (overheids)instelling, bedrijf^h: *secret ~* geheime dienst; **2** krijgsmachtonderdeel^h *(army, navy or airforce): on (active) ~* in actieve dienst; **3** hulp, bijstand, dienst(verlening): *do s.o. a ~* iem een dienst bewijzen; **4** (kerk)dienst; **5** verbinding, dienst *(by bus, train or boat);* **6** onderhoudsbeurt, onderhoud^h, service; **7** servies^h; **8** nutsbedrijf^h; **9** *(sport)* opslag, service(beurt); **10** gasleiding, waterleiding *(in house),* huisaansluiting; **11** dienstbaarheid, dienst, het dienen, het dienstbaar zijn: *in ~* in dienst *(eg of bus or train);* **12** nut^h, dienst: *at your ~* tot uw dienst; **13** bediening, service

²service [sɔːvis] *vb* **1** onderhouden, een (onderhouds)beurt geven; **2** (be)dienen, voorzien van

serviceable [sɔːvissəbl] **1** nuttig, bruikbaar, handig; **2** sterk, stevig, duurzaam

service area wegrestaurant^h *(with filling station)*

service charge 1 bedieningsgeld^h; **2** administratiekosten

service flat verzorgingsflat

serviceman [sɔːvismən] militair, soldaat

service road ventweg, parallelweg

serviette [sɔːvie·et] servet(je)^h, vingerdoekje^h

servile [sɔːvajl] slaafs, onderdanig, kruiperig: *~ imitation* slaafse navolging

servility [sɔːvillitie] slaafsheid, kruiperige houding

serving [sɔːving] portie: *three ~s of ice-cream* drie porties ijs

servitude [sɔːvitjoe:d] slavernij, onderworpenheid

sesame [sessəmie] sesam(kruid^h); sesamzaad^h ‖ *Open ~!* Sesam, open u!

session [sesjən] **1** zitting *(court of law, administration, committee),* vergadering, sessie: *secret ~* geheime zitting; **2** zittingsperiode, zittingstijd; **3** academiejaar^h, semester^h, halfjaar^h; **4** schooltijd; **5** bijeenkomst, partij, vergadering; **6** (opname)sessie: *recording ~* opnamesessie (in studio)

¹set [set] *vb* **1** zetten, plaatsen, stellen, leggen, doen zitten: *~ a trap* een val zetten; *~ free* vrijlaten, bevrijden; *~ pen to paper* beginnen te schrijven; **2** gelijkzetten *(clock, timepiece);* **3** opleggen, opdragen, opgeven, geven *(example),* stellen, opstellen, (samen)stellen *(questions etc): ~ s.o. a good example* iem het goede voorbeeld geven; *~ s.o. a task* iem een taak opleggen; *~ to work* zich aan het werk zetten, beginnen te werken; **4** bepalen *(date),* voorschrijven, aangeven *(size, pace, tone),* vaststellen: *~ the fashion* de mode bepalen; *~ a price on sth.* de prijs van iets bepalen; **5** brengen, aanleiding geven tot, veroorzaken: *that ~ me thinking* dat bracht me aan het denken; **6** stijf doen worden *(cement, jelly etc);* **7** instellen *(camera, lens, appliance);* **8** dekken

(table): ~ *the table* de tafel dekken; **9** zetten *(letters, text);* **10** uitzetten *(watch, nets),* posteren: *~ a watch* een schildwacht uitzetten; **11** zetten *(broken leg),* bij elkaar voegen, samenvoegen; **12** op muziek zetten *(text): ~ to music* op muziek zetten; **13** situeren *(story, play): the novel is ~ in the year 2020* de roman speelt zich af in het jaar 2020; **14** vestigen *(record): ~ a new record* een nieuw record vestigen; *~ (up)on s.o.* iem aanvallen; *against that fact you must ~ that …* daartegenover moet je stellen dat …; *~ s.o. against s.o.* iem opzetten tegen iem; *~ s.o. beside s.o. else* iem met iem anders vergelijken

²set [set] *vb* **1** vast worden, stijf worden *(of cement, jelly),* verharden, stollen, en vaste vorm aannemen, bestendig worden *(of weather);* **2** ondergaan *(of sun, moon): the sun had nearly ~* de zon was bijna onder; **3** aan elkaar groeien *(of broken leg)*

³set *n* **1** stel^h, span^h, servies^h, set *(pots, pans etc),* reeks: *~ of (false) teeth* een (vals) gebit; **2** kring, gezelschap^h, groep, kliek: *the jet ~* de elite; *the smart ~* de chic, de hogere standen *(of:* kringen); **3** toestel^h, radiotoestel^h, tv-toestel^h; **4** stek, loot, jonge plant; **5** set, spel^h, partij; **6** *(maths)* verzameling; **7** vorm, houding *(of head),* ligging *(of hills): the ~ of her head* de houding van haar hoofd; **8** toneelopbouw, scène, (film)decor^h, *(by extension)* studiohal, set: *on (the) ~* op de set, bij de (film)opname

⁴set *adj* **1** vast, bepaald, vastgesteld, stereotiep, routine-, onveranderlijk: *~ phrase* stereotiepe uitdrukking; *~ purpose* vast vooropgesteld doel; **2** voorgeschreven, opgelegd *(book, subject);* **3** strak, onbeweeglijk, stijf *(face),* koppig, hardnekkig: *~ in one's ways* met vaste gewoonten; *~ fair: a)* bestendig *(weather); b)* prettig, goed *(prospect);* **4** klaar, gereed: *get ~, ready, steady, go* op uw plaatsen, klaar voor de start, af; *be all ~ for sth.* helemaal klaar zijn voor iets; **5** volledig en tegen vaste prijs *(meal in restaurant): ~ dinner* dagschotel, dagmenu; **6** geplaatst, gevestigd: *eyes ~ deep in the head* diepliggende ogen; **7** vastbesloten: *her mind is ~ on pleasure* ze wil alleen plezier maken; *~ square* tekendriehoek

set about 1 beginnen (met, aan), aanpakken: *the next day they ~ cleaning the house* de dag daarop begonnen ze met het schoonmaken van het huis; **2** aanvallen

set apart terzijde leggen, reserveren

set aside 1 terzijde zetten, reserveren, sparen *(money);* *~ for* reserveren voor; **2** buiten beschouwing laten, geen aandacht schenken aan: *setting aside the details* afgezien van de details

setback 1 inzinking; **2** tegenslag, nederlaag

set back terugzetten, achteruitzetten: *the accident has set us back by about four weeks* door het ongeluk zijn we ongeveer vier weken achter (op schema) geraakt

set down 1 neerzetten; **2** afzetten, laten afstappen *(from vehicle);* **3** neerschrijven, opschrijven

set in intreden *(season, reaction),* invallen *(dark-*

ness, thaw), beginnen: rain has ~ het is gaan regenen

¹set off vb zich op weg begeven, vertrekken: ~ in pursuit de achtervolging inzetten

²set off vb 1 versieren; 2 doen uitkomen (colours): she wore a dress that ~ her complexion quite well ze droeg een jurk die haar teint goed deed uitkomen; 3 doen ontbranden, tot ontploffing brengen (bomb); 4 doen opwegen, goedmaken: ~ against doen opwegen tegen; 5 doen (laugh, talk), stimuleren: set s.o. off laughing iem aan het lachen brengen; 6 afzetten, afpassen: a small area was ~ for the smokers er was een kleine ruimte afgezet voor de rokers

set on ertoe brengen, aansporen

¹set out vb 1 zich op weg begeven, vertrekken: ~ for Paris vertrekken met bestemming Parijs; 2 zich voornemen, het plan opvatten

²set out vb 1 uitzetten, klaarzetten, opzetten (chessmen): if you ~ the white pieces, I'll do the black ones als jij de witte stukken opzet, doe ik de zwarte; 2 tentoonstellen, uitstallen (goods); 3 verklaren, uiteenzetten

set point setpuntʰ

set square tekendriehoek

sett [set] 1 (dassen)burcht; 2 vierkante straatkei

setting [setting] 1 ondergang (sun, moon); 2 stand, instelling (of instrument, machine); 3 omlijsting, achtergrond: the story has its ~ in Sydney het verhaal speelt zich af in Sydney; 4 montering, aankleding (film, play)

¹settle [setl] vb 1 gaan zitten, zich neerzetten, neerstrijken: ~ back in a chair gemakkelijk gaan zitten in een stoel; 2 neerslaan, bezinken (of dust, dregs); 3 zich vestigen, gaan wonen: ~ in: a) zich installeren (in house); b) zich inwerken; ~ for sth. genoegen nemen met iets; ~ (down) to sth. zich ergens op concentreren, zich ergens toe zetten

²settle [setl] vb 1 kalmeren, (doen) bedaren; 2 opklaren (liquid), helderder worden (maken); 3 (with (up)on) overeenkomen (mbt), een besluit nemen, afspreken: ~ (up)on a date een datum vaststellen; 4 betalen (eg bill), voldoen, vereffenen: ~ a claim schade uitbetalen; ~ up verrekenen (among each other); ~ (an account, old score) with s.o. het iem betaald zetten

³settle [setl] vb 1 regelen, in orde brengen; 2 vestigen (in place of residence, society); 3 koloniseren: their forefathers ~d the land in 1716 hun voorvaderen koloniseerden het land in 1716; 4 zetten, plaatsen, leggen: she ~d herself in the chair zij nestelde zich in haar stoel; 5 (voorgoed) beëindigen, beslissen (argument, doubts), de doorslag geven: that ~s it! dat doet de deur dicht!, dat geeft de doorslag!; let's ~ this once and for all laten we dit nu eens en altijd regelen; 6 schikken, bijleggen, tot een schikking komen: ~ into zich thuis doen voelen in; ~ on vastzetten op

settled [setld] vast, onwrikbaar, gevestigd (opin-

ion), bestendig (weather), onveranderlijk

¹settle down vb 1 een vaste betrekking aannemen, zich vestigen; 2 wennen, zich thuis gaan voelen, ingewerkt raken; 3 (with to) zich concentreren (op), zich toeleggen (op): he finally ~d to his studies eindelijk ging hij zich toeleggen op zijn studie; 4 vast worden (of weather)

²settle down vb kalmeren, tot rust komen (brengen)

settlement [setlmənt] 1 nederzetting, kolonie, groepje kolonisten, plaatsjeʰ; 2 kolonisatie; 3 schikking, overeenkomst; 4 afrekening: in ~ of ter vereffening van

settler [setlə] kolonist

set-to 1 vechtpartij; 2 ruzie: there was a bit of a set-to outside the pub er ontstond ruzie buiten de kroeg

¹set up vb 1 opzetten (eg tent), opstellen, monteren, stichten, oprichten (school), beginnen, aanstellen (committee), opstellen (rules), organiseren; 2 aanheffen, verheffen (voice); 3 veroorzaken; 4 er bovenop helpen, op de been helpen; 5 vestigen: set s.o. up in business iem in een zaak zetten; 6 beramen (hold-up); 7 belazeren, de schuld in de schoenen schuiven

²set up vb zich vestigen: ~ as a dentist zich als tandarts vestigen

set-up 1 opstelling (at film shooting); 2 opbouw, organisatie

seven [sevn] zeven

sevenfold [sevnfoold] 1 zevenvoudig; 2 zevendelig

seven-league: ~ boots zevenmijlslaarzen

seventeen [sevnti:n] zeventien

seventeenth [sevnti:nθ] zeventiende, zeventiende deelʰ

seventh [sevnθ] zevende, zevende deelʰ

seventy [sevntie] zeventig

¹sever [sevvə] vb 1 afbreken: ~ the rope het touw doorsnijden; 2 (af)scheiden: ~ oneself from zich afscheiden van; 3 verbreken (relationship etc)

²sever [sevvə] vb 1 breken, het begeven, losgaan; 2 uiteen gaan, scheiden

several [sevvərəl] 1 verscheidene, enkele, een aantal (ervan): she has written ~ books ze heeft verscheidene boeken geschreven; ~ of my friends verscheidene van mijn vrienden; 2 apart(e), respectievelijk(e), verschillend(e): after their studies the students went their ~ ways na hun studie gingen de studenten elk hun eigen weg

severally [sevvərəlie] 1 afzonderlijk, hoofdelijk: the partners are ~ liable de vennoten zijn hoofdelijk aansprakelijk; 2 elk voor zich, respectievelijk

severance [sevvərəns] 1 verbreking, opzegging (of relations); 2 scheiding, (ver)deling; 3 ontslagʰ, verbreking van arbeidscontract

severe [sivviə] 1 streng, strikt; 2 hevig, bar: ~ conditions barre omstandigheden; 3 zwaar, moeilijk, ernstig: ~ requirements zware eisen; leave (of: let) sth. ~ly alone ergens z'n handen niet aan willen vuilmaken

severity [sivv<u>e</u>rrittie] *(-ies)* **1** strengheid, hardheid; **2** hevigheid, barheid; **3** soberheid, strakheid

sew [soo] naaien, hechten *(wound)*

sewage [s<u>oe</u>:idzj] afvalwater^h, rioolwater^h: *raw ~* ongezuiverd afvalwater

¹sewer [s<u>oe</u>:ə] *n* riool(buis)

²sewer [s<u>oo</u>ə] *n* naaister

sewerage [s<u>oe</u>:əridzj] **1** riolering, rioolstelsel^h; **2** (afval)waterafvoer

sewing [s<u>oo</u>ing] naaiwerk^h

sew up 1 dichtnaaien, hechten; **2** succesvol afsluiten, beklinken, regelen

¹sex [seks] *n* **1** geslacht^h, sekse: *the second ~* de tweede sekse, de vrouw(en); **2** seks, erotiek; **3** seksuele omgang, geslachtsgemeenschap: *have ~ with s.o.* met iem naar bed gaan, vrijen

²sex [seks] *vb* seksen, het geslacht vaststellen van

sexism [s<u>e</u>ksizm] seksisme^h, ongelijke behandeling i.v.m. sekse

¹sexist [s<u>e</u>ksist] *adj* seksistisch

²sexist [s<u>e</u>ksist] *n* seksist

sexless [s<u>e</u>ksləs] **1** onzijdig, geslachtloos; **2** niet opwindend

sex object 1 seksobject^h, lustobject^h; **2** sekssymbool^h

sextant [s<u>e</u>kstənt] sextant *(navigation instrument)*

sexual [s<u>e</u>ksjoeəl] **1** seksueel, geslachts-: *~ harassment* ongewenste intimiteiten *(at work); ~ intercourse* geslachtsgemeenschap; **2** geslachtelijk, mbt het geslacht

sexuality [seksjoe·ælittie] seksualiteit

sexy [s<u>e</u>ksie] sexy, opwindend

s.f. *science fiction* SF

Sgt. *sergeant*

sh [sjsjsj] sst

shabby [sj<u>æ</u>bie] **1** versleten, af(gedragen), kaal; **2** sjofel, armoedig; **3** min, gemeen: *what a ~ way to treat an old friend!* wat een laag-bij-de-grondse manier om een oude vriend te behandelen!

shack [sjæk] **1** hut; **2** hok^h, keet, schuurtje^h

¹shackle [sj<u>æ</u>kl] *n* **1** (hand)boei, keten, kluister; **2** *~s* belemmering; **3** schakel, sluiting

²shackle [sj<u>æ</u>kl] *vb* **1** boeien, ketenen; **2** koppelen, vastmaken; **3** belemmeren, hinderen ‖ *be ~d with sth.* met iets opgezadeld zitten

shack up hokken, samenwonen, samenleven: *~ together* (samen)hokken, samenwonen

¹shade [sjeed] *n* **1** schaduw, lommer^h: *put s.o. (sth.) in the ~* iem (iets) overtreffen; **2** schaduwplek(je^h); **3** schakering, nuance: *~s of meaning* (betekenis)nuances; **4** (zonne)scherm^h, (lampen)kap, zonneklep; **5** schim, geest, spook^h; **6** tikkeltje^h, ietsje^h, beetje^h; **7** (rol)gordijn^h; **8** *~s* duisternis, schemerduister^h; **9** *~s* zonnebril

²shade [sjeed] *vb* **1** beschermen, beschutten, *(fig)* in de schaduw stellen: *~ one's eyes* zijn hand boven de ogen houden; **2** afschermen *(light)*, dimmen; **3** arceren, schaduw aanbrengen in

³shade [sjeed] *vb* geleidelijk veranderen, (doen)

overgaan ‖ *~ away (of: off)* geleidelijk aan (laten) verdwijnen

shading [sj<u>ee</u>ding] arcering

¹shadow [sj<u>æ</u>doo] *n* **1** schaduw, duister^h, duisternis, schemerduister^h; **2** schaduw(beeld^h) *(also fig)*, silhouet^h: *afraid of one's own ~* zo bang als een wezel; *cast a ~ on sth.* een schaduw werpen op iets *(also fig)*; **3** schaduwplek, schaduwhoek, arcering, schaduw *(in painting);* **4** iem die schaduwt, spion, detective: *he is the ~ of his former self* hij is bij lange na niet meer wat hij geweest is; *without the ~ of a doubt* zonder ook maar de geringste twijfel

²shadow [sj<u>æ</u>doo] *vb* schaduwen, volgen *(by detective)*

shadow-boxing het schaduwboksen

shadowy [sj<u>æ</u>dooie] **1** onduidelijk, vaag, schimmig; **2** schaduwrijk, in schaduw gehuld

shady [sj<u>ee</u>die] **1** schaduwrijk; **2** onbetrouwbaar, verdacht, louche

¹shaft [sja:ft] *n* **1** schacht *(of arrow, spear);* **2** steel, stok; **3** lichtstraal, lichtbundel, bliksemstraal, lichtflits; **4** koker, schacht *(lift, mine);* **5** (drijf)as ‖ *get the ~* te grazen genomen worden

²shaft [sja:ft] *vb* te grazen nemen, belazeren

shag [sjæg] **1** warboel, kluwen; **2** shag

shagged (out) [sjægd aut] bekaf, uitgeteld

shaggy [sj<u>æ</u>gie] **1** harig, ruigbehaard; **2** ruig, wild, woest

shah [sja:] sjah

¹shake [sjeek] *vb* **1** schudden, schokken, beven, (t)rillen: *~ with laughter* schudden van het lachen; **2** wankelen; **3** de hand geven: *~ (on it)!* geef me de vijf!, hand erop!

²shake [sjeek] *vb* **1** doen schudden, schokken, doen beven; **2** (uit)schudden, zwaaien, heen en weer schudden: *~ dice* dobbelstenen schudden; *~ off: a)* (van zich) afschudden; *b) (also fig)* ontsnappen aan; *~ before use (of: using)* schudden voor gebruik; **3** geven, schudden *(hand);* **4** schokken, verontrusten, overstuur maken: *mother was tremendously shaken by Paul's death* moeder was enorm getroffen door de dood van Paul; **5** aan het wankelen brengen *(fig)*, verzwakken, verminderen: *these stories have shaken the firm's credit* deze verhalen hebben de firma in diskrediet gebracht

³shake [sjeek] *n* **1** het schudden, handdruk: *he said no with a ~ of the head* hij schudde (van) nee; **2** milkshake; **3** ogenblik^h, momentje^h: *in two ~s (of a lamb's tail)* zo, direct, in een seconde

shakedown afpersing, geld-uit-de-zakklopperij

¹shake down *vb* **1** gewend raken, ingewerkt raken; **2** goed gaan lopen, werken, goed afgesteld zijn

²shake down *vb* **1** (af)schudden, uitschudden; **2** (op de grond) uitspreiden; **3** afpersen, geld uit de zak kloppen

shake up 1 (door elkaar) schudden *(also fig)*, hutselen *(drink);* **2** reorganiseren, orde op zaken stellen in

shake-up radicale reorganisatie ‖ *they need a thor-*

ough ~ ze moeten eens flink wakker geschud worden

shaky [sjeekie] **1** beverig, trillerig, zwak(jes); **2** wankel *(also fig)*, gammel, onbetrouwbaar: *my Swedish is rather* ~ mijn Zweeds is nogal zwak

shall [sjæl] **1** zullen: *how ~ I recognize her?* hoe zal ik haar herkennen?; **2** *(command; also promise, threat, plan etc)* zullen, moeten: *you ~ do as I tell you* doe wat ik zeg; **3** zullen, moeten: ~ *I open the window?* zal ik het raam openzetten?

shallot [sjəlot] sjalot

shallow [sjæloo] **1** ondiep: ~ *dish* plat bord; **2** licht, niet diep *(of breathing):* ~ *arguments* oppervlakkige argumenten

shallows [sjælooz] ondiepte, ondiepe plaats, wad[h]

¹sham [sjæm] *n* **1** komedie, schijn(vertoning), bedrog[h]: *the promise was a* ~ de belofte was maar schijn; **2** imitatie; **3** bedrieger, hypocriet

²sham [sjæm] *adj* **1** namaak-, imitatie-, vals; **2** schijn-, gesimuleerd, pseudo-: *a ~ fight* een schijngevecht

³sham [sjæm] *vb* voorwenden, doen als of: ~ *illness* doen alsof je ziek bent

¹shamble [sjæmbl] *vb* schuifelen, sloffen *(also fig): a shambling gait* een sukkelgangetje

²shamble [sjæmbl] *n* schuifelgang(etje[h])

shambles [sjæmblz] janboel, troep, bende, zooi: *the house is a complete* ~ het huis is een echte varkensstal

¹shame [sjeem] *n* **1** schande, schandaal[h]; **2** zonde ‖ *what a* ~*!* het is een schande!, wat jammer!; **3** schaamte(gevoel[h]): *have no sense of* ~ zich nergens voor schamen; **4** schande, smaad, vernedering: *to my* ~ tot mijn (grote) schande; *(to speaker)* ~*!* schandalig!, hoe durft u!; *put to* ~: *a)* in de schaduw stellen; *b)* beschaamd maken *(of:* doen staan); ~ *on you!* schaam je!, je moest je schamen!

²shame [sjeem] *vb* **1** beschamen: *it ~s me to say this* ik schaam me ervoor dit te (moeten) zeggen; **2** schande aandoen, te schande maken; **3** in de schaduw stellen, overtreffen: *your translation ~s all the other attempts* jouw vertaling stelt alle andere pogingen in de schaduw

shameful [sjeemfoel] **1** beschamend; **2** schandelijk, schandalig

shameless [sjeemləs] schaamteloos, onbeschaamd

¹shampoo [sjæmpoe:] *n* shampoo

²shampoo [sjæmpoe:] *vb* shamponeren, met shampoo reinigen *(car, carpet)*

shamrock [sjæmrok] klaver

shandy [sjændie] shandy

shank [sjængk] **1** (onder)been[h], scheenbeen[h], schenkel; **2** schacht *(of anchor, column, key)*; **3** steel

shanks'(s) pony *go on (of: ride)* ~ met de benenwagen gaan

shanty [sjæntie] **1** barak, hut, keet; **2** zeemansliedje[h]

shanty town sloppenwijk, barakkenkamp[h]

¹shape [sjeep] *n* **1** vorm, gestalte, gedaante, verschijning: *take* ~ (vaste, vastere) vorm aannemen; *in the* ~ *of* in de vorm van; **2** (bak-, giet)vorm, model[h], sjabloon; **3** (goede) conditie, (goede) toestand, vorm: *in bad* ~ in slechte conditie; *(+ negation) in any* ~ *or form* in welke vorm dan ook, van welke aard dan ook; *knock* (of: *lick) sth. into* ~ iets fatsoeneren

²shape [sjeep] *vb* **1** vormen, maken, ontwerpen: ~*d like (a pear)* in de vorm van (een peer), (peer)vormig; **2** bepalen, vormen, vorm (richting) geven aan: *his theories, which* ~*d mathematical thinking in the 1980s* zijn theorieën, die het wiskundig denken in de jaren tachtig richting gaven

³shape [sjeep] *vb* (also with *up)* zich ontwikkelen, zich vormen, vorm aannemen: *we'll see how things* ~ *(up)* we zullen zien hoe de dingen zich ontwikkelen

shapeless [sjeepləs] **1** vorm(e)loos, ongevormd; **2** misvormd, vervormd

shapely [sjeeplie] goedgevormd, welgevormd

¹share [sjeə] *n* **1** aandeel[h], effect[h]; **2** (onder)deel[h], aandeel[h], part[h], gedeelte[h], portie: *get one's fair* ~ zijn rechtmatig (aan)deel krijgen; *go* ~*s (with s.o. in sth.)* de kosten (van iets met iem) delen

²share [sjeə] *vb* delen, deelnemen: ~ *and* ~ *alike* eerlijk delen

³share [sjeə] *vb* **1** (ver)delen: ~ *a bedroom* een slaapkamer delen; ~ *(out) among* verdelen onder; **2** deelgenoot maken van: ~ *a secret with s.o.* iem deelgenoot maken van een geheim

shareholder aandeelhouder

share-out verdeling

shark [sja:k] **1** haai; **2** afzetter, woekeraar

¹sharp [sja:p] *adj* **1** scherp, spits, puntig: *a ~ angle* een scherpe hoek; **2** schril: *a ~ contrast* een schril contrast; **3** abrupt, plotseling, steil: *a ~ fall in prices* een scherpe daling van de prijzen; **4** bijtend, doordringend, snijdend: ~ *frost* bijtende vrieskou; **5** scherp, pikant, sterk: *a ~ flavour* een scherpe smaak; **6** hevig, krachtig: *a ~ blow* een hevige klap; **7** streng, vinnig: *a ~ reproof* een scherp verwijt; **8** scherpzinnig, bijdehand, pienter, vlug: *keep a ~ look-out* scherp uitkijken; *be too ~ for s.o.* iem te slim af zijn; **9** geslepen, sluw: *a ~ salesman* een gehaaid verkoper; **10** stevig, flink, vlug: *at a ~ pace* in een stevig tempo; ~ *practice* oneerlijke praktijken, een vuil zaakje

²sharp [sja:p] *adv* **1** stipt, precies, klokslag: *three o'clock* ~ klokslag drie uur; **2** opeens, plotseling, scherp: *turn ~ right* scherp naar rechts draaien; *look* ~*!* schiet op, haast je!

³sharp [sja:p] *n* (noot met) kruis[h] ‖ *F* ~ f-kruis, fa kruis, fis

sharpen [sja:pən] scherp(er) worden (maken), (zich) (ver)scherpen, slijpen

sharper [sja:pə] afzetter, oplichter

sharp-eyed scherpziend, waakzaam, alert

sharpish [sja:pisj] snel, (nu) meteen, direct: *I expect they want their dinner pretty ~ after such a long* *drive* ik verwacht dat ze wel snel willen eten na zo'n lange rit

sharpshooter scherpschutter

¹shatter [sjætə] *vb* **1** aan gruzelementen slaan, (compleet) vernietigen: *his death ~ed our hopes* zijn dood ontnam ons alle hoop; **2** schokken, in de war brengen: *~ed nerves* geschokte zenuwen; **3** afmatten, totaal uitputten: *I feel completely ~ed* ik ben doodop

²shatter [sjætə] *vb* uiteenspatten, barsten, in stukken (uiteen)vallen

¹shave [sjeev] *vb* **1** (zich) scheren; **2** (also with *off*) (af)schaven, afraspen; **3** scheren langs, schampen, rakelings gaan langs

²shave [sjeev] *n* scheerbeurt: *I badly need a ~* ik moet me nodig weer eens scheren; *a close shave* op het nippertje

shaving [sjeeving] **1** het scheren, scheerbeurt; **2** schijfje, *~s* spaanders, schaafkrullen

shawl [sjo:l] sjaal(tje), omslagdoek, hoofddoek

she [sjie:] zij, ze, *(in some constructions)* die, dat, het || *is it a he or a ~?* is het een jongen of een meisje?

sheaf [sjie:f] *(sheaves)* **1** schoof; **2** bundel: *he produced a ~ of papers from a plastic bag* hij haalde uit een plastic tasje een stapel papieren te voorschijn

shear [sjiə] **1** (af)scheren: *~ing sheep* schapen scheren; **2** ontdoen, plukken, villen: *shorn of* ontdaan van

shears [sjiəz] (grote) schaar, heggenschaar: *a pair of ~* een schaar

sheath [sjie:θ] **1** schede, (bescherm)huls, koker; **2** nauwaansluitende jurk; **3** condoom^h, kapotje^h

sheathe [sjie:ð] in de schede steken, van een omhulsel voorzien: *he carefully sheathed the knife* hij stak het mes zorgvuldig in de schede

sheathing [sjie:ðing] **1** (beschermende) bekleding, omhulling, mantel; **2** bekleding

shebang [sjibæng] zootje^h, zaak(je^h), santenkraam: *the whole ~* het hele zootje

¹shed [sjed] *vb* **1** afwerpen, verliezen, afleggen, afschudden: *the tree had ~ its leaves* de boom had zijn bladeren laten vallen; *the lorry ~ its load* de vrachtwagen verloor zijn lading; **2** storten, vergieten: *~ hot tears* hete tranen schreien

²shed *n* schuur(tje^h), keet, loods

sheen [sjie:n] glans, schittering, (weer)schijn

sheep [sjie:p] *(sheep)* schaap^h *(also fig)*, onnozel kind^h, gedwee persoon: *the black ~* het zwarte schaap; *separate the ~ and the goats* de goeden van de slechten scheiden, het koren van het kaf scheiden

sheepdog (schaap)herdershond *(collie)*

sheepfold schaapskooi

sheepish [sjie:pisj] verlegen, onnozel, dom

¹sheer [sjiə] *adj* **1** dun, doorschijnend, transparant: *~ nylon* dun nylon; **2** erg steil, loodrecht; **3** volkomen, je reinste: *that's ~ nonsense* dat is klinkklare onzin!

²sheer *vb (shipp)* scherp uitwijken, zwenken || *~ off*

uit 't roer lopen, *(inf)* 'm smeren; *~ away from* mijden

sheet [sjie:t] **1** (bedden)laken^h: *fitted ~* hoeslaken; *between the ~s* in bed, tussen de lakens; **2** blad^h, vel^h *(paper)*; **3** plaat: *a ~ of glass* een glasplaat, een, een stuk glas; **4** gordijn^h, muur, vlaag: *a ~ of flame* een vuurzee

sheet ice 1 ijs^h, ijslaag *(on water)*; **2** ijzel

sheeting [sjie:ting] **1** lakenstof^h; **2** bekleding(smateriaal^h)

sheet iron bladstaal^h, plaatijzer^h

sheet lightning weerlicht^h, bliksem

sheik(h) [sjeek] sjeik

shelf [sjelf] *(shelves)* **1** (leg)plank, boekenplank; **2** (rots)richel || *be (put, left) on the ~: a)* afgeschreven worden, in onbruik raken, afgedankt worden; *b)* blijven zitten, niet meer aan een man raken *(of woman)*

shelf-life [sjelflajf] houdbaarheid: *most dairy products have a limited ~* de meeste zuivelproducten zijn beperkt houdbaar

¹shell [sjel] *n* **1** geraamte^h *(of bldg)*, skelet^h, romp *(of ship)*, chassis^h; **2** deegbakje^h, pasteikorst; **3** huls, granaat^h, patroon^h; **4** hard omhulsel^h, schelp, slakkenhuis^h, dop, schaal, schulp: *come out of one's ~* loskomen, ontdooien

²shell [sjel] *vb* **1** van zijn schil ontdoen, schillen, doppen, pellen; **2** beschieten, onder vuur nemen, bombarderen

shellfish schaaldier^h, schelpdier^h

shell out dokken, neertellen, ophoesten

¹shelter [sjeltə] *n* **1** schuilgelegenheid, schuilkelder, bushokje^h, tramhuisje^h; **2** schuilplaats, toevluchtsoord^h, tehuis^h, asiel^h: *~ for battered women* opvang(te)huis voor mishandelde vrouwen; **3** *(with from)* beschutting (tegen), bescherming: *give ~* onderdak verlenen

²shelter [sjeltə] *vb (with from)* schuilen (voor, tegen)

³shelter [sjeltə] *vb* **1** *(with from)* beschutten (tegen), beschermen; **2** huisvesten, onderdak verlenen

¹shelve [sjelv] *vb* **1** op een plank zetten, opbergen; **2** op de lange baan schuiven, opschorten

²shelve [sjelv] *vb* geleidelijk aflopen *(of bottom)*, glooien, (zacht) hellen

shenanigan [sjinænigən] **1** trucje^h, foefje^h; **2** kattenkwaad^h, bedriegerij

¹shepherd [sjeppəd] *n* (schaap)herder

²shepherd [sjeppəd] *vb* hoeden, leiden, in de gaten houden

shepherdess [sjeppədis] herderin

sheriff [sjerrif] sheriff

sherry [sjerrie] sherry

¹shield [sjie:ld] *n* **1** schild^h; **2** beveiliging, bescherming

²shield [sjie:ld] *vb (with from)* beschermen (tegen), in bescherming nemen

¹shift [sjift] *vb* **1** van plaats veranderen, zich verplaatsen, schuiven: *~ing sands* drijfzand; **2** wisselen, veranderen: *the scene ~s* de achtergrond van het verhaal verandert; **3** zich redden, zich behelpen, het klaarspelen: ~ *for oneself* het zelf klaarspelen

²shift [sjift] *vb* **1** verplaatsen, verschuiven, verzetten: ~ *the blame onto* de schuld schuiven op; **2** verwisselen, verruilen, veranderen, schakelen *(acceleration):* ~ *one's ground* plotseling een ander standpunt innemen

³shift [sjift] *n* **1** verschuiving, verandering; **2** ploeg *(workmen);* **3** werktijd, arbeidsduur; **4** redmiddel[h], hulpmiddel[h] || *make* ~ *without* het stellen zonder

shift key hoofdlettertoets

shiftless [sjiftləs] niet vindingrijk, inefficiënt, onbeholpen

shift work ploegendienst

shifty [sjiftie] niet rechtdoorzee, stiekem, onbetrouwbaar

Shiite [sjie:ajt] sjiiet

shilling [sjilling] shilling

shilly-shally [sjilliesjælie] dubben, weifelen, aarzelen

¹shimmer [sjimmə] *vb* glinsteren, flakkeren

²shimmer [sjimmə] *n* flikkering, flauw schijnsel[h]

¹shin [sjin] *n* scheen: *Joe got kicked on the ~s during the match* Joe werd tijdens de wedstrijd tegen zijn schenen geschopt

²shin [sjin] *vb* klauteren, klimmen *(using hands and feet):* ~ *up a tree* in een boom klimmen

shindy [sjindie] herrie, tumult[h], opschudding: *kick up a ~* herrie schoppen

¹shine [sjajn] *vb* schijnen, lichten, gloeien: *he shone his light in my face* hij scheen met zijn lantaarn in mijn gezicht

²shine [sjajn] *vb* **1** glanzen, glimmen, blinken; **2** schitteren, uitblinken: ~ *out* duidelijk naar voren komen

³shine [sjajn] *vb* poetsen *(shoes)*

⁴shine [sjajn] *n* **1** schijn(sel[h]), licht[h], uitstraling; **2** glans, schittering: *take the ~ out of* van zijn glans beroven, maken dat de aardigheid af gaat van; **3** poetsbeurt, het poetsen *(of shoes): take a ~ to s.o.* iem zomaar aardig vinden

shingle [sjinggl] **1** dakspaan, panlat; **2** kiezel[h], grind[h], kiezelstrand[h]; **3** ~*s* gordelroos

shiny [sjajnie] glanzend, glimmend

¹ship [sjip] *n* **1** schip[h], vaartuig[h]: *on board* ~ aan boord; **2** vliegtuig[h], kist; **3** ruimteschip[h]

²ship [sjip] *vb* **1** verschepen, (per schip) verzenden (vervoeren): ~ *off* (of: *out)* verzenden; **2** aan boord nemen, laden; **3** binnenkrijgen: ~ *water* water maken; ~ *off* wegsturen, wegzenden

shipboard scheepsboord[h]: *on* ~ aan boord

shipbuilding scheepsbouw

shipload scheepslading, scheepsvracht

shipmate scheepsmaat, medebemanningslid[h]

shipment [sjipmənt] **1** zending, vracht, scheepslading; **2** vervoer[h] *(not only by ship)*

shipowner reder

shipper [sjippə] expediteur, verzender

shipping [sjipping] **1** verscheping, verzending; **2** scheepvaart

shipshape [sjipsjeep] netjes, in orde, keurig

¹shipwreck *n* schipbreuk, *(fig)* ondergang, mislukking

²shipwreck *vb* schipbreuk (doen) lijden, (doen) mislukken

shipyard scheeps(timmer)werf

shire [sjajjə] graafschap[h]

¹shirk [sjə:k] *vb* zich onttrekken aan

²shirk [sjə:k] *vb* zich drukken

shirt [sjə:t] overhemd[h] || *keep one's ~ on* zich gedeisd houden; *put one's ~ on sth.* al zijn geld op iets zetten *(horses)*

shirtsleeve hemdsmouw: *in one's ~s* in hemdsmouwen

shirty [sjə:tie] nijdig, kwaad, geërgerd

¹shit [sjit] *vb (vulg)* schijten, poepen

²shit [sjit] *vb* schijten op: ~ *oneself* het in zijn broek doen *(also fig)*

³shit [sjit] *n* **1** stront, kak, poep; het poepen: *have a* ~ gaan kakken; **2** rommel, rotzooi; **3** zeurkous; **4** gezeik[h], geklets[h], onzin; **5** hasj

¹shiver [sjivvə] *vb* rillen *(with fear, cold)*, sidderen

²shiver [sjivvə] *n* rilling *(also fig)*, siddering, gevoel[h] van angst (afkeer): *give s.o. the ~s* iem de rillingen geven

shivery [sjivvərie] **1** rillerig, beverig; **2** kil *(of weather)*

shoal [sjool] **1** ondiepte; **2** zandbank; **3** menigte, troep, school *(of fish)*

¹shock [sjok] *n* **1** aardschok; **2** dikke bos[h] *(of hair)*; **3** schok, schrik, (onaangename) verrassing: *come upon s.o. with a* ~ een (grote) schok zijn voor iem; **4** (elektrische) schok; **5** shock: *in a state of* ~ in shocktoestand

²shock [sjok] *vb* een schok veroorzaken

³shock [sjok] *vb* **1** schokken, choqueren, laten schrikken: *be ~ed at* (of: *by)* geschokt zijn door; **2** een schok geven *(also electr)*, een shock veroorzaken bij

shocking [sjokking] **1** stuitend, schokkend, weerzinwekkend; **2** vreselijk, erg: ~ *weather* rotweer

shockproof schokvast

shoddy [sjoddie] prullig, niet degelijk

shoe [sjoe:] **1** schoen; **2** hoefijzer[h]; **3** remschoen, remblok || *(know) where the ~ pinches* (weten) waar de schoen wringt, weten waar de pijn zit; *put oneself in s.o.'s ~s* zich in iemands positie verplaatsen

shoelace (schoen)veter

shoestring 1 (schoen)veter; **2** (te) klein budget[h]: *on a* ~ met erg weinig geld

¹shoo [sjoe:] *interj* ks(t)

²shoo [sjoe:] *vb* ks(t) roepen, wegjagen: ~ *sth. away* (of: *off)* iets wegjagen

¹shoot [sjoe:t] *vb* **1** snel bewegen, (weg)schieten, voortschieten: ~ *ahead* vooruitschieten; **2** schieten *(with weapon):* ~ *at* (of: *for):* a) schieten (op); b) (zich) richten op; **3** afgaan *(of weapon);* **4** steken *(of pain, wound): the pain shot through* (of: *up) his arm*

een stekende pijn ging door zijn arm; **5** uitlopen, ontspruiten; **6** *(sport)* (op doel) schieten; **7** plaatjes schieten, foto's nemen, filmen: ~ *!* zeg op!, zeg het maar!

²**shoot** [sjoe:t] *vb* **1** (af)schieten *(bullet, arrow etc)*, afvuren *(also fig; questions etc):* ~ *down* neerschieten, *(fig)* afkeuren; ~ *off: a)* afschieten, afsteken *(fireworks); b)* afvuren *(gun);* **2** jagen (op); **3** doen bewegen, schuiven *(bolt),* spuiten *(drugs);* **4** (naar doel) schieten *(ball),* schieten; **5** snel passeren: *he shot the traffic lights* hij ging met hoge snelheid door de verkeerslichten; **6** schieten *(pictures),* opnemen *(film);* **7** spelen *(billiards etc)*

³**shoot** [sjoe:t] *n* **1** (jonge) spruit, loot, scheut; **2** jacht(partij)

¹**shooting** [sjoe:ting] *n* **1** jacht; **2** het schieten; **3** opname *(film, sequence)*

²**shooting** [sjoe:ting] *adj* **1** schietend; **2** stekend: ~ *pains* pijnscheuten; ~ *star* vallende ster

shooting gallery schietbaan

shooting match schietwedstrijd: *the whole* ~ het hele zaakje

¹**shoot out** *vb* naar buiten schieten: *the branches are beginning to* ~ de takken beginnen al uit te schieten

²**shoot out** *vb* een vuurgevecht leveren over: *they're going to shoot it out* ze gaan het uitvechten (met de revolver)

shoot-out gevecht^h *(with small arms)*

¹**shoot up** *vb* omhoog schieten *(of plants, children),* snel groeien *(of temperature, prices)*

²**shoot up** *vb* kapot schieten, overhoop schieten

¹**shop** [sjop] *n* **1** winkel, zaak: *mind the* ~ de winkel runnen, *(fig)* de touwtjes in handen hebben; **2** werkplaats, atelier^h; **3** werk^h, zaken, beroep^h: *set up* ~ een zaak opzetten; *talk* ~ over zaken praten; *all over the* ~ door elkaar, her en der verspreid

²**shop** [sjop] *vb* winkelen: ~ *around* rondkijken, zich oriënteren (alvorens te kopen) *(also fig)*

³**shop** [sjop] *vb* verlinken *(to police)*

shop floor 1 werkplaats, werkvloer; **2** arbeiders

shopkeeper winkelier

shoplifter winkeldief

shopping [sjopping] boodschappen; het boodschappen doen: *Mary always does her* ~ *in Leeds* Mary doet haar boodschappen altijd in Leeds

shop-soiled minder geworden *(of goods, because they have lain too long; also fig),* smoezelig

shop steward vakbondsvertegenwoordiger

shopwalker (afdelings)chef

¹**shore** [sjo:] *n* **1** kust, oever *(of lake):* *off the* ~ voor de kust; *on* ~ aan (de) wal, op het land; **2** steunbalk

²**shore** [sjo:] *vb (also fig)* steunen, schragen: ~ *up* (onder)steunen

shoreline waterlijn, oever, kustlijn

¹**short** [sjo:t] *adj* **1** kort, klein, beknopt: ~ *and sweet* kort en bondig; *little* ~ *of* weinig minder dan, bijna; ~ *for* een afkorting van; *in* ~ in het kort; **2** kort(durend): *(at)* ~ *notice* (op) korte termijn; ~ *order* snelbuffet; *in* ~ *order* onmiddellijk; *make* ~ *work of*

snel een einde maken aan; **3** te kort, onvoldoende, karig, krap: ~ *of breath* kortademig; ~ *change* te weinig wisselgeld; ~ *of money* krap bij kas; *in* ~ *supply* schaars, beperkt leverbaar; ~ *weight* ondergewicht; *(be)* ~ *of* (of: *on)* te kort (hebben) aan; **4** kortaf, bits; **5** bros, kruimelig *(eg dough);* **6** onverdund *(hard liquor): a* ~ *drink* (of: *one)* een borrel; ~ *circuit* kortsluiting; ~ *temper* drift(igheid)

²**short** [sjo:t] *adv* **1** niet (ver) genoeg: *four inches* ~ vier inches te kort; *come* (of: *fall)* ~ tekortschieten; *(fig) cut s.o.* ~ iem onderbreken; **2** plotseling: *stop* ~ plotseling ophouden; *be taken* (of: *caught)* ~ nodig moeten; *sell s.o.* ~ iem te kort doen; *nothing* ~ *of: a)* slechts, alleen maar; *b)* niets minder dan; ~ *of* behalve, zonder

³**short** [sjo:t] *n* **1** korte (voor)film; **2** borrel; **3** ~s korte broek; onderbroek

shortage [sjo:tidzj] gebrek^h, tekort^h, schaarste

shortbread zandkoek

short-change 1 te weinig wisselgeld geven aan: *be* ~d te weinig (wisselgeld) terugkrijgen; **2** afzetten

¹**short-circuit** *vb* kortsluiting veroorzaken

²**short-circuit** *vb* **1** kortsluiten; **2** verkorten *(procedure etc),* vereenvoudigen

shortcoming tekortkoming

short cut korte(re) weg

shorten [sjo:tn] verkorten: ~*ed form* verkorting

shortfall tekort^h

shorthand steno(grafie)

short-handed met te weinig personeel

shortish [sjo:tisj] vrij kort, aan de korte kant

¹**shortlist** *vb* voordragen, op de voordracht plaatsen, nomineren

²**shortlist** *n* aanbevelingslijst *(of applicants, candidates)*

short-lived kortdurend, kortlevend

shortly [sjo:tlie] spoedig, binnenkort

short-sighted 1 bijziend; **2** kortzichtig

short-tempered opvliegend

short-term op korte termijn, kortetermijn-

short-winded 1 kortademig; **2** kortdurend

¹**shot** *n* **1** schot^h *(also sport),* worp, stoot; **2** (snedige) opmerking; **3** gok, poging: *it's a long* ~, *but certainly worth trying* het is een hele gok, maar zeker de moeite van het proberen waard; *have* (of: *make) a* ~ *(at sth.)* (ergens) een slag (naar) slaan; **4** *(photo)* opname, kiekje^h; **5** injectie, shot; **6** *(athletics)* (stoot)kogel; **7** borrel; **8** lading *(of firearm),* schroot^h: ~ *in the arm: a)* stimulans, injectie; *b)* borrel(tje); *a* ~ *across the bows* een schot voor de boeg, waarschuwing; *a* ~ *in the dark* een slag in de lucht; *call the* ~s de leiding hebben, het voor het zeggen hebben; *(do sth.) like a* ~ onmiddellijk (iets doen)

²**shot** *adj* doorweven, vol: ~ *(through) with* doorspekt met; *be* ~ *of* klaar zijn met, af zijn van

¹**shotgun** [sjotgun] *n* (jacht)geweer^h

²**shotgun** [sjotgun] *adj* gedwongen: ~ *wedding* (of: *marriage)* moetje

should [sjoed] zou(den), zou(den) moeten, moest(en), mochten: *~ you need any help, please ask the staff* mocht u hulp nodig hebben, wendt u zich dan tot het personeel; *why ~ I listen to him?* waarom zou ik naar hem luisteren?; *the teacher told Sheila that she ~ be more careful* de docent zei tegen Sheila dat zij voorzichtiger moest zijn; *he hoped that he ~ be accepted* hij hoopte dat hij aangenomen zou worden; *if Sheila came, I ~ come too* als Sheila kwam, dan kwam ik ook; *it ~ be easy for you* het moet voor jou gemakkelijk zijn; *yes, I ~ love to* ja, dat zou ik echt graag doen; *I suggest that we ~ leave* ik stel voor dat wij naar huis (zouden) gaan; *(sometimes untranslated) it's surprising he ~ be thought so attractive* het is verbazingwekkend dat hij zo aantrekkelijk wordt gevonden

¹shoulder [sjooldə] *n* **1** schouder: *stand head and ~s above* met kop en schouders uitsteken boven *(also fig)*; **2** (weg)berm; **3** schoft *(of animal)*: *put (of: set) one's ~ to the wheel* zijn schouders ergens onder zetten, ergens hard aan werken; *rub ~s with* omgaan met; *(straight) from the ~* op de man af, recht voor z'n raap

²shoulder [sjooldə] *vb* **1** op zich nemen, op zijn schouders nemen: *~ a great burden* een zware last op zich nemen; **2** duwen, (met de schouders) dringen: *he ~ed his way through the crowd* hij baande zich een weg door de menigte

shoulder blade schouderblad[h]

¹shout [sjaut] *vb* schreeuwen, (uit)roepen, brullen, gillen: *~ oneself hoarse* zich schor schreeuwen; *the audience ~ed down the speaker* het publiek joelde de spreker uit; *~ for joy* het uitroepen van vreugde

²shout [sjaut] *n* schreeuw, kreet, gil: *~ of joy* vreugdekreet

¹shove [sjuv] *vb* (weg)duwen, dringen (tegen), een zet geven, stoppen, leggen: *~ along* heen en weer duwen, vooruitdringen; *~ it in the drawer* stop het in de la; *~ off:* a) afschuiven; b) afduwen *(in boat)*; *let's ~ off* laten we er vandoor gaan

²shove [sjuv] *n* duw, zet, stoot

¹shovel [sjuvl] *n* **1** schop, spade, schep; **2** schoep *(of machine)*; **3** laadschop

²shovel [sjuvl] *vb* (op)scheppen, schuiven, opruimen (met een schep): *~ food into one's mouth* eten in zijn mond proppen; *~ a path through the snow* een pad graven door de sneeuw

¹show [sjoo] *vb* **1** (aan)tonen, laten zien, tentoonstellen, vertonen: *~ one's cards* (of: *hand*) open kaart spelen *(also fig)*; *~ (s.o.) the way:* a) iem de weg wijzen; b) *(also fig)* een voorbeeld stellen; *~ oneself* je (gezicht) laten zien, je ware aard tonen; *he has nothing to ~ for all his work* zijn werk heeft helemaal niets opgeleverd; **2** uitleggen, demonstreren, bewijzen: *he ~ed me how to write* hij leerde me schrijven; **3** te kennen geven, tentoonspreiden: *~ bad taste* van een slechte smaak getuigen; **4** (rond)leiden: *~ s.o. about* (of: *(a)round*) iem rondleiden; *~ her into the waiting room* breng haar naar de wachtkamer;

~ s.o. over the factory iem een rondleiding geven door de fabriek; **5** aanwijzen: *the clock ~s five minutes past* de klok staat op vijf over

²show [sjoo] *vb* (zich) (ver)tonen *(of film): your slip is ~ing* je onderjurk komt eruit; *time will ~* de tijd zal het leren; *it just goes to ~!* zo zie je maar!

³show [sjoo] *n* **1** vertoning, show, uitzending, (televisie)programma[h], concert[h], opvoering: *a ~ in the theatre* een toneelopvoering; **2** spektakel(stuk)[h], grootse vertoning: *a ~ of force* (of: *strength*) een machtsvertoon; *make a ~ of one's learning* te koop lopen met zijn geleerdheid; **3** tentoonstelling; **4** poging, gooi, beurt: *a bad* (of: *poor*) *~* een slechte beurt; *good ~!* goed geprobeerd!; *put up a good ~* een goede prestatie leveren; **5** uiterlijk[h], schijn, opschepperij: *this is all empty ~* dit is allemaal slechts schijn; **6** pracht (en praal); **7** vertoning, demonstratie: *objects on ~* de tentoongestelde voorwerpen; *vote by (a) ~ of hands* d.m.v. handopsteking stemmen; *give the (whole) ~ away* de hele zaak verraden; *steal the ~* de show stelen

show business amusementsbedrijf[h], show business

showcase vitrine *(in shop, museum)*, uitstalkast

showdown 1 *(poker)* het tonen van zijn kaarten *(also fig)*; **2** directe confrontatie, krachtmeting

¹shower [sjauə] *n* **1** bui: *occasional ~s* hier en daar een bui; **2** douche: *have a ~* douchen, een douche nemen; **3** stroom, toevloed, golf: *a ~ of arrows* een regen van pijlen

²shower [sjauə] *vb* **1** (with *with*) overgieten (met), uitstorten, doen neerstromen; **2** (with *with*) overladen (met), overstelpen: *~ questions on s.o.* een heleboel vragen op iem afvuren

³shower [sjauə] *vb* **1** zich douchen; **2** (toe)stromen: *apples ~ed down the tree* het regende appels uit de boom

showery [sjauərie] buiig, regenachtig

showgirl revuemeisje[h]

showing [sjooing] vertoning, voorstelling, voorkomen[h], figuur[+h]: *make a good ~* een goed figuur slaan; *a poor ~* een zwakke vertoning *(eg of football team)*; *on present ~* zoals de zaak er nu voor blijkt te staan

showman [sjoomən] **1** impresario *(organiser of concerts, shows)*; **2** aansteller

show off *vb* opscheppen, indruk proberen te maken

²show off *vb* **1** pronken met, etaleren: *don't ~ your knowledge* loop niet zo te koop met je kennis; **2** goed doen uitkomen: *your white dress shows off your tanned skin* je witte jurk doet je gebruinde huid goed uitkomen

show-off opschepper

showpiece pronkstuk[h], paradepaardje[h]

showroom toonzaal

show trial schijnproces[h]

¹show up *vb* **1** ontmaskeren, aan het licht brengen: *~ an impostor* een bedrieger ontmaskeren; **2** zichtbaar maken: *only strong light shows up her wrinkles* slechts sterk licht toont haar rimpeltjes; **3** in verlegenheid brengen: *the pupil's remark showed him up* de opmerking van de scholier zette hem voor gek

²**show up** *vb* opdagen, verschijnen

show-window etalage

showy [sjooie] opvallend, opzichtig

shrapnel [sjræpnəl] **1** (soort) granaat; **2** granaatscherven

¹**shred** [sjred] *n* **1** stukjeʰ, reepjeʰ, snipper: *not a ~ of clothing* geen draadje kleding; *tear sth. to ~s: a)* iets aan flarden scheuren; *b) (also fig)* niets heel laten van; **2** greintjeʰ: *not a ~ of evidence* niet het minste bewijs, geen enkel bewijs

²**shred** [sjred] *vb* verscheuren, versnipperen, in stukjes snijden

shredder [sjreddə] **1** (grove keuken)schaaf *(for vegetables, cheese)*, rasp; **2** papierversnipperaar

shrew [sjroe:] feeks

shrewd [sjroe:d] slim: *~ guess* intelligente gok; *~ observer* scherp waarnemer

¹**shriek** [sjrie:k] *vb* schreeuwen, gillen: *~ out* uitschreeuwen; *~ with laughter* gieren van het lachen

²**shriek** [sjrie:k] *n* schreeuw, gil, (schrille) kreet

shrift [sjrift]: *make short ~ of* korte metten maken met

shrill [sjril] schel, schril, doordringend, *(fig)* fel: *~ contrast* schril contrast

shrimp [sjrimp] garnaal; *(inf)* klein opdondertjeʰ

shrine [sjrajn] **1** (heiligen)tombe; **2** heiligdomʰ, *(fig)* gedenkplaats

¹**shrink** [sjringk] *vb* **1** krimpen, afnemen, slinken; **2** wegkruipen, ineenkrimpen, *(fig)* huiveren: *~ back* terugdeinzen

²**shrink** [sjringk] *vb* doen krimpen, kleiner maken, doen slinken

³**shrink** [sjringk] *n* zielenknijper *(psychiatrist)*

shrivel [sjrivl] verschrompelen, uitdrogen, inkrimpen

¹**shroud** [sjraud] *n* **1** lijkwa(de), doodskleedʰ; **2** *(fig)* sluier: *wrapped in a ~ of mystery* in een sluier van geheimzinnigheid gehuld

²**shroud** [sjraud] *vb* (om)hullen, verbergen: *mountains ~ed in mist* in mist gehulde bergen

Shrove Tuesday Vastenavond, vette dinsdag *(Tuesday before Ash Wednesday)*

shrub [sjrub] struik, heester

¹**shrug** [sjrug] *vb* (de schouders) ophalen

²**shrug** [sjrug] *n* schouderophalenʰ

shrug off van zich afschudden *(clothing)*, geen belang hechten aan: *she shrugged off all criticism* zij liet alle kritiek langs haar heen gaan

shrunken [sjrungkən] gekrompen, verschrompeld

shucks! [sjuks] **1** onzin!; **2** krijg nou wat!

¹**shudder** [sjuddə] *vb* **1** huiveren, sidderen, beven: *I ~ to think* ik huiver bij de gedachte; **2** trillen

²**shudder** [sjuddə] *n* huivering, rilling

¹**shuffle** [sjufl] *vb* **1** mengen, door elkaar halen, schudden *(cards)*; **2** heen en weer bewegen, herverdelen: *~ one's papers* in zijn papieren rommelen; **3**

schuiven: *try to ~ off one's responsibility* zijn verantwoordelijkheid proberen af te schuiven

²**shuffle** [sjufl] *vb* schuifelen, sloffen: *~ one's feet* met de voeten schuifelen

³**shuffle** [sjufl] *n* **1** schuifelgang; **2** *(dance)* schuifelpas; **3** het schudden *(of cards, dominoes)*

shufti [sjoeftie] kijkjeʰ: *have* (of: *take) a ~ at* een blik werpen op

shun [sjun] mijden, schuwen

shunt [sjunt] afleiden, afvoeren, rangeren, op een dood spoor zetten *(pers)*: *~ a train onto a siding* een trein op een zijspoor rangeren

shush [sjusj] sst!, stilte!

¹**shut** [sjut] *vb* **1** sluiten, dichtdoen, dichtslaan, dichtdraaien, *(fig)* stopzetten: *~ one's eyes to sth.* iets niet willen zien; *~ in by mountains* door bergen ingesloten; *~ down a plant* een fabriek (voorgoed) sluiten; *~ out of* de toegang ontzeggen tot; **2** opsluiten: *~ sth. away* iets (veilig) opbergen; *~ oneself in* zichzelf opsluiten *(eg in room)*

²**shut** [sjut] *vb* sluiten, dichtgaan: *the shop ~s on Sundays* de winkel is 's zondags gesloten

³**shut** [sjut] *adj* dicht, gesloten: *slam the door ~* de deur dichtsmijten

shutdown sluiting, stopzetting *(of business)*

shut-eye slaap, dutjeʰ: *have a bit of ~* een dutje doen

¹**shutter** [sjuttə] *n* **1** blind, (rol)luikʰ: *put up the ~s* de zaak sluiten *(temporarily or permanently)*; **2** sluiter *(also of camera)*

²**shutter** [sjuttə] *vb* met (een) luik(en) sluiten: *~ed windows* vensters met gesloten luiken

¹**shuttle** [sjutl] *n* **1** schuitjeʰ *(of sewing machine)*; **2** pendeldienst

²**shuttle** [sjutl] *vb* pendelen

³**shuttle** [sjutl] *vb* heen en weer vervoeren

shuttlecock pluimbal, shuttle *(badminton)*

shuttle service pendeldienst

¹**shut up** *vb* **1** zwijgen: *shut up!* kop dicht!; **2** sluiten *(shop etc)*

²**shut up** *vb* **1** sluiten, (zorgvuldig) afsluiten: *they ~ the house before they left* ze sloten het huis af voordat ze weggingen; *~ shop* de zaak sluiten; **2** opsluiten, achter slot en grendel zetten, opbergen; **3** doen zwijgen, de mond snoeren: *turn the television on, that usually shuts them up* zet de tv maar aan, meestal houden ze dan hun mond dicht

¹**shy** [sjaj] *adj* **1** verlegen: *give s.o. a ~ look* iem verlegen aankijken; **2** voorzichtig, behoedzaam: *fight* (of: *be) ~ of* uit de weg gaan; **3** schuw, schichtig *(animals)*

²**shy** [sjaj] *vb* **1** schichtig opspringen: *~ at sth.* schichtig worden voor iets *(of horses)*; **2** terugschrikken: *~ away from sth.* iets vermijden, voor iets terugschrikken

³**shy** *vb* gooien, slingeren

⁴**shy** *n (shies)* **1** gooi, worp; **2** gooi, poging, experimentʰ: *have a ~ at sth.* een gooi doen naar iets, het (ook) eens proberen

shyster [sjajstə] gewetenloos mens *(esp lawyer or*

politician)

Siamese [sajjəmie:z] Siamees

Siberian [sajbiəriən] Siberisch

¹sick [sik] *adj* **1** ziek, sukkelend: *fall ~* ziek worden; *go* (of: *report*) *~* zich ziek melden; **2** misselijk, *(fig also)* met walging vervuld: *be ~* overgeven, braken; *be worried ~* doodongerust zijn; *you make me ~!* je doet me walgen!; **3** wee, onpasselijk makend: *a ~ feeling* een wee gevoel; **4** ziekelijk, ongezond, morbide, wrang *(mockery)*: *a ~ joke* een lugubere grap; *a ~ mind* een zieke geest; **5** beu, moe(de): *I am ~ (and tired) of it* ik ben het spuugzat; *~ to death of s.o.* (sth.) iem (iets) spuugzat zijn

²sick [sik] *n* braaksel[h], spuugsel[h]

sickbay ziekenboeg

sickbed ziekbed[h]

sick benefit ziekengeld[h]

sick call ziekenbezoek[h] *(by doctor or clergyman)*

¹sicken [sikkən] *vb* **1** ziek worden; **2** misselijk worden; **3** *(with for)* smachten (naar); **4** de eerste tekenen (ve ziekte) vertonen, onder de leden hebben: *be ~ing for measles* de mazelen onder de leden hebben

²sicken [sikkən] *vb* ziek maken, doen walgen

sickening [sikkəning] **1** ziekmakend, ziekteverwekkend; **2** walgelijk, weerzinwekkend

sickle [sikl] sikkel

sick leave ziekteverlof[h]: *on ~* met ziekteverlof

sick list ziekenlijst: *on the ~* afwezig wegens ziekte

sickly [siklie] **1** ziekelijk, sukkelend; **2** bleek *(face, complexion)*, flauw *(smile)*; **3** walgelijk *(smell)*, wee

sickness [siknəs] **1** ziekte; **2** misselijkheid

sickness benefit ziektegeld[h], uitkering wegens ziekte

sick pay ziekengeld[h]

¹side [sajd] *n* **1** zij(de), (zij)kant, flank, helling *(of mountain)*, oever *(of river)*, richting, aspect[h], trek *(of character)*: *always look on the bright ~ of life* bekijk het leven altijd van de zonnige kant; *take ~s with s.o.* partij voor iem kiezen; *this ~ up* deze kant boven *(on boxes before shipping)*; *at* (of: *by) my ~* naast mij; *~ by ~* zij aan zij; *whose ~ are you on, anyway?* aan wiens kant sta jij eigenlijk?; **2** bladzijde; **3** gedeelte[h], deel[h]: *he went to the far ~ of the room* hij liep tot achter in de kamer; **4** gezichtspunt[h]; **5** ploeg, team[h]: *let the ~ down* niet aan de verwachtingen van de anderen voldoen; *know (on) which ~ one's bread is buttered* weten waar men zijn kaarsje moet laten branden; *the other ~ of the coin* de keerzijde van de medaille; *laugh on the other ~ of one's face* (of: *mouth*) lachen als een boer die kiespijn heeft; *put on* (of: *to*) *one ~*, *set on one ~* terzijde leggen, sparen, reserveren; *take on* (of: *to*) *one ~* terzijde nemen *(for a talk)*; *on the ~: a)* als bijverdienste, zwart; *b)* in het geniep

²side [sajd] *adj* **1** zij-: *~ entrance* zij-ingang; **2** bij-, neven-

³side [sajd] *vb* (with *against, with*) partij kiezen (tegen, voor)

sideboard 1 buffet[h]; **2** dientafel; **3** *~s* bakkebaarden

sideburns bakkebaarden

sidecar zijspan[h]

side dish bijgerecht[h]

side effect 1 bijwerking *(of medicine or therapy)*; **2** neveneffect[h]

sidekick handlanger, ondergeschikte partner

sidelight 1 zijlicht[h], stadslicht[h] *(of car)*; **2** *(fig)* toevallige informatie: *that throws some interesting ~s on the problem* dat werpt een interessant licht op de zaak

¹sideline *n* **1** bijbaan, nevenactiviteit; **2** *~s (sport)* zijlijnen || *be* (of: *sit, stand*) *on the ~s* de zaak van een afstand bekijken

²sideline *vb* van het veld sturen, *(fig)* buiten spel zetten, negeren

sidelong zijdelings

side-saddle dameszadel[h]

sideshow bijkomende voorstelling, extra attractie *(at fairground; in circus)*

side-slip zijwaartse slip *(of car, aeroplane, skier)*

¹sidestep *vb* ontwijken, uit de weg gaan *(also fig; responsibility, problems)*

²sidestep *vb* opzijgaan, uitwijken

sidestroke zijslag *(swimming)*

¹sideswipe *n* **1** zijslag, zijstoot; **2** schimpscheut, hatelijke opmerking

²sideswipe *vb* schampen (langs), zijdelings raken

sidetrack 1 op een zijspoor zetten *(also fig)*, rangeren, opzijschuiven; **2** van zijn onderwerp afbrengen, afleiden

sidewalk *(Am)* stoep, trottoir[h]

sideward [sajdwəd] zijwaarts, zijdelings

siding [sajding] **1** rangeerspoor[h], wisselspoor[h]; **2** afbouwmateriaal[h], buitenbekleding *(of wall)*

sidle [sajdl] zich schuchter bewegen: *~ up to s.o., ~ away from s.o.* schuchter naar iem toelopen, schuchter van iem weglopen

siege [sie:dʒ] beleg[h], belegering, blokkade: *lay ~ to* belegeren; *raise the ~* het beleg opbreken

sieve [siv] *n* zeef: *a memory like a ~* een geheugen als een zeef

²sieve [siv] *vb* ziften *(also fig)*, zeven, schiften

sift [sift] **1** ziften *(also fig)*, strooien *(sugar)*: *~ out* uitzeven; **2** uitpluizen, doorpluizen: *he ~ed through his papers* hij doorzocht zijn papieren

¹sigh [saj] *vb* zuchten: *~ for* smachten naar

²sigh [saj] *n* zucht

¹sight [sajt] *n* **1** (aan)blik, (uit)zicht[h], schouwspel[h], bezienswaardigheid: *I cannot stand* (of: *bear) the ~ of him* ik kan hem niet luchten of zien; *catch ~ of, get a ~ of* in het oog krijgen, een glimp opvangen van; *lose ~ of* uit het oog verliezen *(also fig)*; *see the ~s* de bezienswaardigheden bezoeken; **2** vizier[h]: *have one's ~s set on, set one's ~s on* op het oog hebben, erg willen; **3** boel: *he is a ~ too clever for me* hij is me veel te vlug af; **4** (ge)zicht[h], gezichtsvermogen[h]: *loss of ~* het blind worden; **5** gezicht[h], het zien: *at first ~* op het eerste gezicht; *know s.o. by ~* iem van gezicht kennen; **6** (uit)zicht^h, gezicht(sveld)^h: *come into (of: within) ~ zichtbaar worden; keep in ~ of* binnen het gezichtsveld blijven van; *out of ~, out of mind* uit het oog, uit het hart; *we are (with)in ~ of the end* het einde is in zicht; *stay (of: keep) out of ~* blijf uit het gezicht; *raise one's ~s* meer verwachten; *out of ~!* fantastisch!, te gek!; *second ~* helderziendheid

²sight [sajt] *vb* **1** in zicht krijgen, in het vizier krijgen; **2** waarnemen, zien: *he was last ~ed in London in 1992* hij werd voor het laatst gezien in Londen in 1992

sightseeing het bezoeken van bezienswaardigheden

sightseer [sajtsie:ə] toerist

¹sign [sajn] *n* **1** teken^h, symbool^h; **2** aanwijzing, (ken)teken^h, blijk, voorteken^h; **3** wenk, teken^h, seintje^h; **4** (uithang)bord^h; **5** (ken)teken^h: *~ of the times* teken des tijds; **6** sterrenbeeld^h: *~ of the zodiac* sterrenbeeld

²sign [sajn] *vb* **1** (onder)tekenen: *~ one's name* tekenen; *~ in* tekenen bij aankomst, intekenen; *~ on at the Job Centre* inschrijven op het arbeidsbureau; *~ up for a course* zich voor een cursus inschrijven; **2** signeren, ondertekenen: *~ed copies are available within* gesigneerde exemplaren zijn binnen verkrijgbaar; **3** wenken, een teken geven, gebaren; **4** (with *on, up*) contracteren *(player)*

¹signal [signl] *n* **1** signaal^h *(also fig; also of radio, TV)*, teken^h, sein^h: *~ of distress* noodsignaal; **2** sein(apparaat^h), signaal^h; **3** verkeerslicht^h

²signal [signl] *adj* buitengewoon, glansrijk: *a ~ victory* een glansrijke overwinning

³signal [signl] *vb* (over)seinen, een teken geven

⁴signal [signl] *vb* aankondigen, te kennen geven

signal box seinhuisje^h

signalize [signəlajz] doen opvallen, de aandacht vestigen op, opluisteren

signalman [signəlmən] seiner, *(railways also)* sein(huis)wachter

signatory [signətərie] ondertekenaar

signature [signətsjə] handtekening

signature tune herkenningsmelodie, tune *(of radio, TV)*

signboard 1 uithangbord^h; **2** bord^h met opschrift

signet [signit] zegel^h

significance [signiffikkəns] betekenis, belang^h: *a meeting of great historical ~* een ontmoeting van grote historische betekenis

significant [signiffikkənt] belangrijk; veelbetekenend: *be ~ of* aanduiden, kenmerkend zijn voor

signify [signiffaj] **1** betekenen, beduiden; **2** te kennen geven: *the teacher rose, ~ing that the class was over* de docent stond op, daarmee gaf hij te kennen dat de les afgelopen was

sign language gebarentaal

sign-on herkenningsmelodie *(of radio or TV programme)*, tune

signpost wegwijzer

¹silence [sajləns] *n* stilte, stilzwijgen^h, stilzwijgendheid, zwijgzaamheid: *put (of: reduce) s.o. to ~* iem tot zwijgen brengen; *in ~* in stilte, stilzwijgend; *~!* stil!, zwijg!

²silence [sajləns] *vb* tot zwijgen brengen, het stilzwijgen opleggen, stil doen zijn

silencer [sajlənsə] **1** geluiddemper *(on firearm)*; **2** knalpot

silent [sajlənt] stil, (stil)zwijgend, zwijgzaam, onuitgesproken, stom, rustig: *a ~ film* een stomme film; *keep ~* rustig blijven

silhouette [silloe:ɛt] silhouet^h, beeltenis, schaduwbeeld^h, omtrek

¹silk [silk] *n* **1** zij(de), zijdedraad; **2** King's (Queen's) Counsel

²silk [silk] *adj* zijden, zijde-

silken [silkən] **1** zij(de)achtig; **2** zacht

silkworm zijderups

sill [sil] **1** vensterbank; **2** drempel

¹silly [sillie] *adj* **1** dwaas, dom, onverstandig; **2** verdwaasd, suf, murw: *knock s.o. ~* iem murw slaan

²silly [sillie] *n* domoor: *of course you're coming with us, ~!* natuurlijk mag je met ons mee, dommerdje!

silly season komkommertijd

silo [sajloo] silo, voederkuil, (betonnen) voedersleuf

silt [silt] slib^h, slik

silt up dichtslibben, verzanden

¹silver [silvə] *n* **1** zilver^h; **2** zilvergeld^h; **3** zilver(werk)^h, *(fig)* tafelgerei^h

²silver [silvə] *adj* **1** van zilver, zilveren, zilver-: *~ foil* zilverfolie; **2** verzilverd: *~ plate* verzilverd vaatwerk; **3** zilverachtig: *~ wedding (anniversary)* zilveren bruiloft

silverfish zilvervisje^h, papiermot

silversmith zilversmid

silvery [silvərie] zilverachtig; zilverkleurig

similar [simmillə] *(with to)* gelijk (aan), vergelijkbaar, hetzelfde, *(maths)* gelijkvormig: *in ~ cases* in vergelijkbare gevallen

similarity [simmilæritie] **1** vergelijkbaarheid, overeenkomst; **2** punt^h van overeenkomst, gelijkenis

similarly [simmilləlie] **1** op dezelfde manier, op een vergelijkbare manier; **2** *(at beginning of sentence)* evenzo

simile [simmillie] vergelijking, gelijkenis *(figure of speech)*

¹simmer [simmə] *vb* **1** sudderen, pruttelen; **2** zich inhouden *(of rage, laughter)*: *~ down* bedaren

²simmer [simmə] *vb* aan het sudderen brengen, houden

³simmer [simmə] *n* gesudder^h, gepruttel^h

¹simper [simpə] *vb* onnozel glimlachen, zelfvoldaan grijnslachen

²simper [simpə] *n* onnozele glimlach, zelfvoldane grijnslach

simple [simpl] **1** eenvoudig, eerlijk, simpel: *the ~ life* het natuurlijke leven; *the ~ truth* de nuchtere waarheid; **2** dwaas, onnozel; **3** eenvoudig, gemakkelijk: ~ *solution* eenvoudige oplossing; **4** enkel(voudig): ~ *forms of life* eenvoudige levensvormen

simple-minded 1 argeloos, onnadenkend; **2** zwakzinnig

simpleton [simpltən] dwaas, sul

simplicity [simplissittie] **1** eenvoud, ongecompliceerdheid: *it is ~ itself* het is een koud kunstje; **2** simpelheid

simplification [simpliffikkeesjən] vereenvoudiging

simplify [simpliffaj] **1** vereenvoudigen; **2** (te) eenvoudig voorstellen, simplificeren

simply [simplie] **1** eenvoudig, gewoonweg; **2** stomweg; **3** enkel, maar, slechts: *if you want to call the nurse,* ~ *push the red button* als u de zuster wilt roepen, hoeft u alleen maar op de rode knop te drukken

simulate [simjoeleet] **1** simuleren, voorwenden, doen alsof; **2** imiteren, nabootsen: *~d gold* namaakgoud

simulation [simjoeleesjən] **1** voorwending, veinzerij; **2** nabootsing, imitatie

simultaneity [simltənie:ittie] gelijktijdigheid

simultaneous [simltəniəs] gelijktijdig, simultaan: *~ly with* tegelijk met

¹sin [sin] *n* zonde, *(fig also)* misdaad: *live in* ~ in zonde leven, samenwonen; *for my ~s* voor mijn straf

²sin [sin] *vb* (with *against*) zondigen (tegen)

¹since [sins] *prep* sinds, sedert, van … af: *he has never been the same* ~ *his wife's death* hij is nooit meer dezelfde geweest sinds de dood van zijn vrouw

²since [sins] *adv* **1** sindsdien, van toen af, ondertussen: *I've lived here ever* ~ ik heb hier sindsdien de hele tijd gewoond; **2** geleden: *he left some years* ~ hij is enige jaren geleden weggegaan

³since [sins] *conj* **1** sinds, vanaf de tijd dat: *I haven't seen you* ~ *you were a child* ik heb je niet meer gezien sinds je klein was; **2** aangezien, daar: *~ you don't want me around I might as well leave* aangezien je me niet in de buurt wilt hebben, kan ik net zo goed weggaan

sincere [sinsiə] eerlijk, oprecht, gemeend

sincerely [sinsiəlie] eerlijk, oprecht, gemeend: *yours* ~ met vriendelijke groeten *(complimentary close in letter to acquaintances)*

sincerity [sinserrittie] eerlijkheid, gemeendheid: *in all* ~ in alle oprechtheid

sine [sajn] sinus

sinew [sinjoe] **1** pees; **2** (spier)kracht

sinful [sinfoel] **1** zondig, schuldig; **2** slecht

¹sing [sing] *vb* **1** zingen, suizen *(of wind)*, fluiten *(of bullet)*; **2** gonzen *(of ear)* ‖ ~ *sth. out* iets uitroepen; ~ *out (for)* schreeuwen (om)

²sing [sing] *vb* bezingen

sing. *singular* enk, enkelvoud

¹singe [sindzj] *vb* **1** (ver)schroeien; **2** krullen, golven *(hair)*

²singe [sindzj] *n* **1** schroeiing; **2** schroeiplek

singer [singə] zanger(es)

singing [singing] **1** (ge)zang^h, het zingen; **2** zangkunst

¹single [singgl] *adj* **1** enkel(voudig); **2** ongetrouwd, alleenstaand; **3** enig; **4** afzonderlijk, individueel: *not a* ~ *man helped* niet één man hielp; **5** eenpersoons-: ~ *bed* eenpersoonsbed; **6** enkele reis: *a* ~ *ticket* een (kaartje) enkele reis; *in* ~ *file* achter elkaar (in de rij)

²single [singgl] *n* **1** enkeltje^h, enkele reis; **2** vrijgezel; **3** *(mus)* single; **4** *~s* enkel(spel)^h *(at tennis)*

single-handed alleen, zonder steun

single-minded 1 doelbewust; **2** vastberaden

singleness [singglnəs] concentratie ‖ ~ *of purpose* doelgerichte toewijding

single out uitkiezen, selecteren

singlet [singglit] (onder)hemd^h, sporthemd^h

¹sing-song *n* **1** dreun: *say sth. in a* ~ iets opdreunen; **2** samenzang

²sing-song *adj* eentonig, zangerig

¹singular [singgjoelə] *adj* **1** bijzonder, uitzonderlijk; **2** ongewoon, vreemd: ~ *event* eigenaardige gebeurtenis

²singular [singgjoelə] *n (linguistics)* enkelvoud^h, enkelvoudsvorm

singularity [singgjoelærittie] bijzonderheid; eigenaardigheid

Sinhalese [sinhəlie:z] *(Sinhalese)* Singalees *(inhabitant of Sri Lanka)*

sinister [sinnistə] **1** boosaardig, onguur; **2** onheilspellend, duister, sinister

¹sink [singk] *vb* **1** (weg)zinken, (weg)zakken, verzakken: *her spirits sank* de moed zonk haar in de schoenen; *his voice sank to a whisper* zijn stem daalde tot op fluisterniveau; **2** (neer)dalen: ~ *in one's estimation* in iemands achting dalen; **3** afnemen, verflauwen, verdwijnen; **4** achteruit gaan, zwakker worden: *the sick man is ~ing fast* de zieke man gaat snel achteruit; **5** doordringen, indringen (in): *his words will* ~ *in* zijn woorden zullen inslaan; ~ *or swim* pompen of verzuipen

²sink [singk] *vb* **1** laten zinken, doen zakken: ~ *a ship* een schip tot zinken brengen; **2** vergeten, laten rusten: ~ *the differences* de geschillen vergeten; **3** graven, boren: ~ *a well* een put boren; **4** bederven *(plan etc)*, verpesten: *be sunk in thought* in gedachten verzonken zijn; *be sunk* reddeloos verloren zijn

³sink [singk] *n* **1** gootsteen(bak); **2** wasbak; **3** poel *(van kwaad)*: ~ *of iniquity* poel van verderf

sinner [sinnə] zondaar

sinuous [sinjoeəs] **1** kronkelend, bochtig; **2** lenig, buigzaam

sinus [sajnəs] holte, opening; *(anatomy)* sinus

¹sip [sip] *vb* **1** met kleine teugjes drinken; **2** (with *at*) nippen (aan)

²sip [sip] *n* slokje^h, teugje^h

siphon [sajfən] *(also with off, out)* (over)hevelen *(also fig)*, overtappen: *management ~ed millions* *into plans for the building of a new head office* de directie hevelde miljoenen over naar plannen voor de bouw van een nieuw hoofdkantoor

sir [sə:] meneer, mijnheer *(form of address): Dear Sir* geachte heer; *Dear Sirs* mijne heren *(in letter); no ~!* geen sprake van!

sire [sajjə] **1** vader van dier *(of horse);* **2** Sire, heer *(form of address of emperor, king)*

siren [sajjərən] **1** (alarm)sirene; **2** *(mythology)* sirene; **3** verleidster

sister [sistə] **1** zus(ter); **2** non, zuster; **3** (hoofd)verpleegster

sisterhood [sistəhoed] **1** zusterschap; nonnenorde; **2** vrouwenbeweging

sister-in-law schoonzus(ter)

¹sit [sit] *vb* **1** zitten: *~ tight* rustig blijven zitten, volhouden; **2** zijn, zich bevinden, liggen, staan: *~ heavy on the stomach* zwaar op de maag liggen; **3** poseren, model staan: *~ for a portrait* voor een portret poseren; **4** (zitten te) broeden; **5** zitting hebben: *~ pretty* op rozen zitten; *~ about (of: around)* lanterfanten; *~ back* gemakkelijk gaan zitten, *(fig)* zijn gemak nemen, zich terugtrekken; *~ by* rustig toe zitten te kijken; *~ down* gaan zitten; *~ in* als vervanger optreden; *~ in on* als toehoorder bijwonen; *~ for an exam* een examen afleggen

²sit [sit] *vb* **1** laten zitten; **2** berijden *(horse);* **3** afleggen *(examination)*

sitcom [sitkom] *situation comedy* komische tv-serie

sit-down zittend: *~ meal* zittend genuttigde maaltijd

¹site [sajt] *n* **1** plaats, lokatie; **2** (bouw)terreinʰ

²site [sajt] *vb* plaatsen, situeren: *the farm is beautifully ~d* de boerderij is prachtig gelegen

sit on 1 zitting hebben in; **2** onderzoeken; **3** laten liggen, niets doen aan; **4** terechtwijzen, op z'n kop zitten

sitter [sitə] **1** modelʰ, iem die poseert; **2** broedende vogel, broedhen; **3** babysitter kinderoppas, babysit

sitter-in (baby)oppas

¹sitting [sitting] *n* **1** zitting, vergadering; **2** tafel, gelegenheid om te eten; **3** het zitten; **4** het poseren || *he read the story at one ~* hij las het verhaal in één ruk uit

²sitting [sitting] *adj* zittend: *~ duck (of: target)* makkelijk doel(wit), weerloos slachtoffer; *~ tenant* huidige huurder

sittingroom zitkamer, woonkamer, huiskamer

situated [sitjoe·eetid] **1** geplaatst; **2** gelegen, gesitueerd

situation [sitjoe·eesjən] **1** toestand, situatie, omstandigheden; **2** ligging, plaats; **3** betrekking, baan: *~ vacant* functie aangeboden, vacature

sit up 1 rechtop (gaan) zitten: *that will make him ~ and take notice!* daar zal hij van opkijken!; **2** opblijven, waken *(with sick person)*

six [siks] zes: *arranged by ~es* per zes geschikt; *everything is at ~es and sevens* alles is helemaal in de war; *it's ~ of one and half a dozen of the other, it's ~*

and two threes het is lood om oud ijzer

sixfold [siksfoold] zesvoudig

six-shooter revolver

sixteen [sikstie:n] zestien

sixteenth [sikstie:nθ] zestiende, zestiende deelʰ

sixth [siksθ] zesde, zesde deelʰ

sixth form bovenbouw vwo

sixthly [siksθlie] ten zesde, op de zesde plaats

sixty [sikstie] zestig: *in the sixties* in de jaren zestig

sixty-four thousand dollar question hamvraag

size [sajz] **1** afmeting, formaatʰ, grootte, omvang: *trees of various ~s* bomen van verschillende grootte; **2** maat: *she takes ~ eight* ze heeft maat acht; *cut down to ~* iem op zijn plaats zetten

sizeable [sajzəbl] vrij groot, flink

¹sizzle [sizl] *vb* sissen, knetteren

²sizzle [sizl] *n* gesisʰ, geknetterʰ

sizzling [sizling] snik-: *a ~ hot day* een snikhete dag

¹skate [skeet] *n* **1** schaats: *get (of: put) one's ~s on* opschieten; **2** rolschaats

²skate [skeet] *vb* **1** schaatsen(rijden); **2** rolschaatsen || *~ over (of: round) sth.* ergens luchtig overheen lopen

skateboard skateboardʰ, rol(schaats)plank

skateboarding het skateboarden

skater [skeetə] **1** schaatser; **2** rolschaatser

skating rink 1 ijsbaan, schaatsbaan; **2** rolschaatsbaan

skedaddle [skidædl] ervandoor gaan, 'm smeren

skeleton [skellittən] **1** skeletʰ, geraamteʰ: *the ~ of the building* het geraamte van het gebouw; **2** uitgemergeld persoon (dierʰ); **3** schemaʰ, schets: *~ in the cupboard (of: closet)* onplezierig (familie)geheim, lijk in de kast

skeleton key loper

¹sketch [sketsj] *n* **1** schets, tekening, beknopte beschrijving; **2** sketch, kort toneelstukjeʰ (verhaalʰ)

²sketch [sketsj] *vb* schetsen, tekenen

³sketch [sketsj] *vb (also with in, out)* schetsen, kort beschrijven

sketchy [sketsjie] schetsmatig, ruw, *(fig)* oppervlakkig

skew [skjoe:] schuin, scheef

¹skewer [skjoe:ə] *n* vleespen, spies

²skewer [skjoe:ə] *vb* doorsteken *((as if) with skewer)*

¹ski [skie:] *n* ski

²ski [skie:] *vb* skiën, skilopen

¹skid [skid] *vb* slippen *(also of wheel),* schuiven

²skid [skid] *n* **1** steunblokʰ, steunbalk; **2** glijbaan, glijplank; **3** remschoen, remblokʰ; **4** schuiver, slip, slippartij: *the car went into a ~* de wagen raakte in een slip; *put the ~s under one's plans: a)* iem (iets) ruïneren; *b)* iem achter zijn vodden zitten

skid row achterbuurt

skier [skie:ə] skiër

skiff [skif] skiff

skilful [skilfoel] bekwaam, (des)kundig; vakkundig, ervaren

skill [skil] bekwaamheid; vakkundigheid, vaardig-

heid
skilled [skild] bekwaam; vakkundig: ~ *worker* geschoolde arbeider, vakman
skim [skim] **1** vluchtig inkijken: ~ *over a book* een boek vlug doornemen; **2** afromen *(milk);* **3** scheren
skimmed [skimd] afgeroomd: ~ *milk* taptemelk
¹skimp [skimp] *vb (*with *on)* bezuinigen (op), beknibbelen: *whatever you do, don't* ~ *on your food* wat je ook doet, ga in ieder geval niet bezuinigen op het eten
²skimp [skimp] *vb* **1** karig (toe)bedelen, zuinig zijn met; **2** kort houden
skimpy [skimpie] karig, schaars
¹skin [skin] *n* huid *(also of aeroplane, ship),* velʰ, pels: *have a thick* ~ een olifantshuid hebben; *have a thin* ~ erg gevoelig zijn; ~ *and bone(s)* vel over been; *escape by the* ~ *of one's teeth* op het nippertje ontsnappen; *get under s.o.'s* ~: *a)* iem irriteren; *b)* bezeten zijn van iem; *save one's* ~ er heelhuids afkomen
²skin [skin] *vb* **1** villen, (af)stropen *(also fig);* **2** schillen, pellen; **3** oplichten, afzetten ‖ *keep one's eye* ~*ned* alert zijn, wakker blijven
skin-deep oppervlakkig *(also fig): his politeness is only* ~ zijn beleefdheid is alleen maar buitenkant
skin diver sportduiker
skinflint vrek
skinful [skinfoel] genoeg drank om dronken van te worden: *he has had quite a* ~ *by the look of him* hij heeft zo te zien al het nodige op
skin game 1 oneerlijk gokspelʰ; **2** afzetterij, zwendel
skinny [skinnie] broodmager
skint [skint] platzak, blut
¹skip [skip] *vb* **1** huppelen, (over)springen; **2** touwtjespringen ‖ ~ *over* overslaan, luchtig overheen gaan
²skip [skip] *vb* overslaan, weglaten, wegblijven van
³skip [skip] *n* **1** sprongetjeʰ; **2** afvalcontainer
skipper [skippə] **1** kapitein, schipper; **2** *(sport)* aanvoerder ve team
¹skirmish [skə:misj] *n* **1** schermutseling *(also fig);* **2** woordenwisseling
²skirmish [skə:misj] *vb* **1** schermutselen; **2** (rede)twisten
¹skirt [skə:t] *n* **1** rok; **2** rand, zoom, uiteindeʰ; **3** *(inf)* stukʰ: *what a piece of* ~*!* wat een stuk!
²skirt [skə:t] *vb* **1** begrenzen, lopen langs; **2** ontwijken, omzeilen
skittish [skittisj] **1** schichtig *(of horse),* nerveus; **2** grillig; **3** frivool
skittle [skitl] kegel
skive [skajv] zich aan het werk onttrekken, zich drukken: *were you skiving or were you really ill?* was je je aan het drukken, of was je echt ziek?
skulk [skulk] **1** zich verschuilen; **2** sluipen
skull [skul] schedel; doodshoofdʰ
skullcap petjeʰ, kalotjeʰ, keppeltjeʰ
skunk [skungk] **1** stinkdierʰ; **2** schoft, schooier

sky [skaj] hemel, lucht: *praise s.o. to the skies* iem de hemel in prijzen; *the* ~ *is the limit* het kan niet op *(of money)*
sky-blue hemelsblauw
skydive *(parachuting)* vrije val maken: *skydiving* vrije val
sky-high hemelhoog, *(fig)* buitensporig hoog *(eg prices): blow* ~ in de lucht laten vliegen, opblazen, *(fig)* geen spaan heel laten van
skyjacking (vliegtuig)kaping
¹skylark *n* veldleeuwerik
²skylark *vb* **1** stoeien; **2** pret maken
skylight dakraamʰ
skyline 1 horizon; **2** skyline, silhouetʰ *(seen against sky)*
skyrocket omhoogschieten *(of prices): fuel prices have* ~*ed again* de brandstofprijzen zijn weer huizenhoog gestegen
skyscraper wolkenkrabber
slab [slæb] **1** plaat *(eg iron);* **2** plat rechthoekig stukʰ steen
¹slack [slæk] *adj* **1** slap, los: *reign with a* ~ *hand* met slappe hand regeren; **2** zwak, laks; **3** lui, traag: ~ *water* stil water, dood getijde
²slack [slæk] *n* **1** los (hangend) deel van zeil of touw: *take up* (of: *in) the* ~: *a)* aantrekken *(rope etc); b) (fig)* de teugel(s) kort houden; **2** steenkoolgruisʰ; **3** ~*s* sportpantalon, lange broek; **4** slappe tijd
³slack [slæk] *vb* **1** verslappen, (zich) ontspannen; **2** los(ser) maken, (laten) vieren; **3** de kantjes ervanaf lopen, traag werken ‖ ~ *off* verslappen *(in one's work)*
¹slacken [slækən] *vb* **1** verslappen, (zich) ontspannen; **2** langzamer lopen (rijden); **3** verminderen, afnemen
²slacken [slækən] *vb* los(ser) maken, (laten) vieren: ~ *speed* vaart minderen
slag-heap heuvel van mijnafval
¹slam [slæm] *vb* **1** met een klap dichtslaan; (neer)smijten, dichtsmijten: ~ *the door (in s.o.'s face)* de deur (voor iemands neus) dichtslaan; ~ *down* neersmijten; **2** harde klap met de hand geven; **3** scherp bekritiseren
²slam [slæm] *n* **1** harde slag, *(baseball)* rake slag; **2** slemʰ *(bridge),* alle slagen: *grand* ~ groot slem
¹slander [sla:ndə] *n* laster(praat)
²slander [sla:ndə] *vb* (be)lasteren
slanderous [sla:ndərəs] lasterlijk
slang [slæng] zeer informele taal, jargonʰ, taal van bepaalde sociale klasse of beroep
¹slant [sla:nt] *vb* hellen, schuin aflopen
²slant [sla:nt] *vb* **1** laten hellen, scheef houden; **2** niet objectief weergeven: ~*ed news* nieuwsberichten waarin partij wordt gekozen
³slant [sla:nt] *n* **1** helling, schuinte; **2** gezichtspuntʰ, kijk, optiek ‖ *the top shelf was on a* ~ de bovenste plank hing scheef
¹slap [slæp] *vb* **1** een klap geven, meppen: ~ *s.o. on the back* iem op zijn schouder kloppen, iem felicite-

ren; **2** smijten, kwakken: ~ *down: a)* neersmijten; *b) (inf)* hard aanpakken *(eg a wrong)*

²slap [slæp] *n* klap, mep: ~ *on the back* vriendschappelijke klap op de rug, *(fig)* schouderklopje; ~ *in the face* klap in het gezicht *(also fig);* ~ *on the wrist* vermaning, lichte straf; ~ *and tickle* geflirt

³slap [slæp] *adv* **1** met een klap, regelrecht; **2** eensklaps

slapdash nonchalant, lukraak

slap-happy 1 uitgelaten; **2** nonchalant

slapstick 1 gooi-en-smijtfilm; **2** grove humor

slap-up super-de-luxe, eersteklas

¹slash [slæsj] *vb* **1** houwen; **2** snijden; **3** striemen; **4** drastisch verlagen *(prices);* **5** scherp bekritiseren; **6** een split maken in: ~*ed sleeve* mouw met split

²slash [slæsj] *n* **1** houw, slag; **2** snee, jaap; **3** schuine streep

¹slate [sleet] *n* **1** lei *(rock, writing tablet),* daklei; **2** kandidatenlijst

²slate [sleet] *vb* **1** beleggen *(eg meeting),* vaststellen; **2** scherp bekritiseren; **3** (als kandidaat) voordragen, voorstellen

slatternly [slætənlie] slonzig

¹slaughter [slo:tə] *n* slachting, bloedbad[h]

²slaughter [slo:tə] *vb* **1** slachten, vermoorden; **2** totaal verslaan, inmaken

slaughterhouse slachthuis[h], abattoir[h]

¹Slav [sla:v] *adj* Slavisch

²Slav [sla:v] *n* Slaaf

¹slave [sleev] *n* slaaf, slavin

²slave [sleev] *vb* zich uitsloven, zwoegen: ~ *away (at sth.)* zwoegen (op iets), ploeteren *(eg for examination)*

slaver [slævə] kwijlen *(also fig). that dog is ~ing at the mouth* het kwijl loopt die hond zijn bek uit

slavery [sleevərie] **1** slavernij; **2** slavenarbeid

Slavic [sla:vik] Slavisch

slavish [sleevisj] slaafs, onderdanig

slay [slee] doden, afmaken, slachten

sleaze [slie:z] goorheid, viesheid

sleazy [slie:zie] **1** goor, vies; **2** armoedig, goedkoop: ~ *excuse* waardeloos excuus

¹sled [sled] *n* slee

²sled [sled] *vb* sleeën

sledge [sledzj] slee

sledgehammer voorhamer, moker: ~ *blow* keiharde slag

¹sleek [slie:k] *adj* **1** zacht en glanzend *(of hair);* **2** (te) keurig verzorgd, opgedoft, opgedirkt; **3** mooi gestroomlijnd *(of car)*

²sleek [slie:k] *vb* **1** gladmaken; **2** glanzend maken

¹sleep [slie:p] *n* **1** slaap, nachtrust: *my foot has gone to* ~ mijn voet slaapt; *not lose* ~ *over sth.* niet wakker liggen van iets; *put to* ~*: a)* in slaap brengen; *b)* wegmaken *(anaesthetic); c)* een spuitje geven *(animal);* **2** rust(periode), winterslaap; **3** slaap, oogvuil[h]

²sleep [slie:p] *vb* slapen, rusten: ~ *round the clock* de klok rond slapen; ~ *late* uitslapen; ~ *in: a)* in huis

slapen *(eg as housesitter); b)* uitslapen; ~ *on* (of: *over) sth.* een nachtje over iets slapen; *let ~ing dogs lie* men moet geen slapende honden wakker maken; ~ *around* met jan en alleman naar bed gaan; ~ *with s.o.* met iem naar bed gaan

³sleep [slie:p] *vb* slaapplaats hebben voor: *this hotel ~s eighty (guests)* dit hotel biedt plaats voor tachtig gasten; ~ *off one's hangover* zijn roes uitslapen

sleeper [slie:pə] **1** slaper, slaapkop; **2** dwarsbalk *(of railway);* **3** slaapwagen; slaaptrein

sleepwalker slaapwandelaar

sleepy [slie:pie] **1** slaperig; **2** loom

¹sleet [slie:t] *n* natte sneeuw(bui), natte hagel(bui)

²sleet [slie:t] *vb* sneeuwen en regenen tegelijk

sleeve [slie:v] **1** mouw; **2** koker, mof; **3** hoes *(of gramophone record)* ‖ *have sth. up one's* ~ iets achter de hand houden; *laugh in* (of: *up) one's* ~ in zijn vuistje lachen; *roll up one's ~s* de handen uit de mouwen steken

sleeveless [slie:vləs] mouwloos

sleigh [slee] arrenslee

sleight-of-hand 1 goochelarij, gegoochel[h] *(also fig);* **2** vingervlugheid

slender [slendə] **1** slank, tenger; **2** schaars, karig: *a ~ income* een karig inkomen; **3** zwak, teer

¹slew *vb* (rond)zwenken, met kracht omdraaien

²slew *n (Am)* massa, hoop: *there have been a whole ~ of shooting incidents* er is weer een hele reeks schietpartijen geweest

¹slice [slajs] *n* **1** plak(je[h]), snee(tje[h]), schijf(je[h]): ~ *of cake* plakje cake; **2** deel[h]; **3** schep: ~ *of luck* meevaller

²slice [slajs] *vb* kappen *(hit (ball) with spin)*

³slice [slajs] *vb* **1** (also with *up)* in plakken snijden; **2** snijden, (with *off)* afsnijden: ~*d bread* gesneden brood

¹slick [slik] *adj (inf)* **1** glad, glibberig, glanzend; **2** glad, uitgeslapen, gehaaid; **3** oppervlakkig, zich mooi voordoend; **4** goed (uitgevoerd), kundig, soepel (draaiend, verlopend)

²slick [slik] *n* olievlek *(on surface of sea)*

slicker [slikkə] **1** gladjanus; **2** waterafstotende regenjas

¹slide [slajd] *vb* **1** schuiven: *sliding door* schuifdeur; *sliding scale* variabele schaal, glijdende (loon)schaal; **2** slippen; **3** (uit)glijden; **4** (voort) laten glijden: ~ *over sth.* luchtig over iets heen praten

²slide [slajd] *n* **1** glijbaan; **2** sleehelling; **3** val, achteruitgang *(also fig): a dangerous ~ in oil prices* een gevaarlijke daling van de olieprijzen; **4** (stoom)schuif; **5** dia(positief[h]); **6** (aard)verschuiving, lawine; **7** haarspeld

slide rule rekenliniaal

¹slight [slajt] *adj* **1** tenger, broos; **2** gering, klein, onbeduidend: ~ *cold* lichte verkoudheid; *not in the ~est* niet in het minst

²slight [slajt] *vb* geringschatten, kleineren: ~*ing remarks about his teacher* geringschattende opmerkingen over zijn docent

slightly [slajtlie] een beetje, enigszins: ~ *longer* een beetje langer

¹slim [slim] *adj* **1** slank, tenger; **2** klein, gering: ~ *chance* geringe kans

²slim [slim] *vb* afslanken, aan de (slanke) lijn doen

slime [slajm] slijmʰ

slimy [slajmie] **1** slijmerig *(also fig)*, glibberig; **2** kruiperig

¹sling [sling] *vb* **1** (weg)slingeren, zwaaien, smijten: ~ *s.o. out* iem eruit smijten; **2** ophangen

²sling [sling] *n* **1** slinger; **2** zwaai, slingering; **3** katapult; **4** draagdoek, mitella; **5** draagriem, draagband; **6** lus, (hijs)strop

slink [slingk] (weg)sluipen: ~ *away* (of: *off, out)* zich stilletjes uit de voeten maken; ~ *in* heimelijk binnensluipen

¹slip [slip] *vb* **1** (uit)glijden, slippen; *~ped disc* hernia; *time ~s away* (of: *by)* de tijd gaat ongemerkt voorbij; ~ *through* doorschieten; **2** glippen, (snel) sluipen: ~ *away* wegglippen; ~ *in* naar binnen glippen; ~ *through one's fingers* door zijn vingers glippen; **3** afglijden, vervallen: *let* ~ zich verspreken; ~ *up* zich vergissen; ~ *into of a dress* een jurk aanschieten

²slip [slip] *vb* **1** schuiven, slippen, laten glijden: ~ *in a remark* een opmerking tussendoor plaatsen; **2** ontglippen, ontschieten: ~ *one's attention* ontgaan; ~ *one's memory* (of: *mind)* vergeten; *let ~: a)* zich laten ontvallen; *b)* laten ontsnappen; **3** (opvallend) toestoppen

³slip [slip] *n* **1** misstap *(also fig)*, vergissing, ongelukjeʰ: ~ *of the pen* verschrijving; ~ *of the tongue* verspreking; **2** hoesjeʰ, (kussen)sloop; **3** onderrok, onderjurk; **4** strookjeʰ (papier); **5** stek(jeʰ), ent: *give s.o. the* ~ aan iem ontsnappen

slip-knot 1 schuifknoop; **2** slipsteek

slipover 1 slip-over; **2** pullover

slipper [slipƏ] pantoffel, slipper

slippery [slipƏrie] **1** glad, glibberig; **2** moeilijk te pakken te krijgen, ontwijkend, *(fig also)* moeilijk te begrijpen; **3** glibberig, riskant; **4** onbetrouwbaar, vals || ~ *slope* glibberig pad, gevaarlijke koers

slip road oprit, afrit, invoegstrook, uitvoegstrook

slipshod [slipsjod] onzorgvuldig, slordig

slipstream 1 schroefwind, luchtbeweging door de propeller veroorzaakt; **2** zuiging *(behind car)*

slip-up vergissing, fout(jeʰ)

¹slit [slit] *n* **1** spleet, gleuf, lange snee; **2** split *(eg in dress)*

²slit [slit] *vb* **1** snijden; **2** scheuren

slither [sliðƏ] glijden, glibberen

sliver [slivvƏ] **1** splinter, scherf; **2** dun plakjeʰ

slob [slob] smeerlap, slons, luie stomkop

slobber [slobbƏ] **1** kwijlen; **2** sentimenteel doen, zwijmelen: ~ *over sth.* zwijmelig doen over iets

¹slog [slog] *vb* **1** (with *at*) zwoegen (op), noest doorwerken (aan): ~ *away* (*at*) ijverig doorworstelen (met); **2** ploeteren, sjokken

²slog [slog] *vb* (*cricket, boxing*) hard stoten, uithalen

naar, een ontzettende mep geven || ~ *it out* het uitvechten

³slog [slog] *n* **1** geploeterʰ, gezwoegʰ; **2** *(cricket, boxing)* harde klap, woeste slag, uithaal

slogan [sloogƏn] **1** strijdkreet; **2** mottoʰ; **3** slagzin *(in advertisement)*

¹slop [slop] *vb* **1** (with *over*) overstromen: ~ *about* (of: *around*) rondklotsen; **2** plassen, kliederen; **3** sloffen; **4** morsen (op), kliederen (op): ~ *about* (of: *around*) rondhannesen

²slop [slop] *n* **1** waterige soep, slappe kost; **2** spoeling, dun varkensvoerʰ; **3** ~*s* vuil waswaterʰ

¹slope [sloop] *vb* hellen, schuin aflopen, schuin oplopen, glooien: ~ *down (to)* aflopen (naar); ~ *off* er vandoor gaan

²slope [sloop] *n* helling

sloppy [sloppie] **1** slordig, slonzig, onzorgvuldig; **2** melig, sentimenteel; **3** vies en nat

¹slosh [slosj] *vb* **1** klotsen met: ~ *about* rondklotsen; **2** meppen, een dreun verkopen: ~ *the paint on the wall* de verf op de muur kwakken

²slosh [slosj] *vb* **1** plassen, ploeteren; **2** klotsen

slot [slot] **1** groef, geul, gleuf; **2** plaatsjeʰ, ruimte, zendtijd: *find a ~ for* een plaats inruimen voor *(in programme)*

sloth [slooθ] **1** luiaard; **2** luiheid

slot machine 1 automaat; **2** *(game)* fruitmachine

¹slouch [slautsj] *vb* **1** hangen, erbij hangen; **2** een slappe houding hebben

²slouch [slautsj] *n* **1** slappe houding, ronde rug; **2** zoutzak: *be no ~ at* handig zijn in

¹slough [slau] *n* **1** moerasʰ; **2** modderpoel

²slough [sluf] *n* afgeworpen huid *(of snake etc)*

Slovak [sloovæk] Slowaaks

Slovene [sloovie:n] Sloveens

slovenly [sluvvƏnlie] slonzig, slordig

¹slow [sloo] *adj* **1** langzaam, traag, geleidelijk: ~ *handclap* traag handgeklap *(as sign of boredom)*; ~ *train* boemeltrein; **2** saai, flauw; **3** laat: ~ *on the uptake* traag van begrip

²slow [sloo] *adv* langzaam: *be four minutes* ~ vier minuten achterlopen; *go* ~ het langzaam aan doen

³slow [sloo] *vb* vertragen, inhouden: ~ *(the car) down* snelheid minderen; ~ *down* het kalmer aan doen

slowdown vertraging, vermindering, productievermindering

sludge [sludzj] **1** slijkʰ, modder; **2** olieklont, oliekorst

slug [slug] **1** naakte slak; **2** metaalklomp; **3** kogel; **4** slok

sluggard [slugƏd] luiaard

sluggish [slugisj] traag

¹sluice [sloe:s] *n* **1** sluis; **2** sluiskolk; **3** sluisdeur

²sluice [sloe:s] *vb* (also with *out)* uitstromen

³sluice [sloe:s] *vb* **1** laten uitstromen; **2** (also with *out, down)* overspoelen, water laten stromen over

slum [slum] achterbuurt, slopʰ

slumber [slumbƏ] slaap, sluimer

¹**slump** [slʌmp] *vb* **1** in elkaar zakken: ~ *down to the floor* op de vloer in elkaar zakken; **2** instorten, mislukken, *(fin)* vallen

²**slump** [slʌmp] *n* ineenstorting, snelle daling: *a ~ in sales of violent videogames* een sterke daling in de verkoop van gewelddadige videospelletjes

¹**slur** [slə:] *n* smet, blaam

²**slur** [slə:] *vb* brabbelen, onduidelijk (uit)spreken ‖ *that fact was ~red over* aan dat feit werd achteloos voorbij gegaan

slurp [slə:p] slobberen, (op)slurpen

slush [slʌʃ] **1** sneeuwbrij; **2** dunne modder; **3** gezwijmelʰ, sentimentele onzin

slut [slʌt] *(vulg)* **1** slons; **2** slet, slettebak

sluttish [slʌtisj] *(inf)* **1** slonzig; **2** sletterig

sly [slaj] **1** sluw, geslepen; **2** geniepig; **3** pesterig ‖ *on the ~* in het geniep

¹**smack** [smæk] *n* **1** smaak; **2** vleugjeʰ; **3** trek: *he has a ~ of inflexibility in him* hij heeft iets onverzettelijks; **4** smakkend geluidʰ, smak; **5** klap; **6** klapzoen: *have a ~ at sth.* een poging wagen (te)

²**smack** [smæk] *adv* **1** met een klap: *hit s.o. ~ on the head* iem een rake klap op zijn kop geven; **2** recht, precies: *~ in the middle* precies in het midden

³**smack** [smæk] *vb* (with *of*) rieken (naar)

⁴**smack** [smæk] *vb* **1** slaan; **2** smakken met *(lips);* **3** met een smak neerzetten

smacker [smækə] **1** klap, smak; **2** klapzoen; **3** pondʰ; dollar

¹**smacking** [smæking] *n* pakʰ slaag

²**smacking** [smæking] *adj* energiek, vlug: *at a ~ pace* in een stevig tempo

¹**small** [smo:l] *adj* **1** klein, gering, jong, fijn, onbelangrijk: *~ arms* handvuurwapens; *~ business* kleinbedrijf; *~ change* kleingeld; *~ print* kleine druk, *(fig)* de kleine lettertjes; *~ wonder* geen wonder; *feel* (of: *look) ~* zich schamen; **2** bescheiden: *in a ~ way* op kleine schaal; **3** slap, licht, met weinig alcohol: *~ beer* zwak alcoholisch bier, *(fig)* onbelangrijke zaken; *the ~ hours* de kleine uurtjes

²**small** [smo:l] *n* **1** het smalste gedeelte: *the ~ of the back* lende(streek); **2** *~s* kleine was

small-minded kleingeestig

smallpox pokken

small-scale kleinschalig

small talk gekletsʰ, informeel gesprekjeʰ

small-time gering, onbelangrijk

smarmy [sma:mie] zalvend, vleierig: *be polite and helpful, but never be ~* wees beleefd en hulpvaardig, maar doe nooit kruiperig

¹**smart** [sma:t] *adj* **1** heftig, fel: *at a ~ pace* met flinke pas; **2** bijdehand, slim, gevat: *~ card* chipkaart, smartcard; **3** sluw; **4** keurig, knap: *how ~ you look!* wat zie je er mooi uit!; *~ alec* wijsneus

²**smart** [sma:t] *vb* **1** pijn doen, steken; **2** pijn hebben, lijden: *~ over* (of: *under) an insult* zich gekwetst voelen door een belediging

smarten [sma:tn] (also with *up)* opknappen, (zichzelf) opdoffen

¹**smash** [smæsj] *vb* (also with *up)* breken, kapot vallen

²**smash** [smæsj] *vb* **1** slaan op, beuken tegen; **2** (also with *up)* vernielen, in de prak rijden: *~ in* in elkaar slaan, inslaan; **3** uiteenjagen, verpletteren *(enemy);* **4** *(tennis)* smashen

³**smash** [smæsj] *vb* **1** razen, beuken, botsen: *the car ~ed into the garage door* de auto vloog met een klap tegen de garagedeur; **2** geruïneerd worden, failliet gaan; **3** *(tennis)* een smash slaan

⁴**smash** [smæsj] *n* **1** slag, gerinkelʰ; **2** klap, slag, dreun; **3** ineenstorting, krach, bankroetʰ; **4** topper, groot succesʰ; **5** *(tennis)* smash

smashed [smæsjt] dronken

smasher [smæsjə] **1** iets geweldigs, kanjer: *Lisa is a real ~* Lisa is echt een wereldmeid; **2** dreun, vernietigend antwoordʰ

smash hit geweldig succesʰ

smashing [smæsjing] geweldig

smash-up klap, dreun, botsing

smattering [smætəring] beetjeʰ: *have a ~ of French* een paar woordjes Frans spreken

¹**smear** [smiə] *n* **1** smeerʰ, vlek; **2** verdachtmaking; **3** uitstrijkjeʰ

²**smear** [smiə] *vb* **1** smeren, uitsmeren; besmeren; **2** vlekken maken op; **3** verdacht maken

³**smear** [smiə] *vb* **1** vies worden, uitlopen; **2** afgeven

smear test uitstrijkjeʰ

¹**smell** [smel] *n* **1** reuk, geur, *(fig)* sfeer; **2** vieze lucht ‖ *take a ~ at this* ruik hier eens even aan

²**smell** [smel] *vb* **1** (with *of)* ruiken (naar), geuren (naar); **2** snuffelen; **3** (with *of)* stinken (naar), ruiken (naar) *(also fig);* **4** (with *at)* ruiken (aan)

smell out opsporen, op het spoor komen: *they use sniffer dogs to ~ drug traffickers* ze zetten snuffelhonden in om drugshandelaren op te sporen

smelly [smellie] vies, stinkend

¹**smelt** *n* spiering

²**smelt** *vb* **1** uitsmelten *(ore);* **2** uit erts uitsmelten *(metal)*

¹**smile** [smajl] *vb* **1** (with *at)* glimlachen (naar, tegen); **2** er stralend uitzien *(nature)*

²**smile** [smajl] *vb* glimlachend uiten: *she ~d her approval* ze glimlachte goedkeurend

³**smile** [smajl] *n* glimlach: *wipe the ~ off s.o.'s face* iem het lachen doen vergaan; *be all ~s* stralen, van oor tot oor glimlachen

¹**smirch** [smə:tsj] *vb* **1** bevuilen; **2** *(fig)* een smet werpen op

²**smirch** [smə:tsj] *n* vlek, *(fig)* smet

¹**smirk** [smə:k] *vb* zelfgenoegzaam glimlachen

²**smirk** [smə:k] *n* zelfgenoegzaam lachjeʰ

smite [smajt] **1** slaan; verslaan, vellen; **2** straffen; **3** raken, treffen: *smitten with s.o.* smoorverliefd op iem

smith [smiθ] **1** smid; **2** maker, smeder

smithereens [smiðərie:nz]: *smash into* (of: *to) ~* aan diggelen gooien

smithy [smiðie] smederij

smock [smok] **1** kieltje^h, schortje^h; **2** jak^h, kiel

■**smoke** [smook] *vb* roken: *~d ham* gerookte ham; *no smoking* verboden te roken

■**smoke** [smook] *n* **1** rook; **2** rokertje^h, sigaret; **3** damp; **4** trekje^h || *go up in ~* in rook opgaan, *(fig)* op niets uitlopen

smoke out **1** uitroken *(from hole etc);* **2** te weten komen *(eg plans)*

smoker [smookə] **1** roker; **2** rookcoupé, rookrijtuig^h; **3** mannenbijeenkomst

smokescreen rookgordijn^h, *(also fig)* afleidingsmanoeuvre

smooch [smoe:tsj] vrijen, knuffelen

^1**smooth** [smoe:ð] *adj* **1** glad; **2** soepel, gelijkmatig; **3** gemakkelijk; **4** rustig; **5** overmatig vriendelijk, glad: *~ operator* gladjanus; **6** zacht smakend; **7** zacht, strelend *(of voice, sound): in ~ water* in rustig vaarwater

^2**smooth** [smoe:ð] *vb* **1** gladmaken, effen maken; **2** *(also with out)* gladstrijken, *(fig)* (onregelmatigheden, verschillen) wegnemen: *~ down one's clothes* zijn kleren gladstrijken

smoothie [smoe:ðie] gladde, handige prater

^1**smother** [smuðə] *vb* **1** (uit)doven; **2** smoren, onderdrukken: *all opposition was ~ed* elke vorm van tegenstand werd onderdrukt; **3** *(with in)* overladen (met), overdekken (met) *(fig)*, verstikken: *~ed in cream* rijkelijk met room bedekt

^2**smother** [smuðə] *vb* (ver)stikken, (ver)smoren

smoulder [smooldə] (na)smeulen, gloeien

^1**smudge** [smudzj] *n* vlek, *(fig)* smet

^2**smudge** [smudzj] *vb* vlekken

^3**smudge** [smudzj] *vb* **1** (be)vlekken, vuilmaken; **2** *(fig)* een smet werpen op, bezoedelen

smudgy [smudzjie] **1** vlekkerig, besmeurd; **2** wazig

smug [smug] zelfvoldaan

smuggle [smugl] smokkelen

smuggler [smuglə] smokkelaar

smut [smut] **1** vuiltje^h, stofje^h; **2** roetdeeltje^h; **3** roet^h, kolenstof; **4** vuiligheid: *talk ~* vuile taal uitslaan

smutty [smuttie] vuil, goor, vies

snack [snæk] snack, hapje^h, tussendoortje^h

snack bar snackbar, snelbuffet^h

^1**snag** [snæg] *n* **1** uitsteeksel^h, punt^h, stomp; **2** probleem^h, tegenvaller: *there's a ~ in it somewhere* er schuilt ergens een addertje onder 't gras; **3** (winkel)haak, scheur, haal; **4** boom(stronk)

^2**snag** [snæg] *vb* **1** blijven haken met; **2** scheuren *(clothing);* **3** te pakken krijgen

snail [sneel] (huisjes)slak *(also fig)*, slome: *~ mail* slakkenpost, gewone post

snake [sneek] slang || *a ~ in the grass* een addertje onder het gras

^1**snap** [snæp] *vb* **1** *(also with at)* happen (naar), bijten; **2** (af)breken, (af)knappen, het begeven *(also fig);* **3** (dicht)klappen, dichtslaan: *the door ~ped to* (of: *shut)* de deur sloeg dicht; **4** *(also with out)* snauwen: *~ at: a)* grijpen naar; *b)* aangrijpen *(chance etc); I was only ~ped at* ik werd alleen maar

afgesnauwd; *~ out of it* ermee ophouden; *~ to it* vooruit, schiet 'ns op

^2**snap** [snæp] *vb* **1** (weg)grissen, grijpen, (weg)rukken: *~ up* op de kop tikken; **2** knippen met *(fingers);* **3** kieken, een foto maken van: *~ it up* vooruit, aan de slag

^3**snap** [snæp] *n* **1** klap: *shut a book with a ~* een boek met een klap dichtdoen; **2** hap, beet; **3** knip *(with fingers, scissors);* **4** foto; **5** karweitje^h van niets, kleinigheid; **6** pit, energie: *put some ~ into it!* een beetje meer fut!

^4**snap** [snæp] *adj* **1** impulsief: *~ decision* beslissing van 't moment (zelf); **2** onverwacht, onvoorbereid: *~ check* (onverwachte) controle

^5**snap** [snæp] *interj* klap, knal

snapdragon [snæpdrægən] *(bot)* leeuwenbek

snap election vervroegde verkiezingen

snappy [snæpie] **1** pittig, levendig; **2** chic, net; **3** snauwerig; prikkelbaar || *look ~!, make it ~!* schiet op!

snapshot kiekje^h, snapshot^h, momentopname

snare [sneə] (val)strik, val: *lay a ~ for s.o.* voor iem een valstrik leggen

^1**snarl** [sna:l] *vb* **1** *(with at)* grauwen (tegen), grommen, snauwen; **2** in de war raken (brengen)

^2**snarl** [sna:l] *n* **1** grauw^h, snauw; **2** knoop *(also fig)*, wirwar || *be in a ~* in de war zijn

snarl up **1** in de war raken (brengen), in de knoop raken (brengen): *get snarled up* verstrikt raken; **2** vastlopen *(of traf)*

snarl-up **1** (verkeers)knoop; **2** warboel

^1**snatch** [snætsj] *vb* rukken || *~ at* grijpen naar, (dadelijk) aangrijpen

^2**snatch** [snætsj] *vb* **1** (weg)rukken, (weg)grijpen, bemachtigen: *~ a kiss* een kus stelen; *~ away* wegrukken, wegpakken; *she ~ed the letter out of my hand* ze rukte de brief uit mijn hand; **2** aangrijpen, gebruik maken van

^3**snatch** [snætsj] *n* **1** greep, ruk: *make a ~ at* een greep doen naar; **2** brok^h, stuk^h, fragment^h: *a ~ of conversation* een flard van een gesprek; *sleep in ~es* met tussenpozen slapen

snazzy [snæzie] **1** chic; **2** opzichtig

^1**sneak** [snie:k] *vb* sluipen: *~ away* wegsluipen; *~ (up)on s.o.* naar iem toesluipen; *~ on s.o.* over iem klikken, iem verraden

^2**sneak** [snie:k] *vb* heimelijk doen, smokkelen: *~ a smoke* stiekem roken

^3**sneak** [snie:k] *n* **1** gluiper(d); **2** klikspaan

^4**sneak** [snie:k] *adj* onverwacht, verrassings-: *a ~ preview* een onaangekondigde voorvertoning

sneaker [snie:kə] **1** sluiper; **2** gluiperd; **3** klikspaan; **4** *~s* gympies

sneaking [snie:king] **1** gluiperig; **2** heimelijk; **3** vaag: *a ~ suspicion* een vaag vermoeden

sneak-thief insluiper

^1**sneer** [sniə] *vb* **1** *(with at)* grijnzen (naar), spottend lachen; **2** spotten (met)

^2**sneer** [sniə] *n* **1** grijns(lach); **2** *(with at)* spottende opmerking (over), hatelijkheid

¹sneeze [snie:z] *vb* niezen || *not to be ~d at* de moeite waard, niet niks

²sneeze [snie:z] *n* nies(geluidʰ), ~s genies

snick [snik] knip(jeʰ), inkeping

¹snicker [snikkə] *vb* **1** (zacht) hinniken; **2** giechelen

²snicker [snikkə] *n* **1** hinnikgeluidʰ; **2** giechel

snide [snajd] hatelijk

¹sniff [snif] *vb* **1** snuiven, snuffen; **2** snuffelen || *not to be ~fed at* niet te versmaden

²sniff [snif] *vb* **1** snuiven; **2** besnuffelen; **3** ruiken, de geur opsnuiven van

³sniff [snif] *n* **1** snuivend geluidʰ; **2** luchtjeʰ, snuifjeʰ: *get a ~ of sea air* de zeelucht opsnuiven

sniffer dog snuffelhond *(for explosives, drugs)*

¹sniffle [snifl] *vb* snuffen, snotteren

²sniffle [snifl] *n* gesnuifʰ, gesnotterʰ

sniffy [sniffie] arrogant, hooghartig

¹snigger [snigə] *vb* gniffelen

²snigger [snigə] *n* giechel

¹snip [snip] *vb* (*also with off*) (af)knippen, doorknippen, versnipperen

²snip [snip] *vb* snijden, knippen

³snip [snip] *n* **1** knip: *one ~ of the scissors and 99 balloons flew up into the air* een knip met de schaar en 99 ballonnen gingen de lucht in; **2** snipper, stukjeʰ, fragmentʰ; **3** koopjeʰ, buitenkans

¹snipe [snajp] *vb* (*with at*) sluipschieten, uit een hinderlaag schieten (op)

²snipe [snajp] *n* snip

sniper [snajpə] sluipschutter

snippet [snippit] stukjeʰ, fragmentʰ, knipselʰ

¹snitch [snitsj] *vb* klikken: *he ~ed on John* hij verklikte John

²snitch [snitsj] *vb* gappen

snivel [snivl] **1** een loopneus hebben, snotteren; **2** grienen, janken

snob [snob] snob

snobbery [snobbərie] snobismeʰ

snog [snog] vrijen

¹snooker [snoe:kə] *n* snooker(biljart)ʰ

²snooker [snoe:kə] *vb* in het nauw drijven, in een moeilijke positie brengen, dwarsbomen

snoop [snoe:p] *(inf)* (*with about, around*) rondsnuffelen

snooty [snoe:tie] verwaand

¹snooze [snoe:z] *vb* dutten, een uiltje knappen

²snooze [snoe:z] *n* dutjeʰ

¹snore [sno:] *vb* snurken

²snore [sno:] *n* gesnurkʰ, snurk

¹snort [sno:t] *n* gesnuifʰ: *he gave a ~ of contempt* hij snoof minachtend

²snort [sno:t] *vb* snuiven: *Ian ~ed with rage* Ian snoof van woede

snot [snot] snotʰ

snotty [snottie] **1** snotterig, met snot; **2** verwaand, snobistisch

snout [snaut] snuit

¹snow [snoo] *n* **1** sneeuw *(also on TV screen)*; **2** sneeuwbui; **3** sneeuw, cocaïne

²snow [snoo] *vb* **1** sneeuwen; **2** neerdwarrelen

³snow [snoo] *vb* ondersneeuwen, overdonderen || *be ~ed in* (of: *up*) ingesneeuwd zijn; *be ~ed under* ondergesneeuwd worden, bedolven worden

¹snowball *n* sneeuwbal

²snowball *vb* een sneeuwbaleffect hebben, escaleren

³snowball *vb* **1** (met sneeuwballen) bekogelen; **2** doen escaleren

snowbound ingesneeuwd

snowdrift sneeuwbank

snowdrop sneeuwklokjeʰ

snowflake sneeuwvlok(jeʰ)

snowman sneeuwman, sneeuwpop

snow-white sneeuwwit

snowy [snooie] **1** besneeuwd; sneeuwachtig; **2** sneeuwwit

Snr *Senior* sr.

¹snub [snub] *vb* afstoten, afkatten, met de nek aanzien

²snub [snub] *n* bitse afwijzing: *her remark was clearly meant as a ~* haar opmerking was duidelijk bedoeld om te katten

¹snuff [snuf] *n* snuif(tabak): *take ~* snuiven

²snuff [snuf] *vb* snuiven *(tobacco, cocaine)*

³snuff [snuf] *vb* **1** snuiten; **2** opsnuiven; **3** besnuffelen || *~ it* 't hoekje omgaan; *~ out* een eind maken aan *(expectation, uprising etc)*

snuffle [snufl] snotteren

¹snug [snug] *adj* **1** behaaglijk, beschut, knus; **2** goed ingericht; **3** nauwsluitend; **4** ruim *(income)*

²snug [snug] *n* gelagkamer

snuggle [snugl] zich nestelen: *~ up to s.o.* lekker tegen iem aan gaan liggen; *~ down* lekker onder de dekens kruipen

¹so [soo] *adv* **1** zo, aldus: *(would you) be ~ kind as to leave* zou u zo goed willen zijn weg te gaan; *but even ~* maar toch; *~ far it hasn't happened* tot nu toe is het niet gebeurd; *~ long as you don't tell anybody* als je 't maar aan niemand vertelt; *if ~* als dat zo is; **2** zozeer, zo erg: *she is not ~ stupid* ze is niet zo dom; *~ many came* er kwamen er zo veel; **3** daarom, zodoende: *~ what?* en dan?, wat dan nog?; *~ here we are!* hier zijn we dan!; *~ there you are* daar ben je dus; *~ long!* tot ziens!; *every ~ often* nu en dan; *~ there* nu weet je het

²so [soo] *adj* **1** zo, waar: *is that really ~?* is dat echt waar?; *if ~* als dat zo is; **2** dat, het: *she was skinny but not extremely ~* ze was wel mager maar niet extreem; *'She's the prettiest' 'Yes, ~ she is'* 'Ze is de knapste' 'Dat is ze inderdaad'

³so [soo] *pron* **1** dusdanig, dat: *'You were cheating' 'But ~ were you'* 'Je hebt vals gespeeld' 'Maar jij ook'; **2** iets dergelijks, zo(iets): *six days or ~* zes dagen of zo

⁴so [soo] *conj* **1** zodat, opdat, om: *be careful ~ you don't get hurt* pas op dat je je geen pijn doet; **2** zodat, (en) dus: *he is late, ~ (that) we can't start yet* hij is te laat, zodat we nog niet kunnen beginnen

⁵so [soo] *interj* ziezo

¹soak [sook] *vb* weken, in de week zetten: ~ *off* los-
weken

²soak [sook] *vb* **1** doorweken, (door)drenken: ~*ed to
the skin* doornat; ~*ed through* kletsnat; **2** (onder)dompelen: ~ *oneself in* zich verdiepen in; **3** afzetten: ~ *the rich* de rijken plukken

³soak [sook] *vb* sijpelen, doortrekken: ~ *through the
paper* het papier doordrenken

⁴soak [sook] *n* **1** week, het nat maken; **2** zuipschuit,
drankorgel^h

s̲o̲a̲king [s̲o̲oking] door en door: ~ *wet* doorweekt

soak up 1 opnemen, absorberen; **2** kunnen incasseren *(criticism, blow)*

s̲o̲-and-so [s̲o̲oənsoo] **1** die en die, dinges; **2** dit en
dit; **3** je-weet-wel: *a real* ~ een rotzak

¹soap [soop] *n* **1** zeep; **2** soap

²soap [soop] *vb* (in)zepen

s̲o̲apbox 1 zeepdoos; **2** zeepkist, geïmproviseerd
platform^h

s̲o̲ap opera soap (opera)

s̲o̲apsuds zeepsop

soar [so:] **1** hoog vliegen, *(fig)* een hoge vlucht nemen; **2** (omhoog) rijzen, stijgen: *prices* ~*ed* de prijzen vlogen omhoog; **3** zweven

¹sob [sob] *vb* snikken

²sob [sob] *vb* snikkend vertellen: *sob one's heart out*
hartverscheurend snikken

³sob [sob] *n* snik

¹s̲o̲ber [s̲o̲obə] *adj* **1** nuchter, niet beschonken: *as* ~
as a judge volkomen nuchter; **2** matig, ingetogen: ~
colours gedekte kleuren; **3** beheerst, kalm; **4** verstandig, afgewogen: *in* ~ *fact* in werkelijkheid; **5**
ernstig

²s̲o̲ber [s̲o̲obə] *vb* (with *down, up*) nuchter worden
(maken), (doen) bedaren

sobri̲ety [səbra̲jjətie] **1** nuchterheid; gematigdheid;
2 kalmte; ernst

s̲o̲b story zielig verhaal^h, tranentrekker

so-ca̲lled [sooko̲:ld] zogenaamd

s̲o̲ccer [s̲o̲kkə] voetbal^h

sociabi̲lity [soosjəbi̲llittie] gezelligheid

s̲o̲ciable [s̲o̲osjəbl] gezellig, vriendelijk

¹s̲o̲cial [s̲o̲osjl] *adj* **1** sociaal, maatschappelijk: *man
is a* ~ *animal* de mens is een sociaal wezen; **2** gezellig; vriendelijk; **3** gezelligheids-: *a* ~ *club* een gezel-
ligheidsvereniging

²s̲o̲cial [s̲o̲osjl] *n* gezellige bijeenkomst, feestje^h

s̲o̲cialism [s̲o̲osjəlizm] socialisme^h

¹s̲o̲cialist [s̲o̲osjəlist] *adv* socialistisch

²s̲o̲cialist [s̲o̲osjəlist] *n* socialist

s̲o̲cialize [s̲o̲osjəlajz] gezellig doen, zich aanpassen:
~ *with* omgaan met

social sci̲ence sociale wetenschap(pen), maat-
schappijwetenschappen

social se̲rvice 1 liefdadig werk^h; **2** ~*s* sociale voorzieningen

social work maatschappelijk werk^h

soci̲ety [səsa̲jjətie] **1** vereniging, genootschap^h; **2** de

samenleving, (de) maatschappij; **3** gezelschap^h: *I
try to avoid his* ~ ik probeer zijn gezelschap te ontlopen; **4** society, hogere kringen

sociolo̲gical [soosiəlo̲dzjikl] sociologisch

sociolo̲gist [soosie-o̲llədzjist] socioloog

sociolo̲gy [soosie-o̲llədzjie] sociologie

¹sock [sok] *n* **1** sok; **2** inlegzool(tje^h); **3** (vuist)slag,
oplawaai; **4** windzak ‖ *pull one's* ~*s up* er tegen aan
gaan; *put a* ~ *in it* kop dicht

²sock [sok] *vb* meppen, slaan, dreunen ‖ ~ *it to s.o.: a)*
iem op zijn donder geven; *b)* grote indruk op iem
maken

s̲o̲cket [s̲o̲kkit] **1** holte, (oog)kas, gewrichtsholte; **2**
kandelaar; **3** sok, mof, buis; **4** contactdoos; fitting,
lamphouder

sod [sod] **1** vent; **2** rotklus, ellende; **3** (gras)zode

s̲o̲da [s̲o̲odə] **1** soda, natriumcarbonaat^h: *baking* ~
zuiveringszout; **2** soda(water)^h; **3** priklimonade,
fris^h

s̲o̲dden [s̲o̲dn] **1** doorweekt, doordrenkt; **2** klef *(of
bread etc);* **3** opgeblazen, opgezwollen *(through
drink):* ~ *features* opgeblazen gezicht

s̲o̲dium [s̲o̲odiəm] natrium^h

Sod's La̲w de wet van 'Sod' *(if anything can go
wrong, it will)*

s̲o̲fa [s̲o̲ofə] bank, sofa

soft [soft] **1** zacht, gedempt *(light);* **2** slap *(also fig)*,
week, sentimenteel: *(have) a* ~ *spot for s.o.* een zwak
voor iem hebben; **3** niet-verslavend, soft *(drugs);* **4**
eenvoudig: ~ *option* gemakkelijke weg; **5** onnozel:
have gone ~ *in the head* niet goed wijs zijn geworden; **6** niet-alcoholisch, fris *(drink):* ~ *drink*
fris(drank); **7** zwak, gek, verliefd: *be* ~ *about* gek
zijn op, een zwak hebben voor; ~ *loan* lening op
gunstige voorwaarden

soft co̲py tekst(en) in elektronische vorm *(not on
paper)*

soft dri̲nk fris(drank)

¹s̲o̲ften [s̲o̲ffən] *vb* **1** zacht(er) worden; **2** vertederd
worden

²s̲o̲ften [s̲o̲ffən] *vb* **1** zacht(er) maken, dempen
(light), ontharden *(water);* **2** verwennen, verslappen; **3** vertederen

soften up 1 mild stemmen; **2** verzwakken, murw
maken

s̲o̲ftie [s̲o̲ftie] slappeling, goedzak, dwaas

soft-s̲o̲ap stroop smeren bij, vleien

s̲o̲ftware [s̲o̲ftweə] software, (computer)program-
matuur

s̲o̲ggy [s̲o̲gie] **1** doorweekt; **2** drassig; **3** klef *(of
bread etc)*

¹soil [sojl] *n* **1** grond, land^h, teelaarde; **2** (vader)land^h:
on Dutch ~ op Nederlandse bodem; *native* ~ geboortegrond; **3** (ver)vuil(ing); **4** afval^h; **5** aarde,
grond, land^h

²soil [sojl] *vb* vuilmaken

³soil [sojl] *vb* vuil worden

¹s̲o̲lace [s̲o̲lləs] *n* troost, bemoediging

²s̲o̲lace [s̲o̲lləs] *vb* troosten, opbeuren: ~ *oneself* *(with sth.)* zich troosten (met iets)

solar [soolə] vd zon, zonne-: ~ *eclipse* zonsverduistering

solar system zonnestelsel[h]

soldering iron [sooldəring ajjən] soldeerbout

soldier [sooldzjə] **1** militair, soldaat; **2** strijder, voorvechter

soldier on volhouden

¹sole [sool] *n* **1** zool *(of foot and shoe);* **2** tong *(fish and dish)*

²sole [sool] *adj* **1** enig, enkel; **2** exclusief, uitsluitend: ~ *agent* alleenvertegenwoordiger

solely [soollie] **1** alleen; **2** enkel, uitsluitend

solemn [solləm] **1** plechtig; **2** ernstig: *look as ~ as a judge* doodernstig kijken; **3** (plecht)statig; **4** belangrijk, gewichtig: ~ *warning* dringende waarschuwing

solemnity [səlemnittie] **1** plechtigheid; **2** plechtstatigheid, ceremonieel[h]; **3** ernst

¹solicit [səlissit] *vb* **1** (dringend) verzoeken: ~ *s.o.'s attention* iemands aandacht vragen; **2** aanspreken *(by prostitute)*

²solicit [səlissit] *vb* **1** een verzoek doen; **2** tippelen

solicitor [səlissittə] **1** procureur; **2** rechtskundig adviseur, advocaat *(at lower court);* **3** notaris

solicitous [səlissittəs] **1** *(with about, for)* bezorgd (om), bekommerd; **2** aandachtig, nauwgezet

solicitude [səlissitjoe:d] **1** zorg, bezorgdheid, angst; **2** aandacht, nauwgezetheid

¹solid [sollid] *adj* **1** vast, stevig, solide: ~ *rock* vast gesteente; **2** ononderbroken *(of time): Brugman talked ~ly for three hours* Brugman sprak drie uur aan één stuk; **3** betrouwbaar *(financially);* **4** driedimensionaal: ~ *geometry* stereometrie; **5** unaniem: ~ *vote* eenstemmigheid; **6** gegrond, degelijk: ~ *reasons* gegronde redenen; **7** zuiver, massief, puur: ~ *gold* puur goud

²solid [sollid] *n* **1** vast lichaam[h]; **2** (driedimensionaal) lichaam[h]; **3** ~*s* vast voedsel[h]

solidarity [sollidærittie] solidariteit

solidify [səliddiffaj] hard(er) (doen) worden, (doen) verharden

solidity [səliddittie] **1** hardheid; **2** dichtheid, compactheid

soliloquy [səlilləkwie] alleenspraak, monoloog: *teaching involves more than holding a ~ for fifty minutes* lesgeven houdt meer in dan vijftig minuten lang een monoloog houden

solitary [sollittərie] **1** alleen(levend), solitair; **2** eenzelvig; **3** afgezonderd, eenzaam: ~ *confinement* eenzame opsluiting; **4** enkel: *give me one ~ example* geef mij één enkel voorbeeld

solitude [sollitjoe:d] eenzaamheid

¹solo [sooloo] *n* solo-optreden[h]; solovlucht

²solo [sooloo] *adv* solo, alleen: *fly ~* solo vliegen; *go ~* een solocarrière beginnen, op de solotoer gaan

soloist [soolooist] solist(e)

so long tot ziens

solstice [solstis] zonnestilstand, zonnewende

soluble [soljoebl] **1** oplosbaar; **2** verklaarbaar

solution [səloe:sjən] oplossing, solutie, *(fig)* uitweg: ~ *for* (of: *of, to) a problem* oplossing van een probleem

solve [solv] **1** oplossen, een uitweg vinden voor; **2** verklaren

solvency [solvənsie] solvabiliteit, financiële draagkracht

solvent [solvənt] oplosmiddel[h]

sombre [sombə] somber, duister, zwaarmoedig

¹some [sum] *pron* **1** wat, iets, enkele(n), sommige(n), een aantal, een of ander(e), een: *.she bought ~ oranges* ze kocht een paar sinaasappels; ~ *day you'll understand* ooit zul je het begrijpen; *I've made a cake; would you like ~?* ik heb een cake gebakken, wil je er wat van *(of:* een stukje)?; ~ *say so* er zijn er die dat zeggen; **2** geweldig, fantastisch: *that was ~ holiday* tjonge, nou dat was een fijne vakantie

²some [sum] *adv* **1** ongeveer, zo wat: *it costs ~ fifty pounds* het kost zo'n vijftig pond; **2** *(Am; inf)* enigszins, een beetje: *he was annoyed ~* hij was een tikje geïrriteerd

somebody [sumbədie] iemand

some day [sumdee] op een dag, ooit: *we all must die ~* we moeten allemaal eens sterven

somehow [sumhau] **1** op de een of andere manier, hoe dan ook, ergens: ~ *(or other) you'll have to tell him* op de een of andere wijze zul je het hem moeten vertellen; **2** om de een of andere reden, waarom dan ook

someone [sumwun] iemand

someplace [sumplees] *(Am)* ergens, op een of ander plaats: *do it ~ else* doe het ergens anders

¹somersault [summəso:lt] *n* salto (mortale), buiteling: *turn (of: do) a ~* een salto maken

²somersault [summəso:lt] *vb* een salto maken

something [sumθing] **1** iets, wat: *he dropped ~* hij liet iets vallen; *seventy ~* zeventig en nog wat; *there is ~ in (of: to) it* daar is iets van aan; **2** *(with of)* iets, enigszins: *it came as ~ of a surprise* het kwam een beetje als een verrassing

sometime [sumtajm] ooit, eens: *I'll show it to you ~* ik zal het je wel eens laten zien

sometimes [sumtajmz] soms, af en toe, bij gelegenheid

somewhat [sumwot] enigszins, een beetje: *the soil is ~ moist* de aarde is een beetje vochtig

somewhere [sumweə] **1** ergens (heen): *we're getting ~ at last* dat lijkt er al meer op; **2** ongeveer: ~ *about sixty* zo'n zestig

somnolence [somnələns] slaperigheid

son [sun] zoon, jongen

sonata [səna:tə] sonate

song [song] **1** lied(je[h]), wijsje[h]; **2** gezang[h] || *don't make such a ~ and dance about those old records* maak toch niet zo'n drukte om die oude platen; *go for a ~* bijna voor niets van de hand gaan; *on ~* op dreef, op volle toeren, in topvorm

songbird zangvogel

sonic [sonnik] mbt geluid(sgolven), geluids-: ~ boom (of: bang) supersone knal

son-in-law schoonzoon

sonnet [sonnit] sonnet[h]

sonny [sunnie] jochie[h], mannetje[h]

soon [soe:n] 1 spoedig, gauw, snel (daarna): *speak too* ~ te voorbarig zijn; *the ~er the better* hoe eerder hoe beter; *as* ~ *as* zodra (als), meteen toen; *no ~er had he arrived than she left* nauwelijks was hij aangekomen of zij ging al weg; 2 graag, bereidwillig: *I'd ~er walk* ik loop liever; *I'd (just) as* ~ *stay home* ik blijf net zo lief thuis

soothe [soe:ð] kalmeren, geruststellen, troosten

soothsayer [soe:θseeə] waarzegger

sooty [soetie] 1 roetig, (als) met roet bedekt; 2 roetkleurig

sop [sop] doorweken, soppen

sophisticated [səfistikkeetid] 1 subtiel, ver ontwikkeld: *a* ~ *taste* een verfijnde smaak; 2 wereldwijs, ontwikkeld; 3 ingewikkeld

sophistication [səfistikkeesjən] 1 subtiliteit, raffinement[h]; 2 wereldwijsheid; 3 complexiteit

sopping [sopping] doorweekt, doornat: ~ *with rain* kletsnat van de regen

soppy [soppie] sentimenteel, zoetig

soprano [səpra:noo] sopraan(zangeres)

sorcerer [so:sərə] tovenaar

sorcery [so:sərie] tovenarij

sordid [so:did] 1 vuil (*also fig*), vies: *the* ~ *details* de smerige details; 2 armzalig, beroerd

¹sore [so:] *adj* 1 pijnlijk, irriterend: *a* ~ *throat* keelpijn; 2 onaangenaam, pijnlijk: *a* ~ *point* een teer punt; 3 beledigd, kwaad, nijdig: *don't get* ~ *about the money you lost* maak je niet zo nijdig over het geld dat je verloren hebt; *a sight for* ~ *eyes* een aangenaam iets

²sore [so:] *n* 1 pijnlijke plek, zweer, wond; 2 ~*s* zeer[h], pijnlijk onderwerp[h]: *recall* (of: *reopen*) *old* ~*s* oude wonden openrijten

sorehead zeur(kous)

sorely [so:lie] ernstig, in belangrijke mate, pijnlijk: *he was* ~ *tempted* hij werd in grote verleiding gebracht

sorrel [sorrəl] zuring, soort moeskruid[h]

sorrow [sorroo] verdriet[h], leed[h]: *drown one's* ~*s* zijn verdriet verdrinken

sorrowful [sorroofoel] 1 treurig; 2 bedroefd

¹sorry [sorrie] *adj* 1 droevig, erbarmelijk: *he came home in a* ~ *condition* hij kwam thuis in een trieste toestand; 2 naar, ellendig: *be in a* ~ *plight* in een ellendige situatie verkeren; 3 waardeloos (*excuse etc*); 4 bedroefd; 5 medelijdend: *be* (of: *feel*) ~ *for s.o.* medelijden hebben met iem; 6 berouwvol: *you'll be* ~ het zal je berouwen, hier (of: daar) krijg je spijt van

²sorry [sorrie] *interj* 1 sorry, het spijt me, pardon; 2 wat zegt u?

¹sort [so:t] *n* 1 soort, klas(se), type[h]: *just buy him an*

ice cream, that ~ *of thing* koop maar een ijsje voor hem, of zoiets; *a* ~ *of (a)* een soort van, een of andere; *he is a lawyer of* ~*s* hij is een soort advocaat, hij is zo'n beetje advocaat; *'I'm going alone' 'you'll do nothing of the* ~*!'* 'ik ga alleen' 'daar komt niets van in, daar is geen sprake van!'; *all* ~*s of* allerlei; 2 persoon, type[h], slag: *he is a bad* ~ hij deugt niet; 3 (*comp*) sortering: *be out of* ~*s* zich niet lekker voelen

²sort [so:t] *vb* sorteren, klasseren: ~ *letters* brieven sorteren; ~ *over* (of: *through*) sorteren, klasseren

sort of [so:təv] min of meer, zo ongeveer, een beetje: *I feel* ~ *ill* ik voel me een beetje ziek; *'are you in charge here?' 'well yes, sort of'* 'heeft u hier de leiding?' 'nou, min of meer, ja'

sort out 1 sorteren, indelen, rangschikken; 2 ordenen, regelen: *things will sort themselves out* de zaak komt wel terecht; *sort oneself out* met zichzelf in het reine komen; 3 te pakken krijgen, een opdonder geven: *stop that or I'll come and sort you out* hou daarmee op of je krijgt het met mij aan de stok

so-so zozo, middelmatig

sot [sot] dronkaard

soul [sool] 1 ziel, geest: *poor* ~*!* (arme) stakker!; *with heart and* ~ met hart en ziel; *All Souls' Day* Allerzielen; *not a (living)* ~ geen levende ziel, geen sterveling; 2 soul: *the (life and)* ~ *of the party* de gangmaker van het feest; *she is the* ~ *of kindness* zij is de vriendelijkheid zelf

soul-destroying geestdodend, afstompend

soul mate boezemvriend(in), minnaar, minnares

¹sound [saund] *n* 1 geluid[h], klank, toon: *I don't like the* ~ *of it* het bevalt me niet, het zit me niet lekker; *by the* ~ *of it* (of: *things*) zo te horen; 2 gehoorsafstand; 3 zee-engte, zeestraat; 4 inham, baai, golf

²sound [saund] *adj* 1 gezond, krachtig, gaaf, fit: *be (as)* ~ *as a bell*: *a)* (zo) gezond als een vis zijn; *b)* perfect functioneren (*machine*); *a* ~ *mind in a* ~ *body* een gezonde geest in een gezond lichaam; 2 correct, logisch, gegrond (*argument*), wijs (*advice*); 3 financieel gezond, evenwichtig, betrouwbaar; 4 vast (*sleep*); 5 hard, krachtig: *a* ~ *thrashing* een flink pak ransel

³sound [saund] *adv* vast, diep (*sleep*): ~ *asleep* vast in slaap

⁴sound [saund] *vb* klinken (*also fig*), luiden, galmen: *that* ~*s reasonable* dat klinkt redelijk; ~ *off*: *a)* opscheppen; *b)* zijn mening luid te kennen geven

⁵sound [saund] *vb* 1 laten klinken: ~ *a warning* een waarschuwing laten horen; 2 uiten, uitspreken; 3 blazen (*alarm, retreat*), blazen op (*eg trumpet*); 4 testen (*by percussing lungs*); 5 peilen (*also fig*), onderzoeken, polsen: ~ *s.o. out about* (of: *on*) *sth.* iem over iets polsen

sounding [saunding] peiling (*also fig*): *make* (of: *take*) ~*s* poolshoogte nemen, opiniepeilingen houden

sounding board 1 klankbord[h] (*also fig*), spreekbuis; 2 klankbodem

soundly [saundlie] **1** gezond, stevig; **2** vast *(asleep)*
soundtrack 1 geluidsspoorʰ *(of film with sound);* **2** (cd met) opgenomen filmmuziek
soup [soe:p] soep ‖ *in the ~* in de puree
soup kitchen 1 gaarkeuken *(for poor, homeless);* **2** veldkeuken
soup up opvoeren *(engine, power)*
sour [sauə] **1** zuur, wrang; **2** onvriendelijk, scherp *(tongue);* **3** guur, onaangenaam *(weather)* ‖ *~ grapes* de druiven zijn zuur; *go* (of: *turn) ~* slecht aflopen
source [so:s] bron *(also fig),* oorsprong, oorzaak
sourpuss zuurpruim
souse [saus] **1** doornat maken, (een vloeistof) gieten (over iets); **2** pekelen, marineren
soused [saust] bezopen, dronken
¹south [sauθ] *n* het zuiden *(point of compass),* zuid: *(to the) ~ of* ten zuiden van; *the South* het zuidelijk gedeelte
²south [sauθ] *adj* zuidelijk
³south [sauθ] *adv* in, uit, naar het zuiden: *down ~* in het zuiden
southbound op weg naar het zuiden
south-east zuidoostelijk
south-eastern zuidoostelijk
¹southerly [suðəlie] *n* zuidenwind
²southerly [suðəlie] *adj, adv* zuidelijk
southern [suðn] zuidelijk: *~ lights* zuiderlicht, aurora australis
southerner [suðənə] zuiderling, Amerikaan uit de zuidelijke staten
South Pole zuidpool
southward [sauθwəd] zuid(waarts), zuidelijk
south-west zuidwestelijk
south-western zuidwestelijk
¹sovereign [sovrin] *n* soeverein, vorst
²sovereign [sovrin] *adj* **1** soeverein, onafhankelijk, heersend, oppermachtig; **2** doeltreffend, efficiënt, krachtig *(remedy)*
sovereignty [sovrəntie] soevereiniteit, zelfbeschikking, heerschappij
¹sow [soo] *vb* **1** zaaien *(also fig),* verspreiden; **2** zaaien, (be)planten, poten
²sow [soo] *vb* opwekken, de kiem leggen van: *~ the seeds of doubt* twijfel zaaien
³sow [sau] *n* zeug
soy [soj] soja
spa [spa:] **1** minerale bron; **2** badplaats *(near spring),* kuuroordʰ
¹space [spees] *n* **1** ruimte; **2** afstand, interval; **3** plaats, ruimte, gebiedʰ: *clear a ~ for s.o.* (sth.) ruimte maken voor iem (iets); **4** tijdsspanne: *during the ~ of three years* binnen het bestek van drie jaar; *vanish into ~* in het niet verdwijnen
²space [spees] *vb* uit elkaar plaatsen, over de tijd verdelen: *~ out* over meer ruimte verdelen, spreiden; *~ out payments* betalen in termijnen
spacecraft ruimtevaartuigʰ
spaced out 1 zweverig, high, onder invloed; **2** we-

reldvreemd, excentriek
spaceman ruimtevaarder
space probe ruimtesonde
spacing [speesing] spatie: *single ~* met enkele regelafstand
spacious [speesjəs] ruim, groot
spade [speed] **1** spade, schop; **2** *(cards)* schoppen(s): *the five of ~s* schoppen vijf; *call a ~ a ~* de dingen bij hun naam noemen
Spain [speen] Spanje
¹span [spæn] *n* **1** breedte, wijdte, vleugelbreedte, spanwijdte *(of aeroplane);* **2** (tijd)span(ne); **3** overspanning, spanwijdte
²span [spæn] *vb* overspannen *(also fig),* overbruggen
¹spangle [spænggl] *n* lovertjeʰ, dun blaadjeʰ klatergoud
²spangle [spænggl] *vb* met lovertjes versieren: *~d with stars* met sterren bezaaid
Spaniard [spænjəd] **1** Spanjaard; **2** Spaanse
Spanish [spænisj] Spaans ‖ *~ chestnut* tamme kastanje(boom)
spank [spængk] (een pak) voor de broek geven, een pak slaag geven
¹spanking [spængking] *n* pakʰ voor de broek
²spanking [spængking] *adj* **1** kolossaal, prima; **2** vlug, krachtig
spanner [spænə] moersleutel: *adjustable ~* Engelse sleutel; *throw a ~ into the works* een spaak in het wiel steken
¹spar [spa:] *n* lange paal, rondhoutʰ
²spar [spa:] *vb* **1** boksen; **2** redetwisten
¹spare [speə] *vb* **1** het stellen zonder, missen, overhebben: *enough and to ~* meer dan genoeg; *can you ~ me a few moments?* heb je een paar minuten voor mij?; **2** sparen, ontzien: *~ s.o.'s feelings* iemands gevoelens sparen; **3** sparen, bezuinigen op: *no expense ~d* zonder geld te sparen
²spare [speə] *adj* **1** extra, reserve: *~ room* logeerkamer; *~ tyre* reservewiel, *(mockingly)* zwembandje; **2** vrij *(time);* **3** mager: *go ~* razend worden
³spare [speə] *n* reserve, dubbel, reserveonderdeelʰ, reservewielʰ
¹spark [spa:k] *n* vonk, *(fig)* sprank(jeʰ), greintjeʰ: *a ~ of compassion* een greintje medelijden; *some bright ~ left the tap running* één of andere slimmerik heeft de kraan open laten staan
²spark [spa:k] *vb* **1** ontsteken, doen ontbranden; **2** aanvuren, aanwakkeren; **3** uitlokken: *~ off a war* een oorlog uitlokken
³spark [spa:k] *vb* vonken
¹sparkle [spa:kl] *vb* **1** fonkelen, glinsteren: *sparkling with wit* sprankelend van geest(igheid); **2** parelen, (op)bruisen: *sparkling water* spuitwater; *sparkling wine* mousserende wijn; **3** sprankelen, geestig zijn
²sparkle [spa:kl] *n* fonkeling, glinstering; gefonkelʰ
sparring partner sparringpartner *(also fig),* trainingspartner, oefenmaat
sparrow [spæroo] mus
sparrow hawk sperwer

sparse [spa:s] dun, schaars, karig: *a ~ly populated area* een dunbevolkt gebied

Spartan [spa:tn] Spartaans, *(fig)* zeer hard

spasm [spæzm] **1** kramp, huivering, spasme[h]: *~s of laughter* lachkrampen; **2** aanval, opwelling: *~s of grief* opwellingen van smart

spastic [spæstik] spastisch, krampachtig

spat klappen, ruzietje[h]

spate [speet] **1** hoge waterstand *(of river): the rivers are in ~* de rivieren zijn gezwollen; **2** toevloed, overvloed, stroom: *a ~ of publications* een stroom publicaties

spatial [speesjl] ruimtelijk, ruimte-

¹spatter [spætə] *vb* **1** (be)spatten, (be)sprenkelen, klateren: *the lorry ~ed my clothes with mud* de vrachtauto bespatte mijn kleren met modder; **2** bekladden, besmeuren *(also fig)*

²spatter [spætə] *n* **1** spat(je[h]), vlekje[h]; **2** gespat[h]

spatula [spætjoelə] spatel

¹spawn [spo:n] *vb* kuit schieten

²spawn [spo:n] *n* **1** kuit *(of fish);* **2** kikkerdril[h]

¹speak [spie:k] *vb* spreken, een toespraak houden: *so to ~* (om) zo te zeggen, bij wijze van spreken; *strictly ~ing* strikt genomen; *~ out against sth.* zich tegen iets uitspreken; *~ up for s.o. (sth.)* het voor iem (iets) opnemen; *nothing to ~ of* niets noemenswaard(ig)s; *~ ill of s.o. (sth.)* kwaad spreken over iem (iets); *~ to s.o. (about sth.)* iem (over iets) aanspreken; *(telephone) ~ing!* spreekt u mee!; *that ~s for itself* dat spreekt voor zich; *could you ~ up please* kunt u wat harder spreken, a.u.b.; *~ for sth.: a)* iets bestellen; *b)* van iets getuigen; *c)* een toespraak houden *(of:* pleiten) voor *(also fig)*

²speak [spie:k] *vb* (uit)spreken, zeggen, uitdrukken: *~ one's mind* zijn mening zeggen

speaker [spie:kə] **1** spreker; **2** *Speaker* voorzitter vh Lagerhuis

speaking [spie:king] sprekend, levensecht, treffend: *a ~ likeness* een sprekende gelijkenis

speaking terms: *not be on ~ with s.o.* niet (meer) spreken tegen iem, onenigheid met iem hebben

¹spear [spiə] *n* speer, lans

²spear [spiə] *vb* (met een speer) doorboren, spietsen

¹spearhead *n* speerpunt, *(fig)* spits, leider

²spearhead *vb* de spits zijn van *(also fig)*, leiden, aanvoeren *(eg action, campaign)*

¹special [spesjl] *adj* speciaal, bijzonder, apart, extra || *Special Branch* Politieke Veiligheidspolitie; *~ delivery* expressebestelling

²special [spesjl] *n* iets bijzonders, extra-editie, speciaal gerecht[h] op menu, speciale attractie, (tv-)special, speciaal programma[h]

specialism [spesjəlizm] specialisme[h], specialisatie

specialist [spesjəlist] specialist

speciality [spesjie·ælittie] **1** bijzonder kenmerk[h], bijzonderheid, detail[h]; **2** specialiteit *(subject, product etc)*

specialization [spesjəlajzeesjən] specialisatie

¹specialize [spesjəlajz] *vb* **1** zich specialiseren, gespecialiseerd zijn; **2** in bijzonderheden treden

²specialize [spesjəlajz] *vb* **1** specificeren, speciaal vermelden; **2** beperken

specially [spesjəlie] speciaal, op speciale wijze, bijzonder: *he is not ~ interesting* hij is niet bepaald interessant

species [spie:sjie:z] soort, type[h]: *the (human) ~, our ~* het mensdom, de menselijke soort

specific [spissiffik] **1** specifiek, duidelijk: *be ~ de dingen bij hun naam noemen, er niet omheen draaien; **2** specifiek, soortelijk: *~ gravity* soortelijk gewicht

specification [spessiffikkeesjən] **1** specificatie, gedetailleerde beschrijving; **2** *~s* technische beschrijving

specify [spessiffaj] specificeren, precies vermelden

specimen [spessimmən] **1** monster[h], staaltje[h]; **2** (mooi) exemplaar[h], (rare) knakker, eigenaardige kerel

speck [spek] vlek, stip, plek(je[h]), *(fig)* greintje[h]

¹speckle [spekl] *n* spikkel, stippel, vlekje[h]

²speckle [spekl] *vb* bespikkelen, stippelen

specs [speks] *spectacles* bril

spectacle [spektəkl] **1** schouwspel[h], vertoning; **2** aanblik, gezicht[h]; **3** *~s* bril: *a pair of ~s* een bril

spectacular [spektækjoelə] spectaculair, sensationeel

spectator [spekteetə] toeschouwer, kijker

spectre [spektə] spook[h], geest, schim *(also fig)*

speculate [spekjoeleet] speculeren, berekenen: *~ about (of: on)* overdenken, overpeinzen; *~ in* speculeren in

speculation [spekjoeleesjən] **1** beschouwing, overpeinzing; **2** speculatie

speculative [spekjoelətiv] speculatief, theoretisch, op gissingen berustend

speech [spie:tsj] **1** toespraak, rede(voering), speech: *Queen's (of: King's) ~* troonrede; *maiden ~* eerste redevoering die iem houdt, redenaarsdebuut; **2** opmerking, uitlating; **3** rede: *(in)direct ~* (in)directe rede; *reported ~* indirecte rede; **4** spraak(vermogen[h]), uiting, taal: *freedom of ~* vrijheid van meningsuiting

speech day prijsuitdeling(sdag) *(at school)*

speechless [spie:tsjləs] **1** sprakeloos, verstomd; **2** onbeschrijfelijk: *~ admiration* woordeloze bewondering

¹speed [spie:d] *n* **1** spoed, haast; **2** (rij)snelheid, vaart, gang: *(at) full ~* met volle kracht, in volle vaart; **3** versnelling *(of bicycle);* **4** versnelling(sbak) *(of car);* **5** (sluiter)snelheid; **6** speed, amfetamine

²speed [spie:d] *vb* **1** (te) snel rijden, de maximumsnelheid overschrijden: *~ up* sneller gaan rijden, gas geven; **2** (voorbij)snellen *(also fig)*

³speed [spie:d] *vb* **1** opjagen, haast doen maken: *it needs ~ing up* er moet schot in worden gebracht, er moet tempo in komen; **2** versnellen, opvoeren: *~ up (production)* (de productie) opvoeren; **3** *(with away)* (snel) vervoeren

speed bump verkeersdrempel
speeding [spie:ding] het te hard rijden
speed limit topsnelheid, maximumsnelheid
speedometer [spie:dommittə] snelheidsmeter
speedway 1 (auto)renbaan, speedway(baan); **2** autosnelweg
speedy [spie:die] snel, vlug, prompt
¹spell [spel] vb spellen; ~ out (of: over) uitleggen, nauwkeurig omschrijven
²spell [spel] vb (voor)spellen, betekenen, inhouden: these measures ~ the ruin of deze maatregelen betekenen de ondergang van
³spell [spel] n **1** bezwering(sformule), ban, betovering: put a ~ on (of: over) betoveren; fall under the ~ of in de ban raken van; **2** periode, tijd(je[h]), (werk)beurt; **3** vlaag, aanval, bui: cold ~ koudegolf
spellbound geboeid, gefascineerd: hold one's audience ~ het publiek in zijn ban houden
spelling [spelling] spelling(wijze)
spend [spend] **1** uitgeven, spenderen, besteden: ~ money on geld spenderen aan; **2** doorbrengen, wijden: ~ the evening watching TV de avond doorbrengen met tv kijken; **3** uitputten: the storm had soon spent its force de storm was spoedig uitgeraasd
spendthrift verkwister, verspiller
spent 1 (op)gebruikt, af, leeg: ~ cartridge lege huls; **2** uitgeput, afgemat
sperm [spə:m] **1** spermacel, zaadcel; **2** sperma[h], zaad[h]
sperm whale potvis
spew [spjoe:] (uit)braken, spuwen: ~ out uitspugen; ~ up overgeven
sphere [sfiə] **1** bol, bal, kogel; **2** hemellichaam[h], globe, wereldbol; **3** sfeer, kring, gebied[h], terrein[h]: ~ of influence invloedssfeer
spherical [sferrikl] (bol)rond, bol-
sphinx [sfingks] sfinx
spice [spajs] kruid[h], kruiden, specerij(en): add ~ to kruiden, smaak geven aan
spick and span brandschoon, keurig, in de puntjes; **2** (spik)splinternieuw
spicy [spajsie] **1** gekruid, heet; **2** geurig; **3** pikant (fig), pittig: ~ story gewaagd verhaal
spider [spajdə] spin, spinnenkop
spidery [spajdərie] **1** spinachtig, (fig) krabbelig (handwriting); **2** broodmager: ~ legs spillebenen; **3** ragfijn
spiel [sjpie:l] **1** woordenstroom, (breedsprakig) verhaal[h]; **2** reclametekst (radio)
¹spike [spajk] n **1** (scherpe) punt, pin, piek, prikker (for bills, loose notes etc); **2** (koren)aar; **3** ~s spikes (sports shoe)
²spike [spajk] vb **1** (vast)spijkeren; **2** van spijkers (punten) voorzien: ~d shoes spikes; **3** alcohol toevoegen aan: ~ coffee with cognac wat cognac in de koffie doen
¹spill [spil] vb **1** doen overlopen, laten overstromen, morsen (met), omgooien, verspillen: ~ the wine met wijn morsen; **2** vergieten (blood), doen vloeien

²spill [spil] vb overlopen, overstromen, uitstromen: the milk ~ed de melk liep over
³spill [spil] n **1** val(partij), duik; **2** stukje papier (hout) (to light lamp or stove); **3** het afwerpen (of horseman); **4** verspilling
spillage [spillidzj] lozing (eg of oil into sea)
spillway 1 overlaat; **2** afvoerkanaal[h]
¹spin [spin] vb **1** spinnen (also fig); **2** in elkaar draaien, verzinnen, produceren (story); **3** spineffect geven (ball); **4** snel laten ronddraaien: ~ a coin kruis of munt gooien; ~ a top tollen (game); ~ out: a) uitspinnen (story); b) rekken (time); c) zuinig zijn met (money)
²spin [spin] vb tollen, snel draaien: make s.o.'s head ~ iemands hoofd doen tollen
³spin [spin] n **1** draaibeweging, rotatie, (sport) spin, effect[h] (on ball); **2** ritje[h], tochtje[h]: let's go for a ~ laten we 'n eindje gaan rijden; **3** (terug)val, duik (also fig); **4** spin, tolvlucht: in a (flat) ~ in paniek, van de kaart
spinach [spinnidzj] spinazie
spindle [spindl] **1** spindel, (spin)klos, spoel; **2** as, spil; **3** stang, staaf, pijp
spindly [spindlie] spichtig, stakig
spin-drier centrifuge
spin-dry centrifugeren
spine [spajn] **1** ruggengraat; **2** stekel, doorn; **3** rug (of book)
spine-chiller horrorfilm, horrorroman, horrorverhaal[h], griezel-, gruwelfilm
spineless [spajnləs] **1** zonder ruggengraat (also fig); **2** karakterloos, slap
spin-off (winstgevend) nevenproduct[h] (resultaat[h]), bijproduct[h]
spinster [spinstə] **1** oude vrijster; **2** ongehuwde vrouw
¹spiral [spajjərəl] adj **1** spiraalvormig, schroefvormig: ~ staircase wenteltrap; **2** kronkelend
²spiral [spajjərəl] n spiraal, schroeflijn
spire [spajjə] (toren)spits, piek, punt[h]
¹spirit [spirrit] n **1** geest, ziel, karakter[h], bovennatuurlijk wezen[h]: the Holy Spirit de Heilige Geest; kindred ~s verwante zielen; **2** levenskracht, energie; **3** levenslust, opgewektheid; **4** moed, durf, lef[h]; **5** zin, diepe betekenis: the ~ of the law de geest van de wet; **6** spiritus, alcohol, (sometimes singular) sterkedrank(en): methylated ~ (brand)spiritus; **7** ~s gemoedsgesteldheid, gestesgesteldheid, stemming: be in great (of: high) ~s opgewekt zijn; **8** mens met karakter, karakter[h]; **9** ~s spiritus, geest: public ~ gemeenschapszin
²spirit [spirrit] vb (with away, off) wegtoveren, ontfutselen, (fig) heimelijk laten verdwijnen
spirited [spirrittid] **1** levendig, geanimeerd; **2** bezield, vol energie
spiritless [spirritləs] **1** lusteloos, moedeloos; **2** levenloos, doods, saai
spirit level waterpas
spiritual [spirritsjoeəl] **1** geestelijk, spiritueel; **2**

mentaal, intellectueel; **3** godsdienstig, religieus ‖ ~ *healing* geloofsgenezing

spiritualism [spirritsjoeəlizm] **1** spiritualisme^h; **2** spiritisme^h

¹spit [spit] *vb* **1** spuwen, spugen; **2** sputteren, blazen *(eg cat)*; **3** lichtjes neervallen, druppelen *(rain)* ‖ *he is the ~ting image of his father* hij lijkt als twee druppels water op zijn vader

²spit [spit] *vb (also with out)* (uit)spuwen, (uit)spugen, opgeven ‖ ~ *it out!* voor de dag ermee!

³spit [spit] *n* **1** spuug^h, speeksel^h; **2** spit^h, braadspit^h; **3** landtong; **4** spade, schop: *dig a hole two ~(s) deep* een gat twee spaden diep graven; **5** geblaas^h, gesis^h *(of cat)*: ~ *and polish* (grondig) poetswerk *(eg in army)*

¹spite [spajt] *n* wrok, boosaardigheid: *from* (of: *out of)* ~ uit kwaadaardigheid; *in* ~ *of* ondanks; *in* ~ *of oneself* of men wil of niet

²spite [spajt] *vb* treiteren, pesten

spiteful [spajtfoel] hatelijk

spitfire heethoofd, driftkop

spittle [spitl] speeksel^h, spuug^h

¹splash [splæsj] *vb* **1** (rond)spatten, uiteenspatten: ~ *about* rondspatten; **2** rondspetteren; **3** klateren, kletteren

²splash [splæsj] *vb* **1** (be)spatten; **2** laten spatten; **3** met grote koppen in de krant zetten

³splash [splæsj] *n* **1** plons; **2** vlek, spat; **3** gespetter^h, gespat^h ‖ *make a* ~ opzien baren

⁴splash [splæsj] *adv* met een plons

splatter [splætə] **1** spetteren, (be)spatten; **2** poedelen; **3** klateren, kletteren

¹splay [splee] *vb* **1** *(also with out)* (zich) verwijden, (zich) verbreden; **2** *(also with out)* (zich) uitspreiden

²splay [splee] *vb* naar buiten staan *(of foot)*

spleen [splie:n] **1** milt; **2** zwaarmoedigheid, neerslachtigheid; **3** boze bui ‖ *vent one's* ~ zijn gal spuwen

splendid [splendid] **1** schitterend, prachtig; **2** groots, indrukwekkend; **3** voortreffelijk, uitstekend

splendour [splendə] **1** pracht, praal; **2** glorie, grootsheid

¹splice [splajs] *vb* **1** verbinden, aan elkaar verbinden, een verbinding maken; **2** lassen, koppelen *(film, sound tape)* ‖ *get ~d* trouwen

²splice [splajs] *n* **1** las, verbinding; **2** splits *(of rope)*; **3** houtverbinding

splint [splint] **1** metaalstrook, metaalstrip; **2** spalk

¹splinter [splintə] *n* splinter, scherf

²splinter [splintə] *vb* versplinteren, splinteren

¹split [split] *vb* **1** splijten, splitsen, *(fig)* afsplitsen, scheuren: *George and I have split up* George en ik zijn uit elkaar gegaan; ~ *up into groups* (zich) in groepjes verdelen; **2** delen, onder elkaar verdelen: *let's* ~ *(the bill)* laten we (de kosten) delen

²split [split] *vb (with on)* verraden

³split *n* **1** spleet, kloof, *(fig)* breuk, scheiding; **2** split-

sing; **3** ~*s* spagaat: *do the ~s* een spagaat maken

⁴split *adj* **1** gespleten, gebarsten; **2** gesplitst, gescheurd: *(sport)* ~ *decision* niet-eenstemmige beslissing; ~ *level* met halve verdiepingen; ~ *pea* spliterwt; ~ *second* onderdeel van een seconde, flits

splitting [splitting] fel, scherp, hevig: ~ *headache* barstende hoofdpijn

split-up breuk *(after quarrel)*, echtscheiding, het uit-elkaar-gaan

splodge [splodzj] vlek, plek, veeg

splurge [splə:dzj] **1** uitspatting, het zich te buiten gaan; **2** spektakel^h

¹splutter [spluttə] *vb* **1** sputteren, stamelen, hakkelen; **2** sputteren, sissen; **3** proesten, spetteren

²splutter [spluttə] *n* gesputter^h, gespetter^h

¹spoil [spojl] *vb* **1** bederven, (doen) rotten, beschadigen, verpesten: ~ *the fun* het plezier vergallen; **2** bederven, verwennen, vertroetelen: *be ~ing for a fight* staan te trappelen om te vechten

²spoil [spojl] *n* buit, geplunderde goederen

spoilsport spelbreker

spoke **1** spaak; **2** sport, trede ‖ *put a* ~ *in s.o.'s wheel* iem een spaak in het wiel steken

spokesman [spooksmən] woordvoerder, afgevaardigde

spokesperson [spookspə:sn] woordvoerder

¹sponge [spundzj] *n* **1** klaploper; **2** spons: *(boxing) throw in the* ~ de spons opgooien, *(fig)* de strijd opgeven; **3** wondgaas^h

²sponge [spundzj] *vb* klaplopen, parasiteren: ~ *on s.o.* op iem (parasi)teren

³sponge [spundzj] *vb* **1** sponzen, *(with down, off)* schoon-, afsponzen; **2** afspoelen met een spons

sponge bag toilettasje^h

sponger [spundzjə] **1** sponzenduiker; **2** klaploper

¹sponsor [sponsə] *n* **1** sponsor, geldschieter; **2** peter, meter

²sponsor [sponsə] *vb* propageren, steunen, bevorderen; sponsoren

spontaneity [spontənie:ittie] spontaniteit

spontaneous [sponteeniəs] **1** spontaan, natuurlijk, ongedwongen; **2** uit zichzelf, vanzelf: ~ *combustion* zelfontbranding

¹spoof [spoe:f] *n* **1** poets, bedrog^h; **2** parodie

²spoof [spoe:f] *vb* **1** voor de gek houden, een poets bakken; **2** parodiëren

spook [spoe:k] geest, spook^h

spooky [spoe:kie] spookachtig, griezelig, eng

spool [spoe:l] **1** spoel; **2** klos, garenklos

spoon [spoe:n] lepel

spoon-feed **1** voeren, met een lepel voeren; **2** iets met de lepel ingieten, iem iets voorkauwen

¹sport [spo:t] *n* **1** pret, spel^h, plezier^h: *in* ~ voor de grap; **2** spel^h, tijdverdrijf^h; **3** sport; **4** jacht; **5** sportieve meid (kerel)

²sport [spo:t] *vb* pronken met, vertonen, te koop lopen met: *he was ~ing a bowler hat* hij liep met een hoge hoed

³sport [spo:t] *vb* spelen *(of animals)*, zich vermaken

sporting [spo:ting] **1** sportief, eerlijk, fair: *~ chance* redelijke kans; **2** sport-

sports [spo:ts] **1** sport; **2** sportdag, sportevenement; **3** atletiek

sportsman [spo:tsmən] **1** sportieve man; **2** sportman

sportsmanship [spo:tsmənsjip] sportiviteit, zich als een goede winnaar (verliezer) gedragen

sportswoman 1 sportieve vrouw; **2** sportvrouw

sporty [spo:tie] **1** sportief, sport-; **2** zorgeloos, vrolijk; **3** opvallend, bijzonder *(of clothes)*

¹**spot** [spot] *n* **1** plaats, plek: *they were on the ~* ze waren ter plaatse; **2** vlekjeʰ, stip; **3** puistjeʰ; **4** positie, plaats, functie; **5** spot(jeʰ) *(advertising etc)*; **6** spot(lightʰ); **7** beetjeʰ, wat: *a ~ of bother* een probleempje; **8** onmiddellijke levering: *now he is in a (tight) ~* nu zit hij in de penarie; *he had to leave on the ~* hij moest op staande voet vertrekken; *put s.o. on the ~* iem in het nauw brengen, iem voor het blok zetten

²**spot** [spot] *adv* precies: *arrive ~ on time* precies op tijd komen

³**spot** [spot] *vb* **1** vlekken maken in, bevlekken; **2** herkennen, eruit halen: *~ a mistake* een fout ontdekken

⁴**spot** [spot] *vb* **1** verkleuren, vlekken krijgen; **2** vlekken; **3** spetteren, licht regenen: *it is ~ting with rain* er vallen dikke regendruppels

spot check (onverwachte) steekproef

spotless [spotləs] brandschoon, vlekkeloos, *(fig also)* onberispelijk

¹**spotlight** *n* **1** bundellichtʰ, spotlightʰ; **2** bermlichtʰ *(of car)* || *be in the ~, hold the ~* in het middelpunt van de belangstelling staan

²**spotlight** *vb* **1** beschijnen; **2** onder de aandacht brengen

spotty [spottie] **1** vlekkerig; **2** ongelijkmatig, onregelmatig; **3** puisterig

spouse [spaus] echtgenoot, echtgenote

¹**spout** [spaut] *n* **1** pijp, buis; **2** tuit; **3** stortkoker; **4** straal, opspuitende vloeistof, opspuitend zandʰ || *up the ~: a)* naar de knoppen, verknald *(eg money, life); b)* totaal verkeerd *(eg figures); c)* hopeloos in de knoei, reddeloos verloren *(of person); d)* zwanger

²**spout** [spaut] *vb* **1** spuiten, met kracht uitstoten: *the water ~ed from the broken pipe* het water spoot uit de gebarsten leiding; **2** galmen, spuien: *she was always ~ing German verses* ze liep altijd Duitse verzen te galmen

¹**sprain** [spreen] *vb* verstuiken

²**sprain** [spreen] *n* verstuiking

sprat [spræt] sprot

¹**sprawl** [spro:l] *vb* **1** armen en benen uitspreiden, nonchalant liggen, onderuit zakken; **2** zich uitspreiden, alle kanten op gaan: *~ing suburbs* naar alle kanten uitgroeiende voorsteden

²**sprawl** [spro:l] *n* **1** nonchalante houding; **2** slordige massa, vormeloos geheelʰ: *the ~ of the suburbs* de uitdijende voorsteden

¹**spray** [spree] *n* **1** takjeʰ *(also as corsage)*, twijg; **2** verstuiver, spuitbus; **3** straal, wolk; **4** nevel, wolk van druppels

²**spray** [spree] *vb* (be)sproeien, (be)spuiten, (een vloeistof) verstuiven

¹**spread** [spred] *vb* **1** zich uitstrekken, zich uitspreiden; **2** zich verspreiden, overal bekend worden: *the disease ~ quickly to other villages* de ziekte breidde zich snel uit naar andere dorpen; **3** uitgespreid worden: *cold butter does not ~ easily* koude boter smeert niet gemakkelijk

²**spread** [spred] *vb* **1** uitspreiden, verbreiden, verspreiden, *(fig also)* spreiden, verdelen: *~ out one's arms* zijn armen uitspreiden; **2** uitsmeren, uitstrijken; **3** bedekken, beleggen, besmeren; **4** klaarzetten *(meal)*, dekken *(table)*

³**spread** [spred] *n* **1** wijdte, breedte, *(fig also)* reikwijdte; **2** uitdijing; **3** verbreiding, verspreiding; **4** stuk land, landbezitʰ van één boer; **5** smeerselʰ; **6** (feest)maalʰ, onthaalʰ; **7** dubbele pagina, spread

spreadeagle 1 (zich) met armen en benen wijd neerleggen; **2** volkomen verslaan, verpletteren

spree [sprie:] pretʰ(jeʰ), lol: *spending ~* geldsmijterij

sprig [sprig] **1** twijgjeʰ, takjeʰ; **2** telg, spruit

¹**spring** [spring] *vb* **1** (op)springen: *the first thing that ~s to one's mind* het eerste wat je te binnen schiet; *~ to one's feet* opspringen; **2** (terug)veren; **3** *(also with up)* ontspringen, ontstaan, voorkomen: *~ from* afstammen van; *~ from (of: out of)* voortkomen uit

²**spring** [spring] *vb* **1** springen over *(of horse, obstacle)*; **2** plotseling bekendmaken: *~ sth. on s.o.* iem met iets verrassen

³**spring** [spring] *n* **1** bron *(also fig)*, oorsprong, herkomst; **2** (metalen) veer, springveer; **3** sprong; **4** lente, voorjaarʰ: *in (the) ~* in het voorjaar

spring-clean voorjaarsschoonmaak, grote schoonmaak

spring roll loempia

spring tide springtijʰ, springvloed

springtime lente(tijd), voorjaarʰ

springy [springie] **1** veerkrachtig; **2** elastisch

¹**sprinkle** [springkl] *vb* **1** sprenkelen *(also fig)*, strooien; **2** bestrooien *(also fig)*, besprenkelen: *~ with* bestrooien met

²**sprinkle** [springkl] *n* **1** regenbuitjeʰ; **2** kleine hoeveelheid || *a ~ of houses* enkele (verspreid liggende) huizen

sprinkler [springklə] **1** (tuin)sproeier; **2** blusinstallatie

sprinkling [springkling] kleine hoeveelheid, greintjeʰ

¹**sprint** [sprint] *n* sprint, spurt

²**sprint** [sprint] *vb* sprinten

sprinter [sprintə] **1** *(sport)* sprinter; **2** sprinter *(train)*

sprite [sprajt] **1** (boze) geest; **2** elf(jeʰ)

¹**sprout** [spraut] *vb* **1** (ont)spruiten, uitlopen; **2** de

hoogte in schieten, groeien: ~ *up* de hoogte in schieten

²**sprout** [spraut] *vb* doen ontspruiten

³**sprout** [spraut] *n* 1 spruit, loot, scheut; 2 spruitjeʰ *(vegetable)*

¹**spruce** [sproe:s] *adj* net(jes), keurig

²**spruce** [sproe:s] *vb* opdoffen, opdirken, verfraaien

³**spruce** [sproe:s] *n* spar, sparrenhoutʰ

spry [spraj] levendig, actief: *a ~ old man* een vitale oude man

spud [spud] pieper, aardappel

spunk [spungk] pit, lefʰ, durf

¹**spur** [spə:] *n* 1 spoorʰ *(of horseman): win one's ~s: a)* zijn sporen verdienen; *b) (also fig)* zich onderscheiden; 2 aansporing, prikkel, stimulans: *act on the ~ of the moment* spontaan iets doen; 3 uitloper *(of mountain)*

²**spur** [spə:] *vb* 1 de sporen geven; 2 aansporen, aanmoedigen: *~ on (to)* aanzetten, aansporen (tot)

spurious [spjoeəriəs] 1 onecht, vals, vervalst; 2 onlogisch: *~ argument* verkeerd argument

spurn [spə:n] 1 (weg)trappen; 2 afwijzen, vd hand wijzen

¹**spurt** [spə:t] *n* 1 uitbarsting, losbarsting, vlaag, opwelling: *a ~ of flames* een plotselinge vlammenzee; 2 sprint(jeʰ), spurt: *put on a ~* een sprintje trekken; 3 (krachtige) straal, stroom, vloed

²**spurt** [spə:t] *vb* 1 spurten, sprinten; 2 spuiten, opspatten: *the blood ~ed out* het bloed gutste eruit

¹**sputter** [spʌtə] *vb* sputteren, proesten, stamelen, brabbelen

²**sputter** [spʌtə] *n* gesputterʰ; gestamelʰ

¹**spy** [spaj] *n (spies)* spion(ne), geheim agent(e)

²**spy** [spaj] *vb* spioneren, spieden, loeren, een spion zijn: *~ (up)on* bespioneren, bespieden; *~ into* bespioneren, zijn neus steken in

³**spy** [spaj] *vb* 1 bespioneren, bespieden; 2 ontwaren, in het oog krijgen || *I ~ (with my little eye)* ik zie, ik zie, wat jij niet ziet

spy out 1 verkennen, onderzoeken; 2 opsporen

sq. *square* kwadraatʰ

¹**squabble** [skwɒbl] *vb* kibbelen, overhoop liggen

²**squabble** [skwɒbl] *n* schermutseling, gekibbelʰ

squad [skwod] 1 *(sport)* selectie; 2 sectie

squad car patrouilleauto

squadron [skwɒdrən] 1 eskadronʰ; 2 *(navy, airforce)* eskaderʰ

squadron leader majoor, eskadercommandant *(in airforce)*

squalid [skwɒllid] 1 smerig, vuil, vies, gemeen, laag; 2 ellendig, beroerd

¹**squall** [skwo:l] *n* 1 vlaag, rukwind, windstoot, bui, storm; 2 kreet, gil, schreeuw

²**squall** [skwo:l] *vb* gillen, krijsen, (uit)schreeuwen

squally [skwo:lie] 1 buiig, regenachtig, winderig; 2 stormachtig

squalor [skwɒllə] 1 misère; 2 smerigheid

squander [skwɒndə] (with *on*) verspillen (aan): *~ money* met geld smijten

¹**square** [skweə] *n* 1 vierkantʰ; 2 kwadraatʰ, tweede macht; 3 pleinʰ; 4 veldʰ, hokjeʰ, ruit *(on games' board);* 5 (huizen)blokʰ; 6 oefenpleinʰ, oefenterreinʰ; 7 ouderwets persoon || *be back to ~ one* van voren af aan moeten beginnen; *on the ~: a)* rechtdoorzee; *b)* in een rechte hoek

²**square** [skweə] *adj* 1 vierkant, kwadraat-, in het vierkant, fors, breed *(of figure): ~ brackets* vierkante haakjes; *one ~ metre* één vierkante meter; *three metres ~* drie meter in het vierkant; 2 recht(hoekig); 3 eerlijk, fair, open(hartig) *(eg answer),* regelrecht *(eg refusal): a ~ deal* een rechtvaardige behandeling, een eerlijke transactie; 4 ouderwets; 5 stevig *(of meal);* 6 *(sport, esp golf)* gelijk: *be (all) ~* gelijk staan; *a ~ peg (in a round hole)* de verkeerde persoon (voor iets); *be ~ with* quitte staan met, op gelijke hoogte *(of:* voet) staan met; *all ~* we staan quitte, *(sport)* gelijke stand

³**square** [skweə] *adv* 1 recht(hoekig), rechtop; 2 (regel)recht: *look s.o. ~ in the eye* iem recht in de ogen kijken; 3 eerlijk, rechtvaardig: *play ~* eerlijk spelen; 4 rechtuit, open(hartig): *come ~ out with an answer* onomwonden antwoorden

⁴**square** [skweə] *vb* 1 vierkant maken; 2 rechthoekig maken; 3 rechten *(shoulders),* rechtzetten; 4 in orde brengen, regelen; *~ up* vereffenen; *~ up one's debts* zijn schuld(en) voldoen; 5 omkopen; 6 kwadrateren, tot de tweede macht verheffen: *three ~d equals nine* drie tot de tweede (macht) is negen; 7 *(sport)* op gelijke stand brengen

⁵**square** [skweə] *vb* 1 overeenstemmen, kloppen; 2 in een rechte hoek staan

square-built vierkant, hoekig, breed

squarely [skweəlie] 1 recht(hoekig), rechtop; 2 (regel)recht; 3 eerlijk: *act ~* eerlijk handelen

square up 1 in gevechtshouding gaan staan: *~ to reality* de werkelijkheid onder ogen zien; 2 afrekenen, orde op zaken stellen

¹**squash** [skwosj] *vb* 1 pletten, platdrukken; 2 verpletteren *(only fig),* de mond snoeren; 3 de kop indrukken; 4 wringen: *~ in* erin persen

²**squash** [skwosj] *vb* 1 geplet worden; 2 dringen, zich persen: *can I ~ in next to you?* kan ik er nog bij, naast u?

³**squash** [skwosj] *n* 1 kwast, vruchtendrank; 2 gedrangʰ, oploop; 3 pulp

squashy [skwosjie] 1 zacht, overrijp; 2 drassig

¹**squat** [skwot] *vb* 1 (also with *down)* (neer)hurken; 2 zich tegen de grond drukken *(of animal);* 3 zich illegaal vestigen *(on a stretch of land);* 4 als kraker een leegstaand pand bewonen

²**squat** [skwot] *adj* 1 gedrongen, plomp; 2 gehurkt

³**squat** [skwot] *n* 1 hurkende houding, het hurken; 2 ineengedoken houding *(of animal);* 3 kraakpandʰ; 4 het kraken *(of house)*

squatter [skwɒttə] 1 (illegale) kolonist, landbezetter; 2 kraker

¹**squawk** [skwo:k] *vb* krijsen, schril schreeuwen

²**squawk** [skwo:k] *n* schreeuw, gekrijsʰ

¹squeak [skwie:k] *vb* **1** piepen, knarsen, gilletjes slaken; **2** doorslaan ‖ ~ *through (of: by)* het nog net halen

²squeak [skwie:k] *n* **1** gepiep[h], geknars[h]; **2** klein kansje[h] ‖ *that was a narrow ~* dat was op het nippertje, dat ging *(of:* kon, lukte) nog net

squeaky [skwie:kie] piepend, krakend ‖ ~ *clean* brandschoon

¹squeal [skwie:l] *vb* **1** krijsen, piepen; **2** klikken, doorslaan: ~ *on s.o.* iem aanbrengen

²squeal [skwie:l] *n* **1** gil, schreeuw, gepiep[h]; **2** klacht

squeamish [skwie:misj] **1** (gauw) misselijk; **2** teergevoelig, overgevoelig; **3** (al te) kieskeurig ‖ *this film is not for ~ viewers* deze film is niet geschikt voor al te gevoelige kijkers

squeegee [skwie:dzjie:] rubber wisser[h], schuiver, trekker

¹squeeze [skwie:z] *vb* **1** drukken (op), knijpen (in); (uit)persen, uitknijpen: ~ *a lemon* een citroen uitpersen; **2** duwen, wurmen: *how can she ~ so many things into one single day?* hoe krijgt ze zoveel dingen op één dag gedaan?; **3** tegen zich aan drukken, stevig omhelzen

²squeeze [skwie:z] *vb* dringen, zich wringen: ~ *through* zich erdoorheen wurmen *(also fig)*

³squeeze [skwie:z] *n* **1** samendrukking, pressie, druk: *she gave his hand a little ~* ze kneep even in zijn hand; *put the ~ on s.o.* iem onder druk zetten; **2** gedrang[h]; **3** (stevige) handdruk, (innige) omarming; **4** beperking, schaarste: *it was a close (of: narrow, tight) ~* we zaten als haringen in een ton

squelch [skweltsj] een zuigend geluid maken, ploeteren

squib [skwib] **1** voetzoeker; **2** blindganger; **3** schotschrift[h]

squid [skwid] pijlinktvis

squidgy [skwidzjie] klef

squiggle [skwigl] kronkel(lijn), krabbel

¹squint [skwint] *vb* **1** scheel kijken; **2** gluren, turen: ~ *at sth.* een steelse blik op iets werpen

²squint [skwint] *n* **1** scheel oog[h]; turend oog[h]; **2** (vluchtige) blik: *have (of: take) a ~ at sth.* een blik werpen op iets

squire [skwajjə] **1** landjonker, landheer *(in England);* **2** meneer *(form of address among men)*

squirm [skwə:m] **1** kronkelen, zich in bochten wringen; **2** wel door de grond kunnen gaan: *be ~ing with embarrassment* zich geen raad weten van verlegenheid

squirrel [skwirrəl] eekhoorn

¹squirt [skwə:t] *vb* (krachtig) naar buiten spuiten

²squirt [skwə:t] *vb* (uit)spuiten, uitspuwen

³squirt [skwə:t] *n* **1** straal *(of liquid etc);* **2** spuit(je[h]), waterpistool[h]

sr. *senior* sr., Sen.

St *Saint* St.; H., Sint, Heilige

St. 1 *Street* str., straat; **2** *strait* zee-engte; straat

¹stab [stæb] *vb* (with *at*) (toe)stoten (naar), steken, uithalen (naar): *a ~bing pain* een stekende pijn

²stab [stæb] *vb* (door)steken, neersteken, doorboren: *be ~bed to death* doodgestoken worden

³stab [stæb] *n* **1** steek(wond), stoot, uithaal; **2** pijnscheut, plotse opwelling; **3** poging, gooi: *have (of: make) a ~ at* eens proberen; *a ~ in the back* dolkstoot in de rug

stability [stəbillittie] stabiliteit, duurzaamheid

stabilize [steebillajz] (zich) stabiliseren, in evenwicht blijven (brengen)

¹stable [steebl] *adj* **1** stabiel, vast, duurzaam; **2** standvastig

²stable [steebl] *n* **1** stal, *(fig)* ploeg, groep; **2** (ren)stal ‖ *it is no use shutting the ~ door after the horse has bolted* als het kalf verdronken is, dempt men de put

¹stack [stæk] *n* **1** (hooi)mijt, houtmijt; **2** stapel, hoop: ~*s of money* bergen geld; **3** schoorsteen

²stack [stæk] *vb* **1** (op)stapelen, op een hoop leggen, volstapelen; **2** arrangeren: ~ *the cards* de kaarten vals schikken

¹stack up *vb* **1** opstapelen; **2** ophouden: *traffic was stacked up for miles* het verkeer werd kilometers lang opgehouden

²stack up *vb* **1** een file vormen *(of cars, aeroplanes),* aanschuiven; **2** ervoor staan

stadium [steediəm] stadion[h]

¹staff [sta:f] *n* **1** staf *(also fig),* steun; **2** vlaggenstok; **3** notenbalk; **4** staf *(also mil),* personeel[h], korps[h]

²staff [sta:f] *vb* bemannen, van personeel voorzien

¹stag [stæg] *n* **1** hertenbok; **2** man die alleen op stap is

²stag [stæg] *adj* mannen-: ~ *party* vrijgezellenfeest, hengstenbal

¹stage [steedzj] *n* **1** toneel[h] *(also fig),* podium[h], platform[h]: *put on the ~* opvoeren; *be on the ~* aan het toneel verbonden zijn; **2** fase, stadium[h]: *at this ~* op dit punt, in dit stadium; **3** stopplaats, halte aan het eind ve tariefzone; **4** etappe, traject[h], tariefzone: *by easy ~s* in korte etappes; *in ~s* gefaseerd; **5** postkoets: *set the ~ for* de weg bereiden voor

²stage [steedzj] *vb* **1** opvoeren, ten tonele brengen; **2** produceren; **3** regisseren; **4** organiseren

stagecoach postkoets

stage fright plankenkoorts

stage-manage in scène zetten, opzetten

¹stagger [stægə] *vb* wankelen: ~ *along* moeizaam vooruitkomen

²stagger [stægə] *vb* **1** doen wankelen, *(fig)* onthutsen; **2** zigzagsgewijs aanbrengen: *a ~ed road crossing* een kruising met ver.., ..agende zijwegen; **3** spreiden *(holidays):* ~*ed office hours* glijdende werktijden

³stagger [stægə] *n* wankeling

staggering [stægəring] **1** wankelend; **2** onthutsend, duizelingwekkend

stagnant [stægnənt] **1** stilstaand; **2** stagnerend

stagnate [stægneet] stilstaan, stagneren, stremmen

staid [steed] **1** bezadigd; **2** vast, stellig

¹stain [steen] *vb* vlekken

²**stain** [steen] *vb* **1** bevlekken; **2** kleuren: *~ed glass* gebrandschilderd glas

³**stain** [steen] *n* **1** vlek, smet, schandvlek; **2** kleurstof

stainless [steenləs] roestvrij *(steel)*

stair [steə] **1** *also ~s* trap; **2** trede

staircase trap

stairwell trappenhuis^h

¹**stake** [steek] *n* **1** staak, paal; **2** brandstapel: *go to the ~* op de brandstapel sterven; **3** inzet, *(fig)* belang^h: *have a ~ in sth.* zakelijk belang hebben bij iets; *be at ~* op het spel staan

²**stake** [steek] *vb* **1** *(with off, out)* afpalen *(eg land)*, afbakenen: *~ out a claim* aanspraak maken op; **2** spietsen; **3** *(with on)* verwedden (om), inzetten (op), *(fig)* op het spel zetten: *I'd ~ my life on it* ik durf er mijn hoofd om te verwedden; *~ out* posten bij, in de gaten houden

stale [steel] **1** niet vers, oud(bakken); **2** afgezaagd; **3** (afge)mat, machinaal

stalemate [steelmeet] **1** *(chess)* pat^h; **2** patstelling, dood punt^h

¹**stalk** [sto:k] *n* **1** *(bot)* stengel, steel; **2** stronk

²**stalk** [sto:k] *vb* *(with out)* (uit) schrijden: *the chairman ~ed out in anger* de voorzitter stapte kwaad op

³**stalk** [sto:k] *vb* **1** besluipen; **2** achtervolgen; **3** rondwaren door

¹**stall** [sto:l] *n* **1** box, hok^h, stal; **2** stalletje^h, stand; **3** stallesplaats, *~s* stalles

²**stall** [sto:l] *vb* **1** blijven steken, ingesneeuwd zijn; **2** afslaan *(of engine)*; **3** uitvluchten zoeken, tijd rekken

³**stall** [sto:l] *vb* **1** stallen; **2** ophouden, blokkeren

stallion [stæliən] (dek)hengst

¹**stalwart** [sto:lwət] *adj* **1** stevig, stoer; **2** flink; **3** standvastig, trouw

²**stalwart** [sto:lwət] *n* trouwe aanhanger

stamen [steemən] meeldraad

stamina [stæminnə] uithoudingsvermogen^h

stammer [stæmə] stotteren, stamelen || *speak with a ~* stotteren

¹**stamp** [stæmp] *n* **1** stempel, *(fig)* (ken)merk^h; **2** zegel, postzegel, waarmerk^h; **3** kenmerk^h

²**stamp** [stæmp] *vb* stampen, trappen

³**stamp** [stæmp] *vb* **1** stempelen, persen, waarmerken: *be ~ed on one's memory* in zijn geheugen gegrift zijn; **2** frankeren, een postzegel plakken op: *~ed addressed envelope* antwoordenvelop; **3** fijnstampen; *~ out* uitroeien; *~ on* onderdrukken

¹**stampede** [stæmpie:d] *n* **1** wilde vlucht, op hol slaan *(of animals)*, paniek; **2** stormloop

²**stampede** [stæmpie:d] *vb* op de vlucht slaan, op hol slaan

³**stampede** [stæmpie:d] *vb* op de vlucht jagen, *(fig)* het hoofd doen verliezen: *don't be ~d into selling your house* ga nou niet halsoverkop je huis verkopen

stance [sta:ns] **1** houding, stand; **2** pose, gezindheid: *an obvious anti-American ~* een duidelijke anti-Amerikaanse gezindheid

¹**stand** [stænd] *vb* **1** (rechtop) staan, opstaan: *~ clear of* vrijlaten *(door etc)*; **2** zich bevinden, staan, liggen; **3** stilstaan, halt houden, stoppen *(of vehicles)*; **4** blijven staan, stand houden: *~ and deliver!* je geld of je leven!; **5** gelden, opgaan: *the offer still ~s* het aanbod is nog van kracht; **6** zijn, (ervoor) staan, zich in een bepaalde situatie bevinden: *I want to know where I ~* ik wil weten waar ik aan toe ben; **7** kandidaat zijn, zich kandidaat stellen: *~ for president against Al Gore* kandidaat zijn voor het presidentschap met Al Gore als tegenkandidaat; *I ~ corrected* ik neem mijn woorden terug; *~ to lose sth.* waarschijnlijk iets zullen verliezen; *~ aloof* zich op een afstand houden; *~ apart* zich afzijdig houden; *~ easy!* op de plaats rust!; *~ in (for s.o.)* (iem) vervangen

²**stand** [stænd] *vb* **1** plaatsen, rechtop zetten: *~ everything on its head* alles op zijn kop zetten; **2** verdragen, uitstaan; doorstaan, ondergaan; **3** weerstaan; **4** trakteren (op): *~ s.o. (to) a drink* iem op een drankje trakteren

³**stand** [stænd] *n* **1** stilstand, halt: *bring to a ~* tot staan brengen; **2** stelling *(also mil)*; *(fig)* standpunt^h; **3** plaats, positie, post; **4** statief^h, standaard; **5** stand, kraam; **6** standplaats *(of taxis etc)*; **7** tribune, podium^h, getuigenbank

¹**standard** [stændəd] *n* **1** peil^h, niveau^h: *~ of living* levensstandaard; *below ~* beneden peil, beneden de norm; **2** vaandel^h *(also fig)*, standaard, vlag; **3** maat(staf), norm; **4** standaard(maat); **5** houder *(eg candlestick)*; **6** (munt)standaard: *the gold ~* de gouden standaard; **7** standaer, steun, paal; **8** hoogstammige plant (struik)

²**standard** [stændəd] *adj* **1** normaal, gebruikelijk: *~ size* standaardmaat, standaardgrootte; **2** staand: *~ rose* stamroos

standardization [stændədajzeesjən] standaardisering, normalisering

standardize [stændədajz] standaardiseren, normaliseren

stand aside 1 opzijgaan; **2** zich afzijdig houden

stand back 1 achteruit gaan; **2** op een afstand liggen; **3** afstand nemen; **4** zich op de achtergrond houden

¹**standby** *n* **1** reserve; **2** stand-by

²**standby** *adj* reserve-, nood-

stand by 1 erbij staan; **2** werkloos toezien; **3** gereed staan; **4** bijstaan, steunen; **5** zich houden aan *(promise)*, trouw blijven aan *(somebody)*

stand down zich terugtrekken, aftreden

stand for 1 staan voor, betekenen; **2** goedvinden, zich laten welgevallen

stand-in vervanger

¹**standing** [stænding] *adj* **1** blijvend, van kracht, vast: *~ committee* permanente commissie; *~ joke* vaste grap; *~ order: a)* doorlopende order; *b)* automatische overschrijving; *~ orders* statuten; **2** staand, stilstaand: *~ ovation* staande ovatie; **3** zonder aanloop *(of jump etc)*

²**standing** [stænding] *n* **1** status, rang, positie: *s.o. of* ~ iem van aanzien; **2** reputatie; **3** (tijds)duur: *friendship of long* ~ oude vriendschap

standing room staanplaatsen

stand-off **1** impasse, patstelling; **2** evenwichtʰ; **3** (periode van) nietsdoen

standout *(Am; inf)* uitblinker, schoonheid: *Helen's translation was a* ~ Helens vertaling stak met kop en schouder boven de rest uit

stand out 1 duidelijk uitkomen, in het oog vallen; **2** zich onderscheiden; **3** blijven volhouden: ~ *for* verdedigen

standpoint [stændpojnt] standpuntʰ *(also fig)*: *from a commercial* ~ commercieel gezien

standstill [stændstil] stilstand: *at a* ~ tot stilstand gekomen

¹**stand up** *vb* **1** overeind staan; **2** gaan staan: ~ *and be counted* voor zijn mening uitkomen; ~ *for* opkomen voor; **3** standhouden, overeind blijven, *(fig)* doorstaan: *that won't* ~ *in court* daar blijft niets van overeind in de rechtszaal; ~ *to* trotseren

²**stand up** *vb* laten zitten: *she stood me up* zij is niet op komen dagen

stand-up 1 rechtop staand; **2** lopend *(of supper etc)*; **3** flink *(fight)*, stevig || ~ *comedian* conferencier

stanza [stænzə] coupletʰ, strofe

¹**staple** [steepl] *n* **1** nietjeʰ; **2** krammetjeʰ; **3** hoofdbestanddeelʰ *(also fig)*, hoofdschotel

²**staple** [steepl] *vb* (vast)nieten, hechten

³**staple** [steepl] *adj* **1** voornaamste: ~ *diet* hoofdvoedsel; ~ *products* stapelproducten; **2** belangrijk

stapler [steeplə] nietmachine

¹**star** [sta:] *n* **1** ster: *Star of David* davidster; *shooting* ~ vallende ster; *thank one's (lucky)* ~s zich gelukkig prijzen; **2** asterisk, sterretjeʰ; **3** uitblink(st)er, beroemdheid, (film)ster, vedette: *all-* ~ *cast* sterbezetting; *the Stars and Stripes* (of: *Bars*) Amerikaanse vlag

²**star** [sta:] *vb* (als ster) optreden

³**star** [sta:] *vb* **1** met een sterretje aanduiden; **2** als ster laten optreden: *a film* ~*ring Eddy Murphy* een film met (in de hoofdrol) Eddy Murphy

starboard [sta:bəd] stuurboordʰ, rechts

starch [sta:tsj] **1** zetmeelʰ; **2** stijfselʰ

starchy [sta:tsjie] **1** zetmeelrijk: ~ *food* meelkost; **2** gesteven; **3** stijfjes

¹**stare** [steə] *vb* (with *at*) staren (naar)

²**stare** [steə] *vb* staren naar: *it is staring you in the face* het ligt voor de hand; ~ *s.o. down* (of: *out*) iem aanstaren tot hij de ogen neerslaat

³**stare** [steə] *n* starende blik

starfish zeester

¹**staring** [steəring] *adj* (te) fel *(colour)*

²**staring** [steəring] *adv* volledig: *stark* ~ *mad* knettergek

¹**stark** [sta:k] *adj* **1** grimmig; **2** stijf; onbuigzaam; **3** *(fig)* schril: ~ *contrast* schril contrast; **4** verlaten *(of landscape)*, kaal: ~ *poverty* bittere armoede

²**stark** [sta:k] *adv* volledig: ~ *naked* spiernaakt

starkers [sta:kəz] poedelnaakt

starlet [sta:lit] (film)sterretjeʰ

starling [sta:ling] spreeuw

star-spangled [sta:spænggld] met sterren bezaaid || *the Star-Spangled Banner: a)* het Amerikaanse volkslied; *b)* de Amerikaanse vlag

¹**start** [sta:t] *vb* **1** beginnen, starten, beginnen te lopen: ~*ing next month* vanaf volgende maand; ~ *out* vertrekken, *(fig)* zijn loopbaan beginnen; ~ *(all) over again* (helemaal) opnieuw beginnen; ~ *at* beginnen bij; ~ *from* beginnen bij, *(fig)* uitgaan van; *to* ~ *(off) with* om (mee) te beginnen, in het begin, in de eerste plaats; **2** vertrekken, opstijgen, afvaren: ~ *(out) for* op weg gaan naar; **3** (op)springen, (op)schrikken: ~ *back (from)* terugdeinzen (voor); ~ *at* (op)schrikken van; **4** (plotseling) bewegen, losspringen *(of wood)*, aanslaan *(of engine)*, te voorschijn springen: ~ *for the door* richting deur gaan; **5** startsein geven; **6** uitpuilen *(of eyes)*

²**start** [sta:t] *vb* **1** (doen) beginnen, aan de gang brengen, aanzetten, starten *(engine)*, aansteken *(fire)*, op touw zetten, opzetten *(business etc)*, naar voren brengen *(subject)*; **2** brengen tot, laten: *the dust* ~*ed me coughing* door het stof moest ik hoesten; **3** aannemen, laten beginnen

³**start** [sta:t] *n* **1** schok, ruk: *give s.o. a* ~ iem laten schrikken, iem doen opkijken; *wake up with a* ~ wakker schrikken; **2** start: *from* ~ *to finish* van begin tot eind; *false* ~ valse start *(also fig)*; *get off to a good* ~ goed beginnen, een goede start maken; *make a* ~ *on* beginnen met; *make a fresh (of: new)* ~ opnieuw beginnen; *for a* ~ om te beginnen; *from the (very)* ~ vanaf het (allereerste) begin; **3** startseinʰ; **4** voorsprong, voordeelʰ: *give s.o. a* ~ *(in life)* iem op gang helpen

starter [sta:tə] **1** beginner: *a slow* ~ iem die langzaam op gang komt; **2** startmotor; **3** voorafjeʰ, voorgerechtʰ: *for* ~*s* om te beginnen

starting block startblokʰ

starting point uitgangspuntʰ *(also fig)*

¹**startle** [sta:tl] *vb* **1** doen schrikken, opschrikken; **2** schokken

²**startle** [sta:tl] *vb* (op)schrikken

startling [sta:tling] verrassend

start off *vb* **1** beginnen: *he started off (by) saying that* hij begon met te zeggen dat; **2** vertrekken; **3** beginnen te zeggen

²**start off** *vb* (with *on*) aan de gang laten gaan (met), laten beginnen (met)

¹**start up** *vb* **1** opspringen; **2** een loopbaan beginnen: ~ *in business* in zaken gaan; **3** ontstaan, opkomen

²**start up** *vb* aan de gang brengen, opzetten *(business)*, starten *(engine)*

star turn hoofdnummerʰ

starvation [sta:veesjən] **1** hongerdood; **2** verhongering

¹**starve** [sta:v] *vb* **1** verhongeren: ~ *to death* verhongeren; **2** honger lijden; **3** sterven vd honger

²**starve** [sta:v] *vb* **1** uithongeren; **2** doen kwijnen, *(al-*

so fig) laten hunkeren, onthouden: *be ~d of* behoefte hebben aan; **3** door uithongering dwingen: *be ~d into surrender* door uithongering tot overgave gedwongen worden

stash [stæsj] *(also with away)* verbergen, opbergen

¹state [steet] *n* **1** toestand, staat: *~ of affairs* stand van zaken; *a poor ~ of health* een slechte gezondheidstoestand; **2** (gemoeds)toestand, stemming: *be in a ~* in alle staten zijn; **3** staat, natie, rijk^h; **4** staatsie, praal: *~ banquet* staatsiebanket; **5** *the States* Verenigde Staten: *lie in ~* opgebaard liggen

²state [steet] *vb* **1** (formeel) verklaren, uitdrukken; **2** aangeven, opgeven: *at ~d intervals* op gezette tijden, met regelmatige tussenpozen; **3** vaststellen, specificeren

stateless [steetləs] staatloos

stately [steetlie] **1** statig; **2** waardig; **3** formeel || *~ home* landhuis

statement [steetmənt] **1** verklaring; **2** (bank)afschrift^h

state-of-the-art hypermodern, uiterst geavanceerd

stateroom 1 staatsiezaal; **2** passagiershut; **3** (privé)coupé

statesman [steetsmən] staatsman

statewide over de gehele staat

static [stætik] **1** statisch, stabiel; **2** in rust; **3** atmosferisch

¹station [steesjən] *n* **1** station^h *(also of railway, radio, TV)*, goederenstation^h; **2** standplaats, plaats, post; **3** brandweerkazerne; **4** politiebureau^h; **5** *(mil)* basis, post; **6** positie, rang, status: *marry above one's ~* boven zijn stand trouwen

²station [steesjən] *vb* plaatsen, stationeren: *~ oneself* post vatten

stationary [steesjənərie] stationair, stilstaand, vast

stationer [steesjənə] handelaar in kantoorbenodigdheden, kantoorboekhandel

stationery [steesjənərie] **1** kantoorbenodigdheden; **2** kantoorboekhandel; **3** briefpapier^h en enveloppen: *printed ~* voorbedrukt briefpapier

stationmaster stationschef

statistical [stətistikl] statistisch

statistics [stətistiks] statistiek(en), cijfers, percentages

statue [stætsjoe:] (stand)beeld^h

statuesque [stætsjoe·esk] **1** als een standbeeld; **2** plastisch

statuette [stætsjoe·et] beeldje^h

stature [stætsjə] **1** gestalte, (lichaams)lengte; **2** *(fig)* formaat^h

status [steetəs] status

statute [stætjoe:t] statuut^h, wet

statutory [stætjoetərie] statutair, volgens de wet

¹staunch [sto:ntsj] *adj* **1** betrouwbaar, trouw; **2** solide

²staunch [sto:ntsj] *vb* **1** stelpen; **2** tot staan brengen; **3** waterdicht maken

stave [steev] **1** duig; **2** stok, knuppel; **3** stang, staaf;

4 sport *(of ladder, chair)*

stave in 1 in duigen slaan; **2** een gat slaan in, indrukken, kapotslaan

stave off 1 van zich afhouden, op een afstand houden; **2** voorkomen

¹stay [stee] *vb* **1** blijven, *(with for)* wachten op: *come to ~*, *be here to ~* blijven, *(fig)* zich een blijvende plaats verwerven; **2** verblijven, logeren: *~ the night* de nacht doorbrengen; **3** stilhouden, ophouden; **4** verblijven

²stay [stee] *vb* **1** *(also with up)* (onder)steunen; **2** (het) uithouden *(sport)*: *stay the course* tot het einde toe volhouden

³stay [stee] *vb* blijven: *~ seated* blijven zitten; *~ ahead of the others* de anderen voor blijven; *~ away* wegblijven; *~ behind* (achter)blijven; *~ in (after school)* nablijven; *~ indoors* binnen blijven; *~ on: a)* erop blijven; *b)* aanblijven *(of light etc); c)* (aan)blijven *(in office); ~ up late* laat opblijven

⁴stay [stee] *n* **1** verblijf^h, oponthoud^h; **2** steun *(also fig)*; **3** verbindingsstuk^h *(eg in aeroplane)*; **4** balein^h

stayer [steeə] **1** blijver; **2** volhouder, doorzetter, langeafstandsloper, langeafstandszwemmer

staying power uithoudingsvermogen^h

steadfast [stedfa:st] **1** vast, standvastig; **2** trouw

¹steady [steddie] *adj* **1** vast, vaststaand, stabiel: *(as) ~ as a rock* rotsvast; **2** gestaag, geregeld, vast *(of job, income etc)*, regelmatig *(of life)*, sterk *(of nerves)*; **3** kalm, evenwichtig: *~ on!* kalm aan!, langzaam!; **4** betrouwbaar, oppassend; **5** gematigd *(of climate)*, matig

²steady [steddie] *adv* vast, gestaag || *go ~* vaste verkering hebben

³steady [steddie] *interj* **1** kalm aan, rustig; **2** *(shipp)* recht zo

⁴steady [steddie] *n* vrijer, vaste vriend(in)

⁵steady [steddie] *vb* **1** vastheid geven, steunen: *~ oneself* zich staande houden; **2** bestendigen, stabiliseren

⁶steady [steddie] *vb* **1** vast, bestendig worden; **2** kalm worden

steak [steek] **1** (lapje) vlees^h, runderlapje^h; **2** (vis)moot; **3** visfilet

¹steal [stie:l] *vb* **1** stelen; **2** sluipen: *~ away* er heimelijk vandoor gaan; *~ up on s.o.* iem besluipen; *~ over s.o.* iem bekruipen *(of feeling, thought)*

²steal [stie:l] *vb* (ont)stelen, ontvreemden: *~ a ride* stiekem meerijden

stealth [stelθ] heimelijkheid, geheim^h: *by ~* stiekem, in het geniep

¹steam [stie:m] *n* stoom(kracht), wasem, condensatie, *(fig)* kracht(ige gevoelens), vaart: *blow (of: let, work) off ~* stoom afblazen, zijn agressie kwijtraken; *run out of ~* zijn energie verliezen, futloos worden

²steam [stie:m] *vb* **1** stomen, dampen: *~ing hot milk* gloeiend hete melk; **2** opstomen, *(fig)* energiek werken: *~ ahead (of: away)* doorstomen, er vaart achter zetten

³**steam** [stie:m] *vb* (gaar) stomen, klaarstomen: *~ed
fish* gestoomde vis

steamboat stoomboot

steamer [stie:mə] **1** stoompan, stoomketel; **2**
stoomschipʰ, stoomboot

¹**steamroller** *n* stoomwals *(also fig)*

²**steamroller** *vb* **1** met een stoomwals platwalsen; **2**
verpletteren, vernietigen: *~ all opposition* alle verzet de kop indrukken

¹**steam up** *vb* beslaan, met condensatie bedekt worden: *my glasses are steaming up* mijn bril beslaat

²**steam up** *vb* **1** doen beslaan, met condensatie bedekken; **2** opgewonden maken, opwinden, ergeren:
don't get steamed up about it maak je er niet druk
om

steamy [stie:mie] **1** mbt stoom, dampig; **2** heet, sensueel

steed [stie:d] (strijd)rosʰ, paardʰ

¹**steel** [stie:l] *n* **1** staalʰ *(also fig)*; **2** stukʰ staal: *a man
of ~* een man van staal, een sterke man

²**steel** [stie:l] *vb* stalen, pantseren *(also fig)*, harden,
sterken: *~ oneself to do sth.* zich dwingen iets te
doen

steelworks staalfabriek

steely [stie:lie] stalen, (als) van staal, *(fig)* onbuigzaam: *~ composure* ijzige kalmte

¹**steep** [stie:p] *adj* **1** steil, sterk hellend: *a ~ slope* een
steile helling; **2** scherp (oplopend), snel (stijgend):
a ~ rise in prices scherpe prijsstijgingen; **3** onredelijk *(eg of claim)*, sterk *(story)*

²**steep** [stie:p] *vb* (in)trekken, weken

³**steep** [stie:p] *vb* onderdompelen *(also fig)*

steeple [stie:pl] (toren)spits, bovenste deelʰ ve toren

steeplechase *(equestrian sport, athletics)* steeplechase, hindernisren, hindernisloop

¹**steer** [stiə] *vb* sturen, koers (doen) zetten: *he ~ed
for home* hij ging op huis aan; *~ clear of sth.* uit de
buurt blijven van iets

²**steer** [stiə] *n* **1** jonge os; **2** stierkalfʰ

steersman [stiəzmən] stuurman, roerganger

¹**stem** [stem] *n* **1** stam *(of tree, word)*, basisvorm; **2**
(hoofd)stengel *(of flower)*, steel(tjeʰ); **3** stamvor-
mig deelʰ, steel *(of glass, pipe)*; **4** voorsteven, boeg:
from ~ to stern van de voor- tot de achtersteven,
(fig) van top tot teen

²**stem** [stem] *vb* **1** doen stoppen, stelpen; **2** het hoofd
bieden aan, weerstand bieden aan: *~ the tide (of
public opinion)* tegen het getijde (van de publieke
opinie) ingaan

stem from stammen uit, voortkomen uit: *his bitterness stems from all his disappointments* zijn verbittering komt door al zijn teleurstellingen

stench [stentsj] stank

stencil [stensil] **1** stencilʰ, stencilafdruk; **2** model-
vorm, sjabloon

¹**step** [step] *vb* stappen, gaan: *~ forward* naar voren
komen, zich aanbieden als vrijwilliger; *~ inside*
komt u binnen; *~ on the gas* (of: *it)* flink gas geven,

(fig) opschieten; *~ out of line* uit het gareel raken

²**step** [step] *n* **1** stap, voetstap, (dans)pas: *break ~* uit
de pas gaan; *fall into ~ with* zich aansluiten bij, in
de pas lopen met; *~ by ~* stapje voor stapje, geleidelijk; *out of ~: a)* uit de pas; *b) (also fig)* niet ermee
eens; *c)* uit de toon; **2** stap, daad: *watch* (of: *mind)
your ~* wees voorzichtig, pas op; **3** (trap)trede,
stoepjeʰ; **4** *~s* (stenen) trap, stoep(jeʰ); **5** *~s*
trap(ladder)

step aside 1 opzij stappen, uit de weg gaan; **2** zijn
plaats afstaan

stepbrother stiefbroer, halfbroer

stepdaughter stiefdochter

step down 1 aftreden; **2** zijn plaats afstaan

stepfather stiefvader

step in 1 binnenkomen; **2** tussenbeide komen, inspringen

stepmother stiefmoeder

step off beginnen, starten: *~ on the wrong foot* op
de verkeerde manier beginnen

step out 1 snel(ler) gaan lopen, flink doorstappen;
2 (even) naar buiten gaan

stepping stone [steppingstoon] **1** stapsteen *(eg to
wade through river)*; **2** springplank, hulp: *a ~ to
success* een springplank naar het succes

stepsister stiefzuster

stepson stiefzoon

¹**step up** *vb* doen toenemen, opvoeren: *~ production*
de productie opvoeren

²**step up** *vb* naar voren komen, opstaan

stereotype [sterriətajp] stereotype, stereotiep
beeldʰ

sterile [sterrajl] **1** steriel, onvruchtbaar, *(fig)* weinig
creatief: *a ~ discussion* een zinloze discussie; **2** steriel, kiemvrij

sterility [sterillittie] onvruchtbaarheid, steriliteit

sterilize [sterrillajz] steriliseren; onvruchtbaar maken, kiemvrij maken

¹**sterling** [stə:ling] *n* pondʰ sterling

²**sterling** [stə:ling] *adj* echt, zuiver, onvervalst, *(fig)*
degelijk, betrouwbaar: *a ~ friend* een echte vriend;
~ silver 92,5% zuiver zilver

¹**stern** [stə:n] *adj* streng, hard, onbuigzaam, strikt

²**stern** [stə:n] *n* achterschipʰ, achtersteven

steroid [stiərojd] steroïdeʰ: *anabolic ~s* anabole
steroïden

stethoscope [steθəskoop] stethoscoop

stetson [stetsn] (breedgerande) cowboyhoed

¹**stew** [stjoe:] *n* stoofpot, stoofschotel ‖ *be in a ~* opgewonden zijn

²**stew** [stjoe:] *vb* stoven, smoren ‖ *let s.o. ~ (in one's
own juice)* iem in zijn eigen vet gaar laten koken

steward [stjoe:əd] **1** rentmeester, beheerder; **2** steward, hofmeester; **3** ceremoniemeester, zaalwachter; **4** wedstrijdcommissaris, official

¹**stick** [stik] *vb* **1** klem zitten, vastzitten; **2** blijven steken, (blijven) vastzitten; **3** plakken *(also fig)*,
(vast)kleven, *(inf)* blijven: *it will always ~ in my
mind* dat zal me altijd bijblijven; *~ together* bij el-

kaar blijven; ~ around rondhangen, in de buurt blijven; ~ to the point bij het onderwerp blijven; ~ to one's principles trouw blijven aan zijn principes

²**stick** [stik] vb 1 (vast)steken, (vast)prikken, bevestigen, opprikken; 2 doodsteken, neersteken; 3 steken, zetten, leggen: ~ it in your pocket stop het in je zak; 4 (vast)kleven, vastlijmen, vastplakken; 5 (only negative) pruimen, uitstaan, verdragen: I can't ~ such people ik heb de pest aan zulke mensen

³**stick** [stik] n 1 stok, tak, stukʰ hout; 2 staf, stok(jeʰ); 3 staaf(jeʰ), reep(jeʰ), stukʰ: a ~ of chalk een krijtje; 4 stok, knuppel; 5 stick, hockeystick, (polo)hamer: (fig) wield the big ~ dreigen; 6 stengel, steel (celeriac); 7 figuur⁺ʰ, snuiter, droogstoppel; 8 afranseling (also fig): give s.o. some ~ iem een pak slaag geven

stick at 1 opzien tegen, terugdeinzen voor: ~ nothing nergens voor terugdeinzen; 2 doorgaan (met), volhouden

sticker [stikkə] 1 plakkertjeʰ, zelfklevend etiketʰ, sticker; 2 doorzetter, volhouder

stick-in-the-mud conservatieveling, vastgeroest iemand

stickleback stekelbaars

stickler [stiklə] (with for) (hardnekkig) voorstander (van), ijveraar: ~ for accuracy Pietje Precies

stick out 1 overduidelijk zijn; 2 volhouden, doorbijten: ~ for sth. zich blijven inzetten voor iets; 3 uitsteken, vooruit steken

¹**stick up** vb 1 omhoogstaan, uitsteken; 2 opkomen: ~ for s.o. het voor iem opnemen

²**stick up** vb omhoogsteken, uitsteken: stick 'em up, stick your hands up handen omhoog

stick-up overval

sticky [stikkie] 1 kleverig, plakkerig; 2 pijnlijk, lastig: he will come to (of: meet) a ~ end het zal nog slecht met hem aflopen; 3 zwoel, broeierig, drukkend: she has got ~ fingers ze heeft lange vingers, zij jat

¹**stiff** [stif] adj 1 stijf, stug, gereserveerd; 2 vastberaden, koppig: put up (a) ~ resistance hardnekkig weerstand bieden; 3 stram, stroef: a ~ neck een stijve nek; 4 zwaar, moeilijk, lastig: a ~ climb een flinke klim(partij); 5 sterk, stevig, krachtig: a ~ breeze een stevige bries; 6 (te) groot, overdreven, onredelijk: ~ demands pittige eisen; 7 sterk (alcoholic drink): a ~ drink een stevige borrel; keep a ~ upper lip zich flink houden, geen emoties tonen

²**stiff** [stif] adv door en door, intens: bore s.o. ~ iem gruwelijk vervelen; scare s.o. ~ iem de stuipen op het lijf jagen

³**stiff** [stif] n (inf) lijkʰ, dooie

¹**stiffen** [stiffən] vb 1 verstijven; 2 verstevigen, in kracht toenemen

²**stiffen** [stiffən] vb 1 dikker maken, doen verdikken; 2 verstevigen, krachtiger maken, (also fig) versterken, vastberadener maken

stiff-necked 1 koppig, eigenzinnig; 2 verwaand

¹**stifle** [stajfl] vb 1 verstikken, doen stikken, smoren, (fig also) in de doofpot stoppen: a stifling heat een

verstikkende hitte; 2 onderdrukken: ~ one's laughter zijn lach inhouden

²**stifle** [stajfl] vb stikken, smoren (also fig)

stigma [stigmə] brandmerkʰ, (schand)vlek, stigmaʰ

stigmatize [stigmətajz] stigmatiseren, brandmerken

stile [stajl] 1 overstap; 2 draaihekjeʰ

stiletto heel naaldhak

¹**still** [stil] adv 1 stil: keep ~ (zich) stilhouden; my heart stood ~ mijn hart stond stil (with fright); 2 nog (altijd): is he ~ here? is hij hier nog?; 3 nog (meer): he is ~ taller, he is taller ~ hij is nog groter; 4 toch, niettemin: … but he ~ agreed … maar hij stemde er toch mee in

²**still** [stil] adj 1 stil, onbeweeglijk, rustig, kalm; 2 stil, geluidloos, gedempt; 3 niet mousserend: ~ wine niet-mousserende wijn; ~ picture filmfoto, stilstaand (film)beeld

³**still** [stil] n 1 filmfoto, stilstaand (film)beeldʰ; 2 distilleertoestelʰ

stillborn doodgeboren

still life stillevenʰ

stilt [stilt] 1 stelt; 2 paal, pijler

stilted [stiltid] 1 (als) op stelten; 2 stijf, gekunsteld

stimulant [stimjoelənt] stimulans, opwekkend middelʰ, (fig) prikkel

stimulate [stimjoeleet] stimuleren, opwekken: ~ s.o. (in)to more efforts iem tot meer inspanningen aanmoedigen

¹**sting** [sting] vb 1 steken, bijten, (fig) grieven: a bee ~s een bij steekt; his conscience stung him zijn geweten knaagde; 2 prikkelen, branden, (fig) aansporen: that stung him (in)to action dat zette hem tot actie aan; 3 afzetten, oplichten: ~ s.o. for a few dollars iem een paar dollar lichter maken

²**sting** [sting] n 1 angel; 2 giftand; 3 brandhaar⁺ʰ; 4 steek, beet, prikkel(ing)

stinging [stinging] 1 stekend, bijtend: a ~ reproach een scherp verwijt; 2 prikkelend

stingy [stindzjie] vrekkig, gierig

¹**stink** [stingk] vb 1 stinken: it ~s to high heaven het stinkt uren in de wind; 2 oerslecht zijn, niet deugen: this plan ~s dit plan deugt van geen kanten

²**stink** [stingk] n 1 stank; 2 herrie: create (of: kick up, make, raise) a ~ about sth. herrie schoppen over iets

stinker [stingkə] 1 stinker(d); 2 iets beledigends, iets slechts, moeilijke opdracht, lastig examenʰ

stinking [stingking] 1 stinkend (also fig): ~ rich stinkend rijk; 2 oerslecht, gemeen

¹**stint** [stint] vb zich bekrimpen, zich beperken

²**stint** [stint] vb 1 beperken, inperken; 2 zuinig toebedelen, krap houden: ~ oneself of food zichzelf karig voedsel toebedelen

³**stint** [stint] n portie, karwei(tje)ʰ, taak: do one's daily ~ zijn dagtaak volbrengen; without ~ onbeperkt

stipulate [stipjoeleet] bedingen, bepalen, als voorwaarde stellen: ~ for the best conditions de beste voorwaarden bedingen

¹stir [stə:] *vb* **1** *(with up)* (op)poken, opporren, *(fig)* aanwakkeren, *(fig)* aanstoken, opstoken: ~ *one's curiosity* iemands nieuwsgierigheid prikkelen; **2** *(also with up)* (om)roeren

²stir [stə:] *vb* **1** (zich) (ver)roeren, (zich) bewegen; **2** opstaan, op zijn

³stir [stə:] *n* **1** het roeren, het poken: *give the fire a ~* pook het vuur even op; **2** beroering, opwinding, sensatie: *cause* (of: *make) quite a ~* (veel) opzien baren, (veel) ophef veroorzaken

stirring [stə:ring] opwekkend, stimulerend, bezielend

stirrup [stirrəp] (stijg)beugel

¹stitch [stitsj] *n* **1** steek in de zij; **2** steek: *drop a ~* een steek laten vallen; **3** lapje^h, stukje^h (stof), *(fig)* beetje^h: *not do a ~ of work* geen lor uitvoeren; *not have a ~ on* spiernaakt zijn; **4** *(med)* hechting: *in ~es* slap van het lachen, in een deuk (van het lachen)

²stitch [stitsj] *vb* **1** stikken, (vast)naaien, dichtnaaien: ~ *up a wound* een wond hechten; **2** borduren

stoat [stoot] **1** hermelijn; **2** wezel

¹stock [stok] *n* **1** moederstam *(from which grafts are taken)*; **2** steel; **3** familie, ras^h, geslacht^h, afkomst: *be* (of: *come) of good ~* van goede komaf zijn; **4** aandeel^h, effect^h; **5** voorraad: ~ *in trade: a)* voorhanden voorraad; *b)* kneep (van het vak), truc; *while ~s last* zolang de voorraad strekt; *take ~* de inventaris opmaken; *(fig) take ~ (of the situation)* de toestand bekijken; *out of ~* niet in voorraad; **6** bouillon; **7** aandelen(bezit^h), effecten, fonds^h: *his ~ is falling* zijn ster verbleekt; **8** materiaal^h, materieel^h, grondstof: *rolling ~* rollend materieel *(of railways)*; **9** vee(stapel)^h; **10** ~*s (shipp)* stapel(blokken), helling: *on the ~s* op stapel, *(fig)* in voorbereiding

²stock [stok] *adj* **1** gangbaar: ~ *sizes* gangbare maten; **2** stereotiep, vast: *a ~ remark* een stereotiepe opmerking

³stock [stok] *vb* voorraad inslaan, zich bevoorraden, hamsteren: ~ *up on sugar* suiker inslaan

⁴stock [stok] *vb* van het nodige voorzien: *a well-~ed department store* een goed voorzien warenhuis; **2** in voorraad hebben

stockade [stokkeed] **1** houten omheining; **2** met houten afzetting omheind terrein^h

stock exchange effectenbeurs, beurs(gebouw^h): *the Stock Exchange* de (Londense) Beurs

stockholder aandeelhouder

stocking [stokking] kous

stock-in-trade **1** (goederen)voorraad; **2** gereedschap^h ‖ *that joke is part of his ~* dat is één van zijn standaardgrappen

stockist [stokkist] leverancier (uit voorraad)

stock market (effecten)beurs

¹stockpile *n* voorraad, reserve

²stockpile *vb* voorraden aanleggen (van)

stock size vaste maat, confectiemaat

stock-still doodstil

stocky [stokkie] gedrongen, kort en dik, stevig

stodge [stodzj] zware kost, onverteerbaar eten^h, *(fig)* moeilijke stof

stodgy [stodzjie] **1** zwaar, onverteerbaar *(food); (fig)* moeilijk, droog; **2** saai, vervelend

stoic(al) [stooik(l)] stoïcijns, onaangedaan

¹stoke [stook] *vb* **1** *(also with up)* het vuur opstoken; **2** *(with up)* zich met eten volproppen

²stoke [stook] *vb (also with up)* aanstoken, opstoken *(fire)*, opvullen *(stove)*

stolid [stollid] onverstoorbaar, standvastig

¹stomach [stummək] *n* **1** maag: *on an empty ~* op een nuchtere maag; **2** buik: *lie on one's ~* op zijn buik liggen; **3** eetlust, trek; **4** zin: *I have no ~ for a fight* ik heb geen zin om ruzie te maken

²stomach [stummək] *vb* slikken, pikken, aanvaarden: *you needn't ~ such a remark* zo'n opmerking hoef je niet zomaar te slikken

stomach-ache **1** maagpijn; **2** buikpijn

¹stomp [stomp] *vb* stampen

²stomp [stomp] *n* stomp *(jazz dance, jazz music)*

stone [stoon] **1** steen *(also as hard mineral)*, pit *(of fruit); (semi-)precious ~* (half)edelsteen; **2** stone, 14 Engelse pond^h: *he weighs 14 ~(s)* hij weegt 90 kilo; *leave no ~ unturned* geen middel onbeproefd laten, alles proberen; *rolling ~* zwerver

Stone Age stenen tijdperk^h

stone-cold steenkoud ‖ ~ *sober* broodnuchter; ~ *dead* morsdood

stoned [stoond] **1** stomdronken; **2** stoned, high

stonemason steenhouwer

stone's throw steenworp: *within a ~* op een steenworp afstand

stony [stoonie] **1** steenachtig, vol stenen; **2** keihard, steenhard, *(fig)* gevoelloos

stony-broke platzak, blut

stooge [stoe:dzj] **1** *(theatre)* mikpunt^h, aangever; **2** knechtje^h, slaafje^h; **3** stroman

stool [stoe:l] **1** kruk, bankje^h; **2** voetenbank(je^h); **3** ontlasting

¹stoop [stoe:p] *vb* **1** (zich) bukken, voorover buigen; **2** zich verwaardigen; **3** zich vernederen, zich verlagen: *he wouldn't stoop to lying about his past* hij vond het beneden zijn waardigheid om over zijn verleden te liegen; **4** gebogen lopen, met ronde rug lopen

²stoop [stoe:p] *vb* buigen: ~ *one's head* het hoofd buigen

³stoop [stoe:p] *n* **1** gebukte houding; **2** ronde rug, kromme rug

¹stop [stop] *vb* **1** ophouden, tot een eind komen, stoppen; **2** stilhouden, tot stilstand komen: ~ *short* plotseling halt houden; *they ~ped short of actually smashing the windows* ze gingen niet zover, dat ze de ramen daadwerkelijk ingooiden; ~ *at nothing* tot alles in staat zijn, nergens voor terugschrikken; **3** blijven, verblijven, overblijven: ~ *by* (even) langskomen; ~ *in* binnenblijven; ~ *off* zijn reis onderbreken; ~ *over* de (vlieg)reis onderbreken

²stop [stop] *vb* **1** (af)sluiten, dichten, dichtstoppen:

~ *up a leak* een lek dichten; **2** verhinderen, afhouden, tegenhouden: ~ *thief!* houd de dief!; **3** blokkeren, tegenhouden: ~ *a cheque* een cheque blokkeren; **4** een eind maken aan, stopzetten, beëindigen, ophouden met, staken: ~ *work* het werk neerleggen; ~ *it!* hou op!

³**stop** [stop] *n* **1** einde^h, beëindiging, pauze, onderbreking: *bring to a* ~ stopzetten, een halt toeroepen; *put a* ~ *to* een eind maken aan; **2** halte, stopplaats; **3** afsluiting, blokkade, belemmering; **4** punt^h; **5** diafragma^h, lensopening; **6** pal, plug, begrenzer: *pull out all the* ~*s* alle registers opentrekken, alles uit de kast halen

stopgap 1 noodoplossing; **2** invaller; **3** stoplap
stopover reisonderbreking, kort verblijf^h
stoppage [stoppidzj] **1** verstopping, stremming; **2** inhouding: ~ *of pay* inhouden van loon; **3** staking, (werk)onderbreking, prikactie
stoppage time (extra) bijgetelde tijd *(to make up for interruptions of play)*
stopper [stoppə] stop, plug, kurk: *put the* ~*(s) on sth.* ergens een eind aan maken
storage [sto:ridzj] opslag, bewaring
¹**store** [sto:] *n* **1** voorraad: *in* ~ in voorraad; *there's a surprise in* ~ *for you* je zult voor een verrassing komen te staan; **2** opslagplaats, magazijn^h, pakhuis^h; **3** ~*s (mil)* provisie, goederen, proviand^h; **4** *(Am)* winkel, zaak; **5** warenhuis^h: *set (great)* ~ *by* veel waarde hechten aan
²**store** [sto:] *vb* bevoorraden, inslaan
storehouse pakhuis^h, opslagplaats: *Steve is a* ~ *of information* Steve is een grote bron van informatie
storekeeper 1 *(Am)* winkelier; **2** hoofd vh magazijn
storeroom opslagkamer, voorraadkamer
storey [sto:rie] verdieping, woonlaag: *the second* ~ de eerste verdieping
stork [sto:k] ooievaar
¹**storm** [sto:m] *n* **1** (hevige) bui, noodweer^h; **2** storm(wind), orkaan: ~ *in a teacup* storm in een glas water, veel drukte om niks; **3** uitbarsting, vlaag: ~ *of protests* regen van protesten
²**storm** [sto:m] *vb* **1** stormen, waaien, onweren; **2** *(with at)* tekeergaan (tegen), uitvallen, razen; **3** rennen, denderen: ~ *in* binnen komen stormen
³**storm** [sto:m] *vb (mil)* bestormen, stormlopen op
storm cloud regenwolk, onweerswolk, *(fig)* donkere wolk, teken^h van onheil
stormy [sto:mie] **1** stormachtig, winderig; **2** heftig, ruw: *a* ~ *meeting* een veelbewogen bijeenkomst
story [sto:rie] **1** verhaal^h, relaas^h: *cut a long* ~ *short* om kort te gaan; *the (same) old* ~ het oude liedje; **2** (levens)geschiedenis, historie; **3** vertelling, novelle, verhaal^h; **4** *(journalism)* (materiaal voor) artikel^h, verhaal^h; **5** smoesje^h, praatje^h: *tell stories* jokken; **6** verdieping
¹**storybook** *n* verhalenboek^h
²**storybook** *adv* als in een sprookje, sprookjesachtig: *a* ~ *ending* een gelukkige afloop, een happy end
¹**stout** [staut] *adj* **1** moedig, vastberaden: ~ *resist-*

ance krachtig verzet; **2** solide, stevig; **3** gezet, dik
²**stout** [staut] *n* stout, donker bier^h
stout-hearted dapper, moedig, kloek
stove **1** (elektrische) kachel, gaskachel, kolenkachel; **2** (elektrisch) fornuis^h, gasoven, gasfornuis^h
stow [stoo] opbergen, inpakken || ~ *it!* kap ermee!, hou op!
stowaway [stooəwee] verstekeling
¹**stow away** *vb* zich verbergen *(on ship, aeroplane)*
²**stow away** *vb* opbergen, wegbergen
straddle [strædl] schrijlings zitten (op), met gespreide benen zitten (op), wijdbeens staan (boven)
straggle [strægl] **1** (af)dwalen, achterblijven, van de groep af raken; **2** (wild) uitgroeien, verspreid groeien: *straggling houses* verspreid liggende huizen
straggly [stræglie] **1** (onregelmatig) verspreid, verstrooid, schots en scheef; **2** verwilderd, verward *(hair, beard)*
¹**straight** [street] *adj* **1** recht, steil, sluik *(hair)*, rechtop: *(as)* ~ *as a die* kaarsrecht, *(fig)* goudeerlijk; **2** puur, onverdund, *(fig)* zonder franje, serieus: *a* ~ *rendering of the facts* een letterlijke weergave van de feiten; ~ *whisky* whisky puur; **3** open(hartig), eerlijk, rechtdoorzee: ~ *answer* eerlijk antwoord; **4** strak, in de plooi, correct: *keep a* ~ *face* zijn gezicht in de plooi houden; *keep (s.o.) to the* ~ *and narrow path* (iem) op het rechte pad houden; **5** ordelijk, geordend, netjes: *put (of: set) the record* ~ een fout herstellen; **6** direct, rechtstreeks; **7** hetero(seksueel)
²**straight** [street] *adv* **1** rechtstreeks, meteen, zonder omwegen: *come* ~ *to the point* meteen ter zake raken; **2** recht, rechtop: ~ *on* rechtdoor; *think* ~ helder denken; *tell s.o.* ~ iem eerlijk de waarheid zeggen
³**straight** [street] *n* recht stuk^h *(of racecourse)*
straightaway onmiddellijk
¹**straighten** [streetn] *vb* rechtzetten, rechttrekken *(also fig)*: ~ *one's legs* de benen strekken; ~ *the room* de kamer aan kant brengen; ~ *oneself up* zich oprichten
²**straighten** [streetn] *vb* recht worden, rechttrekken, bijtrekken *(also fig)*: ~ *up* overeind gaan staan
straighten out 1 recht leggen, rechtmaken; **2** op orde brengen: *things will soon straighten themselves out* alles zal gauw op zijn pootjes terechtkomen
straightforward 1 oprecht, open, eerlijk; **2** duidelijk
straight-up eerlijk (waar), serieus
¹**strain** [streen] *vb* **1** zich inspannen, moeite doen, zwoegen; **2** *(with at)* rukken (aan), trekken: ~ *at the leash* aan de teugels trekken, zich los willen rukken *(fig)*
²**strain** [streen] *vb* **1** spannen, (uit)rekken; **2** inspannen, maximaal belasten: ~ *one's eyes* turen, ingespannen kijken; **3** overbelasten; **4** verrekken *(muscles)*, verdraaien; **5** vastklemmen; **6** zeven, la-

ten doorsijpelen; **7** afgieten

³strain [streen] *n* **1** spanning, druk, trek, *(fig)* belasting, inspanning; **2** overbelasting, uitputting; **3** verrekking *(of muscles)*, verstuiking; **4** ~s flard *(of music, poem)*, melodie; **5** stijl, toon *(of expression)*; **6** (karakter)trek, element^h; **7** stam, ras^h, soort

strained [streend] gedwongen, geforceerd, onnatuurlijk

strainer [streenə] **1** zeef; **2** vergiet^h; **3** filter(doek)^h

strait [street] **1** zee-engte, (zee)straat: *the Straits of Dover* het Nauw van Calais; **2** lastige omstandigheden, moeilijkheden: *be in dire ~s* ernstig in het nauw zitten

straitened [streetnd] behoeftig

straitjacket dwangbuis, keurslijf^h *(also fig)*

strait-laced puriteins, bekrompen, preuts

strand [strænd] streng, snoer^h, draad: *a ~ of pearls* een parelsnoer

stranded [strændid] gestrand, aan de grond, vast(gelopen) *(also fig)*

strange [streendzj] **1** vreemd, onbekend, nieuw: *he is ~ to the business* hij heeft nog geen ervaring in deze branch; **2** eigenaardig, onverklaarbaar: *~ to say* vreemd genoeg

stranger [streendzjə] vreemde(ling), onbekende, buitenlander: *be a ~ to* ergens part noch deel aan hebben

strangle [stræŋgl] **1** wurgen; **2** onderdrukken, smoren *(tendency, cry)*

stranglehold wurggreep, verstikkende greep *(also fig)*: *have a ~ on* in zijn greep hebben

¹strap [stræp] *n* **1** riem, band(je^h); **2** strop, band, reep *(also of metal)*

²strap [stræp] *vb* **1** vastbinden, vastgespen; **2** *(also with up)* verbinden, met pleisters afdekken

strapping [stræping] flink, potig, stoer

strategic [strətie:dzjik] strategisch

strategist [strætədzjist] strateeg

strategy [strætədzjie] strategie, plan^h, methode, beleid^h

stratification [strætiffikkeesjən] **1** laagvorming; **2** gelaagdheid, verdeling in lagen

straw [stro:] **1** stro^h; **2** strohalm, strootje^h: *a ~ in the wind* een voorteken, een teken aan de wand; *the last ~, the ~ that broke the camel's back* de druppel die de emmer deed overlopen; *clutch at ~s* zich aan iedere strohalm vastklampen; **3** rietje^h *(for drinking)*

strawberry [stro:bərie] **1** aardbei(plant); **2** donkerroze^h

¹stray [stree] *vb* dwalen, rondzwerven *(also fig)*: *~ from the subject* van het onderwerp afdwalen

²stray [stree] *n* **1** zwerver, verdwaalde *(also fig)*, zwerfdier^h; **2** dakloos kind^h

³stray [stree] *adj* verdwaald, zwervend: *~ bullet* verdwaalde kogel; *~ cats* zwerfkatten

¹streak [strie:k] *n* **1** streep, lijn, strook: *a ~ of light* een streepje licht; **2** (karakter)trek, tikje^h: *there's a ~ of madness in Mel* er zit (ergens) een draadje los

bij Mel; *like a ~ of lightning* bliksemsnel

²streak [strie:k] *vb* **1** (weg)schieten, flitsen, snellen; **2** streaken, naakt rondrennen

³streak [strie:k] *vb* strepen zetten op, strepen maken in: *~ed with grey* met grijze strepen

streaky [strie:kie] gestreept, met strepen, doorregen *(of bacon)*

¹stream [strie:m] *n* **1** stroom, water^h, beek, stroomrichting; **2** (stort)vloed, stroom

²stream [strie:m] *vb* **1** stromen *(also fig)*, vloeien, druipen: *his face was ~ing with sweat* het zweet liep hem langs het gezicht; **2** wapperen, waaien, fladderen

³stream [strie:m] *vb* doen stromen, druipen van: *the wound was ~ing blood* het bloed gutste uit de wond

streamer [strie:mə] wimpel, lint^h, serpentine

streamline stroomlijnen, *(fig)* lijn brengen in, vereenvoudigen: *~ an organization* een organisatie efficiënter maken

street [strie:t] straat, weg, straatweg: *dead-end street* doodlopende straat; *be ~s ahead (of)* ver voorliggen op; *in* (Am: *on*) *the ~* op straat; *that's (right) up my ~* dat is precies in mijn straatje, dat is net iets voor mij

streetcar *(Am)* tram

street level gelijkvloers^h

streetwalker tippelaarster

streetwise door het (straat)leven gehard, door de wol geverfd, slim

strength [strengθ] **1** sterkte *(also fig)*, kracht(en), vermogen^h: *on the ~ of* op grond van, uitgaand van; **2** (getal)sterkte, macht, bezetting: *(bring) up to (full) ~* op (volle) sterkte (brengen); **3** gehalte^h, concentratie, zwaarte *(of tobacco)*, sterkte: *go from ~ to ~* het ene succes na het andere behalen

¹strengthen [strengθən] *vb* sterk(er) maken, versterken, verstevigen

²strengthen [strengθən] *vb* sterk(er) worden, in kracht toenemen

strenuous [strenjoeəs] **1** zwaar, inspannend, vermoeiend; **2** vol energie, onvermoeibaar, ijverig

¹stress [stres] *n* **1** spanning, druk, stress, belasting: *(be) under great ~* onder (grote) druk staan, zwaar belast worden; **2** klem(toon), nadruk, accent^h, *(fig)* gewicht^h, belang^h: *lay ~ on* benadrukken; **3** *(techn)* spanning, druk, (be)last(ing)

²stress [stres] *vb* **1** benadrukken, de nadruk leggen op: *we can't ~ enough that* we kunnen er niet voldoende de nadruk op leggen dat; **2** belasten, onder druk zetten

stress mark klemtoonteken^h, accent^h

¹stretch [stretsj] *vb* **1** *(with out)* zich uitstrekken, (languit) gaan liggen; **2** zich uitstrekken (tot), reiken (tot); zich uitrekken; **3** rekbaar zijn, elastisch zijn; **4** *(with over)* duren, zich uitspreiden (over); **5** (uit)rekken *(also fig)*: *~ s.o.'s patience* iemands geduld op de proef stellen; **6** (aan)spannen, opspannen, strak trekken: *~ a rope* een touw spannen; **7** (uit)strekken, reiken: *~ oneself* zich uitrekken; **8** tot het uiterste inspannen, forceren: *be fully ~ed* zich helemaal geven; **9** ruim interpreteren, het niet zo nauw nemen (met) *(rules)*, geweld aandoen, overdrijven: *~ the rules* de regels vrij interpreteren; **10** verrekken *(muscles)*

²**stretch** [stretsj] *n* **1** (groot) stuk^h *(land, road, sea etc)*, uitgestrektheid, vlakte, eind(je)^h, stuk^h: *~ of road* stuk weg; **2** tijd, periode, *(inf)* straftijd: *ten hours at a ~* tien uur aan een stuk; **3** rek(baarheid), elasticiteit: *not by any ~ of the imagination* met de beste wil van de wereld niet; *at full ~* met inspanning van al zijn krachten; *at a ~* desnoods, als het moet

stretcher [stretsjə] brancard, draagbaar

strew [stroe:] **1** *(with on, over)* uitstrooien (over), *(with with)* bestrooien (met): *books were strewn all over his desk* zijn bureau was bezaaid met boeken; **2** verspreid liggen op

stricken [strikkən] getroffen, geslagen, bedroefd: *~ look* verslagen blik

strict [strikt] strikt, nauwkeurig: *~ parents* strenge ouders; *~ly speaking* strikt genomen

stricture [striktsjə] aanmerking, afkeuring: *pass ~s (up)on* kritiek uitoefenen op

¹**stride** [strajd] *vb* (voort)stappen, grote passen nemen

²**stride** [strajd] *n* **1** pas, stap, schrede: *get into one's ~* op dreef komen; *take sth. in (one's) ~: a)* ergens makkelijk overheen stappen; *b)* iets spelenderwijs doen *(of:* klaren); **2** gang: *make great ~s* grote vooruitgang boeken

strident [strajdənt] schel, schril, scherp

strife [strajf] ruzie, conflict^h: *industrial ~* industriële onrust

¹**strike** [strajk] *vb* **1** slaan, uithalen, treffen, raken, botsen (met, op), stoten (op, tegen), aanvallen, toeslaan, aanslaan *(string, note)*, aansteken *(match)*: *~ a blow* een klap uitdelen; *the clock ~s* de klok slaat; *struck dumb* met stomheid geslagen; *~ down: a)* neerslaan; *b) (also fig)* vellen; *c)* branden *(of sun)*; *~ (up)on: a)* treffen, slaan op; *b)* stoten op, ontdekken; *c)* krijgen, komen op *(idea)*; *struck by lightning* door de bliksem getroffen; **2** staken, in staking gaan; **3** (op pad, weg) gaan, beginnen (met): *~ for home* de weg naar huis inslaan; *~ home to s.o.* grote indruk maken op iem, geheel doordringen tot iem *(of remark)*; *struck on* smoor(verliefd) op; **4** ontdekken, vinden, stoten op: *~ oil* olie aanboren, *(fig)* fortuin maken; **5** een indruk maken op, opvallen, lijken: *did it ever ~ you that* heb je er wel eens aan gedacht dat, is het jou wel eens opgevallen dat; **6** opkomen bij, invallen *(idea)*: *~ terror into s.o.'s heart* iem de schrik op het lijf jagen

³**strike** [strajk] *n* **1** slag, klap; **2** (lucht)aanval; **3** staking: *(out) on ~* in staking; **4** vondst *(of oil etc)*, ont-

dekking, *(fig)* succes^h, vangst

strike off 1 schrappen, royeren; **2** afdraaien, drukken

¹**strike out** *vb* schrappen, doorhalen

²**strike out** *vb* **1** (fel) uithalen *(also fig)*, (fel) tekeergaan; **2** nieuwe wegen inslaan: *~ on one's own* zijn eigen weg inslaan

strike pay stakingsuitkering

striker [strajkə] **1** staker; **2** slagman; **3** *(socc)* spits

strike up 1 gaan spelen (zingen), inzetten, aanheffen; **2** beginnen: *~ a conversation (with)* een gesprek aanknopen (met)

striking [strajking] opvallend, treffend, aantrekkelijk

striking distance bereik^h: *within ~* binnen het bereik, binnen loopafstand

¹**string** [string] *n* **1** koord^h, touw(tje)^h, garen^h: *pull ~s* invloed uitoefenen; **2** draad, band; **3** snaar; **4** *~s* strijkinstrumenten, strijkers; **5** aaneenschakeling, reeks, sliert, streng: *~ of cars* rij auto's; *have two ~s (of: a second ~) to one's bow* twee paarden wedden, meer pijlen op zijn boog hebben; *with no ~s attached: a)* zonder kleine lettertjes; *b)* zonder verplichtingen (achteraf)

²**string** [string] *vb* **1** (vast)binden; **2** (aan elkaar) rijgen, ritsen, aaneenschakelen: *~ words together* woorden aan elkaar rijgen; **3** *(with up)* opknopen, ophangen; **4** bespannen, besnaren: *highly strung* fijnbesnaard, overgevoelig; *strung up* zenuwachtig, gespannen, opgewonden

¹**string along** *vb (with with)* zich aansluiten (bij)

²**string along** *vb* belazeren, misleiden, aan het lijntje houden

stringency [strindzjənsie] strengheid, striktheid: *the ~ of the law* de bindende kracht van de wet

stringent [strindzjənt] stringent, streng, dwingend

string quartet strijkkwartet^h

stringy [stringie] **1** draderig, pezig: *~ arm* pezige arm; **2** mager, lang en dun

¹**strip** [strip] *vb* **1** (also with off) zich uitkleden: *~ped to the waist* met ontbloot bovenlijf; **2** een striptease opvoeren

²**strip** [strip] *vb* **1** uitkleden; **2** (also with off) van iets ontdoen, pellen, (af)schillen, verwijderen, afscheuren, afhalen *(bed)*, afkrabben *(paint)*: *~ down* uit elkaar halen, ontmantelen *(machines)*

³**strip** [strip] *n* **1** strook, strip, reep; **2** kleur(en) *(of sports team)* || *tear s.o. off a ~, tear a ~ (of: ~s) off s.o,* iem uitfoeteren

strip cartoon stripverhaal^h, beeldverhaal^h

stripe [strajp] **1** streep, lijn, strook; **2** streep *(decoration)*; **3** opvatting, mening: *of all political ~s* van alle politieke kleuren

striped [strajpt] gestreept

strip-lighting tl-verlichting, buisverlichting

stripy [strajpie] streperig, met strepen

strive [strajv] **1** *(with after, for)* (na)streven, zich inspannen (voor); **2** vechten

¹**stroke** [strook] *n* **1** slag, klap, stoot: *at a ~* in één

klap; *on the ~ of twelve* klokslag twaalf (uur), op slag van twaalven; **2** aanval, beroerte; **3** haal, streep; **4** schuine streep; **5** streling, aai; **6** *(rowing)* slag(roeier): *~ of (good) luck* buitenkansje, geluk(je); *he has not done a ~ of work* hij heeft geen klap uitgevoerd

²stroke [strook] *vb* **1** aaien, strelen, (glad)strijken; **2** *(rowing)* de slag aangeven in, slag(roeier) zijn

¹stroll [strool] *vb* wandelen, kuieren, slenteren

²stroll [strool] *n* wandeling(etjeʰ), blokjeʰ om: *go for a ~* een blokje om lopen

stroller [stroolə] **1** wandelaar; **2** *(Am)* wandelwagen(tjeʰ), buggy

strong [strong] sterk, krachtig, fors, stevig, zwaar *(beer, cigar)*, geconcentreerd *(solution)*, scherp *(odour, taste)*, drastisch *(measure)*, hoog *(fever, price etc)*, onregelmatig *(verb)*, kras *(language)*: *~ arm of the law* (sterke) arm der wet; *~ language* (of: *stuff)* krasse taal, gevloek; *~ nerves* stalen zenuwen; *hold ~ views* er een uitgesproken mening op nahouden; *(still) going ~* nog steeds actief; *two hundred ~* tweehonderd man sterk; *be ~ in* uitblinken in

strong-arm hardhandig, ruw, gewelddadig: *~ methods* grove middelen

strongbox brandkast, geldkist, safe(loketʰ)

stronghold *(also fig)* bolwerkʰ, vesting

strongly [stronglie] **1** sterk: *feel ~ about sth.* iets uitgesproken belangrijk vinden; **2** met klem, nadrukkelijk

strong-minded vastberaden, stijfkoppig

strongroom (bank)kluis

strong-willed wilskrachtig, vastberaden

structural [struktsjərəl] structureel, bouw-, constructie-: *~ alterations* verbouwing

structure [struktsjə] **1** bouwwerkʰ, constructie, (op)bouw; **2** structuur, samenstelling, constructie

¹struggle [strugl] *vb* worstelen, vechten, *(also fig)* strijden, zich inspannen: *~ to one's feet* overeind krabbelen

²struggle [strugl] *n* **1** worsteling, gevechtʰ, strijd: *put up a ~* zich verzetten; **2** (kracht)inspanning: *quite a ~* een heel karwei

strum [strum] betokkelen, tingelen

¹strut [strut] *vb* pompeus schrijden (op, over), paraderen, heen en weer stappen (op)

²strut [strut] *n* **1** pompeuze gang; **2** stut, steun

¹stub [stub] *n* **1** stomp(jeʰ), eindjeʰ, peuk; **2** recustrook, controlestrook *(of voucher or cheque book)*

²stub [stub] *vb* **1** stoten: *~ one's toe* zijn teen stoten; **2** (with *out*) uitdrukken, uitdoven: *~ out a cigarette* een sigaret uitmaken

stubble [stubl] **1** stoppel(s); **2** stoppelveldʰ; **3** stoppelbaard

stubborn [stubbən] **1** koppig, eigenwijs; **2** weerbarstig: *~ lock* stroef slot

¹stucco [stukkoo] *n* stucʰ, pleister(kalk), gipspleister

²stucco [stukkoo] *vb* pleisteren, stukadoren

stuck 1 vast *(also fig)*, klem, onbeweeglijk, ten einde raad: *be ~ for an answer* met zijn mond vol tanden staan; *get ~ with s.o.* met iem opgezadeld zitten; **2** vastgekleefd, vastgeplakt

stuck-up bekakt, verwaand

¹stud [stud] *n* **1** (sier)spijker, sierknopjeʰ; **2** knoop(jeʰ), overhemds-, boorden-, manchetknoopjeʰ; **3** (ren)stal, fokbedrijfʰ; **4** fokhengst, dekhengst *(also fig)*; **5** nop *(under football shoe)*; *(Belg)* stud

²stud [stud] *vb* **1** (with *with*) beslaan (met), voorzien van spijkers, knopjes; **2** bezetten, bedekken: *~ded with quotations* vol citaten

student [stjoe:dənt] **1** student(e): *~ of law, law ~* student in de rechten, rechtenstudent; **2** kenner: *~ of bird-life* vogelkenner

students' union studentenvereniging

student teacher 1 (leraar-)stagiair(e); **2** iem die studeert voor onderwijzer

stud farm fokbedrijfʰ

studied [studdied] weloverwogen, (wel)doordacht: *~ insult* opzettelijke belediging; *~ smile* gemaakte glimlach

studio [stjoe:die-oo] **1** studio, werkplaats, atelierʰ *(of artist)*; **2** *~s* filmstudio

studio flat eenkamerappartementʰ, studio

studious [stjoe:diəs] **1** leergierig, ijverig; **2** nauwgezet; **3** bestudeerd, weloverwogen, opzettelijk: *~ politeness* bestudeerde beleefdheid

¹study [studdie] *n* **1** studie, onderzoekʰ, aandacht, attentie; **2** studeerkamer, *(Belg)* bureauʰ; **3** *-ies* studie(vakʰ): *graduate studies* postkandidaatsstudie, *(Belg)* derde cyclus

²study [studdie] *vb* studeren, les(sen) volgen, college lopen: *~ to be a doctor* voor dokter studeren

³study [studdie] *vb* **1** (be)studeren, onderzoeken: *~ law* rechten studeren; **2** instuderen, van buiten leren

¹stuff [stuf] *n* **1** materiaalʰ, (grond)stof, elementen: *she has the ~ of an actrice in her* er zit een actrice in haar; **2** spulʰ, goed(jeʰ), waar: *a drop of the hard ~* een lekker neutje; *do you call this ~ coffee?* noem jij deze troep koffie?; **3** troep, rommel: *throw that ~ away!* gooi die rommel weg!; *do your ~* eens tonen wat je kan; *know one's ~* zijn vak verstaan; *that's the ~!* (dat is) je ware!, zo mag ik 't horen

²stuff [stuf] *vb* **1** (op)vullen, volproppen, volstoppen: *~ oneself* zich volproppen, zich overeten; *~ full* volproppen; *my mind is ~ed with facts* mijn denkraam zit vol (met) feiten; **2** (vol)stoppen, dichtstoppen: *~ed nose* verstopte neus; *my nose is completely ~ed up* mijn neus is helemaal verstopt; **3** proppen, stoppen, steken, duwen: *~ sth. in(to)* iets proppen in; **4** opzetten: *~ a bird* een vogel opzetten; **5** farceren, vullen: *~ed pepper* gevulde paprika; *(you can) ~ yourself!* je kan (van mij) de pot op!; *he can ~ his job!* hij kan de pot op met zijn baan

stuffing [stuffing] (op)vulselʰ, vulling, farce ‖ *knock (of: take) the ~ out of s.o.* iem tot moes slaan, iem uitschakelen

stuffy [stuffie] **1** bedompt, benauwd, muf; **2** saai, vervelend; **3** bekrompen, preuts

¹stumble [stumbl] *vb* **1** struikelen, vallen; **2** hakkelen, haperen, stamelen: ~ *in one's speech* hakkelen

²stumble [stumbl] *n* struikeling, misstap, *(fig)* blunder

stumble across tegen het lijf lopen, toevallig ontmoeten, stuiten op, toevallig vinden

stumbling block 1 struikelblok^h; **2** steen des aanstoots

¹stump [stump] *n* **1** stomp(je^h), (boom)stronk, eindje^h, peukje^h; **2** *(cricket)* wicketpaaltje^h

²stump [stump] *vb* stampen

³stump [stump] *vb* voor raadsels stellen, moeilijke vragen stellen: *that ~ed me* daar had ik geen antwoord op

stumper [stumpə] moeilijke vraag

stump up dokken, betalen, neertellen

stumpy [stumpie] gedrongen, kort en dik

stun [stun] **1** bewusteloos slaan; **2** schokken, verwarren, verdoven; **3** versteld doen staan, verbazen: *be ~ned into speechlessness* met stomheid geslagen zijn

stunner [stunnə] schoonheid

stunning [stunning] ongelofelijk mooi, verrukkelijk, prachtig

¹stunt [stunt] *n* **1** stunt, (acrobatische) toer, kunstje^h; **2** (reclame)stunt, attractie; **3** stuntvlucht

²stunt [stunt] *vb* (in zijn groei) belemmeren

stupefaction [stjoe:pifæksjən] verbijstering, (stomme) verbazing

stupefy [stjoe:piffaj] **1** bedwelmen, verdoven: *be stupefied by drink* door de drank versuft zijn; **2** verbijsteren, versteld doen staan

stupendous [stjoe:pendəs] fantastisch, enorm: *a ~ effort* een ongelofelijke inspanning

¹stupid [stjoe:pid] *adj* **1** dom, stom(pzinnig); **2** suf, versuft

²stupid [stjoe:pid] *n* sufferd

stupidity [stjoe:piddittie] domheid, stommiteit, domme opmerking, traagheid (van begrip)

stupor [stjoe:pə] (toestand van) verdoving: *in a drunken ~* in benevelde toestand

sturdy [sta:die] **1** sterk, flink, stevig (gebouwd); **2** vastberaden, krachtig

sturgeon [sta:dzjən] steur

¹stutter [stuttə] *vb* stotteren, stamelen: ~ *out* stotterend uitbrengen

²stutter [stuttə] *n* gestotter^h: *have a ~* stotteren

sty [staj] *(also ~es)* **1** varkensstal, varkenshok^h; **2** strontje^h *(small sore on eyelid)*

style [stajl] **1** genre^h, type^h, model^h, vorm: *in all sizes and ~s* in alle maten en vormen; **2** benaming, (volledige) (aanspreek)titel, (firma)naam: *trade under the ~ of Young & Morris* handel drijven onder de firmanaam Young & Morris; **3** (schrijf)stijl, (schrijf)wijze: *spaghetti Italian ~* spaghetti op zijn Italiaans; **4** stijl, stroming, school: *the new ~ of*

building de nieuwe bouwstijl; **5** manier van doen, levenswijze, stijl: *the balloon sailed into the air* de ballon ging zonder enig probleem schitterend omhoog; **6** mode, stijl: *in ~* in de mode; *cramp s.o.'s ~* iem in zijn doen en laten belemmeren

stylish [stajlisj] **1** modieus, naar de mode (gekleed); **2** stijlvol, elegant, deftig, chic

stylist [stajlist] **1** stilist(e); auteur met (goede) stijl; **2** ontwerp(st)er

stylistic [stajlistik] stilistisch: *a ~ change* een stijlverandering

stylize [stajlajz] stileren: *~d representations* gestileerde afbeeldingen

suave [swa:v] hoffelijk, beleefd, *(depr)* glad

sub [sub] **1** voorschot^h *(wages)*; **2** duikboot; **3** wissel(speler)

sub- [sub] ondergeschikt, bijkomend, hulp-: *~ post office* hulppostkantoor

¹subconscious [subkonsjəs] *adj* onderbewust

²subconscious [subkonsjəs] *n* onderbewustzijn^h, onderbewuste^h

subdivision [subdivvizjən] (onder)verdeling, onderafdeling

subdue [səbdjoe:] **1** onderwerpen, beheersen: ~ *one's passions* zijn hartstochten beteugelen; **2** matigen, verzachten

subdued [səbdjoe:d] getemperd, gematigd, gedempt, ingehouden, stil: ~ *colours* zachte kleuren

¹subject [subdzjikt] *adj* **1** onderworpen: ~ *to foreign rule* onder vreemde heerschappij; **2** afhankelijk: ~ *to your consent* behoudens uw toestemming; **3** onderhevig, blootgesteld: ~ *to change* vatbaar voor wijziging(en)

²subject [subdzjikt] *n* **1** onderdaan, ondergeschikte, **2** onderwerp^h, thema^h: *on the ~ of* omtrent, aangaande, over; **3** (studie)object^h, (school)vak^h; **4** aanleiding, omstandigheid, reden; **5** *(linguistics)* onderwerp^h

³subject [səbdzjekt] *vb* (with *to*) onderwerpen (aan), doen ondergaan

subject index 1 klapper, systematisch register^h; **2** trefwoordenregister^h

subjection [səbdzjeksjən] onderwerping, afhankelijkheid, onderworpenheid

subjective [səbdzjektiv] subjectief

subject matter onderwerp^h, inhoud *(of book)*

subjugation [subdzjoegeesjən] onderwerping, overheersing

subjunctive [səbdzjungktiv] *(linguistics)* aanvoegende wijs

sublime [səblajm] subliem, verheven: *(from) the ~ to the ridiculous* (van) het sublieme tot het potsierlijke

submarine [submərie:n] duikboot, onderzeeër

submerge [səbma:dzj] **1** (doen) duiken *(of submarine)*, onderduiken; **2** (doen) zinken, (doen) ondergaan, overstromen: *~d rocks* blinde klippen

submersion [səbma:sjən] onderdompeling, overstroming

submission [səbmisjən] **1** onderwerping, onderdanigheid: *starve the enemy into* ~ de vijand uithongeren; **2** voorstel[h]

submissive [səbmissiv] onderdanig, onderworpen

[1]**submit** [səbmit] *vb* toegeven, zwichten, zich overgeven: ~ *to s.o.'s wishes* iemands wensen inwilligen; ~ *to defeat* zich gewonnen geven

[2]**submit** [səbmit] *vb* **1** (with *to*) voorleggen (aan): ~ *s.o.'s name for appointment* iem ter benoeming voordragen; **2** onderwerpen, overgeven: ~ *oneself to* zich onderwerpen aan

[1]**subordinate** [səbo:dinnət] *adj* (with *to*) ondergeschikt (aan), onderworpen, afhankelijk: ~ *clause* bijzin, ondergeschikte zin

[2]**subordinate** [səbo:dinneet] *vb* (with *to*) ondergeschikt maken (aan), achterstellen (bij)

subordination [səbo:dinneesjən] **1** ondergeschiktheid; **2** (*linguistics*) onderschikking

[1]**subpoena** [səbpie:nə] *n* dagvaarding

[2]**subpoena** [səbpie:nə] *vb* dagvaarden

[1]**subscribe** [səbskrajb] *vb* **1** (onder)tekenen, zijn handtekening zetten onder: ~ *one's name (to sth.)* (iets) ondertekenen; **2** inschrijven (voor)

[2]**subscribe** [səbskrajb] *vb* **1** (with *to*) intekenen (voor), zich abonneren (op) (*magazine*): ~ *for* (vooraf) bestellen; **2** (with *to*) onderschrijven (*opinion*); **3** (with *to*) (geldelijk) steunen

subscriber [səbskrajbə] **1** ondertekenaar; **2** intekenaar, abonnee

subscription [səbskripsjən] **1** ondertekening; **2** abonnement[h], intekening, inschrijving: *take out a* ~ *to sth.* zich op iets abonneren; **3** contributie, bijdrage, steun

subsequent [subsikwənt] (with *to*) volgend (op), later, aansluitend

subsequently [subsikwəntlie] vervolgens, nadien, daarna

subservient [səbsə:viənt] **1** bevorderlijk, nuttig: ~ *to* bevorderlijk voor; **2** ondergeschikt; **3** kruiperig, onderdanig

subside [səbsajd] **1** (be)zinken, (in)zakken, verzakken; **2** slinken, inkrimpen, afnemen; **3** bedaren

subsidence [səbsajdəns] instorting, verzakking, het wegzakken

subsidiary [səbsiddiərie] **1** helpend, steunend, aanvullings-: ~ *troops* hulptroepen; **2** (with *to*) ondergeschikt (aan), afhankelijk (van): ~ *subject* bijvak

subsidize [subsiddajz] subsidiëren

subsidy [subsiddie] subsidie

subsist [səbsist] (in) leven (blijven): ~ *on welfare* van een uitkering leven

subsistence [səbsistəns] **1** bestaan[h], leven[h]; **2** onderhoud[h], kost, levensonderhoud[h]

subsoil [subsojl] ondergrond

substance [substəns] substantie, wezen[h], essentie, stof, materie, kern, hoofdzaak: *the* ~ *of his remarks* de kern van zijn opmerkingen; *a man of* ~ een rijk man

substantial [səbstænsjl] werkelijk, aanzienlijk, stoffelijk, degelijk: ~ *meal* stevige maaltijd

substantiate [səbstænsjie·eet] van gronden voorzien, bewijzen, verwezenlijken: ~ *a claim* een bewering hard maken

[1]**substitute** [substitjoe:t] *n* vervanger, plaatsvervanger, (*also sport*) invaller

[2]**substitute** [substitjoe:t] *vb* in de plaats stellen (voor), invallen (voor): ~ *A by* (of: *with*) *B* A door B vervangen; ~ *A for B* B vervangen door A

[3]**substitute** [substitjoe:t] *adj* plaatsvervangend

substitution [substitjoe:sjən] vervanging

subtenant [subtennənt] onderhuurder

subterfuge [subtəfjoe:dzj] **1** uitvlucht, voorwendsel[h]; **2** trucje[h], list

subterranean [subtəreeniən] onderaards, ondergronds

subtitle [subtajtl] ondertitel

subtle [sutl] subtiel, fijn, nauwelijks merkbaar, scherp(zinnig): *smile subtly* fijntjes lachen

subtlety [sutltie] subtiliteit, scherpzinnigheid, subtiel onderscheid[h]

subtract [səbtrækt] (with *from*) aftrekken (van), in mindering brengen (op)

subtraction [səbtræksjən] aftrekking, vermindering

suburb [subbə:b] voorstad, buitenwijk

suburban [səbə:bən] van de voorstad, (*fig*) bekrompen

subversive [səbvə:siv] ontwrichtend, ondermijnend

subway [subwee] **1** (voetgangers)tunnel, ondergrondse (door)gang; **2** (*Am*) metro

[1]**succeed** [səksie:d] *vb* slagen, gelukken, succes hebben: ~ *in (doing) sth.* slagen in iets, erin slagen iets te doen

[2]**succeed** [səksie:d] *vb* (op)volgen: ~ *to the property* de bezittingen overerven

success [səkses] succes[h], goede afloop, bijval: *be a* ~, *meet with* ~ succes boeken; *make a* ~ *of it* het er goed afbrengen

successful [səksesfoel] succesvol, geslaagd

succession [səksesjən] **1** reeks, serie, opeenvolging: ~ *of defeats* reeks nederlagen; **2** (troon)opvolging: *law of* ~ successiewet; *in quick* ~ vlak na elkaar

successive [səksessiv] opeenvolgend

successor [səksessə] opvolger: ~ *to the throne* troonopvolger

succinct [səksingkt] beknopt, kort, bondig

succour [sukkə] hulp, steun

[1]**succulent** [sukjoelənt] *adj* sappig

[2]**succulent** [sukjoelənt] *n* vetplant

succumb [səkum] (with *to*) bezwijken (aan, voor): ~ *to one's enemies* zwichten voor zijn vijanden

[1]**such** [sutsj] *adj* **1** zulk(e), zodanig, dergelijke, zo'n: ~ *clothes as he would need* de kleren die hij nodig zou hebben; ~ *as* zoals; *a man* ~ *as Paul* een man als Paul; *I have accepted his help,* ~ *as it is* ik heb zijn

hulp aangenomen, ook al is die vrijwel niets waard; *there's no ~ thing as automatic translation* automatisch vertalen is onmogelijk; **2** die en die, dat en dat: *at ~ (and ~) a place and at ~ (and ~) a time* op die en die plaats en op dat en dat uur

²such [sutsj] *pron* zulke, zo iem (iets), dergelijke(n), zulks: *~ was not my intention* dat was niet mijn bedoeling; *~ being the case* nu de zaken er zo voorstaan

suchlike [sutsjlajk] zo'n, zulk(e), dergelijke: *worms and ~ creatures* wormen en dergelijke beestjes

¹suck [suk] *vb* **1** zuigen (aan, op): *~ sweets* op snoepjes zuigen; *~ in* opzuigen, in zich opnemen; *~ up* opzuigen; **2** likken, vleien: *~ up (to)* iem likken, iem vleien

²suck [suk] *n* slokje[h], teugje[h]

sucker [sukkə] **1** zuiger, uitloper, scheut; **2** onnozele hals, sukkel: *I am a ~ for red-headed women* ik val nu eenmaal op vrouwen met rood haar

suckle [sukl] de borst krijgen (geven), zuigen, zogen

suckling [sukling] **1** zuigeling; **2** jong[h]

suction [suksjən] zuiging, (kiel)zog[h]

Sudan [soe:da:n] Sudan

Sudanese [soe:dənie:z] *(Sudanese)* Sudanees

sudden [sudn] plotseling, haastig, snel, scherp: *~ death (play-off)* beslissende verlenging; *all of a ~* plotseling, ineens

suddenly [sudnlie] plotseling, opeens, ineens

suds [sudz] (zeep)sop, schuim

sue [soe:] **1** (gerechtelijk) vervolgen, dagvaarden: *~ for divorce* (echt)scheiding aanvragen; **2** verzoeken, smeken: *~ for mercy* (iem) om genade smeken

¹suffer [suffə] *vb* **1** lijden, schade lijden, beschadigd worden: *~ from* lijden aan; **2** (with *for*) boeten (voor)

²suffer [suffə] *vb* verdragen, dulden: *not ~ fools (gladly)* weinig geduld hebben met dwazen

suffering [suffəring] pijn, lijden[h]

suffice [səfajs] genoeg zijn (voor), volstaan, voldoen: *your word will ~ (me)* uw woord is me voldoende; *~ (it) to say that* het zij voldoende te zeggen dat

sufficiency [səfisjənsie] **1** voldoende voorraad, toereikende hoeveelheid; **2** toereikendheid

sufficient [səfisjənt] voldoende, genoeg

suffocate [sufføkeet] (doen) stikken, verstikken

suffocation [suffəkeesjən] (ver)stikking

suffrage [sufridzj] stemrecht[h], kiesrecht[h]

suffuse [səfjoe:z] bedekken: *eyes ~d with tears* ogen vol tranen; *~d with light* overgoten door licht

¹sugar [sjoegə] *n* **1** suiker; **2** schat(je[h]), liefje[h]; **3** zoete woordjes, vleierij

²sugar [sjoegə] *vb* **1** zoeten, suiker doen in; **2** aangenamer maken, verzoeten: *~ the pill* de pil vergulden

sugarcane suikerriet[h]

sugar caster suikerstrooier, strooibus

sugary [sjoegərie] **1** suikerachtig, suiker-; **2** suiker-

zoet *(fig)*, stroperig

suggest [sədzjest] suggereren, doen denken aan, duiden op, influisteren, ingeven, opperen, aanvoeren, voorstellen, aanraden: *~ doing sth.* voorstellen iets te doen; *~ sth. to s.o.* iem iets voorstellen

suggestion [sədzjestsjən] **1** suggestie, aanduiding, aanwijzing, mededeling, idee[h], overweging, voorstel[h], raad: *at the ~ of* op aanraden van; **2** zweem, tikje[h]: *a ~ of anger* een zweem van woede

suggestion box ideeënbus

suggestive [sədzjestiv] **1** suggestief, suggererend, veelbetekenend; **2** gewaagd, van verdacht allooi, schuin

suicidal [soe:issajdl] **1** zelfmoord-; **2** met zelfmoordneigingen

suicide [soe:issajd] **1** zelfmoord, zelfdoding: *commit ~* zelfmoord plegen; **2** zelfmoordenaar

suicide squad zelfmoordcommando[h]

¹suit [soe:t] *n* **1** kostuum[h], pak[h]: *bathing ~* badpak; **2** *(cards)* kleur, kaarten van één kleur: *follow ~* kleur bekennen, *(fig)* iemands voorbeeld volgen; **3** stel[h], uitrusting: *~ of armour* wapenrusting; **4** (rechts)geding[h], proces[h], rechtszaak: *criminal ~* strafrechtelijke procedure

²suit [soe:t] *vb* **1** passen (bij), geschikt zijn (voor), staan (bij): *this colour ~s her complexion* deze kleur past bij haar teint; *~ s.o. (down) to the ground: a)* voor iem geknipt zijn, precies bij iem passen; *b)* iem uitstekend van pas komen; **2** gelegen komen (voor), uitkomen (voor), schikken: *that date will ~ (me)* die datum komt (me) goed uit

³suit [soe:t] *vb* **1** aanpassen, geschikt maken: *~ one's style to one's audience* zijn stijl aan zijn publiek aanpassen; **2** goed zijn voor: *I know what ~s me best* ik weet wel wat voor mij het beste is; **3** voldoen, aanstaan, bevredigen: *~ s.o.'s needs* aan iemands behoeften voldoen; *~ yourself!: a)* ga je gang maar!; *b)* moet je zelf weten!

suitability [soe:təbillittie] geschiktheid, gepastheid

suitable [soe:təbl] (with *to, for*) geschikt (voor), gepast, passend

suitcase koffer, *(Belg)* valies[h]

suite [swie:t] **1** stel[h], rij, suite, ameublement[h]: *~ of rooms* suite; *three-piece ~* driedelige zitcombinatie; **2** suite, gevolg[h]

suited [soe:tid] **1** geschikt, (bij elkaar) passend: *well ~ to one another* voor elkaar gemaakt; **2** gericht (op), beantwoordend (aan)

¹sulk [sulk] *vb* mokken, chagrijnig zijn

²sulk [sulk] *n* boze bui: *have a ~, have (a fit of) the ~s* een chagrijnige bui hebben

sulky [sulkie] chagrijnig

sullen [sullən] **1** nors, stuurs, somber: *~ sky* sombere hemel

sulphur [sulfə] zwavel

sulphuric [sulfjoeərik] zwavelachtig, zwavelhoudend: *~ acid* zwavelzuur

sultry [sultrie] **1** zwoel, drukkend; **2** wellustig, sensueel

sum [sum] **1** som, totaal^h, geheel^h, bedrag^h; **2** (reken)som, berekening, optelling: *good at ~s* goed in rekenen; **3** samenvatting, kern, strekking: *in ~* in één woord

summarily [summərillie] **1** summier, in het kort: *deal ~ with* summier behandelen; **2** terstond, zonder vorm van proces

summarize [summərajz] samenvatten

¹summary [summərie] *n* samenvatting, korte inhoud, uittreksel^h

²summary [summərie] *adj* beknopt

summer [summə] zomer, *(fig)* bloeitijd: *in (the) ~* in de zomer

summer school zomercursus, vakantiecursus *(at university)*

summertime zomerseizoen^h, zomer(tijd)

summer time zomertijd

summery [summərie] zomers

summing-up [summing up] samenvatting *(by judge)*

summit [summit] **1** top, hoogste punt^h; **2** toppunt^h, hoogtepunt^h: *at the ~* op het hoogste niveau; **3** topconferentie

summit meeting topconferentie

summon [summən] **1** bijeenroepen, oproepen; **2** dagvaarden

¹summons [summənz] *n* **1** oproep; **2** aanmaning; **3** dagvaarding: *serve a ~ on s.o.* iem dagvaarden

²summons [summənz] *vb* **1** dringend aanmanen; **2** dagvaarden

summon up vergaren, verzamelen: *~ one's courage (to do sth.)* zich vermannen, al zijn moed verzamelen (om iets te doen)

sumptuous [sumptjoeəs] weelderig, luxueus, rijk

sum total 1 totaal^h; **2** resultaat^h

¹sum up *vb* samenvatten

²sum up *vb* beoordelen, doorzien: *sum s.o. up as a fool* iem voor gek verslijten

sun [sun] zon, zonlicht^h, zonneschijn: *a place in the ~* een plaatsje in de zon, *(fig)* een gunstige positie; *beneath* (of: *under*) *the ~* onder de zon, op aarde

sunbeam zonnestraal

sunblind zonnescherm^h

sunburn zonnebrand, roodverbrande huid

sunburnt 1 gebruind; **2** *(Am)* verbrand

sundae [sundee] ijscoupe

Sunday [sundee] zondag, feestdag, rustdag

Sunday best zondagse kleren: *in one's ~* op zijn zondags

sundial zonnewijzer

sundown zonsondergang: *at ~* bij zonsondergang

sundry [sundrie] divers, allerlei, verschillend

sunflower zonnebloem

sunglasses zonnebril: *a pair of ~* een zonnebril

sunken [sungkən] **1** gezonken, onder water, ingevallen: *~ eyes* diepliggende ogen; **2** verzonken, ingegraven, verlaagd: *~ road* holle weg

sunlamp hoogtezon

sunlight zonlicht^h

sunlit door de zon verlicht, in het zonlicht, zonovergoten

sunny [sunnie] zonnig, vrolijk: *on the ~ side of forty* nog geen veertig

sunrise zonsopgang

sun roof 1 plat dak^h *(to sunbathe);* **2** schuifdak^h *(of car)*

sunset zonsondergang, avondrood^h: *at ~* bij zonsondergang

sunshade zonnescherm^h, parasol, zonneklep

sunshine zonneschijn, *(fig)* zonnetje^h

sunstroke zonnesteek

suntanned gebruind, bruin

sunup zonsopgang

super [soe:pə] super, fantastisch

superabundant [soe:pərəbundənt] (zeer, al te) overvloedig, rijkelijk (aanwezig)

superannuated [soe:pərænjoe·eetid] **1** gepensioneerd; **2** verouderd, ouderwets

superannuation [soe:pərænjoe·eesjən] **1** pensionering, pensioen^h; **2** pensioen^h, lijfrente

superb [soe:pə:b] groots, prachtig, voortreffelijk

supercilious [soe:pəsilliəs] uit de hoogte, verwaand

superficial [soe:pəfisjl] oppervlakkig, niet diepgaand, vluchtig: *~ wound* ondiepe wond

superfluous [soe:pə:floeəs] overbodig

superhuman bovenmenselijk, buitengewoon

superimpose [soe:pərimpooz] bovenop leggen, opleggen

superintend [soe:pərintend] toezicht houden (op), controleren, toezien (op)

superintendent [soe:pərintendənt] **1** (hoofd)opzichter, hoofd^h, directeur; **2** hoofdinspecteur *(of police)*

¹superior [soe:piəriə] *adj* **1** superieur, beter, bovenst, opperst, *(fig also)* hoger, hoofd-: *~ to: a)* beter *(quality); b)* hoger *(rank); be ~ to* verheven zijn boven, staan boven; **2** hoger, voornaam, deftig; **3** verwaand, arrogant: *~ smile* hooghartig lachje; *~ court* hogere rechtbank

²superior [soe:piəriə] *n* **1** meerdere, superieur, hogere in rang, chef; **2** overste: *Mother Superior* moeder-overste

superiority [soe:piərie·orrittie] superioriteit, grotere kracht, hogere kwaliteit

¹superlative [soe:pə:lətiv] *adj* voortreffelijk, prachtig

²superlative [soe:pə:lətiv] *n* superlatief *(also linguistics),* overtreffende trap

superman [soe:pəmæn] superman, supermens

supermarket [soe:pə:ma:kit] supermarkt

supernatural [soe:pənætsjərəl] bovennatuurlijk

supernaturalistic [soe:pənætsjrəlistik] bovennatuurlijk, supernaturalistisch

supernumerary [soe:pənjoe:mərərie] **1** extra^h, reserve; **2** figurant

superpower [soe:pəpauə] grootmacht, supermacht

supersede [soe:pəsie:d] vervangen, de plaats doen innemen van; afschaffen

supersonic [soe:pəsɒnnik] supersonisch, sneller dan het geluid

superstition [soe:pəstisjən] bijgeloof[h]

supervise [soe:pəvajz] 1 aan het hoofd staan (van), leiden; 2 toezicht houden (op), controleren

supervision [soe:pəvizjən] supervisie, leiding, toezicht[h]

supervisor [soe:pəvajzə] 1 opzichter, controleur, inspecteur, chef; 2 coördinator

supine [soe:pajn] 1 achteroverliggend, op de rug liggend; 2 lui, traag

supper [suppə] (licht) avondmaal[h], avondeten[h], souper[h]

supplant [səpla:nt] verdringen, vervangen

supple [supl] soepel (also fig), buigzaam, lenig

¹supplement [suplimmənt] n aanvulling, bijvoegsel[h], supplement[h]: pay a ~ bijbetalen

²supplement [suplimment] vb aanvullen, ve supplement voorzien: ~ by (of: with) aanvullen met

supplementary [suplimmentərie] aanvullend, toegevoegd, extra

supplication [suplikkeesjən] smeekbede

supplier [səplajjə] leverancier

¹supply [səplaj] vb 1 leveren, verschaffen, bezorgen, voorzien van: ~ sth. to s.o., ~ s.o. with sth. iem iets bezorgen, iem van iets voorzien; 2 voorzien in, verhelpen, vervullen: ~ a need voorzien in een behoefte

²supply [səplaj] n 1 voorraad, -ies (mond)voorraad, proviand[h], benodigdheden; 2 bevoorrading, aanvoer, toevoer, levering; 3 aanbod[h]: ~ and demand vraag en aanbod

¹support [səpɔ:t] vb 1 (onder)steunen, stutten, dragen; 2 steunen, helpen, bijstaan, verdedigen, bijvallen, subsidiëren; 3 onderhouden, voorzien in de levensbehoeften van: ~ oneself zichzelf onderhouden; 4 verdragen, doorstaan, verduren: ~ing programme bijfilm, voorfilm(pje); ~ing part (of: role) bijrol

²support [səpɔ:t] n 1 steun, hulp, ondersteuning: in ~ of tot steun van; 2 steun(stuk[h]), stut, drager, draagbalk; 3 onderhoud[h], levensonderhoud[h], middelen van bestaan

supporter [səpɔ:tə] 1 verdediger, aanhanger, voorvechter; 2 supporter

supportive [səpɔ:tiv] steunend, helpend, aanmoedigend

suppose [səpooz] (ver)onderstellen, aannemen, denken: he is ~d to be in London hij zou in Londen moeten zijn; I'm not ~d to tell you this ik mag je dit (eigenlijk) niet vertellen; I suppose so ik neem aan van wel; ~ it rains stel dat het regent, en als het nou regent?

supposed [səpoozd] vermeend, vermoedelijk, zogenaamd: his ~ wealth zijn vermeende rijkdom

supposedly [səpoozidlie] vermoedelijk, naar alle waarschijnlijkheid, naar verluidt

supposing [səpoozing] indien, verondersteld dat: ~ it rains, what then? maar wat als het regent?

supposition [suppəzisjən] (ver)onderstelling, vermoeden[h], gissing: in (of: on) the ~ that in de veronderstelling dat

suppository [səpɒzzittərie] zetpil

suppress [səpres] onderdrukken, bedwingen, achterhouden: ~ evidence bewijsstukken achterhouden; ~ feelings gevoelens onderdrukken

suppression [səpresjən] onderdrukking

suppressor [səpressə] onderdrukker

supranational [soe:prənæsjənəl] supranationaal, bovennationaal

supremacy [soe:premməsie] overmacht, superioriteit

supreme [soe:prie:m] opperst, hoogst: Supreme Being Opperwezen, God; Supreme Court hooggerechtshof

¹surcharge [sɔ:tsja:dzj] n 1 toeslag, strafport; 2 extra belasting

²surcharge [sɔ:tsja:dzj] vb 1 extra laten betalen; 2 overladen, overbelasten

¹sure [sjoeə] adj 1 zeker, waar, onbetwistbaar: one thing is ~ één ding staat vast; 2 zeker, veilig, betrouwbaar: ~ proof waterdicht bewijs; 3 zeker, verzekerd, overtuigd: ~ of oneself zelfverzekerd, zelfbewust; you can be ~ of it daar kan je van op aan; ~ card iem (iets) waar men op kan bouwen; ~ thing: a) feit, zekerheid; b) (exclamation) natuurlijk!; be ~ to tell her vergeet vooral niet het haar te vertellen; it is ~ to be a girl het wordt vast een meisje; just to make ~ voor alle zekerheid

²sure [sjoeə] adv zeker, natuurlijk, ongetwijfeld: ~ enough! natuurlijk!; he promised to come and ~ enough he did hij beloofde te komen en ja hoor, hij kwam ook; I don't know for ~ ik ben er niet (zo) zeker van

sure-fire onfeilbaar, zeker: ~ winner zekere winnaar

surely [sjoeəlie] 1 zeker, ongetwijfeld, toch: slowly but ~ langzaam maar zeker; ~ I've met you before? ik heb je toch al eens eerder ontmoet?; ~ you are not suggesting it wasn't an accident? je wilt toch zeker niet beweren dat het geen ongeluk was?; 2 natuurlijk, ga je gang (in reply to request)

surety [sjoeərətie] 1 borgsteller; 2 borg(som): stand ~ for s.o. zich borg stellen voor iem

¹surf [sɔ:f] n branding

²surf [sɔ:f] vb surfen: ~ the Net internetten, (op het net) surfen

¹surface [sɔ:fis] n oppervlak[h], oppervlakte (also fig): come to the ~ te voorschijn komen, bovenkomen

²surface [sɔ:fis] vb aan de oppervlakte komen (also fig), opduiken, verschijnen

³surface [sɔ:fis] vb bedekken, bestraten, asfalteren

surface mail landpost, zeepost

surfboard surfplank

surfeit [sɔ:fit] overdaad, overlading (of stomach): have a ~ of zich ziek eten aan

¹surge [sɔ:dʒ] *vb* **1** golven, deinen, stromen: ~ *by* voorbijstromen; **2** dringen, duwen: *surging crowd* opdringende massa; **3** opwellen, opbruisen *(of feelings)*

²surge [sɔ:dʒ] *n* **1** (hoge) golf; **2** opwelling, vlaag, golf

surgeon [sɔ:dʒən] **1** chirurg; **2** scheepsdokter

surgery [sɔ:dʒərie] **1** behandelkamer, spreekkamer *(of doctor)*; **2** spreekuur[h]; **3** chirurgie, heelkunde: *be in* (of: *have, undergo*) ~ geopereerd worden

surgical [sɔ:dʒikl] chirurgisch, operatief || ~ *stocking* steunkous, elastische kous

¹Surinam [soeərinæm] *adj* Surinaams

²Surinam [soeərinæm] *n* Suriname

Surinamese [soeərinnəmie:z] Surinaams

surly [sɔ:lie] knorrig, nors

surmise [səmajz] gissing, vermoeden[h]

surmount [səmoont] **1** overwinnen, te boven komen; **2** bedekken, overdekken: *peaks ~ed with snow* met sneeuw bedekte toppen

surname [sɔ:neem] achternaam

surpass [səpa:s] overtreffen, te boven gaan: ~ *all expectations* alle verwachtingen overtreffen

¹surplus [sɔ:pləs] *n* overschot[h], teveel[h], rest(ant[h])

²surplus [sɔ:pləs] *adj* overtollig, extra: ~ *grain* graanoverschot

¹surprise [səprajz] *n* verrassing, verbazing, verwondering: *come as a* ~ *(to s.o.)* totaal onverwacht komen (voor iem); *to my great* ~ tot mijn grote verbazing

²surprise [səprajz] *vb* verrassen, verbazen, overvallen, betrappen: *you'd be ~ed!* daar zou je van opkijken!

surprised [səprajzd] verrast, verbaasd: *be ~ at* zich verbazen over

surprising [səprajzing] verrassend, verbazingwekkend

surrealism [səriəlizm] surrealisme[h]

¹surrender [sərendə] *vb* zich overgeven, capituleren

²surrender [sərendə] *vb* overgeven, uitleveren, afstaan, afstand doen van

³surrender [sərendə] *n* overgave

surreptitious [surrəptisjəs] heimelijk, stiekem: ~ *glance* steelse blik

¹surrogate [surrəgət] *adj* plaatsvervangend, surrogaat- || ~ *mother(hood)* draagmoeder(schap)

²surrogate [surrəgət] *n* **1** plaatsvervanger, substituut; **2** vervangend middel[h], surrogaat[h]

surround [səraund] omringen, omsingelen: ~*ed by* (of: *with*) omringd door

surroundings [səraundingz] omgeving, buurt, streek, omtrek

surveillance [sə:veeləns] toezicht[h], bewaking: *under (close)* ~ onder (strenge) bewaking

¹survey [səvee] *vb* **1** overzien, toezien op; **2** onderzoeken; **3** taxeren *(house)*; **4** opmeten, karteren

²survey [sɔ:vee] *n* **1** overzicht[h]: *a ~ of major Dutch writers* een overzicht van belangrijke Nederlandse schrijvers; **2** onderzoek[h]; **3** taxering, taxatierap-

port[h] *(of house)*; **4** opmeting, opname, kartering *(of terrain)*

surveyor [səveeə] **1** opziener, opzichter, inspecteur; **2** landmeter; **3** taxateur

survival [səvajvl] **1** overleving, het overleven: ~ *of the fittest* natuurlijke selectie, (het verschijnsel dat) de sterkste(n) overleven; **2** overblijfsel[h]

survive [səvajv] overleven, voortbestaan, bewaard blijven, langer leven dan, *(fig)* zich (weten te) handhaven: ~ *an earthquake* een aardbeving overleven; ~ *one's children* zijn kinderen overleven

survivor [səvajvə] overlevende

susceptibility [səseptibbillittie] **1** gevoeligheid; **2** *-ies* zwakke plek: *wound s.o. in his susceptibilities* iem op zijn zwakke plek raken

susceptible [səseptibl] *(with to)* vatbaar (voor), gevoelig (voor), onderhevig (aan)

¹suspect [səspekt] *vb* **1** vermoeden, vrezen, geloven, denken; **2** *(with of)* verdenken (van), wantrouwen

²suspect [suspekt] *n* verdachte

³suspect [suspekt] *adj* verdacht

suspend [səspend] **1** (op)hangen; **2** uitstellen: ~*ed sentence* voorwaardelijke straf; **3** schorsen

suspender [səspendə] **1** (sok)ophouder; **2** ~*s (Am)* bretels: *a pair of ~s* bretels

suspense [səspens] spanning, onzekerheid: *hold* (of: *keep) in* ~ in onzekerheid laten

suspension [səspensjən] **1** opschorting *(of verdict, sentence etc)*, onderbreking, uitstel[h] *(of payment)*; **2** vering

suspension bridge hangbrug, kettingbrug

suspicion [səspisjən] **1** vermoeden[h], veronderstelling: *have a ~ that* vermoeden dat; **2** verdenking: *above ~* boven alle verdenking verheven; **3** zweempje[h]: *a ~ of irony* een zweempje ironie

suspicious [səspisjəs] **1** verdacht: *feel ~ about* (of: *of)* iem wantrouwen; **2** wantrouwig, achterdochtig

suss out 1 doorkrijgen *(sth): I can't ~ how to remove that wheel clamp* ik kan er maar niet achter komen hoe ik die wielklem eraf moet halen; **2** doorhebben *(somebody)*

sustain [səsteen] **1** (onder)steunen, dragen, staven, bevestigen: ~*ing food* versterkend voedsel; **2** volhouden, aanhouden: ~ *a note* een noot aanhouden; **3** doorstaan: ~ *an attack* een aanval afslaan; **4** ondergaan, lijden, oplopen: ~ *a defeat* een nederlaag oplopen

sustained [səsteend] voortdurend, aanhoudend

sustenance [sustənəns] voedsel[h] *(also fig)*

SW *South-West(ern)* Z.W., zuidwest

¹swab [swob] *n* **1** zwabber, stokdweil; **2** prop (watten), wattenstokje[h]; **3** uitstrijk(je[h]): *take a* ~ een uitstrijkje maken

²swab [swob] *vb* zwabberen, (op)dweilen, opnemen

¹swagger [swægə] *vb* **1** paraderen, lopen als een pauw; **2** opscheppen, pochen

²swagger [swægə] *n* **1** geparadeer[h], zwier(ige gang); **2** opschepperij

¹**swallow** [swo̲lloo] *vb* slikken

²**swallow** [swo̲lloo] *vb* **1** (door)slikken, inslikken, binnenkrijgen; **2** opslokken, verslinden: *~ up* opslokken, inlijven; **3** *(fig)* slikken, geloven: *~ a story* een verhaal slikken; **4** inslikken *(words or sounds)*; **5** herroepen, terugnemen: *~ one's words* zijn woorden terugnemen; **6** onderdrukken, verbijten: *~ one's pride* zijn trots terzijde schuiven; *~ hard* zich vermannen

³**swallow** [swo̲lloo] *n* **1** zwaluw; **2** slok ‖ *one ~ doesn't make a summer* één zwaluw maakt nog geen zomer

swallow-tailed zwaluwstaartvormig, gevorkt: *~ coat* rok(jas)

¹**swamp** [swomp] *n* moeras(land)ʰ

²**swamp** [swomp] *vb* **1** doen vollopen; **2** onder water doen lopen, overstromen; **3** bedelven, overspoelen: *~ with work* bedelven onder het werk

swan [swon] zwaan ‖ *the Swan of Avon* Shakespeare

¹**swank** [swæŋk] *vb* opscheppen, zich aanstellen: *~ about in a new fur coat* rondparaderen in een nieuwe bontmantel

²**swank** [swæŋk] *n* **1** opschepper; **2** opschepperij

swanky [swæŋkie] **1** opschepperig; **2** chic, modieus, stijlvol

¹**swap** [swop] *vb* ruilen, uitwisselen: *~ jokes* moppen tappen onder elkaar; *~ over* (of: *round*) van plaats verwisselen; *~ for* (in)ruilen tegen

²**swap** [swop] *n* ruil: *do* (of: *make*) *a ~* ruilen

¹**swarm** [swo:m] *n* zwerm, massa: *~ of bees* bijenzwerm; *~s of children* drommen kinderen

²**swarm** [swo:m] *vb* **1** (uit)zwermen, samendrommen: *~ in* naar binnen stromen; *~ about* (of: *round*) samendrommen rond; **2** *(with* with*)* krioelen (van), wemelen; **3** klimmen: *~ up a tree* in een boom klauteren

swarthy [swo:ðie] donker, bruin, zwart(achtig)

swastika [swo̲stikkə] hakenkruisʰ

swat [swot] meppen, (dood)slaan: *~ a fly* een vlieg doodmeppen

swathe [sweeð] **1** zwad(e), hoeveelheid met één maai afgesneden gras (koren); **2** (gemaaide) strook, baan: *cut a wide ~ through* flinke sporen achterlaten in

¹**sway** [swee] *vb* slingeren, (doen) zwaaien, *(fig also)* (doen) aarzelen: *~ to the music* deinen op de maat van de muziek

²**sway** [swee] *vb* beïnvloeden: *be ~ed by* zich laten leiden door

³**sway** [swee] *n* **1** slingering, zwaai, schommeling *(of ship etc)*; **2** invloed, druk, overwichtʰ, dwang: *under the ~ of his arguments* overgehaald door zijn argumenten

swear [sweə] **1** *(with at, about)* vloeken (op, over); **2** zweren, een eed afleggen, met kracht beweren, wedden: *~ an oath* een eed afleggen; *~ to do sth.* plechtig beloven iets te zullen doen; *~ by s.o. (sth.)* bij iem (iets) zweren, volkomen op iem (iets) vertrouwen; **3** beëdigen, de eed afnemen: *sworn translator* beëdigd vertaler; *sworn enemies* gezworen

vijanden; *~ in* beëdigen; *~ to secrecy* (of: *silence*) een eed van geheimhouding afnemen van

swearword vloek, krachtterm

¹**sweat** [swet] *vb* zweten, (doen) (uit)zweten: *~ blood* water en bloed zweten; *~ it out* (tot het einde) volhouden, standhouden, zweten

²**sweat** [swet] *n* **1** zweetʰ: *he was in a cold ~* het klamme zweet brak hem uit; **2** inspanning, karweiʰ: *a frightful ~* een vreselijk karwei; **3** eng gevoelʰ, angst, spanning: *in a ~* benauwd, bang; **4** (oude) rot: *old ~* oude rot

sweated [swettid] door uitbuiting verkregen, uitgebuit: *~ labour* slavenarbeid

sweater [swettə] sweater, sportvestʰ, (wollen) trui

sweat suit trainingspakʰ, joggingpakʰ

sweaty [swettie] **1** zwetend, bezweet, zweterig; **2** broeierig, heet

Swede [swie:d] Zweed(se)

Sweden [swie:dn] Zweden

¹**Swedish** [swie:disj] *adj* Zweeds

²**Swedish** [swie:disj] *n* Zweedsʰ *(language)*

¹**sweep** [swie:p] *vb* **1** vegen: *~ the seas de* zeeën schoonvegen; *be swept from sight* aan het gezicht onttrokken worden; *~ up* aanvegen, uitvegen, bijeenvegen; **2** (laten) slepen; **3** (toe)zwaaien, slaan: *~ aside* (met een zwaai) opzijschuiven, *(fig)* naast zich neerleggen; *~ off* (met een zwaai) afnemen *(hat)*; **4** meesleuren, wegsleuren, meevoeren, afrukken: *~ along* meesleuren, meeslepen; *be swept off one's feet* a) omvergelopen worden; b) *(fig)* overdonderd worden; c) versteld staan, halsoverkop verliefd worden; *be swept out to sea* in zee gesleurd worden; **5** doorkruisen, teisteren, razen over: *the storm swept the country* de storm raasde over het land; **6** afzoeken; **7** bestrijken; **8** (volledig) winnen; **9** zich (snel) (voort)bewegen, vliegen: *~ along* voortsnellen; *~ by* (of: *past*) voorbijschieten; *~ down on* aanvallen; *~ on* voortijlen; *~ round* zich (met een zwaai) omdraaien; *~ from* (of: *out of*) *the room* de kamer uit stuiven; *~ into power* aan de macht komen; **10** zich uitstrekken: *~ down to the sea* zich uitstrekken tot aan de zee

²**sweep** [swie:p] *n* **1** (schoonmaak)beurt, opruiming: *make a clean ~* schoon schip maken; **2** veger, schoorsteenveger, straatveger; **3** veeg, haal (met een borstel), streek; **4** zwaai, slag, draai, bocht: *wide ~* wijde draai; *a ~ of mountain country* een stuk bergland, een berglandschap

sweeper [swie:pə] **1** veger, straatveger, schoorsteenveger; **2** tapijtenroller, (straat)veegmachine; **3** *(socc)* vrije verdediger, laatste man

sweeping [swie:ping] **1** veelomvattend, ingrijpend: *~ changes* ingrijpende veranderingen; **2** radicaal, veralgemenend: *~ condemnation* radicale veroordeling; **3** geweldig, kolossaal: *~ reductions* reusachtige prijsverlagingen

¹**sweet** [swie:t] *adj* zoet, lekker, heerlijk, geurig, melodieus: *~ nature* zachte natuur, beminnelijk karakter; *keep s.o. ~* iem te vriend houden; *be ~ on s.o.*

sweet 842

gek zijn op iem; *how ~ of you* wat aardig van je; *~ nothings* lieve woordjes; *have a ~ tooth* een zoetekauw zijn

²sweet [swie:t] *n* **1** lieveling, schatje^h; **2** snoepje^h, lekkers^h; **3** dessert^h, toetje^h

¹sweeten [swie:tn] *vb* **1** zoeten, zoet(er) maken; **2** verzachten, verlichten, veraangenamen; **3** sussen, omkopen, zoet houden

²sweeten [swie:tn] *vb* zoet(er) worden

sweetener [swie:tənə] **1** zoetstof; **2** smeergeld^h, fooi, steekpenning

sweetheart 1 schat; **2** liefje^h, vriend(in)

sweetie [swie:tie] **1** liefje^h, schatje^h; **2** snoepje^h

sweetness [swie:tnəs] zoetheid: *yesterday Sarah was all ~ and light* gisteren was Sarah een en al beminnelijkheid

sweet-talk vleien

¹swell [swel] *vb* (op)zwellen, bol gaan staan: *~ out* bollen; *~ up* (op)zwellen; *~ with pride* zwellen van trots

²swell [swel] *vb* doen zwellen, bol doen staan: *~ one's funds* wat bijverdienen

³swell [swel] *n* **1** zwelling, het zwellen, volheid; **2** deining

⁴swell [swel] *adj* voortreffelijk, prima: *a ~ teacher* een prima leraar

swelling [swelling] zwelling, het zwellen

sweltering [sweltəring] smoorheet, drukkend

¹swerve [swə:v] *vb* **1** zwenken, plotseling uitwijken: *~ from the path* van het pad afdwalen *(also fig)*; **2** afwijken, afdwalen

²swerve [swə:v] *vb* **1** doen zwenken, opzij doen gaan; **2** doen afwijken

³swerve [swə:v] *n* zwenking, wending

swift [swift] vlug, snel, rap

¹swig [swig] *vb* met grote teugen drinken

²swig [swig] *vb* naar binnen gieten, leegzuipen

³swig [swig] *n* slok

¹swill [swil] *vb* zuipen, gretig drinken

²swill [swil] *vb* **1** af-, door-, uitspoelen: *~ down* afspoelen; *~ out* uitspoelen; **2** opzuipen, gretig opdrinken: *~ down* opzuipen

³swill [swil] *n* **1** spoeling, spoelbeurt: *give a ~* uitspoelen; **2** afval^h; **3** varkensdraf, varkensvoer^h

¹swim [swim] *vb* **1** zwemmen *(also fig)*, baden; **2** vlotten, drijven, zweven: *~ming in butter* drijvend in de boter; **3** duizelen, draaierig worden: *my head is ~ming* het duizelt mij

²swim [swim] *vb* (over)zwemmen: *~ a river* een rivier overzwemmen

³swim [swim] *n* zwempartij: *have (of: go) for a ~* gaan zwemmen, een duik (gaan) nemen; *be in (of: out of) the ~* (niet) op de hoogte zijn, (niet) meedoen

swim-bladder zwemblaas

swimmer [swimmə] zwemmer

swimming [swimming] de zwemsport

swimming costume zwempak^h, badpak^h

swimmingly [swimminglie] vlot, moeiteloos, als

van een leien dakje: *everything goes on* (of: *off*) *~* alles loopt gesmeerd

swimming pool zwembad^h

swimming trunks zwembroek

¹swindle [swindl] *vb* oplichten, afzetten, bedriegen: *~ money out of s.o., ~ s.o. out of money* iem geld afhandig maken

²swindle [swindl] *n* (geval^h van) zwendel, bedrog^h, oplichterij

swindler [swindlə] zwendelaar(ster), oplichter

swine [swajn] zwijn^h, varken^h

¹swing [swing] *vb* **1** met veerkrachtige tred gaan, met zwaaiende gang lopen: *~ along* (of: *by, past*) met veerkrachtige gang voorbijlopen; **2** swingen; **3** opgehangen worden: *~ for it* ervoor gestraft worden; **4** slingeren, schommelen, zwaaien: *(fig) ~ into action* in actie komen; **5** draaien, (doen) zwenken: *~ round* (zich) omdraaien, omgooien; *~ to* dichtslaan *(door etc)*; **6** (op)hangen: *~ from the ceiling* aan het plafond hangen; **7** beïnvloeden, bepalen, manipuleren: *what swung it was the money* wat de doorslag gaf, was het geld; **8** wijsmaken: *you can't ~ that sort of stuff on her* zoiets maak je haar niet wijs

²swing [swing] *n* **1** schommel; **2** schommeling, zwaai, slingerbeweging, forse beweging: *~ in public opinion* kentering in de publieke opinie; **3** (fors) ritme^h; **4** swing(muziek); **5** actie, vaart, gang: *in full ~* in volle actie; *get into the ~ of things* op dreef komen; **6** inspiratie: *go with a ~* van een leien dakje gaan

swing bridge draaibrug

swing door klapdeur, tochtdeur

swingeing [swindzjing] geweldig, enorm: *~ cuts* zeer drastische bezuinigingen

swinging [swinging] **1** schommelend, slingerend, zwaaiend; **2** veerkrachtig: *~ step* veerkrachtige tred; **3** ritmisch, swingend

¹swipe [swajp] *n* **1** mep, (harde) slag: *have* (of: *take*) *a ~ at* uithalen naar; **2** verwijt^h, schimpscheut

²swipe [swajp] *vb* gappen, jatten, stelen

¹swirl [swə:l] *vb* **1** (doen) wervelen, (doen) dwarrelen: *~ about* rondwervelen, ronddwarrelen; **2** (doen) draaien

²swirl [swə:l] *n* **1** (draai)kolk, maalstroom; **2** werveling

¹swish [swisj] *n* **1** zwiep, slag; **2** zoevend geluid^h, geruis^h: *the ~ of a cane* het zoeven van een rietje

²swish [swisj] *adj* chic, modieus

³swish [swisj] *vb* **1** zoeven, suizen, ruisen: *~ past* voorbijzoeven; **2** zwiepen

⁴swish [swisj] *vb* doen zwiepen, slaan met: *~ing tail* zwiepende staart

¹Swiss [swis] *adj* Zwitsers

²Swiss [swis] *n* Zwitsers(e) || *~ roll* opgerolde cake met jam

¹switch [switsj] *n* **1** schakelaar; **2** *(railways)* wissel; **3** ommezwaai, verandering; **4** twijgje^h, loot; **5** (valse) haarlok, (valse) haarvlecht

²**switch** [switsj] *vb* **1** (om)schakelen, veranderen (van), overgaan (op): *~ places* van plaats veranderen; *~ off: a)* uitschakelen, afzetten; *b)* versuffen; *~ over: a)* overschakelen; *b) (radio, TV)* een ander kanaal kiezen; *~ through (to)* doorverbinden; *~ to* overgaan naar; **2** draaien, (doen) omzwaaien: *~ round* omdraaien

³**switch** [switsj] *vb* **1** verwisselen: *~ (a)round* verwisselen; **2** ontsteken

switchback 1 bochtige, heuvelige weg; **2** achtbaan

switchboard schakelbord[h]

switched-on 1 levendig, alert; **2** bij (de tijd), vooruitstrevend; **3** high

switch on 1 inschakelen, aanzetten, aandoen; **2** stimuleren, doen opleven, inspireren

switch-over 1 overschakeling, omschakeling; **2** overgang, verandering

¹**swivel** [swivl] *vb* (rond)draaien: *~ round in one's chair* ronddraaien in zijn stoel

²**swivel** [swivl] *n* (ketting)wartel

swivel chair draaistoel

swizz [swiz] **1** bedrog[h]; **2** ontgoocheling

swollen gezwollen *(also fig)*, opgeblazen

swollen-headed 1 verwaand, arrogant; **2** overmoedig

swoon [swoe:n] **1** in vervoering geraken; **2** bezwijmen, in onmacht vallen

¹**swoop** [swoe:p] *vb* stoten *(of bird of prey)*, (op een prooi) neerschieten, zich storten op *(also fig)*: *~ down* stoten

²**swoop** [swoe:p] *n* **1** duik; **2** veeg, haal: *at one (fell) ~* met één slag, in één klap

¹**swop** [swop] *n* ruil

²**swop** [swop] *vb* ruilen, uitwisselen: *~ for* (in)ruilen tegen

sword [so:d] zwaard[h] || *cross ~s (with)* in conflict komen (met); *put to the ~* over de kling jagen, vermoorden

swordfish zwaardvis

swordsman [so:dzmən] **1** zwaardvechter; **2** schermer

sworn [swo:n] **1** gezworen: *~ enemies* gezworen vijanden; **2** beëdigd: *~ statement* verklaring onder ede

¹**swot** [swot] *n* **1** blokker, stuud, studie(bol); **2** geblok[h], gezwoeg[h]

²**swot** [swot] *vb* blokken op: *~ sth. up, ~ up on sth.* iets erin stampen, iets repeteren: *~ for an exam* blokken voor een examen

sycamore [sikkəmo:] **1** esdoorn; **2** plataan[h]

syllable [silləbl] lettergreep

syllabus [silləbəs] samenvatting, leerplan[h]

sylph [silf] **1** luchtgeest; **2** tengere, elegante dame

symbol [simbl] symbool[h], (lees)teken[h]

symbolic(al) [simbollik(l)] symbolisch: *be ~ of* voorstellen

symbolism [simbəlizm] **1** symbolisme[h]; **2** symboliek, symbolische betekenis

symbolize [simbəlajz] symboliseren, symbool zijn van: *a white dove ~s peace* een witte duif is het symbool van vrede

symmetry [simmətrie] symmetrie

sympathetic [simpəθettik] **1** sympathiek, welwillend: *be (of: feel) ~ to/toward(s) s.o.* iem genegen zijn; **2** meevoelend, deelnemend

sympathize [simpəθajz] **1** sympathiseren: *~ with* sympathiseren met, meevoelen met; **2** meevoelen, deelneming voelen

sympathy [simpəθie] sympathie, genegenheid, deelneming: *letter of ~* condoléancebrief; *feel ~ for* meeleven met; *be in ~ with* gunstig staan tegenover, begrip hebben voor

symphony [simfənie] symfonie

symptom [simptəm] symptoom[h], (ziekte)verschijnsel[h], indicatie

symptomatic [simptəmættik] symptomatisch: *be ~ of* symptomatisch zijn voor, wijzen op

synagogue [sinnəgog] synagoge

sync [singk] synchronisatie: *be out of ~ with* niet gelijk lopen met

synchronic [singkronnik] synchroon

¹**synchronize** [singkrənajz] *vb* **1** synchroniseren *(also film)*, (doen) samenvallen (in de tijd): *~ with* synchroniseren met; **2** gelijk zetten *(clock)*

²**synchronize** [singkrənajz] *vb* **1** gelijktijdig gebeuren; samenvallen; **2** gelijk staan *(of clock)*

syndicate [sindikkət] **1** syndicaat[h], belangengroepering; **2** perssyndicaat[h], persbureau[h]

syndrome [sindroom] syndroom[h], complex[h] van kenmerkende (ziekte)verschijnselen

synod [sinnod] synode

synonym [sinnənim] synoniem[h]

synonymous [sinnonnimməs] synoniem

synopsis [sinnopsis] korte inhoud(sbeschrijving), samenvatting, overzicht[h]

syntax [sintæks] syntaxis, zinsbouw

synthesize [sinθəsajz] **1** maken, samenstellen; **2** bijeenvoegen, tot een geheel maken; **3** synthetisch bereiden, langs kunstmatige weg maken

synthetic [sinθettik] synthetisch, op synthese berustend; kunstmatig vervaardigd

syphilis [siffillis] syfilis

Syria [sirriə] Syrië

¹**Syrian** [sirriən] *adj* Syrisch

²**Syrian** [sirriən] *n* Syriër

¹**syringe** [sirrindzj] *n* (injectie)spuit

²**syringe** [sirrindzj] *vb* **1** inspuiten, een injectie geven; **2** uitspuiten, schoonspuiten

syrup [sirrəp] siroop; stroop

system [sistəm] **1** stelsel[h], systeem[h]; **2** geheel[h], samenstel[h]; **3** methode; **4** gestel[h], lichaam[h], lichaamsgesteldheid; **5** systematiek || *get sth. out of one's ~* iets verwerken

systematic [sistəmættik] systematisch, methodisch

systematize [sistəmətajz] systematiseren, tot een systeem maken

t

t [tie:] t, T || *cross one's t's (and dot one's i's)* de puntjes op de i zetten, op de details letten; *to a T* precies, tot in de puntjes

ta [ta:] *(inf, child language)* dank je

tab [tæb] **1** lus, ophanglusje[h]; **2** etiketje[h], label[h]; **3** klepje[h], flapje[h], lipje[h] *(of tin);* **4** *(inf)* rekening: *pick up the ~* betalen; **5** tabtoets: *keep ~s* (of: *a) ~ on* in de gaten houden

tabby [tæbie] **1** cyperse kat; **2** poes, vrouwtjeskat

tabernacle [tæbənækl] *(rel)* tabernakel[h], (veld)hut, tent

table [teebl] **1** tafel: *lay the ~* de tafel dekken; *at ~* aan tafel; **2** tabel, lijst, tafel: *learn one's ~s* de tafels van vermenigvuldiging leren; *turn the ~s (on s.o.)* de rollen omdraaien; *under the ~* dronken; *drink s.o. under the ~* iem onder de tafel drinken

tablecloth tafelkleed[h]

table-mat onderzetter

tablespoon opscheplepel, eetlepel

tablet [tæblət] **1** (gedenk)plaat, plaquette; **2** tablet[h], pil

table tennis tafeltennis[h]

tabloid [tæblojd] krant(je[h]) *(half size of regular newspaper)*

tabloid press sensatiepers

taboo [təboe:] taboe[h]: *put sth. under ~* iets taboe verklaren

tacit [tæsit] stilzwijgend

taciturn [tæsittə:n] zwijgzaam, (stil)zwijgend

¹tack [tæk] *n* **1** kopspijker(tje[h]), nageltje[h], *(Am)* punaise; **2** koers, boeg *(while navigating);* **3** koers(verandering), strategie, aanpak

²tack [tæk] *vb* **1** vastspijkeren: *(fig) ~ on* toevoegen aan; **2** rijgen

³tack [tæk] *vb* van koers veranderen, het anders aanpakken

¹tackle [tækl] *vb* **1** aanpakken, onder de knie proberen te krijgen: *~ a problem* een probleem aanpakken; **2** aanpakken, een hartig woordje spreken met; **3** tackelen, (de tegenstander) neerleggen

²tackle [tækl] *n* **1** takel; **2** *(sport)* tackle; **3** *(American football)* tackle, stopper; **4** uitrusting, benodigdheden; **5** *(shipp)* takelage, takelwerk[h]

tacky [tækie] **1** plakkerig, kleverig; **2** haveloos, sjofel; **3** smakeloos, ordinair

tact [tækt] tact

tactful [tæktfoel] tactvol, omzichtig

tactic [tæktik] **1** tactische zet, tactiek, manoeuvre; **2** *~s* tactiek

tactical [tæktikl] tactisch *(also mil);* diplomatiek

tactile [tæktajl] **1** tast-: *~ organs* tastorganen; **2** tastbaar, voelbaar

tactless [tæktləs] tactloos

tad [tæd] klein beetje[h]: *just a ~ depressing* een klein beetje deprimerend

Tadzhikistan [ta:dzjikkista:n] Tadzjikistan

¹tag [tæg] *n* **1** etiket[h] *(also fig),* insigne[h], label[h]; **2** stiftje[h] *(at end of shoe-lace etc);* **3** afgezaagd gezegde[h], cliché[h]; **4** flard, rafel, los uiteinde[h]; **5** klit haar

²tag [tæg] *vb (with along)* dicht volgen, slaafs achternalopen || *the children were ~ging along behind their teacher* de kinderen liepen (verveeld) achter hun onderwijzer aan

³tag [tæg] *vb* **1** van een etiket voorzien *(also fig),* etiketteren, merken; **2** vastknopen, toevoegen: *a label had been ~ged on at the top* aan de bovenkant was een kaartje vastgemaakt

¹tail [teel] *n* **1** staart; **2** onderste, achterste deel[h], uiteinde[h], pand[h], sleep *(of clothing),* staart *(of comet, aeroplane);* **3** *~s* munt(zijde); **4** *~s* rokkostuum[h] || *with one's ~ between one's legs* met hangende potjes; *turn ~ and run* hard weglopen; *be on s.o.'s ~* iem op de hielen zitten

²tail [teel] *vb* schaduwen, volgen

tailback file, verkeersopstopping

tailboard laadklep, achterklep

tailcoat jacquet[h], rok, rokkostuum[h]

¹tailgate *n (Am)* achterklep, laadklep, vijfde deur *(of car)*

²tailgate *vb* geen afstand houden, bumperkleven

tail light (rood) achterlicht[h]

tail off 1 geleidelijk afnemen, verminderen; **2** verstommen; **3** uiteenvallen

¹tailor [teelə] *n* kleermaker

²tailor [teelə] *vb* **1** maken *(clothes),* op maat snijden en aan elkaar naaien; **2** aanpassen, op maat knippen: *we ~ our insurance to your needs* wij stemmen onze verzekering af op uw behoeften

tailor-made 1 maat-: *~ suit* maatkostuum[h]; **2** geknipt, precies op maat

tailwind rugwind

¹taint [teent] *n* smet(je[h]), vlekje[h]

²taint [teent] *vb* bederven, rotten, ontaarden

³taint [teent] *vb* besmetten

Taiwan [tajwa:n] Taiwan

Taiwanese [tajwənnie:z] *(Taiwanese)* Taiwanees

¹take [teek] *vb* **1** nemen, grijpen, (beet)pakken: *(fig) ~ my grandfather, he is still working* neem nou mijn opa, die werkt nog steeds; **2** veroveren, innemen, vangen, *(chess, draughts)* slaan: *(chess) he took my bishop* hij sloeg mijn loper; *he took me unawares* hij verraste mij; **3** winnen, (be)halen; **4** nemen, zich verschaffen, gebruiken: *~ the bus* de bus nemen; *this seat is taken* deze stoel is bezet; *do you ~ sugar in your tea?* gebruikt u suiker in de thee?; **5** vereisen, in beslag nemen: *it won't ~ too much time* het zal niet al te veel tijd kosten; *have what it ~s* aan de eisen voldoen; **6** meenemen, brengen: *that bus will ~ you to the station* met die bus kom je bij het station; *~ s.o. around* iem rondleiden; *~ s.o. aside* iem apart nemen; **7** weghalen, wegnemen: *~ five from twelve* trek vijf van twaalf af; **8** krijgen, vatten, voelen: *she took an immediate dislike to him* zij kreeg onmiddellijk een hekel aan hem; *~ fire* vlam vatten; *~ it into one's head* het in zijn hoofd krijgen; **9** opnemen, noteren, meten: *let me ~ your temperature* laat mij even je temperatuur opnemen; **10** begrijpen: *~ for granted* als vanzelfsprekend aannemen; *I ~ it that he'll be back soon* ik neem aan dat hij gauw terugkomt; *~ it badly* het zich erg aantrekken; *what do you ~ me for?* waar zie je me voor aan?; **11** aanvaarden, accepteren: *~ sides* partij kiezen; *you may ~ it from me* je kunt van mij aannemen; **12** maken, doen, nemen *(school subject): ~ a decision* een besluit nemen; *~ an exam* een examen afleggen; *~ notes* aantekeningen maken; *she took a long time over it* zij deed er lang over; **13** raken, treffen; **14** behandelen *(problem etc);* **15** gebruiken, innemen: *~ it or leave it* graag of niet; *~ aback* verrassen, van zijn stuk brengen, overdonderen; *she was rather ~n by* (of: *with) it* zij was er nogal mee in haar schik; *~ it (up)on oneself* het op zich nemen, het wagen

²**take** [teek] *vb* **1** pakken, aanslaan, wortel schieten; **2** effect hebben, inslaan, slagen; **3** bijten *(of fish);* **4** worden: *he was taken ill* hij werd ziek; **5** vlam vatten: *Gerard ~s after his father* Gerard lijkt op zijn vader; *I took against him at first sight* ik mocht hem meteen al niet

³**take** [teek] *n* **1** vangst; **2** opbrengst, ontvangst(en); **3** *(film)* opname

take apart 1 uit elkaar halen, demonteren; **2** een vreselijke uitbrander geven

¹**takeaway** *n* afhaalrestaurant^h

²**takeaway** *adj* afhaal-, meeneem-

take away 1 aftrekken; **2** weghalen; **3** verminderen, verkleinen, afbreuk doen aan: *it takes sth. away from the total effect* het doet een beetje afbreuk aan het geheel

take back 1 terugbrengen, *(fig)* doen denken aan: *it took me back to my childhood* het deed me denken aan mijn jeugd; **2** terugnemen; intrekken

take down 1 afhalen, naar beneden halen; **2** opschrijven, noteren; **3** uit elkaar halen, demonteren, slopen

take-home afhaal-, meeneem-: *~ dinners* afhaalmaaltijden; *~ exam* tentamen dat je thuis maakt

take-home pay nettoloon^h

take in 1 in huis nemen, kamers verhuren aan; **2** naar binnen halen, meenemen; **3** omvatten, betreffen; **4** innemen *(clothing); (shipp)* oprollen *(sailing);* **5** begrijpen, doorzien; **6** (in zich) opnemen *(surroundings etc),* bekijken; **7** bedriegen; **8** geabonneerd zijn op

¹**take off** *vb* **1** uittrekken, uitdoen; **2** meenemen,

wegvoeren: *she took the children off to bed* zij bracht de kinderen naar bed; **3** afhalen, weghalen, verwijderen; **4** verlagen *(price);* **5** nadoen, imiteren; **6** vrij nemen: *take oneself off* ervandoor gaan, zich uit de voeten maken

²**take off** *vb* **1** zich afzetten; **2** opstijgen, starten *(also fig; of project etc);* **3** (snel) populair worden, succes hebben

take-off 1 start, het opstijgen, vertrek^h; **2** parodie, imitatie

¹**take on** *vb* **1** op zich nemen, als uitdaging accepteren; **2** krijgen, aannemen *(colour),* overnemen; in dienst nemen; **3** het opnemen tegen, vechten tegen; **4** aan boord nemen

²**take on** *vb* tekeergaan, zich aanstellen

take out 1 mee naar buiten nemen, mee uit nemen, naar buiten brengen; *(Am) ~ food* een afhaalmaaltijd meenemen; *take s.o. out for a walk* (of: *meal)* iem mee uit wandelen nemen, iem mee uit eten nemen; **2** verwijderen, uithalen; **3** te voorschijn halen; **4** nemen, aanschaffen: *~ an insurance (policy)* een verzekering afsluiten; **5** buiten gevecht stellen *(opponent): take it out of s.o.* veel van iemands krachten vergen; *don't take it out on him* reageer het niet op hem af

takeover overname

take over 1 overnemen, het heft in handen nemen; **2** navolgen, overnemen

take to 1 beginnen te, gaan doen aan, zich toeleggen op; **2** aardig vinden, mogen: *he did not take kindly to it* hij moest er niet veel van hebben; **3** de wijk nemen naar, vluchten naar: *~ one's bed* het bed houden

¹**take up** *vb* **1** optillen, oppakken: *~ the hatchet* de strijdbijl opgraven; **2** absorberen *(also fig),* opnemen, in beslag nemen: *it nearly took up all the room* het nam bijna alle ruimte in beslag; **3** oppikken *(passengers);* **4** ter hand nemen, gaan doen aan: *~ a cause* een zaak omhelzen; *~ gardening* gaan tuinieren; **5** vervolgen *(story),* hervatten; **6** aannemen, aanvaarden, ingaan op: *he took me up on my offer* hij nam mijn aanbod aan; **7** innemen *(position),* aannemen *(attitude): I'll take you up on that* daar zal ik je aan houden

²**take up** *vb* verder gaan *(of story, chapter)* || *~ with* bevriend raken met

taking [teeking] *~s* verdiensten, recette, ontvangsten || *for the ~* voor het grijpen

talcum powder talkpoeder^h

tale [teel] **1** verhaal(tje)^h: *thereby hangs a ~* daar zit een (heel) verhaal aan vast; *tell ~s* kletsen, roddelen; **2** sprookje^h, legende; **3** leugen, smoes(je^h); **4** gerucht^h, roddel, praatje^h

talent [tælənt] **1** talent^h, (natuurlijke) begaafdheid, gave; **2** talent^h, begaafde persoon

talented [tæləntid] getalenteerd, talentvol

taleteller 1 kwaadspreker; **2** roddelaar(ster)

¹**talk** [to:k] *vb* **1** spreken, praten: *now you're ~ing* zo mag ik het horen, dat klinkt al (een stuk) beter; *you*

can (of: *can't*) ~ moet je horen wie het zegt; *do the ~ing* het woord voeren; *(at beginning of sentence) ~ing of plants* over planten gesproken; **2** roddelen, praten: *people will* ~ de mensen roddelen toch (wel); ~ *to s.o.* eens ernstig praten met iem
²**talk** [to:k] *vb* **1** spreken (over), discussiëren over, bespreken: ~ *s.o.'s head off* iem de oren van het hoofd praten; ~ *one's way out of sth.* zich ergens uitpraten; **2** zeggen, uiten: ~ *s.o. round to sth.* iem ompraten tot iets; ~ *s.o. into (doing) sth.* iem overhalen iets te doen; ~ *s.o. out of (doing) sth.* iem iets uit het hoofd praten
³**talk** [to:k] *n* **1** praatje^h, lezing *(on radio);* **2** gesprek^h: *have a* ~ *(to, with s.o.)* (met iem) spreken; **3** ~s besprekingen, onderhandelingen; **4** gepraat^h; **5** gerucht^h, praatjes: *there is* ~ *of* er is sprake van (dat), het gerucht gaat dat; **6** geklets^h: *be all* ~ praats hebben *(but achieving nothing)*
talk about 1 spreken over, bespreken, het hebben over: ~ *problems!* over problemen gesproken!; *know what one is talking about* weten waar men het over heeft; **2** roddelen over: *be talked about* over de tong gaan; **3** spreken van, zijn voornemen uiten (om): *they're talking about emigrating to Australia* zij overwegen naar Australië te emigreren
talkative [to:kətiv] praatgraag, praatziek
talk down neerbuigend praten: ~ *to one's audience* afdalen tot het niveau van zijn gehoor
talking point discussiepunt^h
talking-to uitbrander: *(give s.o.) a good* ~ een hartig woordje (met iem spreken)
talk of 1 spreken over, bespreken: *(at beginning of sentence)* talking of plants over planten gesproken; **2** spreken van, het hebben over: ~ *doing sth.* van plan zijn iets te doen
talk over (uitvoerig) spreken over, uitvoerig bespreken: *talk things over with s.o.* de zaak (uitvoerig) met iem bespreken
talk show praatprogramma^h, talkshow *(on TV)*
tall [to:l] **1** lang *(of person),* groot; hoog *(of tree, mast etc):* *Peter is 6 feet* ~ Peter is 1,80 m (lang); *the pole is 10 feet* ~ de paal is 3 m hoog; **2** overdreven, te groot: ~ *order* onredelijke eis; ~ *story* sterk verhaal; ~ *talk* opschepperij
¹**tally** [tælie] *vb* (with *with*) overeenkomen (met), gelijk zijn, kloppen
²**tally** [tælie] *n* **1** rekening; **2** inkeping; **3** label^h, etiket^h, merk^h; **4** score(bord^h); **5** aantekening: *keep (a)* ~ *(of)* aantekening houden (van)
talon [tælən] klauw *(of bird of prey)*
¹**tame** [teem] *adj* **1** tam, mak; **2** meegaand; **3** oninteressant, saai
²**tame** [teem] *vb* temmen, *(fig)* bedwingen
tamper with 1 knoeien met, verknoeien: ~ *documents* documenten vervalsen; **2** zich bemoeien met; **3** komen aan, zitten aan; **4** omkopen
¹**tan** [tæn] *vb* bruin worden *(sun)*
²**tan** [tæn] *vb* **1** bruinen *(sun);* **2** looien, tanen || ~ *s.o.'s hide,* ~ *the hide off s.o.* iem afranselen

³**tan** [tæn] *adj* geelbruin; zongebruind
tandem [tændəm] tandem || *in* ~ achter elkaar
tang [tæng] **1** scherpe (karakteristieke) lucht, indringende geur; **2** scherpe smaak; smaakje^h *(fig),* zweem, tikje^h
tangent [tændzjənt] raaklijn, tangens || *fly* (of: *go) off at a* ~ een gedachtesprong maken, plotseling van koers veranderen
tangerine (orange) [tændzjərie:n] mandarijn(tje^h)
tangible [tændzjibl] tastbaar *(also fig),* voelbaar, concreet
¹**tangle** [tænggl] *n* **1** knoop, klit *(in hair, wool etc):* *in a* ~ in de war; **2** verwarring, wirwar
²**tangle** [tænggl] *vb* **1** in de knoop raken, klitten; **2** in verwarring raken, in de war raken: ~ *with s.o.* verwikkeld raken in een ruzie met iem
tank [tængk] **1** (voorraad)tank, reservoir^h; **2** tank, pantserwagen
tanker [tængkə] tanker
tank up 1 tanken, (bij)vullen; **2** zich volgieten, zuipen
tannery [tænərie] looierij
tannin [tænin] looizuur^h, tannine
tanning [tæning] pak^h slaag: *give him a good ~!* geef hem een goed pak slaag!
tantalize [tæntəlajz] **1** doen watertanden, kwellen; **2** verwachtingen wekken
tantalizing [tæntəlajzing] (heel) verleidelijk, aantrekkelijk
tantamount [tæntəmaunt] *(with to)* gelijk(waardig) (aan): *be* ~ *to* neerkomen op
tantrum [tæntrəm] woede-uitbarsting, driftbui *(pl, of small child):* *get into a* ~, *throw a* ~ een woedeaanval krijgen
¹**tap** [tæp] *n* **1** kraan, tap(kraan), stop *(of vat):* *turn the* ~ *on* doe de kraan open; *on* ~ uit het vat, van de tap, *(fig)* meteen voorradig, zo voorhanden; **2** tik(je^h), klopje^h: *a* ~ *on a shoulder* een schouderklopje; **3** afluisterapparatuur
²**tap** [tæp] *vb* **1** doen tikken: ~ *s.o. on the shoulder* iem op de schouder kloppen; **2** (af)tappen, afnemen: *her telephone was ~ped* haar telefoon werd afgeluisterd; *(fig)* ~ *a person for information* informatie aan iem ontfutselen; **3** openen, aanbreken *(also fig),* aanboren, aansnijden, *(fig also)* gebruiken: ~ *new sources of energy* nieuwe energiebronnen aanboren
³**tap** [tæp] *vb* tikken, kloppen: ~ *at* (of: *on) the door* op de deur tikken
¹**tape** [teep] *n* **1** lint^h, band^h, koord^h: *insulating* ~ isolatieband; **2** meetlint^h, centimeter; **3** (magneet)band, geluidsband, videoband; **4** (plak)band^h: *adhesive* ~ plakband
²**tape** [teep] *vb* opnemen, een (band)opname maken (van)
³**tape** [teep] *vb* **1** (vast)binden, inpakken, samenbinden; **2** *(Am)* verbinden, met verband omwikkelen: *his knee was ~d up* zijn knie zat in het verband;

have s.o. ~d iem helemaal doorhebben

tape measure meetlint^h, centimeter

¹taper [teepə] *vb* **1** taps toelopen, geleidelijk smaller worden: *this stick ~s off to a point* deze stok loopt scherp toe in een punt; **2** *(with off)* (geleidelijk) kleiner worden, verminderen, afnemen

²taper [teepə] *vb* smal(ler) maken, taps doen toelopen

³taper [teepə] *n* **1** (dunne) kaars; **2** (was)pit, lontje^h; **3** (geleidelijke) versmalling *(eg of long object)*, spits toelopend voorwerp^h

tape recorder bandrecorder

tapestry [tæpistrie] **1** wandtapijt^h; **2** bekledingsstof van muren

tapeworm lintworm

taproom tapperij, gelagkamer

¹tar [ta:] *n* teer^h

²tar [ta:] *vb* teren, met teer insmeren, *(fig)* zwartmaken: *~ and feather s.o.* iem met teer en veren bedekken *(as punishment)*

tarantula [tərǽntjoelə] vogelspin; tarantula

tardy [ta:die] **1** traag, sloom: *~ progress* langzame vooruitgang; *he is ~ in paying* hij is slecht van betalen; **2** (te) laat; **3** weifelend, onwillig

tare [teə] **1** tarra(gewicht^h) *(difference between gross and net weight);* **2** leeg gewicht^h *(of lorry etc)*

¹target [ta:git] *n* **1** doel^h, roos, schietschijf, *(fig)* streven^h, doeleinde^h: *on ~* op de goede weg, in de goede richting; **2** doelwit^h *(of mockery, criticism)*, mikpunt^h

²target [ta:git] *vb* mikken op: *he ~s his audiences carefully* hij neemt zijn publiek zorgvuldig op de korrel

tariff [tærif] (tol)tarief^h, invoerrechten, uitvoerrechten: *postal ~s* posttarieven

¹tarnish [ta:nisj] *vb* dof worden, verkleuren, aanslaan *(of metal); (fig)* aangetast worden

²tarnish [ta:nisj] *vb* dof maken, doen aanslaan, *(fig)* bezoedelen: *a ~ed reputation* een bezoedelde naam

³tarnish [ta:nisj] *n* glansverlies^h, dofheid, *(fig)* smet

tarry [tærie] **1** treuzelen, op zich laten wachten; **2** (ver)blijven, zich ophouden

¹tart [ta:t] *adj* **1** scherp(smakend), zuur, wrang; **2** scherp, sarcastisch

²tart [ta:t] *n (inf)* **1** slet, del; **2** (vruchten)taart(je^h)

tartan [ta:tn] **1** Schotse ruit; **2** doek^h in Schotse ruit; **3** tartan^h, (geruite) Schotse wollen stof

tartar [ta:tə] **1** *Tartar* Tataar; **2** woesteling; **3** tandsteen

tart up opdirken, optutten: *~ a house* een huis kitscherig inrichten

task [ta:sk] taak, karwei^h, opdracht || *take s.o. to ~ (for)* iem onderhanden nemen (vanwege)

task force speciale eenheid *(of army, police)*, gevechtsgroep

taskmaster opdrachtgever: *a hard ~* een harde leermeester

¹taste [teest] *n* **1** kleine hoeveelheid, hapje^h, slokje^h, beetje^h, tikkeltje^h: *have a ~ of this cake* neem eens

een hapje van deze cake; **2** ervaring, ondervinding: *give s.o. a ~ of the whip* iem de zweep laten voelen; **3** smaak, smaakje^h, voorkeur, genoegen^h: *leave a unpleasant ~ in the mouth* een onaangename nasmaak hebben *(also fig); everyone to his ~* ieder zijn meug; *add sugar to ~* suiker toevoegen naar smaak; **4** smaak, smaakzin, schoonheidszin, gevoel^h *(for proper behaviour, fashion, style etc): in good ~: a)* smaakvol; *b)* behoorlijk; *sweet to the ~* zoet van smaak

²taste [teest] *vb* smaken: *the pudding ~d of garlic* de pudding smaakte naar knoflook

³taste [teest] *vb* **1** proeven, keuren; **2** ervaren, ondervinden: *~ defeat* het onderspit delven

tasteful [teestfoel] smaakvol

tasteless [teestləs] **1** smaakloos, mbt water enz.; **2** smakeloos, van een slechte smaak

tasty [teestie] **1** smakelijk; **2** hartig

ta-ta [təta:] dáág

tatter [tætə] flard, lomp, vod^h: *in ~s* aan flarden, kapot *(also fig)*

tattered [tætəd] **1** haveloos, aan flarden *(clothes);* **2** in lompen gekleed *(pers)*

¹tattle [tætl] *n* **1** geklets^h, geroddel^h; **2** geklik^h

²tattle [tætl] *vb* kletsen, roddelen

¹tattoo [tætoe:] *n* **1** tatoeage; **2** taptoe *(drumbeat or clarion call): beat the ~* taptoe slaan; **3** tromgeroffel^h

²tattoo [tætoe:] *vb* tatoeëren

tatty [tætie] slordig, slonzig, sjofel

¹taunt [to:nt] *vb* hekelen: *they ~ed him into losing his temper* ze tergden hem tot hij in woede uitbarstte

²taunt [to:nt] *n* hatelijke opmerking, bespotting: *~s* spot, hoon

Taurus [to:rəs] *(astrology)* (de) Stier

taut [to:t] strak, gespannen

tavern [tævən] taveerne, herberg

tawdry [to:drie] opzichtig, smakeloos, opgedirkt

¹tax [tæks] *n* **1** last, druk, gewicht^h: *be a ~ on* veel vergen van; **2** belasting, rijksbelasting: *value added ~* belasting op de toegevoegde waarde, btw

²tax [tæks] *vb* **1** belasten, belastingen opleggen; **2** veel vergen van, zwaar op de proef stellen: *~ your memory* denk eens goed na

taxation [tækseesjən] **1** belasting(gelden); **2** belastingsysteem^h

tax cut belastingverlaging

tax evasion belastingontduiking

tax-free belastingvrij

¹taxi [tæksie] *n (also ~es)* taxi

²taxi [tæksie] *vb* **1** (doen) taxiën; **2** in een taxi rijden (vervoeren)

taxman **1** belastingontvanger; **2** belastingen, fiscus

taxpayer belastingbetaler

tax with 1 beschuldigen van, ten laste leggen; **2** rekenschap vragen voor, op het matje roepen wegens

T.B. *tuberculosis* tb(c)^h

tea [tie:] **1** thee; lichte maaltijd om 5 uur 's middags; theevisite; **2** theeplant; theebladeren

teabag theezakje^h, theebuiltje^h

^1**teach** [tie:tsj] *vb* onderwijzen, leren, lesgeven: ~ *s.o. chess,* ~ *chess to s.o.* iem leren schaken; *John teaches me (how) to swim* John leert mij zwemmen; ~ *school* onderwijzer zijn

^2**teach** [tie:tsj] *vb* **1** leren, afleren: *I will* ~ *him to betray our plans* ik zal hem leren onze plannen te verraden; **2** doen inzien, leren: *experience taught him that* … bij ondervinding wist hij dat …

teacher [tie:tsjə] **1** leraar, docent(e); **2** onderwijzer(es)

teaching [tie:tsjing] **1** het lesgeven; **2** onderwijs^h; **3** leer, leerstelling

tea cloth theedoek, droogdoek

teacup theekopje^h

teak [tie:k] teakhout^h

^1**team** [tie:m] *n* **1** team^h, (sport)ploeg, elftal^h; **2** span^h *(of draught animals)*

^2**team** [tie:m] *vb* (with *up*) een team vormen: ~ *up with* samenwerken met, samenspelen met

team-mate teamgenoot

team spirit teamgeest

teamster [tie:mstə] **1** voerman, menner; **2** vrachtwagenchauffeur

teamwork groepsarbeid; samenwerking, samenspel^h

^1**tear** [tiə] *n* **1** traan: *move s.o. to* ~s iem aan het huilen brengen; *shed* ~s *over* tranen storten over *(sth not worthy of tears)*; **2** drup(pel)

^2**tear** [teə] *vb* **1** scheuren, stuk gaan: *silk* ~s *easily* zijde scheurt makkelijk; **2** rukken, trekken: ~ *at sth.* aan iets rukken; **3** rennen, *(fig)* stormen, vliegen: *the boy tore across the street* de jongen stormde de straat over

^3**tear** [teə] *vb* **1** (ver)scheuren *(also fig): the girl tore a hole in her coat* het meisje scheurde haar jas; ~ *up* verscheuren, *(fig)* tenietdoen; *(fig) be torn between love and hate* tussen liefde en haat in tweestrijd staan; ~ *in half* (of: *two*) in tweeën scheuren; **2** (uit)rukken, (uit)trekken: ~ *down a building* een gebouw afbreken

^4**tear** [teə] *n* **1** scheur; **2** flard

tear apart 1 verscheuren *(fig);* zich vernietigend uitlaten over; **2** overhoop halen; **3** *(inf)* uitschelden || *the critics tore his latest novel apart* de critici schreven zijn laatste roman de grond in

tearaway herrieschopper

tear away aftrekken, wegtrekken, afscheuren, *(fig)* verwijderen: *(fig) I could hardly tear myself away from the party* ik kon het feest maar met tegenzin verlaten

tearful [tjəfoel] **1** huilend; **2** huilerig

tear into in alle hevigheid aanvallen, heftig tekeergaan tegen

tear-jerker [tjədzjə:kə] tranentrekker, smartlap, sentimentele film, sentimenteel liedje^h

tear off afrukken, aftrekken, afscheuren, *(fig)* verwijderen

tearoom tearoom, theesalon

^1**tease** [tie:z] *vb* **1** plagen, lastig vallen, pesten: ~ *s.o. for sth.* iem lastig vallen om; **2** opgewonden maken, opwinden; **3** ontlokken: ~ *out* ontwarren *(also fig)*

^2**tease** [tie:z] *n* **1** plaaggeest, kwelgeest; **2** plagerij, geplaag^h; flirt

teaser [tie:zə] **1** plaaggeest, plager; **2** moeilijke vraag, probleemgeval^h

teaspoon theelepeltje^h

teat [tie:t] **1** tepel; **2** speen

tea towel theedoek, droogdoek

technical [teknikl] technisch

technicality [teknikælittie] **1** technische term; **2** technisch detail^h, (klein) formeel punt^h: *he lost the case on a* ~ hij verloor de zaak door een vormfout

technician [teknisjən] technicus, specialist: *dental* ~ tandtechnicus

technique [teknie:k] techniek, werkwijze, vaardigheid

technology [teknollədzjie] technologie, techniek

tedious [tie:diəs] vervelend, langdradig, saai

tedium [tie:diəm] **1** verveling; **2** saaiheid, eentonigheid, langdradigheid

tee [tie:] *(golf)* tee || *to a* ~ precies, tot in de puntjes

teem [tie:m] **1** wemelen, krioelen, tieren: ~*ing with* krioelen van; *his head* ~s *with new ideas* zijn hoofd zit vol nieuwe ideeën; *those forests* ~ *with snakes* die bossen krioelen van de slangen; **2** stortregenen, gieten: *it was teeming down* (of: *with*) *rain* het goot

teen [tie:n] **1** tiener; **2** ~s tienerjaren: *boy* (of: *girl*) *in his* (of: *her*) ~s tiener

teenager [tie:needzjə] tiener

teeny(-weeny) [tie:niewie:nie] piepklein

teeter [tie:tə] **1** wankelen, waggelen: *(fig)* ~ *on the edge of collapse* op de rand van de ineenstorting staan; **2** wippen, op de wip spelen

teethe [tie:ð] tandjes krijgen *(esp milk teeth)*

teething troubles kinderziekten *(fig)*

teetotaller [tie:tootələ] geheelonthouder

telebanking [tellibængking] het telebankieren

telecommunications [tellikkəmjoe:nikkeesjənz] **1** telecommunicatietechniek; **2** (telecommunicatie)verbindingen

telefax [tellifæks] telefax

telegram [telligræm] telegram^h: *by* ~ per telegram

telegraph [telligra:f] telegraaf, telegrafie: *by* ~ per telegraaf

telemarketing [tellimma:kəting] telefonische verkoop, telemarketing

telepathy [tilleppəθie] telepathie

^1**telephone** [telliffoon] *n* telefoon, (telefoon)toestel^h: *by* ~ telefonisch; *on* (of: *over*) *the* ~ telefonisch

^2**telephone** [telliffoon] *vb* telefoneren, (op)bellen: *he has just* ~d *through from Beirut* hij heeft zojuist uit Beiroet opgebeld

telephone booth telefooncel

telephone call telefoongesprek^h

telephone directory telefoongids

teleprinter [telliprintə] telex, telexapparaat^h: *by* ~

per telex

¹telescope [tẹlliskoop] *n* telescoop, (astronomische) verrekijker

²telescope [tẹlliskoop] *vb* **1** in elkaar schuiven; **2** ineengedrukt worden: *two cars ~d together in the accident* twee auto's werden bij het ongeval ineengedrukt

³telescope [tẹlliskoop] *vb* in elkaar schuiven, ineendrukken, samendrukken

telescopic [tẹlliskọppik] telescopisch, ineenschuifbaar: *~ lens* telelens

teleselling [tẹllissẹlling] telefonische verkoop, telemarketing

teleshopping [tẹllisjọpping] het telewinkelen, het teleshoppen

television [tẹllivvizjən] televisie, tv(-toestel[h]): *watch ~ tv* kijken; *on (the) ~* op de televisie

television broadcast televisie-uitzending

television commercial reclamespot

television set televisietoestel[h]

teleworking [tẹlliwwɔ:king] telewerken[h], het thuiswerken

¹telex [tẹlleks] *n* **1** telex, telexbericht[h]: *by ~* per telex; **2** telexdienst

²telex [tẹlleks] *vb* telexen

¹tell [tel] *vb* **1** spreken, zeggen, vertellen: *as far as we can ~* voor zover we weten; *you can never ~* je weet maar nooit; **2** het verklappen, het verraden: *don't ~!* verklap het niet!; *~ on s.o.* iem verklikken; **3** (mee)tellen, meespelen, van belang zijn: *his age will ~ against him* zijn leeftijd zal in zijn nadeel pleiten

²tell [tel] *vb* **1** vertellen, zeggen, spreken: *~ a secret* een geheim verklappen; *(inf) ~ s.o. where he gets off, ~ s.o. to get off* iem op zijn plaats, iem op zijn nummer zetten; *you're ~ing me!* vertel mij wat!; **2** weten, kennen, uitmaken: *can you ~ the difference?* weet (of: zie) jij het verschil?; *can she ~ the time yet?* kan ze al klok kijken?; *there is no ~ing what will happen* je weet maar nooit wat er gebeurt; *how can I ~ if (of: whether) it is true or not?* hoe kan ik weten of het waar is of niet?; **3** onderscheiden, uit elkaar houden: *~ truth from lies* de waarheid van leugens onderscheiden; **4** zeggen, bevelen, waarschuwen: *I told you so!* ik had het je nog gezegd!; *all told* alles bij elkaar (genomen), over het geheel; *I'll ~ you what: let's call him now* weet je wat?: laten we hem nu opbellen; *(inf) ~ s.o. off for sth.* iem om iets berispen

teller [tẹllə] **1** verteller; **2** (stemmen)teller *(eg in House of Commons);* **3** kassier

telling [tẹlling] **1** treffend, raak: *a ~ blow* een rake klap; **2** veelbetekenend, veelzeggend

tell-tale 1 roddelaar(ster); **2** verklikker; **3** teken[h], aanduiding: *(fig) a ~ nod* een veelbetekenend knikje

telly [tẹllie] teevee, tv

temerity [timmẹrrittie] roekeloosheid

¹temp [temp] *n, temporary employee* tijdelijk mede-

werk(st)er, uitzendkracht

²temp [temp] *vb* als uitzendkracht werken, werken via een uitzendbureau

¹temper [tempə] *n* **1** humeur[h], stemming: *be in a bad ~* in een slecht humeur zijn, de pest in hebben; **2** kwade bui; **3** driftbui, woedeaanval: *fly (of: get) into a ~* een woedeaanval krijgen; **4** opvliegend karakter[h], drift: *have a ~* opvliegend zijn; **5** kalmte, beheersing: *keep one's ~* zijn kalmte bewaren

²temper [tempə] *vb* temperen, matigen

temperament [tempərəmənt] **1** temperament[h] *(also fig)*, aard, gestel[h], vurigheid; **2** humeurigheid

temperamental [tempərəmẹntl] **1** natuurlijk, aangeboren; **2** grillig, onberekenbaar, vol kuren

temperance [tempərəns] **1** gematigdheid, matigheid; zelfbeheersing; **2** geheelonthouding

temperate [tempərət] **1** matig, gematigd: *~ zone* gematigde luchtstreek; **2** met zelfbeheersing

temperature [tempərətsjə] temperatuur, verhoging, koorts: *have (of: run) a ~* verhoging hebben

tempest [tempist] (hevige) storm *(also fig)*

tempestuous [tempẹstjoeəs] stormachtig *(also fig)*, hartstochtelijk

template [templit] mal, sjabloon

temple [templ] **1** tempel, kerk; **2** slaap *(on head)*

tempo [tẹmpoo] tempo[h]

temporary [tempərərie] tijdelijk, voorlopig: *buildings* noodgebouwen; *~ employment agency* uitzendbureau

tempt [tempt] **1** verleiden, in verleiding brengen: *I am ~ed to believe that it's true* ik ben geneigd te geloven dat het waar is; **2** tarten, tergen: *~ Providence* het noodlot tarten

temptation [temptẹẹsjən] **1** verleidelijkheid; **2** verleiding, verzoeking: *lead us not into ~* leid ons niet in verzoeking

tempting [tempting] verleidelijk

ten [ten] tien: *I bet you ~ to one she'll come* ik wed tien tegen één dat ze komt

tenable [tẹnnəbl] verdedigbaar, houdbaar

tenacious [tinnẹẹsjəs] **1** vasthoudend, hardnekkig; **2** krachtig, goed *(of memory)*

tenacity [tinặsittie] **1** vasthoudendheid, hardnekkigheid; **2** kracht *(of memory)*

tenancy [tẹnnənsie] **1** huur(termijn), pacht(termijn); **2** bewoning, gebruik[h], genot[h]

tenant [tẹnnənt] **1** huurder, pachter; **2** bewoner

¹tend [tend] *vb* **1** gaan *(in certain direction)*, zich richten, zich uitstrekken: *prices are ~ing downwards* de prijzen dalen; **2** neigen, geneigd zijn: *John ~s to get angry* John wordt gauw boos; *it ~s to get hot in here in summer* het wordt hier vaak erg warm in de zomer; *~ to* zwemen naar, *(Am)* aandacht besteden aan

²tend [tend] *vb* **1** verzorgen, zorgen voor, passen op: *~ sheep* schapen hoeden; **2** *(Am)* bedienen: *who's ~ing bar?* wie staat er achter de bar?

tendency [tẹndənsie] **1** neiging, tendens, trend; **2** aanleg: *he has a ~ to grow fat* hij heeft een aanleg tot dik worden

tendentious [tendensjəs] partijdig, vooringenomen

¹tender [tendə] *adj* 1 mals *(of meat);* 2 gevoelig: ~ *spot* gevoelige plek; 3 broos, teer; 4 liefhebbend, teder; 5 pijnlijk, zeer: ~ *place* gevoelige plek; 6 jong, onbedorven: *of ~ age* van prille leeftijd

²tender [tendə] *vb* inschrijven: ~ *for the building of a road* inschrijven op de aanleg van een weg

³tender [tendə] *vb* aanbieden: ~ *one's resignation* zijn ontslag indienen

⁴tender [tendə] *n* 1 verzorger, oppasser; tender; 2 tender *(of locomotive);* 3 offerte, inschrijving: *put out to* ~ aanbesteden (voor inschrijving)

tenderfoot groentjeʰ, nieuwkomer

tender-hearted teerhartig

tendon [tendən] (spier)pees

tendril [tendril] 1 (hecht)rank *(of plant);* 2 streng, sliert

tenement [tennimmənt] 1 pachtgoedʰ; 2 (huur)kamer, appartementʰ

tenement house huurkazerne, etagewoning, flatgebouwʰ

tenfold [tenfoold] tienvoudig

tenner [tennə] tientjeʰ, (briefjeʰ van) tien pond (dollar)

tennis [tennis] tennis(spel)ʰ

tennis court tennisbaan

tenor [tennə] 1 tenor *(singer, part, voice, instrument);* 2 gang *(of one's life),* loop, verloopʰ, (algemene) richting; 3 teneur *(of text, conversation),* strekking: *get the ~ of what is being said* in grote lijnen begrijpen wat er wordt gezegd

¹tense [tens] *n* tijd, werkwoordstijd

²tense [tens] *adj* gespannen, in spanning: *a face ~ with anxiety* een van angst vertrokken gezicht

³tense [tens] *vb* (with *up)* zenuwachtig worden

⁴tense [tens] *vb* (with *up)* gespannen maken: ~ *one's muscles* zijn spieren spannen

tension [tensjən] 1 spanning, gespannenheid, strakheid *(eg of rope),* zenuwachtigheid: *suffer from nervous ~* overspannen zijn; 2 gespannen toestand: *racial ~s* rassenonlusten; 3 trekspanning *(of solid substance);* 4 (elektrische) spanning

tent [tent] tent: *(also fig) pitch one's ~* zijn tent opslaan

tentacle [tentəkl] tentakel, tastorgaanʰ, voelspriet, vangarm

tentative [tentətiv] 1 voorlopig: *a ~ conclusion* een voorzichtige conclusie; 2 aarzelend

tenterhooks: *on ~* ongerust, in gespannen verwachting

tenth [tenθ] tiende, tiende deelʰ

tenuous [tenjoeəs] 1 dun, (rag)fijn; 2 (te) subtiel; 3 vaag, zwak: *a ~ argument* een zwak argument

tenure [tenjə] 1 pachtregeling; 2 ambtstermijn; 3 beschikkingsrechtʰ, eigendomsrechtʰ; 4 vaste aanstelling

tepid [teppid] lauw, halfwarm, *(fig)* koel, mat

term [tə:m] 1 onderwijsperiode, trimesterʰ, semesterʰ, kwartaalʰ; 2 termijn, periode, duur, tijd, ambtstermijn, zittingsperiode *(of court of law, parliament),* huurtermijn, aflossingstermijn, (af)betalingstermijn: *in the short ~* op korte termijn; 3 *(maths)* term, lidʰ; 4 (vak)term, woordʰ, uitdrukking, ~s bewoordingen, manier van uitdrukken: *tell s.o. in no uncertain ~s* in niet mis te verstane bewoordingen te kennen geven; 5 ~*s* voorwaarden *(of agreement, contract),* condities, bepalingen: ~*s of reference* taakomschrijving *(eg of committee); on equal ~s* als gelijken; *to be on friendly ~s with s.o.* op vriendschappelijke voet met iem staan; *come to ~s with* zich verzoenen met, zich neerleggen bij; *in ~s of money* financieel gezien, wat geld betreft; *they are not on speaking ~s* ze spreken niet meer met elkaar, ze hebben onenigheid

¹terminal [tə:minl] *adj* 1 eind-, slot-, laatste: ~ *station* eindstation; 2 terminaal, ongeneeslijk; 3 van (onderwijs)periode, termijn-: ~ *examinations* trimesterexamens, semesterexamens

²terminal [tə:minl] *n* 1 contactklem; 2 eindpuntʰ, eindhalte, eindstationʰ; 3 (computer)terminal

¹terminate [tə:minneet] *vb* eindigen, aflopen

²terminate [tə:minneet] *vb* beëindigen, eindigen, een eind maken aan, (af)sluiten: ~ *a contract* een contract opzeggen; ~ *a pregnancy* een zwangerschap onderbreken

terminology [tə:minnollədzjie] terminologie, (systeemʰ van) vaktermen

terminus [tə:minnəs] eindpuntʰ *(of bus route, railway line),* eindstationʰ, eindhalte

termite [tə:majt] termiet

¹terrace [terrəs] *n* 1 verhoogd vlak oppervlakʰ, (dak)terrasʰ; 2 bordesʰ, (open) tribune, staanplaatsen; 3 rij huizen, huizenblokʰ

²terrace [terrəs] *vb* tot terras(sen) vormen, terrasgewijs aanleggen: ~*d garden* terrastuin; ~*d house* rijtjeshuis

terrain [tərreen] terreinʰ, gebiedʰ *(also fig)*

terrestrial [tirrestriəl] van de aarde, van het land, aards

terrible [terribl] 1 verschrikkelijk, vreselijk; 2 ontzagwekkend, enorm: *a ~ responsibility* een zware verantwoordelijkheid

terribly [terriblie] verschrikkelijk

terrier [terriə] terriër

terrific [tərriffik] geweldig, fantastisch: *at a ~ speed* razendsnel

terrify [terriffaj] schrik aanjagen: *be terrified of s.o. (sth.)* doodsbang zijn voor iem (iets)

terrifying [terriffajjing] angstaanjagend, afschuwelijk

territorial [territto:riəl] territoriaal: ~ *waters* territoriale wateren, driemijlszone

territory [territtərie] 1 territoriumʰ, (stuk) grondgebiedʰ; 2 territoriumʰ, (eigen) woongebiedʰ, (grond)gebiedʰ; 3 (stukʰ) landʰ, gebiedʰ, terreinʰ *(also fig),* districtʰ, werkterreinʰ, *(com)* rayonʰ, handelsgebied[h]: *unknown ~* onbekend gebied

terror [terrə] **1** verschrikking, plaag: *the ~ of the neighbourhood* de schrik van de buurt; **2** lastig iem, rotjoch[h], rotmeid; **3** (gevoel van) schrik: *run away in ~* in paniek wegvluchten

terrorism [terrərizm] terrorisme[h]

¹terrorist [terrərist] *adj* terroristisch, terreur-

²terrorist [terrərist] *n* terrorist

terrorize [terrərajz] terroriseren, schrik aanjagen

terse [tə:s] beknopt, kort

¹test [test] *n* **1** test, toets(ing), proef, toets, proefwerk[h], *(chem)* reactie: *put sth. to the ~* iets op de proef stellen, iets testen; **2** toets, criterium[h], maat(staf); **3** *(chem)* reageermiddel[h]

²test [test] *vb* (d.m.v. een test) onderzoeken: *~ for* onderzoeken (op), het gehalte bepalen van

³test [test] *vb* **1** toetsen, testen, aan een test onderwerpen, nagaan, nakijken, onderzoeken; **2** veel vergen van, hoge eisen stellen aan: *~ s.o.'s patience* iemands geduld zwaar op de proef stellen; *~ing times* zware tijden

testament [testəmənt] **1** *the Testament* Testament[h] *(part of bible)*; **2** testament[h]: *last will and ~* uiterste wil(sbeschikking), testament

testator [testeetə] testateur, erflater

test case proefproces[h]

testicle [testikl] teelbal, zaadbal, testikel

testify [testiffaj] *(with against, for)* getuigen (tegen, voor): *~ to: a)* bevestigen; *b)* getuigenis afleggen van; *c)* een teken zijn *(of:* bewijs) zijn van

testimonial [testimmooniəl] **1** getuigschrift[h], aanbevelingsbrief; **2** huldeblijk, eerbewijs[h]

testimony [testimmənie] (getuigen)verklaring, bewijs[h], (ken)teken[h], blijk

test tube reageerbuis

testy [testie] **1** prikkelbaar, opvliegend; **2** geërgerd, geïrriteerd: *a ~ remark* een knorrige opmerking

tetchy [tetsjie] prikkelbaar *(pers)*, lichtgeraakt

¹tether [teðə] *n* tuier *(rope used to secure grazing animal)* ‖ *at the end of one's ~* uitgeteld, aan het eind van zijn Latijn

²tether [teðə] *vb* vastmaken, tuien, (aan een paal) vastleggen, (vast)binden, *(fig)* aan banden leggen

text [tekst] **1** tekst(gedeelte[h]), gedrukte tekst, inhoud; **2** tekst, onderwerp[h], bijbeltekst

textbook [tekstboek] leerboek[h], studieboek[h], schoolboek[h] ‖ *~ example* schoolvoorbeeld

textile [tekstajl] weefsel[h], textielproduct[h], stof[h]

texture [tekstsjə] textuur, weefselstructuur, *(by extension)* structuur, samenstelling: *the smooth ~ of ivory* de gladheid van ivoor

Thames [temz] Theems

than [ðæn] **1** dan, als: *she's better ~ I am* (of: *~ me)* zij is beter dan ik; *he would sooner die ~ give in* hij zou (nog) liever sterven dan toegeven; *none other ~ Joe* niemand anders dan Joe; **2** of, dan, en, toen

thank [θæŋk] **1** (be)danken, dankbaar zijn: *~ you* dank u (wel), (ja) graag, alstublieft; *no, ~ you* (nee) dank u; **2** danken, (ver)wijten, verantwoordelijk

stellen: *she has herself to ~ for that* het is haar eigen schuld, dat heeft ze aan zichzelf te danken

thankful [θæŋkfoel] dankbaar, erkentelijk, blij

thankless [θæŋkləs] ondankbaar

thanks [θæŋks] dankbaarheid, dankbetuiging, (kort) dankgebed: *a letter of ~* een schriftelijk bedankje; *received with ~* in dank ontvangen; *(inf) ~!* bedankt!, merci!; *no, ~* (nee) dank je (wel), laat maar (zitten)

thanksgiving [θæŋksgivving] dankbetuiging, dankzegging

Thanksgiving (Day) *(Am)* Thanksgiving Day *(national holiday; fourth Thursday in November)*

thanks to dankzij, door (toedoen van)

thank-you bedankje[h], woord[h] van dank: *a ~ letter* een bedankbriefje

¹that [ðæt] *pron* **1** die, dat: *~'s Alice* dat is Alice; *~'s life* zo is het leven; *at ~ point* toen; *do you see ~ house?* zie je dat huis daar?; *don't yell like ~* schreeuw niet zo; *he isn't as stupid as all ~* zo stom is hij ook weer niet; *~'s ~* dat was het dan, zo, dat zit erop; **2** diegene, datgene, hij, zij, dat: *those going by train* diegenen die met de trein gaan; **3** die, dat, wat, welke: *the chair(s) ~ I bought* de stoel(en) die ik gekocht heb; **4** dat, waarop, waarin, waarmee: *the house ~ he lives in* het huis waarin hij woont; *(inf) ~'s it: a)* dat is 't hem nu juist, dat is (nu juist) het probleem; *b)* dat is wat we nodig hebben *(of:* de oplossing, het); *c)* dit *(of:* dat) is het einde; *we left it at ~* we lieten het daarbij

²that [ðæt] *conj* **1** dat, het feit dat: *it was only then ~ I found out that ...* pas toen ontdekte ik dat ...; *she knew ~ he was ill* ze wist dat hij ziek was; **2** *(purpose)* opdat, zodat; **3** *(reason or cause)* omdat: *not ~ I care, but ...* niet dat het mij iets kan schelen, maar ...; **4** *(consequence)* dat, zodat: *so high ~ you cannot see the top* zo hoog dat je de top niet kan zien

³that [ðæt] *adv* **1** zo(danig): *she's about ~ tall* ze is ongeveer zo groot; **2** heel, heel erg, zo: *its not all ~ expensive* het is niet zo heel erg duur

¹thatch [θætsj] *n* **1** strodak[h], rieten dak[h]; **2** dakstro[h], dekriet[h], dakbedekking

²thatch [θætsj] *vb* (een dak) (met stro) bedekken: *~ed roof* strodak

¹thaw [θɔ:] *vb* (ont)dooien, smelten, *(fig)* ontdooien, vriendelijker worden

²thaw [θɔ:] *n* dooi

¹the [ðə] *art* **1** de, het: *she looks after ~ children* zij zorgt voor de kinderen; *~ Italians love spaghetti* (de) Italianen zijn dol op spaghetti; *play ~ piano* piano spelen; *ah, this is ~ life!* ah, dit is pas leven!; *help ~ blind* help de blinden; **2** mijn, jouw *(etc)*: *I've got a pain in ~ leg* ik heb pijn in mijn been; **3** per, voor elk; *paid by ~ week* per week betaald

²the [ðə] *adv* **1** *(with comparative)* hoe, des te: *so much ~ better* des te beter; *~ sooner ~ better* hoe eerder hoe beter; **2** *(with superlative)* de, het: *he finished ~ fastest* hij was het eerste klaar

theatre [θiətə] **1** theater[h], schouwburg; **2** toneel[h],

theatrical

toneelstukken, drama[h]; **3** collegezaal, gehoorzaal, auditorium[h]; **4** operatiekamer; **5** toneel[h], (actie)terrein[h], operatieterrein[h]: ~ *of war* oorlogstoneel

theatrical [θie·ǽtrikl] **1** toneel-, theater-; **2** theatraal, overdreven

thee [ði:] u, gij

theft [θeft] diefstal

their [ðeə] **1** hun, haar: *they studied ~ French* ze leerden hun Frans; ~ *eating biscuits annoyed her* (het feit) dat zij koekjes aten irriteerde haar; **2** zijn, haar: *no-one gave ~ address* niemand gaf zijn adres

theirs [ðeəz] **1** de (het) hunne, van hen: *a friend of ~* een vriend van hen; **2** de (het) zijne, de (het) hare, van hem (haar): *I forgot my book, could somebody lend me ~?* ik ben mijn boek vergeten, kan iemand mij het zijne lenen?

them [ðem] **1** hen, hun, aan hen, ze: *I bought ~ a present* (of: *a present for ~)* ik heb een cadeau voor hen gekocht; **2** zij (ze): *I hate ~ worrying like that* ik vind het vreselijk als ze zich zulke zorgen maken; *it is ~* zij zijn het

theme [θie:m] **1** thema[h], onderwerp[h], gegeven[h]; **2** *(Am)* opstel[h], essay[h]; **3** *(mus)* thema[h], hoofdmelodie, herkenningsmelodie

theme park themapark[h]; pretpark[h]

theme song herkenningsmelodie

themselves [ðəmselvz] **1** zich, zichzelf: *the students kept it to ~* de studenten hielden het voor zich; **2** zelf, zij zelf, hen zelf: *they ~ started* zij zelf zijn ermee begonnen

¹then [ðen] *adv* **1** toen, op dat ogenblik, destijds: *before ~* voor die tijd; *by ~* dan, toen, ondertussen; **2** dan, (onmiddellijk) daarna, verder: ~ *they went home* daarna zijn ze naar huis gegaan; **3** dan (toch), in dat geval: *why did you go ~?* waarom ben je dan gegaan?; ~ *and there* onmiddellijk, dadelijk; *but ~, why did you do it?* maar waarom heb je het dan toch gedaan?

²then [ðen] *adj* toenmalig: *the ~ chairman* de toenmalige voorzitter

thence [ðens] **1** vandaar, van daaruit; **2** daarom, dus, daaruit

theologian [θiəloodzjiən] theoloog, godgeleerde

theological [θiəlodzjikl] theologisch, godgeleerd

theology [θie·ollədzjie] theologie, godgeleerdheid

theorem [θiərəm] (grond)stelling, principe[h], theorie

theoretical [θiərettikl] **1** theoretisch; **2** denkbeeldig, fictief: ~ *amount* fictief bedrag

theoretician [θiərətisjən] theoreticus

theory [θiərie] theorie, leer, veronderstelling: ~ *of evolution* evolutietheorie; *in ~* in theorie, op papier; *(maths)* ~ *of chances* kansrekening

therapeutic(al) [θerrəpjoe:tik(l)] therapeutisch, genezend

therapy [θerrəpie] therapie, geneeswijze, (psychiatrische) behandeling

¹there [ðeə] *adv* **1** daar, er, ginds, *(fig)* op dat punt, wat dat betreft: ~*'s no rush* er is geen haast bij; ~ *I don't agree with you* op dat punt ben ik het niet met je eens; ~ *they come* daar komen ze; *he lives over ~* hij woont daarginds; **2** daar(heen), daar naar toe: ~ *and back* heen en terug; ~ *you are: a)* alstublieft, alsjeblieft; *b)* zie je wel, wat heb ik je gezegd; ~ *and then* onmiddellijk, ter plekke

²there [ðeə] *interj* daar, zie je, nou: ~, *what did I tell you!* nou, wat heb ik je gezegd!

thereabouts [ðeərəbauts] daar ergens, (daar) in de buurt, daaromtrent, *(fig)* rond die tijd, (daar, zo) ongeveer: *twenty years or ~* zo ongeveer twintig jaar

thereafter daarna

thereby daardoor || ~ *hangs a tale* daar zit nog een (heel) verhaal aan vast

therefore daarom, om die reden, dus

thereof daarvan, ervan

thereupon daarop

thermal [θə:ml] **1** thermisch, warmte-; **2** thermaal: ~ *springs* warmwaterbronnen

thermometer [θəmommitə] thermometer

thermos [θə:məs] thermosfles, thermoskan

thermostat [θə:məstæt] thermostaat, warmteregulator

thesis [θie:sis] thesis, (hypo)these, (academisch) proefschrift[h]

they [ðee] **1** zij, ze: ~ *chased each other* ze zaten elkaar achterna; *so ~ say* dat zeggen ze toch; **2** hij (of zij): *everyone is proud of the work ~ do themselves* iedereen is trots op het werk dat hij zelf doet

¹thick [θik] *adj* **1** dik, breed *(line)*, vet *(letter, font)*, zwaar(gebouwd), (op)gezwollen, dubbel *(tongue)*: *two inches ~* twee inch dik; **2** dik, dicht, (with *with)* dicht bezet, bezaaid (met), druk, (with *with)* vol (van, met), overvloedig, weinig vloeibaar (doorzichtig), mistig, betrokken *(weather)*: ~ *on the ground* zeer talrijk; *the sky was ~ with planes* de lucht zag zwart van vliegtuigen; **3** zwaar *(accent)*; **4** dom, traag van begrip; **5** *(inf)* intiem, dik bevriend: *be as ~ as thieves* de beste maatjes met elkaar zijn; **6** *(inf)* sterk (overdreven): *a bit ~* al te kras; *give s.o. a ~ ear* iem een oorveeg geven; *have a ~ skin* een olifantshuid hebben; *lay it on ~* flink overdrijven

²thick [θik] *adv* **1** dik, breed, vet; **2** dik, dicht, dicht opeengepakt, dicht op elkaar, talrijk: *blows came ~ and fast* het regende slagen

³thick [θik] *n* dichtste, drukste gedeelte[h], drukte: *be in the ~ of it* er midden in zitten; *through ~ and thin* door dik en dun

¹thicken [θikkən] *vb* dik(ker) worden, gebonden worden *(of liquid)*, toenemen (in dikte, aantal)

²thicken [θikkən] *vb* dik(ker) maken, indikken, doen toenemen (in dikte, aantal): ~ *gravy with flour* saus binden met bloem

thicket [θikkit] (kreupel)bosje[h], struikgewas[h]

thickheaded [θik'] dom, bot (van verstand)

thickness [θiknəs] **1** dikte, afmeting in de dikte, dik gedeelte, troebelheid, mistigheid: *length, width, and ~* lengte, breedte en dikte; **2** laag

thickset 1 dicht (beplant, bezaaid); **2** zwaar (gebouwd), dik, gedrongen
thick-skinned dikhuidig, *(fig)* ongevoelig
thick-witted dom, bot (van verstand)
thief [θie:f] *(thieves)* dief
thieve [θie:v] stelen
thievish [θie:visj] steels, dieven-, heimelijk
thigh [θaj] dij
thimble [θimbl] vingerhoed
#thin [θin] *adj* **1** dun, smal, fijn, schraal, mager, slank: ~ *air* ijle lucht; **2** dun (bezet, gezaaid), dunbevolkt: *a ~ audience* een klein publiek; *(inf)* ~ *on top* kalend; **3** dun (vloeibaar), slap, waterig: ~ *beer* schraal bier; **4** zwak, armzalig: *a ~ excuse* een mager excuus; *disappear into ~ air* spoorloos verdwijnen; *the ~ end of the wedge* het eerste (kleine) begin; *skate on ~ ice* zich op glad ijs wagen; *have a ~ skin* erg gevoelig zijn; *have a ~ time (of it): a)* een moeilijke tijd doormaken; *b)* weinig succes boeken
²thin [θin] *vb* (ver)dunnen, uitdunnen, vermageren
thine [ðajn] *(possessive pronoun)* van u; uw, de (het) uwe
thing [θing] **1** ding^h, dingetje^h, zaak(je^h), voorwerp^h, iets: *a good ~ too!* (dat is) maar goed ook!; *it's a good ~ that* het is maar goed dat; *it's a good ~ to* je doet er goed aan (om); *a lucky ~ no-one got caught* gelukkig werd (er) niemand gepakt; *make a ~ of* ergens moeilijk over doen; *not a ~ to wear* niks om aan te trekken; *it didn't mean a ~ to me* het zei me totaal niets; *and another ~* bovendien, meer nog; *for one ~: a)* in de eerste plaats, om te beginnen; *b)* immers; **2** schepsel^h, wezen^h, ding^h: *the poor ~* de (arme) stakker; **3** (favoriete) bezigheid: *do one's (own) ~* doen waar men zin in heeft; **4** (dat) wat gepast is: *the very ~ for you* echt iets voor jou; *be not (quite) the ~* niet passen; **5** (dat) wat nodig is: *just the ~ I need* juist wat ik nodig heb; **6** het belangrijkste (punt, kenmerk): *the ~ is that* de kwestie is dat, waar het om gaat is dat; **7** ~*s* spullen: *pack one's* ~*s* zijn boeltje bijeenpakken; **8** ~*s* (algemene) toestand: *that would only make ~ worse* dat zou het allemaal alleen maar verergeren; *how are ~s?*, *(inf) how's ~s?* hoe gaat het (ermee)?; *have a ~ about: a)* geobsedeerd zijn door; *b)* dol zijn op; *c)* als de dood zijn voor; *not know the first ~ about* het minste verstand hebben van; *know a ~ or two about* het een en ander weten over; *let ~s rip* (of: *slide*) de boel maar laten waaien; *well, of all ~s!* wel heb ik ooit!; *I'll do it first ~ in the morning* ik doe het morgenochtend meteen; *the first ~ I knew she had hit him* voor ik wist wat er gebeurde had ze hem een mep gegeven
¹think [θingk] *vb* **1** denken, (erover) nadenken, zich (goed) bedenken; ~ *for oneself* zelfstandig denken; ~ *to oneself* bij zichzelf denken; ~ *back to* terugdenken aan; *yes, I ~ so* ja, ik denk van wel; ~ *twice* er (nog eens) goed over nadenken; ~ *about: a)* denken aan, nadenken over; *b)* overwegen *(idea, proposal, plan)*; *c)* (terug)denken aan; ~ *about moving* er

ernstig over denken om te verhuizen; **2** het verwachten, het vermoeden, het in de gaten hebben: *I thought as much* dat was te verwachten, ik vermoedde al zoiets, dat dacht ik al
²think [θingk] *vb* **1** denken, vinden, geloven: ~ *s.o. pretty* iem mooi vinden; ~ *out for oneself* voor zichzelf beslissen; **2** (na)denken over: ~ *out* overdenken, goed (na)denken over; ~ *over* overdenken, in overweging houden; ~ *through* doordenken, (goed) nadenken over; ~ *up* bedenken, verzinnen; *and to ~ (that)* en dan te moeten bedenken dat; ~ *what you're doing* bedenk wat je doet; **3** overwegen; **4** denken aan, zich herinneren: *he didn't ~ to switch off the headlights* hij vergat de koplampen uit te doen; **5** (in)zien, zich voorstellen, begrijpen: *she couldn't ~ how he did it* ze begreep niet hoe hij het voor elkaar had gekregen; **6** verwachten, vermoeden, bedacht zijn op: *she never thought to see us here* ze had nooit verwacht ons hier te treffen; ~ *nothing of sth.* iets niets bijzonders vinden, zijn hand voor iets niet omdraaien
³think [θingk] *n* **1** gedachte; **2** bedenking, overweging: *have a hard ~ about* diep nadenken over; *have got another ~ coming* het lelijk mis hebben
thinker [θingkə] denker, geleerde, filosoof
thinking [θingking] **1** het (na)denken: *way of ~* denkwijze, zienswijze; **2** mening, oordeel^h
think of 1 denken aan, rekening houden met: *(just, to)* ~ *it!* stel je (eens) voor!; **2** (erover) denken om, van plan zijn: *be thinking of doing sth.* van plan zijn iets te doen; *he would never ~ (doing) such a thing* zoiets zou nooit bij hem opkomen; **3** *(after cannot, could not, try, want etc)* zich herinneren; **4** bedenken, voorstellen, verzinnen, (uit)vinden: ~ *a number* neem een getal in gedachten; **5** aanzien, aanslaan: *think highly of* een hoge dunk hebben van; *think better of it* zich bedenken, ervan afzien
think-tank denktank, groep specialisten
thin-skinned overgevoelig, lichtgeraakt
third [θə:d] derde, derde deel^h, *(mus)* terts: ~ *in line* (als) derde op de lijst; *in ~ (gear)* in zijn drie, in zijn derde versnelling
third-degree derdegraads-
thirdly [θə:dlie] op de derde plaats
third-party tegenover derden: ~ *insurance* aansprakelijkheidsverzekering, WA-verzekering
Third World derde wereld
¹thirst [θə:st] *n* dorst *(also fig)*, sterk verlangen^h
²thirst [θə:st] *vb* sterk verlangen: ~ *after* (of: *for*) snakken naar; ~ *after revenge* op wraak belust zijn
thirsty [θə:stie] **1** dorstig: *be* (of: *feel*) ~ dorst hebben; **2** verlangend: *be ~ for* snakken naar
thirteen [θə:tie:n] dertien
thirteenth [θə:tie:nθ] dertiende, dertiende deel^h
thirtieth [θə:tieəθ] dertigste, dertigste deel^h
thirty [θə:tie] dertig: *he's in his early thirties* hij is voor in de dertig
¹this [ðis] *pron (these)* **1** dit, deze, die, dat: *these are my daughters* dit zijn mijn dochters, *what's all ~?*

wat is hier allemaal aan de hand?, wat heeft dit allemaal te betekenen?; ~ *is where I live* hier woon ik; *do it like ~* doe het zo; **2** nu, dit: ~ *is a good moment to stop* dit is een goed moment om te stoppen; *after* ~ hierna; *at ~* op dit ogenblik; *for all ~* ondanks dit alles; **3** *(what is just over)* laatste, voorbije: *she's so grumpy these days* ze is tegenwoordig zo humeurig; ~ *morning* vanmorgen; **4** *(what is coming)* komende, aanstaande: *where are you travelling ~ summer?* waar ga je de komende zomer naar toe?; **5** *(inf)* een (zekere), zo'n: ~ *fellow came cycling along* er kwam een kerel aanfietsen

²this [ðis] *adv* zo: *I know ~ much, that the idea is crazy* ik weet in elk geval dat het een krankzinnig idee is

thither [ðiðə] daarheen, ginds

thong [θong] **1** (leren) riempje^h; **2** ~s (teen)slipper, sandaal

thorn [θɔ:n] **1** doorn; **2** doornstruik || *a ~ in one's flesh* een doorn in het vlees

thorny [θɔ:nie] **1** doorn(acht)ig, stekelig; **2** lastig; **3** ergerlijk

thorough [θurrə] **1** grondig, diepgaand: *a ~ change* een ingrijpende verandering; **2** echt, volmaakt: *a ~ fool* een volslagen idioot

¹thoroughbred [θurrəbred] *adj* volbloed, rasecht, ras- *(also fig)*

²thoroughbred [θurrəbred] *n* rasdier^h, raspaard^h

thoroughfare [θurrəfeə] **1** (drukke) verkeersweg, verkeersader, belangrijke waterweg; **2** doorgang, doortocht, doorreis: *no ~* geen doorgaand verkeer, verboden toegang, doodlopende weg

thoroughgoing 1 zeer grondig, volledig: ~ *cooperation* verregaande samenwerking; **2** echt, volmaakt

thou [ðau] gij: ~ *shalt not kill* gij zult niet doden

¹though [ðoo] *conj* hoewel: ~ *he smiles I do not trust him* hoewel hij glimlacht vertrouw ik hem niet; ~ *only six, he is a bright lad* hoewel hij nog maar zes jaar is, is hij een slim jongetje; *as ~* alsof

²though [ðoo] *adv* niettemin, desondanks, toch wel: *I really liked the first part,* ~ maar het eerste deel vond ik echt heel goed

thought 1 gedachte: *perish the ~!* ik moet er niet aan denken!; **2** bedoeling, plan^h: *she had no ~ of hurting him* het was niet haar bedoeling om hem pijn te doen; **3** idee^h, opinie; **4** het denken, gedachte: *in ~* in gedachten verzonken; **5** denkwijze; **6** de rede, het denkvermogen; **7** het nadenken, de aandacht: *after serious ~* na rijp beraad; **8** hoop, verwachting: *I had given up all ~ of ever getting away from there* ik had alle hoop opgegeven er nog ooit vandaan te komen; *have second ~s* zich bedenken

thoughtful [θɔ:tfoel] **1** nadenkend; **2** diepzinnig; **3** attent, zorgzaam

thoughtless [θɔ:tləs] **1** gedachteloos; **2** onnadenkend; **3** roekeloos; **4** onattent, zelfzuchtig

thousand [θauznd] duizend, *(fig)* talloos

thousandth [θauzndθ] duizendste^h, duizendste deel^h

thrash [θræsj] **1** geselen, aframmelen; **2** verslaan, niets heel laten van || ~ *out a solution* tot een oplossing komen

thrashing [θræsjing] **1** pak^h rammel; **2** nederlaag

¹thread [θred] *n* **1** draad, *(fig also)* lijn: *lose the ~ of one's story* de draad van zijn verhaal kwijtraken; *take up (of: pick up) the ~s* de draad weer opnemen; **2** garen^h; **3** schroefdraad: *hang by a (single) ~* aan een zijden draad hangen

²thread [θred] *vb* **1** een draad steken in *(needle)*; **2** rijgen *(beads)*; **3** inpassen, inleggen *(film, sound tape etc)*; **4** zich een weg banen door, *(fig)* zich heen worstelen door; **5** banen, zoeken, vinden: ~ *one's way through the crowd* zich een weg banen door de menigte

threadbare [θredbeə] **1** versleten, kaal; **2** armoedig: *a ~ joke* een afgezaagde grap

threat [θret] **1** dreigement^h, bedreiging: *under ~ of* onder bedreiging met; **2** gevaar^h, bedreiging: *they are a ~ to society* ze vormen een gevaar voor de maatschappij

¹threaten [θretn] *vb* **1** bedreigen, een dreigement uiten tegen, een gevaar vormen voor: *peace is ~ed* de vrede is in gevaar; **2** dreigen (met): *they ~ed to kill him* ze dreigden hem te doden

²threaten [θretn] *vb* **1** dreigen (te gebeuren); **2** er dreigend uitzien: *the weather is threatening* de lucht ziet er dreigend uit

three [θrie:] drie, drietal, drietje, maat drie, drie uur: ~ *parts* drievierde, driekwart

three-cornered 1 driehoekig; **2** driehoeks-, tussen drie partijen

¹three-D *adj* driedimensionaal

²three-D *n* driedimensionale vorm

threefold [θrie:foold] drievoudig

three-piece driedelig: ~ *suit* driedelig pak

three-quarter driekwart

threesome [θrie:səm] drietal^h, driemanschap^h

threshold [θresjoold] **1** drempel *(also fig)*, aanvang, begin^h: ~ *of pain* pijndrempel; **2** ingang

thrice [θrajs] drie maal

thrift [θrift] zuinigheid, spaarzaamheid

thrifty [θriftie] zuinig, spaarzaam

¹thrill [θril] *n* **1** beving, golf van ontroering; **2** huivering *(of fear, horror)*: *he felt a ~ of horror* hij huiverde van afgrijzen; **3** opwindende gebeurtenis: *it was quite a ~* het was heel opwindend

²thrill [θril] *vb* **1** doen beven, opwinden: *be ~ed (to bits) with sth.* ontzettend gelukkig met iets zijn; **2** doen huiveren, angst aanjagen

³thrill [θril] *vb* **1** beven, aangegrepen worden; **2** huiveren

thriller [θrillə] iets opwindends, thriller, spannend misdaadverhaal^h

thrilling [θrilling] spannend, opwindend

thrive [θrajv] gedijen, floreren, bloeien: *he seems to ~ on hard work* hard werken schijnt hem goed te doen

throat [θroot] **1** hals; **2** keel, strot: *clear one's ~* zijn keel schrapen; *be at each other's ~s* elkaar in de haren vliegen; *force* (of: *ram, thrust*) *sth. down s.o.'s ~ iem* iets opdringen

¹throb [θrob] *vb* **1** kloppen; **2** bonzen, bonken *(of heart)*

²throb [θrob] *n* klop, geklop[h], gebons[h]

throe [θroo] heftige pijn || *(fig) in the ~s of* worstelend met

throne [θroon] troon, zetel, *(fig also)* macht, heerschappij

¹throng [θrong] *n* menigte, mensenmassa

²throng [θrong] *vb* zich verdringen, toestromen

³throng [θrong] *vb* vullen, overstelpen, overvol maken: *people ~ed the streets* de straten zagen zwart van de mensen

¹throttle [θrotl] *n (techn)* smoorklep

²throttle [θrotl] *vb* **1** doen stikken, (ver)smoren, *(fig also)* onderdrukken; **2** wurgen; **3** gas minderen *(car)*

throttle b<u>a</u>ck afremmen *(also fig)*, (vaart) minderen

¹through [θroo:] *prep* **1** (helemaal) door, via, langs, over, gedurende: *seen ~ a child's eyes* gezien met de ogen van een kind; *he remained calm ~ the whole trial* hij bleef kalm gedurende het hele proces; *~ and ~* helemaal door(heen), *(also fig)*; **2** *(manner)* door middel van: *he spoke ~ his representative* hij sprak via zijn vertegenwoordiger; **3** *(cause)* door, wegens, uit: *he could not travel ~ illness* hij kon wegens ziekte niet reizen; **4** *(Am)* tot en met: *Monday thru Thursday* van maandag tot en met donderdag

²through [θroo:] *adv* **1** door, verder: *go ~ with* doorgaan met; **2** door(heen): *read sth. ~: a)* iets doornemen; *b)* iets uitlezen; **3** klaar, erdoorheen; **4** helemaal, van begin tot eind: *get soaked* (of: *wet*) *~* doornat worden; *~ and ~* door en door, in hart en nieren; *are you ~?: a)* heeft u verbinding? *(telephone); b) (Am)* bent u klaar?; *I will put you ~* ik zal u doorverbinden

³through [θroo:] *adj* doorgaand, doorlopend: *~ train* doorgaande trein; *no ~ road* geen doorgaand verkeer

¹throughout *prep* (helemaal) door, door heel: *~ the country* door, in heel het land

²throughout *adv* helemaal, door en door, steeds: *our aim has been ~ …* ons doel is steeds geweest …

thr<u>ou</u>ghway snelweg

¹throw [θroo] *vb* met iets gooien, werpen

²throw [θroo] *vb* **1** werpen, gooien, *(fig also)* terecht doen komen: *~ dice* dobbelstenen gooien, dobbelen; *the horse threw him* het paard wierp hem af; *~ oneself into sth.* zich ergens op werpen, zich enthousiast ergens in storten; *be thrown (back) upon one's own resources* op zichzelf worden teruggeworpen; **2** richten, (toe)werpen, toezenden: *he threw us a sarcastic look* hij wierp ons een sarcastische blik toe; **3** afschieten *(missile)*; **4** omzetten, veranderen in; **5** draaien *(wood, earthenware)*; **6** snel op zijn plaats brengen, leggen, maken: *~ the switch to 'off'*

de schakelaar op 'uit' zetten; **7** maken, hebben, organiseren: *(inf) ~ a party* een fuif geven; **8** *(inf)* verwarren, van de wijs brengen: *~ open* openstellen; *~ s.o. into confusion* iem in verwarring brengen

³throw [θroo] *n* worp, gooi

throw ab<u>ou</u>t rondsmijten: *throw one's money about* met geld smijten

throw aw<u>a</u>y 1 weggooien; **2** verspelen, missen: *~ a chance* een kans verspelen; **3** vergooien: *throw one's money away on* zijn geld weggooien aan

thr<u>ow</u>-away 1 wegwerp-; **2** zonder nadruk: *a ~ remark* een quasi-nonchalante opmerking

thr<u>ow</u>back 1 terugslag; **2** terugkeer

throw b<u>a</u>ck 1 teruggooien; **2** openslaan, opzij werpen: *~ the blankets* de dekens terugslaan; *be thrown back on* moeten teruggrijpen naar, weer aangewezen zijn op

throw d<u>ow</u>n 1 neergooien; **2** afbreken

throw <u>i</u>n 1 erin gooien, inwerpen; **2** gratis toevoegen: *I'll ~ an extra battery* ik doe er nog een gratis batterij bij; **3** terloops opmerken; **4** *(sport)* ingooien

thr<u>ow</u>-in *(sport)* inworp

throw <u>o</u>ff 1 zich bevrijden van, van zich af schudden; **2** uitgooien, haastig uittrekken: *~ one's mask* zijn masker afwerpen *(also fig)*; **3** uitstoten, *(also fig)* produceren

throw <u>ou</u>t 1 weggooien, wegdoen; **2** verwerpen, afwijzen; **3** uiten, suggereren; **4** geven, uitzenden: *~ heat* warmte uitstralen; **5** in de war brengen: *now all our calculations are thrown out* nu zijn al onze berekeningen fout; **6** wegsturen, eruit gooien

throw <u>o</u>ver in de steek laten: *he threw her over* hij heeft haar laten zitten

throw tog<u>e</u>ther bij elkaar brengen, samenbrengen: *throw people together* mensen met elkaar in contact brengen

¹throw <u>u</u>p *vb (inf)* overgeven, kotsen

²throw <u>u</u>p *vb* **1** omhoog gooien, optillen: *~ one's eyes* de ogen ten hemel slaan; **2** voortbrengen; **3** optrekken, opbouwen: *~ barricades* barricaden opwerpen; **4** opgeven, opzeggen: *~ one's job* zijn baan vaarwel zeggen

thru [θroe:] *see* through

thrum [θrum] **1** tokkelen (op), pingelen (op) *(guitar)*; **2** ronken, brommen, dreunen

thrush [θrusj] lijster

¹thrust [θrust] *n* **1** stoot, duw, zet; **2** steek *(also fig)*; **3** druk, (drijf)kracht; **4** beweging, streven[h], richting; **5** *(mil)* uitval

²thrust *vb* **1** uitvallen, toestoten; **2** dringen, worstelen: *~ in* zich een weg banen naar binnen

³thrust *vb* **1** stoten; **2** steken, stoppen: *he thrust his hands into his pockets* hij stak zijn handen in zijn zakken; **3** duwen, dringen: *she thrust her way through the crowd* ze worstelde zich door de menigte heen; *~ sth. upon s.o.* iem ergens mee opschepen

¹thud [θud] *n* plof, slag, bons

²thud [θud] *vb* (neer)ploffen, bonzen

thug [θug] misdadiger, moordenaar

thuggery [θ<u>u</u>gərie] gewelddadigheid

¹thumb [θum] *n* duim ‖ *give the ~s up* (of: *down*) goedkeuren, afkeuren; *twiddle one's ~s* duimendraaien; *~s down* afgewezen; *~s up!: a)* prima!; *b)* kop op!, hou je taai; *be under s.o.'s ~* bij iem onder de plak zitten

²thumb [θum] *vb* (with *through*) (door)bladeren *(eg book)*

³thumb [θum] *vb* **1** beduimelen, vuile vingerafdrukken achterlaten in; **2** vragen *(lift)*, liften: *~ a ride* liften

¹thump [θump] *n* dreun, klap

²thump [θump] *adv* met een dreun: *the boy ran ~ with his head against the bookcase* de jongen liep 'bam' met zijn hoofd tegen de boekenkast

³thump [θump] *vb* dreunen, bonzen

⁴thump [θump] *vb* **1** dreunen op, beuken: *he was ~ing out a well-known song* timmerend op de toetsen speelde hij een bekend liedje; **2** stompen; **3** een pak slaag geven

thumping [θ<u>u</u>mping] geweldig

¹thunder [θ<u>u</u>ndə] *n* **1** donder, onweerʰ; **2** gedonderʰ *(also fig)* ‖ *steal s.o.'s ~* met de eer gaan strijken

²thunder [θ<u>u</u>ndə] *vb* **1** donderen, onweren; **2** denderen, dreunen; **3** donderen, razen, tekeergaan

³thunder [θ<u>u</u>ndə] *vb* uitbulderen, brullen: *~ out curses* verwensingen uitschreeuwen

thunderbolt **1** bliksemflits; **2** donderslag, schok, klap

thunderclap donderslag *(also fig)*

thundering [θ<u>u</u>ndəring] **1** donderend; **2** kolossaal

thunderstorm onweersbui

thunderstruck (als) door de bliksem getroffen

thundery [θ<u>u</u>ndərie] **1** onweerachtig; **2** dreigend

Thursday [θə:zdee] donderdag

thus [ðus] (al)dus, zo ‖ *~ far* tot hier toe, tot nu toe

thwart [θwo:t] **1** verijdelen, dwarsbomen; **2** tegenwerken, tegenhouden

thy [ðaj] uw

thyme [tajm] tijm

¹tick [tik] *n* **1** tik, getikʰ *(of clock)*; **2** momentjeʰ, ogenblikjeʰ: *in two ticks* in een wip; **3** vink(jeʰ), (merk)teken(tjeʰ) *(used on checklist)*; **4** kredietʰ, pof: *on ~* op de pof

²tick [tik] *vb* tikken: *~ away* (of: *by):* a) tikken; *b)* voorbijgaan *(time); what makes s.o. (sth.) ~* wat iem drijft; *~ over: a)* stationair draaien *(of engine); b) (inf)* zijn gangetje gaan

³tick [tik] *vb* aanstrepen *(on list)* ‖ *~ off* een uitbrander geven

ticker [tikkə] **1** horlogeʰ, klok; **2** hartʰ, rikketik

¹ticket [tikkit] *n* **1** kaart(jeʰ), toegangsbewijsʰ, plaatsbewijsʰ; **2** prijskaartjeʰ, etiketʰ; **3** bon, bekeuring; **4** *(Am)* kandidatenlijst ‖ *that's just the ~* dát is het (precies), precies wat we nodig hebben (of: zoeken)

²ticket [tikkit] *vb* **1** etiketteren, prijzen; **2** bestemmen, aanduiden; **3** *(Am)* een bon geven

¹tickle [tikl] *vb* **1** kietelen, kriebelen, *(fig)* (aange-

naam) prikkelen; **2** amuseren, aan het lachen maken: *be ~d to death* zich kostelijk amuseren

²tickle [tikl] *n* gekietelʰ; kietelend gevoelʰ

ticklish [tiklisj] **1** kittelig, kittelachtig; **2** netelig

tidal [tajdl] getijde-: *~ river* getijderivier

tidal wave getijdegolf, vloedgolf, *(fig)* golf van emotie

tiddler [tidlə] **1** visjeʰ; **2** klein kindʰ, *(fig)* klein broertjeʰ

tiddly [tidlie] **1** aangeschoten; **2** klein

tiddlywinks [tidliewingks] vlooienspel

tide [tajd] **1** getij(de)ʰ, tijʰ: *high ~* vloed; *low ~* eb; *(fig) turn the ~* het getijde doen keren; **2** stroom, stroming *(also fig): (inf; fig) swim* (of: *go) with the ~* met de stroom mee gaan

tidemark hoogwaterlijn

¹tide over *vb* (iem) verder helpen, (iem) voorthelpen *(financially)*

²tide over *vb* helpen over: *she gave me £15 to tide me over the next two days* ze gaf me £15 om me door de volgende twee dagen te helpen

tideway **1** stroombedʰ; **2** eb in stroombed

tidings [tajdingz] tijding(en)

¹tidy [tajdie] *n* opbergdoosjeʰ voor prulletjes

²tidy [tajdie] *adj* **1** netjes, keurig, op orde; **2** proper; **3** aardig (groot): *~ income* aardig inkomen

³tidy [tajdie] *vb* opruimen, schoonmaken: *~ away* opruimen; *~ up* opruimen, in orde brengen

¹tie [taj] *vb* **1** (vast)binden, (vast)knopen: *his hands are ~d* zijn handen zijn gebonden *(fig); ~ a knot* een knoop leggen; *~ back* opbinden, bijeen binden *(eg hair);* **2** (ver)binden; **3** binden, beperken: *~ down* de handen binden, bezighouden; *~ s.o. down to* iem zich laten houden aan; **4** *(sport)* gelijk spelen, staan met: *~d game* gelijkspel

²tie [taj] *vb* **1** vastgemaakt worden; **2** een knoop leggen; **3** *(sport)* gelijk eindigen: *they ~d for a second place* ze deelden de tweede plaats; *~ in (with)* verband houden (met), *(fig)* kloppen

³tie [taj] *n* **1** touw(tjeʰ), koordʰ; **2** (strop)das; **3** band, verbondenheid; **4** *(sport, game)* gelijk spelʰ; **5** *(sport)* (afval)wedstrijd, voorronde

tiebreak(er) beslissingswedstrijd, *(tennis)* tiebreak(er)

tied [tajd] *(vast)*gebonden: *~ house* gebonden café *(selling beer from one particular brewery)*

tie-on hang-: *~ label* hangetiket

tiepin dasspeld

tier [tiə] rij, verdieping, rang *(eg in theatre)*

¹tie up *vb* **1** vastbinden, verbinden, dichtbinden: *~ a dog* een hond vastleggen; *(fig) be tied up with* verband houden met; **2** afmeren; **3** *(druk)* bezighouden, ophouden, stopzetten: *be tied up* bezet zijn; **4** vastzetten, vastleggen *(money)*

²tie up *vb* **1** afgemeerd worden; **2** verband houden; **3** kloppen ‖ *~ with* verband houden met, kloppen met

tiff [tif] ruzietjeʰ

tiger [tajgə] tijger

¹tight [tajt] *adj* **1** strak, nauw(sluitend), krap: ~ *shoes* te nauwe schoenen; **2** propvol: *a ~ schedule* een overladen programma; **3** potdicht; **4** beklemmend: *be in a ~ corner* (of: *place, spot*) in een lastig parket zitten; **5** schaars, krap; **6** gierig; **7** stevig, vast; **8** streng: *keep a ~ grip* (of: *hold*) *on s.o.* iem goed in de hand houden; **9** *(inf)* dronken: *a ~ squeeze* een hele toer

²tight [tajt] *adv* vast, stevig: *hold me ~* hou me stevig vast; *good night, sleep ~* goedenacht, welterusten

¹tighten [tajtn] *vb* **1** aanhalen, spannen, vastsnoeren: *~ one's belt* de buikriem aanhalen *(fig)*; **2** vastklemmen, vastdraaien; **3** verscherpen *(measure)*: *~ up* verscherpen

²tighten [tajtn] *vb* **1** zich spannen, strakker worden; **2** krap worden

tight-fisted krenterig

tight-fitting nauwsluitend

tight-lipped 1 met opeengeklemde lippen; **2** gesloten, stil

tightrope walker koorddanser

tights [tajts] panty: *(a pair of)* ~ een panty

tightwad vrek

tigress [tajgris] tijgerin

tile [tajl] tegel, (dak)pan ‖ *he has a ~ loose* d'r zit een steekje los bij hem; *be (out) on the ~s* aan de zwier zijn

¹till [til] *prep (time)* tot (aan), voor: ~ *tomorrow* tot morgen; *not ~ after dinner* niet vóór het middageten

²till [til] *n* geldlade, kassa

³till [til] *vb* bewerken *(soil)*

⁴till [til] *conj (time)* tot(dat), voordat: *he read ~ Harry arrived* hij las tot Harry (aan)kwam; *it was a long time ~ she came home* het duurde lang voor zij thuis kwam

tiller [tilə] roer^h, roerpen, helmstok

¹tilt [tilt] *vb* **1** scheef staan, (over)hellen: ~ *over* wippen, kantelen; **2** op en neer gaan, wiegelen, schommelen

²tilt [tilt] *vb* scheef houden, zetten, doen (over)hellen, kantelen

³tilt [tilt] *n* **1** schuine stand: *he wore his hat at a ~* hij had zijn hoed schuin op; **2** steekspel^h, *(fig)* woordenwisseling

timber [timbə] **1** balk; **2** (timmer)hout^h

timbered [timbəd] in vakwerk uitgevoerd: *a ~ house* een huis in vakwerk

¹time [tajm] *n* **1** tijd, tijdsduur: *gain ~* tijd winnen; *kill ~* de tijd doden; *lose no ~* geen tijd verliezen, direct doen; *take one's ~* zich niet haasten; *~ and (~) again* steeds opnieuw; *in next to no ~* in een mum van tijd; *let's take some ~ off* (of: ~ *out*) laten we er even tussenuit gaan; *I'm working against ~* ik moet me (vreselijk) haasten, het is een race tegen de klok; *for a ~* een tijdje; *all the ~: a)* de hele tijd, voortdurend; *b)* altijd; **2** tijdstip^h, tijd: *do you have the ~?* weet u hoe laat het is?; *keep (good) ~* goed lopen *(of clock)*; *at the ~* toen, indertijd; *by the ~ the*

police arrived, ... tegen de tijd dat de politie arriveerde, ...); *what ~ is it?, what's the ~?* hoe laat is het?; **3** ~*s* tijdperk^h, periode: *move with the ~s* met zijn tijd meegaan; *at one ~* vroeger, eens; *be behind the ~s* achterlopen, niet meer van deze tijd zijn; *once upon a ~* er was eens; **4** gelegenheid, moment^h: *have ~ on one's hands* genoeg vrije tijd hebben; *any ~* altijd, om 't even wanneer; *every ~* elke keer, altijd, steeds (of: telkens) (weer); *many ~s, many a ~* vaak, dikwijls; **5** keer, maal^+h: *nine ~s out of ten* bijna altijd, negen op de tien keer; *pass the ~ of day with s.o.* iem goedendag zeggen, even met iem staan praten; *I had the ~ of my life* ik heb ontzettend genoten; *since ~ out of mind* sinds onheuglijke tijden; *do ~* zitten *(in prison)*; *I have no ~ for him* ik mag hem niet, ik heb een hekel aan hem; *mark ~ (mil)* pas op de plaats maken, *(fig)* een afwachtende houding aannemen; *play for ~* tijd rekken; *~ will tell* de tijd zal het uitwijzen; *~'s up!* het is de hoogste tijd!; *(and) about ~ too!* (en) het werd ook tijd; *~ after ~* keer op keer; *at all ~s* altijd, te allen tijde; *one at a ~* één tegelijk; *at the same ~: a)* tegelijkertijd; *b)* toch; *at ~s* soms; *for the ~ being* voorlopig; *from ~ to ~* van tijd tot tijd; *in ~: a)* op tijd; *b)* na verloop van tijd; *on ~: a)* op tijd; *b)* op afbetaling; **6** *(mus)* maat: *keep ~* in de maat blijven, de maat houden; **7** tempo^h

²time [tajm] *vb* **1** vaststellen, berekenen *(time, duration)*: *the train is ~d to leave at four o'clock* de trein moet om vier uur vertrekken; **2** het juiste moment kiezen voor (om te): *his visit was ill ~d* zijn bezoek kwam ongelegen; **3** klokken

time-consuming tijdrovend

time-honoured traditioneel

timekeeper 1 uurwerk^h: *my watch is a good ~* mijn horloge loopt altijd op tijd; **2** tijdwaarnemer, tijdopnemer

time lag pauze *(between two consecutive occurrences)*, tijdsverloop^h, vertraging, tijdsinterval

timeless [tajmləs] **1** oneindig, eeuwig; **2** tijd(e)loos

timely [tajmlie] **1** tijdig; **2** van pas komend, gelegen

time out time-out, onderbreking

timepiece uurwerk^h, klok, horloge^h

timer [tajmə] **1** timer *(eg on video)*; **2** tijdopnemer; **3** tijdwaarnemer

timeserving opportunistisch

timeshare deeltijdeigenaarschap^h

time-sharing deeltijdeigenaarschap^h

¹timetable *n* **1** dienstregeling; **2** (les)rooster^h

²timetable *vb* een rooster maken

³timetable *vb* plannen, inroosteren

time warp vervorming van de tijd, tijdsvervorming

time-wasting het tijdrekken, het tijdwinnen, spelbederf^h

time-worn 1 versleten, oud; **2** afgezaagd

timid [timmid] **1** bang, angstig; **2** timide, verlegen

timidity [timmidditie] **1** angst; **2** bedeesdheid

timorous [timmərəs] **1** bang, angstig; **2** timide, bedeesd

timpani [tɪmpənie] pauk(en)

timpanist [tɪmpənist] paukenist

¹tin [tin] *n* **1** tinʰ; **2** blikʰ; **3** blik(jeʰ), conservenblikʰ; **4** bus

²tin [tin] *adj* **1** tinnen: ~ *soldier* tinnen soldaatje; **2** blikken: ~ *can* (leeg) blikje; ~ *whistle* blikken fluitje; **3** prullerig

³tin [tin] *vb* inblikken

tinder [tɪndə] **1** tondel; **2** olie op het vuur

tinderbox 1 tondeldoos; **2** *(fig)* kruitvatʰ

tine [tajn] **1** scherpe puntʰ, tand *(of (pitch)fork)*; **2** geweitak

tinfoil aluminiumfolieʰ

¹tinge [tindzj] *n* tint(jeʰ) *(also fig)*

²tinge [tindzj] *vb* **1** tinten; **2** doortrekken: *comedy ~d with tragedy* tragikomedie

¹tingle [tɪŋgl] *vb* **1** opgewonden zijn, popelen; **2** (laten) tintelen, (doen) suizen *(of ears)*

²tingle [tɪŋgl] *n* tinteling

¹tinker [tɪŋkə] *n* ketellapper

²tinker [tɪŋkə] *vb* **1** ketellappen; **2** (with *at*, *with*) prutsen (aan)

¹tinkle [tɪŋkl] *vb* **1** rinkelen, tingelen; **2** plassen

²tinkle [tɪŋkl] *vb* laten rinkelen

³tinkle [tɪŋkl] *n* **1** gerinkelʰ; **2** plasjeʰ; **3** telefoontjeʰ

tinny [tɪnnie] **1** tin-, blikachtig; **2** metaalachtig *(of sound)*; **3** waardeloos

tin-opener blikopener

tinplate blikʰ

tinpot waardeloos

tinsel [tɪnsl] klatergoudʰ *(also fig)*

¹tint [tint] *n* **1** (pastel)tint; **2** kleurshampoo

²tint [tint] *vb* kleuren

tiny [tajnie] heel klein, nietig

¹tip [tip] *n* **1** tipjeʰ, topjeʰ, puntʰ, filterʰ *(of cigarette)*, pomerans *(on billiard cue)*: *the ~ of the iceberg* het topje van de ijsberg; **2** stortʰ, stortplaats, *(fig)* zwijnenstal; **3** fooi; **4** tip, raad: *give s.o. a ~ on* iem een tip geven over; **5** tik(jeʰ), duwtjeʰ: *have sth. on the ~ of one's tongue* iets voor op de tong hebben liggen

²tip [tip] *vb* **1** doen overhellen: ~ *sth. up* iets schuin houden; **2** doen omslaan, omvergooien: ~ *over* omgooien; **3** (weg)kieperen; **4** overgieten; **5** aantikken, eventjes aanraken; **6** tippen, (als fooi) geven; **7** tippen, als kanshebber aanwijzen

³tip [tip] *vb* **1** kiep(er)en, kantelen: *these bunks ~ up* deze slaapbanken klappen omhoog; **2** omkantelen: ~ *over* omvallen; **3** fooien uitdelen

tip off waarschuwen, een tip geven

tip-off waarschuwing, hint

¹tipple [tɪpl] *n* (sterke)drank, drankjeʰ

²tipple [tɪpl] *vb* aan de drank zijn, pimpelen

tipster [tɪpstə] tipgever, informant

tipsy [tɪpsie] aangeschoten

tiptoe [tɪptoo] op zijn tenen lopen ‖ *on ~*: *a)* op zijn tenen, stilletjes; *b)* vol verwachting

tip-top [tɪptop] tiptop, piekfijn; **2** chic

tip-up: *a ~ seat* een klapstoeltje

¹tire [tajjə] *vb* **1** moe worden; **2** (with *of*) beu worden:

I never ~ of it het verveelt me nooit

²tire [tajjə] *vb* **1** *(also with out)* afmatten, vermoeien; **2** vervelen

³tire [tajjə] *n* **1** hoepel; **2** band

tired [tajjəd] **1** moe: ~ *out* doodop; **2** afgezaagd: *be ~ of sth.* iets beu zijn

tireless [tajjələs] **1** onvermoeibaar; **2** onophoudelijk

tiresome [tajjəsəm] **1** vermoeiend; **2** vervelend, saai

tiro [tajroo] beginneling, beginner

tissue [tɪsjoe:] **1** doekjeʰ, gaasjeʰ; **2** papieren (zak)doekjeʰ, velletje vloeipapierʰ; **3** webʰ, netwerkʰ: ~ *of lies* aaneenschakeling van leugens; **4** (cel)weefselʰ

tissue paper zijdepapierʰ

tit [tit] **1** mees; **2** *(inf)* tiet; tepel; **3** sukkel, klier

titanic [tajtænik] reusachtig

titbit [tɪtbit] **1** lekker hapjeʰ; **2** interessant nieuwtjeʰ, roddeltjeʰ

tit-for-tat vergeldings-, uit wraak

titillate [tɪttilleet] prikkelen, aangenaam opwinden

titivate [tɪttivveet] mooi maken, opdirken

title [tajtl] titel, titelbladʰ, *(sport)* kampioen(schap), *(law)* eigendomsrechtʰ, ondertitel, aftiteling *(of film)*

titled [tajtld] met een (adellijke) titel

title deed eigendomsakte

¹titter [tɪttə] *vb* (onderdrukt, nerveus) giechelen

²titter [tɪttə] *n* gegiechelʰ

tittle [tɪtl] tittel *(also fig)*, puntjeʰ

¹tittle-tattle [tɪtltætl] *n* kletspraat, roddelpraat

²tittle-tattle [tɪtltætl] *vb* kletsen

¹to [toe:] *prep* **1** naar, naar ... toe, tot: *pale ~ clear blue* bleek tot hel blauw; *drink ~ her health* op haar gezondheid drinken; *they remained loyal ~ a man* ze bleven stuk voor stuk trouw; ~ *my mind* volgens mij; *travel ~ Rome* naar Rome reizen; *from bad ~ worse* van kwaad tot erger; **2** *(place; also fig)* tegen, op, in: *I've been ~ my aunt's* ik ben bij mijn tante gaan logeren; *we beat them eleven ~ seven* we hebben ze met elf (tegen) zeven verslagen; **3** *(in comparison)* met, ten opzichte van, voor: *use 50 lbs. ~ the acre* gebruik 50 pond per acre; *superior ~ synthetic fabric* beter dan synthetische stof; *compared ~ Jack* vergeleken bij Jack; *true ~ nature* natuurgetrouw; *I'm new ~ the place* ik ben hier nieuw; *made ~ size* op maat gemaakt; **4** *(time)* tot, tot op, op: *three years ago ~ the day* precies drie jaar geleden; *stay ~ the end* tot het einde blijven; *five (minutes) ~ three* vijf (minuten) voor drie; **5** bij, aan, van: *the key ~ the house* de sleutel van het huis; *there's more ~ it* er zit meer achter

²to [toe:] *adv* **1** *(direction)* (er)heen: ~ *and fro* heen en weer; **2** *(place; also fig)* tegen, bij, eraan: *bring s.o. ~* iem bijbrengen

³to [toe:] *particle (often untranslated)* **1** te: *I don't want ~ apologize* ik wil mij niet verontschuldigen; **2** dat, het: *I don't want ~* dat wil ik niet

toad [tood] *(zoology)* pad

toadstool paddestoel

¹toady [toodie] *n* vleier

²toady [toodie] *vb* vleien: ~ *to s.o.* iem vleien

to-and-fro [toe:ǝnfroo] heen en weer (gaand), schommelend

¹toast [toost] *n* **1** toast: *propose a* ~ *to s.o.* een toast uitbrengen op iem; **2** geroosterde boterham, toast: *have s.o. on* ~ iem helemaal in zijn macht hebben

²toast [toost] *vb* **1** roosteren, toast maken van: *(fig)* ~ *oneself at the fire* zich warmen bij het vuur; **2** toasten op

toaster [toostǝ] broodrooster^h

toastmaster ceremoniemeester *(at dinner)*

tobacco [tǝbækoo] tabak

tobacconist [tǝbækǝnist] tabakshandelaar

¹toboggan [tǝbogǝn] *n* slee

²toboggan [tǝbogǝn] *vb* sleeën, rodelen

tod [tod]: *on one's* ~ in z'n uppie

today [tǝdee] vandaag, tegenwoordig

toddle [todl] **1** waggelen; **2** kuieren: ~ *round* (of: *over)* even aanlopen; **3** (also with *along)* opstappen

toddler [todlǝ] dreumes, hummel

to-do [tǝdoe:] drukte, gedoe^h, ophef

toe [too] teen, neus, punt^h || *turn up one's ~s* de pijp uitgaan; *on one's ~s* alert

toecap neus *(of shoe)*

toehold steunpuntje^h, *(fig)* houvast^h, opstapje^h

toenail teennagel

toff [tof] fijne meneer: *the ~s* de rijkelui

toffee [toffie] toffee

toffee-nosed snobistisch, verwaand

together [tǝgeðǝ] **1** samen, bijeen: *come* ~ samenkomen; **2** tegelijk(ertijd): *all* ~ *now* nu allemaal tegelijk; **3** aaneen, bij elkaar, tegen elkaar: *tie* ~ aan elkaar binden; **4** *(inf)* voor elkaar, geregeld: *get things* ~ de boel regelen; **5** achtereen, zonder tussenpozen: *for hours* ~ uren aan een stuk, uren achter elkaar; ~ *with* met

toggle [togl] **1** knevel, pin; **2** houtje^h *(on duffel coat)*

togs [togz] kloffie, plunje

¹toil [tojl] *n* gezwoeg^h

²toil [tojl] *vb* **1** (with *at, on)* hard werken (aan): ~ *away* ploeteren; **2** moeizaam vooruitkomen

toilet [tojlit] **1** wc, toilet^h; **2** toilet^h, gewaad^h: *make one's* ~ toilet maken; **3** toilettafel, kaptafel

toilet bag toilettas

toiletry [tojlitrie] **1** toiletartikel^h; **2** toiletgerei^h

¹token [tookǝn] *n* **1** teken^h, blijk, bewijs^h: *in* ~ *of* ten teken van; **2** herinnering, aandenken^h; **3** bon, cadeaubon; **4** munt, fiche^h, penning

²token [tookǝn] *adj* symbolisch: ~ *resistance* symbolisch verzet

tolerable [tollǝrǝbl] **1** draaglijk; **2** toelaatbaar; **3** redelijk

tolerance [tollǝrǝns] **1** verdraagzaamheid, tolerantie: ~ *of* (of: *to) hardship* het verdragen van ontberingen; **2** toegestane afwijking, tolerantie, speling

tolerant [tollǝrǝnt] verdraagzaam

tolerate [tollǝreet] **1** tolereren, verdragen; **2** (kunnen) verdragen

toleration [tollǝreesjǝn] verdraagzaamheid

¹toll [tool] *n* **1** tol, *(fig; mostly singular)* prijs: *take a heavy* ~ een zware tol eisen; **2** kosten ve interlokaal telefoongesprek; **3** (klok)gelui^h

²toll [tool] *vb* **1** luiden *(of bell);* **2** slaan *(the hour)*

toll bridge tolbrug

toll road tolweg

tom [tom] kater || *(every) Tom, Dick and Harry* Jan, Piet en Klaas; *peeping Tom* gluurder

tomato [tǝma:too] tomaat

tomb [toe:m] (praal)graf^h; (graf)tombe; grafmonument^h

tombola [tomboolǝ] tombola *(lottery game)*

tomboy wilde meid

tombstone grafsteen

tomcat kater

tome [toom] (dik) boekdeel^h

tomfool stom

tomfoolery **1** dwaasheid, flauw gedrag^h; **2** onzin

tomorrow [tǝmorroo] morgen: ~ *week* morgen over een week

tomtom tamtam, trommel

ton [tun] **1** (metrieke) ton *(weight; approx 1,016 kg)*: *(fig) it weighs (half) a* ~ het weegt loodzwaar; **2** grote hoeveelheid; **3** honderd (pond, mijl per uur): *do the* ~ honderd mijl per uur rijden; *come down like a* ~ *of bricks* flink tekeergaan

¹tone [toon] *n* **1** toon, klank, stem(buiging), tint: *speak in an angry* ~ op boze toon spreken; **2** intonatie, accent^h; **3** *(photo)* toon, tint; **4** *(mus)* (hele) toon, grote seconde; **5** geest, stemming *(also of market)*: *set the* ~ de toon aangeven

²tone [toon] *vb* overeenstemmen: ~ *(in) with* kleuren bij

³tone [toon] *vb* **1** tinten; **2** doen harmoniëren: ~ *(in) with* doen harmoniëren met, laten passen bij

tone-deaf geen (muzikaal) gehoor hebbend

tone down **1** afzwakken *(also fig):* ~ *one's language* op zijn woorden passen; **2** verzachten

toneless [toonlǝs] **1** toonloos, monotoon; **2** kleurloos

toner [toonǝ] inkt *(for printers and copiers)*

tongs [tongz] tang: *pair of* ~ tang

tongue [tung] **1** tong, spraak; **2** taal; **3** tongvormig iets, lipje^h *(of shoe)*, landtong, klepel *(of bell)* || *(speak) with* ~ *in cheek* spottend (spreken); *hold your ~!* houd je mond!; *have lost one's* ~ zijn tong verloren hebben; *set ~s wagging* de tongen in beweging brengen

tongue-in-cheek ironisch, spottend

tongue-tied met de mond vol tanden

tongue-twister tongbreker, moeilijk uit te spreken woord^h (zin)

tonic [tonnik] versterkend middel^h *(also fig)*

tonight [tǝnajt] **1** vanavond; **2** vannacht

tonsil [tonsil] (keel)amandel: *have one's ~s out* zijn amandelen laten knippen

tonsil(l)itis [tonsillajtis] amandelontsteking

tonsure [tonsjə] tonsuur

too [toe:] **1** te (zeer): *~ good to be true* te mooi om waar te zijn; **2** *(inf)* erg, al te: *it's ~ bad* (het is) erg jammer; **3** ook, eveneens: *he, ~, went to Rome* híj ging ook naar Rome; *he went to Rome, ~* hij ging ook naar Róme; **4** bovendien: *they did it; on Sunday ~!* zij hebben het gedaan; en nog wel op zondag!

toolbar *(comp)* werkbalk

¹tool [toe:l] *n* **1** handwerktuig[h], (stuk[h]) gereedschap[h], instrument[h]: *down ~s* het werk neerleggen *(in protest);* **2** werktuig[h] *(only fig)*

²tool [toe:l] *vb* toeren, rijden: *~ along* rondtoeren, voortsnorren

³tool [toe:l] *vb* bewerken

toolbox gereedschapskist

tool-shed gereedschapsschuurtje[h]

¹toot [toe:t] *n* **1** (hoorn)stoot; **2** getoeter[h]

²toot [toe:t] *vb* toeteren, blazen (op)

tooth [toe:θ] *(teeth)* **1** tand *(also of comb, saw)*, kies, *teeth* gebit[h]: *(fig) (fight) ~ and nail* met hand en tand (vechten); *(fig) armed to the teeth* tot de tanden gewapend; *(fig) get one's teeth into sth.* ergens zijn tanden in zetten; **2** *teeth (inf)* kracht, effect[h]: *(inf) be fed up to the (back) teeth* er schoon genoeg van hebben; *kick in the teeth* voor het hoofd stoten; *the sound set his teeth on edge* het geluid ging hem door merg en been

toothache tandpijn, kiespijn

toothbrush tandenborstel

toothed [toe:θt] **1** getand; **2** met tanden

toothless [toe:θləs] **1** tandeloos; **2** krachteloos

toothpaste tandpasta

toothpick tandenstoker

toothsome [toe:θsəm] lekker

toothy [toe:θie] **1** met grote, vooruitstekende tanden; **2** getand

¹tootle [toe:tl] *vb* blazen (op), toeteren (op) *(instrument)*

²tootle [toe:tl] *vb* (rond)toeren

³tootle [toe:tl] *n* getoeter[h]

tootsy [toetsie] *(child language)* voet(je[h])

¹top [top] *n* **1** top, hoogste punt[h]: *from ~ to bottom* van onder tot boven; *from ~ to toe* van top tot teen; *(shout) at the ~ of one's voice* luidkeels (schreeuwen); *on ~* boven(aan); **2** bovenstuk[h], bovenkant, tafelblad[h], dop *(of bottle, fountain pen)*, top(je[h]) *(article of clothing)*, deksel[+h], kroonkurk, room *(on milk)*, bovenrand *(of page);* **3** beste, belangrijkste[h] *(of form, organisation): be* (of: *come out) (at the) ~ of the form* de beste van de klas zijn; **4** oppervlakte; **5** tol *(toy): off the ~ of one's head* onvoorbereid *(speaking); (feel) on ~ of the world* (zich) heel gelukkig (voelen); *(inf) blow one's ~* in woede uitbarsten; *come out on ~* overwinnen; *get on ~ of sth.* iets de baas worden; *go over the ~: a)* te ver gaan; *b)* uit de loopgraven komen; *on ~ of that* daar komt nog bij, bovendien

²top [top] *adj* hoogste, top-: *~ drawer* bovenste la;

(fig) out of the ~ drawer van goede komaf; *~ prices* hoogste prijzen; *at ~ speed* op topsnelheid

³top [top] *vb* **1** van top voorzien, bedekken: *(fig) ~ off* (of: *up) sth.* iets bekronen; **2** de top bereiken van *(eg mountain; also fig);* **3** aan de top staan *(also fig)*, aanvoeren *(list, team);* **4** overtreffen: *to ~ it all* tot overmaat van ramp; *~ and tail* afhalen, doppen; *~ up* bijvullen

topaz [toopæz] topaas[+h]

top boot kaplaars

topcoat 1 overjas; **2** bovenste verflaag, deklaag

top copy origineel[h]

top-down van boven af, van boven naar beneden *(of corporate structure)*

top-drawer van goede komaf

top-dress bestrooien *(of sand, manure etc)*

top flight 1 eersteklas, uitstekend; **2** best mogelijk

top hat hoge hoed

top-heavy *(also fig)* topzwaar

topiary [toopiərie] **1** vormboom; **2** vormsnoei

topic [toppik] onderwerp[h] (van gesprek): *~ of conversation* gespreksthema

topical [toppikl] **1** actueel; **2** plaatselijk *(also med);* **3** naar onderwerp gerangschikt, thematisch

topknot (haar)knotje[h]; **2** strik *(in hair);* **3** kam *(of cock)*

topmost [topmoost] (aller)hoogst

topnotch eersteklas

topper [toppə] hoge hoed

topping [topping] toplaag(je[h]), sierlaagje[h]

¹topple [topl] *vb* (bijna) omvallen, kantelen: *~ down* (of: *over)* omtuimelen

²topple [topl] *vb* (bijna) doen omvallen, omkieperen

tops [tops] je van het: *come out ~* als de beste uit de bus komen

top secret uiterst geheim

topside 1 bovenkant; **2** *(roughly)* biefstuk

topsoil bovenste laag losse (teel)aarde, bovengrond

topsy-turvy [topsietə:vie] ondersteboven (gekeerd), op zijn kop: *the world is going ~* de wereld wordt op zijn kop gezet

¹top-up *adj* aanvullend

²top-up *n* aanvulling

¹torch [to:tsj] *n* **1** toorts, fakkel *(also fig);* **2** zaklamp; **3** soldeerlamp

²torch [to:tsj] *vb* in brand steken

torchlight 1 fakkellicht[h]; **2** licht[h] ve zaklantaarn

torment [to:ment] *n* kwelling

torment [to:ment] *vb* kwellen, plagen: *~ed by mosquitoes* bestookt door muggen

tornado [to:needoo] *(also ~es)* tornado

¹torpedo [to:pie:doo] *n (~es)* torpedo

²torpedo [to:pie:doo] *vb (also fig)* torpederen

torpid [to:pid] **1** gevoelloos; **2** traag; **3** in winterslaap

torrent [torrənt] *(also fig)* stortvloed: *the rain fell in ~s* het stortregende

torrential [tərensjl] *(also fig)* als een stortvloed: *~*

rains stortregens

torrid [torrid] **1** zeer heet, tropisch, verzengend *(heat): the ~ zone* de tropen; **2** intens

torso [to:soo] *(also fig)* torso

tort [to:t] onrechtmatige daad

tortoise [to:təs] landschildpad

tortoiseshell 1 lapjeskat; **2** schildpad *(as material)*

tortuous [to:tsjoeəs] **1** kronkelend, slingerend *(of road);* **2** omslachtig, gecompliceerd, misleidend, bedrieglijk

¹torture [to:tsjə] *vb* martelen: *~d by doubt* gekweld door twijfel

²torture [to:tsjə] *n* marteling, zware kwelling

torture chamber martelkamer, folterkamer

torturer [to:tsjərə] folteraar, beul

Tory [to:rie] conservatief, lid[h] vd conservatieve partij in Groot-Brittannië

tosh [tosj] onzin

¹toss [tos] *vb* tossen, een munt opgooien, loten: *we'll have to ~ for it* we zullen erom moeten tossen

²toss [tos] *vb* **1** slingeren: *the ship was ~ed about* het schip werd heen en weer geslingerd; **2** schudden, (doen) zwaaien, afwerpen; **3** gooien, aangooien, opgooien, in de lucht werpen: *~ hay* hooi keren; **4** een munt opgooien met: *I'll ~ you for it* we loten erom

³toss [tos] *n* **1** worp; **2** beweging, knik, slinger, zwaai, val: *take a ~* van het paard geslingerd worden, *(fig)* vallen; **3** opgooi: *argue the ~* een definitieve beslissing aanvechten; *lose the ~* verliezen bij het tossen

toss off 1 achteroverslaan *(drink);* **2** razendsnel produceren: *~ a speech* voor de vuist weg een toespraak houden

toss up tossen, kruis of munt gooien

toss-up 1 opgooi; **2** *(inf)* twijfelachtige zaak, onbesliste zaak: *it's a ~ whether* het is een gok of, het is nog maar de vraag of

tot [tot] **1** dreumes: *a tiny ~* een kleine hummel; **2** scheutje[h] *(of hard liquor)*

¹total [tootl] *n* totaal[h]

²total [tootl] *adj* totaal, volledig: *~ abstainer* geheelonthouder; *in ~ ignorance* in absolute onwetendheid; *sum ~* totaalbedrag

³total [tootl] *vb (with (up) to)* oplopen (tot)

⁴total [tootl] *vb* **1** bedragen, oplopen tot; **2** *(also with up)* het totaal vaststellen van

totalitarian [tootælittəəriən] totalitair

totality [tootælittie] **1** totaal[h]; **2** totaliteit

tote [toot] (bij zich) dragen *(eg gun),* meevoeren

tote bag (grote) draagtas

totter [tottə] **1** wankelen *(also fig);* **2** wankelend overeind komen: *~ to one's feet* wankelend opstaan

¹tot up *vb (with to)* oplopen (tot), bedragen

²tot up *vb* optellen

¹touch [tutsj] *vb* (elkaar) raken, aan elkaar grenzen

²touch [tutsj] *vb* **1** raken *(also fig),* aanraken: *you haven't ~ed your meal* je hebt nog geen hap gegeten; **2** een tikje geven, aantasten, *(fig)* aankunnen: *he ~ed his cap* hij tikte zijn pet aan; **3** raken, ontroeren:

~ed with pity door medelijden bewogen; **4** treffen, betreffen: *he does not want to ~ politics* hij wil zich niet met politiek inlaten; **5** benaderen, bereiken, *(fig)* evenaren: *the thermometer ~ed 50°* de thermometer liep tot 50° op; *~ s.o. for a fiver* iem vijf pond aftroggelen

³touch [tutsj] *n* **1** aanraking, tik(je[h]), contact[h] *(also fig): I felt a ~ on my shoulder* ik voelde een tikje op mijn schouder; *be in ~ with* contact hebben met; *lose ~ with* uit het oog verliezen; **2** gevoel[h] bij aanraking, tastzin; **3** vleugje[h], snufje[h] *(eg salt),* lichte aanval *(of disease): a ~ of the sun* een lichte zonnesteek; **4** stijl, manier: *put the finishing ~(es) to sth.* de laatste hand leggen aan iets; *lose one's ~* achteruitgaan, het verleren; **5** *(mus)* aanslag; **6** *(sport)* deel[h] van veld buiten de zijlijnen *(football, rugby): play at ~* tikkertje spelen

¹touch-and-go *n* **1** een dubbeltje op zijn kant; **2** veranderlijkheid

²touch-and-go *adj* riskant: *it's a ~ state of affairs* het is een dubbeltje op zijn kant

touch at aandoen: *the ship touched at Port Said* het schip deed Port Said aan

touchdown 1 landing *(aeroplane);* **2** *(rugby, American football)* touch-down

¹touch down *vb* landen

²touch down *vb (rugby, American football)* aan de grond brengen achter de doellijn *(ball; by opponent)*

touched [tutsjt] **1** ontroerd; **2** getikt

touching [tutsjing] ontroerend

touchline zijlijn

touch off 1 afvuren, doen ontploffen; **2** de stoot geven tot

touchpaper lont *(eg of fireworks)*

touchscreen aanraakscherm[h]

touchstone maatstaf

touch-tone toets-, drukknop-: *~ phone* toetstelefoon

touch-type blind typen

touch up 1 retoucheren; **2** bijschaven, *(fig)* opfrissen *(memory)*

touch (up)on terloops behandelen

touchy [tutsjie] **1** overgevoelig, prikkelbaar; **2** netelig

¹tough [tuf] *adj* **1** taai, stoer: *as ~ as old boots: a)* vreselijk taai; *b)* keihard; *~ as nails* spijkerhard; **2** moeilijk, lastig: *a ~ job* een lastig karwei; **3** onbuigzaam: *a ~ guy* (of: *customer)* een keiharde; *get ~ with* hard optreden tegen; **4** ruw; **5** tegenvallend, hard: *it's your ~ luck* het is je eigen stomme schuld; *it's ~ on him* het is een grote tegenvaller voor hem; *~ (luck)!* pech!, jammer!

²tough [tuf] *adv* hard, onverzettelijk: *talk ~* zich keihard opstellen *(during negotations)*

³tough [tuf] *n* woesteling, zware jongen

toughen [tuffən] taai, hard (doen) worden: *~ up* sterker worden

toughie [tuffie] **1** rouwdouw; **2** lastig probleem[h]

toupee [toe:pee] haarstukje^h

¹tour [toeə] *n* **1** reis, rondreis; **2** *(with of)* (kort) bezoek^h (aan): *a guided ~ of* (of: *round*) *the castle* een rondleiding door het kasteel; **3** tournee: *on ~* op tournee; **4** verblijf^h: *the ambassador did a four-year ~ in Washington* de ambassadeur heeft vier jaar Washington als standplaats gehad

²tour [toeə] *vb* **1** (be)reizen, rondreizen; **2** op tournee gaan door

tourism [toeərizm] toerisme^h

tourist [toeərist] toerist

tourist office VVV-kantoor^h

tournament [toeənəmənt] toernooi^h, steekspel^h

tour operator reisorganisator

tousle [tauzl] in de war maken *(hair)*

¹tout [taut] *vb* **1** klanten lokken, werven; **2** sjacheren, handelen *(in information about racehorses)*

²tout [taut] *vb* **1** verhandelen *(information about racehorses)*; **2** op de zwarte markt verkopen *(tickets)*

³tout [taut] *n* **1** klantenlokker; **2** scharrelaar, handelaar *(esp in illegal tickets and information about racehorses)*

¹tow [too] *n* **1** sleep: *take a car in ~* een auto slepen; **2** het (mee)slepen

²tow [too] *vb* (weg)slepen, op sleeptouw nemen, (weg)trekken

towards [təwo:dz] **1** naar, tot, richting: *her window faced ~ the sea* haar raam keek uit op de zee; *he walked ~ the signpost* hij ging op de wegwijzer af; *we're saving ~ buying a house* we sparen om later een huis te kunnen kopen; **2** ten opzichte van, met betrekking tot: *her attitude ~ her parents* haar houding ten opzichte van haar ouders; **3** *(to express time)* voor, vlak voor, naar ... toe: *~ six (o'clock)* tegen zessen

tow bar 1 trekhaak; **2** *(skiing)* sleepbeugel *(of ski lift)*, anker^h

towel [tauəl] handdoek: *throw in the ~* de handdoek in de ring gooien, *(fig)* het opgeven

towelling [tauəling] badstof

¹tower [tauə] *n* **1** toren, (zend)mast; **2** torenflat, kantoorflat || *~ of strength* steun en toeverlaat, rots in de branding

²tower [tauə] *vb* (with over, above) uittorenen (boven), (hoog) uitsteken

tower block torengebouw^h, torenflat

towering [tauəring] **1** torenhoog; **2** enorm, hevig: *he's in a ~ rage* hij is razend

towing zone wegsleepzone

town [taun] **1** stad; **2** gemeente || *go to ~ on something* zich inzetten, veel werk maken van iets, *(inf)* uitspatten, zich uitleven; *(out) on the ~* (aan het) stappen, (een avondje) uit; *he went up to ~ from Nottingham* hij is vanuit Nottingham naar Londen gegaan

town clerk gemeentesecretaris

town council gemeenteraad

town hall stadhuis^h

township [taunsjip] **1** gemeente; **2** kleurlingenwijk, woonstad

townspeople [taunzpie:pl] **1** stedelingen, ingezetenen; **2** stadsmensen

towpath jaagpad^h

towrope sleeptouw^h

toxic [toksik] toxisch, giftig, vergiftigings-

¹toy [toj] *n* speeltje^h, (stuk^h) speelgoed^h, *(fig)* speelbal

²toy [toj] *vb* (with with) spelen (met), zich amuseren (met): *he ~ed with the idea of buying a new car* hij speelde met de gedachte een nieuwe auto te kopen

toyshop speelgoedwinkel

¹trace [trees] *n* spoor^h, voetspoor^h, *(also fig)* overblijfsel^h, vleugje^h: *not a ~ of humour* geen greintje humor; *lose ~ of* uit het oog verliezen; *lost without ~* spoorloos verdwenen; *kick over the ~s* uit de band springen

²trace [trees] *vb* **1** (with out) (uit)tekenen, schetsen, trekken *(line)*; **2** overtrekken; **3** volgen, nagaan; **4** *(with back)* nagaan, naspeuren, opsporen, terugvoeren: *the rumour was ~d back to his aunt* men kwam erachter dat het gerucht afkomstig was van zijn tante; **5** vinden, ontdekken: *I can't ~ that book* ik heb dat boek niet kunnen vinden

tracer [treesə] lichtspoorkogel

tracing paper overtrekpapier^h

¹track [træk] *n* **1** spoor^h: *on the right ~* op het goede spoor *(also fig)*; *go off the beaten ~* ongebaande wegen bewandelen *(fig)*; *be on s.o.'s ~* iem op het spoor zijn; **2** voetspoor^h, (voet)afdruk, prent *(of animals)*: *(fig) cover (up) one's ~s* zijn sporen uitwissen; **3** pad^h, bosweg, landweg, *(fig also)* weg, baan; **4** renbaan, racebaan, wielerbaan; **5** (spoor)rails; **6** rupsband; **7** nummer^h *(on CD, gramophone record)*; (opname)spoor^h *(on cassette) tape)*: *the wrong side of the (railroad) ~s* de achterbuurten; *lose ~ of* uit het oog verliezen, niet meer op de hoogte blijven van; *(inf) make ~s* 'm smeren; *across the ~s* in de achterbuurten; *(inf) in one's ~s* ter plaatse, ter plekke

²track [træk] *vb* **1** het spoor volgen van, volgen; **2** *(with down)* (op)sporen, ontdekken, naspeuren

track events *(athletics)* loopnummers

tracksuit trainingspak^h

tract [trækt] **1** uitgestrekt gebied^h, landstreek; **2** traktaat^h, verhandeling *(rel, ethics)*

traction [træksjən] **1** trekking, het (voort)trekken; **2** trekkracht, aandrijving

tractor [træktə] tractor, (landbouw)trekker

¹trade [treed] *n* **1** handel, zaken: *Department of Trade and Industry (roughly)* Ministerie van Economische Zaken; *do a good ~* goede zaken doen; **2** bedrijfstak, branche; **3** handel, (mensen van) het vak, handelaars; **4** vak^h, ambacht^h, beroep^h: *a butcher by ~* slager van beroep; **5** passaat(wind)

²trade [treed] *vb* handel drijven, handelen, zaken doen || *~ (up)on s.o.'s generosity* misbruik maken van iemands vrijgevigheid

³trade [treed] *vb* verhandelen, uitwisselen, (om)ruilen: ~ *in an old car for a new one* een oude auto voor een nieuwe inruilen

trade association beroepsvereniging

trade fair handelsbeurs

trade-in 1 inruilobject[h]; **2** inruil

trademark handelsmerk[h], *(fig)* typisch kenmerk[h] *(of person)*

trade price (groot)handelsprijs

trader [treedə] **1** handelaar; **2** koopvaardijschip[h]

tradesman [treedzmən] **1** winkelier; **2** leverancier

tradespeople winkeliers *(as group)*

trade(s) union [treed(z) joe:niən] (vak)bond, vakvereniging

trade unionist vakbondslid[h], aanhanger ve vakbond

trade wind passaatwind

trading estate industriegebied[h]

trading post handelsnederzetting

tradition [trədisjən] traditie, overlevering

traditional [trədisjənəl] traditioneel, vanouds gebruikelijk

¹traffic [træfik] *n* **1** verkeer[h], vervoer[h], transport[h]; **2** handel, koophandel: ~ *in drugs* drugshandel

²traffic [træfik] *vb* **1** handel drijven (in), handelen (in), zaken doen (in); **2** zwarte handel drijven (in), sjacheren (met) || ~ *in arms* wapenhandel drijven

trafficator [træfikkeetə] richtingaanwijzer

traffic circle rotonde, (rond) verkeersplein[h]

traffic jam (verkeers)opstopping

trafficker [træfikkə] zwarthandelaar, sjacheraar, dealer *(in drugs etc)*

traffic lane rijstrook

traffic sign verkeersteken[h], verkeersbord[h]

traffic warden parkeercontroleur

tragedy [trædzjiddie] tragedie, drama[h], tragiek, het tragische

tragic [trædzjik] tragisch, droevig

¹trail [treel] *n* **1** sliert, stroom, rij: ~ *s of smoke* rookslierten; **2** spoor[h], pad[h]: *a ~ of destruction* een spoor van vernieling; *blaze a ~ (fig)* de weg banen, baanbrekend werk verrichten; **3** spoor[h], prent *(of animal)*, geur(vlag) *(as trace)*: *be hard* (of: *hot) on s.o.'s ~* iem op de hielen zitten

²trail [treel] *vb* **1** slepen, loshangen: *her gown was ~ing along on the ground* haar japon sleepte over de grond; **2** zich (voort)slepen, strompelen; **3** kruipen *(of plants)*; **4** *(with behind) (sport)* achterliggen, achterstaan, achteraankomen: *his voice ~ed off* zijn stem stierf weg

³trail [treel] *vb* **1** slepen, sleuren; **2** volgen, schaduwen; **3** *(sport)* achterliggen op, achterstaan op

trailer [treelə] **1** aanhangwagen, oplegger; **2** caravan; **3** trailer

¹train [treen] *n* **1** trein: *by ~* per trein; **2** sleep *(of dress); (fig)* nasleep; **3** gevolg[h], stoet, sleep; **4** rij, reeks, opeenvolging, *(fig)* aaneenschakeling: *a ~ of thought* een gedachtegang; *preparations are in ~* de voorbereidingen zijn aan de gang

²train [treen] *vb* **1** (zich) trainen, (zich) oefenen; **2** een opleiding volgen, studeren: *he is ~ing to be a lawyer* hij studeert voor advocaat

³train [treen] *vb* **1** trainen, oefenen, africhten *(animal);* **2** opleiden, scholen; **3** leiden *(plant);* **4** richten, mikken

trainee [treenie:] stagiair(e)

trainer [treenə] **1** trainer, africhter, dompteur; **2** ~*s* trainingsschoenen

training [treening] training, oefening, opleiding: *physical* ~ conditietraining

training college pedagogische academie

traipse [treeps] sjouwen, slepen || ~ *about* rondslenteren

trait [treet] trek(je[h]), karaktertrek, karaktereigenschap

traitor [treetə] (land)verrader, overloper: *turn* ~ een verrader worden

trajectory [trədzjektərie] baan *(of missile)*

tram [træm] tram: *by* ~ met de tram

tramline 1 tramrail; **2** ~*s* dubbele zijlijnen *(in tennis court)*

¹tramp [træmp] *n* **1** getrappel[h], gestamp[h]; **2** voettocht, trektocht; **3** zwerver, landloper; **4** tramp(boot), vrachtzoeker, schip vd wilde vaart

²tramp [træmp] *vb* **1** stappen, marcheren, stampen; **2** lopen, trekken, een voettocht maken

³tramp [træmp] *vb* **1** aflopen, doorlopen; **2** trappen op, stampen op: ~ *down* plattrappen

¹trample [træmpl] *vb* stampen, trappelen, stappen: ~ *(up)on* trappen op, *(fig)* met voeten treden; ~ *on s.o.'s feelings* iemands gevoelens kwetsen

²trample [træmpl] *vb* vertrappen, trappen op

trance [tra:ns] trance: *be in a* ~ in trance zijn

tranquil [trængkwil] kalm, vredig, rustig

tranquillity [trængkwillittie] kalmte, rust(igheid)

tranquillize [trængkwillajz] kalmeren, tot bedaren brengen

tranquillizer [trængkwillajzə] tranquillizer, kalmerend middel[h]

transact [trænzækt] verrichten, afhandelen, afwikkelen: ~ *business with s.o.* met iem zaken doen

transaction [trænzæksjon] **1** transactie, zaak, handelsovereenkomst; **2** afhandeling, afwikkeling

transatlantic [trænzətlæntik] trans-Atlantisch

transceiver [trænsie:və] *(radio)* zendontvanger

transcend [trænsend] **1** te boven gaan; **2** overtreffen: *he ~s himself* hij overtreft zichzelf

transcendent [trænsendənt] superieur, alles (allen) overtreffend, buitengewoon

transcendental [trænsendentl] transcendentaal, bovenzintuiglijk

transcribe [trænskrajb] transcriberen, overschrijven, (in een andere spelling) overbrengen, *(mus)* bewerken: ~ *the music for organ* de muziek voor orgel bewerken

transcription [trænskripsjon] transcriptie, het overschrijven, *(mus)* bewerking, arrangement[h]

¹transfer [trænsfə:] *vb* **1** overstappen: ~ *from the* *train to the bus* van de trein op de bus overstappen; **2** overgeplaatst worden, veranderen *(of place, work, school)*

²transfer [trænsfɔ:] *vb* **1** overmaken, overhandigen, overdragen: *~ one's rights to s.o.* zijn rechten aan iem (anders) overdragen; **2** overplaatsen, verplaatsen, overbrengen; **3** overdrukken; **4** *(sport)* transfereren *(player)*

³transfer [trænsfɔ:] *n* **1** overplaatsing, overdracht, *(sport)* transfer; **2** overgeplaatste, *(sport)* transfer(speler); **3** *(fin)* overdracht, overschrijving, overboeking; **4** overdrukplaatjeʰ; **5** overstapkaartjeʰ

transferable [trænsfɔ:rəbl] **1** verplaatsbaar; **2** overdraagbaar; **3** inwisselbaar, verhandelbaar *(cheque etc)*

transference [trænsfərəns] overplaatsing, overbrenging

transfix [trænsfɪks] **1** doorboren, doorsteken *(eg with lance)*; **2** (vast)spietsen; **3** als aan de grond nagelen, verlammen

¹transform [trænsfɔ:m] *vb* (van vorm, gedaante, karakter) veranderen, een gedaanteverwisseling ondergaan

²transform [trænsfɔ:m] *vb* **1** (van vorm, gedaante, karakter doen) veranderen, her-, omvormen: *stress ~ed him into an aggressive man* door de stress veranderde hij in een agressief man; **2** *(also electr)* omzetten, transformeren

transformation [trænsfəmeesjən] transformatie

transformer [trænsfɔ:mə] *(electr)* transformator

transfuse [trænsfjoe:z] een transfusie geven (van)

transfusion [trænsfjoe:zjən] transfusie

transgenic [trænzdzjennik] transgenetisch *(of crop etc)*

¹transgress [trænzgres] *vb* **1** een overtreding begaan; **2** zondigen

²transgress [trænzgres] *vb* overtreden, inbreuk maken op, schenden

transient [trænziənt] **1** voorbijgaand, kortstondig; **2** doorreizend, doortrekkend

transistor [trænzistə] transistor

transit [trænzit] doorgang, doortocht: *in ~* tijdens het vervoer, onderweg

transition [trænzisjən] overgang: *period of ~* overgangsperiode

transitional [trænzisjənəl] tussenliggend, overgangs-, tussen-

transitive [trænsittiv] transitief, overgankelijk

translate [trænzleet] **1** vertalen: *~ a sentence from English into Dutch* een zin uit het Engels in het Nederlands vertalen; **2** interpreteren, uitleggen, vertolken; **3** omzetten, omvormen *(also biology)*: *~ ideas into actions* ideeën in daden omzetten

translation [trænzleesjən] vertaling

translator [trænzleetə] **1** vertaler; **2** tolk

translucent [trænzloe:snt] doorschijnend

transmission [trænzmisjən] **1** uitzending, programmaʰ; **2** overbrenging, overdracht *(also of dis-*

ease, heredity); **3** transmissie, overbrenging, versnellingsbak; **4** het doorgeven, overlevering

transmit [trænzmit] **1** overbrengen, overdragen *(also of disease, heredity)*: *~ a message* een boodschap overbrengen; **2** overleveren, doorgeven *(traditions etc)*

transmitter [trænzmittə] **1** overbrenger, overdrager; **2** seintoestelʰ, seingever; **3** microfoon *(of telephone)*; **4** zender *(radio, TV)*

transparency [trænspærənsie] **1** dia(positiefʰ), projectieplaatjeʰ; **2** doorzichtigheid

transparent [trænspærənt] **1** doorzichtig *(also fig)*, transparant: *a ~ lie* een doorzichtige leugen; **2** eenvoudig, gemakkelijk te begrijpen

¹transpire [trænspajjə] *vb* **1** transpireren, zweten *(of human being, animal)*; **2** uitlekken, aan het licht komen, bekend worden: *it ~d that the president himself was involved* het lekte uit dat de president er zelf bij betrokken was

²transpire [trænspajjə] *vb* uitwasemen, uitzweten

¹transplant [trænsplant] *vb* **1** verplanten, overplanten; **2** overbrengen, doen verhuizen; **3** transplanteren, overplanten

²transplant [trænspla:nt] *n* **1** getransplanteerd orgaanʰ (weefselʰ), transplantaatʰ; **2** transplantatie

¹transport [trænspo:t] *n* vervoer(middel)ʰ, transportʰ: *public ~* openbaar vervoer; *I'd like to come, but I've no ~* ik zou wel mee willen, maar ik heb geen vervoer

²transport [trænspo:t] *vb* vervoeren, transporteren, overbrengen

transportation [trænspo:teesjən] **1** vervoermiddelʰ, transportmiddelʰ; **2** vervoerʰ, transportʰ, overbrenging

transport cafe wegrestaurantʰ

transpose [trænspooz] **1** anders schikken, (onderling) verwisselen, omzetten; **2** *(mus)* transponeren

¹trap [træp] *n* **1** val, (val)strik, hinderlaag, strikvraag: *lay (of: set) a ~* een val (op)zetten, een strik spannen; **2** sifon, stankafsluiter *(in drainpipe)*; **3** *(inf)* smoel, waffel, bek: *shut your ~!* hou je kop!

²trap [træp] *vb* **1** (ver)strikken, (in een val) vangen, *(fig)* in de val laten lopen: *~ s.o. into a confession* iem door een list tot een bekentenis dwingen; **2** opsluiten: *be ~ped* opgesloten zitten, in de val zitten, vastzitten; **3** opvangen *(eg energy)*

trapdoor valdeur, val, (val)luikʰ

trapeze [trəpie:z] trapeze

trapper [træpə] vallenzetter, pelsjager

trappings [træpingz] (uiterlijke) sieraden, (uiterlijk) vertoon

¹trash [træsj] *n* **1** rotzooi, (oude) rommel, troep; **2** onzin, geklets²ʰ; **3** afvalʰ, vuilʰ, vuilnis; **4** nietsnut(ten), uitschotʰ, tuigʰ

²trash [træsj] *vb* kritiseren, afkraken *(book, film etc)*

trash can vuilnisemmer

trashy [træsjie] waardeloos, kitscherig: *~ novel* flutroman

trauma [trɔ:mə] **1** wond, verwonding, letselʰ; **2**

(psychology) trauma^h

traumatic [tro:mætik] traumatisch, beangstigend

^1**travel** [trævl] *vb* **1** reizen, een reis maken: *~ling circus* rondreizend circus; **2** vertegenwoordiger zijn: *~ in electrical appliances* vertegenwoordiger in huishoudelijke apparaten zijn; **3** zich (voort)bewegen, zich voortplanten, gaan: *news ~s fast* nieuws verspreidt zich snel; *flowers ~ badly* bloemen kunnen slecht tegen vervoer

^2**travel** [trævl] *vb* **1** doorreizen, doortrekken, afreizen *(also as commercial traveller)*; **2** afleggen: *~ 500 miles a day* 500 mijl per dag afleggen

^3**travel** [trævl] *n* **1** (lange, verre) reis, rondreis, het reizen: *on our ~s* tijdens onze rondreis; **2** *~s* reisverhaal^h, reisverhalen, reizen, reisbeschrijving: *Gulliver's Travels* Gullivers Reizen

travel agency reisbureau^h

traveller [trævələ] **1** reiziger, bereisd man; **2** handelsreiziger, vertegenwoordiger

traveller's cheque reischeque

travelog(ue) [trævəlog] (geïllustreerd) reisverhaal^h, reisfilm

^1**traverse** [trævə:s] *vb* **1** (door)kruisen, oversteken, (dwars) trekken door, doorsnijden; **2** dwars beklimmen *(slope)*

^2**traverse** [trævə:s] *vb* schuins klimmen

travesty [trævəstie] travestie, karikatuur, parodie: *~ of justice* karikatuur van rechtvaardigheid

^1**trawl** [tro:l] *vb* met een sleepnet vissen (naar), *(fig)* uitkammen, uitpluizen: *(fig) ~ for* zorgvuldig doorzoeken

^2**trawl** [tro:l] *n* **1** sleepnet^h, trawl; **2** zoektocht, speurtocht *(eg for talent)*

trawler [tro:lə] treiler, trawler

tray [tree] **1** dienblad^h, (presenteer)blad^h; **2** bakje^h, brievenbak(je^h)

treacherous [tretsjərəs] verraderlijk, onbetrouwbaar: *~ ice* verraderlijk ijs; *~ memory* onbetrouwbaar geheugen

treachery [tretsjərie] verraad^h, ontrouw, onbetrouwbaarheid

treacle [trie:kl] (suiker)stroop *(also fig)*

treacly [trie:klie] stroperig, kleverig, *(fig)* (honing)zoet, vleiend

^1**tread** [tred] *vb* treden, stappen, lopen, wandelen: *~ in the mud* in de modder trappen

^2**tread** [tred] *vb* **1** betreden, bewandelen, begaan; **2** trappen, (ver)trappen, in-, stuk-, uit-, vasttrappen, *(fig)* onderdrukken: *~ grapes* (met de voeten) druiven persen; *~ water* watertrappelen; **3** heen en weer lopen in, lopen door; **4** (zich) banen, platlopen

^3**tread** [tred] *n* **1** tred, pas, gang: *a heavy ~* een zware stap; **2** trede, opstapje^h; **3** loopvlak^h *(of tyre);* **4** profiel^h *(of tyre)*

treadle [tredl] trapper, pedaal^h

treadmill tredmolen *(also fig)*

treason [trie:zən] hoogverraad^h, landverraad^h

^1**treasure** [trezjə] *n* **1** schat, kostbaarheid, *(inf)* juweel^h, parel: *my secretary is a ~* ik heb een juweel van een secretaresse; **2** schat(ten), rijkdom: *~ of ideas* schat aan ideeën

^2**treasure** [trezjə] *vb* **1** (with *up*) verzamelen, bewaren; **2** waarderen, op prijs stellen

treasure house schatkamer: *the museum is a ~ of paintings* dit museum heeft een schat aan schilderijen

treasurer [trezjərə] penningmeester

treasure trove (gevonden) schat, (waardevolle) vondst, rijke bron *(also fig)*

treasury [trezjrie] **1** schatkamer, schatkist, *(fig)* bron; **2** *the Treasury* Ministerie^h van Financiën

^1**treat** [trie:t] *vb* **1** behandelen *(also med): ~ s.o. kindly* iem vriendelijk behandelen; **2** beschouwen, afdoen: *~ sth. as a joke* iets als een grapje opvatten; **3** aan de orde stellen, behandelen *(subject);* **4** trakteren, onthalen

^2**treat** [trie:t] *vb* **1** trakteren; **2** (with *with*) onderhandelen (met), (vredes)besprekingen voeren (met), zaken doen (met)

^3**treat** [trie:t] *n* traktatie, (feestelijk) onthaal^h, feest^h, plezier^h: *it's my ~* ik trakteer

treatise [trie:tis] verhandeling, beschouwing

treatment [trie:tmənt] behandeling, verzorging

treaty [trie:tie] verdrag^h, overeenkomst

^1**treble** [trebl] *adj* driemaal, drievoudig, driedubbel: || *~ recorder* altblokfluit

^2**treble** [trebl] *vb* verdrievoudigen, met drie vermenigvuldigen

tree [trie:] boom: *family ~* stamboom

trefoil [treffojl] *(bot)* klaver(blad^h)

trellis [trellis] latwerk^h, traliewerk^h

^1**tremble** [trembl] *vb* **1** beven, rillen, bibberen: *in fear and trembling* met angst en beven; **2** schudden *(bldg, earth),* trillen; **3** huiveren, in angst zitten: *I ~ to think* ik moet er niet aan denken, ik huiver bij de gedachte

^2**tremble** [trembl] *n* trilling, huivering, rilling: *be all of a ~* over zijn hele lichaam beven

tremendous [trimmendəs] **1** enorm, geweldig; **2** fantastisch

tremor [tremmə] **1** aardschok, lichte aardbeving; **2** huivering, siddering

tremulous [tremjoeləs] **1** trillend, sidderend; **2** schuchter, nerveus: *~ voice* onvaste stem

trench [trentsj] **1** geul, greppel; **2** loopgraaf; **3** *(geology)* trog

trenchant [trentsjənt] scherp, krachtig: *~ remark* spitse opmerking

^1**trend** [trend] *n* tendens, neiging, trend: *set the ~* de toon aangeven

^2**trend** [trend] *vb* overhellen, geneigd zijn: *prices are ~ing downwards* de prijzen lijken te gaan zakken

trendsetter trendsetter, voorloper

trendy [trendie] in, modieus, trendy

trepidation [treppiddeesjən] ongerustheid, angst

^1**trespass** [trespəs] *vb* **1** op verboden terrein komen; **2** *(rel)* een overtreding begaan, zondigen

^2**trespass** [trespəs] *n* **1** overtreding, inbreuk, schending; **2** *(rel)* zonde, schuld

trespasser [trespəsə] overtreder: *~s will be prosecuted* verboden toegang voor onbevoegden

trespass (up)on 1 wederrechtelijk betreden *(grounds);* **2** beslag leggen op, inbreuk maken op, misbruik maken van *(time, hospitality)*

trestle [tresl] schraag, onderstel[h]

trestle table schragentafel

trial [trajjəl] **1** (gerechtelijk) onderzoek[h], proces[h], rechtszaak; **2** proef, experiment[h]: *give sth. a ~* iets testen; *by ~ and error* met vallen en opstaan; **3** poging; **4** beproeving *(also fig)*, probleem[h]: *~s and tribulations* zorgen en problemen

triangle [trajænggl] driehoek, triangel

triangular [trajængggjoelə] **1** driehoekig; **2** driezijdig

tribal [trajbl] stam(men)-, ve stam

tribe [trajb] **1** stam, volksstam; **2** groep, geslacht[h] *(related things)*

tribesman [trajbzmən] **1** stamlid[h]; **2** stamgenoot

tribulation [tribjoeleesjən] **1** bron van ellende; **2** beproeving, rampspoed

tribunal [trajbjoe:nl] **1** rechtbank, gerecht[h], tribunaal[h]; **2** *(roughly)* commissie, raad, raad van onderzoek

tribune [tribjoe:n] **1** volksleider, demagoog; **2** podium[h], tribune

tributary [tribjoetərie] **1** schatplichtige; belastingplichtige *(state, person);* **2** zijrivier

tribute [tribjoe:t] **1** bijdrage, belasting; **2** hulde, eerbetoon[h]: *pay (a) ~ to s.o.* iem eer bewijzen

trice [trajs] ogenblik[h], moment[h]: *in a ~* in een wip

¹trick [trik] *n* **1** truc *(also fig)*, foefje[h], kneep: *know the ~s of the trade* het klappen van de zweep kennen; *magic ~s* goocheltrucs; **2** handigheid, slag: *get (of: learn) the ~ of it* de slag te pakken krijgen (van iets); **3** streek, kattenkwaad[h]: *play a ~ (up)on s.o., play s.o. a ~* iem een streek leveren; **4** aanwensel[h], tic: *you have the ~ of pulling your hair when you're nervous* je hebt de vreemde gewoonte om aan je haren te trekken als je zenuwachtig bent; **5** *(cards)* slag: *this poison should do the ~* met dit vergif moet het lukken; *not (of: never) miss a ~* overal van op de hoogte zijn; *be up to s.o.'s ~s* iem doorhebben; *how's ~s?* hoe staat het ermee?

²trick [trik] *vb* **1** bedriegen, misleiden: *~ s.o. into sth.* iem iets aanpraten, iem ergens inluizen; **2** oplichten, afzetten: *~ s.o. out of his money* iem zijn geld afhandig maken

trickery [trikkərie] bedrog[h]

¹trickle [trikl] *vb* **1** druppelen; **2** druppelsgewijs komen (gaan): *the first guests ~d in* at ten o'clock om tien uur druppelden de eerste gasten binnen

²trickle [trikl] *n* **1** stroompje[h], straaltje[h]; **2** het druppelen

trickster [trikstə] oplichter, bedrieger

tricky [trikkie] **1** sluw, listig; **2** lastig, moeilijk: *~ question* lastige vraag

tricycle [trajsikl] driewieler

trident [trajdənt] drietand

tried beproefd, betrouwbaar

triennial [trajjenniəl] **1** driejaarlijks, om de drie jaar terugkomend; **2** driejarig, drie jaar durend

trifle [trajfl] **1** kleinigheid, wissewasje[h]; **2** habbekrats, prikje[h], schijntje[h]; **3** beetje[h]: *he's a ~ slow* hij is ietwat langzaam

trifle with 1 niet serieus nemen: *she is not a woman to be trifled with* zij is geen vrouw die met zich laat spotten; **2** spelen met

trifling [trajfling] **1** onbelangrijk: *of ~ importance* van weinig belang; **2** waardeloos

¹trigger [trigə] *n* trekker, pal *(of pistol):* *pull the ~* de trekker overhalen, *(fig)* het startschot geven

²trigger [trigə] *vb* teweegbrengen, veroorzaken: *~ off: a)* op gang brengen; *b)* ten gevolge hebben

trigger-happy 1 schietgraag, snel schietend; **2** strijdlustig

trigonometry [trigənommitrie] trigonometrie, driehoeksmeting

¹trill [tril] *vb* trillen, kwinkeleren, vibreren ‖ *~ the r* een rollende r maken

²trill [tril] *n* **1** roller, triller *(of birds);* **2** met trilling geproduceerde klank, rollende medeklinker *(eg rolling r)*

trillion [trilliən] **1** triljoen *(10¹⁸);* *(fig)* talloos; **2** *(Am)* biljoen *(10¹²)*, miljoen maal miljoen, *(fig)* talloos

¹trim [trim] *adj* **1** net(jes), goed verzorgd: *a ~ garden* een keurig onderhouden tuin; **2** in vorm, in goede conditie

²trim [trim] *vb* **1** in orde brengen, net(jes) maken, (bij)knippen *(eg of hair);* **2** afknippen, *(fig)* besnoeien: *~ (down) the expenditure* de uitgaven beperken; **3** versieren: *a coat ~med with fur* een jas afgezet met bont; **4** naar de wind zetten *(of sails); (fig)* aanpassen; schikken: *he ~s his opinions to the circumstances* hij past zijn mening aan de omstandigheden aan

³trim [trim] *n* **1** versiering, sierstrip(pen) *(on car);* **2** het bijknippen; **3** staat (van gereedheid), conditie: *the players were in (good)* ~ de spelers waren in (goede) vorm

trimmer [trimmə] **1** snoeimes[h], tuinschaar, tondeuse; **2** weerhaan *(fig)*, opportunist

trimmings [trimmingz] **1** garnituur, toebehoren[h]; **2** (af)snoeisel[h], afknipsel[h]; **3** opsmuk, franje: *tell us the story without the ~s* vertel ons het verhaal zonder opsmuk

Trinity [trinnittie] Drie-eenheid

trinket [tringkit] **1** kleinood[h]; **2** prul[h], snuisterij

trio [trie:oo] **1** drietal[h]; **2** *(mus)* trio[h]

¹trip [trip] *vb* **1** (also with *up*) struikelen, uitglijden; **2** huppelen, trippelen: *the girl ~ped across the room* het meisje huppelde door de kamer; **3** *(*with *up)* een fout begaan: *the man ~ped up after a few questions* de man versprak zich na een paar vragen

²trip [trip] *vb* **1** (also with *up*) laten struikelen, beentje lichten; **2** *(*also with *up)* op een fout betrappen;

3 *(also with up)* erin laten lopen, strikken, zich laten verspreken

³trip [trip] *n* **1** tocht, reis, uitstapje^h; **2** misstap *(also fig)*, val, vergissing; **3** trip *(on LSD; also fig)*, reuze ervaring

tripe [trajp] **1** pens; **2** *(inf)* onzin

¹triple [tripl] *adj* drievoudig; driedubbel

²triple [tripl] *vb* verdrievoudigen

triplet [triplit] **1** één ve drieling, ~s drieling; **2** drietal^h, drie, trio^h

triplicate [triplikkət] triplicaat^h, derde exemplaar^h: *in* ~ in drievoud

tripod [trajpod] driepoot, statief^h

tripper [trippə] dagjesmens

triptych [triptik] drieluik^h

tripwire struikeldraad, valstrik

trite [trajt] afgezaagd, cliché

¹triumph [trajjəmf] *n* triomf, overwinning, groot succes^h

²triumph [trajjəmf] *vb* zegevieren: ~ *over difficulties* moeilijkheden overwinnen

triumphal [trajjumfl] triomf-, zege-: ~ *arch* triomfboog

triumphant [trajjumfənt] **1** zegevierend; **2** triomfantelijk

trivet [trivvit] drievoet, *(Am)* onderzetter *(for pots and pans etc)*

trivial [trivviəl] **1** onbelangrijk; **2** gewoon, alledaags; **3** oppervlakkig

triviality [trivvie·ælittie] **1** iets onbelangrijks; **2** onbelangrijkheid

Trojan [troodzjən] Trojaan || *work like a* ~ werken als een paard

trolley [trollie] **1** tweewielig (vierwielig) karretje^h, winkelwagentje^h; **2** tram; **3** theewagen || *off one's* ~ (stapel)gek

trolley bus trolleybus

trolley car tram

trollop [trolləp] *(inf)* **1** slons, sloddervos; **2** slet, sloerie

trombone [tromboon] trombone, schuiftrompet

¹troop [troe:p] *n* **1** troep, menigte; **2** *(mil)* troep, peloton^h; **3** ~s troepen(macht), strijdmachten

²troop [troe:p] *vb* **1** als groep gaan: *his children ~ed in* zijn kinderen marcheerden naar binnen; **2** samenscholen

trooper [troe:pə] **1** cavalerist; **2** gewoon soldaat; **3** (staats)politieagent || *swear like a* ~ vloeken als een ketter

trophy [troofie] **1** prijs, trofee; **2** trofee, zegeteken^h *(also fig)*, aandenken^h

tropic [troppik] keerkring: ~ *of Cancer* kreeftskeerkring; ~ *of Capricorn* steenbokskeerkring; *the ~s* de tropen

tropical [troppikl] tropisch, *(fig)* heet, drukkend

¹trot [trot] *vb* **1** draven *(also of person)*; **2** *(inf)* lopen, (weg)gaan

²trot [trot] *vb*: ~ *out* voor de dag komen met

³trot [trot] *n* **1** draf(je^h), haastige beweging: *be on the*

~ ronddraven, niet stilzitten; **2** ~s *(vulg)* diarree: *have the ~s* aan de dunne zijn

trotter [trottə] **1** draver *(horse)*; **2** varkenspoot

¹trouble [trubl] *n* **1** zorg, bezorgdheid: *that is the least of my ~s!* dat is mij een zorg!; **2** tegenslag, narigheid, probleem^h: *get into* ~ in moeilijkheden raken; **3** ongemak^h, overlast: *I do not want to be any* ~ ik wil (u) niet tot last zijn; **4** moeite, inspanning: *save oneself the* ~ zich de moeite besparen; **5** kwaal, ongemak^h: *he suffers from back* ~ hij heeft rugklachten; **6** onlust, onrust; **7** pech, mankement^h: *the car has got engine* ~ de wagen heeft motorpech

²trouble [trubl] *vb* **1** verontrusten: *what ~s me is …* wat me dwars zit is …; **2** lastig vallen, storen: *I hope I'm not troubling you* ik hoop dat ik niet stoor; **3** kwellen

³trouble [trubl] *vb* moeite doen: *do not ~ to explain* doe geen moeite het uit te leggen

troublemaker [trublmeekə] onruststoker, herrieschopper

troubleshooter [trublsjoe:tə] probleemoplosser, puinruimer

troublesome [trublsəm] lastig

trough [trof] **1** trog, drinkbak, eetbak; **2** goot; **3** laagte(punt^h), diepte(punt^h) *(on meter, in statistics etc)*

trounce [trauns] afrossen, afstraffen, *(sport; fig)* inmaken

troupe [troe:p] troep, groep *(esp actors, artists)*

trouser [trauzə] broek(s)-: ~ *buttons* broeksknopen

trousers [trauzəz] (lange) broek: *a pair of* ~ een (lange) broek; *wear the* ~ de broek aan hebben

trousseau [troe:soo] uitzet

trout [traut] (zee)forel || *old* ~ oude tang

trowel [trauəl] troffel || *lay it on with a* ~ het er dik op leggen, aandikken

Troy [troj] Troje

truant [troe:ənt] **1** spijbelaar: *play* ~ spijbelen; **2** lijntrekker

truce [troe:s] (tijdelijk) bestand^h, (tijdelijke) wapenstilstand

truck [truk] **1** vrachtwagen, truck; **2** handkar, bagagekar *(esp railways)*; **3** open goederenwagen; **4** ruilhandel, ruilverkeer^h || *have no* ~ *with* geen zaken doen met, niets te maken willen hebben met

trucker [trukkə] *(Am)* vrachtwagenchauffeur

truckle [trukl] kruipen, kruiperig doen: ~ *to s.o.* voor iem kruipen

truckle bed (laag) rolbed^h

truculence [trukjoeləns] **1** vechtlust, agressiviteit; **2** gewelddadigheid

truculent [trukjoelənt] vechtlustig, agressief

¹trudge [trudzj] *vb* sjokken, slepen: ~ *along* zich voortslepen

²trudge [trudzj] *vb* afsjokken, afsukkelen *(distance)*

³trudge [trudzj] *n* (trek)tocht, mars

¹true [troe:] *adj* **1** waar, juist: *come* ~ werkelijkheid worden; **2** echt, waar: ~ *to life* levensecht; **3** trouw:

a ~ *friend* een trouwe vriend

²**true** [troe:] *adv* **1** waarheidsgetrouw: *ring* ~ echt klinken; **2** juist

true-blue 1 betrouwbaar, eerlijk, loyaal; **2** onwrikbaar, aarts- *(of conservative politician)*

true-born (ras)echt, geboren

truffle [trʉfl] truffel *(also bonbon)*

truism [troe:izm] **1** waarheid als een koe; **2** afgezaagd gezegde[h]

truly [troe:lie] **1** oprecht, waarlijk: *I am ~ grateful to you* ik ben u oprecht dankbaar; **2** echt, werkelijk; **3** trouw, toegewijd; **4** terecht, juist: *yours ~: a)* hoogachtend *(complimentary close in letters); b)* de ondergetekende, ik

¹**trump** [trump] *n* troef *(also fig)*, troefkaart: *spades are ~s* schoppen is troef; *come* (of: *turn) up ~s: a)* voor een meevaller zorgen; *b)* geluk hebben met

²**trump** [trump] *vb* troeven, troef (uit)spelen ‖ ~ *up* verzinnen; *the charge was clearly ~ed up* de beschuldiging was duidelijk verzonnen

trump card troefkaart *(also fig): that was my ~* dat was mijn laatste redmiddel

¹**trumpet** [trumpit] *n* **1** trompet: *(fig) blow one's own ~* zijn eigen lof zingen; **2** trompetgeluid[h], getrompetter[h] *(eg of elephant)*

²**trumpet** [trumpit] *vb* **1** trompet spelen; **2** trompetteren

truncate [trungkeet] beknotten *(also fig)*, aftoppen, besnoeien: ~ *a story* een verhaal inkorten

trunk [trungk] **1** (boom)stam; **2** romp, torso; **3** (hut)koffer *(oft also piece of furniture);* **4** slurf, snuit *(of elephant);* **5** kofferbak *(of car);* **6** ~s korte broek, zwembroek *(for men)*

trunk call interlokaal (telefoon)gesprek[h]

trunk road hoofdweg

¹**truss** [trus] *n* **1** dakkap, dakspant[h]; **2** breukband; **3** bundel, bos[h], pak[h]

²**truss** [trus] *vb* (stevig) inbinden: ~ *up: a)* inbinden, opmaken *(chicken); b)* knevelen

¹**trust** [trust] *n* **1** vertrouwen[h]: *a position of ~* een vertrouwenspositie; **2** (goede) hoop, verwachting; **3** zorg, hoede: *commit a child to s.o.'s ~* een kind aan iemands zorgen toevertrouwen; **4** trust, kartel[h]; **5** *(law)* trust, machtiging tot beheer van goederen voor een begunstigde: *hold property in* (of: *under)* ~ eigendom in bewaring hebben

²**trust** [trust] *vb* **1** vertrouwen: *you should not ~ in him* je mag hem niet vertrouwen; **2** vertrouwen hebben, hopen

³**trust** [trust] *vb* **1** vertrouwen op, aannemen, hopen: *I ~ everything is all right with him* ik hoop maar dat alles met hem in orde is; **2** toevertrouwen: *he ~ed his car to a friend* hij gaf zijn auto bij een vriend in bewaring

trustee [trustie:] beheerder, bewindvoerder *(of capital, estate)*, bestuurder, commissaris *(of institution, school)*

trusting [trusting] vertrouwend, vriendelijk

trustworthy [trustwɔ:ðie] betrouwbaar

truth [troe:θ] **1** waarheid: *to tell the ~, …* om de waarheid te zeggen, …; **2** echtheid; **3** oprechtheid

truthful [troe:θfoel] **1** eerlijk, oprecht; **2** waar, (waarheids)getrouw

¹**try** [traj] *vb* **1** proberen, uitproberen, op de proef stellen, *(also fig)* vermoeien: ~ *s.o.'s patience* iemands geduld op de proef stellen; ~ *to be on time* proberen op tijd te komen; *tried and found wanting* gewogen en te licht bevonden; ~ *on* aanpassen *(clothes);* ~ *out* testen, de proef nemen met; ~ *sth. on s.o.* iets op iem uitproberen; *just ~ and stop me!* probeer me maar eens tegen te houden!; **2** berechten, verhoren: ~ *s.o. for murder* iem voor moord berechten

²**try** [traj] *n (tries)* **1** poging: *give it a ~* het eens proberen, een poging wagen; **2** *(rugby)* try

trying [trajjing] moeilijk, zwaar: ~ *person to deal with* lastige klant

try-out test, proef: *give s.o. a ~* het met iem proberen

tsar [za:] tsaar

T-shirt T-shirt[h]

T.T. 1 *teetotaller* **2** *Tourist Trophy* TT *(motorcycle race)*

tub [tub] tobbe, (was)kuip, ton

tubby [tubbie] tonvormig, rond, dik

tube [tjoe:b] **1** buis(je[h]), pijp, slang, huls, koker, tube; **2** binnenband; **3** metro; **4** *(Am)* televisie

tuberculosis [tjoebə:kjoeloosis] tuberculose

tubular [tjoe:bjoelə] buisvormig

¹**tuck** [tuk] *vb* **1** plooien; **2** inkorten, innemen; **3** (with *up)* opstoppen, optrekken; **4** intrekken: *with his legs ~ed up under him* in kleermakerszit; **5** *(also with away)* (ver)stoppen, wegstoppen, verschuilen: ~ *away* (of: *in)* verorberen; **6** (with *in)* instoppen, *(also with up)* toedekken, wikkelen: ~ *one's shirt into one's trousers* zijn hemd in zijn broek stoppen

²**tuck** [tuk] *vb* plooien maken ‖ ~ *in!* val aan, tast toe!; ~ *into* flink smullen van

³**tuck** [tuk] *n* **1** plooi; **2** zoetigheid

tuck-in smulpartij

tuck shop snoepwinkeltje[h]

Tuesday [tjoe:zdee] dinsdag

tuft [tuft] bosje[h], kwastje[h]; kuifje[h]

¹**tug** [tug] *vb* (with *at)* rukken (aan)

²**tug** [tug] *vb* **1** rukken aan; **2** slepen *(tug boat)*

³**tug** [tug] *n* **1** ruk, haal: *give a ~ at* (heftig) rukken aan; **2** (felle) strijd, conflict[h]: *(inf)* ~ *of love* touwtrekkerij om (de voogdij over) een kind *(between divorced parents);* **3** sleepboot

tuition [tjoe·isjən] **1** schoolgeld[h], lesgeld[h]; **2** onderwijs[h]

tulip [tjoe:lip] tulp

¹**tumble** [tumbl] *vb* **1** vallen, tuimelen, struikelen: ~ *down* neerploffen; ~ *down the stairs* van de trap rollen; **2** rollen, woelen: ~ *about* rondtollen; **3** stormen, lopen: ~ *into* (of: *out of) bed* in zijn bed ploffen, uit zijn bed springen; **4** (snel) zakken, kelderen: *tumbling prices* dalende prijzen; ~ *to* snappen

²**tumble** [tumbl] *vb* **1** doen vallen, omgooien; **2** in de war brengen; **3** drogen *(in tumble drier)*

³**tumble** [tumbl] *n* **1** val(partij): *have* (of: *take) a ~* vallen; **2** warboel: *in a ~* overhoop

tumbledown bouwvallig

tumble-dryer droogtrommel

tumbler [tumblə] **1** duikelaar; **2** acrobaat; **3** tuimelglasʰ, (groot) bekerglasʰ; **4** *(techn)* tuimelaar *(of lock);* **5** droogtrommel

tummy [tummie] buik(jeʰ)

tummy button navel

tumour [tjoe:mə] tumor

tumult [tjoe:mult] tumultʰ: *in a ~* totaal verward

tumultuous [tjoe:multjoeəs] tumultueus, wanordelijk

tun [tun] vatʰ

tuna [tjoe:nə] tonijn

tundra [tundrə] toendra

¹**tune** [tjoe:n] *n* **1** wijsjeʰ, melodie, *(fig)* toon; **2** juiste toonhoogte: *sing out of ~* vals zingen; **3** overeenstemming: *it is in ~ with the spirit of the time* het is in overeenstemming met de tijdgeest; *call the ~* de lakens uitdelen; *change one's ~, sing another* (of: *dance to another) ~* een andere toon aanslaan, een toontje lager gaan zingen; *to the ~ of £1000* voor het bedrag van £1000

²**tune** [tjoe:n] *vb* **1** stemmen; **2** afstemmen *(also fig),* instellen: *~ oneself to* zich aanpassen aan; *~d to* afgestemd op; **3** afstellen *(engine)*

³**tune** [tjoe:n] *vb* **1** (with *with)* harmoniëren (met); **2** zingen

tune in afstemmen, de radio (televisie) aanzetten: *~ to* afstemmen op

¹**tune up** *vb* stemmen *(of orchestra)*

²**tune up** *vb* in gereedheid brengen, afstellen

tunic [tjoe:nik] **1** tunica; **2** tuniek, (korte) uniformjas

tunnel [tunl] **1** tunnel; **2** onderaardse gang *(of mole etc)*

tunny [tunnie] tonijn

turban [tə:bən] tulband

turbid [tə:bid] **1** troebel, drabbig; **2** verward: *~ emotions* verwarde emoties

turbine [tə:bajn] turbine

turbot [tə:bət] tarbot

turbulence [tə:bjoeləns] **1** wildheid; **2** beroering, onrust

turbulent [tə:bjoelənt] **1** wild; **2** woelig; oproerig

turd [tə:d] **1** drol; **2** verachtelijk persoon

turf [tə:f] **1** graszode, plag; **2** gras(veld)ʰ; **3** renbaan, racebaan, paardenrennenʰ

turgid [tə:dzjid] **1** *(med)* (op)gezwollen; **2** hoogdravend

Turk [tə:k] Turk(se)

turkey [tə:kie] **1** kalkoen; **2** *(Am)* flop ‖ *talk ~* geen blad voor de mond nemen

Turkish [tə:kisj] Turks ‖ *~ bath* Turks bad; *~ delight* Turks fruit; *~ towel* ruwe badhanddoek

turmoil [tə:mojl] beroering: *the whole country was in (a) ~* het gehele land was in opschudding

¹**turn** [tə:n] *vb* **1** woelen, draaien: *toss and ~ all night* de hele nacht (liggen) draaien en woelen; **2** zich richten, zich wenden: *his thoughts ~ed to his mother* hij dacht aan zijn moeder; *~ away (from)* zich afwenden (van), weggaan (van); *~ to drink* aan de drank raken; **3** van richting veranderen, afslaan, een draai maken, (zich) omkeren: *the aeroplane ~ed sharply* het vliegtuig maakte een scherpe bocht; *~ about* zich omkeren; *about ~!* rechtsom(keert)! *(order to troops);* ~ *(a)round: a)* zich omdraaien; *b)* een ommekeer maken, van gedachten *(of:* mening) veranderen; *~ back* terugkeren, omkeren; **4** draaien *(of head, stomach),* tollen, duizelen: *my head is ~ing* het duizelt mij; **5** gisten, bederven: *~ to* aan het werk gaan; *~ into* veranderen in, worden; *~ on: a)* draaien om, afhangen van; *b)* gaan over *(of conversation); water ~s to ice* water wordt ijs; *~ (up)on s.o.* iem aanvallen, zich tegen iem keren

²**turn** [tə:n] *vb* **1** (rond)draaien, doen draaien: *the wheels ~ fast* de wielen draaien snel; **2** omdraaien, (doen) omkeren, omploegen, omspitten, omslaan, keren *(collar),* omvouwen: *the car ~ed* de auto keerde; *~ about* omkeren, omdraaien; *~ (a)round* ronddraaien, omkeren; *~ back* omvouwen, omslaan; *~ sth. inside out* iets binnenstebuiten keren, *(fig)* grondig doorzoeken, overhoophalen; *~ upside down* ondersteboven keren; *~ to page seven* sla bladzijde zeven op; **3** draaien *(on lathe, at pottery etc),* vormen, maken: *~ a phrase* iets mooi zeggen; **4** verzuren, zuur worden (maken): *the warm weather ~ed the milk* door het warme weer verzuurde de melk; **5** maken, draaien, beschrijven *(circle etc);* **6** overdenken, overwegen, **7** omgaan *(corner),* omdraaien, omzeilen *(cape),* omtrekken; **8** (doen) veranderen (van), omzetten, verzetten, (ver)maken, ken, een wending geven aan *(conversation),* bocht laten maken, draaien, afwenden, omleiden: *~ the car into the garage* de auto de garage indraaien; *~ into* veranderen in, (ver)maken tot, omzetten in; *~ the conversation to sth. different* het gesprek op iets anders brengen; **9** richten, wenden: *~ your attention to the subject* richt je aandacht op het onderwerp; **10** doen worden, maken: *the sun ~ed the papers yellow* de zon maakte de kranten geel; *(Am) loose* loslaten, vrijlaten; **11** verdraaien, verzwikken *(ankle etc);* **12** misselijk maken: *Chinese food ~s my stomach* Chinees eten maakt mijn maag van streek; **13** worden *(time, age),* passeren, geweest zijn: *it is* (of: *has) ~ed six o'clock* het is zes uur geweest; **14** (weg)sturen, (weg)zenden: *~ s.o. adrift* iem aan zijn lot overlaten; *~ away* wegsturen, wegjagen, ontslaan, *(fig)* verwerpen, afwijzen; *we were ~ed back at the entrance* bij de ingang werden we teruggestuurd; **15** zetten, doen, brengen, laten gaan: *~ s.o. into the street* iem op straat zetten; **16** omzetten, draaien, een omzet hebben van, maken *(profit)*

³**turn** [tə:n] *vb* worden: *~ traitor* verrader worden;

the milk ~ed sour de melk werd zuur

⁴turn [tə:n] *n* **1** draai, slag, omwenteling, *(fig)* ommekeer, kentering *(of season)*, wisseling: *a few ~s of the screwdriver will do* een paar slagen met de schroevendraaier is genoeg; *~ of the tide* getijwisseling, kentering; **2** bocht, draai, kromming, afslag: *the next right ~* de volgende afslag rechts; **3** wending, draai, (verandering van) richting: *take a ~ for the worse* een ongunstige wending nemen; **4** beurt: *take ~s at sth.* iets om beurten doen, elkaar aflossen met iets; *~ and ~ about* om en om, om de beurt; *by ~s* om en om, om de beurt; *in ~* om de beurt, achtereenvolgens, op zijn beurt; *take it in ~(s) to do sth.* iets om beurten doen; *out of ~: a)* vóór zijn beurt, niet op zijn beurt; *b)* op een ongeschikt moment; **5** dienst, daad: *do s.o. a bad* (of: *ill*) *~* iem een slechte dienst bewijzen; **6** aanleg, neiging: *be of a musical ~ (of mind)* muzikaal aangelegd zijn; **7** korte bezigheid, wandelingetje^h, ommetje^h, ritje^h, tochtje^h, nummer(tje)^h *(in circus, show)*, artiest *(in show)*; **8** korte tijd *(of participation, work)*, poos: *take a ~ at the wheel* het stuur een tijdje overnemen; **9** slag, winding *(in rope etc)*; **10** schok, draai, schrik: *she gave him quite a ~* zij joeg hem flink de stuipen op het lijf; **11** aanval, vlaag *(of rage, illness)*: *~ of the century* eeuwwisseling; *~ of phrase* formulering; *at every ~* bij elke stap, overal

turnabout ommekeer

turncoat overloper, afvallige, deserteur

¹turn down *vb* **1** omvouwen, omslaan: *~ the sheets* de lakens omslaan; **2** (om)keren, omdraaien *(card)*; **3** afwijzen *(plan, person)*, verwerpen: *they turned your suggestion down* ze wezen je voorstel van de hand; **4** lager zetten *(gas, light)*; zachter zetten *(radio, volume)*

²turn down *vb* achteruitgaan, een recessie doormaken: *our economy is turning down* onze economie gaat achteruit

¹turn in *vb* **1** binnengaan, indraaien; **2** naar binnen staan: *his feet ~* zijn voeten staan naar binnen; **3** onder de wol kruipen, erin duiken

²turn in *vb* **1** naar binnen vouwen, naar binnen omslaan; **2** overleveren, uitleveren *(to police)*; **3** inleveren, geven

turning [tə:ning] afsplitsing, aftakking, zijstraat, afslag; bocht: *the next ~ on* (of: *to*) *the right* de volgende straat rechts

turning point keerpunt^h *(also fig)*: *~ in* (of: *of*) *s.o.'s life* keerpunt in iemands leven

turnip [tə:nip] raap, knol *(fodder)*

¹turn off *vb* **1** afsluiten *(gas, water)*: *~ the gas* draai het gas uit; **2** uitzetten, afzetten, uitdoen *(eg light)*; **3** weerzin opwekken bij, doen afknappen: *it really turns me off* ik word er niet goed van

²turn off *vb* **1** afslaan; **2** *(inf)* interesse verliezen, afhaken

turn-off 1 afslag; **2** afknapper

¹turn on *vb* **1** aanzetten, aandoen *(radio etc)*; *(fig)* laten werken; **2** opendraaien, openzetten *(water, gas)*;

3 enthousiast maken, opwinden

²turn on *vb* enthousiast raken

turnout 1 opkomst, publiek^h, menigte; **2** kleding; **3** opruimbeurt: *your kitchen needs a good ~* jouw keuken heeft een flinke schoonmaakbeurt nodig; **4** productie

¹turn out *vb* **1** (op)komen, verschijnen; **2** zich ontwikkelen, aflopen: *things will ~ all right* het zal goed aflopen; **3** naar buiten staan *(of feet etc)*; **4** *(mil)* aantreden *(of watch)*

²turn out *vb* **1** uitdoen, uitdraaien *(light, stove etc)*; **2** eruit gooien, wegsturen; **3** produceren, afleveren; **4** leegmaken, opruimen, een beurt geven: *~ your handbag* je handtas omkeren; **5** uitrusten, kleden; **6** optrommelen, bijeenroepen

³turn out *vb* blijken (te zijn), uiteindelijk zijn: *the man turned out to be my neighbour* de man bleek mijn buurman te zijn

turnover 1 omzetsnelheid *(of articles)*; **2** omzet; **3** verloop^h *(of staff)*; **4** (appel)flap

¹turn over *vb* **1** zich omkeren; **2** kantelen, omvallen; **3** aanslaan, starten *(of (car) engine)*

²turn over *vb* **1** omkeren, omdraaien, op zijn kop zetten; **2** omslaan *(page)*, doorbladeren: *please ~* zie ommezijde; **3** starten *(car etc)*; **4** overwegen: *turn sth. over in one's mind* iets (goed) overdenken; **5** overgeven, uitleveren, overleveren *(to police)*

turnstile tourniquet^h, draaihek^h

¹turn up *vb* **1** verschijnen, komen (opdagen); te voorschijn komen, voor de dag komen: *your brooch has turned up* je broche is terecht; **2** zich voordoen: *the opportunity will ~* de gelegenheid doet zich wel voor; **3** naar boven gedraaid zijn

²turn up *vb* **1** vinden; **2** blootleggen, aan de oppervlakte brengen; **3** naar boven draaien, opzetten *(collar)*, omslaan *(sleeve, pipe)*, omhoogslaan, om(hoog)vouwen, opslaan *(eyes)*: *turn one's collar up* zijn kraag opzetten; **4** hoger draaien, harder zetten *(radio)*

turpentine [tə:pəntajn] terpentijn(olie)

turquoise [tə:kwojz] turkoois^{+h}

turret [turrit] **1** torentje^h; **2** geschutkoepel

turtle [tə:tl] **1** (zee)schildpad; **2** *(Am)* zoetwaterschildpad

turtledove tortelduif

turtleneck 1 col; **2** coltrui

¹tussle [tusl] *n* vechtpartij, worsteling

²tussle [tusl] *vb* (with *with*) vechten (met), worstelen (met)

tutelage [tjoe:tillidzj] voogdijschap^h

¹tutor [tjoe:tə] *n* **1** privéleraar; **2** studiebegeleider, *(roughly)* mentor; **3** *(Am)* docent

²tutor [tjoe:tə] *vb* **1** als privéleraar werken; **2** *(Am)* college krijgen ge docent

³tutor [tjoe:tə] *vb* (with *in*) (privé)les geven (in)

tuxedo [tuksie:doo] *(Am)* smoking(kostuum^h)

TV *television* tv

¹twang [twæng] *vb* **1** geplukt worden *(of string)*; **2** snorren, zoeven *(of arrow)*; **3** spelen *(on instru-*

ment), rammen, zagen *(on violin)*: ~*ing on a guitar* jengelend op een gitaar

²**twang** [twæng] *vb* **1** scherp laten weerklinken; **2** nasaal uitspreken; **3** bespelen, jengelen op, krassen op

³**twang** [twæng] *n* **1** tjing, ploink *(of string)*; **2** neusgeluid^h: *speak with a* ~ door de neus praten

¹**tweak** [twie:k] *vb* beetpakken (en omdraaien), knijpen in, trekken aan *(ear, nose)*

²**tweak** [twie:k] *n* ruk *(on ear, nose)*

twee [twie:] **1** fijntjes, popp(er)ig; **2** zoetelijk

¹**tweet** [twie:t] *vb* tjilpen, tjirpen

²**tweet** [twie:t] *n* tjiep, tjilp, getjilp^h *(of bird)*

tweezers [twie:zəz] pincet: *a pair of* ~ een pincet

twelfth [twelfθ] twaalfde, twaalfde deel^h

Twelfth Night driekoningenavond

twelve [twelv] twaalf

twentieth [twentieəθ] twintigste, twintigste deel^h

twenty [twentie] twintig: *in the twenties* in de jaren twintig

twice [twajs] tweemaal, twee keer: ~ *a day* tweemaal per dag; ~ *as good* dubbel zo goed; *once or* ~ een keer of twee

¹**twiddle** [twidl] *vb* zitten te draaien (met, aan), spelen (met), friemelen (met)

²**twiddle** [twidl] *n* draai; krul, kronkel

¹**twig** [twig] *n* twijg, takje^h

²**twig** [twig] *vb* (het) snappen, (het) begrijpen

twilight [twajlajt] **1** schemering *(also fig)*, vage voorstelling; **2** schemerlicht^h

¹**twin** [twin] *n* **1** (een ve) tweeling; **2** bijbehorende, tegenhanger; **3** ~*s* tweeling

²**twin** [twin] *adj* tweeling-: ~ *beds* lits-jumeaux; ~ *towers* twee identieke torens naast elkaar

¹**twine** [twajn] *n* streng, vlecht

²**twine** [twajn] *vb* zich wikkelen, zich winden: *the vines* ~*d (themselves) round the tree* de ranken slingerden zich om de boom

³**twine** [twajn] *vb* **1** wikkelen, winden, vlechten: *she* ~*d her arms (a)round my neck* zij sloeg haar armen om mijn nek; **2** omwikkelen

twin-engined tweemotorig

twinge [twindzj] **1** scheut, steek; **2** *(fig)* knaging *(of conscience)*, kwelling; ~*s of conscience* gewetenswroeging

¹**twinkle** [twingkl] *vb* **1** schitteren, fonkelen *(of star)*: *his eyes* ~*d with amusement* zijn ogen schitterden van plezier; **2** trillen

²**twinkle** [twingkl] *vb* knipperen met *(eyes)*

³**twinkle** [twingkl] *n* **1** schittering, fonkeling: *a mischievous* ~ een ondeugende flikkering; **2** knipoog; **3** trilling: *in a* ~ in een oogwenk

twinkling [twingkling]: *in the* ~ *of an eye* in een ogenblik *(of:* mum van tijd)

¹**twirl** [twə:l] *vb* snel (doen) draaien, (doen) tollen, (doen) krullen

²**twirl** [twə:l] *n* **1** draai, pirouette; **2** krul

¹**twist** [twist] *vb* **1** draaien, zich wentelen: *the corners of his mouth* ~*ed down* zijn mondhoeken trokken naar beneden; **2** kronkelen, zich winden; **3** zich wringen

²**twist** [twist] *vb* **1** samendraaien, samenstrengelen, *(tobacco)* spinnen: ~ *flowers into a garland* bloemen tot een krans samenvlechten; **2** vlechten *(eg rope)*; **3** winden, draaien om: ~ *the lid off a jar* het deksel van een jampot afdraaien; **4** verdraaien, verwringen, vertrekken *(face)*, verrekken *(muscle)*, verstuiken *(foot)*, omdraaien *(arm)*; **5** *(fig)* verdraaien *(story, words etc)*: *a* ~*ed mind* een verwrongen geest; **6** wringen, afwringen, uitwringen

³**twist** [twist] *n* **1** draai, draaibeweging, bocht, kromming, *(fig)* wending: *a road full of* ~*s and turns* een weg vol draaien en bochten; *give the truth a* ~ de waarheid een beetje verdraaien; **2** verdraaiing, vertrekking *(of face)*; **3** afwijking, *(of character)* trek

twister [twistə] **1** bedrieger; **2** *(Am)* wervelwind

¹**twit** [twit] *n* sufferd, domkop

²**twit** [twit] *vb* **1** bespotten; **2** verwijten: ~ *s.o. about* *(of:* on) *his clumsiness* iem (een beetje spottend) zijn onhandigheid verwijten

¹**twitch** [twitsj] *vb* **1** trekken, trillen: *a* ~*ing muscle* een trillende spier; **2** (with *at)* rukken (aan)

²**twitch** [twitsj] *vb* **1** vertrekken: *(fig) he didn't* ~ *an eyelid* hij vertrok geen spier; **2** trekken aan

³**twitch** [twitsj] *n* **1** trek, kramp; **2** ruk

¹**twitter** [twitə] *vb* tjilpen, kwetteren

²**twitter** [witə] *n* getjilp^h, gekwetter^h ‖ *all of a* ~ opgewonden

two [toe:] twee, tweetal: ~ *years old* twee jaar oud; ~ *or three* een paar, een stuk of wat; ~ *by* ~ twee aan twee; *arranged in* ~*s* per twee gerangschikt; *cut in* ~ in tweeën gesneden; *an apple or* ~ een paar appelen; *in* ~ ~*s* in een paar tellen

two-bit *(Am)* klein, waardeloos

two-earner tweeverdiener(s)-: ~ *couple* tweeverdieners

two-edged *(also fig)* tweesnijdend

two-faced met twee gezichten, *(fig)* onoprecht

twofold [toe:foold] tweevoudig

two-handed **1** voor twee handen: ~ *sword* tweehandig zwaard; **2** voor twee personen: ~ *saw* trekzaag

twopence [tuppəns] (Brits muntstuk van) twee pence ‖ *I don't care* ~ ik geef er geen zier om

twopenny [tuppənie] twee pence kostend (waard)

twosome [toe:səm] **1** tweetal^h; **2** spel^h voor twee

two-stroke tweetakt-

¹**two-time** *vb* dubbel spel spelen

²**two-time** *vb* bedriegen, ontrouw zijn

two-way **1** tweerichtings-: ~ *traffic* tweerichtingsverkeer; **2** wederzijds

tycoon [tajkoe:n] magnaat

¹**type** [tajp] *n* **1** type^h, soort, model^h; **2** zetsel^h: *in* ~ gezet; *in italic* ~ in cursief (schrift); **3** drukletter, type^h

²**type** [tajp] *vb* typen, tikken: ~ *out* uittikken

typecast steeds een zelfde soort rol geven *(actor)*: *be* ~ *as a villain* altijd maar weer de schurk spelen

typewriter schrijfmachine

typhoid [tajfojd] tyfus

wringen

typhoon [tajfoe:n] tyfoon
typhus [tajfəs] vlektyfus
typical [tippikl] typisch, typerend, kenmerkend: *be*
~ *of* karakteriseren, kenmerkend zijn voor
typify [tippiffaj] **1** typeren, karakteriseren; **2** symboliseren
typography [tajpografie] typografie
tyrannical [tirænikl] tiranniek
¹tyrannize [tirrənajz] *vb* (with *over)* als een tiran regeren (over), *(fig)* de tiran spelen
²tyrannize [tirrənajz] *vb* tiranniseren
tyranny [tirrənie] **1** tirannie; **2** tirannieke daad
tyrant [tajjərənt] tiran
tyre [tajjə] band

u

u [joe:] u, U
ubiquitous [joe:bikwittɔs] overal aanwezig
udder [uddə] uier
U.F.O. [joe:effoo] *unidentified flying object* ufo, vliegende schotel
Uganda [joe:gændə] Uganda
Ugandan [joe:gændən] Ugandees
ugh [oech] bah
ugly [uglie] **1** lelijk, afstotend: *(fig)* ~ *duckling* lelijk eendje; *(inf) (as)* ~ *as sin* (zo) lelijk als de nacht; **2** dreigend: *an* ~ *look* een dreigende blik; **3** *(inf)* vervelend, lastig *(of character): an* ~ *customer* een lastig mens
uh [ɔ:] eh
U.K. *United Kingdom* UK; VK, Verenigd Koninkrijk
Ukraine [joe:kreen] Oekraïne
ulcer [ulsə] (open) zweer; maagzweer
ulterior [ultjɔriə] verborgen: *an* ~ *motive* een bijbedoeling
¹ultimate [ultimmət] *n* maximumʰ, *(fig)* toppuntʰ, (het) einde
²ultimate [ultimmət] *adj* **1** ultiem, uiteindelijk, laatst; **2** fundamenteel; **3** uiterst, maximaal: *the* ~ *chic* het toppunt van chic
ultimately [ultimmətlie] uiteindelijk
ultimatum [ultimmeetəm] ultimatumʰ
ultra [ultrə] extremistisch, radicaal
ultramarine [ultrəmɔrie:n] ultramarijnʰ, lazuur(blauw)ʰ
ultramodern [ultrəmoddən] hypermodern
ultrasound scan echoscopie
ultraviolet [ultrəvajjəlit] ultravioletʰ
Ulysses [joe:lissie:z] Odysseus
um [um] hm, h'm
umbilical [umbillikl] navel-: ~ *cord* navelstreng
umbrage [umbridzj] ergernis: *give* ~ ergeren; *take* ~ *at* (of: *over)* zich ergeren aan
¹umbrella [umbrellə] *n* **1** paraplu, *(fig)* bescherming, overkoepelende organisatie: *under the* ~ *of the EU* onder de bescherming van de EU; **2** (tuin)parasol, zonneschermʰ
²umbrella [umbrellə] *adj* algemeen, verzamel-: ~ *term* overkoepelende term
¹umpire [umpajjə] *n* scheidsrechter, umpire
²umpire [umpajjə] *vb* als scheidsrechter optreden (in)

umpteen [umptie:n] *(inf)* een hoop, heel wat, tig
umpteenth [umptie:nθ] *(inf)* zoveelste
U.N. *United Nations* VN, Verenigde Naties
unabated [unnəbeetid] onverminderd
unable [unneebl] niet in staat: *he was* ~ *to come* hij was verhinderd
unabridged [unnəbridzjd] onverkort, niet ingekort
unacceptable [unnəkseptəbl] onaanvaardbaar
unaccompanied [unnəkumpənied] **1** onvergezeld; **2** *(mus)* zonder begeleiding
unaccountable [unnəkauntəbl] onverklaarbaar
unaccustomed [unnəkustəmd] **1** ongewoon, ongebruikelijk; **2** niet gewend: *he is* ~ *to writing letters* hij is niet gewend brieven te schrijven
unaffected [unnəfektid] **1** ongedwongen, natuurlijk; **2** onaangetast, *(fig)* niet beïnvloed, ongewijzigd
unaided [unneedid] zonder hulp
unambiguous [unæmbigjoeəs] ondubbelzinnig
unanimity [joe:nənimmittie] **1** eenstemmigheid, unanimiteit; **2** eensgezindheid
unanimous [joe:nænimmɔs] **1** eenstemmig, unaniem; **2** eensgezind
unannounced [unnənaunst] onaangekondigd
unanswerable [unna:nsərəbl] **1** onweerlegbaar; **2** niet te beantwoorden
unapproachable [unnəprootsjəbl] ontoegankelijk, onbenaderbaar
unarmed [unna:md] ongewapend
unashamed [unnəsjeemd] **1** zich niet schamend; **2** onbeschaamd
unasked [unna:skt] ongevraagd
unattached [unnətætsjt] **1** los; niet gebonden, onafhankelijk; **2** alleenstaand, ongetrouwd
unattended [unnətendid] **1** niet begeleid; **2** onbeheerd: *leave sth.* ~ iets onbeheerd laten (staan)
unauthorized [unno:θərajzd] **1** onbevoegd; **2** ongeoorloofd; **3** niet geautoriseerd, onofficieel: *an* ~ *biography* een onofficiële biografie
unavailing [unnəveeling] vergeefs, nutteloos
unavoidable [unnəvojdəbl] onvermijdelijk
unaware [unnəweə] (with *of*) zich niet bewust (van): *be* ~ *that* niet weten dat
unawares [unnəweəz] **1** onverwacht(s): *catch s.o.* ~ iem verrassen; **2** onbewust
unbalance [unbæləns] uit zijn evenwicht brengen, in verwarring brengen
unbalanced [unbælənst] **1** niet in evenwicht, onevenwichtig; **2** in de war
unbar [unba:] ontgrendelen, *(fig)* openstellen, vrij maken
unbearable [unbeərəbl] **1** ondraaglijk; **2** onuitstaanbaar
unbeaten [unbie:tn] **1** niet verslagen, ongeslagen *(sport);* **2** onovertroffen, ongebroken *(record)*
unbecoming [unbikkumming] **1** niet (goed) staand; **2** ongepast, onbehoorlijk: *your conduct is* ~ *for* (of: *to) a gentleman!* zo gedraagt een heer zich

niet!

unbelief [unbillie:f] ongeloof^h, ongelovigheid
unbelievable [unbillie:vəbl] ongelofelijk
unbeliever [unbillie:və] ongelovige
unbending [unbending] onbuigzaam, onverzettelijk
unbias(s)ed [unbajjəst] 1 onbevooroordeeld; 2 zuiver, niet vertekend
unbind [unbajnd] 1 losmaken; 2 bevrijden
unblushing [unblusjing] 1 schaamteloos; 2 niet blozend
unborn [unbo:n] 1 (nog) ongeboren; 2 toekomstig
unbosom [unboezəm] uiten: ~ oneself (to) zijn hart uitstorten (bij)
unbowed [unbaud] 1 ongebogen; 2 ongebroken (fig), niet onderworpen
unbridled [unbrajdld] ongebreideld: ~ tongue losse tong
unbroken [unbrookən] 1 ongebroken, heel; 2 ongedresseerd; 3 ononderbroken; 4 onovertroffen, ongebroken (record)
unbuckle [unbukl] losgespen
unburden [unbə:dn] 1 ontlasten, van een last bevrijden: ~ one's conscience zijn geweten ontlasten; ~ oneself (of: one's heart) to s.o. zijn hart uitstorten bij iem; 2 zich bevrijden van, opbiechten
uncalled-for [unko:ld fo:] 1 ongewenst, ongepast; 2 onnodig: that remark was ~ die opmerking was nergens voor nodig; 3 ongegrond
uncanny [unkænie] geheimzinnig, griezelig
uncaring [unkəring] onverschillig, ongevoelig
unceasing [unsie:sing] onophoudelijk
unceremonious [unserrimmooniəs] 1 informeel, ongedwongen; 2 niet erg beleefd
uncertain [unsə:tən] 1 onzeker: in no ~ terms in niet mis te verstane bewoordingen; be ~ of (of: about) s.o.'s intentions twijfelen aan iemands bedoelingen; 2 onbepaald, vaag; 3 veranderlijk: a woman with an ~ temper een wispelturige vrouw
uncertainty [unsə:təntie] 1 onzekerheid, twijfel(achtigheid); 2 onduidelijkheid, vaagheid; 3 veranderlijkheid, onbetrouwbaarheid
unchallenged [untsjælindzjd] onbetwist, zonder tegenspraak: we cannot let this pass ~ we kunnen dit niet zo maar laten passeren
uncharitable [untsjærittəbl] harteloos, liefdeloos: an ~ judg(e)ment een hard oordeel
unchecked [untsjekt] 1 ongehinderd; 2 ongecontroleerd
unclassified [unklæsiffajd] 1 ongeordend, niet ingedeeld; 2 niet geheim (vertrouwelijk)
uncle [ungkl] oom
unclean [unklie:n] 1 vuil; bevuild (fig), bevlekt; 2 onkuis
Uncle Sam [unkl sæm] (inf) Uncle Sam, de Amerikaanse regering, het Amerikaanse volk
uncoil [unkojl] (zich) ontrollen
uncoloured [unkulləd] ongekleurd (also fig), objectief

uncomfortable [unkumfətəbl] 1 ongemakkelijk, oncomfortabel: ~ situation pijnlijke situatie; 2 niet op zijn gemak, verlegen
uncommitted [unkəmittid] 1 niet-gebonden, neutraal: he wants to remain ~ hij wil zich niet vastleggen; 2 zonder verplichting(en)
uncommon [unkommən] ongewoon
uncompromising [unkomprəmajzing] 1 onbuigzaam, niet toegeeflijk; 2 vastberaden
unconcerned [unkənsə:nd] 1 onbezorgd; 2 onverschillig
unconditional [unkəndisjənəl] onvoorwaardelijk
¹**unconscious** [unkonsjəs] adj 1 onbewust, niet wetend: be ~ of sth. zich ergens niet bewust van zijn; 2 bewusteloos
²**unconscious** [unkonsjəs] n het onbewuste, het onderbewuste
uncontested [unkəntestid] onbetwist: ~ election verkiezing zonder tegenkandidaten
uncontrollable [unkəntrooləbl] 1 niet te beheersen, onbedwingbaar; 2 onbeheerst: ~ laughter onbedaarlijk gelach
unconventional [unkənvensjənəl] 1 onconventioneel, ongebruikelijk; 2 natuurlijk; 3 niet-conventioneel, nucleair, atoom-
unconvincing [unkənvinsing] niet overtuigend
uncork [unko:k] ontkurken
uncouple [unkupl] ontkoppelen, afkoppelen, loskoppelen
uncouth [unkoe:θ] ongemanierd, grof
¹**uncover** [unkuvvə] vb 1 het (hoofd)deksel afnemen van, opgraven; 2 aan het licht brengen, ontdekken
²**uncover** [unkuvvə] vb zijn hoofddeksel afnemen
unction [ungksjən] zalving
unctuous [ungktjoeəs] zalvend, vleierig
uncut [unkut] 1 ongesneden, ongemaaid; 2 onverkort, ongecensureerd (book, film); 3 ongeslepen (diamond)
undaunted [undo:ntid] onverschrokken: ~ by niet ontmoedigd door
undecided [undissajdid] 1 onbeslist: the match was left ~ de wedstrijd eindigde onbeslist; 2 weifelend, besluiteloos: be ~ about in tweestrijd staan over
undeniable [undinnajjəbl] onbetwistbaar: that is undeniably true dat is ontegenzeglijk waar
¹**under** [undə] prep 1 (place) onder, (fig) onder het gezag van, onder toezicht van: ~ the cliffs aan de voet van de klippen; he wrote ~ another name hij schreef onder een andere naam; a place ~ the sun een plekje onder de zon; 2 (circumstance) onder, in, in een toestand van, krachtens, tijdens: ~ construction in aanbouw; the issue ~ discussion het probleem dat ter discussie staat; collapse ~ the strain het onder de spanning begeven; 3 minder dan: ~ age minderjarig; just ~ a minute net iets minder dan een minuut, net binnen de minuut; children ~ six kinderen beneden de zes jaar
²**under** [undə] adv 1 onder, eronder, hieronder,

daaronder, (naar) beneden, omlaag: *groups of nine and* ~ groepen van negen en minder; **2** in bedwang, onder controle; **3** bewusteloos: *the drug put her* ~ *for the day* door het verdovingsmiddel raakte zij de hele dag buiten bewustzijn

under-age [ʌndəreedʒj] minderjarig

undercarriage [ʌndəkæridʒj] **1** onderstel[h] *(of wagon)*, chassis[h]; **2** landingsgestel[h]

underclothes [ʌndəklooðz] ondergoed

undercover [ʌndəkʌvvə] geheim

undercurrent [ʌndəkurrənt] onderstroom *(also fig)*, verborgen gedachten, gevoelens

underdeveloped onderontwikkeld *(also econ, photo)*, (nog) onvoldoende ontwikkeld

underdog [ʌndədog] underdog, (verwachte) verliezer

underdone niet (helemaal) gaar

underestimate onderschatten, te laag schatten

underexposure onderbelichting

underfloor [ʌndəfloː] onder de vloer: ~ *heating* vloerverwarming

underfoot [ʌndəfoet] **1** onder de voet(en), op de grond, *(fig)* onderdrukt: *crush* (of: *trample*) *sth.* ~ iets vertrappen; **2** in de weg, voor de voeten

undergo [ʌndəgoo] ondergaan, doorstaan

undergraduate [ʌndəgrædjoeət] *(inf)* student(e) *(who does not have a degree yet)*

¹**underground** [ʌndəgraund] *n* metro, ondergrondse: *by* ~ met de ondergrondse

²**underground** [ʌndəgraund] *adj* ondergronds, (zich) onder de grond (bevindend), *(fig)* clandestien

³**underground** [ʌndəgraund] *adv* ondergronds, onder de grond, *(fig)* clandestien: *go* ~ onderduiken, ondergronds gaan werken

undergrowth [ʌndəgrooθ] kreupelhout[h]

underhand [ʌndəhænd] **1** onderhands, clandestien; **2** achterbaks

underhanded **1** onderhands; **2** achterbaks

underlie [ʌndəlaj] **1** liggen onder, zich bevinden onder; **2** ten grondslag liggen aan, verklaren: *underlying principles* grondprincipes; **3** schuil gaan achter: *underlying meaning* werkelijke betekenis

underline [ʌndəlajn] onderstrepen *(also fig)*, benadrukken

undermine [ʌndəmajn] ondermijnen, ondergraven *(also fig)*, verzwakken

¹**underneath** [ʌndəniːθ] *prep (place)* beneden, (vlak) onder: ~ *his coat he wore a suit* onder zijn jas droeg hij een pak

²**underneath** [ʌndəniːθ] *adv (place; also fig)* onderaan, eronder, aan de onderkant: *what's written* ~? wat staat er aan de onderkant geschreven?

³**underneath** [ʌndəniːθ] *n* onderkant

underpants [ʌndəpænts] onderbroek

underprivileged (kans)arm, sociaal zwak

underrate **1** te laag schatten *(costs)*; **2** onderschatten, onderwaarderen

underscore [ʌndəskoː] onderstrepen *(also fig)*, benadrukken

undersea [ʌndəsiː] onderzees, onderzee-, onderwater-

under-secretary [ʌndəsekrətərie] **1** ondersecretaris, tweede secretaris; **2** staatssecretaris: *permanent* ~ *(roughly)* secretaris-generaal *(of ministry)*

underside [ʌndəsajd] onderkant, onderzijde

undersigned [ʌndəsajnd] ondertekend (hebbend): *I, the* ~ ik, ondergetekende

undersized te klein, onder de normale grootte

understand [ʌndəstænd] **1** (het) begrijpen, inzien, verstand hebben van, (goed) op de hoogte zijn: *give s.o. to* ~ *that* iem te verstaan geven dat; ~ *each other (of: one another)* elkaar begrijpen, op één lijn zitten; *I simply don't* ~ ik snap het gewoon niet; ~ *about* verstand hebben van; **2** (het) begrijpen, (er) begrip hebben voor: *he begged her to* ~ hij smeekte haar begrip voor de situatie te hebben; **3** begrijpen, (er)uit opmaken, vernemen: *I understood that you knew him* ik had begrepen dat je hem kende; **4** verstaan *(language)*; **5** opvatten: *as I* ~ *it* zoals ik het zie; **6** als vanzelfsprekend aannemen: *that is understood!* (dat spreekt) vanzelf!

understandable [ʌndəstændəbl] begrijpelijk

understandably [ʌndəstændəblie] **1** begrijpelijk; **2** begrijpelijkerwijs: ~, *we were all annoyed* begrijpelijkerwijs waren we allemaal geïrriteerd

¹**understanding** [ʌndəstænding] **1** afspraak, overeenkomst: *come to* (of: *reach*) *an* ~ het eens worden; *on the* ~ *that* met dien verstande dat; **2** (onderling) begrip[h], verstandhouding; **3** verstand[h], intelligentie, begrip[h]; **4** interpretatie, beoordeling, opvatting: *a wrong* ~ *of the situation* een verkeerde beoordeling van de situatie

²**understanding** [ʌndəstænding] *adj* begripvol, welwillend

understatement understatement[h], (te) zwakke aanduiding

undertake [ʌndəteek] **1** ondernemen; **2** op zich nemen, beloven, zich verplichten tot; **3** garanderen, instaan voor

undertaker [ʌndəteekə] begrafenisondernemer

¹**undertaking** [ʌndəteeking] *n* **1** onderneming: *translating the Bible is quite an* ~ het is een hele onderneming om de bijbel te vertalen; **2** (plechtige) belofte, garantie

²**undertaking** [ʌndəteeking] *n* het verzorgen van begrafenissen

undertone [ʌndətoon] **1** gedempte toon: *speak in* ~s (of: *an* ~) met gedempte stem spreken; **2** ondertoon *(fig)*; **3** lichte tint, zweem: *red with a slight* ~ *of yellow* rood met een klein beetje geel erin

undervalue onderwaarderen

underwater [ʌndəwoːtə] onder water

underwear [ʌndəweə] ondergoed[h]

underworld [ʌndəwoːld] onderwereld

underwrite [ʌndərajt] **1** ondertekenen *(policy)*, afsluiten *(insurance)*; (door ondertekening) op zich nemen *(risk, liability)*; **2** verzekeren *(shipp)*; zich

nadrukken

garant stellen voor; **3** onderschrijven, goedvinden

undies [ˈundiez] *(inf)* (dames)ondergoed

undisputed [undispˈjoeːtid] onbetwist

undistinguished [undistˈinggwisjt] niet bijzonder, alledaags, gewoon

¹undo [undˈoeː] *vb* **1** losmaken, losknopen; **2** uitkleden; **3** tenietdoen, ongedaan maken: *this mistake can never be undone* deze fout kan nooit goedgemaakt worden

²undo [undˈoeː] *vb* losgaan

undomesticated [undəmˈestikkeetid] **1** ongetemd, wild; **2** niet huishoudelijk (aangelegd)

undone [undˈun] **1** ongedaan, onafgemaakt; **2** los(gegaan): *come ~* losgaan, losraken

undoubted [undˈautid] ongetwijfeld

undreamed [undrˈieːmd] onvoorstelbaar: *~ of* onvoorstelbaar

undress [undrˈes] (zich) uitkleden

undue [undjˈoeː] **1** overmatig: *exercise ~ influence upon s.o.* te grote invloed op iem uitoefenen; **2** onbehoorlijk

unduly [undjˈoeːlie] **1** uitermate, overmatig; **2** onbehoorlijk; **3** onrechtmatig

undying [undˈajjing] onsterfelijk, eeuwig

unearth [unnˈaːθ] **1** opgraven, *(fig)* opdiepen; **2** onthullen

unearthly [unnˈaːθlie] **1** bovenaards; **2** bovennatuurlijk, mysterieus; **3** angstaanjagend, eng; **4** *(inf)* onmogelijk *(time): wake s.o. up at an ~ hour* iem op een belachelijk vroeg uur wakker maken

uneasy [unnˈieːzie] **1** onbehaaglijk: *~ conscience* bezwaard geweten; *be ~ with* zich niet op zijn gemak voelen met; **2** bezorgd: *be ~ about, grow ~ at* zich zorgen maken over; **3** onrustig *(eg during sleep);* **4** verontrustend

uneconomic(al) [unnieːkənˈommik(l)] **1** oneconomisch, onrendabel; **2** verkwistend

uneducated [unnˈedjoekeetid] ongeschoold, onontwikkeld

unemployed [unnimplˈojd] **1** ongebruikt; **2** werkloos, zonder werk

unemployment [unnimplˈojmənt] werkloosheid: *~ benefit* werkloosheidsuitkering

unending [unnˈending] **1** oneindig, eindeloos; **2** onophoudelijk

unenviable [unnˈenviəbl] niet benijdenswaard(ig), onplezierig *(task)*

unequal [unnˈieːkwəl] ongelijk(waardig): *~ in size* ongelijk in grootte

unerring [unnˈaːring] onfeilbaar: *~ devotion* niet aflatende toewijding

uneven [unnˈieːvn] **1** ongelijk, oneffen *(eg surface);* onregelmatig; **2** van ongelijke kwaliteit

uneventful [unnivvˈentfoel] onbewogen, rustig, saai: *~ day* dag zonder belangrijke gebeurtenissen

unexpected [unnikspˈektid] onverwacht

unfailing [unfˈeeling] onuitputtelijk, onophoudelijk

unfair [unfˈeə] oneerlijk, onrechtvaardig: *~ compe-*tition oneerlijke concurrentie

unfaithful [unfˈeeθfoel] ontrouw, overspelig

unfamiliar [unfəmˈilliə] **1** onbekend, niet vertrouwd; **2** ongewoon, vreemd

¹unfasten [unfˈaːsn] *vb* losmaken, losknopen

²unfasten [unfˈaːsn] *vb* losgaan

unfavourable [unfˈeevərəbl] ongunstig

unfeeling [unfˈieːling] gevoelloos *(also fig)*, hardvochtig

unfinished [unfˈinnisjt] **1** onaf, onvoltooid: *~ business* onafgedane kwestie(s); **2** onbewerkt *(eg wood)*

unfit [unfˈit] **1** ongeschikt; **2** in slechte conditie

unflinching [unflˈintsjing] **1** onbevreesd; **2** vastberaden

unfold [unfˈoold] **1** (zich) openvouwen; **2** (zich) uitspreiden; **3** (zich) openbaren, (zich) ontvouwen

unforeseeable [unfoːsˈieːəbl] onvoorspelbaar

unforgettable [unfəgˈettəbl] onvergetelijk

unforgivable [unfəgˈivvəbl] onvergeeflijk

unfortunate [unfˈoːtsjənət] ongelukkig, betreurenswaardig

unfriendly [unfrˈendlie] onvriendelijk, vijandig: *~ area* onherbergzaam gebied; *~ reception* koele ontvangst

unfurl [unfˈaːl] (zich) ontrollen, (zich) ontvouwen *(eg of flag)*

ungainly [ungˈeenlie] lomp

unget-at-able [ungetˈætəbl] *(inf)* onbereikbaar

ungodly [ungˈodlie] **1** goddeloos; **2** *(inf)* afgrijselijk

ungrateful [ungrˈeetfoel] ondankbaar

unguarded [ungˈaːdid] **1** onbewaakt: *in an ~ moment* op een onbewaakt ogenblik; **2** onbedachtzaam; **3** achteloos

unguent [ˈunggwənt] zalf

unhappy [unhˈæpie] **1** ongelukkig, bedroefd; **2** ongepast

unharmed [unhˈaːmd] ongedeerd, onbeschadigd

unhealthy [unhˈelθie] ongezond *(also fig)*, ziekelijk

unheard [unhˈaːd] niet gehoord, ongehoord: *his advice went ~* naar zijn raad werd niet geluisterd

unheard-of [unhˈaːdov] ongekend, buitengewoon

unheeded [unhˈieːdid] genegeerd, in de wind geslagen: *his remark went ~* er werd geen acht geslagen op zijn opmerking

unhinge [unhˈindzj] **1** uit de scharnieren tillen *(door);* **2** *(inf)* uit zijn evenwicht brengen: *his mind is ~d* hij is geestelijk uit evenwicht

unholy [unhˈoolie] **1** goddeloos; **2** *(inf)* verschrikkelijk: *(inf) at an ~ hour* op een onchristelijk tijdstip; *~ noise* heidens lawaai

unicorn [ˈjoeːnikkoːn] eenhoorn

unidentified [unnajdˈentifajd] niet geïdentificeerd: *~ flying object* vliegende schotel

unification [joeːnifˈikkeesjən] eenmaking, unificatie

¹uniform [ˈjoeːniffoːm] *adj* uniform, eensluidend

²uniform [ˈjoeːniffoːm] *n* uniform[h]

uniformity [joeːnifˈoːmittie] **1** uniformiteit; **2** gelijkmatigheid

unify [joe:niffaj] (zich) verenigen, tot één maken

unilateral [joe:nilætərəl] eenzijdig, van één kant

unimpeachable [unnimpie:tsjabl] **1** onbetwistbaar; **2** onberispelijk

unimportant [unnimpo:tənt] onbelangrijk

unintentional [unnintensjənəl] onbedoeld, onopzettelijk

uninterested [unnjntrəstid] **1** ongeïnteresseerd; **2** zonder belangen

uninterrupted [unnintəruptid] ononderbroken, doorlopend

union [joe:niən] **1** verbond[h], unie; **2** (vak)bond, vakvereniging; **3** studentenvereniging; **4** huwelijk[h]; **5** verbinding, koppelstuk[h]

unionist [joe:niənist] vakbondslid[h]

Union Jack Britse vlag

union leader vakbondsleider

unique [joe:nie:k] uniek, (inf) opmerkelijk

unisex [joe:nisseks] uniseks-

unison [joe:nisn] **1** koor[h], het tegelijk spreken: speak in ~ in koor spreken; **2** harmonie: work in ~ eendrachtig samenwerken

unit [joe:nit] **1** eenheid, onderdeel[h], afdeling, meetgrootheid, (techn) apparaat[h], module: ~ of account rekeneenheid; **2** combineerbaar onderdeel[h] (of furniture), unit, blok[h]

¹**unite** [joe:najt] vb **1** zich verenigen, samenwerken, fuseren: they ~d in fighting the enemy samen bestreden zij de vijand; **2** zich verbinden, aaneengroeien; **3** zich mengen

²**unite** [joe:najt] vb **1** verbinden; verenigen, tot een geheel maken; **2** in de echt verbinden

united [joe:najtid] **1** verenigd: United Kingdom Verenigd Koninkrijk; United Nations Verenigde Naties; United States Verenigde Staten; **2** saamhorig, hecht, harmonieus; **3** gezamenlijk: with their ~ powers met vereende krachten

unity [joe:nittie] **1** geheel[h], eenheid, samenhang; **2** samenwerking; **3** harmonie: at (of: in) ~ eendrachtig, eensgezind

universal [joe:nivvə:sl] **1** universeel, algemeen: ~ rule algemeen geldende regel; **2** algeheel, alomvattend: ~ agreement algemene instemming

universe [joe:nivvə:s] **1** heelal[h]; **2** wereld, (also) gebied[h]

university [joe:nivvə:sittie] universiteit, hogeschool

unjust [undzjust] onrechtvaardig

unjustifiable [undzjustiffajjəbl] niet te verantwoorden

unkempt [unkempt] **1** ongekamd; **2** onverzorgd

unkind [unkajnd] **1** onaardig, onvriendelijk; **2** ruw

unknown [unnoon] onbekend: ~ quantity onbekende grootheid, (fig) onzekere factor; ~ to us buiten ons medeweten, zonder dat wij het wisten

unlawful [unlo:foel] onwettig, illegaal

unleaded [unleddid] loodvrij

unleash [unlie:sj] losmaken vd riem (dog); (also fig)

ontketenen: ~ one's rage (up)on s.o. zijn woede op iem koelen

unless [unles] tenzij, behalve, zonder dat: I won't go ~ you come with me ik ga niet tenzij jij meekomt

¹**unlike** [unlajk] prep **1** anders dan, in tegenstelling tot; **2** niet typisch voor: that's ~ John dat is niets voor John

²**unlike** [unlajk] adj, adv **1** verschillend, niet gelijkend; **2** ongelijkwaardig; **3** (maths) tegengesteld

unlikely [unlajklie] **1** onwaarschijnlijk; **2** weinig belovend, niet hoopgevend: he is ~ to succeed hij heeft weinig kans van slagen

unlimited [unljmmittid] onbeperkt, ongelimiteerd

unload [unlood] **1** lossen, uitladen, leegmaken; **2** wegdoen, zich ontdoen van: ~ responsibilities onto s.o. de verantwoordelijkheid op iem afschuiven; **3** ontladen (firearm; also fig), afreageren

unlock [unlok] **1** openmaken, opendoen, vh slot doen; **2** losmaken, bevrijden, de vrije loop laten

unloose(n) [unlo:s(ən)] **1** losmaken, losknopen, vrijlaten: old memories were unloose(ne)d oude herinneringen kwamen boven; **2** ontspannen

unlucky [unlukkie] ongelukkig: be ~ pech hebben

unmanageable [unmænidzjəbl] **1** onhandelbaar; **2** onhanteerbaar, niet te besturen

unmannerly [unmænəlie] ongemanierd, ruw, onbeschaafd

unmarried [unmæried] ongetrouwd

unmask [unma:sk] het masker afnemen, ontmaskeren, onthullen

unmentionable [unmensjənəbl] **1** taboe; **2** niet (nader) te noemen; **3** niet te beschrijven

unmindful [unmajndfoel] zorgeloos, vergeetachtig: ~ of zonder acht te slaan op

unmistakable [unmisteekəbl] onmiskenbaar, ondubbelzinnig

unmitigated [unmittigeetid] **1** onverminderd, onverzacht; **2** absoluut, volkomen: ~ disaster regelrechte ramp

unnatural [unnætsjərəl] onnatuurlijk, abnormaal

unnecessary [unnessəsərie] **1** onnodig, niet noodzakelijk; **2** overbodig

unnerve [unnə:v] **1** van zijn stuk brengen, ontmoedigen; **2** nerveus maken

UNO [joe:noo] United Nations Organisation VN, Verenigde Naties

unobtrusive [unnəbtroe:siv] **1** onopvallend; **2** discreet, voorzichtig

unoccupied [unnokjoepajd] **1** leeg, onbezet, vrij; **2** niet bezig, werkeloos

unofficial [unnəfjsjəl] onofficieel, officieus, niet bevestigd || ~ strike wilde staking

unpack [unpæk] uitpakken: ~ one's suitcase zijn koffer uitpakken

unpaid [unpeed] onbetaald

unparalleled [unpærəleld] zonder weerga, ongeëvenaard

unpick [unpik] lostornen: ~ a seam een naad lostornen

unpleasant [unpl_e_zzənt] onaangenaam, onplezierig

unpleasantness [unpl_e_zzəntnəs] **1** onaangenaam voorval[h]; **2** wrijving, woorden, ruzie; **3** onaangenaamheid

unpopular [unp_o_pjoelə] impopulair

unprecedented [unpr_e_ssiddentid] ongekend, nooit eerder voorgekomen

unpredictable [unpridd_i_ktəbl] onvoorspelbaar

unprepared [unpripp_e_əd] **1** onvoorbereid, geïmproviseerd; **2** onverwacht(s)

unprofessional [unprəf_e_sjənəl] **1** niet professioneel, onprofessioneel, niet beroeps, amateur-; **2** amateuristisch

unproved [unpr_oe_:vd] niet bewezen

unprovoked [unprəv_oo_kt] niet uitgelokt, zonder aanleiding

unqualified [unkw_o_lliffajd] **1** niet gekwalificeerd, onbevoegd; **2** onvoorwaardelijk: ~ *success* onverdeeld succes

unquestionably [unkw_e_stsjənəblie] ongetwijfeld, zonder twijfel: *they are ~ the best team of the U.S.A.* dat ze het beste team van Amerika zijn, staat buiten kijf

unquestioned [unkw_e_stsjənd] **1** niet ondervraagd; **2** onbetwistbaar; **3** onbetwist, niet tegengesproken

unquestioning [unkw_e_stsjəning] onvoorwaardelijk

unquote [unkw_oo_t] een citaat beëindigen, aanhalingstekens sluiten: *he said (quote) 'Over my dead body' (~)* hij zei (aanhalingstekens openen) 'Over mijn lijk' (aanhalingstekens sluiten)

¹unravel [unr_æ_vl] *vb* ontrafelen *(also fig)*, uithalen, *(fig also)* uitzoeken, oplossen

²unravel [unr_æ_vl] *vb* rafelen, rafelig worden

unreal [unr_i_əl] **1** onwerkelijk, denkbeeldig; **2** onecht, onwaar, vals

unreasonable [unr_ie_:zənəbl] **1** redeloos, verstandeloos; **2** onredelijk; **3** buitensporig, overdreven

unreasoning [unr_ie_:zəning] redeloos, irrationeel, onnadenkend

unrelenting [unrill_e_nting] **1** onverminderd, voortdurend; **2** meedogenloos, onverbiddelijk

unreliable [unrill_a_jjəbl] onbetrouwbaar

unrelieved [unrill_ie_:vd] **1** eentonig, vlak, saai: ~ *by* niet afgewisseld met; **2** hevig, sterk, intens

unreserved [unrizzə_:vd] **1** onverdeeld, geheel, onvoorwaardelijk; **2** openhartig, eerlijk

unrest [unr_e_st] onrust, beroering

unrewarding [unriww_oo_:ding] niet lonend, niet de moeite waard, *(fig)* ondankbaar

unrivalled [unr_a_jvld] ongeëvenaard

unroll [unr_oo_l] (zich) uitrollen, (zich) ontrollen, *(also fig)* (zich) tonen, (zich) onthullen

unruffled [unr_u_fld] kalm, onverstoord

unruly [unr_oe_:lie] onhandelbaar, weerspannig

unsatisfactory [uns_æ_tisfæktərie] onbevredigend

unsavoury [uns_ee_vərie] **1** onsmakelijk, vies, *(also fig)* weerzinwekkend; **2** smakeloos, flauw

unscathed [unsk_ee_ðd] ongedeerd, onbeschadigd: *return ~* heelhuids terugkeren

unscramble [unskr_æ_mbl] **1** ontcijferen, decoderen; **2** ontwarren, uit elkaar halen

¹unscrew [unskr_oe_:] *vb* **1** losschroeven; **2** losdraaien, eraf draaien: *can you ~ this bottle?* krijg jij deze fles open?

²unscrew [unskr_oe_:] *vb* **1** losraken; **2** losgeschroefd worden

unscrupulous [unskr_oe_:pjoeləs] zonder scrupules, immoreel, gewetenloos

unseasonable [uns_ie_:zənəbl] abnormaal voor het seizoen: *an ~ summer* een slechte zomer

unseat [uns_ie_:t] **1** afwerpen, uit het zadel werpen; doen vallen, ten val brengen; **2** zijn positie afnemen, *(pol)* zijn zetel doen verliezen

unseeing [uns_ie_:ing] niet(s) ziend, wezenloos

unseemly [uns_ie_:mlie] **1** onbehoorlijk; **2** onaantrekkelijk, lelijk

unseen [uns_ie_:n] **1** onzichtbaar; **2** onvoorbereid: *questions on an ~ text* vragen over een niet bestudeerde tekst

¹unsettle [uns_e_tl] *vb* **1** onvast worden; (aan het) wankelen (slaan) *(fig)*, op losse schroeven komen te staan, onzeker worden; **2** van streek raken; **3** wisselvallig worden *(of weather)*

²unsettle [uns_e_tl] *vb* **1** doen loskomen, los maken; **2** doen wankelen *(fig)*, op losse schroeven zetten: *unsettling changes* veranderingen die alles op losse schroeven zetten; **3** van streek maken

unsettled [uns_e_tld] **1** onzeker, verwar(ren)d: ~ *times* onzekere tijden; **2** wisselvallig, veranderlijk *(weather)*; **3** onbeslist, (nog) niet uitgemaakt: *this issue is still ~* deze kwestie is nog niet afgedaan; **4** in de war

unshrinkable [unsjr_i_nkəbl] krimpvrij

unskilled [unsk_i_ld] **1** ongeschoold; **2** onervaren, onbedreven

unsociable [uns_oo_sjəbl] **1** terughoudend, teruggetrokken; **2** ongezellig

unsocial [uns_oo_sjl] asociaal, onmaatschappelijk: ~ *hours* ongebruikelijke werktijden

unsophisticated [unsəf_i_stikkeetid] **1** onbedorven, echt, eerlijk; **2** onervaren, naïef; **3** ongedwongen, ongecompliceerd

unsound [uns_au_nd] **1** ongezond, ziek(elijk): *of ~ mind* krankzinnig, ontoerekeningsvatbaar; **2** ongaaf; **3** onstevig, zwak; **4** ondeugdelijk; **5** ongegrond, ongeldig; **6** onbetrouwbaar, vals

unsparing [unsp_ee_ring] **1** kwistig, gul, vrijgevig: ~ *of* kwistig met; **2** meedogenloos, ongenadig

unspeakable [unsp_ie_:kəbl] **1** onuitsprekelijk, onuitspreekbaar, onbeschrijf(e)lijk; **2** afschuwelijk

unstable [unst_ee_bl] **1** veranderlijk, wisselvallig; onevenwichtig, wispelturig; **2** onstabiel *(also science, chem)*, labiel; **3** onvast, los

unstamped [unst_æ_mpt] ongefrankeerd

unsteady [unst_e_ddie] **1** onvast, wankel: *her voice was ~* haar stem was onvast; **2** veranderlijk, wisselvallig; **3** onregelmatig

unstinted [unstintid] royaal, gul, kwistig

unstuck [unstuk] los || *(inf)* come *(badly)* ~ in het honderd lopen, mislukken

unstudied [unstuddied] **1** ongekunsteld, natuurlijk; **2** ongestudeerd, ongeschoold

unsuccessful [unsəksesfoel] **1** niet succesvol, zonder succes; **2** niet geslaagd, afgewezen: *be* ~ niet slagen, mislukken

unsure [unsjoeə] **1** onzeker, onvast; **2** onbetrouwbaar, twijfelachtig

unsuspecting [unsəspekting] **1** nietsvermoedend; **2** niet achterdochtig, argeloos

unswerving [unswə:ving] **1** recht, rechtdoor, rechtaan; **2** onwankelbaar

untangle [untænggl] **1** ontwarren; **2** ophelderen, oplossen

untenable [untennəbl] onhoudbaar *(also fig)*, niet te verdedigen

unthinkable [unθingkəbl] **1** ondenkbaar, onvoorstelbaar; **2** onaanvaardbaar: *it's* ~! geen sprake van!, daar komt niets van in!; **3** onwaarschijnlijk

unthinking [unθingking] **1** onnadenkend: ~ *moment* onbewaakt ogenblik; **2** onbewust, onbedoeld

untidy [untajdie] slordig

untie [untaj] **1** losknopen, losmaken; **2** bevrijden *(person who is tied up)*, vrijlaten

until [əntil] tot, totdat, voor, (+ *negation)* niet voor: *I cannot leave* ~ *Sunday* ik kan niet voor zondag vertrekken, ik kan pas zondag vertrekken; *I did not know about it* ~ *today* ik wist er tot vandaag niets van; *I was very lonely* ~ *I met Karen* ik was erg eenzaam tot ik Karen ontmoette

untimely [untajmlie] **1** ongelegen, ongeschikt; **2** voortijdig, te vroeg: ~ *death* te vroege dood

untold [untoold] **1** niet verteld; **2** onnoemelijk, onmetelijk

untoward [untəwo:d] **1** ongelegen, ongewenst: ~ *circumstances* ongunstige omstandigheden; **2** ongepast

untried [untrajd] **1** niet geprobeerd, onbeproefd; **2** niet getest

untrue [untroe:] **1** onwaar, niet waar; **2** ontrouw, niet loyaal; **3** afwijkend *(from norm)*, onzuiver, scheef: ~ *tone* onzuivere toon

¹unused [unjoe:zd] *adj* ongebruikt, onbenut: ~ *opportunity* onbenutte gelegenheid

²unused [unjoe:st] *adj* niet gewend: ~ *to hard work* er niet aan gewend hard te (moeten) werken

unusual [unjoe:zjoeəl] **1** ongebruikelijk, ongewoon; **2** opmerkelijk, buitengewoon

unutterable [unnuttərəbl] onuitsprekelijk *(also fig)*, onbeschrijfelijk: ~ *idiot* volslagen idioot

unvarnished [unva:nisjt] onverbloemd

¹unveil [unveel] *vb* onthullen, ontsluieren, *(fig)* openbaren, aan het licht brengen

²unveil [unveel] *vb* de sluier afdoen, de sluier laten vallen

unwanted [unwontid] **1** ongewenst; **2** onnodig

unwarranted [unworrəntid] ongerechtvaardigd, ongewettigd, ongegrond

unwell [unwel] onwel, ziek

unwieldy [unwie:ldie] **1** onhandelbaar, onhandig, onpraktisch, niet gemakkelijk te hanteren; **2** onbehouwen, lomp

unwilling [unwilling] onwillig

¹unwind [unwajnd] *vb* **1** zich afwikkelen *(also fig)*, zich ontrollen; **2** *(inf)* zich ontspannen

²unwind [unwajnd] *vb* **1** afwikkelen, ontrollen; **2** ontwarren

unwitting [unwitting] **1** onwetend, onbewust; **2** onopzettelijk, ongewild

unworthy [unwə:ðie] **1** onwaardig; **2** ongepast: *that attitude is* ~ *of you* die houding siert je niet

unwrap [unræp] openmaken, uitpakken

unwritten [unritn] **1** ongeschreven; **2** mondeling overgeleverd || ~ *law* ongeschreven wet, gewoonterecht

unzip [unzip] openritsen, losmaken

¹up [up] *adv* **1** *(place or direction)* omhoog, op-, uit-: *six floors* ~ zes hoog; ~ *the republic* leve de republiek; *live* ~ *in the hills* boven in de bergen wonen; *turn* ~ *the music* zet de muziek harder; *he went* ~ *north* hij ging naar het noorden; ~ *and down* op en neer, heen en weer; ~ *till* (of: *to) now* tot nu toe; ~ *to and including* tot en met; *from £4* ~ vanaf vier pond; *children from six years* ~ kinderen van zes jaar en ouder; **2** te voorschijn, zichtbaar: *it will turn* ~ het zal wel aan het licht komen; **3** helemaal, op, door-: *full* ~ (helemaal) vol; **4** *(place or direction)* in, naar: *he went* ~ *to Cambridge* hij ging in Cambridge studeren; *(sport) be two (goals)* ~ twee goals voorstaan; *I don't feel* ~ *to it* ik voel er mij niet toe in staat

²up [up] *prep* **1** *(place or direction)* op, boven in, omhoog: ~ *(the) river* stroomopwaarts; *(theatre)* ~ *stage* achter op de scène; ~ *the stairs* de trap op; **2** *(direction towards a central point)* naar, in: ~ *the street* verderop in de straat; ~ *the valley* (verder) het dal in; ~ *and down the country* door het gehele land

³up [up] *adj* **1** omhoog-, opgaand, hoog, hoger(geplaatst): *an* ~ *stroke* opwaartse uithaal *(with pen)*; **2** op, uit bed, wakker; **3** actief, gezond; **4** gestegen, omhooggegaan: *the temperature is* ~ *eight degrees* de temperatuur ligt acht graden hoger; **5** naar een hoger gelegen plaats gaand *(of train)*: *the* ~ *line* de Londenlijn; **6** in aanmerking komend (voor), ter studie: *the house is* ~ *for sale* het huis staat te koop; **7** verkiesbaar gesteld, kandidaat: *Senator Smith is* ~ *for re-election* senator Smith stelt zich herkiesbaar; **8** om, voorbij: *time is* ~ de tijd is om; **9** met voorsprong, vóór op tegenstrever: *road* ~ werk in uitvoering *(warning sign)*; **10** duurder (geworden), in prijs gestegen: *coffee is* ~ *again* de koffie is weer eens duurder geworden; **11** *(after noun)* naar boven lopend, omhooggericht: *what is* ~? wat gebeurt er (hier)?; ~ *and about* (of: *around)* weer op de been, (druk) in de weer

⁴up [up] *n* **1** (opgaande) helling; **2** opwaartse beweging ‖ *~s and downs* wisselvalligheden, voor- en tegenspoed; *(inf) on the ~-and-~* gestaag stijgend, *(Am)* eerlijk, openhartig

⁵up [up] *vb (inf)* onverwacht doen, plotseling beginnen: *she ~ped and left* zij vertrok plotseling

⁶up [up] *vb (inf)* (plotseling) de hoogte in jagen, verhogen, (abrupt) doen stijgen: *he ~ped the offer* hij deed een hoger bod

upbraid [upbreed] verwijten, een (fikse) uitbrander geven: *~ s.o. for doing sth.* (of: *with sth.*) iem iets verwijten

upbringing [upbringing] opvoeding

upcoming *(Am)* voor de deur staand; aanstaande

up-country 1 in, naar, uit het binnenland; **2** achtergebleven, naïef

¹update *vb* moderniseren, bijwerken, herzien

²update *n* herziening, moderne versie

upend *n* **1** op zijn kop zetten, ondersteboven zetten; **2** omverslaan

¹upgrade *vb* **1** bevorderen, promotie geven; **2** verbeteren, opwaarderen

²upgrade *n* (oplopende) helling ‖ *on the ~: a)* oplopend, toenemend; *b)* vooruitgang boekend

upheaval [uphie:vl] omwenteling, opschudding: *social ~* sociale beroering

¹uphill *adj* **1** hellend, oplopend, (berg)opwaarts; **2** (uiterst) moeilijk, zwaar

²uphill *adv* **1** bergop, naar boven, omhoog; **2** moeizaam, tegen de stroom in

uphold [uphoold] **1** ophouden, rechthouden, hoog houden; **2** (moreel) steunen, goedkeuren; **3** (her)bevestigen, blijven bij

upholster [uphoolstə] stofferen *(room, seats)*, bekleden

upholstery [uphoolstərie] stoffering, bekleding

upland [upländ] **1** hoogland[h], plateau[h]; **2** binnenland[h]

upmarket voor de betere inkomensklasse, uit de duurdere prijsklasse: *an ~ bookshop* een exclusieve boekhandel

upon [əpon] *see* on

¹upper [uppə] *adj* **1** hoger, boven-, opper-: *~ arm* bovenarm; *~ atmosphere* hogere atmosfeer *(above troposphere)*; *~ lip* bovenlip; **2** hoger gelegen: *~ reaches of the Nile* bovenloop van de Nijl; **3** belangrijker, hoger geplaatst, superieur: *the ~ class* de hogere stand, de aristocratie; *have the ~ hand* de overhand hebben; *the Upper House* het Hogerhuis, Senaat, Eerste Kamer; *(inf) he is wrong in the ~ storey* hij is niet goed bij zijn hoofd

²upper [uppə] *n* **1** bovenleer[h] *(of footwear)*; **2** *(Am; inf)* pepmiddel[h], *(fig)* stimulans, leuke ervaring ‖ *(inf) be (down) on one's ~s* berooid zijn, straatarm zijn

upper-class uit de hogere stand, aristocratisch

uppermost [uppəmoost] hoogst, bovenst, belangrijkst

uppish [uppisj] *(inf)* verwaand, arrogant

¹upright *adj* **1** recht(opstaand), loodrecht staand, kaarsrecht; **2** oprecht, rechtdoorzee ‖ *~ piano* pianino, gewone piano

²upright *adv* rechtop, verticaal

³upright *n* stijl, staander, stut

uprising [uprajzing] opstand

uproar [upro:] tumult[h], rumoer[h], herrie

uproarious [upro:riəs] **1** luidruchtig, uitgelaten; **2** lachwekkend

uproot 1 ontwortelen *(also fig)*, uit zijn vertrouwde omgeving wegrukken *(persons);* **2** uitroeien

¹upset [upset] *vb* **1** omkantelen, omslaan, omvallen; **2** overlopen; **3** verstoord worden, in de war raken

²upset [upset] *vb* **1** omstoten, omverwerpen, omgooien; **2** doen overlopen; **3** in de war sturen, verstoren, van zijn stuk brengen: *a very ~ting experience* een heel nare ervaring; **4** ziek maken, van streek maken *(stomach)*

³upset [upset] *adj* van streek, overstuur, geërgerd

⁴upset [upset] *n* **1** omverwerping, verstoring, totale ommekeer; **2** ontsteltenis: *Sheila has had a terrible ~* Sheila heeft een flinke klap gekregen; **3** lichte (maag)stoornis; **4** *(sport)* verrassende nederlaag (wending)

upside down 1 ondersteboven, omgekeerd; **2** compleet in de war

¹upstage *adj (inf)* hooghartig, afstandelijk

²upstage *vb (inf)* meer aandacht trekken dan, de show stelen van, in de schaduw stellen

¹upstairs *adv* naar de bovenverdieping(en), de trap op, naar boven

²upstairs *adj* mbt de bovenverdieping(en), boven-

upstanding 1 recht overeind (staand); **2** flinkgebouwd; **3** eerlijk, oprecht

¹upstate *adj (Am)* meer naar het binnenland gelegen, provinciaal, provincie-, afgelegen

²upstate *adv* uit, naar, in het binnenland, noordelijk

upstream tegen de stroom in(gaand), stroomopwaarts

upsurge [upsə:dzj] **1** opwelling, vlaag; **2** plotselinge toename

uptake [upteek] opname *(of food, liquid)* ‖ *slow* (of: *quick) on the ~* niet zo vlug van begrip

uptight *(inf)* **1** zenuwachtig, gespannen; **2** kwaad

up-to-date 1 bijgewerkt, op de hoogte; **2** modern, bij(detijds), hedendaags

uptown 1 in, naar, van de bovenstad; **2** *(Am)* in, naar, van de betere woonwijk(en)

upturn 1 beroering; **2** verbetering, ommekeer

upward [upwəd] stijgend, opwaarts, toenemend

upwards [upwədz] (naar) omhoog, naar boven, in stijgende lijn: *from the knees ~* boven de knieën; *~ of twenty people* meer dan twintig mensen

uranium [joereeniəm] uranium[h]

urban [ə:bən] stedelijk, stads-

urbanize [ə:bənajz] verstedelijken, urbaniseren

urchin [ə:tsjin] rakker, boefje[h], kwajongen

¹urge [ə:dzj] *vb* **1** drijven, aansporen: *~ on* voortdrijven; **2** dringend verzoeken, bidden, smeken; **3** bepleiten, aandringen op; **4** trachten te overtuigen: *she ~d (up)on us the need for secrecy* zij drukte ons de noodzaak van geheimhouding op het hart

²urge [ə:dzj] *n* drang, impuls, neiging, behoefte

urgency [ə:dzjɔnsie] **1** (aan)drang, pressie; **2** urgentie, dringende noodzaak

urgent [ə:dzjənt] **1** urgent, dringend; **2** aanhoudend, hardnekkig

urinal [joeərinl] **1** urinaalʰ, (pis)fles; **2** urinoirʰ, openbare waterplaats

urinate [joeərinneet] urineren, wateren

urine [joeərin] urine, plas

urn [ə:n] urn

us [us] **1** (voor, aan) ons: *all of ~ enjoyed it* wij genoten er allen van; *he helps them more than ~* hij helpt hen meer dan ons; **2** wij, ons: *~ girls refused to join in* wij meisjes weigerden mee te doen; *they are stronger than ~* ze zijn sterker dan wij; **3** *(referring to 1st person singular)* mij: *let ~ hear it again* laat het nog eens horen

U.S. *United States* VS; Verenigde Staten

U.S.A. 1 *United States of America* VS; Verenigde Staten; **2** *United States Army*

usable [joe:zəbl] bruikbaar

usage [joe:sidzj] gebruikʰ, behandeling, gewoonte, taalgebruikʰ

¹use [joe:s] *n* **1** gebruikʰ, toepassing: *make a good ~ of* goed gebruik maken van; *in ~* in gebruik; *out of ~* in onbruik; **2** nutʰ, bruikbaarheid: *have no ~ for: a)* niet kunnen gebruiken; *b)* niets moeten hebben van; *this will be of ~* dit zal goed van pas komen; *it is no ~ arguing* tegenspreken heeft geen zin; *what is the ~ of it?* wat heeft het voor zin?

²use [joe:z] *vb* **1** gebruiken: *~ up* opmaken; **2** behandelen: *he was ill ~d* hij werd slecht behandeld

used [joe:zd] gebruikt, tweedehands

¹used to [joe:stoe] *vb* had(den) de gewoonte te, deed, deden: *the summers ~ be hotter* de zomers waren vroeger warmer; *my father ~ say: 'Money doesn't buy you happiness.'* mijn vader zei altijd: 'Met geld koop je geen geluk.'

²used to [joe:st toe] *adj* gewend aan, gewoon aan

useful [joe:sfoel] bruikbaar, nuttig: *come in ~* goed van pas komen; *make oneself ~* zich verdienstelijk maken

useless [joe:sləs] **1** nutteloos, vergeefs; **2** onbruikbaar, waardeloos, hopeloos

user [joe:zə] gebruiker, verbruiker, verslaafde *(alcohol, drugs)*

user-friendly gebruikersvriendelijk

¹usher [usjə] *n* **1** portierʰ, zaalwachter; **2** plaatsaanwijzer; **3** ceremoniemeester

²usher [usjə] *vb* **1** als portier, plaatsaanwijzer optreden voor, voorgaan, brengen naar: *~ out* uitlaten, naar buiten geleiden; *~ into* binnenleiden in; **2** *(with in)* aankondigen, *(fig)* inluiden, de voorbode zijn van

usual [joe:zjoeəl] gebruikelijk, gewoon: *business as ~* de zaken gaan gewoon door, alles gaat zijn gange-

tje; *as ~* zoals gebruikelijk; *it is ~ to* het is de gewoonte om

usually [joe:zjoeəlie] gewoonlijk

usurp [joe:zə:p] onrechtmatig in bezit nemen, zich toe-eigenen; zich aanmatigen

usury [joe:zjərie] woeker, woekerrente

utensil [joe:tensl] **1** gebruiksvoorwerpʰ: *cooking ~s* keukengerei; **2** *~s* werktuigen *(also fig)*, gereedschapʰ

uterus [joe:tərəs] baarmoeder

utility [joe:tillittie] **1** (openbare) voorziening, nutsbedrijfʰ, waterleidings-, gas-, elektriciteitsbedrijfʰ; **2** nutʰ, nuttigheid

utility room *(roughly)* bijkeuken

utilize [joe:tillajz] gebruiken, gebruik maken van

¹utmost [utmoost] *adj* uiterst, hoogst: *of the ~ importance* van het (aller)grootste belang

²utmost [utmoost] *n* **1** uiterste (grens); **2** uiterste best, al het mogelijke: *do one's ~* zijn uiterste best doen

¹utter [uttə] *adj* uiterst, absoluut, volslagen

²utter [uttə] *vb* **1** uiten, slaken *(eg sigh, cry)*; **2** uitspreken, zeggen; **3** in omloop brengen *(counterfeit money)*

utterance [uttərəns] uiting *(also linguistics)*, uitlating, woorden: *give ~ to* uitdrukking geven aan

utterly [uttəlie] **1** uiterst, absoluut; **2** volkomen, volslagen: *~ mad* volslagen krankzinnig

U-turn (totale) ommezwaai: *(traf) no ~s* keren verboden

uvula [joe:vjoelə] huig

uxorious [ukso:riəs] **1** dol op zijn echtgenote; **2** slaafs *(towards wife)*

Uzbek [oezbek] Oezbeeks

Uzbekistan [oezbekkista:n] Oezbekistan

V

v *versus* van

V *volt(s)* V

vacancy [veekənsie] 1 vacature; 2 lege plaats, leegte, ruimte: *no vacancies* vol *(in hotel);* 3 afwezigheid

vacant [veekənt] 1 leeg; leeg(staand) *(of house),* onbewoond: *~ possession* leeg te aanvaarden; 2 vacant *(of position),* open(staand); 3 afwezig *(of mind)*

vacate [vəkeet] 1 vrij maken, ontruimen *(house);* 2 opgeven *(position),* neerleggen *(office)*

¹**vacation** [vəkeesjən] *n* 1 vakantie *(esp of court of law and universities): long ~* zomervakantie; 2 ontruiming *(of house)*

²**vacation** [vəkeesjən] *vb (Am)* vakantie hebben, houden

vaccinate [væksinneet] *(with against)* vaccineren (tegen), inenten

vaccination [væksinneesjən] (koepok)inenting, vaccinatie

vaccine [væksie:n] vaccinʰ, entstof

vacillate [væsilleet] *(with between)* aarzelen (tussen), onzeker zijn

vacuity [vəkjoe:ittie] 1 leegheid; 2 saaiheid; 3 dwaasheid

¹**vacuum** [vækjoeəm] *n* vacuümʰ, leegte: *~ cleaner* stofzuiger

²**vacuum** [vækjoeəm] *vb* stofzuigen

vagabond [vægəbond] vagebond, landloper

vagina [vədzjajnə] vagina

vagrancy [veegrənsie] landloperij

¹**vagrant** [veegrənt] *adj* (rond)zwervend, rondtrekkend

²**vagrant** [veegrənt] *n* landloper, zwerver

vague [veeg] 1 vaag, onduidelijk, onscherp: *be ~ about sth.* vaag zijn over iets; 2 gering: *I haven't the ~st idea* ik heb geen flauw idee

vain [veen] 1 ijdel, verwaand; 2 zinloos, nutteloos, vals *(hope),* vergeefs *(effort, attempt): in ~* tevergeefs; 3 triviaal, leeg: *take God's name in ~* Gods naam ijdel gebruiken

vale [veel] vallei, dalʰ

valentine [vælantajn] 1 liefjeʰ *(chosen on St Valentine's Day, 14 February);* 2 valentijnskaart

valerian [vəliəriən] valeriaan

valet [vælee] 1 lijfknecht, (persoonlijke) bediende; 2 hotelbediende

valiant [væliənt] moedig, heldhaftig

valid [vælid] 1 redelijk *(of arguments etc),* steekhoudend, gegrond; 2 geldig *(of ticket)*

validate [væliddeet] bevestigen, bekrachtigen

validity [vəliddittie] 1 (rechts)geldigheid, het van kracht zijn; 2 redelijkheid *(of arguments etc)*

valley [vælie] dalʰ, vallei

valour [vælə] (helden)moed, dapperheid

¹**valuable** [væljoeəbl] *adj* 1 waardevol, nuttig; 2 kostbaar

²**valuable** [væljoeəbl] *n* kostbaarheid

valuation [væljoe·eesjən] 1 schatting; 2 waarde, beoordeling

¹**value** [væljoe:] *n* 1 (gevoels)waarde, betekenis; 2 maatstaf, waarde; 3 (gelds)waarde, valuta, prijs: *(get) ~ for money* waar voor zijn geld (krijgen); *to the ~ of* ter waarde van; 4 nutʰ, waarde: *of great ~* erg nuttig

²**value** [væljoe:] *vb* 1 *(with at)* taxeren (op), schatten; 2 waarderen, op prijs stellen

value added tax belasting op de toegevoegde waarde, btw

valve [vælv] 1 klep, ventielʰ *(also music),* schuif; 2 klep(vliesʰ) *(of heart, blood vessels)*

vamp [væmp]: *~ up* opkalefateren, opknappen

vampire [væmpajjə] 1 vampier: *~ bat* vampier *(kind of bat);* 2 uitzuiger *(fig)*

van [væn] 1 bestelwagen, bus(jeʰ), *(in compounds oft)* wagen; 2 (goederen)wagon

vandal [vændl] vandaal

vandalism [vændəlizm] vandalismeʰ, vernielzucht

vane [veen] 1 vin, bladʰ, schoep *(of screw),* vleugel; 2 windwijzer, weerhaantjeʰ

vanguard [vænga:d] voorhoede *(also fig),* spits

vanilla [vənillə] vanille

vanish [vænisj] (plotseling) verdwijnen

vanity [vænittie] 1 ijdelheid, verbeelding; 2 leegheid

vanquish [vængkwisj] overwinnen *(also fig),* verslaan, bedwingen

vantage [va:ntidzj] *(Am)* voordeelʰ *(tennis),* voorsprong

vapid [væpid] 1 duf, flauw; 2 smakeloos, verschaald *(beer)*

vaporize [veepərajz] (laten) verdampen

vaporizer [veepərajzə] verstuiver

vapour [veepə] damp, gasʰ, wasem

variability [veəriəbillittie] veranderlijkheid, onbestendigheid

¹**variable** [veəriəbl] *adj* veranderlijk, wisselend, onbestendig

²**variable** [veəriəbl] *n* variabele (grootheid); variabele waarde

variance [veəriəns] verschilʰ, afwijking, *(fig)* verschilʰ van mening: *be at ~* het oneens zijn; *at ~ with* in strijd met, in tegenspraak met

¹**variant** [veəriənt] *adj* afwijkend, alternatief

²**variant** [veəriənt] *n* variant, afwijkende vorm

variation [veərie·eesjən] variatie *(also music),*

(af)wisseling, afwijking

varicoloured [ve̯əriekulləd] veelkleurig

varied [ve̯əried] gevarieerd, afwisselend

variegated [ve̯ərigeetid] (onregelmatig) gekleurd, (bont) geschakeerd

variety [vəra̯jjətie] **1** verscheidenheid, afwisseling, variatie, verandering, assortiment[h]: *they sell a wide ~ of toys* ze verkopen allerlei verschillende soorten speelgoed; **2** variëteit *(biology)*, verscheidenheid, ras[h], (onder)soort: *~ is the spice of life* verandering van spijs doet eten; **3** variété[h]

various [ve̯əriəs] **1** gevarieerd, uiteenlopend, verschillend (van soort): *their ~ social backgrounds* hun verschillende sociale achtergrond; **2** verscheiden, divers: *he mentioned ~ reasons* hij noemde diverse redenen

¹varnish [va̠:nisj] *n* vernis[+h], vernislaag *(also fig)*, lak, glazuur[h] *(of earthenware): a ~ of civilization* een dun laagje beschaving

²varnish [va̠:nisj] *vb* vernissen, lakken, *(fig)* mooier voorstellen: *she tried to ~ over his misbehaviour* ze probeerde zijn wangedrag te verbloemen

varsity [va̠:sittie] **1** universiteit *(Oxford and Cambridge)*; **2** *(Am)* universiteitsteam[h] *(eg of sport)*

vary [ve̯ərie] variëren, (doen) veranderen: *with ~ing success* met wisselend succes; *prices ~ from 15 to 95 pounds* de prijzen lopen uiteen van 15 tot 95 pond

vase [va:z] vaas

vast [va:st] enorm (groot), geweldig: *~ auditorium* kolossale aula; *~ly exaggerated* vreselijk overdreven

vat [væt] vat[h], ton, kuip

VAT [vie:eetie:] *value added tax* btw, belasting op de toegevoegde waarde

¹vault [vo:lt] *n* **1** gewelf[h], boog, (gewelfde) grafkelder (wijnkelder); **2** (bank)kluis; **3** sprong, *(athletics)* polsstoksprong

²vault [vo:lt] *vb (also fig)* springen (op, over), een sprong maken, *(athletics)* polsstokhoogspringen

vaunt [vo:nt] opscheppen (over) ‖ *her much-vaunted secretary* haar veelgeprezen secretaris

V.D. *venereal disease* soa, seksueel overdraagbare aandoening

veal [vie:l] kalfsvlees[h]

veer [viə] van richting (doen) veranderen, omlopen, (met de klok mee)draaien *(of wind); (fig)* een andere kant (doen) opgaan: *the car ~ed off the road* de auto schoot (plotseling) van de weg af

¹vegetable [ve̯dzjətəbl] *n* **1** groente, eetbaar gewas[h]; **2** plant, *(fig)* vegeterend mens

²vegetable [ve̯dzjətəbl] *adj* plantaardig, groente- ‖ *~ marrow* pompoen

¹vegetarian [vedzjitte̯əriən] *adj* vegetarisch

²vegetarian [vedzjitte̯əriən] *n* vegetariër

vegetate [ve̯dzjitteet] **1** groeien, spruiten *((as if) of plant)*; **2** vegeteren *(fig)*

vegetation [vedzjitte̯esjən] **1** vegetatie, (planten)groei; **2** *(med)* vegetatie, woekering

vehemence [vi̯əməns] felheid, hevigheid

vehement [vi̯əmənt] fel, heftig, krachtig

vehicle [vie̠:ikl] **1** voertuig[h] *(also fig)*, middel[h], medium[h]: *language is the ~ of thought* taal is het voertuig van de gedachte; **2** oplosmiddel[h], bindmiddel[h]; **3** drager, overbrenger

¹veil [veel] *n* sluier: *draw a ~ over sth.* een sluier over iets trekken, *(also fig)* iets in de doofpot stoppen; *take the ~* non worden

²veil [veel] *vb* (ver)sluieren *(also fig): ~ed threat* verholen dreigement

vein [veen] **1** ader, bloedvat[h], ertsader, nerf; **2** vleugje[h], klein beetje[h]: *a ~ of irony* een vleugje ironie; **3** gemoedstoestand, bui: *in the same ~* in dezelfde geest, van hetzelfde soort

velcro [ve̯lkroo] klittenband[h]

velocity [villo̯ssittie] snelheid

¹velvet [ve̯lvit] *n* fluweel[h]

²velvet [ve̯lvit] *adj* fluwelen

vend [vend] **1** verkopen; **2** venten, aan de man brengen

vendetta [vende̯ttə] bloedwraak

vending machine automaat *(for soft drinks, sweets, cigarettes etc)*

vendor [ve̯ndə] verkoper

¹veneer [vinniə] *n* **1** fineer[h]; **2** *(fig)* vernisje[h], dun laagje[h] (vernis)

²veneer [vinniə] *vb* **1** fineren; **2** *(fig)* een vernisje geven

venerable [ve̯nnərəbl] **1** eerbiedwaardig; **2** hoogeerwaarde *(title of archdeacon)*; **3** *(Roman Catholicism)* eerwaardig

venerate [ve̯nnəreet] aanbidden

veneration [vennəre̯esjən] verering, diepe eerbied

Venetian [vinnie̠:sjən] Venetiaans ‖ *~ blind* jaloezie

vengeance [ve̯ndzjəns] wraak: *take ~ (up)on s.o.* zich op iem wreken; *work with a ~* werken dat de stukken eraf vliegen

venial [vie̠:niəl] vergeeflijk, onbetekenend

Venice [ve̯nnis] Venetië

venom [ve̯nnəm] **1** vergif[h]; **2** venijn[h], boosaardigheid

venomous [ve̯nnəməs] **1** (ver)giftig; **2** venijnig, boosaardig

¹vent [vent] *n* **1** (lucht)opening, (ventilatie)gat[h], luchtgat[h]; **2** *(also fig)* uitlaat, uitweg: *give ~ to one's feelings* zijn hart luchten; **3** split *(in coat etc)*

²vent [vent] *vb* **1** uiten *(feelings)*, luchten; **2** afreageren: *~ sth. on s.o. (sth.)* iets afreageren op iem (iets)

ventilate [ve̯ntilleet] **1** ventileren, luchten; **2** (in het openbaar) bespreken, naar buiten brengen *(opinion)*

ventilation [ventille̠esjən] **1** ventilatie, luchtverversing, ventilatie(systeem[h]); **2** openbare discussie; **3** uiting, het naar buiten brengen *(of opinion etc)*

ventriloquist [ventri̯lləkwist] buikspreker

¹venture [ve̯ntsjə] *n* (gevaarlijke) onderneming, gewaagd project[h], speculatie, avontuurlijke reis

(stap)

²**venture** [vɛntsjə] *vb* **1** (aan)durven, wagen (iets te doen), durven (te beweren); **2** (zich) wagen, riskeren: ~ *one's life* zijn leven op het spel zetten; *nothing~d, nothing gained* wie niet waagt, die niet wint; ~ *out of doors* zich op straat wagen

venue [vɛnjoe:] **1** plaats van samenkomst, ontmoetingsplaats, trefpunt[h]; **2** plaats van handeling, lokatie, terrein[h], toneel[h]

veracity [vərǽsittie] **1** oprechtheid, eerlijkheid; **2** geloofwaardigheid, nauwkeurigheid

veranda(h) [vərǽndə] veranda

verb [vɔ:b] werkwoord[h]

verbal [vɔ:bl] **1** mondeling, gesproken, verbaal: ~ *agreement* mondelinge overeenkomst; **2** van woorden, woord(en)-; **3** woordelijk, woord voor woord: ~ *translation* letterlijke vertaling

verbatim [vɔ:beetim] woordelijk, woord voor woord

verbose [vɔ:boos] breedsprakig

verdict [vɔ:dikt] **1** oordeel[h], vonnis[h], beslissing: ~ *on* oordeel over; **2** (jury)uitspraak: *bring in a* ~ uitspraak doen

verge [vɔ:dзj] rand, kant *(fig)*, berm: *bring s.o. to the* ~ *of despair* iem op de rand van de wanhoop brengen

verge on grenzen aan: *verging on the tragic* op het randje van het tragische

verifiable [vɛrriffajjəbl] verifieerbaar: *his story is hardly* ~ de waarheid van zijn verhaal kan moeilijk bewezen worden

verification [vɛrriffikkeesjən] **1** verificatie, onderzoek[h]; **2** bevestiging

verify [vɛrriffaj] **1** verifiëren, de juistheid nagaan van; **2** waarmaken, bevestigen

veritable [vɛrrittəbl] waar, echt, werkelijk

vermilion [vəmilliən] vermiljoen[h]

vermin [vɔ:min] **1** ongedierte[h]; **2** gespuis[h]

verminous [vɔ:minnəs] **1** vol (met) ongedierte; **2** door ongedierte overgebracht *(disease)*; **3** vies

¹**vernacular** [vənǽkjoelə] *adj* in de landstaal

²**vernacular** [vənǽkjoelə] *n* landstaal, streektaal

versatile [vɔ:sətajl] **1** veelzijdig, *(also)* flexibel *(of mind)*; **2** ruim toepasbaar, veelzijdig bruikbaar

versatility [vɔ:sətillittie] **1** veelzijdigheid; **2** ruime toepasbaarheid

verse [vɔ:s] **1** vers[h], versregel, dichtregel, bijbelvers[h]; **2** vers[h], couplet[h], strofe; **3** versvorm, verzen; gedichten: *blank* ~ onberijmde verzen

versed [vɔ:st] bedreven, ervaren

versification [vɔ:siffikkeesjən] **1** verskunst; **2** versbouw

¹**versify** [vɔ:siffaj] *vb* **1** rijmen, dichten; **2** rijmelen

²**versify** [vɔ:siffaj] *vb* op rijm zetten

version [vɔ:sjən] **1** versie, variant, interpretatie, lezing, vertaling; **2** *Version* bijbelvertaling

versus [vɔ:səs] **1** tegen, contra; **2** vergeleken met, tegenover

vertebra [vɔ:tibrə] (ruggen)wervel

¹**vertebrate** [vɔ:tibreet] *adj* gewerveld

²**vertebrate** [vɔ:tibreet] *n* gewerveld dier[h]

¹**vertical** [vɔ:tikl] *adj* verticaal, loodrecht

²**vertical** [vɔ:tikl] *n* **1** loodlijn; **2** loodrecht vlak[h]; **3** loodrechte stand: *out of the* ~ niet loodrecht, uit het lood

vertigo [vɔ:tigoo] duizeligheid, draaierigheid

verve [vɔ:v] vuur[h], geestdrift

¹**very** [vɛrrie] *adv* **1** heel, erg: *that is* ~ *difficult* dat is erg moeilijk; *the* ~ *last day* de allerlaatste dag; **2** helemaal: *keep this for your* ~ *own* houd dit helemaal voor jezelf; **3** precies: *in the* ~ *same hotel* in precies hetzelfde hotel

²**very** [vɛrrie] *adj* **1** absoluut, uiterst: *from the* ~ *beginning* vanaf het allereerste begin; **2** zelf, juist, precies: *the* ~ *man he needed* precies de man die hij nodig had; *he died in this* ~ *room* hij stierf in deze zelfde kamer; *this is the* ~ *thing for me* dat is net iets voor mij; **3** enkel, alleen (al): *the* ~ *fact that* ... alleen al het feit dat ...

vessel [vɛsl] **1** vat[h] *(for liquid)*; **2** *(anatomy, botany)* vat[h], kanaal[h], buis *(for blood, fluid)*; **3** vaartuig[h], schip[h]

¹**vest** [vɛst] *n* **1** (onder)hemd[h]; **2** *(Am)* vest[h]

²**vest** [vɛst] *vb* toekennen, bekleden: ~*ed interests* gevestigde belangen

vestibule [vɛstibjoe:l] **1** vestibule, hal[h]; **2** kerkportaal[h]

vestige [vɛstidzj] spoor[h]: *not a* ~ *of regret* geen spoor van spijt

vestment [vɛstmənt] **1** (ambts)kleed[h], ambtsgewaad[h]; **2** *(rel)* liturgisch gewaad[h], misgewaad[h]

¹**vet** [vɛt] *n, veterinary surgeon* dierenarts, veearts

²**vet** [vɛt] *vb* **1** medisch behandelen *(animal)*; **2** grondig onderzoeken, (medisch) keuren, *(fig)* doorlichten

¹**veteran** [vɛttərən] *adj* **1** door en door ervaren; **2** veteranen- ‖ ~ *car* oldtimer *(from before 1916)*

²**veteran** [vɛttərən] *n* veteraan, oudgediende *(also fig)*, oud-soldaat

veterinarian [vɛttərinneəriən] *(Am)* dierenarts, veearts

veterinary [vɛttərinnərie] veeartsenij-: ~ *surgeon* dierenarts, veearts

¹**veto** [vie:too] *n* veto(recht)[h]

²**veto** [vie:too] *vb* zijn veto uitspreken over, zijn toestemming weigeren

vex [vɛks] **1** ergeren, plagen, irriteren; **2** in de war brengen

vexation [vɛkseesjən] **1** ergernis, irritatie; **2** kwelling

vexatious [vɛkseesjəs] vervelend, ergerlijk

vexed [vɛkst] **1** geërgerd, geïrriteerd; **2** hachelijk, netelig: ~ *question* lastige kwestie

VHF *very high frequency* FM

via [vajjə] **1** via, door, langs: *he left* ~ *the garden* hij vertrok door de tuin; **2** *(means)* door middel van

viability [vajjəbillittie] **1** levensvatbaarheid; **2** doenlijkheid, uitvoerbaarheid

viable [vajjəbl] **1** levensvatbaar *(also fig);* **2** uitvoerbaar

viaduct [vajjədukt] viaduct[h]

vibes [vajbz] *vibrations* vibraties, uitstralende gevoelens

vibrant [vajbrənt] **1** trillend; **2** helder *(of colour);* **3** levendig, krachtig *(of voice)*

vibrate [vajbreet] (doen) trillen *(also fig)*

vibration [vajbreesjən] trilling

vicar [vikkə] **1** predikant, dominee *(Anglican Church);* **2** *(Roman Catholicism)* plaatsvervanger, vicaris

vicarage [vikkəridzj] pastorie

vicarious [vikkeəriəs] **1** afgevaardigd; **2** indirect

vice [vajs] **1** gebrek[h], onvolmaaktheid, slechte gewoonte; **2** ondeugd; **3** ontucht, prostitutie; **4** handschroef, bankschroef

vice-chairman vice-president, vice-voorzitter

vice-chancellor 1 vice-kanselier *(of court of law);* **2** rector magnificus *(of university)*

viceroy [vajsroj] onderkoning

vicinity [vissinnittie] **1** buurt, wijk; **2** nabijheid, buurt, omgeving

vicious [visjəs] **1** wreed, boosaardig, gemeen: ~ *blow* gemene mep; **2** gevaarlijk, gewelddadig: ~*(-looking) knife* gevaarlijk (uitziend) mes; **3** vol kuren *(of animals):* ~ *circle: a)* vicieuze cirkel; *b) (also fig)* cirkelredenering

vicissitudes [vississitjoe:dz] wisselvalligheden

victim [viktim] **1** slachtoffer[h], dupe: *fall* ~ *to s.o. (sth.)* aan iem (iets) ten prooi vallen; **2** offer[h] *(human, animal)*

victimize [viktimmajz] **1** slachtofferen, doen lijden; **2** represailles nemen tegen *(eg a few persons),* (onverdiend) straffen

victor [viktə] overwinnaar, winnaar

Victorian [vikto:riən] Victoriaans, *(roughly)* (overdreven) preuts, schijnheilig

victorious [vikto:riəs] **1** zegevierend: *be* ~ overwinnen, de overwinning behalen; **2** overwinnings-

victory [viktərie] overwinning, zege

victualler [vitlə] leverancier van levensmiddelen || *licensed* ~ caféhouder met vergunning

victuals [vitlz] levensmiddelen, proviand

¹video [viddie·oo] *n* video(film), videorecorder

²video [viddie·oo] *vb* op (de) video opnemen

videodisc videoplaat, beeldplaat

videophone beeldtelefoon

video recorder videorecorder

¹videotape *n* videoband

²videotape *vb* op videoband opnemen

videotex [viddie·ooteks] videotex, viditel

vie [vaj] rivaliseren

Vienna [vie·ennə] Wenen

¹Viennese [vie·ənie:z] *n (Viennese)* Wener; Weense

²Viennese [vie·ənie:z] *adj* Weens

¹view [vjoe:] *n* **1** bezichtiging, inspectie, *(fig)* overzicht[h]: *a general* ~ *of the subject* een algemeen overzicht van het onderwerp; **2** zienswijze, opvatting:

take a dim (of: poor) ~ of s.o.'s conduct iemands gedrag maar matig waarderen; *in my* ~ volgens mij, zoals ik het zie; **3** uitzicht[h], gezicht[h], *(fig)* vooruitzicht[h]; **4** gezicht[h], afbeelding, *(fig)* beeld[h]; **5** bedoeling: *with a* ~ *to doing sth.* met de bedoeling iets te doen; **6** zicht[h], gezicht(svermogen)[h]; **7** zicht[h], uitzicht[h], gezichtsveld[h]: *come into* ~ in zicht komen; *have in* ~ op het oog hebben; *in* ~ *of* vanwege, gezien

²view [vjoe:] *vb* tv kijken

³view [vjoe:] *vb* **1** bekijken, beschouwen *(also fig):* ~ *a house* een huis bezichtigen; **2** inspecteren

viewer [vjoe:ə] **1** kijker, tv-kijker; **2** viewer *(for viewing slides)*

viewpoint gezichtspunt[h], oogpunt[h] *(also fig)*

vigil [vidzjil] waak, (nacht)wake: *keep* ~ waken

vigilance [vidzjilləns] waakzaamheid, oplettendheid

vigilant [vidzjillənt] waakzaam, oplettend, alert

vigorous [vigərəs] **1** krachtig, sterk, vol energie; **2** krachtig, gespierd *(language);* **3** groeizaam, gezond *(plants)*

vigour [vigə] **1** kracht, sterkte; **2** energie, vitaliteit; **3** groeikracht, levenskracht *(of plants, animals)*

Viking [vajking] viking, Noorman

vile [vajl] **1** gemeen; **2** walgelijk, afschuwelijk *(eg food);* **3** gemeen, beroerd *(weather)*

villa [villə] villa, landhuis[h]

village [villidzj] dorp[h]: ~ *green: a)* dorpsplein; *b)* dorpsweide

villager [villidzjə] dorpsbewoner

villain [villən] **1** boef, schurk, slechterik: *heroes and* ~*s* helden en schurken; **2** rakker, deugniet

villainous [villənəs] schurkachtig, gemeen, doortrapt, heel slecht

villainy [villənie] **1** schurkenstreek; **2** schurkachtigheid, doortraptheid

vim [vim] fut, pit

vindicate [vindikkeet] **1** rechtvaardigen; **2** van verdenking zuiveren, rehabiliteren

vindication [vindikkeesjən] **1** rechtvaardiging; **2** rehabilitatie

vindictive [vindiktiv] straffend, rancuneus, wraakzuchtig

vine [vajn] **1** wijnstok, wingerd; **2** *(Am)* kruiper, klimplant

vinegar [vinnigə] azijn

vineyard [vinjəd] wijngaard

¹vintage [vintidzj] **1** wijnoogst, wijnpluk; **2** wijntijd, (goed) wijnjaar[h]; **3** jaar[h], jaargang, bouwjaar[h], lichting: *they belong to the 1960* ~ zij zijn van de lichting van 1960

²vintage [vintidzj] *adj* **1** uitstekend, voortreffelijk: *a* ~ *silent film* een klassieke stomme film; **2** oud, antiek: ~ *car* auto uit de periode 1916-1930, klassieke auto

vinyl [vajnil] vinyl[h]

viola [vie·oolə] altviool

violate [vajjəleet] **1** overtreden, inbreuk maken op,

breken: ~ *a treaty* een verdrag schenden; **2** schenden, ontheiligen; **3** verkrachten

violation [vajjəleesjən] **1** overtreding *(also sport)*; **2** schending, schennis; **3** verkrachting

violence [vajjələns] **1** geweld[h]: *acts of* ~ gewelddadigheden; **2** gewelddadigheid: *crimes of* ~ geweldmisdrijven; **3** hevigheid, heftigheid

violent [vajjələnt] **1** hevig, heftig, wild: ~ *contrast* schril contrast; **2** gewelddadig: ~ *death* gewelddadige dood; **3** hel, schreeuwend *(colour)*

[1]violet [vajjəlit] *n* viooltje[h]

[2]violet [vajjəlit] *adj* violet, paars(achtig blauw)

violin [vajjəlin] **1** viool; **2** violist(e)

violinist [vajjəlinnist] violist(e)

VIP [vie:ajpie:] *very important person* vip; hooggeplaatst persoon, beroemdheid

viper [vajpə] adder *(also fig)*, serpent[h], verrader

[1]virgin [və:dzjin] *n* maagd *(also of man)*

[2]virgin [və:dzjin] *adj* maagdelijk, ongerept: ~ *snow* vers gevallen sneeuw

virginity [və:dzjinnittie] maagdelijkheid, het (nog) maagd zijn, *(fig)* ongereptheid

virile [virrajl] **1** mannelijk; **2** potent

virility [virrillittie] **1** mannelijkheid, kracht; **2** potentie

virtual [və:tjoeəl] feitelijk, eigenlijk, praktisch: *to them it was a* ~ *defeat* voor hen kwam het neer op een nederlaag; ~ *reality* virtuele werkelijkheid

virtually [və:tjoeəlie] praktisch, feitelijk: *my work is* ~ *finished* mijn werk is zo goed als af

virtue [və:tsjoe:] **1** deugd: *make a* ~ *of necessity* van de nood een deugd maken; **2** verdienste, goede eigenschap: *by* (of: *in) *~ *of* op grond van

virtuosity [və:tjoe-ossittie] virtuositeit, meesterschap[h]

virtuous [və:tjoeəs] **1** deugdzaam; **2** kuis

virulence [virroeləns] **1** kwaadaardigheid, virulentie; **2** venijnigheid

virulent [virroelənt] **1** (zeer) giftig, dodelijk *(poison)*; **2** kwaadaardig *(disease)*; **3** venijnig, kwaadaardig

virus [vajjərəs] virus[h]

visa [vie:zə] visum[h]

viscosity [viskossittie] kleverigheid; taaiheid, stroperigheid

viscount [vajkaunt] burggraaf *(title between baron and earl)*

viscountess [vajkauntis] burggravin

viscous [viskəs] **1** kleverig; **2** taai *(also fig)*

visibility [vizzibbillittie] **1** zicht[h] *(meteorology)*; **2** zichtbaarheid

visible [vizzibl] zichtbaar, waarneembaar, merkbaar

vision [vizjən] **1** gezicht(svermogen)[h], het zien: *field of* ~ gezichtsveld; **2** visie, inzicht[h]: *a man of* ~ een man met visie; **3** visioen[h], droom(beeld[h]); **4** (droom)verschijning; **5** (vluchtige) blik, glimp

[1]visionary [vizjənərie] *adj* **1** visioenen hebbend; **2** dromerig, onrealistisch; **3** denkbeeldig

[2]visionary [vizjənərie] *n* **1** ziener, profeet; **2** dromer, idealist

[1]visit [vizzit] *vb* **1** bezoeken, op visite gaan bij; **2** *(Am)* logeren bij, verblijven bij; **3** inspecteren, onderzoeken; **4** bezoeken, treffen, teisteren: *the village was ~ed by the plague* het dorp werd getroffen door de pest

[2]visit [vizzit] *vb* **1** een bezoek afleggen, op bezoek gaan; **2** *(Am)* logeren, verblijven || *(Am)* ~ *with* een praatje (gaan) maken met

[3]visit [vizzit] *n* bezoek[h], visite *(also of doctor)*, (tijdelijk) verblijf[h]: *pay s.o. a* ~ iem een bezoek(je) brengen

visitation [vizzitteesjən] **1** (officieel) bezoek[h], huisbezoek[h]; **2** beproeving

visiting [vizzitting] bezoekend, gast-: ~ *professor* gasthoogleraar; *(sport) the* ~ *team* de gasten

visiting hours bezoekuur, bezoektijd

visitor [vizzittə] bezoeker, gast, toerist

visor [vajzə] **1** klep *(of hat)*; **2** zonneklep *(of car)*; **3** vizier[h] *(of helmet)*

vista [vistə] **1** uitzicht[h], doorkijk(je[h]), (ver)gezicht[h]; **2** perspectief[h], vooruitzicht[h]: *open up new ~s* (of: *a new ~)* nieuwe perspectieven openen

visual [vizjoeəl] **1** visueel: ~ *aids* visuele hulpmiddelen; ~ *arts* beeldende kunsten; ~ *display unit* (beeld)scherm, monitor; **2** gezichts-, oog-; **3** zichtbaar; **4** optisch

visualize [vizjoeəlajz] **1** zich voorstellen; **2** visualiseren, zichtbaar maken

vital [vajtl] **1** essentieel, van wezenlijk belang, onmisbaar: ~ *importance* van vitaal belang; **2** vitaal, levenskrachtig, levens-: ~ *parts* vitale delen; ~ *statistics: a)* bevolkingsstatistiek; *b)* belangrijkste feiten

vitality [vajtælittie] vitaliteit, levenskracht

vitamin [vittəmin] vitamine

vitiate [visjie-eet] **1** schaden, schenden, verzwakken; **2** bederven, vervuilen *(also fig)*

vitreous [vitriəs] glas-, glazen, van glas; glasachtig, glazig

vitriol [vitriəl] *(chem)* zwavelzuur[h], *(fig)* venijn[h]

viva [vajvə] mondeling (her)examen[h]

vivacious [vivveesjəs] levendig, opgewekt

vivacity [vivæsittie] levendigheid, opgewektheid

vivid [vivvid] **1** helder *(colour, light)*, sterk; **2** levendig, krachtig: *a ~ imagination* een levendige fantasie

vivisection [vivvisseksjən] vivisectie

vixen [viksn] **1** wijfjesvos; **2** feeks

viz. [viz] *videlicet* nl.; namelijk, te weten, d.w.z.

vocabulary [vəkæbjoelərie] woordenlijst; woordenschat

[1]vocal [vookl] *adj* **1** gesproken, mondeling, vocaal, gezongen: ~ *group* zanggroep; **2** zich duidelijk uitend, welbespraakt; **3** stem-: ~ *cords* (of: *chords)* stembanden

[2]vocal [vookl] *n* **1** lied(je[h]), (pop)song; **2** ~*s* zang: ~*s: Michael Jackson* zang: Michael Jackson

vocalist [vookəlist] vocalist(e), zanger(es)
vocation [vookeesjən] **1** beroep^h, betrekking; **2** roeping; **3** aanleg, talent^h: *have a ~ for* aanleg hebben voor
vocational [vookeesjənəl] beroeps-, vak-: *~ training* beroepsonderwijs
vociferate [vəsifəreet] schreeuwen, heftig protesteren
vociferous [vəsifərəs] schreeuwend; lawaaierig, luidruchtig
vogue [voog] **1** mode: *be in ~* in de mode zijn, in zijn; **2** populariteit
^{1}**voice** [vojs] *n* **1** stem, (stem)geluid^h, uiting, mening: *speak in a low ~* op gedempte toon spreken; *give ~ to* uitdrukking geven aan; *raise one's ~: a)* zijn stem verheffen; *b)* protest aantekenen; *in (good) ~* goed bij stem; **2** vorm: *active ~* bedrijvende vorm
^{2}**voice** [vojs] *vb* uiten, verwoorden
voice-over commentaarstem *(with film, documentary)*
^{1}**void** [vojd] *adj* **1** leeg, verlaten: *~ of* zonder, vrij van; **2** nietig, ongeldig: *null and ~* ongeldig, van nul en gener waarde
^{2}**void** [vojd] *n* leegte, (lege) ruimte, vacuüm^h
vol. [vol] *volume* (boek)deel^h
volatile [volətajl] **1** vluchtig, (snel) vervliegend; **2** veranderlijk, wispelturig
volcanic [volkænik] vulkanisch *(also fig)*, explosief
volcano [volkeenoo] *(also ~es)* vulkaan *(also fig)*, explosieve situatie
volition [vəlisjən] wil, wilskracht: *by (of: of) one's own ~* uit eigen wil, vrijwillig
^{1}**volley** [vollie] *n* **1** salvo^h *(also fig)*, (stort)vloed, regen: *a ~ of oaths* (of: *curses)* een scheldkanonnade; **2** *(sport)* volley^h, *(socc)* omhaal
^{2}**volley** [vollie] *vb* **1** (gelijktijdig) losbranden, een salvo afvuren *(also fig)*; **2** in een salvo afgeschoten worden, (tegelijk) door de lucht vliegen; **3** *(sport)* volleren, een volley maken, *(socc)* omhalen
^{3}**volley** [vollie] *vb* **1** *(sport)* uit de lucht slaan (schieten), *(socc)* direct op de slof nemen; **2** *(tennis)* volleren, met een volley passeren
volleyball volleybal^h
volt [voolt] volt
voltage [vooltidzj] voltage^h
volume [voljoe:m] **1** (boek)deel^h, band, bundel: *speak ~s* boekdelen spreken; **2** jaargang; **3** hoeveelheid, omvang, volume^h; **4** volume^h, inhoud; **5** volume^h, (geluids)sterkte: *turn down the ~* het geluid zachter zetten
voluminous [vəljoe:minnəs] omvangrijk, lijvig, wijd *(eg clothing, book)*
voluntary [volləntərie] **1** vrijwillig, uit eigen beweging: *~ worker* vrijwilliger; **2** vrijwilligers-: *~ organization (roughly)* stichting; **3** gefinancierd door vrijwillige giften *(church, school)*
^{1}**volunteer** [volləntiə] *n* vrijwilliger
^{2}**volunteer** [volləntiə] *vb* zich (als vrijwilliger) aanmelden, uit eigen beweging meedoen

^{3}**volunteer** [volləntiə] *vb* **1** (vrijwillig, uit eigen beweging) aanbieden; **2** uit zichzelf zeggen *(remark, information)*
voluptuous [vəluptjoeəs] **1** sensueel, wellustig; **2** weelderig, overvloedig
^{1}**vomit** [vommit] *vb* (uit)braken *(also fig)*, overgeven
^{2}**vomit** [vommit] *n* braaksel^h, overgeefsel^h
voracious [vəreesjəs] vraatzuchtig *(also fig)*: *a ~ reader* een alleslezer
vortex [vo:teks] werveling *(also fig)*, maalstroom
^{1}**vote** [voot] *n* **1** stem, uitspraak: *cast (of: record) one's ~* zijn stem uitbrengen; *casting ~* beslissende stem *(by chairman, when votes are equally divided)*; **2** stemming: *~ of censure* motie van afkeuring; *~ of confidence* motie van vertrouwen; *put sth. to the ~* iets in stemming brengen; **3** stemmenaantal^h: *the floating ~* de zwevende kiezers; **4** stemrecht^h; **5** stembriefje^h
^{2}**vote** [voot] *vb* stemmen, een stemming houden
^{3}**vote** [voot] *vb* **1** bij stemming verkiezen, stemmen op; **2** bij stemming bepalen, beslissen: *~ s.o. out of office* (of: *power)* iem wegstemmen; **3** (geld) toestaan; **4** uitroepen tot, het ermee eens zijn dat: *the play was ~d a success* het stuk werd algemeen als een succes beschouwd; **5** voorstellen: *I ~ we leave now* ik stel voor dat we nu weggaan
vote in verkiezen: *the Conservatives were voted in again* de conservatieven werden opnieuw verkozen
voter [vootə] **1** kiezer: *floating ~* zwevende kiezer; **2** stemgerechtigde
voucher [vautsjə] bon, waardebon, cadeaubon, consumptiebon
vouch for [vautsj] instaan voor, waarborgen, borg staan voor
^{1}**vow** [vau] *n* gelofte, eed, plechtige belofte: *make (of: take) a ~* plechtig beloven
^{2}**vow** [vau] *vb* (plechtig) beloven, gelofte afleggen van, zweren
vowel [vauəl] *(linguistics)* klinker
^{1}**voyage** [vojjidzj] *n* lange reis, zeereis, bootreis: *~ home* thuisreis, terugreis; *~ out* heenreis
^{2}**voyage** [vojjidzj] *vb* reizen
voyager [vojjidzjə] (ontdekkings)reiziger
vs. *versus* van, vs.
vulcanization [vulkənajzəisjən] vulkanisatie
vulgar [vulgə] **1** vulgair, laag (bij de grond), ordinair; **2** alledaags, gewoon; **3** algemeen (bekend, aangenomen), vh volk: *~ tongue* volkstaal; *~ fraction* gewone breuk
vulgarity [vulgærittie] **1** *-ties* platte uitdrukking, grove opmerking; **2** *-ties* smakeloze, onbeschaafde daad; **3** platheid; vulgair gedrag^h
vulgarize [vulgərajz] **1** populariseren, gemeengoed maken; **2** verlagen, onbeschaafd maken
vulnerable [vulnərəbl] kwetsbaar *(also fig)*, gevoelig
vulture [vultsjə] **1** gier; **2** aasgier *(only fig)*

W

W 1 *watt(s)* W; **2** *west(ern)* W

wacky [wǽkie] mesjogge, kierewiet

wad [wod] **1** prop *(cotton wool, paper etc)*, dot, (op)vulsel^h; **2** pak^h *(letters, money etc)*; **3** pak(je^h), rolletje^h *(banknotes)*

¹waddle [wodl] *vb* waggelen

²waddle [wodl] *n* waggelende gang, eendengang

wade [weed] waden: ~ *through a boring book* een vervelend boek doorworstelen; ~ *in* aanpakken; ~ *into s.o. (sth.)* iem (iets) hard aanpakken

wader [weedə] **1** wader; **2** waadvogel; **3** ~*s* lieslaarzen

wafer [weefə] **1** wafel(tje^h); **2** hostie; ouwel

¹waffle [wofl] *n* **1** wafel; **2** gewauwel^h, gezwets^h, onzin

²waffle [wofl] *vb* wauwelen, kletsen

¹waft [woft] *vb* zweven, drijven, waaien

²waft [woft] *vb* voeren, dragen, doen zweven

¹wag [wæg] *vb* **1** schudden *(head)*, heen en weer bewegen: ~ *one's finger at s.o.* iem met de vinger dreigen; **2** kwispelen *(tail)*

²wag [wæg] *vb* **1** waggelen, wiebelen, schommelen *(while walking):* *set the tongues* ~*ging* de tongen in beweging brengen; **2** kwispelen

³wag [wæg] *n* **1** waggeling, kwispeling; **2** grappenmaker

¹wage [weedzj] *n* loon^h, arbeidsloon^h: *minimum* ~ minimumloon

²wage [weedzj] *vb* voeren *(war, campaign):* ~ *war against* (of: *on*) oorlog voeren tegen

wage-cut loonsverlaging

¹wager [weedzjə] *n* weddenschap: *lay* (of: *make*) *a* ~ een weddenschap aangaan

²wager [weedzjə] *vb* **1** een weddenschap aangaan; **2** verwedden, wedden (om, met), op het spel zetten: *I'll* ~ *(you £10) that he'll come* ik wed (tien pond met u) dat hij komt

wages floor minimumloon^h

waggish [wægisj] guitig, ondeugend

¹waggle [wægl] *vb* **1** waggelen, wiebelen, schommelen; **2** kwispelen

²waggle [wægl] *vb* **1** schudden *(head)*, heen en weer bewegen; **2** kwispelen (met)

³waggle [wægl] *n* waggeling, schommeling

waggoner [wægənə] vrachtrijder, voerman

wagon [wægən] **1** wagen, boerenwagen; *(Am)* wagentje^h, kar *(with ice cream, hot dogs etc)*; **2** dienwagen(tje^h), theewagen; **3** *(Am)* stationcar *(type of car)*; **4** goederenwagon; **5** vrachtwagen ‖ *go on the (water)* ~ geheelonthouder worden

wagtail kwikstaart

¹wail [weel] *vb* **1** klagen, jammeren, huilen *(also of wind)*; **2** loeien, huilen *(of siren)*

²wail [weel] *n* **1** geweeklaag^h, gejammer^h; **2** geloei^h, gehuil^h *(of siren)*

waist [weest] **1** middel^h, taille *(also of article of clothing):* *stripped to the* ~ met ontbloot bovenlijf; **2** smal(ler) gedeelte^h, vernauwing

waistcoat [weestkoot] vest^h *(of suit)*

waistline middel^h, taille *(also of article of clothing)*

¹wait [weet] *vb* **1** wachten: ~ *a minute!* wacht even!; *I'll do it while you* ~ het is zo klaar, u kunt erop wachten; **2** bedienen (aan tafel): ~ *at s.o.* iem bedienen; ~ *and see* (de dingen) afwachten; ~ *for me!* niet zo vlug!

²wait [weet] *vb* afwachten, wachten op: ~ *one's turn* zijn beurt afwachten

³wait [weet] *n* **1** wachttijd, (het) wachten, oponthoud^h; **2** hinderlaag: *lie in* ~ *for s.o.* voor iem op de loer liggen

waiter [weetə] kelner

waitress [weetris] serveerster

waive [weev] **1** afzien van, afstand doen van *(rights, privileges)*; **2** uitstellen, opschorten *(problem)*

¹wake [week] *vb* ontwaken, wakker worden *(also fig):* *in his waking hours* wanneer hij wakker is; ~ *up* ontwaken, wakker worden; ~ *up to sth.* iets gaan inzien

²wake [week] *vb* **1** *(also with up)* wekken, wakker maken *(also fig)*; **2** bewust maken, doordringen: ~ *s.o. up to sth.* iem van iets doordringen

³wake [week] *n* **1** kielwater^h, (kiel)zog^h; **2** *(fig)* spoor^h, nasleep: *in the* ~ *of* in het spoor van, in de voetstappen van

wakeful [weekfoel] **1** wakend, waakzaam; **2** slapeloos: ~ *nights* slapeloze nachten

¹waken [weekən] *vb* **1** wekken, wakker maken; **2** opwekken

²waken [weekən] *vb* ontwaken, wakker worden

¹walk [wo:k] *vb* **1** lopen: ~ *in one's sleep* slaapwandelen; **2** stappen, stapvoets gaan *(of horse)*; **3** (rond)waren, verschijnen: ~ *away* (of: *off*) *with: a)* er vandoor gaan met, stelen; *b)* gemakkelijk winnen; ~ *off* opstappen, er vandoor gaan; ~ *out: a)* het werk onderbreken, staken; *b)* opstappen, weglopen *(eg at consultation);* ~ *out on s.o.* iem in de steek laten; ~ *tall* het hoofd hoog dragen, trots zijn; ~ *up!* kom erin!, komt dat zien! *(eg at circus);* ~ *up to s.o.* op iem afgaan; *(inf)* ~ *over* met gemak achter zich laten; ~ *(all) over s.o.* met iem de vloer (aan)vegen

²walk [wo:k] *vb* **1** lopen, gaan, te voet afleggen *(distance);* **2** lopen door, langs, op, bewandelen; **3** meelopen met: ~ *s.o. home* iem naar huis brengen; **4** laten lopen, uitlaten *(eg dog)*, stapvoets laten lopen *(horse):* ~ *s.o. off his feet* iem de benen uit zijn lijf la-

ten lopen
³**walk** [wo:k] *n* **1** gang, manier van gaan; **2** stap, stapvoetse gang *(of horse);* **3** wandeling: *have* (of: *take) a ~,* go *for a ~* een wandeling (gaan) maken; **4** levenswandel: *~ of life: a)* beroep, roeping; *b)* (maatschappelijke) rang *(of:* stand); **5** wandelgang, voetpad[h]; **6** wandelafstand: *it is ten minutes' ~* het is tien minuten lopen

walker [wo:kə] wandelaar, voetganger

walking papers ontslag(brief): *get one's ~* zijn ontslag krijgen

walkout 1 staking, werkonderbreking; **2** het weglopen *(from a meeting by way of protest)*

walkover gemakkelijke overwinning

walkway 1 gang, wandelgang; **2** wandelweg, promenade

¹**wall** [wo:l] *n* muur, wand: *(fig) a writing on the ~* een teken aan de wand; *drive* (of: *push) s.o. to the ~* iem in het nauw drijven; *drive s.o. up the ~* iem stapelgek maken

²**wall** [wo:l] *vb* **1** ommuren; **2** dichtmetselen

wallet [wollit] portefeuille

wallflower 1 muurbloem; **2** muurbloempje[h]

¹**Walloon** [woloe:n] *adj* Waals

²**Walloon** [woloe:n] *n* Waal *(inhabitant of the Walloon provinces in Belgium)*

¹**wallop** [woləp] *vb* aframmelen, hard slaan

²**wallop** [woləp] *n* **1** dreun, mep; **2** bier[h]

¹**walloping** [woləping] *adj* reusachtig, enorm

²**walloping** [woləping] *n* **1** aframmeling; **2** zware nederlaag

wallow [woloo] **1** (zich) wentelen, (zich) rollen: *~ in the mud* zich in het slijk wentelen *(fig); (fig) ~ in self-pity* zwelgen in zelfmedelijden; **2** rollen, slingeren *(of ship)*

wall painting 1 muurschildering, fresco[h]; **2** muurschilderkunst

wallpaper behang[h]

wall-to-wall kamerbreed *(eg carpet)*

wally [wollie] sukkel, stommeling

walnut [wo:lnut] walnoot

walrus [wo:lrəs] walrus

¹**waltz** [wo:ls] *n* wals *(dance (music))*

²**waltz** [wo:ls] *vb* walsen, de wals dansen, *(fig)* (rond)dansen ‖ *~ off with* er vandoor gaan met

wan [won] **1** bleek, flets *(complexion);* **2** flauw, zwak *(light, smile)*

wand [wond] toverstokje[h], toverstaf

wander [wondə] **1** (rond)zwerven, (rond)dwalen: *~ about* rondzwerven; **2** kronkelen, (zich) slingeren *(of river, road);* **3** verdwalen, op de verkeerde weg raken *(also fig);* **4** afdwalen *(also fig): ~ from* (of: *off) one's subject* van zijn onderwerp afdwalen; **5** kuieren

wanderer [wondərə] zwerver

¹**wane** [ween] *vb* afnemen, verminderen, *(fig)* vervallen

²**wane** [ween] *n: on the ~* aan het afnemen *(also fig)*

¹**wangle** [wænggl] *vb* zich eruit draaien, zich redden: *~ (oneself) out of a situation* zich uit een situatie weten te redden

²**wangle** [wænggl] *vb* weten los te krijgen, klaarspelen: *~ a well-paid job out of s.o.* een goed betaalde baan van iem weten los te krijgen

³**wangle** [wænggl] *n* (slinkse) streek, smoesje[h]

¹**want** [wont] *vb* **1** (graag) willen, wensen: *I ~ it (to be) done today* ik wil dat het vandaag gedaan wordt; *~ in* naar binnen willen; **2** moeten, hoeven: *you ~ to see a psychiatrist* je moet naar een psychiater; *in that case you ~ room 12A, it's just around the corner* in dat geval moet u kamer 12A hebben, die is net om de hoek; **3** nodig hebben, vergen, vereisen; **4** zoeken, vragen *(pers): ~ed, experienced mechanic* gevraagd: ervaren monteur; *~ed by the police (for a crime)* gezocht door de politie (voor een misdaad)

²**want** [wont] *vb* behoeftig zijn ‖ *he does not ~ for anything, he ~s for nothing* hij komt niets te kort

³**want** [wont] *n* **1** behoefte: *meet a long-felt ~* in een lang gevoelde behoefte voorzien; **2** gebrek[h], gemis[h]: *drink water for ~ of anything better* water drinken bij gebrek aan iets beters; **3** tekort[h], nood; **4** armoede, behoeftigheid: *live in ~* in armoede leven

wanting [wonting] **1** te kort, niet voorhanden: *a few pages are ~* er ontbreken een paar bladzijden; **2** onvoldoende: *be ~ in sth.: a)* in iets tekortschieten; *b)* iets missen

wanton [wontən] **1** lichtzinnig *(of woman);* **2** moedwillig; **3** buitensporig, onverantwoord

¹**war** [wo:] *n* oorlog: *~ of nerves* zenuw(en)oorlog; *wage ~ on* (of: *against)* oorlog voeren tegen *(also fig); have been in the ~s* er gehavend uitzien

²**war** [wo:] *vb* strijd voeren, strijden *(oft fig): ~ against* strijden tegen

¹**warble** [wo:bl] *vb* **1** kwelen; **2** zingen *(of bird)*

²**warble** [wo:bl] *n* gekweel[h], gezang[h]

ward [wo:d] **1** (ziekenhuis)afdeling; **2** (stads)wijk *(as part of consituency);* **3** pupil *(minor under guardianship); (fig)* beschermeling: *~ of court* onder bescherming van het gerecht staande minderjarige; **4** voogdijschap[h], hoede, curatele; **5** afdeling van gevangenis

warden [wo:dn] **1** hoofd[h], beheerder, bestuurder *(of schools, hospitals etc);* **2** *(Am)* gevangenisdirecteur; **3** wachter, opzichter, bewaker, suppoost, conciërge, portier[h]

warder [wo:də] cipier, gevangenbewaarder

ward off afweren, afwenden

wardrobe [wo:droob] **1** kleerkast, hangkast; **2** garderobe *(also in theatre)*

wardroom officierenkajuit, officiersmess

ware [weə] **1** (koop)waar, goederen; **2** aardewerk[h]

warehouse pakhuis[h], opslagplaats, magazijn[h]

warfare [wo:feə] oorlog(voering), strijd *(also fig)*

warhorse 1 oorlogspaard[h], strijdros[h]; **2** ijzervreter; **3** oude rot *(in politics)*

warlike [wo:lajk] **1** krijgshaftig, strijdlustig; **2** militair, oorlogs-

warlord militair leider

¹**warm** [wo:m] *adj* **1** warm *(also fig)*, innemend: ~ *greetings* hartelijke groeten; *give a ~ welcome to* hartelijk welkom heten; *keep a place ~ for s.o.* een plaats voor iem openhouden; **2** warmbloedig, hartstochtelijk, vurig: *a ~ supporter* een vurig aanhanger; **3** verhit *(also fig)*, geanimeerd, heftig: *a ~ discussion* een geanimeerde discussie; *make things ~ for s.o.: a)* het iem moeilijk maken; *b)* iem straffen

²**warm** [wo:m] *vb* warm worden *(also fig)*, in de stemming (ge)raken: ~ *to* (of: *toward(s)*) *s.o.* iets gaan voelen voor iem

³**warm** [wo:m] *vb* **1** (ver)warmen; **2** opwarmen *(also fig)*, warm maken

⁴**warm** [wo:m] *n* warmte: *come in and have a ~!* kom binnen en warm je wat!

warm-hearted warm, hartelijk

warmonger [wo:munggə] oorlogs(aan)stoker

warmth [wo:mθ] *(also fig)* warmte, hartelijkheid, vuur[h]

¹**warm up** *vb* **1** warm(er) worden *(also fig)*, op temperatuur komen, *(fig)* in de stemming raken; **2** *(sport)* een warming-up doen, de spieren losmaken

²**warm up** *vb* **1** opwarmen *(also fig)*, warm maken, in de stemming brengen; **2** (ver)warmen

warm-up opwarming(stijd)

warn [wo:n] **1** waarschuwen: ~ *s.o. of sth.* iem op iets opmerkzaam maken, iem voor iets waarschuwen; **2** waarschuwen: *the doctor warned him off drink* de dokter waarschuwde hem geen alcohol te drinken; ~ *s.o. off* iem weren

warning [wo:ning] waarschuwing(steken[h]), *(fig)* afschrikwekkend voorbeeld[h]: *give a ~* waarschuwen

¹**warp** [wo:p] *vb* krom trekken *(of wood)*

²**warp** [wo:p] *vb* **1** krom trekken *(wood)*; **2** scheeftrekken, bevooroordeeld maken

³**warp** [wo:p] *n* **1** schering *(in weaving)*; **2** kromtrekking *(in wood)*

warpath oorlogspad[h]: *go on the ~* op het oorlogspad gaan

¹**warrant** [worrənt] *n* **1** bevel(schrift)[h], aanhoudingsbevel[h]: ~ *of arrest* arrestatiebevel; **2** machtiging, volmacht; **3** (waar)borg; **4** rechtvaardiging, grond: *no ~ for* geen grond tot

²**warrant** [worrənt] *vb* **1** garanderen: ~ed pure gegarandeerd zuiver; **2** verzekeren: *I* (of: *I'll*) ~ *(you)* dat kan ik je verzekeren

³**warrant** [worrənt] *vb* **1** rechtvaardigen; **2** machtigen

warranty [worrəntie] (schriftelijke) garantie

warren [worrən] **1** konijnenpark[h]; **2** doolhof *(of streets)*, wirwar

warrior [worriə] **1** strijder, krijger; **2** soldaat

Warsaw [wo:so:] Warschau

warship oorlogsschip[h]

wart [wo:t] wrat: ~*s and all* met alle gebreken

wartime oorlogstijd

wary [weərie] **1** omzichtig, alert: ~ *of* op zijn hoede voor; **2** voorzichtig

¹**wash** [wosj] *vb* **1** zich wassen, zich opfrissen; **2** gewassen (kunnen) worden; **3** geloofwaardig zijn: *that argument won't ~* dat argument gaat niet op; **4** breken *(of wave): the stain will ~ off* de vlek gaat er (in de was) wel uit

²**wash** [wosj] *vb* **1** wassen, *(fig)* zuiveren: ~ *clean* schoonwassen; ~ *off* (eraf) wassen; **2** wassen, de was doen; **3** meesleuren *(of water)*, wegspoelen: *be ~ed overboard* overboord slaan

³**wash** [wosj] *n* **1** wasbeurt, het wassen: *have a ~* zich wassen; **2** vieze, waterige troep, slootwater[h], slappe thee; **3** was(goed[h]); **4** golfslag; **5** zog[h], kielwater[h]; **6** spoelwater[h]: *it'll come out in the ~* het zal wel loslopen

washable [wosjəbl] wasbaar

wash away afwassen, wegspoelen, uitwassen, *(fig)* reinigen, zuiveren: ~ *s.o.'s sins* iem reinigen van zijn zonden

wash down 1 wegspoelen *(food, with drink)*; **2** (helemaal) schoonmaken: ~ *with ammonia* schoonmaken met ammonia

washed-out 1 verbleekt *(in the wash)*; **2** uitgeput; **3** *(sport)* afgelast *(wegens regen)*

washed-up verslagen, geruïneerd

washer [wosjə] **1** wasser; **2** (sluit)ring, afdichtingsring; **3** leertje[h]; **4** wasmachine, wasautomaat

washing [wosjing] was(goed[h])

washing-up afwas, vaat: *it's your turn to do the ~* jij bent aan de beurt om af te wassen

wash-leather zeem, zeemleer[h]

¹**wash out** *vb* (in de was) eruit gaan *(of stains)*

²**wash out** *vb* **1** uitwassen, uitspoelen; **2** wegspoelen; **3** onmogelijk maken *(of rain, the match)*

wash-out flop, mislukking

washroom 1 wasruimte, waslokaal[h]; **2** *(Am)* toilet[h]

washstand wastafel

¹**wash up** *vb* **1** *(Am)* zich opfrissen; **2** afwassen, de vaat doen

²**wash up** *vb* doen aanspoelen *(of tide)*

washy [wosjie] **1** waterig *(of liquid)*, slap; **2** bleek, kleurloos

wasp [wosp] wesp

waspish [wospisj] *(oft depr)* **1** wespachtig; **2** giftig, nijdig; **3** dun, slank *(like a wasp)*

wastage [weestidzj] **1** verspilling, verlies[h] *(through leakage)*; **2** verloop[h] *(of staff)*

¹**waste** [weest] *n* **1** woestenij, woestijn *(also fig)*; **2** verspilling; **3** afval(product)[h], puin[h], vuilnis: *go to ~, run to ~* verloren gaan, verspild worden

²**waste** [weest] *vb* **1** verspild worden; **2** *(with away)* wegteren, wegkwijnen

³**waste** [weest] *vb* **1** verspillen, verkwisten: *you didn't ~ time* je liet er geen gras over groeien; ~ *time on sth.* tijd verspillen aan iets; **2** verwoesten

⁴**waste** [weest] *adj* **1** woest, braak(liggend), verlaten: *lay ~* verwoesten; **2** afval-, overtollig

wastebasket *(Am)* afvalbak, prullenmand

wasteful [weestfoel] verspillend, spilziek

wasteland woestenij, onbewoonbaar gebied[h]: *(fig)*

a cultural ~ een cultureel onderontwikkeld gebied

wastepaper papierafval[h]

wastepipe afvoer(buis)

¹watch [wotsj] *n* **1** horloge[h]; **2** *~es* (nacht)wake; **3** bewaker, wachtpost, nachtwaker; **4** waaktijd, wachtkwartier[h]; wacht(dienst); bewaking, uitkijk: *keep ~ over* waken over; **5** wacht, waakzaamheid, hoede: *keep (a) close ~ on* (nauwlettend) in de gaten houden, de wacht houden

²watch [wotsj] *vb* **1** (toe)kijken; **2** wachten: *~ for one's chance* zijn kans afwachten; **3** uitkijken: *~ out* uitkijken, oppassen; *~ (out) for* uitkijken naar, loeren op; **4** de wacht houden

³watch [wotsj] *vb* **1** bekijken, kijken naar; **2** afwachten *(chance, opportunity): ~ one's chance* zijn kans afwachten; **3** gadeslaan, letten op: *~ one's weight* op zijn gewicht letten; *~ it!* pas op!, voorzichtig!; *~ yourself* pas op!; **4** bewaken, hoeden *(cattle);* **5** verzorgen, zorgen voor

watchdog waakhond *(also fig)*, (be)waker

watchful [wɑtsjfoel] waakzaam, oplettend

watchmaker horlogemaker

watchman [wotsjmən] bewaker, nachtwaker

watchword 1 wachtwoord[h]; **2** leus, slogan

¹water [wo:tə] *n* **1** water[h]: *tread ~* watertrappelen; *spend money like ~* geld uitgeven als water; **2** water[h], waterstand: *at high ~* bij hoogwater; **3** urine: *make* (of: *pass*) *~* wateren; **4** water[h]; **5** *~s* mineraalwater[h], *(fig)* (water)kuur: *drink* (of: *take*) *the ~s* een kuur doen; *~ on the brain* waterhoofd; *run like ~ off a duck's back* niet het minste effect hebben; *hold ~* steek houden; *fish in troubled ~s* in troebel water vissen

²water [wo:tə] *vb* **1** water geven, begieten: *~ the plants* de planten water geven; **2** van water voorzien, bespoelen, besproeien; *~ down* aanlengen, *(fig)* afzwakken; *a ~ed-down version* een verwaterde versie

³water [wo:tə] *vb* **1** tranen, lopen, wateren: *my eyes ~ed* mijn ogen traanden; **2** watertanden: *make the mouth ~* doen watertanden; **3** water drinken *(of animals)*

water biscuit (cream)cracker

water-borne 1 drijvend, vlot; **2** over water vervoerd, zee-: *~ trade* zeehandel

water-butt regenton

watercolour 1 aquarel, waterverfschilderij[h]; **2** waterverf

waterfall waterval

waterfowl watervogel

waterfront waterkant *(of city district etc): on the ~* aan de waterkant

water heater boiler; *(Am)* geiser

watering place 1 waterplaats; **2** kuuroord[h], badplaats

water level (grond)waterpeil[h]

waterline waterlijn *(of ship)*

waterlogged 1 vol water (gelopen) *(ship);* **2** met water doortrokken *(soil, wood)*

Waterloo [wo:təloe:] (verpletterende) nederlaag, beslissende slag: *meet one's ~* verpletterend verslagen worden

waterman [wo:təmən] veerman

watermark 1 watermerk[h] *(in paper);* **2** waterpeil[h]

water-meadow uiterwaard

water-power waterkracht, hydraulische kracht

¹waterproof *adj* waterdicht

²waterproof *n* (waterdichte) regenjas

³waterproof *vb* waterdicht maken

watershed 1 waterscheiding; **2** *(fig)* keerpunt[h]

¹water-ski *n* waterski

²water-ski *vb* waterskiën

water snake ringslang

waterspout 1 waterspuwer, spuier; **2** waterhoos

water-table grondwaterspiegel

watertight *(also fig)* waterdicht

waterway 1 waterweg; **2** vaarwater[h]

waterwheel waterrad[h]

water wings (zwem)vleugels

waterworks 1 waterleiding(bedrijf); **2** waterlanders, tranen

watery [wo:tərie] **1** waterachtig, water-, vol water; **2** nat, vochtig, tranend: *~ eye* waterig oog, traanoog; **3** waterig, smakeloos, flauw, slap, bleek

watt [wot] watt

wattle [wotl] **1** lel, halskwab *(esp of birds);* **2** hordewerk[h], gevlochten rijswerk[h]

¹wave [weev] *vb* **1** (toe)wuiven, zwaaien: *(fig) ~ sth. aside* iets van tafel vegen; *~ s.o. on* iem gebaren verder te gaan; *~ at* (of: *to*) *s.o.* naar iem zwaaien; **2** krullen, golven

²wave [weev] *vb* **1** golven, fluctueren; **2** wapperen *(of flag)*

³wave [weev] *n* **1** golf *(also fig)*, vloed, *(fig)* opwelling: *~ of violence* golf van geweld; **2** (haar)golf; **3** wuivend gebaar[h]; **4** golf(beweging), verkeersgolf, aanvalsgolf

wavelength golflengte *(λ; also fig): be on the same ~* op dezelfde golflengte zitten *(fig)*

waver [weevə] **1** onzeker worden, wankelen; **2** aarzelen: *~ between* aarzelen tussen; **3** flikkeren *(of light)*, flakkeren *(of candle)*

wavy [weevie] golvend, deinend

¹wax [wæks] *n* **1** (bijen)was: *(fig) be ~ in s.o.'s hands* als was in iemands handen zijn; **2** (boen)was; **3** oorsmeer[h]

²wax [wæks] *vb* wassen, opkomen, toenemen *(of water, moon)*

waxen [wæksn] **1** glad als was; **2** week als was

waxwork 1 wassen beeld[h]; **2** *~s* wassenbeeldententoonstelling, wassenbeeldenmuseum[h]

waxy [wæksie] **1** wasachtig, bleek; **2** woedend, opvliegend

¹way [wee] *n* **1** weg; route: *(fig) things are going his ~* het zit hem mee; *lose the* (of: *one's*) *~* verdwalen, de weg kwijtraken; *(fig) pave the ~ (for sth., s.o.)* de weg effenen (voor iets, iem); *(fig) pay one's ~* geen schulden maken, zonder verlies werken; *work one's*

~ *through college* werkstudent zijn; ~ *in* ingang; ~ *out* uitgang, *(fig)* uitweg; *better weather is on the ~* er is beter weer op komst; *on the ~ out* op weg naar buiten, *(inf; fig)* uit (de mode) rakend; *that's the ~ (it is, goes)* zo gaat het nu eenmaal; **2** manier, wijze, gewoonte, gebruik^h, *(depr)* hebbelijkheid: ~ *of life* levenswijze; ~ *of thinking* denkwijze; *in a big ~: a)* op grote schaal; *b)* grandioos; *c)* met enthousiasme; *go the right ~ about sth.* iets op de juiste wijze aanpakken; *(fig) find a ~* een manier vinden, er raad op weten; *set in one's ~s* met vast(geroest)e gewoontes; *one ~ and another* alles bij elkaar (genomen); *one ~ or another* (of: *the other)* op de een of andere manier; *there are no two ~s about it* er is geen twijfel (over) mogelijk; **3** richting: *look the other ~* de andere kant opkijken *(also fig); (fig) I don't know which ~ to turn* ik weet me geen raad; *the other ~ around* (of: *about)* andersom; **4** opzicht^h: *in a ~* in zekere zin; *in more ~s than one* in meerdere opzichten; **5** afstand, eind^h, stuk^h: *a long ~ away* (of: *off)* een heel eind weg, ver weg; *go a long ~ to meet s.o.* iem een heel eind tegemoet komen *(also fig);* **6** (voort)gang, snelheid, vaart: *be under ~* onderweg zijn; *gather ~* vaart krijgen *(of ship); negotiations are well under ~* onderhandelingen zijn in volle gang; **7** ruimte *(also fig),* plaats, gelegenheid: *clear the ~: a)* de weg banen; *b) (also fig)* ruim baan maken; *give ~: a)* toegeven, meegeven; *b) (also fig)* wijken, voorrang geven; *c)* doorzakken, bezwijken; *make ~ for* plaats maken voor; *put s.o. in the ~ of sth.* iem op weg helpen (met iets), iem aan iets helpen; *out of the* (of: *one's)* ~ uit de weg *(also fig); get sth. out of the ~* iets uit de weg ruimen, iets afhandelen; *~s and means* geldmiddelen; *make ~* opschieten *(also fig); make one's (own)* ~ *(in life, in the world)* in de wereld vooruitkomen; *(fig) go one's own ~* zijn eigen weg gaan; *go out of one's* (of: *the)* ~ *to …* zijn (uiterste) best doen om …; *have a ~ with elderly people* met ouderen om weten te gaan; *you can't have it both ~s* óf het een óf het ander; *see one's ~ (clear) to doing sth.* zijn kans schoon zien om iets te doen; *by the ~* terloops, trouwens, à propos; *they had done nothing out of the ~* zij hadden niets bijzonders gedaan; *by ~ of example* als voorbeeld; *any ~* in ieder geval, hoe dan ook; *either ~* hoe dan ook; *(inf) every which ~* overal, in alle hoeken en gaten; *(Am; inf) no ~!* geen sprake van!

²way [wee] *adv* ver, lang, een eind: ~ *back* ver terug, (al) lang geleden

waylay [weelee] **1** belagen, opwachten; **2** onderscheppen

way-out te gek, geavanceerd, excentriek

wayside kant vd weg, berm: *(fig) fall by the ~* afvallen, uitvallen

wayward [weewəd] eigenzinnig, koppig

W.C. *water closet* wc

we [wie:] wij

weak [wie:k] **1** zwak, slap, week *(constitution),*

broos: *a ~ argument* een zwakke redenering; *go ~ at the knees: a)* slappe knieën krijgen *(when in love); b)* op zijn benen staan te trillen *(with fear);* ~ *at* (of: *in) physics* zwak in natuurkunde; **2** flauw, zwak, matig *(offer, market, Stock Exchange): a ~ demand (for)* weinig vraag (naar); *have a ~ spot for* een speciaal plekje in zijn hart hebben voor

¹weaken [wie:kən] *vb* toegeven, zwichten

²weaken [wie:kən] *vb* verzwakken, afzwakken, (doen) verslappen

weak-kneed 1 besluiteloos, slap, niet wilskrachtig; **2** bangelijk, timide, laf

weakling [wie:kling] zwakkeling, slappeling

weak-minded 1 zwakzinnig, *(fig)* achterlijk; **2** zwak *(of will, character)*

weakness [wie:knəs] **1** zwakte, slapheid, zwakheid; **2** zwak punt^h; **3** zwakheid, zonde, fout; **4** zwak^h, voorliefde: *he has a ~ for blonde women* hij valt op blonde vrouwen

weal [wie:l] striem, streep

wealth [welθ] **1** overvloed, rijkdom; **2** rijkdom(men), bezit^h, bezittingen, vermogen^h

wealthy [welθie] rijk, vermogend

wean [wie:n] spenen *(child, young)* ‖ ~ *s.o. (away) from sth.* iem iets afleren

weapon [weppən] wapen^h

weaponry [weppənrie] wapentuig^h

¹wear [weər] *vb* **1** dragen *(on one's body),* aan hebben; **2** vertonen, hebben, tentoonspreiden, voeren *(colour, flag): he ~s a beard* hij heeft een baard; **3** uitputten; **4** *(inf; oft with negation)* aanvaarden, toestaan: *they won't ~ it* zij nemen het niet

²wear [weər] *vb (also fig)* verslijten, (af)slijten, uitslijten: *worn clothes* afgedragen kleren; ~ *thin* dun worden, slijten; *my patience is ~ing thin* mijn geduld is aan het opraken

³wear [weər] *vb* **1** goed blijven *(also fig): this sweater ~s well* deze trui ziet er nog goed uit; **2** (also with *on, away)* voortkruipen *(of time),* voortduren: *the meeting wore on* (of: *away)* de vergadering ging maar door

⁴wear [weər] *n* **1** dracht, het aanhebben *(clothing);* **2** het gedragen worden *(of clothing),* gebruik^h; **3** slijtage: *show (signs of)* ~ slijtageplekken vertonen; **4** sterkte, kwaliteit; **5** (passende) kleding, tenue^h: *sports~* sporttenue; *normal ~ and tear* normale slijtage

wear down 1 (af)slijten, verslijten; **2** verzwakken, afmatten: ~ *resistance* tegenstand (geleidelijk) overwinnen

wearing [weəring] vermoeiend, slopend

wearisome [wiəriesəm] **1** vermoeiend; **2** vervelend, langdradig

¹wear off *vb* (geleidelijk) minder worden: *the novelty will soon ~* het nieuwtje zal er (wel) gauw af gaan

²wear off *vb* verslijten, afslijten

¹wear out *vb* afgemat raken: *his patience wore out* zijn geduld raakte op

²wear out *vb* verslijten, afdragen

³**wear out** vb uitputten: *wear oneself out* uitgeput raken, zich uitsloven

¹**weary** [wiərie] adj **1** moe, lusteloos: ~ *of* moe van *(also fig);* **2** vermoeiend

²**weary** [wiərie] vb moe worden: ~ *of* moe worden, genoeg krijgen van

³**weary** [wiərie] vb vermoeien

¹**weasel** [wie:zl] n wezel

²**weasel** [wie:zl] vb (also with *out)* zich drukken, er tussenuit knijpen: ~ *out (of one's duty)* zich onttrekken (aan zijn plicht); ~ *words* dubbelzinnig spreken

¹**weather** [weðə] n weerʰ: *wet* ~ nat weer; *(be, feel) under the ~:* a) (zich) niet lekker (voelen); b) dronken (zijn)

²**weather** [weðə] vb verweren

³**weather** [weðə] vb **1** doen verweren; **2** doorstaan *(storm; also fig),* te boven komen

weather-beaten 1 (door storm) beschadigd (geteisterd); **2** verweerd *(of face)*

weatherboard 1 waterdorpel; **2** houten buitenbekleding *(of overlapping planks)*

weathercock weerhaan, windwijzer, *(fig)* draaier, opportunist

weather eye: *keep a* ~ *open (for)* op zijn hoede zijn (voor), oppassen (voor)

weather forecast weer(s)voorspelling, weerberichtʰ

weatherglass barometer

weatherproof weerbestendig, tegen weer en wind bestand

weathervane windwijzer

¹**weave** [wie:v] vb zigzaggen, (zich) slingeren, *(traf)* weven, van rijstrook wisselen

²**weave** [wie:v] vb zich slingerend banen: *they were weaving their way through the full hall* zij baanden zich zigzaggend een weg door de volle hal

³**weave** vb **1** vlechten, weven; **2** verweven, verwerken; **3** maken *(story),* ophangen

⁴**weave** n **1** weefselʰ; **2** (weef)patroonʰ

web [web] **1** (spinnen)webʰ; **2** webʰ, weefselʰ, net(werk)ʰ *(also fig);* **3** val, netten; **4** weefselʰ; **5** (zwem)vliesʰ

webbing [webbing] **1** singel(band), geweven band; **2** omboordselʰ

¹**wed** [wed] vb trouwen, huwen: ~*ded couple* getrouwd paar

²**wed** [wed] vb paren: ~ *to* paren aan

wedded [weddid] **1** huwelijks-, vh huwelijk: ~ *life* huwelijksleven; **2** verslingerd, getrouwd: *(fig)* ~ *to his job* getrouwd met zijn werk

wedding [wedding] **1** huwelijkʰ, huwelijksplechtigheid, bruiloft; **2** koppeling, het samengaan: *the* ~ *of two great minds* het samengaan van twee grote geesten

wedding breakfast bruiloftsmaalʰ, maaltijd of lunch na trouwerij

wedding ring trouwring

¹**wedge** [wedzj] n **1** wig *(also fig): drive a* ~ *between*

the parties tweedracht zaaien tussen de partijen; **2** wigvorm; **3** hoek, puntʰ *(of cheese, cake)*

²**wedge** [wedzj] vb vastzetten, vastklemmen: *we were* ~*d (in) between the police and the rioters* we zaten ingeklemd tussen de politie en de relschoppers

wedlock [wedlok] huwelijkʰ, huwelijkse staat || *born out of* ~ buiten huwelijk geboren, onecht

Wednesday [wednzdee] woensdag

wee [wie:] klein: *a* ~ *bit* een klein beetje, ietsje, een pietsje *(also iron)*

¹**weed** [wie:d] n **1** onkruidʰ; **2** tabak, marihuana, hasj, sigaret; **3** lange slapjanus

²**weed** [wie:d] vb **1** wieden, verwijderen, schoffelen; **2** wieden *(only fig),* zuiveren: *the manager* ~*ed out the most troublesome employees* de manager zette de lastigste werknemers aan de kant

weedkiller onkruidverdelger

weedy [wie:die] **1** vol onkruid; **2** slungelig

week [wie:k] week; werkweek: *a* ~ *(on) Sunday, Sunday* ~ zondag over een week; *yesterday* ~ gisteren een week geleden; *most people work a 38-hour* ~ de meeste mensen hebben een 38-urige werkweek; ~ *in,* ~ *out* week in, week uit, wekenlang

weekday doordeweekse dag, werkdag, weekdag

weekend weekendʰ, weekeindeʰ

¹**weekly** [wie:klie] adj wekelijks: *she earns £150* ~ zij verdient 150 pond in de week

²**weekly** [wie:klie] n weekbladʰ

weeny [wie:nie] heel klein, piepklein

¹**weep** [wie:p] vb wenen, huilen: ~ *for* (of: *with) joy* van vreugde schreien; *no-one will* ~ *over his resignation* niemand zal een traan laten om zijn vertrek

²**weep** [wie:p] vb **1** storten, schreien *(tears);* **2** huilen, schreien: ~ *oneself to sleep* zichzelf in slaap huilen

³**weep** [wie:p] n huilbui: *let them have their* ~ laat ze maar (uit)huilen

weeping [wie:ping] met hangende takken, treur-: ~ *willow* treurwilg

weepy [wie:pie] **1** huilerig, snotterig; **2** sentimenteel

wee(-wee) [wie:(wie:)] plasjeʰ: *do (a)* ~, *have a* ~ een plasje plegen

¹**weigh** [wee] vb **1** wegen: *it* ~*s four kilos* het weegt vier kilo; *the greengrocer* ~*ed a of potatoes* de groenteman woog een zak aardappelen; ~ *in* (laten) wegen, zich laten wegen; ~ *out* afwegen; **2** overwegen, afwegen: ~ *one's words* zijn woorden wegen; ~ *up:* a) wikken en wegen; b) schatten; c) zich een mening vormen over; ~ *up the situation* de situatie opnemen; **3** lichten *(anchor, ship):* ~ *down* beladen, *(fig)* deprimeren; *his marriage problems* ~ *him down* hij gaat gebukt onder zijn huwelijksproblemen

²**weigh** [wee] vb drukken, een last zijn: *his unemployment* ~*s (up)on him* hij gaat gebukt onder zijn werkloosheid; ~ *in with* aan komen zetten met, te berde brengen

weighbridge weegbrug

weigh-in gewichtscontrole *(of boxer before fight; of jockey after race)*, wegen na de wedren

¹weight [weet] *n* **1** gewicht^h *(for scales)*; gewichtsklasse, zwaarte: *~s and measures* maten en gewichten; *lose ~* afvallen, vermageren; *put on ~* aankomen, zwaarder worden; *over ~* te zwaar; *under ~* te licht; **2** gewicht^h, zwaar voorwerp^h; **3** (zware) last, *(fig)* druk, belasting: *his departure is a ~ off my mind* zijn vertrek is een pak van mijn hart; **4** belang^h, invloed: *worth one's ~ in gold* zijn gewicht in goud waard; **5** grootste deel^h, hoofddeel^h, grootste nadruk: *the ~ of evidence is against them* het grootste gedeelte van het bewijsmateriaal spreekt in hun nadeel; *carry ~* gewicht in de schaal leggen, van belang zijn; *give ~ to* versterken, extra bewijs leveren voor; *pull one's ~ (fig)* (ieder) zijn steentje bijdragen; *throw one's ~ about* (of: *around*) zich laten gelden, gewichtig doen

²weight [weet] *vb* **1** verzwaren *(also of material)*; **2** beladen *(also fig)*, gebukt doen gaan: *~ed down with many parcels* beladen met veel pakjes

weightlifter gewichtheffer

weight-watcher lijner, iem die goed op zijn lichaamsgewicht let

weighty [weetie] **1** zwaar; **2** belangrijk, zwaarwegend; **3** invloedrijk, gezaghebbend

weir [wiə] **1** (stuw)dam; **2** (vis)weer^h

weird [wiəd] raar, gek, vreemd, eng

weirdo [wiədoo] *(~es)* rare (snuiter)

¹welcome [welkəm] *vb* **1** verwelkomen, welkom heten; **2** (gunstig) onthalen: *we'd ~ a change* we zouden een verandering toejuichen

²welcome [welkəm] *adj* **1** welkom, aangenaam: *~ change* welkome verandering; **2** *(roughly)* vrij: *you're ~ to the use of my books* je mag mijn boeken gerust gebruiken; *'thank you' - 'you're ~'* 'dank u' - 'geen dank'; *~ home, ~ back* welkom thuis

³welcome [welkəm] *n* **1** welkom^h, verwelkoming; **2** onthaal^h: *they gave the speaker a hearty ~* zij heetten de spreker hartelijk welkom; *bid s.o. ~* iem welkom heten; *outstay one's ~* langer blijven dan men welkom is, blijven plakken

¹weld [weld] *vb* **1** lassen; **2** samenvoegen, aaneensmeden ‖ *this iron ~s well* dit ijzer laat zich goed lassen

²weld [weld] *n* las(naad)

welfare [welfeə] **1** welzijn^h, welvaart, voorspoed; **2** maatschappelijk werk^h, welzijnszorg; **3** bijstand: *be on ~* van de bijstand leven

welfare state verzorgingsstaat, welvaartsstaat

welfare work maatschappelijk werk^h, welzijnszorg

¹well [wel] *adv* **1** op de juiste manier, goed, naar wens: *behave ~* zich goed gedragen; **2** zorgvuldig, grondig, door en door: *~ cooked* goed gaar; **3** ver, ruim, zeer, een eind: *~ in advance* ruim van tevoren; *the exhibition was ~ worth visiting* de tentoonstelling was een bezoek meer dan waard; **4** gunstig, vriendelijk, goedkeurend: *treat s.o. ~* iem vriendelijk behandelen; **5** redelijkerwijze, met recht: *I can-*

not very *~ refuse to help him* ik kan moeilijk weigeren om hem te helpen; **6** verstandig: *be ~ off: a)* er warmpjes bijzitten; *b)* geluk hebben; *~ and truly* helemaal; *be ~ out of it* er goed van af komen *(of sth unpleasant); as ~* ook, evenzeer, net zo lief *(of:* goed); *as ~ as* zowel ... als, en, niet alleen ... maar ook; *in theory as ~ as in practice* zowel in theorie als in de praktijk; *wish s.o. ~* iem succes toewensen; *leave (of: let) ~ alone* laat maar zo, het is wel goed zo

²well [wel] *adj* **1** gezond, goed, beter, wel: *she's feeling ~ again* zij voelt zich weer goed; **2** goed, in orde, naar wens: *all's ~ that ends well* eind goed, al goed; *~ enough* goed genoeg; **3** raadzaam, wenselijk: *it would be (just) as ~ to confess your little accident* je kan het beste je ongelukje maar opbiechten; *all very ~ (, but)* alles goed en wel (maar), dat kan wel zijn (maar) *(but); she's ~ in with my boss* zij staat in een goed blaadje bij mijn baas

³well [wel] *interj* **1** zo, nou, wel: *~, what a surprise* zó, wat een verrassing; **2** nou ja, goed dan, jawel *(but): ~, if she loves the boy* nou ja, als ze van de jongen houdt; **3** goed, nu: *oh ~, you can't win them all* nou ja, je kan niet altijd winnen; *~ then?* wel?, nu?

⁴well [wel] *n* **1** put; diepe ruimte, diepte, kuil; **2** boorput, oliebron; **3** koker, schacht

⁵well [wel] *vb* vloeien, (op)wellen

well-advised verstandig, raadzaam

well-appointed goed ingericht, goed voorzien

well-being welzijn^h, gezondheid, weldadig gevoel^h

well-bred welopgevoed, beschaafd, welgemanierd

well-disposed (with *towards*) welwillend (jegens), vriendelijk (tegen), gunstig gezind

well-fed 1 goed gevoed; **2** weldoorvoed, dik, gezet

well-heeled rijk, vermogend

well-informed 1 goed op de hoogte, onderlegd; **2** goed ingelicht, welingelicht

wellington [welingtən] rubberlaars, kaplaars

well-known bekend, overal bekend

well-meaning goedbedoeld, welgemeend

well-nigh bijna, vrijwel: *it's ~ impossible* het is vrijwel onmogelijk

well off rijk, welgesteld: *you don't know when you're ~* je hebt geen idee hoe goed je 't hebt

well-oiled dronken, in de olie

well-preserved goed geconserveerd *(of elderly person): grandfather looks ~ at 93* grootvader ziet er nog goed uit op zijn 93e

well-read [welred] belezen

wellspring (onuitputtelijke) bron

well-timed op het juiste moment (gedaan, gezegd, komend)

well-to-do rijk, bemiddeld

well-tried beproefd

well-worn afgezaagd, cliché(matig), alledaags

welsh [welsj] zijn woord niet houden, verplichtingen niet nakomen: *~ on debts* schulden niet (af)betalen

¹Welsh [welsj] *adj* Wels, van Wales, in het Wels ‖ *~ rabbit, ~ rarebit* toast met gesmolten kaas

²**Welsh** [welsj] *n* bewoners van Wales

welsher [wɛlsjə] bedrieger, oplichter *(of bookmaker)*

Welshman [wɛlsjmən] bewoner van Wales

¹**welter** [wɛltə] *n* mengelmoes^h, enorm aantal^h, enorme hoeveelheid

²**welter** [wɛltə] *vb* zich rollen, zich wentelen *(also fig)*

welterweight (bokser uit het) weltergewicht

¹**west** [west] *n* het westen: *the West* het westelijk gedeelte

²**west** [west] *adj* westelijk, west(en)-: ~ *wind* westenwind

³**west** [west] *adv* in, uit, naar het westen, ten westen

westbound in westelijke richting (gaand, reizend)

West Country het zuidwesten van Engeland

¹**westerly** [wɛstəlie] *n* westenwind

²**westerly** [wɛstəlie] *adj* westelijk

¹**western** [wɛstən] *adj* westelijk, west(en)-

²**western** [wɛstən] *n* western, wildwestfilm, wildwestroman

westerner [wɛstənə] westerling

westward(s) [wɛstwəd] westwaarts, westelijk

¹**wet** [wet] *adj* **1** nat, vochtig: ~ *paint* nat, pas geverfd; ~ *through, wringing* ~ kletsnat, helemaal doorweekt; **2** regenachtig, nat; **3** *(inf)* slap, sullig, sloom: ~ *blanket*: *a)* domper, koude douche; *b)* spelbreker; ~ *dream* natte droom; *he is still* ~ *behind the ears* hij is nog niet droog achter de oren

²**wet** [wet] *vb* **1** nat maken, bevochtigen; **2** plassen in *(bed etc)*: ~ *the bed* bedwateren; *he has* ~ *his pants again* hij heeft weer in zijn broek geplast

³**wet** [wet] *n* **1** nat weer^h, regen; **2** nattigheid, vocht^h, vochtigheid; **3** sukkel, doetje^h

wetting [wɛtting] het nat (gemaakt) worden: *get a* ~ een bui op zijn kop krijgen

¹**whack** [wæk] *vb* een mep geven, een dreun verkopen

²**whack** [wæk] *n* **1** klap, mep, dreun; **2** (aan)deel^h, portie; **3** poging: *let me have a* ~ *at it* laat mij het eens proberen

whacked [wækt] doodmoe, uitgeteld, kapot

whacking [wæking] *(inf)* enorm, kolossaal

whale [weel] walvis || *a* ~ *of a time* een reusachtige tijd; *they had a* ~ *of a time* ze hebben een geweldige lol gehad

whalebone balein^h

whaling [weeling] walvisvangst

wham [wæm] klap, slag, dreun || ~! knal!, boem!

wharf [wo:f] *(also wharves)* kade, aanlegsteiger

what [wot] **1** wat: ~*'s the English for 'gezellig'?* wat is 'gezellig' in het Engels?; *no matter* ~ hoe dan ook; ~ *do you call that?* hoe heet dat?; *books, clothes, records and* ~ *have you* boeken, kleren, platen en wat nog allemaal; ~ *of it?* en wat (zou dat) dan nog?; ~ *about an ice-cream?* wat zou je denken van een ijsje?; ~ *did he do that for?* waarom deed hij dat?; ~ *if I die?* stel dat ik doodga, wat dan?; **2** wat, dat(gene) wat, hetgeen: ~*'s more* bovendien, erger nog; *say* ~ *you will* wat je ook zegt; **3** welke, wat voor;

welke (ook), die, dat: ~ *work we did was worthwhile* het beetje werk dat we deden was de moeite waard; ~ *books do you read?* wat voor boeken lees je?; **4** *(in exclamations)* wat (voor), welk (een): ~ *a delicious meal!* wat een lekkere maaltijd!; *and* ~ *not* en wat al niet, enzovoorts enzovoorts; *so* ~? nou en?, wat dan nog?

whatever 1 alles wat, wat ook: *I'll stay* ~ *happens* ik blijf, wat er ook gebeurt; **2** om het even wat (welke), wat (welke) dan ook: *have you found your scarf or* ~ heb je je sjaal of wat je ook kwijt was gevonden; *any colour* ~ om het even welke kleur; **3** *(in questions and negations)* helemaal, totaal, überhaupt: *no-one* ~ helemaal niemand; **4** wat (toch): ~ *happened?* wat is er in 's hemelsnaam gebeurd?; ~ *for?* waarom toch?

whatnot [wotnot] wat al niet, noem maar op: *she bought books, records and* ~ ze kocht boeken, platen en noem maar op

wheat [wie:t] tarwe || *separate the* ~ *from the chaff* het kaf van het koren scheiden

wheaten [wie:tn] tarwe-: ~ *products* tarweproducten

wheatmeal tarwemeel^h, volkoren tarwemeel^h

¹**wheedle** [wie:dl] *vb* flikflooien, vleien

²**wheedle** [wie:dl] *vb* **1** *(with into)* met gevlei overhalen (tot); **2** *(with out of)* aftroggelen, afvleien: ~ *a promise out of s.o.* iem zover krijgen dat hij een belofte doet

¹**wheel** [wie:l] *n* **1** wiel^h, rad^h, draaischijf; **2** stuur^h, stuurrad^h, stuurwiel^h, roer^h: *at (of: behind) the* ~ aan het roer, achter het stuur, *(fig)* aan de leiding; **3** auto, kar: *on* ~*s* per auto, met de wagen; *there are* ~*s within* ~*s* het zit zeer ingewikkeld in elkaar

²**wheel** [wie:l] *vb* **1** rollen, rijden; **2** *(also with (a)round, about)* zich omkeren, zich omdraaien, van richting veranderen; **3** cirkelen, in rondjes vliegen *(of birds)* || ~*ing and dealing* ritselen, gesjacher, gemarchandeer

³**wheel** [wie:l] *vb* duwen, trekken *(sth on wheels)*, (ver)rijden, rollen: *they* ~*ed the patient back to his room* ze reden de patiënt terug naar zijn kamer

wheelbarrow kruiwagen

wheelchair rolstoel

wheelhouse stuurhut, stuurhuis^h

¹**wheeze** [wie:z] *vb* **1** piepen, fluiten(d ademhalen); **2** hijgen, puffen

²**wheeze** [wie:z] *n* **1** gepiep^h *(of breathing)*; **2** grap, geintje^h; **3** plannetje^h, idee^h

whelp [welp] jong^h, puppy, welp

¹**when** [wen] *adv* **1** *(interrogative)* wanneer: ~ *will I see you?* wanneer zie ik je weer?; **2** wanneer, waarop, dat: *the day* ~ *I went to Paris* de dag waarop ik naar Parijs ging; *(when pouring) say* ~ zeg maar ho; *since* ~ *has he been here?* sinds wanneer is hij al hier?

²**when** [wen] *conj* **1** toen: *she came* ~ *he called* ze kwam toen hij riep; ~ *I was a little girl* toen ik een klein meisje was; **2** als, wanneer: *he laughs* ~ *you*

tickle him hij lacht (telkens) als je hem kietelt; **3** als (het zo is dat): *why use gas ~ it can explode?* waarom gas gebruiken als (je weet dat) het kan ontploffen?; **4** hoewel, terwijl, ondanks (het feit) dat: *the part was plastic when it ought to have been made of leather* het onderdeel was van plastic hoewel het van leer had moeten zijn

when̲e̲ver 1 telkens wanneer, wanneer ook, om het even wanneer: *~ we meet he turns away* iedere keer als wij elkaar tegenkomen, draait hij zich om; **2** wanneer (toch, in 's hemelsnaam): *~ did I say that?* wanneer in 's hemelsnaam heb ik dat gezegd?

where [weə] **1** *(interrogative)* waar, waar(heen, -in, -op) *(also fig):* ~ *are you going?* waar ga je naar toe?; **2** (al)waar, waarheen: *Rome, ~ once Caesar reigned* Rome, alwaar eens Caesar heerste; **3** daar waar, in die omstandigheden waar, waarbij: *nothing has changed ~ Rita is concerned* er is niets veranderd wat Rita betreft; **4** terwijl, daar waar: *~ she was shy her brother was talkative* terwijl zij verlegen was, was haar broer spraakzaam

where̲abouts [we̲ərəbauts] verblijfplaats, plaats waar iem (iets) zich bevindt

where̲a̲s [weəræz] hoewel, daar waar, terwijl

where̲of waarvan: *the things ~ he spoke* de dingen waarover hij sprak

where̲upo̲n waarna, waarop: *he emptied his glass, ~ he left* hij dronk zijn glas leeg, waarna hij vertrok

where̲ver [weərevvə] **1** waar (toch, in 's hemelsnaam): ~ *can John be?* waar kan John toch zijn?; **2** waar ook, overal waar: *I'll think of you ~ you go* ik zal aan je denken waar je ook naar toe gaat

where̲with̲al middelen, (benodigde) geld[h]: *I don't have the ~* ik heb er geen geld voor

whet [wet] wetten, slijpen, (aan)scherpen

whether [we̲ðə] **1** of: *she wondered ~ he would be in* ze vroeg zich af of hij thuis zou zijn; *he wasn't sure ~ to buy it* hij wist niet of hij het wel zou kopen; **2** (with *or*) of(wel), zij het, hetzij: ~ *he is ill or not I shall tell him* of hij nu ziek is of niet, ik zal het hem zeggen

whe̲tstone wetsteen, slijpsteen

which [witsj] **1** welk(e): *~ colour do you prefer?* welke kleur vind je het mooist?; **2** welke (ervan), wie, wat: *he could not tell ~ was ~* hij kon ze niet uit elkaar houden; **3** die, dat, welke, wat: *the clothes ~ you ordered* de kleren die je besteld hebt; **4** wat, hetgeen, (iets) wat: *he said they were spying on him, ~ is sheer nonsense* hij zei dat ze hem bespioneerden, wat klinkklare onzin is

which̲ever om het even welk(e), welk(e) ook, die(gene) die: *~ way you do it* hoe je het ook doet

¹whiff [wif] *n* **1** vleug *(of smell)*, zweem, flard *(of smoke)*, zuchtje[h] *(of air, wind)*, spoor[h] *(also fig);* **2** teug, het opsnuiven, het inademen; **3** sigaartje[h]

²whiff [wif] *vb* (onaangenaam) ruiken, rieken

¹while [wajl] *n* tijd(je[h]), poos(je[h]): *a good ~* geruime tijd; *worth ~* de moeite waard; *they will make it worth your ~* je zult er geen spijt van hebben; *(eve-*

ry) once in a ~ af en toe, een enkele keer; *we haven't seen her for a long ~* wij hebben haar lang niet gezien; *(for) a ~* een tijdje, een ogenblik

²while [wajl] *conj* **1** terwijl, zo lang als: ~ *I cook the meal you can clear up* terwijl ik het eten maak kun jij opruimen; **2** *(contrast)* terwijl, hoewel, daar waar: ~ *she has the talent she does not have the perseverance* hoewel ze het talent heeft, zet ze niet door

whilst [wajlst] *see* while **2**

whim [wim] gril, opwelling, bevlieging

¹whimper [wi̲mpə] *vb* janken, jammeren

²whimper [wi̲mpə] *n* zacht gejank[h], gejammer[h]: *without a ~* zonder een kik te geven

whimsical [wi̲mzikl] grillig, eigenaardig, fantastisch

whimsica̲lity [wimzikælittie] **1** gril, kuur; **2** grilligheid

whimsy [wi̲mzie] **1** gril, kuur, opwelling; **2** eigenaardigheid

¹whine [wajn] *vb* **1** janken, jengelen; **2** zeuren, zaniken

²whine [wajn] *n* gejammer[h], gejengel[h]

whinge [windzj] mopperen, klagen, zeuren

¹whinny [wi̲nnie] *vb* hinniken

²whinny [wi̲nnie] *n* hinnikend geluid[h], gehinnik[h]

¹whip [wip] *n* zweep, karwats, gesel

²whip [wip] *vb* **1** snel bewegen, snellen, schieten: *she ~ped off her coat* zij gooide haar jas uit; ~ *up: a)* snel oppakken; *b)* snel in elkaar draaien *(of:* flansen); *he ~ped round the corner* hij schoot de hoek om; **2** overhands naaien; **3** zwepen *(also fig),* (met de zweep) slaan, ranselen: *the rain ~ped the windows* de regen striemde tegen de ramen; **4** kloppen *(fresh cream etc),* stijf slaan: *~ped cream* slagroom; **5** verslaan, kloppen, in de pan hakken

whip hand: *have (got) the ~ of* (of: *over)* de overhand hebben over

whiplash injury zweepslagtrauma[h]

whipping [wi̲pping] pak[h] slaag, aframmeling

whippy [wi̲ppie] veerkrachtig, buigzaam

whip-round inzameling: *have a ~* de pet laten rondgaan

¹whirl [wə:l] *vb* **1** tollen, rondtuimelen: *my head ~s* het duizelt mij; **2** stormen, snellen, stuiven

²whirl [wə:l] *vb* ronddraaien, wervelen, (doen) dwarrelen: *he ~ed round* hij draaide zich vliegensvlug om

³whirl [wə:l] *n* **1** werveling, draaikolk; **2** verwarring, roes: *my thoughts are in a ~* het duizelt mij; **3** drukte, gewoel[h], maalstroom: *a ~ of activity* koortsachtige bedrijvigheid; **4** poging: *give it a ~* probeer het eens een keer

whirligig [wə̲:ligig] **1** tol *(toy),* molentje[h]; **2** draaimolen, carrousel

whirlpool 1 draaikolk; **2** wervelbad[h], bubbelbad[h]

¹whirlwind *n* wervelwind, windhoos

²whirlwind *adj* bliksem-, zeer snel: *a ~ campaign* een bliksemcampagne

¹whirr [wə:] *vb* gonzen, zoemen, snorren

²**whirr** [wɔ:] *n* gegons^h, gezoem^h, gesnor^h

¹**whisk** [wisk] *n* **1** kwast, plumeau, borstel; **2** garde, (eier)klopper

²**whisk** [wisk] *vb* **1** zwaaien, zwiepen; **2** *(also with up)* (op)kloppen, stijf slaan

whisk away 1 wegvegen, wegslaan; **2** snel wegvoeren, snel weghalen: *the children were whisked off to bed* de kinderen werden snel in bed gestopt

whisker [wiskə] **1** snorhaar^h, snorharen *(of cat etc)*; **2** ~*s* bakkebaard(en) ‖ *win by a* ~ met een neuslengte winnen

whiskey [wiskie] *(Am, Ireland)* (glas^h) whisky

whisky [wiskie] (glas^h) whisky

¹**whisper** [wispə] *vb* fluisteren, ruisen, roddelen

²**whisper** [wispə] *n* **1** gefluister^h, geruis^h *(of wind)*: *in a* ~, *in* ~*s* fluisterend; **2** gerucht^h, insinuatie; **3** het fluisteren, fluistering

¹**whistle** [wisl] *vb* fluiten, een fluitsignaal geven ‖ ~ *up* in elkaar flansen, uit het niets te voorschijn roepen

²**whistle** [wisl] *n* **1** fluit, fluitje^h; **2** gefluit^h, fluitend geluid^h ‖ *wet one's* ~ de keel smeren *(with drink)*; *blow the* ~ *on sth.: a)* een boekje opendoen over iets; *b)* een eind maken aan

whit [wit] grein^h, sikkepit: *not a* ~ geen zier, geen steek

¹**white** [wajt] *adj* **1** wit, bleek, blank: ~ *Christmas* witte kerst; ~ *coffee* koffie met melk; ~ *as a sheet* lijkbleek, wit als een doek; ~ *tie: a)* wit strikje *(of dress suit); b)* rokkostuum; **2** blank *(of human being)*: ~ *ant* termiet; ~ *elephant: a)* witte olifant; *b)* kostbaar maar nutteloos bezit *(of:* geschenk); *c)* weggegooid geld; ~ *ensign* Britse marinevlag; *show the* ~ *feather* zich lafhartig gedragen; ~ *hope* iem van wie men grote verwachtingen heeft; ~ *lie* leugentje om bestwil; *White Paper* witboek; ~ *spirit* terpentine; *bleed s.o.* ~ iem uitkleden, iem het vel over de oren halen

²**white** [wajt] *n* **1** wit^h *(also chess, draughts)*, het witte; **2** oogwit^h; **3** blanke

white-collar witte boorden-, hoofd-: ~ *job* kantoorbaan; ~ *staff* administratief personeel

Whitehall [wajtho:l] Whitehall, *(fig)* de (Britse) regering, Londen

white-hot witheet, witgloeiend

White House [wajt haus] Witte Huis, *(fig)* Amerikaanse president

¹**whiten** [wajtn] *vb* witten, bleken

²**whiten** [wajtn] *vb* wit worden, opbleken

¹**whitewash** *vb* **1** witten; **2** vergoelijken; **3** witwassen

²**whitewash** *n* **1** witkalk, witsel^h; **2** vergoelijking, dekmantel

whither [wiðə] **1** *(interrogative)* waarheen, waar naar toe; **2** naar daar waar, naar ergens waar: *he knew* ~ *she had gone* hij wist waar zij heengegaan was

Whit Monday [witmundee] pinkstermaandag, tweede pinksterdag

Whitsun [witsn] Pinksteren

Whit Sunday pinksterzondag

whittle [witl] *(with away, down)* (af)snijden *(wood)*, snippers afsnijden van, besnoeien, *(fig)* reduceren, beknibbelen

¹**whiz(z)** [wiz] *vb* zoeven, fluiten, suizen: *they ~ed past* zij zoefden voorbij

²**whiz(z)** [wiz] *n (whizzes)* gefluit^h, het zoeven, gesuis^h

whiz(z)kid briljant jongmens^h, genie^h, wonder^h

who [hoe:] **1** die, wie: *anyone* ~ *disagrees* wie niet akkoord gaat; **2** om het even wie, wie dan ook; **3** wie: ~ *cares* wat maakt het uit; ~ *knows what he'll do next* wie weet wat hij nog zal doen

whodun(n)it [hoe:dunnit] detective(roman), detectivefilm

whoever 1 wie (toch): ~ *can that be?* wie kan dat toch zijn?; **2** om het even wie, wie (dan) ook, al wie: ~ *you meet, don't speak to them* wie je ook tegenkomt, spreek hen niet aan

¹**whole** [hool] *adj* **1** (ge)heel, totaal, volledig: ~ *number* heel getal; *swallow sth.* ~ iets in zijn geheel doorslikken, *(fig)* iets voor zoete koek aannemen; **2** geheel, gaaf, gezond: *go (the)* ~ *hog* tot het einde toe doorgaan, geen half werk doen; *a* ~ *lot of people* een heleboel mensen; *(Am) the* ~ *shebang* het hele zootje

²**whole** [hool] *n* geheel^h, totaal^h: *on the* ~ alles bij elkaar, in het algemeen; *the* ~ *of Boston* heel Boston

³**whole** [hool] *adv* totaal, geheel: *a* ~ *new life* een totaal nieuw leven

wholehearted hartgrondig

¹**wholesale** [hoolseel] *n* groothandel

²**wholesale** [hoolseel] *adj* **1** in het groot, groothandel-, grossiers-: *sell* ~ in het groot verkopen; **2** massaal, op grote schaal: ~ *slaughter* massamoord

wholesaler [hoolseelə] groothandelaar, grossier

wholesome [hoolsəm] **1** gezond, heilzaam; **2** nuttig *(advice)*

wholewheat volkoren

wholly [hoolie] geheel, volledig, totaal

whom [hoe:m] **1** wie: *tell* ~ *you like* zeg het aan wie je wil; **2** die, wie: *your father is a man for* ~ *I have immense respect* jouw vader is iemand voor wie ik enorm veel respect heb

¹**whoop** [woe:p] *vb* schreeuwen, roepen, een kreet slaken *(with joy)* ‖ ~ *it up* uitbundig feestvieren

²**whoop** [woe:p] *n* uitroep, kreet *(with joy)*

whoopee [woepie:]: *make* ~ keet maken, aan de zwier gaan

whooping cough [hoe:ping kof] kinkhoest

¹**whoosh** [woe:sj] *n* gesuis^h, geruis^h, gesis^h

²**whoosh** [woe:sj] *vb* suizen, ruisen, sissen

whop [woop] afranselen, slaan, *(fig)* verslaan

whopper [woppə] **1** kanjer; **2** grove leugen

whopping [wopping] *(inf)* kolossaal, geweldig: *a* ~ *(great) lie* een kolossale leugen

whore [ho:] *(inf)* hoer

whorehouse bordeel^h

whorl [wo:l] **1** krans *(of leaves around stem)*; **2** spiraal *(of shell, fingerprint)*

whose [hoe:z] van wie, wat, welke, waarvan, wiens, wier: *~ cap is this?* wiens pet is dit?, wie zijn pet is dit?; *a writer ~ books are all bestsellers* een schrijver wiens boeken allemaal bestsellers zijn; *children ~ parents work at home* kinderen wier, van wie de ouders thuis werken

¹why [waj] *adv* waarom, om welke reden: *~ not ask him?* waarom vraag je het (hem) niet gewoon?; *the ~s and wherefores* het hoe en waarom

²why [waj] *interj (when surprised)* wel allemachtig: *~, if it isn't Mr Smith* wie we daar hebben! Meneer Smith!; *~, a child could answer that* nou zeg, een kind zou dat weten

wick [wik] wiek, pit, kousje[h] *(of lamp)*, katoen[h] || *get on s.o.'s ~* iem op de zenuwen werken

wicked [wikkid] **1** slecht, verdorven, zondig: *~ prices* schandelijk hoge prijzen; **2** kwaadaardig, gemeen *(tongue)*; **3** schadelijk, kwalijk *(cough)*, gevaarlijk *(storm)*, streng *(winter)*

wicker [wikkə] vlechtwerk[h]

wicket [wikkit] deurtje[h], hekje[h] || *(fig) bat* (of: *be) on a sticky ~* zich in een moeilijk parket bevinden

¹wide [wajd] *adj* **1** wijd, breed; **2** ruim, uitgestrekt, veelomvattend, rijk *(experience)*, algemeen *(knowledge): he has ~ interests* hij heeft een brede interesse; **3** wijd open *(eyes): keep your eyes ~* houd je ogen wijd open; **4** ernaast, mis, ver naast *(shot, guess): ~ of the mark* compleet ernaast, irrelevant; *the dart went ~ of the target* het pijltje ging ver naast het doel; *~ boy* gladde jongen; *give s.o. (sth.) a ~ berth* iem (iets) uit de weg blijven

²wide [wajd] *adv* **1** wijd, breed; **2** helemaal, volledig

wide-angle groothoek-

widely [wajdlie] **1** wijd (uiteen), ver uit elkaar; **2** breed, over een groot gebied, *(also fig)* op vele gebieden: *~ known* wijd en zijd bekend; **3** sterk, heel, erg: *differ ~* sterk verschillen

widen [wajdn] breder worden, maken

wide-ranging breed opgezet, van grote omvang

¹widow [widdoo] *n* weduwe

²widow [widdoo] *vb* tot weduwe (weduwnaar) maken: *her ~ed father* haar vader, die weduwnaar is

widower [widdooə] weduwnaar

width [witθ] breedte

wield [wie:ld] **1** uitoefenen, bezitten *(power, influence)*; **2** hanteren, gebruiken *(tools)*

wife [wajf] *(wives)* vrouw, echtgenote: *(inf) the ~* vrouwlief, mijn vrouw

wig [wig] pruik

¹wiggle [wigl] *vb* **1** wiebelen; **2** wriemelen, kronkelen

²wiggle [wigl] *vb* doen wiebelen, op en neer bewegen, heen en weer bewegen: *~ one's toes* zijn tenen bewegen

³wiggle [wigl] *n* gewiebel[h]

¹wild [wajld] *adj* **1** wild, ongetemd: *~ flower* wilde bloem; **2** barbaars, onbeschaafd: *the Wild West* het wilde Westen; *run ~* verwilderen *(eg of garden)*; **3** onbeheerst, losbandig; **4** stormachtig, guur *(of weather, sea)*; **5** woest, onherbergzaam *(of region)*; **6** dol, waanzinnig: *the ~est nonsense* je reinste onzin; **7** woest, woedend: *~ with anger* razend van woede; **8** wanordelijk, verward *(of hair)*; **9** fantastisch *(of idea)*, buitensporig: *the ~est dreams* de stoutste dromen; **10** roekeloos, gewaagd; **11** woest, enthousiast: *she's ~ about him* ze is weg van hem; *a ~ guess* een gok in het wilde weg; *~ horses wouldn't drag it from me!* voor geen geld ter wereld vertel ik het; *~ camping* vrij kamperen

²wild [wajld] *n* **1** woestenij, wildernis: *(out) in the ~s* in de wildernis; **2** (vrije) natuur, natuurlijke staat: *in the ~* in het wild

wild card jokerteken[h]

¹wildcat *n* **1** wilde kat, boskat; **2** heethoofd, kat *(woman)*

²wildcat *adj* **1** onsolide *(bank, firm)*, (financieel) onbetrouwbaar; **2** wild, onofficieel *(of strike)*

wilderness [wildənəs] wildernis *(also fig)*

wildfire [wajldfajjə]: *spread like ~* als een lopend vuurtje (rondgaan)

wildfowl wild gevogelte[h] *(waterfowl)*

wild-goose chase dwaze onderneming: *be on a ~* met een dwaze onderneming bezig zijn; *send s.o. on a ~* iem misleiden

wile [wajl] list, (sluwe) streek

wilful [wilfoel] **1** koppig, eigenzinnig; **2** opzettelijk, expres: *~ murder* moord met voorbedachten rade

wiliness [wajlienəs] sluwheid

¹will [wil] *vb* **1** willen, wensen, verlangen: *God ~ing* als God het wil; *whether she ~ or no* of ze wil of niet; **2** willen; zullen: *(emphatically) I said I would do it and I ~* ik heb gezegd dat ik het zou doen en ik zal het ook doen; *~ you hurry up, please?* wil je opschieten, alsjeblieft?; *that ~ be John* dat zal John wel zijn; *I ~ lend you a hand* ik zal je een handje helpen; **3** *(habit, repetition)* plegen, kunnen: *accidents ~ happen* ongelukken zijn niet te vermijden; **4** kunnen, in staat zijn te: *this ~ do* zo is het genoeg; **5** zullen, moeten: *you ~ do as I say* je zult doen wat ik zeg

²will [wil] *n* **1** testament[h]: *his last ~ (and testament)* zijn laatste wilsbeschikking; *she has a ~ of her own* ze heeft een eigen willetje; *he did it of his own free ~* hij deed het uit vrije wil; **2** wil, wilskracht, wens, verlangen[h]: *good ~* goede wil; *at ~* naar goeddunken; *with a ~* vastberaden, enthousiast

willies [williez] kriebels, de zenuwen: *give s.o. the ~* iem op de zenuwen werken

willing [willing] gewillig, bereid(willig): *~ workers* werkwilligen; *I am ~ to admit that ...* ik geef grif toe dat ...

willow [willoo] wilg

willowy [willooie] slank, soepel, elegant

will power wilskracht: *by sheer ~* door louter wilskracht

willy-nilly [willienillie] goedschiks of kwaadschiks: *~, he was sent to Spain for a year* hij werd voor een jaar naar Spanje gestuurd, of hij nu wilde of niet

wilt [wilt] **1** (doen) verwelken, (doen) verdorren; **2** hangerig worden, lusteloos worden

wily [wajlie] sluw, listig, slim

wimp [wimp] sul, doetje[h]

[1]**win** [win] *vb* **1** winnen *(competition, prize etc)*: *you can't ~ 'em all* je kunt niet altijd winnen; **2** verkrijgen, verwerven, behalen *(victory, fame, honour)*, winnen *(friendship, confidence)*, ontginnen *(mine, vein)*, winnen *(ore, oil)*: *~ back* terugwinnen; **3** overreden, overhalen: *~ s.o. over* iem overhalen

[2]**win** [win] *vb* zegevieren, de overwinning behalen, (het) winnen: *~ hands down* op zijn gemak winnen; *~ out* (of: *through)* zich erdoorheen slaan, het (uiteindelijk) winnen

[3]**win** [win] *n* overwinning

[1]**wince** [wins] *vb* huiveren, ineenkrimpen *(of pain etc)*, terugdeinzen: *~ at s.o.'s words* van iemands woorden huiveren

[2]**wince** [wins] *n* huivering *(of pain, fear)*

[1]**winch** [wintsj] *n* windas, lier

[2]**winch** [wintsj] *vb* opwinden met een windas

[1]**wind** [wind] *n* **1** wind, luchtstroom, tocht, rukwind: *(fig) take the ~ from* (of: *out of) s.o.'s sails* iem de wind uit de zeilen nemen; *fair ~* gunstige wind; **2** windstreek, windrichting; **3** adem(haling), lucht: *get back* (of: *recover) one's ~* (weer) op adem komen; **4** (buik)wind, darmgassen: *break ~* een wind laten; *get ~ of sth.* ergens lucht van krijgen; *(see) how the ~ blows* (of: *lies)* (kijken) uit welke hoek de wind waait; *(inf) get* (of: *have) the ~ up* hem knijpen, in de rats zitten; *(inf) put the ~ up* de stuipen op het lijf jagen; *(sail) near the ~* scherp (bij de wind) (zeilen), *(fig)* de grens van het toelaatbare (raken); *there's sth. in the ~* er is iets aan de hand; *second ~* het weer op adem komen, (nieuwe) energie (voor tweede krachtsinspanning); **5** *~s* blazers(sectie)

[2]**wind** [wind] *vb* buiten adem brengen, naar adem laten snakken *(after thump)*

[3]**wind** [wajnd] *vb* winden, spoelen, draaien || *~ on (a film)* (een filmpje) doorspoelen

[4]**wind** [wajnd] *vb* **1** kronkelen, zich slingeren: *the river ~s through the landscape* de rivier kronkelt door het landschap; **2** spiralen, zich draaien: *~ing staircase* (of: *stairs)* wenteltrap

[5]**wind** [wajnd] *vb* **1** winden, wikkelen, (op)rollen: *~ back* terugspoelen; *~ in* binnenhalen, inhalen *(of (fishing) line)*; **2** omwinden, omwikkelen; **3** opwinden: *~ one's watch* zijn horloge opwinden

windbag [windbæg] *(inf)* kletsmajoor

windbreak beschutting (tegen de wind)

windchill gevoelstemperatuur, windverkilling

[1]**wind down** [wajnd daun] *vb* zich ontspannen, uitrusten

[2]**wind down** [wajnd daun] *vb* **1** omlaagdraaien: *~ a car window* een portierraampje naar beneden draaien; **2** terugschroeven, verminderen

windfall **1** afgewaaide vrucht; **2** meevaller, mazzeltje[h], erfenisje[h]

wind farm windmolenpark[h]

winding-up [wajndingup] liquidatie, opheffing

wind instrument blaasinstrument[h]

windmill [windmil] **1** windmolen, windturbine; **2** (speelgoed)molentje[h] || *fight (of: tilt) at ~s* tegen windmolens vechten

window [windoo] **1** raam[h], venster[h], ruit; **2** etalage

window dressing 1 het etaleren, etalage; **2** etalage(-inrichting), etalagemateriaal[h]

window-pane (venster)ruit

window-shop etalages kijken: *go ~ping* etalages gaan kijken

windowsill vensterbank, raamkozijn[h]

windpipe luchtpijp

windscreen voorruit *(of car)*

windshield 1 windscherm[h] *(of motorcycle, scooter)*; **2** *(Am)* voorruit *(of car)*

windshield wiper *(Am)* ruitenwisser

windsock windzak *(at airport)*

windsurfing windsurfen

windswept 1 winderig, door de wind geteisterd; **2** verwaaid, verfomfaaid

[1]**wind up** [wajnd up] *vb* **1** eindigen (als), terechtkomen (in), worden (tot): *he'll ~ in prison* hij belandt nog eens in de gevangenis; **2** sluiten, zich opheffen

[2]**wind up** [wajnd up] *vb* besluiten, beëindigen, afronden: *~ a conversation* een gesprek beëindigen; *winding up* tot besluit, samenvattend

[3]**wind up** [wajnd up] *vb* **1** opwinden, opdraaien *(of spring mechanism)*: *~ an alarm* een wekker opwinden; **2** omhoogdraaien, ophalen, ophijsen; **3** opwinden, opzwepen: *get wound up* opgewonden raken

[1]**windward** [windwəd] *adj* **1** loef-, wind-: *~ side* loefzijde, windzijde; **2** windwaarts, tegen de wind (in)

[2]**windward** [windwəd] *adv* windwaarts, tegen de wind in

[3]**windward** [windwəd] *n* loef(zijde)

windy [windie] **1** winderig, open, onbeschut; **2** winderig, opgeblazen, gezwollen *(of words)*; **3** bang

wine [wajn] wijn

[1]**wing** [wing] *n* **1** vleugel: *(fig) spread* (of: *stretch) one's ~s* op eigen benen gaan staan; *(fig) take under one's ~s* onder zijn vleugels nemen; **2** *(architecture)* vleugel, zijstuk[h]; **3** *(mil)* vleugel, flank; **4** *(pol; fig)* (partij)vleugel; **5** *(football, rugby; fig)* vleugel(speler); **6** *~s* coulisse: *in the ~s* achter de schermen; *clip s.o.'s ~s* iem kortwieken; *on the ~* in de vlucht

[2]**wing** [wing] *vb* vliegen, (als) op vleugels gaan

[3]**wing** [wing] *vb* **1** van vleugels voorzien, *(fig)* vleugels geven, voortjagen; **2** vleugellam maken, aan de vleugel verwonden

winger [wingə] *(football, rugby)* vleugelspeler, buitenspeler

wingspan vleugelspanning, *(aviation)* spanwijdte

[1]**wink** [wingk] *vb* **1** knipperen (met) (de ogen): *~ at s.o.* iem een knipoog geven; **2** twinkelen

[2]**wink** [wingk] *n* **1** knipperbeweging *(with eyes)*, knipoog(je[h]): *give s.o. a ~* iem een knipoog geven;

2 ogenblik^h *(of sleep):* not get a ~ *(of sleep),* not sleep a ~ geen oog dichtdoen; *tip s.o. the* ~ iem een hint geven; *forty* ~s dutje

winker [wingkə] richtingaanwijzer, knipperlicht^h

winkle out lospeuteren, uitpersen: *winkle information out of s.o.* informatie van iem lospeuteren

winner [winnə] **1** winnaar; **2** (kas)succes^h: *be onto a* ~ een lot uit de loterij hebben

winning [winning] **1** winnend, zegevierend; **2** innemend, aantrekkelijk *(smile etc)*

winnow [winnoo] **1** wannen, van kaf ontdoen: ~ *the chaff (from the grain)* het kaf (uit het koren) wannen; **2** (uit)ziften, schiften

wino [wajnoo] *(also* ~es) zuiplap, dronkenlap

winsome [winsəm] aantrekkelijk, charmant

winter [wintə] winter: *in* ~ 's winters, in de winter; *last* ~ afgelopen winter

winter sports [wintə spo:ts] wintersporten

wintry winters, winter-, guur

¹wipe [wajp] *vb* **1** (af)vegen, (weg)wrijven, (uit)wissen: ~ *one's feet* (of: *shoes)* zijn voeten vegen; ~ *away* wegvegen, wrijven; ~ *down, give a wipe-down* afnemen *(with damp cloth); please* ~ *that grin off your face* haal die grijns van je gezicht; **2** (af)drogen, droog wrijven: ~ *one's hands* zijn handen afdrogen

²wipe [wajp] *n* veeg: *give sth. a* ~ iets even afvegen

wipe off 1 afvegen, wegvegen, uitwissen; **2** tenietdoen *(debt etc)*

wipe out 1 uitvegen, uitdrogen, (van binnen) schoonmaken; **2** vereffenen, uitwissen; **3** wegvagen, met de grond gelijk maken, uitroeien, vernietigen; **4** uitvegen, wegvegen, uitwissen

wipe up 1 afdrogen: *help to* ~ *(the dishes)* helpen met afdrogen; **2** opnemen, opdweilen

¹wire [wajjə] *n* **1** metaalkabel; telefoon-, telegraafkabel, telefoonlijn; **2** *(Am)* telegram^h: *by* ~ telegrafisch, per telegram; **3** metaaldraad: *barbed* ~ prikkeldraad

²wire [wajjə] *vb (Am)* telegraferen: ~ *(to) s.o.* iem een telegram sturen

³wire [wajjə] *vb* **1** met een draad vastmaken; **2** bedraden

wired [wajjə:d] **1** (met draad) verstevigd *(of clothing);* **2** op het alarmsysteem aangesloten; **3** voorzien van afluisterapparatuur

¹wireless [wajjələs] *n* **1** radiotelefonie; **2** radio: *on the* ~ op de radio

²wireless [wajjələs] *adj* draadloos, radio-

wiretapping het afluisteren

wiring [wajjəring] bedrading

wiry [wajjərie] **1** draad-, als draad; **2** taai, buigzaam als draad, weerbarstig *(hair);* **3** pezig

wisdom [wizdəm] wijsheid

wisdom tooth verstandskies

wise [wajz] wijs, verstandig || *it is easy to be* ~ *after the event* achteraf is het (altijd) makkelijk praten; *be* ~ *to sth.* iets in de gaten hebben; *without anyone's being the* ~r onopgemerkt, zonder dat er een

haan naar kraait; *come away none the* ~r niets wijzer zijn geworden

¹wisecrack *n* grappige opmerking

²wisecrack *vb* een grappige opmerking maken

wiseguy wijsneus, betweter

wisely [wajzlie] wijselijk: *he* ~ *kept his mouth shut* hij hield wijselijk zijn mond

¹wise up *vb (Am)* in de gaten krijgen, door krijgen: ~ *to what is going on* in de smiezen krijgen wat er gaande is

²wise up *vb (Am)* uit de droom helpen: *get wised up* uit de droom geholpen worden

¹wish [wisj] *vb* **1** wensen, willen, verlangen: *what more can you* ~ *for?* wat wil je nog meer?; **2** (toe)wensen: ~ *s.o. well* iem het beste wensen; ~ *away* wegwensen, wensen dat iets niet bestond; *I wouldn't wish that on my worst enemy* dat zou ik mijn ergste vijand nog niet toewensen

²wish [wisj] *n* **1** verlangen^h, behoefte, zin; **2** wens: *best* (of: *good) ~es* beste wensen; *express a* ~ *to* de wens te kennen geven te; *make a* ~ een wens doen

wishful [wisjfoel] wensend, verlangend: ~ *thinking* wishful thinking, *(roughly)* vrome wens, ijdele hoop

wishy-washy [wisjiewosjie] **1** waterig, slap, dun; **2** krachteloos, slap, armzalig

wisp [wisp] **1** bosje^h, bundeltje^h: ~ *of hay* bosje hooi; **2** pluimpje^h, plukje^h: ~ *of hair* plukje haar, piek; **3** sliert, kringel, (rook)pluim(pje^h): ~s *of music* flarden muziek

wistful [wistfoel] **1** weemoedig, droefgeestig; **2** smachtend

¹wit [wit] *n* **1** gevat iem; **2** scherpzinnigheid; **3** geestigheid; **4** ~s verstand^h, benul^h, intelligentie: *have enough* ~ (of: *have the* ~(s)) *to say no* zo verstandig zijn nee te zeggen; *at one's* ~s' *end* ten einde raad; *have one's* ~s *about one* alert zijn, bijdehand zijn; *live by* (of: *on) one's* ~s op ongeregelde manier aan de kost komen

²wit [wit] *vb: to* ~ te weten, namelijk, dat wil zeggen

witch [witsj] heks

witchcraft tove(na)rij, hekserij

witch doctor medicijnman

witchery [witsjərie] **1** betovering, bekoring, charme; **2** tovenarij

with [wið] **1** met: *a conversation* ~ *Jill* een gesprek met Jill; *compared* ~ *Mary* vergeleken bij Mary; *angry* ~ *Sheila* kwaad op Sheila; **2** *(direction)* mee met, overeenkomstig (met): *it changes* ~ *the seasons* het verandert met de seizoenen; *sail* ~ *the wind* met de wind zeilen; *come* ~ *me* kom met mij mee; **3** *(accompaniment, cohesion, characteristic)* (samen) met, bij, inclusief, hebbende: *she can sing* ~ *the best of them* ze kan zingen als de beste; *I like it* ~ *sauce* ik eet het graag met saus; *what is* ~ *him?* wat is er met hem (aan de hand)?; *spring is* ~ *us* het is lente; *it's all right* ~ *me* ik vind het goed, mij is het om het even; **4** *(place; also fig)* bij, toevertrouwd aan: *she stayed* ~ *her aunt* ze logeerde bij haar tante; **5** *(con-*

trast) niettegenstaande, ondanks: *a nice girl, ~ all her faults* een leuk meisje, ondanks haar gebreken; **6** *(means or cause)* met, met behulp van, door middel van: *they woke her ~ their noise* zij maakten haar wakker met hun lawaai; *pleased ~ the results* tevreden over de resultaten; *filled ~ water* vol water; *sick ~ worry* ziek van de zorgen; **7** *(time)* bij, tegelijkertijd met, samen met: *~ his death all changed* met zijn dood veranderde alles; *he arrived ~ Mary* hij kwam tegelijkertijd met Mary aan; *she's not ~ it: a)* ze heeft geen benul; *b)* ze is hopeloos ouderwets; *I'm ~ you there* dat ben ik met je eens; *away (*of: *down) ~ him!* weg met hem!; *it's all over ~ him* het is met hem afgelopen; *what's up ~ him?* wat heeft hij?

¹withdraw [wiðdrọ:] *vb* **1** terugtrekken: *~ one's hand* zijn hand terugtrekken; **2** onttrekken aan, niet laten deelnemen: *~ a team from a tournament* een ploeg uit een toernooi terugtrekken; **3** terugnemen *(remark, promise)*, herroepen: *~ an offer* op een aanbod terugkomen; **4** opnemen *(from bank account):* *~ a hundred pounds* honderd pond opnemen

²withdraw [wiðdrọ:] *vb* **1** uit de weg gaan, opzijgaan; **2** zich terugtrekken: *the army withdrew* het leger trok terug; **3** zich onttrekken aan, niet deelnemen

withdrawal [wiðdrọ:əl] **1** terugtrekking, terugtocht, het (zich) terugtrekken; **2** intrekking *(eg of promise);* **3** opname *(from bank account);* **4** ontwenning *(from drug)*

withdrawn 1 teruggetrokken, op zichzelf (levend); **2** (kop)schuw, bescheiden, verlegen

¹wither [wiðə] *vb* **1** verwelken, verdorren: *~ed leaves* dorre bla(de)ren; **2** vergaan: *my hopes ~ed (away)* mijn hoop vervloog

²wither [wiðə] *vb* **1** doen verwelken; doen vergaan; **2** vernietigen, wegvagen

withhold [wiθhọọld] onthouden, niet geven, toestaan, inhouden: *~ one's consent* zijn toestemming weigeren

within [wiðịn] *(place)* binnen in, in: *~ the organization* binnen de organisatie; *he came to ~ five feet from the goal* hij kwam tot op anderhalve meter van het doel; *he returned ~ an hour* hij kwam binnen het uur terug; *inquire ~* informeer binnen

without [wiðạut] zonder: *she left ~ a word* zij vertrok zonder een woord te zeggen; *it goes ~ saying* het spreekt vanzelf; *he had to do ~* hij moest het zonder stellen

withstand [wiθstænd] **1** weerstaan, het hoofd bieden: *~ an attack* een aanval weerstaan; **2** bestand zijn tegen, opgewassen zijn tegen: *~ wind and weather* bestand zijn tegen weer en wind

¹witness [witnis] *n* **1** (oog)getuige; medeondertekenaar; **2** getuigenis, getuigenverklaring, (ken)tekenʰ, bewijsʰ: *bear (*of: *give) ~ (on behalf of s.o.)* getuigen (ten gunste van iem); *bear ~ of (*of: *to)* staven, bewijzen

²witness [witnis] *vb* **1** getuige zijn van, bij: *~ an accident* getuige zijn van een ongeluk; *~ a signature* (als getuige) medeondertekenen; **2** getuigen van, een teken zijn van

³witness [witnis] *vb* getuigen, als getuige verklaren: *~ against s.o.* getuigen tegen iem

witness box getuigenbank

witter on [wittər ọn] kletsen, wauwelen

witticism [wittisizm] geestige opmerking

witty [wittie] geestig

¹wizard [wizzəd] *n* **1** tovenaar: *he's a ~ with a microwave oven* hij kan toveren met een magnetron; **2** genieʰ

²wizard [wizzəd] *adj* waanzinnig, te gek, eindeloos

wizened [wizzənd] verschrompeld, gerimpeld, verweerd

wk *week*

¹wobble [wobl] *vb* waggelen, wankelen

²wobble [wobl] *vb* wiebelen (met): *don't ~ your chair* zit niet met je stoel te wiebelen

³wobble [wobl] *n* **1** schommeling, afwijking; **2** beving, trilling

wobbly [woblie] wankel, onvast, wiebelig

woe [woo] **1** ramp(spoed), narigheid, ellende; **2** smart, weeʰ: *tale of ~* smartelijk verhaal

woeful [woofoel] smartelijk, verdrietig

¹wolf [woelf] *n (wolves)* **1** wolf; **2** versierder ‖ *keep the ~ from the door* (nog) brood op de plank hebben; *~ in sheep's clothing* wolf in schaapskleren; *cry ~ (too often)* (te vaak) (lichtvaardig) loos alarm slaan

²wolf [woelf] *vb (also with down)* (op)schrokken, naar binnen schrokken *(food)*

wolf cub wolfsjongʰ, wolfjeʰ

woman [woemən] *(women)* **1** vrouw, vrouwspersoon, de vrouw, het vrouwelijke geslacht; **2** werkster, (dienst)meid; **3** maîtresse; **4** vrouw, echtgenote

womanhood [woemənhoed] **1** vrouwelijkheid, het vrouw-zijn; **2** de vrouwen, het vrouwelijk geslacht

womanish [woemənisj] **1** vrouwelijk, vrouw(en)-; **2** *(depr)* verwijfd

womanizer [woemənajzə] rokkenjager, versierder

womanly [woemənlie] vrouwelijk

womb [woe:m] baarmoeder, *(also fig)* schoot

¹wonder [wundə] *vb* **1** *(with at)* verbaasd staan (van), verrast zijn, zich verbazen, (vreemd) opkijken: *I don't ~ at her hesitation* haar aarzeling verbaast me niet; *I shouldn't ~ if* het zou me niet verbazen als; **2** benieuwd zijn, zich iets afvragen: *I ~ who will win* ik ben benieuwd wie er gaat winnen; *I ~ whether she noticed* ik vraag me af of ze het gemerkt heeft; **3** iets betwijfelen, zich iets afvragen: *Is that so? I ~* O ja? Ik betwijfel het (ten zeerste), ik moet het nog zien

²wonder [wundə] *n* **1** wonderʰ, volmaakt voorwerpʰ; **2** wonderʰ, mirakelʰ: *(fig) do (*of: *work) ~s* wonderen doen; *~s never cease* de wonderen zijn de wereld nog niet uit; **3** verwondering, verbazing, bewondering: *it is little (*of: *no) ~ that* het is geen wonder dat

wonderful [wʌndəfoel] schitterend, geweldig, fantastisch

wonderland sprookjesland[h], wonderschoon gebied[h]

wondrous [wʌndrəs] wonder(baarlijk): ~ *tales* wondere vertellingen

wonky [wʌngkie] krakkemikkig, wankel, *(fig)* slap

woo [woe:] **1** dingen naar (de gunst van), voor zich trachten te winnen: ~ *the voters* dingen naar de gunst van de kiezers; **2** het hof maken, dingen naar de hand van

¹wood [woed] *n* **1** hout[h]: *I haven't had the flu this winter yet, touch* ~ ik heb deze winter nog geen griep gehad, laat ik het afkloppen; **2** bos[h]: *a walk in the ~s* een wandeling in het bos; *he can't see the ~ for the trees* hij ziet door de bomen het bos niet meer; *out of the ~(s)* in veilige haven, buiten gevaar, uit de problemen

²wood [woed] *adj* houten

woodcarving houtsnijwerk[h]

woodcraft houtsnijkunst, houtbewerking

woodcut 1 houtsnede; **2** hout(snede)blok[h]

woodcutter houthakker

wooded [woedid] bebost, bosrijk

wooden [woedn] **1** houten: ~ *horse* houten paard, paard van Troje; ~ *shoe* klomp; **2** houterig, stijf, harkerig

wooden-headed dom, stom

woodlouse pissebed

woodman [woedmən] **1** houtvester; boswachter; **2** houthakker

woodpecker specht

woodsman [woedzmən] **1** houtvester; boswachter; **2** houthakker

woodwinds hout[h]

woodwork 1 houtbewerking, timmermanskunst; **2** houtwerk[h] || *crawl (come) out of the* ~ plotseling te voorschijn komen

woof [woef] **1** woef(geluid[h]), waf, geblaf[h]; **2** inslag *(of fabric)*

woofer [woe:fə] woofer, lagetonenluidspreker

¹wool [woel] *n* wol || *pull the* ~ *over s.o.'s eyes* iem zand in de ogen strooien

²wool [woel] *adj* wollen, van wol

¹wool-gathering *adj* verstrooid, afwezig, aan het dagdromen

²wool-gathering *n* verstrooidheid, afwezigheid

woollen [woelən] wollen, van wol

¹woolly [woelie] *adj* **1** wollen, wollig, van wol; **2** onduidelijk, vaag, wollig, warrig

²woolly [woelie] *n* wolletje[h], trui, wollen kledingstuk[h], ondergoed[h]

woozy [woe:zie] wazig, licht in het hoofd

¹word [wə:d] *n* **1** woord[h], (gesproken) uiting, ~s tekst, woorden *(to song):* *have a* ~ *in s.o.'s ear* iem iets toefluisteren; *by* ~ *of mouth* mondeling; *put* ~s *in(to) s.o.'s mouth* iem woorden in de mond leggen; *right from the* ~ *go* vanaf het begin; ~s *fail me* woor-

den schieten mij tekort; *say the* ~ een seintje geven; *take s.o. at his* ~ iem aan zijn woord houden; ~ *for* ~ woord voor woord, woordelijk; *in other* ~s met andere woorden; *put into* ~s onder woorden brengen; *have a* ~ *with s.o.* iem (even) spreken; *have* ~s *with s.o.* woorden hebben met iem; **2** (ere)woord[h], belofte: *he is as good as his* ~ wat hij belooft doet hij; *I give you my* ~ *for it* ik verzeker het je op mijn erewoord; *keep one's* ~ (zijn) woord houden; *take s.o.'s* ~ *for it* iem op zijn woord geloven; **3** (wacht)woord[h], bevel[h]: *his* ~ *is law* zijn wil is wet; **4** nieuws[h], bericht[h], boodschap: *the* ~ *got round that* het bericht deed de ronde dat; *send* ~ *of* berichten; *eat one's* ~s zijn woorden inslikken, iets terugnemen; *I could not get a* ~ *in edgeways* ik kon er geen speld tussen krijgen; *weigh one's* ~s zijn woorden wegen

²word [wə:d] *vb* verwoorden, onder woorden brengen: *I received a carefully* ~ed *letter* ik kreeg een brief die in zorgvuldige bewoordingen gesteld was

wordplay woord(en)spel[h], woordspelingen

word processor tekstverwerker

word wrap woordomslag, automatische tekstoverloop naar volgende regel op scherm

¹work [wə:k] *n* **1** werk(stuk)[h], arbeid: *a* ~ *of art* een kunstwerk; *have one's* ~ *cut out (for one)* ergens de handen aan vol hebben; *set to* ~ aan het werk gaan; *set about one's* ~ *in the wrong way* verkeerd te werk gaan; *at* ~ aan het werk, op het werk; *men at* ~ werk in uitvoering; *out of* ~ werkloos; **2** borduur-, hand-, naaldwerk[h]; **3** ~s oeuvre[h], werken, verzameld werk[h]: *Joyce's collected* ~s de verzamelde werken van Joyce; **4** ~s mechanisme[h] *(of clock etc);* **5** ~s zooi, bups, mikmak; **6** ~s fabriek, bedrijf[h], werkplaats: *give s.o. the* ~s: *a)* iem flink onder handen nemen; *b)* iem om zeep helpen; *(inf) gum up the* ~s de boel in de war sturen; *shoot the* ~s alles op alles zetten, alles riskeren

²work [wə:k] *vb* **1** werken, functioneren: *the scheme didn't* ~ het plan werkte niet; ~ *away* (druk) aan het werk zijn; ~ *at* werken aan, zijn best doen op; *it* ~ *by electricity* het loopt op elektriciteit; ~ *on* werken aan iets, bezig zijn met iets; ~ *to* werken volgens; **2** gisten, werken; **3** raken *(in a condition):* *the boy's socks* ~ed *down* de sokken van de jongen zakten af; ~ *round to* toe werken naar, aansturen op

³work [wə:k] *vb* **1** verrichten, tot stand brengen, bewerkstelligen: ~ *miracles* (of: *wonders*) wonderen verrichten; **2** laten werken, aan het werk hebben: ~ *s.o. hard* iem hard laten werken; **3** in werking zetten, aanzetten, bedienen, bewerken, in bedrijf houden: ~ *a mine* een mijn exploiteren; **4** zich banen *(a path through sth):* ~ *one's way to the top* zich naar de top werken; **5** bewerken, kneden, werken met: ~ *clay* kleien, boetseren

workable [wə:kəbl] **1** bedrijfsklaar, gebruiksklaar, bruikbaar; **2** uitvoerbaar, haalbaar, werkbaar

workaholic [wə:kəhollik] werkverslaafde, workaholic

workbench werkbank
workbook 1 werkboek(je[h]); **2** handleiding, instructieboekje[b]
worker [wɔ:kə] werker, arbeider, werknemer
workhorse werkpaard[h] *(also fig)*, werkezel
work in 1 insteken; **2** verwerken: *try to ~ some more details* probeer nog een paar bijzonderheden op te nemen; *~ with* (kunnen) samenwerken met
working [wɔ:king] werkend, werk-: *the ~ class* de arbeidersklasse; *~ man* arbeider; *~ mother* buitenshuis werkende moeder
working knowledge praktijkkennis, praktische beheersing: *~ of German* voldoende beheersing van het Duits
working week werkweek
workload werk[h], werklast, werkbelasting
workman [wɔ:kmən] werkman, arbeider
workmanship [wɔ:kmənʃip] **1** vakmanschap[h], vakkundigheid; **2** (hand)werk[h], afwerking
work off wegwerken: *~ steam* stoom afblazen
workout training
¹work out *vb* **1** uitwerken, opstellen *(plan etc)*; **2** uitrekenen, uitwerken, berekenen, uitzoeken: *work things out* de dingen op een rijtje zetten; *try if you can work it out for yourself* probeer eens of je er zelf achter kunt komen; **3** hoogte krijgen van, doorgronden, doorzien
²work out *vb* **1** zich ontwikkelen, verlopen, (gunstig) uitvallen; **2** oplosbaar zijn, uitkomen; **3** trainen ‖ *~ at* (of: *to)* uitkomen op, bedragen
workplace werk[h], werkplek: *at* (of: *in) the ~* op het werk
work placement stage: *do a ~ at a department store* stage lopen bij een warenhuis
workshop 1 werkplaats, atelier[h]; **2** workshop; **3** werkgroep
workstation 1 werkplek; **2** werkstation[h]
worktop werkblad[h], aanrecht[h]
work-to-rule stiptheidsactie
¹work up *vb* **1** opbouwen, uitbouwen; **2** stimuleren: *~ an appetite* zich inspannen zodat men honger krijgt; **3** woedend (nerveus) maken: *don't get worked up* maak je niet druk; **4** opwerken, omhoogwerken: *work one's way up from* zich omhoogwerken vanuit; **5** (om)vormen: *he's working up his notes into a book* hij is bezig zijn aantekeningenmateriaal uit te werken tot een boek; *work s.o. up* iem opjuinen
²work up *vb* (with *to)* toe werken (naar)
world [wɔ:ld] wereld, *(fig)* hoop, boel, menigte: *make a ~ of difference* een hoop verschil uitmaken; *it will do you a ~ of good* daar zul je reuze van opknappen; *come into the ~* geboren worden; *all the ~ knows, the whole ~ knows* de hele wereld weet het; *why in the ~ did you do this?* waarom heb je dat in 's hemelsnaam gedaan?; *out of this ~: a)* niet van deze wereld; *b)* te gek; *the other ~* het hiernamaals; *the Third World* de derde wereld; *I'd give the ~ to …* ik zou er alles (ter wereld) voor over hebben om …;

think the ~ of s.o. een zeer hoge dunk van iem hebben, iem op handen dragen; *they are ~s apart* ze verschillen als dag en nacht; *not for (all) the ~* voor geen goud; *it is for all the ~ like* (of: *as if)* het lijkt sprekend op
world-beater superkampioen
WorldCup wereldbeker, wereldkampioenschap(pen) *(socc)*
worldly [wɔ:ldlie] werelds, aards, wereldwijs: *~ wisdom* wereldwijsheid; *~ goods* wereldse goederen
worldly-wise wereldwijs
world record wereldrecord[h]
world war wereldoorlog
worldwide wereldwijd, over de hele wereld
¹worm [wɔ:m] *n* **1** worm, hazelworm; **2** schroefdraad
²worm [wɔ:m] *vb* **1** ontwormen *(dog, cat etc)*; **2** wurmen: *~ one's way into* zich weten in te dringen in; **3** ontfutselen, ontlokken: *~ a secret out of s.o.* iem een geheim ontfutselen
worn-out 1 afgedragen, (tot op de draad) versleten; **2** uitgeput, doodop, bekaf
worried [wʌrried] bezorgd, ongerust: *a ~ look* een zorgelijk gezicht
worrisome [wʌrriesəm] **1** zorgwekkend, onrustbarend; **2** zorgelijk, tobberig
¹worry [wʌrrie] *n* **1** (voorwerp[h] van) zorg; **2** zorgenkind[h], bron van zorgen; **3** (be)zorg(dheid), ongerustheid
²worry [wʌrrie] *vb* (with *about, over)* zich zorgen maken (over): *I should ~* (zal) mij een zorg (zijn); *not to ~!* maak je geen zorgen!; *~ at: a)* zich het hoofd breken over *(problem); b)* aandringen bij *(somebody)*
³worry [wʌrrie] *vb* lastig vallen, hinderen, storen: *the rain doesn't ~ him* de regen deert hem niet; *oh, that doesn't ~ me* o, daar zit ik niet (zo) mee, daar geef ik niks om; *you'll ~ yourself to death* je maakt je veel te druk
worrying [wʌrrie·ing] zorgwekkend, zorgelijk
¹worse [wɔ:s] *adj, adv* **1** slechter, erger, minder (goed): *to make things ~* tot overmaat van ramp; *~ still* erger nog; **2** zieker, zwakker: *today mother was much ~ than yesterday* vandaag was moeder zieker dan gisteren; *the ~ for drink* (of: *liquor)* aangeschoten; *he is none the ~ for* hij is niet minder geworden van, hij heeft niet geleden onder; *I like him none the ~ for it* ik mag hem er niet minder om
²worse [wɔ:s] *n* iets slechters, slechtere dingen: *a change for the ~* een verandering ten kwade, een verslechtering
worsen [wɔ:sn] verergeren, verslechteren, bemoeilijken
¹worship [wɔ:ʃip] *n* **1** verering, aanbidding; **2** eredienst, godsdienst(oefening) ‖ *Your Worship* Edelachtbare
²worship [wɔ:ʃip] *vb* **1** naar de kerk gaan; **2** van eerbied vervuld zijn, in aanbidding verzonken zijn
³worship [wɔ:ʃip] *vb (also fig)* aanbidden, vereren

worshipper [wɔːˈsjippə] 1 kerkganger, gelovige; 2 aanbidder, vereerder

worst [wɔːst] 1 slechtst, ergst: *come off* ~ aan het kortste eind trekken; 2 ziekst, zwakst: *if the* ~ *comes to the* ~ in het ergste geval; *so you want to fight, OK, we'll fight. Do your* ~*!* dus jij wil vechten, goed, dan vechten we. Kom maar op!; *at (the)* ~ in het ergste geval

¹**worth** [wɔːθ] *adj* waard: *land* ~ *100,000 dollars* land met een waarde van 100.000 dollar; *it is* ~ *(one's) while* het is de moeite waard; ~ *seeing* bezienswaardig; *for what it's* ~ voor wat het waard is; *it's* ~ *it* het is de moeite waard; *for all one is* ~ uit alle macht

²**worth** [wɔːθ] *n* 1 waarde, kwaliteit: *of great* ~ van grote waarde; 2 markt-, tegenwaarde: *I want a dollar's* ~ *of apples* mag ik voor een dollar appels?

worthwhile de moeite waard, waardevol, nuttig

worthy [ˈwɔːðie] 1 waardig, waardevol; 2 waard: *in clothes* ~ *of the occasion* in bij de gelegenheid passende kleding; *he isn't* ~ *of her* hij is haar niet waard; 3 *(oft iron)* achtenswaardig, braaf

would [woed] 1 willen, zullen, wensen: *he* ~ *not hear of it* hij wilde er niet van horen; *I wish he* ~ *leave me alone* ik wilde dat hij me met rust liet; *I* ~ *like to show you this* ik zou je dit graag laten zien; *he* ~ *sooner die than surrender* hij zou liever sterven dan zich overgeven; 2 gewoonlijk, steeds, altijd: *we* ~ *walk to school together* we liepen gewoonlijk samen naar school; 3 zou(den): *I* ~ *try it anyway (if I were you)* ik zou het toch maar proberen (als ik jou was); *he was writing the book that* ~ *bring him fame* hij was het boek aan het schrijven dat hem beroemd zou maken; 4 *(supposition)* moeten, zullen, zou(den), moest(en): *he* ~ *be in bed by now* hij zal nu wel in bed liggen; ~ *you please shut the door?* wil je de deur sluiten alsjeblieft?; 5 *(doubt or uncertainty)* zou kunnen: *we* ~ *suggest the following* we zouden het volgende willen voorstellen

would-be 1 *(depr)* zogenaamd; 2 toekomstig, potentieel, mogelijk: *a* ~ *buyer* een mogelijke koper, een gegadigde

¹**wound** [woeːnd] *n* wond, verwonding, *(fig)* belediging ‖ *lick one's* ~*s* zijn wonden likken *(after defeat)*

²**wound** [woeːnd] *vb* (ver)wonden, *(fig)* grieven, krenken: *when he suddenly left her, she felt* ~*ed and betrayed* toen hij plotseling bij haar wegging, voelde ze zich gekwetst en verraden

wow [wau] 1 klapper, groot succesʰ, sensatie; 2 wow *(of stereo equipment)*

wrack [ræk] verwoesting, vervalʰ, ruïne

wraith [reeθ] (geest)verschijning, schim, spookʰ, spookgestalte

¹**wrangle** [ˈrænggl] *vb* ruzie maken, ruziën: ~ *with s.o. about sth.* met iem om iets ruziën

²**wrangle** [ˈrænggl] *n* ruzie

¹**wrap** [ræp] *vb* 1 inpakken, verpakken; 2 wikkelen, omslaan, vouwen; 3 (om)hullen, bedekken: ~*ped in mist* in nevelen gehuld

²**wrap** [ræp] *vb* zich wikkelen

³**wrap** [ræp] *n* 1 omslag(doekʰ), omgeslagen kledingstukʰ, sjaal, stola; 2 (reis)deken ‖ *take the* ~*s off* onthullen; *under* ~*s* geheim

wrapper [ˈræpə] 1 (stof)omslagʰ, kaft; 2 adresband(jeʰ); 3 papiertjeʰ, pakpapierʰ, wikkel

¹**wrap up** *vb* 1 zich (warm) (aan)kleden; 2 zijn mond houden: ~*!* kop dicht!

²**wrap up** *vb* 1 verpakken, inpakken; 2 warm aankleden, (goed, stevig) inpakken; 3 afwikkelen, afronden, sluiten: ~ *a deal* een overeenkomst sluiten; *be wrapped up in* opgaan in; *wrap it up!* hou op!

wrathful [ˈrɔθfoel] woedend

wreak [rieːk] 1 uitstorten: ~ *vengeance (up)on* wraak nemen op; 2 veroorzaken, aanrichten

wreath [rieːθ] (rouw)krans, (ere)krans

¹**wreathe** [rieːð] *vb* 1 omkransen, om(k)ringen, omhullen: ~*d in* om(k)ringd door, gehuld in; *(fig) a face* ~ *in smiles* een in glimlachen gehuld gelaat; 2 (om)wikkelen, (om)strengelen; 3 (be)kransen, met een krans tooien

²**wreathe** [rieːð] *vb* kringelen, kronkelen

¹**wreck** [rek] *n* 1 wrakʰ *(also fig)*, ruïne; 2 schipbreuk *(also fig)*, ondergang, vernietiging

²**wreck** [rek] *vb* 1 schipbreuk doen lijden, doen stranden, aan de grond doen lopen, *(fig)* doen mislukken *(plan etc): the ship was* ~*ed on the rocks* het schip liep op de rotsen; 2 ruïneren, verwoesten, te gronde richten

wreckage [ˈrekidzj] wrakgoedʰ, wrakstukken, brokstukken, restanten

wrecker [ˈrekə] 1 berger, bergingsmaatschappij; 2 *(Am)* sloper, sloopbedrijfʰ; 3 *(Am)* takelwagen

wren [ren] winterkoninkjeʰ

¹**wrench** [rentsj] *n* 1 ruk, draai; 2 verrekking, verstuiking; 3 moersleutel

²**wrench** [rentsj] *vb* 1 (los)wringen, (los)wrikken, een ruk geven aan: ~ *open* openwrikken, openrukken; ~ *away* (of: *off*) losrukken, wegrukken, loswrikken; 2 verzwikken, verstuiken; 3 vertekenen, verdraaien *(facts etc)*

wrest [rest] 1 (los)rukken, (los)wringen, (los)wrikken: *(fig)* ~ *a confession from s.o.* een bekentenis uit iem persen; 2 zich meester maken van, zich toe-eigenen; 3 verdraaien, geweld aandoen *(meaning, facts)*

wrestle [ˈresl] worstelen (met, tegen) *(also fig)*: ~ *with problems* met problemen kampen

wretch [retsj] 1 stakker, zielepoot; 2 ellendeling, klier; 3 schurk, boef, schooier

wretched [ˈretsjid] 1 beklagenswaardig, zielig, droevig; 2 ellendig, ongelukkig; 3 verachtelijk, laag; 4 waardeloos, beroerd, rot-

¹**wriggle** [ˈrigl] *vb* kronkelen, wriemelen, *(fig)* zich in allerlei bochten wringen: ~ *out of sth.* ergens onderuit proberen te komen

²**wriggle** [ˈrigl] *vb* 1 wriemelen met, wriemelend heen en weer bewegen; 2 kronkelend afleggen

³**wriggle** [ˈrigl] *n* kronkelbeweging, gekronkelʰ, gewriemelʰ

wring [ring] **1** omdraaien: ~ *a hen's neck* een kip de nek omdraaien; **2** (uit)wringen, (uit)persen, samenknijpen: ~ *s.o.'s hand* iem stevig de hand drukken; **3** afpersen, afdwingen: ~ *a confession from* (of: *out of) s.o.* iem een bekentenis afdwingen

¹wrinkle [rɪngkl] *n* **1** rimpel, plooi, kreuk; **2** foefje[h], kunstje[h]; **3** tip, idee[h]

²wrinkle [rɪngkl] *vb* rimpelen, rimpels (doen) krijgen, kreuke(le)n

wrist [rist] **1** pols(gewricht[h]); **2** pols(stuk[h]) *(of clothing)*, manchet

wristband **1** horlogebandje[h], pols(arm)band; **2** manchet

wristlet [rɪstlit] **1** horlogeband(je[h]); **2** polsband(je[h]) *(sport)*; **3** armband(je[h])

writ [rit] **1** bevelschrift[h], dwangbevel[h], gerechtelijk schrijven[h]: *serve a ~ on* een dagvaarding betekenen aan; **2** de Schrift *(bible)*

write [rajt] schrijven, (weg)schrijven: ~ *a cheque* een cheque uitschrijven; ~ *back* terugschrijven, antwoorden; ~ *about* (of: *on) a subject* over een onderwerp schrijven; ~ *away for* over de post bestellen; *nothing to* ~ *home about* niet(s) om over naar huis te schrijven; *envy was written all over his face* de jaloezie stond hem op het gezicht te lezen

write down **1** neerschrijven, opschrijven, op papier vastleggen; **2** beschrijven, uitmaken voor, beschouwen (als): *write s.o. down a bore* (of: *as) a bore* iem uitmaken voor een vervelende vent

¹write in *vb* schrijven, schriftelijk verzoeken: ~ *for a free catalogue* schrijven om een gratis catalogus

²write in *vb* bijschrijven, invoegen, toevoegen, inlassen

¹write off *vb* schrijven, over de post bestellen: ~ *for sth.,* ~ *to order sth.* schrijven om iets te bestellen

²write off *vb* **1** afschrijven *(also fig)*, afvoeren: ~ *losses* verliezen afschrijven; **2** (op)schrijven, in elkaar draaien

write-off **1** afschrijving; **2** total loss, weggooier *(fig)*

write out **1** uitschrijven, voluit schrijven; **2** schrijven, uitschrijven *(cheque etc)*; **3** schrappen, uitschrijven *(part in TV series):* her part was written out haar rol werd geschrapt

writer [rajtə] schrijver, schrijfster, auteur: *the (present)* ~ ondergetekende

write up **1** bijwerken *(diary)*; **2** uitwerken, uitschrijven

writhe [rajð] wringen, kronkelen, (ineen)krimpen: ~ *with pain* kronkelen van de pijn

writing [rajting] **1** schrijven[h]: *in* ~ schriftelijk; **2** (hand)schrift[h]; **3** schrift[h], schriftuur: *put sth. down in* ~ iets op schrift stellen; **4** ~*s* werken, geschriften: *the* ~ *on the wall* het teken aan de wand

writing pad schrijfblok[h], blocnote

¹wrong [rong] *adj* **1** verkeerd, fout, onjuist: ~ *number* verkeerd verbonden; *(the)* ~ *way round* achterstevoren, de verkeerde kant op; *go down the* ~ *way* in het verkeerde keelgat schieten *(of food)*; **2** slecht, verkeerd, niet goed: *you're* ~ *to do this, it's* ~

of you to do this u doet hier verkeerd aan; **3** in de verkeerde richting, de verkeerde kant op: *get hold of the* ~ *end of the stick* het bij het verkeerde eind hebben; *come to the* ~ *shop* aan het verkeerde adres (gekomen) zijn; *get on the* ~ *side of s.o.* iemands sympathie verliezen; *on the* ~ *side of sixty* de zestig gepasseerd; *(Am) the* ~ *side of the tracks* de achterbuurten, de zelfkant; *bark up the* ~ *tree* op het verkeerde spoor zijn, aan het verkeerde adres zijn; *you're* ~ je hebt ongelijk, je vergist je

²wrong [rong] *n* **1** kwaad[h], onrecht[h]: *right and* ~ juist en onjuist; **2** misstand, wantoestand; **3** onrechtmatige daad: *be in the* ~: *a)* het mis hebben; *b)* de schuldige zijn, het gedaan hebben

³wrong [rong] *vb* **1** onrecht doen, onrechtvaardig behandelen, onredelijk zijn tegen: ~ *a person* iem te kort doen; **2** onbillijk beoordelen

wrongdoing [rongdoe:ing] **1** wandaad, overtreding; **2** wangedrag[h], misdadigheid

wrongful [rongfoel] **1** onterecht, onbillijk; **2** onrechtmatig, onwettig

wrong-headed **1** dwars(liggerig), eigenwijs; **2** foutief, verkeerd

wrought-up gespannen, nerveus, opgewonden

wry [raj] **1** (ver)zuur(d), wrang: ~ *mouth* zuinig mondje; **2** (licht) ironisch, spottend, droog, laconiek *(of humour):* ~ *smile* spottend lachje

wt. *weight* gewicht

WYSIWYG [wizziwwig] *(comp)* What You See Is What You Get

X

xenophobia [zennəfoobiə] xenofobie, vreemdelingenhaat, vreemdelingenangst
XL *extra large* XL, extra groot *(clothing)*
Xmas [krismɔs] kerst, Kerstmis
¹X-ray *n* **1** röntgenstraal; **2** röntgenfoto
²X-ray *vb* **1** doorlichten *(also fig);* **2** bestralen
xylophone [zajləfoon] xylofoon

y

yacht [jot] jacht[h] *(ship)*
yachting [jɔtting] (wedstrijd)zeilen[h]
yahoo [ja:hoe:] varken[h], schoft
yak [jæk] jak, knorbuffel
yammer [jæmə] **1** jammeren; **2** kakelen
1yank [jæŋk] *vb* een ruk geven aan, trekken
2yank [jæŋk] *n* ruk, sjor
Yank(ee) [jæŋkie] *(Am)* yank(ee), *(hist)* noorderling
yard [ja:d] **1** Engelse el *(91.4 cm): by the ~* per yard, *(fig)* ellenlang; **2** *(shipp)* ra; **3** (omheind) terrein[h], binnenplaats, erf[h]; **4** *(Am)* plaatsje[h], (achter)tuin, gazon[h]: *the Yard* Scotland Yard
yardstick meetlat, *(fig)* maatstaf
yarn [ja:n] **1** lang verhaal[h], (langdradig) verhaal[h]; **2** garen[h], draad || *spin a ~* een lang verhaal vertellen
1yawn [jo:n] *vb* geeuwen, gapen *(also fig)*, wijd geopend zijn: *~ing hole* gapend gat
2yawn [jo:n] *n* geeuw, gaap
yd(s) *yard(s)*
1ye [jie:] *pron* gij, u, jullie, jij
2ye [jie:] *art* de: *~ olde Spanish Inn* de oude Spaanse uitspanning
yea [jee] **1** stem vóór: *~s and nays* stemmen vóór en tegen; **2** voorstemmer
year [jiə] **1** jaar[h]: *a ~ from today* vandaag over een jaar; *all the ~ round* het hele jaar door; *for many ~s* sinds jaar en dag; *over the ~s* met de jaren; **2** lange tijd, *(fig)* eeuw; **3** *~s* jaren, leeftijd; **4** *~s* eeuwigheid *(only fig)*, eeuwen: *it has been ~s* het is eeuwen geleden
yearling [jiəling] eenjarig dier[h], eenjarig renpaard[h]
yearly [jiəlie] jaarlijks, elk jaar: *a ~ income* een jaarinkomen
yearn [jə:n] smachten, verlangen: *~ after* (of: *for)* smachten naar
yeast [jie:st] gist, *(fig)* desem
1yell [jel] *vb* gillen, schreeuwen: *~ one's head off* tekeergaan, tieren
2yell [jel] *n* gil, kreet, schreeuw; aanmoedigingskreet
1yellow [jelloo] *adj* **1** geel(achtig); **2** laf || *(socc) show s.o. a ~ card* iem een gele kaart geven; *~ pages* gouden gids
2yellow [jelloo] *n* **1** geel[h]; **2** eigeel[h], dooier
1yelp [jelp] *vb* **1** keffen; **2** janken; **3** gillen
2yelp [jelp] *n* **1** gekef[h]; **2** gejank[h]; **3** gil

yen [jen] **1** yen *(Japanese currency)*; **2** verlangen[h]
yeoman [joomən] kleine landeigenaar
yep [jep] *(Am; inf)* ja
1yes [jes] *adv* ja, jawel *(after negative sentence)*
2yes [jes] *n* ja[h]: *say ~* ja zeggen, het jawoord geven
yesterday [jestədee] gisteren: *~'s weather was terrible* het weer van gisteren was afgrijselijk; *the day before ~* eergisteren; *I saw him ~ week* ik heb hem gisteren een week geleden gezien
1yet [jet] *adv* **1** nog, tot nu toe, nog altijd: *she has ~ to ring up* ze heeft nog steeds niet opgebeld; *as ~* tot nu toe; **2** *(in interrogative sentences)* al; **3** opnieuw, nog: *~ again* nog een keer; **4** toch nog, uiteindelijk: *he'll beat you ~* hij zal jou nog wel verslaan; **5** toch: *and ~ she refused* en toch weigerde zij (het)
2yet [jet] *conj* maar (toch), doch: *strange ~ true* raar maar waar
yew [joe:] taxus(boom); taxushout[h]
Yid [jid] *(depr)* jood[h], jid
Yiddish [jiddisj] Jiddisch
1yield [jie:ld] *vb* **1** opbrengst hebben, vrucht dragen *(of tree)*; **2** zich overgeven *(to enemy)*; **3** toegeven, wijken: *~ to temptation* voor de verleiding bezwijken; **4** voorrang verlenen
2yield [jie:ld] *vb* **1** voortbrengen *(fruit; also fig: profit, results)*, opleveren, opbrengen; **2** overgeven, opgeven, afstaan: *~ (up) one's position to the enemy* zijn positie aan de vijand overgeven; **3** toegeven
3yield [jie:ld] *n* opbrengst, productie, oogst, rendement[h]
yielding [jie:lding] **1** meegevend, buigzaam; **2** meegaand
yobbo [jobboo] vandaal
yodel [joodl] jodelen
yoga [joogə] yoga
yogurt [jogət] yoghurt
1yoke [jook] *n* **1** juk[h] *(also fig)*, heerschappij, slavernij: *throw off the ~* zich van het juk bevrijden; **2** koppel[h], span[h], paar[h]; **3** draagjuk[h]; **4** verbintenis, juk[h] *(of marriage)*
2yoke [jook] *vb* **1** onder het juk brengen, inspannen, voorspannen; **2** koppelen, verbinden: *~d in marriage* in de echt verbonden
yokel [jookl] boerenkinkel
yolk [jook] dooier
yonder [jondə] ginds, daar ginder
yore [jo:]: *of ~* (van) vroeger, uit het verleden
you [joe] **1** jij, jou, je, *(form)* u: *I saw ~ chasing her* ik heb gezien hoe je haar achterna zat; *Mrs Walters to ~* voor jou ben ik mevr. Walters; **2** jullie, u: *what are ~ two up to?* wat voeren jullie twee uit?; **3** je, men: *~ can't always get what you want* je kunt niet altijd krijgen wat je wilt; *that's fame for ~* dat noem ik nou nog eens beroemd zijn
1young [jung] *adj* **1** jong, pasgeboren, klein, nieuw, vers, fris: *~ child* klein kind, kindje; *a ~ family* een gezin met kleine kinderen; **2** vroeg, net begonnen: *the day (of: night) is (still) ~* het is nog vroeg; **3** junior, jong(er)e: *the ~er Smith, Smith the ~er* de jon-

gere Smith; **4** jeugdig: *one's ~ day(s)* iemands jonge jaren; *~ blood* nieuw, vers bloed, nieuwe ideeën; *Young Turk* revolutionair, rebel; *~ turk* wildebras

²young [jung] *n* **1** de jongelui, de jeugd; **2** jongen *(of animal)*

youngster [jungstə] **1** jongmens[h]; **2** jochie[h], kereltje[h]

your [jo:] **1** jouw, jullie, uw, van jou, jullie: *this is ~ day* dit is jullie grote dag; *I was surprised at ~ leaving so hastily* ik was verbaasd dat je zo haastig vertrok; **2** zo'n (fameuze), een: *so this is ~ Hyde Park!* dit is dus dat (beroemde) Hyde Park van jullie!

yours [jo:z] van jou, van jullie, de, het jouwe, de, het uwe: *take what is ~* neem wat van jou is; *a friend of ~* een vriend van jou; *sincerely ~* met vriendelijke groeten

yourself [jəs̱elf] **1** je, zich: *you are not ~* je bent niet in je gewone doen; *then you came to ~* toen kwam je bij; **2** je zelf, zelf: *it's easier to do it ~* het is gemakkelijker om het zelf te doen; *you ~ told me* je hebt het me zelf gezegd

yourselves [jəs̱elvz] **1** zich, jullie: *you ought to be ashamed of ~* jullie zouden je moeten schamen; **2** zelf: *finish it ~* maak het zelf af

youth [joe:θ] **1** jeugd, jonge jaren; **2** jongeman, jongen; **3** tiener, *~s* jongelui

youthful [joe:θfoel] jeugdig, jong, jeugd-

youth hostel jeugdherberg

¹yowl [jaul] *vb* janken *(of animals)*

²yowl [jaul] *n* gejank[h] *(of animals)*

yu(c)k [juk] bah, gadsie

yucky [jukkie] smerig

¹Yugoslav [joe:goosla:v] *adj* Joegoslavisch, van Joegoslavië

²Yugoslav [joe:goosla:v] *n* Joegoslaaf

Yugoslavia [joe:goosla:viə] Joegoslavië

yuletide 1 *Yuletide* Kerstmis, kerst; **2** kersttijd

yummy [jummie] **1** lekker, heerlijk; **2** prachtig *(eg of colours)*

yuppie [juppie] *young urban professional* yup(pie)

Z

z [zed] z, Z

¹**zany** [zeenie] *n* idioot, halvegare

²**zany** [zeenie] *adj* 1 grappig, zot, leuk; 2 idioot, krankzinnig, absurd

¹**zap** [zæp] *vb (inf)* 1 snel gaan, zoeven, racen: *he was ~ping off in his car to London* hij scheurde weg in zijn wagen naar Londen; 2 zappen, kanaalzwemmen *(TV)*

²**zap** [zæp] *vb* raken, treffen

³**zap** [zæp] *n* pit, pep ‖ *~!* zoef!, flits!, wam!

zeal [zie:l] ijver, geestdrift: *show ~ for sth.* voor iets enthousiast zijn

zealot [zellət] fanatiekeling

zealous [zelləs] 1 ijverig, vurig, enthousiast; 2 verlangend, gretig

zebra [zie:brə] zebra: *~ crossing* zebra(pad)

zenith [zenniθ] toppuntʰ, top, piek

¹**zero** [zjəroo] *num* nul, nulpunt, laagste punt, beginpunt: *his chances of recovery were ~* hij had geen enkele kans op herstel

²**zero** [zjəroo] *vb* het vizier instellen, scherpstellen: *~ in on: a)* het vuur richten op; *b)* zijn aandacht richten op *(problem); c)* inhaken op *(eg on new market)*

zest [zest] 1 iets extra's, jeu, pit: *give (of: add) ~ to* meer smaak geven aan, wat meer pit geven; 2 animoʰ, enthousiasmeʰ: *~ for life* levenslust, levensvreugde

zillion [zilliən] eindeloos groot getalʰ

zinc [zingk] zinkʰ

¹**zip** [zip] *n* 1 snerpend geluidʰ, gescheurʰ *(of clothing);* 2 rits(sluiting); 3 pit, fut: *she's still full of ~* zij zit nog vol energie

²**zip** [zip] *vb* ritsen: *~ up* dichtritsen

³**zip** [zip] *vb* 1 zoeven, scheuren: *bullets ~ped over them* kogels floten over hen heen; 2 snel gaan: *~ by* voorbijsnellen; 3 vast-, los-, ingeritst worden

Zip code *(Am)* postcode

zipper [zippə] rits(sluiting)

zippy [zippie] energiek, levendig, vitaal

zodiac [zoodie·æk] dierenriem

zombie [zombie] levenloos iem, robot, automaat, zoutzak

zone [zoon] 1 streek, gebiedʰ, terreinʰ, zone; 2 luchtstreek; 3 ring, kring, streep; 4 *(Am)* post-, telefoon-, treindistrictʰ

zoo [zoe:] *zoological garden* dierentuin

zoological [zooəlodzjikl] zoölogisch, dierkundig

zoologist [zoe:olladzjist] zoöloog, dierkundige

zoology [zoe:olladzjie] 1 dierkunde, zoölogie; 2 dierenlevenʰ, fauna, dierenwereld *(in certain region)*

¹**zoom** [zoe:m] *vb* 1 zoemen, snorren; 2 snel stijgen *(also fig),* de hoogte in schieten; 3 *(inf)* zoeven, hard rijden; 4 *(photo)* zoomen: *~ in (on)* inzoomen (op); *~ out* uitzoomen

²**zoom** [zoe:m] *n* 1 gezoemʰ; 2 *(photo)* zoom

zoom lens zoomlens, zoomobjectiefʰ

zucchini [zoekienie] *(Am)* courgette